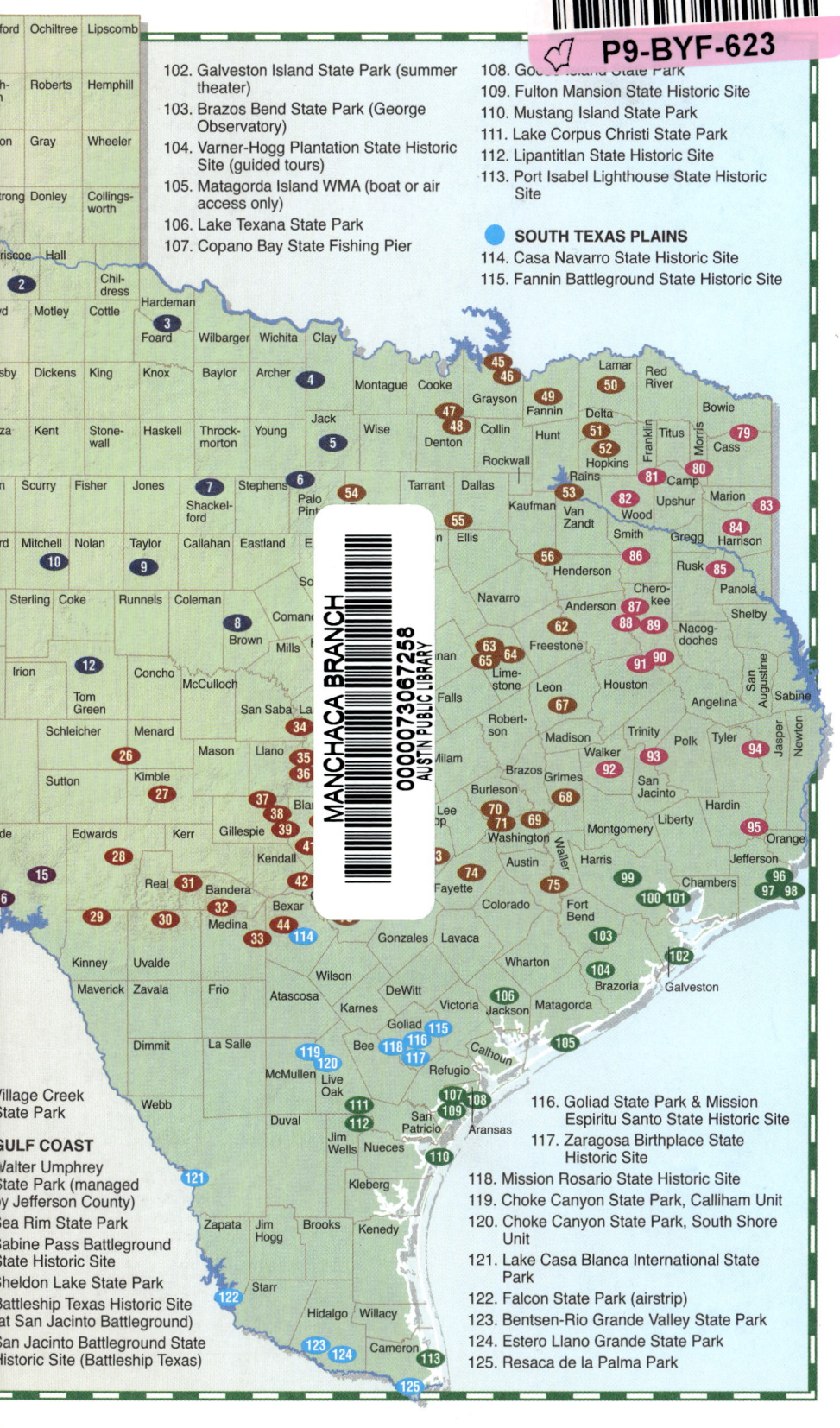

102. Galveston Island State Park (summer theater)
103. Brazos Bend State Park (George Observatory)
104. Varner-Hogg Plantation State Historic Site (guided tours)
105. Matagorda Island WMA (boat or air access only)
106. Lake Texana State Park
107. Copano Bay State Fishing Pier

108. Goose Island State Park
109. Fulton Mansion State Historic Site
110. Mustang Island State Park
111. Lake Corpus Christi State Park
112. Lipantitlan State Historic Site
113. Port Isabel Lighthouse State Historic Site

● **SOUTH TEXAS PLAINS**
114. Casa Navarro State Historic Site
115. Fannin Battleground State Historic Site

116. Goliad State Park & Mission Espiritu Santo State Historic Site
117. Zaragosa Birthplace State Historic Site
118. Mission Rosario State Historic Site
119. Choke Canyon State Park, Calliham Unit
120. Choke Canyon State Park, South Shore Unit
121. Lake Casa Blanca International State Park
122. Falcon State Park (airstrip)
123. Bentsen-Rio Grande Valley State Park
124. Estero Llano Grande State Park
125. Resaca de la Palma Park

Village Creek State Park

GULF COAST
Walter Umphrey State Park (managed by Jefferson County)
Sea Rim State Park
Sabine Pass Battleground State Historic Site
Sheldon Lake State Park
Battleship Texas Historic Site (at San Jacinto Battleground)
San Jacinto Battleground State Historic Site (Battleship Texas)

TEXAS ALMANAC

2012–2013

Published by

Texas State Historical Association

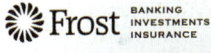

TEXAS ALMANAC
2012 — 2013

Editor	Elizabeth Cruce Alvarez
Associate Editor	Robert Plocheck
Cover Artwork	"Willie Nelson" by Lamberto® Alvarez Lamberto Art & Design www.lamberto.com
Cover Design	David Timmons Design Austin, Texas
Interior Designs	Shelley Kirby M Street Creative Dallas, Texas

ISBN (hardcover) 978-0-87611-247-2
ISBN (flexbound) 978-0-87611-248-9

Library of Congress Control Number: 2011929467

Copyright © 2012

The Texas State Historical Association
University of North Texas
1155 Union Circle #311580, Denton, Texas, 76203-5017
(940) 369-5200

www.TexasAlmanac.com

Distributed by Texas A&M University Press Consortium
4354 TAMU, College Station, Texas, 77843-4354

To order by telephone, call (800) 826-8911

To order online, log onto:

http://www.tamupress.com/product/Texas-Almanac-20122013,6826.aspx

THE SOURCE FOR ALL THINGS TEXAN SINCE 1857

Preface

With the publication of the 66th edition of the Texas Almanac, there are many people to thank for various aspects of this work.

We first want to thank Willie Nelson for his kindness in allowing us to use his likeness on the cover. Our friend Carl Cornelius, mayor of Carl's Corner and friend of Willie's, served as a go-between, arranging the permission for us to use Willie's image on the cover. We thank both Willie and Carl for their enthusiasm for this project. We also thank artist Lamberto Alvarez for creating the extraordinary painting of Willie Nelson and then donating the image for use on the cover and in marketing materials. *(See "About the Cover," below.)*

Since converting the Almanac to a four-color book with the 2006–2007 edition, there has been much emphasis on running as many photographs from around the state as we can fit. Associate Editor Robert Plocheck has taken many beautiful photos on his frequent travels to all corners of Texas. We also are indebted to many others who have contributed photos. We thank Dr. Ron Billings of the Texas Forest Service for the many photos he has allowed us to use from his travels to Texas State Forests, as well as to many cities, towns, and rural settings across Texas. We appreciate the Texas Parks and Wildlife Department for the generous use of their beautiful photos of our wonderful state parks. These gorgeous photos offer inspiration to visit as many of our treasured state parks as possible. Many thanks to the Mission-Aransas National Estuarine Research Reserve for submitting several photos of lovely scenes along the Texas Gulf Coast, the U.S. Fish and Wildlife Service for some incredible shots of wildlife, and the USDA for several great photos used in the Agriculture section.

Each edition of the Almanac includes a wealth of updated facts, figures, and articles. We have hundreds of sources who submit updated information for each edition, including state agencies, county and city officials, and business representatives. As always, we are very appreciative of the time it takes them to prepare and submit their updated information. One of the surveys we send out every two years goes to the 1,215 mayors of Texas, seeking the names of newly elected mayors and the city managers. The surveys are mailed in May after the mayoral elections and then come flooding back in during the next few weeks for input in the Local Government section. It's a big job, and since I have been editor, beginning with the 2004–2005 edition, I have had help from my daughter, Veronica Alvarez, with inputting all of those names. Once again, with this edition, she spent much time opening and sorting surveys, and updating names. I thank her very much for her time and accuracy in this incredibly detailed project.

We hope all Texas Almanac readers will also visit our newly redesigned website at **www.TexasAlmanac.com.** The website includes the Almanac's Searchable Texas Town Database,© new County and Town data pages, articles from past Almanacs, and links to all Texas Almanacs from 1857 through 2004–2005: **www.TexasAlmanac.com/archive.** The Almanac Archive will soon contain all other editions, as well. Lastly, thank you to all of the Almanac readers who have purchased this edition. We appreciate you and hope you enjoy the new Texas Almanac.

Lamberto Alvarez photo

Elizabeth Cruce Alvarez
Editor, 2011

About the Cover

The painting gracing the cover of this edition of the Texas Almanac was created by artist Lamberto Alvarez of Southlake, Texas. Lamberto, in addition to being my husband, is an artist and illustrator who has spent his life creating beautiful and meaningful works of art for publications, businesses, and private art lovers. His start as an artist and photographer in the newspaper industry gave him a sense of the newsworthiness of people and events. His evolution into the world of fine art took him into the realm of portrait painting, abstracts, landscapes, and experimentation with a wide variety of media, including concrete. The combination of his news background and fine art instincts is what led Lamberto to create the painting of Willie Nelson that is on the cover. When he met Willie for the first time at Carl's Corner in Hill County, Lamberto was taking photographs and sensed the historic nature of the event where Willie was opening Willie's Place at Carl's Corner, an entertainment business that also had a biodiesel component. Although the entertainment venue is now closed, Willie's continued support of the biodiesel movement gave Lamberto a sense of a man who loves people and the land around him. The painting came about from Lamberto's own photographs and depicts Willie Nelson as he is now — a larger-than-life Texan with an eye on the environmental future of Texas and the nation.

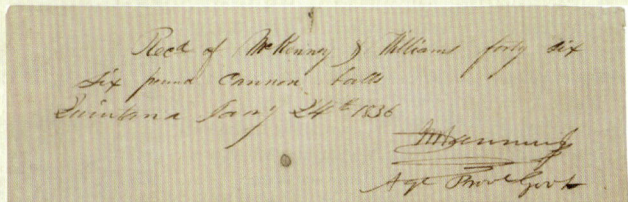

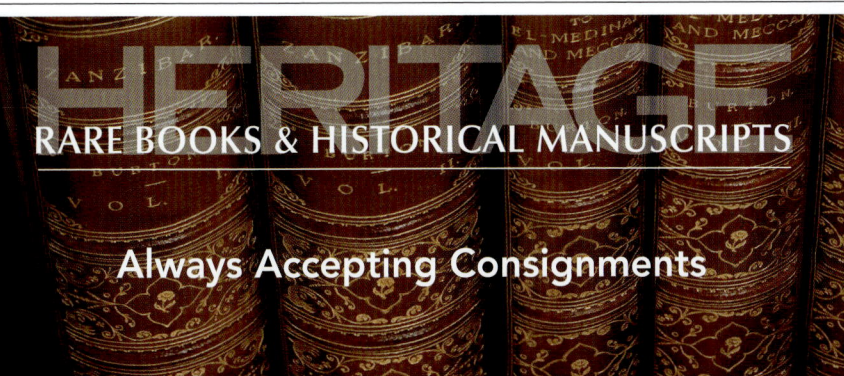

Enduring Icons That Are Part of Texas

An enduring icon of the Texas music scene, Willie Nelson is a testament to creativity, individuality, and endurance — qualities admired by all Texans regardless of their political persuasion.

Nelson's music has been the soundtrack to my life, beginning with memories of my uncles sitting around our living room in the 1950s playing and singing "Hello Walls," and continuing through my college days in Austin in the 1970s with the rise of redneck rock and outlaw country, both of which Nelson instigated.

The last time I saw Nelson in person was at the John T. Floore Country Store in Helotes in the 2000s, and he hadn't lost a step or skipped a beat. The hole in his guitar, Trigger, had grown larger, but the music inspired that crowd the same way it had in Austin in the 1970s.

Like Nelson, the Texas Almanac is also a testament to endurance. Published since 1857, it has found new life with the Texas State Historical Association, a 501(c)(3) charitable organization founded in 1897 and located in Denton at the University of North Texas.

We are proud to present the second TSHA edition of the Texas Almanac, and we hope you will also take a look at the Almanac's new website and digital archive, a collection of 54 past editions of the Texas Almanac going back to 1857, at www.texasalmanac.com.

It's difficult to imagine Texas music without the influence of Willie Nelson, and it's difficult to imagine Texas without the Almanac. The TSHA looks forward to publishing it for many years to come.

Kent Calder
Executive Director
Texas State Historical Association

TABLE OF CONTENTS

INDEX OF MAPS

INDEX OF TABLES

Contents

TEXAS
The Lone Star State

On this and the following page is a demographic and geographic profile of the second-largest, second-most-populous state in the United States. Look in the Index to find more-detailed information about each subject.

The Government

Capital: Austin

Government: Bicameral Legislature

28th State to enter the Union: Dec. 29, 1845

Present Constitution adopted: 1876

State motto: Friendship (1930)

State symbols:
    Flower: Bluebonnet (1901)
    Bird: Mockingbird (1927)
    Tree: Pecan (1919)
    Song: "Texas, Our Texas" (1929)

Origin of name: Texas, or Tejas, was the Spanish pronunciation of a Caddo Indian word meaning "friends" or "allies."

Nickname: Texas is called the Lone Star State because of the design of the state flag: a broad vertical blue stripe at left centered by a single white star, and at right, horizontal bars of white (top) and red.

The People

Population, 2010 U.S. Census......... 25,145,561

Population, 2000 U.S. Census......... 20,851,820

Population increase, 2000–2010........... 20.6%

Population, 1990 U.S. Census........... 16,986,510

Population increase, 1990–2000........... 22.8%

Ethnicity, 2008 *(for explanation of categories, see page 232):*

	Number	Percent
Anglo	11,337,714	45.3%
Hispanic	8,791,986	37.6%
Black	2,782,876	11.8%
Other	991,804	5.3%

Population density (2010)..............96.3 per sq. mi.

Voting-age population (2010) 18,789,238

(U.S. Census Bureau, State Data Center, Texas Secretary of State.)

On an Average Day in Texas in 2008:

There were 1,107 resident live births.
There were 448 resident deaths.
There were 659 more births than deaths.
There were 484 marriages.
There were 217 divorces.

(2008 Texas Vital Statistics, Dept. of State Health Services)

Ten Largest Cities

City	Population
Houston (Harris Co.)	2,099,451
San Antonio (Bexar Co.)	1,327,407
Dallas (Dallas Co.)	1,197,816
Austin (Travis Co.)	790,390
Fort Worth (Tarrant Co.)	741,206
El Paso (El Paso Co.)	649,121
Arlington (Tarrant Co.)	365,438
Corpus Christi (Nueces Co.)	305,215
Plano (Collin Co.)	259,841
Laredo (Webb Co.)	236,091

(January 2010 U.S. Census Bureau.)

Number of counties 254
Largest by pop.......... 4,092,459.............Harris Co.
Smallest by pop......................82............Loving Co.

Number of incorporated cities.................... 1,215
Number of cities of 100,000 pop. or more......29
Number of cities of 50,000 pop. or more........63
Number of cities of 10,000 pop. or more..... 246

Business

Gross State Product (2010)...........$1.286 trillion
Per Capita Personal Income (2009)........ $38,609
Civilian Labor Force (Feb. 2011)........12,150,757

(GSP: Texas Comptroller of Public Accounts and U.S. Bureau of Economic Analysis; per capita income: U.S. Bureau of Economic Analysis; civilian labor force: Texas Workforce Commission.)

The Natural Environment

Area (total) .... 268,596 sq. miles
(171,901,440 acres)

Land area .... 261,232 sq. miles
(167,188,480 acres)

Water area .... 7,365 sq. miles
(4,713,600 acres)

Geographic center: About 15 miles northeast of Brady in northern McCulloch County.

Highest point: Guadalupe Peak (8,749 ft.) in Culberson County in far West Texas.

Lowest point: Gulf of Mexico (sea level).

Normal average annual precipitation range:
From 60.57 inches at Jasper County in far East Texas to 9.43 inches at El Paso, in far West Texas.

Record highest temperature:
Seymour, Baylor Co., Aug. 12, 1936 .... 120°F
Monahans, Ward Co., June 28, 1994 ..... 120°F

Record lowest temperature:
Tulia, Swisher Co., Feb. 12, 1899 .... −23°F
Seminole, Gaines Co., Feb. 8, 1933 .... −23°F

Principal Products

Manufactures: Chemicals and allied products, petroleum and coal products, food and kindred products, transportation equipment.

Farm products: Cattle, cotton, vegetables, fruits, nursery and greenhouse, dairy products.

Minerals: Petroleum, natural gas, and natural gas liquids.

Finance (as of 12/31/2010):
Number of banks 567
Total deposits $248,753,645,000
Number of savings & loan associations 19
Total assets $53,980,441,000
Number of savings banks 29
Total assets $8,559,443,000

(Banks: Federal Reserve Bank of Dallas; savings and loans and savings banks: Texas Savings and Loan Department.)

Agriculture:
Total farm marketings, 2009 .... $16.6 billion
Number of farms, 2010 247,500
Land in farms (acres, 2010) .... 130.4 million
Cropland (acres, 2007) 33,667,177
Harvested land (acres, 2007) 19,174,301
Irrigated land (acres, 2007) 5,010,416

(The Statistical Abstract of the United States 2010; 2007 Census of Agriculture.)

Guadalupe Peak, the highest point in Texas, with El Capitan in the foreground. Photo by Robert Plocheck.

TEXAS' Rank Among the United States

Texas' rank among the United States in selected categories are given below. Others categories are covered in other sections, such as Agriculture, Business, Transportation, Science and Health.

Source (unless otherwise noted): The 2011 Statistical Abstract, U.S. Census Bureau; www.census.gov/compendia/statab

Ten Most Populous States, 2010

Rank	State	Population 2010	%Change 2000–2010
1.	California	37,253,956	10.0
2.	**Texas**	**25,145,561**	**20.6**
3.	New York	19,378,102	2.1
4.	Florida	18,801,310	17.6
5.	Illinois	12,830,632	3.3
6.	Pennsylvania	12,702,379	3.4
7.	Ohio	11,536,504	1.6
8.	Michigan	9,883,640	–0.6
9.	Georgia	9,687,653	18.3
10.	North Carolina	9,535,483	18.5

(United States, 308,745,538 9.7)

Ten Fastest Growing States, 2010

Rank	State	Population Change 2000–2010
1.	Nevada	35.1%
2.	Arizona	24.6%
3.	Utah	23.8%
4.	Idaho	21.1%
5.	**Texas**	**20.6%**
6.	North Carolina	18.5%
7.	Georgia	18.3%
8.	Florida	17.6%
9.	Colorado	16.9%
10.	South Carolina	15.3%

Unauthorized Immigrants, 2009

Rank	State	Estimated
1.	California	2,600,000
2.	**Texas**	**1,680,000**
3.	Florida	720,000
4.	New York	550,000
5.	Illinois	540,000
6.	Georgia	480,000
7.	Arizona	460,000
8.	North Carolina	370,000
9.	New Jersey	360,000
10.	Nevada	260,000
	Other states	2,730,000

(United States 10,750,000)

States with Most Live Births, 2007

Rank	State	Births
1.	California	566,414
2.	**Texas**	**407,625**
3.	New York	253,451
4.	Florida	239,165
5.	Illinois	180,836
6.	Georgia	151,137
7.	Ohio	150,879

(United States 4,316,233)

. . . Highest Birth Rates, 2007

Rank	State	Births per 1,000 Pop.
1.	Utah	20.8
2.	**Texas**	**17.1**
3.	Idaho	16.7
4.	Arizona	16.2
4.	Alaska	16.2
5.	Nevada	16.1
5.	Mississippi	15.9

(United States 14.3)

States with Most Farms, 2009

Rank	State	No. of Farms
1.	**Texas**	**247,500**
2.	Missouri	108,000
3.	Iowa	93,000
4.	Oklahoma	87,000
5.	Kentucky	86,000
6.	California	82,000
7.	Minnesota	81,000
8.	Tennessee	79,000

(United States 2,200,000)

. . . Most Land in Farms, 2009

Rank	State	Farm Acreage
1.	**Texas**	**130,400,000**
2.	Montana	60,800,000
3.	Kansas	46,200,000
4.	Nebraska	45,600,000
5.	South Dakota	43,700,000
6.	New Mexico	43,000,000
7.	North Dakota	39,600,000

(United States 919,800,000)

FLAGS OF TEXAS

United States
1845-Present

Spain
1519-1821

France
1685-1690

Republic
Republic: 1836-1845; State: 1845-Present

Mexico
1821-1836

Confederate States of America
1861-1865

Texas often is called the **Lone Star State** because of its state flag with a single star. The state flag was also the **flag of the Republic of Texas**.

The following information about historic Texas flags, the current flag, and other Texas symbols may be supplemented by information from the **Texas State Library & Archives** in Austin. (On the web: **www. texasalmanac.com/topics/flags-symbols** and **www. tsl.state.tx.us/ref/abouttx/index.html#flags**)

Six Flags of Texas

Six different flags have flown over Texas during eight changes of sovereignty. The accepted sequence of these flags follows:

Spanish — 1519–1821

French — 1685–1690

Mexican — 1821–1836

Republic of Texas — 1836–1845

Confederate States of America — 1861–1865

United States — 1845 to the present.

Evolution of the Lone Star Flag

The Convention at Washington-on-the-Brazos in March 1836 allegedly adopted a flag for the Republic that was designed by **Lorenzo de Zavala.** The design of de Zavala's flag is unknown, but the convention journals state that a "Rainbow and star of five points above the western horizon; and a star of six points sinking below" was added to de Zavala's flag.

There was a suggestion the letters "T E X A S" be placed around the star in the flag, but there is no evidence that the Convention ever approved a final flag design. Probably because of the hasty dispersion of the Convention and loss of part of the Convention notes, nothing further was done with the Convention's proposals for a national flag.

A so-called **"Zavala flag"** is sometimes flown in Texas today that consists of a blue field with a white five-pointed star in the center and the letters "T E X A S" between the star points, but there is no historical evidence to support this flag's design.

The **first official flag of the Republic,** known as

the **National Standard of Texas** or **David G. Burnet's flag,** was adopted by the Texas Congress and approved by President Sam Houston on Dec. 10, 1836. The design "shall be an azure ground with a large golden star central."

The Lone Star Flag

On Jan. 25, 1839, President Mirabeau B. Lamar approved the adoption by Congress of a new national flag. This flag consisted of "a blue perpendicular stripe of the width of one third of the whole length of the flag, with a white star of five points in the centre thereof, and two horizontal stripes of equal breadth, the upper stripe white, the lower red, of the length of two thirds of the length of the whole flag." This is the **Lone Star Flag,** which later became the state flag.

Although Senator William H. Wharton proposed the adoption of the Lone Star Flag in 1838, no one knows who actually designed the flag. The legislature in 1879 inadvertently repealed the law establishing the state flag, but the legislature adopted a new law in 1933 that legally re-established the flag's design.

The red, white, and blue of the state flag stand, respectively, for bravery, purity, and loyalty. The proper **finial** for use with the state flag is either **a star or a spearhead.** Texas is one of only two states that has a flag that formerly served as the flag of an independent nation. The other is Hawaii.

Rules for Display of the State Flag

The Texas Flag Code was first adopted in 1933 and completely revised in 1993. Laws governing display of the state flag are found in sections 3100.051 through 3100.072 of the Texas Government Code. (On the web: **www.tsl.state.tx.us/ref/abouttx/flagcode.html**). A summary of those rules follows:

★ The Texas flag should be displayed on state and national holidays and on special occasions of historical significance, and it should be displayed at every school on regular school days. **When flown out-of-doors,** the Texas flag should not be flown earlier than sunrise nor later than sunset unless properly illuminated. It should not be left out in inclement weather unless a weatherproof flag is used. It should be flown with the white stripe uppermost **except in case of distress.**

★ No flag other than the **United States flag** should be placed above or, if on the same level, to the state flag's right (observer's left). The state flag should be underneath the national flag when the two are flown from the same halyard. **When flown from adjacent flagpoles,** the national flag and the state flag should be of approximately the same size and on flagpoles of equal height; the national flag should be on the flag's own right (observer's left).

★ If the state flag is displayed with the flag of another U.S. state, a nation other than the U.S., or an international organization, the state flag should be, from an observer's perspective, to the left of the other flag on a separate flagpole or flagstaff, and the state flag should not be above the other flag on the same flagpole or flagstaff or on a taller flagpole or flagstaff. If the state flag and the U.S. flag are displayed from crossed flagstaffs, the state flag should be, from an observer's perspective, to the right of the U.S. flag and the state flag's flagstaff should be behind the U.S.

flag's flagstaff.

★ **When the flag is displayed horizontally,** the white stripe should be above the red stripe and, from an observer's perspective, to the right of the blue stripe. **When the flag is displayed vertically,** the blue stripe should be uppermost and the white stripe should be to the state flag's right (observer's left).

★ If the state and national flags are both **carried in a procession,** the national flag should be on the marching right and state flag should be on the national flag's left (observer's right).

★ **On Memorial Day,** the state flag should be displayed at half-staff until noon and at that time raised to the peak of the flagpole. **On Peace Officers Memorial Day** (May 15), the state flag should be displayed at half-staff all day, unless that day is also Armed Forces Day.

★ The state flag should not touch anything beneath it or be dipped to any person or things except the U.S. flag. Advertising should not be fastened to a flagpole, flagstaff, or halyard on which the state flag is displayed.

★ If a state flag is no longer used or useful as an emblem for display, it should be destroyed, preferably by burning. A **flag retirement ceremony** is set out in the Texas Government Code at the Texas State Library & Archives website mentioned earlier.

Pledge to the Texas Flag

Honor the Texas flag;
I pledge allegiance to thee,
Texas, one state under
God, one and indivisible.

A pledge to the Texas flag was adopted in 1933 by the 43rd Legislature. It contained a phrase, "Flag of 1836," which inadvertently referred to the **David G. Burnet flag** instead of the Lone Star Flag adopted in 1839. In 2007, the 80th Legislature changed the pledge to its current form:

A person reciting the pledge to the state flag should face the flag, place the right hand over the heart, and remove any easily removable hat.

The pledge to the Texas flag may be recited at all public and private meetings at which the Pledge of Allegiance to the national flag is recited and at state historical events and celebrations.

The pledge to the Texas flag should be recited after the pledge of allegiance to the United States flag, if both are recited.

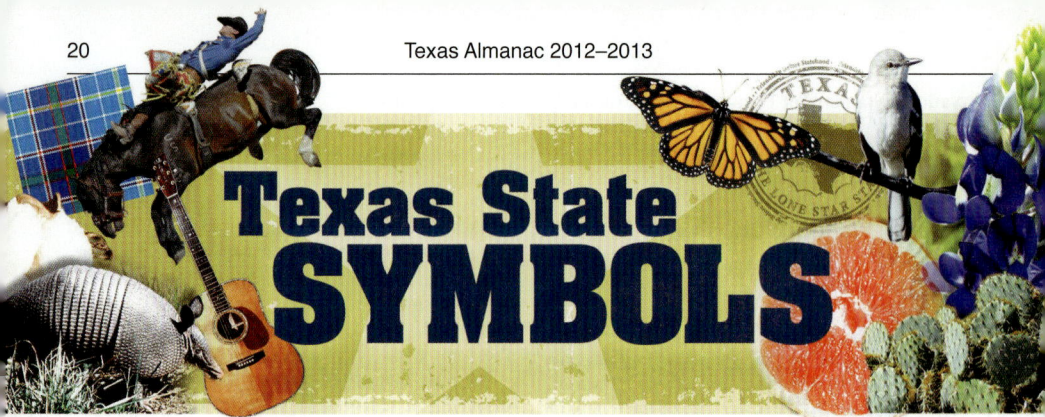

Texas State SYMBOLS

State Song

The state song of Texas is **"Texas, Our Texas."** The music was written by the late William J. Marsh (who died Feb. 1, 1971, in Fort Worth at age 90), and the words by Marsh and Gladys Yoakum Wright, also of Fort Worth. It was the winner of a state song contest sponsored by the 41st Legislature and was adopted in 1929. The wording has been changed once: Shortly after Alaska became a state in January 1959, the word "Largest" in the third line was changed by Mr. Marsh to "Boldest."

The text follows:

Texas, Our Texas

Texas, our Texas! All hail the mighty State!
Texas, our Texas! So wonderful, so great!
Boldest and grandest, Withstanding
    ev'ry test;
O Empire wide and glorious, You stand
    supremely blest.

Chorus

God bless you Texas!
And keep you brave and strong,
That you may grow in power and worth,
Thro'out the ages long.

Refrain

Texas, O Texas! Your freeborn single star,
Sends out its radiance to nations near
    and far.
Emblem of freedom! It sets our
    hearts aglow,
With thoughts of San Jacinto and
    glorious Alamo.

Texas, dear Texas! From tyrant grip
    now free,
Shines forth in splendor your star
    of destiny!
Mother of heroes! We come your
    children true,
Proclaiming our allegiance, our faith,
    our love for you.

State Motto

The state motto is **"Friendship."** The word Texas, or Tejas, was the Spanish pronunciation of a Caddo Indian word meaning "friends" or "allies" (41st Legislature in 1930).

State Citizenship Designation

The people of Texas usually call themselves Texans. However, **Texian** was generally used in the early period of the state's history.

State Seal

The design of the **obverse (front)** of the State Seal consists of "a star of five points encircled by olive and live oak branches, and the words, 'The State of Texas.'" (State Constitution, Art. IV, Sec. 19.) This design is a slight modification of the Great Seal of the Republic of Texas, adopted by the Congress of the Republic, Dec. 10, 1836, and readopted with modifications in 1839.

An official design for the **reverse (back)** of the seal was adopted by the 57th Legislature in 1961, but there were discrepancies between the written description and the artistic rendering that was adopted at the same time. To resolve the problems, the 72nd Legislature in 1991 adopted an official design.

Front of Seal

Back of Seal

The 73rd Legislature in 1993 finally adopted the reverse by law. The current description is in the Texas Government Code, section 3101.001:

"(b) The reverse side of the state seal contains a shield displaying a depiction of:

(1) the Alamo; (2) the cannon of the Battle of Gonzales; and (3) Vince's Bridge.

(c) The shield on the reverse side of the state seal is encircled by:

(1) live oak and olive branches; and (2) the unfurled flags of: (A) the Kingdom of France; (B) the

Kingdom of Spain; (C) the United Mexican States; (D) the Republic of Texas; (E) the Confederate States of America; and (F) the United States of America.

(d) Above the shield is emblazoned the motto, "REMEMBER THE ALAMO," and beneath the shield are the words, "TEXAS ONE AND INDIVISIBLE."

(e) A white five-pointed star hangs over the shield, centered between the flags."

Texas State Symbols

State Bird — The **mockingbird** (*Mimus polyglottos*) is the state bird of Texas, adopted by the 40th Legislature of 1927 at the request of the Texas Federation of Women's Clubs.

State Flower — The state flower of Texas is the **bluebonnet,** also called **buffalo clover, wolf flower,** and *el conejo* (the rabbit). The bluebonnet was adopted as the state flower, at the request of the Society of Colonial Dames in Texas, by the 27th Legislature in 1901. The original resolution made *Lupinus subcarnosus* the state flower, but a resolution by the 62nd Legislature in 1971 provided legal status as the state flower of Texas for "*Lupinus Texensis* and any other variety of bluebonnet."

State Tree — The **pecan tree** (*Carya illinoinensis*) is the state tree of Texas. The sentiment that led to its official adoption probably grew out of the request of Gov. James Stephen Hogg that a pecan tree be planted at his grave. The 36th Legislature in 1919 adopted the pecan tree.

Other Symbols

(In 2001, the Texas Legislature placed restrictions on the adoption of future symbols by requiring that a joint resolution to designate a symbol must specify the item's historical or cultural significance to the state.)

State Air Force — The **Commemorative Air Force** (formerly known as the Confederate Air Force), based in Midland at Midland International Airport, was proclaimed the state air force of Texas by the 71st Legislature in 1989.

State Amphibian — The **Texas toad** was named the state amphibian by the 81st Legislature in 2009.

State Bluebonnet City — The city of **Ennis** in Ellis County was named the state bluebonnet city by the 75th Legislature in 1997.

State Bluebonnet Festival — The **Chappell Hill Bluebonnet Festival,** held in April, was named state bluebonnet festival by the 75th Legislature in 1997.

State Bluebonnet Trail — The city of **Ennis** was named state bluebonnet trail by the 75th Legislature in 1997.

State Bread — *Pan de campo*, translated "camp bread" and often called cowboy bread, was named the state bread by the 79th Legislature in 2005. It is a simple baking-powder bread that was a staple of early Texans and often baked in a Dutch oven.

State Cooking Implement — The **cast iron Dutch oven** was named the cooking implement of Texas by the 79th Legislature in 2005.

State Dinosaur — *Paluxysaurus jonesi* was designated the state dinosaur by the 81st Legislature in 2009.

State Dish — **Chili** was proclaimed the Texas state dish by the 65th Legislature in 1977.

State Dog Breed — The **Blue Lacy** was

State Tree — Pecan Tree

State Cooking Implement — Cast Iron Dutch Oven

State Dog Breed — Blue Lacy

State Fish — Guadalupe Bass

(below)
State Gemstone Cut — Lone Star Cut

State Grass — Sideoats Grama

designated the state dog breed by the 79th Legislature in 2005. The Blue Lacy is a herding and hunting breed descended from greyhound, scent-hound, and coyote stock and developed by the Lacy brothers, who left Kentucky and settled near Marble Falls in 1858.

State Epic Poem — **"The Legend of Old Stone Ranch,"** written by John Worth Cloud, was named the epic poem of Texas by the 61st Legislature in 1969. The work is a 400-page history of the Albany–Fort Griffin area written in verse form.

State Fiber and Fabric — **Cotton** was designated the state fiber and fabric by the 75th Legislature in 1997.

State Fish — The **Guadalupe bass,** a member of the genus *Micropterus* within the sunfish family, was named the state fish of Texas by the 71st Legislature in 1989. It is one of a group of fish collectively known as black bass.

State Flower Song — **"Bluebonnets,"** written by Julia D. Booth and Lora C. Crockett, was named the state flower song by the 43rd Legislature in 1933.

State Folk Dance — The **square dance** was designated the state folk dance by the 72nd Legislature in 1991.

State Fruit — **Texas red grapefruit** was designated the state fruit by the 73rd Legislature in 1993.

State Gem — **Texas blue topaz,** the state gem of Texas, is found in the Llano uplift area in Central Texas, especially west to northwest of Mason. It was designated by the 61st Legislature in 1969.

State Gemstone Cut — The **Lone Star Cut** was named the state gemstone cut by the 65th Legislature in 1977.

State Grass — **Sideoats grama** (*Bouteloua curtipendula*), a native grass found on many different Texas soils, was designated the state grass of Texas by the 62nd Legislature in 1971.

State Health Nut — The **pecan** was designated the state nut by the 77th Legislature in 2001.

State Horse — The **American Quarter Horse** was named state horse by the 81st Legislature in 2009.

State Insect — The **Monarch butterfly** (*Danaus plexippus*) was designated the state insect by the 74th Legislature in 1995.

State Mammals — The **armadillo** (*Dasypus novemcinctus*) was designated the state **small mammal**; the **longhorn** was designated the state **large mammal**; and the **Mexican free-tailed bat** (*Tadarida brasiliensis*) was designated the state flying mammal by the 74th Legislature in 1995.

State Music — **Western swing** was named the state's official music by the 82nd Legislature in 2011.

State Musical Instrument — The **guitar** was named the state musical instrument by the 75th Legislature in 1997.

State Native Pepper — The **chiltepin** was named the native pepper of Texas by the 75th Legislature in 1997.

State Native Shrub — **Texas purple sage** (*Leucophyllum frutescens*) was designated the state native shrub by the 79th Legislature in 2005.

State Pepper — The **jalapeño pepper** was designated the state pepper by the 74th Legislature in 1995.

State Plant — The **prickly pear cactus** was

State Railroad —
Texas State Railroad

named the state plant by the 74th Legislature in 1995.

State Plays — The four official state plays of Texas are *The Lone Star, Texas, Beyond the Sundown*, and *Fandangle*. They were designated by the 66th Legislature in 1979.

State Precious Metal — **Silver** was named the official precious metal by the 80th Legislature in 2007.

State Railroad — The **Texas State Railroad** was designated the state railroad by the 78th Legislature in 2003. It is a steam-powered tourist excursion train that runs between the towns of Rusk and Palestine.

State Reptile — The **Texas horned lizard** (*Phrynosoma cornutum*) was named the state reptile by the 73rd Legislature in 1993.

State Shell — The **lightning whelk** (*Busycon perversum pulleyi*) was named the state seashell by the 70th Legislature in 1987. One of the few shells that open on the left side, the lightning whelk is named for its colored stripes and is found only on the Gulf Coast.

State Ship — The battleship **USS Texas** was designated the state ship by the 74th Legislature in 1995. The USS Texas was launched on May 18, 1912, from Newport News, Virginia, and commissioned on March 12, 1914. In 1919, it became the first U.S. battleship to launch an aircraft, and in 1939, it received the first commercial radar in the U.S. Navy. In 1940, the Texas was designated flagship of the U.S. Atlantic Fleet and was the last of the battleships to participate in both World Wars I and II. It was decommissioned on April 21, 1948, and is a National Historic Landmark and a National Mechanical Engineering Landmark.

State Shoe — The **cowboy boot** was named the state shoe by the 80th Legislature in 2007.

State Shrub — The **crape myrtle** (*Lagerstroemia indica*) was designated the official state shrub by the 75th Legislature in 1997.

State Snack — **Tortilla chips and salsa** was designated the state snack by the 78th Legislature in 2003.

State Sport — **Rodeo** was named the state sport of Texas by the 75th Legislature in 1997.

State Stone — **Petrified palmwood**, found in Texas principally near the Gulf Coast, was designated the state stone by the 61st Legislature in 1969.

State Tall Ship — The **Elissa** was named the state tall ship by the 79th Legislature in 2005. The 1877 ship makes its home at the Texas Seaport Museum at the port of Galveston.

State Tartan — The **Texas Bluebonnet Tartan** was named the official state tartan by the 71st Texas Legislature in 1989.

State Tie — The **bolo tie** was designated the state tie by the 80th Legislature in 2007.

State Vegetable — The **Texas sweet onion** was designated the state vegetable by the 75th Legislature in 1997.

State Vehicle — The **chuck wagon** was named the state vehicle by the 79th Legislature in 2005. Texas rancher Charles Goodnight is credited with inventing the chuck wagon to carry food and supplies for the cowboys on trail drives.

State 10K — The **Texas Roundup 10K** was named the state 10K by the 79th Legislature in 2005 to encourage Texans to exercise and incorporate physical activity into their daily lives. ☆

State Insect — Monarch Butterfly

(below)
*State Pepper —
Jalapeño Pepper*

State Native Pepper — Chiltepin

State Reptile — Texas Horned Lizard

State Seashell — Lightning Whelk

(below) *State Stone —
Petrified Palmwood*

State Tartan — Texas Bluebonnet

State Tall Ship — The Elissa

History

The Union ship the Westfield *explodes in Galveston Bay in 1863. Engraving courtesy of the Library of Congress.*

The Civil War on the Home Front

**Willie Nelson and the Birth
 of the Austin Music Scene**

A Brief Sketch of Texas History

Section Sponsored by
H-E-B

The Civil War on the Home Front

Conflict Began as Texan vs. Texan

By Mike Cox

In a reflective mood, on Aug. 30, 1914, W.D. McDonald wrote a long letter to the *Trenton Tribune,* his old hometown newspaper in Fannin County. He noted it had been 54 years that month since his honorable discharge from Company C, First U.S. Cavalry, and 52 years since he enlisted in the Confederate Army to fight against some of the same men with whom he had once chased hostile Indians.

Married Sept. 1, 1861 — only four months into the Civil War — McDonald built a log cabin near Honey Grove and settled into domestic life. "We . . . were happy," he wrote. "But listen, we hear patriotic men and women all over our Southland saying: 'Your homes are in danger of being destroyed.' I, with every fibre of my being going on to that six-months bride in love said, 'Here am I; send me.' "

On Feb. 22, 1862, McDonald enlisted in Company D, 16th Texas Cavalry, "and for three years and four months I did the best I could to protect that log cabin home and that wife."

Unlike many thousands of Texans who fought for the South, McDonald survived unscathed. Late in life, he and his wife moved to Abilene, a West Texas town that had not even existed during the Civil War.

As a young Federal cavalry trooper, McDonald had followed in newspapers the growing sectional crisis that led to what would be the nation's deadliest war. The election of that "Black Republican" Abraham Lincoln as president in the fall of 1860 climaxed nearly a decade of political strife between the slave-reliant South and the more urbanized North. Starting with South Carolina, the Southern states began seceding from the Union as the not-even-century-old nation edged steadily toward fratricidal war.

In Texas, a secession convention composed of 177 locally elected delegates convened in Austin on Jan. 28, 1861. Only five days later, by a vote of 166 to 8, the body adopted an ordinance of secession.

Future governor James W. Throckmorton drew boos when he cast his vote against the measure.

"Mr. President, when the rabble hiss, well may the patriots tremble," he retorted, addressing Oran M. Roberts, the convention's presiding officer. In addition to

> *"Mr. President, when the rabble hiss, well may the patriots tremble."*
> *— James W. Throckmorton*

James W. Throckmorton drew boos when he voted against secession. Photo courtesy of the Texas State Library & Archives.

voting for leaving the Union, the convention created a Committee of Public Safety, which claimed all Federal military installations in Texas, including the U.S. arsenal in San Antonio. U.S. Army Gen. David E. Twiggs, the ranking military officer in Texas, surrendered his entire 3,000-soldier command and relinquished all military property, including 10,000 rifles.

The last chance for Texas to avoid the coming hostilities came with a statewide referendum on Feb. 23, 1861, but 46,153 Texans voted for secession, with only 13,020 voting against leaving the Union. Texas would be the nascent Confederate States of America's seventh star, with four more breakaway states soon to join the confederation.

The nation's long war of words over states rights and the extension of slavery ended on April 12, when Confederate artillery began bombarding Fort Sumter, a Federal harbor defense installation off Charleston, South Carolina. Three days later, President Lincoln signed a proclamation calling for 75,000 militiamen to put down a rebellion. Then, on April 19, he ordered a naval blockade of the Southern states from the mouth of the Rio Grande to South Carolina. Lincoln extended the blockade to Virginia a week later following the secession of that commonwealth and North Carolina.

The first fighting in Texas was Texan versus Texan, as a vicious war within a war broke out in the Hill Country, where many of the liberal-minded German settlers who had come to the state in the mid-1840s opposed slavery and remained loyal to the Union. Confederate militiamen, some more outlaw than soldier, terrorized Gillespie and surrounding counties, lynching Unionists and stealing what they could under the guise of military authority. When the German-Texans in Gillespie County organized as the Union Loyal League to defend themselves against what they called *Die Hangerbande* (the Hanging Bandits) things only got worse.

By the summer of 1862, the South instituted mandatory military service for all white males 18–35. Needless to say, the German immigrants had no interest in fighting for the Confederacy. James Duff, a dishonorably discharged U.S. Army soldier who now led Confederate forces in the Hill Country, declared the region in open rebellion against the Confederacy. Faced with hanging or conscription, 68 German men decided to ride for Mexico. They made it as far as the Nueces River, when, on Aug. 10, Duff and his men caught up with them. A sharp battle ended with 19 Germans and 12 Confederates dead. An additional nine wounded German-Texans were later executed. The bloody incident broke the spirit of German resistance, but hangings and murders of suspected Union sympathizers continued throughout the war.

The next outbreak of internal strife came along the Red River in North Texas, another pocket of pro-Union sentiment. On Oct. 1, 1862, a roundup of suspected Unionists led to the hanging of seven men following their hasty trial for treason. Fourteen more were lynched without benefit of a court proceeding. When one of the leaders of the Unionist cleanup was murdered, his killer was soon hanged. But 19 others suspected of Union complicity also got lynched in Gainesville, with five more hanged in Sherman. The event became known as the

FUNERAL OF GERMAN PATRIOTS AT COMFORT, TEXAS, August 20, 1865.—[See Page 89.]

The funeral at Comfort for German settlers who refused to fight for the Confederacy. They were killed in battle with Confederate troops or executed after being captured. This wood engraving was published Jan. 20, 1866, in Harper's Weekly. *Print courtesy of the Library of Congress.*

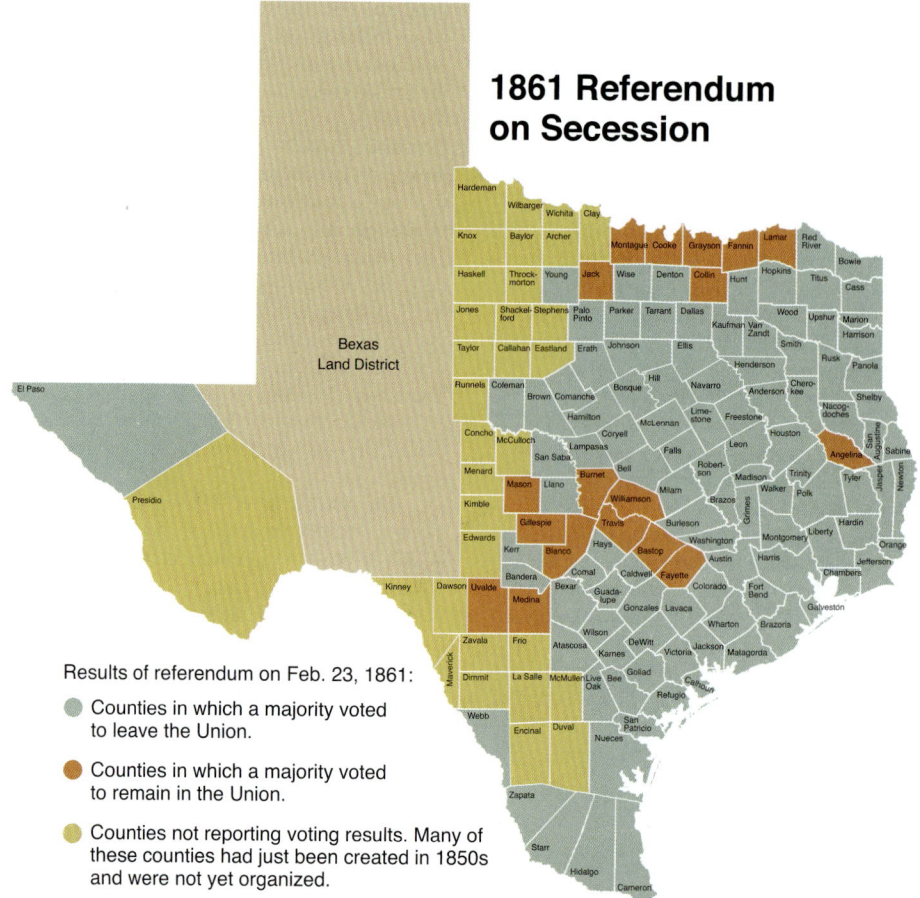

1861 Referendum on Secession

Results of referendum on Feb. 23, 1861:

- Counties in which a majority voted to leave the Union.
- Counties in which a majority voted to remain in the Union.
- Counties not reporting voting results. Many of these counties had just been created in 1850s and were not yet organized.

Great Hanging at Gainesville and still stands as one of the worst episodes of vigilantism in U.S. history.

The same month the hangings began in North Texas, the U.S. Navy captured Galveston, which ranked as Texas' largest and most prosperous city. One of the busiest ports on the Gulf of Mexico, its capture had been a key objective of Federal war planners. Federal control of the port, which came on Oct. 8, 1862, made it even harder for blockade-runners to escape with cotton to sell in the foreign market and for the South to receive badly needed supplies.

Earlier that year, on Aug. 16–18, 1862, the U.S. Navy shelled Corpus Christi and attacked by land, but an attempt to take the town failed. One possible factor in that came to light when Confederate defenders noticed that an inordinate number of Federal shells had not exploded on impact. Examining one of the still-intact rounds, someone discovered it held whiskey, not gunpowder. Though not mentioned in the official record of the engagement, the enduring

legend is that some of the Yankee seaman had been emptying shells to hide their clandestine whiskey supply. Elsewhere along the Texas coast, Federal naval forces conducted periodic offensive operations from 1862 to 1864.

Attacking by land and sea, Confederate forces under Generals John B. Magruder, the ranking CSA officer in Texas, and William B. Scurry retook Galveston on New Year's Day 1863.

While rebel soldiers defeated the 43rd Massachusetts Volunteers on land, two Confederate vessels armored with bales of cotton took on a much larger and better-armed Federal flotilla. One of the "cottonclads" ran aground, but the other, though badly battered by Union cannon fire, rammed the Federal gunboat *Harriet Lane*. Capt. Henry Lubbock, the brother of Texas Gov. Francis Lubbock, boarded the Union vessel, killed most of her officers (including the grandfather of future U.S. Army Gen. Jonathan Wainwright), and called for the surrender of the rest of the Federal fleet. Commodore William Renshaw declined to lower his flag, but accidentally ran his flagship, the *West-field*, aground. As he prepared to scuttle his ship rather than have her pass into rebel hands, the vessel's powder magazine exploded before he meant it to, killing him and most of his officers and sailors. *(See engraving on page 25.)* Seeing this, the remaining Union vessels soon stood to sea, leaving Galveston back in Confederate control for the rest of the war.

Loss of Galveston severely crimped Federal plans for a Texas invasion, but the North did not give up. In September 1863, red-headed 27-year-old Houston bartender Dick Dowling proved he could do more than mix a stiff drink. Commanding 47 mostly Irish soldiers known as Dowling's Davis (as in Jefferson Davis) Guards, the withering artillery fire Dowling directed stood off an invading force

Lt. Dick Dowling

of 20 warships and 5,000 Union soldiers during the Battle of Sabine Pass. In appreciation, the Confederate government presented Dowling and his men silver medals, the only such awards conferred on any Confederate soldiers during the war.

Dowling's victory would not affect the war's outcome, but it had huge significance for Texas. Historians agree that the one-sided,

A statue of Confederate hero Dick Dowling stands in Hermann Park in Houston. It was the first public monument in the City of Houston and was unveiled on March 17 (Saint Patrick's Day), 1905. Photo courtesy of the Houston Arts Alliance.

short-lived battle spared the state from a Union invasion that would have visited on Texas the same level of devastation and misery experienced by other Confederate states, such as what

A soldier can be seen standing in a Confederate lookout tower at Bolivar Point on Galveston Island. This stereo card was created between 1863 and 1864 by photographer George N. Barnard. Courtesy of the Library of Congress.

Georgia saw when Gen. William T. Sherman made his infamous march to the sea.

Throughout the Civil War, Texas had to contend with another problem none of its sister Confederate states faced: An ongoing threat from hostile Indians. The withdrawal of Federal forces at the beginning of the war had left Texas' western frontier exposed to raids from Comanches and Kiowas, effectively contracting the settled portion of the state by a hundred miles. Texas garrisoned some of the abandoned Federal forts with state troops and mounted regular patrols to look for and occasionally skirmish with Indian war parties.

A Civil War re-enactment is conducted at Dallas Heritage Village in Old City Park. Photo courtesy of Dallas Heritage Village.

In West Texas, Fort Chadbourne, Camp Colorado, Fort McKavett, Fort Mason, and Camp Verde also served at various times as prisoner-of-war camps. The Confederacy also had four such camps in East Texas, the largest being Camp Ford at Tyler. The state prison at Huntsville also housed Federal prisoners.

The North tried one more time to invade Texas, this time along the Red River through Louisiana in the spring of 1864. Confederate troops, many of them from Texas, defeated Union forces in western Louisiana at the battles of Mansfield and Pleasant Hill.

If anything, given the destruction of telegraph lines in the South, at the end of the war news traveled even slower than it had early on in the conflict. Though rumors were afloat in Brownsville that Gen. Robert E. Lee had surrendered the Army of Northern Virginia, no official word had been received by Gen. James E. Slaughter and Col. John Salmon "RIP" Ford, who commanded Confederate troops in the Rio Grande Valley.

The two officers learned on May 12, 1865, that 1,600 Federal troops under Lt. Col. David Branson were on the march from Brazos Santiago to Brownsville to take the town. Slaughter proposed retreat, but Ford famously declared: "Retreat, hell!"

That night, Ford's men skirmished with Union forces at Palmito Ranch, a dozen miles east of Brownsville. Fearing Confederate reinforcements, the Federals torched the ranch and withdrew to Palmito Hill, four miles distant.

John Creed Moore raised and trained the Second Texas Infantry for the Confederate Army. He served at the Battle of Shiloh and in Georgia and Alabama. After the war, he returned to Texas to teach mathematics at Coronal Institute and served as superintendent of schools at Mexia and East Dallas. Photo courtesy of the Library of Congress.

Black Soldier Was First Native Texan to Win Medal of Honor

The first recipient of the Medal of Honor who was born in Texas was Milton M. Holland. The nation's highest military honor (originally called the Congressional Medal of Honor) was instituted at the beginning of the Civil War to recognize the heroic actions of Union soldiers in that struggle.

Holland was born in Panola County in August 1844 (some sources say Austin). Along with two brothers, he was sent to school in Athens County, Ohio, before the Civil War by his "owner."

When the Civil War broke out, he worked as a civilian for the quartermaster corps until blacks were allowed to join the army in 1863. The young man raised a company of African-Americans in Athens, and the group was mustered into the 5th Regiment, U.S. Colored Troops. Holland attained the rank of sergeant-major, the highest rank open to blacks at the time.

When the officers of his unit were either killed or wounded in an advance on Richmond, Virginia, on Sept. 29, 1864, Holland assumed command and led a courageous charge that allowed a white military unit to return to the Union line. The actions of Holland and his regiment earned the highest praise from Gen. Ulysses S. Grant.

Milton M. Holland. Photo courtesy of the Library of Congress.

Holland was presented with his Medal of Honor on April, 6, 1865. His citation states: "Took command of Company C, after all the officers had been killed or wounded, and gallantly led it." In all, 23 black soldiers and sailors won the Medal of Honor during the Civil War. Because Holland entered the Union army in Ohio, his military service and heroism are credited to that state in U.S. military records.

Holland did not return to Texas after the war, migrating instead to Washington, D.C. In the 1890s, he founded the Alpha Insurance Company in Washington, D.C., one of the first black-owned insurance companies in the nation. He died in 1910 in Silver Springs, Maryland.

Milton's brother, William, did return to Texas and taught for a time in Austin. A staunch Republican, William Holland served in the 15th Legislature, where he authored legislation creating Prairie View Normal, the first college for blacks in Texas and now Prairie View A&M University. *(See page 473: 19th Century African-American Legislators and Constitutional Convention Delegates.)*

— From the Texas Almanac 1994–1995 and the Richmond Battlefield website, National Park Service; www.nps.gov/rich/historyculture/holland.htm

On May 13, supported by a battery of 12-pounders, Ford's command advanced on the Union troops. Soon, those who were not killed or wounded surrendered. This was not only the final fighting in Texas, it was the last land battle of the Civil War.

Gen. E. Kirby Smith formally surrendered what little remained of the CSA's Trans-Mississippi Department on June 2. Seventeen days later, U.S. Gen. Gordon Granger arrived at Galveston. The same day, June 19, he issued an order advising Texans that the Emancipation Proclamation was in effect. That marked the end of slavery in Texas for more than 200,000 African-Americans, a figure that included thousands of slaves moved by their "owners" into Texas from other Confederate states for "safekeeping" during the war.

While Texas had been spared the devastation seen in much of the South, it paid a dear price for its decision to join the Confederacy. Of the 65,000–70,000 Texans (more than 10 percent of the state's population) who served in the Confederate military, an estimated 24,000 died. Thousands more came home with life-altering wounds, from missing arms or legs to blindness. Countless others suffered from the psychological trauma they had endured, a condition that more than a century later would come to be called Post-Traumatic Stress Disorder.

Texas' elected officials were far slower in providing assistance to these veterans than their predecessors in office had been in contributing men and treasure to the war effort. A home for Confederate veterans in Austin that opened in 1886 with money raised by the Daughters of the Confederacy did not begin receiving state

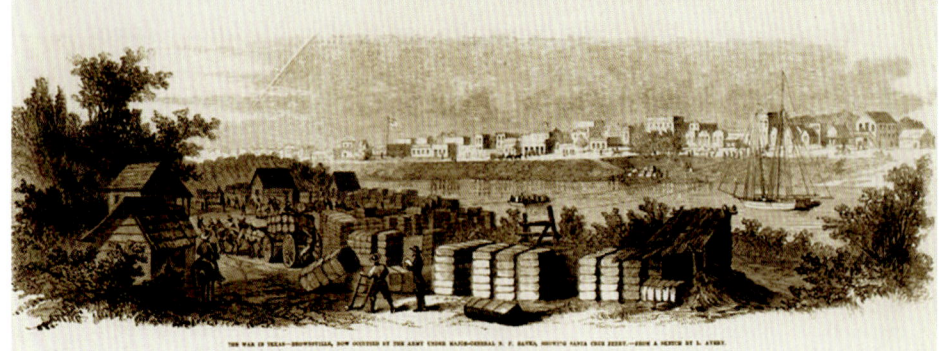

A view of Brownsville, showing the Santa Cruz Ferry, during its occupation by the Union Army under Major-General Nathaniel P. Banks. Banks' troops occupied Brownsville from November 1863 until Confederate troops commanded by John S. "RIP" Ford reoccupied the town on July 30, 1864. This illustration by L. Avery was published Dec. 5, 1863, in Frank Leslie's illustrated newspaper. Courtesy of the Library of Congress.

funds until 1891.

The last survivor of the war was Mississippi-born Walter Williams. He came to Texas at age 14 and served under Confederate Gen. John Bell Hood. Williams died at age 117 in 1959 and is buried in Franklin in Robertson County.

Aside from the thousands of lives lost and economic and social upheaval, the Civil War changed the Texas map. Of Texas' 254 counties, 29 are named for Confederate veterans. Ten of the tens of thousands of Texans who served in the military during the war would become governors.

Not every Texan who went to war fought for the South. Some 2,000 men from the Lone Star State joined the Federal military. One of those Texas Unionists was Edmund J. Davis, who as a brigadier general commanded the Federal 1st Texas Cavalry during the war and served as governor during Reconstruction.

Texas' economy did not fully recover from the impact of the Civil War until World War II, when Japan and Germany threatened the nation that Lincoln and his armies had saved from division.

The Civil War claimed its last life in Texas nearly 145 years after Appomattox when a 62-year-old Victoria man drowned on Jan. 1, 2010, after his 14-foot aluminum boat struck the submerged wreckage of the *Mary Summers,* a Confederate blockade runner sunk during the war at the confluence of the Navidad and Lavaca rivers to prevent Union vessels from navigating up either stream.

Lewis Maverick, one of the three sons of Texas pioneer Samuel Maverick and his wife, Mary, who had fought for the South, survived the war. Like many of the soldiers on both sides, he kept a diary. Back in Texas from the battle-scarred Deep South, his wartime journal ended on May 31, 1865, with this: "Alas under what gloomy circumstances we return, how different from our fond hope."

Mike Cox is an author and Texana writer living in a Austin.

Non-commissioned officers from the 19th Iowa Infantry were prisoners at Camp Ford, near Tyler, and were exchanged for Confederate prisoners at the end of the war. They were photographed on their arrival at New Orleans. Photo courtesy of the Library of Congress.

Timeline of Secession and the Civil War

1861

Feb. 1 — The Secession Convention approves an ordinance withdrawing Texas from the Union because "the power of the Federal Government is sought to be made a weapon with which to strike down the interests and prosperity of the people of Texas and her Sister slaveholding States"; the action is ratified by the voters on Feb. 23 in a referendum vote. Secession is official on March 2.

Feb. 13 — Robert E. Lee is ordered to return to Washington from regimental headquarters at Fort Mason in West Texas to assume command of the Union Army. Instead, Lee resigns his commission; he assumes command of Confederate forces by June 1862.

March 1 — Texas is accepted as a state by the provisional government of the Confederate States of America, even before its secession from the Union is official.

March 5 — The Secession Convention approves an ordinance accepting Confederate statehood.

March 16 — Sam Houston resigns as governor in protest against secession.

1862

March 28 — Battle of Glorieta. Gen. H.H. Sibley's brigade is forced to return to Texas, ending the attempt to take New Mexico.

Aug. 10 — About 68 Union loyalists, mostly German immigrants from the area of Comfort in Central Texas, start for Mexico in an attempt to reach U.S. troops; 19 are killed by Confederates on the Nueces River. Eight others are killed on Oct. 18 at the Rio Grande. Others drown attempting to swim the river. (The loyalists' deaths are commemorated in Comfort by the Treue der Union [True to the Union] monument.)

Aug. 16–18 — U.S. Navy bombards Corpus Christi, attempts to take the city are repulsed.

Oct. 8 — Federal forces capture Galveston.

October — Forty-two men thought to be Union sympathizers are hanged at various times during October in Gainesville.

1863

Jan. 1 — Confederate forces retake Galveston.

July 26 — Sam Houston dies in Huntsville from pneumonia at age 70.

Sept. 8 — The Battle of Sabine Pass. Federal forces are repulsed by a unit led by Lt. Dick Dowling.

Nov. 2–6 — Federal forces take Brownsville.

1864

July 30 — Confederate forces reoccupy Brownsville.

1865

May 13 — The Battle of Palmito Ranch is fought near Brownsville, the last land battle of the Civil War. After the Confederate's victory, they learned the western rebel states had authorized the disbanding of armies and accepted a truce with the Union forces a few days later.

For more information about the Civil War in Texas, see the pages 53–56 and the Handbook of Civil War Texas at www.tshaonline.org/handbook/civil-war.

Artist Jim Franklin created this poster for the opening of the Armadillo World Headquarters in 1970. It is part of the Texas Poster Art Collection at the Dolph Briscoe Center for American History, The University of Texas at Austin. Used by permission.

Willie Nelson and the Birth of the Austin Music Scene

By Joe Nick Patoski

Over the summer of 1970, a loose collective of hippies, free spirits, and dreamers refashioned the old National Guard armory building at the corner of South First Street and Barton Springs, just across the Colorado River from downtown Austin, into a concert hall and beer garden.

The Armadillo World Headquarters was all about music, a shared tolerance for marijuana, psychedelic drugs, and cold beer, and like its namesake had a hard-shell interior with a docile disposition. During its first two years of operation, the Armadillo brought in a parade of touring talent who otherwise would have bypassed Texas, including Ry Cooder, Captain Beefheart, Taj Mahal, Dr. John the Night Tripper, Frank Zappa, the Flying Burrito Brothers, the New Riders of the Purple Sage, Bill Monroe, and especially Commander Cody and His Lost Planet Airmen.

But it wasn't until the night of Aug. 12, 1972, when Willie Nelson walked onto the stage of the Armadillo that everything changed. That performance in front of a mixed crowd of hippies and rednecks is recognized as the starting point of the modern Austin music scene.

A vibrant music community was already in the making, articulated by several outsiders who relocated to Austin like Nelson did to make music unfettered by commercial restraints. Most prominent were Jerry Jeff Walker, a New York folkie from the Greenwich Village scene who had written a hit song about a New Orleans street dancer called "Mr. Bojangles," another singer-songwriter from Houston named Guy Clark, whose vivid story songs had been covered by Walker, and a lanky Fort Worth kid with high cheekbones and a taste for liquor named Townes Van Zandt, considered by his peers as the purist songwriter of all.

Walker also fronted the Lost Gonzo Band. Their live recording *Viva Terlingua!* — made in 1973 in the old Hill Country dancehall at Luckenbach (pop. 3) with fiddler Sweet Mary Egan and a harmonica player named Mickey Raphael — set the standard for rowdy Texas-style country rock. It was the first "made-in-Austin" album to go gold.

The Lost Gonzos — Gary P. Nunn, Bob Livingston, Michael McGeary, Herb Steiner, Craig Hillis, and Kelly Dunn — performed as the Cosmic Cowboy Orchestra whenever they supported Micheal Murphey, the flaxen-haired, buckskin-loving singer-songwriter from Dallas with the two best-selling albums in Austin, *Geronimo's Cadillac* and *Cosmic Cowboy Souvenir*. Murphey came out of the same Rubiyat Club folk scene in Dallas where a husky-voiced belter named B.W. Stevenson from Murphey's high school, Adamson, developed his robust singing style that led to several hit singles, notably "My Maria," No. 9 on Billboard's pop singles chart and No. 1 on the adult contemporary chart in 1973.

Another Adamson grad and Rubiyat regular, Ray Wylie Hubbard, was beginning to make forays down to Austin from Red River, New Mexico, where he had a music club, while another Rubiyat vet, Willis Alan Ramsey, recorded his debut album for Leon Russell's Shelter Records showcasing a country/folk/rock songcraft so exquisite he would never make another album.

Jerry Jeff Walker frequently worked as a solo act at Castle Creek, a listening room a block from the State Capitol that showcased singer-songwriters. Walker arranged for a friend of his from Florida named Jimmy Buffett to sit in between sets before getting his own gig. Castle Creek inspired a song Buffett was crafting called "Wasting Away In Margaritaville" that would become his calling card.

A San Antonio native named Doug Sahm came to Austin from the other direction, relocating from San Francisco where his rock 'n' roll Tex-Mex flavored band, the Sir Douglas Quintet, had gone after their 1966 pop hit "She's About a Mover." A homesick Sahm chose Austin over San Antonio for its tolerance of people who looked and acted different. Besides, he had been playing the city since he was a seven-year-old lap steel guitar prodigy who sang country.

Music-making had historically been a provincial and low-key affair in Austin. Scholz' Garten, established by August Scholz in 1866 and still the home of the Saengerrunde German singing club, was the city's oldest drinking establishment.

The abiding appreciation of folk music and traditional music could be traced to 1909 when University of Texas assistant extension school director John Lomax and professor Leonidas Payne co-founded the Texas Folklore Society. Within six months, there were 92 charter members.

Fifty-five years later, Kenneth Threadgill's filling station and beer joint on North Lamar served as the informal meeting place for folk music aficionados, including a young University of Texas student named Janis Joplin who showed up to sing and play at the weekly hootenannies. When properly inspired and lubricated, Mr. Threadgill would cut loose with yodels in the style of Jimmie

Willie Nelson during his first performance at the Armadillo World Headquarters in 1972. Photo by Burton Wilson; used with his permission.

Freda & the Firedogs hang out in the Armadillo World Headquarters Beer Garden on July 30, 1972. "Freda" is famed blues performer Marcia Ball. Photo by Burton Wilson; used with his permission.

Rodgers, country music's first star.

Before Willie, traditional country music had been largely limited to a few bars and dancehalls such as Big G's, Dessau Hall, Big Gil's, and the Broken Spoke, and bands such as Dolores and the Bluebonnet Boys, the Moods of Country Music, Johnny Lyons and Janet Lynn & the Country Nu-Notes, Jess DeMaine and the Country Music Revue featuring Mary Margaret Kyle, and Bert Rivera and the Night Riders, whose leader had several years road experience as Hank Thompson's steel guitar player.

In 1970, Freda & the Firedogs, a band of like-minded college students led by a dark-haired Cajun pianist named Marcia Ball, aka Freda, tapped into the traditional country zeitgeist and started drawing an unusually strange mix of students, bikers, Mexican families, hippies, hillbillies, and old-time country music fans to the Split Rail Drive-Inn on South Lamar.

Similarly, a small clutch of white kids were drawn to East Austin to soak up the African-American sounds of performers such as Erbie Bowser, Blues Boy Hubbard, T.D. Bell, Hosea Hargrove, and barrelhouse pianist Robert Shaw at clubs including the Victory Lounge,

the IL, Charlie's Playhouse, Ernie's Chicken Shack, and Marie's Tea Room Number 2. The white blues kids had their own playhouse, the One Knite on Red River Street, a half block from the police station where the Storm, featuring Dallas' Jimmie Vaughan on guitar and Lubbock's Lewis Cowdrey on harmonica, and the Nightcrawlers, the band headed by Irving drummer Doyle Bramhall and including Jimmie Vaughan's little brother Stevie, were part of the weekly lineup.

Mexican-Americans had their own music scenes in clubs along East Sixth Street and in *salons de baile* on the edge of town where *conjunto* combos fronted by Johnny Degollado (El Montopolis Kid) and accordion maestro Camilo Cantu and Tejano big bands such as Ruben Ramos, aka El Gato Negro, and the Mexican Revolution played for dancers.

Rock 'n' roll bands played cover versions of popular songs at fraternity and sorority parties at The University of Texas, but by the mid-1960s, some bands began to dabble in original music, most significantly the 13th Floor Elevators, a pioneering psychedelic band led by a yowling Travis High School dropout named Roky Erickson that had a national Top

40 hit in 1966 called "You're Gonna Miss Me" distinguished by an electric jug. The Elevators and like-minded rock bands worked in such places as the Old New Orleans around the UT campus.

By the late 1960s, Austin had its first hippie venue, the Vulcan Gas Company at 300 Congress Avenue, inspired by music ballrooms in San Francisco where many Austin musicians and hangers-on had migrated. The Vulcan was the predecessor to the Armadillo, featuring local and touring psychedelic rock, folk, and blues artists and led to the discovery of an albino blues guitarist from Beaumont named Johnny Winter, who opened for blues giant Muddy Waters. House bands included Shiva's Headband and the Conqueroo, an eclectic folk-rock-blues-jazz group. Vulcan shows were promoted with posters created by Gilbert Shelton, the creator of the Furry Freak Brothers, and other underground artists, and Jim Franklin, who made the armadillo into the iconic symbol of Texas hippies.

Willie Nelson became Austin's music catalyst through his Nashville connections and extensive body of recorded work, and because he represented the kind of country music the rock 'n' rollers and the folkies were trying to project in their own sounds. At 39, he was older than the student-aged musicians and had experience with publishing and recording contracts. And while he came to town clean-shaven with his hair barely covering the tops of his ears, he adapted quickly, letting his hair grow long, cultivating a beard, dressing on stage in blue jeans, tennis shoes, and T-shirts, with a bandanna around his neck or head, and an earring in his lobe.

With bass player Bee Spears wearing a headband and moccasins in Indian fashion and drummer Paul English performing with a black cape with red lining draped over his shoulders, and new addition Mickey Raphael, an Afro-haired harmonica player who had been playing with B.W. Stevenson, Willie Nelson and band fit right in in Austin.

Nelson's groundbreaking Armadillo performance in 1972 opened with a string of early songwriting hits — "Crazy," "Hello Walls," "Funny How Time Slips Away," and "Nightlife" — to introduce himself to those in the audience who had never heard him before, then demon-

The Vulcan Gas Company in Austin was the predecessor to the Armadillo and featured local and touring psychedelic rock, folk, and blues artists. Photo by Burton Wilson; used with his permission.

When Willie Nelson first performed at the Armadillo World Headquarters in 1972, artist Micael Priest created his "Willie Nelson in Concert with Greezy Wheels" poster. It is part of the Texas Poster Art Collection at the Dolph Briscoe Center for American History, The University of Texas at Austin. Used by permission.

strated his guitar-playing prowess as his band alternated sets with young country-rockers Greezy Wheels until closing time at midnight. Afterward, the show moved to a suite at the Crest Hotel across Town Lake that writers Edwin "Bud" Shrake and Gary "Jap" Cartwright had rented, where a guitar pulling ensued featuring Willie Nelson, with University of Texas football coach Darrell K Royal calling out requests and making sure the audience adhered to his rule to respect musicians and the music they were making: "If I can hear you, then you are too loud. If you wish to socialize, please go out on to the front or back porch." Those who failed to observe the rule were asked to leave.

Willie Nelson's first show at the Armadillo coincided with the appearance of KOKE-FM, an Austin radio station that coined the phrase "progressive country" to explain its eclectic playlist, which included Ernest Tubb and classic Texas honky-tonk, Bob Wills and the Made-in-Texas sound called western swing, Nashville rebel Waylon Jennings, as well as the Byrds, the Rolling Stones, Creedence Clearwater Revival, and lots of Willie Nelson, who also sang jingles for the station and played impromptu shows on the air with friends such as Kris Kristofferson. Progressive country would also be labeled as redneck rock, Texas music, and outlaw country. Whatever it was, the music sounded like nowhere else but Austin.

In 1974, Willie added television to his Austin portfolio when he agreed to perform in front of cameras at Studio 6A on the campus of The University of Texas at Austin for KLRN-TV (now KRLU-TV), the Public Broadcasting Service television channel serving San Antonio and Austin. KLRN program director Bill Arhos, producer Paul Bosner, and director Bruce Scafe secured grant money to film a pilot for a live music series focusing on original Texas music. The pilot led to the first broadcast of *Austin City Limits* in 1976. The series is the longest running music program on American television.

Willie would proceed to further invest in the Austin music scene by buying the old Terrace Motor Inn on Academy Street, just off South Congress Avenue, and by helping transform the Terrace's convention center into the Texas Opera House, later known as the Austin Opry House, where he built a recording studio, before moving his operations to near Spicewood in the Hill Country west of the city where his empire included the most modern recording facility in Texas, a golf course, a western town, and condominiums.

Joe Nick Patoski is a writer and historian who has been writing about Texas and Texans for four decades. His biography Willie Nelson: An Epic Life *was published by Little, Brown & Company in 2008 and was recognized with the 2009 TCU Texas Book Award for the best book written about Texas.*

Willie Nelson's Fourth of July picnic in 1973 near Dripping Springs was the first of many more to come. Photo by Burton Wilson; used with his permission.

A Brief Sketch of TEXAS HISTORY

This two-part sketch of Texas' past, from prehistoric times to 1980, is based on "A Concise History of Texas" by former Texas Almanac editor Mike Kingston. Mr. Kingston's history was published in the 1986–1987 edition of the Texas Almanac, which marked Texas' sesquicentennial. Robert Plocheck, associate editor of the Texas Almanac, edited and expanded Mr. Kingston's history.

Prehistory to Annexation

Prehistoric Texas

Early Texans are believed to have been descendants of Asian groups that migrated across the Bering Strait during the Ice Ages of the past 50,000 years.

At intermittent periods, enough water accumulated in massive glaciers worldwide to lower the sea level several hundred feet. During these periods, the Bering Strait became a 1,300-mile-wide land bridge between North America and Asia.

These early adventurers worked their way southward for thousands of years, eventually getting as far as Tierra del Fuego in South America about 10,000 years ago.

Biologically, they were completely modern homo sapiens. No evidence has been found to indicate that any evolutionary change occurred in the New World.

Four basic stages reflecting cultural advancement of early inhabitants are used by archeologists in classifying evidence. These stages are:

- **Paleo-Indian** (20,000 to 7,000 years ago)
- **Archaic** (7,000 years ago to about the time of Christ)
- **Woodland** (time of Christ to 800–1,000 years ago)
- **Neo-American or Late Prehistoric** (800–1,000 years ago until European contact).

Not all early people advanced through all these stages in Texas. Much cultural change occurred in adaptation to changes in climate. The Caddo tribes of East Texas, for example, reached the Neo-American stage before the Spanish and French explorers made contact in the 1500s and 1600s.

Others, such as the Karankawas of the Gulf Coast, advanced no further than the Archaic stage of civilization at the same time. Still others advanced and then regressed in the face of a changing climate.

The earliest confirmed evidence indicates that humans were in Texas sometime between 10,000 and 13,000 years ago.

Paleo-Indians were successful big-game hunters. Artifacts from this period are found across the state but not in great number, indicating that they were a small, nomadic population.

As Texas' climate changed at the end of the Ice Age about 7,000 years ago, inhabitants adapted. Apparently the state experienced an extended period of warming and drying, and the population during the **Archaic** period increased.

These Texans began to harvest fruits and nuts, and to exploit rivers for food, as indicated by the freshwater mussel shells in ancient garbage heaps.

The **Woodland** stage is distinguished by the development of settled societies, with crops and local wild plants providing much of their diet. The bow and arrow came into use, and the first pottery is associated with this period.

Pre-Caddoan tribes in East Texas had formed villages and were building distinctive mounds for burials and for ritual.

The **Neo-American** period is best exemplified by the highly civilized Caddoes, who had a complex culture with well-defined social stratification. They were fully agricultural and participated in trade over a wide area of North America.

The Spanish Explorations

Spain's exploration of North America was one of the first acts of a vigorous nation that was emerging from centuries of campaigns to oust the Islamic Moors from the Iberian Peninsula.

In early **1492**, the Spanish forces retook the province of Granada, completing the reconquista or reconquest. Later in the year, the Catholic royals of the united country, Ferdinand and Isabella, took a major stride toward shaping world history by commissioning Christopher Columbus for the voyage that was to bring Europeans to America.

As early as **1519, Capt. Alonso Alvarez de Pineda**, in the service of the governor of Jamaica, mapped the coast of Texas.

The **first recorded exploration of today's Texas** was made in the 1530s by **Alvar Núñez Cabeza de Vaca**, along with two other Spaniards and a Moorish slave named Estevanico. They were members of an expedition commanded by Panfilo de Narváez that left Cuba in 1528 to explore what is now the southeastern United States. Ill-fated from the beginning, many members of the expedition lost their lives, and others, including Cabeza de Vaca, were shipwrecked on the Texas coast. Eventually the band wandered into Mexico in 1536.

In **1540**, Francisco Vázquez de Coronado was commissioned to lead an exploration of the American Southwest. The quest took him to the land of the Pueblo Indians in what is now New Mexico. Native Americans, who had learned it was best to keep Europeans away from their homes, would suggest vast riches could be found in other areas. So Coronado pursued a fruitless search for gold and silver across the **High Plains of Texas**, Oklahoma and Kansas.

While Coronado was investigating Texas from the west, Luis de Moscoso Alvarado approached from the east. He assumed leadership of Hernando de Soto's expedition when the commander died on the banks of the Mississippi River. In **1542**, Moscoso's group ventured as far west as **Central Texas** before returning to the Mississippi.

Forty years passed after the Coronado and Moscoso expeditions before Fray Agustín Rodríguez, a Franciscan missionary, and Francisco Sánchez Chamuscado, a soldier, led an expedition into Texas and New Mexico.

Following the Río Conchos in Mexico to its confluence with the Rio Grande near present-day **Presidio** and then turning northwestward up the great river's valley, the explorers passed through the El Paso area in **1581**.

Juan de Oñate was granted the right to develop this area populated by Pueblo Indians in 1598. He blazed a trail across the desert from Santa Barbara, Chihuahua, to intersect the Rio Grande at the Pass of the North. For the next 200 years, this was the supply route from the interior of Mexico that served the northern colonies.

Texas was attractive to the Spanish in the 1600s. Small expeditions found trade possibilities, and missionaries ventured into the territory. Frays Juan de Salas and Diego López responded to a request by the Jumano Indians for religious instruction in **1629**, and for a brief time priests lived with the Indians near present-day **San Angelo**.

The first permanent settlement in Texas was established in **1681–1682** after New Mexico's Indians rebelled and drove Spanish settlers southward. The colonists retreated to the **El Paso** area, where the missions of Corpus Christi de la Isleta and Nuestra Señora del Socorro — each named for a community in New Mexico — were established. Ysleta pueblo originally was located on the south side of the Rio Grande, but as the river changed its course, the pueblo ended up on the north bank. Now part of El Paso, the community is considered the oldest European settlement in Texas.

French Exploration

In 1682, **René Robert Cavelier, Sieur de La Salle**, explored the Mississippi River to its mouth at the Gulf of Mexico. La Salle claimed the vast territory drained by the river for France.

Two years later, La Salle returned to the New World with four ships and enough colonists to establish his country's claim. Guided by erroneous maps, this second expedition overshot the mouth of the Mississippi by 400 miles and ended up on the Texas coast. Though short of supplies because of the loss of two of the ships, the French colonists established Fort Saint Louis on Garcitas Creek several miles inland from Lavaca Bay.

Francisco Vasquez de Coronado explored the Texas High Plains looking for gold and silver. This drawing by Frederic Remington entitled "Coronado's March – Colorado" is courtesy of the Library of Congress.

In 1718, Spanish officials allowed missionaries to found a mission at San Pedro Springs. That mission, called San Antonio de Valero, was later to be known as the Alamo. Photo courtesy of Downtown San Antonio.org.

In 1687, La Salle and a group of soldiers began an overland trip to find French outposts on the Mississippi River. Somewhere west of the Trinity River, the explorer was murdered by some of his men. His grave has never been found. *(A more detailed account of La Salle's expedition can be found in the Texas Almanac 1998–1999 and on the Texas Almanac website.)*

In 1689, Spanish authorities sent **Capt. Alonso de León**, the governor of Coahuila (which at various times included Texas in its jurisdiction), into Texas to confront the French. He headed eastward from present-day **Eagle Pass** and eventually found the tattered remnants of Fort Saint Louis.

Indians had destroyed the settlement and killed many colonists. León continued tracking survivors of the ill-fated colony into East Texas.

Spanish Rule

Father **Damián Massanet** accompanied León on this journey. The priest was fascinated with tales about the "Tejas" Indians of the region.

Tejas meant *friendly*, but at the time the term was considered a tribal name. Actually these Indians were members of the Caddo Confederacy that controlled parts of four present states: Texas, Louisiana, Arkansas and Oklahoma.

The Caddo religion acknowledged one supreme god, and when a Tejas chief asked Father Massanet to stay and instruct his people in his faith, the Spaniards promised to return and establish a mission.

The pledge was redeemed in **1690** when the mission San Francisco de los Tejas was founded near present-day Weches in Houston County.

Twin disasters struck this missionary effort. Spanish government officials quickly lost interest when the French threat at colonization diminished. And as was the case with many New World Indians who had no resistance to European diseases, the Tejas soon were felled by an epidemic. The Indians blamed the new

religion and resisted conversion. The mission languished, and it was difficult to supply it from other Spanish outposts in northern Mexico. In 1693, the Spanish officials closed the mission effort in **East Texas.**

Although Spain had not made a determined effort to settle Texas, great changes were coming to the territory. Spain introduced horses into the Southwest. By the late 1600s, Comanches were using the horses to expand their range southward across the plains, displacing the Apaches. In the **1720s**, the **Apaches** moved onto the lower Texas Plains, usurping the traditional hunting grounds of the Jumanos and others. The nomadic Coahuiltecan bands were particularly hard hit.

In 1709, Fray Antonio de San Buenaventura y Olivares had made an initial request to establish a mission at San Pedro Springs (today's San Antonio) to minister to the Coahuiltecans. Spanish officials denied the request. However, new fears over the French movement into East Texas changed that.

Another Franciscan, **Father Francisco Hidalgo**, who had earlier served at the missions in East Texas, returned to them when he and **Father Antonio Margil de Jesús** accompanied **Capt. Diego Ramón** on an expedition to the area in 1716. In that year, the mission of San Francisco de los Neches was established near the site of the old San Francisco de los Tejas mission. Nuestra Señora de Guadalupe was located at the present-day site of Nacogdoches, and Nuestra Señora de los Dolores was placed near present-day San Augustine.

The East Texas missions did little better on the second try, and supplying the frontier missions remained difficult. It became apparent that a way station between northern Mexico and East Texas was needed.

In 1718, Spanish officials consented to Fray Olivares' request to found a mission at San Pedro Springs. That mission, called **San Antonio de Valero**, was later to be known as the **Alamo**. Because the Indians of the region often did not get along with each other, other missions were established to serve each group.

These missions flourished and each became an early ranching center. But the large herds of cattle and horses attracted trouble. The San Antonio missions began to face the wrath of the Apaches. The mission system, which attempted to convert the Indians to Christianity and to "civilize" them, was partially successful in subduing minor tribes but not larger tribes like the Apaches.

The Spanish realized that more stable colonization efforts must be made. Indians from Mexico, such as the Tlascalans who fought with Cortés against the Aztecs, were brought into Texas to serve as examples of "good" Indians for the wayward natives.

In **1731**, Spanish colonists from the **Canary Islands** were brought to Texas and founded the **Villa of San Fernando de Béxar**, the first civil jurisdiction in the province and today's **San Antonio**.

In the late 1730s, Spanish officials became concerned over the vulnerability of the large area between the Sierra Madre Oriental and the Gulf Coast in northern Mexico. The area was unsettled, a haven for runaway Indian slaves and marauders, and it was a wide-open pathway for the English or French to travel from the Gulf to the rich silver mines in Durango.

For seven years, the search for the right colonizer went on before **José de Escandón** was selected in 1746. A professional military man and successful administrator, Escandón earned a high reputation by subduing Indians in central Mexico. On receiving the assignment, he launched a broad land survey of the area running from the mountains to the Gulf and from the Río Pánuco in Tamaulipas, Mexico, to the Nueces River in Texas.

In 1747, he began placing colonists in settlements throughout the area. **Tomás Sánchez** received a land grant on the Rio Grande in 1755 from which **Laredo** developed. And other small Texas communities along the river sprang up as a result of Escandón's well-executed plan. Many old Hispanic families in Texas hold title to their land based on grants in this period.

In the following decades, a few other Spanish colonists settled around the old missions and frontier forts. **Antonio Gil Ybarbo** led one group that settled **Nacogdoches** in the **1760s and 1770s.**

The Demise of Spain

Spain's final 60 years of control of the province of Texas were marked with a few successes and a multitude of failures, all of which could be attributed to a breakdown in the administrative system.

Charles III, the fourth of the Bourbon line of kings, took the Spanish throne in 1759. He launched a series of reforms in the New World. The king's choice of administrators was excellent. In 1765, José de Gálvez was dispatched to New Spain (an area that then included all of modern Mexico and much of today's American West) with instructions to improve both the economy and the defense of the area.

Gálvez initially toured parts of the vast region, gaining first-hand insight into the practical problems of the colony. There were many that could be traced to Spain's basic concepts of colonial government. Texas, in particular, suffered from the mercantilist economic system that attempted to funnel all colonial trade through ports in Mexico.

But administrative reforms by Gálvez and his nephew, Bernardo Gálvez, namesake of Galveston, were to be followed by ill-advised policies by successors.

Problems with the Comanches, Apaches and "Norteños," as the Spanish called some tribes, continued to plague the province, too.

About the same time, Spain undertook the administration of the Louisiana Territory. One of the terms of the cession by France was that the region would enjoy certain trading privileges denied to other Spanish dependencies. So although Texas and Louisiana were neighbors, trade between the two provinces was banned.

The Spanish crown further complicated matters by placing the administration of Louisiana under authorities in Cuba, while Texas remained under the authorities in Mexico City.

The death of Charles III in 1788 and the beginning of the French Revolution a year later weakened Spain's hold on the New World dominions. Charles IV was not as good a sovereign as his predecessor, and his choice of ministers was poor. The quality of frontier administrators declined, and relations with Indians soured further.

Charles IV's major blunder, however, was to side with French royalty during the revolution, earning Spain the enmity of Napoleon Bonaparte. Spain also allied with England in an effort to thwart Napoleon, and in this losing cause, the Spanish were forced to cede Louisiana back to France.

In 1803, Napoleon broke a promise to retain the territory and sold it to the United States. Spain's problems in the New World thereby took on an altogether different dimension. Now, Anglo-Americans cast longing eyes on the vast undeveloped territory of Texas.

With certain exceptions for royalists who left the American colonies during the revolution, Spain had maintained a strict prohibition against Anglo or other non-Spanish settlers in their New World territories. But they were unprepared to police the eastern border of Texas after removing the presidios in the 1760s. What had been a provincial line became virtually overnight an international boundary, and an ill-defined one at that.

American Immigrants

Around **1800, Anglo-Americans** began to probe the Spanish frontier. Some settled in East Texas and others crossed the Red River and were tolerated by authorities.

Others, however, were thought to have nefarious designs. Philip Nolan was the first of the American filibusters to test Spanish resolve. Several times he entered Texas to capture wild horses to sell in the United States.

But in 1801, the Spanish perceived an attempted insurrection by Nolan and his followers. He was killed in a battle near present-day Waco, and his company was taken captive to work in the mines in northern Mexico.

Spanish officials were beginning to realize that the economic potential of Texas must be developed if the

Anglo-Americans were to be neutralized. But Spain's centuries-long role in the history of Texas was almost over.

Resistance to Spanish rule had developed in the New World colonies. Liberal ideas from the American and French revolutions had grown popular, despite the crown's attempts to prevent their dissemination.

In Spain, three sovereigns — Charles IV, Napoleon's brother Joseph Bonaparte, and Ferdinand VII — claimed the throne, often issuing different edicts simultaneously. Since the time of Philip II, Spain had been a tightly centralized monarchy with the crown making most decisions. Now, chaos reigned in the colonies.

As Spain's grip on the New World slipped between 1790 and 1820, Texas was almost forgotten, an internal province of little importance. Colonization was ignored; the Spanish government had larger problems in Europe and in Mexico.

Spain's mercantile economic policy penalized colonists in the area, charging them high prices for trade goods and paying low prices for products sent to markets in the interior of New Spain. As a result, settlers from central Mexico had no incentives to come to Texas. Indeed, men of ambition in the province often prospered by turning to illegal trade with Louisiana or to smuggling. On the positive side, however, Indians of the province had been mollified through annual gifts and by developing a dependence on Spain for trade goods.

Ranching flourished. In **1795**, a census found **69 families** living on 45 ranches in the **San Antonio** area. A census in **1803** indicated that there were **100,000 head of cattle** in Texas. But aside from a few additional families in Nacogdoches and La Bahía (near present-day Goliad), the province was thinly populated.

The largest group of early immigrants from the United States was not Anglo, but Indian.

As early as **1818, Cherokees** of the southeastern United States came to Texas, settling north of Nacogdoches on lands between the Trinity and Sabine rivers. The Cherokees had been among the first U.S. Indians to accept the federal government's offers of resettlement. As American pioneers entered the newly acquired lands of Georgia, Alabama and other areas of the Southeast, the Indians were systematically removed, through legal means or otherwise.

Some of the displaced groups settled on land provided in Arkansas Territory, but others, such as the Cherokees, came to Texas. These Cherokees were among the "Five Civilized Tribes" that had adopted agriculture and many Anglo customs in an unsuccessful attempt to get along with their new neighbors. Alabama and Coushatta tribes had exercised squatters' rights in present-day Sabine County in the early 1800s, and soon after the Cherokees arrived, groups of Shawnee, Delaware and Kickapoo Indians came from the United States.

A **second wave of Anglo** immigrants began to arrive in Texas, larger than the first and of a different character. These Anglos were not so interested in agricultural opportunities as in other schemes to quickly recoup their fortunes.

Spain recognized the danger represented by the unregulated colonization by Americans. The Spanish Cortes' colonization law of 1813 attempted to build a buffer between the eastern frontier and northern Mexico. Special permission was required for Americans to settle within 52 miles of the international boundary, although this prohibition often was ignored.

As initially envisioned, Americans would be allowed to settle the interior of Texas. Colonists from Europe and Mexico would be placed along the eastern frontier to limit contact between the Americans and the United States. Spanish officials felt that the Americans already in Texas illegally would be stable if given a stake in the province through land ownership.

Moses Austin, a former Spanish subject in the vast Louisiana Territory, applied for the first empresario grant from the Spanish government. With the intercession of Baron de Bastrop, a friend of Austin's from Missouri Territory, the request was approved in January **1821**.

Austin agreed to settle **300 families** on land bounded by the Brazos and Colorado rivers on the east and west, by El Camino Real (the old military road running from San Antonio to Nacogdoches) on the north, and by the Gulf Coast.

But Austin died in June 1821, leaving the work to his son, **Stephen F. Austin**. Problems began as soon as the first authorized colonists arrived in Texas the following December when it was learned that Mexico had gained independence from Spain.

Mexico, 1810–1836

Mexico's war for independence, 1810–1821, was savage and bloody in the interior provinces, and Texas suffered as well.

In early 1812, Mexican revolutionary **José Bernardo Gutiérrez de Lara** traveled to Natchitoches, La., where, with the help of U.S. agents, an expedition was organized. **Augustus W. Magee**, a West Point graduate, commanded the troop, which entered Texas in August 1812. This "Republican Army of the North" easily took Nacogdoches, where it gathered recruits.

After withstanding a siege at La Bahía, the army took San Antonio and proclaimed the First Republic of Texas in April 1813. A few months later, the republican forces were bloodily subdued at the Battle of Medina River.

Royalist Gen. Joaquín de Arredondo executed a staggering number of more than 300 republicans, including some Americans, at San Antonio, and a young lieutenant, **Antonio López de Santa Anna**, was recognized for valor under fire.

When the war finally ended in Mexico in 1821, little more had been achieved than separation from Spain.

Sensing that liberal reforms in Spain would reduce the authority of royalists in the New World, Mexican conservatives had led the revolt against the mother country. They also achieved early victories in the debate over the form of government the newly independent Mexico should adopt.

An independent Mexico was torn between advocates of centralist and federalist forms of government.

The former royalists won the opening debates, settling Emperor Agustín de Iturbide on the new Mexican throne. But he was overthrown and the Constitution of

1824, a federalist document, was adopted.

The Mexican election of 1828 was a turning point in the history of the country when the legally elected administration of Manuel Gómez Pedraza was overthrown by supporters of Vicente Guerrero, who in turn was ousted by his own vice president Anastasio Bustamante. Mexico's most chaotic political period followed. Between 1833 and 1855, the Mexican presidency changed hands 36 times.

Texas, 1821–1833

Mexico's **land policy,** like Spain's, differed from the U.S. approach. Whereas the United States sold land directly to settlers or to speculators who dealt with the pioneers, the Mexicans retained tight control of the property transfer until predetermined agreements for development were fulfilled.

But a 4,428-acre *sitio* — a square league — and a 177-acre *labor* could be obtained for only surveying costs and administrative fees as low as $50. The empresario was rewarded with grants of large tracts of land, but only when he fulfilled his quota of families to be brought to the colonies.

Considering the prices the U.S. government charged, Texas' land was indeed a bargain and a major attraction to those Americans looking for a new start.

More than 25 empresarios were commissioned to settle colonists. Empresarios included **Green DeWitt** and **Martín de León,** who in 1824 founded the city of Guadalupe Victoria (present-day Victoria).

By 1830, Texas boasted an estimated population of 15,000, with Anglo-Americans outnumbering Hispanics by a margin of four to one.

Stephen F. Austin was easily the most successful empresario. After his initial success, Austin was authorized in 1825 to bring 900 more families to Texas, and in 1831, he and his partner, **Samuel Williams,** received another concession to bring 800 Mexican and European families. Through Austin's efforts, 1,540 land titles were issued to settlers.

In the early years of colonization, the settlers busied themselves clearing land, planting crops, building homes and fending off Indian attacks. Many were successful in establishing a subsistence economy.

One weakness of the Mexican colonial policy was that it did not provide the factors for a market economy. Although towns were established, credit, banks and good roads were not provided by the government.

Ports were established at Galveston and Matagorda bays after Mexican independence, but the colonists felt they needed more, particularly one at the mouth of the Brazos. And foreign ships were barred from coastwise trade, which posed a particular hardship because Mexico had few merchant ships.

To settle in Texas, pioneers had to become Mexican citizens and to embrace Roman Catholicism. Most of the Americans were Protestants, if they adhered to any religion, and they were fiercely defensive of the right to **religious freedom** enjoyed in the United States.

Although no more than one-fourth of the Americans ever swore allegiance to the Catholic Church, the requirement was a long-standing irritation.

Slavery, too, was a point of contention. Mexico prohibited the introduction of slavery after December 1827. Nevertheless, several efforts were made to evade the government policy. Austin got the state Legislature to recognize labor contracts under which slaves were technically free but bound themselves to their masters for life. Often entire families were covered by a single contract. While many early Anglo colonists were not slaveholders, they were Southerners, and the ownership of slaves was a cultural institution that they supported. The problem was never settled during Texas' colonial period despite the tensions it generated.

Most of the early Anglo-American colonists in Texas intended to fulfill their pledge to become good Mexican citizens. But the political turmoil following the 1828 presidential election raised doubts in the Americans' minds about the ability of Mexico to make representative government function properly.

On a tour of Texas in 1827 and 1828, Gen. Manuel Mier y Terán noted that the Texans "carried their constitutions in their pockets." And he feared the Americans' desire for more rights and liberties than the government was prepared to offer would lead to rebellion. Unrest increased in Texas when Gen. Mier y Terán began reinforcing existing garrisons and establishing new ones.

But a major factor in the discontent of Americans came with the **decree of April 6, 1830,** when the Mexican government in essence banned further American immigration into Texas and tried to control slavery. (For an account of how Texans opposed this decree at Fort Anahuac, see Texas History Features on the *Texas Almanac* Web site.)

Austin protested that the prohibition against American immigration would not stop the flow of Anglos into Texas; it would stop only stable, prosperous Americans from coming.

Austin's predictions were fulfilled. Illegal immigrants continued to come. By 1836, the estimated number of people in Texas had reached 35,000.

Prelude to Revolution

In the midst of all the turmoil, Texas was prospering. By 1834, some 7,000 bales of cotton with a value of $315,000 were shipped to New Orleans. In the middle of the decade, Texas exports, including cotton and beaver, otter and deer skins, amounted to $500,000.

Trade ratios were out of balance, however, because $630,000 in manufactured goods were imported. And, there was little currency in Texas. Ninety percent of the business transactions were conducted with barter or credit.

In 1833 and 1834, the **Coahuila y Texas** legislature was diligently trying to respond to the complaints of the Texas colonists. The English language was recognized for official purposes. Religious toleration was approved. The court system was revised, providing Texas with an appellate court and trial by jury.

In Mexico City, however, a different scenario was developing. **Santa Anna** assumed supreme authority in April 1834 and began dismantling the federalist government. Among the most offensive changes dictated by Santa Anna was the reduction of the state militias to one man per each 500 population. The intent was to eliminate possible armed opposition to the emerging centralist government.

But liberals in the state of Zacatecas in central

Mexico rebelled. Santa Anna's response was particularly brutal, as he tried to make an example of the rebels. Troops were allowed to sack the state capital after the victory over the insurgents.

Trouble also was brewing closer to the Texans. In March 1833, the Coahuila y Texas legislature moved the state capital from Saltillo to Monclova. The Monclova legislature in 1834 gave the governor authority to sell 400 *sitios* — or 1.77 million acres of land — to finance the government and to provide for protection. A year later the lawmakers criticized Santa Anna's reputation on federalism. Seeing a chance to regain lost prestige, Saltillo declared for Santa Anna and set up an opposition government. In the spring of 1835, Santa Anna sent his brother-in-law, Martín Perfecto de Cos, to break up the state government at Monclova.

Texans were appalled by the breakdown in state government, coming on the heels of so many assurances that the political situation was to improve.

Texas politics were polarizing. A "war party" advocated breaking away from Mexico altogether, while a "peace party" urged calm and riding out the political storm. Most of the settlers, however, aligned with neither group.

In January 1835, Santa Anna sent a detachment of soldiers to Anahuac to reinforce the customs office, but duties were being charged irregularly at various ports on the coast. William B. Travis, in an act not supported by all colonists, led a contingent of armed colonists against the Mexican soldiers, who withdrew without a fight.

Although some members of the peace party wrote Mexican Gen. **Martín Perfecto de Cos**, stationed at Matamoros, apologizing for the action, he was not compromising. Cos demanded that the group be arrested and turned over to him. The Texans refused.

The committees of correspondence, organized at the Convention of 1832 (which had asked that Texas be separated from Coahuila), began organizing another meeting. Because the term "convention" aroused visions of revolution in the eyes of Mexican officials, the gathering at Washington-on-the-Brazos in October 1835 was called a "consultation." But with the breakdown of the state government and with Santa Anna's repeal of the Constitution of 1824, the American settlers felt well within their rights to provide a new framework with which to govern Texas.

Fresh from brutally putting down the rebellion in Zacatecas, Santa Anna turned his attention to Texas. Gen. Cos was determined to regarrison the state, and the settlers were equally determined to keep soldiers out.

Col. **Domingo de Ugartechea**, headquartered at San Antonio, became concerned about armed rebellion when he heard of the incident at Anahuac. He recalled a six-pound cannon that had been given DeWitt colonists to fight Indians.

Ugartechea ordered Cpl. Casimira de León with five men to Gonzales to retrieve the weapon. No problems were expected, but officials at Gonzales refused to surrender the weapon. When the Mexicans reinforced Cpl. León's men, a call was sent out for volunteers to help the Gonzales officials. Dozens responded.

Oct. 2, 1835, the Texans challenged the Mexicans with a **"come-and-take-it" flag** over the cannon. After a brief skirmish, the Mexicans withdrew, but the first rounds in the Texas Revolution had been fired.

Winning Independence

As 1836 opened, Texans felt in control of their destiny and secure in their land and their liberties. The Mexican army had been driven from their soil.

But tragedy loomed. Easy victories over government forces at Anahuac, Nacogdoches, Goliad, Gonzales and San Antonio in the fall of 1835 had given them a false sense of security. That independent mood was their undoing, for no government worthy of the name coordinated the defense of Texas. Consequently, as the Mexican counterattack developed, no one was in charge. Sam Houston was titular commander-in-chief of the Texas forces, but he had little authority.

Some even thought the Mexicans would not try to re-enter Texas. Few Texans counted on the energy and determination of Santa Anna, the dictator of Mexico.

The status of the strongholds along the San Antonio River was of concern to Houston. In mid-January, Houston sent **James Bowie** to San Antonio to determine if the Alamo was defensible. If not, Bowie had orders to destroy it and withdraw the men and artillery to Gonzales and Copano.

On Feb. 8, David Crockett of Tennessee, bringing 12 men with him, arrived to aid the revolutionaries.

On Feb. 12, 1836, Santa Anna's main force crossed the Rio Grande headed for San Antonio. The Mexican battle plan had been debated. But Mexico's national pride had been bruised by the series of defeats the nation's army had suffered in 1835, capped by Gen. Cos's ouster from San Antonio in December.

On Feb. 11, the Consultation's "governor of the government" **Henry Smith**, sent **William B. Travis** to San Antonio. Immediately a split in command at the **Alamo** garrison arose. Most were American volunteers who looked to the Houston-appointed Bowie as their leader. Travis had only a handful of Texas army regulars. Bowie and Travis agreed to share the command of 150 men.

Arriving at the Alamo on Feb. 23, Santa Anna left no doubt regarding his attitude toward the defenders. He hoisted a blood-red flag, the traditional Mexican symbol of no quarter, no surrender, no mercy. Travis and Bowie defiantly answered the display with a cannon shot.

Immediately the Mexicans began surrounding the Alamo and bombarding it. Throughout the first night and nights to come, Santa Anna kept up a continual din to destroy the defenders' morale.

On Feb. 24, Bowie became ill and relinquished his share of command to Travis. Although the Mexican bombardment of the Alamo continued, none of the defenders was killed. In fact, they conducted several successful forays outside the fortress to burn buildings that were providing cover for the Mexican gunners and to gather firewood.

Messengers also successfully moved through the Mexican lines at will, and 32 reinforcements from Gonzales made it into the Alamo without a loss on March 1.

Historians disagree over which flag flew over the defenders of the Alamo.

Mexican sources have said that Santa Anna was

outraged when he saw flying over the fortress a Mexican tricolor, identical to the ones carried by his troops except with the numbers "1 8 2 4" emblazoned upon it. Some Texas historians have accepted this version because the defenders of the Alamo could not have known that Texas' independence had been declared on March 2. To the knowledge of the Alamo's defenders, the last official position taken by Texas was in support of the Constitution of 1824, which the flag symbolized. But the only flag found after the battle, according to historian Walter Lord, was one flown by the **New Orleans Greys**.

By March 5, Santa Anna had 4,000 men in camp, a force he felt sufficient to subdue the Alamo.

Historians disagree on the date, but the story goes that on March 3 or 5, Travis called his command together and explained the bleak outlook. He then asked those willing to die for freedom to stay and fight; those not willing could try to get through enemy lines to safety. Even the sick Jim Bowie vowed to stay. Only Louis (Moses) Rose, a veteran of Napoleon's retreat from Moscow slipped out of the Alamo that night.

At dawn March 6, Santa Anna's forces attacked. When the fighting stopped between 8:30 and 9 a.m., all the defenders were dead. Only a few women, children and black slaves survived the assault. **Davy Crockett**'s fate is still debated. Mexican officer Enrique de la Peña held that Crockett was captured with a few other defenders and was executed by Santa Anna.

Santa Anna's victory came at the cost of almost one-third his forces killed or wounded. Their deaths in such number set back Santa Anna's timetable. The fall of the Alamo also brutally shook Texans out of their lethargy.

Sam Houston, finally given command of the entire Texas army, left the convention at **Washington-on-the-Brazos** on the day of the fall of the Alamo.

On March 11, he arrived at Gonzales to begin organizing the troops. Two days later, **Susanna Dickinson**, the wife of one of the victims of the Alamo, and two slaves arrived at Houston's position at Gonzales with the news of the fall of the San Antonio fortress.

Houston then ordered **James Fannin** to abandon the old presidio **La Bahía** at Goliad and to retreat to Victoria. Fannin had arrived at the fort in late January with more than 400 men. As a former West Pointer, he had a background in military planning, but Fannin had refused Travis' pleas for help, and after receiving Houston's orders, Fannin waited for scouting parties to return.

Finally, on March 19, he left, but too late. Forward elements of Gen. José de Urrea's troops caught Fannin's command on an open prairie. After a brief skirmish Fannin surrendered.

Santa Anna was furious when Gen. Urrea appealed for clemency for the captives. The Mexican leader issued orders for their execution. On March 27, a Palm Sunday, most of the prisoners were divided into groups and marched out of Goliad, thinking they were being transferred to other facilities. When the execu-

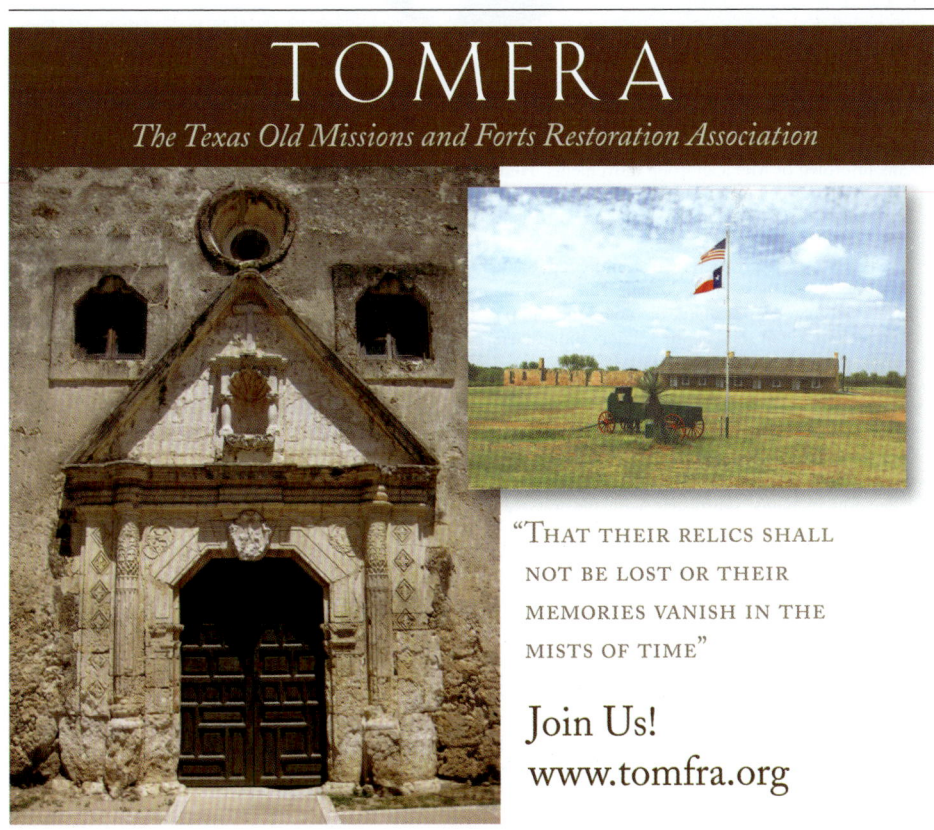

tions began, many escaped. But about 350 were killed.

On March 17, Houston reached the Colorado near the present city of La Grange and began receiving reinforcements. Within a week, the small force of several hundred had become almost respectable, with 1,200-1,400 men in camp.

By the time Houston reached the Colorado, the convention at Washington-on-the-Brazos was completing work. **David Burnet**, a New Jersey native, was named interim president of the new Texas government, and **Lorenzo de Zavala**, a Yucatán native, was named vice president.

On March 27, Houston moved his men to San Felipe on the Brazos. The Texas army was impatient for a fight, and there was talk in the ranks that, if action did not develop soon, a new commander should be elected.

As the army marched farther back toward the San Jacinto River, two Mexican couriers were captured and gave Houston the information he had hoped for. Santa Anna in his haste had led the small Mexican force in front of Houston. Now the Texans had an opportunity to win the war.

Throughout the revolt, Houston's intelligence system had operated efficiently. Scouts, commanded by **Erastus "Deaf" Smith**, kept the Texans informed of Mexican troop movements. **Hendrick Arnold**, a free black, was a valuable spy, posing as a runaway slave to enter Mexican camps to gain information.

Early on April 21, Gen. Cos reinforced Santa Anna's troops with more than 500 men. The new arrivals, who had marched all night, disrupted the camp's routine for a time, but soon all the soldiers and officers settled down for a midday rest.

About 3 p.m., Houston ordered his men to parade and the battle was launched at 4:30 p.m.

A company of Mexican-Texans, commanded by Juan Seguín, had served as the rear guard for Houston's army through much of the retreat across Texas and had fought many skirmishes with the Mexican army in the process.

Perhaps fearing the Mexican-Texans would be mistaken for Santa Anna's soldiers, Houston had assigned the company to guard duty as the battle approached. But after the men protested, they fought in the battle of San Jacinto.

Historians disagree widely on the number of troops on each side. Houston probably had about 900 while Santa Anna had between 1,100 and 1,300.

But the Texans had the decided psychological advantage. Two thirds of the fledgling Republic's army were "old Texans" who had family and land to defend. They had an investment of years of toil in building

Lorenzo de Zavala was the first vice president of the Republic of Texas. Courtesy of the Texas State Library & Archives.

their homes. And they were eager to avenge the massacre of men at the Alamo and Goliad.

In less than 20 minutes they set the Mexican army to rout. More than 600 Mexicans were killed and hundreds more wounded or captured. Only nine of the Texans died in the fight.

It was not until the following day that Santa Anna was captured. One Texan noticed that a grubby soldier his patrol found in the high grass had a silk shirt under his filthy jacket. Although denying he was an officer, he was taken back to camp, where he was acknowledged with cries of "El Presidente" by other prisoners.

Santa Anna introduced himself when taken to the wounded Houston.

President Burnet took charge of Santa Anna, and on May 14 the dictator signed **two treaties at Velasco**, a public document and a secret one. The public agreement declared that hostilities would cease, that the Mexican army would withdraw to south of the **Rio Grande**, that prisoners would be released and that Santa Anna would be shipped to Veracruz as soon as possible.

In the secret treaty, Santa Anna agreed to recognize Texas' independence, to give diplomatic recognition, to negotiate a commercial treaty and to set the Rio Grande as the new Republic's boundary.

Republic of Texas, 1836–1845

Sam Houston was easily the most dominant figure throughout the nearly 10-year history of the Republic of Texas. While he was roundly criticized for the retreat across Texas during the revolution, the victory at San Jacinto endeared him to most of the new nation's inhabitants.

Houston handily defeated Henry Smith and Stephen F. Austin in the election called in September 1836 by the interim government, and he was inaugurated as president on Oct. 22.

In the same September election, voters overwhelmingly approved a proposal to request annexation to the United States.

The first cabinet appointed by the new president represented an attempt to heal old political wounds. Austin was named secretary of state and Smith was secretary of the treasury. But Texas suffered a major tragedy in late December 1836 when Austin, the acknowledged **"Father of Texas,"** died of pneumonia.

A host of problems faced the new government. Santa Anna was still in custody, and public opinion favored his execution. Texas' leadership wisely kept Santa Anna alive, first to keep from giving the Mexicans an emotional rallying point for launching another invasion. Second, the Texas leaders hoped that the dictator would keep his promise to work for recognition of Texas.

Santa Anna was released in November 1836 and made his way to Washington, D.C. Houston hoped the dictator could persuade U.S. President **Andrew Jackson** to recognize Texas. Jackson refused to see Santa Anna, who returned to Mexico, where he had fallen from power.

Another major challenge was the Texas army. The new commander, Felix Huston, favored an invasion of Mexico, and the troops, made up now mostly of American volunteers who came to Texas after the battle of San Jacinto, were rebellious and ready to fight.

President Houston tried to replace Felix Huston with **Albert Sidney Johnston**, but Huston seriously wounded Johnston in a duel. In May 1837, Huston was asked to the capital in Columbia to discuss the invasion. While Huston was away from the troops, Houston sent **Thomas J. Rusk**, the secretary of war, to furlough the army without pay — but with generous land grants. Only 600 men were retained in the army.

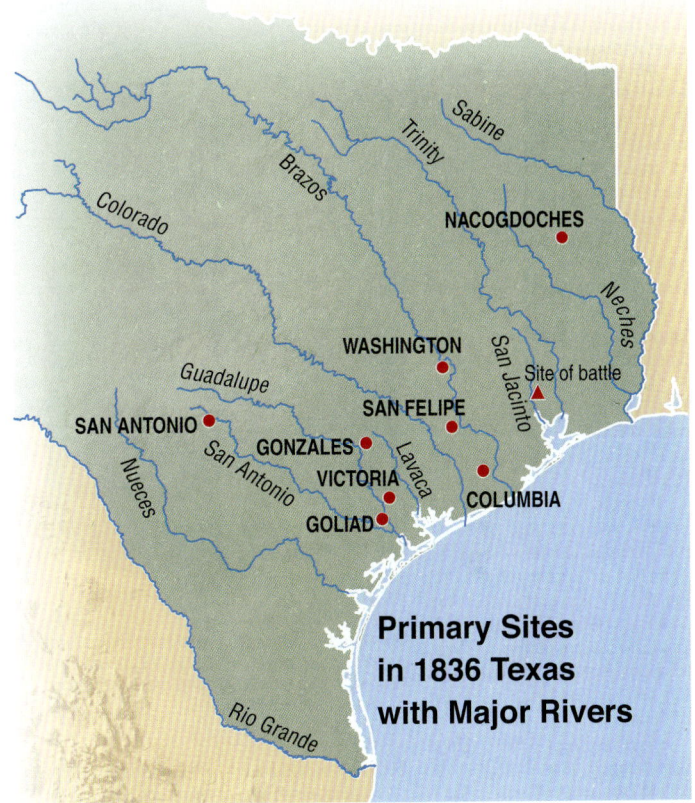

Primary Sites in 1836 Texas with Major Rivers

The Republic's other problems were less tractable. The economy needed attention, Indians still were a threat, Mexico remained warlike, foreign relations had to be developed, and relations with the United States had to be solidified.

The greatest disappointment in Houston's first term was the failure to have the Republic annexed to the United States. Henry Morfit, President Jackson's agent, toured the new Republic in the summer of 1836. Although impressed, Morfit reported that Texas' best chance at continued independence lay in the "stupidity of the rulers of Mexico and the financial embarrassment of the Mexican government." He recommended that annexation be delayed.

Houston's foreign policy achieved initial success when **J. Pinckney Henderson** negotiated a trade treaty with Great Britain. Although the agreement was short of outright diplomatic recognition, it was progress. In the next few years, France, Belgium, The Netherlands and some German states recognized the new Republic.

Under the constitution, Houston's first term lasted only two years, and he could not succeed himself. His successor, **Mirabeau B. Lamar**, had grand visions and was a spendthrift. Houston's first term cost Texas only about $500,000, while President Lamar and the Congress spent $5 million in the next three years.

Early in 1839, Lamar gained recognition as the **"Father of Education"** in Texas when the Congress granted each of the existing 23 counties three leagues of land to be used for education. Fifty leagues of land were set aside for a university.

Despite the lip service paid to education, the government did not have the money for several years to set up a school system. Most education during the Republic was provided by private schools and churches.

Lamar's Indian policies differed greatly from those under Houston. Houston had lived with Cherokees as a youth, was adopted as a member of a tribe and advocated Indian rights long before coming to Texas. Lamar reflected more the frontier attitude toward American Indians. His first experience in public life was as secretary to Gov. George Troup of Georgia, who successfully opposed the federal government's policy of assimilation of Indians at the time. Indians were simply removed from Georgia.

Texans first tried to negotiate the Cherokees' removal from the region, but in July 1839, the Indians were forcibly ejected from Texas at the **Battle of the Neches River** in Van Zandt County. Houston's close friend, the aging Cherokee chief **Philip Bowles**, was killed in the battle while Houston was visiting former President Jackson in Tennessee. The Cherokees moved on to Arkansas and Indian Territory.

Houston was returned to the presidency of the Republic in 1841. His second administration was even more frugal than his first; soon income almost matched expenditures.

Houston re-entered negotiations with the Indians in Central Texas in an attempt to quell the raids on settlements. A number of trading posts were opened along the frontier to pacify the Indians.

War fever reached a high pitch in Texas in 1842, and Houston grew increasingly unpopular because he would not launch an offensive war against Mexico.

In March 1842, Gen. **Rafael Vásquez** staged guerrilla raids on San Antonio, Victoria and Goliad, but quickly left the Republic.

A force of 3,500 Texas volunteers gathered at San Antonio demanding that Mexico be punished. Houston urged calm, but the clamor increased when Mexican **Gen. Adrian Woll** captured San Antonio in September. He raised the Mexican flag and declared the reconquest of Texas.

Ranger Capt. **Jack Hays** was camped nearby. Within days 600 volunteers had joined him, eager to drive the Mexican invaders from Texas soil. Gen. Woll withdrew after the **Battle of Salado**.

Alexander Somervell was ordered by Houston to follow with 700 troops and harass the Mexican army. He reached Laredo in December and found no Mexican troops. Somervell crossed the Rio Grande to find military targets. A few days later, the commander returned home, but 300 soldiers decided to continue the raid under the command of William S. Fisher. On Christmas day, this group attacked the village of **Mier**,

As Sam Houston completed his second term as president of the Republic of Texas, the United States was becoming more interested in annexation. File image.

only to be defeated by a Mexican force that outnumbered them 10-to-1.

After attempting mass escape, the survivors of the Mier expedition were marched to Mexico City where Santa Anna, again in political power, ordered their execution. When officers refused to carry out the order, it was amended to require execution of one of every 10 Texans. The prisoners drew beans to determine who would be shot; bearers of **black beans** were executed. Texans again were outraged by the treatment of prisoners, but the war fever soon subsided.

As Houston completed his second term, the United States was becoming more interested in annexation. Texas had seriously flirted with Great Britain and France, and the Americans did not want a rival republic with close foreign ties on the North American continent. Houston orchestrated the early stages of the final steps toward annexation. It was left to his successor, **Anson Jones**, to complete the process.

The Republic of Texas' main claim to fame is simply endurance. Its settlers, unlike other Americans who had military help, had cleared a large region of Indians by themselves, had established farms and communities and had persevered through extreme economic hardship.

Adroit political leadership had gained the Republic recognition from many foreign countries. Although dreams of empire may have dimmed, Texans had established an identity on a major portion of the North American continent. The frontier had been pushed to a line running from Corpus Christi through San Antonio and Austin to the Red River.

The U.S. presidential campaign of 1844 was to make Texas a part of the Union. ☆

Annexation to 1980

Annexation

Annexation to the United States was far from automatic for Texas once independence from Mexico was gained in 1836. Sam Houston noted that Texas "was more coy than forward" as negotiations reached a climax in 1845.

William H. Wharton was Texas' first representative in Washington. His instructions were to gain diplomatic recognition of the new Republic's independence.

After some squabbles, the U.S. Congress appropriated funds for a minister to Texas, and President Andrew Jackson recognized the new country in one of his last acts in office in March 1837.

Texas President **Mirabeau B. Lamar** (1838–41) opposed annexation. He held visions of empire in which Texas would rival the United States for supremacy on the North American continent.

During his administration, Great Britain began a close relationship with Texas and made strenuous efforts to get Mexico to recognize the Republic. This relationship between Great Britain and Texas raised fears in the United States that Britain might attempt to make Texas part of its empire.

Southerners feared for the future of slavery in Texas, which had renounced the importation of slaves as a concession to get a trade treaty with Great Britain, and American newspapers noted that trade with Texas had suffered after the Republic received recognition from European countries.

In Houston's second term in the Texas presidency, he instructed **Isaac Van Zandt**, his minister in Washington, to renew the annexation negotiations. Although U.S. President **John Tyler** and his cabinet were eager to annex Texas, they were worried about ratification in the U.S. Senate. The annexation question was put off.

In January 1844, Houston again gave Van Zandt instructions to propose annexation talks. This time the United States agreed to Houston's standing stipulation that, for serious negotiations to take place, the United States must provide military protection to Texas. U.S. naval forces were ordered to the Gulf of Mexico and U.S. troops were positioned on the southwest border close to Texas.

On April 11, 1844, Texas and the United States signed a treaty for annexation. Texas would enter the Union as a territory, not a state, under terms of the treaty. The United States would assume Texas' debt up to $10 million and would negotiate Texas' southwestern boundary with Mexico.

On June 8, 1844, the U.S. Senate rejected the treaty with a vote of 35-16, with much of the opposition coming from the slavery abolition wing of the Whig Party.

But **westward expansion** became a major issue in the U.S. presidential election that year. James K. Polk, the Democratic nominee, was a supporter of expansion, and the party's platform called for adding Oregon and Texas to the Union.

After Polk won the election in November, President Tyler declared that the people had spoken on the issue of annexation, and he resubmitted the matter to Congress.

Several bills were introduced in the U.S. House of Representatives containing various proposals.

In **February 1845**, the U.S. Congress approved a resolution that would bring Texas into the Union as a state. Texas would cede its public property, such as forts and custom houses, to the United States, but it could keep its public lands and must retain its public debt. The region could be divided into four new states in addition to the original Texas. And the United States would negotiate the Rio Grande boundary claim.

British officials asked the Texas government to delay consideration of the U.S. offer for 90 days to attempt to get Mexico to recognize the Republic. The delay did no good: Texans' minds were made up.

President Anson Jones, who succeeded Houston in 1844, called a convention to write a **state constitution** in Austin on July 4, 1845.

Mexico finally recognized Texas' independence, but the recognition was rejected. **Texas voters overwhelmingly accepted** the U.S. proposal and approved the new constitution in a referendum.

On **Dec. 29, 1845**, the U.S. Congress accepted the state constitution, and Texas became the 28th state in the Union. The first meeting of the Texas Legislature took place on Feb. 16, 1846.

1845–1860

The entry of Texas into the Union touched off the **War with Mexico**, a war that some historians now think was planned by President James K. Polk to obtain the vast American Southwest.

Gen. **Zachary Taylor** was sent to Corpus Christi, just above the Nueces River, in July 1845. In February 1846, right after Texas formally entered the Union, the general was ordered to move troops into the disputed area south of the Nueces to the mouth of the Rio Grande. Mexican officials protested the move, claiming the status of the territory was under negotiation.

After Gen. Taylor refused to leave, Mexican President **Mariano Paredes** declared the opening of a defensive war against the United States on April 24, 1846. After initial encounters at **Palo Alto and Resaca de la Palma**, both a few miles north of today's **Brownsville**, the war was fought south of the Rio Grande.

President Polk devised a plan to raise 50,000 volunteers from every section of the United States to fight the war. About 5,000 Texans saw action in Mexico.

Steamboats provided an important supply link for U.S. forces along the Rio Grande. Historical figures such as **Richard King**, founder of the legendary King Ranch, and **Mifflin Kenedy**, another rancher and businessman, first came to the **Lower Rio Grande Valley** as steamboat operators during the war.

Much farther up the Rio Grande, the war was hardly noticed. U.S. forces moved south from Santa Fe, which had been secured in December 1846. After a minor skirmish with Mexican forces north of El Paso, the U.S. military established American jurisdiction in this part of Texas.

Gen. **Winfield Scott** brought the war to a close in March 1847 with the capture of Mexico City.

When the **Treaty of Guadalupe Hidalgo** was signed on Feb. 2, 1848, the United States had acquired the American Southwest for development. And in Texas, the Rio Grande became an international boundary.

Europeans, of whom the vast majority were **German**, rather than Anglos, were the first whites to push the Texas frontier into west Central Texas after annexation. **John O. Meusebach** became leader of the German immigration movement in Texas, and he led a wagon train of some 120 settlers to the site of **Fredericksburg** in May 1846.

Germans also migrated to the major cities, such as San Antonio and Galveston, and by 1850 there were more people of German birth or parentage in Texas than there were Mexican-Texans.

The estimated population of 150,000 at annexation grew to 212,592, including 58,161 slaves, in the first U.S. census count in Texas in 1850.

As the state's population grew, the regions developed distinct population characteristics. The southeast and eastern sections attracted immigrants from the Lower South, the principal slaveholding states. Major plantations developed in these areas.

North Texas got more Upper Southerners and Midwesterners. These immigrants were mostly small farmers and few owned slaves.

Mexican-Texans had difficulty with Anglo immigrants. The **"cart war"** broke out in 1857. Mexican teamsters controlled the transportation of goods from the Gulf coast to San Antonio and could charge lower rates than their competition.

A campaign of terror was launched by Anglo haulers, especially around Goliad, in an attempt to drive the Mexican-Texans out of business. Intervention by the U.S. and Mexican governments finally brought the situation under control, but it stands as an example of the attitudes held by Anglo-Texans toward Mexican-Texans.

Cotton was by far the state's largest money crop, but corn, sweet potatoes, wheat and sugar also were produced. **Saw milling** and grain milling became the major industries, employing 40 percent of the manufacturing workers.

Land disputes and the public-debt issue were settled with the **Compromise of 1850**. Texas gave up claims to territory extending to Santa Fe and beyond in exchange for $10 million from the federal government. That sum was used to pay off the debt of the Republic.

Personalities, especially Sam Houston, dominated elections during early statehood, but, for most Texans, politics were unimportant. Voter turnouts were low in the 1850s until the movement toward secession gained strength.

Secession

Texas' population almost tripled in the decade between 1850 and 1860, when 604,215 people were counted, including 182,921 slaves. Many of these new settlers came from the Lower South, a region familiar with slavery. Although three-quarters of the Texas population and two-thirds of the farmers did not own slaves, slaveowners controlled 60 to 70 percent of the wealth of the state and dominated the politics.

In 1850, 41 percent of the state's officeholders were from the slaveholding class; a decade later, more than 50 percent of the officeholders had slaves.

In addition to the political power of the slaveholders, they also provided role models for new immigrants to the state. After these newcomers got their first land, they saw slave ownership as another step up the economic ladder, whether they owned slaves or not. Slave ownership was an economic goal.

This attitude prevailed even in areas of Texas where slaveholding was not widespread or even practical. These factors were the wind that fanned the flames of the secessionist movement throughout the late 1850s.

The appearance of the **Know-Nothing Party**, which based its platform on a pro-American, anti-immigrant foundation, began to move Texas toward party politics. Because of the large number of foreign-born settlers, the party attracted many Anglo voters. In 1854, the Know-Nothings elected candidates to city offices in San Antonio, and a year later, the mayor of Galveston was elected with the party's backing. Also in 1855, the Know-Nothings elected 20 representatives and five senators to the Legislature.

The successes spurred the **Democrats** to serious party organization for the first time. In 1857, **Hardin Runnels** was nominated for governor at the Democratic convention held in Waco. **Sam Houston** sought the governorship as an independent, but he also got Know-Nothing backing. Democrats were organized, however, and Houston was dealt the only election defeat in his political career.

Runnels was a strong states'-rights Democrat who irritated many Texans during his administration by advocating reopening the slave trade. His popularity on the frontier also dropped when Indian raids became more severe.

Most Texans still were ambivalent about secession. The Union was seen as a protector of physical and economic stability. No threats to person or property were perceived in remaining attached to the United States.

In 1859, Houston again challenged Runnels, basing his campaign on Unionism. Combined with Houston's personal popularity, his position on the secession issue apparently satisfied most voters, for they gave him a solid victory over the more radical Runnels. In

Compromise of 1850

Land given up in Compromise of 1850

WYOMING

COLORADO

NEW MEXICO

KANSAS

OKLAHOMA

TEXAS

Gulf of Mexico

0 ▬▬▬▬ 200 MILES

addition, Unionists **A.J. Hamilton** and **John H. Reagan** won the state's two congressional seats. Texans gave the states'-rights Democrats a sound whipping at the polls.

Within a few months, however, events were to change radically the political atmosphere of the state. On the frontier, the army could not control Indian raids, and with the later refusal of a Republican-controlled Congress to provide essential aid in fighting Indians, the federal government fell into disrepute.

Secessionists played on the growing distrust. Then in the summer of 1860, a series of fires in the cities around the state aroused fears that an abolitionist plot was afoot and that a slave uprising might be at hand — a traditional concern in a slaveholding society.

Vigilantes lynched blacks and Northerners across Texas, and a siege mentality developed.

When **Abraham Lincoln** was elected president (he was not on the ballot in Texas), secessionists went to work in earnest.

Pleas were made to Gov. Houston to call the Legislature into session to consider secession. Houston refused, hoping the passions would cool. They did not. Finally, **Oran M. Roberts** and other secessionist leaders issued a call to the counties to hold elections and send delegates to a convention in Austin. Ninety-two of 122 counties responded, and on Jan. 28, 1861, the meeting convened.

Only eight delegates voted against secession, while 166 supported it. An election was called for

Feb. 23, 1861, and the ensuing campaign was marked by intolerance and violence. Opponents of secession were often intimidated — except the governor, who courageously stumped the state opposing withdrawal from the Union. Houston also argued that if Texas did secede it should revert to its status as an independent republic and not join the Confederacy.

Only one-fourth of the state's population had been in Texas during the days of independence, and the argument carried no weight. On election day, 76 percent of 61,000 voters favored secession.

President Lincoln, who took office within a couple of weeks, reportedly sent the Texas governor a letter offering 50,000 federal troops to keep Texas in the Union. But after a meeting with other Unionists, Houston declined the offer. "I love Texas too well to bring strife and bloodshed upon her," the governor declared. On March 16, Houston refused to take an oath of loyalty to the Confederacy and was replaced in office by **Lt. Gov. Edward Clark.**

See page 28 for results of the Referendum on Ordinance of Secession of 1861.

Civil War

Texas did not suffer the devastation of its Southern colleagues in the Civil War. On but a few occasions did Union troops occupy territory in Texas, except in the El Paso area.

The state's cotton was important to the Confederate war effort because it could be transported from Gulf ports when other Southern shipping lanes were blockaded.

Some goods became difficult to buy, but unlike other states of the Confederacy, Texas still received consumer goods because of the trade that was carried on through Mexico during the war.

Although accurate figures are not available, historians estimate that between 70,000 and 90,000 Texans fought for the South, and between 2,000 and 3,000, including some former slaves, saw service in the Union army.

Texans became disenchanted with the Confederate government early in the war. State taxes were levied for the first time since the Compromise of 1850, and by war's end, the Confederacy had collected more than $37 million from the state.

But most of the complaints about the government centered on Brig. Gen. **Paul O. Hebert**, the Confederate commander of the Department of Texas.

In April 1862, Gen. Hebert declared martial law without notifying state officials. Opposition to the South's new conscription law, which exempted persons owning more than 15 slaves among other categories of exemptions, prompted the action.

The violence against suspected Union sympathizers reached its zenith with the **"Great Hanging at Gainesville,"** when 40 men were tried and hanged at Gainesville in October 1862. Two others were shot as they tried to escape. Although the affair reached its climax in Cooke County, men were killed in neighboring Grayson, Wise and Denton counties. Most were accused of treason or insurrection, but evidently few had actually conspired against the Confederacy, and many were innocent of the abolitionist sentiments for which they were tried.

In November 1862, Gen. Hebert prohibited the export of cotton except under government control, and this proved a disastrous policy. The final blow came when the commander failed to defend **Galveston** and it fell into Union hands in the fall of 1862.

Maj. Gen. **John B. Magruder**, who replaced Hebert, was much more popular. The new commander's first actions were to combat the Union offensive against Texas ports. Sabine Pass had been closed in September 1862 by the Union blockade, and Galveston was in Northern hands.

On Jan. 1, 1863, Magruder retook Galveston with the help of two steamboats lined with cotton bales. Sharpshooters aboard proved devastating in battles against the Union fleet. Three weeks later, Magruder used two other cotton-clad steamboats to break the Union blockade of Sabine Pass, and two of the state's major ports were reopened.

Late in 1863, the Union launched a major offensive against the Texas coast that was partly successful. On Sept. 8, however, Lt. **Dick Dowling** and 42 men fought off a 1,500-man Union invasion force at **Sabine Pass**. In a brief battle, Dowling's command sank two Union gunboats and put the other invasion ships to flight.

Federal forces were more successful at the mouth of the Rio Grande. On Nov. 1, 1863, 7,000 Union troops landed at **Brazos Santiago**, and five days later, Union forces entered Brownsville. Texas Unionists led by **E.J. Davis** were active in the Valley, moving as far upriver as Rio Grande City. Confederate Col. **John S. "Rip" Ford**, commanding state troops, finally pushed the Union soldiers out of Brownsville in July 1864, reopening the important port for the Confederacy.

Most Texans never saw a Union soldier during the war. The only ones they might have seen were in the **prisoner-of-war camps**. The largest, **Camp Ford**, near Tyler, housed 5,000 prisoners. Others operated in Kerr County and at Hempstead.

As the war dragged on, the mood of Texans changed. Those on the homefront began to feel they were sacrificing loved ones and suffering hardship so cotton speculators could profit. Public order broke down as refugees flocked to Texas. And slaves from other states were sent to Texas for safekeeping. When the war ended, there were an estimated 400,000 slaves in Texas, more than double the number counted in the 1860 census.

Morale was low in Texas in early 1865. Soldiers at Galveston and Houston began to mutiny. At Austin, Confederate soldiers raided the state treasury in March and found only $5,000 in specie. Units began breaking up, and the army was beginning to dissolve before Gen. **Robert E. Lee** surrendered at **Appomattox** in April 1865. He surrendered the Army of Northern Virginia, and while this assured Union victory, the surrender of other Confederate units was to follow until the last unit gave up in Oklahoma at the end of June.

The last land battle of the Civil War was fought at **Palmito Ranch** near Brownsville on May 13, 1865. After the Confederate's victory, they learned the governors of the Western Rebel states had authorized the disbanding of armies, and, a few days later, they accepted a truce with the Union forces.

A man representing the Freedman's Bureau stands between armed groups of white and black Americans. Wood carving by Alfred R. Waud, first published in Harper's Weekly on July 25, 1868. Image courtesy of the Library of Congress.

Reconstruction

On June 19, 1865, **Gen. Gordon Granger**, under the command of Gen. Philip M. Sheridan, arrived in Galveston with 1,800 federal troops to begin the Union occupation of Texas. Gen. Granger proclaimed the emancipation of the slaves.

A.J. Hamilton, a Unionist and former congressman from Texas, was named provisional governor by President Andrew Johnson.

Texas was in turmoil. Thousands of the state's men had died in the conflict. Indian raids had caused as much damage as the skirmishes with the Union army, causing the frontier to recede up to 100 miles eastward in some areas.

Even worse, confusion reigned. No one knew what to expect from the conquering forces.

Gen. Granger dispatched troops to the population centers of the state to restore civil authority. But only a handful of the 50,000 federal troops that came to Texas was stationed in the interior. Most were sent to the Rio Grande as a show of force against the French forces in Mexico, and clandestine aid was supplied to Mexican President Benito Juarez in his fight against the French and Mexican royalists.

The **frontier forts**, most of which were built during the early 1850s by the federal government to protect western settlements, had been abandoned by the U.S. Army after secession. These were not remanned, and a prohibition against a militia denied settlers a means of self-defense against Indian raids. *(For an overview of the frontier forts, see Texas Almanac 2004–2005 or www.TexasAlmanac.com.)*

Thousands of freed black slaves migrated to the cities, where they felt the federal soldiers would provide protection. Still others traveled the countryside, seeking family members and loved ones from whom they had been separated during the war.

The **Freedman's Bureau**, authorized by Congress in March 1865, began operation in September 1865 under Gen. E.M. Gregory. It had the responsibility to provide education, relief aid, labor supervision and judicial protection for the newly freed slaves.

The bureau was most successful in opening schools for blacks. Education was a priority because 95 percent of the freed slaves were illiterate.

The agency also was partially successful in getting blacks back to work on plantations under reasonable labor contracts.

Some plantation owners harbored hopes that they would be paid for their property loss when the slaves were freed. In some cases, the slaves were not released from plantations for up to a year.

To add to the confusion, some former slaves had the false notion that the federal government was going to parcel out the plantation lands to them. These blacks simply bided their time, waiting for the division of land.

Under pressure from President Johnson, Gov. Hamilton called for an election of delegates to a constitutional convention in January 1866. Hamilton told the gathering what was expected: Former slaves were to be given civil rights; the secession ordinance had to be repealed; Civil War debt had to be repudiated; and slavery was to be abolished with ratification of the Thirteenth Amendment.

Many delegates to the convention were former secessionists, and there was little support for compromise.

J.W. Throckmorton, a Unionist and one of eight men who had opposed secession in the convention of 1861, was elected chairman of the convention. But a coalition of conservative Unionists and Democrats controlled the meeting. As a consequence, Texas took limited steps toward appeasing the victorious North.

Slavery was abolished, and blacks were given some civil rights. But they still could not vote and were barred from testifying in trials against whites.

No action was taken on the Thirteenth Amendment because, the argument went, the amendment already had been ratified.

Otherwise, the constitution that was written followed closely the constitution of 1845. President Johnson in August 1866 accepted the new constitution and declared insurrection over in Texas, the last of the states of the Confederacy so accepted under **Presidential Reconstruction**.

Throckmorton was elected governor in June, along with other state and local officials. However, Texans had not learned a lesson from the war.

When the Legislature met, a series of laws limiting the rights of blacks were passed. In labor disputes, for example, the employers were to be the final arbitrators. The codes also bound an entire family's labor, not just the head of the household, to an employer.

Funding for black education would be limited to what could be provided by black taxpayers. Since few blacks owned land or had jobs, that provision effectively denied education to black children. However, the thrust of the laws and the attitude of the legislators was clear: Blacks simply were not to be considered full citizens.

Many of the laws later were overturned by the Freedman's Bureau or military authorities when, in March 1867, Congress began a **Reconstruction plan** of its own. The Southern states were declared to have no legal government and the former Confederacy was divided into districts to be administered by the military until satisfactory Reconstruction was effected. Texas and Louisiana made up the Fifth Military District under the command of Gen. Philip H. Sheridan.

Gov. Throckmorton clashed often with Gen. Sheridan. The governor thought the state had gone far enough in establishing rights for the newly freed slaves and other matters. Finally in August 1867, Throckmorton and other state officials were removed from office by Sheridan because they were considered an "impediment to the reconstruction." **E.M. Pease**, the former two-term governor and a Unionist, was named provisional governor by military authorities.

A **new constitutional convention** was called by Gen. Winfield S. Hancock, who replaced Sheridan in November 1867. For the first time, blacks were allowed to participate in the elections that selected delegates. A total of 59,633 whites and 49,497 blacks registered. The elected delegates met on June 1, 1868. Deliberations, however, got bogged down on partisan political matters, and the convention spent $200,000, an astronomical sum for the time.

This constitution of 1869, as it came to be known, granted full rights of citizenship to blacks, created a system of education, delegated broad powers to the governor and generally reflected the views of the state's Unionists.

Gov. Pease, disgusted with the convention and with military authorities, resigned in September 1869. Texas had no chief executive until January 1870, when the newly elected **E.J. Davis** took office.

Meeting in February 1870, the Legislature created a **state militia** under the governor's control; created a **state police force**, also controlled by the governor; postponed the 1870 general election to 1872; enabled the governor to appoint more than 8,500 local office-holders; and granted subsidized **bonds for railroad construction** at a rate of $10,000 a mile.

For the first time, a system of public education was created. The law required compulsory attendance at school for four months a year, set aside one-quarter of the state's annual revenue for education and levied a poll tax to support education. Schools also were to be integrated, which enraged many white Texans.

The Davis administration was the most unpopular

in Texas' history. In fairness, historians have noted that Davis did not feel that whites could be trusted to assure the rights of the newly freed blacks.

Violence was rampant in Texas. One study found that between the close of the Civil War and mid-1868, 1,035 people were murdered in Texas, including 486 blacks, mostly victims of white violence.

Gov. Davis argued that he needed broad police powers to restore order. Despite their unpopularity, the state police and militia — blacks made up 40 percent of the police and a majority of the militia — brought the lawlessness under control in many areas.

Democrats, aided by moderate Republicans, regained control of the Legislature in the 1872 elections, and, in 1873, the lawmakers set about stripping the governor of many of his powers.

The political turmoil ended with the gubernatorial election of 1873, when **Richard Coke** easily defeated Davis. Davis tried to get federal authorities to keep him in office, but President Grant refused to intervene.

In January of 1874, Democrats were in control of state government again. The end of Reconstruction concluded the turbulent Civil War era, although the attitudes that developed during the period lasted well into the 20th century.

Capital and Labor

A **constitutional convention** was called in 1875 to rewrite the 1869 constitution, a hated vestige of Radical Republican rule.

Every avenue to cutting spending at any level of government was explored. Salaries of public officials were slashed. The number of offices was reduced. Judgeships, along with most other offices, were made elective rather than appointive.

The state road program was curtailed, and the immigration bureau was eliminated.

Perhaps the worst change was the destruction of the statewide school system. The new charter created a "community system" without a power of taxation, and schools were segregated by race.

Despite the basic reactionary character, the new constitution also was visionary. Following the lead of several other states, the Democrats declared railroads to be common carriers and subject to regulation.

To meet the dual challenge of lawlessness and Indian insurrection, Gov. Coke in 1874 re-established the **Texas Rangers**.

While cowboys and cattle drives are romantic subjects for movies on the Texas of this period, the fact is that the simple cotton farmer was the backbone of the state's economy.

But neither the farmer nor the cattleman prospered throughout the last quarter of the 19th century. At the root of their problems was federal monetary policy and the lingering effects of the Civil War.

Although the issuance of paper money had brought about a business boom in the Union during the war, inflation also increased. Silver was demonetized in 1873. Congress passed the Specie Resumption Act in 1875 that returned the nation to the gold standard in 1879. Almost immediately a contraction in currency began. Between 1873 and 1891, the amount of national bank notes in circulation declined from $339 million to $168 million.

The reduction in the money supply was devastating in the defeated South. Land values plummeted. In 1870, Texas land was valued at an average of $2.62 an acre, compared with the national average of $18.26 an acre. With the money supply declining and the national economy growing, farm prices dropped. In 1870, a bushel of wheat brought $1. In the 1890s, wheat was 60 cents a bushel. Except for a brief spurt in the early 1880s, cattle prices followed those of crops.

Between 1880 and 1890, the number of farms in Texas doubled, but the number of tenants tripled. By 1900, almost half the state's farmers were tenants.

The much-criticized crop-lien system was developed following the war to meet credit needs of the small farmers. Merchants would extend credit to farmers through the year in exchange for liens on their crops. But the result of the crop-lien system, particularly when small farmers did not have enough acreage to operate efficiently, was a state of continual debt and despair.

The work ethic held that a man would benefit from his toil. When this apparently failed, farmers looked to the monetary system and the railroads as the causes. Their discontent hence became the source of the agrarian revolt that developed in the 1880s and 1890s.

The entry of the Texas & Pacific and the Missouri-Kansas-Texas **railroads** from the northeast changed trade patterns in the state.

Since the days of the Republic, trade generally had flowed to Gulf ports, primarily Galveston. Jefferson in Northeast Texas served as a gateway to the Mississippi River, but it never carried the volume of trade that was common at Galveston.

The earliest railroad systems in the state also were centered around Houston and Galveston, again directing trade southward. With the T&P and Katy lines, North Texas had direct access to markets in St. Louis and the East.

Problems developed with the railroads, however. In 1882, Jay Gould and Collis P. Huntington, owner of the Southern Pacific, entered into a secret agreement that amounted to creation of a monopoly of rail service in Texas. They agreed to stop competitive track extensions; to divide under a pooling arrangement freight moving from New Orleans and El Paso; to purchase all competing railroads in Texas; and to share the track between Sierra Blanca and El Paso.

The Legislature made weak attempts to regulate railroads, as provided by the state constitution. Gould thwarted an attempt to create a commission to regulate the railroads in 1881 with a visit to the state during the Legislature's debate.

The railroad tycoon subdued the lawmakers' interest with thinly disguised threats that capital would abandon Texas if the state interfered with railroad business.

As the 19th century closed, Texas remained an agricultural state. But the industrial base was growing. Between 1870 and 1900, the per capita value of manu-

Apache Indian prisoners are photographed during a rest stop beside the Southern Pacific Railway near the Nueces River in Texas on Sept. 10, 1886. Among those who are on their way to exile in Florida are Natchez (center front) and, to the right, Geronimo and his son in matching shirts. Photo by A.J. McDonald; courtesy of the U.S. National Archives and Records Administration.

factured goods in the United States rose from $109 to $171. In Texas, these per capita values increased from $14 to $39, but manufacturing values in Texas industry still were only one-half of annual agricultural values.

In 1886, a new breed of Texas politician appeared. **James Stephen Hogg** was not a Confederate veteran, and he was not tied to party policies of the past.

As a reform-minded attorney general, Hogg had actively enforced the state's few railroad regulatory laws. With farmers' support, Hogg was elected governor in 1890, and at the same time, a debate on the constitutionality of a **railroad commission** was settled when voters amended the constitution to provide for one. The reform mood of the state was evident. Voters returned only 22 of the 106 members of the Texas House in 1890.

Despite his reputation as a reformer, Hogg accepted the growing use of **Jim Crow laws** to limit blacks' access to public services. In 1891, the Legislature responded to public demands and required railroads to provide separate accommodations for blacks and whites.

The stage was being set for one of the major political campaigns in Texas history, however. Farmers did not think that Hogg had gone far enough in his reform program, and they were distressed that Hogg had not appointed a farmer to the railroad commission. Many began to look elsewhere for the solutions to their problems. The **People's Party** in Texas was formed in August 1891.

The 1892 general election was one of the most spirited in the state's history. Gov. Hogg's supporters shut conservative Democrats out of the convention in Houston, so the conservatives bolted and nominated railroad attorney George Clark for governor.

The People's Party, or **Populists**, for the first time had a presidential candidate, James Weaver, and a gubernatorial candidate, T.L. Nugent.

Texas Republicans also broke ranks. The party's strength centered in the black vote. After the death of former Gov. E.J. Davis in 1883, **Norris Wright Cuney**, a black, was party leader. Cuney was considered one of the most astute politicians of the period, and he controlled federal patronage.

White Republicans revolted against the black leadership, and these "Lily-whites" nominated **Andrew Jackson Houston**, son of Sam Houston, for governor.

Black Republicans recognized that alone their strength was limited, and throughout the latter part of the 19th century, they practiced fusion politics, backing candidates of third parties when they deemed it appropriate. Cuney led the Republicans into a coalition with the conservative Democrats in 1892, backing George Clark.

The election also marked the first time major Democratic candidates courted the black vote. Gov. Hogg's supporters organized black voter clubs, and the governor got about half of the black vote.

Black farmers were in a quandary. Their financial problems were the same as those small farmers who backed the Populists.

White Populists varied in their sympathy with the racial concerns of blacks. On the local level, some whites showed sympathy with black concerns about education, voting, and law enforcement. Black farmers also were reluctant to abandon the Republican Party because it was their only political base in Texas.

Hogg was re-elected in 1892 with a 43 percent plurality in a field of five candidates.

Populists continued to run well in state races until 1898. Historians have placed the beginning of the party's demise in the 1896 presidential election in which national Populists fused with the Democrats and supported **William Jennings Bryan**.

Although the Populist philosophy lived on, the party declined in importance after 1898. Farmers remained active in politics, but most returned to the Democratic Party, which usurped many of the Populists' issues.

Oil

Seldom can a people's history be profoundly changed by a single event on a single day. But Texas' entrance into the industrial age can be linked directly to the discovery of oil at **Spindletop**, three miles from **Beaumont**, on Jan. 10, 1901.

From that day, Texas' progress from a rural, agricultural state to a modern industrial giant was steady.

1900–1920

One of the greatest natural disasters ever to strike the state occurred on Sept. 8, 1900, when a **hurricane devastated Galveston**, killing 6,000 people. (For a more detailed account, see "After the Great Storm" in the *Texas Almanac 1998–1999*). In rebuilding from that disaster, Galveston's civic leaders fashioned the **commission form of municipal government**.

Amarillo later refined the system into the council-manager organization that is widely used today.

The great Galveston storm also reinforced arguments by Houston's leadership that an inland port should be built for protection against such tragedies and disruptions of trade. The **Houston Ship Channel** was soon a reality.

The reform spirit in government was not dead after the departure of Jim Hogg. In 1901, the Legislature prohibited the issuing of railroad passes to public officials. More than 270,000 passes were issued to officials that year, and farmers claimed that the free rides increased their freight rates and influenced public policy as well.

In 1903, state Sen. **A.W. Terrell** got a major **election-reform law** approved, a measure that was further modified two years later. A was established to replace a hodgepodge of practices for nominating candidates that had led to charges of irregularities after each election.

Also in the reform spirit, the Legislature in 1903 prohibited abuse of **child labor** and set minimum ages at which children could work in certain industries. The action preceded federal child-labor laws by 13 years.

However, the state, for the first time, imposed the **poll tax** as a requirement for voting. Historians differ on whether the levy was designed to keep blacks or poor whites — or both — from voting. Certainly the poll tax cut election turnouts. Black voter participation dropped from about 100,000 in the 1890s to an estimated 5,000 in 1906.

The Democratic State Executive Committee also recommended that county committees limit participa-

Children who worked as messengers in San Antonio in 1913. The messengers and their contact with Red Light districts in most large cities in Texas was considered one of the worst phases of child labor in the state. Photo by Lewis Wickes Hine; courtesy of the Library of Congress.

tion in primaries to whites only, and most accepted the suggestion.

The election of **Thomas M. Campbell** as governor in 1906 marked the start of a progressive period in Texas politics. Interest revived in controlling corporate influence.

Under Campbell, the state's **antitrust laws** were strengthened and a **pure food and drug bill** was passed. Life insurance companies were required to invest in Texas 75 percent of their reserves on policies in the state. Less than one percent of the reserves had been invested prior to the law.

Some companies left Texas. But the law was beneficial in the capital-starved economy. In 1904, voters amended the constitution to allow the state to charter **banks** for the first time, and this eased some of the farmers' credit problems. In 1909, the Legislature approved a bank-deposit insurance plan that predated the federal program.

With corporate influence under acceptable control, attention turned to the issue of prohibition of alcohol. Progressives and prohibitionists joined forces against the conservative establishment to exert a major influence in state government for the next two decades.

Prohibitionists had long been active in Texas. They had the **local-option clause** written into the Constitution of 1876, which allowed counties or their subdivisions to be voted dry. But in 1887, a prohibition amendment to the state constitution had been defeated by a two-to-one margin, and public attention had turned to other problems.

In the early 20th century, the prohibition movement gathered strength. Most of Texas already was dry because of local option. When voters rejected a prohibition amendment by a slim margin in 1911, the state had 167 dry counties and 82 wet or partially wet counties. The heavily populated counties, however, were wet. Prohibition continued to be a major issue.

Problems along the U.S.-Mexico border escalated in 1911 as the decade-long **Mexican Revolution** broke out. Soon the revolutionaries controlled some northern Mexican states, including Chihuahua. Juarez and El Paso were major contact points. El Paso residents could stand on rooftops to observe the fighting between revolutionaries and government troops. Some Americans were killed.

After pleas to the federal government got no action, Gov. Oscar Colquitt sent state militia and Texas Rangers into the Valley in 1913 to protect Texans after Matamoros fell to the rebels. Unfortunately, the Rangers killed many innocent Mexican-Texans during the operation. In addition to problems caused by the fighting and raids, thousands of Mexican refugees flooded Texas border towns to escape the violence of the revolution.

In 1914, **James E. Ferguson** entered Texas politics and for the next three decades, "Farmer Jim" was one of the most dominating and colorful figures on the political stage. Ferguson, a banker from Temple, skirted the prohibition issue by pledging to veto any legislation pertaining to alcoholic beverages.

His strength was among farmers, however. Sixty-two percent of Texas' farmers were tenants, and Ferguson pledged to back legislation to limit tenant rents. Ferguson also was a dynamic orator. He easily won the primary and beat out three opponents in the general election.

Ferguson's first administration was successful. The Legislature passed the law limiting tenants' rents, although it was poorly enforced, and aid to rural schools was improved.

In 1915, the border problems heated up. A Mexican national was arrested in the Lower Rio Grande Valley carrying a document outlining plans for Mexican-Americans, Indians, Japanese and blacks in Texas and the Southwest to eliminate all Anglo males over age 16 and create a new republic. The document, whose author was never determined, started a bloodbath in the Valley. Mexican soldiers participated in raids across the Rio Grande, and Gov. Ferguson sent in the Texas Rangers.

Historians differ on the number of people who were killed, but a safe assessment would be hundreds. Gov. Ferguson and Mexican President Venustiano Carranza met at Nuevo Laredo in November 1915 in an attempt to improve relations. The raids continued.

Pancho Villa raided Columbus, N.M., in early 1916; two small Texas villages in the Big Bend, Glenn Springs and Boquillas, also were attacked. In July, President **Woodrow Wilson** determined that the hostilities were critical and activated the National Guard. Soon 100,000 U.S. troops were stationed along the border. **Fort Bliss** in El Paso housed 60,000 men, and **Fort Duncan** near Eagle Pass was home to 16,000.

With the exception of Gen. John J. Pershing's pursuit of Villa into Northern Mexico, few U.S. troops crossed into Mexico. But the service along the border gave soldiers basic training that was put to use when the United States entered World War I in 1917.

Ferguson was easily re-elected in 1916, and he worked well with the Legislature the following year. But after the Legislature adjourned, the governor got into a dispute with the board of regents of the **University of Texas**. The disagreement culminated in the governor's vetoing all appropriations for the school. As the controversy swirled, the Travis County grand jury indicted Ferguson for misappropriation of funds and for embezzlement. In July 1917, Speaker of the Texas House F.O. Fuller called a special session of the Legislature to consider **impeachment** of the governor.

The Texas House voted 21 articles of impeachment, and the Senate in August 1917 convicted Ferguson on 10 of the charges. The Senate's judgment not only removed Ferguson from office, but also barred him from seeking office again. Ferguson resigned the day before the Senate rendered the decision in an attempt to avoid the prohibition against seeking further office.

Texas participated actively in **World War I**. Almost 200,000 young Texans, including 31,000 blacks, volunteered for military service, and 450 Texas women served in the nurses' corps. Five thousand lost their lives overseas, either fighting or in the **influenza pandemic** that swept the globe.

Texas also was a major training ground during the conflict, with 250,000 soldiers getting basic training in the state. On the negative side, the war frenzy opened a period of intolerance and nativism in the state. German-Texans were suspect because of their ancestry. A law was passed to prohibit speaking against the war effort. Persons who failed to participate in patriotic activities often were punished. Gov. William P. Hobby even vetoed the appropriation for the German department at the University of Texas.

Ferguson's removal from office was a devastating blow to the anti-prohibitionists. Word that the former governor had received a $156,000 loan from members of the brewers' association while in office provided ammunition for the progressives. In February 1918, a special session of the Legislature prohibited saloons within a 10-mile radius of military posts and ratified the national prohibition amendment, which had been introduced in Congress by Texas Sen. **Morris Sheppard**.

Women also were given the **right to vote in state primaries** at the same session.

Although national prohibition was to become effective in early 1920, the Legislature presented a prohibition amendment to voters in May 1919, and it was approved, bringing prohibition to Texas earlier than to the rest of the nation. At the same time, a woman suffrage amendment, which would have granted women the right to vote in all elections, was defeated.

Although World War I ended in November 1918, it brought many changes to Texas. Rising prices during the war had increased the militancy of labor unions.

Blacks also became more militant after the war.

Discrimination against black soldiers led in 1917 to a riot in Houston in which several people were killed.

With the election of Mexican President Alvaro Obregón in 1920, the fighting along the border subsided. In 1919, state Rep. J.T. Canales of Brownsville initiated an investigation of the **Texas Rangers'** role in the border problems. As a result of the study, the Rangers' manpower was reduced from 1,000 members to 76, and stringent limitations were placed on the agency's activities. Standards for members of the force also were upgraded.

By 1920, although still a rural state, the face of Texas was changing. Nearly one-third of the population was in the cities. **Pat M. Neff** won the gubernatorial election of 1920, beating Sen. Joseph W. Bailey in the primary. As a former prosecuting attorney in McLennan County, Neff made law and order the major thrust of his administration. During his tenure the state took full responsibility for developing a **highway system**, a **gasoline tax** was imposed, and a state **park board** was established.

In 1921, a group of West Texans threatened to form a new state because Neff vetoed the creation of a new college in their area. Two years later, **Texas Technological College** (now Texas Tech University) was authorized in Lubbock and opened its doors in 1925.

Although still predominantly a rural state, Texas cities were growing. In 1900, only 17 percent of the population lived in urban areas; by 1920, that figure had almost doubled to 32 percent. A discontent developed with the growth of the cities. Rural Texans had long seen cities as hotbeds of vice and immorality. Simple rural values were cherished, and it seemed that those values were threatened in a changing world. After World War I, this transition accelerated.

KKK and Minorities

In addition, "foreigners" in the state became suspect; nativism reasserted itself. German-Texans were associated with the enemy in the war, and Mexican-Texans were mostly Roman Catholics and likened to the troublemakers along the border. Texas was a fertile ground for the new **Ku Klux Klan** that entered the state in late 1920. The Klan's philosophy was a mixture of patriotism, law-and-order, nativism, white supremacy and Victorian morals. Its influence spread quickly across the state, and reports of Klan violence and murder were rampant.

Prohibition had brought a widespread disrespect for law. Peace officers and other officials often ignored speakeasies and gambling. The Klan seemed to many Texans to be an appropriate instrument for restoring law and order and for maintaining morality in towns and cities. By 1922, many of the state's large communities were under direct Klan influence, and a Klan-backed candidate, Earle Mayfield, was elected to the U.S. Senate, giving Texas the reputation as the most powerful Klan bastion in the Union. Hiram Wesley Evans of Dallas also was elected imperial wizard of the national Klan in that year.

The Klan became more directly involved in politics and planned to elect the next governor in 1924. Judge Felix Robertson of Dallas got the organization's backing in the Democratic primary. Former governor Jim Ferguson filed to run for the office, but the Texas

Supreme Court ruled that he could not because of his impeachment conviction. So Ferguson placed his wife, Miriam A. Ferguson, on the ballot. Several other prominent Democrats also entered the race.

The Fergusons made no secret that Jim would have a big influence on his wife's administration. One campaign slogan was, "Two governors for the price of one." Mrs. Ferguson easily won the runoff against Robertson when many Texans decided that "Ferguson-ism" was preferable to the Klan in the governor's office.

Minorities began organizing in Texas to seek their civil rights. The National Association for the Advancement of Colored People (**NAACP**) opened a Texas chapter in 1912, and by 1919, there were chapters in 31 Texas communities. Similarly, Mexican-Texans formed Orden Hijos de America in 1921, and in 1929, the **League of United Latin American Citizens** (LU-LAC) was organized in Corpus Christi.

The Klan dominated the Legislature in 1923, passing a law barring blacks from participation in the Democratic primary. Although blacks had in fact been barred from voting in primaries for years, this law gave **Dr. Lawrence A. Nixon**, a black dentist from El Paso, the opportunity to go to court to fight the all-white primary. In 1927, the U.S. Supreme Court overturned the statute, but that was only the beginning of several court battles, which were not resolved until 1944.

Disgruntled Democrats and Klansmen tried to beat Mrs. Ferguson in the general election in 1924, but she was too strong. Voters also sent 91 new members to the Texas House, purging it of many of the Klan-backed representatives. After that election, the Klan's power ebbed rapidly in Texas.

Mrs. Ferguson named Emma Grigsby Meharg as Texas' first woman secretary of state in 1925. The governors Ferguson administration was stormy. Jim was accused of cronyism in awarding highway contracts and in other matters. And "Ma" returned to her husband's practice of liberal clemency for prisoners. In two years, Mrs. Ferguson extended clemency to 3,595 inmates.

Although Jim Ferguson was at his bombastic best in the 1926 Democratic primary, young Attorney General **Dan Moody** had little trouble winning the nomination and the general election.

At age 33, Moody was the youngest person ever to become governor of Texas. Like many governors during this period, he was more progressive than the Legislature, and much of his program did not pass. Moody was successful in some government reorganization. He also cleaned up the highway department, which had been criticized under the Fergusons, and abandoned the liberal clemency policy for prisoners. And Moody worked at changing Texas' image as an anti-business state. "The day of the political trust-buster is gone," he told one Eastern journalist.

Progressives and prohibitionists still had a major influence on the Democratic Party, and 1928 was a watershed year for them. Moody easily won renomination and re-election. But the state party was drifting away from the direction of national Democrats. When **Al Smith**, a wet and a Roman Catholic, won the presidential nomination at the national Democratic convention in Houston, Texans were hard-pressed to remain faithful to the "party of the fathers." Moody, who had been considered a potential national figure, ruined his political career trying to straddle the fence, angering both wets and drys, Catholics and Protestants. Former governor O.B. Colquitt led an exodus of so-called "**Hoovercrats**" from the state Democratic convention in 1928, and for the first time in its history, Texas gave its electoral votes to a Republican, Herbert Hoover, in the general election.

Through the 1920s, oil continued to increase in importance in Texas' economy. New discoveries were made at Mexia in 1920, Luling in 1922, Big Lake in Reagan Conty in 1923, in the Wortham Field in 1924 and in Borger in 1926. But oil still did not dominate the state's economic life.

As late as **1929**, meat packing, cottonseed processing and various milling operations exceeded the added value of petroleum refining. And as the 1920s ended, lumbering and food processing shared major economic roles with the petroleum industry. During the decade, Texas grew between 35 and 42 percent of U.S. cotton and 20-30 percent of the world crop. Irrigation and mechanization opened the South Plains to cotton growing. Eight years later, more than 1.1 million bales were grown in the region, mostly around Lubbock.

But Texas, with the rest of the nation, was on the threshhold of a major economic disaster that would have irreversible consequences. The **Great Depression** was at hand.

Depression Years

Historians have noted that the state's economic collapse was not as severe as that which struck the industrialized states. Texas' economy had sputtered through the decade of the 1920s, primarily because of the fluctuation of the price of cotton and other agricultural products. But agricultural prices were improving toward the end of the decade.

The Fergusons attempted a political comeback in the gubernatorial election of 1930. But Texans elected **Ross S. Sterling**, the founder of Humble Oil Co. Early in the Depression, Texans remained optimistic that the economic problems were temporary, another of the cyclical downturns the nation experienced periodically. Indeed, some Texans even felt that the hardships would be beneficial, ridding the economy of speculators and poor businessmen. Those attitudes gave way to increasing concern as the poor business conditions dragged on.

A piece of good luck turned into a near economic disaster for the state in late 1930. **C.M. "Dad" Joiner** struck oil near Kilgore, and soon the **East Texas oil boom** was in full swing. Millions of barrrels of new oil flooded the market, making producers and small landowners wealthy. Soon the glut of new oil drove market prices down from $1.10 a barrel in 1930 to 10 cents in 1931. Many wells had to be shut in around the state because they could not produce oil profitably at the low prices.

The Texas Railroad Commission attempted in the spring of 1931 to control production through proration, which assigned production quotas to each well (called the allowable). The first proration order limited each well to about 1,000 barrels a day of production. **Proration** had two goals: to protect reserves through conservation and to maintain prices by limiting production. But, on July 28, a federal court ruled that proration was an illegal attempt to fix prices.

In August 1931, Gov. Sterling placed four counties of the East Texas field under martial law and briefly shut down oil production there altogether. A federal court later ruled the governor's actions illegal. Gov. Sterling was roundly criticized for sending troops. Opponents said the action was taken to aid the major oil companies to the disadvantage of independent producers.

In 1932, Gov. Sterling appointed **Ernest O. Thompson** to a vacancy on the railroad commission. Thompson, who had led a coalition in favor of output regulation, is credited with fashioning a compromise between independents and major oil companies. In April 1933, the railroad commission prorated production on the basis, in part, of bottom-hole pressure in each well, and the courts upheld this approach. But enforcement remained a problem.

Finally in 1935, Texas' Sen. **Tom Connally** authored the Hot Oil Act, which involved the federal government in regulation by prohibiting oil produced in violation of state law from being sold in interstate commerce. Thereafter, Texas' producers accepted the concept of proration. Since Texas was the nation's largest oil producer, the railroad commission could set the national price of oil through proration for several decades thereafter.

Despite these problems, the oil boom helped East Texas weather the Depression better than other parts of the state. Farmers were hit particularly hard in 1931. Bumper crops had produced the familiar reduction in prices. Cotton dropped from 18 cents per pound in 1928 to six cents in 1931. That year Louisiana Gov. **Huey Long** proposed a ban on growing cotton in 1932 to eliminate the surplus. The Louisiana legislature enacted the ban, but Texas was the key state to the plan since it led the nation in cotton production. Gov. Sterling was cool to the idea, but responded to public support of it by calling a special session of the Legislature. The lawmakers passed a **cotton acreage limitation** bill in 1931, but the law was declared unconstitutional the following year.

One feature of the Depression had become the number of transients drifting from city to city looking for work. Local governments and private agencies tried to provide relief for the unemployed, but the effort was soon overwhelmed by the number of persons needing help. In Houston, blacks and Mexican-Texans were warned not to apply for relief because there was not enough money to take care of whites, and many Mexicans returned to Mexico voluntarily and otherwise.

To relieve the local governments, Gov. Sterling proposed a bond program to repay counties for highways they had built and to start a public-works program. Texans' long-held faith in self-reliance and rugged individualism was put to a severe test.

By **1932**, many were looking to the federal government to provide relief from the effects of the Depression.

U.S. Speaker of the House **John Nance Garner** of Texas was a presidential candidate when the Democrats held their national convention. To avoid a dead-locked convention, Garner maneuvered the Texans to change strategy. On the fourth ballot, the Texas delegation voted for the eventual nominee, New York Gov. **Franklin D. Roosevelt**. Garner got the second place on the ticket that swept into office in the general election.

In Texas, **Miriam Ferguson** was successful in unseating Gov. Sterling in the Democratic primary, winning by about 4,000 votes. Her second administration was less turbulent than the first. State government costs were reduced, and voters approved $20 million in so-called "bread bonds" to help provide relief. In 1933, **horse racing** came to the state, authorized through a rider on an appropriations bill legalizing pari-mutuel betting. The law was repealed in 1937. Prohibition also was repealed in 1933, although much of Texas remained dry under the **local-option** laws and the prohibition against open saloons.

State government faced a series of financial problems during Mrs. Ferguson's second term. The annual deficit climbed to $14 million, and the state had to default on the interest payments on some bonds. Voters aggravated the situation by approving a $3,000 **homestead exemption**. Many property owners were losing their homes because they could not pay taxes. And while the exemption saved their homesteads, it worsened the state's financial problems.

Many Texas banks failed during the Depression, as did banks nationally. One of Roosevelt's first actions was to declare a national bank holiday in 1933. Gov. Ferguson closed state banks at the same time, although she had to "assume" authority that was not in the law.

The New Deal

In Washington, Texans played an important role in shaping Roosevelt's **New Deal**. As vice president, Garner presided over the Senate and maneuvered legislation through the upper house. **Texans** also chaired major committees in the House: **Sam Rayburn**, Interstate and Foreign Commerce; **Hatton W. Sumners**, Judiciary; **Fritz G. Lanham**, Public Buildings and Grounds; **J.J. Mansfield**, Rivers and Harbors; and **James P. Buchanan**, Appropriations. With this influence, the Texas delegation supported the president's early social programs. In addition, **Jesse Jones** of Houston served as director of the Reconstruction Finance Corporation, the Federal Loan Administration and as Secretary of Commerce. Jones was one of the most influential men in Washington and second only to Roosevelt in wielding financial power to effect recovery.

Poor conservation practices had left many of the state's farmlands open to erosion. During the **Dust Bowl** days of the early and mid-1930s, for example, the weather bureau in Amarillo reported 192 dust storms within a three-year period. Cooperation between state and federal agencies helped improve farmers' conservation efforts and reduced the erosion problem by the end of the decade.

Mrs. Ferguson did not seek re-election in 1934, and Attorney General **James V. Allred** was elected. Under his administration, several social-welfare programs were initiated, including old-age pensions, teachers' retirement and worker's compensation. Allred was re-elected in 1936.

Some of the New Deal's luster dimmed when the

nation was struck by another recession in 1937.

Although Texas' economic condition improved toward the end of the decade, a full recovery was not realized until the beginning of World War II — when the state went through another industrial revolution.

Tragedy struck the small East Texas town of **New London** in Rusk County on March 18, 1937. At 3:05 p.m., natural gas, which had seeped undetected into an enclosed area beneath a school building from a faulty pipe connection, exploded when a shop teacher turned on a sander. Approximately 298 of the 540 students and teachers in the school died, and all but 130 of the survivors were injured. The disaster prompted the Legislature to pass a law requiring that a malodorant be added to gas so leaks could be detected by smell.

National Youth Administration trainees for war jobs watch the Navy planes they are learning to service at the Naval Air Base at Corpus Christi. Photo taken in August 1942 by Howard R. Hollem; courtesy of the Library of Congress.

In 1938, voters elected one of the most colorful figures in the state's political history to the governor's office. **W. Lee "Pappy" O'Daniel**, a flour salesman and leader of a radio hillbilly band, came from nowhere to defeat a field of much better known candidates in the Democratic primary and to easily win the general election. When re-elected two years later, O'Daniel became the first candidate to poll more than one million votes in a Texas election.

But O'Daniel's skills of state did not equal his campaigning ability, and throughout his administration, the governor and the Legislature were in conflict. In early **1941**, long-time U.S. Senator Morris Sheppard died, and O'Daniel wanted the office. He appointed Andrew Jackson Houston, Sam Houston's aged son, to fill the vacancy. Houston died after only 24 days in office. O'Daniel won the special election for the post in a close race with a young congressman, **Lyndon B. Johnson**.

Lt. Gov. **Coke R. Stevenson** succeeded O'Daniel as governor and brought a broad knowledge of government to the office. Stevenson was elected to two full terms. Thanks to frugal management and greatly increasing revenues during the war years, he left the state treasury with a surplus in 1947. Voters also solved the continuing deficit problem by approving a pay-as-you-go amendment to the constitution in 1942. It requires the state comptroller to certify that tax revenues will be available to support appropriations. Otherwise the money cannot be spent.

World War II

As in every war after Texas entered the Union, young Texans flocked to military service when the United States entered World War II. More than 750,000 served, including 12,000 women in the auxiliary services. In December 1942, U.S. Secretary of the Navy Frank Knox said Texas contributed the largest percentage of its male population to the armed forces of any state. Thirty Texans won Congressional Medals of Honor in the fighting. **Audie Murphy**, a young farm boy from Farmersville, became one of the most decorated soldiers of the war. Dallas-born **Sam Dealey** was the most-decorated Navy man.

Important contributions also were made at home. Texas was the site of 15 training posts, at which more than one and a quarter million men were trained, and of several prisoner-of-war camps.

World War II irrevocably changed the face of Texas. During the decade of the 1940s, the state's population switched from predominantly rural to 60 percent urban. The number of **manufacturing** workers almost doubled. And as had been the dream of Texas leaders for more than a century, the state began to attract new industries.

Conservatives vs. Liberals

The state's politics became increasingly controlled by conservative Democrats after Gov. Allred left office. In 1946, **Beauford H. Jester**, a member of the railroad commission, gained the governorship. Under Jester in 1947, the Legislature passed the state's right-to-work law, prohibiting mandatory union membership, and reorganized public education with passage of the **Gilmer-Aikin Act**.

During the Jester administration several major constitutional amendments were adopted. Also, one of Texas' greatest tragedies occurred on April 16, 1947, when the French ship SS *Grandcamp,* carrying a load of ammonium nitrate, exploded at **Texas City**. More than 500 died and 4,000 sustained injuries. Property damage exceeded $200 million.

In **1948**, Sen. W. Lee O'Daniel did not seek re-election. Congressman Lyndon Johnson and former Gov. Coke Stevenson vied for the Democratic nomination. In the runoff, Johnson won by a mere **87 votes** in the closest — and most hotly disputed — statewide election in Texas' history. Johnson quickly rose to a leadership position in the U.S. Senate, and, with House Speaker Sam Rayburn, gave Texas substantial influence in national political affairs.

Although re-elected in 1948, Jester died in July 1949, the only Texas governor to die in office, and Lt. Gov. **Allan Shivers** succeeded him. During Shivers' administration, state spending more than doubled, reaching $805.7 million in 1956, as the governor increased appropriations for public-health institutions, school salaries, retirement benefits, highways and old-age pensions.

Shivers broke with tradition, successfully winning three full terms as governor after completing Jester's unexpired term. Shivers also led a revolt by Texas Democrats against the national party in **1952**. The governor, who gained both the Democratic and Republican nominations for the office under the law that allowed cross-filing that year, supported Republican Dwight Eisenhower for the presidency. Many Texas Democrats broke with the national party over the so-called "**Tidelands issue.**" Texas claimed land 12 miles out into the Gulf as state lands. The issue was important because revenue from oil and natural gas production from the area supported public education in the state.

Major oil companies also backed Texas' position because state royalties on minerals produced from the land were much lower than federal royalties. President Harry S. Truman vetoed legislation that would have given Texas title to the land. Democratic presidential nominee Adlai Stevenson was no more sympathetic to the issue, and Texas gave its electoral votes to Republican Dwight Eisenhower in an election that attracted a two million-vote turnout for the first time in Texas. President Eisenhower signed a measure into law guaranteeing Texas' tidelands.

Scandal struck state government in 1954 when irregularities were discovered in the handling of funds in the veterans' land program in the General Land Office. Land Commissioner Bascom Giles was convicted of several charges and sent to prison. Several insurance companies also went bankrupt in the mid-1950s, prompting a reorganization of the State Board of Insurance in 1957.

In 1954, the U.S. Supreme Court ruled unconstitutional the segregation of schools, and for the next quarter-century, **school integration** became a major political issue. By the late 1960s, most institutions were integrated, but the state's major cities continued to wage court battles against forced busing of students to attain racial balance. Blacks and Mexican-Texans also made gains in voting rights during the 1950s.

Shivers had easily defeated **Ralph W. Yarborough** in the Democratic primary in 1952, but the divisions between the party's loyalists and those who bolted ranks to join Republicans in presidential races were growing. Shivers barely led the first 1954 primary over Yarborough and won the nomination with 53 percent of the vote in the runoff. Yarborough ran an equally close race against **Price Daniel**, a U.S. Senator who sought the governorship in 1956. Upon election as governor, Daniel left the Senate, and Yarborough won a special election to fill the vacancy in 1957. Yarborough won re-election in 1964 before losing to **Lloyd Bentsen** in 1970 in the Democratic primary. Although a liberal, Yarborough proved to be unusually durable in Texas' conservative political climate.

The state budget topped $1 billion for the first time in 1958. The Legislature met for 205 days in regular and special sessions in 1961–62 and levied, over Gov. Daniel's opposition, the state's first broad-based **sales tax in 1962**.

Technological Growth

Through the 1950s and 1960s, Texas' industrial base had expanded and diversified. Petroleum production and refining remained the cornerstones, but other industries grew. Attracted by cheap electricity, the aluminum industry came to Texas. Starting from the base developed during World War II, defense industries and associated high-tech firms, specializing in electronics and computers, centered on the Dallas–Fort Worth area and Houston. One of the most important scientific breakthroughs of the century came in 1958 in Dallas. **Jack Kilby**, an engineer at **Texas Instruments**, developed and patented the integrated circuit that became the central part of computers.

Sen. Lyndon Johnson unsuccessfully sought the Democratic presidential nomination in 1960, and **John F. Kennedy** subsequently selected the Texan as his running mate. Johnson is credited with keeping several Southern states, including Texas, in the Democratic column in the close election. Kennedy was a Roman Catholic and a liberal, a combination normally rejected by the Southern states. When Johnson left the Senate to assume his new office in 1961, **John Tower** won a special election that attracted more than 70 candidates. Tower became the first Republican since Reconstruction to serve as a Texas senator.

During the early 1960s, Harris County was chosen as the site for the National Aeronautics and Space Administration's manned spacecraft center. The acquisition of **NASA** further diversified Texas' industrial base.

In 1962, **John B. Connally**, a former aide to LBJ and Secretary of the Navy under Kennedy, returned to Texas to seek the governorship. Gov. Daniel sought an unprecedented fourth term and was defeated in the Democratic primary. Connally won a close Democratic runoff over liberal **Don Yarborough** and was elected easily. As governor, Connally concentrated on improving **public education, state services** and **water development**. He was re-elected in 1964 and 1966.

The Assassination

One of the major tragedies in the nation's history occurred in Dallas on **Nov. 22, 1963**, when President Kennedy was assassinated while riding in a motorcade. Gov. Connally also was seriously wounded. Lyndon Johnson was administered the oath of the presidency by Federal Judge Sarah T. Hughes of Dallas aboard Air Force One at Love Field. Lee Harvey Oswald was arrested for the murder of the president on the afternoon of the assassination, but Oswald was killed by Dallas nightclub operator Jack Ruby two days later.

An extensive investigation into the assassination of President Kennedy was conducted by the Warren Commission. The panel concluded that Oswald was the killer and that he acted alone. Ruby, who was convicted of killing Oswald, died of cancer in the Dallas County jail in 1967 while the case was being appealed.

The assassination damaged the Republican Party in Texas, however. Building strength in Texas' conservative political atmosphere in 1962, eight Republicans, the most in decades, had been elected to the Texas House. And two Republicans — Ed Foreman of Odessa and Bruce Alger of Dallas — served in Congress. All were defeated in the 1964 general election.

In the emotional aftermath of the tragedy, Johnson, who won the presidency outright in a **landslide election in 1964**, persuaded the Congress to pass a series of civil-rights and social-welfare programs that changed the face of the nation. Texas was particularly affected by the civil-rights legislation and a series of lawsuits challenging election practices. During the 1960s, the state constitutional limitation of urban representation in the Legislature was overturned. The poll tax was declared unconstitutional, and the practice of electing officials from at-large districts fell to the so-called "one-man, one-vote" ruling. As a result, more Republican, minority and liberal officials were elected, particularly from urban areas. In 1966, **Curtis Graves** and **Barbara Jordan** of Houston and **Joe Lockridge** of Dallas became the first blacks to serve in the Texas Legislature since 1898.

Lyndon Johnson did not seek re-election in 1968. The nation had become involved in an unpopular war in Vietnam, and Johnson bowed out of the race in the interest of national unity.

Sharpstown Scandal

Democrats stayed firmly in control of state government. **Preston Smith** was elected governor, and **Ben Barnes** gained the lieutenant governorship. Both were re-elected in 1970. Although state spending continued to increase, particularly on education, the Legislature otherwise was quiet. A minimum-wage law was approved, and public kindergartens were authorized in 1969.

At a special session, the **Sharpstown scandal**, one of the state's major scandals developed. Gov. Smith allowed the lawmakers to consider special banking legislation supported by Houston banker Frank Sharp. Several public officials were implicated in receiving favors from the banker for seeing that the legislation passed. Texas House Speaker Gus Mutscher and Rep. Tommy Shannon were convicted of conspiracy to accept bribes in a trial held in Abilene.

Voters in **1972** demanded a new leadership in the state capital. Smith and Barnes were defeated in the Democratic primary, and **Dolph Briscoe** was elected governor. In the fall, Texans gave presidential candidate Richard Nixon the state's electoral votes. Nixon carried 246 counties over Democrat George McGovern and received more than 65 percent of the popular vote.

The Legislature in 1973 was dominated by a reform atmosphere in the wake of the Sharpstown scandal. Price Daniel Jr., son of the former governor, was selected speaker of the House, and several laws concerning ethics and disclosure of campaign donations and spending were passed. Open meetings and open records statutes also were approved.

By 1970, Texas had become an even more urban state. The census found almost 11.2 million people in the state, ranking it sixth nationally. Three Texas cities, Houston, Dallas and San Antonio, were among the 10 largest in the nation.

Through the first half of the 1970s, several major changes were made in state policy. **Liquor-by-the-drink** became legal and the age of majority was lowered from 20 to 18, giving young people the right to vote. Also, the state's first Public Utilities Commission was created, hearing its initial case in September 1976.

Prosperity

Texas entered a period of unparalleled prosperity in 1973 when the Organization of Petroleum Exporting Countries (OPEC) boycotted the U.S. market. Severe energy shortages resulted, and the price of oil and natural gas skyrocketed. The federal government had allowed foreign oil to be imported through the 1960s, severely reducing the incentives to find and produce domestic oil. Consequently, domestic producers could not compensate for the loss in foreign oil as a result of the boycott.

The Texas Railroad Commission had long complained about the importation of foreign oil, and in 1972, the panel had removed proration controls from wells in the state, allowing 100 percent production. For the rest of the decade, domestic producers mounted a major exploration effort, drilling thousands of wells. Nevertheless, **Texas' oil and gas production peaked in 1970** and has been declining since. Newly discovered oil and gas have not replaced the declining reserves. While Texans suffered from the inflation that followed, the state prospered. Tax revenues at all levels of government increased, and state revenues, basically derived from oil and gas taxes, spiraled, as did the state budget.

With the new revenue from inflation and petroleum taxes, state spending rose from $2.95 billion in 1970 to $8.6 billion in 1979, and education led the advance, moving from 42 percent of the budget to 51.5 percent. But there was no increase in state tax rates.

It was no surprise that **education** was one of the major beneficiaries of increased state spending. After World War II, more emphasis was placed on education across the state. **Community colleges** sprang up in many cities, and a total of 109 colleges were established between the end of the war and 1980. Quantity did not assure quality, however, and Texas' public and higher education seldom were ranked among national leaders.

In 1972, voters approved an amendment authorizing the Legislature to sit as a **constitutional convention** to rewrite the 1876 charter. The lawmakers met for several months and spent $5 million, but they failed to propose anything to be considered by voters. The public was outraged, and in 1975, the Legislature presented the work of the convention to voters in the form of eight constitutional amendments. All were defeated in a special election in November 1975.

Texas voters participated in their **first presidential primary in 1976**. Jimmy Carter of Georgia won the Democratic primary, and eventually the presidency. Ronald Reagan carried the state's Republicans, but lost the party's nomination to President Gerald Ford.

The state proved politically volatile in **1978**. First, Attorney General **John Hill** defeated Gov. Dolph Briscoe in the Democratic primary. A political newcomer, Dallas businessman **William P. Clements**, upset Hill in the general election, giving Texas its first Republican governor since Reconstruction. Also for the first time since Reconstruction, state officials were elected to **four-year terms.** ☆

University of North Texas Press

CAPTAIN JOHN R. HUGHES
Lone Star Ranger
CHUCK PARSONS

The first full modern bio of this Ranger Captain who served from 1887 until 1915. Known as the "Border Boss" for his years on the southwest Texas border, Hughes received more honors than any other Ranger. 464 pp. 50 b&w illus. $29.95 hardcover.

RAWHIDE RANGER, IRA ATEN
Enforcing Law on the Texas Frontier
BOB ALEXANDER

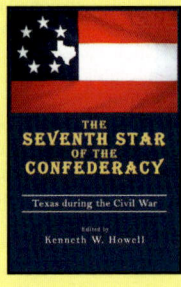

At age twenty-three, Aten joined Company D of the Texas Rangers and proceeded to make his mark in nineteenth-century Texas as the epitome of a frontier lawman and peace officer. 528 pp. 100 b&w illus. $32.95 hardcover.

VENGEANCE IS MINE
The Scandalous Love Triangle That Triggered the Boyce-Sneed Feud
BILL NEAL

The 1912 Boyce-Sneed feud began in West Texas with a love triangle between Lena Snyder Sneed, the headstrong high-spirited wife; Al Boyce, Jr., the romantic reckless lover; and John Beal Sneed, the arrogant vindictive husband. 336 pp. 36 b&w illus. $24.95 hardcover.

WRITTEN IN BLOOD
The History of Fort Worth's Fallen Lawmen Volume 2, 1910-1928
RICHARD F. SELCER AND KEVIN S. FOSTER

Selcer and Foster are back, covering more line-of-duty deaths of fallen officers from all branches of law enforcement in an even bloodier era. 464 pp. 45 b&w illus. $39.95 hardcover and $19.95 paperback. **Volume 1** also available.

BLOODY BILL LONGLEY
The Mythology of a Gunfighter, Second Edition
RICK MILLER

Miller's thorough research shows the murderous Longley was not the self-proclaimed "worst outlaw" in Texas, and debunks the popular legend that he escaped his execution by hanging. 385 pp. 38 b&w illus. $29.95 hardcover.

NEW IN PAPERBACK!

THE SEVENTH STAR OF THE CONFEDERACY
Texas during the Civil War
KENNETH W. HOWELL

"Howell has managed to gather eighteen of the very best Texas Civil War historians for this fine publication." —**Jerry Thompson.** 464 pp. 23 b&w illus. 4 maps. $18.95 paperback.

THE BIG THICKET GUIDEBOOK
Exploring the Backroads and History of Southeast Texas
LORRAINE G. BONNEY

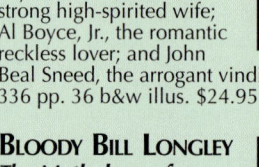

Fifteen tours take you down the backroads, along the historical paths, and guide you through the scenic landscape of this diverse ecosystem. 848 pp. 100 b&w illus. 16 maps. $29.95 hardcover.

WINCHESTER WARRIORS

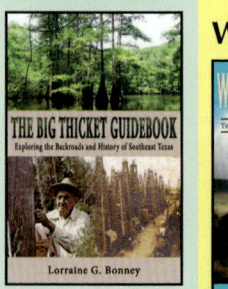

Texas Rangers of Company D, 1874-1901
BOB ALEXANDER
Alexander puts a human face on the Rangers as the company transforms into career lawmen. Generously illustrated. 464 pp. 100 b&w illus. $19.95 paperback.

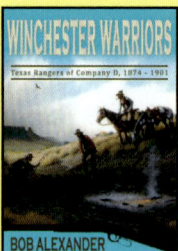

TO ORDER CALL 1-800-826-8911 OR VISIT *www.tamupress.com*

Environment

Elephant Rock near Shafter in Presidio County. Photo by Ron Billings; Texas Forest Service.

Physical Regions

Geology

Soils

Aquifers, Rivers, Lakes

Plant Life

Forests & Grasslands

Wildlife

The Physical State of Texas

The Area of Texas

Texas occupies about 7 percent of the total water and land area of the United States. Second in size among the states, **Texas has a land and water area of 268,596 square miles,** as compared with Alaska's 665,384 square miles, according to the United States Bureau of the Census. California, the third-largest state, has 163,695 square miles. Texas is as large as all of New England, New York, Delaware, Pennsylvania, Ohio, and Virginia combined.

The **state's total area** consists of 261,232 square miles of land and 7,365 square miles of water.

Length and Breadth

The **longest straight-line distance** in a general north-south direction is 801 miles from the northwest corner of the Panhandle to the extreme southern tip of Texas on the Rio Grande southeast of Brownsville. The greatest east-west distance is 773 miles from the extreme eastward bend in the Sabine River in Newton County to the extreme western bulge of the Rio Grande just northwest of El Paso.

The **geographic center** of Texas is southwest of Mercury in northern McCulloch County at approximately 99° 20' West longitude and 31° 08' North latitude.

Texas' Boundary Lines

The boundary of Texas by segments, including only larger river bends and only the great arc of the coastline, is as follows:

BOUNDARY	MILES
Rio Grande	889.0
Coastline	367.0
Sabine River, Lake, and Pass	180.0
Sabine River to Red River	106.5
Red River	480.0
East Panhandle line	133.6
North Panhandle line	167.0
West Panhandle line	310.2
Along 32nd parallel	209.0
TOTAL	2,842.3

Following the smaller meanderings of the rivers and the tidewater coastline, the following are the boundary measurements:

BOUNDARY	MILES
Rio Grande	1,254.0
Coastline (tidewater)	624.0
Sabine River, Lake, and Pass	292.0
Sabine River to Red River	106.5
Red River	726.0
East Panhandle line	133.6
North Panhandle line	167.0
West Panhandle line	310.2
Along 32nd parallel	209.0
TOTAL	3,822.3

Latitude and Longitude

The extremes of latitude and longitude in Texas are as follows:

— From **25° 50' North latitude** at the extreme southern turn of the Rio Grande on the south line of Cameron County to **36° 30' North latitude** along the north line of the Panhandle, and

— From **93° 31' West longitude** at the extreme eastern point of the Sabine River on the east line of Newton County to **106° 38' West longitude** at the extreme westward point of the Rio Grande on the western edge of El Paso.

Named Mountain Peaks in Texas
Above 8,000 Feet

The highest point in the state is **Guadalupe Peak** at **8,749 feet** above sea level. Its twin, **El Capitan**, stands at **8,085** feet and also is located in Culberson County near the New Mexico state line.

Both are in Guadalupe Mountains National Park, which includes the scenic McKittrick Canyon.

The elevations used on this page are from various sources, including the U.S. Geological Survey, the National Park Service, and the Texas Department of Transportation.

The named peaks above 8,000 feet and the counties in which they are located are listed below.

NAME	COUNTY	ELEVATION
Guadalupe Peak	Culberson	8,749
Bush Mountain	Culberson	8,631
Shumard Peak	Culberson	8,615
Bartlett Peak	Culberson	8,508
Mount Livermore (Baldy Peak)	Jeff Davis	8,378
Hunter Peak (Pine Top Mtn.)	Culberson	8,368
El Capitan	Culberson	8,085

Elevation Highs and Lows

HIGHEST TOWN: Fort Davis in Jeff Davis County is the **highest town** of any size in Texas at 5,050 feet above sea level, and the county has the **highest average elevation.**

HIGHEST HIGHWAY: The **highest state highway point** also is in Jeff Davis County at **McDonald Observatory** on **Mount Locke,** where the road reaches 6,781 feet above sea level, as determined by the Texas Department of Transportation.

HIGHEST RAILWAY: The **highest railway point** is Paisano Pass, 14 miles east of Marfa in Presidio County, which is 5,074 above sea level.

LOWEST POINT: Sea level is the **lowest elevation** determined in Texas, and it can be found in all the coastal counties. No point in the state has been found by the geological survey to be below sea level. ☆

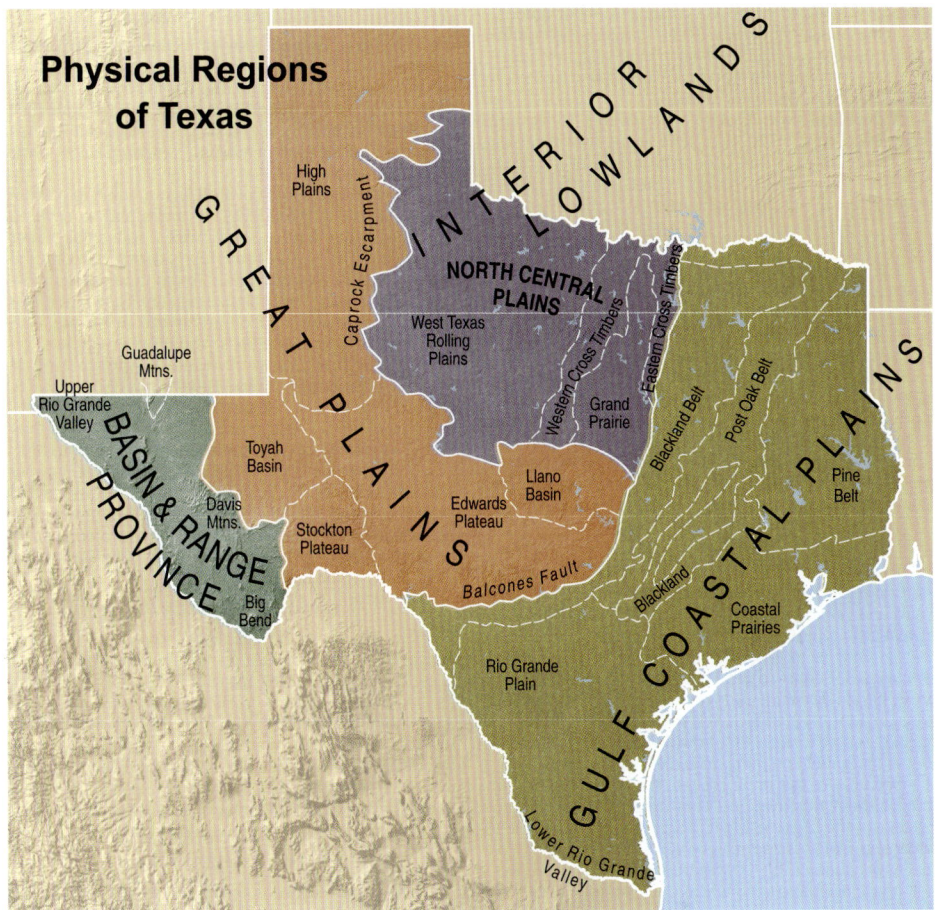

Physical Regions of Texas

Physical Regions

This section was reviewed by Dr. David R. Butler, Texas State University System Regents' Professor of Geography at Texas State University–San Marcos.

The principal physical regions of Texas are usually listed as follows (*see also,* the maps for Vegetational Areas and Soils):

I. GULF COASTAL PLAINS

Texas' Gulf Coastal Plains are the western extension of the coastal plain extending from the Atlantic Ocean to beyond the Rio Grande. Its characteristic rolling to hilly surface covered with a heavy growth of pine and hardwoods extends into East Texas. In the increasingly arid west, however, its forests become secondary in nature, consisting largely of post oaks and, farther west, prairies and brushlands.

The interior limit of the Gulf Coastal Plains in Texas is the line of the **Balcones Fault and Escarpment**. This geologic fault or shearing of underground strata extends eastward from a point on the Rio Grande near Del Rio. It extends to the northwestern part of Bexar County, where it turns northeastward and extends through Comal, Hays, and Travis counties, intersecting the Colorado River immediately north of Austin. The fault line is a single, definite geologic feature, accompanied by a line of southward- and eastward-facing hills.

The resemblance of the hills to balconies when viewed from the plain below accounts for the Spanish name for this area: *balcones.*

North of Waco, features of the fault zone are sufficiently inconspicuous that the interior boundary of the Coastal Plain follows the traditional geologic contact between upper and lower Cretaceous rocks. This contact is along the eastern edge of the **Eastern Cross Timbers**.

This fault line is usually accepted as the boundary between lowland and upland Texas. Below the fault line, the surface is characteristically coastal plains. Above the Balcones Fault, the surface is characteristically interior rolling plains.

A. Pine Belt or "Piney Woods"

The Pine Belt, called the **"Piney Woods,"** extends 75 to 125 miles into Texas from the east. From north to south, it extends from the Red River to within about 25 miles of the Gulf Coast. Interspersed among the pines are hardwood timbers, usually in valleys of rivers and creeks. This area is the source of practically all of Texas' **commercial timber production** (*see Texas Forest Resources, page 107*). It was settled early in Texas' history and is one of the oldest farming areas in the state.

This area's soils and climate are adaptable to the production of a variety of fruit and vegetable crops. Cattle raising is widespread, along with the development of pastures planted to improved grasses. Lumber production is the principal industry. There is a large **iron-and-steel industry** near Daingerfield in Morris County based on nearby iron deposits. Iron deposits are also worked in Rusk and one or two other counties.

A **great oil field** discovered in Gregg, Rusk, and Smith counties in 1931 has done more than anything else to contribute to the economic growth of the area. This area has a variety of clays, lignite, and other minerals as potentials for development.

B. Post Oak Belt

The main Post Oak Belt of Texas is wedged between the Pine Belt on the east, Blacklands on the west, and the Coastal Prairies on the south, covering a considerable area in East-Central Texas. The principal industry is diversified farming and livestock raising.

Throughout, it is spotty in character, with some insular areas of blackland soil and some that closely resemble those of the Pine Belt. There is a small, isolated area of loblolly pines in Bastrop, Caldwell, Fayette, and Lee counties known as the **"Lost Pines,"** the westernmost southern pines in the United States. The Post Oak Belt has lignite, commercial clays, and some other minerals.

C. Blackland Belt

The Blackland Belt stretches from the Rio Grande to the Red River, lying just below the line of the **Balcones Fault** and varying in width from 15 to 70 miles. It is narrowest below the segment of the Balcones Fault from the Rio Grande to Bexar County and gradually widens as it runs northeast to the Red River. Its rolling prairie, easily turned by the plow, developed rapidly as a farming area until the 1930s and was the principal cotton-producing area of Texas. Now, however, other Texas areas that are irrigated and mechanized lead in farming.

Because of the early growth, the Blackland Belt is still the **most thickly populated area in the state** and contains within it and along its border more of the state's large and middle-sized cities than any other area. Primarily because of this concentration of population, this belt has the most diversified manufacturing industry of the state.

D. Coastal Prairies

The Texas Coastal Prairies extend westward along the coast from the Sabine River, reaching inland 30 to 60 miles. Between the Sabine and Galveston Bay, the line of demarcation between the prairies and the Pine Belt forests to the north is very distinct. The Coastal Prairies extend along the Gulf of Mexico from the Sabine to the Lower Rio Grande Valley.

The eastern half is covered with a heavy growth of grass; the western half, which is more arid, is covered with short grass and, in some places, with small timber and brush. The soil is heavy clay. Grass supports the **densest cattle population in Texas,** and cattle ranching is the principal agricultural industry. Rice is a major crop, grown under irrigation from wells and rivers. Cotton, grain sorghum, and truck crops also are grown.

Coastal Prairie areas have seen the greatest industrial development in Texas history since World War II. Chief concentration has been from Orange and Beaumont to Houston, and much of the development has been in **petrochemicals and the aerospace industry**.

Corpus Christi, in the Coastal Bend, and Brownsville, in the Lower Rio Grande Valley, have seaports and agricultural and industrial sections. **Cotton, grain, vegetables, and citrus fruits** are the principal crops. Cattle production is significant, with the famed King Ranch and other large ranches located here.

E. Lower Rio Grande Valley

The deep alluvial soils and distinctive economy cause the Lower Rio Grande Valley to be classified as a subregion of the Gulf Coastal Plains. **"The Valley,"** as it is called locally, is Texas' greatest citrus and winter vegetable growing region because of the normal absence of freezing weather and the rich delta soils of the Rio Grande. Despite occasional damaging freezes, the Lower Valley ranks high among the nation's fruit and truck-farming regions. Much of the acreage is irrigated, although dry-land farming also is practiced.

F. Rio Grande Plain

This area may be roughly defined as lying south of San Antonio between the Rio Grande and the Gulf

These barrier island dunes are within the Texas Coastal Prairies, which extend along the Gulf of Mexico from the Sabine River to the Lower Rio Grande Valley. Photo by Chad Leister, Mission-Aransas NERR.

The Ray Roberts-Lewisville Lake State Park Greenbelt lies in the North Central Plains near the boundary of the Grand Prairie and the Eastern Cross Timbers. Photo by Robert Plocheck.

Coast. The Rio Grande Plain shows characteristics of both the Gulf Coastal Plains and the North Mexico Plains because there is similarity of topography, climate, and plant life all the way from the Balcones Escarpment in Texas to the Sierra Madre Oriental in Mexico, which runs past Monterrey about 160 miles south of Laredo.

The Rio Grande Plain is partly prairie, but much of it is covered with a dense growth of **prickly pear, mesquite, dwarf oak, catclaw, guajillo, huisache, blackbrush, cenizo,** and other cactus and wild shrubs. It is devoted primarily to raising cattle, sheep, and goats. The **Texas Angora goat and mohair industry** centers in this area and on the Edwards Plateau, which borders it on the north. San Antonio and Laredo are its chief commercial centers, with San Antonio dominating trade.

There is some farming, and the **Winter Garden,** centering in Dimmit and Zavala counties north of Laredo, is irrigated from wells and streams to produce vegetables in late winter and early spring. Primarily, however, the central and western part of the Rio Grande Plain is devoted to **livestock raising.**

The rainfall is less than 25 inches annually, and the hot summers cause heavy evaporation, so that cultivation without irrigation is limited.

Over a large area in the central and western parts of the Rio Grande Plain, the growth of **small oaks, mesquite, prickly pear (Opuntia) cactus,** and a variety of wild shrubs is very dense, and it is often called the **Brush Country.** It is also referred to as the **chaparral** and the **monte.** (*Monte* is a Spanish word, one meaning of which is dense brush.)

II. INTERIOR LOWLANDS

North Central Plains

The North Central Plains of Texas are a southwestern extension into Texas of the **interior, or central, lowlands** that extend northward to the Canadian border, paralleling the Great Plains to the West. The North Central Plains of Texas extend from the **Blackland Belt** on the east to the **Caprock Escarpment** on the west. From north to south, they extend from the Red River to the Colorado River.

A. West Texas Rolling Plains

The West Texas Rolling Plains, approximately the western two-thirds of the North Central Plains in Texas, rise from east to west in altitude from about 750 feet to 2,000 feet at the base of the **Caprock Escarpment**. Annual rainfall ranges from about 30 inches on the east to 20 inches on the west. In general, as one progresses westward in Texas, the precipitation not only declines but also becomes more variable from year to year. Temperature varies rather widely between summer's heat and winter's cold.

This area still has a **large cattle-raising industry** with many of the state's largest ranches. However, there is much level, cultivable land.

B. Grand Prairie

Near the eastern edge of the North Central Plains is the **Grand Prairie,** extending south from the Red River in an irregular band through Cooke, Montague, Wise, Denton, Tarrant, Parker, Hood, Johnson, Bosque, Coryell, and some adjacent counties.

It is a limestone-based area, usually treeless except along the numerous streams, and adapted primarily to raising livestock and growing staple crops. Sometimes called the **Fort Worth Prairie,** it has an agricultural economy and largely rural population, with no large cities, except Fort Worth on its eastern boundary.

C. Eastern and Western Cross Timbers

Hanging over the top of the Grand Prairie and dropping down on each side are the Eastern and Western Cross Timbers. The two southward-extending bands are connected by a narrow strip along the Red River.

The **Eastern Cross Timbers** extend southward from the Red River through eastern Denton County and along the boundary between Dallas and Tarrant counties. It then stretches through Johnson County to the Brazos River and into Hill County.

The much larger **Western Cross Timbers** extend from the Red River south through Clay, Montague, Jack, Wise, Parker, Palo Pinto, Hood, Erath, Eastland, Comanche, Brown, and Mills counties to the Colorado River, where they meet the **Llano Basin.**

Their soils are adapted to fruit and vegetable crops, which reach considerable commercial production in some areas in Parker, Erath, Eastland, and Comanche counties.

The Lake Buchanan lighthouse stands near the dam in the Llano Basin. This area, part of the Great Plains region, is in the Highland Lakes Country. Photo by Ron Billings; Texas Forest Service.

III. GREAT PLAINS

A. High Plains

The Great Plains, which lie to the east of the base of the Rocky Mountains, extend into northwestern Texas. This area, commonly known as the **High Plains**, is a vast, flat, high plain covered with thick layers of alluvial material. It is also known as the **Staked Plains** or the Spanish equivalent, *Llano Estacado.*

Historians differ as to the origin of this name. Some say it came from the fact that the explorer Coronado's expedition used stakes to mark its route across the trackless sea of grass so that it would be guided on its return trip. Others think that the *estacado* refers to the **palisaded appearance** of the Caprock in many places, especially the west-facing escarpment in New Mexico.

The **Caprock Escarpment** is the dividing line between the High Plains and the lower West Texas Rolling Plains. Like the Balcones Escarpment, the Caprock Escarpment is a striking physical feature, rising abruptly 200, 500, and in some places almost 1,000 feet above the plains. Unlike the **Balcones Escarpment**, the Caprock was caused by surface erosion.

Where rivers issue from the eastern face of the Caprock, there frequently are notable canyons, such as **Palo Duro Canyon** on the **Prairie Dog Town Fork of the Red River**, **Blanco Canyon on the White River**, as well as the breaks along the Canadian River as it crosses the Panhandle north of Amarillo.

Along the eastern edge of the Panhandle, there is a gradual descent of the land's surface from high to low plains; but at the Red River, the Caprock Escarpment becomes a striking surface feature. It continues as an east-facing wall south through Briscoe, Floyd, Motley, Dickens, Crosby, Garza, and Borden counties, gradually decreasing in elevation. South of Borden County, the escarpment is less obvious, and the boundary between the High Plains and the **Edwards Plateau** occurs where the alluvial cover of the High Plains disappears.

Stretching over the largest level plain of its kind in the United States, the High Plains rise gradually from about 2,700 feet on the east to more than 4,000 in spots along the New Mexico border.

Chiefly because of climate and the resultant agriculture, subdivisions are called the North Plains and South Plains. The **North Plains,** from Hale County north, has primarily **wheat and grain sorghum farming,** but with significant ranching and petroleum developments. Amarillo is the largest city, with Plainview on the south and Borger on the north as important commercial centers.

The **South Plains,** also a leading grain sorghum region, **leads Texas in cotton production.** Lubbock is the principal city, and Lubbock County is one of the state's largest cotton producers. Irrigation from underground reservoirs, centered around Lubbock and Plainview, waters much of the crop acreage.

B. Edwards Plateau

Geographers usually consider that the Great Plains at the foot of the Rocky Mountains actually continue southward from the High Plains of Texas to the Rio Grande and the Balcones Escarpment. This southern and lower extension of the Great Plains in Texas is known as the **Edwards Plateau.**

It lies between the Rio Grande and the Colorado River. Its southeastern border is the Balcones Escarpment from the Rio Grande at Del Rio eastward to San Antonio and thence to Austin on the Colorado River. Its upper boundary is the Pecos River, though the **Stockton Plateau** is geologically and topographically classed with the Edwards Plateau.

The Edwards Plateau varies from about 750 feet high at its southern and eastern borders to about 2,700 feet in places. Almost the entire surface is a thin, limestone-based soil covered with a medium to thick growth of **cedar, small oak,** and **mesquite** and a varying growth of **prickly pear.** Grass for cattle, weeds for sheep, and tree foliage for the browsing goats support three industries — **cattle, goat,** and **sheep raising** — upon which the area's economy depends. It is the **nation's leading**

Angora goat and mohair producing region and one of the nation's leading sheep and wool areas. A few crops are grown.

Hill Country

The Hill Country is a popular name for the **eastern portion of the Edwards Plateau** south of the Llano Basin. Its notable large springs include **Barton Springs** at Austin, **San Marcos Springs** at San Marcos, **Comal Springs** at New Braunfels, several springs at San Antonio, and a number of others.

The Hill Country is characterized by rugged hills with relatively steep slopes and thin soils overlying limestone bedrock. High gradient streams combine with these steep hillslopes and occasionally heavy precipitation to produce an area with a significant flash-flood hazard.

C. Toyah Basin

To the northwest of the Edwards and Stockton plateaus is the Toyah Basin, a broad, flat remnant of **an old sea floor** that occupied the region as recently as Quaternary time.

Located in the **Pecos River Valley,** this region, in relatively recent time, has become important for many agricultural products as a result of irrigation. Additional economic activity is afforded by **local oil fields.**

D. Llano Basin

The Llano Basin lies at the junction of the Colorado and Llano rivers in Burnet and Llano counties. Earlier, this was known as the **"Central Mineral Region"** because of evidence there of a large number of minerals.

On the Colorado River in this area, a succession of dams impounds two large and five small reservoirs. Uppermost is **Lake Buchanan**, one of the large reservoirs, between Burnet and Llano counties. Below it in the western part of Travis County is **Lake Travis**.

Between these two large reservoirs are three smaller ones, **Inks, L.B. Johnson** (formerly Granite Shoals), and **Marble Falls** reservoirs, used primarily to produce electric power from the overflow from Lake Buchanan. **Lake Austin** is along the western part of the city of Austin. Still another small lake, **Lady Bird Lake** (formerly Town Lake), is formed by a low-water dam in Austin.

The recreational area around these lakes has been called the **Highland Lakes Country**. This is an interesting area with Precambrian and Paleozoic rocks found on the surface. Granitic domes, exemplified by **Enchanted Rock** north of Fredericksburg, form the core of this area of ancient rocks.

IV. BASIN and RANGE PROVINCE

The Basin and Range province, with its center in Nevada, surrounds the Colorado Plateau on the west and south and enters far West Texas from southern New Mexico on the east. It consists of broad interior **drainage basins** interspersed with scattered **fault-block mountain ranges.**

Although this is the only part of Texas regarded as mountainous, these should not be confused with the Rocky Mountains. Of all the independent ranges in West Texas, only the Davis Mountains resemble the Rockies, and there is much debate about this.

Texas west of the Edwards Plateau, bounded on the north by New Mexico and on the south by the Rio Grande, is distinctive in its physical and economic conditions. Traversed from north to south by fault-block mountains, it contains all of Texas' true mountains and also is very interesting geologically.

A. Guadalupe Mountains

Highest of the Trans-Pecos Mountains is the **Guadalupe Range**, which enters Texas from New Mexico. It abruptly ends about 20 miles south of the boundary line, where **Guadalupe Peak**, (8,749 feet, highest in Texas) and **El Capitan** (8,085 feet) are situated. El Capitan, because of perspective, appears to the observer on the plain below to be higher than Guadalupe.

Lying just west of the Guadalupe Range and extending to the **Hueco Mountains** a short distance east of El Paso is the **Diablo Plateau** or basin. It has no drainage outlet to the sea. The runoff from the scant rain that falls on its surface drains into a series of salt lakes that lie

Hueco Tanks State Park near El Paso lies within the Hueco Mountains, one of several fault-block mountain ranges that traverse the Basin and Range Province of West Texas. Photo by Robert Plocheck.

just west of the Guadalupe Mountains. These lakes are dry during periods of low rainfall, exposing bottoms of solid salt; for years they were a source of **commercial salt**. West of the Hueco Mountains are the **Franklin Mountains** in El Paso, with the Hueco Bolson (a down-dropped area approximately 4,000 feet above sea level) separating the two fault-block ranges.

B. Davis Mountains

The Davis Mountains are principally in Jeff Davis County. The highest peak, **Mount Livermore** (8,378 feet), is **one of the highest in Texas**; there are several others more than 7,000 feet high. These mountains intercept the moisture-bearing winds and receive more precipitation than elsewhere in the Trans-Pecos, so they have **more vegetation** than the other Trans-Pecos mountains. Noteworthy are the **San Solomon Springs** at the northern base of these mountains.

C. Big Bend

South of the Davis Mountains lies the Big Bend country, so called because it is encompassed on three sides by a great southward swing of the Rio Grande. It is a

San Elizario Mission in the Upper Rio Grande Valley is the oldest mission in Texas. Photo by Robert Plocheck.

mountainous country of scant rainfall and sparse population. Its principal mountains, the **Chisos**, rise to 7,825 feet in **Mount Emory**.

Along the Rio Grande are the **Santa Elena, Mariscal,** and **Boquillas canyons** with rim elevations of 3,500 to 3,775 feet. They are among the noteworthy canyons of the North American continent.

Because of its remarkable topography and plant and animal life, the southern part of this region along the Rio Grande is home to **Big Bend National Park**, with headquarters in the Chisos Basin, a deep valley in the Chisos Mountains. It is a favorite recreation area.

D. Upper Rio Grande Valley

The Upper Rio Grande Valley, or El Paso Valley, is a narrow strip of irrigated land running down the river from El Paso for a distance of 75 miles or more.

In this area are the historic towns and missions of **Ysleta, Socorro,** and **San Elizario, oldest in Texas**. Cotton is the chief product of this valley, much of it is the long-staple variety.

This limited area has a dense urban and rural population, in marked contrast to the territory surrounding it. ☆

Santa Elena Canyon in Big Bend National Park reveals limestone that was deposited in shallow Mesozoic seas. Photo by Robert Plocheck.

Geology of Texas

Source: Bureau of Economic Geology, The University of Texas at Austin; www.beg.utexas.edu/

History in the Rocks

Mountains, seas, coastal plains, rocky plateaus, high plains, forests — all of this **physiographic variety** in Texas is controlled by the varied rocks and structures that underlie and crop out across the state. The fascinating geologic history of Texas is recorded in the rocks — both those exposed at the surface and those penetrated by holes drilled in search of oil and natural gas.

The rocks reveal a dynamic, ever-changing earth — ancient mountains, seas, volcanoes, earthquake belts, rivers, hurricanes, and winds. Today, the volcanoes and great earthquake belts are no longer active, but rivers and streams, wind and rain, and the slow, inexorable alterations of rocks at or near the surface continue to change the face of Texas.

The geologic history of Texas, as documented by the rocks, began more than a billion years ago. Its legacy is the mineral wealth and varied land forms of modern Texas.

Geologic Time Travel

The story preserved in rocks requires an understanding of the origin of strata and how they have been deformed. **Stratigraphy** is the study of the composition, sequence, and origin of rocks: what rocks are made of, how they were formed, and the order in which the layers were formed.

Structural geology reveals the architecture of rocks: the locations of the mountains, volcanoes, sedimentary basins, and earthquake belts.

The **map on the following page** shows where rocks of various geologic ages are visible **on the surface** of Texas today. History concerns events through time, but geologic time is such a grandiose concept, most find it difficult to comprehend. So geologists have named the various chapters of earth history.

Precambrian Eon

Precambrian rocks, more than 600 million years old, are exposed at the surface in the **Llano Uplift of Central Texas** and in scattered outcrops in West Texas, around and north of **Van Horn** and **near El Paso.**

These rocks, some more than a billion years old, include complexly deformed rocks that were originally formed by cooling from a liquid state, as well as rocks that were altered from pre-existing rocks.

Precambrian rocks, often called the **"basement complex,"** are thought to form the foundation of continental masses. They underlie all of Texas. The outcrop in Central Texas is only the exposed part of the **Texas Craton**, which is primarily buried by younger rocks. (A craton is a stable, almost immovable portion of the earth's crust that forms the nuclear mass of a continent.)

Paleozoic Era

During the early part of the Paleozoic Era (approximately 600 million to 350 million years ago), broad, relatively **shallow seas** repeatedly inundated the Texas Craton and much of North and West Texas. The evidence for these events is found exposed around the Llano Uplift and in far West Texas near Van Horn and El Paso, and also in the subsurface throughout most of West and North Texas. The evidence includes early Paleozoic rocks — **sandstones, shales, and limestones,** similar to sediments that form in seas today — and the fossils of animals, similar to modern crustaceans — the **brachiopods, clams, snails, and related organisms** that live in modern marine environments.

By late Paleozoic (approximately 350 million to 240 million years ago), the Texas Craton was bordered on the east and south by a long, deep marine basin called the **Ouachita Trough.** Sediments slowly accumulated in this trough until late in the Paleozoic Era. Plate-tectonic theory postulates that the collision of the North American Plate (upon which the Texas Craton is located) with the European and African–South American plates uplifted the thick sediments that had accumulated in the trough to form the **Ouachita Mountains.**

At that time, the Ouachitas extended across Texas. Today, the Texas portion of the old mountain range is mostly buried by younger rocks. Ancient remnants can be seen in the **Marathon Basin of West Texas** due to uplift and erosion of younger sediments. The public can see the remains of this once-majestic Ouachita Mountain range at Post Park, just south of Marathon in Brewster County. Other remnants at the surface are exposed in southeastern Oklahoma and southwestern Arkansas.

During the **Pennsylvanian Period,** however, the Ouachita Mountains bordered the eastern margin of shallow inland seas that covered most of West Texas. Rivers flowed westward from the mountains to the seas bringing sediment to form deltas along an ever-changing coastline.

The sediments were then reworked by the waves and currents of the inland sea. Today, these fluvial, delta, and shallow **marine deposits** compose the late Paleozoic rocks that crop out and underlie the surface of North-Central Texas.

Broad marine shelves divided the West Texas seas into several sub-basins, or deeper areas, that received more sediments than accumulated on the limestone shelves. **Limestone reefs** rimmed the deeper basins. Today, these reef limestones are important oil reservoirs in West Texas.

These seas gradually withdrew from Texas, and by the late **Permian Period,** all that was left in West Texas were shallow basins and wide tidal flats in which salt, gypsum, and red muds accumulated in a hot, arid land. Strata deposited during the Permian Period are exposed today along the edge of the Panhandle, as far east as Wichita Falls and south to Concho County, and in the Trans-Pecos.

Mesozoic Era

Approximately 240 million years ago, the major geologic events in Texas shifted from West Texas to East and Southeast Texas. The European and African–South

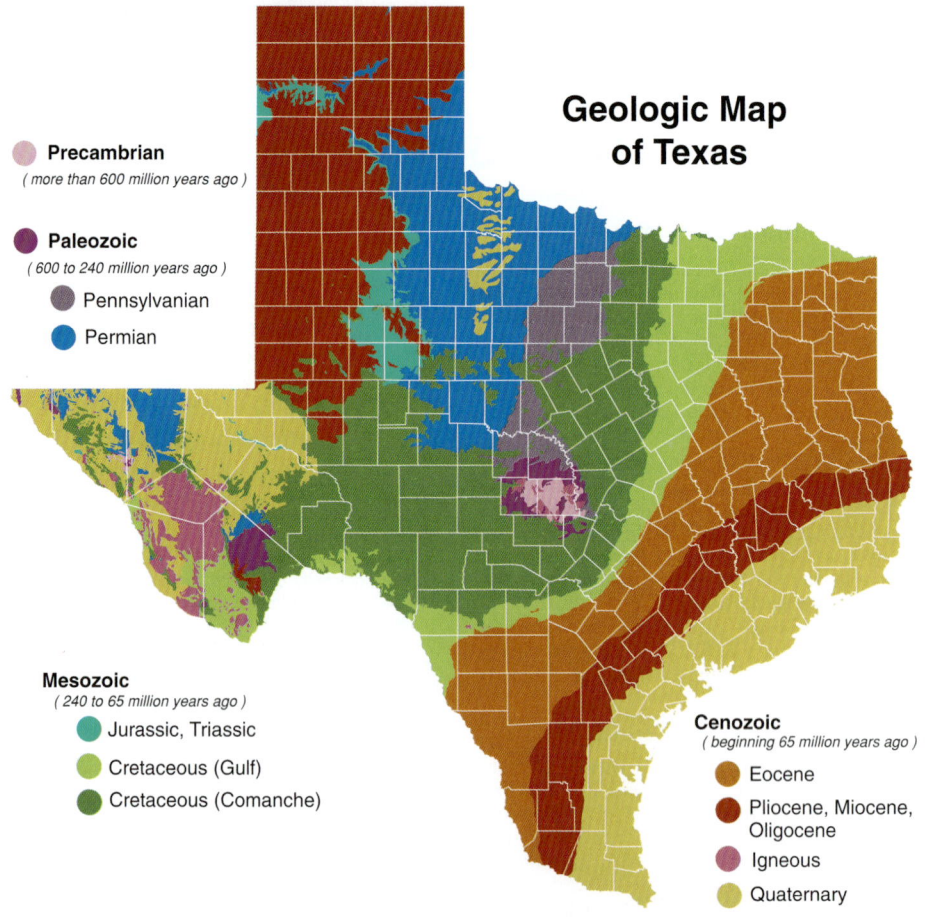

Geologic Map of Texas

Precambrian
(more than 600 million years ago)

Paleozoic
(600 to 240 million years ago)

Pennsylvanian

Permian

Mesozoic
(240 to 65 million years ago)

Jurassic, Triassic

Cretaceous (Gulf)

Cretaceous (Comanche)

Cenozoic
(beginning 65 million years ago)

Eocene

Pliocene, Miocene, Oligocene

Igneous

Quaternary

Sedimentary strata are seen at the Lighthouse formation in Palo Duro Canyon State Park near Canyon in the Panhandle region of Texas. Photo by Ron Billings; Texas Forest Service.

American plates, which had collided with the North American plate to form the Ouachita Mountains, began to separate from North America.

A series of faulted basins, or rifts, extending from Mexico to Nova Scotia were formed. These **rifted basins** received sediments from adjacent uplifts. As Europe and the southern continents continued to drift away from North America, the Texas basins were eventually buried beneath **thick deposits of marine salt** within the newly formed East Texas and Gulf Coast basins.

Jurassic and Cretaceous rocks in East and Southeast Texas document a sequence of broad limestone shelves at the edge of the developing Gulf of Mexico. From time to time, the shelves were buried beneath **deltaic sandstones and shales,** which built the northwestern margin of the widening Gulf of Mexico to the south and southeast.

As the underlying salt was buried more deeply by dense sediments, the salt became unstable and moved toward areas of least pressure. As the salt moved, it arched or pierced overlying sediments forming, in some cases, columns known as **"salt domes."** In some cases, these salt domes moved to the surface; others remain beneath a sedimentary overburden. This mobile salt formed numerous structures that would later serve to trap oil and natural gas.

By the early **Cretaceous** (approximately 140 million years ago), the shallow Mesozoic seas covered a large part of Texas, eventually extending west to the Trans-Pecos area and north almost to present-day state boundaries. Today, the limestone deposited in those seas is exposed in the walls of the magnificent canyons of the Rio Grande in the **Big Bend National Park area** and in the canyons and headwaters of streams that drain the Edwards Plateau, as well as in Central Texas from San Antonio to Dallas.

Animals of many types lived in the shallow Mesozoic seas, tidal pools, and coastal swamps. Today, these lower Cretaceous rocks are some of the most fossiliferous in the state. **Tracks of dinosaurs** occur in several

places, and remains of **terrestrial, aquatic, and flying reptiles** have been collected from Cretaceous rocks in many areas.

During most of the late Cretaceous, much of Texas lay beneath marine waters that were deeper than those of the early Cretaceous seas, except where rivers, deltas, and shallow marine shelves existed.

River delta and strandline sandstones are the reservoir rocks for the most prolific oil field in Texas. When discovered in 1930, this **East Texas oil field** contained recoverable reserves estimated at 5.6 billion barrels.

The chalky rock that we now call the **"Austin Chalk"** was deposited when the Texas seas became deeper. Today, the chalk (and other Upper Cretaceous rocks) crops out in a wide band that extends from near Eagle Pass on the Rio Grande, east to San Antonio, north to Dallas, and east to the Texarkana area. The Austin Chalk and other upper Cretaceous rocks dip southeastward beneath the East Texas and Gulf Coast basins.

The late Cretaceous was the time of the **last major seaway across Texas,** because mountains were forming in the western United States that influenced areas as far away as Texas.

A **chain of volcanoes** formed beneath the late Cretaceous seas in an area roughly parallel to and south and east of the old, buried Ouachita Mountains. The eruptions of these volcanoes were primarily on the sea floor and great clouds of steam and ash likely accompanied them.

Between eruptions, invertebrate marine animals built reefs on the shallow volcanic cones. **Pilot Knob,** located southeast of Austin, is one of these **old volcanoes** that is now exposed at the surface.

Cenozoic Era

At the dawn of the Cenozoic Era, approximately 65 million years ago, deltas fed by rivers were in the northern and northwestern margins of the East Texas Basin. These streams flowed eastward, draining areas to the north and west. Although there were minor incursions of the seas, the Cenozoic rocks principally document extensive seaward building by broad deltas, marshy lagoons, sandy barrier islands, and embayments.

Thick vegetation covered the levees and areas between the streams. **Coastal plains** were taking shape under the same processes still at work today.

The Mesozoic marine salt became buried by thick sediments in the coastal plain area. The salt began to form ridges and domes in the Houston and Rio Grande areas. The heavy load of sand, silt, and mud deposited by the deltas eventually caused some areas of the coast to subside and form **large fault systems,** essentially parallel to the coast.

Many of these coastal faults moved slowly and probably generated little earthquake activity. However, **movement along the Balcones and Luling-Mexia-Talco zones,** a complex system of faults along the western and northern edge of the basins, likely generated large earthquakes millions of years ago.

Predecessors of modern animals roamed the Texas Cenozoic coastal plains and woodlands. Bones and teeth of **horses, camels, sloths, giant armadillos, mammoths, mastodons, bats, rats, large cats,** and other modern or extinct mammals have been excavated from coastal plain deposits.

Vegetation in the area included varieties of plants and trees both similar and dissimilar to modern ones. **Fossil palmwood,** the **Texas "state stone,"** is found in sediments of early Cenozoic age.

The Cenozoic Era in Trans-Pecos Texas was entirely different. There, **extensive volcanic eruptions** formed great calderas and produced copious lava flows. These eruptions ejected great clouds of volcanic ash and rock particles into the air — many times the amount of material ejected by the 1980 eruption of Mount St. Helens.

Ash from the eruptions drifted eastward and is found in many of the sand-and-siltstones of the Gulf Coastal Plains. **Lava** flowed over older Paleozoic and Mesozoic rocks, and igneous intrusions melted their way upward into crustal rocks. These volcanic and intrusive igneous rocks are well exposed in arid areas of the Trans-Pecos today.

In the Texas Panhandle, streams originating in the recently elevated southern Rocky Mountains brought floods of gravel and sand into Texas. As the braided streams crisscrossed the area, they formed **great alluvial fans.**

These fans, which were deposited on the older Paleozoic and Mesozoic rocks, occur from northwestern Texas into Nebraska. Between 1 million and 2 million years ago, the streams of the Panhandle were isolated from their Rocky Mountain source, and the eastern edge of this sheet of alluvial material began to retreat westward, forming the **Caprock of the modern High Plains.**

Late in the Cenozoic Era, **a great Ice Age** descended on the northern North American continent. For more than 2 million years, there were successive advances and retreats of the thick sheets of glacial ice. Four periods of extensive glaciation were separated by warmer interglacial periods. Although the glaciers never reached as far south as Texas, the state's climate and sea level underwent major changes with each period of glacial advance and retreat.

Sea level during times of glacial advance was 300 to 450 feet lower than during the warmer interglacial periods because so much sea water was captured in the ice sheets. The climate was both more humid and cooler than today, and the major Texas rivers carried more water and more sand and gravel to the sea. These deposits underlie the outer 50 miles or more of the Gulf Coastal Plain.

Approximately 3,000 years ago, sea level reached its modern position. The rivers, deltas, lagoons, beaches, and barrier islands that we know as coastal Texas today have formed since that time. ☆

Oil and natural gas, as well as nonfuel minerals, are important to the Texas economy. For a more detailed discussion, see pages 627–636 and 637–644.

The Waco Mammoth Site contains the remains of 22 Columbian mammoths, which were first discovered in 1978. During the Cenozoic Era, mammoths roamed Texas' coastal plains and woodlands. Waco Mammoth Site opened to the public in 2009 and includes a dig shelter, a suspended walkway, which provides an overhead view of the mammoths, a scenic trailway, a welcome center, and a gift shop. It is open Tuesday through Saturday. Photo by Bill C. Foster.

Cattle graze in a well-managed pasture on Copita fine sandy loam in Zapata County. For livestock producers, knowledge of the ecological sites on their rangeland provides information that can help them improve their range grasses and maximize profits. Photo courtesy of the USDA-Natural Resources Conservation Service.

Soils of Texas

Source: Natural Resources Conservation Service, U.S. Department of Agriculture, Temple, Texas; www.tx.nrcs.usda.gov/

One of Texas' most important natural resources is its soil. Texas soils are complex because of the wide diversity of climate, vegetation, geology, and landscape. **More than 1,300 different kinds of soil** are recognized in Texas. Each has a specific set of properties that affect its use.

Soil maps and information about soils and their uses are available for nearly all of the state's 254 counties. Texas' official soil information site is the the **Web Soil Survey**: **http://websoilsurvey.nrcs.usda.gov.**

For more information, contact the **Natural Resources Conservation Service** at 101 S. Main, Temple 76501-7602; (254) 742-9800; or visit **www.tx.nrcs. usda.gov;** click on "Information About: Soils."

Web Soil Survey — An Electronic Tool

For decades, soil scientists with the U.S. Department of Agriculture Natural Resources Conservation Service have been studying Texas soils and **mapping its properties, qualities, and characteristics.** Soils information that was once available only through paper maps or books is now easily accessed online through the **Web Soil Survey,** which also offers a soil survey application that can be downloaded.

As the state's population continues to move from rural to urban areas, the Web Soil Survey is a tool landowners can use to make land-use and management decisions. This free tool allows landowners to analyze soil data and maps. It is used by farmers and ranchers to find information about soil properties and qualities to optimize agricultural production, and by homeowners and commercial builders looking for information on the suitability or the limitations of a building site.

The Web Soil Survey includes downloadable soils data, archived soil surveys, and soil survey status information. In four steps, landowners can define an area of interest, view and print a soil map, explore soil information, and use a free shopping cart to collect a variety of thematic maps and reports for a printable **Custom Soil Resource report.** The site includes a glossary of words and definitions.

Major Soil Areas

Texas can be divided into 21 **Major Land Resource Areas** that have similar or related soils, vegetation, topography, climate, and land uses. Following are brief descriptions of these areas:

Trans-Pecos Soils

The 18.7 million acres of the Trans-Pecos, mostly west of the Pecos River, are diverse plains and valleys intermixed with mountains. Surface drainage is slow to rapid. This arid region is used mainly as **rangeland.** A small amount of irrigated cropland lies on the more fertile soils along the Rio Grande and the Pecos River. **Vineyards** are a more recent use of these soils, as is the disposal of large volumes of municipal wastes.

Upland soils are mostly well-drained, light reddish-brown to brown clay loams, clays, and sands (some have a large amount of gypsum or other salts). Many areas have shallow soils and rock outcrops, and sizable areas have deep sands. **Bottomland soils** are deep, well-drained, dark grayish-brown to reddish-brown silt loams, loams, clay loams, and clays. The lack of soil moisture and wind erosion are the major soil-management problems. Only irrigated crops can be grown on these soils, and most areas lack an adequate source of good water.

Upper Pecos, Canadian Valleys, and Plains Soils

The Upper Pecos, Canadian Valleys, and Plains area occupies a little over a half-million acres and is in the northwest part of Texas near the Texas–New Mexico border. It is characterized by broad rolling plains and tablelands broken by drainageways and tributaries of the Canadian River. It includes the **Canadian Breaks**, which are rough, steep lands below the adjacent High Plains. The average annual precipitation is about 15 inches, but it fluctuates widely from year to year. Surface drainage is slow to rapid.

The soils are well drained and alkaline. The mostly reddish-brown clay loams and sandy loams were formed mostly in material weathered from sandstone and shale. Depths range from shallow to very deep.

The area is used mainly as **rangeland** and **wildlife habitat.** Native vegetation is mid- to short-grass prairie species, such as hairy grama, sideoats grama, little bluestem, alkali sacaton, vine-mesquite, and galleta in the plains and tablelands. Juniper and mesquite grow on the relatively higher breaks. Soil management problems include low soil moisture and brush control.

High Plains Soils

The High Plains area comprises a vast high plateau of more than 19.4 million acres in northwestern Texas. It lies in the southern part of the Great Plains province that includes large, similar areas in Oklahoma and New Mexico. The flat, nearly level treeless plain has few streams to cause local relief. However, several major rivers originate in the High Plains or cross the area. The largest is the **Canadian River,** which has cut a deep valley across the Panhandle section.

Playas, small intermittent lakes scattered through the area, lie up to 20 feet below the surrounding plains. A 1965 survey counted more than 19,000 playas in 44 counties occupying some 340,000 acres. Most runoff from rainfall is collected in the playas, but only 10 to 40 percent of this water percolates back to the **Ogallala Aquifer.** The aquifer is virtually the exclusive water source in this area.

Upland soils are mostly well-drained, deep, neutral to alkaline clay loams and sandy loams in shades of brown or red. Sandy soils are in the southern part. Many soils have large amounts of lime at various depths and some are shallow over **caliche.** Soils of bottomlands are minor in extent.

The area is used mostly for **cropland,** but significant areas of rangeland are in the southwestern and extreme northern parts. **Millions of cattle** populate the many large feedlots in the area. The soils are moderately productive, and the flat surface encourages irrigation and mechanization. Limited soil moisture, constant danger of wind erosion, and irrigation water management are the major soil-management problems, but the region is Texas' leading producer of three important crops: **cotton, grain sorghums,** and **wheat.**

Rolling Plains Soils

The Rolling Plains include 21.7 million acres east of the High Plains in northwestern Texas. The area lies west of the North Central Prairies and extends from the edge of the Edwards Plateau in Tom Green County northward into Oklahoma. The landscape is nearly level to strongly rolling, and surface drainage is moderate to rapid. Outcrops of red beds, geologic materials, and associated reddish soils have led some scientists to use the name **"Red Plains."** Limestone underlies the soils in the southeastern part. The eastern part contains large areas of badlands.

Upland soils are mostly deep, pale-brown through reddish-brown to dark grayish-brown, neutral to alkaline sandy loams, clay loams, and clays; some are deep sands.

Many soils have a large amount of lime in the lower part, and a few others are saline; some are shallow and stony. **Bottomland soils** are mostly reddish-brown and sandy to clayey; some are saline.

This area is used mostly for **rangeland,** but **cotton, grain sorghums,** and **wheat** are important crops. The major soil-management problems are brush control, wind erosion, low fertility, and lack of soil mosture. Salt spots are a concern in some areas.

North Central Prairie Soils

The North Central Prairie occupies about 7 million acres in North Central Texas. Adjacent to this area on the north is the rather small area (less than 1 million acres) called **Rolling Red Prairies,** which extends into Oklahoma and is included here because the soils and land use are similar. This area lies between the Western Cross Timbers and the Rolling Plains. It is predominantly **grassland intermixed with small wooded areas.** The landscape is undulating with slow to rapid surface drainage.

Upland soils are mostly deep, well-drained, brown or reddish-brown, slightly acid loams over neutral to alkaline, clayey subsoils. Some soils are shallow or moderately deep to shale. **Bottomland soils** are mostly well-drained, dark-brown or gray loams and clays.

This area is used mostly as **rangeland,** but **wheat, grain sorghums,** and other crops are grown on the better soils. Brush control, wind and water erosion, and limited soil moisture are the major management concerns.

Edwards Plateau Soils

The 22.7 million acres of the Edwards Plateau are in South Central Texas east of the Trans-Pecos and west of the Blackland Prairie. Uplands are nearly level to undulating except near large stream valleys, where the landscape is hilly with deep canyons and steep slopes. There are many **cedar brakes** in this area. Surface drainage is rapid.

Upland soils are mostly shallow, stony, or gravelly, dark alkaline clays and clay loams underlain by limestone. Lighter-colored soils are on steep sideslopes and deep, less-stony soils are in the valleys. **Bottomland soils** are mostly deep, dark-gray or brown, alkaline loams and clays.

Raising **beef cattle** is the main enterprise in this region, but it is also the center of Texas' and the nation's **mohair** and **wool production.** The area is a **major deer habitat,** and hunting leases produce income. Cropland is mostly in the valleys on the deeper soils and is used mainly for growing forage crops and hay. The major soil-management concerns are brush control, large stones, low fertility, excess lime, and limited soil moisture.

Central or Llano Basin Soils

The Central Basin, also known as the Llano Basin, occupies a relatively small area in Central Texas. It includes parts or all of Llano, Mason, Gillespie, and adjoining counties. The total area is about 1.6 million acres of undulating to hilly landscape.

Upland soils are mostly shallow, reddish-brown to brown, mostly gravelly and stony, neutral to slightly acid sandy loams over granite, limestone, gneiss, and schist bedrock. Large boulders are on the soil surface in some areas. Deeper, less stony sandy-loam soils are in the valleys. **Bottomland soils** are minor areas of deep, dark-gray or brown loams and clays.

Ranching is the main enterprise, with some farms producing **peaches, grain sorghum,** and **wheat.** The area provides excellent **deer habitat,** and hunting leas-

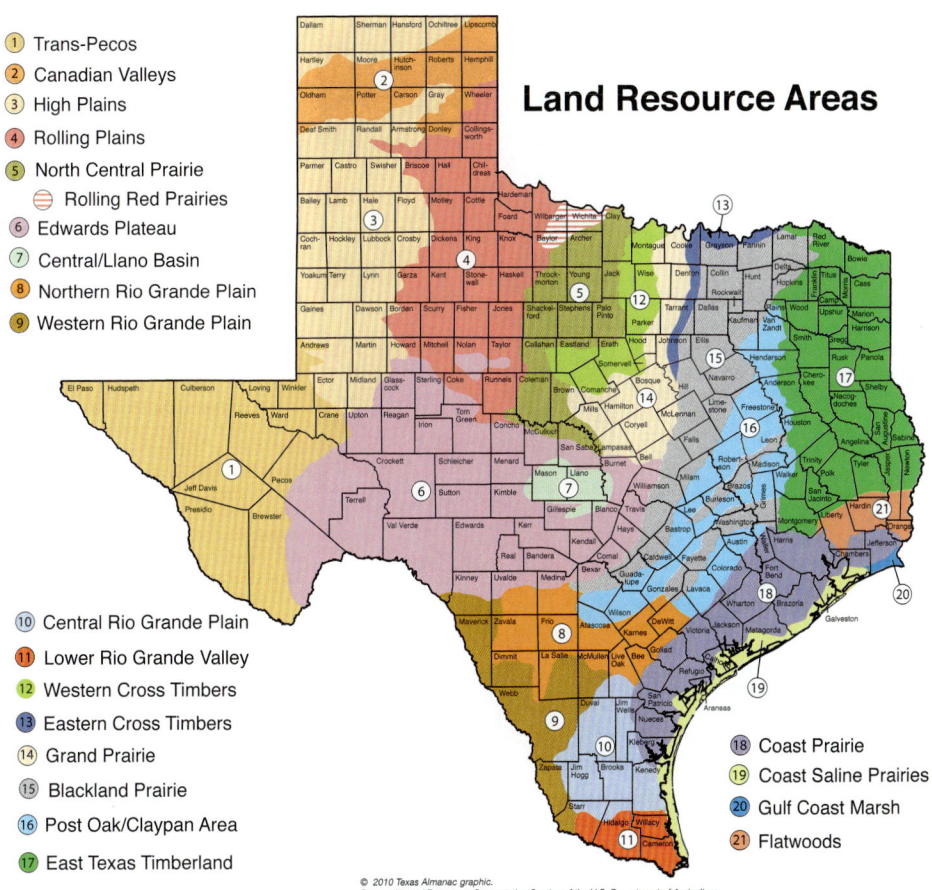

Land Resource Areas

1 Trans-Pecos
2 Canadian Valleys
3 High Plains
4 Rolling Plains
5 North Central Prairie
  ⊖ Rolling Red Prairies
6 Edwards Plateau
7 Central/Llano Basin
8 Northern Rio Grande Plain
9 Western Rio Grande Plain

10 Central Rio Grande Plain
11 Lower Rio Grande Valley
12 Western Cross Timbers
13 Eastern Cross Timbers
14 Grand Prairie
15 Blackland Prairie
16 Post Oak/Claypan Area
17 East Texas Timberland

18 Coast Prairie
19 Coast Saline Prairies
20 Gulf Coast Marsh
21 Flatwoods

© 2010 Texas Almanac graphic.
Source: Natural Resources Conservation Service of the U.S. Department of Agriculture.

es are a major source of income. Brush control, large stones, and limited soil moisture are soil-management concerns.

Northern Rio Grande Plain Soils

The Northern Rio Grande Plain comprises about 6.3 million acres in South Texas extending from Uvalde to Beeville. The landscape is nearly level to rolling, mostly brush-covered plains with slow to rapid surface drainage.

The major **upland soils** are deep, reddish-brown or dark grayish-brown, neutral to alkaline loams and clays. **Bottomland soils** are mostly dark-colored loams.

The area is mostly rangeland with significant areas of cropland. **Grain sorghums, cotton, corn,** and **small grains** are the major crops. Crops are irrigated in the western part, especially in the **Winter Garden** area, where vegetables such as spinach, carrots, and cabbage are grown. Much of the area is good **deer and dove habitat;** hunting leases are a major source of income. Brush control, soil fertility, and irrigation-water management are the major soil-management concerns.

Western Rio Grande Plain Soils

The Western Rio Grande Plain comprises about 5.3 million acres in an area of southwestern Texas from Del Rio to Rio Grande City. The landscape is nearly level to undulating except near the Rio Grande where it is hilly. Surface drainage is slow to rapid.

The major soils are mostly deep, brown or gray alkaline clays and loams. Some are saline.

Most of the soils are used for **rangeland.** Irrigated **grain sorghums** and **vegetables** are grown along the Rio Grande. **Hunting leases** are a major source of income. Brush control and limited soil moisture are the major soil-management problems.

Central Rio Grande Plain Soils

The Central Rio Grande Plain comprises about 5.9 million acres in an area of South Texas from Live Oak County to Hidalgo County. It Includes the **South Texas Sand Sheet,** an area of deep, sandy soils and active sand dunes. The landscape is nearly level to gently undulating. Surface drainage is slow to rapid. **Upland soils** are mostly deep, light-colored, neutral to alkaline sands and loams. Many are saline or sodic. Bottomland soils are of minor extent.

Most of the area is used for raising **beef cattle.** A few areas, mostly in the northeast part, are used for growing **grain sorghums, cotton,** and small grains. **Hunting leases** are a major source of income. Brush control is the major soil-management problem on rangeland; wind erosion and limited soil moisture are major concerns on cropland.

Lower Rio Grande Valley Soils

The Lower Rio Grande Valley comprises about 2.1 million acres in extreme southern Texas. The landscape is level to gently sloping with slow surface drainage.

Upland soils are mostly deep, grayish-brown, neutral to alkaline loams; coastal areas are mostly gray, silty clay loam and silty clay; some are saline. Bottomland soils are minor in extent.

Most of the soils are used for growing **irrigated vegetables** and **citrus,** along with **cotton, grain sorghums,** and **sugar cane.** Some areas are used for growing **beef cattle.** Irrigation water management and wind erosion are the major soil-management problems on cropland; brush control is the major problem on rangeland.

Western Cross Timbers Soils

The Western Cross Timbers area comprises about 2.6 million acres. It includes the wooded section west of the Grand Prairie and extends from the Red River southward to the north edge of Brown County. The landscape is undulating and is dissected by many drainageways including the **Brazos and Red rivers.** Surface drainage is rapid.

Upland soils are mostly deep, grayish-brown, slightly acid loams with loamy and clayey subsoils. **Bottomland soils** along the major rivers are deep, reddish-brown, neutral to alkaline silt loams and clays.

The area is used mostly for grazing **beef and dairy cattle** on native range and improved pastures. Crops are **peanuts, grain sorghums, small grains, peaches, pecans,** and **vegetables.** The major soil-management problem on grazing lands is brush control. Waste management on dairy farms is a more recent concern. Wind and water erosion are the major problems on cropland.

Eastern Cross Timbers Soils

The Eastern Cross Timbers area comprises about 1 million acres in a long narrow strip of wooded land that separates the northern parts of the Blackland Prairie and Grand Prairie and extends from the Red River southward to Hill County. The landscape is gently undulating to rolling and is dissected by many streams, including the **Red and Trinity rivers.** Sandstone-capped hills are prominent in some areas. Surface runoff is moderate to rapid.

The **upland soils** are mostly deep, light-colored, slightly acid sandy loams and loamy sands with reddish loamy or clayey subsoils. **Bottomland soils** are reddish-brown to dark gray, slightly acid to alkaline loams or gray clays.

Grassland consisting of native range and improved pastures is the major land use. **Peanuts, grain sorghums, small grains, peaches, pecans,** and **vegetables** are grown in some areas. Brush control, water erosion, and low fertility are the major soil concerns in management.

Grand Prairie Soils

The Grand Prairie comprises about 6.3 million acres in North Central Texas. It extends from the Red River to about the Colorado River. It lies between the Eastern and Western Cross Timbers in the northern part and just west of the Blackland Prairie in the southern part. The landscape is undulating to hilly and is dissected by many streams including the **Red, Trinity, and Brazos rivers.** Surface drainage is rapid.

Vertical profile of Houston black clay, which occurs on about 1.5 million acres in the Blackland Prairie. It is used extensively for crops and forage grasses. Its high shrink-swell potential affects building site development. Photo courtesy of the USDA-Natural Resources Conservation Service.

Upland soils are mostly dark-gray, alkaline clays; some are shallow over limestone and some are stony. Some areas have light-colored loamy soils over chalky limestone. **Bottomland soils** along the Red and Brazos rivers are reddish silt loams and clays. Other bottomlands have dark-gray loams and clays.

Land use is a mixture of rangeland, pastureland, and cropland. The area is mainly used for growing **beef cattle.** Some **small grain, grain sorghums, corn,** and **hay** are grown. Brush control and water erosion are the major management concerns.

Blackland Prairie Soils

The Blackland Prairies consist of about 12.6 million acres of east-central Texas extending southwesterly from the Red River to Bexar County. There are smaller areas to the southeast. The landscape is undulating with few scattered wooded areas that are mostly in the bottomlands. Surface drainage is moderate to rapid.

Both **upland** and **bottomland** soils are deep, dark-gray to black alkaline clays. Some soils in the western part are shallow to moderately deep over chalk. Some soils on the eastern edge are neutral to slightly acid, grayish clays and loams over mottled clay subsoils (sometimes called graylands). Blackland soils are known as **"cracking clays"** because of the large, deep cracks that form in dry weather. This high shrink-swell property can cause serious damage to foundations, highways, and other structures and is a safety hazard in pits and trenches.

Land use is divided about equally between cropland and grassland. **Cotton, grain sorghums, corn, wheat, oats,** and **hay** are grown. **Grassland** is mostly improved pastures, with native range on the shallower and steeper soils. Water erosion, cotton root rot, soil tilth, and brush control are the major management problems.

Claypan Area Soils

The Claypan Area consists of about 6.1 million acres in east-central Texas just east of the Blackland Prairie. The landscape is a gently undulating to rolling, moderately dissected woodland also known as the **Post Oak Belt** or **Post Oak Savannah.** Surface drainage is moderate.

Upland soils commonly have a thin, light-colored, acid sandy loam surface layer over dense, mottled red, yellow, and gray claypan subsoils. Some deep, sandy soils with less clayey subsoils exist. **Bottomlands** are deep, highly fertile, reddish-brown to dark-gray loamy to clayey soils.

Land use is mainly **rangeland.** Some areas are in improved pastures. Most cropland is in bottomlands that are protected from flooding. Major crops are **cotton, grain sorghums, corn, hay,** and **forage crops,** most of which are irrigated. Brush control on rangeland and irrigation water management on cropland are the major soil-management problems. Water erosion is a serious problem on the highly erosive claypan soils, especially where they are overgrazed.

East Texas Timberland Soils

The East Texas Timberlands area comprises about 16.1 million acres of the forested eastern part of the state. The land is gently undulating to hilly and well dissected by many streams. Surface drainage is moderate to rapid.

This area has many kinds of **upland soils** but most are deep, light-colored, acid sands and loams over loamy and clayey subsoils. Deep sands are in scattered areas, and red clays are in areas of "redlands." **Bottomland soils** are mostly brown to dark-gray, acid loams and some clays.

The land is used mostly for growing **commercial pine timber** and for **woodland grazing.** Improved pastures are scattered throughout and are used for grazing **beef and dairy cattle** and for hay production. Some **commercial hardwoods** are in the bottomlands. Woodland management problems include seedling survival, invasion of hardwoods in pine stands, effects of logging on water quality, and control of the southern pine beetle. Lime and fertilizers are necessary for productive cropland and pastures.

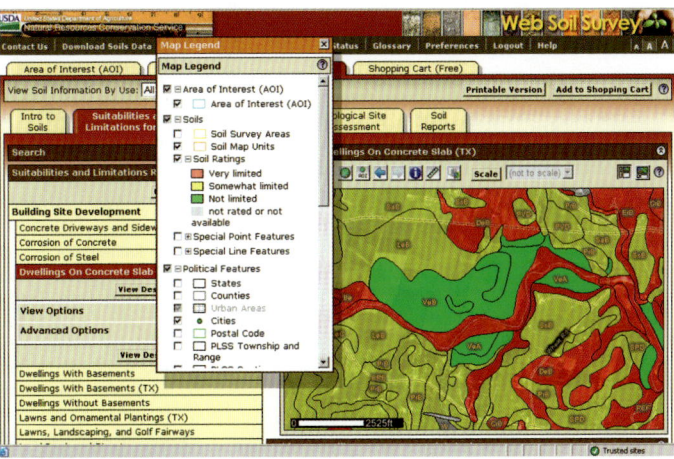

The Web Soil Survey provides maps showing the suitability and limitations of soils for over a hundred different uses. The colors on this map indicate which areas are suitable for dwellings on a concrete slab. Photo courtesy of the USDA-Natural Resources Conservation Service.

Coast Prairie Soils

The Coast Prairie includes about 8.7 million acres near the Gulf Coast. It ranges from 30 miles to 80 miles in width and parallels the coast from the Sabine River in Orange County in Southeast Texas to Baffin Bay in Kleberg County in South Texas. The landscape is level to gently undulating with slow surface drainage.

Upland soils are mostly deep, dark-gray, neutral to slightly acid clay loams and clays. Lighter-colored and more-sandy soils are in a strip on the northwestern edge. Some soils in the southern part are alkaline; some are saline and sodic. **Bottomland soils** are mostly deep, dark-colored clays and loams along small streams but are greatly varied along the rivers.

Land use is mainly **grazing lands** and **cropland.** Some hardwood timber is in the bottomlands. Many areas are also managed for **wetland wildlife habitat.** The nearly level topography and productive soils encourage farming. **Rice, grain sorghums, cotton, corn,** and **hay** are the main crops. Brush management on grasslands and removal of excess water on cropland are the major management concerns.

Coast Saline Prairies Soils

The Coast Saline Prairies area includes about 3.2 million acres along a narrow strip of wet lowlands adjacent to the coast; it includes the **barrier islands** that extend from Mexico to Louisiana. The surface is at or only a few feet above sea level with many areas of **saltwater marsh.** Surface drainage is very slow.

The soils are mostly deep, dark-colored clays and loams; many are saline and sodic. Light-colored sandy soils are on the barrier islands. The water table is at or near the surface of most soils.

Cattle grazing is the chief economic use of the various salt-tolerant cordgrasses and sedges. Many areas are managed for **wetland wildlife.** Recreation is popular on the barrier islands. Providing fresh water and access to grazing areas are the major management concerns.

Gulf Coast Marsh Soils

This 150,000-acre area lies in the extreme southeastern corner of Texas. The area can be subdivided into four parts: **freshwater, intermediate, brackish,** and **saline (saltwater) marsh.** The degree of salinity of this system grades landward from saltwater marshes along the coast to freshwater marshes inland. Surface drainage is very slow.

This area contains many lakes, bayous, tidal channels, and man-made canals. About one-half of the marsh is fresh; one-half is salty. Most of it is susceptible to flooding either by fresh water drained from lands adjacent to the marsh or by saltwater from the Gulf of Mexico. Most of the soils are poorly drained, continuously saturated, soft, and can carry little weight. In general, the organic soils have a thick layer of dark gray, relatively undecomposed organic material over a gray, clayey subsoil. The mineral soils have a surface of dark gray, highly decomposed organic material over a gray, clayey subsoil.

Most of the almost treeless and uninhabited area is in marsh vegetation, such as grasses, sedges, and rushes. It is used mainly for **wildlife habitat.** Part of the fertile and productive estuarine complex supports marine life of the Gulf of Mexico. It also provides **wintering ground for waterfowl** and **habitat for many furbearing animals** and **alligators.** A significant acreage is firm enough to support livestock and is used for **winter grazing of cattle.** The major management problems are providing fresh water and access to grazing areas.

Flatwoods Soils

The Flatwoods area includes about 2.5 million acres of woodland in humid Southeast Texas just north of the Coast Prairie and extending into Louisiana. The landscape is level to gently undulating. Surface drainage is slow.

Upland soils are mostly deep, light-colored, acid loams with gray, loamy, or clayey subsoils. **Bottomland soils** are deep, dark-colored, acid clays and loams. The water table is near the surface at least part of the year.

The land is mainly used for **forest,** although **cattle** are grazed in some areas. Woodland management problems include seedling survival, invasion of hardwoods in pine stands, effects of logging on water quality, and control of the southern pine beetle. ☆

Water Resources

Sources: Texas Water Development Board, www.twdb.state.tx.us; U.S. Geological Survey, http://tx.usgs.gov/

Historically, Texas has had a wealth of fresh to slightly saline water, which underlies more than 81 percent of the state. About 60 percent of the approximately 16 million acre-feet of water used yearly in Texas is derived from underground formations that make up **9 major and 21 minor aquifers.**

Nearly 80 percent of the groundwater produced in 2008 was used for irrigating crops, especially in the Panhandle region. Groundwater also supplies about 35 percent of the state's municipal needs.

Major Aquifers of Texas

Ogallala

The Ogallala aquifer extends through 48 counties of the Texas Panhandle and is the southernmost extension of the largest aquifer **(High Plains aquifer)** in North America. The Ogallala Formation of late Miocene to early Pliocene age consists of heterogeneous sequences of coarse-grained sand and gravel in the lower part, grading upward into clay, silt, and fine sand. In Texas, the Panhandle is the most extensive region irrigated with groundwater. In 2008, almost 96 percent of the water pumped from the Ogallala was used for irrigation.

Water-level declines are occurring in part of the region because of extensive pumping that far exceeds recharge. Water-conservation measures by agricultural and municipal users are being promoted. Computer models of the northern and southern portions of the Ogallala aquifer were completed by the Texas Water Development Board and its contractor. Several agencies are investigating playa recharge and agricultural re-use projects over the aquifer.

Gulf Coast Aquifer

The Gulf Coast aquifer forms an irregularly shaped belt that parallels the Texas coastline and extends through 54 counties from the Rio Grande northeastward to the Louisiana border. The **aquifer system** is composed of the Catahoula, Oakville, Fleming, Goliad, Willis, Lissie, Bentley, Montgomery, and Beaumont formations.

This system has been divided into three major water-producing components referred to as the **Chicot, Evangeline,** and **Jasper** aquifers. In 2008, municipal uses accounted for 62 percent and irrigation accounted for 25 percent of the total pumpage from the aquifer.

Water quality is generally good northeast of the San Antonio River basin, but deteriorates to the southwest. Years of heavy pumpage have caused significant water-level declines in portions of the aquifer. Some of these declines have resulted in significant **land-surface subsidence**, particularly in the Houston-Galveston area.

Edwards (Balcones Fault Zone)

The Edwards (BFZ) aquifer forms a narrow belt extending through 13 counties from a groundwater divide in Kinney County through the San Antonio area northeastward to the Leon River in Bell County. A poorly defined groundwater divide in Hays County hydrologically separates the aquifer into the **San Antonio and Austin regions.** Water in the aquifer occurs in fractures, honeycomb zones (or intergranular pores), and solution channels in the Edwards and associated limestone formations of Cretaceous age.

In 2008, about 72 percent of pumpage from the aquifer was for municipal use. Irrigation was the principal use in Medina and Uvalde counties. Until recently, San

Water Regulation

In Texas, water law historically has been different for surface water and groundwater. **Surface water** belongs to the state and, except for limited amounts of water for household and on-farm livestock use, requires permits for use.

In general, **groundwater** is considered the property of the surface landowner by "right of capture," meaning the landowner may pump as much water from beneath his land as he can for any beneficial use. This right may be limited only through the creation of ground-water conservation districts, which may make rules to protect and conserve groundwater supplies within their boundaries.

The **Texas Commission on Environmental Quality** is responsible for permitting and adjudicating surface-water rights and uses. It is the primary regulator of surface water and polices contamination and pollution of both surface and groundwater.

The **Texas Water Development Board** collects data on occurrence, availability, and water quality within the state; plans for future supply and use; and administers the state's funds for grants and loans to finance future water development and supply.

In January 2007, the Texas Water Development Board released a comprehensive **statewide water plan**, which the 75th Texas Legislature in 1997 required the board to complete every five years. The TWDB divided the state into 16 regional water-planning areas, and each area's Regional Water Planning Group is required to adopt a water plan that addresses conservation of water supplies, and that looks at how to meet future water needs and how to respond to future droughts.

Antonio was one of the largest cities in the world that relied solely on a single groundwater source for its municipal supply. The aquifer now provides approximately 90 percent of the city's drinking water. The aquifer also feeds several well-known **recreational springs** and underlies some of Texas' most environmentally sensitive areas.

In 1993, the Edwards Aquifer Authority (EAA) was created by the legislature to regulate aquifer pumpage to benefit all users from Uvalde County through a portion of Hays County. Barton Springs–Edwards Aquifer Conservation District provides aquifer management for the rest of Hays and southern Travis counties, and the Kinney County Groundwater Conservation District manages the aquifer segment within Kinney County.

The EAA has an active program to educate the public on water conservation and also operates several active groundwater recharge sites. The San Antonio River Authority also has a number of flood-control structures that effectively recharge the aquifer.

Conservation districts are promoting more-efficient irrigation techniques, and market-based, voluntary transfers of unused agricultural water rights to municipal uses are more common.

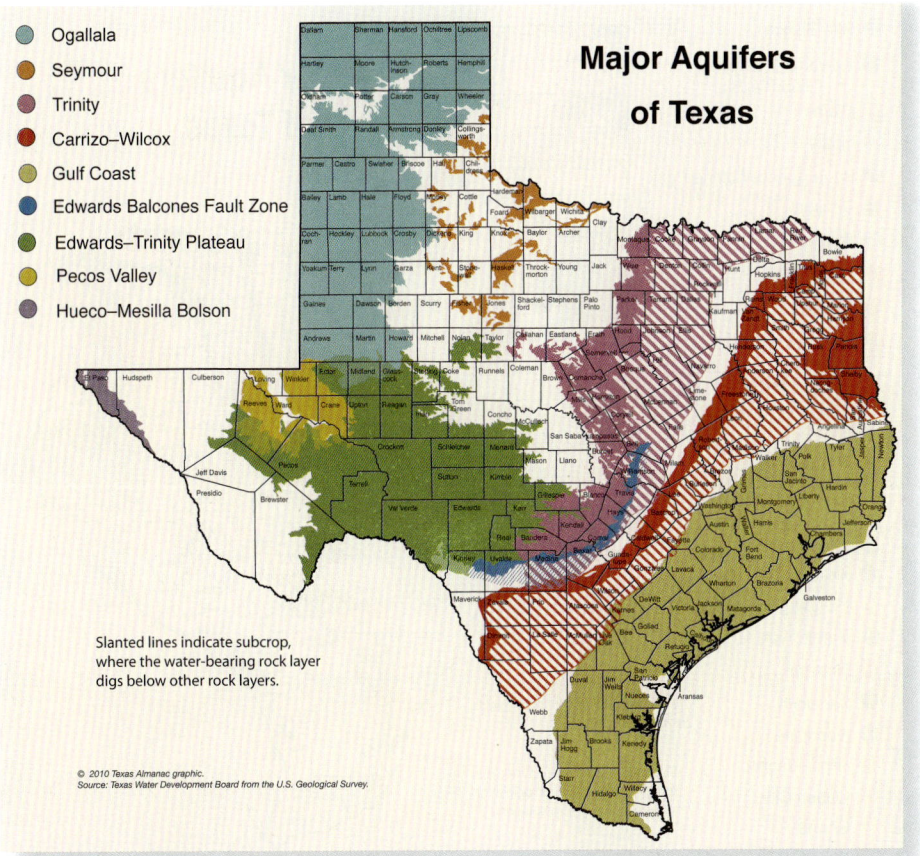

Major Aquifers of Texas

- ● Ogallala
- ● Seymour
- ● Trinity
- ● Carrizo–Wilcox
- ● Gulf Coast
- ● Edwards Balcones Fault Zone
- ● Edwards–Trinity Plateau
- ● Pecos Valley
- ● Hueco–Mesilla Bolson

Slanted lines indicate subcrop, where the water-bearing rock layer digs below other rock layers.

© 2010 Texas Almanac graphic.
Source: Texas Water Development Board from the U.S. Geological Survey.

Carrizo-Wilcox

Extending from the Rio Grande in South Texas northeastward into Arkansas and Louisiana, the Carrizo-Wilcox aquifer provides water to all or parts of 66 counties. The **Wilcox Group** and overlying **Carrizo Sand** form a hydrologically connected system of sand locally interbedded with clay, silt, lignite, and gravel.

Throughout most of its extent in Texas, the aquifer yields fresh to slightly saline water that is used mainly for irrigation in the **Winter Garden District** of South Texas, and for public supply and industrial use in Central and Northeast Texas. In 2008, irrigation accounted for 43 percent of water pumped from the aquifer, and municipal supply accounted for 47 percent.

Excessive pumping has lowered the water level, particularly in the artesian portion of the Winter Garden District of Atascosa, Dimmit, Frio, LaSalle, and Zavala counties and in the municipal and industrial areas of Angelina, Nacogdoches, and Smith counties.

Trinity

The Trinity Aquifer consists of basal Cretaceous-age Trinity Group formations extending through 61 counties from the Red River in North Texas to the Hill Country of Central Texas. The aquifer is comprised of the **Twin Mountains, Glen Rose, Paluxy, Hosston,** and **Hensell formations.** Where the Glen Rose thins or is absent, the Twin Mountains and Paluxy formations coalesce to form the **Antlers Formation.** In the south, the Trinity includes the Glen Rose and underlying **Travis Peak** formations. Water from the Antlers portion is used mainly for irriga-

tion in the outcrop area of North and Central Texas.

Elsewhere, water from the Trinity Aquifer is used primarily for municipal and domestic supply. Municipal use accounted for 63 percent of the total aquifer use in 2008. Extensive development of the Trinity Aquifer in the Dallas-Fort Worth and Waco areas has resulted in water-level declines of 350 to more than 1,000 feet.

Edwards-Trinity Plateau

This aquifer underlies the Edwards Plateau, extending through 40 counties from the Hill Country of Central Texas westward to the Trans-Pecos region. It consists of sandstone and limestone formations of the Trinity formations, and limestones and dolomites of the Edwards and associated limestone formations. Groundwater movement is generally toward the southeast.

Near the plateau's edge, flow is toward the main streams, where the water issues from springs. Irrigation, mainly in the northwestern portion of the region, accounted for about 79 percent of total aquifer use in 2008 and has resulted in significant water-level declines in Glasscock and Reagan counties. Elsewhere, the aquifer supplies fresh but hard water for municipal, domestic, and livestock use.

Seymour

This aquifer consists of isolated areas of alluvium found in parts of 25 north-central and Panhandle counties in the upper Red River and Brazos River basins. Eastward-flowing streams during the Quaternary Period deposited discontinuous beds of poorly sorted gravel, sand, silt, and clay that were later dissected by erosion,

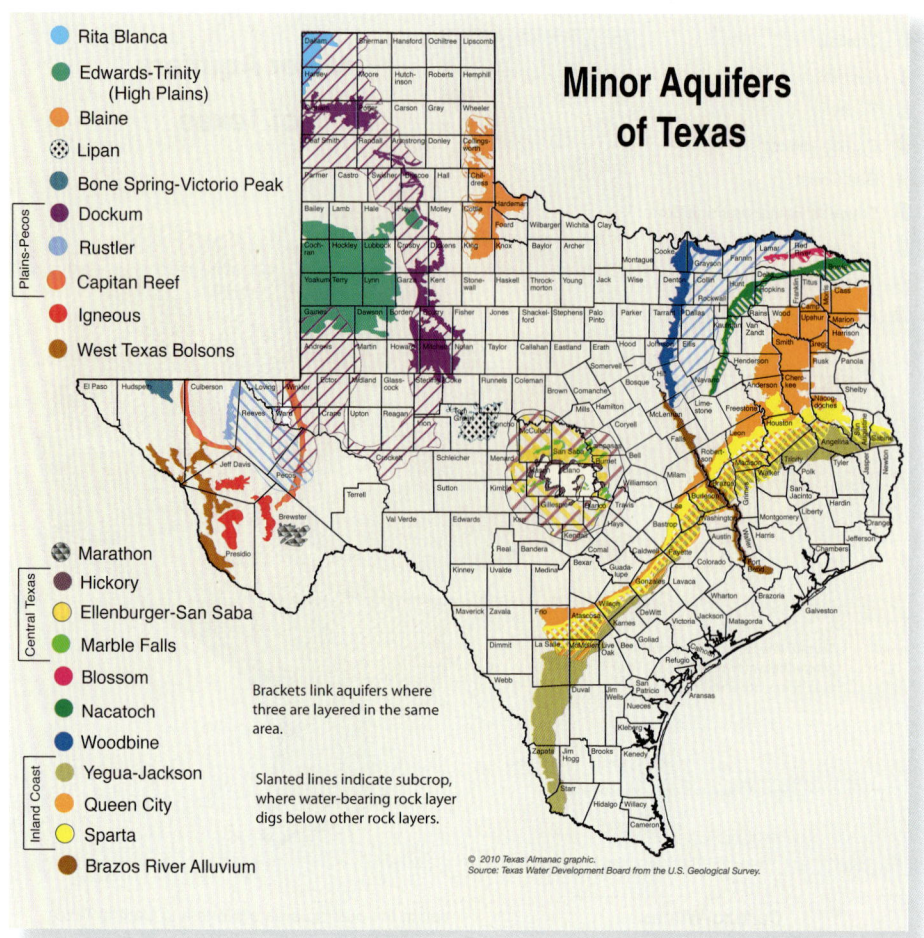

Minor Aquifers of Texas

Plains-Pecos
- Rita Blanca
- Edwards-Trinity (High Plains)
- Blaine
- Lipan
- Bone Spring-Victorio Peak
- Dockum
- Rustler
- Capitan Reef
- Igneous
- West Texas Bolsons

Central Texas
- Marathon
- Hickory
- Ellenburger-San Saba
- Marble Falls
- Blossom
- Nacatoch
- Woodbine

Inland Coast
- Yegua-Jackson
- Queen City
- Sparta
- Brazos River Alluvium

Brackets link aquifers where three are layered in the same area.

Slanted lines indicate subcrop, where water-bearing rock layer digs below other rock layers.

© 2010 Texas Almanac graphic.
Source: Texas Water Development Board from the U.S. Geological Survey.

resulting in the isolated remnants of the formation. Individual accumulations vary greatly in thickness, but most of the Seymour is less than 100 feet.

The lower, more permeable part of the aquifer produces the greatest amount of groundwater. Irrigation pumpage accounted for 94 percent of the total use from the aquifer in 2008. Water quality generally ranges from fresh to slightly saline. However, the salinity has increased in many heavily pumped areas to the point where the water has become unsuitable for domestic and municipal use. Natural salt pollution in the upper reaches of the Red and Brazos river basins precludes the full utilization of these water resources.

Hueco-Mesilla Bolson

These aquifers are located in El Paso and Hudspeth counties in far West Texas and occur in Tertiary and Quaternary basin-fill deposits that extend northward into New Mexico and westward into Mexico. The Hueco Bolson, located on the eastern side of the **Franklin Mountains,** consists of up to 9,000 feet of clay, silt, sand, and gravel and is an important source of drinking water for both El Paso and Juarez, Mexico.

Located west of the Franklin Mountains, the Mesilla Bolson reaches up to 2,000 feet in thickness and contains three separate water-producing zones.

Historical large-scale groundwater withdrawals, especially for the municipal uses of El Paso and Juarez, have caused major water-level declines and significantly

changed the direction of flow, causing a deterioration of the chemical quality of the groundwater in the aquifer, according to El Paso Water Utilities and the USGS.

Municpal water use in 2008 accounted for 87 percent of total use from the Hueco-Mesilla Bolson. El Paso, however, has reduced its use of groundwater from the Hueco Bolson since 1989, and observation wells indicate that water levels have stabilized. El Paso and Fort Bliss also have built the **world's largest inland desalination plant** in El Paso County, which uses brackish groundwater from the Hueco Bolson.

Pecos Valley

Located in the upper Pecos River Valley of West Texas, this aquifer, formerly called the Cenozoic Pecos Alluvium, extends through 12 counties. In 2008, 72 percent of groundwater pumped from the aquifer was used for irrigation, and the rest is withdrawn for industrial uses, power supply, and municipal use. Consisting of up to 1,500 feet of alluvial fill, the aquifer occupies two hydrologically separate basins: the **Pecos Trough** in the west and the **Monument Draw Trough** in the east.

Water is generally hard and contains dissolved-solids concentrations ranging from less than 300 to more than 5,000 parts per million. Water-level declines in excess of 200 feet have occurred in Reeves and Pecos counties but have slowed since the mid-1970s with the decrease in irrigation pumpage. Declines continue in Ward County due to increased municipal and industrial pumping. ☆

Major Rivers of Texas

There are 11,247 named Texas streams identified in the U.S. Geological Survey Geographic Names Information System. Their combined length is about 80,000 miles, and they drain 263,513 square miles within Texas. **Fourteen major rivers** are described in this section, starting with the southernmost and moving northward:

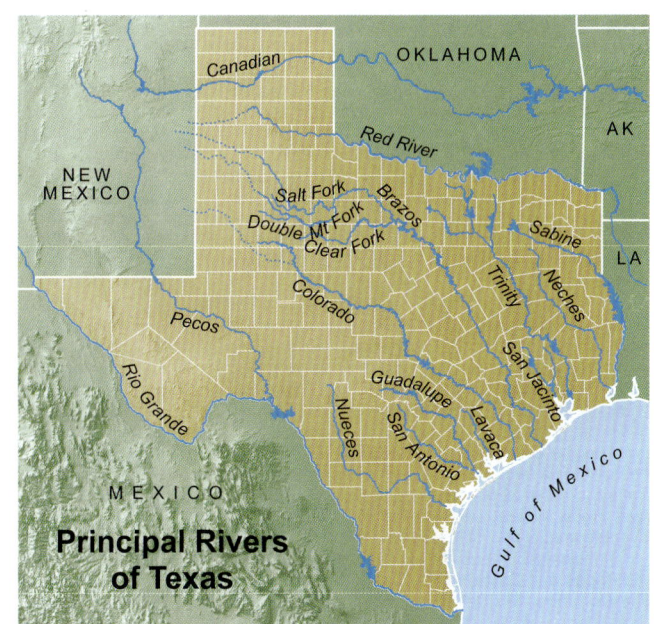

Principal Rivers of Texas

Rio Grande

The Pueblo Indians called this river **P'osoge**, which means the "river of great water." In 1582, **Antonio de Espejo** of Nueva Vizcaya, Mexico, followed the course of the **Río Conchos** to its confluence with a great river, which Espejo named **Río del Norte (River of the North)**. The name **Rio Grande** was first given the stream apparently by the explorer **Juan de Oñate**, who arrived on its banks near present-day El Paso in 1598.

Thereafter the names were often consolidated as **Río Grande del Norte**. It was shown also on early Spanish maps as **Río San Buenaventura** and **Río Ganapetuan**. In its lower course, it early acquired the name **Río Bravo**, which is its name on most Mexican maps. At times it has also been known as **Río Turbio**, probably because of its muddy appearance during its frequent rises. Some people erroneously call this watercourse the Rio Grande River.

This river **forms the boundary of Texas** and the international U.S.-Mexican border for **889** or **1,254** river miles, depending upon method of measurement. (See **Texas Boundary Lines, page 68.**)

The **U.S. Geological Survey** figure for the total length from its headwaters to its mouth on the Gulf of Mexico is **1,900** miles.

According to the USGS, the Rio Grande is tied with the St. Lawrence River (also 1,900 miles) as the **fourth-longest** North American river, exceeded only by the Missouri-Mississippi, McKenzie-Peace, and Yukon rivers. Since all of these except the Missouri-Mississippi are partly in Canada, the Rio Grande is the **second-longest river entirely within or bordering the United States**. It is **Texas' longest river.**

The snow-fed flow of the Rio Grande is used for irrigation in Colorado below the San Juan Mountains, where the river rises at the Continental Divide. Turning south, it flows through a canyon in northern New Mexico and again irrigates a broad valley of central New Mexico. Southern New Mexico impounds Rio Grande waters in Elephant Butte Reservoir for irrigation of the valley above and below El Paso.

The valley near El Paso is thought to be the **oldest irrigated area in Texas** because Indians were irrigating crops here when Spanish explorers arrived in the early 1500s.

From source to mouth, the Rio Grande drops 12,000 feet to sea level as a mountain torrent, desert stream, and meandering coastal river. Along its banks and in its valley, Europeans established some of their first North American settlements. Here are situated **three of the oldest towns in Texas — Ysleta, Socorro, and San Elizario.**

Because of the extensive irrigation, the Rio Grande virtually ends at the lower end of the El Paso valley, except in seasons of above-normal flow.

The river starts again as a perennially flowing

AVERAGE ANNUAL FLOW		
	RIVER	ACRE-FEET*
1.	Brazos	6,074,000
2.	Sabine	5,864,000
3.	Trinity	5,727,000
4.	Neches	4,323,000
5.	Red	3,464,000
6.	Colorado	1,904,000

*One acre-foot equals 325,851 gallons of water.
Source: Texas Water Development Board, 2007 State Water Plan.

LENGTHS OF MAJOR RIVERS		
	RIVER	LENGTH-MILES*
1.	Rio Grande	1,900
2.	Red	1,290
3.	Brazos	1,280
4.	Pecos	926
5.	Canadian	906
6.	Colorado	865

*Length from the original headwaters where the name defines the complete length to its outflow point. *Source: U.S. Geological Survey, 2008.*

stream where the Río Conchos of Mexico flows into it at Presidio-Ojinaga. Through the **Big Bend,** the Rio Grande flows through three successive **canyons,** the **Santa Elena,** the **Mariscal,** and the **Boquillas.** The Santa Elena has a river bed elevation of 2,145 feet and a canyon-rim elevation of 3,661. Corresponding figures for Mariscal are 1,925 and 3,625, and for Boquillas, 1,850 and 3,490. The river here flows for about 100 miles around the base of the **Chisos Mountains** as the southern boundary of **Big Bend National Park**.

Below the Big Bend, the Rio Grande gradually emerges from mountains onto the Coastal Plains. A 191.2-mile strip on the U.S. side from Big Bend National Park downstream to the Terrell–Val Verde county line has federal designation as the **Rio Grande Wild and Scenic River**.

At the confluence of the Rio Grande and Devils River, the United States and Mexico have built **Amistad Dam,** to impound 3,151,267 acre-feet of water, of which Texas' share is 56.2 percent. **Falcon Reservoir**, also an international project, impounds 2,646,187 acre-feet of water, of which Texas' share in Zapata and Starr counties is 58.6 percent.

The Rio Grande, where it joins the Gulf of Mexico, has created a fertile delta called the **Lower Rio Grande Valley**, a major vegetable- and fruit-growing area. The river drains 49,387 square miles of Texas and has an average annual flow of 645,500 acre-feet.

Principal tributaries flowing from the Texas side are the **Pecos** and **Devils** rivers. On the Mexican side are **Río Conchos, Río Salado,** and **Río San Juan**. About three-fourths of the water running into the Rio Grande below El Paso comes from the Mexican side.

Pecos River

The Pecos, one of the major tributaries of the Rio Grande, rises on the western slope of the Santa Fe Mountains in the **Sangre de Cristo Range** of northern New Mexico. It enters Texas as the boundary between Loving and Reeves counties and flows **350 miles** south-

east as the boundary for several other counties, entering Val Verde County at its northwestern corner and angles across that county to its mouth on the **Rio Grande**, northwest of Del Rio.

According to the Handbook of Texas, the origins of the river's several names began with Antonio de Espejo, who called the river the **Río de las Vacas** ("river of the cows") because of the number of buffalo in the vicinity. Gaspar Castaño de Sosa, who followed the Pecos northward, called it the **Río Salado** because of its salty taste, which caused it to be shunned by men and animals alike.

It is believed that the name "Pecos" first appears in Juan de Oñate's reports concerning the Indian pueblo of Cicuye, now known as the **Pecos Pueblo** in New Mexico, and is of unknown origin.

Through most of its **926-mile-long** course from its headwaters, the Pecos River parallels the Rio Grande. The total drainage area of the Pecos in New Mexico and Texas is about 44,000 square miles. Most of its tributaries flow from the west; these include the **Delaware River** and **Toyah Creek**.

The topography of the river valley in Texas ranges from semi-arid irrigated farmlands, desert with sparse vegetation, and, in the lowermost reaches of the river, deep canyons.

Nueces River

The Nueces River rises in two forks in Edwards and Real counties and flows **315 miles** to Nueces Bay on the Gulf near Corpus Christi. Draining 16,700 square miles, it is a beautiful, **spring-fed stream** flowing through **canyons** until it issues from the **Balcones Escarpment** onto the Coastal Plains in northern Uvalde County.

Alonso de León, in 1689, gave it its name. **Nueces**, plural of *nuez*, means nuts in Spanish. (More than a century earlier, Cabeza de Vaca had referred to a **Río de las Nueces** in this region, but that is now thought to have been the Guadalupe.)

The original Indian name for this river seems to

The sun rises on the Trinity River near Riverside in Walker County. Photo by Ron Billings; Texas Forest Service.

Texas River Basins

1. Canadian
2. Red
3. Brazos
4. Colorado
5. Rio Grande
6. Trinity
7. Neches
8. Sabine
9. Nueces
10. San Antonio
11. Guadalupe
12. Lavaca
13. San Jacinto
14. Sulphur
15. Cypress

Sulphur and Cypress are sometimes included in the Red River basin. See Sulphur River and [Big] Cypress [Creek] in the Secondary Streams of Texas.

— Main River
----- Tributary

© 2010 Texas Almanac graphic.
Sources: Bureau of Economic Geology of the University of Texas at Austin and the U.S. Geological Survey.

have been **Chotilapacquen.** Crossing Texas in 1691, Terán de los Rios named the river **San Diego**.

The Nueces was the boundary line between the Spanish provinces of Texas and Nuevo Santander. After the Texas Revolution of 1836, both Texas and Mexico claimed the territory between the Nueces and the Rio Grande, a dispute that was settled in 1848 by the **Treaty of Guadalupe Hidalgo,** which fixed the international boundary at the Rio Grande.

Average runoff of the Nueces is about 539,700 acre-feet a year. Principal water conservation projects are **Lake Corpus Christi** and **Choke Canyon Reservoir**. Principal tributaries of the Nueces are the **Frio** and the **Atascosa**.

San Antonio River

The San Antonio River has at its source **large springs** within and near the city limits of San Antonio. It flows **180 miles** across the Coastal Plains to a junction with the **Guadalupe** near the Gulf Coast. Its channel through San Antonio has been developed into a parkway known as the **River Walk.**

Its principal tributaries are the **Medina River** and **Cibolo Creek,** both spring-fed streams, and this, with its own spring origin, gives it remarkably clear water and makes it one of the steadiest of Texas rivers. Including the Medina River headwaters, it is **238 miles** in length.

The river was first named the **León** by Alonso de

León in 1689; the name was not for himself, but he called it "lion" because its channel was filled with a rampaging flood.

Because of its limited and arid drainage area (4,180 square miles) the average runoff of the San Antonio River is relatively small, about 562,700 acre-feet annually.

Guadalupe River

The Guadalupe rises in its North and South forks in western Kerr County. A **spring-fed stream,** it flows eastward through the Hill Country until it issues from the **Balcones Escarpment** near New Braunfels. It then crosses the Coastal Plains to San Antonio Bay. Its total length is **409 miles**, and its drainage area is 5,953 square miles. Its principal tributaries are the **San Marcos**, another spring-fed stream, which joins it in Gonzales County; the **San Antonio**, which joins it just above its mouth on San Antonio Bay; and the **Comal**, which joins it at New Braunfels.

There has been power development on the Guadalupe near Gonzales and Cuero for many years, and there is also power generation at **Canyon Lake**. Because of its springs and its considerable drainage area, the Guadalupe has an average annual runoff of more than 1.42 million acre-feet.

The name Guadalupe is derived from **Nuestra Señora de Guadalupe,** the name given the stream by

Alonso de León.

Lavaca River

The Lavaca rises in extreme southeastern Fayette County and flows **117 miles** into the Gulf through Lavaca Bay. Without a spring-water source and with only a small watershed, including that of its principal tributary, the **Navidad,** its flow is intermittent. Runoff averages about 277,000 acre-feet yearly.

The Spanish called it the Lavaca (cow) because of the numerous bison found near it. It is the principal stream running to the Gulf between the Guadalupe and the Colorado, and drains 2,309 square miles. The principal lake on the **Navidad** is **Lake Texana.**

Colorado River

Rising in east-central Dawson County, the Colorado River, which flows **865 miles** to Matagorda Bay, is the **longest river within Texas**. Its drainage area, which extends into New Mexico, is 42,318 square miles.

Its average annual runoff reaches a volume of 1.9 million acre-feet near the Gulf. Its name is a Spanish word meaning **"reddish."** There is evidence that Spanish explorers originally named the muddy Brazos "Colorado," but Spanish mapmakers later transposed the two names.

The river flows through a rolling, mostly prairie terrain to the vicinity of San Saba County, where it enters the rugged **Hill Country** and **Llano Basin**. It passes through a picturesque series of **canyons** until it issues from the **Balcones Escarpment** at Austin and flows across the Coastal Plains.

In the Hill Country, a remarkable series of reservoirs has been built to provide hydoelectric power. The largest of these are **Lake Buchanan** in Burnet and Llano counties and **Lake Travis** in Travis County. Between the two in Burnet County are three smaller reservoirs: **Inks, Lyndon B. Johnson** (formerly Granite Shoals), and **Marble Falls**. Below Lake Travis is the older **Lake Austin**, largely filled with silt, whose dam is used to produce power from waters flowing down from the lakes above. **Lady Bird Lake** (formerly Town Lake) is in the City of Austin. This entire area is known as the **Highland Lakes Country**.

As early as the 1820s, Anglo-Americans settled on the banks of the lower Colorado, and in 1839, the **Capital Commission of the Republic of Texas** chose the picturesque area where the river flows from the **Balcones Escarpment** as the site of a new capital of the Republic — now **Austin**, capital of the state.

The early colonists encouraged navigation along the lower channel with some success. However, a **natural log raft** that formed 10 miles from the Gulf blocked river traffic after 1839, although shallow-draught vessels occasionally ventured as far upstream as Austin.

Conservation and utilization of the waters of the Colorado are under jurisdiction of three agencies created by the Legislature; the **Lower, Central,** and **Upper Colorado River Authorities**.

The principal tributaries of the Colorado River are the several prongs of the **Concho River** on its upper course, **Pecan Bayou (farthest west "bayou" in the United States)**, and the **Llano, San Saba,** and **Pedernales** rivers. All except Pecan Bayou flow into the Colorado from the **Edwards Plateau** and are spring-fed, perennially flowing rivers. In the numerous mussels found along these streams, **pearls** occasionally have been found. On early Spanish maps, the Middle Concho was called **Río de las Perlas**.

Brazos River

The Brazos River proper is considered to begin where the **Double Mountain** and **Salt Forks** flow together in **northeastern Stonewall County;** it then flows **840 miles** across Texas. The **U.S. Geological Survey** puts the **total length** from the New Mexico source of its longest upper prong at **1,280 miles.**

With a drainage area of about 42,865 square miles, it is the second-largest river basin in Texas, after the Rio Grande. It flows directly into the Gulf southwest of Freeport in Brazoria County. **Its average annual flow exceeds 6 million acre-feet, the largest volume of any river in the state.**

The Brazos' third upper fork is the **Clear Fork**, which joins the main stream in Young County, just above **Possum Kingdom Lake**. The Brazos crosses most of the main physiographic regions of Texas — High Plains, West Texas Rolling Plains, Western Cross Timbers, Grand Prairie, and Gulf Coastal Plains.

The original name of this river was **Brazos de Dios**, meaning "Arms of God." There are several legends as to why. One is that the Coronado expedition, wandering on the trackless **Llano Estacado**, exhausted its water and was threatened with death from thirst. Arriving at the bank of the river, they gave it the name "Brazos de Dios" in thankfulness. Another is that a ship exhausted its water supply, and its crew was saved when they found the mouth of the Brazos. Still another story is that miners on the San Saba were forced by drought to seek water near present-day Waco and in gratitude called it Brazos de Dios.

Much early Anglo-American colonization of Texas took place in the Brazos Valley. Along its channel were **San Felipe de Austin**, capital of Austin's colony; **Washington-on-the-Brazos**, where Texans declared independence from Mexico; and other historic settlements. There was some navigation of the **lower channel** of the Brazos in this period. Near its mouth it intersects the **Gulf Intracoastal Waterway,** which provides connection with the commerce on the Mississippi.

Most of the Brazos Valley lies within the boundaries of the **Brazos River Authority**, which conducts a multipurpose program for development. A large reservoir on the main channel of the Brazos is **Lake Whitney** (554,203 acre-feet capacity), where it is the boundary line between Hill and Bosque counties. **Lake Waco** on the Bosque and **Belton Lake** on the Leon are among the principal reservoirs on its tributaries. In addition to its three upper forks, other chief tributaries are the **Paluxy, Little,** and **Navasota** rivers.

San Jacinto River

The San Jacinto is a short river with a drainage basin of 3,936 square miles and an average annual runoff of nearly 1.36 million acre-feet. It is formed by the junction of its East and West forks in northeastern Harris County and runs to the Gulf through Galveston Bay. Its total length, including the East Fork, is about **85 miles**.

Lake Conroe is on the West Fork, and **Lake Houston** is at the junction of the West Fork and the East Fork. The **Houston Ship Channel** runs through the lower course of the San Jacinto and its tributary, **Buffalo Bayou,** connecting the Port of Houston to the Gulf.

There are two stories concerning the origin of its name. One is that when early explorers discovered it, its channel was choked with hyacinth ("**jacinto**" is the Spanish word for hyacinth). The other is that it was discovered on Aug. 17, St. Hyacinth's Day. The **Battle of San Jacinto** was fought on the bank of this river on April 21, 1836, when Texas won its independence from Mexico. **San Jacinto Battleground State Historic Site and monument** commemorate the battle.

Trinity River

The Trinity rises in its East Fork, Elm Fork, West Fork, and Clear Fork in Grayson, Montague, Archer, and Parker counties, respectively. The main stream begins with the junction of the Elm and West forks at Dallas.

Cowboys cast long shadows as they ride along the Rio Grande near Candelaria in Presidio County. File photo.

Its length is **550 miles**, and its drainage area is 17,913 square miles. Because of moderate to heavy rainfall over its drainage area, it has a average annual flow of 5.7 million acre-feet near its mouth on Trinity Bay.

The Trinity derives its name from the Spanish "**Trinidad.**" Alonso de León named it **La Santísima Trinidad** (the Most Holy Trinity).

Navigation was developed along its lower course with several riverport towns, such as **Sebastopol** in Trinity County. For many years, there has been a basin-wide movement for navigation, conservation, and utilization of its water. The **Trinity River Authority** is a state agency and the **Trinity Improvement Association** is a publicly supported nonprofit organization that has advocated its development.

The Trinity has in its valley **more large cities, greater population, and more industrial development** than any other river basin in Texas. On the Coastal Plains, there is large use of its waters for **rice irrigation**. Large reservoirs on the Elm Fork are **Lewisville Lake** and **Ray Roberts Lake**. There are four reservoirs above Fort Worth: **Lake Worth**, **Eagle Mountain Lake,** and **Lake Bridgeport** on the West Fork and **Benbrook Lake** on the Clear Fork.

Lake Lavon in southeast Collin County and **Lake Ray Hubbard** in Collin, Dallas, Kaufman, and Rockwall counties are on the East Fork. **Lake Livingston** is in Polk, San Jacinto, Trinity, and Walker counties.Two other reservoirs in the Trinity basin below the Dallas–Fort Worth area are **Cedar Creek Reservoir** and **Richland-Chambers Reservoir**.

Neches River

The Neches rises in Van Zandt County in East Texas and flows **416 miles** to **Sabine Lake** near Port Arthur. It has a drainage area of 9,937 square miles. Abundant rainfall over its entire basin gives it an average annual flow near the Gulf of about 4.3 million acre-feet a year. The river takes its name from the **Neches Indians,** who

the early Spanish explorers found living along its banks. Principal tributary of the Neches, and comparable with the Neches in length and flow above their confluence, is the **Angelina River,** so named for **Angelina (Little Angel),** a Hainai Indian girl who converted to Christianity and played an important role in the early development of this region.

Both the Neches and the Angelina run most of their courses in the **Piney Woods,** and there was much settlement along them as early as the 1820s.

Sam Rayburn Reservoir, near Jasper on the Angelina River, was completed and dedicated in 1965. It has a storage capacity of 2.87 million acre-feet. Reservoirs located on the Neches River include **Lake Palestine** in the upper basin and **B. A. Steinhagen Lake** located at the junction of the Neches and the Angelina rivers.

Sabine River

The Sabine River is formed by three forks rising in Collin and Hunt counties. From its sources to its mouth on **Sabine Lake,** it flows approximately **360 miles** and drains 7,570 square miles.

Sabine comes from the **Spanish word** for cypress, as does the name of the **Sabinal River,** which flows into the Frio River in Southwest Texas. The Sabine has an average annual flow volume of 5.86 million acre-feet, the second-largest in the state after the Brazos.

Throughout most of Texas history, the lower Sabine has been the **eastern Texas boundary line,** though for a while there was doubt as to whether the Sabine or the Arroyo Hondo, east of the Sabine in Louisiana, was the boundary. For a number of years, the outlaw-infested **neutral ground** lay between them. There was also a **boundary dispute** in which it was alleged that the Neches was really the Sabine and, therefore, the boundary.

Travelers over the part of the **Camino Real** known as the **Old San Antonio Road** crossed the Sabine at the **Gaines Ferry** in Sabine County, and there were crossings for the **Atascosito Road** and other travel and trade routes of that day.

Two of Texas' largest reservoirs have been created by dams on the Sabine River. The first of these is **Lake Tawakoni,** in Hunt, Rains, and Van Zandt counties, with a storage capacity of 888,126 acre-feet.

Toledo Bend Reservoir impounds 4.47 million acre-feet of water on the Sabine in Newton, Panola, Sabine, and Shelby counties. It is the **largest lake** lying wholly or partly in Texas and the **9th-largest reservoir (in capacity by volume) in the United States**. This is a joint project of Texas and Louisiana, through the **Sabine River Authority**.

Red River

The Red River, with a length of **1,290 miles** from its headwaters, is exceeded in length only by the Rio Grande among rivers associated with Texas. Its original source is water in Curry County, New Mexico, near the Texas boundary, forming a definite channel as it crosses Deaf Smith County, Texas, in tributaries that flow into the **Prairie Dog Town Fork of the Red River**. These waters carve the spectacular **Palo Duro Canyon** of the High Plains before the Red River leaves the **Caprock Escarpment,** flowing eastward.

Where the Red River crosses the 100th meridian at the bottom of the Panhandle, the river becomes the **Texas-Oklahoma boundary** and is soon joined by Buck Creek to form the main channel, according to the U.S. Geological Survey. Its length in Texas is **695 miles,** before it flows into Arkansas, where it swings south to flow through Louisiana.

The Red River, which drains 24,297 square miles in Texas, is a part of the **Mississippi drainage basin,** and at one time it emptied all of its water into the Mississippi. In recent years, however, part of its water, especially at flood stage, has flowed to the Gulf via the **Atchafalaya River** in Louisiana.

The Red River takes its name from the red color of the current. This caused every explorer who came to its banks to call it "red" regardless of the language he spoke — **Río Rojo** or **Río Roxo** in Spanish, **Rivière Rouge** in French. At an early date, the river became the axis for French advance from Louisiana northwestward as far as present-day Montague County. There was consistent **early navigation** of the river from its mouth on the Mississippi to Shreveport, above which navigation was blocked by a **natural log raft**.

A number of important gateways into Texas from the North were established along the stream, such as **Pecan Point** and **Jonesborough** in Red River County, **Colbert's Ferry** and **Preston** in Grayson County, and later, **Doan's Store Crossing** in Wilbarger County. The river was a menace to the early traveler because of both its variable current and its **quicksands,** which brought disaster to many a trail-herd cow, as well as ox team and covered wagon.

The largest water conservation project on the Red River is **Lake Texoma,** with a conservation storage capacity of 2.51 million acre-feet.

Red River water's high content of salt and other minerals limits its usefulness along its upper reaches. Ten **salt springs** and tributaries in Texas and Oklahoma contribute most of these minerals.

The uppermost tributaries of the Red River in Texas are **Tierra Blanca Creek,** which rises in Curry County, N.M., and flows easterly across Deaf Smith and Randall counties to meet **Palo Duro Creek** and form the **Prairie Dog Town Fork** a few miles east of Canyon.

Other principal tributaries in Texas are the **Pease** and the **Wichita** in North Central Texas and the **Sulphur** in Northeast Texas, which flows through **Wright Patman Lake,** then into the Red River after it has crossed the boundary line into Arkansas.

The last major tributary in Northeast Texas is the **Cypress Creek system,** which flows into Louisiana before joining with the Red River. Major reservoirs in this basin are **Lake O' the Pines** and **Caddo Lake.**

From Oklahoma, the principal tributary is the **Washita,** which has its headwaters in Roberts County, Texas. The **Ouachita,** a river with the same pronunciation though spelled differently, is the principal tributary to the Red River's lower course in Arkansas.

The Red River **boundary dispute,** a long-standing feud between Oklahoma and Texas, was finally settled in **2000** when the boundary was set at the vegetation line on the south bank, except for Lake Texoma, where the boundary was set within the channel of the lake.

Canadian River

The Canadian River heads near **Raton Pass** in northern New Mexico near the Colorado boundary line and flows into Texas on the west line of Oldham County. It crosses the Texas Panhandle into Oklahoma and there flows into the Arkansas River, a total distance of **906 miles**. It drains 12,865 square miles in Texas, and much of its **213-mile course across the Panhandle** is in a deep gorge.

A tributary, the **North Canadian River,** drips briefly into the Texas Panhandle in Sherman County before it joins the main channel in Oklahoma.

One of several theories as to how the Canadian got its name is that some early explorers thought it flowed into Canada. **Lake Meredith,** formed by **Sanford Dam,** provides water for several Panhandle cities.

Because of the **deep gorge** and the **quicksand** that occurs in many places, the Canadian River has been a particularly difficult stream to bridge. It is known, especially in its lower course in Oklahoma, as outstanding among the streams of the country for the great amount of quicksand in its channel. ☆

Secondary Streams of Texas

In addition to the principal rivers just discussed, Texas has many other streams of various size. The following list gives a few of these streams as designated by the U.S. Geological Survey, with additional information from the new Handbook of Texas and previous Texas Almanacs.

Alamito Creek — Formed by confluence of North, South forks 3 mi. N Marfa in Presidio County. Flows SE 82 mi. to Rio Grande 5 mi. S Presidio.

Angelina River — Rises in central Rusk County; flows SE 120 mi. through Cherokee, Nacogdoches, Angelina, San Augustine counties into Sam Rayburn Reservoir, then into Jasper County to the Neches River 12 mi.

west of Jasper. A meandering stream through forested country.

Aransas River — Formed 2 mi. N Skidmore in SC Bee County by union of Poesta and Aransas creeks; flows SE 40 mi. forming boundary between San Patricio and Refugio counties; then briefly into Aransas County where it empties into Copano Bay.

Atascosa River — Formed NW Atascosa County by confluence of North, West prongs, flows SE 92 mi. through Atascosa and Live Oak counties into Frio River 2 mi. NW Three Rivers.

Attoyac Bayou — Rises 2.8 mi. NE Mount Enterprise in SE Rusk County; flows SE 67 mi. through Shelby, San Augustine and Nacogdoches counties into Angelina River at Sam Rayburn Reservoir.

Tubing is a popular activity on the Frio River. Photo by Ron Billings; Texas Forest Service.

Barton Creek — Rises NE of Henly in NW Hays County; flows E 40 mi. through Travis County to Colorado River at Lady Bird Lake in Austin.

Beals Creek — Formed by confluence of Sulphur Springs and Mustang draws 4 mi. W Big Spring SW Howard County; flows E 55 mi. into Mitchell County to mouth on Colorado River.

Big Cypress Creek — Forms in SE Hopkins County E of Pickton; flows SE 60 mi. to mouth on Big Cypress Bayou 3 mi. E Jefferson in Marion County and just before the bayou flows into Caddo Lake. The creek forms the boundary lines between Camp and Titus, Camp and Morris, and Morris and Upshur counties. It passes through Lake Cypress Springs, Lake Bob Sandlin, and Lake O' the Pines. Part of the Red River drainage basin.

Blackwater Draw — Rises in Curry County, N.M.; flows into Texas in extreme NW Bailey County; flows SE through Lamb, Hale, and Lubbock counties to junction with Yellow House Draw to form North Fork of the Double Mountain Fork Brazos River. Length, 100 mi.

Blanco Creek — Rises near the intersection of Bee, Goliad and Karnes county lines in extreme S Karnes County; flows SE 45 mi. forming boundary of Bee and Goliad counties. Joins Medio Creek in Refugio County to form Mission River.

Blanco Creek — Rises E of Concan in Uvalde County; flows S 44 mi. to Frio River.

Blanco River — Rises W Lindendale in NE Kendall County; flows E 44 mi. through Blanco and Hay counties; joins San Marcos River, a tributary of the Guadalupe; fed by many springs.

Bosque River — Flows from Lake Waco in McLennan County 5 mi. into Brazos River.

Bosque River, North — Formed at Stephenville by the union of North, South forks in Erath County; flows generally SE 96 mi. through Hamilton, Bosque and McLennan counties into Lake Waco.

Bosque River, South — Rises near Coryell-McLennan

county line; flows NE 24 mi. into Lake Waco.

Brady Creek — Rises 14 mi. SW Eden in SW Concho County; flows 90 mi. through McCulloch and San Saba counties into San Saba River 10 mi. SW of Richland Springs.

Brazos River, Clear Fork — Rises 8 mi. E Snyder in Scurry County; flows NE 180 mi. through Fisher, Jones, Haskell, Throckmorton, Shackelford and Stephens counties into Brazos River in S Young County; drainage area 5,728 sq. mi.

Brazos River, Double Mountain Fork — Rises 12 mi. SE Tahoka, Lynn County; flows E 175 mi. through Garza, Kent, Fisher and Haskell counties to confluence with Salt Fork of the Brazos, north of Old Glory in Stonewall County.

Brazos River, North Fork Double Mountain Fork— Formed by union of Yellow House and Blackwater draws in Lubbock; flows SE 75 miles through Crosby, Garza and Kent counties to junction with Double Mountain Fork Brazos River.

Brazos River, Salt Fork — Rises in SE Crosby County; flows 150 mi. through Garza and Kent counties to confluence with Double Mountain Fork in NE Stonewall County to form the main stream of Brazos River.

Buck Creek — Also called Spiller Creek. Rises SE Donley County; flows SE 49 mi. through Collingsworth and Childress counties to Texas-Oklahoma boundary; then 3 mi. through Oklahoma to junction with Prairie Dog Town Fork of Red River NW Hardeman County to form main stream of the Red River.

Buffalo Bayou — Rises in extreme N Fort Bend County; flows E 46 mi. through Houston into San Jacinto River in Harris County. Part of Houston Ship Channel.

California Creek — Rises 10 mi. NE Roby in Fisher County; flows NE 70 mi. through Jones County into Paint Creek in E Haskell County.

Caney Creek — Rises near Wharton in Wharton County; flows 75 mi. through Matagorda County into east end of Matagorda Bay. Centuries ago, the current Caney

Creek channel was the channel for the Colorado River.

Capote/Wildhorse Draw — Rises N of Van Horn in Culberson County; runs 86 mi. S through Jeff Davis County to SW of Marfa in Presidio County. One of a number of streams in this area with no outlet to the sea.

Cedar Bayou — Rises 11 mi. NW Liberty in Liberty County; flows 46 mi. S as boundary between Harris County and Liberty and Chambers counties, and into Trinity Bay.

Chambers Creek — Formed SW Waxahachie in Ellis County by union North, South forks; flows SE 45 mi. through Navarro County into Richland Creek at Richland-Chambers Reservoir.

Cibolo Creek — Rises 7 mi. W Boerne in Kendall County; flows SE through Bexar, Comal, Guadalupe and Wilson counties into San Antonio River in Karnes County; 96 mi. in length. Spring-fed, perennially flowing stream.

Coleto Creek — Formed SW of Mission Valley in NW Victoria County by union of Twelve Mile and Fifteen Mile creeks forming boundary between Victoria and Goliad counties. From Coleto Creek Reservoir flows to Guadalupe River in Victoria County.

Comal River — Rises in Comal Springs in City of New Braunfels and flows SE about 2.5 miles to Guadalupe River. Shortest river in Texas.

Concho River — Formed at San Angelo by conjunction North, South Concho rivers; flows E 24 mi. through Tom Green County, then 29 mi. through Concho County into Colorado River 12 mi. NE Paint Rock. Drainage basin, including North and South Concho, 6,613 sq. mi. A spring-fed stream.

Concho River, Middle — Rises SW Sterling County; flows S, then E 66 mi. through Tom Green panhandle, Irion and Reagan counties into South Concho River at Lake Nasworthy near Tankersley in Tom Green County.

Concho River, North — Rises in S Howard County; flows 137 mi. through Glasscock, Sterling and Coke counties to confluence with South Concho to form Concho River in Tom Green County. Drainage basin, 1,510 sq. mi.

Concho River, South — Rises in C Schleicher County; flows N through Lake Nasworthy to confluence with North Concho River in Tom Green County; length, 41 mi.; drainage basin area 3, 866 sq. mi. Perennial flow from springs.

Cowleech Fork Sabine River — Rises 2 mi. NW Celeste NW Hunt County; flows SE 40 mi. to Lake Tawakoni.

Deep Creek — Rises SE Baird, Callahan County; flows N 55 mi. into Hubbard Creek in Shackelford County near McCatherine Mountain.

Deep Creek — Rises 4 mi. N Fluvanna NW Scurry County; flows SSE 70 mi. to mouth on Colorado River in extreme N Mitchell County.

Delaware River — Rises eastern slope Delaware Mountains in N Culberson County; flows in NE course; crosses Texas-New Mexico state line and enters Pecos River; length, 50 mi.

Devils River — Formed SW Sutton County by union Dry Devils River and Granger Draw; flows SE 95 mi. through Val Verde County into Rio Grande at Amistad Reservoir. Spring-fed, perennially flowing stream throughout most of its course.

Elm Creek — Rises 3 mi. SE Nolan in Nolan County; flows NE 60 mi., passes through Lake Abilene, Buffalo Gap and Abilene in Taylor County and through Lake Fort Phantom Hill into Clear Fork Brazos River near Nugent SE Jones County.

Frio River — Formed at Leakey in Real County by union of West and East Frio rivers; flows S 190 mi. through Uvalde, Medina, Frio, La Salle, McMullen counties (Choke Canyon Reservoir); joins Nueces River S of Three Rivers in Live Oak County. Drainage area, 7,310 sq. mi. Fed by springs in northern part, where it flows through picturesque canyon.

Greens Bayou — Rises 9 mi. W Aldine, C Harris County; flows ESE into Houston Ship Channel; 42 mi. long.

Hondo Creek — Rises 7.5 mi. NW Tarpley C Bandera

County; flows SSE 67 mi. through Medina and Frio counties to Frio River 5 mi. NW Pearsall.

Howard Draw — Rises at Crockett-Reagan county line; flows SSW 45 mi. through Val Verde County to Pecos River near Pandale.

Hubbard Creek — Rises 3 mi. NW Baird N Callahan County; flows NE 62 mi. through Shackelford County; then into Stephens County (Hubbard Creek Reservoir) and joins Clear Fork of the Brazos River 10 NW Breckenridge.

James River — Rises SE Kimble County; flows NE 37 mi. to join Llano River in Mason County.

Jim Ned Creek — Rises 10 mi. NW Tuscola SC Taylor County; flows SE 71 mi. through Callahan and Coleman counties to Brown County to join Pecan Bayou, a tributary of Colorado River.

Johnson Draw — Rises NE Crockett County; runs SSE 66 miles to mouth on Devils River in Val Verde County.

Lampasas River — Rises NW Mills County; flows SE 100 miles through Hamilton, Lampasas, Burnet and Bell counties (Stillhouse Hollow Lake); unites with Leon River to form Little River.

Leon River — Formed by confluence North, Middle and South Forks in NC Eastland County; flows SE 185 mi. through Comanche, Hamilton and Coryell counties to junction with Lampasas River to form Little River in Bell County.

Leona River — Rises N Uvalde in central Uvalde County; flows SE 83 mi. through Zavala County into Frio River in Frio County.

Limpia Creek — Heads in the Davis Mountains on the NE slope of Mount Livermore in Jeff Davis County and flows 52 mi. E, NE and E through Limpia Canyon to disappear at the head of Barrilla Draw in Pecos County. Part of course through Limpia Canyon noted for its scenic beauty.

Little Brazos River — Rises 5 mi. SW Thornton, SW Limestone County; flows 72 mi. SE through Falls and Robertson counties into Brazos River in Brazos County.

Little River — Formed central Bell County by union Leon, Lampasas rivers; flows 75 mi. SE through Milam County into Brazos River.

Llano River — Formed C Kimble County by union North, South Llano rivers; flows E 100 mi. through Mason, Llano counties to Colorado River. Drainage area, including North, South Llano rivers, 4,460 sq. mi. A spring-fed stream of the Edwards Plateau, known for scenic beauty.

Llano River, North — Rises C Sutton County; flows E 40 mi. to union with South Llano River at Junction in Kimble County.

Llano River, South — Rises in NC Edwards County; flows 55 mi. NE to confluence with North Llano River at Junction in Kimble County.

Los Olmos Creek — Rises central Duval County; flows SE 71 mi. through Jim Wells and Brooks counties; forms boundary between Kenedy and Kleberg counties; into Baffin Bay.

Madera Canyon — Rises N slope Mount Livermore, Jeff Davis County, at altitude of 7,500 ft.; flows 40 mi. NE to join Aguja Creek at Reeves County line to form Toyah Creek, tributary through Pecos River to Rio Grande. Intermittent stream. Noteworthy for its beauty.

Medina River — Rises in North, West prongs in W Bandera County; flows SE 116 mi. through Medina and Bexar counties to San Antonio River. A spring-fed stream. Scenically beautiful along upper course.

Medio Creek — Rises S Karnes County; flows SE 2 mi. through Karnes County, then 7 mi. along boundary Karnes and Bee counties, then SE 37 mi. through Bee County, SE 7 mi. through Refugio County to junction with Blanco Creek to form Mission River.

Mission River — Formed by confluence of Blanco and Medio creeks in C Refugio County; flows SE 24 mi. to mouth on Mission Bay, an inlet of Copano Bay.

Mulberry Creek — Rises NW Armstrong County at Fair-

Visitors to South Llano River State Park play in the Llano River near Junction in Kimble County. Photo courtesy of the Texas Parks and Wildlife Department.

view; flows SE 58 mi. through Donley and Briscoe counties into Prairie Dog Town Fork Red River in NW Hall County.

Navasota River — Rises SE Hill County; flows SE 125 mi. through Limestone County and along boundary Leon, Madison, Robertson, Brazos and Grimes counties to Brazos River near Navasota.

Navidad River — Forms at juncture of East and West Navidad rivers in NE Lavaca County; flows 74 mi. through Lavaca and Jackson counties into Lake Texana near Ganado; then joins Lavaca River.

Nolan River — Rises in NW Johnson County; flows S 30 mi. through Lake Pat Cleburne and into Hill County where is empties into Brazos River at Lake Whitney.

Onion Creek — Rises 1 mi. W of Hays-Blanco county line SE Blanco County; flows SE 37 mi. through N Hays County; then 22 mi. through S Travis County into Colorado River near Garfield.

Paint Creek — Rises in extreme NW Jones County near Tuxedo; flows NE, then SE 53 mi. through SE corner of Stonewall County; then across S Haskell County (Lake Stamford) and into W Throckmorton County to mouth on Clear Fork Brazos River.

Palo Blanco Creek — Rises SE Hebbronville in N Jim Hogg County; flows SE 59 mi. through Duval and Brooks, where it passes through Laguna Salada; then into NW Kenedy County.

Palo Duro Creek — Rises in W Deaf Smith County; flows E 45 mi. into C Randall County to junction with Tierra Blanca Creek near Canyon to form the Prairie Dog Town Fork of the Red River. Lends its name to the notable canyon.

Paluxy River — Formed in E Erath County by convergence of North and South branches at Bluff Dale; flows SE 29 mi. through Hood and Somervell counties to mouth on Brazos River. Dinosaur Valley State Park at a large bend of the river in Somervell County is site of 100-million-year-old dinosaur tracks.

Pease River — Formed by union of North and Middle Pease rivers in NE Cottle County; flows E 100 mi. through Hardeman, Foard and Wilbarger counties into Red River 8 mi. NE of Vernon.

Pease River, Middle — Rises 8 mi. NW Matador in WC Motley County; flows E 63 miles into North Pease River to form the Pease River in NE Cottle County.

Pease River, North — Rises 9 mi. SE Cedar Hill in E Floyd County; flows E 60 mi. through Motley, Hall and Cottle counties. Joins Middle Pease to form Pease River.

Pease River, South — Also called Tongue River. Rises 11 mi. SW Roaring Springs in SW Motley County; flows ENE 40 mi. to mouth on Middle Pease River in W Cottle County.

Pecan Bayou — Formed by union of South, North prongs in SC Callahan County; flows SE 90 mi. through Coleman, Brown (Lake Brownwood) and Mills counties into Colorado River SW Goldthwaite. Westernmost bayou.

Pedernales River — Rises NE corner of Kerr County; flows E 106 mi. through Kimble, Gillespie, Blanco, Hays and Travis counties into Colorado River at Lake Travis. Spring-fed; a beautiful stream.

Pine Island Bayou — Rises near Rye NE Liberty County; flows 76 mi. SE through Hardin and Jefferson counties into Neches River.

Red River, Prairie Dog Town Fork — Formed by union of Palo Duro and Tierra Blanca creeks in Randall County; flows E 160 mi. through Armstrong, Briscoe, Hall, and Childress counties to junction with Buck Creek to form Red River in NW corner of Hardeman County. Palo Duro Canyon is along course of this stream as it descends from Great Plains.

Red River, North Fork — Rises W Gray County; flows SE 180 mi. through Wheeler County into Oklahoma to junction with the Red River NE Vernon in Wilbarger County.

Red River, Salt Fork — Rises N Armstrong County; flows SE 155 mi. through Donley and Collingsworth counties and into Oklahoma. It joins the Red River opposite the northernmost point of Wilbarger County.

Richland Creek — Rises 3.5 mi. E Itasca N Hill County; flows E 50 mi. through Ellis and Navarro counties, through Navarro Mills Lake and Richland-Chambers Reservoir; then into the Trinity River in Freestone County.

Running Water Draw — Rises 24 mi. WNW Clovis, N.M.;

flows ESE into Texas in C Parmer County; then through Castro, Lamb, Hale and Floyd counties to join Callahan Draw 8 mi. W Floydada at head of White River, a tributary of the Brazos River.

Sabana River — Rises at Callahan-Eastland county line; flows SE 50 through Comanche County into Leon River at Proctor Lake.

Sabinal River — Rises 7 mi. N Vanderpool in NW Bandera County; flows S 60 mi. to junction with Frio River in SE Uvalde County. The West Sabinal River, which rises in Real County, joins the main stream at the Bandera-Uvalde county line.

San Bernard River — Rises 1 mi. S New Ulm in W Austin County; flows SE, forming boundary Austin and Colorado counties, 31 mi.; Austin and Wharton counties, 8 mi.; Wharton and Fort Bend counties, 28 mi.; approaches Gulf of Mexico in Brazoria County. Total length, 120 mi. (For more than 100 years locals have reported hearing the wail of a violin from the river. The mystery has never been solved, although some say the musical sounds are caused by escaping gas. The phenomenon has caused the stream to be called the Singing River — *Handbook of Texas*.)

San Gabriel River — Formed at Georgetown in C Williamson County by union of North and South forks; flows NE 50 mi. into Milam County to join Little River. Originally called San Xavier River.

San Jacinto River, East — Rises E Walker County; flows SE and S 69 mi. through San Jacinto, Liberty, Montgomery and Harris counties into Lake Houston and San Jacinto River.

San Jacinto River, West — Rises E Grimes County NE Shiro; flows SE 90 mi. through Walker County; into Lake Conroe in Montgomery County; then through Montgomery County to Lake Houston in Harris County.

San Marcos River — Formed near N limits City of San Marcos, Hays County, by several large springs, although watershed extends about 10 mi. NE of springs; Blanco River joins the San Marcos River 4 mi. downstream; flows SE 59 mi. as boundary between Guadalupe and Caldwell counties; then through Gonzales County to join Guadalupe River 2 mi. W Gonzales.

Sandy Creek — Rises SW Colorado County; flows SSE 42 mi. through Lavaca, Wharton and Jackson counties into Lake Texana.

San Saba River — Formed W Fort McKavett at Schleicher-Menard county line by union of North Valley and Middle Valley prongs; flows NE 140 mi. through Menard, Mason, McCulloch and San Saba counties into Colorado River 8 mi. NE San Saba. One of the picturesque streams of the Edwards Plateau.

Spring Creek — Rises NE Waller County near Fields Store; flows E 64 mi. forming boundary between Waller and Harris counties, and Montgomery and Harris counties to junction with West Fork San Jacinto River and Lake Houston.

Sulphur River — Formed E Delta County by junction North, South branches; flows E 183 miles forming boundary between Franklin and Red River counties; Titus and Red River counties; Morris and Red River and Bowie counties; then between Bowie and Cass counties, where it flows into Wright Patman Lake; continues on into Red River in S Miller County, Ark.

Sulphur River, North — Rises 1 mi. SW Gober S Fannin County; flows SE, E 54 mi. as boundary between Delta and Lamar counties and to union with South Sulphur River to form Sulphur River.

Sulphur River, South — Rises N Leonard S Fannin County; flows ESE 50 mi. through Hunt County; then as boundary between Hopkins and Delta counties (through Cooper Lake) to union with North Sulphur to form Sulphur River.

Sulphur Springs Draw — Rises in E Lea County, N.M.; enters Texas W Yoakum County at Bronco; flows SE 100 mi. through Terry, Gaines, Dawson, Martin, and

Howard counties to confluence with Mustang Creek to form Beals Creek, a tributary of Colorado River.

Sweetwater Creek — Rises 2 mi. W Maryneal C Nolan County; flows NE 45 mi. through Fisher and Jones counties into Clear Fork Brazos River.

Terlingua Creek — Rises WC Brewster County; flows S 83 mi. into Rio Grande just E Santa Elena Canyon.

Tierra Blanca Creek — Rises N Curry County, N.M.; flows E across Texas state line in SW Deaf Smith County and 75 mi. through Deaf Smith, Parmer and Randall counties to junction with Palo Duro Creek where it forms Prairie Dog Town Fork Red River.

Toyah Creek — Forms near boundary Jeff Davis-Reeves counties; flows NE 50 mi. into Pecos River NC Reeves County.

Trinity River, Clear Fork — Rises NW Poolville in NW Parker County; flows SE 56 mi. through Tarrant County into West Fork Trinity River at Fort Worth.

Trinity River, East Fork — Rises 1.5 mi. NW Dorchester in SC Grayson County; flows through Collin County (Lake Lavon and Lake Ray Hubbard); then Rockwall and Dallas counties into Trinity River in SE Kaufman County.

Trinity River, Elm Fork — Rises 1 mi. NW Saint Jo in E Montague County; flows 85 mi. SE through Cooke, Denton counties (Ray Roberts Lake and Lewisville Lake) to junction with West Fork to form Trinity River proper at Irving in WC Dallas County.

Trinity River, West Fork — Rises in SC Archer County; flows SE 145 mi. through Jack, Wise (Lake Bridgeport) and Tarrant (Eagle Mountain Lake and Lake Worth) counties to conjunction with Elm Fork to form Trinity River proper in WC Dallas County.

Tule Creek — Formed in Swisher County by union of North, Middle and South Tule draws; flows E 40 mi. through Mackenzie Reservoir and Briscoe County into Prairie Dog Town Fork Red River. Remarkably beautiful Tule Canyon along lower course.

Turkey Creek — Rises near Turkey Mountain EC Kinney County; flows SE 54 mi. through Uvalde, Zavala, Dimmit counties to Nueces River.

Washita River — Rises SE Roberts County; flows E 35 mi. through Hemphill County to Oklahoma state line, then SE to Red River at Lake Texhoma. Total length, 295 mi.

White River — Formed 8 mi. W Floydada in WC Floyd County by union of Running Water and Callahan draws; flows SE 62 mi. through Blanco Canyon and White River Lake in Crosby County; then through Garza and Kent counties into Salt Fork Brazos River; principal tributary to Salt Fork.

Wichita River — Formed NE Knox County by union North, South Wichita rivers; flows NE 90 mi. through Baylor (Lake Kemp and Lake Diversion), Archer, Wichita and Clay counties to Red River N Byers.

Wichita River, Little — Formed in C Archer County by union of its North, Middle and South forks; flows NE 62 mi. through Clay County (Lake Arrowhead) into Red River.

Wichita River, North — Rises 6 mi. E East Afton in NE Dickens County; flows E through King, Cottle, Foard counties; then as boundary for Foard and Knox counties; then briefly into Baylor County to junction with South Wichita River to form Wichita River proper NE Vera in Knox County. Length, 100 mi.

Wichita River, South — Rises 10 mi. E Dickens in EC Dickens County; flows E 85 mi. through King and Knox counties to junction with North Wichita to form Wichita River.

Yellow House Draw — Rises in SE Bailey County; flows SE 80 mi. through Cochran, Hockley and Lubbock counties to confluence with Blackwater Draw at Lubbock to form the North Fork of Double Mountain Fork Brazos River. ☆

Artificial Lakes and Reservoirs

Sources: U.S. Geological Survey, Texas Water Development Board, New Handbook of Texas, Texas Parks & Wildlife, U.S. Army Corps of Engineers, previous Texas Almanacs, various river basin authorities, websites of owner of reservoirs.

The large increase in the number of reservoirs in Texas during the past half-century has greatly improved water conservation and supplies.

As late as 1913, Texas had only four major reservoirs with a total storage capacity of 277,600 acre-feet. Most of this capacity was in Medina Lake in southwest Texas, with 254,000 acre-feet* capacity, created by a dam completed in May 1913.

By January 2007, Texas had 196 major reservoirs (those with a normal capacity of 5,000 acre-feet or larger), with a total conservation surface area of 1,666,856 acres and a conservation storage capacity of 37,179,139 acre-feet.

According to the U.S. Statistical Abstract of 2008, Texas has **5,607 square miles of inland water,** ranking it first in the 48 contiguous states, followed by Florida, with 5,373 sq. mi.; Minnesota, 4,782; and Louisiana, 4,433.

There are about **6,736 reservoirs** in Texas with a normal storage capacity of 10 acre-feet or larger.

Natural Lakes

There are many natural lakes in Texas, though none is of great size. The largest designated natural lake touching the border of Texas is Sabine Lake, into which the Sabine and Neches rivers discharge. It is more properly a bay of the Gulf of Mexico. Also near the coast, in Calhoun County, is Green Lake, which at about 10,000 acre-feet is one of the state's largest natural freshwater lakes.

Caddo Lake, on the Texas-Louisiana border, was a natural lake originally, but its present capacity and surface area are largely due to dams built to raise the surface of the original body of water. Natural Dam Lake, in Howard County, has a similar history.

In East Texas, there are many small natural lakes formed by "horse-shoe" bends that have been eliminated from the main channel of a river. There are also a number of these "horse-shoe" lakes along the Rio Grande in the lower valley, where they are called *resacas*.

On the South Plains and west of San Angelo are lakes, such as Big Lake in Reagan County, that are usually dry.

The table that begins below lists reservoirs in Texas having more than 5,000 acre-feet capacity. With few exceptions, the listed reservoirs are those that were completed by Jan. 1, 2011. *Reservoirs that are normally dry are in italics.*

Some industrial cooling reservoirs are not included in this table.

Conservation storage capacity as of 2011 is used; the surface area used is that area at conservation elevation only. Because sediment deposition constantly reduces reservoir volumes over time, these are figures from the most recent surveys available.

Various methods of computing capacity area are used, and detailed information may be obtained from

the Texas Water Development Board, Austin, from the U.S. Army Corps of Engineers, or from local sources. Boundary reservoir capacities include water designated for Texas and non-Texas water, as well.

Information is in the following order: **(1)** Name of lake or reservoir; **(2)** year of first impounding of water; **(3)** county or counties in which it is located; **(4)** river or creek on which it is located; **(5)** location with respect to some city or town; **(6)** purpose of reservoir; **(7)** owner of reservoir.

Some of these items, when not listed, are not available. For the larger lakes and reservoirs, the dam impounding water to form the lake bears the same name, unless otherwise indicated.

Lakes and Reservoirs, Date of Origin	Surface Area (Acres)	Storage Capacity (Acre-Ft.*)
Abilene, L. — (1919) Taylor Co.; Elm Cr.; 6 mi. NW Tuscola; (M-In.-R); City of Abilene..................................	595	6,099
Addicks Reservoir — (1948) Harris Co.; South Mayde Cr.; 1 mi. E of Addicks; (FC only) USAE.....................	16,423	200,840
Alan Henry, L.— (1993) Garza Co.; Double Mountain Fork Brazos River; 10 mi. E Justiceburg; (M-In.-Ir.); City of Lubbock	2,741	94,808
Alcoa L. — (1952) Milam Co.; Sandy Cr.; 7 mi. SW Rockdale; (In.-R); Alcoa Aluminum (also called Sandow L.)	914	15,650
Amistad Reservoir, International — (1969) Val Verde Co.; Rio Grande; an international project of the U.S. and Mexico; 12 mi. NW Del Rio; (C-R-Ir.-P-FC); International Boundary and Water Com. (Texas'share of conservation capacity is 56.2 percent.) (Formerly Diablo Reservoir)	65,597	3,274,057
Amon G. Carter, L. — (1961) Montague Co.; Big Sandy Cr.; 6 mi. S Bowie; (M-In.); City of Bowie..................	1,540	27,500
Anahuac, L. — (1936, 1954) Chambers Co.; Turtle Bayou; near Anahuac; (Ir.-Mi.); Chambers-Liberty Counties Navigation District. (also called Turtle Bayou Reservoir).................................	5,035	33,348
Anzalduas Channel Dam — Hidalgo Co.; Rio Grande; 11 mi. upstream from Hidalgo; (Ir.-FC); United States and Mexico..	1,472	13,910
Aquilla L. — (1983) Hill Co.; Aquilla Cr.; 10.2 mi. W of Hillsboro; (FC-M-Ir.-In.-R); USAE-Brazos R. Auth........	3,066	44,566
Arlington, L. — (1957) Tarrant Co.; Village Cr.; 7 mi. W Arlington; (M-In.); City of Arlington	1,926	40,188
Arrowhead, L. — (1966) Clay-Archer counties.; Little Wichita R.; 13 mi. SE Wichita Falls; (M); City of Wichita Falls	14,969	235,997
Athens, L. — (1962) Henderson Co.; 8 mi. E Athens; (M-FC-R); Athens Mun. Water Authority (formerly Flat Creek Reservoir)	1,799	29,475

*An acre-foot is the amount of water necessary to cover an acre of surface area with water one foot deep. The **years** in the table refer to first impounding of water. **Double years** refer to later, larger dams. **Abbreviations are:** L., lake; R., river; Co., county; Cr., creek; (C) conservation; (FC) flood control; (R) recreation; (P) power; (M) municipal; (D) domestic; (Ir.) irrigation; (In.) industry; (Mi.) mining, including oil production; (FH) fish hatchery; USAE, United States Army Corps of Engineers; WC&ID, Water Control and Improvement District; WID, Water Improvement District; USBR, United States Bureau of Reclamation; Auth., Authority; LCRA, Lower Colorado River Authority; TP&WD, Texas Parks & Wildlife Dept.; USDA, United States Department of Agriculture; Imp., impounded.

Lakes and Reservoirs, Date of Origin	Surface Area (Acres)	Storage Capacity (Acre-Ft.*)
Austin, L. — (1893, 1915, 1939) Travis Co.; Colorado R.; W Austin city limits; (M-In.-P); City of Austin, leased to LCRA (Imp. by Tom Miller Dam)........................	1,599	24,644
(In 1893, the first dam was completed. It broke in 1900. In 1915, a second dam was partially built but not completed. In 1939, the present Tom Miller Dam was completed.)		
Ballinger/Moonen, L. — (1947) Runnels Co.; Valley Creek; 5 mi. W Ballinger; (M); City of Ballinger	500	6,850
Balmorhea, L. — (1917) Reeves Co.; Sandia Cr.; 3 mi. SE Balmorhea; (Ir.); Reeves Co. WID No. 1	573	6,350
Bardwell L. — (1965) Ellis Co.; Waxahachie Cr.; 3 mi. SE Bardwell; (FC-C-R); USAE....................................	3,138	46,472
Barker Reservoir — *(1945) Harris Co.; above Buffalo Bayou ; (FC only) USAE..............................*	*16,739*	*209,013*
Bastrop, L. — (1964) Bastrop Co.; Spicer Cr.; 3 mi. NE Bastrop; (In.); LCRA..	906	16,590
Baylor Creek L. — (1950) Childress Co.; 10 mi. NW Childress; (M-R); City of Childress	610	9,220
Belton L. — (1954) Bell-Coryell counties; Leon R.; 3 mi. N. Belton; (M-FC-In.-Ir.); USAE-Brazos R. Auth.	12,135	435,225
Benbrook L. — (1952) Tarrant Co.; Clear Fk. Trinity R.; 10 mi. SW Fort Worth; (FC-R); USAE......................	3,635	85,648
Big Creek Reservoir — (1987) Delta Co; Big Creek; 1 mi. N Cooper; (M); City of Cooper..........................	512	4,890
Bivins L. — (1927) Randall Co.; Palo Duro Cr.; 8 mi. NW Canyon; (M); Amarillo; City of Amarillo (also called Amarillo City Lake)............	379	5,122
Bob Sandlin, L. — (1977) Titus-Wood-Camp-Franklin counties; Big Cypress Cr.; 5 mi. SW Mount Pleasant; (In.-M-R); Titus Co. FWSD No. 1 (Imp. by Fort Sherman Dam)	9,004	201,733
Bonham, L. — (1969) Fannin Co.; Timber Cr.; 5 mi. NE Bonham; (M); Bonham Mun. Water Auth.	1,012	11,038
Brady Creek Reservoir — (1963) McCulloch Co.; Brady Cr.; 3 mi. W Brady; (M-In.); City of Brady....................	2,020	30,430
Brandy Branch Reservoir — (1983) Harrison Co.; Brandy Br.; 10 mi. SW Marshall; (In.); AEP- Southwestern Electric Power Co.......	1,242	29,513
Braunig L., Victor — (1962) Bexar Co.; Arroyo Seco; 15 mi. SE San Antonio; (In.); Pub. Svc. Bd./San Antonio.................	1,350	26,500
Brazoria Reservoir — (1954) Brazoria Co.; off-channel reservoir; 1 mi. NE Brazoria; (In.); Dow Chemical Co.	1,865	21,970
Bridgeport, L. — (1932) Wise-Jack counties; W. Fk. of Trinity R.; 4 mi. W Bridgeport; (M-In.-FC-R); Tarrant Regional Water Dist.	11,954	366,236
Brownwood, L. — (1933) Brown Co.; Pecan Bayou; 8 mi. N Brownwood; (M-In.-Ir.); Brown Co. WC&ID No. 1	6,587	131,429
Bryan L. — (1977) Brazos Co.; unnamed stream; 6 mi. NW Bryan; (R-In.); City of Bryan	829	15,227
Buchanan, L. — (1937) Burnet-Llano-San Saba counties; Colorado R.; 13 mi. W Burnet; (M-Ir.-Mi-P); LCRA...............	22,137	886,626
Buffalo Lake — *(1938) Randall Co.; Tierra Blanca Cr.; 2 mi. S. Umbarger; (R); U.S. Fish and Wildlife Service; (Imp. by Umbarger Dam)...........*	*1,900*	*18,150*
Caddo L. — (1873, 1914, 1971) Harrison-Marion counties, Texas, and Caddo Parish, La. An original natural lake, whose surface and capacity were increased by construction of dams	26,800	129,000
(In November 1873, the U.S. Army used nitroglycerin charges to remove the last portion of the Red River raft, a natural logjam. This resulted in the gradual depletion of Caddo water. In 1914, a dam was completed near Mooringsport, La. In 1971, a larger replacement dam was completed.)		
Calaveras L. — (1969) Bexar Co.; Calaveras Cr.; 15 mi. SE San Antonio; (In.); Pub. Svc. Bd. of San Antonio..................	3,624	63,200
Camp Creek L. — (1949) Robertson Co.; 13 mi. E Franklin; (R); Camp Creek Water Co.	750	7,000
Canyon L. — (1964) Comal Co.; Guadalupe R.; 12 mi. NW New Braunfels; (M-In.-P-FC); Guadalupe- Blanco R. Authority & USAE................	8,308	378,852
Casa Blanca L. — (1951) Webb Co.; Chacon Cr.; 3 mi. NE Laredo; (R); Webb Co.; (Imp. by Country Club Dam).................	1,680	20,000
Cedar Creek Reservoir — (1965) Henderson-Kaufman counties; Cedar Cr.; 3 mi. NE Trinidad; (M-R); Tarrant Regional Water Dist.; (also called Joe B. Hogsett, L.).................	32,873	644,785
Champion Creek Reservoir — (1959) Mitchell Co.; 7 mi. S. Colorado City; (M-In.); City of Colorado City	1,560	42,500
Cherokee, L. — (1948) Gregg-Rusk counties; Cherokee Bayou; 12 mi. SE Longview; (M-In.-R); Cherokee Water Co.............	3,467	43,297
Choke Canyon Reservoir — (1982) Live Oak-McMullen counties; Frio R.; 4 mi. W Three Rivers; (M-In.-R-FC); City of Corpus Christi-USBR	25,989	695,271
Cisco, L. — (1923) Eastland Co.; Sandy Cr.; 4 mi. N. Cisco; (M); City of Cisco (Imp. by Williamson Dam).......	10,450	26,000
Cleburne, L. Pat — (1964) Johnson Co.; Nolan R.; 4 mi. S. Cleburne; (M); City of Cleburne	1,558	26,008
Clyde, L. — (1970) Callahan Co.; N. Prong Pecan Bayou; 6 mi. S. Clyde; (M); City of Clyde and USDA Soil Conservation Service..............	449	5,748
Coffee Mill L. — (1939) Fannin Co.; Coffee Mill Cr.; 12 mi. NW Honey Grove; (R); U.S. Forest Service..........	650	8,000
Coleman, L. — (1966) Coleman Co.; Jim Ned Cr.; 14 mi. N. Coleman; (M-In.); City of Coleman	1,811	38,094
Coleto Creek Reservoir — (1980) Goliad–Victoria counties; Coleto Cr.; 12 mi. SW Victoria; (In); Guadalupe–Blanco River Auth........	3,100	31,040
Colorado City, L. — (1949) Mitchell Co.; Morgan Cr.; 4 mi. SW Colorado City; (M-In.-P); TXU..................	1,612	31,805
Conroe, L. — (1973) Montgomery-Walker counties; W. Fk. San Jacinto R.; 7 mi. NW Conroe; (M-In.-Mi.); San Jacinto River Authority, City of Houston and Texas Water Dev. Bd.	20,118	416,228
Cooper, L./Olney— (1953) Archer Co.; Mesquite Crk; 8 mi. E Megargel; (W-R); City of Olney; (see L. Olney)	446	6,650
Cooper Lake — (1991) Delta-Hopkins counties; Sulphur R.; 3 mi.SE Cooper; (FC-M-R); USAE; (also called Jim Chapman Lake)	17,958	298,930

An acre-foot is the amount of water necessary to cover an acre of surface area with water one foot deep. The **years in the table refer to first impounding of water. **Double years** refer to later, larger dams. **Abbreviations are:** L., lake; R., river; Co., county; Cr., creek; (C) conservation; (FC) flood control; (R) recreation; (P) power; (M) municipal; (D) domestic; (Ir.) irrigation; (In.) industry; (Mi.) mining, including oil production; (FH) fish hatchery; USAE, United States Army Corps of Engineers; WC&ID, Water Control and Improvement District; WID, Water Improvement District; USBR, United States Bureau of Reclamation; Auth., Authority; LCRA, Lower Colorado River Authority; TP&WD, Texas Parks & Wildlife Dept.; USDA, United States Department of Agriculture; Imp., impounded.*

Possum Kingdom Lake has a surface area of more than 16,000 acres in Palo Pinto, Young, Stephens, and Jack counties. It was formed by the Brazos River in 1941. Photo courtesy of the Texas Parks and Wildlife Department.

Lakes and Reservoirs, Date of Origin	Surface Area (Acres)	Storage Capacity (Acre-Ft.*)
Corpus Christi, L. — (1930) Live Oak-San Patricio-Jim Wells counties; Nueces R.; 4 mi. SW Mathis; (P-M-In.-Ir.-Mi.-R.); Lower Nueces River WSD (Imp. by Wesley E. Seale Dam)	18,256	257,260
Cox Creek Reservoir — Calhoun Co.; Cox Creek; 2 mi. E Point Comfort; (In); Alcoa Alumninum; (Also called Raw Water Lake and Recycle Lake)	541	5,034
Crook, L. — (1923) Lamar Co.; Pine Cr.; 5 Mi. N. Paris; (M); City of Paris	1,060	9,210
Cypress Springs, L. — (1970) Franklin Co.; Big Cypress Cr.; 8 mi. SE Mount Vernon; (In-M); Franklin Co. WD and Texas Water Development Board (formerly Franklin Co. L.); (Imp. by Franklin Co. Dam)	3,252	66,756
Daniel, L. — (1948) Stephens Co.; Gunsolus Cr.; 7 mi. S Breckenridge; (M-In.); City of Breckenridge; (Imp. by Gunsolus Creek Dam)	924	9,515
Davis, L. — Knox Co.; Double Dutchman Cr.; 5 mi. SE Benjamin; (Ir); League Ranch	585	5,454
Delta Lake Res. Units 1 and 2 — (1939) Hidalgo Co.; Rio Grande (off channel); 4 mi. N. Monte Alto; (Ir.); Hidalgo-Willacy counties WC&ID No. 1 (formerly Monte Alto Reservoir)	2,371	14,000
Diversion, L. — (1924) Archer-Baylor counties; Wichita R.; 14 mi. W Holliday; (M-In.); City of Wichita Falls and Wichita Co. WID No. 2	3,133	40,000
Dunlap, L. — (1928) Guadalupe Co.; Guadalupe R.; 9 mi. NW Seguin; (P); Guadalupe-Blanco R. Auth.; (Imp. by TP-1 Dam)	410	5,900
Eagle L. — (1900) Colorado Co.; Colorado R. (off channel); in Eagle Lake; (Ir.); Lakeside Irrigation Co.	1,200	9,600
Eagle Mountain Lake — (1934) Tarrant-Wise counties; W. Fk. Trinity R.; 14 mi. NW Fort Worth; (M-In.-Ir.); Tarrant Regional Water Dist.	8,694	179,880
Eagle Nest Lake — (1951) Brazoria Co.; off-channel Brazos R.; 12 mi. WNW Angleton; (Ir.); T.M. Smith, et al. (also called Manor Lake)	—	18,000
Eastman Lakes — 8 lakes; Harrison Co.; Sabine R. basin; NW of Longview; Texas Eastman Co.	—	8,135
Electra, L. — (1950) Wilbarger Co.; Camp Cr. and Beaver Cr.; 7 mi. SW Electra; (In.-M); City of Electra	731	5,626
Ellison Creek Reservoir — (1943) Morris Co.; Ellison Cr.; 8 mi. S. Daingerfield; (P-In.); Lone Star Steel	1,516	24,700
Fairfield L. — (1970) Freestone Co.; Big Brown Cr.; 11 mi. NE Fairfield; (In.); TXU; (formerly Big Brown Creek Reservoir)	2,159	44,169
Falcon Reservoir, International — (1954) Starr-Zapata counties; Rio Grande; (International—U.S.-Mexico); 3 mi. W Falcon Heights; (M-In.-Ir.-FC-P-R); International Boundary and Water Com.; (Texas' share of total conservation capacity is 58.6 per cent)	85,194	2,646,187
Fayette Co. Reservoir — (1958) Fayette Co.; Cedar Cr.; 8.5 mi. E. La Grange; (In.); LCRA (also called Cedar Creek Reservoir)	2,400	71,400
Forest Grove Reservoir — (1982) Henderson Co.; Caney Cr.; 7 mi. NW Athens; (In.); TXU, Agent	1,502	20,038
Fort Phantom Hill, Lake — (1938) Jones Co.; Elm Cr.; 5 mi. S. Nugent; (M-R); City of Abilene	4,213	70,036
Georgetown, L. — (1980) Williamson Co.; N. Fk. San Gabriel R.; 3.5 mi. W Georgetown; (FC-M-In.); USAE	1,287	36,904
Gibbons Creek Reservoir — (1981) Grimes Co.; Gibbons Cr.; 9.5 mi NW Anderson; (In.); Texas Mun. Power Agency	2,770	27,603
Gilmer Reservoir — (2001) Upshur Co.; Kelsey Creek; 15 mi. N of Longview; 4 mi. W of Gilmer; (M); City of Gilmer.	1,010	12,720
Gladewater, L. — (1952) Upshur Co.; Glade Cr.; in Gladewater; (M-R); City of Gladewater	481	4,738
Gonzales, Lake — (1931) Gonzales Co.; Guadalupe R.; 4.5 mi. SE Belmont; (P); Guadalupe-Blanco R. Auth. (also called H-4 Reservoir)	696	6,500
Graham, L. — (1929) Young Co.; Flint and Salt Creeks; 2 mi. NW Graham; (M-In.); City of Graham	2,444	45,302

*An acre-foot is the amount of water necessary to cover an acre of surface area with water one foot deep. The **years** in the table refer to first impounding of water. **Double years** refer to later, larger dams. **Abbreviations are:** L., lake; R., river; Co., county; Cr., creek; (C) conservation; (FC) flood control; (R) recreation; (P) power; (M) municipal; (D) domestic; (Ir.) irrigation; (In.) industry; (Mi.) mining, including oil production; (FH) fish hatchery; USAE, United States Army Corps of Engineers; WC&ID, Water Control and Improvement District; WID, Water Improvement District; USBR, United States Bureau of Reclamation; Auth., Authority; LCRA, Lower Colorado River Authority; TP&WD, Texas Parks & Wildlife Dept.; USDA, United States Department of Agriculture; Imp., impounded.

Lakes and Reservoirs, Date of Origin	Surface Area (Acres)	Storage Capacity (Acre-Ft.*)
Granbury, L. — (1969) Hood Co.; Brazos R.; 8 mi. SE Granbury; (M-In.-Ir.-P); Brazos River Authority (Imp. by DeCordova Bend Dam)	7,945	129,011
Granger L. — (1980) Williamson Co.; San Gabriel R.; 10 mi. NE Taylor; (FC-M-In.); USAE (formerly Laneport L.)	4,064	50,779
Grapevine L. — (1952) Tarrant-Denton counties; Denton Cr.; 2 mi. NE Grapevine; (M-FC-In.-R.); USAE	6,893	164,703
Greenbelt L. — (1967) Donley Co.; Salt Fk. Red R.; 5 mi. N Clarendon; (M-In.); Greenbelt M&I Water Auth.	2,025	60,400
Greenville City Lakes — 6 lakes; Hunt Co.; Conleech Fork, Sabine R.; 2 mi. Greenville; (M-Other); City of Greenville	—	6,864
Halbert, L. — (1921) Navarro Co.; Elm Cr.; 4 mi. SE Corsicana; (M-In-R); City of Corsicana	603	6,033
Harris Reservoir, William — (1947) Brazoria Co.; off-channel between Brazos R. and Oyster Cr.; 8 mi. NW Angleton; (In.); Dow Chemical Co.	1,663	9,200
Hawkins, L. — (1962) Wood Co.; Little Sandy Cr.; 3 mi. NW Hawkins; (FC-R); Wood County; (Imp. by Wood Co. Dam No. 3)	800	11,890
Holbrook, L. — (1962) Wood Co.; Keys Cr.; 4 mi. NW Mineola; (FC-R); Wood County; (Imp. by Wood Co. Dam No. 2)	653	7,990
Hords Creek L. — (1948) Coleman Co.; Hords Cr.; 5 mi. NW Valera; (M-FC); City of Coleman and USAE	504	8,112
Houston, L. — (1954) Harris Co.; San Jacinto R.; 4 mi. N Sheldon; (M-In.-Ir.-Mi.-R); City of Houston	11,854	133,990
Houston County L. — (1966) Houston Co.; Little Elkhart Cr.; 10 mi. NW Crockett; (M-In.); Houston Co. WC&ID No. 1	1,330	17,665
Hubbard Creek Reservoir — (1962) Stephens Co.; 6 mi. NW Breckenridge; (M-In.-Mi.); West Central Texas Mun. Water Authority	14,922	324,983
Imperial Reservoir — (1912) Reeves-Pecos counties; Pecos R.; 35 mi. N Fort Stockton; (Ir.); Pecos County WC&ID No. 2	1,530	6,000
Inks L. — (1938) Burnet-Llano counties; Colorado R.; 12 mi. W Burnet; (M-Ir.-Mi.-P); LCRA	788	14,074
Jacksonville, L. — (1959) Cherokee Co.; Gum Cr.; 5 mi. SW Jacksonville; (M-R); City of Jacksonville; (Imp. by Buckner Dam)	1,165	25,732
J. B. Thomas, L. — (1952) Scurry-Borden counties; Colorado R.; 16 mi. SW Snyder; (M- In.-R); Colorado River Mun. Water Dist.; (Imp. by Colorado R. Dam)	7,282	200,604
J. D. Murphree Wildlife Management Area Impoundments — Jefferson Co.; off-channel reservoirs between Big Hill and Taylor bayous; at Port Acres; (FH-R); TP&WD (formerly Big Hill Reservoir)	6,881	13,500
Joe Pool Lake — (1986) Dallas-Tarrant-Ellis counties; Mountain Cr.; 14 mi. SW Dallas; (FC-M-R); USAE-Trinity River Auth. (formerly Lakeview Lake)	7,470	176,900
Johnson Creek Reservoir — (1961) Marion Co.; 13 mi. NW Jefferson; (In.); AEP-Southwestern Electric Power Co.	650	10,100
Kemp, L. — (1923) Baylor Co.; Wichita R.; 6 mi. N Mabelle; (M-P-Ir.); City of Wichita Falls; Wichita Co. WID 2	15,357	245,434
Kickapoo, L. — (1945) Archer Co.; N. Fk. Little Wichita R.; 10 mi. NW Archer City; (M); City of Wichita Falls	6,028	85,825
Kiowa, L. — (1967) Cooke Co.; Indian Cr.; 8 mi. SE Gainesville; (R); Lake Kiowa, Inc.	560	7,000
Kirby, L. — (1928) Taylor Co.; Cedar Cr.; 5 mi. S. Abilene; (M); City of Abilene	740	7,620
Kurth, L. — (1950) Angelina Co.; off-channel reservoir; 8 mi. N Lufkin; (In.); Abitibi Consolidated Industries.	726	14,769
Lady Bird Lake (Town Lake) — (1960) Travis Co.; Colorado R.; within Austin city limits; (R); City of Austin	468	7,338
Lake Creek L. — (1952) McLennan Co.; Manos Cr.; 4 mi. SW Riesel; (In.); TXU	550	8,400
Lake Fork Reservoir — (1980) Wood-Rains counties; Lake Fork Cr.; 5 mi. W Quitman; (M-In.); Sabine River Authority	27,264	636,133
Lake O' the Pines — (1959) Marion-Upshur-Morris counties; Cypress Cr.; 9 mi. W Jefferson; (FC-C-R-In.-M); USAE (Imp. by Ferrell's Bridge Dam)	16,919	241,363
Lavon, L. — (1953) Collin Co.; East Fk. Trinity R.; 2 mi. W Lavon; (M-FC-In.); USAE	21,357	458,569
Leon, Lake — (1954) Eastland Co.; Leon R.; 7 mi. S Ranger; (M-In.); Eastland Co. Water Supply Dist.	1,590	27,290
Lewis Creek Reservoir — Montgomery Co.; Lewis Cr.; 10 mi. NW Conroe; (In.); Entergy	1,010	16,400
Lewisville L. — (1929, 1954) Denton Co.; Elm Fk. Trinity R.; 2 mi. NE Lewisville; (M-FC-In.-R); USAE; (also called Lake Dallas and Garza-Little Elm)	27,175	598,902
Limestone, L. — (1978) Leon-Limestone-Robertson cos.; Navasota R.; 7 mi. NW Marquez; (M-In.-Ir.); Brazos River Authority	12,553	208,017
Livingston, L. — (1969) Polk-San Jacinto-Trinity-Walker counties; Trinity R.; 6 mi. SW Livingston; (M-In.-Ir.); City of Houston and Trinity River Authority	83,277	1,741,900
Loma Alta Lake — Cameron Co.; off-channel Rio Grande; 8 mi. NE Brownsville; (M-In.); Brownsville Navigation Dist.	2,490	26,500
Lost Creek Reservoir — (1990) Jack Co.; Lost Cr.; 4 mi. NE Jacksboro; (M); City of Jacksboro	413	11,961
Lyndon B. Johnson, L. — (1951) Burnet-Llano counties; Colorado R.; 5 mi. SW Marble Falls; (P); LCRA; (Imp. by Alvin Wirtz Dam); (formerly Granite Shoals L.)	6,273	133,090
Mackenzie Reservoir — (1974) Briscoe Co.; Tule Cr.; 9 mi. NW Silverton; (M); Mackenzie Mun. Water Auth.	896	46,545
Marble Falls, L. — (1951) Burnet Co.; Colorado R.; 1.25 mi. SE Marble Falls; (P); LCRA; (Imp. by Max Starcke Dam)	608	7,486
Martin Creek L. — (1974) Rusk-Panola counties; Martin Cr.; 17 mi. NE Henderson; (P); TXU	4,981	75,116
Medina L. — (1913) Medina-Bandera counties; Medina R.; 8 mi. W Rio Medina; (Ir.); Bexar- Medina-Atascosa Co. WID No. 1	6,066	254,823

*An acre-foot is the amount of water necessary to cover an acre of surface area with water one foot deep. The **years** in the table refer to first impounding of water. **Double years** refer to later, larger dams. **Abbreviations are:** L., lake; R., river; Co., county; Cr., creek; (C) conservation; (FC) flood control; (R) recreation; (P) power; (M) municipal; (D) domestic; (Ir.) irrigation; (In.) industry; (Mi.) mining, including oil production; (FH) fish hatchery; USAE, United States Army Corps of Engineers; WC&ID, Water Control and Improvement District; WID, Water Improvement District; USBR, United States Bureau of Reclamation; Auth., Authority; LCRA, Lower Colorado River Authority; TP&WD, Texas Parks & Wildlife Dept.; USDA, United States Department of Agriculture; Imp., impounded.

Lakes and Reservoirs, Date of Origin	Surface Area (Acres)	Storage Capacity (Acre-Ft.*)
Meredith, L. — (1965) Moore-Potter-Hutchinson counties; Canadian R.; 10 mi. NW Borger; (M-In.- FC-R); cooperative project for municipal water supply by Amarillo, Lubbock and other High Plains cities. Canadian R. Municipal Water Authority-USBR; (Imp. by Sanford Dam)	16,411	817,970
Millers Creek Reservoir — (1990) Baylor-Throckmorton counties.; Millers Cr.; 9 mi. SE Goree; (M); North Central Texas Mun. Water Auth. and Texas Water Development Board	2,268	29,171
Mineral Wells, L. — (1920) Parker Co.; Rock Cr.; 4 mi. E Mineral Wells; (M); Palo Pinto Co. Mun. WD No. 1	440	7,065
Mitchell County Reservoir — (1993) Mitchell Co.; branch of Beals Creek (Mi.-In.); Colorado River MWD	1,463	27,266
Monticello Reservoir — (1972) Titus Co.; Blundell Cr.; 2.5 mi. E. Monticello; (In.); TXU	2,001	34,740
Moss L., Hubert H. — (1960) Cooke Co.; Fish Cr.; 10 mi. NW Gainesville; (M-In.); City of Gainesville	1,140	24,155
Mountain Creek L. — (1937) Dallas Co.; Mountain Cr.; 4 mi. SE Grand Prairie; (In.); TXU	2,710	22,840
Murvaul, L. — (1958) Panola Co.; Murvaul Bayou; 10 mi. W Carthage; (M-In.-R); Panola Co. Fresh Water Supply Dist. No. 1	3,529	38,284
Mustang Lake East/West — Brazoria Co.; Mustang Bayou; 6 mi. S Alvin; (Ir.-In.-R); Chocolate Bayou Land & Water Co.	—	6,451
Nacogdoches, L. — (1976) Nacogdoches Co.; Bayo Loco Cr.; 10 mi. W Nacogdoches; (M); City of Nacogdoches	2,212	39,523
Nasworthy, L. — (1930) Tom Green Co.; S Concho R.; 6 mi. SW San Angelo; (M-In.-Ir); City of San Angelo	1,380	10,108
Natural Dam L. — (1957, 1989) Howard Co.; Sulphur Springs Draw; 8 mi. W Big Spring; An original natural lake, whose surface and capacity were increased by construction of dams; (FC); Wilkinson Ranch & Colorado River MWD	3,605	54,560
Navarro Mills L. — (1963) Navarro-Hill counties; Richland Cr.; 16 mi. SW Corsicana; (M-FC); USAE	4,736	49,827
Nocona, L. — (1960) Montague Co.; 8 mi. NE Nocona; (M-In.-Mi.); No. Montague County Water Supply District (also known as Farmers Creek Reservoir)	1,362	21,749
North Fk. Buffalo Creek Reservoir — (1964) Wichita Co.; 5 mi. NW Iowa Park; (M); Wichita Co. WC&ID No.3	1,392	15,400
North L. — (1957) Dallas Co.; S. Fork Grapevine Cr.; 2 mi. SE Coppell; (In.); TXU	800	17,000
Oak Creek Reservoir — (1952) Coke Co.; 5 mi. SE Blackwell; (M-In.); City of Sweetwater	2,375	39,360
O. C. Fisher L. — (1952) Tom Green Co.; N. Concho R.; 3 mi. NW San Angelo; (M-FC-C- Ir.-R-In.-Mi); USAE —Upper Colo. River Auth. (formerly San Angelo L.)	5,440	115,743
O. H. Ivie Reservoir — (1990) Coleman-Concho-Runnels counties; 24 mi. SE Ballinger; (M-In.), Colorado R. Mun. Water Dist. (formerly Stacy Reservoir)	19,149	554,340
Olmos Reservoir — (1926) Bexar Co.; Olmos Cr.; in San Antonio; (FC only), City of San Antonio	1,050	15,500
Olney, L./Cooper — (1935) Archer Co.; Mesquite Crk; 8 mi. E Megargel; (W-R); City of Olney; (see L. Cooper)	446	6,650
Palestine, L. — (1962) Anderson-Cherokee-Henderson-Smith counties; Neches R.; 4 mi. E Frankston; (M-In.-R); Upper Neches R. MWA (Imp. by Blackburn Crossing Dam)	22,656	373,202
Palo Duro Reservoir — (1991) Hansford Co.; Palo Duro Cr.; 12 mi. N Spearman; (M-R); Palo Duro River Auth.	2,413	61,239
Palo Pinto, L. — (1964) Palo Pinto Co.; 15 mi. SW Mineral Wells; (M-In.); Palo Pinto Co. Muni. Water Dist. 1	2,176	27,215
Pat Mayse L. — (1967) Lamar Co.; Sanders Cr.; 2 mi. SW Arthur City; (M-In.-FC); USAE	5,638	117844
Pinkston Reservoir — (1976) Shelby Co.; Sandy Cr.; 12.5 mi. SW Center; (M); City of Center; (formerly Sandy Creek Reservoir)	523	7,380
Possum Kingdom L. — (1941) Palo Pinto-Young-Stephens-Jack counties; Brazos R.; 11 mi. SW Graford; (M-In.-Ir.-Mi.-P-R); Brazos R. Authority; (Imp. by Morris Sheppard Dam)	16,716	540,340
Proctor L. — (1963) Comanche Co.; Leon R.; 9 mi. NE Comanche; (M-In.-Ir.-FC); USAE- Brazos River Auth.	4,537	55,457
Quitman, L. — (1962) Wood Co.; Dry Cr.; 4 mi. N Quitman; (FC-R); Wood County (Imp. by Wood Co. Dam No.1)	814	7,440
Randell L. — (1909) Grayson Co.; Shawnee Cr.; 4 mi. NW Denison; (M); City of Denison	280	6,290
Ray Hubbard, L. — (1968) Collin-Dallas-Kaufman-Rockwall counties; (formerly Forney Reservoir); E. Fk. Trinity R.; 15 mi. E Dallas; (M); City of Dallas	20,963	452,040
Ray Roberts, L. — (1987) Denton-Cooke-Grayson counties; Elm Fk. Trinity R.; 11 mi. NE Denton; (FC-M-D); City of Denton, Dallas, USAE; (also known as Aubrey Reservoir)	29,350	788,490
Red Bluff Reservoir — (1937) Loving-Reeves counties, Texas; and Eddy Co.; N.M.; Pecos R.; 5 mi. N Orla; (Ir.-P); Red Bluff Water Power Control District.	11,193	153,670
Red Draw Reservoir — (1985) Howard Co.; Red Draw; 5 mi. E Bi Spring; (Mi.-In.); Colorado River MWD	374	8,538
Richland-Chambers Reservoir — (1987) Freestone-Navarro counties; Richland Cr.; 20 mi. SE Corsicana; (M); Tarrant Regional Water Dist.	43,384	1,112,763
Rita Blanca, L. — (1940) Hartley Co.; Rita Blanca Cr.; 2 mi. S Dalhart; (R) City of Dalhart	524	12,100
River Crest L. — (1953) Red River Co.; off-channel reservoir; 7 mi. SE Bogata; (In.); TXU	555	7,000
Sam Rayburn Reservoir — (1965) Jasper-Angelina-Sabine-Nacogdoches-San Augustine counties; Angelina R.; (M-P-In.-Ir.-R); USAE; (formerly McGee Bend Reservoir)	112,590	2,876,033
San Bernard Reservoirs #1, #2, #3 — Brazoria Co.; Off-Channel San Bernard R.; 3 mi. N Sweeney; (In.); ConocoPhillips	—	8,610
Santa Rosa L. — (1929) Wilbarger Co.; Beaver Cr.; 15 mi. S Vernon; (Mi.); W. T. Waggoner Estate	1,500	11,570
Sheldon Reservoir — (1943) Harris Co.; Carpenters Bayou; 2 mi. SW Sheldon; (R-FH); TP&WD	1,244	4,224

*An acre-foot is the amount of water necessary to cover an acre of surface area with water one foot deep. The **years** in the table refer to first impounding of water. **Double years** refer to later, larger dams. **Abbreviations are:** L., lake; R., river; Co., county; Cr., creek; (C) conservation; (FC) flood control; (R) recreation; (P) power; (M) municipal; (D) domestic; (Ir.) irrigation; (In.) industry; (Mi.) mining, including oil production; (FH) fish hatchery; USAE, United States Army Corps of Engineers; WC&ID, Water Control and Improvement District; WID, Water Improvement District; USBR, United States Bureau of Reclamation; Auth., Authority; LCRA, Lower Colorado River Authority; TP&WD, Texas Parks & Wildlife Dept.; USDA, United States Department of Agriculture; Imp., impounded.

Lakes and Reservoirs, Date of Origin	Surface Area (Acres)	Storage Capacity (Acre-Ft.*)
Smithers L. — (1957) Fort Bend Co.; Dry Creek; 10 mi. SE Richmond; (In.); Texas Genco	2,480	18,700
Somerville L. — (1967) Burleson-Washington-Lee counties; Yegua Cr.; 2 mi. S Somerville; (M-In.-Ir.- FC); USAE-Brazos River Authority	11,555	147,104
South Texas Project Reservoir — (1983) Matagorda Co.; off-channel Colorado R.; 16 mi. S Bay City; (In.); STP Nuclear Operating Co.	7,000	202,600
Spence Reservoir, E. V. — (1969) Coke Co.; Colorado R.; 2 mi. W. Robert Lee; (M-In.-Mi); Colorado R. Mun. Water Dist.; (Imp. by Robert Lee Dam)	14,640	517,272
Squaw Creek Reservoir — (1983) Somervell-Hood counties; Squaw Cr.; 4.5 mi. N Glen Rose; (In.); TXU	3,297	151,273
Stamford, L. — (1953) Haskell Co.; Paint Cr.; 10 mi. SE Haskell; (M-In.); City of Stamford	5,124	51,573
Steinhagen L., B. A. — (1951) Tyler-Jasper counties; Neches R.; 1/2 mi. N Town Bluff; (FC-R-C); USAE (also called Town Bluff Reservoir and Dam B. Reservoir);(Imp. by Town Bluff Dam)	10,687	66,972
Stillhouse Hollow L. — (1968) Bell Co.; Lampasas R.; 5 mi. SW Belton; (M-In.-Ir.-FC); USAE- Brazos River Authority; (also called Lampasas Reservoir)	6,484	227,825
Striker Creek Reservoir — (1957) Rusk-Cherokee counties; Striker Cr.; 18 mi. SW Henderson; (M -In.); Angelina-Nacogdoches WC&ID No. 1	1,920	22,865
Sulphur Springs, L. — (1950) Hopkins Co.; White Oak Cr.; 2 mi. N Sulphur Springs; (M); Sulphur Springs WD; (formerly called White Oak Creek Reservoir)	1,340	14,160
Sulphur Springs Draw Reservoir — (1992) Martin Co.; Sulphur Springs Draw; 12 mi. NE Stanton; (FC); Colorado River MWD	970	7,997
Sweetwater, L. — (1930) Nolan Co.; Bitter Creek; 6 mi. SE Sweetwater (M-R); City of Sweetwater	630	11,900
Tawakoni, L. — (1960) Rains-Van Zandt-Hunt counties; Sabine R.; 9 mi. NE Wills Point; (M-In.-Ir-R); Sabine River Authority; (Imp. by Iron Bridge Dam)	37,879	888,140
Terrell City L. — (1955) Kaufman Co.; Muddy Cedar Cr.; 6 mi. E Terrell; (M-R); City of Terrell	849	8,594
Texana, L. — (1980) Jackson Co.; Navidad R. and Sandy Cr.; 6.8 mi. SE Edna; (M-Ir); USBR, Lavaca-Navidad R. Auth., Texas Water Dev. Bd.; (formerly Palmetto Bend Reservoir)	9,727	161,085
Texoma, L. — (1943) Grayson-Cooke cos., Texas; Bryan-Marshall-Love cos., Okla.; (Imp. by Denison Dam) on Red R. below confluence of Red and Washita rivers; (P-FC-C-R); USAE	74,686	2,516,232
Toledo Bend Reservoir — (1967) Newton-Panola-Sabine-Shelby counties; Sabine R.; 14 mi. NE Burkeville; (M-In.-Ir.-PR); Sabine River Authority (Texas' share of capacity is half amount shown)	181,600	4,477,000
Tradinghouse Creek Reservoir — (1968) McLennan Co.; Tradinghouse Cr.; 9 mi. E Waco; (In.); TXU	2,010	37,800
Travis, L. — (1942) Travis-Burnet counties; Colorado R.; 13 mi. NW Austin; (M-In.-Ir.- Mi.-P-FC-R); LCRA: (Imp. by Mansfield Dam)	19,199	1,134,863
Trinidad L. — (1923) Henderson Co.; off-channel reservoir Trinity R.; 2 mi. S. Trinidad; (P); TXU.	740	7,450
Truscott Brine L. — (1987) Knox Co.; Bluff Cr.; 26 mi. NNW Knox City; (Chlorine Control); Red River Auth.	3,146	111,147
Twin Buttes Reservoir — (1963) Tom Green Co.; Concho R.; 8 mi. SW San Angelo; (M-In. -FC-Ir.-R.); City of San Angelo-USBR-Tom Green Co. WC&ID No. 1	9,080	186,200
Twin Oaks Reservoir — (1982) Robertson Co.; Duck Cr.; 12 mi. N. Franklin; (In) TXU	2,330	30,319
Tyler, L. /Lake Tyler East — (1949/1967) Smith Co.; Prairie and Mud Creeks.; 12 mi. SE Tyler; (M-In); City of Tyler; (Imp. by Whitehouse and Mud Creek dams)	4,737	80,198
Upper Nueces L. — (1926, 1948) Zavala Co.; Nueces R.; 6 mi. N Crystal City; (Ir.); Zavala-Dimmit Co. WID No. 1	316	5,200
Valley Acres Reservoir — (1956) Hidalgo Co.; off-channel Rio Grande; 7 mi. N Mercedes; (Ir-M-FC); Valley Acres Water Dist.	325	1,950
Valley L. — (1961) Fannin-Grayson counties; 2.5 mi. N Savoy; (P); TXU; (formerly Brushy Creek Reservoir)	1,080	16,400
Waco, L. — (1929) McLennan Co.; Bosque R.; 2 mi. W Waco; (M-FC-C-R); City of Waco-USAE Brazos River Authority	8,437	144,830
Walter E. Long, L. — (1967) Travis Co.; Decker Cr.; 9 mi. E Austin; (M-In.-R); City of Austin; (formerly Decker Lake)	1,269	33,940
Waxahachie, L. — (1956) Ellis Co.; S Prong Waxahachie Cr.; 4 mi. SE Waxahachie; (M-In); Ellis County WC&ID No. 1; (Imp. by S. Prong Dam)	656	11,386
Weatherford, L. — (1956) Parker Co.; Clear Fork Trinity River; 7 mi. E Weatherford; (M-In.); City of Weatherford	1,112	17,812
Welsh Reservoir — (1976) Titus Co.; Swauano Cr.; 11 mi. SE Mount Pleasant; (R-In.); AEP-Southwestern Electric Power Co.; (formerly Swauano Creek Reservoir)	1,269	20,242
White River L. — (1963) Crosby Co.; 16 mi. SE Crosbyton; (M-In.-Mi.); White River Municipal Water Dist.	1,642	31,846
White Rock L. — (1911) Dallas Co.; White Rock Cr.; within NE Dallas city limits; (R); City of Dallas	1,088	9,004
Whitney, L. — (1951) Hill-Bosque-Johnson counties; Brazos R.; 5.5 mi. SW Whitney (FC-P); USAE	23,220	554,203
Wichita, L. — (1901) Wichita Co.; Holliday Cr.; 6 mi. SW Wichita Falls; (M-P-R); City of Wichita Falls	2,200	14,000
Winnsboro, L. — (1962) Wood Co.; Big Sandy Cr.; 6 mi. SW Winnsboro; (FC-R); Wood County; (Imp. by Wood Co. Dam No. 4)	806	8,100
Winters, L. — (1983) Runnels Co.; Elm Cr.; 4.5 mi. E Winters; (M); City of Winters (also known as Elm Creek Lake and New Lake Winters)	643	8,374
Worth, L. — (1914) Tarrant Co.; W. Fk. Trinity R.; in NW Fort Worth; (M); City of Fort Worth	3,458	33,495
Wright Patman L. — (1957) Bowie-Cass-Morris-Titus-Red River counties; Sulphur R.; 8 mi. SW Texarkana; (FC-M); USAE; (formerly Texarkana Lake)	24,438	122,640

*An acre-foot is the amount of water necessary to cover an acre of surface area with water one foot deep. The **years** in the table refer to first impounding of water. **Double years** refer to later, larger dams. **Abbreviations are:** L., lake; R., river; Co., county; Cr., creek; (C) conservation; (FC) flood control; (R) recreation; (P) power; (M) municipal; (D) domestic; (Ir.) irrigation; (In.) industry; (Mi.) mining, including oil production; (FH) fish hatchery; USAE, United States Army Corps of Engineers; WC&ID, Water Control and Improvement District; WID, Water Improvement District; USBR, United States Bureau of Reclamation; Auth., Authority; LCRA, Lower Colorado River Authority; TP&WD, Texas Parks & Wildlife Dept.; USDA, United States Department of Agriculture; Imp., impounded.

Bluebonnets grow along railroad tracks in San Saba County in the Edwards Plateau vegetational area. Photo by Ron Billings; Texas Forest Service.

Texas Plant Life

This article was updated for the Texas Almanac by Stephan L. Hatch, Director, S.M. Tracy Herbarium and Professor, Department of Rangeland Ecology and Management, Texas A&M University.

Vegetational Diversity

The types of plants found in Texas vary widely from one region to the next. This is due to the amount and frequency of rainfall, diversity of soils, and the number of frost-free days. From the forests of East Texas to the deserts of West Texas, from the grassy plains of North Texas to the semi-arid brushlands of South Texas, plant species change continuously.

More than 100 million acres of Texas are devoted to **grazing,** both for domestic and wild animals. This is the **largest single use of land** in the state. More than 80 percent of the acreage is devoted to range in the Edwards Plateau, Cross Timbers and Prairies, South Texas Plains, and Trans-Pecos Mountains and Basins.

Sideoats grama, which occurs on more different soils in Texas than any other native grass, was officially designated as the **state grass of Texas** by the Texas Legislature in 1971.

The **10 principal plant life areas** of Texas, starting in the east, are:

1. Piney Woods

Most of this area of some 16 million acres ranges from about 50 to 700 feet above sea level and receives 40 to 56 inches of rain yearly. Many rivers, creeks, and bayous drain the region. Nearly all of Texas' commercial timber comes from this area. There are three native species of **pine,** the principal timber: longleaf, shortleaf, and loblolly. An introduced species, the slash pine, also is widely grown. Hardwoods include **oaks, elm, hickory, magnolia, sweet and black gum, tupelo,** and others.

The area is interspersed with native and improved grasslands. **Cattle** are the primary grazing animals.

Deer and **quail** are abundant in properly managed habitats. Primary forage plants, under proper grazing management, include species of **bluestems, rossettegrass, panicums, paspalums, blackseed needlegrass, Canada and Virginia wildryes, purpletop, broadleaf and spike woodoats, switchcane, lovegrasses, indiangrass,** and numerous **legume** species.

Highly disturbed areas have understory and overstory of undesirable woody plants that suppress growth of pine and desirable grasses. The primary forage grasses have been reduced, and the grasslands have been invaded by **threeawns, annual grasses, weeds, broomsedge bluestem, red lovegrass,** and shrubby woody species.

2. Gulf Prairies and Marshes

The Gulf Prairies and Marshes cover approximately 10 million acres. There are two subunits: (a) the marsh and salt grasses immediately at tidewater, and (b) a little farther inland, a strip of bluestems and tall grasses, with some gramas in the western part. Many of these grasses make excellent grazing.

Oaks, elm, and other hardwoods grow to some extent, especially along streams, and the area has some **post oak** and brushy extensions along its borders. Much of the Gulf Prairies is fertile farmland, and the area is well suited for **cattle.**

Principal grasses of the Gulf Prairies are **tall bunchgrasses,** including **big bluestem, little bluestem, seacoast bluestem, indiangrass, eastern gamagrass, Texas wintergrass, switchgrass,** and **gulf cordgrass. Saltgrass** occurs on moist saline sites.

Heavy grazing has changed the native vegetation in many cases so the predominant grasses are the less desirable **broomsedge bluestem, smutgrass, threeawns, tumblegrass,** and many other inferior grasses.

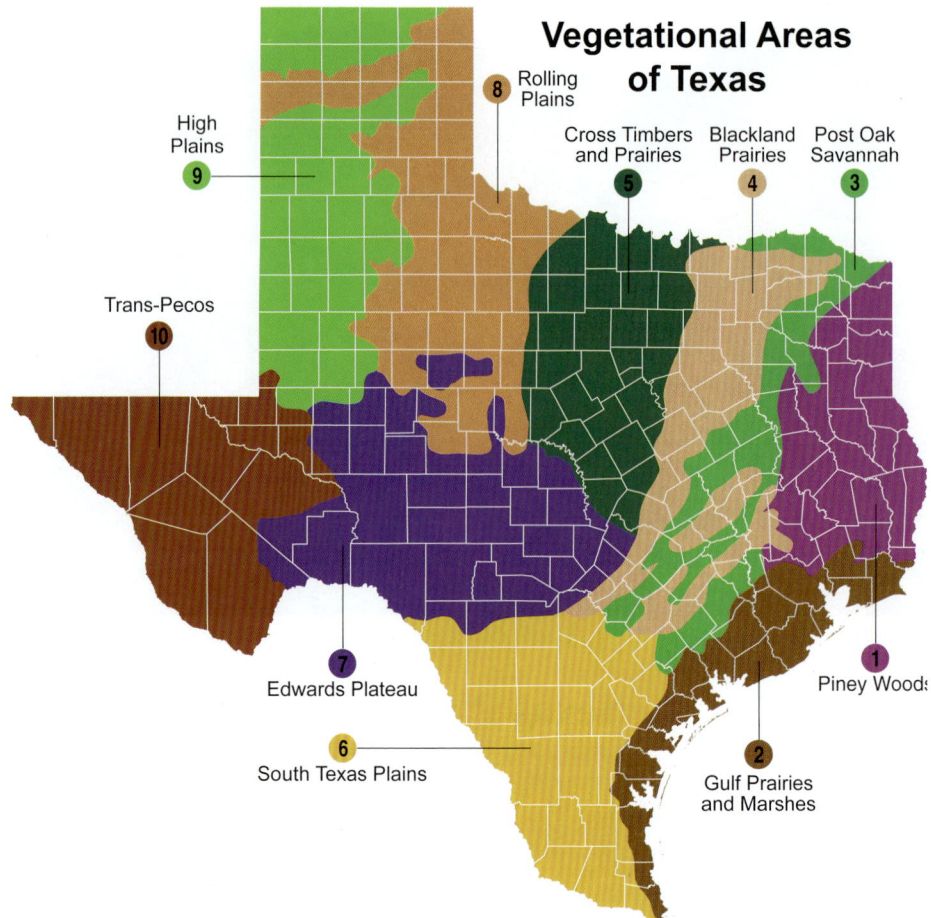

Vegetational Areas of Texas

8 Rolling Plains

High Plains 9

Cross Timbers and Prairies 5

Blackland Prairies 4

Post Oak Savannah 3

Trans-Pecos 10

Edwards Plateau 7

Piney Woods 1

South Texas Plains 6

Gulf Prairies and Marshes 2

Other plants that have invaded the productive grasslands include **oak underbrush, Macartney rose, huisache, mesquite, prickly pear, ragweed, bitter sneezeweed, broomweed,** and others.

Vegetation of the Gulf Marshes consists primarily of **sedges, bullrush, flat-sedges, beakrush** and other rushes, **smooth cordgrass, marshhay cordgrass, marsh millet,** and **maidencane.** The marshes are grazed best during winter.

3. Post Oak Savannah

This secondary forest area, also called the **Post Oak Belt,** covers some 7 million acres. It is immediately west of the primary forest region, with less annual rainfall and a little higher elevation. Principal trees are **post oak, blackjack oak,** and **elm. Pecans, walnuts,** and other kinds of water-demanding trees grow along streams. The southwestern extension of this belt is often poorly defined, with large areas of prairie.

The upland soils are **sandy** and **sandy loam,** while the bottomlands are **sandy loams** and **clays.**

The original vegetation consisted mainly of **little bluestem, big bluestem, indiangrass, switchgrass, purpletop, silver bluestem, Texas wintergrass, spike woodoats, longleaf woodoats, post oak,** and **blackjack oak.** The area is still largely native or improved grasslands, with **small farms** located throughout. Intensive grazing has contributed to dense stands of a woody understory of **yaupon, greenbriar,** and **oak** brush.

Mesquite has become a serious problem. Good forage plants have been replaced by such plants as **split-beard bluestem, red lovegrass, broomsedge bluestem, broomweed, bullnettle,** and **western ragweed.**

4. Blackland Prairies

This area of about 12 million acres, while called a "prairie," has much timber along the streams, including a variety of **oaks, pecan, elm, bois d'arc,** and **mesquite.** In its native state, it was largely a grassy plain — the first native grassland in the westward extension of the Southern Forest Region.

Most of this fertile area has been cultivated, and only small acreages of grassland remain in original vegetation. In heavily grazed pastures, the tall bunchgrass has been replaced by **buffalograss, Texas grama,** and other less productive grasses. **Mesquite, lotebush,** and other woody plants have invaded the grasslands.

The original grass vegetation includes **big** and **little bluestem, indiangrass, switchgrass, sideoats grama, hairy grama, tall dropseed, Texas wintergrass,** and **buffalograss.** Non-grass vegetation is largely legumes and composites.

5. Cross Timbers and Prairies

Approximately 15 million acres of alternating woodlands and prairies, often called the **Western Cross Timbers,** constitute this region. Sharp changes in the vegetational cover are associated with different soils and topography, but the grass composition is rather uniform.

The prairie grasses are **big bluestem, little bluestem, indiangrass, switchgrass, Canada wildrye, sideoats grama, hairy grama, tall grama, tall dropseed, Texas wintergrass, blue grama,** and **buffalograss.**

On Cross Timbers soils, the vegetation is composed of **big bluestem, little bluestem, hooded windmillgrass, sand lovegrass, indiangrass, switchgrass,** and many species of legumes. The woody vegetation includes **shinnery, blackjack, post,** and **live oaks.**

The entire area has been invaded heavily by woody brush plants of oaks, mesquite, juniper, and other unpalatable plants that furnish little forage for livestock.

6. South Texas Plains

South of San Antonio, between the coast and the Rio Grande, are some 21 million acres of subtropical dryland vegetation, consisting of small trees, shrubs, cactus, weeds, and grasses. The area is noteworthy for extensive brushlands and is known as the **Brush Country,** or the Spanish equivalents of **chaparral** or **monte.** Principal plants are **mesquite, small live oak, post oak, prickly pear (Opuntia) cactus, catclaw, blackbrush, whitebrush, guajillo, huisache, cenizo,** and others that often grow very densely.

The original vegetation was mainly perennial warm-season **bunchgrasses** in **savannahs** of **post oak, live oak,** and **mesquite.** Other brush species form dense thickets on the ridges and along streams. Long-continued grazing has contributed to the dense cover of brush. Most of the desirable grasses have only persisted under the protection of brush and cacti.

There are distinct differences in the original plant communities on various soils. Dominant grasses on the sandy loam soils are **seacoast bluestem, bristlegrass, paspalum, windmillgrass, silver bluestem, big sandbur,** and **tanglehead.** Dominant grasses on the clay and clay loams are **silver bluestem, Arizona cottontop, buffalograss, common curlymesquite, bristlegrass, pappusgrass, gramas, plains lovegrass, Texas cupgrass, vinemesquite,** other **panicums,** and **Texas wintergrass.**

Low saline areas are characterized by **gulf cordgrass, saltgrass, alkali sacaton,** and **switchgrass.** In the post oak and live oak savannahs, the grasses are mainly **seacoast bluestem, indiangrass, switchgrass, crinkleawn, paspalums,** and **panicums.** Today much of the area has been reseeded to **buffelgrass.**

7. Edwards Plateau

These 25 million acres are rolling to mountainous, with woodlands in the eastern part and grassy prairies in the west. There is a good deal of brushy growth in the central and eastern areas. The combination of grasses, weeds, and small trees is ideal for **cattle, sheep, goats, deer,** and **wild turkey.**

This limestone-based area is characterized by the large number of **springfed, perennially flowing streams** that originate in its interior and flow across the **Balcones Escarpment,** which bounds it on the south and east. The soils are shallow, ranging from sands to clays, and are calcareous in reaction. This area is predominantly rangeland, with cultivation confined to the deeper soils.

In the east-central portion is the well-marked **Central** or **Llano Basin,** centering in Mason, Llano, and Burnet counties, with a mixture of granitic and sandy soils. The western portion of the area comprises the semi-arid **Stockton Plateau.**

Noteworthy is the growth of **cypress** along the perennially flowing streams. Separated by many miles from the cypress growth of the moist Southern Forest Belt, they constitute one of Texas' several **"islands"** of **vegetation.** These trees, which grow to stately proportions, were commercialized in the past.

A family crosses a wooden boardwalk through a cypress slough in Big Thicket National Preserve in Hardin County. The preserve, located in the Piney Woods region, is composed of 15 units in seven counties. Texas Almanac file photo.

The principal grasses of the clay soils are **cane bluestem, silver bluestem, little bluestem, sideoats grama, hairy grama, indiangrass, common curlymesquite, buffalograss, fall witchgrass, plains lovegrass, wildryes,** and **Texas wintergrass.**

The rocky areas support tall or mid-grasses with an overstory of **live oak, shinnery oak, juniper,** and **mesquite.** The heavy clay soils have a mixture of **tobosagrass, buffalograss, sideoats grama,** and **mesquite.**

Throughout the Edwards Plateau, **live oak, shinnery oak, mesquite,** and **juniper** dominate the woody vegetation. Woody plants have invaded to the degree that they must be controlled before range forage plants can re-establish.

8. Rolling Plains

This is a region of approximately 24 million acres of alternating woodlands and prairies. The area is half **mesquite woodland** and half **prairie.** Mesquite trees have steadily invaded and increased in the grasslands for many years, despite constant control efforts.

Soils range from coarse sands along outwash terraces adjacent to streams to tight or compact clays on redbed clays and shales. Rough broken lands on steep slopes are found in the western portion. About two-thirds of the area is **rangeland,** but cultivation is important in certain localities.

The original vegetation includes **big, little, sand and silver bluestems, Texas wintergrass, indiangrass, switchgrass, sideoats and blue gramas, wildryes, tobosagrass,** and **buffalograss** on the clay soils.

The sandy soils support **tall bunchgrasses,** mainly **sand bluestem. Sand shinnery oak, sand sagebrush,** and **mesquite** are the dominant woody plants.

Continued heavy grazing contributes to the increase in woody plants, low-value grasses such as **red grama, red lovegrass, tumblegrass, gummy lovegrass, Texas grama, sand dropseed,** and **sandbur,** with **western ragweed, croton,** and many other weedy forbs. **Yucca** is a problem plant on certain rangelands.

9. High Plains

The High Plains, some 19 million treeless acres, are an extension of the Great Plains to the north. Its level nature and porous soils prevent drainage over wide areas.

The relatively light rainfall flows into the numerous shallow **"playa"** lakes or sinks into the ground to feed the great **underground aquifer** that is the source of wa-

ter for the countless wells that irrigate the surface of the plains. A large part of this area is under irrigated farming, but native grassland remains in about one-half of the High Plains.

Blue grama and **buffalograss** comprise the principal vegetation on the clay and clay loam "hardland" soils. Important grasses on the sandy loam "sandy land" soils are **little bluestem, western wheatgrass, indiangrass, switchgrass,** and **sand reedgrass. Sand shinnery oak, sand sagebrush, mesquite,** and **yucca** are conspicuous invading brushy plants.

Above, red cactus flowers bloom in the desert near Fort Davis in Jeff Davis County. Photo by Janet Morrow. Below, a butterfly lights on a thistle in the Rita Blanca National Grassland in Dallam County. Photo courtesy of the U.S. Forest Service.

10. Trans-Pecos Mountains and Basins

With as little as eight inches of annual rainfall, long hot summers, and usually cloudless skies to encourage evaporation, this 18-million-acre area produces only drought-resistant vegetation without irrigation. Grass is usually short and sparse.

The principal vegetation consists of **lechuguilla, ocotillo, yucca, cenizo, prickly pear,** and other arid land plants. In the more arid areas, **gyp** and **chino grama,** and **tobosagrass** prevail. There is some **mesquite.** The vegetation includes **creosotetarbush, desert shrub, grama grassland, yucca and juniper savannahs, pine oak forest,** and **saline flats.**

The mountains are 3,000 to 8,749 feet in elevation and support **piñon pine, juniper,** and some **ponderosa pine** and other forest vegetation on a few of the higher slopes. The grass vegetation, especially on the higher mountain slopes, includes many **southwestern** and **Rocky Mountain species** not present elsewhere in Texas. On the desert flats, **black grama, burrograss,** and **fluffgrass** are frequent.

More productive sites have numerous species of **grama, muhly, Arizona cottontop, dropseed,** and **perennial threeawn grasses.** At the higher elevations, **plains bristlegrass, little bluestem, Texas bluestem, sideoats grama, chino grama, blue grama, piñon ricegrass, wolftail,** and several species of **needlegrass** are frequent.

The common invaders on all depleted ranges are **woody plants, burrograss, fluffgrass, hairy erioneuron, ear muhly, sand muhly, red grama, broom snakeweed, croton, cacti,** and several poisonous plants. ☆

For Further Reading

Hatch, S.L., K.N. Gandhi, and L.E. Brown, *Checklist of the Vascular Plants of Texas;* MP1655, Texas Agricultural Experiment Station, College Station, 1990.

A mixture of hardwoods and pines like these in Davy Crockett National Forest are found throughout much of the 43-county Texas timber region. Photo by Ron Billings; Texas Forest Service.

Texas Forest Resources

Source: Texas Forest Service, Texas A&M University System. On the web: txforestservice.tamu.edu

Texas has an abundance and a great diversity of forest resources. Forest land covers roughly 38 percent of the state's land area. According to 2009 figures from the **Forest Inventory and Analysis (FIA),** there are 63.3 million acres of forests and woodlands in Texas, a number much larger than previous Forest Service estimates.

East Texas Piney Woods

The East Texas pine-hardwood region, often called the **Piney Woods,** is the principal forest region in Texas. The 43-county region forms the western edge of the southern pine region, extending from Bowie and Red River counties in northeast Texas to Jefferson, Harris, and Waller counties in southeast Texas. The counties contain 12.1 million acres of forestland of which 11.9 million acres are classified as productive timberland and produce nearly all of the state's commercial timber.

Following is a summary of the findings of the Forest Inventory of East Texas, completed in 2009 by the Texas Forest Service (TFS) in cooperation with the USDA Forest Service Southern Research Station.

Timberland Acreage and Ownership

Nearly all (11.9 million of 12.1 million acres) of the East Texas forest is classified as "timberland," which is suitable for production of timber products and not reserved as parks or wilderness areas. Texas timberland acreage remained stable between 2008 and 2009. This is a result of a balance between new timberland acres coming from agricultural lands, which are either intentionally planted with trees or have naturally reverted to forest, and previous forested land that is converted to other uses, such as commercial or residential areas.

Ninety-two percent of East Texas timberland is owned by approximately 210,000 private individuals, families, partnerships, corporations, forest-products companies, and timber investment groups. The remaining 8 percent is owned by federal, state, and local governments. The following table shows acreage of timberland by ownership:

Ownership Class	Thous. Acres
Private	11,028.8
Public:	
National forest	689.4
Misc. federal	255.9
State & local	167.0
Total	**11,964.9**

East Texas has undergone major shifts in private ownership during the past decade, primarily a transfer of land from forest industry owners to non-industrial private owners. Information from several sources, such as the FIA, National Woodland Owner Survey, and timberland transaction records, suggests that the forest industry now accounts for no more than 50 thousand acres. Non-industrial private corporations, which include timber investment corporations, account for 3.0 million to 3.4 million acres, and family forest landowners account for 7.5 million to 8.0 million acres.

Forest Types

Six major forest types are found in the East Texas Piney Woods. Two pine-forest types are most common. The **loblolly-shortleaf** and **longleaf-slash** forest types are dominated by the four species of southern yellow pine. In these forests, the various pine trees make up at least 50 percent of the trees.

Oak-hickory is the second most common forest type. These are upland hardwood forests in which oaks or hickories make up at least 50 percent of the trees and

Logs are processed at a sawmill in Nacogdoches County. The East Texas timber region produced 479,840,840 cubic feet of timber in 2009. Photo by Ron Billings; Texas Forest Service.

pine species are less than 25 percent. **Oak-pine** is a mixed-forest type in which more than 50 percent of the trees are hardwoods, but pines make up 25 percent to 49 percent of the trees.

Two forest types, **oak-gum-cypress** and **elm-ash-cottonwood,** are bottomland types that are commonly found along creeks, river bottoms, swamps, and other wet areas. The oak-gum-cypress forests are typically made up of many species including blackgum, sweetgum, oaks, and southern cypress. The elm-ash-cottonwood bottomland forests are dominated by those trees but also contain many other species, such as willow, sycamore, and maple.

Other forest types found in East Texas include small acreages of mesquite, exotic hardwoods, red cedar, and unproductive lands that are considered forested but do not meet stocking requirements. The following table shows the breakdown in acreage by forest type:

Forest Type Group	Thous. Acres
Southern Pine:	
Loblolly-shortleaf	5,079.0
Longleaf-slash	190.4
Oak-hickory	3,003.3
Oak-pine	1,431.8
Bottomland Hardwood:	
Oak-gum-cypress	1,386.2
Elm-ash-cottonwood	638.5
Other	411.9
Total	**12,141.1**

Southern pine plantations, established by tree planting and usually managed intensively to maximize timber production, are an important source of wood fiber. Texas forests include 2.5 million acres of **pine plantations,** 62 percent of which are on industrially managed land, 34 percent on non-industrial private land, and 4 percent on public land. Genetically superior tree seedlings are usually planted to improve survival and growth.

Timber Volume and Number of Trees

Texas timberland contains about **16 billion cubic feet of timber "growing-stock" volume.** One billion cubic feet of growing stock produces roughly enough lumber to build a 2,000-square-foot home for one out of every three Texans. The inventory of softwood increased slightly from 9.3 billion cubic feet in 2008 to 9.4 billion cubic feet in 2009. The hardwood inventory decreased slightly from 6.6 billion cubic feet in 2008 to 6.5 billion cubic feet in 2009.

There are an estimated **7.7 billion live trees in East Texas,** according to the 2009 survey. This includes 2.1 billion softwoods and 5.6 billion hardwoods. The predominant species are loblolly and shortleaf pine; 2 billion pine trees are found in East Texas.

Timber Growth and Removals

Between 2004 and 2009, an annual average of 719 million cubic feet of growing stock timber was removed from the inventory, either through harvest or land-use changes. Meanwhile, 846.3 million cubic feet of growing stock were added to the inventory through growth each year.

For pine, an average of 551.7 million cubic feet was removed during those years, while 611.8 million cubic feet were added by growth. For hardwoods, 166.2 million cubic feet were removed, while 223.6 million cubic feet were added by growth.

The 2009 Timber Harvest

Total Removals

Total removals of growing stock in East Texas in 2009, including both pine and hardwood, decreased 11.6 percent from 2008. The total volume of growing stock that was removed from the 43-county timber region was 468.8 million cubic feet in 2009, compared to 530.2 million cubic feet in 2008. Included in the total growing stock removals are timber harvested for industrial use and an estimate of logging residue.

Industrial roundwood harvest in Texas in 2009, the portion of the total removal that was subsequently utilized in the **manufacture of wood products,** totaled 396.4 million cubic feet for pine and 83.4 million cubic feet for hardwood. The pine industrial roundwood har-

Beyond the Piney Woods: Texas' Other Tree Regions

In addition to the 12 million acres of timberland in East Texas, there are an additional 51 million acres of land in the remainder of Texas that are considered forestland. These forests consist of mesquite woodlands, oak-hickory forests, juniper woodlands, and other western forest types. These forests do not have the commercial timber value of the East Texas Piney Woods but are environmentally important with benefits of wildlife habitat, improved water quality, recreation, and aesthetics.

Following is a brief description of these areas.

• **Post Oak Belt**: The Post Oak Belt forms a band of wooded savannah mixed with pasture and cropland immediately west of the Piney Woods. It extends from Lamar and Red River counties southwest as far as Bee and Atascosa counties. Predominant species include post oak, blackjack oak, and elm. An interesting area called the "**Lost Pines**" forms an isolated island of southern-pine forest in Bastrop, Caldwell, Fayette, and Lee counties just a few miles southeast of Austin.

• **Eastern and Western Cross Timbers**: The Eastern and Western Cross Timbers cover an area of about 3 million acres in North-Central Texas.

The term "cross timbers" originated with the early settlers who, in their travels from east to west, crossed alternating patches of oak forest and prairies and so affixed the name "cross timbers" to these forests.

• **Cedar Brakes**: Farther south in the Edwards Plateau region are the cedar brakes, which extend over 3.7 million acres. Cedar, live oak, and mesquite dominate these steep slopes and rolling hills. Mesquite is harvested for cooking wood, knick-knacks, and woodworking. Live oak in this region is declining because of the oak wilt disease.

• **Mountain Forests**: The mountain forests of the Trans-Pecos region, including Jeff Davis County and the Big Bend, are rugged and picturesque. Several western tree species, including piñon pine, ponderosa pine, southwestern white pine, and even Douglas fir are found there, along with aspen and several species of oak.

• **Coastal Forests**: The coastal forests of the southern Gulf Coast are characterized by a mix of brush and short, scrubby trees. Common species include mesquite, live oak, and acacia. Some of these scrub forests are particularly important as migratory bird habitat.

---

vest was down 10 percent from 2008, and the hardwood roundwood harvest was down 14.6 percent. The combined harvest dropped 10.8 percent in 2009 to 479.8 million cubic feet. Top producing counties included Jasper, Newton, Tyler, San Augustine, and Cherokee.

Total Harvest Value

Stumpage value of the East Texas timber harvest in 2009 was $214.9 million, a 33.8-percent decrease from 2008. The delivered value of timber was down 26.2 percent to $494.8 million. Pine timber accounted for 82.3 percent of the total stumpage value and 80.2 percent of the total delivered value.

The harvest of **sawlogs for production of lumber** was down 10.1 percent in 2009 to 1.2 billion board feet. The pine sawlog harvest totaled 1.0 billion board feet, down 10.8 percent, and the hardwood sawlog harvest decreased 8.3 percent to 204 million board feet. Jasper,

Cherokee, Angelina, Newton, and Polk counties were the top producers of sawlogs.

Timber cut for the production of **structural panels,** including both plywood and OSB (oriented strand board) and hardwood veneer, totaled 91.6 million cubic feet, a 11.7 percent decrease from 2008. Polk, Angelina, Cherokee, Trinity, and Houston counties were the top producers of veneer and panel roundwood.

The harvest of timber for the manufacture of **pulp and paper products** decreased to 2.3 million cords in 2009, a 10.6-percent reduction from 2008. Jasper, Tyler, Newton, San Augustine, and Cass counties were the top producers of pulpwood.

Other roundwood harvest, including posts, poles, and pilings, totaled 1.9 million cubic feet in 2009.

Import-Export Trends

Texas was a **net exporter** of timber products in

Texas Forest Products Production 1999–2009

| Year | Lumber* (thousand board feet) | | Paper (short tons) | | | Structural Panel |
	Pine	Hardwood	Paper	Paperboard*	Total Paper Products	Pine (thousand square feet*)
1999	1,279,487	225,570	1,079,397	1,979,592	3,058,989	3,260,055
2000	1,410,999	184,172	955,117	2,037,148	2,992,265	3,265,644
2001	1,293,823	213,795	599,902	2,083,326	2,683,228	2,732,940
2002	1,425,613	223,932	551,367	2,179,423	2,730,790	2,818,356
2003	1,490,311	287,062	255,462	2,170,185	2,425,647	2,723,225
2004	1,591,109	324,663	0**	2,560,480	2,560,480	2,859,012
2005	1,733,314	230,090	0**	2,512,262	2,512,262	3,249,558
2006	1,676,461	240,214	0**	2,781,865	2,781,865	2,935,637
2007	1,550,716	180,713	0**	2,788,308	2,788,308	2,503,941
2008	1,406,103	213,191	0**	2,329,347	2,329,347	2,204,544
2009	1,237,801	171,514	0**	2,007,054	2,007,054	1,958,794
	*Includes tie volumes.		*Includes fiberboard and miscellaneous products. **There was no paper or market pulp production due to the closure of a major paper mill.			*3/8-inch basis

2009. Total import from other states was 61.7 million cubic feet, while the total export was 64.7 million cubic feet. Texas mills utilized 86.5 percent of the timber harvested in the state in 2009. The remainder was processed mainly by mills in Arkansas, Louisiana, and Oklahoma.

Production of Forest Products

LUMBER — Texas sawmills produced 1.4 billion board feet of lumber in 2009, a decrease of 13 percent from 2008. Production of pine lumber decreased 12 percent to 1.2 billion board feet in 2009, while hardwood lumber production dropped 19.5 percent, to 171.5 million board feet in 2009.

STRUCTURAL PANEL PRODUCTS — Production of structural panels, including plywood and OSB, decreased to 2 billion square feet in 2009.

PAPER PRODUCTS — Production of paperboard totaled 2 million tons in 2009. There was no paper production in Texas in 2009.

TREATED WOOD — There was a 22.1 percent increase in the volume of wood processed by Texas wood treaters in 2009 over 2008. The total volume treated in 2009 was 46.2 million cubic feet. Among major treated products, lumber accounted for 69.6 percent of the total volume; crossties accounted for 15.6 percent; utility poles and fence posts each accounted for 7.1 percent and 4.0 percent, respectively.

PRIMARY MILL RESIDUE — Total mill residue, including chips, sawdust, shavings, and bark produced in primary mills, such as sawmills, panel mills, and chip mills, was 5.6 million short tons in 2009, a decrease of 3.4 percent from 2008. Of this residue, 83 percent was from pine species and 17 percent was from hardwood species. Chips accounted for 52.2 percent of mill residue, followed by bark (29.5 percent), sawdust (13 percent), and shavings (5.4 percent).

Total Timber Production and Value by County in Texas, 2009

County	Pine	Hardwood	Total	Stumpage Value	Delivered Value
	Cubic feet			Thousand dollars	
Anderson	12,553,297	2,173,132	14,726,429	$ 7,607	$ 15,985
Angelina	20,858,637	2,239,974	23,098,611	11,837	24,919
Bowie	4,852,769	2,033,561	6,886,330	2,877	7,010
Camp	234,120	138,079	372,199	151	390
Cass	14,860,870	6,238,280	21,099,150	8,324	20,919
Chambers	350,354	968,417	1,318,771	492	1,348
Cherokee	19,246,092	5,747,091	24,993,183	12,415	27,218
Franklin	229,813	342,995	572,808	309	692
Gregg	510,300	2,405,881	2,916,181	1,891	3,907
Grimes	904,718	839	905,557	596	1,070
Hardin	22,576,676	1,748,773	24,325,449	9,656	23,681
Harris	2,721,662	147,550	2,869,212	1,914	3,449
Harrison	6,113,298	2,922,874	9,036,172	4,420	9,752
Henderson	770,881	871,350	1,642,231	859	1,909
Houston	13,013,654	349,359	13,363,013	7,337	14,623
Jasper	38,997,118	1,819,590	40,816,708	16,401	39,664
Jefferson	91,721	90,769	182,490	133	246
Leon	1,598,036	133,086	1,731,122	1,148	2,077
Liberty	12,721,193	4,323,305	17,044,498	8,006	18,115
Madison	3,303	0	3,303	1	3
Marion	6,108,314	2,883,881	8,992,195	4,087	9,469
Montgomery	4,383,828	529,492	4,913,320	3,102	5,799
Morris	1,334,455	1,174,036	2,508,491	903	2,476
Nacogdoches	17,124,312	2,624,454	19,748,766	9,187	20,578
Newton	31,455,434	1,237,312	32,692,746	12,476	31,163
Orange	1,383,086	50,185	1,433,271	648	1,453
Panola	11,652,446	5,619,239	17,271,685	8,535	19,025
Polk	22,624,637	2,134,959	24,759,596	11,344	25,502
Red River	4,813,679	3,045,756	7,859,435	2,571	7,570
Rusk	9,358,585	4,990,346	14,348,931	6,919	15,715
Sabine	13,821,616	1,067,664	14,889,280	6,448	14,911
San Augustine	26,609,426	2,889,906	29,499,332	10,320	27,500
San Jacinto	9,982,408	753,361	10,735,769	5,890	11,796
Shelby	10,466,181	2,407,418	12,873,599	4,924	12,483
Smith	2,217,978	3,178,419	5,396,397	3,122	6,629
Titus	279,546	796,780	1,076,326	674	1,398
Trinity	11,775,113	575,991	12,351,104	6,492	13,355
Tyler	24,611,928	5,201,155	29,813,083	10,454	28,167
Upshur	2,086,755	2,054,800	4,141,555	1,971	4,579
Van Zandt	97,431	105,904	203,335	127	256
Walker	5,865,024	303,956	6,168,980	3,835	7,146
Waller	73,441	1,342	74,783	44	85
Wood	885,149	1,135,321	2,020,470	764	2,040
Other Counties	4,184,362	3,980,612	8,164,974	3,669	8,746
Totals	**396,403,646**	**83,437,194**	**479,840,840**	**$214,880**	**$494,818**

Texas Forest Service firefighters work to put out the Putnam wildfire in March 2011 in Callahan County. In 2009, forest service and local fire departments responded to 17,488 fires. Photo by Ron Billings; Texas Forest Service.

Reforestation

A total of 112,422 acres was planted during the winter 2008 and spring 2009 planting season, a 29.9-percent increase over the 2007–2008 season. Industrial landowners, including acres planted by Timber Investment Management Organizations (TIMOs) and timberland Real Estate Investment Trusts (REITs), planted 81,067 acres, up 35.6 percent from the previous season.

The Family Forest owners planted 30,791 acres in 2008–2009, up 18.6 percent over 2007–2008. Public landowners only planted 464 acres. The divestiture of industry lands into the non-industrial private sector will eventually lead to a sharp reduction in industry reforestation acreage. Non-industrial ownerships typically reforest less than industry.

Fire Protection

During the 2009 fire season, Texas Forest Service and local fire departments responded to 17,488 fires that burned 726,502 acres and destroyed 436 homes. Wildfire suppression efforts were credited with saving 13,602 homes valued at more than $500 million.

Texas has a tiered approach to emergencies, such as wildland fires, with response coming from local, district, state, and federal levels. When a fire surpasses the capabilities of local fire departments, the TFS steps in to help. On average, TFS personnel respond to 15 percent of the wildland fires that burn across the state; however, those fires burn 70 percent of total acres lost to wildland fires each year.

Forest Pests

The **southern pine beetle** is the most destructive insect pest in the 12 million acres of commercial forests in East Texas. Typically, this bark beetle kills more timber annually than forest fires.

This destructive insect is currently at very low levels in East Texas but is expected to return to outbreak status. When outbreaks occur, the TFS coordinates all direct control activity on state and private forestlands. These activities include detecting infestations from the air, checking infestations on the ground to evaluate the need for control, notifying landowners, and providing technical assistance when control is warranted.

Recent efforts have focused on rating the susceptibility of pine stands to future southern pine beetle outbreaks, as well as prevention of infestations. Since 2003, the TFS has offered federal cost shares to private forest landowners in East Texas as an incentive to thin the young pine stands that are most susceptible to bark beetles. Thinning dense forests to promote vigorous tree growth is the preferred long-run method to reduce tree losses caused by bark beetles.

Extensive mortality of live oaks in Central Texas is caused by a vascular wilt disease called **oak wilt**. A suppression project, administered by TFS Forest Pest Management personnel, provides technical assistance and education for affected landowners.

Invasive (non-native) insects, diseases, and plants are a problem for Texas' forest landowners. The **soapberry borer,** a wood-boring beetle introduced from Mexico, has killed western soapberry trees in some 44 counties in Central Texas. Invasive plants, such as **Japanese climbing fern, Chinese tallow, and non-native privets,** have also spread rapidly.

Urban Forests

Because an estimated 86 percent of Texans now live in urban areas, urban trees and forests play an important role in their lives.

Trees reduce the urban heat island effect by shading and evaporative cooling. They also purify the air by absorbing pollutants, slowing the chemical reactions that produce harmful ozone, and filtering dust. Urban forests reduce storm water runoff and soil erosion, and they buffer against noise, glare, and strong winds, while providing habitat for urban wildlife.

Environmental benefits from a single tree may be worth more than $275 each year. The value to real estate and the emotional and psychological benefits raise the value of our urban trees even higher. ☆

Public Forests and Grasslands in Texas

Sources: U.S. Forest Service, Lufkin and Albuquerque, NM; www.fs.fed.us/r8/texas/ and the Texas Forest Service, Texas A&M University System; txforestservice.tamu.edu

There are **four national forests** and all or part of **five national grasslands** in Texas. These federally owned lands are administered by the U.S. Department of Agriculture Forest Service and by district rangers.

The national forests cover 637,472 acres in parts of 12 Texas counties. The national grasslands cover 117,394 acres in six Texas counties. Two of these grasslands extend into Oklahoma, as well.

The four East Texas forests and two North Texas grasslands are under the supervision of the National Forests and Grasslands in Texas (2221 North Raguet St., Lufkin 75904; (936) 639-8501).

The three West Texas grasslands (Black Kettle, McClellan Creek, and Rita Blanca) are administered by the Forest Supervisor in Albuquerque, N.M., as units of the Cibola National Forest.

The following list gives the name of the forest or grassland, the administrative district(s) for each, the acreage in each county, total acreage, and named places within each forest:

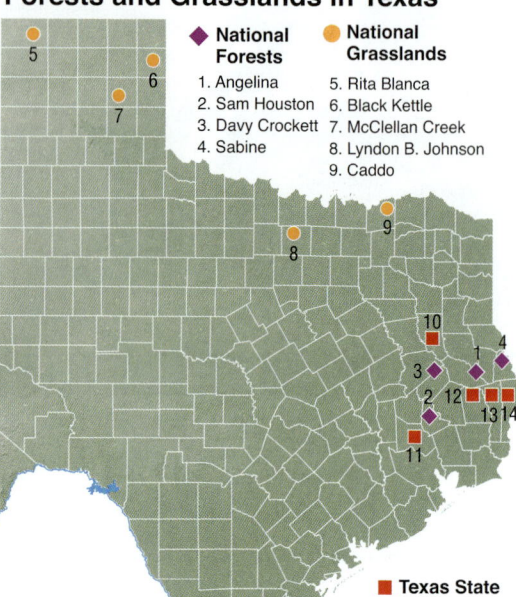

Forests and Grasslands in Texas

◆ National Forests
1. Angelina
2. Sam Houston
3. Davy Crockett
4. Sabine

● National Grasslands
5. Rita Blanca
6. Black Kettle
7. McClellan Creek
8. Lyndon B. Johnson
9. Caddo

■ Texas State Forests
10. Fairchild
11. Jones
12. Kirby
13. Masterson
14. Siecke

National Forests

Angelina National Forest — Angelina Ranger District (Zavalla); Angelina County, 58,520 acres; Jasper, 21,013; Nacogdoches, 9,238; San Augustine, 64,389. Total, 153,160 acres. Contains the Aldridge Sawmill Historic Site, and Upland Island and Turkey Hill Wilderness.

Davy Crockett National Forest — Davy Crockett District (Ratcliff); Houston County, 93,320 acres; Trinity, 67,313. Total, 160,633 acres. Contains the Big Slough Wilderness.

Sabine National Forest — Sabine District (Hemphill); Jasper County, 64 acres; Newton, 1,781; Sabine, 95,454; San Augustine, 4,287; Shelby, 59,212. Total, 160,798 acres. Contains the Indian Mounds Wilderness.

Sam Houston National Forest — Sam Houston District (New Waverly); Montgomery County, 47,801 acres; San Jacinto, 60,632; Walker, 54,597. Total, 163,030 acres. Contains the Little Lake Creek Wilderness.

National Grasslands

Lyndon B. Johnson National Grassland and **Caddo National Grassland** — District Ranger at Decatur; Fannin County, 17,873 acres; Montague, 61; Wise, 20,252. Total, 38,186 acres.

Black Kettle National Grassland — Lake Marvin District Ranger in Cheyenne, Okla.; Hemphill County, 576 acres; Roger Mills County, Okla., 30,724 acres. Total, 31,300 acres.

McClellan Creek National Grassland — District Ranger in Cheyenne, Okla.; Gray County, 1,449 acres. Total, 1,449 acres.

Rita Blanca National Grassland — District Ranger at Clayton, N.M.; Dallam County, 77,183 acres; Cimar-

ron County, Okla., 15,639 acres. Total, 92,822 acres.

Establishment of National Forests and Grasslands

National forests in Texas were established by invitation of the Texas Legislature by an Act of 1933, authorizing the purchase of lands in Texas for the establishment of national forests. President Franklin D. Roosevelt proclaimed these purchases on Oct. 15, 1936.

The national grasslands were originally submarginal Dust Bowl project lands, purchased by the federal government primarily under the Bankhead-Jones Farm Tenant Act (1937). Today they are well covered with grasses and native shrubs.

Forests and Grasslands Uses

The national forests are managed to achieve sustainable conditions and provide wildlife habitat, outdoor recreation, water, wood, minerals, and forage for public use while retaining the aesthetic, historic, and spiritual qualities of the land.

In 1960, the Multiple Use–Sustained Yield Act put into law what had been practiced in Texas for almost 30 years: that resources on public lands will be managed so that they are used in ways that best meet the needs of the people, that the benefits obtained will exist indefinitely, and that each natural resource will be managed in balance with other resources.

However, even the most carefully planned system of management cannot foresee factors that can cause drastic changes in a forest. Fire, storms, insects, and disease, for example, can prompt managers to deviate from land management plans and can alter the way a forest is managed.

1. Timber Production

About 486,000 acres of the national forests in Texas are suitable for timber production. Sales of sawtimber, pulpwood, and other forest products are initiated to implement forest plans and objectives. The estimated net growth is more than 200 million board feet per year and is valued at $40 million. A portion of this growth is normally removed by cutting.

2. Cattle Grazing

Permits to graze cattle on national grasslands are granted to the public for an annual fee. About 600 head of cattle are grazed on the Caddo–Lyndon B. Johnson National Grasslands annually. On the Rita Blanca National Grasslands, 5,425 head of cattle are grazed each year, most of them in Texas.

3. Hunting and Fishing

State hunting and fishing laws and regulations apply to all national forest land. Game law enforcement is carried out by the Texas Parks and Wildlife Department.

A wide variety of fishing opportunities are available on the Angelina, Sabine, Neches, and San Jacinto rivers; the Sam Rayburn and Toledo Bend reservoirs; Lake Conroe; and many small streams. Hunting is not permitted on the McClellan Creek National Grassland nor at the Lake Marvin Unit of the Black Kettle National Grassland.

Dogwoods bloom in the Stephen F. Austin Experimental Forest, located within the Angelina National Forest, eight miles southwest of Nacogdoches. Photo by Ron Billings; Texas Forest Service.

4. Recreational Facilities

An estimated 3 million people visit the recreational areas in the national forests and grasslands in Texas each year, primarily for picnicking, swimming, fishing, camping, boating, and nature enjoyment.

The Sabine and Angelina National Forests are on the shores of Toledo Bend and Sam Rayburn reservoirs, two large East Texas lakes featuring fishing and other water sports. Lake Conroe and Lake Livingston offer water-related outdoor recreation opportunities on and near the Sam Houston National Forest.

Recreational activities offered in the National Forests and Grasslands are listed in the Recreation section on page 182.

State Forests

Texas has **five state forests**, all of which are used primarily for demonstration and research. They are all game sanctuaries with no firearms or hunting allowed.

Recreational opportunities, such as horseback riding, hiking, bird watching, and picnicking, are available in all but the Masterson Forest. *See page 179 for recreation information.*

I.D. Fairchild State Forest — Texas' largest forest is located west of Rusk in Cherokee County. This forest was transferred from the state prison system in 1925. Additional land was obtained in 1963 from the Texas State Hospitals and Special Schools for a total acreage of 2,740.

W. Goodrich Jones State Forest — Located south of Conroe in Montgomery County, it comprises 1,733 acres. It was purchased in 1926 and named for the founder of the Texas Forestry Association.

John Henry Kirby Memorial State Forest — This 600-acre forest in Tyler County was donated by lumberman John Henry Kirby in 1929, as well as later donors. Revenue from this forest is given to the Association of Former Students of Texas A&M University for student-loan purposes.

Paul N. Masterson Memorial Forest — Mrs. Leonora O'Neal Masterson of Beaumont donated this 519 acres in Jasper County in 1984 in honor of her husband, who was a tree farmer and an active member of the Texas Forestry Association.

E.O. Siecke State Forest — The first state forest, it was purchased by the state in 1924. It contains 1,722 acres of pine land in Newton County. An additional 100 acres was obtained by a 99-year lease in 1946. ☆

National Wildlife Refuges

Source: U.S. Fish and Wildlife Service, U.S. Department of the Interior.

Texas has more than 470,000 acres in 17 national wildlife refuges. Their descriptions, with date of acquisition in parentheses, follow.

Included in this acreage are two conservation easement refuges, which may be visited at different times of the year for bird watching and wildlife viewing, as well as hunting and fishing. Write or call before visiting to check on facilities and days and hours of operation. On the web: www.fws.gov/southwest/.

Anahuac (1963): The more than 34,000 acres of this refuge are located along the upper Gulf Coast in Chambers County. Fresh and saltwater marshes and miles of beautiful, sweeping coastal prairie provide wintering habitat for large flocks of waterfowl, including geese, 27 species of ducks, and six species of rails. Roseate spoonbills, great and snowy egrets, and white-faced ibis are among the other birds frequenting the refuge. Other species include alligator, muskrat, and bobcat. Fishing, bird watching, auto tours, and hunting are available. Office: Box 278, Anahuac 77514; (409) 267-3337.

Aransas (1937): This refuge complex comprises 115,000 acres including Blackjack Peninsula, Matagorda Island, and three satellite units in Aransas and Refugio counties. Besides providing wintering grounds for the largest wild flock of endangered whooping cranes, the refuge is home to more than 390 species of waterfowl and other migratory birds. Refuge Tour Loop is open daily, sunrise to sunset. Claude F. Lard Visitor Center is open daily, 8:30 a.m. to 4:30 p.m. Other facilities include a 40-foot observation tower and walking trails. Office: Box 100, Austwell 77950; (361) 286-3559.

Attwater Prairie Chicken (1972): Established in Colorado County to preserve habitat for the endangered Attwater's prairie chicken (a ground-dwelling grouse), the refuge comprises 10,528 acres of native tallgrass prairie, sandy knolls, and wooded areas. A 5-mile auto tour loop is available year-round. Two hiking trails, the Pipit and Sycamore trails, traverse the prairie, potholes,

and riparian areas. The auto tour loop can also serve as a hiking trail. Refuge open sunrise to sunset. Office: Box 519, Eagle Lake 77434; (979) 234-3021.

Balcones Canyonlands (1992): This 25,000-acre refuge is located in Burnet, Travis, and Williamson counties northwest of Austin. It was established to protect the nesting habitat of two endangered birds: black-capped vireo and golden-cheeked warbler. The Shin Oak Observation Deck is open almost year around (excluding a few weekends in the fall). Hunting available. Open Monday–Friday, 8:00 a.m.–4:30 p.m Office: 24518 FM-1431, Marble Falls, 78654; (512) 339-9432.

Big Boggy (1983): This refuge occupies 5,000 acres of coastal prairie and salt marsh along East Matagorda Bay for the benefit of wintering waterfowl. The refuge is only open to waterfowl hunting in season. Office: 6801 County Road 306, Brazoria, 77422; (979) 964-3639.

Brazoria (1966): The 43,388 acres of this refuge, located along the Gulf Coast in Brazoria County, serve as haven for wintering waterfowl and a wide variety of other migratory birds. The refuge also supports many marsh and water birds, from roseate spoonbills and great blue herons to white-faced ibis and sandhill cranes. Brazoria Refuge is within the Freeport Christmas Bird Count circle, which frequently achieves the highest number of species seen in a 24-hour period. Open daily sunrise to sunset. Hunting and fishing also available. Office: 24907 FM 2004, Angleton, 77515; (979) 922-1037.

Buffalo Lake (1958): Comprising 7,664 acres in the Central Flyway in Randall County in the Panhandle, this refuge contains some of the best remaining shortgrass prairie in the United States. Buffalo Lake is now dry; a marsh area is artificially maintained for the numerous birds, reptiles, and mammals. Available activities include picnicking, auto tour, birding, photography, and hiking. Office: Box 179, Umbarger 79091; (806) 499-3382.

Caddo Lake (2000): Established on portions of the 8,5000-acre Longhorn Army Ammunition Plant in Harrison County, this refuge contains a mature flooded bald cypress forest, with some trees nearly 400 years old.

Black-necked stilt at the Aransas National Wildlife Refuge. Photo by Carolyn Rose, Mission-Aransas NERR.

The wetlands support a diverse plant community. The bottomland hardwood forest ecosystem provides essential habitat for migratory and resident wildlife. The wetlands of Caddo Lake are important to migratory birds within the Central Flyway. The area supports one of the highest breeding populations of wood ducks and prothonotary warblers. Bird watching, hunting, equestrian use, auto tour, hiking, and biking are available. Office: (903) 679-9144.

Hagerman (1946): Hagerman National Wildlife Refuge lies on the Big Mineral arm of Lake Texoma in Grayson County. The 4,500 acres of marsh and water and 6,900 acres of upland and farmland provide a feeding and resting place for migrating waterfowl. Bird watching, fishing, and hunting are available. Office: 6465 Refuge Road, Sherman, 75092-5817; (903) 786-2826.

Laguna Atascosa: (1946): This refuge is the southernmost waterfowl refuge in the Central Flyway and contains more than 45,000 acres fronting on the Laguna Madre in the Lower Rio Grande Valley in Cameron and Willacy counties. Open lagoons, coastal prairies, salt flats, and brushlands support a wide diversity of wildlife. The United States' largest concentration of redhead ducks winters here, along with many other species of waterfowl and shorebirds. White-tailed deer, javelina, and armadillo can be found, along with endangered ocelot. Bird watching and nature study are popular; auto-tour roads and nature trails are available. Camping and fishing are permitted within Adolph Thomae Jr. County Park. Hunting also available. Office: 22817 Ocelot Road, Los Fresnos, 78566; (956) 748-3607.

Lower Rio Grande Valley (1979): Part of the 180,000 acre South Texas Refuge Complex, this refuge lies within Cameron, Hidalgo, Starr, and Willacy counties. It is comprised of more than 100 separate tracts of land, some fallow farm fields connecting healthy habitat that can become travel corridors for wildlife. The refuge includes 11 different habitat types, including sabal palm forest, tidal flats, coastal brushland, mid-delta thorn forest, woodland potholes and basins, upland thorn scrub, flood forest, barretal, riparian woodland, and Chihuahuan thorn forest. Nearly 500 species of birds and over 300 butterfly species have been found there, as well as four of the five cats that occur within the United States: jaguarundi, ocelot, bobcat, and mountain lion. Seasonal hunting and canoe tours are available. Office: 3325 Green Jay Road, Alamo, 78516 ; (956) 784-7500.

McFaddin (1980): This refuge's 55,000 acres in Jefferson and Chambers counties are of great importance to wintering populations of migratory waterfowl. One of the densest populations of alligators in Texas is found here. Activities on the refuge include wildlife observation, hunting, fishing, and crabbing. Seven boat ramps provide access to inland lakes and waterways; limited roadways. Open daily from sunrise until sunset. Office: 7950

Volunteers plant trees on the Anahuac National Wildlife Refuge in areas damaged in September 2008 by Hurricane Ike. Photo by Steve Hillebrand; U.S. Fish & Wildlife Service.

S. Gulfway Dr., Sabine Pass, 77655; (409) 971-2909.

Muleshoe (1935): Oldest of the national refuges in Texas, Muleshoe provides winter habitat for waterfowl and the continent's largest wintering population of sandhill cranes. Comprising 5,809 acres in the High Plains of Bailey County, the refuge contains playa lakes, marsh areas, caliche outcroppings, and native grasslands. A nature trail, campground, and picnic area are available. Office: Box 549, Muleshoe 79347; 806-946-3341.

San Bernard (1968): Located in Brazoria and Matagorda counties on the Gulf Coast near Freeport, this refuge's 27,414 acres attract migrating waterfowl, including thousands of white-fronted and Canada geese and several duck species, which spend the winter on the refuge. Habitats, consisting of coastal prairies, salt-mud flats, and saltwater and freshwater ponds and potholes, also attract yellow rails, roseate spoonbills, reddish egrets, and American bitterns. Visitors enjoy auto and hiking trails, photography, bird watching, fishing, and waterfowl hunting in season. Office: 6801 County Road 306, Brazoria, 77422; (979) 964-4011.

Santa Ana (1943): Santa Ana is located on the north bank of the Rio Grande in Hidalgo County. Santa Ana's 2,088 acres of subtropical forest and native brushland are at an ecological crossroads of subtropical, Gulf Coast, Great Plains, and Chihuahuan desert habitats. Santa Ana attracts birders from across the United States who can view many species of Mexican birds as they reach the northern edge of their ranges in South Texas. Also found at Santa Ana are ocelot and jaguarundi, endangered members of the cat family. Visitors enjoy a tram or auto drive, bicycling and hiking trails, and a tower overlook. Office: 3325 Green Jay Road, Alamo, 78516; (956) 784-7500.

Texas Point (1980): Texas Point's 8,900 acres are located in Jefferson County on the upper Gulf Coast, 12 miles east of McFaddin NWR, where they serve a large wintering population of waterfowl and migratory birds. The endangered southern bald eagle and peregrine falcon may occasionally be seen during peak fall and spring migrations. Alligators are commonly observed during the spring, summer, and fall months. Activities include wildlife observation, hunting, fishing, and crabbing. Access to the refuge is by boat and on foot only. Open daily from sunrise until sunset. Office: 7950 S. Gulfway Dr., Sabine Pass, 77655; (409) 971-2909.

Trinity River (1994): Established to protect remnant bottomland hardwood forests and associated wetlands, this refuge, located in northern Liberty County off State Highway 787 about 15 miles east of Cleveland, provides habitat for wintering, migrating, and breeding waterfowl and a variety of other wetland-dependent wildlife. A tract south of Liberty includes Champion Lake. Office: Box 10015, Liberty 77575; (936) 336-9786. ☆

Texas Wildlife Management Areas

Source: Texas Parks and Wildlife Department; http://www.tpwd.state.tx.us/huntwild/hunt/wma/.

Texas Parks and Wildlife Department is responsible for managing 49 wildlife management areas (WMAs) in the state totaling 768,175 acres. Thirty of the WMAs are owned in fee title, while 19 are managed under license agreements with other agencies.

Wildlife management areas are used principally for hunting, but many are also used for research, fishing, wildlife viewing, hiking, camping, bicycling, and horseback riding, when those activities are compatible with the primary goals for which the WMA was established. See the table on the following page for activities available in Texas' WMAs.

Access to WMAs at times designated for public use is provided through various permits, depending on the activity.

Hunting permits include the drawn Special Permit ($80 or $130), Regular Daily Permit ($20), or Annual Public Hunting Permit ($48).

A Limited Public Use Permit ($12) allows access for such activities as birdwatching, hiking, camping, or picnicking.

On most WMAs, restrooms and drinking water are not provided; check with the TPWD about facilities before visiting a WMA.

For further information, contact the Texas Parks and Wildlife Department, 4200 Smith School Rd., Austin 78744; or call 1-800-792-1112 and choose menu #5, selection #1. ☆

Texas Wildlife Management Areas

1. Alabama Creek
2. Alazan Bayou
3. Angelina-Neches/Dam B
4. Atkinson Island
5. Bannister
6. Big Lake Bottom
7. Black Gap
8. Blue Elbow Swamp-Tony Houseman
9. Caddo Lake
10. Caddo National Grasslands
11. Candy Cain Abshier
12. Cedar Creek Islands
13. Chaparral
14. Cooper
15. D.R. Wintermann
16. Elephant Mountain

Gene Howe
17. Gene Howe Unit
18. W.A. "Pat" Murphy Unit
19. Granger
20. Guadalupe Delta
21. Gus Engeling
22. J.D. Murphree
23. James E. Daughtrey
24. Justin Hurst
25. Keechi Creek

26. Kerr

Las Palomas
27. Anacua Unit
28. Lower Rio Grande Valley Units
29. Lower Neches
30. M.O. Neasloney
31. Mad Island
32. Mason Mountain
33. Matador

34. Matagorda Island
35. McGillivray & Leona McKie Muse
36. Moore Plantation
37. Nannie M. Stringfellow
38. Nature Center
39. North Toledo Bend
40. Old Sabine Bottom
41. Pat Mayse

Playa Lakes
42. Armstong Unit
43. Taylor Lakes Unit

44. Ray Roberts Lake
45. Redhead Pond
46. Richland Creek
47. Sam Houston National Forest
48. Sierra Diablo
49. Somerville
50. Tawakoni
51. Welder Flats
52. White Oak Creek

Texas Wildlife Management Areas (Acreage)	County	Day Use Only	Hunting	Fishing	Camping	Wildlife Viewing	Hiking	Interpretive Trail	Auto Tour	Bicycling	Equestrian	Comments
Alabama Creek (14,561)	Trinity		★	★	★	★	★		★	★	★	In Davy Crockett Nat. Forest
Alazan Bayou (2,063)	Nacogdoches		★	★	★	★					★	
Angelina-Neches/Dam B (12,636)	Jasper/Tyler		★	★	★	★	★			★		
Atkinson Island (150)	Harris	★		★		★						Boat access only
Bannister (25,695)	San Augustine		★	★	★	★	★			★	★	In Angelina National Forest
Big Lake Bottom (3,894)	Anderson	★	★	★		★						2,870 acres available to public
Black Gap (103,000)	Brewster	★	★	★	★	★	★		★	★	★	NW of Big Bend National Park
Blue Elbow Swamp-Tony Houseman (3,987)	Orange		★	★	★	★	★					
Caddo Lake WMA (8,005)	Marion/Harrison		★	★	★	★					★	
Caddo Natl Grasslands (16,140)	Fannin		★	★	★	★	★			★	★	
Candy Cain Abshier (207)	Chambers	★				★						Excellent birding spring and fall
Cedar Creek Islands (160)	Henderson	★			★		★					Camp in Purvis Creek SP, Fairfield Lake SP; do not disturb rookeries in spring & summer
Chaparral (15,200)	La Salle/Dimmit		★		★	★	★		★	★		
Cooper (19,280)	Delta/Hopkins	★	★	★		★	★					Camping at Cooper Lake SP
D.R. Wintermann (246)	Wharton	★				★						Restricted access; bird refuge
Elephant Mountain (23,147)	Brewster		★		★	★	★		★			
Gene Howe Unit (5,887)	Hemphill		★	★	★	★	★			★	★	Riding March–August only
W.A. "Pat" Murphy Unit (432)	Hemphill		★	★		★	★					
Granger (10,888)	Williamson		★	★	★	★	★			★		Primitive camping only
Guadalupe Delta (6,593)	Calhoun/Refugio		★	★		★	★			★		Freshwater Marsh
Gus Engling (10,958)	Anderson		★	★	★	★	★		★	★	★	
J.D. Murphree (24,250)	Jefferson	★	★	★		★						Access by boat only
James E. Daughtrey (4,400)	Live Oak/McMullen	★	★			★						Primitive camping only
Justin Hurst (11,938)	Brazoria		★	★		★	★	★		★		On Texas Coastal Birding Trail
Keechi Creek (1,500)	Leon		★									
Kerr (6,493)	Kerr		★	★		★			★	★		On Guadalupe River
Las Palomas:												
Anacua Unit (222)	Cameron		★			★						
Lower Rio Grande Valley Units (3,311)	Cameron/Hidalgo	★	★			★	★					Also Starr & Willacy counties
Lower Neches (7,998)	Orange	★	★	★		★	★					Coastal marsh
M.O. Neasloney (100)	Gonzales	★				★	★	★				
Mad Island (7,200)	Matagorda		★			★						Coastal wetlands
Mason Mountain (5,301)	Mason		★									Restricted access
Matador (28,183)	Cottle		★	★	★	★	★	★	★		★	Primitive camping; tours
Matagorda Island (56,688)	Calhoun		★	★	★	★	★			★		
McGillivray & Leona McKie Muse (1,972)	Brown		★			★						
Moore Plantation (26,772)	Sabine/Jasper		★	★	★	★	★	★		★	★	In Sabine National Forest
Nannie M. Stringfellow (3,664)	Brazoria		★			★						Open for special hunts only
Nature Center (82)	Smith	★				★	★	★				Primarily for school groups
North Toledo Bend (3,650)	Shelby		★	★	★	★	★				★	Limited use of horses
Old Sabine Bottom (5,158)	Smith		★	★	★	★	★			★	★	Canoeing
Pat Mayse (8,925)	Lamar		★	★	★	★	★				★	
Playa Lakes:		★	★			★	★					
Armstrong Unit (160)	Casto	★				★						
Taylor Lakes Unit (527)	Donley	★	★			★	★					Hunting only on Donley Co. unit
Ray Roberts Lake WMA (41,303)	Cooke/Denton	★	★	★		★	★					Also Grayson County
Redhead Pond (37)	Nueces	★				★						Freshwater wetland
Richland Creek (13,797)	Freestone/Navarro		★	★	★	★	★			★	★	
Sam Houston Natl Forest (161,508)	San Jacinto/Walker		★	★	★	★	★		★	★	★	Also Montgomery County
Sierra Diablo (11,624)	Hudspeth/Culberson		★									Restricted acess
Somerville (11,630)	Burleson/Lee	★	★	★		★	★			★		Camping at nearby state park
Tawakoni (9,756)	Hunt/Van Zandt		★	★	★	★	★			★		
Welder Flats (1,480)	Calhoun	★		★		★						Boat access only
White Oak Creek (25,777)	Bowie/Cass/Morris	★	★	★		★	★				★	Also Titus County; camp in Atlanta and Daingerfield SPs

A rehabilitated brown pelican is released into the Gulf of Mexico by TPWD employees. The pelican is one of many that were cleaned up after being contaminated by the British Petroleum oil spill that lasted for five months in 2010. Photo courtesy of the Texas Parks & Wildlife Department.

Texas' Threatened and Endangered Species

Endangered species are those the Texas Parks and Wildlife Department (TPWD) has named as being at risk of statewide extinction. Threatened species are likely to become endangered in the future. The following species are either endangered or threatened as of July 2011. This list varies slightly from the federal list. Contact Endangered Resources Branch, Texas Parks and Wildlife, 4200 Smith School Road, Austin 78744; 800-792-1112; www.tpwd.state.tx.us/nature/endang/endang.htm.

Endangered Species

MAMMALS — Bats: Mexican long-nosed bat. **Marine Mammels**: West Indian manatee; finback and humpback whales. **Carnivores**: jaguar; jaguarundi; ocelot; gray and red wolves.
BIRDS — Waterbirds: Whooping crane; "Eastern" brown pelican. **Raptors**: Northern aplomado falcon. **Upland Birds**: Attwater's greater prairie chicken. **Shorebirds**: Eskimo curlew; interior least tern. **Woodpeckers**: red-cockaded woodpeckers. **Songbirds**: southwestern willow flycatcher; black-capped vireo; golden-cheeked warbler.
REPTILES — Turtles: Atlantic hawksbill, Kemp's Ridley, leatherback, and sea turtles.
AMPHIBIANS — Salamanders: Barton Springs and Texas blind salamanders. **Frogs & Toads**: Houston toad.
FISHES — Minnows: Rio Grande silvery minnow. **Killifishes**: Comanche Springs and Leon Springs pupfishes. **Livebearers**: Big Bend, Clear Creek, Pecos, and San Marcos gambusias. **Perches**: Fountain darter. **Coastal Fishes**: smalltooth sawfish.
INVERTEBRATES — Crustaceans: Peck's cave amphipod. **Mollusks & Snails**: Pecos assiminea snail.
PLANTS — Cacti: Black lace, Nellie's Cory, Sneed's pincushion, star, and Tobusch fishhook cacti; Davis' green pitaya. **Trees, Shrubs, Sub-shrubs**: Texas ayenia; Johnston's frankenia; Walker's manioc; Texas snowbells. **Wildflowers**: South Texas ambrosia; Zapata and white bladderpod; Terlingua Creek cat's-eye; ashy dogweed; Texas trailing phlox; Texas poppy-mallow; Texas prairie dawn; slender rushpea; large-fruited sand-verbena. **Orchids**: Navasota ladies'-tresses. **Grasses**: little aguja pondweed; Texas wild-rice.

Threatened Species

MAMMALS — Bats: Rafinesque's big-eared, southern yellow, and spotted bats. **Carnivores**: black and Louisiana black bears; white-nosed coati; margay. **Marine Mammals**: Atlantic spotted and rough-toothed dolphins; dwarf sperm, false killer, Gervais' beaked, goose-beaked, killer, pygmy killer, pygmy sperm, and short-finned pilot whales. **Rodents**: Palo Duro mouse; Coues' rice rat and Texas kangaroo rat.

BIRDS — Waterbirds: reddish egret; white-faced ibis; wood stork. **Raptors**: bald eagle; American peregrine falcon; common black, gray, white-tailed, and zone-tailed hawks; swallow-tailed kite; Mexican spotted owl; cactus ferruginous pygmy-owl. **Shorebirds**: piping plover; sooty tern. **Songbirds**: rose-throated becard; tropical parula; Bachman's, Texas Botteri's, and Arizona Botteri's sparrows; northern beardless tyrannulet.
REPTILES — Turtles: loggerhead and green sea turtles; Texas tortoise; alligator snapping, Cagle's map, and Chihuahuan mud turtles. **Lizards**: reticulated gecko; mountain short-horned, reticulate collared, and Texas horned lizards. **Snakes**: speckled racer; black-striped, Brazos water, Chihuahuan desert lyre, Louisiana pine, northern cat-eyed, smooth green, scarlet, Texas indigo, and Trans-Pecos black-headed snakes; timber (canebrake) rattlesnake.
AMPHIBIANS — Salamanders: black-spotted newt; Blanco blind, Cascade Caverns, Comal blind, and San Marcos salamanders; South Texas siren (large form). **Frogs & Toads**: sheep and white-lipped frogs; Mexican treefrog; Mexican burrowing toad.
FISHES — Large River Fish: paddlefish and shovelnose sturgeon. **Minnows**: Rio Grande chub; Devils River minnow; Arkansas River, bluehead, bluntnose, Chihuahua, and proserpine shiners; Mexican stoneroller. **Suckers**: blue sucker and creek chubsucker. **Catfishes**: toothless blindcat and widemouth blindcat. **Killifishes**: Conchos and Pecos pupfishes. **Livebearers**: blotched and San Felipe gambusias. **Killifishes**: Conchos and Pecos pupfishes. **Perches**: blackside and Rio Grande darters. **Coastal Fishes**: opossum pipefish; river and Mexican goby.
INVERTEBRATES — Mollusks & Snails: Texas fatmucket; Mexican and Texas fawnsfoot; Texas heelsplitter; Southern hickorynut; Texas hornshell; salina mucket; golden orb; Louisiana, Texas, and triangle pigtoe; smooth and Texas pimpleback; sandbank pocketbook; false spike.
PLANTS — Cacti: Bunched cory, Chisos Mountains hedgehog, and Lloyd's mariposa cacti. **Trees, Shrubs, Sub-shrubs**: Hinckley's oak. **Wildflowers**: Pecos sunflower; earth fruit. ☆

Texas Wildlife

Source: Texas Parks and Wildlife Department, Austin; www.nsrl.ttu.edu/tmot1/

The wide variation of soils, climate, topography, and vegetation in Texas have resulted in an unusually rich diversity of animal life. The Texas environment supports **141 species of native terrestrial mammals,** a number exceeded in the United States only by California and New Mexico. In addition to native species, there are also 12 exotics or non-native species that have been introduced by man either accidentally (house mouse, roof rat, Norway rat) or intentionally (nutria, red fox, feral pig, axis deer, fallow deer, sika deer, nilgai, barbary sheep, and blackbuck) and have become established in the environment.

A few of the leading land mammals of Texas are described here. Those marked by an asterisk (*) are non-native species. Information was provided by the Nongame and Urban Program, Texas Parks and Wildlife Department, and updated using the online version of *The Mammals of Texas* by David J. Schmidly and the late William B. Davis: www.nsrl.ttu.edu/tmot1/. The print version was first published in 1947 and updated in 1994 by Texas Parks and Wildlife Press, Austin,. The online version is maintained by Texas Tech University. For additional wildlife information on the web: **www.tpwd.state.tx.us/huntwild/wild/species/**.

Mammals

Armadillo — The **nine-banded armadillo** *(Dasypus novemcinctus)* is one of Texas' most interesting mammals. It is found in most of the state except the western Trans-Pecos. It is now common as far north and east as Oklahoma and Mississippi.

Badger — The **badger** *(Taxidea taxus)* is found throughout the state except the extreme eastern region. It is a fierce fighter, and it is valuable in helping control the rodent population.

Bat — Thirty-two species of these winged mammals have been found in Texas, more than in any other state in the United States. Of these, 27 species are known residents, though they are seldom seen by the casual observer. The **Mexican,** or **Brazilian, free-tailed bat** *(Tadarida brasiliensis)* and the **cave myotis** *(Myotis velifer)* constitute most of the cave-dwelling bats of Central and West Texas.

They have some economic value for their deposits of nitrogen-rich **guano.** Some commercial guano has been produced from **James River Bat Cave,** Mason County; **Beaver Creek Cavern,** Burnet County; and from large deposits in other caves including **Devil's Sinkhole,** Edwards County; **Blowout Cave,** Blanco County; and **Bandera Bat Cave,** Bandera County. The largest concentration of bats in the world is found at **Bracken Cave** in Comal County, which is thought to hold between 20 million and 40 million bats. The **big brown bat** *(Eptesicus fuscus),* the **red bat** *(Lasiurus borealis),* and the **evening bat** *(Nycticeius humeralis)* are found in East and Southeast Texas. The evening and big brown bats are forest and woodland dwelling mammals.

The rarer species of Texas bats have been found along the Rio Grande and in the Trans-Pecos. Bats can be observed at dusk near a water source, and many species may also be found foraging on insects attracted to street lights. Everywhere bats occur, they are the main predators of night-flying insects, including mosquitoes and many crop pests. On the web: **www.batcon.org/**

Bear — The **black bear** *(Ursus americanus),* formerly common throughout most of the state, is now surviving in remnant populations in mountainous areas of the Trans-Pecos. Some are fleeing the drought and wildfires in Mexico and moving into the Big Bend area.

Beaver — The **American beaver** *(Castor canadensis)* is found over most of the state except for the Llano Estacado and parts of the Trans-Pecos.

Bighorn — (See **Sheep.**)

A bison herd resides at San Angelo State Park. Photo courtesy of Texas Parks & Wildlife Deparment.

A coyote wanders near the Cottonwood Campground in Big Bend National Park. Coyotes are found throughout the state but are most numerous in the brush country of Southwest Texas. Photo by Ron Billings; Texas Forest Service.

Bison — The largest of native terrestrial wild mammals of North America, the **American bison** *(Bos bison)*, commonly called **buffalo**, was formerly found in the western two-thirds of the state. Today, it is extirpated or confined on ranches. Deliberate slaughter of this majestic animal for hides and to eliminate the Plains Indians' main food source reached a peak about 1877–78, and the bison was almost eradicated by 1885. Estimates of the number of buffalo killed vary, but as many as 200,000 hides were sold in Fort Worth at a single two-day sale. Except for the interest of the late **Col. Charles Goodnight** and a few other foresighted men, the bison might be extinct.

Cat — The **jaguar** *(Felis onca)* is probably now extinct in Texas and, along with the **ocelot, jaguarundi,** and **margay,** is listed as endangered or threatened by both federal and state wildlife agencies. The **mountain lion** *(Felis concolor)*, also known as **cougar** and **puma,** was once found statewide. It is now found in the mountainous areas of the Trans-Pecos and the dense Rio Grande Plain brushland. The **ocelot** *(Felis pardalis)*, also known as the **leopard cat,** is found usually along the border. The **red-and-gray cat,** or **jaguarundi** *(Felis yagouaroundi Geoffroy)* is found, rarely, in extreme South Texas. The **margay** *(Felis wiedii)* was reported in the 1850s near Eagle Pass. The **bobcat** *(Lynx rufus)* is found throughout the state in large numbers.

Chipmunk — The **gray-footed chipmunk** *(Tamias canipes)* is found at high altitudes in the Guadalupe and Sierra Diablo ranges of the Trans-Pecos. (*See also,* **Ground Squirrel,** with which the chipmunk is often confused in public reference.)

Coati — The **white-nosed coati** *(Nasua narica)*, a relative of the raccoon, is occasionally found in southern Texas from Brownsville to the Big Bend. It inhabits woodland areas and feeds both on the ground and in trees. The coati, which is on the list of threatened species, is also found occasionally in Big Bend National Park.

Coyote — The **coyote** *(Canis latrans)* exists in great numbers in Texas. It is the most destructive predator of Texas livestock. On the other hand, it is probably the most valuable predator in the balance of nature. It is a protection to crops and range lands by its control of rodents and rabbits. It is found throughout the state but is most numerous in the brush country of Southwest Texas. It is the second-most important fur-bearing animal in the state.

Deer — The **white-tailed deer** *(Odocoileus virginianus)*, found throughout the state in brushy or wooded areas, is the most important Texas game animal. Its numbers in Texas are estimated at more than 3 million. The **mule deer** *(Odocoileus heminous)* is found principally in the Trans-Pecos and Panhandle areas. It has increased in number in recent years. The little **Del Carmen deer** *(white-tailed subspecies)* is found in limited numbers in the high valleys of the Chisos Mountains in the Big Bend. The only native **elk** in Texas *(Cervus merriami)*, found in the southern Guadalupe Mountains, became extinct about the turn of the 20th century. The **wapiti** or **elk** *(Cervus elaphus)*, was introduced into the same area about 1928. There are currently several herds totalling several hundred individuals.

A number of exotic deer species have been introduced, mostly for hunting purposes. The **axis deer*** *(Cervus axix)* is the most numerous of the exotics. Native to India, it is found mostly in Central and South Texas, both free-ranging and confined on ranches. **Blackbuck*** *(Antilope cervicapra)*, also native to India, is the second-most numerous exotic deer in the state and is found on ranches in 86 counties. **Fallow deer*** *(Cervus dama)*, native to the Mediterranean, has been introduced to 93 counties, while the **nilgai*** *(Boselaphus tragocamelus)*, native of India and Pakistan, is found mostly on ranches in Kenedy and Willacy counties. The **sika deer*** *(Cervus nippon)*, native of southern Siberia, Japan, and China, has been introduced in 77 counties in Central and South Texas.

Dolphin — The **Atlantic spotted dolphin** *(Stenella frontalis)* is rather small, long-snouted, and spotted; it is purplish gray, appearing blackish at a distance, usually with numerous small white or gray spots on its sides and back. In the Gulf of Mexico, this dolphin is second in abundance only to the **bottlenose dolphin.** The bottlenose *(Tursiops truncatus)* is stout and short-beaked with sloping forehead, projecting lower jaw, and high dorsal fin. Other species, such as the Clymene, the Common dolphin, the Pantropical Spotted, Risso's, Rough-toothed, Spinner, and Striped are unusual and known in Texas only through strandings along Gulf beaches.

Ferret — The **black-footed ferret** *(Mustela nigripes)* was formerly found widely ranging through the West Texas country of the prairie dog on which it preyed. It is now considered extinct in Texas. It is of the same genus as the weasel and the mink.

Fox — The **common gray fox** (Urocyon cinereoargenteus) is found throughout most of the state, primarily in the woods of East Texas, in broken parts of the Edwards Plateau, and in the rough country at the foot of the High Plains. The **kit** or **Swift fox** (Vulpes velox) is found in the western one-third of the state. A second species of **kit fox** (Vulpes macrotis) is found in the Trans-Pecos and is fairly numerous in some localities. The **red fox**[*] (Vulpes vulpes), which ranges across Central Texas, was introduced for sport.

Gopher — Nine species of pocket gopher occur in Texas. The **Botta's pocket gopher** (Thomomys bottae) is found from the Trans-Pecos eastward across the Edwards Plateau. The **plains pocket gopher** (Geomys bursarius) is found from Midland and Tom Green counties east and north to McLennan, Dallas, and Grayson counties. The **desert pocket gopher** (Geomys arenarius) is found only in the Trans-Pecos, while the **yellow-faced pocket gopher** (Cratogeomys castanops) is found in the western one-third of the state, with occasional sightings along the Rio Grande in Maverick and Cameron counties. The **Texas pocket gopher** (Geomys personatus) is found in South Texas from San Patricio County to Val Verde County. **Attwater's pocket gopher** (Geomys attwateri) and **Baird's pocket gopher** (Geomys breviceps) are both found generally in South-Central and Coastal Texas from the Brazos River to the San Antonio River and south to Matagorda and San Patricio counties. **Jones' pocket gopher** (Geomys knoxjonesi) is found only in far West Texas, while the **Llano pocket gopher** (Geomys texensis) is found only

A green jay finds a perch on a javelina in the Laguna Atascosa National Wildlife Refuge. Photo by Steve Hillebrand; U.S. Fish & Wildlife Service.

in two isolated areas of the Hill Country.

Ground Squirrel — Five or more species of ground squirrel live in Texas, mostly in the western part of the state. The **rock squirrel** (Spermophilus variegatus) is found throughout the Edwards Plateau and Trans-Pecos. The **Mexican ground squirrel** (Spermophilus mexicanus) occurs throughout much of South Texas, the Trans-Pecos, and almost to the Red River just east of the Panhandle. The **spotted ground squirrel** (Spermophilus spilosoma) is found generally in the western half of the state. The **thirteen-lined ground squirrel** (Spermophilus tridecemlineatus) is found in a narrow strip from Dallas and Tarrant counties to the Gulf. The **Texas antelope squirrel** (Ammospermophilus interpres) is found along the Rio Grande from El Paso to Val Verde County.

Hog, Feral — (See **Pig, Feral**.)

Javelina — The **javelina** or **collared peccary** (Tayassu tajacu) is found in brushy semi-desert areas where prickly pear, a favorite food, is found. The javelina was hunted commercially for its hide until 1939. They are harmless to livestock and to people, though they can defend themselves ferociously when attacked by hunting dogs.

Mink — The **mink** (Mustela vison) is found in the eastern half of the state, always near streams, lakes, or other water sources. Although it is an economically important fur-bearing animal in the eastern United States, it ranked only 13th in numbers and 9th in economic value to trappers in Texas in 1988–89, according to a Texas Parks and Wildlife Department survey.

Mole — The **eastern mole** (Scalopus aquaticus) is

Mule deer roam through Palo Duro Canyon State Park in the Panhandle. Photo by Ron Billings; Texas Forest Service.

found in the eastern two-thirds of Texas. Moles cannot see and spend most of their life in underground burrows they excavate for themselves or usurp from other mammals, such as pocket gophers. The burrowing of moles can damage lawns, row crops, and the greens of golf courses. Benefits, however, are aerating soil and eating larval insects that destroy roots of grass and crops.

Muskrat — The **common muskrat** *(Ondatra zibethica)* occurs in aquatic habitats in the northern, southeastern, and southwestern parts of the state. Although the muskrat was once economically valuable for its fur, its numbers have declined, mostly because of the loss of habitat.

Nutria* — This introduced species *(Myocastor coypus)*, native to South America, is found in the eastern two-thirds of the state. The fur is not highly valued and, because nutria are in competition with muskrats, their spread is discouraged. They have been used widely in Texas as a cure-all for ponds choked with vegetation, with spotty results.

Opossum — A **marsupial**, the **Virginia opossum** *(Didelphis virginiana)* is found in nearly all parts of the state. The opossum has economic value for its pelt, and its meat is considered a delicacy by some. It is one of the chief contributors to the Texas fur crop.

Otter — A few **river otter** *(Lutra canadensis)* are found in the eastern quarter of the state. It has probably been extirpated from the Panhandle, North-Central, and South Texas.

Pig, Feral* — Feral pigs are found throughout Texas but especially in areas of the Rio Grande and Coastal Plains, as well as in the woods of East Texas. They are descendants of escaped domestic hogs or of European wild hogs that were imported for sport. Their rooting habits can extensively destroy vegetation and soil.

Porcupine — The **yellow-haired porcupine** *(Erethizon dorsatum)* is found from the western half of the state east to Bosque County. It is adapted to a variety of habitats and, in recent years, has expanded into South Texas. Porcupines are expert at climbing trees but are as much at home in rocks as on the ground or in trees. They have a relatively long lifespan; one marked female lived more than 10 years under natural conditions.

Prairie Dog — Until recent years, probably no sight

The black-tailed jack rabbit is found throughout Texas except the Big Thicket area of East Texas. Photo courtesy of Texas Parks & Wildlife Department.

was so universal in West Texas as the **black-tailed prairie dog** *(Cynomys ludovicianus)*. Naturalists estimated its population in the hundreds of millions, and prairie-dog towns often covered many acres with thickly spaced burrows. Its destruction of range grasses and cultivated crops has caused farmers and ranchers to destroy many of them, and it is extirpated from much of its former range. It is being propagated in several public zoos, notably in the **prairie dog town in Mackenzie Park** at Lubbock. It has been honored in Texas by the naming of the **Prairie Dog Town Fork** of the Red River, one segment of which is located the beautiful **Palo Duro Canyon.**

Pronghorn — The **Pronghorn** *(Antilocapra americana)* formerly was found in the western two-thirds of the state. It is currently found only in limited areas from the Panhandle to the Trans-Pecos. Despite management efforts, its numbers have been decreasing in recent years.

Rabbit — The **black-tailed jack rabbit** *(Lepus californicus)* is found throughout Texas except the Big Thicket area of East Texas. It breeds rapidly, and its long hind legs make it one of the world's faster-running animals. The **Eastern cottontail** *(Sylvilagus floridanus)* is found mostly in the eastern three-quarters of the state. The **desert cottontail** *(Sylvilagus auduboni)* is found in the western half of the state, usually on the open range. The **swamp rabbit** *(Sylvilagus aquaticus)* is found in East Texas and the coastal area.

Raccoon — The **raccoon** *(Procyon lotor)* is found throughout Texas, especially in woodlands and near water. It is strictly nocturnal. A raccoon makes its den in a large hollow tree or hollow log, in which it spends the daylight hours sleeping and in which it also rears its young. In western areas, dens usually are in crevices of rocky bluffs.

Rats and Mice — There are 40 to 50 species of rats and mice in Texas of varying characteristics, habitats, and economic destructiveness. The **Norway rat*** *(Rattus norvegicus)* and the **roof rat*** *(Rattus rattus),* both non-native species, are probably the most common and most destructive. They also are instrumental in the transmission of several dread diseases, including bubonic plague and typhus. The **common house mouse*** *(Mus musculis)* is estimated in the hundreds of millions annually. The **Mexican vole** *(Microtus mexicanus guadalupensis),* also called the **Guadalupe Mountain**

A Mexican ground squirrel among cactus flowers in the Lower Rio Grande Valley National Wildlife Refuge. Photo by Larry Ditto; U.S. Fish & Wildlife Service.

vole, is found only in the higher elevations of Guadalupe Mountains National Park and just over the border into New Mexico.

Ringtail — The **ringtail** *(Bassariscus astutus)* is a cat-sized carnivore resembling a small fox with a long raccoon-like tail. It found statewide but is rare in the Lower Valley and the Coastal Plains. Ringtails are nocturnal and live in a variety of habitats, preferring rocky areas, such as rock piles, stone fences, and canyon walls.

Sheep — The **mountain sheep** *(Ovis canadensis),* or **desert bighorn,** formerly was found in isolated areas of the mountainous Trans-Pecos, but the last native sheep were seen in 1959. Recently, they have been introduced into the same areas with success. The **barbary sheep*** *(Ammotragus lervia),* or **aoudad,** first introduced to the Palo Duro Canyon area in 1957–58, has become firmly established. Private introductions have brought it into the Edwards Plateau, Trans-Pecos, South Texas, Rolling Plains, and Post Oak Savannah regions.

Shrew — The **shrew** is one of the smallest mammals. Four species are found in Texas: the **southern short-tailed shrew** *(Blarina Carolinensis),* found in the eastern one-fourth of the state; the **least shrew** *(Cryptotis parva),* in eastern and central areas; **Elliot's short-tailed shrew** *(Blarina hylophaga),* known only in Aransas, Montague, and Bastrop counties; and the **desert shrew** *(Notiosorex crawfordi),* found in the western two-thirds of the state.

Skunk — There are six species of skunk in Texas. The **Eastern spotted skunk** *(Spilogale putorius)* is found in the eastern half of the state, the Gulf area, and across North-Central Texas to the Panhandle. A small skunk, it is often erroneously called civet cat. The **Western spotted skunk** *(Spilogale gracilis)* is found in the southwestern part of the state north to Garza and Howard counties and east to Bexar and Duval counties. The **striped skunk** *(Mephitis mephitis)* is found statewide, mostly in brush or wooded areas. The **hooded skunk** *(Mephitis macroura)* is found in limited numbers in the Big Bend and adjacent parts of the Trans-Pecos. The **eastern hog-nosed skunk** *(Conepatus leuconotus),* found in the Gulf Coastal Plains, ranges southward into Mexico. The **common hog-nosed skunk** *(Conepatus mesoleucus)* is found in southwestern, central, and southern Texas, north to Collin and Lubbock counties.

Squirrel — The **eastern fox squirrel** *(Sciurus niger)* is found in the eastern two-thirds of the state. The **eastern gray squirrel** *(Sciurus carolinensis)* is found generally in the eastern third of the state. The **flying squirrel** *(Glaucomys volans)* is found in wooded areas of East Texas. The fox and gray squirrels are important small game animals. *See also,* **Ground Squirrel.**

Whale — Some species that are found in the Gulf of Mexico include: **dwarf sperm whale** *(Kogia simus);* **pygmy sperm whale** *(Kogia breviceps),* found near the Texas coast where strandings occur relatively frequently; **short-finned pilot whale** *(Globicephala macrorhynchus),* common in the Gulf where there are numerous strandings and sightings; **sperm whale** *(Physeter macrocephalus),* an endangered species and the most numerous of the great whales in the Gulf, where sightings are relatively common. Other species are known in Texas only through strandings on Gulf beaches.

Weasel — The **long-tailed weasel** *(Mustela frenata),* akin to the mink, is found statewide, but is scarce in West Texas and the far north Panhandle. In general, their destruction of mice, ground squirrels, and pocket gophers benefits agriculture. But on occasion they enter poultry houses and wantonly kill chickens.

Wolf — The **red wolf** *(Canis rufus)* was once found throughout the eastern half of the state. It has now been extirpated from the wild, with the only known remnants of the population now in captive propagation. The **gray wolf** *(Canis lupus)* once had a wide range over the western two-thirds of the state. It is now considered extinct in Texas. The **red wolf** and **gray wolf** are on the federal and state endangered species lists.

Reptiles and Arachnids

Most of the more than **100 species and subspecies of snakes** found in Texas are beneficial, as also are other reptiles. There are **16 poisonous species and subspecies.**

Poisonous reptiles include three species of **copperheads** *(southern, broad-banded, and Trans-Pecos);* one kind of **cottonmouth** *(western);* 11 kinds of **rattlesnakes** *(canebrake, western massasauga, desert massasauga, western pigmy, western diamondback, timber, banded rock, mottled rock, northern blacktailed, Mojave, and prairie);* and the **Texas coral snake.**

Also noteworthy are the **horned lizard,** also called **horned toad,** which is on the list of threatened species; the **vinegarone,** a type of whip scorpion; **tarantula,** a hairy spider; and **alligator.** ☆

Box turtles sun themselves at the Lady Bird Johnson Wildflower Center near Austin. Photo by Ron Billings; Texas Forest Service.

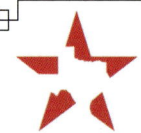

Texas State Historical Association

Our Newest Books

Arsenal of Defense: Fort Worth's Military Legacy
J'NELL L. PATE
$39.95
With this book, Pate, one of Fort Worth's most respected historians, details the military's massive impact on the city and adds to our understanding of the development of the community popularly known as "Cowtown."

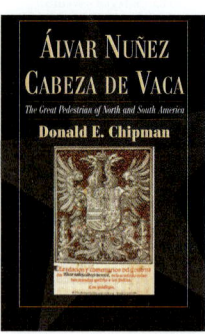

Álvar Nuñez Cabeza de Vaca: The Great Pedestrian of North and South America
DONALD E. CHIPMAN
$12.95
In this short, lively book, Chipman details the fascinating life of the man who spent years wandering through Texas and the modern Borderlands and left us the first written record of Texas. Spring 2012.

They Called It the War Effort: Oral Histories from World War II Orange, Texas, 2nd ed.
LOUIS FAIRCHILD
$39.95
A greatly revised and expanded edition of the classic history in which Southeast Texans, white and black, describe the World War II home-front experience in their own words. Spring 2012.

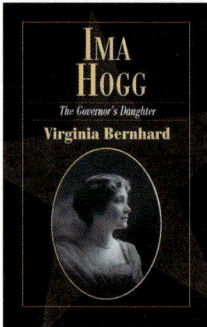

Ima Hogg: The Governor's Daughter
VIRGINIA BERNHARD
$15.95
A new edition of the classic biography of th Texas governor James Stephen Hogg's daughter, who became one of Houston's great cultural leaders, founding the Houston Symphony, and whose beautiful home, Bayou Bend, has become a treasured historic site.

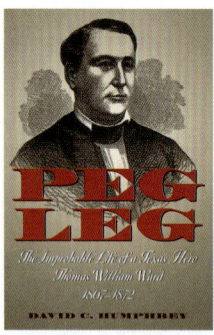

Peg Leg: The Improbable Life of a Texas Hero, Thomas William Ward, 1807–1872
DAVID C. HUMPHREY
$39.95
The warts-and-all biography of a determined hero of the Texas Revolution who endured the trauma of two amputations "reads like a novel" (Jerry Turner, *Mexia News*) and won a Spur Award from the Western Writers of America.

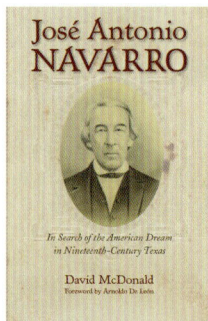

José Antonio Navarro: In Search of the American Dream in Nineteenth-Century Texas
DAVID MCDONALD
$49.95 (hardcover), $24.95 (paperback)
This long overdue biography of the leading Tejano political figure of the nineteenth century has been called "groundbreaking" by Mike Cox of the *Austin American-Statesman* and won the Summerfield G. Roberts Award from the Sons of the Republic of Texas.

TO ORDER VISIT WWW.TSHAONLINE.ORG OR CALL 940-399-5200

Weather

Sunrise at Rockport in Aransas County. Photo by Ron Billings; Texas Forest Service.

Weather

Source: Unless otherwise noted, this information is provided by Texas State Climatologist John W. Nielsen-Gammon and Assistant State Climatologist Brent McRoberts, Texas A&M University, College Station.

Weather Highlights 2009

March 25: With hail ranging from quarter to teacup size, a **thunderstorm** pummeled the Austin area. In Austin's history, the top three most destructive hailstorms have occurred on March 25 (1993, 2005, 2009). This storm, the most costly, was estimated at $160 million in damage.

April 16: A severe weather outbreak over the South Plains region of West Texas produced **13 tornados and a catastrophic series of hail storms.** In Lubbock, more than 3,000 homes and 1,100 vehicles were damaged. Authorities estimated $41.3 million in losses for that day's severe weather.

April 18: In Harris and Galveston counties, heavy rainfall was a result of several intense thunderstorms positioned over the Houston area. The highest one-hour rainfall total was 6.90 inches at Bay Area Boulevard and Clear Creek, which surpassed the record set by Tropical Storm Allison in 2001. This **fatal flash flood** event claimed five lives, all children under age 7, who were trapped in a submerged vehicle. Property damage was estimated at $7.5 million.

Dec. 23–24: A rare, but dangerous weather event occurred just prior to Christmas Eve. A series of supercell thunderstorms hit northeast Texas and produced an astonishing 12 tornados, costly hail storms, and prolific rainmakers that caused numerous reports of flash flooding. An **EF3 twister** ravaged the city of Lufkin and destroyed several businesses, homes, and vehicles. This tornado alone caused $10 million in damage, and the events of that afternoon into the early morning wreaked destruction estimated at over $12 million.

Climatic Data Regions of Texas

High Plains
Low Rolling Plains
Trans-Pecos
North Central
East Texas
Edwards Plateau
South Central
Upper Coast
South Texas
Lower Valley

above-average temperatures for the month.

February's trend followed closely to that of January: precipitation deficits and warm temperatures. Although generally wetter than January, only five stations received at least 50 percent of their normal precipitation. West Texas was especially dry, and a significant portion of statewide rainfall was caused by a line of severe storms that moved through the state mid-month. La Niña conditions dominated February, bringing warm conditions to Texas. Several locations recorded temperatures well into the 90s. Maximum monthly temperatures across the state averaged almost 7 degrees above normal, with some stations reporting temperatures more than 9 degrees above average.

March was one of the wettest months since August 2008. All but six first-order weather stations received at least their normal monthly precipitation. Of the six that did not, Victoria and Amarillo received at least 80 percent of

Monthly Summaries 2009

As La Niña conditions developed in the Pacific Ocean, Texas experienced an extraordinarily dry **January.** No state weather station received even half its normal monthly precipitation. Except for Dallas-Fort Worth, no station received more than a third of its average January precipitation. Nine of 19 first-order stations in Texas received less than a 10th of their average precipitation. Hardest hit were Southwest Texas, the Edwards Plateau, and the Panhandle, including Brownsville, El Paso, San Angelo, and Amarillo. Temperatures also were abnormal, and every first-order station recorded

	Average Temperatures 2009										Precipitation 2009 (Inches)									
	High Plains	Low Plains	North Central	East Texas	Trans-Pecos	Edwards Plateau	South Central	Upper Coast	South Texas	Lower Valley	High Plains	Low Plains	North Central	East Texas	Trans-Pecos	Edwards Plateau	South Central	Upper Coast	South Texas	Lower Valley
Jan.	40.1	43.6	46.8	47.4	47.5	47.8	54.2	54.7	57.5	63.4	0.03	0.09	0.78	1.63	0.01	0.26	0.36	0.37	0.10	0.14
Feb.	46.8	52.1	55.1	55.4	53.2	56.2	62.0	61.5	63.9	68.9	0.49	0.45	0.96	1.61	0.04	0.30	0.50	1.11	0.20	0.46
Mar.	52.6	57.5	58.9	58.3	59.0	60.8	64.2	63.5	67.6	69.9	0.70	0.85	4.01	6.18	0.47	2.37	2.18	3.25	0.70	0.37
April	57.7	62.6	63.3	63.2	64.9	65.3	69.7	68.6	73.8	76.2	1.86	2.50	4.64	5.54	0.26	3.19	3.87	7.20	1.02	0.05
May	66.4	69.7	71.7	72.5	74.5	74.6	78.3	77.4	81.8	81.8	1.10	1.84	3.67	5.18	1.49	1.99	1.82	2.15	2.19	2.20
June	76.6	81.0	82.1	81.8	80.8	82.8	84.7	83.1	86.5	85.3	3.05	2.98	2.71	1.32	2.75	1.79	0.36	0.79	0.33	1.03
July	79.0	82.5	84.8	83.9	83.1	84.6	87.6	85.9	89.3	88.5	3.85	4.10	3.49	6.86	1.99	2.32	0.68	2.66	0.70	0.18
Aug.	77.8	82.7	84.2	82.2	81.3	84.2	87.0	85.2	88.2	87.9	2.12	1.85	1.75	3.06	1.60	0.93	1.25	2.21	0.52	0.54
Sep.	67.9	71.8	74.1	74.7	72.7	73.8	78.3	78.6	79.8	82.1	1.18	3.37	7.16	6.71	1.27	4.10	6.36	4.69	5.46	6.04
Oct.	55.7	58.9	61.6	63.1	64.5	64.6	70.5	71.5	73.4	77.7	1.67	2.33	9.36	14.45	1.17	4.01	7.41	10.13	2.92	2.92
Nov.	51.0	55.7	58.2	58.7	55.1	56.6	61.8	62.6	63.0	67.9	0.12	0.10	1.29	2.18	0.30	1.03	4.18	3.21	2.08	0.95
Dec.	34.6	38.8	41.5	43.5	43.8	43.6	48.4	50.4	50.3	55.8	0.77	1.46	2.04	4.72	0.76	1.58	3.41	5.92	2.46	5.13
Ann.	58.9	63.1	65.2	65.4	65.0	66.2	70.6	70.3	72.9	75.5	16.94	21.42	41.86	59.44	12.11	23.87	32.38	43.69	18.68	20.01

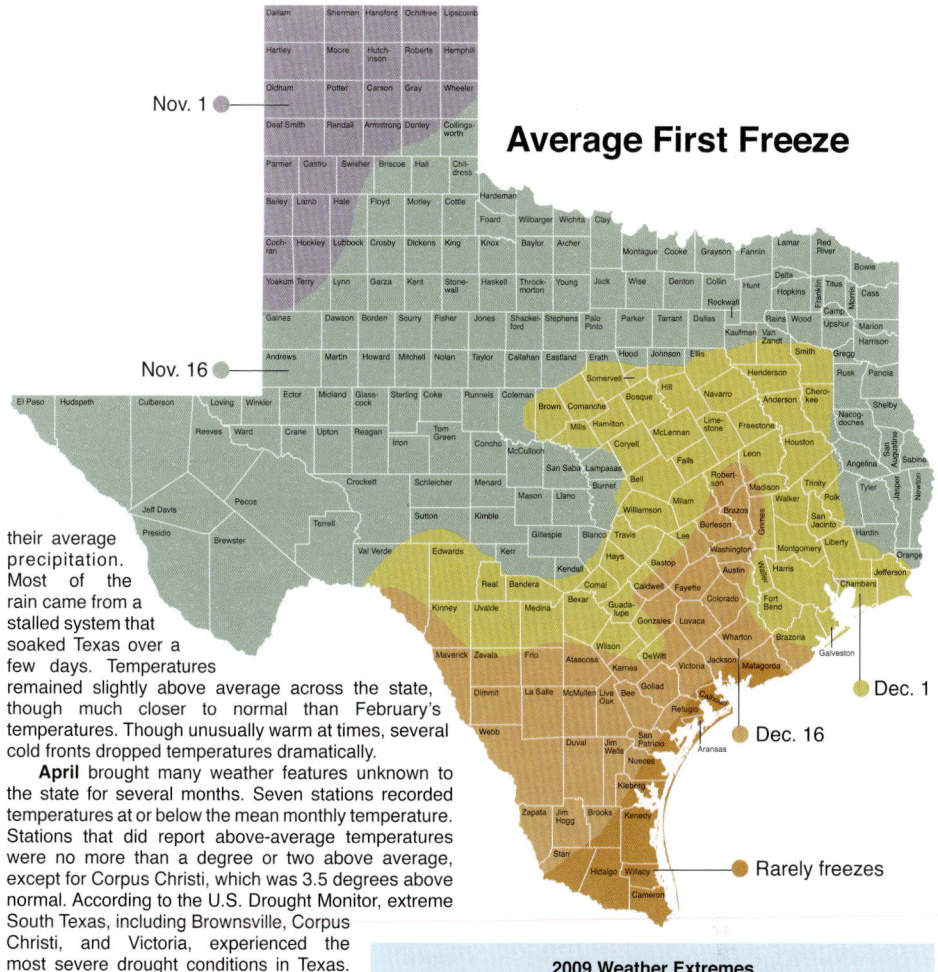

Average First Freeze

Nov. 1

Nov. 16

Dec. 1

Dec. 16

Rarely freezes

their average precipitation. Most of the rain came from a stalled system that soaked Texas over a few days. Temperatures remained slightly above average across the state, though much closer to normal than February's temperatures. Though unusually warm at times, several cold fronts dropped temperatures dramatically.

April brought many weather features unknown to the state for several months. Seven stations recorded temperatures at or below the mean monthly temperature. Stations that did report above-average temperatures were no more than a degree or two above average, except for Corpus Christi, which was 3.5 degrees above normal. According to the U.S. Drought Monitor, extreme South Texas, including Brownsville, Corpus Christi, and Victoria, experienced the most severe drought conditions in Texas. East Texas was not only relatively cool, but experienced a torrential rainfall event, and some communities reported almost 6 inches of rain in one hour. Rainfall totals reached near record levels in Houston, where flooding was a major concern during the last part of April.

May conditions followed those of the first three months of 2009: warm temperatures and little rainfall. Only the Panhandle remained cooler than average, while portions of South and West Texas had mean monthly temperatures nearly 4 degrees above average. Only extreme West, Northeast, and South Texas, as well as the Abilene area, received their normal monthly precipitation. The Upper Coast was especially dry; cities such as Houston and Galveston received about 5 percent of normal precipitation. Most weather stations reported less than a third of their normal rainfall for May. During mid-month, a cold front swept through the state, bringing abundant lightning, five tornadoes, and golf-ball-sized hail to Central Texas.

June was a record-breaking month for many areas of Texas, especially in the southeast. Houston and Galveston experienced their driest May and June in recorded history, about 5 percent of their normal precipitation for the two months. Southeast Texas and the Gulf Coast region were the driest areas of Texas

2009 Weather Extremes	
Lowest Temp.: Bravo,* Hartley Co., Dec. 10	–3° F
Highest Temp.: Hebbronville, Jim Hogg Co., July 9	118°F
24-hour Precip: Jarrell, Williamson Co., Sept. 12	14.33"
Monthly Precip.: Broaddus, San Augustine Co., October	22.87"
Least Annual Precip.: Tornillo, El Paso Co.	5.53"
Greatest Annual Precip.: New Boston, Bowie Co.	81.87"

Bravo was located at the Hartley-Oldham county line, near the state line.

relative to normal; most of these areas received about a quarter of normal June precipitation. The Panhandle and Central Texas received closer to average rainfall, while Northeast and West Texas received slightly more than average. Temperatures were exceedingly high for most of the state, a sign of things to come for July.

July went down in the record books as the hottest month ever recorded for several cities in Central and South Texas, and it was perhaps the hottest month ever for the state as a whole. July continued a trend of unprecedented dryness that had areas from Central Texas to the Coastal Bend suffering through a drought worse than any since the 1950s. The Office of the State Climatologist concluded that Bastrop, Caldwell, and Lee counties in Central Texas, and Victoria, Bee, San Patricio, Live Oak, Jim Wells, and Duval counties were in the midst of their worst drought since precipitation records began to be kept in 1895. July was remarkable for its persistent and record-setting warmth in areas where

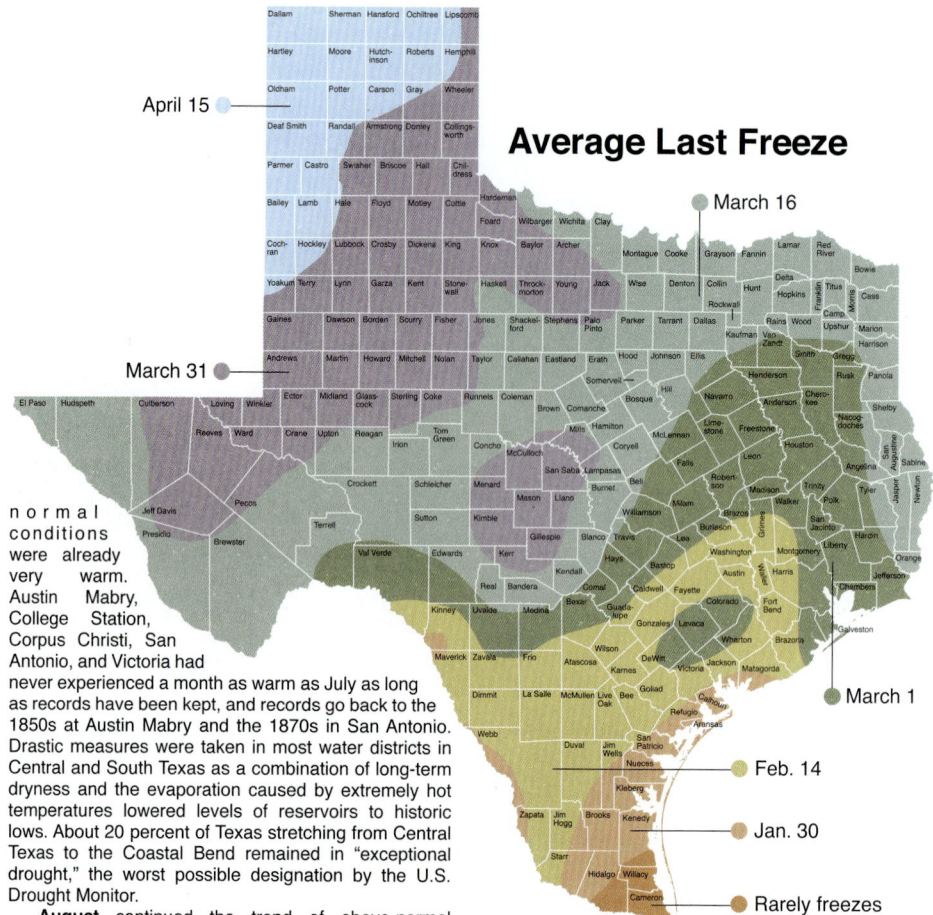

Average Last Freeze

April 15
March 31
March 16
March 1
Feb. 14
Jan. 30
Rarely freezes

n o r m a l conditions were already very warm. Austin Mabry, College Station, Corpus Christi, San Antonio, and Victoria had never experienced a month as warm as July as long as records have been kept, and records go back to the 1850s at Austin Mabry and the 1870s in San Antonio. Drastic measures were taken in most water districts in Central and South Texas as a combination of long-term dryness and the evaporation caused by extremely hot temperatures lowered levels of reservoirs to historic lows. About 20 percent of Texas stretching from Central Texas to the Coastal Bend remained in "exceptional drought," the worst possible designation by the U.S. Drought Monitor.

August continued the trend of above-normal temperatures across most of Texas, although areas of the Panhandle got some break from the extreme heat gripping the rest of the state. Average daytime temperatures topped 100 degrees in Austin, Del Rio, and San Antonio, all of which were part of a larger area in Central and South Texas that received only a small fraction of precipitation expected in a normal August. Rainfall was plentiful in the Panhandle and in extreme Northeast Texas. The South Central, Coastal Bend, and Lower Valley regions remained in exceptional drought the entire summer, and these conditions devastated agriculture and forced careful conservation of water resources in these areas.

Just like August, **September** began hot and humid, with average to slightly above average temperatures across the state. During the second week, an area of low pressure drew moisture from the Gulf of Mexico, providing much needed rain to many parts of Texas. While September rains that fell in the south did a great deal to improve the drought there, large long-term precipitation deficits remained in most of South Texas. For example, the 6.27 inches of precipitation in Corpus Christi was more than had fallen the first eight months of 2009 (4.10 inches).

October was a fairly wet month for East Texas, while the western and southern areas were drier than normal. All of Texas was affected by several cold fronts, with a progressive weather pattern that was seemingly different every day. For the month, a combination of these fronts and rainy days kept temperatures below

normal in North and Central Texas. The rest of the state saw temperatures near normal. Unsettled weather in the last third of the month was brought by remnants of **Hurricane Rick.** Much of the state's eastern half saw heavy rainfall, and several tornadoes were reported on the 29th in Northeast Texas near the Texas-Louisiana border. The rains in South-Central Texas were extremely beneficial, greatly improving the drought conditions present at the beginning of the month. Although portions of South Texas saw improvement in drought conditions, Corpus Christi and much of the Coastal Bend did not receive enough rainfall to break an exceptional drought that had been present for some time.

November was not nearly as wet as October over most of the state. As the month began, most of the state saw high temperatures in the 70s, while high temperatures in South Texas were still in the 80s. Starting on the 8th, East Texas felt the indirect effect of **Hurricane Ida,** with the Coastal Bend area hardest hit. Much of the weather action in November took place as the month (and hurricane season) came to a close. On the 29th, a tornado briefly touched down in New Boston, causing damage to four homes and knocking down trees and power lines. In the cold sector of the storm, Amarillo reported 2 inches of snow.

December was one of the coldest months of the year on average in Texas and was unusually frigid across the entire state. The monthly average mean temperature of 42.9 degrees was the fifth coldest December statewide

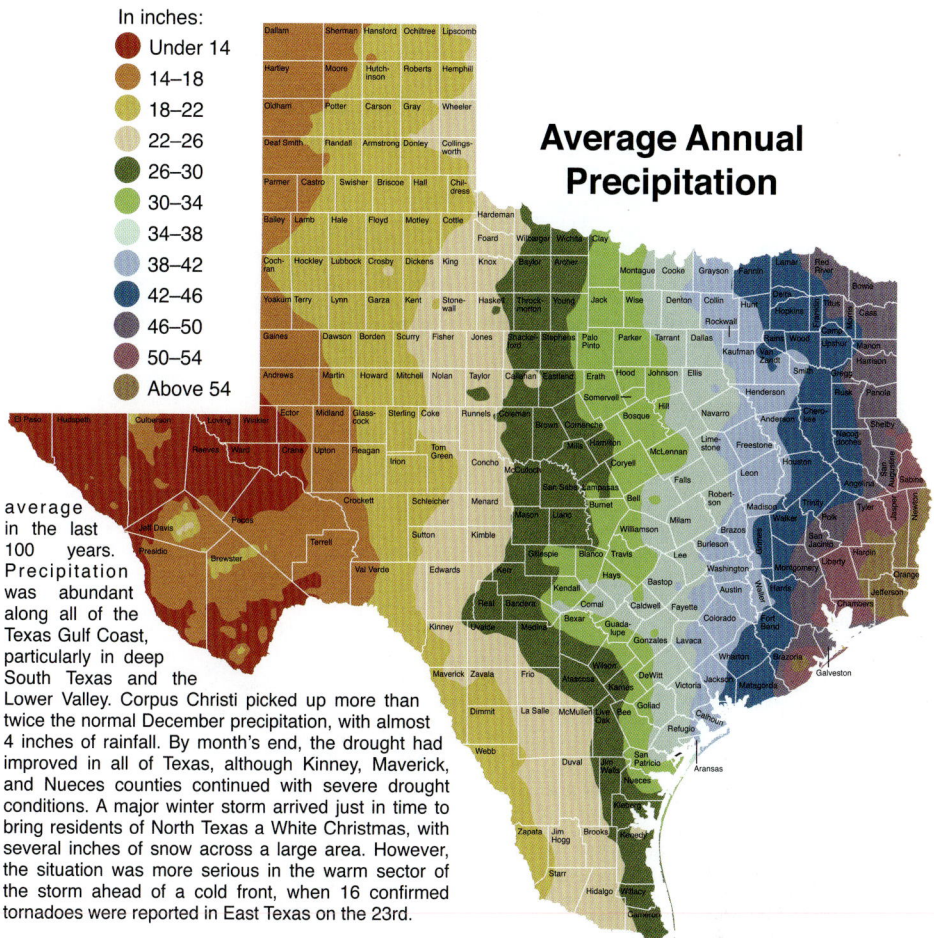

Average Annual Precipitation

In inches:
- Under 14
- 14–18
- 18–22
- 22–26
- 26–30
- 30–34
- 34–38
- 38–42
- 42–46
- 46–50
- 50–54
- Above 54

average in the last 100 years. Precipitation was abundant along all of the Texas Gulf Coast, particularly in deep South Texas and the Lower Valley. Corpus Christi picked up more than twice the normal December precipitation, with almost 4 inches of rainfall. By month's end, the drought had improved in all of Texas, although Kinney, Maverick, and Nueces counties continued with severe drought conditions. A major winter storm arrived just in time to bring residents of North Texas a White Christmas, with several inches of snow across a large area. However, the situation was more serious in the warm sector of the storm ahead of a cold front, when 16 confirmed tornadoes were reported in East Texas on the 23rd.

Weather Highlights 2010

Jan. 20: Rare events produced a costly day of severe storms over northeast Texas in mid-winter. Supercell storms produced **10 tornadoes**, including an EF3 twister that hit Crossroads and Jonesville in Harrison County. With maximum winds estimated at 150–160 mph, this single storm caused an estimated $1.5 million in damage. An EF2 tornado in Van Zandt County caused destruction estimated at $1 million; the overall economic loss for that day was over $4 million.

Feb. 11–12: In North Texas, a **record snowfall** blanketed the entire region. With an average of 8–12 inches across numerous counties, the snow caused major tree damage, and falling limbs were the primary cause of widespread power outages. More than 500,000 homes, businesses, and schools were without power for several days as this powerful snowstorm left its mark. The most snow was measured at 14.4 inches in northwest Tarrant County, and economic losses were estimated at over $22 million.

June 30: Hurricane Alex made landfall just south of Cameron County around 8 p.m., reaching wind speeds of 109 mph and central pressure of 946 millibars, making it a Category 2 storm. Around 9,000 electric customers were without power in the Lower Rio Grande Valley, and they were drenched with 6–9 inches of rain, with some areas receiving 10 inches or more. As Alex traveled inland, it continued to wreak havoc with flash floods. Along the Sierra Madre Oriental foothills, Alex created record flows and fatal floods, which set a record of 88,000 cubic feet per second. Alex and Tropical Depression No. 2, which followed two weeks later, lead to record flooding along the Rio Grande and into the Rio Grande Valley, with damage estimates at more than $1.35 billion.

Sept. 6–7: Tropical Storm Hermine left the ocean about 40 miles south of Brownsville at 8:30 p.m. with peak sustained winds at around 65 mph. After making landfall, Hermine tracked north by northwestward and entered Texas through Cameron County around midnight. Sustained winds between 50–60 mph caused widespread damage to trees and power lines. Around 5 a.m., the core exited Deep South Texas near Falfurrias, leaving a swath of damage from flash floods and strong winds. A federal state of emergency was declared in Cameron, Willacy, and Kenedy counties, and the estimated damage was $12.3 million.

Monthly Summaries 2010

Signs of El Niño still building in the Pacific Ocean were seen statewide in **January,** another wet and cold month for Texas. Some areas saw the coldest temperatures in two decades. All first-order weather stations received rain, and all but six received more than normal rainfall. Waco received 5.30 inches of precipitation, including 4.50 inches falling in a 24-hour period on Jan. 28–29. Several storm systems passed though the state, including an outbreak of severe weather on the 20th. The

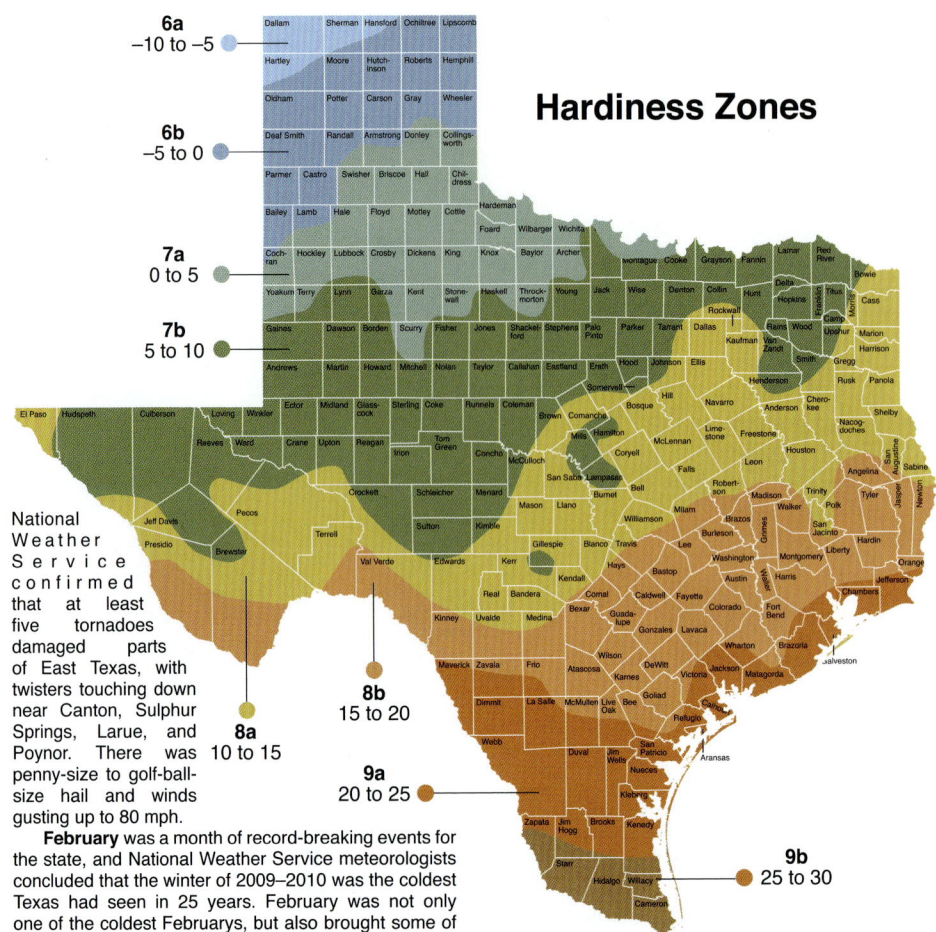

Hardiness Zones

6a
−10 to −5

6b
−5 to 0

7a
0 to 5

7b
5 to 10

8a
10 to 15

8b
15 to 20

9a
20 to 25

9b
25 to 30

National Weather Service confirmed that at least five tornadoes damaged parts of East Texas, with twisters touching down near Canton, Sulphur Springs, Larue, and Poynor. There was penny-size to golf-ball-size hail and winds gusting up to 80 mph.

February was a month of record-breaking events for the state, and National Weather Service meteorologists concluded that the winter of 2009–2010 was the coldest Texas had seen in 25 years. February was not only one of the coldest Februarys, but also brought some of the heaviest snowfall ever seen in North Texas. A snowstorm on Feb. 11–12 brought 12.5 inches of snow to Dallas-Fort Worth International Airport in a 24-hour period, breaking the old record of 12.1 inches in January 1964. This included 11.2 inches on the 11th, which shattered the previous record of 7.8 inches for a single calendar day. This snow event lasted just 24 hours and brought the snow total for the Dallas-Fort Worth area up to 15 inches for the year, 2 inches shy of the all-time record of 17.5 inches set in 1977–1978. The snow caused minimal problems for the NBA All-Star game held that weekend at the new Cowboys Stadium in Arlington.

March continued a string of colder-than-normal months across all of Texas, though precipitation was not quite as abundant as in the first two months of 2010. The coldest temperatures relative to normal were along the Upper Texas Coast and in South-Central Texas. The maximum temperature reached 87 degrees in San Angelo on the 14th, which was the highest reading in the continental United States for that day. However, a cold front pushed through and held temperatures in the 40s most of the next day with cloudy skies and drizzle, weather more typical of the past winter. The month's coldest morning was the 21st, the first full day of spring.

2010 Weather Extremes	
Lowest Temp.: Lipscomb, Lipscomb Co., Jan. 8	−6° F
Highest Temp.: Lajitas, Brewster Co., June 7–8	115°F
Castolon, Brewster Co., June 7–8	115°F
Rio Grande Village, Brewster Co., June 6–7	115°F
Presidio, Presidio Co., June 7	115°F
24-hour Precip: Georgetown Lake, Williamson Co., Sept. 8	14.57"
Monthly Precip: Calliham, McMullen Co., April	23.27"
Least Annual Precip.: Agua Fria,* Brewster Co.	4.71"
Greatest Annual Precip.: West Columbia, Brazoria Co.	59.63"

Agua Fria was in southwest Brewster County near TX 118 north of Study Butte.

The temperature in Amarillo dipped to 20 degrees, with temperatures in outlying areas dropping into the teens. The month ended on a warm note as several stations in West Texas reported temperatures in the 90s on the 31st. Childress topped out at 98 degrees, which was the third-warmest March reported in records dating to 1948.

April was filled with severe weather for many parts of Texas. During mid-month, El Paso received a heavy downpour of rain that was accompanied by golf-ball-size hail. A severe thunderstorm hit on the 17th that spawned a tornado at King Ranch in the Lower Valley and caused flooding as more than 10 inches of rain fell in a few hours near Choke Canyon Lake. No damage was associated with the tornado, but the Coast Guard was called in to help with water rescues due to the severe flooding. Two Houston residents were struck by lightning while playing soccer on the 18th, and 2.47 inches of rain fell at Houston Intercontinental Airport. At month's end, several more tornadoes hit across the state. The National Weather Service confirmed that eight tornadoes touched down in the Panhandle on the 23rd alone. Two tornadoes touched down near the town of Goodlight and another, near Jericho, was on the ground for about eight minutes. Just two days later, an EF1 tornado touched down in Mabank.

May was drier than normal across most of Texas, particularly in North-Central and East Texas. Rainfall throughout the month was characterized by isolated locations picking up excessive amounts of precipitation. Flooding was an issue in Del Rio, which set May records after receiving 7.12 inches of rain on the 24th in a 24-hour period and 10.45 inches for the entire month. Flooding was reported in the Permian Basin when Midland International Airport received 1.40 inches of its monthly total of 1.65 inches on the 14th. Victoria picked up 6.02 inches in 24 hours from May 14–15, which was over 85 percent of its monthly precipitation. Galveston received 3.65 inches over the same 24-hour period and 3.66 inches for the month. Following the excessive rainfall on the weekend of the 14th–16th, rain was scarce across most of the state for the rest of May. El Paso received only a hundredth of an inch of rain during the entire month. By the end of the month, East Texas had moderate drought conditions as dryness in May, normally one of the wettest months of the year, combined with much warmer than normal temperatures.

June was drier than normal across most of Texas, although a few regions received above-normal precipitation. A storm system on the June 9–10 dumped several inches of rain in an area stretching from Austin–San Antonio northeastward to Texarkana. This same storm system was responsible for several flooding deaths at a campground in Arkansas. College Station picked up 4.27 inches of rain on the 9th, and extensive flooding was reported along the Guadalupe and Comal rivers in Central Texas. Tyler received 8.14 inches on the 10th, and 8 to 12 inches of rain caused extensive damage to homes and washed out roadways in Hill and Navarro counties. Severe thunderstorms in the Panhandle on the 13th dumped over 6 inches of rain in Hansford County, and in Moore County, a storm dropped a massive 6-inch hailstone that was caught on video. Toward month's end, a tropical system that eventually became **Hurricane Alex** formed in the Gulf of Mexico and threatened the Lower Gulf Coast. Alex made landfall on the evening of the 30th in northern Mexico as a Category-2 hurricane with 105-mph winds. Hurricane Alex's most significant impact was excessive rain, which led to flooding on South Padre Island. On the 30th, McAllen set a daily rainfall record for the month

with 6.66 inches of rain, while Brownsville recorded 5.86 inches of precipitation, setting a 24-hour rainfall record for June. In addition to the flooding rains in the Lower Valley, several tornadoes were reported, one of which overturned a mobile home.

In **July,** precipitation was abundant across most of Texas, with most of the rain falling early in the month. July began with the remnants of **Hurricane Alex,** which made landfall in northern Mexico on June 30th and dropped several inches of rain across South Texas. During the first week, moisture from the Gulf of Mexico streamed into the state and helped provide fuel for heavy rains across all of Texas, with the exception of the Trans-Pecos. Rainfall totals during the first week were impressive across the Upper Coast, the Edwards Plateau, the Panhandle, and the Lower Valley, the latter of which was directly impacted by the landfall of Hurricane Alex. During a 24-hour period ending on the 1st, Brownsville picked up 6.14 inches of precipitation and Corpus Christi received 4 inches. During the July 2–3, Houston Intercontinental Airport picked up 5.45 inches of precipitation, a record for the month. As the remnants of Alex moved to the west, Lubbock received 4.38 inches of rain on the 2nd–3rd, also a record for July. A few days later, a frontal boundary stalled across the Panhandle, dumping excessive amounts of rain. Amarillo broke its all-time 24-hour precipitation record when 7.25 inches of rain fell on the 7th–8th, and on the 8th, the maximum temperature was only 71 degrees. Amarillo also set a July record with a monthly precipitation total of 8.02 inches.

Dry and hot describes the weather in **August,** as the trend of above-normal temperatures continued across most of the state. Average daytime temperatures topped 100 degrees in College Station, Dallas-Fort Worth, San Angelo, Austin, Waco, and Wichita Falls. No weather station saw an average daily high temperatures below 90 degrees, while daily average minimum temperatures were all at least 69 degrees. One record was set, as the minimum temperature on the 26th dropped to 48 degrees in Amarillo. Both College Station and Houston saw some of their warmest daily minimums ever recorded. College Station never dropped below 72 degrees, and in Houston, the daily low temperature never dipped below 74 degrees. Only Amarillo, Corpus Christi, Houston, Lubbock, Port Arthur, Wichita Falls, and San Angelo received more than an inch of rain, and no station had above-normal amounts of precipitation. The 3.34 inches of rain in Port Arthur was the largest amount recorded at a first-order station during August. Although Port Arthur received the most precipitation, this was only 69 percent of its normal rainfall for the month. Plenty of sunshine and warm temperatures, which averaged 100.6 degrees, helped keep Austin from receiving any

Average Temperatures 2010

	High Plains	Low Plains	North Central	East Texas	Trans-Pecos	Edwards Plateau	South Central	Upper Coast	South Texas	Lower Valley
Jan.	36.6	39.9	42.5	43.2	43.3	44.3	49.9	49.7	52.8	58.4
Feb.	35.2	39.1	40.5	42.0	46.2	44.6	48.6	48.8	51.9	56.6
Mar.	48.0	51.8	53.3	53.6	54.0	54.3	59.1	59.0	61.6	65.5
April	58.6	62.4	64.7	65.7	64.6	64.5	68.5	68.7	71.1	73.9
May	65.7	70.1	73.9	76.0	73.6	73.8	77.9	78.2	79.2	81.2
June	79.4	82.4	83.6	83.2	83.3	82.4	83.0	83.6	84.4	85.2
July	77.3	80.4	83.7	83.5	78.9	81.0	83.2	83.6	83.5	84.1
Aug.	79.1	84.3	87.3	86.8	82.0	84.7	85.9	86.0	86.5	86.9
Sep.	73.8	76.4	78.3	79.1	76.2	77.6	79.9	80.6	81.2	82.3
Oct.	61.8	65.3	66.5	66.8	67.3	67.1	70.3	71.8	72.2	75.8
Nov.	47.9	53.0	56.8	57.7	54.6	57.7	62.1	62.3	64.4	68.1
Dec.	42.0	45.3	47.4	47.4	49.1	48.4	54.5	55.1	57.3	62.1
Ann.	58.8	62.5	64.9	65.4	64.4	65.0	68.6	69.0	70.5	73.3

Precipitation 2010
(Inches)

	High Plains	Low Plains	North Central	East Texas	Trans-Pecos	Edwards Plateau	South Central	Upper Coast	South Texas	Lower Valley
Jan.	1.37	1.86	3.37	3.04	1.11	2.95	3.42	3.33	2.67	0.62
Feb.	1.72	2.10	3.30	4.36	1.00	2.58	3.84	3.92	3.11	3.52
Mar.	1.64	1.56	3.66	3.39	0.29	1.91	2.20	2.25	0.85	0.40
April	3.00	4.73	2.93	1.46	1.24	3.08	2.07	1.04	5.55	3.56
May	1.97	2.32	2.14	1.84	0.58	2.87	3.11	3.80	3.33	1.95
June	2.74	2.78	2.82	4.42	1.60	1.77	4.17	4.01	3.02	3.77
July	4.61	5.91	3.89	4.61	4.39	4.61	5.56	10.88	5.27	7.85
Aug.	2.00	0.97	0.86	1.34	1.98	1.20	0.47	2.02	0.36	0.24
Sep.	1.63	3.67	8.30	2.74	1.61	4.06	9.92	7.54	7.76	7.98
Oct.	1.19	1.33	1.24	2.03	0.14	0.35	0.06	0.20	0.06	0.00
Nov.	0.73	0.38	1.29	3.17	0.00	0.11	1.16	3.54	0.40	0.05
Dec.	0.18	0.40	1.58	1.31	0.02	0.58	0.77	2.74	0.14	0.05
Ann.	22.78	28.01	35.38	33.71	13.96	26.07	36.75	45.27	32.52	29.99

precipitation during the entire month.

From heat to tropical storms, Texas saw it all during **September.** According to the National Weather Service, the summer of 2010 (June through August) was the fourth-warmest in U.S. history. The summer heat extended into September across much of Texas. Temperatures remained high until a cold front passed through the state near the autumnal equinox. Seven of the 19 first-order stations saw an absolute maximum temperature of 100 degrees or more, and every station recorded a positive average minimum temperature departure for the month. All 19 stations received at least four days of rain, with Corpus Christi receiving the most at 15.86 inches. The Austin, Dallas-Fort Worth, and Waco areas broke new monthly records for maximum rain totals in 24 hours. Austin had 7.39 inches, Dallas-Fort Worth had 5.75 inches, and Waco had 5.89 inches.

Two things severely lacking during **October** were precipitation and the normal cooler autumn temperatures. Average maximum temperatures were stuck in the 80s across the state, and all average maximum temperatures were above normal for this time of year. Only El Paso saw one day that was below its daily average temperatures. During the rest of the month, El Paso recorded average temperatures 3.5 degrees above normal. Brownsville saw the state's highest average maximum temperature at 87.4 degrees, while Del Rio saw the state's absolute maximum temperature of 99 degrees. Mean average temperatures were above normal at all major stations except Corpus Christi, San Antonio, Victoria, and Waco. Although the state recorded warmer-than-normal average maximum temperatures, the majority of the state saw lower-than-normal average minimum temperatures.

La Niña was the name of the game during **November,** and just like October, precipitation was rare and temperatures stayed above normal across all of Texas. Absolute monthly maximum temperatures ranged from the lower 60s to the lower 80s. Brownsville had the highest monthly average maximum temperature in the state at 80.7 degrees. Corpus Christi, Brownsville, Del Rio, and Victoria all had daily absolute maximum temperatures that reached 90 degrees. Houston set a daily absolute maximum temperature record for the month when it topped out at 89 degrees. Galveston was the only station that did not have above-normal maximum temperatures. Every first-order station had an absolute minimum temperature that fell below the freezing mark except Brownsville. The lowest absolute minimum temperature was in Amarillo at 15 degrees.

December was drier and warmer than normal across most of Texas, leading to an increase in drought conditions in terms of severity and spatial coverage. The main culprit was moderate-to-strong La Niña conditions persisting in the Pacific Ocean, which were a significant contrast to the El Niño that brought cooler and wetter-than-normal weather in the winter of 2009–2010. Because the first few months of 2010 brought above-normal precipitation throughout Texas, there was a regeneration of vegetation following the 2008–2009 drought. However, drought conditions that developed over the summer dried out much of the vegetation, leaving it as fuel susceptible to wildfires. Numerous wildfires were reported during December, including one that destroyed more than 900 acres of grasslands in Oldham and Deaf Smith counties. ☆

Meteorological Data

Source: Updated as of July 2011 by the National Climatic Data Center. Additional data for these locations are listed by county in the table of Texas temperature, freeze, growing season, and precipitation records, beginning on page 144.

City	Temperature						Precipitation						Relative Humidity		Wind			Sun
	Record High	Month & Year	Record Low	Month & Year	No. Days Max. 90° and Above	No. Days Min. 32° and Below	Maximum in 24 Hours	Month & Year	Snowfall (Mean Annual)	Max. Snowfall in 24 Hours	Month & Year	6:00 a.m., CST	Noon, CST	Speed, MPH (Mean Annual)	Highest MPH	Month & Year	Percent Possible Sunshine
Abilene	111	8/1943	-9	1/1947	95	50	6.70	9/1961	4.9	9.3	4/1996	72	57	11.9	55	4/1998	71
Amarillo	108	6/1998+	-16	2/1899	64	110	6.75	5/1951	16.8	20.6	3/1934	72	53	13.5	60	6/1994	73
Austin	112	9/2000	-2	1/1949	109	18	15.00	9/1931	1.0	9.7	11/1937	81	64	8.5	52	5/1997	60
Brownsville	106	3/1984	16	12/1989	124	2	12.19	9/1967	**	**	3/1993	89	69	11.3	51	9/1996	60
Corpus Christi	109	9/2000	13	12/1989	107	5	8.92	8/1980	**	2.3	12/2004	89	70	12.0	56	5/1999	60
Dallas-Fort Worth	113	6/1980	-2	1/1949	97	36	5.91	10/1959	2.7	12.7	1/1964	78	62	10.7	73	8/1959	61
Del Rio	112	6/1988	10	12/1989	129	15	17.03	8/1998	0.9	8.6	1/1985	73	65	9.4	60	8/1970	84
El Paso	114	6/1994	-8	1/1962	107	57	6.50	7/1881	5.5	16.8	12/1987	55	27	8.8	84	3/1977	84
Galveston	104	9/2000	8	2/1899	30	5	13.91	10/1901	0.2	15.4	2/1895	72	72	11.0	*100	9/1900	62
†Houston	109	9/2000+	7	12/1989	100	16	11.02	6/2001	0.4	2.0	1/1963	88	69	7.6	51	8/1983	59
Lubbock	114	6/1994	-17	2/1933	81	91	7.46	9/2008	10.4	16.3	1/1983	72	52	12.4	70	3/1952	72
Midland-Odessa	116	6/1994	-11	2/1985+	101	63	5.99	7/1961	4.7	9.8	12/1998	70	51	11.1	67	2/1996	74
Port Arthur-Beaumont	108	8/2000	3	2/1899	84	13	17.16	9/1980	0.3	4.4	2/1960	90	71	9.6	105	8/2005	58
San Angelo	111	7/1960+	-4	12/1989	108	51	6.25	9/1980	3.3	7.4	1/1978	75	57	10.3	75	4/1969	70
San Antonio	111	9/2000	0	1/1949	113	21	13.35	10/1998	0.7	13.2	1/1985	82	61	9.1	51	9/2010	60
Victoria	111	9/2000	9	12/1989	106	10	9.87	4/1991	0.1	2.1	1/1985	89	69	9.9	99	7/1963	49
Waco	112	8/1969	-5	1/1949	109	33	7.98	12/1997	1.6	7.0	1/1949	82	64	11.0	69	6/1961	59
Wichita Falls	117	6/1980	-12	1/1947	103	63	6.22	9/1980	6.0	9.7	3/1989	78	58	11.6	69	6/2002	60
§Shreveport, LA	109	9/2000+	3	1/1962	90	35	10.44	4/1991	1.5	5.6	1/1982	85	65	8.3	63	5/2000	63

*100 mph recorded at 6:15 p.m., Sept. 8, 1900, just before the anemometer blew away. Maximum velocity was estimated to be 120 mph from the northeast between 7:30 p.m. and 8:30 p.m.

†The official Houston station was moved from near downtown to Intercontinental Airport, 12 miles north of the old station.

+ Also recorded on earlier dates, months, or years.

§Shreveport is included because it is near the boundary line and its data can be considered representative of Texas' east border.

**Trace is an amount too small to measure.

Texas Is Tornado Capital

An average of 132 tornadoes touch Texas soil each year. The annual total varies considerably, and certain areas are struck more often than others. Tornadoes occur with greatest frequency in the Red River Valley of North Texas.

Tornadoes may occur in any month and at any hour of the day, but they occur with greatest frequency during the late spring and early summer months, and between the hours of 4 p.m. and 8 p.m.

In the period 1951–2010, nearly 62.7 percent of all Texas tornadoes occurred within the three-month period of April, May, and June, with almost **one-third of the total tornadoes occurring in May**.

More tornadoes have been recorded in Texas than in any other state, which is partly due to the state's size.

Between 1951 and 2010, 7,900 funnel clouds reached the ground, thus becoming tornadoes. Texas ranks 11th among the 50 states in the density of tornadoes, with an average of 5.7 tornadoes per 10,000 square miles per year during this period.

The greatest outbreak of tornadoes on record in Texas was associated with **Hurricane Beulah in September 1967**. Within a five-day period, Sept. 19–23, 115 known tornadoes, all in Texas, were spawned by this great hurricane. Sixty-seven occurred on Sept. 20, a Texas **record for a single day**.

In addition to Hurricane Beulah's 115 tornadoes, there were another 9 tornadoes in September for a total of 124, which is a Texas record for a single month.

The greatest number of tornadoes in Texas in a single year is 232, also in 1967. The second-highest number in a single year is 1995, when 223 tornadoes occurred in Texas.

In 1982, there were 123 tornadoes formed in May, making it the worst outbreak of spring tornadoes in Texas. On average, May has the highest number of tornadoes per month with 39.38. January has the lowest average with 2.33.

A rare winter tornado outbreak occurred on Dec. 29, 2006. There were 27 tornadoes on this day, which is the largest monthly total for December. On average, December has 3.12 tornadoes. ☆

Occurrences by Month, Year

Source: Office of State Climatologist

Year	Jan.	Feb.	March	April	May	June	July	Aug.	Sept.	Oct.	Nov.	Dec.	TOTAL
1951	0	0	1	1	5	7	1	0	0	0	0	0	15
1952	0	1	3	4	2	1	0	1	0	0	0	1	13
1953	0	2	2	3	6	2	3	5	0	2	1	6	32
1954	0	3	1	23	21	14	5	1	4	5	0	0	77
1955	0	0	7	15	42	32	1	5	2	0	0	0	104
1956	0	3	5	3	17	5	6	4	2	9	2	0	56
1957	0	1	21	69	33	5	0	3	2	6	5	0	145
1958	2	0	7	12	15	13	10	7	0	0	8	0	74
1959	0	0	8	4	32	14	10	3	4	5	6	0	86
1960	4	1	0	8	29	14	3	4	2	11	1	0	77
1961	0	1	21	15	24	30	9	2	12	0	10	0	124
1962	0	4	12	9	25	56	12	15	7	2	0	1	143
1963	0	0	3	9	19	24	8	4	6	4	5	0	82
1964	0	1	6	22	15	11	9	7	3	1	3	0	78
1965	2	5	3	7	43	24	2	9	4	6	0	3	108
1966	0	4	1	21	22	15	3	8	3	0	0	0	77
1967	0	2	11	17	34	22	10	5	124	2	0	5	232
1968	2	1	3	13	47	21	4	8	5	8	11	16	139
1969	0	1	1	16	65	16	6	7	6	8	1	0	127
1970	1	3	5	23	23	9	5	20	9	20	0	3	121
1971	0	20	10	24	27	33	7	20	7	16	4	23	191
1972	1	0	19	13	43	12	19	13	8	9	7	0	144
1973	14	1	29	25	21	24	4	8	5	3	9	4	147
1974	2	1	8	19	18	26	3	9	6	22	2	0	116
1975	5	2	9	12	50	18	10	3	3	3	1	1	117
1976	1	1	8	53	63	11	16	6	13	4	0	0	176
1977	0	0	3	34	50	4	5	5	12	0	6	4	123
1978	0	0	0	34	65	10	13	6	6	1	2	0	137
1979	1	2	24	33	39	14	12	10	4	15	3	0	157
1980	0	2	7	26	44	21	2	34	10	5	0	2	153
1981	0	7	7	9	71	26	5	20	5	23	3	0	176
1982	0	0	6	27	123	36	4	0	3	0	3	1	203
1983	5	7	24	1	62	35	4	22	5	0	7	14	186
1984	0	13	9	18	19	19	0	4	1	5	2	5	95
1985	0	0	5	41	28	5	3	1	1	3	1	2	90
1986	0	12	4	21	50	24	3	5	4	7	1	0	131
1987	1	1	7	0	54	19	11	3	8	0	16	4	124
1988	0	0	0	11	7	7	6	2	42	4	10	0	89
1989	3	0	5	3	70	63	0	6	3	6	1	0	160
1990	3	3	4	56	62	20	5	2	3	0	0	0	158
1991	20	5	2	39	72	36	1	2	3	8	4	0	192
1992	0	5	13	22	43	66	4	4	4	7	21	0	189
1993	1	4	5	17	39	4	4	0	12	23	8	0	117
1994	0	1	1	48	88	2	1	4	3	9	8	0	165
1995	6	0	13	36	66	75	11	3	2	1	0	10	223
1996	7	1	2	21	33	9	3	8	33	8	4	1	130
1997	0	6	7	31	59	50	2	2	1	16	3	0	177
1998	24	15	4	9	11	6	3	5	3	28	1	0	109
1999	22	0	22	23	70	26	3	8	0	0	0	4	178
2000	0	7	49	33	23	8	3	0	0	10	20	1	154
2001	0	0	4	12	36	12	0	7	15	24	27	5	142
2002	0	0	44	25	61	5	1	4	13	8	0	22	183
2003	0	0	4	31	50	29	6	1	4	12	29	0	166
2004	1	1	27	25	29	34	1	5	0	4	55	2	184
2005	0	0	6	7	27	46	15	4	2	0	0	2	109
2006	0	1	4	20	43	7	3	3	0	9	0	27	117
2007	2	1	56	61	43	21	8	4	14	2	1	3	216
2008	0	3	15	48	33	9	5	1	2	3	1	3	123
2009	0	5	4	48	18	32	2	4	1	4	1	12	131
2010	10	0	0	19	34	23	3	1	12	10	0	0	112
Total	140	160	591	1,329	2,363	1262	318	367	468	401	314	187	7,900

This table was compiled by the National Climatic Data Center, Environmental Data Service, and the National Oceanic and Atmospheric Administration.

A controlled burn on Sunday, April 17, 2011, devours fuel on the mountains around McDonald Observatory to starve the Rock House wildfire. The Hobby-Eberly Telescope dome is at right. Months of drought caused wildfires to rage across much of West Texas early in 2011. Photo by Frank Cianciolo; McDonald Observatory.

Extreme Weather Records in Texas

Temperature

Lowest	-23°F	Tulia	Feb. 12, 1899
	-23°F	Seminole	Feb. 8, 1933
Highest	120°F	Seymour	Aug. 12, 1936
	120°F	Monahans	June 28, 1994
Coldest Winter			1898–1899

Wind Velocity

Highest sustained wind

145 mph SE	Matagorda	Sept. 11, 1961
145 mph NE	Port Lavaca	Sept. 11, 1961

Highest peak gust

180 mph SW	Aransas Pass	Aug. 3, 1970
180 mph WSW	Robstown	Aug. 3, 1970

These winds occurred during Hurricane Carla in 1961 and Hurricane Celia in 1970.

Tornadoes

Since 1950, there have been six tornadoes of the F5 category, that is, with winds between 261–318 mph.

Waco	McLennan County	May 11, 1953
Wichita Falls	Wichita County	April 3, 1964
Lubbock	Lubbock County	May 11, 1970
Valley Mills	McLennan County	May 6, 1973
Brownwood	Brown County	April 19, 1976
Jarrell	Williamson County	May 27, 1997

Rainfall

Wettest year statewide		1941	42.62 in.
Driest year statewide		1917	14.30 in.
Most annual	Clarksville	1873	109.38 in.
Least annual	Presidio	1956	1.64 in.
Most in 24 hours†	Alvin	July 25-26, 1979	43.00 in.
Most in 18 hours	Thrall	Sept. 9, 1921	36.40 in.

†Unofficial estimate of rainfall during Tropical Storm Claudette. Greatest 24-hour rainfall at an official site occurred at Albany, Shackelford County, Aug. 4, 1978: 29.05 inches.

Hail

(Hailstones six inches or greater, since 1950)

8.00 in.	Winkler County	May 31, 1960
7.50 in.	Young County	April 14, 1965
6.00 in.	Ward County	May 10, 1991
7.05 in.	Burleson County	Dec. 17, 1995

Snowfall

65.0 in.	Season	Romero*	1923-24
61.0 in.	Month	Vega	Feb. 1956
61.0 in.	Single storm	Vega	Feb. 1-8, 1956
24.0 in.	24 hours	Plainview	Feb. 3-4, 1956
24.2 in.	Annual average	Vega	

*Romero was in southwestern Hartley County.

Source: National Weather Service, Dallas/Fort Worth.

Texas Droughts, 1892–2010

The following table shows the extent of drought by major region, 1892–2010, by listing the **percent of normal precipitation**. *Drought here is arbitrarily defined as when there is less than 75 percent of normal precipitation.

Year	High Plains	Low Rolling Plains	North Central	East Texas	Trans-Pecos	Edwards Plateau	South Central	Upper Coast	South Texas	Lower Valley
1892					68				73	
1893			67	70		49	56	64	53	59
1894					68					
1897							73		72	
1898									69	51
1901		71	70			60	62	70	44	
1902									65	73
1907										65
1909			72	68	67	74	70			
1910	59	59	64	69	43	65	69	74	59	
1911										70
1916		73		74	70		73	69		
1917	58	50	63	59	44	46	42	50	32	48
1920										71
1921						72				73
1922					68					
1924			73	73		71		72		
1925			72					72		
1927									74	74
1933	72				62	68				
1934	66					46	69			
1937								72		
1939							69			72
1943			72							
1948			73	74	62		71	67		
1950							68		74	64
1951					61	53				
1952	68	66			73				56	70
1953	69					49	73			
1954	70	71	68	73		50	50	57	71	
1956	51	57	61	68	44	43	55	62	53	53
1962							68		67	65
1963			63	68		65	61	73		
1964	74				69					63
1970	65	63					72			
1988					67	62	67	68		
1989							72		66	64
1990										73
1994							68			
1996							71		60	70
1998		69					71			
1999			73			67	69	69		
2000							74			67
2001						56				
2003	65	71								
2005			68	66						72
2006						66				
2008						66	61			
2009										
2010				70						

Drought Frequency

This table shows the number of years of drought and the **number of separate droughts** by region. For example, the High Plains has had 10 drought years, consisting of five 1-year droughts, one 2-year drought and one 3-year drought, a total of 7 droughts.

Years of Drought	High Plains	Low Rolling Plains	North Central	East Texas	Trans-Pecos	Edwards Plateau	South Central	Upper Coast	South Texas	Lower Valley
1	5	8	10	8	7	10	14	10	10	15
2	1	1	2	2	5	5	2	2	3	2
3	1	...	...	...	1	...	...	...	...	...
Total Droughts	7	9	12	10	13	15	16	12	13	17
Drought Years	10	10	14	12	20	20	18	14	16	19

Drought Definitions

*Drought has proven to be difficult to define and there is no universally accepted definition. The most commonly used drought definitions are based on meteorological, agricultural, hydrological and socioeconomic effects.

Meteorological drought is often defined by a period of substantially **diminished precipitation** duration and/or intensity. The commonly used definition of meteorological drought is an interval of time, generally on the order of months or years, during which the actual moisture supply at a given place consistently falls below the climatically appropriate moisture supply.

Agricultural drought occurs when there is **inadequate soil moisture** to meet the needs of a particular crop at a particular time. Agricultural drought usually occurs after or during meteorological drought but before hydrological drought and can also affect livestock and other dry-land agricultural operations.

Hydrological drought refers to **deficiencies in surface and subsurface water** supplies. It is measured as streamflow and as lake, reservoir and groundwater levels. There is usually a delay between lack of rain and less measurable water in streams, lakes and reservoirs. Therefore, hydrological measurements tend to lag other drought indicators.

Socioeconomic drought occurs when physical water shortages start to affect the health, well-being, and **quality of life** of the people, or when the drought starts to affect the **supply and demand** of an economic product.

Source: New Mexico Drought Planning Team Web site.

Normal Annual Rainfall by Texas Climatic Region

Listed below is the normal annual rainfall in inches for five 30-year periods in each geographical region (See map, p. 126). Normals are given **in the same order** as the regions appear in the tables above.

Region	Normal Rainfall in Inches									
	HP	LRP	NC	ET	TP	EP	SC	UC	ST	LV
1931–1960	18.51	22.99	32.93	45.96	12.03	25.91	33.24	46.19	22.33	24.27
1941–1970	18.59	23.18	32.94	45.37	11.57	23.94	33.03	46.43	21.95	23.44
1951–1980	17.73	22.80	32.14	44.65	11.65	23.52	34.03	45.93	22.91	24.73
1961–1990	18.88	23.77	33.99	45.67	13.01	24.00	34.49	47.63	23.47	25.31
1971–2000	19.64	24.51	35.23	48.08	13.19	24.73	36.21	50.31	24.08	25.43

Three separate funnels can be seen as a tornado touches down near Jarrell in Williamson County on May 27, 1997. The half-mile-wide EF5 tornado claimed 27 lives, injured 12, and caused more than $40 million in damage. Photo by Scott Beckwith.

Significant and Destructive Weather

Source: This list of significant weather events in Texas since 1766 was compiled from ESSA-Weather Bureau information, previous Texas Almanacs, the Handbook of Texas, The Dallas Morning News and other sources.

Sept. 4, 1766: Hurricane. Galveston Bay. Spanish Mission Nuestra Señora de la Luz destroyed.

Sept. 12, 1818: Hurricane. Galveston Island. Salt water flowed four feet deep. Only six buildings remained habitable. Of the six vessels and two barges in the harbor, even the two not seriously damaged were reduced to dismasted hulks. **Pirate Jean Lafitte** moved to one hulk so his **Red House** might serve as a hospital.

Aug. 6, 1844: Hurricane. Mouth of Rio Grande. All houses destroyed at the mouth of the river and at **Brazos Santiago**, eight miles north; 70 lives lost.

Sept. 19, 1854: Hurricane. It struck near **Matagorda**, and moved inland, northwestward over **Columbus**. Main impact fell in **Matagorda and Lavaca bays**. Almost all buildings in Matagorda were destroyed. Four lives were lost in town; more lives were lost on the peninsula.

Oct. 3, 1867: Hurricane. This hurricane moved inland **south of Galveston**, but raked the entire Texas coast **from the Rio Grande to the Sabine. Bagdad and Clarksville**, towns at the mouth of the Rio Grande, were destroyed. Much of Galveston was flooded and property damage there was estimated at $1 million.

Sept. 16, 1875: Hurricane. Struck **Indianola**, Calhoun County. Three-fourths of town swept away; 176 lives lost. Flooding from the bay caused nearly all destruction.

Aug. 13, 1880: Hurricane. Center struck **Matamoros, Mexico; lower Texas coast** affected.

Oct. 12–13, 1880: Hurricane. Brownsville. City nearly destroyed, many lives lost.

Dec. 29, 1880: Snow. Brownsville. A rare snowstorm in the Lower Rio Grande Valley.

Aug. 23–24, 1882: Torrential rains caused **flooding** on the **North and South Concho and Bosque rivers** (South Concho reported 45 feet above normal level), destroying **Benficklen**, then county seat of Tom Green County, leaving only the courthouse and jail. More than 50 persons drowned in **Tom Green and Erath counties**, with property damage at

$200,000 and 10,000 to 15,000 head of livestock lost.

Aug. 19–21, 1886: Hurricane. Indianola. Every house destroyed or damaged. Indianola was never rebuilt.

Oct. 12, 1886: Hurricane. Sabine, Jefferson County. Hurricane passed over Sabine. The inundation extended 20 miles inland and nearly every house in the vicinity was moved from its foundation; 150 persons were drowned.

April 28, 1893: Tornado. Cisco, Eastland County; 23 killed, 93 injured; damage $400,000.

Feb. 1895: Freeze/Snow. Coastal Texas. What is probably the greatest heavy-snow anomaly in the climatic history of the U.S. resulted from a snowstorm along the Texas coast on the 14th–15th. **Houston; Orange; Stafford,** Fort Bend County; and **Columbus**, Colorado County, each reported a snowfall of 20 inches. **Galveston** had a snowfall of 15.4 inches. Snow fell as far south as the Lower Rio Grande Valley, where **Brownsville** received 5 inches. The Lower Valley had lows of **22°F** the 14th through the 17th, destroying the vegetable crops.

May 15, 1896: Tornadoes, Sherman, Grayson County; **Justin** and **Gribble Springs**, Denton County; 76 killed; damage $225,000.

Sept. 12, 1897: Hurricane. Many houses in Port Arthur were demolished; 13 killed, damage $150,000.

May 1, 1898: Tornado. Mobeetie, Wheeler County. Four killed, several injured; damage $35,000.

Feb. 11–13, 1899: Freeze. A disastrous cold wave throughout the state. Newspapers described it as the worst freeze ever known in the state. **Brownsville's** temperature reach 16°F on the 12th and remained below freezing through the 13th. Much destruction of vegetable crops.

June 27–July 1, 1899: Rainstorm. A storm, centered over **the Brazos River watershed**, precipitated an average of 17 inches over 7,000 square miles. At **Hearne**, the gage overflowed at 24 inches; estimated total rainfall was 30 inches. At **Turnersville**, Coryell County, 33 inches were recorded in three days. This rain caused the **worst Brazos**

River flood on record. Between 30 and 35 lives were lost. Property damage was estimated at $9 million.

April 5–8, 1900: Rainstorm. This storm began in two centers, over **Val Verde County** on the Rio Grande, and over **Swisher County** on the High Plains, and converged in the vicinity of **Travis County**, causing disastrous floods in the **Colorado, Brazos and Guadalupe rivers**. McDonald Dam on the Colorado River at Austin crumbled suddenly. A wall of water swept through the city taking at least 23 lives. Damage was estimated at $1.25 million.

Sept. 8–9, 1900: Hurricane. Galveston. The Great Galveston Storm was the **worst natural disaster in U.S. history** in terms of human life. Loss of life at Galveston has been estimated at 6,000 to 8,000, but the exact number has never been exactly determined. The island was completely inundated; not a single structure escaped damage. Most of the loss of life was due to drowning by storm tides that reached 15 feet or more. The anemometer blew away when the wind reached 100 mph at 6:15 p.m. on the 8th. Wind reached an estimated maximum velocity of 120 mph between 7:30 and 8:30 p.m. Property damage has been estimated at $30 million to $40 million.

May 18, 1902: Tornado. Goliad. This tornado cut a 250-yard-wide path through town, turning 150 buildings into rubble. Several churches were destroyed, one of which was holding services; all 40 worshippers were either killed or injured. This tornado killed 114, injured 230, and caused an estimated $200,000 in damages.

April 26, 1906: Tornado. Bellevue, Clay County, demolished; considerable damage done at **Stoneburg**, seven miles east in Montague County; 17 killed, 20 injured; damage $300,000.

May 6, 1907: Tornado. North of **Sulphur Springs**, Hopkins County; five killed, 19 injured.

May 13, 1908: Tornado. Linden, Cass County. Four killed, seven injured; damage $75,000.

May 22–25, 1908: Rainstorm; unique because it originated on the Pacific Coast. It moved first into **North Texas** and southern Oklahoma and thence to **Central Texas**, precipitating as much as 10 inches. Heaviest floods were in the upper Trinity basin, but flooding was general as far south as the Nueces. Property damage exceeded $5 million and 11 lives were lost in the Dallas vicinity.

March 23, 1909: Tornado. **Slidell**, Wise County; 11 killed, 10 injured; damage $30,000.

May 30, 1909: Tornado. Zephyr, Brown County; 28 killed, many injured; damage $90,000.

July 21, 1909: Hurricane. Velasco, Brazoria County. One-half of town destroyed, 41 lives lost; damage $2,000,000.

Dec. 1–5, 1913: Rainstorm. This caused the **second major Brazos River flood**, and caused more deaths than the storm of 1899. It formed over **Central Texas** and spread both southwest and northeast with precipitation of 15 inches at **San Marcos** and 11 inches at **Kaufman**. Floods caused loss of 177 lives and $8.54 million damage.

April 20–26, 1915: Rainstorm. Originated over Central Texas and spread into North and East Texas with precipitation up to 17 inches, causing floods in **Trinity, Brazos, Colorado and Guadalupe rivers**. More than 40 lives lost and $2.33 million damage.

Aug. 16–19, 1915: Hurricane. Galveston. Peak wind gusts of 120 miles recorded at Galveston; tide ranged 9.5 to 14.3 feet above mean sea level in the city, and up to 16.1 feet near the causeway. Business section flooded with 5 to 6 feet of water. At least 275 lives lost, damage $56 million. A new seawall prevented a repetition of the 1900 disaster.

Aug. 18, 1916: Hurricane. Corpus Christi. Maximum wind speed 100 mph. 20 Lives lost; damage $1.6 million.

Jan. 10–12, 1918: Blizzard. This was the most severe since that of February, 1899; it was accompanied by zero degree temperature in North Texas and temperatures from 7° to 12° below freezing along the lower coast.

April 9, 1919: Tornado. Leonard, Ector and Ravenna in Fannin County; 20 killed, 45 injured; damage $125,000.

April 9, 1919: Tornado. Henderson, Van Zandt, Wood, Camp, and Red River counties, 42 killed, 150 injured; damage $450,000.

May 7, 1919: Windstorms. Starr, Hidalgo, Willacy and Cameron counties. Violent thunderstorms with high winds, hail and rain occurred between **Rio Grande City** and the coast, killing 10 persons. Damage to property and crops was $500,000. Seven were killed at **Mission**.

Sept. 14, 1919: Hurricane. Near **Corpus Christi**. Center moved inland south of Corpus Christi; tides 16 feet above normal in that area and 8.8 feet above normal at **Galveston**. Extreme wind at Corpus Christi measured at 110 mph; 284 lives lost; damage $20.3 million.

April 13, 1921: Tornado. Melissa, Collin County, and **Petty**, Lamar County. Melissa was practically destroyed; 12 killed, 80 injured; damage $500,000.

April 15, 1921: Tornado. Wood, Cass and Bowie counties; 10 killed, 50 injured; damage $85,000.

Sept. 8–10, 1921: Rainstorm. Probably the **greatest rainstorm in Texas history**, it entered Mexico as a hurricane from the Gulf. Torrential rains fell as the storm moved northeasterly across Texas. **Record floods** occurred in **Bexar, Travis, Williamson, Bell and Milam counties**, killing 215 persons, with property losses over $19 million. Five to nine feet of water stood in downtown **San Antonio**. A total of 23.98 inches was measured at the U.S. Weather Bureau station at **Taylor** during a period of 35 hours, with a 24-hour maximum of 23.11 on September 9-10. The **greatest rainfall recorded in United States history during 18 consecutive hours** (measured at an unofficial weather-monitoring site) fell at Thrall, Williamson County, 36.40 inches fell on Sept. 9.

April 8, 1922: Tornado. Rowena, Runnels County. Seven killed, 52 injured; damage $55,000.

April 8, 1922: Tornado. Oplin, Callahan County. Five killed, 30 injured; damage $15,000.

April 23–28, 1922: Rainstorm. An exceptional storm entered Texas from the west and moved from the **Panhandle** to **North Central and East Texas**. Rains up to 12.6 inches over Parker, Tarrant and Dallas counties caused severe floods in the Upper Trinity at **Fort Worth**; 11 lives were lost; damage was estimated at $1 million.

May 4, 1922: Tornado. Austin, Travis County; 12 killed, 50 injured; damage $500,000.

May 14, 1923: Tornado. Howard and Mitchell counties; 23 killed, 100 injured; damage $50,000.

April 12, 1927: Tornado. Edwards, Real and Uvalde counties; 74 killed, 205 injured; damage $1.23 million. Most of damage was in **Rocksprings** where 72 deaths occurred and town was practically destroyed.

May 9, 1927: Tornado. Garland; eleven killed; damage $100,000.

May 9, 1927: Tornado. Nevada, Collin County; **Wolfe City**, Hunt County; and **Tigertown**, Lamar County; 28 killed, over 200 injured; damage $900,000.

Jan. 4, 1929: Tornado. Near **Bay City**, Matagorda County. Five killed, 14 injured.

April 24, 1929: Tornado. Slocum, Anderson County; seven killed, 20 injured; damage $200,000.

May 24–31, 1929: Rainstorm. Beginning over **Caldwell County**, a storm spread over much of **Central and Coastal Texas** with maximum rainfall of 12.9 inches, **causing floods in Colorado, Guadalupe, Brazos, Trinity, Neches and Sabine rivers**. Much damage at **Houston** from overflow of bayous. Damage estimated at $6 million.

May 6, 1930: Tornado. Bynum, Irene and Mertens in Hill County; **Ennis**, Ellis County; and **Frost**, Navarro County; 41 killed; damage $2.1 million.

May 6, 1930: Tornado. Kenedy and Runge in Karnes County; **Nordheim**, DeWitt County; 36 killed, 34 injured; damage $127,000.

June 30–July 2, 1932: Rainstorm. Torrential rains fell over the upper watersheds of the **Nueces and Guadalupe rivers**, causing destructive floods. Seven persons drowned; property losses exceeded $500,000.

Aug. 13, 1932: Hurricane. Near **Freeport**, Brazoria County. Wind speed at **East Columbia** estimated at 100 mph; 40 lives lost, 200 injured; damage $7.5 million.

March 30, 1933: Tornado. Angelina, Nacogdoches and San Augustine counties; 10 killed, 56 injured; damage $200,000.

April 26, 1933: Tornado. Bowie County near Texarkana. Five killed, 38 injured; damage $14,000.

April 29, 1933: Dust storm. Panhandle, South Plains. The dust storm extended from **Sweetwater** north to Central Kansas and from Albuquerque, N.M., to Oklahoma. Newspaper accounts described it as the worst sandstorm in years; "as dark as any night" in **Perryton**. Thousands of acres of small grain crops were blown from the soil.

July 22–25, 1933: Tropical Storm. One of the greatest U.S. storms in area and general rainfall. The storm reached the vicinity of **Freeport** late on July 22 and moved very slowly overland across eastern Texas, July 22-25. The storm center moved into northern Louisiana on the 25th. Rainfall averaged 12.50 inches over an area of about 25,000 square miles. Twenty inches or more fell in a small area of eastern Texas and western Louisiana surrounding Logansport, La. The 4-day total at Logansport was 22.30 inches. Property damage was estimated at $1.12 million.

July 30, 1933: Tornado. Oak Cliff section of Dallas, Dallas County. Five killed, 30 injured; damage $500,000.

Sept. 4–5, 1933: Hurricane. Near **Brownsville**. Center passed inland a short distance north of Brownsville, where an extreme wind of 106 mph was measured before the anemometer blew away. Peak wind gusts were estimated at 120 to 125 mph. 40 known dead, 500 injured; damage $16,903,100. About 90 percent of the citrus crop in the **Lower Rio Grande Valley** was destroyed.

July 25, 1934: Hurricane. Near **Seadrift**, Calhoun County, 19 lives lost, many minor injuries; damage $4.5 million. About 85 percent of damage was in crops.

Jan.–March 1935: Dust storms. Amarillo. Seven times, the visibility in Amarillo declined to zero from dust storms. One of these complete blackouts lasted eleven hours. One of the storms raged for 3 1/2 days.

Sept. 15–18, 1936: Rainstorm. Excessive rains over the **North Concho and Middle Concho rivers** caused a sharp rise in the Concho River, which overflowed **San Angelo**. Much of the business district and 500 homes were flooded. Four persons drowned and property losses estimated at $5 million. Four-day storm rainfall at San Angelo measured 25.19 inches; 11.75 inches fell on the 15th.

June 10, 1938: Tornado. Clyde, Callahan County; 14 killed, 9 injured; damage $85,000.

Sept. 23, 1941: Hurricane. Center moved inland near Matagorda, and passed over **Houston** about midnight. Extremely high tides along coast in the **Matagorda to Galveston** area. Heaviest property and crop losses were in counties from Matagorda County to the Sabine River. Four lives lost. Damage was $6.5 million.

April 28, 1942: Tornado. Crowell, Foard County; 11 killed, 250 injured; damage $1.5 million.

Aug. 30, 1942: Hurricane. Matagorda Bay. Highest wind estimated 115 mph at **Seadrift**. Tide at **Matagorda**,14.7 feet. Storm moved west-north-westward and finally diminished over the **Edwards Plateau**; eight lives lost, property damage estimated at $11.5 million, and crop damage estimated at $15 million.

May 10, 1943: Tornado. Laird Hill, Rusk County, and **Kilgore**, Gregg County. Four killed, 25 injured; damage $1 million.

July 27, 1943: Hurricane. Near **Galveston**. Center moved inland across **Bolivar Peninsula and Trinity Bay**. A wind gust of 104 mph was recorded at **Texas City**; 19 lives lost; damage estimated at $16.6 million.

Aug. 26–27, 1945: Hurricane. Aransas-San Antonio Bay area. At **Port O'Connor**, the wind reached 105 mph when the cups were torn from the anemometer. Peak gusts of 135 mph were estimated at **Seadrift, Port O'Connor and Port Lavaca**; three killed, 25 injured; damage $20.1 million.

Jan. 4, 1946: Tornado. Near **Lufkin**, Angelina County and **Nacogdoches**, Nacogdoches County; 13 killed, 250 injured; damage $2.1 million.

Jan. 4, 1946: Tornado. Near **Palestine**, Anderson County; 15 killed, 60 injured; damage $500,000.

May 18, 1946: Tornado. Clay, Montague and Denton counties. Four killed, damage $112,000.

April 9, 1947: Tornado. White Deer, Carson County; **Glazier**, Hemphill County; and **Higgins**, Lipscomb County;

68 killed, 201 injured; damage $1.55 million. Glazier completely destroyed. **One of the largest tornadoes on record.** Width of path, 1 mile at Higgins; length of path, 221 miles across portions of Texas, Oklahoma and Kansas. This tornado also struck Woodward, Okla.

May 3, 1948: Tornado. McKinney, Collin County; three killed, 43 injured; $2 million damage.

May 15, 1949: Tornado. Amarillo and vicinity; six killed, 83 injured. Total damage from tornado, wind and hail, $5.3 million. Total destruction over one-block by three-block area in southern part of city; airport and 45 airplanes damaged; 28 railroad boxcars blown off track.

Jan.–Feb. 1951: Freeze. On Jan. 31.–Feb. 3 and again on Feb. 13–17, cold waves swept over the entire state, bringing **snow and sleet.** Heavy damage was done in the **Lower Rio Grande Valley** to truck and citrus crops, notably in the earlier of these northers. During the norther of Jan. 31–Feb. 3, the temperature went to −19°F in Dalhart.

Sept. 8–10, 1952: Rainstorm. Heavy rains over the **Colorado and Guadalupe River watersheds** in southwestern Texas caused major flooding. From 23 to 26 inches fell between **Kerrville, Blanco and Boerne.** Highest stages ever known occurred in the **Pedernales River**; five lives lost, three injured; 17 homes destroyed, 454 damaged. Property loss several million dollars.

March 13, 1953: Tornado. Jud and O'Brien, Haskell County; and **Knox City**, Knox County; 17 killed, 25 injured; damage $600,000.

May 11, 1953: Tornado. Near **San Angelo**, Tom Green County; eleven killed, 159 injured; damage $3.24 million.

May 11, 1953: Tornado. Waco, McLennan County; 114 killed, 597 injured; damage $41.15 million. **One of two most disastrous tornadoes**; 150 homes destroyed, 900 homes damaged; 185 other buildings destroyed; 500 other buildings damaged.

Feb. 1–5, 1956: Blizzard. Northwestern Texas. A major blizzard moved into the Panhandle and South Plains on Feb. 1. Snow and high winds continued through Feb. 5. **Snowfall was the heaviest on record in Texas.** Twenty deaths were attributed to the blizzard.

April 2, 1957: Tornado. Dallas, Dallas County; 10 killed, 200 injured; damage $4 million. Moving through Oak Cliff and West Dallas, it damaged 574 buildings, largely homes.

April–May, 1957: Torrential Rains. Excessive flooding occurred throughout the area **east of the Pecos River to the Sabine River** during the last 10 days of April; 17 lives were lost, and several hundred homes were destroyed. During May, more than 4,000 persons were evacuated from unprotected lowlands on the **West Fork of the Trinity above Fort Worth** and along creeks in Fort Worth. Twenty-nine houses at **Christoval** were damaged or destroyed and 83 houses at **San Angelo** were damaged. Five persons were drowned in floods in **South Central Texas.**

May 15, 1957: Tornado. Silverton, Briscoe County; 21 killed, 80 injured; damage $500,000.

June 27, 1957: Hurricane Audrey. Center crossed the Gulf coast near the Texas-Louisiana line. **Orange** was in the western portion of the eye between 9 and 10 a.m. In Texas, nine lives were lost, 450 persons injured; property damage was $8 million. Damage was extensive in **Jefferson and Orange counties**, with less in **Chambers and Galveston counties**. Maximum wind reported in Texas, 85 m.p.h. at **Sabine Pass**, with gusts to 100 m.p.h.

Oct. 28, 1960: Rainstorm. Rains of 7-10 inches fell in **South Central Texas**; 11 died from drowning in flash floods. In **Austin** about 300 families were driven from their homes. Damage in Austin was estimated at $2.5 million.

Sept. 8–14, 1961: Hurricane Carla. Port O'Connor; maximum wind gust at **Port Lavaca** estimated at 175 mph. Highest tide was 18.5 feet at Port Lavaca. Most damage was to **coastal counties between Corpus Christi and Port Arthur** and inland **Jackson, Harris and Wharton counties**. In Texas, 34 persons died; seven in a tornado that swept across **Galveston Island**; 465 persons were injured. Property and crop damage conservatively estimated at $300 million. The evacuation of an estimated 250,000 persons kept loss of life low. **Hurricane Carla was the largest hurricane of record.**

Jan. 9–12, 1962: Freeze. A disastrous cold wave comparable to the cold waves of 1899 and 1951. Low temperatures ranged from **-15°F in the Panhandle to 10°F at Rio Grande City.** Agricultural losses were estimated at $50 million.

Sept. 7, 1962: Rainstorm. Fort Worth. Rains fell over the Big Fossil and Denton Creek watersheds ranging up to 11 inches of fall in three hours. Extensive damage from flash flooding occurred in **Richland Hills and Haltom City.**

Sept. 16–20, 1963: Hurricane Cindy. Rains of 15 to 23.5 inches fell in portions of **Jefferson, Newton and Orange counties** when Hurricane Cindy became stationary west of **Port Arthur.** Flooding from the excessive rainfall resulted in total property damage of $11.6 million and agricultural losses of $500,000.

April 3, 1964: Tornado. Wichita Falls. Seven killed, 111 injured; damage $15 million; 225 homes destroyed, 50 with major damage, and 200 with minor damage. Sixteen other buildings received major damage.

Sept. 21–23, 1964: Rainstorm. Collin, Dallas and Tarrant counties. Rains of more than 12 inches fell during the first eight hours of the 21st. Flash flooding of tributaries of the Trinity River and smaller creeks and streams resulted in two drownings and an estimated $3 million property damage. Flooding of homes occurred in all sections of **McKinney.** In **Fort Worth,** there was considerable damage to residences along Big Fossil and White Rock creeks.

Jan. 25, 1965: Dust Storm. West Texas. The worst dust storm since February 1956 developed on the **southern High Plains.** Winds, gusting up to 75 mph at **Lubbock,** sent dust billowing to 31,000 feet in the area **from the Texas-New Mexico border eastward to a line from Tulia to Abilene.** Ground visibility was reduced to about 100 yards in many sections. The worst hit was the **Muleshoe, Seminole, Plains, Morton** area on the South Plains. The rain gage at Reese Air Force Base, Lubbock, contained 3 inches of fine sand.

June 2, 1965: Tornado. Hale Center, Hale County. Four killed, 76 injured; damage $8 million.

June 11, 1965: Rainstorm. Sanderson, Terrell County. Torrential rains of up to eight inches in two hours near Sanderson caused a major flash flood that swept through the town. As a result, 26 persons drowned and property losses were estimated at $2.72 million.

April 22–29, 1966: Flooding. Northeast Texas. Twenty to 26 inches of rain fell in portions of Wood, Smith, Morris, Upshur, Gregg, Marion and Harrison counties. Nineteen persons drowned in the rampaging rivers and creeks that swept away bridges, roads and dams, and caused an estimated $12 million damage.

April 28, 1966: Flash flooding. Dallas County. Flash flooding from torrential rains in Dallas County resulted in 14 persons drowned and property losses at $15 million.

Sept. 18–23, 1967: Hurricane Beulah. Near **Brownsville.** The **third largest hurricane of record,** Hurricane Beulah moved inland near the mouth of the Rio Grande on the 20th. Wind gusts of 136 mph were reported during Beulah's passage. Rains 10 to 20 inches over much of the area **south of San Antonio** resulted in record-breaking floods. An unofficial gaging station at **Falfurrias** registered the highest accumulated rainfall, 36 inches. The resultant stream overflow and surface runoff inundated 1.4 million acres. Beulah spawned 115 tornadoes, all in Texas, the **greatest number of tornadoes on record for any hurricane.** Hurricane Beulah caused 13 deaths and 37 injuries, of which five deaths and 34 injuries were attributed to tornadoes. Property losses were estimated at $100 million and crop losses at $50 million.

April 18, 1970: Tornado. Near **Clarendon,** Donley County. Seventeen killed, 42 injured; damage $2.1 million. Fourteen persons were killed at a resort community at Green Belt Reservoir, 7 miles north of Clarendon.

May 11, 1970: Tornado. Lubbock, Lubbock County. Twenty-six killed, 500 injured; damage $135 million. Fifteen square miles, almost one-quarter of the city of Lubbock, suffered damage.

Aug. 3–5, 1970: Hurricane Celia. Corpus Christi. Hurricane Celia was a unique but severe storm. Measured in dollars, it was **the costliest in the state's history to that time.** Sustained wind speeds reached 130 mph, but it was great bursts of kinetic energy of short duration that appeared to cause the severe damage. Wind gusts of 161 mph were measured at the **Corpus Christi** National Weather Service Office. At **Aransas Pass,** peak wind gusts were estimated as high as 180 mph, after the wind equipment had been blown away. Celia caused 11 deaths in Texas, at least 466 injuries, and total property and crop damage in Texas estimated at $453.77 million. Hurricane Celia crossed the Texas coastline midway between Corpus Christi and Aransas Pass about 3:30 p.m. CST on Aug. 3. Hardest hit was the metropolitan area of **Corpus Christi,** including **Robstown, Aransas Pass, Port Aransas** and small towns on the north side of Corpus Christi Bay.

Feb. 20–22, 1971: Blizzard. Panhandle. Paralyzing blizzard, worst since March 22–25, 1957, storm transformed Panhandle into one vast snowfield as 6 to 26 inches of snow were whipped by 40 to 60 mph winds into drifts up to 12 feet high. At **Follett,** 3-day snowfall was 26 inches. Three persons killed; property and livestock losses were $3.1 million.

Sept. 9–13, 1971: Hurricane Fern. Coastal Bend. Ten to 26 inches of rain resulted in some of worst flooding since Hurricane Beulah in 1967. Two persons killed; losses were $30.2 million.

May 11–12, 1972: Rainstorm. South Central Texas. Seventeen drowned at **New Braunfels,** one at **McQueeney.** New Braunfels and **Seguin** hardest hit. Property damage $17.5 million.

June 12–13, 1973: Rainstorm. Southeastern Texas. Ten drowned. Over $50 million in property and crop damage. From 10-15 inches of rain recorded.

Nov. 23–24, 1974: Flash Flooding. Central Texas. Over $1 million in property damage. Thirteen people killed, 10 in **Travis County.**

Jan. 31–Feb. 1, 1975: Flooding. Nacogdoches County. Widespread heavy rain caused flash flooding here, resulting in three deaths; damage over $5.5 million.

May 23, 1975: Rainstorm. Austin area. Heavy rains, high winds and hail resulted in over $5 million property damage; 40 people injured. Four deaths caused by drowning.

April 19, 1976: Tornado. Brownwood. An F-5 tornado destroyed a few homes and airplanes. Nine persons were injured.

June 15, 1976: Rainstorm. Harris County. Rains in excess of 13 inches caused damage estimated at near $25 million. Eight deaths were storm-related, including three drownings.

Aug. 1–4, 1978: Heavy Rains, Flooding. Edwards Plateau, Low Rolling Plains. Remnants of **Tropical Storm Amelia** caused some of the worst flooding of this century. As much as 30 inches of rain fell near **Albany** in Shackelford County, where six drownings were reported. In **Bandera, Kerr, Kendall and Gillespie counties,** 27 people drowned and the damage total was at least $50 million.

Dec. 30–31, 1978: Ice Storm. North Central Texas. Possibly the **worst ice storm in 30 years** that hit Dallas County particularly hard. Damage estimates reached $14 million, and six deaths were storm-related.

April 10, 1979: The worst single tornado in Texas' history hit Wichita Falls. Earlier on the same day, **several tornadoes** hit farther west. The destruction in Wichita Falls resulted in 42 dead, 1,740 injured, over 3,000 homes destroyed and damage of approximately $400 million. An estimated 20,000 persons were left homeless by this storm. In all, the tornadoes on April 10 killed 53 people, injured 1,812 and caused over $500 million damages.

May 3, 1979: Thunderstorms. Dallas County was hit by a wave of the most destructive thunderstorms in many years; 37 injuries and $5 million in damages resulted.

July 25–26, 1979: Tropical storm Claudette caused over $750 million in property and crop damages, but fortunately only few injuries. Near **Alvin,** an estimated 43 inches of rain fell, a new state record for 24 hours.

Aug. 24, 1979: One of the worst **hailstorms** in **West Texas** in the past 100 years; $200 million in crops, mostly cotton, destroyed.

Sept. 18–20, 1979: Coastal flooding from heavy rain,

18 inches in 24 hours at **Aransas Pass**, and 13 inches at **Rockport**.

Aug. 9–11, 1980: Hurricane Allen hit **South Texas** and left three dead, causing $650 million to $750 million in property and crop damages. Over 250,000 coastal residents had to be evacuated. The worst damage occurred along **Padre Island** and in **Corpus Christi**. Over 20 inches of rain fell in **extreme South Texas**, and 29 tornadoes occurred; one of the worst hurricane-related outbreaks.

Summer 1980: One of the hottest summers in the history of the Lone Star State.

Sept. 5–8, 1980: Hurricane Danielle brought rain and flooding to Southeast and Central Texas. Seventeen inches of rain fell at **Port Arthur**, and 25 inches near **Junction**.

May 24–25, 1981: Severe flooding in Austin claimed 13 lives, injured about 100 and caused $40 million in damage. Up to 5.5 inches of rain fell in one hour west of the city.

Oct. 11–14, 1981: Record rains in North Central Texas caused by the remains of **Pacific Hurricane Norma**. Over 20 inches fell in some locations.

April 2, 1982: A tornado outbreak in Northeast Texas. The most severe tornado struck **Paris**; 10 people were killed, 170 injured and 1,000 left homeless. Over $50 million in damages resulted. A total of seven tornadoes that day left 11 dead and 174 injured.

May, 1982: Texas recorded **123 tornadoes**, the most ever in May, and one less than the most recorded in any single month in the state. One death and 23 injuries occurred.

Dec. 1982: Heavy snow. El Paso recorded 18.2 inches of snow, the most in any month there.

Aug. 15–21, 1983: Hurricane Alicia was the first hurricane to make landfall in the continental U.S. in three years (Aug. 18), and **one of the costliest in Texas history** ($3 billion). Alicia caused widespread damage to a large section of **Southeast Texas**, including coastal areas near **Galveston** and the entire **Houston** area. Alicia spawned 22 tornadoes, and highest winds were estimated near 130 mph. In all, 18 people were killed and 1,800 injured as a result of the tropical storm.

Jan. 12–13, 1985: A record-breaking snowstorm struck **West and South Central Texas** with up to 15 inches of snow that fell at many locations **between San Antonio and the Rio Grande**. San Antonio recorded 13.2 inches of snow for Jan. 12 (the greatest in a day) and 13.5 inches for the two-day total. **Eagle Pass** reported 14.5 inches of snow.

June 26, 1986: Hurricane Bonnie made landfall between **High Island and Sabine Pass** around 3:45 a.m. The highest wind measured in the area was a gust of 97 m.p.h., which was recorded at the **Sea Rim State Park**. As much as 13 inches of rain fell in **Ace** in southern Polk County. There were several reports of funnel clouds, but no confirmed tornadoes. While the storm caused no major structural damage, there was widespread minor damage. Numerous injuries were reported.

May 22, 1987: A strong, **multiple-vortex tornado** struck the town of **Saragosa**, Reeves County. Of the town's 183 inhabitants, 30 were killed and 121 were injured. Eighty-five percent of the town's structures were destroyed, while total damage topped $1.3 million.

Oct. 15–19, 1994: Extreme amounts of rainfall, up to 28.90 inches over a 4-day period, fell throughout southeastern part of the state. Seventeen lives were lost, most of them victims of flash flooding. Many rivers reached record flood levels. **Houston** was cut off from many other parts of the state, as numerous roads, including Interstate 10, were under water. Damage was estimated to be near $700 million; 26 counties were declared disaster areas.

May 5, 1995: A thunderstorm moved across the **Dallas/Fort Worth** area with 70 mph wind gusts and rainfall rates of almost three inches in 30 minutes (five inches in one hour). Twenty people lost their lives as a result of this storm, 109 people were injured by large hail and, with more than $2 billion in damage, NOAA dubbed it the **"costliest thunderstorm event in history."**

May 28, 1995: A **supercell thunderstorm** produced extreme winds and giant hail in **San Angelo**, injuring at least 80 people and causing about $120 million in damage. Sixty-one homes were destroyed, and more than 9,000 were slightly

damaged. In some areas, hail was six inches deep, with drifts to two feet.

Feb. 21, 1996: Anomalously **high temperatures** were reported over the **entire state**, breaking records in nearly every region of the state. Temperatures near 100°F shattered previous records by as many as 10°F as Texans experienced heat more characteristic of mid-summer than winter.

May 10, 1996: Hail up to five inches in diameter fell in **Howard County**, causing injuries to 48 people and $30 million worth of property damage.

May 27, 1997: Tornado. Jarrell. A half-mile-wide F-5 tornado struck Jarrell, Williamson County, leveling the Double Creek subdisivion, claiming 27 lives, injuring 12 others, and causing more than $40 million in damage.

March–May, 1998: According to the Climate Prediction Center, this three-month period ranks as the **seventh driest** for a region including Texas, Oklahoma, Arkansas, Louisiana and Mississippi. May 1998 has been ranked as both the **warmest and the driest May** in this region.

Aug. 22–25, 1998: Tropical Storm Charley brought torrential rains and flash floods to the **Hill Country**. Thirteen people lost their lives and more than 200 were injured.

Oct. 17–19, 1998: Rainstorm. Hill Country. A massive, devastating flood set all-time records for rainfall and river levels, resulted in the deaths of 25 people, injured more than 2,000 others, and caused more than $500 million damage from the Hill Country to the counties **south and east of San Antonio**.

Jan. 22, 1999: Hail. Brazos County. Golf ball- and softball-sized **hail** fell in the **Bryan-College Station** area, resulting in $10 million in damage to cars, homes and offices.

May 1999: Storms, Tornadoes. East, Central, West Texas. Numerous severe weather outbreaks caused **damaging winds, large hail, dangerous lightning, and numerous tornadoes**. An F-3 tornado moved through downtown area and high school of **De Kalb**, Bowie County, on the 4th, injuring 22 people and causing $125 million in damage to the community. On the same day, **two F-2 tornadoes** roared through **Kilgore** simultaneously. On the 11th, an **F-4** tornado moved through parts of **Loyal Valley**, Mason County, and **Castell**, Llano County, taking the life of one and injuring six. The 25th saw storms produce **2.5-inch hail** in **Levelland** and **Amarillo**. The total cost of damages caused by May storms was more than $157 million.

August 1999: Excessive heat throughout the month resulted in 16 fatalities in the **Dallas/Fort Worth** area. The airport reported 26 consecutive days of 100°F or greater temperatures.

January–October 2000: Drought. A **severe drought** plagued **most of Texas**. Some regions experienced little to no rain for several months during the summer. **Abilene** saw no rain for **72 consecutive days,** while **Dallas** had **no rain for 84 consecutive days** during the summer. During July, aquifers hit all-time lows, and lakes and streams fell to critical levels. Most regions had to cut back or stop agricultural activities because of the drought, which resulted in $515 million in agricultural loss, according to USDA figures.

March 28, 2000: Tornado. Fort Worth. A supercell over Fort Worth produced an F-3 tornado, which injured 80 people and caused significant damage. Flooding claimed the lives of two people.

May 20, 2000: Rainstorm. Southeast Texas. A flash flood in the **Liberty** and **Dayton** area was caused by 18.3 inches of rain's falling in five hours. Up to 80 people had to be rescued from the flood waters; property damage totalled an estimated $10 million.

July 2000: Excessive heat resulted from a high-pressure ridge, particularly from the 12th to the 21st. **Dallas/Fort Worth** airport reported a **10-day average of 103.3°F**. College Station had **12 consecutive days of 100°F or greater** temperatures. The heat caused 34 deaths in North and Southeast Texas, primarily among the elderly.

Aug. 2, 2000: Storm. Houston. Lightning struck a tree at Astroworld in Houston injuring 17 teens.

Sept. 5, 2000: Excessive heat resulted in at least eight **all-time high temperature** records around the state, one of which was **Possum Kingdom Lake**, which reached 114°F. This day is being regarded as the **hottest day ever in Texas,**

considering the state as a whole.

Dec. 13 and 24-25, 2000: Ice/Snow. Two major winter storms blanketed **Northeast Texas** with up to six inches of ice from each storm. Eight inches of snow fell in the **Panhandle**, while areas in North Texas received 12 inches. Thousands of motorists were stranded on Interstate 20 and had to be rescued by the National Guard; 235,000 people lost electric service from the first storm alone. Roads were treacherous, driving was halted in several counties, and the total cost of damages from both storms reached more than $156 million.

Jan. 1–31, 2001: Drought. South Texas. The U.S. Department of Agriculture Farm Service Agency received a **Presidential Disaster Declaration** in December 2000 because of **persistent drought** conditions in **South Texas;** $125 million in damage was reported in the region.

May 2001: Storms. San Antonio, High Plains. Numerous storms causing excessive damage. **Four-inch hail** caused nearly $150 million in damages in **San Antonio** on the 6th. On the 30th, supercell **thunderstorms** in the **High Plains** region produced winds over 100 mph and golf-ball-sized hail caused more than $186 million in damage. All told, storms caused 36 injuries and more than $358 million in damage to property and agriculture.

June–December 2001: Drought. Significant drought-like conditions occurred in Texas from early summer through December. After the yearly drought report was filed, it was determined that the total crop damage across the South Plains region was about $420 million. Consequential losses occurred to crops such as cotton, wheat, grain sorghum and corn.

June 5–10, 2001: Tropical Storm Allison hit the **Houston** area, which dumped large amounts of rain on the city. The storm made landfall on the western end of **Galveston Island** and over the next five days produced record rainfall. These amazing amounts of precipitation led to devastating flooding across southeastern Texas. Some weather stations in the Houston area reported more than 40 inches of rain total and more than 18 inches in a 24-hour period. Twenty-two deaths and $5.2 billion in damage resulted.

July–August 2001: Excessive heat plagued Texas during July and August, which resulted in 17 deaths in the Houston area.

Oct. 12, 2001: Tornado. Hondo. An F2 tornado caused $20 million in damage. The tornado injured 25 people and damaged the National Guard Armory and a large hangar at the Hondo Airport, as well as nearly two dozen aircraft. Some 150 homes in Hondo and 50 on its outskirts were damaged, and nearly 100 mobile homes were damaged.

Nov. 15, 2001: Rainstorms. Central Texas. Storms caused **flash flooding** and some weak **tornadoes** in the Edwards Plateau, South Central and southern portions of North Central regions. Flash flooding caused 8 deaths and 198 injuries.

March 2002: Storms. Central Texas. Several **violent storms** occurred, which produced hail, tornadoes and strong winds. Hail 1-3/4 inches in diameter caused $16 million in damage to **San Angelo** on the 19th, while 30 people where injured on the same day by an **F2 tornado** in **Somerset**, Bexar County, that also caused $2 million in damage. For the month, there were three fatalities, 64 injuries and more than $37.5 million in damage.

June 30–July 7, 2002: Rainstorm. Central Texas. Excessive rainfall occurred in the **South Central** and **Edwards Plateau** regions, with some areas reporting more than 30 inches of rain. In the South Central region alone nearly $250 million dollars worth of damage was reported from this significant weather event. In Central Texas, 29 counties were devastated by the flooding and declared federal disaster areas by President George W. Bush. The total event damage was estimated at more than $2 billion.

Sept. 5–7, 2002: Tropical Storm Fay. Coastal Plains. The storm made landfall along the coast on the 6th. This system produced extremely heavy rainfall, strong damaging wind gusts and tornadoes. Ten to 20 inches of rain fell in eastern **Wharton County. Brazoria County** was hit the hardest from this system with about 1,500 homes flooded. Tropical Storm Fay produced five tornadoes, flooded many

areas and caused significant wind damage. Damage of $4.5 million was reported.

Oct. 24, 2002: Raintorms. South Texas. Severe thunderstorms in South Texas produced heavy rain, causing flooding and two tornadoes in **Corpus Christi**. The most extensive damage occurred across **Del Mar College**. The storm caused one death, 26 injuries and total damages exceeded more then $85 million in damage.

Feb. 24–26, 2003: Snow/Ice. North Central Texas. A severe cold front brought **freezing rain, sleet** and **snow** to the **North Central Texas**. Snow accumulations were as high as **5 inches** resulting in $15 million in damages. Most schools and businesses were closed for this period.

April 8, 2003: Rainstorm. Brownsville. A severe thunderstorm caused one of the **most destructive hail events in the history of Brownsville.** Hail exceeded 2.75 inches in diameter and caused $50 million in damages to the city. At least 5 injuries were reported.

July 14–16, 2003: Hurricane Claudette. Port O'Connor. The hurricane made landfall near Port O'Connor in the late morning hours of the 14th. At landfall, wind speeds were more than 90 mph. The system, which moved westward toward Big Bend and northern Mexico, caused 1 death and 2 injuries, and total damages were estimated at more than $100 million.

Sept. 2003: Floods. Upper Coast, South Texas. Persistent flooding during the month caused more than $2 million in damages. The remnants of **Tropical Storm Grace** caused flash flooding along the Upper Coast region near **Galveston** early in September, with rainfall estimates in Matagorda County ranging from 6 to 12 inches. During the second half of the month, **South Texas** was hit with a **deluge of rain caused by a tropical wave** combined with approaching cold fronts, and monthly rainfall totals ranged from 7 to 15 inches throughout the deep south.

June 1–9, 2004: Floods. North Central Texas. Flash flooding due to an upper air disturbance and associated cold front caused damage to more than 1,000 homes through **North Central Texas.** This was the first of many days in which heavy rains fell throughout the state. Estimated damages were more $7.5 million.

June 21, 2004: Tornadoes. Panhandle. Severe weather kicked up just ahead of a frontal boundary causing damage to **Amarillo** and the surrounding area. Eight tornadoes were reported around the Panhandle, and there were many reports of hail, topping out at 4.25 inches in diameter in Potter County. Thousands of homes were damaged, and the total damage was estimated at more than $150 million.

July 28–29, 2004: Rainstorm. North Central Texas. A stationary front lead to torrential rainfall in **Dallas and Waco**. Hundreds of homes were damaged by flash flooding, as 24-hour rainfall totals for the two cities approached 5 inches. Outlying areas of the cities reported as much as 7 inches of rain in a 12-hour period on the 29th. Damage estimates topped $20 million.

Sept. 14, 2004: Storm. Grapeland. A lightning strike during football practice at Grapeland High School, Houston County, caused one death and injuries to 40 players and coaches.

Dec. 24–26, 2004: Snow. Coastal Texas. Large portions of Southeast and South Texas saw their **first white Christmas in recorded history**. A cold front past over the state a few days prior to Christmas Eve dropping temperatures below freezing. Another cold front brought snow, and it accumulated Christmas Eve night and into Christmas day. Galveston and Houston recorded 4 inches of snow, while areas even further south, such as **Victoria, had 12 inches. Brownsville recorded 1.5 inches of snow.**

March 25, 2005: Hail. Austin. In the evening of March 25, the **most destructive hailstorm in 10 years** struck the greater Austin area. The storm knocked out power to 5,000 homes in northwest Austin. Hail of 2 inches in diameter was reported near the Travis County Exposition Center. Total damage was estimated at $100 million.

May 2005–December 2006: Drought. In May, portions of North Central Texas were upgraded from moderate to **severe drought.** By the end of the May, the drought had made significant agricultural and hydrological impacts on

Firefighters on Second Street in Roma patrol a neighborhood by boat after Hurricane Alex flooded communities in Starr County in July 2010. Photo by Daniel Llargues; FEMA.

the region. In November, many Central Texas counties were added to the drought. The Texas Cooperative Extension estimated statewide drought losses at $4.1 billion, $1.9 billion in North Texas alone.

June 9, 2005: Tornado. Petersburg. An **F-3 tornado** affected the Petersburg area in southeast Hale County across to portions of southwest and south-central Floyd County. Total damage was estimated at $70 million.

Sept. 23, 2005: Hurrican Rita. Southeast Texas. The eye of **Hurricane Rita** moved ashore in extreme southwest Louisiana between Sabine Pass and Johnson's Bayou in Cameron Parish with maximum sustained winds of 120 mph, category-3 strength. On Sept. 22, Rita had strengthened to a peak intensity of 175 mph winds. In Southeast Texas, Rita resulted in 3 fatalities, 3 injuries, and $159.5 million in property and crop damage. Property damage was estimated at $2.1 billion.

Dec. 27, 2005: **Wildfire. Cross Plains.** A wildfire in Callahan County caused $11 million in property damages. The fire started just west of Cross Plains and quickly moved east, fanned by winds gusting near 40 mph. The fire moved into Cross Plains quickly and two elderly people were unable to escape the flames; 16 firefighters were also injured while fighting this fire.

Jan. 1, 2006: Wildfires. North Texas. Several wildfires exploded across North Texas due to low humidity, strong winds and the ongoing drought. Fires were reported in Montague, Eastland and Palo Pinto counties. Five injuries were reported as well as $10.8 million in property damage.

March 12–18, 2006: Wildfires. Borger. A wildfire now known as the **Borger wildfire** start four miles southwest of Borger, Hutchinson County. The wildfire burned a total of 479,500 acres. In all, seven people were killed and 28 structures were lost with total property damage at $49.9 million and crop damage at $45.4 million. A second wildfire known as the **Interstate-40 wildfire** burned 427,696 acres. The Texas Forest Service named the two wildfires the East Amarillo Complex. In all, 12 people were killed, total property damage was $49.9 million and crop damage was $45.4 million.

March 19, 2006: Tornado. Uvalde. An **F-2 tornado** moved through the Uvalde area causing $1.5 million in property damage. It was the strongest tornado in South Central Texas since Oct. 12, 2001.

April 11–13, 2006: Wildfire. Canadian. A wildfire 10 miles north of Canadian, Hemphill County, burned 18,000 acres and destroyed crops. Two injuries were reported. Total crop damage was estimated at $90 million.

April 18, 2006: Hail. Gillespie County. Hailstones as large as 2.5 inches in diameter destroyed windows in homes and car windshields between Harper and Doss in Gillespie County. The hail also damaged 70 percent of the area peach crop, an estimated loss of $5 million.

April 20, 2006: Hail. San Marcos. Hailstones as large at 4.25 inches in diameter (grapefruit-size) was reported south of San Marcos. Damage from this storm was estimated at $100 million with up to 10,000 vehicles damaged and another 7,000 vehicles at homes.

May 4, 2006: Hail. Snyder. Lime-to-baseball-size **hail** fell across Snyder in Scurry County for a least 15 minutes. The hail was blown sideways at times by 60-to-70-mph winds. Total damage was estimated at $15 million.

May 5, 2006: Tornado. Waco. A **tornado** with peak intensity estimated at **low F-2**. Total damage was $3 million.

May 9, 2006: Tornado. Childress. An **F-2 tornado** resulted in significant damage along a one-and-one-half mile path through the north side of Childress during the evening hours. An instrument at Childress High School measured a wind gust of 109 mph. Property damage was estimated at $5.7 million.

Aug. 1, 2006: Thunderstorms. El Paso. Storms in a saturated atmosphere repeatedly developed and moved over mainly the northwest third of El Paso County, concentrating in an area near the Franklin Mountains. Rainfall reports varied from 4–6 inches within 15 hours, with an isolated report of about 8 inches on the western slope of the mountain range. Antecedent conditions from 4 days of heavy rains, combined with terrain effects of the mountains, led to excessive runoff and flooding not seen on such a large scale in the El Paso area in more than 100 years. Property damage was estimated at $180 million.

March 29, 2007: Floods. Corsicana. Flash flooding along Interstate 45 submerged two cars in Navarro County, north of Corsicana, and two feet of water was reported on I-45 and Texas 31, east of town. Damage to businesses, roads and bridges was estimated at $19 million.

April 13, 2007: Hail. Colleyville. Teacup-size hail was reported in Colleyville as strong storms developed in Tarrant County. Hail damage to 5,500 cars and 3,500 homes and businesses was estimated at $10 million.

April 24, 2007: Tornado. Eagle Pass. A large tornado crossed the Rio Grande from Mexico near 6 p.m., striking Rosita Valley, near Eagle Pass. Ten deaths were reported, including a family of five in a mobile home. Golf-ball size hail and the tornado struck Rosita Valley Elementary School, leaving only the interior walls standing. Damage indicated wind speeds near 140 mph and an F-3 level, with a path one-quarter mile wide and four miles long. The tornado also destroyed one 59 manufactured homes and 57 houses. Total damage was estimated at $80 million.

June 17–18, 2007: Floods. North Texas. Torrential rain fell as an upper-level low lingered for several days. In Tarrant County, one person drowned after her rescue boat capsized. Hundreds of people were rescued from high water. In Grayson County, a woman died in floodwaters as she drove under an overpass, and another death occurred in Cooke County. Three people in Cooke County died when a mobile home was carried away by floodwaters. Damage was estimated at $30 million in Tarrant County, $20 million in Grayson County and $28 million in Cooke County.

June 27, 2007: Floods. Marble Falls. Two lines of thunderstorms produced 10–19 inches of rain in southern Burnet County. Hardest hit was Marble Falls, where two young men died in the early morning when their jeep was swept into high water east of town. Damage to more than 315 homes and businesses was $130 million.

Sept. 13, 2007: Hurricane. Jefferson County. Hurricane Humberto made landfall around 1 a.m. in rural southwestern Jefferson County near McFaddin National Wildlife Refuge. Minimum pressure was around 985 millibars, with maximum winds at 90 mph. Some flash flooding occurred in urban areas between Beaumont and Orange, as 11 inches of rain fell in Jefferson County. Coastal storm tides were 3–5 feet, with the highest storm surge occurring at Texas Point. Humberto caused one death, 12 injuries and $25 million in damage.

March 31, 2008: Hail. Northeast Texas. Severe thunderstorms developed across the Red River valley of northeast Texas, many producing large hail that damaged car windows, skylights and roofs in Texarkana and elsewhere in Bowie County. Damage was estimated at $120 million.

April 10, 2008: Tornadoes. Johnson County. A lone supercell thunderstorm evolved in the afternoon on April 9, producing tornadoes and large hail. A tornado touched down near Happy Hill and traveled northeast 3 miles to Pleasant Point, where it dissipated. The F-1 tornado, with maximum wind speeds of 90–95 mph, destroyed three homes and damaged more than 30 homes and other buildings. Damage was $25 million.

May 14, 2008: Hail. Austin. A severe thunderstorm southwest of Austin moved northeast across downtown Austin causing extensive damage from winds and large hail. Large trees and branches were knocked down, and baseball-size hail and 70–80 mph winds blew out windows in apartments and office buildings, including the State Capitol. Total damage was estimated at $50 million.

August 18, 2008: Floods. Wichita Falls. An unseasonably strong upper-level storm system moved over North Texas, and several waves of heavy thunderstorms caused high precipitation and widespread flooding in the Iowa Park, Burkburnett and Wichita Falls areas. In Wichita Falls, many homes were flooded and residents were evacuated by boat. At least 118 homes were flooded, 19 of which were destroyed. Burkburnett and Iowa Park were isolated for a few hours because of street flooding. Damage was estimated at $25 million, and Gov. Rick Perry declared Wichita County a disaster area.

Sept. 12, 2008: Hurricane. Galveston. The eye of **Hurricane Ike** moved ashore near the city of Galveston. The central pressure was 951.6 millibars, with maximum sustained winds around 110 mph, which made Hurricane Ike a strong Category-2 storm. There were 12 deaths directly related to Ike, with 11 occurring in Galveston County from drowning due to storm surge. There were at least another 25 fatalities indirectly related to Ike, either due to carbon monoxide poisoning from generators, accidents while clearing debris, or house fires from candles. The majority of property damage at the coast was a result of storm tide. Damage was typical of a Category-3 or -4 storm, and collectively, damage amounts were near $14 billion in the counties of Harris, Chambers, Galveston, Liberty, Polk, Matagorda, Brazoria, Fort Bend, San Jacinto, and Montgomery, with an estimated $8 billion of that due to storm surge in coastal Galveston, Harris, and Chambers counties.

Jan. 19, 2009: Wildfire. Hidalgo County. With the aid of strong gusts, low humidity, a lack of rain, and warm temperatures, a wildfire spread across Hidalgo County and consumed four buildings at the Moore Air Force Base. By the time the wildfire had been contained, it had spread to 2,560 acres, and the damage at the air force base was estimated at $10 million.

March 30, 2009: Hail. Northeast Tarrant County. Ping-pong- to baseball-size hail fell on numerous cities in northeast Tarrant County due to a strong line of severe storms. Much of the damage was to automobiles, and the overall estimated damage was $95 million.

April 11, 2009: Hail. Midland. Up to golf-ball-size hail caused tremendous damage to homes and vehicles during a severe storm. There was an estimated $160 million in roof repair. A woman was pelted in the stomach by a hailstone that broke through the window in her dining room.

May 2, 2009: Thunderstorm Wind. Irving. The National Weather Service determined that a microburst caused the Dallas Cowboys' bubble practice facility to collapse from winds estimated at 70 mph. Twelve people were injured, including one coach who was paralyzed from the waist down. The damage was estimated at $5 million.

June 11, 2009: Thunderstorm Wind. Burnet. A peak wind of 67 mph was measured at the Burnet Airport and numerous planes were flipped or blown across the tarmac. Damage in the entire city was estimated at $5 million.

Sept. 16, 2009: Hail. El Paso. A series of supercell storms produced golf-ball-size and possibly tennis-ball-size hail that caused extensive damage. The most costly hailstorm in recorded history for the El Paso area, the estimated damage was $150 million.

Dec. 23, 2009: Tornado. Lufkin. An EF3 tornado touched down in Lufkin and caused extensive damage to structures, homes, and vehicles as it tore through the city. The twister and heavy rains caused damage estimated at $10 million.

June 9, 2010: Flash Flood. New Braunfels. Storms produced rains in excess of 11 inches, which caused the Guadalupe River to rise over 20 feet in just two hours. Campers, vehicles, boats, homes, and businesses suffered extensive damages along the riverbanks. This flash flood resulted in one death and over $10 million in damage.

July 2, 2010: Tornado. Hebbronville. An EF1 tornado that developed along the residual shear left behind from Hurricane Alex caused considerable damage in Hebbronville. Over half of the town's population lost power. and the tornado was reported to be as wide as a football field. The estimated damage was $1.5 million.

July 4, 2010: Flood. Terry, Lubbock, Garza, and Lynn Counties. A series of thunderstorms erupted in the early morning of the Fourth of July over the west South Texas Plains. Local flooding caused numerous roadway closures and damage to over 100 vehicles. While there were no injuries, local officials estimated that over 300 homes and businesses were affected and the economic losses were around $16.5 million.

July 8, 2010: Flood. Starr County. Another storm that formed in the aftermath of Hurricane Alex, this system dumped an estimated 50 inches or more of rain on the lower Rio Grande Valley over 10 days leading up to July 8. Falcon Reservoir rose during days of rain and finally spilled over on the 8th. The Rio Grande was nearly 2 miles wide at some points. The estimated cost was around $37 million.

Oct. 24, 2010: Tornado. Rice, Navarro County. An intense EF2 tornado struck the town of Rice with maximum winds of 135 mph. Vehicles were overturned on Interstate 45 and 11 train cars were derailed when the tornado hit the railroad tracks. The football, baseball, and softball fields of the local high school were damaged. and the intermediate school lost the gymnasium roof and suffered a caved in wall. The economic loss was estimated at $1 million. ☆

Texas Temperature, Freeze, Growing Season and Precipitation Records by County

Data in the table below are from the office of the Texas State Climatologist, Texas A&M University, College Station. Because of the small change in averages, data are revised only at intervals of 10 years. Data below are the latest compilations, as of Feb. 1, 2004, and reflect data compiled during 1971–2000. The table shows temperature, freeze, growing season and precipitation for each county in Texas. Data for counties where a National Weather Service Station has not been maintained long enough to establish a reliable mean are interpolated from isoline charts prepared from mean values from stations with long-established records. Mean maximum temperature for July is computed from the sum of the daily maxima. Mean minimum January is computed from the sum of the daily minima. Weather stations shown in italics do not measure all categories and some data are from the period 1961–1990. An asterisk (*) preceding a record high or low or rainfall extreme denotes a figure that also occurred on an earlier date.

COUNTY AND STATION	July Mean Max. (F.)	January Mean Min. (F.)	Record Highest (F.)	Year	Record Lowest (F.)	Year	Last in Spring	First in Fall	Growing Season (Days)	Jan.	Feb.	Mar.	Apr.	May	June	July	Aug.	Sept.	Oct.	Nov.	Dec.	Annual	Highest Daily Rainfall (In.)	Mo.-Year
Anderson, Palestine	93.9	37.4	114	1954	-4	1930	Mar. 15	Nov. 18	247	3.60	3.34	3.87	3.80	4.51	4.53	2.55	3.23	3.45	4.90	4.44	4.16	46.38	9.10	08-1991
Andrews, Andrews	94.5	30.4	113	1994	-1	1985	Mar. 29	Nov. 10	226	0.48	0.51	0.52	0.85	1.78	2.12	2.25	1.77	2.21	1.43	0.64	0.59	15.15	7.60	07-1914
Angelina, Lufkin	93.5	37.9	*110	2000	-2	1951	Mar. 13	Nov. 15	247	4.45	3.17	3.53	3.13	5.29	4.18	2.60	3.08	4.08	4.13	4.54	4.44	46.62	7.47	10-1994
Aransas, Rockport	90.1	44.9	105	2000	12	1983	Feb. 2	Dec. 20	318	2.40	2.18	2.36	2.07	3.66	3.50	2.43	3.13	5.53	4.23	2.56	1.91	35.96	8.15	09-1979
Archer, Archer City	97.0	26.7	114	1980	*-10	1989	Mar. 28	Nov. 9	225	1.13	1.75	2.05	2.46	4.33	3.46	1.79	2.66	3.11	3.39	1.90	1.75	29.78	7.95	10-1981
Armstrong, Claude	90.5	21.2	*108	1980	-16	1905	Apr. 19	Oct. 20	184	0.51	0.58	1.23	1.60	3.34	3.33	3.08	3.00	2.37	1.91	0.82	0.62	22.39	10.27	05-1982
Atascosa, Poteet	95.9	39.0	*110	2000	0	1949	Feb. 25	Dec. 2	279	1.27	1.83	1.54	2.50	4.09	4.06	1.64	2.69	2.90	3.04	1.79	1.65	29.00	8.75	07-1949
Austin, Sealy	94.9	40.7	111	2000	0	1989	Feb. 18	Dec. 8	291	3.14	2.81	2.61	3.22	4.71	3.85	1.93	3.06	4.33	4.44	3.68	2.90	40.68	11.00	08-1945
Bailey, Muleshoe	91.9	20.2	*110	1944	-21	1933	Apr. 17	Oct. 21	186	0.43	0.50	0.64	1.01	2.04	2.49	2.09	3.07	2.34	1.50	0.67	0.59	17.37	5.25	05-1951
Bandera, Medina	93.9	33.3	109	1980	5	1989	Mar. 22	Nov. 10	233	1.72	1.91	2.27	2.69	4.35	4.29	2.55	3.08	3.66	4.14	2.84	2.28	35.78	9.86	08-1971
Bastrop, Smithville	95.4	36.7	*111	2000	-14	1930	Mar. 4	Nov. 20	260	2.73	2.32	2.56	3.00	5.12	3.66	2.01	2.25	3.56	4.70	3.29	2.84	38.04	16.05	06-1940
Baylor, Seymour	96.5	27.7	120	1936	-14	1947	Mar. 30	Nov. 6	220	1.05	1.56	1.90	1.84	4.13	3.63	1.86	2.58	3.51	2.86	1.48	1.41	27.79	6.20	05-1989
Bee, Beeville	94.6	43.1	111	1939	8	1983	Feb. 14	Dec. 6	294	1.94	1.84	1.90	2.68	3.49	4.19	2.69	3.02	4.30	3.60	2.00	1.83	33.48	10.61	09-1967
Bell, Temple	95.0	34.9	112	1947	*-4	1949	Mar. 3	Nov. 22	264	1.91	2.70	2.65	2.81	4.56	3.71	1.82	2.20	4.00	3.73	2.58	2.68	35.81	9.62	10-1998
Bexar, San Antonio	94.6	38.6	111	2000	-6	1949	Feb. 28	Nov. 25	270	1.66	1.75	1.89	2.60	4.72	4.30	2.03	2.57	3.00	3.86	2.66	1.96	32.92	11.26	10-1998
Blanco, Blanco	93.7	34.0	*110	2000	-6	1949	Mar. 20	Nov. 11	235	1.79	2.08	2.69	2.69	4.51	4.18	2.02	2.38	3.26	4.18	2.37	2.37	34.75	17.47	09-1952
Borden, Gail	94.6	29.8	116	1994	-1	1989	Mar. 27	Nov. 8	226	0.58	0.73	0.66	1.20	2.80	2.81	2.35	2.52	2.83	1.77	0.74	0.59	19.68	9.13	10-1960
Bosque, Lake Whitney	96.2	32.7	113	2000	*-3	1989	Mar. 15	Nov. 17	247	1.93	2.39	2.87	3.18	4.29	3.96	2.03	2.37	2.76	3.95	2.67	2.67	35.07	6.22	10-1971
Bowie, Texarkana	93.1	30.7	108	2000	*-6	1989	Mar. 20	Nov. 14	238	3.91	3.80	4.46	4.23	4.97	4.82	3.62	2.41	3.77	4.61	5.69	4.95	51.24	5.45	03-1989
Brazoria, Angleton	91.8	43.7	107	2000	*7	1989	Feb. 15	Dec. 5	290	4.76	3.50	3.76	3.74	5.20	6.44	4.24	4.83	7.49	4.25	4.86	4.17	57.24	14.36	07-1979
Brazos, College Station	95.6	39.8	112	2000	2	1989	Mar. 2	Nov. 29	271	3.32	2.38	3.20	3.20	5.05	3.79	1.92	2.92	3.91	4.22	3.18	3.23	39.67	6.23	09-1983
Brewster, Alpine	88.7	31.3	107	1972	-3	1983	Apr. 8	Nov. 1	207	0.45	0.50	0.34	0.58	1.25	2.18	2.63	2.92	3.23	1.58	0.45	0.67	17.19	3.13	06-1968
Brewster, Chisos Basin	84.2	36.1	103	1972	-9	1949	Mar. 16	Nov. 17	246	0.55	0.69	0.36	0.61	1.60	2.42	3.55	2.76	2.71	1.72	0.66	0.58	19.17	4.29	10-1966
Briscoe, Silverton	90.9	21.6	*109	1994	-9	1963	Apr. 14	Oct. 22	190	0.57	0.78	1.17	1.59	3.22	3.96	2.30	2.76	2.67	1.68	0.90	0.74	22.34	5.25	06-1979
Brooks, Falfurrias	97.0	43.9	115	1998	9	1962	Feb. 6	Dec. 13	311	1.12	1.56	0.86	1.48	2.95	3.25	1.84	2.91	3.84	3.22	1.31	1.08	25.42	10.00	09-1967
Brown, Brownwood	95.0	29.6	111	1964	-6	1989	Mar. 25	Nov. 11	231	1.28	2.09	2.07	2.45	3.62	3.75	1.80	2.28	2.67	3.01	1.62	1.68	28.32	*6.60	06-2000

COUNTY AND STATION	TEMPERATURE						AVERAGE FREEZE DATES		Growing Season	MEAN PRECIPITATION													EXTREMES	
	Mean Max. July (F.)	Mean Min. January (F.)	Record Highest (F.)	Year	Record Lowest (F.)	Year	Last in Spring (Mo. Day)	First in Fall (Mo. Day)	Days	January (In.)	February (In.)	March (In.)	April (In.)	May (In.)	June (In.)	July (In.)	August (In.)	September (In.)	October (In.)	November (In.)	December (In.)	Annual (In.)	Highest Daily Rainfall (In.)	Mo.-Year
Burleson, Somerville	96.7	36.4	114	2000	3	1989	Mar. 3	Nov. 23	264	2.93	2.53	2.62	2.92	4.39	4.21	1.78	2.43	3.59	4.33	3.63	3.14	38.50	15.25	10-1994
Burnet, Burnet	93.6	33.3	*114	1917	*-4	1989	Mar. 20	Nov. 12	237	1.61	2.16	2.33	2.48	4.58	4.09	2.04	2.06	3.15	3.46	2.32	2.15	32.43	9.80	09-1936
Caldwell, Luling	95.8	36.9	*110	2000	-3	1949	Mar. 7	Nov. 20	258	2.27	2.20	2.22	3.06	5.44	4.29	1.70	2.32	3.70	4.36	3.00	2.30	36.86	10.53	10-1998
Calhoun, Port O'Connor	88.2	47.9	105	2000	10	1989	Jan. 29	Dec. 31	338	3.07	2.20	1.73	1.55	3.70	2.77	3.05	2.94	4.97	4.45	2.53	1.82	34.78	12.50	07-1976
Callahan, Putnam	94.9	31.1	110	1964	*15	1901	Mar. 13	Nov. 13	234	1.17	1.55	1.76	1.80	3.13	3.25	1.77	2.99	2.79	3.03	1.64	1.41	25.52	5.00	08-1978
Cameron, Brownsville	92.4	50.5	106	1984	15	1951	Dec. 25	Jan. 24	>365	1.36	1.18	0.93	1.96	2.48	2.93	1.77	2.10	5.31	3.78	1.75	1.11	27.55	12.09	09-1967
Camp, Pittsburg	94.0	32.0	109		-3		Mar. 21	Nov. 14	238	3.30	3.40	4.40	3.70	4.60	3.90	3.30	2.10	3.30	4.40	4.80	3.90	45.10		
Carson, Panhandle	90.8	19.3	109	1964	*-10	1963	Apr. 18	Oct. 22	186	0.62	0.73	1.43	1.80	3.10	3.54	2.67	2.78	2.21	1.71	0.98	0.64	22.21	8.05	05-1951
Cass, Wright Patman Dam	94.0	31.0	103		8		Mar. 19	Nov. 11	237	3.70	3.60	4.40	4.00	4.50	4.50	3.30	2.60	3.50	4.30	5.30	4.80	48.20		
Castro, Dimmitt	90.1	20.4	111	1983	-9	1986	Apr. 25	Oct. 16	172	0.50	0.51	0.81	0.99	2.76	3.12	2.40	3.06	2.57	1.58	0.71	0.70	19.71	4.38	10-1998
Chambers, Anahuac	91.9	41.7	110	1943	8	1989	Feb. 12	Dec. 9	299	4.84	2.83	3.33	3.56	5.22	5.88	4.59	4.74	6.42	4.06	4.31	4.30	54.08	15.87	08-1945
Cherokee, Rusk	92.8	36.8	117	2000	*-5	1982	Mar. 10	Nov. 21	255	4.41	3.64	4.12	3.86	4.69	4.34	2.05	2.38	4.01	4.94	4.63	4.53	48.50	10.00	06-2001
Childress, Childress	95.3	35.3	110	1951	-8	1989	Apr. 1	Nov. 6	218	0.50	0.95	1.41	2.01	3.46	3.51	1.74	2.38	2.51	2.07	1.06	0.86	22.65	5.32	10-1983
Clay, Henrietta	95.0	26.8	*116	1951	*-8	1989	Mar. 30	Nov. 5	220	1.53	2.08	2.45	2.71	4.39	3.72	2.61	2.40	3.35	3.35	1.77	2.17	31.66	6.07	06-1959
Cochran, Morton	91.4	23.1	*110	1994	-12	1963	Apr. 14	Oct. 24	193	0.50	0.58	0.64	0.89	1.92	2.52	1.44	2.97	2.66	1.64	0.79	0.62	18.34	4.69	07-1960
Coke, Robert Lee	94.6	29.0	114	2000	*4	1989	Mar. 26	Nov. 11	230	0.81	1.22	1.05	1.72	3.24	2.90	1.77	2.58	3.46	2.73	1.15	1.00	23.00	8.40	10-1957
Coleman, Coleman	94.7	35.5	114	1936	*2	1930	Mar. 23	Nov. 13	234	1.03	1.75	1.84	2.19	4.11	4.05	1.77	2.28	3.25	3.08	1.57	1.48	28.00	8.55	07-1932
Collin, McKinney	93.7	31.1	118	1936	-7	1930	Mar. 21	Nov. 11	235	2.43	2.91	3.37	3.65	5.68	4.11	2.36	2.16	3.15	4.24	3.71	3.24	41.01	12.10	09-1964
Collingsworth, Wellington	92.7	27.0	113	1994	-6	1989	Apr. 1	Nov. 4	216	0.62	0.73	1.47	2.07	3.88	3.47	2.25	1.85	2.58	2.37	0.89	0.62	22.80	9.50	10-1986
Colorado, Columbus	97.9	36.8	116	2000	*4	1989	Mar. 11	Nov. 16	250	3.61	2.84	2.93	3.57	5.75	5.03	2.64	3.07	3.92	4.16	3.99	3.21	44.72	10.00	06-1973
Comal, New Braunfels	96.3	35.5	112	2000	*2	1932	Mar. 4	Nov. 21	261	1.88	1.98	2.57	2.90	5.01	4.81	1.72	2.32	3.46	4.38	2.44	1.00	35.74	8.55	06-1973
Comanche, Proctor Reservoir	94.7	30.6	113	2000	-8	1989	Mar. 20	Nov. 15	238	1.34	2.02	2.13	2.81	4.75	3.98	1.70	2.63	3.01	3.32	2.07	1.77	31.12	8.37	06-1988
Concho, Paint Rock	95.5	31.9	111	1978	-7	1985	Mar. 31	Nov. 6	219	1.04	1.52	1.35	1.56	3.31	3.77	1.84	2.05	3.55	2.81	1.41	1.29	25.50	8.25	09-1980
Cooke, Gainesville	97.4	28.0	112		-6		Mar. 27	Nov. 8	226	1.80	2.20	3.40	3.20	4.60	3.70	2.00	2.40	4.50	4.60	2.51	1.90	36.90	8.35	06-1964
Coryell, Gatesville	95.0	33.5	*112	2000	-6	1949	Mar. 24	Nov. 13	234	1.65	2.35	2.93	2.90	4.38	3.66	1.72	2.53	2.87	3.30	2.35	2.35	33.43	6.65	06-1991
Cottle, Paducah	96.4	26.2	118	1994	*-7	1989	Mar. 29	Nov. 5	221	0.82	1.11	1.31	1.92	3.85	3.67	1.48	2.63	2.96	2.06	1.08	0.98	24.11	5.55	08-1986
Crane, Crane	96.8	30.6	115	1994	-6	1985	Mar. 23	Nov. 11	232	0.57	0.59	0.34	0.84	1.86	1.71	1.57	2.02	2.95	1.64	0.68	0.70	15.38	5.80	10-1959
Crockett, Ozona	93.0	27.7	*109	1969	-8	1951	Apr. 1	Nov. 2	215	0.70	0.78	1.06	1.36	2.44	1.94	2.05	2.27	2.92	2.25	0.99	0.67	18.95	5.78	06-1913
Crosby, Crosbyton	92.5	25.3	113	1994	*-10	1930	Apr. 2	Nov. 1	212	0.68	0.96	1.87	1.87	3.05	3.10	2.11	3.05	3.46	1.91	0.95	0.84	22.95	7.00	08-1966
Culberson, Van Horn	91.7	27.8	112	1969	-7	1962	Apr. 4	Nov. 5	215	0.39	0.33	0.16	0.24	0.71	1.25	3.11	2.23	2.23	1.27	0.46	0.53	11.98	4.52	08-1985
Dallam, Dalhart	90.0	19.0	*107	1990	-21	1959	Apr. 23	Oct. 16	175	0.52	0.40	1.08	1.35	2.72	2.27	2.43	2.99	1.56	1.32	0.71	0.54	18.57	6.02	03-1977
Dallas, Dallas	96.1	36.4	115	1909	-12	1989	Mar. 3	Nov. 25	267	1.89	2.31	3.13	3.46	5.30	3.92	2.19	2.17	2.65	4.65	2.61	2.53	37.05	6.24	10-1985
Dawson, Lamesa	92.9	26.0	114	1994	-12	1933	Apr. 4	Nov. 5	214	0.57	0.77	0.73	0.88	2.35	2.81	2.00	2.00	3.42	1.76	0.82	0.77	19.07		
Deaf Smith, Hereford	91.6	21.1	111	1910	-17	1951	Apr. 19	Oct. 19	182	0.50	0.50	0.98	1.02	2.12	2.90	2.06	3.22	2.25	1.59	0.77	0.74	18.65	*5.30	10-1976

COUNTY AND STATION	Mean Max. July F.	Mean Min. January F.	Record Highest F.	Year	Record Lowest F.	Year	Last in Spring Mo. Day	First in Fall Mo. Day	Growing Season Days	Jan. In.	Feb. In.	Mar. In.	Apr. In.	May In.	June In.	July In.	Aug. In.	Sept. In.	Oct. In.	Nov. In.	Dec. In.	Annual In.	Highest Daily Rainfall In.	Mo.-Year
Delta, Cooper	94.0	30.0	110		-1	1949	Mar. 25	Nov. 13	233	2.70	3.20	4.10	3.60	5.40	4.00	2.90	2.10	3.90	4.80	4.30	4.00	45.00	7.30	05-1982
Denton, Denton	94.1	32.0	*113	1954	*-3	1989	Mar. 18	Nov. 16	243	1.94	2.55	2.82	3.30	5.41	3.29	2.53	2.26	3.35	4.81	2.87	2.66	37.79	12.40	06-1940
DeWitt, Cuero	95.1	41.3	113	2000	7	1989	Feb. 28	Nov. 25	270	2.30	1.95	2.32	2.96	4.74	4.51	2.18	2.25	4.31	3.67	2.66	2.23	36.08	4.70	08-1996
Dickens, Spur	95.4	25.5	117	1994	-17	1933	Apr. 2	Nov. 4	215	0.55	0.70	0.84	1.53	3.18	2.68	1.74	2.12	2.17	1.66	0.82	0.69	18.68	8.78	07-1990
Dimmit, Carrizo Springs	98.3	39.6	114	1942	10	1989	Feb. 14	Dec. 4	292	1.00	0.94	0.89	1.47	2.96	2.78	1.26	2.33	1.95	2.66	1.10	0.87	20.21	9.25	05-2001
Donley, Clarendon	94.7	22.4	117	1936	*-11	1989	Apr. 11	Oct. 25	196	0.64	0.81	1.43	2.25	3.60	3.70	1.54	2.81	2.69	1.78	0.94	0.85	23.89	7.85	09-1971
Duval, Freer	97.3	42.5	116	1998	12	1963	Feb. 13	Dec. 8	297	1.15	1.31	1.58	1.69	3.63	3.68	1.54	2.25	3.06	2.92	1.54	1.05	25.40	7.00	10-1957
Eastland, Eastland	94.9	26.7	*115	1943	*-6	1973	Apr. 1	Nov. 8	221	1.20	1.73	1.93	2.27	3.72	3.40	1.73	2.29	2.67	3.25	1.72	1.62	27.53	4.53	04-1969
Ector, Penwell	96.0	28.7	116	1994	-12	1985	Mar. 30	Nov. 7	222	0.42	0.58	0.42	0.61	2.11	1.56	1.30	1.46	2.35	1.24	0.63	0.61	13.29	9.50	09-1935
Edwards, Rocksprings	91.6	34.3	*108	1980	*3	1951	Mar. 18	Nov. 17	243	0.77	0.81	1.75	2.23	3.23	3.07	2.05	2.84	2.44	3.41	1.03	3.22	24.76	10.80	09-1958
Ellis, Waxahachie	96.0	35.0	115	1909	-4	1989	Mar. 14	Nov. 18	248	2.11	2.85	3.21	3.89	4.85	3.51	2.28	2.26	3.16	4.43	3.04	3.22	38.81	9.71	09-1974
El Paso, El Paso	94.5	32.9	114	1994	-8	1962	Mar. 22	Nov. 8	230	0.45	0.39	0.26	0.23	0.38	0.87	1.49	1.75	1.61	0.81	0.42	0.77	9.43	2.26	05-1956
Erath, Stephenville	93.6	30.0	111	1925	-8	1989	Mar. 22	Nov. 13	235	1.31	1.86	2.35	2.53	4.35	3.41	1.47	2.41	2.80	3.28	1.97	1.97	29.71	11.90	07-1903
Falls, Marlin	95.0	37.0	*112	1969	-7	1949	Mar. 10	Nov. 17	251	2.49	2.60	3.30	3.19	5.35	3.55	1.92	1.97	3.08	3.90	3.17	3.30	37.99	13.30	07-1903
Fannin, Bonham	92.6	30.2	115	1936	*-5	1930	Mar. 27	Nov. 8	225	2.39	3.01	3.76	3.41	5.57	4.50	3.45	2.13	3.45	5.40	3.94	3.55	44.56	9.41	06-1940
Fayette, La Grange	95.9	41.4	110	2000	3	1989	Feb. 26	Nov. 23	269	3.05	2.88	2.55	2.99	4.82	4.41	2.25	2.81	3.68	4.47	3.36	3.04	40.31	6.85	08-1972
Fisher, Rotan	94.2	27.2	116	1994	*-5	1989	Mar. 29	Nov. 9	225	0.80	0.95	1.30	1.72	3.68	2.74	1.92	2.76	3.45	2.30	1.13	1.07	24.22	6.51	09-1942
Floyd, Floydada	92.3	23.2	111	1994	-9	1963	Apr. 8	Oct. 30	205	0.45	0.72	0.98	1.58	3.01	3.74	2.00	2.50	2.88	1.62	0.84	0.63	20.95	6.85	08-1972
Foard, Crowell	97.0	24.0	114		-7		Apr. 2	Nov. 7	219	1.00	1.40	1.60	2.10	4.30	3.70	1.70	2.40	3.30	2.40	1.50	1.00	26.40	8.65	
Fort Bend, Sugar Land	93.7	41.6	108	1989	*6	1989	Feb. 15	Dec. 10	294	4.06	2.98	3.24	3.48	4.69	5.51	3.30	4.29	5.82	4.03	4.58	3.36	49.34	10.60	06-2001
Franklin, Mount Vernon	92.8	32.2	*108	2000	-1	1989	Mar. 22	Nov. 12	235	2.83	3.41	4.23	3.56	4.71	4.79	3.82	2.19	3.75	4.77	5.10	4.49	47.65	6.10	07-1990
Freestone, Fairfield	95.0	36.9	113	2000	-2	1989	Mar. 19	Nov. 17	242	2.84	3.29	3.29	3.38	5.04	3.79	2.14	2.56	3.48	4.64	4.16	3.70	42.31	4.31	01-1999
Frio, Pearsall	97.5	37.9	113	2000	*7	1989	Feb. 22	Nov. 25	275	1.30	1.45	1.30	2.15	3.33	3.68	1.58	2.61	2.29	3.20	1.60	1.24	25.73	7.84	08-1946
Gaines, Seminole	94.1	26.7	114	1994	-9	1962	Apr. 2	Nov. 3	215	0.64	0.72	0.61	0.91	2.39	2.45	2.44	2.31	2.73	1.39	0.90	0.71	18.20	5.40	05-1999
Galveston, Galveston	88.7	49.7	102	1999	*14	1989	Jan. 19	Jan. 9	358	4.08	2.61	2.76	2.56	3.70	4.04	3.45	4.22	5.76	3.49	3.64	3.53	43.84	13.63	07-1900
Garza, Post	94.0	27.8	115	1994	*-1	1989	Mar. 30	Nov. 9	223	0.58	0.98	0.76	1.43	3.01	2.83	2.00	2.88	3.07	2.05	0.89	0.78	21.29	6.75	10-1926
Gillespie, Fredericksburg	93.1	36.1	*109	2000	-5	1949	Mar. 18	Nov. 12	238	1.36	1.91	1.86	2.40	4.29	3.97	2.00	2.74	3.07	3.72	2.19	2.14	31.65	8.03	07-1999
Glasscock, Garden City	94.0	26.7	114	1994	-3	1989	Apr. 3	Nov. 3	213	0.73	0.71	0.70	1.14	2.18	1.91	1.86	2.02	2.97	1.66	0.75	0.69	17.32	8.75	07-1945
Goliad, Goliad	95.5	43.3	*112	1998	*4	1962	Feb. 25	Nov. 26	273	2.34	2.11	2.00	3.19	4.49	4.96	2.85	3.49	4.56	4.26	2.19	2.14	38.58	9.16	09-1967
Gonzales, Gonzales	93.9	38.7	111	2000	-8	1989	Feb. 26	Dec. 1	277	2.36	2.83	2.76	3.04	5.43	4.24	1.60	2.68	3.20	3.87	2.84	2.46	36.02	16.31	08-1981
Gray, Pampa	92.0	21.9	111	1980	*-2	1989	Apr. 13	Oct. 25	195	0.57	0.83	1.50	1.95	3.37	3.52	2.85	2.38	2.29	1.58	1.20	0.70	22.74	3.54	07-1982
Grayson, Sherman	92.7	32.2	113	1936	-4	1930	Mar. 22	Nov. 14	236	2.11	2.63	3.44	3.49	5.41	4.37	2.34	2.25	4.01	5.15	3.81	3.03	42.04	8.40	08-1920
Gregg, Longview	94.5	33.7	113	1936		1989	Mar. 19	Nov. 15	240	3.79	3.93	4.11	4.19	4.79	5.03	2.83	2.71	3.81	4.34	4.75	4.78	49.06	8.70	03-1989
Grimes, Richards	96.0	40.0	108		4		Mar. 1	Dec. 4	278	4.10	3.00	3.30	3.40	5.20	3.90	2.20	2.60	4.20	4.40	4.10	4.30	44.70	6.50	

COUNTY AND STATION	TEMPERATURE Mean Max. July (F.)	Mean Min. January (F.)	Record Highest (F.)	Record Highest Year	Record Lowest (F.)	Record Lowest Year	AVERAGE FREEZE DATES Last in Spring (Mo. Day)	First in Fall (Mo. Day)	Growing Season (Days)	MEAN PRECIPITATION January (In.)	February (In.)	March (In.)	April (In.)	May (In.)	June (In.)	July (In.)	August (In.)	September (In.)	October (In.)	November (In.)	December (In.)	Annual (In.)	EXTREMES Highest Daily Rainfall (In.)	Mo.-Year
Guadalupe, New Braunfels	95.0	36.0	110		0		Mar. 6	Nov. 28	267	1.90	2.20	1.80	2.60	5.00	4.10	2.00	2.50	4.10	3.50	2.80	2.00	34.50		
Hale, Plainview	91.0	24.4	111	1994	-8	1933	Apr. 4	Oct. 31	209	0.59	0.63	0.80	1.52	2.91	3.05	2.45	2.38	2.28	1.72	0.84	0.73	19.90	7.00	07-1960
Hall, Memphis	95.7	25.5	*117	1944	-11	1930	Apr. 1	Nov. 4	217	0.57	0.88	1.52	2.04	3.93	3.51	1.88	2.25	2.45	1.77	0.96	0.75	22.51	8.80	06-1960
Hamilton, Hamilton	94.3	33.4	109	1964	-3	1959	Mar. 16	Nov. 15	243	1.64	1.76	2.61	2.72	3.70	3.71	1.53	1.57	2.85	2.90	1.01	1.60	28.59	8.20	10-1959
Hansford, Spearman	95.5	22.4	111	1936	-22	1959	Apr. 16	Oct. 23	189	0.53	0.62	1.52	1.58	2.83	2.97	2.77	2.38	2.08	1.35	1.01	0.66	20.30	5.80	05-1965
Hardeman, Quanah	96.5	24.6	*119	1994	-15	1989	Apr. 4	Nov. 2	211	0.96	1.17	1.65	2.08	3.86	3.73	2.42	2.57	3.43	2.37	1.40	1.12	26.76	8.03	08-1995
Hardin, Evadale	93.0	37.0	102		12		Mar. 31	Nov. 14	246	5.40	3.70	4.20	4.00	5.50	5.50	4.10	4.20	4.50	5.36	5.00	5.10	56.50		
Harris, Houston	93.6	45.2	108	2000	9	1989	Feb. 8	Dec. 20	308	4.25	3.01	3.19	3.46	5.11	6.84	4.36	4.54	5.62	5.26	4.54	3.78	53.96	9.95	10-1949
Harrison, Marshall	92.4	33.4	112	1909	-5	1930	Mar. 20	Nov. 12	236	4.38	4.07	4.33	4.35	5.07	5.23	3.02	2.68	3.89	4.66	4.59	4.95	51.22	8.58	03-1989
Hartley, Channing	90.9	20.0	*108	1981	-9	1979	Apr. 19	Oct. 19	182	0.35	0.45	0.76	1.10	1.88	2.30	2.59	3.50	1.66	1.33	0.61	0.67	17.20	3.80	12-1997
Haskell, Haskell	96.1	28.8	*115	1994	*-6	1989	Mar. 27	Nov. 12	229	0.96	1.47	1.46	1.99	3.32	3.26	1.61	2.74	2.96	2.53	1.26	1.37	24.93	14.29	08-1978
Hays, San Marcos	95.1	38.6	*111	2000	-2	1949	Feb. 28	Nov. 24	268	2.05	2.21	2.09	2.85	5.31	4.84	2.12	2.65	3.46	4.03	3.17	2.41	37.19	15.78	10-1998
Hemphill, Canadian	93.9	18.8	*112	1994	*-14	1942	Apr. 10	Oct. 16	188	0.46	0.71	1.70	1.72	3.75	3.33	2.19	2.36	2.36	1.47	0.94	0.69	21.68	5.15	10-1985
Henderson, Athens	93.4	35.2	*109	2000	-6	1985	Mar. 19	Nov. 14	239	2.96	3.37	3.70	3.47	4.82	3.95	1.74	2.43	3.07	4.70	3.94	3.88	42.03	7.19	04-1986
Hidalgo, McAllen	95.5	48.2	109	1999	17	1962	Jan. 05	Jan. 30	>365	1.20	1.37	0.95	1.36	2.51	2.49	1.70	2.31	4.00	2.76	0.95	1.01	22.61	7.81	08-1980
Hill, Hillsboro	95.2	35.2	113	1917	-6	1989	Mar. 19	Nov. 14	240	2.19	2.67	3.21	3.24	4.65	4.07	2.08	2.19	2.92	4.15	2.70	3.08	37.15	11.30	09-1936
Hockley, Levelland	92.7	23.7	115	1994	-16	1963	Apr. 08	Oct. 27	201	0.59	0.63	0.58	1.03	2.35	2.78	2.22	2.87	3.24	1.62	0.85	0.82	19.58	4.23	06-1999
Hood, Cresson	97.0	33.0	110		-6		Mar. 26	Nov. 13	232	1.60	2.20	2.60	2.90	4.70	3.90	1.70	2.40	2.60	3.90	2.30	2.30	33.10		
Hopkins, Sulphur Springs	94.8	31.1	115	1969	-4	1989	Mar. 25	Nov. 12	232	2.88	3.20	4.27	4.34	5.00	4.64	3.22	2.35	3.35	5.21	4.77	4.46	47.69	8.11	07-1994
Houston, Crockett	93.3	35.9	114	1909	*0	1989	Mar. 10	Nov. 18	252	4.00	3.10	3.45	3.87	4.66	4.46	2.84	2.81	4.12	4.22	3.93	4.02	45.48	9.11	06-2001
Howard, Big Spring	94.3	29.6	114	1994	*-5	1985	Mar. 23	Nov. 13	235	0.72	0.81	0.73	1.34	3.05	2.58	2.11	2.38	3.51	1.78	0.77	0.67	20.12	4.84	05-1994
Hudspeth, Sierra Blanca	92.0	25.1	*109	1994	-10	1985	Apr. 18	Oct. 29	193	0.49	0.41	0.26	0.29	0.53	1.11	3.82	2.29	2.19	1.15	0.44	0.66	11.93	3.32	09-1978
Hunt, Greenville	93.3	31.2	116	1936	-4	1930	Mar. 23	Nov. 13	235	2.51	3.16	3.67	3.79	5.47	4.03	2.96	2.18	3.56	4.91	3.98	3.48	43.70	6.95	09-1936
Hutchinson, Borger	92.6	23.4	*108	1998	-12	1951	Apr. 14	Oct. 25	193	0.65	0.69	1.56	1.77	3.08	3.20	2.69	3.16	2.00	1.60	0.88	0.70	21.98	3.79	05-1959
Irion, Funk Ranch	95.0	32.0	108		12		Mar. 27	Nov. 11	229	0.70	1.10	1.00	1.60	2.50	2.50	1.40	1.90	3.10	2.10	1.00	1.00	19.90		
Jack, Jacksboro	94.4	29.7	*113	1980	-7	1989	Mar. 21	Nov. 14	237	1.28	1.79	2.38	2.60	4.96	3.18	2.26	2.15	3.18	3.78	2.05	1.83	31.44	9.60	04-1957
Jackson, Edna	94.0	42.0	105		17		Feb. 19	Dec. 6	290	3.10	2.40	2.00	3.10	5.30	4.60	2.90	2.60	4.90	5.00	3.40	2.80	42.10	9.04	03-1999
Jasper, Sam Rayburn Dam	94.5	35.2	109	2000	7	1989	Mar. 17	Nov. 14	241	5.94	4.55	5.29	4.51	5.53	5.81	4.24	3.92	3.97	4.84	5.88	6.09	60.57	5.30	08-1932
Jeff Davis, Fort Davis	89.5	28.4	*107	1998	*0	1985	Apr. 9	Nov. 2	206	0.43	0.35	0.34	0.50	1.46	1.79	3.30	2.97	2.76	1.29	1.22	0.53	15.86	4.13	05-1984
Jeff Davis, Mount Locke	84.5	32.4	*104	1994	-10	1962	Apr. 17	Oct. 26	191	0.53	0.49	0.33	0.60	1.73	2.56	3.82	4.02	3.29	1.71	0.56	0.73	20.37	12.09	09-1963
Jefferson, Beaumont	91.6	42.9	108	2000	12	1989	Feb. 14	Dec. 6	295	5.69	3.35	3.75	3.84	5.83	6.58	5.23	4.85	6.10	4.67	4.75	5.25	59.89	9.40	09-1971
Jim Hogg, Hebbronville	97.5	43.8	111	1998	*12	1989	Feb. 8	Dec. 11	307	1.12	1.40	1.14	1.69	3.33	3.13	1.44	2.28	3.68	2.22	1.22	1.10	23.75	12.14	09-1971
Jim Wells, Alice	96.1	44.1	*111	1998	*12	1971	Jan. 29	Dec. 15	320	1.21	1.51	1.34	1.65	3.16	3.41	2.18	2.70	4.52	3.55	1.76	1.21	27.52	9.02	05-1989
Johnson, Cleburne	97.0	34.0	114	1939	-5	1989	Mar. 18	Nov. 13	240	1.90	2.29	3.07	3.53	5.11	3.90	2.18	2.36	2.88	3.92	2.54	2.57	36.25		

County and Station	TEMPERATURE						AVERAGE FREEZE DATES		Growing Season	MEAN PRECIPITATION													EXTREMES	
	July Mean Max °F	January Mean Min °F	Record Highest °F	Year	Record Lowest °F	Year	Last in Spring Mo. Day	First in Fall Mo. Day	Days	January In.	February In.	March In.	April In.	May In.	June In.	July In.	August In.	September In.	October In.	November In.	December In.	Annual In.	Highest Daily Rainfall In.	Mo.-Year
Jones, Anson	96.3	30.7	114	1994	−12	1989	Mar. 28	Nov. 12	228	1.03	1.51	1.21	1.94	3.20	3.13	2.04	2.94	3.93	2.55	1.22	1.30	26.00	5.60	09-1988
Karnes, Karnes City	95.0	41.0	112		7		Feb. 24	Dec. 2	281	1.50	1.70	1.50	2.50	3.20	3.70	2.40	2.40	3.40	3.00	1.90	1.50	28.40		
Kaufman, Kaufman	94.6	32.3	113	1936	*−3	1989	Mar. 19	Nov. 14	240	2.74	3.04	3.37	3.06	4.45	3.31	2.12	1.98	2.77	4.81	3.80	3.45	38.90	13.66	08-1908
Kendall, Boerne	91.9	34.3	112	1925	−4	1949	Mar. 20	Nov. 13	238	1.79	2.24	2.57	2.87	4.66	4.77	2.23	3.05	3.61	4.09	3.11	2.37	37.36	9.04	10-1913
Kenedy, Sarita	95.7	45.0	110		14		Feb. 2	Dec. 18	319	1.10	1.80	1.30	1.60	2.70	3.30	1.50	3.40	4.70	3.40	1.90	1.20	27.90		
Kent, Jayton	95.7	24.9	116	1994	−6	1985	Apr. 2	Nov. 7	218	0.91	1.14	1.12	1.73	3.35	3.21	1.59	2.81	3.04	2.17	0.90	0.97	22.94	6.50	06-1991
Kerr, Kerrville	92.0	32.0	110		−7		Apr. 6	Nov. 6	216	1.30	1.80	2.10	2.30	4.20	4.00	2.20	2.30	3.90	3.80	2.60	2.10	32.60		
Kimble, Junction	94.8	29.3	*110	1984	−11	1929	Apr. 2	Nov. 1	212	0.77	1.43	1.42	1.95	3.23	3.10	1.55	2.20	2.28	2.68	1.37	1.26	23.24	6.10	09-1980
King, Guthrie	96.7	23.9	119	1994	−10	1989	Apr. 6	Nov. 4	211	1.03	1.28	1.26	1.79	3.90	3.17	1.94	2.87	3.25	2.38	1.12	1.01	25.00	8.85	07-1986
Kinney, Brackettville	95.5	37.3	111	1988	4	1962	Mar. 5	Nov. 15	255	0.77	1.16	1.10	1.99	2.87	3.18	1.90	2.29	2.77	2.49	1.41	0.97	22.79	6.20	05-1991
Kleberg, Kingsville	95.5	43.4	*111	2000	10	1989	Feb. 10	Dec. 11	303	1.44	1.71	1.24	1.80	3.53	4.02	1.97	3.05	3.98	3.72	1.50	1.07	29.03	6.67	12-1991
Knox, Munday	96.5	28.1	*117	1994	*−9	1989	Mar. 28	Nov. 12	228	1.00	1.54	1.69	1.91	3.85	3.46	1.70	2.68	3.22	2.73	1.38	1.20	26.36	8.00	06-1930
Lamar, Paris	94.3	29.9	115	1936	*−5	1930	Mar. 18	Nov. 14	240	2.63	3.00	4.11	3.56	5.63	4.25	3.89	2.39	4.42	5.04	4.70	4.20	47.82	7.61	06-1928
Lamb, Littlefield	92.0	22.7	112	1994	−6	1979	Apr. 11	Oct. 25	196	0.55	0.52	0.75	1.11	2.24	3.04	2.44	2.80	2.26	1.52	0.69	0.77	18.69	6.95	05-1957
Lampasas, Lampasas	94.1	30.4	*112	1917	−12	1949	Apr. 1	Nov. 07	219	1.50	2.34	2.31	2.48	4.37	3.49	1.68	2.42	2.61	3.33	2.32	2.23	31.08	9.50	10-1986
La Salle, Fowlerton	98.9	39.1	113	1998	9	1962	Feb. 27	Nov. 26	271	0.93	1.08	1.46	1.84	2.73	2.61	1.53	2.19	2.71	3.15	1.22	1.11	22.56	11.30	07-1936
Lavaca, Hallettsville	94.4	41.8	*111	1980	5	1989	Feb. 25	Nov. 29	277	2.91	2.50	2.46	3.44	5.75	5.02	2.28	2.95	4.49	4.07	3.53	2.83	42.23	11.30	07-1936
Lee, Lexington	93.6	37.3	111	2000	−3	1949	Mar. 1	Nov. 22	265	2.60	2.53	2.54	2.48	4.82	3.78	2.06	2.06	3.26	4.69	3.82	2.78	36.02	10.13	10-1994
Leon, Centerville	94.7	34.3	*111	1954	−3	1949	Mar. 17	Nov. 14	242	3.40	3.18	3.51	3.29	4.77	4.12	2.48	2.62	3.50	4.79	3.82	3.60	43.08	8.50	10-1994
Liberty, Liberty	92.2	40.3	108	1913	7	1989	Feb. 18	Dec. 1	285	4.91	3.74	3.84	4.01	5.80	6.88	4.46	4.34	5.92	5.77	5.84	5.01	60.52	18.50	10-1994
Limestone, Mexia	95.8	33.7	112	1909	−5	1989	Mar. 6	Nov. 20	258	2.44	3.08	3.45	3.14	4.91	3.89	1.99	2.56	4.16	4.29	3.64	3.85	41.40	11.80	09-1932
Lipscomb, Lipscomb	96.2	16.2	114	1978	*−18	1974	Apr. 23	Oct. 11	170	0.54	0.81	1.91	2.00	3.85	3.28	1.60	2.52	1.97	1.46	1.12	0.81	22.57	6.62	05-1951
Live Oak, Choke Canyon Dam	97.0	42.0	109		12		Feb. 20	Dec. 6	289	1.20	1.10	1.80	2.40	2.80	2.70	1.60	1.40	2.10	2.00	1.70	1.20	22.00		
Llano, Llano	96.0	32.3	115	1933	−7	1929	Mar. 18	Nov. 12	238	1.08	1.80	1.90	2.19	3.94	3.40	1.84	2.03	2.14	2.88	2.23	1.90	27.33	12.53	09-1952
Loving, Mentone	91.9	24.4	114	1994	−14		Apr. 8	Nov. 8	222	0.50	0.30	0.30	0.20	1.10	0.90	1.80	1.40	1.20	1.00	0.30	0.30	9.10	5.70	06-1967
Lubbock, Lubbock	92.2	25.1	111	1994	−15	1933	Apr. 3	Nov. 1	211	0.50	0.71	0.76	1.29	2.31	2.98	2.13	2.36	2.57	1.70	0.71	0.67	18.69	8.32	08-1945
Lynn, Tahoka	92.2	25.1	111	1994	−15	1933	Apr. 4	Nov. 4	213	0.66	0.79	0.71	1.48	2.74	3.22	2.62	2.23	2.65	1.73	0.86	0.79	20.48	8.00	04-1921
Madison, Madisonville	96.0	35.8	112	2000	−2	1949	Mar. 7	Nov. 18	255	3.81	2.83	3.24	3.26	5.06	3.89	2.72	2.95	4.20	4.41	4.01	3.62	44.00	9.10	09-1952
Marion, Jefferson	93.1	31.4	108	2000	−5	1989	Mar. 25	Nov. 6	225	4.13	3.96	4.41	4.07	4.60	4.84	2.89	2.93	3.40	4.64	4.68	4.71	49.26	7.45	09-1961
Martin, Lenorah	94.0	30.0	109		−8		Apr. 5	Nov. 5	215	0.70	0.70	0.70	1.20	2.40	2.50	2.00	1.60	3.10	1.80	0.80	0.70	18.20		
Mason, Mason	94.9	30.8	109	1962	*3	1985	Mar. 26	Nov. 9	227	0.91	1.97	1.74	2.05	3.31	4.00	2.00	2.52	3.00	3.01	2.07	1.37	27.95	8.95	06-1936
Matagorda, Bay City	92.4	45.7	*109	2000	*7	1989	Feb. 11	Dec. 13	306	3.89	2.97	3.00	3.18	4.90	4.68	3.89	3.48	5.61	5.13	3.97	3.33	48.03	15.60	07-1971
Maverick, Eagle Pass	98.1	40.1	*115	1944	*10	1962	Feb. 12	Dec. 5	295	0.80	0.94	0.72	1.75	2.95	3.49	2.03	2.01	2.57	2.33	1.08	0.81	21.48		
McCulloch, Brady	94.5	32.3	*110	1980	−2	1989	Mar. 21	Nov. 11	235	1.01	1.68	1.63	1.92	3.60	3.26	2.68	2.57	3.26	2.68	1.73	1.61	27.63	6.51	07-1971

COUNTY AND STATION	TEMPERATURE — Mean Max. July (F.)	Mean Min. January (F.)	Record Highest (F.)	Year	Record Lowest (F.)	Year	FREEZE — Last in Spring	First in Fall	Growing Season (Days)	January (In.)	February (In.)	March (In.)	April (In.)	May (In.)	June (In.)	July (In.)	August (In.)	September (In.)	October (In.)	November (In.)	December (In.)	Annual (In.)	Highest Daily Rainfall (In.)	Mo.-Year
McLennan, Waco	96.7	35.1	112	1969	-5	1949	Mar. 13	Nov. 19	250	1.90	2.43	2.48	2.99	4.46	3.08	2.23	1.85	2.88	3.67	2.61	2.76	33.34	7.98	12-1997
McMullen, Tilden	98.7	40.1	119	1910	5	1989	Feb. 21	Dec. 3	284	1.15	1.27	1.33	1.95	3.10	3.37	1.52	2.56	2.91	2.14	1.38	1.19	23.87	6.93	09-1967
Medina, Hondo	95.0	38.0	112		4		Mar. 6	Nov. 24	263	1.30	1.50	1.60	2.70	3.80	3.60	1.40	1.50	2.80	2.90	1.80	1.40	26.30	6.03	09-1936
Menard, Menard	94.8	30.7	114	1927	-6	1929	Apr. 7	Oct. 29	204	0.97	1.48	1.60	1.72	3.22	3.38	2.14	1.50	2.69	2.57	1.51	1.28	24.90	4.75	05-1968
Midland, Midland	94.3	29.6	116	1994	-11	1985	Mar. 30	Nov. 12	226	0.53	0.58	0.42	0.73	1.79	1.71	1.89	1.77	2.31	1.77	0.65	0.65	14.80	12.45	09-1921
Milam, Cameron	95.7	39.2	114	1917	-7	1930	Mar. 7	Nov. 22	260	2.29	2.53	2.45	2.88	5.01	3.22	1.94	1.95	3.54	3.73	3.12	2.86	35.52	7.20	10-1969
Mills, Goldthwaite	92.0	35.2	110	1964	-7	1989	Mar. 20	Nov. 15	239	1.26	2.10	2.04	2.28	3.85	3.81	1.76	1.95	2.79	3.11	2.05	1.78	28.78	8.65	04-1900
Mitchell, Colorado City	95.9	27.0	115	1907	-7	1947	Mar. 25	Nov. 7	226	0.44	0.89	1.07	1.33	2.49	2.84	1.23	2.27	2.79	2.22	0.90	0.64	19.43	10.25	05-1989
Montague, Bowie	94.7	28.3	115	1980	-11	1989	Mar. 21	Nov. 12	236	1.47	2.13	2.62	3.42	5.04	3.42	1.81	2.27	3.67	4.20	2.18	2.02	33.72		
Montgomery, Conroe	94.3	40.0	109	2000	3	1989	Feb. 27	Nov. 25	270	4.21	2.97	2.94	3.85	5.50	4.58	3.22	3.73	4.46	4.70	4.79	4.37	49.32	14.35	10-1994
Moore, Dumas	91.7	20.8	*109	1980	*-18	1959	Apr. 18	Oct. 22	186	0.47	0.58	1.13	1.31	2.74	2.41	2.42	2.47	1.95	1.11	0.66	0.50	17.75	4.10	05-1988
Morris, Daingerfield	95.0	33.7	112	1998	4	1962	Mar. 3	Nov. 22	263	3.54	3.35	4.64	4.32	4.43	4.24	2.98	3.40	3.29	4.35	4.84	4.39	46.76	7.48	04-1966
Motley, Matador	94.8	27.3	116	1994	-5	1989	Apr. 1	Nov. 8	221	0.67	0.90	1.21	1.09	3.16	3.60	2.10	2.41	3.11	2.09	0.99	0.85	23.54	5.30	10-1983
Nacogdoches, Nacogdoches	94.0	36.0	110		0		Mar. 16	Nov. 12	243	4.40	3.90	4.20	4.10	4.80	4.10	2.90	3.10	3.70	4.00	4.60	4.60	48.40	9.96	05-1968
Navarro, Corsicana	94.5	34.0	113	1954	-5	1949	Mar. 9	Nov. 23	259	2.49	3.08	3.34	3.39	4.95	3.40	2.16	2.37	3.04	4.33	3.33	3.60	39.48	8.28	09-1980
Newton, Toledo Bend Dam	94.0	35.0	107		7		Mar. 24	Nov. 9	228	5.70	4.40	4.80	4.00	4.90	5.00	3.60	3.40	3.58	4.10	5.00	6.10	54.90	7.92	10-1995
Nolan, Roscoe	93.8	28.9	113	1994	-11	1947	Mar. 31	Nov. 10	223	1.03	1.18	1.11	1.52	3.04	3.09	1.89	2.59	3.58	2.53	0.99	0.99	23.54	7.11	05-1989
Nueces, Corpus Christi	93.2	46.2	109	2000	13	1989	Feb. 3	Dec. 23	319	1.62	1.84	1.74	2.05	3.48	3.53	2.00	3.54	5.03	3.94	1.74	1.75	32.26	4.50	09-1990
Ochiltree, Perryton	91.4	18.4	111	1981	-17	1988	Apr. 25	Oct. 17	174	0.47	0.62	1.71	1.80	3.33	2.97	2.74	3.20	1.89	1.38	1.09	0.66	20.88	6.65	10-1981
Oldham, Boys Ranch	92.3	20.5	110	1982	-11	1983	Apr. 13	Oct. 16	186	0.49	0.28	0.89	1.13	2.47	2.18	2.96	3.20	1.94	1.48	0.66	0.50	18.18	9.25	04-1991
Orange, Orange	91.0	41.0	104		10		Mar. 16	Nov. 11	240	6.00	3.60	3.90	3.92	5.70	6.20	5.30	4.70	5.60	4.60	4.60	5.20	59.00	7.05	07-1962
Palo Pinto, Mineral Wells	97.3	33.4	*114	1980	-8	1989	Mar. 23	Nov. 13	233	1.42	1.99	2.69	2.75	4.59	3.25	2.25	2.34	2.80	3.81	2.16	1.74	31.79	3.90	10-1986
Panola, Carthage	93.7	33.9	*109	2000	*1	1989	Mar. 17	Nov. 14	242	4.76	3.88	4.00	4.36	5.05	4.95	3.25	2.92	3.75	4.65	4.93	5.01	51.51	5.22	10-1986
Parker, Weatherford	95.2	29.0	119	1980	*-10	1989	Mar. 29	Nov. 8	223	1.50	2.36	2.79	2.84	4.76	3.93	2.11	2.60	2.85	4.19	2.61	2.16	34.70		
Parmer, Friona	89.8	21.7	*108	1980	-15	1963	Apr. 19	Oct. 20	183	0.56	0.53	0.91	1.09	2.19	2.50	2.24	2.89	1.69	1.60	0.80	0.79	15.79		
Pecos, Fort Stockton	95.8	31.4	117	1994	-6	1985	Mar. 26	Nov. 12	230	0.50	0.47	0.38	0.72	1.59	1.70	1.34	1.95	2.75	1.45	0.61	0.60	14.06		
Polk, Livingston	94.1	35.8	*111	2000	*3	1989	Mar. 17	Nov. 13	241	4.64	3.47	3.89	3.92	5.54	5.20	3.55	3.41	4.73	3.82	4.76	4.92	51.85	10.47	10-1994
Potter, Amarillo	91.0	22.6	*108	1998	-14	1951	Apr. 18	Oct. 20	185	0.63	0.55	1.13	1.33	2.50	3.28	2.68	2.94	1.88	1.50	0.68	0.61	19.71	4.92	06-1984
Presidio, Marfa	88.9	23.9	*106	1994	-2	1972	Apr. 11	Oct. 30	201	0.41	0.47	0.24	0.38	0.66	1.80	2.83	2.70	1.69	0.99	0.39	0.59	15.79	2.93	05-1984
Presidio, Presidio	100.8	34.5	*117	1960	4	1962	Mar. 5	Nov. 20	260	0.31	0.36	0.15	0.38	0.66	1.51	2.01	1.82	1.69	0.99	0.37	0.51	10.76	3.30	04-1979
Rains, Emory	92.4	31.6	110	1964	-5	1989	Mar. 22	Nov. 12	234	3.04	3.34	3.88	3.72	5.31	4.19	2.33	2.23	2.98	4.66	3.89	3.93	43.50	5.65	06-1992
Randall, Canyon	92.6	23.7	*109	1981	-14	1951	Apr. 13	Oct. 22	191	0.46	0.52	0.99	1.08	2.89	2.96	2.39	2.84	1.97	1.78	0.69	0.62	19.19	7.87	08-1968
Reagan, Big Lake	93.4	29.1	110	1998	*1	1998	Apr. 1	Nov. 5	218	0.68	0.92	0.81	1.42	2.39	1.99	1.79	2.18	1.92	1.92	0.88	0.84	18.79	4.85	07-1990
Real, Camp Wood	94.2	33.1	*109	2000	*5	1989	Mar. 22	Nov. 11	233	1.11	1.44	1.55	2.41	3.16	3.68	2.09	3.07	2.87	3.46	1.77	1.38	27.99	8.37	11-2001

COUNTY AND STATION	TEMP Mean Max. July F.	TEMP Mean Min. January F.	Record Highest F.	Record Highest Year	Record Lowest F.	Record Lowest Year	Freeze Last in Spring	Freeze First in Fall	Growing Season Days	Jan In.	Feb In.	Mar In.	Apr In.	May In.	June In.	July In.	Aug In.	Sept In.	Oct In.	Nov In.	Dec In.	Annual In.	Highest Daily Rainfall In.	Highest Daily Rainfall Mo-Year
Red River, Clarksville	92.2	29.7	115	1936	-7	1930	Mar. 28	Nov. 9	226	2.65	3.17	4.50	4.02	5.43	4.00	3.23	2.07	3.83	4.99	5.43	4.51	47.83	8.30	05-1933
Reeves, Balmorhea	94.7	30.1	112	1939	-9	1933	Mar. 30	Nov. 9	223	0.58	0.56	0.24	0.63	1.45	1.24	1.78	2.29	3.08	1.19	0.54	0.61	14.19	4.13	07-1973
Reeves, Pecos	98.5	28.1	118	1968	-9	1962	Mar. 26	Nov. 7	225	0.47	0.45	0.34	0.47	1.25	1.24	1.35	1.62	2.24	1.10	0.47	0.61	11.61	4.38	05-1992
Refugio, Refugio	94.0	45.0	106		8		Feb. 14	Dec. 15	304	2.50	2.20	1.50	1.90	4.30	4.80	3.30	3.50	7.00	5.20	2.30	1.60	40.10		
Roberts, Miami	92.4	20.6	114	1917	*-15	1942	Apr. 15	Oct. 19	186	0.68	0.83	1.74	2.19	3.77	3.26	2.39	2.40	2.38	1.64	1.12	0.90	23.30	5.58	10-1985
Robertson, Franklin	95.1	38.2	112	2000	-1	1989	Mar. 9	Nov. 19	254	3.03	2.86	2.90	3.03	4.81	2.95	2.04	2.60	3.65	4.38	3.26	3.52	39.03	7.48	07-1979
Rockwall, Rockwall	96.0	33.0	118		-7		Mar. 23	Nov. 14	236	2.10	2.70	3.50	3.60	5.30	3.70	2.30	2.00	3.00	4.60	3.40	3.20	39.40		
Runnels, Ballinger	94.3	28.5	116	1907	-6	1949	Mar. 28	Nov. 9	225	0.94	1.32	1.27	1.80	3.38	3.15	1.39	2.40	3.08	2.52	1.31	1.20	23.76	7.05	05-1946
Rusk, Henderson	93.1	33.1	*111	2000	-1	1989	Mar. 20	Nov. 15	239	4.08	3.78	4.00	3.91	4.73	4.87	2.81	2.75	3.71	4.68	4.67	4.23	48.22	11.05	03-1989
Sabine, Hemphill	93.0	36.0	104		8		Mar. 21	Nov. 12	236	5.50	4.00	5.00	4.20	5.00	5.00	3.80	3.90	3.80	3.90	5.00	6.00	54.40		
San Augustine, Broaddus	93.0	35.0	106		9		Mar. 19	Nov. 12	238	5.30	4.10	4.40	3.40	4.60	4.50	3.00	3.90	4.60	3.60	4.40	5.70	51.10		
San Jacinto, Coldspring	93.8	37.5	110	1998	-11	1985	Mar. 11	Nov. 22	255	4.63	3.44	3.61	3.73	5.40	5.93	2.95	3.52	4.45	4.40	4.89	4.82	51.77	13.50	06-1973
San Patricio, Sinton	91.7	44.2	109	2000	10	1989	Feb. 7	Dec. 13	308	1.91	2.02	1.91	1.99	4.07	3.97	2.98	3.16	5.61	4.61	2.04	1.27	35.54	12.35	04-1930
San Saba, San Saba	95.8	33.4	112	1978	-1	1989	Mar. 20	Nov. 11	236	1.09	1.94	1.96	2.13	3.92	3.62	1.87	2.29	2.38	2.82	2.04	1.66	27.72	11.20	10-1969
Schleicher, Eldorado	93.0	28.0	107		3		Mar. 28	Nov. 12	229	0.70	0.90	0.70	2.50	2.50	1.90	1.60	2.10	2.38	2.10	1.00	0.60	19.00		
Scurry, Snyder	94.6	26.7	115	1936	-11	1936	Apr. 1	Nov. 7	219	0.69	1.03	1.09	1.69	3.01	3.06	2.04	2.55	3.30	2.34	0.91	0.80	22.51	5.26	07-1948
Shackelford, Albany	95.4	28.4	115	1972	-8	1947	Mar. 28	Nov. 6	222	1.01	1.65	1.95	2.34	3.76	3.45	1.91	3.04	3.17	3.00	1.55	1.62	28.45	5.80	07-1953
Shelby, Center	93.9	34.9	112	2000	0	1951	Mar. 20	Nov. 10	234	5.04	4.13	4.21	4.41	5.04	4.81	3.04	3.76	4.20	4.64	4.68	5.05	53.01	9.66	11-1940
Sherman, Stratford	91.1	18.5	*108	1953	*-20	1933	Apr. 26	Oct. 15	171	0.48	0.44	1.21	1.46	2.85	2.26	2.31	2.67	1.71	1.15	0.79	0.56	17.89	5.60	08-1992
Smith, Tyler	94.0	38.0	108		0		Mar. 7	Nov. 21	259	3.30	3.70	4.00	3.70	4.50	3.70	2.20	2.60	3.30	5.10	4.50	4.80	45.40		
Somervell, Glen Rose	97.3	28.9	115	1984	-15	1989	Apr. 11	Oct. 29	200	1.64	2.28	2.80	2.91	5.20	4.02	2.19	2.18	3.15	3.83	2.24	2.38	34.82	8.48	07-1995
Starr, Rio Grande City	99.1	44.5	116	1998	10	1962	Feb. 9	Dec. 14	309	0.97	1.10	0.74	2.17	2.42	2.94	1.27	1.97	4.68	2.48	0.90	0.92	21.61	12.51	09-1967
Stephens, Breckenridge	96.8	30.9	114	1936	-7	1989	Mar. 29	Nov. 10	226	1.30	1.39	2.05	2.22	3.53	3.12	1.86	2.06	2.93	3.44	1.56	1.63	27.04	15.70	10-1981
Sterling, Sterling City	94.7	27.4	112	1994	-13	1985	Apr. 4	Nov. 3	212	0.85	0.91	0.91	1.43	2.79	2.33	1.40	1.87	3.29	1.84	0.85	0.93	19.40	6.53	07-1948
Stonewall, Aspermont	97.4	27.2	117	1994	-10	1989	Mar. 30	Nov. 8	223	0.90	1.31	1.32	1.65	3.44	2.94	1.32	2.77	3.04	2.35	1.17	1.03	33.24	6.92	04-1930
Sutton, Sonora	94.7	27.2	109	1980	-8	1951	Apr. 4	Nov. 3	213	0.84	1.16	1.18	1.57	2.57	2.54	1.93	2.93	3.07	2.53	1.26	0.82	22.40	7.92	09-1976
Swisher, Tulia	91.1	22.2	*110	1994	*-10	1951	Apr. 14	Oct. 24	193	0.59	0.72	1.05	1.31	2.99	3.42	2.32	2.65	2.86	1.63	0.87	0.76	20.71	5.18	06-1985
Tarrant, Benbrook	96.6	31.4	111	1954	-6	1989	Mar. 15	Nov. 17	247	1.70	2.19	2.67	3.17	4.58	3.56	2.29	2.03	2.91	4.14	2.35	2.47	34.01	6.36	10-1991
Taylor, Abilene	94.8	31.8	110	1978	*-7	1989	Mar. 24	Nov. 12	232	0.97	1.13	1.41	1.67	2.83	3.06	1.70	2.63	2.91	2.90	1.30	1.27	23.78	6.30	08-1978
Terrell, Sanderson	91.9	30.5	110	1969	3	1989	Mar. 22	Nov. 10	233	0.39	0.59	0.40	0.86	1.74	2.09	1.52	1.87	2.41	1.75	0.81	0.51	14.94	5.35	06-1965
Terry, Brownfield	92.5	26.1	*111	1994	*-8	1963	Apr. 3	Nov. 3	213	0.54	0.68	0.64	0.95	2.90	3.00	2.31	2.15	2.78	1.50	0.79	0.65	18.89	5.05	10-1983
Throckmorton, Throckmorton	97.0	28.0	114		-11		Mar. 31	Nov. 6	220	1.00	1.50	1.60	2.10	3.30	3.50	1.80	2.60	3.30	2.90	1.50	1.50	26.60		
Titus, Mount Pleasant	94.2	29.3	118	1936	-12	1951	Mar. 29	Nov. 5	220	3.27	3.54	4.42	3.77	5.02	4.89	3.75	2.05	3.56	4.74	5.07	4.49	48.57	8.06	11-1994
Tom Green, San Angelo	94.4	31.8	111	1960	-4	1989	Mar. 28	Nov. 13	230	0.82	1.18	0.99	1.60	3.09	2.52	1.10	2.05	2.95	2.57	1.10	0.94	20.91	6.24	09-1980

COUNTY AND STATION	TEMPERATURE						AVERAGE FREEZE DATES		Growing Season	MEAN PRECIPITATION													EXTREMES	
	Mean Max. July (F.)	Mean Min. January (F.)	Record Highest (F.)	Year	Record Lowest (F.)	Year	Last in Spring (Mo. Day)	First in Fall (Mo. Day)	Days	January (In.)	February (In.)	March (In.)	April (In.)	May (In.)	June (In.)	July (In.)	August (In.)	September (In.)	October (In.)	November (In.)	December (In.)	Annual (In.)	Highest Daily Rainfall (In.)	Mo.-Year
Travis, Austin	95.0	40.0	112	2000	-2	1949	Feb. 17	Dec. 6	291	1.89	1.99	2.14	2.51	5.03	3.81	1.97	2.31	2.91	3.97	2.68	2.44	33.65	8.00	06-1941
Trinity, Groveton	94.8	37.1	111	2000	1	1989	Mar. 14	Nov. 14	244	4.17	3.21	3.67	3.13	5.11	5.01	3.48	3.25	4.10	4.07	4.49	4.41	48.10	12.10	10-1994
Tyler, Town Bluff Dam	92.1	38.3	109	2000	6	1989	Mar. 9	Nov. 19	255	5.08	4.02	4.56	4.41	5.61	5.74	3.46	3.42	4.17	3.68	5.08	5.56	54.79	7.50	09-1996
Upshur, Gilmer	93.4	31.4	114	1936	*-4	1989	Mar. 29	Nov. 5	220	3.51	3.58	4.38	4.12	4.41	4.13	3.04	2.50	3.84	4.47	4.75	4.35	47.08	7.88	04-1966
Upton, McCamey	95.6	33.1	*113	1994	-2	1962	Mar. 20	Nov. 12	236	0.47	0.56	0.41	0.93	1.61	1.55	0.94	1.95	2.68	2.06	0.59	0.70	14.45	9.13	10-1986
Uvalde, Uvalde	96.0	37.0	111		6		Mar. 10	Nov. 21	255	1.00	1.10	1.00	2.00	3.30	3.50	1.20	2.60	2.30	2.40	1.60	1.30	23.30		
Val Verde, Del Rio	96.2	39.7	112	1988	10	1989	Feb. 19	Dec. 1	284	0.57	0.96	0.96	1.71	2.31	2.34	2.02	2.16	2.06	2.00	0.96	0.75	18.80	17.03	08-1998
Van Zandt, Wills Point	93.3	31.4	115	1909	*-2	1989	Mar. 14	Nov. 18	248	3.10	3.22	3.74	3.68	4.74	4.45	2.16	2.26	3.39	4.78	4.23	3.93	43.68	7.08	06-1945
Victoria, Victoria	93.4	43.6	111	2000	9	1989	Feb. 9	Dec. 11	305	2.44	2.04	2.25	2.97	5.12	4.96	2.90	3.05	5.00	4.26	2.64	2.47	40.10	9.87	04-1991
Walker, Huntsville	93.8	39.0	108	2000	2	1989	Feb. 23	Nov. 30	279	4.28	3.14	3.47	3.50	5.08	4.66	2.67	3.69	4.73	4.32	4.87	4.10	48.51	10.21	10-1994
Waller, Hempstead	95.0	38.0	107		13		Feb. 28	Dec. 4	283	2.80	2.90	2.10	3.90	4.70	3.60	2.00	2.40	4.60	4.00	3.20	3.00	38.20		
Ward, Monahans	98.6	26.5	*118	1994	-9	1962	Apr. 1	Nov. 7	219	0.51	0.57	0.27	0.55	1.80	1.43	1.31	1.65	2.55	1.39	0.53	0.67	13.23	4.40	09-1980
Washington, Brenham	96.7	39.3	113	2000	*-2	1930	Feb. 20	Dec. 5	288	3.41	2.78	2.93	3.39	5.14	4.66	1.93	3.14	4.83	4.48	4.17	3.29	44.15	10.38	10-1994
Webb, Laredo	101.6	41.8	*114	1998	11	1983	Feb. 9	Dec. 5	299	0.76	0.94	0.92	1.55	2.73	2.99	1.79	2.42	2.73	2.72	1.13	0.85	21.53	6.65	07-1981
Wharton, Pierce	94.3	41.8	112	2000	4	1949	Feb. 19	Dec. 6	290	3.42	2.84	2.74	3.18	5.18	4.69	3.10	3.57	5.81	4.61	3.55	3.23	45.92	8.85	11-1943
Wheeler, Shamrock	93.3	22.9	113	1980	-13	1984	Apr. 6	Oct. 27	203	0.56	0.84	1.88	2.62	3.92	3.74	2.17	2.27	2.83	1.92	1.17	0.83	24.32	8.24	06-1995
Wichita, Wichita Falls	97.2	28.9	117	1980	-12	1947	Mar. 28	Nov. 9	225	1.12	1.58	2.27	2.62	3.92	3.69	1.58	2.39	3.19	3.11	1.68	1.68	28.83	6.19	09-1980
Wilbarger, Vernon	97.2	25.7	119	1943	-9	1989	Mar. 30	Nov. 9	223	1.09	1.34	1.98	2.36	4.11	3.82	1.94	3.07	3.54	2.70	1.48	1.12	28.55	14.82	08-1995
Willacy, Raymondville	95.3	47.5	109	1916	*14	1962	Jan. 19	Jan. 1	347	1.36	1.59	1.44	1.53	2.80	3.22	1.91	3.06	5.40	3.17	1.38	1.11	27.97	9.90	09-1975
Williamson, Taylor	95.3	35.8	*112	2000	-5	1949	Mar. 5	Nov. 20	259	2.09	2.38	2.63	2.68	5.19	3.78	1.62	2.09	3.30	3.83	2.95	2.57	35.11	*6.00	09-1958
Wilson, Floresville	95.7	38.4	111	2000	5	1985	Mar. 8	Nov. 21	257	1.58	1.60	1.65	2.53	3.69	3.24	1.60	2.54	3.39	2.75	2.24	1.57	27.60	9.25	09-1967
Winkler, Wink	96.1	27.8	117	1994	-14	1962	Apr. 2	Nov. 4	215	0.41	0.48	0.32	0.53	1.34	1.83	1.95	1.29	2.14	1.51	0.55	0.57	12.92	5.64	10-1940
Wise, Bridgeport	98.0	30.5	*115	1980	-8	1989	Mar. 30	Nov. 7	222	1.53	2.06	2.63	2.83	5.53	3.54	2.26	2.01	2.97	4.37	2.28	2.01	34.02	9.07	10-1919
Wood, Mineola	93.1	31.2	*110	2000	1	1983	Apr. 1	Nov. 7	219	3.33	3.43	4.05	3.98	4.71	3.99	2.92	2.23	3.67	4.99	4.50	4.08	45.88	6.42	12-1982
Yoakum, Plains	91.7	25.1	111	1994	*-12	1951	Apr. 5	Oct. 29	206	0.49	0.72	0.60	1.15	2.38	2.55	2.34	2.75	3.67	1.24	0.75	0.77	18.41	6.11	07-1960
Young, Graham	96.6	27.1	117	1936	*-8	1989	Apr. 2	Nov. 6	217	1.16	1.79	2.22	2.45	4.52	3.60	2.17	2.32	3.64	3.79	1.88	1.81	31.35	8.22	10-1981
Zapata, Zapata	98.0	45.4	116	1998	13	1911	Jan. 24	Dec. 25	337	0.70	1.04	0.79	1.39	2.27	2.67	1.55	1.80	3.65	1.85	0.94	0.88	19.53	6.10	04-1966
Zavala, Crystal City	97.1	42.6	115	2000	*11	1989	Feb. 16	Dec. 6	292	0.93	1.08	1.08	1.75	2.41	3.25	1.67	2.03	2.10	2.44	1.12	0.84	20.70	6.83	10-1959

Calendar

McDonald Observatory in Jeff Davis County. Photo by Frank Cianciolo; McDonald Observatory.

Seasons

Morning & Evening Stars

Eclipses & Transit of Venus

Major Meteor Showers

Chronological Eras & Cycles

Calendars for 2012 & 2013

Astronomical Calendars for 2012 & 2013

An Explanation of Texas Time

The subsequent calendars were calculated principally from data on the **U.S. Naval Observatory's website** (http://www.usno.navy.mil/USNO) and from its publications ***Astronomical Phenomena for 2012*** and ***Astronomical Phenomena for 2013.***

Times listed here are **Central Standard Time,** except for the period from 2:00 a.m. on the second Sunday in March until 2:00 a.m. on the first Sunday in November, when **Daylight Saving Time,** which is one hour later than Central Standard Time, is in effect.

All of Texas is in the Central Time Zone, except El Paso and Hudspeth counties and the northwest corner of Culberson County, which observe Mountain Time. Mountain Time is one hour earlier than Central Time.

All times are calculated for the intersection of 99° 20' west longitude and 31° 08' north latitude, which is closest to the **town of Mercury** and is about 15 miles northeast of Brady, McCulloch County. This point is the **approximate geographical center** of the state.

How to Adjust Rise & Set Times

To adjust the time of sunrise or sunset, moonrise or moonset for any point in Texas, apply the following rule: **Add four minutes** to the time given in this calendar for each degree of longitude that the place lies west of the 99th meridian; **subtract four minutes** for each degree of longitude the place lies east of the 99th meridian.

At times there will be considerable variation for distances north and south of the line of 31° 08' north latitude, but the rule for calculating it is complicated. The formula given above will get sufficiently close results.

The **accompanying map** shows the intersection for which all times given here are calculated, with some major Texas cities and their longitudes. These make it convenient to calculate time at any given point.

Planetary Configurations & Phenomena

The phenomena and planetary configurations of the heavens for 2012 and 2013 are given in the center column of the calendars on pages 155–162. Below is an explanation of the symbols used in those tables:

☉ The Sun	● The Earth	⛢ Uranus
☾ The Moon	♂ Mars	♆ Neptune
☿ Mercury	♃ Jupiter	♇ Pluto
♀ Venus	♄ Saturn	

Aspects: Conjunction & Opposition

☌ This symbol, appearing between symbols for heavenly bodies, means they are **"in conjunction,"** that is, having the same longitude in the sky and appearing near each other. For example, ♀ ☌ ☾ means Venus is **north** or **south** of the moon by a few degrees. Conjunctions listed in this calendar are separated by **10 degrees** or less. **Inferior** and **superior conjuctions** mean an inner plant, Venus or Mercury, is in line with the Sun, either between the Earth and the Sun **(inferior)** or on the opposite side of the Sun **(superior).**

☍ This symbol means that the heavenly body listed is in **"opposition"** to the Sun, or that they differ by 180 degrees of longitude.

Common Astronomical Terms

★ **Aphelion** — Point at which a planet's orbit is farthest from the sun.

★ **Perihelion** — Point at which a planet's orbit is nearest the sun.

★ **Apogee** — That point of the moon's orbit farthest from the earth.

★ **Perigee** — That point of the moon's orbit nearest the earth.

The Seasons

2012

Spring — Tuesday, **March 20,** at 12:14 a.m. (CDT);
Summer — Wednesday, **June 20,** at 6:09 p.m. (CDT);
Autumn — Saturday, **Sept. 22,** at 9:49 a.m. (CDT);
Winter — Friday, **Dec. 21,** at 5:12 a.m. (CST).

2013

Spring — Wednesday, **March 20,** at 6:02 a.m. (CDT);
Summer — Friday, **June 21,** at 12:04 a.m. (CDT);
Autumn — Sunday, **Sept. 22,** at 3:44 p.m. (CDT);
Winter — Saturday, **Dec. 21,** at 11:11 a.m. (CST).

Morning & Evening Stars

Morning Stars, 2012

Venus ♀ — June 13 – Dec. 31
Mars ♂ — Jan. 1 – March 3
Jupiter ♃ — May 28 – Dec. 3
Saturn ♄ — Jan. 1 – April 15; Nov. 12 – Dec. 31

Evening Stars, 2012

Venus ♀ — Jan. 1 – May 30
Mars ♂ — March 3 – Dec. 31
Jupiter ♃ — Jan. 1 – April 29; Dec. 3 – Dec. 31
Saturn ♄ — April 15 – Oct. 8

Morning Stars, 2013

Venus ♀ — Jan. 1 – Feb. 16
Mars ♂ — June 20 – Dec. 31
Jupiter ♃ — July 4 – Dec. 31
Saturn ♄ — Jan. 1 – April 28; Nov. 24 – Dec. 31

Evening Stars, 2013

Venus ♀ — May. 7 – Dec. 31
Mars ♂ — Jan. 1 – Feb. 9
Jupiter ♃ — Jan. 1 – June 5
Saturn ♄ — April 28 – Oct. 20

Major Meteor Showers

These are approximate dates. Listen to local news/weather broadcasts several days beforehand to determine peak observation days and hours. Generally, viewing is best between midnight and dawn of the date listed.

Meteor shower dates are provided by McDonald Observatory, The University of Texas at Austin.

Meteor Shower	Peak 2012	Peak 2013
Quadrantid	Jan. 3	Jan. 4
Lyrid	April 21	April 22
Eta Aquarid	May 5	May 6
Perseid	Aug. 12	Aug. 13
Orionid	Oct. 21	Oct. 22
Leonid	Nov. 17	Nov. 18
Geminid	Dec. 13	Dec. 14

Eclipses & Transit of Venus

2012

May 20 — Sun, annular eclipse, visible in North America except easternmost areas, Hawaii, eastern Europe, Greenland, China, Russia, southeast Asia, Philippines, Indonesia, Arctic Ocean, north Pacific Ocean.

June 4 — Moon, partial eclipse, visible in western and central parts of North and South America, Pacific Ocean, Antarctica, Australasia, Japan, eastern Asia.

June 5 — Transit of Venus, visible in North America, Greenland, northwest South America, Australasia, Asia, eastern Africa, eastern Europe.

Nov. 13 — Sun, total eclipse, visible in Australasia, Polynesia, southern Pacific Ocean, Antarctica, extreme southern South America.

Nov. 28 — Moon, penumbral eclipse, North America except the East, east Africa, Europe, Asia, Australia, Greenland, Indian and Pacific oceans.

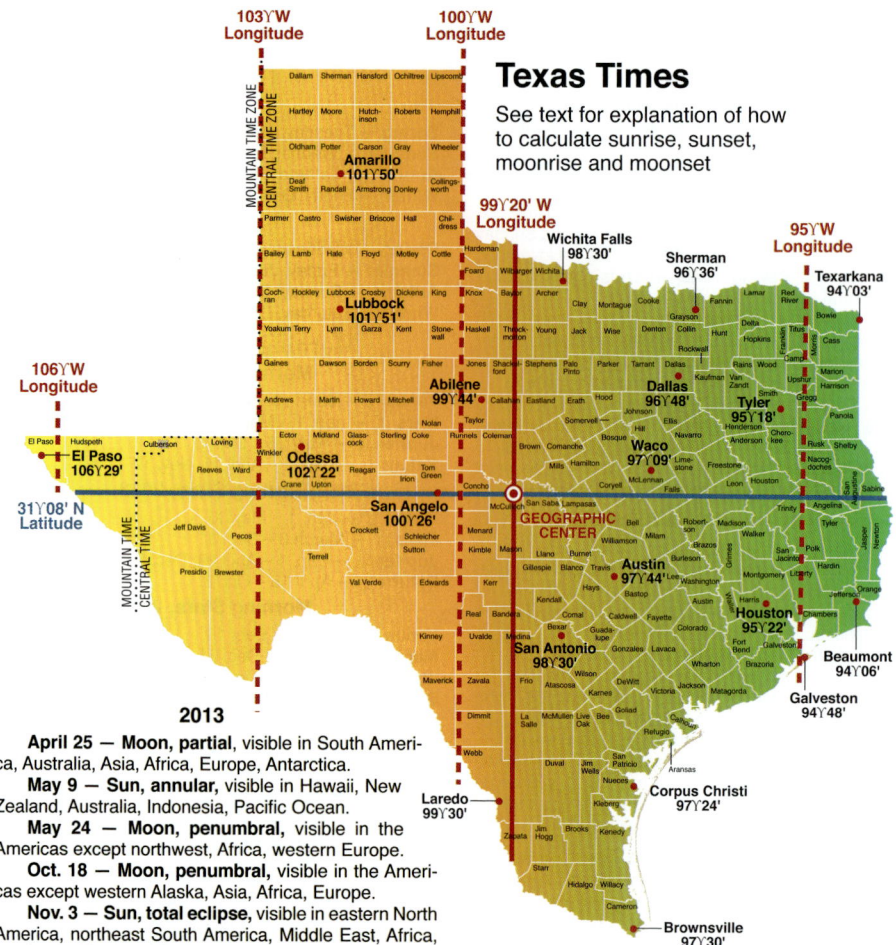

Texas Times

See text for explanation of how to calculate sunrise, sunset, moonrise and moonset

103°W Longitude

100°W Longitude

99°20' W Longitude

95°W Longitude

106°W Longitude

31°08' N Latitude

GEOGRAPHIC CENTER

Amarillo 101°50'

Wichita Falls 98°30'

Sherman 96°36'

Texarkana 94°03'

Lubbock 101°51'

Dallas 96°48'

Tyler 95°18'

Abilene 99°44'

El Paso 106°29'

Odessa 102°22'

Waco 97°09'

San Angelo 100°26'

Austin 97°44'

Houston 95°22'

San Antonio 98°30'

Beaumont 94°06'

Galveston 94°48'

Laredo 99°30'

Corpus Christi 97°24'

Brownsville 97°30'

2013

April 25 — Moon, partial, visible in South America, Australia, Asia, Africa, Europe, Antarctica.

May 9 — Sun, annular, visible in Hawaii, New Zealand, Australia, Indonesia, Pacific Ocean.

May 24 — Moon, penumbral, visible in the Americas except northwest, Africa, western Europe.

Oct. 18 — Moon, penumbral, visible in the Americas except western Alaska, Asia, Africa, Europe.

Nov. 3 — Sun, total eclipse, visible in eastern North America, northeast South America, Middle East, Africa, southwest Europe, Atlantic and west Indian oceans.

Chronological Eras & Cycles

Chronological Eras, 2012

The year 2012 of the **Christian** era comprises the latter part of the 236th and the beginning of the 237th year of the independence of the United States of America, and corresponds to the year 6725 of the Julian period. All dates, below, are given in terms of the Gregorian calendar, in which Jan. 14, 2012, corresponds to Jan. 1, 2012, of the Julian calendar:

Era	Year	Begins
Byzantine	7521	Sept. 14
Jewish (A.M.)*	5773	Sept. 16
Chinese (rén chén)	4649	Jan. 23
Roman (A.U.C.)	2765	Jan. 14
Nabonassar	2761	April 20
Japanese	2672	Jan. 1
Grecian (Seleucidæ)	2324	Sept. 14 or Oct. 14
Indian (Saka)	1934	March 21
Diocletian (Coptic)	1729	Sept. 11
Islamic (Hegira)*	1434	Nov. 14

Year begins at sunset.

Chronological Cycles, 2012

Dominical Letter	AG	Julian Period	6725
Epact	6	Roman Indiction	5
Golden Number or Lunar Cycle	XVIII	Solar Cycle	5

Chronological Eras, 2013

The year 2013 of the **Christian** era comprises the latter part of the 237th and the beginning of the 238th year of the independence of the United States of America, and corresponds to the year 6726 of the Julian period. All dates, below, are given in terms of the Gregorian calendar, in which Jan. 14, 2013, corresponds to Jan. 1, 2013, of the Julian calendar:

Era	Year	Begins
Byzantine	7522	Sept. 14
Jewish (A.M.)*	5774	Sept. 4
Chinese (gui si)	4650	Feb. 10
Roman (A.U.C.)	2766	Jan. 14
Nabonassar	2762	April 20
Japanese	2673	Jan. 1
Grecian (Seleucidæ)	2325	Sept. 14 or Oct. 14
Indian (Saka)	1935	March 22
Diocletian (Coptic)	1730	Sept. 11
Islamic (Hegira)*	1435	Nov. 4

Year begins at sunset.

Chronological Cycles, 2013

Dominical Letter	F	Julian Period	6726
Epact	17	Roman Indiction	6
Golden Number or Lunar Cycle	XIX	Solar Cycle	6

2012

Times are **Central Standard Time,** except from March 11 to Nov. 4, during which **Daylight Saving Time** is observed. **Boldface times for moonrise and moonset indicate p.m.** Times are figured for the point **99° 20' West and 31° 08' North,** the approximate geographical center of the state. **See page 153** for explanation of **how to get the approximate time at any other Texas point.** (On the web: http://www.usno.navy.mil/astronomy) Please note: Not all eclipses are visible in United States. For visibility, see listing beginning on **page 153.**

1st Month — January 2012 — 31 Days

Moon's Phases — *First Qtr.,* Jan. 1, 12:15 a.m.; *Full,* Jan. 9, 1:30 a.m.; *Last Qtr.,* Jan. 16, 3:08 a.m.; *New,* Jan. 23, 1:39 a.m.; *First Qtr.,* Jan. 30, 10:10 p.m.

Day of Year	Day of Month	Day of Week	Planetary Configurations and Phenomena	Sunrise	Sunset	Moonrise	Moonset
1	1	Su.	First qtr. ☾	7:36	5:46	**12:22**	12:47
2	2	Mo.	☾at apogee; ♃☌☾(9pm)	7:36	5:47	**12:55**	1:41
3	3	Tu.		7:36	5:47	**1:30**	2:35
4	4	We.	● at perihelion (6 pm)	7:36	5:48	**2:10**	3:29
5	5	Th.		7:37	5:49	**2:54**	4:23
6	6	Fr.		7:37	5:50	**3:43**	5:17
7	7	Sa.		7:37	5:50	**4:37**	6:08
8	8	Su.		7:37	5:51	**5:35**	6:57
9	9	Mo.	Full ☾	7:37	5:52	**6:36**	7:41
10	10	Tu.		7:37	5:53	**7:38**	8:23
11	11	We.		7:37	5:54	**8:40**	9:01
12	12	Th.		7:37	5:55	**9:42**	9:38
13	13	Fr.	♀☌♆ (1 am)	7:37	5:55	**10:45**	10:13
14	14	Sa.	♂☌☾ (1 am)	7:37	5:56	**11:49**	10:49
15	15	Su.		7:36	5:57		11:26
16	16	Mo.	Last qtr.☾; ♄☌☾ (1 pm)	7:36	5:58	12:54	**12:07**
17	17	Tu.	☾ at perigee (3 pm)	7:36	5:59	2:00	**12:52**
18	18	We.		7:36	6:00	3:06	**1:42**
19	19	Th.		7:36	6:01	4:10	**2:38**
20	20	Fr.		7:35	6:02	5:10	**3:39**
21	21	Sa.		7:35	6:02	6:04	**4:42**
22	22	Su.		7:35	6:03	6:52	**5:46**
23	23	Mo.	New ☾	7:34	6:04	7:35	**6:48**
24	24	Tu.	♂ stationary (7 pm)	7:34	6:05	8:13	**7:48**
25	25	We.	♆☌☾ (6 am)	7:33	6:06	8:47	**8:46**
26	26	Th.	♀☌☾ (1 pm)	7:33	6:07	9:19	**9:42**
27	27	Fr.	♅☌☾ (8 pm)	7:32	6:08	9:50	**10:36**
28	28	Sa.		7:32	6:09	10:21	**11:30**
29	29	Su.		7:31	6:10	10:54	
30	30	Mo.	First qtr. ☾ at apogee	7:31	6:11	11:28	12:24
31	31	Tu.		7:30	6:11	**12:06**	1:18

2nd Month — February 2012 — 29 Days

Moon's Phases — *Full,* Feb. 7, 3:54 p.m.; *Last Qtr.,* Feb. 14, 11:04 a.m.; *New,* Feb. 21, 4:35 p.m.; *First Qtr.,* Feb. 29, 7:21 p.m.

Day of Year	Day of Month	Day of Week	Planetary Configurations and Phenomena	Sunrise	Sunset	Moonrise	Moonset
32	1	We.		7:30	6:12	**12:47**	2:12
33	2	Th.		7:29	6:13	**1:34**	3:05
34	3	Fr.		7:28	6:14	**2:25**	3:57
35	4	Sa.		7:28	6:15	**3:21**	4:47
36	5	Su.		7:27	6:16	**4:21**	5:34
37	6	Mo.		7:26	6:17	**5:23**	6:17
38	7	Tu.	Full ☾; ☿ in superior ☌	7:26	6:18	**6:26**	6:57
39	8	We.	♄ stationary (6 am)	7:25	6:18	**7:30**	7:36
40	9	Th.	♀☌♅ (11 pm)	7:24	6:19	**8:35**	8:13
41	10	Fr.	♂☌☾ (6 am)	7:23	6:20	**9:40**	8:49
42	11	Sa.	☾ at perigee (1 pm)	7:22	6:21	**10:46**	9:27
43	12	Su.	♄☌☾ (7 pm)	7:22	6:22	**11:52**	10:08
44	13	Mo.		7:21	6:23		10:52
45	14	Tu.	Last qtr. ☾	7:20	6:24	12:58	11:40
46	15	We.		7:19	6:24	2:02	**12:34**
47	16	Th.		7:18	6:25	3:03	**1:31**
48	17	Fr.		7:17	6:26	3:58	**2:32**
49	18	Sa.		7:16	6:27	4:47	**3:34**
50	19	Su.	♆☌☉ (3 pm)	7:15	6:28	5:31	**4:35**
51	20	Mo.		7:14	6:28	6:10	**5:35**
52	21	Tu.	New ☾	7:13	6:29	6:45	**6:34**
53	22	We.	Pallas ☌ ☉ (12 pm)	7:12	6:30	7:18	**7:30**
54	23	Th.		7:11	6:31	7:50	**8:25**
55	24	Fr.	♅☌☾ (7 am)	7:10	6:32	8:21	**9:20**
56	25	Sa.	♀☌☾ (4 pm)	7:09	6:32	8:53	**10:14**
57	26	Su.		7:08	6:33	9:27	**11:08**
58	27	Mo.	☾at apogee;♃☌☾(12am)	7:07	6:34	10:03	
59	28	Tu.		7:06	6:35	10:43	12:02
60	29	We.	First qtr. ☾	7:05	6:35	11:27	12:55

† *Daylight Saving Time begins at 2 a.m.*

3rd Month — March 2012 — 31 Days

Moon's Phases — *Full,* March 8, 3:39 a.m.; *Last Qtr.,* March 14, 8:25 p.m.; *New,* March 22, 9:37 a.m; *First Qtr.,* March 30, 2:41 p.m.

Day of Year	Day of Month	Day of Week	Planetary Configurations and Phenomena	Sunrise	Sunset	Moonrise	Moonset
61	1	Th.		7:03	6:36	**12:15**	1:47
62	2	Fr.		7:02	6:37	**1:08**	2:36
63	3	Sa.	♂ ☍	7:01	6:38	**2:05**	3:24
64	4	Su.		7:00	6:38	**3:05**	4:08
65	5	Mo.	♂ closest approach	6:59	6:39	**4:07**	4:49
66	6	Tu.		6:58	6:40	**5:11**	5:29
67	7	We.		6:56	6:40	**6:16**	6:07
68	8	Th.	Full ☾; ♂☌☾ (12 am)	6:55	6:41	**7:23**	6:45
69	9	Fr.		6:54	6:42	**8:30**	7:23
70	10	Sa.	☾ at perigee (4 am)	6:53	6:42	**9:39**	8:04
71	†11	Su.	**DST begins;** ♄☌☾(2am)	7:52	7:43	**11:47**	9:48
72	12	Mo.		7:50	7:44		10:37
73	13	Tu.		7:49	7:45	12:54	11:30
74	14	We.	Last qtr. ☾	7:48	7:45	1:57	**12:27**
75	15	Th.	♀☌♃ (6 am)	7:47	7:46	2:54	**1:27**
76	16	Fr.		7:45	7:47	3:45	**2:28**
77	17	Sa.		7:44	7:47	4:30	**3:29**
78	18	Su.		7:43	7:48	5:10	**4:28**
79	19	Mo.		7:42	7:49	5:46	**5:26**
80	20	Tu.	**Equinox;** ♆☌☾ (2 am)	7:40	7:49	6:19	**6:22**
81	21	We.	☿ in inferior ☌ (2 pm)	7:39	7:50	6:51	**7:17**
82	22	Th.	New ☾	7:38	7:50	7:22	**8:12**
83	23	Fr.		7:37	7:51	7:54	**9:06**
84	24	Sa.	♅☌☉ (1 pm)	7:35	7:52	8:27	**10:00**
85	25	Su.	♃☌☾ (7 pm)	7:34	7:52	9:02	**10:54**
86	26	Mo.	☾at apogee; ♀☌☾(1 pm)	7:33	7:53	9:41	**11:47**
87	27	Tu.	♀ gr. elongation E (3 am)	7:32	7:54	10:23	
88	28	We.		7:30	7:54	11:09	12:39
89	29	Th.		7:29	7:55	11:59	1:29
90	30	Fr.	First qtr. ☾	7:28	7:56	**12:53**	2:16
91	31	Sa.		7:27	7:56	**1:50**	3:00

Astronomical Calendar for 2012

4th Month — April 2012 — 30 Days

Moon's Phases — *Full*, April 6, 2:19 p.m.; *Last Qtr.*, April 13, 5:50 a.m.; *New*, April 21, 2:18 a.m.; *First Qtr.*, April 29, 4:57 a.m.

Day of Year	Day of Month	Day of Week	Planetary Configurations and Phenomena	Sunrise	Sunset	Moon-rise	Moon-set
92	1	Su.		7:25	7:57	**2:49**	3:42
93	2	Mo.		7:24	7:58	**3:51**	4:21
94	3	Tu.	☿ stationary; ♂ ☌ ☾ (10pm)	7:23	7:58	**4:54**	4:59
95	4	We.		7:22	7:59	**6:00**	5:36
96	5	Th.		7:21	8:00	**7:07**	6:14
97	6	Fr.	Full ☾	7:19	8:00	**8:16**	6:55
98	7	Sa.	☾ at perigee; ♄ ☌ ☾	7:18	8:01	**9:27**	7:38
99	8	Su.		7:17	8:01	**10:37**	8:26
100	9	Mo.	Vesta ☌ ☉ (7 pm)	7:16	8:02	**11:44**	9:20
101	10	Tu.	♇ stationary	7:15	8:03		10:18
102	11	We.		7:13	8:03	12:46	11:19
103	12	Th.	♇ ☌ ☾ (4 am)	7:12	8:04	1:41	**12:22**
104	13	Fr.	Last qtr. ☾	7:11	8:05	2:28	**1:23**
105	14	Sa.		7:10	8:05	3:10	**2:24**
106	15	Su.	♂ stationary; ♄ ☍	7:09	8:06	3:47	**3:22**
107	16	Mo.	♆ ☌ ☾; ♀ ☌ Aldebaran	7:08	8:07	4:21	**4:18**
108	17	Tu.		7:07	8:07	4:53	**5:13**
109	18	We.	☿ gr. elong. W; ☿ ☌ ☾	7:05	8:08	5:24	**6:07**
110	19	Th.	♅ ☌ ☾ (3 am)	7:04	8:09	5:55	**7:00**
111	20	Fr.		7:03	8:09	6:28	**7:54**
112	21	Sa.	New ☾; ☿ ☌ ♅ (9 pm)	7:02	8:10	7:03	**8:48**
113	22	Su.	☾ at apogee; ♃ ☌ ☾ (2 pm)	7:01	8:11	7:40	**9:41**
114	23	Mo.		7:00	8:11	8:21	**10:34**
115	24	Tu.	♀ ☌ ☾ (9 pm)	6:59	8:12	9:06	**11:24**
116	25	We.		6:58	8:13	9:54	
117	26	Th.	Ceres ☌ ☉ (9 am)	6:57	8:13	10:46	12:12
118	27	Fr.		6:56	8:14	11:41	12:56
119	28	Sa.		6:55	8:15	**12:38**	1:38
120	29	Su.	First qtr. ☾	6:54	8:15	**1:37**	2:17
121	30	Mo.	♀ greatest illumination	6:53	8:16	**2:37**	2:54

5th Month — May 2012 — 31 Days

Moon's Phases — *Full*, May 5, 10:35 p.m.; *Last Qtr.*, May 12, 4:47 p.m.; *New*, May 20, 6:47 p.m.; *First Qtr.*, May 28, 3:16 p.m.

Day of Year	Day of Month	Day of Week	Planetary Configurations and Phenomena	Sunrise	Sunset	Moon-rise	Moon-set
122	1	Tu.	♂ ☌ ☾ (9 am)	6:52	8:17	**3:40**	3:30
123	2	We.		6:51	8:17	**4:44**	4:07
124	3	Th.		6:51	8:18	**5:51**	4:45
125	4	Fr.	♄ ☌ ☾ (5 pm)	6:50	8:19	**7:01**	5:26
126	5	Sa.	Full ☾ at perigee (11pm)	6:49	8:20	**8:12**	6:12
127	6	Su.		6:48	8:20	**9:22**	7:03
128	7	Mo.		6:47	8:21	**10:29**	8:00
129	8	Tu.		6:46	8:22	**11:29**	9:02
130	9	We.	♇ ☌ ☾ (12 pm)	6:46	8:22		10:07
131	10	Th.		6:45	8:23	12:21	11:12
132	11	Fr.		6:44	8:24	1:07	**12:15**
133	12	Sa.	Last qtr. ☾	6:43	8:24	1:47	**1:15**
134	13	Su.	♃ ☌ ☉ (8 am); ♆ ☌ ☾	6:43	8:25	2:22	**2:12**
135	14	Mo.		6:42	8:26	2:55	**3:08**
136	15	Tu.	♀ stationary; Pallas ☌ ☾	6:41	8:26	3:26	**4:02**
137	16	We.	♅ ☌ ☾ (12 pm)	6:41	8:27	3:58	**4:56**
138	17	Th.		6:40	8:28	4:30	**5:49**
139	18	Fr.		6:40	8:28	5:04	**6:43**
140	19	Sa.	☾ at apogee; Juno ☍	6:39	8:29	5:40	**7:36**
141	20	Su.	New ☾; eclipse ☉ (3 pm)	6:39	8:30	6:20	**8:29**
142	21	Mo.		6:38	8:30	7:04	**9:20**
143	22	Tu.	♀ ☌ ☾ (4 pm)	6:38	8:31	7:51	**10:09**
144	23	We.		6:37	8:32	8:42	**10:55**
145	24	Th.		6:37	8:32	9:36	**11:37**
146	25	Fr.		6:36	8:33	10:32	
147	26	Sa.		6:36	8:33	11:30	12:17
148	27	Su.	☿ in superior ☌ (6 am)	6:35	8:34	**12:28**	12:54
149	28	Mo.	First qtr. ☾	6:35	8:35	**1:28**	1:29
150	29	Tu.	♂ ☌ ☾ (6 am)	6:35	8:35	**2:29**	2:04
151	30	We.		6:35	8:36	**3:33**	2:40
152	31	Th.		6:34	8:36	**4:39**	3:18

6th Month — June 2012 — 30 Days

Moon's Phases — *Full*, June 4, 6:12 a.m.; *Last Qtr.*, June 11, 5:41 a.m.; *New*, June 19, 10:02 a.m.; *First Qtr.*, June 26, 10:30 p.m.

Day of Year	Day of Month	Day of Week	Planetary Configurations and Phenomena	Sunrise	Sunset	Moon-rise	Moon-set
153	1	Fr.	♄ ☌ ☾ (12 am)	6:34	8:37	**5:48**	4:00
154	2	Sa.		6:34	8:37	**6:57**	4:48
155	3	Su.	☾ at perigee (8 am)	6:34	8:38	**8:06**	5:41
156	4	Mo.	Full ☾; eclipse ☾ (3 am)	6:33	8:38	**9:10**	6:41
157	5	Tu.	♀ inf. ☌-transit ☉; ♇ ☌ ☾	6:33	8:39	**10:08**	7:46
158	6	We.		6:33	8:39	**10:58**	8:52
159	7	Th.		6:33	8:40	**11:42**	9:58
160	8	Fr.		6:33	8:40		11:02
161	9	Sa.		6:33	8:41	12:20	**12:02**
162	10	Su.	♆ ☌ ☾ (12 am)	6:33	8:41	12:55	**1:00**
163	11	Mo.	Last qtr. ☾	6:33	8:41	1:28	**1:56**
164	12	Tu.	♅ ☌ ☾ (8 pm)	6:33	8:42	1:59	**2:50**
165	13	We.		6:33	8:42	2:31	**3:44**
166	14	Th.		6:33	8:43	3:04	**4:37**
167	15	Fr.	♀ ☌ Aldebaran (1 am)	6:33	8:43	3:40	**5:31**
168	16	Sa.	☾ at apogee	6:33	8:43	4:18	**6:24**
169	17	Su.	♃ ☌ ☾ (3 am); ♀ ☌ ☾ (8 pm)	6:33	8:43	5:01	**7:16**
170	18	Mo.		6:34	8:44	5:47	**8:06**
171	19	Tu.	New ☾	6:34	8:44	6:38	**8:53**
172	20	We.	**Solstice** (6:09 pm)	6:34	8:44	7:31	**9:37**
173	21	Th.	☿ ☌ Pollux; ☿ ☌ ☾ (2 pm)	6:34	8:44	8:27	**10:18**
174	22	Fr.		6:34	8:45	9:25	**10:56**
175	23	Sa.		6:35	8:45	10:23	**11:31**
176	24	Su.		6:35	8:45	11:22	
177	25	Mo.		6:35	8:45	**12:22**	12:06
178	26	Tu.	First qtr. ☾; ♄ ♀ stationary	6:36	8:45	**1:23**	12:41
179	27	We.		6:36	8:45	**2:26**	1:17
180	28	Th.	♄ ☌ ☾ (7 am)	6:36	8:45	**3:31**	1:56
181	29	Fr.	♇ ☍	6:37	8:45	**4:38**	2:39
182	30	Sa.	☿ gr. elongation E (9 pm)	6:37	8:45	**5:46**	3:28

☉ The Sun ● The Earth ☾ The Moon ☿ Mercury ♀ Venus ♂ Mars ♃ Jupiter ♄ Saturn ♆ Neptune ♅ Uranus ♇ Pluto ☌ = in conjunction ☍ = opposition to the ☉

Astronomical Calendar for 2012

7th Month — July 2012 — 31 Days

Moon's Phases — *Full,* July 3, 1:52 p.m.; *Last Qtr.,* July 10, 8:48 p.m.; *New,* July 18, 11:24 p.m.; *First Qtr.,* July 26, 3:56 a.m.

Day of Year	Day of Month	Day of Week	Planetary Configurations and Phenomena	Sunrise	Sunset	Moonrise	Moonset
183	1	Su.	☾ at perigee (1 pm)	6:37	8:45	**6:51**	4:23
184	2	Mo.		6:38	8:45	**7:52**	5:25
185	3	Tu.	Full ☾; ♇ ☌ ☾ (7 am)	6:38	8:45	**8:46**	6:30
186	4	We.	● at aphelion (10 pm)	6:39	8:45	**9:33**	7:37
187	5	Th.		6:39	8:45	**10:15**	8:43
188	6	Fr.		6:40	8:45	**10:52**	9:46
189	7	Sa.	♆ ☌ ☾ (9 am)	6:40	8:45	**11:26**	10:46
190	8	Su.		6:41	8:44	**11:59**	11:44
191	9	Mo.	♀ ☌ Aldebaran (2 pm)	6:41	8:44		**12:41**
192	10	Tu.	Last qtr. ☾; ♅ ☌ ☾ (4 am)	6:42	8:44	12:32	**1:35**
193	11	We.		6:42	8:44	1:05	**2:30**
194	12	Th.	♀ greatest illumination	6:43	8:43	1:39	**3:23**
195	13	Fr.	☾ at apogee (12 pm)	6:43	8:43	2:17	**4:17**
196	14	Sa.	☿ stationary (12 am)	6:44	8:43	2:58	**5:09**
197	15	Su.	♀ ☌ ☾ (10 am)	6:44	8:42	3:42	**6:00**
198	16	Mo.		6:45	8:42	4:31	**6:49**
199	17	Tu.		6:45	8:41	5:24	**7:34**
200	18	We.	New ☾	6:46	8:41	6:20	**8:17**
201	19	Th.	Juno stationary (9 am)	6:47	8:40	7:17	**8:56**
202	20	Fr.		6:47	8:40	8:16	**9:33**
203	21	Sa.		6:48	8:39	9:16	**10:09**
204	22	Su.		6:48	8:39	10:16	**10:44**
205	23	Mo.		6:49	8:38	11:17	**11:19**
206	24	Tu.	♂ ☌ ☾ (5 pm)	6:50	8:38	**12:19**	**11:57**
207	25	We.	♄ ☌ ☾ (2 pm)	6:50	8:37	**1:23**	
208	26	Th.	First qtr. ☾	6:51	8:36	**2:28**	12:38
209	27	Fr.		6:52	8:36	**3:33**	1:24
210	28	Sa.	☿ in inferior ☌ (3 pm)	6:52	8:35	**4:38**	2:15
211	29	Su.	☾ at perigee (3 am)	6:53	8:34	**5:38**	3:12
212	30	Mo.	♇ ☌ ☾ (3 pm)	6:53	8:34	**6:34**	4:14
213	31	Tu.		6:54	8:33	**7:24**	5:18

8th Month — August 2012 — 31 Days

Moon's Phases — *Full,* Aug. 1, 10:27 p.m.; *Last Qtr.,* Aug. 9, 1:55 p.m.; *New,* Aug. 17, 10:54 a.m.; *First Qtr.,* Aug. 24, 8:54 a.m.; *Full,* Aug. 31, 8:58 a.m.

Day of Year	Day of Month	Day of Week	Planetary Configurations and Phenomena	Sunrise	Sunset	Moonrise	Moonset
214	1	We.	Full ☾	6:55	8:32	**8:08**	6:24
215	2	Th.		6:55	8:31	**8:47**	7:28
216	3	Fr.	♃ ☌ Aldebaran (12 am)	6:56	8:31	**9:23**	8:30
217	4	Sa.		6:57	8:30	**9:57**	9:30
218	5	Su.		6:57	8:29	**10:30**	10:28
219	6	Mo.	♅ ☌ ☾ (12 pm)	6:58	8:28	**11:04**	11:24
220	7	Tu.	☿ stationary (12 pm)	6:58	8:27	**11:38**	**12:19**
221	8	We.		6:59	8:26		**1:14**
222	9	Th.	Last qtr. ☾	7:00	8:25	12:15	**2:08**
223	10	Fr.	☾ at apogee (6 am)	7:00	8:24	12:54	**3:00**
224	11	Sa.	♃ ☌ ☾ (4 pm)	7:01	8:23	1:37	**3:52**
225	12	Su.	♂ ☌ Spica (7 pm)	7:02	8:22	2:24	**4:41**
226	13	Mo.	♀ ☌ ☾ (3 pm)	7:02	8:21	3:15	**5:28**
227	14	Tu.		7:03	8:20	4:09	**6:12**
228	15	We.	♀ gr. elong. W (4 am)	7:03	8:19	5:06	**6:53**
229	16	Th.	☿ gr. elong. W (7 am)	7:04	8:18	6:05	**7:31**
230	17	Fr.	New ☾; ♂ ☌ ♄ (4 am)	7:05	8:17	7:05	**8:08**
231	18	Sa.		7:05	8:16	8:06	**8:44**
232	19	Su.		7:06	8:15	9:08	**9:21**
233	20	Mo.		7:07	8:14	10:11	**9:58**
234	21	Tu.	♄ ☌ ☾ (10 pm)	7:07	8:13	11:16	**10:39**
235	22	We.	♂ ☌ ☾ (3 am)	7:08	8:12	**12:21**	**11:23**
236	23	Th.	☾ at perigee (2 pm)	7:08	8:11	**1:26**	
237	24	Fr.	First qtr. ☾; ♆ ☍	7:09	8:10	**2:30**	12:12
238	25	Sa.		7:10	8:08	**3:31**	1:06
239	26	Su.	♇ ☌ ☾ (9 pm)	7:10	8:07	**4:27**	2:05
240	27	Mo.		7:11	8:06	**5:17**	3:08
241	28	Tu.		7:11	8:05	**6:03**	4:11
242	29	We.		7:12	8:04	**6:43**	5:14
243	30	Th.		7:13	8:02	**7:20**	6:16
244	31	Fr.	Full ☾; ♆ ☌ ☾ (12 am)	7:13	8:01	**7:55**	7:16

9th Month — September 2012 — 30 Days

Moon's Phases — *Last Qtr.,* Sept. 8, 8:15 a.m.; *New,* Sept. 15, 9:11 p.m. *First Qtr.,* Sept. 22, 2:41 p.m.; *Full,* Sept. 29, 10:19 p.m.

Day of Year	Day of Month	Day of Week	Planetary Configurations and Phenomena	Sunrise	Sunset	Moonrise	Moonset
245	1	Sa.	♀ ☌ Pollux (5 pm)	7:14	8:00	**8:29**	8:15
246	2	Su.	♅ ☌ ☾ (7 pm)	7:14	7:59	**9:02**	9:12
247	3	Mo.		7:15	7:58	**9:36**	10:08
248	4	Tu.		7:15	7:56	**10:12**	11:03
249	5	We.		7:16	7:55	**10:51**	11:58
250	6	Th.		7:17	7:54	**11:32**	**12:51**
251	7	Fr.	☾ at apogee (1 am)	7:17	7:52		**1:43**
252	8	Sa.	Last qtr. ☾; ♃ ☌ ☾ (6 am)	7:18	7:51	12:17	**2:33**
253	9	Su.	Ceres ☌ ☾ (4 am)	7:18	7:50	1:06	**3:20**
254	10	Mo.	☿ in superior ☌	7:19	7:49	1:58	**4:04**
255	11	Tu.		7:20	7:47	2:53	**4:46**
256	12	We.	♀ ☌ ☾ (12 pm)	7:20	7:46	3:51	**5:26**
257	13	Th.		7:21	7:45	4:50	**6:04**
258	14	Fr.		7:21	7:44	5:51	**6:40**
259	15	Sa.	New ☾	7:22	7:42	6:53	**7:17**
260	16	Su.		7:22	7:41	7:57	**7:56**
261	17	Mo.	♇ stationary (4 pm)	7:23	7:40	9:03	**8:36**
262	18	Tu.	☾ at perigee; ♄ ☌ ☾ (9am)	7:24	7:38	10:10	**9:20**
263	19	We.	♂ ☌ ☾ (4 pm)	7:24	7:37	11:17	**10:09**
264	20	Th.		7:25	7:36	**12:22**	**11:03**
265	21	Fr.		7:25	7:35	**1:25**	
266	22	Sa.	**Equinox;** First qtr. ☾	7:26	7:33	**2:23**	12:01
267	23	Su.	♇ ☌ ☾ (2 am)	7:27	7:32	**3:15**	1:02
268	24	Mo.	Pallas ☍	7:27	7:31	**4:01**	2:04
269	25	Tu.		7:28	7:29	**4:42**	3:07
270	26	We.		7:28	7:28	**5:19**	4:08
271	27	Th.	♆ ☌ ☾ (6 am)	7:29	7:27	**5:54**	5:07
272	28	Fr.		7:29	7:26	**6:28**	6:05
273	29	Sa.	Full ☾; ♅ ☍	7:30	7:24	**7:01**	7:02
274	30	Su.	♅ ☌ ☾ (12am) ☿ ☌ Spica (9pm)	7:31	7:23	**7:35**	7:58

Bright stars = Aldebaran, Antares, Spica, Pollux, Regulus. ★ **Minor planets or asteroids =** Ceres, Pallas, Juno, Vesta ★ ☌ = in conjunction by 10° or < ★ ☍ = opposition to ☉

Astronomical Calendar for 2012

10th Month — October 2012 — 31 Days

Moon's Phases — *Last Qtr.*, Oct. 8, 2:33 a.m.; *New*, Oct. 15, 7:03 a.m.; *First Qtr.*, Oct. 21, 10:32 p.m.; *Full*, Oct. 29, 2:49 p.m.

Day of Year	Day of Month	Day of Week	Planetary Configurations and Phenomena	Sunrise	Sunset	Moonrise	Moonset
275	1	Mo.		7:31	7:22	**8:11**	8:53
276	2	Tu.		7:32	7:20	**8:48**	9:48
277	3	We.	♀ ☌ Regulus (3 am)	7:33	7:19	**9:29**	10:42
278	4	Th.	☾ at apogee (8 pm)	7:33	7:18	**10:12**	11:35
279	5	Fr.		7:34	7:17	**10:59**	**12:25**
280	6	Sa.	☿ ☌ ♄ (2 am)	7:34	7:16	**11:49**	**1:13**
281	7	Su.	Ceres ☌ ☾ (12 am)	7:35	7:14		**1:58**
282	8	Mo.	Last qtr. ☾	7:36	7:13	12:42	**2:40**
283	9	Tu.		7:36	7:12	1:38	**3:20**
284	10	We.		7:37	7:11	2:35	**3:57**
285	11	Th.		7:38	7:10	3:34	**4:34**
286	12	Fr.	♀ ☌ ☾ (2 pm)	7:38	7:08	4:34	**5:10**
287	13	Sa.		7:39	7:07	5:37	**5:48**
288	14	Su.		7:40	7:06	6:42	**6:28**
289	15	Mo.	New ☾	7:40	7:05	7:50	**7:12**
290	16	Tu.	☾at perigee; ☿☌☾(9pm)	7:41	7:04	8:59	**8:00**
291	17	We.		7:42	7:03	10:07	**8:53**
292	18	Th.		7:43	7:02	11:14	**9:52**
293	19	Fr.		7:43	7:01	**12:15**	**10:54**
294	20	Sa.	♂ ☌ Antares (1 am)	7:44	7:00	**1:10**	**11:58**
295	21	Su.	First qtr. ☾	7:45	6:59	**1:59**	
296	22	Mo.		7:45	6:58	**2:42**	1:01
297	23	Tu.		7:46	6:57	**3:20**	2:02
298	24	We.		7:47	6:56	**3:56**	3:02
299	25	Th.	♄ ☌ ☉	7:48	6:55	**4:29**	4:00
300	26	Fr.	☿ gr. elongation E (5pm)	7:49	6:54	**5:02**	4:56
301	27	Sa.	⛢ ☌ ☾ (5 am)	7:49	6:53	**5:36**	5:51
302	28	Su.		7:50	6:52	**6:10**	6:46
303	29	Mo.	Full ☾	7:51	6:51	**6:47**	7:41
304	30	Tu.		7:52	6:50	**7:26**	8:35
305	31	We.	Ceres stationary (4 pm)	7:52	6:49	**8:09**	9:28

11th Month — November 2012 — 30 Days

Moon's Phases — *Last Qtr.*, Nov. 6, 6:36 p.m.; *New*, Nov. 13, 4:08 p.m.; *First Qtr.*, Nov. 20, 8:31 a.m.; *Full*, Nov. 28, 8:46 a.m.

Day of Year	Day of Month	Day of Week	Planetary Configurations and Phenomena	Sunrise	Sunset	Moonrise	Moonset
306	1	Th.	☾at apogee; ♃☌☾(8pm)	7:53	6:48	**8:55**	10:19
307	2	Fr.		7:54	6:47	**9:44**	11:08
308	3	Sa.		7:55	6:47	**10:35**	11:54
309	† 4	Su.	**DST ends**	6:56	5:46	**10:29**	11:36
310	5	Mo.		6:56	5:45	**11:24**	**12:16**
311	6	Tu.	Last qtr. ☾; ☿ stationary	6:57	5:44		**12:53**
312	7	We.		6:58	5:44	12:20	**1:29**
313	8	Th.		6:59	5:43	1:18	**2:05**
314	9	Fr.		7:00	5:42	2:18	**2:41**
315	10	Sa.		7:01	5:42	3:20	**3:18**
316	11	Su.	♆ stationary; ♀☌☾(12pm)	7:01	5:41	4:25	**3:59**
317	12	Mo.	♄ ☌ ☾ (3 pm)	7:02	5:40	5:33	**4:45**
318	13	Tu.	New ☾	7:03	5:40	6:43	**5:37**
319	14	We.	☾ at perigee (4 am)	7:04	5:39	7:52	**6:34**
320	15	Th.	♀ ☌ Spica (5 pm)	7:05	5:39	8:59	**7:37**
321	16	Fr.	♇ ☌ ☾ (5 pm)	7:06	5:38	9:59	**8:43**
322	17	Sa.	☿ in inferior ☌ (10 am)	7:07	5:38	10:53	**9:49**
323	18	Su.		7:07	5:38	11:39	**10:53**
324	19	Mo.		7:08	5:37	**12:20**	**11:55**
325	20	Tu.	First qtr. ☾; ♆☌☾(4 pm)	7:09	5:37	**12:57**	
326	21	We.		7:10	5:36	**1:31**	12:54
327	22	Th.		7:11	5:36	**2:05**	1:51
328	23	Fr.		7:12	5:36	**2:37**	2:47
329	24	Sa.		7:13	5:36	**3:11**	3:41
330	25	Su.		7:13	5:35	**3:47**	4:36
331	26	Mo.	☿stationary; ♀☌♄(11pm)	7:14	5:35	**4:25**	5:30
332	27	Tu.		7:15	5:35	**5:07**	6:23
333	28	We.	Full☾;apogee;eclipse☾☌♃	7:16	5:35	**5:51**	7:15
334	29	Th.		7:17	5:35	**6:39**	8:04
335	30	Fr.		7:18	5:35	**7:30**	8:51

† Daylight Saving Time ends at 2 a.m.

12th Month — December 2012 — 31 Days

Moon's Phases — *Last Qtr.*, Dec. 6, 9:31 a.m.; *New*, Dec. 13, 2:42 a.m.; *First Qtr.*, Dec. 19, 11:19 p.m.; *Full*, Dec. 28, 4:21 a.m.

Day of Year	Day of Month	Day of Week	Planetary Configurations and Phenomena	Sunrise	Sunset	Moonrise	Moonset
336	1	Sa.		7:18	5:35	**8:23**	9:35
337	2	Su.	♃ ☍	7:19	5:35	**9:17**	10:16
338	3	Mo.		7:20	5:35	**10:13**	10:53
339	4	Tu.	♀ gr. elong. W (5 pm)	7:21	5:35	**11:09**	11:29
340	5	We.		7:22	5:35		**12:03**
341	6	Th.	Last qtr. ☾	7:22	5:35	12:06	**12:38**
342	7	Fr.	♃ ☌ Aldebaran (2 pm)	7:23	5:35	1:05	**1:13**
343	8	Sa.		7:24	5:35	2:06	**1:51**
344	9	Su.	Vesta ☍; Spica ☌☾ (6am)	7:25	5:35	3:10	**2:33**
345	10	Mo.	♄ ☌ ☾ (6 am)	7:25	5:35	4:17	**3:20**
346	11	Tu.	♀ ☌ ☾ (8 am)	7:26	5:36	5:26	**4:13**
347	12	We.	☾ at perigee (5 pm)	7:27	5:36	6:34	**5:14**
348	13	Th.	New ☾; ⛢ stationary	7:27	5:36	7:39	**6:19**
349	14	Fr.	♇ ☌ ☾ (6 am)	7:28	5:37	8:38	**7:27**
350	15	Sa.	♂ ☌ ☾ (4 am)	7:29	5:37	9:29	**8:35**
351	16	Su.		7:29	5:37	10:15	**9:41**
352	17	Mo.	☿ ☌ Antares (9 am)	7:30	5:38	10:55	**10:43**
353	18	Tu.	♆ ☌☾ (12 am); Ceres ☍	7:30	5:38	11:31	**11:43**
354	19	We.	First qtr. ☾	7:31	5:39	**12:06**	
355	20	Th.	⛢ ☌ ☾ (2 pm)	7:31	5:39	**12:39**	12:40
356	21	Fr.	**Solstice** (5:12 am)	7:32	5:40	**1:13**	1:36
357	22	Sa.	Juno ☌ ☉ (12 pm)	7:32	5:40	**1:48**	2:30
358	23	Su.	♀ ☌ Antares (5 am)	7:33	5:41	**2:25**	3:24
359	24	Mo.		7:33	5:41	**3:05**	4:18
360	25	Tu.	☾at apogee; ♃☌☾(6 pm)	7:34	5:42	**3:49**	5:10
361	26	We.		7:34	5:42	**4:35**	6:01
362	27	Th.		7:35	5:43	**5:26**	6:49
363	28	Fr.	Full ☾	7:35	5:44	**6:18**	7:34
364	29	Sa.		7:35	5:44	**7:13**	8:16
365	30	Su.	♇ ☌ ☉ (8 am)	7:35	5:45	**8:08**	8:55
366	31	Mo.		7:36	5:46	**9:04**	9:31

☉ The Sun ● The Earth ☾ The Moon ☿ Mercury ♀ Venus ♂ Mars ♃ Jupiter ♄ Saturn ♆ Neptune ⛢ Uranus ♇ Pluto ☌ = in conjunction ☍ = opposition to the ☉

2013

Times are **Central Standard Time,** except from March 10 to Nov. 3, during which **Daylight Saving Time** is observed. **Boldface times for moonrise and moonset indicate p.m.** Times are figured for the point **99° 20' West and 31° 08' North,** the approximate geographical center of the state. **See page 153 for explanation of how to get the approximate time at any other Texas point. (On the web: http://www.usno.navy.mil/astronomy)** Please note: Not all eclipses are visible in United States. For visibility, see listing beginning on **page 154.**

1st Month — January 2013 — 31 Days

Moon's Phases — *Last Qtr.,* Jan. 4, 9:58 p.m.; *New,* Jan. 11, 1:44 p.m.; *First Qtr.,* Jan. 18, 5:45 p.m. *Full,* Jan. 26, 10:38 p.m.

Day of Year	Day of Month	Day of Week	Planetary Configurations and Phenomena	Sunrise	Sunset	Moon-rise	Moon-set
1	1	Tu.	● at perihelion (11 pm)	7:36	5:46	**10:00**	10:06
2	2	We.		7:36	5:47	**10:58**	10:40
3	3	Th.		7:36	5:48	**11:57**	11:14
4	4	Fr.	Last qtr. ☾	7:36	5:49		11:50
5	5	Sa.		7:37	5:49	12:58	**12:28**
6	6	Su.		7:37	5:50	2:01	**1:11**
7	7	Mo.		7:37	5:51	3:06	**1:59**
8	8	Tu.		7:37	5:52	4:12	**2:54**
9	9	We.		7:37	5:53	5:17	**3:56**
10	10	Th.	☾at perigee; ♀☌☾(6 am)	7:37	5:54	6:18	**5:02**
11	11	Fr.	New ☾	7:37	5:54	7:14	**6:10**
12	12	Sa.		7:37	5:55	8:03	**7:18**
13	13	Su.	♂ ☌ ☾ (6 am)	7:37	5:56	8:47	**8:24**
14	14	Mo.	♆ ☌ ☾ (11 am)	7:36	5:57	9:26	**9:27**
15	15	Tu.		7:36	5:58	10:03	**10:27**
16	16	We.	⛢ ☌ ☾ (11 pm)	7:36	5:59	10:38	**11:25**
17	17	Th.		7:36	6:00	11:12	
18	18	Fr.	First qtr.☾; ☿ superior ☌	7:36	6:00	11:48	12:21
19	19	Sa.		7:35	6:01	**12:24**	1:17
20	20	Su.		7:35	6:02	**1:03**	2:11
21	21	Mo.	♃ ☌ ☾ (9 pm)	7:35	6:03	**1:45**	3:03
22	22	Tu.	☾ at apogee (5 am)	7:34	6:04	**2:31**	3:55
23	23	We.		7:34	6:05	**3:20**	4:44
24	24	Th.		7:33	6:06	**4:12**	5:30
25	25	Fr.		7:33	6:07	**5:06**	6:13
26	26	Sa.	Full ☾	7:33	6:08	**6:01**	6:54
27	27	Su.	Vesta stationary (12 pm)	7:32	6:09	**6:58**	7:32
28	28	Mo.		7:32	6:09	**7:55**	8:08
29	29	Tu.		7:31	6:10	**8:53**	8:43
30	30	We.	♃ stationary (10 am)	7:30	6:11	**9:51**	9:17
31	31	Th.		7:30	6:12	**10:51**	9:52

2nd Month — February 2013 — 28 Days

Moon's Phases — *Last Qtr.,* Feb. 3, 7:56 a.m.; *New,* Feb. 10, 1:20 a.m.; *First Qtr.,* Feb. 17, 2:31 p.m.; *Full,* Feb. 25, 2:26 p.m.

Day of Year	Day of Month	Day of Week	Planetary Configurations and Phenomena	Sunrise	Sunset	Moon-rise	Moon-set
32	1	Fr.		7:29	6:13	**11:53**	10:30
33	2	Sa.		7:29	6:14		11:10
34	3	Su.	Last qtr. ☾; ♄☌☾ (4 am)	7:28	6:15	12:56	11:55
35	4	Mo.	Ceres stationary (11 am)	7:27	6:16	2:00	**12:46**
36	5	Tu.		7:26	6:17	3:03	**1:42**
37	6	We.		7:26	6:17	4:04	**2:44**
38	7	Th.	☾ at perigee (6 am)	7:25	6:18	5:00	**3:49**
39	8	Fr.	☿ ☌ ♂ (3 pm)	7:24	6:19	5:51	**4:56**
40	9	Sa.		7:23	6:20	6:37	**6:02**
41	10	Su.	New ☾	7:23	6:21	7:19	**7:07**
42	11	Mo.	☿ ☌ ☾ (12 pm)	7:22	6:22	7:57	**8:09**
43	12	Tu.		7:21	6:23	8:34	**9:09**
44	13	We.	⛢ ☌ ☾ (10 am)	7:20	6:23	9:09	**10:08**
45	14	Th.		7:19	6:24	9:45	**11:05**
46	15	Fr.		7:18	6:25	10:22	
47	16	Sa.	☿ gr. elongation E (3pm)	7:17	6:26	11:00	12:00
48	17	Su.	First qtr. ☾	7:16	6:27	11:42	12:54
49	18	Mo.	Vesta ☌ ☾ (3 pm)	7:15	6:27	**12:26**	1:46
50	19	Tu.	☾at apogee; ♄ stationary	7:14	6:28	**1:13**	2:36
51	20	We.		7:13	6:29	**2:03**	3:24
52	21	Th.	♆ ☌ ☉	7:12	6:30	**2:56**	4:08
53	22	Fr.	☿ stationary (1 pm)	7:11	6:31	**3:51**	4:50
54	23	Sa.		7:10	6:31	**4:47**	5:29
55	24	Su.		7:09	6:32	**5:45**	6:06
56	25	Mo.	Full ☾	7:08	6:33	**6:43**	6:42
57	26	Tu.		7:07	6:34	**7:43**	7:17
58	27	We.		7:06	6:34	**8:44**	7:53
59	28	Th.		7:05	6:35	**9:46**	8:31

† *Daylight Saving Time begins at 2 a.m.*

3rd Month — March 2013 — 31 Days

Moon's Phases — *Last Qtr.,* March 4, 3:53 p.m.; *New,* March 11, 2:51 p.m; *First Qtr.,* March 19, 12:27 p.m.; *Full,* March 27, 4:27 a.m.

Day of Year	Day of Month	Day of Week	Planetary Configurations and Phenomena	Sunrise	Sunset	Moon-rise	Moon-set
60	1	Fr.	Spica ☌ ☾ (1 am)	7:04	6:36	**10:49**	9:11
61	2	Sa.	♄ ☌ ☾ (9 am)	7:03	6:37	**11:53**	9:55
62	3	Su.		7:01	6:37		10:44
63	4	Mo.	Last qtr. ☾; ☿ inferior ☌	7:00	6:38	12:56	11:38
64	5	Tu.	☾ at perigee (5 pm)	6:59	6:39	1:56	**12:36**
65	6	We.		6:58	6:40	2:53	**1:38**
66	7	Th.		6:57	6:40	3:44	**2:42**
67	8	Fr.		6:56	6:41	4:31	**3:47**
68	9	Sa.		6:54	6:42	5:13	**4:50**
69	†10	Su.	**DST begins;** ♆☌☾(11am)	7:53	7:42	6:52	**6:53**
70	11	Mo.	New ☾	7:52	7:43	7:29	**7:53**
71	12	Tu.		7:51	7:44	8:05	**8:53**
72	13	We.		7:49	7:44	8:41	**9:51**
73	14	Th.		7:48	7:45	9:18	**10:47**
74	15	Fr.		7:47	7:46	9:56	**11:43**
75	16	Sa.	☿ stationary (4 pm)	7:46	7:46	10:37	
76	17	Su.	♃ ☌ ☾ (8 pm)	7:45	7:47	11:20	12:36
77	18	Mo.	☾ at apogee (10 pm)	7:43	7:48	**12:06**	1:27
78	19	Tu.	First qtr. ☾	7:42	7:48	**12:55**	2:16
79	20	We.	**Equinox** (6.02 am)	7:41	7:49	**1:46**	3:01
80	21	Th.		7:40	7:50	**2:40**	3:44
81	22	Fr.		7:38	7:50	**3:35**	4:24
82	23	Sa.		7:37	7:51	**4:31**	5:01
83	24	Su.	♃ ☌ Aldebaran (1 pm)	7:36	7:52	**5:29**	5:38
84	25	Mo.		7:35	7:52	**6:29**	6:13
85	26	Tu.		7:33	7:53	**7:30**	6:50
86	27	We.	Full ☾	7:32	7:54	**8:33**	7:27
87	28	Th.	♀ in superior ☌; ⛢ ☌ ☉	7:31	7:54	**9:37**	8:07
88	29	Fr.		7:30	7:55	**10:43**	8:51
89	30	Sa.	☾ at perigee (11 pm)	7:28	7:56	**11:48**	9:40
90	31	Su.	☿ gr. elongation W (5pm)	7:27	7:56		10:33

Astronomical Calendar for 2013

4th Month — April 2013 — 30 Days

Moon's Phases — *Last Qtr.,* April 2, 11:37 p.m.; *New,* April 10, 4:35 a.m.; *First Qtr.,* April 18, 7:31 a.m.; *Full,* April 25, 2:57 p.m.

Day of Year	Day of Month	Day of Week	Planetary Configurations and Phenomena	Sunrise	Sunset	Moon-rise	Moon-set
91	1	Mo.		7:26	7:57	12:50	11:31
92	2	Tu.	Last qtr. ☾	7:25	7:57	1:48	**12:33**
93	3	We.		7:23	7:58	2:41	**1:36**
94	4	Th.		7:22	7:59	3:29	**2:39**
95	5	Fr.		7:21	7:59	4:11	**3:42**
96	6	Sa.	♆ ☌ ☾ (8 pm)	7:20	8:00	4:51	**4:43**
97	7	Su.		7:18	8:01	5:27	**5:43**
98	8	Mo.	☿ ☌ ☾ (5 am)	7:17	8:01	6:03	**6:41**
99	9	Tu.		7:16	8:02	6:38	**7:39**
100	10	We.	New ☾	7:15	8:03	7:15	**8:36**
101	11	Th.		7:14	8:03	7:52	**9:32**
102	12	Fr.	♇ stationary (2 pm)	7:13	8:04	8:32	**10:26**
103	13	Sa.		7:11	8:05	9:15	**11:19**
104	14	Su.	♃ ☌ ☾ (1 pm)	7:10	8:05	10:00	
105	15	Mo.	☾ at apogee (5 pm)	7:09	8:06	10:48	12:09
106	16	Tu.		7:08	8:07	11:38	12:55
107	17	We.	♂ ☌ ☉ (7 pm)	7:07	8:07	**12:30**	1:39
108	18	Th.	First qtr. ☾	7:06	8:08	**1:24**	2:19
109	19	Fr.	☿ ☌ ⛢ (4 pm)	7:05	8:09	**2:18**	2:57
110	20	Sa.		7:04	8:09	**3:14**	3:33
111	21	Su.		7:02	8:10	**4:12**	4:08
112	22	Mo.		7:01	8:11	**5:12**	4:44
113	23	Tu.		7:00	8:11	**6:14**	5:20
114	24	We.	Spica ☌ ☾ (7 pm)	6:59	8:12	**7:18**	5:59
115	25	Th.	Full ☾; ♄ ☌ ☾ (9 pm)	6:58	8:13	**8:25**	6:42
116	26	Fr.		6:57	8:13	**9:32**	7:30
117	27	Sa.	☾ at perigee (3 pm)	6:56	8:14	**10:38**	8:23
118	28	Su.	♄ ☍	6:55	8:15	**11:40**	9:21
119	29	Mo.		6:54	8:15		10:23
120	30	Tu.		6:53	8:16	12:36	11:28

5th Month — May 2013 — 31 Days

Moon's Phases — *Last Qtr.,* May 2, 6:14 a.m.; *New,* May 9, 7:28 p.m.; *First Qtr.,* May 17, 11:35 p.m.; *Full,* May 24, 11:25 p.m.; *Last Qtr.,* May 31, 1:58 p.m.

Day of Year	Day of Month	Day of Week	Planetary Configurations and Phenomena	Sunrise	Sunset	Moon-rise	Moon-set
121	1	We.		6:53	8:17	1:27	**12:33**
122	2	Th.	Last qtr. ☾	6:52	8:17	2:11	**1:36**
123	3	Fr.		6:51	8:18	2:52	**2:37**
124	4	Sa.	♆ ☌ ☾ (2 am)	6:50	8:19	3:29	**3:37**
125	5	Su.		6:49	8:19	4:04	**4:35**
126	6	Mo.	⛢ ☌ ☾ (7 pm)	6:48	8:20	4:39	**5:32**
127	7	Tu.		6:47	8:21	5:14	**6:29**
128	8	We.		6:47	8:21	5:51	**7:24**
129	9	Th.	New ☾	6:46	8:22	6:30	**8:19**
130	10	Fr.	Pallas ☌ ☉ (4 pm)	6:45	8:23	7:11	**9:12**
131	11	Sa.	☿ in superior ☌	6:44	8:23	7:55	**10:03**
132	12	Su.	♃ ☌ ☾ (8 am)	6:44	8:24	8:42	**10:51**
133	13	Mo.	☾ at apogee (9 am)	6:43	8:25	9:31	**11:35**
134	14	Tu.		6:42	8:25	10:23	
135	15	We.		6:42	8:26	11:15	12:16
136	16	Th.		6:41	8:27	**12:09**	12:55
137	17	Fr.	First qtr. ☾	6:40	8:27	**1:03**	1:31
138	18	Sa.	♀ ☌ Aldebaran (5 am)	6:40	8:28	**1:59**	2:06
139	19	Su.		6:39	8:29	**2:56**	2:40
140	20	Mo.	☿ ☌ Aldebaran (8 pm)	6:39	8:29	**3:55**	3:15
141	21	Tu.		6:38	8:30	**4:57**	3:52
142	22	We.	Spica ☌ ☾ (6 am)	6:38	8:31	**6:02**	4:32
143	23	Th.	♄ ☌ ☾ (5 am)	6:37	8:31	**7:09**	5:16
144	24	Fr.	Full ☾; eclipse ☾; ☿☌♀	6:37	8:32	**8:17**	6:07
145	25	Sa.	☾ at perigee (9 pm)	6:36	8:33	**9:23**	7:03
146	26	Su.		6:36	8:33	**10:24**	8:06
147	27	Mo.	☿ ☌ ♃ (5 am)	6:36	8:34	**11:19**	9:12
148	28	Tu.	♀ ☌ ♃ (4 pm)	6:35	8:34		10:19
149	29	We.		6:35	8:35	12:08	11:26
150	30	Th.		6:35	8:35	12:51	**12:29**
151	31	Fr.	Last qtr. ☾; ♆☌☾ (9 am)	6:34	8:36	1:30	**1:31**

6th Month — June 2013 — 30 Days

Moon's Phases — *New,* June 8, 10:56 a.m.; *First Qtr.,* June 16, 12:24 p.m.; *Full,* June 23, 6:32 a.m.; *Last Qtr.,* June 29, 11:54 p.m.

Day of Year	Day of Month	Day of Week	Planetary Configurations and Phenomena	Sunrise	Sunset	Moon-rise	Moon-set
152	1	Sa.		6:34	8:37	2:06	**2:30**
153	2	Su.		6:34	8:37	2:41	**3:27**
154	3	Mo.	⛢ ☌ ☾ (3 am)	6:34	8:38	3:16	**4:24**
155	4	Tu.		6:33	8:38	3:52	**5:19**
156	5	We.		6:33	8:39	4:30	**6:14**
157	6	Th.		6:33	8:39	5:10	**7:07**
158	7	Fr.	♆ stationary (1 pm)	6:33	8:40	5:52	**7:59**
159	8	Sa.	New ☾	6:33	8:40	6:38	**8:47**
160	9	Su.	☾ at apogee (5 pm)	6:33	8:41	7:27	**9:33**
161	10	Mo.	♀☌☾(6 am); ☿☌☾(6 pm)	6:33	8:41	8:18	**10:16**
162	11	Tu.		6:33	8:41	9:10	**10:55**
163	12	We.	☿ gr. elong. E (12 pm)	6:33	8:42	10:03	**11:32**
164	13	Th.	Juno stationary (8 am)	6:33	8:42	10:57	
165	14	Fr.		6:33	8:42	11:51	12:06
166	15	Sa.		6:33	8:43	**12:46**	12:40
167	16	Su.	First qtr. ☾	6:33	8:43	**1:43**	1:14
168	17	Mo.		6:33	8:43	**2:42**	1:49
169	18	Tu.	Spica ☌ ☾ (3 pm)	6:33	8:44	**3:43**	2:26
170	19	We.	♃ ☌ ☉ (11 am)	6:34	8:44	**4:48**	3:06
171	20	Th.	☿ ☌ ♀ (1 pm)	6:34	8:44	**5:54**	3:53
172	21	Fr.	**Solstice** (12:04 am)	6:34	8:44	**7:01**	4:45
173	22	Sa.	♀ ☌ Pollux (8 pm)	6:34	8:45	**8:05**	5:44
174	23	Su.	Full ☾ at perigee (6 am)	6:35	8:45	**9:04**	6:49
175	24	Mo.		6:35	8:45	**9:57**	7:58
176	25	Tu.	☿ stationary (6 pm)	6:35	8:45	**10:45**	9:07
177	26	We.		6:35	8:45	**11:27**	10:14
178	27	Th.	♆ ☌ ☾ (4 pm)	6:36	8:45		11:19
179	28	Fr.		6:36	8:45	12:06	**12:21**
180	29	Sa.	Last qtr. ☾	6:36	8:45	12:42	**1:20**
181	30	Su.	⛢ ☌ ☾ (10 am)	6:37	8:45	1:18	**2:18**

☉ The Sun ● The Earth ☾ The Moon ☿ Mercury ♀ Venus ♂ Mars ♃ Jupiter ♄ Saturn ♆ Neptune ⛢ Uranus ♇ Pluto ☌ = in conjunction ☍ = opposition to the ☉

Astronomical Calendar for 2013

7th Month — July 2013 — 31 Days

Moon's Phases — *New,* July 8, 2:14 a.m.; *First Qtr.,* July 15, 10:18 p.m.; *Full,* July 22, 1:16 p.m.; *Last Qtr.,* July 29, 12:43 p.m.

Day of Year	Day of Month	Day of Week	Planetary Configurations and Phenomena	Sunrise	Sunset	Moonrise	Moonset
182	1	Mo.	♇ ☍	6:37	8:45	1:54	**3:14**
183	2	Tu.		6:38	8:45	2:31	**4:09**
184	3	We.		6:38	8:45	3:10	**5:03**
185	4	Th.		6:38	8:45	3:51	**5:55**
186	5	Fr.	● at aphelion (10 am)	6:39	8:45	4:36	**6:44**
187	6	Sa.	☾ at apogee; ♂☌☾ (7am)	6:39	8:45	5:24	**7:31**
188	7	Su.		6:40	8:45	6:14	**8:15**
189	8	Mo.	New ☾; ♄ stationary	6:40	8:44	7:05	**8:55**
190	9	Tu.	☿ in inferior ☌	6:41	8:44	7:58	**9:33**
191	10	We.	♀ ☌ ☾ (6 pm)	6:41	8:44	8:52	**10:09**
192	11	Th.		6:42	8:44	9:46	**10:43**
193	12	Fr.		6:42	8:43	10:41	**11:16**
194	13	Sa.		6:43	8:43	11:37	**11:50**
195	14	Su.		6:44	8:43	**12:33**	
196	15	Mo.	First qtr. ☾; Spica ☌ ☾	6:44	8:42	**1:32**	12:25
197	16	Tu.	♄ ☌ ☾ (8 pm)	6:45	8:42	**2:33**	1:03
198	17	We.	♅ stationary (7 pm)	6:45	8:41	**3:37**	1:45
199	18	Th.		6:46	8:41	**4:41**	2:33
200	19	Fr.		6:46	8:41	**5:45**	3:27
201	20	Sa.	☿ stationary (9 pm)	6:47	8:40	**6:46**	4:28
202	21	Su.	☾ at perigee (3 pm)	6:48	8:40	**7:42**	5:34
203	22	Mo.	Full ☾; ♀☌Regulus; ♂☌♃	6:48	8:39	**8:33**	6:42
204	23	Tu.		6:49	8:38	**9:19**	7:52
205	24	We.		6:49	8:38	**10:00**	8:59
206	25	Th.	♆ ☌ ☾ (1 am)	6:50	8:37	**10:39**	10:04
207	26	Fr.		6:51	8:37	**11:16**	11:07
208	27	Sa.	♅ ☌ ☾ (5 pm)	6:51	8:36	**11:53**	**12:07**
209	28	Su.		6:52	8:35		**1:05**
210	29	Mo.	Last qtr. ☾	6:53	8:35	12:30	**2:02**
211	30	Tu.	♀ gr. elong. W (4 am)	6:53	8:34	1:09	**2:57**
212	31	We.		6:54	8:33	1:50	**3:50**

8th Month — August 2013 — 31 Days

Moon's Phases — *New,* Aug. 6, 4:51 p.m.; *First Qtr.,* Aug. 14, 5:56 a.m.; *Full,* Aug. 20, 8:45 p.m.; *Last Qtr.,* Aug. 28, 4:35 a.m.

Day of Year	Day of Month	Day of Week	Planetary Configurations and Phenomena	Sunrise	Sunset	Moonrise	Moonset
213	1	Th.		6:54	8:32	2:34	**4:40**
214	2	Fr.		6:55	8:32	3:20	**5:28**
215	3	Sa.	☾ at apogee; ♃☌☾ (5 pm)	6:56	8:31	4:09	**6:13**
216	4	Su.	♂☌☾ (6 am); ☿☌ Pollux	6:56	8:30	5:01	**6:55**
217	5	Mo.	☿☌☾ (4 am); Vesta ☌ ☉	6:57	8:29	5:53	**7:34**
218	6	Tu.	New ☾	6:58	8:28	6:47	**8:10**
219	7	We.		6:58	8:27	7:42	**8:45**
220	8	Th.		6:59	8:26	8:36	**9:19**
221	9	Fr.	♀ ☌ ☾ (9 pm)	7:00	8:26	9:32	**9:53**
222	10	Sa.		7:00	8:25	10:29	**10:28**
223	11	Su.		7:01	8:24	11:26	**11:05**
224	12	Mo.	Spica ☌ ☾ (4 am)	7:01	8:23	**12:26**	**11:45**
225	13	Tu.	♄ ☌ ☾ (3 am)	7:02	8:22	**1:27**	
226	14	We.	First qtr. ☾	7:03	8:21	**2:29**	12:29
227	15	Th.		7:03	8:20	**3:31**	1:19
228	16	Fr.		7:04	8:19	**4:31**	2:15
229	17	Sa.	Ceres ☌ ☉	7:05	8:18	**5:28**	3:16
230	18	Su.		7:05	8:16	**6:20**	4:22
231	19	Mo.	☾ at perigee (8 pm)	7:06	8:15	**7:08**	5:29
232	20	Tu.	Full ☾	7:06	8:14	**7:52**	6:37
233	21	We.	♆ ☌ ☾ (10 am)	7:07	8:13	**8:32**	7:43
234	22	Th.		7:08	8:12	**9:11**	8:48
235	23	Fr.		7:08	8:11	**9:49**	9:51
236	24	Sa.	♅☌☾ (2 am); ☿ superior ☌	7:09	8:10	**10:27**	10:51
237	25	Su.		7:09	8:09	**11:06**	11:50
238	26	Mo.	♆ ☍	7:10	8:07	**11:47**	**12:47**
239	27	Tu.		7:11	8:06		**1:41**
240	28	We.	Last qtr. ☾	7:11	8:05	12:30	**2:33**
241	29	Th.		7:12	8:04	1:16	**3:23**
242	30	Fr.	☾ at apogee (7 pm)	7:12	8:03	2:04	**4:09**
243	31	Sa.	♃ ☌ ☾ (12 pm)	7:13	8:01	2:54	**4:52**

9th Month — September 2013 — 30 Days

Moon's Phases — *New,* Sept. 5, 6:36 a.m. *First Qtr.,* Sept. 12, 12:08 p.m.; *Full,* Sept. 19, 6:13 a.m.; *Last Qtr.,* Sept. 26, 10:55 p.m.

Day of Year	Day of Month	Day of Week	Planetary Configurations and Phenomena	Sunrise	Sunset	Moonrise	Moonset
244	1	Su.		7:14	8:00	3:46	**5:32**
245	2	Mo.	♂ ☌ ☾ (5 am)	7:14	7:59	4:40	**6:09**
246	3	Tu.		7:15	7:58	5:34	**6:45**
247	4	We.		7:15	7:57	6:29	**7:20**
248	5	Th.	New ☾; ♀☌ Spica (8 am)	7:16	7:55	7:25	**7:54**
249	6	Fr.		7:16	7:54	8:22	**8:29**
250	7	Sa.		7:17	7:53	9:21	**9:06**
251	8	Su.	♀ ☌ ☾ (4 pm)	7:18	7:52	10:20	**9:46**
252	9	Mo.	♄ ☌ ☾ (12 pm)	7:18	7:50	11:21	**10:29**
253	10	Tu.		7:19	7:49	**12:23**	**11:17**
254	11	We.		7:19	7:48	**1:24**	
255	12	Th.	First qtr. ☾	7:20	7:46	**2:24**	12:10
256	13	Fr.		7:21	7:45	**3:20**	1:08
257	14	Sa.		7:21	7:44	**4:12**	2:10
258	15	Su.	☾ at perigee (12 pm)	7:22	7:43	**5:00**	3:15
259	16	Mo.		7:22	7:41	**5:44**	4:20
260	17	Tu.	♆ ☌ ☾ (6 pm)	7:23	7:40	**6:25**	5:25
261	18	We.		7:23	7:39	**7:05**	6:30
262	19	Th.	Full ☾; ♀ ☌ ♄ (7 pm)	7:24	7:37	**7:43**	7:33
263	20	Fr.	♇ stationary (12 am)	7:25	7:36	**8:21**	8:34
264	21	Sa.		7:25	7:35	**9:00**	9:35
265	22	Su.	**Equinox** (3:44 pm)	7:26	7:34	**9:41**	10:33
266	23	Mo.		7:26	7:32	**10:24**	11:30
267	24	Tu.	☿ ☌ Spica (2 pm)	7:27	7:31	**11:10**	**12:24**
268	25	We.		7:28	7:30	**11:57**	**1:14**
269	26	Th.	Last qtr. ☾	7:28	7:28		**2:02**
270	27	Fr.	☾ at apogee (1 pm)	7:29	7:27	12:47	**2:46**
271	28	Sa.	♃ ☌ ☾ (4 am)	7:29	7:26	1:38	**3:27**
272	29	Su.		7:30	7:25	2:31	**4:06**
273	30	Mo.		7:31	7:23	3:24	**4:42**

Bright stars = Aldebaran, Antares, Spica, Pollux, Regulus. ★ **Minor planets or asteroids =** Ceres, Pallas, Juno, Vesta ★ ☌ = in conjunction by 10° or < ★ ☍ = opposition to ☉

Astronomical Calendar for 2013

10th Month — October 2013 — 31 Days

Moon's Phases — *New,* Oct. 4, 7:35 p.m.; *First Qtr.,* Oct. 11, 6:02 p.m.; *Full,* Oct. 18, 6:38 p.m.; *Last Qtr.,* Oct. 26, 6:40 p.m.

Day of Year	Day of Month	Day of Week	Planetary Configurations and Phenomena	Sunrise	Sunset	Moonrise	Moonset
274	1	Tu.	♂ ☌ ☾ (1 am)	7:31	7:22	4:19	**5:17**
275	2	We.		7:32	7:21	5:14	**5:52**
276	3	Th.	♅ ☍	7:32	7:20	6:11	**6:27**
277	4	Fr.	New ☾	7:33	7:18	7:10	**7:04**
278	5	Sa.		7:34	7:17	8:10	**7:44**
279	6	Su.	☿ ☌ ☾ (5 pm)	7:34	7:16	9:12	**8:27**
280	7	Mo.		7:35	7:15	10:15	**9:14**
281	8	Tu.	♀ ☌ ☾ (7 am)	7:36	7:13	11:18	**10:06**
282	9	We.	☿ gr. elongation E	7:36	7:12	**12:18**	**11:03**
283	10	Th.	☾ at perigee (6 pm)	7:37	7:11	**1:16**	
284	11	Fr.	First qtr. ☾	7:38	7:10	**2:09**	12:04
285	12	Sa.	Juno ☌ ☾ (9 pm)	7:38	7:09	**2:57**	1:07
286	13	Su.		7:39	7:08	**3:42**	2:11
287	14	Mo.	♂ ☌ Regulus (5 pm)	7:40	7:06	**4:22**	3:15
288	15	Tu.	♆ ☌ ☾ (1 am)	7:40	7:05	**5:01**	4:17
289	16	We.	♀ ☌ Antares (11 am)	7:41	7:04	**5:39**	5:19
290	17	Th.	♅ ☌ ☾ (4 pm)	7:42	7:03	**6:16**	6:20
291	18	Fr.	Full ☾; eclipse ☾ (4 pm)	7:42	7:02	**6:55**	7:20
292	19	Sa.		7:43	7:01	**7:35**	8:19
293	20	Su.		7:44	7:00	**8:17**	9:17
294	21	Mo.	☿ stationary (10 am)	7:45	6:59	**9:02**	10:12
295	22	Tu.		7:45	6:58	**9:49**	11:05
296	23	We.		7:46	6:57	**10:38**	11:55
297	24	Th.		7:47	6:56	**11:29**	**12:40**
298	25	Fr.	☾ at apogee (9 am)	7:48	6:55		**1:23**
299	26	Sa.	Last qtr. ☾	7:48	6:54	12:21	**2:02**
300	27	Su.		7:49	6:53	1:14	**2:39**
301	28	Mo.		7:50	6:52	2:07	**3:14**
302	29	Tu.	♂ ☌ ☾ (8 pm)	7:51	6:51	3:01	**3:48**
303	30	We.		7:51	6:50	3:57	**4:23**
304	31	Th.		7:52	6:49	4:54	**4:59**

11th Month — November 2013 — 30 Days

Moon's Phases — *New,* Nov. 3, 6:50 a.m.; *First Qtr.,* Nov. 9, 11:57 p.m.; *Full,* Nov. 17, 9:16 a.m.; *Last Qtr.,* Nov. 25, 1:28 p.m.

Day of Year	Day of Month	Day of Week	Planetary Configurations and Phenomena	Sunrise	Sunset	Moonrise	Moonset
305	1	Fr.	♀ gr. elongation E	7:53	6:48	5:54	**5:37**
306	2	Sa.	Spica ☌ ☾ (2 am)	7:54	6:48	6:56	**6:19**
307	† 3	Su.	**DST ends;** eclipse ☉	6:55	5:47	6:59	**6:05**
308	4	Mo.		6:55	5:46	8:04	**6:57**
309	5	Tu.		6:56	5:45	9:08	**7:54**
310	6	We.	☾ at perigee; ♀ ☌ ☾ (7pm)	6:57	5:45	10:09	**8:56**
311	7	Th.	♃ stationary (1 am)	6:58	5:44	11:05	**10:00**
312	8	Fr.		6:59	5:43	11:56	**11:04**
313	9	Sa.	First qtr. ☾	7:00	5:42	**12:41**	
314	10	Su.	☿ stationary (8 am)	7:00	5:42	**1:23**	12:08
315	11	Mo.	♆ ☌ ☾ (5 am)	7:01	5:41	**2:02**	1:11
316	12	Tu.		7:02	5:41	**2:39**	2:12
317	13	We.	♅ ☌ ☾ (9 pm)	7:03	5:40	**3:16**	3:12
318	14	Th.		7:04	5:40	**3:53**	4:11
319	15	Fr.		7:05	5:39	**4:32**	5:09
320	16	Sa.		7:06	5:39	**5:12**	6:07
321	17	Su.	Full ☾; ☿ gr. elong. W	7:06	5:38	**5:56**	7:03
322	18	Mo.		7:07	5:38	**6:42**	7:56
323	19	Tu.		7:08	5:37	**7:31**	8:47
324	20	We.		7:09	5:37	**8:21**	9:35
325	21	Th.	♃ ☌ ☾ (11 pm)	7:10	5:37	**9:12**	10:19
326	22	Fr.	☾ at apogee (4 am)	7:11	5:36	**10:05**	10:59
327	23	Sa.		7:12	5:36	**10:57**	11:37
328	24	Su.		7:12	5:36	**11:50**	**12:12**
329	25	Mo.	Last qtr. ☾; ☿ ☌ ♄ (10 pm)	7:13	5:35		**12:46**
330	26	Tu.		7:14	5:35	12:44	**1:19**
331	27	We.	♂ ☌ ☾ (10 am)	7:15	5:35	1:39	**1:54**
332	28	Th.		7:16	5:35	2:37	**2:30**
333	29	Fr.	Spica ☌ ☾ (11 am)	7:17	5:35	3:36	**3:09**
334	30	Sa.		7:17	5:35	4:38	**3:53**

† Daylight Saving Time ends at 2 a.m.

12th Month — December 2013 — 31 Days

Moon's Phases — *New,* Dec. 2, 6:22 p.m.; *First Qtr.,* Dec. 9, 9:12 a.m.; *Full,* Dec. 17, 3:28 a.m.; *Last Qtr.,* Dec. 25, 7:48 a.m.

Day of Year	Day of Month	Day of Week	Planetary Configurations and Phenomena	Sunrise	Sunset	Moonrise	Moonset
335	1	Su.	♄ ☌ ☾ (4 am)	7:18	5:35	5:43	**4:42**
336	2	Mo.	New ☾	7:19	5:35	6:48	**5:37**
337	3	Tu.		7:20	5:35	7:53	**6:39**
338	4	We.	☾ at perigee (4 am)	7:21	5:35	8:53	**7:44**
339	5	Th.	♀ ☌ ☾ (6 pm)	7:21	5:35	9:48	**8:51**
340	6	Fr.	♀ gr. illumination	7:22	5:35	10:38	**9:58**
341	7	Sa.		7:23	5:35	11:22	**11:03**
342	8	Su.	♆ ☌ ☾ (11 am)	7:24	5:35	**12:03**	
343	9	Mo.	First qtr. ☾	7:24	5:35	**12:41**	12:06
344	10	Tu.		7:25	5:35	**1:18**	1:07
345	11	We.	♅ ☌ ☾ (1 am)	7:26	5:36	**1:54**	2:06
346	12	Th.		7:27	5:36	**2:32**	3:04
347	13	Fr.		7:27	5:36	**3:11**	4:01
348	14	Sa.		7:28	5:37	**3:53**	4:56
349	15	Su.		7:28	5:37	**4:38**	5:50
350	16	Mo.		7:29	5:37	**5:25**	6:42
351	17	Tu.	Full ☾; ♅ stationary	7:30	5:38	**6:15**	7:31
352	18	We.		7:30	5:38	**7:06**	8:16
353	19	Th.	☾ at apogee; ♃ ☌ ☾ (1am)	7:31	5:38	**7:58**	8:58
354	20	Fr.	♀ stationary	7:31	5:39	**8:50**	9:36
355	21	Sa.	**Solstice** (11:11 am)	7:32	5:39	**9:43**	10:12
356	22	Su.		7:32	5:40	**10:36**	10:46
357	23	Mo.		7:33	5:40	**11:30**	11:20
358	24	Tu.		7:33	5:41		11:53
359	25	We.	Last qtr. ☾	7:34	5:42	12:24	**12:27**
360	26	Th.		7:34	5:42	1:21	**1:03**
361	27	Fr.		7:34	5:43	2:20	**1:43**
362	28	Sa.		7:35	5:43	3:21	**2:28**
363	29	Su.	☿ in superior ☌	7:35	5:44	4:25	**3:19**
364	30	Mo.		7:35	5:45	5:29	**4:16**
365	31	Tu.		7:36	5:46	6:32	**5:20**

☉ The Sun ● The Earth ☾ The Moon ☿ Mercury ♀ Venus ♂ Mars ♃ Jupiter ♄ Saturn ♆ Neptune ♅ Uranus ♇ Pluto ☌ = in conjunction ☍ = opposition to the ☉

206-Year Calendar, A.D. 1894–2099, Inclusive

Using this calendar, you can find the day of the week for any day of the month and year for the period 1894–2099, inclusive. **To find any day of the week,** first look in the table of Common Years or Leap Years for the year required. Under each month are numbers that refer to the corresponding numbers at the head of each column in the Table of Days, below. For example, to find what day of the week March 2 fell on in the year 1918, find 1918 in the table of Common Years. In a parallel line under March is the number 5. Look at column 5 in the Table of Days; there, it shows that March 2 fell on Saturday.

Common Years, 1894 to 2099

											Jan.	Feb.	Mar.	Apr.	May	June	July	Aug.	Sept.	Oct.	Nov.	Dec.
1894	1900	...	...	...	...	...	...	...	...	...												
1906	1917	1923	1934	1945	1951	1962	1973	1979	1990	...	1	4	4	7	2	5	7	3	6	1	4	6
2001	2007	2018	2029	2035	2046	2057	2063	2074	2085	2091												
1895	...	...	...	...	...	...	...	...	...	...												
1901	1907	1918	1929	1935	1946	1957	1963	1974	1985	1991	2	5	5	1	3	6	1	4	7	2	5	7
2002	2013	2019	2030	2041	2047	2058	2069	2075	2086	2097												
1897	...	...	...	...	...	...	...	...	...	...												
1909	1915	1926	1937	1943	1954	1965	1971	1982	1993	1999	5	1	1	4	6	2	4	7	3	5	1	3
2012	2021	2027	2038	2049	2055	2066	2077	2083	2094	2100												
1898	1910	1921	1927	1938	1949	1955	1966	1977	1983	1994	6	2	2	5	7	3	5	1	4	6	2	4
2005	2011	2022	2033	2039	2050	2061	2067	2078	2089	2095												
1899	1905	1911	1922	1933	1939	1950	1961	1967	1978	1989	7	3	3	6	1	4	6	2	5	7	3	5
1995	2006	2017	2023	2034	2045	2051	2062	2073	2079	2090												
1902	1913	1919	1930	1941	1947	1958	1969	1975	1986	1997	3	6	6	2	4	7	2	5	1	3	6	1
2003	2014	2025	2031	2042	2053	2059	2070	2081	2087	2098												
1903	1914	1925	1931	1942	1953	1959	1970	1981	1987	1998	4	7	7	3	5	1	3	6	2	4	7	2
2009	2015	2026	2037	2043	2054	2065	2071	2082	2093	2099												

Leap Years, 1896 to 2096

									Jan.	Feb. (29)	Mar.	Apr.	May	June	July	Aug.	Sept.	Oct.	Nov.	Dec.
...	...	1920	1948	1976	2004	2032	2060	2088	4	7	1	4	6	2	4	7	3	5	1	3
...	...	1924	1952	1980	2008	2036	2064	2092	2	5	6	2	4	7	2	5	1	3	6	1
...	...	1928	1956	1984	2012	2040	2068	2096	7	3	4	7	2	5	7	3	6	1	4	6
...	1904	1932	1960	1988	2016	2044	2072	...	5	1	2	5	7	3	5	1	4	6	2	4
1896	1908	1936	1964	1992	2020	2048	2076	...	3	6	7	3	5	1	3	6	2	4	7	2
...	1912	1940	1968	1996	2024	2052	2080	...	1	4	5	1	3	6	1	4	7	2	5	7
...	1916	1944	1972	2000	2028	2056	2084	...	6	2	3	6	1	4	6	2	5	7	3	5

Table of Days

1		2		3		4		5		6		7	
Mon.	1	Tues	1	Wed.	1	Thurs.	1	Fri.	1	Sat.	1	SUN.	1
Tues.	2	Wed.	2	Thurs.	2	Fri.	2	Sat.	2	SUN.	2	Mon.	2
Wed.	3	Thurs.	3	Fri.	3	Sat.	3	SUN.	3	Mon.	3	Tues.	3
Thurs.	4	Fri.	4	Sat.	4	SUN.	4	Mon.	4	Tues.	4	Wed.	4
Fri.	5	Sat.	5	SUN.	5	Mon.	5	Tues.	5	Wed.	5	Thurs.	5
Sat.	6	SUN.	6	Mon.	6	Tues.	6	Wed.	6	Thurs.	6	Fri.	6
SUN.	7	Mon.	7	Tues.	7	Wed.	7	Thurs.	7	Fri.	7	Sat.	7
Mon.	8	Tues.	8	Wed.	8	Thurs.	8	Fri.	8	Sat.	8	SUN.	8
Tues.	9	Wed.	9	Thurs.	9	Fri.	9	Sat.	9	SUN.	9	Mon.	9
Wed.	10	Thurs.	10	Fri.	10	Sat.	10	SUN.	10	Mon.	10	Tues.	10
Thurs.	11	Fri.	11	Sat.	11	SUN.	11	Mon.	11	Tues.	11	Wed.	11
Fri.	12	Sat.	12	SUN.	12	Mon.	12	Tues.	12	Wed.	12	Thurs.	12
Sat.	13	SUN.	13	Mon.	13	Tues.	13	Wed.	13	Thurs.	13	Fri.	13
SUN.	14	Mon.	14	Tues.	14	Wed.	14	Thurs.	14	Fri.	14	Sat.	14
Mon.	15	Tues.	15	Wed.	15	Thurs.	15	Fri.	15	Sat.	15	SUN.	15
Tues.	16	Wed.	16	Thurs.	16	Fri.	16	Sat.	16	SUN.	16	Mon.	16
Wed.	17	Thurs.	17	Fri.	17	Sat.	17	SUN.	17	Mon.	17	Tues.	17
Thurs.	18	Fri.	18	Sat.	18	SUN.	18	Mon.	18	Tues.	18	Wed.	18
Fri.	19	Sat.	19	SUN.	19	Mon.	19	Tues.	19	Wed.	19	Thurs.	19
Sat.	20	SUN.	20	Mon.	20	Tues.	20	Wed.	20	Thurs.	20	Fri.	20
SUN.	21	Mon.	21	Tues.	21	Wed.	21	Thurs.	21	Fri.	21	Sat.	21
Mon.	22	Tues.	22	Wed.	22	Thurs.	22	Fri.	22	Sat.	22	SUN.	22
Tues.	23	Wed.	23	Thurs.	23	Fri.	23	Sat.	23	SUN.	23	Mon.	23
Wed.	24	Thurs.	24	Fri.	24	Sat.	24	SUN.	24	Mon.	24	Tues.	24
Thurs.	25	Fri.	25	Sat.	25	SUN.	25	Mon.	25	Tues.	25	Wed.	25
Fri.	26	Sat.	26	SUN.	26	Mon.	26	Tues.	26	Wed.	26	Thurs.	26
Sat.	27	SUN.	27	Mon.	27	Tues.	27	Wed.	27	Thurs.	27	Fri.	27
SUN.	28	Mon.	28	Tues.	28	Wed.	28	Thurs.	28	Fri.	28	Sat.	28
Mon.	29	Tues.	29	Wed.	29	Thurs.	29	Fri.	29	Sat.	29	SUN.	29
Tues.	30	Wed.	30	Thurs.	30	Fri.	30	Sat.	30	SUN.	30	Mon.	30
Wed.	31	Thurs.	31	Fri.	31	Sat.	31	SUN.	31	Mon.	31	Tues.	31

Beginning of the Year

The Athenians began the year in June; the Macedonians, in September; the Romans, first in March and later in January; the Persians, on Aug. 11; and the ancient Mexicans, on Feb. 23. The Chinese year, which begins in late January or early February, is similar to the Mohammedan year. Both have 12 months of 29 and 30 days alternating, while in every 19 years, there are seven years that have 13 months. This does not quite fit the planetary movements, hence the Chinese have formed a cycle of 60 years, in which period 22 intercalary (added to the calendar) months occur.

Recreation

Canoeing on Inks Lake in Burnett County. Photo courtesy of Texas Parks & Wildlife Department.

Texas State Parks & Historic Sites

Texas State Forests

National Parks, Historic Sites,
   Recreation Areas

Birding, Fishing, Hunting

Fairs & Festivals

Texas State Parks & Historic Sites

Texas' diverse system of state parks and historic sites offers contrasting attractions — mountains and canyons, arid deserts and lush forests, spring-fed streams, sandy dunes, saltwater surf and fascinating historic sites.

The state park information was provided by **Texas Parks and Wildlife** (TPW) and the historic site information was provided by the **Texas Historical Commission**. Additional information and brochures on individual parks are available from the TPW's Austin headquarters, 4200 Smith School Rd., Austin 78744; 1-800-792-1112; **www.tpwd.state.tx.us/park/**, and the historical commission, **www.thc.state.tx.us/hsites/hsdefault.shtml**.

The TPW's **Central Reservation Center** can take reservations for almost all state parks. Exceptions are Indian Lodge, the Texas State Railroad, and facilities not operated by the TPW. Call the center during usual business hours at 512-389-8900. The TDD line is 512-389-8915.

The **Texas State Parks Pass**, currently costing $60 per year, waives entrance fees for all members and all passengers in member's vehicle to all state parks when entrance fees are required, as well as other benefits. For further information, contact TPW 512-389-8900.

Texas State Parklands Passport is a windshield decal granting discounted entrance to state parks for Texas residents who are senior citizens or are collecting Social Security disability payments and free entrance for disabled U.S. veterans. Available at state parks with proper identification. Details can be obtained at numbers or addresses above.

The following information is a brief glimpse of what each park has to offer. Refer to the **chart on pages 166–167** for a more complete list of available activities and facilities. Entrance fees to state parks range from $1 to $5 per person. There are also fees for tours and some activities. For up-to-date information, call the information number listed above before you go. Road abbreviations used in this list are: IH - interstate highway, US - U.S. Highway, TX - state highway, FM - farm-to-market road, PR - park road.

A boater shoves off from a pier at Wright Patman Lake in Atlanta State Park, Cass County, in northeast Texas. Photo courtesy of Texas Parks & Wildlife Department.

List of State Parks & Historic Sites

Abilene State Park, 16 miles southwest of Abilene on FM 89 and PR 32 in Taylor County, consists of 529.4 acres that were deeded by the City of Abilene in 1933. A part of the **official Texas longhorn herd** and bison are located in the park. Large groves of pecan trees that once shaded bands of Comanches now shade visitors at picnic tables. Activities include camping, hiking, picnicking, nature study, biking, lake swimming and fishing. In addition to **Lake Abilene, Buffalo Gap**, the original Taylor County seat (1878) and one of the early frontier settlements, is nearby. Buffalo Gap was on the **Western**, or **Goodnight-Loving, Trail**, over which pioneer Texas cattlemen drove herds to railheads in Kansas.

Acton State Historic Site is a .01-acre cemetery plot in Hood County where **Davy Crockett's** second wife, Elizabeth, was buried in 1860. It is 4.5 miles east of Granbury on US 377 to FM 167 south, then 2.4 miles south to Acton. Nearby attractions include **Cleburne, Dinosaur Valley** and **Lake Whitney state parks**.

Admiral Nimitz State Historic Site (see **National Museum of the Pacific War**).

Atlanta State Park is 1,475 acres located 11 miles northwest of Atlanta on FM 1154 in Cass County; adjacent to **Wright Patman Dam** and **Reservoir**. Land acquired from the U.S. Army in 1954 by license to 2004 with option to renew to 2054. Camping, biking and hiking in pine forests, as well as water activities, such as boating, fishing, lake swimming. Nearby are historic town of **Jefferson** and the **Caddo Lake** and **Daingerfield state parks**.

Balmorhea State Park is 45.9 acres four miles southwest of Balmorhea on TX 17 between Balmorhea and Toyahvale in Reeves County. Deeded in 1934-35 by private owners and Reeves Co. Water Imp. Dist. No. 1 and built by the Civilian Conservation Corps (CCC). Swimming pool (1-3/4 acres) fed by artesian **San Solomon Springs**; also provides water to **aquatic refuge** in park. Activities include swimming, picnicking, camping, scuba and skin diving. Motel rooms available at **San Solomon Springs Courts**. Nearby are city of Pecos, **Fort Davis National Historic Site, Davis Mountains State Park** and **McDonald Observatory**.

Barton Warnock Environmental Education Center consists of 99.9 acres in Brewster County. Originally built by the Lajitas Foundation in 1982 as the Lajitas Museum Desert Gardens, the TPW purchased it in 1990 and renamed it for Texas botanist Dr. Barton Warnock. The center is also the eastern entrance station to **Big Bend Ranch State Park**. Self-guiding botanical and museum tours. On FM 170 one mile east of Lajitas.

Bastrop State Park is 3,503.7 acres one mile east of Bastrop on TX 21 or from TX 71. The park was acquired by deeds from the City of Bastrop and private owners in 1933-35; additional acreage acquired in 1979. Site of famous "Lost Pines," isolated region of loblolly pine and hardwoods. **Swimming pool, cabins** and **lodge** are among facilities. Fishing at Lake Bastrop, backpacking, picnicking, canoeing, bicycling, hiking. Golf course adjacent to park. **State capitol** at Austin 32 miles away; 13-mile drive through forest leads to **Buescher State Park.**

Battleship *Texas* State Historic Site (see **San Jacinto Battleground State Historic Site** and **Battleship Texas**)

Bentsen-Rio Grande Valley State Park, a scenic park, is along the Rio Grande five miles southwest of Mission off FM 2062 in Hidalgo County. The 760 acres of **subtropical resaca woodlands and brushlands** were acquired from private owners in 1944. Park is excellent base from which to tour **Lower Rio Grande Valley** of Texas and adjacent **Mexico**; most attractions within an hour's drive. Hiking trails provide chance to study unique plants and animals of park. Many birds unique to southern United States found here, including **pauraque, groove-billed ani, green kingfisher, rose-throated becard** and **tropical parula**. Birdwatching tours guided by park naturalists offered daily December–March. Park is one of last natural refuges in Texas for **ocelot** and **jaguarundi**. Trees include **cedar elm, anaqua, ebony** and **Mexican ash**. Camping, hiking, picnicking, boating, fishing also available. Nearby are **Santa Ana National Wildlife Refuge, Falcon State Park** and **Sabal Palm Sanctuary.**

Big Bend Ranch State Park, more than 299,008 acres of **Chihuahuan Desert wilderness** in Brewster and Presidio counties along the Rio Grande, was purchased from private owners in 1988. The purchase more than doubled the size of the state park system, which comprised at that time 220,000 acres. Eastern entrance at Barton Warnock Environmental Education Center one mile east of Lajitas on FM 170; western entrance is at **Fort Leaton State Historic Park** four miles east of Presidio on FM 170. The area includes **extinct volcanoes**, several **waterfalls**, two **mountain ranges**, at least **11 rare species of plants and animals**, and **90 major archaeological sites**. There is little development. Vehicular access limited; wilderness backpacking, hiking, scenic drive, picnicking, fishing and swimming. There are longhorns in the park, although they are not part of the official **state longhorn herd**.

Big Spring State Park is 382 acres located on FM 700 within the city limits of Big Spring in Howard County. Both city and park were named for a natural spring that was replaced by an artificial one. The park was deeded by the City of Big Spring in 1934 and 1935. Drive to top of **Scenic Mountain** provides panoramic view of surrounding country and look at **prairie dog colony**. The "big spring," nearby in a city park, provided watering place for herds of bison, antelope and wild horses. Used extensively also as campsite for early Indians, explorers and settlers.

Blanco State Park is 104.6 acres along the Blanco River four blocks south of Blanco's town square in Blanco County. The land was deeded by private owners in 1933. Park area was used as campsite by early explorers and settlers. Fishing, camping, swimming, picnicking, boating. **LBJ Ranch** and **LBJ State Historic Site, Pedernales Falls** and **Guadalupe River state parks** are nearby.

Bonham State Park is a 261-acre park located two miles southeast of Bonham on TX 78, then two miles southeast on FM 271 in Fannin County. It includes a 65-acre lake, **rolling prairies** and **woodlands**. The land was acquired in 1933 from the City of Bonham. Swimming, camping, mountain-bike trail, lighted fishing pier, boating. **Sam Rayburn Memorial Library** in Bonham. **Sam Rayburn Home** and **Valley Lake** nearby.

Brazos Bend State Park in Fort Bend County, eight miles east of Damon off FM 1462 on FM 762, approximately 28 miles south of Houston. The 4,897-acre park was purchased from private owners in 1976–77. **George Observatory** in park. **Observation platform** for spotting and photographing the **270 species of birds, 23 species of mammals, and 21 species of reptiles and amphibians, including American alligator**, that frequent the park. Interpretive and educational programs every weekend. Backpacking, camping, hiking, biking, fishing. Creekfield Lake Nature Trail.

Buescher State Park, a scenic area, is 1,016.7 acres 2 miles northwest of Smithville off TX 71 to FM 153 in Bastrop County. Acquired between 1933 and 1936, about one-third deeded by private owner; heirs donated a third; balance from City of Smithville. **El Camino Real** once ran near park, connecting **San Antonio de Béxar** with **Spanish missions in East Texas**. Park land was part of **Stephen F. Austin's colonial grant**. Some **250 spe-**

Bastrop State Park features cabins built by the Civilian Conservation Corps. Photo by Ron Billings; Texas Forest Service.

The observation platform at Brazos Bend State Park is great for photographing the many species of birds, mammals, reptiles, and amphibians that frequent the park. Photo courtesy of Texas Parks & Wildlife Department.

cies of birds can be seen. Camping, fishing, hiking, boating. Scenic park road connects with **Bastrop State Park** through **Lost Pines** area.

Caddo Lake State Park, north of Karnack one mile off TX 43 to FM 2198 in Harrison County, consists of 483.85 acres along **Cypress Bayou**, which runs into Caddo Lake. A scenic area, it was acquired from private owners in 1933. Nearby Karnack is childhood home of Lady Bird Johnson. Close by is old city of **Jefferson**, famous as commercial center of Northeast Texas during last half of 19th century. Caddo Indian legend attributes formation of Caddo Lake to **a huge flood**. Cypress trees, **American lotus** and lily pads, as well as **71 species of fish**, predominate in lake. **Nutria, beaver, mink, squirrel, armadillo, alligator** and **turtle** abound. Activities include camping, hiking, swimming, fishing, canoeing. Screened shelters, cabins.

Caddo Mounds State Historic Site in Cherokee County six miles southwest of Alto on TX 21. Total of 93.8 acres acquired in 1975. Open for day visits only, park offers exhibits and interpretive trails through reconstructed **Caddo dwellings and ceremonial areas**, including two temple mounds, a burial mound and a village area typical of people who lived in region for 500 years beginning about A.D. 800. Open Tuesday–Sunday. Nearby are **Jim Hogg** and **Mission Tejas State historic sites** and **Texas State Railroad**.

Caprock Canyons State Park and Trailway, 100 miles southeast of Amarillo and 3.5 miles north of Quitaque off FM 1065 and TX 86 in Briscoe, Floyd and Hall counties, has 15,313 acres. Purchased in 1975. Scenic escarpment's canyons provided camping areas for **Indians of Folsom culture** more than 10,000 years ago. **Mesquite** and **cacti** in the **badlands** give way to **tall grasses, cottonwood** and **plum thickets** in the bottomlands. Wildlife includes **aoudad sheep, coyote, bobcat, porcupine** and **fox**. Activities include scenic drive, camping, hiking, mountain-bike riding, horse riding and horse camping. A **64.25-mile trailway** (hike, bike and equestrian trail) extends from South Plains to Estelline.

Casa Navarro State Historic Site, on .7 acre at corner of S. Laredo and W. Nueva streets in downtown San Antonio, was acquired by donation from San Antonio Conservation Society Foundation in 1975. The furnished **Navarro House** three-building complex, built about 1848, was home of statesman, rancher and Texas patriot **José Antonio Navarro**. Guided tours; exhibits. Open Wednesday through Sunday.

Cedar Hill State Park, an urban park on 1,826 acres 10 miles southwest of Dallas via US 67 and FM 1382 on **Joe Pool Lake**, was acquired by long-term lease from the Army Corp of Engineers in 1982. Camping mostly in wooded areas. Fishing from two lighted jetties and a perch pond for children. Swimming, boating, bicycling, birdwatching and picnicking. Vegetation includes several sections of **tall-grass prairie**. Penn Farm Agricultural History Center includes reconstructed buildings of the **19th-century Penn Farm** and exhibits; self-guided tours.

Choke Canyon State Park consists of two units, South Shore and Calliham, located on 26,000-acre **Choke Canyon Reservoir**. Park acquired in 1981 in a 50-year agreement among Bureau of Reclamation, City of Corpus Christi and Nueces River Authority. Thickets of **mesquite** and **blackbrush acacia** predominate, supporting populations of **javelina, coyote, skunk** and **alligator**, as well as the **crested caracara**. The 385-acre **South Shore Unit** is located 3.5 miles west of Three Rivers on TX 72 in Live Oak County; the 1,100-acre **Calliham Unit** is located 12 miles west of Three Rivers, on TX 72, in McMullen County. Both units offer camping, picnicking, boating, fishing, lake swimming, and baseball and volleyball areas. The Calliham Unit also has a hiking trail, wildlife educational center, screened shelters, rentable **gym and kitchen**. **Sports complex** includes swimming pool and tennis, volleyball, shuffleboard and basketball courts. Across dam from South Shore is North Shore Equestrian and Camping Area; 18 miles of horseback riding trails.

Cleburne State Park is a 528-acre park located 10 miles southwest of Cleburne via US 67 and PR 21 in Johnson County with 116-acre spring-fed lake; acquired from the City of Cleburne and private owners in 1935 and 1936. **Oak, elm, mesquite, cedar** and **redbud** cover white rocky hills. Bluebonnets in spring. Activities include camping, picnicking, hiking, bicycling, canoeing, swimming, boating, fishing. Nearby are **Fossil Rim Wildlife Center** and **dinosaur tracks** in Paluxy River at **Dinosaur Valley State Park**.

Colorado Bend State Park, a 5,328.3-acre facility, is 28 miles west of Lampasas in Lampasas and San Saba counties. Access is from Lampasas to Bend on FM 580 west, then follow signs (access road subject to flooding). Park site was purchased partly in 1984, with balance acquired in 1987. Primitive camping, fishing, swimming, hiking, biking and picnicking; guided tours to Gorman Falls; crawling cave tours require reservations. Rare and endangered species here include **golden-cheeked warbler, black-capped vireo** and **bald eagle**.

Confederate Reunion Grounds State Historic Site, located in Limestone County on the Navasota River, is 77.1 acres in size. Acquired 1983 by deed from Joseph E. Johnston Camp No. 94 CSA. Entrance is 6 miles south of Mexia on TX 14, then 2.5 miles west on FM 2705. **Historic buildings**, two **scenic footbridges** span creek; hiking trail. Nearby are **Fort Parker State Park** and **Old Fort Parker**.

Cooper Lake State Park, comprises 3,026 acres three miles southeast of Cooper in Delta and Hopkins counties acquired in 1991 by 25-year lease from Army Corps of Engineers. Two units, **Doctors Creek** and **South Sulphur**, adjoin 19,300-surface-acre Cooper Lake. Fishing, boating, camping, picnicking, swimming. Screened shelters and cabins. South Sulphur offers equestrian camping and horseback riding trails. Access to Doctors Creek Unit is via TX 24 east from Commerce to Cooper, then east on TX 154 to FM 1529 to park. To South Sulphur Unit, take IH 30 to Exit 122 west of Sulphur Springs to TX 19, then TX 71, then FM 3505.

One of the 14 cabins available to rent at Cooper Lake State Park. See table on page 183. Photo by Robert Plocheck.

Copper Breaks State Park, 12 miles south of Quanah on TX 6 in Hardeman County, was acquired by purchase from private owner in 1970. Park features rugged scenic beauty on 1,898.8 acres, two lakes, **grass-covered mesas** and juniper breaks. Nearby **medicine mounds** were important ceremonial sites of Comanche Indians. Nearby **Pease River** was site of 1860 battle in which **Cynthia Ann Parker** was recovered from Comanches. Part of **state longhorn herd** lives at park. Abundant wildlife. Nature, hiking and equestrian trails; natural and historical exhibits; summer programs; horseback riding; camping, equestrian camping.

Daingerfield State Park, off TX 49 and PR 17 southeast of Daingerfield in Morris County, is a 550.9-acre recreational area that includes an 80-surface-acre lake; deeded in 1935 by private owners. This area is center of iron industry in Texas; nearby is Lone Star Steel Co. In spring, **dogwood, redbuds** and **wisteria** bloom; in fall, brilliant foliage of **sweetgum, oaks** and **maples** contrast with dark green pines. Campsites, lodge and cabins.

Davis Mountains State Park is 2,709 acres in Jeff Davis County, 4 miles northwest of Fort Davis via TX 118 and PR 3. The scenic area was deeded in 1933-1937 by private owners. First European, **Antonio de Espejo**, came to area in 1583. Extremes of altitude produce both **plains grasslands** and **piñon-juniper-oak woodlands. Montezuma quail**, rare in Texas, visit park. Scenic drives, camping and hiking. **Indian Lodge**, built by the Civilian Conservation Corps during the early 1930s, has 39 rooms, restaurant and swimming pool (reservations: 432-426-3254). Four-mile hiking trail leads to **Fort Davis National Historic Site**. Other nearby points of interest include **McDonald Observatory** and 74-mile scenic loop through **Davis Mountains**. Nearby are scenic **Limpia, Madera, Musquiz** and **Keesey canyons; Camino del Rio;** ghost town of Shafter; **Big Bend National Park; Big Bend Ranch State Park; Fort Davis National Historic Site;** and **Fort Leaton State Historic Site**.

Devil's River State Natural Area comprises 19,988.6 acres in Val Verde County, 22 miles off US 277, about 65 miles north of Del Rio on graded road. It is an **ecological and archaeological crossroads**. Ecologically, it is in a **transitional area** between the **Edwards Plateau**, the **Trans-Pecos desert** and the **South Texas brush country**. Archaeological studies suggest occupation and use by cultures from both east and west. Camping, hiking and mountain biking. Canyon and pictograph-site tours by prearrangement only. **Dolan Falls** is nearby and is accessible only through The Nature Conservancy of Texas.

Devil's Sinkhole State Natural Area, comprising 1,859.7 acres about 6 miles northeast of Rocksprings on US 377 in Edwards County, is a **vertical cavern**. The sinkhole, discovered by Anglo settlers in 1867, is a registered **National Natural Landmark**; it was purchased in 1985 from private owners. The cavern opening is about 40 by 60 feet, with a vertical drop of about 140 feet. Access by prearranged tour with Devil's Sinkhole Society (830-683-BATS). Bats can be viewed in summer leaving cave at dusk; no access to cave itself. Contact **Kickapoo Cavern State Park** to arrange a tour.

Dinosaur Valley State Park, located off US 67 four miles west of Glen Rose in Somervell County, is a 1,524.72-acre scenic park. Land was acquired from private owners in 1968. **Dinosaur tracks** in bed of Paluxy River and two full-scale dinosaur models, originally created for New York World's Fair in 1964–65, on display. Part of state **longhorn herd** is in park. Camping, picnicking, hiking, mountain biking, swimming, fishing.

Eisenhower Birthplace State Historic Site is 6 acres off US 75 at 609 S. Lamar, Denison, Grayson County. The property was acquired in 1958 from the Eisenhower Birthplace Foundation. Restoration of home of President Dwight Eisenhower includes furnishings of period and some personal effects of Gen. Eisenhower. Guided tour; call for schedule. Park open daily, except Christmas Day and New Year's Day; call for hours. Town of Denison established on **Butterfield Overland Mail** Route in 1858.

Eisenhower State Park, 423.1 acres five miles northwest of Denison via US 75 to TX 91N to FM 1310 on the shores of **Lake Texoma** in Grayson County, was acquired by an Army lease in 1954. Named for the 34th U.S. president, **Dwight D. Eisenhower**. First Anglo settlers came to area in 1835; **Fort Johnson** was established in area in 1840; **Colbert's Ferry** established on Red River in 1853 and operated until 1931. Areas of **tall-grass prairie** exist. Hiking, camping, picnicking, fishing, swimming.

Enchanted Rock State Natural Area is 1,643.5 acres on Big Sandy Creek 18 miles north of Fredericksburg on FM 965 on the line between Gillespie and Llano counties. Acquired in 1978 by The Nature Conservancy of Texas; state acquired from TNCT in 1984. Enchanted Rock is huge **pink granite boulder** rising 425 feet above ground and covering 640 acres. It is **second-largest batholith** (underground rock

Parks text continues on page 172

☆ Texas State Parks & State Historic Sites ☆

Park / †Type of Park / Special Features	Nearest Town	Day Use Only	Historic Site/Museum	Exhibit/Interp-retive Center	Restrooms	Showers	Trailer Dump Stn.	Camping ††	Screened Shelters	Cabins	Group Facilities	Nature Trail	Hiking Trail	Picnicking	Boat Ramp	Fishing	Swimming	Canoe Rentals	Miscellaneous
Abilene SP	BUFFALO GAP				★	★	★	15	★		BG	★		★		☆	★		L
Acton SHS ▲ Grave of Davy Crockett's Wife	GRANBURY	★	★																
Atlanta SP	ATLANTA				★	★	★	14			DG	★	★	★	★	☆	☆	★	
Balmorhea SP San Solomon Springs Courts	BALMORHEA			★	★	★	★	14			DG			★			★		I
Barton Warnock Environmental Ed. Center	LAJITAS	★		★	★							★							
Bastrop SP	BASTROP				★	★	★	10		★	BG	★	★			☆	★	★	G
Battleship *Texas* SHS San Jacinto Battleground	DEER PARK	★	★	★															
Bentsen–Rio Grande Valley SP	MISSION				★	★		10			BG	★	★	★	★	☆			
Big Bend Ranch SP	PRESIDIO				★	★	★	1			NG	★	★			☆	☆		B1, L, E
Big Spring SP	BIG SPRING				★	★		13			BG	★	★	★					
Blanco SP	BLANCO				★	★	★	16	★		DG	★		★		☆	☆		
Bonham SP	BONHAM				★	★	★	14			BG	★		★	★	★	☆		B1
Brazos Bend SP George Observatory	RICHMOND			★	★	★	★	4	★		BG	★	★	★		★			B1, B2
Buescher SP	SMITHVILLE				★	★	★	14	★		BG	★		★	★		☆		B2
Caddo Lake SP	KARNACK				★	★	★	15	★	★	BG	★		★	★	★		★	
Caddo Mounds SHS ▲	ALTO	★	★	★	★									★					
Caprock Canyons SP & TW	QUITAQUE				★	★	★	8			BG	★	★	★	★	★	☆		B1, E
Casa Navarro SHS ▲	SAN ANTONIO	★	★	★	★														
Cedar Hill SP	CEDAR HILL				★	★	★	12			DG	★	★	★	★	★	☆		B1
Choke Canyon SP, Calliham Unit	CALLIHAM				★	★	★	10	★		BG	★		★	★	★	★		
South Shore Unit	THREE RIVERS				★	★	★	8						★	★	★	★		B1, E
Cleburne SP	CLEBURNE				★	★	★	16	★		BG	★	★	★	★	☆	☆		
Colorado Bend SP Cave Tours	BEND				★			1				★	★	★	★	☆	★		B1
Confederate Reunion Grounds SHS ▲	MEXIA				★	★	★	1			BG	★		★		☆			
Cooper Lake SP, Doctors Creek Unit	COOPER				★	★	★	4	★		DG	★		★	★	★			
South Sulphur Unit	SULPHUR SPRINGS				★	★	★	14	★	★	DG	★		★	★	★	★		B1, E
Copper Breaks SP	QUANAH				★	★	★	10			BG	★		★	★	★	☆		B1, E, L
Daingerfield SP	DAINGERFIELD				★	★	★	15		★	BG	★		★	★	★	☆	★	
Davis Mountains SP Indian Lodge	FORT DAVIS			★	★	★	★	11			DG	★	★						I, E
Devils River SNA Reservations Required	DEL RIO							1			BG								B1, E
Devil's Sinkhole SNA	ROCKSPRINGS	*(No access to cavern. Tours of SNA by special request only.)*																	
Dinosaur Valley SP Dinosaur Footprints	GLEN ROSE			★	★	★	★	12			DG	★	★	★		☆	☆		B1, E, L
Eisenhower SP Marina	DENISON				★	★	★	15	★		BG	★		★	★	★	☆		B1
Eisenhower Birthplace SHS ▲	DENISON	★	★	★							DG								
Enchanted Rock SNA	FREDERICKSBURG				★	★	★	9			DG	★	★	★					R
Estero Llano Grande SP	WESLACO																		
Fairfield Lake SP	FAIRFIELD				★		★	11			DG	★		★	★	★			B1
Falcon SP Airstrip	ZAPATA				★	★	★	15	★		BG	★		★	★	☆	☆		B1
Fannin Battleground SHS ▲	GOLIAD	★	★	★	★						DG			★					
Fanthorp Inn SHS	ANDERSON	★	★	★	★									★					
Fort Boggy SP	CENTERVILLE	★									DG	★		★	★	☆	☆		
Fort Griffin SHS ▲	ALBANY	★	★	★	★		★	10			BG	★	★	★			☆		L, E
Fort Lancaster SHS ▲	OZONA	★	★	★	★									☆					
Fort Leaton SHS	PRESIDIO	★	★	★	★									★					
Fort McKavett SHS ▲	FORT McKAVETT	★	★	★	★							★		★					
Fort Parker SP	MEXIA				★	★	★	14	★		BG	★		★	★	★	☆	★	B1
Fort Richardson SP & Lost Creek Res. TW	JACKSBORO				★	★	★	10	★		DG	★	★	★	★	★			E
Franklin Mountains SP Wyler Aerial Tramway	EL PASO	★						6			DG	★	★	★					B1, E, R
Fulton Mansion SHS ▲	FULTON	★	★	★										★					
Galveston Island SP Summer Theater	GALVESTON			★	★	★	★	4	★			★		★		☆	☆		B1
Garner SP	CONCAN				★	★	★	14	★	★	BG	★		★	★	☆	☆	★	B2
Goliad SP & Mission Espiritu Santo HS	GOLIAD	★	★	★	★			11	★		DG	★	★	★		★	★		B1
Goose Island SP	ROCKPORT				★	★	★	14			BG			★	★	★			
Government Canyon SNA	SAN ANTONIO																		
Gov. Hogg Shrine ▲	QUITMAN	★	★	★	★						DG	★		★					
Guadalupe River SP & Honey Creek SNA	BOERNE				★	★	★	13				★		★		☆	☆		E
Hill Country SNA	BANDERA							6			NG	★				☆	☆		B1, E
Hueco Tanks SP & HS Indian Pictographs	EL PASO			★	★	★	★	14			DG	★	★	★					R
Huntsville SP	HUNTSVILLE				★	★	★	14	★		DG	★		★	★	★	☆	★	B1, B2
Inks Lake SP	BURNET				★	★	★	10	★		BG	★		★	★	★	☆	★	G
Jim Hogg HS ▲	RUSK	★	★	★	★							★		★					
Kickapoo Cavern SP Reservations Required	BRACKETTVILLE				★		★	6			NG	★	★						B1
Lake Arrowhead SP	WICHITA FALLS				★	★	★	10			DG	★	★	★	★		☆		E

† — TYPES OF PARKS

SP	State Park	HS	Historic Site
SHS	State Historic Site	TW	Trailway
SNA	State Natural Area		

†† — TYPES OF CAMPING

1–Primitive/Backpacking; 2–Walk-in Tent; 3–Tent; 4–Water & Electric; 5–Water, Electric & Sewer; 6–1 & 2; 7–1, 2 & 4; 8–1, 2, 3 & 4; 9–1 & 3; 10–1, 3 & 4; 11–1, 3, 4 & 5; 12–1 & 4; 13–2, 3 & 4; 14–3 & 4; 15–3, 4 & 5; 16–4 & 5; 17–1, 3 & 5.

☆ Texas State Parks & State Historic Sites ☆

Park / †Type of Park / Special Features	NEAREST TOWN	Day Use Only	Historic Site/Museum	Exhibit/Interpretive Center	Restrooms	Showers	Trailer Dump Stn.	Camping ††	Screened Shelters	Cabins	Group Facilities	Nature Trail	Hiking Trail	Picnicking	Boat Ramp	Fishing	Swimming	Canoe Rentals	Miscellaneous
Lake Bob Sandlin SP	MOUNT PLEASANT				★	★	★	10	★		DG	★	★	★	★	★	☆		B1
Lake Brownwood SP	BROWNWOOD				★	★	★	15	★	★	BG	★	★	★	★	★	☆		
Lake Casa Blanca International SP	LAREDO				★	★	★	14			DG			★	★	☆	☆		B1
Lake Colorado City SP	COLORADO CITY				★	★	★	14		★	BG	★	★	★	★	★	☆		
Lake Corpus Christi SP	MATHIS				★	★	★	15	★		DG			★	★	★	☆		
Lake Livingston SP	LIVINGSTON				★	★	★	15	★		DG	★	★	★	★	★	☆		B1, B2, E
Lake Mineral Wells SP & TW	MINERAL WELLS				★	★	★	10	★		DG	★	★	★	★	★	☆	★	B1, E, R
Lake Somerville SP & TW, Birch Creek Unit	SOMERVILLE			★	★	★	★	10			BG	★	★	★	★	★	☆	★	B1, E
Nails Creek Unit	LEDBETTER			★	★	★	★	10			DG	★	★	★	★	★	☆	★	B1, E
Lake Tawakoni SP	WILLS POINT				★	★	★	4				★	★	★	☆	☆			
Lake Texana SP	EDNA			★	★	★	★	14			DG	★	★	★	★	★	☆	★	B1
Lake Whitney SP (Airstrip)	WHITNEY				★	★	★	15	★		BG	★	★	★	☆	☆			B1
Landmark Inn SHS ▲ (Hotel Rooms)	CASTROVILLE	★	★	★							DG	★		★		☆			I
Lipantitlan SHS	SAN PATRICIO	★												★					
Lockhart SP	LOCKHART				★	★		16			BG			★			★		G
Longhorn Cavern SP ▲ (Cavern Tours)	BURNET	★	★	★	★							★	★	★					
Lost Maples SNA	VANDERPOOL				★	★	★	12				★	★	★		☆	☆		
Lyndon B. Johnson SP & HS	STONEWALL	★	★	★	★						DG	★		★		☆	★		L
Magoffin Home SHS ▲	EL PASO	★	★	★	★														
Martin Creek Lake SP	TATUM				★	★	★	12	★		DG	★	★	★	★	★	☆		B1
Martin Dies Jr. SP	JASPER				★	★	★	14	★		BG	★	★	★	★	★	☆	★	B1
McKinney Falls SP	AUSTIN	★		★	★	★	★	13	★		BG	★	★			☆	☆		B1, B2
Meridian SP	MERIDIAN				★	★	★	13	★		BG	★	★	★	★	☆	☆		
Mission Tejas SP	WECHES			★	★	★	★	15			BG	★	★	★		☆			
Monahans Sandhills SP	MONAHANS			★	★	★	★	14			DG	★		★					E
Monument Hill & Kreische Brewery SHS	LA GRANGE	★	★	★	★							★		★					
Mother Neff SP	MOODY				★	★	★	10			BG	★	★	★		☆			
Mustang Island SP	PORT ARANSAS				★	★	★	12						★		☆	☆		B1
National Museum of the Pacific War ▲	FREDERICKSBURG	★	★	★	★							★							E
Old Fort Parker ▲	GROESBECK	★	★	★				1											E
Palmetto SP	LULING				★	★	★	15			BC	★	★	★		★	☆	★	
Palo Duro Canyon SP (Summer Drama: "Texas")	CANYON			★	★	★	★	8	★			★	★	★		★			B1, E, L
Pedernales Falls SP	JOHNSON CITY				★	★	★	9			NG	★	★	★		☆	☆		B1, E
Port Isabel Lighthouse SHS ▲	PORT ISABEL	★	★		★														
Possum Kingdom SP	CADDO				★	★	★	10		★		★	★	★	★	★	☆	★	
Purtis Creek SP	EUSTACE				★	★	★	10			★	★	★	★	★	★	☆	★	P
Ray Roberts Lake SP, Isle du Bois Unit	PILOT POINT				★	★	★	13			DG	★	★	★	★	★	☆	★	B1, B2, E
Johnson Branch Unit	VALLEY VIEW				★	★	★	7			DG	★	★	★	★	★	☆		B1, B2
Jordan Unit (Lantana Resort)	PILOT POINT																		
Resaca de la Palma SP	BROWNSVILLE																		
Sabine Pass Battleground SHS ▲	SABINE PASS	★	★		★		★	12						★	★	☆			
Sam Bell Maxey House SHS ▲	PARIS	★	★	★	★														
Sam Rayburn House SHS ▲	BONHAM																		
San Angelo SP	SAN ANGELO				★	★	★	8		★	BG	★	★	★	★	★	☆		B1, E, L
San Felipe de Austin SHS ▲	SAN FELIPE																		
San Jacinto Battleground SHS (Battleship Texas)	HOUSTON	★	★	★	★						DG	★		★			☆		
Sea Rim SP	PORT ARTHUR				★	★	★	10			★			★	★	★	☆	★	B1
Sebastopol House SHS	SEGUIN	★	★	★										★					
Seminole Canyon SP & HS (Indian Pictographs)	LANGTRY	★	★	★	★	★		14				★	★	★					B1
Sheldon Lake SP (Environmental Learning Center)	HOUSTON	★										★	☆	★	★	★			
South Llano River SP	JUNCTION			★	★	★	★	10				★	★	★		☆	☆		B1
Starr Family Home SHS ▲	MARSHALL	★	★	★	★														
Stephen F. Austin SP	SAN FELIPE			★	★	★	★	15	★		BG	★	★	★		☆			G
Texas State Railroad ▲	PALESTINE & RUSK	★	★	★	★														
Tyler SP	TYLER				★	★	★	15	★		BG	★	★	★	★	★	☆	★	B1
Varner-Hogg Plantation SHS ▲	WEST COLUMBIA	★	★	★	★							★		★		☆			
Village Creek SP	LUMBERTON				★	★	★	13			BG	★	★	★		☆	☆	★	B1
Walter Umphrey SP ▲	PORT ARTHUR					(Managed by Jefferson County)													
Washington-on-the-Brazos SHS — Barrington Living History Farm (Anson Jones Home)	WASHINGTON	★	★	★	★						DG	★	★						
Wyler Aerial Tramway at Franklin Mts. SP	EL PASO	★		★	★														

Facilities

▲ Facilities not operated by Parks & Wildlife Department.

★ Facilities or services available for activity.

☆ Permitted but facilities not provided.

Miscellaneous Codes

& Some handicap accessible facilities

B1 Mountain Biking
B2 Surfaced Bike Trail
DG Day-Use Group Facilities
NG Overnight Group Facilities
BG Both Day & Night Group Facilities

E Equestrian Facilities and/or Trails
G Golf
I Hotel-Type Facilities
L Texas Longhorn Herd
R Rock Climbing

formation uncovered by erosion) in the United States. Indians believed **ghost fires** flickered at top and were awed by weird creaking and groaning, which geologists say resulted from rock's heating and expanding by day, cooling and contracting at night. Enchanted Rock is a **National Natural Landmark** and is on the **National Register of Historic Places**. Activities include hiking, geological study, camping, **rock climbing** and star gazing.

Estero Llano Grande State Park, part of the World Birding Center network, is a 176-acre wetlands refuge 3.2 miles southeast of Weslaco off FM 1015. Birds seen here include **waders, shorebirds** and **migrating waterfowl**, as well as coastal species such as **Roseate spoonbill** and **Ibis**. Rare spottings include **red-crowned parrots** and **green parakeets**. Opened daily. Guided tours offered.

Fairfield Lake State Park is 1,460 acres adjacent to Lake Fairfield, 6 miles northeast of the city of Fairfield off FM 2570 and FM 3285 in Freestone County. It was leased from Texas Utilities in 1971–72. Surrounding woods offer sanctuary for many species of birds and wildlife. Camping, hiking, backpacking, nature study, water-related activities available. Extensive schedule of tours, seminars and other activities.

Falcon State Park is 572.6 acres located 15 miles north of Roma off US 83 and FM 2098 at southern end of Falcon Reservoir in Starr and Zapata counties. Park leased from International Boundary and Water Commission in 1949. Gently rolling hills covered by **mesquite, huisache, wild olive, ebony, cactus**. Excellent **birding** and **fishing**. Camping and water activities also. Nearby are **Mexico, Fort Ringgold** in Rio Grande City and historic city of **Roma. Bentsen-Rio Grande Valley State Park** is 65 miles away.

Fannin Battleground State Historic Site, 9 miles east of Goliad in Goliad County off US 59 to PR 27. The 13.6-acre park site was acquired by the state in 1914; transferred to TPW by legislative enactment in 1965. At this site on March 20, 1836, **Col. James Fannin** surrendered to Mexican **Gen. José Urrea** after **Battle of Coleto**; 342 massacred and 28 escaped near what is now **Goliad State Park**. Near Fannin site is **Gen. Ignacio Zaragoza's Birthplace** and partially restored **Mission Nuestra Señora del Espíritu Santo de Zúñiga** (see also **Goliad State Park** in this list).

Fanthorp Inn State Historic Site includes a historic double-pen cedar-log dogtrot house and 1.4 acres in Anderson, county seat of Grimes County, south of TX 90. Acquired by purchase in 1977 from a Fanthorp descendant and opened to the public in 1987. Inn records report visits from many prominent civic and military leaders, including **Sam Houston, Anson Jones**, and generals **Ulysses S. Grant, Robert E. Lee** and **Stonewall Jackson**. Originally built in 1834, it has been restored to its 1850 use as a family home and travelers' hotel. Tours available Friday, Saturday, Sunday. Call TPW for stagecoach-ride schedule. No dining or overnight facilities.

Fort Boggy State Park is 1,847 acres of wooded, rolling hills in Leon County near Boggy Creek, about 4 miles south of Centerville on TX 75. Land donated to TPWD in 1985 by Eileen Crain Sullivan. Area once home to Keechi and Kickapoo tribes. Log fort was built by settlers in 1840s; first settlement north of the Old San Antonio Road and between the Navasota and Trinity rivers. Swimming beach, fishing, picnicking, nature trails for hiking and mountain biking. Fifteen-acre lake open to small craft. Open-air group pavilion overlooking lake can be reserved ($50 per day). Nearby attractions include **Rusk/Palestine, Fort Parker**, and **Texas State Railroad state**

parks, and **Old Fort Parker Historic Site**. Open Wed.–Sun. for day use only; entrance fee. For reservations, call 512-389-8900.

Fort Griffin State Historic Site is 506.2 acres 15 miles north of Albany off US 283 in Shackelford County. The state was deeded the land by the county in 1935. Portion of **state longhorn herd** resides in park. On bluff overlooking townsite of **Fort Griffin** and **Clear Fork of Brazos River** valley are partially restored ruins of **Old Fort Griffin**, restored bakery, replicas of enlisted men's huts. Fort constructed in 1867, deactivated 1881. Camping, equestrian camping, hiking. Nearby are **Albany** with restored courthouse square, **Abilene** and **Possum Kingdom state parks**. Albany annually holds "Fandangle" musical show in commemoration of frontier times.

More Travel Information

Call the **Texas Department of Transportation**'s toll-free number: **1-800-888-8TEX** for:

- The **Texas State Travel Guide**, a free, full-color publication with information about attractions, activities, history and historic sites.
- The official **Texas state highway map**.

On the Internet: **www.traveltex.com**

Fort Lancaster State Historic Site, 81.6-acres located about 8 miles east of Sheffield on TX 290 in Crockett County. Acquired in 1968 by deed from Crockett County; Henry Meadows donated 41 acres in 1975. **Fort Lancaster** established Aug. 20, 1855, to guard San Antonio-El Paso Road and protect movement of supplies and immigrants from Indian hostilities. Site of part of Camel Corps experiment. Fort abandoned March 19, 1861, after Texas seceded from Union. Exhibits on history, natural history and archaeology; nature trail, picnicking. Open daily; day use only.

Fort Leaton State Historic Site, 4 miles southeast of Presidio in Presidio County on FM 170, was acquired in 1967 from private owners. Consists of 23.4 acres, 5 of which are on site of **trading post**. In 1848, **Ben Leaton** built fortified adobe trading post known as Fort Leaton near present Presidio. Ben Leaton died in 1851. Guided tours; exhibits trace history, natural history and archaeological history of area. Serves as western entrance to **Big Bend Ranch State Park**. Day use only.

Fort McKavett State Historic Site, 79.5 acres acquired from 1967 through the mid-1970s from Fort McKavett Restoration, Inc., Menard County and private individuals, is located 23 miles west of Menard off US 190 and FM 864. Originally called **Camp San Saba**, the fort was built by War Department in 1852 to protect frontier settlers and travelers on Upper El Paso Road from Indians. Camp later renamed for **Capt. Henry McKavett**, killed at Battle of Monterrey, Sept. 21, 1846. Fort abandoned March 1859; reoccupied April 1868. A **Buffalo Soldier** post. Abandoned again June 30, 1883. Once called by Gen. Wm. T. Sherman, "the prettiest post in Texas." More than 25 restored buildings, ruins of many others. Interpretive exhibits. Day use only.

Fort Parker State Park includes 1,458.8 acres, including 758.78 land acres and 700-acre lake between Mexia and Groesbeck off TX 14 in Limestone County. Named for the former private fort built near present park in 1836, the site was acquired from private owners and the City of Mexia 1935-1937. Camping, fishing, swimming, canoeing, picnicking. Nearby is **Old Fort Parker Historic Site**, which is operated by the City of Groesbeck.

Fort Richardson State Park, Historic Site, and Lost Creek Reservoir Trailway, located one-half mile south of Jacksboro off US 281 in Jack County, contains 454 acres. Acquired in 1968 from City of Jacksboro. Fort founded in 1867, northernmost of line of federal forts established after Civil War for protection from Indians; originally named **Fort Jacksboro**. In April 1867, fort was moved to its present location from 20 miles farther south; on Nov. 19, 1867, made permanent post at Jacksboro and named for **Israel Richardson**, who was fatally wounded at Battle of Antietam. Expeditions sent from Fort Richardson arrested Indians responsible for **Warren Wagon Train Massacre** in

Fort McKavett State Historic Site in Menard County dates from 1852. Photo by Robert Plocheck.

1871 and fought Comanches in **Palo Duro Canyon**. Fort abandoned in May 1878. Park contains seven restored buildings and two replicas. Interpretive center, picnicking, camping, fishing; **ten-mile trailway**.

Franklin Mountains State Park, created by an act of the legislature in 1979 to protect the mountain range as a wilderness preserve and acquired by TPW in 1981, comprises 24,247.56 acres, all within El Paso city limits. **Largest urban park in the nation**. It includes virtually an entire **Chihuahuan Desert mountain range**, with an elevation of 7,192 feet at the summit. The park is habitat for many Chihuahuan Desert plants including **sotol, lechuguilla, ocotillo, cholla** and **barrel cactus**, and such animals as **mule deer, fox** and an occasional **cougar**. Camping, mountain biking, nature study, hiking, picnicking, rock-climbing. **Wyler Aerial Tramway**, an aerial cable-car tramway on 195 acres of rugged mountain on east side of Franklin Mountains. Purchase tickets at tramway station on McKinley Ave. Check with park for fees and hours; 915-566-6622. Other area attractions include **Hueco Tanks State Historic Site and Magoffin Home State Historic Site.**

Fulton Mansion State Historic Site in Fulton is 3.5 miles north of Rockport off TX Business 35 on South Fulton Beach Rd. in Aransas County. The 2.3 acre-property was acquired by purchase from private owner in 1976. Three-story wooden structure, built in 1874-1877, was home of **George W. Fulton**, prominent in South Texas for economic and commercial influence; mansion derives significance from its innovative construction and Victorian design. Call ahead for days and hours of guided tours; open Wednesday–Sunday; 800-792-1112.

Galveston Island State Park, on the west end of Galveston Island on FM 3005, is a 2,013.1-acre site acquired in 1969 from private owners. Camping, birding, nature study, swimming, bicycling and fishing amid **sand dunes and grassland**. Musical productions in **amphitheater** during summer.

Garner State Park is 1,419.8 acres of recreational facilities on US 83 on the Frio River in Uvalde County 9 miles south of Leakey. Named for **John Nance Garner**, U.S. Vice President, 1933-1941, the park was deeded in 1934-

36 by private owners. Camping, hiking, picnicking, river recreation, miniature golf, biking, boat rentals. Cabins available. Nearby is **John Nance "Cactus Jack" Garner Museum** in Uvalde. Nearby also are ruins of historic **Mission Nuestra Señora de la Candelaria del Cañon**, founded in 1749; **Camp Sabinal** (a U.S. Cavalry post and later Texas Ranger camp) established 1856; **Fort Inge**, established 1849.

Goliad State Park and **Mission Espíritu Santo Historic Site** are 188.3 acres one-fourth mile south of Goliad on US 183 and 77A, along the San Antonio River in Goliad County. The land was deeded to the state in 1931 by the City and County of Goliad; transferred to TPW 1949. Nearby are the sites of several battles in the Texas fight for independence from Mexico. The park includes a replica of **Mission Nuestra Señora del Espíritu Santo de Zúñiga**, originally established 1722 and settled at its present site in 1749. **Gen. Ignacio Zaragoza Birthplace State Historic Site**, which is located near **Presidio la Bahía**, across the river. Gen. Zaragoza was the Mexican national hero who led troops against the French at historic **Battle of Puebla** on May 5, 1862. The restored presidio and chapel, **Nuestra Señora de Loreto de la Bahía**, dates to 1749. Adjacent is a memorial shaft marking the common burial site of **Fannin** and victims of Goliad massacre (1836). Located four miles west of Goliad on US 59 is the **Mission Rosario State Historic Site** which contains ruins of **Nuestra Señora del Rosario** mission, established 1754. At Goliad State Park are camping, picnicking, historical exhibits, nature trail. (See also **Fannin Battleground State Historic Site.**)

Goose Island State Park, 321.4 acres 10 miles northeast of Rockport on TX 35 and PR 13 on St. Charles and Aransas bays in Aransas County, was deeded by private owners in 1931-1935 plus an additional seven acres donated in the early 1990s by Sun Oil Co. Located here is "Big Tree" estimated to be a 1,000-year-old **live oak**. Fishing, picnicking and camping, plus excellent birding; no swimming. Rare and endangered **whooping cranes** can be viewed during winter just across St. Charles Bay in **Aransas National Wildlife Refuge**.

Government Canyon State Natural Area is an 8,622-acre

area in Bexar County, northwest of San Antonio, 3.5 miles northwest of Loop 1604 and FM 471, then 1.6 miles north on Galm Road. Day use only. No camping. Open Friday–Monday. Trees such as **mounatin laurel, Ashe juniper, Mexican buckeye** and **Escarpment black cherry.**

Gov. Hogg Shrine Historic Site is a 26.7-acre tract on TX 37 about six blocks south of the Wood County Courthouse in Quitman. Named for **James Stephen Hogg,** first native-born governor of Texas, the park includes museums housing items that belonged to the Hogg and Stinson families. Seventeen acres deeded by the Wood County Old Settlers Reunion Association in 1946; 4.74 acres gift of Miss Ima Hogg in 1970; 3 acres purchased **Gov. James Stephen Hogg Memorial Shrine** created in 1941. Three museums: Gov. Hogg's wedding held in **Stinson Home; Honeymoon Cottage; Miss Ima Hogg Museum** houses both park headquarters and display of representative history of entire Northeast Texas area. Operated by City of Quitman.

Guadalupe River State Park comprises 1,938.7 acres on cypress-shaded Guadalupe River in Kendall and Comal counties, 13 miles east of Boerne on TX 46. Acquired by deed from private owners in 1974. Park has four miles of river frontage with several **white-water rapids** and is located in a stretch of **Guadalupe River** noted for canoeing, tubing. Picnicking, camping, hiking, nature study. Trees include **sycamore, elm, basswood, pecan, walnut, persimmon, willow** and **hackberry** (see also **Honey Creek State Natural Area**).

Hill Country State Natural Area in Bandera and Medina counties, 9 miles west of Bandera on FM 1077. The 5,369.8-acre site acquired by gift from Merrick Bar-O-Ranch and purchased in 1976. Park is located in typical Texas Hill Country on West Verde Creek and contains several **spring-fed streams.** Primitive and equestrian camping, hiking, horseback riding, mountain biking, fishing. Group lodge.

Honey Creek State Natural Area consists of 2,293.7 acres adjacent to **Guadalupe River State Park** (above); entrance is in the park. Acquired from The Nature Conservancy of Texas in 1985 with an addition from private individual in 1988. Diverse plant life includes **agarita, Texas persimmon** and **Ashe juniper** in hills, and **cedar elm, Spanish oak, pecan, walnut** and **Mexican buckeye** in bottomlands. Abundant wildlife includes **ringtail, leopard frog, green kingfisher, golden-cheeked warbler** and **canyon wren.** Schedule varies; call 830-796-4413 for details.

Hueco Tanks State Park and Historic Site, located 32 miles northeast of El Paso in El Paso County on FM 2775 just north of US 62-180, was obtained from the county in 1969, with additional 121 acres purchased in 1970. Featured in this 860.3-acre park are large **natural rock basins** that provided water for archaic hunters, Plains Indians, Butterfield Overland Mail coach horses and passengers, and other travelers in this arid region. In park are **Indian pictographs, old ranch house** and relocated **ruins of stage station.** Rock climbing, picnicking, camping, hiking. Wildlife includes **gray fox, bobcat, prairie falcons, golden eagles.** Visitation is limited. Pictograph tours are by advanced request. Call 1-800-792-112, (Option 3).

Huntsville State Park is 2,083.2-acre recreational area off IH 45 and PR 40 six miles south of Huntsville in Walker County, acquired by deeds from private owners in 1937. Heavily wooded park adjoins **Sam Houston National Forest** and encloses **Lake Raven.** Hiking, camping, fishing, biking, paddle boats, canoeing. At nearby Huntsville are **Sam Houston's old homestead (Steamboat House),** containing some of his personal effects, and **his grave.** Approximately 50 miles away is **Alabama-Coushatta Indian Reservation** in Polk County.

Inks Lake State Park is 1,201 acres of recreational facilities along Inks Lake, 9 miles west of Burnet on the Colorado River off TX 29 on PR 4 in Burnet County. Acquired by deeds from the Lower Colorado River Authority and pri-

vate owners in 1940. Camping, hiking, fishing, swimming, boating, golf. **Deer, turkey** and other wildlife abundant. Nearby are **Longhorn Cavern State Park, LBJ Ranch, LBJ State Historic Site, Pedernales Falls State Park** and **Enchanted Rock State Natural Area. Granite Mountain** quarry at nearby Marble Falls furnished red granite for **Texas state capitol. Buchanan Dam,** considered the largest multi-arch dam in the nation, located 4 miles from park.

Jim Hogg Historic Site is 178.4 acres of East Texas Pineywoods in Cherokee County, 2 miles east of Rusk off U.S. 84 E. and Fire Tower Road. Memorial to Texas' first native-born governor, James Stephen Hogg, 1891–1895. Remnants of 1880s iron ore mining. Scale replica of Hogg birthplace. Picnicking, historical study, nature study, hiking and bird watching. Self-guided and guided museum tours and nature trail tours. Operated by the City of Rusk; 903-683-4850. Area attractions: **Caddoan Mounds** and **Mission Tejas State** historic sites, **Rusk/Palestine, Texas State Railroad** and **Tyler state parks** and historic Nacogdoches. Day use only; entrance fee.

Kickapoo Cavern State Park is located about 22 miles north of Brackettville on RM 674 on the Kinney/Edwards county line in the southern Edwards Plateau. The park (6,368.4 acres) contains **15 known caves,** two of which are large enough to be significant: **Kickapoo Cavern,** about 1/4 mile in length, has impressive formations, and **Green Cave,** slightly shorter, supports a nursery colony of **Brazilian freetail bats** in summer. Birds include rare species such as **black-capped vireo, varied bunting** and **Montezuma quail.** Reptiles and amphibians include **barking frog, mottled rock rattlesnake** and **Texas alligator lizard.** Tours of Kickapoo and observation of bats available only by special arrangement. Group lodge; primitive camping; hiking and mountain-biking trails. Open only by reservation.

Kreische Brewery State Historic Site (see Monument Hill and Kreische Brewery State Historic Sites).

Lake Arrowhead State Park consists of 524 acres in Clay County, about 14 miles south of Wichita Falls on US 281 to FM 1954, then 8 miles to park. Acquired in 1970 from the City of Wichita Falls. **Lake Arrowhead** is a reservoir on the Little Wichita River with 106 miles of shoreline. The land surrounding the lake is generally semiarid, gently rolling prairie, much of which has been invaded by mesquite in recent decades. Fishing, camping, lake swimming, picnicking, horseback-riding area.

Lake Bob Sandlin State Park, on the wooded shoreline of 9,400-acre Lake Bob Sandlin, is located 12 miles southwest of Mount Pleasant off FM 21 in Titus County. Activities in the 639.8-acre park include picnicking, camping, mountain biking, hiking, swimming, fishing and boating. **Oak, hickory, dogwood, redbud, maple** and **pine** produce spectacular fall color. Eagles can sometimes be spotted in winter months.

Lake Brownwood State Park in Brown County is 537.5 acres acquired from Brown County Water Improvement District No. 1 in 1934. Park reached from TX 279 to PR 15, 16 miles northwest of Brownwood on Lake Brownwood near **geographical center of Texas.** Water sports, hiking, camping. Cabins available.

Lake Casa Blanca International State Park, located one mile east of Laredo off US 59 on Loop 20, was formerly operated by the City of Laredo and Webb County and was acquired by TPW in 1990. Park includes 371 acres on Lake Casa Blanca. **Recreation hall** can be reserved. Camping, picnicking, fishing, ball fields, playgrounds, amphitheater, and tennis courts. County-operated golf course nearby.

Lake Colorado City State Park, 500 acres leased for 99 years from a utility company. It is located in Mitchell County 11 miles southwest of Colorado City off IH 20 on FM 2836. Water sports, picnicking, camping, hiking. Part of **state longhorn herd** can be seen in park.

Lake Corpus Christi State Park, a 14,112-acre park in San Patricio, Jim Wells and Live Oak counties. Located 35

Equestrian trails wind through the Hill Country State Natural Area in Bandera and Medina counties. Photo courtesy of Texas Parks & Wildlife Department.

miles northwest of Corpus Christi and four miles southwest of Mathis off TX 359 and Park Road 25. Was leased from City of Corpus Christi in 1934. Camping, picnicking, birding, water sports. Nearby are **Padre Island National Seashore; Mustang Island, Choke Canyon, Goliad and Goose Island state parks; Aransas National Wildlife Refuge, and Fulton Mansion State Historic Site**.

Lake Livingston State Park, in Polk County, about one mile southwest of Livingston on FM 3126 and PR 65, contains 635.5 acres along Lake Livingston. Acquired by deed from private landowners in 1971. Near ghost town of **Swartwout**, steamboat landing on Trinity River in 1830s and 1850s. Camping, picnicking, swimming pool, fishing, mountain biking and stables.

Lake Mineral Wells State Park and Trailway, located 4 miles east of Mineral Wells on US 180 in Parker County, consists of 3,282.5 acres encompassing Lake Mineral Wells. In 1975, the City of Mineral Wells donated 1,095 land acres and the lake to TPW; the federal government transferred additional land from Fort Wolters army post. Popular for **rock-climbing/rappelling**. Swimming, fishing, boating, camping; the 20-mile **Lake Mineral Wells State Trailway** avaiable for hiking, bicycling, equestrian use.

Lake Somerville State Park, northwest of Brenham in Lee and Burleson counties, was leased from the federal government in 1969. **Birch Creek Unit** (2,365 acres reached from TX 60 and PR 57) and **Nails Creek Unit** (3,155 acres reached from US 290 and FM 180), are connected by a **13-mile trailway system**, with **equestrian and primitive camp sites**, rest benches, shelters and drinking water. Also camping, birding, picnicking, volleyball and water sports. **Somerville Wildlife Management Area**, 3,180 acres is nearby.

Lake Tawakoni State Park is a 376.3-acre park in Hunt County along the shore of its namesake reservoir. It was acquired in 1984 through a 50-year lease agreement with the Sabine River Authority and opened in 2001. Includes a swimming beach, half-mile trail, picnic sites, boat ramp

and campsites. A **40-acre tallgrass prairie** managed in the post-oak woodlands. The park is reached from IH 20 on TX 47 north to FM 2475 about 20 miles past Wills Point.

Lake Texana State Park is 575 acres, 6.5 miles east of Edna on TX 111, halfway between Houston and Corpus Christi in Jackson County, with camping, boating, fishing and picnicking facilities. It was acquired by a 50-year lease agreement with the Bureau of Reclamation in 1977. Good birding in the **oak/pecan woodlands**. **Alligators** are often found in park coves.

Lake Whitney State Park is 1,280.7 acres along the east shore of Lake Whitney west of Hillsboro via TX 22 and FM 1244 in Hill County. Acquired in 1954 by a Department of the Army lease. Located near ruins of **Towash**, early Texas settlement inundated by the lake. Towash Village named for chief of Hainai Indians. Park noted for **bluebonnets** in spring. Camping, hiking, birding, picnicking, water activities.

Landmark Inn State Historic Site, 4.7 acres in Castroville, Medina County, about 15 miles west of San Antonio, was acquired through donation by Miss Ruth Lawler in 1974. Castroville, settled in the 1840s by Alsatian farmers, is called **Little Alsace of Texas**. Landmark Inn built about 1844 as residence and store for **Cesar Monod**, mayor of Castroville 1851-1864. Special workshops, tours and events held at inn; grounds may be rented for receptions, family reunions and weddings. Overnight lodging; all rooms air-conditioned and nonsmoking.

Lipantitlan State Historic Site is 5 acres 9 miles east of Orange Grove in Nueces County off Texas 359, FM 624 and FM 70. The property was deeded by private owners in 1937. Fort constructed here in 1833 by Mexican government fell to Texas forces in 1835. Only facilities are picnic tables. **Lake Corpus Christi State Park** is nearby.

Lockhart State Park is 263.7 acres 4 miles south of Lockhart via US 183, FM 20 and PR 10 in Caldwell County. The land was deeded by private owners between 1934 and 1937. Camping, picnicking, hiking, fishing, 9-hole golf course. After Comanche raid at Linnville, **Battle of Plum Creek** (1840) was fought in area.

Longhorn Cavern State Park, off US 281 and PR 4 about 6 miles west and 6 miles south of Burnet in Burnet County, is 645.62 acres dedicated as a natural landmark in 1971. It was acquired in 1932-1937 from private owners. The cave has been used as a shelter since prehistoric times. Among legends about the cave is that the outlaw **Sam Bass** hid stolen money there. Confederates made gunpowder in the cave during the Civil War. Nature trail; guided tours of cave; picnicking, hiking. Cavern operated by concession agreement. **Inks Lake State Park** and **Lyndon B. Johnson Ranch** located nearby.

Lost Maples State Natural Area consists of 2,174.2 scenic acres on the Sabinal River in Bandera and Real counties, 5 miles north of Vanderpool on FM 187. Acquired by purchase from private owners in 1973-1974. Outstanding example of Edwards Plateau flora and fauna, features isolated stand of uncommon **Uvalde bigtooth maple. Rare golden-cheeked warbler, black-capped vireo** and **green kingfisher** nest and feed in park. Fall foliage can be spectacular (late Oct. through early Nov.). Hiking trails, camping, fishing, picnicking, birding.

Lyndon B. Johnson State Park & Historic Site, off US 290 in Gillespie County 14 miles west of Johnson City near Stonewall, contains 717.9 acres. Acquired in 1965 with private donations. **Home of Lyndon B. Johnson** located north bank of **Pedernales River** across Ranch Road 1 from park; portion of **official Texas longhorn herd** maintained at park. Wildlife exhibit includes **turkey, deer and bison.** **Living-history demonstrations** at restored **Sauer-Beckmann house.** Reconstruction of **Johnson birthplace** is open to public. Historic structures, swimming pool, tennis courts, baseball field, picnicking. Day use only. Nearby is family cemetery where former president and relatives are buried. In Johnson City is **boyhood home of President Johnson.** (See **National Parks.**)

Magoffin Home State Historic Site, in El Paso, is a 19-room territorial-style adobe on a 1.5-acre site. Purchased by the state and City of El Paso in 1976, it is operated by TPW. Home was built in 1875 by El Pasoan **Joseph Magoffin.** Furnished with original family artifacts. Guided tours; call for schedule. Day use only.

Martin Creek Lake State Park, 286.9 acres, is located 4 miles south of Tatum off TX 43 and CR 2183 in Rusk County. It was deeded to the TPW by Texas Utilities in 1976. Water activities; also cabins, camping, picnicking. Roadbed of **Trammel's Trace**, old Indian trail that became major route for settlers moving to Texas from Arkansas, can be seen. **Hardwood and pine** forest shelters abundant wildlife including **swamp rabbits, gophers, nutria** and numerous species of land birds and waterfowl.

Martin Dies Jr. State Park is 705 acres in Jasper and Tyler counties on B. A. Steinhagen Reservoir between Woodville and Jasper via US 190. Land leased for 5 years from Corps of Engineers in 1964. Located at edge of **Big Thicket.** Plant and animal life varied and abundant. Winter **bald eagle census** conducted at nearby Sam Rayburn Reservoir. Camping, hiking, mountain biking, water activities. Wildscape/herb garden. Park is approximately 30 miles from **Alabama and Coushatta Indian Reservation.**

McKinney Falls State Park is 744.4 acres 13 miles southeast of the state Capitol in Austin off US 183. Acquired in 1970 by gift from private owners. Named for Thomas F. McKinney, **one of Stephen F. Austin's first 300 colonists,** who built his home here in the mid-1800s on Onion Creek. Ruins of his homestead can be viewed. Swimming, hiking, biking, camping, picnicking, fishing, guided tours.

Meridian State Park in Bosque County is a 505.4-acre park. The heavily wooded land, on TX 22 three miles southwest of Meridian, was acquired from private owners in 1933-1935. **Texas-Santa Fe expedition** of 1841 passed through Bosque County near present site of park on Bee Creek. **Endangered golden-cheeked warbler** nests here. Camping, picnicking, hiking, fishing, lake swimming, birding, bicycling.

Mission Tejas State Park is a 363.5-acre park in Houston County. Situated 12 miles west of Alto via TX 21 and PR 44, the park was acquired from the Texas Forest Service in 1957. In the park is a representation of **Mission San Francisco de los Tejas,** the first mission in East Texas (1690). It was abandoned, then re-established 1716; abandoned again 1719; re-established again 1721; abandoned for last time in 1730 when the mission was moved to San Antonio. Also in park is restored **Rice Family Log Home,** built about 1828. Camping, hiking, fishing, picnicking.

Monahans Sandhills State Park consists of 3,840 acres of sand dunes, some up to 70 feet high, in Ward and Winkler counties 5 miles northeast of Monahans on IH 20 to PR 41. Land leased by state from private foundation until 2056. Dunes used as meeting place by raiding Indians.

Mother Neff State Park was the first official state park in Texas. Photo courtesy of Texas Parks & Wildlife Department.

Jetties offer a great view at Mustang Island State Park. Photo courtesy of Texas Parks & Wildlife Department.

Camping, hiking, picnicking, sand-surfing. Scheduled tours. **Odessa meteor crater** is nearby, as is **Balmorhea State Park**.

Monument Hill State Historic Site and **Kreische Brewery State Historic Site** are operated as one park unit. Monument Hill consists of 40.4 acres one mile south of La Grange on US 77 to Spur Road 92 in Fayette County. Monument and tomb area acquired by state in 1907; additional acreage acquired from the Archdiocese of San Antonio in 1956. Brewery and home purchased from private owners in 1977. Monument is dedicated to **Capt. Nicholas Dawson** and his men, who fought at **Salado Creek** in 1842, in Mexican **Gen. Adrián Woll's** invasion of Texas, and to the men of the **"black bean lottery"** (1843) of the **Mier Expedition**. Remains were brought to **Monument Hill** for reburial in 1848. Kreische Complex, on 36 acres, is linked to Monument Hill through interpretive trail. **Kreische Brewery State Historic Site** includes the brewery and stone-and-wood house built between 1850-1855 on Colorado River. One of **first commercial breweries** in state, it closed in 1884. Smokehouse and barn also in complex. Guided tours of brewery and house; call for schedule. Also picnicking, nature study.

Mother Neff State Park was the **first official state park** in Texas. It originated with 6 acres donated by Mrs. I. E. Neff, mother of **Pat M. Neff**, governor of Texas from 1921 to 1925. Gov. Neff and Frank Smith donated remainder in 1934. The park, located 8 miles west of Moody on FM 107 and TX 236, now contains 259 acres along the Leon River in Coryell County. Heavily wooded. Camping, picnicking, fishing, hiking.

Mustang Island State Park, 3,954 acres on Gulf of Mexico in Nueces County, 14 miles south of Port Aransas on TX 361, was acquired from private owners in 1972. Mustang Island is a barrier island with a complicated ecosystem, dependent upon the sand dune. The foundation plants of the dunes are **sea oats, beach panic grass and soil-bind morning glory**. Beach camping, picnicking; sun, sand and water activities. Excellent birding. **Padre Island National Seashore** 14 miles south.

National Museum of the Pacific War and **Admiral Nimitz State Historic Site** is on 7 acres in downtown Fredericksburg. First established as a state agency in 1969 by Texas Legislature; transferred to TPW in 1981. George Bush Gallery opened in 1999. Named for **Adm. Chester W. Nimitz** of World War II fame, it includes the **Pacific War Museum** in the **Nimitz Steamboat Hotel**; the **Japanese Garden of Peace**, donated by the people of Japan; the **History Walk of the Pacific War**, featuring planes, boats and other equipment from World War II; and other special exhibits. Nearby is **Kerrville State Park**.

Old Fort Parker is a 37.5-acre park 4 miles north of Groesbeck on TX 14 in Limestone County. Deeded by private owners in 1936 and originally constructed by the Civilian Conservation Corps (CCC); rebuilt in 1967. Reconstructed fort is pioneer memorial and site of Cynthia Ann Parker abduction on May 19, 1836, by Comanche Indians. Nearby Fort Parker Cemetery has graves of those killed at the fort in the 1836 raid. Historical study and picnicking. Living History events throughout year. Primitive skills classes/campouts by appointment. Groups welcome. Operated by the City of Groesbeck, 254-729-5253.

Palmetto State Park, a scenic park, is 270.3 acres 8 miles southeast of Luling on US 183 and PR 11 along the San Marcos River in Gonzales County. Land deeded in 1934-1936 by private owners and City of Gonzales. Named for **tropical dwarf palmetto** found there. Diverse plant and animal life; excellent birding. Also picnicking, fishing, hiking, pedal boats, swimming. Nearby **Gonzales** and **Ottine** important in early Texas history. Gonzales settled 1825 as center of **Green DeWitt's colonies**.

Palo Duro Canyon State Park consists of 16,402 acres 12 miles east of Canyon on TX 217 in Armstrong and Randall counties. The land was deeded by private owners in 1933 and is the scene of the annual summer production of the musical drama, "Texas." Spectacular one-million-year-old **scenic canyon** exposes rocks spanning about 200 million years of geological time. **Coronado** may have visited canyon in 1541. Canyon officially discovered by **Capt. R. B. Marcy** in 1852. Scene of decisive battle in 1874 between Comanche and Kiowa Indians and U.S. Army troops under **Gen. Ranald Mackenzie**. Also scene of ranching enterprise started by **Charles Goodnight** in 1876. Part of **state longhorn herd** is kept here. Camping, mountain biking, scenic drives, horseback and hiking trails, horse rentals.

Pedernales Falls State Park, 5,211.7 acres in Blanco County about 9 miles east of Johnson City on FM 2766 along Pedernales River, was acquired from private owners in 1970. Typical **Edwards Plateau** terrain, with **live oaks, deer, turkey** and **stone hills**. Camping, picnicking, hiking, swimming, tubing. Falls main scenic attraction.

Port Isabel Lighthouse State Historic Site consists of 0.9 acre in Port Isabel, Cameron County. Acquired by purchase from private owners in 1950, site includes **lighthouse** constructed in 1852; visitors can climb to top. Park is near sites of Civil War battle of **Palmito Ranch** (1865), and Mexican War battles of **Palo Alto** and **Resaca de la Palma** (1846). Operated by City of Port Isabel.

Possum Kingdom State Park, west of Mineral Wells via US 180 and PR 33 in Palo Pinto County, is 1,528.7 acres adjacent to **Possum Kingdom Lake**, in **Palo Pinto Mountains** and **Brazos River Valley**. Rugged canyons home to **deer**, other wildlife. Acquired from the Brazos River Authority in 1940. Camping, picnicking, swimming, fishing, boating. Cabins available.

Purtis Creek State Park is 1,582.4 acres in Henderson and Van Zandt counties 3.5 miles north of Eustace on FM 316. Acquired in 1977 from private owners. Fishing, camping, hiking, picnicking, paddle boats and canoes.

Ray Roberts Lake State Park (Isle du Bois Unit), consists of 2,263 acres on the south side of Ray Roberts Lake on FM 455 in Denton County. **Johnson Branch Unit** contains 1,514 acres on north side of lake in Denton and Cooke counties 7 miles east of IH 30 on FM 3002. There are also six satellite parks. Land acquired in 1984 by lease from Department of the Army. Abundant and varied plant and animal life. Fishing, camping, picnicking, swimming, hiking, biking; tours of 19-century farm buildings at Johnson Branch. Includes Lantana Ridge Lodge on the east side of the lake. It is a full-service lodging facility with restaurant.

Resaca de la Palma State Park, part of the World Birding Center network, is 1,700 semi-tropical acres off US 281, four miles west of Brownsville in Cameron County. Opened Monday-Friday, by appointment and reservations. Birding and natural history tours offered. Colorful neo-tropical and neartic migrant birds have been noted here.

Sabine Pass Battleground State Historic Site in Jefferson County 1.5 miles south of Sabine Pass on Dick Dowling Road, contains 57.6 acres acquired from Kountze County Trust in 1972. **Lt. Richard W. Dowling**, with small Confederate force, repelled an attempted 1863 invasion of Texas by Union gunboats. **Monument, World War II ammunition bunkers**. Fishing, picnicking, camping.

Sam Bell Maxey House State Historic Site, at the corner of South Church and Washington streets in Paris, Lamar County, was donated by City of Paris in 1976. Consists of .4 acre with 1868 Victorian Italianate-style frame house, plus outbuildings. Most of furnishings accumulated by Maxey family. Maxey served in Mexican and Civil wars and was two-term U.S. Senator. House is on the **National Register of Historic Places**. Open for tours Friday through Sunday.

San Angelo State Park, on **O.C. Fisher Reservoir** adjacent to the city of San Angelo in Tom Green County, contains 7,677 acres of land, most of which will remain undeveloped. Leased from U.S. Corps of Engineers in 1995. Access is from US 87 or 67, then FM 2288. Highly diversified plant and animal life. Activities include boating, water activities, hiking, mountain biking, horseback riding, camping, picnicking. Part of **state longhorn herd** in park. Nearby is **Fort Concho**.

San Jacinto Battleground State Historic Site and **Battleship *Texas* State Historic Site** are located 20 miles east of downtown Houston off TX 225 east to TX 134 to PR 1836 in east Harris County. The park is 1,200 acres with 570-foot-tall monument erected in 1936-1939 in honor of Texans who defeated Mexican **Gen. Antonio López de Santa Anna** on April 21, 1836, to win Texas' independence from Mexico. The park is original site of Texans' camp acquired in 1883. Subsequent acquisitions made in 1897, 1899 and 1985. Park transferred to TPW in 1965. Park registered as **National Historic Landmark**. Elevator ride to observation tower near top of monument; museum. Monument known as **tallest free-standing concrete structure in the world** at the time it was erected. Interpretive trail around battleground. Adjacent to park is the **U.S.S. Texas**, commissioned in 1914. The battleship, the only survivor of the dreadnought class and the only surviving veteran of two world wars, was donated to people of Texas by U.S. Navy. Ship was moored in the Houston Ship Channel at the **San Jacinto Battleground** on San Jacinto Day, 1948. Extensive repairs were done 1988-1990. Some renovation is on-going, but ship is open

for tours. Ship closed Christmas Eve and Christmas Day.

Sea Rim State Park in Jefferson County, 20 miles south of Port Arthur, off TX 87, contains 4,141 acres of marshland and 5.2 miles of **Gulf beach** shoreline, acquired from private owners in 1972. It is prime wintering area for **waterfowl**. Wetlands also shelter such wildlife as river otter, nutria, alligator, mink, muskrat. Camping, fishing, swimming; wildlife observation; nature trail; boating. **Airboat tours of marsh**. Near **McFaddin National Wildlife Refuge**.

Sebastopol House State Historic Site at 704 Zorn Street in Seguin, Guadalupe County, was acquired by purchase in 1976 from Seguin Conservation Society; approximately 2.2 acres. Built about 1856 by **Col. Joshua W. Young** of **limecrete**, concrete made from local gravel and lime, the Greek Revival-style house, which was restored to its 1880 appearance by the TPW, is on National Register of Historic Places. Tours available Friday and Sunday. Also of interest in the area is historic **Seguin**, founded 1838.

Seminole Canyon State Historic Site in Val Verde County, 9 miles west of Comstock off US 90, contains 2,172.5 acres; acquired by purchase from private owners 1973-1977. **Fate Bell Shelter** in canyon contains several important **prehistoric Indian pictographs**. Historic interpretive center. Tours of rock-art sites Wednesday-Sunday; also hiking, mountain biking, camping.

Sheldon Lake State Park and Environmental Learning Center, 2,800 acres in Harris County on Garrett Road 20 miles east of Beltway 8. Acquired by purchase in 1952 from the City of Houston. Freshwater marsh habitat. Activities include nature study, birding, fishing. Wildscape gardens of native plants.

South Llano River State Park, 5 miles south of Junction in Kimble County off US 377, is a 524-acre site. Land donated to the TPW by private owner in 1977. Wooded bottomland along the winding South Llano River is **largest and oldest winter roosting site for the Rio Grande turkey** in Central Texas. Roosting area closed to visitors October-March. Other animals include **wood ducks, javelina, fox, beaver, bobcat** and **armadillo**. Camping, picnicking, tubing, swimming and fishing, hiking, mountain biking.

Starr Family Home State Historic Site, 3.1 acres at 407 W. Travis in Marshall, Harrison County. Greek Revival-style mansion, **Maplecroft**, built 1870-1871, was home to four generations of Starr family, powerful and economically influential Texans. Two other family homes also in park. Acquired by gift in 1976; additional land donated in 1982. Maplecroft is on National Register of Historic Places. Tours Friday–Sunday or by appointment. Special events during year.

Stephen F. Austin State Park is 663.3 acres along the Brazos River in San Felipe, Austin County, named for the "**Father of Texas**." The area was deeded by the San Felipe de Austin Corporation and the **San Felipe** Park Association in 1940. Site of township of San Felipe was seat of government where conventions of 1832 and 1833 and Consultation of 1835 held. These led to **Texas Declaration of Independence**. San Felipe was home of **Stephen F. Austin** and other famous early Texans; home of **Texas' first Anglo newspaper (the Texas Gazette)** founded in 1829; postal system of Texas originated here. Area called "Cradle of Texas Liberty." Museum. Camping, picnicking, golf, fishing, hiking.

Texas State Railroad, in Anderson and Cherokee counties between the cities of Palestine and Rusk, adjacent to US 84, contains 499 acres. Operated by American Heritage Railways since 2007. Trains run seasonal schedules on 25.5 miles of track. Call for information and reservations: 1-888-987-2461. Railroad built by the State of Texas to support the **state-owned iron works** at Rusk. Begun in 1893, and built largely by inmates from the state prison system, the railroad was gradually extended until it reached Palestine in 1909 and established regular rail service between the towns. **Rusk and Palestine Parks** are adjacent to the two **Texas State Railroad Depot**s. Fishing, picnicking, camping, tennis courts, playground. **Train rides** in restored passenger cars.

Tyler State Park is 985.5 acres two miles north of IH 20 on FM 14 north of Tyler in Smith County. Includes 64-acre lake. The land was deeded by private owners in 1934–1935. Heavily wooded. Camping, hiking, fishing, boating, lake swimming. Nearby Tyler called R**ose Capital of Nation, with Tyler Rose Garden and annual Tyler Rose Festival.** Also in Tyler are **Caldwell Children's Zoo** and **Goodman Museum**.

Varner-Hogg Plantation State Historic Site is 66 acres in Brazoria County two miles north of West Columbia on FM 2852. Land originally owned by Martin Varner, a member of Stephen F. Austin's **"Old Three Hundred"** colony; later was home of Texas governor **James Stephen Hogg**. Property was deeded to the state in 1957 by Miss Ima Hogg, Gov. Hogg's daughter. **First rum distillery** in Texas established in 1829 by Varner. Mansion tours Tuesday through Saturday. Also picnicking, fishing.

Village Creek State Park, comprising 1,004 heavily forested acres, is located in Lumberton, Hardin County, 10 miles north of Beaumont off US 69 and FM 3513. Purchased in 1979 from private owner, the park contains abundant flora and fauna typical of the Big Thicket area. **The 200 species of birds** found here include wood ducks, egrets and herons. Activities include fishing, camping, canoeing, swimming, hiking and picnicking. Nearby is the **Big Thicket National Preserve**.

Walter Umphrey State Park is operated by Jefferson County on the south end of Please Island off TX 82. For RV site reservations, contact SGS Causeway Bait & Tackle, 409-985-4811.

Washington-on-the-Brazos State Historic Site consists of 293.1 acres 7 miles southwest of Navasota in Washington County on TX 105 and FM 1155. Land acquired by deed from private owners in 1916, 1976 and 1996. Park includes the site of the signing on March 2, 1836, of the **Texas Declaration of Independence** from Mexico, as well as the site of the later **signing of the Constitution of the Republic of Texas**. In 1842 and 1845, the land included the **capitol of the Republic. Star of the Republic Museum**. Activities include picnicking and birding. **Barrington Living History Farm** is the home of **Anson Jones, the last president of the Republic of Texas.** Activities are guided by entries that Jones made in his daybook while living there. For further information, contact 916-878-2214 or link to barrington.farm@tpwd. state.tx.us**.**

Recreation in the State Forests

All Texas State Forests are game sanctuaries with no firearms or hunting allowed. For general information about the Texas State Forests, *see page 112 in the Environment section.*

I.D. Fairchild State Forest

Located in Cherokee County, recreation includes hiking, horseback riding, picnicking, wildlife viewing and biking.

Special attractions are a **historical fire tower** site with plaque, Red Cockaded Woodpecker Management

Area and a pond with picnic area. Forest management demonstration sites throughout the forest. There are no restroom facilities in this forest.

Open year-round during daylight hours. Obtain information and maps at the Palestine District Office, 2203 West Spring St. (US-287 West) or call (903) 729-7738 weekdays.

W. Goodrich Jones State Forest

The Texas Forestry Museum is located in Lufkin and is open Monday through Saturday. Photo by Ron Billings; Texas Forest Service.

Recreational opportunities in this forest, located in Montgomery County, include bird watching, hiking, horseback riding, picnicking, wildlife viewing and biking.

Special attractions include **Sweetleaf Nature Trail** with State Champion Sweetleaf Tree, Red Cockaded Woodpecker Management Area, two small lakes with limited fishing and picnicking. Forest management demonstration sites throughout the forest.

Open year-round during daylight hours. Information, maps, permits and restrooms available at the Conroe District Office on FM 1488, 1.5 miles west of I-45. Call (936) 273-2261 for information.

John Henry Kirby Memorial State Forest

Located in Tyler County, forest resource educational opportunities at this forest include demonstrations and nature study. Group education tours available by appointment.

Recreational opportunities include hiking, picnicking, bird and wildlife watching. Special attractions are forest management demonstration sites, small picnic area and **John Henry Kirby Monument.**

Open year-round to foot traffic during daylight hours. Contact the district office prior to entry. Special arrangements are needed for vehicle access. Information and maps can be obtained at the Woodville District Office on Hwy. 69 south or by calling (409) 283-3785 weekdays. No restroom facilities are available in this forest.

Masterson State Forest

All use of this forest in Jasper County is by reservation only. Group resource education tours are available by appointment. No public facilities are available. Information and maps can be obtained at the Kirbyville District Office, FM 82, 4.5 miles southeast of Kirbyville; call weekdays at (409) 423-2890.

E.O. Siecke State Forest

Recreational opportunities in this Newton County forest include hiking, bird watching, nature study, horseback riding, picnicking and wildlife viewing.

Special attractions are a **historic fire tower,** the oldest slash pine stand in Texas** and a **trout creek.** Forest management demonstration sites throughout.

Open year-round during daylight hours. Limited access by vehicle. Information, maps and restrooms are available at the Kirbyville District Office, located at the state forest on FM 82, 4.5 miles southeast of Kirbyville. Call (409) 423-2890 weekdays for information. ☆

The Chisos Basin Campground is situated with a view of "The Window," a formation of the Chisos Mountains in Big Bend National Park. Photo by Robert Plocheck.

National Parks, Historic Sites, Recreation Areas

Below are listed the facilities in and the activities that can be enjoyed at the two national parks, a national seashore, a biological preserve, several historic sites, memorials and recreation areas in Texas. They are under supervision of the **U.S. Department of Interior**. On the Web: **www.nps.gov/parks/search.htm**; under "Select State," choose "Texas." In addition, the recreational opportunities in the national forests and national grasslands in Texas, under the jurisdiction of the **U.S. Department of Agriculture**, are listed at the end of the article.

Alibates Flint Quarries National Monument consists of 1,371 acres in Potter County. For more than 10,000 years, **pre-Columbian Indians** dug agatized limestone from the quarries to make projectile points, knives, scrapers and other tools. The area is presently undeveloped. You may visit the flint quarries on guided walking tours with a park ranger. Tours are at 10:00 a.m. and 2:00 p.m. from Memorial Day to Labor Day. Off-season tours can be arranged by writing to Lake Meredith National Recreation Area, Box 1460, Fritch 79036, or by calling 806-857-3151.

Amistad National Recreation Area is located on the U.S. side of Amistad Reservoir, an international reservoir on the Texas-Mexico border. The 57,292-acre park's attractions include boating, water skiing, swimming, fishing, camping and archaeological sites. If lake level is normal, visitors can see 4000-year-old prehistoric pictographs in Panther and Parida caves, which are accessible only by boat. Check with park before visiting. The area is one of the densest concentrations of **Archaic rock art** in North America — more than 300 sites. Commercial campgrounds, motels and restaurants nearby. Marinas located at Diablo East and Rough Canyon. Open year round. NPS Administration, 4121 Hwy. 90 W, Del Rio 78840; 830-775-7491.

Big Bend National Park, established in 1944, has spectacular mountain and **desert scenery** and a variety of unusual geological structures. It is the nation's largest protected area of Chihuahuan Desert. Located in the great bend of the Rio Grande, the 801,000-acre park, which is part of the international boundary between the United States and Mexico, was designated a U.S. Biosphere Reserve in 1976. Hiking, birding and float trips are popular. Numerous campsites are located in park, and the Chisos Mountain Lodge has accommodations for approximately 345 guests. Write for reservations to National Park Concessions, Inc., Big Bend National Park, Texas 79834; 915-477-2291; www.chisosmountainslodge.com. Park open year round; facilities most crowded during spring break. PO Box 129, Big Bend National Park 79834; 915-477-2251.

Big Thicket National Preserve, established in 1974, consists of 15 separate units totalling 97,000 acres of diverse flora and fauna, often nicknamed the "biological crossroads of North America." The preserve, which includes parts of seven East Texas counties, has been designated an "International Biosphere Reserve" by the United Nations Educational, Scientific and Cultural Organization (UNESCO). The preserve includes **four different ecological systems:** Southeastern swamps, Eastern forests, Central Plains and Southwestern deserts. The visitor information station is located on FM 420, seven miles north of Kountze; phone 409-951-6725. Open daily from 9 a.m. to 5 p.m. Naturalist activities are available by reservation only; reservations are made through the station. Eight trails, ranging in length from one-half mile to 18 miles, visit a variety of forest communities. The two shortest trails are handicapped accessible. Trails are open year round, but flooding may occur after heavy rains. Horses permitted on the Big Sandy Horse Trail only. Boating and canoeing are popular on preserve corridor units. Park headquarters are at 3785 Milam, Beaumont 77701; 409-246-2337.

Chamizal National Memorial, established in 1963 and opened to the public in 1973, stands as a monument to Mexican-American friendship and goodwill. The memorial, on 52 acres in El Paso, commemorates the peaceful settlement on Aug. 29, 1963, of a 99-year-old boundary dispute between the United States and Mexico. Chamizal uses the **visual and performing arts** as a medium of interchange, helping people better understand not only other cultures but their own, as well. It hosts a variety of programs throughout the year, including: the fall Chamizal Festival musical event; the Siglo de Oro drama festival (early March); the Oñate Historical Festival celebrating the First Thanksgiving (April); and Music Under the Stars (Sundays, June-August). The park has a 1.8-mile walking trail and picnic areas. Phone: 915-532-7273.

Fort Davis National Historic Site in Jeff Davis County was a key post in the West Texas defense system, guarding immigrants and tradesmen on the San Antonio-El Paso road from 1854 to 1891. At one time, Fort Davis was manned by black troops, called **"Buffalo Soldiers"** (because of their curly hair) who fought with great distinction in the Indian Wars. Henry O. Flipper, the first black graduate of West Point, served at Fort Davis in the early 1880s. The 474-acre historic site is located on the north edge of the town of Fort Davis in the Davis Mountains, the second-highest mountain range in the state. The site includes a museum, an auditorium with daily audio-visual programs, restored and refurnished buildings, picnic area and hiking trails. Open year round except Christmas Day. PO Box 1379, Fort Davis 79734; 915-426-3224.

Guadalupe Mountains National Park, established in 1972, includes 86,416 acres in Hudspeth and Culberson counties. The Park contains one of the most extensive fossil reefs on record. Deep canyons cut through this reef and provide a rare opportunity for geological study. Special points of interest are **McKittrick Canyon,** a fragile riparian environment, and **Guadalupe Peak,** the highest in Texas. Camping, hiking on 80 miles of trails, Frijole Ranch Museum, summer amphitheater programs. Orientation, free information and natural history exhibits available at Visitor Center. Open year round. Lodging at Van Horn, Texas, and White's City or Carlsbad, NM. HC 60, Box 400, Salt Flat 79847; 915-828-3251.

Lake Meredith National Recreation Area, 30 miles northeast of Amarillo, centers on a reservoir on the Canadian River, in Moore, Hutchinson and Potter counties. The 50,000-acre recreational area is popular for **water-based activities.** Boat ramps, picnic areas, unimproved campsites. Commercial lodging and trailer hookups available in nearby towns. Open year round. PO Box 1460, Fritch 79036; 806-857-3151.

Lyndon B. Johnson National Historic Site includes two separate districts 14 miles apart. The Johnson City District comprises the boyhood home of the 36th President of United States and the Johnson Settlement, where his grandparents resided during the late 1800s. The LBJ Ranch District can be visited only by taking the National Park Service bus tour starting at the LBJ State Historic Site. The tour includes the reconstructed **LBJ Birthplace,** old school, family cemetery, show barn and a view of the **Texas White House.** Site in Blanco and Gillespie counties was established in 1969, and contains 1,570 acres, 674 of which are federal. Open year round except Thanksgiving, Christmas Day and New Year's Day. No camping on site; commercial campgrounds, motels in area. PO Box 329, Johnson City 78636; 830-868-7128.

Pratt Cabin sits in McKittrick Canyon in Guadalupe Mountains National Park. Photo by Robert Plocheck.

Lake Whitney is one of 29 Texas lakes that are operated by the U.S. Corps of Engineers. Most of these lakes have swim areas, boat ramps, picnic and camp sites, and rental units; see table on next page. Photo courtesy of Texas Parks & Wildlife Department.

Padre Island National Seashore consists of a 67.5-mile stretch of a barrier island along the Gulf Coast; noted for **white-sand beaches,** excellent fishing and abundant bird and marine life. Contains 133,000 acres in Kleberg, Willacy and Kenedy counties. Open year round. One paved campground (fee charged) located north of Malaquite Beach; unpaved (primitive) campground area south on beach. Five miles of beach are accessible by regular vehicles; 55 miles are accessible only by 4x4 vehicles. Off-road vehicles prohibited. Camping permitted in two designated areas. Commercial lodging available on the island outside the National Seashore boundaries. PO Box 181300, Corpus Christi 78480; 361-949-8068.

Palo Alto Battlefield National Historic Site, Brownsville, preserves the site of the first major battle in the Mexican-American War. Fought on May 8, 1846, it is recognized for the innovative use of light or "flying" artillery. Participating in the battle were **three future presidents:** General Zachary Taylor and Ulysses S. Grant on the U.S. side, and Gen. Mariano Arista on the Mexican. Historical markers are located at the junction of Farm-to-Market roads 1847 and 511. Access to the 3,400-acre site is currently limited. Exhibits at the visitors center interpret the battle as well as the causes and consequences of the war. Phone 956-541-2785.

Rio Grande Wild and Scenic River is a 196-mile strip on the U.S. shore of the Rio Grande in the Chihuahuan Desert, beginning in Big Bend National Park and continuing downstream to the Terrell-Val Verde County line. There are federal facilities in Big Bend National Park only. Contact Big Bend National Park for more information.

San Antonio Missions National Historical Park preserves four Spanish Colonial Missions — **Concepción, San José, San Juan** and **Espada** — as well as the Espada dam and aqueduct, which are two of the best-preserved remains in the United States of the Spanish Colonial irrigation system, and **Rancho de las Cabras,** the colonial ranch of Mission Espada. All were crucial elements to Spanish settlement on the Texas frontier. When Franciscan attempts to establish a chain of missions in East Texas in the late 1600s failed, the Spanish Crown ordered three missions transferred to the San Antonio River valley in 1731.

The missions are located within the city limits of San Antonio, while Rancho de las Cabras is located 25 miles south in Wilson County near Floresville. The four missions, which are **still in use as active parishes,** are open to the public from 9 a.m. to 5 p.m. daily except Thanksgiving, Christmas and New Year's. Public roadways connect the sites; a hike-bike trail is being developed. The visitor center for the mission complex is at San José. For more information, write to 2202 Roosevelt Ave., San Antonio 78210; 210-534-8833 or 210-932-1001.

Recreation in the National Forests

For general information about the National Forests and National Grasslands, ***see page 112 in the Environment section.***

An estimated 3 million people visit the National Forests in Texas for recreation annually. These visitors use established recreation areas primarily for hiking, picnicking, swimming, fishing, camping, boating and nature enjoyment. In the following list of some of these areas, Forest Service Road is abbreviated FSR:

Angelina National Forest

Boykin Springs, 14 miles southeast of Zavalla, has a 6-acre lake and facilities for hiking, swimming, picnicking, fishing, and camping. Bouton Lake, 14 miles southeast of Zavalla off Texas 63 and FSR 303, has a 9-acre natural lake with primitive facilities for camping, picnicking, and fishing.

Caney Creek on Sam Rayburn Reservoir, 10 miles southeast of Zavalla off FM 2743, offers fishing, boating, and camping. Sandy Creek, 15.5 miles east of Zavalla on Sam Rayburn, offers fishing, boating, and camping.

Recreational Facilities, Corps of Engineers Lakes, 2010

Source: Fort Worth District, Corps of Engineers

Reservoir	Swim Areas	Boat Ramps	Picnic Sites	Camp Sites	Rental Units	Visitor Hours, 2010
Aquilla	0	3	0	0	0	321,443
Bardwell	3	6	47	154	0	565,801
Belton	4	20	385	266	0	9,511,895
Benbrook	3	15	139	185	0	2,960,326
Buffalo Bayou[1, 3]	0	0	848	0	0	12,024,430
Canyon	6	17	190	452	24	2,535,980
Cooper	2	5	110	184	14	4,075,678
Georgetown	1	3	82	251	0	3,398,754
Granger	2	5	129	143	0	1,106,311
Grapevine	2	12	231	160	18	8,051,052
Hords Creek	4	9	8	139	0	635,242
Joe Pool	3	7	315	556	8	7,715,315
Lake O' the Pines	7	32	164	442	0	10,569,613
Lavon	2	19	199	280	0	4,465,801
Lewisville	8	21	339	405	5	14,858,942
Navarro Mills	3	6	26	255	0	5,079,449
O.C. Fisher	0	13	75	71	0	638,077
Pat Mayse[2]	3	10	0	211	3	1,264,896
Proctor	6	7	49	219	0	2,413,388
Ray Roberts	2	10	281	356	30	19,490,353
Sam Rayburn	7	31	26	708	68	15,063,678
Somerville	2	12	112	809	21	12,611,767
Stillhouse Hollow	3	5	83	73	0	1,274,316
Texoma[2, 4]	6	27	116	825	269	84,891,234
Town Bluff [5]	1	15	89	365	3	4,666,073
Waco	2	12	148	216	2	3,227,657
Wallisville[1]	0	2	10	0	0	266,756
Whitney	6	32	101	815	0	5,244,821
Wright Patman	4	20	183	543	0	9,763,598
Totals	92	376	4,485	9,083	465	248,692,646

All above lakes managed by the Fort Worth District, U.S. Army Corps of Engineers, with the following exceptions:
[1] Managed by Galveston District, USACE.
[2] Managed by Tulsa District, USACE.
[3] Includes both Addicks and Barker Dams.
[4] Figures for facilities are for Texas side of lake. Visitation is for entire lake.
[5] Also called B.A. Steinhagen Lake and Dam B. Revervoir.

The Sawmill Hiking Trail is 2.5 miles long and winds from Aldridge Sawmill trail head to Boykin Springs Recreation Area.

Davy Crockett National Forest

Ratcliff Lake, 25 miles west of Lufkin on Texas 7, is a 45-acre lake with facilities for picnicking, hiking, swimming, boating, fishing, and camping. There is also an amphitheater.

The 20-mile-long 4C National Recreation Trail connects Ratcliff Recreation Area to the Neches Bluff overlook. The Piney Creek Horse Trail is 54 miles long and can be entered approximately 5.5 miles south of Kennard off County Road 4625. There are two horse camps along this trail system.

Sabine National Forest

Indian Mounds Recreation Area, located 12 miles southeast of Hemphill off FM 83 about, has camping facilities and a boat ramp. Lakeview, on Toledo Bend Reservoir, 21 miles from Pineland, offers camping, hiking, and fishing and can be reached via Texas 87, FM 2928,

and FSR 120.

Ragtown, 26 miles southeast of Center and accessible by Texas 87 and Texas 139, County Road 3184, and FSR 132, is also on Toledo Bend and has facilities for hiking, camping, and boating. Red Hill Lake, 3 miles north of Milam on Texas 87, has facilities for fishing, swimming, camping, and picnicking. Willow Oak Recreation Area on Toledo Bend, 13 miles south of Hemphill off Texas 87, offers fishing, picnicking, camping, and boating.

Trail Between the Lakes is 28 miles long from Lakeview Recreation Area on Toledo Bend to U.S. 96 near Sam Rayburn Reservoir.

Sam Houston National Forest

Cagle Recreation Area is located on the shores of Lake Conroe, 50 miles north of Houston and 5 miles west of I-45 at FM 1375. Cagle offers camping, fishing, hiking, birding, and other recreational opportunities in a forested lakeside setting.

Double Lake, 3 miles south of Coldspring on FM 2025, has facilities for picnicking, hiking, camping, swimming, and fishing.

Stubblefield Lake, 15 miles west-northwest of New Waverly off Texas 1375 on the shores of Lake Conroe, has facilities for camping, hiking, picnicking, and fishing.

The Lone Star Hiking Trail, approximately 128 miles long, is located in Sam Houston National Forest in Montgomery, Walker, and San Jacinto counties.

Recreation on the National Grasslands

North Texas

Lake Davy Crockett Recreation Area (Caddo National Grassland), 12 miles north of Honey Grove (Fannin County) on FM 409, just off FM 100, has a boat-launch ramp and camping sites on a 450-acre lake.

Coffee Mill Lake Recreation Area has camping and picnicking facilities on a 650-acre lake. This area is 4 miles west of Lake Davy Crockett Recreation Area.

The Caddo Multi-Use Trail system, also 4 miles west of Lake Crockett, offers camping, hiking, and horseback riding on 35 miles of trails.

Black Creek Lake Recreation Area (Lyndon B. Johnson National Grassland) is 8 miles north of Decatur (Wise County) and has camping, picnic facilities, and a boat-launch ramp on a 35-acre lake.

Cottonwood Lake, 13 miles north of Decatur, is around 40 acres and offers hiking, boating, and fishing.

The Cottonwood-Black Creek Hiking Trail is 4 miles long and connects the two lakes. It is rated moderately difficult. There are nearly 75 miles of multipurpose trails that run in the Cottonwood Lake vicinity.

TADRA Horse Trail, 10 miles north of Decatur, has camping and 75 miles of horse trails. Restrooms and and parking facilities are available.

West Texas

Lake McClellan (McClellan Creek National Grassland) in Gray County, and Lake Marvin, which is part of the Black Kettle National Grassland in Hemphill County, receive more than 28,000 recreation visitors annually.

These areas provide camping, picnicking, fishing, birdwatching, and boating facilities. Concessionaires operate facilities at Lake McClellan, and a nominal fee is charged for use of the areas.

At the Rita Blanca National Grassland (Dallam County), about 4,500 visitors a year enjoy picnicking and hunting. Thompson Grove Picnic Area is 14 miles northeast of Texline. ☆

Visitors to Longhorn Cavern State Park await the start of a cavern tour beneath a land bridge that marks the entrance to the Central Texas show cave near Burnet. Photo courtesy of the Texas Parks & Wildlife Department.

National Natural Landmarks in Texas

Nineteen Texas natural areas have been listed on the **National Registry of Natural Landmarks**.

The registry was established by the Secretary of the Interior in 1962 to identify and encourage the preservation of geological and ecological features that represent nationally significant examples of the nation's natural heritage.

The registry currently lists a total of 587 national natural landmarks. Texas areas on the list, as of August 2001, and their characteristics, are these (year of listing in parentheses):

Attwater Prairie Chicken Preserve, Colorado County, 55 miles west of Houston in the national wildlife refuge, is rejuvenated Gulf Coastal Prairie, which is habitat for Attwater's prairie chickens. (1968)

Bayside Resaca Area, Cameron County, Laguna Atascosa National Wildlife Refuge, 28 miles north of Brownsville. Excellent example of a resaca, supporting coastal salt-marsh vegetation and rare birds. (1980)

Catfish Creek, Anderson County, 20 miles northwest of Palestine, is undisturbed riparian habitat. (1983)

Cave Without a Name, Kendall County, 12 miles northeast of Boerne, is a cave of several rooms that are filled with spectacular formations. (2009)

Caverns of Sonora, Sutton County, 16 miles southwest of Sonora, has unusual geological formations. (1965)

Devil's Sink Hole, Edwards County, 9 miles northeast of Rocksprings, is a deep, bell-shaped, collapsed limestone sink with cave passages extending below the regional water table. (1972)

Dinosaur Valley, Somervell County, in Dinosaur Valley State Park, four miles west of Glen Rose, contains fossil footprints exposed in bed of Paluxy River. (1968)

Enchanted Rock, Gillespie and Llano counties, 12 miles southwest of Oxford, is a classic batholith, composed of coarse-grained pink granite. (1971)

Ezell's Cave, Hays County, within the city limits of San Marcos, houses at least 36 species of cave creatures. (1971)

Fort Worth Nature Center and Refuge, Tarrant County, within the Fort Worth city limits. Contains remnants of the Grand Prairie and a portion of the Cross Timbers, with limestone ledges and marshes. Refuge for migratory birds and other wildlife, and home to 11 buffalo raised by the center's staff. Educational programs offered for youth and adults. Self-guided hiking. (1980)

Greenwood Canyon, Montague County, along a tributary of Braden Branch, is a rich source of Cretaceous fossils. (1975)

High Plains Natural Area, Randall County, Buffalo Lake National Wildlife Refuge, 26 miles southwest of Amarillo, is a grama-buffalo shortgrass area. (1980)

Little Blanco River Bluff, Blanco County, comprises an Edwards Plateau limestone-bluff plant community. (1982)

Longhorn Cavern, Burnet County, 11 miles southwest of Burnet. Formed at least 450 million years ago, cave contains several unusual geologic features. (1971)

Lost Maples State Natural Area, Bandera and Real counties, 61 miles northwest of San Antonio, contains Edwards Plateau fauna and flora, including unusual bigtooth maple. Largest known nesting population of golden-cheeked warbler. (1980)

Muleshoe National Wildlife Refuge, Bailey County, 59 miles northwest of Lubbock, contains playa lakes and typical High Plains shortgrass grama grasslands. (1980)

Natural Bridge Caverns, Comal County, 16 miles west of New Braunfels, is a multilevel cavern system, with beautiful and unusual geological formations. (1971)

Odessa Meteor Crater, Ector County, 10 miles southwest of Odessa, is one of only two known meteor sites in the country. (1965)

Palo Duro Canyon State Park, Armstrong and Randall counties, 22 miles south-southwest of Amarillo. Cut by waters of the Red River, it contains cross-sectional views of sedimentary rocks representing four geological periods. (1976)

Santa Ana National Wildlife Refuge, Hidalgo County, 7 miles south of Alamo, is a lowland forested area with jungle-like vegetation. It is habitat for more than 300 species of birds and some rare mammals. (1966) ☆

Sea Center Texas

Source: Texas Parks and Wildlife Department; www.tpwd.state.tx.us/seacenter

In addition to its approximately 125 parks, the Texas Parks and Wildlife Department also operates Sea Center Texas — a marine aquarium, fish hatchery, and nature center that both educates and entertains visitors. The visitor center opened in 1996 and has interpretive displays, a "touch tank," and native Texas habitat exhibits depicting a salt marsh, bay, jetty, reef, and open Gulf waters. The Gulf aquarium features "Cooper," a 50-pound grouper; a green moray eel; a nurse shark; and other offshore species.

Sea Center is said to be the world's largest redfish hatchery and is one of three marine hatcheries on the Texas coast that produces juvenile red drum and spotted seatrout for enhancing natural populations in Texas bays. The hatchery has the capability to produce 15 million juvenile fish yearly. It is also a testing ground for production of other marine species, such as flounder. Guided hatchery tours and educational programs are available by reservation.

A half-acre youth fishing pond introduces youngsters to saltwater fishing through scheduled activities. The pond is handicap accessible and stocked with a variety of marine fish.

The center's wetland area is part of the Great Texas Coastal Birding Trail, where more than 150 species of birds have been identified. The wetland consists of a one-acre salt marsh and a three-acre freshwater marsh. Damselflies, dragonflies, butterflies, turtles, and frogs are frequently sited off the boardwalk. Adjacent to the butterfly and hummingbird gardens, a small outdoor pavilion provides visitors with a quiet resting place.

Sea Center Texas is operated in partnership with The Dow Chemical Company and the Coastal Conservation Association. It is located in Lake Jackson, 50 miles south of Houston, off of Texas 288.

Admission and parking are free. It is open from 9 a.m. to 4 p.m. Tuesday through Saturday, and from 1 p.m. to 4 p.m. Sunday. It is closed Mondays and some holidays. Reservations are required for group tours, nature tours, and hatchery tours. For more information, call 979-292-0100 or email seacenter@tpwd.state.tx.us. ☆

A Sea Center volunteer explains a "touch tank" exhibit to schoolchildren at the visitor center. Sea Center is open Tuesday through Sunday. Admission and parking are free. Photo courtesy of Texas Parks & Wildlife Department.

Texas State Aquarium

The Texas State Aquarium, located on 7.3 acres on the southernmost tip of Corpus Christi Beach in Corpus Christi, is operated by the Texas State Aquarium Association, a nonprofit, self-supporting organization established in 1978. Efforts to fund a public aquarium in South Texas first began in 1952. Several nonprofit organizations founded over the years eventually grew into the Texas State Aquarium Association.

Since 1978 the association has raised more than $28 million in private and public funding for the construction and operation of the aquarium. The city of Corpus Christi provided $14.5 million, of which $4 million came from a bond issue.

In 1985 the Sixty-ninth Texas Legislature declared the project the "Official Aquarium of the State of Texas." Construction of the first phase of the project, the Jesse H. and Mary Gibbs Jones Gulf of Mexico Exhibit Building, began in September 1988 and was completed in July 1990.

In 2003, Dolphin Bay opened to house its Atlantic bottlenose dolphins. The same year, the Environmental Discovery Center opened, featuring an expanded library, a Family Learning Center and the Flint Hills Resources Distance Learning Studio.

The aquarium's exhibits and research focus on the plants and animals of the Gulf of Mexico and the Caribbean. The Texas State Aquarium is the first facility in the United States to do so.

There is an admission and parking fee. Open daily 9 a.m. to 5 p.m., Labor Day through March 1, and until 6 p.m. March 1 through Labor Day. For more information call 1-800-477-GULF. www.texasstateaquarium.org.— *New Handbook of Texas and Texas State Aquarium.* ☆

Fishing and canoeing are popular activities at Palmetto State Park in Gonzales County. Photo courtesy of Texas Parks & Wildlife Department.

Recreational Fishing in Texas

Source: Texas Parks and Wildlife Department; www.tpwd.state.tx.us/fishboat/

Freshwater Fishing

Freshwater fishing in Texas continues to increase in popularity and revenue. There were an estimated 1.854 million freshwater recreational anglers as of Aug. 31, 2010, with annual expenditures of $2.39 billion, an increase over the $1.49 billion in 2008.

Texas anglers can fish for 268 species of freshwater fish, including 78 species that inhabit areas with low salinity and can be found in rivers entering the Gulf of Mexico. Only 25 of the total number of fish species are not native, but were introduced into the state.

The most popular fish for recreational fishing are largemouth bass; catfish; crappie; and striped, white, and hybrid striped bass.

The Texas Parks and Wildlife Department operates field stations, fish hatcheries, and research facilities to support the conservation and management of fishery resources. The hatcheries operated by TPWD raise largemouth and smallmouth bass, as well as catfish, striped and hybrid striped bass, and sunfish.

TPWD has continued its programs of stocking fish in public waters to increase angling opportunities. Many conservation-minded anglers who desire continued quality fishing practice catch-and-release fishing.

Texas Freshwater Fisheries Center

The Texas Freshwater Fisheries Center in Athens, about 75 miles southeast of Dallas, is an $18 million hatchery and educational center, where visitors can learn about the underwater life.

The interactive Visitors Center includes aquarium displays of fish in their natural environment. Visitors get an "eye-to-eye" view of three authentically designed Texas freshwater habitats: a Hill Country stream, an East Texas pond, and a reservoir. A marsh exhibit features live American alligators.

A casting pond stocked with rainbow trout in the winter and catfish in the summer provides a place for visitors to learn how to bait a hook, cast a line, and land a fish. The center has conference facilities and hosts groups by appointment.

The Texas Freshwater Fisheries Center is open Tuesday through Saturday, 9 a.m. to 4 p.m., and Sunday, 1 to 4 p.m. It is closed on Monday. Admission is charged.

The Center is located 4.5 miles east of Athens on FM 2495 at Lake Athens. Address: 5550 FM 2495, Athens 75752, or call 903-676-2277.

Saltwater Fishing

There are about 1.1 million saltwater anglers in Texas (16 years old and older) who spend an estimated $981 million annually on fishing-related expenditures. In 2010, anglers harvested 1.73 million fish from both Texas bays and the Gulf of Mexico off Texas.

The most popular saltwater sport fish in Texas bays are spotted seatrout, sand seatrout, Atlantic croaker, red drum, southern flounder, black drum, sheepshead, and gafftopsail catfish.

Offshore, some of the fish that anglers target are red snapper, king mackerel, Spanish mackerel, dolphin (fish), cobia, tarpon, and yellowfin tuna. ☆

For Commercial Fishing data, see page 620.

Licenses & Game Harvests

Source: Texas Parks and Wildlife Department; www.tpwd.state.tx.us/hunt/hunt.htm

Licenses and Revenue

Texas Parks and Wildlife Department reported the following totals for hunting and fishing licenses, stamps, and permits for the 2008–2009 and the 2009–2010 seasons, which begin Sept. 1 and end Aug. 31:

2008–2009 Season	Volume	Revenue
Hunting Licenses	511,494	$21,044,187
Fishing Licenses	1,255,289	$33,531,538
Combined Licenses	618,812	$34,973,036
TOTALS	**2,385,595**	**$89,548,761**
2009–2010 Season	Volume	Revenue
Hunting Licenses	511,522	$23,334,354
Fishing Licenses	1,223,101	$33,920,596
Combined Licenses	614,074	$32,898,574
TOTALS	**2,348,697**	**$90,153,524**

More than 1.1 million white-tail deer were harvested in the past two hunting seasons. Photo by Ray Sasser.

Game Harvest Estimates

During the **2008–2009 license year,** TPWD estimated that hunters harvested:

- 619,650 – white-tailed deer
- 9,278 – mule deer
- 19,198 – wild turkey in the fall
- 19,548 – wild turkey in the spring
- 4,869,866 – mourning dove
- 1,065,940 – bobwhite quail
- 32,942 – javelina

During the **2009–2010 license year,** TPWD estimated that hunters harvested:

- 559,357 – white-tailed deer
- 12,746 – mule deer
- 16,511 – wild turkey in the fall
- 20,555 – wild turkey in the spring
- 6,239,521 – mourning dove
- 584,533 – bobwhite quail
- 28,367 – javelina

As of the 2005–2006 hunting year, rabbits and squirrels are no longer surveyed. ☆

Hunting Licenses

A hunting license is required of Texas residents and non-residents who hunt any legal bird or animal. Hunting licenses and stamp endorsements are valid during the period Sept. 1 through the following Aug. 31 of each year, except licenses issued for a specific number of days or time periods.

A hunting license (except the non-resident special hunting license and non-resident 5-day special hunting license) is valid for taking all legal species of wildlife in Texas including deer, turkey, javelina, antelope, aoudad (sheep), and all small game and migratory game birds. Stamp endorsement requirements apply.

Special licenses and tags are required for taking alligators, and a trapper's license is required to hunt fur-bearing animals.

In addition to a valid hunting license:

★ An Upland Game Bird Stamp Endorsement is required to hunt turkey, pheasant, quail, lesser prairie chicken, or chachalaca. Non-residents who purchase the non-resident spring turkey license are exempt from this stamp endorsement requirement.

★ A Migratory Game Bird Endorsement and HIP (Harvest Information Program) Certification is required to hunt any migratory game birds, including waterfowl, coot, rail, gallinule, snipe, dove, sandhill crane, and woodcock.

★ A valid Federal Duck Stamp is required of waterfowl hunters age 16 or older.

On the Web, information from TPWD on hunting: www.tpwd.state.tx.us/huntwild/.

Hunting Leases

Hunting leases are important to the economies of many Texas towns. The Texas Parks and Wildlife Department has launched Hunt Texas, a free online connection between landowners and hunters, at **www.tpwd.state.tx.us/exptexas/programs/hunt-texas/.** Through the website, landowners can register their leases and hunters can search by county, game type, length of lease terms, costs, and weapons allowed.

Fishing Licenses

All **fishing licenses and stamp endorsements** are valid only during the period Sept. 1 through the following Aug. 31, except licenses issued for a specific number of days or time periods. If you own any valid freshwater fishing package, you will be able to purchase a saltwater stamp and also fish saltwater. If you own any valid saltwater fishing package, you will be able to purchase a freshwater stamp and also fish freshwater. An all-water fishing package is available that enables you to fish both fresh and salt water.

Detailed information concerning licenses, stamps, seasons, regulations, and related information can be obtained from Texas Parks and Wildlife Department, 4200 Smith School Road, Austin 78744; (800) 792-1112 or 512-389-4800.

On the Web, information from TPWD: www.tpwd.state.tx.us/business/licenses/.

Birding in Texas

World Birding Center

The World Birding Center comprises nine birding education centers and observation sites in the Lower Rio Grande Valley designed to protect wildlife habitat and offer visitors a view of more than 500 species of birds. The center has partnered with the Texas Parks and Wildlife Department, the U.S. Fish and Wildlife Service and nine communities to turn 10,000 acres back into natural areas for birds, butterflies and other wildlife.

This area in Cameron, Hidalgo and Starr counties is a natural migratory path for millions of birds that move between the Americas. The nine WBC sites are situated along the border with Mexico:

Bentsen–Rio Grande Valley State Park

This is the World Birding Center Headquarters and comprises the 760-acre Bentsen-RGV State Park and 1,700 acres of adjoining federal refuge land near **Mission.** The site offers: daily tram service; 4 nature trails ranging in length from 1/4 mile to 2 miles; 2-story high Hawk Observation Tower with a 210-foot-long handicapped access ramp; 2 observation decks; 2 accessible bird blinds; primitive camping sites (by reservation); rest areas; picnic sites with tables; exhibit hall; park store; coffee bar; meeting room (available for rental); catering kitchen; bike rentals (1 and 2 seat bikes). Access within the park is by foot, bike and tram only; (956) 585-1107. **Hours:** 6 a.m. to 10 p.m., seven days a week.

Edinburg Scenic Wetlands

This 40-acre wetlands in **Edinburg** is an oasis for water-loving birds, butterflies and other wildlife. The site is currently offering:walking trails, nature tours and classes; (956) 381-9922. **Hours:** 8 a.m. – 5 p.m., Monday through Wednesday; 8 a.m.–6 p.m., Thursday through Saturday. Closed Sunday.

Estero Llano Grande State Park

This 176-acre refuge in **Weslaco** attracts a wide array of South Texas wildlife with its varied landscape of shallow lake, woodlands and thorn forest; 956-565-3919. **Hours:** 8 a.m.–5 p.m., Monday through Friday; 8 a.m.–7:30 p.m., Saturday and Sunday through August.

Bird Sighting Regions

Panhandle-Plains

North Central

East Texas Timberlands

Trans-Pecos

Central Plateau

Central Prairie

Coastal Prairie

Rio Grande Brushlands

Source: Texas Ornithological Society

Roseate spoonbills line the bank while a shorebird feeds at Aransas National Wildlife Refuge. Photo by Steve Hillebrand; U.S. Fish & Wildlife Service.

Birdwatchers find plenty of wildlife to photograph on an observation deck at the Laguna Atascosa National Wildlife Refuge. Photo by Steve Hillebrand; U.S. Fish & Wildlife Service.

Harlingen Arroyo Colorado

This site in **Harlingen** is connected by an arroyo waterway, as well as hike-and-bike trails meandering through the city, Hugh Ramsey Nature Park to the east and the Harlingen Thicket to the west; (956) 427-8873. **Hours:** Office, 8 a.m.–5:00 p.m., Monday through Friday. Nature trails are open seven days a week, sunrise to sunset.

Old Hidalgo Pumphouse

Visitors to this museum in **Hidalgo** on the Rio Grande can learn about the steam-driven irrigation pumps that transformed Hidalgo County into a year-round farming area. The museum's grounds feature hummingbird gardens, walking trails and historic tours; (956) 843-8686. **Hours:** 10 a.m.–5 p.m., Monday through Friday; 1 p.m.–5 p.m., Sunday. Closed Saturday.

Quinta Mazatlan

This 1930s country estate in **McAllen** is a historic Spanish Revival adobe hacienda surrounded by lush tropical landscaping and native woodland. It is also an urban oasis, where quiet trails wind through more than 15 acres of birding habitat; (956) 688-3370. **Hours:** 8 a.m.–5 p.m., Tuesday through Saturday. Open until sunset on Thursdays. Closed Mondays and holidays.

A Young American Kestrel at Aransas National Wildlife Refuge. Photo by Steve Hillebrand; U.S. Fish & Wildlife Service.

Resaca de la Palma State Park

More than 1,700 acres of newly opened wilderness near **Brownsville**, this site comprises the largest tract of native habitat in the World Birding Center network. The park offers birding tours and natural history tours. Admission is by appointment and reservation only; (956) 565-3919.

Roma Bluffs

History and nature meet on scenic bluffs above the Rio Grande, where the World Birding Center in **Roma** is located on the old plaza of a once-thriving steamboat port. Part of a national historic district, the WBC Roma Bluffs includes a riverside nature area of three acres in Starr County. The site offers: walking trails, canoe trips, birding tours, natural history tours and classes; (956) 849-4930. **Hours:** 8 a.m.–4:00 p.m. Tuesday through Saturday, although trails are open seven days a week and are free to the public.

South Padre Island Birding and Nature Center

At the southern tip of the world's longest barrier island, **South Padre Island** Birding and Nature Center is a slender thread of land between the shallow Laguna Madre and the Gulf of Mexico. This site offers: a nature trail boardwalk and birding tours; 1-800-SOPADRE. **Hours:** 9 a.m.–5 p.m., seven days a week.

Great Texas Coastal Birding Trail

The Great Texas Coastal Birding Trail winds its way through 43 Texas counties along the entire Texas coastal region. The trail, completed in April 2000, is divided into upper, central and lower coastal regions. It includes 308 wildlife-viewing sites and such amenities as boardwalks, parking pullouts, kiosks, observation platforms and landscaping to attract native wildlife.

Color-coded maps are available, and signs mark each site. Trail maps contain information about the birds and habitats likely to be found at each site, the best season to visit, and food and lodging.

For information, contact: Nature Tourism Coordinator, Texas Parks and Wildlife Department, 4200 Smith School Road, Austin, TX 78744; 512-389-4396. On the Web: www.tpwd.state.tx.us/huntwild/wild/wildlife_trails/. ☆

The Cinco de Mayo Celebration takes place each year at the Texas Freshwater Fisheries Center in Henderson County. Photo by Larry Hodge.

Fairs, Festivals, and Special Events

Fairs, festivals, and other special events provide year-round recreation in Texas. Some are of national interest, while many attract visitors from across the state. Each county profile in the Counties section also lists events in the Recreation paragraph and following town names. Information here was furnished by event coordinators.

Abilene — West Texas Fair & Rodeo; September; 1700 Hwy. 36, 79602; www.taylorcountyexpocenter.com. *Since 1897.*

Albany — Fort Griffin Fandangle; June; PO Box 155, 76430; www.fortgriffinfandangle.org. *Since 1938.*

Alvarado — Johnson County Pioneers & Old Settlers Reunion; August; PO Box 217, 76009. *Since 1893.*

Amarillo — Tri-State Fair; September; PO Box 31087, 79120.

Anderson — Grimes County Fair; June; PO Box 435, 77830.

Angleton — Brazoria County Fair; October; PO Box 818, 77516; www.bcfa.org. *Since 1939.*

Aransas Pass — Shrimporee; June, 130 W. Goodnight, 78336; www.aransaspass.org. *Since 1949.*

Arlington — Texas Scottish Festival; June; PO Box 511, 76634; www.texasscottishfestival.com. *Since 1986.*

Athens — Cinco de Mayo Celebration; May; Texas Freshwater Fisheries Center, 5550 FM 2495; 75752. www.athenstx.org; (903) 670-2266.

Athens — Texas Fiddlers' Asso. Reunion; May (last Fri.); PO Box 1441, 75751. *Since 1932.*

Austin — Star of Texas Fair & Rodeo; March; 9100 Decker Lake Rd. 78724; www.rodeoaustin.com. *Since 1937.*

Austin — Austin Fine Arts Festival; April; PO Box 5705, 78763; www.austinfineartsfestival.org.

Bay City — Matagorda County Fair & Livestock Show; February; PO Box 1803, 77404; www.matagorda-countyfair.com. *Since 1945.*

Bay City — Bay City Rice Festival; October; PO Box 867; 77404; www.baycitylions.org.

Beaumont — South Texas State Fair; October; 7250 Wespark Cr., 77705; www.ymbl.org. *Since 1943.*

Bellville — Austin County Fair; October; PO Box 141,

77418; www.austincountyfair.com.

Belton — 4th of July Celebration & PRCA Rodeo; July; PO Box 659, 76513; www.beltonchamber.com.

Belton — Central Texas State Fair; Aug.-Sept.; PO Box 206, 76513; www.centraltexasstatefair.com.

Big Spring — Howard County Fair; September; PO Box 2356, 79721. *Since 1973*

Boerne — Boerne Berges Fest; June; PO Box 748, 78006; www.bergesfest.com.

Boerne — Kendall County Fair; September (Labor Day Wknd.); PO Box 954, 78006; www.kcfa.org. *Since 1906.*

Brackettville — Gunfighter Competition; July; PO Box 528, 78832; www.alamovillage.com.

Brackettville — Western Horse Races & BBQ; September (Labor Day); PO Box 528, 78832; www.alamovillage.com.

Brenham — Washington County Fair; September; 1305 E. Blue Bell Rd., 77833; www.washingtoncofair.com. *Since 1870.*

Brownsville — Charro Days Fiesta; February; PO Box 3247, 78523-3247; www.charrodaysfiesta.com. *Since 1938.*

Burnet — Burnet Bluebonnet Festival; April; 229 S. Pierce; 78611. 222.burnetchamber.org. *Since 1986.*

Burton — Cotton Gin Festival; April (3rd wknd.); PO Box 98; 77835; www.cottonginmuseum.org. *Since 1990.*

Caldwell — Kolache Festival; September; 301 N. Main Street; 77836; (979) 567-0000.

Caldwell — Burleson County Fair; September; PO Box 634, 77836; (979) 567-9319.

Canyon — TEXAS! Musical Drama; June–August; 1514 5th Ave., 79015; www.texas-show.com. *Since 1966.*

Chappell Hill — Bluebonnet Festival; April; 152 Cnty. Rd. 4145, 76634; http://clifton.centraltx.com/heritage.htm.

Clifton — Norse Smorgasbord; November; 152 Cnty. Rd. 4145, 76634; http://clifton.centraltx.com/heritage.htm.

Clute — Great Texas Mosquito Festival; July; PO Box 997, 77531; www.mosquitofestival.com. *Since 1981.*

Columbus — Colorado County Fair; September; PO Box 506, 78933; www.coloradocountyfair.org.

Conroe — Montgomery County Fair; March–April; PO Box 869, 77305-0869; www.mcfa.org. *Since 1957.*

Corpus Christi — Bayfest; September–October; PO Box 1858, 78403-1858; www.bayfesttexas.com.

Corpus Christi — Buc Days; April–May; PO Box 30404, 78463; www.bucdays.com.

Corsicana — Derrick Days; April; 120 N. 12th St., 75110; www.corsicana.org. *Since 1976.*

Crowell — Cynthia Ann Parker Festival; May; PO Box 452, 79227; www.crowelltex.com/CAP/cappage1.html.

Dalhart — XIT Rodeo & Reunion; August (1st full wknd.); PO Box 967, 79022. *Since 1936.*

Dallas — State Fair of Texas; September–October; PO Box 150009, 75315; www.bigtex.com. *Since 1886.*

Decatur — Wise County Old Settlers Reunion; July (last full week); PO Box 203, 76234.

De Leon — De Leon Peach & Melon Festival; August; PO Box 44, 76444-0044; www.cctc.net/~pmdeleon/index.htm. *Since 1917.*

Denton — North Texas State Fair & Rodeo; August; PO Box 1695, 76202; www.ntfair.com. *Since 1929.*

Edna — Jackson County Youth Fair; October; PO Box 457, 77957; www.jcyf.org. *Since 1949.*

Ennis — National Polka Festival; May; PO Box 1177, 75120-1237; www.visitennis.org/festivals.html.

Fairfield — Freestone County Fair; June; PO Box 196; 75840.

Flatonia — Czhilispiel; October (4th full wknd.); PO Box 610, 78941; www.flatoniachamber.com. *Since 1973.*

Fort Worth — Pioneer Days; September; 131 E. Exchange Ave., Ste 100B, 76106; www.fortworthstockyards.org.

Fort Worth — Southwestern Exposition & Livestock Show; January-February; PO Box 150, 76101; www.fwssr.com. *Since 1897.*

Fredericksburg — Night in Old Fredericksburg; July; 302 E. Austin, 78624; www.fredericksburg-texas.com. *Since 1963.*

Fredericksburg — Oktoberfest; October (1st wknd.); PO Box 222, 78624; www.Oktoberfestinfbg.com.

Freer — Freer Rattlesnake Roundup; May; PO Box 717, 78357; www.freerrattlesnake.com. *Since 1966.*

Galveston — Dickens on The Strand; December; 502 20th St., 77550; www.dickensonthestrand.org. *Since 1973.*

Galveston — Galveston Historic Homes Tour; May; 502 20th St., 77550-2014; www.galvestonhistory.org. *Since 1974.*

Gilmer — East Texas Yamboree; October; PO Box 854, 75644; www.yamboree.com. *Since 1937.*

Glen Flora — Wharton County Youth Fair; April; PO Box 167, 77443; www.whartoncountyyouthfair.org. *Since 1976.*

Graham — Art Splash on the Square; May; PO Box 1684, 76450; www.art-splash.com.

Graham — Red, White & You Parade & Festivities; July; PO Box 299; 76450; www.visitgraham.com.

Granbury — Annual July 4th Celebration; July; 116 W. Bridge St., 76048; www.granburychamber.com.

Granbury — Harvest Moon Festival; October; 116 W. Bridge St., 76048; www.hgma.com. *Since 1977.*

Grand Prairie — National Championship Pow-Wow; September; 2602 Mayfield Rd, 75052; www.tradersvillage.com. *Since 1963.*

Greenville — Hunt County Fair; June; PO Box 1071, 75403; www.huntcountyfair.com. *Since 1970.*

Groesbeck — Limestone County Fair; March–April; PO Box 965, 76642.

Hallettsville — Hallettsville Kolache Fest; September; PO Box 313, 77964; www.hallettsville.com. *Since*

Kolaches are the main attraction at the Kolache Festival held each September in Caldwell, Burleson County. Photo by Ron Billings; Texas Forest Service.

1995.

Helotes — Helotes Cornyval; May (1st wknd.); PO Box 376, 78023; www.cornyval.com. *Since 1967.*

Hempstead — Waller County Fair; September–October; PO Box 911, 77445. www.wallercountyfair.com. *Since 1946.*

Hico — Hico Old Settler Reunion; July; PO Box 93, 76457; www.hico-tx.com. *Since 1887.*

Hidalgo — BorderFest; March; PO Box 722; 78557; www.borderfest. com.

Hondo — Medina County Fair; September (3rd wknd.); PO Box 4, 78861. *Since 1980.*

Houston — Harris County Fair; October; 1 Abercrombie Dr, 77084-4233; www.harriscountyfair.net. *Since 1977.*

Houston — Houston International Festival; April–May; 1111 Bagby St., Ste. 2550, 77002; www.ifest.org.

Houston — Houston Livestock Show and Rodeo; March; PO Box 20070; 77225-0070; www.hlsr.com.

Hughes Springs — Wildflower Trails of Texas; April; PO Box 805, 75656. *Since 1970.*

Huntsville — Walker County Fair & Rodeo; March–April; PO Box 1817, 77342; www.walkercountyfair.com. *Since 1979.*

Jefferson — Historical Pilgrimage and Spring Festival; May (1st wknd.); PO Box 301, 75657-0301; www.theexcelsiorhouse.com. *Since 1947.*

Johnson City — Blanco County Fair; August; PO Box 261, 78636-0261; www.lbjcountry.com/

Kenedy — Bluebonnet Days; April; 205 South 2nd St., 78119-2729.

Kerrville — Kerr County Fair; October; PO Box 290842, 78029; www.kerrcountyfair.com. *Since 1980.*

Kerrville — Kerrville Folk Festival; May–June; PO Box 291466, 78029; www.kerrvillefolkfestival.com. *Since 1972.*

Kerrville — The Official Texas State Arts & Crafts Fair; May (Memorial wknd.); 4000 Riverside Dr., 78028, www.tacef.org. *Since 1972.*

Kerrville — Kerrville Wine and Music Festival; September (Labor Day wknd.); PO Box 291466; 78029; www.kerrvillefolkfestival.com. *Since 1991.*

Killeen — Take 190 West: Killeen Salutes the Arts; February; www.take190west.com.

LaGrange — Fayette County Fair; September (Labor Day wknd.); PO Box 544, 78945; www.fayettecountyfair.net. *Since 1926.*

Laredo — Border Olympics; January–March; PO Box 450037, 78044-0037; http://borderolympics.net. *Since 1947.*

Laredo — Laredo International Fair & Expo; March; PO Box 1770, 78043; www.laredofair.com. *Since 1963.*

Laredo — Washington's Birthday Celebration; January–February; 1819 E. Hillside Rd., 78041-3383; www.wbcalaredo.com. *Since 1898.*

Longview — Gregg County Fair & Exposition; September; 1511 Judson Rd., Ste. F, 75601; www.greggcountyfair.com. *Since 1951.*

Lubbock — 4th on Broadway Festival; July; PO Box 1643, 79408; www.broadwayfestivals.com. *Since 1991.*

Lubbock — Lights on Broadway Celebration; December; PO Box 1643, 79408; www.broadwayfestivals.com.

Lubbock — Panhandle-South Plains Fair; September; PO Box 208, 79408; www.southplainsfair.com. *Since 1914.*

Lufkin — Texas Forest Festival; September; 1615 S. Chestnut St., 75901; www.texasforestfestival.com.

Luling — Luling Watermelon Thump; June (last full wknd); PO Box 710, 78648-0710; www.watermelonthump.com. *Since 1953.*

Marshall — Fire Ant Festival; October; PO Box 520, 75671; www.marshall-chamber.com. *Since 1984.*

Marshall — Stagecoach Days Festival; May; PO Box 520, 75671; www.marshall-chamber.com. Since 1973.

Dickens on the Strand has been held each December in Galveston since 1973. Photo courtesy of the Galveston Historical Foundation.

Marshall — Wonderland of Lights; November–December; PO Box 520, 75671; www.marshalltxchamber.com.

Mercedes — Rio Grande Valley Livestock Show; March; 1000 N. Texas; www.rgvlivestockshow.com. *Since 1940.*

Mesquite — Mesquite Championship Rodeo; April–September (each Fri. & Sat.); 1818 Rodeo Dr, 75149-3800; www.mesquiterodeo.com. *Since 1958.*

Monahans — Butterfield-Overland Stage Coach and Wagon Festival; July; 401 S. Dwight Ave., 79756 www.butterfield.ws/. *Since 1994.*

Mount Pleasant — Titus County Fair; September; PO Box 1232, 75456-1232; www.tituscountyfair.com.

Nacogdoches — Piney Woods Fair; October; 3805 NW Stallings Dr., 75964; www.nacexpo.net. *Since 1978.*

Nederland — Nederland Heritage Festival; March; PO Box 1176, 77627; www.nederlandhf.org. *Since 1973.*

New Braunfels — Comal County Fair; September; PO Box 310223, 78131-0223; www.comalcountyfair.org. *Since 1894.*

New Braunfels — Wurstfest; October–November; PO Box 310309, 78131-0309; www.wurstfest.com.

Odessa — Permian Basin Fair & Expo; September; 218 W. 46th St., 79764; www.permianbasinfair.com.

Palestine — Dogwood Trails Festival; March–April; PO Box 2828, 75802-2828; www.visitpalestine.com.

Paris — Red River Valley Fair; August–September; 570 E. Center St., 75460; www.rrvfair.org. *Since 1911.*

Pasadena — Pasadena Livestock Show & Rodeo; September–October; 7601 Red Bluff Rd., 77507-1035; www.pasadenarodeo.com.

Plantersville — Texas Renaissance Festival; October–November (8 weekends); 21778 FM 1774, 77363; www.texrenfest.com. *Since 1975.*

Port Aransas — Whooping Crane Festival; February (last weekend); 403 West Cotter, 78373; www.whoopingcranefestival.org. *Since 1996.*

Port Arthur — CalOILcade; October; PO Box 2336, 77643; www.portarthur.com/cavoilcade. *Since 1953.*

Port Lavaca — Calhoun County Fair; October (3rd wknd.); PO Box 42, 77979-0042. *Since 1963.*

Poteet — Poteet Strawberry Festival; April; PO Box 227, 78065; www.strawberryfestival.com. *Since 1948.*

Refugio — Refugio County Fair & Rodeo & Livestock Show; March; PO Box 88, 78377. *Since 1961.*

Rio Grande City — Starr County Fair; March (1st full wknd.); PO Box 841, 78582. *Since 1961.*

Rosenberg — Fort Bend County Fair; September–October; PO Box 428, 77471; www.fbcfa.org. *Since 1937.*

Salado — Salado Scottish Games and Competitions; November (2nd wknd); PO Box 36, 76571-0036; www.ctam-salado.org.

San Angelo — San Angelo Stock Show & Rodeo; February; 200 W 43rd St., 76903; www.sanangelorodeo.com. *Since 1932.*

San Antonio — Fiesta San Antonio; April; 2611 Broadway St.; 78215; www.fiesta-sa.org. *Since 1891.*

San Antonio — Texas Folklife Festival; June; 801 S. Bowie, 78205; www.texasfolklifefestival.org. *Since 1972.*

Sanderson — Cinco de Mayo Celebration; May (1st Sat.); PO Box 598, 79848.

Sanderson — 4th of July Celebration; July; PO Box 4810, 79848-4810; www.sandersontx.info. *Since 1908.*

Sanderson — Prickly Pear Pachanga; October; PO Box 410, 79848; www.sandersontx.info. *Since 2001.*

Santa Fe — Galveston County Fair & Rodeo; April; PO Box 889, 77510; www.galvestoncountyfair.com.

Schulenburg — Schulenburg Festival; August (1st full wknd.); PO Box 115; 78956; www.schulenburgfestival.com. *Since 1976.*

Seguin — Guadalupe Agricultural & Livestock Fair; October (2nd wknd); PO Box 334, 78155; www.guadalupecountyfairandrodeo.com. *Since 1885.*

Shamrock — St. Patrick's Day Celebration; March; PO Box 588, 79079. www.shamrocktx.net/site/index-2.html. *Since 1947.*

Stamford — Texas Cowboy Reunion; July; PO Box 948, 79553; www.tcrrodeo.com. *Since 1933.*

Sulphur Springs — Hopkins County Fall Festival; September (3rd Sat.); PO Box 177, 75483. **Sweetwater** — Rattlesnake Roundup; March; PO Box 416, 79556-0416; www.rattlesnakeroundup.net. *Since 1958.*

Terlingua — Terlingua International Chili Championship; November; PO Box 39, 79852; www.chili.org. *Since 1947.*

Texarkana — Four States Fair; September; 3700 E. 50th St., Texarkana AR, 75504; www.fourstatesfair.com.

Tyler — East Texas State Fair; September; 2112 W. Front St., 75702; www.etstatefair.com. *Since 1914.*

Tyler — Texas Rose Festival; Ocober (3rd wknd.); PO Box 8224, 75711; www.texasrosefestival.com. *Since 1933.*

Waco — Heart O' Texas Fair & Rodeo; October; 4601 Bosque Blvd.; 76710; www.hotfair.com. *Since 1954.*

Waxahachie — Gingerbread Trail Tour of Homes; June (1st full wknd); PO Box 706, 75168; www.-rootsweb.com/~txecm/ginger.htm. *Since 1969.*

Waxahachie — Scarborough Renaissance Festival; April–May; PO Box 538, 75168-0538; www.scarboroughrenfest.com. *Since 1980.*

Weatherford — Parker County Peach Festival; July (2nd Sat.); PO Box 310, 76086; www.weatherford-chamber.com. *Since 1985.*

Weatherford — Christmas on the Square; December; PO Box 310, 76086; www.weatherford-chamber.com. *Since 1988.*

West — Westfest; September (Labor Day wknd.); PO Box 123, 76691; www.westfest.com. *Since 1976.*

Winnsboro — Autumn Trails Festival; October (every wknd.); PO Box 464; 75494.

Woodville — Tyler County Dogwood Festival; March–April; PO Box 2151, 75979-2151; www.tylercountydogwoodfestival.org. Since 1944.

Yorktown — Yorktown's Fiesta En La Calle Festival; April (1st Sat.); PO Box 488, 78164-0488; www.yorktowntx.com.

Yorktown — Yorktown's Annual Western Days Celebration; October (3rd full wknd.); PO Box 488, 78164-0488; www.yorktowntx.com. *Since 1959.* ☆

Since 1947, the Terlingua International Chili Championship has been held each November in Brewster County. Photo by Ron Billings; Texas Forest Service.

Sports

The Dallas Cowboys vs. the Houston Texans in a 2010 preseason game. Photo by MC Glasgow (CC).

High School Football Champions
Boys High School Basketball Champions
Girls High School Basketball Champions
Texas Sports Hall of Fame
Professional Football in Texas
Olympic Medalists from Texas

Southlake Carroll enters Texas Stadium for the 2005 title game against Katy. Photo by Philip Shoffner (CC).

STATE: High School Football Championships

The University Interscholastic League, which governs literary and athletic competition among schools in Texas, was organized in 1910 as a division of the University of Texas extension service. Initially, it sponsored forensic competition.

By 1920, the UIL organized the structure of the high school football game in response to the growing popularity of the sport in Texas. Town football teams had begun competing around the state in the early 1890s.

From 1920 until 1947, the UIL named only one state football champion for the larger schools. Smaller schools were limited to regional titles.

Beginning in 1948, champions were named by divisions based on school enrollment, with the introduction of City, AA and A divisions.

Over the years, other adjustments have been made in determining the divisions, so that today the divisions range from 6-Man competition for the smaller schools to the largest 5A schools.

In the 1990s, subdivisions were added within 2A-5A divisions, with the larger schools included in the Division I. Subdivisions were added to the two other divisions for the season competition in 2006.

Following are listed the champions by UIL division, along with the runner up, and the points scored by each team in the championship game. Included in years 1940-68 are the teams competing in the Prairie View Interscholastic League (PVIL, first called the Interscholastic League of Colored Schools). Between 1965 and 1968, the schools were integrated into the UIL. (OT refers to overtime.) *Source: The University Interscholastic League at* www.uil.utexas.edu.

Division	Champion over Runner Up (with score)
2010	
6-man I	Garden City 82 – Throckmorton 68
6-man II	Richland Springs 46 – Sterling 0
A I	Mart 28 – Goldthwaite 7
A II	Falls City 32 – Windthorst 7
AA I	Daingerfield 33 – Cameron Yoe 27
AA II	Idalou 20 – Lexington 3
AAA I	Henderson 28 – Chapel Hill 21
AAA II	Carthage 47 – Coldspring-Oakhurst 22
AAAA I	Lake Travis 27 – Denton Ryan 7
AAAA II	Aledo 69 – La Marque 34
AAAAA I	Palestine 28 – Euless Trinity 24
AAAAA II	Cibolo Steele 24 – Denton Guyer 21
2009	
6-man I	Garden City 122 – Strawn 88

Division	Champion over Runner Up (with score)
6-man II	Borden County 28 – Highland 14
A I	Goldthwaite 29 – Canadian 25
A II	Cayuga 38 – Albany 24
AA I	Pilot Point 35 – Kirbyville 18
AA II	Daingerfield 64 – Bushland 14
AAA I	Gilmer 43 – Wylie (Abilene) 26
AAA II	Carthage 13 – Graham 12
AAAA I	Lake Travis 24 – Longview 17
AAAA II	Aledo 35 – Brenham 21
AAAAA I	Euless Trinity 41 – Westlake (Austin) 38
AAAAA II	Abilene 28 – Katy 17
2008	
6-man I	Strawn 58 – Follett 29
6-man II	Borden County 54 – Woodson 8

UIL high school football championships

Division	Champion over Runner Up (with score)
A I	Canadian 38 – Mart 7
A II	Stratford 24 – Cayuga 13
AA I	Muleshoe 48 – Kirbyville 26
AA II	Daingerfield 26 – Cisco 8
AAA I	Prosper 17 – La Vega (Waco) 10
AAA II	Carthage 49 – Celina 37
AAAA I	Lake Travis 48 – Longview 23
AAAA II	Sulphur Springs 69 – Dayton 49
AAAAA I	Allen 21 – Fort Bend Hightower 14
AAAAA II	Katy 17 – Wylie (Dallas) 3
2007	
6-man I	Richland Springs 98 – Rule 54
6-man II	Motley County 44 – Woodson 38
A I	Munday 26 – Bremond 6
A II	Alto 22 – Seymour 0
AA I	Farmersville 27 – Tatum 24 (OT)
AA II	Canadian 40 – Elysian Fields 25
AAA I	LIberty Hill 38 – Gilmer 13
AAA II	Celina 21 – China Spring 14
AAAA I	Lamar Consolidated 20 – Copperas Cove 14
AAAA II	Lake Travis 36 – Highland Park (Dallas) 34
AAAAA I	Euless Trinity 13 – Converse Judson 10
AAAAA II	Katy 28 – Pflugerville 7
2006	
6-man I	Richland Springs 78 – Rule 58
6-man II	Northside (Wilbarger Co.) 60 – Jayton 41
A I	Alto 42 – McCamey 13
A II	Chilton 20 – Windthorst 10
AA I	Tatum 32 – Littlefield 14
AA II	Mart 23 – Cisco 13
AAA I	Liberty-Eylau (Texarkana) 35 – Robinson 34
AAA II	LIberty Hill 22 – Celina 19
AAAA I	Alamo Heights 40 – Copperas Cove 28
AAAA II	La Marque 34 – Waco 14
AAAAA I	Southlake Carroll 43 – Westlake (Austin) 29
AAAAA II	Cedar Hill 51 – Cypress Falls 17
2005	
6-man	Throckmorton 68 – Turkey Valley 22
A	Stratford 21 – Big Sandy 20
AA I	Newton 28 – Argyle 20
AA II	Celina 28 – Omaha Paul Pewitt 12
AAA I	Wimberley 21 – Gainesville 7
AAA II	Tatum 38 – Hutto 34
AAAA I	Highland Park (Dallas) 59 – Marshall 0
AAAA II	Lewisville Hebron 28 – Calallen 0
AAAAA I	Euless Trinity 28 – Converse Judson 14
AAAAA II	Southlake Carroll 34 – Katy 20
2004	
6-man	Richland Springs 58 – Turkey Valley 38
A	Shiner 33 – Stratford 19
AA I	Boyd 17 – Newton 14
AA II	Crawford 28 – Troup 14
AAA I	Wylie (Abilene) 17 – Cuero 14
AAA II	Gilmer 49 – Jasper 47
AAAA I	Ennis 23 – Marshall 21
AAAA II	Kilgore 33 – Dallas Lincoln 27 (OT2)
AAAAA I	Tyler Lee 28 – Spring Westfield 21
AAAAA II	Southlake Carroll 27 – Smithson Valley 24
2003	
6-man	Strawn 67 – Fort Davis 62
A	Windthorst 28 – Shiner 27
AA I	San Augustine 28 – Tuscola Jim Ned 7

Division	Champion over Runner Up (with score)
AA II	Garrison 27 – Bangs 0
AAA I	Gainesville 35 – Burnet 24
AAA II	Atlanta 34 – Marlin 0
AAAA I	North Crowley 20 – Bay City 6
AAAA II	La Marque 43 – Denton Ryan 35 (OT3)
AAAAA I	North Shore (Houston) 23 – Woodlands 7
AAAAA II	Katy 16 – Southlake Carroll 15
2002	
6-man	Calvert 51 – Sanderson 46
A	Petrolia 39 – Celeste 18
AA I	Corrigan-Camden 33 – Bangs 14
AA II	Rosebud-Lott 34 – Cisco 0
AAA I	Everman 35 – Burnet 14
AAA II	Bandera 27 – Greenwood 24 (OT2)
AAAA I	Texarkana 42 – New Braunfels 11
AAAA II	Denton Ryan 38 – Brenham 8
AAAAA I	Converse Judson 33 – Midland 32
AAAAA II	Southlake Carroll 45 – Smithson Valley 14
2001	
6-man	Whitharral 27 – Richland Springs 20
A	Burkeville 27 – Celeste 8
AA I	Blanco 16 – Van Alstyne 0
AA II	Celina 41 – Garrison 35
AAA I	Everman 25 – Sinton 14
AAA II	Commerce 14 – La Grange 11
AAAA I	Denton Ryan 42 – Smithson Valley 35 (OT)
AAAA II	Ennis 21 – Bay City 0
AAAAA I	Mesquite 14 – San Antonio Taft 13
AAAAA II	Lufkin 38 – Westlake (Austin) 24
2000	
6-man	Panther Creek 42 – Highland 36
A	Stratford 49 – Burkeville 14
AA I	Sonora 27 – Blanco 24
AA II	Celina 21 – Mart 17
AAA I	Gatesville 14 – Wylie (Abilene) 10
AAA II	La Grange 20 – Forney 17
AAAA I	Bay City 24 – Denton Ryan 2
AAAA II	Ennis 38 – West Orange-Stark 24
AAAAA I	Midland Lee 33 – Westlake (Austin) 21
AAAAA II	Katy 35 – Tyler John Tyler 20
1999	
6-man	Gordon 54 – Groom 34
A	Bartlett 35 – Aspermont 6
AA I	Mart 40 – Boyd 7
AA II	Celina 38 – Elysian Fields 7
AAA I	Liberty-Eylau (Texarkana) 49 – Mathis 6
AAA II	Commerce 17 – Sealy 10
AAAA I	Texas City 27 – Hereford 14
AAAA II	Stephenville 28 – Port Neches-Groves 18
AAAAA I	Midland Lee 42 – Aldine Eisenhower 21
AAAAA II	Garland 37 – Katy 25
1998	
6-man	Trinidad 62 – Borden County 16
A	Tenaha 20 – Wheeler 13
AA I	Omaha Paul Pewitt 28 – Brookshire-Royal 26
AA II	Celina 21 – Elysian Fields 0
AAA I	Aledo 14 – Cuero 7
AAA II	Newton 21 – Daingerfield 0
AAAA I	Grapevine 22 – Bay City 0
AAAA II	Stephenville 34 – La Marque 7
AAAAA I	Duncanville 24 – Converse Judson 21
AAAAA II	Midland Lee 54 – San Antonio MacArthur 0

UIL high school football championships

Division	Champion over Runner Up (with score)
1997	
6-man	Borden County 48 – Panther Creek 16
A	Granger 40 – Wheeler 0
AA	Stanton 33 – Rogers 7
AAA	Sealy 28 – Commerce 21
AAAA I	Texas City 37 – Corsicana 34
AAAA II	La Marque 17 – Denison 0
AAAAA I	Katy 24 – Longview 3
AAAAA II	Flower Mound Marcus 59 – Alief Hastings 20
1996	
6-man	Gordon 51 – Whitharral 50
A	Windthorst 41 – Tenaha 12
AA	Iraan 14 – Groveton 7
AAA	Sealy 36 – Tatum 27
AAAA I	Grapevine 34 – Hays Consolidated 19
AAAA II	La Marque 34 – Denison 3
AAAAA I	Lewisville 58 – Converse Judson 34
AAAAA II	Westlake (Austin) 55 – Abilene Cooper 15
1995	
6-man	Amherst 78 – Milford 42
A	Thorndale 14 – Roscoe 7
AA	Celina 32 – Alto 28
AAA	Sealy 21 – Commerce 20
AAAA	La Marque 31 – Denison 8
AAAAA I	Converse Judson 31 – Odessa Permian 28
AAAAA II	SA Roosevelt 17 – Flower Mound Marcus 10
1994	
6-man	Amherst 30 – Milford 20
A	Thorndale 36 – Crawford 13
AA	Goldthwaite 20 – Schulenburg 16
AAA	Sealy 36 – Atlanta 15
AAAA	Stephenville 32 – La Marque 17
AAAAA I	Plano 28 – Katy 7
AAAAA II	Tyler John Tyler 35 – Westlake (Austin) 24
1993	
6-man	Panther Creek 56 – Dell City 28
A	Sudan 54 – Bremond 0
AA	Goldthwaite 21 – Omaha Paul Pewitt 8
AAA	Southlake Carroll 14 – Cuero 6
AAAA	Stephenville 26 – La Marque 13
AAAAA I	Converse Judson 36 – Plano 13
AAAAA II	Lewisville 43 – Aldine MacArthur 37
1992	
6-man	Panther Creek 54 – Fort Hancock 26
A	Bartlett 33 – Sudan 26
AA	Schulenburg 35 – Goldthwaite 20
AAA	Southlake Carroll 48 – Coldspring 0
AAAA	Waxahachie 28 – A&M Consolidated 24
AAAAA I	Converse Judson 52 – Euless Trinity 0
AAAAA II	Temple 38 – Houston Yates 20
1991	
6-man	Fort Hancock 64 – Christoval 14
A	Memphis 21 – Oakwood 14
AA	Schulenburg 21 – Albany 0
AAA	Groesbeck 7 – Burnet 0
AAAA	A&M Consolidated 35 – Carthage 16
AAAAA I	Killeen 14 – Fort Bend Dulles 10
AAAAA II	Odessa Permian 27 – SA Marshall 14
1990	
6-man	Fort Hancock 66 – Christoval 17
A	Bartlett 36 – Munday 28
AA	Groveton 25 – De Leon 19

Division	Champion over Runner Up (with score)
AAA	Vernon 41 – Crockett 20
AAAA	Wilmer-Hutchins 19 – Westlake (Austin) 7
AAAAA I	Marshall 21 – Converse Judson 19
AAAAA II	Aldine 27 – Arlington Lamar 10
1989	
6-man	Fort Hancock 48 – Jayton-Girard
A	Thorndale 42 – Sudan 24
AA	Groveton 20 – Lorena 13
AAA	Mexia 22 – Vernon 21
AAAA	Chapel Hill (Tyler) 14 – A&M Consolidated 0
AAAAA	Odessa Permian 28 – Aldine 14
1988	
6-man	Fort Hancock 76 – Zephyr 30
A	White Deer 14 – Flatonia 13
AA	Corrigan-Camden 35 – Quanah 14
AAA	Southlake Carroll 42 – Navasota 8
AAAA	Paris 31 – West Orange-Stark 13
AAAAA	Converse Judson 1 – Dallas Carter 0 *(Game score: Dallas Carter 31, Converse Judson 14. Carter stripped of title.)*
1987	
6-man	Lohn 58 – Wellman 30
A	Wheeler 23 – Bremond 21
AA	Lorena 8 – Refugio 7
AAA	Cuero 14 – McGregor 6
AAAA	West Orange-Stark 17 – Rockwall 7
AAAAA	Plano 28 – Houston Stratford 21
1986	
6-man	Fort Hancock 50 – Christoval 36
A	Burkeville 33 – Throckmorton 7
AA	Shiner 18 – Mart 0
AAA	Jefferson 24 – Cuero 0
AAAA	West Orange-Stark 21 – McKinney 9
AAAAA	Plano 24 – La Marque 7
1985	
6-man	Jayton 64 – Christoval 14
A	Goldthwaite 24 – Runge 7
AA	Electra 29 – Groveton 13
AAA	Daingerfield 47 – Cuero 22
AAAA	Sweetwater 17 – Tomball 7
AAAAA	Houston Yates 37 – Odessa Permian 0
1984	
6-man	Jayton 44 – May 28
A	Munday 13 – Union Hill 0
AA	Groveton 38 – Panhandle 7
AAA	Medina Valley 21 – Daingerfield 13
AAAA	Denison 27 – Tomball 13
AAAAA	Odessa Permian 21 – Beaumont French 21 (co-champions)
1983	
6-man	Highland 67 – Mozelle 50
A	Knox City 27 – Bremond 20
AA	Boyd 16 – Groveton 8
AAA	Daingerfield 42 – Sweeny 0
AAAA	Bay City 30 – Lubbock Estacado 0
AAAAA	Converse Judson 25 – Midland Lee 21
1982	
6-man	Highland 60 – Mullin 13
A	Union Hill 13 – Roscoe 0
AA	Eastland 28 – East Bernard 6
AAA	Refugio 22 – Littlefield 21
AAAA	Fort Bend Willowridge 22 – Corsicana 17
AAAAA	Beaumont West Brook 21 – Hurst Bell

UIL high school football championships

Division	Champion over Runner Up (with score)
1981	
6-man	Whitharral 56 – Mullin 36
A	Bremond 12 – Wink 9
AA	Pilot Point 32 – Garrison 0
AAA	Cameron 26 – Gilmer 3
AAAA	Brownwood 24 – Fort Bend Willowridge 9
AAAAA	Lake Highlands (Dallas) 19 – Houston Yates 6
1980	
6-man	Milford 36 – Highland 16
A	Valley View 7 – Rankin 6
AA	Pilot Point 0 – Tidehaven 0 (co-champions)
AAA	Pittsburg 13 – Van Vleck 2
AAAA	Huntsville 19 – Paris 0
AAAAA	Odessa Permian 28 – Port Arthur Jefferson 19
1979	
6-man	Milford 53 – Cotton Center 34
B	Wheeler 33 – High Island 21
A	Hull-Daisetta 28 – China Spring 18
AA	Van 25 – McGregor 0
AAA	McKinney 20 – Bay City 7
AAAA	Temple 28 – Houston Memorial 6
1978	
6-man	Cherokee 29 – Cotton Center 27
B	Union Hill 14 – Wheeler 7
A	China Spring 42 – Lexington 3
AA	Sealy 42 – Wylie (Dallas) 20
AAA	Brownwood 21 – Gainesville 12
AAAA	Houston Stratford 29 – Plano 13
1977	
6-man	May 42 – Marathon 35
B	Wheeler 35 – Lone Oak 13
A	East Bernard 27 – Seagraves 10
AA	Wylie (Dallas) 22 – Bellville 14
AAA	Dickinson 40 – Brownwood 28
AAAA	Plano 13 – Port Neches-Groves 10
1976	
6-man	Marathon 62 – May 16
B	Gorman 18 – Ben Bolt-Palito Blanco 6
A	Barbers Hill 17 - De Leon 8
AA	Rockdale 23 – Childress 6
AAA	Beaumont Hebert 35 – Gainesville 7
AAAA	San Antonio Churchill 10 – Temple 0
1975	
6-man	Cherokee 40 – Marathon 26
8-man	Leakey 32 – Follett 14
B	Big Sandy 26 – Groom 2
A	De Leon 28 – Schulenburg 15
AA	La Grange 27 – Childress 6
AAA	Ennis 13 – Cuero 10
AAAA	Port Neches-Groves 20 – Odessa Permian 10
1974	
6-man	Marathon 60 – Cherokee 58
8-man	Follett 28 – La Pryor 22
B	Big Sandy 0 – Celina 0 (co-champions)
A	Grapeland 19 – Aledo 18
AA	Newton 56 – Spearman 26
AAA	Cuero 19 – Gainesville 7
AAAA	Brazoswood (Clute) 22 – Mesquite 12
1973	
6-man	Cherokee 43 – Marathon 12
8-man	Goree 52 – La Pryor 22
B	Big Sandy 25 – Rule 0

Division	Champion over Runner Up (with score)
A	Troup 28 – Vega 7
AA	Friendswood 28 – Hooks 15
AAA	Cuero 21 – Mount Pleasant 7
AAAA	Tyler John Tyler 21 – Austin Reagan 14
1972	
6-man	O'Brien 60 – Jarrell 14
8-man	Goree 28 – Harrold 24
B	Chilton 6 – Windthorst 0
A	Schulenburg 14 – Clarendon 10
AA	Boling 20 – Rockwall 0
AAA	Uvalde 33 – Lewisville 27
AAAA	Odessa Permian 37 – Baytown Sterling 7
1971	
A	Barbers Hill 3 – Sonora 3 (co-champions)
AA	Jacksboro 20 – Rosebud-Lott 14
AAA	Plano 21 – Gregory-Portland 20
AAAA	San Antonio Lee 28 – Wichita Falls 27
1970	
A	Sonora 45 – Pflugerville 6
AA	Refugio 7 – Iowa Park 7 (co-champions)
AAA	Brownwood 14 – Cuero 0
AAAA	Austin Reagan 21 – Odessa Permian 14
1969	
A	Mart 28 – Sonora 0
AA	Iowa Park 31 – Klein 14
AAA	Brownwood 34 – West Columbia 16
AAAA	Wichita Falls 28 – San Antonio Lee 20
1968	
A	Sonora 9 – Poth 0
AA	Daingerfield 7 – Lufkin Dunbar 6
AAA	Lubbock Estacado 14 – Refugio 0
AAAA	Austin Reagan 17 – Odessa Permian 11
PVIL AAA	Corsicana Jackson 31 – Gladewater Weldon 6
1967	
A	Tidehaven 7 – Clifton 6
AA	Plano 27 – San Antonio Randolph 8
AAA	Brownwood 36 – El Campo 12
AAAA	Austin Reagan 20 – Abilene Cooper 19
PVIL AA	Jasper Rowe 55 – Hallsville Galilee 12
PVIL AAA	Lufkin Dunbar 44 – Texarkana Dunbar 24
1966	
A	Sonora 40 – Schulenburg 14
AA	Sweeny 29 – Granbury 7
AAA	Bridge City 30 – McKinney 6
AAAA	San Angelo Central 21 – Spring Branch (Houston) 14
PVIL AA	Bay City Hilliard 42 – Denton Moore 0
PVIL AAA	Lufkin Dunbar 14 – Wichita Falls Washington 7
PVILAAAA	Beaumont Hebert 14 – Dallas Madison 3
1965	
A	Wills Point 14 – White Deer 0
AA	Plano 20 – Edna 17
AAA	Brownwood 14 – Bridge City 0
AAAA	Odessa Permian 11 – San Antonio Lee 6
PVIL A	Sweeny Carver 21 – Cameron Price 14
PVIL AA	Conroe Washington 33 – Sherman Douglas 12
PVIL AAA	Wichita Falls Washington 31 – Nacogdoches Campbell 0
PVILAAAA	Houston Yates 18 – Fort Worth Terrell 0
1964	
A	Archer City 13 – Ingleside 6
AA	Palacios 12 – Marlin 0

UIL high school football championships

Division	Champion over Runner Up (with score)
AAA	Palestine 24 – San Marcos 15
AAAA	Garland 26 – Galena Park 21
PVIL A	Bartlett Washington 8 – Garland Carver 6
PVIL AA	Sherman Douglas 32 – Conroe Washington 18
PVIL AAA	Lufkin Dunbar 20 – Marlin Washington 7
PVILAAAA	Waco Moore 16 – Houston Yates 14
1963	
A	Petersburg 20 – George West 12
AA	Rockwall 7 – Fort Bend Dulles 6
AAA	Corsicana 7 – Pharr-San Juan-Alamo 0
AAAA	Garland 17 – Corpus Christi Miller 0
PVIL A	Smithville Brown 38 – Mineola McFarland 6
PVIL AA	Lubbock Dunbar 19 – Conroe Washington 14
PVIL AAA	FW Kirkpatrick 46 – Gladewater Weldon 14
PVILAAAA	Galveston Central 34 – Dallas Madison 14
1962	
A	Rotan 39 – Ingleside 6
AA	Jacksboro 52 – Rockdale 0
AAA	Dumas 14 – Pharr-San Juan-Alamo 3
AAAA	San Antonio Brackenridge 30 – Borger 26
PVIL A	Taylor Price 42 – Dayton Colbert 6
PVIL AA	Wharton Training 40 – Lubbock Dunbar 6
PVIL AAA	Fort Worth Kirkpatrick 6 – Galena Park Fidelity Manor 0
PVILAAAA	Houston Yates 18 – Fort Worth Dunbar 15
1961	
A	Albany 18 – Hull-Daisetta 12
AA	Donna 28 – Quanah 21
AAA	Dumas 6 – Nederland 0
AAAA	Wichita Falls 21 – Galena Park
PVIL A	Richardson Hamilton Park 24 – Sweeny Carver 0
PVIL AA	Midland Carver 42 – Conroe Washington 16
PVIL AAA	Baytown Carver 21 – Fort Worth Kirkpatrick 6
PVILAAAA	Austin Anderson 20 – Houston Yates 13
1960	
A	Albany 20 – Crosby 0
AA	Denver City 26 – Bellville 21
AAA	Brownwood 26 – Port Lavaca 6
AAAA	Corpus Christi Miller 13 – Wichita Falls 6
PVIL A	Freeport Lanier 28 – West Dunbar 24
PVIL AA	Conroe Washington 16 – Midland Carver 6
PVIL AAA	Corpus Christi Coles 38 – Wichita Falls Washington 21
PVILAAAA	Houston Washington 6 – Waco Moore 6 (co-champions)
1959	
A	Katy 16 – Sundown 6
AA	Brady 1 – Stamford 0 *(Game score: Stamford 19, Brady 14. Stamford stripped of title.)*
AAA	Breckenridge 20 – Cleburne 20 (co-champs)
AAAA	Corpus Christi Ray 20 – Wichita Falls 6
PVIL A	West Dunbar 42 – Livingston Dunbar 12
PVIL AA	Bay City Hilliard 22 – FW Kirkpatrick 14
PVIL AAA	Beaumont Hebert 37 – Dallas Lincoln 0
1958	
A	White Deer 44 – Elgin 22
AA	Stamford 23 – Angleton 0
AAA	Breckenridge 42 – Kingsville 14
AAAA	Wichita Falls 48 – Pasadena 6
PVIL A	Livingston Dunbar 26 – Grand Prairie Dal-Worth 24

Division	Champion over Runner Up (with score)
PVIL AA	Baytown Carver 17 – Denton Moore 14
PVIL AAA	Dallas Washington 35 – Houston Washington 0
1957	
A	Mart 7 – White Oak 7 (co-champions)
AA	Terrell 41 – Brady 6
AAA	Nederland 20 – Sweetwater 7
AAAA	Highland Park (Dallas) 21 – Port Arthur 9
PVIL A	Galena Park Fidelity Manor 29 – Vernon Washington 6
PVIL AA	Corsicana Jackson 46 – Denton Moore 0
PVIL AAA	Austin Anderson 22 – Dallas Washington 14
1956	
A	Stinnett 35 – Hondo 13
AA	Stamford 26 – Brady 13
AAA	Garland 3 – Nederland 0
AAAA	Abilene 14 – Corpus Christi Ray 0
PVIL A	Sealy Austin County 19 – Kaufman Pyle 18
PVIL AA	Corsicana Jackson 18 – Denton Moore 0
PVIL AAA	Austin Anderson 26 – Dallas Washington 7
1955	
A	Deer Park 7 – Stinnett 0
AA	Stamford 34 – Hillsboro 7
AAA	Port Neches 20 – Garland 14
AAAA	Abilene 33 – Tyler 13
PVIL A	Rockdale Aycock 21 – West Dunbar 7
PVIL AA	Baytown Carver 33 – Gladewater Weldon 13
PVIL AAA	Port Arthur Lincoln 9 – Dallas Lincoln 6
1954	
A	Deer Park 26 – Albany 6
AA	Phillips 21 – Killeen 13
AAA	Breckenridge 20 – Port Neches 7
AAAA	Abilene 14 – Houston S.F. Austin 7
PVIL A	Livingston Dunbar 25 – College Station Lincoln 20
PVIL AA	Orange Wallace 39 – Greenville Carver 0
PVIL AAA	Houston Wheatley 13 – Waco Moore 0
1953	
A	Ranger 34 – Luling 21
AA	Huntsville 40 – Ballinger 6
AAA	Port Neches 24 – Big Spring 13
AAAA	Houston Lamar 33 – Odessa 7
PVIL A	Livingston Dunbar (winner) – West Columbia Brown *(no score available)*
PVIL AA	Corsicana Jackson 19 – Abilene Woodson 0
PVIL AAA	Port Arthur Lincoln 38 – Dallas Washington 7
1952	
A	Wink 26 – Deer Park 20
AA	Terrell 61 – Yoakum 13
AAA	Breckenridge 28 – Temple 20
AAAA	Lubbock 12 – Baytown Lee 7
PVIL A	Arp Industrial (winner) – Lockhart Carver *(no score available)*
PVIL AA	Amarillo Carver 7 – Palestine Lincoln 0
PVIL AAA	Waco Moore 14 – Corpus Christi Coles 0
1951	
A	Giddings 25 – Newcastle 9
AA	Arlington 7 – La Vega (Waco) 0
AAA	Breckenridge 20 – Temple 14
AAAA	Lubbock 14 – Baytown Lee 12
PVIL A	Huntsville Sam Houston 7 – Hillsboro Peabody 6
PVIL AA	Houston Yates 6 – Waco Moore (co-champs)

UIL high school football championships

Division	Champion over Runner Up (with score)
1950	
A	Wharton 13 – Kermit 9
AA	Wichita Falls 14 – Austin 13
City	Dallas Sunset 14 – Houston Reagan 6
PVIL A	San Angelo Blackshear 32 – Huntsville Sam Houston 0
PVIL AA	Dallas Washington 24 – Houston Yates 21
1949	
A	Littlefield 13 – Mexia 0
AA	Wichita Falls 34 – Austin 13
City	San Antonio Jefferson 31 – Dallas Sunset 13
PVIL A	Orange Wallace 34 – Victoria Gross 13
PVIL AA	Dallas Lincoln 13 – Port Arthur Lincoln 13 (co-champions)
1948	
A	Monahans 14 – New Braunfels 0
AA	Waco 21 – Amarillo 0
City	FW Arlington Heights 20 – Houston Lamar 0
PVIL A	Denison Terrell 13 – Orange Wallace 0
PVIL AA	Corpus Christi Coles 6 – Dallas Washington 0
1947	
UIL	San Antonio Brackenridge 22 – Highland Park (Dallas) 13
PVIL A	Denison Terrell 6 – Taylor Price 6 (co-champions)
PVIL AA	Fort Worth Terrell 13 – Corpus Christi Coles 6
1946	
UIL	Odessa 21 – San Antonio Jefferson 14
PVIL	Dallas Washington 19 – Galveston Central 19 (co-champions)
1945	
UIL	Highland Park (Dallas) 7 – Waco 7 (co-champions)
PVIL	Wichita Falls Washington 12 – Austin Anderson 2
1944	
UIL	Port Arthur 20 – Highland Park (Dallas) 7

Division	Champion over Runner Up (with score)
PVIL	Houston Wheatley 7 – Fort Worth Terrell 6
1943	
UIL	San Angelo 26 – Lufkin 13
PVIL	Wichita Falls Washington 7 – Houston Yates 7 (co-champions)
1942	
UIL	Austin 20 – Dallas Sunset 7
PVIL	Austin Anderson 20 – Paris Gibbons 0
1941	
UIL	Wichita Falls 13 – Temple 0
PVIL	Dallas Washington 12 – Houston Wheatley 0
1940	
UIL	Amarillo 20 – Temple 7
PVIL	Fort Worth Terrell 26 – Austin Anderson 0
UIL	
1939	Lubbock 20 – Waco 14
1938	Corpus Christi 20 – Lubbock 6
1937	Longview 19 – Wichita Falls 12
1936	Amarillo 10 – Kerrville Tivy 6
1935	Amarillo 13 – Greenville 0
1934	Amarillo 48 – Corpus Christi 0
1933	Greenville 21 – Dallas Tech 0
1932	Corsicana 0 – Fort Worth Masonic Home 0 *(Corsicana awarded title on penetrations, 3-0.)*
1931	Abilene 13 – Beaumont 0
1930	Tyler 25 – Amarillo 13
1929	Port Arthur 0 – Breckenridge 0 (co-champs)
1928	Abilene 38 – Port Arthur 0
1927	Waco 21 – Abilene 14
1926	Waco 20 – Dallas Oak Cliff 7
1925	Waco 20 – Dallas Forest Avenue 7
1924	Dallas Oak Cliff 31 – Waco 0
1923	Abilene 3 – Waco 0
1922	Waco 13 – Abilene 10
1921	Bryan 35 – Dallas Oak Cliff 13
1920	Houston Heights 0 – Cleburne 0 (co-champs)

Boys High School Basketball Champions

The University Interscholastic League basketball championships began in 1921 when El Paso High School, coached by Luther Coblentz, won over the Brackenridge team from San Antonio.

The Prairie View Interscholastic League began basketball championships in 1940 when Houston Yates defeated Houston Wheatley. The PVIL began to merge with the UIL at the start of the 1967-68 school year and disbanded at the end of the 1969-70 school year.

Today, the UIL has divisions determined by the school size from 1A to 5A. Girls basketball championships have been awarded by the UIL since 1951.

Following are the champions by UIL division, along with the runner up, and the points scored by each team in the championship game. Included in years 1940-70 are the teams competing in the Prairie View Interscholastic League (PVIL, first called the Interscholastic League of Colored Schools). (OT refers to overtime.) *Sources: The University Interscholastic League at www.uil.utexas.edu, and* The Dallas Morning News.

Division	Champion over Runner Up (with score)
2011	
A Div. I	Eula 64 – Tenaha 49
A Div. II	Paducah 45 – Bronte 30
AA	Idalou 55 – Tatum 54
AAA	Corpus Christi West Oso 61 – Burkburnett 57
AAAA	Dallas Kimball 58 – La Marque 64
AAAAA	Flower Mound Marcus 40 – Garland Lakeview Centennial 38
2010	
A Div. I	Cayuga 82 – Bronte 60

Division	Champion over Runner Up (with score)
A Div. II	Nazareth 52 – Lenorah Grady 43
AA	Ponder 66 – Idalou 40
AAA	Lubbock Estacado 69 – Dallas Madison 63
AAAA	Houston Yates 92 – Lancaster 73
AAAAA	Fort Bend Bush 65 – Garland Lakeview Centennial 58
2009	
A Div. I	Roscoe 52 – Plains 48
A Div. II	Slocum 45 – Nazareth 27
AA	Ponder 51 – New Waverly 39

UIL boys basketball championships

Division	Champion over Runner Up (with score)
AAA	Dallas Madison 68 – Lubbock Estacado 66
AAAA	Houston Yates 94 – Dallas Kimball 78
AAAAA	DeSoto 59 – Cedar Hill 47
2008	
A Div. I	Thorndale 53 – Dallardsville Big Sandy 42
A Div. II	Laneville 56 – Goodrich 50
AA	Ponder 72 – Tuscola Jim Ned 51
AAA	Kennedale 61 – Burkburnet 59
AAAA	Dallas South Oak Cliff 80 – Fort Worth Southwest 77
AAAAA	North Crowley 73 – Fort Bend Dulles 67
2007	
A Div. I	Thorndale 39 – Martins Mill 37
A Div. II	Nazareth 52 – Laneville 43
AA	Kountze 71 – Shallowater 57
AAA	Hardin-Jefferson 56 – Wylie (Abilene) 44
AAAA	Dallas S. Oak Cliff 54 – Beaumont Ozen 42
AAAAA	Duncanville 60 – Kingwood 46
2006	
A Div. I	Bogata Rivercrest 57 – Gruver 49
A Div. II	Nazareth 53 – Lipan 48
AA	Arp 65 – Ponder 49
AAA	Dallas Roosevelt 61 – Carrollton Ranchview 46
AAAA	Ft. Worth Dunbar 2 – Dallas S. Oak Cliff 0 *(Game score: South Oak Cliff 76, Dunbar 58. South Oak Cliff stripped of title.)*
AAAAA	Plano 60 – Kingwood 58 (OT)
2005	
A	Morton 69 – Lipan 53
AA	Kountze 77 – Tuscola Jim Ned 64
AAA	Van 62 – Graham 41
AAAA	San Antonio Houston 2 – Dallas S. Oak Cliff 0 *(Game score: South Oak Cliff 64, SA Houston 43. South Oak Cliff stripped of title.)*
AAAAA	Kingwood 54 – DeSoto 52
2004	
A	Normangee 50 – Lenorah Grady 37
AA	Shallowater 47 – Argyle 42 (OT)
AAA	Kountze 73 – Greenwood 54
AAAA	Houston Jones 63 – Dallas Lincoln 61
AAAAA	Houston Milby 72 – Cedar Hill 67
2003	
A	Nazareth 52 – Tenaha 47
AA	Brock 81 – Hitchcock 52
AAA	Everman 72 – Tatum 44
AAAA	Fort Worth Dunbar 66 – Beaumont Ozen 54
AAAAA	DeSoto 94 – Corpus Christi Ray 73
2002	
A	Brock 70 – Nazareth 50
AA	Little River-Academy 49 – Frankston 48
AAA	Gainesville 79 – Kountze 62
AAAA	Dallas Lincoln 71 – Beaumont Ozen 51
AAAAA	San Antonio Jay 54 – Dallas Kimball 53
2001	
A	Evadale 66 – Goodrich 60
AA	Ponder 50 – Danbury 49
AAA	Mexia 74 – West Oso (Corpus Christi) 49
AAAA	Beaumont Ozen 58 – San Antonio Lanier 42
AAAAA	Fort Bend Willowridge 65 – Bryan 58
2000	
A	Brookeland 63 – Moulton 53
AA	Peaster 67 – Van Vleck 58
AAA	Waco La Vega 60 – Gainesville 47

Division	Champion over Runner Up (with score)
AAAA	Denton Ryan 80 – Dallas Madison 69
AAAAA	Fort Bend Willowridge 59 – Klein Forest 52
1999	
A	Moulton 54 – Brookeland 49
AA	Peaster 66 – Wellington 62 (OT)
AAA	Mexia 77 – Seminole 71 (OT)
AAAA	Crowley 60 – Port Arthur Lincoln 51
AAAAA	Duncanville 78 – Dallas Kimball 61
1998	
A	Moulton 67 – Goodrich 44
AA	Krum 64 – Little River-Academy 52
AAA	Clarksville 90 – Crockett 83
AAAA	Houston Waltrip 67 – Highland Park (Dallas) 60
AAAAA	Midland 63 – San Antonio Taft 51
1997	
A	Wortham 50 – Nazareth 42
AA	Italy 71 – Vanderbilt Industrial 63
AAA	Dallas Madison 64 – Tulia 58
AAAA	San Antonio Fox Tech 68 – Dallas Lincoln 59
AAAAA	Dallas Kimball 64 – North Shore (Houston) 53
1996	
A	Avinger 51 – Anderson-Shiro 48
AA	Krum 53 – Winnie East Chambers 39
AAA	Sinton 66 – Graham 59
AAAA	Pampa Arthur 82 – Dallas Madison 68
AAAAA	Dallas Kimball 72 – Euless Trinity 64
1995	
A	Sudan 74 – Calvert 71
AA	La Poynor 60 – Maypearl 56
AAA	Clarksville 87 – Madisonville 69
AAAA	Port Arthur Lincoln 57 – Austin Anderson 56
AAAAA	San Antonio E. Central 108 – Dallas Carter 86
1994	
A	Lipan 62 – Nazareth 60
AA	Krum 56 – Troup 45
AAA	Ferris 84 – Littlefield 66
AAAA	Plainview 54 – Austin Anderson 52
AAAAA	Fort Bend Willowridge 50 – Plano East 44
1993	
A	Laneville 77 – Brock 68
AA	Troup 69 – Amarillo Highland Park 49
AAA	Southlake Carroll 66 – Ferris 56
AAAA	Dallas Lincoln 46 – Port Arthur Lincoln 45
AAAAA	Fort Worth Dunbar 74 – Converse Judson 64
1992	
A	Laneville 51 – Petersburg 49
AA	Troup 60 – Krum 48
AAA	Stafford 73 – Groesbeck 72
AAAA	Dallas South Oak Cliff 73 – Georgetown 60
AAAAA	Longview 71 – Victoria 67 (OT)
1991	
A	Moulton 53 – Bronte 44
AA	Abernathy 55 – Troup 46
AAA	Hardin-Jefferson 75 – Clarksville 68
AAAA	Port Arthur Lincoln 77 – Alamo Heights 68
AAAAA	Duncanville 65 – San Antonio Jay 38
1990	
A	Santo 67 – Moulton 64
AA	Ingram Moore 73 – Troup 72
AAA	Navasota 71 – Lamesa 54
AAAA	Dallas Lincoln 87 – Boerne 77
AAAAA	Dallas Kimball 59 – Clear Lake (Houston) 56

UIL boys basketball championships

Division	Champion over Runner Up (with score)
1989	
A	Ladonia Fannindel 75 – Moulton 58
AA	Edgewood 48 – Tidehaven 46
AAA	San Antonio Cole 66 – Clarksville 60
AAAA	Port Arthur Lincoln 86 – Austin Travis 72
AAAAA	Clear Lake (Houston) 86 – San Antonio Jay 69
1988	
A	Paducah 99 – Dallardsville Big Sandy 61
AA	Archer City 80 – Liberty Hill 69
AAA	Sweeny 59 – West Oso (Corpus Christi) 50
AAAA	Port Arthur Lincoln 66 – Wichita Falls Hirschi 59
AAAAA	Houston Sam Houston 73 – FW Dunbar 68
1987	
A	Paducah 71 – Bronte 39
AA	Morton 84 – Liberty Hill 72
AAA	Sweeny 66 – Hughes Springs 64
AAAA	Dallas Hillcrest 54 – Cleburne 42
AAAAA	La Porte 64 – San Antonio Holmes 58
1986	
A	Nazareth 53 – Archer City 49
AA	Morton 73 – Dripping Springs 59
AAA	Cleveland 57 – Dimmitt 56
AAAA	Port Arthur Lincoln 55 – Mansfield 39
AAAAA	Amarillo 68 – Dallas Kimball 63
1985	
A	La Poynor 47 – Nazareth 41
AA	Grapeland 63 – Morton 56
AAA	Sweeny 55 – Brownsboro 43
AAAA	Bay City 65 – Lamesa 63
AAAAA	Houston Madison 86 – Conroe 69
1984	
A	Snook 39 – Nazareth 30
AA	Shelbyville 73 – Somerville 67
AAA	New Boston 76 – Hardin-Jefferson 65
AAAA	Port Arthur Lincoln – Flour Bluff 52
AAAAA	Bryan 68 – Houston Memorial 56
1983	
A	Snook 76 – Nacogdoches Central Heights 40
AA	Morton 91 – Bartlett 69
AAA	Dimmitt 81 – Van Vleck 54
AAAA	Waxahachie 79 – Borger 66
AAAAA	Bryan 71 – Fort Worth Paschal 54
1982	
A	Snook 52 – Greenwood 45
AA	Shelbyville 46 – Nixon 39
AAA	Dimmitt 60 – Linden Kildare 59
AAAA	Beaumont Hebert 76 – Waxahachie 71
AAAAA	San Antonio Churchill 75 – Galveston Ball 74
1981	
A	Snook 41 – Midway (Henrietta) 33
AA	Liberty City Sabine 62 – Shallowater 42
AAA	Altair Rice 56 – North Lamar (Paris) 52
AAAA	Beaumont Hebert 59 – Canyon 57
AAAAA	Port Arthur Lincoln 92 – San Antonio Marshall 84
1980	
B	Snook 59 – Petty West Lamar 58
A	Liberty City Sabine 69 – Bartlett 68
AA	Abernathy 64 – Boling 58
AAA	Beaumont Hebert 88 – Snyder 53
AAAA	Houston Kashmere 70 – Plano 69
1979	
B	Snook 57 – Krum 56

Division	Champion over Runner Up (with score)
A	Vega 52 – La Poynor 44
AA	Seminole 47 – Altair Rice 42
AAA	Huntsville 48 – Mineral Wells 45
AAAA	Lufkin 75 – Fort Worth Dunbar 74
1978	
B	Krum 69 – Avinger 68
A	Snook 63 – Coppell 62
AA	Whitehouse 60 – Dimmitt 59
AAA	Huntsville 55 – Mineral Wells 49
AAAA	Houston Wheatley 84 – SA Fox Tech 83
1977	
B	Avinger 68 – Hedley 62
A	Broaddus 84 – Whitewright 71
AA	Morton 63 – Kountze 60
AAA	Daingerfield 72 – Borger 68
AAAA	Dallas S.Oak Cliff 78 – Ft. Worth Dunbar 71
1976	
B	Richards 57 – Brookeland 47
A	Broaddus 82 – Crowell 46
AA	Mart 57 – Moulton 52
AAA	Odessa Ector 78 – Waxahachie 75
AAAA	El Paso Eastwood 74 – Tyler 62
1975	
B	La Poynor 52 – Spade 42
A	Brookshire Royal 62 – Whitewright 57
AA	Dimmitt 49 – Van Vleck 43
AAA	Lamesa 59 – South Grand Prairie 55
AAAA	Houston Kashmere 60 – Ft. Worth Paschal 58
1974	
B	Huckabay 49 – La Poynor 48
A	Huntington 41 – Snook 39
AA	Bowie 76 – Friona 66
AAA	Gonzales 77 – Crosby 62
AAAA	Houston Kashmere 91 – Dallas S. Oak Cliff 87
1973	
B	La Poynor 72 – Brock 52
A	Kennard 77 – Petrolia 67
AA	San Augustine 60 – Grand Saline 58
AAA	Longview Pine Tree 45 – Lamesa 38
AAAA	Houston Wheatley 84 – Midland 78
1972	
B	La Poynor 53 – Snook 44
A	Pottsboro 61 – Garrison 60
AA	Morton 62 – Whitehouse 59
AAA	Odessa Ector 71 – Henderson 64
AAAA	Dallas Roosevelt 68 – SA Jefferson 63
1971	
B	Krum 52 – Snook 51
A	Van Horn 68 – Pottsboro 67
AA	Hughes Spring 64 – Friendswood 60
AAA	Dumas 65 – Fort Worth Como 59
AAAA	Cypress-Fairbanks 70 – Houston Wheatley 58
1970	
B	Chester 75 – Midway (Henrietta) 53
A	Kennard 72 – Clarendon 64
AA	Kountze 75 – Taft 73
AAA	Kerrville Tivy 81 – Cypress-Fairbanks 68
AAAA	Houston Wheatley 108 – Carrollton Turner 80
PVIL AAA	Jacksonville Douglas 88 – Kilgore Dansby 69
1969	
B	Snook 50 – Brookeland 41
A	Friendswood 51 – Pineland W. Sabine 49

UIL boys basketball championships

Division	Champion over Runner Up (with score)
AA	FW Kirkpatrick 63 – Spring Klein 54
AAA	Kerrville Tivy 55 – Perryton 54
AAAA	Houston Wheatley 52 – Houston Memorial 47
PVIL A	Houston Carverdale 78 – Madisonville Marion 66
PVIL AAA	Jacksonvill Douglas 69 – Crockett Bunch 45

1968

B	Kennard 64 – Friendswood 49
A	Aspermont 52 – Louise 50
AA	Kirbyville 57 – Mexia 52
AAA	Lake Highlands (Dallas) 51 – Lubbock Dunbar 49
AAAA	Houston Wheatley 85 – Dallas Jefferson 80
PVIL A	E. Liberty Center 67 – Mt. Enterprise Concord 56
PVIL AA	Crockett Bunch 67 – Texarkana Macedonia 62
PVIL AAA	Tyler Emmett 114 – Carthage Turner 90

1967

B	Kennard 51 – Krum 47
A	Brownsboro 68 – Archer City 59
AA	Hardin-Jefferson 59 – Dimmitt 51
AAA	Lamesa 60 – South San Antonio 56
AAAA	San Antonio Lee 70 – Houston Memorial 69
PVIL A	Mt. Enterprise Concord 61 – W. Kirbyville 39
PVIL AA	San Augustine Lincoln 87 – Mexia Dunbar 77
PVIL AAA	Fort Worth Kirkpatrick 68 – Galena Park Fidelity Manor 66
PVILAAAA	Fort Worth Terrell 92 – Houston Yates 67

1966

B	Snook 64 – Channing 40
A	Gruver 63 – Honey Grove 62
AA	Lake Worth 60 – Crane 42
AAA	San Antonio Marshall 64 – Clear Creek 60
AAAA	Houston Memorial 73 – Dallas Samuell 68
PVIL A	Center Daniels (winner) — Taylor Hughes
PVIL AA	Cy-Fair Carverdale 70 – Gilmer Valley View 67
PVIL AAA	Galena Park Fidelity Manor 61 – Bryan Kemp 45
PVILAAAA	Houston Wheatley 87 – Fort Worth Terrell 74

1965

B	Snook 48 – Deweyville 44
A	Pineland W. Sabine 51 – Woodsboro 48
AA	FW Lake Worth 60 – Port Authur Austin 49
AAA	San Marcos 87 – Waxahachie 63
AAAA	Houston Jones 64 – Dallas Jefferson 59
PVIL A	Arp Industrial 63 – Sweeny Carver 38
PVIL AA	Cypress-Fairbanks Carverdale 75 – Grand Prairie Dal-Worth 72
PVIL AAA	Lubbock Dunbar 82 – Carthage Turner 66
PVILAAAA	Fort Worth Terrell 81 – Houston Worthing 80

1964

B	McAdoo 66 – Hutto 65
A	Talco 75 – Henrietta 60
AA	Canyon 52 – Lancaster 51
AAA	Graham 60 – Clear Creek 50
AAAA	Houston Austin 50 – Dallas Adamson 42
PVIL A	Commerce Norris 51 – Larue Central 46
PVIL AA	Daingerfield Rhoads 57 – Midland Carver 55
PVIL AAA	Fort Worth Kirkpatrick 65 – Galena Park Fidelity Manor 61
PVILAAAA	Beaumont Pollard 58 – Houston Kashmere 55

1963

B	McAdoo 53 – Prairie Valley 35
A	Pineland W. Sabine 66 – Woodsboro 51
AA	Buna 47 – Canyon 41

Division	Champion over Runner Up (with score)
AAA	Clear Creek 62 – Seminole 57
AAAA	San Angelo 62 – Spring Branch (Houston) 49
PVIL A	W. Kirbyville 64 – Smithville Brown 45
PVIL AA	Midland Carver 47 – Fairfield Dogan 36
PVIL AAA	Carthge Turner 68 – Bryan Kemp 48
PVILAAAA	FW Terrell 87 – Galventon Central 83 (OT2)

1962

B	Huntington 60 – Roxton 56
A	White Deer 59 – Woodsboro 39
AA	Buna 49 – Jacksboro 30
AAA	Dumas 58 – Waxahachie 38
AAAA	Dallas Jefferson 69 – Houston Jeff Davis 46
PVIL A	Colorado City Wallace – Bruceville Sunset 56
PVIL AA	Lubbock Dunbar 63 Galena Park Fidelity Manor 52
PVIL AAA	Fort Worth Como 75 – Carthage Turner 56
PVILAAAA	Houston Worthing 62 – Dallas Madison 56 (OT)

1961

B	Frankston 60 – Hutto 44
A	Simms Bowie 53 – Brownsboro 52
AA	Buna 60 – Dimmitt 36
AAA	South San Antonio 67 – Clear Creek 54
AAAA	Houston Austin 68 – Amarillo Palo Duro 60
PVIL A	Prairie View 75 – Neches Clemons 48
PVIL AA	Galena Park Fidelity Manor 63 Daingerfield Rhoads 48
PVIL AAA	FW Kirkpatrick 67 – Corpus Christi Coles 45
PVILAAAA	Houston Wheatley 98 – Dallas Madison 48

1960

B	McAdoo 58 – Midway (Henrietta) 42
A	Huntington 61 – Sunray 46
AA	Linden-Kildare 52 – Dimmitt 44
AAA	Lamesa 56 – South San Antonio 54
AAAA	Beaumont South Park 41 – Austin 36
PVIL A	College Station Lincoln 69 – Ladonia Clark 56
PVIL AAA	Lubbock Dunbar 74 – Houston Elmore 71
PVILAAAA	Houston Kashmere - Dallas Madison (co-champions, game called off.)

1959

B	Midway (Henrietta) 65 – Kyle 58
A	Huntington 63 – Plains 43
AA	Buna 53 – Bowie 48
AAA	Houston Smiley 58 – Hereford 42
AAAA	Pampa 65 – Dallas Jefferson 52
PVIL A	Center Daniels (winner) – Linden Fairview
PVIL AAA	Navasota Carver 66 – Amarillo Carver 58
PVILAAAA	Houston Wheatley 70 – Dallas Madison 55

1958

B	Blossom 67 – Dallardsville Big Sandy 61
A	Simms Bowie 48 – Brownsboro 47
AA	Belton 58 – New London 56
AAA	Waxahachie 77 – South San Antonio 63
AAAA	Pampa 48 – Port Arthur 47
PVIL A	Woodville Scott 67 – Fairfield Dogan 40
PVIL AAA	Temple Dunbar 66 – Aldine Carver 45
PVILAAAA	Houston Wheatley 63 – Beaumont Hebert 39

1957

B	Dallardsville Big Sandy 80 – Meadows 59
A	White Oak 66 – McGregor 51
AA	Buna 74 – Seminole 45
AAA	Houston Smiley 52 – Pecos 35
AAAA	Port Arthur 67 – Pampa 51
PVIL A	Woodville Scott 75 – Fairfield Dogan 54

UIL boys basketball championships

Division	Champion over Runner Up (with score)
PVIL AAA	Lubbock Dunbar 98 – Baytown Carver 79
PVILAAAA	Fort Worth Terrell 73 – Houston Wheatley 69
1956	
B	Pollok Central 74 – Krum 68
A	Buna 52 – Troup 42
AA	Jacksonville 70 – Phillips 68
AAA	Amarillo Palo Duro 59 – Beaumont French 51
AAAA	Laredo 65 – North Dallas 54
PVIL A	Rockdale Aycock 53 – Daingerfield Rhoads 51
PVIL AAA	Orange Wallace 49 – Lufkin Dunbar 46
PVILAAAA	Port Arthur Lincoln 76 – Galveston Central 64
1955	
B	Avoca 47 – Dallardsville Big Sandy 41
A	Buna 58 – Dickinson 49
AA	Seminole 50 – San Marcos 49
AAA	Victoria 60 – Beaumont French 51
AAAA	Dallas Crozier Tech 59 – Waco 57
PVIL A	Palestine Green Bay 64 – Daingerfield Rhoads 48
PVIL AAA	Victoria Goss 71 – Odessa Blackshear 48
PVILAAAA	Houston Wheatley 58 – Houston Yates 45
1954	
B	Cayuga 79 – Dallardsville Big Sandy 54
A	Sweeny 92 – Sundown 67
AA	Bowie 70 – Spring Branch (Houston) 40
AAA	Alamo Heights 67 – Galena Park 60
AAAA	Pampa 47 – Dallas Crozier Tech 44
PVIL A	Palestine Green Bay 80 – Tyler Stanton 48
PVIL AAA	Paris Gibbons 62 – Odessa Blackshear 60
PVILAAAA	Houston Wheatley 63 – Beaumont Pollard 47
1953	
B	Cayuga 66 – Dallardsville Big Sandy 50
A	White Oak 69 – Denver City 53
AA	Bowie 81 – Dumas 44
AAA	Beaumont South Park 83 – SA Edison 54
AAAA	Pampa 61 – Austin 47
PVIL A	Center Daniels 55 – Palestine Green Bay 33
PVIL AAA	Lubbock Dunbar 67 – Odessa Blackshear 55
PVILAAAA	Houston Wheatley 62 – Fort Worth Terrell 43
1952	
B	Dallardsville Big Sandy 62 – Laneville 41
A	Dimmitt 62 – Plano 40
AA	Bowie 65 – Levelland 59
AAA	Alamo Heights 49 – Gladewater 45
AAAA	Fort Worth Polytechnic 56 – Borger 51
Div. I (3A v. 4A)	Alamo Heights 54 – Fort Worth Polytecnic 46
Div. II (1A v. 2A)	Dimmitt 59 – Bowie 54
PVIL A	West Columbia Brown (winner) – Livingston Dunbar (No score available.)
PVILAAAA	Houston Wheatley 56 – Houston Washington 50
1951	
B	Cayuga 44 – Dallardsville Big Sandy 38
A	Bowie 54 – Brenham 34
AA	Lubbock 44 – Austin 43
City	Houston Lamar 78 – Alamo Heights 52
PVIL A	Huntsville S. Houston 58 – Atlanta Pruitt 56
PVILAAAA	Houston Wheatley 61 – Austin Anderson 51
1950	
B	Gruver 43 – Waelder 34
A	Canyon 49 – South San Antonio 25

Division	Champion over Runner Up (with score)
AA	Corpus Christi 40 – Vernon 34
City	Houston Milby 40 – Dallas Crozier Tech 39
PVIL A	W. Columbia Brown 72 – Hallsville Galilee 34
PVILAAAA	Houston Wheatley 54 –Houston Yates 47
1949	
B	Martins Mill 39 – Dallardsville Big Sandy 33
A	Memphis 27 – Beaumont French 25
AA	Texas City 30 – Brownwood 28
City	Fort Worth Paschal 41 – Houston Milby 40
PVIL A	Arp Industrial 59 – Wharton Training 38
PVILAAAA	Houston Yates (winner) – San Antonio Wheatley (No score available.)
1948	
B	Maydell 35 – Johnson City 22
A	Mount Vernon 44 – East Mountain 43
AA	Dallas Crozier Tech 29 – Lufkin 28
PVIL A	W. Columbia Brown 65 – Hallsville Galilee 42
PVILAAAA	Houston Wheatley 46 – Dallas Lincoln 26
1947	
B	Johnson City 16 – Marfa 14
A	East Mountain 35 – Bowie 22
AA	El Paso 27 – San Antonio Jefferson 22
PVILAAAA	Houston Yates 40 – Beaumont Hebert 33
1946	
B	Stratford 29 – Perrin 18
A	Pasadena 50 – Levelland 35
AA	Dallas Crozier Tech 32 – Houston Jeff Davis 28
PVILAAAA	Houston Washington 40 –Galveston Central 33
1945	
B	Prairie Lea 35 – Mount Enterprise 33
A	San Antonio Lanier 30 – Quitman 24
AA	Fort Worth Paschal 43 – Lufkin 29
PVILAAAA	Houston Yates 42 – Beaumont Hebert 16
1944	
B	Prairie Lea 30 – Blossom 26
A	Nocona 33 – Mount Vernon 22
AA	Sunset 29 – Childress 20
PVILAAAA	Galveston Central 40 – Dallas Lincoln 29
1943	
B	Slidell 36 – Sidney 23
A	San Antonio Lanier 30 – Beaumont French 18
AA	Houston Jeff Davis 40 – Austin 27
PVILAAAA	Houston Yates 35 – Beaumont Hebert 15
1942	
B	Slidell 32 – Fayetteville 22
A	Van 35 – Nederland 27
AA	Houston Jeff Davis 55 – Lufkin 35
PVILAAAA	Houston Wheatley 31 – Houston Yates 30
1941	
UIL	El Paso 27 – Abilene 20
PVIL	Dallas Washington 26 – Houston Wheatley 25
1940	
UIL	San Marcos 22 – El Paso 21
PVIL	Houston Yates 32 – Houston Wheatley 19
UIL	
1939	Livingston 37 – San Antonio Lanier 35
1938	Dallas Wilson 41 – Abilene 27
1937	Carey 26 – Gober 18
1936	Cushing 33 – El Paso 29
1935	Denton 38 – Lamesa 23
1934	Athens 28 – Lamesa 22
1933	Athens 36 – Houston Jeff Davis 20

UIL boys basketball championships

Division	Champion over Runner Up (with score)	Division	Champion over Runner Up (with score)
1932	Temple 30 – Houston San Jacinto 23	1926	San Antonio Brackenridge 29 – Corsicana 23
1931	Athens 25 – Houston San Jacinto 22	1925	Beaumont 14 – San Antonio Brackenridge 12
1930	Denton 30 – Estelline 11	1924	Dallas Oak Cliff 29 – El Paso 18
1929	Athens 22 – Denton 11	1923	Dallas Oak Cliff 17 – El Paso 15
1928	Austin 33 – Temple 13 *(Austin disqualified.)*	1922	Lindale 27 – El Paso 15 *(Lindale disqualified.)*
1927	Athens 23 – Denton 14	1921	El Paso 25 – San Antonio Brackenridge 11

Girls High School Basketball Champions

Following are listed the champions by UIL division, along with the runner up, and the points scored by each team in the championship game. (OT refers to overtime.) *Sources: The University Interscholastic League at* www.uil.utexas.edu, *and* The Dallas Morning News.

Division	Champion over Runner Up (with score)	Division	Champion over Runner Up (with score)
2011		A Div. II	Roby 44 – Neches 34
A Div. I	Smyer 52 – Martins Mill 49	AA	Brock 61 – Woodville 32
A Div. II	Neches 65 – Whitharral 44	AAA	Robinson 49 – Argyle 33
AA	Brock 47 – Winnsboro 26	AAAA	Midway (Waco) 50 – Mansfield Timberview 27
AAA	Wylie (Abilene) 66 – Lucas Lovejoy 58	AAAAA	Mansfield Summit 52 — Houston Nimitz 43
AAAA	Canyon 44 – Austin LBJ 39	**2008**	
AAAAA	Irving MacArthur 74 – Georgetown 51	A Div. I	Martins Mill 48 – Sudan 43
2010		A Div. II	Follett 71 – Kennard 51
A Div. I	Smyer 49 – Martins Mill 41	AA	Tuscola Jim Ned 65 – Poth 49
A Div. II	Neches 61 – McLean 32	AAA	Canyon 59 – Kennedale 43
AA	Brock 38 – Wall 33	AAAA	Dallas Lincoln 50 – Dickinson 47
AAA	Liberty–Eylau (Texarkana) 70 – Wylie (Abilene) 68 (OT)	AAAAA	Cypress-Fairbanks 50 – DeSoto 33
AAAA	Mansfield Timberview 55 – Frisco Wakeland 39	**2007**	
AAAAA	Cypress-Fairbanks 65 – Fort Bend Hightower 41	A Div. I	Lindsay 43 – Sundown 36
2009		A Div. II	Nazareth 61 – Garden City 31
A Div. I	Sudan 71 – Roscoe 38	AA	Poth 72 – Winnsboro 70 (OT2)
		AAA	Canyon 53 – Crockett 38

Denton High School girls basketball team of 1911. Denton Public Liberary/UNTPortal to Texas History.

UIL girls basketball championships

Division	Champion over Runner Up (with score)
AAAA	Fort Worth Dunbar 62 – Dickinson 51
AAAAA	Rockwall 59 – Cypress-Fairbanks 54 (OT)
2006	
A Div. I	Martins Mill 61 – Elkhart Slocum 30
A Div. II	Kennard 44 – Springlake-Earth 26
AA	Argyle 51 – Wall 33
AAA	China Spring 57 – Wylie (Abilene) 54
AAAA	Waxahachie 52 – Kerrvile Tivy 48
AAAAA	Plano West 54 – Rockwall 47
2005	
A	Seagraves 56 – Nazareth 51
AA	Brock 64 – Canadian 30
AAA	Canyon 66 – Cleveland 46
AAAA	Fort Worth Dunbar 56 – Angleton 50
AAAAA	Arlington Bowie 69 – Humble 62 (OT)
2004	
A	Archer City 59 – Fayetteville 47
AA	Shallowater 44 – Aubrey 37
AAA	Canyon 63 – Winnsboro 33
AAAA	Dallas Lincoln 57 – Plainview 35
AAAAA	Spring Westfield 66 – Duncanville 49
2003	
A	Priddy 66 – La Poynor 63
AA	Brock 55 – Shallowater 36
AAA	Canyon 76 – Kountze 45
AAAA	Plainview 50 – Dallas Lincoln 42
AAAAA	Duncanville 47 – Georgetown 27
2002	
A Div. I	Brock 58 – La Poynor 26
A Div. II	Nazareth 67 – Dodd City 42
AA	Buffalo 48 – Abernathy 43
AAA	Llano 67 – Liberty-Eylau (Texarkana) 51
AAAA	Plainview 68 – Dallas Lincoln 40
AAAAA	Mansfield 47 – San Antonio Taft 42
2001	
A	Nazareth 61 – Kennard 44
AA	Nacogdoches Central Heights 57 – Boyd 56
AAA	Winnsboro 51 – Wylie (Abilene) 48
AAAA	Plainview 51 – Dallas Lincoln 40
AAAAA	Mansfield 62 – Spring Westfield 49
2000	
A	Nazareth 72 – Valley View 56
AA	Farwell 47 – Brock 35
AAA	Winnsboro 54 – Smithville 51
AAAA	Canyon 74 – Waxahachie 54
AAAAA	Mansfield 69 – Plano 43
1999	
A	Vega 70 – Valley View 64
AA	Hughes Springs 61 – Salado 33
AAA	Winnsboro 56 – Hudson 48
AAAA	Dallas Lincoln 52 – Canyon 49
AAAAA	Mansfield 65 – Corpus Christi Carroll 46
1998	
A	Karnack 69 – Nazareth 45
AA	Hamilton 54 – Ozona 45
AAA	Comanche 65 – Winnsboro 56
AAAA	Canyon Randall 52 – Bay City 23
AAAAA	Alief Elsik 58 – Amarillo Palo Duro 38
1997	
A	Whiteface 59 – Celeste 39
AA	Poth 54 – Shallowater 50
AAA	Barbers Hill 66 – Dripping Springs 45

Division	Champion over Runner Up (with score)
AAAA	Levelland 36 – Cedar Hill 33
AAAAA	Duncanville 44 – Alief Elsik 33
1996	
A	Nazareth 43 – Celeste 30
AA	Ozona 45 – Gunter 39
AAA	Groesbeck 63 – Slaton 61
AAAA	Canyon 60 – Cedar Hill 34
AAAAA	Westlake (Austin) 64 – Alief Elsik 60 (OT2)
1995	
A	Sudan 66 – Alvord 42
AA	Ozona 61 – Cooper 47
AAA	Bowie 65 – Dripping Springs 50
AAAA	Cleburne 55 – Silsbee 50
AAAAA	Westlake (Austin) 59 – Duncanville 56 (OT)
1994	
A	Sudan 40 – Jayton 36
AA	Tuscola Jim Ned 31 – Hemphill 29
AAA	Dripping Springs 64 – La Vega (Waco) 56
AAAA	Midway (Waco) 52 – Dallas Lincoln 40
AAAAA	Amarillo 62 – Conroe 46
1993	
A	Celeste 63 – Muenster 38
AA	Marion 69 – Hamilton 63
AAA	Dimmitt 59 – Dripping Springs 51
AAAA	Westlake (Austin) 48 – Levelland 40
AAAAA	Amarillo 68 – Corpus Christi King 65
1992	
A	Celeste 70 – Brock 57
AA	Panhandle 52 – Marion 49
AAA	Canyon 49 – Winnsboro 29
AAAA	Canyon Randall 43 – Georgetown 42
AAAAA	San Marcos 45 – Duncanville 43
1991	
A	Nazareth 50 – Moulton 30
AA	Abernathy 37 – Honey Grove 32
AAA	Tulia 58 – Winnsboro 39
AAAA	Levelland 51 – Dallas Lincoln 30
AAAAA	Amarillo Tascosa 54 – Victoria 41
1990	
A	Nazareth 53 – Moulton 34
AA	Tatum 61 – Marion 50
AAA	Wylie (Abilene) 51 – Edna 37
AAAA	Calallen 46 – Midway (Waco) 39
AAAAA	Duncanville 74 – Houston Yates 51
1989	
A	Nazareth 57 – La Poynor 33
AA	Grapeland 54 – Abernathy 47
AAA	Hardin-Jefferson 46 – Canyon 44
AAAA	Levelland 45 – West Orange-Stark 24
AAAAA	Duncanville 42 – Victoria 38
1988	
A	Nazareth 64 – La Poynor 28
AA	Godley 60 – Grapeland 58
AAA	Brownfield 49 – Hardin-Jefferson 40
AAAA	Levelland 38 – Calallen 35
AAAAA	Duncanville 60 – North Mesquite 46
1987	
A	Sudan 55 – Moulton 26
AA	Morton 68 – Paris 53
AAA	Slaton 43 – Sweeny 40
AAAA	Levelland 41 – Calallen 30
AAAAA	Plainview 59 – Austin Lanier 47

UIL girls basketball championships

Division	Champion over Runner Up (with score)
1986	
A	Snook 36 – Nazareth 33
AA	Abernathy 51 – Rogers 42
AAA	Hardin-Jefferson 72 – Ingleside 53
AAAA	Levelland 44 – A&M Consolidated 43
AAAAA	Victoria 57 – Tyler Lee 44
1985	
A	Nazareth 56 – Priddy 48
AA	Troy 80 – Abernathy 72
AAA	Vernon 52 – Sweeny 51
AAAA	Waco Richfield 44 – Sweetwater 35
AAAAA	Dallas South Oak Cliff 60 – Victoria 46
1984	
A	Nazareth 64 – Petty West Lamar 32
AA	Pollock Central 37 – Hale Center 36
AAA	Abernathy 67 – Groesbeck 57
AAAA	Waco Richfield 56 – Levelland 43
AAAAA	Longview 72 – Houston Yates 52
1983	
A	Sudan 46 – La Poynor 34
AA	Hardin 41 – Hale Center 39
AAA	Barbers Hill 86 – Sweeny 81
AAAA	Levelland 41 – Calallen 28
AAAAA	Houston Yates 58 – Victoria 56
1982	
A	Nazareth 64 – Dime Box 37
AA	Hardin 69 – Phillips 61
AAA	Barbers Hill 68 – Sweeny 53
AAAA	Del Valle (Austin) 76 – Carthage 64
AAAAA	Victoria 46 – Dallas South Oak Cliff 45
1981	
A	Nazareth 84 – Colmesneil 39
AA	Hardin 61 – New Deal 46
AAA	Abernathy 61 – Sweeny 59
AAAA	Canyon 64 – Bay City 53
AAAAA	Lubbock Monterey 71 – Duncanville 70
1980	
B	Nazareth 56 – Brock 50
A	Bogata Rivercrest 68 – Panhandle 41
AA	Slaton 75 – Kyle Hays 44
AAA	Dumas 53 – Flour Bluff 43
AAAA	Dallas S.Oak Cliff 74 – Lubbock Monterrey 49
1979	
B	Nazareth 46 – Brock 43
A	Hale Center 46 – Bogota Rivercrest 29
AA	Slaton 68 – Pflugerville 54
AAA	Georgetown 51 – Sweeny 49
AAAA	Victoria 43 – Dallas South Oak Cliff 41
1978	
B	Nazareth 47 – Graford 39
A	Robert Lee 44 – Cushing 41
AA	Slaton 55 – Granbury 45
AAA	Canyon 59 – Tuloso-Midway 37
AAAA	Dallas South Oak Cliff 70 – Victoria 62
1977	
B	Nazareth 73 – May 54
A	Cooper 85 – Deweyville 69
AA	Spearman 61 – Robinson 58
AAA	Canyon 58 – Midway (Waco) 54
AAAA	Dallas S.Oak Cliff 79 – Schertz Clemens 65
1976	
B	Neches 53 – Crawford 49

Division	Champion over Runner Up (with score)
A	Stratford 60 – Archer City 57
AA	Phillips 83 – Bellville 69
AAA	Midway (Waco) 64 – Canyon 59
AAAA	Duncanville 70 – Victoria 69
1975	
B	Crawford 45 – Neches 44
A	Southlake Carroll 50 – Vega 48
AA	George West 52 – Bellville 51
AAA	Midway (Waco) 60 – Canyon 52
1974	
B	Poolville 60 – Klondike 54
A	Grandview 52 – Shiner 36
AA	Slaton 51 – Comanche 45
AAA	Canyon 65 – Conroe 41
1973	
B	Neches 49 – Poolville 45
A	Grandview 39 – Turkey Valley 37
AA	Midway (Waco) 65 – Comanche 46
AAA	Angleton 57 – Canyon 55
1972	
B	Round Top-Carmine 54 – Huckabay 48
A	Claude 57 – Southlake Carroll 55
AA	Spearman 50 – Robinson 49
AAA	Canyon 59 – Rockdale 36
1971	
B	Round Top-Carmine 48 – Grandview 33
A	Claude 46 – Glen Rose 33
AA	Spearman 52 – Buna 47
AAA	Victoria 55 – Canyon 51
1970	
B	Follett 59 – Trent 50
A	Wylie (Abilene) 80 – Grandview 57
AA	Robinson 57 – Spearman 49
AAA	Tuloso-Midway 66 – Canyon 54
1969	
B	Klondike 62 – High Island 48
A	Stratford 42 – Deweyville 37
AA	Midway (Waco) 66 – Spearman 55
AAA	Canyon 59 – Angleton 42
1968	
B	High Island 53 – Klondike 40
A	Springlake-Earth 75 – George West 65
AA	Bogata Rivercrest 56 – Gregory-Portland 54
AAA	Stephenville 39 – West Orange 27
1967	
B	High Island 48 – Quitaque 39
A	Springlake-Earth 105 – Cross Plains 52
AA	Little Cypress (Orange) 52 – Spearman 43
AAA	Tulia 70 – Victoria 57
1966	
B	Round Top-Carmine 57 – Deport 32
A	Jourdanton 79 – Springlake-Earth 74
AA	Spearman 50 – Little Cypress (Orange) 46
AAA	Tulia 76 – Victoria 75
1965	
B	Trent 69 – Round Top-Carmine 65
A	Roosevelt (Lubbock) 77 – Jourdanton 71
AA	Edna 60 – Friona 57
AAA	Victoria 63 – Weslaco 46
1964	
B	Trent 76 – Burkeville 27
A	Baird 85 – Jourdanton 68

UIL girls basketball championships

Division	Champion over Runner Up (with score)
AA	Friona 50 – Clear Creek 45
1963	
B	Slidell 71 – Wells 65
A	Sundown 51 – Moulton 48
AA	West 49 – Little Cypress (Orange) 42
1962	
B	Claude 55 – Wells 41
A	Sundown 51 – Ladonia Fannindel 46
AA	Devine 38 – Tulia 37
1961	
B	Midway (Henrietta) 54 – Claude 48
A	Sundown 50 – Moulton 46
AA	Buna 66 – Spearman 47
1960	
B	North Hopkins 42 – Claude 38
A	Cooper 60 – Moulton 51
AA	Buna 66 – Spearman 63
1959	
B	North Hopkins 64 – Bovina 47
A	Pollok Central 58 – Sudan 57
AA	Abernathy 59 – Buna 57
1958	
B	North Hopkins 86 – Collinsville 28
A	Cooper 59 – Moulton 53
AA	Abernathy 64 – Fort Worth Brewer 53

Division	Champion over Runner Up (with score)
1957	
B	Roosevelt (Lubbock) 56 – Hawley 40
A	Ropesville 64 – Cooper 51
AA	Buna 69 – Seagoville 31
1956	
B	Collinsville 83 – North Hopkins 75
A	Buna 54 – New Deal 44
AA	Angleton 51 – Seagoville 48
1955	
B	Midway (Waco) 58 – Cotton Center 50
A	Dimmitt 62 – Granbury 44
AA	Bowie 54 – Angleton 52
1954	
B	Winnie East Chambers 46 – Claude 45
A	Dimmitt 66 – Granbury 60
1953	
B	New Deal 58 – Whitesboro 44
A	Claude 40 – Bryson 30
1952	
B	Claude 47 – Duncanville 42
A	Hamilton 27 – Morton 19
1951	
B	Claude 42 – Clyde Denton Valley 40
A	Comanche 50 – McLean 49

American League Champions 2010

ABOVE, opening day of the Texas Rangers championship season at the Ballpark in Arlington. RIGHT, slugger/outfielder Josh Hamilton. Photos by Red3biggs (CC).

In their first pennant since moving to North Texas in 1972, the Texas Rangers defeated the New York Yankees four games to two in the American League Championship series.

The Rangers beat the Tampa Bay Rays in the first round of the 2010 playoffs, 3 games to 2.

The AL champs then faced the National League champion San Francisco Gaints in the World Series, losing four games to one.

The Rangers' Josh Hamilton was named the American League Most Valuable Player after setting a series record for intentional walks.

The Yankees had been the team's nemesis three

separate times in the playoffs in the 1990s when they stopped the Rangers attempts to reach the World Series.

During the 2010 season, the Rangers had a record of 90 wins and 72 loses, spending most of the year at the top of the American League West Division. Their best record was in 1999 when they had 95 wins and 67 loses.

Texas' other major-league baseball team, the Houston Astros, won the National League pennant in 2005. They were swept in the World Series by the Chicago White Sox.

Texas Private Schools Football Championships

Private schools are barred from participation in the University Interscholastic League (UIL), which was made up of public schools exclusively until 2003 when Dallas Jesuit and Strake Jesuit of Houston were admitted. The two schools, which had been part of the TCIL (see following) until 2000, were forced into independent status when the TCIL ceased operations and TAPPS, made up of mostly smaller schools, would not allow admittance to their league because of the large size of the two schools.

The UIL in 2003 altered its provisions for membership for private schools with several stipulations, including that a private school must not qualify for membership in organizations similar to the UIL, thereby allowing for the admission of the Dallas Jesuit and Strake Jesuit only.

TCIL: Texas Christian Interscholastic League

The TCIL was organized as the Texas Catholic Interscholastic League in 1935 when St. Mary's University in San Antonio was asked to sponsor a boys's basketball tournament for private Catholic schools.

Other boys' sports have been added thorugh the years, and girls' competition was initiated in 1971.

The name of the organization was changed to Texas Christian Interscholastic League in 1976 when non-Catholic schools joined. In 1999-2000, the TCIL ceased to exist and most schools joined the Texas Association of Private and Parochial Schools (TAPPS).

The known TCIL champions are as follows:

Division	Champion
1999	Dallas Jesuit
1998	Dallas Jesuit
1997	Dallas Jesuit
1996	Houston St. Thomas
1995	Dallas Jesuit
1994	Houston Strake Jesuit
1993	Dallas Jesuit / Beaumont Kelly (co-champs)
1992	Beaumont Kelly
1991	Dallas Jesuit
1990	
AAA	San Antonio St. Anthony
AAAA	San Antonio Central Catholic/ Dallas Jesuit (co-champs)
1989	
AAAA	Houston St. Thomas
1988	
AAA	Dallas Bishop Lynch
AAAA	Houston St. Thomas
1987	
AAA	Beaumont Kelly
AAAA	Dallas Jesuit
1986	
AAAA	Dallas Jesuit
1985	
AAAA	Houston St. Thomas
1984	
AAA	Houston Marian Christian
AAAA	Houston St. Thomas
1983	
AAA	Houston St. Pius
AAAA	Houston St. Thomas
1982	
AAA	Houston St. Pius
AAAA	Dallas Jesuit
1981	
AAA	Houston Marian Christian
AAAA	Houston St. Thomas
1980	
AAA	Brownsville St. Joseph
AAAA	Houston Strake Jesuit
1979	
AAA	Beaumont Kelly

Division	Champion
AAAA	Houston Strake Jesuit
1978	
AAA	Houston St. Pius
AAAA	Dallas Jesuit
1977	
AA	Brownsville St. Joseph
AAA	Houston St. Pius
AAAA	Houston Strake Jesuit
1976	
AA	Victoria St. Joseph
AAA	Houston Marian Christian/ Galveston O'Connell (co-champs)
AAAA	Houston Strake Jesuit
1975	
AAA	Waco Reicher
AAAA	Dallas Jesuit
1974	
AAA	Waco Reicher
AAAA	Dallas Jesuit
1973	
AAA	Galveston O'Connell
AAAA	Houston St. Thomas
1972	
AAA	Galveston O'Connell
AAAA	Houston St. Thomas
1971	
AAA	Houston St. Pius
AAAA	Houston St. Thomas
1970	
AAA	Houston St. Pius
AAAA	San Antonio Central Catholic
1969	
AAA	Fredericksburg St. Mary's
AAAA	Houston St. Thomas
1968	
AAA	Fredericksburg St. Mary's
AAAA	Houston St. Thomas
1967	
AAA	Corpus Christi Academy
AAAA	Dallas Jesuit
1966	
AAA	Fredericksburg St. Mary's
AAAA	Houston St. Thomas

Private high school football championships

Division	Champion
1965	
AAA	Victoria St. Joseph
AAAA	Houston St. Thomas
1964	
AAA	Corpus Christi Academy
AAAA	Houston St. Thomas
1963	
AAA	Schulenburg Forest
AAAA	Waco Reicher
1962	
AAA	Brownsville St. Joseph
AAAA	Waco Reicher
1961	
AAA	Corpus Christi Academy
AAAA	Galveston Kirwin

Division	Champion
1960	
AAA	Corpus Christi Academy
AAAA	Dallas Jesuit
1959	Dallas Jesuit
1958	Dallas Jesuit
1957	Dallas Jesuit
1956	Dallas Jesuit
1955	Beaumont St. Anthony
1954	Dallas Jesuit
1953	Houston St. Thomas
1952	Port Arthur Bishop Byrne
1951	Port Arthur Bishop Byrne
1950	Houston St. Thomas

TAPPS: Texas Association of Private and Parochial Schools

The Texas Association of Private and Parochial Schools is by far the largest group of private schools in the state with more than 225 member institutions.

The interscholastic competition began in 1978 and was significantly expanded when the Texas Christian Interscholastic League ceased to exist in 2000.

Listed below are previous state champions, runners-up and the game scores.

YEAR	Division	Champion	Runner Up
2010	6-Man Division I	Bulverde Bracken Chrisitian 52	Dallas Covenant 38
	6-Man Division II	Brenham Christian 52	Dallas Tyler Street Christian 12
	Division IV	Shiner St. Paul 48	Colleyville Covenant 41
	Division III	Austin Regents 38	Bullard Brook Hill 7
	Division II	Dallas Parish Episcopal 49	Fort Worth Christian 41
	Division I	Plano Prestonwood 38	Fort Worth Nolan Catholic 35
2009	6-Man Division I	Greenville Christian 72	Dallas Covenant 40
	6-Man Division II	Duncanville Christway 56	Brenham Christian 52
	Division IV	Richardson Canyon Creek 46	Friscoe Legacy 34
	Division III	Waco Reicher 35	Bullard Brook Hill 28
	Division II	Plano Prestonwood 35	Argyle Liberty Christian 17
	Division I	Fort Worth Nolan 21	Addison Trinity Christian 20 (OT)
2008	6-Man Division I	Greenville Christian 72	Rockwall Heritage 48
	6-Man Division II	Fredericksburg Heritage 46	Duncanville Christway 0
	Division IV	Richardson Canyon Creek 33	Frisco Legacy 30
	Division III	Waco Reicher 49	Austin Regents 17
	Division II	Dallas Christian 44	Trinity Christian Cedar Hill 13
	Division I	Fort Worth Nolan 20	Dallas Bishop Lynch 0
2007	6-Man Division I	Greenville Christian 70	Denton Calvary 22
	6-Man Division II	Fredericksburg Heritage 26	Fort Worth Glenview 20 (OT)
	Division IV	Hallettsville Sacred Heart 39	Fort Worth Calvary 8
	Division III	Waco Reicher 41	Grapevine Faith 7
	Division II	Argyle Liberty Christian 28	Dallas Christian 7
	Division I	Houston St. Pius 38	Fort Worth Nolan 14
2006	6-Man Division I	Rockwall Heritage 79	Greenville Christian 43
	6-Man Division II	Fort Worth Glenview 68	Dallas Covenant 18
	Division IV	Colleyville Covenant 27	Hallettsville Sacred Heart 26
	Division III	Austin Regents 16	Trinity Christian Cedar Hill 13
	Division II	Midland Christian 21	Denton Liberty Christian 14
	Division I	Houston St. Pius 35	Addison Trinity Christian 14
2005	6-Man Division I	Abilene Christian 38	Rockwall Heritage 16
	6-Man Division II	Fredericksburg Heritage 44	Arlington St. Alban's 32
	Division IV	Carrollton American Heritage 27	Cedar Hill Trinity Christian 20
	Division III	Plano Prestonwood 46	Houston Northland 14
	Division II	Arlington Grace Prep 42	Denton Liberty Christian 18
	Division I	Fort Worth Nolan 28	Addison Trinity Christian 25

Private high school football championships

YEAR	Division	Champion	Runner Up
2004	6-Man Division I	Greenville Christian 74	Denton Calvary 56
	6-Man Division II	Fredericksburg Heritage 44	Granbury Happy Hill 24
	Division IV	Lubbock Christian 54	Muenster Sacred Heart 31
	Division III	Waco Reicher 39	Plano Prestonwood 13
	Division II	Midland Christian 16	Arlington Grace Prep 13
	Division I	Fort Worth Nolan 14	Houston St. Pius 0
2003	6-Man A	Granbury Happy Hill 62	Marble Falls Faith 20
	6-Man AA	Austin Regents 60	Abilene Christian 12
	AA	Muenster Sacred Heart 42	Hallettsville Sacred Heart 12
	AAA	San Antonio Cornerstone 35	Fort Worth Southwest 27
	AAAA	Arlington Grace Prep 20	Dallas Christian 19
	AAAAA	Dallas Bishop Lynch 31	San Antonio Central 8
2002	6-Man A	Granbury Happy Hill 78	Arlington St. Alban's 36
	6-Man AA	Austin Regents 36	Abilene Christian 26
	AA	Hallettsville Sacred Heart 36	Colleyville Covenant 3
	AAA	Rowlett Rockwall Christian 31	Arlington Pantego Christian 3
	AAAA	Arlington Grace Prep 15	Dallas Christian 6
	AAAAA	Dallas Bishop Lynch 50	Victoria St. Joseph 28
2001	6-Man	Austin Regents 60	Greenville Christian 56
	AA	Rockwall Christian 48	Hallettsville Sacred Heart 21
	AAA	San Antonio Cornerstone 34	Arlington Pantego Christian 28
	AAAA	Midland Christian 20	Denton Liberty Christian 14
	AAAAA	San Antonio Central Catholic 38	Houston St. Thomas 28
2000	6-Man	El Paso Jesus Chapel 70	Dallas Metropolitan 46
	AA	Hallettsville Sacred Heart 13	Rockwall Christian 6
	AAA	Katy Faith West 13	Galveston O'Connell 6
	AAAA	Midland Christian 48	Fort Worth Christian 24
	AAAAA	Addison Trinity Christian 42	Dallas Bishop Lynch 13
1999	6-Man	El Paso Jesus Chapel 57	Watauga Harvest Christian 20
	AA	Carrollton American Heritage 28	Bryan Allen Academy 24
	AAA	Arlington Grace Prep 49	Fort Worth Southwest 0
	AAAA	Houston Second Baptist 31	Dallas Christian 14
	AAAAA	Houston St. Pius 49	San Antonio Central Catholic 30

TCIL/TAPPS

Gary Kubiak, head coach of the NFL Houston Texans, is one of the athletes to come out of the football programs of Texas' private and parochial schools. Kubiak was quarterback for Houston St. Pius 1975–1978.
He went on to play for Texas A&M and in the NFL.

Photo by Brit (CC).

Private high school football championships

YEAR	Division	Champion	Runner Up
	6-Man	El Paso Jesus Chapel 72	Greenville Christian 52
	AA	Bryan Allen Academy 35	Carrollton American Heritage 6
1998	AAA	Arlington Grace Prep 35	Houston Christian 17
	AAAA	Dallas Christian 33	Houston Second Baptist 20
	AAAAA	Beaumont Kelly 26	Houston St. Pius 7
	6-Man	Waxahachie Cornerstone 40	Bryan Allen Academy 34
	AA	Shiner St. Paul 27	Balch Springs Christian 0
1997	AAA	Pantego Christian 32	Halletsville Sacred Heart 25
	AAAA	Dallas Christian 21 (OT)	Houston Northwest Academy 14
	AAAAA	Dallas Bishop Lynch 20	Addiston Trinity Christian 13
	6-Man	Bryan Allen Academy 30	Abilene Christian 12
	AA	Waco Parkview Christian 34	Shiner St. Paul 6
1996	AAA	Halletsville Sacred Heart 46	Arlington Pantego Christian 7
	AAAA	Denton Liberty Christian 35	Houston Northwest Academy 0
	AAAAA	Addison Trinity Christian 19	Houston Second Baptist 17
	6-Man	Midland Christian 64	Abilene Christian 18
	A	Fort Worth Masonic Home 28	Shiner St. Paul 7
1995	AA	Tyler Gorman 35	Halletsville Sacred Heart 18
	AAA	Dallas Christian 35	Fort Worth Christian 12
	Super AAA	Dallas Bishop Lynch 55	Fort Worth Nolan 7
	6-Man	Midland Christian 57	Bryan Allen Academy 28
	A	Muenster Sacred Heart 14	Waco Parkview Christian 14
1994		(Muenster Sacred Heart wins on first downs)	
	AA	Denton Liberty Christian 15	Dallas Tyler Street Christian 0
	AAA	Cedar Hill Trinity Christian 19	Dallas Christian 7
	Super AAA	Dallas Bishop Lynch 43	Addison Trinity Christian 42
	6-Man	Midland Christian 74	El Paso Jesus Chapel 34
	A	Dallas Tyler Street Christian 58	Muenster Sacred Heart 7
	AA	Dallas Lexington Academy 21	Lubbock Christian 21
1993		(Lexington Academy wins on penetrations)	
	AAA	Cedar Hill Trinity Christian 48	Galveston O'Connell 12
	Super AAA	Houston St. Pius 26	Addison Trinity Christian 26
		(Co-Champions)	
	6-Man	Midland Christian 46	Houston Southwest Christian 0
	A	Shiner St. Paul 8	Dallas Tyler Street Christian 6
1992	AA	Hallettsviile Sacred Heart 31	Waco Christian 8
	AAA	Fort Worth Christian 29	Cedar Hill Trinity Christian 12
	Super AAA	Addison Trinity Christian 31	Dallas Bishop Lynch 14
	6-Man	Midland Christian 44	El Paso Jesus Chapel 39
1991	A	Waco Parkview Christian 43	Dallas Lexington Academy 6
	AA	Cedar Hill Trinity Christian 24	Tyler Gorman 9
	AAA	Addison Trinity Christian 49	Fort Worth Christian 0
	6-Man	El Paso Jesus Chapel 58	Midland Christian 34
1990	A	Dallas Lexington Academy 46	Waco Parkview Christian 6
	AA	Hallettsville Sacred Heart 21	Cedar Hill Trinity Christian 14
	AAA	Dallas Bishop Dunne 39	Fort Worth Nolan 0
	A	Dallas Temple Christian 16	Dallas Lexington Academy 0
1989	AA	Waco Christian 26	Fort Worth Temple Christian 7
	AAA	Dallas Christian 26	Dallas Bishop Dunne 22
	A	Dallas Temple Christian 23	Dallas Lexington Academy 6
1988	AA	Fort Worth Temple Christian 41	Tyler Gorman 0
	AAA	Dallas Bishop Dunne 35	Houston St. Pius 26
1987	Division II	Abilene Christian 34	Richardson Canyon Creek 8
	Division I	Dallas Christian 19	Addison Trinity Christian 14
1986	Division II	Arlington Texas Christian 29	Richardson Canyon Creek 21
	Division I	Dallas Christian 36	Houston Northwest Academy 35
1985	Division II	Arlington Texas Christian 17	Richardson Canyon Creek 7
	Division I	Dallas Christian 16	Lubbock Christian 0
1984	Division II	DeSoto Brook Hollow Christian 48	Dallas Tyler Street Christian 37
	Division I	Dallas Bishop Dunne 33	Dallas First Baptist 0

Private high school football championships

YEAR	Division	Champion	Runner Up
1983	Division II	Houston Greenwood Village 20	Dallas Oak Cliff Christian 8
	Division I	Fort Worth Country Day 10	Lubbock Christian 8
1982	Division II	Abilene Christian 26	Arlington Bethel Baptist 6
	Division I	Houston Northwest Academy 36	Dallas Christian 22
1981	Division II	Farmers Branch Heritage 14	Arlington Bethel Baptist 7
	Division I	Fort Worth Country Day 33	Abilene Christian 7
1980		Fort Worth Christian 20	Bryan Allen Academy 18
1979		Houston Northwest Academy 27	Addison Trinity Christian 7
1978		Fort Worth Christian 34	Lubbock Christian 2
1977		Harlingen Marine Military 20	Fort Worth Christian 0
1976		Houston St. Pius 20	Fort Worth Christian 7
1975		Houston Northwest Academy 13	Harlingen Marine Military 10
1974		Houston Northwest Academy 34	Bryan Allen Academy 22
1973		Houston St. Pius 19	San Antonio Texas Military 0

Private High School Boys Basketball Champions

TCIL: Texas Christian Interscholastic League

Following are listed the boys basketball team champions of the TCIL, as information was available. *Sources: Various press reports and Internet websites.*

Division	Champion	Division	Champion
2000		**1987**	
AAAA	Dallas Jesuit	AAA	Corpus Christi Incarnate Word
1999		AAAA	Dallas Bishop Lynch
AAA	San Antonio Antonian	**1986**	
AAAA	Dallas Jesuit	AAA	Galveston O'Connell
1998		AAAA	Dallas Jesuit
AAA	San Antonio Antonian	**1985**	
AAAA	Houston Strake Jesuit	AAA	San Antonio St. Gerard
1997		AAAA	Dallas Jesuit
AAA	San Antonio Antonian	**1984**	
AAAA	Dallas Jesuit	AAA	N/A
1996		AAAA	San Antonio Central Catholic
AAA	San Antonio Antonian	**1983**	
AAAA	Houston Strake Jesuit	AAA	Houston Marian Christian
1995		AAAA	Dallas Jesuit
AAA	San Antonio Antonian	**1982**	
AAAA	Houston Strake Jesuit	AAA	Galveston O'Connell
1994		AAAA	San Antonio Central Catholic
AAA	San Antonio Holy Cross	**1981**	
AAAA	Houston Strake Jesuit	AAA	Corpus Christi Incarnate Word
1993		AAAA	San Antonio St. Gerard
AAA	San Antonio St. Gerard	**1980**	
AAAA	Houston Strake Jesuit	AAA	Corpus Christi Incarnate Word
1992		AAAA	Dallas Bishop Lynch
AAA	San Antonio Holy Cross	**1979**	
AAAA	Dallas Jesuit	AAA	Lubbock Christ the King
1991		AAAA	Dallas Bishop Dunne
AAA	San Antonio Holy Cross	**1978**	
AAAA	San Antonio Central Catholic	AAA	Houston St. Pius
1990		AAAA	Fort Worth Nolan
AAA	Beaumont Kelly	**1977**	
AAAA	Houston St. Thomas	AAA	San Antonio Healy-Murphy
1989		AAAA	Houston Strake Jesuit
AAA	N/A	**1976**	
AAAA	Dallas Jesuit	AAA	Galveston O'Connell
1988		AAAA	Houston Strake Jesuit
AAA	Houston Marian Christian	**1975**	
AAAA	Houston Strake Jesuit	AAA	San Antonio Healy-Murphy

Private schools boys basketball championships

Division	Champion
AAAA	San Antonio Central Catholic
1974	
AAA	San Antonio Healy-Murphy
AAAA	San Antonio Central Catholic
1973	
AAA	Laredo St. Joseph
AAAA	Houston Mount Carmel
1972	
AAA	Laredo St. Joseph
AAAA	Dallas Bishop Dunne
1971	
AAA	San Antonio St. Peter Claver
AAAA	Dallas Jesuit
1970	
AAA	Wichita Falls Notre Dame
AAAA	Dallas Jesuit
1969	
AAA	San Antonio St. Anthony
AAAA	Houston Mount Carmel
1968	
AAA	San Antonio Central Catholic
AAAA	San Antonio Antonian
1967	
AAA	San Antonio St. Anthony
AAAA	San Antonio Central Catholic
1966	
AAA	San Antonio St. Peter Claver
AAAA	San Antonio Central Catholic
1965	
AAA	San Antonio St. Peter Claver
AAAA	San Antonio Central Catholic
1964	
AAA	Dallas St. Peter's Academy
AAAA	San Antonio Central Catholic
1963	
AAA	San Antonio St. Peter Claver
AAAA	Houston St. Thomas
1962	
AAA	Port Arthur Sacred Heart
AAAA	Dallas Jesuit
1961	
AAA	San Antonio St. Peter Claver
AAAA	San Antonio Central Catholic

Division	Champion
1960	
AAA	Port Arthur Sacred Heart
AAAA	El Paso Cathedral
1959	
AAA	Port Arthur Sacred Heart
AAAA	Dallas Jesuit
1958	
AAA	Brownsville St. Joseph
AAAA	Houston St. Thomas
1957	
AAA	Brownsville St. Joseph
AAAA	El Paso Cathedral
1956	
AAA	Victoria St. Joseph
AAAA	Houston St. Thomas
1955	
AAA	San Antonio St. Gerard
AAAA	Dallas Jesuit
1954	Houston St. Thomas
1953	Houston St. Thomas
1952	Houston St. Thomas
1951	San Antonio Central Catholic
1950	El Paso Cathedral
1949	San Antonio Central Catholic
1948	San Antonio Central Catholic
1947	no tournament
1946	San Antonio Central Catholic
1943-45	no tournaments
1942	El Paso Cathedral
1941	El Paso Cathedral
1940	El Paso Cathedral
1939	El Paso Cathedral
1938	El Paso Cathedral
1937	San Antonio Central Catholic
1936	El Paso Cathedral
1935	Abilene St. Joseph

TAPPS: Texas Association of Private and Parochial Schools

Following are listed the boys basketball team champions of the TAPPS, as information was available. *Sources: Various press reports and Internet websites.*

Division	Champion
2011	
A	Boerne Geneva
AA	Kingwood Northeast
AAA	Conroe The Woodlands
AAAA	Arlington Grace Prep
AAAAA	Houston St. Thomas
2010	
A	Dallas Tyler Street
AA	Rowlett Rockwall Christian
AAA	Bullard Brook Hill
AAAA	Houston Second Baptist
AAAAA	Plano Prestonwood

Division	Champion
2009	
A	Dallas Tyler Street
AA	Kingwood Northwest
AAA	The Woodlands Christian
AAAA	Houston Westbury Christian
AAAAA	Addison Trinity Christian
2008	
A	Dickinson Living Faith
AA	Sherman Texoma
AAA	The Woodlands Christian
AAAA	Cedar Hill Trinity Christian
AAAAA	Midland Christian

Private schools boys basketball championships

Division	Champion
AAAAAA	Houston St. Thomas
2007	
A	Dickinson LIving Faith
AA	DeSoto Canterbury
AAA	Fort Worth Bethesda
AAAA	Cypress Christian
AAAAA	Midland Christian
AAAAAA	Houston St. Pius
2006	
A	DeSoto Canterbury
AA	Grand Prairie Shady Grove
AAA	Fort Worth Lake Country
AAAA	Cypress Christian
AAAAA	Houston Westbury Christian
AAAAAA	Beaumont Kelly
2005	
A	Sherman Texoma
AA	Colleyville Covenant
AAA	Grapevine Faith
AAAA	Cypress Christian
AAAAA	Houston Westbury Christian
AAAAAA	Beaumont Kelly
2004	
A	Fort Worth Ambassadors
AA	Kingwood Northeast
AAA	Carrollton Chrisitan
AAAA	Houston Westbury Christian
AAAAA	Austin St. Michael's
2003	
A	Fort Worth Ambassadors
AA	Kingwood Northeast
AAA	Cypress Christian
AAAA	Houston Westbury Christian
AAAAA	Austin St. Michael's
2002	
A	Fort Worth Ambassadors
AA	Kingwood Northeast
AAA	Arlington Grace Prep
AAAA	Tyler Grace Community
AAAAA	Dallas Bishop Lynch
2001	
A	Cleveland Christian Heritage
AA	Houston Sweetwater Christian
AAA	Houston Westbury Christian
AAAA	Houston Christian
AAAAA	Harlingen Marine Military
2000	
A	Cleveland Christian Heritage
AA	Carrollton American Heritage
AAA	Houston Westbury Christian
AAAA	Houston Second Baptist
AAAAA	Addison Trinity Christian
1999	
A	Cleveland Christian Heritage
AA	Waco Christian
AAA	Houston Westbury Christian
AAAA	Lubbock Trinity Christian
AAAAA	San Antonio Antonian
1998	
A	Beaumont Living Waters
AA	Bulverde Bracken Christian
AAA	Grand Prairie Shady Grove

Division	Champion
AAAA	Houston Westbury Christian
AAAAA	San Antonio Central Catholic
1997	
A	Beaumont Living Waters
AA	Waxahachie Cornerstone
AAA	Grand Prairie Shady Grove
AAAA	Houston Westbury Christian
AAAAA	Houston Second Baptist
1996	
A	West Houston Christian
AA	Houston Westbury Christian
AAA	Dallas Christian
1995	
A	Cleveland Christian Heritage
AA	Houston Westbury Christian
AAA	Houston St. Pius
1994	
A	Dallas Tyler Street
AA	Houston Westbury Christian
AAA	Addison Trinity Christian
1993	
A	Dallas Tyler Street
AA	Grapevine Faith Christian
AAA	Austin Hyde Park Baptist
1992	
A	Dallas Lexington Academy
AA	Houston Westbury Christian
AAA	Houston Academy Hall
1991	
A	Conroe Lifestyle Christian
AA	Houston Westbury Christian
AAA	Corpus Christi Incarnate Word
1990	
A	Dallas Lakehill Prep
AA	Lubbock Christian
AAA	Corpus Christi Incarnate Word
1989	
A	Amarillo Christian
AA	Lubbock Christian
AAA	Houston Marian Christian
1988	
Division II	Tomball Concordia Lutheran
Division I	Austin Hyde Park Baptist
1987	
Division II	Dallas Tyler Street
Division I	Dallas First Baptist
1986	
Division II	Dallas Tyler Street
Division I	Dallas First Baptist
1985	
Division II	Dallas Tyler Street
Division I	Dallas First Baptist
1984	Garland Christian
1983	Houston Life Christian
1982	Highlands Chinquapin
1981	Abilene Christian
1980	Houston Northwest Academy
1979	Abilene Christian
1978	Abilene Christian

Private High School Girls Basketball Champions

TCIL: Texas Christian Interscholastic League

Following are listed the girls basketball team champions of the TCIL, as information was available. *Sources: Various press reports and Internet websites.*

Division	Champion
1998	
AAA	
AAAA	St. Michael's
1997	
AAA	
AAAA	St. Michael's
1992	
AAA	
AAAA	Dallas Bishop Lynch
1991	
AAA	
AAAA	Dallas Bishop Lynch
1990	
AAA	
AAAA	Dallas Bishop Lynch
1989	
AAA	
AAAA	Dallas Bishop Lynch
1988	
AAA	
AAAA	Houston St. Agnes
1986	
AAA	Dallas Ursuline
AAAA	Dallas Bishop Lynch
1983	
AAA	Muenster Sacred Heart
AAAA	Dallas Bishop Lynch
1982	
AAA	Houston Lutheran
AAAA	Dallas Bishop Lynch
1981	
AAA	Corpus Christi Incarnate Word
AAAA	Houston Mount Carmel

Division	Champion
1980	
AAA	Corpus Christi Incarnate Word
AAAA	Houston Mount Carmel
1979	
AAA	Lubbock Christ the King
AAAA	Dallas Bishop Lynch
1978	
AAA	Lubbock Christ the King
AAAA	Houston Mount Carmel
1977	
AAA	Ennis St. John
AAAA	Dallas Bishop Lynch
1976	
AAA	Ennis St. John
AAAA	Dallas Bishop Lynch
1975	
AAA	Ennis St. John
AAAA	Dallas Bishop Dunne
1974	
AAA	
AAAA	Corpus Christi Incarnate Word
1973	
AAA	
AAAA	Corpus Christi Incarnate Word
1972	
AAA	
AAAA	Corpus Christi Incarnate Word
1971	
AAA	
AAAA	Amarillo Alamo Catholic

TAPPS: Texas Association of Private and Parochial Schools

Following are listed the girls basketball team champions of the TAPPS, as information was available. *Sources: Various press reports and Internet websites.*

Division	Champion
2011	
A	Granbury Happy Hill
AA	Sherman Texoma Christian
AAA	Tomball Rosehill
AAAA	Houston Westbury Christian
AAAAA	Argyle Liberty Christian
2010	
A	Boerne Geneva
AA	Sherman Texoma
AAA	Amarillo San Jacinto
AAAA	Houston Westbury Christian
AAAAA	Dallas Bishop Lynch
2009	
A	Plainview Christian
AA	Sherman Texoma

Division	Champion
AAA	Amarillo San Jacinto
AAAA	Houston Westbury Christian
AAAAA	Dallas Bishop Lynch
2008	
A	San Antonio Christian Academy
AA	Sherman Texoma
AAA	Midland Classical
AAAA	Fort Wroth Lake Country
AAAAA	Argyle Liberty Christian
AAAAAA	Dallas Bishop Lynch
2007	
A	San Antonio Believers
AA	Muenster Sacred Heart
AAA	Amarillo San Jacinto
AAAA	Grapevine Faith Christian

Private schools girls basketball championships

Division	Champion
AAAAA	Argyle Liberty Christian
AAAAAA	Dallas Bishop Lynch
2006	
A	Sherman Texoma
AA	Colleyville Covenant
AAA	Lubbock Christian
AAAA	Lubbock Trinity
AAAAA	Fort Worth Christian
AAAAAA	Dallas Bishop Lynch
2005	
A	San Antonio Believers
AA	Midland Classical
AAA	Fort Worth Lake Country
AAAA	Lubbock Trinity
AAAAA	Fort Worth Christian
AAAAAA	Dallas Bishop Lynch
2004	
A	McKinney Christian
AA	Muenster Sacred Heart
AAA	Fort Worth Lake Country
AAAA	Lubbock Trinity
AAAAA	Dallas Bishop Lynch
2003	
A	San Antonio Believers
AA	Muenster Sacred Heart
AAA	Fort Worth Lake Country
AAAA	Lubbock Trinity
AAAAA	Dallas Bishop Lynch
2002	
A	San Antonio Believers
AA	Muenster Sacred Heart
AAA	Houston Westbury Christian
AAAA	Fort Worth Christian
AAAAA	Dallas Bishop Lynch
2001	
A	Conroe Covenant
AA	Muenster Sacred Heart
AAA	Houston Westbury Christian
AAAA	Austin St. Michael's
AAAAA	Addison Trinity Christian
2000	
A	Round Rock Christian
AA	Muenster Sacred Heart
AAA	Houston Westbury Christian
AAAA	Dallas Bishop Dunne
AAAAA	Dallas Bishop Lynch
1999	
A	Shiner St. Paul
AA	Muenster Sacred Heart
AAA	Lubbock Christian
AAAA	Austin St. Michael's
AAAAA	Dallas Bishop Lynch
1998	
A	Dallas Lakewood Presbyterian
AA	Muenster Sacred Heart
AAA	Wichita Falls Notre Dame
AAAA	League City Bay Area Christian
AAAAA	Dallas Bishop Lynch
1997	
A	La Marque Abundant Life
AA	Katy Faith West

Division	Champion
AAA	Dallas Lexington Academy
AAAA	Houston Westbury Christian
AAAAA	Dallas Bishop Lynch
1996	
A	Cedar Park Hilltop Baptist
AA	Lubbock Christian
AAA	Dallas Bishop Lynch
1995	
A	Cedar Park Hilltop Baptist
AA	Waco Vanguard
AAA	Dallas Bishop Lynch
1994	
A	Lubbock Trinity
AA	Waco Vanguard
AAA	Dallas Bishop Lynch
1993	
A	Shiner St. Paul
AA	Waco Vanguard
AAA	Dallas Bishop Lynch
1992	
A	Midland Christian
AA	Waco Vanguard
AAA	Dallas Bishop Lynch
1991	
A	Denton Selwyn
AA	Lubbock Christian
AAA	Dallas Bishop Lynch
1990	
A	Muenster Sacred Heart
AA	Lubbock Christian
AAA	Corpus Christi Incarnate Word
1989	
A	Muenster Sacred Heart
AA	Hallettsville Sacred Heart
AAA	Houston Northwest Academy
1988	
Division II	Muenster Sacred Heart
Division I	Fort Worth Nolan
1987	
Division II	Lubbock Christian
Division I	Fort Worth Nolan
1986	
Division II	Dallas Tyler Street
Division I	Fort Worth Nolan
1985	
Division II	Dallas Tyler Street
Division I	Fort Worth Nolan
1984	Houston Northwest Academy
1983	Fort Worth Country Day
1982	Houston Northwest Academy
1981	Lubbock Christian
1980	Lubbock Christian
1979	Abilene Christian

NBA Champions 2011

The Maverick's Dirk Nowitzki (41) is guarded by Rashad Lewis in a game of the 2011 championship season. Coach Rick Carlisle, at right. Photos by Keith Allison (CC).

The Dallas Mavericks defeated the Miami Heat four games to two in the National Basketball Assocation Championship series in June 2011.

Lead by Dirk Nowitzki and coached by Rick Carlisle, the Mavericks reversed the outcome of their last trip to the finals in 2006 when they lost to Miami.

Nowitzki was also named the Most Valuable Player of the 2011 NBA finals.

Since their inaugural season in 1980, the Mavs have won three division titles (1987, 2007, 2010), two conference championships (2006 and 2011) and been to the playoffs 16 times.

Professional Football in Texas

Professional football first arrived in Texas in the fall of 1952 when a 16-member syndicate purchased the National Football League franchise that had been known as the New York Yanks. The team, coached by Jim Phelan, enjoyed little success playing in the Cotton Bowl as the Dallas Texans. By the end of the season, after the league had bought back the franchise, the Texans were playing "home" games elsewhere, including Akron, Ohio, where they had their only victory, 27-23, over the Chicago Bears of George Halas.

Dallas Texans (NFL)

Year	Win	Loss	Tie
– 1951 played as the New York Yanks			
1952	1	11	0

1953 — remnants of the team became the new Baltimore Colts, including Pro Football Hall of Famers Art Donovan and Gino Marchetti.

The coin toss at the AFL championship game in 1962 between the Dallas Texans and the Houston Oilers.

Big-time professional football returned to Texas when Bud Adams of Houston and Lamar Hunt of Dallas started the American Football League in 1959. In October 1959, Adams announced the Houston team would be known as the Oilers. Hunt's team was named the Texans and played in the Cotton Bowl. AFL play began in 1960.

The Oilers were an immediate success, winning the first AFL championship by defeating the Los Angeles Chargers in January 1961.

The Dallas Texans, meanwhile, had difficulties. They found themselves battling for ticket sales with the new National Football League expansion team owned by Clint Murchison Jr., the Dallas Cowboys.

In May of 1963 the Cowboys had their first major victory when Hunt announced he was moving his team to Kansas City, where it would be renamed the Chiefs.

When the city of Houston declined to build a new stadium for the Oilers, who had been playing in the Astrodome, Adams moved his team in 1997 to Nashville, where it was renamed the Tennessee Titans.

Dallas Texans (AFL)

Year	Win	Loss	Tie	Playoffs
1960	8	6	0	
1961	6	8	0	
1962	11	3	0	won AFL championship over Houston Oilers
1963 — team moved to Kansas City to become the Chiefs				

Houston Oilers (AFL–NFL)

Year	Win	Loss	Tie	Playoffs
1960	10	4	0	won AFL championship over Los Angeles Chargers
1961	10	3	1	won AFL championship over San Diego Chargers
1962	11	3	0	lost AFL championship to Dallas Texans
1963	6	8	0	
1964	4	10	0	
1965	4	10	0	
1966	3	11	0	
1967	9	4	1	lost AFL championship to Oakland Raiders
1968	7	7	0	
1969	6	6	2	lost divisional playoff to Oakland Raiders
AFL, NFL merge				
1970	3	10	1	
1971	4	9	1	
1972	1	13	0	
1973	1	13	0	
1974	7	7	0	
1975	10	4	0	
1976	5	9	0	
1977	8	6	0	
1978	10	6	0	2nd AFC Central; lost AFC championship to Pittsburgh Steelers
1979	11	5	0	2nd AFC Central; lost AFC championship to Pittsburgh Steelers
1980	11	5	0	2nd AFC Central; lost wild-card playoff to Oakland Raiders
1981	7	9	0	
1982	1	8	0	(players' strike)
1983	2	13	0	
1984	3	13	0	
1985	5	11	0	
1986	5	11	0	
1987	9	6	0	2nd AFC Central; lost divisional playoff to Denver Broncos
1988	10	6	0	3rd AFC Central; lost divisional playoff to Buffalo Bills
1989	9	7	0	2nd AFC Central; lost wild-card playoff to Pittsburgh Steelers
1990	9	7	0	2nd AFC Central; lost wild-card playoff to Cincinnati Bengals
1991	11	5	0	1st AFC Central; lost divisonal playoff to Denver Broncos
1992	10	6	0	2nd AFC Central; lost wild-card playoff to Buffalo Bills
1993	12	4	0	1st AFC Central; lost divisional playoff to Kansas City Chiefs
1994	2	14	0	
1995	7	9	0	
1996	8	8	0	

1997 — moved to Tennessee, renamed the Titans in 1999.

Dallas Cowboys (NFL)

The National Football League expanded to 13 teams in January 1960 when Dallas businessman Clint Murchison Jr. was granted a franchise.

His Dallas Cowboys (originally to be called the Dallas Rangers) were organized too late to take part in the college draft that year and did not win a single game in the 1960 season.

Since that first year, the Cowboys have developed into one of the most popular teams in the NFL.

Under head coaches Tom Landry, Jimmy Johnson and Barry Switzer, the Cowboys have gone to the Super Bowl eight times, winning five times, and have advanced to the playoffs 30 times. The team now plays at the new Cowboys Stadium in Arlington.

Year	Win	Loss	Tie	Playoffs
1960	0	11	1	
1961	4	9	1	
1962	5	8	1	
1963	4	10	0	

Chuck Howley intercepts a Bob Griese pass during the Cowboys' first Super Bowl victory in January 1972. Dallas beat the Miami Dolphins 24–3. Cowboy quarterback Roger Staubach (12) stands on the sidelines.

Year	Win	Loss	Tie	Playoffs
1964	5	8	1	
1965	7	7	0	
1966	10	3	1	1st Eastern Conf.; lost NFL championship to Green Bay Packers
1967	9	5	0	1st Capitol Div.; lost NFL championship to Green Bay Packers
1968	12	2	0	1st Capitol Div.; lost divisional playoff to Cleveland Browns
1969	11	2	1	1st Capitol Div.; lost divisional playoff to Cleveland Browns
AFL, NFL merge				
1970	10	4	0	1st NFC East; lost Super Bowl to Baltimore Colts
1971	11	3	0	1st NFC East; won Super Bowl over Miami Dolphins
1972	10	4	0	2nd NFC East; lost NFC championship to Washington Redskins
1973	10	4	0	1st NFC East; lost NFC championship to Minnesota Vikings
1974	8	6	0	
1975	10	4	0	2nd NFC East; lost Super Bowl to Pittsburgh Steelers
1976	11	3	0	1st NFC East; lost divisional playoff to Los Angeles Rams
1977	12	2	0	1st NFC East; won Super Bowl over Denver Broncos
1978	12	4	0	1st NFC East; lost Super Bowl to Pittsburgh Steelers
1979	11	5	0	1st NFC East; lost divisional playoff to Los Angeles Rams
1980	12	4	0	2nd NFC East; lost NFC championship to Philadelphia Eagles
1981	12	4	0	1st NFC East; lost NFC championship to San Francisco 49ers
1982	6	3	0	(players' strike); lost NFC championship to Washington Redskins
1983	12	4	0	2nd NFC East; lost wild-card playoff to Los Angeles Rams
1984	9	7	0	
1985	10	6	0	1st NFC East; lost divisional playoff to Los Angeles Rams
1986	7	9	0	
1987	7	8	0	
1988	3	13	0	
1989	1	15	0	
1990	7	9	0	
1991	11	5	0	2nd NFC East; lost divisional playoff to Detroit Lions
1992	13	3	0	1st NFC East; won Super Bowl over Buffalo Bills
1993	13	3	0	1st NFC East; won Super Bowl over Buffalo Bills
1994	12	4	0	1st NFC East; lost NFC championship to San Francisco 49ers

Year	Win	Loss	Tie	Playoffs
1995	12	4	0	1st NFC East; won Super Bowl over Pittsburgh Steelers
1996	10	6	0	1st NFC East; lost divisional playoff to Carolina Panthers
1997	6	10	0	
1998	10	6	0	1st NFC East; lost wild-card playoff to Arizona Cardinals
1999	8	8	0	2nd NFC East; lost wild-card playoff to Minnesota Vikings
2000	5	11	0	
2001	5	11	0	
2002	5	11	0	
2003	10	6	0	2nd NFC East; lost wild-card playoff to Carolina Panthers
2004	6	10	0	
2005	9	7	0	
2006	9	7	0	2nd NFC East; lost wild-card playoff to Seattle Seahawks
2007	13	3	0	1st NFC East; lost divisional playoff to New York Giants
2008	9	7	0	
2009	11	5	0	1st NFC East; lost divisional playoff to Minnesota Vikings
2010	6	10	0	

Reliant Stadium, home of the Houston Texans, has a retractable roof.

Houston Texans (NFL)

After Bud Adams moved to Tennessee, Houston decided to build a new football stadium in order to get a National Football League expansion franchise.

On Oct. 6, 1999, the NFL team owners voted 29-0 to award their 32nd franchise to Houston and businessman Bob McNair.

In September 2002, the Texans became the first NFL team in 41 years to win their expansion debut, stunning the Dallas Cowboys 19-10 before 69,604 at the brand-new Reliant Stadium in Houston.

Year	Win	Loss	Tie	Playoffs
2002	4	12	0	
2003	5	11	0	
2004	7	9	0	
2005	2	14	0	
2006	6	10	0	
2007	8	8	0	
2008	8	8	0	
2009	9	7	0	
2010	6	10	0	

Other professional football leagues

The United States Football League played for three seasons, 1983-85, with teams in San Antonio and Houston after the initial season.

The Gamblers, who played in the Astrodome, were coached by former NFL head coach Jack Pardee. The most notable player was future Buffalo Bills quarterback Jim Kelly.

The San Antonio Gunslingers, owned by oilman Clint Manges, were quarterbacked by Rick Neuheisel. Their home games were in Alamo Stadium.

Houston Gamblers (USFL)

Year	Win	Loss	Tie	Playoffs
1984	13	5	0	lost quarterfinal to Arizona Wranglers
1985	10	8	0	lost quarterfinal to Birmingham Stallions

San Antonio Gunslingers (USFL)

Year	Win	Loss	Tie	Playoffs
1984	7	11	0	
1985	10	13	0	

San Antonio Wings and Houston Texans (WFL)

The World Football League played in 1974 and part of 1975, with teams briefly in Houston and San Antonio.

In 1974, the Texans played in the Houston Astrodome for eleven games, going 3-7-1, before the franchise moved to northern Louisiana to become the Shreveport Steamer. The team finished the year with a 7-12-1 record overall.

In 1975, the San Antonio Wings were the brief, last incarnation of the Washington-Baltimore Ambassadors, Virginia Ambassadors, Florida Blazers. The Wings played home games in 23,000-seat Alamo Stadium and finished with a 7-6 record before the league disbanded in October 1975.

San Antonio Riders (WLAF)

The World League of American Football was founded in 1990 with the support of the National Football League. The San Antonio Riders played in 1991 in Alamo Stadium with a 4-6 record and in 1992 in Bobcat Stadium in San Marcos with a 7-3 record.

When the NFL suspended the league after the 1992 season, the San Antonio and Sacramento teams were accepted into the Canadian Football League, but the San Antonio franchise folded before the beginning of the 1993 season.

The NFL revived the WLAF with European teams in 1995. It existed as NFL Europe until 2007.

Houston Outlaws (RFL)

The Regional Football League existed for one season in 1999. The Houston Outlaws played most of their home games at Memorial Stadium in Pasadena and went 7-2. They were defeated 14-12 by the Mobile Admirals before 5,500 fans in Mobile in the only championship game.

San Antonio Matadors and Houston Marshals (SFL)

The Spring Football League played for less than a month in 2000. Besides the teams in San Antonio and Houston, there were teams in Los Angeles and Miami.

The San Antonio Matadors and the Houston Marshals, both with 2-0 records, were declared league co-champions before the league folded.

Go to texasalmanac/topics/sports.com for more Texas sports information.

Texas Sports Hall of Fame

The Texas Sports Hall of Fame was organized in 1951 by the Texas Sports Writers Association. Each year the honorees are inducted into the Hall of Fame at a gala dinner.

The hall of fame was originally in Grand Prairie in the Dallas-Fort Worth area.

The Hall of Fame was closed in 1986 for financial reasons, but in 1991 it was reopened in Waco.

In addition to memorabilia, the new location also houses archives.

Under the current selection process, dues-paying members of the Texas Sports Hall of Fame can nominate any number of individuals. (Anyone can become a member.)

The selection committee, chaired by Dave Campbell, founder of *Texas Football Magazine,* reviews all nominees and creates the "Official Voting Membership" ballot.

Ballots are then mailed to the voting membership, former Texas Sports Hall of Fame inductees and the media selection committee.

The results of the balloting are announced in the fall with the induction banquet following in the winter.

The hall of fame web site is at www.tshof.org.

Bela Karolyi. Photo by Taty2007 (GFDL).

Year	Inductee	Sport	Texas connection, career
	From the Texas Sports Hall of Fame, The Handbook of Texas, The Dallas Morning News and other sources.		
2010	Charley Johnson	Football	Big Spring, pro quarterback 1961-75, Houston Oilers
	Donna Lopiano	Womens Sports	Softball All-American, UT women's athletic director 1975-92
	Clint Murchison	Football	initial owner of Dallas Cowboys 1960-1984
	Drew Pearson	Football	Dallas Cowboys receiver 1973-1983
	John Randle	Football	Hearne, Texas A&I lineman, NFL 1990-03, Minnesota Vikings
	Jim Sundberg	Baseball	MLB catcher 1974-89, executive, Texas Rangers
	Emmitt Thomas	Football	Angleton, Bishop College, Kansas City Chiefs 1966-78
	Willie Willis	Baseball	Austin, Negro League shortstop 1920s-30s
	Laura Wilkinson	Swimming	Spring, Olympic Gold in diving 2000, UT All-American
2009	Bud Adams	Football	Houston Oilers owner, co-founder AFL 1960
	Lance Berkman	Baseball	Waco, New Braunfels Canyon, Rice, Houston Astros
	Lawrence Elkins	Football	Brownwood, Baylor receiver, Houston Oilers 1965-68
	Burt Hooton	Baseball	UT, Cubs, Dodgers, Texas Rangers 1985, Astros coach
	Chuck Howley	Football	Dallas Cowboys linebacker 1961-73
	Tommy Kramer	Football	San Antonio, Rice quarterback, Minnesota Vikings 1977-89
	Harvey Martin	Football	East Texas State, Dallas Cowboys defensive end 1973-83
	Kim Mulkey	Basketball	Baylor women's coach 2000-
	Dan Reeves	Football	Dallas Cowboys running back/QB 1965-72, NFL coach
	Max Williams	Basketball	Avoca, SMU, coach Dallas Chaparrals 1969-70
2008	Rolando Blackman	Basketball	Olympics 1980, Dallas Mavericks 1981-92
	Bill Bradley	Football	Palestine, UT, Philadelphia Eagles defensive back 1969-76
	Lee Roy Jordan	Football	Dallas Cowboys linebacker 1963-76
	Abe Lemons	Basketball	UT coach 1977-82
	Kyle Rote Jr.	Soccer	Dallas Tornado 1973-78, Houston Hurricane 1979
	LaDainian Tomlinson	Football	Waco, TCU, San Diego Chargers running back 2001-
	Steve Worster	Football	Bridge City, UT fullback 1968-70
2007	Leta Andrews	Basketball	Granbury 1954-55, coach 1962- at Calallen, Granbury, others
	Ray Childress	Football	Richardson, A&M tackle, Houston Oilers 1985-95
	Spike Dykes	Basketball	coach at Coahoma, Midland Lee, others, Texas Tech 1986-99
	Mia Hamm	Soccer	Wichita Falls, college/national/Olympics 1989-2004
	Abner Haynes	Football	North Texas, Dallas Texans running back, AFL 1960-67
	Michael Irvin	Football	Dallas Cowboys receiver 1988-99
	Mike Modano	Hockey	Dallas Stars 1993-2010
	Jim Ray Smith	Football	West Columbia, Baylor, Cleveland 1956-62, Cowboys 1962-64

Year	Inductee	Sport	Texas connection, career
2006	DeLoss Dodds	Athletics	UT athletic director, 1981-
	Rafer Johnson	Olympics	Olympic decathlon 1956, 1960, Hillsboro native
	Jerry Jones	Football	Dallas Cowboys owner, 1989-
	Roosevelt Leaks	Football	UT running back 1972-74, Brenham
	Warren Moon	Football	Houston Oilers quarterback, 1984-93
	Don Perkins	Football	Dallas Cowboys running back, 1961-68
	Billy Sims	Football	Oklahoma, Heisman 1978, Hooks native
2005	Bobby Bragan	Baseball	Fort Worth Cats manager, Houston Colt .45s coach
	Tim Brown	Football	Notre Dame, Heisman, NFL 1988-04, from Dallas
	Augie Garrido	Baseball	UT coach, 1997-
	Zina Garrison	Tennis	Houston, Olympics 1988, pro 1982-96
	Bela Karolyi	Gymnastics	Trainer, Olympics coach, Houston resident
	Martha Karolyi	Gymnastics	Trainer, Olympics coach, Houston resident
	James Segrest	Track	Coach, Odessa College 1973-94
	R.C. Slocum	Football	A&M coach, 1989-2003
	Emmitt Smith	Football	Dallas Cowboys running back, 1990-2002
2004	Jeff Bagwell	Baseball	Houston Astros, 1991-2004
	Craig Biggio	Baseball	Houston Astros, 1988-2007
	Wayne Graham	Baseball	Coach, San Jacinto Jr. College, Rice 1992-
	Harley Redin	Basketball	Coach, Wayland Baptist 1946-73, U.S. national teams
	Mary Lou Retton	Gymnastics	Olympics 1984, Houston resident
	Rayfield Wright	Football	Dallas Cowboys tackle, 1967-79
2003	Elvin Bethea	Football	Houston Oilers lineman, 1968-83
	Carroll Dawson	Basketball	Alba, coach Baylor 1973-77, Houston Rockets exec.
	Bob Hayes	Football	Dallas Cowboys receiver 1965-74
	Robert Hughes	Basketball	Winningest coach 1958- 2005, Fort Worth high schools
	Rudy Tomjanovich	Basketball	Player, coach, Houston Rockets beginning 1970
	Stanley Williams	Football	Cisco, Baylor 1949-51, All America
	Bill Yeoman	Football	Coach, University of Houston, 1962-86

Zina Garrison. File Photo.

LaDainian Tomlinson. Photo by Dirk (CC).

Lance Berkman. Photo by Mojo (CC).

Go to texasalmanac/topics/sports.com for the complete list of inductees from 1951.

Texas Olympic Medalists

This is a list of athletes with Texas connections who have won medals in Olympic Games. This includes those born here or have lived in Texas, as well as U.S. team members who spent their collegiate careers at Texas universities.

Information included is: the athlete's name, the sport and the year, as well as the types of medals (G-Gold, S-Silver, B-Bronze).

If the athlete won more than one of the same kind of medal in any one year, the number is noted before the letter code; i.e., 2G indicates that the athlete won two gold medals in the games indicated.

The symbol (†) following the medal code indicates that the athlete participated in preliminary contests only; the medal was awarded because of membership on a winning team. Years in which the athlete participated in the Games but did not win a medal are not included.

Track indicates all track and field events except those noted separately.

Source: United States Olympic Committee

Olympian	Sport	Year	Medal
Abdallah, Nia Nicole	Taekwondo	2004	S
Allen, Chad	Baseball	1996	B
Armstrong, Lance	Cycling	2000	B
Arnette, Jay Hoyland	Basketball	1960	G
Austin, Charles	Track	1996	G
Baker, Walter Thane	Track	1956	G,S,B
		1952	S
Baptiste, Kirk	Track	1984	S
Barr, Beth	Swimming	1988	S
Bassham, Lanny Robert	Shooting	1976	G
		1972	S
Bates, Michael D.	Track	1992	B
Beck, Robert Lee	Pentathlon	1960	2B
Bedforth, B.J.	Swimming	2000	G
Berens, Ricky	Swimming	2008	G
Berube, Ryan Thomas	Swimming	1996	G
Brew, Derrick K.	Track	2004	G, B
Brown, Earlene Dennis	Track	1960	B
Browning, David (Skippy)	Diving	1952	G
Buckner, William Quinn	Basketball	1976	G
Buford-Bailey, Tonja	Track	1996	B
Burrell, Leroy Russel	Track	1992	G
Carey, Rick	Swimming	1984	3G
Carlisle, Daniel T.	Shooting	1984	B
Carter, Michael D.	Shotput	1984	S
Clay, Bryan E.	Decathlon	2008	G
		2004	S
Cline, Nancy Lieberman	Basketball	1976	S
Cohen, Tiffany	Swimming	1984	G
Corbelli, Laurie Flachmeier	Volleyball	1984	S
Cotton, John	Baseball	2000	G
Crocker, Ian	Swimming	2008	G
		2004	G,S,B
		2000	G
Cross-Battle, Tara	Volleyball	1992	B
Davis, Clarissa G.	Basketball	1992	B
Davis, Jack Wells	Track	1956	S
		1952	S
Davis, Josh C.	Swimming	2000	2S
		1996	3G
Davis, W.F. (Buddy)	High Jump	1952	G
DeLoach, Joseph N. Jr.	Track	1988	G
Dersch, Hans	Swimming	1992	G
Didrikson, Mildred (Babe)	Track	1932	2G, S

Olympian	Sport	Year	Medal
Donie, Scott R.	Diving	1992	S
Drexler, Clyde	Basketball	1992	G
Dusing, Nate	Swimming	2004	B
		2000	S
Eller, Glenn	Shooting	2008	G
Ethridge, Mary (Kamie)	Basketball	1988	G
Farmer-Patrick, Sandra	Track	1992	S
Finn-Burrell, Michelle Bonae	Track	1992	G
Forbes, James Ricardo	Basketball	1972	S
Ford, Gilbert (Gib)	Basketball	1956	B
Foreman, George	Boxing	1968	G
Fortenberry, Joe Cephis	Basketball	1936	G
Garrison, Zina	Tennis	1988	G, B
George, Chris	Baseball	2000	G
Gjertson, Doug	Swimming	1992	G, B
		1988	G
Glenesk, Dean William	Pentathlon	1984	S
Goldblatt, Scott	Swimming	2004	G
		2000	B
Gonzáles, Paul G. Jr.	Boxing	1984	G
Guidry, Carlette D.	Track	1996	G†
		1992	G
Hall, Gary Jr.	Swimming	2004	G, B
		2000	2G,S,B
		1996	2G, 2S
Hamm, Mia	Soccer	2004	G
		2000	S
		1996	G
Hannan, Tommy	Swimming	2000	G
Hansen, Brendan	Swimming	2008	G
		2004	G,S,B
Hansen, Fred Morgan	Track	1964	G
Harkrider, Kiplan P.	Baseball	1996	B
Hartwell, Erin Wesley	Cycling	1996	S
		1992	B
Hays, Todd	Bobsled	2002	S
Heath, Michael Steward	Swimming	1984	2G, S
Hedgepeth, Whitney L.	Swimming	1996	G, 2S
Hedrick, Chad	Speed Skating	2010	S,B
		2006	G,S,B
Heidenreich, Jerry	Swimming	1972	2G,S,B
Henry, James Edward	Diving	1968	B

Bryan Clay, who won medals in 2004 and 2008, was born in Austin. Photo by Eckhard Pecher (CC).

Nastia Liukin, who was born in Russia, graduated from Spring Creek Academy in Plano and attended Southern Methodist University. Photo by Bryan Allison (CC).

Olympian	Sport	Year	Medal
Hill, Denean E.	Track	1992	S
		1988	S
		1984	G
Hill, Grant Henry	Basketball	1996	G
Homfeld, Conrad E.	Equestrian	1984	G, S
Hooper, Darrow	Shotput	1952	S
Horton, Jonathan	Gymnastics	2008	S
Howard, Sherri Francis	Track	1988	S
		1984	G
Jackson, Lucious Brown	Basketball	1964	G
Jacobs, Chris	Swimming	1988	2G, S
Johnson, Michael	Track	2000	2G
		1996	2G
		1992	G
Johnson, Rafer L.	Decathlon	1960	G
		1956	S
Jones, John Wesley(Lamb)	Track	1976	G
Jordan, Shaun	Swimming	1992	G
		1988	G
Juarez, Ricardo Rocky	Boxing	2000	S
Julich, Robert William	Cycling	2004	B
Keeler, Kathryn Elliott	Rowing	1984	G
Kern, Douglas James	Sailing	1992	S
Kiefer, Adolph	Swimming	1936	G
King, Judith Brown	Track	1984	S
Kleine, Megan	Swimming	1992	G†
Kolius, John Waldrip	Sailing	1976	S
Lane, Colleen	Swimming	2004	S
Langkop, Dorothy Franey	Speed Skating	1932	B
Leetch, Brian Joseph	Ice Hockey	2002	S
Lewis, F. (Carl) Carlton	Track	1996	G
		1992	2G
		1988	2G, S
		1984	4G
Lienhard, William Barner	Basketball	1952	G

Olympian	Sport	Year	Medal
Lipinski, Tara K.	Figure Skating	1998	G
Liukin, Nastia	Gymnastics	2008	G,3S,B
Lloyd, Andrea	Basketball	1988	G
Losey, Robert G. (Greg)	Pentathlon	1984	S
Lopez, Diana	Taekwondo	2008	B
Lopez, Mark	Taekwondo	2008	S
Lopez, Steve	Taekwondo	2008	B
Lowe, Sara Elizabeth	Swimming	2004	B
Magers, Rose Mary	Volleyball	1984	S
Malone, Jordan	Speed Skating	2010	B
Marsh, Michael L.	Track	1996	S
		1992	2G
Marshall, Christine	Swimming	2008	B
Matson, James Randel (Randy)	Shotput	1968	G
		1964	G
Matson, Ollie G.	Track	1952	S, B
McFalls, Jennifer Yvonne	Softball	2000	G
McFarlane, Tracey	Swimming	1988	S
McKenzie, Kim	Track	1984	B
Meadows, Earle	Track	1936	G
Mills, Ronald P.	Swimming	1968	B
Mitchell, Betsy	Swimming	1988	S
		1984	G, S
Moceanu, Dominique H.	Gymnastics	1996	G
Montgomery, James P.	Swimming	1976	3G, B
Moore, James Warren	Pentathlon	1964	S
Morrow, Bobby Joe	Track	1956	3G
Munoz, Felipe	Swimming	1968	G
Neilson-Bell, Sandy	Swimming	1972	3G
Nelson, Lianne Bennion	Rowing	2004	S
Newhouse, Frederick V.	Track	1976	G, S
Nott/Cunningham, Tara Lee	Weightlifting	2004	G
Okafor, Emeka	Basketball	2004	B
Olajuwon, Hakeem	Basketball	1996	G
Olsen, Justin	Bobsled	2010	G

Olympian	Sport	Year	Medal
Osterman, Catherine (Cat)	Softball	2008	S
		2004	G
Paddock, Charles W.	Track	1924	S
		1920	2G, S
Patton, Darvis	Track	2004	S
Peirsol, Aaron	Swimming	2008	2G, S
		2004	3G
		2000	S
Perry, Nanceen L.	Track	2000	B
Pesthy, Paul Karoly	Fencing	1964	S
Phenix, Erin	Swimming	2000	G
Postma, Joan Spillane	Swimming	1960	G
Potter, Cynthia Ann	Diving	1976	B
Rambo, John Barnett	Track	1964	B
Rauch, Jamie	Swimming	2000	S
Retton, Mary Lou	Gymnastics	1984	G,2S,2B
Richards, Robert E.	Track	1956	G
		1952	G
		1948	B
Richards, Sanya	Track	2008	G, B
		2004	G
Ritter, Louise	Track	1988	G
Robertson, Alvin Cyrrale	Basketball	1984	G
Robinson, David M.	Basketball	1996	G
		1992	G
		1988	B
Robinson, Moushaumi	Track	2004	G
Robinson, Robert J.	Basketball	1948	G
Robinzine, Kevin B.	Track	1988	G
Roe, Frederick	Polo	1924	S
Russell, Douglas Albert	Swimming	1968	2G
Russell, John William	Equestrian	1952	B
Schneider, Marcus B.	Rowing	1996	B
Slay, Brandon Douglas	Wrestling	2000	G
Smith, Dean	Track	1952	G
Smith, Lamont	Track	1996	G
Smith, Owen Guinn	Track	1948	G
Smith, Tommie C.	Track	1968	G
Southern, S. Edward	Track	1956	S
Steinseifer, Carrie	Swimming	1984	2G

Olympian	Sport	Year	Medal
Sterkle, Jill Ann	Swimming	1988	2B
		1984	G
		1976	G
Stevenson, Toby	Pole Vault	2004	S
Stulce, Michael S.	Shotput	1992	G
Swoopes, Sheryl Denise	Basketball	2004	G
		2000	G
		1996	G
Sykora, Stacy	Volleyball	2008	S
Taylor, Robert	Track	1972	G, S
Teagarden, Taylor	Baseball	2008	B
Tisdale, Wayman L.	Basketball	1984	G
Valdez, Jesse	Boxing	1972	B
Van, Allen	Ice Hockey	1952	S
Vollmer, Dana	Swimming	2004	G
Walker, Laura Anne	Swimming	1988	B
Walker, Neil	Swimming	2004	G, B
		2000	G, S
Walters, Dave	Swimming	2008	G
Wariner, Jeremy	Track	2008	G, S
		2004	2G
Weatherspoon, Teresa G.	Basketball	1992	B
		1988	G
Weber-Gale, Garrett	Swimming	2008	2G
Wells, Rhoshii S.	Boxing	1996	B
Wells, Wayne A.	Wrestling	1972	G
Whitfield, Malvin G.	Track	1952	G, S
		1948	G, S
Wilkinson, Laura A.	Diving	2000	G
Williams, Christa L.	Softball	2000	G
		1996	G
Williamson, Darold	Track	2004	G
Wilson, Craig Martin	Water Polo	1988	S
		1984	S
Wolfe, Rowland (Flip)	Gymnastics	1932	G
Wrightson, Bernard C.	Diving	1968	G
Wylie, Paul Stanton	Figure Skating	1992	S
Young, Earl Verdelle	Track	1960	2G
Zmeskal, Kim	Gymnastics	1992	B

Sanya Richards, who won medals in 2004 and 2008, lives in Austin. Photo by Andre Zehetbauer (CC).

Jeremy Wariner, who won medals in 2004 and 2008, graduated from Lamar High School in Arlington and attended Baylor University. Photo by Phil McElhinney (CC).

Counties

The Donley County Courthouse in Clarendon. Photo by Robert Plocheck.

History

Maps

Vital Statistics

Recreation

Population

Cities and Towns

Climate

Counties of Texas

These pages describe Texas' 254 counties and hundreds of towns. Descriptions are based on reports from chambers of commerce, the Texas Cooperative Extension, federal and state agencies, the *New Handbook of Texas* and other sources. Consult the index for other county information.

County maps are based on those of the Texas Department of Transportation and are copyrighted, 2011, as are the entire contents.

Physical Features: Descriptions are from U.S. Geological Survey and local sources.

Economy: From information provided by local chambers of commerce and county extension agents.

History: From Texas statutes, *Fulmore's History and Geography of Texas as Told in County Names*, WPA Historical Records Survey, Texas Centennial Commission Report and the *New Handbook of Texas*.

Ethnicity: Percentage estimates of 2008 from the Texas State Data Center, University of Texas at San Antonio. **Anglo** refers to non-Hispanic whites; **Black** refers to non-Hispanic blacks; **Hispanic** refers to Hispanics of all races; **Other** is composed of persons from all other racial groups who are non-Hispanic.

Vital Statistics: From the Texas Department of State Health Services Annual Report 2008, except for marriages/divorces, which are from 2007.

Recreation: From information provided by local chambers of commerce and county extension agents. Attempts were made to note activities unique to the area or that point to ethnic or cultural heritage.

Minerals: From county extension agents.

Agriculture: Condensed from information provided to the Texas Almanac by county extension agents in 2010. Market value (total cash receipts) of agricultural products sold is from the **2007 Census of Agriculture** of the U.S. Department of Agriculture for that year.

Cities: Towns listed include the county seat, incorporated cities and towns with post offices, as well as certain census designated places (CDP). Population figures for incorporated towns and CDPs are from the 2010 U.S. Census. Population estimates for other towns are from local officials received through a survey from the Texas Almanac.

Sources of DATA LISTS

Population (of county): The county population as of April 1, 2010, U.S. Census Bureau. The line following gives the percentage of increase or decrease from the 2000 U.S. census count.

Area: Total area in square miles, including water surfaces, as determined in the 2000 U.S. census.

Land Area: The land area in square miles as determined by the U.S. Census Bureau in 2000.

Altitude (ft.): Principally from U.S. Geological Survey topographic maps, including **revisions available in 2008**. Not all of the surface of Texas has been precisely surveyed for elevation; in some cases data are from the Texas Railroad Commission or the Texas Department of Transportation.

Climate: Provided by the National Oceanic and Atmospheric Administration state climatologist, College Station. Data are revised at 10-year intervals to cover the previous three decades. Listed are the latest compilations, as of Jan. 1, 2003, and pertain to a particular site within the county (usually the county seat). The data include: **Rainfall** (annual mean in inches); **Temperature** (in degrees Fahrenheit); January mean minimum and July mean maximum.

Workforce/Wages: Prepared by the Texas Workforce Commission, Austin, in cooperation with the Bureau of Labor Statistics of the U.S. Department of Labor. The data are computed from reports by all establishments subject to the Texas Unemployment Compensation Act.

(Agricultural employers are subject to the act if they employ as many as three workers for 20 weeks or pay cash wages of $6,250 in a quarter. Employers who pay $1,000 in wages in a quarter for domestic services are subject also. Still not mandatorily covered are self-employed, unpaid family workers, and those employed by churches and some small nonprofit organizations.)

The work/wage data include (state total, lowest county and highest county included here):

Civilian labor force as of January 2011. Texas, 12,150,757; Loving County, 52; Harris County, 2,017,690.

Unemployed: The unemployment rate (percentage of workforce) as of January 2011. Texas, 8.5; Hemphill County, 3.3; Starr County, 19.5.

Total Wages paid in the fourth quarter of 2010. Texas, $131,021,680,279; Loving County $503,346; Harris County, $32,270,669,921.

Average Weekly Wage as of the fourth quarter of 2010. Texas, $1,372; Delta County, $443; Carson County, $1,461.

Property Values: Appraised gross market value of real and personal property in each county appraisal district in 2009 as reported to the State Property Tax Board.

Retail Sales: Figures for 2010 as reported to the state Comptroller of Public Accounts.

Anderson County

Physical Features: Forested, hilly East Texas county, slopes to Trinity and Neches rivers; sandy, clay, black soils; pines, hardwoods.

Economy: Manufacturing, distribution, agribusiness, tourism; hunting and fishing leases; prison units.

History: Comanche, Waco, other tribes. Anglo-American settlers arrived in 1830s. Antebellum slaveholding area. County created and organized from Houston County in 1846; named for K.L. Anderson, last vice president of the Republic of Texas.

Race/Ethnicity, 2008: (In percent) Anglo, 61.5; Black, 23.0; Hispanic, 14.6; Other, 0.9.

Vital Statistics, 2008: Births, 667; deaths, 622; marriages, 436; divorces, 173.

Recreation: Fishing, hunting, streams, lakes; dogwood trails; historic sites; railroad park; museums.

Minerals: Oil and gas.

Agriculture: Cattle, hay, truck vegetables, melons, pecans, peaches. Market value $39.4 million. Timber sold.

PALESTINE (18,712), county seat; clothing, metal, wood products; transportation and agribusiness center; scientific balloon station; historic bakery; library; vocational-technical facilities; hospitals; community college; dulcimer festival in March, hot pepper festival in October.

Other towns include: **Cayuga** (137); **Elkhart** (1,371); **Frankston** (1,229), tourism, packaging industry, oil and gas, commuters to Tyler; depot museum, Square Fair in October; **Montalba** (110); **Neches** (175); and **Tennessee Colony** (300) site of state prisons.

Population	**58,458**
Change fm 2000	6.08
Area (sq. mi.)	1,077.95
Land Area (sq. mi.)	1,070.79
Altitude (ft.)	174-773
Rainfall (in.)	46.38
Jan. mean min.	37.4
July mean max.	93.9
Civ. Labor	20,992
Unemployed	9.9
Wages	$176,357,659
Av. Weekly Wage	$767
Prop. Value	$3,516,718,761
Retail Sales	$1,221,118,966

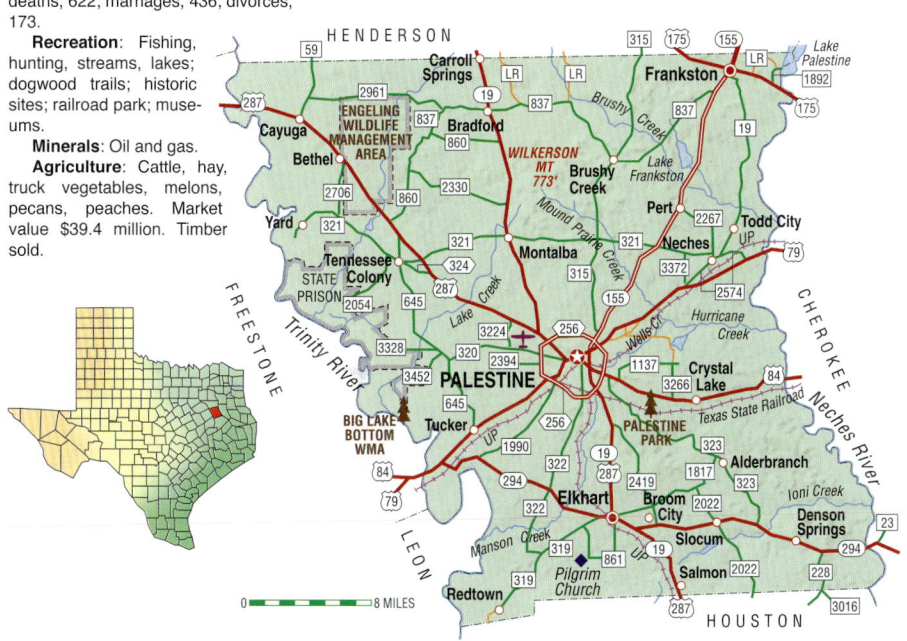

Railroad Abbreviations

AAT..Austin Area Terminal Railroad
AGC.. Alamo Gulf Coast Railway
ATK.. AMTRAK
ANR....................................Angelina & Neches River Railroad
ATCX ....Austin & Texas Central Railroad
BLR.. Blacklands Railroad
BNSF.. BNSF Railroad
BOP.. Border Pacific Railroad
BRG.................... Brownsville & Rio Grande Int'l Railroad
CMC .... CMC Railroad
DART...Dallas Area Rapid Transit
DGNO....................Dallas, Garland & Northeastern Railroad
FWWR.................... Fort Worth & Western Railroad/Tarantula
GCSR .... Gulf, Colorado & San Saba RailwayCorp.
GRR.. Georgetown Railroad
GVSR ....Galveston Railroad
KCS ....Kansas City Southern Railway
KRR...Kiamichi Railroad Company
MCSA ....Moscow, Camden & San Augustine RR
PCN.................................... Point Comfort & Northern Railway
PNR........................ Panhandle Northern Railroad Company
PTRA.................................Port Terminal Railroad Association

PVS ....Pecos Valley Southern Railway
RC ....Rusk County Rural Rail Transportation District
RSS ....Rockdale, Sandow & Southern Railroad
RVSC...Rio Valley Switching
SAW .... South Plains Switching LTD
SRN .... Sabine River & Northern Railroad Company
SSC ....Southern Switching (Lone Star Railroad)
SW.......................................Southwestern Shortline Railroad
TCT...................................Texas City Terminal Railway
TIBR ....Timber Rock Railroad
TM .... The Texas Mexican Railway Company
TN...Texas & Northern Railway
TNER............................Texas Northeastern Railroad
TNMR .... Texas & New Mexico Railroad
TNW ....Texas North Western Railway
TP .... Texas Pacifico Transportation
TSE.........................Texas South-Eastern Railroad Company
TXGN....................Texas, Gonzales & Northern Railway
TXR .... Texas Rock Crusher Railway
TSSR ....Texas State Railroad
UP........................... Union Pacific Railroad Company
WTJR...................Wichita, Tillman & Jackson Railway
WTLR .... West Texas & Lubbock Railroad

Andrews County

Physical Features: South Plains, drain to playas; grass, mesquite, shin oak; red clay, sandy soils.

Economy: Natural resources/mining; manufacturing; trade, construction; government/services; agribusiness.

History: Apache, Comanche area until U.S. Army campaigns of 1875. Ranching developed around 1900. Oil boom in 1940s. County created 1876 from Bexar Territory; organized 1910; named for Texas Revolutionary soldier Richard Andrews.

Race/Ethnicity, 2008: (In percent) Anglo, 51.0; Black, 1.8; Hispanic, 45.8; Other, 1.4.

Vital Statistics, 2008: Births, 231; deaths, 130; marriages, 115; divorces, 63.

Recreation: Prairie dog town, wetlands, bird viewing; museum; camper facilities; Fall Fiesta in September.

Minerals: Oil and gas.

Agriculture: Beef, cotton, sorghums, grains, corn, hay; significant irrigation. Market value $15.9 million.

ANDREWS (11,088) county seat; trade center, amphitheatre, hospital.

Other towns include, **McKinney Acres** (815).

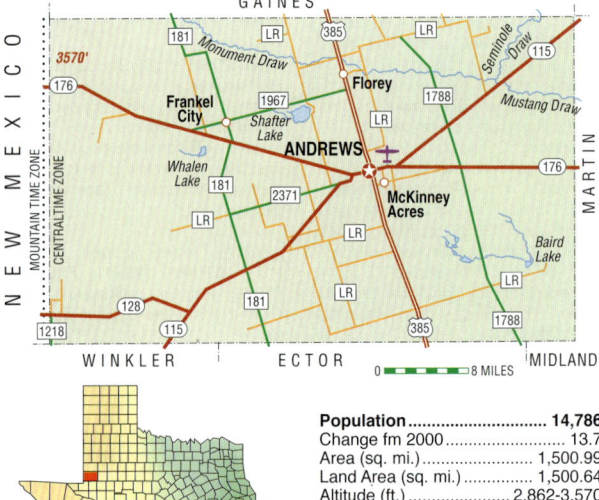

Population	14,786
Change fm 2000	13.7
Area (sq. mi.)	1,500.99
Land Area (sq. mi.)	1,500.64
Altitude (ft.)	2,862-3,570
Rainfall (in.)	15.15
Jan. mean min.	30.4
July mean max.	94.5
Civ. Labor	7,082
Unemployed	5.9
Wages	$53,023,789
Av. Weekly Wage	$1,025
Prop. Value	$3,599,181,992
Retail Sales	$152,460,556

Angelina County

Physical Features: Rolling, hilly East Texas county; black, red, gray soils; Angelina National Forest.

Economy: Timber; manufacturers of iron and steel castings, truck trailers, mobile homes; government/services; wood and paper products.

History: Caddoan area. First land deed to Vicente Micheli 1801. Anglo-American setters arrived in 1820s. County created and organized in 1846 from Nacogdoches County; named for legendary Indian maiden Angelina.

Race/Ethnicity, 2008: (In percent) Anglo, 63.5; Black, 14.4; Hispanic, 20.9; Other, 1.2.

Vital Statistics, 2008: Births, 1,265; deaths, 847; marriages, 696; divorces, 478.

Recreation: Sam Rayburn Reservoir; national, state forests, parks; locomotive exhibit; Forest Festival; bike ride in fall.

Minerals: Limited output of natural gas and oil.

Agriculture: Poultry, beef, horticulture, limited fruits and vegetables. Market value $29.4 million. A leading timber-producing county.

LUFKIN (35,067) county seat; manufacturing; Angelina College; hospitals; U.S., Texas Forest centers; zoo; Expo Center and Texas Forestry Museum.

Other towns include: **Burke** (737); **Diboll** (4,776); **Hudson** (4,731); **Huntington** (2,118); **Pollok** (400); **Zavalla** (713).

For explanation of sources, abbreviations and symbols, see p. 232 and foldout map.

Population	86,771
Change from 2000	8.29
Area (sq. mi.)	864.45
Land Area (sq. mi.)	801.56
Altitude (ft.)	102-460
Rainfall (in.)	46.62
Jan. mean min.	37.9
July mean max.	93.5
Civ. Labor	39,814
Unemployed	8.2
Wages	$332,786,940
Av. Weekly Wage	$724
Prop. Value	$4,578,195,149
Retail Sales	$1,008,282,301

Aransas County

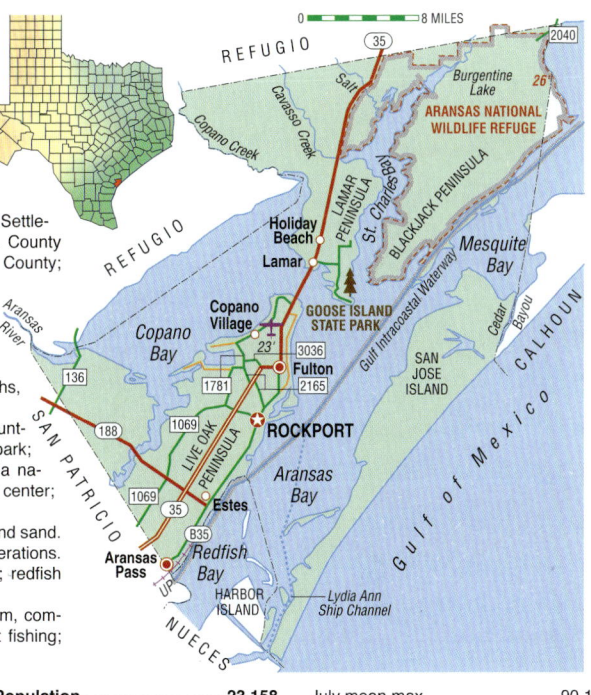

Physical Features: Coastal plains; sandy loam, coastal clays; bays, inlets; mesquites, oaks.

Economy: Tourism, recreational fishing, commercial shrimping, hunting.

History: Karankawa, Coahuiltecan area. Settlement by Irish and Mexicans began in 1829. County created and organized in 1871 from Refugio County; named for Rio Nuestra Señora de Aranzazu, derived from a Spanish palace.

Race/Ethnicity, 2008: (In percent) Anglo, 73.3; Black, 1.5; Hispanic, 21.4; Other, 3.8.

Vital Statistics, 2008: Births, 263; deaths, 345; marriages, 238; divorces, 107.

Recreation: Sport fishing, waterfowl hunting; Fulton Mansion; state marine lab; state park; Texas Maritime Museum; bird sanctuaries (a nationally known birding hotspot); Rockport art center; hummingbird festival in September.

Minerals: Oil and gas, also oystershell and sand.

Agriculture: Cotton, hay, cow-calf operations. Market value $1.7 million. Fishing, hunting; redfish hatchery.

ROCKPORT (8,766) county seat; tourism, commercial oyster and shrimp harvesting, sport fishing; commuting to Corpus Christi and Victoria, retirement residences; Festival of Wines in May.

Fulton (1,358) tourism, oyster harvesting, Oysterfest in March.

Also, **Holiday Beach** (514) and **Lamar** (636).

Part of **Aransas Pass**.

Population	23,158	July mean max.	90.1
Change fm 2000	2.94	Civ. Labor	11,836
Area (sq. mi.)	527.95	Unemployed	8.3
Land Area (sq. mi.)	251.86	Wages	$44,124,468
Altitude (ft.)	sea level-26	Av. Weekly Wage	$627
Rainfall (in.)	35.96	Prop. Value	$3,149,425,299
Jan. mean min.	44.9	Retail Sales	$232,327,589

A commercial fisherman repairs his boat at Rockport-Fulton. Photo by Robert Plocheck.

Archer County

Physical Features: Northwestern county, rolling to hilly, drained by Wichita, Trinity River forks; black, red loams, sandy soils; mesquites, post oaks.

Economy: Cattle, milk production, oil, hunting leases. Part of Wichita Falls metropolitan area.

History: Caddo, Comanche, Kiowas and other tribes in area until 1875; Anglo-American settlement developed soon afterward. County created from Fannin Land District, 1858; organized 1880. Named for Dr. B.T. Archer, Republic commissioner to United States.

Race/Ethnicity, 2008: (In percent) Anglo, 92.9; Black, 0.2; Hispanic, 6.3; Other, 0.7.

Vital Statistics, 2008: Births, 78; deaths, 79; marriages, 38; divorces, 51.

Recreation: Hunting of deer, turkey, dove, feral hog, coyote; fishing in area lakes, rodeo in June.

Minerals: Oil and natural gas.

Agriculture: Cow/calf, stocker cattle, dairy, wheat, hay, silage and horses. Market value $61 million.

ARCHER CITY (1,834) county seat; cattle, oil field service center; museum; book center; Royal Theatre productions; some manufacturing.

Other towns include: **Holliday** (1,758) Mayfest in spring; **Lakeside City** (997); **Megargel** (203); **Scotland** (501); **Windthorst** (409), biannual German sausage festival (also in Scotland).

Population	**9,054**
Change fm 2000	2.26
Area (sq. mi.)	925.78
Land Area (sq. mi.)	909.70
Altitude (ft.)	900-1,355
Rainfall (in.)	29.78
Jan. mean min.	26.7
July mean max.	97.0
Civ. Labor	4,948
Unemployed	5.4
Wages	$16,612,384
Av. Weekly Wage	$648
Prop. Value	$906,753,409
Retail Sales	$53,166,158

Armstrong County

Physical Features: Partly on High Plains, broken by Palo Duro Canyon. Chocolate loam, gray soils.

Economy: Agribusiness, tourism, and commuting to Amarillo.

History: Apache, then Comanche territory until U.S. Army campaigns of 1874-75. Anglo-Americans began ranching soon afterward. County created from Bexar District in 1876; organized in 1890; the name honors pioneer Texas family.

Race/Ethnicity, 2008: (In percent) Anglo, 92.6; Black, 0.3; Hispanic, 6.7; Other, 0.4.

Vital Statistics, 2008: Births, 23; deaths, 15; marriages, 4; divorces, 3.

Recreation: Palo Duro Canyon State Park; Goodnight Ranch Home.

Minerals: Sand, gravel.

Agriculture: Stocker cattle, cow-calf operations; wheat, sorghum, cotton and hay; some irrigation. Market value $37.4 million.

CLAUDE (1,196) county seat; farm, ranch supplies; glass company; medical center; Caprock Roundup in July.

Also, **Goodnight** (20), and **Washburn** (120).

Population	**1,901**
Change fm 2000	–11.5
Area (sq. mi.)	913.81
Land Area (sq. mi.)	913.63
Altitude (ft.)	2,300-3,535
Rainfall (in.)	22.39
Jan. mean min.	21.2
July mean max.	90.5
Civ. Labor	1,061
Unemployed	4.3
Wages	$3,147,255
Av. Weekly Wage	$659
Prop. Value	$185,294,600
Retail Sales	$3,619,756

For explanation of sources, abbreviations and symbols, see p. 232 and foldout map.

Atascosa County

Physical Features: On grassy prairie south of San Antonio, drained by Atascosa River, tributaries; mesquites, other brush.

Economy: Coal plant, oil, commuters to San Antonio.

History: Inhabited by Coahuiltecan Indians; later Apaches, Comanches in area. Families from Mexico established ranches in the mid-1700s. Anglo-Americans arrived in the 1840s. County created from Bexar District in 1856 and organized that same year. Atascosa means boggy in Spanish.

Race/Ethnicity, 2008: (In percent) Anglo, 37.7; Black, 0.4; Hispanic, 61.2; Other, 0.7.

Vital Statistics, 2008: Births, 648; deaths, 368; marriages, 289; divorces, 55.

Recreation: Quail, deer hunting; museums; river park; theater group.

Minerals: Lignite, oil, gas.

Agriculture: Beef cattle, peanuts, vegetable farming. 25,000 acres irrigated. Market value $50.3 million.

JOURDANTON (3,871) county seat; coal mining; hospital; park, walking trail; chili cookoff in May, Czech Day in July.

PLEASANTON (8,934) farming, oil-field drilling, health services; cowboy homecoming in August, Longhorn museum; hospital.

Other towns include: **Campbellton** (350); **Charlotte** (1,715); **Christine** (390); **Leming** (946).

Also, **Lytle** (2,492) greenhouse, peanuts processed; **Peggy** (22); **Poteet** (3,260) strawberry "capital," festival in April.

Population	44,911
Change frm 2000	16.27
Area (sq. mi.)	1,235.61
Land Area (sq. mi.)	1,232.12
Altitude (ft.)	180-784
Rainfall (in.)	29.00
Jan. mean min.	39.0
July mean max.	95.9
Civ. Labor	19,750
Unemployed	8.7
Wages	$85,177,700
Av. Weekly Wage	$699
Prop. Value	$2,923,422,523
Retail Sales	$424,378,541

The Royal Theatre, focus of 'The Last Picture Show,' in Archer City at Archer County. Photo by Robert Plocheck.

Austin County

Physical Features: Level to hilly, drained by San Bernard, Brazos rivers; black prairie to sandy upland soils.

Economy: Agribusiness; tourism, government/services; metal, other manufacturing; commuting to Houston.

History: Tonkawa Indians; reduced by diseases. Birthplace of Anglo-American colonization, 1821, and German mother colony at Industry, 1831. County created and organized in 1837; named for Stephen F. Austin, father of Texas.

Race/Ethnicity, 2008: (In percent) Anglo, 68.2; Black, 10.8; Hispanic, 20.4; Other, 0.7.

Vital Statistics, 2008: Births, 400; deaths, 260; marriages, 195; divorces, 110.

Recreation: Fishing, hunting; state park, Pioneer Trail; Bellville Country Livin' festival in April; Lone Star Raceway Park.

Minerals: Oil and natural gas.

Agriculture: Beef production and hay. Also rice, corn, sorghum, nursery crops, grapes, pecans. Market value $30.9 million.

BELLVILLE (4,097) county seat; varied manufacturing; hospital; oil.

SEALY (6,019) oil-field and military vehicle manufacturing, varied industries; Blinn College branch; polka fest in March.

Other towns include: **Bleiblerville** (125); **Brazos Country** (469); **Cat Spring** (200); **Frydek** (900) Grotto celebration in April; **Industry** (304); **Kenney** (957); **New Ulm** (974) retail, art festival in April; **San Felipe** (747) colonial capital of Texas; **Wallis** (1,252) autofest in October.

Population	28,417
Change fm 2000	20.46

Area (sq. mi.)	656.37
Land Area (sq. mi.)	652.59

Altitude (ft.)	70-463
Rainfall (in.)	40.68
Jan. mean min.	40.7
July mean max.	94.9
Civ. Labor	13,589
Unemployed	9.0
Wages	$128,426,208
Av. Weekly Wage	$869
Prop. Value	$4,025,862,308
Retail Sales	$2,119,983,211

Bailey County

Physical Features: High Plains county, sandy loam soils; mesquite brush; drains to draws forming upper watershed of Brazos River, playas.

Economy: Farm supply manufacturing; electric generating plant; food-processing plants.

History: Settlement began after 1900. County created from Bexar District 1876, organized 1917. Named for Alamo hero Peter J. Bailey.

Race/Ethnicity, 2008: (In percent) Anglo, 45.0; Black, 1.2; Hispanic, 53.4; Other, 0.4.

Vital Statistics, 2008: Births, 110; deaths, 50; marriages, 46; divorces, 18.

Recreation: Muleshoe National Wildlife Refuge; "Old Pete," the national mule memorial; historical building park; museum; motorcycle rally; mule deer, sandhill crane, pheasant hunting.

Minerals: Insignificant.

Agriculture: Feedlot, dairy cattle; cotton, wheat, sorghum, corn, vegetables; 100,000 acres irrigated. Market value $234 million.

MULESHOE (5,158) county seat; agribusiness center; feed-corn milling; hospital; livestock show.

Other towns include: **Enochs** (80); **Maple** (75).

Population	7,165
Change fm 2000	8.66
Area (sq. mi.)	827.38
Land Area (sq. mi.)	826.69
Altitude (ft.)	3,660-4,120

Rainfall (in.)	17.37
Jan. mean min.	20.2
July mean max.	91.9
Civ. Labor	3,245
Unemployed	7.4

Wages	$23,439,851
Av. Weekly Wage	$660
Prop. Value	$493,927,868
Retail Sales	$31,506,166

Bandera County

Physical Features: Scenic southwestern county of cedar-covered hills on the Edwards Plateau; Medina, Sabinal Rivers; limestone, sandy soils; species of oaks, walnuts, native cherry and Uvalde maple.

Economy: Tourism, hunting, fishing, ranching supplies, forest products.

History: Apache, then Comanche territory. White settlement began in early 1850s, including Mormons and Poles. County created, organized, from Bexar, Uvalde counties, 1856; named for Bandera (flag) Mountains.

Race/Ethnicity, 2008: (In percent) Anglo, 85.4; Black, 0.3; Hispanic, 13.5; Other, 0.8.

Vital Statistics, 2008: Births, 188; deaths, 178; marriages, 128; divorces, 71.

Recreation: RV parks, resort ranches; Lost Maples and Hill Country State Natural Areas; rodeo on Memorial Day weekend; Medina Lake.

Minerals: Not significant.

Agriculture: Beef cattle, sheep, goats, horses, apples. Market value $7 million. Hunting and nature tourism important.

BANDERA (857) county seat; tourism, dude ranches, Frontier Times Museum; Celebrate Bandera weekend of Labor Day.

Other towns include: **Medina** (850) apple growing; **Pipe Creek** (130); **Tarpley** (30); **Vanderpool** (20).

Also, the community of **Lakehills** (5,150) on Medina Lake, Cajun Fest in September, and **Lake Medina Shores** (1,235).

Population	20,485
Change fm 2000	16.1
Area (sq. mi.)	797.54
Land Area (sq. mi.)	791.73
Altitude (ft.)	1,064-2,340
Rainfall (in.)	35.78
Jan. mean min.	33.3
July mean max.	93.9
Civ. Labor	9,979
Unemployed	7.8
Wages	$20,749,012
Av. Weekly Wage	$551
Prop. Value	$3,157,664,274
Retail Sales	$89,719,661

For explanation of sources, abbreviations and symbols, see p. 232 and foldout map.

A hiking trail along a creek in Lost Maples State Natural Area. Photo by Robert Plocheck.

Physical Features: Rolling; alluvial, sandy, loam soils; varied timber, Lost Pines; bisected by Colorado River.

Economy: Government/services; tourism; agribusiness; biotechnology research; computer-related industries; commuters to Austin.

History: Tonkawa Indian area; Comanches also present. Spanish fort established 1804. County created 1836; organized in 1837; named for Baron de Bastrop, who aided Moses and Stephen F. Austin in establishing colony in 1820s.

Race/Ethnicity, 2008: (In percent) Anglo, 61.2; Black, 7.8; Hispanic, 30.1; Other, 1.0.

Vital Statistics, 2008: Births, 980; deaths, 515; marriages, 424; divorces, 251.

Recreation: Fishing, hunting, canoeing; state parks; Lake Bastrop; historic sites; museum; railroad park; natural science center; nature trails.

Minerals: LIgnite and clay.

Agriculture: Hay, beef cattle, nursery/turf grass, pecans, vegetables. Market value $38.2 million. Pine for lumber, oak for firewood.

BASTROP (7,218) county seat; government/services, tourism, hospitals, University of Texas cancer research center, federal prison; riverwalk; Pedal Thru the Pines in March.

ELGIN (8,135) sausage plants, brick plant; horse, cattle breeding; medical research; library; Western Days in June, Hogeye festival in October.

Smithville (3,817) government/services, hospital, M.D. Anderson research facility, railroad; recycling center; jamboree on weekend after Easter.

Other towns: **Cedar Creek** (145);

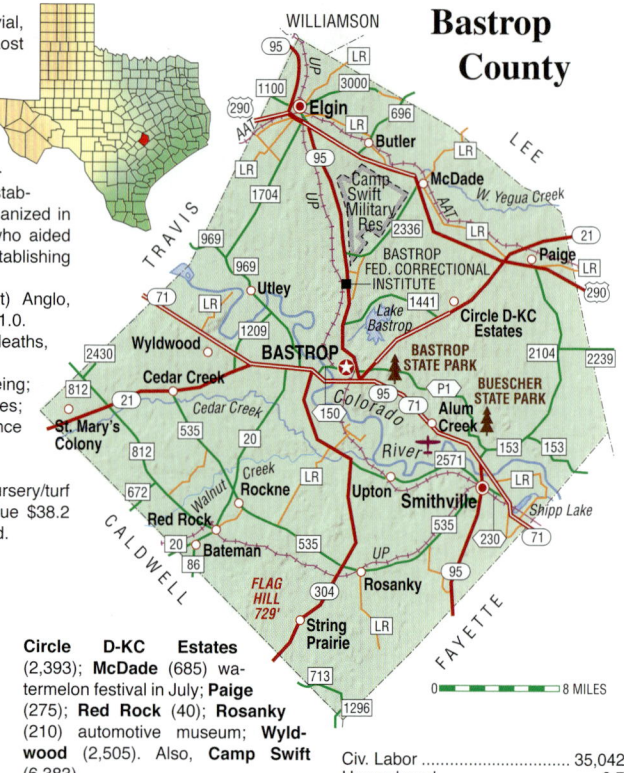

Bastrop County

Circle D-KC Estates (2,393); **McDade** (685) watermelon festival in July; **Paige** (275); **Red Rock** (40); **Rosanky** (210) automotive museum; **Wyldwood** (2,505). Also, **Camp Swift** (6,383).

Population 74,171
Change fm 2000 .... 28.47
Area (sq. mi.) 895.92
Land Area (sq. mi.) 888.35
Altitude (ft.) 300-729
Rainfall (in.) 38.04
Jan. mean min. 36.7
July mean max. 95.4

Civ. Labor 35,042
Unemployed 8.7
Wages $123,125,688
Av. Weekly Wage $664
Prop. Value $5,998,114,882
Retail Sales $811,914,271

For explanation of sources, abbreviations and symbols, see p. 232 and foldout map.

Fishing cabins line Lake Kemp in Baylor County. Photo by Robert Plocheck.

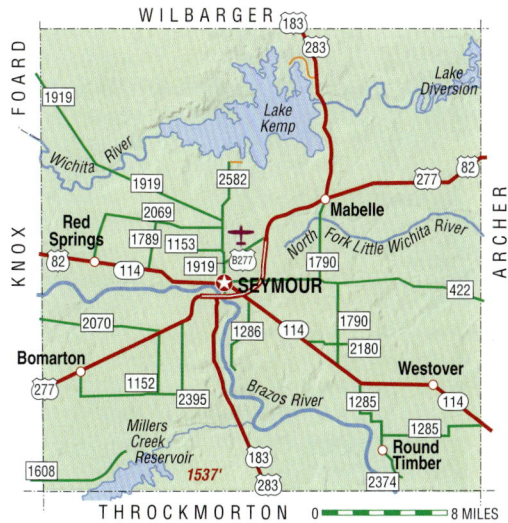

Baylor County

Physical Features: Northwest county; level to hilly; drains to Brazos, Wichita rivers; sandy, loam, red soils; grassy, mesquites, cedars.

Economy: Agribusiness; retail/service; health services.

History: Comanches, with Wichitas and other tribes; removed in 1874-75. Anglo-Americans settled in the 1870s. County created from Fannin County 1858; organized 1879. Named for H.W. Baylor, Texas Ranger surgeon.

Race/Ethnicity, 2008: (In percent) Anglo, 85.1; Black, 3.5; Hispanic, 10.3; Other, 1.1.

Vital Statistics, 2008: Births, 38; deaths, 56; marriages, 32; divorces, 21.

Recreation: Lakes; hunting; settlers reunion, rodeo, go-cart races in July.

Minerals: Oil, gas produced.

Agriculture: Wheat, cattle, cow-calf operations, grain sorghum, cotton, hay. Market value $42.9 million.

SEYMOUR (2,740) county seat; agribusiness; hospital; dove hunters' breakfast in September.

Population	3,726
Change fm 2000	−8.97
Area (sq. mi.)	901.01
Land Area (sq. mi.)	870.77
Altitude (ft.)	1,053-1,537
Rainfall (in.)	27.79
Jan. mean min.	27.7
July mean max.	96.5

Civ. Labor	1,783	Av. Weekly Wage	$548
Unemployed	6.7	Prop. Value	$656,449,690
Wages	$8,485,252	Retail Sales	$23,176,284

Bee County

Physical Features: South Coastal Plain, level to rolling; black clay, sandy, loam soils; brushy.

Economy: Agriculture, government/services; hunting leases; oil and gas business.

History: Karankawa, Apache, Pawnee territory. First Spanish land grant, 1789. Irish settlers arrived 1826-29. County created from Karnes, Live Oak, Goliad, Refugio, San Patricio, 1857; organized 1858; named for Gen. Barnard Bee.

Race/Ethnicity, 2008: (In percent) Anglo, 32.7; Black, 9.1; Hispanic, 57.4; Other, 0.8.

Vital Statistics, 2008: Births, 414; deaths, 223; marriages, 195; divorces, 108.

Recreation: Hunting, birding, camping; historical sites, antiques; rodeo/roping events.

Minerals: Oil, gas produced.

Agriculture: Beef cattle, corn, cotton and grain sorghhum. Market value $39.2 million. Hunting leases.

BEEVILLE (12,863) county seat; aircraft maintenance, waste-bind manufacturing, retail center; Costal Bend College; hospital; art museum; Diez y Seis festival in September.

Other towns and places include: **Blue Berry Hill** (866); **Mineral** (65); **Normanna** (113); **Pawnee** (166); **Pettus** (558); **Skidmore** (925); **Tuleta** (288); **Tynan** (278).

Population	31,861
Change fm 2000	−1.54
Area (sq. mi.)	880.31
Land Area (sq. mi.)	880.14
Altitude (ft.)	39-540
Rainfall (in.)	33.48
Jan. mean min.	43.1
July mean max.	94.6
Civ. Labor	12,480
Unemployed	9.5
Wages	$78,942,758
Av. Weekly Wage	$691
Prop. Value	$2,002,239,460
Retail Sales	$256,651,131

Bell County

Physical Features: Central Texas Blackland, level to hilly; black to light soils in west; mixed timber.

Economy: Fort Hood; manufacturing includes computers, plastic goods, furniture, clothing; agribusiness; distribution center; tourism.

History: Tonkawas, Lipan Apaches; reduced by disease and advancing frontier by 1840s. Comanches raided into 1870s. Settled in 1830s as part of Robertson's colony. A few slaveholders in 1850s. County created from Milam County in 1850; named for Gov. P.H. Bell.

Race/Ethnicity, 2008: (In percent) Anglo, 50.4; Black, 23.2; Hispanic, 21.0; Other, 5.4.

Vital Statistics, 2008: Births, 6,346; deaths, 1,863; marriages, 4,128; divorces, 2,016.

Recreation: Fishing, hunting; lakes; historic sites; exposition center; Salado gathering of Scottish clans in November.

Minerals: Gravel.

Agriculture: Beef, corn, sorghum, wheat, cotton. Market value $61.7 million.

BELTON (18,216) county seat; University of Mary Hardin-Baylor; government/services; manufacturing; museum, nature center.

Population	310,235
Change fm 2000	30.37
Area (sq. mi.)	1,087.93
Land Area (sq. mi.)	1,059.72
Altitude (ft.)	390-1,227
Rainfall (in.)	35.81
Jan. mean min.	34.9
July mean max.	95.0
Civ. Labor	132,134
Unemployed	7.9
Wages	$1,065,704,132
Av. Weekly Wage	$768
Prop. Value	$14,640,684,306
Retail Sales	$4,091,441,772

KILLEEN (127,921) Fort Hood; colleges; regional airport; retail center, varied manufacturing; hospital; museums, planetarium; Four Winds Powwow in September.

TEMPLE (66,102) Major medical center with two hospitals and VA hospital; diversified industries; rail, wholesale distribution center; retail center; Temple College; Czech museum; early-day tractor, engine show in October.

Other towns include: **Harker Heights** (26,700) Founder's Day in October; **Heidenheimer** (224); **Holland** (1,121) corn festival in June; **Little River-Academy** (1,961); **Morgan's Point Resort** (4,170); **Nolanville** (4,259); **Pendelton** (369); **Rogers** (1,218); **Salado** (2,126) tourism, civic center, amphitheathre, art fair in August; **Troy** (1,645). Also, part of **Bartlett**.

Fort Hood has a population of 29,589.

Mission Espada in San Antonio, established in 1731. Photo by Robert Plocheck.

Bexar County

Physical Features: On edge of Balcones Escarpment, Coastal Plain; heavy black to thin limestone soils; spring-fed streams; underground water; mesquite, other brush.

Economy: Medical/biomedical research and services; government center with large federal payroll, military bases; tourism; education center.

History: Coahuiltecan Indian area; also Lipan Apaches and Tonkawas present. Mission San Antonio de Valero (Alamo) founded in 1718. Canary Islanders arrived in 1731. Anglo-American settlers began arriving in late 1820s. County created 1836 from Spanish municipality named to honor the duke of Bexar; a colonial capital of Texas.

Race/Ethnicity, 2008: (In percent) Anglo, 30.8; Black, 7.9; Hispanic, 58.2; Other, 3.1.

Vital Statistics, 2008: Births, 27,220; deaths, 10,722; marriages, 12,200; divorces, 4,160.

Recreation: Historic sites include the Alamo, other missions, Casa Navarro, La Villita; River Walk, El Mercado (market), Tower of the Americas, Brackenridge Park, zoo, Sea World, HemisFair Park, Institute of Texan Cultures; museums, symphony orchestra; hunting, fishing; NBA Spurs; Fiesta in April, Folklife Festival in June.

Minerals: Gravel, sand, limestone.

Agriculture: Nursery crops, beef cattle, grain sorghum, hay, corn. Market value $84.2 million.

Education: Fourteen colleges including Our Lady of the Lake, St. Mary's University, Trinity University and the University of Texas at San Antonio.

SAN ANTONIO (1,327,407) county seat; Texas' second largest city; varied manufacturing with emphasis on high-tech industries; other products include construction equipment, concrete and dairy products; industrial warehousing. **Leon Springs** is now part of San Antonio.

Other towns include: **Alamo Heights** (7,031); **Balcones Heights** (2,941); **Castle Hills** (4,116); **China Grove** (1,179); **Converse** (18,198); **Elmendorf** (1,488); **Fair Oaks Ranch** (5,986); **Grey Forest** (473) **Helotes** (7,341); **Hill Country Village** (985); **Hollywood Park** (3,062).

Also, **Kirby** (8,000); **Leon Valley** (10,151); **Live Oak** (13,131); **Macdona** (559); **Olmos Park** (2,237); **St. Hedwig** (2,094); **Selma** (5,540, parts in Guadalupe and Comal counties); **Shavano Park** (3,035); **Somerset** (1,631); **Terrell Hills** (4,878); **Universal City** (18,530); **Von Ormy** (1,085); **Windcrest** (5,364).

Part of **Schertz**. **Lackland Air Force Base** has a population fo 9,918.

Population	**1,714,773**
Change fm 2000	23.11
Area (sq. mi.)	1,256.66
Land Area (sq. mi.)	1,246.82
Altitude (ft.)	400-1,896
Rainfall (in.)	32.92
Jan. mean min.	38.6
July mean max.	94.6
Civ. Labor	775,976
Unemployed	7.9
Wages	$8,177,600,806
Av. Weekly Wage	$866
Fed. Wages	$347,876,629
Prop. Value	$108,468,097,872
Retail Sales	$21,619,183,658

For explanation of sources, abbreviations and symbols, see p. 232 and foldout map.

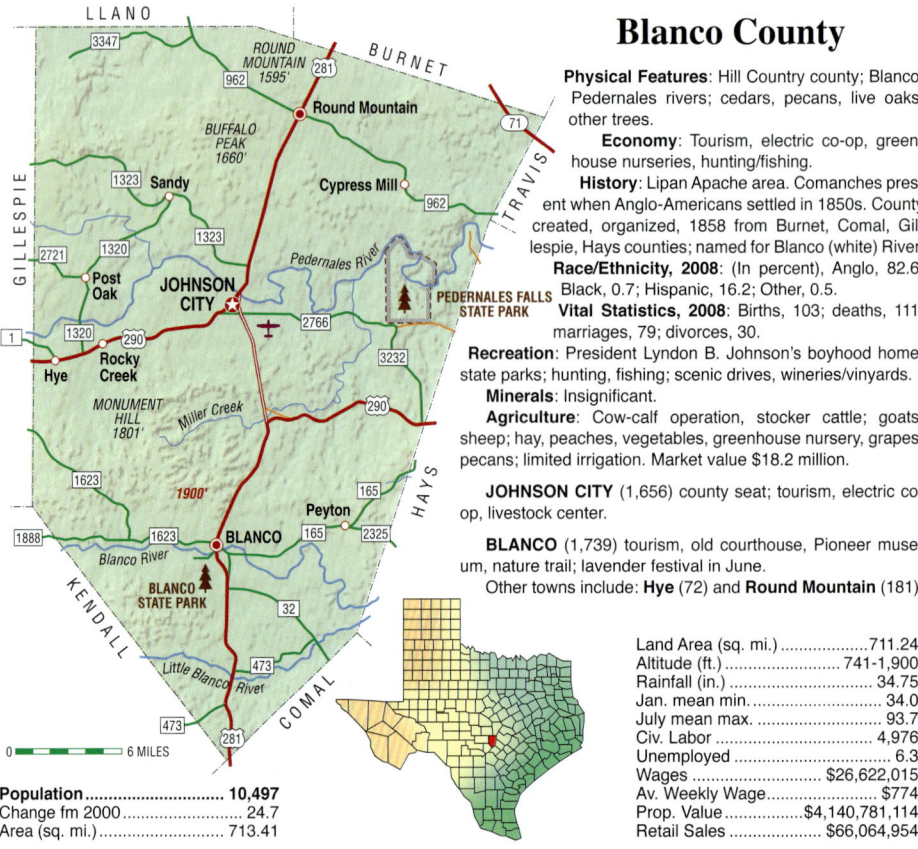

Blanco County

Physical Features: Hill Country county; Blanco, Pedernales rivers; cedars, pecans, live oaks, other trees.

Economy: Tourism, electric co-op, greenhouse nurseries, hunting/fishing.

History: Lipan Apache area. Comanches present when Anglo-Americans settled in 1850s. County created, organized, 1858 from Burnet, Comal, Gillespie, Hays counties; named for Blanco (white) River.

Race/Ethnicity, 2008: (In percent), Anglo, 82.6; Black, 0.7; Hispanic, 16.2; Other, 0.5.

Vital Statistics, 2008: Births, 103; deaths, 111; marriages, 79; divorces, 30.

Recreation: President Lyndon B. Johnson's boyhood home; state parks; hunting, fishing; scenic drives, wineries/vinyards.

Minerals: Insignificant.

Agriculture: Cow-calf operation, stocker cattle; goats, sheep; hay, peaches, vegetables, greenhouse nursery, grapes, pecans; limited irrigation. Market value $18.2 million.

JOHNSON CITY (1,656) county seat; tourism, electric co-op, livestock center.

BLANCO (1,739) tourism, old courthouse, Pioneer museum, nature trail; lavender festival in June.

Other towns include: **Hye** (72) and **Round Mountain** (181).

Land Area (sq. mi.) 711.24
Altitude (ft.) 741-1,900
Rainfall (in.) 34.75
Jan. mean min. 34.0
July mean max. 93.7
Civ. Labor 4,976
Unemployed 6.3
Wages $26,622,015
Av. Weekly Wage...................... $774
Prop. Value $4,140,781,114
Retail Sales $66,064,954

Population 10,497
Change fm 2000 .... 24.7
Area (sq. mi.) 713.41

Borden County

Physical Features: Rolling surface, broken by Caprock Escarpment; drains to Colorado River; sandy loam, clay soils.

Economy: Agriculture and hunting leases; oil; wind turbines.

History: Comanche area. Anglo-Americans settled in 1870s. County created 1876 from Bexar District, organized 1891; named for Gail Borden, patriot, inventor, editor.

Race/Ethnicity, 2008: (In percent) Anglo, 85.8; Black, 0.0; Hispanic, 13.8; Other, 0.4.

Vital Statistics, 2008: Births, 5; deaths, 2; marriages, 1; divorce, 3.

Recreation: Fishing; quail and deer hunting; Lake J.B. Thomas; museum; Coyote Opry in September; junior livestock show in January, ranch horse competition in September.

Minerals: Oil, gas, caliche, sand, gravel.

Agriculture: Beef cattle, cotton, wheat, hay, pecans, oats; some irrigation. Market value $13.2 million.

GAIL (231) county seat; museum, antique shop, ambulance service; "star" construction atop Gail Mountain.

Population 641
Change fm 2000 .... −12.07
Area (sq. mi.) 906.04
Land Area (sq. mi.) 898.80

Altitude (ft.) 2,258-2,990
Rainfall (in.) 19.68
Jan. mean min. 29.8
July mean max. 94.6
Civ. Labor 488
Unemployed 5.4

Wages $1,327,357
Av. Weekly Wage....................... $562
Prop. Value $1,135,096,795
Retail Sales $130,485

For explanation of sources, abbreviations and symbols, see p. 232 and foldout page.

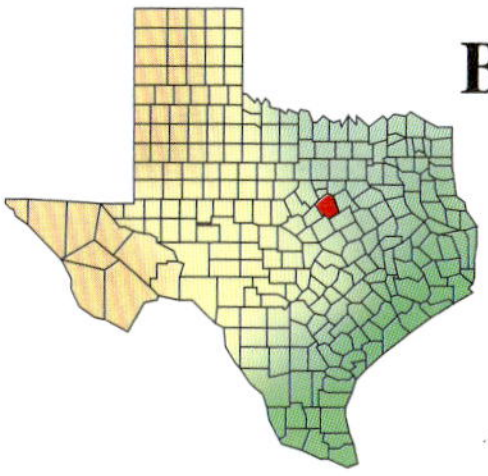

Bosque County

0 ▬▬▬ 6 MILES

Physical Features: Hilly, broken by Brazos, Bosque rivers; limestone to alluvial soils; cedars, oaks, mesquites.

Economy: Agribusiness, government/services, small industries, tourism.

History: Tonkawa, Waco and Tawakoni Indians. Settlers from England and Norway arrived in 1850s. County created, organized, 1854 from Milam District, McLennan County; named for Bosque (woods) River.

Race/Ethnicity, 2008: (In percent) Anglo, 81.4; Black, 2.0; Hispanic, 16.0; Other, 0.6.

Vital Statistics, 2008: Births, 190; deaths, 251; marriages, 105; divorces, 61.

Recreation: Lake, state park, museum at Clifton, fine art conservatory; fishing, hunting; scenic routes, Norwegian smorgasbord at Norse in November.

Minerals: Limestone, gas & oil.

Agriculture: Beef cattle, forages, small grains, turkeys (second in production). Market value $42.8 million. Hunting leases.

MERIDIAN (1,493) county seat; food processing, government/services, tourism; retirement home, community college, national championship barbecue cook-off in October.

CLIFTON (3,442) retirement/health care, limestone sales, light manufacturing; hospital, nursing school; library; Norwegian historic district; Norwegian Country Christmas.

Other towns include: **Cranfills Gap** (281) Lutefisk dinner in December; **Iredell** (339); **Kopperl** (225); **Laguna Park** (1,276); **Morgan** (490); **Valley Mills** (1,203); **Walnut Springs** (827).

Population	**18,212**
Change fm 2000	5.86
Area (sq. mi.)	1,002.63
Land Area (sq. mi.)	989.18

Altitude (ft.)	410-1,284
Rainfall (in.)	35.07
Jan. mean min.	32.7
July mean max.	96.2
Civ. Labor	8,209
Unemployed	9.2
Wages	$30,832,330
Av. Weekly Wage	$651
Prop. Value	$2,568,061,361
Retail Sales	$85,341,427

Mushaway Peak near Gail in Borden County. Photo by Robert Plocheck.

Bowie County

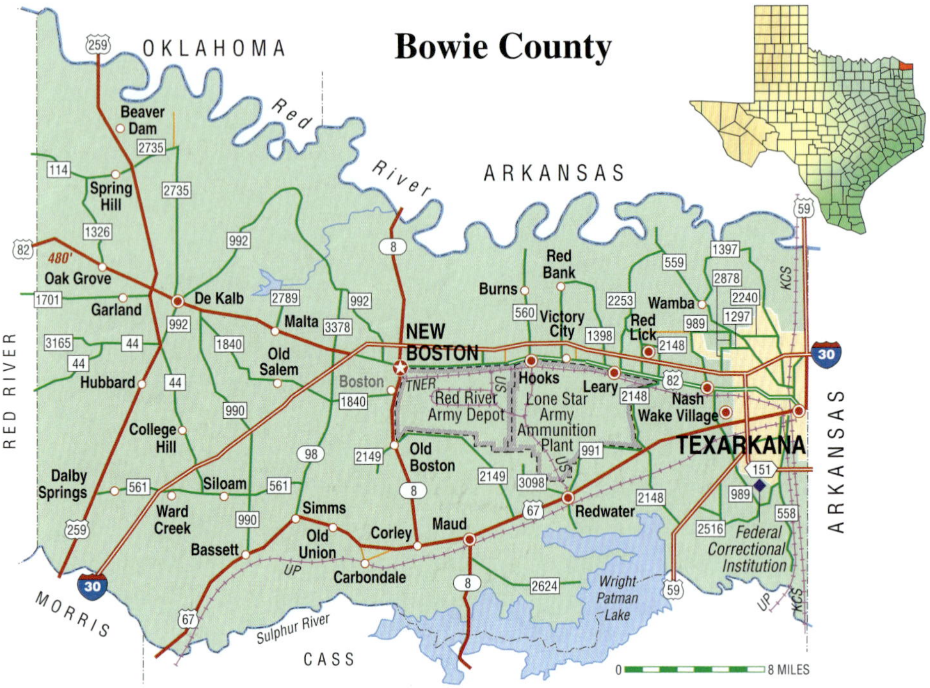

[Map of Bowie County, Texas showing cities, roads, rivers, and surrounding states Oklahoma and Arkansas. Cities include Beaver Dam, Spring Hill, Oak Grove, Garland, De Kalb, Hubbard, College Hill, Dalby Springs, Ward Creek, Bassett, Old Union, Carbondale, Simms, Corley, Maud, Redwater, Old Boston, NEW BOSTON, Boston, Malta, Old Salem, Burns, Red Bank, Victory City, Red Lick, Wamba, Hooks, Leary, Nash, Wake Village, TEXARKANA. Features include Red River Army Depot, Lone Star Army Ammunition Plant, Wright Patman Lake, Federal Correctional Institution.]

Physical Features: Forested hills at northeast corner of state; clay, sandy, alluvial soils; drained by Red and Sulphur rivers.

Economy: Government/services, lumber, manufacturing, agribusiness.

History: Caddo area, abandoned in 1790s after trouble with Osage tribe. Anglo-Americans began arriving 1815-20. County created, organized, 1840 from Red River County; named for Alamo hero James Bowie.

Race/Ethnicity, 2008: (In percent) Anglo, 66.9; Black, 25.4; Hispanic, 6.3; Other, 1.4.

Vital Statistics, 2008: Births, 1,172; deaths, 936; marriages, 608; divorces, 335.

Recreation: Lakes, Crystal Springs beach; hunting, fishing; historic sites; Four-States Fair in Sep-tember, Octoberfest.

Minerals: Oil, gas, sand, gravel.

Agriculture: Beef cattle, pecans, hay, corn, poultry, soybeans, dairy, nurseries, wheat, rice, horses, milo. Market value $48.4 million. Pine timber, hardwoods, pulpwood harvested.

NEW BOSTON (4,550) site of county courthouse; army depot, lumber mill, steel manufacture, agribusiness; state prison; Pioneer Days in August.

The area of **Boston**, officially designated as the county seat, has been annexed by New Boston.

TEXARKANA (36,411 in Texas, 29,624 in Arkansas) rubber company, paper manufacturing, distribution; hospitals; tourism; colleges; federal prison; Perot Theatre; Quadrangle Festival in September.

Other towns include: **De Kalb** (1,899) agriculture, government/ services, commuting to Texarkana, Oktoberfest; **Hooks** (2,769); **Leary** (495); **Maud** (1,056); **Nash** (2,960); **Red Lick** (1,008); **Redwater** (1,057); **Simms** (240); **Wake Village** (5,492).

Population	92,565
Change fm 2000	3.65
Area (sq. mi.)	922.77
Land Area (sq. mi.)	887.87
Altitude (ft.)	200-480
Rainfall (in.)	51.24
Jan. mean min.	30.7
July mean max.	93.1
Civ. Labor	45,347
Unemployed	8.5
Wages	$424,924,461
Av. Weekly Wage	$765
Prop. Value	$5,662,424,921
Retail Sales	$1,434,214,127

Grassy dunes along the coast near West Bay in Brazoria County. Photo by Robert Plocheck.

Brazoria County

Physical Features: Flat Coastal Plain, coastal soils, drained by Brazos and San Bernard rivers.

Economy: Petroleum and chemical industry, fishing, tourism, agribusiness. Part of Houston metropolitan area.

History: Karankawa area. Part of Austin's "Old Three Hundred" colony of families arriving in early 1820s. County created 1836 from Municipality of Brazoria, organized in 1837; name derived from Brazos River.

Race/Ethnicity, 2008: (In percent) Anglo, 59.3; Black, 9.2; Hispanic, 27.9; Other, 3.6.

Vital Statistics, 2008: Births, 5,020; deaths, 1,930; marriages, 1,673; divorces, 1,335.

Recreation: Beaches, water sports; fishing, hunting; wildlife refuges, historic sites; state and county parks; replica of the first capitol of the Republic of Texas at West Columbia.

Minerals: Oil, gas, sand, gravel.

Agriculture: Cattle, hay, rice, soybeans, sorghum, nurseries, corn, cotton, aquaculture, bees (second in number of colonies). 20,000 acres of rice irrigated. Market value $55.1 million.

ANGLETON (18,862) county seat; banking and distribution center for oil, chemical, agricultural area; fish-processing plant; hospital.

BRAZOSPORT (57,288) is a community of eight cities; chemical complex, deepwater seaport, commercial fishing, tourism; college; hospital; Bra-

zosport cities include: **Clute** (11,211) mosquito festival in July, **Freeport** (12,049) blues festival in August, **Jones Creek** (2,020), **Lake Jackson** (26,849) museum, sea center, Gulf Coast Bird Observatory, **Oyster Creek** (1,111), **Quintana** (56) Neotropical Bird Sanctuary, **Richwood** (3,510), **Surfside Beach** (482).

ALVIN (24,236) petrochemical processing, agribusiness, rail, trucking; junior college; hospital; Crawfest and Shrimp Boil in April.

PEARLAND (91,252, partly in Fort Bend, Harris counties) trucking, metal fabrication, oilfield, chemical production; commuting to Houston, NASA; community college; Hindu temple, Winter Fest in January.

Other towns include: **Bailey's Prairie** (727); **Bonney** (310); **Brazoria** (3,019) government/services, retail, manufacturing; library; No-Name Festival in June, Santa Anna Ball in July; **Brookside Village** (1,523).

Also, **Damon** (552); **Danbury** (1,715); **Danciger** (357); **Hillcrest Village** (730); **Holiday Lakes** (1,107); **Iowa Colony**

(1,170); **Liverpool** (482); **Manvel** (5,179); **Old Ocean** (150); **Rosharon** (1,152); **Sandy Point** (250); **Sweeny** (3,684) petrochemicals, government/services, hospital, library, Pride Day in May, Levi Jordan Plantation; **West Columbia** (3,905) chemical industry, retail, cattle, rice farming, museum, historic sites, plantation, San Jacinto Festival in April, Stephen F. Austin funeral procession re-eactment in October.

Population	313,166
Change fm 2000	29.53
Area (sq. mi.)	1,597.44
Land Area (sq. mi.)	1,386.40
Altitude (ft.)	sea level-146
Rainfall (in.)	57.24
Jan. mean min.	43.7
July mean max.	91.8
Civ. Labor	149,893
Unemployed	9.5
Wages	$1,017,651,775
Av. Weekly Wage	$897
Prop. Value	$27,194,056,832
Retail Sales	$3,070,089,351

County adopted by:
Columbia Historical Museum
Capital Park of Republic of Texas

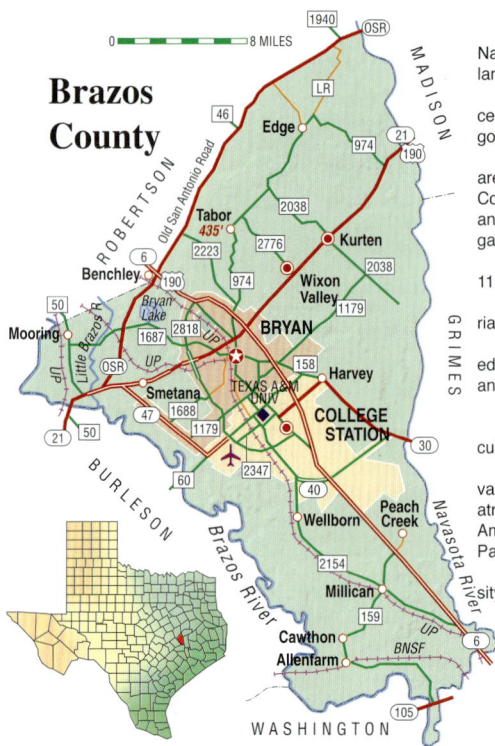

Brazos County

Physical Features: South central county between Brazos, Navasota rivers; rich bottom soils, sandy, clays on rolling uplands; oak trees.

Economy: Texas A&M University; market and medical center; agribusiness; computers, research and development; government/services; winery; industrial parks; tourism.

History: Bidais and Tonkawas; Comanches hunted in area. Part of Stephen F. Austin's second colony, late 1820s. County created 1841 from Robertson, Washington counties and named Navasota; renamed for Brazos River in 1842, organized 1843.

Race/Ethnicity, 2008: (In percent) Anglo, 61.5; Black, 11.4; Hispanic, 22.0; Other, 5.1.

Vital Statistics, 2008: Births, 2,614; deaths, 839; marriages, 1,394; divorces, 368.

Recreation: Fishing, hunting; raceway; many events related to Texas A&M activities; George Bush Presidential Library and Museum; winery harvest weekends in August.

Minerals: Sand and gravel, lignite, gas, oil.

Agriculture: Cattle, poultry, cotton, hay, horses and horticulture. Market value $54.5 million.

BRYAN (76,201) county seat; defense electronics, other varied manufacturing, agribusiness center; hospitals, psychiatric facilities; Blinn College extension; Brazos Valley African American Museum; steak & grape festival in June, Fiestas Patrias in September.

COLLEGE STATION (93,857) home of Texas A&M University, varied high-tech manufacturing, research; hospital.

Other towns include: **Kurten** (398); **Millican** (240); **Wellborn** (400); **Wixon Valley** (254).

County adopted by:
BrazosCountyHistory.org
BrazosValleyMuseum.org

Population	194,851	Unemployed	6.3
Change fm 2000	27.84	Wages	$813,676,377
Area (sq. mi.)	590.29	Av. Weekly Wage	$712
Land Area (sq. mi.)	585.78	Prop. Value	$12,172,589,574
Altitude (ft.)	157-435	Retail Sales	$2,354,927,513

Rainfall (in.)	39.67
Jan. mean min.	39.8
July mean max.	95.6
Civ. Labor	98,547

Ocotillo plants in the desert of Big Bend National Park. Photo by Robert Plocheck.

Brewster County

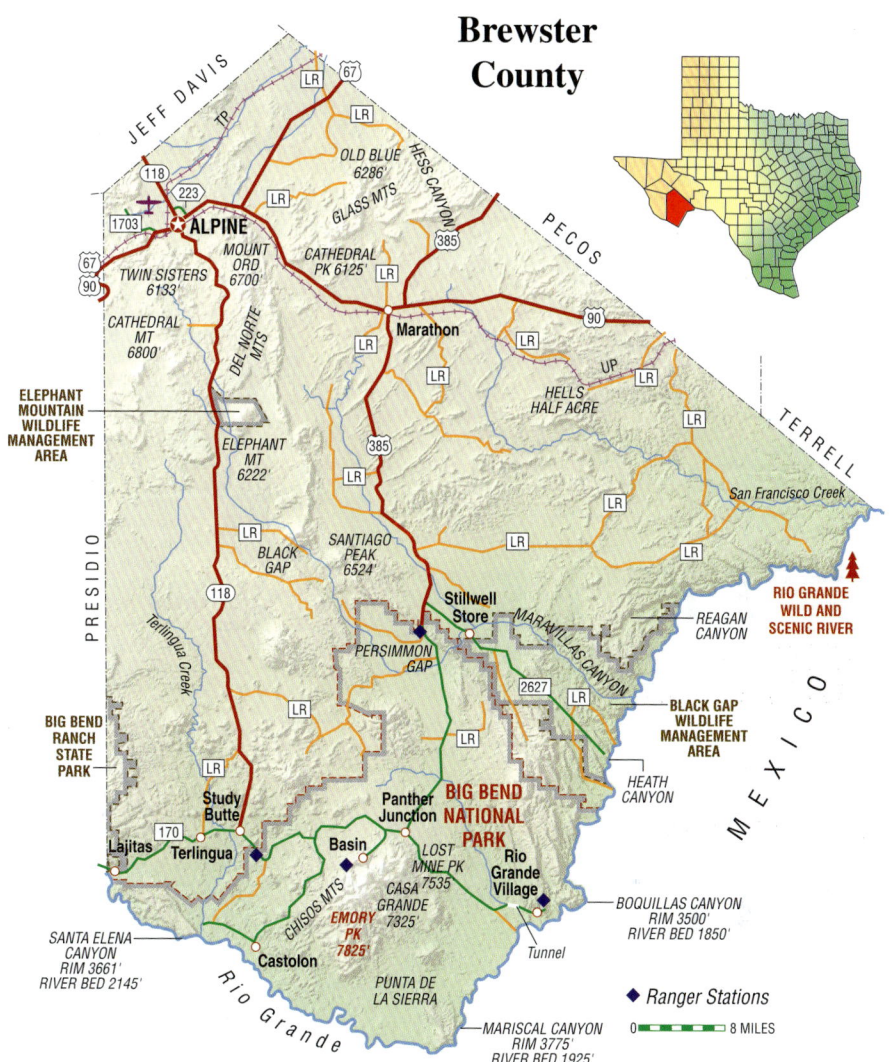

JEFF DAVIS

TP

67

LR

LR

OLD BLUE
6286'

HESS CANYON

118

223

LR

GLASS MTS

PECOS

1703

ALPINE

MOUNT
ORD
6700'

CATHEDRAL
PK 6125'

385

LR

67
90

TWIN SISTERS
6133'

DEL NORTE MTS

Marathon

LR

90

UP

CATHEDRAL
MT
6800'

LR

LR

HELLS
HALF ACRE

LR

ELEPHANT
MOUNTAIN
WILDLIFE
MANAGEMENT
AREA

ELEPHANT
MT
6222'

385

LR

LR

TERRELL

San Francisco Creek

PRESIDIO

Terlingua Creek

118

LR

BLACK
GAP

SANTIAGO
PEAK
6524'

Stillwell
Store

MARAVILLAS CANYON

LR

LR

REAGAN
CANYON

RIO GRANDE
WILD AND
SCENIC RIVER

PERSIMMON
GAP

2627

LR

BLACK GAP
WILDLIFE
MANAGEMENT
AREA

MEXICO

BIG BEND
RANCH
STATE
PARK

LR

LR

LR

HEATH
CANYON

Study
Butte

170

Panther
Junction

BIG BEND
NATIONAL
PARK

Lajitas   Terlingua

Basin

LOST
MINE PK

Rio
Grande
Village

BOQUILLAS CANYON
RIM 3500'
RIVER BED 1850'

SANTA ELENA
CANYON
RIM 3661'
RIVER BED 2145'

CHISOS MTS

EMORY
PK
7825'

CASA
GRANDE
7325'

7535

Castolon

PUNTA DE
LA SIERRA

Tunnel

Rio Grande

MARISCAL CANYON
RIM 3775'
RIVER BED 1925'

◆ Ranger Stations

0 ▬▬▬▬▬ 8 MILES

Physical Features: Largest county, with area slightly less than that of Connecticut plus Rhode Island; mountains, canyons, distinctive geology, plant life, animals.

Economy: Agriculture, tourism, government/services, Sul Ross State University, mining.

History: Pueblo culture had begun when Spanish explored in the 1500s. Mescalero Apaches in Chisos; Comanches raided in area. Ranching developed in northern part in the 1880s; Mexican agricultural communites were along river. County created, organized, 1887 from Presidio County; named for Henry P. Brewster, Republic secretary of war.

Race/Ethnicity, 2008: (In percent) Anglo, 50.3; Black, 1.2; Hispanic, 47.3; Other, 1.3.

Vital Statistics, 2008: Births, 112;

deaths, 85; marriages, 63; divorces, 0.

Recreation: Big Bend National Park, Big Bend Ranch State Park, Rio Grande Wild and Scenic River; ghost towns, scenic drives; hunting; museum; rockhound areas; cavalry post, Barton Warnock Environmental Education Center at Lajitas; Terlingua chili cookoff in November.

Minerals: Bentonite.

Agriculture: Beef cattle, meat goats, horses. Market value $9.6 million. Hunting leases important.

ALPINE (5,905) county seat; ranch trade center, tourism, varied manufacturing; Sul Ross State University; hospital.

Marathon (430) tourism, ranching center, Gage Hotel, Marathon Basin quilt show in October.

Also, **Basin** (30) and **Study Butte** (233), and **Terlingua** (58).

Population	**9,232**
Change fm 2000	4.13
Area (sq. mi.)	6,192.78
Land Area (sq. mi.)	6,192.61
Altitude (ft.)	1,400-7,825
Rainfall (in.) Alpine	17.19
Rainfall (in.) Big Bend	19.17
Jan. mean min. Alpine	31.3
Jan. mean min. Big Bend	36.1
July mean max. Alpine	88.7
July mean max. Big Bend	84.2
Civ. Labor	5,350
Unemployed	6.3
Wages	$39,853,674
Av. Weekly Wage	$677
Prop. Value	$850,136,947
Retail Sales	$87,498,875

Briscoe County

Physical Features: Partly on High Plains, broken by Caprock Escarpment, fork of Red River; sandy, loam soils.

Economy: Agribusiness, government/services, banking.

History: Apaches, displaced by Comanches around 1700. Ranchers settled in 1880s. County created from Bexar District, 1876, organized 1892; named for Andrew Briscoe, Republic of Texas soldier.

Race/Ethnicity, 2008: (In percent) Anglo, 71.4; Black, 2.4; Hispanic, 26.0; Other, 0.2.

Vital Statistics, 2008: Births, 23; deaths, 28; marriages, 9; divorces, 6.

Recreation: Hunting, fishing; scenic drives; museum; state park, trailway, Clarity tunnel, Mackenzie Reservoir.

Minerals: Insignificant.

Agriculture: Cotton, cattle, wheat, corn. Some 32,000 acres irrigated. Market value $27.9 million.

SILVERTON (731) county seat; agribusiness center, irrigation supplies manufactured; clinics.

Quitaque (411) trade center, agribusiness, nature tourism.

Population 1,637	July mean max. 90.9
Change fm 2000 .... −8.55	Civ. Labor 667
Area (sq. mi.) 901.59	Unemployed 6.3
Land Area (sq. mi.) 900.25	Wages $2,988,247
Altitude (ft.) 2,064-3,370	Av. Weekly Wage $549
Rainfall (in.) 22.34	Prop. Value $251,443,348
Jan. mean min. 21.6	Retail Sales $5,119,884

Brooks County

Physical Features: On Rio Grande plain; level to rolling; brushy; light to dark sandy loam soils.

Economy: Oil, gas, hunting leases, cattle, watermelons and hay.

History: Coahuiltecan Indians. Spanish land grants date to around 1800. County created from Hidalgo, Starr, Zapata counties, 1911, organized in 1912. Named for J.A. Brooks, Texas Ranger and legislator.

Race/Ethnicity, 2008: (In percent) Anglo, 7.5; Black, 0.1; Hispanic, 92.1; Other, 0.3.

Vital Statistics, 2008: Births, 145; deaths, 85; marriages, 40; divorces, 26.

Recreation: Hunting, fishing; Heritage Museum, Don Pedrito shrine; Fiesta del Campo in October.

Minerals: Oil, gas production; uranium.

Agriculture: Beef cow-calf operations, stocker; crops include hay, squash, watermelons, habanero peppers. Market value $19.1 million.

FALFURRIAS (4,981) county seat; oil and gas, agriculture, government/services.

Other towns include: **Encino** (143).

Population 7,223	Rainfall (in.) 25.42
Change fm 2000 .... −9.44	Jan. mean min. 43.9
Area (sq. mi.) 943.61	July mean max. 97.0
Land Area (sq. mi.) 943.28	Civ. Labor 3,175
Altitude (ft.) 46-431	Unemployed 9.8

Wages $23,982,529
Av. Weekly Wage $753
Prop. Value $1,616,263,636
Retail Sales $61,782,662

For explanation of sources, abbreviations and symbols, see p. 232 and foldout map.

Brown County

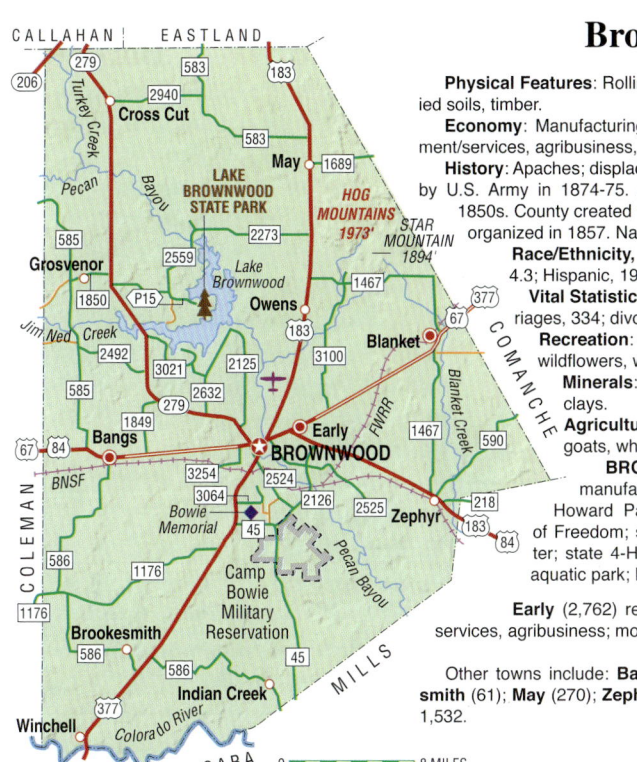

Physical Features: Rolling, hilly; drains to Colorado River; varied soils, timber.

Economy: Manufacturing plants, distribution centers, government/services, agribusiness, medical, education.

History: Apaches; displaced by Comanches who were removed by U.S. Army in 1874-75. Anglo-Americans first settled in mid-1850s. County created 1856 from Comanche, Travis counties, organized in 1857. Named for frontiersman Henry S. Brown.

Race/Ethnicity, 2008: (In percent) Anglo, 75.6; Black, 4.3; Hispanic, 19.2; Other, 0.9.

Vital Statistics, 2008: Births, 489; deaths, 514; marriages, 334; divorces, 115.

Recreation: State park; museums; fishing, hunting; wildflowers, walking trails.

Minerals: Oil, gas, paving materials, gravel, clays.

Agriculture: Cattle, hay, peanuts, pecans, meat goats, wheat, hogs. Market value $35.9 million.

BROWNWOOD (19,288) county seat; manufacturing, retail trade, distribution center; Howard Payne University, MacArthur Academy of Freedom; state substance abuse treatment center; state 4-H Club center; hospital; train museum; aquatic park; Reunion Celebration in September.

Early (2,762) retail, light manufacturing, government/services, agribusiness; motorcycle rally in October.

Other towns include: **Bangs** (1,603); **Blanket** (390); **Brookesmith** (61); **May** (270); **Zephyr** (201). **Lake Brownwood** area has 1,532.

Population	38,106
Change fm 2000	1.15
Area (sq. mi.)	956.94
Land Area (sq. mi.)	943.85
Altitude (ft.)	1,230-1,973
Rainfall (in.)	28.32
Jan. mean min.	29.6
July mean max.	95.0
Civ. Labor	18,488
Unemployed	7.9
Wages	$124,664,673
Av. Weekly Wage	$641
Prop. Value	$3,216,968,915
Retail Sales	$450,113,246

Downtown Falfurrias, Brooks County. Photo by Robert Plocheck.

Physical Features: Rolling to hilly; drains to Brazos, Yegua Creek, Somerville Lake; loam and heavy bottom soils; oaks, other trees.

Economy: Oil and gas, tourism, commuters to Texas A&M University, agribusiness.

History: Tonkawas and Caddoes roamed the area. Mexicans and Anglo-Americans settled around fort in 1830. Black freedmen migration increased until 1910. Germans, Czechs, Italians migrated in 1870s-80s. County created, organized, 1846 from Milam, Washington counties; named for Edward Burleson, a hero of the Texas Revolution.

Race/Ethnicity, 2008: (In percent) Anglo, 67.2; Black, 15.1; Hispanic, 17.2; Other, 0.5.

Vital Statistics, 2008: Births, 190; deaths, 172; marriages, 60; divorces, 54.

Recreation: Fishing, hunting; lake recreation; historic sites; Czech heritage museum.

Minerals: Oil, gas, sand, gravel.

Agriculture: Cattle, cotton, corn, hay, sorghum, broiler production, soybeans; some irrigation. Market value $56.4 million.

CALDWELL (4,104) county seat; agribusiness, oil and gas, manufacturing, distribution center, tourism; hospital; civic center, museum; Kolache Festival in September.

Somerville (1,376) tourism, railroad center, some manufacturing; museum; Country Cajun festival in March.

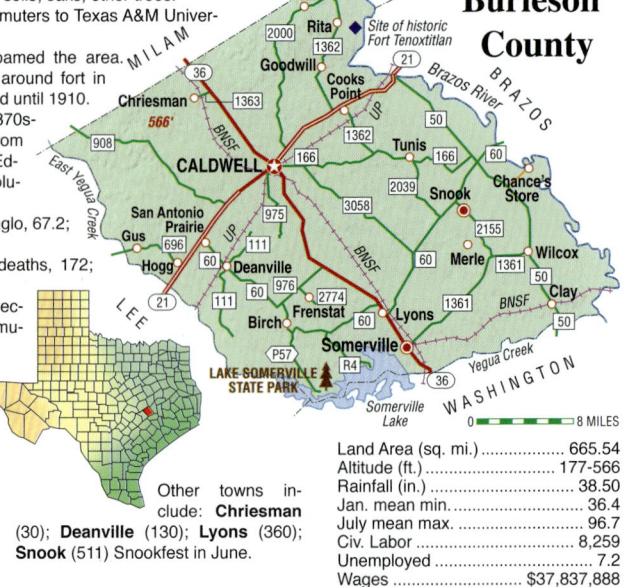

Burleson County

Other towns include: **Chriesman** (30); **Deanville** (130); **Lyons** (360); **Snook** (511) Snookfest in June.

Population	**17,187**
Change fm 2000	4.35
Area (sq. mi.)	677.78

Land Area (sq. mi.)	665.54
Altitude (ft.)	177-566
Rainfall (in.)	38.50
Jan. mean min.	36.4
July mean max.	96.7
Civ. Labor	8,259
Unemployed	7.2
Wages	$37,837,888
Av. Weekly Wage	$771
Prop. Value	$2,092,043,670
Retail Sales	$162,883,514

Burnet County

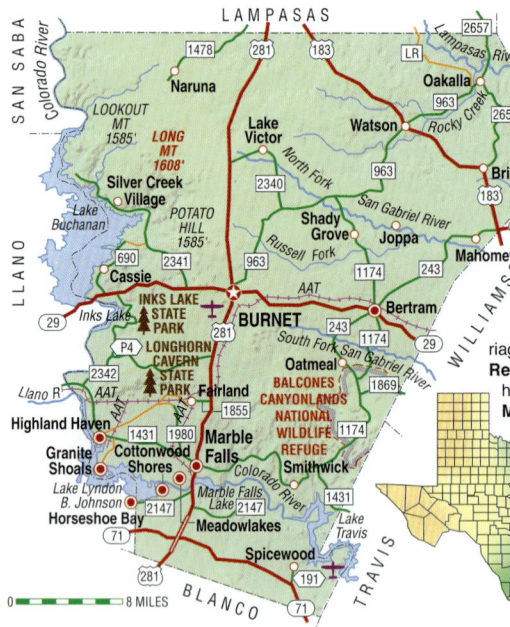

Physical Features: Scenic Hill Country county with lakes; caves; sandy, red, black waxy soils; cedars, other trees.

Economy: Tourism, stone processing, hunting leases.

History: Tonkawas, Lipan Apaches. Comanches raided in area. Frontier settlers arrived in the late 1840s. County created from Bell, Travis, Williamson counties, 1852; organized 1854; named for David G. Burnet, provisional president of the Republic.

Race/Ethnicity, 2008: (In percent) Anglo, 80.7; Black, 1.2; Hispanic, 17.3; Other, 0.7.

Vital Statistics, 2008: Births, 531; deaths, 393; marriages, 336; divorces, 191.

Recreation: Water sports on lakes; sites of historic forts; hunting; state parks; wildflowers; birding; scenic train ride.

Minerals: Granite, limestone.

Agriculture: Cattle, goats, grapes, hay. Market value $12.3 million. Deer, wild hog and turkey hunting leases.

BURNET (5,987) county seat; tourism, government/services, varied industries, ranching; hospital; museums; vineyards; Bluebonnet festival in April.

MARBLE FALLS (6,077) tourism, retail, manufacturing; granite, limestone quarries; August drag boat race.

Other towns include: **Bertram** (1,353) Oatmeal festival on Labor Day; **Briggs** (172); **Cottonwood Shores** (1,123); **Granite Shoals** (4,910); **Highland Haven** (431); **Meadowlakes** (1,777); **Spicewood** (2,000).

Also, part of **Horseshoe Bay** (3,418).

Population	**42,750**
Change fm 2000	25.19
Area (sq. mi.)	1,020.96
Land Area (sq. mi.)	996.04
Altitude (ft.)	682-1,608
Rainfall (in.)	32.43
Jan. mean min.	33.3
July mean max.	93.6
Civ. Labor	22,199
Unemployed	7.0

Wages	$117,319,137
Av. Weekly Wage	$740
Prop. Value	$6,317,576,980
Retail Sales	$568,058,143

For explanation of sources, abbreviations and symbols, see p. 232 and foldout map.

Caldwell County

Physical Features: Varied soils ranging from black clay to waxy; level, draining to San Marcos River.

Economy: Petroleum, varied manufacturing, government/services; part of Austin metro area, also near San Antonio.

History: Tonkawa area. Part of the DeWitt colony, Anglo-Americans settled in the 1830s. Mexican migration increased after 1890. County created, organized, from Bastrop, Gonzales counties, 1848; named for frontiersman Mathew Caldwell.

Race/Ethnicity, 2008: (In percent) Anglo, 46.2; Black, 8.5; Hispanic, 44.6; Other, 0.7.

Vital Statistics, 2008: Births, 497; deaths, 257; marriages, 168; divorces, 130.

Recreation: Fishing, state park, nature trails, museums; Luling Watermelon Thump and Lockhart Chisholm Trail roundup in June.

Minerals: Oil, gas, sand, gravel.

Agriculture: Eggs, beef cattle, broilers, hay, nurseries, cotton. Market value $47 million.

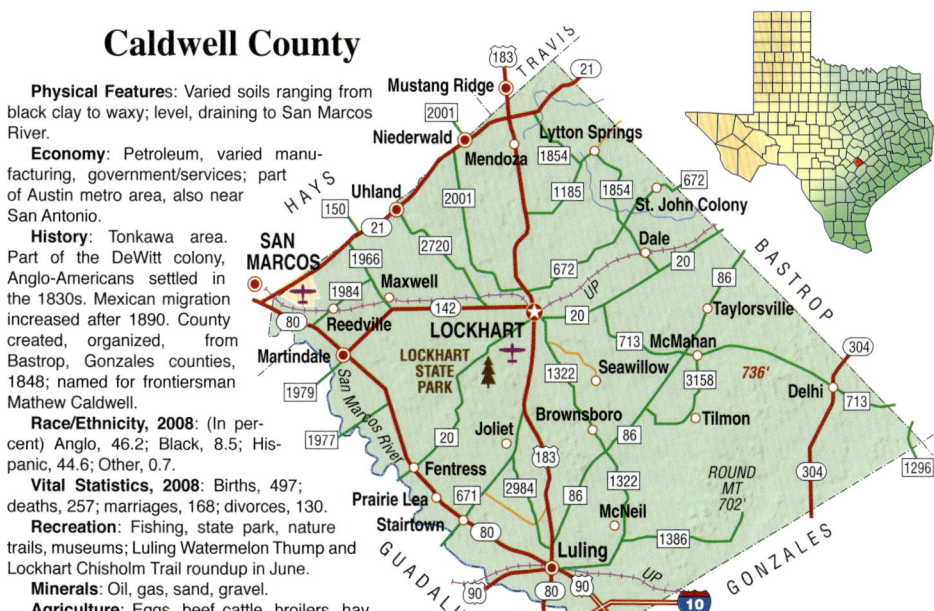

LOCKHART (12,698) county seat; petroleum, agribusiness center, tourism, light manufacturing, prison.

Luling (5,411) oil, tourism, agriculture; oil museum; hospitals, barbecue cook-off in April.

Other towns include: **Dale** (500); **Fentress** (291); **Martindale** (1,116); **Maxwell** (500); part of **Mustang Ridge** (861, mostly in Travis County), and **Prairie Lea** (255).

Also, part of **Niederwald** (565), part of **Uhland** (1,014) and a small part of **San Marcos** (44,894), all mostly in Hays County.

Population	38,066
Change fm 2000	18.24
Area (sq. mi.)	547.41

Land Area (sq. mi.)	545.73
Altitude (ft.)	315-736
Rainfall (in.)	36.86
Jan. mean min.	36.9
July mean max.	95.8
Civ. Labor	16,118
Unemployed	9.2
Wages	$57,383,491
Av. Weekly Wage	$634
Prop. Value	$2,234,476,871
Retail Sales	$293,936,019

Luling has decorated oil well pumpjacks with cartoon characters like Snoopy. Photo by Robert Plocheck.

Calhoun County

Physical Features: Sandy, broken by bays; partly on Matagorda Island.

Economy: Aluminum, plastics plants; marine construction; agribusinesses; petroleum; tourism; fish processing.

History: Karankawa area. Empresario Martín De León brought 41 families in 1825. County created and organized from Jackson, Matagorda, Victoria counties, 1846. Named for John C. Calhoun, U.S. statesman.

Race/Ethnicity, 2008: (In percent) Anglo, 48.4; Black, 2.7; Hispanic, 44.6; Other, 4.4.

Vital Statistics, 2008: Births, 321; deaths, 188; marriages, 161; divorces, 35.

Recreation: Beaches, fishing, water sports, duck, goose hunting; historic sites, county park.

Minerals: Oil, gas.

Agriculture: Cotton, cattle, corn, grain sorghum. Market value $29 million. Commercial fishing.

PORT LAVACA (12,248) county seat; commercial seafood operations, offshore drilling, tourist center; some manufacturing; convention center; hospital; La Salle Days in April.

Other towns include: **Long Mott** (76); **Point Comfort** (737) aluminum, plastic plants, deepwater port; **Port O'Connor** (1,253) tourist center, seafood processing, manufacturing, library, lighted boat parade in December; **Seadrift** (1,364) commercial fishing, processing plants, Bayfront Park, Shrimpfest in June.

Population		21,381
Change fm 2000		3.55
Area (sq. mi.)		1,032.16
Land Area (sq. mi.)		512.31
Altitude (ft.)		sea level-56
Rainfall (in.)		34.78
Jan. mean min.		47.9
July mean max.		88.2

Civ. Labor	9,666	Av. Weekly Wage	$1,048
Unemployed	10.2	Prop. Value	$4,061,520,191
Wages	$138,477,657	Retail Sales	$203,565,216

Callahan County

Physical Features: On divide between Brazos, Colorado rivers; level to rolling.

Economy: Ranching; feed and fertilizer business; many residents commute to Abilene; 200,000 acres in hunting leases.

History: Comanche territory until 1870s. Anglo-American settlement began around 1860. County created 1858 from Bexar, Bosque, Travis counties; organized 1877. Named for Texas Ranger J.H. Callahan.

Race/Ethnicity, 2008: (In percent) Anglo, 91.7; Black, 0.3; Hispanic, 6.9; Other, 1.1.

Vital Statistics, 2008: Births, 154; deaths, 162; marriages, 47; divorces, 54.

Recreation: Hunting, lakes; museums; Cross Plains Hunters' Feed at deer season.

Minerals: Oil and gas.

Agriculture: Cattle, wheat, sorghum, oats. Market value $25.4 million. Hunting leases important.

BAIRD (1,496) county seat; ranching/agricultural trade center, antiques shops, some manufacturing, shipping; historic sites; Market Daze in June.

Clyde (3,713) steel water systems manufacturing, government/services; library; Pecan Festival in October.

Other towns include: **Cross Plains** (982) oil and gas, agriculture, and government/services, home of creator of Conan the Barbarian, museum, Barbarian Festival in June; **Putnam** (94).

Population		13,544
Change fm 2000		4.95
Area (sq. mi.)		901.26
Land Area (sq. mi.)		898.62
Altitude (ft.)		1,350-2,204
Rainfall (in.)		25.52
Jan. mean min.		31.1
July mean max.		94.9
Civ. Labor		7,129
Unemployed		6.9

Wages	$19,844,231
Av. Weekly Wage	$725
Prop. Value	$1,277,371,840
Retail Sales	$51,233,284

Cameron County

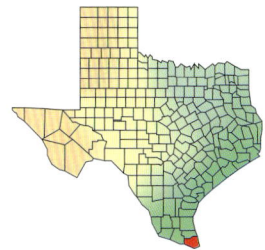

Physical Features: Southernmost county in rich Rio Grande Valley soils; flat landscape; semitropical climate.

Economy: Agribusiness, tourism, seafood processing, shipping, manufacturing, government/services.

History: Coahuiltecan Indian area. Spanish land grants date to 1781. County created from Nueces County, 1848; named for Capt. Ewen Cameron of Mier Expedition.

Race/Ethnicity, 2008: (In percent) Anglo, 11.8; Black, 0.3; Hispanic, 87.1; Other, 0.8.

Vital Statistics, 2008: Births, 8,119; deaths, 2,172; marriages, 2,507; divorces, 660.

Recreation: South Padre Island: year-round resort; fishing, hunting, water sports; historical sites, Palo Alto visitors center; gateway to Mexico, state parks; wildlife refuge; recreational vehicle center.

Minerals: Natural gas, oil.

Agriculture: Cotton, grain sorghums, vegetables. Ranked second in sugar cane acreage. Wholesale nursery plants raised. Small feedlot and cow-calf operations; 200,000 acres irrigated, mostly cotton and grain sorghums Market value $112.4 million. Ranked second in value of aquaculture.

BROWNSVILLE (175,023) county seat; international trade, varied industries, shipping, tourism; college, hospitals, crippled children health center; Gladys Porter Zoo, historic Fort Brown; University of Texas at Brownsville.

Harlingen (64,849) health care, manufacturing, agribusiness, food processing, ecotourism, education; hospitals; nature center; greyhound races; birding festival in November.

San Benito (24,250) varied manufacturing, bottling; tourism; hospital; recreation facilities.

South Padre Island (2,816) beaches, tourism/convention center, birding, Coast Guard station, Sand Castle Days in October.

Other towns include: **Bayview** (383); **Bluetown** (356); **Cameron Park** (6,963); **Combes** (2,895); Encantada-Ranchito El Calaboz (2,255); **Indian Lake** (640); **La Feria** (7,302); **Laguna Heights** (3,488); **Laguna Vista** (3,117); **Laureles** (3,692); **Los Fresnos** (5,542) Little Graceland Museum, Butterfly Farm, library; **Los Indios** (1,083); **Olmito** (1,210); **Palm Valley** (1,304).

Also, **Port Isabel** (5,006) tourist center, fishing, museums, old lighthouse, Shrimp Cook-Off in November; **Primera** (4,070); **Rancho Viejo** (2,437); **Rangerville** (289); **Rio Hondo** (2,356); **Santa Maria** (733); **Santa Rosa** (2,873).

Population	**406,220**
Change fm 2000	21.18
Area (sq. mi.)	1,276.33
Land Area (sq. mi.)	905.76
Altitude (ft.)	sea level-67
Rainfall (in.)	27.55
Jan. mean min.	50.5
July mean max.	92.4
Civ. Labor	159,656
Unemployed	12.4
Wages	$993,484,601
Av. Weekly Wage	$610
Prop. Value	$16,814,992,080
Retail Sales	$3,442,024,445

For explanation of sources, abbreviations and symbols, see p. 232 and foldout map.

Camp County

Population	12,401
Change fm 2000	7.38
Area (sq. mi.)	203.20
Land Area (sq. mi.)	197.51
Altitude (ft.)	236-538
Rainfall (in.)	45.10
Jan. mean min.	32.0
July mean max.	94.0
Civ. Labor	6,013
Unemployed	9.2
Wages	$35,186,693
Av. Weekly Wage	$628
Prop. Value	$900,441,887
Retail Sales	$97,213,157

Physical Features: East Texas county with forested hills; drains to Cypress Creek on north; Lake O' the Pines, Lake Bob Sandlin; third smallest county in Texas.

Economy: Agribusiness, chicken processing, timber industries, light manufacturing, retirement center.

History: Caddo area. Anglo-American settlers arrived in late 1830s. Antebellum slaveholding area. County created, organized, from Upshur County 1874; named for jurist J.L. Camp.

Race/Ethnicity, 2008: (In percent) Anglo, 61.8; Black, 17.8; Hispanic, 19.9; Other, 0.5.

Vital Statistics, 2008: Births, 179; deaths, 135; marriages, 162; divorces, 34.

Recreation: Water sports, fishing on lakes; farmstead and airship museum; Pittsburg hot links; Chickfest in September.

Minerals: Oil, gas, clays, coal.

Agriculture: Poultry and products important; beef, dairy cattle, horses; peaches (second in acreage), hay, blueberries, vegetables. Market value $143.1 million. Forestry.

PITTSBURG (4,497) county seat; agribusiness, timber, tourism, food processing, light manufacturing, commuting to Longview, Tyler; hospital; community college; Prayer Tower.

Other towns include: **Leesburg** (128) and **Rocky Mound** (75).

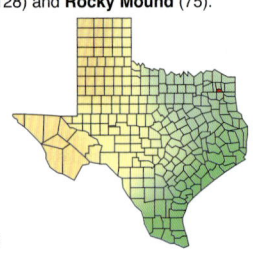

Carson County

Physical Features: In center of Panhandle on level, some broken land; loam soils.

Economy: Pantex nuclear weapons assembly/disassembly facility (U.S. Department of Energy), commuting to Amarillo, petrochemical plants, agribusiness.

History: Apaches, displaced by Comanches. Anglo-American ranchers settled in the 1880s. German, Polish farmers arrived around 1910. County created from Bexar District, 1876; organized 1888. Named for Republic secretary of state S.P. Carson.

Race/Ethnicity, 2008: (In percent) Anglo, 90.8; Black, 0.8; Hispanic, 7.5; Other, 0.9.

Vital Statistics, 2008: Births, 69; deaths, 66; marriages, 44; divorces, 22.

Recreation: Museum, The Cross at Groom; Square House Barbecue in fall.

Minerals: Oil, gas production.

Agriculture: Cattle, cotton, wheat, sorghum, corn, hay, soybeans. Market value $93.7 million.

PANHANDLE (2,452) county seat; government/services, agribusiness, petroleum center, commuters to Amarillo; Veterans Day celebration, car show in June.

Other towns include: **Groom** (574) farming center, government/services, Groom Day festival in August; **Skellytown** (473); **White Deer** (1,000) Polish Sausage festival in November.

Population	6,182
Change fm 2000	–5.13
Area (sq. mi.)	924.10
Land Area (sq. mi.)	923.19
Altitude (ft.)	2,926-3,595
Rainfall (in.)	22.21
Jan. mean min.	19.3
July mean max.	90.8
Civ. Labor	3,261
Unemployed	5.6
Wages	$92,096,340
Av. Weekly Wage	$1,461
Prop. Value	$1,235,737,050
Retail Sales	$163,852,802

For explanation of sources, abbreviations and symbols, see p. 232 and foldout map.

Cass County

Physical Features: Forested Northeast county rolling to hilly; drained by Cypress Bayou, Sulphur River.

Economy: Timber, paper industries; varied manufacturing; agribusiness; government/services.

History: Caddoes, displaced by other tribes in 1790s. Anglo-Americans arrived in 1830s. Antebellum slaveholding area. County created, organized, 1846 from Bowie County; named for U.S. Sen. Lewis Cass.

Race/Ethnicity, 2008: (In percent) Anglo, 76.6; Black, 20.5; Hispanic, 2.1; Other, 0.7.

Vital Statistics, 2008: Births, 367; deaths, 405; marriages, 215; divorces, 123.

Recreation: Fishing, hunting, water sports; state, county parks; lake, wildflower trails.

Minerals: Oil, iron ore.

Agriculture: Poultry, cattle, nurseries, forage, watermelons. Market value $68.8 million. Timber important.

LINDEN (1,988) county seat, timber, agribusiness, tourism; oldest courthouse still in use as courthouse, hospital; Rock and Roll Hall of Fame.

ATLANTA (5,675) Paper and timber industries, government/services, varied manufacturing, hospital, library; Forest Festival in August.

Other towns include: **Avinger** (444) timber, paper industry, steel plant, early cemetery, Glory Days celebration in

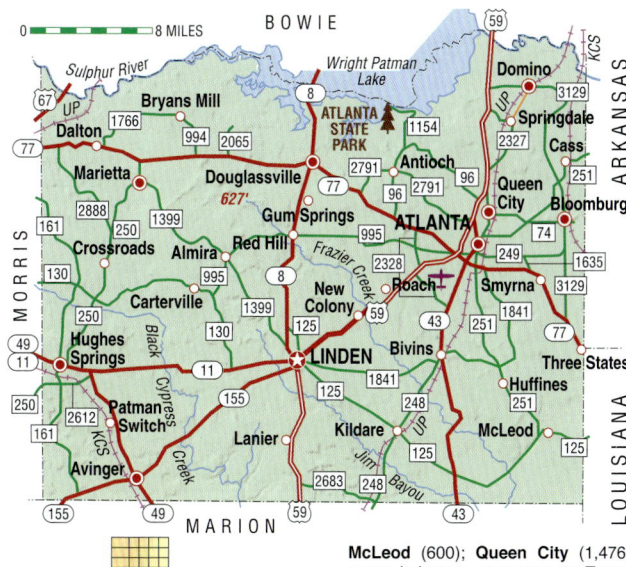

October; **Bivins** (215); **Bloomburg** (404); **Domino** (93); **Douglassville** (229); **Hughes Springs** (1,760) varied manufacturing, warehousing, trucking school, Pumpkin Glow in October; **Kildare** (104); **Marietta** (134);

McLeod (600); **Queen City** (1,476) paper industry, commuters to Texarkana, government/services, historic sites.

Population	30,464
Change fm 2000	0.09
Area (sq. mi.)	960.35
Land Area (sq. mi.)	937.35
Altitude (ft.)	167-627
Rainfall (in.)	48.20
Jan. mean min.	31.0
July mean max.	94.0
Civ. Labor	13,479
Unemployed	11.4
Wages	$67,569,101
Av. Weekly Wage	$677
Prop. Value	$2,127,065,966
Retail Sales	$245,385,001

Kite flying near Port Isabel, Cameron County. Photo by Robert Plocheck.

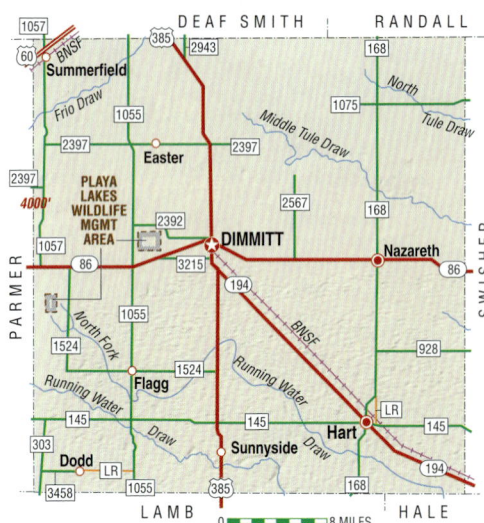

Castro County

Physical Features: Flat Panhandle county, drains to creeks, draws and playas; underground water.

Economy: Agribusiness.

History: Apaches, displaced by Comanches in 1720s. Anglo-American ranchers began settling in 1880s. Germans settled after 1900. Mexican migration increased after 1950. County created 1876 from Bexar District, organized 1891. Named for Henri Castro, Texas colonizer.

Race/Ethnicity, 2008: (In percent) Anglo, 40.5; Black, 2.6; Hispanic, 56.6; Other, 0.3.

Vital Statistics, 2008: Births, 152; deaths, 64; marriages, 51; divorces, 13.

Recreation: Pheasant hunting; Italian POW camp site; Dimmitt Harvest Days celebrated in August.

Minerals: Insignificant.

Agriculture: Beef cattle, dairies, corn, cotton, wheat, sheep. Market value $973.4 million; second in state.

DIMMITT (4,393) county seat; agribusiness center; library, hospital; quilt festival in April.

Other towns include: **Hart** (1,114) and **Nazareth** (311).

Population		8,062
Change fm 2000		–2.69
Area (sq. mi.)		899.32
Land Area (sq. mi.)		898.31
Altitude (ft.)		3,565-4,000

Rainfall (in.)		19.71
Jan. mean min.		20.4
July mean max.		90.1
Civ. Labor		3,595
Unemployed		5.9

Wages		$21,177,868
Av. Weekly Wage		$620
Prop. Value		$674,830,460
Retail Sales		$35,794,221

Chambers County

Physical Features: Gulf coastal plain, coastal soils; some forests.

Economy: Chemical plants, agribusiness, seafood processing, distribution facilities.

History: Karankawa and other coastal tribes. Nuestra Señora de la Luz Mission established near present Wallisville in 1756. County created, organized, 1858 from Liberty, Jefferson counties. Named for Gen. T. J. Chambers, surveyor.

Race/Ethnicity, 2008: (In percent) Anglo, 74.7; Black, 9.4; Hispanic, 14.8; Other, 1.1.

Vital Statistics, 2008: Births, 448; deaths, 224; marriages, 166; divorces, 165.

Recreation: Fishing, hunting; water sports; camping; county parks; wildlife refuge; historic sites; Wallisville Heritage Museum; Texas Gatorfest in September.

Minerals: Oil, gas.

Agriculture: Rice, beef, forages, soybeans, aquaculture, corn, winter wheat, grain sorghum; significant irrigation. Market value $17.6 million.

ANAHUAC (2,243) county seat; canal connects with Houston Ship Channel; agribusiness; hospital; library.

WINNIE (3,254) oil and gas; hospital; government/services; Texas Rice Festival in October.

Other towns include: **Beach City** (2,198), **Cove** (510), **Hankamer** (226), **Mont Belvieu** (3,835), **Old River-Winfree** (1,245), **Stowell** (1,756) and **Wallisville** (452).

Population		35,096
Change fm 2000		34.82
Area (sq. mi.)		871.99
Land Area (sq. mi.)		599.31
Altitude (ft.)		sea level-82
Rainfall (in.)		54.08
Jan. mean min.		41.7
July mean max.		91.9
Civ. Labor		15,728
Unemployed		10.4
Wages		$123,451,371
Av. Weekly Wage		$999
Prop. Value		$6,929,543,790
Retail Sales		$1,824,950,335

For explanation of sources, abbreviations and symbols, see p. 232 and foldout map.

Cherokee County

Physical Features: East Texas county; hilly, partly forested; drains to Angelina, Neches rivers; many streams, lakes; sandy, clay soils.

Economy: Government/services, varied manufacturing, agribusiness.

History: Caddo tribes attracted Spanish missionaries around 1720. Cherokees began settling area around 1820, and soon afterward Anglo-Americans began to arrive. Cherokees forced to Indian Territory 1839. Named for Indian tribe; created, organized, 1846 from Nacogdoches County.

Race/Ethnicity, 2008: (In percent) Anglo, 65.3; Black, 15.6; Hispanic, 18.4; Other, 0.8.

Vital Statistics, 2008: Births, 741; deaths, 547; marriages, 379; divorces, 151.

Recreation: Water sports; fishing, hunting; historic sites and parks; Texas State Railroad; nature trails through forests; lakes.

Minerals: Gas, oil.

Agriculture: Nurseries (first in state in value of sales), hay, beef cattle, dairies, poultry. Market value $140.3 million. Timber, hunting income significant.

RUSK (5,551) county seat; agribusiness, tourism, state mental hospital, prison unit; heritage festival in October.

JACKSONVILLE (14,544) varied manufacturing, plastics, agribusiness, tourism, retail center; hospitals; junior colleges; Love's Lookout; Tomato Fest in June.

Other towns include: **Alto** (1,225) farming, timber, light manufacturing, pecan festival in November; **Cuney** (140);

Gallatin (419); **Maydelle** (250); **New Summerfield** (1,111); **Reklaw** (379, partly in Rusk County); **Wells** (790). Part of **Bullard** and part of **Troup**.

Population	50,845	Altitude (ft.)	187-775
Change fm 2000	8.97	Rainfall (in.)	48.50
Area (sq. mi.)	1,061.93	Jan. mean min.	36.8
Land Area (sq. mi.)	1,052.22	uly mean max.	92.8
		Civ. Labor	20,560

Unemployed	9.7
Wages	$121,437,627
Av. Weekly Wage	$621
Prop. Value	$3,296,694,158
Retail Sales	$386,497,896

A country road near Charlie, Clay County. Photo by Robert Plocheck.

Childress County

Physical Features: Rolling prairie, at corner of Panhandle, draining to fork of Red River; mixed soils.

Economy: Government/services, retail trade, tourism, agriculture.

History: Apaches, displaced by Comanches. Ranchers arrived around 1880. County created 1876 from Bexar, Young districts; organized 1887; named for writer of Texas Declaration of Independence, George C. Childress.

Race/Ethnicity, 2008: (In percent) Anglo, 62.0; Black, 14.1; Hispanic, 23.3; Other, 0.7.

Vital Statistics, 2008: Births, 90; deaths, 71; marriages, 62; divorces, 23.

Recreation: Recreation on lakes and creek, fishing; hunting of deer, turkey, wild hog, quail, dove; parks; county museum.

Agriculture: Cotton, beef cattle, wheat, hay, sorghum, peanuts; 6,000 acres irrigated. Market value $25.9 million. Hunting leases.

CHILDRESS (6,105) county seat; agribusiness, hospital, prison unit; settlers reunion and rodeo in July. Other towns include: **Tell** (15).

Population	**7,041**	Altitude (ft.)	1,560-2,060
Change fm 2000	−8.42	Rainfall (in.)	22.65
Area (sq. mi.)	713.61	Jan. mean min.	26.8
Land Area (sq. mi.)	710.34	July mean max.	95.3
		Civ. Labor	3,183

Unemployed	7.5
Wages	$17,454,795
Av. Weekly Wage	$533
Prop. Value	$510,284,430
Retail Sales	$76,554,592

Clay County

Physical Features: Hilly, rolling; Northwest county drains to Red, Trinity rivers, lake; sandy loam, chocolate soils; mesquites, post oaks.

Economy: Oil, agribusiness, varied manufacturing.

History: Wichitas arrived from north-central plains in mid-1700s, followed by Apaches and Comanches. Ranching attempts began in 1850s. County created from Cooke County, 1857; Indians forced disorganization, 1862; reorganized, 1873; named for Henry Clay, U.S. statesman.

Race/Ethnicity, 2008: (In percent) Anglo, 94.6; Black, 0.4; Hispanic, 3.9; Other, 1.1.

Vital Statistics, 2008: Births, 108; deaths, 104; marriages, 71; divorces, 45.

Recreation: Fishing, water sports; state park; pioneer reunion.

Minerals: Oil and gas, stone.

Agriculture: Beef and dairy cattle, horses raised; wheat, cotton, pecan, peaches. Market value $56.9 million. Oaks, cedar, elms sold to nurseries, mesquite cut for firewood.

HENRIETTA (3,141) county seat; oil; agribusiness, government/services, manufacturing, tourism; hospital; museum; Turkey Fest in April.

Other towns include: **Bellevue** (362), **Bluegrove** (135), **Byers** (496), **Dean** (493), **Jolly** (172), **Petrolia** (686).

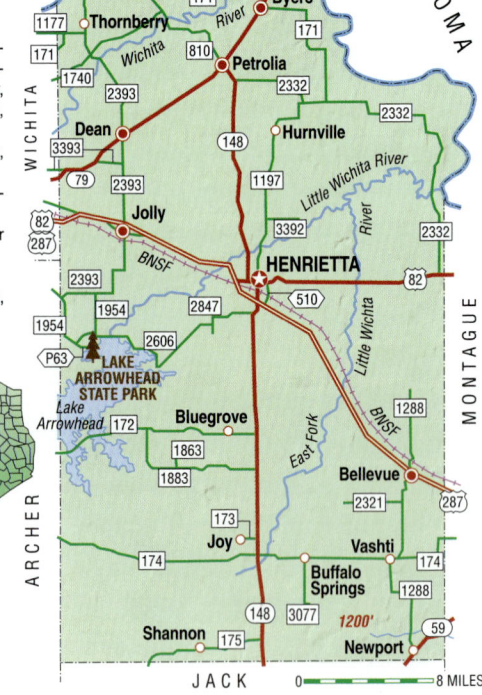

Population	**10,752**
Change fm 2000	−2.31
Area (sq. mi.)	1,116.17
Land Area (sq. mi.)	1,097.82
Altitude (ft.)	791-1,200
Rainfall (in.)	31.66
Jan. mean min.	26.8
July mean max.	95.0
Civ. Labor	6,028

Unemployed	6.7
Wages	$12,981,204
Av. Weekly Wage	$636
Prop. Value	$1,378,872,593
Retail Sales	$62,497,607

Cochran County

Physical Features: South Plains bordering New Mexico with small lakes (playas); underground water; loam, sandy loam soils.

Economy: Agribusiness, government/services, retail.

History: Hunting area for various Indian tribes. Ranches operated in the 1880s but population in 1900 was still only 25. Farming began in the 1920s. County created from Bexar, Young districts, 1876; organized 1924; named for Robert Cochran, who died at the Alamo.

Race/Ethnicity 2008: (In percent) Anglo, 46.2; Black, 5.2; Hispanic, 47.9; Other, 0.7.

Vital Statistics, 2008: Births, 67; deaths, 30; marriages, 6; divorces, 5.

Recreation: Museum; Last Frontier Trail Drive and Buffalo Soldier Day in June.

Minerals: Insignificant.

Agriculture: Cotton, peanuts, sorghum, peas, sunflowers, wheat. Crops 60 percent irrigated. Market value $91.7 million.

MORTON (2,006) county seat; oil, farm center, meat packing, light manufacture; hospital.

Other towns include: **Bledsoe** (126), **Whiteface** (449).

For explanation of sources, abbreviations and symbols, see p. 232 and foldout map.

Population **3,127**	Altitude (ft.) 3,565-4,000	Unemployed 9.3
Change fm 2000 .... −16.17	Rainfall (in.) 18.34	Wages $7,660,524
Area (sq. mi.) 775.31	Jan. temp. min. 23.1	Av. Weekly Wage $687
Land Area (sq. mi.) 775.22	July temp. max. 91.4	Prop. Value $667,857,680
	Civ. Labor 1,349	Retail Sales $22,519,847

The 1937 Childress County Courthouse in Modern style. Photo by Robert Plocheck.

Coke County

Physical Features: West Texas prairie, hills, Colorado River valley; sandy loam, red soils; reservoirs.

Economy: Oil and gas, government/services, agriculture.

History: From 1700 to 1870s, Comanches roamed the area. Ranches began operating after the Civil War. County created, organized, 1889 from Tom Green County; named for Gov. Richard Coke.

Race/Ethnicity, 2008: (In percent) Anglo, 77.4; Black, 1.8; Hispanic, 19.9; Other, 0.9.

Vital Statistics, 2008: Births, 31; deaths, 52; marriages, 13; divorces, 10.

Recreation: Hunting, fishing, Caliche Loop birdwatching trail; lakes; Sumac hiking trail; historic sites, Fort Chadbourne, county museum, Fort Chadbourne Days in May; amphitheater.

Minerals: Oil, gas.

Agriculture: Beef cattle, small grains, sheep and goats, hay. Market value $13.6 million.

ROBERT LEE (1,049) county seat; oil and gas, wind farms, ranching, government/services; old jail museum.

BRONTE (999) ranching, oil.

Other towns include: **Silver** (34) and **Tennyson** (46). Also, a small part of **Blackwell** (311).

Population	3,320
Change fm 2000	–14.08
Area (sq. mi.)	927.97
Land Area (sq. mi.)	898.81
Altitude (ft.)	1,700-2,608
Rainfall (in.)	23.00
Jan. mean min.	29.0
July mean max.	96.4
Civ. Labor	1,362
Unemployed	8.1
Wages	$5,450,770
Av. Weekly Wage	$577
Prop. Value	$793,843,770
Retail Sales	$19,287,799

Coleman County

Physical Features: Hilly, rolling; drains to Colorado River, Pecan Bayou; lakes; mesquite, oaks.

Economy: Agribusiness, petroleum, ecotourism, varied manufacturing.

History: Presence of Apaches and Comanches brought military outpost, Camp Colorado, before the Civl War. Settlers arrived after organization. County created 1858 from Brown, Travis counties; organized 1864; named for Houston's aide, R.M. Coleman.

Race/Ethnicity, 2008: (In percent), Anglo, 80.4; Black, 2.6; Hispanic, 16.3; Other, 0.7.

Vital Statistics, 2008: Births, 112; deaths, 135; marriages, 69; divorces, 61.

Recreation: Fishing, hunting; water sports; city park, historic sites; lakes; Santa Anna Peak; Santa Anna bison cook-off in May.

Minerals: Oil, gas, stone, clays.

Agriculture: Cattle, wheat, sheep, hay, grain sorghum, goats, oats, cotton. Market value $20 million. Mesquite for firewood and furniture.

COLEMAN (4,709) county seat; varied manufacturing; hospital, library, museums; Fiesta de la Paloma in October.

Santa Anna (1,099) agribusiness, some manufacturing, tourism.

Other towns include: **Burkett** (30), **Goldsboro** (30), **Gouldbusk** (70), **Novice** (139), **Rockwood** (53), **Talpa** (127), and **Valera** (80).

For explanation of sources, abbreviations and symbols, see p. 232 and foldout map.

Population	8,895
Change fm 2000	–3.68
Area (sq. mi.)	1,281.45
Land Area (sq. mi.)	1,260.20
Altitude (ft.)	1,289-2,250
Rainfall (in.)	28.70
Jan. mean min.	30.0
July mean max.	93.7
Civ. Labor	4,318
Unemployed	7.1
Wages	$15,15,857,635
Av. Weekly Wage	$568
Prop. Value	$1,304,741,766
Retail Sales	$54,934,032

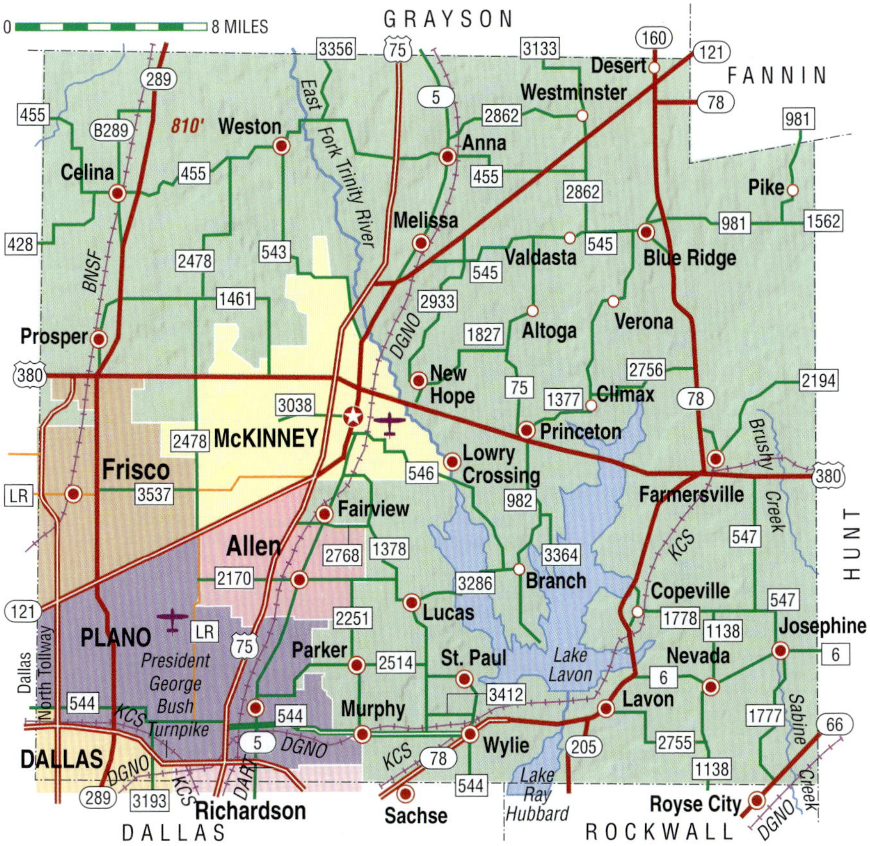

Map

G R A Y S O N

F A N N I N

0 ——— 8 MILES

455
289
B289
810' Weston
Celina
455
428
2478
1461
BNSF
Prosper
380
2478 McKINNEY
3038
Frisco
3537
LR
121
PLANO
President George Bush Turnpike
544
DALLAS
289 3193
Richardson
D A L L A S

D E N T O N

3356
75
East Fork Trinity River
5
Anna
2862
Melissa
543
2933
1827
New Hope
75
3038
Lowry Crossing
546
Fairview
2768 1378
3286
Lucas
2251
Parker
2514
St. Paul
3412
Murphy
544
KCS
DGNO
5
KCS
78
Wylie
544
Sachse
Lake Ray Hubbard

3133
Desert
Westminster
2862
455
2862
Valdasta
545
545
Altoga
1377 Climax
Princeton
982
3364
Branch
Copeville
1778 1138
Nevada
6
Lavon
205
2755
1138

160
121
78
981
Pike
981 1562
545 Blue Ridge
Verona
2756
78 2194
380
Brushy Creek
Farmersville
547
KCS
547
Josephine
6
1777
66
Royse City
Sabine Creek
DGNO

R O C K W A L L

H U N T

Physical Features: Heavy, black clay soil; level to rolling; drains to Trinity, Lake Lavon.

Economy: Government/services, manufacturing plants, retail and wholesale center, many residents work in Dallas.

History: Caddo area until 1850s. Settlers of Peters colony arrived in early 1840s. County created, organized, from Fannin County 1846. Named for pioneer settler Collin McKinney.

Race/Ethnicity, 2008: (In percent) Anglo, 72.4; Black, 5.6; Hispanic, 13.3; Other, 8.7.

Vital Statistics, 2008: Births, 11,028; deaths, 2,937; marriages, 4,766; divorces, 2,154.

Recreation: Fishing, water sports; historic sites; old homes restoration, tours; natural science museum.

Minerals: Insignificant.

Agriculture: Landscape nurseries, corn, wheat, cattle, hay, grain sorghum. Market value $61.1 million.

McKINNEY (131,117) county seat; agribusiness, trade center, varied industry; hospital, community college; museums.

PLANO (259,841) telecommunications, manufacturing, newspaper printing, medical services, research center, commercial and financial center; com-

Collin County

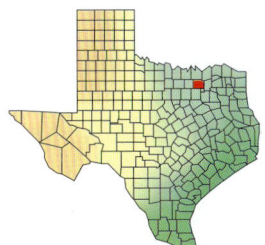

munity college; hospitals; balloon festival in September.

Frisco (116,989) technical, areospace industry, hospital, community college.

Other towns include: **Allen** (84,246) manufacturing, wholesale trade, hospital, community college, nature conservatory, natatorium, historic dam, Stampede radeo in October; **Anna** (8,249) **Blue Ridge** (822); **Celina** (6,028) museum, historic town square, Fun Day in September; **Copeville** (243).

Also, **Fairview** (7,248) government/services, retail center, commuters, museum, old mill site, wildlife

sanctuary; **Farmersville** (3,301) agriculture, light industries, Audie Murphy Day in June.

Also, **Josephine** (812); **Lavon** (2,219); **Lowry Crossing** (1,711); **Lucas** (5,166); **Melissa** (4,695) industrial plants, library, old town; **Murphy** (17,708); **Nevada** (822); **New Hope** (614); **Parker** (3,811); **Princeton** (6,807) manufacturing, commuters, Spring Onion festival in April.

Also, **Prosper** (9,423); **St. Paul** (1,066); **Westminster** (861); **Weston** (563); **Wylie** (41,427) manufacturing, retail, hospital, historic sites, big cat sanctuary, July Jubilee.

Also, part of **Dallas**, part of **Richardson** and part of **Sachse**.

Population	782,341
Change fm 2000	59.12
Area (sq. mi.)	885.85
Land Area (sq. mi.)	847.56
Altitude (ft.)	434-810
Rainfall (in.)	41.01
Jan. mean min.	31.1
July mean max.	92.7
Civ. Labor	423,740
Unemployed	7.6
Wages	$4,121,226,643
Av. Weekly Wage	$1,091
Prop. Value	$84,552,357,870
Retail Sales	$11,687,768,949

Collingsworth County

Physical Features: Panhandle county of rolling, broken terrain, draining to Red River forks; sandy and loam soils.

Economy: Agribusiness.

History: Apaches, displaced by Comanches. Ranchers from England arrived in late 1870s. County created 1876, from Bexar and Young districts, organized 1890. Named for Republic of Texas' first chief justice, James Collinsworth (name misspelled in law).

Race/Ethnicity, 2008: (In percent) Anglo, 66.5; Black, 5.7; Hispanic, 25.9; Other, 1.9.

Vital Statistics, 2008: Births, 50; deaths, 43; marriages, 26; divorces, 12.

Recreation: Deer, quail hunting; children's camp, county museum, pioneer park; Wellington peanut festival in September.

Minerals: Gas, oil production.

Agriculture: Cotton, peanuts (second in acreage), cow-calf operations, wheat, stocker cattle; 22,000 acres irrigated. Market value $50.3 million.

WELLINGTON (2,189) county seat; peanut-processing plants, varied manufacturing, agriculture; hospital, library; restored Ritz Theatre.

Other towns include: **Dodson** (109), **Quail** (19), **Samnorwood** (51).

Population	3,057
Change fm 2000	–4.65
Area (sq. mi.)	919.44
Land Area (sq. mi.)	918.80
Altitude (ft.)	1,750-2,840
Rainfall (in.)	22.80
Jan. mean min.	27.0
July mean max.	97.9
Civ. Labor	1,371
Unemployed	6.1
Wages	$7,180,426
Av. Weekly Wage	$589
Prop. Value	$477,121,190
Retail Sales	$13,165,689

Colorado County

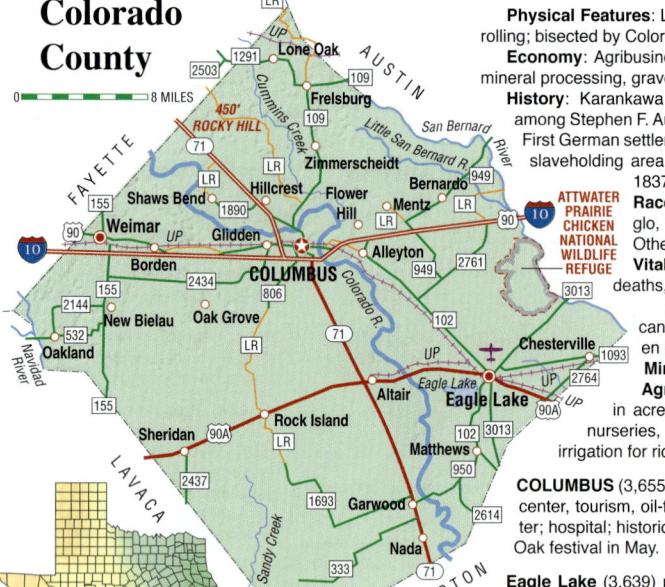

Physical Features: Located in three soil areas; level to rolling; bisected by Colorado River; oaks.

Economy: Agribusiness, oil-field services, ecotourism, mineral processing, gravel mining.

History: Karankawa and other tribes. Anglo settlers among Stephen F. Austin's Old Three Hundred families. First German settlers arrived around 1840. Antebellum slaveholding area. County created 1836, organized 1837; named for river.

Race/Ethnicity, 2008: (In percent) Anglo, 59.8; Black, 15.5; Hispanic, 24.1; Other, 0.5.

Vital Statistics, 2008: Births, 278; deaths, 254; marriages, 142; divorces, 67.

Recreation: Hunting, bicycling, canoeing; historic sites; prairie chicken refuge; opera house in Columbus.

Minerals: Gas, oil.

Agriculture: Rice (second in state in acres), cattle, corn, cotton, soybeans, nurseries, hay, poultry, sorghum; significant irrigation for rice. Market value $72 million.

COLUMBUS (3,655) county seat; mining, agribusiness center, tourism, oil-field servicing, timber-treating center; hospital; historical sites, homes, walking tour; Live Oak festival in May.

Eagle Lake (3,639) rice drying center; hospital; goose hunting; Prairie Edge museum.

Weimar (2,151) agriculture, light industry, meat processing, retail; hospital, library; "Gedenke" (remember) celebration on Mother's Day weekend.

Other towns include: **Altair** (30), **Garwood** (975), **Glidden** (661), **Nada** (165), **Oakland** (80), **Rock Island** (160), **Sheridan** (225).

Population	20,874
Change fm 2000	2.37
Area (sq. mi.)	973.59
Land Area (sq. mi.)	962.95
Altitude (ft.)	125-450
Rainfall (in.)	44.72
Jan. mean min.	36.8
July mean max.	96.3
Civ. Labor	10,325
Unemployed	8.2
Wages	$62,419,203
Av. Weekly Wage	$756
Prop. Value	$3,557,985,758
Retail Sales	$237,448,473

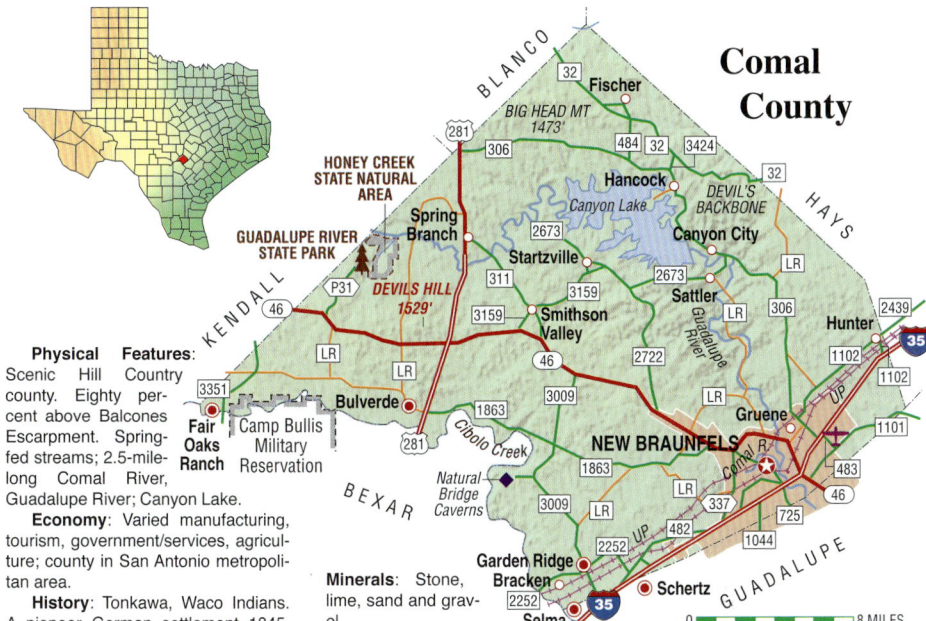

Comal County

Physical Features: Scenic Hill Country county. Eighty percent above Balcones Escarpment. Spring-fed streams; 2.5-mile-long Comal River, Guadalupe River; Canyon Lake.

Economy: Varied manufacturing, tourism, government/services, agriculture; county in San Antonio metropolitan area.

History: Tonkawa, Waco Indians. A pioneer German settlement 1845. Mexican migration peaked during Mexican Revolution. County created from Bexar, Gonzales, Travis counties and organized in 1846; named for river, a name for Spanish earthenware or metal pan used for cooking tortillas.

Race/Ethnicity, 2008: (In percent) Anglo, 75.2; Black, 0.9; Hispanic, 22.9; Other, 1.0.

Vital Statistics, 2008: Births, 1,336; deaths, 838; marriages, 746; divorces, 343.

Recreation: Fishing, hunting; historic sites; scenic drives; lake facilities; Prince Solms Park, other county parks; Landa Park with 76 species of trees; Gruene historic area; caverns; river resorts; river tubing; Schlitterbahn water park; Wurstfest in November, Wasselfest in December.

Minerals: Stone, lime, sand and gravel.

Agriculture: Cattle, goats, sheep, hogs, horses; nursery, hay, corn, sorghum, wheat. Market value $6.6 million.

NEW BRAUNFELS (57,740) county seat; manufacturing, retail, distribution center; picturesque city, making it a tourist center; Conservation Plaza; rose garden; hospital; library; mental health and retardation center. **Gruene** is now part of New Braunfels.

Other towns include: **Bulverde** (4,630); **Garden Ridge** (3,259); the retirement and recreation community around **Canyon Lake** (21,262), which includes **Startzville, Sattler, Smithson Valley, Canyon City, Fischer** and **Spring Branch**.

Also in the county, parts of **Fair Oaks Ranch** (5,986), **Selma** (5,540) and **Schertz** (31,465).

Population	108,472
Change fm 2000	39.03
Area (sq. mi.)	574.59
Land Area (sq. mi.)	561.45
Altitude (ft.)	560-1,529
Rainfall (in.)	35.74
Jan. mean min.	35.5
July mean max.	94.7
Civ. Labor	58,113
Unemployed	7.2
Wages	$372,077,485
Av. Weekly Wage	$728
Prop. Value	$13,928,668,353
Retail Sales	$1,461,367,461

For explanation of sources, abbreviations and symbols, see p. 232 and foldout page.

A cove of Canyon Lake, Comal County. Photo by Robert Plocheck.

Comanche County

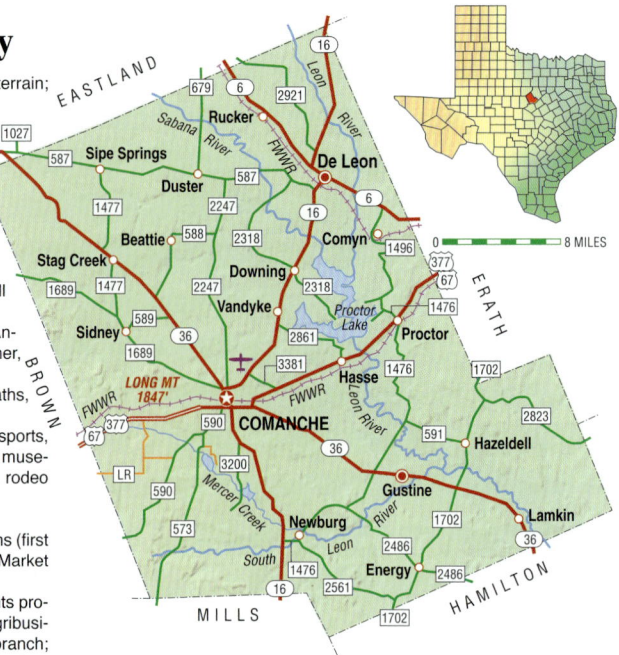

Physical Features: Rolling, hilly terrain; sandy, loam, waxy soils; drains to Leon River, Proctor Lake; pecans, oaks, mesquites, cedars.

Economy: Dairies, peanut-, pecan-shelling plants, manufacturing.

History: Comanche area. Anglo-American settlers arrived in 1854 on land granted earlier to Stephen F. Austin and Samuel May Williams. County created, organized, 1856 from Bosque, Coryell counties; named for Indian tribe.

Race/Ethnicity, 2008: (In percent) Anglo, 73.8; Black, 0.5; Hispanic, 25.2; Other, 0.5.

Vital Statistics, 2008: Births, 210; deaths, 188; marriages, 90; divorces, 50.

Recreation: Hunting, fishing, water sports, nature tourism; parks, community center, museums; Comanche Pow-Wow in September, rodeo in July.

Minerals: Limited gas, oil, stone, clay.

Agriculture: Dairies, beef cattle, pecans (first in state in acreage), hay, wildlife, melons. Market value $144.9 million.

COMANCHE (4,335) county seat; plants process feed, food; varied manufacturing; agribusiness; winery; hospital; Ranger College branch; library; state's oldest courthouse, "Old Cora," on display on town square.

De Leon (2,246) pecans, light manufacturing; hospital; car museum, Peach and Melon Festival in August.

Other towns include: **Energy** (70), **Gustine** (476), **Proctor** (228) and **Sidney** (148).

Population	13,974
Change fm 2000	–0.37
Area (sq. mi.)	947.67
Land Area (sq. mi.)	937.69
Altitude (ft.)	1,020-1,847
Rainfall (in.)	31.12
Jan. mean min.	30.6
July mean max.	95.5
Civ. Labor	6,718
Unemployed	6.9
Wages	$27,849,075
Av. Weekly Wage	$588
Prop. Value	$1,851,810,356
Retail Sales	$111,929,063

Concho County

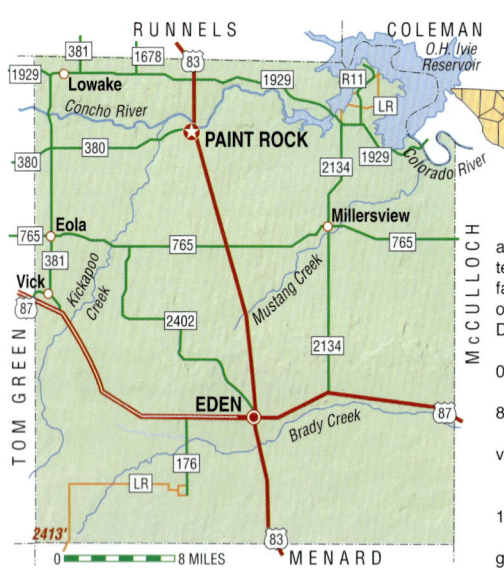

Physical Features: On Edwards Plateau; rough, broken to south; level in north; sandy, loam and dark soils; drains to creeks and Colorado River.

Economy: Agribusiness, manufacturing.

History: Athabascan-speaking Plains Indians, then Jumanos in 1600s, absorbed by Lipan Apaches 1700s. Comanches raided after 1800. Anglo-Americans began ranching around 1850; farming after the Civil War. Mexican-Americans employed on sheep ranches 1920s-30s. County created from Bexar District, 1858, organized 1879; named for river.

Race/Ethnicity, 2008: (In percent) Anglo, 55.2; Black, 0.9; Hispanic, 43.6; Other, 0.3.

Vital Statistics, 2008: Births, 25; deaths, 39; marriages, 8; divorces, 9.

Recreation: Famed for 1,500 Indian pictographs; reservoir.

Minerals: Oil, gas, stone.

Agriculture: Sheep, cattle, goats; wheat, feed grains; 10,000 acres irrigated for cotton. Market value $21.2 million.

PAINT ROCK (273) county seat; named for Indian pictographs nearby; farming, ranching center.

EDEN (2,766) steel fabrication, detention center; hospital; fall fest.

Other towns include: **Eola** (215), **Lowake** (40) and **Millersview** (80).

For explanation of sources, abbreviations and symbols, see p. 232 and foldout page.

Population	4,087
Change fm 2000	3.05
Area (sq. mi.)	993.69
Land Area (sq. mi.)	991.45
Altitude (ft.)	1,421-2,413
Rainfall (in.)	25.50
Jan. mean min.	31.9
July mean max.	97.4
Civ. Labor	1,274
Unemployed	8.2
Wages	$7,023,786
Av. Weekly Wage	$620
Prop. Value	$674,765,070
Retail Sales	$16,549,372

Cooke County

Physical Features: North Texas county; drains to Red, Trinity rivers, lakes; sandy, red, loam soils.

Economy: Oil and gas, varied manufacturing, commuting to northern Dallas-Fort Worth metroplex.

History: Frontier between Caddoes and Comanches. Anglo-Americans arrived in late 1840s. Germans settled western part around 1890. County created, organized, 1848 from Fannin County; named for Capt. W.G. Cooke of the Texas Revolution.

Race/Ethnicity, 2008: (In percent) Anglo, 81.6; Black, 3.3; Hispanic, 13.7; Other, 1.4.

Vital Statistics, 2008: Births, 538; deaths, 430; marriages, 615; divorces, 155.

Recreation: Water sports; hunting, fishing; zoo; museum; park, Gainsville Depot Day/car show in October.

Minerals: Oil, natural gas, sand, gravel.

Agriculture: Beef cattle, horses, forages, wheat. Market value $58.3 million. Hunting leases important.

GAINESVILLE (16,002) county seat; tourism, plastics, agribusiness, aircraft and steel fabrication; Victorian homes, walking tours; hospital; community college, juvenile correction unit; Camp Sweeney for diabetic children.

Muenster (1,544) varied manufacturing, food processing, oil and gas, agriculture; hospital; Germanfest in April.

Other towns include: **Callisburg** (353), **Era** (150), **Lindsay** (1,018) 1919 Romanesque-style church, **Myra** (150), **Oak Ridge** (141), **Rosston** (75), **Valley View** (757) and the residential community around **Lake Kiowa** (1,906).

For explanation of sources, abbreviations and symbols, see p. 232 and foldout page.

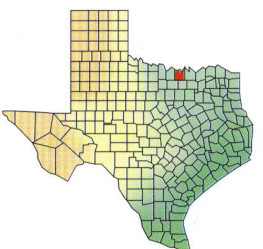

Population	38,437
Change fm 2000	5.7
Area (sq. mi.)	898.81
Land Area (sq. mi.)	873.64
Altitude (ft.)	617-1,217
Rainfall (in.)	36.90
Jan. mean min.	28.0
July mean max.	95.0
Civ. Labor	21,659
Unemployed	6.4
Wages	$159,894,439
Av. Weekly Wage	$810
Prop. Value	$4,672,759,030
Retail Sales	$595,953,933

A hay field along FM 3002 in southern Cooke County. Photo by Robert Plocheck.

Coryell County

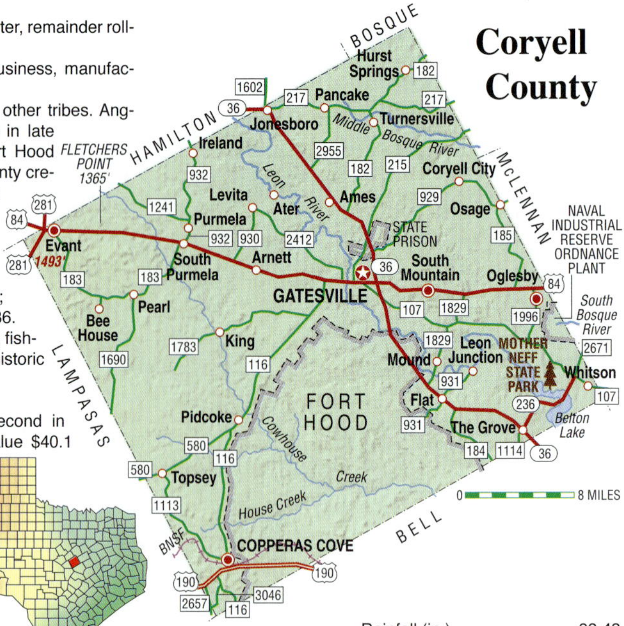

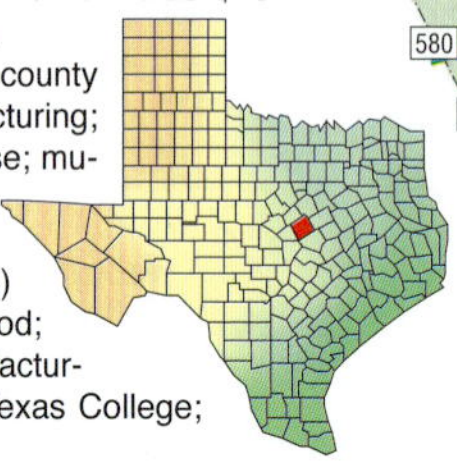

Physical Features: Leon Valley in center, remainder rolling, hilly.

Economy: Fort Hood, prisons, agribusiness, manufacturing.

History: Tonkawa area, later various other tribes. Anglo-Americans settled around Fort Gates in late 1840s. Permanent establishment of Fort Hood in 1950 changed cultural geography. County created from Bell County, organized, 1854; named for local pioneer James Coryell.

Race/Ethnicity, 2008: (In percent) Anglo, 57.9; Black, 22.4; Hispanic, 15.3; Other, 4.4.

Vital Statistics, 2008: Births, 1,047; deaths, 372; marriages, 456; divorces, 236.

Recreation: State park; deer hunting; fishing; lakes, Leon River; bluebonnet area; historic homes; log jail; Shivaree in June.

Minerals: Oil and gas.

Agriculture: Beef, forages, oats (second in acreage), wildlife, row crops. Market value $40.1 million. Hunting leases, timber.

GATESVILLE (15,751) county seat; prisons, varied manufacturing; hospital; refurbished courthouse; museum; branch Central Texas College.

COPPERAS COVE (32,032) business center for Fort Hood; industrial filters, other manufacturing; hospital, library; Central Texas College; Spurfest in September.

Other towns include: **Evant** (426, partly in Hamilton County), **Flat** (210), **Jonesboro** (125), **Mound** (125), **Oglesby** (484), **Purmela** (50), **South Mountain** (384). Part of **Fort Hood**.

Population	75,388
Change fm 2000	0.55
Area (sq. mi.)	1,056.73
Land Area (sq. mi.)	1,051.76
Altitude (ft.)	600-1,493

Rainfall (in.)	33.43
Jan. mean min.	33.5
July mean max.	96.4
Civ. Labor	25,272
Unemployed	9.4
Wages	$130,160,151
Av. Weekly Wage.................	$670
Prop. Value..........	$3,239,836,254
Retail Sales	$472,369,632

The Cottle County Courthouse in Paducah. Photo by Robert Plocheck.

Cottle County

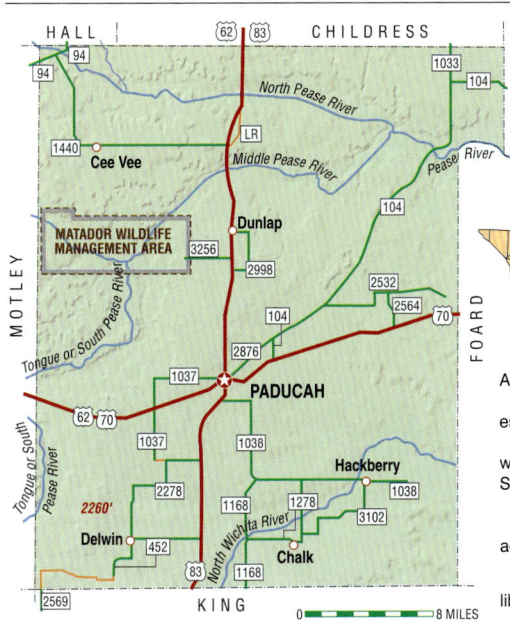

Physical Features: Northwest county below Caprock, rough in west, level in east; gray, black, sandy and loam soils; drains to Pease River.

Economy: Agribusiness, government/services.

History: Around 1700, Apaches were displaced by Comanches, who in turn were driven out by U.S. Army 1870s. Anglo-American settlers arrived in 1880s. County created 1876 from Fannin County; organized 1892; named for George W. Cottle, Alamo hero.

Race/Ethnicity, 2008: (In percent) Anglo, 65.6; Black, 10.7; Hispanic, 23.3; Other, 0.3.

Vital Statistics, 2008: Births, 15; deaths, 29; marriages, 7; divorces, 1.

Recreation: Hunting of quail, dove, wild hogs, deer; wildlife management area; museum, Fiestas Patrias in September, horse and colt show in April.

Minerals: Oil, natural gas.

Agriculture: Beef cattle, cotton, peanuts, wheat. 3,000 acres irrigated. Market value $17.5 million.

PADUCAH (1,186) county seat; government/services, library.

Other towns include: **Cee Vee** (45).

Population	**1,505**
Change fm 2000	−20.96
Area (sq. mi.)	901.59
Land Area (sq. mi.)	901.18
Altitude (ft.)	1,470-2,260
Rainfall (in.)	24.11
Jan. mean min.	26.2
July mean max.	96.8
Civ. Labor	737
Unemployed	5.8
Wages	$3,696,398
Av. Weekly Wage	$655
Prop. Value	$538,162,050
Retail Sales	$12,031,301

Crane County

Physical Features: Rolling prairie, Pecos Valley, some hills; sandy, loam soils; Juan Cordona Lake (intermittent).

Economy: Oil and gas; agriculture; government/services.

History: Lipan Apache area. Ranching developed in the 1890s. Oil discovered in 1926. County created from Tom Green County in 1887, organized in 1927; named for Baylor University president W. C. Crane.

Race/Ethnicity, 2008: (In percent) Anglo, 48.7; Black, 3.1; Hispanic, 47.5; Other, 0.7.

Vital Statistics, 2008: Births, 60; deaths, 34; marriages, 32; divorces, 7.

Recreation: Museum of the Desert Southwest; sites of pioneer trails and historic Horsehead Crossing on Pecos River; hunting of mule deer, quail; camping park; rodeo in May.

Minerals: Oil, gas production.

Agriculture: Cattle ranching, goats. Market value $1.7 million.

CRANE (3,353) county seat; oil-well servicing and production, foundry, steel, surfboard manufacturing; hospital.

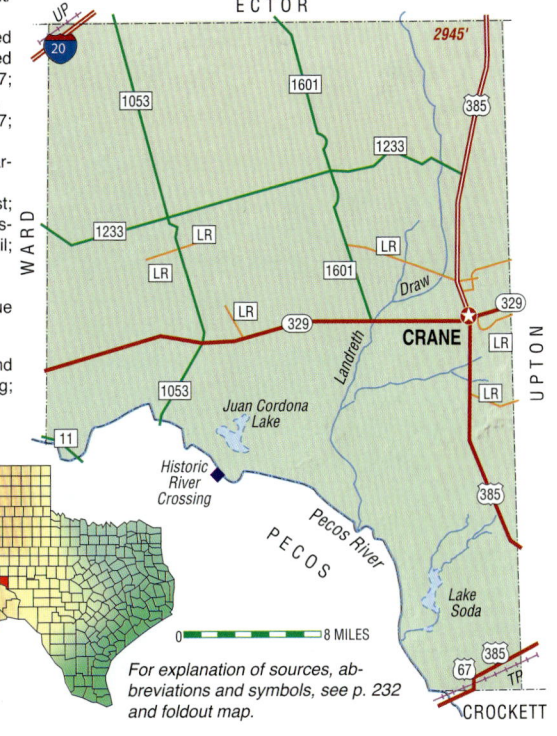

For explanation of sources, abbreviations and symbols, see p. 232 and foldout map.

Population	**4,375**
Change fm 2000	9.48
Area (sq. mi.)	785.59
Land Area (sq. mi.)	785.56
Altitude (ft.)	2,290-2,945
Rainfall (in.)	15.38
Jan. mean min.	30.6
July mean max.	95.3
Civ. Labor	1,576
Unemployed	8.9
Wages	$20,562,975
Av. Weekly Wage	$1,085
Prop. Value	$2,164,635,510
Retail Sales	$32,146,208

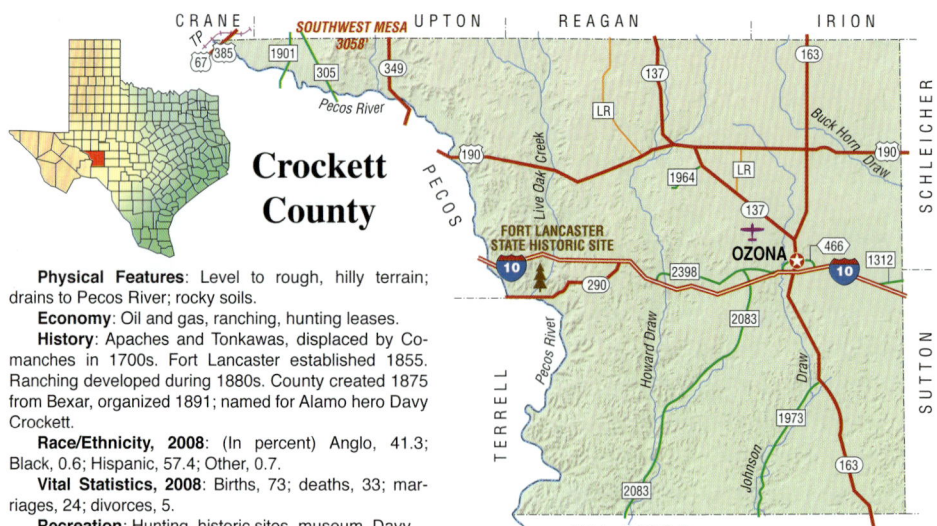

Crockett County

Physical Features: Level to rough, hilly terrain; drains to Pecos River; rocky soils.

Economy: Oil and gas, ranching, hunting leases.

History: Apaches and Tonkawas, displaced by Comanches in 1700s. Fort Lancaster established 1855. Ranching developed during 1880s. County created 1875 from Bexar, organized 1891; named for Alamo hero Davy Crockett.

Race/Ethnicity, 2008: (In percent) Anglo, 41.3; Black, 0.6; Hispanic, 57.4; Other, 0.7.

Vital Statistics, 2008: Births, 73; deaths, 33; marriages, 24; divorces, 5.

Recreation: Hunting, historic sites, museum, Davy Crockett statue in park; Davy Crockett festival in August, Deerfest in December.

Minerals: Oil, gas production.

Agriculture: Sheep (first in numbers), goats; beef cattle. Market value $13.6 million.

OZONA (3,225) county seat; trade center for ranching, hunting leases, tourism.

Population	3,719
Change fm 2000	–9.27
Area (sq. mi.)	2,807.43
Land Area (sq. mi.)	2,807.42
Altitude (ft.)	1,720-3,058
Rainfall (in.)	18.95
Jan. mean min.	27.7
July mean max.	93.0
Civ. Labor	1,983
Unemployed	6.3
Wages	$11,775,493
Av. Weekly Wage	$626
Prop. Value	$2,437,871,380
Retail Sales	$31,742,691

Crosby County

Physical Features: Flat, rich soil above Caprock, broken below; drains into Brazos River forks and playas.

Economy: Agribusiness, tourism, commuters to Lubbock.

History: Comanches, driven out by U.S. Army in 1870s; ranching developed soon afterward. Quaker colony founded in 1879. County created from Bexar District 1876, organized 1886; named for Texas Land Commissioner Stephen Crosby.

Race/Ethnicity, 2008: (In percent) Anglo, 41.8; Black, 3.8; Hispanic, 54.0; Other, 0.3.

Vital Statistics, 2008: Births, 79; deaths, 64; marriages, 38; divorces, 12.

Recreation: White River Lake; Silver Falls Park; hunting.

Minerals: Sand, gravel, oil, gas.

Agriculture: Cotton, beef cattle, sorghum; about 200,000 acres irrigated. Market value $92.7 million.

CROSBYTON (1,741) county seat; agribusiness center; hospital, Pioneer Museum, Prairie Ladies Multi-Cultural Center, library; Cowboy Gathering in October.

Other towns include: **Lorenzo** (1,147); **Ralls** (1,944) government/services, agribusiness, museums, Cotton Boll Fest in September.

Population	6,059
Change fm 2000	–14.32
Area (sq. mi.)	901.69
Land Area (sq. mi.)	899.51
Altitude (ft.)	2,250-3,235
Rainfall (in.)	22.95
Jan. mean min.	25.3
July mean max.	92.5
Civ. Labor	2,644
Unemployed	8.8
Wages	$20,709,381
Av. Weekly Wage	$964
Prop. Value	$655,160,660
Retail Sales	$156,654,973

For explanation of sources, abbreviations and symbols, see p. 232 and foldout map.

Irrigated cotton field near Lobo, Culberson County. Photo by Robert Plocheck.

Culberson County

Physical Features: Contains Texas' highest mountain; slopes toward Pecos Valley on east, Diablo Bolson on west; salt lakes; unique vegetation in canyons.

Economy: Tourism, government/services, talc mining and processing, agribusiness, sulfur mining.

History: Apaches arrived about 600 years ago. U.S. military frontier after Civil War. Ranching developed after 1880. Mexican migration increased after 1920. County created from El Paso County 1911, organized 1912; named for D.B. Culberson, Texas congressman.

Race/Ethnicity, 2008: (In percent) Anglo, 24.7; Black, 0.6; Hispanic, 73.6; Other, 1.1.

Vital Statistics, 2008: Births, 40; deaths, 14; marriages, 1; divorces, 2.

Recreation: National park; Guadalupe and El Capitan, twin peaks; scenic canyons and mountains; classic car museum, antique saloon bar; frontier days in June, big buck tournament.

Minerals: Sulfur, talc, marble, oil.

Agriculture: Beef cattle; crops include cotton, vegetables, melons, pecans; 4,000 acres in irrigation. Market value $15.1 million.

VAN HORN (2,063) county seat; agribusiness, tourism, rock crushing, government/services; hospital.

Other towns: **Kent** (30).

Population	**2,398**
Change fm 2000	−19.39
Area (sq. mi.)	3,812.71
Land Area (sq. mi.)	3,812.46
Altitude (ft.)	2,900-8,749
Rainfall (in.)	11.98
Jan. mean min.	27.8
July mean max.	91.7
Civ. Labor	1,675
Unemployed	4.8
Wages	$8,063,401
Av. Weekly Wage	$571
Prop. Value	$378,859,140
Retail Sales	$97,882,863

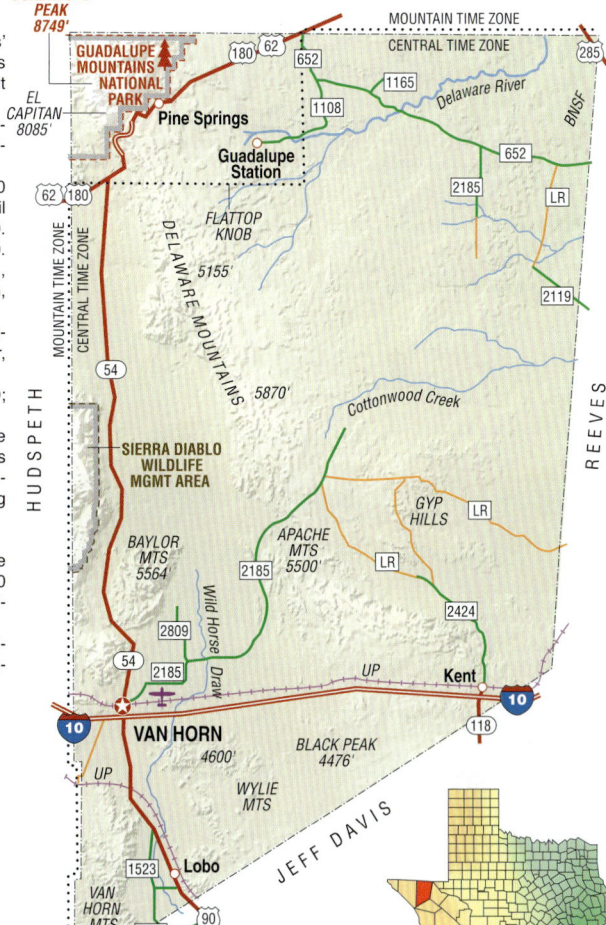

Dallam County

Physical Features: Prairie, broken by creeks; playas; sandy, loam soils; Rita Blanca National Grassland.

Economy: Agribusiness, dairies, cheese manufacturing, tourism.

History: Earliest Plains Apaches; displaced by Comanches and Kiowas. Ranching developed in late 19th century. Farming began after 1900. County created from Bexar District, 1876, organized 1891. Named for lawyer-editor James W. Dallam.

Race/Ethnicity, 2008: (In percent) Anglo, 65.3; Black, 1.6; Hispanic, 32.1; Other, 0.9.

Vital Statistics, 2008: Births, 120; deaths, 55; marriages, 79; divorces, 32.

Recreation: XIT museum, XIT rodeo in August, pheasant hunting, wildlife, grasslands.

Minerals: Petroleum.

Agriculture: First in production of grain (corn, wheat, sorghum). Cattle, hogs (second in number), dairies, potatoes, sunflowers, beans; substantial irrigation. Market value $552.9 million.

DALHART (7,930, partly in Hartley County) county seat; government/services; agribusiness center for parts of Texas, New Mexico, Oklahoma; railroad; cheese plant; grain operations; hospital; prison; Rita Blanca Lake.

Other towns include: **Kerrick** (35) and **Texline** (507).

Population	**6,703**
Change fm 2000	7.73
Area (sq. mi.)	1,505.26
Land Area (sq. mi.)	1,504.69
Altitude (ft.)	3,655-4,780
Rainfall (in.)	18.57
Jan. mean min.	19.0
July mean max.	90.0
Civ. Labor	3,704
Unemployed	4.5
Wages	$38,442,579
Av. Weekly Wage	$802
Prop. Value	$880,577,207
Retail Sales	$77,239,907

For explanation of sources, abbreviations and symbols, see p. 232 and foldout map.

Rita Blanca Lake Park in Dalhart. Photo by Robert Plocheck.

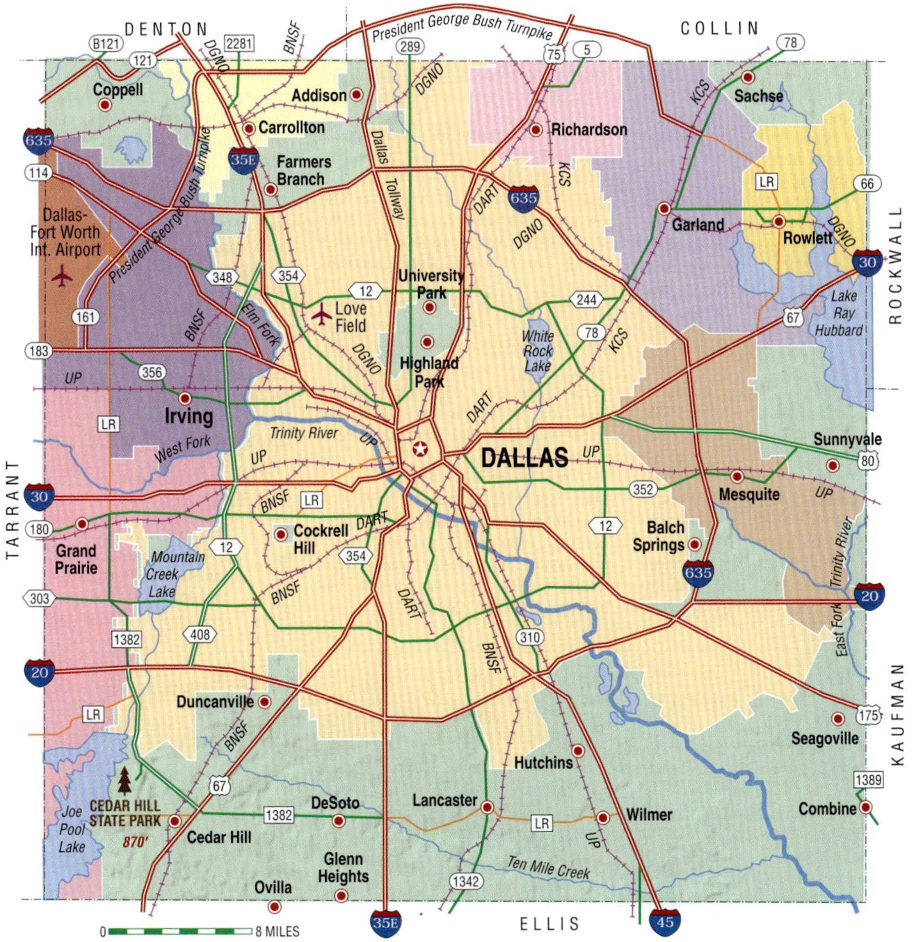

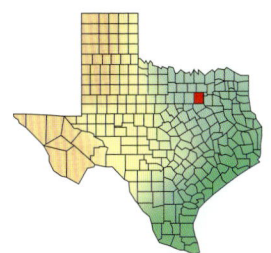

Dallas County

Physical Features: Mostly flat, heavy blackland soils, sandy clays in west; drains to Trinity River.

Economy: A national center for telecommunications, transportation, electronics manufacturing, data processing, conventions and trade shows; foreign-trade zone located at D/FW International Airport, U.S. Customs port of entry; government/services.

History: Caddoan tribal area. Anglo-Americans began arriving in 1840. Antebellum slaveholding area. County created in 1846 from Nacogdoches and Robertson counties, organized the same year; named for U.S. Vice President George Mifflin Dallas.

Race/Ethnicity, 2008: (In percent) Anglo, 33.5; Black, 20.3; Hispanic, 40.2; Other, 5.9.

Vital Statistics, 2008: Births, 43,064; deaths, 13,964; marriages, 14,521; divorces, 8,271.

Recreation: One of the state's top tourist destinations and one of the nation's most popular conven-

tion centers; State Fair, museums, zoo, West End shopping and tourist district, historical sites, including Sixth Floor museum in the old Texas School Book Depository, site of the assassination of President Kennedy.

Also, the Morton H. Meyerson Symphony Center; performing arts; professional sports; Texas broadcast museum; lakes, state park, Audobon center; theme and amusement parks.

Minerals: Sand, gravel, oil and gas.

Population	2,368,139
Change fm 2000	6.73
Area (sq. mi.)	908.56
Land Area (sq. mi.)	879.60
Altitude (ft.)	350-870
Rainfall (in.)	37.05
Jan. mean min.	36.4
July mean max.	96.1
Civ. Labor	1,172,318
Unemployed	9.0
Wages	$21,638,802,651
Av. Weekly Wage	$1,167
Prop. Value	$197,209,361,610
Retail Sales	$47,991,431,979

Agriculture: Horticultural crops, wheat, hay, corn, soybeans (fourth in acreage), horses. Market value $35.2 million.

Education: Southern Methodist University, University of Dallas, Dallas Baptist University, University of Texas at Dallas, University of Texas Southwestern Medical Center and many other education centers.

DALLAS (1,197,816) county seat; center of state's largest consolidated metropolitan area and third-largest city in Texas; D/FW International

Airport is one of the world's busiest; headquarters for the U.S. Army and Air Force Exchange Service; Federal Reserve Bank; a leader in fashions and in computer operations; hospitals; many hotels in downtown area offer adequate accommodations for most conventions.

Garland (226,876) varied manufacturing, community college branch, hospitals, performing arts center.

Irving (216,290) telecommunications; varied light manufacturing, food processing; distribution center; Boy Scout headquarters and museum; North Lake College; hospitals.

Other cities include: **Addison** (13,056) general aviation airport, theater center; **Balch Springs** (23,728); part of **Carrollton** (119,907) residential community, distribution center, hospital; **Cedar Hill** (45,028) residential, light manufacturing, retail, Northwood University, state park, Country Day on the Hill in October; **Cockrell Hill** (4,193); **Coppell** (38,659) distribution, varied manufacturing, office

center, hike and bike trails; **DeSoto** (49,047) residential community, light industry and distribution, hospitals; Toad Holler Creekfest in June.

Also, **Duncanville** (38,524) varied manufacturing, many commuters to Dallas; Sandra Meadows Classic girls basketball tournament in December; **Farmers Branch** (28,616) distribution center, varied manufacturing, Brookhaven College, hospital.

Also, **Glenn Heights** (11,278, partly in Ellis County); most of **Grand Prairie** (175,396) wholesale trade, aerospace, entertainment, hospital, library, Joe Pool Reservoir, Indian pow-wow in September, Lone Star horse-racing track; **Highland Park** (8,564).

Also, **Hutchins** (5,338) varied manufacturing; **Lancaster** (36,361) residential, industrial, distribution center, Cedar Valley College, Commemorative Air Force museum, Bear Creek nature preserve, depot, historic town square, Oktoberfest.

Also, **Mesquite** (139,824) varied industries; hospitals; championship rodeo, rodeo parade in spring; community college, historical parks; most of **Richardson** (99,223) telecommunications, software development, financial services, hospital, library, Wildflower Music Festival in May; **Rowlett** (56,199) residential, manufacturing, government/services, hospital, library, park, hike and bike trails.

Also, **Sachse** (20,229, partly in Collin County) commuting to Dallas, government/services, Fallfest in October; **Seagoville** (14,835) rural/suburban setting, federal prison, Seagofest in October; **Sunnyvale** (5,130) tile manufacturing, hospital, Samuell Farm, Sunnyfest on July 4; **University Park** (23,068); **Wilmer** (3,682).

Part of **Combine** (1,942) and part of **Ovilla** (3,492).

County adopted by:
J.P. Bryan in honor of the Reeder, Petty and Vonder Hoya families

Dawson County

Physical Features: South Plains county, broken on the east; loam and sandy soils.

Economy: Agriculture, farm and gin equipment manufacturing, peanut plant, government/services.

History: Comanche, Kiowa area. Ranching developed in 1880s. Farming began after 1900. Hispanic population increased after 1940. County created from Bexar District, 1876, organized 1905; named for Nicholas M. Dawson, San Jacinto veteran.

Race/Ethnicity, 2008: (In percent) Anglo, 38.5; Black, 8.3; Hispanic, 52.8; Other, 0.5.

Vital Statistics, 2008: Births, 226; deaths, 139; marriages, 80; divorces, 43.

Recreation: Parks, museum, campground; Lamesa poetry and music fest in May.

Minerals: Oil, natural gas.

Agriculture: First in cotton acreage; peanuts, sorghums, watermelons, alfalfa, grapes. 70,000 acres irrigated. Market value $112.3 million.

LAMESA (9,422) county seat; agribusiness, food processing, oil-field services, some manufacturing, computerized cotton-classing office; hospital; library; Howard College branch; prison unit; chicken-fried steak festival in April.

Other towns include: **Ackerly** (220, partly in Martin County), **Los Ybañez** (19) and **Welch** (222). Also, **O'Donnell** (831, mostly in Lynn County) bust of Dan Blocker.

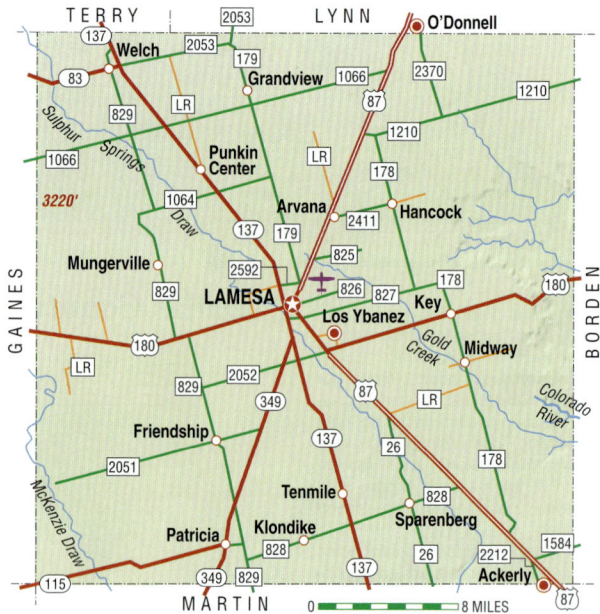

Population	13,833
Change fm 2000	−7.69
Area (sq. mi.)	902.12
Land Area (sq. mi.)	902.06
Altitude (ft.)	2,580-3,220
Rainfall (in.)	19.07
Jan. mean min.	26.0
July mean max.	92.9
Civ. Labor	5,367
Unemployed	8.4
Wages	$40,901,740
Av. Weekly Wage	$641
Prop. Value	$1,184,849,200
Retail Sales	$147,077,686

Deaf Smith County

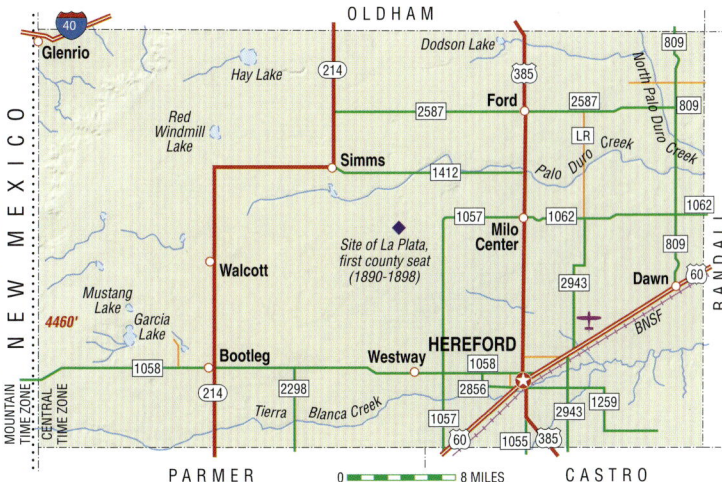

Physical Features: High Plains county, partly broken; chocolate and sandy loam soils; drains to Palo Duro and Tierra Blanca creeks.

Economy: Agriculture, varied industries, meat packing, offset printing.

History: Apaches, displaced by Comanches, Kiowas. Ranching developed after U.S. Army drove out Indians 1874-75. Farming began after 1900. Hispanic settlement increased after 1950. County created 1876, from Bexar District; organized 1890. Named for famed scout in Texas Revolution, Erastus (Deaf) Smith.

Race/Ethnicity, 2008: (In percent) Anglo, 34.8; Black, 1.4; Hispanic, 63.2; Other, 0.6.

Vital Statistics, 2008: Births, 362; deaths, 149; marriages, 161; divorces, 16.

Recreation: Museum, tours, POW camp chapel; Cinco de Mayo, Pioneer Days in May.

Minerals: Insignificant.

Agriculture: Leading agricultural county, dairies, feedlot operations, cotton, wheat, sorghum, corn; 50 percent irrigated. Market value $1.15 billion, first in state.

HEREFORD (15,370) county seat; cattle feeding, agriculture, trucking; hospital; Amarillo College branch; aquatic center. Other towns include: **Dawn** (52).

Population	19,372
Change fm 2000	4.37
Area (sq. mi.)	1,498.26
Land Area (sq. mi.)	1,497.34
Altitude (ft.)	3,650-4,460
Rainfall (in.)	18.65
Jan. mean min.	21.1
July mean max.	91.6
Civ. Labor	9,132
Unemployed	6.1
Wages	$65,800,771
Av. Weekly Wage	$697
Prop. Value	$1,445,691,331
Retail Sales	$308,465,222

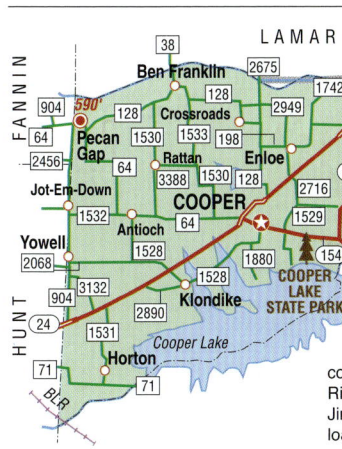

Population	5,231
Change fm 2000	−1.8
Area (sq. mi.)	277.92
Land Area (sq. mi.)	277.08
Altitude (ft.)	322-590
Rainfall (in.)	45.00
Jan. mean min.	30.0
July mean max.	94.0
Civ. Labor	2,344
Unemployed	10.6
Wages	$7,981,239
Av. Weekly Wage	$443
Prop. Value	$351,978,952
Retail Sales	$10,921,858

Physical Features: Northeastern county between two forks of Sulphur River; Cooper Lake (also designated Jim Chapman Lake); black, sandy loam soils.

Economy: Agriculture, government/services, retirement location.

History: Caddo area, but disease, other tribes caused displacement around 1790. Anglo-Americans arrived in 1820s. County created and organized in 1870 from Lamar, Hopkins counties. Greek letter delta origin of name, because of shape of the county.

Race/Ethnicity, 2008: (In percent) Anglo, 87.2; Black, 9.0; Hispanic, 3.1; Other, 0.7.

Vital Statistics, 2008: Births, 52; deaths, 74; marriages, 37; divorces, 17.

Delta County

Recreation: Fishing, hunting; lake, state park; Cooper Chiggerfest in October.

Minerals: Insignificant.

Agriculture: Beef, hay, soybeans, wheat, corn, sorghum, cotton. Market value $17.2 million.

COOPER (1,969) county seat; commuters, industrial park, some manufacturing, agribusiness; museum, library; post office mural.

Other towns include: **Ben Franklin** (60), **Enloe** (90), **Klondike** (175), **Lake Creek** (55) and **Pecan Gap** (203).

For explanation of sources, abbreviations and symbols, see p. 232 and foldout map.

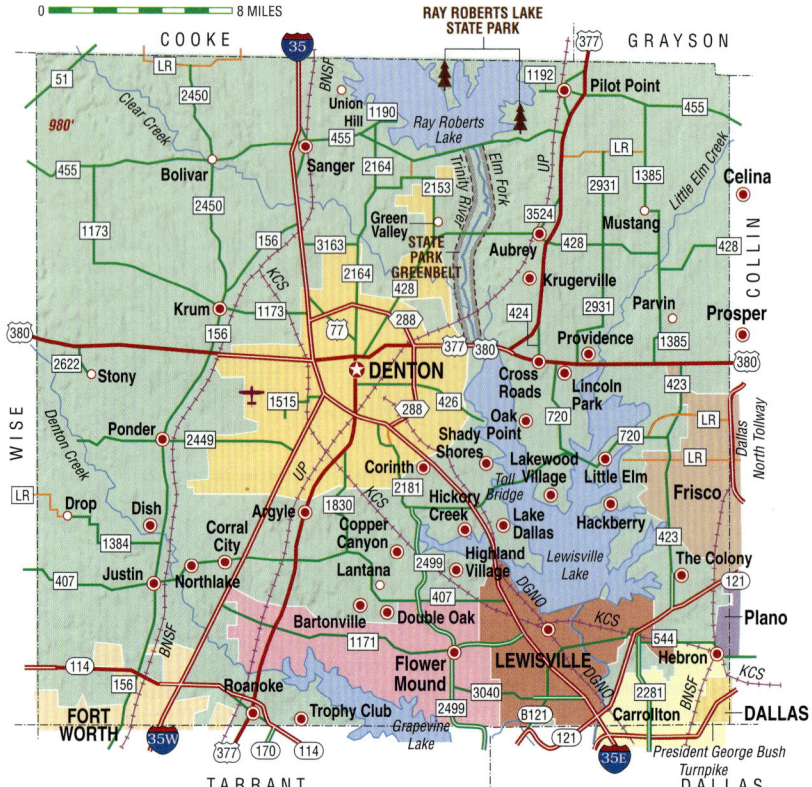

Denton County

Physical Features: North Texas county; partly hilly, draining to Elm Fork of Trinity River, lakes; Blackland and Grand Prairie soils and terrain.

Economy: Varied industries, colleges, horse industry, tourism, government/services; part of Dallas-Fort Worth metropolitan area.

History: Land grant from Texas Congress 1841 for Peters colony. County created out of Fannin County 1846; named for John B. Denton, pioneer Methodist minister.

Race/Ethnicity, 2008: (In percent) Anglo, 71.7; Black, 7.0; Hispanic, 15.8; Other, 5.6.

Vital Statistics, 2008: Births, 9,397; deaths, 2,548; marriages, 3,861; divorces, 2,495.

Recreation: Lake activities, parks; universities' cultural, athletic activities, including "Texas Women; A Celebration of History"; "First Ladies of Texas" collection of memorabilia; Little Chapel in the Woods; Texas Motor Speedway; Denton Jazz Festival in April.

Minerals: Natural gas.

Education: University of North Texas and Texas Woman's University.

Agriculture: Second in number of horses. Eggs, nurseries, turf, cattle; also, hay, sorghum, wheat, peanuts grown. Market value $79.2 million.

DENTON (113,383) county seat; universities, manufacturers of trucks (Peterbilt), medical, aviation; hospitals;

historic courthouse square; storytelling festival in March.

LEWISVILLE (95,290) commuting to Dallas-Fort Worth, retail center, electronics and varied industries; hospital, library; Celtic Feis & Scottish Highland Games in March.

Flower Mound (64,669) residential community, library, mound of native grasses, bike classic in spring.

Carrollton (119,907, also in Dallas County), hospital.

Other towns include: **Argyle** (3,282) horse farms/training, bluegrass festival in March; **Aubrey** (2,595) horse farms/training, cabinet construction, peanut festival in October; **Bartonville** (1,469); **Copper Canyon** (1,334); **Corinth** (19,935); **Corral City** (27); **Cross Roads** (1,563); **Dish** (201); **Double Oak** (2,867).

Also, **Hackberry** (968); **Hebron** (415); **Hickory Creek** (3,247); **Highland Village** (15,056); **Justin** (3,246); **Krugerville** (1,662); **Krum** (4,157) commuters, old grain mill; **Lake Dallas** (7,105) light manufacturing, marina, historic downtown, Mardi Gras.

Also, **Lakewood Village** (545); **Lantana** (6,874); **Lincoln Park** (308);

Little Elm (25,898) light manufacturing, lake activities, summer concert series; **Northlake** (1,724); **Oak Point** (2,786); **Pilot Point** (3,856) light manufacturing, horse ranches, Fireman's Fest in April; **Ponder** (1,395); **Providence** (4,786).

Also, **Roanoke** (5,962); **Sanger** (6,916) distribution center, commuters, government/services, lakes, Sellabration in September; **Shady Shores** (2,612) park; **The Colony** (36,328) tourism, IBM offices, chili cook-off in June, Las Vegas Night in April; and **Trophy Club** (8,204) commuters, retail, park.

Parts of **Dallas**, **Fort Worth**, **Frisco**, **Plano**, **Coppell**, **Celina**, **Prosper**, **Southlake**, **Westlake**.

Population	662,614
Change fm 2000	53.04
Area (sq. mi.)	957.88
Land Area (sq. mi.)	888.54
Altitude (ft.)	433-980
Rainfall (in.)	37.79
Jan. mean min.	32.0
July mean max.	94.1
Civ. Labor	359,215
Unemployed	7.8
Wages	$1,903,384,119
Av. Weekly Wage	$836
Prop. Value	$62,395,015,227
Retail Sales	$8,860,400,001

For explanation of sources, abbreviations and symbols, see p. 232 and foldout map.

DeWitt County

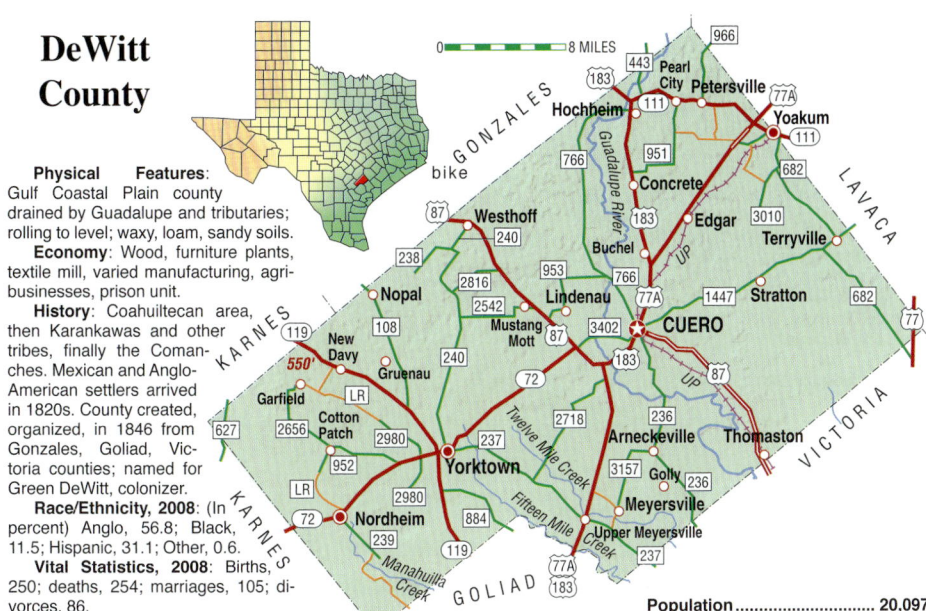

Physical Features: Gulf Coastal Plain county drained by Guadalupe and tributaries; rolling to level; waxy, loam, sandy soils.

Economy: Wood, furniture plants, textile mill, varied manufacturing, agribusinesses, prison unit.

History: Coahuiltecan area, then Karankawas and other tribes, finally the Comanches. Mexican and Anglo-American settlers arrived in 1820s. County created, organized, in 1846 from Gonzales, Goliad, Victoria counties; named for Green DeWitt, colonizer.

Race/Ethnicity, 2008: (In percent) Anglo, 56.8; Black, 11.5; Hispanic, 31.1; Other, 0.6.

Vital Statistics, 2008: Births, 250; deaths, 254; marriages, 105; divorces, 86.

Recreation: Hunting, fishing, birding, historic homes, museums, wildflowers, German dance halls.

Minerals: Oil and natural gas.

Agriculture: Cattle, dairy products, poultry, swine, corn, sorghum, cotton, hay, pecans. Market value $41 million.

CUERO (6,841) county seat; agriculture, leather products, food processing; hospital; Turkeyfest in October.

Yorktown (2,092) agribusiness, oil and gas; library, museum, park, hike/trail; Western Days in October, German feasts, spring and fall.

Other towns include: **Hochheim** (70), **Meyersville** (110), **Nordheim** (307), **Thomaston** (45), **Westhoff** (410).

Part of **Yoakum** (5,815) cattle, leather, meat processing; hospital, museum, Tom Tom festival in June.

Population	**20,097**
Change fm 2000	0.42
Area (sq. mi.)	910.47
Land Area (sq. mi.)	909.18
Altitude (ft.)	100-550
Rainfall (in.)	36.08
Jan. mean min.	41.3
July mean max.	95.1
Civ. Labor	9,253
Unemployed	7.8
Wages	$56,919,183
Av. Weekly Wage	$659
Prop. Value	$1,865,359,320
Retail Sales	$166,093,588

Old downtown Aubrey, Denton County. Photo by Robert Plocheck.

Dickens County

Physical Features: West Texas county; broken land, Caprock in northwest; sandy, chocolate, red soils; drains to Croton, Duck creeks.

Economy: Agriculture, government services/prison unit, hunting leases.

History: Comanches driven out by U.S. Army 1874-75. Ranching and some farming began in late 1880s. County created 1876, from Bexar District; organized 1891; named for Alamo hero who is variously listed as James R. Demkins or Dimpkins and J. Dickens.

Race/Ethnicity, 2008: (In percent) Anglo, 64.8; Black, 8.3; Hispanic, 26.4; Other, 0.5.

Vital Statistics, 2008: Births, 22; deaths, 19; marriages, 12; divorces, 7.

Recreation: Hunting, fishing; Soldiers Mound site, Dickens Springs; downtown Spur.

Agriculture: Cattle, horses, cotton, hay, small grains. Some irrigation. Market value $21.1 million. Hunting leases important.

Minerals: Oil, gas.

DICKENS (286) county seat, market for ranching country.

SPUR (1,318) agribusiness and shipping center, oil and gas, state prison; homecoming in October.

Other towns include: **Afton** (15) and **McAdoo** (75).

Population	**2,444**
Change fm 2000	–11.51
Area (sq. mi.)	905.21
Land Area (sq. mi.)	904.21

Altitude (ft.)	1,800-3,037
Rainfall (in.)	18.68
Jan. mean min.	25.5
July mean max.	95.4
Civ. Labor	1,003
Unemployed	16,0
Wages	$4,039,121
Av. Weekly Wage	$624
Prop. Value	$802,000,440
Retail Sales	$12,906,878

Population	**9,996**
Change fm 2000	–2.46
Area (sq. mi.)	1,334.48
Land Area (sq. mi.)	1,330.91
Altitude (ft.)	410-871
Rainfall (in.)	20.21
Jan. mean min.	39.6
July mean max.	98.3
Civ. Labor	4,244
Unemployed	9.9
Wages	$33,874,458
Av. Weekly Wage	$803
Prop. Value	$1,598,439,576
Retail Sales	$93,574,682

Dimmit County

Physical Features: Southwest county; level to rolling; much brush; sandy, loam, red soils; drained by Nueces River.

Economy: Government/services, agriculture, oil and gas, tourism.

History: Coahuiltecan area, later Comanches. John Townsend, a black man from Nacogdoches, led first attempt at settlement before the Civil War. Texas Rangers forced out Indians in 1877. Mexican migration increased after 1910. County created 1858 from Bexar, Maverick, Uvalde, Webb counties; organized 1880. Named for Philip Dimitt of Texas Revolution; law misspelled name.

Race/Ethnicity, 2008: (In percent) Anglo, 12.1; Black, 0.7; Hispanic, 86.3; Other, 0.9.

Vital Statistics, 2008: Births, 181; deaths, 83; marriages, 39; divorces, 5.

Recreation: Hunting, fishing, campsites, wildlife area; winter haven for tourists.

Minerals: Oil, natural gas.

Agriculture: Onions, pecans, cantaloupes, olives, tomatoes, tangerines, cattle, goats, horses, hay. Market value $21.7 million.

CARRIZO SPRINGS (5,368) county seat; agribusiness center, feedlot, food processing, oil, gas processing, hunting center; hospital; historic Baptist church; Brush Country Day in October.

Other towns include: **Asherton** (1,084), **Big Wells** (697) Cinco de Mayo, and **Catarina** (118) Camino Real festival in April.

For explanation of sources, abbreviations and symbols, see p. 232 and foldout map.

Donley County

Physical Features: Panhandle county bisected by Red River Salt Fork; rolling to level; clay, loam, sandy soils.

Economy: Agribusiness, government/services, tourism.

History: Apaches displaced by Kiowas and Comanches, who were driven out in 1874-75 by U.S. Army. Methodist colony from New York settled in 1878. County created in 1876, organized 1882, out of Bexar District; named for Texas Supreme Court Justice S.P. Donley.

Race/Ethnicity, 2008: (In percent) Anglo, 86.7; Black, 5.2; Hispanic, 7.1; Other, 1.0.

Vital Statistics, 2008: Births, 40; deaths, 54; marriages, 31; divorces, 8.

Recreation: Lake, hunting, fishing, camping, water sports; Col. Goodnight Chuckwagon cook-off in September.

Minerals: Small amount of natural gas.

Agriculture: Cattle top revenue source; cotton, peanuts, alfalfa, wheat, hay, melons; 11,000 acres irrigated. Market value $85.8 million.

CLARENDON (2,026) county seat; agribusiness, tourism, medical center; Saints Roost museum, library, junior college.

Other towns include: **Hedley** (329) cotton festival in October, **Howardwick** (402) and **Lelia Lake** (70).

Population	**3,677**
Change fm 2000	–3.95
Area (sq. mi.)	933.05
Land Area (sq. mi.)	929.77
Altitude (ft.)	2,080-3,268
Rainfall (in.)	23.89
Jan. mean min.	22.4

July mean max.	94.7
Civ. Labor	1,924
Unemployed	6.9
Wages	$6,878,527
Av. Weekly Wage	$500
Prop. Value	$497,467,408
Retail Sales	$22,423,224

For explanation of sources, abbreviations and symbols, see p. 232 and foldout map.

A hay field in northeast Donley County. Photo by Robert Plocheck.

Duval County

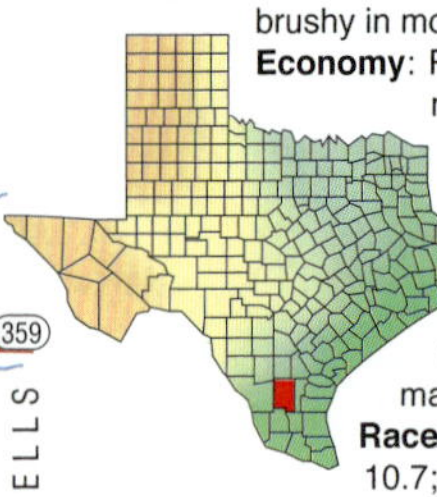

Physical Features: South Texas county; level to hilly, brushy in most areas; varied soils.

Economy: Ranching, petroleum, tourism, government/services.

History: Coahuiltecans, displaced by Comanche bands. Mexican settlement began in 1812. County created from Live Oak, Nueces, Starr counties, 1858, organized 1876; named for Burr H. Duval, a victim of Goliad massacre.

Race/Ethnicity, 2008: (In percent) Anglo, 10.7; Black, 0.4; Hispanic, 88.5; Other, 0.3.

Vital Statistics, 2008: Births, 192; deaths, 105; marriages, 64; divorces, 27.

Recreation: Hunting, tourist crossroads.

Minerals: Oil, gas, salt, sand, gravel, uranium.

Agriculture: Most income from beef cattle; grains, cotton, vegetables, hay, dairy. Market value $14.8 million.

SAN DIEGO (4,488, part in Jim Wells County) county seat; ranching, oil field, tourist center; hospital.

Freer (2,818) oil and gas, construction, ranching and hunting; rattlesnake roundup in May.

Benavides (1,362) serves truck-farming area.

Other towns include: **Concepcion** (62) and **Realitos** (184).

Jan. mean min.	42.5
July mean max.	97.3
Civ. Labor	5,288
Unemployed	11.0
Wages	$30,578,483
Av. Weekly Wage	$754
Prop. Value	$2,306,170,961
Retail Sales	$67,197,830

Population	**11,782**	Land Area (sq. mi.)	1,792.71
Change fm 2000	−10.2	Altitude (ft.)	180-842
Area (sq. mi.)	1,795.67	Rainfall (in.)	25.40

A replica of Stonehenge on the UT-Permian Basin campus in Odessa, Ector County. Photo by Robert Plocheck.

STEPHENS

PALO PINTO

Morton Valley
RANGER
Lake Cisco
CISCO
EASTLAND
North Fork
Middle Fork
Olden
Punkin Center
Staff
Chaney
Scranton
Pleasant Hill
South Fork
Leon River
Carbon
Kokomo
Desdemona
Nimrod
Sabanno
Sabana River
COYOTE PEAK
1882'
Okra
Pioneer
Rising Star
Gorman
COMANCHE
ERATH
S. Fork Palo Pinto Creek
Leon River
FWWR
CALLAHAN
BROWN

1980'

0 8 MILES

Population	18,583
Change fm 2000	1.56
Area (sq. mi.)	931.90
Land Area (sq. mi.)	926.01
Altitude (ft.)	960-1,980
Rainfall (in.)	27.53
Jan. mean min.	26.7
July mean max.	94.9
Civ. Labor	8,840
Unemployed	7.9
Wages	$58,218,289
Av. Weekly Wage	$647
Prop. Value	$1,878,193,540
Retail Sales	$257,840,087

Eastland County

Physical Features: Hilly, rolling; sandy, loam soils; drains to Leon River forks.

Economy: Agribusiness, education, petroleum industries, varied manufacturing.

History: Plains Indian area. Frank Sánchez among first settlers in 1850s. County created from Bosque, Coryell, Travis counties, 1858, organized 1873; named for W.M. Eastland, Mier Expedition casualty.

Race/Ethnicity, 2008: (In percent) Anglo, 83.7; Black, 2.4; Hispanic, 13.2; Other, 0.7.

Vital Statistics, 2008: Births, 206; deaths, 262; marriages, 138; divorces, 71.

Recreation: Lakes, water sports; fishing, hunting; museums; historic sites and displays.

Minerals: Oil, natural gas.

Agriculture: Beef cattle, forage and hay. 20,000 acres irrigated. Market value $28 million.

EASTLAND (3,960) county seat; tourism, government/services, petroleum industries, varied manufacturing; hospital, library; Old Ripfest in September.

CISCO (3,899) manufacturing, oilfield services; Conrad Hilton's first hotel restored, museums; community college; folklife festival in April.

RANGER (2,468) oil center, varied manufacturing, junior college.

Other towns include: **Carbon** (272) livestock equipment manufacturing; **Desdemona** (180); **Gorman** (1,083) peanut processing, agribusiness, hospital; **Olden** (113), and **Rising Star** (835) cap manufacturing, plant nursery; Octoberfest.

Ector County

Physical Features: West Texas county; level to rolling, some sand dunes; meteor crater; desert vegetation.

Economy: Center for Permian Basin oil field operations, plastics, electric generation plants.

History: First settlers in late 1880s. Oil boom in 1926. County created from Tom Green County, 1887; organized 1891; named for jurist M.D. Ector.

Race/Ethnicity, 2008: (In percent) Anglo, 41.9; Black, 4.8; Hispanic, 51.8; Other, 1.5.

Vital Statistics, 2008: Births, 2,688; deaths, 1,170; marriages, 974; divorces, 712.

Recreation: Globe Theatre replica; presidential museum and Bush childhood home; art institute; second-largest U.S. meteor crater; Stonehenge replica.

Minerals: More than 3 billion barrels of oil produced since 1926; gas, cement, stone.

Agriculture: Beef cattle, horses are chief producers; pecans, hay, poultry; minor irrigation. Market value $3.6 million.

Education: University of Texas of Permian Basin, Texas Tech University Health Sciences Center, Odessa (junior) College.

ODESSA (99,940, small part in Midland County) county seat; oil and gas, manufacturing, ranching; hospitals; cultural center; Permian Basin Fair and Expo in September.

Other towns include: **Gardendale** (1,574),

ANDREWS

Gardendale
Goldsmith
Notrees
3360'
West Odessa
Monahans Draw
ODESSA
UT PERMIAN BASIN
Penwell
ODESSA CRATER
Pleasant Farms
UP
Landreth Draw
WINKLER
WARD
CRANE
UPTON
MIDLAND

0 8 MILES

Goldsmith (257), **Notrees** (20), **Penwell** (41), and **West Odessa** (22,707).

Population	137,130
Change fm 2000	13.22
Area (sq. mi.)	901.68
Land Area (sq. mi.)	901.06
Altitude (ft.)	2,780-3,360
Rainfall (in.)	13.29
Jan. mean min.	28.7
July mean max.	96.0
Civ. Labor	73,220
Unemployed	7.0
Wages	$752,573,597
Av. Weekly Wage	$947
Prop. Value	$10,968,132,983
Retail Sales	$2,346,969,621

Edwards County

Physical Features: Rolling, hilly; caves; spring-fed streams; rocky, thin soils; drained by Llano, Nueces rivers; varied timber.

Economy: Hunting leases, tourism, oil and gas production, ranching.

History: Apache area. First land sold in 1876. County created from Bexar District, 1858; organized in 1883; named for Nacogdoches empresario Hayden Edwards.

Race/Ethnicity, 2008: (In percent) Anglo, 51.0; Black, 0.2; Hispanic, 48.3; Other, 0.6.

Vital Statistics, 2008: Births, 23; deaths, 11; marriages, 1; divorces, 4.

Recreation: Hunting, fishing; scenic drives; Devil's Sinkhole, Kickapoo Cavern state parks.

Minerals: Gas.

Agriculture: Second in number of goats. Mohair-wool production, Angora goats, sheep, cattle, some pecans. Market value $8.8 million. Cedar harvested for oil.

ROCKSPRINGS (1,182) county seat; government/services, hunting, ranching, oil, gas, hunters' barbecue in November.

Other towns include: **Barksdale** (100).

Population	**2,002**
Change fm 2000	−7.4
Area (sq. mi.)	2,119.95
Land Area (sq. mi.)	2,119.75
Altitude (ft.)	1,480-2,415
Rainfall (in.)	24.76
Jan. mean min.	34.3
July mean max.	91.6
Civ. Labor	1,007
Unemployed	7.0
Wages	$3,291,422
Av. Weekly Wage	$632
Prop. Value	$1,694,631,232
Retail Sales	$15,677,063

For explanation of sources, abbreviations and symbols, see p. 232 and foldout map.

The Bardwell Dam and Lake in Ellis County. Photo by U.S. Army Corps of Engineers.

Ellis County

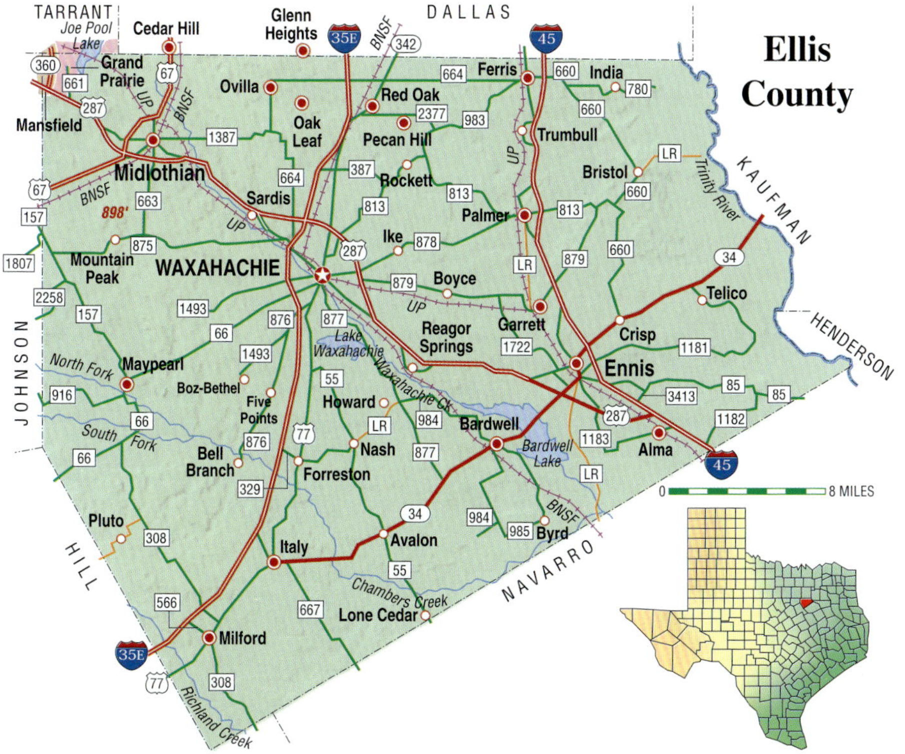

(Map of Ellis County showing cities including Cedar Hill, Glenn Heights, Ferris, India, Grand Prairie, Ovilla, Red Oak, Trumbull, Mansfield, Oak Leaf, Pecan Hill, Bristol, Midlothian, Rockett, Palmer, Sardis, Ike, Mountain Peak, Waxahachie, Boyce, Telico, Maypearl, Reagor Springs, Garrett, Crisp, Ennis, Boz-Bethel, Howard, Five Points, Bardwell, Alma, Bell Branch, Nash, Forreston, Pluto, Italy, Avalon, Byrd, Lone Cedar, Milford. Surrounding counties: TARRANT, DALLAS, KAUFMAN, HENDERSON, NAVARRO, HILL, JOHNSON. Lakes: Joe Pool Lake, Lake Waxahachie, Bardwell Lake. Rivers: Trinity River, Chambers Creek, Richland Creek)

0 — 8 MILES

Physical Features: Blackland soils; level to rolling; Chambers Creek, Trinity River.

Economy: Cement, steel production, warehousing and distribution, government/services; many residents work in Dallas and Fort Worth.

History: Tonkawa tribal area. Part of the Peters colony settled in 1843. County created in 1849 and organized in 1850, from Navarro County. Named for Richard Ellis, president of convention that declared Texas' independence.

Race/Ethnicity, 2008: (In percent) Anglo, 64.8; Black, 9.2; Hispanic, 24.9; Other, 1.1.

Vital Statistics, 2008: Births, 2,095; deaths, 941; marriages, 993; divorces, 416.

Recreation: Lakes, fishing, hunting; bluebonnet trails, historic homes, courthouse; Medieval-theme Scarborough Faire in spring.

Minerals: Cement, gas, sand, gravel.

Agriculture: Cattle, cotton, corn, hay, nurseries. Market value $49.4 million.

WAXAHACHIE (29,621) county seat; manufacturing, steel, aluminum, tourism; hospital; colleges, museums; hike/bike trail; Crape Myrtle festival in July.

Ennis (18,513) manufacturing, distribution, agribusiness, tourism; hospital; bluebonnet trails, National Polka Festival in May.

Midlothian (18,307) cement plants, steel plant, distribution center, manufacturing; heritage park, cabin; spring fling in Apirl.

Other towns include: **Alma** (331); **Avalon** (400); **Bardwell** (649); **Bristol** (668); **Ferris** (2,436); **Forreston** (400); **Garrett** (806); **Howard** (60); **Italy** (1,863); **Maypearl** (934).

Also, **Milford** (728); **Oak Leaf** (1,298); **Ovilla** (3,492); **Palmer** (2,000); **Pecan Hill** (626); and **Red Oak** (10,769) manufacturing, Founders Day in September.

Also, **Glenn Heights** (11,278, mostly in Dallas County). And, small parts of **Grand Prairie** and **Mansfield**.

Population	149,610
Change fm 2000	34.35
Area (sq. mi.)	951.66
Land Area (sq. mi.)	939.91
Altitude (ft.)	300-898
Rainfall (in.)	38.81
Jan. mean min.	35.0
July mean max.	96.0
Civ. Labor	72,771
Unemployed	8.7
Wages	$362,292,695
Av. Weekly Wage	$730
Prop. Value	$12,270,988,294
Retail Sales	$1,213,697,881

For explanation of sources, abbreviations and symbols, see p. 232 and foldout map.

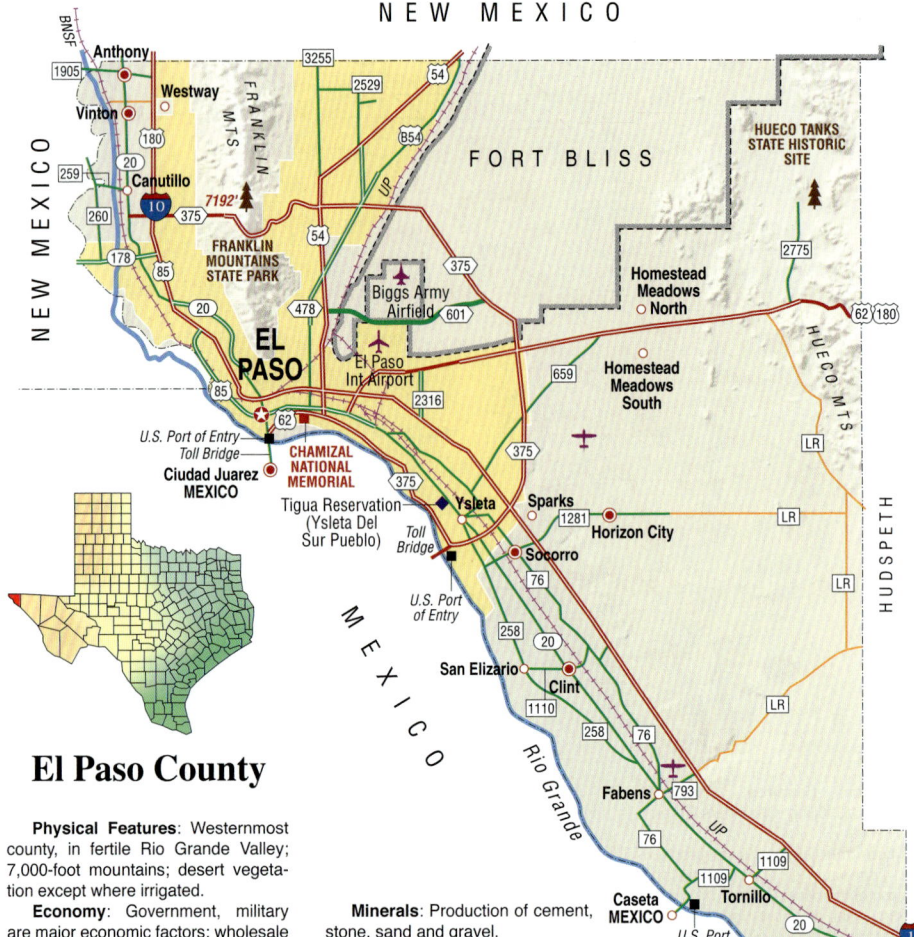

El Paso County

Physical Features: Westernmost county, in fertile Rio Grande Valley; 7,000-foot mountains; desert vegetation except where irrigated.

Economy: Government, military are major economic factors; wholesale and retail distribution center, education, tourism, maquiladora plants, varied manufacturing, oil refining, cotton, food processing.

History: Various Indian tribes inhabited the valley before Spanish civilization arrived in late 1650s. Agriculture in area dates to at least 100 A.D. Spanish along with Tigua and Piro tribes fleeing Santa Fe uprising of 1680 sought refuge in area. County created from Bexar District, 1849; organized 1850; named for historic pass (Paso del Norte), lowest all-weather pass through Rocky Mountains.

Race/Ethnicity, 2008: (In percent) Anglo, 12.0; Black, 2.6; Hispanic, 83.4; Other, 1.9.

Vital Statistics, 2008: Births, 14,013; deaths, 4,524; marriages, 5,921; divorces, 39.

Recreation: Gateway to Mexico; Chamizal Museum; major tourist center; December Sun Carnival with football game; state parks, mountain tramway, missions and other historic sites.

For explanation of sources, abbreviations and symbols, see p. 232 and foldout map.

Minerals: Production of cement, stone, sand and gravel.

Agriculture: Dairies, cattle, cotton, pecans (third in acreage), onions, forage, peppers. Third in colonies of bees. 50,000 acres irrigated, mostly cotton. Market value $47.5 million.

Education: University of Texas at El Paso, UT School of Nursing at El Paso, Texas Tech University Health Sciences Center, El Paso Community College.

EL PASO (649,121) county seat; Texas' sixth-largest city, fifth-largest metro area, largest U.S. city on Mexican border.

A center for government operations. Federal installations include Fort Bliss, William Beaumont General Hospital, La Tuna federal prison, and headquarters of the U.S. Army Air Defense Command.

Manufactured products include clothing, electronics, auto equipment, plastics; trade and distribution; refining; processing oil, food, cotton and other farm products.

Hospitals; museums; convention center; theater, symphony orchestra.

Other towns include: **Anthony** (5,011 in Texas, 9,360 in New Mexi-

co); **Canutillo** (6,321); **Clint** (926); **Fabens** (8,257); **Homestead Meadows North** (5,247); **Homestead Meadows South** (7,427); **Horizon City** (16,735); **Prado Verde** (246); **San Elizario** (13,603); **Socorro** (32,013) settled in 1680; **Sparks** (4,529); **Tornillo** (1,568); **Vinton** (1,971); **Westway** (4,188), and **Ysleta** (now within El Paso) settled in 1680, called the oldest town in Texas.

And, **Fort Bliss** (8,591).

Population	800,647
Change fm 2000	17.81
Area (sq. mi.)	1,014.68
Land Area (sq. mi.)	1,013.11
Altitude (ft.)	3,520-7,192
Rainfall (in.)	9.43
Jan. mean min.	32.9
July mean max.	94.5
Civ. Labor	321,774
Unemployed	10.4
Wages	$2,459,897,516
Av. Weekly Wage	$692
Prop. Value	$37,946,549,556
Retail Sales	$8,666,520,080

Erath County

Physical Features: On Rolling Plains; clay loam, sandy soils; drains to Bosque, Paluxy rivers.

Economy: Agricultural, industrial and educational enterprises.

History: Caddo and Anadarko Indians moved to Oklahoma in 1860. Anglo-American settlement began 1854-55. County created from Bosque, Coryell counties in 1856, organized the same year; named for George B. Erath, Texas Revolution figure.

Race/Ethnicity, 2008: (In percent) Anglo, 77.7; Black, 0.9; Hispanic, 20.5; Other, 0.8.

Vital Statistics, 2008: Births, 507; deaths, 281; marriages, 324; divorces, 126.

Recreation: Old courthouse, log cabins, museums; nearby lakes, hunting, Bosque River Park; university fine arts center; Dairy Fest in June.

Minerals: Gas, oil.

Agriculture: First in milk and dairy products. Beef cattle, horticulture industry, horses raised. Market value $250.2 million.

STEPHENVILLE (17,123) county seat; Tarleton State University, varied manufacturing; hospital, mental health center; Texas A&M research and extension center.

Dublin (3,654) dairies, food processing, varied manufacturing, tourism; library; old Dr Pepper plant; grist mill, St. Patrick's Day celebration.

Other towns include: **Bluff Dale** (400); **Lingleville** (100); **Morgan Mill** (206); **Thurber** (48) former coal-mining town; Gordon Center for Industrial History of Texas.

Population	37,890
Change fm 2000	14.81
Area (sq. mi.)	1,089.80
Land Area (sq. mi.)	1,086.33
Altitude (ft.)	820-1,670
Rainfall (in.)	29.71
Jan. mean min.	30.0
July mean max.	93.6
Civ. Labor	19,321
Unemployed	6.6
Wages	$115,637,493
Av. Weekly Wage	$571
Prop. Value	$3,916,534,130
Retail Sales	$435,377,675

For explanation of sources, abbreviations and symbols, see p. 232 and foldout map.

The landscape along U.S. 67 west of Chalk Mountain. Photo by Robert Plocheck.

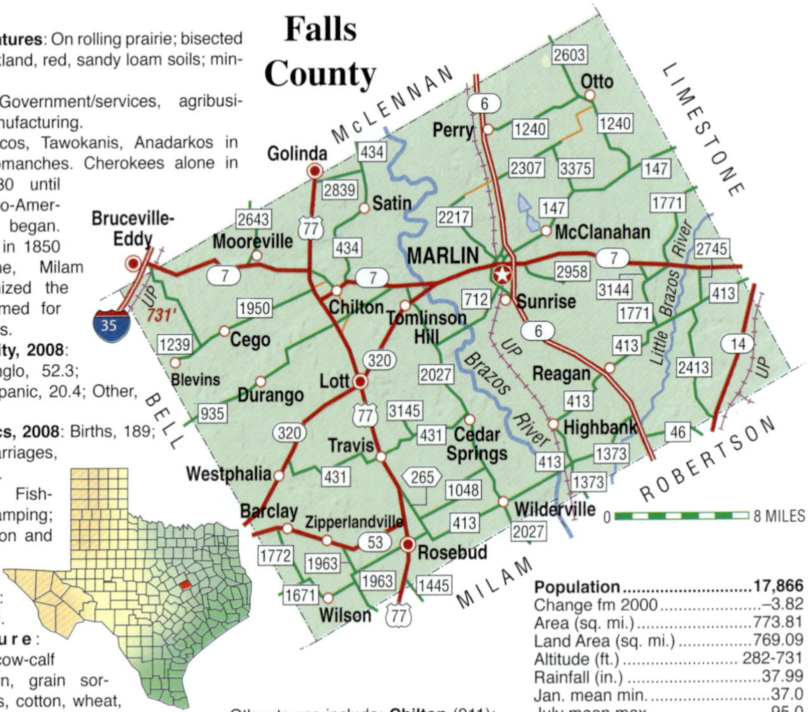

Physical Features: On rolling prairie; bisected by Brazos; blackland, red, sandy loam soils; mineral springs.

Economy: Government/services, agribusiness, varied manufacturing.

History: Wacos, Tawokanis, Anadarkos in conflict with Comanches. Cherokees alone in area from 1830 until 1835 when Anglo-American settlement began. County created in 1850 from Limestone, Milam counties, organized the same year; named for Brazos River falls.

Race/Ethnicity, 2008: (In percent) Anglo, 52.3; Black, 26.9; Hispanic, 20.4; Other, 0.4.

Vital Statistics, 2008: Births, 189; deaths, 204; marriages, 81; divorces, 23.

Recreation: Fishing, hunting, camping; Highland Mansion and Falls on the Brazos.

Minerals: Gravel, sand, oil.

Agriculture: Stocker cattle, cow-calf operations, corn, grain sorghum, soybeans, cotton, wheat, oats, goats, sheep, horses. Some cotton irrigated. Market value $126.8 million.

MARLIN (5,967) county seat; agriculture, prison; hospital; museum.

Falls County

Other towns include: **Chilton** (911); **Golinda** (559); **Lott** (759); **Reagan** (208); **Rosebud** (1,412) feed, fertilizer processing, clothing manufactured; **Satin** (86). Part of **Bruceville-Eddy** (1,475).

Population	17,866
Change fm 2000	–3.82
Area (sq. mi.)	773.81
Land Area (sq. mi.)	769.09
Altitude (ft.)	282-731
Rainfall (in.)	37.99
Jan. mean min.	37.0
July mean max.	95.0
Civ. Labor	6,643
Unemployed	10.0
Wages	$27,911,536
Av. Weekly Wage	$663
Prop. Value	$990,731,630
Retail Sales	$81,264,016

A goat farm south of Bonham in Fannin County. Photo by Robert Plocheck.

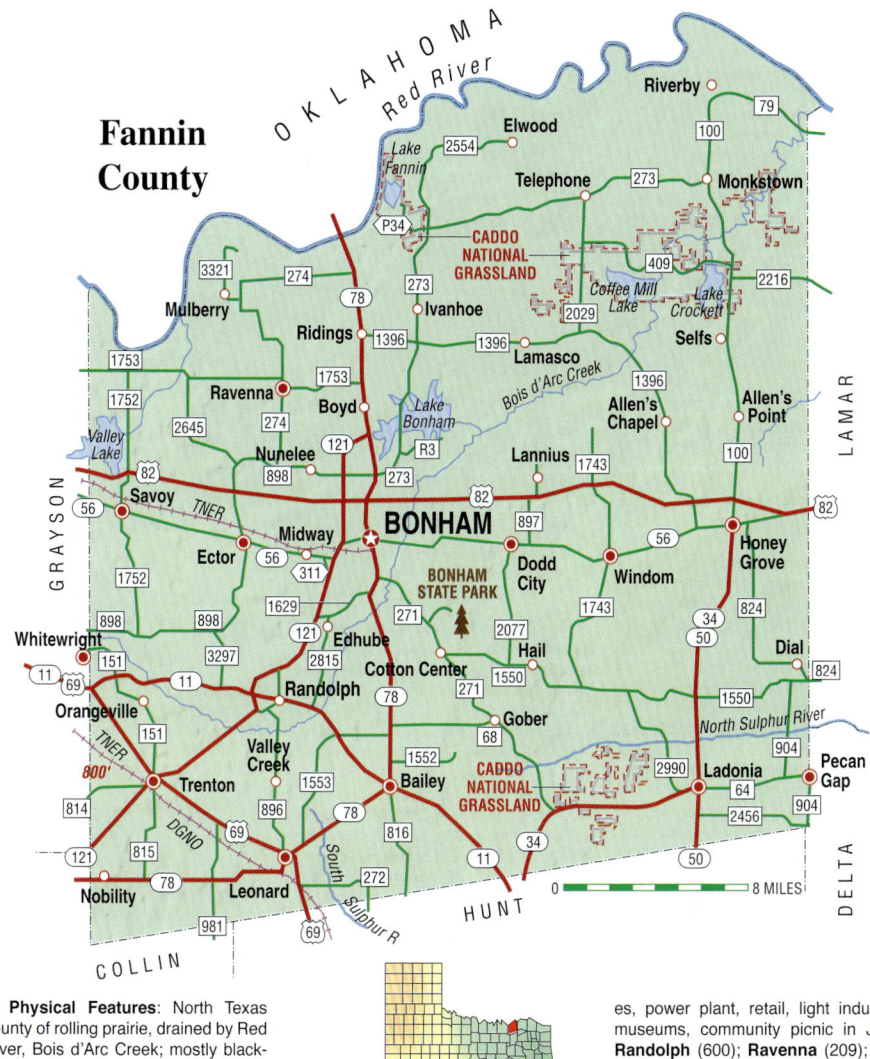

Fannin County

OKLAHOMA
Red River
Riverby
79
Elwood
100
Lake Fannin
2554
Telephone 273
Monkstown
P34
409
CADDO NATIONAL GRASSLAND
2216
3321 274 273
Coffee Mill Lake
Lake Crockett
Mulberry
78
Ivanhoe
2029
Selfs
Ridings 1396
1396
Lamasco
1753
Bois d'Arc Creek
1396
Allen's Point
1752
Ravenna 1753
Boyd
Lake Bonham
Allen's Chapel
100
Valley Lake
2645 274
Nunelee 121
R3
Lannius 1743
LAMAR
898
273
82
82
56
Savoy TNER
Midway
82
897
Honey Grove
Ector 56
BONHAM
56
311
824
1752
BONHAM STATE PARK
Dodd City
Windom
1743
1629
271
34 50
Whitewright
151
898 898
121 Edhube
2077
Dial
3297
2815
Hail
824
Orangeville
151
Randolph
78
271
1550
1550
TNER
Valley Creek
Gober
68
North Sulphur River
800'
Trenton 1553
1552
Bailey
CADDO NATIONAL GRASSLAND
2990
Ladonia
904
Pecan Gap
814
896
78
816
64
2456 904
121
815
DGNO
69
272
34
50
DELTA
Nobility
78
Leonard
South Sulphur R
0   8 MILES
981
69
COLLIN
HUNT

Physical Features: North Texas county of rolling prairie, drained by Red River, Bois d'Arc Creek; mostly black-land soils; national grassland.

Economy: Commuting to DFW metroplex, agribusiness.

History: Caddoes who joined with Cherokees. Anglo-American settlement began in 1836. County created from Red River County, 1837, organized 1838; named for James W. Fannin, a victim of Goliad massacre.

Race/Ethnicity, 2008: (In percent) Anglo, 84.3; Black, 7.8; Hispanic, 6.8; Other, 1.2.

Vital Statistics, 2008: Births, 404; deaths, 422; marriages, 205; divorces, 117.

Recreation: Water activities on lakes; hunting; birding; state park, fossil beds; winery; Sam Rayburn home, library.

Minerals: Sand.

Agriculture: Beef cattle, wheat, corn. Market value $48.7 million. Hunting important.

BONHAM (10,127) county seat; varied manufacturing, veterans hospital/private hospital, state jail; Sam Rayburn birthday celebration in January.

Other towns include: **Bailey** (289); **Dodd City** (369); **Ector** (695); **Gober** (146); **Honey Grove** (1,668) agribusiness center, varied manufacturing, tourism, historic buildings, library, Davy Crockett Festival in October; **Ivanhoe** (110).

Also, **Ladonia** (612) restored historical downtown, tourism, varied manufacturing, commuters, rodeo; **Leonard** (1,990) government/servic-

es, power plant, retail, light industry, museums, community picnic in July; **Randolph** (600); **Ravenna** (209); **Savoy** (831); **Telephone** (210); **Trenton** (635); **Windom** (199).

Also, part of **Pecan Gap** (203) and part of **Whitewright** (1,604).

Population	**33,915**
Change fm 2000	8.56
Area (sq. mi.)	899.16
Land Area (sq. mi.)	891.45
Altitude (ft.)	450-800
Rainfall (in.)	44.56
Jan. mean min.	30.2
July mean max.	92.6
Civ. Labor	13,938
Unemployed	10.1
Wages	$59,219,542
Av. Weekly Wage	$676
Prop. Value	$2,488,211,366
Retail Sales	$182,766,677

For explanation of sources, abbreviations and symbols, see p. 232 and foldout map.

Fayette County

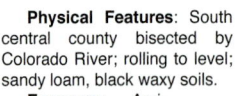

Physical Features: South central county bisected by Colorado River; rolling to level; sandy loam, black waxy soils.

Economy: Agri-business, production of electricity, mineral production, government/services, small manufacturing, tourism.

History: Lipan Apaches and Tonkawas. Austin's colonists arrived in 1822. Germans and Czechs began arriving in 1840s. County created from Bastrop, Colorado counties, 1837; organized, 1838; named for hero of American Revolution, Marquis de Lafayette.

Race/Ethnicity, 2008: (In percent) Anglo, 74.4; Black, 7.0; Hispanic, 18.0; Other, 0.6.

Vital Statistics, 2008: Births, 279; deaths, 300; marriages, 138; divorces, 67.

Recreation: Monument Hill, Kreische brewery, Faison Home Museum, other historic sites including "Painted Churches"; hunting, fishing, lake; German and Czech ethnic foods; Prazska Pout in August, Octoberfests.

Minerals: Oil, gas, sand, gravel, bentonite clay.

Agriculture: Beef cattle, corn, hay, sorghum, pecans, dairies. Market value $52.8 million. Firewood sold.

LA GRANGE (4,641) county seat; electric-power generation, varied manufacturing, food processing, retail trade, tourism; hospital, library, museum, archives; Czech heritage center; Texas Independence Day observance.

Schulenburg (2,852) varied manufacturing, food processing; festival in August.

Round Top (90) music center, tourism; old Lutheran church, Cadillac museum; antiques shows, International Festival Institute, July-August; Schuetzenfest in September, and **Winedale** (67), historic restorations including Winedale Inn.

Other towns include: **Carmine** (250); **Ellinger** (386) Tomato Festival in May; **Fayetteville** (258) tourism, antiques, old precinct courthouse, Lickskillet festival in October; **Flatonia** (1,383) farm market, varied manufacturing, antiques, Czhilispiel in October; **Ledbetter** (83); **Muldoon** (95); **Plum** (145); **Warda** (121); **Warrenton** (186) antique Cadillac museum; **West Point** (213), and **Winchester** (232).

Population	**24,554**
Change fm 2000	12.61
Area (sq. mi.)	959.84
Land Area (sq. mi.)	950.03
Altitude (ft.)	200-590
Rainfall (in.)	40.31
Jan. mean min.	41.4
July mean max.	95.9
Civ. Labor	11,996
Unemployed	6.5
Wages	$83,054,096
Av. Weekly Wage	$759
Prop. Value	$4,411,447,235
Retail Sales	$309,325,825

For explanation of sources, abbreviations and symbols, see p. 232 and fold-out map.

The concert hall of the Round Top International Festival Institute in Fayette County. Photo by Robert Plocheck.

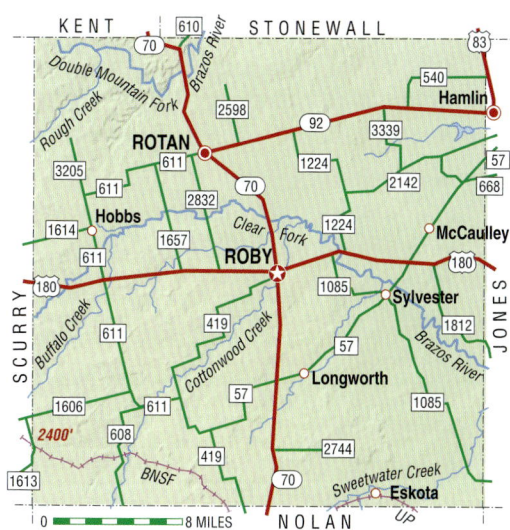

Fisher County

Physical Features: On rolling prairie; mesquite; red, sandy loam soils; drains to forks of Brazos River.

Economy: Agribusiness, hunting, gypsum.

History: Lipan Apaches, disrupted by Comanches and other tribes around 1700. Ranching began in 1876. County created from Bexar District, 1876; organized 1886; named for S.R. Fisher, Republic of Texas secretary of navy.

Race/Ethnicity, 2008: (In percent) Anglo, 72.4; Black, 2.8; Hispanic, 24.1; Other, 0.7.

Vital Statistics, 2008: Births, 41; deaths, 55; marriages, 25; divorces, 7.

Recreation: Quail, dove, turkey hunting; wildlife viewing; county fair, rodeo in August in Roby.

Minerals: Gypsum, oil.

Agriculture: Cattle, cotton, hay, wheat, sorghum, horses, sheep, goats. Irrigation for cotton and alfalfa. Market value $50.5 million.

Population	3,974
Change fm 2000	−8.52
Area (sq. mi.)	901.74
Land Area (sq. mi.)	901.16
Altitude (ft.)	1,720-2,405
Rainfall (in.)	24.22
Jan. mean min.	27.2
July mean max.	94.2
Civ. Labor	1,978
Unemployed	6.7
Wages	$8,017,327
Av. Weekly Wage	$658
Prop. Value	$687,906,769
Retail Sales	$12,399,351

ROBY (643) county seat; agribusiness, cotton gin; hospital between Roby and Rotan.

ROTAN (1,508) gypsum plant, oil mill, agribusiness.

Other towns include: **McCaulley** (96) and **Sylvester** (79). Part of **Hamlin** (2,124).

Floyd County

Physical Features: Flat High Plains, broken by Caprock on east, by White River on south; many playas; red, black loam soils.

Economy: Cotton, wind farm, varied manufacturing, government/services.

History: Plains Apaches and later Comanches. First white settlers arrived in 1884. County created from Bexar District, 1876; organized in 1890. Named for Dolphin Ward Floyd, who died at the Alamo.

Race/Ethnicity, 2008: (In percent) Anglo, 44.8; Black, 3.6; Hispanic, 51.1; Other, 0.5.

Vital Statistics, 2008: Births, 92; deaths, 72; marriages, 28; divorces, 17.

Recreation: Hunting of pheasant, deer, quail; fishing; Blanco Canyon; Floydada Punkin Day in October; museum.

Minerals: Not significant.

Agriculture: Cotton, wheat, sorghum, corn; pumpkins (first in state in production). Some 260,000 acres irrigated. Market value $263 million.

FLOYDADA (3,038) county seat; agriculture, varied manufacturing; Texas A&M engineering extension.

Lockney (1,842) agriculture center; manufacturing; hospital.

Other towns include: **Aiken** (52), **Dougherty** (91), and **South Plains** (67).

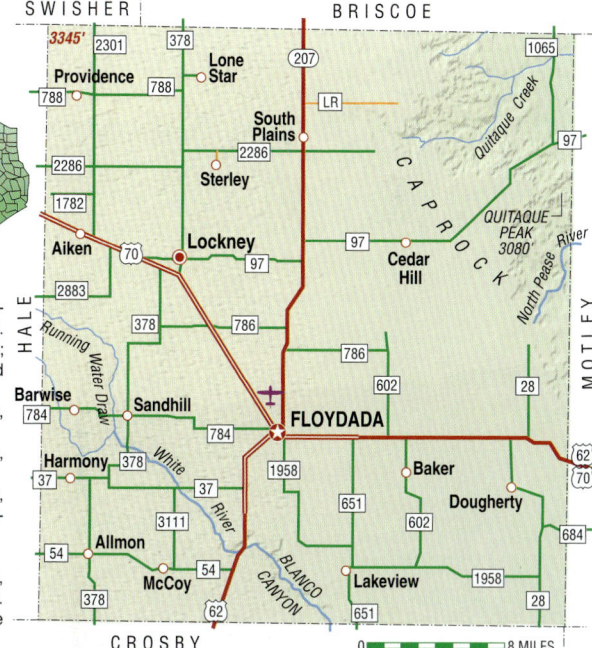

Population	6,446
Change fm 2000	−17.05
Area (sq. mi.)	992.51
Land Area (sq. mi.)	992.19
Altitude (ft.)	2,440-3,345
Rainfall (in.)	20.95
Jan. mean min.	23.2
July mean max.	92.3
Civ. Labor	3,045
Unemployed	10.2
Wages	$17,055,019
Av. Weekly Wage	$666
Prop. Value	$512,803,560
Retail Sales	$35,274,785

For explanation of sources, abbreviations and symbols, see p. 232 and foldout map.

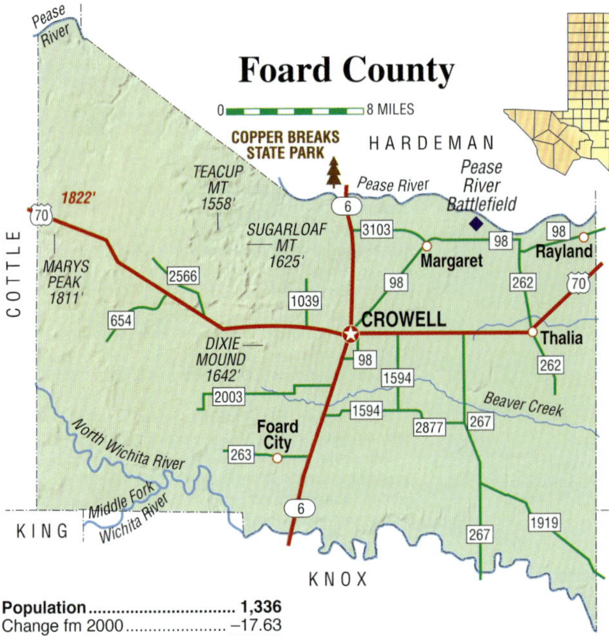

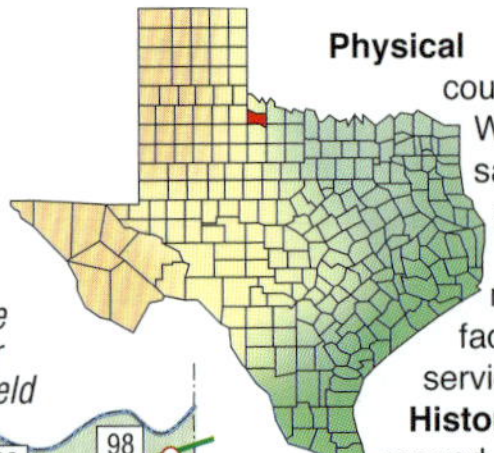

Foard County

0 ━━━━━ 8 MILES

Physical Features: Northwest county drains to North Wichita, Pease rivers; sandy, loam soils, rolling surface.

Economy: Agribusiness, clothes manufacturing, government/service.

History: Comanches, Kiowas ranged the area until driven away in 1870s. Ranching began in 1880. County created out of Cottle, Hardeman, King, Knox counties, 1891, organized the same year; named for Maj. Robert L. Foard of Confederate army.

Race/Ethnicity, 2008: (In percent) Anglo, 77.1; Black, 3.9; Hispanic, 18.2; Other, 0.8.

Vital Statistics, 2008: Births, 12; deaths, 19; marriages,4; divorces, 4.

Recreation: Three museums; hunting; astronomy and ecotourism foundation; wild hog cook-off in November.

Minerals: Natural gas, some oil.

Agriculture: Wheat, cattle, alfalfa, cotton, sorghum, dairies. Market value $17.6 million. Hunting leases important.

CROWELL (948) county seat; retail center, clothing manufacturing; library.

Population	1,336
Change fm 2000	−17.63
Area (sq. mi.)	707.69
Land Area (sq. mi.)	706.68
Altitude (ft.)	1,210-1,822
Rainfall (in.)	26.40
Jan. mean min.	24.0
July mean max.	97.0

Civ. Labor	712
Unemployed	7.7
Wages	$2,157,374
Av. Weekly Wage	$472

Prop. Value	$340,413,240
Retail Sales	$7,198,846

The Caprock at Blanco Canyon, Floyd County. Photo by Robert Plocheck.

Physical Features: On Gulf Coastal Plain; drained by Brazos, San Bernard rivers; level to rolling; rich alluvial soils.

Economy: Agribusiness, petrochemicals, technology, government/services; many residents work in Houston.

History: Karankawas retreated to Mexico by 1850s. Named for river bend where some of Austin's colonists settled 1824. Antebellum plantations made it one of six Texas counties with black majority in 1850. County created 1837 from Austin County; organized 1838.

Race/Ethnicity, 2008: (In percent) Anglo, 40.5; Black, 22.4; Hispanic, 23.0; Other, 14.1.

Vital Statistics, 2008: Births, 7,806; deaths, 2,091; marriages, 2,473; divorces, 1,324.

Recreation: Many historic sites, museums, memorials, parks; George Ranch historical park; state park with George Observatory; fishing, waterfowl hunting.

Minerals: Oil, gas, sulphur, salt, clays, sand and gravel.

Fort Bend County

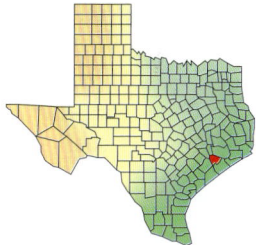

Agriculture: Nursery crops, cotton, sorghum, corn, hay, cattle, horses; irrigation for rice. Market value $94.5 million.

RICHMOND (11,679) county seat; foundry; University of Houston branch, Wharton County Junior College branch; Richmond State supported-living center, hospital.

SUGAR LAND (78,817) government/services, prisons, commuting to Houston; hospitals; University of Houston branch; Museum of Southern History.

MISSOURI CITY (67,358, part in Harris County) hospital.

ROSENBERG (30,618) varied industry, railroad museum.

Other towns include: **Arcola** (1,642); **Beasley** (641); **Cinco Ranch** (18,274); **Fairchilds** (923); **Fresno** (19,069); **Fulshear** (1,134); **Guy** (239); **Katy** (14,102, mostly in Harris County) hospital; **Kendleton** (380); **Meadows Place** (4,660); **Mission Bend** (36,501).

Also, **Needville** (2,823); **New Territory** (15,186); **Orchard** (352); **Pecan Grove** (15,963); **Pleak** (1,044); **Simonton** (814); **Stafford** (17,693, partly in Harris County); **Thompsons** (246); **Weston Lakes** (2,482).

Also, part of **Houston**.

Population	585,375
Change fm 2000	65.15
Area (sq. mi.)	886.05
Land Area (sq. mi.)	874.64
Altitude (ft.)	46-158
Rainfall (in.)	49.34
Jan. mean min.	41.6
July mean max.	93.7
Civ. Labor	282,491
Unemployed	8.1
Wages	$1,688,064,583
Av. Weekly Wage	$981
Prop. Value	$50,560,586,070
Retail Sales	$5,841,024,405

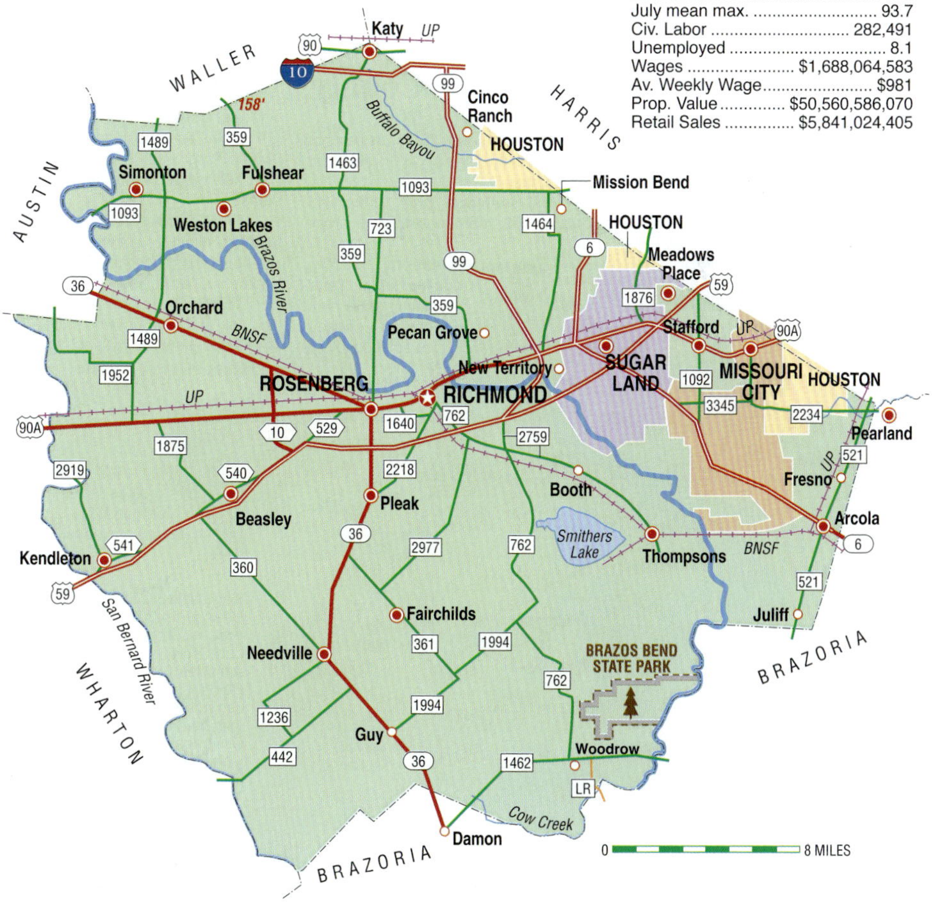

Physical Features: Small Northeast county with many wooded hills; drained by numerous streams; alluvial to sandy clay soils; two lakes.

Economy: Agriculture, government/ services, retirement area, distribution.

History: Caddoes abandoned the area in 1790s because of disease and other tribes. First white settlers arrived around 1818. County created in 1875 from Titus County, organized the same year; named for jurist B.C. Franklin.

Race/Ethnicity, 2008: (In percent) Anglo, 83.9; Black, 4.1; Hispanic, 11.3; Other, 0.8.

Vital Statistics, 2008: Births, 151; deaths, 109; marriages, 57; divorces, 15.

Population	10,605
Change fm 2000	12.13
Area (sq. mi.)	294.77
Land Area (sq. mi.)	285.66
Altitude (ft.)	300-600
Rainfall (in.)	47.65
Jan. mean min.	32.2
July mean max.	92.8
Civ. Labor	5,319
Unemployed	8.1
Wages	$25,479,556
Av. Weekly Wage	$680
Prop. Value	$1,514,722,310
Retail Sales	$88,488,969

Franklin County

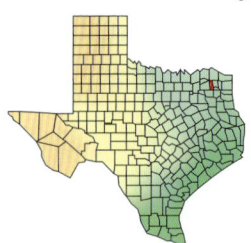

Recreation: Fishing, water sports; historic homes; wild hog hunting, horse stables; stew cook-off in October.

Minerals: Lignite coal, oil and natural gas.

Agriculture: Beef cattle, milk production, poultry, hay. Market value $85.8 million. Timber marketed.

MOUNT VERNON (2,662) county seat; distribution center, manufacturing, tourism, antiques; hospital; museum with Don Meredith exhibit; Labor Day rodeo.

Other towns include: **Scroggins** (150), and **Winnsboro** (3,434, mostly in Wood County) commercial center, Autumn Trails.

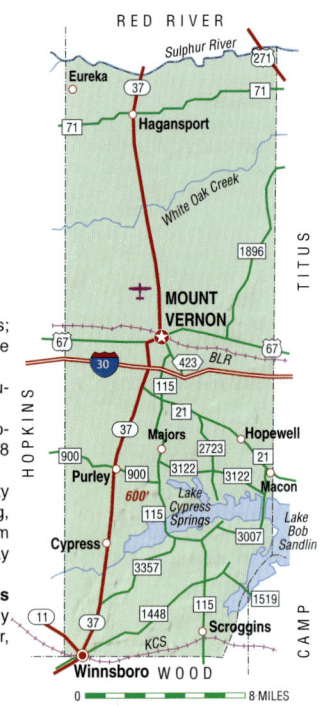

Physical Features: East central county bounded by the Trinity River; rolling Blackland, sandy, loam soils.

Economy: Natural gas, mining, electricity generation, agriculture.

History: Caddo and Tawakoni area. David G. Burnet received land grant in 1825. Seven Mexican citizens received grants in 1833. In 1860, more than half population was black. County created 1850 from Limestone County; organized 1851. Named for indigenous stone.

Freestone County

Race/Ethnicity, 2008: (In percent) Anglo, 70.0; Black, 18.5; Hispanic, 10.9; Other, 0.7.

Vital Statistics, 2008: Births, 243; deaths, 199; marriages, 133; divorces, 64.

Recreation: Fishing, hunting; lakes; historic sites; state park; Teague amateur rodeo in July.

Minerals: Natural gas, oil and lignite coal.

Agriculture: Beef cattle, peaches (third in acreage), hay, blueberries, horticulture. First in number of ducks. Market value $33.9 million. Hunting leases.

FAIRFIELD (2,951) county seat; lignite mining, government/services, trade center; hospital, museum; wild game supper in July.

TEAGUE (3,560) railroad terminal, oil and gas, government/services, electric generating plant, agriculture; library, museum; Parkfest in October.

Other towns include: **Donie** (250), **Kirvin** (129), **Streetman** (247), **Wortham** (1,073) agribusiness, blues festivals in September, Blind Lemon Jefferson gravesite.

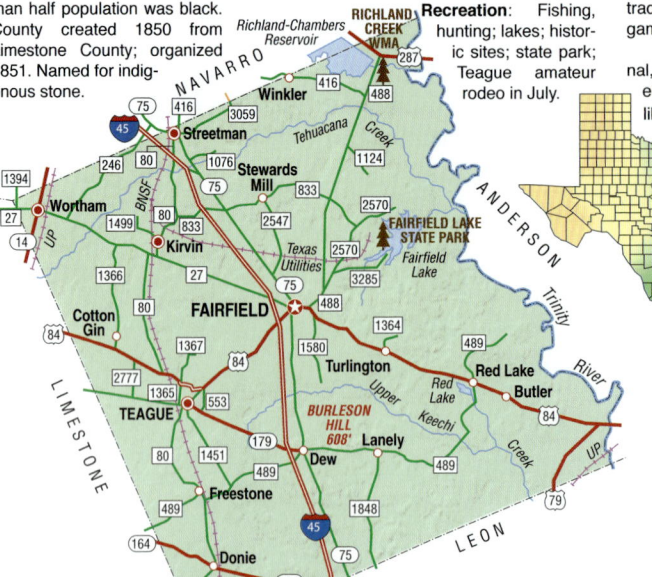

Population	19,816
Change fm 2000	10.91
Area (sq. mi.)	892.13
Land Area (sq. mi.)	877.43
Altitude (ft.)	200-608
Rainfall (in.)	42.31
Jan. mean min.	36.4
July mean max.	95.0
Civ. Labor	10,272
Unemployed	6.9
Wages	$54,135,024
Av. Weekly Wage	$729
Prop. Value	$6,358,090,640
Retail Sales	$172,498,411

For explanation of sources, abbreviations and symbols, see p. 232 and foldout map.

Frio County

Physical Features: South Texas county of rolling terrain with much brush; bisected by Frio River; sandy, red sandy loam soils.

Economy: Agribusiness, oil-field services, hunting leases.

History: Coahuiltecans; many taken into San Antonio missions. Comanche hunters kept settlers out until after the Civil War. Mexican citizens recruited for labor after 1900. County created 1858 from Atascosa, Bexar, Uvalde counties, organized in 1871; named for Frio (cold) River.

Race/Ethnicity, 2008: (In percent) Anglo, 19.2; Black, 4.1; Hispanic, 76.0; Other, 0.6.

Vital Statistics, 2008: Births, 264; deaths, 94; marriages, 89; divorces, 9.

Recreation: Hunting, Big Foot Wallace Museum, Winter Garden area, Pearsall potato fest in May.

Minerals: Oil, natural gas, stone.

Agriculture: Peanuts, potatoes, sorghum, cotton, corn, spinach, cucumbers, watermelons. Second in vegetables harvested. Market value $70.3 million. Hunting leases.

PEARSALL (9,146) county seat; agriculture center, oil and gas, food processing, shipping; old jail museum; hospital; Pioneer Days in April.

Dilley (3,894) shipping center for melons and peanuts; hospital.

Other towns include: **Bigfoot** (450), **Hilltop** (287); **Moore** (475) and **North Pearsall** (614).

Population 17,217
Change fm 2000 .... 5.94

Area (sq. mi.) 1,134.28
Land Area (sq. mi.) 1,133.02
Altitude (ft.) 400-763
Rainfall (in.) 25.73
Jan. mean min. 37.9
July mean max. 97.5
Civ. Labor 7,750
Unemployed 7.6
Wages $39,254,566
Av. Weekly Wage $610
Prop. Value $1,642,834,110
Retail Sales $111,230,183

For explanation of sources, abbreviations and symbols, see p. 232 and fold-out map.

Sunlight flows through an old church in Streetman, Freestone County. Photo by Robert Plocheck.

Gaines County

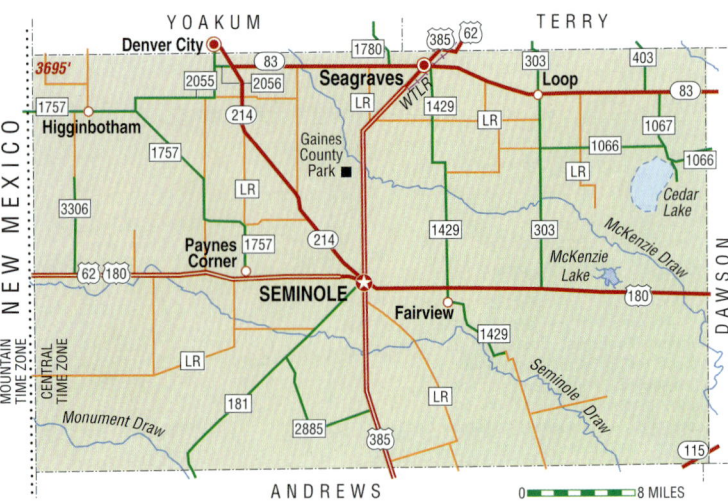

Physical Features: On South Plains, drains to draws; playas; underground water.

Economy: Oil and natural gas, cotton, peanuts.

History: Comanche country until U.S. Army campaigns of 1875. Ranchers arrived in the 1880s; farming began around 1900. County created from Bexar District, 1876; organized in 1905; named for James Gaines, signer of Texas Declaration of Independence.

Race/Ethnicity, 2008: (In percent) Anglo, 56.8; Black, 2.3; Hispanic, 40.5; Other, 0.5.

Vital Statistics, 2008: Births, 328; deaths, 105; marriages, 144; divorces, 25.

Recreation: Cedar Lake one of largest alkali lakes on Texas plains.

Minerals: Oil, gas.

Agriculture: Cotton (third in acreage), peanuts (first in acreage), small grains, pecans, paprika, rosemary; cattle, sheep, hogs; substantial irrigation. Market value $193.2 million.

SEMINOLE (6,430) county seat; farming, oil and natural gas, ranching, market center; hospital, library, museum; Go Nuts produce fair in September.

Seagraves (2,417) market for three-county area; cotton, peanut farming; library, museum; Celebrate Seagraves in July.

Other towns include: **Loop** (225). Also, part of **Denver City** (4,479).

Population	**17,526**
Change fm 2000	21.15
Area (sq. mi.)	1,502.84
Land Area (sq. mi.)	1,502.35
Altitude (ft.)	2,935-3,695
Rainfall (in.)	18.20
Jan. mean min.	26.7
July mean max.	94.1
Civ. Labor	6,874
Unemployed	6.1
Wages	$56,244,693
Av. Weekly Wage	$812
Prop. Value	$4,868,046,022
Retail Sales	$161,423,825

For explanation of sources, abbreviations and symbols, see p. 232 and foldout map.

Tankers in Galveston Bay. Photo by Robert Plocheck.

Physical Features: Partly island, partly coastal plain; flat, artificial drainage; sandy, loam, clay soils; broken by bays.

Economy: Port activities dominate economy; insurance and finance center, petrochemical plants, varied manufacturing, tourism, medical education, oceanographic research, ship building, commercial fishing.

History: Karankawa and other tribes roamed the area until 1850. French, Spanish and American settlement began in 1815 and reached 1,000 by 1817. County created from Brazoria County in 1838; organized in 1839; named for the Spanish governor of Louisiana Count Bernardo de Gálvez.

Race/Ethnicity, 2008: (In percent) Anglo, 58.5; Black, 14.9; Hispanic, 22.7; Other, 3.9.

Vital Statistics, 2008: Births, 4,198; deaths, 2,416; marriages, 2,270; divorces, 1,098.

Recreation: One of Texas' most historic cities; popular tourist and convention center; fishing, surfing, boating, sailing and other water sports, ocean cruises; state park; historic homes tour in spring, Moody Gardens; Mardi Gras celebration; Rosenberg Library; museums; restored sailing ship, "Elissa," railroad museum; Dickens on the Strand in early December.

Minerals: Oil, gas, clays, sand and gravel.

Agriculture: Cattle, aquaculture, nursery crops, rice, hay, horses, soy-

Galveston County

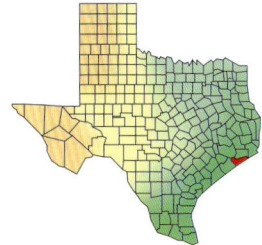

beans, grain sorghum. Market value $8.3 million.

GALVESTON (47,743) county seat; tourist center, shipyard, other industries, insurance, port container facility; University of Texas Medical Branch; National Maritime Research Center; Texas A&M University at Galveston; Galveston College; hospitals.

League City (83,560) residential community, commuters to Houston, hospital.

Texas City (45,099) refining, petrochemical plants, port, rail shipping; College of the Mainland; hospital, library; dike; Cinco de Mayo, Shrimp Boil in August.

Bolivar Peninsula (2,417) includes: **Port Bolivar** (700) lighthouse, free ferry; **Crystal Beach** (800) seafood industry, sport fishing, tourism, Fort Travis Seashore Park, shorebird sanctuary, Crab Festival in

May; **Gilchrist** (400) and **High Island** (300).

Other towns include: **Bacliff** (8,619); **Bayou Vista** (1,537); **Clear Lake Shores** (1,063).

Also, **Dickinson** (18,680) manufacturing, commuters, strawberry festival in May; **Friendswood** (35,805), partly in Harris County); **Hitchcock** (6,961) residential community, tourism, fishing and shrimping, Good Ole Days in August, WWII blimp base, museum.

Also, **Jamaica Beach** (983); **Kemah** (1,773) tourism, boating, commuters, museum, Blessing of Fleet in August; **La Marque** (14,509) refining, greyhound racing, farming, hospital, library, Gulf Coast Grill-off in October; **San Leon** (4,970); **Santa Fe** (12,222); **Tiki Island** (968).

Population	**291,309**
Change fm 2000	16.45
Area (sq. mi.)	872.93
Land Area (sq. mi.)	398.47
Altitude (ft.)	sea level-40
Rainfall (in.)	43.84
Jan. mean min.	49.7
July mean max.	88.7
Civ. Labor	144,173
Unemployed	9.6
Wages	$1,112,627,993
Av. Weekly Wage	$902
Prop. Value	$23,882,539,108
Retail Sales	$2,783,497,774

For explanation of sources, abbreviations and symbols, see p. 232 and foldout map.

Garza County

Physical Features: On edge of Caprock; rough, broken land, with playas, gullies, canyons, Brazos River forks, Lake Alan Henry; sandy, loam, clay soils.

Economy: Agriculture, oil and natural gas, prison, retail trade, government/services, hunting leases.

History: Kiowas and Comanches yielded to U.S. Army in 1875. Ranching began in the 1870s, farming in the 1890s. C.W. Post, the cereal millionaire, established enterprises in 1906. County created from Bexar District, 1876; organized in 1907; named for early Texas family.

Race/Ethnicity, 2008: (In percent) Anglo, 53.2; Black, 5.1; Hispanic, 41.1; Other, 0.5.

Vital Statistics, 2008: Births, 81; deaths, 55; marriages, 39; divorces, 20.

Recreation: Scenic areas, lake activities, Post-Garza Museum, trade days monthly.

Minerals: Oil, gas, sand, gravel.

Agriculture: Cotton, beef cattle, hay; 12,800 acres irrigated. Market value $27.4 million. Hunting leases.

POST (5,376) county seat; founded by C.W. Post; agriculture, tourism, government/services, prisons; Garza Theatre, gospel theater.

Population	6,461
Change fm 2000	32.61
Area (sq. mi.)	896.19
Land Area (sq. mi.)	895.56
Altitude (ft.)	2,140-3,030
Rainfall (in.)	21.29
Jan. mean min.	27.8
July mean max.	94.0
Civ. Labor	2,492
Unemployed	5.7
Wages	$16,520,613
Av. Weekly Wage	$702
Prop. Value	$971,702,540
Retail Sales	$38,199,204

For explanation of sources, abbreviations and symbols, see p. 232 and foldout map.

Gillespie County

Physical Features: Picturesque Edwards Plateau area with hills, broken by spring-fed streams.

Economy: Tourism, government/services, agriculture, wine and specialty foods, hunting leases.

History: German settlement founded 1846 in heart of Comanche country. County created, organized, 1848 from Bexar, Travis counties; named for Texas Ranger Capt. R.A. Gillespie. Birthplace of President Lyndon B. Johnson and Fleet Admiral Chester W. Nimitz.

Race/Ethnicity, 2008: (In percent) Anglo, 81.5; Black, 0.1; Hispanic, 17.9; Other, 0.5.

Vital Statistics, 2008: Births, 296; deaths, 322; marriages, 172; divorces, 79.

Recreation: Among leading deer-hunting areas; numerous historic sites and tourist attractions include LBJ Ranch, Nimitz Hotel and Pacific war museum; Pioneer Museum Complex, Enchanted Rock.

Minerals: Sand, gravel, gypsum, limestone rock.

Agriculture: Beef cattle, peaches (first in acreage), grapes, sheep and goats, hay, grain sorghum, oats, wheat. Market value $28.6 million. Hunting leases important.

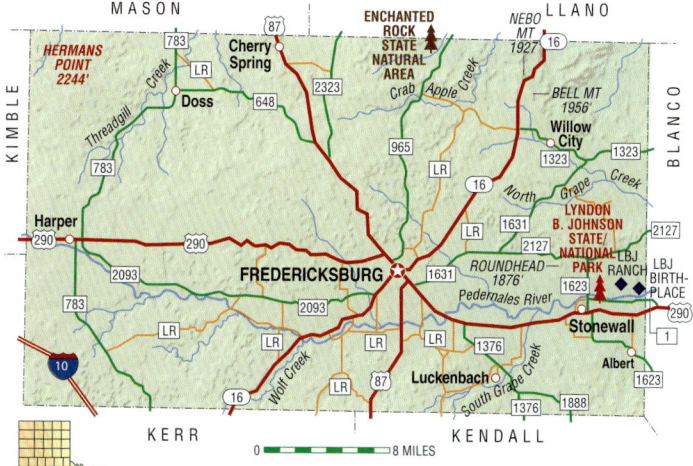

FREDERICKSBURG (10,530) the county seat; agribusiness, tourism, wineries, food processing; museum; tourist attractions; hospital; Oktoberfest.

Other towns include: **Doss** (100); **Harper** (1,192) ranching, deer hunting, Dachshund Hounds Downs race and Trades Day in October; **Luckenbach** (25) saloon, general store and dance hall; **Stonewall** (505) agribusiness, wineries, tourism, hunting, Peach Jamboree in June, and **Willow City** (22) scenic drive.

County adopted by:
Fischer & Wieser
www.jelly.com

Population	24,837
Change fm 2000	19.33
Area (sq. mi.)	1,061.48
Land Area (sq. mi.)	1,061.06
Altitude (ft.)	1,040-2,244
Rainfall (in.)	31.65
Jan. mean min.	36.1
July mean max.	93.1
Civ. Labor	13,502
Unemployed	5.2
Wages	$75,318,779
Av. Weekly Wage	$617
Prop. Value	$6,797,456326
Retail Sales	$380,035,431

Glasscock County

Physical Features: Western county on rolling plains, broken by small streams; sandy, loam soils.

Economy: Farming, ranching, hunting leases, oil and gas, quarries.

History: Hunting area for Kickapoos and Lipan Apaches. Anglo-American sheep ranchers and Mexican-American shepherds or pastores moved into the area in 1880s. County created 1887 from Tom Green County; organized, 1893; named for Texas pioneer George W. Glasscock.

Race/Ethnicity, 2008: (In percent) Anglo, 67.5; Black, 0.6; Hispanic, 31.7; Other, 0.1.

Vital Statistics, 2008: Births, 17; deaths, 2; marriages, 8; divorces, 1.

Recreation: Hunting of deer, quail, turkey, fox, bobcat, coyote; St. Lawrence Fall Festival in October.

Minerals: Oil, gas, stone/rock.

Agriculture: Cotton, watermelons, wheat, sorghum, hay; 60,000 acres irrigated. Cattle, goats, sheep, hogs raised. Market value $46.3 million.

GARDEN CITY (334), county seat; serves sparsely settled ranching, oil area.

Also, **St. Lawrence** (90), farming.

Population	1,226
Change fm 2000	−12.8

Area (sq. mi.)	900.93
Land Area (sq. mi.)	900.75
Altitude (ft.)	2,470-2,785
Rainfall (in.)	17.32
Jan. mean min.	26.7
July mean max.	94.0

Civ. Labor	603
Unemployed	5.5
Wages	$3,636,317
Av. Weekly Wage	$645
Prop. Value	$1,233,117,050
Retail Sales	$4,963,517

Physical Features: Coastal Plain county; rolling, brushy; bisected by San Antonio River; sandy, loam, alluvial soils.

Economy: Government/services, oil/gas, agriculture, electricity-generating plant, tourism.

History: Karankawas, Comanches and other tribes in area in historic period. La Bahía presidio/mission established 1749. County created 1836 from Spanish municipality; organized 1837; name is anagram of (H)idalgo. Birthplace of Gen. Ignacio Zaragoza, hero of Battle of Puebla (Mexico).

Race/Ethnicity, 2008: (In percent) Anglo, 58.2; Black, 4.5; Hispanic, 37.0; Other, 0.3.

Vital Statistics, 2008: Births, 81; deaths, 78; marriages, 39; divorces, 7.

Recreation: Missions, restored Presidio La Bahía, Fannin Battleground; Old Market House museum; lake, fishing, hunting (deer, quail, dove, hogs), camping, canoeing, birding.

Minerals: Production of oil, gas.

Agriculture: Beef cattle, stocker operations and fed cattle are top revenue producers; corn, grain sorghum, cotton, hay; minor irrigation for pasture. Market value $20 million. Hunting leases.

GOLIAD (1,908) county seat; one of state's oldest towns; oil, gas center; agriculture; tourism; library; Zaragoza Birthplace State Historic Site, statue; Goliad Massacre re-enactment in March, Diez y Seis in September.

Other towns include: **Berclair** (253), **Fannin** (359) and **Weesatche** (411).

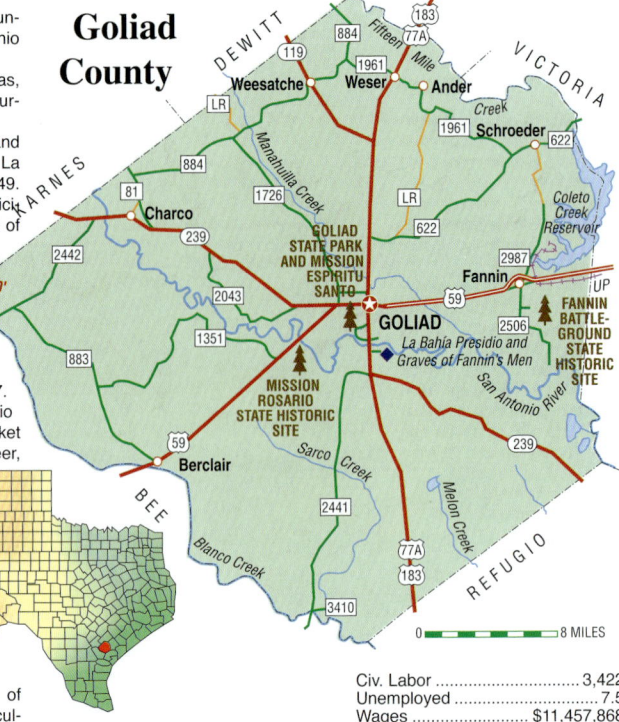

Goliad County

Population	7,210
Change fm 2000	4.07
Area (sq. mi.)	859.35
Land Area (sq. mi.)	853.52
Altitude (ft.)	50-420
Rainfall (in.)	38.58
Jan. mean min.	43.3
July mean max.	95.5

Civ. Labor	3,422
Unemployed	7.5
Wages	$11,457,868
Av. Weekly Wage	$604
Prop. Value	$1,907,894,530
Retail Sales	$29,592,498

For explanation of sources, abbreviations and symbols, see p. 232, and foldout map.

Panhandle landscape along U.S. 60 northeast of Pampa, Gray County. Photo by Robert Plocheck

Gonzales County

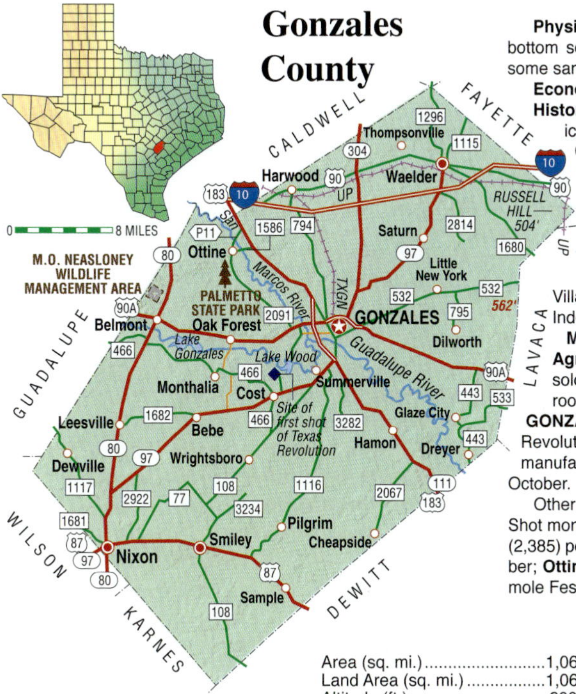

Physical Features: South central county; rolling, rich bottom soils along Guadalupe River and its tributaries; some sandy areas; many oaks, pecans.

Economy: Agribusiness, hunting leases.

History: Coahuiltecan area. Among first Anglo-American settlements; the DeWitt colony late 1820s. County created 1836; organized 1837; named for Coahuila y Texas Gov. Rafael Gonzales.

Race/Ethnicity, 2008: (In percent) Anglo, 46.6; Black, 8.5; Hispanic, 44.4; Other, 0.6.

Vital Statistics, 2008: Births, 330; deaths, 186; marriages, 112; divorces, 61.

Recreation: Historic sites, homes, Pioneer Village Living History Center, state park, museums, Independence Day.

Minerals: Gas, oil, clay, gravel.

Agriculture: Major poultry county (leader in turkeys sold); cattle; hay, corn, sorghum, pecans, mushrooms. Market value $404 million.

GONZALES (7,237) county seat; first shot in Texas Revolution fired here; shipping, processing center, manufacturing; hospital; "Come and Take It" festival in October.

Other towns include: **Belmont** (55); **Cost** (84) First Shot monument; **Harwood** (118); **Leesville** (152); **Nixon** (2,385) poultry-processing plant, Feather Fest in September; **Ottine** (80); **Smiley** (549); **Waelder** (1,065) Guacamole Fest in September; **Wrightsboro** (10).

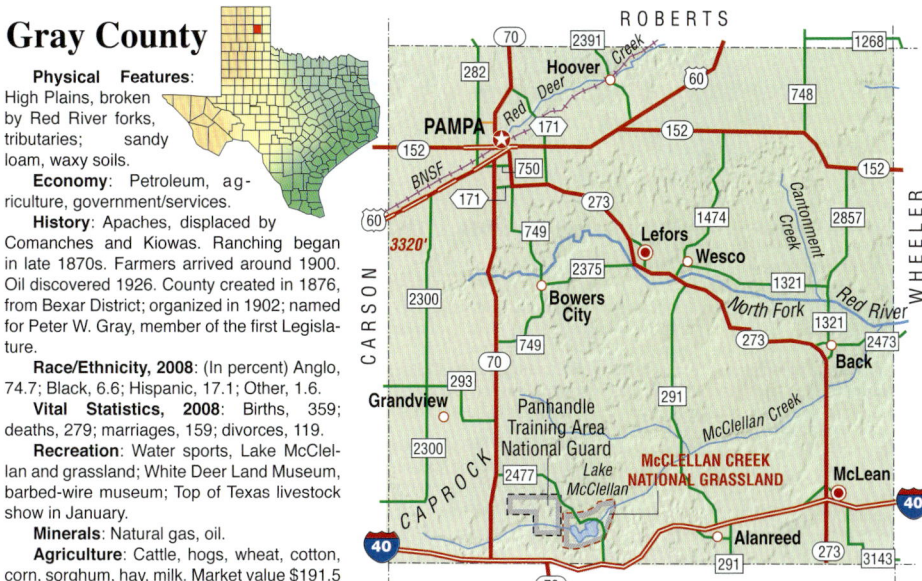

Population	19,807
Change fm 2000	6.33
Area (sq. mi.)	1,069.82
Land Area (sq. mi.)	1,067.75
Altitude (ft.)	200-562
Rainfall (in.)	36.02
Jan. mean min.	38.7
July mean max.	93.9
Civ. Labor	9,892
Unemployed	6.6
Wages	$57,242,593
Av. Weekly Wage	$685
Prop. Value	$3,079,943,810
Retail Sales	$354,378,780

Gray County

Physical Features: High Plains, broken by Red River forks, tributaries; sandy loam, waxy soils.

Economy: Petroleum, agriculture, government/services.

History: Apaches, displaced by Comanches and Kiowas. Ranching began in late 1870s. Farmers arrived around 1900. Oil discovered 1926. County created in 1876, from Bexar District; organized in 1902; named for Peter W. Gray, member of the first Legislature.

Race/Ethnicity, 2008: (In percent) Anglo, 74.7; Black, 6.6; Hispanic, 17.1; Other, 1.6.

Vital Statistics, 2008: Births, 359; deaths, 279; marriages, 159; divorces, 119.

Recreation: Water sports, Lake McClellan and grassland; White Deer Land Museum, barbed-wire museum; Top of Texas livestock show in January.

Minerals: Natural gas, oil.

Agriculture: Cattle, hogs, wheat, cotton, corn, sorghum, hay, milk. Market value $191.5 million.

PAMPA (17,994) county seat; petroleum, agriculture; hospital; college; prison; Woody Guthrie museum; Mud Bog car show in June.

Other towns include: **Alanreed** (48); **Lefors** (497); **McLean** (778) commercial center for southern part of county.

Population	22,535
Change fm 2000	–0.92
Area (sq. mi.)	929.25
Land Area (sq. mi.)	928.28
Altitude (ft.)	2,450-3,320
Rainfall (in.)	22.74
Jan. mean min.	21.9
July mean max.	92.0
Civ. Labor	10,726
Unemployed	7.9
Wages	$97,391,491
Av. Weekly Wage	$893
Prop. Value	$1,818,609,515
Retail Sales	$234,003,639

For explanation of sources, abbreviations and symbols, see p. 232, and foldout map.

Grayson County

Physical Features: North Texas county; level, some low hills; sandy loam, blackland soils; drains to Red River and tributaries of Trinity River.

Economy: A manufacturing, distribution and trade center for northern Texas and southern Oklahoma; nature tourism, mineral production.

History: Caddo and Tonkawa area. Preston Bend trading post established 1836-37. Peters colony settlers arrived in 1840s. County created 1846 from Fannin County; named for Republic Atty. Gen. Peter W. Grayson.

Race/Ethnicity, 2008: (In percent) Anglo, 80.8; Black, 6.2; Hispanic, 10.2; Other, 2.8.

Vital Statistics, 2008: Births, 1,590; deaths, 1,267; marriages, 922; divorces, 574.

Recreation: Lakes, fishing, hunting, water sports, state park, cultural activities, wildlife refuge, Pioneer Village, railroad museum.

For explanation of sources, abbreviations and symbols, see p. 232 and foldout map.

Minerals: Oil, gas, gravel, sand.

Agriculture: Wheat, corn, hay, beef cattle, horses (third in number). Market value $52.8 million.

Education: Austin College in Sherman and Grayson County College located between Sherman and Denison.

SHERMAN (38,521) county seat; varied manufacturing, processors and distributors for major companies; Austin College; hospital.

DENISON (22,682) manufacturing, food processing, medical services, tourism; hospital; Eisenhower birthplace; Arts & Wine Renaissance in April, Main Street Fall festival in October.

Other towns include: **Bells** (1,392); **Collinsville** (1,624); **Dorchester** (148); **Gordonville** (165); **Gunter** (1,498); **Howe** (2,600) distribution, varied manufacturing, museum, Founders' Day in May; **Knollwood** (226); **Potts-**

boro (2,160) lake activities, marinas, Frontier Days in September; **Sadler** (343).

Also, **Southmayd** (992); **Tioga** (803) Gene Autry museum, festival in September; **Tom Bean** (1,045); **Van Alstyne** (3,046) window screen, electronics, saddle, tack manufacturing; **Whitesboro** (3,793) agribusiness, tourism, manufacturing, library, Peanut Festival in October; **Whitewright** (1,604) agribusiness, tourism, manufacturing, museum, Wine & Rose tour in May.

Population	120,877
Change fm 2000	9.3
Area (sq. mi.)	979.19
Land Area (sq. mi.)	933.51
Altitude (ft.)	500-930
Rainfall (in.)	42.04
Jan. mean min.	32.2
July mean max.	92.7
Civ. Labor	57,170
Unemployed	8.8
Wages	$424,560,916
Av. Weekly Wage	$776
Prop. Value	$9,270,112,691
Retail Sales	$1,440,386,358

Gregg County

Physical Features: A populous, leading petroleum county, heart of the famed East Texas oil field; bisected by the Sabine River; hilly, timbered; with sandy, clay, alluvial soils.

Economy: Oil but with significant other manufacturing; tourism, conventions, agri-business and lignite coal production.

History: Caddoes; later Cherokees, who were driven out in 1838 by President Lamar. First land grants issued in 1835 by Republic of Mexico. County created and organized in 1873 from Rusk, Upshur counties; named for Confederate Gen. John Gregg. In U.S. censuses 1880-1910, blacks were more numerous than whites. Oil discovered in 1931.

Race/Ethnicity, 2008: (In percent) Anglo, 62.2; Black, 20.6; Hispanic, 15.5; Other, 1.7.

Vital Statistics, 2008: Births, 2,002; deaths, 1,224; marriages, 1,416; divorces, 442.

Recreation: Water activities on lakes, hunting, varied cultural events, East Texas Oil Museum in Kilgore.

Minerals: Leading oil-producing county with more than 3 billion barrels produced since 1931; also, sand, gravel and natural gas.

Agriculture: Cattle, horses, hay, nursery crops. Market value $3.8 million. Timber sales.

LONGVIEW (80,455, small part in Harrison County) county seat; chemical manufacturing, oil industry, distribution and retail center; hospitals; LeTourneau University, UT-Tyler Longview center; convention center; balloon race in July.

Kilgore (12,975, part in Rusk County), oil, distribution center; Kilgore

College, Rangerette museum; Shakespeare festival in summer.

Gladewater (6,441, part in Upshur County) oil, manufacturing, tourism, antiques, agriculture; library, airport, skydiving; Gusher Days in April; daffodils in February-March.

Other towns include: **Clarksville City** (865); **Easton** (510, partly in Rusk County); **Judson** (1,057); **Lakeport** (974); **Liberty City** (2,351) oil, tourism, government/services, Honor America Night in November; **Warren City** (298); **White Oak** (6,489) oil and gas, industrial park, commuting to Longview, Tyler; Roughneck Days in spring.

Population	121,730
Change fm 2000	9.29
Area (sq. mi.)	276.37
Land Area (sq. mi.)	274.03
Altitude (ft.)	240-530
Rainfall (in.)	49.06
Jan. mean min.	33.7
July mean max.	94.5
Civ. Labor	66,857
Unemployed	7.0
Wages	$852,855,214
Av. Weekly Wage	$874
Prop. Value	$9,633,366,742
Retail Sales	$2,640,407,785

For explanation of sources, abbreviations and symbols, see p. 232 and foldout map.

A freight train moves along the Union Pacific line in northern Grayson County. Photo by Robert Plocheck.

Grimes County

Physical Features: Rich bottom soils along Brazos, Navasota rivers; remainder hilly, partly forested.

Economy: Varied manufacturing, agribusiness, tourism.

History: Bidais (customs similar to the Caddoes) lived peacefully with Anglo-American settlers who arrived in 1820s, but tribe was removed to Indian Territory. Planter agriculture reflected in 1860 census, which listed 77 persons owning 20 or more slaves. County created from Montgomery County in 1846, organized the same year; named for Jesse Grimes, who signed Texas Declaration of Independence.

Race/Ethnicity, 2008: (In percent) Anglo, 63.0; Black, 17.9; Hispanic,18.5; Other, 0.6.

Vital Statistics, 2008: Births, 330; deaths, 248; marriages, 130; divorces, 49.

Recreation: Hunting, fishing; Gibbons Creek Reservoir; historic sites; fall

Renaissance Festival at Plantersville.

Minerals: Lignite coal, natural gas.

Agriculture: Cattle, forage, horses, poultry; berries, pecans, honey sales significant. Market value $49.9 million. Some timber sold, Christmas tree farms.

ANDERSON (222) county seat; rural center; Fanthorp Inn historic site; Go-Texan weekend in February.

NAVASOTA (7,049) agribusiness center for parts of three counties; varied manufacturing; food, wood processing; hospital; prisons; La Salle statue; Blues Fest in August.

Other towns include: **Bedias** (443); **Iola** (401); **Plantersville** (260); **Richards** (300); **Roans Prairie** (64); **Shiro** (210); **Todd Mission** (107).

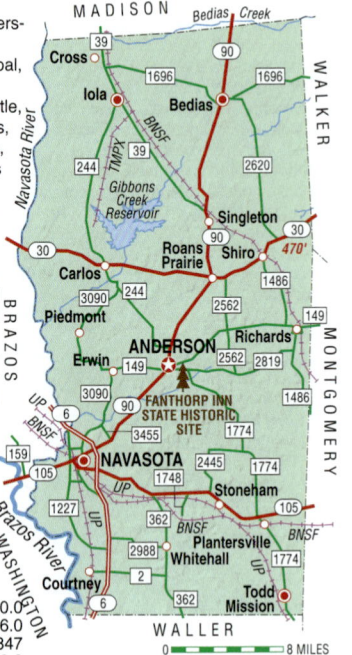

Population	26,604
Change fm 2000	12.96
Area (sq. mi.)	801.16
Land Area (sq. mi.)	793.60
Altitude (ft.)	150-470
Rainfall (in.)	44.70
Jan. mean min.	40.0
July mean max.	96.0
Civ. Labor	11,847
Unemployed	8.8
Wages	$82,222,999
Av. Weekly Wage	$847
Prop. Value	$3,628,334,427
Retail Sales	$167,898,961

Guadalupe County

Physical Features: South central county bisected by Guadalupe River; level to rolling surface; sandy, loam, blackland soils.

Economy: Varied manufacturing, commuting to San Antonio, agribusiness, tourism.

History: Karankawas, Comanches, other tribes until 1850s. Spanish land grant in 1806 to José de la Baume. DeWitt colonists arrived in 1827. County created, organized, 1846 from Bexar, Gonzales counties; named for river.

Race/Ethnicity, 2008: (In percent) Anglo, 55.8; Black, 5.2; Hispanic, 37.1; Other, 1.9.

Vital Statistics, 2008: Births, 1,654; deaths, 833; marriages, 530; divorces, 432.

Recreation: Fishing, hunting, river floating; Sebastopol site, other historic sites; river drive; Fiestas Juan Seguin in June, Diez y Seis in September in Seguin.

Minerals: Oil, gas, gravel, clays.

Agriculture: Nursery crops, cattle, hay, row crops. Market value $41.2 million.

SEGUIN (25,175) county seat; steel production, varied manufacturing, government/services; hospital, museums; Texas Lutheran University; Pecan Fest in early fall.

Other towns include: **Cibolo** (15,349), **Geronimo** (1,032), **Kingsbury** (782), **Marion** (1,066), **Mc-**

Queeney (2,545), **New Berlin** (511), **Redwood** (4,338), **Santa Clara** (725); **Schertz** (31,465, parts in Bexar and Comal counties), **Staples** (267).

Also, part of **New Braunfels**, part of **Selma**, and a small part of **San Marcos.**

For explanation of sources, abbreviations and symbols, see p. 232 and foldout map.

Population	131,533
Change fm 2000	47.75
Area (sq. mi.)	714.17
Land Area (sq. mi.)	711.14
Altitude (ft.)	350-952
Rainfall (in.)	34.50
Jan. mean min.	35.5
July mean max.	94.7
Civ. Labor	60,855
Unemployed	7.4
Wages	$279,161,536
Av. Weekly Wage	$730
Prop. Value	$10,619,038,403
Retail Sales	$978,925,120

Hale County

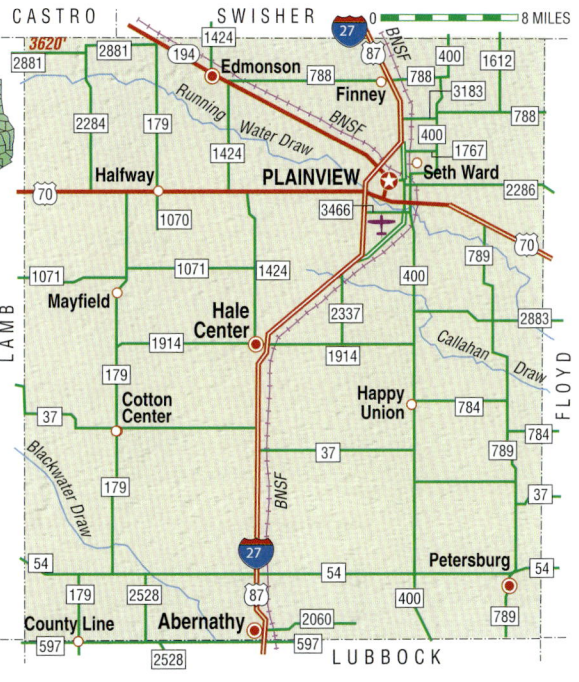

Physical Features: High Plains; fertile sandy, loam soils; playas; large underground water supply.

Economy: Agribusiness, food processing/distribution, manufacturing, government/services.

History: Comanche hunters driven out by U.S. Army in 1875. Ranching began in 1880s. First motor-driven irrigation well drilled in 1911. County created from Bexar District, 1876; organized 1888; named for Lt. J.C. Hale, who died at San Jacinto.

Race/Ethnicity, 2008: (In percent), Anglo, 40.6; Black, 6.0; Hispanic, 52.6; Other, 0.8.

Vital Statistics, 2008: Births, 637; deaths, 281; marriages, 205; divorces, 89.

Recreation: Llano Estacado Museum; art gallery, antiques stores; pheasant hunting; Plainview Cattle Drive in September.

Minerals: Some oil.

Agriculture: Cotton, fed beef, sorghum, dairies, corn, vegetables, wheat. Market value $364.4 million. Irrigation of 448,000 acres.

PLAINVIEW (22,194) county seat; distribution center, food processing; Wayland Baptist University; hospital, library, mental health center; state prisons.

Hale Center (2,252) trade center; farm museum, library, parks, murals, cacti gardens.

Abernathy (2,805, part in Lubbock County) government/services, farm supplies, textile plant, gins.

Other towns include: **Cotton Center** (300), **Edmonson** (111), **Petersburg** (1,202), **Seth Ward** (2,025).

Population	36,273
Change fm 2000	−0.9
Area (sq. mi.)	1,004.77
Land Area (sq. mi.)	1,004.65
Altitude (ft.)	3,180-3,620
Rainfall (in.)	19.90
Jan. mean min.	24.4
July mean max.	91.0
Civ. Labor	17,443
Unemployed	7.7
Wages	$120,788,482
Av. Weekly Wage	$630
Prop. Value	$2,265,683,596
Retail Sales	$2,196,004,683

For explanation of sources, abbreviations and symbols, see p. 232 and foldout map.

Downtown Plainview, Hale County. Photo by Robert Plocheck.

Hall County

Physical Features: Rolling to hilly, broken by Red River forks, tributaries; red and black sandy loam.

Economy: Agriculture, farm, ranch supplies, marketing for large rural area.

History: Apaches displaced by Comanches, who were removed to Indian Territory in 1875. Ranching began in 1880s. Farming expanded after 1910. County created 1876 from Bexar, Young districts; organized 1890; named for Republic of Texas secretary of war W.D.C. Hall.

Race/Ethnicity, 2008: (In percent) Anglo, 56.9; Black, 8.8; Hispanic, 33.9; Other, 0.5.

Vital Statistics, 2008: Births, 40; deaths, 40; marriages, 21; divorces, 9.

Recreation: Hunting of deer, wild hog, turkey, quail, dove; Rails to Trails system; Bob Wills museum; Memphis Picnic festival in September.

Minerals: None.

Agriculture: Cotton, cattle, peanuts, wheat, sorghum, alfalfa hay. Market value $43.5 million. Hunting leases.

MEMPHIS (2,290) county seat; agriculture, retail; historic buildings.

Other towns include: **Estelline** (145), motorcyle rally/chili cookoff in August, **Lakeview** (107), **Turkey** (421) Bob Wills Day in April.

Population **3,353**	July mean max. 95.7
Change fm 2000 .... −11.34	Civ. Labor 1,366
Area (sq. mi.) 904.08	Unemployed 9.0
Land Area (sq. mi.) 903.09	Wages $6,892,076
Altitude (ft.) 1,750-2,550	Av. Weekly Wage.............. $544
Rainfall (in.) 22.51	Prop. Value $427,234,740
Jan. mean min. 25.5	Retail Sales $35,532,700

Hamilton County

Physical Features: Hilly north central county broken by scenic valleys; loam soils.

Economy: Agribusiness, varied manufacturing, and government/services.

History: Waco and Tawakoni Indian area. Anglo-American settlers arrived in mid-1850s. County created, organized 1858, from Bosque, Comanche, Lampasas counties; named for South Carolina Gov. James Hamilton, who aided Texas Revolution and Republic.

Race/Ethnicity, 2008: (In percent) Anglo, 90.3; Black, 0.1; Hispanic, 8.9; Other, 0.7.

Vital Statistics, 2008: Births, 108; deaths, 128; marriages, 57; divorces, 42.

Recreation: Deer, quail, duck hunting; Linear Pecan Creek park in Hamilton.

Minerals: Natural gas.

Agriculture: Beef, milk, hay. Market value $51.4 million. Hunting leases important.

HAMILTON (3,095) county seat; varied manufacturing; hospital; Central Texas College branch; historical homes; dove festival on Labor Day.

Hico (1,379) tourism, agriculture, varied manufacturing; antiques shops, Billy the Kid museum; steak cookoff in May.

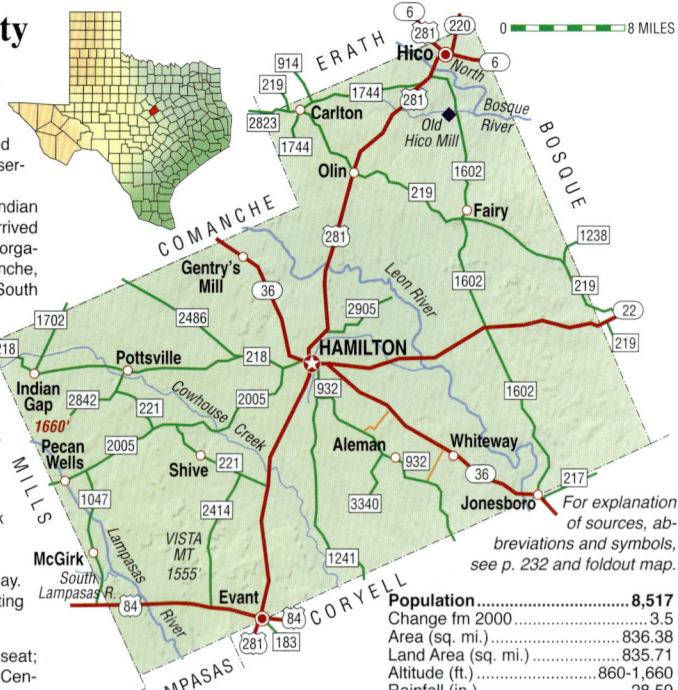

For explanation of sources, abbreviations and symbols, see p. 232 and foldout map.

Other towns include: **Carlton** (75), **Evant** (426, partly in Coryell County), **Jonesboro** (125, partly in Coryell County); **Pottsville** (105).

Population **8,517**	
Change fm 2000 .... 3.5	
Area (sq. mi.) 836.38	
Land Area (sq. mi.) 835.71	
Altitude (ft.) 860-1,660	
Rainfall (in.) 28.59	
Jan. mean min. 33.4	
July mean max. 94.3	
Civ. Labor 4,510	
Unemployed 6.3	
Wages $22,864,663	
Av. Weekly Wage...................... $647	
Prop. Value $1,761,312,203	
Retail Sales $75,129,108	

Hansford County

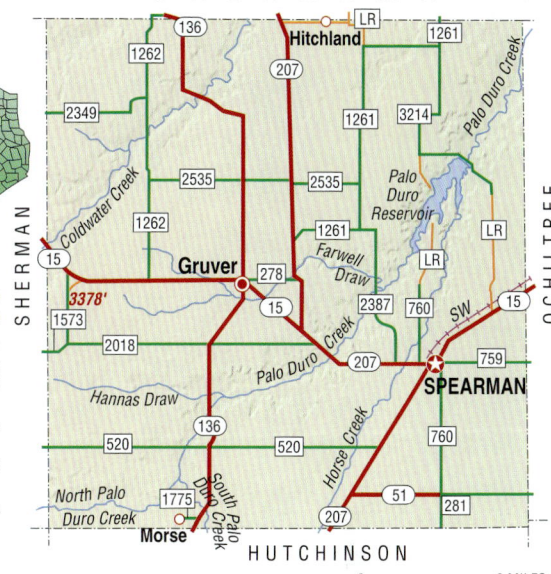

Physical Features: High Plains, many playas, creeks, draws; sandy, loam, black soils; underground water.

Economy: Agribusinesses; oil, natural gas operations; wind energy.

History: Apaches, pushed out by Comanches around 1700. U.S. Army removed Comanches in 1874-75, and ranching began soon afterward. Farmers, including Norwegians, moved in around 1900. County created in 1876, from Bexar, Young districts; organized in 1889; named for jurist J.M. Hansford.

Race/Ethnicity, 2008: (In percent) Anglo, 59.6; Black, 0.2; Hispanic, 39.7; Other, 0.6.

Vital Statistics, 2008: Births, 102; deaths, 63; marriages, 29; divorces, 12.

Recreation: Stationmasters House Museum, hunting, lake activities, ecotourism.

Minerals: Production of gas, oil.

Agriculture: Large cattle-feeding operations; corn, wheat (second in acreage), sorghum; hogs. Substantial irrigation. Market value $589.8 million.

SPEARMAN (3,368) county seat; farming, cattle production, oil and natural gas, wind energy, biofuels; hospital, library, windmill collection; Heritage Days in May/June.

Other towns include: **Gruver** (1,194) farm and ranch market, natural gas production, Fourth of July barbecue; and **Morse** (147).

Population	**5,613**
Change fm 2000	4.55
Area (sq. mi.)	920.40
Land Area (sq. mi.)	919.80
Altitude (ft.)	2,750-3,378
Rainfall (in.)	20.30
Jan. mean min.	22.4
July mean max.	95.5

Civ. Labor	2,731
Unemployed	4.8
Wages	$21,368,718
Av. Weekly Wage	$811
Prop. Value	$1,188,464,479
Retail Sales	$32,126,386

For explanation of sources, abbreviations and symbols, see p. 232 and foldout map.

A truck moves over the High Plains of the Panhandle near Gruver, Hansford County. Photo by Robert Plocheck.

Big sky at Medicine Mound, Hardeman County. Photo by Robert Plocheck.

Hardeman County

Physical Features: Rolling, broken area on divide between Pease, Red rivers; sandy, loam soils.

Economy: Agriculture, gypsum production, oil and natural gas.

History: Apaches, later the semi-sedentary Wichitas and Comanche hunters. Ranching began in late the 1870s. Farming expanded after 1900. County created in 1858 from Fannin County; recreated in 1876, organized in 1884; named for pioneer brothers Bailey and T.J. Hardeman.

Race/Ethnicity, 2008: (In percent) Anglo, 76.5; Black, 4.9; Hispanic, 17.8; Other, 0.9.

Vital Statistics, 2008: Births, 60; deaths, 23; marriages, 31; divorces, 23.

Recreation: state park; lake activities; Medicine Mound aborigine gathering site; Quanah Parker monument; hunting of deer, quail, wild hogs.

Minerals: Oil, natural gas, gypsum.

Agriculture: Wheat, cattle, cotton. Market value $24 million. Hunting leases.

QUANAH (2,641) county seat; agribusiness, manufacturing, ranching; hospital; historical sites; Fall Festival in September.

Other towns include: **Chillicothe** (707) farm market center, hospital.

For explanation of sources, abbreviations and symbols, see p. 232 and foldout map.

Area (sq. mi.)	697.00
Land Area (sq. mi.)	695.38
Altitude (ft.)	1,250-1,850
Rainfall (in.)	26.76
Jan. mean min.	24.6
July mean max.	96.5

Population **4,139**
Change fm 2000 ....–12.38

Civ. Labor	2,182
Unemployed	7.0
Wages	$9,664,652
Av. Weekly Wage	$618
Prop. Value	$602,805,700
Retail Sales	$24,849,716

Hardin County

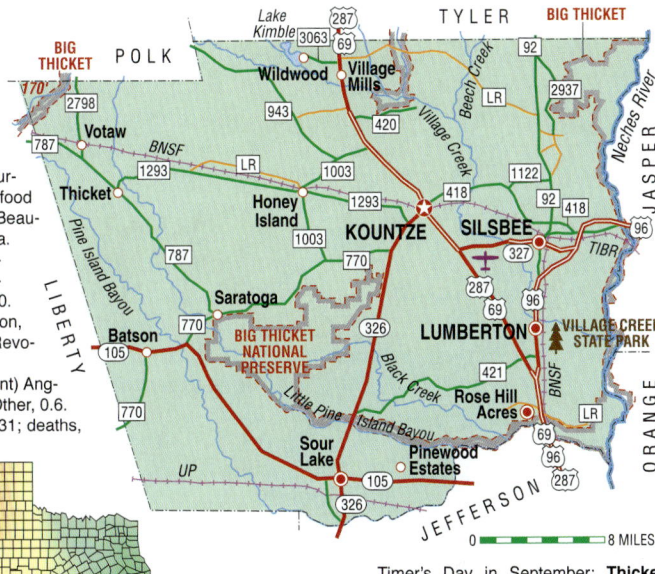

Physical Features: Southeast county; timbered; many streams; sandy, loam soils; Big Thicket covers much of area.

Economy: Paper manufacturing, wood processing, minerals, food processing, oil and gas; county in Beaumont-Port Arthur-Orange metro area.

History: Lorenzo de Zavala received first land grant in 1829. Anglo-American settlers arrived in 1830. County created 1858 from Jefferson, Liberty counties. Named for Texas Revolutionary leader William Hardin.

Race/Ethnicity, 2008: (In percent) Anglo, 88.6; Black, 7.5; Hispanic, 3.3; Other, 0.6.

Vital Statistics, 2008: Births, 731; deaths, 514; marriages, 404; divorces, 262.

Recreation: Big Thicket with rare plant, animal life; national preserve; Red Cloud Water Park in Silsbee; hunting, fishing; state park; Cajun Country Music Festival in October in Kountze.

Minerals: Oil, gas, sand, gravel.

Agriculture: Beef cattle, hay, blueberries (first in acreage), bees (first in number of colonies) and rice; market value $6.3 million. Timber provides most income; more than 85 percent of county forested. Hunting leases.

KOUNTZE (2,123) county seat; government/services, retail center, commuting to Beaumont; library, museum.

SILSBEE (6,611) forest products, rail center, oil, gas; library, Ice House museum; Dulcimer Festival in fall.

LUMBERTON (11,943) construction, government/services, tourism, retail; library, Lamar University extension; Village Creek Festival in April.

Other towns and places include: **Batson** (140); **Pinewood Estates** (1,678); **Rose Hill Acres** (441); **Saratoga** (1,000) Big Thicket Museum; **Sour Lake** (1,813) oil, lumbering; Old

For explanation of sources, abbreviations and symbols, see p. 232 and foldout map.

Timer's Day in September; **Thicket** (306); **Village Mills** (1,700); **Votaw** (160); and **Wildwood** (1,235).

Population	54,635
Change fm 2000	13.65
Area (sq. mi.)	897.37
Land Area (sq. mi.)	894.33
Altitude (ft.)	7-170
Rainfall (in.)	56.50
Jan. mean min.	37.0
July mean max.	93.0
Civ. Labor	27,678
Unemployed	9.5
Wages	$115,852,784
Av. Weekly Wage	$713
Prop. Value	$3,274,399.930
Retail Sales	$547,490,825

The city skyline beyond the Houston Police Officers Memorial. Photo by Robert Plocheck.

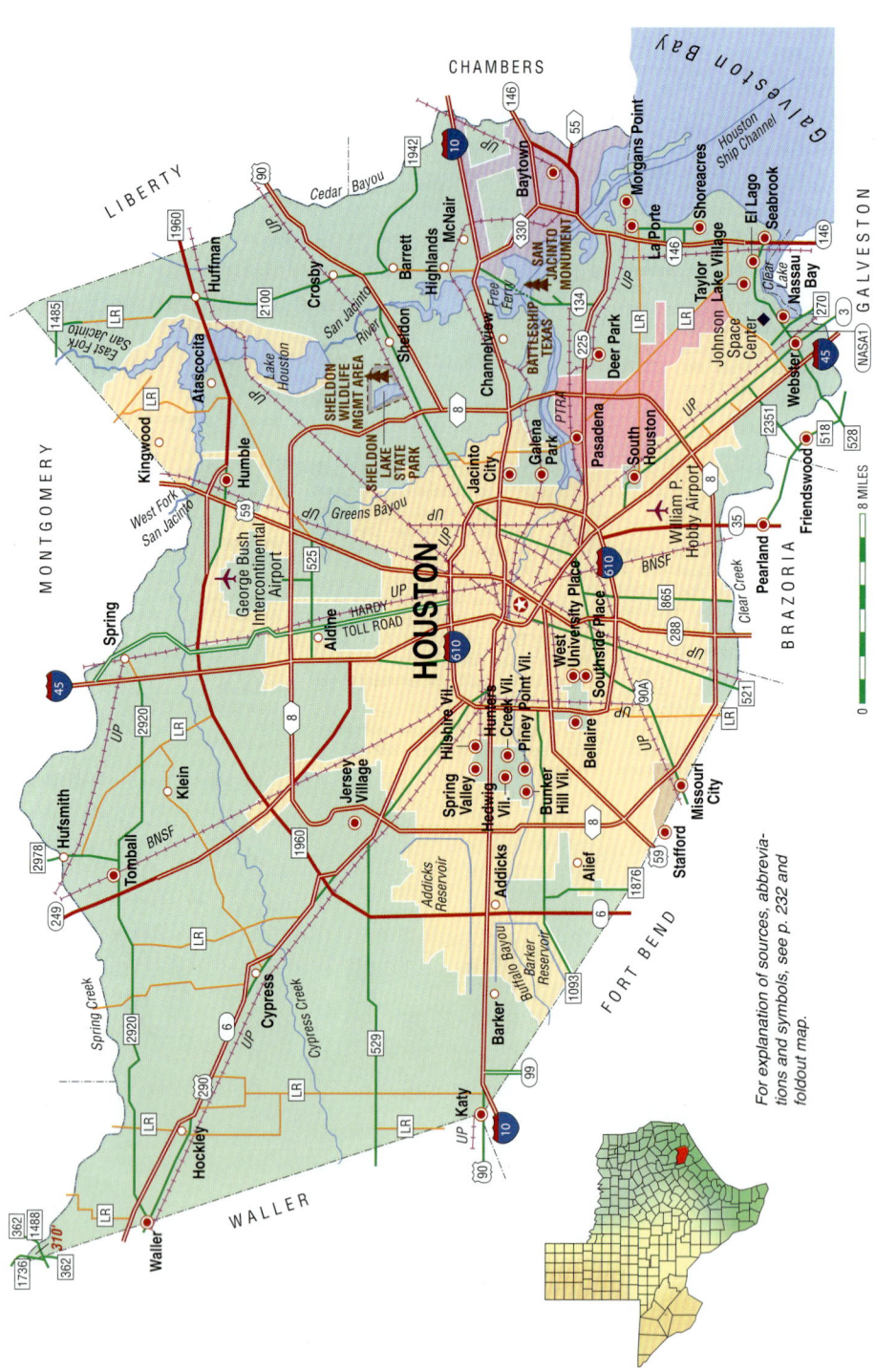

For explanation of sources, abbreviations and symbols, see p. 232 and foldout map.

Physical Features: Largest county in eastern half of state; level; typically coastal surface and soils; many bayous, lakes, canals for artificial drainage; partly forested.

Economy: Highly industrialized county with largest population; more than 92 foreign governments maintain offices in Houston; corporate management center; nation's largest concentration of petrochemical plants; largest U.S. wheat-exporting port, among top U.S. ports in the value of foreign trade and total tonnage.

Petroleum refining, chemicals, food, fabricated metal products, non-electrical machinery, primary metals, scientific instruments; paper and allied products, printing and publishing; center for energy, space and medical research; center of international business.

History: Orcoquiza villages visited by Spanish authorities in 1746. Pioneer settlers arrived by boat from Louisiana in 1822. Antebellum planters brought black slaves. Mexican migration increased after Mexican Revolution. County created 1836, organized 1837; named for John R. Harris, founder of Harrisburg (now part of Houston) in 1824.

Race/Ethnicity, 2008: (In percent) Anglo, 32.4; Black, 18.4; Hispanic, 42.0; Other, 7.2.

Vital Statistics, 2008: Births, 71,353; deaths, 21,922; marriages, 29,577; divorces, 13,943.

Recreation: Professional baseball, basketball, football, soccer; rodeo and livestock show; Jones Hall for the Performing Arts; Nina Vance Alley Theatre; Convention Center; Toyota Center, a 19,000-seat sports and entertainment center; Reliant Stadium and downtown ballpark.

Sam Houston Park, with restored early Houston homes, church, stores; Museum of Fine Arts, Contemporary Arts Museum, Rice Museum; Wortham Theater; Hobby Center for Performing Arts; museum of natural science, planetarium, zoo in Hermann Park.

San Jacinto Battleground, Battleship Texas; Johnson Space Center.

Fishing, boating, other freshwater and saltwater activities.

Minerals: Among leading oil, gas, petrochemical areas; production of petroleum, cement, natural gas, salt, lime, sulfur, sand and gravel, clays, stone.

Agriculture: Nursery crops, grass (third in acreage of sod), cattle, hay, horses, vegetables, Christmas trees, goats, rice, corn. Market value $62.5 million. Substantial income from forest products.

Harris County

Education: Houston is a major center of higher education, with more than 300,000 students enrolled in 28 colleges and universities in the county. Among these are Rice University, the University of Houston, Texas Southern University, University of St. Thomas, Houston Baptist University.

Medical schools include Houston Baptist University School of Nursing, University of Texas Health Science Center, Baylor College of Medicine, Institute of Religion and Human Development, Texas Chiropractic College, Texas Woman's University-Houston Center.

Refineries line the Houston Ship Channel. Photo by Robert Plocheck.

HOUSTON (2,099,451) county seat; largest Texas city; fourth-largest in nation.

A leading center for manufacture of petroleum equipment, agricultural chemicals, fertilizers, pesticides, oil and gas pipeline transmission; a leading scientific center; manufacture of machinery, fabricated metals; a major distribution, shipping center; engineering and research center; food processing; 85 hospitals.

Plants make apparel, lumber and wood products; furniture, paper, chemical, petroleum and coal products; publishing center; one of the nation's largest public school systems; prominent corporate center; Go Texan Days (rodeo) in February/March, international festival in March/April.

Pasadena (149,043) residential city with large industrial area manufacturing petrochemicals and other petroleum-related products; civic center; San Jacinto College, Texas Chiropractic College; hospitals; historical museum; Strawberry Festival in May.

Baytown (71,802) refining, petrochemical center; commuters to Houston; Lee College; hospital, museum, library; historical homes; Chili When It's Chilly cookoff in January.

The **Clear Lake Area** — which includes **El Lago** (2,706); **Nassau Bay** (4,002); **Seabrook** (11,952); **Taylor Lake Village** (3,544); **Webster** (10,400) — tourism, Johnson Space Center, University of Houston-Clear Lake, commuting to Houston; Bayport Industrial Complex includes Port of Bayport; 12 major marinas; hospitals; Christmas lighted boat parade.

Other towns include: **Aldine** (15,869); **Atascocita** (65,844); **Barrett** (3,199); **Bellaire** (16,855) residential city with several major office buildings; **Bunker Hill Village** (3,633); **Channelview** (38,289) hospital; **Crosby** (2,299) government/services, chemical plant, Czech Fest in October; **Deer Park** (32,010) ship-channel industries, Totally Texas celebration in April; **Galena Park** (10,887); **Hedwig Village** (2,557); **Highlands** (7,522), commuters, heritage museum, Jamboree in October; **Hilshire Village** (746); **Hockley** (400); **Huffman** (15,000); **Humble** (15,133) oil-field equipment manufactured, retail center, hospital; **Hunters Creek Village** (4,367); **Jacinto City** (10,553); **Jersey Village** (7,620).

Also, **Katy** (14,102, partly in Fort Bend, Waller counties) corporate headquarters, distribution center, hospitals, museums, park; Rice Harvest festival in October; **Klein** (45,000); **La Porte** (33,800) petrochemical industry; depot museum; Sylvan Beach Festival in April; Galveston Bay; **Morgan's Point** (339); **Piney Point Village** (3,125); **Sheldon** (1,990); **Shoreacres** (1,493); **South Houston** (16,983).

Also, **Southside Place** (1,715); **Spring** (54,298); **Spring Valley** (3,715); **Tomball** (10,753) computers, oil equipment, retail center, antiques, hospital, sports medical center, museum, junior college, parks, Germanfest in March; **West University Place** (14,787).

Parts of **Friendswood**, **Missouri City**, **Pearland**, **Stafford** and **Waller**.

Addicks, **Alief** and **Kingwood** are now within the city limits of Houston.

Population	**4,092,459**
Change fm 2000	20.35
Area (sq. mi.)	1,777.69
Land Area (sq. mi.)	1,728.83
Altitude (ft.)	sea level-310
Rainfall (in.)	53.96
Jan. mean min.	45.2
July mean max.	93.6
Civ. Labor	2,017,690
Unemployed	8.8
Wages	$32,270,669,921
Av. Weekly Wage	$1,231
Prop. Value	$340,679,006,490
Retail Sales	$67,825,950,837

Harrison County

Physical Features: East Texas county; hilly, rolling; over half forested; Sabine River; Caddo Lake.

Economy: Oil, gas processing, lumbering, pottery, other varied manufacturing.

History: Agriculturist Caddo Indians whose numbers were reduced by disease. Anglo-Americans arrived in the 1830s. In 1850, the county had more slaves than any other in the state. County created in 1839 from Shelby County; organized in 1842. Named for eloquent advocate of Texas Revolution, Jonas Harrison.

Race/Ethnicity, 2008: (In percent) Anglo, 66.9; Black, 23.2; Hispanic, 9.1; Other, 0.8.

Vital Statistics, 2008: Births, 886; deaths, 559; marriages, 485; divorces, 120.

Recreation: Fishing, other water activities on Caddo and other lakes; hunting; plantation homes, historic sites; Stagecoach Days in May; Old Courthouse Museum; Old World Store; state park, performing arts; Fire Ant festival in October.

Minerals: Oil, gas, lignite coal, clays, sand and gravel.

Agriculture: Cattle, hay. Also, poultry, nursery plants, horses, vegetables, watermelons. Market value $14.1 million. Hunting leases important. Substantial timber industry.

MARSHALL (23,523) county seat; petroleum and lumber processing, varied manufacturing; civic center; historic sites, including Starr Family State Historic Site; hospital; Wiley College, East Texas Baptist University; Wonderland of Lights in December.

Other towns include: **Elysian Fields** (500); **Hallsville** (3,577) Western Days in October, museum; **Harleton** (390); **Jonesville** (70); **Karnack** (350); **Nesbitt** (281); **Scottsville** (376);

For explanation of sources, abbreviations and symbols, see p. 232 and foldout map.

Uncertain (94) tourism, fishing, hunting, Mayhaw Festival in May; **Waskom** (2,160) oil, gas, ranching, Armadillo Daze in April; **Woodlawn** (550). Also, part of **Longview**.

Population	**65,631**
Change fm 2000	5.67
Area (sq. mi.)	915.09
Land Area (sq. mi.)	898.71
Altitude (ft.)	168-600
Rainfall (in.)	51.22
Jan. mean min.	33.4
July mean max.	92.4
Civ. Labor	32,677
Unemployed	8.7
Wages	$254,395,907
Av. Weekly Wage	$869
Prop. Value	$7,571,087,290
Retail Sales	$643,148,166

The Hartley County Courthouse in Channing. Photo by Robert Plocheck.

Hartley County

Physical Features: Panhandle High Plains; drains to Canadian River tributaries, playas; sandy, loam, chocolate soils; lake.

Economy: Agriculture, dairies, gas production.

History: Apaches, pushed out by Comanches around 1700. U.S. Army removed Indians in 1875. Pastores (Hispanic sheepmen) in area until 1880s. Cattle ranching began in 1880s. Farming expanded after 1900. County created 1876 from Bexar, Young districts; organized 1891; named for Texas pioneers O.C. and R.K. Hartley.

Race/Ethnicity, 2008: (In percent) Anglo, 78.2; Black, 7.4; Hispanic, 13.8; Other, 0.6.

Vital Statistics, 2008: Births, 60; deaths, 54; marriages, 1; divorces, 13.

Recreation: Rita Blanca Lake activities; ranch museum; XIT Rodeo and Reunion at Dalhart in August.

Minerals: Sand, gravel, natural gas.

Agriculture: Cattle, corn (second in acreage), wheat, hay, dairy cows, vegetables. 110,000 acres irrigated.

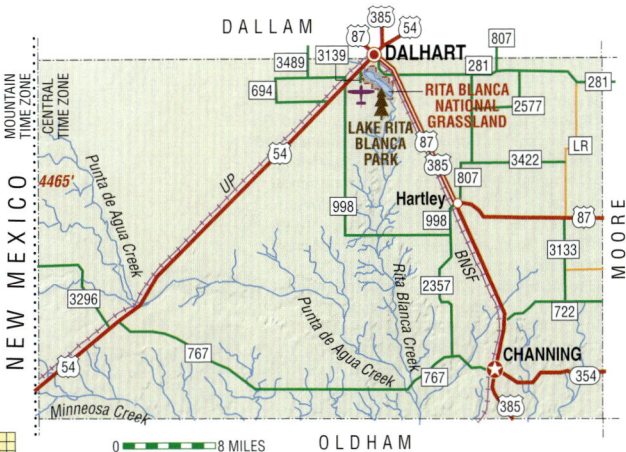

Market value $724.5 million. Hunting leases.

CHANNING (363) county seat, old XIT Ranch general headquarters; Roundup in July.

DALHART (7,930, mostly in Dallam County) cattle production, dairies, cheese plant; hospital.

Also, **Hartley** (540).

Population	6,062
Change fm 2000	9.48
Area (sq. mi.)	1,463.20
Land Area (sq. mi.)	1,462.25
Altitude (ft.)	3,340-4,465
Rainfall (in.)	17.20
Jan. mean min.	20.0
July mean max.	90.9
Civ. Labor	2,459
Unemployed	5.5
Wages	$15,265,392
Av. Weekly Wage	$672
Prop. Value	$1,021,058,542
Retail Sales	$28,638,580

Haskell County

Physical Features: Northwest county; rolling; broken areas; drained by Brazos tributaries; lake; sandy loam, gray, black soils.

Economy: Agribusiness, oil-field operations.

History: Apaches until 1700, then Comanche area. Ranching began in late 1870s after Indians removed. Farming expanded after 1900. County created 1858, from Milam, Fannin counties; re-created 1876; organized 1885; named for Goliad victim C.R. Haskell.

Race/Ethnicity, 2008: (In percent) Anglo, 71.5; Black, 3.0; Hispanic, 24.9; Other, 0.5.

Vital Statistics, 2008: Births, 66; deaths, 95; marriages, 35; divorces, 13.

Recreation: Lake Stamford activities, bass tournament in August; Haskell arts & crafts show in November; hunting of deer, geese, wild hog.

Minerals: Oil and gas.

Agriculture: Wheat, cotton, peanuts; 28,000 acres irrigated. Beef cattle raised. Market value $67.7 million.

HASKELL (3,322) county seat; farming center; hospital; city park; Wild Horse Prairie Days in June.

Other towns include: **O'Brien** (106), **Rochester** (324), **Rule** (636), **Weinert** (172).

Also, **Stamford** (3,124, mostly in Jones County).

Population	5,899
Change fm 2000	−3.18
Area (sq. mi.)	910.25
Land Area (sq. mi.)	902.97
Altitude (ft.)	1,340-1,795
Rainfall (in.)	24.93
Jan. mean min.	28.8
July mean max.	96.1
Civ. Labor	3,021
Unemployed	5.3
Wages	$16,002,367
Av. Weekly Wage	$616
Prop. Value	$575,990,576
Retail Sales	$72,858,096

For explanation of sources, abbreviations and symbols, see p. 232 and foldout map.

Hays County

Physical Features: Hilly in west, blackland in east; bisected by Blanco River; on edge of Balcones Escarpment.

Economy: Education, tourism, retirement area, some manufacturing; part of Austin metropolitan area.

History: Tonkawa area, also Apache and Comanche presence. Spanish authorities attempted first permanent settlement in 1807. Mexican land grants in early 1830s to Juan Martín Veramendi, Juan Vicente Campos and Thomas Jefferson Chambers. County created, organized, 1843 from Travis County; named for Capt. Jack Hays, famous Texas Ranger.

Race/Ethnicity, 2008: (In percent) Anglo, 63.5; Black, 3.5; Hispanic, 31.6; Other, 1.5.

Vital Statistics, 2008: Births, 2,089; deaths, 739; marriages, 960; divorces, 415.

Recreation: Fishing, hunting; college cultural, athletic events; African-American museum, LBJ museum; Cypress Creek and Blanco River resorts, guest ranches, Wonder World park, Aquarena center.

Minerals: Sand, gravel, cement produced.

Agriculture: Beef cattle, goats, exotic wildlife; greenhouse nurseries; hay, corn, sorghum, wheat and cotton. Market value $11.4 million.

SAN MARCOS (44,894) county seat; Texas State University, Gary Job Corps center; government/services, distribution center, outlet center; hospital, sports medicine, physical therapy center; Scheib Center for mentally handicapped; San Marcos River; Cinco de Mayo festival.

Other towns include: **Bear Creek** (382); **Buda** (7,295) retail, government/services, Stagecoach park, Wiener Dog races in April; **Driftwood** (144); **Dripping Springs** (1,788); **Hays** (217); **Kyle** (28,016); **Mountain City** (648.

Also, **Niederwald** (565, partly in Caldwell County); **Uhland** (1,014, partly in Caldwell County); **Wimberley** (2,626) tourism, retirement community, artists, concert series, Country Pie Social and Fair in April; **Woodcreek** (1,457).

For explanation of sources, abbreviations and symbols, see p. 232 and foldout map.

Population	157,107
Change fm 2000	60.99
Area (sq. mi.)	679.79
Land Area (sq. mi.)	677.87
Altitude (ft.)	550-1,620
Rainfall (in.)	37.19
Jan. mean min.	38.6
July mean max.	95.1
Civ. Labor	80,787
Unemployed	7.4
Wages	$424,828,163
Av. Weekly Wage	$650
Prop. Value	$13,780,640,259
Retail Sales	$2,141,378,244

Hemphill County

Physical Features: Panhandle county; sloping surface, broken by Canadian, Washita rivers; sandy, red, dark soils.

Economy: Oil and gas, agriculture, tourism and hunting, government/services.

History: Apaches, who were pushed out by Comanches, Kiowas. Tribes removed to Indian Territory in 1875. Ranching began in late 1870s. Farmers began to arrive after 1900. County created from Bexar, Young districts, 1876; organized 1887; named for Republic of Texas Justice John Hemphill.

Race/Ethnicity, 2008: Anglo, 77.8; Black, 1.5; Hispanic, 19.5; Other, 1.2.

Vital Statistics, 2008: Births, 62; deaths, 26; marriages, 25; divorces, 6.

Recreation: Lake Marvin; fall foliage tour; hunting, fishing; Indian Battleground, wildlife management area; museum; 4th of July rodeo; prairie chicken viewing in April.

Minerals: Oil, natural gas, caliche.

Agriculture: Beef cattle, wheat, horses, hay, alfalfa, avocados; some irrigation. Market value $117.7 million. Hunting leases, nature tourism.

CANADIAN (2,649) county seat; oil, gas production; hospital.

Population	3,807
Change fm 2000	13.61
Area (sq. mi.)	912.06
Land Area (sq. mi.)	909.68
Altitude (ft.)	2,170-3,000
Rainfall (in.)	21.68
Jan. mean min.	18.8
July mean max.	93.9
Civ. Labor	2,531
Unemployed	3.3
Wages	$25,081,797
Av. Weekly Wage	$945
Prop. Value	$2,331,636,090
Retail Sales	$32,298,562

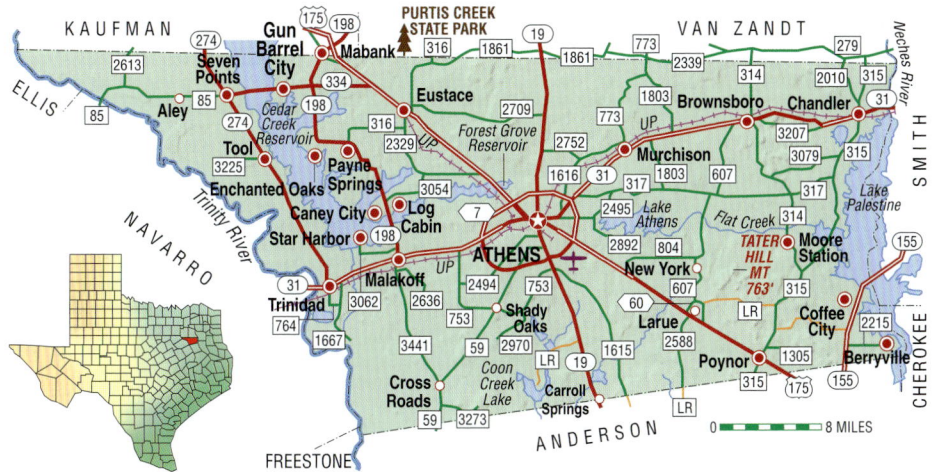

Henderson County

Physical Features: East Texas county bounded by Neches, Trinity rivers; hilly, rolling; one-third forested; sandy, loam, clay soils; commercial timber; Cedar Creek, other lakes.

Economy: Agribusiness, retail trade, varied manufacturing, minerals, recreation, tourism.

History: Caddo area. Cherokee, other tribes migrated into the area in 1819-20 ahead of white settlement. Cherokees forced into Indian Territory in 1839. Anglo-American settlers arrived in 1840s. County created 1846 from Nacogdoches, Houston counties and named for Gov. J. Pinckney Henderson.

Race/Ethnicity, 2008: (In percent) Anglo, 82.4; Black, 6.4; Hispanic, 10.2; Other, 0.9.

Vital Statistics, 2008: Births, 1,029; deaths, 894; marriages, 556; divorces, 130.

Recreation: Cedar Creek Reservoir, Lake Palestine, other lakes; Purtis Creek State Park; hunting, fishing, birdwatching; East Texas Arboretum.

Minerals: Oil, gas, clays, lignite, sulfur, sand and gravel.

Agriculture: Nurseries, cattle, hay, horses, rabbits. Market value $44.5 million. Hunting leases and fishing.

ATHENS (12,710) county seat; agribusiness center, varied manufacturing, tourism, state fish hatchery and museum, hospital, mental health center; Trinity Valley Community College; Texas Fiddlers' Contest in May.

Gun Barrel City (5,672) recreation, retirement, retail center.

Malakoff (2,324) brick factory, varied industry, tourism, library, Cornbread Festival in April.

Other towns include: **Berryville** (975); **Brownsboro** (1,039); **Caney City** (217); **Chandler** (2,734) commuting to Tyler, retail trade, tourism, Pow Wow Festival in October; **Coffee City** (278); **Enchanted Oaks** (326); **Eustace** (991); **Larue** (250); **Log Cabin** (714); **Moore Station** (201); **Murchison** (594); **Payne Springs** (767); **Poynor** (305); **Seven Points** (1,455) agribusiness, retail trade, recreation, Monte Carlo celebration in November; **Star Harbor** (444); **Tool** (2,240), and **Trinidad** (886).

Also, **Mabank** (3,035, mostly in Kaufman County).

Population	78,532
Change fm 2000	7.17
Area (sq. mi.)	949.00
Land Area (sq. mi.)	874.24
Altitude (ft.)	256-763
Rainfall (in.)	42.03
Jan. mean min.	35.2
July mean max.	93.4
Civ. Labor	35,887
Unemployed	8.9
Wages	$128,698,947
Av. Weekly Wage	$629
Prop. Value	$6,812,850,400
Retail Sales	$675,420,967

For explanation of sources, abbreviations and symbols, see p. 232 and foldout map.

The heights of downtown Canadian, Hemphiill County. Photo by Robert Plocheck.

Physical Features: Rich alluvial soils along Rio Grande; sandy, loam soils in north; semitropical vegetation.

Economy: Food processing and shipping, other agribusinesses, tourism, mineral operations.

History: Coahuiltecan and Karankawa area. Comanches forced Apaches southward into valley in 1700s; Comanches arrived in valley in 1800s. Spanish settlement occurred 1750-1800. County created, organized, 1852 from Cameron, Starr counties; named for leader of Mexico's independence movement, Father Miguel Hidalgo y Costillo.

Race/Ethnicity, 2008: (In percent) Anglo, 7.6; Black, 0.3; Hispanic, 91.2; Other, 0.9.

Vital Statistics, 2008: Births, 17,082; deaths, 3,382; marriages, 4,762; divorces, 100.

Recreation: Winter resort, retirement area; fishing, hunting; gateway to Mexico; historical sites; Bentsen-Rio Grande Valley State Park; museums; All-Valley Winter Vegetable Show at Pharr.

Minerals: Oil, gas, stone, sand and gravel.

Agriculture: Ninety percent of farm cash receipts from crops (ranked first in state), principally from sugar cane (first in acreage), grain, vegetables (first in acreage), citrus, cotton; livestock includes cattle; 270,000 acres irrigated. Market value $314.3 million.

EDINBURG (71,100) county seat; vegetable processing and packing, petroleum operations, tourism, clothing; planetarium; the University of Texas-Pan American; hospitals; behavorial health center; museum;

Hidalgo County

Population	**774,769**
Change fm 2000	36.05
Area (sq. mi.)	1,582.66
Land Area (sq. mi.)	1,569.75
Altitude (ft.)	28–376
Rainfall (in.)	22.61
Jan. mean min.	48.2
July mean max.	95.5
Civ. Labor	312,901
Unemployed	12.8
Wages	$1,769,784,659
Av. Weekly Wage	$611
Prop. Value	$32,500,440,315
Retail Sales	$7,744,168,815

Texas Cook'em High Steaks July 4 weekend, Fiesta Edinburg in February.

McALLEN (129,877) government/services; food processing and shipping, varied manufacturing, tourism; community college; hospitals; Palmfest in October.

Mission (77,058) citrus groves, agricultural processing and distribution; hospital; community college; international butterfly park; Citrus Fiesta in January.

Pharr (70,400) agriculture, trading center; trucking; tourism; old clock, juke box museums; folklife festival in February.

Other towns include: **Abram** (2,067); **Alamo** (18,353) live steam museum; **Alton** (12,341); **Doffing** (5,091); **Donna** (15,798) citrus center, varied manufacturing; **Edcouch** (3,161); **Elsa** (5,660); **Granjeno** (293); **Hargill** (877); **Hidalgo** (11,198) trade zone, shipping, winter resort, agribusiness, historical sites, library, Borderfest in March; **La Blanca** (2,488); **La Homa** (11,985); **La Joya** (3,985); **La Villa** (1,957); **Los Ebanos** (335).

Also, **Mercedes** (15,570) "boot capital," citrus, and vegetable center, food processing, tourism, recreation vehicle show in January, Hispanic Fest July 4; **Mila Doce** (6,222); **Monte Alto** (1,924); **North Alamo** (3,235); **Nurillo** (7,344); **Palmhurst** (2,607); **Palmview** (5,460); **Palmview South** (5,575); **Peñitas** (4,403); **Progreso** (5,507); **Progreso Lakes** (240); **San Carlos** (3,130); **San Juan** (33,856) retirement area, trucking, Shrine of Our Lady of San Juan, Spring Fiesta in February; **San Manuel-Linn** (801); **South Alamo** (3,361); **Sullivan City** (4,002); **Weslaco** (35,670) agriculture, nature tourism, South Texas College, hospital, Dragonfly Days in May.

Hill County

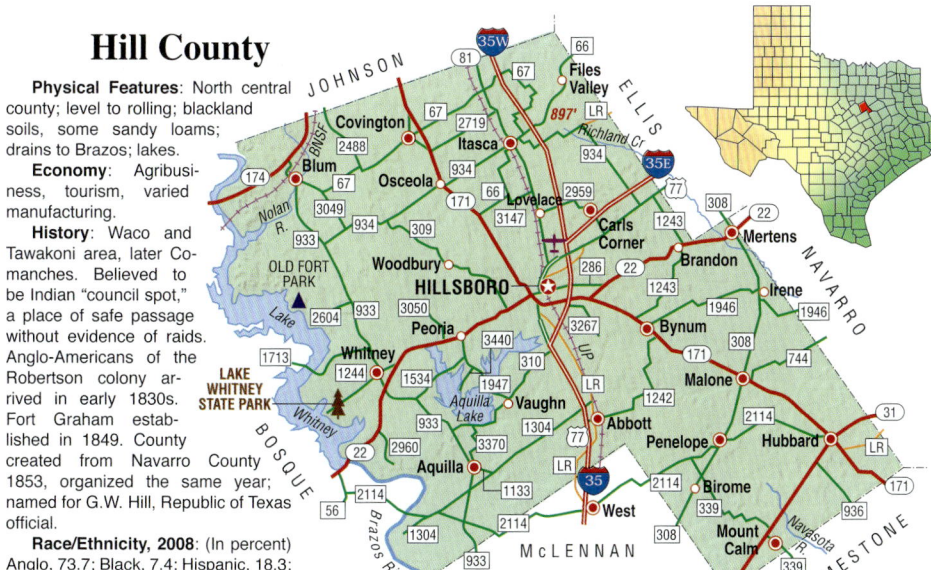

Physical Features: North central county; level to rolling; blackland soils, some sandy loams; drains to Brazos; lakes.

Economy: Agribusiness, tourism, varied manufacturing.

History: Waco and Tawakoni area, later Comanches. Believed to be Indian "council spot," a place of safe passage without evidence of raids. Anglo-Americans of the Robertson colony arrived in early 1830s. Fort Graham established in 1849. County created from Navarro County 1853, organized the same year; named for G.W. Hill, Republic of Texas official.

Race/Ethnicity, 2008: (In percent) Anglo, 73.7; Black, 7.4; Hispanic, 18.3; Other, 0.5.

Vital Statistics, 2008: Births, 450; deaths, 416; marriages, 248; divorces, 148.

Recreation: Lake activities; excursion boat on Lake Whitney; Texas Heritage Museum including Confederate and Audie Murphy exhibits, historic structures, rebuilt frontier fort barracks; motorcycle track.

Minerals: Gas, limestone.

Agriculture: Corn, cattle, sorghum, wheat, cotton, dairies, turkeys. Market value $74.2 million. Some firewood marketed.

HILLSBORO (8,456) county seat; agribusiness, varied manufacturing, retail, outlet center, tourism, antiques malls; Hill College; hospital; Cell Block museum, restored courthouse; Cotton Pickin Fair in September.

Whitney (2,807) tourism, varied manufacturing; medical center; Pioneer Days in October.

Other towns include: **Abbott** (356); **Aquilla** (109); **Blum** (444); **Brandon** (75); **Bynum** (199); **Carl's Corner** (173); **Covington** (269); **Hubbard** (1,423) agriculture, machine shop, antiques, museum, library, Magnolias & Mistletoe Victorian Christmas celebration; **Irene** (170); **Itasca** (1,644); **Malone** (269); **Mertens** (125); **Mount Calm** (320); **Penelope** (198).

Population	**35,089**
Change fm 2000	8.56
Area (sq. mi.)	985.65
Land Area (sq. mi.)	962.36
Altitude (ft.)	417-897
Rainfall (in.)	37.15
Jan. mean min.	35.2
July mean max.	95.2
Civ. Labor	16,043
Unemployed	8.8
Wages	$71,467,707
Av. Weekly Wage	$597
Prop. Value	$2,949,746,267
Retail Sales	$377,192,458

For explanation of sources, abbreviations and symbols, see p. 232 and foldout map.

Tram awaits birders at Bentsen-Rio Grande Valley State Park, Hidalgo County. Photo by Robert Plocheck.

Hockley County

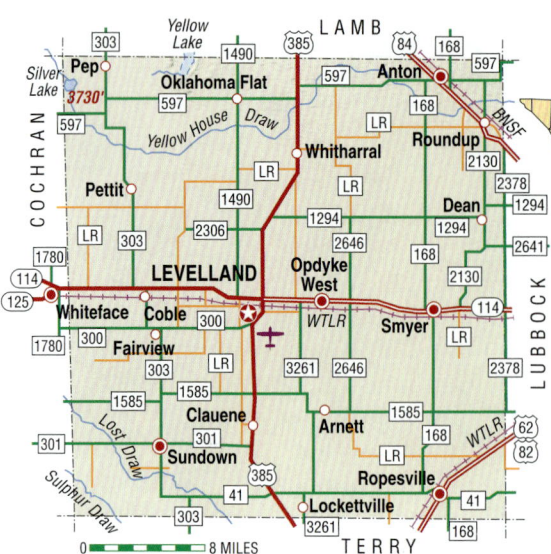

Physical Features: South Plains, numerous playas, drains to Yellow House Draw; loam, sandy loam soils.

Economy: Extensive oil, gas production and services; manufacturing; varied agribusiness.

History: Comanches displaced Apaches in early 1700s. Large ranches of 1880s brought few residents. Homesteaders arrived after 1900. County created 1876, from Bexar, Young districts; organized 1921. Named for Republic of Texas secretary of war Gen. G.W. Hockley.

Race/Ethnicity, 2008: Anglo, 53.1; Black, 4.1; Hispanic, 42.2; Other, 0.6.

Vital Statistics, 2008: Births, 380; deaths, 192; marriages, 157; divorces, 53.

Recreation: Early Settlers' Day in July; Marigolds Arts, Crafts Festival in November.

Minerals: Oil, gas, stone; one of leading oil counties with more than 1 billion barrels produced.

Agriculture: Cotton, grain sorghum; cattle, hogs raised; substantial irrigation. Market value $107.7 million.

LEVELLAND (13,542) county seat; oil, cotton, cattle center; government/services; hospital; South Plains College; Hot Burrito & Bluegrass music festival in July.

Other towns include: **Anton** (1,126); **Opdyke West** (174); **Pep** (3); **Ropesville** (434); **Smyer** (474); **Sundown** (1,397); **Whitharral** (158).

Population............................ 22,935	July mean max. 92.7
Change fm 2000 .... 0.96	Civ. Labor 12,166
Area (sq. mi.)......................... 908.55	Unemployed 6.4
Land Area (sq. mi.) 908.28	Wages $92,845,046
Altitude (ft.) 3,300-3,730	Av. Weekly Wage.................... $747
Rainfall (in.) 19.58	Prop. Value $3,681,197,664
Jan. mean min. 23.7	Retail Sales $208,644,349

Hood County

Physical Features: Hilly; broken by Paluxy, Brazos rivers; sandy loam soils.

Economy: Tourism, commuting to Fort Worth, nuclear power plant, agriculture.

History: Lipan Apache and Comanche area. Anglo-American settlers arrived in late 1840s. County created, organized, 1866 from Johnson and Erath counties; named for Confederate Gen. John B. Hood.

Race/Ethnicity, 2008: (In percent) Anglo, 88.2; Black, 0.3; Hispanic, 10.5; Other, 1.0.

Vital Statistics, 2008: Births, 584; deaths, 558; marriages, 335; divorces, 198.

Recreation: Lakes, fishing, scenic areas; summer theater; Gen. Granbury's Bean & Rib cookoff in March; Acton historic site.

Minerals: Oil, gas, stone.

Agriculture: Hay, turfgrass, beef cattle, nursery crops, pecans, peaches; some irrigation. Market value $18.9 million.

GRANBURY (7,978) county seat; tourism, real estate, power plants; historic downtown area, opera house; hospital; library; Civil War re-enactment in October.

Other towns include: **Acton** (1,129) grave of Elizabeth Crockett, wife of Davy; **Brazos Bend** (305); **Cresson** (741); **DeCordova** (2,683); **Lipan** (480); **Oak Trail Shores** (2,755); **Paluxy** (76); **Pecan Plantation** (5,294); **Tolar** (681).

Population............................ 51,182	Rainfall (in.) 33.10
Change fm 2000 .... 24.53	Jan. mean min. 33.0
Area (sq. mi.)......................... 436.80	July mean max. 97.0
Land Area (sq. mi.) 421.61	Civ. Labor 26,239
Altitude (ft.) 600-1,230	Unemployed 7.8
	Wages $114,159,175
	Av. Weekly Wage.................... $690
	Prop. Value $6,476,090,070
	Retail Sales $538,347,782

For explanation of sources, abbreviations and symbols, see p. 232 and foldout map.

Hopkins County

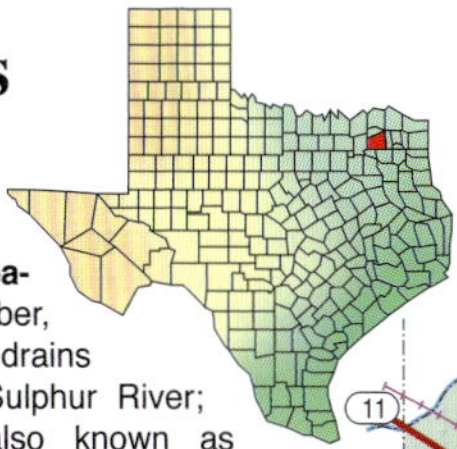

Physical Features: Varied timber, including pines; drains north to South Sulphur River; Cooper Lake (also known as Jim Chapman Lake); light, sandy to heavier black soils.

Economy: Agribusiness, feed mills; varied manufacturing.

History: Caddo area, displaced by Cherokees, who in turn were forced out by President Lamar in 1839. First Anglo-American settlement in 1837. County created in 1846 from Lamar, Nacogdoches counties, organized the same year; named for pioneer Hopkins family.

Race/Ethnicity, 2008: (In percent) Anglo, 78.3; Black, 8.3; Hispanic, 12.4; Other, 1.0.

Vital Statistics, 2008: Births, 482; deaths, 354; marriages, 256; divorces, 185.

Recreation: Fishing, hunting; state park, lake activities; dairy museum; dairy festival in June; stew contest in September.

Minerals: Lignite coal.

Agriculture: Dairies, beef cattle, hay. Market value $208.3 million. Firewood and hardwood lumber marketed.

SULPHUR SPRINGS (15,449) county seat; dairy farming, equine center, food processing and distribution, varied manufacturing, tourism; hospital; library, heritage park, music box gallery, civic center.

Other towns include: **Brashear** (280), **Como** (702), **Cumby** (777), **Dike** (170), **Pickton** (300), **Saltillo** (200), **Sulphur Bluff** (280), **Tira** (297).

For explanation of sources, abbreviations and symbols, see p. 232 and foldout map.

Population	**35,161**
Change fm 2000	10.02
Area (sq. mi.)	792.74
Land Area (sq. mi.)	782.40
Altitude (ft.)	340-649
Rainfall (in.)	47.69
Jan. mean min.	31.1
July mean max.	94.8
Civ. Labor	17,751
Unemployed	7.4
Wages	$100,647,638
Av. Weekly Wage	$673
Prop. Value	$2,416,799,693
Retail Sales	$416,590,606

The Hopkins County Courthouse in Sulphur Springs. Photo by Robert Plocheck.

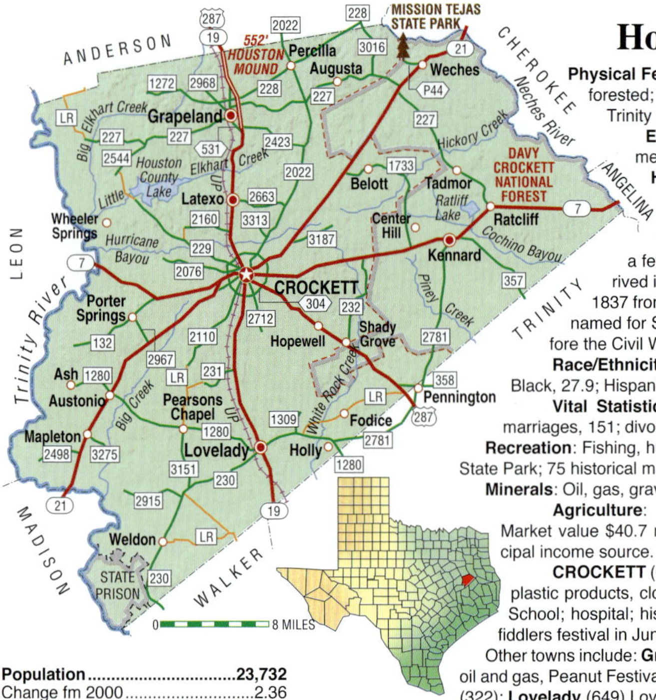

Houston County

Physical Features: East Texas county over half forested; rolling terrain, draining to Neches, Trinity rivers; timber production.

Economy: Livestock, timber, government/services, manufacturing, tourism.

History: Caddo group attracted mission San Francisco de los Tejas, 1690. Spanish town of Bucareli established in 1774. Both lasted only a few years. Anglo-American settlers arrived in 1820s. County created, organized, 1837 from Nacogdoches County by Republic; named for Sam Houston. Cotton plantations before the Civil War had many slaves.

Race/Ethnicity, 2008: (In percent) Anglo, 62.2; Black, 27.9; Hispanic, 9.4; Other, 0.5.

Vital Statistics, 2008: Births, 270; deaths, 311; marriages, 151; divorces, 66.

Recreation: Fishing, hunting; national forest; Mission Tejas State Park; 75 historical markers; Houston County Lake.

Minerals: Oil, gas, gravel.

Agriculture: Cattle, hay, watermelons, cotton. Market value $40.7 million. Hunting leases. Timber principal income source.

CROCKETT (6,950), county seat; timber, steel and plastic products, clothing manufacturing, Crockett State School; hospital; historic sites; Black Expo in February; fiddlers festival in June.

Other towns include: **Grapeland** (1,489) steel, agribusiness, oil and gas, Peanut Festival in October; **Kennard** (337); **Latexo** (322); **Lovelady** (649) Lovefest in February; **Ratcliff** (106).

Population	23,732
Change fm 2000	2.36
Area (sq. mi.)	1,236.83
Land Area (sq. mi.)	1,230.89
Altitude (ft.)	150-552
Rainfall (in.)	45.48
Jan. mean min.	35.9

July mean max.	93.3
Civ. Labor	8,517
Unemployed	10.6

Wages	$66,540,673
Av. Weekly Wage	$788
Prop. Value	$2,594,022,840
Retail Sales	$162,006,146

Howard County

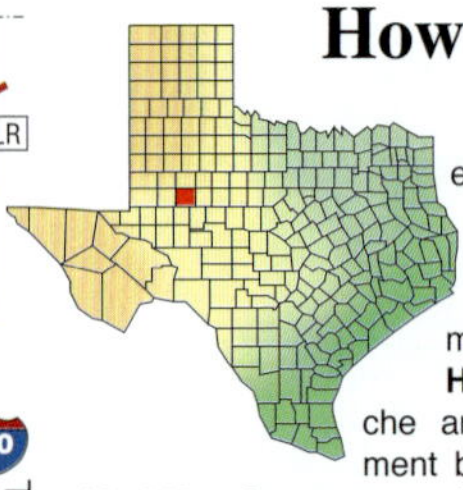

Physical Features: On edge of Llano Estacado; sandy loam soils.

Economy: Agriculture, petrochemicals, government/services.

History: Pawnee and Comanche area. Anglo-American settlement began in 1870. Oil boom in mid-1920s. County named for V.E. Howard, legislator; created 1876 from Bexar, Young districts; organized 1882.

Race/Ethnicity, 2008: (In percent), Anglo, 51.9; Black, 4.8; Hispanic, 42.1; Other, 1.2.

Vital Statistics, 2008: Births, 455; deaths, 348; marriages, 252; divorces, 31.

Recreation: Lakes, state park; campground in Comanche Trail Park, Native Plant Trail, museum, historical sites, Pow Wow in April, Pops in the Park in July.

Minerals: Oil, gas, sand, gravel and stone.

Agriculture: Cotton, beef, hay. Market value $40.9 million.

BIG SPRING (27,282) county seat; agriculture, petrochemicals, varied manufacturing; hospitals including a state institution and Veterans Administration hospital; federal prison; Howard College; railroad plaza.

Other towns include: **Coahoma** (817), **Forsan** (210), **Knott** (200), and **Sand Springs** (835)..

Population	35,012
Change fm 2000	4.12
Area (sq. mi.)	904.19
Land Area (sq. mi.)	902.84
Altitude (ft.)	2,180-2,800
Rainfall (in.)	20.12
Jan. mean min.	29.6
July mean max.	94.3
Civ. Labor	14,133

Unemployed	7.2
Wages	$123,987,316
Av. Weekly Wage	$787
Prop. Value	$2,909,581,171
Retail Sales	$397,200,343

For explanation of sources, abbreviations and symbols, see p. 232 and foldout map.

The Guadalupe Mountains beyond the irrigated fields of Dell City. Photo by Robert Plocheck.

Hudspeth County

Physical Features: Plateau, basin terrain, draining to salt lakes; Rio Grande; mostly rocky, alkaline, clay soils and sandy loam soils, except alluvial along Rio Grande; desert, mountain vegetation. Fertile agricultural valley.

Economy: Agribusiness, mining, tourism, hunting leases.

History: Mescalero Apache area. Fort Quitman established in 1858 to protect routes to west. Railroad in 1881 brought Anglo-American settlers. Political turmoil in Mexico (1912-29) brought more settlers from Mexico. County named for Texas political leader Claude B. Hudspeth; created 1917 from El Paso County, organized the same year.

Race/Ethnicity, 2008: (In percent) Anglo, 21.2; Black, 0.2; Hispanic, 77.5; Other, 1.1.

Vital Statistics, 2008: Births, 44; deaths, 20; marriages,1; divorces, 0.

Recreation: Scenic drives; fort ruins; hot springs; salt basin; white sands; hunting; birding; part of Guadalupe Mountains National Park, containing unique plant life, canyons.

Minerals: Talc, stone, gypsum.

Agriculture: Most income from cotton, vegetables, hay, alfalfa; beef cattle raised; 35,000 acres irrigated. Market value $31.1 million.

SIERRA BLANCA (553) county seat; ranching center, tourist stop on interstate highway; adobe courthouse; 4th of July fair, livestock show in January.

Other towns include: **Dell City** (365) feedlots, vegetable packing, gypsum, trade center, airport, some of largest water wells in state, Wild West Chili Fest in September; and **Fort Hancock** (1,750).

For explanation of sources, abbreviations and symbols, see p. 232 and foldout map.

Population	....	**3,476**
Change fm 2000	....	3.95
Area (sq. mi.)	....	4,571.93
Land Area (sq. mi.)	....	4,571.00
Altitude (ft.)	....	3,117-7,484

Rainfall (in.)	....	11.93
Jan. mean min.	....	25.1
July mean max.	....	92.0
Civ. Labor	....	1,799
Unemployed	....	5.8

Wages	....	$14,860,879
Av. Weekly Wage	....	$956
Prop. Value	....	$473,986,242
Retail Sales	....	$7,681,890

Population	86,129
Change fm 2000	12.45
Area (sq. mi.)	882.02
Land Area (sq. mi.)	841.16
Altitude (ft.)	437-730
Rainfall (in.)	43.70
Jan. mean min.	31.2
July mean max.	93.3
Civ. Labor	37.499
Unemployed	9.3
Wages	$303,318,608
Av. Weekly Wage	$831
Prop. Value	$5,444,129,407
Retail Sales	$957,771,056

Hunt County

Physical Features: Level to rolling surface; Sabine, Sulphur rivers; Lake Tawakoni; mostly heavy Blackland soil, some loam, sandy loams.

Economy: Education, varied manufacturing, agribusiness; several Fortune 500 companies in county; many residents employed in Dallas area.

History: Caddo Indians gone by the 1790s. Kiowa bands in the area when Anglo-American settlers arrived in 1839. County named for Memucan Hunt, Republic secretary of navy; created in 1846 from Fannin, Nacogdoches counties, organized the same year.

Race/Ethnicity, 2008: (In percent) Anglo, 74.7; Black, 10.6; Hispanic, 12.8; Other, 1.9.

Vital Statistics, 2008: Births, 1,102; deaths, 845; marriages, 616; divorces, 297.

Recreation: Lake Tawakoni sports, catfish tournament in August; Texas A&M University-Commerce events.

Minerals: Sand and white rock, gas, oil.

Agriculture: Cattle, forage, greenhouse crops, top revenue sources; horses, wheat, oats, cotton, grain sorghum. Market value $40.5 million. Some firewood sold.

GREENVILLE (25,557) county seat; varied manufacturing, government/services, commuters to Dallas; hospital; branch of Paris Junior College; cotton museum, Audie Murphy exhibit; Native American Pow-wow in January.

Commerce (8,078) Texas A&M University-Commerce, varied manufacturing, tourism; hospital; planetarium, children's museum; Bois d'Arc Bash in September.

Other towns include: **Caddo Mills** (1,338); **Campbell** (638); **Celeste** (814); **Hawk Cove** (483); **Lone Oak** (598); **Merit** (225); **Neyland-ville** (97); **Quinlan** (1,394); **West Tawakoni** (1,576) tourist center, light industry, Lakefest in October; **Wolfe City** (1,412) manufacturing, antiques shops, commuters to Dallas, museum, library, car and truck show in October.

County adopted:
In memory of
Rafael and Lenora Cavazos

A small stone memorial at the battleground of Adobe Walls, Hutchinson County. Photo by Robert Plocheck.

Hutchinson County

Physical Features: High Plains, broken by Canadian River and tributaries, Lake Meredith; fertile valleys along streams.

Economy: Oil, gas, petrochemicals, agribusiness, varied manufacturing, tourism.

History: Antelope Creek Indian area. Later Comanches were driven out in U.S. cavalry campaigns of 1874–1875. Adobe Walls site of two Indian attacks, 1864 and 1874. Ranching began in the late 1870s. Oil boom in the early 1920s. County created in 1876 from Bexar Territory; organized in 1901; named for pioneer jurist Anderson Hutchinson.

Race/Ethnicity, 2008: (In percent) Anglo, 76.9; Black, 2.8; Hispanic, 18.5; Other, 1.8.

Vital Statistics, 2008: Births, 308; deaths, 251; marriages, 168; divorces, 106.

Recreation: Lake activities, fishing, camping; Adobe Walls, historic Indian battle site.

Minerals: Gas, oil, sand, gravel.

Agriculture: Cattle, corn, wheat, grain sorghum; about 45,000 acres irrigated. Market value $49.6 million.

STINNETT (1,881) county seat; petroleum refining, farm center.

BORGER (13,251) petroleum refining, petrochemicals, carbon-black production, oil-field servicing, varied manufacturing, retail center; Frank Phillips College; museum; hospital; downtown beach bash in June.

Other cities include: **Fritch** (2,117), **Sanford** (164).

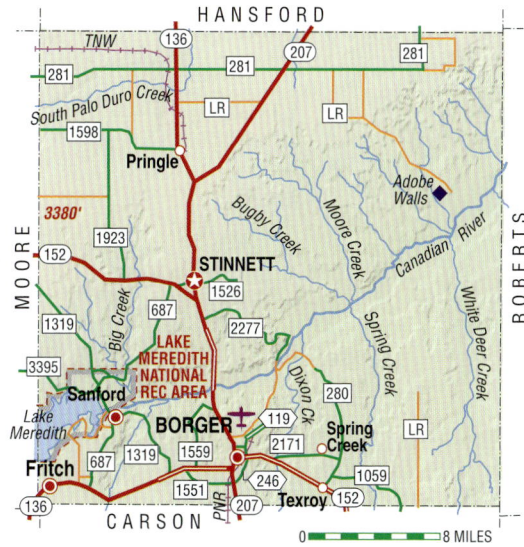

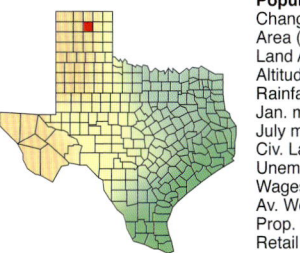

Population	**22,150**
Change fm 2000	–7.16
Area (sq. mi.)	894.95
Land Area (sq. mi.)	887.37
Altitude (ft.)	2,600-3,380
Rainfall (in.)	21.98
Jan. mean min.	23.4
July mean max.	92.6
Civ. Labor	11,307
Unemployed	8.0
Wages	$105,686,439
Av. Weekly Wage	$970
Prop. Value	$2,782,868,080
Retail Sales	$176,343,563

Irion County

Physical Features: West Texas county with hilly surface, broken by Middle Concho, tributaries; clay, sandy soils.

Economy: Ranching, oil, gas production, wildlife recreation.

History: Tonkawa Indian area. Anglo-American settlement began in late 1870s. County named for Republic leader R.A. Irion; created, organized, 1889 from Tom Green County.

Race/Ethnicity, 2008: (In percent) Anglo, 75.1; Black, 0.2; Hispanic, 24.2; Other, 0.5.

Vital Statistics, 2008: Births 11; deaths, 12; marriages, 0; divorces, 5.

Recreation: Hunting; historic sites, including Dove Creek battlefield and stagecoach stops, old Sherwood courthouse built 1900; hunters appreciation dinner in November.

Minerals: Oil, gas.

Agriculture: Beef cattle, sheep, goats; hay, wheat. Market value $6.1 million.

MERTZON (781) county seat; farm center. wool warehousing.

Other towns include: **Barnhart** (110).

Population	1,599
Change fm 2000	–9.71
Area (sq. mi.)	1,051.59
Land Area (sq. mi.)	1,051.48
Altitude (ft.)	2,000-2,750
Rainfall (in.)	19.90
Jan. mean min.	32.0
July mean max.	95.0
Civ. Labor	946
Unemployed	5.8
Wages	$7,248,973
Av. Weekly Wage	$995
Prop. Value	$924,714,210
Retail Sales	$5,285,148

For explanation of sources, abbreviations and symbols, see p. 232 and foldout map.

Jack County

Physical Features: Rolling Cross Timbers, broken by West Fork of the Trinity, other streams; sandy, dark brown, loam soils; lakes.

Economy: Petroleum production, oil-field services, livestock, manufacturing, tourism.

History: Caddo and Comanche borderland. Anglo-American settlers arrived in 1855, part of Peters Colony. County named for brothers P.C. and W.H. Jack, leaders in Texas' independence effort; created 1856 from Cooke County; organized 1857 with Mesquiteville (orginal name of Jacksboro) as county seat.

Race/Ethnicity, 2008: (In percent) Anglo, 85.2; Black, 4.9; Hispanic, 8.9; Other, 0.9.

Vital Statistics, 2008: Births, 105; deaths, 86; marriages, 67; divorces, 35.

Recreation: Hunting, wildlife leases; fishing; lake activities; Fort Richardson, Texas 4-H Museum (county is birthplace of 4-H clubs in Texas), other historic sites; Lost Creek Reservoir State Trailway.

Minerals: Oil, gas.

Agriculture: Cattle, hay, wheat, goats, sheep. Market value $18.3 million. Firewood sold.

JACKSBORO (4,511) county seat; agribusiness, varied manufacturing, tourism; petroleum production and services; hospital, hospice; library; Old Mesquiteville Festival in fall.

Other towns include: **Bryson** (539), **Jermyn** (75), **Perrin** (398).

Prop. Value $2,028,493,390
Retail Sales $43,331,958

Population 9,044	Jan. mean min. 29.7
Change fm 2000 .... 3.21	July mean max. 94.4
Area (sq. mi.) 920.11	Civ. Labor 5,066
Land Area (sq. mi.) 916.61	Unemployed 6.1
Altitude (ft.) 836-1,510	Wages $31,994,982
Rainfall (in.) 31.44	Av. Weekly Wage $901

Jackson County

Physical Features: South coastal county of prairie and motts of trees; loam, clay, black soils; drains to creeks, rivers, bays.

Economy: Petroleum production, plastics manufacturing, agribusiness.

History: Karankawa area. Lipan Apaches and Tonkawas arrived later. Six of Austin's Old Three Hundred families settled in the 1820s. Mexican municipality, created 1835, became original county the following year; named for U.S. President Andrew Jackson. Oil discovered in 1934.

Race/Ethnicity, 2008: (In percent) Anglo, 63.2; Black, 7.6; Hispanic, 28.3; Other, 0.9.

Vital Statistics, 2008: Births, 217; deaths, 171; marriages, 101; divorces, 25.

Recreation: Hunting, fishing, birding (southern bald eagle in area); historic sites; Texana Museum; Lake Texana, Brackenridge Plantation campground, state park; Chili Spill in November at Lake Texana, county fair, rodeo in April.

Minerals: Oil and natural gas.

Agriculture: Beef cattle, corn, rice, sorghum, cotton; 13,000 acres of rice irrigated. Market value $62.6 million.

EDNA (5,499) county seat; oil and gas, chemical plants, agriculture; hospital, library, museums.

Other towns include: **Francitas** (125); **Ganado** (2,003) oil and gas, agriculture, historic movie theater, Crawfish Festival in May; **LaSalle** (110); **La Ward** (213); **Lolita** (555); **Vanderbilt** (395).

Population 14,075	Jan. mean min. 42.0
Change fm 2000 .... −2.2	July mean max. 94.0
Area (sq. mi.) 857.03	Civ. Labor 6,836
Land Area (sq. mi.) 829.49	Unemployed 7.6
Altitude (ft.) .... sea level-155	Wages $47,993,746
Rainfall (in.) 42.10	Av. Weekly Wage $718

For explanation of sources, abbreviations and symbols, see p. 232 and foldout map.

Prop. Value $1,929,250,183
Retail Sales $158,998,572

Jasper County

Physical Features: East Texas county; hilly to level; national forest; lakes; Neches River.

Economy: Timber industries; prison, government/services.

History: Caddo and Atakapa tribal area. Land grants to John R. Bevil and Lorenzo de Zavala in 1829. County created in 1836, organized in 1837, from Mexican municipality; named for Sgt. William Jasper of American Revolution.

Race/Ethnicity, 2008: (In percent) Anglo, 76.5; Black, 17.8; Hispanic, 4.9; Other, 0.8.

Vital Statistics, 2008: Births, 494; deaths, 422; marriages, 324; divorces, 224.

Recreation: Lake activities; hunting; fishing; state park, Big Thicket.

Minerals: Oil, gas produced.

Agriculture: Beef cattle, plant nurseries, fruits, vegetables. Market value $6.7 million. Timber is major income producer. Hunter leases important.

JASPER (7,590) county seat; tourism, government/services, hospital; Angelina College extension; museum; Azalea Festival in March, October Fest.

Other towns include: **Browndell** (197); **Buna** (2,142) timber, oil, polka dot house, Redbud Festival in March; **Evadale** (1,483); **Kirbyville** (2,142) government/services, retail, commuters, museum, Calaboose museum, Magnolia Festival in April; **Sam Rayburn** (600).

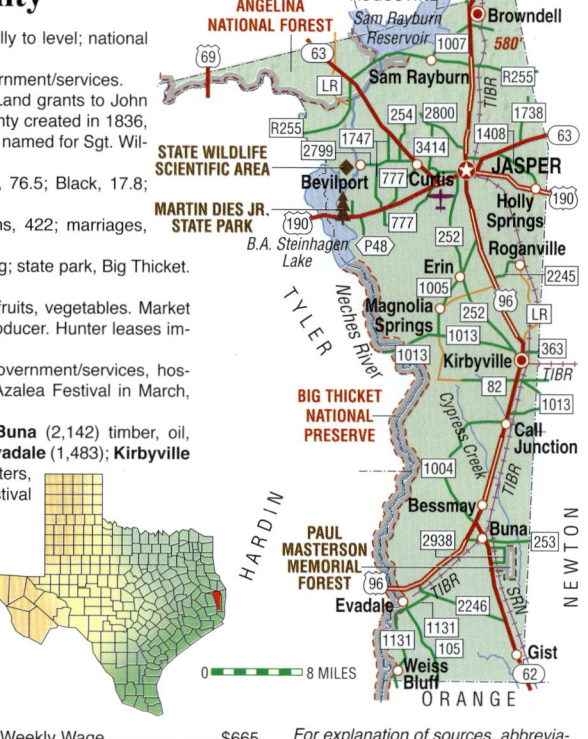

Population	35,710
Change fm 2000	0.3
Area (sq. mi.)	969.62
Land Area (sq. mi.)	937.40
Altitude (ft.)	10-580
Rainfall (in.)	60.57
Jan. mean min.	35.2
July mean max.	94.5
Civ. Labor	15,875
Unemployed	12.7
Wages	$88,797,117

Av. Weekly Wage	$665
Prop. Value	$2,526,383,594
Retail Sales	$354,514,601

For explanation of sources, abbreviations and symbols, see p. 232 and foldout map.

Porch of Fort Richardson at Jacksboro, Jack County. Photo by Robert Plocheck.

View to the southwest from the summit at Davis Mountains State Park. Photo by Robert Plocheck.

Jeff Davis County

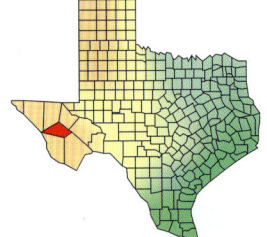

Physical Features: Highest average elevation in Texas; peaks (Mt. Livermore, 8,378 ft.), canyons, plateaus; intermountain wash, clay, loam soils; cedars, oaks in highlands.

Economy: Tourism, agriculture, McDonald Observatory.

History: Mescalero Apaches in area when Antonio de Espejo explored in 1583. U.S. Army established Fort Davis in 1854 to protect routes to west. Civilian settlers followed, including Manuel Músquiz, a political refugee from Mexico. County named for Jefferson Davis, U.S. war secretary, Confederate president; created, organized, 1887 from Presidio County.

Race/Ethnicity, 2008: (In percent) Anglo, 62.9; Black, 1.1; Hispanic, 35.6; Other, 0.5.

Vital Statistics, 2008: Births, 19; deaths, 13; marriages, 1; divorces, 0.

Recreation: Scenic drives including loop along Limpia Creek, Mt. Livermore, Blue Mountain; hunting; Fort Davis National Historic Site; state park; McDonald Observatory on Mt.

Locke; solar power park; Chihuahuan Desert Research Institute; hummingbird festival in August.

Minerals: Not significant.

Agriculture: Greenhouse tomatoes, beef cattle, horses, meat goats. Market value $10.4 million. Hunting leases important.

FORT DAVIS (1,201), county seat; ranch center, trade, tourism, government/services; library; Overland Trail museum; "Coolest July 4th in Texas."

Other town: **Valentine** (134).

Population	**2,342**
Change fm 2000	6.12
Area (sq. mi.)	2,264.60
Land Area (sq. mi.)	2,264.43
Altitude (ft.)	3,162-8,378
Rainfall (in.) Fort Davis	15.86
Rainfall (in.) Mt. Locke	20.37
Jan. mean min. Fort Davis	28.4
Jan. mean min. Mt. Locke	32.4
July mean max. Fort Davis	89.5
July mean max. Mt. Locke	84.5
Civ. Labor	1,159
Unemployed	5.9
Wages	$7,715,632
Av. Weekly Wage	$614
Prop. Value	$476,948,990
Retail Sales	$7,653,523

For explanation of sources, abbreviations and symbols, see p. 232 and foldout map.

Jefferson County

Physical Features: Gulf Coast grassy plain, with timber in northwest; beach sands, sandy loams, black clay soils; drains to Neches River, Gulf of Mexico.

Economy: Government/services, petrochemical and other chemical plants, shipbuilding, steel mill, port activity, oil-field supplies.

History: Atakapas and Orcoquizas, whose numbers were reduced by epidemics or migration before Anglo-American settlers arrived in 1820s. Cajuns arrived in 1840s; Europeans in 1850s. Antebellum slaveholding area. County created 1836 from Mexican municipality; organized 1837; named for U.S. President Thomas Jefferson.

Race/Ethnicity, 2008: (In percent) Anglo, 44.3; Black, 34.9; Hispanic, 15.8; Other, 4.9.

Vital Statistics, 2008: Births, 3,574; deaths, 2,586; marriages, 2,299; divorces, 1,005.

Recreation: Beaches, fresh and saltwater fishing; duck, goose hunting; water activities; Dick Dowling Monument and Park; Spindletop site, energy, fire museums; saltwater lake; wildlife refuge; Lamar University events; historic sites; South Texas Fair in March.

Minerals: Large producer of oil, gas, sulfur, salt, sand and gravel.

Agriculture: Rice, soybeans; crawfish; beef cattle; hay; considerable rice irrigated. Market value $26.8 million. Timber sales significant.

BEAUMONT (118,296) county seat; oil and gas production, government/services, engineering and industrial services, port; Lamar University, Institute of Technology; hospitals; Neches River Festival in April.

PORT ARTHUR (53,818) oil, chemical activities, shrimping and crawfishing, shipping, offshore marine, tourism; hospitals; museum; prison; Asian New Year Tet, Janis Joplin Birthday Bash in January. **Sabine Pass** and **Port Acres** are now within the city limits of Port Arthur.

Other towns include: **Bevil Oaks** (1,274); **Central Gardens** (4,347); **China** (1,160); **Fannett** (2,252); **Groves** (16,144) retail center, some manufacturing, government/services, tourism; hospital, pecan festival in September; **Hamshire** (759).

Also, **Nederland** (17,547) manufacturing, transportation, petrochemical refining; Windmill and French museum; hospital; Tex Ritter memorial and park, heritage festival in March (city founded by Dutch immigrants in 1898).

Also, **Nome** (588); **Port Neches** (13,040) chemical and synthetic rubber industry, manufacturing, library, riverfront park with La Maison Beausoleil, RiverFest in May; **Taylor Landing** (228).

Population	252,273
Change fm 2000	0.09
Area (sq. mi.)	1,111.26
Land Area (sq. mi.)	903.55
Altitude (ft.)	sea level-49
Rainfall (in.)	59.89
Jan. mean min.	42.9
July mean max.	91.6
Civ. Labor	119,431
Unemployed	12.0
Wages	$1,516,766,312
Av. Weekly Wage	$953
Prop. Value	$25,124,672,428
Retail Sales	$3,436,871,729

For explanation of sources, symbols and abbreviations, see p. 232 and foldout map.

Jim Hogg County

Physical Features: South Texas county on rolling plain, with heavy brush cover; white blow sand and sandy loam; hilly, broken.

Economy: Oil, cattle operations.

History: Coahuiltecan area, then Lipan Apache. Spanish land grant in 1805 to Xavier Vela. County named for Gov. James Stephen Hogg; created, organized 1913 from Brooks, Duval counties.

Race/Ethnicity, 2008: (In percent) Anglo, 8.5; Black, 0.4; Hispanic, 90.6; Other, 0.5.

Vital Statistics, 2008: Births, 96; deaths, 50; marriages, 36; divorces, 4.

Recreation: White-tailed deer and bobwhite hunting.

Minerals: Oil and gas.

Agriculture: Cattle, hay, milk goats; some irrigation. Market value $7.4 million.

HEBBRONVILLE (4,558) county seat; ranching, oil-field center.

Other towns include: **Guerra** (6), **Las Lomitas** (244) and **South Fork Estates** (70), and **Thompsonville** (46).

Population...............................**5,300**	Altitude (ft.)............................ 230-878	Unemployed 7.8
Change fm 2000............................0.36	Rainfall (in.) 23.75	Wages $18,507,512
Area (sq. mi.).........................1,136.16	Jan. mean min...............................43.8	Av. Weekly Wage........................$683
Land Area (sq. mi.) 1,136.11	July mean max. 97.5	Prop. Value $664,967,550
	Civ. Labor 2,959	Retail Sales $32,957,824

Jim Wells County

Physical Features: South Coastal Plains; level to rolling; sandy to dark soils; grassy with mesquite brush.

Economy: Oil and gas production, agriculture, nature tourism.

History: Coahuiltecans, driven out by Lipan Apaches in 1775. Tomás Sánchez established settlement in 1754. Anglo-American settlement in 1878. County created 1911 from Nueces County; organized 1912; named for developer J.B. Wells Jr.

Race/Ethnicity, 2008: (In percent) Anglo, 21.1; Black, 0.5; Hispanic, 77.7; Other, 0.7.

Vital Statistics, 2008: Births, 684; deaths, 339; marriages, 283; divorces, 133.

Recreation: Hunting; fiestas; Tejano Roots hall of fame; South Texas museum.

Minerals: Oil, gas, caliche.

Agriculture: Cattle, sorghum, corn, cotton, dairies, goats, wheat, watermelons, sunflowers, peas, hay, sesame. Market value $61 million.

ALICE (19,104) county seat; oil-field service center, agribusiness, government/services; hospital; Bee County College extension; Fiesta Bandana (from original name of city) in May.

Other towns include: **Alfred** (91); **Ben Bolt** (1,600); **Orange Grove** (1,318); **Pernitas Point** (274, partly in Live Oak County); **Premont** (2,653) wildflower tour in spring; **Rancho Alegre** (1,704); **Sandia** (379).

Population **40,838**
Change fm 2000.....................3.85
Area (sq. mi.).......................868.22
Land Area (sq. mi.) 864.52
Altitude (ft.) 50-450
Rainfall (in.) 27.52
Jan. mean min......................44.1
July mean max. 96.1
Civ. Labor 21,012
Unemployed 8.1
Wages $187,955,252
Av. Weekly Wage.................$823
Prop. Value $2,036,249,101
Retail Sales $500,323,275

For explanation of sources, symbols and abbreviations, see p. 232 and foldout map.

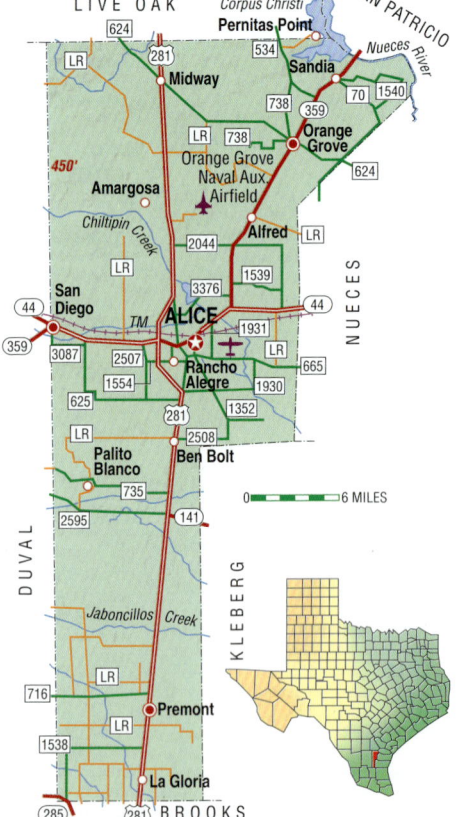

Johnson County

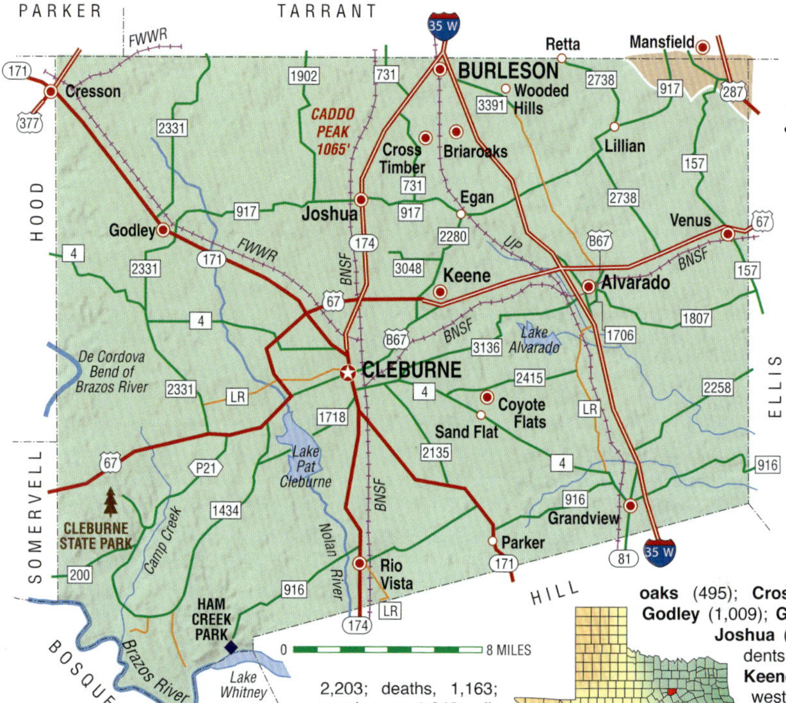

PARKER · TARRANT

Cresson · Retta · Mansfield · BURLESON · Wooded Hills · Briaroaks · Cross Timber · Lillian · Egan · Venus · Joshua · Godley · Keene · Alvarado · CLEBURNE · De Cordova Bend of Brazos River · CLEBURNE STATE PARK · Lake Pat Cleburne · Coyote Flats · Sand Flat · Grandview · Parker · Rio Vista · HAM CREEK PARK · Lake Whitney

CADDO PEAK 1065'

Lake Alvarado

HOOD · SOMERVELL · BOSQUE · HILL · ELLIS

0 — 8 MILES

For explanation of sources, symbols and abbreviations, see p. 232 and foldout map.

Physical Features: North central county drained by tributaries of Trinity, Brazos rivers; lake; hilly, rolling, many soil types.

Economy: Agribusiness, railroad shops; manufacturing, distribution, lake activities, many residents employed in Fort Worth; part of Fort Worth-Arlington metropolitan area.

History: No permanent Indian villages existed in area. Anglo-American settlers arrived in 1840s. County named for Col. M.T. Johnson of Mexican War, Confederacy; created, organized 1854. Formed from McLennan, Hill, Navarro counties.

Race/Ethnicity, 2008: (In percent) Anglo, 77.5; Black, 2.8; Hispanic, 17.8; Other, 1.9.

Vital Statistics, 2008: Births, 2,203; deaths, 1,163; marriages, 1,242; divorces, 547.

Recreation: Bird, deer hunting; water activities on Lake Pat Cleburne; state park; sports complex; museum; Chisholm Trail; Goatneck bike ride in July.

Minerals: Limestone, sand and gravel.

Agriculture: Cattle, hay, horses (fourth in numbers), dairies, cotton, sorghum, wheat, oats, hogs. Market value $62 million.

CLEBURNE (29,337) county seat; manufacturing, oil and gas; hospital, library, museum; Hill College campus; Whistle Stop Christmas.

BURLESON (36,690, part in Tarrant County) agriculture, retail center; hospital.

Other towns include: **Alvarado** (3,785) County Pioneer Days; **Briar-** oaks (495); **Cross Timber** (268); **Godley** (1,009); **Grandview** (1,561); **Joshua** (5,910) many residents work in Fort Worth; **Keene** (6,106) Southwestern Adventist University; **Lillian** (1,160); **Rio Vista** (873), and **Venus** (2,960).

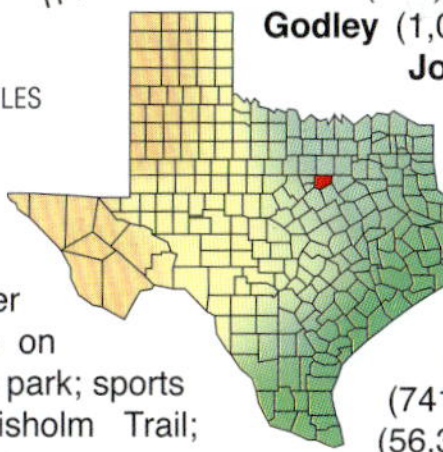

Also, part of **Cresson** (741); and part of **Mansfield** (56,368, mostly in Tarrant County).

Population	150,934
Change fm 2000	19.02
Area (sq. mi.)	734.46
Land Area (sq. mi.)	729.42
Altitude (ft.)	500-1,065
Rainfall (in.)	36.25
Jan. mean min.	34.0
July mean max.	97.0
Civ. Labor	75,245
Unemployed	8.3
Wages	$381,676,375
Av. Weekly Wage	$744
Prop. Value	$14,639,358,048
Retail Sales	$3,453,554,160

The state prison at Venus, Johnson County. Photo by Robert Plocheck.

Jones County

Physical Features: West Texas Rolling Plains; drained by Brazos River fork, tributaries; Lake Fort Phantom Hill.

Economy: Agribusiness; government/services; varied manufacturing.

History: Comanches and other tribes hunted in area. Military presence began in 1851. Ranching established in 1870s. County named for the last president of the Republic, Anson Jones; created 1858 from Bexar, Bosque counties; re-created 1876; organized 1881.

Race/Ethnicity, 2008: (In percent) Anglo, 64.4; Black, 11.4; Hispanic, 23.3; Other, 0.9.

Vital Statistics, 2008: Births, 184; deaths, 210; marriages, 62; divorces, 36.

Recreation: Lake activities, hunting, Fort Phantom Hill, Cowboy Reunion July 4 in Stamford.

Minerals: Oil, gas, sand and gravel, stone.

Agriculture: Cotton, wheat, sesame and peanuts; cattle. Some 10,000 acres irrigated for peanuts and hay. Market value $59.2 million.

ANSON (2,430) county seat; farming center, government/services; hospital; old courthouse, opera house, museums; Mesquite Daze festivals in April and October.

STAMFORD (3,124) trade center for three counties, hospital, historic homes, cowboy museum.

HAMLIN (2,124) farm and ranching, feed mill, oil/gas, electricity/steam plant using mesquite trees; hospital; museums; dove cookoff in October.

Other towns include: **Hawley** (634), **Lueders** (346) limestone quarries.

Part of **Abilene**.

Population **20,202**
Change fm 2000 .... –2.81
Area (sq. mi.) 937.13

Land Area (sq. mi.) 930.99
Altitude (ft.) 1,480–1,970
Rainfall (in.) 26.00
Jan. mean min. 30.7
July mean max. 96.3
Civ. Labor 7,732
Unemployed 7.8
Wages $31,540,104
Av. Weekly Wage $617
Prop. Value $957,039,450
Retail Sales $153,329,941

Karnes County

Physical Features: Sandy loam, dark clay, alluvial soils in rolling terrain; traversed by San Antonio River; mesquite, oak trees.

Economy: Oil and gas, agribusiness.

History: Coahuiltecan Indian area. Spanish ranching began around 1750. Anglo-Americans arrived in 1840s; Polish in 1850s. County created, organized, 1854 from Bexar, Goliad, San Patricio counties; named for Texas Revolutionary figure Henry W. Karnes.

Race/Ethnicity, 2008: (In percent) Anglo, 39.7; Black, 9.2; Hispanic, 50.5; Other, 0.7.

Vital Statistics, 2008: Births, 160; deaths, 136; marriages, 1; divorces, 22.

Recreation: Panna Maria, nation's oldest Polish settlement, founded 1854; Old Helena restored courthouse, museum; dove hunting, nature tourism, guest ranches.

Minerals: Oil, gas, uranium.

Agriculture: Beef cattle, grain, cotton, hay. Market value $24.6 million.

KARNES CITY (3,042) county seat; oil and gas, agribusiness, tourism, processing center, oil-field servicing, manufacturing; library; Lonesome Dove Fest in September.

KENEDY (3,296) farm and oil center, library, dove/quail hunting, prison, hospital; Bluebonnet Days in April.

Other towns include: **Falls City** (611) ranching, sausage making, library, city park on river; **Gillett** (120); **Hobson** (135); **Panna Maria** (45); **Runge** (1,031) oil and gas services, farming, museum, library; cowboy breakfast in December.

For explanation of sources, abbreviations and symbols, see p. 232 and foldout map.

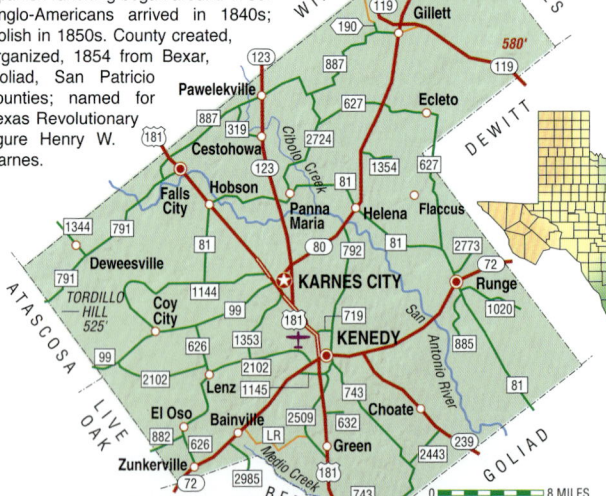

Population **14,824**
Change fm 2000 .... –4.03
Area (sq. mi.) 753.58
Land Area (sq. mi.) 750.32

Altitude (ft.) 180–580
Rainfall (in.) 28.40

Jan. mean min. 41.0
July mean max. 95.0
Civ. Labor 5,470
Unemployed 9.1
Wages $30,724,266
Av. Weekly Wage $629
Prop. Value $1,340,968,518
Retail Sales $119,900,063

Kaufman County

Physical Features: North Blackland prairie, draining to Trinity River, Cedar Creek and Lake.

Economy: varied manufacturing, trade center, government/services, antiques center, commuting to Dallas.

History: Caddo and Cherokee Indians; removed by 1840 when Anglo-American settlement began. County created from Henderson County and organized, 1848; named for member of Texas and U.S. congresses D.S. Kaufman.

Race/Ethnicity, 2008: (In percent) Anglo, 72.5; Black, 10.0; Hispanic, 16.3; Other, 1.2.

Vital Statistics, 2008: Births, 1,500; deaths, 784; marriages, 716; divorces, 400.

Recreation: Lake activities; Porter Farm near Terrell is site of origin of U.S.-Texas Agricultural Extension program; antique centers near Forney; historic homes at Terrell.

Minerals: Oil, gas, stone, sand.

Agriculture: Nursery crops; beef cattle, horses, goats, hogs, sheep; wheat, hay, sorghum, oats, peaches. Market value $43.7 million.

KAUFMAN (6,703) county seat; government/services, manufacturing and distribution, commuters to Dallas; hospital; Caboodle Fest in October.

TERRELL (15,816) agribusiness, varied manufacturing, outlet center; private hospital, state hospital; community college, Southwestern Christian College; British flying school museum, Heritage Jubilee in April.

Other towns include: **Combine** (1,942, partly in Dallas County); **Cottonwood** (185); **Crandall** (2,858); **Elmo** (768); **Forney** (14,661) important antiques center, light industrial, commuters to Dallas, historic homes, Jackrabbit Stampede bike race in September; **Grays Prairie** (337); **Kemp** (1,154); **Lawrence** (259); **Mabank** (3,035, partly in Henderson County) varied manufacturing, tourism, retail trade, Western Week in June; **Oak Grove** (603); **Oak Ridge** (495); **Post Oak Bend** (595); **Rosser** (332); **Scurry** (681); **Talty** (1,535).

For explanation of sources, abbreviations and symbols, see p. 232 and foldout map.

Population	103,350
Change fm 2000	44.92
Area (sq. mi.)	806.81
Land Area (sq. mi.)	786.04
Altitude (ft.)	300-611
Rainfall (in.)	38.90
Jan. mean min.	32.3
July mean max.	94.6
Civ. Labor	48,170
Unemployed	9.2
Wages	$245,169,195
Av. Weekly Wage	$714
Prop. Value	$8,302,016,074
Retail Sales	$1,114,744,474

Panna Maria in Karnes County, the oldest Polish community in the nation. Photo by Robert Plocheck.

Kendall County

Physical Features: Hill Country, plateau, with springfed streams; caves; scenic drives.

Economy: Government/services, agribusiness, commuters to San Antonio, tourism, retirement area, some manufacturing.

History: Lipan Apaches, Kiowas and Comanches in area when German settlers arrived in 1840s. County created from Blanco, Kerr counties 1862; named for pioneer journalist-sheepman and early contributor to Texas Almanac, George W. Kendall.

Race/Ethnicity, 2008: (In percent) Anglo, 80.9; Black, 0.2; Hispanic, 18.3; Other, 0.5.

Vital Statistics, 2008: Births, 357; deaths, 283; marriages, 400; divorces, 72.

Recreation: Hunting, fishing, exotic wildlife, state park; Cascade Cavern, Cave Without a Name; historic sites.

Minerals: Limestone rock, caliche.

Agriculture: Cattle, goats, sheep, hay. Market value $7.6 million. Cedar posts, firewood sold.

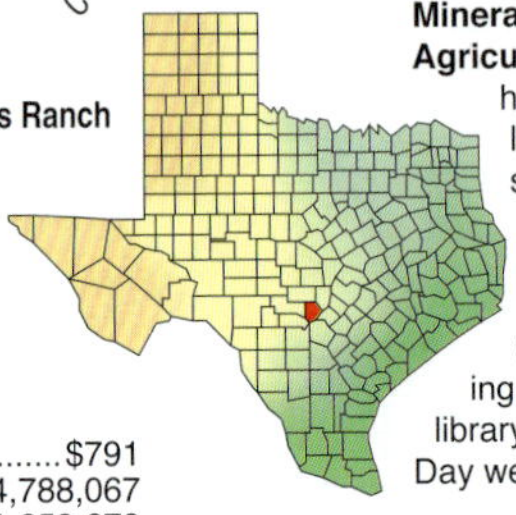

BOERNE (10,471) county seat; tourism, antiques, some manufacturing, ranching, commuting to San Antonio; library; Berges Fest on Father's Day weekend.

Other towns include: **Comfort** (2,363) tourism, ranching, Civil War monument honoring Unionists, library, mountain bike trail; **Kendalia** (149); **Sisterdale** (110); **Waring** (73). Part of **Fair Oaks Ranch** (5,986).

Population	33,410
Change fm 2000	40.72
Area (sq. mi.)	663.04
Land Area (sq. mi.)	662.44
Altitude (ft.)	1,000-2,080
Rainfall (in.)	37.36
Jan. mean min.	34.3
July mean max.	91.9
Civ. Labor	16,929
Unemployed	6.6
Wages	$110,156,371

Av. Weekly Wage	$791
Prop. Value	$6,414,788,067
Retail Sales	$851,659,670

For explanation of sources, abbreviations and symbols, see p. 232 and foldout map.

The Kenedy County Courthouse in Sarita. Photo by Robert Plocheck.

Kenedy County

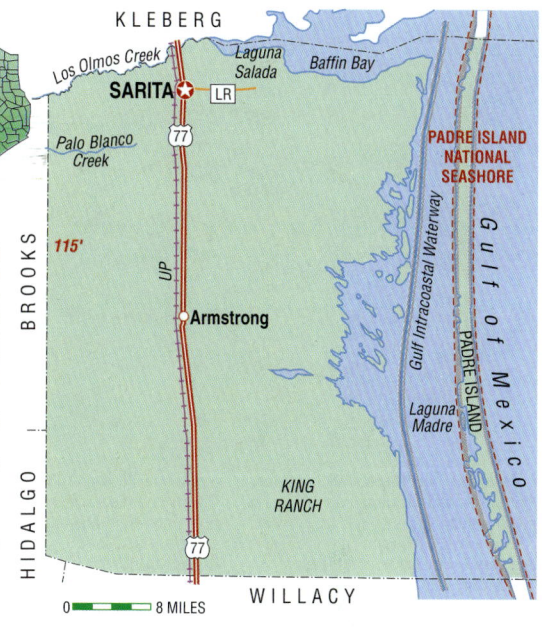

Physical Features: Gulf coastal county; flat, sandy terrain, some loam soils; motts of live oaks.

Economy: Oil, ranching, hunting leases, nature tourism.

History: Coahuiltecan Indians who assimilated or were driven out by Lipan Apaches. Spanish ranching began in the 1790s. Anglo-Americans arrived after the Mexican War. Among last counties created in 1921 from Cameron, Hidalgo, Willacy counties, organized the same year; named for pioneer steamboat operator and cattleman, Capt. Mifflin Kenedy.

Race/Ethnicity, 2008: (In percent) Anglo, 21.0; Black, 0.0; Hispanic, 78.5; Other, 0.5.

Vital Statistics, 2008: Births, 5; deaths, 6; marriages, 4; divorces, 0.

Recreation: Hunting, fishing, bird watching.

Minerals: Oil, gas.

Agriculture: Beef cattle. Market value $19 million. Hunting leases.

SARITA (238) county seat; cattle-shipping point, ranch headquarters, gas processing; one of state's least populous counties.

Also, **Armstrong** (4).

Population......................................416
Change fm 2000...........................0.48

Area (sq. mi.).........................1,945.60	Civ. Labor 231
Land Area (sq. mi.)...............1,456.77	Unemployed 4.3
Altitude (ft.) .... sea level-115	Wages $6,197,480
Rainfall (in.) 27.90	Av. Weekly Wage.....................$1,128
Jan. mean min. 45.0	Prop. Value $2,048,551,109
July mean max. 95.0	Retail Sales ....NA

Kent County

Physical Features: Rolling, broken terrain; lake; drains to Salt and Double Mountain forks of Brazos River; sandy, loam soils.

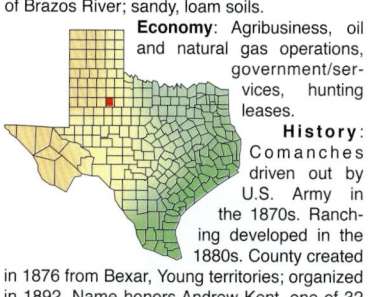

Economy: Agribusiness, oil and natural gas operations, government/services, hunting leases.

History: Comanches driven out by U.S. Army in the 1870s. Ranching developed in the 1880s. County created in 1876 from Bexar, Young territories; organized in 1892. Name honors Andrew Kent, one of 32 volunteers from Gonzales who died at the Alamo.

Race/Ethnicity, 2008: (In percent) Anglo, 90.8; Black, 0.2; Hispanic, 8.9; Other, 0.0.

Vital Statistics, 2008: Births, 6; deaths, 10; marriages, 4; divorces, 4.

Recreation: Hunting, fishing; scenic croton breaks and salt flat; Winterfest in December.

Minerals: Oil, gas.

Agriculture: Cattle, cotton, wheat, sorghum. Market value $6.8 million.

JAYTON (534) county seat; oil-field services, farming, ranching center; Summerfest in August.

Other towns include: **Girard** (50).

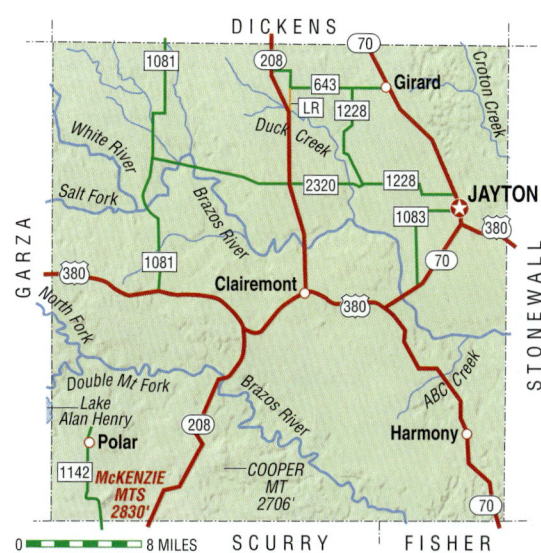

Population.............................808	Wages $2,204,536
Change fm 2000..................−5.94	Av. Weekly Wage.................$554
Area (sq. mi.).....................902.91	Prop. Value $964,763,720
Land Area (sq. mi.) 902.33	Retail Sales $12,354,985
Altitude (ft.) 1,740-2,830	
Rainfall (in.) 22.94	
Jan. mean min. 24.9	*For explanation of symbols,*
July mean max. 95.7	*sources and abbreviations, see*
Civ. Labor 428	*p. 232 and foldout map.*
Unemployed 6.3	

Kerr County

Physical Features: Picturesque, hills, spring-fed streams; dams, lakes on Guadalupe River.

Economy: Tourism, medical services, agribusiness, hunting leases.

History: Lipan Apaches, Kiowas and Comanches in area. Anglo-American settlers arrived in late 1840s. County created 1856 from Bexar County; named for member of Austin's Colony, James Kerr.

Race/Ethnicity, 2008: (In percent) Anglo, 75.3; Black, 1.7; Hispanic, 22.0; Other, 1.0.

Vital Statistics, 2008: Births, 588; deaths, 670; marriages, 352; divorces, 226.

Recreation: Youth camps, dude ranches, park, Cailloux and Point theaters, wildlife management area, Cowboy Artists Museum, Kerrville Folk Festival in May/June.

Minerals: none.

Agriculture: Cattle, hay, goats, horses; deer (first in numbers as livestock). Market value $13.4 million. Hunting leases important.

KERRVILLE (22,347) county seat; tourist center, youth camps, agribusiness, aircraft and parts, varied manufacturing; Schreiner University; state hospital, veterans hospital, private hospital; retirement center; retail trade; state arts, crafts show in May.

Other towns include: **Camp Verde** (41); **Center Point** (800); **Hunt** (708) youth camps, hospital; **Ingram** (1,804) camps, cabins; **Mountain Home** (96).

Population	**49,625**
Change fm 2000	13.68
Area (sq. mi.)	1,107.66
Land Area (sq. mi.)	1,106.12
Altitude (ft.)	1,400–2,420
Rainfall (in.)	32.60
Jan. mean min.	32.0
July mean max.	92.0
Civ. Labor	23,007
Unemployed	6.7
Wages	$161,037,112
Av. Weekly Wage	$717
Prop. Value	$5,794,007,230
Retail Sales	$719,039,955

For explanation of symbols, sources and abbreviations, see p. 232 and foldout map.

Tubing on the South Llano River near Junction, Kimble County. Photo by Ron Billings; Texas Forest Service.

Kimble County

Population	4,607
Change fm 2000	3.11
Area (sq. mi.)	1,250.92
Land Area (sq. mi.)	1,250.70
Altitude (ft.)	1,476-2,460
Rainfall (in.)	23.24
Jan. mean min.	29.3
July mean max.	94.8
Civ. Labor	1,958
Unemployed	8.0
Wages	$9,846,910
Av. Weekly Wage	$540
Prop. Value	$2,011,959,701
Retail Sales	$58,768,153

Physical Features: Picturesque Edwards Plateau; rugged, broken by numerous streams; drains to Llano River; sandy, gray, chocolate loam soils.

Economy: Livestock production and market, tourism, cedar oil and wood products, metal building materials.

History: Apache, Kiowas and Comanche stronghold until 1870s. Military outposts protected first Anglo-American settlers in 1850s. County created from Bexar County 1858; organized 1876. Named for George C. Kimble, a Gonzales volunteer who died at the Alamo.

Race/Ethnicity, 2008: (In percent) Anglo, 75.6; Black, 0.1; Hispanic, 23.4; Other, 0.9.

Vital Statistics, 2008: Births, 44; deaths, 57; marriages, 31; divorces, 20.

Recreation: Hunting, fishing in spring-fed streams; nature tourism; among leading deer counties; state park; Kimble Kounty Kow Kick on Labor Day, Wild Game dinner on Thanksgiving Saturday.

Minerals: gravel.

Agriculture: Cattle, meat goats, sheep, Angora goats, pecans. Market value $8.4 million. Hunting leases important. Firewood, cedar sold.

JUNCTION (2,574) county seat; tourism, varied manufacturing, livestock production; two museums; Texas Tech University center; hospital; library; airport.

Other towns include: **London** (180); **Roosevelt** (14).

King County

Physical Features: Hilly, broken by Wichita, Brazos tributaries; extensive grassland; dark loam to red soils.

Economy: Oil and gas, ranching, government/services, horse sales, hunting leases.

History: Apache area until Comanches moved in about 1700. Comanches removed by U.S. Army in 1874–1875 after which ranching began. County created in 1876 from Bexar District; organized in 1891; named for William P. King, a volunteer from Gonzales who died at the Alamo.

Race/Ethnicity, 2008: (In percent) Anglo, 90.0; Black, 0.0; Hispanic, 9.1; Other, 0.8.

Vital Statistics, 2008: Births, 0; deaths, 1; marriages, 2; divorces, 0.

Recreation: 6666 Ranch visits, hunting, roping and ranch horse competitions.

Minerals: Oil, gas.

Agriculture: Cattle, horses, wheat, hay, cotton. Market value $17.9 million. Hunting leases important.

GUTHRIE (160) county seat; ranch-supply center, government/services; community center complex, library; Thanksgiving community supper.

Population	286
Change fm 2000	−19.66
Area (sq. mi.)	913.33
Land Area (sq. mi.)	912.29
Altitude (ft.)	1,450-2,250
Rainfall (in.)	25.00
Jan. mean min.	23.9
July mean max.	96.7
Civ. Labor	180
Unemployed	7.2
Wages	$1,434,999
Av. Weekly Wage	$968
Prop. Value	$666,129,940
Retail Sales	NA

For explanation of symbols, sources and abbreviations, see p. 232 and foldout map.

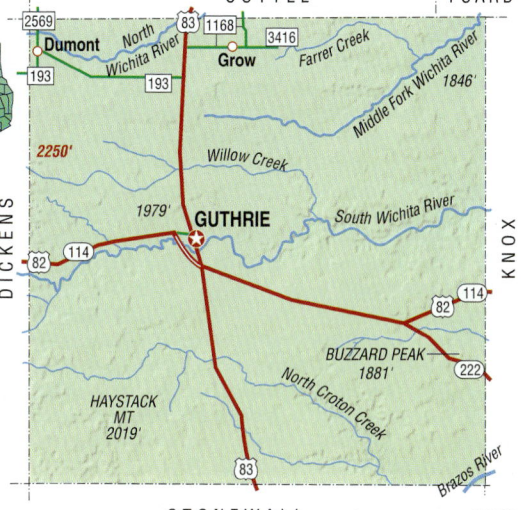

Kinney County

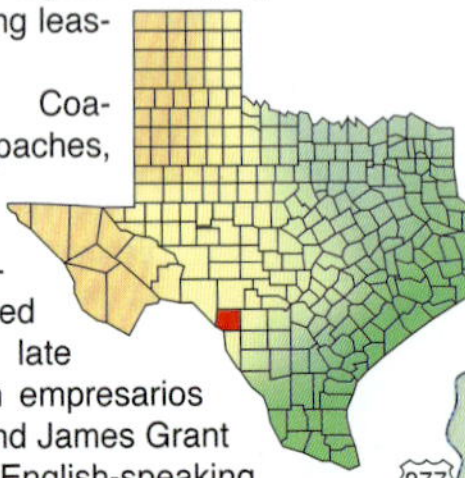

Physical Features: Hilly, broken by Rio Grande tributaries; Anacacho Mountains; Nueces Canyon.

Economy: Agribusiness, government/services, hunting leases.

History: Coahuiltecans, Apaches, Comanches in area. Spanish Franciscans established settlement in late 1700s. English empresarios John Beales and James Grant established English-speaking colony in 1834. Black Seminoles served as army scouts in 1870s. County created from Bexar County 1850; organized 1874; named for H.L. Kinney, founder of Corpus Christi.

Race/Ethnicity, 2008: (In percent) Anglo, 43.4; Black, 1.4; Hispanic, 54.9; Other, 0.3.

Vital Statistics, 2008: Births, 37; deaths, 39; marriages, 17; divorces, 2.

Recreation: Hunting; old Fort Clark Springs; state park; Cinco de Mayo, Juneteenth.

Minerals: Not significant.

Agriculture: Cattle, goats, hay, grain sorghum, cotton, corn, oats, wheat. Market value $6.4 million.

BRACKETTVILLE (1,688) county seat; agriculture, tourism; museum.

Other towns include: **Fort Clark Springs** (1,228); **Spofford** (95).

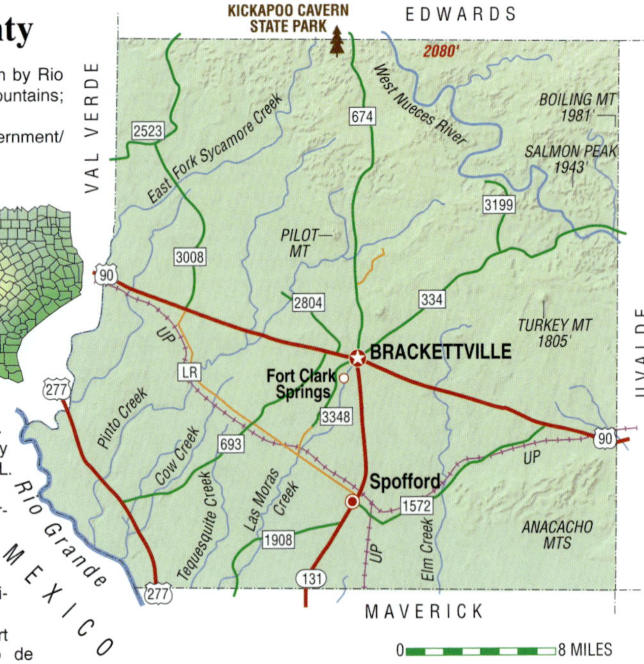

Population	3,598
Change fm 2000	6.48
Area (sq. mi.)	1,365.31
Land Area (sq. mi.)	1,363.44
Altitude (ft.)	790-2,080
Rainfall (in.)	22.79
Jan. mean min.	37.3
July mean max.	95.5
Civ. Labor	1,483

Unemployed	9.5
Wages	$7,848,174
Av. Weekly Wage	$779
Prop. Value	$1,195,614,650
Retail Sales	$10,421,354

For explanation of sources, symbols and abbreviations, see p. 232 and foldout map.

The community of Vattmann, Kleberg County. Photo by Robert Plocheck.

Physical Features: Coastal plain, broken by bays; sandy, loam, clay soils; tree motts.

Economy: Oil and gas, Naval air station, chemicals and plastics, agriculture, Texas A&M University-Kingsville.

History: Coahuiltecan and Karankawa area. Spanish land grants date to 1750s. In 1853 Richard King purchased Santa Gertrudis land grant. County created, organized, 1913 from Nueces County; named for San Jacinto veteran and rancher Robert Kleberg.

Race/Ethnicity, 2008: (In percent) Anglo, 26.2; Black, 3.9; Hispanic, 67.6; Other, 2.3.

Kleberg County

Vital Statistics, 2008: Births, 511; deaths, 195; marriages, 245; divorces, 114.

Recreation: Fishing, hunting, water sports, park Baffin Bay; wildlife sanctuary; winter bird watching; university events, museum; King Ranch headquarters, tours; La Posada celebration in November.

Minerals: Oil, gas, uranium.

Agriculture: Cotton, beef cattle, grain sorghum. Market value $65 million. Hunting leases/eco-tourism.

KINGSVILLE (26,213) county seat; government/services, oil, gas, agribusiness, tourism, chemical plant, university, Coastal Bend College branch; hospital; ranching heritage festival in February. King Ranch Breakfast in November.

Other towns include: **Riviera** (689).

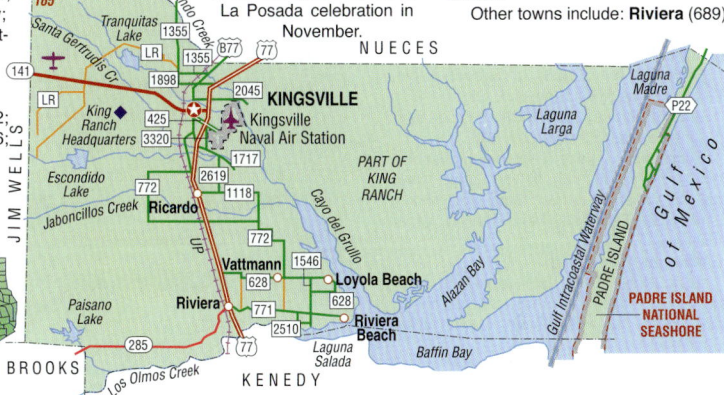

Population		32,061
Change fm 2000		1.62
Area (sq. mi.)		1,090.29
Land Area (sq. mi.)		870.97

Altitude (ft.)		sea level-165
Rainfall (in.)		29.03
Jan. mean min.		43.4
July mean max.		95.5
Civ. Labor		17,201

Unemployed		7.5
Wages		$115,983,415
Av. Weekly Wage		$708
Prop. Value		$2,051,022,655
Retail Sales		$445,501,722

Knox County

Physical Features: Eroded breaks on West Texas Rolling Plains; Brazos, Wichita rivers; sandy, loam soils.

Economy: Oil, agriculture, government/services.

History: Indian conscripts used during Spanish period to mine copper deposits along the Brazos. Ranching, farming developed in 1880s. German colony settled in 1895. County created from Bexar, Young territories 1858; re-created 1876; organized 1886; named for U.S. Secretary of War Henry Knox.

Race/Ethnicity, 2008: (In percent) Anglo, 62.4; Black, 7.9; Hispanic, 29.0; Other, 0.7.

Vital Statistics, 2008: Births, 53; deaths, 57; marriages, 0; divorces, 6.

Recreation: Lake activities, fishing, hunting; Knox City seedless watermelon festival in July.

Minerals: Oil, gas.

Agriculture: Wheat, cattle, cotton. Some cotton irrigated. Market value $38.4 million.

BENJAMIN (258) county seat; ranching, farm center; veterans memorial.

MUNDAY (1,300) portable buildings, other manufacturing; A&M vegetable research station.

KNOX CITY (1,130) agribusiness, petroleum center; USDA plant materials research center; hospital.

Other towns include: **Goree** (203); **Rhineland** (120) old church established by German immigrants.

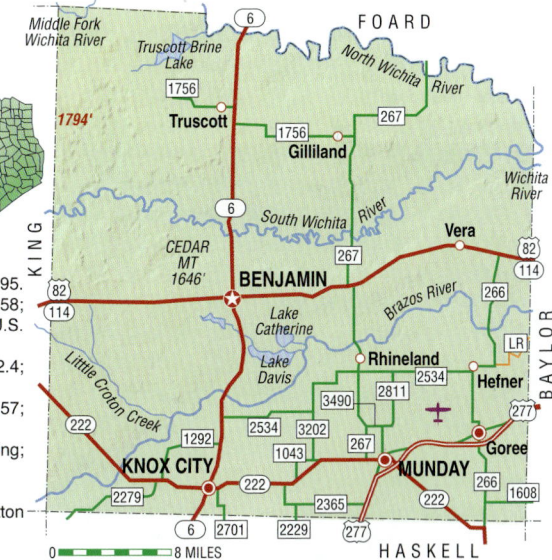

Population		3,719
Change fm 2000		−12.56
Area (sq. mi.)		855.43
Land Area (sq. mi.)		849.00
Altitude (ft.)		1,200-1,794
Rainfall (in.)		26.36
Jan. mean min.		28.1
July mean max.		96.5
Civ. Labor		1,767

Unemployed		5.9
Wages		$12,521,930
Av. Weekly Wage		$735
Prop. Value		$420,116,898
Retail Sales		$27,479,658

For explanation of sources, symbols and abbreviations, see p. 232 and foldout map.

Lamar County

Physical Features: North Texas county on divide between Red, Sulphur rivers; soils chiefly blackland, except along Red; pines, hardwoods.

Economy: Varied manufacturing, agribusiness, medical, government/services.

History: Caddo Indian area. First Anglo-American settlers arrived about 1815. County created 1840 from Red River County; organized 1841; named for second president of Republic, Mirabeau B. Lamar.

Race/Ethnicity, 2008: (In percent) Anglo, 79.5; Black, 14.5; Hispanic, 4.1; Other, 1.9.

Vital Statistics, 2008: Births, 673; deaths, 612; marriages, 421; divorces, 308.

Recreation: Lake activities; Gambill goose refuge; hunting, fishing; state park; Trail de Paris rail-to-trail; Sam Bell Maxey Home; State Sen. A.M. Aikin Archives, other museums.

Minerals: Negligible.

Agriculture: Beef, hay (second in acreage), dairy, soybeans (second in acreage), wheat, corn, sorghum, cotton. Market value $60.4 million.

PARIS (25,171) county seat; varied manufacturing, food processing, government/services; hospitals; junior college; museums; Tour de Paris bicycle rally in July; archery pro-am tournament in March.

Other towns include: **Arthur City** (180), **Blossom** (1,494), **Brookston** (130), **Chicota** (150), **Cunningham** (110), **Deport** (578, partly in Red River County), **Pattonville** (180), **Petty** (130), **Powderly** (1,178), **Reno** (3,166), **Roxton** (650), **Sumner** (95), **Sun Valley** (69), **Toco** (75).

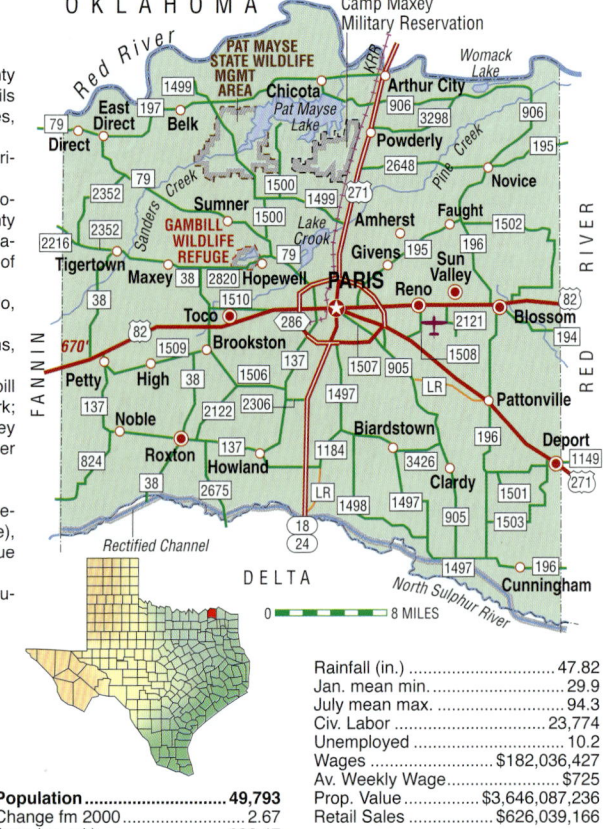

Population 49,793
Change fm 2000 .... 2.67
Area (sq. mi.) 932.47
Land Area (sq. mi.) 916.81
Altitude (ft.) 335-670

Rainfall (in.) 47.82
Jan. mean min. 29.9
July mean max. 94.3
Civ. Labor 23,774
Unemployed 10.2
Wages $182,036,427
Av. Weekly Wage....................... $725
Prop. Value $3,646,087,236
Retail Sales $626,039,166

For explanation of sources, symbols and abbreviations, see p. 232 and foldout map.

Autumn in Roxton, Lamar County. Photo by Robert Plocheck.

Lamb County

Physical Features: Rich, red, brown soils on the High Plains; some hills; drains to upper Brazos River tributaries; numerous playas.

Economy: Agribusiness; distribution center; denim textiles.

History: Apaches, displaced by Comanches around 1700. U.S. Army pushed Comanches into Indian Territory in 1875. Ranching began in 1880s; farming after 1900. County created 1876 from Bexar District; organized 1908; named for Lt. G.A. Lamb, who died in battle of San Jacinto.

Race/Ethnicity, 2008: (In percent) Anglo, 45.4; Black, 4.5; Hispanic, 49.6; Other, 0.5.

Vital Statistics, 2008: Births, 250; deaths, 159; marriages, 72; divorces, 32.

Recreation: Waylon Jennings Birthday Bash in June at Littlefield, museums, Earth Day in April.

Minerals: Oil, stone, gas.

Agriculture: Fed cattle; cotton, corn, wheat, grain sorghum, vegetables, soybeans, hay; sheep. 385,000 acres irrigated. Market value $406.3 million.

LITTLEFIELD (6,372) county seat; textile mill, agribusiness, manufacturing; hospital, prison.

Olton (2,215) agribusiness, retail center; Sandcrawl museum; pheasant hunt in winter; Sandhills Celebration in August.

Other towns include: **Amherst** (721); **Earth** (1,065) farming center, dairies, feed lot, supplies; **Fieldton** (20); **Spade** (73); **Springlake** (108); **Sudan** (958) farming center, government/services, Homecoming Day in fall.

Population 13,977
Change fm 2000 .... –4.98
Area (sq. mi.) 1,017.73

Land Area (sq. mi.) 1,016.21
Altitude (ft.) 3,390-3,870
Rainfall (in.) 18.69
Jan. mean min. 22.7
July mean max. 92.0
Civ. Labor 6,841
Unemployed 7.6
Wages $38,591,088
Av. Weekly Wage $634
Prop. Value $1,027,764,031
Retail Sales $84,727,891

Lampasas County

Physical Features: Central Texas on edge of Hill Country; Colorado, Lampasas rivers; cedars, oaks, pecans.

Economy: Many employed at Fort Hood, several industrial plants, agribusinesses, tourism.

History: Mineral springs attracted first Anglo-Americans in 1853. Frontier confrontations between settlers, Comanches continued into 1870s. County created, organized, 1856 from Bell, Travis counties. Named for river. Some have speculated that an early expedition named river for city of Lampazos in Mexico.

Race/Ethnicity, 2008: (In percent) Anglo, 78.9; Black, 3.0; Hispanic, 16.8; Other, 1.3.

Vital Statistics, 2008: Births, 267; deaths, 225; marriages, 151; divorces, 104.

Recreation: Scenic drives; state park; deer hunting, fishing in streams; Hancock Springs free-flow swim area at Lampasas.

Minerals: Sand and gravel, stone.

Agriculture: Beef cattle, hay, goats, exotic animals. Market value $14 million. Hunting leases, ecotourism.

LAMPASAS (6,681) county seat; commuters to Ft. Hood, industrial plants, agriculture, tourism; historic downtown; hospital; college extensions; museum; Spring Ho in July.

Other towns include: **Bend** (115, partly in San Saba County); **Izoro** (17); **Kempner** (1,089); **Lometa** (856) market and shipping point; Diamondback Jubilee in March.

Population 19,677
Change fm 2000 .... 10.78
Area (sq. mi.) 713.96
Land Area (sq. mi.) 712.04
Altitude (ft.) 800-1,669
Rainfall (in.) 31.08
Jan. mean min. 30.4
July mean max. 94.1
Civ. Labor 10,943
Unemployed 7.2
Wages $37,208,576
Av. Weekly Wage $612
Prop. Value $1,989,069,380
Retail Sales $167,513,727

For explanation of sources, symbols and abbreviations, see p. 232 and foldout map.

La Salle County

Physical Features: Brushy plain, broken by Nueces, Frio rivers and their tributaries; chocolate, dark gray, sandy loam soils.

Economy: Agribusiness, hunting leases, tourism, government services.

History: Coahuiltecans, squeezed out by migrating Apaches. U.S. military outpost in 1850s; settlers of Mexican descent established nearby village. Anglo-American ranching developed in 1870s. County created from Bexar District 1858; organized 1880; named for Robert Cavelier Sieur de La Salle, French explorer who died in Texas.

Race/Ethnicity, 2008: (In percent) Anglo, 16.5; Black, 2.9; Hispanic, 80.2; Other, 0.4.

Vital Statistics, 2008: Births, 100; deaths, 44; marriages, 14; divorces, 1.

Recreation: Nature trails; school where Lyndon B. Johnson taught; wildlife management area; deer, bird, javelina hunting, fishing; wild hog cookoff in March.

Minerals: Oil, gas.

Agriculture: Beef cattle, peanuts, watermelons, grain sorghum. Market value $31 million.

COTULLA (3,603) county seat; livestock, state prison; hunting center; Brush Country museum; Cinco de Mayo celebration.

Other towns include: **Encinal** (559), **Fowlerton** (55).

Population	6,886
Change fm 2000	17.39
Area (sq. mi.)	1,494.23
Land Area (sq. mi.)	1,488.85
Altitude (ft.)	255-650
Rainfall (in.)	22.56
Jan. mean min.	39.1
July mean max.	98.9
Civ. Labor	3,159
Unemployed	7.9
Wages	$24,810,665
Av. Weekly Wage	$979
Prop. Value	$1,441,215,026
Retail Sales	$94,490,255

Lavaca County

Physical Features: Coastal Plains county; north rolling; sandy loam, black waxy soils; drains to Lavaca, Navidad rivers.

Economy: Varied manufacturing, oil and gas production, agribusinesses, tourism.

History: Coahuiltecan area; later Comanches until 1850s. Anglo-Americans first settled in 1831. Germans and Czechs arrived 1880-1900. County created 1846 from Colorado, Jackson, Gonzales, Victoria counties. Name is Spanish word for cow, la vaca, from name of river.

Race/Ethnicity, 2008: (In percent) Anglo, 77.9; Black, 7.6; Hispanic, 14.1; Other, 0.5.

Vital Statistics, 2008: Births, 234; deaths, 233; marriages, 105; divorces, 30.

Recreation: Deer, other hunting, fishing; wildflower trails, historic sites, churches; Hallettsville fiddlers frolics in April.

Minerals: Some oil, gas.

Agriculture: Cattle, forage, poultry, rice, corn, sorghum. Market value $58.9 million. Hunting leases.

HALLETTSVILLE (2,550) county seat; retail center; varied manufacturing; agribusiness; museum; library, hospital; domino, "42" tournaments; Kolache Fest in September.

Yoakum (5,815, partly in DeWitt County); cattle, leather, meat processing; hospital; museum; Tom Tom festival in June.

Shiner (2,069) Spoetzl brewery, varied manufacturing; museum; clinic; Half Moon Holidays in July.

Other towns include: **Moulton** (886) agribusiness, Town & Country Jamboree in July; **Sublime** (75); **Sweet Home** (360).

For explanation of sources, symbols and abbreviations, see p. 232 and foldout map.

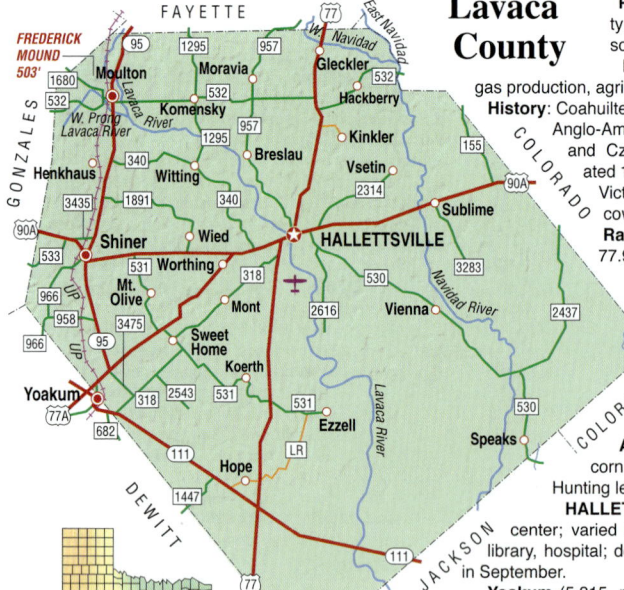

Population	19,263
Change fm 2000	0.28
Area (sq. mi.)	970.35
Land Area (sq. mi.)	969.90
Altitude (ft.)	85-503
Rainfall (in.)	42.23
Jan. mean min.	41.8
July mean max.	94.4
Civ. Labor	9,861
Unemployed	6.6
Wages	$50,118,797
Av. Weekly Wage	$642
Prop. Value	$2,959,872,935
Retail Sales	$210,991,031

Lee County

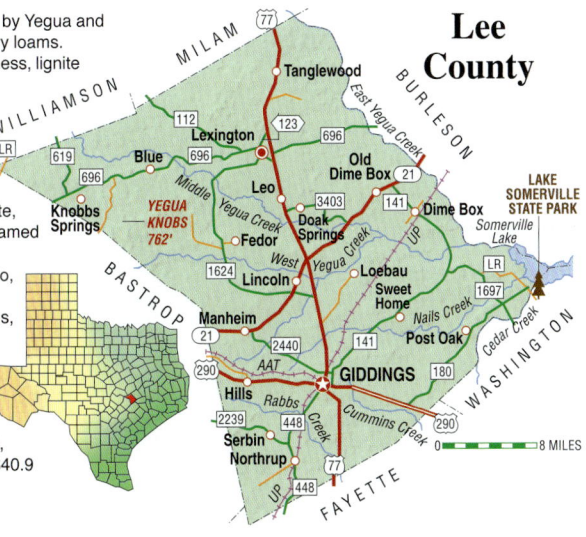

Physical Features: Rolling terrain, broken by Yegua and its tributaries; red to black soils, sandy to heavy loams.

Economy: Varied manufacturing, agribusiness, lignite coal operations, government/services.

History: Tonkawas; removed in 1855 to Brazos Reservation. Most Anglo-American settlement occurred after Texas Revolution. Slaveholding area. Germans, Wends, other Europeans began arriving in 1850s. County created from Bastrop, Burleson, Fayette, Washington counties and organized in 1874; named for Confederate Gen. Robert E. Lee.

Race/Ethnicity, 2008: (In percent) Anglo, 64.0; Black, 11.6; Hispanic, 23.7; Other, 0.6.

Vital Statistics, 2008: Births, 215; deaths, 174; marriages, 102; divorces, 49.

Recreation: Fishing, hunting; state park; pioneer village; historic sites.

Minerals: Lignite coal, iron ore, gravel.

Agriculture: Beef cattle, hay, nurseries, poultry, peanuts, goats, horses, aquaculture, corn; 25,000 acres irrigated. Market value $40.9 million. Firewood.

GIDDINGS (4,881) county seat; agriculture, government/services, oil-field operations, light manufacturing, hospital; Charcoal Challenge barbecue cookoff in May.

Other towns include: **Dime Box** (381); **Lexington** (1,177) livestock-marketing center, log cabins heritage center, Chocolate Lovers festival in October; **Lincoln** (336); **Serbin** (109) Wendish museum.

Population	16,612
Change fm 2000	6.1
Area (sq. mi.)	634.03
Land Area (sq. mi.)	628.50
Altitude (ft.)	238-762
Rainfall (in.)	36.02
Jan. mean min.	37.3
July mean max.	93.6
Civ. Labor	9,295
Unemployed	6.6
Wages	$64,440,090
Av. Weekly Wage	$854
Prop. Value	$2,532,590,438
Retail Sales	$283,382,634

Leon County

Physical Features: Hilly, rolling, almost half covered by timber; drains to Navasota, Trinity rivers and tributaries; sandy, dark, alluvial soils.

Economy: Oil, gas, agribusiness.

History: Bidais band, absorbed into Kickapoos and other groups. Permanent settlement by Anglo-Americans occurred after Texas Revolution; Germans arrived in the 1870s. County created, organized, 1846 from Robertson County; named for founder of Victoria, Martín de León.

Race/Ethnicity, 2008: (In percent) Anglo, 79.8; Black, 10.0; Hispanic, 9.6; Other, 0.6.

Vital Statistics, 2008: Births, 203; deaths, 198; marriages, 101; divorces, 55.

Recreation: Hilltop Lakes resort area; sites of Camino Real, Fort Boggy State Park; deer hunting.

Minerals: Oil, gas, lignite coal.

Agriculture: Cow-calf production, hogs, poultry. Hay, watermelons, vegetables, small grains. Christmas trees. Market value $85.8 million. Hardwoods, pine marketed.

CENTERVILLE (892) county seat; farm center, hunting, tourism, oil, natural gas; timber.

BUFFALO (1,856) coal mining, oil and natural gas; library; May Spring Fest with fiddlers' contest.

Other towns include: **Concord** (28); **Flynn** (81); **Hilltop Lakes** (1,101) resort, retirement center; **Jewett** (1,167) electricity-generating plant, steel mill, strip mining, civic center, museum, library, Classic Coon Hunt in January.

Also, **Leona** (175) candle factory; **Marquez** (263); **Normangee** (685, partly in Madison County) farming, tourism; library, museum, city park; **Oakwood** (510).

Population	16,801
Change fm 2000	9.56
Area (sq. mi.)	1,080.38
Land Area (sq. mi.)	1,072.04
Altitude (ft.)	150-630
Rainfall (in.)	43.08
Jan. mean min.	34.3
July mean max.	94.7
Civ. Labor	8,206
Unemployed	8.0
Wages	$55,552,470
Av. Weekly Wage	$803
Prop. Value	$3,423,187,430
Retail Sales	$169,708,007

For explanation of sources, symbols and abbreviations, see p. 232 and foldout map.

Liberty County

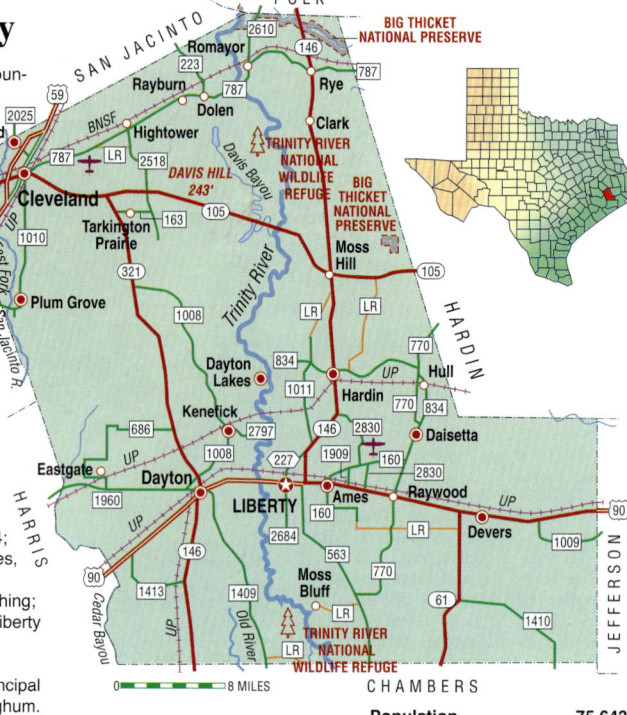

Physical Features: Coastal Plain county east of Houston; 60 percent in pine, hardwood timber; bisected by Trinity River; sandy, loam, black soils; Big Thicket.

Economy: Agribusiness; chemical plants; varied manufacturing; tourism; forest industries; prisons; many residents work in Houston; part of Houston metropolitan area.

History: Karankawa area until 1740s. Spanish established Atascosito settlement in 1756. Settlers from Louisiana began arriving in 1810s. County named for Spanish municipality, Libertad; created 1836, organized 1837.

Race/Ethnicity, 2008: (In percent) Anglo, 70.7; Black, 12.8; Hispanic, 15.5; Other, 1.0.

Vital Statistics, 2008: Births, 1,084; deaths, 707; marriages, 656; divorces, 215.

Recreation: Big Thicket; hunting, fishing; historic sites; Trinity Valley exposition; Liberty Opry.

Minerals: Oil, gas.

Agriculture: Beef cattle; rice is principal crop. Also nursery crops, corn, hay, sorghum. Market value $25.1 million. Some lumbering.

LIBERTY (8,397) county seat; petroleum-related industry, agribusiness; library, museum, regional historical resource depository; Liberty Bell; hospital; Jubilee in March.

Cleveland (7,675) forest products processed, shipped; tourism; library; museum; hospital.

Dayton (7,242) rice, oil center.

Other towns include: **Ames** (1,003);

Daisetta (966); **Dayton Lakes** (93); **Devers** (447); **Hardin** (819); **Hull** (800); **Kenefick** (563); **North Cleveland** (247); **Plum Grove** (600); **Raywood** (231); **Romayor** (135); **Rye** (150).

County adopted:
In honor of
John Price Daniel

Population	75,643
Change fm 2000	7.82
Area (sq. mi.)	1,176.22
Land Area (sq. mi.)	1,159.68
Altitude (ft.)	3-243
Rainfall (in.)	60.52
Jan. mean min.	40.3
July mean max.	92.2
Civ. Labor	32,394
Unemployed	11.9
Wages	$153,397,234
Av. Weekly Wage	$720
Prop. Value	$4,969,615,584
Retail Sales	$1,305,919,213

The business district of Lipscomb, county seat of Lipscomb County. Photo by Robert Plocheck.

Limestone County

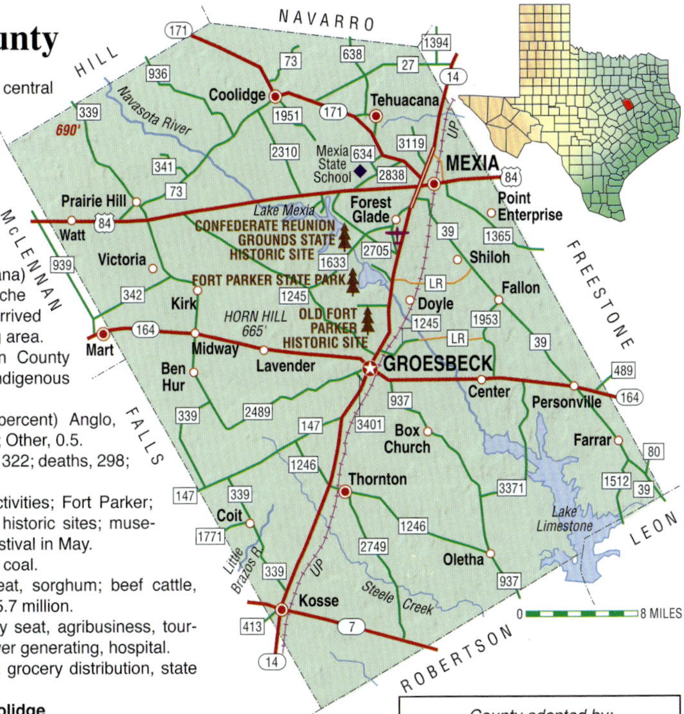

Physical Features: East central county on divide between Brazos and Trinity rivers; borders Blacklands, level to rolling; drained by Navasota and tributaries.

Economy: Government/services, electricity-generating plant.

History: Tawakoni (Tehuacana) and Waco area, later Comanche raiders. First Anglo-Americans arrived in 1833. Antebellum slaveholding area. County created from Robertson County and organized 1846; named for indigenous rock.

Race/Ethnicity, 2008: (In percent) Anglo, 62.4; Black, 19.3; Hispanic, 17.8; Other, 0.5.

Vital Statistics, 2008: Births, 322; deaths, 298; marriages, 179; divorces, 37.

Recreation: Fishing, lake activities; Fort Parker; Confederate Reunion Grounds; historic sites; museum; hunting; Groesbeck fiddle festival in May.

Minerals: Natural gas, lignite coal.

Agriculture: Hay, corn, wheat, sorghum; beef cattle, horses, poultry. Market value $45.7 million.

GROESBECK (4,328) county seat, agribusiness, tourism, hunting, mining, prison, power generating, hospital.

MEXIA (7,459) agribusiness, grocery distribution, state school, hospital.

Other towns include: **Coolidge** (955), **Kosse** (464), **Prairie Hill** (150), **Tehuacana** (283), **Thornton** (526).

Population	**23,384**
Change fm 2000	6.05
Area (sq. mi.)	933.15
Land Area (sq. mi.)	908.88

Altitude (ft.)	363-690
Rainfall (in.)	41.40
Jan. mean min.	33.7
July mean max.	95.8
Civ. Labor	11,961
Unemployed	7.1
Wages	$66,064,850

Av. Weekly Wage	$581
Prop. Value	$2,996,507,448
Retail Sales	$253,832,326

Lipscomb County

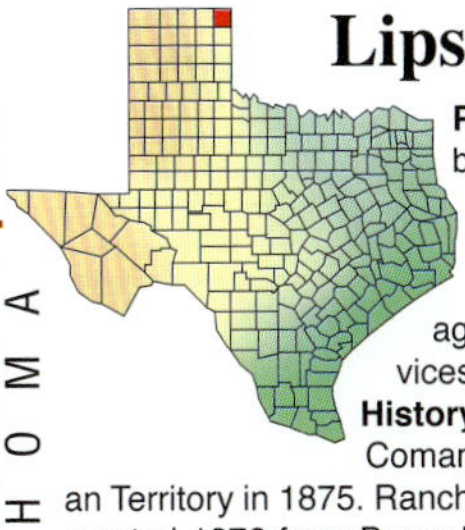

Physical Features: High Plains, broken in east; drains to tributaries of Canadian, Wolf Creek; sandy loam, black soils.

Economy: Oil, gas operations, agribusinesses, government/services.

History: Apaches, later Kiowas and Comanches who were driven into Indian Territory in 1875. Ranching began in late 1870s. County created 1876 from Bexar District; organized 1887; named for A.S. Lipscomb, Republic of Texas leader.

Race/Ethnicity, 2008: (In percent) Anglo, 73.6; Black, 0.5; Hispanic, 24.4; Other, 1.5.

Vital Statistics, 2008: Births, 46; deaths, 32; marriages, 37; divorces, 7.

Recreation: Hunting; Wolf Creek museum; prairie chicken booming grounds..

Minerals: Oil, natural gas.

Agriculture: Cattle, corn, wheat, grain sorghum, hay, sunflowers. Some 25,000 acres irrigated. Market value $80.5 million.

LIPSCOMB (37), county seat; livestock center.

BOOKER (1,516, partly in Ochiltree County) trade center, library.

Other towns include: **Darrouzett** (350) Deutsches Fest in July; **Follett** (459); **Higgins** (397) library, Will Rogers Day in August.

Population	**3,302**
Change fm 2000	8.01
Area (sq. mi.)	932.22
Land Area (sq. mi.)	932.11
Altitude (ft.)	2,220-2,892
Rainfall (in.)	22.57
Jan. mean min.	16.2

July mean max.	94.2
Civ. Labor	1,606
Unemployed	5.3
Wages	$11,909,712
Av. Weekly Wage	$763
Prop. Value	$1,260,845,766
Retail Sales	$27,868,333

Live Oak County

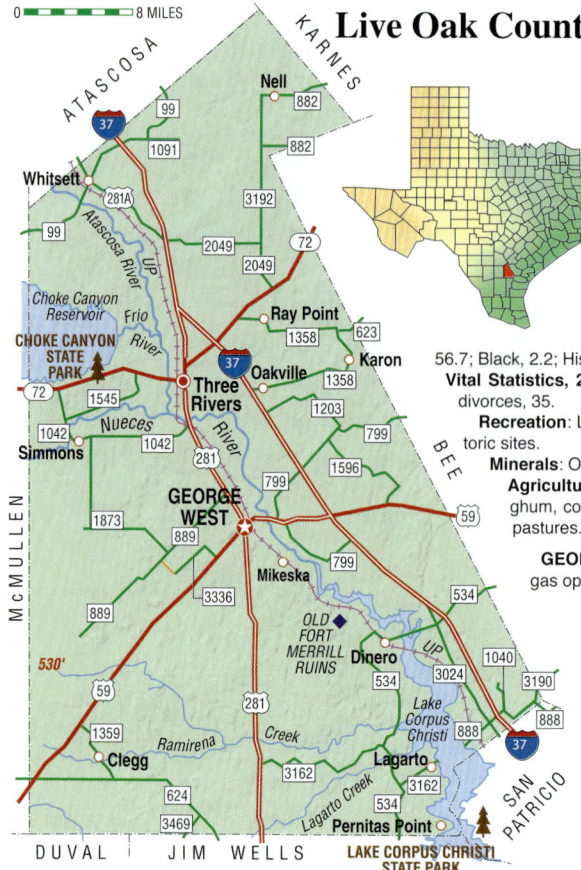

Physical Features: Brushy plains between San Antonio and Corpus Christi, partly broken by Nueces River and its tributaries; black waxy, gray sandy, other soils.

Economy: Oil, government/services, tourism, agribusinesses.

History: Coahuiltecans squeezed out by Lipan Apaches and Spanish. Spanish ranching started in the 1810s. Settlers from Ireland arrived in 1835. County named for predominant tree; created in 1856 from Nueces, San Patricio counties, organized the same year.

Race/Ethnicity, 2008: (In percent) Anglo, 56.7; Black, 2.2; Hispanic, 40.6; Other, 0.4.

Vital Statistics, 2008: Births, 117; deaths, 116; marriages, 59; divorces, 35.

Recreation: Lakes; water activities; state park; hunting; historic sites.

Minerals: Oil, gas, sand, gravel.

Agriculture: Cow-calf operations; hogs; corn, grain sorghum, cotton; some irrigation for hay, coastal Bermuda pastures. Market value $21 million.

GEORGE WEST (2,445) county seat, oil and natural gas operations, museum, Storyfest in November.

Three Rivers (1,848) agribusinesses, refinery, federal prison, tourism, salsa festival in April.

Other towns include: **Dinero** (344); **Lagarto** (735), **Pernitas Point** (274, partly in Jim Wells County), **Whitsett** (200).

Altitude (ft.)	94–530
Rainfall (in.)	22.00
Jan. mean min.	42.0
July mean max.	97.0
Civ. Labor	5,276
Unemployed	6.6
Wages	$31,745,719
Av. Weekly Wage	$769
Prop. Value	$2,006,078,490
Retail Sales	$114,990,613

For explanation of sources, symbols and abbreviations, see p. 232 and foldout map.

Population	11,531
Change fm 2000	–6.32
Area (sq. mi.)	1,078.83
Land Area (sq. mi.)	1,036.30

The Loving County Courthouse in Mentone. Photo by Robert Plocheck.

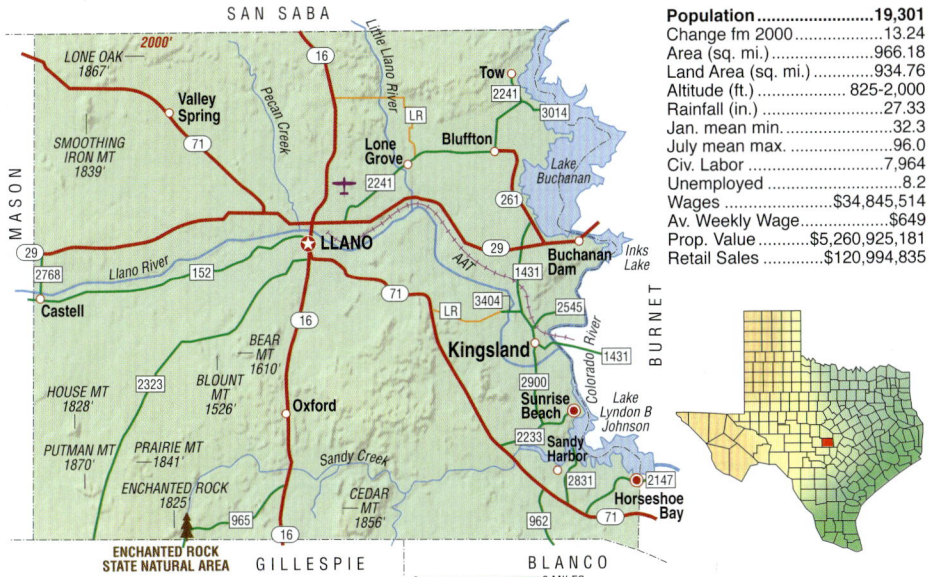

Population 19,301
Change fm 2000 .... 13.24
Area (sq. mi.) 966.18
Land Area (sq. mi.) 934.76
Altitude (ft.) 825-2,000
Rainfall (in.) 27.33
Jan. mean min. 32.3
July mean max. 96.0
Civ. Labor 7,964
Unemployed 8.2
Wages $34,845,514
Av. Weekly Wage $649
Prop. Value $5,260,925,181
Retail Sales $120,994,835

Llano County

Physical Features: Central county drains to Colorado, Llano rivers; rolling to hilly; Highland lakes.

Economy: Tourism, retirement center, ranch trading center, vineyards.

History: Tonkawa tribes, later Comanches. Anglo-American and German settlers arrived in the 1840s. County name is Spanish for plains; created in 1856 from Bexar District and Gillespie County, organized the same year.

Race/Ethnicity, 2008: (In percent) Anglo, 93.0; Black, 0.3; Hispanic, 5.9; Other, 0.8.

Vital Statistics, 2008: Births, 159; deaths, 283; marriages, 118; divorces, 70.

Recreation: Leading deer-hunting county; fishing, lake activities, major tourist area, Enchanted Rock, eagles' nest along Highway 29, bluebonnet festival, Hill Country Wine Trail in spring.

Minerals: Granite, vermiculite, llanite.

Agriculture: Beef cattle, sheep, goats. Market value $11.8 million. Deer-hunting, wildlife leases.

LLANO (3,232) county seat; agriculture, hunting, tourism; hospital; historic district; museum; Texas gold panning championship in September.

Kingsland (6,030) tourism, retirement community, recreaton, vineyards; library; archaeological center; AquaBoom on July 4.

Other towns include: **Bluffton** (75); **Buchanan Dam** (1,519) hydroelectric industry, tourism, fishing, water sports; **Castell** (72); **Horseshoe Bay** (3,418, partly in Burnet County); **Sunrise Beach** (713); **Tow** (305); **Valley Spring** (50).

Loving County

Physical Features: Flat desert terrain with a few low-rolling hills; slopes to Pecos River; Red Bluff Reservoir; sandy, loam, clay soils.

Economy: Petroleum operations; cattle.

History: Land developers began operations in late 19th century. Oil discovered in 1925. County created in 1887 from Tom Green County; organized in 1931, the last county organized. Named for Oliver Loving, trail driver. Loving is Texas' least populous county.

Race/Ethnicity, 2008: (In percent) Anglo, 87.9; Black, 0.0; Hispanic, 12.1; Other, 0.0.

Vital Statistics, 2008: Births, 0; deaths, 1; marriages, 3; divorces, 0.

Recreation: NA.

Minerals: Oil, gas.

Agriculture: Some cattle. Market value not available.

MENTONE (19) county seat, oil-field supply center; only town.

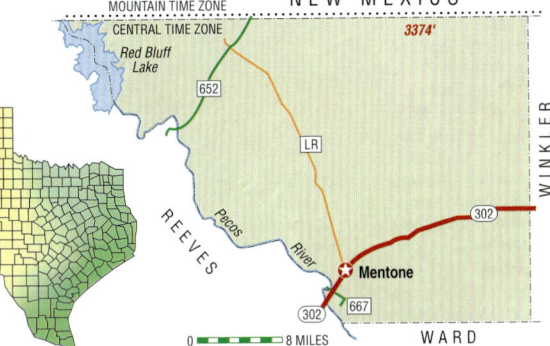

Population 82
Change fm 2000 .... 22.39
Area (sq. mi.) 676.85
Land Area (sq. mi.) 673.08
Altitude (ft.) 2,660-3,374
Rainfall (in.) 9.10
Jan. mean min. 28.0
July mean max. 96.0
Civ. Labor 52
Unemployed 7.7
Wages $503,346
Av. Weekly Wage $671
Prop. Value $788,736,320
Retail Sales .... NA

For explanation of sources, symbols and abbreviations, see p. 232 and foldout map.

Lubbock County

Physical Features: South Plains, broken by 1,500 playas, upper Brazos River tributaries; rich soils with underground water.

Economy: Among world's largest cottonseed processing centers, a leading agribusiness center, cattle feedlots, varied manufacturing, higher education center, medical center, government/services.

History: Evidence of human habitation for 12,000 years. In historic period, Apache Indians, followed by Comanche hunters. Sheep raisers from Midwest arrived in late 1870s. Cotton farms brought in Mexican laborers in 1940s-60s. County named for Col. Tom S. Lubbock, an organizer of Confederate Terry's Rangers; county created 1876 from Bexar District; organized 1891.

Race/Ethnicity, 2008: (In percent) Anglo, 57.2; Black, 8.0; Hispanic, 32.4; Other, 2.4.

Vital Statistics, 2008: Births, 4,331; deaths, 2,157; marriages, 2,085; divorces, 1,098.

Recreation: Lubbock Lake archaeological site; Texas Tech events; civic center; Buddy Holly statue, Walk of Fame, festival in September; planetarium; Ranching Heritage Center; Panhandle-South Plains Fair; wine festivals; Buffalo Springs Lake.

Minerals: Oil, gas, stone, sand and gravel.

Agriculture: The leading cotton-producing county. Fed beef, cow-calf operations; poultry, eggs; hogs. Other crops, nursery, grain sorghum, wheat, sunflowers, soybeans, hay, vegetables; more than 230,000 acres irrigated, mostly cotton. Market value $209 million.

Education: Texas Tech University with law and medical schools; Lubbock Christian University; South Plains College branch; Wayland Baptist University off-campus center.

LUBBOCK (229,573) county seat; center for large agricultural area; manufacturing includes electronics, earth-moving equipment, food containers, fire-protection equipment, clothing, other products; distribution center for South Plains; feedlots; museum; government/services; hospitals, psychiatric hospital; state school for retarded; wind power center.

Other towns include: **Buffalo Springs** (453); **Idalou** (2,250); **New Deal** (794); **Ransom Canyon** (1,096); **Shallowater** (2,484); **Slaton** (6,121) agribusiness, government/services, varied manufacturing, railroad, Harvey House museum, sausagefest in October; **Wolfforth** (3,670) retail, government/services.

Also, part of **Abernathy** (2,805).

Population	278,831
Change fm 2000	14.92
Area (sq. mi.)	900.70
Land Area (sq. mi.)	899.49
Altitude (ft.)	2,821-3,402
Rainfall (in.)	18.69
Jan. mean min.	24.4
July mean max.	91.9
Civ. Labor	143,851
Unemployed	6.3
Wages	$1,209,470,389
Av. Weekly Wage	$745
Prop. Value	$15,329,188,575
Retail Sales	$4,285,067,067

For explanation of sources, abbreviations and symbols, see p. 232 and foldout map.

Lynn County

Physical Features: South Plains, broken by Caprock Escarpment, playas, draws; sandy loam, black, gray soils.

Economy: Agribusiness.

History: Apaches, ousted by Comanches who were removed to Indian Territory in 1875. Ranching began in the 1880s. Farming developed after 1900. County created in 1876 from Bexar District; organized in 1903; named for Alamo victim W. Lynn.

Race/Ethnicity, 2008: (In percent) Anglo, 47.8; Black, 2.8; Hispanic, 48.7; Other, 0.7.

Vital Statistics, 2008: Births, 95; deaths, 52; marriages, 32; divorces, 8.

Recreation: Pioneer museum in Tahoka; Dan Blocker museum in O'Donnell; sandhill crane migration in winter.

Minerals: Oil, natural gas.

Agriculture: Cotton produces largest income (second in acreage); 77,000 acres irrigated. Also, ranching, grain sorghum. Market value $98.9 million.

TAHOKA (2,673) county seat; agricultural center, electric and telephone cooperatives; hospital; museum; Harvest Festival in the fall.

O'Donnell (831, partly in Dawson County) commercial center, bust of Dan Blocker.

Other towns include: **New Home** (334); **Wilson** (489).

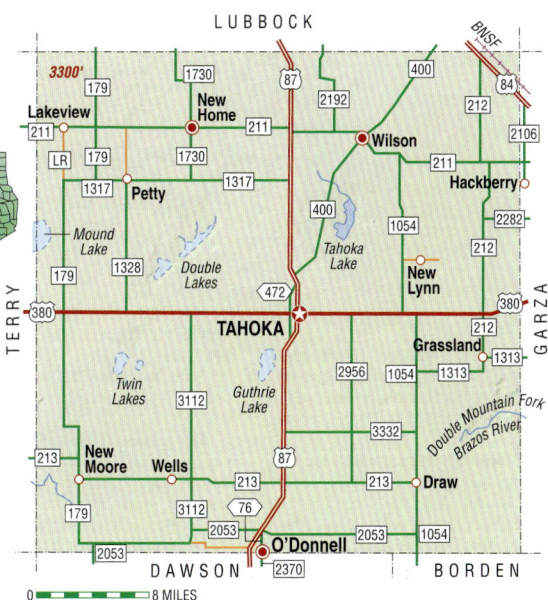

Population **5,915**	July mean max. 92.2
Change fm 2000 ....–9.70	Civ. Labor 2,769
Area (sq. mi.) 893.46	Unemployed 7.0
Land Area (sq. mi.) 891.88	Wages $12,535,764
Altitude (ft.) 2,660-3,300	Av. Weekly Wage................$611
Rainfall (in.) 20.48	Prop. Value $531,147,130
Jan. mean min. 25.1	Retail Sales $18,391,611

Madison County

Physical Features: Hilly, draining to Trinity, Navasota rivers, Bedias Creek; one-fifth of area timbered; alluvial, loam, sandy soils.

Economy: Prison, government/services, varied manufacturing, agribusiness, oil production.

History: Caddo, Bidai Indian area; Kickapoos migrated from east. Spanish settlements established in 1774 and 1805. Anglo-Americans arrived in 1829. Census of 1860 showed 30 percent of population was black. County named for U.S. President James Madison; created from Grimes, Leon, Walker counties 1853; organized 1854.

Race/Ethnicity, 2008: (In percent) Anglo, 60.3; Black, 21.6; Hispanic, 17.4; Other, 0.7.

Vital Statistics, 2008: Births, 172; deaths, 136; marriages, 128; divorces, 43.

Recreation: Fishing, hunting; Spanish Bluff where survivors of the Gutíerrez-Magee expedition were executed in 1813; other historic sites.

Minerals: sand, oil.

Agriculture: Nursery crops, cattle, horses, poultry raised; forage for livestock. Market value $83.3 million.

MADISONVILLE (4,396) county seat; farm-trade center, varied manufacturing; hospital, library; Spring Fling in April.

Other towns, **Midway** (288); **Normangee** (685, mostly in Leon County); **North Zulch** (600).

Population **13,664**	
Change fm 2000 ....5.6	
Area (sq. mi.) 472.44	
Land Area (sq. mi.) 469.65	
Altitude (ft.) 131-420	
Rainfall (in.) 44.00	
Jan. mean min. 35.8	
July mean max. 96.0	
Civ. Labor 5,601	
Unemployed 8.3	
Wages $33,792,388	
Av. Weekly Wage.......................$613	
Prop. Value $1,358,781,614	
Retail Sales $195,350,044	

County adopted by:
"True Texan"
Tony Madison

Marion County

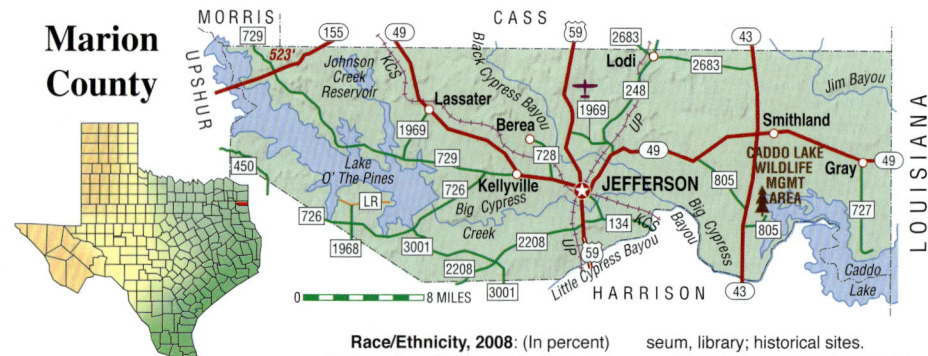

Physical Features: Northeastern county; hilly, three-quarters forested with pines, hardwoods; drains to Caddo Lake, Lake O' the Pines, Cypress Bayou.

Economy: Agriculture, tourism, forestry, food processing.

History: Caddoes forced out in 1790s. Kickapoo in area when settlers arrived from Deep South around 1840. Antebellum slaveholding area. County created 1860 from Cass County, organized the same year; named for Gen. Francis Marion of American Revolution.

Race/Ethnicity, 2008: (In percent) Anglo, 73.5; Black, 23.1; Hispanic, 2.4; Other, 1.0.

Vital Statistics, 2008: Births, 124; deaths, 147; marriages, 85; divorces, 64.

Recreation: Lake activities, hunting, Excelsior Hotel, 84 medallions on historic sites including Jay Gould railroad car, museum, historical homes tour in May, Spring Festival.

Minerals: Iron ore, natural gas, oil.

Agriculture: Beef cattle, hay. Market value $4.2 million. Forestry is most important industry.

JEFFERSON (2,106) county seat; tourism, syrup works, forestry; museum, library; historical sites.

Other towns include: **Lodi** (175).

Population	10,546
Change fm 2000	–3.61
Area (sq. mi.)	420.36
Land Area (sq. mi.)	381.21
Altitude (ft.)	168-523
Rainfall (in.)	49.26
Jan. mean min.	31.4
July mean max.	93.1
Civ. Labor	5,051
Unemployed	9.9
Wages	$13,835,997
Av. Weekly Wage	$561
Prop. Value	$954,194,810
Retail Sales	$67,677,155

Martin County

Physical Features: South Plains; sandy, loam soils, broken by playas, creeks.

Economy: Oil and natural gas production, agribusiness.

History: Apaches, ousted by Comanches who in turn were forced out by U.S. Army in 1875. Farming began in 1881. County created from Bexar District in 1876; organized in 1884; named for Wylie Martin, senator of Republic of Texas.

Race/Ethnicity, 2008: (In percent) Anglo, 54.0; Black, 1.7; Hispanic, 44.0; Other, 0.3.

Vital Statistics, 2008: Births, 94; deaths, 42; marriages, 43; divorces, 19.

Recreation: Museum, settlers reunion in July.

Minerals: Oil, gas.

Agriculture: Cotton, beef cattle, milo, wheat, horses, meat goats. Market value $52.9 million.

STANTON (2,492) county seat; farm, ranch, oil center; varied manufacturing; electric co-op; communting to Midland, Big Spring; hospital; restored monastery, other historic buildings; Old Sorehead trade days April, June, October.

Other towns include: **Ackerly** (220, partly in Dawson County); **Lenorah** (83); **Tarzan** (30). A small part of **Midland**.

Population	4,799
Change fm 2000	1.12
Area (sq. mi.)	915.62
Land Area (sq. mi.)	914.78
Altitude (ft.)	2,470-2,976
Rainfall (in.)	18.20
Jan. mean min.	30.0
July mean max.	94.0
Civ. Labor	2,257
Unemployed	5.8
Wages	$15,497,989
Av. Weekly Wage	$808
Prop. Value	$1,927,627,456
Retail Sales	$61,932,977

For explanation of sources, symbols and abbreviations, see p. 232 and foldout map.

Mason County

Physical Features: Central county; hilly, draining to Llano and San Saba rivers and their tributaries; limestone, red soils; varied timber.

Economy: Sand plants, tourism, hunting.

History: Lipan Apaches, driven south by Comanches around 1790. German settlers arrived in mid-1840s, followed by Anglo-Americans. Mexican immigration increased after 1930. County created from Bexar, Gillespie counties in 1858, organized the same year; named for Mexican War victim U.S. Army Lt. G.T. Mason.

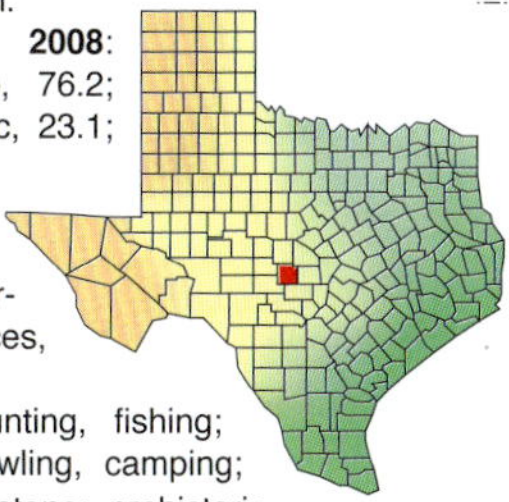

Race/Ethnicity, 2008: (In percent) Anglo, 76.2; Black, 0.1; Hispanic, 23.1; Other, 0.6.

Vital Statistics, 2008: Births, 31; deaths, 49; marriages, 27; divorces, 22.

Recreation: Hunting, fishing; kayaking, rock crawling, camping; historic homes of stone; prehistoric Indian artifacts exhibit; Fort Mason, where Robert E. Lee served; bat cave; wildflower drives in spring, Mason Apple Fest in September.

Minerals: Sand, topaz, granite.

Agriculture: Hay, cattle, grapes, meat goats, sheep. Market value $48 million. Hunting leases important.

MASON (2,114) county seat; agriculture, hunting, nature tourism; museums, historical district, homes, rock fences built by German settlers; wild game dinner in November.

Other towns include: **Art** (14), **Fredonia** (55), **Pontotoc** (125).

Population	4,012
Change fm 2000	7.33
Area (sq. mi.)	932.18
Land Area (sq. mi.)	932.07
Altitude (ft.)	1,180-2,217
Rainfall (in.)	27.95
Jan. mean min.	30.8
July mean max.	94.9
Civ. Labor	2,341
Unemployed	5.4
Wages	$7,840,361
Av. Weekly Wage	$551
Prop. Value	$1,423,253,020
Retail Sales	$23,937,161

For explanation of sources, symbols and abbreviations, see p. 232 and foldout map.

![Bluebonnets surround the church in Art, Mason County. Photo by Joe Michael Feist.]

Bluebonnets surround the church in Art, Mason County. Photo by Joe Michael Feist.

Matagorda County

Population	36,702
Change fm 2000	–3.31
Area (sq. mi.)	1,612.19
Land Area (sq. mi.)	1,114.46
Altitude (ft.)	sea level-70
Rainfall (in.)	48.03
Jan. mean min.	45.7
July mean max.	92.4
Civ. Labor	18,124
Unemployed	12.5
Wages	$120,554,209
Av. Weekly Wage	$861
Prop. Value	$5,423,834,676
Retail Sales	$309,592,968

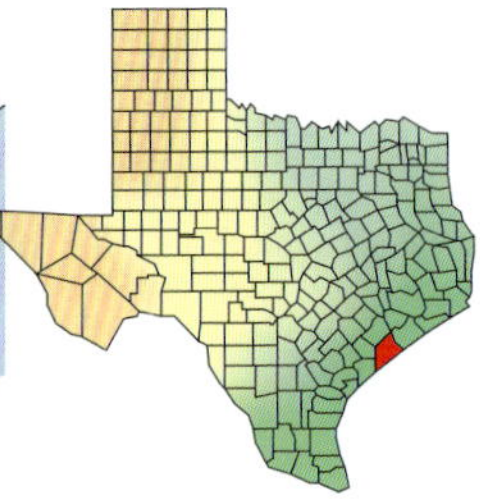

Map locations and labels: WHARTON, BRAZORIA, Pledger, 1301, 60, BNSF, 1728, Sugar Valley, Linnville Bayou, 70', 3156, 35, Van Vleck, UP, 1162, Clemville, 2540, Cedar Lane, 521, 3086, 1468, 2175, BAY CITY, 457, Cedar, Lake Creek, 2611, 71, Markham, 2431, Midfield, 111, 458, 71, 456, UP, 2668, Live Oak Bayou, Cedar Lake, Blessing, 459, Elmaton, 3057, 521, Sargent, 616, 35, 2853, 1486, 2078, Wadsworth, Lake Austin, Caney Creek, 457, 1862, 521, 521, 521, Chinquapin, 1095, South Texas Project Reservoir, 60, Matagorda, San Bernard National Wildlife Refuge, 35, Collegeport, Matagorda, East Matagorda Bay, 3280, Palacios, 2031, Big Boggy National Wildlife Refuge, Gulf Intracoastal Waterway, Palacios Channel, Matagorda Bay, MATAGORDA PENINSULA, Tres Palacios Bay, Port Lavaca Ship Channel, Gulf of Mexico, JACKSON, CALHOUN, Tres Palacios R., Colorado River, 0　8 MILES

Physical Features: Gulf Coastal Plain; flat, broken by bays; many different soils; drains to Colorado River, creeks, coast.

Economy: Nuclear power plant, petrochemicals, agribusiness.

History: Karankawa Indian area, Tonkawas arrived later. Anglo-Americans arrived in 1822. Mexican immigration increased after 1920. An original county, created in 1836 from Spanish municipality, named for canebrake; organized in 1837; settled by Austin colonists.

Race/Ethnicity, 2008: (In percent) Anglo, 47.6; Black, 12.3; Hispanic, 36.5; Other, 3.6.

Vital Statistics, 2008: Births, 547; deaths, 334; marriages, 285; divorces, 147.

Recreation: Fishing, water sports, hunting, birding; historic sites, museums; Bay City rice festival in October.

Minerals: Oil and gas.

Agriculture: Cattle, rice (third in acreage), cotton, sorghum, soybeans; 24,000 acres irrigated for rice. Market value $106.8 million. First in value of aquaculture.

BAY CITY (17,614) county seat; nuclear power plant; petrochemicals; agribusiness; hospital, junior college branch.

Palacios (4,718) tourism, seafood industry; hospital; Marine Education Center; public fishing piers; Bay Festival on Labor Day.

Other towns include: **Blessing** (927) historic sites; **Cedar Lane** (300); **Collegeport** (80); **Elmaton** (160); **Markham** (1,082); **Matagorda** (503), early Texas town, first Episcopal church in state.

Also, **Midfield** (305); **Pledger** (265); **Sargent** (900) retirement and recreation community, fishing, birding, commercial fishing, barbecue cookoff in April; **Van Vleck** (1,844); **Wadsworth** (160).

For explanation of sources, symbols and abbreviations, see p. 232 and foldout map.

Fishing the old channel of the Colorado River on the Matagorda Peninsula. Photo by Robert Plocheck.

Maverick County

Physical Features: Southwestern county on Rio Grande; broken, rolling surface, with dense brush; clay, sandy, alluvial soils.

Economy: Oil, government/services, agribusiness, tourism.

History: Coahuiltecan Indian area; later Comanches in area. Spanish ranching began in 1760s. First Anglo-Americans arrived in 1834. County named for Sam A. Maverick, whose name is now a synonym for unbranded cattle; created 1856 from Kinney County; organized 1871.

Race/Ethnicity, 2008: (In percent) Anglo, 3.0; Black, 0.1; Hispanic, 95.5; Other, 1.4.

Vital Statistics, 2008: Births, 1,033; deaths, 327; marriages, 494; divorces, 41.

Recreation: Tourist gateway to Mexico; white-tailed deer, bird hunting; fishing; historic sites, Fort Duncan museum.

Minerals: Oil, gas, sand, gravel.

Agriculture: Cattle feedlots; pecans, vegetables, sorghum, wheat; goats, sheep. Some irrigation from Rio Grande. Market value $26.1 million.

EAGLE PASS (26,248) county seat; government/services, retail center, tourism; hospital; junior college, Sul Ross college branch; entry point to Piedras Negras, Mex., Nacho Festival in Piedras Negras in October.

Other communities include: **Chula Vista** (3,818), **Eidson Road** (8,960), **El Indio** (190), **Las Quintas Fronterizas** (3,290), **Rosita** (2,704), all immediately south of Eagle Pass.

Also, **Elm Creek** (2,469) and **Quemado** (230).

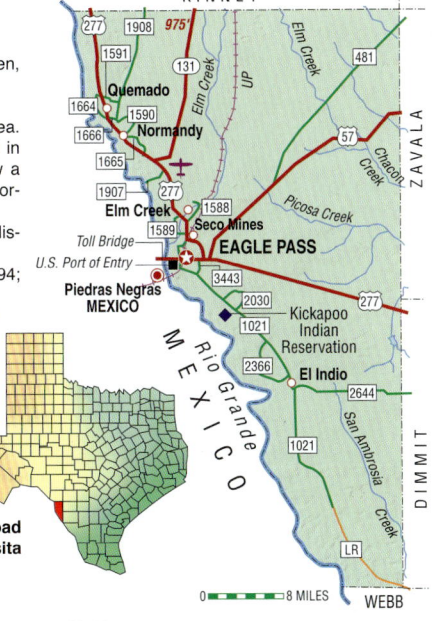

Population	54,258	Rainfall (in.)	21.48	Wages	$123,501,523
Change fm 2000	14.72	Jan. mean min.	40.1	Av. Weekly Wage	$573
Area (sq. mi.)	1,291.74	July mean max.	98.1	Prop. Value	$3,113,013,147
Land Area (sq. mi.)	1,280.08	Civ. Labor	23,976	Retail Sales	$616,291,503
Altitude (ft.)	550-975	Unemployed	17.6		

McCulloch County

Physical Features: Hilly and rolling; drains to Colorado, Brady Creek and Lake, San Saba River; black loams to sandy soils.

Economy: Agribusiness, manufacturing, tourism, hunting leases.

History: Apache area. First Anglo-American settlers arrived in late 1850s, but Comanche raids delayed further settlement until 1870s. County created from Bexar District 1856; organized 1876; named for San Jacinto veteran Gen. Ben McCulloch.

Race/Ethnicity, 2008: (In percent) Anglo, 68.7; Black, 1.6; Hispanic, 29.2; Other, 0.5.

Vital Statistics, 2008: Births, 104; deaths, 99; marriages, 53; divorces, 33.

Recreation: Hunting; lake activities; museum, restored Santa Fe depot, goat cookoff on Labor Day, muzzle-loading rifle association state championship; rodeos; golf, tennis tournaments.

Minerals: Sand, gravel, gas and oil.

Agriculture: Beef cattle provide most income; wheat, sheep, goats, hay, cotton, sorghum, hogs, dairy cattle; some irrigation for peanuts. Market value $18.1 million.

BRADY (5,528) county seat; silica sand, oil-field equipment, ranching, tourism, other manufacturing; hospital; Heart of Texas car show in April, Cinco de Mayo.

Other towns: **Doole** (74), **Lohn** (149), **Melvin** (178), **Mercury** (166), **Rochelle** (163) and **Voca** (56).

For explanation of sources, symbols and abbreviations, see p. 232 and foldout map.

Population	8,283	July mean max.	94.5	
Change fm 2000	0.95	Civ. Labor	3,906	
Area (sq. mi.)	1,073.35	Unemployed	6.8	
Land Area (sq. mi.)	1,069.31	Wages	$28,096,585	
Altitude (ft.)	1,280-2,021	Av. Weekly Wage	$697	
Rainfall (in.)	27.63	Prop. Value	$1,466,898,450	
Jan. mean min.	32.3	Retail Sales	$93,755,915	

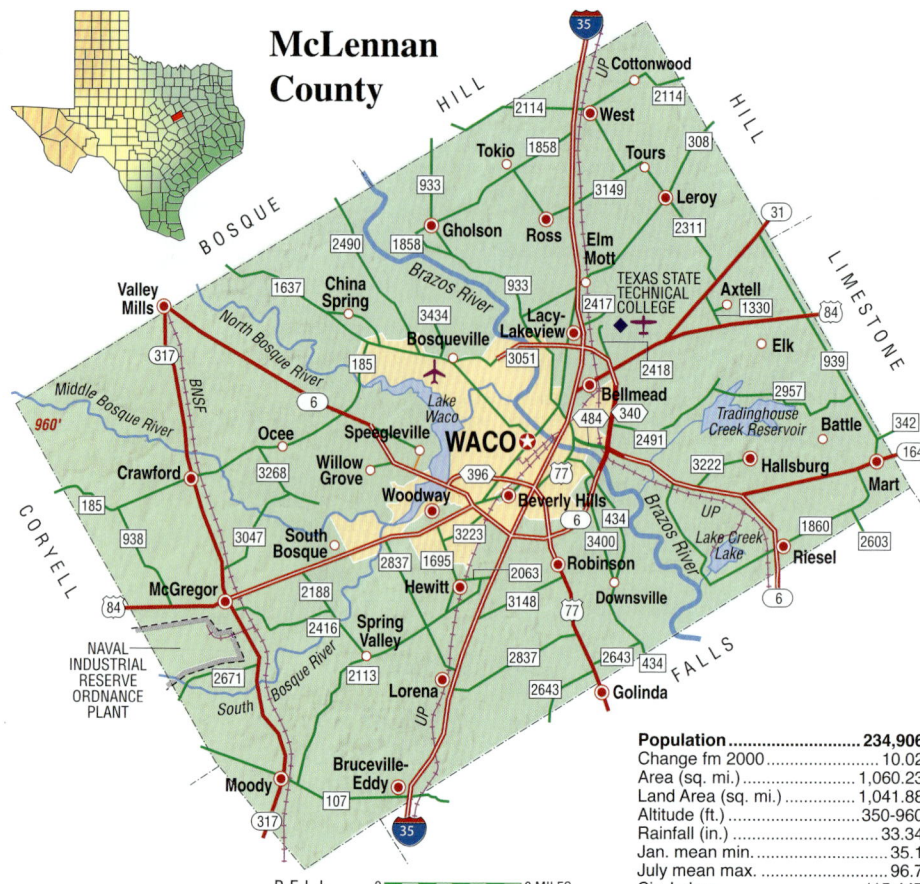

McLennan County

Population **234,906**
Change fm 2000 .... 10.02
Area (sq. mi.) 1,060.23
Land Area (sq. mi.) 1,041.88
Altitude (ft.) 350-960
Rainfall (in.) 33.34
Jan. mean min. 35.1
July mean max. 96.7
Civ. Labor 115,447
Unemployed 7.7
Wages $1,029,849,325
Av. Weekly Wage........................ $791
Prop. Value $13,748,019,080
Retail Sales $3,184,734,405

Physical Features: Central Texas county of mostly Blackland prairie, but rolling hills in west; drains to Bosque, Brazos rivers and Lake Waco; heavy, loam, sandy soils.

Economy: A leading distribution, government center for Central Texas; diversified manufacturing; education; aerospace; health care; banking, insurance headquarters.

History: Tonkawas, Wichitas and Wacos in area. Anglo-American settlers arrived in 1840s. Indians removed to Brazos reservations in 1854. County created from Milam County in 1850; named for settler, Neil McLennan Sr.

Race/Ethnicity, 2008: (In percent) Anglo, 57.5; Black, 15.5; Hispanic, 25.0; Other, 2.0.

Vital Statistics, 2008: Births, 3,503; deaths, 2,057; marriages, 1,869; divorces, 940.

Recreation: Texas Ranger Hall of Fame; Texas Sports Hall of Fame; Dr Pepper Museum; Cameron Park; drag boat races April and May; zoo; historic sites, homes; museums; li-

braries, art center; symphony; civic theater; Baylor University events; Heart o' Texas Fair in October.

Minerals: Sand and gravel.

Agriculture: Beef cattle, corn, wheat, hay, oats, sorghum, soybeans, turkeys, dairy cattle. Market value $104.7 million.

Education: Baylor University; community college; Texas State Technical College.

WACO (124,805) county seat; higher education, government/services, varied manufacturing; hospitals; riverside park, zoo.

Hewitt (13,549) iron works, other manufacturing; hamburger cookoff in September.

West (2,807) famous for Czech foods; varied manufacturing; Westfest Labor Day weekend.

Other towns include: **Axtell** (300); **Bellmead** (9,901); **Beverly Hills** (1,995); **Bruceville-Eddy** (1,475, partly in Falls County); **China Spring** (1,281); **Crawford**

(717); **Elm Mott** (300); **Gholson** (1,061); **Hallsburg** (507); **Lacy-Lakeview** (6,489); **Leroy** (337); **Lorena** (1,691); **Mart** (2,209) agricultural center, some manufacturing, museum, juvenile correction facility; **McGregor** (4,987) agriculture, manufacturing, distribution; private telephone museum; Frontier Founders Day in September; **Moody** (1,371) agriculture, commuting to Waco, Temple; library; Cotton Harvest fest in September; **Riesel** (1,007); **Robinson** (10,509); **Ross** (283); **Woodway** (8,452).

Part of **Golinda** (559, mostly in Falls County) and part of **Valley Mills** (1,203, mostly in Bosque County).

County adopted by:
**Watson Caufield and
Mary Maxwell Arnold**

McMullen County

Physical Features: Southern county of brushy plain, sloping to Frio, Nueces rivers and tributaries; saline clay soils.

Economy: Government/services, retail, agriculture, oil and gas services.

History: Coahuiltecans, squeezed out by Lipan Apaches and other tribes. Anglo-American settlers arrived in 1858. Sheep ranching of 1870s attracted Mexican laborers. County created from Atascosa, Bexar, Live Oak counties 1858; organized 1862, reorganized 1877; named for Nueces River pioneer-empresario John McMullen.

Race/Ethnicity, 2008: (In percent) Anglo, 64.8; Black, 0.8; Hispanic, 34.0; Other, 0.3.

Vital Statistics, 2008: Births, 9; deaths, 8; marriages, 5; divorces, 0.

Recreation: Hunting, wildlife viewing; lake activities, state park; Labor Day rodeo.

Minerals: Gas, oil, lignite, caliche, kaolinite.

Agriculture: Beef cattle. Market value $8.8 million. Wildlife enterprises important.

TILDEN (261), county seat; oil, gas, lignite mining, ranch center, government/services. Other towns include: **Calliham** (100).

Population 707	Jan. mean min. 40.1	Wages $2,869,201
Change fm 2000 .... –16.92	July mean max. 98.7	Av. Weekly Wage $724
Area (sq. mi.) 1,142.60	Civ. Labor 369	Prop. Value $1,372,365,859
Land Area (sq. mi.) 1,113.00	Unemployed 6.8	Retail Sales $8,548,466
Altitude (ft.) 150-642		
Rainfall (in.) 23.87		

Medina County

Physical Features: Southwestern county with scenic hills in north; south has fertile valleys, rolling surface; Medina River, Lake.

Economy: Agribusiness, tourism, commuters to San Antonio.

History: Lipan Apaches and Comanches. Settled by Alsatians led by Henri Castro in 1844. Mexican immigration increased after 1900. County created and organized in 1848 from Bexar; named for river, probably for Spanish engineer Pedro Medina.

Race/Ethnicity, 2008: (In percent) Anglo, 50.0; Black, 1.7; Hispanic, 47.5; Other, 0.8.

Vital Statistics, 2008: Births, 597; deaths, 403; marriages, 245; divorces, 109.

Recreation: A leading deer area; scenic drives, camping, fishing, historic buildings, museum, market trail days most months.

Minerals: Oil and gas.

Agriculture: Cattle, corn, cotton, sorghum, wheat, vegetables, hay; 40,000 acres irrigated. Market value $80.9 million.

HONDO (8,803) county seat; flight training center, aerospace industry, agribusiness, varied manufacturing, hunting leases; hospital; prisons; wild game festival in January.

Castroville (2,680) farming; tourism; commuting to San Antonio; Landmark Inn, museum; St. Louis Day celebration in August.

Devine (4,350) commuters, shipping for truck crop-livestock; fall festival in October.

Other towns: **D'Hanis** (847), **La Coste** (1,119), **Natalia** (1,431), **Riomedina** (60), **Yancey** (209). Also, **Lytle** (2,492, mostly in Atascosa County).

Population 46,006	Unemployed 8.2	
Change fm 2000 .... 17.05	Wages $60,355,700	
Area (sq. mi.) 1,334.53	Av. Weekly Wage $568	
Land Area (sq. mi.) 1,327.76	Prop. Value $3,959,401,364	
Altitude (ft.) 570-1,995	Retail Sales $305,843,929	
Rainfall (in.) 26.30		
Jan. mean min. 38.0	*For explanation of sources, abbreviations and symbols, see p. 232 and foldout map.*	
July mean max. 95.0		
Civ. Labor 20,277		

Menard County

Physical Features: West central county of rolling topography, draining to San Saba River and tributaries; limestone soils.

Economy: Agribusiness, tourism, oil, gas production.

History: Apaches, followed by Comanches in 18th century. Mission Santa Cruz de San Sabá established in 1757. A few Anglo-American and German settlers arrived in 1840s. County created from Bexar County in 1858, organized 1871; named for Galveston's founder, Michel B. Menard.

Race/Ethnicity, 2008: (In percent) Anglo, 65.2; Black, 0.3; Hispanic, 33.4; Other, 1.0.

Vital Statistics, 2008: Births, 29; deaths, 42; marriages, 7; divorces, 6.

Recreation: Hunting, fishing; historic sites, including Spanish presidio, mission, irrigation ditches; U.S. fort; railroad museum; Jim Bowie day in September.

Minerals: Oil, gas.

Agriculture: Cattle, wildlife, goats, sheep, pecans. Market value $7.9 million.

MENARD (1,471) county seat; agribusiness, government/services. Other towns include: **Fort McKavett** (50); **Hext** (75).

Population	2,242
Change fm 2000	–5.0
Area (sq. mi.)	902.25
Land Area (sq. mi.)	901.91
Altitude (ft.)	1,690-2,436
Rainfall (in.)	24.90
Jan. mean min.	30.7
July mean max.	94.8
Civ. Labor	1,017
Unemployed	8.4
Wages	$2,870,286
Av. Weekly Wage	$488
Prop. Value	$1,055,076,600
Retail Sales	$13,929,844

Midland County

Physical Features: Flat western county, broken by draws; sandy, loam soils with native grasses.

Economy: Among leading petroleum-producing counties; distribution, administrative center for oil industry; varied manufacturing; government/services.

History: Comanches in area in 19th century. Sheep ranching developed in 1880s. Permian Basin oil boom began in 1920s. County created from Tom Green County in 1885, organized the same year; name came from midway location on railroad between El Paso and Fort Worth. Chihuahua Trail and Emigrant Road were pioneer trails that crossed county.

Race/Ethnicity, 2008: (In percent) Anglo, 54.0; Black, 7.1; Hispanic, 37.0; Other, 1.9.

Vital Statistics, 2008: Births, 2,278; deaths, 1,047; marriages, 1,218; divorces, 544.

Recreation: Permian Basin Petroleum Museum, Library, Hall of Fame; Museum of Southwest; Commemorative Air Force and Museum; community theater; metropolitan events; homes of Presidents Bush.

Minerals: Oil, natural gas.

Agriculture: Beef cattle, horses, sheep and goats; cotton, hay, pecans; 20,000 acres irrigated. Market value $15.4 million.

MIDLAND (111,147) county seat; petroleum, petrochemical center; varied manufacturing; livestock sale center; hospitals; cultural activities; community college; polo club, Texas League baseball; Celebration of the Arts in May.

Part of **Odessa**.

Population	136,872
Change fm 2000	17.98
Area (sq. mi.)	901.97
Land Area (sq. mi.)	900.25
Altitude (ft.)	2,550-2,980
Rainfall (in.)	14.80
Jan. mean min.	29.6
July mean max.	94.3
Civ. Labor	77,478
Unemployed	5.0
Wages	$966,395,684
Av. Weekly Wage	$1,076
Prop. Value	$12,539,717,280
Retail Sales	$2,359,998,318

For explanation of sources, abbreviations and symbols, see p. 232 and foldout map.

Milam County

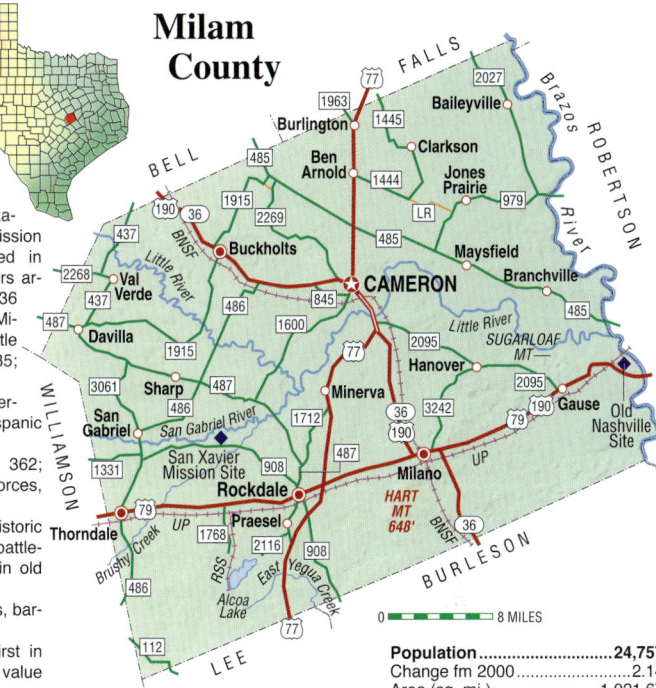

Physical Features: East central county of partly level Blackland; southeast rolling to Post Oak Belt; Brazos, Little rivers.

Economy: Lignite mining, aluminum, other manufacturing, agribusiness.

History: Lipan Apaches, Tonkawas and Comanches in area. Mission San Francisco Xavier established in 1745–1748. Anglo-American settlers arrived in 1834. County created in 1836 from municipality named for Ben Milam, a leader who died at the battle for San Antonio in December 1835; organized in 1837.

Race/Ethnicity, 2008: (In percent) Anglo, 65.3; Black, 11.4; Hispanic 22.5; Other, 0.7.

Vital Statistics, 2008: Births, 362; deaths, 283; marriages, 166; divorces, 105.

Recreation: Fishing, hunting; historic sites include Fort Sullivan, Indian battlegrounds, mission sites; museum in old jail at Cameron, El Camino Real.

Minerals: Large lignite deposits, barite, limited oil and gas production.

Agriculture: Cattle, poultry (first in number of turkeys), corn. Market value $105.3 million.

CAMERON (5,552) county seat; government/services, manufacturing; hospital, library; dewberry festival in April.

ROCKDALE (5,595) aluminum plant, government/services; hospital, juvenile detention center.

Other towns include: **Buckholts** (515); **Burlington** (100); **Davilla** (191); **Gause** (425); **Milano** (428); **Thorndale** (1,336) agribusiness, farming, ranching, antiques, barbecue cook-off in June.

For explanation of sources, abbreviations and symbols, see p. 232 and foldout map.

Population	**24,757**
Change fm 2000	2.14
Area (sq. mi.)	1,021.67
Land Area (sq. mi.)	1,016.71
Altitude (ft.)	250-648
Rainfall (in.)	35.52
Jan. mean min.	39.2
July mean max.	95.7
Civ. Labor	10,783
Unemployed	11.1
Wages	$56,241,810
Av. Weekly Wage	$785
Prop. Value	$2,657,591,155
Retail Sales	$172,075,086

The San Saba River in Menard County. Photo by Robert Plocheck.

Mills County

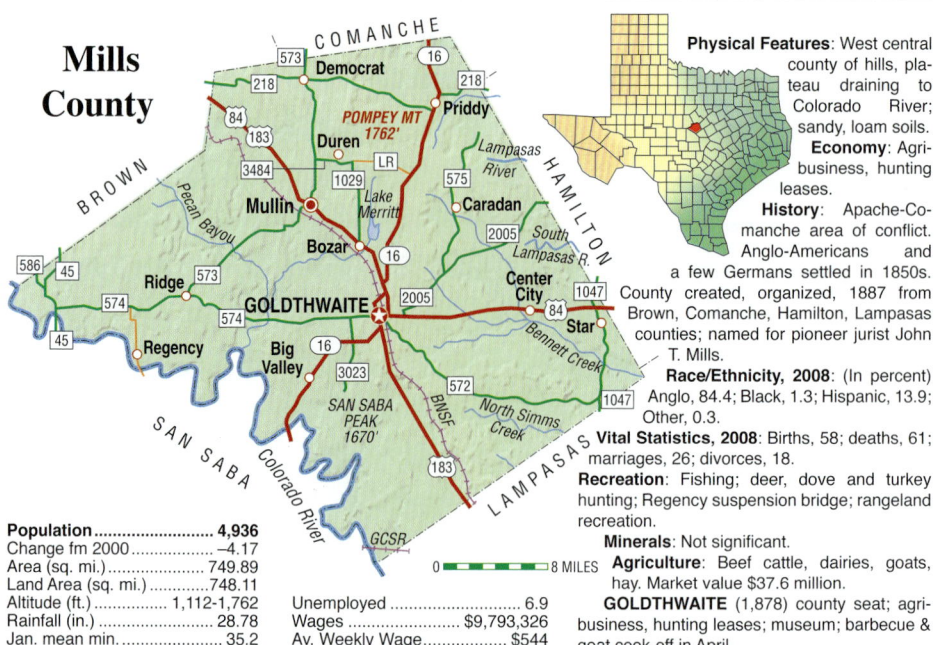

Physical Features: West central county of hills, plateau draining to Colorado River; sandy, loam soils.

Economy: Agribusiness, hunting leases.

History: Apache-Comanche area of conflict. Anglo-Americans and a few Germans settled in 1850s. County created, organized, 1887 from Brown, Comanche, Hamilton, Lampasas counties; named for pioneer jurist John T. Mills.

Race/Ethnicity, 2008: (In percent) Anglo, 84.4; Black, 1.3; Hispanic, 13.9; Other, 0.3.

Vital Statistics, 2008: Births, 58; deaths, 61; marriages, 26; divorces, 18.

Recreation: Fishing; deer, dove and turkey hunting; Regency suspension bridge; rangeland recreation.

Minerals: Not significant.

Agriculture: Beef cattle, dairies, goats, hay. Market value $37.6 million.

GOLDTHWAITE (1,878) county seat; agribusiness, hunting leases; museum; barbecue & goat cook-off in April.

Other towns include: **Mullin** (179); **Priddy** (215); **Star** (97).

Population	4,936
Change fm 2000	–4.17
Area (sq. mi.)	749.89
Land Area (sq. mi.)	748.11
Altitude (ft.)	1,112-1,762
Rainfall (in.)	28.78
Jan. mean min.	35.2
July mean max.	92.0
Civ. Labor	2,320
Unemployed	6.9
Wages	$9,793,326
Av. Weekly Wage	$544
Prop. Value	$1,180,651,840
Retail Sales	$81,397,476

Mitchell County

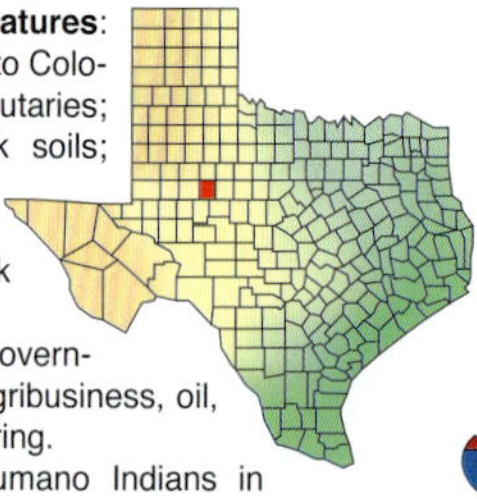

Physical Features: Rolling, draining to Colorado and tributaries; sandy, red, dark soils; Lake Colorado City and Champion Creek Reservoir.

Economy: Government/services, agribusiness, oil, some manufacturing.

History: Jumano Indians in area; Comanches arrived about 1780. Anglo-American settlers arrived in late 1870s after Comanches were forced into Indian Territory. County created 1876 from Bexar District; organized 1881; named for pioneer brothers Asa and Eli Mitchell.

Race/Ethnicity, 2008: (In percent) Anglo, 52.4; Black, 12.6; Hispanic, 34.3; Other, 0.8.

Vital Statistics, 2008: Births, 104; deaths, 96; marriages, 62; divorces, 24.

Recreation: Lake activities, state park, museums, hunting, Colorado City playhouse.

Minerals: Oil.

Agriculture: Cotton principal crop, grains also produced. Cattle, sheep, goats, hogs raised. Market value $27.3 million.

COLORADO CITY (4,146) county seat; government/services, agriculture, oil, manufacturing; hospital; boar goat cook-off in October.

Other towns include: **Loraine** (602) and **Westbrook** (253), trade centers. The community around **Lake Colorado City** (588).

Population	9,403
Change fm 2000	–3.04
Area (sq. mi.)	915.90
Land Area (sq. mi.)	910.04
Altitude (ft.)	1,930-2,574
Rainfall (in.)	19.43
Jan. mean min.	27.0
July mean max.	95.9
Civ. Labor	3,633
Unemployed	8.2
Wages	$20,316,291
Av. Weekly Wage	$686
Prop. Value	$1,249,454,073
Retail Sales	$47,721,258

For explanation of sources, abbreviations and symbols, see p. 232 and foldout map.

Montague County

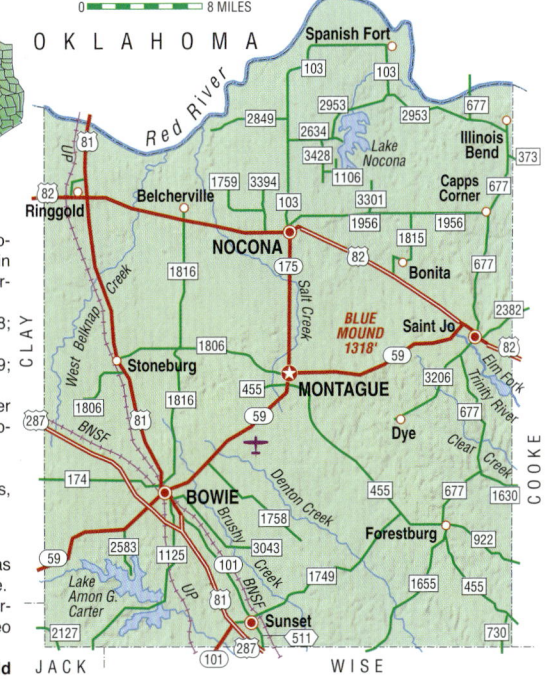

Physical Features: Rolling, draining to tributaries of Trinity, Red rivers; sandy loams, red, black soils; Lake Nocona, Lake Amon G. Carter.

Economy: Agribusiness, oil, varied manufacturing, government/services.

History: Kiowas and Wichitas who allied with Comanches. Anglo-American settlements developed in 1850s. County created from Cooke County 1857, organized 1858; named for pioneer Daniel Montague.

Race/Ethnicity, 2008: (In percent) Anglo, 91.8; Black, 0.1; Hispanic, 7.1; Other, 1.0.

Vital Statistics, 2008: Births, 251; deaths, 309; marriages, 145; divorces, 70.

Recreation: Lake activities; quail, turkey, deer hunting; scenic drives; museums; historical sites, motorcycle dirt track.

Minerals: Oil, rock, limestone, sand.

Agriculture: Beef, hay, wheat, dairies, pecans, peaches, melons. Market value $36.6 million.

MONTAGUE (304) county seat.

BOWIE (5,218) varied manufacturing, oil and gas operations; hospital; library; Jim Bowie Days in June.

NOCONA (3,033) athletic goods, boot manufacturing; hospital; Fun Day each May, Chisholm Trail rodeo in September.

Other towns include: **Forestburg** (50); **Ringgold** (100); **Saint Jo** (1,043) ranching, oil and gas, machine shops; rodeo in August; **Sunset** (497).

For explanation of sources, abbreviations and symbols, see p. 232 and foldout map.

Population	**19,719**
Change fm 2000	3.15
Area (sq. mi.)	938.44
Land Area (sq. mi.)	930.66
Altitude (ft.)	715-1,318
Rainfall (in.)	33.72
Jan. mean min.	28.3
July mean max.	94.7
Civ. Labor	10,264
Unemployed	7.0
Wages	$40,531,903
Av. Weekly Wage	$645
Prop. Value	$2,642,053,500
Retail Sales	$181,465,566

The Montague County Courthouse in Montague. Photo by Robert Plocheck.

Montgomery County

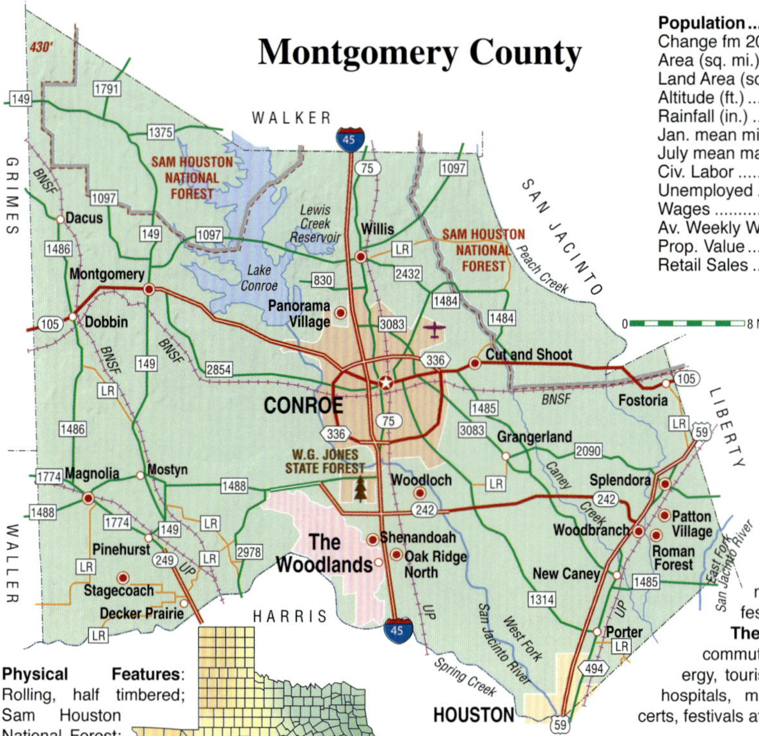

Population **455,746**
Change fm 2000 .... 55.14
Area (sq. mi.) 1,076.81
Land Area (sq. mi.) 1,044.03
Altitude (ft.) 50-430
Rainfall (in.) 49.32
Jan. mean min. 40.0
July mean max. 94.3
Civ. Labor 224,469
Unemployed 7.7
Wages $1,553,835,802
Av. Weekly Wage $918
Prop. Value $37,332,459,797
Retail Sales $7,375,470,465

For explanation of sources, symbols and abbreviations, see p. 232 and foldout map.

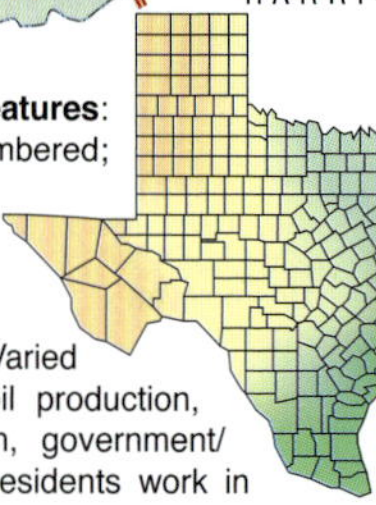

Physical Features:
Rolling, half timbered; Sam Houston National Forest; loam, sandy, alluvial soils.

Economy: Varied manufacturing, oil production, medical research, government/ services, many residents work in Houston.

History: Orcoquisacs and Bidais, removed from area by 1850s. Anglo-Americans arrived in 1820s as part of Austin's colony. County created 1837 from Washington County; named for Richard Montgomery, American Revolution general.

Race/Ethnicity, 2008: (In percent) Anglo, 77.7; Black, 3.6; Hispanic, 16.6; Other, 2.0.

Vital Statistics, 2008: Births, 6,412; deaths, 2,671; marriages, 2,943; divorces, 1,547.

Recreation: Hunting, fishing; Lake Conroe activities; national and state forests; hiking, boating, horseback riding; historic sites.

Minerals: Natural gas.

Agriculture: Greenhouse plants, hay, beef cattle, horses. Market value $42.6 million. Timber important.

CONROE (56,207) county seat; retail/wholesale center, government/ services, manufacturing, commuters to Houston; hospitals, community college,

County adopted:
**In honor of
Timothy Houston Daniel**

museum; Cajun catfish festival in October.

The Woodlands (93,847) commuters to Houston, energy, tourism; college branches, hospitals, museums, parks, concerts, festivals at Mitchell Pavilion.

Other towns include: **Cut and Shoot** (1,070); **Dobbin** (310); **Grangerland** (300); **Magnolia** (1,393); **Montgomery** (621) commuters to Houston and Conroe, antiques stores, pioneer museum, historic homes tour in April; **New Caney** (6,800); **Oak Ridge North** (3,049); **Panorama Village** (2,170).

Also, **Patton Village** (1,557); **Pinehurst** (4,624); **Porter** (4,200); **Porter Heights** (1,653); **Roman Forest** (1,538); **Shenandoah** (2,134); **Splendora** 1,615); **Stagecoach** (538); **Willis** (5,662) commuters to Conroe and Houston; **Woodbranch** (1,282); **Woodloch** (207).

Also, part of **Houston** [Kingwood], hospital.

Lake Meredith is in three counties of the Texas Panhandle including Moore County. Photo by Robert Plocheck.

Moore County

Physical Features: Flat to rolling, broken by creeks; sandy loams; lake.

Economy: Varied agribusiness, petroleum, natural gas.

History: Comanches, removed to Indian Territory in 1874-75; ranching began soon afterward. Farming developed after 1910. Oil boom in 1920s. County created 1876 from Bexar District; organized 1892; named for Republic of Texas navy commander E.W. Moore.

Race/Ethnicity, 2008: (In percent) Anglo, 43.9; Black, 0.4; Hispanic, 54.3; Other, 1.4.

Vital Statistics, 2008: Births, 429; deaths, 138; marriages, 133; divorces, 76.

Recreation: Lake Meredith activities; pheasant, deer, quail hunting; historical museum; arts center; free overnight RV park; Dogie Days in June.

Minerals: Oil and gas.

Agriculture: Fed beef, corn, wheat, stocker cattle, sorghum, cotton, soybeans, sunflowers. Market value $463.2 million. Irrigation of 162,000 acres.

DUMAS (14,691) county seat; tourism, retail trade, varied agribusiness; hospital, hospice, retirement complex.

Other towns include: **Cactus**

(3,179), **Sunray** (1,926). Small part of **Fritch**.

Population	21,904
Change fm 2000	8.86
Area (sq. mi.)	909.61
Land Area (sq. mi.)	899.66
Altitude (ft.)	2,915-3,825
Rainfall (in.)	17.75
Jan. mean min.	20.8
July mean max.	91.7
Civ. Labor	11,693
Unemployed	5.0
Wages	$97,107,888
Av. Weekly Wage	$726
Prop. Value	$3,349,902,911
Retail Sales	$365,818,868

Morris County

Physical Features: East Texas county of forested hills; drains to streams, lakes.

Economy: Steel manufacturing, agriculture, timber, government/services.

History: Caddo Indians until 1790s. Kickapoo and other tribes in area 1820s-30s. Anglo-American settlement began in mid-1830s. Antebellum slaveholding area. County named for legislator-jurist W.W. Morris; created from Titus County and organized in 1875.

Race/Ethnicity, 2008: (In percent) Anglo, 69.4; Black, 25.2; Hispanic, 4.5; Other, 0.9.

Vital Statistics, 2008: Births, 177; deaths, 168; marriages, 98; divorces, 61.

Recreation: Activities on Lake O' the Pines, small lakes; fishing, hunting; state park.

Minerals: Iron ore.

Agriculture: Beef cattle, broiler production, hay. Market value $38.6 million. Timber industry significant.

DAINGERFIELD (2,560) county seat; varied manufacturing, government/services; library, museum, city park, historic theater; Northeast Texas Community College; Daingerfield Days in October.

Other towns include: **Cason** (173); **Lone Star** (1,581) oil-field equipment manufactured, catfish farming, Starfest in September; **Naples** (1,378) trailer manufacturing, livestock, watermelon festival in July; **Omaha** (1,021), retail center, government/services, commuters, fall festival in October.

Population	12,934
Change fm 2000	-0.87
Area (sq. mi.)	258.64
Land Area (sq. mi.)	254.51
Altitude (ft.)	228-614
Rainfall (in.)	46.76
Jan. mean min.	33.7
July mean max.	95.0
Civ. Labor	6,132
Unemployed	12.4
Wages	$50,991,047
Av. Weekly Wage	$906
Prop. Value	$1,145,074,800
Retail Sales	$68,766,078

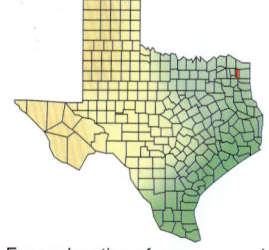

For explanation of sources, symbols and abbreviations, see p. 232 and foldout map.

Motley County

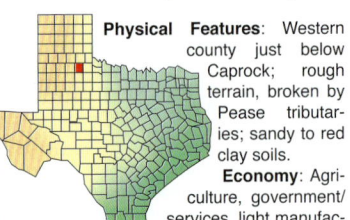

Physical Features: Western county just below Caprock; rough terrain, broken by Pease tributaries; sandy to red clay soils.

Economy: Agriculture, government/services, light manufacturing.

History: Comanches, removed to Indian Territory by U.S. Army in 1874-75. Ranching began in late 1870s. County created out of Bexar District 1876; organized 1891; named for Dr. J.W. Mottley, signer of Texas Declaration of Independence (name misspelled in statute).

Race/Ethnicity, 2008: (In percent) Anglo, 81.6; Black, 3.8; Hispanic, 13.9; Other, 0.7.

Vital Statistics, 2008: Births, 7; deaths, 22; marriages, 4; divorces, 0.

Recreation: Quail, dove, turkey, deer, feral hog hunting; Matador Ranch headquarters; spring-fed pool at Roaring Springs; Motley-Dickens settlers reunion in August at Roaring Springs.

Minerals: Minimal.

Agriculture: Beef cattle, cotton, wheat, sorghum, hay. Some irrigation. Market value $16.4 million. Hunting leases important.

MATADOR (719) county seat; ranching, farming, government/services; museum, historic oil-derrick gas station; motorcycle races in April.

Other towns include: **Flomot** (181) bluegrass festival in May, and **Roaring Springs** (234).

Population	1,210
Change fm 2000	−15.15
Area (sq. mi.)	989.81
Land Area (sq. mi.)	989.38
Altitude (ft.)	1,800-3,083
Rainfall (in.)	22.90
Jan. mean min.	27.3
July mean max.	94.8
Civ. Labor	689
Unemployed	6.1

Wages	$2,584,846
Av. Weekly Wage	$535
Prop. Value	$285,480,140
Retail Sales	$5,595,549

For explanation of sources, symbols and abbreviations, see p. 232 and foldout map.

Downtown Roaring Springs, Motley County. Photo by Robert Plocheck.

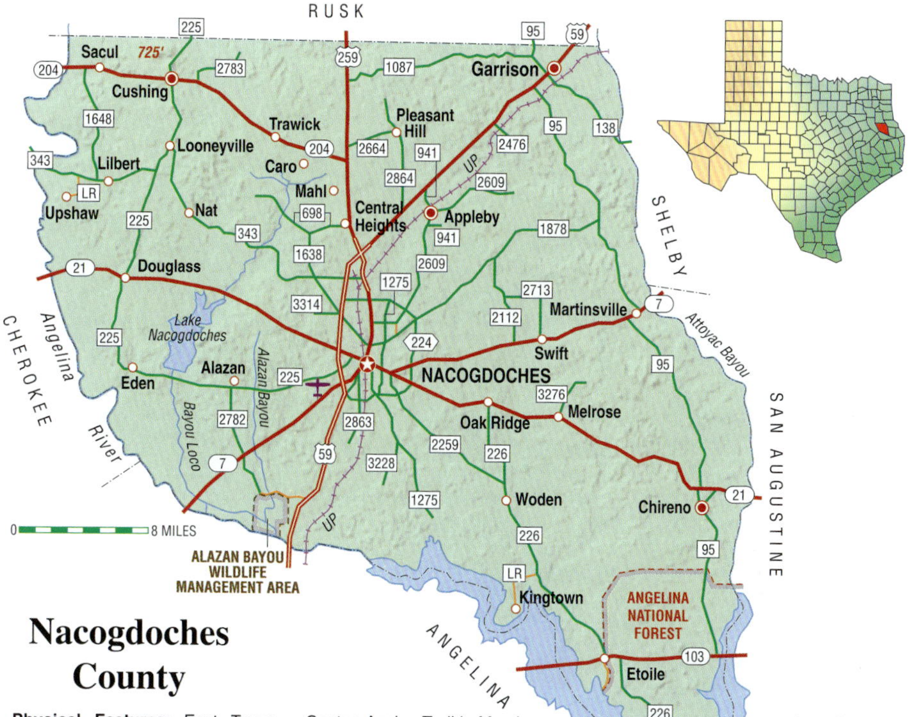

Nacogdoches County

Physical Features: East Texas county on divide between streams; hilly; two-thirds forested; red, gray, sandy soils; Sam Rayburn Reservoir.

Economy: Agribusiness, timber, manufacturing, education, tourism.

History: Caddo tribes, joined by displaced Cherokees in 1820s. Indians moved west of Brazos by 1840. Spanish missions established in 1716. Spanish settlers arrived in mid-1700s. Anglo-Americans arrived in 1820s. Original county of Republic 1836, organized in 1837.

Race/Ethnicity, 2008: (In percent) Anglo, 65.8; Black, 16.9; Hispanic, 16.0; Other, 1.3.

Vital Statistics, 2008: Births, 1,016; deaths, 567; marriages, 476; divorces, 25.

Recreation: Lake, river activities; Stephen F. Austin State University events; Angelina National Forest; historic sites; tourist attractions include the Old Stone Fort, pioneer homes, museums, Millard's Crossing Historic Village, Piney Woods Native Plant Center; Azalea Trail in March, Blueberry Festival in June.

Minerals: First Texas oil discovered here, 1866; gas, oil, clay, stone.

Agriculture: A leading poultry-producing county (second in number of broilers); beef cattle raised. Market value $317.2 million. Substantial timber sold.

NACOGDOCHES (32,996) county seat; varied manufacturing, lumber mills, wood products, trade center; hospitals; Stephen F. Austin State University; Nine Flags Festival in November/December.

Other towns include: **Appleby** (474), **Chireno** (386), **Cushing** (612), **Douglass** (380), **Etoile** (700), **Garrison** (895), **Martinsville** (350), **Sacul** (150), **Woden** (400).

For explanation of sources, symbols and abbreviations, see p. 232 and foldout map.

Population	64,524
Change fm 2000	8.99
Area (sq. mi.)	981.33
Land Area (sq. mi.)	946.77
Altitude (ft.)	164-725
Rainfall (in.)	48.40
Jan. mean min.	36.0
July mean max.	94.0
Civ. Labor	31,848
Unemployed	7.1
Wages	$204,499,515
Av. Weekly Wage	$675
Prop. Value	$4,973,861,450
Retail Sales	$747,733,875

An historical home at Chireno. Photo by Robert Plocheck.

Navarro County

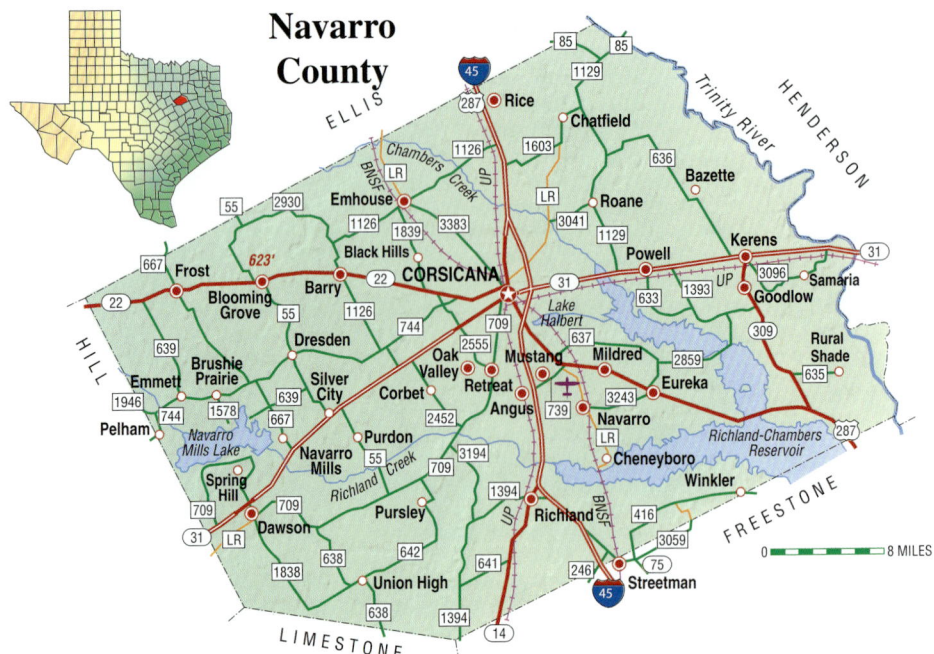

Physical Features: Level Blackland, some rolling; drains to creeks, Trinity River; Navarro Mills Lake, Richland-Chambers Reservoir.

Economy: Diversified manufacturing, agribusinesses, oil-field operations, distribution.

History: Kickapoo and Comanche area. Anglo-Americans settled in late 1830s. Antebellum slaveholding area. County created from Robertson County, organized in 1846; named for Republic of Texas leader José Antonio Navarro.

Race/Ethnicity, 2008: (In percent) Anglo, 59.5; Black, 15.9; Hispanic, 23.3; Other, 1.2.

Vital Statistics, 2008: Births, 708; deaths, 520; marriages, 382; divorces, 196.

Recreation: Lake activities; Pioneer Village; historic buildings; youth exposition, Derrick Days in April.

Minerals: Longest continuous Texas oil flow; more than 200 million barrels produced since 1895; natural gas, sand and gravel also produced.

Agriculture: Beef cattle, cotton, sorghum, corn, wheat, sunflowers, herbs, horses, dairies. Market value $52.4 million.

CORSICANA (23,770) county seat; major distribution center, pecans, candy, fruitcakes; varied manufacturing; agribusiness; hospital; Navarro College; Texas Youth Commission facility.

Other towns include: **Angus** (414); **Barry** (242); **Blooming Grove** (821); **Chatfield** (40); **Dawson** (807); **Emhouse** (133); **Eureka** (307); **Frost** (643); **Goodlow** (200).

Also, **Kerens** (1,573) some manufacturing, nature tourism, Cotton Harvest Festival in October; **Mildred** (368); **Mustang** (21); **Navarro** (210); **Oak Valley** (368); **Powell** (136); **Purdon** (133); **Retreat** (377); **Rice** (923); **Richland** (264).

Population	47,735
Change fm 2000	5.79
Area (sq. mi.)	1,086.17
Land Area (sq. mi.)	1,070.66
Altitude (ft.)	250-623
Rainfall (in.)	39.48
Jan. mean min.	34.0
July mean max.	94.5
Civ. Labor	21,737
Unemployed	9.5
Wages	$136,503,574
Av. Weekly Wage	$644
Prop. Value	$3,481,490,390
Retail Sales	$534,043,900

For explanation of sources, symbols and abbreviations, see p. 232 and foldout map.

Wind turbines amid cotton fields of Nolan County. Photo by Robert Plocheck.

Newton County

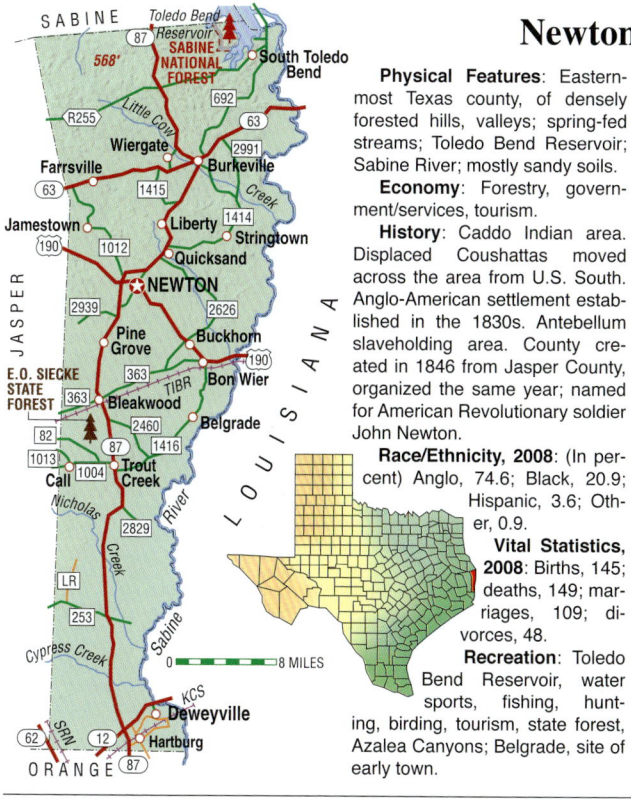

Physical Features: Easternmost Texas county, of densely forested hills, valleys; spring-fed streams; Toledo Bend Reservoir; Sabine River; mostly sandy soils.

Economy: Forestry, government/services, tourism.

History: Caddo Indian area. Displaced Coushattas moved across the area from U.S. South. Anglo-American settlement established in the 1830s. Antebellum slaveholding area. County created in 1846 from Jasper County, organized the same year; named for American Revolutionary soldier John Newton.

Race/Ethnicity, 2008: (In percent) Anglo, 74.6; Black, 20.9; Hispanic, 3.6; Other, 0.9.

Vital Statistics, 2008: Births, 145; deaths, 149; marriages, 109; divorces, 48.

Recreation: Toledo Bend Reservoir, water sports, fishing, hunting, birding, tourism, state forest, Azalea Canyons; Belgrade, site of early town.

Minerals: Oil, gas.

Agriculture: Cattle, hay, nursery crops, vegetables, goats, hogs. Market value $2 million. Hunting leases. Major forestry area.

NEWTON (2,478) county seat; lumber manufacturing, plywood mill, private prison unit, tourist center; genealogical library, museum; Wild Azalea festival in March.

Deweyville (1,023) power plant, commercial center for forestry, farming area.

Other towns include: **Bon Wier** (375); **Burkeville** (603); **Call** (493); **South Toledo Bend** (524); **Wiergate** (350).

Population	14,445
Change fm 2000	–4.16
Area (sq. mi.)	939.51
Land Area (sq. mi.)	932.69
Altitude (ft.)	10-568
Rainfall (in.)	54.90
Jan. mean min.	35.0
July mean max.	94.0
Civ. Labor	5,887
Unemployed	14.3
Wages	$12,632,446
Av. Weekly Wage	$560
Prop. Value	$1,472,392,492
Retail Sales	$38,567,993

Nolan County

Physical Features: On divide between Brazos, Colorado watersheds; mostly red sandy loams, some waxy, sandy soils; lakes.

Economy: Farms/ranches, oil/gas, wind energy, government/services.

History: Anglo-American settlement began in the late 1870s. County created from Bexar, Young districts 1876; organized 1881; named for adventurer Philip Nolan, who was killed near Waco.

Race/Ethnicity, 2008: (In percent) Anglo, 62.7; Black, 5.3; Hispanic, 31.6; Other, 0.5.

Vital Statistics, 2008: Births, 236; deaths, 189; marriages, 111; divorces, 59.

Recreation: Lakes, hunting, pioneer museum; rattlesnake roundup in March, Soap Box Derby in June.

Minerals: Oil, gas.

Agriculture: Beef cattle, cotton, sorghum. Market value $37.1 million. Twenty percent irrigated.

SWEETWATER (10,906) county seat; wind energy, varied manufacturing, gypsum; hospital; Texas State Technical College; WWII museum.

Other towns include: **Blackwell** (311, partly in Coke County), Oak Creek Reservoir to south; **Maryneal** (50); **Nolan** (60); **Roscoe** (1,322).

Population	15,216
Change fm 2000	–3.71
Area (sq. mi.)	913.93
Land Area (sq. mi.)	911.98
Altitude (ft.)	1,896-2,603

Rainfall (in.)	23.54
Jan. mean min.	28.9
July mean max.	93.8
Civ. Labor	7,785
Unemployed	7.1
Wages	$53,272,473
Av. Weekly Wage	$680
Prop. Value	$3,212,144,999
Retail Sales	$202,013,754

Nueces County

Physical Features: Southern Gulf Coast county; flat, rich soils, broken by bays, Nueces River, Petronila Creek; includes Mustang Island, north tip of Padre Island.

Economy: Petroleum processing, deepwater port facility, agriculture, tourism.

History: Coahuiltecan, Karankawa and other tribes who succumbed to disease or fled by 1840s. Spanish settlers arrived in 1760s. Settlers from Ireland arrived around 1830. County name is Spanish for nuts; county named for river; created 1846 out of San Patricio County.

Race/Ethnicity, 2008: (In percent) Anglo, 31.4; Black, 4.0; Hispanic, 62.3; Other, 2.3.

Vital Statistics, 2008: Births, 4,971; deaths, 2,581; marriages, 2,272; divorces, 1,361.

Recreation: Major resort area; beaches, fishing, water sports, birding; Padre Island National Seashore, Mustang Island State Park, Lipantitlan State Historic Site; Art Museum of South Texas, Corpus Christi Museum of Science and History; Texas State Aquarium; professional baseball, hockey; greyhound race track.

Minerals: Oil, gas, sand, gravel.

Agriculture: Grain sorghum (first in acreage), cotton, cattle, wheat, hay, nurseries/turfgrass. Market value $110.9 million.

CORPUS CHRISTI (305,215) county seat; seaport, naval bases, varied manufacturing, petroleum processing, tourism; hospitals; museums; Army depot; Texas A&M University-Corpus Christi, Del Mar College; replica of Columbus' ship on display, USS Lexington museum, Harbor Lights; Buccaneer Days in April.

Port Aransas (3,480) deepwater port, tourism, marine research, Coast Guard base, fishing industry; University of Texas Marine Science Institute; museum; Celebration of Whooping Cranes in February; Texas Sand Fest in April.

Robstown (11,487) agriculture, transportation, tourism, petroleum processing; regional fairgrounds; Cottonfest in October, Fiesta Mexicana in March.

Population	340,223
Change fm 2000	8.47
Area (sq. mi.)	1,166.42
Land Area (sq. mi.)	835.82
Altitude (ft.)	sea level-150
Rainfall (in.)	32.26
Jan. mean min.	46.2
July mean max.	93.2
Civ. Labor	169,663
Unemployed	8.4
Wages	$1,632,587,171
Av. Weekly Wage	$826
Prop. Value	$21,418,298,688
Retail Sales	$3,988,342,693

Other towns include: **Agua Dulce** (812); **Banquete** (726); **Bishop** (3,134) petrochemicals, agriculture, pharmaceuticals, plastics, nature trail, Old Tyme Faire in April; **Chapman Ranch** (200); **Driscoll** (739); **La Paloma-Lost Creek** (408); **North San Pedro** (895); **Petronila** (113); **Rancho Banquete** (424); **Sandy Hollow-Escondidas** (296); **Spring Gardens** (563); **Tierra Grande** (356); **Tierra Verde** (277).

Annaville, Calallen and **Flour Bluff** are now part of Corpus Christi.

For explanation of sources, symbols and abbreviations, see p. 232 and foldout map.

The Port Aransas ferry, Nueces County. Photo by Robert Plocheck.

Ochiltree County

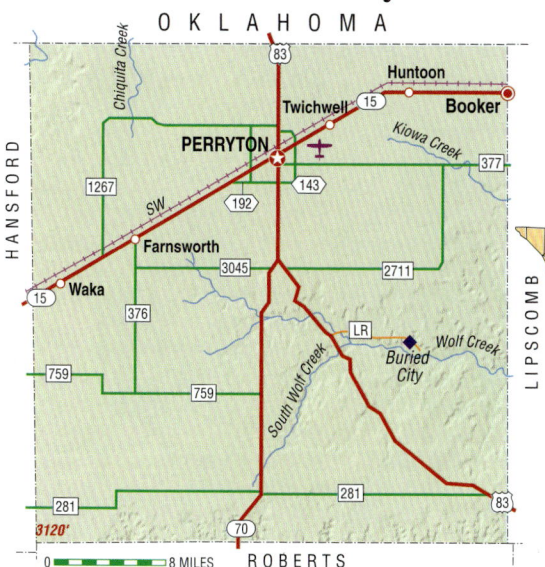

Physical Features: Panhandle county bordering Oklahoma; level, broken by creeks; deep loam, clay soils.

Economy: Oil/gas, agribusiness, center of large feedlot and swine operations.

History: Apaches, pushed out by Comanches in late 1700s. Comanches removed to Indian Territory in 1874-75. Ranching developed in 1880s; farming after 1900. Created from Bexar District 1876, organized 1889; named for Republic of Texas leader W.B. Ochiltree.

Race/Ethnicity, 2008: (In percent) Anglo, 58.3; Black, 0.1; Hispanic, 40.5; Other, 1.1.

Vital Statistics, 2008: Births, 197; deaths, 68; marriages, 99; divorces, 27.

Recreation: Wolf Creek park; Museum of the Plains; Prehistoric settlement site of "Buried City"; pheasant hunting, also deer and dove; Wheatheart of the Nation celebration in August.

Minerals: Oil, natural gas, caliche.

Agriculture: Cattle, swine (first in number), wheat (first in acreage), corn, grain sorghum, cotton; 80,000 acres irrigated. Market value $395.1 million.

Population **10,223**	July mean max. 91.4
Change fm 2000 ....13.51	Civ. Labor 5,594
Area (sq. mi.) 918.07	Unemployed 4.6
Land Area (sq. mi.) 917.56	Wages $53,550,829
Altitude (ft.) 2,550-3,120	Av. Weekly Wage..................$886
Rainfall (in.) 20.88	Prop. Value $1,250,363,728
Jan. mean min. 18.4	Retail Sales $108,419,390

PERRYTON (8,802) county seat; oil/gas, cattle feeding, grain center; hospital; college.

Other towns include: **Farnsworth** (130); **Waka** (65). Also, **Booker** (1,516, mostly in Lipscomb County).

Oldham County

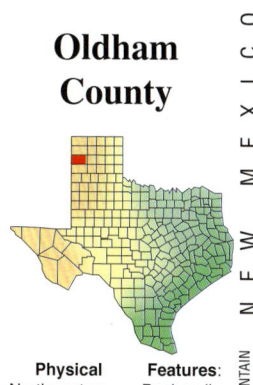

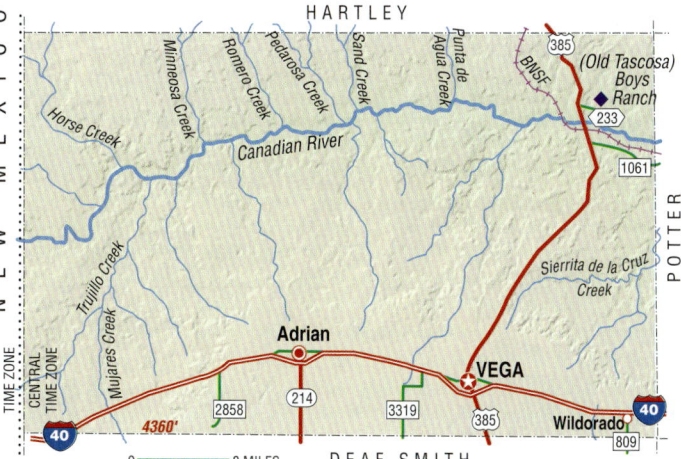

Physical Features: Northwestern Panhandle county; level, broken by Canadian River and tributaries.

Economy: Agriculture, wind energy, sand, gravel.

History: Apaches; followed later by Comanches, Kiowas. U.S. Army removed Indians in 1875. Anglo ranchers and Spanish pastores (sheep men) from New Mexico were in area in 1870s. County created 1876 from Bexar District; organized 1880; named for editor-Confederate senator W.S. Oldham.

Race/Ethnicity, 2008: (In percent) Anglo, 84.6; Black, 2.4; Hispanic, 11.4; Other, 1.5.

Vital Statistics, 2008: Births, 22; deaths, 14; marriages, 16; divorces, 1.

Recreation: Old Tascosa, Cal Farley's Boys Ranch, Boot Hill Cemetery, museums; midway point on old Route 66; County Roundup in August, Boys Ranch rodeo Labor Day weekend.

Minerals: Sand and gravel, oil, natural gas, stone.

Agriculture: Beef cattle; crops include wheat, grain sorghum. Market value $119.4 million.

VEGA (884) county seat; ranch trade center; museums.

Other towns: **Adrian** (166); **Wildorado** (210). Also, Cal Farley's **Boys Ranch** (282).

Population **2,052**	
Change fm 2000 ....−6.09	
Area (sq. mi.) 1,501.42	
Land Area (sq. mi.) 1,500.63	
Altitude (ft.) 3,140-4,360	
Rainfall (in.) 18.18	
Jan. mean min. 20.5	
July mean max. 92.3	
Civ. Labor 927	
Unemployed 6.0	
Wages $5,839,984	
Av. Weekly Wage....................$599	
Prop. Value $352,043,116	
Retail Sales $17,289,628	

Orange County

Physical Features: In southeastern corner of the state; bounded by Sabine, Neches rivers, Sabine Lake; coastal soils; two-thirds timbered.

Economy: Petrochemicals, varied manufacturing, agribusiness, tourism, lumber processing.

History: Atakapan Indian area. French traders in area by 1720. Anglo-American settlement began in 1820s. County created, organized, from Jefferson County in 1852; named for early orange grove.

Race/Ethnicity, 2008: (In percent) Anglo, 83.2; Black, 9.6; Hispanic, 5.2; Other, 2.1.

Vital Statistics, 2008: Births, 1,152; deaths, 921; marriages, 714; divorces, 286.

Recreation: Fishing, hunting, water sports, birding, county park, museums; historical homes, crawfish and crab festivals in spring.

Minerals: Salt, oil, gas, clays, sand and gravel.

Agriculture: Cattle, hay, Christmas trees and rice are top revenue sources; honey a significant revenue producer; fruits, berries, vegetables. Also, crawfishing. Market value not available. Hunting leases. Timber important.

ORANGE (18,595) county seat; seaport, petrochemical plants, varied manufacturing, food and timber processing shipping; hospital, theater, museums; Lamar State College-Orange; Mardi Gras/gumbo festival in February.

Bridge City (7,840) varied manufacturing, ship repair yard, steel fabrication, fish farming, government/services; library; tall bridge and newer suspension bridge over Neches; stop for Monarch butterfly in fall during its migration to Mexico.

Vidor (10,579) steel processing, railroad-car refinishing; library; barbecue festival in April.

Other towns include: **Mauriceville** (3,252); **Orangefield** (725); **Pine Forest** (487); **Pinehurst** (2,097); **Rose City** (502); **West Orange** (3,443).

Population	81,837
Change fm 2000	–3.68
Area (sq. mi.)	379.54
Land Area (sq. mi.)	356.40
Altitude (ft.)	sea level-35
Rainfall (in.)	59.00
Jan. mean min.	41.0
July mean max.	91.0
Civ. Labor	42,530
Unemployed	11.7
Wages	$241,126,064
Av. Weekly Wage	$864
Prop. Value	$5,370,102,368
Retail Sales	$833,287,757

For explanation of sources, symbols and abbreviations, see p. 232 and foldout map.

Possum Kingdom Lake, Palo Pinto County. Photo by Robert Plocheck.

Palo Pinto County

Physical Features: North central county; broken, hilly, parts wooded; Possum Kingdom, Palo Pinto lakes; sandy, gray, black soils.

Economy: Varied manufacturing, tourism, petroleum, agribusiness.

History: Anglo-American ranchers arrived in 1850s. Conflicts between settlers and numerous Indian tribes who had sought refuge on Brazos resulted in Texas Rangers removing Indians in 1856. County created 1856 from Bosque, Navarro counties; organized 1857; named for creek (in Spanish name means painted blue).

Race/Ethnicity, 2008: (In percent) Anglo, 77.1; Black, 2.6; Hispanic, 19.2; Other, 1.2.

Vital Statistics, 2008: Births, 399; deaths, 323; marriages, 230; divorces, 172.

Recreation: Lake activities, hunting, fishing, state park, Rails to Trails hiking, biking, fossil park.

Minerals: Oil, gas, clays.

Agriculture: Cattle, dairy products, nursery crops, hay, wheat. Market value $23.5 million. Cedar posts marketed.

PALO PINTO (333) county seat.

MINERAL WELLS (16,788, part in Parker County) oil and gas, manufacturing, tourism; hospital, Weatherford College branch; art center; state park east of city in Parker County; Crazy Water Festival in October.

Other towns include: **Gordon** (478); **Graford** (584) retirement/recreation area, Possum Fest in October; **Mingus** (235); **Santo** (445), and **Strawn** (653).

Population	28,111
Change fm 2000	4.02
Area (sq. mi.)	985.50
Land Area (sq. mi.)	952.93
Altitude (ft.)	782-1,530
Rainfall (in.)	31.79
Jan. mean min.	33.4
July mean max.	97.3
Civ. Labor	14,039
Unemployed	8.3
Wages	$85,993,704
Av. Weekly Wage	$814
Prop. Value	$3,723,373,830
Retail Sales	$314,524,241

Panola County

Physical Features: East Texas county; sixty percent forested, rolling plain; broken by Sabine, Murvaul Creek, Toledo Bend Reservoir.

Economy: Gas processing, oil-field operation, agribusiness, food processing.

History: Caddo area. Anglo-American settlement established in 1833. Antebellum slaveholding area. County name is Indian word for cotton; created, organized, from Harrison, Shelby counties 1846.

Race/Ethnicity, 2008: (In percent) Anglo, 75.7; Black, 18.8; Hispanic, 4.8; Other, 0.6.

Vital Statistics, 2008: Births, 312; deaths, 220; marriages, 244; divorces, 111.

Recreation: Lake fishing, water activities, hunting; Jim Reeves memorial, Tex Ritter museum and Texas Country Music Hall of Fame.

Minerals: Oil, natural gas.

Agriculture: Broilers, cattle, forages. Market value $63.4 million. Timber sales significant.

CARTHAGE (6,779) county seat; petroleum processing, poultry, sawmills; hospital, junior college; Oil & Gas Blast in October.

Other towns include: **Beckville** (847), **Clayton** (125), **DeBerry** (200), **Gary** (311), **Long Branch** (150), **Panola** (305). Also, **Tatum** (1,385, mostly in Rusk County).

Population	23,796
Change fm 2000	4.57
Area (sq. mi.)	821.34
Land Area (sq. mi.)	800.92
Altitude (ft.)	172-548
Rainfall (in.)	51.51
Jan. mean min.	33.9
July mean max.	93.7
Civ. Labor	14,089
Unemployed	7.3
Wages	$95,220,979
Av. Weekly Wage	$831
Prop. Value	$5,753,579,400
Retail Sales	$227,778,065

County adopted in memory of:
Gladys Whitfield Parker
1883–1982

Parker County

Physical Features: Hilly, broken by Brazos, Trinity tributaries, lakes; varied soils.

Economy: Agriculture, varied manufacturing, government/services, commuters.

History: Comanche and Kiowa area in late 1840s when Anglo-American settlers arrived. County named for pioneer legislator Isaac Parker; created, organized, 1855 from Bosque, Navarro counties.

Race/Ethnicity, 2008: (In percent) Anglo, 86.2; Black, 2.1; Hispanic, 10.4; Other, 1.2.

Vital Statistics, 2008: Births, 1,387; deaths, 882; marriages, 750; divorces, 400.

Recreation: Water sports; state park and trailway; nature trails; hunting; Peach Festival in July and frontier rodeo days in June; first Monday trade days monthly.

Minerals: Gas, oil, stone, sand, gravel, clays.

Agriculture: Beef cattle, greenhouse horticultural, hay, horses (first in number), peaches, pecans. Market value $60 million.

WEATHERFORD (25,250) county seat; manufacturing, retail, commuters to Fort Worth, government/services, equine industry; hospital, Weatherford College; museums, gardens.

Other towns include: **Aledo** (2,716); **Annetta** (1,288), **Annetta North** (518) and **Annetta South** (526); **Cool** (157); **Dennis** (300); **Hudson Oaks** (1,662); **Millsap** (403); **Peaster** (1,000); **Poolville** (520); **Reno** (2,494); **Sanctuary** (329); **Springtown** (2,658) commuters, government/services, Wild West Festival in September; **Whitt** (38); **Willow Park** (3,982).

Part of **Azle** (10,947); **Briar**, (5,655); **Cresson** (741). Also, part of **Fort Worth** and **Mineral Wells**.

Population	116,927
Change fm 2000	32.13
Area (sq. mi.)	910.09
Land Area (sq. mi.)	903.51
Altitude (ft.)	700-1,362
Rainfall (in.)	34.70
Jan. mean min.	29.0
July mean max.	95.2
Civ. Labor	55,012
Unemployed	8.0
Wages	$252,876,217
Av. Weekly Wage	$746
Prop. Value	$12,531,809,530
Retail Sales	$1,582,850,626

Parmer County

Physical Features: Western High Plains, broken by draws, playas; sandy, clay, loam soils.

Economy: Cattle feeding, grain elevators, meat-packing plant, other agribusiness.

History: Apaches, pushed out in late 1700s by Comanches, Kiowas. U.S. Army removed Indians in 1874-75. Anglo-Americans arrived in 1880s. Mexican migration increased after 1950. County named for Republic figure Martin Parmer; created from Bexar District 1876, organized 1907.

Race/Ethnicity, 2008: (In percent) Anglo, 43.4; Black, 1.0; Hispanic, 55.1; Other, 0.5.

Vital Statistics, 2008: Births, 140; deaths, 92; marriages, 31; divorces, 36.

Recreation: Hunting, Border Town Days in July at Farwell.

Minerals: Not significant.

Agriculture: Beef cattle (third in numbers), dairies (second in value of sales); crops include wheat, corn, cotton, grain sorghum, alfalfa; apples and potatoes also raised; 190,000 acres irrigated. Market value $937.7 million, third in state.

FARWELL (1,363) county seat; agribusiness center, grain storage, plants make farm equipment.

FRIONA (4,123) cattle, farming, dairies; hospital; museum; Cheeseburger Festival in July.

Other towns include: **Bovina** (1,868) farm trade center; **Lazbuddie** (248).

Population	10,269
Change fm 2000	2.53
Area (sq. mi.)	885.17
Land Area (sq. mi.)	881.66
Altitude (ft.)	3,785-4,440
Rainfall (in.)	18.38
Jan. mean min.	21.7
July mean max.	89.8
Civ. Labor	4,633
Unemployed	4.8
Wages	$44,660,293
Av. Weekly Wage	$651
Prop. Value	$928,010,749
Retail Sales	$48,490,741

For explanation of sources, symbols and abbreviations, see p. 232 and foldout map.

Pecos County

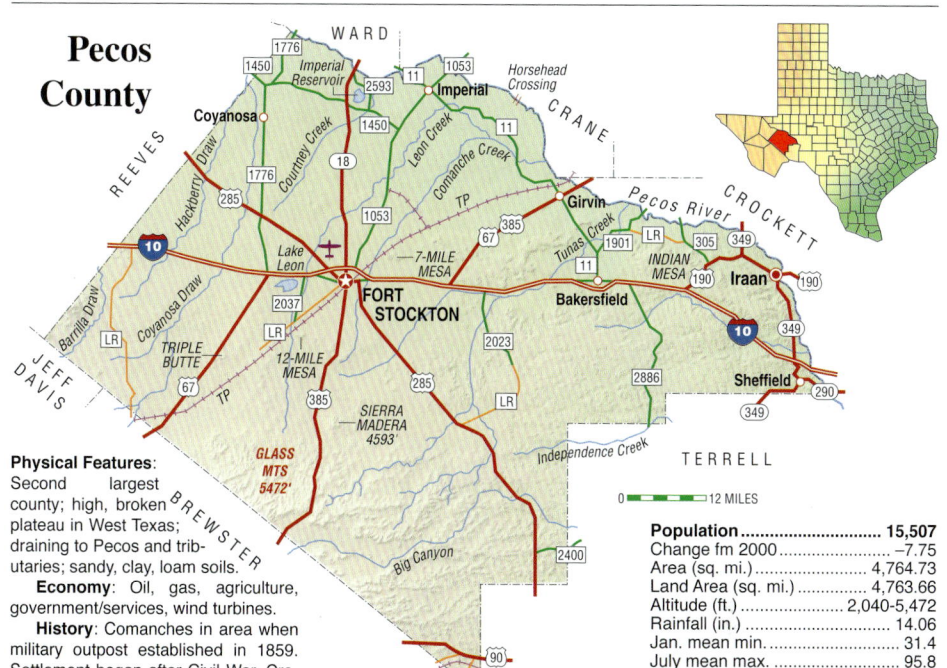

Physical Features:
Second largest county; high, broken plateau in West Texas; draining to Pecos and tributaries; sandy, clay, loam soils.

Economy: Oil, gas, agriculture, government/services, wind turbines.

History: Comanches in area when military outpost established in 1859. Settlement began after Civil War. Created from Presidio County 1871; organized 1872; named for Pecos River, name origin uncertain.

Race/Ethnicity, 2008: (In percent) Anglo, 30.9; Black, 3.8; Hispanic, 64.5; Other, 0.7.

Vital Statistics, 2008: Births, 241; deaths, 125; marriages, 106; divorces, 42.

Recreation: Old Fort Stockton, Annie Riggs Museum, stagecoach stop, scenic drives, Dinosaur Track Roadside Park, cattle-trail sites, archaeological museum with oil and ranch-heritage collections; Comanche Springs Water Carnival in summer.

Minerals: Gas, oil, gravel, caliche.

Agriculture: Cattle, alfalfa, pecans, sheep, goats, onions, peppers, melons. Market value $27.5 million. Aquaculture firm producing shrimp. Hunting.

FORT STOCKTON (8,283) county seat, distribution center for petroleum industry, government/services, agriculture, tourism, manufacturing, winery, prisons, spaceport launching small satellites; hospital; historical tours.

Iraan (1,229) oil and natural gas center, tourism, ranching, meat processing; hospital; Alley Oop park.

Other towns include: **Coyanosa** (163); **Girvin** (20); **Imperial** (278) center for irrigated farming; **Sheffield** (322) oil, gas center.

For explanation of sources, symbols and abbreviations, see p. 232 and foldout map.

Population	**15,507**
Change fm 2000	−7.75
Area (sq. mi.)	4,764.73
Land Area (sq. mi.)	4,763.66
Altitude (ft.)	2,040-5,472
Rainfall (in.)	14.06
Jan. mean min.	31.4
July mean max.	95.8
Civ. Labor	9,758
Unemployed	5.9
Wages	$65,396,091
Av. Weekly Wage	$842
Prop. Value	$4,245,902,450
Retail Sales	$139,150,357

U.S. 190 heading west into the Pecos Valley at Iraan, Pecos County. Photo by Robert Plocheck.

Polk County

Population	45,413
Change fm 2000	10.41
Area (sq. mi.)	1,109.81
Land Area (sq. mi.)	1,057.26
Altitude (ft.)	68-484
Rainfall (in.)	51.85
Jan. mean min.	35.8
July mean max.	94.1
Civ. Labor	18,427
Unemployed	10.7
Wages	$96,039,009
Av. Weekly Wage	$689
Prop. Value	$4,062,672,374
Retail Sales	$428,743,447

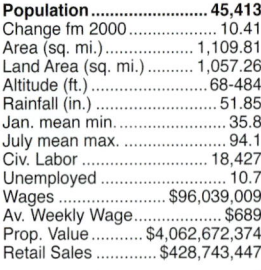

Physical Features: Rolling; densely forested, with Big Thicket, unique plant, animal life; Neches, Trinity rivers, tributaries.

Economy: Timber, lumber, tourism, manufacturing.

History: Caddo area; Alabama and Coushatta Indians arrived from Louisiana in late 1700s. Anglo-American and Hispanic families received land grants in early 1830s. County named for U.S. President James K. Polk; created from Liberty County, organized 1846.

Race/Ethnicity, 2008: (In percent) Anglo, 75.2; Black, 11.8; Hispanic, 10.7; Other, 2.3.

Vital Statistics, 2008: Births, 527; deaths, 597; marriages, 340; divorces, 134.

Recreation: Lake and state park, water activities, fishing, hunting, Alabama-Coushatta Reservation, museum, Big Thicket, woodland trails, champion trees, historic homes.

Minerals: Oil, gas, sand, gravel.

Agriculture: Hay, greenhouse nurseries, vegetables; also cattle, horses. Market value $9.9 million. Timber and hardwood.

LIVINGSTON (5,335) county seat; lumber, tourism, oil; museum, hospital; Civil War reenactment in February. **West Livingston** (8,071), prison.

Other towns include: **Ace** (40); **Camden** (1,200); **Corrigan** (1,595) plywood plant; **Dallardsville** (350); **Goodrich** (271); **Leggett** (500); **Moscow** (170) historic sites; **Onalaska** (1,764); **Seven Oaks** (111).

Potter County

Physical Features: Panhandle county; mostly level, part rolling; broken by Canadian River and tributaries; sandy, sandy loam, chocolate loam, clay soils; Lake Meredith.

Economy: Transportation and distribution hub for large area, manufacturing, agribusiness, tourism, government/services, petrochemicals, gas processing.

History: Apaches, pushed out by Comanches in 1700s. Comanches removed to Indian Territory in 1874-75. Ranching began in late 1870s. Oil boom in 1920s. County named for Robert Potter, Republic leader; created 1876 from Bexar District; organized 1887.

Race/Ethnicity, 2008: (In percent) Anglo, 49.8; Black, 9.9; Hispanic, 36.2; Other, 4.1.

Vital Statistics, 2008: Births, 2,199; deaths, 1,229; marriages, 1,559; divorces, 392.

Recreation: Lake activities, Alibates Flint Quarries National Monument, hunting, fishing, Wildcat Bluff nature center, Cadillac Ranch, professional sports events, Tri-State Fair in September.

Minerals: Natural gas, oil, helium.

Agriculture: Beef cattle production and processing; wheat, sorghum, cotton. Market value $29.9 million.

AMARILLO (190,695 total, part in Randall County) county seat; hub for northern Panhandle oil and ranching, distribution and marketing center, tourism, manufacturing, food processing, prison; hospitals; Amarillo College, Texas Tech University medical, engineering, pharmacy schools; Quarter Horse Hall of Fame, museum.

Other towns include: **Bishop Hills** (193) and **Bushland** (1,485).

Population	121,073
Change fm 2000	6.63
Area (sq. mi.)	921.98
Land Area (sq. mi.)	909.24
Altitude (ft.)	2,915-3,910
Rainfall (in.)	19.71
Jan. mean min.	22.6
July mean max.	91.0
Civ. Labor	58,173
Unemployed	6.6
Wages	$815,970,513
Av. Weekly Wage	$839
Prop. Value	$6,752,456,283
Retail Sales	$2,412,851,701

For explanation of sources, symbols and abbreviations, see p. 232 and foldout map.

The Chinati Mountains along U.S. 67 near Shafter, Presidio County. Photo by Robert Plocheck.

Presidio County

Physical Features: Rugged, some of Texas' tallest mountains; clays, loams, sandy loams on uplands; intermountain wash; timber sparse; Capote Falls, state's highest.

Economy: Government/services, ranching, hunting leases, tourism.

History: Presidio area has been cultivated farmland since at least 1200 A.D. Spanish explorers of the 1500s encountered villages of permanent dwellings along Rio Grande. Jumanos, Apaches and Comanches were in area when Spanish missions began in the 1680s. Anglo-Americans arrived in the 1840s. County created in 1850 from Bexar District; organized in 1875; named for Spanish Presidio del Norte (fort of the north).

Race/Ethnicity, 2008: (In percent) Anglo, 13.3; Black, 0.2; Hispanic, 86.1; Other, 0.4.

Vital Statistics, 2008: Births, 133; deaths, 49; marriages, 61; divorces, 0.

Recreation: Hunting; scenic drives along Rio Grande, in mountains; ghost towns, mysterious Marfa Lights; Fort D.A. Russell; Big Bend Ranch State Park; hot springs; Cibolo Creek Ranch Resort; Chinati Foundation art festival in fall, Marfa film festival in May.

(Chinati Mountains State Natural Area not yet open to public.)

Minerals: Sand, gravel, silver, zeolite.

Agriculture: Beef cattle, tomatoes, hay, onions, melons. 5,500 acres irrigated near Rio Grande. Market value not available.

MARFA (1,981) county seat; Border Patrol headquarters, tourism, ranching; art center, gateway to mountainous area; Paisano Hotel, headquarters for movie, *Giant*; Marfa Lights festival Labor Day weekend.

PRESIDIO (4,426) international bridge to Ojinaga, Mex., gateway to Mexico's West Coast by rail; Fort Leaton historic site; asado cook-off in February.

Other towns include: **Redford** (90); **Shafter** (57) old mining town.

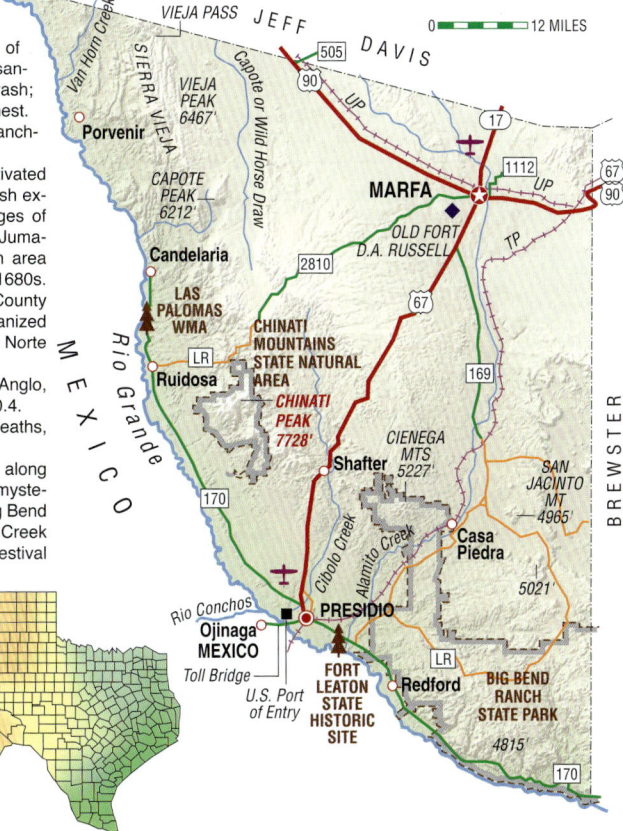

Population	7,818
Change fm 2000	7.04
Area (sq. mi.)	3,856.26
Land Area (sq. mi.)	3,855.51
Altitude (ft.)	2,400-7,728
Rainfall (in.) Marfa	15.79
Rainfall (in.) Presidio	10.76
Jan. mean min. Marfa	23.9
Jan. mean min. Presidio	34.5

July mean max. Marfa	88.9
July mean max. Presidio	100.8
Civ. Labor	3,950
Unemployed	17.4
Wages	$21,321,852
Av. Weekly Wage	$720
Prop. Value	$385,620,550
Retail Sales	$44,252,612

For explanation of sources, symbols, see p. 232 and foldout map.

Rains County

Physical Features: Northeastern county; rolling; partly Blackland, sandy loams, sandy soils; Sabine River, Lake Tawakoni.

Economy: Agribusiness, some manufacturing.

History: Caddo area. In 1700s, Tawakoni Indians entered the area. Anglo-Americans arrived in 1840s. County, county seat named for Emory Rains, Republic leader; created, organized, 1870 from Hopkins, Hunt and Wood counties; birthplace of National Farmers Union, 1902.

Race/Ethnicity, 2008: (In percent) Anglo, 90.6; Black, 2.4; Hispanic, 5.8; Other, 1.1.

Vital Statistics, 2008: Births, 123; deaths, 116; marriages, 74; divorces, 54.

Recreation: Lake Tawakoni and Lake Fork Reservoir activities; birding, Eagle Fest in February.

Minerals: Gas, oil.

Agriculture: Beef, forages, dairies, vegetables (second in sweet potato acreage), fruits, nurseries. Market value $13.9 million.

EMORY (1,239) county seat; local trade, tourism, government/services, commuting to Greenville and Dallas; African-American museum.

Other towns include: **East Tawakoni** (883) and **Point** (820), manufacturing, tourism, tamale fest on July 4. Part of **Alba** (504), mostly in Wood County.

Population	10,914
Change fm 2000	19.42
Area (sq. mi.)	258.87
Land Area (sq. mi.)	232.05
Altitude (ft.)	340-570
Rainfall (in.)	43.50
Jan. mean min.	31.6
July mean max.	92.4
Civ. Labor	5,156
Unemployed	9.1
Wages	$11,766,786
Av. Weekly Wage	$552
Prop. Value	$871,243,870
Retail Sales	$103,312,546

Randall County

Physical Features: Panhandle county; level, but broken by scenic Palo Duro Canyon, Buffalo Lake; silty clay, loam soils.

Economy: Agribusiness, education, tourism, part of Amarillo metro area.

History: Comanche Indians removed in mid-1870s; ranching began soon afterward. County created 1876 from Bexar District; organized 1889; named for Confederate Gen. Horace Randal (name misspelled in statute).

Race/Ethnicity, 2008: (In percent) Anglo, 82.1; Black, 1.9; Hispanic, 13.8; Other, 2.2.

Vital Statistics, 2008: Births, 1,556; deaths, 903; marriages, 412; divorces, 404.

Recreation: State park, with *Texas* outdoor musical drama each summer; Panhandle-Plains Historical Museum; West Texas A&M University events; aoudad sheep, migratory waterfowl hunting in season; Buffalo Lake National Wildlife Refuge; cowboy breakfasts at ranches.

Minerals: Not significant.

Agriculture: Grain sorghum, beef cattle, wheat, silage, cotton, dairies, hay. Market value $393.4 million.

CANYON (13,303) county seat; West Texas A&M University, tourism, commuting to Amarillo, ranching, farm center, light manufacturing, gateway to state park.

AMARILLO (190,695, mostly in Potter County) hub for northern Panhandle oil and ranching, distribution and marketing center, manufacturing; hospitals.

Other towns include: **Lake Tanglewood** (796); **Palisades** (325); **Timbercreek Canyon** (418); **Umbarger** (327) German sausage festival in November. Part of **Happy** (678, mostly in Swisher County).

Population	120,725
Change fm 2000	15.74
Area (sq. mi.)	922.42
Land Area (sq. mi.)	914.43
Altitude (ft.)	2,700-3,890
Rainfall (in.)	19.19
Jan. mean min.	23.7
July mean max.	92.6
Civ. Labor	69,768
Unemployed	5.2
Wages	$247,264,560
Av. Weekly Wage	$658
Prop. Value	$7,783,134,562
Retail Sales	$1,241,599,618

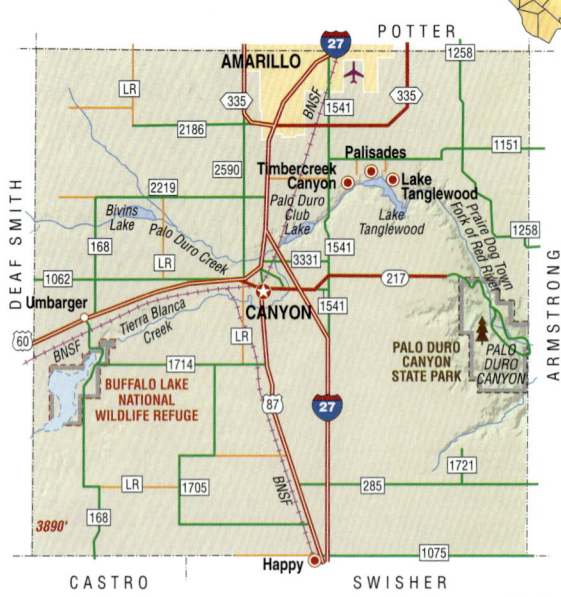

For explanation of sources, abbreviations and symbols, see p. 232 and foldout map.

Reagan County

Physical Features: Western county; level to hilly, broken by draws, Big Lake (intermittent); sandy, loam, clay soils.

Economy: Oil and gas production, hunting, ranching.

History: Comanche bands in area until the mid-1870s. Ranching began in the 1880s. Hispanic migration increased after 1950. County named for U.S. Sen. John H. Reagan, first chairman of the Texas Railroad Commission; county created in 1903 from Tom Green County, organized the same year.

Race/Ethnicity, 2008: (In percent) Anglo, 43.0; Black, 2.9; Hispanic, 53.4; Other, 0.7.

Vital Statistics, 2008: Births, 59; deaths, 30; marriages, 22; divorces, 11.

Recreation: Site of 1923 discovery well Santa Rita No. 1 on University of Texas land, Texon reunion in June.

Minerals: Gas, oil.

Agriculture: Cotton, beef cattle, sheep, goats. Market value $16.5 million. Hunting leases are important.

BIG LAKE (2,936) county seat; center for oil and gas activities, agriculture, government/services; hospital; Spring bluegrass festival, St. Rita festival in August.

Population **3,367**
Change fm 2000 .... 1.23

Area (sq. mi.)	1,175.98
Land Area (sq. mi.)	1,175.30
Altitude (ft.)	2,370-2,960
Rainfall (in.)	18.79
Jan. mean min.	29.1
July mean max.	93.4
Civ. Labor	2,680
Unemployed	3.5
Wages	$27,010,295

Av. Weekly Wage	$990
Prop. Value	$1,823,297,059
Retail Sales	$17,495,730

For explanation of sources, abbreviations and symbols, see p. 232 and foldout map.

The Cadillac Ranch, the roadside sculpture, in Amarillo. Photo by Robert Plocheck.

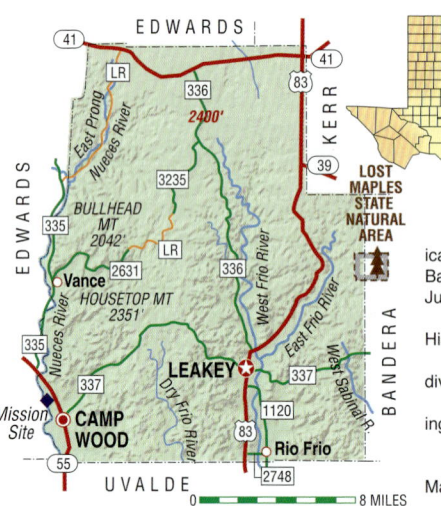

Real County

Physical Features: Hill Country, spring-fed streams, scenic canyons; Frio, Nueces rivers; cedars, pecans, walnuts, many live oaks.

Economy: Ranching, tourism, government/services, cedar cutting.

History: Tonkawa area; Lipan Apaches arrived in early 1700s; later, Comanche hunters in area. Spanish mission established 1762. Anglo-Americans arrived in 1850s. County created, organized, 1913 from Bandera, Edwards, Kerr counties; named for legislator-ranchman Julius Real.

Race/Ethnicity, 2008: (In percent) Anglo, 74.8; Black, 0.3; Hispanic, 24.2; Other, 0.7.

Vital Statistics, 2008: Births, 34; deaths, 39; marriages, 16; divorces, 4.

Recreation: Tourist and hunting center, birding, fishing, camping, scenic drives, state natural area.

Minerals: Not significant.

Agriculture: Goats, sheep, beef cattle produce most income. Market value $2.8 million. Cedar posts processed.

LEAKEY (425) county seat; tourism, ranching; museums; July Jubilee.

CAMP WOOD (706) tourist and ranching hub for parts of three counties; San Lorenzo de la Santa Cruz mission site; museum; settlers reunion in August.

Population	**3,309**
Change fm 2000	8.60
Area (sq. mi.)	700.04
Land Area (sq. mi.)	699.91
Altitude (ft.)	1,400-2,400
Rainfall (in.)	27.99
Jan. mean min.	33.1
July mean max.	94.2
Civ. Labor	1,521
Unemployed	6.3
Wages	$4,473,044
Av. Weekly Wage	$510
Prop. Value	$940,966,041
Retail Sales	$15,038,765

Red River County

Physical Features: On Red-Sulphur rivers' divide; 39 different soil types; half timbered.

Economy: Manufacturing, government/services, agriculture.

History: Caddo Indians abandoned area in 1790s. One of the oldest counties; settlers were moving in from the United States in 1810s. Kickapoo and other tribes arrived in 1820s. Antebellum slaveholding area. County created 1836 as original county of the Republic; organized 1837; named for Red River, its northern boundary.

Race/Ethnicity, 2008: (In percent) Anglo, 74.5; Black, 18.5; Hispanic, 6.3; Other, 0.7.

Vital Statistics, 2008: Births, 159; deaths, 195; marriages, 69; divorces, 67.

Recreation: Historical sites include pioneer homes, birthplace of John Nance Garner; water activities; hunting of deer, turkey, duck, small game.

Minerals: Small oil flow.

Agriculture: Beef cattle, corn, soybeans, wheat, sorghum, hay. Market value $35.9 million. Timber sales substantial.

CLARKSVILLE (3,285) county seat; varied manufacturing; hospital; library; Historical Society bazaar in October.

Other towns include: **Annona** (315); **Avery** (482); **Bagwell** (150); **Bogata** (1,153); **Detroit** (732) commercial center in west. Part of **Deport** (578).

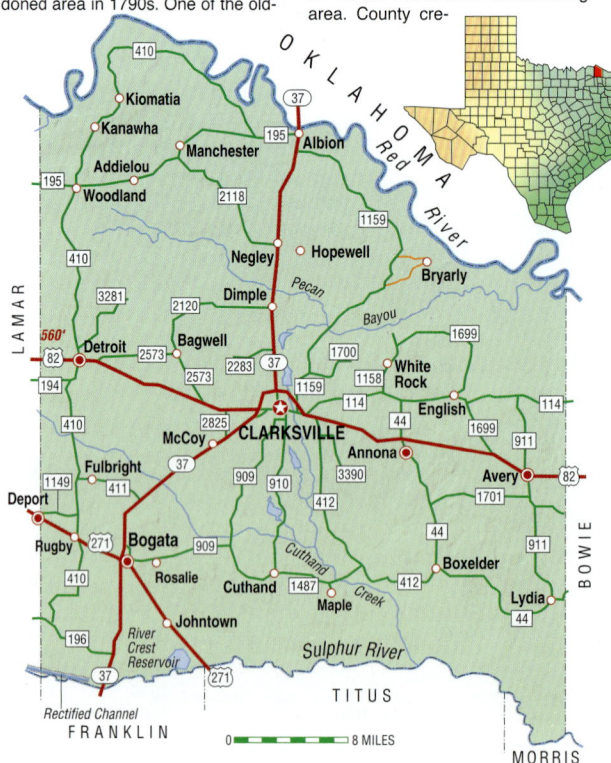

Population	**12,860**
Change fm 2000	−10.16
Area (sq. mi.)	1,057.61
Land Area (sq. mi.)	1,050.18
Altitude (ft.)	260-560
Rainfall (in.)	47.83
Jan. mean min.	29.7
July mean max.	92.2
Civ. Labor	5,840
Unemployed	12.2
Wages	$19,603,092
Av. Weekly Wage	$566
Prop. Value	$1,311,573,080
Retail Sales	$45,931,175

For explanation of sources, abbreviations and symbols, see p. 232 and foldout map.

Reeves County

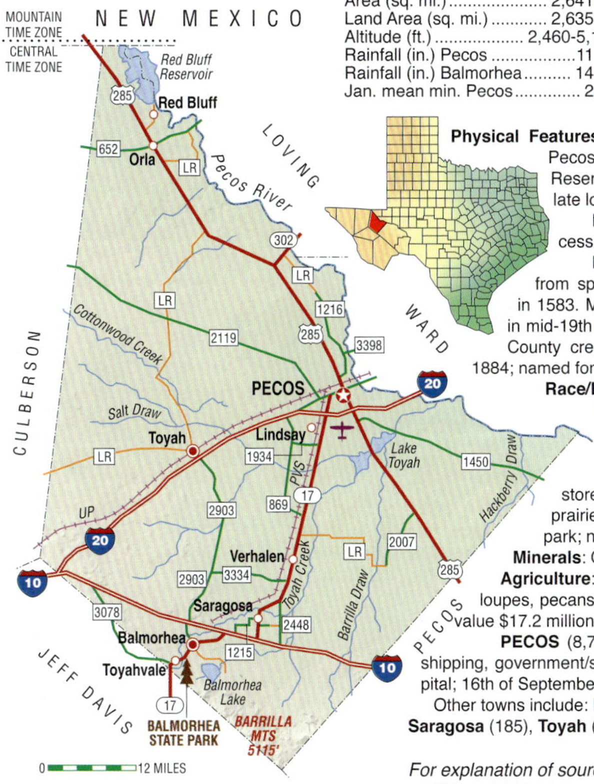

MOUNTAIN
TIME ZONE
CENTRAL
TIME ZONE

N E W   M E X I C O

Population	13,783
Change fm 2000	4.92
Area (sq. mi.)	2,641.95
Land Area (sq. mi.)	2,635.88
Altitude (ft.)	2,460-5,115
Rainfall (in.) Pecos	11.61
Rainfall (in.) Balmorhea	14.19
Jan. mean min. Pecos	28.1

Jan. mean min. Balmorhea	30.1
July mean max. Pecos	98.5
July mean max. Balmorhea	94.7
Civ. Labor	4,797
Unemployed	9.9
Wages	$35,959,215
Av. Weekly Wage	$683
Prop. Value	$815,283,050
Retail Sales	$101,876,784

Physical Features: Rolling plains, broken by many draws, Pecos River, Balmorhea, Toyah lakes, Red Bluff Reservoir; Barrilla Mountains on the south; chocolate loam, clay, sandy, mountain wash soils.

Economy: Agriculture, tourism, food processing, government/services, gravel.

History: Jumanos were irrigating crops from springs (Balmorhea) when Spanish explored in 1583. Mexican farmers supplied nearby Fort Davis in mid-19th century. Anglo-Americans arrived in 1870s. County created 1883 from Pecos County; organized 1884; named for Confederate Col. George R. Reeves.

Race/Ethnicity, 2008: (In percent) Anglo, 22.1; Black, 1.9; Hispanic, 75.3; Other, 0.8.

Vital Statistics, 2008: Births, 216; deaths, 118; marriages, 56; divorces, 20.

Recreation: Replica of Judge Roy Bean store, West of Pecos museum; park with javelina, prairie dogs; scenic drives; water activities; state park; night in old Pecos, cantaloupe festival in July.

Minerals: Oil, gas, gravel.

Agriculture: Ranching, dairies, hay, cotton, cantaloupes, pecans, pistachios, 15,000 arcres irrigated. Market value $17.2 million.

PECOS (8,780) county seat; food processing, produce shipping, government/services, prison, tourism, agribusiness; hospital; 16th of September fiesta.

Other towns include: **Balmorhea** (479), **Lindsay** (271); **Orla** (80), **Saragosa** (185), **Toyah** (90), **Toyahvale** (60).

For explanation of sources, abbreviations and symbols, see p. 232 and foldout map.

0 ▬▬▬▬▬ 12 MILES

Rain clouds over La Calera chapel outside Toyahvale. Photo by Robert Plocheck.

Refugio County

Physical Features: Coastal plain, broken by streams, bays; sandy, loam, black soils; mesquite, oak, huisache motts.

Economy: Petroleum, petrochemical production, agribusinesses, tourism, commuting to Corpus Christi, Victoria.

History: Karankawa area. Spanish mission, for which the county is named, Our Lady of Refuge, established in 1793. Colonists from Ireland and United States arrived in 1830s. Original county of the Republic created 1836, organized 1837.

Race/Ethnicity, 2008: (In percent) Anglo, 43.6; Black, 7.0; Hispanic, 48.4; Other, 0.9.

Vital Statistics, 2008: Births, 87; deaths, 87; marriages, 44; divorces, 19.

Recreation: Water activities, hunting, fishing, historic sites, wildlife refuge, home of the whooping crane; Refugio Festival of Flags in October.

Minerals: Oil, natural gas.

Agriculture: Cotton, beef cattle, sorghum, corn, soybeans, horses. Market value $29.4 million. Hunting leases are important.

REFUGIO (2,890) county seat; petroleum, agribusiness center; hospital; museum, historic homes.

Other towns include: **Austwell** (147); **Bayside** (325) resorts; **Tivoli** (479); **Woodsboro** (1,512) commercial center.

Population	7,383
Change fm 2000	–5.69
Area (sq. mi.)	818.64
Land Area (sq. mi.)	770.21
Altitude (ft.)	sea level-100
Rainfall (in.)	40.10
Jan. mean min.	45.0
July mean max.	94.0
Civ. Labor	4,220
Unemployed	6.9
Wages	$21,973,750
Av. Weekly Wage	$744
Prop. Value	$1,571,023,430
Retail Sales	$61,590,522

Roberts County

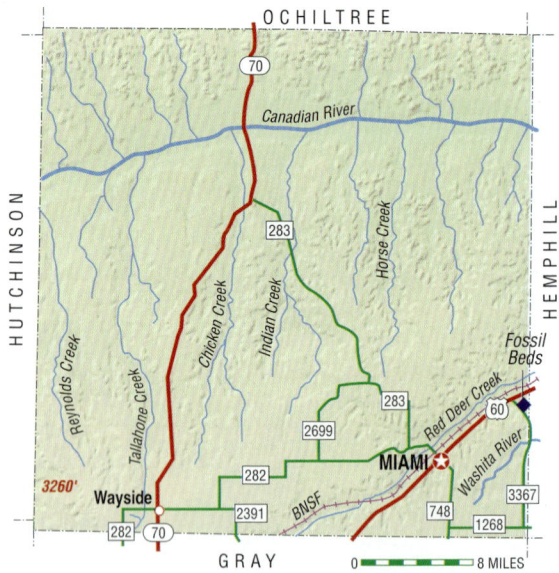

Physical Features: Rolling, broken by Canadian and tributaries; Red Deer Creek; black, sandy loam, alluvial soils.

Economy: Oil-field operations, agribusiness.

History: Apaches; pushed out by Comanches who were removed in 1874-75 by U.S. Army. Ranching began in late 1870s. County created 1876 from Bexar District; organized 1889; named for Texas leaders John S. Roberts and Gov. O.M. Roberts.

Race/Ethnicity, 2008: (In percent) Anglo, 95.9; Black, 0.5; Hispanic, 3.6; Other, 0.1.

Vital Statistics, 2008: Births, 8; deaths, 5; marriages, 0; divorces, 2.

Recreation: Scenic drives, hunting, museum; national cow-calling contest in June.

Minerals: Production of gas, oil.

Agriculture: Beef cattle; wheat, sorghum, corn, soybeans, hay; 10,000 acres irrigated. Market value $16.7 million.

MIAMI (597) county seat; ranching, oil center, some manufacturing.

Population	929
Change fm 2000	4.74
Area (sq. mi.)	924.19
Land Area (sq. mi.)	924.09
Altitude (ft.)	2,380-3,260
Rainfall (in.)	23.30
Jan. mean min.	20.6
July mean max.	92.4
Civ. Labor	563
Unemployed	5.2
Wages	$2,045,743
Av. Weekly Wage	$598
Prop. Value	$908,724,962
Retail Sales	$2,143,055

For explanation of sources, symbols and abbreviations, see p. 232 and foldout map.

Physical Features: Rolling in north and east, draining to bottoms along Brazos, Navasota rivers; sandy soils, heavy in bottoms.

Economy: Agribusiness, government/services, oil and gas.

History: Tawakoni, Waco, Comanche and other tribes. Anglo-Americans arrived in the 1820s. Antebellum slaveholding area. County created in 1837, organized in 1838, subdivided into many others later; named for pioneer Sterling Clack Robertson.

Race/Ethnicity, 2008: (In percent) Anglo, 58.2; Black, 23.5; Hispanic, 17.7; Other, 0.6.

Vital Statistics, 2008: Births, 226; deaths, 202s; marriages, 89; divorces, 34.

Recreation: Hunting, fishing; historic sites; dogwood trails, wildlife preserves.

Minerals: Gas, oil, lignite coal.

Agriculture: Poultry, beef cattle, cotton, hay, corn; 20,000 acres of cropland irrigated. Market value $116 million.

FRANKLIN (1,564) county seat; oil and gas, power plants, mining, agriculture; Carnegie library.

HEARNE (4,459) agribusiness, varied manufacturing; depot museum, World War II POW camp.

Other towns include: **Bremond** (929) power plant, coal mining, Polish Days in June; **Calvert** (1,192) agriculture, tourism, antiques, Maypole festival, tour of homes; **Mumford** (170); **New Baden** (150); **Wheelock** (225).

Robertson County

For explanation of sources, symbols and abbreviations, see p. 232 and foldout map.

Population		16,622
Change fm 2000		3.89
Area (sq. mi.)		865.67
Land Area (sq. mi.)		854.56
Altitude (ft.)		230-610

Rainfall (in.)		39.03
Jan. mean min.		38.2
July mean max.		95.1
Civ. Labor		7,425

Unemployed		9.4
Wages		$34,484,228
Av. Weekly Wage		$728
Prop. Value		$5,672,187,340
Retail Sales		$74,981,564

Landscape along FM 283 in central Roberts County. Photo by Robert Plocheck.

Rockwall County

Physical Features: Rolling prairie, mostly Blackland soil; Lake Ray Hubbard. Texas' smallest county.

Economy: Industrial employment in local plants and in Dallas; in Dallas metropolitan area; residential development around Lake Ray Hubbard.

History: Caddo area. Cherokees arrived in 1820s. Anglo-American settlers arrived in 1840s. County created, organized, 1873 from Kaufman; named for wall-like rock formation.

Race/Ethnicity, 2008: (In percent) Anglo, 79.4; Black, 3.5; Hispanic, 15.2; Other, 1.9.

Vital Statistics, 2008: Births, 1,011; deaths, 368; marriages, 1,281; divorces, 295.

Recreation: Lake activities; proximity to Dallas; unusual rock outcrop.

Minerals: Not significant.

Agriculture: Small grains, cattle, horticulture, horses. Market value $3.9 million.

ROCKWALL (37,490) county seat; commuters, varied manufacturing, government/services, retail; hospital; harbor retail/entearnment district; Founders Day in April.

Other towns include: **Fate** (6,357); **Heath** (6,921); **McLendon-Chisholm** (1,373) chili cookoff in October; **Mo-**bile City (188); **Royse City** (9,349) government/services, varied manufacturing, agribusiness, museum, library, Funfest in October.

Part of **Rowlett** (56,199) hospital, and part of **Wylie** (41,349).

Population	78,337
Change fm 2000	81.84
Area (sq. mi.)	148.70
Land Area (sq. mi.)	128.79
Altitude (ft.)	430-624
Rainfall (in.)	39.40
Jan. mean min.	33.0
July mean max.	96.0
Civ. Labor	40,370
Unemployed	8.0
Wages	$196,945,432
Av. Weekly Wage	$707
Prop. Value	$7,596,217,488
Retail Sales	$1,048,773,215

Runnels County

Physical Features: Level to rolling; bisected by Colorado and tributaries; sandy loam, black waxy soils.

Economy: Agribusiness, oil, government/services, manufacturing.

History: Spanish explorers found Jumanos in area in 1650s; later, Apaches and Comanches driven out in 1870s by U.S. military. First Anglo-Americans arrived in 1850s; Germans, Czechs around 1900. County named for planter-legislator H.G. Runnels; created 1858 from Bexar, Travis counties; organized 1880.

Race/Ethnicity, 2008: (In percent) Anglo, 64.0; Black, 1.5; Hispanic, 33.7; Other, 0.7.

Vital Statistics, 2008: Births, 125; deaths, 180; marriages, 68; divorces, 26.

Recreation: Deer, dove and turkey hunting; O.H. Ivie Reservoir; fishing; antique car museum; historical markers in county.

Minerals: Oil, gas, sand.

Agriculture: Beef cattle, cotton, wheat, grain sorghum, dairies, sheep and goats. Market value $53.8 million.

BALLINGER (3,767) county seat; varied manufacturing, oil-field services, meat processing; Carnegie Library, hospital, Western Texas College extension; the Cross, 100-ft. tall atop hill south of city; Festival of Ethnic Cultures in April.

Other towns include: **Miles** (829); **Norton** (50); **Rowena** (349); **Wingate** (100); **Winters** (2,562) manufacturing, museum, hospital.

Population	10,501
Change fm 2000	–8.65
Area (sq. mi.)	1,057.13
Land Area (sq. mi.)	1,050.73
Altitude (ft.)	1,915-2,301
Rainfall (in.)	23.76
Jan. mean min.	28.5
July mean max.	94.3
Civ. Labor	4,557
Unemployed	8.3
Wages	$23,206,820
Av. Weekly Wage	$608
Prop. Value	$1,144,471,490
Retail Sales	$68,014,897

For explanation of sources, abbreviations and symbols, see p. 232 and foldout map.

Rusk County

Physical Features: East Texas county on Sabine-Angelina divide; varied deep, sandy soils; over half in pines, hardwoods; lakes.

Economy: Lignite mining, electricity generation, oil and gas, lumbering, brick production, agribusiness, government/services.

History: Caddo area. Cherokees settled in 1820s; removed in 1839. First Anglo-Americans arrived in 1829. Antebellum slaveholding area. County named for Republic, state leader Thomas J. Rusk; created from Nacogdoches County in 1843, organized the same year.

Race/Ethnicity, 2008: (In percent) Anglo, 68.5; Black, 18.5; Hispanic, 12.3; Other, 0.7.

Vital Statistics, 2008: Births, 647; deaths, 504; marriages, 340; divorces, 231.

Recreation: Water sports, state park, historic homes and sites, scenic drives, site of East Texas Field discovery oil well; Henderson syrup festival in November.

Minerals: Oil, natural gas, lignite, clays.
Agriculture: Beef cattle, hay, broilers, nursery plants. Market value $56.1 million. Timber income substantial.

HENDERSON (13,712) county seat; power plant, mining, lumber, state jails; hospital, museum.

Other towns include: **Joinerville** (140); **Laird Hill** (300); **Laneville** (169); **Minden** (150); **Mount Enterprise** (447); **New London** (998) site of 1937 school explosion that killed 293 students and faculty; **Overton** (2,554, partly in Smith County) oil, lumbering center, petroleum processing, prison, A&M research center, blue grass festival in July; **Price** (275); **Tatum** (1,385, partly in Panola County); **Turnertown-Selman City** (271).

Also, part of **Easton** (510), part of **Reklaw** (379), and part of **Kilgore** (12,975).

Population	53,330
Change fm 2000	12.58
Area (sq. mi.)	938.62
Land Area (sq. mi.)	923.55
Altitude (ft.)	250-710
Rainfall (in.)	48.22
Jan. mean min.	33.1
July mean max.	93.1
Civ. Labor	24,948
Unemployed	7.6
Wages	$144,434,705
Av. Weekly Wage	$819
Prop. Value	$6,920,061,830
Retail Sales	$352,561,457

For explanation of sources, abbreviations and symbols, see p. 232 and foldout map.

A plant nursery growing poinsettias near Price, Rusk County. Photo by Robert Plocheck.

Sabine County

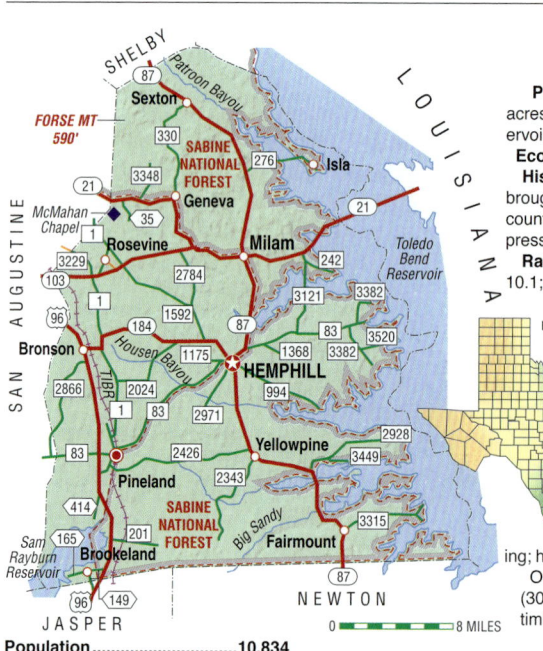

Physical Features: Eighty percent forested; 114,498 acres in national forest; Sabine River, Toledo Bend Reservoir on east; Sam Rayburn Reservoir on southwest.

Economy: Timber, government/services, tourism.

History: Caddo area. Spanish land grants in 1790s brought first Spanish and Anglo settlers. An original county, created 1836; organized 1837. Name means cypress in Spanish.

Race/Ethnicity, 2008: (In percent) Anglo, 87.3; Black, 10.1; Hispanic, 2.2; Other, 0.4.

Vital Statistics, 2008: Births, 107; deaths, 166; marriages, 72; divorces, 21.

Recreation: Lake activities, hunting, campsites, marinas, historic homes; McMahan's Chapel, pioneer Protestant church; Sabine National Forest.

Minerals: Glauconite, oil.

Agriculture: Beef cattle; forage, fruit raised. Market value $8.5 million. Significant timber industry.

HEMPHILL (1,198) county seat; timber, livestock center, retail, tourism, manufacturing; hospital; jail museum, library; Deerfest in September. Other towns include: **Bronson** (377); **Brookeland** (300); **Geneva** (200); **Milam** (1,480); **Pineland** (850) timber processing.

Population		10,834
Change fm 2000		3.49
Area (sq. mi.)		576.61
Land Area (sq. mi.)		490.27
Altitude (ft.)		164-590
Rainfall (in.)		54.40
Jan. mean min.		36.0
July mean max.		93.0
Civ. Labor		3,534
Unemployed		17.0
Wages		$21,460,215
Av. Weekly Wage		$826
Prop. Value		$780,264,992
Retail Sales		$62,422,001

San Augustine County

Physical Features: Hilly East Texas county, 80 percent forested with 66,799 acres in Angelina National Forest, 4,317 in Sabine National Forest; Sam Rayburn Reservoir; varied soils, sandy to black alluvial.

Economy: Lumbering, poultry, varied manufacturing.

History: Presence of Ais Indians attracted Spanish mission in 1717. First Anglos and Indians from U.S. southern states arrived around 1800. Antebellum slaveholding area. County created and named for Mexican municipality in 1836; an original county; organized 1837.

Race/Ethnicity, 2008: (In percent) Anglo, 65.4; Black, 30.1; Hispanic, 4.2; Other, 0.3.

Vital Statistics, 2008: Births, 99; deaths, 150; marriages, 64; divorces, 9.

Recreation: Lake activities, historic homes, tourist facilities in national forests; San Augustine sassafras festival in October.

Minerals: Small amount of oil.

Agriculture: Poultry, cattle, horses; watermelons, peas, corn, truck crops. Market value $55.7 million. Timber sales significant.

SAN AUGUSTINE (2,108) county seat; oil and gas, poultry farms, logging, tourism; hospital; Mission Dolores museum. Other towns include: **Broaddus** (207).

Population		8,865
Change fm 2000		–0.91
Area (sq. mi.)		592.21
Land Area (sq. mi.)		527.87
Altitude (ft.)		164-590
Rainfall (in.)		51.10
Jan. mean min.		35.0
July mean max.		93.0
Civ. Labor		3,739
Unemployed		12.7
Wages		$13,323,702
Av. Weekly Wage		$610
Prop. Value		$599,845,853
Retail Sales		$56,646,216

For explanation of sources, abbreviations and symbols, see p. 232 and foldout map.

San Jacinto County

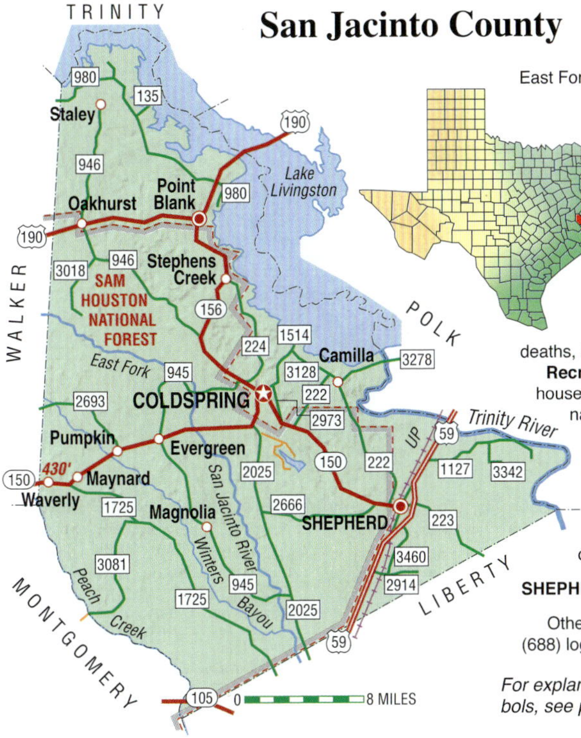

Physical Features: East Texas county north of Houston; rolling hills; 80 percent forested; Sam Houston National Forest; Trinity, East Fork San Jacinto rivers.

Economy: Timber and oil.

History: Atakapa Indian area. Anglo-Americans arrived in the 1820s. Land grants issued to Mexican families in the early 1830s. County created from Liberty, Montgomery, Polk, and Walker counties in 1869; organized in 1870; named for the battle.

Race/Ethnicity, 2008: (In percent) Anglo, 82.2; Black, 12.3; Hispanic, 4.9; Other, 0.7.

Vital Statistics, 2008: Births, 280; deaths, 283; marriages, 120; divorces, 131.

Recreation: Lake activities, hunting, old courthouse and jail. Approximately 60 percent of county in national forest.

Minerals: Oil, rock, gravel and iron ore.

Agriculture: Beef cattle and forages. Market value $6.9 million. Timber is the principal product.

COLDSPRING (853) county seat; lumbering, oil, farming center, tourism; historic sites.

SHEPHERD (2,319) lumbering, tourism, ranching.

Other towns include: **Oakhurst** (233); **Point Blank** (688) logging, agribusiness, construction.

For explanation of sources, abbreviations and symbols, see p. 232 and foldout map.

Population 26,384	Rainfall (in.) 51.77	Wages $15,15,827,184
Change fm 2000 .... 18.6	Jan. mean min. 37.5	Av. Weekly Wage........................ $586
Area (sq. mi.) 627.90	July mean max. 93.8	Prop. Value $2,071,572,605
Land Area (sq. mi.) 570.65	Civ. Labor 10,490	Retail Sales $53,364,487
Altitude (ft.) 62-430	Unemployed 11.4	

Loblolly pine and flaming sumac in Sabine County. Photo by Ron Billings; Texas Forest Service.

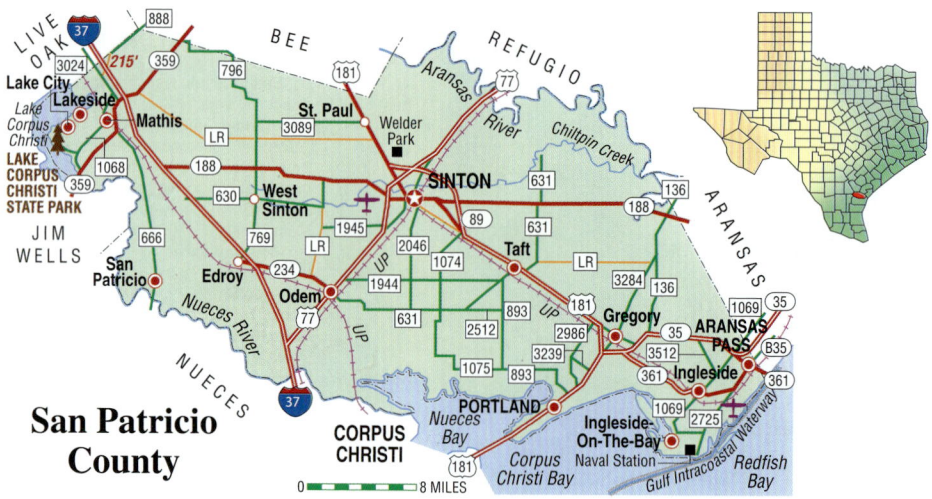

San Patricio County

Physical Features: Grassy, coastal prairie draining to Aransas, Nueces rivers and to bays; sandy loam, clay, black loam soils; lake.

Economy: Oil, petrochemicals, agribusiness, manufacturing, tourism, in Corpus Christi metropolitan area.

History: Karankawa area. Mexican sheep herders in area before colonization. Settled by Irish families in 1830 (name is Spanish for St. Patrick). Created, named for municipality 1836; organized 1837, reorganized 1847.

Race/Ethnicity, 2008: (In percent) Anglo, 43.2; Black, 3.1; Hispanic, 52.1; Other, 1.5.

Vital Statistics, 2008: Births, 1,118; deaths, 526; marriages, 367; divorces, 219.

Recreation: Water activities, hunting, Corpus Christi Bay, state park, Welder Wildlife Foundation and Park, birdwatching.

Minerals: Oil, gas, gravel, caliche.

Agriculture: Cotton, grain sorghum, beef cattle, corn. Market value $109.2 million. Fisheries income significant.

SINTON (5,665) county seat; oil, agribusiness, tourism; Go Texan Days in October.

ARANSAS PASS (8,204, part in Aransas County) deepwater port, shrimping, tourism, offshore oil-well servicing, aluminum and chemical plants; hospital; Shrimporee in May.

PORTLAND (15,099) retail center, petrochemicals, commuters to Corpus Christi; Indian Point pier; Windfest in April.

Other towns include: **Edroy** (331); **Gregory** (1,907); **Ingleside** (9,387) offshore well servicing, chemical and manufacturing plants, commuters, birding, Round Up Days in April; **Ingleside-on-the-Bay** (615); **Lake City** (509); **Lakeside** (312); **Mathis** (4,942); **Odem** (2,389); **St. Paul** (584);

San Patricio (395); **Taft** (3,048) agriculture, drug rehabilitation center, commuters, wind farm, blackland museum, barbecue, tamale and hot sauce cook-off in December; **Taft Southwest** (1,460).

Population	64,804
Change fm 2000	–3.48
Area (sq. mi.)	707.06
Land Area (sq. mi.)	691.65
Altitude (ft.)	sea level-215
Rainfall (in.)	35.54
Jan. mean min.	44.2
July mean max.	91.7
Civ. Labor	31,569
Unemployed	10.7
Wages	$180,421,389
Av. Weekly Wage	$801
Prop. Value	$4,471,852,347
Retail Sales	$713,109,690

For explanation of sources, abbreviations and symbols, see p. 232 and foldout map.

Downtown Eldorado, Schleicher County. Photo by Robert Plocheck.

San Saba County

Physical Features: West central county; hilly, rolling; bisected by San Saba River; Colorado River on east; black, gray sandy loam, alluvial soils.

Economy: Pecan processing and retail trade, tourism, hunting leases.

History: Apaches and Comanches in the area when Spanish explored. Anglo-American settlers arrived in the 1850s. County created from Bexar District in 1856, organized the same year; named for river.

Race/Ethnicity, 2008: (In percent) Anglo, 72.6; Black, 2.3; Hispanic, 24.5; Other, 0.6.

Vital Statistics, 2008: Births, 71; deaths, 62; marriages, 28; divorces, 15.

Recreation: State park with Gorman Falls; deer hunting; historic sites; fishing; scenic drives; wildflower trail.

Minerals: Rock quarry, limestone and sand rock.

Agriculture: Beef cattle, pecans (second in acreage), wheat, hay, some sheep and goats. Market value $28.6 million. Hunting, wildlife leases.

SAN SABA (3,099) county seat; claims title "Pecan Capital of the World"; stone processing, varied manufacturing, prison; Cow Camp cookoff in May.

Other towns include: **Bend** (115, partly in Lampasas County); **Cherokee** (175); **Richland Springs** (338).

Population	6,131
Change fm 2000	–0.89
Area (sq. mi.)	1,138.25
Land Area (sq. mi.)	1,134.47
Altitude (ft.)	1,020-1,980
Rainfall (in.)	27.72
Jan. mean min.	33.4
July mean max.	95.8
Civ. Labor	2,204
Unemployed	9.2
Wages	$12,877,126
Av. Weekly Wage	$577
Prop. Value	$1,349,792,170
Retail Sales	$50,271,316

Schleicher County

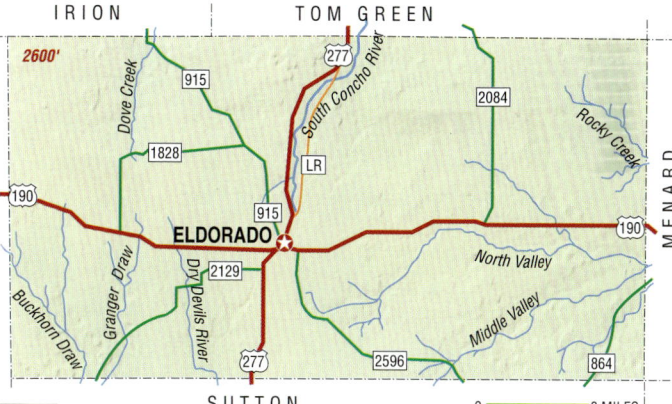

Physical Features: West central county on edge of Edwards Plateau, broken by Devils, Concho, San Saba tributaries; part hilly; black soils.

Economy: Oil, ranching, hunting.

History: Jumanos in area in the 1630s. Later, Apaches and Comanches; removed in the 1870s. Ranching began in the 1870s. Census of 1890 showed third of population from Mexico. County named for Gustav Schleicher, founder of German colony; county created from Crockett County in 1887, organized in 1901.

Race/Ethnicity, 2008: (In percent) Anglo, 49.4; Black, 1.4; Hispanic, 48.7; Other, 0.5.

Vital Statistics, 2008: Births, 52; deaths, 37; marriages, 17; divorces, 4.

Recreation: Hunting, livestock show in January, youth and open rodeos, mountain bike events.

Minerals: Oil, natural gas.

Agriculture: Beef cattle, sheep, goats, cotton, hay. Market value $13.6 million. Hunting leases important.

ELDORADO (1,951) county seat; oil activities, center for livestock, mohair marketing, woolen mill, government/services; hospital.

For explanation of sources, abbreviations and symbols, see p. 232 and foldout map.

Population	3,461
Change fm 2000	17.92
Area (sq. mi.)	1,310.65
Land Area (sq. mi.)	1,310.61
Altitude (ft.)	2,070-2,600
Rainfall (in.)	19.00
Jan. mean min.	28.0
July mean max.	93.0
Civ. Labor	1,491
Unemployed	7.4
Wages	$8,532,879
Av. Weekly Wage	$767
Prop. Value	$656,050,394
Retail Sales	$10,637,666

Scurry County

Physical Features: Plains county below Caprock, some hills; drained by Colorado, Brazos tributaries; lake; sandy, loam soils.

Economy: Oil, government/services, agribusiness, manufacturing.

History: Apaches; displaced later by Comanches who were relocated to Indian Territory in 1875. Ranching began in late 1870s. County created from Bexar District 1876; organized 1884; named for Confederate Gen. W.R. Scurry.

Race/Ethnicity, 2008: (In percent) Anglo, 60.5; Black, 6.6; Hispanic, 32.4; Other, 0.5.

Vital Statistics, 2008: Births, 279; deaths, 170; marriages, 126; divorces, 72.

Recreation: Lake J.B. Thomas water recreation; Towle Memorial Park; museums, community theater, White Buffalo Days and Bikefest in October.

Minerals: Oil, gas.

Agriculture: Cotton, wheat, cattle, hay. Market value $43.4 million.

SNYDER (11,202) county seat; textiles, brick plant, cotton, oil center; Western Texas College, hospital, museum; Western Swing days in July.

Other towns include: **Dunn** (75);

Fluvanna (180); **Hermleigh** (345); **Ira** (250).

Population	16,921
Change fm 2000	3.42
Area (sq. mi.)	907.53
Land Area (sq. mi.)	902.50
Altitude (ft.)	1,800-2,840

Rainfall (in.)	22.51
Jan. mean min.	26.7
July mean max.	94.6
Civ. Labor	8,067
Unemployed	6.2
Wages	$81,807,517
Av. Weekly Wage	$880
Prop. Value	$3,938,394,908
Retail Sales	$197,595,809

Shackelford County

Physical Features: Rolling, hilly, drained by tributaries of Brazos; sandy and chocolate loam soils; lake.

Economy: Oil and ranching, some manufacturing, hunting leases.

History: Apaches; driven out by Comanches. First Anglo-American settlers arrived soon after establishment of military outpost in the 1850s. County created from Bosque County in 1858; organized in 1874; named for Dr. Jack Shackelford (sometimes referred to as John), Texas Revolutionary hero.

Race/Ethnicity, 2008: (In percent) Anglo, 90.6; Black, 0.4; Hispanic, 8.7; Other, 0.4.

Vital Statistics, 2009: Births, 36; deaths, 33; marriages, 17; divorces, 12.

Recreation: Fort Griffin State Park, courthouse historical district, hunting, lake, outdoor activities, June Fandangle musical about area history.

Minerals: Oil, natural gas.

Agriculture: Beef cattle, wheat, hay, cotton. Market value $16.1 million. Hunting leases.

ALBANY (2,034) county seat; tourism, hunting, oil, ranching; historical district, Old Jail art center.

Other town: **Moran** (270).

Population	3,378
Change fm 2000	2.3
Area (sq. mi.)	915.54
Land Area (sq. mi.)	913.95
Altitude (ft.)	1,150-2,000
Rainfall (in.)	28.45
Jan. mean min.	28.4
July mean max.	95.4
Civ. Labor	2,244
Unemployed	4.8

Wages	$12,118,944
Av. Weekly Wage	$788
Prop. Value	$1,598,079,306
Retail Sales	$15,361,209

For explanation of sources, abbreviations and symbols, see p. 232 and foldout map.

Shelby County

Physical Features: East Texas county; partly hills, much bottomland; well-timbered, 67,762 acres in national forest; Attoyac Bayou and Toledo Bend, other streams; sandy, clay, alluvial soils.

Economy: Poultry, timber, cattle, tourism.

History: Caddo Indian area. First Anglo-Americans settled in the 1810s. Antebellum slaveholding area. Original county of Republic, created in 1836; organized in 1837; named for Isaac Shelby of American Revolution.

Race/Ethnicity, 2008: (In percent) Anglo, 65.4; Black, 19.9; Hispanic, 14.1; Other, 0.6.

Vital Statistics, 2008: Births, 420; deaths, 283; marriages, 193; divorces, 38.

Recreation: Toledo Bend Reservoir activities; Sabine National Forest; hunting, fishing; camping; historic sites, restored 1885 courthouse.

Minerals: Natural gas, oil.

Agriculture: County first in poultry and egg production. Beef cattle. Market value $403.1 million. Timber sales significant.

CENTER (5,193) county seat; poultry, timber, oil and gas, tourism; hospital, Panola College extension, museum; What-A-Melon festival in July, poultry festival in October.

Other towns: **Huxley** (385); **Joaquin** (824); **Shelbyville** (600); **Tenaha** (1,150); **Timpson** (1,155) livestock, timber, farming, commuters, genealogy library, Frontier Days in July.

Population	25,448
Change fm 2000	0.89
Area (sq. mi.)	834.53
Land Area (sq. mi.)	794.11
Altitude (ft.)	174-630
Rainfall (in.)	53.01
Jan. mean min.	34.9
July mean max.	93.9
Civ. Labor	13,029
Unemployed	8.7
Wages	$74,092,512
Av. Weekly Wage	$666
Prop. Value	$2,164,139,522
Retail Sales	$300,752,430

For explanation of sources, abbreviations and symbols, see p. 232 and foldout map.

The school gym built by the WPA in 1938–1939 in Moran, Shackelford County. Photo by Robert Plocheck.

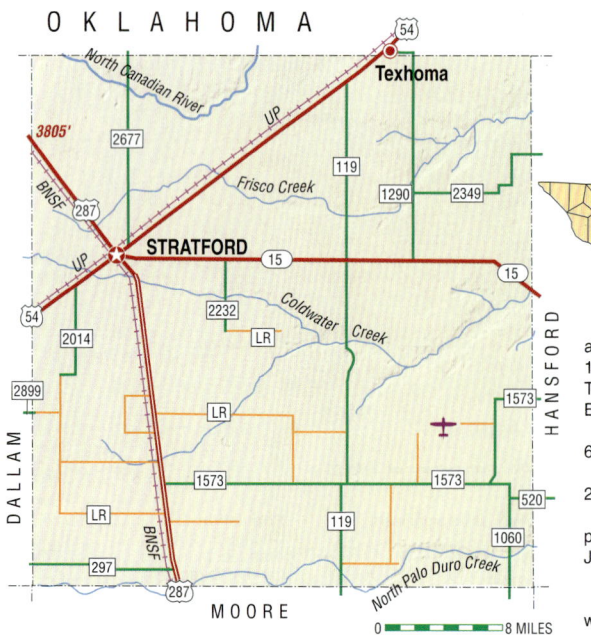

Sherman County

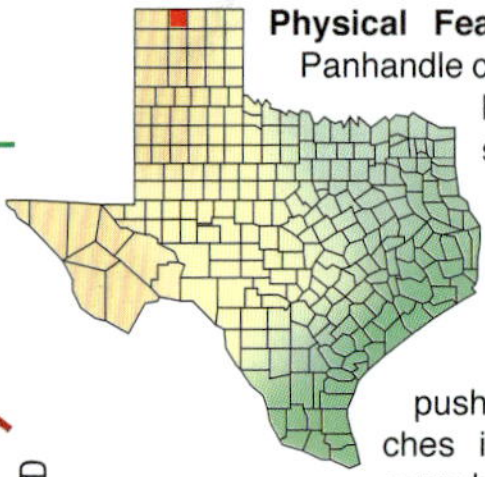

Physical Features: A northern Panhandle county; level, broken by creeks, playas; sandy to dark loam soils; underground water.

Economy: Agribusiness, tourism.

History: Apaches, pushed out by Comanches in the 1700s. Comanches removed to Indian Territory in 1875. Ranching began around 1880; farming after 1900. County named for Texas Gen. Sidney Sherman; created from Bexar District in 1876; organized in 1889.

Race/Ethnicity, 2008: (In percent) Anglo, 69.0; Black, 0.4; Hispanic, 30.0; Other, 0.5.

Vital Statistics, 2008: Births, 39; deaths, 21; marriages, 27; divorces, 7.

Recreation: Depot museum; pheasant, pronghorn hunting, jamboree and rodeo in July, carriage driving event in September.

Minerals: Natural gas, oil.

Agriculture: Beef and stocker cattle, wheat, corn, milo, cotton; 145,000 acres irrigated. Market value $448.9 million.

Population	3,034
Change fm 2000	–4.77
Area (sq. mi.)	923.20
Land Area (sq. mi.)	923.03
Altitude (ft.)	3,200-3,805
Rainfall (in.)	17.89
Jan. mean min.	18.5
July mean max.	91.1
Civ. Labor	1,426
Unemployed	5.2
Wages	$8,027,236
Av. Weekly Wage	$695
Prop. Value	$1,015,341,320
Retail Sales	$14,634,755

For explanation of sources, abbreviations and symbols, see p. 232 and foldout map.

STRATFORD (2,017) county seat; agribusiness, petroleum, tourism, birdseed packaging; VA clinic; science and art museum.

Texhoma (1,295 [with 346 in Texas]) other principal town.

A train moves north out of Stratford, Sherman County. Photo by Robert Plocheck.

Smith County

W O O D

Sabine River

U P S H U R

V A N   Z A N D T

Jamestown
Friendship
Garden Valley
Hideaway
Mount Sylvan
New Harmony
Lindale
Red Springs
Winona
Starrville
OLD SABINE BOTTOM WMA
TYLER STATE PARK
Hopewell
Swan
Shady Grove
GOODMAN MT 631'

G R E G G

TYLER

University of Texas at Tyler
New Chapel Hill
Overton
Noonday
Gresham
Flint
Whitehouse
Omen
Arp
Lake Tyler
Lake Tyler East

H E N D E R S O N

R U S K

Lake Palestine
Coffee City
Bullard
Troup

C H E R O K E E

0 _____ 8 MILES

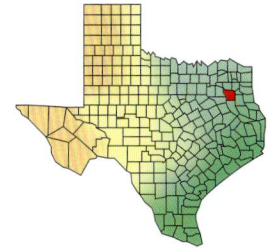

Physical Features: Populous East Texas county of rolling hills, many timbered; Sabine, Neches, other streams; Tyler, Palestine lakes; alluvial, gray, sandy loam, clay soils.

Economy: Medical facilities, education, government/services, agribusiness, petroleum production, manufacturing, distribution center, tourism.

History: Caddoes of area reduced by disease and other tribes in 1790s. Cherokees settled in 1820s; removed in 1839. In late 1820s, first Anglo-American settlers arrived. Antebellum slaveholding area. County named for Texas Revolutionary Gen. James Smith; county created 1846 from Nacogdoches County, organized the same year.

Race/Ethnicity, 2008: (In percent) Anglo, 61.9; Black, 18.7; Hispanic, 17.6; Other, 1.8.

Vital Statistics, 2008: Births, 3,027; deaths, 1,860; marriages, 1,744; divorces, 487.

Recreation: Activities on Palestine, Tyler lakes; Rose Garden; state park; Goodman Museum; Caldwell Zoo; collegiate events; Juneteenth celebration, Rose Festival in October,

Azalea Trail, East Texas Fair in September/October.

Minerals: Oil, gas.

Agriculture: Horticultural crops and nurseries, beef cattle, forages, fruits and vegetables, horses, Christmas trees (first in acreage). Market value $68 million. Timber sales substantial.

TYLER (96,900) county seat; claims title, "Rose Capital of the Nation"; administrative center for oil production, varied manufacturing; University of Texas at Tyler, Tyler Junior College, Texas College, University of Texas Health Center; hospitals, nursing school.

Other towns include: **Arp** (970) Strawberry Festival in April; **Bullard**

(2,463, part in Cherokee County); **Flint** (2,500); **Hideaway** (3,083); **Lindale** (4,818) distribution center, foundry, varied manufacturing, Country Fest in October; **New Chapel Hill** (594); **Noonday** (777) Sweet Onion festival in June; **Troup** (1,869, part in Cherokee County); **Whitehouse** (7,660) commuters to Tyler, government/services, Yesteryear festival in June; **Winona** (576).

Part of **Overton** (2,554, mostly in Rusk County).

Population	**209,714**
Change fm 2000	20.04
Area (sq. mi.)	949.45
Land Area (sq. mi.)	928.38
Altitude (ft.)	275-671
Rainfall (in.)	45.40
Jan. mean min.	38.0
July mean max.	94.0
Civ. Labor	101,674
Unemployed	8.2
Wages	$999,331,815
Av. Weekly Wage	$829
Prop. Value	$15,702,258,769
Retail Sales	$3,157,431,580

For explanation of sources, symbols and abbreviations, see p. 232 and foldout map.

Somervell County

Physical Features: Hilly terrain southwest of Fort Worth; Brazos, Paluxy rivers; gray, dark, alluvial soils; second-smallest county.

Economy: Tourism, nuclear power plant, government/services, commuters, natural gas.

History: Wichita, Tonkawa area; Comanches later. Anglo-Americans arrived in 1850s. County created as Somerville County in 1875 from Hood County, organized the same year. Spelling was changed 1876; named for Republic of Texas Gen. Alexander Somervell.

Race/Ethnicity, 2008: (In percent) Anglo, 83.3; Black, 0.2; Hispanic, 15.7; Other, 0.8.

Vital Statistics, 2008: Births, 111; deaths, 80; marriages, 83; divorces, 33.

Recreation: Fishing, hunting; unique geological formations; dinosaur tracks in state park; Glen Rose Big Rocks Park; Fossil Rim Wildlife Center; nature trails, museums; exposition center; Paluxy Pedal bicycle ride in October.

Minerals: Sand, gravel, silica, natural gas.

Agriculture: Cattle, hay, horses, nurseries. Market value $4.5 million. Hunting leases important.

GLEN ROSE (2,444) county seat; nuclear power plant, tourism, farm trade center; hospital; Hill College branch.

Other towns include: **Nemo** (56); **Rainbow** (121).

County adopted by:
Becky Madole Cornell

Population	**8,490**
Change fm 2000	24.69
Area (sq. mi.)	191.90
Land Area (sq. mi.)	187.17
Altitude (ft.)	550-1,310
Rainfall (in.)	34.82
Jan. mean min.	28.9
July mean max.	97.3
Civ. Labor	4,266
Unemployed	8.6
Wages	$56,408,962
Av. Weekly Wage	$1,095
Prop. Value	$3,957,685,783
Retail Sales	$46,176,913

Starr County

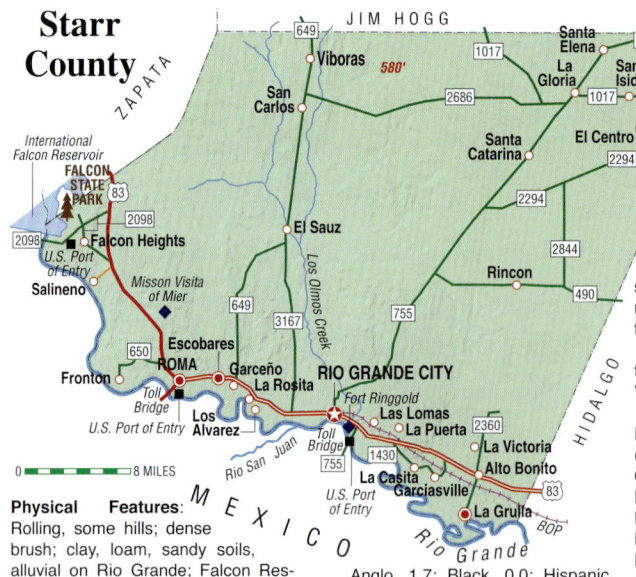

RIO GRANDE CITY (13,834) county seat; government/services, tourism, agriculture; hospital, college extensions; trolley tours; Vaquero Days in February.

ROMA-Los Saenz (9,765) agriculture center; La Purísima Concepcíon Visita.

Other towns include: **Delmita** (50); **Escobares** (1,188); **Falcon Heights** (53); **Fronton** (180); **Garceño** (420); **Garciasville** (46); **La Casita** (128); **La Grulla** (1,622); **La Puerta** (632); **La Rosita** (85); **Las Lomas** (3,147); **La Victoria** (171); **Los Alvarez** (303); **North Escobares** (118); **Salineño** (201); **San Isidro** (240); **Santa Elena** (64).

Physical Features: Rolling, some hills; dense brush; clay, loam, sandy soils; alluvial on Rio Grande; Falcon Reservoir.

Economy: Vegetable packing, other agribusiness, oil processing, tourism, government/services.

History: Coahuiltecan Indian area. Settlers from Spanish villages that were established in 1749 on south bank began to move across river soon afterward. Fort Ringgold established in 1848. County named for Dr. J.H. Starr, secretary of treasury of the Republic; county created from Nueces and organized in 1848.

Race/Ethnicity, 2008: (In percent) Anglo, 1.7; Black, 0.0; Hispanic, 97.9; Other, 0.3.

Vital Statistics, 2008: Births, 1,335; deaths, 364; marriages, 376; divorces, 13.

Recreation: Falcon Reservoir activities; deer, white-wing dove hunting; access to Mexico; historic houses, Lee House at Fort Ringgold; grotto at Rio Grande City; Roma Fest in November.

Minerals: Oil, gas, sand, gravel.

Agriculture: Beef and fed cattle; vegetables, cotton, sorghum; 18,000 acres irrigated for vegetables. Market value $64.4 million.

Population	**60,968**
Change fm 2000	13.75
Area (sq. mi.)	1,229.28
Land Area (sq. mi.)	1,223.02
Altitude (ft.)	125-580
Rainfall (in.)	21.61
Jan. mean min.	44.5
July mean max.	99.1
Civ. Labor	26,226
Unemployed	19.5
Wages	$96,039,635
Av. Weekly Wage	$513
Prop. Value	$2,853,771,520
Retail Sales	$401,148,667

Stephens County

Physical Features: West central county; broken, hilly; Hubbard Creek Reservoir, Possum Kingdom, Daniel lakes; Brazos River; loam, sandy soils.

Economy: Oil, agribusiness, manufacturing, recreation.

History: Comanches, Tonkawas in area when Anglo-American settlement began in 1850s. County created as Buchanan 1858 from Bosque; renamed 1861 for Confederate Vice President Alexander H. Stephens; organized 1876.

Race/Ethnicity, 2008: (In percent) Anglo, 77.7; Black, 3.0; Hispanic, 18.7; Other, 0.5.

Vital Statistics, 2008: Births, 136; deaths, 116; marriages, 71; divorces, 41.

Recreation: Lakes activities, hunting, campsites, historical points, Swenson Museum, Sandefer Oil Museum, aviation museum, festival and car show in fall.

Minerals: Oil, gas, stone.

Agriculture: Cattle, hogs, goats, sheep; wheat, oats, hay, peanuts, grain sorghums, cotton, pecans. Market value $12.4 million.

BRECKENRIDGE (5,780) county seat; oil, agriculture, oil-field equipment, aircraft parts; hospital, prison, Texas State Technical College branch, library.

Other towns include: **Caddo** (70) gateway to Possum Kingdom State Park.

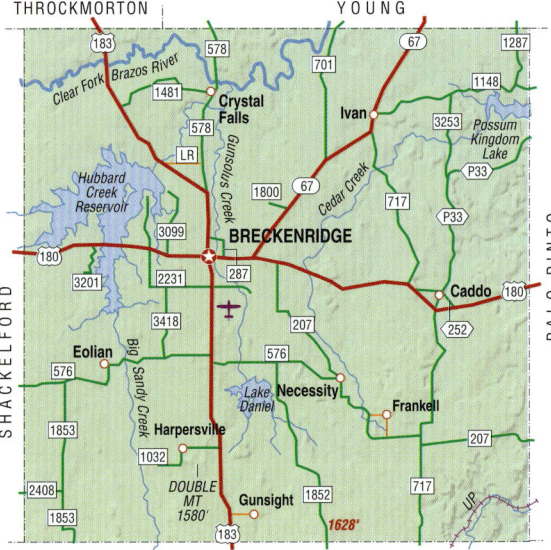

Population 9,630	
Change fm 2000 .... −0.46	
Area (sq. mi.) 921.48	
Land Area (sq. mi.) 894.64	
Altitude (ft.) 995-1,628	
Rainfall (in.) 27.04	
Jan. mean min. 30.9	
July mean max. 96.8	
Civ. Labor 4,669	
Unemployed 8.7	

Wages $29,552,074
Av. Weekly Wage............ $716
Prop. Value $1,421,988,215
Retail Sales $116,972,911

For explanation of sources, symbols and abbreviations, see p. 232 and foldout map.

Downtown Breckenridge, Stephens County. Photo by Robert Plocheck.

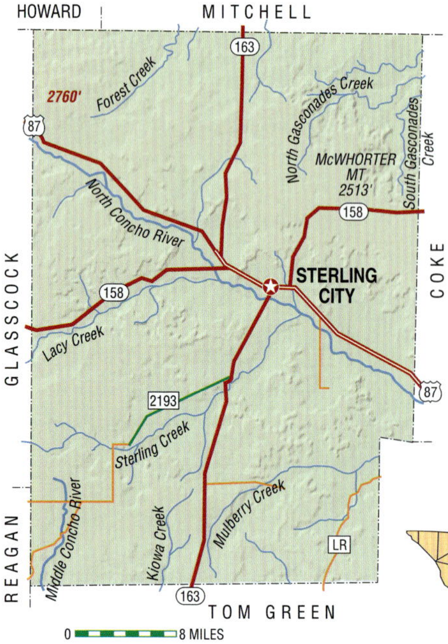

Sterling County

Physical Features: Central prairie, surrounded by hills, broken by Concho River and tributaries; sandy to black soils.

Economy: Ranching, oil and gas, hunting leases.

History: Ranching began in late 1870s after Comanches, Kickapoos and other tribes removed by U.S. Army. County named for buffalo hunter W.S. Sterling; created, organized, 1891 from Tom Green County.

Race/Ethnicity, 2008: (In percent) Anglo, 65.9; Black, 0.0; Hispanic, 33.7; Other, 0.3.

Vital Statistics, 2008: Births, 12; deaths, 12; marriages, 9; divorces, 3.

Recreation: Hunting of deer, quail, turkey, dove; hunters appreciation dinner in November; junior livestock show in January.

Minerals: Oil, natural gas.

Agriculture: Meat goats, sheep, beef cattle, wheat, hay; about 1,000 acres irrigated. Market value not available.

STERLING CITY (888) county seat; farm, ranch trade center; oil-field services.

Population	1,143
Change fm 2000	–17.95
Area (sq. mi.)	923.49
Land Area (sq. mi.)	923.36
Altitude (ft.)	2,000-2,760
Rainfall (in.)	19.40
Jan. mean min.	27.4
July mean max.	94.7
Civ. Labor	739
Unemployed	5.7
Wages	$4,866,630
Av. Weekly Wage	$727
Prop. Value	$1,623,927,155
Retail Sales	$3,327,028

Stonewall County

Physical Features: Western county on Rolling Plains below Caprock, bisected by Brazos forks; sandy loam, sandy, other soils; some hills.

Economy: Agribusiness, light fabrication, government/services.

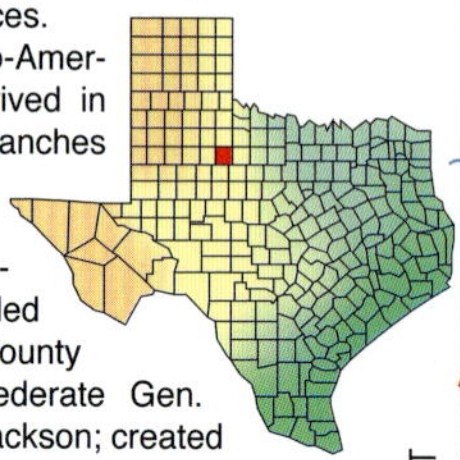

History: Anglo-American ranchers arrived in 1870s after Comanches and other tribes removed by U.S. Army. German farmers settled after 1900. County named for Confederate Gen. T.J. (Stonewall) Jackson; created from Bexar District 1876, organized 1888.

Race/Ethnicity, 2008: (In percent) Anglo, 82.7; Black, 3.1; Hispanic, 13.4; Other, 0.8.

Vital Statistics, 2008: Births, 20; deaths, 23; marriages, 2; divorces, 2.

Recreation: Deer, quail, feral hog, turkey hunting; rodeos in June, September.

Minerals: Gypsum, gravel, oil.

Agriculture: Beef cattle, wheat, cotton, peanuts, hay. Also, grain sorghum, meat goats and swine. Market value $13.7 million.

ASPERMONT (919) county seat; oil field and ranching center, light fabrication; hospital; livestock show in February, Springfest.

Other towns include: **Old Glory** (100) farming center.

For explanation of sources, symbols and abbreviations, see p. 232 and foldout map.

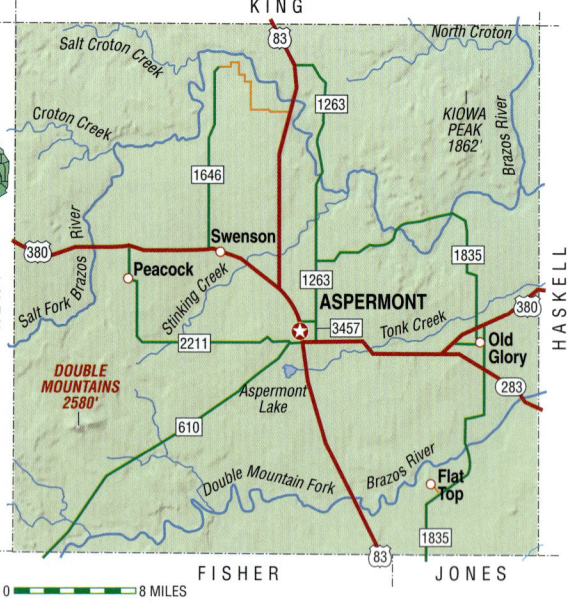

Population	1,490	July mean max.	97.4
Change fm 2000	–11.99	Civ. Labor	778
Area (sq. mi.)	920.23	Unemployed	5.1
Land Area (sq. mi.)	918.67	Wages	$4289,264
Altitude (ft.)	1,450-2,580	Av. Weekly Wage	$617
Rainfall (in.)	23.24	Prop. Value	$503,759,622
Jan. mean min.	27.2	Retail Sales	$7,222,150

Sutton County

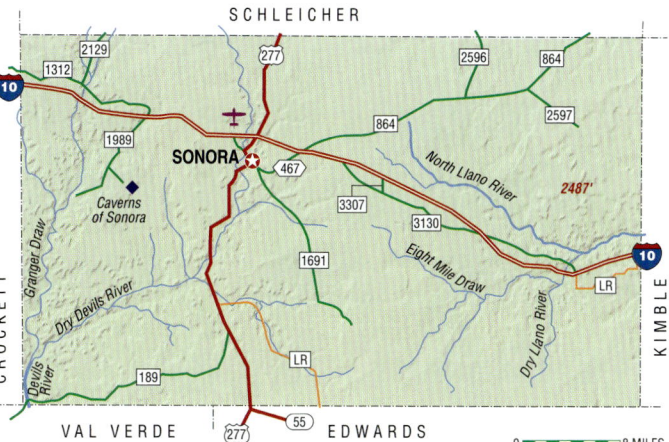

Physical Features: Southwestern county; level in west, rugged terrain in east, broken by tributaries of Devils, Llano rivers; black, red loam soils.

Economy: Natural gas, hunting, tourism, agriculture.

History: Lipan Apaches drove out Tonkawas in 1600s. Comanches, military outpost and disease forced Apaches south. Anglo-Americans settled in 1870s. Mexican immigration increased after 1890. County created from Crockett 1887; organized 1890; named for Confederate Col. John S. Sutton.

Race/Ethnicity, 2008: (In percent) Anglo, 45.1; Black, 0.3; Hispanic, 54.0; Other, 0.5.

Vital Statistics, 2008: Births, 70; deaths, 31; marriages, 35; divorces, 10.

Recreation: Hunting, Meirs Museum, ranch museum, Caverns of Sonora, wildlife santuary, Cinco de Mayo.

Minerals: Oil, natural gas.

Agriculture: Meat goats, sheep, cattle, Angora goats (first in number of goats). Exotic wildlife. Wheat and oats raised for grazing, hay; minor irrigation. Market value $9.6 million. Hunting leases important.

SONORA (3,027) county seat; oil and gas, ranching, tourism; hospital; wool and mohair show in June.

Population	4,128
Change fm 2000	1.25
Area (sq. mi.)	1,454.40
Land Area (sq. mi.)	1,453.76
Altitude (ft.)	1,840-2,487
Rainfall (in.)	22.40
Jan. mean min.	27.2
July mean max.	94.7
Civ. Labor	2,974
Unemployed	5.3
Wages	$32,626,984
Av. Weekly Wage	$1,123
Prop. Value	$1,946,405,486
Retail Sales	$29,887,984

Swisher County

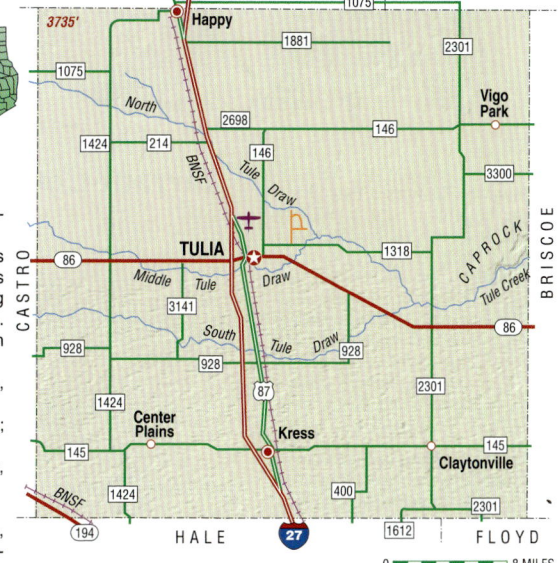

Physical Features: High Plains; level, broken by Tule Canyon and Creek; playas; large underground water supply; rich soils.

Economy: Feedlots, grain storage, manufacturing, tourism, prison.

History: Apaches; displaced by Comanches around 1700. U.S. Army removed Comanches in 1874. Ranching began in late 1870s. Farming developed after 1900. County named for J.G. Swisher of Texas Revolution; county created from Bexar, Young territories 1876; organized 1890.

Race/Ethnicity, 2008: (In percent) Anglo, 54.4; Black, 6.0; Hispanic, 39.1; Other, 0.5.

Vital Statistics, 2008: Births, 115; deaths, 73; marriages, 38; divorces, 28.

Recreation: Mackenzie battle site, depot, Ozark Trail marker festival in May.

Minerals: Not significant.

Agriculture: Stocker cattle, feedlots. Cotton, corn, wheat, sorghum. Some 400,000 acres irrigated. Market value $453.7 million.

TULIA (4,967) county seat; wind energy, feedlots, manufacturing, cotton storage, prison; hospital, library, museum; stock show in January.

Other towns include: **Happy** (678, partly in Randall County); **Kress** (715); **Vigo Park** (36).

Population	7,854
Change fm 2000	–6.25
Area (sq. mi.)	900.68
Land Area (sq. mi.)	900.43
Altitude (ft.)	3,160-3,735
Rainfall (in.)	20.71
Jan. mean min.	22.2
July mean max.	91.1
Civ. Labor	3,536
Unemployed	6.8
Wages	$17,638,769
Av. Weekly Wage	$611
Prop. Value	$516,455,107
Retail Sales	$50,501,969

For explanation of sources, symbols and abbreviations, see p. 232 and foldout map.

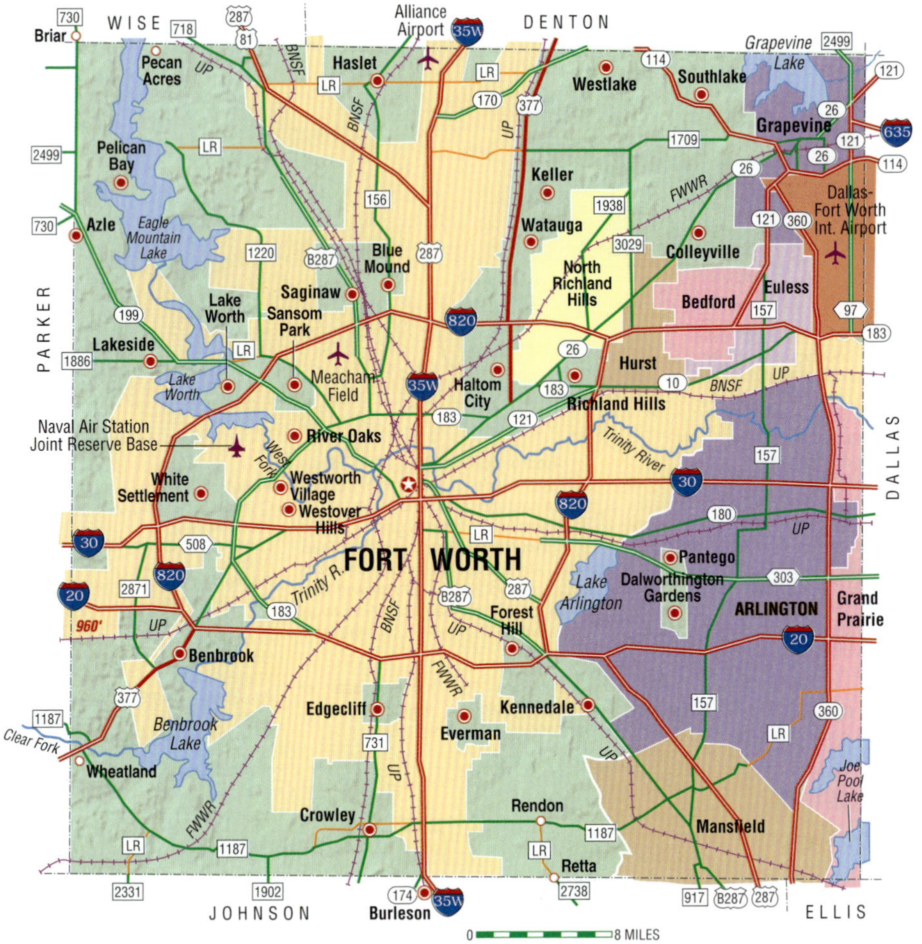

Tarrant County

Physical Features: Part Blackland, level to rolling; drains to Trinity; Worth, Grapevine, Eagle Mountain, Benbrook lakes.

Economy: Tourism, planes, helicopters, foods, mobile homes, electronic equipment, chemicals, plastics among products of more than 1,000 factories, large federal expenditure, D/FW International Airport, economy closely associated with Dallas urban area.

History: Caddoes in area. Comanches, other tribes arrived about 1700. Anglo-Americans settled in the 1840s. Named for Gen. Edward H. Tarrant, who helped drive Indians from the area. County created in 1849 from Navarro County; organized in 1850.

Race/Ethnicity, 2008: (In percent) Anglo, 52.3; Black, 13.9; Hispanic, 27.5; Other, 6.3.

Vital Statistics, 2008: Births, 29,333; deaths, 10,726; marriages, 12,705; divorces, 7,267.

Recreation: Scott Theatre; Amon G.

Carter Museum; Kimbell Art Museum; Modern Art Museum; Museum of Science and History; Casa Manana; Botanic Gardens; Fort Worth Zoo; Log Cabin Village, all in Fort Worth.

Also, Six Flags Over Texas at Arlington; Southwestern Exposition, Stock Show; Convention Center; Stockyards Historical District; Texas Rangers and Dallas Cowboys at Arlington, other athletic events.

Minerals: Production of cement, sand, gravel, stone, gas.

Agriculture: Hay, beef cattle, wheat, horses, horticulture. Market value $61.4 million. Firewood marketed.

Education: Texas Christian University, University of Texas at Arlington, Texas Wesleyan University, Southwestern Baptist Theological Seminary and several other academic centers including a junior college system with five campus and various centers.

FORT WORTH (741,206, parts in Denton, Parker and Wise counties) county seat; a major mercantile, commercial and financial center; airplane, helicopter and other plants.

A cultural center with renowned art museums, Bass Performance Hall; many conventions held in downtown center; agribusiness center for wide area with grain-storage and feed-mill operations; adjacent to D/FW International Airport; hospitals.

ARLINGTON (365,438) UT-Arlington, General Motors assembly plant, tourism, Texas Rangers baseball team, Dallas Cowboys football stadium, retail; hospitals, bowling museum and hall of fame, performing arts pavilion, country music review; Texas Scottish festival in June.

Other towns include: **Hurst** (37,337); **Euless** (51,277); **Bedford** (46,979) helicopter plant, hospital, Celtic festival in fall; **North Richland Hills** (63,343) hospital.

Azle (10,947, partly in Parker County) government/services, varied industries, natural gas, hospital, commuters to Fort Worth, Jumpin' Jack Jamboree in September with car show-Weiner Dog race; **Benbrook** (21,234) varied manufacturing, hospitals; **Blue Mound** (2,394); **Briar** (5,665, parts in Wise and Parker counties).

Also, **Colleyville** (22,807) medical services, financial offices, commuters, government/services, nature center, barbecue cook-off in April, Sousa event in July; **Crowley** (12,838) varied manufacturing, government/services, hospital; **Dalworthington Gardens** (2,259); **Edgecliff** (2,776); **Everman** (6,108); **Forest Hill** (12,355).

Also, **Grapevine** (46,334) manufacturing, distribution, near the D/FW International Airport, tourist center, hospital, Grapefest in September; **Haltom City** (42,409) light manufacturing, food processing, medical center; library; **Haslet** (1,517) commuters, government/services, chili fest and rodeo

Largest U.S. Media Markets

Rank	TV Homes
1. New York	7.52 million
2. Los Angeles	5.67 million
3. Chicago	3.50 million
4. Philadelphia	3.02 million
5. Dallas/Fort Worth	2.59 million
6. San Francisco	2.52 million
7. Boston	2.46 million
8. Atlanta	2.41 million
9. Washington, D.C.	2.39 million
10. Houston	2.18 million

Source: Nielsen Media Research, 2011.

in May; **Keller** (39,627) Bear Creek Park, Wild West Fest.

Also, **Kennedale** (6,763) commuters, printing, manufacturing, library, drag strip, custom car show in May; **Lakeside** (1,307); **Lake Worth** (4,584) retail, tourism, auction house, museum, nature center.

Also, **Mansfield** (56,368, partly in Johnson and Ellis counties) varied manufacturing, retail centers, government/services, commuters, hospital, community college, library, museum,

> County adopted:
> **In honor of**
> **Dr. David R. Murph**

parks, pecan festival in September; **Pantego** (2,394); **Pelican Bay** (1,547); **Rendon** (12,552); **Richland Hills** (7,801).

Also, **River Oaks** (7,427); **Saginaw** (19,806) grain milling, manufacturing, distribution, library, aquatic center; **Sansom Park** (4,686); **Southlake** (26,575) technology, financial, retail center, hospital, parks, Oktoberfest; **Watauga** (23,497); **Westlake** (992); **Westover Hills** (682); **Westworth Village** (2,472).

Also, **White Settlement** (16,116) aircraft manufacturing, drilling equipment, technological services, Civil War museum, parks, historical sites; industrial park; White Settlement Day parade in fall.

Also, part of **Burleson** (36,690); part of **Grand Prairie** (175,396), and part of **Pecan Acres** (4,099).

Population	1,809,034
Change fm 2000	25.09
Area (sq. mi.)	897.48
Land Area (sq. mi.)	863.42
Altitude (ft.)	420-960
Rainfall (in.)	34.01
Jan. mean min.	31.4
July mean max.	96.6
Civ. Labor	907,005
Unemployed	8.5
Wages	$9,597,519,345
Av. Weekly Wage	$976
Prop. Value	$163,770,266,884
Retail Sales	$23,844,708,138

Dusk falls at Town Center in Southlake, Tarrant County. Photo by Lamberto Alvarez.

Physical Features: Prairies, with Callahan Divide, draining to Colorado tributaries, Brazos forks; Lakes Abilene, Kirby; mostly loam soils.

Economy: Agribusiness, oil and gas, education, Dyess Air Force Base.

History: Comanches in area about 1700. Anglo-American settlers arrived in 1870s. Named for Alamo heroes Edward, James and George Taylor, brothers; county created from Bexar, Travis counties 1858; organized 1878.

Race/Ethnicity, 2008: (In percent) Anglo, 68.1; Black, 7.7; Hispanic, 21.5; Other, 2.8.

Vital Statistics, 2008: Births, 2,121; deaths, 1,205; marriages, 1,307; divorces, 609.

Recreation: Abilene State Park, lake activities, Nelson Park Zoo, college events, Buffalo Gap historical tour and arts festival in April, Western Heritage ranch rodeo in May and West Texas Fair in September at Abilene.

Minerals: Oil, natural gas.

Taylor County

Agriculture: Beef cattle, small grain, cotton, milo. Market value $50.6 million.

Education: Abilene Christian University, Hardin-Simmons University, McMurry University, Texas Tech University pharmacy school and branch campus, Cisco Junior College branch.

ABILENE (117,063, a small part in Jones County) county seat; distribution center, manufacturing, wind energy, meat and dairy processing, oil-field service center; hospitals, Abilene State School,

West Texas Rehabilitation Center; Fort Phantom Hill (in Jones County). **Wylie** is now part of Abilene.

Other communities include: **Buffalo Gap** (464) historic sites; **Impact** (35); **Lawn** (314); **Merkel** (2,590) agribusiness center, clothing manufacturing, oil-field services; **Ovalo** (225); **Potosi** (2,991); **Trent** (337); **Tuscola** (742); **Tye** (1,242).

Population	**131,506**
Change fm 2000	3.91
Area (sq. mi.)	919.25
Land Area (sq. mi.)	915.63
Altitude (ft.)	1,640-2,490
Rainfall (in.)	23.78
Jan. mean min.	31.8
July mean max.	94.8
Civ. Labor	68,118
Unemployed	6.6
Wages	$525,365,690
Av. Weekly Wage	$707
Prop. Value	$7,518,899,186
Retail Sales	$1,986,083,195

For explanation of sources, abbreviations and symbols, see p. 232 and foldout map.

JONES

NOLAN

CALLAHAN

RUNNELS   COLEMAN

0 _____ 8 MILES

Terrell County

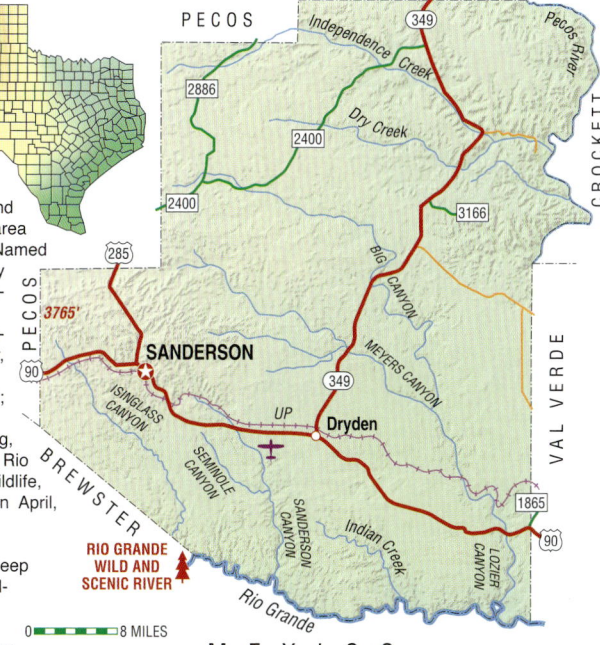

Physical Features: Trans-Pecos southwestern county; semi-mountainous, many canyons; rocky, limestone soils.

Economy: Ranching, hunting leases, oil and gas exploration, tourism.

History: Coahuiltecans, Jumanos and other tribes left many pictographs in area caves. Sheep ranching began in 1880s. Named for Confederate Gen. A.W. Terrell; county created 1905 from Pecos County, organized the same year.

Race/Ethnicity, 2008: (In percent) Anglo, 48.1; Black, 0.00; Hispanic, 59.6; Other, 2.3.

Vital Statistics, 2008: Births, 12; deaths, 11; marriages, 5; divorces, 1.

Recreation: Nature tourism, hunting, especially white-tailed and mule deer, Rio Grande Wild and Scenic River, varied wildlife, hiking trail; Big Bend open road race in April, Prickly Pear Pachanga in October.

Minerals: Gas, oil, limestone.

Agriculture: Goats (meat, Angora); sheep (meat, wool); some beef cattle. Market value $4 million. Wildlife leases important.

SANDERSON (837) county seat; ranching, hunting, oil and gas, tourism, government/services; museum.

Other town: **Dryden** (13).

Population	**984**
Change fm 2000	–8.97
Area (sq. mi.)	2,357.75
Land Area (sq. mi.)	2,357.72

Altitude (ft.)	1,180-3,765
Rainfall (in.)	14.94
Jan. mean min.	30.5
July mean max.	91.9
Civ. Labor	361
Unemployed	10.0
Wages	$3,734,583
Av. Weekly Wage	$835

Prop. Value	$1,150,545,623
Retail Sales	$2,579,915

For explanation of sources, abbreviations and symbols, see p. 232 and foldout map.

Wind turbines along FM 126 in Taylor County. Photo by Robert Plocheck.

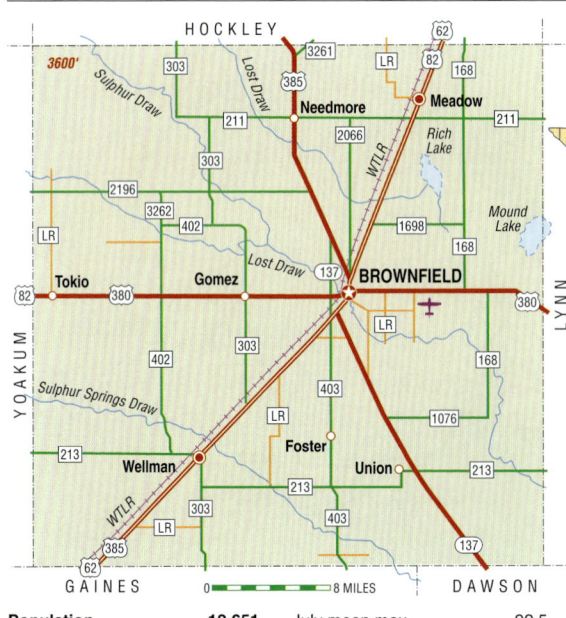

Terry County

Physical Features: South Plains, broken by draws, playas; sandy, sandy loam, loam soils.

Economy: Government/services, oil-field services, agribusiness.

History: Comanches removed in 1870s by U.S. Army. Ranching developed in 1890s; farming after 1900. Oil discovered in 1940. County named for Confederate Col. B.F. Terry, head of the Eighth Texas Cavalry (Terry's Texas Rangers). Created from Bexar District 1876; organized 1904.

Race/Ethnicity, 2008: (In percent), Anglo, 45.5; Black, 5.1; Hispanic, 48.8; Other, 0.6.

Vital Statistics, 2008: Births, 210; deaths, 130; marriages, 95; divorces, 43.

Recreation: Museum, aquatic center, quilt show in April, harvest festival in October.

Minerals: Oil, salt mining.

Agriculture: Cotton, peanuts (third in acreage), grain sorghum, guar, wheat, melons, cucumbers, sesame. 170,000 acres irrigated. Market value $124.8 million.

BROWNFIELD (9,657) county seat; oilfield services, wind energy, agribusiness, minerals and peanut processing; hospital; prison.

Other towns include: **Meadow** (593); **Tokio** (5); **Wellman** (203).

Population.......................**12,651**	July mean max. 92.5
Change fm 2000.................−0.86	Civ. Labor 5,788
Area (sq. mi.)....................890.93	Unemployed 7.6
Land Area (sq. mi.)...........889.88	Wages $40,309,540
Altitude (ft.) 3,080-3,600	Av. Weekly Wage.................$749
Rainfall (in.) 18.89	Prop. Value..........$1,081,949,880
Jan. mean min. 26.1	Retail Sales $132,965,074

Throckmorton County

Physical Features: Northwest county southwest of Wichita Falls; rolling, between Brazos forks; red to black soils.

Economy: Oil, agribusiness, hunting.

History: Site of Comanche Indian Reservation 1854–1859. Ranching developed after the Civil War. County named for Dr. W.E. Throckmorton, father of Gov. J.W. Throckmorton; county created from Fannin in 1858; organized in 1879.

Race/Ethnicity, 2008: (In percent) Anglo, 89.0; Black, 0.1; Hispanic, 10.4; Other, 0.6.

Vital Statistics, 2008: Births, 22; deaths, 17; marriages, 9; divorces, 3.

Recreation: Hunting, fishing; historic sites include Camp Cooper, site of former Comanche reservation, restored ranch home; Millers Creek Reservoir; wild game dinner in January.

Minerals: Natural gas, oil.

Agriculture: Beef cattle, horses, wheat, hay. Market value $21.9 million. Mesquite firewood sold. Hunting leases important.

THROCKMORTON (828) county seat; varied manufacturing, oil-field services; hospital; Old Jail museum.

Other towns include: **Elbert** (30), **Woodson** (264).

Population **1,641**	Unemployed 5.4
Change fm 2000 ....−11.3	Wages $3,705,470
Area (sq. mi.) 915.47	Av. Weekly Wage.....................$580
Land Area (sq. mi.) 912.34	Prop. Value $509,836,502
Altitude (ft.) 1,100-1,730	Retail Sales $8,744,679
Rainfall (in.) 26.60	
Jan. mean min. 28.0	*For explanation of sources, abbreviations and symbols, see p. 232 and foldout map.*
July mean max. 97.0	
Civ. Labor 1,092	

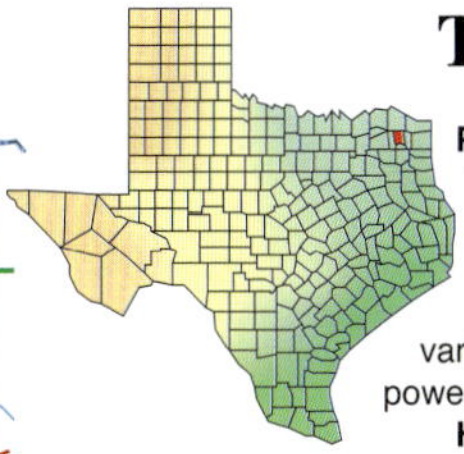

Titus County

Physical Features: Northeast Texas county; hilly, timbered; drains to Big Cypress Creek, Sulphur River.

Economy: Agribusiness, varied manufacturing, electric power generation, .

History: Caddo area. Cherokees and other tribes settled in 1820s. Anglo-American settlers arrived in 1840s. Named for pioneer settler A.J. Titus; county created from Bowie, Red River counties in 1846, organized the same year.

Race/Ethnicity, 2008: (In percent) Anglo, 52.1; Black, 10.5; Hispanic, 36.4; Other, 1.0.

Vital Statistics, 2008: Births, 600; deaths, 269; marriages, 260; divorces, 81.

Recreation: Fishing, hunting, lake activities, state park, rodeo, railroad museum, flower gardens.

Minerals: Lignite coal mining.

Agriculture: Poultry, beef cattle, hay, horticulture, horses. Market value $79.5 million. Timber sales significant.

MOUNT PLEASANT (15,564) county seat; tourism, varied manufacturing, food-processing plants; hospital; Northeast Texas Community College; jubilee and outhouse races in May.

Other towns include: **Cookville** (105), **Millers Cove** (149), **Talco** (516), **Winfield** (524).

For explanation of sources, abbreviations and symbols, see p. 232 and foldout map.

Population	32,334
Change fm 2000	14.99
Area (sq. mi.)	425.69
Land Area (sq. mi.)	410.54
Altitude (ft.)	250-530
Rainfall (in.)	48.57

Jan. mean min.	29.3
July mean max.	94.2
Civ. Labor	14,565
Unemployed	8.1
Wages	$142,634,545
Av. Weekly Wage	$678
Prop. Value	$3,771,824,379
Retail Sales	$503,011,331

The Throckmorton County Courthouse. Photo by Robert Plocheck.

Tom Green County

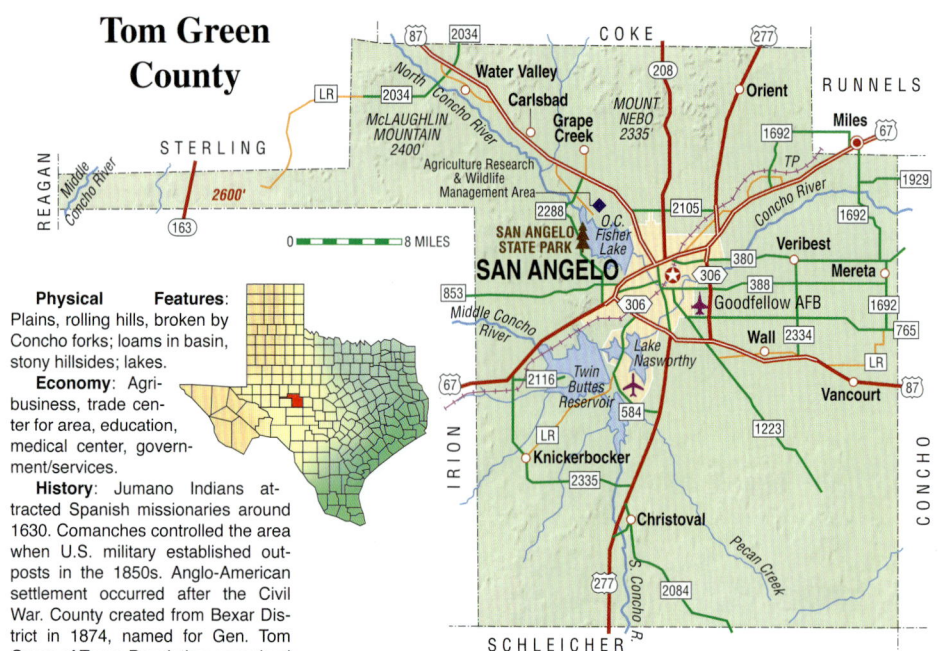

Physical Features:
Plains, rolling hills, broken by Concho forks; loams in basin, stony hillsides; lakes.

Economy: Agribusiness, trade center for area, education, medical center, government/services.

History: Jumano Indians attracted Spanish missionaries around 1630. Comanches controlled the area when U.S. military established outposts in the 1850s. Anglo-American settlement occurred after the Civil War. County created from Bexar District in 1874, named for Gen. Tom Green of Texas Revolution; organized in 1875; twelve other counties created from original.

Race/Ethnicity, 2008: (In percent) Anglo, 56.9; Black, 4.3; Hispanic, 36.9; Other, 1.9.

Vital Statistics, 2008: Births, 1,635; deaths, 1,072; marriages, 999; divorces, 418.

Recreation: Water sports, hunting, Fort Concho museum, symphony, baseball team, Christmas at Old Fort Concho, February rodeo.

Minerals: Oil, natural gas.

Agriculture: Cotton, cattle, goats, sheep, small grains, milo. About 30,000 acres irrigated. Market value $133 million; first in sheep and goat production.

SAN ANGELO (93,200) county seat; government/services, retail, transportation, education; hospitals, Angelo State University, Howard Junior College branch; riverwalk; Museum of Fine Arts, drag boat races in June.

Other towns include: **Carlsbad** (719); **Christoval** (504); **Grape Creek** (3,154); **Knickerbocker** (94); **Mereta** (131); **Vancourt** (131); **Veribest** (115); **Wall** (329); **Water Valley** (203).

Population	110,224
Change fm 2000	5.97
Area (sq. mi.)	1,540.54
Land Area (sq. mi.)	1,522.10
Altitude (ft.)	1,675-2,600
Rainfall (in.)	20.91
Jan. mean min.	31.8
July mean max.	94.4
Civ. Labor	54,099
Unemployed	6.7
Wages	$405,344,501
Av. Weekly Wage	$701
Prop. Value	$5,952,318,649
Retail Sales	$1,427,714,628

County adopted by:
Becky Madole Cornell

The Bob Bullock Texas State History Museum in Austin. Photo by Robert Plocheck.

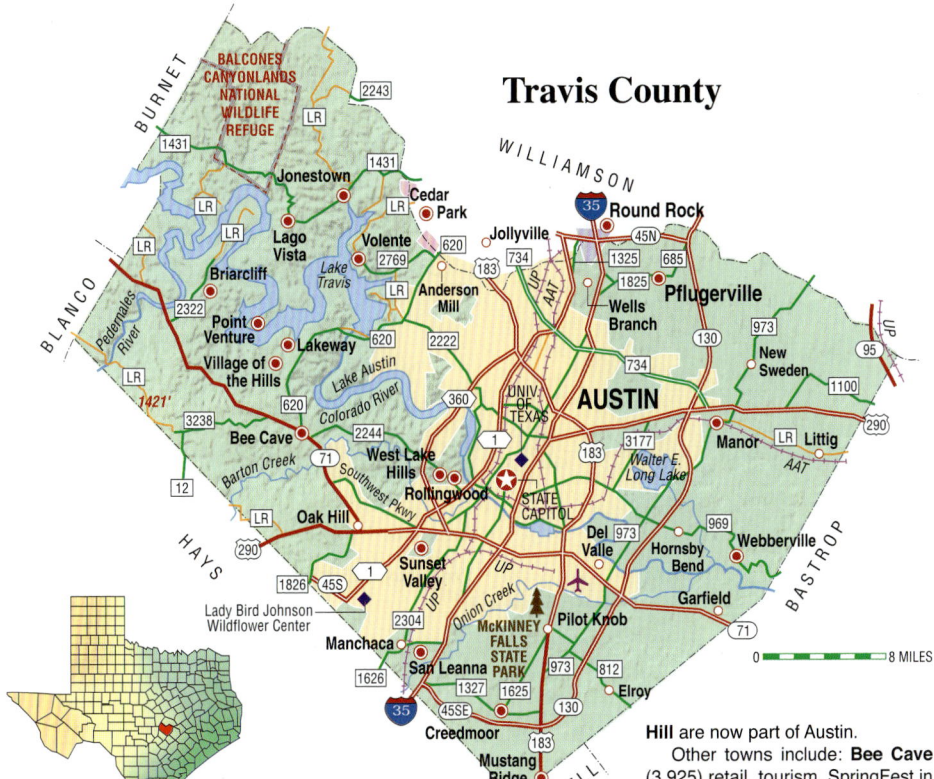

Travis County

Physical Features
Central county of scenic hills, broken by Colorado River and lakes; cedars, pecans, other trees; diverse soils, mineral deposits.

Economy: Government/services, education, technology, research and industry.

History: Tonkawa and Lipan Apache area; Comanches, Kiowas arrived about 1700. Spanish missions from East Texas temporarily relocated near Barton Springs in 1730 before removing to San Antonio. Anglo-Americans arrived in early 1830s. County created 1840, when Austin became Republic's capital, from Bastrop County; organized 1843; named for Alamo commander Col. William B. Travis; many other counties created from its original area.

Race/Ethnicity, 2008: (In percent) Anglo, 49.2; Black, 9.2; Hispanic, 35.3; Other, 6.2.

Vital Statistics, 2008: Births, 16,512; deaths, 4,519; marriages, 7,830; divorces, 2,886.

Recreation: Colorado River lakes, hunting, fishing; McKinney Falls State Park; Lady Bird John-son Wildflower Center; collegiate, metropolitan, governmental events; official buildings and historic sites; museums; Sixth St. restoration area; scenic drives; many city parks; South by Southwest film, music festival in March.

Minerals: Production of lime, stone, sand, gravel, oil and gas.

Agriculture: Cattle, nursery crops, hogs; sorghum, corn, cotton, small grains, pecans. Market value $22.8 million.

Education: University of Texas, St. Edward's University, Concordia Lutheran University, Huston-Tillotson College, Austin Community College, Episcopal and Presbyterian seminaries.

AUSTIN (790,390, partly in Williamson County) county seat and state capital; state and federal payrolls, IRS center, tourism, Lyndon B. Johnson Library, research, high-tech industries; hospitals, including state institutions for blind, deaf, mental illnesses; popular retirement area. **Anderson Mill, Del Valle** and **Oak Hill** are now part of Austin.

Other towns include: **Bee Cave** (3,925) retail, tourism, SpringFest in April; **Briarcliff** (1,438); **Creedmoor** (202); **Garfield** (1,698); **Jonestown** (1,834) tourism, retail, commuters, Chili Pod chili cook-off in April; **Lago Vista** (6,041) residential real estate, retail, tourism, lake activities; **Lakeway** (11,391) residential real estate, retail, tourism, lake activities; **Manchaca** (1,133); **Manor** (5,037); **Mustang Ridge** (861, partly in Caldwell County).

Also, **Pflugerville** (46,936) high-tech industries, agriculture, government/services, Deutchenfest in May; **Point Venture** (800); **Rollingwood** (1,412); **San Leanna** (497); **Sunset Valley** (749); **The Hills** (2,472) residential community; **Volente** (520); **Webberville** (392); **Wells Branch** (12,120); **West Lake Hills** (3,063).

Also, part of **Cedar Park**, part of **Jollyville** and part of **Round Rock**, all mostly in Williamson County.

Population	1,024,266
Change fm 2000	26.1
Area (sq. mi.)	1,022.06
Land Area (sq. mi.)	989.30
Altitude (ft.)	400-1,421
Rainfall (in.)	33.65
Jan. mean min.	40.0
July mean max.	95.0
Civ. Labor	557,298
Unemployed	7.0
Wages	$8,185,275,492
Av. Weekly Wage	$1,099
Prop. Value	$121,677,580,934
Retail Sales	$14,397,166,162

> *County adopted:*
> **In honor of**
> **Judge Bill Aleshire**

Trinity County

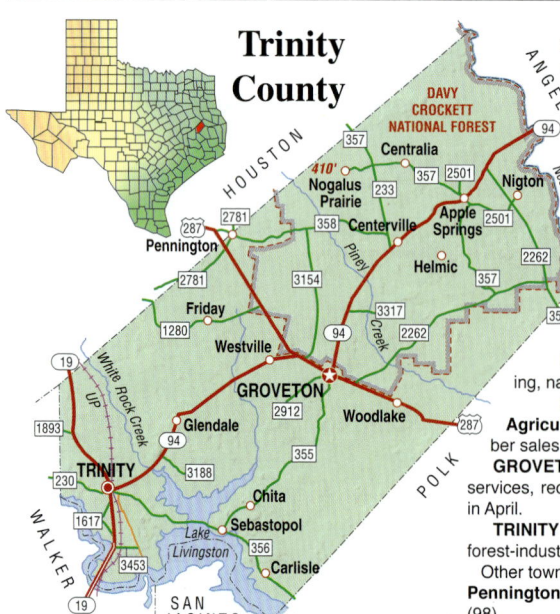

Physical Features: Heavily forested East Texas county of hills, between Neches and Trinity (Lake Livingston) rivers; rich alluvial soils, sandy upland; 67,910 acres in national forest.

Economy: Agriculture, government/services.

History: Caddoes, reduced by disease in late 1700s. Kickapoo, Alabama, Coushatta in area when Anglo-Americans settled in 1840s. Named for river; county created, organized, in 1850 out of Houston County.

Race/Ethnicity, 2008: (In percent) Anglo, 80.7; Black, 12.5; Hispanic, 6.2; Other, 0.6.

Vital Statistics, 2008: Births, 164; deaths, 208; marriages, 63; divorces, 34.

Recreation: Lake activities, fishing, hiking, hunting, national forest, historic site.

Minerals: Oil and gas.

Agriculture: Beef cattle. Market value $9.2 million. Timber sales significant. Hunting leases, fishing.

GROVETON (1,057) county seat; logging, government/services, recreation; museum, library; Bear Chase marathon in April.

TRINITY (2,697) government/services, steel fabrication, forest-industries center, commuters; hospital.

Other towns include: **Apple Springs** (350); **Centralia** (190); **Pennington** (67); **Sebastopol** (120) historic town; **Woodlake** (98).

Av. Weekly Wage	$546
Prop. Value	$1,151,675,898
Retail Sales	$71,013,723

County adopted in honor of:
Bess Courtney Brannen
Carl Andrew Brannen

Population	14,585	Rainfall (in.)	48.10
Change fm 2000	5.85	Jan. mean min.	37.1
Area (sq. mi.)	714.00	July mean max.	94.8
Land Area (sq. mi.)	692.84	Civ. Labor	5,872
Altitude (ft.)	131-410	Unemployed	9.4
		Wages	$15,966,119

Tyler County

Physical Features: Hilly East Texas county; densely timbered; drains to Neches River; B.A. Steinhagen Lake; Big Thicket is unique plant and animal area.

Economy: Lumbering, government/services, some manufacturing, tourism, hunting leases.

History: Caddoan area. Cherokees, Alabama and Coushatta pushed into area from U.S. South in 1820s. Anglo-Americans settled in 1830s. Named for U.S. President John Tyler; county created, organized, in 1846 from Liberty County.

Race/Ethnicity, 2008: (In percent) Anglo, 84.2; Black, 11.8; Hispanic, 3.3; Other, 0.7.

Vital Statistics, 2008: Births, 225; deaths, 229; marriages, 131; divorces, 110.

Recreation: Big Thicket National Preserve; Heritage Village; lake activities; Allan Shivers Museum; state forest; historic sites; dogwood festival in spring; rodeo, frontier frolics in September; gospel music fest in June.

Minerals: Oil, natural gas.

Agriculture: Beef cattle, hay, nursery crops, blueberries, horses. Market value $21.8 million. Timber sales significant.

WOODVILLE (2,586) county seat; lumber, cattle market, varied manufacturing, tourism; hospital, prison.

Other towns include: **Chester** (312) **Colmesneil** (596), **Doucette** (160), **Fred** (299), **Hillister** (250), **Ivanhoe** (887), **Ivanhoe North** (538), **Spurger** (590), **Warren** (757).

Population	21,766	July mean max.	92.1
Change fm 2000	4.29	Civ. Labor	8,644
Area (sq. mi.)	935.71	Unemployed	11.3
Land Area (sq. mi.)	922.90	Wages	$30,496,951
Altitude (ft.)	50-461	Av. Weekly Wage	$595
Rainfall (in.)	54.79	Prop. Value	$2,108,296,883
Jan. mean min.	38.3	Retail Sales	$107,389,781

Upshur County

Physical Features: East Texas county; rolling to hilly, over half forested; drains to Sabine River, Little Cypress Creek, Lake O' the Pines, Lake Gilmer, Lake Gladewater.

Economy: Manufacturing, oil, gas, agribusiness, timber.

History: Caddoes; reduced by epidemics in 1700s. Cherokees in area in 1820s. Anglo-American settlement in mid-1830s. County created from Harrison, Nacogdoches counties in 1846, organized the same year; named for U.S. Secretary of State A.P. Upshur.

Race/Ethnicity, 2008: (In percent) Anglo, 82.4; Black, 10.1; Hispanic, 6.5; Other, 1.0.

Vital Statistics, 2008: Births, 489; deaths, 404; marriages, 225; divorces, 192.

Recreation: Scenic trails, hunting, fishing, fall foliage, Gilmer East Texas Yamboree in October.

Minerals: Oil, gas, sand, gravel.

Agriculture: Dairies, beef cattle, hay, vegetable crops, poultry. Market value $48.9 million. Timber a major product.

GILMER (4,905) county seat; manufacturing, communications, electric power; hospital; museums; Texas Motorized Trails.

Other towns include: **Big Sandy** (1,343); **Diana** (585); **East Mountain** (797); **Ore City** (1,144); **Union Grove** (357).

Part of **Gladewater** (6,441).

Population	39,309
Change fm 2000	11.39
Area (sq. mi.)	592.67
Land Area (sq. mi.)	587.64
Altitude (ft.)	228-685
Rainfall (in.)	47.08
Jan. mean min.	31.4
July mean max.	93.4
Civ. Labor	20,390
Unemployed	8.2

Wages	$55,688,540
Av. Weekly Wage	$649
Prop. Value	$2,966,468,044
Retail Sales	$287,461,323

For explanation of sources, symbols and abbreviations, see p. 232 and foldout map.

The Trinity County Courthouse in Groveton. Photo by Ron Billings; Texas Forest Service.

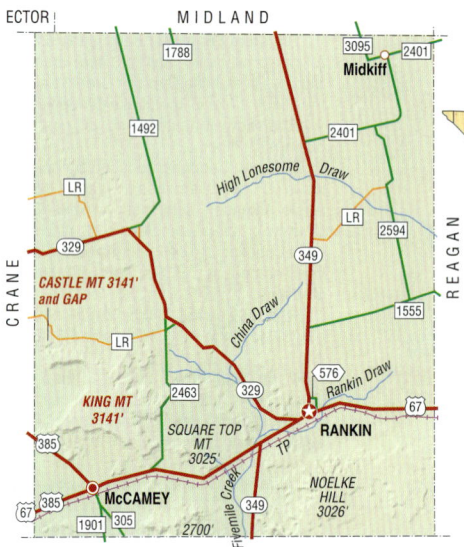

Population	3,355
Change fm 2000	–1.44
Area (sq. mi.)	1,241.83
Land Area (sq. mi.)	1,241.68
Altitude (ft.)	2,310-3,141
Rainfall (in.)	14.45
Jan. mean min.	33.1
July mean max.	95.6
Civ. Labor	1,858
Unemployed	4.6
Wages	$20,055,268
Av. Weekly Wage	$1,013
Prop. Value	$3,535,085,429
Retail Sales	$20,682,544

Upton County

Physical Features: Western county; north flat, south rolling, hilly; limestone, sandy loam soils, drains to creeks.

Economy: Oil, wind turbines, farming, ranching.

History: Apache and Comanche area until tribes removed by U.S. Army in 1870s. Sheep, cattle ranching developed in 1880s. Oil discovered in 1925. County created in 1887 from Tom Green County; organized 1910; name honors brothers John and William Upton, Confederate colonels.

Race/Ethnicity, 2008: (In percent) Anglo, 50.7; Black, 1.4; Hispanic, 47.0; Other, 0.9.

Vital Statistics, 2008: Births, 55; deaths, 29; marriages, 4; divorces, 9.

Recreation: Historic sites, Mendoza Trail museum, scenic areas; McCamey chili cookoff in October, pecan show in November.

Minerals: Oil, natural gas.

Agriculture: Cotton, sheep, goats, cattle, watermelons, pecans. Extensive irrigation. Market value $8.6 million.

RANKIN (778) county seat, oil, ranching, farming; hospital; Barbados cookoff in May, All Kid rodeo in June.

McCAMEY (1,887) oil, gas, wind; hospital; Wind Energy bluegrass festival in September.

Other town: **Midkiff** (182).

Uvalde County

Physical Features: Edwards Plateau, rolling hills below escarpment; spring-fed Sabinal, Frio, Leona, Nueces rivers; cypress, cedar, other trees, including maple groves.

Economy: Agribusinesses, hunting leases, light manufacturing, tourism.

History: Spanish mission Nuestra Señora de la Candelaria founded in 1762 for Lipan Apaches near present-day Montell; Comanches harassed mission. U.S. military outpost established in 1849. County created from Bexar 1850; re-created, organized 1856; named for 1778 governor of Coahuila, Juan de Ugalde, with name Anglicized.

Race/Ethnicity, 2008: (In percent) Anglo, 29.3; Black, 0.3; Hispanic, 69.7; Other, 0.7.

Vital Statistics, 2008: Births, 438; deaths, 227; marriages, 148; divorces, 72.

Recreation: Deer, turkey hunting; Garner State Park; water activities on rivers; John Nance Garner museum; Uvalde Memorial Park; scenic trails, historic sites.

Minerals: Asphalt, stone, sand, gravel.

Agriculture: Cattle, vegetables, corn, cotton, sorghum, sheep, goats, hay, wheat. Substantial irrigation. Market value $77.7 million.

UVALDE (15,751) county seat; vegetable, wool, mohair processing, tourism; opera house; junior college, A&M research center; hospital; Fort Inge Day in April.

Sabinal (1,695) farm, ranch center, tourism, retirement area.

Other towns include: **Concan** (225); **Knippa** (689); **Utopia** (277) resort; **Uvalde Estates** (2,171).

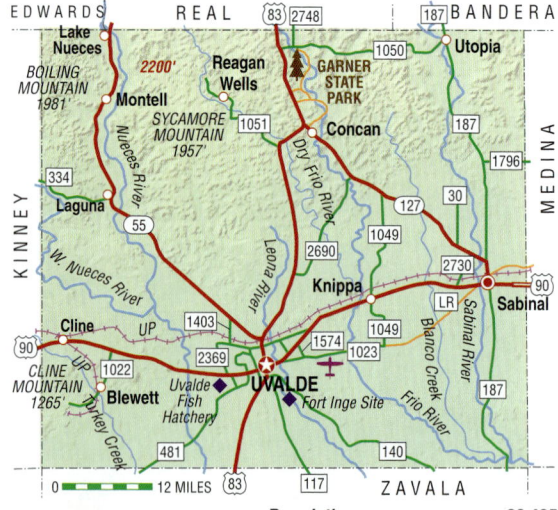

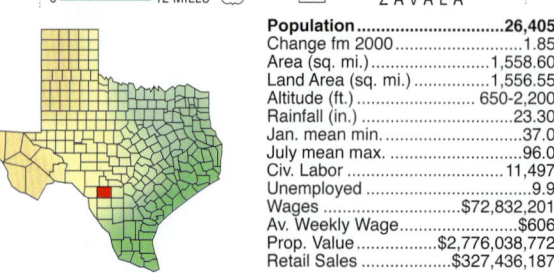

Population	26,405
Change fm 2000	1.85
Area (sq. mi.)	1,558.60
Land Area (sq. mi.)	1,556.55
Altitude (ft.)	650-2,200
Rainfall (in.)	23.30
Jan. mean min.	37.0
July mean max.	96.0
Civ. Labor	11,497
Unemployed	9.9
Wages	$72,832,201
Av. Weekly Wage	$606
Prop. Value	$2,776,038,772
Retail Sales	$327,436,187

For explanation of sources, abbreviations and symbols, see p. 232 and foldout map.

Val Verde County

Physical Features: Southwestern county bordering Mexico, rolling, hilly; brushy; Devils, Pecos rivers, Rio Grande and Amistad Reservoir; limestone, alluvial soils.

Economy: Agribusiness, tourism, trade center, military, Border Patrol, hunting leases, fishing.

History: Apaches, Coahuiltecans, Jumanos present when Spanish came through in the late 1500s. Comanches arrived later. U.S. military outposts established in the 1850s to protect settlers. Only county named for a Civil War battle; Val Verde means green valley. Created, organized, 1885 from Crockett, Kinney, Pecos counties.

Race/Ethnicity, 2008: (In percent) Anglo, 19.9; Black, 1.5; Hispanic, 77.6; Other, 1.1.

Vital Statistics, 2008: Births, 951; deaths, 324; marriages, 369; divorces, 144.

Recreation: Gateway to Mexico; deer hunting, fishing; Amistad lake activities; two state parks; Langtry restoration of Judge Roy Bean's saloon; ancient pictographs; San Felipe Springs; winery.

Minerals: Production sand and gravel, gas, oil.

Agriculture: Sheep (second in numbers), Angora and meat goats (third in numbers); cattle; minor irrigation. Market value $12 million.

DEL RIO (35,591) county seat; government/services including federal agencies and military, agribusiness, tourism; hospital, extension colleges; Fiesta de Amistad in October.

Laughlin Air Force Base (1,569).

Other towns and places include:

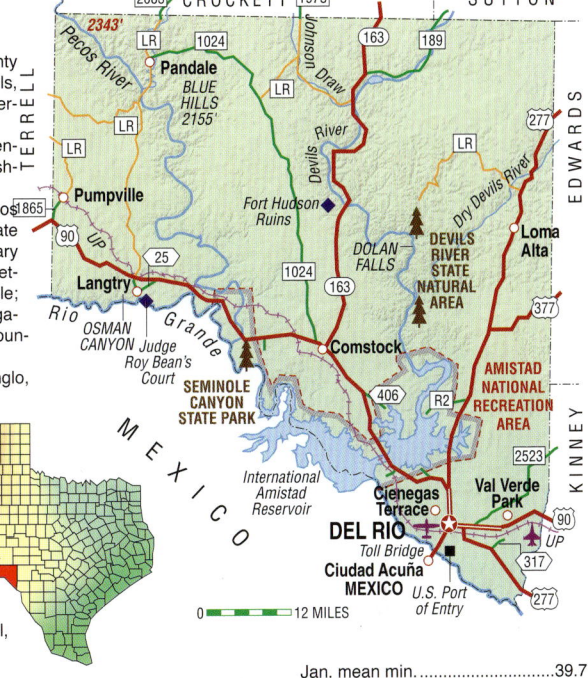

Cienegas Terrace (3,424); **Comstock** (344); **Langtry** (30); **Val Verde Park** (2,384).

Population 48,879
Change fm 2000 .... 8.97
Area (sq. mi.) 3,232.40
Land Area (sq. mi.) 3,170.38
Altitude (ft.) 845-2,343
Rainfall (in.) 18.80

Jan. mean min. 39.7
July mean max. 96.2
Civ. Labor 21,209
Unemployed 9.8
Wages $148,831,379
Av. Weekly Wage $677
Prop. Value $2,174,938,894
Retail Sales $510,159,703

For explanation of sources, abbreviations and symbols, see p. 232 and foldout map.

Boats moored at Amistad Reservoir, Val Verde County. Photo by Robert Plocheck.

Van Zandt County

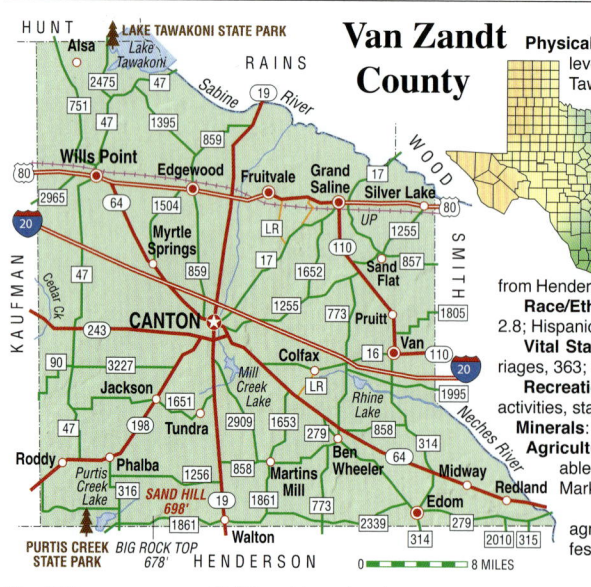

Physical Features: Eastern county in three soil belts; level to rolling; Sabine, Neches rivers; Lake Tawakoni; partly forested.

Economy: Agriculture, goverment/services, commuters to Dallas.

History: Caddoes, reduced by epidemics before settlers arrived. Cherokees settled in 1820s; removed in 1839 under policies of President Lamar; Anglo-American settlement followed. County named for Republic leader Isaac Van Zandt; created from Henderson County in 1848, organized the same year.

Race/Ethnicity, 2008: (In percent) Anglo, 87.7; Black, 2.8; Hispanic, 8.7; Other, 0.7.

Vital Statistics, 2008: Births, 617; deaths, 651; marriages, 363; divorces, 223.

Recreation: Canton First Monday trades days, lake activities, state parks, historic sites.

Minerals: Oil, gas.

Agriculture: Nurseries, cattle, dairies, forages, vegatables. First in nursery and sweet potato acreage. Market value $95.2 million.

CANTON (3,581) county seat; tourism, agribusiness, commuters; museums, bluegrass festival in June.

Wills Point (3,524) government/services, retail, tourism, commuters, depot museum, bluebird festival in April.

Other towns include: **Ben Wheeler** (504); **Edgewood** (1,441) commuters, heritage park, antiques; **Edom** (375) arts and crafts; **Fruitvale** (408); **Grand Saline** (3,136) salt plant, hospital, Salt Palace museum, birding, Bloomin' Festival in March; **Van** (2,632) oil center, hay, cattle, oil festival in October.

Population	52,579
Change fm 2000	9.22
Area (sq. mi.)	859.48
Land Area (sq. mi.)	848.64
Altitude (ft.)	330-698
Rainfall (in.)	43.68
Jan. mean min.	31.4
July mean max.	93.3
Civ. Labor	25,568
Unemployed	7.9
Wages	$77,116,278
Av. Weekly Wage	$620
Prop. Value	$3,851,581,794
Retail Sales	$404,318,842

For explanation of sources, abbreviations and symbols, see p. 232 and foldout map.

Victoria County

Physical Features: Rolling prairies, intersected by many streams; sandy loams, clays, alluvial soils.

Economy: Petrochemical plants, government/services, oil, manufacturing, agribusiness, tourism.

History: Karankawas, other tribes in area when Spanish explored in 1528. Comanches and Tawakonis arrived later. La Salle's camp on Garcitas Creek 1685-1687. Spanish ranching developed in the 1750s. Anglo-Americans arrived after 1836. An original county, created in 1836 from Mexican municipality named for President Guadalupe Victoria of Mexico.

Race/Ethnicity, 2008: (In percent) Anglo, 46.4; Black, 6.3; Hispanic, 46.0; Other, 1.4.

Vital Statistics, 2008: Births, 1,429; deaths, 737; marriages, 710; divorces, 278.

Recreation: Fishing, hunting; saltwater activities, historic homes, sites, riverside park, Coleto Creek Reservoir and park, zoo, Czech festival in September at Victoria.

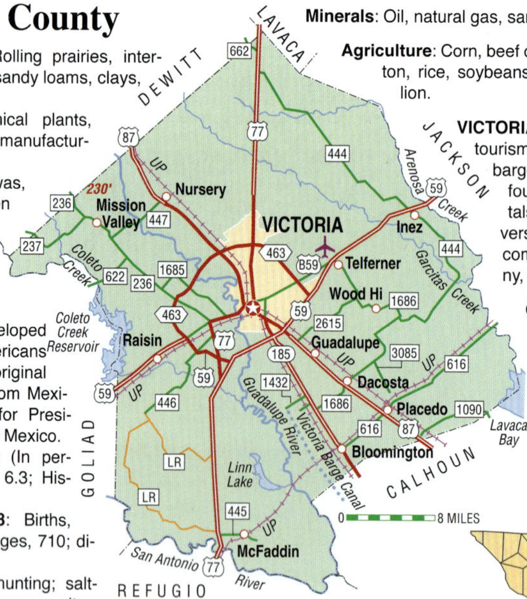

Minerals: Oil, natural gas, sand, gravel.

Agriculture: Corn, beef cattle, grain sorghums, cotton, rice, soybeans. Market value $43.4 million.

VICTORIA (62,592) county seat; tourism, agribusiness center, on barge canal, petrochemicals, foundry equipment; hospitals; Victoria College, University of Houston at Victoria; community theater, symphony, museums.

Other towns include: **Bloomington** (2,459), **Inez** (2,098), **McFaddin** (50), **Nursery** (450), **Placedo** (692), **Telferner** (700).

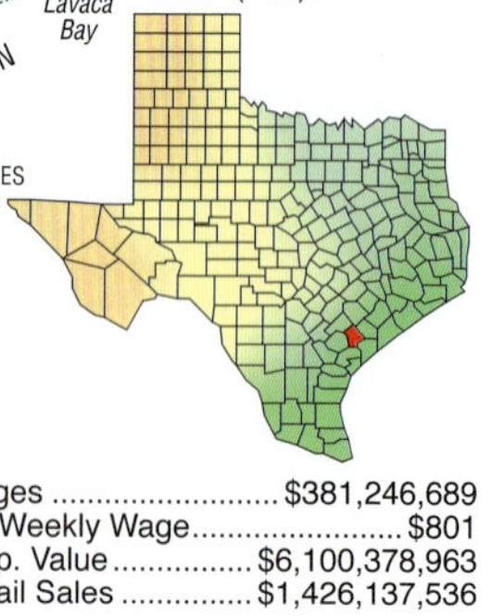

Population	86,793
Change fm 2000	3.22
Area (sq. mi.)	888.73
Land Area (sq. mi.)	882.50
Altitude (ft.)	sea level-230
Rainfall (in.)	40.10
Jan. mean min.	43.6
July mean max.	93.4
Civ. Labor	45,672
Unemployed	7.1
Wages	$381,246,689
Av. Weekly Wage	$801
Prop. Value	$6,100,378,963
Retail Sales	$1,426,137,536

Walker County

Physical Features: South central county north of Houston of rolling hills; more than 70 percent forested; national forest; San Jacinto, Trinity rivers.

Economy: State employment in prison system, education.

History: Coahuiltecans, Bidais in area when Spanish explored around 1690. Later, area became trading ground for many Indian tribes. Anglo-Americans settled in the 1830s. Antebellum slaveholding area. County created in 1846 from Montgomery County, organized the same year; first named for U.S. Secretary of Treasury R.J. Walker; renamed in 1863 for Texas Ranger Capt. S.H. Walker.

Race/Ethnicity, 2008: (In percent) Anglo, 59.9; Black, 23.2; Hispanic, 15.4; Other, 1.4.

Vital Statistics, 2008: Births, 642; deaths, 452; marriages, 452; divorces, 204.

Recreation: Fishing, hunting, lake activities; Sam Houston museum, homes, grave; prison museum; other historic sites, state park, Sam Houston National Forest; Sam Houston folk festival in spring.

Minerals: Clays, gas, oil, sand and gravel, stone.

Agriculture: Cattle, nursery plants, poultry, cotton, hay. Market value $26.9 million. Timber sales substantial; Christmas trees.

HUNTSVILLE (38,548) county seat; state prison system, Sam Houston State University, forest products, varied manufacturing; hospital; museums, arts center.

Other towns include: **Dodge** (150), **New Waverly** (1,032), **Riverside** (510).

Population	67,861
Change fm 2000	9.88
Area (sq. mi.)	801.44
Land Area (sq. mi.)	787.45
Altitude (ft.)	131-500
Rainfall (in.)	48.51
Jan. mean min.	39.0
July mean max.	93.8
Civ. Labor	27,954
Unemployed	8.0

Wages	$206,827,483
Av. Weekly Wage	$677
Prop. Value	$3,122,869,751
Retail Sales	$720,729,717

For explanation of sources, symbols and abbreviations, see p. 525 and foldout map.

Oil and football at Van High School, Van Zandt County. Photo by Robert Plocheck.

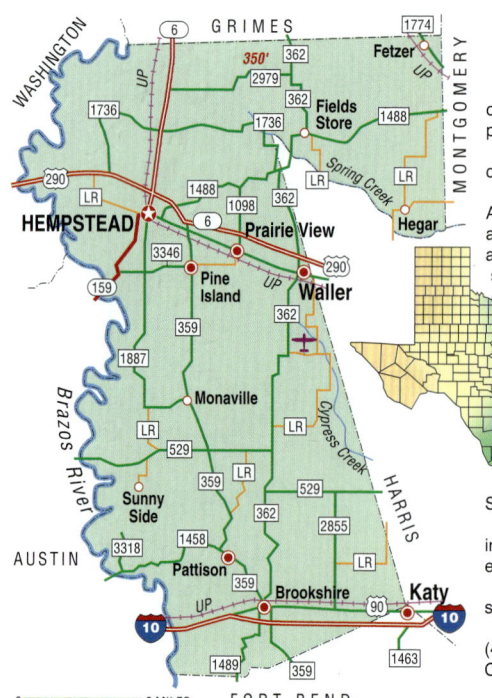

Waller County

Physical Features: South central county near Houston on rolling prairie; drains to Brazos; alluvial soils; about 20 percent forested.

Economy: Agribusiness, construction, education, part of Houston metropolitan area.

History: Bidais Indians reduced to about 100 when Anglo-Americans settled in 1820s. Antebellum slaveholding area. County named for Edwin Waller, Republic leader; created in 1873 from Austin, Grimes counties, organized the same year.

Race/Ethnicity, 2008: (In percent), Anglo, 47.4; Black, 26.5; Hispanic, 25.4; Other, 0.7.

Vital Statistics, 2008: Births, 618; deaths, 255; marriages, 285; divorces, 143.

Recreation: Fishing, hunting; historic sites; museum.

Minerals: Oil, gas.

Agriculture: Cattle, hay, nurseries, rice, turf grass, horses, corn, watermelons, goats, berries. 10,000 acres irrigated. Market value $55.1 million. Some timber marketed.

HEMPSTEAD (5,770) county seat; varied manufacturing, commuting to Houston, agribusiness center, large vegetable market; watermelon fest in July.

Prairie View (5,576) home of Prairie View A&M University.

Other towns include: **Brookshire** (4,702), **Pattison** (472), **Pine Island** (988), **Waller** (2,326, partly in Harris County) agriculture, education, construction.

Also, part of **Katy** (14,102, mostly in Harris County) hospitals.

Population	43,205		
Change fm 2000	32.28	Rainfall (in.)	38.20
Area (sq. mi.)	518.49	Jan. mean min.	38.0
Land Area (sq. mi.)	513.63	July mean max.	95.0
Altitude (ft.)	100-350	Civ. Labor	16,803
		Unemployed	9.3
		Wages	$154,194,999
		Av. Weekly Wage	$847
		Prop. Value	$19,863,747,780
		Retail Sales	$378,114,695

Ward County

Physical Features: Western county on Pecos River; plain covered by grass, brush; sandy, loam soils.

Economy: Oil, gas, government/services.

History: Jumano Indians in area when Spanish explored in 1580s. Comanches arrived later. Railroad stations established in 1880s. Oil discovered in 1920s. County named for Republic leader Thomas W. Ward; county created from Tom Green County in 1887; organized in 1892.

Race/Ethnicity, 2008: (In percent) Anglo, 48.8; Black, 4.9; Hispanic, 45.4; Other, 0.8.

Vital Statistics, 2008: Births, 185; deaths, 114; marriages, 74; divorces, 39.

Recreation: Sandhills state park, camel treks, Million Barrel museum in Monahans, county park, Butterfield stagecoach festival in July.

Minerals: Oil, gas, caliche, sand, gravel.

Agriculture: Beef cattle, alfalfa, horses, cotton, goats. Market value

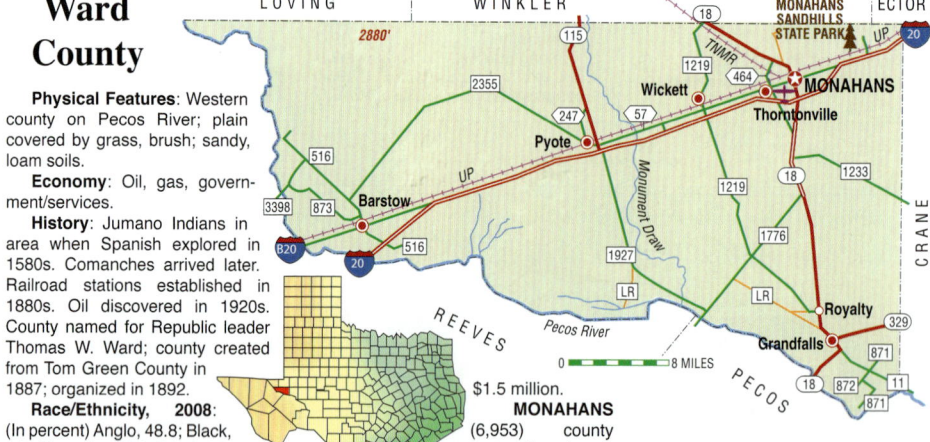

$1.5 million.

MONAHANS (6,953) county seat; oil and gas, ranching; hospital, nursing school extension.

Other towns: **Barstow** (349); **Grandfalls** (360); **Pyote** (114) Rattlesnake bomber base museum; **Thorntonville** (476); **Wickett** (498).

For explanation of sources, abbreviations and symbols, see p. 232 and foldout map.

Population	10,658
Change fm 2000	−2.3
Area (sq. mi.)	835.74
Land Area (sq. mi.)	835.49
Altitude (ft.)	2,400-2,880
Rainfall (in.)	13.23
Jan. mean min.	26.5
July mean max.	98.6
Civ. Labor	4,925
Unemployed	7.7
Wages	$44,532,304
Av. Weekly Wage	$952
Prop. Value	$1,776,968,448
Retail Sales	$93,622,777

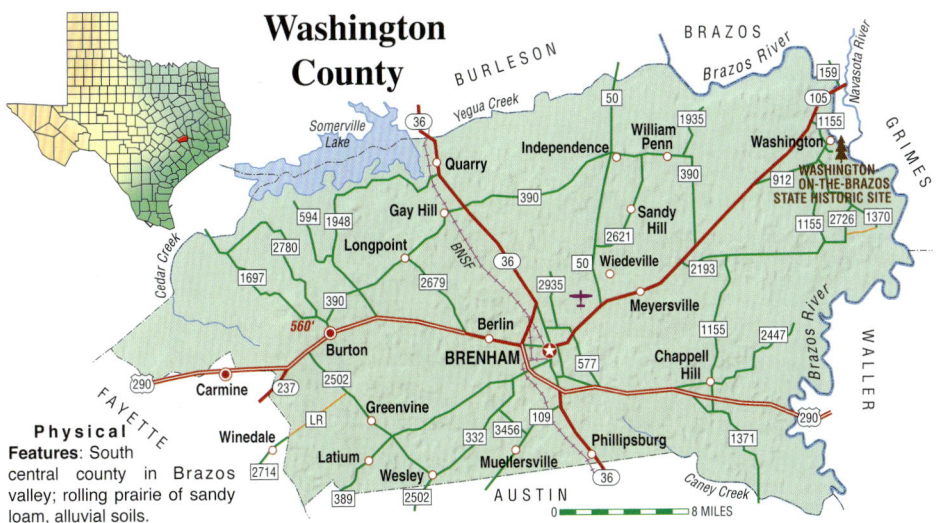

Washington County

For explanation of sources, abbreviations and symbols, see p. 232 and foldout map.

Physical Features: South central county in Brazos valley; rolling prairie of sandy loam, alluvial soils.

Economy: Agribusiness, oil, tourism, manufacturing, government/services.

History: Coahuiltecan tribes and Tonkawas in area when Anglo-American settlers arrived in 1821. Antebellum slaveholding area. Germans arrived around 1870. County named for George Washington; an original county, created in 1836, organized in 1837.

Race/Ethnicity, 2008: (In percent), Anglo, 68.1; Black, 18.4; Hispanic, 11.9; Other, 1.6.

Vital Statistics, 2008: Births, 460; deaths, 362; marriages, 233; divorces, 107.

Recreation: Many historic sites, including Washington-on-the-Brazos, Texas Baptist Historical Museum, Star of Republic Museum; wildflowers, Somerville Lake, fishing, hunting, birding; antique rose nursery.

Minerals: Oil, gas and stone.

Agriculture: Cattle, poultry, dairy products, hogs, horses; hay, corn, sorghum, cotton, small grains, nursery crops. Market value $44.8 million.

BRENHAM (15,716) county seat; Blue Bell creamery, retail, tourism; hospital; Blinn College; Maifest.

Other towns include: **Burton** (300) agriculture, tourism, national landmark cotton gin, festival in April; **Chappell Hill** (750) sausage production, tourism, historic homes, Scarecrow festival in October; **Washington** (100) site of signing of Texas Declaration of Independence.

Population	**33,718**
Change fm 2000	11.01
Area (sq. mi.)	621.35
Land Area (sq. mi.)	609.22
Altitude (ft.)	150-560
Rainfall (in.)	44.15
Jan. mean min.	39.3
July mean max.	96.7
Civ. Labor	16,723
Unemployed	6.5
Wages	$135,215,978
Av. Weekly Wage	$713
Prop. Value	$5,042,873,475
Retail Sales	$437,896,292

The Baptist church in Independence, Washington County, was established in 1839. Photo by Robert Plocheck.

Webb County

Physical Features: Southwestern county on Rio Grande: rolling, some hills; much brush; sandy, gray soils; alluvial along river.

Economy: International trade, manufacturing, tourism, government/services, natural gas, oil.

History: Coahuiltecan groups squeezed out by Comanches, Apaches and Spanish settlers. Laredo founded in 1755 by Tomás Sánchez. County named for Republic leader James Webb; created, organized, 1848 from Nueces and Bexar counties.

Race/Ethnicity, 2008: (In percent) Anglo, 3.9; Black, 0.1; Hispanic, 95.2; Other, 0.8.

Vital Statistics, 2008: Births, 5,897; deaths, 1,137; marriages, 1,762; divorces, 246.

Recreation: Tourist gateway to Mexico; hunting, fishing; Lake Casa Blanca park, water recreation; historic sites; Museum of Republic of the Rio Grande; Fort McIntosh; minor league baseball, hockey; Washington's Birthday celebration.

Minerals: Natural gas, oil, coal.

Agriculture: Onions, melons, nursery crops, cattle, horses, goats. About 4,500 acres irrigated. Market value $24.7 million. Mesquite sold. Hunting leases important.

LAREDO (236,091) county seat; international trade, retail center, government/services; rail, highway gateway to Mexico; Texas A&M International University, community college; hospitals; entertainment/sports arena; "El Grito" on Sept. 15; Jalapeño festival in February.

Other towns and places include: **Bruni** (379); **El Cenizo** (3,273); **Mirando City** (375); **Oilton** (353); **Rio Bravo** (4,794).

For explanation of sources, abbreviations and symbols, see p. 232 and foldout map.

Population	250,304
Change fm 2000	29.61
Area (sq. mi.)	3,375.53
Land Area (sq. mi.)	3,356.83
Altitude (ft.)	310-940
Rainfall (in.)	21.53
Jan. mean min.	43.7
July mean max.	101.6
Civ. Labor	95,585
Unemployed	8.7
Wages	$736,699,467
Av. Weekly Wage	$653
Prop. Value	$15,567,486,388
Retail Sales	$2,941,272,143

A service station along the old Route 66 in Shamrock, Wheeler County. Photo by Robert Plocheck.

Wharton County

Physical Features: Gulf prairie; bisected by Colorado River; alluvial, black, sandy loam soils.

Economy: Oil, agribusiness, hunting, varied manufacturing, government/services.

History: Karankawas in area until 1840s. Anglo-American colonists settled in 1823. Czechs, Germans arrived in 1880s. Mexican migration increased after 1950. County named for John A. and William H. Wharton, brothers active in the Texas Revolution; created, organized, 1846 from Colorado, Matagorda and Jackson counties.

Race/Ethnicity, 2008: (In percent) Anglo, 47.8; Black, 14.8; Hispanic, 36.8; Other, 0.6.

Vital Statistics, 2008: Births, 642; deaths, 370; marriages, 298; divorces, 152.

Recreation: Waterfowl hunting, fishing, big-game, birding; art, historical museums; riverfront park at Wharton; historic sites; Plaza Theater at Wharton.

Minerals: Oil, gas.

Agriculture: Top rice-producing county; cotton, milo, corn, sorghum, soybeans (first in acreage); 130,000 acres irrigated. Market value $240.2 million.

WHARTON (8,832) county seat; health care, plastics, government/services; hospitals, junior college; Juneteenth, wine and arts festival in October.

EL CAMPO (11,602) rice processing, plastic, styrofoam processing; hospital; Polka Expo in November.

Other towns include: **Boling** (1,122); **Danevang** (61); **East Bernard** (2,272) commuters, agribusiness, retail, klobase-kolache festival in June; **Egypt** (26); **Glen Flora** (210); **Hungerford** (347); **Lane City** (111); **Lissie** (72); **Louise** (995); **Pierce** (51).

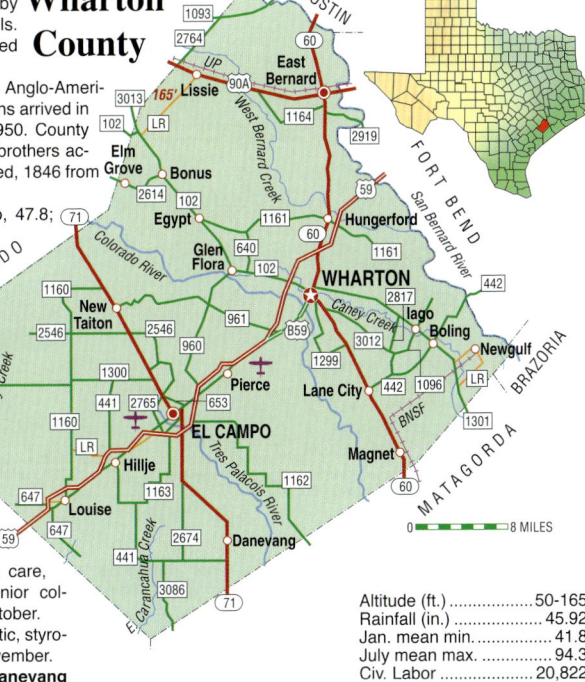

Population	41,280
Change fm 2000	0.22
Area (sq. mi.)	1,094.43
Land Area (sq. mi.)	1,090.13

Altitude (ft.)	50-165
Rainfall (in.)	45.92
Jan. mean min.	41.8
July mean max.	94.3
Civ. Labor	20,822
Unemployed	8.9
Wages	$123,345,595
Av. Weekly Wage	$650
Prop. Value	$4,137,802,888
Retail Sales	$533,318,342

Wheeler County

Physical Features: Panhandle county adjoining Oklahoma. Plain, on edge of Caprock; Red River, Sweetwater Creek; some canyons; red sandy loam, black clay soils.

Economy: Oil, gas, agribusiness, tourism.

History: Apaches, displaced by Kiowas, Comanches around 1700. Military outpost established in 1875 after Indians forced into Oklahoma. Ranching began in late 1870s. Oil boom in 1920s. County named for pioneer jurist R.T. Wheeler; county created from Bexar, Young districts 1876; organized 1879.

Race/Ethnicity, 2008: (In percent) Anglo, 79.9; Black, 3.3; Hispanic, 15.4; Other, 1.5.

Vital Statistics, 2008: Births, 66; deaths, 47; marriages, 115; divorces, 16.

Recreation: Pioneer West museum at Shamrock; historic sites; Old Mobeetie jail, trading post, Fort Elliott.

Minerals: Oil, natural gas.

Agriculture: Fed beef, cow-calf and stocker cattle, swine, horses; wheat, rye (second in acreage), grain sorghum, cotton. Market value $129.5 million.

WHEELER (1,592) county seat; agribusiness, petroleum center, tourism, slaughter plant; hospital, library.

SHAMROCK (1,910) tourism, agribusiness, antiques shops; hospital, library, old Route 66 sites; St. Patrick's Day event.

Other towns include: **Allison** (135); **Briscoe** (135); **Mobeetie** (101).

Population	5,410
Change fm 2000	-2.39
Area (sq. mi.)	915.34
Land Area (sq. mi.)	914.26
Altitude (ft.)	2,005-3,000
Rainfall (in.)	24.32

Jan. mean min.	22.9
July mean max.	93.3
Civ. Labor	3,249
Unemployed	4.2
Wages	$20,095,075
Av. Weekly Wage	$687
Prop. Value	$2,383,399,950
Retail Sales	$52,442,640

For explanation of sources, abbreviations and symbols, see p. 232 and foldout map.

Wichita County

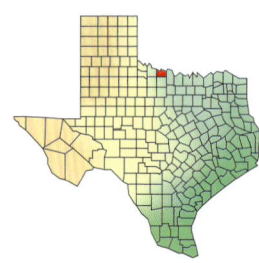

Physical Features: North-west county in prairie bordering Oklahoma; drained by Red, Wichita rivers; lakes; sandy, loam soils.

Economy: Manufacturing, retail trade center for large area, air base, government/services, agriculture.

History: Wichitas and other Caddoan tribes in area in 1700s; Comanches, Apaches also present until 1850s. Anglo-American settlement increased after 1870. County named for tribe; created from Young Territory 1858; organized 1882.

Race/Ethnicity, 2008: (In percent) Anglo, 68.7; Black, 11.2; Hispanic, 16.1; Other, 4.0.

Vital Statistics, 2008: Births, 1,893; deaths, 1,255; marriages, 1,859; divorces, 728.

Recreation: Museums; historic sites; Texas-Oklahoma High School Oil Bowl football game; collegiate activities; water sports on lakes; Fiestas Patrias parade, Ranch Round-up in August.

Minerals: Oil.

Agriculture: Beef cattle, horticul-ture, wheat, hay. Seventy-five percent of hay irrigated; 10 percent of wheat/cotton. Market value $27.2 million.

WICHITA FALLS (104,553) county seat; distribution center for large area of Texas and Oklahoma, government/services, varied manufacturing, oilfield services; hospitals, including North Texas state hospital; Midwestern State University, vocational-technical training center; hiking trails; Hotter'n Hell bicycle race in August; Sheppard Air Force Base.

Other cities include: **Burkburnett** (10,811) some manufacturing, Trails and Tales of Boomtown USA display

For explanation of sources, abbreviations and symbols, see p. 232 and foldout map.

and tours; **Cashion** (348); **Electra** (2,791) oil, agriculture, manufacturing, commuters to Wichita Falls; hospital; goat barbecue in May; **Iowa Park** (6,355) manufacturing, prison, Parkfest in May; **Kamay** (640); **Pleasant Valley** (336).

Population 131,500
Change fm 2000 .... −1.3
Area (sq. mi.) 633.01
Land Area (sq. mi.) 627.66
Altitude (ft.) 912-1,240
Rainfall (in.) 28.83
Jan. mean min. 28.9
July mean max. 97.2
Civ. Labor 61,338
Unemployed 8.0
Wages $504,974,776
Av. Weekly Wage $726
Prop. Value $6,707,839,079
Retail Sales $1,603,886,643

The entrance to the Waggoner Ranch in southern Wilbarger County. Photo by Robert Plocheck.

Wilbarger County

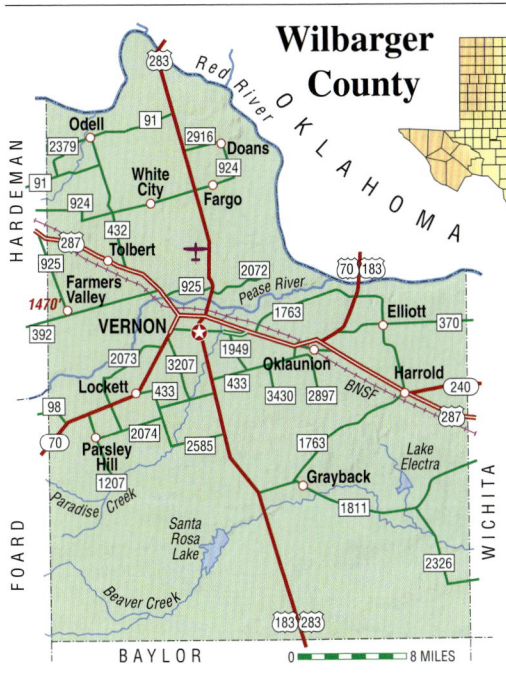

Physical Features: Gently rolling prairie draining to Red, Pease rivers, tributaries; sandy, loam, waxy soils; Santa Rosa Lake.

Economy: Agribusiness, electricity generating plant, government/services.

History: Anglo-American settlement developed after removal of Comanches into Indian Territory in 1875. County named for pioneers Josiah and Mathias Wilbarger; created from Bexar District 1858; organized 1881.

Race/Ethnicity, 2008: (In percent) Anglo, 63.8; Black, 9.6; Hispanic, 25.2; Other, 1.4.

Vital Statistics, 2008: Births, 215; deaths, 166; marriages, 206; divorces, 31.

Recreation: Doan's Crossing, on route of cattle drives; Waggoner Ranch, other historic sites; hunting, fishing; Red River Valley Museum; Santa Rosa roundup in May.

Minerals: Oil.

Agriculture: Wheat, cattle, cotton, alfalfa, peanuts; 25,000 acres irrigated. Market value $42.9 million.

VERNON (11,002) county seat; government/services, agribusiness, manufacturing, electricity-generating plant; college; state hospital/mental health center, private hospital, prison; museums; vintage car show in August.

Other towns include: **Harrold** (200); **Lockett** (150) A&M extension center; **Odell** (100); **Oklaunion** (138).

Population	13,535
Change fm 2000	–7.77
Area (sq. mi.)	978.10
Land Area (sq. mi.)	971.06
Altitude (ft.)	1,030-1,470
Rainfall (in.)	28.55
Jan. mean min.	25.7
July mean max.	97.2
Civ. Labor	7,829
Unemployed	6.3
Wages	$54,568,018
Av. Weekly Wage	$608
Prop. Value	$1,437,223,490
Retail Sales	$113,001,444

Willacy County

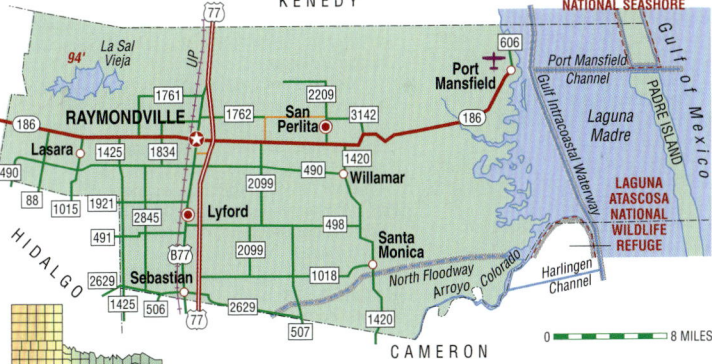

Physical Features: Flat coastal prairie sloping toward Gulf; alluvial, sandy, marshy soils; Padre Island; La Sal Vieja, salt lake; wildlife refuge.

Economy: Agribusiness, oil, government/services.

History: Coahuiltecan area when Spanish explored in 1500s. Spanish ranching began in 1790s. County named for Texas legislator John G. Willacy; created in 1911 from Cameron, Hidalgo counties; reorganized in 1921.

Race/Ethnicity, 2008: (In percent) Anglo, 9.9; Black, 1.8; Hispanic, 88.0; Other, 0.3.

Vital Statistics, 2008: Births, 330; deaths, 116; marriages, 112; divorces, 53.

Recreation: Fresh and saltwater fishing, hunting of deer, turkey, dove; mild climate attracts many winter tourists.

Minerals: Oil, natural gas.

Agriculture: Cotton, sorghum, corn, vegetables, sugar cane; 20 percent of cropland irrigated. Livestock includes cattle, horses, goats, hogs. Market value $51.2 million.

RAYMONDVILLE (11,284) county seat; agribusiness, oil center, food processing, tourism, enterprise zone, prison; historial museum; Boot Fest in October.

Other towns include: **Lasara** (1,039); **Lyford** (2,611); **Port Mansfield** (226) sport-fishing, birding, tourism, fishing tournament in July; **San Perlita** (573); **Sebastian** (1,917).

Population	22,134
Change fm 2000	10.22
Area (sq. mi.)	784.23
Land Area (sq. mi.)	596.68
Altitude (ft.)	sea level-94
Rainfall (in.)	27.97
Jan. mean min.	47.5
July mean max.	95.3
Civ. Labor	9,356
Unemployed	13.6
Wages	$37,773,568
Av. Weekly Wage	$669
Prop. Value	$980,713,765
Retail Sales	$95,938,566

For explanation of sources, abbreviations and symbols, see p. 232 and foldout map.

Williamson County

Physical Features: Central county near Austin. Level to rolling; mostly Blackland soil, some loam, sand; drained by San Gabriel and tributaries.

Economy: Agribusinesses, varied manufacturing, education center, government/services; the county is part of Austin metropolitan area.

History: Tonkawa area; later, other tribes. Comanches raided until 1860s. Anglo-American settlement began in late 1830s. County named for Robert M. Williamson, pioneer leader; created from Milam and organized in 1848.

Race/Ethnicity, 2008: (In percent) Anglo, 69.9; Black, 5.8; Hispanic, 20.7; Other, 3.6.

Vital Statistics, 2008: Births, 6,443; deaths, 1,762; marriages, 2,112; divorces, 724.

Recreation: Lake recreation; Inner Space Cavern; historic sites; deer hunting, fishing; Gov. Dan Moody Museum at Taylor; San Gabriel Park; old settlers park; walking tours, rattlesnake sacking, barbecue cookoff, frontier days in summer; Round Rock minor league baseball.

Minerals: Building stone, sand and gravel.

Agriculture: Corn, cattle, sorghum, cotton, wheat, hay, nusery crops. Market value $190.4 million.

GEORGETOWN (47,400) county seat; education, health, government/services, manufacturing, retail; hospital; Southwestern University; Red Poppy festival in April.

ROUND ROCK (99,887, part in Travis County) semiconductor, varied manufacturing, tourism and distribution center; hospital; Texas Baptist Children's Home.

Cedar Park (48,937, part in Travis County) limestone mining, commuting to Austin, hospital, community college extension, steam-engine train; Cedar Chopper festival in the spring.

Taylor (15,191) agribusiness, publishing center, varied manufacturing including cottonseed and meat processing; hospital.

Other towns include: **Andice** (300); **Bartlett** (1,623, partly in Bell County) cotton, corn production, commuters, prison, first rural electrification in nation in 1933, clinic, library, Friendship

For explanation of sources, abbreviations and symbols, see p. 232 and foldout map.

Fest in September; **Brushy Creek** (21,764); **Coupland** (280); **Florence** (1,136).

Also, **Granger** (1,419); **Hutto** (14,698) agriculture, manufacturing, government/services, commuters to Austin, museum, Olde Tyme Days in October; **Jarrell** (984); **Jollyville** (16,151, partly in Travis County); **Leander** (26,521); **Liberty Hill** (967) artisans center; **Schwertner** (175); **Thrall** (839); **Walburg** (277); **Weir** (450).

Also, part of **Austin**.

Population	**422,679**
Change fm 2000	69.09
Area (sq. mi.)	1,134.74
Land Area (sq. mi.)	1,122.77
Altitude (ft.)	400-1,360
Rainfall (in.)	35.11
Jan. mean min.	35.8
July mean max.	95.3
Civ. Labor	218,258
Unemployed	7.5
Wages	$1,409,337,392
Av. Weekly Wage	$887
Prop. Value	$38,793,312,852
Retail Sales	$6,073,030,533

Wilson County

Physical Features: Upper Coastal Plains; mostly sandy soils, some heavier; San Antonio River, Cibolo Creek.

Economy: Agribusiness, commuters to San Antonio; part of San Antonio metropolitan area.

History: Coahuiltecan Indians in area when Spanish began ranching around 1750. Anglo-American settlers arrived in the 1840s. Germans, Polish settled in the 1850s. County created from Bexar, Karnes counties and organized in 1860; named for James C. Wilson, member of the Mier Expedition.

Race/Ethnicity, 2008: (In percent) Anglo, 60.0; Black, 1.0; Hispanic, 38.4; Other, 0.6.

Vital Statistics, 2008: Births, 485; deaths, 326; marriages, 245; divorces, 137.

Recreation: Mission ranch ruins, historic homes; Stockdale watermelon jubilee in June; Floresville peanut festival in October.

Minerals: Oil, gas, clays.

Agriculture: Cattle, dairies, hogs, poultry; peanuts, sorghum, corn, small grains, vegetables, watermelons, fruit. Market value $52.9 million.

FLORESVILLE
(6,448) county seat; agribusiness; hospital, veterans home; Heritage Days in spring.

Other towns include: **La Vernia** (1,034); **Pandora** (110); **Poth** (1,908) agriculture, commuting to San Antonio, bicycle ride in September; **Stockdale** (1,442) agriculture, commuting to San Antonio, museum, nature center, watermelon jubilee in June; **Sutherland Springs** (420).

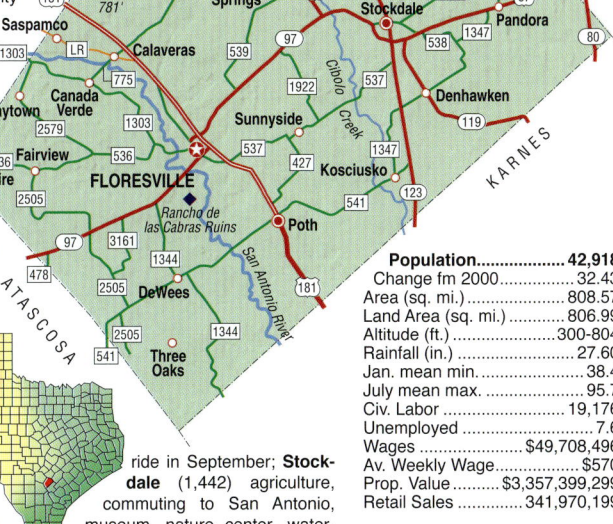

Population	42,918
Change fm 2000	32.43
Area (sq. mi.)	808.57
Land Area (sq. mi.)	806.99
Altitude (ft.)	300-804
Rainfall (in.)	27.60
Jan. mean min.	38.4
July mean max.	95.7
Civ. Labor	19,176
Unemployed	7.6
Wages	$49,708,496
Av. Weekly Wage	$570
Prop. Value	$3,357,399,299
Retail Sales	341,970,199

Part of **Nixon** (2,385, mostly in Gonzales County).

Winkler County

Physical Features: Western county adjoining New Mexico on plains, partly sandy hills.

Economy: Oil, natural gas, ranching, prison, some farming.

History: Apache area until arrival of Comanches in 1700s. Anglo-Americans began ranching in 1880s. Oil discovered 1926. Mexican migration increased after 1960. County named for Confederate Col. C.M. Winkler; created from Tom Green County in 1887; organized in 1910.

Race/Ethnicity, 2008: (In percent) Anglo, 48.9; Black, 1.8; Hispanic, 48.8; Other, 0.5.

Vital Statistics, 2008: Births, 133; deaths, 66; marriages, 34; divorces, 32.

Recreation: Monahans Sandhills State Park; museum; zoo; wooden oil derrick; Roy Orbison festival in June at Wink; Wink Sink, large sinkhole.

Minerals: Oil, gas.

Agriculture: Major producer of chip potatoes; meat goats, beef cattle. Market value $3.3 million.

KERMIT (5,708) county seat; oil, gas, ranching, some farming; hospital; Celebration Days in August.

Wink (940) oil, gas, ranching.

Population	7,110
Change fm 2000	−0.88
Area (sq. mi.)	841.24
Land Area (sq. mi.)	841.05
Altitude (ft.)	2,665-3,400
Rainfall (in.)	12.92
Jan. mean min.	27.8
July mean max.	96.1
Civ. Labor	3,349
Unemployed	7.6

Wages	$29,284,237
Av. Weekly Wage	$945
Prop. Value	$1,626,031,933
Retail Sales	$58,441,096

For explanation of sources, abbreviations and symbols, see p. 232 and foldout map.

Wise County

Physical Features: Northwest county of rolling prairie, some oaks; clay, loam, sandy soils; lakes.

Economy: Petroleum, sand and gravel, agribusiness, many residents work in Fort Worth.

History: Caddo Indian groups. Delaware tribe present when Anglo-Americans arrived in 1850s. County created, organized, 1856 from Cooke County; named for Virginian, U.S. Sen. Henry A. Wise, who favored annexation of Texas.

Race/Ethnicity, 2008: (In percent) Anglo, 84.4; Black, 1.1; Hispanic, 13.6; Other, 0.9.

Vital Statistics, 2008: Births, 816; deaths, 474; marriages, 465; divorces, 284.

Recreation: Lake activities, hunting, exotic deer preserve, historical sites, Lyndon B. Johnson National Grassland, heritage museum; Decatur Chisholm trail days in June, Bridgeport Butterfield stage days in July.

Minerals: Natural gas, oil, sand, gravel.

Agriculture: Beef cattle, hay, dairies, horses, wheat, goats. Market value $41.1 million.

DECATUR (6,042) county seat; petroleum center, dairying, cattle marketing, some manufacturing; hospital.

BRIDGEPORT (5,976) trade center for lake resort, oil and gas production, manufacturing, prison release facility; time-share housing, art community.

Other towns include: **Alvord** (1,334); **Aurora** (1,220) sand and gravel, manufacturing, equestrian cen-

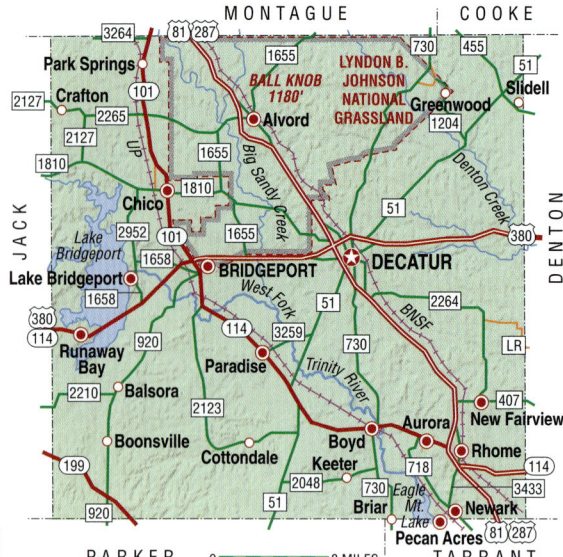

ter, "alien crash" site; **Boyd** (1,207) chili cookoff in May; **Briar** (5,665, mostly in Tarrant County); **Chico** (1,002); **Greenwood** (76); **Lake Bridgeport** (340); **Newark** (1,005); **New Fairview** (1,258); **Paradise** (441); **Pecan Acres** (4,099, partly in Tarrant County); **Rhome** (1,522); **Runaway Bay** (1,286) tourism, fishing, boating, Spring Fest at Easter; **Slidell** (175).

Population	**59,127**
Change fm 2000	21.18
Area (sq. mi.)	922.77
Land Area (sq. mi.)	904.61
Altitude (ft.)	649-1,180
Rainfall (in.)	34.02
Jan. mean min.	30.5
July mean max.	98.0
Civ. Labor	28,114
Unemployed	8,0
Wages	$216,679,433
Av. Weekly Wage	$869
Prop. Value	$9,366,440,990
Retail Sales	$506,643,134

For explanation of sources, abbreviations and symbols, see p. 232 and foldout map.

The Wise County Courthouse in Decatur. Photo by Robert Plocheck.

Wood County

Physical Features: Hilly northeastern county almost half forested; sandy to alluvial soils; drained by Sabine and tributaries; many lakes.

Economy: Agribusiness, oil, gas, tourism.

History: Caddo Indians, reduced by disease. Anglo-American settlement developed in 1840s. County created, organized, from Van Zandt County 1850; named for Gov. George T. Wood.

Race/Ethnicity, 2008: (In percent) Anglo, 86.4; Black, 5.6; Hispanic, 7.3; Other, 0.7.

Vital Statistics, 2008: Births, 438; deaths, 583; marriages, 206; divorces, 84.

Recreation: Autumn trails; lake activities; hunting, bass fishing, birding; Gov. Hogg shrine and museum; historic sites; scenic drives; Mineola depot; autumn trails.

Minerals: Gas, oil, sand, gravel.

Agriculture: Cattle, dairies, poultry, forages, vegetables, nurseries. Market value $104 million. Timber production significant.

QUITMAN (1,809) county seat; tourism, food processing, some manufacturing; hospital; botanical gardens; dogwood festival.

MINEOLA (4,515) agribusiness, some manufacturing, railroad center, antiques shops; museum, library; nature preserve; Ironhorse Fall Fest.

Winnsboro (3,434, partly in Franklin County) poultry production, dairies, distribution, prison; hospital.

Other towns include: **Alba** (504, partly in Rains County); **Golden** (398) Sweet

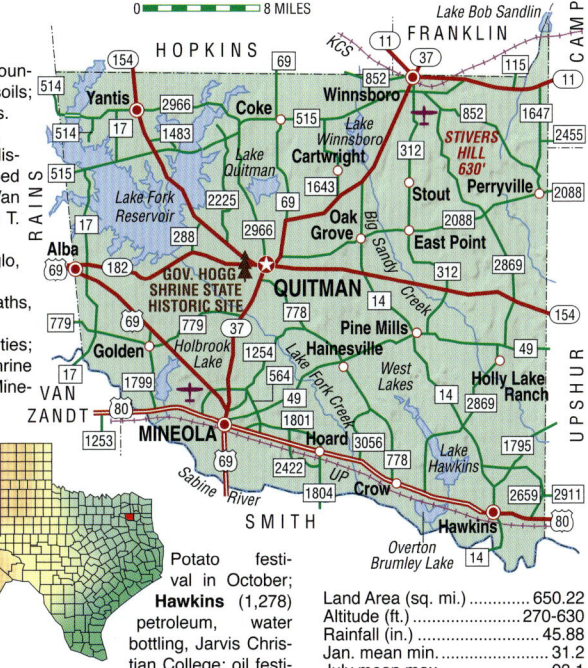

Potato festival in October; **Hawkins** (1,278) petroleum, water bottling, Jarvis Christian College; oil festival in October; **Holly Lake Ranch** (2,774); **Yantis** (400).

Population	41,964
Change fm 2000	14.18
Area (sq. mi.)	695.80
Land Area (sq. mi.)	650.22
Altitude (ft.)	270-630
Rainfall (in.)	45.88
Jan. mean min.	31.2
July mean max.	93.1
Civ. Labor	18,067
Unemployed	8.9
Wages	$74,670,411
Av. Weekly Wage	$633
Prop. Value	$3,632,091,721
Retail Sales	$367,610,448

Yoakum County

Physical Features: Western county is level to rolling; playas, draws; sandy, loam, chocolate soils.

Economy: Oil, gas, agriculture.

History: Comanche hunting area. Anglo-Americans began ranching in 1890s. Oil discovered 1936. Mexican migration increased in 1950s. County named for Henderson Yoakum, pioneer historian; created from Bexar District in 1876; organized in 1907.

Race/Ethnicity, 2008: (In percent) Anglo, 46.6; Black, 1.2; Hispanic, 51.6; Other, 0.6.

Vital Statistics, 2008: Births, 151; deaths, 58; marriages, 54; divorces, 26.

Recreation: Tsa Mo Ga museum at Plains; Plains watermelon roundup on Labor Day weekend.

Minerals: Oil, natural gas.

Agriculture: Cotton, peanuts (second in acreage), sorghum, wheat, watermelons, cattle. 100,000 acres irrigated. Market value $90.1 million.

PLAINS (1,481) county seat; oil, agribusiness center.

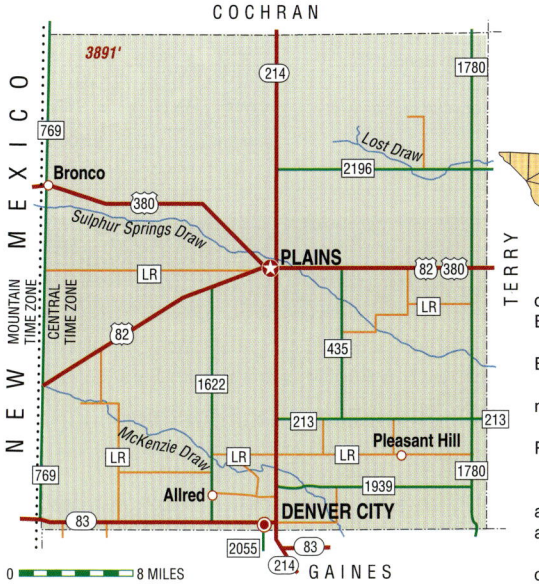

DENVER CITY (4,479) center for oil, agriculture activities in two counties; hospital, library, museum.

Population	7,879
Change fm 2000	7.61
Area (sq. mi.)	799.76
Land Area (sq. mi.)	799.75
Altitude (ft.)	3,400-3,891
Rainfall (in.)	18.41
Jan. mean min.	25.1
July mean max.	91.7
Civ. Labor	3,948
Unemployed	5.9
Wages	$43,664,741
Av. Weekly Wage	$990
Prop. Value	$3,784,408,279
Retail Sales	$74,032,660

For explanation of sources, abbreviations and symbols, see p. 232 and foldout map.

Young County

Physical Features: Hilly, broken; drained by Brazos and tributaries; Possum Kingdom Lake, Lake Graham.

Economy: Oil, agribusiness, tourism, hunting leases.

History: U.S. military outpost established in 1851. Site of Brazos Indian Reservation 1854–1859 with Caddoes, Wacos, other tribes. Anglo-American settlers arrived in the 1850s. County named for early Texan, Col. W.C. Young; created in 1856 from Bosque, Fannin counties, organized the same year; reorganized 1874.

Race/Ethnicity, 2008: (In percent) Anglo, 83.2; Black, 1.5; Hispanic, 14.5; Other, 0.8.

Vital Statistics, 2008: Births, 261; deaths, 258; marriages, 156; divorces, 101.

Recreation: Lake activities; hunting; Fort Belknap; marker at oak tree in Graham where ranchers formed forerunner of Texas and Southwestern Cattle Raisers Association.

Minerals: Oil, natural gas, sand, gravel.

Agriculture: Beef cattle; wheat chief crop, also hay, cotton, pecans, nursery plants. Market value $21.2 million.

GRAHAM (8,903) county seat; oil, gas, agriculture, tourism, government/services; hospital; old post office museum/art center; Western heritage days in September.

Other towns include:

Loving (300); **Newcastle** (585) old coal-mining town; **Olney** (3,285) aluminum, varied manufacturing, hospital; One-Arm Dove Hunt in September; **South Bend** (140).

For explanation of sources, abbreviations and symbols, see p. 232 and foldout map.

Population	18,550
Change fm 2000	3.38
Area (sq. mi.)	930.84
Land Area (sq. mi.)	922.33
Altitude (ft.)	995-1,522
Rainfall (in.)	31.35
Jan. mean min.	27.1
July mean max.	96.6
Civ. Labor	9,651
Unemployed	7.1
Wages	$64,644,879
Av. Weekly Wage	$752
Prop. Value	$1,718,748,910
Retail Sales	$197,585,712

Zapata County

Physical Features: South Texas county of rolling, brushy topography; broken by tributaries of Rio Grande; Falcon Reservoir.

Economy: Natural gas, oil, ranching, Falcon Reservoir activities, government/services.

History: Coahuiltecan Indians in area when the ranch settlement of Nuestra Señora de los Dolores was established in 1750. Anglo-American migration increased after 1980. County named for Col. Antonio Zapata, pioneer rancher; created 1858 from Starr, Webb counties.

Race/Ethnicity, 2008: (In percent) Anglo, 10.6; Black, 0.1; Hispanic, 89.0; Other, 0.2.

Vital Statistics, 2008: Births, 317; deaths, 85; marriages, 0; divorces, 0.

Recreation: Lake, state park, Dolores Hacienda historic site, rock hunting, hang gliding encampment June/July.

Minerals: Natural gas, oil, caliche.

Agriculture: Cattle; onions (third in acreage), cantaloupes, melons, goats. Market value $13,1 million. Hunting/wildlife leases important.

ZAPATA (5,089) county seat; tourism, agribusiness, oil, retirement center; clinic; fajita cook-off in November.

Other towns include: **Falcon** (191); **Lopeño** (174); **Medina** (3,935), and **San Ygnacio** (667) historic buildings, museum.

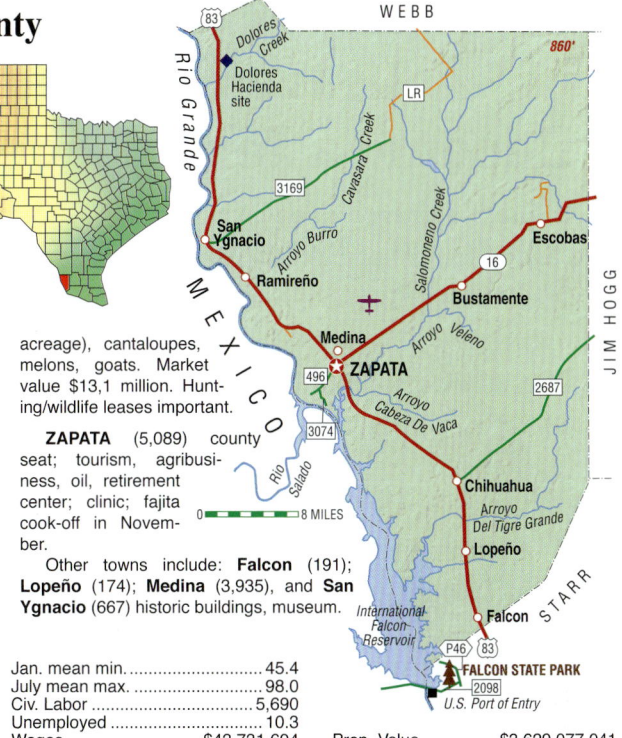

Population	14,018
Change fm 2000	15.07
Area (sq. mi.)	1,058.10
Land Area (sq. mi.)	996.76
Altitude (ft.)	301-860
Rainfall (in.)	19.53

Jan. mean min.	45.4
July mean max.	98.0
Civ. Labor	5,690
Unemployed	10.3
Wages	$43,731,694
Av. Weekly Wage	$868

Prop. Value	$3,629,077,041
Retail Sales	$87,280,330

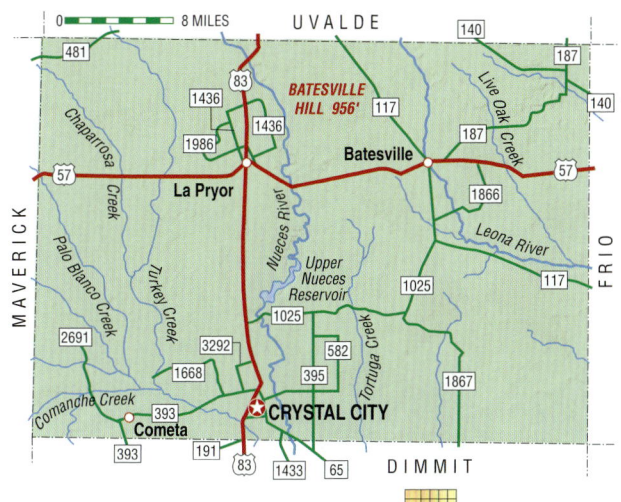

Zavala County

Physical Features: Southwestern county near Mexican border; rolling plains broken by much brush; Nueces, Leona, other streams.

Economy: Agribusiness, food packaging, leading county in Winter Garden truck-farming area, and government/services.

History: Coahuiltecan area; Apaches, Comanches arrived later. Ranching developed in the late 1860s. County created from Maverick and Uvalde counties in 1858; organized in 1884; named for Texas Revolutionary leader Lorenzo de Zavala.

Race/Ethnicity, 2008: (In percent) Anglo, 7.6; Black, 0.3; Hispanic, 91.8; Other, 0.2.

Vital Statistics, 2008: Births, 222; deaths, 90; marriages, 47; divorces, 0.

Recreation: Hunting, fishing; spinach festival in November.

Minerals: Oil, natural gas.

Agriculture: Cattle, grains, vegetables, cotton, pecans. About 50,000 acres irrigated. Market value $59.8 million. Hunting leases important.

CRYSTAL CITY (7,136) county seat; agribusiness, food processing, oil-field services; site of Japanese detention center. Home of Popeye statue.

Other towns include: **Batesville** (1,068) and **La Pryor** (1,643).

Population	11,677
Change fm 2000	0.66
Area (sq. mi.)	1,301.72
Land Area (sq. mi.)	1,298.48
Altitude (ft.)	540-956
Rainfall (in.)	20.70
Jan. mean min.	42.6
July mean max.	97.1
Civ. Labor	4,066
Unemployed	16.3
Wages	$19,164,056
Av. Weekly Wage	$476
Prop. Value	$1,415,422,941
Retail Sales	$39,751,938

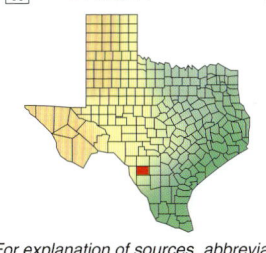

For explanation of sources, abbreviations and symbols, see p. 232 and foldout map.

Population

A sign proclaims the population on entry into Iraan. Photo by Robert Plocheck.

2010 U.S. Census of Towns

2000 U.S. Census of Towns

State Growth Analysis

Metro Areas

Center of Population by Decade

Recent Population Growth in Texas

The population of Texas on April 1, 2010, was 25,145,561 according to the U.S. Census, an increase of 4,293,741 persons from the 2000 census. That new count makes it the second largest state after California, which has a popultion of 37,253, 956.

As it has in every decade, the Texas' rate of increase, 20.6 percent, outpaced that of the nation as a whole, 9.7 percent.

The population growth in Texas between 2000 and 2010 was the largest of any state in raw numbers, and was the third largest in percentage terms, exceeded only by Arizona and Nevada.

According to the Texas State Data Center, the population of Texas grows rapidly through both natural increase (the excess of births over deaths) and in-migration.

For the past two decades, in-migration from other states and other countries has contributed approximately half of the state's population growth in any given year. Estimated net in-migration from other states to Texas between 2000 and 2008 was 710,000, and net international migration to the state was 850,000.

The Hispanic population of Texas grew by 41.9 percent in the last decade, while the non-Hispanic white population grew by only 4.2 percent. So, the racial and ethnic composition has changed.

In 2000, non-Hispanic whites made up 53 percent of the population, Hispanics made up 32 percent, blacks were 11 percent, while 4 percent were classified as "other," mainly Asian descent.

In 2010, non-Hispanic whites made up 45 percent of the population of the state, blacks remained at 11 percent, "other" was at 6 percent, while the Hispanic portion increased to 38 percent of the state's population.

Metropolitan counties on the Texas-Mexico border have grown more quickly than the state as a whole since 2000. Hidalgo County in the McAllen-Edinburg-Mission metropolitan area has experienced the most rapid growth (36%) between 2000 and 2010, and is a net in-migration area for both domestic and international migrants.

All other border counties experienced net domestic out-migration, offset by international migration and a high birth rate.

A large majority of population growth in the state occurs in its four largest metropolitan areas: Dallas-Fort Worth-Arlington, Houston-Baytown-Sugar Land, San Antonio and Austin-Round Rock, which experienced 40. 7 percent growth.

Other statistics from the Office of the State Demographer:

— Youth: Approximately 28 percent of Texas's population is under 18 and only 10 percent is older than 65.

— Urban: Texas has three of the 10 largest cities in the nation and several of the metropolitan areas in the state are among the most rapidly growing.

— Rural: Texas is the second largest state in terms of square miles and approximately 17 percent of the population lives in rural areas.

— Workers: Texas has a civilian labor force of more than 12 million and an unemployment rate lower than most states.

— Family: Texas ranks third among states for the percent of households that are married-couple families with children.

— Multi-generational: Texas ranks third among states for percent of households which are multi-generational.

— Growing: Among cities with more than 100,000 population, four of the 10 fastest growing areas are in Texas. ☆

Sources: U.S. Bureau of the Census and the Office of the State Demographer, Texas State Data Center.

Population change, 1850–2010

Year	Total Population		Percent change	
	Texas	U.S.	Texas	U.S.
1850	212,592	23,191,876	...	...
1860	604,215	31,443,321	184.2	35.6
1870	818,579	39,181,449	35.5	26.6
1880	1,591,749	50,155,783	94.5	26.0
1890	2,235,527	62,947,714	40.4	25.5
1900	3,048,710	75,994,575	36.4	20.7
1910	3,896,542	91,972,266	27.8	21.0
1920	4,663,228	105,710,620	19.7	14.9
1930	5,824,715	122,775,046	24.9	16.1
1940	6,414,824	131,669,275	10.1	7.2
1950	7,711,194	150,697,361	20.2	14.5
1960	9,579,677	179,323,175	24.2	19.0
1970	11,196,730	203,302,031	16.9	13.4
1980	14,229,191	226,545,805	27.1	11.4
1990	16,986,510	248,709,873	19.4	9.8
2000	20,851,820	281,421,906	22.8	13.2
2010	25,145,561	308,745,538	20.6	9.7

Source: U.S. Census.

Rank	METRO AREA	2010 Population
1.	New York	18,897,109
2.	Los Angeles	12,828,837
3.	Chicago	9,461,105
4.	**Dallas-Fort Worth**	**6,371,733**
5.	Philadelphia	5,965,343
6.	**Houston**	**5,946,800**
7.	Washington, D.C.	5,582,170
8.	Miami	5,564,635
9.	Atlanta	5,268,860
10.	Boston	4,552,402

Source: U.S. Census.

Counties of Significant Population Change: 2000 to 2010

Fastest Growing by Percent Gain			Fastest Growing by Most Persons Gained		
Rank, County	Major cities	Percent	Rank, County	Major cities	Number
1. Rockwall	Rockwall	81.84	1. Harris	Houston	691,881
2. Williamson	Round Rock	69.09	2. Tarrant	Fort Worth	362,815
3. Fort Bend	Sugar Land	65.15	3. Bexar	San Antonio	321,842
4. Hays	San Marcos	60.99	4. Collin	Plano	290,666
5. Collin	Plano	59.12	5. Fort Bend	Sugar Land	230,923
6. Montgomery	The Woodlands-Conroe	55.14	6. Denton	Denton-Lewisville	229,638
7. Denton	Denton-Lewisville	53.04	7. Travis	Austin	211,986
8. Guadalupe	Seguin	47.75	8. Hidalgo	McAllen	205,306
9. Kaufman	Terrell-Kaufman	44.92	9. Williamson	Round Rock	172,712
10. Kendall	Boerne	40.72	10. Montgomery	The Woodlands-Conroe	161,978

Chart shows Rockwall County increased in population by 81.84 percent since 2000, while Harris County (Houston) gained 691,881 people, etc. Source: U.S. Bureau of the Census.

Fastest Declining by Percent Loss			Fasting Declining by Most Persons Lost		
Rank, County	Major cities	Percent	Rank, County	Major cities	Number
1. Cottle	Paducah	−20.96	1. Orange	Orange	−3,129
2. King	Guthrie	−19.66	2. San Patricio	Aransas Pass-Sinton	−2,334
3. Culberson	Van Horn	−19.40	3. Hutchinson	Borger-Stinnett	−1,707
4. Sterling	Sterling City	−17.95	4. Red River	Clarksville	−1,454
5. Foard	Crowell	−17.63	5. Duval	San Diego-Freer	−1,338
6. Floyd	Floydada	−17.05	6. Floyd	Floydada	−1,325
7. McMullen	Tilden	−16.92	7. Pecos	Fort Stockton	−1,302
8. Cochran	Morton	−16.17	8. Matagorda	Bay City	−1,255
9. Motley	Matador	−15.15	9. Dawson	Lamesa	−1,152
10. Crosby	Crosbyton	−14.32	10. Wilbarger	Vernon	−1,141

Chart shows Cottle County declined in population by 20.96 percent since the 2000 census, while Orange County declined by 3,129 people, etc. Source: U.S. Bureau of the Census.

Largest Counties by Population 2010					
Rank, County	Major cities	Population	Rank, County	Major cities	Population
1. Harris	Houston	4,092,459	16. Bell	Temple, Killeen	310,235
2. Dallas	Dallas	2,368,139	17. Galveston	Galveston	291,309
3. Tarrant	Fort Worth	1,809,034	18. Lubbock	Lubbock	278,831
4. Bexar	San Antonio	1,714,733	19. Jefferson	Beaumont	252,273
5. Travis	Austin	1,024,266	20. Webb	Laredo	250,304
6. El Paso	El Paso	800,647	21. McLennan	Waco	234,906
7. Collin	Plano	782,341	22. Smith	Tyler	209,714
8. Hidalgo	McAllen	774,769	23. Brazos	Bryan-College Station	194,851
9. Denton	Denton-Lewisville	662,614	24. Hays	San Marcos	157,107
10. Fort Bend	Sugar Land	585,375	25. Johnson	Cleburne-Burleson	150,934
11. Montgomery	Woodlands-Conroe	455,746	26. Ellis	Waxahachie	149,610
12. Williamson	Round Rock	422,679	27. Ector	Odessa	137,130
13. Cameron	Brownsville	406,220	28. Midland	Midland	136,872
14. Nueces	Corpus Christi	340,223	29. Guadalupe	Seguin	131,533
15. Brazoria	Brazosport	313,166	30. Taylor	Abilene	131,506

Source: U.S. Bureau of the Census.

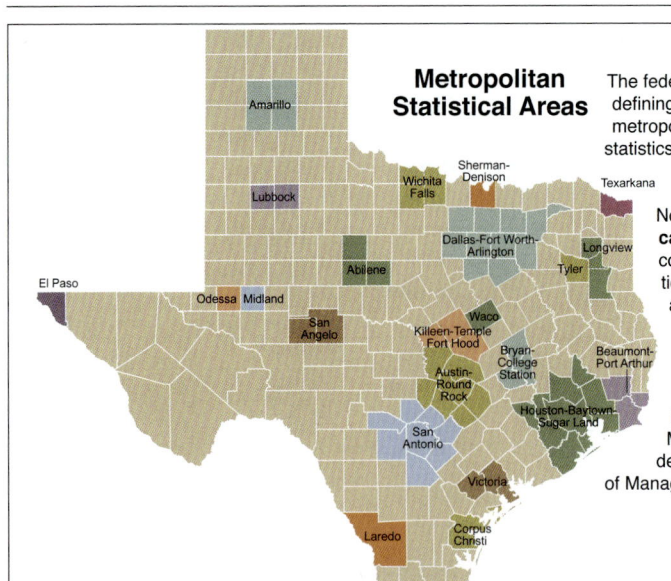

Metropolitan Statistical Areas

The federal government in 1949 began defining geographic units as standard metropolitan areas for the gathering of statistics.

Now called **Metropolitan Statistical Areas** (MSAs), these may be composed of one or more counties. Metropolitan Divisions (MD) are sub-units of a larger MSA classification.

Following are the 25 Texas metro areas listed in descending order by population. The MSAs are based on the 2010 designations of the federal Office of Management and Budget.

Metropolitan Statistical Areas	2010 Population	Percent change 2000-2010
1. **Dallas-Fort Worth-Arlington** (Dallas-Plano-Irving MD and Fort Worth-Arlington MD) Dallas-Plano-Irving MD (Collin, Dallas, Delta, Denton, Ellis, Hunt, Kaufman, Rockwall counties) Fort Worth-Arlington MD (Johnson, Parker, Tarrant, Wise counties)	6,371,773	23.4
2. **Houston-Baytown-Sugar Land** (Austin, Brazoria, Chambers, Fort Bend, Galveston, Harris, Liberty, Montgomery, San Jacinto, Waller counties)	5,962,549	26.4
3. **San Antonio** (Atascosa, Bandera, Bexar, Comal, Guadalupe, Kendall, Medina, Wilson counties)	2,142,508	25.2
4. **Austin-Round Rock** (Bastrop, Burnet, Caldwell, Hays, Travis, Williamson counties)	1,759,039	40.7
5. **El Paso** (El Paso County)	800,647	17.8
6. **McAllen-Edinburg-Mission** (Hidalgo County)	774,769	36.1
7. **Corpus Christi** (Aransas, Nueces, San Patricio counties)	428,185	6.2
8. **Brownsville-Harlingen** (Cameron County)	406,220	21.2
9. **Killeen-Temple-Fort Hood** (Bell, Coryell, Lampasas counties)	405,300	22.6
10. **Beaumont-Port Arthur** (Hardin, Jefferson, Orange counties)	388,745	0.9
11. **Lubbock** (Crosby, Lubbock counties)	284,890	14.1
12. **Laredo** (Webb County)	250,304	29.6
13. **Amarillo** (Armstrong, Carson, Potter, Randall counties)	249,881	10.3
14. **Waco** (McLennan County)	234,906	10.0
15. **Bryan-College Station** (Brazos, Burleson, Robertson counties)	228,660	23.7
16. **Longview** (Gregg, Rusk, Upshur counties)	214,369	10.5
17. **Tyler** (Smith County)	209,714	20.0
18. **Abilene** (Callahan, Jones, Taylor counties)	165,252	3.1
19. **Wichita Falls** (Archer, Clay, Wichita counties)	151,306	– 0.1
20. **Odessa** (Ector County)	137,130	13.2
21. **Midland** (Midland County)	136,872	18.0
22. **Texarkana** (Bowie County, TX, and Miller County, AR)	136,027	4.8
23. **Sherman-Denison** (Grayson County)	120,877	9.3
24. **Victoria** (Calhoun, Goliad, Victoria counties)	115,384	3.3
25. **San Angelo** (Irion, Tom Green counties)	111,823	5.7

Population 2000 and 2010

Population: Numbers in parentheses are from the 2000 U.S. census. The Census Bureau counts only incorporated cities and a few unincorporated towns called Census Designated Places.

Population figures at the far right for incorporated cities and CDPs are from the U.S. Census of 2010. Names of the incorporated cities are in capital letters, e.g., "ABBOTT".

The population figure given for all other towns is an estimate received from local officials through a Texas Almanac survey.

When no 2000 census was conducted for the town, these places show "(nc)" for "not counted" in place of a 2000 population figure.

Location: The county in which the town is located follows the name of town. If more than one county is listed, the town is principally in the first-named county, e.g., "ABERNATHY, Hale-Lubbock".

Businesses: For incorporated cities, the number following the county name indicates the number of business in the city as of January 2010 as reported by the state comptroller. For unincorporated towns, it is the number of businesses within the postal zip code as reported by the U.S. Bureau of the Census for 2006.

For example, "ABBOTT, Hill, 28" means Abbott in Hill County had 28 businesses.

Post Offices: Places with post offices, as of Nov. 2008, are marked with an asterisk (*), e.g., "*Afton".

Town, County ....Pop. 2010	Town, County ....Pop. 2010	Town, County ....Pop. 2010
*ABBOTT, Hill, 28, (300).............356	*ALAMO, Hidalgo, 523,	*ALTO, Cherokee, 68,
*ABERNATHY, Hale-Lubbock, 77,	(14,760)...........................18,353	(1,190)............................1,225
(2,839)................................2,805	Alamo Alto, El Paso......................19	Alto Bonito, Starr, (569)................342
*ABILENE, Taylor-Jones, 4,012,	Alamo Beach, Calhoun................100	Altoga, Collin 137
(115,930) 117,063	ALAMO HEIGHTS, Bexar, 359,	*ALTON, Hidalgo, 309,
Ables Springs, Kaufman.................20	(7,319)..............................7,031	(4,384)...........................12,341
Abner, Kaufman.............................75	*Alanreed, Gray, 3 48	Alum Creek, Bastrop 70
Abram, Hidalgo, (nc)..................2,067	Alazan, Nacogdoches..................100	*ALVARADO, Johnson, 208,
*ACADEMY [Little River-], Bell, 36,	*ALBA, Wood-Rains, 55,	(3,288)................................3,785
(1,645)................................1,961	(430)..................................504	*ALVIN, Brazoria, 1,019,
Acala, Hudspeth 25	*ALBANY, Shackelford, 116,	(21,413)...........................24,236
*Ace, Polk.....................................40	(1,921)................................2,034	*ALVORD, Wise, 59, (1,007) 1,334
*ACKERLY, Dawson-Martin, 14,	Albert, Gillespie 25	Amargosa, Jim Wells,(nc).............291
(245)....................................220	Albion, Red River..........................52	*AMARILLO, Potter-Randall, 6,759,
Acme, Hardeman............................14	Alderbranch, Anderson....................5	(173,627).......................190,695
Acton, Hood..............................1,129	Aldine, Harris, (13,979)............15,869	Amaya, Zavala, (nc) 93
Acuff, Lubbock.............................152	*ALEDO, Parker, 267,	Ambia, Lamar 16
Acworth, Red River........................50	(1,726)................................2,716	Ambrose, Grayson..........................90
Adams Gardens, Cameron...........200	Aleman, Hamilton 50	Ames, Coryell 10
Adams Store, Panola....................12	Alexander, Erath 40	AMES, Liberty, 8, (1,079) 1,003
Adamsville, Lampasas...................41	Aley, Henderson 45	Amherst, Lamar............................125
Addicks, Harris, ... [part of Houston]	Alfred, Jim Wells, (451) 91	*AMHERST, Lamb, 14, (791).......721
Addielou, Red River.......................31	Algerita, San Saba........................10	Amistad, Val Verde, (nc) 53
*ADDISON, Dallas, 1,903,	Algoa, Galveston 135	Ammannsville, Fayette 137
(14,166)............................13,056	*ALICE, Jim Wells, 806,	Amphion, Atascosa........................26
Adell, Parker...............................100	(19,010)..........................19,104	Amsterdam, Brazoria 193
*Adkins, Bexar, 89 400	Alice Acres, Jim Wells, (491)........490	Anadarko, Rusk.............................30
Admiral, Callahan 18	*Alief, Harris............. [part of Houston]	*ANAHUAC, Chambers, 75,
Adobes, Presidio 5	Allamoore, Hudspeth.....................25	(2,210)................................2,243
*ADRIAN, Oldham, 13, (159)........166	*ALLEN, Collin, 2,415,	Anchor, Brazoria............................80
Advance, Parker 100	(43,554)..........................84,246	*ANDERSON, Grimes, 45,
*Afton, Dickens, 1 15	Allenfarm, Brazos 35	(257)..................................222
Agnes, Parker................................60	Allenhurst, Matagorda 72	Anderson Mill, Williamson-Travis,
*AGUA DULCE, Nueces, 20,	Allen's Chapel, Fannin...................41	(8,953)..............[part of Austin]
(737)...................................812	Allen's Point, Fannin......................76	Ander-Weser-Kilgore, Goliad.......322
Agua Dulce, El Paso, (738) 3,014	Allentown, Angelina 800	*Andice, Williamson.....................300
Agua Nueva, Jim Hogg....................5	Alleyton, Colorado, 17 165	*ANDREWS, Andrews, 438,
Aguilares, Webb, (nc)....................21	*Allison, Wheeler, 3 135	(9,652)............................11,088
*Aiken, Floyd, 1 52	Allmon, Floyd................................24	*ANGLETON, Brazoria, 614,
Aiken, Shelby..............................150	Allred, Yoakum..............................90	(18,130)...........................18,862
Aikin Grove, Red River.................15	ALMA, Ellis, 7, (302)....................331	ANGUS, Navarro, 15, (334).........414
Airport Road Addition, Brooks,	Almira, Cass 30	*ANNA, Collin, 185, (1,225).......8,249
(132).....................................161	*ALPINE, Brewster, 371,	Annaville, Nueces
Airville, Bell..................................65	(5,786)..............................5,905	...............[part of Corpus Christi]
Alabama-Coushatta, Polk,	Alsa, Van Zandt 30	ANNETTA, Parker, 25,
(480)....................................572	*Altair, Colorado, 11.......................30	(1,108)................................1,288

CITIES & TOWNS

Town, County .... Pop. 2010

ANNETTA NORTH, Parker, 20,
   (467) 518
ANNETTA SOUTH, Parker, 11,
   (555) 526
*ANNONA, Red River, 9, (282) 315
*ANSON, Jones, 95, (2,556) 2,430
Antelope, Jack 65
*ANTHONY, El Paso, 133,
   (3,850) 5,011
Antioch, Cass 45
Antioch, Delta 10
Antioch, Madison 15
Antioch Colony, Hays 25
*ANTON, Hockley, 17, (1,200) ... 1,126
APPLEBY, Nacogdoches,
   (444) 474
*Apple Springs, Trinity, 13 350
*AQUILLA, Hill, 6, (136) 109
*ARANSAS PASS, San Patricio-
   Aransas, 382, (8,138) 8,204
Arbala, Hopkins 41
Arcadia, Shelby 35
*ARCHER CITY, Archer, 77,
   (1,848) 1,834
ARCOLA, Fort Bend, 62,
   (1,048) 1,642
Arden, Irion 7
Argo, Titus 200
*ARGYLE, Denton, 214,
   (2,365) 3,282
*ARLINGTON, Tarrant, 10,955,
   (332,969) 365,438
Armstrong, Bell 25
*Armstrong, Kenedy, 1 4
Arneckeville, DeWitt 50
Arnett, Coryell 15
Arnett, Hockley 5
*ARP, Smith, 61, (901) 970
Arroyo City, Cameron 250
Arroyo Colorado Estates,
   Cameron, (755) 997
Arroyo Gardens, Cameron, (nc) ... 456
*Art, Mason, 2 14
Artesia Wells, La Salle, 2 35
*Arthur City, Lamar, 10 180
Arvana, Dawson 25
Asa, McLennan 46
Ash, Houston 19
Ashby, Matagorda 60
*ASHERTON, Dimmit, 12,
   (1,342) 1,084
Ashland, Upshur 45
Ashtola, Donley 20
Ashwood, Matagorda 132
Asia, Polk 83
*ASPERMONT, Stonewall, 62,
   (1,021) 919
Atascocita, Harris, (35,757) 65,844
*Atascosa, Bexar, 31 600
Ater, Coryell 12
*ATHENS, Henderson, 624,
   (11,297) 12,710
*ATLANTA, Cass, 253,
   (5,745) 5,675
Atlas, Lamar 28
Atoy, Cherokee 50
*AUBREY, Denton, 150,
   (1,500) 2,595
Augusta, Houston 40
AURORA, Wise, 16, (853) 1,220
*AUSTIN, Travis-Williamson,
   33,537, (656,562) 790,390

Austonio, Houston 37
*AUSTWELL, Refugio, 4, (192) 147
Authon, Parker 15
*Avalon, Ellis, 6 400
*AVERY, Red River, 20, (462) 482
*AVINGER, Cass, 20, (464) 444
*Avoca, Jones, 4 121
*Axtell, McLennan, 23 300
*AZLE, Tarrant-Parker, 578,
   (9,600) 10,947

B

Back, Gray 6
*Bacliff, Galveston, 82,
   (6,962) 8,619
*Bagwell, Red River, 3 150
*BAILEY, Fannin, 7, (213) 289
BAILEY'S PRAIRIE, Brazoria, 11,
   (694) 727
Baileyville, Milam 32
Bainer, Lamb 10
Bainville, Karnes 8
*BAIRD, Callahan, 69, (1,623) ... 1,496
Baker, Floyd 28
Bakersfield, Pecos 11
*BALCH SPRINGS, Dallas, 611,
   (19,375) 23,728
BALCONES HEIGHTS, Bexar, 127,
   (3,016) 2,941
Bald Hill, Angelina 100

Bald Prairie, Robertson 40
*BALLINGER, Runnels, 210,
   (4,243) 3,767
*BALMORHEA, Reeves, 22,
   (527) 479
Balsora, Wise 50
*BANDERA, Bandera, 281,
   (957) 857
Bandera Falls, Bandera 90
*BANGS, Brown, 40, (1,620) 1,603
*Banquete, Nueces, 4, (nc) 726
Barbarosa, Guadalupe 46
Barclay, Falls 58
*BARDWELL, Ellis, 10, (583) 649
*Barker, Harris 2,500
*Barksdale, Edwards, 5 100
Barnes, Polk 75
*Barnhart, Irion, 6 110
Barnum, Polk 50
*Barrett, Harris, (2,872) 3,199
*BARRY, Navarro, 0, (209) 242
*BARSTOW, Ward, 2, (406) 349
*BARTLETT, Williamson-Bell, 63,
   (1,675) 1,623
Barton Corners, Lipscomb 4
Barton Creek, Travis,
   (1,589) 3,077
BARTONVILLE, Denton, 94,
   (1,093) 1,469

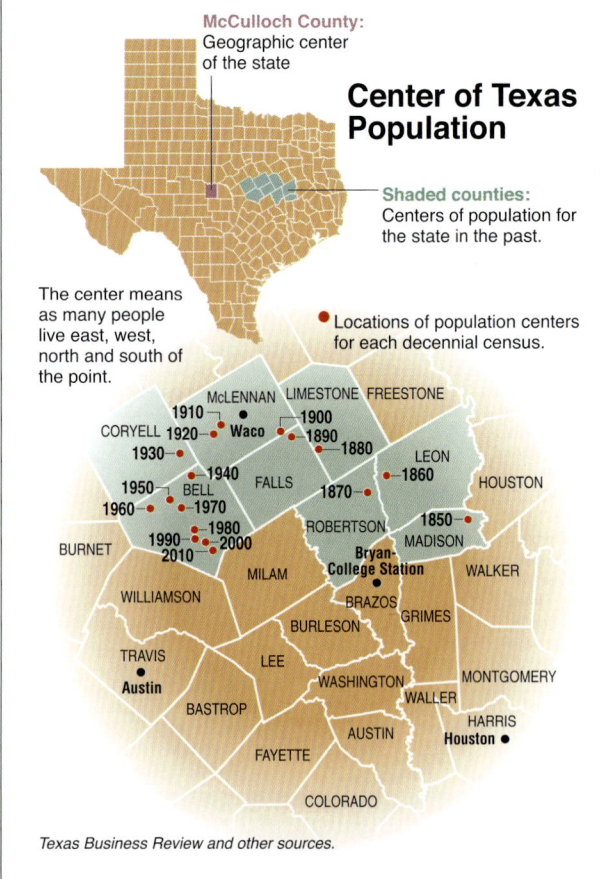

McCulloch County:
Geographic center of the state

Center of Texas Population

Shaded counties:
Centers of population for the state in the past.

The center means as many people live east, west, north and south of the point.

Locations of population centers for each decennial census.

Texas Business Review and other sources.

Town, County .... Pop. 2010	Town, County .... Pop. 2010	Town, County .... Pop. 2010
Barwise, Floyd 16	Ben Hur, Limestone 42	*Bledsoe, Cochran, 3 126
*Basin, Brewster, 5 30	*BENJAMIN, Knox, 13, (264) 258	*Bleiblerville, Austin, 5 125
Bassett, Bowie 373	Bennett, Parker 40	*Blessing, Matagorda, 23,
*BASTROP, Bastrop, 663,	Benoit, Runnels 10	(861) 927
(5,340) 7,218	Bentonville, Jim Wells 15	Blevins, Falls 36
Bateman, Bastrop 12	*Ben Wheeler, Van Zandt, 61 504	Blewett, Uvalde 10
Batesville, Red River 14	*Berclair, Goliad, 1 253	Blodgett, Titus 60
*Batesville, Zavala, 10,	Berea, Houston 41	*BLOOMBURG, Cass, 10,
(1,298) 1,068	Berea, Marion 200	(375) 404
*Batson, Hardin, 13 140	Bergheim, Kendall, 17 1,213	*BLOOMING GROVE, Navarro, 18,
Battle, McLennan 100	Berlin, Washington 40	(833) 821
Bausell-Ellis, Willacy, (112) 120	Bernardo, Colorado 155	*Bloomington, Victoria, 10,
Baxter, Henderson 150	BERRYVILLE, Henderson, 10,	(2,562) 2,459
*BAY CITY, Matagorda, 585,	(891) 975	*BLOSSOM, Lamar, 43,
(18,667) 17,614	*BERTRAM, Burnet, 86,	(1,439) 1,494
Baylor Lake, Childress 27	(1,122) 1,353	Blue, Lee 75
BAYOU VISTA, Galveston, 26,	Bessmay, Jasper 400	Blue Berry Hill, Bee, (982) 866
(1,644) 1,537	Best, Reagan 2	*Bluegrove, Clay, 2 135
*BAYSIDE, Refugio, 10, (360) 325	Bethany, Panola 50	BLUE MOUND, Tarrant, 46,
*BAYTOWN, Harris, 1,931,	Bethel, Anderson 75	(2,388) 2,394
(66,430) 71,802	Bethel, Henderson 125	*BLUE RIDGE, Collin, 33,
BAYVIEW, Cameron, 15, (323) 383	Bethel, Runnels 20	(672) 822
Bazette, Navarro 30	Bethlehem, Upshur 75	Bluetown, Cameron, (nc) 356
BEACH CITY, Chambers, 0,	Bettie, Upshur 110	*Bluff Dale, Erath, 19 400
(1,645) 2,198	Beulah, Limestone 12	*Bluffton, Llano, 5 75
BEAR CREEK, Hays, 0,	BEVERLY HILLS, McLennan, 100,	*BLUM, Hill, 22, (399) 444
(360) 382	(2,113) 1,995	Bluntzer, Nueces 150
*BEASLEY, Fort Bend, 17,	BEVIL OAKS, Jefferson, 26,	*BOERNE, Kendall, 1,321,
(590) 641	(1,346) 1,274	(6,178) 10,471
Beattie, Comanche 48	Bevilport, Jasper 12	*BOGATA, Red River, 40,
*BEAUMONT, Jefferson, 4,125,	Beyersville, Williamson 80	(1,396) 1,153
(113,866) 118,296	Biardstown, Lamar 75	Bois d'Arc, Anderson 25
Beaver Dam, Bowie 55	*Bigfoot, Frio, 2, (304) 450	Bois d'Arc, Rains 10
Bebe, Gonzales 42	Big Hill, Limestone 9	Bold Springs, Polk 100
Becker, Kaufman 300	*BIG LAKE, Reagan, 155,	Boles Home, Hunt 100
*BECKVILLE, Panola, 34, (752) ... 847	(2,885) 2,936	*Boling, Wharton, 25,
Becton, Lubbock 62	*BIG SANDY, Upshur, 104,	(1,271) 1,122
*BEDFORD, Tarrant, 1,561,	(1,288) 1,343	Bolivar, Denton 140
(47,152) 46,979	*BIG SPRING, Howard, 689,	Bolivar Peninsula, Galveston,
*BEDIAS, Grimes, 36, (nc) 443	(25,233) 27,282	(3,853) 2,417
BEE CAVE, Travis, 315,	Big Thicket Estates, Liberty-Polk,	Bomarton, Baylor 15
(656) 3,925	(nc) 742	Bonami, Jasper 12
Bee House, Coryell 15	Big Valley, Mills 35	Bonanza, Hopkins 26
*BEEVILLE, Bee, 512,	*BIG WELLS, Dimmit, 16,	Bonanza Hills, Webb, (nc) 37
(13,129) 12,863	(704) 697	*BONHAM, Fannin, 398,
Belcherville, Montague 25	Biloxi, Newton 75	(9,990) 10,127
Belfalls, Bell 30	Birch, Burleson 200	Bonita, Montague 25
Belgrade, Newton 20	Birome, Hill 30	BONNEY, Brazoria, 0, (384) 310
Belk, Lamar 58	Birthright, Hopkins 100	Bonnie View, Refugio 97
*BELLAIRE, Harris, 803,	Biry, Medina 24	Bonus, Wharton 44
(15,642) 16,855	*BISHOP, Nueces, 76, (3,305) .. 3,134	*Bon Wier, Newton, 10 375
Bell Branch, Ellis 125	BISHOP HILLS, Potter, 0, (210) ... 193	*BOOKER, Lipscomb-Ochiltree, 45,
*BELLEVUE, Clay, 15, (386) 362	*Bivins, Cass, 11 215	(1,315) 1,516
*BELLMEAD, McLennan, 255,	Bixby, Cameron, (356) 504	Boonsville, Wise 52
(9,214) 9,901	Black, Parmer, (nc) 100	Booth, Fort Bend 118
*BELLS, Grayson, 44, (1,190) ... 1,392	Blackfoot, Anderson 50	Bootleg, Deaf Smith 10
*BELLVILLE, Austin, 318,	Black Hill, Atascosa 60	Borden, Colorado 60
(3,794) 4,097	Black Hills, Navarro 80	*BORGER, Hutchinson, 448,
Belmena, Milam 15	Black Jack, Cherokee 47	(14,302) 13,251
*Belmont, Gonzales, 2 55	Black Jack, Robertson 45	Bosqueville, McLennan 200
Belott, Houston 101	Black Oak, Hopkins 150	Boston, Bowie ... [part of New Boston]
*BELTON, Bell, 755,	*BLACKWELL, Nolan-Coke, 13,	Botines, Webb, (132) 117
(14,623) 18,216	(360) 311	*BOVINA, Parmer, 27, (1,874)... 1,868
Ben Arnold, Milam 100	Blair, Taylor 25	Bowers City, Gray 26
*BENAVIDES, Duval, 27,	Blanchard, Polk 500	*BOWIE, Montague, 326,
(1,686) 1,362	*BLANCO, Blanco, 243,	(5,219) 5,218
*Ben Bolt, Jim Wells, 2 1,600	(1,505) 1,739	Bowman, Archer 200
*BENBROOK, Tarrant, 729,	Blanconia, Bee 100	Bowser, San Saba 20
(20,208) 21,234	Bland Lake, San Augustine 80	Box Canyon, Val Verde, (nc) 34
Benchley, Robertson 110	*BLANKET, Brown, 24, (402) 390	Box Church, Limestone 45
*Bend, San Saba-Lampasas, 3 115	Blanton, Hill 5	Boxelder, Red River 100
*Ben Franklin, Delta 60	Bleakwood, Newton 450	Boxwood, Upshur 20

Town, County .... Pop. 2010	Town, County .... Pop. 2010	Town, County .... Pop. 2010
Boyce, Ellis 125	Brownsboro, Caldwell 50	*BURTON, Washington, 54,
Boyd, Fannin 105	*BROWNSBORO, Henderson, 56,	(359) 300
*BOYD, Wise, 126, (1,099) 1,207	(796) 1,039	*Bushland, Potter, 10 1,485
*Boys Ranch, Oldham, 3, (nc) 282	*BROWNSVILLE, Cameron, 4,852,	Bustamante, Zapata 10
Boz-Bethel, Ellis 100	(139,722) 175,023	Busterville, Hockley 6
Bozar, Mills 9	*BROWNWOOD, Brown, 774,	Butler, Bastrop 40
Brachfield, Rusk 40	(18,813) 19,288	Butler, Freestone 67
Bracken, Comal 95	Broyles Chapel, Anderson 40	Butterfield, El Paso, (61) 114
*BRACKETTVILLE, Kinney, 71,	*BRUCEVILLE-EDDY, McLennan-	*BYERS, Clay, 12, (517) 496
(1,876) 1,688	Falls, 30, (1,490) 1,475	*BYNUM, Hill, 5, (225) 199
Brad, Palo Pinto 16	Brumley, Upshur 75	Byrd, Ellis 30
Bradford, Anderson 60	Brundage, Dimmit, (31) 27	Byrdtown, Lamar 22
Bradshaw, Taylor 61	*Bruni, Webb, 8, (412) 379	**C**
*BRADY, McCulloch, 296,	Brushie Prairie, Navarro 35	*CACTUS, Moore, 34, (2,538) ... 3,179
(5,523) 5,528	Brushy Creek, Anderson 125	*Caddo, Stephens, 4 70
Branch, Collin 530	Brushy Creek, Williamson,	*CADDO MILLS, Hunt, 104,
Branchville, Milam 127	(15,371) 21,764	(1,149) 1,338
*Brandon, Hill, 1 75	*BRYAN, Brazos, 2,466,	Cade Chapel, Navarro 25
*Brashear, Hopkins, 7 280	(65,660) 76,201	Cadiz, Bee 15
*BRAZORIA, Brazoria, 224,	Bryans Mill, Cass 150	Calallen, Nueces
(2,787) 3,019	Bryarly, Red River 3	.... [part of Corpus Chrisiti]
Brazos, Palo Pinto 97	Bryce, Rusk 15	Calaveras, Wilson 100
BRAZOS BEND, Hood, 0, (nc) 305	*BRYSON, Jack, 16, (528) 539	*CALDWELL, Burleson, 327,
BRAZOS COUNTRY, Austin, 13,	*Buchanan Dam, Llano, 42,	(3,449) 4,104
(nc) 469	(1,688) 1,519	Caledonia, Rusk 75
Brazos Point, Bosque 20	Buchanan Lake Village, Llano,	Calf Creek, McCulloch 23
Brazosport, Brazoria,	(nc) 692	Calina, Limestone 10
(59,440) 57,288	Buchel, DeWitt 45	*Call, Newton, 3 493
*BRECKENRIDGE, Stephens, 293,	Buckeye, Matagorda 16	Callendar Lake, Van Zandt,
(5,868) 5,780	*BUCKHOLTS, Milam, 15,	(nc) 1,039
*BREMOND, Robertson, 48,	(387) 515	*Calliham, McMullen, 2 100
(876) 929	Buckhorn, Austin 50	CALLISBURG, Cooke, 0, (365) 353
*BRENHAM, Washington, 999,	Buckhorn, Newton 80	Call Junction, Jasper 50
(13,507) 15,716	Buckner, Parker 10	*CALVERT, Robertson, 74,
Breslau, Lavaca 65	*BUDA, Hays, 497, (2,404) 7,295	(1,426) 1,192
Briar, Tarrant-Wise-Parker,	Buena Vista, Shelby 20	*Camden, Polk, 2 1,200
(5,350) 5,665	*BUFFALO, Leon, 152,	*CAMERON, Milam, 211,
BRIARCLIFF, Travis, 44, (895) .. 1,438	(1,804) 1,856	(5,634) 5,552
BRIAROAKS, Johnson, 7, (493) ... 495	*BUFFALO GAP, Taylor, 43,	Cameron Park, Cameron,
Brice, Hall 20	(463) 464	(5,961) 6,963
*BRIDGE CITY, Orange, 231,	Buffalo Mop, Limestone 21	Camilla, San Jacinto 200
(8,651) 7,840	Buffalo Springs, Clay 45	Camp Air, Mason 12
*BRIDGEPORT, Wise, 292,	BUFFALO SPRINGS, Lubbock, 0,	*CAMPBELL, Hunt, 48, (734) 638
(4,309) 5,976	(493) 453	*Campbellton, Atascosa, 4 350
Bridges Chapel, Titus 90	Buford, Mitchell 30	Camp Creek Lake, Robertson 350
*Briggs, Burnet, 8 172	Bula, Bailey 35	Campo Alto, Hidalgo 500
Bright Star, Rains 75	Bulcher, Cooke 3	Camp Ruby, Polk 35
Brinker, Hopkins 100	*BULLARD, Smith-Cherokee, 156,	Camp San Saba, McCulloch 36
*Briscoe, Wheeler, 6 135	(1,150) 2,463	Camp Seale, Polk 53
Bristol, Ellis, (nc) 668	Bull Run, Newton 90	Camp Springs, Scurry 10
*BROADDUS, San Augustine, 26,	*BULVERDE, Comal, 451,	Camp Swift, Bastrop, (4,731) 6,383
(189) 207	(3,761) 4,630	Camp Switch, Gregg 70
Broadway, Lamar 25	*Buna, Jasper, 88, (2,269) 2,142	Campti, Shelby 25
Brock, Parker 2,000	Buncombe, Panola 95	*Camp Verde, Kerr 41
Brock Junction, Parker 100	Bunger, Young 40	*CAMP WOOD, Real, 46,
Bronco, Yoakum 30	BUNKER HILL VILLAGE, Harris,	(822) 706
*Bronson, Sabine, 6 377	65, (3,654) 3,633	Canada Verde, Wilson 40
*BRONTE, Coke, 51, (1,076) 999	Bunyan, Erath 20	*CANADIAN, Hemphill, 153,
*Brookeland, Sabine, 27 300	*BURKBURNETT, Wichita, 256,	(2,233) 2,649
*Brookesmith, Brown, 3 61	(10,927) 10,811	Candelaria, Presidio 55
Brooks, Panola 40	BURKE, Angelina, 0, (315) 737	CANEY CITY, Henderson, 13,
Brookshier, Runnels 15	*Burkett, Coleman, 2 30	(236) 217
*BROOKSHIRE, Waller, 169,	*Burkeville, Newton, 14 603	Cannon, Grayson 50
(3,450) 4,702	Burleigh, Austin 150	*CANTON, Van Zandt, 894,
BROOKSIDE VILLAGE, Brazoria,	*BURLESON, Johnson-Tarrant,	(3,292) 3,581
42, (1,960) 1,523	1,317, (20,976) 36,690	Cantu Addition, Brooks, (217) 188
*Brookston, Lamar, 16 130	*Burlington, Milam, 7 100	*Canutillo, El Paso, 111,
Broom City, Anderson 20	*BURNET, Burnet, 422,	(5,129) 6,321
BROWNDELL, Jasper, 2, (219) ... 197	(4,735) 5,987	*CANYON, Randall, 411,
*BROWNFIELD, Terry, 292,	Burns, Bowie 400	(12,875) 13,303
(9,488) 9,657	Burns City, Cooke 45	Canyon City, Comal 600
Browning, Smith 25	Burrantown, Houston 70	Canyon Creek, Hood, (nc) 916

Town, County .... Pop. 2010	Town, County .... Pop. 2010	Town, County .... Pop. 2010
*Canyon Lake, Comal, 247, (16,870) 21,262	*Cee Vee, Cottle, 1 45	China Grove, Scurry 15
Cape Royale, San Jacinto, (nc).... 670	Cego, Falls 42	*China Spring, McLennan, 54, (nc) 1,281
Caplen, Galveston 60	Cele, Travis 20	Chinati, Presidio 8
Capps Corner, Montague 30	*CELESTE, Hunt, 30, (817).......... 814	Chinquapin, Matagorda 6
Cap Rock, Crosby 6	*CELINA, Collin-Denton, 234, (1,861) 6,028	*CHIRENO, Nacogdoches, 22, (405) 386
Caps, Taylor.................................. 300	Center, Limestone 76	CHISHOLM [McLendon-], Rockwall, 3, (914) 1,373
Caradan, Mills................................. 20	*CENTER, Shelby, 350, (5,678) 5,193	Chita, Trinity 81
Carancahua, Jackson.................... 375	Center City, Mills............................ 27	Choate, Karnes.............................. 30
*CARBON, Eastland, 7, (224) 272	Center Grove, Houston................... 39	Chocolate Bayou, Brazoria............. 60
Carbondale, Bowie 30	Center Grove, Titus 65	Choice, Shelby 35
Carey, Childress 15	Center Hill, Houston 105	*Chriesman, Burleson..................... 30
Carlisle, Trinity 68	Center Plains, Swisher 20	*CHRISTINE, Atascosa, (436)...... 390
Carlos, Grimes 60	Center Point, Camp 41	*Christoval, Tom Green, 19, (422) 504
*Carlsbad, Tom Green, 7, (nc)...... 719	*Center Point, Kerr, 45................. 800	Chula Vista, Cameron, (nc) 288
CARL'S CORNER, Hill, 5, (134) 173	Center Point, Upshur 50	Chula Vista, Maverick, (nc)........ 3,818
Carlson, Travis 20	Centerview, Leon 20	Chula Vista, Zavala, (400) 450
*Carlton, Hamilton, 2 75	*CENTERVILLE, Leon, 96, (903) 892	Church Hill, Rusk 20
*CARMINE, Fayette, 46, (228) 250	Centerville, Trinity 60	Churchill, Brazoria 90
Carmona, Polk................................ 50	Central, Angelina 1,400	*CIBOLO, Guadalupe, 386, (3,035) 15,349
Caro, Nacogdoches........................ 70	Central Gardens, Jefferson, (4,106) 4,347	Cienegas Terrace, Val Verde, (2,878) 3,424
Carricitos, Cameron...................... 147	Central Heights, Nacogdoches...... 300	Cinco Ranch, Fort Bend-Harris, (11,196) 18,274
Carrizo Hill, Dimmit, (548) 582	Central High, Cherokee 30	Cipres, Hidalgo 20
*CARRIZO SPRINGS, Dimmit, 158, (5,655) 5,368	*Centralia, Trinity 190	Circle, Lamb 6
Carroll, Smith................................. 60	Cesar Chavez, Hidalgo, (1,469) 1,929	Circle Back, Bailey......................... 10
Carroll Springs, Anderson-Henderson 20	Cestohowa, Karnes 110	Circle D-KC Estates, Bastrop, (2,010) 2,393
*CARROLLTON, Dallas-Denton, 5,189, (109,576) 119,907	Chalk, Cottle 17	Circleville, Williamson..................... 50
Carson, Fannin............................... 22	Chalk Hill, Rusk 200	*CISCO, Eastland, 166, (3,851) 3,899
Carta Valley, Edwards 12	Chalk Mountain, Erath 25	Cistern, Fayette 137
Carterville, Cass 39	Chambliss, Collin 29	Citrus City, Hidalgo, (941)......... 2,321
*CARTHAGE, Panola, 381, (6,664) 6,779	Champion, Nolan 10	Citrus Grove, Matagorda 30
Cartwright, Wood 144	Champions, Harris................... 21,250	Clairemont, Kent 12
Casa Piedra, Presidio...................... 8	Chances Store, Burleson............... 15	Clairette, Erath 55
Cash, Hunt..................................... 56	*CHANDLER, Henderson, 131, (2,099) 2,734	Clara, Wichita 100
CASHION, Wichita, 0, (346)......... 348	Chaney, Eastland 35	Clardy, Lamar 160
*Cason, Morris, 2.......................... 173	*Channelview, Harris, 387, (29,685) 38,289	*CLARENDON, Donley, 92, (1,974) 2,026
Cass, Cass 100	*CHANNING, Hartley, 13, (356) ... 363	Clareville, Bee 25
Cassie, Burnet.............................. 496	Chapman, Rusk.............................. 20	Clark, Liberty 75
Cassin, Bexar 200	*Chapman Ranch, Nueces, 3....... 200	Clarkson, Milam 10
*Castell, Llano, 1 72	Chappel, San Saba 25	*CLARKSVILLE, Red River, 149, (3,883) 3,285
CASTLE HILLS, Bexar, 359, (4,202) 4,116	*Chappell Hill, Washington, 35 750	CLARKSVILLE CITY, Gregg, 18, (806) 865
Castolon, Brewster 8	Charco, Goliad................................ 96	*CLAUDE, Armstrong, 52, (1,313) 1,196
*CASTROVILLE, Medina, 246, (2,664) 2,680	Charleston, Delta 150	Clauene, Hockley 10
*Catarina, Dimmit, 6, (135) 118	Charlie, Clay 70	Clawson, Angelina 1,500
*Cat Spring, Austin, 17 200	*CHARLOTTE, Atascosa, 33, (1,637) 1,715	Clay, Burleson 61
Cavazos, Cameron........................ 282	*Chatfield, Navarro, 2 40	Clays Corner, Parmer 15
Caviness, Lamar............................. 90	Cheapside, Gonzales 5	*Clayton, Panola, 3...................... 125
Cawthon, Brazos 75	Cheek, Jefferson 1,096	Claytonville, Swisher 85
Cayote, Bosque 75	Cheneyboro, Navarro 100	Clear Creek, Burnet........................ 78
*Cayuga, Anderson, 4.................. 137	*Cherokee, San Saba, 12............ 175	CLEAR LAKE SHORES, Galveston, 97, (1,205) 1,063
Cedar Bayou, Harris 1,555	Cherry Spring, Gillespie................. 75	*CLEBURNE, Johnson, 1,170, (26,005) 29,337
*Cedar Creek, Bastrop, 98 145	*CHESTER, Tyler, 14, (265) 312	Clegg, Live Oak 125
*CEDAR HILL, Dallas-Ellis, 1,267, (32,093) 45,028	Chesterville, Colorado 50	Clemville, Matagorda...................... 25
Cedar Hill, Floyd 24	*CHICO, Wise, 70, (947) 1,002	Cleo, Kimble 3
Cedar Lake, Matagorda................ 160	*Chicota, Lamar, 1 150	Cleveland, Austin 125
*Cedar Lane, Matagorda, 3 300	Chihuahua, Zapata, (95)................. 84	*CLEVELAND, Liberty, 456, (7,605) 7,675
*CEDAR PARK, Williamson-Travis, 1,938, (26,049) 48,937	*CHILDRESS, Childress, 217, (6,778) 6,105	Cliffside, Potter 206
Cedar Point, Polk, (nc) 630	*CHILLICOTHE, Hardeman, 18, (798) 707	
Cedar Shores, Bosque 270	*Chilton, Falls, 13, (nc) 911	
Cedar Springs, Falls....................... 90	*CHINA, Jefferson, 45, (1,112) 1,160	
Cedar Springs, Upshur................. 100	CHINA GROVE, Bexar, 55, (1,247) 1,179	
Cedarvale, Kaufman....................... 50		
Cedar Valley, Bell 14		

Town, County ....Pop. 2010	Town, County ....Pop. 2010	Town, County ....Pop. 2010

*CLIFTON, Bosque, 224,
(3,542) 3,442
Climax, Collin....................................82
Cline, Uvalde 15
*CLINT, El Paso, 60, (980) 926
Clinton, Hunt...................................150
Close City, Garza.............................94
Cloverleaf, Harris, (23,508) 22,942
*CLUTE, Brazoria, 382,
(10,424) 11,211
*CLYDE, Callahan, 150,
(3,345) 3,713
*COAHOMA, Howard, 27,
(932) 817
Coble, Hockley 11
Cochran, Austin 200
COCKRELL HILL, Dallas, 106,
(4,443) 4,193
COFFEE CITY, Henderson, 19,
(193) 278
Coffeeville, Upshur 50
Cofferville, Lamb 4
Coit, Limestone................................25
Coke, Wood......................................53
*COLDSPRING, San Jacinto, 107,
(691) 853
*COLEMAN, Coleman, 229,
(5,127) 4,709
Colfax, Van Zandt 94
Colita, Polk 50
College Hill, Bowie..........................116
College Mound, Kaufman.............500
*Collegeport, Matagorda, 1.............80
*COLLEGE STATION, Brazos,
2,226, (67,890) 93,857
*COLLEYVILLE, Tarrant, 1,157,
(19,636) 22,807
*COLLINSVILLE, Grayson, 48,
(1,235) 1,624
*COLMESNEIL, Tyler, 36, (638) ...596
Colony, Rains 70
Colorado Acres, Webb, (nc) 296
*COLORADO CITY, Mitchell, 174,
(4,281) 4,146
Coltharp, Houston............................40
Colton, Travis...................................50

*COLUMBUS, Colorado, 311,
(3,916) 3,655
*COMANCHE, Comanche, 211,
(4,482) 4,335
*COMBES, Cameron, 42,
(2,553) 2,895
COMBINE, Kaufman-Dallas, 54,
(1,788) 1,942
Cometa, Zavala 10
*Comfort, Kendall, 123,
(2,358) 2,363
*COMMERCE, Hunt, 209,
(7,669) 8,078
*COMO, Hopkins, 20, (621).........702
*Comstock, Val Verde, 3...............344
Comyn, Comanche...........................30
*Concan, Uvalde, 28....................225
*Concepcion, Duval, 2, (61)...........62
Concord, Cherokee 50
*Concord, Leon, 3...........................28
Concord, Madison 50
Concord, Rusk.................................23
Concrete, DeWitt 46
Cone, Crosby...................................50
Conlen, Dallam 14
Connor, Madison 20
*CONROE, Montgomery, 2,816,
(36,811) 56,207
Content, Bell 25
*CONVERSE, Bexar, 452,
(11,508) 18,198
Conway, Carson 20
Cooks Point, Burleson 60
*Cookville, Titus, 14.......................105
COOL, Parker, 7, (162).................157
*COOLIDGE, Limestone, 17,
(848) 955
*COOPER, Delta, 77,
(2,150) 1,969
Cooper, Houston..............................27
Copano Village, Aransas 210
*Copeville, Collin, 6 243
*COPPELL, Dallas-Denton, 1,432,
(35,958) 38,659
*COPPERAS COVE, Coryell,
591, (29,592) 32,032

COPPER CANYON, Denton, 49,
(1,216) 1,334
Corbet, Navarro 80
Cordele, Jackson.............................51
CORINTH, Denton, 554,
(11,325) 19,935
Corinth, Jones 10
Corinth, Leon...................................50
Corley, Bowie...................................35
Cornersville, Hopkins....................200
Cornett, Cass...................................30
Cornudas, Hudspeth.........................5
*CORPUS CHRISTI, Nueces,
9,862, (277,454) 305,215
CORRAL CITY, Denton, 2, (89)......27
*CORRIGAN, Polk, 69,
(1,721) 1,595
*CORSICANA, Navarro, 974,
(24,485) 23,770
Coryell City, Coryell 70
*Cost, Gonzales, 4...........................84
Cotton Center, Fannin 33
*Cotton Center, Hale, 5.................300
*Cottondale, Wise 300
Cotton Gin, Freestone 28
Cotton Patch, DeWitt.......................11
Cottonwood, Callahan 55
COTTONWOOD, Kaufman, 0,
(181) 185
Cottonwood, Madison....................40
Cottonwood, McLennan.................150
Cottonwood, Somervell 24
COTTONWOOD SHORES, Burnet,
33, (877)..............................1,123
*COTULLA, La Salle, 104,
(3,614) 3,603
Couch, Karnes.................................10
Coughran, Atascosa 20
Country Acres, San Patricio,
(289) 185
County Line, Lubbock....................59
County Line, Rains 40
*Coupland, Williamson, 25 280
Courtney, Grimes.............................60
COVE, Chambers, 18, (323) 510
Cove Springs, Cherokee 40

The main street in Chireno, Nacogdoches County. Photo by Robert Plocheck.

Town, County ....Pop. 2010	Town, County ....Pop. 2010	Town, County ....Pop. 2010

*COVINGTON, Hill, 14, (282) 269
Cox, Upshur.................................... 30
*Coyanosa, Pecos, 6, (138).......... 163
Coy City, Karnes............................ 30
Coyote Acres, Jim Wells, (389) 508
COYOTE FLATS, Johnson, 0,
   (nc) 312
Crabbs Prairie, Walker 240
Craft, Cherokee 21
Crafton, Wise................................. 100
*CRANDALL, Kaufman, 94,
   (2,774) 2,858
*CRANE, Crane, 104, (3,191) ... 3,353
*CRANFILLS GAP, Bosque, 18,
   (335) 281
*CRAWFORD, McLennan, 38,
   (705) 717
Creath, Houston 20
Crecy, Trinity 15
CREEDMOOR, Travis, 24,
   (211) 202
Crescent Heights, Henderson 180
*CRESSON, Hood-Johnson-Parker,
   77, (nc) 741
Crews, Runnels 30
Crisp, Ellis.................................... 115
*CROCKETT, Houston, 318,
   (7,141) 6,950
*Crosby, Harris, 341, (1,714) 2,299
*CROSBYTON, Crosby, 54,
   (1,874) 1,741
Cross, Grimes................................ 53
Cross, McMullen............................. 25
Cross Cut, Brown 22
Cross Mountain, Bexar,
   (1,524) 3,124
*CROSS PLAINS, Callahan, 69,
   (1,068) 982
Crossroads, Cass........................... 60
Crossroads, Delta 20
CROSS ROADS, Denton, 50,
   (603) 1,563
Crossroads, Harrison.................... 100
Cross Roads, Henderson 160
Crossroads, Hopkins 50
Cross Roads, Madison 75
Cross Roads, Milam 35
CROSS TIMBER, Johnson, 0,
   (277) 268
Croton, Dickens............................. 7
Crow, Wood 178
*CROWELL, Foard, 50, (1,141).... 948
*CROWLEY, Tarrant, 340,
   (7,467) 12,838
Crown, Atascosa............................ 10
Cruz Calle, Duval.......................... 12
Cryer Creek, Navarro 15
Crystal Beach, Galveston 800
*CRYSTAL CITY, Zavala, 129,
   (7,190) 7,136
Crystal Falls, Stephens.................. 10
Crystal Lake, Anderson 20
Cuadrilla, El Paso 67
*CUERO, DeWitt, 301,
   (6,571) 6,841
Cuevitas, Hidalgo, (37).................. 40
*CUMBY, Hopkins, 59, (616) 777
Cumings, Fort Bend, (683) 981
Cundiff, Jack.................................. 45
*CUNEY, Cherokee, 8, (145) 140
*Cunningham, Lamar.................... 110
Currie, Navarro 25

Curtis, Jasper 150
*CUSHING, Nacogdoches, 34,
   (637).. 612
Cusseta, Cass 30
*CUT AND SHOOT, Montgomery,
   64, (1,158) 1,070
Cuthand, Red River....................... 116
Cyclone, Bell.................................. 47
Cypress, Franklin........................... 20
Cypress Creek, Kerr 200
*Cypress [-Fairbanks], Harris,
   1,029, ... 27,000
Cypress Mill, Blanco 200

D

Dacosta, Victoria 89
Dacus, Montgomery 190
Daffan, Travis 500
*DAINGERFIELD, Morris, 103,
   (2,517)................................... 2,560
*DAISETTA, Liberty, 17,
   (1,034) 966
Dalby Springs, Bowie 141
*Dale, Caldwell, 29 500
*DALHART, Dallam-Hartley, 296,
   (7,237)................................... 7,930
*Dallardsville, Polk, 1 350
*DALLAS, Dallas-Collin-Denton,
   44,144, (1,188,580) 1,197,816
Dalton, Cass 50
DALWORTHINGTON GARDENS,
   Tarrant, 164, (2,186)............. 2,259
*Damon, Brazoria, 23, (535)........ 552
*DANBURY, Brazoria, 49,
   (1,611) 1,715
*Danciger, Brazoria...................... 357
*Danevang, Wharton, 6 61
Daniels, Panola 75
Danville, Gregg 200
Darby Hill, San Jacinto 50
Darco, Harrison 10
Darden, Polk................................ 320
*DARROUZETT, Lipscomb,
   18, (303) 350
Datura, Limestone 2
*Davila, Milam, 1 191
Davis, Atascosa.............................. 8
Davis Prairie, Limestone............... 17
*Dawn, Deaf Smith, 3 52
*DAWSON, Navarro, 22,
   (852) 807
*DAYTON, Liberty, 366,
   (5,709) 7,242
DAYTON LAKES, Liberty, 0,
   (101) 93
Deadwood, Panola 106
DEAN, Clay, 1, (341) 493
Dean, Hockley 20
*Deanville, Burleson, 6 130
*DeBerry, Panola, 23 200
*DECATUR, Wise, 467,
   (5,201) 6,042
Decker Prairie, Montgomery...... 2,000
DeCORDOVA, Hood, 0,
   (nc) 2,683
*DEER PARK, Harris, 1,028,
   (28,520) 32,010
*DE KALB, Bowie, 88,
   (1,769) 1,899
*DE LEON, Comanche, 103,
   (2,433) 2,246
Delhi, Caldwell............................. 300
Delia, Limestone 20

*DELL CITY, Hudspeth, 19,
   (413)....................................... 365
Del Mar Heights, Cameron,
   (259) 113
*Delmita, Starr, 2 50
Delray, Panola 45
*DEL RIO, Val Verde, 988,
   (33,867) 35,591
Delrose, Upshur............................. 35
Del Sol, San Patricio, (nc) 239
*Del Valle, Travis, 93 ... [part of Austin]
Delwin, Cottle 12
Demi-John, Brazoria..................... 300
Democrat, Mills.............................. 8
Denhawken, Wilson...................... 52
*DENISON, Grayson, 975,
   (22,773) 22,682
Denning, San Augustine 100
*Dennis, Parker, 3........................ 300
Denson Springs, Anderson.......... 100
Denton, Callahan............................ 6
*DENTON, Denton, 3,432,
   (80,537) 113,383
*DENVER CITY, Yoakum, 173,
   (3,985) 4,479
*DEPORT, Lamar-Red River, 12,
   (718)....................................... 578
Derby, Frio.................................... 50
*Desdemona, Eastland, 7............. 180
Desert, Collin................................. 35
*DESOTO, Dallas, 1,162,
   (37,646) 49,047
*DETROIT, Red River, 25,
   (776) 732
*DEVERS, Liberty, 17, (416) 447
*DEVINE, Medina, 252,
   (4,140) 4,350
Dew, Freestone 150
DeWees, Wilson 60
Deweesville, Karnes 12
*Deweyville, Newton, 17,
   (1,190) 1,023
Dewville, Gonzales 30
Dexter, Cooke 12
*D'Hanis, Medina, 20, (nc)........... 847
Dial, Fannin 76
Dialville, Cherokee....................... 200
*Diana, Upshur, 41 585
*DIBOLL, Angelina, 134,
   (5,470) 4,776
Dicey, Parker 40
*DICKENS, Dickens, 16, (332)..... 286
*DICKINSON, Galveston, 566,
   (17,093) 18,680
*Dike, Hopkins, 3......................... 170
*DILLEY, Frio, 62, (3,674).......... 3,894
Dilworth, Gonzales 18
Dilworth, Red River....................... 25
*Dime Box, Lee, 20....................... 381
*DIMMITT, Castro, 142,
   (4,375) 4,393
Dimple, Red River 60
*Dinero, Live Oak, 2 344
Ding Dong, Bell............................ 301
Direct, Lamar................................. 85
Dirgin, Rusk.................................. 50
DISH, Denton, 0, (345)................. 201
Divide, Kerr................................. 250
Divot, Frio..................................... 30
Dixie, Grayson 17
Dixon, Hunt................................... 31
Dixon-Hopewell, Houston 10

CITIES & TOWNS

Town, County ....Pop. 2010	Town, County ....Pop. 2010	Town, County ....Pop. 2010
Doak Springs, Lee 50	Duren, Mills..................................... 15	El Camino Angosto, Cameron,
Doans, Wilbarger.............................. 20	Duster, Comanche........................ 25	(254) 253
*Dobbin, Montgomery, 7 310	Dye, Montague 30	*EL CAMPO, Wharton, 610,
Dobrowolski, Atascosa 10	**E**	(10,945) 11,602
Dodd, Castro 12	Eagle, Chambers........................... 50	EL CENIZO, Webb, 42,
*DODD CITY, Fannin, 24,	*EAGLE LAKE, Colorado, 130,	(3,545) 3,273
(419) 369	(3,664) 3,639	El Centro, Starr............................... 10
*Dodge, Walker, 1 150	*EAGLE PASS, Maverick, 889,	*ELDORADO, Schleicher, 79,
*DODSON, Collingsworth, 0,	(22,413) 26,248	(1,951) 1,951
(115) 109	*EARLY, Brown, 181,	Eldorado Center, Navarro............. 20
Dodson Prairie, Palo Pinto 18	(2,588) 2,762	Eldridge, Colorado......................... 20
Doffing, Hidalgo, (4,256)............ 5,091	*EARTH, Lamb, 27, (1,109)....... 1,065	*ELECTRA, Wichita, 81,
Dog Ridge, Bell.............................. 215	East Afton, Dickens 13	(3,168) 2,791
Dogwood City, Smith 800	*EAST BERNARD, Wharton, 106,	Elevation, Milam 12
Dolen, Liberty 75	(1,729) 2,272	*ELGIN, Bastrop, 412,
DOMINO, Cass, 3, (52) 93	East Caney, Hopkins 100	(5,700) 8,135
*Donie, Freestone, 6..................... 250	East Columbia, Brazoria................ 95	Eliasville, Young............................ 150
*DONNA, Hidalgo, 440,	East Delta, Delta............................ 60	*El Indio, Maverick, 2, (263) 190
(14,768) 15,798	East Direct, Lamar.......................... 48	Elk, McLennan 150
*Doole, McCulloch.......................... 74	Easter, Castro................................. 26	*ELKHART, Anderson, 65,
Doolittle, Hidalgo, (2,358).......... 2,769	Easterly, Robertson 61	(1,215) 1,371
DORCHESTER, Grayson, 0,	Eastgate, Liberty........................... 200	EL LAGO, Harris, 81, (3,075) 2,706
(109) 148	East Hamilton, Shelby 25	*Ellinger, Fayette, 4 386
Dorras, Stonewall 20	*EASTLAND, Eastland, 250,	Elliott, Robertson 55
Doss, Cass 15	(3,769) 3,960	Elliott, Wilbarger 50
*Doss, Gillespie, 8 100	EAST MOUNTAIN, Upshur,	Ellis [Bausell-], Willacy, (112)....... 120
Dot, Falls 17	14, (580) 797	*Elmaton, Matagorda, 2............... 160
Dotson, Panola................................ 35	*EASTON, Gregg-Rusk, 5,	Elm Creek, Maverick, (1,928).... 2,469
Double Bayou, Chambers 400	(524) 510	*ELMENDORF, Bexar, 68,
DOUBLE OAK, Denton, 120,	East Point, Wood............................ 40	(664) 1,488
(2,179) 2,867	East Sweden, McCulloch................ 40	Elm Grove, Cherokee 50
*Doucette, Tyler, 4 160	EAST TAWAKONI, Rains, 15,	Elm Grove, San Saba 15
*Dougherty, Floyd, 1 91	(775) 883	Elm Grove, Wharton 76
Dougherty, Rains............................. 75	Ebenezer, Camp............................ 55	Elm Grove Camp, Guadalupe 88
*Douglass, Nacogdoches, 19 380	Ebenezer, Jasper........................... 50	*Elm Mott, McLennan, 68 300
*DOUGLASSVILLE, Cass, 8,	Echo, Coleman 16	*Elmo, Kaufman, 3, (nc) 768
(175) 229	Ecleto, Karnes 22	Elmont, Grayson 15
Downing, Comanche 30	*ECTOR, Fannin, 26, (600) 695	Elm Ridge, Milam 25
Downsville, McLennan................... 150	*EDCOUCH, Hidalgo, 46,	Elmwood, Anderson 25
Doyle, Limestone............................ 50	(3,342) 3,161	Eloise, Falls 29
Doyle, San Patricio, (285)............. 254	*EDDY [Bruceville-], McLennan-Falls,	El Oso, Karnes 35
Dozier, Collingsworth........................ 4	30, (1,490)........................... 1,475	*EL PASO, El Paso, 16,765,
Drane, Navarro 16	*EDEN, Concho, 50, (2,561) 2,766	(563,662) 649,121
Drasco, Runnels 15	Eden, Nacogdoches 100	El Refugio, Starr, (221) 331
Draw, Lynn 18	Edgar, DeWitt 8	Elroy, Travis.................................. 125
Dreka, Shelby 30	Edge, Brazos 100	*ELSA, Hidalgo, 128, (5,549) 5,660
Dresden, Navarro 25	EDGECLIFF, Tarrant, 0,	El Sauz, Starr 50
Dreyer, Gonzales............................ 20	(2,550) 2,776	Elton, Dickens 4
*Driftwood, Hays, 32, (nc)............ 144	Edgewater Estates, San Patricio,	El Toro, Jackson 136
*DRIPPING SPRINGS, Hays,	(nc) 72	El Venadito, Cameron................... 207
475, (1,548) 1,788	*EDGEWOOD, Van Zandt, 94,	Elwood, Fannin 31
*DRISCOLL, Nueces, 15, (825).... 739	(1,348) 1,441	Elwood, Madison 50
Drop, Denton 90	Edgeworth, Bell 15	*Elysian Fields, Harrison, 5 500
*Dryden, Terrell, 3........................... 13	Edhube, Fannin 40	Emberson, Lamar 80
Dubina, Fayette 272	*EDINBURG, Hidalgo, 1,720,	Emerald Bay, Smith, (nc)............ 1,047
*DUBLIN, Erath, 157,	(48,465) 77,100	EMHOUSE, Navarro, 3, (159) 133
(3,754) 3,654	*EDMONSON, Hale, 5,	Emmett, Navarro 100
Dudley, Callahan 25	(123) 111	*EMORY, Rains, 172, (1,021).... 1,239
Duffau, Erath 76	*EDNA, Jackson, 265,	Encantada-Ranchito El Calaboz,
*DUMAS, Moore, 392,	(5,899) 5,499	Cameron, (2,100) 2,255
(13,747) 14,691	Edna Hill, Erath.............................. 32	ENCHANTED OAKS, Henderson,
Dumont, King................................... 19	EDOM, Van Zandt, 15, (322)........ 375	0, (357) 326
Dunbar, Rains.................................. 40	*Edroy, San Patricio, 3,	*ENCINAL, La Salle, 18, (629) 559
*DUNCANVILLE, Dallas, 1,246,	(420) 331	*Encino, Brooks, 8, (177).............. 143
(36,081) 38,524	Egan, Johnson.............................. 133	*Energy, Comanche, 1................... 70
Dundee, Archer............................... 12	*Egypt, Wharton, 2 26	Engle, Fayette 141
Dunlap, Callahan 25	Eidson Road, Maverick,	English, Red River 100
Dunlap, Cottle 10	(9,348) 8,960	Enloe, Delta, 4................................ 90
Dunlap, Travis.................................. 80	Elam Springs, Upshur.................... 50	*ENNIS, Ellis, 731,
Dunlay, Medina 145	El Arroyo, Starr 500	(16,045) 18,513
*Dunn, Scurry 75	Elbert, Throckmorton, (56).............. 30	Enoch, Upshur................................ 25
Duplex, Fannin 25	Elbow, Howard................................ 10	*Enochs, Bailey 80
Durango, Falls 54		

Town, County ....Pop. 2010	Town, County ....Pop. 2010	Town, County ....Pop. 2010
Enon, Upshur.................................. 204	Falman, San Patricio, (nc).............. 76	*FOLLETT, Lipscomb, 27,
*Eola, Concho, 3............................ 215	Famuliner, Cochran 5	(412)... 459
Eolian, Stephens 9	Fannett, Jefferson, (nc) 2,252	Folsom, Shelby.................................30
*Era, Cooke, 7 150	*Fannin, Goliad, 4............................359	Ford, Deaf Smith 25
Ericksdahl, Jones 35	Fargo, Wilbarger 169	Fords Corner, San Augustine 30
Erin, Jasper...................................... 70	Farmers Academy, Titus 75	Fordtran, Victoria 18
Erna, Menard................................... 27	*FARMERS BRANCH, Dallas,	Forest, Cherokee............................85
Erwin, Grimes 52	1,919, (27,508) 28,616	*Forestburg, Montague, 4...............50
Escobares, Starr, 25, (1,954)..... 1,188	Farmers Valley, Wilbarger 30	Forest Chapel, Lamar 105
Escobas, Zapata............................... 2	*FARMERSVILLE, Collin, 196,	Forest Glade, Limestone 340
Escondidas [Sandy Hollow-],	(3,118) 3,301	Forest Grove, Milam 60
Nueces, (433).........................357	Farmington, Grayson...................... 40	Forest Heights, Orange 250
Eskota, Fisher.................................. 32	*Farnsworth, Ochiltree, 6............. 130	Forest Hill, Lamar 50
Esperanza, Hudspeth.....................75	Farrar, Limestone 51	FOREST HILL, Tarrant, 314,
Espey, Atascosa 55	Farrsville, Newton 152	(12,949) 12,355
Estacado, Lubbock-Crosby 32	*FARWELL, Parmer, 46,	Forest Hill, Wood 30
*ESTELLINE, Hall, 6, (168) 145	(1,364) 1,363	*FORNEY, Kaufman, 611,
Estes, Aransas................................ 50	Fashing, Atascosa 35	(5,588) 14,661
Ethel, Grayson................................ 40	*FATE, Rockwall, 111,	*Forreston, Ellis, 3 400
*Etoile, Nacogdoches, 10 700	(497) 6,357	*FORSAN, Howard, 8, (226) 210
Eula, Callahan 125	Faught, Lamar 25	Fort Bliss, El Paso, (8,264)........ 8,591
*EULESS, Tarrant, 1,490,	Faulkner, Lamar.............................. 10	Fort Clark Springs, Kinney,
(46,005) 51,277	Fawil, Newton 183	(nc) 1,228
Eulogy, Bosque............................... 10	*FAYETTEVILLE, Fayette, 59,	*Fort Davis, Jeff Davis, 63,
Eureka, Franklin 18	(261) 258	(1,050)................................... 1,201
EUREKA, Navarro, 9, (340).........307	Faysville, Hidalgo, (348)............... 439	*Fort Hancock, Hudspeth, 14,
*EUSTACE, Henderson, 44,	Fedor, Lee 92	(1,713)................................... 1,750
(798) 991	*Fentress, Caldwell, 8.................. 291	Fort Hood, Bell-Coryell,
*Evadale, Jasper, 18, (1,430) 1,483	*FERRIS, Ellis, 95, (2,175) 2,436	(33,711) 29,589
*EVANT, Coryell-Hamilton, 29,	Fetzer, Waller 150	*Fort McKavett, Menard, 1.............. 50
(393) 426	Fields Store, Waller 500	Fort Parker, Limestone 2
Evergreen, San Jacinto 150	*Fieldton, Lamb, 4 20	Fort Parker State Park,
EVERMAN, Tarrant, 110,	Fife, McCulloch................................ 32	Limestone 30
(5,836) 6,108	Fifth Street, Fort Bend,	Fort Spunky, Hood 15
Ewell, Upshur 20	(2,059) 2,486	*FORT STOCKTON, Pecos, 305,
Ezzell, Lavaca 55	Files Valley, Hill............................... 60	(7,846) 8,283
F	Fincastle, Henderson...................... 75	*FORT WORTH, Tarrant-Denton-
*Fabens, El Paso, 76,	Finney, Hale.................................... 18	Parker-Wise, 20,321,
(8,043) 8,257	*Fischer, Comal, 12 200	(534,694) 741,206
Fabrica, Maverick, (nc) 923	Fisk, Coleman.................................. 40	Foster, Terry...................................... 6
FAIRCHILDS, Fort Bend, 0,	Five Points, Ellis 25	Fostoria, Montgomery................... 586
(678) 923	Flaccus, Karnes 15	Fouke, Wood 30
*FAIRFIELD, Freestone, 235,	Flagg, Castro 26	Four Corners, Brazoria 30
(3,094) 2,951	*Flat, Coryell, 2 210	Four Corners, Chambers................ 18
Fairland, Burnet 340	Flat Fork, Shelby 10	Four Corners, Fort Bend,
Fairlie, Hunt 80	*FLATONIA, Fayette, 100,	(2,954) 12,382
Fairmount, Sabine 1,500	(1,377) 1,383	Four Corners, Montgomery 500
Fair Oaks, Limestone 15	Flat Prairie, Trinity........................... 33	Four Points, Webb, (nc)................. 18
*FAIR OAKS RANCH, Bexar-Comal-	Flats, Rains.................................... 100	*Fowlerton, La Salle, 2, (62)......... 55
Kendall, 137, (4,695) 5,986	Flat Top, Stonewall 5	Frame Switch, Williamson 25
Fair Play, Panola 80	*Flint, Smith, 146 2,500	*Francitas, Jackson 125
Fairview, Armstrong 75	Flo, Leon... 12	Frankel City, Andrews....................... 2
Fairview, Cass 20	*Flomot, Motley, 2.......................... 181	Frankell, Stephens............................ 8
FAIRVIEW, Collin, 222,	Flora, Hopkins 20	*FRANKLIN, Robertson, 82,
(2,644) 7,248	*FLORENCE, Williamson, 74,	(1,470) 1,564
Fairview, Gaines........................... 160	(1,054) 1,136	*FRANKSTON, Anderson, 111,
Fairview, Hockley............................ 20	*FLORESVILLE, Wilson, 319,	(1,209)................................... 1,229
Fairview, Hood................................ 30	(5,868) 6,448	*Fred, Tyler, 8 299
Fairview, Howard.............................. 5	Florey, Andrews 25	*FREDERICKSBURG, Gillespie,
Fairview, Wilson.............................. 95	Flour Bluff, Nueces,	1,193, (8,911) 10,530
Fairy, Hamilton................................ 40	.... [part of Corpus Christi]	*Fredonia, Mason, 3 55
Falcon, Zapata, (184) 191	Flowella, Brooks, (134)................. 118	Freedom, Rains 60
*Falcon Heights, Starr, (335) 53	Flower Hill, Colorado 20	*FREEPORT, Brazoria, 321,
Falcon Lake Estates, Zapata,	*FLOWER MOUND, Denton,	(12,708) 12,049
(830) 1,036	2,402, (50,702) 64,669	*FREER, Duval, 103, (3,241) 2,818
Falcon Mesa, Zapata, (506) 405	Floyd, Hunt 90	Freestone, Freestone 100
Falcon Village, Starr, (78) 47	*FLOYDADA, Floyd, 116,	Frelsburg, Colorado 75
*FALFURRIAS, Brooks, 144,	(3,676) 3,038	Frenstat, Burleson 50
(5,297) 4,981	*Fluvanna, Scurry, 3 180	Fresno, Collingsworth..................... 10
Fallon, Limestone 100	*Flynn, Leon, 5 81	*Fresno, Fort Bend, 78,
*FALLS CITY, Karnes, 38,	Foard City, Foard............................ 10	(6,603) 19,069
(591) 611	Fodice, Houston 49	Freyburg, Fayette 148

Town, County .... Pop. 2010	Town, County .... Pop. 2010	Town, County .... Pop. 2010
Friday, Trinity 99	*Geneva, Sabine 200	Goodsprings, Rusk 40
Friendship, Dawson 40	Geneview, Stonewall 3	Goodwill, Burleson 12
Friendship, Smith 200	Gentry's Mill, Hamilton 20	Goodwin, San Augustine 70
Friendship, Upshur 25	George's Creek, Somervell 43	*GORDON, Palo Pinto, 31,
Friendship Village, Bowie 200	*GEORGETOWN, Williamson,	(451) 478
*FRIENDSWOOD, Galveston-Harris,	1,961, (28,339) 47,400	*Gordonville, Grayson, 21 165
1,269, (29,037) 35,805	*GEORGE WEST, Live Oak, 145,	*GOREE, Knox, 4, (321) 203
Frio Town, Frio 9	(2,524) 2,445	*GORMAN, Eastland, 36,
*FRIONA, Parmer, 83,	Georgia, Lamar 55	(1,236) 1,083
(3,854) 4,123	Germany, Houston 23	Goshen, Walker 250
*FRISCO, Collin-Denton, 3,827,	*Geronimo, Guadalupe, 4,	Gould, Cherokee 20
(33,714) 116,989	(619) 1,032	*Gouldbusk, Coleman, 2 70
*FRITCH, Hutchinson-Moore, 70,	GHOLSON, McLennan, 17,	Graceton, Upshur 100
(2,235) 2,117	(922) 1,061	*GRAFORD, Palo Pinto, 33,
Frog, Kaufman 90	Gibtown, Jack 20	(578) 584
Fronton, Starr, (599) 180	*GIDDINGS, Lee, 326, (5,105) .. 4,881	Graham, Garza 139
*FROST, Navarro, 26, (648) 643	*Gilchrist, Galveston, 12 400	*GRAHAM, Young, 572,
Fruitland, Montague 20	*Gillett, Karnes, 4 120	(8,716) 8,903
*FRUITVALE, Van Zandt, 9,	Gilliland, Knox 20	*GRANBURY, Hood, 1,159,
(418) 408	*GILMER, Upshur, 397,	(5,718) 7,978
Frydek, Austin 900	(4,799) 4,905	Grand Acres, Cameron, (203) 49
Fulbright, Red River 150	Gilpin, Dickens 2	Grand Bluff, Panola 115
*FULSHEAR, Fort Bend, 147,	Ginger, Rains 96	*GRANDFALLS, Ward, 8,
(716) 1,134	*Girard, Kent, (62) 50	(391) 360
*FULTON, Aransas, 96,	Girlstown USA, Cochran 98	*GRAND PRAIRIE, Dallas-Tarrant-
(1,553) 1,358	*Girvin, Pecos 20	Ellis, 4,537, (127,427) 175,396
Funston, Jones 26	Gist, Jasper 20	*GRAND SALINE, Van Zandt,
Furrh, Panola 40	Givens, Lamar 135	145, (3,028) 3,136
G	*GLADEWATER, Gregg-Upshur,	Grandview, Dawson 12
Gadston, Lamar 35	372, (6,078) 6,441	Grandview, Gray 13
*Gail, Borden, 3, (nc) 231	Glaze City, Gonzales 10	*GRANDVIEW, Johnson, 87,
*GAINESVILLE, Cooke, 843,	Glazier, Hemphill 48	(1,358) 1,561
(15,538) 16,002	Glecker, Lavaca 78	*GRANGER, Williamson, 43,
Galena, Smith 50	Glen Cove, Coleman 40	(1,299) 1,419
*GALENA PARK, Harris, 173,	Glendale, Trinity 175	Grangerland, Montgomery 300
(10,592) 10,887	Glenfawn, Rusk 100	*GRANITE SHOALS, Burnet,
Galilee, Smith 150	*Glen Flora, Wharton, 3 210	77, (2,040) 4,910
*GALLATIN, Cherokee, 2,	Glenn, Dickens 4	GRANJENO, Hidalgo, 2,
(378) 419	GLENN HEIGHTS, Dallas-Ellis,	(313) 293
Galloway, Panola 71	142, (7,224) 11,278	Grape Creek, Tom Green,
*GALVESTON, Galveston, 1,654,	Glenrio, Deaf Smith 10	(3,138) 3,154
(57,247) 47,743	*GLEN ROSE, Somervell, 215,	*GRAPELAND, Houston, 92,
*GANADO, Jackson, 86,	(2,122) 2,444	(1,451) 1,489
(1,915) 2,003	Glenwood, Upshur 150	*GRAPEVINE, Tarrant, 2,737,
Garceño, Starr, (1,438) 420	Glidden, Colorado, 2, (nc) 661	(42,059) 46,334
*Garciasville, Starr, 5, (nc) 46	Globe, Lamar 60	Grassland, Lynn 40
*Garden City, Glasscock, 19,	Glory, Lamar 30	Gray, Marion 12
(nc) 334	*Gober, Fannin 146	Grayback, Wilbarger 10
*Gardendale, Ector, 18,	*GODLEY, Johnson, 46,	GRAYS PRAIRIE, Kaufman, 6,
(1,197) 1,574	(879) 1,009	(296) 337
Gardendale, La Salle 40	*Golden, Wood, 6 398	Graytown, Wilson 85
GARDEN RIDGE, Comal, 139,	Goldfinch, Frio 35	Greatwood, Fort Bend,
(1,882) 3,259	*Goldsboro, Coleman 30	(6,640) 11,538
Garden Valley, Smith 150	*GOLDSMITH, Ector, 19, (253) 257	Green, Karnes 50
Garfield, DeWitt 16	*GOLDTHWAITE, Mills, 99,	Green Hill, Titus 150
Garfield, Travis, (1,660) 1,698	(1,802) 1,878	Green Lake, Calhoun 51
Garland, Bowie 125	*GOLIAD, Goliad, 139,	Greenpond, Hopkins 150
*GARLAND, Dallas, 6,722,	(1,975) 1,908	Green's Creek, Erath 75
(215,768) 226,876	GOLINDA, Falls-McLennan, 8,	Green Valley, Denton 55
Garner, Parker 196	(423) 559	Green Valley Farms, Cameron,
Garner State Park .... Uvalde 50	Golly, DeWitt 41	(720) 1,272
GARRETT, Ellis, 7, (448) 806	Gomez, Terry 6	Greenview, Hopkins 25
*GARRISON, Nacogdoches, 57,	*GONZALES, Gonzales, 371,	*GREENVILLE, Hunt, 959,
(844) 895	(7,202) 7,237	(23,960) 25,557
*Garwood, Colorado, 20 975	Goober Hill, Shelby 30	Greenvine, Washington 35
*GARY, Panola, 14, (303) 311	Goodland, Bailey 10	Greenwood, Hopkins 100
Gastonia, Kaufman 100	Goodlett, Hardeman 80	Greenwood, Midland 2,000
*GATESVILLE, Coryell, 419,	GOODLOW, Navarro, 3, (264) 200	Greenwood, Red River 20
(15,591) 15,751	Good Neighbor, Hopkins 40	*Greenwood, Wise, 5 76
*Gause, Milam, 6 425	Goodnight, Armstrong 20	*GREGORY, San Patricio, 35,
Gay Hill, Washington 40	*GOODRICH, Polk, 21,	(2,318) 1,907
	(243) 271	Gresham, Smith 1,000

Town, County ....Pop. 2010	Town, County ....Pop. 2010	Town, County ....Pop. 2010
GREY FOREST, Bexar, 22, (418) 483	Hagerville, Houston 70	Harmony, Grimes........................ 12
Grice, Upshur 20	Hail, Fannin 30	Harmony, Kent............................ 10
Griffith, Cochran 12	Hainesville, Wood...................... 95	Harmony, Nacogdoches 50
Grigsby, Shelby 15	*HALE CENTER, Hale, 43, (2,263) 2,252	*Harper, Gillespie, 39, (1,006) 1,192
Grit, Mason 15	Halfway, Hale 165	Harpersville, Stephens 5
*GROESBECK, Limestone, 182, (4,291) 4,328	Hall, San Saba............................ 15	Harrison, McLennan 100
*GROOM, Carson, 37, (587) 574	*HALLETTSVILLE, Lavaca, 200, (2,345) 2,550	*Harrold, Wilbarger, 2 200
Grosvenor, Brown....................... 24	Halls Bluff, Houston 67	*HART, Castro, 38, (1,198)...... 1,114
*GROVES, Jefferson, 375, (15,733) 16,144	HALLSBURG, McLennan, 6, (518) 507	Hartburg, Newton 893
*GROVETON, Trinity, 46, (1,107) 1,057	*HALLSVILLE, Harrison, 110, (2,772) 3,577	Hart Camp, Lamb 4
Grow, King................................... 9	*HALTOM CITY, Tarrant, 1,449, (39,018) 42,409	*Hartley, Hartley, 16, (441) 540
Gruenau, DeWitt......................... 18	Hamby, Taylor 100	Harvard, Camp 48
Gruene, Comal, ... [part of New Braunfels]	*HAMILTON, Hamilton, 210, (2,977) 3,095	Harvey, Brazos 1,000
Grulla, Starr, ... (see La Grulla)	*HAMLIN, Jones-Fisher, 76, (2,248) 2,124	Harwell Point, Burnet................ 138
*GRUVER, Hansford, 48, (1,162) 1,194	Hammond, Robertson 44	*Harwood, Gonzales, 9............. 118
Guadalupe, Victoria 70	Hamon, Gonzales........................ 20	*HASKELL, Haskell, 125, (3,106) 3,322
Guadalupe Station, Culberson 10	*Hamshire, Jefferson, 9 759	Haslam, Shelby 100
*Guerra, Jim Hogg, (8) 6	Hancock, Comal 400	*HASLET, Tarrant, 177, (1,134) 1,517
Gum Springs, Cass 50	Hancock, Dawson....................... 30	Hasse, Comanche 50
*GUN BARREL CITY, Henderson, 305, (5,145) 5,672	*Hankamer, Chambers, 8 226	Hatchel, Runnels 6
Gunsight, Stephens 6	Hannibal, Erath........................... 25	Hatchettville, Hopkins 20
*GUNTER, Grayson, 65, (1,230) 1,498	Hanover, Milam........................... 25	Havana, Hidalgo, (452)............. 407
Gus, Burleson.............................. 50	*HAPPY, Swisher-Randall, 20, (647) 678	HAWK COVE, Hunt, 4, (457)...... 483
*GUSTINE, Comanche, 17, (457) 476	Happy Union, Hale 25	*HAWKINS, Wood, 88, (1,331) 1,278
*Guthrie, King, 1, (nc) 160	Happy Valley, Taylor 12	*HAWLEY, Jones, 27, (646)...... 634
*Guy, Fort Bend, 8 239	Harbin, Erath.............................. 21	Hawthorne, Walker 100
Guys Store, Leon........................ 20	*HARDIN, Liberty, 18, (755) 819	Haynesville, Wichita 65
H	Hare, Williamson 60	HAYS, Hays, 4, (233) 217
Haciendito, Presidio..................... 10	*Hargill, Hidalgo, 7, (nc)............ 877	Hazeldell, Comanche 12
Hackberry, Cottle........................ 30	*HARKER HEIGHTS, Bell, 596, (17,308) 26,700	*HEARNE, Robertson, 145, (4,690) 4,459
HACKBERRY, Denton, 16, (544) 968	Harkeyville, San Saba 12	HEATH, Rockwall, 227, (4,149) 6,921
Hackberry, Edwards 3	*Harleton, Harrison, 16 390	*Hebbronville, Jim Hogg, 108, (4,498) 4,558
Hackberry, Garza 5	*HARLINGEN, Cameron, 2,262, (57,564) 64,849	HEBRON, Denton, 45, (874) 415
Hackberry, Lavaca...................... 40	Harmon, Lamar........................... 12	Heckville, Lubbock....................... 91
Hagansport, Franklin 40	Harmony, Floyd 42	*HEDLEY, Donley, 7, (379)....... 329
		Hedwigs Hill, Mason 12
		HEDWIG VILLAGE, Harris, 259, (2,334) 2,557

The old business district of Graford, Palo Pinto County. Photo by Robert Plocheck.

Town, County ....Pop. 2010	Town, County ....Pop. 2010	Town, County ....Pop. 2010
Hefner, Knox...................................3	Hinkles Ferry, Brazoria 35	*HUBBARD, Hill, 60, (1,586) 1,423
Hegar, Waller................................100	Hiram, Kaufman.............................75	Huber, Shelby 15
Heidelberg, Hidalgo, (1,586)......1,725	*HITCHCOCK, Galveston, 177,	Huckabay, Erath 150
*Heidenheimer, Bell, 8..................224	(6,386) 6,961	HUDSON, Angelina, 78,
Helena, Karnes...............................35	Hitchland, Hansford.......................15	(3,792) 4,731
Helmic, Trinity................................86	Hix, Burleson 35	Hudson Bend, Travis, (2,369)....2,981
*HELOTES, Bexar, 536,	Hoard, Wood 45	HUDSON OAKS, Parker, 130,
(4,285) 7,341	Hobbs, Fisher 32	(1,637) 1,662
*HEMPHILL, Sabine, 132,	*Hobson, Karnes, 8 135	Huffines, Cass 140
(1,106) 1,198	*Hochheim, DeWitt 70	*Huffman, Harris, 133 15,000
*HEMPSTEAD, Waller, 266,	*Hockley, Harris, 97 400	Hufsmith, Harris............................500
(4,691) 5,770	Hodges, Jones..............................150	*HUGHES SPRINGS, Cass, 67,
*HENDERSON, Rusk, 580,	Hogansville, Rains 200	(1,856) 1,760
(11,273) 13,712	Hogg, Burleson 20	*Hull, Liberty, 17 800
Henkhaus, Lavaca...........................88	Holiday Beach, Aransas, (nc) 514	*HUMBLE, Harris, 1,932,
Henly, Hays 140	HOLIDAY LAKES, Brazoria, 7,	(14,579) 15,133
*HENRIETTA, Clay, 137,	(1,095) 1,107	*Hungerford, Wharton, 11,
(3,264) 3,141	*HOLLAND, Bell, 48, (1,102).....1,121	(645) 347
Henry's Chapel, Cherokee 75	Holland Quarters, Panola 40	*Hunt, Kerr, 46 708
*HEREFORD, Deaf Smith, 476,	*HOLLIDAY, Archer, 70,	Hunter, Comal................................40
(14,597) 15,370	(1,632) 1,758	HUNTERS CREEK VILLAGE,
Hermits Cove, Rains 40	Holly, Houston 95	Harris, 107, (4,374) 4,367
*Hermleigh, Scurry, 8, (393) 345	Holly Grove, Polk 20	*HUNTINGTON, Angelina, 121,
Herty, Angelina 605	Holly Lake Ranch, Wood,	(2,068) 2,118
Hester, Navarro 35	(nc) 2,774	Huntoon, Ochiltree..........................22
*HEWITT, McLennan, 384,	Holly Springs, Jasper......................50	*HUNTSVILLE, Walker, 1,063,
(11,085) 13,549	HOLLYWOOD PARK, Bexar, 127,	(35,078) 38,548
*Hext, Menard.................................75	(2,983) 3,062	Hurley, Wood 30
HICKORY CREEK, Denton, 108,	Holman, Fayette 101	Hurlwood, Lubbock 152
(2,078) 3,247	Homer, Angelina 360	Hurnville, Clay 10
Hickory Creek, Houston..................31	Homestead Meadows North,	*HURST, Tarrant, 1,745,
Hickory Creek, Hunt 40	El Paso, (4,232).................5,247	(36,273) 37,337
*HICO, Hamilton, 131, (1,341)...1,379	Homestead Meadows South,	Hurstown, Shelby 20
*HIDALGO, Hidalgo, 476,	El Paso, (6,807).................7,247	Hurst Springs, Coryell....................10
(7,322) 11,198	*HONDO, Medina, 313,	*HUTCHINS, Dallas, 115,
Hidden Acres [Lakeshore Gardens-],	(7,897) 8,803	(2,805) 5,338
San Patricio, (720)................504	*HONEY GROVE, Fannin, 69,	*HUTTO, Williamson, 352,
HIDEAWAY, Smith, 0, (2,619)...3,083	(1,746) 1,668	(1,250) 14,698
Higginbotham, Gaines 21	Honey Island, Hardin 401	HUXLEY, Shelby, 4, (298) 385
*HIGGINS, Lipscomb, 17,	Hood, Cooke 13	*Hye, Blanco, 4................................72
(425) 397	Hooker Ridge, Rains 250	Hylton, Nolan 6
High, Lamar 14	*HOOKS, Bowie, 68, (2,973).....2,769	
Highbank, Falls 68	Hoover, Gray 5	**I**
High Hill, Fayette 176	Hoover, Lamar 20	*Iago, Wharton, 25, (nc) 161
*High Island, Galveston, 3............300	Hope, Lavaca 45	Ida, Grayson 30
Highland, Erath 60	Hopewell, Franklin 50	*IDALOU, Lubbock, 83,
HIGHLAND HAVEN, Burnet, 0,	Hopewell, Houston 22	(2,157) 2,250
(450) 431	Hopewell [Dixon-], Houston 10	Iglesia Antigua, Cameron, (nc) 413
HIGHLAND PARK, Dallas, 427,	Hopewell, Lamar.............................90	Ike, Ellis 50
(8,842) 8,564	Hopewell, Red River......................152	Illinois Bend, Montague 40
*Highlands, Harris, 122,	Hopewell, Smith..............................45	IMPACT, Taylor, 0, (39) 35
(7,089) 7,522	HORIZON CITY, El Paso, 214,	*Imperial, Pecos, 4, (428) 278
HIGHLAND VILLAGE, Denton,	(5,233) 16,735	Inadale, Scurry 6
515, (12,173) 15,056	Hornsby Bend, Travis, (nc) 6,791	Independence, Washington..........140
Hightower, Liberty 225	HORSESHOE BAY, Llano-Burnet,	India, Ellis 30
HILL COUNTRY VILLAGE, Bexar,	147, (3,337).........................3,418	Indian Creek, Brown 28
94, (1,028) 985	Hortense, Polk 20	Indian Creek, Smith 300
Hillcrest, Colorado 25	Horton, Delta 40	Indian Gap, Hamilton......................35
HILLCREST VILLAGE, Brazoria, 0,	Horton, Panola 200	Indian Hill, Newton............................7
(722) 730	*HOUSTON, Harris-Fort Bend-	Indian Hills, Hidalgo, (2,036) 2,591
*Hillister, Tyler, 10 250	Montgomery, 87,247,	INDIAN LAKE, Cameron, 0,
Hillje, Wharton 51	(1,953,631) 2,099,451	(541) 640
Hills, Lee 20	Howard, Ellis 60	Indianola, Calhoun.........................200
*HILLSBORO, Hill, 408,	HOWARDWICK, Donley, 13,	Indian Rock, Upshur........................45
(8,232) 8,456	(437) 402	Indian Springs, Polk, (nc) 785
Hillside Acres, Webb, (nc) 30	*HOWE, Grayson, 82,	Indio, Presidio....................................5
Hilltop, Frio, (300) 287	(2,478) 2,600	*INDUSTRY, Austin, 34,
*Hilltop Lakes, Leon, (nc) 1,101	Howland, Lamar 65	(304) 304
HILSHIRE VILLAGE, Harris, 25,	Hoxie, Williamson 60	*Inez, Victoria, 34, (1,787).........2,098
(720) 746	Hoyte, Milam 20	*INGLESIDE, San Patricio, 230,
Hinckley, Lamar 40	Hub, Parmer 25	(9,388) 9,387
Hindes, Atascosa............................14	Hubbard, Bowie 269	INGLESIDE-ON-THE-BAY,
		San Patricio, 14, (659)..........615

Town, County ....Pop. 2010	Town, County ....Pop. 2010	Town, County ....Pop. 2010
*INGRAM, Kerr, 159, (1,740) 1,804	JONESTOWN, Travis, 108, (1,681) 1,834	Kent, Culberson...............................30
*IOLA, Grimes, 13, (nc) 401	*Jonesville, Harrison, 4...................70	Kentucky Town, Grayson...............20
IOWA COLONY, Brazoria, 19, (804) 1,170	Joplin, Jack.....................................15	*KERENS, Navarro, 64, (1,681) 1,573
*IOWA PARK, Wichita, 187, (6,431) 6,355	Joppa, Burnet..................................84	*KERMIT, Winkler, 182, (5,714) 5,708
*Ira, Scurry, 13.............................250	Jordans Store, Shelby 20	*Kerrick, Dallam, 1.........................35
*IRAAN, Pecos, 58, (1,238).......1,229	*JOSEPHINE, Collin, 23, (594) 812	*KERRVILLE, Kerr, 1,486, (20,425).............................22,347
*IREDELL, Bosque, 20, (360).......339	*JOSHUA, Johnson, 253, (4,528) 5,910	Kerrville South, Kerr 6,600
Ireland, Coryell 60	Josserand, Trinity 29	Key, Dawson....................................20
*Irene, Hill......................................170	Jot-Em-Down, Delta 8	Kiam, Polk 24
Ironton, Cherokee..........................110	*JOURDANTON, Atascosa, 144, (3,732) 3,871	Kicaster, Wilson 190
*IRVING, Dallas, 6,832, (191,615) 216,290	Joy, Clay 110	Kickapoo Indian Reservation, Maverick, (nc).........................366
Isla, Sabine...................................350	Jozye, Madison................................36	*Kildare, Cass, 1...........................104
Israel, Polk......................................25	Juarez, Cameron, (nc)..............1,017	*KILGORE, Gregg-Rusk, 861, (11,301) 12,975
*ITALY, Ellis, 49, (1,993) 1,863	Jud, Haskell....................................60	*KILLEEN, Bell, 2,334, (86,911) 127,921
*ITASCA, Hill, 57, (1,503) 1,644	*Judson, Gregg, 8.......................1,057	King, Coryell 30
Ivan, Stephens...............................15	Juliff, Fort Bend 250	King Ranch Headquarters, Kleberg 191
*Ivanhoe, Fannin, 9 110	Jumbo, Panola.................................60	*Kingsbury, Guadalupe, 20, (652) 782
IVANHOE, Tyler, 0, (nc) 887	*JUNCTION, Kimble, 165, (2,618) 2,574	*Kingsland, Llano, 152, (4,584) 6,030
IVANHOE NORTH, Tyler, 0, (nc) ..538	Justiceburg, Garza, 1 76	Kingston, Hunt...............................140
Izoro, Lampasas.............................17	*JUSTIN, Denton, 186, (1,891) 3,246	*KINGSVILLE, Kleberg, 655, (25,575).............................26,213
J		Kingtown, Nacogdoches..............300
*JACINTO CITY, Harris, 219, (10,302) 10,553	**K**	Kingwood, Harris-Montgomery, ...[part of Houston]
*JACKSBORO, Jack, 176, (4,533) 4,511	Kalgary, Crosby 2	Kinkler, Lavaca...............................75
Jackson, Shelby..............................50	*Kamay, Wichita, 7 640	Kiomatia, Red River.........................50
Jackson, Van Zandt.........................25	Kamey, Calhoun 25	KIRBY, Bexar, 139, (8,673)........8,000
*JACKSONVILLE, Cherokee, 737, (13,868) 14,544	Kanawha, Red River 90	*KIRBYVILLE, Jasper, 142, (2,085) 2,142
Jacobia, Hunt..................................60	*Karnack, Harrison, 21 350	Kirk, Limestone 10
Jakes Colony, Guadalupe...............95	*KARNES CITY, Karnes, 89, (3,457) 3,042	Kirkland, Childress...........................25
JAMAICA BEACH, Galveston, 38, (1,075) 983	Karon, Live Oak...............................25	Kirtley, Fayette 93
James, Shelby 75	Katemcy, Mason 80	*KIRVIN, Freestone, 0, (122).......129
Jamestown, Newton 196	*KATY, Harris-Waller-Fort Bend, 2,412, (11,775) 14,102	Kittrell, Walker 126
Jamestown, Smith 75	*KAUFMAN, Kaufman, 327, (6,490) 6,703	Klein, Harris 45,000
*JARRELL, Williamson, 89, (1,319) 984	K-Bar Ranch, Jim Wells, (350) 358	Klondike, Dawson............................50
*JASPER, Jasper, 488, (7,657) 7,590	Keechi, Leon....................................15	*Klondike, Delta, 3 175
*JAYTON, Kent, 19, (513) 534	*KEENE, Johnson, 119, (5,003) 6,106	Klump, Washington..........................20
Jean, Young 110	Keeter, Wise 250	Knapp, Scurry..................................10
*JEFFERSON, Marion, 239, (2,024) 2,106	Keith, Grimes..................................50	*Knickerbocker, Tom Green............94
Jenkins, Morris 350	*KELLER, Tarrant, 1,482, (27,345).............................39,627	*Knippa, Uvalde, 15, (739) 689
Jennings, Lamar 85	Kellers Corner, Cameron 123	Knobbs Springs, Lee 20
*Jermyn, Jack, 4.............................75	Kellerville, Wheeler 50	KNOLLWOOD, Grayson, 7, (375) 226
JERSEY VILLAGE, Harris, 265, (6,880) 7,620	Kellogg, Hunt...................................20	*Knott, Howard 200
*JEWETT, Leon, 71, (861).........1,167	Kellyville, Marion.............................75	*KNOX CITY, Knox, 53, (1,219) 1,130
JF Villarreal, Starr, (nc)................104	Kelsey, Upshur 50	Koerth, Lavaca................................45
Jiba, Kaufman.................................50	Kelton, Wheeler...............................34	Kokomo, Eastland 25
*JOAQUIN, Shelby, 37, (925) 824	*KEMAH, Galveston, 301, (2,330) 1,773	Komensky, Lavaca...........................75
Joe Lee, Bell 8	Kemper City, Victoria 16	*Kopperl, Bosque, 9.....................225
*JOHNSON CITY, Blanco, 134, (1,191) 1,656	*KEMP, Kaufman, 94, (1,133)....1,154	Kosciusko, Wilson 390
Johnsville, Erath 45	*KEMPNER, Lampasas, 67, (1,004) 1,089	*KOSSE, Limestone, 22, (497).....464
Johntown, Red River 175	*Kendalia, Kendall, 6 149	*KOUNTZE, Hardin, 115, (2,115) 2,123
*Joinerville, Rusk 140	*KENDLETON, Fort Bend, 4, (466) 380	*KRESS, Swisher, 19, (826).........715
Joliet, Caldwell..............................192	*KENEDY, Karnes, 114, (3,487) 3,296	KRUGERVILLE, Denton, 58, (903) 1,662
JOLLY, Clay, 6, (188) 172	KENEFICK, Liberty, 11, (667).......563	*KRUM, Denton, 141, (1,979)...4,157
Jollyville, Williamson-Travis, (15,813) 16,151	*KENNARD, Houston, 16, (317) 337	*KURTEN, Brazos, 2, (237).........398
Jonah, Williamson 60	*KENNEDALE, Tarrant, 342, (5,850) 6,763	*KYLE, Hays, 574, (5,314) 28,016
*Jonesboro, Coryell-Hamilton, 6...125	*Kenney, Austin, 2 957	Kyote, Atascosa..............................34
JONES CREEK, Brazoria, 22, (2,130) 2,020	Kenser, Hunt..................................100	
Jones Prairie, Milam.......................20	Kensing, Delta 30	

Town, County ....Pop. 2010	Town, County ....Pop. 2010	Town, County ....Pop. 2010

L

LaBelle, Jefferson 40
*La Blanca, Hidalgo, 12,
  (2,351) 2,488
La Casita, Starr, 5, (nc) 128
Laceola, Madison 10
Lackland Air Force Base, Bexar,
  (7,123) 9,918
La Coma, Webb, (nc) 48
*LA COSTE, Medina, 40,
  (1,255) 1,119
Lacy, Trinity 44
LACY-LAKEVIEW, McLennan,
  129, (5,764) 6,489
*LADONIA, Fannin, 24,
  (667) 612
LaFayette, Upshur 80
*LA FERIA, Cameron, 194,
  (6,115) 7,302
La Feria North, Cameron, (168) ... 212
Lagarto, Live Oak 735
La Gloria, Jim Wells 70
La Gloria, Starr 102
Lago, Cameron, (246) 204
*LAGO VISTA, Travis, 307,
  (4,507) 6,041
*LA GRANGE, Fayette, 428,
  (4,478) 4,641
*LA GRULLA, Starr, 6, (1,211)... 1,622
Laguna, Uvalde 20
Laguna Heights, Cameron,
  (1,990) 3,488
*Laguna Park, Bosque, (nc) 1,276
Laguna Seca, Hidalgo, (251) 266
Laguna Vista, Burnet 94
LAGUNA VISTA, Cameron, 52,
  (1,658) 3,117
La Homa, Hidalgo, (10,433) 11,985
*Laird Hill, Rusk, 4 300
La Isla, El Paso 27
Lajitas, Brewster 75
*LA JOYA, Hidalgo, 71,
  (3,303) 3,985
La Junta, Parker 300
Lake Arrowhead, Clay 250
LAKE BRIDGEPORT, Wise, 8,
  (372) 340
Lake Brownwood, Brown,
  (1,694) 1,532
Lake Bryan, Brazos, (nc) 1,728
Lake Cherokee, Rusk 3,071
Lake Cisco, Eastland 300
LAKE CITY, San Patricio, 0,
  (526) 509
Lake Colorado City, Mitchell,
  (nc) 588
*Lake Creek, Delta, 4 55
*LAKE DALLAS, Denton, 267,
  (6,166) 7,105
Lake Dunlap, Guadalupe,
  (nc) 1,934
Lakehills, Bandera, (4,668) 5,150
*LAKE JACKSON, Brazoria,
  790, (26,386) 26,849
Lake Kiowa, Cooke, (1,883) 1,906
Lake Leon, Eastland 75
Lake Medina Shores, Bandera,
  (nc) 1,235
Lake Meredith Estates,
  Hutchinson, (nc) 437
Lake Murvaul, Panola 300
Lake Nueces, Uvalde 60

LAKEPORT, Gregg, 15, (861) 974
Lakeshore Gardens-Hidden Acres,
  San Patricio, (720) 504
LAKESIDE, San Patricio, (333) 312
LAKESIDE, Tarrant, 43,
  (1,040) 1,307
LAKESIDE CITY, Archer, 24,
  (984) 997
Lakeside Village, Bosque 226
LAKE TANGLEWOOD, Randall,
  19, (825) 796
Lake Victor, Burnet 265
Lakeview, Floyd 39
*LAKEVIEW, Hall, 4, (152) 107
Lakeview, Lynn 15
LAKEVIEW [Lacy-], McLennan,
  129, (5,764) 6,489
Lakeview, Orange 75
Lake View, Val Verde, (167) 199
*LAKEWAY, Travis, 701,
  (8,002) 11,391
Lakewood Harbor, Bosque 250
LAKEWOOD VILLAGE, Denton,
  0, (342) 545
*LAKE WORTH, Tarrant, 280,
  (4,618) 4,584
Lamar, Aransas, (nc) 636
*LA MARQUE, Galveston, 400,
  (13,682) 14,509
Lamasco, Fannin 32
*LAMESA, Dawson, 332,
  (9,952) 9,422
Lamkin, Comanche 87
*LAMPASAS, Lampasas, 387,
  (6,786) 6,681
Lanark, Cass 30
*LANCASTER, Dallas, 728,
  (25,894) 36,361
Landrum Station, Cameron 125
*Lane City, Wharton, 4 111
Lanely, Freestone 27
Laneport, Williamson 40
*Laneville, Rusk, 11 169
*Langtry, Val Verde 30
Lanier, Cass 80
Lannius, Fannin 79
Lantana, Cameron 137
Lantana, Denton, (nc) 6,874
La Paloma, Cameron, (354) 2,903
La Paloma Addition, San Patricio,
  (nc) 330
La Paloma-Lost Creek, Nueces,
  (323) 408
La Parita, Atascosa 48
*LA PORTE, Harris, 930,
  (31,880) 33,800
La Presa, Webb, (508) 319
*La Pryor, Zavala, 13, (1,491).... 1,643
La Puerta, Starr, (1,636) 632
*LAREDO, Webb, 6,626,
  (176,576) 236,091
Laredo Ranchettes, Webb,
  (1,845) 22
La Reforma, Starr 45
Lariat, Parmer 100
La Rosita, Starr, (1,729) 85
*Larue, Henderson, 20 250
*LaSalle, Jackson 110
Lasana, Cameron, (135) 84
*Lasara, Willacy, 3, (1,024)........ 1,039
Las Escobas, Starr 10
Las Haciendas, Webb, (nc) 7

Las Lomas, Starr, (2,684) 3,147
Las Lomitas, Jim Hogg, (267) 244
Las Palmas, Zapata, (nc) 67
Las Palmas II, Cameron, (nc) 1,605
Las Pilas, Webb, (nc) 28
Las Quintas Fronterizas,
  Maverick, (2,030) 3,290
Las Rusias, Cameron 225
Lassater, Marion 60
Las Yescas, Cameron 221
Latch, Upshur 50
Latex, Harrison 75
*LATEXO, Houston, 6, (272) 322
La Tina Ranch, Cameron, (nc) 618
Latium, Washington 30
Laughlin Air Force Base,
  Val Verde, (2,225) 1,569
Laurel, Newton 357
Laureles, Cameron, (3,285) 3,692
Lavender, Limestone 30
*LA VERNIA, Wilson, 150,
  (931) 1,034
La Victoria, Starr, (1,683) 171
*LA VILLA, Hidalgo, 18,
  (1,305) 1,957
*LAVON, Collin, 101, (387)........ 2,219
*LA WARD, Jackson, 15,
  (200) 213
*LAWN, Taylor, 9, (353) 314
Lawrence, Kaufman 259
*Lazbuddie, Parmer, 8 248
*LEAGUE CITY, Galveston-Harris,
  2,282, (45,444) 83,560
Leagueville, Henderson 50
*LEAKEY, Real, 74, (387) 425
*LEANDER, Williamson, 863,
  (7,596) 26,521
LEARY, Bowie, 10, (555) 495
*Ledbetter, Fayette, 14 83
Leedale, Bell 24
*Leesburg, Camp, 16 128
*Leesville, Gonzales, 3 152
*LEFORS, Gray, 13, (559) 497
*Leggett, Polk, 6 500
Lehman, Cochran 6
Leigh, Harrison 60
Lela, Wheeler 135
*Lelia Lake, Donley, 2 70
*Leming, Atascosa, 7, (nc) 946
*Lenorah, Martin, 3 83
Lenz, Karnes 50
Leo, Cooke 20
Leo, Lee 10
*LEONA, Leon, 10, (181) 175
*LEONARD, Fannin, 104,
  (1,846) 1,990
Leon Junction, Coryell 50
Leon Springs, Bexar,
  .... [part of San Antonio]
*LEON VALLEY, Bexar, 517,
  (9,239) 10,151
*LEROY, McLennan, 9, (335) 337
Lesley, Hall 25
*LEVELLAND, Hockley, 491,
  (12,866) 13,542
Leverett's Chapel, Rusk 400
Levi, McLennan 50
Levita, Coryell 70
*LEWISVILLE, Denton, 3,653,
  (77,737) 95,290
*LEXINGTON, Lee, 92,
  (1,178) 1,177

CITIES & TOWNS

Town, County .... Pop. 2010	Town, County .... Pop. 2010	Town, County .... Pop. 2010
*LIBERTY, Liberty, 449, (8,033) 8,397	*LLANO, Llano, 280, (3,325) 3,232	Longworth, Fisher......................... 47
Liberty, Lubbock 228	Llano Grande, Hidalgo, (3,333) 3,008	Looneyville, Nacogdoches.............. 50
Liberty, Milam 40	Lobo, Culberson 15	*Loop, Gaines, 5, (nc)................... 225
Liberty, Newton 128	Locker, San Saba 16	*Lopeño, Zapata, 2, (140)............. 174
Liberty City, Gregg, (1,935) 2,351	Lockett, Wilbarger........................ 150	Lopezville, Hidalgo, (4,476)....... 4,333
Liberty Hill, Houston 73	Lockettville, Hockley 20	*LORAINE, Mitchell, 16, (656) 602
Liberty Hill, Milam 25	*LOCKHART, Caldwell, 429, (11,615) 12,698	*LORENA, McLennan, 140, (1,433) 1,691
*LIBERTY HILL, Williamson, 279, (1,409) 967	*LOCKNEY, Floyd, 64, (2,056) .. 1,842	*LORENZO, Crosby, 25, (1,372) 1,147
Lilbert, Nacogdoches.................... 100	Locust, Grayson 118	Los Altos, Webb, (nc) 140
*Lillian, Johnson, 10 1,160	*Lodi, Marion 175	Los Alvarez, Starr, (1,434)........... 303
*Lincoln, Lee, 13........................... 336	Loebau, Lee.................................. 35	Los Angeles, La Salle 20
LINCOLN PARK, Denton, 7, (517) 308	Logan, Panola 40	Los Angeles Subdivision, Willacy, (86) 121
*LINDALE, Smith, 410, (2,954) 4,818	LOG CABIN, Henderson, 3, (733) 714	Los Arcos, Webb, (nc) 127
*LINDEN, Cass, 89, (2,256) 1,988	*Lohn, McCulloch 149	Los Barreras, Starr 75
Lindenau, DeWitt............................ 50	Loire, Wilson 50	Los Centenarios, Webb, (nc)........... 87
Lindendale, Kendall 70	Lois, Cooke................................... 10	Los Corralitos, Webb, (nc)............. 35
*LINDSAY, Cooke, 26, (788) 1,018	*Lolita, Jackson, 8, (548) 555	*Los Ebanos, Hidalgo, 1, (403) 335
Lindsay, Reeves, (394)................. 271	Loma Alta, McMullen 25	Los Escondidos, Burnet................. 80
*Lingleville, Erath, 1...................... 100	Loma Alta, Val Verde 30	*LOS FRESNOS, Cameron, 150, (4,512) 5,542
Linn Flat, Nacogdoches................. 60	Loma Grande, Zavala, (nc).......... 107	Los Fresnos, Webb, (nc) 67
*Linn [San Manuel-], Hidalgo, 11, (958) 801	Loma Linda, San Patricio, (nc) 122	Los Huisaches, Webb, (nc) 17
Linwood, Cherokee......................... 40	Loma Linda East, Jim Wells, (214) 254	*LOS INDIOS, Cameron, 27, (1,149) 1,083
*LIPAN, Hood, 41, (425) 480	Lomax, Howard 25	Los Lobos, Zapata, (nc)................... 9
*Lipscomb, Lipscomb, 2, (44)........ 37	*LOMETA, Lampasas, 39, (782) 856	Los Minerales, Webb, (nc)............. 20
*Lissie, Wharton, 4 72	*London, Kimble, 6 180	Los Nopalitos, Webb, (nc) 62
Littig, Travis 35	Lone Camp, Palo Pinto................. 110	Losoya, Bexar............................... 500
Little Cypress, Orange................. 900	Lone Cedar, Ellis 18	LOS SAENZ [Roma-], Starr, 218, (9,617) 9,765
*LITTLE ELM, Denton, 578, (3,646) 25,898	Lone Grove, Llano 50	Lost Creek [La Paloma-], Nueces, (323) 408
*LITTLEFIELD, Lamb, 221, (6,507) 6,372	Lone Oak, Colorado 50	Lost Creek, Travis, (4,729) 4,509
Little Hope, Wood 25	*LONE OAK, Hunt, 40, (521) 598	Lost Prairie, Limestone.................... 2
Little Midland, Burnet...................... 82	Lone Pine, Houston 81	Los Veteranos I, Webb, (nc)........... 24
Little New York, Gonzales.............. 15	Lone Star, Cherokee....................... 20	Los Veteranos II, Webb, (nc)......... 24
*LITTLE RIVER-ACADEMY, Bell, 36, (1,645) 1,961	Lone Star, Floyd 42	LOS YBANEZ, Dawson, 3, (32) 19
Lively, Kaufman 50	Lone Star, Lamar............................ 35	*LOTT, Falls, 44, (724) 759
LIVE OAK, Bexar, 375, (9,156) 13,131	*LONE STAR, Morris, 43, (1,631) 1,581	*Louise, Wharton, 32, (977).......... 995
*LIVERPOOL, Brazoria, 21, (404) 482	*Long Branch, Panola, 4.............. 150	Lovelace, Hill 30
*LIVINGSTON, Polk, 605, (5,433) 5,335	Long Lake, Anderson...................... 15	*LOVELADY, Houston, 30, (608) 649
	Long Mott, Calhoun 76	*Loving, Young, 1........................... 300
	Longpoint, Washington................... 30	
	*LONGVIEW, Gregg-Harrison, 3,796, (73,344) 80,455	

The remains of Lobo, Culberson County. Photo by Robert Plocheck.

Town, County ....Pop. 2010	Town, County ....Pop. 2010	Town, County ....Pop. 2010
*Lowake, Concho, 2 40	Mapleton, Houston 32	McCoy, Red River....................... 175
LOWRY CROSSING, Collin, 40,	*Marathon, Brewster, 15,	*McDade, Bastrop, 13, (nc) 685
(1,229) 1,711	(455) 430	*McFaddin, Victoria, 1 50
Loyal Valley, Mason...................... 52	*MARBLE FALLS, Burnet, 696,	McGirk, Hamilton 18
Loyola Beach, Kleberg 195	(4,959) 6,077	*McGREGOR, McLennan, 207,
*Lozano, Cameron, 1, (324) 404	*MARFA, Presidio, 140,	(4,727) 4,987
*LUBBOCK, Lubbock, 7,704,	(2,121) 1,981	*McKINNEY, Collin, 3,973,
(199,564) 229,573	Margaret, Foard............................. 50	(54,369) 131,117
LUCAS, Collin, 161,	Marie, Runnels 10	McKinney Acres, Andrews, (nc).... 815
(2,890) 5,166	*MARIETTA, Cass, 4, (112).......... 134	*McLEAN, Gray, 30, (830) 778
Luckenbach, Gillespie 25	*MARION, Guadalupe, 104,	McLENDON-CHISHOLM,
*LUEDERS, Jones, 10, (300) 346	(1,099) 1,066	Rockwall, 3, (914)............... 1,373
Luella, Grayson 639	*Markham, Matagorda, 14,	*McLeod, Cass, 4 600
*LUFKIN, Angelina, 1,738,	(1,138) 1,082	McMahan, Caldwell 125
(32,709) 35,067	Markley, Young 50	McMillan, San Saba....................... 15
*LULING, Caldwell, 250,	*MARLIN, Falls, 186, (6,628)..... 5,967	McNair, Harris 2,039
(5,080) 5,411	Marlow, Milam............................... 45	McNary, Hudspeth 250
*LUMBERTON, Hardin, 424,	*MARQUEZ, Leon, 36, (220)........ 263	McNeil, Caldwell 100
(8,731) 11,943	Mars, Van Zandt 20	*McQueeney, Guadalupe, 36,
Lums Chapel, Lamb 6	*MARSHALL, Harrison, 945,	(2,527) 2,545
Luther, Howard 3	(23,935) 23,523	*MEADOW, Terry, 13, (658)........ 593
Lutie, Collingsworth 10	Marston, Polk................................ 25	Meadow Grove, Bell 22
Lydia, Red River 109	*MART, McLennan, 63,	MEADOWLAKES, Burnet, 24,
*LYFORD, Willacy, 30, (1,973) .. 2,611	(2,273) 2,209	(1,293) 1,777
Lynn Grove, Grimes 25	*MARTINDALE, Caldwell, 52,	MEADOWS PLACE, Fort Bend,
*Lyons, Burleson, 9 360	(953) 1,116	105, (4,912) 4,660
*LYTLE, Atascosa-Medina-Bexar,	Martins Mill, Van Zandt 158	Mecca, Madison 48
161, (2,383) 2,492	Martin Springs, Hopkins 200	Medicine Mound, Hardeman 50
Lytton Springs, Caldwell 500	*Martinsville, Nacogdoches, 2 350	Medill, Lamar................................. 50
M	Marvin, Lamar................................ 48	*Medina, Bandera, 3 850
*MABANK, Kaufman-Henderson,	Maryetta, Jack.................................. 7	Medina, Zapata, (2,960) 3,935
223, (2,151) 3,035	*Maryneal, Nolan, 3 50	Meeker, Jefferson 2,280
Mabelle, Baylor............................... 9	Marysville, Cooke 12	Meeks, Bell 6
Mabry, Red River 60	*MASON, Mason, 196,	*MEGARGEL, Archer, 10,
*Macdona, Bexar, 3, (nc) 559	(2,134) 2,114	(248) 203
Macon, Franklin 21	Massey Lake, Anderson 30	*MELISSA, Collin, 125,
Macune, San Augustine.................. 50	Masterson, Moore, 1......................... 2	(1,350) 4,695
*MADISONVILLE, Madison, 215,	*MATADOR, Motley, 42,	Melrose, Nacogdoches 400
(4,159) 4,396	(740) 719	*MELVIN, McCulloch, 8, (155)..... 178
Madras, Red River......................... 61	*Matagorda, Matagorda, 23,	*MEMPHIS, Hall, 87,
Magnet, Wharton 42	(nc) 503	(2,479) 2,290
*MAGNOLIA, Montgomery, 536,	*MATHIS, San Patricio, 155,	*MENARD, Menard, 77,
(1,111) 1,393	(5,034) 4,942	(1,653) 1,471
Magnolia, San Jacinto 330	Matthews, Colorado....................... 25	Mendoza, Caldwell 100
Magnolia Beach, Calhoun 250	*MAUD, Bowie, 35, (1,028) 1,056	Menlow, Hill 12
Magnolia Springs, Jasper.............. 20	*Mauriceville, Orange, 16,	*Mentone, Loving, 2, (nc) 19
Maha, Travis 200	(2,743) 3,252	Mentz, Colorado 100
Mahl, Nacogdoches...................... 150	Maverick, Runnels 35	*MERCEDES, Hidalgo, 510,
Mahomet, Burnet 97	Maxdale, Bell 25	(13,649) 15,570
Majors, Franklin 13	Maxey, Lamar................................ 70	Mercury, McCulloch 166
*MALAKOFF, Henderson, 126,	*Maxwell, Caldwell, 29.................. 500	*Mereta, Tom Green, 4 131
(2,257) 2,324	*May, Brown, 17 270	*MERIDIAN, Bosque, 80,
Mallard, Montague 12	*Maydelle, Cherokee, 1 250	(1,491) 1,493
*MALONE, Hill, 17, (278).............. 269	Mayfield, Hale............................... 26	*Merit, Hunt, 3.............................. 225
Malta, Bowie 297	Mayfield, Hill 25	*MERKEL, Taylor, 114,
Malvern, Leon 12	Mayflower, Newton 50	(2,637) 2,590
Mambrino, Hood 74	Maynard, San Jacinto.................. 150	Merle, Burleson 10
*Manchaca, Travis, 92, (nc) 1,133	*MAYPEARL, Ellis, 43, (746)....... 934	Merriman, Eastland 14
Manchester, Red River 185	Maysfield, Milam.......................... 140	*MERTENS, Hill, 4, (146) 125
Mangum, Eastland......................... 15	*McAdoo, Dickens, 2 75	*MERTZON, Irion, 60, (839) 781
Manheim, Lee................................ 50	*McALLEN, Hidalgo, 5,401,	*MESQUITE, Dallas-Kaufman,
Mankin, Henderson 30	(106,414) 129,877	3,428, (124,523) 139,824
Mankins, Archer 10	McBeth, Brazoria 60	Metcalf Gap, Palo Pinto 6
*MANOR, Travis, 197,	*McCAMEY, Upton, 58,	*MEXIA, Limestone, 318,
(1,204) 5,037	(1,805) 1,887	(6,563) 7,459
*MANSFIELD, Tarrant-Johnson-	*McCaulley, Fisher, 1..................... 96	*Meyersville, DeWitt, 10 110
Ellis, 1,863, (28,031) 56,368	McClanahan, Falls 42	Meyersville, Washington................ 15
*MANVEL, Brazoria, 225,	McCook, Hidalgo 50	*MIAMI, Roberts, 31, (588).......... 597
(3,046) 5,179	McCoy, Atascosa 30	Mico, Medina 107
*Maple, Bailey, 1 75	McCoy, Floyd 20	Midcity, Lamar............................... 50
Maple, Red River 30	McCoy, Kaufman 20	Middleton, Leon 26
Maple Springs, Titus 25	McCoy, Panola 30	*Midfield, Matagorda, 6................ 305

Town, County ....Pop. 2010	Town, County ....Pop. 2010	Town, County ....Pop. 2010
*Midkiff, Upton, 9 182	Mont, Lavaca 30	*Muldoon, Fayette, 3 95
*MIDLAND, Midland-Martin, 4,557, (94,996) 111,147	*Montague, Montague, 13, (nc) 304	*MULESHOE, Bailey, 196, (4,530) 5,158
*MIDLOTHIAN, Ellis, 650, (7,480) 18,037	*Montalba, Anderson, 16 110	*MULLIN, Mills, 6, (175) 179
Midway, Dawson........................... 20	*MONT BELVIEU, Chambers, 160, (2,324) 3,835	Mullins Prairie, Fayette................ 107
Midway, Fannin............................. 51	Monte Alto, Hidalgo, (1,611) 1,924	*Mumford, Robertson 170
Midway, Jim Wells 24	Monte Grande, Cameron................ 97	*MUNDAY, Knox, 47, (1,527)..... 1,300
Midway, Limestone 9	Montell, Uvalde............................. 20	Munger, Limestone 5
*MIDWAY, Madison, 13, (288) 228	*MONTGOMERY, Montgomery, 471, (489) 621	Mungerville, Dawson 20
Midway, Polk.............................. 525	Monthalia, Gonzales...................... 32	Muniz, Hidalgo, (1,106) 1,370
Midway, Red River........................ 40	Monticello, Titus............................ 20	*MURCHISON, Henderson, 49, (592) 594
Midway, Titus 110	*MOODY, McLennan, 82, (1,400) 1,371	MURPHY, Collin, 445, (3,099) 17,708
Midway, Upshur 20	*Moore, Frio, 11, (644)................. 475	Murray, Young............................... 45
Midway, Van Zandt 31	Moore's Crossing, Travis 25	Murvaul, Panola.......................... 150
Midway North, Hidalgo, (3,946) 4,752	MOORE STATION, Henderson, 0, (184) 201	Mustang, Denton 25
Midway South, Hidalgo, (1,711) 2,239	Mooreville, Falls............................ 96	MUSTANG, Navarro, 1, (47).......... 21
Midyett, Panola........................... 150	Mooring, Brazos 80	Mustang Mott, DeWitt 20
Mikeska, Live Oak 10	Morales, Jackson........................... 72	MUSTANG RIDGE, Travis-Caldwell , 23, (785) 861
Mila Doce, Hidalgo, (4,907) 6,222	*MORAN, Shackelford, 7, (233) ... 270	*Myra, Cooke, 2........................... 150
*Milam, Sabine, 7, (1,329)......... 1,480	Moravia, Lavaca 165	Myrtle Springs, Van Zandt, (nc) 828
*MILANO, Milam, 29, (400) 428	*MORGAN, Bosque, 11, (485)...... 490	**N**
Milburn, McCulloch 8	Morgan Creek, Burnet 126	*NACOGDOCHES, Nacogdoches, 1,380, (29,914) 32,996
MILDRED, Navarro, 6, (405) 368	Morgan Farm Area, San Patricio, (484) 463	*Nada, Colorado, 10 165
*MILES, Runnels, 46, (850).......... 829	*Morgan Mill, Erath, 6 206	*NAPLES, Morris, 60, (1,410) 1,378
*MILFORD, Ellis, 26, (685)........... 728	MORGAN'S POINT, Harris, 15, (336) 339	Naruna, Burnet 95
Mill Creek, Washington.................. 40	MORGAN'S POINT RESORT, Bell, 60, (2,989) 4,170	*NASH, Bowie, 87, (2,169)........ 2,960
Miller Grove, Hopkins 115	Morning Glory, El Paso, (627) 651	Nash, Ellis..................................... 40
MILLERS COVE, Titus, 6, (120) 149	*Morse, Hansford, 4, (172) 147	NASSAU BAY, Harris, 162, (4,170) 4,002
*Millersview, Concho, 2 80	*MORTON, Cochran, 49, (2,249) 2,006	Nat, Nacogdoches.......................... 50
Millett, La Salle 60	Morton, Harrison............................ 75	*NATALIA, Medina, 63, (1,663) 1,431
Millheim, Austin........................... 170	Morton Valley, Eastland 46	NAVARRO, Navarro, 0, (191) 210
*Millican, Brazos, 8, (108)............ 240	*Moscow, Polk, 10 170	Navarro Mills, Navarro 90
*MILLSAP, Parker, 44, (353)......... 403	Mosheim, Bosque........................... 75	*NAVASOTA, Grimes, 369, (6,789) 7,049
Milo Center, Deaf Smith................... 5	Moss Bluff, Liberty 65	Navidad, Jackson 227
Milton, Lamar................................ 50	Moss Hill, Liberty 180	*NAZARETH, Castro, 12, (356).... 311
Mims, Brazoria.............................. 90	Mostyn, Montgomery 90	Necessity, Stephens 10
*Minden, Rusk, 3 150	*MOULTON, Lavaca, 63, (944) 886	Nechanitz, Fayette......................... 57
*MINEOLA, Wood, 420, (4,550) 4,515	*Mound, Coryell, 2 125	*Neches, Anderson, 8.................. 175
Mineral, Bee 65	Mound City, Anderson-Houston...... 60	*NEDERLAND, Jefferson, 668, (17,422) 17,547
*MINERAL WELLS, Palo Pinto-Parker, 657, (16,946)........ 16,788	MOUNTAIN CITY, Hays, 28, (671) 648	Needmore, Bailey........................... 45
Minerva, Milam 100	*Mountain Home, Kerr, 16 96	Needmore, Terry.............................. 7
Mings Chapel, Upshur 50	Mountain Peak, Ellis 300	*NEEDVILLE, Fort Bend, 150, (2,609) 2,823
*MINGUS, Palo Pinto, 18, (246) 235	Mountain Springs, Cooke 600	Negley, Red River......................... 136
Minter, Lamar................................ 78	Mount Bethel, Panola 65	Neinda, Jones................................ 21
*Mirando City, Webb, 15, (493) 375	*MOUNT CALM, Hill, 16, (310)..... 320	Nell, Live Oak 60
*MISSION, Hidalgo, 1,756, (45,408) 77,058	*MOUNT ENTERPRISE, Rusk, 49, (525) 447	Nelson City, Kendall 50
Mission Bend, Fort Bend-Harris, (30,831) 36,501	Mount Haven, Cherokee................. 30	Nelsonville, Austin 200
Mission Valley, Victoria 225	Mount Hermon, Shelby................... 80	Nelta, Hopkins............................... 36
*MISSOURI CITY, Fort Bend-Harris, 1,874, (52,913) 67,358	Mount Olive, Cherokee 50	*Nemo, Somervell, 13.................... 56
Mixon, Cherokee............................ 50	*MOUNT PLEASANT, Titus, 764, (13,935) 15,564	Nesbitt, Harrison, (302) 281
*MOBEETIE, Wheeler, 8, (107).... 101	Mount Rose, Falls.......................... 26	Neuville, Shelby............................. 65
MOBILE CITY, Rockwall, 2, (196) 188	Mount Selman, Cherokee............. 325	*NEVADA, Collin, 42, (563) 822
Moffat, Bell............................... 1,406	Mount Sylvan, Smith.................... 181	*NEWARK, Wise, 47, (887) 1,005
Moffett, Angelina.......................... 100	*MOUNT VERNON, Franklin, 156, (2,286) 2,662	*New Baden, Robertson, 4........... 150
Moline, Lampasas 32	Mount Vernon, Houston................. 43	NEW BERLIN, Guadalupe, 17, (467) 511
*MONAHANS, Ward, 260, (6,821) 6,953	Mozelle, Coleman 15	New Bielau, Colorado.................... 75
Monaville, Waller 180	Muellersville, Washington.............. 20	*NEW BOSTON, Bowie, 195, (4,808) 4,550
Monkstown, Fannin 35	*MUENSTER, Cooke, 146, (1,556) 1,544	*NEW BRAUNFELS, Comal-Guadalupe, 2,823,
Monroe, Rusk 96	Mulberry, Fannin.......................... 141	
Monroe City, Chambers 11		

Town, County ....Pop. 2010	Town, County ....Pop. 2010	Town, County ....Pop. 2010
(36,494) 57,740	*NOME, Jefferson, 23, (515) 588	*Odell, Wilbarger 100
New Bremen, Austin 125	Noodle, Jones.................................. 40	*ODEM, San Patricio, 67,
Newburg, Comanche...................... 32	NOONDAY, Smith, 57, (515) 777	(2,499) 2,389
Newby, Leon.................................. 40	Nopal, DeWitt 25	*ODESSA, Ector-Midland, 3,922,
*New Caney, Montgomery, 185,	*NORDHEIM, DeWitt, 15,	(90,943) 99,940
.... 6,800	(323) 307	*O'DONNELL, Lynn-Dawson, 16,
*NEWCASTLE, Young, 26,	Norman, Williamson 40	(1,011) 831
(575) 585	Normandy, Maverick..................... 114	Oenaville, Bell............................... 108
NEW CHAPEL HILL, Smith, 12,	*NORMANGEE, Leon-Madison,	O'Farrell, Cass................................ 20
(553) 594	54, (719) 685	Ogburn, Wood 10
New Colony, Bell 12	*Normanna, Bee, (121)................. 113	*OGLESBY, Coryell, 19, (458)...... 484
New Colony, Cass 65	Norse, Bosque............................. 110	*Oilton, Webb, 2, (310)............... 353
New Corn Hill, Williamson 475	North Alamo, Hidalgo, (2,601) ... 3,235	Oklahoma, Montgomery 800
New Davy, DeWitt........................... 20	NORTH CLEVELAND, Liberty, 3,	Oklahoma Flat, Hockley 4
*NEW DEAL, Lubbock, 24,	(263) 247	Oklahoma Lane, Parmer 25
(708) 794	North Escobares, Starr, (1,692).... 118	*Oklaunion, Wilbarger, 4.............. 138
NEW FAIRVIEW, Wise, 15,	Northfield, Motley............................ 15	Okra, Eastland................................ 20
(877) 1,258	NORTHLAKE, Denton, 39,	Ola, Kaufman................................. 65
Newgulf, Wharton 10	(921) 1,724	Old Boston, Bowie 100
New Harmony, Shelby 40	North Pearsall, Frio, (561) 614	Old Center, Panola 83
New Harmony, Smith.................... 350	*NORTH RICHLAND HILLS, Tarrant,	Old Dime Box, Lee 225
*NEW HOME, Lynn, 7, (320)........ 334	2,035, (55,635) 63,343	*Olden, Eastland, 6...................... 113
New Hope, Cherokee...................... 50	Northrup, Lee.................................. 86	Oldenburg, Fayette 92
NEW HOPE, Collin, 18, (662)....... 614	North San Pedro, Nueces, (920) .. 895	*Old Glory, Stonewall, 3.............. 100
New Hope, Jones 9	North Star, Archer 10	Old Midway, Leon 12
New Hope, San Augustine.............. 75	*North Zulch, Madison, 14 600	*Old Ocean, Brazoria, 15............. 150
New Hope, Smith............................ 75	*Norton, Runnels........................... 50	OLD RIVER-WINFREE, Chambers,
New Hope, Wood 15	*Notrees, Ector, 2 20	17, (1,364) 1,245
Newlin, Hall................................... 27	*NOVICE, Coleman, 0, (142)........ 139	Old Salem, Bowie 50
*NEW LONDON, Rusk, 16,	Novice, Lamar 35	Old Union, Bowie 238
(987) 998	Noxville, Kimble................................ 3	Old Union, Limestone 25
New Lynn, Lynn 4	Nugent, Jones 50	Oletha, Limestone 53
New Moore, Lynn 10	Nunelee, Fannin 90	Olfen, Runnels............................... 35
New Mountain, Upshur.................... 20	Nurillo, Hidalgo, (5,056).............. 7,344	Olin, Hamilton 15
Newport, Clay-Jack 75	*Nursery, Victoria, 5...................... 450	Olivarez, Hidalgo, (2,445).......... 3,827
New Salem, Palo Pinto................... 89	**O**	Olivia, Calhoun 215
New Salem, Rusk 55	Oakalla, Burnet............................... 99	Ollie, Polk 5
Newsome, Camp 113	Oakdale, Polk 25	*Olmito, Cameron, 50,
*NEW SUMMERFIELD, Cherokee,	Oak Forest, Gonzales...................... 24	(1,198) 1,210
23, (998) 1,111	Oak Grove, Bowie 294	Olmos, Guadalupe.......................... 65
New Sweden, Travis........................ 60	Oak Grove, Colorado...................... 40	OLMOS PARK, Bexar, 118,
New Taiton, Wharton 10	OAK GROVE, Kaufman, (710) 603	(2,343) 2,237
New Territory, Fort Bend,	Oak Grove, Wood 140	*OLNEY, Young, 130, (3,396).... 3,285
(13,861) 15,186	Oak Hill, Hood 247	*OLTON, Lamb, 61, (2,288)....... 2,215
*NEWTON, Newton, 84,	Oak Hill, Rusk............................... 200	*OMAHA, Morris, 37, (999)........ 1,021
(2,459) 2,478	Oak Hill, Travis .... [part of Austin]	Omen, Smith................................ 150
*New Ulm, Austin, 37..................... 974	*Oakhurst, San Jacinto, 11,	*ONALASKA, Polk, 115,
*NEW WAVERLY, Walker, 93,	(230) 233	(1,174) 1,764
(950) 1,032	Oak Island, Chambers, (nc).......... 363	Opdyke, Hockley 50
New Wehdem, Austin 414	Oakland, Cherokee......................... 50	OPDYKE WEST, Hockley, 4,
New Willard, Polk 160	*Oakland, Colorado 80	(188) 174
New York, Henderson..................... 60	Oakland, Van Zandt........................ 26	Oplin, Callahan 75
NEYLANDVILLE, Hunt, 1, (56)....... 97	OAK LEAF, Ellis, 26, (1,209) 1,298	O'Quinn, Fayette 191
NIEDERWALD, Hays-Caldwell,	OAK POINT, Denton, 99,	Oran, Palo Pinto 61
21, (584) 565	(1,747) 2,786	*ORANGE, Orange, 709,
Nigton, Trinity................................ 87	OAK RIDGE, Cooke, (224)........... 141	(18,643) 18,595
Nimrod, Eastland 45	Oak Ridge, Grayson 161	Orangedale, Bee 40
Nineveh, Leon 50	OAK RIDGE, Kaufman, 10,	*Orangefield, Orange, 9.............. 725
Nix, Lampasas 6	(400) 495	*ORANGE GROVE, Jim Wells,
*NIXON, Gonzales-Wilson, 62,	Oak Ridge, Nacogdoches.............. 225	109, (1,288) 1,318
(2,186) 2,385	OAK RIDGE NORTH, Montgomery,	Orangeville, Fannin 60
Noack, Williamson 70	192, (2,991) 3,049	Orason, Cameron, (nc)................. 129
Nobility, Fannin 100	Oak Trail Shores, Hood,	*ORCHARD, Fort Bend, 16,
Noble, Lamar 14	(2,475) 2,755	(408) 352
Nockernut, Wilson 20	OAK VALLEY, Navarro, 2,	*ORE CITY, Upshur, 58,
*NOCONA, Montague, 138,	(401) 368	(1,106) 1,144
(3,198) 3,033	Oakville, Live Oak, 4..................... 260	Orient, Tom Green 57
Nocona Hills, Montague, (nc) 675	*OAKWOOD, Leon, 32, (471)....... 510	*Orla, Reeves, 2 80
Nogalus Prairie, Trinity 109	Oatmeal, Burnet 74	Osage, Colorado 50
*Nolan, Nolan, 2 60	*O'BRIEN, Haskell, 4, (132) 106	Osage, Coryell 30
*NOLANVILLE, Bell, 43,	Ocee, McLennan 84	Oscar, Bell 58
(2,150) 4,259	Odds, Limestone 24	Osceola, Hill 95

CITIES & TOWNS

Town, County ....Pop. 2010	Town, County ....Pop. 2010	Town, County ....Pop. 2010
Otey, Brazoria...............................318	Parsley Hill, Wilbarger 25	*PETERSBURG, Hale, 40,
*Ottine, Gonzales, 1 80	Parvin, Denton...............................44	(1,262)...............................1,202
Otto, Falls 48	*PASADENA, Harris, 3,389,	Peter's Prairie, Red River...............40
*Ovalo, Taylor, 2 225	(141,674)......................149,043	Petersville, DeWitt 38
*OVERTON, Rusk-Smith, 97,	Patillo, Erath 10	*PETROLIA, Clay, 14, (782)........686
(2,350)...............................2,554	Patman Switch, Cass 40	PETRONILA, Nueces, 3, (83).......113
*OVILLA, Ellis-Dallas, 129,	Patonia, Polk 15	Petteway, Robertson 25
(3,405)...............................3,492	Patricia, Dawson.............................50	Pettibone, Milam 25
Owens, Brown 16	Patroon, Shelby 25	Pettit, Hockley................................30
Owens, Crosby 4	*PATTISON, Waller, 40,	*Pettus, Bee, 14, (608) 558
Owentown, Smith 100	(447)......................................472	*Petty, Lamar, 2 130
Owl Creek, Bell.............................130	PATTON VILLAGE, Montgomery,	Petty, Lynn......................................8
Owl Ranch, Jim Wells, (nc) 225	10, (1,391) 1,557	Peyton, Blanco 30
Oxford, Llano 18	*Pattonville, Lamar, 6.....................180	*PFLUGERVILLE, Travis, 1,411,
OYSTER CREEK, Brazoria, 41,	Pattonfield, Upshur 20	(16,335)..........................46,936
(1,192)................................1,111	Pawelekville, Karnes 110	Phalba, Van Zandt..........................73
*Ozona, Crockett, 122,	*Pawnee, Bee, 3, (201) 166	*PHARR, Hidalgo, 1,612,
(3,436)...............................3,225	Paxton, Shelby 50	(46,660) 70,400
P	Paynes Corner, Gaines 18	Phelps, Walker................................98
Pacio, Delta 35	PAYNE SPRINGS, Henderson,	Phillipsburg, Washington 75
Padgett, Young 28	21, (683)..............................767	Pickens, Henderson 20
*PADUCAH, Cottle, 56,	Peach Creek, Brazos.....................150	Pickett, Navarro..............................30
(1,498)...............................1,186	Peacock, Stonewall.......................100	*Pickton, Hopkins, 4 300
*Paige, Bastrop, 24.......................275	Peadenville, Palo Pinto..................15	Pidcoke, Coryell.............................50
Paint Creek, Haskell 150	Pearl, Coryell..................................50	Piedmont, Grimes...........................50
*PAINT ROCK, Concho, 12,	*PEARLAND, Brazoria-Harris-Fort	Piedmont, Upshur...........................20
(320)....................................273	Bend, 2,952, (37,640).......91,252	*Pierce, Wharton, 3 51
Paisano Park, San Patricio,	Pearl City, DeWitt, 4	Pike, Collin.....................................47
(182)....................................130	*PEARSALL, Frio, 224,	Pilgrim, Gonzales 22
*PALACIOS, Matagorda, 151,	(7,157)...............................9,146	Pilgrim Rest, Rains 72
(5,153)...............................4,718	Pearson, Medina 24	Pilot Grove, Grayson 48
*PALESTINE, Anderson, 800,	Pearsons Chapel, Houston.............95	Pilot Knob, Travis...........................500
(17,598)...........................18,712	Pear Valley, McCulloch...................37	*PILOT POINT, Denton, 189,
PALISADES, Randall, 0, (352) 325	*Peaster, Parker, 1......................1,000	(3,538)...............................3,856
Palito Blanco, Jim Wells 750	Pecan Acres, Tarrant-Wise,	Pine, Camp......................................78
*PALMER, Ellis, 62, (1,774).......2,000	(2,289)...............................4,099	Pine Branch, Red River 40
PALMHURST, Hidalgo, 93,	*PECAN GAP, Delta-Fannin, 7,	Pine Forest, Hopkins 100
(4,872)...............................2,607	(214)....................................203	PINE FOREST, Orange, 14,
PALM VALLEY, Cameron, 16,	Pecan Grove, Fort Bend,	(632)....................................487
(1,298)...............................1,304	(13,551)...........................15,963	Pine Grove, Cherokee 30
PALMVIEW, Hidalgo, 186,	PECAN HILL, Ellis, 7, (672)..........626	Pine Grove, Newton 180
(4,107)...............................5,460	Pecan Plantation, Hood,	Pine Harbor, Marion, (nc) 810
Palmview South, Hidalgo,	(3,544)...............................5,294	Pinehill, Rusk.................................70
(6,219)...............................5,575	Pecan Wells, Hamilton 6	*Pinehurst, Montgomery, 109,
Paloduro, Armstrong.......................10	*PECOS, Reeves, 249,	(4,266)...............................4,624
Paloma Creek, Denton, (nc) 2,501	(9,501)...............................8,780	PINEHURST, Orange, 161,
Paloma Creek South, Denton,	Peeltown, Kaufman 75	(2,274)...............................2,097
(nc) 2,753	Peerless, Hopkins 90	Pine Island, Jefferson 350
*Palo Pinto, Palo Pinto, 15, (nc) ...333	*Peggy, Atascosa, 2.......................22	PINE ISLAND, Waller, 0, (849).....988
*Paluxy, Hood 76	Pelham, Navarro..............................75	*PINELAND, Sabine, 32,
*PAMPA, Gray, 639,	PELICAN BAY, Tarrant, 7,	(980)....................................850
(17,887) 17,994	(1,505)...............................1,547	Pine Mills, Wood............................75
Pancake, Coryell 11	*Pendleton, Bell, 1 369	Pine Prairie, Walker......................450
Pandale, Val Verde 25	*PENELOPE, Hill, 6, (211)............198	Pine Springs, Culberson 20
*Pandora, Wilson, 2 110	*PEÑITAS, Hidalgo, 84,	Pine Springs, Smith 150
*PANHANDLE, Carson, 67,	(1,167)...............................4,403	Pineview, Wood..............................10
(2,589)...............................2,452	Pennington, Trinity-Houston, 5......67	Pinewood Estates, Hardin,
*Panna Maria, Karnes, 5 45	*Penwell, Ector, 4 41	(1,633)...............................1,678
*Panola, Panola, 3.........................305	Peoria, Hill 105	Piney, Austin 60
PANORAMA VILLAGE, Montgomery,	*Pep, Hockley.................................30	PINEY POINT VILLAGE, Harris,
39, (1,965).........................2,170	Percilla, Houston 95	65, (3,380).........................3,125
*PANTEGO, Tarrant, 392,	Perezville, Hidalgo, (5,444).......5,376	Pin Hook, Lamar.............................48
(2,318)...............................2,394	Pernitas Point, Live Oak-Jim	Pioneer, Eastland...........................20
Panther Junction, Brewster 130	Wells, (269)..........................274	*Pipe Creek, Bandera, 124...........130
Papalote, Bee..................................75	*Perrin, Jack, 9, (nc).....................398	Pitner Junction, Rusk.....................20
*PARADISE, Wise, 49, (459)........441	Perry, Falls 76	*PITTSBURG, Camp, 249,
*PARIS, Lamar, 1,176,	*PERRYTON, Ochiltree, 392,	(4,347)...............................4,497
(25,898)...........................25,171	(7,774)...............................8,802	*Placedo, Victoria, 6, (nc) 692
Park, Fayette 25	Perryville, Wood 35	Placid, McCulloch...........................32
PARKER, Collin, 72, (1,379)......3,811	Personville, Limestone 50	Plain, Houston 30
Parker, Johnson..............................93	Pert, Anderson................................20	*PLAINS, Yoakum, 51,
Park Springs, Wise 90	Peters, Austin 150	(1,450)...............................1,481

CITIES & TOWNS

Town, County ....Pop. 2010	Town, County ....Pop. 2010	Town, County ....Pop. 2010
*PLAINVIEW, Hale, 802, (22,336) 22,194	*POST, Garza, 172, (3,708) 5,376	Purves, Erath..................................50
*PLANO, Collin-Denton, 10,812, (222,030) 259,841	Post Oak, Blanco............................10	*PUTNAM, Callahan, 8, (88) 94
*Plantersville, Grimes, 37 260	Postoak, Jack 20	*PYOTE, Ward, 8, (131) 114
Plaska, Hall......................................20	Postoak, Lamar 65	**Q**
PLEAK, Fort Bend, 30, (947).....1,044	Post Oak, Lee................................100	*Quail, Collingsworth, 1, (33)..........19
Pleasant Farms, Ector.................800	POST OAK BEND, Kaufman, 10, (404)...............................595	Quail Creek, Victoria, (nc) 1,628
Pleasant Grove, Falls 35	Post Oak Point, Austin....................60	*QUANAH, Hardeman, 96, (3,022)..............................2,641
Pleasant Grove, Limestone 20	*POTEET, Atascosa, 126, (3,305) 3,260	Quarry, Washington.........................60
Pleasant Grove, Upshur 35	*POTH, Wilson, 49, (1,850).......1,908	Quarterway, Hale 24
Pleasant Grove, Wood 30	Potosi, Taylor, (1,664)...............2,991	*QUEEN CITY, Cass, 67, (1,613)..............................1,476
Pleasant Hill, Eastland...................15	*POTTSBORO, Grayson, 121, (1,579)..............................2,160	*Quemado, Maverick, 11, (243)....230
Pleasant Hill, Nacogdoches..........250	*Pottsville, Hamilton, 1.................105	Quicksand, Newton 50
Pleasant Hill, Polk, (nc) 522	*Powderly, Lamar, 37, (nc) 1,178	Quihi, Medina 125
Pleasant Hill, Yoakum....................30	*POWELL, Navarro, 13, (105)......136	*QUINLAN, Hunt, 174, (1,370)..............................1,394
*PLEASANTON, Atascosa, 434, (8,266) 8,934	*POYNOR, Henderson, 20, (314) 305	QUINTANA, Brazoria, 2, (38) 56
Pleasant Valley, Garza 5	Prado Verde, El Paso, (200).........246	*QUITAQUE, Briscoe, 17, (432)...............................411
PLEASANT VALLEY, Wichita, 0, (408) 336	Praesel, Milam..............................115	*QUITMAN, Wood, 201, (2,030)..............................1,809
*Pledger, Matagorda, 1.................265	Praha, Fayette 90	**R**
Pluck, Polk.......................................53	Prairie Chapel, McLennan..............35	Rabbs Prairie, Fayette....................79
*Plum, Fayette, 5 145	Prairie Dell, Bell 34	Raccoon Bend, Austin 775
PLUM GROVE, Liberty, 1, (930)...............................600	*Prairie Hill, Limestone, 2 150	Rachal, Brooks 36
Pluto, Ellis.......................................30	Prairie Hill, Washington 20	Radar Base, Maverick, (162)........762
Poetry, Kaufman 90	*Prairie Lea, Caldwell, 10 255	Radium, Jones................................10
*POINT, Rains, 42, (792)...............820	Prairie Point, Cooke........................22	Ragtown, Lamar 30
*POINT BLANK, San Jacinto, 5, (559)...............................688	*PRAIRIE VIEW, Waller, 31, (4,410)..............................5,576	*Rainbow, Somervell, 10 121
*POINT COMFORT, Calhoun, 43, (781) 737	Prairieville, Kaufman......................75	Raisin, Victoria................................50
Point Enterprise, Limestone 200	*PREMONT, Jim Wells, 68, (2,772)..............................2,653	Raleigh, Navarro.............................40
POINT VENTURE, Travis, 27, (nc) 800	*PRESIDIO, Presidio, 97, (4,167)..............................4,426	*RALLS, Crosby, 60, (2,252)..............................1,944
Polar, Kent.......................................15	Preston, Grayson, (nc) 2,096	Ramireno, Zapata, (nc)...................35
*Pollok, Angelina, 27....................400	*Price, Rusk, 5...............................275	Ramirez, Duval 42
*PONDER, Denton, 67, (507) 1,395	*Priddy, Mills, 11 215	Ranchette Estates, Willacy, (133)...............................152
Ponta, Cherokee..............................50	PRIMERA, Cameron, 30, (2,723)..............................4,070	Ranchito El Calaboz [Encantada-], Cameron, (2,100)..............2,284
*Pontotoc, Mason, 4 125	Primrose, Van Zandt........................26	Ranchitos East, Webb, (nc)..........212
Poole, Rains.....................................50	*PRINCETON, Collin, 178, (3,477)..............................6,807	Ranchitos Las Lomas, Webb, (334)...............................266
*Poolville, Parker, 24 520	Pringle, Hutchinson 20	Rancho Alegre, Jim Wells, (1,775)..............................1,704
Port Acres, Jefferson, ...[part of Port Arthur]	Pritchett, Upshur...........................125	Rancho Banquete, Nueces, (469)...............................424
Port Alto, Calhoun...........................45	*Proctor, Comanche, 6 228	Rancho Chico, San Patricio, (309)...............................396
*PORT ARANSAS, Nueces, 403, (3,370) 3,480	*PROGRESO, Hidalgo, 53, (4,851)..............................5,507	Rancho Penitas West, Webb, (520)...............................573
*PORT ARTHUR, Jefferson, 1,245, (57,755)..........................53,818	PROGRESO LAKES, Hidalgo, 10, (234)...............................240	RANCHO VIEJO, Cameron, 37, (1,754)..............................2,437
*Port Bolivar, Galveston, 82..........700	Progress, Bailey 49	Rand, Kaufman................................70
*Porter, Montgomery, 290..........4,200	Prospect, Rains 40	Randado, Jim Hogg...........................6
Porter Heights, Montgomery, (1,490) 1,653	*PROSPER, Collin-Denton, 299, (2,097)..............................9,423	*Randolph, Fannin, 2, 600
Porter Springs.................Houston, 50	PROVIDENCE, Denton, (nc) 4,786	Randolph Air Force Base, Bexar, (nc) 1,241
*PORT ISABEL, Cameron, 253, (4,865)..............................5,006	Providence, Floyd...........................78	*RANGER, Eastland, 85, (2,584)..............................2,468
*PORTLAND, San Patricio, 467, (14,827) 15,099	Providence, Polk...........................350	RANGERVILLE, Cameron, 0, (203)...............................289
*PORT LAVACA, Calhoun, 457, (12,035) 12,248	Pruitt, Cass.....................................25	Rankin, Ellis....................................10
*Port Mansfield, Willacy, 9, (415) 226	Pruitt, Van Zandt.............................45	*RANKIN, Upton, 36, (800)...........778
*PORT NECHES, Jefferson, 373, (13,601) 13,040	Pueblo Nuevo, Webb, (nc) 521	RANSOM CANYON, Lubbock, 39, (1,011)..............................1,096
*Port O'Connor , Calhoun, 39, (nc) 1,253	Puerto Rico, Hidalgo.......................50	Ratamosa, Cameron, (218)..........254
Port Sullivan, Milam........................15	Pullman, Potter...............................31	*Ratcliff, Houston, 3......................106
Porvenir, Presidio 3	Pumphrey, Runnels 15	Ratibor, Bell 22
Posey, Hopkins...............................12	Pumpkin, San Jacinto...................150	Rattan, Delta...................................10
Posey, Lubbock 225	Pumpville, Val Verde.......................25	*RAVENNA, Fannin, 13, (215)......209
	Punkin Center, Dawson 30	Rayburn, Liberty 60
	Punkin Center, Eastland 12	
	*Purdon, Navarro, 9......................133	
	Purley, Franklin.............................100	
	*Purmela, Coryell, 4........................50	
	Pursley, Navarro 40	

Town, County ....Pop. 2010	Town, County ....Pop. 2010	Town, County ....Pop. 2010
Rayland, Foard 30	Reilly Springs, Hopkins...................75	*RIO GRANDE CITY, Starr, 399,
*RAYMONDVILLE, Willacy, 195,	Rek Hill, Fayette 168	(11,923) 13,834
(9,733) 11,284	*REKLAW, Cherokee-Rusk, 5,	Rio Grande Village, Brewster 12
Ray Point, Live Oak......................200	(327) 379	*RIO HONDO, Cameron, 56,
*Raywood, Liberty, 11 231	Relampago, Hidalgo, (104)...........132	(1,942) 2,356
Razor, Lamar..................................20	Rendon, Tarrant, (9,022) 12,552	*Riomedina, Medina, 10 60
*Reagan, Falls, 2 208	*RENO, Lamar, 105, (2,767) 3,166	Rios, Duval 75
Reagan Wells, Uvalde 20	RENO, Parker-Tarrant, 23,	*RIO VISTA, Johnson, 43,
Reagor Springs, Ellis...................250	(2,441) 2,494	(656) 873
*Realitos, Duval, 2, (209)..............184	Retreat, Grimes 25	*RISING STAR, Eastland, 33,
Red Bank, Bowie 125	RETREAT, Navarro, 0, (339) 377	(835) 835
Red Bluff, Jackson.........................45	Retta, Tarrant-Johnson 780	Rita, Burleson 50
Red Bluff, Reeves..........................40	Reynard, Houston............................75	Riverby, Fannin..............................15
Redfield, Nacogdoches, (nc) 441	Rhea, Parmer 98	River Crest Estates, Angelina.......250
*Redford, Presidio, (132)...............90	Rhineland, Knox 120	River Hill, Panola 125
Red Hill, Cass................................28	*RHOME, Wise, 88, (551) 1,522	RIVER OAKS, Tarrant, 148,
Red Hill, Limestone 20	Rhonesboro, Upshur 40	(6,985) 7,427
Red Lake, Freestone 50	Ricardo, Kleberg..........................1,641	Rivers End, Brazoria......................90
Redland, Angelina, (nc) 1,047	*RICE, Navarro, 42, (798) 923	*RIVERSIDE, Walker, 34, (425) ...510
Redland, Leon 35	Rice's Crossing, Williamson 130	*Riviera, Kleberg, 28, (nc) 689
Redland, Van Zandt........................45	*Richards, Grimes, 8 300	Riviera Beach, Kleberg.................155
RED LICK, Bowie, 0,	*RICHARDSON, Dallas-Collin,	Roach, Cass...................................50
(853) 1,008	4,885, (91,802)................99,223	Roane, Navarro 120
*RED OAK, Ellis, 470,	*RICHLAND, Navarro, 6, (291).....264	*ROANOKE, Denton, 336,
(4,301) 10,769	Richland, Rains 100	(2,810) 5,962
Red Ranger, Bell 30	*RICHLAND HILLS, Tarrant, 435,	*Roans Prairie, Grimes, 4..............64
*Red Rock, Bastrop, 17.................40	(8,132) 7,801	*ROARING SPRINGS, Motley,
Red Springs, Baylor.......................42	*RICHLAND SPRINGS, San Saba,	13, (265) 234
Red Springs, Smith.......................350	8, (350) 338	Robbins, Leon 20
Redtown, Anderson 30	*RICHMOND, Fort Bend, 751,	*ROBERT LEE, Coke, 50,
Redtown, Angelina.......................500	(11,081) 11,679	(1,171) 1,049
*REDWATER, Bowie, 19,	RICHWOOD, Brazoria, 74,	Robertson, Crosby.........................10
(872) 1,057	(3,012) 3,510	ROBINSON, McLennan, 352,
Redwood, Guadalupe,	Riderville, Panola...........................50	(7,845) 10,509
(3,586) 4,338	Ridge, Mills 25	*ROBSTOWN, Nueces, 364,
Reeds Settlement, Red River.........50	Ridge, Robertson............................67	(12,727) 11,487
Reedville, Caldwell 432	Ridgeway, Hopkins 54	*ROBY, Fisher, 17, (673) 643
Reese, Cherokee...........................75	Ridings, Fannin.............................200	*Rochelle, McCulloch, 5 163
Refuge, Houston 20	*RIESEL, McLennan, 45,	*ROCHESTER, Haskell, 13,
*REFUGIO, Refugio, 127,	(973) 1,007	(378) 324
(2,941) 2,890	Rincon, Starr....................................5	Rock Bluff, Burnet...........................90
Regency, Mills 25	*Ringgold, Montague....................100	Rock Creek, Somervell....................70
Rehburg, Washington.....................20	RIO BRAVO, Webb, 61,	*ROCKDALE, Milam, 251,
Reid Hope King, Cameron,	(5,553) 4,794	(5,439) 5,595
(802) 786	*Rio Frio, Real, 5 50	Rockett, Ellis.................................300

The school in Sabine Pass, Jefferson County. Photo by Robert Plocheck.

Town, County ....Pop. 2010	Town, County ....Pop. 2010	Town, County ....Pop. 2010
Rockford, Lamar 30	*ROWLETT, Dallas-Rockwall,	San Carlos I, Webb, (nc) 316
Rockhouse, Austin 100	1,715, (44,503) 56,199	San Carlos II, Webb, (nc) 261
*Rock Island, Colorado, 1 160	*ROXTON, Lamar, 21, (694) 650	Sanco, Coke 15
Rockland, Tyler 98	Royalty, Ward 27	SANCTUARY, Parker, 29, (256) ... 329
Rockne, Bastrop 190	*ROYSE CITY, Rockwall-Collin,	Sand Branch, Dallas 400
*ROCKPORT, Aransas, 662,	378, (2,957) 9,349	*Sanderson, Terrell, 19, (861) 837
(7,385) 8,766	Rucker, Comanche 28	Sand Flat, Johnson 133
*ROCKSPRINGS, Edwards,	Rugby, Red River 24	Sand Flat, Leon 32
58, (1,285) 1,182	Ruidosa, Presidio 18	Sand Flat, Rains 100
*ROCKWALL, Rockwall, 1,791,	*RULE, Haskell, 14, (698) 636	Sand Flat, Smith 100
(17,976) 37,490	Rumley, Lampasas 8	Sand Flat, Van Zandt 25
*Rockwood, Coleman, 2 53	RUNAWAY BAY, Wise, 35,	Sandhill, Floyd 33
Rocky Branch, Morris 135	(1,104) 1,286	Sand Hill, Upshur 75
Rocky Creek, Blanco 20	*RUNGE, Karnes, 25, (1,080) ... 1,031	*Sandia, Jim Wells, 38, (431) 379
ROCKY MOUND, Camp, 0, (93) 75	Rural Shade, Navarro 30	*SAN DIEGO, Duval-Jim Wells,
Rocky Point, Burnet 152	*RUSK, Cherokee, 186,	103, (4,753) 4,488
Roddy, Van Zandt 29	(5,085) 5,551	Sandlin, Stonewall 3
Rodney, Navarro 15	Russell, Leon 27	Sandoval, Williamson 60
Roeder, Titus 110	Rutersville, Fayette 137	Sand Springs, Howard, (nc) 835
Roganville, Jasper 70	Ruth Springs, Henderson 120	Sandusky, Grayson 15
*ROGERS, Bell, 40, (1,117) ... 1,218	*Rye, Liberty, 4 150	Sandy, Blanco 150
Rogers, Taylor 151	**S**	Sandy, Limestone 5
Rolling Hills, Potter 1,000	Sabanno, Eastland 12	Sandy Harbor, Llano 85
Rolling Meadows, Gregg 362	*SABINAL, Uvalde, 68,	Sandy Hill, Washington 50
ROLLINGWOOD, Travis, 126,	(1,586) 1,695	Sandy Hollow-Escondidas, Nueces,
(1,403) 1,412	*Sabine Pass, Jefferson, 21,	(433) 296
Roma Creek, Starr, (610) 350	...................[part of Port Arthur]	SANDY POINT, Brazoria, 0,
*ROMA-Los Saenz, Starr, 218,	*SACHSE, Dallas-Collin, 547,	(nc) 250
(9,617) 9,765	(9,751) 20,229	*San Elizario, El Paso, 41,
ROMAN FOREST, Montgomery,	Sacul, Nacogdoches, 2 150	(11,046) 13,603
(1,279) 1,538	*SADLER, Grayson, 11, (404) 343	*SAN FELIPE, Austin, 26, (868) ... 747
*Romayor, Liberty, 4 135	Sagerton, Haskell 171	*SANFORD, Hutchinson, 11,
*Roosevelt, Kimble, 2 14	*SAGINAW, Tarrant, 497,	(203) 164
Roosevelt, Lubbock 362	(12,374) 19,806	San Gabriel, Milam 70
*ROPESVILLE, Hockley, 13,	St. Francis, Potter 39	*SANGER, Denton, 238,
(517) 434	*ST. HEDWIG, Bexar, 93,	(4,534) 6,916
Rosalie, Red River 100	(1,875) 2,094	*San Isidro, Starr, 7, (270) 240
*Rosanky, Bastrop, 13 210	*SAINT JO, Montague, 48,	San Jose, Duval 15
*ROSCOE, Nolan, 35, (1,378)... 1,322	(977) 1,043	*SAN JUAN, Hidalgo, 618,
*ROSEBUD, Falls, 65,	St. John Colony, Caldwell 150	(26,229) 33,856
(1,493) 1,412	St. Lawrence, Glasscock 90	SAN LEANNA, Travis, 0, (384) 497
ROSE CITY, Orange, 34, (519) 502	St. Mary's Colony, Bastrop 50	San Leon, Galveston, (4,365)..... 4,970
Rose Hill, Harris 3,500	ST. PAUL, Collin, 30, (630) 1,066	*San Manuel-Linn, Hidalgo,
Rose Hill, San Jacinto 30	St. Paul, San Patricio, (542) 584	11, (958) 801
ROSE HILL ACRES, Hardin, 0,	*SALADO, Bell, 334,	*SAN MARCOS, Hays-Caldwell,
(480) 441	(3,475) 2,126	1,781, (34,733) 44,894
*ROSENBERG, Fort Bend, 1,022,	Salem, Cherokee 20	SAN PATRICIO, San Patricio, 0,
(24,043) 30,618	Salem, Grimes 54	(318) 395
Rosevine, Sabine 50	Salem, Newton 218	San Pedro, Cameron, (668) 530
Rosewood, Upshur 100	Salesville, Palo Pinto 88	*SAN PERLITA, Willacy, 3,
*Rosharon, Brazoria, 101,	Saline, Menard 70	(680) 573
(nc) 1,152	*Salineño, Starr, 1, (304) 201	San Roman, Starr 5
Rosita, Duval 25	Salmon, Anderson 20	*SAN SABA, San Saba, 157,
Rosita, Maverick, (2,574)........... 2,704	Salt Flat, Hudspeth, 1 8	(2,637) 3,099
*ROSS, McLennan, 9, (228) 283	Salt Gap, McCulloch 25	SANSOM PARK, Tarrant, 99,
*ROSSER, Kaufman, 9, (379) 332	*Saltillo, Hopkins, 6 200	(4,181) 4,686
*Rosston, Cooke, 1 75	Samaria, Navarro 90	*SANTA ANNA, Coleman, 52,
Rossville, Atascosa 200	*Samnorwood, Collingsworth,	(1,081) 1,099
*ROTAN, Fisher, 54, (1,611)... 1,508	(39) 51	Santa Anna, Starr 20
Rough Creek, San Saba 15	Sample, Gonzales 16	Santa Catarina, Starr 15
Round House, Navarro 40	Sam Rayburn, Jasper 600	SANTA CLARA, Guadalupe, 23,
*ROUND MOUNTAIN, Blanco, 9,	*SAN ANGELO, Tom Green,	(889) 725
(111) 181	3,585, (88,439) 93,200	Santa Cruz, Starr, (630)................. 54
Round Mountain, Travis.................. 59	*SAN ANTONIO, Bexar, 42,351,	*Santa Elena, Starr, 1 64
Round Prairie, Navarro 40	(1,144,646) 1,327,407	*SANTA FE, Galveston, 420,
*ROUND ROCK, Williamson-Travis,	San Antonio Prairie, Burleson........ 20	(9,548) 12,222
3,522, (61,136) 99,887	*SAN AUGUSTINE, San Augustine,	*Santa Maria, Cameron, 3,
Round Timber, Baylor 2	118, (2,475) 2,108	(846) 733
*ROUND TOP, Fayette, 68, (77)..... 90	*SAN BENITO, Cameron, 604,	Santa Monica, Willacy,
Roundup, Hockley 20	(23,444) 24,250	(78) 83
Rowden, Callahan 15	San Carlos, Hidalgo, (2,650) 3,130	*SANTA ROSA, Cameron, 29,
*Rowena, Runnels, 8.................... 349	San Carlos, Starr 10	(2,833) 2,873

Town, County .... Pop. 2010	Town, County .... Pop. 2010	Town, County .... Pop. 2010
*Santo, Palo Pinto, 23 445	94, (1,145) 1,455	Silver City, Red River 25
*San Ygnacio, Zapata, 4, (853) 667	Seven Sisters, Duval 25	Silver Creek Village, Burnet 300
*Saragosa, Reeves, 2 185	Sexton, Sabine 29	Silver Lake, Van Zandt 42
*Saratoga, Hardin, 11 1,000	*SEYMOUR, Baylor, 126,	*SILVERTON, Briscoe, 42,
Sardis, Ellis 60	(2,908) 2,740	(771) 731
Sargent, Matagorda 900	Shadybrook, Cherokee, (nc) 1,967	Silver Valley, Coleman 20
*Sarita, Kenedy, 2, (nc) 238	Shady Grove , Burnet 114	Simmons, Live Oak 65
Saron, Trinity 5	Shady Grove, Cherokee 30	*Simms, Bowie, 9 240
Saspamco, Wilson 300	Shady Grove, Houston 83	Simms, Deaf Smith 10
*Satin, Falls, 1 86	Shady Grove, Panola 45	*SIMONTON, Fort Bend, 39,
Sattler, Comal 1,000	Shady Grove, Smith 250	(718) 814
Saturn, Gonzales 15	Shady Grove, Upshur 40	Simpsonville, Matagorda 6
Savannah, Denton, (nc) 3,318	Shady Hollow, Travis, (5,140) 5,004	Simpsonville, Upshur 100
*SAVOY, Fannin, 26, (850) 831	Shady Oaks, Henderson 300	Sinclair City, Smith 50
Scenic Oaks, Bexar, (3,279) 4,957	SHADY SHORES, Denton,	Singleton, Grimes 47
Schattel, Frio 30	72, (1,461) 2,612	*SINTON, San Patricio, 202,
*SCHERTZ, Guadalupe-Comal-	Shafter, Presidio, 57	(5,676) 5,665
Bexar, 982, (18,694) 31,465	*SHALLOWATER, Lubbock, 95,	Sipe Springs, Comanche 70
Schicke Point, Calhoun 70	(2,086) 2,484	Sisterdale, Kendall 110
Schroeder, Goliad 347	*SHAMROCK, Wheeler, 106,	Sivells Bend, Cooke 36
*SCHULENBURG, Fayette, 225,	(2,029) 1,910	Six Mile, Calhoun 300
(2,699) 2,852	Shangri La, Burnet 108	Skeeterville, San Saba 10
Schumansville, Guadalupe 678	Shankleville, Newton 35	*SKELLYTOWN, Carson, 14,
Schwab City, Polk 120	Shannon, Clay 20	(610) 473
*Schwertner, Williamson, 3 175	Sharp, Milam 52	*Skidmore, Bee, 11, (1,013) 925
Scissors, Hidalgo, (2,805) 3,186	SHAVANO PARK, Bexar, 102,	Slate Shoals, Lamar 10
*SCOTLAND, Archer, 9, (438) 501	(1,754) 3,035	*SLATON, Lubbock, 171,
*SCOTTSVILLE, Harrison, 11,	Shawnee Prairie, Angelina 20	(6,109) 6,121
(263) 376	Shaws Bend, Colorado 100	Slayden, Gonzales 10
Scranton, Eastland 40	*Sheffield, Pecos, 10 322	Slide, Lubbock 245
Scrappin Valley, Newton 25	Shelby, Austin 300	*Slidell, Wise, 4 175
*Scroggins, Franklin, 18 150	*Shelbyville, Shelby, 23 600	Sloan, San Saba 30
*SCURRY, Kaufman, 54, (nc) 681	Sheldon, Harris, (1,831) 1,990	Slocum, Anderson 250
*SEABROOK, Harris, 477,	SHENANDOAH, Montgomery,	Smetana, Brazos, 80
(9,443) 11,952	244, (1,503) 2,134	*SMILEY, Gonzales, 12, (453) 549
*SEADRIFT, Calhoun, 46,	Shep, Taylor 25	Smithland, Marion-Cass 179
(1,352) 1,364	*SHEPHERD, San Jacinto, 82,	Smith Point, Chambers 180
*SEAGOVILLE, Dallas, 387,	(2,029) 2,319	Smithson Valley, Comal 400
(10,823) 14,835	*Sheridan, Colorado, 15 225	*SMITHVILLE, Bastrop, 269,
*SEAGRAVES, Gaines, 59,	*SHERMAN, Grayson, 1,646,	(3,901) 3,817
(2,334) 2,417	(35,082) 38,521	Smithwick, Burnet 102
Seale, Robertson 60	Sherry, Red River 15	*SMYER, Hockley, 5, (480) 474
*SEALY, Austin, 361, (5,248) 6,019	Sherwood, Irion 170	Smyrna, Cass 215
Seaton, Bell 60	Sherwood Shores, Bell 774	Smyrna, Rains 25
Seawillow, Caldwell 100	Sherwood Shores, Burnet 920	*SNOOK, Burleson, 24, (568) 511
*Sebastian, Willacy, 15,	Sherwood Shores, Grayson 1,590	Snow Hill, Collin 23
(1,864) 1,917	Shields, Coleman 8	Snow Hill, Upshur 75
Sebastopol, Trinity 120	Shiloh, Leon 30	*SNYDER, Scurry, 469,
Seco Mines, Maverick, (nc) 560	Shiloh, Limestone 250	(10,783) 11,202
Security, Montgomery 200	*SHINER, Lavaca, 145,	*SOCORRO, El Paso, 610,
Sedalia, Collin 24	(2,070) 2,069	(27,152) 32,013
Segno, Polk 80	Shirley, Hopkins 20	Soldier Mound, Dickens 10
Segovia, Kimble 12	*Shiro, Grimes, 3 210	Solis, Cameron, (545) 512
*SEGUIN, Guadalupe, 1,205,	Shive, Hamilton 60	*SOMERSET, Bexar, 65,
(22,011) 25,175	SHOREACRES, Harris, 27,	(1,550) 1,631
Sejita, Duval 24	(1,488) 1,493	*SOMERVILLE, Burleson, 85,
Selden, Erath 55	Short, Shelby 15	(1,704) 1,376
Selfs, Fannin 30	Shovel Mountain, Burnet 148	Sommer's Mill, Bell 27
SELMA, Bexar-Guadalupe-Comal,	*Sidney, Comanche, 4 148	*SONORA, Sutton, 174,
292, (788) 5,540	Sienna Plantation, Fort Bend,	(2,924) 3,027
*Selman City [Turnertown-], Rusk,	(1,896) 13,721	*SOUR LAKE, Hardin, 101,
.... 8, 271	*Sierra Blanca, Hudspeth, 12,	(1,667) 1,813
*SEMINOLE, Gaines, 281,	(533) 553	South Alamo, Hidalgo, (3,101) ... 3,361
(5,910) 6,430	Siesta Acres, Maverick, (nc) 1,885	*South Bend, Young, 2 140
Sempronius, Austin 25	Siesta Shores, Zapata, (890) 1,382	South Bosque, McLennan 1,523
Senate, Jack 20	Silas, Shelby 75	South Brice, Hall 10
Serbin, Lee 109	Siloam, Bowie 50	South Fork Estates, Jim Hogg,
Serenada, Williamson, (1,847) .. 1,641	*SILSBEE, Hardin, 302,	(47) 70
Seth Ward, Hale, (1,926) 2,025	(6,393) 6,611	*SOUTH HOUSTON, Harris, 668,
SEVEN OAKS, Polk, 2, (131) 111	*Silver, Coke, 2 34	(15,833) 16,983
Seven Pines, Gregg-Upshur 50	Silver City, Milam 25	*SOUTHLAKE, Tarrant-Denton,
*SEVEN POINTS, Henderson,	Silver City, Navarro 100	1,611, (21,519) 26,575

CITIES & TOWNS

CITIES & TOWNS

Town, County .... Pop. 2010	Town, County .... Pop. 2010	Town, County .... Pop. 2010
Southland, Garza.......................... 157	Starrville, Smith 75	(339)... 497
South La Paloma , Jim Wells, (nc) 345	Startzville, Comal...................... 5,000	Sunset Acres, Webb, (nc)............... 23
*SOUTHMAYD, Grayson, 27, (992) 992	Steele Hill, Dickens.......................... 4	Sunset Oaks, Burnet 198
SOUTH MOUNTAIN, Coryell, 0, (412) 384	Stephens Creek, San Jacinto 385	SUNSET VALLEY, Travis, 136, (365) 749
*SOUTH PADRE ISLAND, Cameron, 347, (2,422) 2,816	*STEPHENVILLE, Erath, 807, (14,921) 17,123	SUN VALLEY, Lamar, 4, (51).......... 69
*South Plains, Floyd 67	Sterley, Floyd 31	SURFSIDE BEACH, Brazoria, 24, (763) 482
South Point, Cameron, (1,118).. 1,376	*STERLING CITY, Sterling, 41, (1,081) 888	*Sutherland Springs, Wilson, 4..... 420
South Purmela, Coryell.................. 10	Stewards Mill, Freestone 22	Swamp City, Gregg......................... 8
South Shore, Bell.......................... 80	Stewart, Rusk 15	Swan, Smith 150
SOUTHSIDE PLACE, Harris, 71, (1,547)................................. 1,715	Stiles, Reagan 4	*SWEENY, Brazoria, 105, (3,624)................................. 3,684
South Sulphur, Hunt 60	Stillwell Store, Brewster 2	Sweet Home, Guadalupe 294
South Toledo Bend, Newton, (576) 524	*STINNETT, Hutchinson, 50, (1,936)................................. 1,881	*Sweet Home, Lavaca, 7 360
Southton, Bexar.......................... 113	Stith, Jones................................... 50	Sweet Home, Lee 30
*Spade, Lamb, 4, (100) 73	*STOCKDALE, Wilson, 72, (1,398)................................. 1,442	Sweet Union, Cherokee................. 40
Spanish Fort, Montague 50	Stockman, Shelby........................ 55	*SWEETWATER, Nolan, 423, (11,415)........................... 10,906
Sparenberg, Dawson..................... 40	Stoneburg, Montague.................... 51	Swenson, Stonewall 80
Sparks, Bell 40	Stoneham, Grimes........................ 15	Swift, Nacogdoches..................... 210
Sparks, El Paso, (2,974)............ 4,529	*Stonewall, Gillespie, 28, (469) 505	Swiss Alp, Fayette 17
Speaks, Lavaca............................ 60	Stony, Denton 25	Sylvan, Lamar............................... 68
*SPEARMAN, Hansford, 115, (3,021)................................. 3,368	Stout, Wood................................. 302	*Sylvester, Fisher, 2....................... 79
Speegleville, McLennan 1,655	*Stowell, Chambers, 9, (1,572)................................. 1,756	**T**
*Spicewood, Burnet, 187.......... 2,000	Stranger, Falls 27	Tabor, Brazos............................. 150
Spider Mountain, Burnet................ 92	*STRATFORD, Sherman, 79, (1,991)................................. 2,017	Tadmor, Houston 67
*SPLENDORA, Montgomery, 145, (1,275) 1,615	Stratton, DeWitt 25	*TAFT, San Patricio, 89, (3,396)................................. 3,048
SPOFFORD, Kinney, 0, (75) 95	*STRAWN, Palo Pinto, 31, (739)..................................... 653	Taft Southwest, San Patricio, (1,721)................................. 1,460
Spraberry, Midland 46	Streeter, Mason 85	*TAHOKA, Lynn, 75, (2,910)...... 2,673
*Spring, Harris, 444, (36,385).. 54,298	*STREETMAN, Freestone, 22, (203)..................................... 247	*TALCO, Titus, 18, (570)............. 516
*Spring Branch, Comal, 213...... 2,000	String Prairie, Bastrop 40	*Talpa, Coleman, 2 127
Spring Creek, Hutchinson............ 139	Stringtown, Newton 20	TALTY, Kaufman, 28, (1,028)..... 1,535
Spring Creek, San Saba................ 20	Structure, Williamson.................... 50	Tamina, Montgomery 900
Springdale, Cass 55	Stubblefield, Houston 15	Tanglewood, Lee 60
Springfield, Anderson 30	Stubbs, Kaufman.......................... 50	Tanquecitos South Acres, Webb, (nc) 233
Spring Gardens, Nueces, (693).... 563	*Study Butte, Brewster, 35, (nc) 233	Tanquecitos South Acres II, Webb, (nc) 50
Spring Hill, Bowie 209	Sturgeon, Cooke........................... 10	Tarkington Prairie, Liberty............. 300
Spring Hill, Navarro 60	Styx, Kaufman.............................. 50	*Tarpley, Bandera, 3 30
Spring Hill, San Jacinto 38	*Sublime, Lavaca.......................... 75	*Tarzan, Martin, 3 30
*SPRINGLAKE, Lamb, (135)........ 108	*SUDAN, Lamb, 23, (1,039) 958	Tascosa Hills, Potter 90
*SPRINGTOWN, Parker, 269, (2,062)................................. 2,658	Sugar Hill, Titus 150	*TATUM, Rusk-Panola, 73, (1,175)................................. 1,385
SPRING VALLEY, Harris, 122, (3,611) 3,715	*SUGAR LAND, Fort Bend, 3,407, (63,328)........... 78,817	*TAYLOR, Williamson, 507, (13,575)........................... 15,191
Spring Valley, McLennan 400	Sugar Valley, Matagorda 47	TAYLOR LAKE VILLAGE, Harris, 78, (3,694)...................... 3,544
*SPUR, Dickens, 54, (1,088)..... 1,318	*SULLIVAN CITY, Hidalgo, 75, (3,998)............................. 4,002	TAYLOR LANDING, Jefferson, 0, (nc) 228
*Spurger, Tyler, 11 590	*Sulphur Bluff, Hopkins, 4........... 280	Taylorsville, Caldwell 20
Stacy, McCulloch 20	*SULPHUR SPRINGS, Hopkins, 790, (14,551)................... 15,449	Taylor Town, Lamar 40
Staff, Eastland 65	Summerfield, Castro 48	Tazewell, Hopkins.......................... 20
*STAFFORD, Fort Bend-Harris, 1,479, (15,681)................ 17,693	Summerville, Gonzales.................. 45	*TEAGUE, Freestone, 112, (4,557)................................. 3,560
Stag Creek, Comanche 45	*Sumner, Lamar, 30....................... 95	Teaselville, Smith......................... 150
STAGECOACH, Montgomery, 26, (455)..................................... 538	*SUNDOWN, Hockley, 56, (1,505)................................. 1,397	*TEHUACANA, Limestone, 2, (307)..................................... 283
Stairtown, Caldwell........................ 35	Sunnyside, Castro......................... 64	Telegraph, Kimble 3
Staley, San Jacinto 55	Sunny Side, Waller 250	*Telephone, Fannin, 11 210
*STAMFORD, Jones-Haskell, 129, (3,636)................................. 3,124	Sunnyside, Wilson 100	*Telferner, Victoria, 8 700
Stampede, Bell 6	SUNNYVALE, Dallas, 227, (2,693)................................. 5,130	Telico, Ellis 115
Stamps, Upshur............................ 45	*SUNRAY, Moore, 49, (1,950)................................. 1,926	*Tell, Childress, 2........................... 15
*STANTON, Martin, 101, (2,556)................................. 2,492	Sunrise, Falls 845	*TEMPLE, Bell, 1,976, (54,514)........................... 66,102
*Staples, Guadalupe, 6, (nc) 267	*SUNRISE BEACH, Llano, 29, (704)..................................... 713	*TENAHA, Shelby, 32, (1,046) .. 1,150
*Star, Mills, 1............................... 97	*SUNSET, Montague, 20,	Tenmile, Dawson 30
STAR HARBOR, Henderson, 6, (416)..................................... 444		*Tennessee Colony, Anderson, 12 300
Star Route, Cochran...................... 15		

Town, County .... Pop. 2010	Town, County .... Pop. 2010	Town, County .... Pop. 2010
*Tennyson, Coke, 1 46	TOCO, Lamar, 2, (89).................... 75	*Tynan, Bee, 4, (301).................... 278
Terlingua, Brewster, (nc)................ 58	Todd City, Anderson..................... 10	Type, Williamson 40
*TERRELL, Kaufman, 790,	TODD MISSION, Grimes, 86,	**U**
(13,606) 15,816	(146) 107	UHLAND, Hays-Caldwell, 16,
TERRELL HILLS, Bexar, 123,	Tokio, McLennan 250	(386) 1,014
(5,019) 4,878	*Tokio, Terry 6	*Umbarger, Randall, 6 327
Terry Chapel, Falls........................ 30	*TOLAR, Hood, 45, (504) 681	UNCERTAIN, Harrison, 9,
Terryville, DeWitt.......................... 40	Tolbert, Wilbarger 15	(150) 94
*TEXARKANA, Bowie-(Miller, Ark.),	Tolette, Lamar.............................. 40	Union, Scurry 20
2,331, (61,230)............... 66,035	Tolosa, Kaufman 65	Union, Terry 8
*TEXAS CITY, Galveston, 989,	*TOMBALL, Harris, 1,290,	Union, Wilson 52
(41,512) 45,099	(9,089) 10,753	Union Grove, Bell 12
TEXHOMA, Sherman-(Texas Co.,	*TOM BEAN, Grayson, 24,	UNION GROVE, Upshur, 3,
Okla.), 22, (1,306) 1,295	(941) 1,045	(346) 357
*TEXLINE, Dallam, 25, (511)........ 507	Tomlinson Hill, Falls...................... 64	Union High, Navarro 30
Texroy, Hutchinson 30	TOOL, Henderson, 63,	Union Hill, Denton......................... 25
Thalia, Foard 50	(2,275) 2,240	UNION VALLEY, Hunt, (nc) 307
*THE COLONY, Denton, 917,	Topsey, Coryell 35	Unity, Lamar 60
(26,531) 36,328	*Tornillo, El Paso, 20,	*UNIVERSAL CITY, Bexar, 631,
Thedford, Smith 65	(1,609) 1,568	(14,849) 18,530
The Grove, Coryell 100	Tours, McLennan 130	UNIVERSITY PARK, Dallas, 878,
THE HILLS, Travis, 0,	*Tow, Llano, 7 305	(23,324) 23,068
(1,492) 2,472	Town Bluff, Tyler 429	Upper Meyersville, DeWitt............. 33
Thelma, Bexar 150	*TOYAH, Reeves, 5, (100) 90	Upshaw, Nacogdoches................. 400
Thelma, Limestone 20	*Toyahvale, Reeves, 1................. 60	Upton, Bastrop............................. 25
Theon, Williamson 30	Tradewinds, San Patricio,	Urbana, San Jacinto 25
Thermo, Hopkins 56	(163) 180	Utley, Bastrop 30
*The Woodlands, Montgomery,	Travis, Falls 48	*Utopia, Uvalde, 32, (241) 227
538, (55,649) 93,847	Travis Ranch, Kaufman,	*UVALDE, Uvalde, 576,
*Thicket, Hardin, 7....................... 306	(nc) 2,556	(14,929) 15,751
*Thomaston, DeWitt, 2 45	Trawick, Nacogdoches 375	Uvalde Estates, Uvalde,
*THOMPSONS, Fort Bend, 7,	Treasure Island, Brazoria 152	(1,972) 2,171
(236)..................................... 246	Treasure Island, Guadalupe 172	**V**
Thompsonville, Gonzales 30	*TRENT, Taylor, 8, (318).............. 337	Valdasta, Collin............................ 82
Thompsonville, Jim Hogg, (nc)....... 46	*TRENTON, Fannin, 47,	*VALENTINE, Jeff Davis, 1,
Thornberry, Clay 75	(662) 635	(187) 134
*THORNDALE, Milam, 69,	Trickham, Coleman 29	*Valera, Coleman, 3...................... 80
(1,278) 1,336	Trimmer, Bell 390	Valle de Oro, Potter 250
*THORNTON, Limestone, 21,	*TRINIDAD, Henderson, 29,	Valle Vista, Starr, (nc) 469
(525)..................................... 526	(1,091) 886	Valley Creek, Fannin 110
THORNTONVILLE, Ward, 8,	*TRINITY, Trinity, 162, (2,721)... 2,697	*VALLEY MILLS, Bosque-McLennan,
(442)..................................... 476	TROPHY CLUB, Denton, 236,	79, (1,123)...................... 1,203
Thorp Spring, Hood 222	(6,350) 8,024	*Valley Spring, Llano 50
*THRALL, Williamson, 28,	*TROUP, Smith-Cherokee, 113,	*VALLEY VIEW, Cooke, 55,
(710)..................................... 839	(1,949) 1,869	(737) 757
Three League, Martin 20	Trout Creek, Newton 70	Valley View, Runnels 10
Three Oaks, Wilson 150	*TROY, Bell, 77, (1,378) 1,645	Valley View, Upshur...................... 75
*THREE RIVERS, Live Oak, 115,	Truby, Jones 26	Valley View, Wichita.................... 210
(1,878) 1,848	Trumbull, Ellis 100	Valley Wells, Dimmit 21
Three States, Cass....................... 45	Truscott, Knox 50	Val Verde, Milam 25
*THROCKMORTON, Throckmorton,	Tucker, Anderson......................... 304	Val Verde Park, Val Verde,
46, (905) 828	*Tuleta, Bee, 7, (292) 288	(1,945) 2,384
Thunderbird Bay, Brown, (nc)....... 663	*TULIA, Swisher, 153,	*VAN, Van Zandt, 111,
Thurber, Erath.............................. 48	(5,117) 4,967	(2,362) 2,632
Tidwell, Hunt................................ 50	Tulip, Fannin 10	*VAN ALSTYNE, Grayson, 158,
Tierra Bonita, Cameron, (160)...... 141	Tulsita, Bee, (20) 14	(2,502) 3,046
Tierra Grande, Nueces, (362)........ 356	Tundra, Van Zandt 34	Vance, Real 20
Tierra Verde, Nueces, (nc) 277	Tunis, Burleson 150	*Vancourt, Tom Green, 1 131
Tigertown, Lamar......................... 400	*TURKEY, Hall, 20, (494) 421	Vandalia, Red River...................... 35
TIKI ISLAND, Galveston, 20,	Turlington, Freestone 27	*Vanderbilt, Jackson, 7,
(1,016) 968	Turnersville, Coryell 125	(411) 395
*Tilden, McMullen, 15, (nc)........... 261	Turnersville, Travis 90	*Vanderpool, Bandera, 2 20
Tilmon, Caldwell 117	*Turnertown-Selman City, Rusk,	Vandyke, Comanche 20
TIMBERCREEK CANYON, Randall,	8 271	*VAN HORN, Culberson, 84,
0, (406) 418	Turtle Bayou, Chambers................ 42	(2,435) 2,063
Timberwood, Bexar, (5,889) 13,447	*TUSCOLA, Taylor, 56, (714) 742	*Van Vleck, Matagorda, 27,
*TIMPSON, Shelby, 57,	Tuxedo, Jones 42	(1,411) 1,844
(1,094) 1,155	Twichell, Ochiltree 22	Vasco, Delta 20
Tin Top, Parker 500	Twitty, Wheeler 12	Vashti, Clay 70
*TIOGA, Grayson, 33, (754)......... 803	*TYE, Taylor, 54, (1,158) 1,242	Vattmann, Kleberg 25
TIRA, Hopkins, 0, (248)................ 297	*TYLER, Smith, 4,649,	Vaughan, Hill 75
*Tivoli, Refugio, 7, (nc) 479	(83,650) 96,900	Veach, San Augustine 12

CITIES & TOWNS

Town, County .... Pop. 2010	Town, County .... Pop. 2010	Town, County .... Pop. 2010
Vealmoor, Howard 5	Wagner, Hunt.................................... 75	Wayside, Roberts 105
*VEGA, Oldham, 37, (936) 884	*Waka, Ochiltree, 2......................... 65	Wealthy, Leon.................................. 12
*VENUS, Johnson, 61,	Wakefield, Polk................................ 25	*WEATHERFORD, Parker, 1,518,
(1,892)................................. 2,960	*WAKE VILLAGE, Bowie, 102,	(19,000) 25,250
Vera, Knox 30	(5,129) 5,492	Weatherly, Hall 8
Verdi, Atascosa.............................. 110	*Walburg, Williamson, 4 277	Weaver, Hopkins 35
Verhalen, Reeves 12	Walcott, Deaf Smith........................... 5	WEBBERVILLE, Travis, 12,
*Veribest, Tom Green, 3 115	Waldeck, Fayette 34	(nc) 392
*VERNON, Wilbarger, 384,	Waldrip, McCulloch 15	Webbville, Coleman......................... 15
(11,660) 11,002	Walhalla, Fayette 38	*WEBSTER, Harris, 801,
Verona, Collin 34	*Wall, Tom Green, 10.................... 329	(9,083) 10,400
Vessey, Red River 15	*WALLER, Waller-Harris, 232,	Weches, Houston 46
Viboras, Starr................................... 22	(2,092) 2,326	Weedhaven, Jackson 35
Vick, Concho 20	*WALLIS, Austin, 61,	Weeping Mary, Cherokee 85
Victoria, Limestone 25	(1,172) 1,252	*Weesatche, Goliad, 3.................. 411
*VICTORIA, Victoria, 2,897,	*Wallisville, Chambers, 11 452	*WEIMAR, Colorado, 180,
(60,603) 62,592	Walnut Bend, Cooke....................... 45	(1,981) 2,151
Victory City, Bowie........................ 250	Walnut Grove, Panola 125	*WEINERT, Haskell, 5, (177)........ 172
*VIDOR, Orange, 487,	*WALNUT SPRINGS, Bosque,	*WEIR, Williamson, 18, (591)........ 450
(11,440) 10,579	18, (755) 827	Weiss Bluff, Jasper......................... 60
Vienna, Lavaca 40	Walton, Van Zandt 35	*Welch, Dawson, 8, (nc) 222
View, Taylor 350	Wamba, Bowie 430	Welcome, Austin............................ 300
Vigo Park, Swisher 36	Waneta, Houston 19	Weldon, Houston 131
Villa del Sol, Cameron, (132)........ 175	Waples, Hood 155	Welfare, Kendall 10
*Village Mills, Hardin, 11 1,700	*Warda, Fayette, 7........................ 121	*Wellborn, Brazos, 7................... 400
Villa Nueva North, Cameron......... 374	Ward Creek, Bowie....................... 164	*WELLINGTON, Collingsworth,
Villa Nueva South, Cameron 402	*Waring, Kendall, 11 73	83, (2,275) 2,189
Villa Pancho, Cameron, (386) 788	*Warren, Tyler, 15, (nc)................. 757	*WELLMAN, Terry, 2, (203) 203
Villarreal, Starr, (nc)..................... 131	WARREN CITY, Gregg-Upshur, 6,	*WELLS, Cherokee, 16, (769)...... 790
Villa Verde, Hidalgo, (891)........... 874	(343) 298	Wells, Lynn 10
Vincent, Howard 10	*Warrenton, Fayette, 3 186	Wells Branch, Travis,
Vineyard, Jack 19	Warsaw, Kaufman 100	(11,271) 12,120
VINTON, El Paso, 96,	Washburn, Armstrong 120	Wesco, Gray..................................... 7
(1,892)................................. 1,971	*Washington, Washington, 17 100	*WESLACO, Hidalgo, 1,025,
Violet, Nueces 160	*WASKOM, Harrison, 78,	(26,935) 35,670
Vistula, Houston 21	(2,068) 2,160	Wesley, Washington 65
*Voca, McCulloch, 3 56	Wastella, Nolan 12	Wesley Grove, Walker.................... 25
VOLENTE, Travis, 27, (nc)........... 520	*WATAUGA, Tarrant, 626,	*WEST, McLennan, 179,
Volga, Houston 9	(21,908) 23,497	(2,692) 2,807
*VON ORMY, Bexar, 68, (nc)..... 1,085	Waterloo, Williamson..................... 70	*WESTBROOK, Mitchell, 12,
Voss, Coleman, 1 20	Waterman, Shelby 40	(203) 253
*Votaw, Hardin, 4 160	*Water Valley, Tom Green, 2......... 203	*WEST COLUMBIA, Brazoria, 169,
Vsetin, Lavaca 45	Watson, Burnet 148	(4,255) 3,905
W	Watt, Limestone............................. 25	Westcott, San Jacinto.................... 25
*WACO, McLennan, 4,450,	Waverly, San Jacinto 200	Westdale, Jim Wells, (295)........... 372
(113,726) 124,805	*WAXAHACHIE, Ellis, 1,115,	Western Lake, Parker, (nc)........ 1,525
*Wadsworth, Matagorda, 12......... 160	(21,426) 29,621	*Westhoff, DeWitt, 4 410
*WAELDER, Gonzales, 24,	Wayne, Cass 15	WESTLAKE, Tarrant-Denton, 63,
(947) 1,065	Wayside, Armstrong, 2 35	(207) 992

The main street in Van Horn, Culberson County. Photo by Robert Plocheck.

CITIES & TOWNS

Town, County .... Pop. 2010	Town, County .... Pop. 2010	Town, County .... Pop. 2010
*WEST LAKE HILLS, Travis, 429, (3,116) 3,063	Whon, Coleman 35	WOODCREEK, Hays, 37, (1,274) 1,457
West Livingston, Polk, (6,612) 8,071	*WICHITA FALLS, Wichita, 3,217, (104,197) 104,553	Wooded Hills, Johnson 580
West Mineola, Wood 20	*WICKETT, Ward, 33, (455) 498	Wood Hi, Victoria 35
*Westminster, Collin, 3, (390) 861	Wied, Lavaca 65	*Woodlake, Trinity, 1 98
West Mountain, Upshur 325	Wiedeville, Washington 35	Woodland, Red River 128
West Odessa, Ector, (17,799) 22,707	*Wiergate, Newton, 2 350	*Woodlawn, Harrison, 6 550
*WESTON, Collin, 16, (635) 563	Wigginsville, Montgomery 100	WOODLOCH, Montgomery, 0, (247) 207
WESTON LAKES, Fort Bend, 0, (nc) 2,482	Wilcox, Burleson 39	Woodrow, Fort Bend 190
WEST ORANGE, Orange, 98, (4,111) 3,443	Wilderville, Falls 45	Woodrow, Lubbock 2,034
Westover, Baylor 18	*Wildorado, Oldham, 9 210	Woods, Panola 65
WESTOVER HILLS, Tarrant, (658) 682	Wild Peach, Brazoria, (2,498).... 2,452	*WOODSBORO, Refugio, 50, (1,685) 1,512
Westphalia, Falls 186	Wildwood, Hardin, (nc) 1,235	*WOODSON, Throckmorton, 14, (296) 264
*West Point, Fayette, 6 213	Wilkins, Upshur 75	Wood Springs, Smith 200
West Sharyland, Hidalgo, (2,947) 2,309	Willamar, Willacy, (15) 15	Woodville, Cherokee 20
West Sinton, San Patricio 318	William Penn, Washington 40	*WOODVILLE, Tyler, 184, (2,415) 2,586
WEST TAWAKONI, Hunt, 56, (1,462) 1,576	*WILLIS, Montgomery, 410, (3,985) 5,662	Woodward, La Salle 10
WEST UNIVERSITY PLACE, Harris, 319, (14,211) 14,787	*Willow City, Gillespie, 3 22	WOODWAY, McLennan, 308, (8,733) 8,452
Westville, Trinity 46	Willow Grove, McLennan 100	Woosley, Rains 47
Westway, Deaf Smith 15	WILLOW PARK, Parker, 152, (2,849) 3,982	*WORTHAM, Freestone, 50, (1,082) 1,073
Westway, El Paso, (3,829) 4,188	Willow Springs, Fayette 74	Worthing, Lavaca 55
Westwood Shores, Trinity, (nc).. 1,162	Willow Springs, Rains 50	Wright City, Smith 172
WESTWORTH VILLAGE, Tarrant, 51, (2,124) 2,472	*WILLS POINT, Van Zandt, 251, (3,496) 3,524	*Wrightsboro, Gonzales 10
*WHARTON, Wharton, 372, (9,237) 8,832	*WILMER, Dallas, 49, (3,393) 3,682	Wyldwood, Bastrop, (2,310) 2,505
Wheatland, Tarrant 175	Wilmeth, Runnels 15	*WYLIE, Collin-Rockwall-Dallas, 1,052, (15,132) 41,427
*WHEELER, Wheeler, 68, (1,378) 1,592	Wilson, Falls 42	Wylie, Taylor .... [part of Abilene]
Wheeler Springs, Houston 89	*WILSON, Lynn, 18, (532) 489	**Y**
*Wheelock, Robertson, 7 225	*WIMBERLEY, Hays, 656, (3,797) 2,626	*Yancey, Medina, 7 209
White City, San Augustine 20	Winchell, Brown 20	*YANTIS, Wood, 47, (321) 388
White City, Wilbarger 40	Winchester, Fayette 232	Yard, Anderson 50
*WHITE DEER, Carson, 43, (1,060) 1,000	WINDCREST, Bexar, 248, (5,105) 5,364	Yarrellton, Milam 35
*WHITEFACE, Cochran, 17, (465) 449	Windemere, Travis, (6,868) 1,037	Yellowpine, Sabine 97
Whiteflat, Motley 4	*WINDOM, Fannin, 14, (245) 199	*YOAKUM, Lavaca-DeWitt, 248, (5,731) 5,815
White Hall, Bell 262	*WINDTHORST, Archer, 43, (440) 409	*YORKTOWN, DeWitt, 119, (2,271) 2,092
White Hall, Grimes 30	Winedale, Fayette 67	Youngsport, Bell 49
*WHITEHOUSE, Smith, 281, (5,346) 7,660	*WINFIELD, Titus, 28, (499) 524	Yowell, Delta-Hunt 30
*WHITE OAK, Gregg, 256, (5,624) 6,489	WINFREE [Old River-], Chambers, 17, (1,364) 1,245	*Ysleta del Sur Pueblo, El Paso, (nc) 350
White Oak, Titus 100	*Wingate, Runnels, 4 100	Yznaga, Cameron, (103) 91
White River Lake, Crosby 83	*WINK, Winkler, 28, (919) 940	**Z**
White Rock, Hunt 80	Winkler, Navarro-Freestone 26	Zabcikville, Bell 76
White Rock, Red River 90	*Winnie, Chambers, 137, (2,914) 3,254	*Zapata, Zapata, 164, (4,856) 5,089
White Rock, Robertson 80	*WINNSBORO, Wood-Franklin, 301, (3,584) 3,434	Zapata Ranch, Willacy, (88) 108
White Rock, San Augustine 60	*WINONA, Smith, 42, (582) 576	*ZAVALLA, Angelina, 41, (647) 713
*WHITESBORO, Grayson, 185, (3,760) 3,793	Winter Haven, Dimmit 123	*Zephyr, Brown, 11 201
*WHITE SETTLEMENT, Tarrant, 325, (14,831) 16,116	*WINTERS, Runnels, 90, (2,880) 2,562	Zimmerscheidt, Colorado 50
White Star, Motley 6	Witting, Lavaca 90	Zion Hill, Guadalupe 595
Whiteway, Hamilton 8	WIXON VALLEY, Brazos, 12, (235) 254	Zipperlandville, Falls 22
*WHITEWRIGHT, Grayson-Fannin, 79, (1,740) 1,604	Wizard Wells, Jack 69	Zorn, Guadalupe 287
*Whitharral, Hockley 158	*Woden, Nacogdoches, 3 400	Zuehl, Guadalupe, (346) 376
Whitman, Washington 25	*WOLFE CITY, Hunt, 52, (1,566) 1,412	Zunkerville, Karnes 15
*WHITNEY, Hill, 203, (1,833) 2,087	*WOLFFORTH, Lubbock, 150, (2,554) 3,670	
*Whitsett, Live Oak, 3 200	Womack, Bosque 25	
Whitson, Coryell 50	Woodbine, Cooke 250	
*Whitt, Parker 38	WOODBRANCH, Montgomery, 0, (1,305) 1,282	
	Woodbury, Hill 45	

CITIES & TOWNS

TSHA EDUCATIONAL SERVICES

The hallmark of TSHA's education program remains its student programs. These currently include the following:

Junior Historians of Texas

Since 1939, Junior Historians has fostered an interest in state and local history through activities, trips, research and more. Usually organized into clubs or chapters, these elementary and secondary students serve their schools and communities while learning history. Chapters receive a variety of materials and benefits including newsletters, notification of upcoming opportunities, and the group's journal, the *Texas Historian,* through their affiliation with TSHA and its partner organization National History Club. A collegiate version of this program exists as the Walter Prescott Webb Historical Society.

Texas History Day

Texas History Day, a yearlong program for students in Grades 6-12, is affiliated with National History Day. Students in the junior division (Grades 6-8) and the senior division (Grades 9-12) prepare projects based on an annual theme while developing critical thinking skills. Though primarily a teaching methodology, the contest aspect of the program coordinated by the TSHA helps provide motivation for students who have consistently been recognized as some the best in the nation.

Texas Quiz Show

The Texas Quiz Show is an annual academic competition for middle school students about all things Texas, conducted in a game show format. The program is designed to provide a fun and easy way to recognize Texas History Month, as required by public law in HB 294, while encouraging students to do additional research and reading in Texas history. Most questions are drawn from the *Texas Almanac* and *Handbook of Texas Online.*

In addition to student oriented programs, TSHA provides services to educators and others including: workshops, travel seminars, lesson plans, a Speakers Bureau, and other resources. TSHA is proud to provide Teaching Texas, a new resource to assist educators in finding the multitude of resources available to teach social studies in Texas located at www.TeachingTexas.org.

For information about all TSHA education programs, visit
www.TSHAonline.org/education

www.tshaonline.org   940-369-5200

Elections

A voter marks a ballot. Photo by Lars Plougmann (CC).

Legislative Budget Cuts School Funds, State Jobs

By Carolyn Barta

An overwhelming Republican majority influenced by the grassroots tea party movement dominated the 82nd Legislature, resulting in a no tax-increase budget with record spending cuts and a conservative social issues agenda.

Gov. Rick Perry said Texas stood in stark contrast to other states after lawmakers approved a $172 billion two-year budget that slashed $15.2 billion or 8.1 percent from previous spending levels.

Lopsided elections in 2010 reflecting an anti-Washington sentiment and a recessionary economy with lowered anticipated sales tax revenue set the stage for a contentious 140-day regular session and an immediate 30-day special session required to finish the work.

Republicans won an impressive 99 Texas House seats in 2010, and two party-switches provided a super majority of 101 House members to the Democrats' 49 – compared to a previous 76-74 Republican majority. In the Texas Senate, Republicans maintained a 19-12 edge.

Perry – campaigning for states rights and against an over-reaching, spendthrift federal government – easily won re-election to become the nation's longest serving governor, beating GOP challenger Kay Bailey Hutchison in the primary and then defeating Democrat and former Houston mayor Bill White.

Presiding officers for both houses also were Re-publican. David Dewhurst was re-elected lieutenant governor and held the Senate gavel. Joe Straus of San Antonio won a second term as House speaker.

The governor and dozens of legislators were backed by tea party activists, who demanded a leaner government and more conservative approach to issues such as immigration and abortion. Some called this Legislature the most conservative ever, albeit it activist conservatism.

While lawmakers delivered on less spending, they were unable to pass two of Perry's priorities, a "sanctuary cities" bill that would have denied state funding to cities that prohibit its law enforcement officers from asking the immigration status of people they arrest, and an "anti-groping" bill that would have criminalized intrusive airport pat-downs by Transportation Security Administration agents.

Republican successes included new laws requiring unsuccessful plantiffs to pay for meritless lawsuits, voters to present photo identification at polling places, and women seeking abortions to have a mandatory sonogram.

Perry's austerity stance, promotion of Texas' job growth, national presence as head of the Republican Governors Association, and his evangelical/conservative appeal led to speculation of presidential aspirations.

The grueling budget battle that consumed the regular session resulted from a projected shortfall of $23

The Texas Senate chamber from the visitors gallery. Photo by Robert Plocheck.

billion to maintain current services with inflation and population growth. The Senate and Democrats in both houses wanted to tap more of the state's Rainy Day Fund, but the House and governor refused to touch more than one-third or $3.2 billion of the fund, leaving $6.5 billion for future needs.

The budget chopped $4 billion from public schools, $1 billion from higher education, including financial aid to some 41,000 students, and eliminated 5,700 state agency jobs. Accounting maneuvers and deferred payments, including $4 billion to $5 billion to pay Medicaid bills, helped to balance the books.

Democrats were powerless to do much more than raise parliamentary roadblocks to cuts to education and human services. Nothing worked until a late-night Senate filibuster before the regular session's last day halted action on the allocation of public school funds.

That required a special session, where lawmakers reduced state aid to education by 6 percent from what was needed to provide for 150,000 new students. Basic funding to districts was cut 3.3 percent across the board the first year and funds were redistributed in the biennium's second year to shrink disparities among districts. Some districts faced 8-to-9 percent cuts.

Teachers demanded more funding in several rallies at the Capitol. The Legislature's response was to give school districts more cost-trimming flexibility, allowing teacher furlough days and salary cuts in lieu of firing personnel or raising local taxes.

Other big items that passed in the special session were congressional redistricting, hurricane insurance reforms, and comprehensive health care legislation allowing Texas to join with other states in a "health care compact" to turn Medicaid and Medicare into state-run block grant programs.

It promised to save money by increasing Medicaid managed care and defunded Planned Parenthood programs – a popular conservative target -- that provided family planning for thousands of poor women.

Congressional redistricting, usually controversial, was ho-hum. A new map was needed to create four new seats, reflecting Texas' gain in population from 20.9 million to 25 million. Democrats criticized the adopted Republican plan for not creating more Hispanic districts, since Hispanics made up 65 percent of the 2010 census population increase, and also for carving up Austin and putting it in a district with San Antonio.

Immigration was a hot topic with more than 50 bills introduced, but little progress was made in the immigrant crackdown as business leaders argued that workers were needed. Opponents of the controversial sanctuary cities legislation complained the law would lead to racial profiling.

Lawmakers also debated, to considerable public attention, legislation allowing 21-year-old college students to carry concealed weapons on college campuses. It failed.

While this Legislature will be remembered for producing a balanced budget with no new taxes but near unprecedented cuts to education, it also tinkered with widespread issues. Other bills passed included regulation of payday lenders; increased speed limits to 75 mph on some major highways outside urban areas; decriminalizing catfish noodling, or bare-handed catching of catfish; the "pork chopper" bill that allowed hunters to shoot feral hogs from helicopters to control the wild hog population, and more regulation of puppy mills and cockfighting.

Lawmakers also declared Western swing the official music of Texas.

Carolyn Barta, a retired Dallas Morning News political writer, teaches journalism at Southern Methodist University.

Texas Election Turnout by Voting Age Population

Year	2008	2004	2000	1996	1992	1988	1984	1980	1976	1972
Major Candidates	Obama McCain	Bush Kerry	Bush Gore	Clinton Dole	Clinton Bush Perot	Bush Dukakis	Reagan Mondale	Reagan Carter	Carter Ford	Nixon McGovern
Percent of VAP that voted	45.6	46.1	44.3	41.0	47.6	44.3	47.6	45.6	46.1	44.9
Percent of registered voters that voted	59.5	56.6	51.8	53.2	72.9	66.2	68.3	68.4	64.8	66.6

The **voting age population (VAP)** refers to the total number of persons of voting age regardless of citizenship, military status, felony conviction or mental state. The Bureau of the Census is the source for the VAP estimates.

Since the National Voter Registration Act of 1993, non-voters cannot be removed from registration rolls of a county until two federal elections have been held. So, for instance, if a person moved in December 2004 from one county to another, that person could be counted as a non-voter in the previous county of residence through the general election of November 2008.

These are called "suspense voters" on county rolls and have affected the statistical reports of the percentage of registered voters participating in elections.

In the early 1970s, various election reforms were enacted by the Legislature, including eliminating the requirement for an annual registration and allowing for a continuing voter registration system.

The presidential elections have a larger voter turnout than off-year and state elections. — RP

Sources: Federal Election Commission and the Texas Secretary of State office.

2010 Gubernatorial Election Results by County

Following are the official results by county in the race for governor. The leading candidates were incumbant Gov. Rick Perry, Republican, and former Houston Mayor Bill White, Democrat.

The total number of voters in the Nov. 2 election, was 4,979,870, was 38 percent of the registered voters. The voting age population was estimated at 18,789,238. The statewide turnout in the previous gubernatorial election in 2006 was 33.64 percent of registered voters. *Source: Texas Secretary of State.*

County	GOVERNORS RACE (votes and percentage of total vote)			
	Perry	%	White	%
Statewide	2,737,481	54.97	2,106,395	42.29
Anderson	6,973	63.6	3,643	33.21
Andrews	2,906	71.7	987	24.4
Angelina	11,942	61.9	6,892	35.7
Aransas	4,829	70.0	1,892	27.4
Archer	2,107	73.5	672	23.5
Armstrong	499	75.5	135	20.4
Atascosa	4,450	52.8	3,714	44.1
Austin	5,901	68.0	2,525	29.1
Bailey	810	73.2	241	21.8
Bandera	4,745	70.5	1,646	24.5
Bastrop	9,426	49.7	8,587	45.3
Baylor	739	66.0	339	30.5
Bee	2,994	52.1	2,612	45.4
Bell	26,318	56.6	17,159	36.9
Bexar	146,760	48.5	148,452	48.8
Blanco	2,589	65.3	1,200	30.3
Borden	241	72.2	74	22.2
Bosque	3,691	62.6	1,956	33.2
Bowie	13,886	61.3	8,274	36.5
Brazoria	43,360	61.4	25,450	36.0
Brazos	23,809	63.2	12,733	33.8
Brewster	1,316	48.0	1,315	48.0
Briscoe	314	64.7	143	29.5
Brooks	260	21.6	936	77.7
Brown	7,115	75.5	1,951	20.7
Burleson	683	66.2	346	33.5
Burnet	8,302	68.8	3,929	27.3
Caldwell	4,035	48.6	3,913	47.2
Calhoun	2,573	56.6	1,870	41.1
Callahan	2,701	76.0	747	21.0
Cameron	16,722	40.8	23,474	57.3
Camp	1,666	53.9	1,337	43.3
Carson	1,369	71.8	446	23.4
Cass	4,404	60.7	2,667	36.8
Castro	834	59.9	515	37.0
Chambers	7,106	71.7	2,537	25.6
Cherokee	7,373	64.0	3,768	32.7
Childress	774	70.2	293	26.6
Clay	2,407	69.7	943	27.3
Cochran	387	67.9	160	28.1
Coke	793	72.9	260	23.9
Coleman	1,935	73.3	617	23.4
Collin	100,359	64.1	51,890	33.1
Collingsworth	547	65.4	259	30.9
Colorado	3,845	61.5	2,256	36.1
Comal	24,916	72.1	8,271	23.9
Comanche	2,250	61.7	1,250	34.3
Concho	566	65.0	269	30.9
Cooke	6,261	67.9	2,573	27.9

County	GOVERNORS RACE (votes and percentage of total vote)			
	Perry	%	White	%
Coryell	5,984	62.3	3,146	32.7
Cottle	291	67.1	113	26.0
Crane	599	73.9	184	22.7
Crockett	616	64.9	302	31.8
Crosby	709	60.3	428	36.4
Culberson	323	44.1	388	52.9
Dallam	683	73.4	195	21.0
Dallas	180,665	42.6	234,478	55.2
Dawson	1,824	61.7	988	33.4
Deaf Smith	1,792	71.8	633	25.6
Delta	864	55.6	640	41.2
Denton	83,726	63.8	43,073	32.8
DeWitt	3,162	69.4	1,230	27.0
Dickens	590	67.3	241	27.5
Dimmit	604	30.5	1,350	68.1
Donley	781	67.4	333	28.8
Duval	738	24.5	2,213	73.5
Eastland	3,224	73.4	999	22.7
Ector	14,466	73.9	4,481	22.9
Edwards	556	59.1	366	38.9
Ellis	20,411	65.8	9,236	29.8
El Paso	32,536	36.8	54,247	61.3
Erath	5,990	68.9	2,385	27.4
Falls	1,854	46.7	1,940	48.8
Fannin	4,453	60.8	2,599	35.5
Fayette	5,256	65.4	2,534	31.5
Fisher	686	51.5	607	45.5
Floyd	1,023	66.9	471	30.8
Foard	148	47.0	153	48.6
Fort Bend	71,658	51.5	65,432	47.0
Franklin	2,203	64.5	1,095	32.0
Freestone	3,326	66.3	1,563	31.2
Frio	940	44.9	1,110	53.0
Gaines	1,847	75.9	507	20.8
Galveston	43,051	56.7	31,186	41.1
Garza	879	70.3	311	24.9
Gillespie	7,008	74.2	2,034	21.5
Glasscock	320	81.6	45	11.5
Goliad	1,438	55.3	1,031	39.7
Gonzales	3,062	58.1	2,056	39.0
Gray	3,777	80.4	766	16.3
Grayson	18,308	68.1	7,771	28.9
Gregg	17,259	67.9	7,607	29.9
Grimes	3,663	59.6	2,276	37.0
Guadalupe	19,837	65.3	9,488	31.2
Hale	3,974	65.4	1,875	30.9
Hall	522	68.5	217	28.5
Hamilton	1,671	62.9	871	32.8
Hansford	1,126	85.0	163	12.3
Hardeman	612	66.4	290	31.5

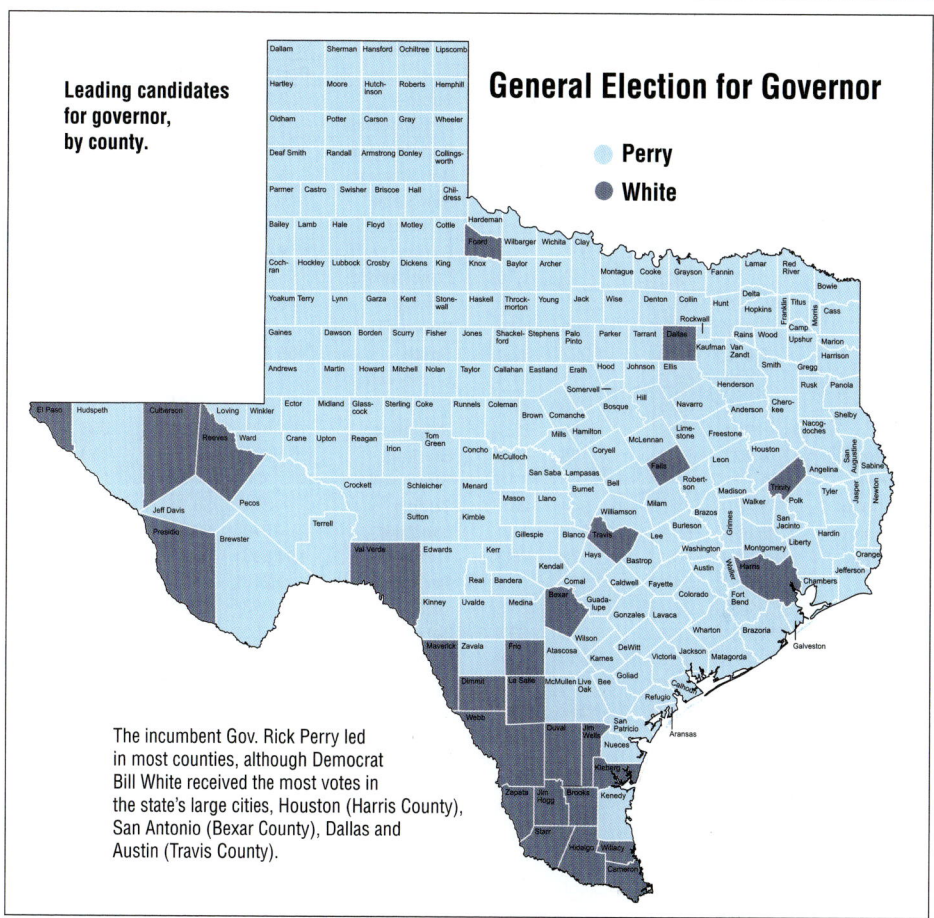

Leading candidates for governor, by county.

General Election for Governor

- Perry
- White

The incumbent Gov. Rick Perry led in most counties, although Democrat Bill White received the most votes in the state's large cities, Houston (Harris County), San Antonio (Bexar County), Dallas and Austin (Travis County).

County	GOVERNORS RACE (votes and percentage of total vote)			
	Perry	%	White	%
Hardin	10,652	73.4	3,553	24.5
Harris	379,516	48.1	395,952	50.2
Harrison	10,508	60.5	6,464	37.2
Hartley	1,041	78.1	251	18.8
Haskell	262	67.0	117	29.9
Hays	20,499	51.8	17,333	43.8
Hemphill	764	69.4	286	26.0
Henderson	12,342	65.4	5,957	31.6
Hidalgo	23,232	31.8	48,895	66.8
Hill	5,447	60.7	3,187	35.5
Hockley	3,085	72.9	963	22.7
Hood	11,490	71.6	3.954	24.6
Hopkins	5,457	62.0	3,111	35.4
Houston	3,822	62.7	2,096	34.4
Howard	4,054	67.7	1,695	28.3
Hudspeth	376	56.0	276	41.1
Hunt	11,593	65.1	5,465	30.7
Hutchinson	4,166	78.4	947	17.8
Irion	476	73.6	153	23.6
Jack	1,604	74.5	475	22.1
Jackson	2,218	60.5	1,352	36.9
Jasper	5,689	67.7	2,557	30.4

County	GOVERNORS RACE (votes and percentage of total vote)			
	Perry	%	White	%
Jeff Davis	539	54.9	384	39.1
Jefferson	27,710	50.5	26,437	48.2
Jim Hogg	288	27.0	777	72.7
Jim Wells	2,657	41.4	3,674	57.2
Johnson	20,827	67.4	8,716	28.2
Jones	2,444	63.4	1,267	32.9
Karnes	1,730	57.3	1,211	40.1
Kaufman	12,990	65.2	6,363	31.9
Kendall	9,744	75.7	2,702	21.0
Kenedy	109	54.8	88	44.2
Kent	189	63.0	101	33.7
Kerr	12,025	72.9	3,913	23.7
Kimble	1,042	78.5	231	17.4
King	93	78.8	23	19.5
Kinney	769	56.8	533	39.4
Kleberg	2,660	47.1	2,859	50.6
Knox	547	61.8	312	35.3
Lamar	7,329	61.4	4,290	36.0
Lamb	1,873	69.2	740	27.4
Lampasas	3,487	70.1	1,239	24.9
La Salle	534	41.0	744	57.2
Lavaca	4,383	68.0	1,904	29.5

County	GOVERNORS RACE (votes and percentage of total vote)			
	Perry	%	White	%
Lee	2,600	60.7	1,491	34.8
Leon	3,820	75.9	1,092	21.7
Liberty	10,309	63.9	5,467	33.9
Limestone	3,197	57.4	2,198	39.4
Lipscomb	644	74.1	195	22.4
Live Oak	2,034	73.0	656	23.5
Llano	5,330	71.8	1,835	24.7
Loving	51	75.0	12	17.6
Lubbock	35,578	66.3	15,887	29.6
Lynn	857	66.1	375	28.9
Madison	2,042	64.5	1,027	32.4
Marion	1,474	54.5	1,121	41.4
Martin	858	72.5	275	23.2
Mason	994	70.3	355	25.1
Matagorda	4,923	57.2	3,448	40.1
Maverick	1,877	26.2	5,142	71.9
McCulloch	1,479	71.0	544	26.1
McLennan	30,694	56.1	22,515	41.1
McMullen	216	70.1	78	25.3
Medina	7,077	64.1	3,578	32.4
Menard	410	70.1	154	26.3
Midland	21,864	78.5	5,085	18.3
Milam	3,225	53.8	2,539	42.4
Mills	1,110	67.3	460	27.9
Mitchell	966	61.0	582	36.7
Montague	3,806	69.9	1413	25.9
Montgomery	86,178	75.2	25,919	22.6
Moore	2,643	75.7	693	19.9
Morris	1,715	49.9	16,33	47.6
Motley	385	72.1	113	21.2
Nacgdoches	8,216	62.6	4,553	34.7
Navarro	6,033	61.7	3,450	35.3
Newton	2,033	60.7	1,247	37.3
Nolan	2,104	60.4	1,235	35.4
Nueces	32,593	52.7	27,921	45.1
Ochiltree	1,679	88.6	188	9.9
Oldham	525	75.6	140	20.2
Orange	12,750	66.7	5,928	31.0
Palo Pinto	4,139	64.5	2,041	31.8
Panola	4,348	67.2	2,004	31.0
Parker	22,167	72.9	7,000	23.0
Parmer	1,293	77.5	324	19.4
Pecos	1,794	54.4	1,405	42.6
Polk	7,989	63.6	4,203	33.5
Potter	10,631	66.4	4,716	29.4
Presidio	325	27.3	842	70.6
Rains	1,835	67.6	827	30.5
Randall	23,381	75.9	6,233	20.2
Reagan	405	76.1	112	21.1
Real	901	72.4	290	23.3
Red River	1,764	56.5	1,293	41.4
Reeves	740	38.7	1,131	59.1
Refugio	1,091	61.9	630	35.8
Roberts	282	79.9	54	15.3
Robertson	2,663	53.6	2,175	43.8
Rockwall	13,550	72.0	4,705	25.0
Runnels	2,017	76.0	569	21.4
Rusk	8,087	67.1	3,643	30.2

County	GOVERNORS RACE (votes and percentage of total vote)			
	Perry	%	White	%
Sabine	2,387	69.5	971	28.3
San Augustine	1,508	59.0	995	38.9
San Jacinto	4,284	59.5	2,704	37.5
San Patricio	5,452	71.7	1,808	23.8
San Saba	1,305	73.0	406	22.7
Schleicher	567	73.4	184	23.8
Scurry	2,424	70.0	881	25.4
Shackelford	824	78.4	192	18.3
Shelby	3,669	63.6	1,991	34.5
Sherman	504	76.1	143	21.6
Smith	35,565	68.8	14,641	28.3
Somervell	1,757	64.1	900	32.8
Starr	737	19.8	2,970	79.7
Stephens	1,823	73.9	553	22.4
Sterling	298	77.6	69	18.0
Stonewall	329	54.8	241	40.2
Sutton	371	58.0	243	38.0
Swisher	818	52.9	657	42.5
Tarrant	194,583	56.0	142,392	41.0
Taylor	19,216	71.7	6,652	24.8
Terrell	293	50.8	257	44.5
Terry	1,663	64.7	802	31.2
Throckmorton	513	73.6	164	23.5
Titus	3,594	57.0	2,538	40.2
Tom Green	16,005	70.5	6,003	26.4
Travis	87,509	36.7	142,345	59.8
Trinity	2,189	46.9	2,338	50.0
Tyler	3,434	61.7	1,964	35.3
Upshur	6,529	66.1	2,906	29.4
Upton	566	68.1	224	27.0
Uvalde	3,144	51.4	2,848	46.5
Val Verde	3,365	47.1	3,636	50.9
Van Zandt	8.797	67.9	3,686	28.5
Victoria	12,560	64.5	6,266	32.2
Walker	7,232	54.0	5,695	42.5
Waller	5,862	56.2	4,306	41.3
Ward	1,593	59.6	955	35.7
Washington	6,939	65.6	3,387	32.0
Webb	6,774	23.0	22,322	75.6
Wharton	5,243	52.7	4,486	45.1
Wheeler	1,172	76.1	321	20.8
Wichita	17,483	68.6	7,210	28.3
Wilbarger	1,813	65.6	865	31.3
Willacy	929	36.8	1,560	61.7
Williamson	59,271	58.6	37,319	36.9
Wilson	6,925	61.3	3,881	34.3
Winkler	827	73.1	260	23.0
Wise	8,972	70.5	3,103	24.4
Wood	8,994	71.8	3,106	24.8
Yoakum	1,218	72.5	376	22.4
Young	4,025	74.9	1,212	22.6
Zapata	319	25.9	902	73.2
Zavala	532	21.2	1,939	77.2

General Election, 2010

Below are the voting results for the general election held November 2, 2010, for all statewide races and for contested congressional (see map on p. 548), state senate, courts of appeals and state board of education races. These are official returns as canvassed by the State Canvassing Board. Abbreviations used are (Dem.) Democrat, (Rep.) Republican, (Lib.) Libertarian, (Grn.) Green, (Ind.) Independent and (W-I) Write-in.

Governor

Rick Perry (Rep.)	2,737,481	54.97%
Bill White (Dem.)	2,106,395	42.29%
Kathie Glass (Lib.)	109,211	2.19%
Deb Shafto (Grn.)	19,516	0.39%
Andy Barron (W-I)	7,267	0.14%
Total vote	4,979,870	

Lieutenant Governor

David Dewhurst (Rep.)	3,049,109	61.78%
Linda Chavez-Thompson (Dem.)	1,719,202	34.83%
Scott Jameson (Lib.)	122,142	2.47%
Herb Gonzales Jr. (Grn.)	44,903	0.90%
Total vote	4,935,356	

Attorney General

Greg Abbott (Rep.)	3,151,064	64.05%
Barbara Ann Rodnofsky (Dem.)	1,655,859	33.66%
Jon Roland (Lib.)	112,118	2.27%
Total vote	4,919,041	

Comptroller of Public Accounts

Susan Combs (Rep.)	3,307,935	83.16%
Mary J. Ruwart (Lib.)	417,523	10.49%
Edward Lindsay (Grn.)	252,233	6.34%
Total vote	3,977,691	

Commissioner of General Land Office

Jerry Patterson (Rep.)	3,001,736	61.66%
Hector Uribe (Dem.)	1,717,518	35.28%
James L. Holdar (Lib.)	148,271	3.04%
Total Vote	4,867,525	

Commissioner of Agriculture

Todd Staples (Rep.)	2,953,775	60.82%
Hank Gilbert (Dem.)	1,738,456	35.79%
Rick Donaldson (Lib.)	164,035	3.37%
Total vote	4,856,266	

Railroad Commissioner

David Porter (Rep.)	2,880,765	59.40%
Jeff Weems (Dem.)	1,757,183	36.23%
Roger Gary (Lib.)	138,978	2.86%
Art Browning (Grn.)	72,291	1.49%
Total vote	4,849,217	

U.S. HOUSE OF REPRESENTATIVES
District 1

Louie Gohmert (Rep.)	129,398	89.72%
Charles F. Parkes III (Lib.)	14,811	10.27%
Total Vote	144,209	

District 2

Ted Poe (Rep.)	130,020	88.61%
David W. Smith (Lib.)	16,711	11.38%
Total Vote	146,731	

District 3

Sam Johnson (Rep.)	101,180	66.28%
John Lingenfelder (Dem.)	47,848	31.34%
Christopher J. Claytor (Lib.)	3,602	2.35%
Harry Pierce (W-I)	22	0.01%
Total Vote	152,652	

District 4

Ralph M. Hall (Rep.)	136,338	73.18%
VaLinda Hathcox (Dem.)	40,975	21.99%
Jim D. Prindle (Lib.)	4,729	2.53%
Shane Shepard (Ind.)	4,244	2.27%
Total Vote	186,286	

District 5

Jeb Hensarling (Rep.)	106,742	70.52%
Tom Berry (Dem.)	41,649	27.51%
Ken Ashby (Lib.)	2,958	1.95%
Total Vote	151,349	

District 6

Joe L. Barton (Rep.)	107,140	65.90%
David E. Cozard (Dem.)	50,717	31.19%
Byron Severns (Lib.)	4,700	2.89%
Total Vote	162,557	

District 7

John Culberson (Rep.)	143,655	81.44%
Bob Townsend (Lib.)	31,704	17.97%
Lissa Squiers (W-I)	1,019	0.57%
Total Vote	176,378	

District 8

Kevin Brady (Rep.)	161,417	80.26%
Kent Hargett (Dem.)	34,694	17.25%
Bruce West (Lib.)	4,988	2.48%
Total Vote	201,099	

District 9

Steve Mueller (Rep.)	24,201	22.88%
Al Green (Dem.)	80,107	75.73%
Michael W. Hope (Lib.)	1,459	1.37%
Total Vote	105,767	

District 10

Michael T. McCaul (Rep.)	144,980	64.67%
Ted Ankrum (Dem.)	74,086	33.04%
Jeremiah "JP" Perkins (Lib.)	5,105	2.27%
Total Vote	224,171	

District 11

Mike Conaway (Rep.)	125,581	80.84%
James Quillian (Dem.)	23,989	15.44%
James A. Powell (Lib.)	4,321	2.78%
Jim Howe (Grn.)	1,449	0.93%
Total Vote	155,340	

District 12

Kay Granger (Rep.)	109,882	71.85%
Tracy Smith (Dem.)	38,434	25.13%
Matthew Solodow (Lib.)	4,601	3.00%
Total Vote	152,917	

District 13

Mac Thornberry (Rep.)	113,201	87.04%
John T. Burwell Jr. (Lib.)	5,650	4.34%
Keith Dyer (Ind.)	11,192	8.60%
Total Vote	130,043	

District 14

Ron Paul (Rep.)	140,623	75.99%
Robert Pruett (Dem.)	44,431	24.00%
Total Vote	185,054	

District 15

Eddie Zamora (Rep.)	39.964	41.59%
Rubén Hinojosa (Dem.)	53,546	55.73%
Aaron I. Cohn (Lib.)	2,570	2.67%
Total Vote	96,080	

District 16

Tim Besco (Rep.)	31,051	36.57%
Silvestre Reyes (Dem.)	49,301	58.07%
Bill Collins (Lib..)	4,319	5.08%
Tim Collins (W-I)	221	0.26%
Total Vote	84,892	

District 17

Bill Flores (Rep.)	106,696	61.80%
Chet Edwards (Dem.)	63,138	36.57%

Richard B. Kelly (Lib.)................................2,808 .... 1.62%
    Total Vote 172,642

District 18
John Faulk (Rep.)......................................33,067 ...... 27.25%
Sheila Jackson Lee (Dem.) ....85,108 ...... 70.15%
Mike Taylor (Lib.) ....3,118 .... 2.57%
Charles B. "ChuckM" Meyer (W-I) ....28 ...... 0.02%
    Total Vote 121,321

District 19
Randy Neugebauer (Rep.) ....106,059 ...... 77.77%
Andy Wilson (Dem.)................................25,984 ...... 19.05%
Richard "Chip" Peterson (Lib.)..................4,315 .... 3.16%
    Total Vote 136,358

District 20
Clayton Trotter (Rep.)............................31,757 ...... 34.44%
Charles A. Gonzalez (Dem.)...................58,645 ...... 63.61%
Michael "Commander" Idrogo (Lib.)..........1,783 .... 1.93%
    Total Vote 92,185

District 21
Lamar Smith (Rep.) ....162,924 ...... 68.87%
Lainey Melnick (Dem.)...........................65,927 ...... 27.87%
James Arthur Strohm (Lib.)......................7,694 .... 3.25%
    Total Vote 236,545

District 22
Pete Olson (Rep.)................................140,537 ...... 67.49%
Kesha Rogers (Dem.)............................62,082 ...... 29.81%
Steven Susman (Lib.)..............................5,538 .... 2.65%
Johnny Williams (W-I)...................................66 ...... 0.03%
    Total Vote 208,223

District 23
Francisco "Quico" Canseco (Rep.).........74,853 ...... 49.39%
Ciro D. Rodriguez (Dem.)......................67,348 ...... 44.44%
Martin Nitschke (Lib.)...............................2,482 .... 1.63%
Ed Scharf (Grn.) ....1,419 .... 0.93%
Craig T. Stephens (Ind.)...........................5,432 .... 3.58%
    Total Vote 151,534

District 24
Kenny E Marchant (Rep.) ....100,078 ...... 81.57%
David Sparks (Lib.)................................22,609 ...... 18.42%
    Total Vote 122,687

District 25
Donna Campbell (Rep.)...........................84,849 ...... 44.83%
Lloyd Doggett (Dem.) ....99,967 ...... 52.82%
Jim Stutsman (Lib.)...................................4,431 .... 2.34%
    Total Vote 189,247

District 26
Michael C. Burgess (Rep.) ....120,984 ...... 67.05%
Neil L. Durrance (Dem.)..........................55,385 ...... 30.69%
Mark Boler (Lib.) ....4,062 .... 2.25%
    Total Vote 180,431

District 27
R. Blake Farenthold (Rep.).....................51,001 ...... 47.84%
Solomon P. Ortiz (Dem.)........................50,226 ...... 47.11%
Ed Mishou (Lib.) ....5,372 .... 5.03%
    Total Vote 106,599

District 28
Bryan Underwood (Rep.)........................46,740 ...... 41.95%
Henry Cuellar (Dem.)..............................62,773 ...... 56.34%
Stephen Kaat (Lib.).................................1,889 .... 1.69%
    Total Vote 111,402

District 29
Roy Morales (Rep.) ....22,825 ...... 34.09%
Gene Green (Dem.)................................43,257 ...... 64.61%
Brad Walters (Lib.)......................................866 .... 1.29%
    Total Vote 66,948

District 30
Stephen E. Broden (Rep.) ....24,668 ...... 21.64%
Eddie Bernice Johnson (Dem.)...............86,322 ...... 75.73%
J.B. Oswalt (Lib.) ....2,988 .... 2.62%
    Total Vote 113,978

District 31
John R. Carter (Rep.) ....126,384 ...... 82.53%
Bill Oliver (Lib.) ....26,735 ...... 17.46%
    Total Vote 153,119

District 32
Pete Sessions (Rep.)..............................59,433 ...... 62.61%
Grier Raggio (Dem.)...............................44,258 ...... 34.88%
John Jay Myers (Lib.) ....3,178 .... 2.50%
    Total Vote 126,869

STATE COURTS
Justice, Supreme Court, Place 3
Debra Lehrmann (Rep.)....................2,907,796 ...... 59.87%
Jim Sharp (Dem.) ....1,809,498 ...... 37.26%
William Bryan Strange III (Lib.).............138,857 .... 2.85%
    Total Vote 4,856,151

Justice, Supreme Court, Place 5
Paul Green (Rep.) ....2,903,359 ...... 60.02%
Bill Moody (Dem.) ....1,789,646 ...... 36.99%
Tom Oxford (Lib.) ....144,306 .... 2.98%
    Total Vote 4,837,311

Justice, Supreme Court, Place 9
Eva Guzman (Rep.).........................2,919,054 ...... 60.34%
Blake Bailey (Dem.).........................1,722,753 ...... 35.61%
Jack Armstrong (Lib.).........................195,234 .... 4.03%
    Total Vote 4,837,041

Judge, Court of Criminal Appeals, Place 2
Lawrence "Larry" Meyers (Rep.)........3,189,842 ...... 82.34%
J. Randell Stevens (Lib.) ....684,005 ...... 17.65%
    Total Vote 3,873,847

Judge, Court of Criminal Appeals, Place 5
Cheryl Johnson (Rep.).......................3,207,376 ...... 82.90%
Dave Howard (Lib.).............................661,160 ...... 17.09%
    Total Vote 3,868,536

Judge, Court of Criminal Appeals, Place 6
Michael E. Keasler (Rep.)..................2,906,012 ...... 60.48%
Keith Hampton (Dem.).......................1,759,365 ...... 36.61%
Robert Ravee Virasin (Lib.) ....139,299 .... 2.89%
    Total Vote 4,804,676

COURTS OF APPEALS
Chief Justice, First District
Sherry Radack (Rep.)...........................653,669 ...... 59.76%
Morris Overstreet (Dem.)......................440,141 ...... 40.23%
    Total Vote 1,093,810

Justice, First District, Place 4
Evelyn Keyes (Rep.)............................645,927 ...... 59.24%
Michael Gomez (Dem.)........................444,390 ...... 40.75%
    Total Vote 1,090,317

Justice, First District, Place 8
Michael Massengale (Rep.)..................633,406 ...... 58.26%
Robert Ray (Dem.) ....453,799 ...... 41.73%
    Total Vote 1,087,205

Justice, Third District, Place 4
Melissa Goodwin (Rep.) ....314,280 ...... 57.14%
Kurt Kuhn (Dem.)................................235,733 ...... 42.85%
    Total Vote 550,013

Justice, Fourth District, Place 2
Marialyn Barnard (Rep.) ....268,383 ......56.11%
Rebeca C. Martinez (Dem.).................209,931 ...... 43.88%
    Total Vote 478,314

Justice, Fifth District, Place 4
Lana Myers (Rep.)...............................371,450 ...... 58.32%
Bonnie Lee Goldstein (Dem.) ....265,463 ...... 41.67%
    Total Vote 636,913

Justice, Fifth District, Place 12
Robert M. "Bob" Fillmore (Rep.) ....370,734 ...... 58.30%
Lawrence J. Praeger (Dem.) ....265,167 ...... 41.69%
    Total Vote 635,901

Gov. Rick Perry. Photo by Jim Greenhill (CC).

Justice, Ninth District, Place 2
Charles A. Kreger (Rep.) .... 182,770 ...... 73.78%
Ron M. Mangus (Dem.) .... 64,943 ...... 26.21%
Total Vote 247,713

Justice, Thirteenth District, Place 3
Greg Perkes (Rep.) .... 136,403 ...... 50.80%
Linda Yañez (Dem.) .... 132,096 ...... 49.19%
Total Vote 268,499

Justice, Fourteenth District, Place 2
Sharon McCally (Rep.) .... 647,290 ...... 59.51%
Norma Venso (Dem.) .... 440,355 ...... 40.48%
Total Vote 1,087,645

Justice, Fourteenth District, Place 5
Martha Hill Jamison (Rep.) .... 644,556 ...... 59.30%
Wallyi Kronzer (Dem.) .... 442,373 ...... 40.69%
Total Vote 1,086,929

Justice, Fourteenth District, Place 9
Tracy Elizabeth Christopher (Rep.) ...... 642,850 ...... 59.17%
Tim Riley (Dem.) .... 443,447 ...... 40.82%
Total Vote 1,086,297

STATE BOARD OF EDUCATION
District 1
Carlos "Charlie" Garza (Rep.) .... 112,167 ...... 51.14%
Rene Nunez (Dem.) .... 107,130 ...... 48.85%
Total Vote 219,297

District 3
Tony Cunningham (Rep.) .... 91,256 ...... 41.11%
Michael Soto (Dem.) .... 123,596 ...... 55.68%
Dean Kareem Kigley (Lib.) .... 6,604 ...... 2.97%
Deborah L. Parrish (W-I) .... 491 ...... 0.22%
Total Vote 221,947

District 5
Ken Mercer (Rep.) .... 262,699 ...... 59.30%
Rebecca Bell-Metereau (Dem.) .... 160,233 ...... 36.17%
Mark Loewe (Lib.) .... 20,052 ...... 4.52%
Total Vote 442,984

District 9
Thomas Ratliff (Rep.) .... 268,694 ...... 84.25%
Jeff McGee (Lib.) .... 35,473 ...... 11.12%
Paul Cardwell (Grn.) .... 14,753 ...... 4.62%
Total Vote 318,920

District 10
Marsha Farney (Rep.) .... 255,874 ...... 55.85%
Judy Jennings (Dem.) .... 183,385 ...... 40.03%
Jessica Dreesen (Lib.) .... 18,848 ...... 4.11%
Total Vote 458,107

District 12
George M. Clayton (Rep.) .... 203,922 ...... 81.23%
Amie Parsons (Lib.) .... 47,112 ...... 18.76%
Total Vote 251,034

District 15
Bob Craig (Rep.) .... 229,510 ...... 89.04%
John Pekowski (Lib.) .... 28,224 ...... 10.95%
Total Vote 257,734

STATE SENATE
District 2
Robert F. Deuell (Rep.) .... 105,779 ...... 66.38%
Kathleen Maria Shaw (Dem.) .... 53,566 ...... 33.61%
Total Vote 159,345

District 3
Robert Nichols (Rep.) .... 153,906 ...... 88.90%
David Scott (Lib.) .... 19,211 ...... 11.09%
Total Vote 173,117

District 5
Steve Ogden (Rep.) .... 145,170 ...... 71.26%
Stephen Wyman (Dem.) .... 58,525 ...... 28.73%
Total Vote 203,695

District 7
Dan Patrick (Rep.) .... 184,704 ...... 86.41%
Lee Coughran (Dem.) .... 29,048 ...... 13.58%
Total Vote 213,752

District 8
Florence Shapiro (Rep.) .... 136,369 ...... 84.02%
Ed Kless (Lib.) .... 25,935 ...... 15.97%
Total Vote 162,304

District 12
Jane Nelson (Rep.) .... 148,592 ...... 86.14%
Mark F. Frohman (Lib.) .... 23,894 ...... 13.85%
Total Vote 172,486

District 13
Michael Mauldin (Rep.) .... 31,596 ...... 21.82%
Rodney Ellis (Dem.) .... 113,155 ...... 78.17%
Total Vote 144,751

District 14
Mary Lou Sarafine (Rep.) .... 68,100 ...... 35.66%
Kirk Watson (Dem.) .... 115,949 ...... 60.72%
Kent Phillips (Lib.) .... 6,884 ...... 3.60%
Total Vote 190,933

District 15
Bill Walker (Rep.) .... 52,959 ...... 40.72%
John Whitmire (Dem.) .... 77,096 ...... 59.27%
Total Vote 130,055

District 17
Joan Huffman (Rep.) .... 112,595 ...... 83.15%
Phil Kurtz (Lib.) .... 22,802 ...... 16.84%
Total Vote 135,397

District 18
Glenn Hegar (Rep.) .... 146,087 ...... 70.42%
Patricia "Pat" Olney .... 61,345 ...... 29.57%
Total Vote 207,432

District 19
Dick Bowen (Rep.) .... 53,024 ...... 45.08%
Carlos I. Uresti (Dem.) .... 61,327 ...... 52.13%
Mette A. Baker (Lib.) .... 3,269 ...... 2.77%
Total Vote 117,620

District 25
Jeff Wentworth (Rep.) .... 192,965 ...... 82.17%
Arthur Maxwell Thomas IV (Lib.) .... 40,972 ...... 17.44%
Eric R. Anderson (W-I) .... 885 ...... 0.37%
Total Vote 234,822

District 29
Dan Chavez (Rep.) .... 33,303 ...... 39.75%
Jose R. Rodriguez (Dem.) .... 50,460 ...... 60.24%
Total Vote 83,763

Texas Primary Elections, 2010

Below are the official returns for the contested races only in the Republican and Democratic Party primaries held March 2, 2010. Included are statewide races and selected district races. The runoffs were held on April 13.

DEMOCRATIC PRIMARY

Governor

Bill White	517,487	76.03%
Farouk Shami	87,411	12.84%
Star Locke	6,276	0.92%
Clement E. Glenn	9,836	1.44%
Bill Dear	6,551	0.96%
Felix Rodriguez Alvarado	33,714	4.95%
Alma Ludivina Aguado	19,273	2.83%
Total vote	680,548	

Lieutenant Governor

Linda Chavez-Thompson	314,972	53.13%
Ronnie Earle	205,516	34.67%
Marc Katz	72,235	12.18%
Total Vote	592,723	

Commissioner of General Land Office

Hector Uribe	292,729	51.71%
Bill Burton	273,349	48.28%
Total Vote	566,078	

Commissioner of Agriculture

Richard "Kinky" Friedman	283,614	47.69%
Hank Gilbert	311,087	52.30%
Total Vote	594,701	

U.S. HOUSE OF REPRESENTATIVES
District 14

Jeff Cherry	4,498	27.34%
Winston Cochran	5,112	31.07%
Robert Pruett	6,842	41.58%
Total Vote	16,452	

District 15

Rubén Hinojosa	37,430	83.71%
Doug "La Peria" Purl	7,282	16.28%
Total Vote	44,712	

District 18

Sheila Jackson Lee	21,570	66.96%
Jarvis Johnson	9,133	28.35%
Sean Roberts	1,508	4.68%
Total Vote	32,211	

District 22

Doug Blatt	3,956	27.70%
Kesha Rogers	7,467	52.28%
Freddie John Wieder Jr.	2,858	20.01%
Total Vote	14,281	

District 23

Ciro D. Rodriguez	34,104	83.37%
Miguel Ortiz	6,799	16.62%
Total Vote	40,903	

STATE SENATE
District 19

Carlos Uresti	25,969	76.16%
Luis C. Juarez Jr.	8,125	23.83%
Total Vote	34,094	

District 29

Jose R. Rodriguez	22,253	69.49%
Liza Montelongo	6,388	19.94%
Louis Irwin	3,382	10.56%
Total Vote	32,023	

STATE BOARD OF EDUCATION
District 5

Rebecca Bell-Metereau	23,060	61.89%
Robert M. Bohmfalk	2,253	6.04%

Daniel Boone	8,365	22.45%
Josiah James Ingalls	3,576	9.59%
Total Vote	37,254	

DEMOCRATIC RUNOFF
U.S. HOUSE OF REPRESENTATIVES
District 14

Winston Cochran	1,309	45.38%
Robert Pruett	1,575	54.61%
Total Vote	2,884	

REPUBLICAN PRIMARY

Governor

Rick Perry	759,296	51.14%
Kay Bailey Hutchison	450,087	30.31%
Debra Medina	275,159	18.53%
Total vote	1,484,542	

Railroad Commissioner

Victor G. Carrillo	474,409	39.26%
David Porter	733,746	60.73%
Total Vote	1,208,155	

Justice, Supreme Court, Place 3

Jeff Brown	188,238	16.75%
Rick Green	212,976	18.95%
Debra Lehrmann	204,779	18.22%
Jim Moseley	203,838	18.14%
Rebecca Simmons	202,750	18.04%
Rick Strange	111,092	9.88%
Total Vote	1,123,673	

Justice, Supreme Court, Place 9

Eva Guzman	722,258	65,29%
Rose Vela	383,936	34.70%
Total Vote	1,106,194	

U.S. HOUSE OF REPRESENTATIVES
District 4

Ralph M. Hall	39,579	57.35%
Steve Clark	20,496	29.70%
John Cooper	3,748	5.43%
Lou Gigliotti	1,044	1.51%
Jerry Ray "Tea" Hall	3,190	4.62%
Joshua Kowert	947	1.37%
Total Vote	69,004	

District 8

Kevin Brady	52.595	79.30%
Scott Baker	8,614	12.98%
Melecio Franco	1,565	2.35%
Tyler Russell	3,542	5.34%
Total Vote	66,316	

District 9

Dave Bannen	2,317	33.35%
Steve Mueller	4,629	66.64%
Total Vote	6,946	

District 10

Michael McCaul	46,881	82.86%
Rick Martin	5,038	8.90%
Joe Petronis	4,656	8.22%
Total Vote	56,575	

District 11

Mike Conaway	55,610	77.36%
Al Cowan	6,680	9.29%
Chris Younts	9,586	13.33%
Total Vote	71,876	

District 12

Kay Granger	40,325	69.97%
Mike Brasovan	10,943	18.98%
Matthew W. Kelly	6,361	11.03%
Total Vote	57,629	

District 14

Ron Paul	45,990	80.76%
John Gay	3,004	5.27%
Tim Graney	5,499	9.65%
Gerald D. Wall	2,448	4.29%
Total Vote	56,941	

District 15

Daniel Garza	3,310	25,63%
Paul B. Haring	5,401	41.82%
Eddie Zamora	4,201	32.53%
Total Vote	12,912	

District 17

Rob Curnock	18,679	28.73%
Timothy Delasandro	3,119	4.79%
Bill Flores	21,479	33.04%
Dave McIntyre	11,870	18.26%
Chuck Wilson	9,853	15.15%
Total Vote	65,000	

District 18

Tex Christopher	1,199	13.13%
John Faulk	5,188	56.82%
Brenda Page	2,743	30.04%
Total Vote	9,130	

District 20

Joseph "Jaime" Martinez	3,510	29.68%
Charles A. Shipp Jr.	2,479	20.96%
Alan Strack	1,997	16.88%
Clayton Trotter	3,838	32.45%
Total Vote	11,824	

District 21

Lamar Smith	61,923	81.38%
Stephen Schoppe	14,166	18.61%
Total Vote	76,089	

District 23

Francisco "Quico" Canseco	9,250	32.15%
Joseph Mack "Doc" Gould	1,459	5.07%
Will Hurd	9,695	33.70%
Mike Kueber	1,990	6.91%
Robert "Doc" Lowry	6,369	22.14%
Total Vote	28,763	

District 24

Kenny E. Marchant	33,283	84.08%

Political Party Organizations

DEMOCRATIC State Executive Committee
www.txdemocrats.org
Chairman, Boyd Richie, 505 W. 12th St., Ste. 200, Austin 78701.

REPUBLICAN State Executive Committee
www.texasgop.org
Chairman, Steve Munisteri, 1108 Lavaca, Ste. 500, Austin 78701.

LIBERTARIAN State Executive Committee
www.lptexas.org
Chair, Patrick Dixon, P.O. Box 41059, Austin 78704.

GREEN State Executive Committee
txgreens.org
Co-Chairs, Dustin Morrow and Christine Morshedi, P.O. Box 271080, Houston 77277-1080.

Former Houston mayor Bill White, the Democratic nominee for governor. Photo by Ed Schipul (CC).

Frank Roszell	6,298	15.91%
Total Vote	39,581	

District 25

Donna Campbell	23,955	69.44%
George Morovich	10,541	30.55%
Total Vote	34,496	

District 26

Michael C. Burgess	44,047	85.80%
James Herford	7,284	14.19%
Total Vote	51,331	

District 27

James Duerr	6,368	32.40%
R. Blake Farenthold	5,921	30.12%
Jessica Puente-Bradshaw	3,097	15.75%
William "Willie" Vaden	4,268	21.71%
Total Vote	19,654	

District 28

Daniel Chavez	4,792	26.01%
Bryan Underwood	13,629	73.98%
Total Vote	18,421	

District 29

Frank "Mazz" Mazzapica	307	4.33%
Roy Morales	4,137	58.35%
Tom Stevens	657	9.26%
Eric Story	1,514	21.35%
George A. Young	474	6.68%
Total Vote	7,089	

District 30

Stephen E. Broden	3,681	49.51%
Sheldon Goldstein	2,809	37.78%
Charles Lingerfelt	944	12.69%
Total Vote	7,434	

District 31

John R. Carter	52,321	89.85%
Raymond Yamka	5,910	10.14%
Total Vote	58,231	

District 32

Pete Sessions	30,509	83.71%
David Smith	16.28	16.28%
Total Vote	36,446	

STATE SENATE
District 2

Robert F. Deuell	38,086	70.95%
Sharon Russell	15,588	29.04%
Total Vote	53,674	

District 5

Steve Ogden	47,699	68.27%
Ben Bius	22,165	31.72%
Total Vote	69,864	

District 19
Dick Bowen	14,050	73.50%
Robert Sol Mayer	5,065	26.49%
Total Vote	19,115	

District 22
Kip Averitt	37,719	60.08%
Darren Yancy	25,060	39.91%
Total Vote	62,779	

Prop. 1 – Require a valid photo ID to cast a ballot
In Favor	1,329,933	92.88%
Against	101,903	7.11%
Total Vote	1,431,836	

Prop. 2 – Limit spending increases of all government bodies in the state to the combined increase of population and inflation
In Favor	1,291,322	91.92%
Against	113,455	8.07%
Total Vote	1,404,777	

Prop. 3 – Congress should cut income taxes rather than spend on economic stimulus
In Favor	1,316,283	93.09%
Against	97,652	6.90%
Total Vote	1,413,935	

Prop. 4 – The word "God," prayers and Ten Commandments should be allowed at public gatherings, government buildings, schools
In Favor	1,376,450	95.15%
Against	70,088	4.84%
Total Vote	1,446,538	

Prop. 5 – Require sonograms to be shown to expecting mothers before elective abortion
In Favor	971,137	68.69%
Against	442,518	31.30%
Total Vote	1,413,655	

COURTS OF APPEALS
Chief Justice, Sixth District
H.D. Bailey	25,092	48.47%
Josh Morriss	26,672	51.52%
Total Vote	51,764	

Justice, First District, Place 4
Evelyn Keyes	120,471	63.19%
Don Self	70,153	36.80%
Total Vote	190,624	

Justice, First District, Place 8 (unexpired)
Michael Massengale	131,829	70.37%
Gael Harrison	55,482	29.62%
Total Vote	187,311	

Justice, Third District, Place 4
Scott Field	58,810	47.00%
Melissa Goodwin	66,301	52.99%
Total Vote	125,111	

Justice, Tenth District, Place 3
Felipe Reyna	25,752	32.07%
Al Scoggins	54,536	67.92%
Total Vote	80,288	

Justice, Fourteenth District, Place 2
Leslie Brock Yates	93,342	48.24%
Sharon McCally	100,134	51.75%
Total Vote	193,476	

STATE BOARD OF EDUCATION
District 3
Tony Cunningham	18,649	58.36%
Joanie Muenzler	13,305	41.63%
Total Vote	31,954	

District 5
Ken Mercer	73,569	69.05%

Tim Tuggey	32,962	30.94%
Total Vote	106,531	

District 9
Don McLeroy	57,901	49.82%
Thomas Ratliff	58,303	50.17%
Total Vote	116,204	

District 10
Marsha Farney	37,459	35.50%
Rebecca Osborne	30,781	29.17%
Brian Russell	37,261	35.31%
Total Vote	105,501	

District 12
Geraldine "Tincy" Miller	34,903	48.16%
George M. Clayton	37,559	51.83%
Total Vote	72,462	

District 15
Bob Craig	76,476	64.30%
Randy Rives	42,455	35.69%
Total Vote	118,931	

REPUBLICAN RUNOFF
Justice, Supreme Court, Place 3
Rick Green	161,644	48.15%
Debra Lehrmann	174,023	51.84%
Total Vote	335,667	

U.S. HOUSE OF REPRESENTATIVES
District 15
Paul B. Haring	1,187	43.24%
Eddie Zamora	1,558	56.75%
Total Vote	2,745	

District 17
Rob Curnock	11,730	34.86%
Bill Flores	21,913	65.13%
Total Vote	33,643	

District 20
Joseph "Jaime" Martinez	957	28.25%
Clayton Trotter	2,430	71.74%
Total Vote	3,387	

District 23
Francisco "Quico" Canseco	7,210	52.63%
Will Hurd	6,488	47.36%
Total Vote	13,698	

District 27
James Duerr	4,496	48.66%
R. Blake Farenthold	4,742	51.33%
Total Vote	9,238	

District 30
Stephen E. Broden	2,126	67.51%
Sheldon Goldstein	1,023	32.48%
Total Vote	3,149	

STATE BOARD OF EDUCATION
District 10
Marsha Farney	23,789	61.78%
Brian Russell	14,716	38.21%
Total Vote	38,505	

Special Elections
STATE SENATE
District 22
Held May 8, 2010
Gayle R. Avant (Democrat)	3,968	13.29%
Brian Birdwell (Republican)	10,900	36.51%
David Sibley (Republican)	13,423	44.96%
Darren Yancy (Republican)	1,560	5.22%
Total Vote	29,851	

Runoff held June 22, 2010
Brian Birdwell (Republican)	14,218	57.89%
David Sibley (Republican)	10,339	42.10%
Total Vote	24,557	

2010 Gubernatorial Primaries: Results by County

Below are the results by county in the party primaries for governor that were held March 2, 2010.

This table lists the principal candidates in the Democratic primary, Bill White and Farouk Shami, who together received 88.87 percent of the total 680,548 votes cast, and in the Republican primary, where 1,484,542 votes were cast, Rick Perry, Kay Bailey Hutchison, and Debra Medina.

Along side the number of votes received by each candidate is listed the percent of the total vote received by each candidate.

When no votes are reported, no primary was held in that county by the party.

Source: Texas Secretary of State.

DEMOCRATIC PRIMARY				County	REPUBLICAN PRIMARY					
White	%	Shami	%		Perry	%	Hutchison	%	Medina	%
517,486	76.03	87,411	12.84	Statewide	759,296	51.14	450,087	30.31	275,159	18.53
944	80.8	60	5.1	Anderson	2,245	49.7	1,237	27.4	1,034	22.9
166	67.8	24	9.8	Andrews	684	54.2	226	17.9	351	27.8
2,768	88.2	97	3.1	Angelina	2,698	53.4	1,643	32.5	712	14.1
344	77.1	74	16.6	Aransas	1,614	65.3	600	24.3	257	10.4
164	83.2	9	4.6	Archer	592	49.9	376	31.7	219	18.4
0	-	0	-	Armstrong	239	48.7	195	39.7	57	11.6
1,250	69.6	254	14.4	Atascosa	957	44.8	727	34.0	452	21.2
487	89.2	35	6.4	Austin	1,946	38.3	1,966	38.7	1,172	23.1
44	64.7	6	8.8	Bailey	376	45.0	386	46.2	73	8.7
246	82.8	40	13.5	Bandera	1,479	45.6	971	29.9	796	24.5
2,485	86.7	184	6.4	Bastrop	2,581	45.1	1,378	24.1	1,769	30.9
197	87.6	1	0.4	Baylor	140	47.6	108	36.7	46	15.6
582	61.8	173	18.4	Bee	706	40.4	467	26.7	576	32.9
2,487	82.8	236	7.9	Bell	7,660	51.7	4,456	30.0	2,713	18.3
32,126	76.3	5,651	13.4	Bexar	34,831	52.2	22,010	33.0	9,927	14.9
262	93.2	14	5.0	Blanco	877	49.4	476	26.8	421	23.7
94	68.1	13	9.4	Borden	58	58.6	18	18.2	23	23.2
775	91.4	31	3.7	Bosque	970	42.5	722	31.6	591	25.9
3,349	79.4	244	5.8	Bowie	3,562	53.0	2,640	39.3	524	7.8
4,683	90.4	277	5.3	Brazoria	12,634	54.5	5,672	24.5	4,869	21.0
1,722	76.2	121	5.4	Brazos	8,661	52.3	5,898	35.6	1,990	12.0
962	59.7	230	14.3	Brewster	210	47.1	106	23.8	130	29.1
47	72.3	6	9.2	Briscoe	108	45.0	88	36.7	44	18.3
1,235	44.6	850	30.7	Brooks	0	-	0	-	0	-
377	80.0	36	7.6	Brown	2,682	49.3	1,491	27.4	1,269	23.3
370	82.8	15	3.4	Burleson	873	52.5	492	29.6	297	17.9
797	92.6	24	2.8	Burnet	3,203	53.5	1,439	24.0	1,347	22.5
1,849	76.0	214	8.8	Caldwell	1,000	50.1	422	21.1	575	28.8
1,517	72.8	126	6.0	Calhoun	534	52.3	249	24.4	238	23.3
160	82.9	20	10.4	Callahan	712	46.4	378	24.6	444	28.9
8,949	57.6	3,667	23.6	Cameron	3,176	69.0	966	21.0	459	10.0
507	86.1	42	7.1	Camp	561	53.8	302	29.0	179	17.2
89	82.4	10	9.3	Carson	556	52.6	392	37.1	109	10.3
2,170	82.3	171	6.5	Cass	695	51.3	455	33.6	206	15.2
166	65.1	19	7.5	Castro	249	47.9	225	43.3	46	8.9
681	84.2	59	7.3	Chambers	2,628	57.2	1,197	26.1	767	16.7
732	83.8	68	7.8	Cherokee	2,681	49.1	1,775	32.5	999	18.3
62	73.8	8	9.5	Childress	349	52.2	261	39.0	59	8.8
370	89.4	8	1.9	Clay	499	45.7	364	33.3	230	21.0
0	-	0	-	Cochran	265	47.6	214	38.4	78	14.0
196	72.3	29	10.7	Coke	116	37.2	130	41.7	66	21.2
117	81.8	9	6.3	Coleman	578	43.7	403	30.5	341	25.8
5,023	82.8	536	8.8	Collin	27,636	48.5	17,959	31.5	11,339	19.9
89	82.4	3	2.8	Collingsworth	129	44.2	143	49.0	20	6.8
479	90.2	32	6.0	Colorado	1,259	40.1	1,024	32.6	855	27.2
1,369	88.0	114	7.3	Comal	7,672	50.7	4,604	30.4	2,867	18.9
735	81.8	36	4.0	Comanche	591	44.5	366	27.6	370	27.9
26	50.0	7	13.5	Concho	154	27.7	311	56.0	90	16.2
320	87.0	21	5.7	Cooke	1,674	32.7	1,959	38.3	1,485	29.0
471	77.2	60	9.8	Coryell	2,258	45.5	1,869	37.6	838	16.9

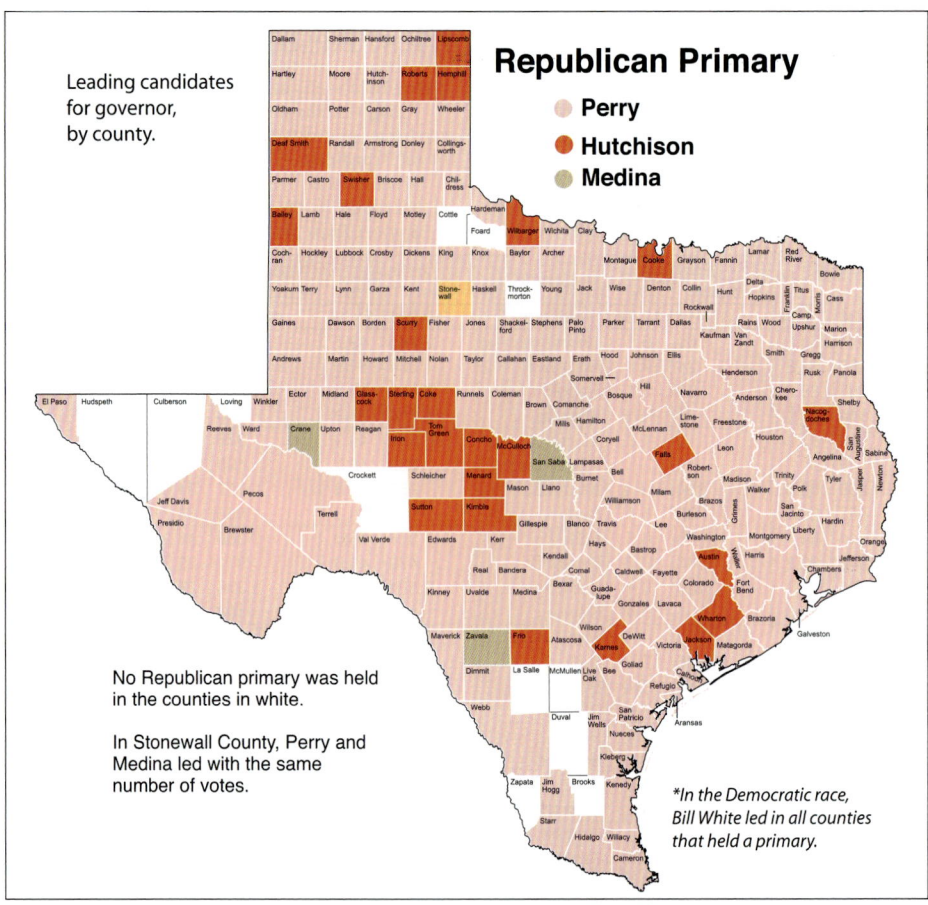

Republican Primary

Leading candidates for governor, by county.

● Perry
● Hutchison
● Medina

No Republican primary was held in the counties in white.

In Stonewall County, Perry and Medina led with the same number of votes.

*In the Democratic race, Bill White led in all counties that held a primary.

DEMOCRATIC PRIMARY				County	REPUBLICAN PRIMARY					
White	%	Shami	%		Perry	%	Hutchison	%	Medina	%
257	72.2	16	4.5	Cottle	0	-	0	-	0	-
80	69.6	18	15.7	Crane	198	39.8	31	6.2	269	54.0
243	37.9	97	15.1	Crockett	0	-	0	-	0	-
214	82.9	20	7.8	Crosby	190	54.8	118	34.0	39	11.2
233	38.5	134	22.1	Culberson	0	-	0	-	0	-
13	68.4	5	26.3	Dallam	277	47.6	201	34.5	104	17.9
43,430	80.4	5,129	9.5	Dallas	45,427	46.8	33,513	34.5	18,118	18.7
294	44.4	47	7.1	Dawson	671	50.7	464	35.0	189	14.3
36	42.9	12	14.3	Deaf Smith	682	42.4	727	45.2	200	12.4
179	85.6	7	3.3	Delta	350	46.1	224	29.5	185	24.4
3,968	85.5	318	6.9	Denton	19,997	47.3	12,558	29.7	9,706	23.0
347	84.0	29	7.0	DeWitt	1,030	42.2	887	36.3	887	36.3
233	66.6	28	8.0	Dickens	139	56.5	79	32.1	28	11.4
810	49.7	337	20.7	Dimmit	69	55.2	32	25.8	23	18.5
110	83.3	10	7.6	Donley	279	46.9	247	41.5	69	11.6
1,917	47.3	1,327	32.7	Duval	0	-	0	-	0	-
197	83.5	20	8.5	Eastland	1,188	45.0	778	29.5	673	25.5
780	59.0	258	19.5	Ector	4,994	55.9	1,406	15.7	2,536	28.4
224	56.3	60	15.1	Edwards	121	54.8	56	25.3	44	19.9
1,389	86.0	106	6.6	Ellis	5,873	41.8	4,186	29.8	3,994	28.4
20,088	58.7	9,879	28.8	El Paso	8,813	57.3	5,413	35.2	1,160	7.5
431	87.2	19	3.8	Erath	2,151	46.6	1,253	27.1	1,215	26.3
585	85.5	34	5.0	Falls	399	34.2	561	48.1	207	17.7
616	86.0	28	3.9	Fannin	1,371	45.2	865	28.5	794	26.2
1,009	91.4	55	5.0	Fayette	1,448	38.4	1,388	36.8	933	24.8

DEMOCRATIC PRIMARY				County	REPUBLICAN PRIMARY					
White	%	Shami	%		Perry	%	Hutchison	%	Medina	%
697	75.8	56	6.1	Fisher	42	53.2	24	30.4	13	16.5
65	62.5	10	9.6	Floyd	404	48.0	351	41.7	86	10.2
206	70.5	10	3.4	Foard	0	-	0	-	0	-
13,272	90.6	1,026	7.0	Fort Bend	18,678	58.2	8,971	27.9	4,452	13.9
309	85.6	16	4.4	Franklin	823	49.4	482	28.9	360	21.6
962	84.5	42	3.7	Freestone	881	54.2	419	25.8	324	20.0
1,459	57.5	376	14.8	Frio	46	37.7	48	39.3	28	23.0
50	54.3	17	18.5	Gaines	949	50.4	632	33.6	301	16.0
7,398	89.6	504	6.1	Galveston	9,208	58.3	4,319	27.3	2,270	14.4
69	55.2	20	16.0	Garza	288	54.5	202	38.3	38	7.2
342	93.4	16	4.4	Gillespie	2,505	46.0	1,727	31.7	1,210	22.2
0	-	0	-	Glasscock	111	28.5	171	44.0	107	27.5
343	58.9	53	9.1	Goliad	412	35.3	389	33.3	366	31.5
652	72.2	89	9.9	Gonzales	907	51.3	509	28.8	351	19.9
65	78.3	7	8.4	Gray	1,928	56.7	1,095	32.2	376	11.1
1,436	80.4	119	6.7	Grayson	5,425	46.3	4,271	36.5	2,016	17.2
1,344	78.6	156	9.1	Gregg	5,921	51.7	4,044	35.3	1,483	13.0
512	72.0	35	4.9	Grimes	1,140	42.2	1,012	37.5	548	20.3
1,499	80.7	193	10.4	Guadalupe	5,950	50.9	3,583	30.6	2,162	18.5
212	57.9	46	12.6	Hale	1,428	44.7	1,361	42.6	407	12.7
174	87.4	8	4.0	Hall	131	53.5	91	37.1	23	9.4
202	93.5	4	1.9	Hamilton	509	46.1	359	32.5	237	21.4
0	-	0	-	Hansford	492	52.2	351	37.2	100	10.6
366	85.7	3.	0.7	Hardeman	96	63.2	41	27.0	15	9.9
1,953	78.0	332	13.3	Hardin	3,427	64.9	1,104	20.9	750	14.2
89,378	90.0	6,953	7.0	Harris	96,262	60.9	42,502	26.9	19,366	12.2
1,921	78.5	208	8.5	Harrison	2,334	52.7	1,596	36.0	503	11.3
0	-	0	-	Hartley	391	52.1	261	34.8	98	13.1
786	79.2	80	8.1	Haskell	140	71.1	35	17.8	22	11.2
4,733	85.0	453	8.1	Hays	3,049	50.0	1,345	22.1	1,703	27.9
18	85.7	1	4.8	Hemphill	293	39.9	348	47.3	94	12.8
1,286	88.4	61	4.2	Henderson	4,017	47.0	2,379	27.8	2,158	25.2
21,353	60.0	8,344	23.5	Hidalgo	3,300	65.8	1,014	20.2	701	14.0
700	89.4	23	2.9	Hill	1,725	39.7	1,725	36.6	1,118	23.7
0	-	0	-	Hockley	1,317	44.3	1,163	39.1	493	16.6
609	91.0	18	2.7	Hood	3,800	48.6	2,092	26.8	1,924	24.6
1,226	90.3	41	3.0	Hopkins	1,716	51.3	853	25.5	775	23.2
588	89.0	31	4.9	Houston	1,328	48.3	948	34.5	474	17.2
339	76.7	54	12.2	Howard	1,505	45.1	1,063	31.9	768	23.0
223	43.2	126	24.4	Hudspeth	0	-	0	-	0	-
1,012	79.1	99	7.7	Hunt	4,190	44.0	2,364	24.8	2,972	31.2
122	66.7	25	13.7	Hutchinson	1,657	55.4	1,020	34.1	313	10.5
94	53.7	28	16.0	Irion	61	34.7	72	40.9	43	24.4
302	84.8	16	4.5	Jack	481	52.6	208	22.8	225	24.6
524	82.4	42	6.6	Jackson	492	38.9	503	39.7	271	21.4
1,224	81.6	163	10.9	Jasper	1,417	67.9	471	22.6	199	9.5
137	74.9	16	8.7	Jeff Davis	159	48.8	75	23.0	92	28.2
12,600	75.9	2,788	16.8	Jefferson	5,820	65.2	2,039	22.8	1,074	12.0
803	40.3	761	38.2	Jim Hogg	11	68.8	1	6.3	4	25.0
2,349	49.0	1,519	31.7	Jim Wells	487	58.3	179	21.4	170	20.3
1,215	90.0	44	3.3	Johnson	6,456	47.9	3,406	25.3	3,608	26.8
320	80.8	29	7.3	Jones	645	41.9	481	31.2	414	26.9
1,361	75.4	190	10.5	Karnes	236	35.4	262	39.3	169	25.3
1,105	85.1	87	6.7	Kaufman	4,756	45.7	3,111	29.9	2,538	24.4
364	89.9	23	5.7	Kendall	3,175	51.6	1,857	30.2	1,127	18.3
64	46.0	33	23.7	Kenedy	5	50.0	4	40.0	1	10.0
126	73.3	17	9.9	Kent	23	43.4	19	35.8	11	20.8
674	86.7	68	8.8	Kerr	4,283	51.5	2,521	30.3	1,513	18.2
19	67.9	2	7.1	Kimble	533	37.9	583	41.4	291	20.7
14	87.5	0	-	King	21	38.2	18	32.7	16	29.1
306	52.6	93	16.0	Kinney	159	53.0	78	26.0	63	21.0

DEMOCRATIC PRIMARY				County	REPUBLICAN PRIMARY					
White	%	Shami	%		Perry	%	Hutchison	%	Medina	%
1,950	58.7	711	21.4	Kleberg	541	58.1	275	29.5	115	12.4
135	71.4	4	2.1	Knox	121	44.3	77	28.2	75	27.5
1,743	87.2	105	5.3	Lamar	2,425	53.6	1,432	31.7	664	14.7
302	69.6	47	10.8	Lamb	680	47.8	538	37.8	205	14.4
240	83.9	23	8.0	Lampasas	1,239	52.1	650	27.3	490	20.6
800	57.7	181	13.1	La Salle	0	-	0	-	0	-
1,119	87.6	74	5.8	Lavaca	1,091	46.9	723	31.1	513	22.0
960	85.8	45	4.0	Lee	470	39.9	317	26.9	392	33.2
253	82.1	24	7.8	Leon	1,625	56.8	787	27.5	449	15.7
2,030	88.8	123	5.4	Liberty	3,486	58.3	1,520	25.4	977	16.3
844	82.5	64	6.3	Limestone	937	49.4	539	28.4	422	22.2
31	83.8	0	-	Lipscomb	193	39.1	245	49.7	193	11.2
402	75.3	56	10.5	Live Oak	493	48.7	237	23.4	283	27.9
475	94.2	13	2.6	Llano	2,054	52.8	1,009	26.0	825	21.2
13	54.2	5	20.8	Loving	0	-	0	-	0	-
2,283	53.6	639	15.0	Lubbock	15,679	50.3	12,173	39.0	3,332	10.68
126	66.7	25	13.2	Lynn	249	47.8	207	39.7	65	12.5
346	84.4	18	4.4	Madison	917	52.4	558	31.9	275	15.7
607	79.7	73	9.6	Marion	290	47.5	198	32.5	122	20.0
35	81.4	4	9.3	Martin	264	38.9	204	30.0	211	31.1
65	87.8	5	6.8	Mason	333	40.6	318	38.7	170	20.7
2,234	83.8	190	7.1	Matagorda	1,118	52.0	573	26.7	458	21.3
1,714	31.3	1,434	26.2	Maverick	38	64.4	8	13.6	13	22.0
101	56.1	27	15.0	McCulloch	401	37.3	465	43.3	208	19.4
3,198	87.8	220	6.0	McLennan	8,313	45.6	7,082	38.8	2,839	15.6
205	74.0	26	9.4	McMullen	0	-	0	-	0	-
598	79.0	107	14.1	Medina	1,961	47.1	1,343	32.3	857	20.6
23	62.2	8	21.6	Menard	106	33.0	175	54.5	40	12.5
669	77.0	111	12.8	Midland	6,791	54.1	2,607	20.8	3,154	25.1
1,287	81.0	102	6.4	Milam	854	51.2	442	26.5	371	22.3
485	82.5	42	7.1	Mills	183	42.9	126	29.5	118	27.6
363	72.9	46	9.2	Mitchell	183	39.1	138	29.5	147	31.4
258	87.8	5	7.7	Montague	1,624	46.6	1,157	33.2	703	20.2
4,056	90.4	289	6.4	Montgomery	26,280	64.6	8,483	20.8	5,927	14.6
38	50.7	7	9.3	Moore	1,176	50.7	831	35.8	311	13.4
1,253	78.6	89	5.6	Morris	239	58.3	111	27.1	60	14.6
141	67.8	26	12.5	Motley	53	55.8	33	34.7	9	9.5
1,158	88.1	54	4.1	Nacogdoches	2,065	38.3	2,438	45.2	885	16.4
1,223	85.6	60	4.2	Navarro	1,908	47.7	1,087	27.2	1,001	25.1
1,380	73.0	236	12.5	Newton	306	72.9	69	16.4	45	10.7
775	70.6	112	10.2	Nolan	341	50.4	207	30.6	128	18.9
6,954	65.7	2,530	23.9	Nueces	9,044	61.2	3,828	25.9	1,909	12.9
11	84.6	1	7.7	Ochiltree	646	47.7	569	42.0	140	10.3
87	79.1	9	8.2	Oldham	169	52.8	110	34.4	41	12.8
3,562	81.8	524	12.0	Orange	3,058	68.8	860	19.3	527	11.9
485	87.4	26	4.7	Palo Pinto	1,233	44.4	747	26.9	794	28.6
837	82.8	65	6.4	Panola	1,022	52.5	742	38.1	183	9.4
1,163	88.8	57	4.4	Parker	6,668	43.3	4,107	26.7	4,632	30.1
20	66.7	1	3.3	Parmer	609	44.9	593	43.7	154	11.4
982	51.0	280	14.5	Pecos	288	53.0	103	19.0	152	28.0
925	89.6	54	5.2	Polk	2,585	49.7	1,788	34.4	824	15.9
604	72.0	105	12.5	Potter	4,024	51.7	2,893	37.2	859	11.0
431	50.5	138	16.2	Presidio	15	60.0	4	16.0	6	24.0
218	88.3	7	2.8	Rains	822	48.4	457	26.9	420	24.7
733	74.7	100	10.2	Randall	7,809	53.7	5,218	35.9	1,522	10.5
6	60.0	0	-	Reagan	265	41.8	245	38.6	124	19.6
9	64.3	1	7.1	Real	491	49.1	265	26.5	244	24.4
587	87.4	19	2.8	Red River	408	50.7	249	31.0	147	18.3
753	39.4	461	24.1	Reeves	27	61.4	7	15.9	10	22.7
614	63.5	185	19.1	Refugio	201	55.1	103	28.2	61	16.7
0	-	0	-	Roberts	98	40.3	114	46.9	31	12.8

DEMOCRATIC PRIMARY				County	REPUBLICAN PRIMARY					
White	%	Shami	%		Perry	%	Hutchison	%	Medina	%
806	78.3	63	6.1	Robertson	661	52.5	396	31.5	201	16.0
590	82.1	40	5.6	Rockwall	4,734	49.6	2,677	28.1	2,125	22.3
115	69.7	20	12.1	Runnels	757	42.3	702	39.5	329	18.4
558	86.1	29	4.5	Rusk	2,892	48.2	2,018	33.6	1,093	18.2
886	84.1	49	4.6	Sabine	506	54.7	252	27.2	167	18.1
1,458	80.8	96	5.3	SanAugustine	155	52.4	71	24.0	70	23.6
1,455	85.6	106	6.2	San Jacinto	1,180	58.1	474	23.3	378	18.6
1,244	62.7	437	22.0	San Patricio	2,073	60.3	817	23.8	548	15.9
81	88.0	4	4.3	San Saba	401	36.6	277	25.3	491	38.2
44	73.3	5	8.3	Schleicher	146	45.9	141	44.3	31	9.7
114	61.3	12	6.5	Scurry	1,022	40.3	1,054	41.6	458	18.1
5	83.3	1	16.7	Shackelford	323	54.7	149	25.2	119	20.1
702	88.6	36	4.5	Shelby	1,054	52.1	763	37.7	205	10.1
11	78.6	1	7.1	Sherman	258	53.1	172	35.4	56	11.5
2,365	82.0	264	9.2	Smith	10,490	54.0	4,661	24.0	4,280	22.0
584	85.1	31	4.5	Somervell	475	50.3	224	23.7	246	26.0
1,899	43.3	1,560	35.6	Starr	27	65.9	6	14.6	8	19.5
236	84.0	16	5.7	Stephens	379	49.0	210	27.2	184	23.8
0	-	0	-	Sterling	55	26.7	125	60.7	26	12.6
338	73.3	38	8.2	Stonewall	12	42.9	4	14.3	12	42.9
48	38.7	17	13.7	Sutton	191	43.1	195	44.0	57	12.9
304	83.1	20	5.5	Swisher	134	45.3	137	46.3	25	8.4
19,857	85.5	1,578	6.8	Tarrant	51,669	47.6	31,655	29.1	35,281	23.3
871	72.8	156	13.0	Taylor	5,677	44.3	4,640	36.2	2,503	19.5
201	52.8	48	12.6	Terrell	16	50.0	9	28.1	7	21.9
518	59.3	94	10.8	Terry	467	57.9	281	34.9	58	7.2
190	62.9	24	7.9	Throckmorton	0	-	0	-	0	-
1,573	82.7	98	5.2	Titus	884	59.6	412	27.8	188	12.7
750	66.4	199	17.6	Tom Green	4,114	41.4	4,562	45.9	1,268	12.8
34,426	90.2	2,384	6.2	Travis	23,856	47.3	15,497	30.7	11,074	22.0
2,176	83.3	156	6.0	Trinity	303	40.6	297	39.8	147	19.7
1,154	80.0	179	12.4	Tyler	781	59.6	359	27.4	171	13.0
803	87.3	54	5.9	Upshur	2,147	47.4	1,396	30.6	995	22.0
369	61.0	57	9.4	Upton	2	66.7	0	-	1	33.3
1,802	57.5	631	20.1	Uvalde	728	51.6	371	26.3	311	22.1
1,638	59.3	377	13.6	Val Verde	854	59.9	365	25.6	207	14.5
680	87.7	34	4.4	Van Zandt	3,357	48.6	1,676	24.3	1,876	27.2
2,143	56.9	337	9.0	Victoria	3,342	43.7	2,933	38.4	1,371	17.9
1,314	91.9	70	4.9	Walker	2,300	40.8	2,294	40.7	1,045	18.5
769	80.3	68	7.1	Waller	1,830	40.9	1,708	38.2	937	20.9
385	50.6	95	12.5	Ward	338	48.1	103	14.7	262	37.3
622	90.8	38	5.5	Washington	2,871	47.3	2,096	34.5	1,109	18.3
15,732	56.8	7,257	26.2	Webb	1,224	55.9	399	32.6	141	11.5
1,014	87.3	81	7.0	Wharton	1,131	23.2	1,977	40.5	1,773	36.3
205	77.4	17	6.4	Wheeler	362	53.1	252	37.0	68	10.0
1,164	75.7	87	5.7	Wichita	6,893	50.3	4,891	35.7	1,919	14.0
237	83.2	11	3.9	Wilbarger	357	33.6	596	56.2	108	10.2
1,610	54.5	650	22.0	Willacy	60	61.2	23	23.5	15	15.3
6,383	90.0	388	5.5	Williamson	17,712	52.6	8,294	24.6	7,651	22.7
1,638	74.2	262	11.9	Wilson	1,519	40.6	1,350	36.1	872	23.3
58	74.4	8	10.3	Winkler	352	52.9	114	17.1	199	29.9
544	87.9	30	4.8	Wise	2,909	41.6	1,932	27.6	2,155	30.8
671	87.7	49	6.4	Wood	3,039	50.6	1,462	24.4	1,501	25.0
33	50.0	8	12.1	Yoakum	688	50.3	515	37.6	165	12.1
243	86.5	8	2.8	Young	1,304	52.0	785	31.3	421	16.8
1,803	56.4	791	24.7	Zapata	0	-	0	-	0	-
994	38.0	713	27.2	Zavala	3	18.8	2	12.5	11	68.8

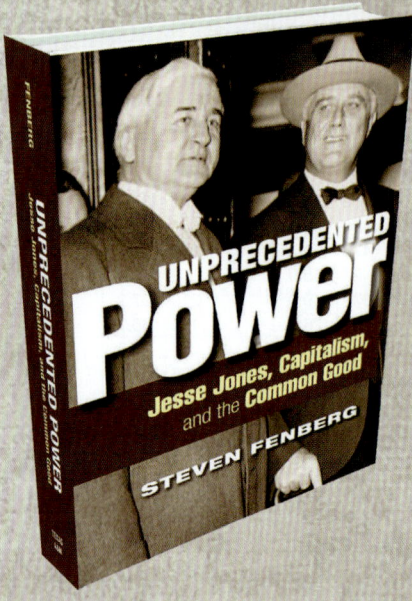

Government

The State Capitol and the Texas Cowboy Statue. Photo by Ron Billings; Texas Forest Service.

Historical Documents

Constitutional Amendments, 2009 and 2011

African-American Legislators of the 19th Century

Chief Government Officials, 1691–2011

State Government

Local Government

Federal Government

Crime in Texas, 2010

Declaration of Independence of the Republic of Texas

The Declaration of Independence of the Republic of Texas was adopted in general convention at Washington-on-the-Brazos, March 2, 1836.

Richard Ellis, president of the convention, appointed a committee of five to write the declaration for submission to the convention. However, there is much evidence that George C. Childress, one of the members, wrote the document with little or no help from the other members. Childress is therefore generally accepted as the author.

The text of the declaration is followed by the names of the signers of the document. The names are presented here as the signers actually signed the document.

Our thanks to the staff of the Texas State Archives for furnishing a photocopy of the signatures.

UNANIMOUS

Declaration of Independence,

BY THE

DELEGATES OF THE PEOPLE OF TEXAS,

IN GENERAL CONVENTION,

AT THE TOWN OF WASHINGTON,

ON THE SECOND DAY OF MARCH, 1836.

When a government has ceased to protect the lives, liberty and property of the people from whom its legitimate powers are derived, and for the advancement of whose happiness it was instituted; and so far from being a guarantee for the enjoyment of those inestimable and inalienable rights, becomes an instrument in the hands of evil rulers for their oppression; when the Federal Republican Constitution of their country, which they have sworn to support, no longer has a substantial existence, and the whole nature of their government has been forcibly changed without their consent, from a restricted federative republic, composed of sovereign states, to a consolidated central military despotism, in which every interest is disregarded but that of the army and the priesthood — both the eternal enemies of civil liberty, and the ever-ready minions of power, and the usual instruments of tyrants; When long after the spirit of the Constitution has departed, moderation is at length, so far lost, by those in power that even the semblance of freedom is removed, and the forms, themselves, of the constitution discontinued; and so far from their petitions and remonstrances being regarded, the agents who bear them are thrown into dungeons; and mercenary armies sent forth to force a new government upon them at the point of the bayonet. When in consequence of such acts of malfeasance and abdication, on the part of the government, anarchy prevails, and civil society is dissolved into its original elements: In such a crisis, the first law of nature, the right of self-preservation — the inherent and inalienable right of the people to appeal to first principles and take their political affairs into their own hands in extreme cases — enjoins it as a right towards themselves and a sacred obligation to their posterity, to abolish such government and create another in its stead, calculated to rescue them from impending dangers, and to secure their future welfare and happiness.

Nations, as well as individuals, are amenable for their acts to the public opinion of mankind. A statement of a part of our grievances is, therefore, submitted to an impartial world, in justification of the hazardous but unavoidable step now taken of severing our political connection with the Mexican people, and assuming an independent attitude among the nations of the earth.

The Mexican government, by its colonization laws, invited and induced the Anglo-American population of Texas to colonize its wilderness under the pledged faith of a written constitution, that they should continue to enjoy that constitutional liberty and republican government to which they had been habituated in the land of their birth, the United States of America. In this expectation they have been cruelly disappointed, inasmuch as the Mexican nation has acquiesced in the late changes made in the government by General Antonio Lopez de Santa Anna, who, having overturned the constitution of his country, now offers us the cruel alternative either to abandon our homes, acquired by so many privations, or submit to the most intolerable of all tyranny, the combined despotism of the sword and the priesthood.

It has sacrificed our welfare to the state of Coahuila, by which our interests have been continually depressed, through a jealous and partial course of legislation carried on at a far distant seat of government, by a hostile majority, in an unknown tongue; and this too, notwithstanding we have petitioned in the humblest terms, for the establishment of a separate state government, and have, in accordance with the provisions of the national constitution, presented the general Congress, a republican constitution which was without just cause contemptuously rejected.

It incarcerated in a dungeon, for a long time, one of our citizens, for no other cause but a zealous endeavor to procure the acceptance of our constitution and the establishment of a state government.

It has failed and refused to secure on a firm basis, the right of trial by jury; that palladium of civil liberty, and only safe guarantee for the life, liberty, and property of the citizen.

It has failed to establish any public system of education, although possessed of almost boundless resources (the public domain) and, although, it is an axiom, in political science, that unless a people are educated and enlightened it is idle to expect the continuance of civil liberty, or the capacity for self-government.

It has suffered the military commandants stationed among us to exercise arbitrary acts of oppression and tyranny; thus trampling upon the most sacred rights of the citizen and rendering the military superior to the civil power.

It has dissolved by force of arms, the state Congress of Coahuila and Texas, and obliged our representatives to fly for their lives from the seat of government; thus depriving us of the fundamental political right of representation.

It has demanded the surrender of a number of our citizens, and ordered military detachments to seize and carry them into the Interior for trial; in contempt of the civil authorities, and in defiance of the laws and constitution.

It has made piratical attacks upon our commerce; by commissioning foreign desperadoes, and authorizing them to seize our vessels, and convey the property of our citizens to far distant ports of confiscation.

It denies us the right of worshiping the Almighty according to the dictates of our own consciences, by the support of a national religion calculated to promote the temporal interests of its human functionaries rather than the glory of the true and living God.

It has demanded us to deliver up our arms; which are essential to our defense, the rightful property of freemen, and formidable only to tyrannical governments.

It has invaded our country, both by sea and by land, with intent to lay waste our territory and drive us from our homes; and has now a large mercenary army advancing to carry on against us a war of extermination.

It has, through its emissaries, incited the merciless savage, with the tomahawk and scalping knife, to massacre the inhabitants of our defenseless frontiers.

It hath been, during the whole time of our connection with it, the contemptible sport and victim of successive military revolutions and hath continually exhibited every characteristic of a weak, corrupt and tyrannical government.

These, and other grievances, were patiently borne by the people of Texas until they reached that point at which forbearance ceases to be a virtue. We then took up arms in defense of the national constitution. We appealed to our Mexican brethren for assistance. Our appeal has been made in vain. Though months have elapsed, no sympathetic response has yet been heard from the Interior. We are, therefore, forced to the melancholy conclusion that the Mexican people have acquiesced in the destruction of their liberty, and the substitution therefor of a military government — that they are unfit to be free and incapable of self-government.

The necessity of self-preservation, therefore, now decrees our eternal political separation.

We, therefore, the delegates, with plenary powers, of the people of Texas, in solemn convention assembled, appealing to a candid world for the necessities of our condition, do hereby resolve and DECLARE that our political connection with the Mexican nation has forever ended; and that the people of Texas do now constitute a FREE, SOVEREIGN and INDEPENDENT REPUBLIC, and are fully invested with all the rights and attributes which properly belong to the independent nations; and, conscious of the rectitude of our intentions, we fearlessly and confidently commit the issue to the decision of the Supreme Arbiter of the destinies of nations.

RICHARD ELLIS, president of the convention and Delegate from Red River.

Charles B Stewart

Tho⁵ Barnett
John S.D. Byrom

Franᶜᵒ Ruiz
J. Antonio Navarro
Jesse B. Badgett
Wᵐ D. Lacey
William Menefee
Jnᵒ Fisher
Mathew Caldwell
William Mottley
Lorenzo de Zavala
Stephen H. Everitt
Geo W Smyth

Elijah Stapp
Claiborne West

Wᵐ B Scates

M.B. Menard
A.B. Hardin
J.W. Bunton
Tho⁵ J. Gasley
R. M. Coleman
Sterling C. Robertson
Benj Briggs Goodrich
G.W. Barnett
James G. Swisher
Jesse Grimes
S. Rhoads Fisher
John W. Moore
John W. Bower
Samˡ A Maverick from Bejar
Sam P. Carson
A. Briscoe
J.B. Woods
Jas Collinsworth
Edwin Waller
Asa Brigham
Geo. C. Childress
Bailey Hardeman
Rob. Potter

Thomas Jefferson Rusk
Chas. S. Taylor
John S. Roberts

Robert Hamilton
Collin McKinney
Albert H Latimer
James Power

Sam Houston
David Thomas

Edwᵈ Conrad
Martin Parmer
Edwin O. LeGrand
Stephen W. Blount
Ja⁵ Gaines
Wᵐ Clark, Jr
Sydney O. Penington
Wᵐ Carrol Crawford
Jnᵒ Turner

Test. H.S. Kimble, Secretary

Documents Concerning the Annexation
of Texas to the United States

For an overview of the subject, please see these discussions: *The New Handbook of Texas,* Texas State Historical Association, Austin, 1996; Vol. 1, pages 192–193. On the web: **www.tshaonline.org/handbook/online/articles/AA/ mga2.html**. Also see, the Texas State Library and Archives website: **www.tsl.state.tx.us/ref/abouttx/annexation/ index.html** and the Texas Almanac website: **www.texasalmanac.com/history/timeline/annexation/.**

Joint Resolution for Annexing

Texas to the United States

Resolved

by the Senate and House of Representatives of the United States of America in Congress assembled, That Congress doth consent that the territory properly included within and rightfully belonging to the Republic of Texas, may be erected into a new State to be called the State of Texas, with a republican form of government adopted by the people of said Republic, by deputies in convention assembled, with the consent of the existing Government in order that the same may by admitted as one of the States of this Union.

2. And be it further resolved, That the foregoing consent of Congress is given upon the following conditions, to wit: First, said state to be formed, subject to the adjustment by this government of all questions of boundary that may arise with other government, --and the Constitution thereof, with the proper evidence of its adoption by the people of said Republic of Texas, shall be transmitted to the President of the United States, to be laid before Congress for its final action on, or before the first day of January, one thousand eight hundred and forty-six. Second, said state when admitted into the Union, after ceding to the United States all public edifices, fortifications, barracks, ports and harbors, navy and navy yards, docks, magazines and armaments, and all other means pertaining to the public defense, belonging to the said Republic of Texas, shall retain funds, debts, taxes and dues of every kind which may belong to, or be due and owing to the said Republic; and shall also retain all the vacant and unappropriated lands lying within its limits, to be applied to the payment of the debts and liabilities of said Republic of Texas, and the residue of said lands, after discharging said debts and liabilities, to be disposed of as said State may direct; but in no event are said debts and liabilities to become a charge upon the Government of the United States. Third — New States

of convenient size not exceeding four in number, in addition to said State of Texas and having sufficient population, may, hereafter by the consent of said State, be formed out of the territory thereof, which shall be entitled to admission under the provisions of the Federal Constitution; and such states as may be formed out of the territory lying south of thirty-six degrees thirty minutes north latitude, commonly known as the Missouri Compromise Line, shall be admitted into the Union, with or without slavery, as the people of each State, asking admission shall desire; and in such State or States as shall be formed out of said territory, north of said Missouri Compromise Line, slavery, or involuntary servitude (except for crime) shall be prohibited.

3. And be it further resolved, That if the President of the United States shall in his judgment and discretion deem it most advisable, instead of proceeding to submit the foregoing resolution of the Republic of Texas, as an overture on the part of the United States for admission, to negotiate with the Republic; then,

Be it resolved, That a State, to be formed out of the present Republic of Texas, with suitable extent and boundaries, and with two representatives in Congress, until the next appointment of representation, shall be admitted into the Union, by virtue of this act, on an equal footing with the existing States, as soon as the terms and conditions of such admission, and the cession of the remaining Texian territory to the United States shall be agreed upon by the governments of Texas and the United States: And that the sum of one hundred thousand dollars be, and the same is hereby, appropriated to defray the expenses of missions and negotiations, to agree upon the terms of said admission and cession, either by treaty to be submitted to the Senate, or by articles to be submitted to the two houses of Congress, as the President may direct.

Approved, March 1, 1845.

Source: Peters, Richard, ed., The Public Statutes at Large of the United States of America, v.5, pp. 797–798, Boston, Chas. C. Little and Jas. Brown, 1850.

Twenty-Ninth Congress:
Session 1 — Resolutions
[No. 1.] Joint Resolution for the Admission of the State of Texas into the Union.

Whereas

the Congress of the United States, by a joint resolution approved March the first, eighteen hundred and forty-five, did consent that the territory properly included within, and rightfully belonging to, the Republic of Texas, might be erected into a new State, to be called _The State of Texas,_ with a republican form of government, to be adopted by the people of said republic, by deputies in convention assembled, with the consent of the existing government, in order that the same might be admitted as one of the States of the Union; which consent of Congress was given upon certain conditions specified in the first and second sections of said joint resolution; and whereas the people of the said Republic of Texas, by deputies in convention assembled, with the consent of the existing government, did adopt a constitution, and erect a new State with a republican form of government, and, in the name of the people of Texas, and by their authority, did ordain and declare that they assented to and accepted the proposals, conditions, and guaranties contained in said first and second sections of said resolution: and whereas the said constitution, with the proper evidence of its adoption by the people of the Republic of Texas, has been transmitted to the President of the United States and laid before Congress, in conformity to the provisions of said joint resolution:

Therefore—

Resolved by the Senate and House of Representatives of the United States of America in Congress assembled, That the State of Texas shall be one, and is hereby declared to be one, of the United States of America, and admitted into the Union on an equal footing with the original States in all respects whatever.

Sec. 2. And be it further resolved, That until the representatives in Congress shall be apportioned according to an actual enumeration of the inhabitants of the United States, the State of Texas shall be entitled to choose two representatives.

Approved, December 29, 1845.

SOURCE: Minot, Geo., ed., Statutes at Large and Treaties of the United States of America from Dec. 1, 1845, to March 3, 1851, V. IX, p. 108

Constitution of Texas

The complete official text of the Constitution of Texas, including the original document, which was adopted on Feb. 15, 1876, plus all amendments approved since that time, is available on the State of Texas website at this address: **http://www.constitution.legis. state.tx.us.** An index at that site points you to the Article and Section of the Constitution that deals with a particular subject.

For election information, upcoming elections, amendment or other election votes and voter registration information, go to: **www.sos.state.tx.us/elections/index.shtml.**

According to the **Legislative Reference Library of Texas**: "The Texas Constitution is one of the longest in the nation and is still growing. As of 2009 (81st Legislature), the Texas Legislature has passed a total of 643 amendments. Of these, 467 have been adopted and 176 have been defeated by Texas voters. Thus, **the Texas Constitution has been amended 467 times since its adoption in 1876.**"

Amendment of the Texas Constitution requires a two-thirds favorable vote by both the Texas House of Representatives and the Texas Senate, followed by a majority vote of approval by voters in a statewide election.

Prior to 1973, amendments to the constitution could not be submitted by a special session of the Legislature. But the constitution was amended in 1972 to allow submission of amendments if the special session was opened to the subject by the governor.

Constitutional amendments are not subject to a gubernatorial veto. Once submitted, voters have the final decision on whether to change the constitution as proposed.

The following table lists the total number of amendments submitted to voters by the Texas Legislature and shows the year in which the Legislature approved them for submission to voters; e.g., the 70th Legislature in 1987 approved 28 bills proposing amendments to be submitted to voters — 25 in 1987

Constitutional Amendments Submitted to Voters by the Texas Legislature

Year	No.	Year	No.	Year	No.
1879	1	1929	7	1977	15
1881	2	1931	9	1978	1
1883	5	1933	12	1979	12
1887	6	1935	13	1981	10
1889	2	1937	7	1982	3
1891	5	1939	4	1983	19
1893	2	1941	5	1985	17
1895	2	1943	3	1986	1
1897	5	1945	8	1987	28
1899	1	1947	9	1989	21
1901	1	1949	10	1990	1
1903	3	1951	7	1991	15
1905	3	1953	11	1993	18
1907	9	1955	9	1995	14
1909	4	1957	12	1997	15
1911	5	1959	4	1999	17
1913	7	1961	14	2001	20
1915	7	1963	7	2003	22
1917	3	1965	27	2005	9
1919	13	1967	20	2007	17
1921	5	1969	16	2009	11
1923	2	1971	18	2011	10
1925	4	1973	9		
1927	8	1975	12		

and 3 in 1988.

For more information on bills and constitutional amendments, see the Legislative Reference Library of Texas website at: **www.lrl.state.tx.us/legis/lrlhome. cfm**.

Amendments, 2009

*The following 11 amendments were submitted to the voters by the 81st Legislature in an election on **Nov. 3, 2009:***

HJR 7 — Authorizing the state to contribute money, property, and other resources for the establishment, maintenance, and operation of veterans hospitals in this state. **Passed:** 789,703 for; 265,627 against.

HJR 14 — Prohibiting the taking, damaging, or destroying of private property for public use unless the action is for the ownership, use, and enjoyment of the property by the State, a political subdivision of the State, the public at large, or entities granted the power of eminent domain under law or for the elimination of urban blight on a particular parcel of property, but not for certain economic development or enhancement of tax revenue purposes, and to limit the legislature's authority to grant the power of eminent domain to an entity. **Passed:** 848,651 for; 198,822 against.

HJR 14 — Establishing the national research university fund to enable emerging research universities in this state to achieve national prominence as major research universities and transferring the balance of the higher education fund to the national research university fund. **Passed:** 593,773 for; 453,319 against.

HJR 36 — Authorizing the legislature to provide for the ad valorem taxation of a residence homestead solely on the basis of the property's value as a residence homestead. **Passed:** 722,427 for; 336,559 against.

HJR 36 — Authorizing the legislature to authorize a single board of equalization for two or more adjoining appraisal entities that elect to provide for consolidated equalizations. **Passed:** 631,365 for; 390,080 against.

HJR 36 — Providing for uniform standards and procedures for the appraisal of property for ad valorem tax purposes. **Passed:** 691,294 for; 363,703 against.

HJR 85 — Providing that elected members of the governing boards of emergency services districts may serve terms not to exceed four years. **Passed:** 759,059 for; 279,566 against.

HJR 102 — Protecting the right of the public, individually and collectively, to access and use the public beaches bordering the seaward shore of the Gulf of Mexico. **Passed:** 805,362 for; 241,522 against.

HJR 116 — Authorizing the Veterans' Land Board to issue general obligation bonds in amounts equal to or less than amounts previously authorized. **Passed:** 672,285 for; 351,036 against.

HJR 127 — Allowing an officer or enlisted member of the Texas State Guard or other state militia or military force to hold other civil offices. **Passed:** 764,994 for; 281,855 against.

HJR 132 — Authorizing the financing, including through tax increment financing, of the acquisition by municipalities and counties of buffer areas or open spaces adjacent to a military installation for the prevention of encroachment or for the construction of roadways, utilities, or other infrastructure to protect or promote the mission of the military installation. **Passed:** 580,030 for; 470,746 against.

Amendments, 2011

*The following 10 amendments were submitted to the voters by the 82nd Legislature in an election on **Nov. 8, 2011:***

SJR 4 — Providing for the issuance of additional general obligation bonds by the Texas Water Development Board in an amount not to exceed $6 billion at any time outstanding.

SJR 9 — Authorizing the governor to grant a pardon to a person who successfully completes a term of deferred adjudication community supervision.

SJR 14 — Authorizing the legislature to provide for an exemption from ad valorem taxation of all or part of the market value of the residence homestead of the surviving spouse of a 100 percent or totally disabled veteran.

SJR 16 — Providing for the appraisal for ad valorem tax purposes of open-space land devoted to water-stewardship purposes on the basis of its productive capacity.

SJR 26 — Authorizing the legislature to allow cities or counties to enter into interlocal contracts with other cities or counties without the imposition of a tax or the provision of a sinking fund.

SJR 28 — Authorizing the legislature to permit conservation and reclamation districts in El Paso County to issue bonds supported by ad valorem taxes to fund the development and maintenance of parks and recreational facilities.

SJR 37 — Changing the length of the unexpired term that causes the automatic resignation of certain elected county or district officeholders if they become candidates for another office.

SJR 50 — Providing for the issuance of general obligation bonds of the State of Texas to finance educational loans to students.

HJR 63 — Authorizing the legislature to permit a county to issue bonds or notes to finance the development or redevelopment of an unproductive, undeveloped, or blighted area and to pledge for repayment of the bonds or notes increases in ad valorem taxes imposed by the county on property in the area. The amendment does not provide authority for increasing ad valorem tax rates.

HJR 109 — Clarifying references to the permanent school fund, allowing the General Land Office to distribute revenue from permanent school fund land or other properties to the available school fund to provide additional funding for public education, and providing for an increase in the market value of the permanent school fund for the purpose of allowing increased distributions from the available school fund. ☆

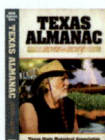

Monument Dedicated to 19th Century African-American Legislators and Constitutional Convention Delegates

During the era of Reconstruction in Texas, 52 African-American men served Texas either in the State Legislature or as delegates to the Constitutional Convention. On March 30, 2010, a monument dedicated to these men was unveiled during a ceremony at the Texas State Cemetery in Austin *(see photo, above)*. An online exhibit about these pioneering men can be found at www.tsl.state.tx.us/exhibits/forever/index.html.

Project Director Larry A. Thomas stands next to the monument dedicated to the 52 African-American state legislators and constitutional convention delegates of the 19th century, who are listed at right. The monument is installed in the Texas State Cemetery in Austin. Photos courtesy of Larry A. Thomas.

David Abner, Sr.
Richard Allen
Edward Anderson
Alexander Asberry
Houston A.P. Bassett
Thomas Beck
Edward Brown
Charles W. Bryant
D.W. Burley
Walter Moses Burton
Silas Cotton
Stephen Curtis
Bird Davis
Goldstein Dupree
Robert J. Evans
Jacob E. Freeman
Matthew Gaines
Harriel G. Geiger
Melvin Goddin
Bedford A. Guy
Nathan H. Haller
Jeremiah J. Hamilton
William H. Holland
Wiley W. Johnson
Mitchell Kendall
Robert A. Kerr
Doc C. Lewis

Ralph Long
Lloyd Henry McCabe
James McWashington
Elias Mayes
David Medlock
John Mitchell
Henry Moore
Robert J. Moore
Sheppard Mullens
Edward Patton
Henry Phelps
William Reynolds
Walter E. Ripton
Meshack R. Roberts
George Thompson Ruby
Alonzo Sledge
Robert Lloyd Smith
Henry Sneed
James H. Stewart
James H. Washington
Benjamin O. Watrous
Allen W. Wilder
Benjamin Franklin Williams
Richard Williams
George W. Wyatt

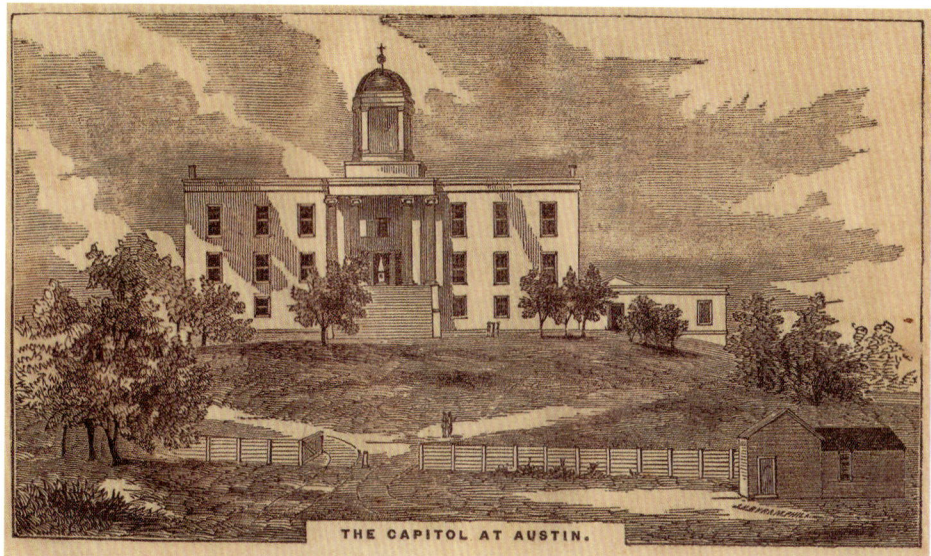

"The Capitol at Austin" from the Texas Almanac 1858. Search the Almanac Archive: www.TexasAlmanac.com/archive.

Texas' Chief Governmental Officials

On this and the following pages are lists of the principal administrative officials who have served the Republic and State of Texas with dates of their tenures of office. In a few instances, there are disputes as to the exact dates of tenures. Dates listed here are those that appear the most authentic.

★ ★ ★ ★ ★ ★ ★

Governors and Presidents

*Spanish Royal Governors

Domingo Terán de los Rios	1691–1692
Gregorio de Salinas Varona	1692–1697
Francisco Cuerbo y Valdés	1698–1702
Mathías de Aguirre	1703–1705
Martín de Alarcón	1705–1708
Simón Padilla y Córdova	1708–1712
Pedro Fermin de Echevers y Subisa	1712–1714
Juan Valdéz	1714–1716
Martín de Alarcón	1716–1719
José de Azlor y Virto de Vera, Marqués de San Miguel de Aguayo	1719–1722
Fernando Pérez de Almazán	1722–1727
Melchor de Mediavilla y Azcona	1727–1731
Juan Antonio Bustillo y Ceballos	1731–1734
Manuel de Sandoval	1734–1736
Carlos Benites Franquis de Lugo	1736–1737
Joseph Fernández de Jáuregui y Urrutia	1737–1737
Prudencio de Orobio y Basterra	1737–1741
Tomás Felipe Winthuisen (or Winthuysen)	1741–1743
Justo Boneo y Morales	1743–1744
Francisco García Larios	1744–1748
Pedro del Barrio Junco y Espriella	1748–1750
Jacinto de Barrios y Jáuregui	1751–1759
Angel de Martos y Navarrete	1759–1767
Hugo Oconór	1767–1770
Juan María Vicencio, Barón de Ripperdá	1770–1778
Domingo Cabello y Robles	1778–1786
Rafael Martínez Pacheco	1787–1790
Manuel Muñoz	1790–1799
Juan Bautista de Elguezábal	1799–1805
Antonio Cordero y Bustamante	1805–1808

Manuel María de Salcedo	1808–1813
Juan Bautista de las Casas (revolutionary gov.)	1811–1811
Cristóbal Domínguez, Benito de Armiñan, Mariano Varela, Juan Ignacio Pérez, Manuel Pardo	1813–1817
Antonio María Martínez	1817–1821

Some authorities would include Texas under administrations of several earlier Spanish Governors. The late Dr. C.E. Castañeda, Latin-American librarian of The University of Texas and authority on the history of Texas and the Southwest, would include the following four: Francisco de Garay, 1523–26; Pánfilo de Narváez, 1526–28; Nuño de Guzmán, 1528–30; Hernando de Soto, 1538–43.

Governors Under Mexican Rule

The first two Governors under Mexican rule, Trespalacios and García, were of Texas only as Texas was then constituted. Beginning with Gonzáles, 1824, the Governors were for the joint State of Coahuila y Texas.

José Felix Trespalacios	1822–1823
Luciano García	1823–1824
Rafael Gonzáles	1824–1826
Victor Blanco	1826–1827
José María Viesca	1827–1830
Ramón Eca y Músquiz	1830–1831
José María Letona	1831–1832
Ramón Eca y Músquiz	1832–1832
Juan Martín de Veramendi	1832–1833
Juan José de Vidáurri y Villasenor	1833–1834
Juan José Elguezábal	1834–1835
José María Cantú	1835–1835
Agustín M. Viesca	1835–1835
Marciel Borrego	1835–1835
Ramón Eca y Músquiz	1835–1835

Provisional Colonial Governor, Before Independence

Henry Smith (Impeached)	1835

James W. Robinson served as acting Governor just prior to March 2, 1836, after Smith was impeached.

Presidents of the Republic of Texas

David G. Burnet .... Mar. 16, 1836–Oct. 22, 1836
(provisional President)
Sam Houston .... Oct. 22, 1836–Dec. 10, 1838
Mirabeau B. Lamar .... Dec. 10, 1838–Dec. 13, 1841
Sam Houston .... Dec. 13, 1841–Dec. 9, 1844
Anson Jones .... Dec. 9, 1844–Feb. 19, 1846

Governors Since Annexation

J. Pinckney Henderson.... Feb. 19, 1846–Dec. 21, 1847

(Albert C. Horton served as acting Governor while Henderson was away in the Mexican War.)

George T. Wood .... Dec. 21, 1847–Dec. 21, 1849
Peter Hansbrough Bell .... Dec. 21, 1849–Nov. 23, 1853
J. W. Henderson .... Nov. 23, 1853–Dec. 21, 1853
Elisha M. Pease............... Dec. 21, 1853–Dec. 21, 1857
Hardin R. Runnels .... Dec. 21, 1857–Dec. 21, 1859
Sam Houston (resigned because of state's secession
from the Union) .... Dec. 21, 1859–Mar. 16, 1861
Edward Clark .... Mar. 16, 1861–Nov. 7, 1861
Francis R. Lubbock (resigned to enter Confederate
Army) .... Nov. 7, 1861–Nov. 5, 1863
Pendleton Murrah (administration terminated by
fall of Confederacy)..... Nov. 5, 1863–June 17, 1865
Fletcher S. Stockdale (Lt. Gov. performed some duties
of office on Murrah's departure, but is sometimes
included in list of Governors. Hamilton's appoint-
ment was for immediate succession, as shown by
the dates.)
Andrew J. Hamilton (Provisional, appointed by
President Johnson).....June 17, 1865–Aug. 9, 1866
James W. Throckmorton...... Aug. 9, 1866–Aug. 8, 1867
Elisha M. Pease (appointed July 30, 1867, under
martial law) .... Aug. 8, 1867–Sept. 30, 1869

Interregnum

Pease resigned and vacated office Sept. 30, 1869; no successor was named until Jan. 8, 1870. Some historians extend Pease's term until Jan. 8, 1870, but in reality Texas was without a head of its civil government from Sept. 30, 1869, until Jan. 8, 1870.

Edmund J. Davis (appointed provisional Governor
after being elected) ...... Jan. 8, 1870–Jan. 15, 1874
Richard Coke (resigned to enter United States
Senate) .... Jan. 15, 1874–Dec. 1, 1876
Richard B. Hubbard............Dec. 1, 1876–Jan. 21, 1879
Oran M. Roberts .... Jan. 21, 1879–Jan. 16, 1883
John Ireland .... Jan. 16, 1883–Jan. 18, 1887
Lawrence Sullivan Ross ... Jan. 18, 1887–Jan. 20, 1891
James Stephen Hogg....... Jan. 20, 1891–Jan. 15, 1895
Charles A. Culberson........ Jan. 15, 1895–Jan. 17, 1899
Joseph D. Sayers .... Jan. 17, 1899–Jan. 20, 1903
S. W. T. Lanham .... Jan. 20, 1903–Jan. 15, 1907
Thos. Mitchell Campbell ....Jan. 15, 1907–Jan. 17, 1911
Oscar Branch Colquitt ....Jan. 17, 1911–Jan. 19, 1915
James E. Ferguson
(impeached)................Jan. 19, 1915–Aug. 25, 1917
William Pettus Hobby ....Aug. 25, 1917–Jan. 18, 1921
Pat Morris Neff.................. Jan. 18, 1921–Jan. 20, 1925
Miriam A. Ferguson .... Jan. 20, 1925–Jan. 17, 1927
Dan Moody .... Jan. 17, 1927–Jan. 20, 1931
Ross S. Sterling................ Jan. 20, 1931–Jan. 17, 1933
Miriam A. Ferguson .... Jan. 17, 1933–Jan. 15, 1935
James V. Allred................. Jan. 15, 1935–Jan. 17, 1939
W. Lee O'Daniel (*resigned to enter United States
Senate*) ....Jan. 17, 1939–Aug. 4, 1941
Coke R. Stevenson............Aug. 4, 1941–Jan. 21, 1947
Beauford H. Jester............Jan. 21, 1947–July 11, 1949

Allan Shivers (*Lt. Governor succeeded on death of
Governor Jester. Elected in 1950 and re-elected
in 1952 and 1954*)....... July 11, 1949–Jan. 15, 1957
Price Daniel .... Jan. 15, 1957–Jan. 15, 1963
John Connally................... Jan. 15, 1963–Jan. 21, 1969
Preston Smith .... Jan. 21, 1969–Jan. 16, 1973
*Dolph Briscoe................. Jan. 16, 1973–Jan. 16, 1979
**William P. Clements....... Jan. 16, 1979–Jan. 18, 1983
Mark White .... Jan. 18, 1983–Jan. 20, 1987
**William P. Clements....... Jan. 20, 1987–Jan. 15, 1991
Ann W. Richards.............. Jan. 15, 1991–Jan. 17, 1995
**George W. Bush ....Jan. 17, 1995–Dec. 21, 2000
**Rick Perry   (*Lt. Gov. succeeded on inauguration of
Bush as U.S. President*) ....Dec. 21, 2000–present

*Effective in 1975, term of office was raised to 4 years, according to a constitutional amendment approved by Texas voters in 1972. See introduction to State Government chapter in this edition for other state officials whose terms were raised to four years.
**Republicans.

★ ★ ★ ★ ★ ★ ★

Vice Presidents and Lieutenant Governors
Vice Presidents of the Republic

	Date Elected
Lorenzo de Zavala (*provisional Vice President*)	
Mirabeau B. Lamar	Sept. 5, 1836
David G. Burnet	Sept. 3, 1838
Edward Burleson	Sept. 6, 1841
Kenneth L. Anderson	Sept. 2, 1844

State Lieutenant Governors

Albert C. Horton.................................... 1846–1847
John A. Greer 1847–1851
J. W. Henderson ....Aug. 4, 1851
D. C. Dickson.. 1853–1855
H. R. Runnels ....Aug. 6, 1855
F. R. Lubbock................................Aug. 4, 1857
Edward Clark ....Aug. 1, 1859
John M. Crockett 1861–1863
Fletcher S. Stockdale 1863–1866
George W. Jones...1866

(Jones was removed by General Sheridan.)

J. W. Flanagan...1869

(Flanagan was appointed U.S. Senator and was never inaugurated as Lt. Gov.)

R. B. Hubbard.. 1873–1876
J. D. Sayers.. 1878–1880
L. J. Storey 1880–1882
Marion Martin.. 1882–1884
Barnett Gibbs.. 1884–1886
T. B. Wheeler 1886–1890
George C. Pendleton.............................. 1890–1892
M. M. Crane..................... Jan. 17, 1893–Jan. 25, 1895
George T. Jester 1895–1898
J. N. Browning 1898–1902
George D. Neal...................................... 1902–1906
A. B. Davidson...................................... 1906–1912
Will H. Mayes.. 1912–1914
William Pettus Hobby 1914–1917
W. A. Johnson (*served Hobby's unexpired
term and until*............................... Jan. 1920)
Lynch Davidson 1920–1922
T. W. Davidson...................................... 1922–1924
Barry Miller 1924–1931
Edgar E. Witt 1931–1935
Walter Woodul 1935–1939
Coke R. Stevenson................................ 1939–1941
John Lee Smith............................. 1943–Jan. 21, 1947
Allan Shivers..................... Jan. 21, 1947–July 11, 1949

(Shivers succeeded to the governorship on death of Governor Beauford H. Jester.)

Ben Ramsey 1951–Sept. 18, 1961

(Ben Ramsey resigned to become a member of the State Railroad Commission.)

Preston Smith 1963–1969
Ben Barnes 1969–1973
William P. Hobby Jr. 1973–1991
Robert D. Bullock 1991–1999
Rick Perry 1999–Dec. 21, 2000
*Bill Ratliff ....Dec. 28, 2000–Jan. 21, 2003
David Dewhurst .... Jan. 21, 2003–present

*Elected by Senate when Rick Perry succeeded to governorship on election of George W. Bush as U.S. President.

★ ★ ★ ★ ★ ★ ★

Secretaries of State

Of the Republic

Raines Yearbook for Texas, 1901, gives the following record of Secretaries of State during the era of the Republic of Texas:

Under David G. Burnet — Samuel P. Carson, James Collingsworth and W. H. Jack.

Under Sam Houston (first term) — Stephen F. Austin, 1836. J. Pinckney Henderson and Dr. Robert A. Irion, 1837–38.

Under Mirabeau B. Lamar — Bernard Bee appointed Dec. 16, 1838; James Webb appointed Feb. 6, 1839; D. G. Burnet appointed Acting Secretary of State, May 31, 1839; N. Amory appointed Acting Secretary of State, July 23, 1839; D. G. Burnet appointed Acting Secretary of State, Aug. 5, 1839; Abner S. Lipscomb appointed Secretary of State, Jan. 31, 1840, and resigned Jan. 22, 1841; Joseph Waples appointed Acting Secretary of State, Jan. 23, 1841, and served until Feb. 8, 1841; James S. Mayfield appointed Feb. 8, 1841; Joseph Waples appointed April 30, 1841, and served until May 25, 1841; Samuel A. Roberts appointed May 25, 1841; reappointed Sept. 7, 1841.

Under Sam Houston (second term) — E. Lawrence Stickney, Acting Secretary of State until Anson Jones appointed Dec. 13, 1841. Jones served as Secretary of State throughout this term except during the summer and part of this term of 1842, when Joseph Waples filled the position as Acting Secretary of State.

Under Anson Jones — Ebenezer Allen served from Dec. 10, 1844, until Feb. 5, 1845, when Ashbel Smith became Secretary of State. Allen was again named Acting Secretary of State, March 31, 1845, and later named Secretary of State.

(In addition to the above, documents in the Texas State Archives indicate that Joseph C. Eldredge, Chief Clerk of the State Department during much of the Republic's existence, signed a number of documents in the absence of the office-holder in the capacity of "Acting Secretary of State.")

State Secretaries of State

Charles Mariner .... Feb. 20, 1846–May 4, 1846
David G. Burnet .... May 4, 1846–Jan. 1, 1848
Washington D. Miller .... Jan. 1, 1848–Jan. 2, 1850
James Webb .... Jan. 2, 1850–Nov. 14, 1851
Thomas H. Duval .... Nov. 14, 1851–Dec. 22, 1853
Edward Clark .... Dec. 22, 1853–Dec. 1857
T. S. Anderson .... Dec. 1857–Dec. 27, 1859
E. W. Cave ....Dec. 27, 1859–Mar. 16, 1861
Bird Holland ....Mar. 16, 1861–Nov. 1861
Charles West .... Nov. 1861–Sept. 1862
Robert J. Townes .... Sept. 1862–May 2, 1865
Charles R. Pryor ....May 2, 1865–Aug. 1865
James H. Bell .... Aug. 1865–Aug. 1866
John A. Green .... Aug. 1866–Aug. 1867
D. W. C. Phillips ....Aug. 1867–Jan. 1870
J. P. Newcomb .... Jan. 1, 1870–Jan. 17, 1874
George Clark .... Jan. 17, 1874–Jan. 27, 1874
A. W. DeBerry ....Jan. 27, 1874–Dec. 1, 1876
Isham G. Searcy ....Dec. 1, 1876–Jan. 23, 1879
J. D. Templeton .... Jan. 23, 1879–Jan. 22, 1881
T. H. Bowman .... Jan. 22, 1881–Jan. 18, 1883
J. W. Baines .... Jan. 18, 1883–Jan. 21, 1887
John M. Moore .... Jan. 21, 1887–Jan. 22, 1891
George W. Smith .... Jan. 22, 1891–Jan. 17, 1895
Allison Mayfield .... Jan. 17, 1895–Jan. 5, 1897
J. W. Madden .... Jan. 5, 1897–Jan. 18, 1899
D. H. Hardy .... Jan. 18, 1899–Jan. 19, 1901
John G. Tod .... Jan. 19, 1901–Jan., 1903
J. R. Curl ....Jan. 1903–April 1905
O. K. Shannon .... April 1905–Jan. 1907
L. T. Dashiel ....Jan. 1907–Feb. 1908
W. R. Davie ....Feb. 1908–Jan. 1909
W. B. Townsend ....Jan. 1909–Jan. 1911
C. C. McDonald ....Jan. 1911–Dec. 1912
J. T. Bowman ....Dec. 1912–Jan. 1913
John L. Wortham .... Jan. 1913–June 1913
F. C. Weinert................................June 1913–Nov. 1914
D. A. Gregg ....Nov. 1914–Jan. 1915
John G. McKay ....Jan. 1915–Dec. 1916
C. J. Bartlett.................................. Dec. 1916–Nov. 1917
George F. Howard ....Nov. 1917–Nov. 1920
C. D. Mims....................................Nov. 1920–Jan. 1921
S. L. Staples .... Jan. 1921–Aug. 1924
J. D. Strickland ....Sept. 1924–Jan. 1, 1925
Henry Hutchings .... Jan. 1, 1925–Jan. 20, 1925
Mrs. Emma G. Meharg .... Jan. 20, 1925–Jan. 1927
Mrs. Jane Y. McCallum .... Jan. 1927–Jan. 1933

Early Leaders of Texas

The presidents of the Republic of Texas and the state's first Governor, from far left: David G. Burnet, provisional president; Sam Houston, second and fourth presidents; Mirabeau B. Lamar, third president; Anson Jones, the Republic's last president; and J. Pinckney Henderson, the Lone Star State's first governor.

W. W. Heath	Jan. 1933–Jan. 1935
Gerald C. Mann	Jan. 1935–Aug. 31, 1935
R. B. Stanford	Aug. 31, 1935–Aug. 25, 1936
B. P. Matocha	Aug. 25, 1936–Jan. 18, 1937
Edward Clark	Jan. 18, 1937–Jan. 1939
Tom L. Beauchamp	Jan. 1939–Oct. 1939
M. O. Flowers	Oct. 26, 1939–Feb. 25, 1941
William J. Lawson	Feb. 25, 1941–Jan. 1943
Sidney Latham	Jan. 1943–Feb. 1945
Claude Isbell	Feb. 1945–Jan. 1947
Paul H. Brown	Jan. 1947–Jan. 19, 1949
Ben Ramsey	Jan. 19, 1949–Feb. 9, 1950
John Ben Shepperd	Feb. 9, 1950–April 30, 1952
Jack Ross	April 30, 1952–Jan. 9, 1953
Howard A. Carney	Jan. 9, 1953–Apr. 30, 1954
C. E. Fulgham	May 1, 1954–Feb. 15, 1955
Al Muldrow	Feb. 16, 1955–Nov. 1, 1955
Tom Reavley	Nov. 1, 1955–Jan. 16, 1957
Zollie Steakley	Jan. 16, 1957–Jan. 2, 1962
P. Frank Lake	Jan. 2, 1962–Jan. 15, 1963
Crawford C. Martin	Jan. 15, 1963–March 12, 1966
John L. Hill	March 12, 1966–Jan. 22, 1968
Roy Barrera	March 7, 1968–Jan. 23, 1969
Martin Dies Jr.	Jan. 23, 1969–Sept. 1, 1971
Robert D. (Bob) Bullock	Sept. 1, 1971–Jan. 2, 1973
V. Larry Teaver Jr.	Jan. 2, 1973–Jan. 19, 1973
Mark W. White Jr.	Jan. 19, 1973–Oct. 27,1977
Steven C. Oaks	Oct. 27, 1977–Jan. 16, 1979
George W. Strake Jr.	Jan. 16, 1979–Oct. 6, 1981
David A. Dean	Oct. 22, 1981–Jan. 18, 1983
John Fainter	Jan. 18, 1983–July 31, 1984
Myra A. McDaniel	Sept. 6, 1984–Jan. 26, 1987
Jack Rains	Jan. 26, 1987–June 15, 1989
George Bayoud Jr.	June 19, 1989–Jan. 15, 1991
John Hannah Jr.	Jan. 17, 1991–March 11, 1994
Ronald Kirk	April 4, 1994–Jan. 10, 1995
Antonio O. "Tony" Garza Jr.	Jan. 18, 1995–Dec. 2, 1997
Alberto R. Gonzales	Dec. 2, 1997–Jan. 10, 1999
Elton Bomer	Jan. 11, 1999–Dec. 31, 2000
Henry Cuellar	Jan. 2, 2001–Oct. 5, 2001
Gwyn Shea	Jan. 2, 2002–Aug. 4, 2003
Geoff Connor	Sept. 26, 2003–Jan. 1, 2005
J. Roger Williams	Jan. 1, 2005–July 1, 2007
Phil Wilson	July 1, 2007–July 6, 2008
Esperanza (Hope) Andrade	July 23, 2008–present

★ ★ ★ ★ ★ ★ ★

Attorneys General
Of the Republic

David Thomas and
  Peter W. Grayson .... Mar. 2–Oct. 22, 1836
J. Pinckney Henderson, Peter W. Grayson,
  John Birdsall, A. S. Thurston 1836–1838

J. C. Watrous	Dec. 1838–June 1, 1840
Joseph Webb and F. A. Morris	1840–1841
George W. Terrell, Ebenezer Allen	1841–1844
Ebenezer Allen	1844–1846

*Of the State

Volney E. Howard	Feb. 21, 1846–May 7, 1846
John W. Harris	May 7, 1846–Oct. 31, 1849
Henry P. Brewster	Oct. 31, 1849–Jan. 15, 1850
A. J. Hamilton	Jan. 15, 1850–Aug. 5, 1850
Ebenezer Allen	Aug. 5, 1850–Aug. 2, 1852
Thomas J. Jennings	Aug. 2, 1852–Aug. 4, 1856
James Willie	Aug. 4, 1856–Aug. 2, 1858
Malcolm D. Graham	Aug. 2, 1858–Aug. 6, 1860
George M. Flournoy	Aug. 6, 1860–Jan. 15, 1862
N. G. Shelley	Feb. 3, 1862–Aug. 1, 1864
B. E. Tarver	Aug. 1, 1864–Dec. 11, 1865
Wm. Alexander	Dec. 11, 1865–June 25, 1866
W. M. Walton	June 25, 1866–Aug. 27, 1867
Wm. Alexander	Aug. 27, 1867–Nov. 5, 1867
Ezekiel B. Turner	Nov. 5, 1867–July 11, 1870
Wm. Alexander	July 11, 1870–Jan. 27, 1874
George Clark	Jan. 27, 1874–Apr. 25, 1876
H. H. Boone	Apr. 25, 1876–Nov. 5, 1878
George McCormick	Nov. 5, 1878–Nov. 2, 1880
J. H. McLeary	Nov. 2, 1880–Nov. 7, 1882
John D. Templeton	Nov. 7, 1882–Nov. 2, 1886
James S. Hogg	Nov. 2, 1886–Nov. 4, 1890
C. A. Culberson	Nov. 4, 1890–Nov. 6, 1894
M. M. Crane	Nov. 6, 1894–Nov. 8, 1898
Thomas S. Smith	Nov. 8, 1898–Mar. 15,1901
C. K. Bell	Mar. 20, 1901–Jan., 1904
R. V. Davidson	Jan. 1904–Dec. 31, 1909
Jewel P. Lightfoot	Jan. 1, 1910–Aug. 31, 1912
James D. Walthall	Sept. 1, 1912–Jan. 1, 1913
B. F. Looney	Jan. 1, 1913–Jan., 1919
C. M. Cureton	Jan. 1919–Dec. 1921
W. A. Keeling	Dec. 1921–Jan. 1925
Dan Moody	Jan. 1925–Jan. 1927
Claude Pollard	Jan. 1927–Sept. 1929
R. L. Bobbitt (Apptd.)	Sept. 1929–Jan. 1931
James V. Allred	Jan. 1931–Jan. 1935
William McCraw	Jan. 1935–Jan. 1939
Gerald C. Mann (resigned)	Jan. 1939–Jan. 1944
Grover Sellers	Jan. 1944–Jan. 1947
Price Daniel	Jan. 1947–Jan. 1953
John Ben Shepperd	Jan. 1953–Jan. 1, 1957
Will Wilson	Jan. 1, 1957–Jan. 15, 1963
Waggoner Carr	Jan. 15, 1963–Jan. 1, 1967
Crawford C. Martin	Jan. 1, 1967–Dec. 29, 1972
John Hill	Jan. 1, 1973–Jan. 16, 1979
Mark White	Jan. 16, 1979–Jan. 18, 1983
Jim Mattox	Jan. 18, 1983–Jan. 15, 1991
Dan Morales	Jan. 15, 1991–Jan. 13, 1999
John Cornyn	Jan. 13, 1999–Dec. 2, 2002

Greg Abbott................................Dec. 2, 2002–present

The first few Attorneys General held office by appointment of the Governor. The office was made elective in 1850 by constitutional amendment. Ebenezer Allen was the first elected Attorney General.

★ ★ ★ ★ ★ ★

Treasurers
Of the Republic

Asa Brigham	1838–1840
James W. Simmons	1840–1841
Asa Brigham	1841–1844
Moses Johnson	1844–1846

Of the State

James H. Raymond	Feb. 24, 1846–Aug. 2, 1858
*C. H. Randolph	Aug. 2, 1858–June 1865
*Samuel Harris	Oct. 2, 1865–June 25, 1866
W. M. Royston	June 25, 1866–Sept. 1, 1867
John Y. Allen	Sept. 1, 1867–Jan. 1869
S. L. Staples	Jan. 1869–Jan. 1874
**George W. Honey	Jan. 1869–Jan. 1874
**B. Graham (short term)	beginning May 27, 1872
A. J. Dorn	Jan. 1874–Jan. 1879
F. R. Lubbock	Jan. 1879–Jan. 1891
W. B. Wortham	Jan. 1891–Jan. 1899
John W. Robbins	Jan. 1899–Jan. 1907
Sam Sparks	Jan. 1907–Jan. 1912
J. M. Edwards	Jan. 1912–Jan. 1919
John W. Baker	Jan. 1919–Jan. 1921
G. N. Holton	July 1921–Nov. 21, 1921
C. V. Terrell	Nov. 21, 1921–Aug. 15, 1924
S. L. Staples	Aug. 16, 1924–Jan. 15, 1925
W. Gregory Hatcher	Jan. 16, 1925–Jan. 1, 1931
Charley Lockhart	Jan. 1, 1931–Oct. 25, 1941
Jesse James	Oct. 25, 1941–Sept. 29, 1977
Warren G. Harding	Oct. 7, 1977–Jan. 3, 1983
Ann Richards	Jan. 3, 1983–Jan. 2, 1991
Kay Bailey Hutchison	Jan. 2, 1991–June 1993
†Martha Whitehead	June 1993–Aug. 1996

Randolph fled to Mexico upon collapse of Confederacy. No exact date is available for his departure from office or for Harris' succession to the post. It is believed Harris took office Oct. 2, 1865.

**Honey was removed from office for a short period in 1872 and B. Graham served in his place.*

† The office of Treasurer was eliminated by constitutional amendment in an election Nov. 7, 1995, effective the last day of August 1996.

★ ★ ★ ★ ★ ★

Railroad Commission of Texas

(After the first three names in the following list, each commissioner's name is followed by a surname in parentheses. The name in parentheses is the name of the commissioner whom that commissioner succeeded.)

John H. Reagan	June 10, 1891–Jan. 20, 1903
L. L. Foster	June 10, 1891–April 30, 1895
W. P. McLean	June 10, 1891–Nov. 20, 1894
L. J. Storey (McLean)	Nov. 21, 1894–Mar. 28,1909
N. A. Stedman (Foster)	May 1, 1895–Jan. 4, 1897
Allison Mayfield (Stedman)	Jan. 5, 1897–Jan. 23, 1923
O. B. Colquitt (Reagan)	Jan. 21, 1903–Jan. 17, 1911
William D. Williams (Storey)	April 28, 1909–Oct. 1, 1916
John L. Wortham (Colquitt)	Jan. 21, 1911–Jan. 1, 1913
Earle B. Mayfield (Wortham)	Jan. 2, 1913–March 1, 1923
Charles Hurdleston (Williams)	Oct. 10, 1916–Dec. 31,1918
Clarence Gilmore (Hurdleston)	Jan. 1, 1919–Jan. 1, 1929
N. A. Nabors (A. Mayfield)	March 1, 1923–Jan. 18, 1925

William Splawn (E. Mayfield)

	March 1, 1923–Aug. 1, 1924
C. V. Terrell (Splawn)	Aug. 15, 1924–Jan. 1, 1939
Lon A. Smith (Nabors)	Jan. 29, 1925–Jan. 1, 1941
Pat M. Neff (Gilmore)	Jan. 1, 1929–Jan. 1, 1933
Ernest O. Thompson (Neff)	Jan. 1, 1933–Jan. 8, 1965
G. A. (Jerry) Sadler (Terrell)	Jan. 1, 1939–Jan. 1, 1943
Olin Culberson (Smith)	Jan. 1, 1941–June 22, 1961
Beauford Jester (Sadler)	Jan. 1, 1943–Jan. 21, 1947
William J. Murray Jr. (Jester)	Jan. 21, 1947–Apr. 10, 1963
Ben Ramsey (Culberson)	Sept. 18, 1961–Dec. 31, 1976
Jim C. Langdon (Murray)	May 28, 1963–Dec. 31, 1977
Byron Tunnell (Thompson)	Jan. 11, 1965–Sept. 15, 1973
Mack Wallace (Tunnell)	Sept. 18, 1973–Sept. 22, 1987
Jon Newton (Ramsey)	Jan. 10, 1977–Jan. 4, 1979
John H. Poerner (Langdon)	Jan. 2, 1978–Jan. 1, 1981
James E. Nugent (Newton)	Jan. 4, 1979–Jan. 3,1995
Buddy Temple (Poerner)	Jan. 2, 1981–March 2, 1986
Clark Jobe (Temple)	March 3, 1986–Jan. 5, 1987
John Sharp (Jobe	Jan. 6, 1987–Jan. 2, 1991
Kent Hance (Wallace)	Sept. 23, 1987–Jan. 2, 1991
*Robert Krueger (Hance)	Jan. 3, 1991–Jan. 22, 1993
Lena Guerrero (Sharp)	Jan. 23, 1991–Sept. 25, 1992
James Wallace (Guerrero)	Oct. 2, 1992–Jan. 4, 1993
Barry Williamson (Wallace)	Jan. 5, 1993–Jan. 4, 1999
Mary Scott Nabors (Krueger)	Feb. 9, 1993–Dec. 9, 1994
Carole K. Rylander (Nabors)	Dec. 10, 1994–Jan. 4, 1999
Charles Matthews (Nugent)	Jan. 3, 1995–Jan. 31, 2005
Antonio Garza (Williamson)	Jan. 4, 1999–Nov. 18, 2002
Michael Williams (Rylander)	Jan. 4, 1999–July 8, 2011
Victor G. Carrillo (Garza)	Feb. 19, 2003–Jan. 1, 2011
Elizabeth A. Jones (Matthews)	Feb. 2, 2005–present
David Porter (Carrillo)	Jan. 1, 2011–present
Barry T. Smitherman (Williams)	July 8, 2011–present

* Robert Krueger resigned when Gov. Ann Richards appointed him interim U.S. Senator on the resignation of Sen. Lloyd Bentsen.

★ ★ ★ ★ ★ ★

Comptroller of Public Accounts
Of the Republic

John H. Money	Dec. 30, 1835–Jan. 17, 1836
H. C. Hudson	Jan. 17, 1836–Oct. 22, 1836
E. M. Pease	June 1837–Dec. 1837
F. R. Lubbock	Dec. 1837–Jan. 1839
Jas. W. Simmons	Jan. 15, 1839–Sept. 30, 1840
Jas. B. Shaw	Sept. 30, 1840–Dec. 24, 1841
F. R. Lubbock	Dec. 24, 1841–Jan. 1, 1842
Jas. B. Shaw	Jan. 1, 1842–Jan. 1, 1846

Of the State

Jas. B. Shaw	Feb. 24, 1846–Aug. 2, 1858
Clement R. Johns	Aug. 2, 1858–Aug. 1, 1864
Willis L. Robards	Aug. 1, 1864–Oct. 12, 1865
Albert R. Latimer	Oct. 12, 1865–Mar. 27, 1866
Robert H. Taylor	Mar. 27, 1866–June 25, 1866
Willis L. Robards	June 25, 1866–Aug. 27, 1867
Morgan C. Hamilton	Aug. 27, 1867–Jan. 8, 1870
A. Bledsoe	Jan. 8, 1870–Jan. 20, 1874
Stephen H. Darden	Jan. 20, 1974–Nov. 2, 1880
W. M. Brown	Nov. 2, 1880–Jan. 16, 1883
W. J. Swain	Jan. 16, 1883–Jan. 18, 1887
John D. McCall	Jan. 18, 1887–Jan. 15, 1895
R. W. Finley	Jan. 15, 1895–Jan. 15, 1901
R. M. Love	Jan. 15, 1901–Jan. 1903
J. W. Stephen	Jan. 1903–Jan. 1911
W. P. Lane	Jan. 1911–Jan. 1915
H. B. Terrell	Jan. 1915–Jan. 1920
M. L. Wiginton	Jan. 1920–Jan. 1921

Lon A. Smith .... Jan. 1921–Jan. 1925
S. H. Terrell.................................... Jan. 1925–Jan. 1931
Geo. H. Sheppard................. Jan., 1931–Jan. 17, 1949
Robert S. Calvert.................. Jan. 17, 1949–Jan., 1975
Robert D. (Bob) Bullock............ Jan. 1975–Jan. 3, 1991
John Sharp .... Jan. 3, 1991–Jan. 2, 1999
Carole Keeton Strayhorn ..... Jan. 2, 1999–Jan. 1, 2007
Susan Combs............................. Jan. 1, 2007–present

★ ★ ★ ★ ★ ★ ★

U.S. Senators from Texas

U.S. Senators were selected by the legislatures of the states until the U.S. Constitution was amended in 1913 to require popular elections. In Texas, the first senator chosen by the voters in a general election was Charles A. Culberson in 1916. Because of political pressures, however, the rules of the Democratic Party of Texas were changed in 1904 to require that all candidates for office stand before voters in the primary. Consequently, Texas' senators faced voters in 1906, 1910 and 1912 before the U.S. Constitution was changed.

Following is the succession of Texas representatives in the United States Senate since the annexation of Texas to the Union in 1845:

Houston Succession

Sam Houston.....................Feb. 21, 1846–Mar. 4, 1859
John Hemphill.....................Mar. 4, 1859–July 11, 1861

Louis T. Wigfall and W. S. Oldham took their seats in the Confederate Senate, Nov. 16, 1861, and served until the Confederacy collapsed. After that event, the State Legislature on Aug. 21, 1866, elected David G. Burnet and Oran M. Roberts to the United States Senate, anticipating immediate readmission to the Union, but they were not allowed to take their seats.

†Morgan C. Hamilton..........Feb. 22, 1870–Mar. 3, 1877
Richard Coke........................Mar. 4, 1877–Mar. 3, 1895
Horace Chilton ....Mar. 3, 1895–Mar. 3, 1901
Joseph W. Bailey................. Mar. 3, 1901–Jan. 8, 1913
Rienzi Melville Johnston.......Jan. 8, 1913–Feb. 3, 1913
‡Morris Sheppard (died)..... Feb. 13, 1913–Apr. 9, 1941
Andrew J. Houston .... June 2–26, 1941
W. Lee O'Daniel...................Aug. 4, 1941–Jan. 3, 1949
Lyndon B. Johnson............. Jan. 3, 1949–Jan. 20, 1961
William A. Blakley .... Jan. 20, 1961–June 15, 1961
†John G. Tower .... June 15, 1961–Jan. 21, 1985
†Phil Gramm.....................Jan. 21, 1985–Dec. 2, 2002
†**John Cornyn** ....Dec. 2, 2002–present

Rusk Succession

Thomas J. Rusk (*died*) ...... Feb 21, 1846–July 29, 1857
J. Pinckney Henderson (*died*)
.... Nov. 9, 1857–June 4, 1858
Matthias Ward (*appointed interim*)
.... Sept. 29, 1858–Dec. 5, 1859
Louis T. Wigfall ....Dec. 5, 1859–March 23, 1861

Succession was broken by the expulsion of Texas Senators following secession of Texas from Union. See note above under "Houston Succession" on Louis T. Wigfall, W. S. Oldham, Burnet and Roberts.

†James W. Flanagan..........Feb. 22, 1870–Mar. 3, 1875
Samuel B. Maxey .... Mar. 3, 1875–Mar. 3, 1887
John H. Reagan (*resigned*)Mar. 3, 1887–June 10, 1891
Horace Chilton (*filled vacancy on appointment*)
.... Dec. 7, 1891–Mar. 30,1892
Roger Q. Mills....................Mar. 30, 1892–Mar. 3, 1899
‡Charles A. Culberson.......... Mar. 3, 1899–Mar. 4, 1923
Earle B. Mayfield .... Mar. 4, 1923–Mar. 4, 1929
Tom Connally........................ Mar. 4, 1929–Jan. 3, 1953
Price Daniel .... Jan. 3, 1953–Jan. 15, 1957
William A. Blakley ....Jan. 15, 1957–Apr. 27, 1957

Ralph W. Yarborough ....Apr. 27, 1957–Jan. 12, 1971
§Lloyd Bentsen................ Jan. 12, 1971–Jan. 20, 1993
Robert Krueger............... Jan. 20, 1993–June 14, 1993
†**Kay Bailey Hutchison**........... June 14, 1993–present

† Republicans
‡ First election to U.S. Senate held in 1916. Prior to that time, senators were appointed by the Legislature.
§ Resigned from Senate when appointed U.S. Secretary of Treasury by Pres. Bill Clinton.

★ ★ ★ ★ ★ ★ ★

Commissioners of the General Land Office

Of the Republic

John P. Borden .... Aug. 23, 1837–Dec. 12, 1840
H. W. Raglin .... Dec. 12, 1840–Jan. 4, 1841
*Thomas William Ward ...... Jan. 4, 1841–Mar. 20, 1848

Of the State

George W. Smyth ....Mar. 20, 1848–Aug. 4, 1851
Stephen Crosby...................Aug. 4, 1851–Mar. 1, 1858
Francis M. White.................. Mar. 1, 1858–Mar. 1, 1862
Stephen Crosby.................Mar. 1, 1862–Sept. 1, 1865
Francis M. White................. Sept. 1, 1865–Aug. 7, 1866
Stephen Crosby................. Aug. 7, 1866–Aug. 27, 1867
Joseph Spence.................Aug. 27, 1867–Jan. 19, 1870
Jacob Kuechler................. Jan. 19, 1870–Jan. 20, 1874
J. J. Groos .... Jan. 20, 1874–June 15, 1878
W. C. Walsh......................July 30, 1878–Jan. 10, 1887
R. M. Hall .... Jan. 10, 1887–Jan. 16, 1891
W. L. McGaughey .... Jan. 16, 1891–Jan. 26, 1895
A. J. Baker....................... Jan. 26, 1895–Jan. 16, 1899
George W. Finger .... Jan. 16, 1899–May 4, 1899
Charles Rogan..................May 11, 1899–Jan. 10, 1903
John J. Terrell..................Jan. 10, 1903–Jan. 11, 1909
J. T. Robison.........................Jan, 1909–Sept. 11, 1929
J. H. Walker .... Sept. 11, 1929–Jan., 1937
William H. McDonald .... Jan 1937–Jan. 1939
Bascom Giles .... Jan. 1939–Jan. 5, 1955
J. Earl Rudder.....................Jan. 5, 1955–Feb. 1, 1958
Bill Allcorn ....Feb. 1, 1958–Jan. 1, 1961
Jerry Sadler .... Jan. 1, 1961–Jan. 1, 1971
Bob Armstrong...................... Jan. 1, 1971–Jan. 1, 1983
Garry Mauro .... Jan. 1, 1983–Jan. 7, 1999
David Dewhurst .... Jan. 7, 1999–Jan. 3, 2003
Jerry Patterson .... Jan. 3, 2003–present

*Part of term after annexation.

★ ★ ★ ★ ★ ★ ★

Speaker of the Texas House

The Speaker of the Texas House of Representatives is the presiding officer of the lower chamber of the State Legislature. The official is elected at the beginning of each regular session by a vote of the members of the House.

Speaker, Residence	Year Elected	Legis- lature
William E. Crump, Bellville	1846	1st
William H. Bourland, Paris	1846	1st
James W. Henderson, Houston	1847	2nd
Charles G. Keenan, Huntsville	1849	3rd
David C. Dickson, Anderson	1851	4th
Hardin R. Runnels, Boston	1853	5th
Hamilton P. Bee, Laredo	1855	6th
William S. Taylor, Larissa	1857	7th
Matt F. Locke, Lafayette	1858	7th
Marion DeKalb Taylor, Jefferson	1859	8th
Constantine W. Buckley, Richmond	1861	9th
Nicholas H. Darnell, Dallas	1861	9th
Constantine W. Buckley, Richmond	1863	9th
Marion DeKalb Taylor, Jefferson	1863	10th

Speaker, Residence	Year Elected	Legislature
Nathaniel M. Burford, Dallas	1866	11th
Ira H. Evans, Corpus Christi	1870	12th
William H. Sinclair, Galveston	1871	12th
Marion DeKalb Taylor, Jefferson	1873	13th
Guy M. Bryan, Galveston	1874	14th
Thomas R. Bonner, Tyler	1876	15th
John H. Cochran, Dallas	1879	16th
George R. Reeves, Pottsboro	1881	17th
Charles R. Gibson, Waxahachie	1883	18th
Lafayette L. Foster, Groesbeck	1885	19th
George C. Pendleton, Belton	1887	20th
Frank P. Alexander, Greenville	1889	21st
Robert T. Milner, Henderson	1891	22nd
John H. Cochran, Dallas	1893	23rd
Thomas Slater Smith, Hillsboro	1895	24th
L. Travis Dashiell, Jewett	1897	25th
J. S. Sherrill, Greenville	1899	26th
Robert E. Prince, Corsicana	1901	27th
Pat M. Neff, Waco	1903	28th
Francis W. Seabury, Rio Grande City	1905	29th
Thomas B. Love, Lancaster	1907	30th
Austin M. Kennedy, Waco	1909	31st
John W. Marshall, Whitesboro	1909	31st
Sam Rayburn, Bonham	1911	32nd
Chester H. Terrell, San Antonio	1913	33rd
John W. Woods, Rotan	1915	34th
Franklin O. Fuller, Coldspring	1917	35th
R. Ewing Thomason, El Paso	1919	36th
Charles G. Thomas, Lewisville	1921	37th
Richard E. Seagler, Palestine	1923	38th
Lee Satterwhite, Amarillo	1925	39th
Robert L. Bobbitt, Laredo	1927	40th
W. S. Barron, Bryan	1929	41st
Fred H. Minor, Denton	1931	42nd
Coke R. Stevenson, Junction	1933	43rd
	1935	44th
Robert W. Calvert, Hillsboro	1937	45th
R. Emmett Morse, Houston	1939	46th
Homer L. Leonard, McAllen	1941	47th
Price Daniel, Liberty	1943	48th
Claud H. Gilmer, Rocksprings	1945	49th
William O. Reed, Dallas	1947	50th
Durwood Manford, Smiley	1949	51st
Reuben Senterfitt, San Saba	1951	52nd
	1953	53rd
Jim T. Lindsey, Texarkana	1955	54th
Waggoner Carr, Lubbock	1957	55th
	1959	56th
James A. Turman, Gober	1961	57th
Byron M. Tunnell, Tyler	1963	58th
Ben Barnes, DeLeon	1965	59th
	1967	60th
Gus F. Mutscher, Brenham	1969	61st
	1971	62nd
Rayford Price, Palestine	1972	62nd
Price Daniel Jr., Liberty	1973	63rd
Bill Clayton, Springlake	1975	64th
	1977	65th
	1979	66th
	1981	67th
Gibson D. Lewis, Fort Worth	1983	68th
	1985	69th
	1987	70th
	1989	71st
	1991	72nd
James M. (Pete) Laney, Hale Center	1993	73rd
"	1995	74th
"	1997	75th
"	1999	76th
"	2001	77th

Speaker, Residence	Year Elected	Legislature
Tom Craddick, Midland	2003	78th
''	2005	79th
''	2007	80th
Joe Straus, San Antonio	2009	81st
''	2011	82nd

★ ★ ★ ★ ★ ★ ★

Chief Justice of the Supreme Court
Republic of Texas

James Collinsworth .... Dec. 16, 1836–July 23, 1838
John Birdsall .... Nov. 19–Dec. 12, 1838
Thomas J. Rusk................. Dec. 12, 1838–Dec. 5, 1840
John Hemphill.................... Dec. 5, 1840–Dec. 29, 1845

Under the Constitutions of 1845 and 1861

John Hemphill.................... Mar. 2, 1846–Oct. 10, 1858
Royall T. Wheeler .... Oct. 11, 1858–April 1864
Oran M. Roberts .... Nov. 1, 1864–June 30, 1866

Under the Constitution of 1866
(Presidential Reconstruction)

*George F. Moore .... Aug. 16, 1866–Sept. 10, 1867

*Removed under Congressional Reconstruction by military authorities who appointed members of the next court.

Under the Constitution of 1866
(Congressional Reconstruction)

Amos Morrill...................... Sept. 10, 1867–July 5, 1870

Under the Constitution of 1869

Lemuel D. Evans .... July 5, 1870–Aug. 31, 1873
Wesley Ogden .... Aug. 31, 1873–Jan. 29, 1874
Oran M. Roberts .... Jan. 29, 1874–Apr. 18, 1876

Under the Constitution of 1876

Oran M. Roberts .... Apr. 18, 1876–Oct. 1, 1878
George F. Moore.................. Nov. 5, 1878–Nov. 1, 1881
Robert S. Gould................. Nov. 1, 1881–Dec. 23, 1882
Asa H. Willie .... Dec. 23, 1882–Mar. 3, 1888
John W. Stayton .... Mar. 3, 1888–July 5, 1894
Reuben R. Gaines .... July 10, 1894–Jan. 5, 1911
Thomas J. Brown................. Jan. 7, 1911–May 26, 1915
Nelson Phillips .... June 1, 1915–Nov. 16, 1921
C. M. Cureton .... Dec. 2, 1921–Apr. 8, 1940
†Hortense Sparks Ward ..... Jan. 8, 1925–May 23, 1925
W. F. Moore .... Apr. 17, 1940–Jan. 1, 1941
James P. Alexander .... Jan. 1, 1941–Jan. 1, 1948
J. E. Hickman .... Jan. 5, 1948–Jan. 3, 1961
Robert W. Calvert .... Jan. 3, 1961–Oct. 4, 1972
Joe R. Greenhill.................. Oct. 4, 1972–Oct. 25, 1982
Jack Pope........................... Nov. 29, 1982–Jan. 5, 1985
John L. Hill Jr. .... Jan. 5, 1985–Jan. 4, 1988
Thomas R. Phillips................ Jan. 4, 1988–Sept. 3 2004
Wallace B. Jefferson .... Sept. 14, 2004–present

†Mrs. Ward served as Chief Justice of a special Supreme Court to hear one case in 1925.

Presiding Judges, Court of Appeals (1876–1891) and Court of Criminal Appeals (1891–present)

Mat D. Ector........................ May 6, 1876–Oct. 29, 1879
John P. White..................... Nov. 9, 1879–Apr. 26, 1892
James M. Hurt .... May 4, 1892–Dec. 31, 1898
W. L. Davidson .... Jan. 2, 1899–June 27, 1913
A. C. Prendergast .... June 27, 1913–Dec. 31, 1916
W. L. Davidson .... Jan. 1, 1917–Jan. 25, 1921
Wright C. Morrow................ Feb. 8, 1921–Oct. 16, 1939
Frank Lee Hawkins............. Oct. 16, 1939–Jan. 2, 1951

Harry N. Graves	Jan. 2, 1951–Dec. 31, 1954
W. A. Morrison	Jan. 1, 1955–Jan. 2, 1961
Kenneth K. Woodley	Jan. 3, 1961–Jan. 4, 1965
W. T. McDonald	Jan. 4, 1965–June 25, 1966
W. A. Morrison	June 25, 1966–Jan. 1, 1967
Kenneth K. Woodley	Jan. 1, 1967–Jan. 1, 1971
John F. Onion Jr.	Jan. 1, 1971–Jan. 1, 1989
Michael J. McCormick	Jan. 1, 1989–Jan. 1, 2001
Sharon Keller	Jan. 1, 2001–present

★ ★ ★ ★ ★ ★ ★

Administrators of Public Education
Superintendents of Public Instruction

Pryor Lea	Nov. 10, 1866–Sept. 12, 1867
Edwin M. Wheelock	Sept. 12, 1867–May 6, 1871
Jacob C. DeGress	May 6, 1871–Jan. 20, 1874
O. H. Hollingsworth	Jan. 20, 1874–May 6, 1884
B. M. Baker	May 6, 1884–Jan. 18, 1887
O. H. Cooper	Jan 18, 1887–Sept. 1, 1890
H. C. Pritchett	Sept. 1, 1890–Sept. 15, 1891
J. M. Carlisle	Sept. 15, 1891–Jan. 10, 1899
J. S. Kendall	Jan. 10, 1899–July 2, 1901
Arthur Lefevre	July 2, 1901–Jan. 12, 1905
R. B. Cousins	Jan. 12, 1905–Jan. 1, 1910

F. M. Bralley	Jan. 1, 1910–Sept. 1, 1913
W. F. Doughty	Sept. 1, 1913–Jan. 1, 1919
Annie Webb Blanton	Jan. 1, 1919–Jan. 16, 1923
S. M. N. Marrs	Jan. 16, 1923–April 28, 1932
C. N. Shaver	April 28, 1932–Oct. 1, 1932
L. W. Rogers	Oct. 1, 1932–Jan. 16, 1933
L. A. Woods	Jan. 16, 1933–*1951

State Commissioner of Education

J. W. Edgar	May 31, 1951–June 30, 1974
Marlin L. Brockette	July 1, 1974–Sept. 1, 1979
Alton O. Bowen	Sept. 1, 1979–June 1, 1981
Raymon Bynum	June 1, 1981–Oct. 31, 1984
W. N. Kirby	April 13, 1985–July 1, 1991
Lionel R. Meno	July 1, 1991–March 1, 1995
Michael A. Moses	March 9, 1995–Aug. 18, 1999
Jim Nelson	Aug. 18, 1999–March 25, 2002
Felipe Alanis	March 25, 2002–July 31, 2003
Shirley J. Neeley	Jan. 12, 2004–July 1, 2007
Robert Scott	July 1, 2007–present

*The office of State Superintendent of Public Instruction was abolished by the Gilmer-Aikin act of 1949 and the office of Commissioner of Education created, appointed by a new State Board of Education elected by the people.

First Ladies of Texas

Martha Evans Gindratt Wood	1847–49
† Bell Administration	1849–53
Lucadia Christiana Niles Pease	1853-57; 1867–69
‡ Runnels Administration	1857–59
Margaret Moffette Lea Houston	1859–61
Martha Evans Clark	1861
Adele Barron Lubbock	1861–1863
Susie Ellen Taylor Murrah	1863–1865
Mary Jane Bowen Hamilton	1865–1866
Annie Rattan Throckmorton	1866–1867
Ann Elizabeth Britton Davis	1870–1874
Mary Home Coke	1874–1876
Janie Roberts Hubbard	1876–1879
Frances Wickliff Edwards Roberts	1879–1883
Anne Maria Penn Ireland	1883–1887
Elizabeth Dorothy Tinsley Ross	1887–1891
Sarah Stinson Hogg	1891–1895
Sally Harrison Culberson	1895–1899
Orlene Walton Sayers	1899–1903
Sarah Beona Meng Lanham	1903–1907
Fannie Brunner Campbell	1907–1911
Alice Fuller Murrell Colquitt	1911–1915
§ Miriam A. Wallace Ferguson	1915–1917
Willie Cooper Hobby	1917–1921
Myrtle Mainer Neff	1921–1925
Mildred Paxton Moody	1927–1931
Maud Gage Sterling	1931–1933
Jo Betsy Miller Allred	1935–1939
Merle Estella Butcher O'Daniel	1939–1941
**Fay Wright Stevenson	1941–1942
**Edith Will Scott Stevenson	1942–1946
Mabel Buchanan Jester	1946–1949
Marialice Shary Shivers	1949–1957
Jean Houston Baldwin Daniel	1957–1963
Idanell Brill Connally	1963–1969
Ima Mae Smith	1969–1973
Betty Jane Slaughter Briscoe	1973–1979
Rita Crocker Bass Clements	1979–1983
Linda Gale Thompson White	1983–1987
Rita Crocker Bass Clements	1987–1991
Laura Welch Bush	1995–2000
Anita Thigpen Perry	2000–present

Anita Thigpen Perry. Photo courtesy of the Office of the First Lady.

†Gov. Peter Hansbrough Bell was not married while in office

‡Gov. Hardin R. Runnels never married.

§Miriam A. Wallace Ferguson was Mistress of the Mansion while her husband, James E. Ferguson, was governor, 1915–1917. She served as both Governor and Mistress of the Mansion, 1925–1927 and 1933–1935.

**Mrs. Coke R. (Fay Wright) Stevenson, the governor's wife, died in the Governor's Mansion Jan. 3, 1942. His mother, Edith Stevenson, served as Mistress of the Mansion thereafter.

During Ann Richards' term as governor, 1991–1995, she was not married. ☆

State Government

Texas state government is divided into executive, legislative and judicial branches under the Texas Constitution adopted in 1876.

The chief executive is the Governor, whose term is for four years. Other elected state officials with executive responsibilities include the Lieutenant Governor, Attorney General, Comptroller of Public Accounts, Commissioner of the General Land Office and Commissioner of Agriculture. The terms of those officials are also four years.

The Secretary of State and the Commissioner of Education are appointed by the Governor.

Except for making numerous appointments and calling special sessions of the Legislature, the Governor's powers are limited in comparison with those in most states.

Current state executives "not-to-exceed" salaries are for the 2010–2011 biennium (maximum possible salaries; actual salaries can be lower); salaries for the 2012–2013 biennium were not available from the State Auditor at press time.

The Governor's office welcomes comments and concerns, which are relayed to government officials who may offer assistance. Send a message at: http://www2.governor.state.tx.us/contact/ or call the **Citizen's Opinion Hotline (1-800-252-9600).**

Governor Rick Perry
P.O. Box 12428, Austin 78711
(512) 463-2000
www.governor.state.tx.us
Salary: $150,000

Lt. Governor David Dewhurst
P.O. Box 12068, Austin 78711
(512) 463-0001
www.senate.state.tx.us
Salary: Same as Senator when serving as President of the Senate; same as Governor when serving as Governor

**Attorney General
Greg Abbott**
P.O. Box 12548, Austin 78711
(512) 463-2100
www.oag.state.tx.us
Salary: $150,000

**Comptroller of Public
Accounts Susan Combs**
P.O. Box 13528, Austin 78711
(512) 463-4600
www.windows.state.tx.us
Salary: $150,000

**Texas Land Commissioner
Jerry Patterson**
P.O. Box 12873, Austin 78711
(512) 463-5256
www.glo.texas.gov
Salary: $137,500

Agriculture Commissioner
Todd Staples
P.O. Box 12847, Austin 78711
(512) 463-7476
www.texasagriculture.gov
Salary: $137,500

Secretary of State
Esperanza (Hope) Andrade
P.O. Box 12697, Austin 78711
(512) 463-5770
www.sos.state.tx.us
Salary: $125,880

Education Commissioner
Robert P. Scott
1701 N. Congress Ave.
Austin 78701
(512) 463-8985
www.tea.state.tx.us
Salary: $186,300

State Government Income and Expenditures

Taxes are the state government's primary source of income. On this and the following pages are summaries of state income and expenditures, percent change from previous year, tax collections, tax revenue by type of tax, a summary of the state budget for the 2012–2013 biennium, Texas Lottery income and expenditures, and the amount of federal payments to state agencies. Totals may not sum due to rounding.

State Revenues by Source and Expenditures by Function

Amounts (in Millions) and Percent Change from Previous Year

Revenues by Source	2010	%	2009	%	2008	%	2007	%	2006	%
Tax Collections	$35,369	−6.5	$37,823	−8.5	$41,358	11.9	$36,956	10.2	$33,544	12.4
Federal Income	36,857	19.4	30,860	17.6	26,238	7.6	24,376	−1.4	24,726	8.4
Licenses, Fees, Permits, Fines, Penalties	6,863	−4.7	7,198	−29.6	10,228	47.9	6,914	15.3	5,999	−2.5
Interest & Other Investment Income	1,059	−21.4	1,347	−41.7	2,309	−2.7	2,373	21.7	1,949	27.5
Net Lottery Proceeds	1,634	3.3	1,582	−1.0	1,597	2.9	1,552	−2.1	1,585	0.0
Sales of Goods & Services	408	−4.6	428	−13.8	496	−8.0	539	9.4	492	43.1
Settlements of Claims	557	−1.3	565	3.0	548	2.0	538	−1.4	545	−1.1
Land Income	761	−3.5	788	−25.0	1,050	39.8	751	−12.7	861	31.6
Contributions to Employee Benefits	0.17	−37.5	0.27	−98.2	15	−93.7	238	7.7	221	12.0
Other Revenues	3,850	4.2	3,696	17.6	3,143	6.4	2,953	18.3	2,497	16.4
Total Net Revenues	**$87,357**	**3.6**	**$84,286**	**−3.1**	**$86,983**	**12.7**	**$77,189**	**6.6**	**$72,421**	**10.0**
Expenditures by Function	**2010**	**%**	**2009**	**%**	**2008**	**%**	**2007**	**%**	**2006**	**%**
General Government – Total	$ 3,618	25.9	$ 2,872	14.3	$2,514	8.1	$2,325	−3.6	$2,412	8.9
Executive	3,212	29.7	2,476	15.4	2,146	8.9	1,970	−5.9	2,094	9.7
Legislative	131	−7.5	142	15.2	123	−4.9	129	11.2	116	−4.4
Judicial	275	7.9	255	4.0	245	8.8	225	11.9	201	9.1
Education	32,418	−2.1	33,121	7.6	30,776	16.9	26,324	13.5	23,185	6.1
Employee Benefits	3,342	14.1	2,928	−1.7	2,980	5.1	2,836	4.7	2,709	−1.3
Health and Human Services	36,301	8.4	33,492	12.8	29,681	6.4	27,895	9.6	25,458	4.7
Public Safety and Corrections	4,704	−6.7	5,043	24.6	4,048	7.1	3,778	−10.4	4,218	27.8
Transportation	5,972	−11.2	6,723	−12.3	7,668	0.8	7,609	4.0	7,316	10.2
Natural Resources/Recreational Services	1,813	−12.4	2,069	−1.6	2,103	10.8	1,898	16.2	1,634	−2.3
Regulatory Agencies	333	−6.7	356	18.2	301	29.3	233	1.6	229	−16.1
Lottery Winnings Paid*	487	−0.9	491	16.2	423	8.5	390	−18.1	476	6.1
Debt Service – Interest	881	−12.4	1,005	3.4	973	16.1	837	6.6	785	25.6
Capital Outlay	566	19.4	474	1.2	468	25.0	375	−8.6	410	−33.7
Total Net Expenditures	**$90,434**	**2.1**	**$ 88,576**	**8.1**	**$81,936**	**10.0**	**$74,501**	**8.2**	**$68,833**	**6.4**

* Does not include payments made by retailers. All amounts rounded. Revenue and expenditures exclude trust funds. Fiscal years end August 31. Source: 2010 State of Texas Annual Cash Report, Revenue and Expenditures of State Funds for the Year Ending August 31, 2010, Comptroller of Public Accounts' Office.

State Government Budget Summary
2012–2013 Biennium

Source: Legislative Budget Board; www.lbb.state.tx.us.

The Legislative Budget Board's (LBB) recommended baseline appropriations for state government operations for the 2012–2013 biennium total $158.7 billion from all fund sources. The recommendations provide a $28.8 billion, or 15.4 percent, decrease from the 2010–2011 biennial level.

General Revenue Funds, including funds dedicated within the General Revenue Fund, total $79.7 billion for the 2012–2013 biennium, a decrease of $8.8 billion, or 9.9 percent, from the anticipated 2010–2011 biennial spending level.

The LBB recommended appropriations for the 2012–2013 biennium are within the Comptroller's 2012–2013 Biennial Revenue Estimate. ☆

Article (Governmental Division) (all funds in millions)	Estimated/ Budgeted for 2010–2011*	Recommended 2012–2013 Budget	Biennial Change	Percentage Change
Art. I — General Government	$ 4,807.9	$ 4,359.9	$ −448.0	−9.3
Art. II — Health and Human Services	65,477.6	49,370.4	−16,107.2	−24.6
Art. III — Education	76,441.5	69,819.9	−6,621.6	−8.7
Public Education	53,701.5	48,278.4	−5,423.1	−10.1
Higher Education	22,740.0	21,541.5	−1,198.5	−5.3
Art. IV — The Judiciary	673.9	604.2	− 69.7	−10.3
Art. V — Public Safety & Criminal Justice	12,073.9	10,743.5	−1,330.5	−11.0
Art. VI — Natural Resources	3,649.0	3,079.9	−569.1	−15.6
Art. VII — Business & Economic Dev.	23,202.8	19,888.7	−3,314.0	−14.3
Art. VIII — Regulatory	798.7	522.1	−276.6	−34.6
Art. IX — General Provisions	0.0	−70.9	−70.9	NA
Art. X — The Legislature	372.8	335.5	−37.2	−10.0
Total	**$ 187,498.1**	**$ 158,653.4**	**$−28,844.7**	**−15.4**

All funds in millions.
*Includes anticipated supplemental spending adjustments.
Notes: *Excludes interagency contracts. Biennial change and percentage change are calculated on actual amounts before rounding. Therefore, table and figure totals may not sum due to rounding.*

State Tax Collections
1996–2010

Fiscal Year‡	State Tax Collections	Resident Population*	Per Capita Tax Collections	Taxes as % of Personal Income
1996	19,762,504,350	18,966,000	1,042.00	4.7
1997	21,187,868,237	19,312,000	1,097.13	4.7
1998	22,634,019,740	20,104,000	1,126.00	4.4
1999	23,614,611,235	20,507,000	1,152.00	4.4
2000	25,283,768,842	20,904,000	1,210.00	4.4
2001	27,230,212,416	21,317,000	1,277.00	4.5
2002	26,279,146,493	21,673,000	1,213.00	4.2
2003	26,126,675,424	22,052,000	1,185.00	4.1
2004	27,913,001,645	22,409,000	1,246.00	4.1
2005	29,838,277,614	22,808,000	1,308.00	4.0
2006	33,544,497,547	23,339,000	1,437.00	4.1
2007	36,955,629,884	23,778,000	1,554.00	4.3
2008	41,357,928,953	24,246,000	1,706.00	4.5
2009	37,822,453,013	24,722,000	1,530.00	4.2
2010	35,368,901,064	25,196,000	1,404.00	3.8

‡ Fiscal years end August 31.
* Revised fiscal year estimates

Sources: Tax collection data, Texas Comptroller of Public Accounts, Annual Cash Reports of various years. Population and personal income figures: U.S. Dept. of Commerce (Bureau of the Census and Bureau of Economic Analysis), adjusted to Texas fiscal years by Comptroller of Public Accounts.

Tax Revenues
2009–2010

Below are listed the major taxes and the amounts each contributed to the state in fiscal years 2009 and 2010.

Type of Tax	FY 2009	FY 2010
Sales	$21,014,065,089	$19,630,305,704
Motor Vehicle Sales and Rentals*	2,600,939,347	2,630,137,405
Motor Fuels	3,032,770,482	3,041,973,016
Franchise	4,250,332,029	3,856,865,935
Insurance	1,257,314,168	1,324,703,043
Natural Gas Production	1,407,739,109	725,538,388
Cigarette &Tobacco	1,556,793,276	1,388,764,873
Alcoholic Beverages	796,948,327	809,233,737
Oil Production	884,510,773	1,008,664,357
Inheritance	2,004,064	81,458
Utility	518,883,903	478,742,739
Hotel	343,544,448	330,809,436
Other Taxes	156,607,998	143,080,974
Totals	**$37,822,453,013**	**$35,368,901,064**

*Includes tax on manufactured housing sales and taxes on interstate motor carriers.

Source: 2008 State of Texas Annual Cash Report, Revenue and Expenditures of State Funds for the Year Ending August 31, 2008, Texas Comptroller of Public Accounts.

Federal Revenue by State Agency

Source: Texas Comptroller of Public Accounts, 2008 State of Texas Annual Cash Report, Revenue and Expenditures of State Funds for the Year Ending Aug. 31, 2010.

Texas received $36.9 billion in federal funds during fiscal 2010, an increase of 19.4 percent over fiscal 2009. The increase was attributable in large part to funds received under the American Recovery and Reinvestment Act, including Medicaid. Federal funds accounted for 42.2 percent of total net revenue, the largest source of revenue in fiscal 2010.

State Agency	2010	2009	2008	2007
Health and Human Services Commission	$20,791,035,173	$17,986,889,565	$14,943,839,631	$14,035,890,889
Texas Education Agency	6,793,852,227	4,459,537,218	4,268,435,111	4,342,879,281
Texas Department of Transportation	2,700,037,782	2,715,159,247	2,690,057,920	1,974,299,512
Department of State Health Services*	1,119,463,885	1,103,725,404	1,066,202,614	978,045,778
Texas Workforce Commission	1,069,280,389	944,252,203	881,300,645	961,052,202
Texas Department of Public Safety	843,634,124	1,191,527,865	321,177,791	378,228,787
Texas Department of Housing and Community Affairs	699,836,513	302,247,875	164,054,834	165,741,641
Texas Higher Education Coordinating Board	533,047,447	−63,119,137	85,016,320	14,954,678
Department of Assistive and Rehabilitative Services	472,313,359	445,955,913	410,578,731	378,867,613
Department of Family and Protective Services	439,105,171	427,157,366	345,358,433	366,446,983
Department of Agriculture	366,217,623	335,083,929	277,766,746	32,973,604
Attorney General	209,910,019	257,765,050	202,161,262	214,241,329
Office of Rural Community Affairs	132,585,818	134,751,702	106,691,789	99,845,076
Department of Aging and Disability Services	126,079,938	114,850,924	107,734,327	107,533,280
All Other Agencies	560,227,324	504,146,080	367,951,531	325,051,848
Total All Agencies	**$36,856,626,791**	**$30,859,931,204**	**$ 26,238,327,684**	**$ 24,376,052,502**

As of Sept. 1, 2004, several agencies were incorporated into the Dept.of State Health Services, including the Dept. of Human Services, Texas Dept. of Health, Texas Rehabilitation Commission, and Texas Commission on Alcohol and Drug Abuse.

Texas Lottery

Source: Texas Lottery Commission; www.txlottery.org/

The State Lottery Act was passed by the Texas Legislature in July 1991. Texas voters approved a constitutional amendment authorizing a state lottery in an election on Nov. 5, 1991, by a vote of 1,326,154 to 728,994. Sales — since the first ticket was sold on May 29, 1992, through 2010 — totaled more than $58 billion. During the same period, more than $34 billion was paid out in prizes.

The Texas Lottery® offers players a wide range of choices, including about 80 instant ticket scratch-off games and seven online games.

About 27 percent of all lottery revenue is transferred to the Foundation School Fund, which supports public education in Texas. Before September 1997, revenues were deposited in the General Revenue Fund.

Texas Lottery transfers to the state from May 1992 to August 2010 totaled $18,248,560,192, with $12,674,802,658 going to the **Foundation School Fund,** $7,328,844 to the **Fund for Veterans' Assistance** administered by the Texas Veterans Commission, and $5,245,360,807 to the **General Revenue Fund.**

Who Plays the Texas Lottery

The Texas Lottery Commission executive director is required to conduct a biennial demographic survey of lottery players to determine the income, age, sex, race, education, and frequency of participation of players. The following information is drawn from the survey, conducted in August 2010 by the Center for Public Policy at the University of Houston. A total of 1,691 usable interviews were completed with Texans ages 18 and older. All demographic information and participation rates were self-reported and not independently verified. The data has·a plus/minus 2.4 percent margin of error at a confidence level of 95 percent.

Around 34 percent of Texans reported purchasing at least one Texas Lottery ticket in 12 months preceding the survey, down from 38.8 percent in the previous survey. Of those, 67.3 percent played Lotto Texas®; 53.8 percent, "scratch off" or instant games; 39.9 percent, Mega Millions®; 21.9 percent, Powerball®; 16.6 percent, Cash Five®; 9.4 percent, Texas Two Step®; 14.7 percent, Pick 3™ day draw; less than 2 percent, Pick 3 night draw or Daily 4™.

Texas Lottery Financial Data

Start-up to Aug. 31, 2010. All dollar amounts in millions.

Period	Sales	Value of Prizes Won	Retailer Commissions	Administration	To State of Texas
Start-up– FY 1993	$2,448	$1,250	$122	$170	$812
FY 1994	2,760	1,529	138	167	869
FY 1995	3,037	1,689	152	188	927
FY 1996	3,432	1,951	172	217	1,158
FY 1997	3,745	2,152	187	236	1,189
FY 1998	3,090	1,648	155	198	1,157
FY 1999	2,572	1,329	129	169	969
FY 2000	2,657	1,509	133	172	918
FY 2001	2,825	1,643	141	173	865
FY 2002	2,966	1,715	148	167	957
FY 2003	3,131	1,845	157	158	955
FY 2004	3,488	2,069	174	181	1,044
FY 2005	3,662	2,228	183	179	1,077
FY 2006	3,775	2,311	189	185	1,085
FY 2007	3,774	2,315	189	183	1,091
FY 2008	3,671	2,281	184	167	1,037
FY 2009	3,720	2,300	186	192	1,043
FY 2010	3,738	2,366	187	172	1,095
All figures accrued.					

Age: The 35–44 and 45–54 age groups had the highest participation rates. The 25–34 age group reported spending more on average than those in other age categories.

Educational Level: Respondents with some college education and those with a college degree were more likely to play lottery games in the past year than other educational groups.

Income Level: Respondents in the $20,000 to $29,999 income category had the highest past-year lottery participation rate (45.8 percent), while nearly every income category at or above $30,000 had a similar participation rate of at least 36 percent.

Ethnic Background: Past-year lottery participation and spending varied across racial and ethnic origin, with non-whites exhibiting greater participation rates and greater median spending than whites.

Sex: Males were more likely than females to play the lottery and averaged $11 per month. Females reported spending $6 per month on average. ✩

The Capitol Fountain on the State Capitol grounds. Ron Billings photo; Texas Forest Service.

Texas Legislature

The Texas Legislature has **181 members: 31 in the Senate** and **150 in the House of Representatives**. Regular sessions convene on the second Tuesday of January in odd-numbered years, but the governor may call special sessions. Article III of the Texas Constitution deals with the legislative branch. On the Web: **www.capitol.state.tx.us.**

The following lists are of members of the **82nd Legislature**, which convened for its Regular Session on Jan. 11, 2011, and adjourned on May 30, 2011. The **83rd Legislature** is scheduled to convene on Jan. 8, 2013, and adjourn May 27, 2013.

State Senate

Thirty-one members of the State Senate are elected to four-year, overlapping terms. Salary: The salary of all members of the Legislature, both Senators and Representatives, is $7,200 per year and $124 per diem during legislative sessions; mileage allowance at same rate provided by law for state employees. The per diem payment applies during each regular and special session of the Legislature.

Senatorial Districts include one or more whole counties and some counties have more than one Senator.

The **address of Senators** is Texas Senate, P.O. Box 12068, Austin 78711-2068; phone (512) 463-0200; Fax: 512-463-0326. On the Web: **www.senate.state. tx.us.**

President of the Senate: Lt. Gov. David Dewhurst; **President Pro Tempore: Mike Jackson; Secretary of the Senate:** Patsy Spaw; **Sergeant-at-Arms:** Rick De-Leon.

Texas State Senators

District, Member, Party-Hometown, Occupation

1. Kevin P. Eltife, R-Tyler; businessman.
2. Robert F. Deuell, R-Greenville; family physician.
3. Robert Nichols, R-Jacksonville; engineer.
4. Tommy Williams, R-The Woodlands; businessman.
5. Steve Ogden, R-Bryan; oil and gas producer.
6. Mario Gallegos Jr., D-Houston; retired firefighter.
7. Dan Patrick, R-Houston; broadcasting.
8. Florence Shapiro, R-Plano; former small business owner.
9. Chris Harris, R-Arlington; attorney.
10. Wendy R. Davis, D-Fort Worth; attorney.
11. Mike Jackson, R-La Porte; businessman.
12. Jane Nelson, R-Flower Mound; businesswoman.
13. Rodney Ellis, D-Houston; attorney, investment banker.
14. Kirk Watson, D-Austin; attorney.
15. **John Whitmire, D-Houston; attorney (Dean of the Senate).**
16. **John J. Carona, R-Dallas; businessman.**
17. **Joan Huffman, R-Houston; attorney.**
18. **Glenn Hegar Jr., R-Katy; farmer.**
19. **Carlos I. Uresti, D-San Antonio; attorney.**
20. Juan (Chuy) Hinojosa, D-McAllen; attorney.
21. Judith Zaffirini, D-Laredo; communications specialist, former educator.
22. Brian Birdwell, R-Granbury; retired military.
23. Royce West, D-Dallas; attorney.
24. Troy Fraser, R-Horseshoe Bay; businessman.
25. Jeff Wentworth, R-San Antonio; attorney, Realtor.
26. Leticia Van de Putte, D-San Antonio; pharmacist.
27. Eddie Lucio Jr., D-Brownsville; advertising executive.
28. Robert Duncan, R-Lubbock; attorney.
29. José R. Rodriguez, D-El Paso; former El Paso County attorney.
30. Craig Estes, R-Wichita Falls; state senator.
31. Kel Seliger, R-Amarillo; business owner.

House of Representatives

This is a list of the 150 members of the House of Representatives in the 82nd Legislature. They were elected for two-year terms from the districts shown below. Representatives and senators receive the same salary (see State Senate). The **address of all Representatives** is House of Representatives, P.O. Box 2910, Austin, 78768-2910; phone: (512) 463-1000; Fax: (512) 463-5896. On the web: **www.house. state.tx.us/**

Speaker Joe Straus

Speaker, Joe Straus III (R-San Antonio). **Speaker Pro Tempore**, Craig Eiland (D-Galveston). **Chief Clerk**, Robert Haney. **Sergeant-at-Arms**, Rod Welsh.

Texas State Representatives

District, Member, Party-Hometown, Occupation

1. George Lavender, R-Texarkana, sales.
2. Dan Flynn, R-Van; attorney, businessman.
3. Erwin Cain, R-Como; small business owner.
4. Lance Gooden, R-Terrell; insurance consultant
5. Bryan Hughes, R-Mineola; attorney.
6. Leo Berman, R-Tyler; retired U.S. Army Lt. Col. and oil and gas executive.
7. David Simpson, R-Longview; businessman.
8. Byron C. Cook, R-Corsicana; businessman, rancher.
9. Wayne Christian, R-Center; investment sales.
10. Jim Pitts, R-Waxahachie; attorney.
11. Charles L. (Chuck) Hopson, R-Jacksonville; pharmacist.
12. James White, R-Hillister, educator.
13. Lois W. Kolkhorst, R-Brenham; business owner, investor.
14. Fred H. Brown, R-College Station; businessman.
15. Rob Eissler, R-The Woodlands; executive recruiter.
16. Brandon Creighton, R-Conroe; attorney, real estate developer.
17. Tim Kleinschmidt, R-Lexington; attorney, rancher.
18. John C. Otto, R-Dayton; CPA.
19. Mike Hamilton, R-Mauriceville; self-employed/catering.
20. Charles Schwertner, R-Georgetown; orthopedic surgeon.
21. Allan B. Ritter, R-Nederland; business owner.
22. Joseph (Joe) Deshotel, D-Beaumont; attorney, businessman.
23. Craig Eiland, D-Galveston; attorney.
24. Larry Taylor, R-Friendswood; insurance agency owner.
25. Dennis H. Bonnen, R-Angleton; banking.
26. Charlie Howard, R-Sugar Land; Realtor, investor.
27. Ron Reynolds, D-Missouri City; attorney.
28. John Zerwas, R-Richmond; physician.
29. Randy Weber, R-Pearland; small business owner.
30. Geanie W. Morrison, R-Victoria; state representative.
31. Ryan Guillen, D-Rio Grande City; Investor.
32. Todd Hunter, R-Corpus Christi; attorney.

33. Raul Torres, R-Corpus Christi; CPA.
34. Connie Scott, R-Corpus Christi; housewife.
35. Jose Aliseda, R-Beeville; attorney.
36. Sergio Muñoz Jr., D-Palmview; attorney.
37. Rene O. Oliveira, D-Brownsville; attorney.
38. Eddie Lucio III, D-Brownsville; attorney.
39. Armando A. (Mando) Martinez, D-Weslaco; firefighter, paramedic.
40. Aaron Peña, R-Edinburg; attorney.
41. Veronica Gonzales, D-McAllen; attorney.
42. Richard Peña Raymond, D-Laredo; businessman.
43. Jose Manuel (J.M.) Lozano, D-Kingsville; restauranteur.
44. John Kuempel, R-Seguin; salesman.
45. Jason A. Isaac, R-Dripping Springs; small business owner.
46. Dawnna M. Dukes, D-Austin; business consultant, marketing.
47. Paul D. Workman, R-Austin; commercial contractor.
48. Donna Howard, D-Austin; nursing, public health.
49. Elliott Naishtat, D-Austin; attorney.
50. Mark Strama, D-Austin; small business owner.
51. Eddie Rodriguez, D-Austin; state representative.
52. Larry Gonzales, R-Round Rock; owner of graphic design company.
53. Harvey Hilderbran, R-Kerrville; businessman.
54. Jimmie Don Aycock, R-Killeen; veterinarian, rancher.
55. Ralph Sheffield, R-Temple; restaurant owner.
56. Charles (Doc) Anderson, R-Waco; veterinarian.
57. Marva Beck, R-Centerville; retired rancher.
58. Rob D. Orr, R-Burleson; real estate broker.
59. Sid Miller, R-Stephenville; nurseryman, rancher.
60. James L. (Jim) Keffer, R-Eastland; businessman.
61. Phil S. King, R-Weatherford; attorney.
62. Larry Phillips, R-Sherman; attorney.
63. Tan Parker, R-Flower Mound; businessman.
64. Myra Crownover, R-Denton; ranching, businesswoman.
65. Burt R. Solomons, R-Carrollton; attorney.
66. Van Taylor, R-Plano; real estate.
67. Jerry Madden, R-Richardson; retired insurance broker, engineer.
68. Richard (Rick) L. Hardcastle, R-Vernon; rancher.
69. Lanham Lyne, R-Wichita Falls; company president.
70. Ken Paxton, R-McKinney; attorney.
71. Susan King, R-Abilene; surgical nurse.
72. Drew Darby, R-San Angelo; attorney, businessman.
73. Doug Miller, R-New Braunfels; insurance agent.
74. Pete P. Gallego, D-Alpine; attorney.
75. Inocente (Chente) Quintanilla, D-Tornillo; retired assistant superintendent, educator.
76. Naomi Gonzalez, D-El Paso; attorney.
77. Marisa Marquez, D-El Paso; community relations manager.
78. Dee Margo, R-El Paso; company chairman.
79. Joseph (Joe) C. Pickett, D-El Paso; real estate.
80. Tracy O. King, D-Batesville; businessman.
81. Tryon D. Lewis, R-Odessa; attorney.
82. Tom Craddick, R-Midland; investor, sales representative.
83. Charles Perry, R-Lubbock; CPA, land developer.
84. John Frullo, R-Lubbock; small business owner.
85. Jim Landtroop, R-Plainview; insurance agent.
86. John T. Smithee, R-Amarillo; attorney.
87. Four Price, R-Amarillo; attorney.
88. Warren D. Chisum, R-Pampa; oil and gas producer, rancher.
89. Jodie Laubenberg, R-Parker; state representative.
90. Lon Burnam, D-Fort Worth; independent consultant.

91. Kelly G. Hancock, R-North Richland Hills; business owner.
92. Todd Smith, R-Euless; attorney.
93. Barbara Nash, R-Arlington; real estate investor.
94. Diane Patrick, R-Arlington; university professor.
95. Marc Veasey, D-Fort Worth; real estate.
96. William (Bill) Zedler, R-Arlington; consultant.
97. Mark M. Shelton, R-Fort Worth; pediatrician.
98. Vicki Truitt, R-Keller; small business owner.
99. Charlie L. Geren, R-Fort Worth; restaurant owner, real estate broker, rancher.
100. Eric Johnson, D-Dallas; attorney.
101. Cindy Burkett, R-Mesquite; company vice president.
102. Stefani Carter, R-Dallas; attorney.
103. Rafael Anchiá, D-Dallas; attorney.
104. Roberto R. Alonzo, D-Dallas; attorney.
105. Linda Harper-Brown, R-Irving; corporate president.
106. Rodney Anderson, R-Grand Prairie; title company vice president.
107. Kenneth Sheets, R-Dallas; attorney.
108. Dan Branch, R-Dallas; attorney.
109. Helen Giddings, D-Dallas; small business owner.
110. Barbara Mallory Caraway, D-Dallas; small business owner.
111. Yvonne Davis, D-Dallas; small business owner.
112. Angie Chen Button, R-Garland; CPA, marketing executive.
113. Joe Driver, R-Garland; insurance agent.
114. Will Hartnett, R-Dallas; probate attorney, businessman.
115. Jim L. Jackson, R-Carrollton; retired.
116. Trey Martinez Fischer, D-San Antonio; attorney.
117. John V. Garza, R-San Antonio; real estate.
118. Joe Farias, D-San Antonio; retired.
119. Roland Gutierrez, D-San Antonio; attorney.
120. Ruth Jones McClendon, D-San Antonio; business-woman.
121. Joe Straus III, R-San Antonio; insurance, investments (**Speaker of the House**).
122. Lyle Larson, R-San Antonio; small business owner.
123. Michael (Mike) Villarreal, D-San Antonio; small business owner, investment banker.
124. Jose Menendez, D-San Antonio; company vice president.
125. Joaquin Castro, D-San Antonio; attorney.
126. Patricia F. Harless, R-Spring; automobile dealer.
127. Dan Huberty, R-Houston; company vice president.
128. Wayne Smith, R-Baytown; civil engineer.
129. John E. Davis, R-Houston; roofing sales.
130. Allen Fletcher, R-Tomball; small business owner.
131. Alma A. Allen, D-Houston; educator.
132. William A. (Bill) Callegari, R-Katy; professional engineer.
133. Jim Murphy, R-Houston; commercial real estate.
134. Sarah Davis, R-West University Place; attorney.
135. Gary Elkins, R-Houston; business consultant.
136. Beverly Woolley, R-Houston; small business owner (**Speaker Pro Tem).**
137. Scott Hochberg, D-Houston; software consultant.
138. Dwayne Bohac, R-Houston; businessman.
139. Sylvester Turner, D-Houston; attorney.
140. Armando Lucio Walle, D-Houston; consultant.
141. Senfronia Thompson, D-Houston; attorney.
142. Harold V. Dutton Jr., D-Houston; attorney.
143. Ana E. Hernandez, D-Houston; attorney.
144. Ken Legler, R-Pasadena; company president.
145. Carol Alvarado, D-Houston; small business consultant.
146. Borris L. Miles, D-Houston; insurance agent.
147. Garnet Coleman, D-Houston; business consultant.
148. Jessica Farrar, D-Houston; architect.
149. Hubert Vo, D-Houston; Realtor, developer.
150. Debbie Riddle, R-Tomball; horse breeder. ☆

The State Capitol shines at night. File photo.

The State Supreme Court Building. Ron Billings photo; Texas Forest Service.

Texas State Judiciary

The judiciary of the state consists of 9 members of the State Supreme Court; 9 members of the Court of Criminal Appeals; 80 of the Courts of Appeals; 443 of the State District Courts; 13 of the Criminal District Courts; 505 County Court judges; 819 Justices of the Peace; and 1,531 Municipal Courts judges.

In addition to its system of formal courts, the State of Texas has established 17 **Alternative Dispute Resolution Centers**. The centers help ease the caseload of Texas courts by using mediation, arbitration, negotiation and moderated settlement conferences to handle disputes without resorting to more costly, time-consuming court actions.

Centers are located in Amarillo, Austin, Beaumont, Bryan, Conroe, Corpus Christi, Dallas, Denton, El Paso, Fort Worth, Houston, Kerrville, Lubbock, Paris, Richmond, San Antonio and Waco. For the fiscal year ending Aug. 31, 2005, the mediation sections of the centers had closed 18,292 cases and had 2,997 cases pending.

(The list of U.S. District Courts in Texas can be found in the Federal Government section, page 555.)

State Higher Courts

The state's higher courts are listed below and are current as of July 2009. Notations in parentheses indicate dates of expiration of terms of office. Judges of the Supreme Court, Court of Criminal Appeals and Courts of Appeals are elected to 6-year, overlapping terms. District Court judges are elected to 4-year terms.

The salaries for judges fiscal years 2008–2009 were as follows: Chief Justice of the Supreme Court and the Presiding Judge of the Court of Criminal Appeals: each $152,500; Justices, $150,000; Chief Justices of the Courts of Appeals, $140,000; justices, $137,500 from the state. A supplemental amount may be paid by counties, not to exceed $15,000 per year, and total salary must be at least $1,000 less than that received by Supreme Court justices. District Court judges receive $137,500 from the state, plus supplemental pay from various subdivisions. Their total salary must be $1,000 less than that received by justices of the Court of Appeals in which the district court is located.

Below is information on the Supreme Court, Court of Criminal Appeals and Courts of Appeals. The information was furnished by each court as of July 2011. Elsewhere in this section are names of county court judges by counties, District Court judges by district number, and the district numbers of the District Court(s) in each county.

Supreme Court

Chief Justice, Wallace B. Jefferson (12/31/12). **Associate Justices**: Paul W. Green (12/31/16); Eva M. Guzman (12/31/16); Nathan L. Hecht (12/31/12); Phil Johnson (12/31/14); Debra H. Lehrmann (12/31/16); David M. Medina (12/31/12); Dale Wainwright (12/31/14); and Don R. Willett (12/31/12).

Clerk of Court, Blake A. Hawthorne. Location of court, Austin. Web: **www.supreme.courts.state.tx.us.**

Court of Criminal Appeals

Presiding Judge, Sharon Keller (12/31/12). **Judges**: Elsa Alcala (12/31/12); Cathy Cochran (12/31/14); Barbara Parker Hervey (12/31/12); Cheryl Johnson (12/31/16); Michael E. Keasler (12/31/16); Lawrence E. Meyers (12/31/16); Tom Price (12/31/14); and Paul Womack (12/31/14). State Prosecuting Attorney, Lisa C. McMinn.

Clerk of Court, Louise Pearson. Location of court, Austin. Web: **www.cca.courts.state.tx.us.**

Courts of Appeals

These courts have jurisdiction within their respective supreme judicial districts. A constitutional amendment approved in 1978 raised the number of associate justices for Courts of Appeals where needed. Judges are elected from the district for 6-year terms. An amendment adopted in 1980 changed the name of the old Courts of Civil Appeals to the Courts of Appeals and changed the jurisdiction of the courts. Web: **www.courts.state.tx.us/courts/coa.asp.**

First District — Houston:* Chief Justice Sherry Radack (12/31/16). **Justices**: Jane Nenninger Bland (12/31/12); Harvey G. Brown (12/31/14); Laura Carter Higley (12/31/14); Rebeca Huddle (12/31/12); Terry Jennings (12/31/12); Evelyn Keyes (12/31/16); Michael C. Massengale (12/31/14); and Jim Sharp (12/31/14). **Clerk of Court**, Karinne McCullough. Counties in the First District: Austin, Brazoria, Chambers, Colorado, Fort Bend, Galveston, Grimes, Harris, Waller, Washington.

Second District — Fort Worth: Chief Justice. Terrie Livingston (12/31/12). **Justices**: Lee Ann Dauphinot (12/31/12); Lee Gabriel (12/31/14); Anne L. Gardner (12/31/16); Bob McCoy (12/31/12); Bill Meier (12/31/14); and Sue Walker (12/31/12). **Clerk of Court**, Debra Spisak. Counties in Second District: Archer, Clay, Cooke, Denton, Hood, Jack, Montague, Parker, Tarrant, Wichita, Wise, Young.

Third District — Austin: Chief Justice J. Woodfin (Woodie) Jones (12/31/14). **Justices**: Melissa Goodwin (12/31/16); Diane Henson (12/31/12); Robert H. Pemberton (12/31/12); David Puryear (12/31/12); Jeff L. Rose (12/31/16). **Clerk of Court**, Jeffrey D. Kyle. Counties in the Third District: Bastrop, Bell, Blanco, Burnet, Caldwell, Coke, Comal, Concho, Fayette, Hays, Irion, Lampasas, Lee, Llano, McCulloch, Milam, Mills, Runnels, San Saba, Schleicher, Sterling, Tom Green, Travis, Williamson.

Fourth District — San Antonio: Chief Justice Catherine Stone (12/31/14). **Justices**: Karen Anne Angelini (12/31/12); Marialyn Barnard (12/31/12); Steve Hilbig (12/31/12); Sandee Bryan Marion (12/31/12); Rebecca Simmons (12/31/12); and Phylis J. Speedlin (12/31/12). **Clerk of Court**, Keith E. Hottle. Counties in the Fourth District: Atascosa, Bandera, Bexar, Brooks, Dimmit, Duval, Edwards, Frio, Gillespie, Guadalupe, Jim Hogg, Jim Wells, Karnes, Kendall, Kerr, Kimble, Kinney, La Salle, Mason, Maverick, McMullen, Medina, Menard, Real, Starr, Sutton, Uvalde, Val Verde, Webb, Wilson, Zapata, Zavala.

Fifth District — Dallas: Chief Justice Carolyn I. Wright (12/31/12). **Justices**: David L. Bridges (12/31/14); Kerry P. FitzGerald (12/31/14); Molly Meredith Francis (12/31/12); Douglas S. Lang (11/14/12); Elizabeth Lang-Miers (12/31/12); Robert M. Fillmore (12/31/16); Joseph B. Morris (12/31/12); Jim A. Moseley (12/31/12); Mary Murphy (12/31/14); Lana Myers (12/31/16); Michael J. O'Neill (12/31/16); Martin E. Richter (12/31/12). **Clerk of Court**, Lisa Matz. Counties in the Fifth District: Collin, Dallas, Grayson, Hunt, Kaufman, Rockwall.

Sixth District — Texarkana: Chief Justice Josh R. Morris III (12/31/16). **Justices**: Jack Carter (12/31/14); and Bailey C. Moseley (12/31/12). **Clerk of Court**, Debbie Autrey. Counties in the Sixth District: Bowie, Camp, Cass, Delta, Fannin, Franklin, Gregg, Harrison, Hopkins, Hunt, Lamar, Marion, Morris, Panola, Red River, Rusk, Titus, Upshur, Wood.

Seventh District — Amarillo: Chief Justice Brian P. Quinn (12/31/14). **Justices**: James T. Campbell (12/31/16); Mackey Hancock (12/31/12); and Patrick A. Pirtle (12/31/12). **Clerk of Court**, Peggy Culp. Counties in the Seventh District: Armstrong, Bailey, Briscoe, Carson, Castro, Childress, Cochran, Collingsworth, Cottle,

Crosby, Dallam, Deaf Smith, Dickens, Donley, Floyd, Foard, Garza, Gray, Hale, Hall, Hansford, Hardeman, Hartley, Hemphill, Hockley, Hutchinson, Kent, King, Lamb, Lipscomb, Lubbock, Lynn, Moore, Motley, Ochiltree, Oldham, Parmer, Potter, Randall, Roberts, Sherman, Swisher, Terry, Wheeler, Wilbarger, Yoakum.

Eighth District — El Paso: Chief Justice David Wellington Chew (12/31/14). **Justices**: Ann Crawford McClure (12/31/12); and Guadalupe Rivera (12/31/14). **Clerk of Court**, Denise Pacheco. Counties in the Eighth District: Andrews, Brewster, Crane, Crockett, Culberson, El Paso, Hudspeth, Jeff Davis, Loving, Pecos, Presidio, Reagan, Reeves, Terrell, Upton, Ward, Winkler.

Ninth District — Beaumont: Chief Justice Steve McKeithen (12/31/14). **Justices**: David B. Gaultney (12/31/14); Henry Hollis Horton (12/31/12); and Charles Kreger (12/31/16). **Clerk of Court**, Carol Anne Flores. Counties in the Ninth District: Hardin, Jasper, Jefferson, Liberty, Montgomery, Newton, Orange, Polk, San Jacinto, Tyler.

Tenth District — Waco: Chief Justice Thomas W. Gray (12/31/12). **Justices**: Rex D. Davis (12/31/14) and Al Scoggins, Jr. (12/31/16). **Clerk of Court**, Sharri Roessler. Counties in the Tenth District: Bosque, Brazos, Burleson, Coryell, Ellis, Falls, Freestone, Hamilton, Hill, Johnson, Leon, Limestone, Madison, McLennan, Navarro, Robertson, Somervell, Walker.

Eleventh District — Eastland: Chief Justice Jim R. Wright (12/31/12). **Justices**: Daniel (Eric) Kalenak (12/31/12) and Terry McCall (12/31/16). **Clerk of Court**, Sherry Williamson. Counties in the Eleventh District: Baylor, Borden, Brown, Callahan, Coleman, Comanche, Dawson, Eastland, Ector, Erath, Fisher, Gaines, Glasscock, Haskell, Howard, Jones, Knox, Martin, Midland, Mitchell, Nolan, Palo Pinto, Scurry, Shackelford, Stephens, Stonewall, Taylor, Throckmorton.

Twelfth District — Tyler: Chief Justice Jim Worthen (12/31/14). **Justices**: Sam Griffith (12/31/12) and Brian T. Hoyle (12/31/16). **Clerk of Court**, Cathy S. Lusk. Counties in the Twelfth District: Anderson, Angelina, Cherokee, Gregg, Henderson, Houston, Nacogdoches, Rains, Rusk, Sabine, San Augustine, Shelby, Smith, Trinity, Upshur, Van Zandt, Wood.

Thirteenth District — Corpus Christi: Chief Justice Rogelio Valdez (12/31/12). **Justices**: Gina M. Benavides (12/31/12); Dori Contreras Garza (12/31/12); Greg Perkes (12/31/14); Nelda V. Rodriguez (12/31/12); Rose Vela (12/31/12). **Clerk of Court**, Dorian E. Ramirez. Counties in the Thirteenth District: Aransas, Bee, Calhoun, Cameron, DeWitt, Goliad, Gonzales, Hidalgo, Jackson, Kenedy, Kleberg, Lavaca, Live Oak, Matagorda, Nueces, Refugio, San Patricio, Victoria, Wharton, Willacy.

Fourteenth District—Houston†: Chief Justice Adele Hedges (12/31/14). **Justices**: John S. Anderson (12/31/12); William Boyce (12/31/14); Jeff Brown (12/31/14); Tracy E. Christopher (12/31/16); Kem Thompson Frost (12/31/14); Martha Hill Jamison (12/31/12); Charles W. Seymore (12/31/12); and Leslie Brock Yates (12/31/16). **Clerk of Court**, Christopher A. Prine. Counties in the Fourteenth District: Austin, Brazoria, Chambers, Colorado, Fort Bend, Galveston, Grimes, Harris, Waller, Washington. ☆

*The location of the First Court of Appeals was changed from Galveston to Houston by the 55th Legislature, with the provision that all cases originated in Galveston County be tried in that city and with the further provision that any case may, at the discretion of the court, be tried in either city.

†Because of the heavy workload of the Houston area Court of Appeals, the 60th Legislature in 1967 provided for the establishment of a Fourteenth Appeals Court in Houston.

District Judges in Texas

Below are the names of all district judges in Texas, as of July 2011, listed in district court order. To determine which judges have jurisdiction in specific counties, refer to the table on pages 494–495.

Sources: Texas Judicial System Directory 2011, Office of Court Administration, and county clerks.

Court	Judge	Court	Judge	Court	Judge
1	Gary H. Gatlin (D)	61	Alfred (Al) Bennett (D)	123	Guy William Griffin (D)
1A	Jerome P. Owens Jr. (D)	62	Robert Scott McDowell (D)	124	F. Alfonso Charles (R)
2	Dwight L. Phifer (D)	63	Enrique Fernandez (D)	125	Kyle Carter (D)
3	Mark A. Calhoon (R)	64	Robert W. Kinkaid Jr. (R)	126	Darlene Byrne (D)
4	J. Clay Gossett (D)	65	Yahara Lisa Gutierrez (D)	127	R.K. Sandill (D)
5	Ralph K. Burgess (R)	66	F.B. (Bob) McGregor Jr. (D)	128	Courtney Burch-Arkeen (R)
6	Eric S. Clifford (R)	67	Donald J. Cosby (R)	129	Michael Paul Gomez (D)
7	Kerry L. Russell (R)	68	Martin J. Hoffman (D)	130	Craig Estlinbaum (D)
8	Robert E. Newsom (D)	69	Ronald E. Enns (R)	131	John D. Gabriel Jr. (D)
9	Frederick E. Edwards (R)	70	W. Denn Whalen (R)	132	Ernie B. Armstrong (R)
10	David Edward Garner (D)	71	William Todd Hughley (R)	133	Jaclanel McFarland (D)
11	Mike Miller (D)	72	Ruben Gonzales Reyes (R)	134	Dale B. Tillery (D)
12	Donald L. Kraemer (R)	73	Renée McElhaney (R)	135	K. Stephen Williams (R)
13	James Lagomarsino (R)	74	Gary Coley (R)	136	Milton G. Shuffield (D)
14	Eric V. Moyé (D)	75	Mark Morefield (R)	137	John (Trey) McClendon (R)
15	Jim Patrick Fallon (R)	76	Kerry (Dan) Woodson (R)	138	Arturo Cisneros Nelson (D)
16	Carmen Rivera-Worley (R)	77	Patrick (Pat) Simmons (D)	139	Jose Roberto Flores (D)
17	Melody Wilkinson (R)	78	W. Bernard Fudge (R)	140	Jim Bob Darnell (R)
18	John Edward Neill (R)	79	Richard Clark Terrell (D)	141	John P. Chupp (R)
19	Ralph T. Strother (R)	80	Larry Weiman (D)	142	George (Jody) Gillls (R)
20	John Youngblood	81	Donna S. Rayes (D)	143	Bob Parks (D)
21	Terry Flenniken (D)	82	Robert Miller Stem (D)	144	Angus McGinty (R)
22	Anna Martinez Boling (R)	83	Carl Pendergrass (R)	145	Campbell Cox II (R)
23	Ben Hardin (R)	84	William D. Smith (R)	146	Jack R. (Rick) Morris (R)
24	Joseph Patrick Kelly (D)	85	J.D. Langley (R)	147	Clifford A. Brown
25	Dwight E. Peschel (R)	86	Howard Tygrett (R)	148	Guy Williams (D)
25A	Wm. C. (Bud) Kirkendall (R)	87	Deborah Oakes Evans (R)	149	Terri Tipton Holder (R)
26	Billy Ray Stubblefield (R)	88	Earl B. Stover III (D)	150	Janet P. Littlejohn (R)
27	Joe Carroll (R)	89	Mark Thomas Price (R)	151	Mike Engelhart (D)
28	Nanette Hasette (D)	90	Stephen O. Crawford (R)	152	Robert Schaffer (D)
29	Jerry D. Ray (R)	91	Steven R. Herod (R)	153	Kenneth Charles Curry (R)
30	Robert P. Brotherton (R)	92	Ricardo P. Rodriguez Jr. (D)	154	Felix Klein (R)
31	Steven R. Emmert (R)	93	Rodolfo (Rudy) Delgado (D)	155	Jeff Steinhauser (R)
32	Glen N. Harrison (R)	94	Bobby Galvan (D)	156	Joel B. Johnson (D)
33	Guilford (Gil) L. Jones III (R)	95	Ken Molberg (D)	157	Randall William Wilson (R)
34	William E. Moody (D)	96	R.H. Wallace Jr. (R)	158	Steve Burgess (R)
35	William Stephen Ellis (D)	97	Roger E. Towery (R)	159	Paul E. White (R)
36	Michael E. Welborn (D)	98	Rhonda Hurley (D)	160	Jim Jordan (D)
37	David A. Berchelmann Jr. (R)	99	William Charles Sowder (R)	161	John W. Smith (R)
38	Camile G. DuBose (D)	100	Stuart M. Messer (R)	162	Lorraine A. Raggio (D)
39	Shane Hadaway (D)	101	Martin (Marty) Lowy (D)	163	Dennis Robert Powell (D)
40	Bob Carroll (R)	102	Bobby Lockhart (D)	164	Alexandra Smoots-Hogan (D)
41	Mary Anne Bramblett (D)	103	Janet L. Leal (D)	165	Josefina Muniz Rendon (D)
42	John Wilson Weeks (R)	104	Lee Hamilton (R)	166	Martha B. Tanner (D)
43	Trey Loftin (R)	105	Angelica Hernandez	167	Mike F. Lynch (R)
44	Carlos Cortez (D)	106	Carter T. Schildknecht (R)	168	Marcos Lizarraga (D)
45	Barbara H. Nellermoe (D)	107	Benjamin Euresti Jr. (D)	169	Gordon G. Adams (R)
46	Dan Mike Bird (D)	108	Douglas Woodburn (R)	170	Jim Meyer (R)
47	Daniel Schaap (R)	109	Martin Muncy (R)	171	Bonnie Rangel (D)
48	David Lettimore Evans (R)	110	William P. Smith (R)	172	Donald J. Floyd (D)
49	Jose (Joe) A. Lopez (D)	111	Monica Zapata Notzon (D)	173	Willis Daniel Moore (R)
50	William Hawkins Heatly (D)	112	Pedro (Pete) Gomez Jr. (D)	174	Ruben Guerrero (D)
51	Barbara Lane Walther (R)	113	John Donovan (R)	175	Mary D. Roman (D)
52	Trent D. Farrell (R)	114	Christi Kennedy (R)	176	Shawna L. Reagin (D)
53	Scott H. Jenkins (D)	115	Lauren L. Parish (D)	177	Kevin Fine (D)
54	Matt E. Johnson (R)	116	Tonya Parker (D)	178	David Mendoza (D)
55	Jeff Shadwick (R)	117	Sandra L. Watts (D)	179	Randy Roll (D)
56	Lonnie Cox (R)	118	Timothy Yeats (R)	180	Marc Brown (R)
57	Antonia (Toni) Arteaga (D)	119	Garland (Ben) Woodward (R)	181	John Boyd Board (R)
58	Robert J. Wortham (D)	120	Maria A. Salas-Mendoza (D)	182	Jeannie S. Barr (R)
59	Rayburn (Rim) M. Nall Jr. (R)	121	Kelly Glen Moore (R)	183	Vanessa Velasquez (R)
60	James Gary Sanderson (D)	122	John A. Ellisor (D)	184	Jan Krocker (D)

Court	Judge	Court	Judge	Court	Judge
185	Susan Brown (R)	253	Chap B. Cain III (R)	321	Carole W. Clark (R)
186	Maria Teresa Herr (D)	254	James Martin (D)	322	Nancy L. Berger (R)
187	Raymond C. Angelini (R)	255	Lori Chrisman Hockett (D)	323	Jean Hudson Boyd (R)
188	David Scott Brabham (R)	256	Davis Lopez (D)	324	Jerome Scott Hennigan (R)
189	William Rambo Burke Jr. (R)	257	Judy Lynn Warne (R)	325	Judith G. Wells (R)
190	Patricia J. Kerrigan (R)	258	Elizabeth E. Coker (D)	326	Aleta Hacker (D)
191	Gena Slaughter (D)	259	Brooks H. Hagler (D)	327	Linda Yee Chew (D)
192	Craig Smith (D)	260	Buddie J. Hahn (D)	328	Ronald R. Pope (R)
193	Carl H. Ginsberg (D)	261	Lora J. Livingston (D)	329	Randy M. Clapp (D)
194	Ernest B. White (D)	262	Denise Bradley (R)	330	Andrea Plumlee (D)
195	Fred Tinsley (D)	263	Jim Wallace (R)	331	David Crain (D)
196	Stephen Tittle (R)	264	Martha Jane Trudo (R)	332	Mario E. Ramirez Jr. (D)
197	Migdalia Lopez (D)	265	Mark C. Stoltz (D)	333	Joseph J. Halbach Jr. (R)
198	Melvin (Rex) Emerson (R)	266	Donald Richard Jones (D)	334	Kenneth Wise (R)
199	Robert T. Dry Jr. (R)	267	Juergen (Skipper) Koetter (R)	335	Reva L. Towslee-Corbett (R)
200	Gisela D. Triana (D)	268	Brady Gifford Elliott (R)	336	Laurine Jean Blake (R)
201	Amy Clark Meachum (D)	269	Daniel E. Hinde (R)	337	Herb Ritchie (D)
202	Leon F. Pesek Jr. (D)	270	Brent G. Gamble (R)	338	Hazel B. Jones (D)
203	Teresa Hawthorne (D)	271	John H. Fostel (D)	339	Maria T. (Terri) Jackson (D)
204	Lena Levario (D)	272	Travis B. Bryan III (R)	340	Jay Weatherby (D)
205	Kathleen H. Olivares (D)	273	Charles Ramsey Mitchell (D)	341	Elma Salinas Ender (D)
206	Rose Guerra Reyna (D)	274	Gary L. Steel (R)	342	James Wade Birdwell (R)
207	Jack Hollis Robison (R)	275	Juan R. Partida (D)	343	Janna K. Whatley (D)
208	Denise M. Collins (D)	276	Robert Rolston (D)	344	Carroll E. Wilborn Jr. (R)
209	Michael T. McSpadden (R)	277	Ken Anderson (R)	345	Stephen A. Yelenosky (D)
210	Gonzalo Garcia (D)	278	Kenneth H. Keeling (R)	346	Angie Juarez Barill (D)
211	L. Dee Shipman Jr. (R)	279	Jeffrey Randall Shelton (D)	347	Nelva Gonzales-Ramos (D)
212	Susan Elizabeth Criss (D)	280	Lynn Bradshaw Hull (R)	348	Dana Michelle Womack (R)
213	Louis E. Sturns (R)	281	Sylvia A. Matthews (R)	349	Pamela Foster Fletcher (R)
214	José Longoria (D)	282	Andy Chatham (R)	350	Thomas Michael Wheeler (R)
215	Steven E. Kirkland (D)	283	Rick Magnis (D)	351	Mark Kent Ellis (R)
216	N. Keith Williams (R)	284	Cara Cordell Wood (R)	352	Bonnie Sudderth (R)
217	Barry Randolph Bryan (R)	285	Richard Price (R)	353	Tim Sulak (D)
218	Stella H. Saxon (D)	286	Jay Michael (Pat) Phelan (R)	354	Richard (Rick) Beacom (R)
219	Scott J. Becker (R)	287	Gordon Houston Green (D)	355	Ralph H. Walton Jr. (R)
220	Phil Robertson (R)	288	Solomon (Sol) Casseb III (R)	356	Steven Thomas (R)
221	Lisa Benge Michalk (R)	289	Carmen Kelsey (D)	357	Leonel Alejandro (D)
222	Roland Saul (R)	290	Melisa Skinner (R)	358	Bill McCoy (R)
223	Phil Vanderpool (R)	291	Susan Lynn Hawk (R)	359	Kathleen A. Hamilton (R)
224	Cathy Stryker (R)	292	Larry Mitchell (D)	360	Michael Sinha (R)
225	Peter Sakai (D)	293	Cynthia L. Muniz (D)	361	Steve Lee Smith (R)
226	Sid L. Harle (R)	294	Teresa Drum (R)	362	R. Bruce McFarling (R)
227	Philip A. Kazen Jr. (D)	295	Caroline Baker (R)	363	Tracy F. Holmes (D)
228	Marc Christopher Carter (R)	296	John R. Roach Jr. (R)	364	Bradley S. Underwood (R)
229	AnaLisa Garza (D)	297	Leo Everett Young Jr. (R)	365	Amado Jose Abascal III (D)
230	Belinda Joy Hill (R)	298	Emily G. Tobolowsky (D)	366	Raymond (Ray) Wheless (R)
231	Randy Catterton (R)	299	Charlie F. Baird (D)	367	Margaret Barnes (R)
232	Mary Lou Keel (R)	300	K. Randall Hufstetler (R)	368	Alfred B. (Burt) Carnes (R)
233	William Wren Harris (R)	301	Lynn Cherry (D)	369	Bascom W. Bentley III (R)
234	Mauricio (Reece) Rondon (R)	302	Tena T. Callahan (D)	370	Noe Gonzalez (D)
235	Janelle M. Haverkamp (R)	303	Dennise Garcia (D)	371	Mollee Bennett Westfall (R)
236	Thomas Wilson Lowe III (R)	304	William A. Mazur Jr. (D)	372	David Scott Wisch (R)
237	Leslie (Les) Hatch (R)	305	Cheryl Lee Shannon (R)	377	Robert C. Cheshire (R)
238	John Gary Hyde (R)	306	Janis L. Yarbrough (D)	378	Joe Grubbs (R)
239	Patrick Edward Sebesta (R)	307	Tim Womack (R)	379	Ron Rangel (D)
240	Thomas R. Culver III (R)	308	James Lombardino (R)	380	Suzanne H. Wooten (R)
241	Jack M. Skeen Jr. (R)	309	Sherill Dean (R)	381	Jose Luis Garza (D)
242	Edward L. Self (R)	310	Lisa Ann Millard (R)	382	Brett Hall (R)
243	Bill D. Hicks (R)	311	Denise Pratt (R)	383	Mike Herrera (D)
244	William Stacy Trotter (R)	312	David Farr (D)	384	Patrick Michael Garcia (D)
245	Roy L. Moore (R)	313	Glenn Devlin (R)	385	Robin Malone Darr (R)
246	Jim York (R)	314	John Franklin Phillips (R)	386	Laura Lee Parker (R)
247	Bonnie Crane Hellums (R)	315	Michael H. Schneider Jr. (R)	387	Robert J. Kern (R)
248	Joan Campbell (R)	316	John W. LaGrone (R)	388	Patricia A. Macias (D)
249	Dennis Wayne Bridewell (R)	317	Larry Edward Thorne III (D)	389	Leticia (Letty) Lopez (D)
250	John K. Dietz (D)	318	Dean Rucker (R)	390	Julie Harris Kocurek (D)
251	Anna E. Estevez (R)	319	Thomas F. Greenwell (R)	391	Thomas J. Gossett (R)
252	Layne W. Walker (D)	320	Don R. Emerson (R)	392	Carter William Tarrance (R)

Court	Judge	Court	Judge	Court	Judge
393	Doug Robison (R)	416	John Christopher Oldner (R)	439	David Rakow (R)
394	Kenneth Daly DeHart (D)	417	Cynthia M. Wheless (R)	441	Rodney W. Satterwhite (R)
395	Michael Paul Jergins (R)	418	Tracy A. Gilbert (R)	444	David A. Sanchez (D)
396	George W. Gallagher (R)	419	Orlinda L. Naranjo (D)	445	J. Rolando Olvera (D)
397	Brian Keith Gary (R)	420	Edwin Allen Klein (R)	448	Regina B. Arditti (D)
398	Aida Salinas Flores (D)	421	Todd Alexander Blomerth (R)	449	Jesse Contreras (D)
399	Juanita Vasquez-Gardner (R)	422	B. Michael Chitty (R)	506	Albert (Buddy) McCaig Jr. (R)
400	Clifford James Vacek (R)	423	Chris Duggan (D)		
401	Mark Joseph Rusch (R)	424	Daniel H. Mills (R)	**Criminal District Courts**		
402	George Timothy Boswell (R)	425	Mark J. Silverstone (R)	Dallas 1	Robert D. Burns III (D)
403	Brenda P. Kennedy (D)	426	Fancy H. Jezek (R)	Dallas 2	Don Adams (D)
404	Elia Cornejo-Lopez (D)	427	Jim Coronado (D)	Dallas 3	Gracie Lewis (D)
405	Wayne Mallia (D)	428	William R. Henry (R)	Dallas 4	John Coleman Creuzot (D)
406	Oscar (O.J.) Hale Jr. (D)	429	Jill R. Willis (R)	Dallas 5	Carter Thompson (D)
407	Karen Pozza (D)	430	Israel Ramon Jr. (D)	Dallas 6	Jeanine L. Howard (D)
408	Larry E. Noll (D)	431	Jonathan Bailey (R)	Dallas 7	Michael Reuss Snipes (D)
409	Sam Medrano Jr. (D)	432	Ruben Gonzalez Jr. (R)	El Paso	Manuel Baranza (D)
410	K. Michael Mayes (R)	433	Dibrell (Dib) Waldrip (R)	Jefferson	John B. Stevens Jr. (D)
411	Robert Hill Trapp (D)	434	James H. Shoemake (R)	Tarrant 1	Sharen Wilson (R)
412	W. Edwin Denman (R)	435	Michael Thomas Seiler (R)	Tarrant 2	Wayne Francis Salvant (R)
413	William C. Bosworth Jr. (R)	436	Lisa Jarrett (R)	Tarrant 3	Robb Caralano (R)
414	Vicki Lynn Menard (R)	437	Lori I. Valenzuela (R)	Tarrant 4	Michael R. Thomas (R)
415	Graham Quisenberry (R)	438	Victor H. Negrón Jr. (R)		

Administrative Judicial Districts of Texas

There are **nine administrative judicial districts** in the state for administrative purposes. An active or retired district judge or an active or retired appellate judge with judicial experience in a district court serves as the Presiding Judge upon appointment by the Governor. They receive extra compensation of $5,000, paid by counties in the that administrative district.

The Presiding Judge convenes an annual conference of the judges in the administrative district to consult on the state of business in the courts. This conference is empowered to adopt rules for the administration of cases in the district.

The Presiding Judge may assign active or retired district judges residing within the administrative district to any of the district courts within the administrative district. The Presiding Judge of one administrative district may request the Presiding Judge of another administrative district to assign a judge from that district to sit in a district court located in the administrative district of the Presiding Judge making the request.

The Chief Justice of the Supreme Court of Texas convenes an annual conference of the nine Presiding Judges to determine the need for assignment of judges and to promote the uniform administration of the assignment of judges.

The Chief Justice is empowered to assign judges of one administrative district for service in another whenever necessary for the prompt and efficient administration of justice.

First District — John David Ovard, Dallas (2/1/13): Anderson, Bowie, Camp, Cass, Cherokee, Collin, Dallas, Delta, Ellis, Fannin, Franklin, Grayson, Gregg, Harrison, Henderson, Hopkins, Houston, Hunt, Kaufman, Lamar, Marion, Morris, Nacogdoches, Panola, Rains, Red River, Rockwall, Rusk, Shelby, Smith, Titus, Upshur, Van Zandt and Wood.

Second District — Olen Underwood, Willis (4/3/13): Angelina, Bastrop, Brazoria, Brazos, Burleson, Chambers, Fort Bend, Freestone, Galveston, Grimes, Hardin, Harris, Jasper, Jefferson, Lee, Leon, Liberty, Limestone, Madison, Matagorda, Montgomery, Newton, Orange, Polk, Robertson, Sabine, San Augustine, San Jacinto, Trinity, Tyler, Walker, Waller, Washington and Wharton.

Third District — Billy Ray Stubblefield, Georgetown (2/3/14): Austin, Bell, Blanco, Bosque, Burnet, Caldwell, Colorado, Comal, Comanche, Coryell, Falls, Fayette, Gonzales, Guadalupe, Hamilton, Hays, Hill, Johnson, Lampasas, Lavaca, Llano, McLennan, Mason, Milam, Navarro, San Saba, Travis and Williamson.

Fourth District — David Peeples, San Antonio (10/8/12): Aransas, Atascosa, Bee, Bexar, Calhoun, DeWitt, Dimmit, Frio, Goliad, Jackson, Karnes, LaSalle, Live Oak, Maverick, McMullen, Refugio, San Patricio, Victoria, Webb, Wilson, Zapata and Zavala.

Fifth District — J. Rolando Olvera, Brownsville (12/31/14): Brooks, Cameron, Duval, Hidalgo, Jim Hogg, Jim Wells, Kenedy, Kleberg, Nueces, Starr and Willacy.

Sixth District — Stephen B. Ables, Kerrville (11/10/12): Bandera, Brewster, Crockett, Culberson, Edwards, El Paso, Gillespie, Hudspeth, Jeff Davis, Kendall, Kerr, Kimble, Kinney, Mason, Medina, Pecos, Presidio, Reagan, Real, Sutton, Terrell, Upton, Uvalde and Val Verde.

Seventh District — Dean Rucker, Midland (12/31/14): Andrews, Borden, Brown, Callahan, Coke, Coleman, Concho, Crane, Dawson, Ector, Fisher, Gaines, Garza, Glasscock, Haskell, Howard, Irion, Jones, Kent, Loving, Lynn, Martin, McCulloch, Menard, Midland, Mills, Mitchell, Nolan, Reeves, Runnels, Schleicher, Scurry, Shackelford, Sterling, Stonewall, Taylor, Throckmorton, Tom Green, Ward and Winkler.

Eighth District — Roger Jeffrey Walker, Fort Worth (12/31/14): Archer, Clay, Cooke, Denton, Eastland, Erath, Hood, Jack, Johnson, Montague, Palo Pinto, Parker, Somervell, Stephens, Tarrant, Wichita, Wise and Young.

Ninth District — Kelly G. Moore, Brownfield (11/10/12): Armstrong, Bailey, Baylor, Briscoe, Carson, Castro, Childress, Cochran, Collingsworth, Cottle, Crosby, Dallam, Deaf Smith, Dickens, Donley, Floyd, Foard, Gray, Hale, Hall, Hansford, Hardeman, Hartley, Hemphill, Hockley, Hutchinson, King, Knox, Lamb, Lipscomb, Lubbock, Moore, Motley, Ochiltree, Oldham, Parmer, Potter, Randall, Roberts, Sherman, Swisher, Terry, Wheeler, Wilbarger and Yoakum. ☆

Texas Courts by County

Below are listed the state district court or courts, court of appeals district, administrative judicial district, and U.S. judicial district for each county in Texas as of July 2011. For the names of the district court judges, see table by district number on page 491. Lists of other judges in the Texas court system begin on page. 489.

County	State Dist. Court(s)	Ct. of App'ls Dist.	Adm. Jud. Dist.	U.S. Jud. Dist.
Anderson	3, 87, 349, 369	12	1	E-Tyler
Andrews	109	8	7	W-Midland
Angelina	159, 217	12	2	E-Lufkin
Aransas	36, 156, 343	13	4	S-C.Christi
Archer	97	2	8	N-W. Falls
Armstrong	47	7	9	N-Amarillo
Atascosa	81, 218	4	4	W-San Ant.
Austin	155	1, 14	3	S-Houston
Bailey	287	7	9	N-Lubbock
Bandera	216	4	6	W-San Ant.
Bastrop	21, 335, 423	3	2	W-Austin
Baylor	50	11	9	N-W. Falls
Bee	36, 156, 343	13	4	S-C.Christi
Bell	27, 146, 169, 264, 426	3	3	W-Waco
Bexar	37, 45, 57, 73, 131, 144, 150, 166, 175, 186, 187, 224, 225, 226, 227, 285, 288, 289, 290, 379, 386, 399, 407, 408, 436, 437, 438	4	4	W-San Ant.
Blanco	33, 424	3	3	W-Austin
Borden	132	11	7	N-Lubbock
Bosque	220	10	3	W-Waco
Bowie	5, 102, 202	6	1	E-Texark.
Brazoria	23, 149, 239, 300, 412	1, 14	2	S-Galves.
Brazos	85, 272, 361	10	2	S-Houston
Brewster	394	8	6	W-Pecos
Briscoe	110	7	9	N-Amarillo
Brooks	79	4	5	S-C.Christi
Brown	35	11	7	N-S. Angelo
Burleson	21, 335	10	2	W-Austin
Burnet	33, 424	3	3	W-Austin
Caldwell	22, 207, 421	3	3	W-Austin
Calhoun	24, 135, 267	13	4	S-Victoria
Callahan	42	11	7	N-Abilene
Cameron	103, 107, 138, 197, 357, 404, 444, 445	13	5	S-Browns-ville
Camp	76, 276	6	1	E-Marshall
Carson	100	7	9	N-Amarillo
Cass	5	6	1	E-Marshall
Castro	64, 242	7	9	N-Amarillo
Chambers	253, 344	1, 14	2	S-Galves.
Cherokee	2, 369	12	1	E-Tyler
Childress	100	7	9	N-Amarillo
Clay	97	2	8	N-W. Falls
Cochran	286	7	9	N-Lubbock
Coke	51	3	7	N-S. Angelo
Coleman	42	11	7	N-S. Angelo
Collin	199, 219, 296, 366, 380, 401, 416, 417, 429	5	1	E-Sherman
Collingsworth	100	7	9	N-Amarillo
Colorado	25, 25-A	1, 14	3	S-Houston
Comal	22, 207, 274, 433	3	3	W-San Ant.
Comanche	220	11	3	N-Ft. Worth
Concho	119	3	7	N-S. Angelo
Cooke	235	2	8	E-Sherman
Coryell	52	10	3	W-Waco
Cottle	50	7	9	N-W. Falls
Crane	109	8	7	W-Midland
Crockett	112	8	6	N-S. Angelo
Crosby	72	7	9	N-Lubbock
Culberson	205, 394	8	6	W-Pecos
Dallam	69	7	9	N-Amarillo
Dallas	14, 44, 68, 95, 101, 116, 134, 160, 162, 191, 192, 193, 194, 195, 203, 204, 254, 255, 256, 265, 282, 283, 291, 292, 298, 301, 302, 303,	5	1	N-Dallas

County	State Dist. Court(s)	Ct. of App'ls Dist.	Adm. Jud. Dist.	U.S. Jud. Dist.
Dallas continued	304, 305, 330, 363, Cr. 1, Cr. 2, Cr. 3, Cr. 4, Cr. 5, Cr. 6, Cr. 7	5	1	N-Dallas
Dawson	106	11	7	N-Lubbock
Deaf Smith	222	7	9	N-Amarillo
Delta	8, 62	6	1	E-Sherman
Denton	16, 158, 211, 362, 367, 393, 431	2	8	E-Sherman
DeWitt	24, 135, 267	13	4	S-Victoria
Dickens	110	7	9	N-Lubbock
Dimmit	293, 365	4	4	W-San Ant.
Donley	100	7	9	N-Amarillo
Duval	229	4	5	S-C.Christi
Eastland	91	11	8	N-Abilene
Ector	70, 161, 244, 358	11	7	W-Midland
Edwards	63	4	6	W-Del Rio
Ellis	40, 378	10	1	N-Dallas
El Paso	34, 41, 65, 120, 168, 171, 205, 210, 243, 327, 346, 383, 384, 388, 409, 448, Cr. 1	8	6	W-El Paso
Erath	266	11	8	N-Ft. Worth
Falls	82	10	3	W-Waco
Fannin	336	6	1	E-Sherman
Fayette	155	3	3	S-Houston
Fisher	32	11	7	N-Abilene
Floyd	110	7	9	N-Lubbock
Foard	46	7	9	N-W. Falls
Fort Bend	240, 268, 328, 387, 400, 434	1, 14	2	S-Houston
Franklin	8, 62	6	1	E-Texark.
Freestone	77, 87	10	2	W-Waco
Frio	81, 218	4	4	W-San Ant.
Gaines	106	11	7	N-Lubbock
Galveston	10, 56, 122, 212, 306, 405	1, 14	2	S-Galves.
Garza	106	7	7	N-Lubbock
Gillespie	216	4	6	W-Austin
Glasscock	118	11	7	N-S. Angelo
Goliad	24, 135, 267	13	4	S-Victoria
Gonzales	25, 25-A	13	3	W-San Ant.
Gray	31, 223	7	9	N-Amarillo
Grayson	15, 59, 397	5	1	E-Sherman
Gregg	124, 188, 307	6, 12	1	E-Tyler
Grimes	12, 506	1, 14	2	S-Houston
Guadalupe	25, 25-A, 274	4	3	W-San Ant.
Hale	64, 242	7	9	N-Lubbock
Hall	100	7	9	N-Amarillo
Hamilton	220	10	3	W-Waco
Hansford	84	7	9	N-Amarillo
Hardeman	46	7	9	N-W. Falls
Hardin	88, 356	9	2	E-B'mont.
Harris	11, 55, 61, 80, 113, 125, 127, 129, 133, 151, 152, 157, 164, 165, 174, 176, 177, 178, 179, 180, 182, 183, 184, 185, 189, 190, 208, 209, 215, 228, 230, 232, 234, 245, 246, 247, 248, 257, 262, 263, 269, 270, 280, 281, 295, 308, 309, 310, 311, 312, 313, 314, 315, 333, 334, 337, 338, 339, 351	1, 14	2	S-Houston
Harrison	71	6	1	E-Marshall
Hartley	69	7	9	N-Amarillo
Haskell	39	11	7	N-Abilene
Hays	22, 207, 274, 428	3	3	W-Austin
Hemphill	31	7	9	N-Amarillo

County	Districts			Region
Henderson	3, 173, 392	12	1	E-Tyler
Hidalgo	92, 93, 139, 206, 275, 332, 370, 389, 398, 430, 449	13	5	S-McAllen
Hill	66	10	3	W-Waco
Hockley	286	7	9	N-Lubbock
Hood	355	2	8	N-Ft. Worth
Hopkins	8, 62	6	1	E-Sherman
Houston	3, 349	12	1	E-Lufkin
Howard	118	11	7	N-Abilene
Hudspeth	205, 394	8	6	W-Pecos
Hunt	196, 354	5, 6	1	N-Dallas
Hutchinson	84, 316	7	9	N-Amarillo
Irion	51	3	7	N-S. Angelo
Jack	271	2	8	N-Ft. Worth
Jackson	24, 135, 267	13	4	S-Victoria
Jasper	1, 1-A	9	2	E-B'mont.
Jeff Davis	394	8	6	W-Pecos
Jefferson	58, 60, 136, 172, 252, 279, 317, Cr. 1	9	2	E-B'mont.
Jim Hogg	229	4	5	S-Laredo
Jim Wells	79	4	5	S-C.Christi
Johnson	18, 249, 413	10	8	N-Dallas
Jones	259	11	7	N-Abilene
Karnes	81, 218	4	4	W-San Ant.
Kaufman	86, 422	5	1	N-Dallas
Kendall	216	4	6	W-San Ant.
Kenedy	105	13	5	S-C.Christi
Kent	39	7	7	N-Lubbock
Kerr	198, 216	4	6	W-San Ant.
Kimble	198	4	6	W-Austin
King	50	7	9	N-W. Falls
Kinney	63	4	6	W-Del Rio
Kleberg	105	13	5	S-C.Christi
Knox	50	11	9	N-W. Falls
Lamar	6, 62	6	1	E-Sherman
Lamb	154	7	9	N-Lubbock
Lampasas	27	3	3	W-Austin
La Salle	81, 218	4	4	S-Laredo
Lavaca	25, 25-A	13	3	S-Victoria
Lee	21, 335	3	2	W-Austin
Leon	12, 87, 278	10	2	W-Waco
Liberty	75, 253	9	2	E-B'mont.
Limestone	77, 87	10	2	W-Waco
Lipscomb	31	7	9	N-Amarillo
Live Oak	36, 156, 343	13	4	S-C.Christi
Llano	33, 424	3	3	W-Austin
Loving	143	8	7	W-Pecos
Lubbock	72, 99, 137, 140, 237, 364	7	9	N-Lubbock
Lynn	106	7	7	N-Lubbock
Madison	12, 278	10	2	S-Houston
Marion	115, 276	6	1	E-Marshall
Martin	118	11	7	W-Midland
Mason	198	4	6	W-Austin
Matagorda	23, 130	13	2	S-Galves.
Maverick	293, 365	4	4	W-Del Rio
McCulloch	198	3	7	W-Austin
McLennan	19, 54, 74, 170, 414	10	3	W-Waco
McMullen	36, 156, 343	4	4	S-Laredo
Medina	38	4	6	W-San Ant.
Menard	198	4	7	N-S. Angelo
Midland	142, 238, 318, 385, 441	11	7	W-Midland
Milam	20	3	3	W-Waco
Mills	35	3	7	N-S. Angelo
Mitchell	32	11	7	N-Abilene
Montague	97	2	8	N-W. Falls
Montgomery	9, 221, 284, 359, 410, 418, 435	9	2	S-Houston
Moore	69	7	9	N-Amarillo
Morris	76, 276	6	1	E-Marshall
Motley	110	7	9	N-Lubbock
Nacogdoches	145, 420	12	1	E-Lufkin
Navarro	13	10	3	N-Dallas
Newton	1, 1-A	9	2	E-B'mont.
Nolan	32	11	7	N-Abilene
Nueces	28, 94, 105, 117, 148, 214, 319, 347	13	5	S-C.Christi
Ochiltree	84	7	9	N-Amarillo
Oldham	222	7	9	N-Amarillo
Orange	128, 163, 260	9	2	E-B'mont.
Palo Pinto	29	11	8	N-Ft. Worth
Panola	123	6	1	E-Tyler
Parker	43, 415	2	8	N-Ft. Worth
Parmer	287	7	9	N-Amarillo
Pecos	83, 112	8	6	W-Pecos
Polk	258, 411	9	2	E-Lufkin
Potter	47, 108, 181, 251, 320	7	9	N-Amarillo
Presidio	394	8	6	W-Pecos
Rains	8, 354	12	1	E-Tyler
Randall	47, 181, 251	7	9	N-Amarillo
Reagan	112	8	6	N-S. Angelo
Real	38	4	6	W-San Ant.
Red River	6, 102	6	1	E-Texark.
Reeves	143	8	7	W-Pecos
Refugio	24, 135, 267	13	4	S-Victoria
Roberts	31	7	9	N-Amarillo
Robertson	82	10	2	W-Waco
Rockwall	382, 439	5	1	N-Dallas
Runnels	119	3	7	N-S. Angelo
Rusk	4	6, 12	1	E-Tyler
Sabine	1, 273	12	2	E-Lufkin
San Augustine	1, 273	12	2	E-Lufkin
San Jacinto	258, 411	9	2	S-Houston
San Patricio	36, 156, 343	13	4	S-C.Christi
San Saba	33, 424	3	3	W-Austin
Schleicher	51	3	7	N-S. Angelo
Scurry	132	11	7	N-Lubbock
Shackelford	259	11	7	N-Abilene
Shelby	123, 273	12	1	E-Lufkin
Sherman	69	7	9	N-Amarillo
Smith	7, 114, 241, 321	12	1	E-Tyler
Somervell	18, 249	10	8	W-Waco
Starr	229, 381	4	5	S-McAllen
Stephens	90	11	8	N-Abilene
Sterling	51	3	7	N-S. Angelo
Stonewall	39	11	7	N-Abilene
Sutton	112	4	6	N-S. Angelo
Swisher	64, 242	7	9	N-Amarillo
Tarrant	17, 48, 67, 96, 141, 153, 213, 231, 233, 236, 297, 322, 323, 324, 325, 342, 348, 352, 360, 371, 372, 396, 432, Cr. 1, Cr. 2, Cr. 3, Cr. 4	2	8	N-Ft. Worth
Taylor	42, 104, 326, 350	11	7	N-Abilene
Terrell	63, 83	8	6	W-Del Rio
Terry	121	7	9	N-Lubbock
Throckmorton	39	11	7	N-Abilene
Titus	76, 276	6	1	E-Texark.
Tom Green	51, 119, 340, 391	3	7	N-S. Angelo
Travis	53, 98, 126, 147, 167, 200, 201, 250, 261, 299, 331, 345, 353, 390, 403, 419, 427	3	3	W-Austin
Trinity	258, 411	12	2	E-Lufkin
Tyler	1-A, 88	9	2	E-Lufkin
Upshur	115	6, 12	1	E-Marshall
Upton	112	8	6	W-Midland
Uvalde	38	4	6	W-Del Rio
Val Verde	63, 83	4	6	W-Del Rio
Van Zandt	294	12	1	E-Tyler
Victoria	24, 135, 267, 377	13	4	S-Victoria
Walker	12, 278	10	2	S-Houston
Waller	155, 506	1, 14	2	S-Houston
Ward	143	8	7	W-Pecos
Washington	21, 335	1, 14	2	W-Austin
Webb	49, 111, 341, 406	4	4	S-Laredo
Wharton	23, 329	13	2	S-Houston
Wheeler	31	7	9	N-Amarillo
Wichita	30, 78, 89	2	8	N-W. Falls
Wilbarger	46	7	9	N-W. Falls
Willacy	197	13	5	S-Brownsville
Williamson	26, 277, 368, 395, 425	3	3	W-Austin
Wilson	81, 218	4	4	W-San Ant.
Winkler	109	8	7	W-Pecos
Wise	271	2	8	N-Ft. Worth
Wood	402	6, 12	1	E-Tyler
Yoakum	121	7	9	N-Lubbock
Young	90	2	8	N-W. Falls
Zapata	49	4	4	S-Laredo
Zavala	293, 365	4	4	W-Del Rio

Texas State Agencies

On the following pages is information about several of the many state agencies in Texas. Information was supplied to the Texas Almanac by the agencies, their websites, and from news reports. The web address for more information about state agencies, boards, and commissions is: www.tsl.state.tx.us/apps/lrs/agencies/.

Texas Commission on Environmental Quality

Source: Texas Commission on Environmental Quality; www.tceq.texas.gov

The Texas Commission on Environmental Quality (TCEQ) is the state's leading environmental agency. Known as the Texas Natural Resource Conservation Commission until September 2002, this agency works to protect Texas' human and natural resources in a manner consistent with sustainable economic development.

The TCEQ has about 2,900 employees; of those, about 1,000 work in the 16 regional offices.

The TCEQ command center is a mobile unit that travels to sites in Texas for environmental monitoring. Photo courtesy of TCEQ.

The operating budget for the 2009 fiscal year was $522.7 million, of which 88.3 percent ($461.5 million) was generated by program fees. The remaining revenues came from federal funds ($42.2 million or 8.1 percent); state general revenue ($10.4 million or 2.0 percent); and other sources ($8.6 million or 1.6 percent).

One of the TCEQ's major functions is issuing permits and other authorizations for the control of air pollution, the safe operation of water and wastewater utilities, and the management of hazardous and nonhazardous waste. More than 126,000 environmental permit applications are received annually.

The agency promotes voluntary compliance with environmental laws through pollution prevention programs, regulatory workshops, and assistance to businesses and local governments. But when environmental laws are violated, the TCEQ has the authority to levy penalties as much as $25,000 a day per violation for administrative cases. In a typical year, the agency investigates more than 100,000 regulated entities for compliance with state and federal laws, and responds to about 7,000 complaints.

In fiscal year 2010, the TCEQ issued 1,640 administrative orders, which yielded $11.3 million in fines, and directed another $3.5 million to supplemental environmental projects benefitting some of the communities in which the environmental violations occurred.

Air Quality

Texas is home to some of the largest U.S. cities, with several metropolitan populations of greater than 1 million people. With these concentrated populations, vehicular traffic and other emissions can create air quality among the most challenging in the country.

The state has a fast-growing population and a large industrial base, especially along the Gulf Coast. The TCEQ measures air quality across the state for compliance with federal standards, as well as localized compounds of concern. Texas' air toxic monitoring network is the most comprehensive in the country with over 70 monitors located across the state. The TCEQ is responsible for developing a state implementation plan to bring metropolitan areas into compliance with federal air quality standards, such as the ozone standard. The leading areas of concern for ozone issues are Houston and Dallas-Fort Worth.

Water Quality

Surface water bodies in Texas are routinely monitored to determine whether they support their designated uses. The TCEQ coordinates a comprehensive sampling program to collect water quality data. The agency also conducts special studies to determine sources of pollution, to assess the effectiveness of water quality management measures, and to evaluate and update water quality standards.

The TCEQ also is responsible for most state and federal regulatory programs that protect groundwater, and for state and federal storm water permits. It is the primary Texas agency authorized to enforce the federal Safe Drinking Water Act, and it administers the supervision program for the state's 6,980 public water systems.

Waste Management

Waste management projects at the TCEQ include Superfund projects, pesticide collections, and waste tire recycling. In 2011, there were 111 Superfund sites in the state and federal Superfund programs. Another major clean-up program focuses on leaking petroleum storage tanks. As of 2011, more than 24,000 such sites were corrected, and work continues at another 1,900 sites. The TCEQ also issues permits for municipal landfill operations and monitors landfill capacity.

Pollution Prevention

The TCEQ offers services to anyone interested in environmental stewardship. Staff members host workshops on recycling and disposal opportunities, and on regulatory and pollution prevention topics. They also offer free on-site technical assistance for regulatory compliance. Contact the TCEQ at PO Box 13087, Austin, 78711; (512) 239-1000; www.tceq.texas.gov. ☆

Health and Human Services Commission

Source: Texas Health and Human Services Commission; www.hhs.state.tx.us

The Texas Health and Human Services Commission (HHSC) is the oversight agency for the state's health and human services system. HHSC also administers state and federal programs that provide financial, health, and social services to Texans.

In 2003, the 78th Texas Legislature mandated an unprecedented transformation of the state's health and human services system to create an integrated, effective, and accessible health and human services enterprise that protects public health and brings high-quality services and support to Texans in need. The transformation blended 12 agencies into five. creating a system that is client-centered, efficient in its use of public resources, and focused on accountability.

The Health and Human Services Commission coordinates administrative functions across the system, determines eligibility for its programs, and administers Medicaid, the Children's Health Insurance Program, Temporary Assistance for Needy Families, SNAP food benefits (formerly know as food stamps), and family violence, disaster assistance, and refugee resettlement programs.

The HHSC executive commissioner is Thomas M. Suehs. The executive commissioner is appointed by the governor and confirmed by the Senate.

The state's health and human services agencies spend more than $25 billion per year to administer more than 200 programs, employ more than 50,000 state workers, and operate from more than 1,000 locations. The HHSC includes four agencies, which operate under the oversight of HHSC. The four new departments under HHSC are:

The Department of Family and Protective Services includes child and adult protective services, childcare licensing, and child abuse prevention and early intervention services. DFPS began services Feb. 1, 2004.

The Department of Assistive and Rehabilitative Services provides rehabilitation services, including vocational rehabilitation and independent living programs; disability determination services; services for the blind, visually impaired, deaf and hard of hearing; and early childhood intervention services. DARS began services March 1, 2004.

The Department of Aging and Disability Services is responsible for aging services; community-based services and state-supported living centers for people with cognitive and development disabilities; community care programs for people with disabilities; and inspection of nursing homes and other long-term care facilities. DADS began services Sept. 1, 2004.

The Department of State Health Services includes public health programs, including immunizations, bioterrorism preparedness, and state laboratory services; Kidney Health Care program; Children with Special Health Care Needs; Women, Infants & Children (WIC); mental health services; substance abuse services; and regulatory services for a variety of health care professionals, facilities, and consumer health protection. DSHS began services on Sept. 1, 2004.

AGENCY EXPENDITURES FOR THE 2010–2011 BIENNIUM	
Department of Aging and Disability Services	$13,641,741,218
Department of Assistive and Rehabilitative Services	$1,348,849,904
Department of Family and Protective Services	$2,740,323,715
Department of State Health Services	$6,140,158,720
Health and Human Services Commission	$40,782,618,434

Other HHSC programs

The Family Violence program educates the public about domestic violence and offers emergency shelter and services to victims and their children.

The Disaster Assistance program processes grant applications for victims of presidentially declared disasters, such as tornados, floods, and hurricanes.

The Refugee Resettlement program is federally funded and provides cash, health care, and social services to eligible refugees to help them quickly become self-sufficient after arriving in the United States. ☆

Major HHSC Programs at a Glance

The **Medicaid** program provides healthcare coverage for one out of every three children in Texas, pays for half of all births and accounts for 25 percent of the state's total budget. In 2010, an average of 3.3 million Texans received healthcare coverage through Medicaid.

The **Children's Health Insurance Program (CHIP)** is designed for families who earn too much money to qualify for Medicaid health care, yet cannot afford private insurance.

The **Temporary Assistance for Needy Families (TANF)** program provides basic financial assistance for needy children and the parents or caretakers with whom they live. As a condition of eligibility, caretakers must sign and abide by a personal-responsibility agreement. Time limits for benefits have been set by both state and federal welfare-reform legislation.

SNAP food benefits, formerly known as food stamps, is a federally funded program that assists low-income families, the elderly, and single adults obtain a nutritionally adequate diet. Those eligible for food benefits include households receiving TANF or federal Supplemental Security Income benefits, and non-public assistance households having incomes below 130 percent of the poverty level. In 2011, more than 3.5 million Texans received SNAP food benefits, and the average monthly benefit amount was about $300.

Both SNAP and TANF benefits are delivered via the electronic benefit transfer (EBT) system, through which clients access benefits at about 12,000 retail locations statewide with the Lone Star card.

Information about Medicaid, CHIP, and other health and human services programs can be found at www.hhsc.state.tx.us, www.211texas.org, or by calling 2-1-1, a toll-free local resource for information on health and human service programs.

The General Land Office

Source: General Land Office of Texas. On the Web: www.glo.state.tx.us

History of the General Land Office

The Texas General Land Office (GLO) is one of the oldest governmental entities in the state, dating back to the Republic of Texas. The first General Land Office was established in 1836 in the Republic's constitution, and the first Texas Congress enacted the provision into law in 1837. The GLO was established to oversee distribution of public lands, register titles, issue patents on land and maintain records of land granted.

In the early years of statehood, beginning in 1845, Texas established the precedent of using its vast public domain for public benefit. The first use was to sell or trade land to eliminate the huge debt remaining from Texas' War for Independence and early years of the Republic.

Texas also gave away land to settlers as homesteads; to veterans as compensation for service; for internal improvements, including building railroads, shipbuilding and improving rivers for navigation; and to build the state Capitol.

The public domain was closed in 1898 when the Texas Supreme Court declared there was no more vacant and unappropriated land in Texas. In 1900, all remaining unappropriated land was set aside by the Texas Legislature to benefit public schools.

Today, 19.9 million acres of land and minerals, owned by the Permanent School Fund, the Permanent University Fund, various other state agencies or the Veterans Land Board, are managed by the General Land Office and the Commissioner of the Texas General Land Office. This includes over 4 million acres of submerged coastal lands, which consist of bays, inlets and the area from the Texas shoreline to the three-marine-league line (10.36 miles) in the Gulf of Mexico. It is estimated that more than 1 million acres make up the public domain of the state's riverbeds and another 1.7 million acres are excess lands belonging to the Permanent School Fund.

The General Land Office is the steward of the Texas Gulf Coast, serving as the premier state agency for protecting and renourishing the coast and fighting coastal erosion. In 1999, the legislature created the Coastal Erosion Planning and Response Act and put the GLO in charge of facilitating restoration and preservation of eroding beaches, dunes, wetlands and other bay shorelines along the Texas coast.

The Permanent University Fund holds title to 2.1 million fee acres, and other state agencies or special schools hold title to another 2.3 million acres. The Permanent School Fund owns mineral rights alone in almost 7.4 million acres covered under the Relinquishment Act, the Free Royalty Act and the various sales acts, and it has outright ownership to about 747,522 upland acres, mostly west of the Pecos River.

Veterans Land Board Programs

Veterans Land Program

In 1946, the Texas Legislature created a bond program to aid veterans in purchasing land. Up to $1.5 billion in bonding authority has been authorized over the

Distribution of the Public Lands of Texas

PURPOSE	ACRES
Settlers	**68,027,108**
Spain and Mexico	24,583,923
Spanish and Mexican Grants south of the Nueces River, recognized by Act of Feb. 10, 1852	3,741,241
Headrights	30,360,002
Republic colonies	4,494,806
Preemption land	4,847,136
Military	**9,874,262**
Bounty	5,354,250
Battle donations	1,162,240
Veterans donations	1,377,920
Confederate	1,979,852
Improvements	**37,155,714**
Road	27,716
Navigation	4,261,760
Irrigation	584,000
Ships	17,000
Manufacturing	111,360
Railroads	32,153,878
Education	**52,329,168**
University, public school and eleemosynary institutions	52,329,168
Total of distributed lands	**167,386,252**

years in a series of constitutional amendments.

The Veterans Land Board has liens on more than 557,511 acres of land in active veterans accounts.

Veterans Housing Assistance Program

The 68th Legislature created the Veterans Housing Assistance Program, which also is funded through bond proceeds. Over the years, Texans have passed constitutional amendments authorizing the sale of up to $2.5 billion in bonds to finance this program.

Veterans Home Improvement Program

In 1986, the Veterans Land Board implemented the Veterans Home Improvement Program, which is funded through the Veterans Housing Assistance Program. It allows Texas veterans to borrow up to $25,000 to make substantial home repairs and improvements.

Texas State Veterans Homes

In 1997, the 75th Legislature approved legislation authorizing the Veterans Land Board to construct and operate Texas State Veterans Homes under a cost-sharing program with the U.S. Department of Veterans Affairs. The homes provide affordable, quality, long-term care for Texas' veterans.

Texas State Veterans Cemeteries

The Veterans Land Board owns and operates several cemeteries under USDVA guidelines. The USDVA funds the design and construction of the cemeteries, but the land must be donated.

For more information on any of these veterans programs, call 1-800-252-VETS (8387), or visit the Texas Veterans Land Board Web site at www.texas-veterans.com.

Voices of Veterans Oral History Program

The Voices of Veterans oral history program seeks to record the stories of Texas veterans and archive the transcripts in the Office of Veterans Records for future researchers and historians. Any veteran interested in including his or her story in the Voices of Veterans program should contact the Veterans Land Board at 1-800-252-VETS. ☆

Texas Historical Commission

The Texas Historical Commission protects and preserves the state's historic and prehistoric resources. The Texas State Legislature established the Texas State Historical Survey Committee in 1953 to identify important historic sites across the state.

The Texas Legislature changed the agency's name to the Texas Historical Commission in 1973 and increased its mission and its protective powers. Today the agency's concerns include archaeology, architecture, history, economic development, heritage tourism, public administration and urban planning. The commission:

• Provides leadership, training and preservation planning through its Visionaries in Preservation Program for county historical commissions, heritage organizations and museums in Texas' 254 counties;

• Assists citizens in obtaining historical designations for buildings, cemeteries, sites and other properties important to the state's historic and prehistoric past;

• Works with communities to help protect Texas' diverse architectural heritage, including historic county courthouses and other public buildings;

• Administers the historical marker program. There are more than 11,000 historical markers across Texas;

• Assists cities in the revitalization of their historic downtowns through the Texas Main Street Program;

• Promotes travel to historic and cultural sites though its award-winning Texas Heritage Trails Program;

• Works with property owners to save archaeological sites on private land;

• Ensures that archaeological sites are protected when land is developed for highways and projects.

Mailing address: PO Box 12276, Austin 78711-2276; (512) 463-6100; www.thc.state.tx.us.

Railroad Commission of Texas

The Railroad Commission of Texas has primary regulatory jurisdiction over the oil and natural gas industry, pipeline transporters, the natural gas and hazardous liquid pipeline industry, natural gas utilities, the liquefied petroleum gas (LP-gas) industry, rail industry, and coal and uranium surface mining operations. It also promotes the use of LP-gas as an alternative fuel in Texas through research and education.

The commission exercises its statutory responsibilities under provisions of the Texas Constitution, the Texas Natural Resources Code, the Texas Water Code, the Texas Utilities Code, the Coal and Uranium Surface Mining and Reclamation Acts, the Pipeline Safety Acts, and the Railroad Safety Act.

The commission has regulatory and enforcement responsibilities under federal law, including the Federal Railroad Safety Act, the Local Rail Freight Assistance Act, the Surface Coal Mining Control and Reclamation Act, Safe Drinking Water Act, the Pipeline Safety Acts, the Resource Conservation Recovery Act, and the Clean Water Act.

The Railroad Commission was established by the Texas Legislature in 1891 and given jurisdiction over rates and operations of railroads, terminals, wharves and express companies. In 1917, the legislature declared pipelines to be common carriers and gave the commission regulatory authority over them. It was also given the responsibility to administer conservation laws relating to oil and natural gas production.

The Railroad Commission exists to protect the environment, public safety, and the rights of mineral interest owners; to prevent waste of natural resources, and to assure fair and equitable utility rates in those industries over which it has authority. Mailing address: PO Box 12967, Austin 78711-2967; (512) 463-7288; www.rrc.state.tx.us.

Texas Workforce Commission

The Texas Workforce Commission (TWC) is the state government agency charged with overseeing and providing workforce development services to employers and job seekers of Texas.

For employers, TWC offers recruiting, retention, training and retraining, outplacement services and information on labor law and labor market statistics.

For job seekers, TWC offers career development information, job search resources, training programs, and, as appropriate, unemployment benefits. While targeted populations receive intensive assistance to overcome barriers to employment, all Texans can benefit from the services offered by TWC and our network of workforce partners.

The Texas Workforce Commission is part of a local and state network dedicated to developing the workforce of Texas. The network is composed of the statewide efforts of the commission coupled with planning and service provision on a regional level by 28 local workforce boards. This network gives customers access to local workforce solutions and statewide services in a single location—Texas Workforce Centers.

Primary services of the Texas Workforce Commission and our network partners are funded by federal tax revenue and are generally free to all Texans. Mailing address: 101 E. 15th Street, Austin 78778; (512) 463-2222; www.twc.state.tx.us.

Texas Youth Commission

The Texas Youth Commission operates correctional facilities and halfway houses to provide for the care, custody and rehabilitation of chronically delinquent or serious youth offenders.

In 2007, however, widespread sexual and physical abuse was uncovered at many of the TYC facilities. After a number of supervisors were dismissed, the entire TYC board resigned on March 15, 2007, and their powers were transferred to a conservator. The 80th Texas Legislature approved a bill to overhaul the troubled agency. The legislation:

• Authorizes the governor to appoint an executive commissioner once the agency is out of conservatorship, and to appoint an ombudsman;

• Establishes an advisory board to the commission consisting of 9 members, with the governor, lieutenant governor and speaker each appointing 3 members;

• Requires TYC to maintain a ratio of one correctional officer for every 12 youth;

• Controls size of future population by requiring misdemeanor offenders to be held in local county probation detention centers instead of TYC;

• Requires TYC to evaluate lengths of stay unique to each offense and to discharge youths at age 19;

• Establishes inspector generals, who must be peace officers, to investigate allegations of criminal conduct in the agency and all contract facilities;

• Requires ombudsman and the TYC chief inspector general to submit reports on investigations to the executive commissioner, advisory board, governor, lieutenant governor, speaker, Texas Department of Criminal Justice Special Prosecution Unit, state auditor, and appropriate legislative committees with TYC oversight;

• Requires TYC to implement strict guidelines to separate and group committed youth by age; and

• Authorizes TDCJ Special Prosecution Unit for crimes that occur in the agency or contract facilities.

In 2009, Gov. Rick Perry appointed Cheryln K. Townsend executive commissioner of TYC. She is now executive director. A board of directors was appointed in September 2009.

Mailing address: PO Box 4260, Austin 78765; (512) 424-6130; www.tyc.state.tx.us. ☆

Texas Department of Criminal Justice

Source: Texas Department of Criminal Justice. On the Web: www.tdcj.state.tx.us

The Texas Board of Criminal Justice (TBCJ or board) is composed of nine non-salaried members who are appointed by the governor for staggered six-year terms. The board governs primarily by employing the executive director, setting rules and policies that guide the Texas Department of Criminal Justice (TDCJ), and by considering other agency actions at its regularly scheduled meetings.

Board members serve in a separate capacity as the Board of Trustees for the **Windham School District** by hiring a superintendent and providing similar oversight. The Windham School District is a separate entity whose primary funding source comes from the Texas Education Agency (TEA).

In addition to hiring the TDCJ executive director, the board is responsible for appointing an inspector general, a director of internal audits, a director of state counsel for offenders, and a prison rape elimination act ombudsman.

The executive director is appointed by the board and is responsible for the administration and enforcement of the statutes relative to the criminal justice system.

The Correctional Institutions Division, Private Facility Contract Monitoring and Oversight Division, Parole Division, and Community Justice Assistance Division are most involved in the everyday confinement and supervision of convicted felons.

The actual supervision of probationers is the responsibility of local community supervision and corrections departments (CSCD). Victim Services coordinates a central mechanism for crime victims to participate in the criminal justice process.

The remaining divisions (Office of the General Counsel, Administrative Review and Risk Management, Business and Finance, Information Technology, Manufacturing and Logistics, Facilities, Rehabilitation Programs, Reentry and Integration Programs, Health Services and Human Resources) support the overall operation of the TDCJ. The Reentry and Integration Division was created in August 2009 to expand the TDCJ's reentry initiative.

The Correctional Institutions Division (CID) is responsible for the confinement of adult felony and state jail offenders who are sentenced to incarceration in a secure state-operated correctional facility. Institutional facilities house offenders convicted of first-, second-, and third-degree felonies.

State jail facilities house offenders convicted of a state jail felony, which consists of certain felonies previously considered non-violent third-degree felonies or Class C misdemeanors. Punishment can be up to two years incarceration in a state jail facility and a fine not to exceed $10,000, with possible community supervision following release from the state jail.

Private Facility Contract Monitoring and Oversight Division is responsible for oversight and monitoring of contracts for privately operated secure facilities, as well as community-based facilities, which include substance abuse treatment services.

The **Parole Division** supervises all offenders

Inmate Profile
As of Fiscal Year 2008

AGE – SEX – ETHNICITY

Male: 92.1%	Hispanic: 32.3%
Black: 36.2%	Other: 0.5%
White: 31.0%	Average age: 37

AVERAGE SENTENCES

Prison: 19.2 years   State jail: 1 year

AVERAGE PART OF SENTENCE SERVED
Based on offenders released in Fiscal Year 2010

Prison: 58.3%   State jail: 99.4%

EDUCATION

Average IQ: 90.6

No high school diploma or GED: 43.1%

Average education achievement score: 8.1

On-Hand Population
As of May 31, 2011

PRISONERS	
Correctional Institutions Division	141,087
State Jails	11,528
SAFP (Substance Abuse)	3,325
TOTAL:	**155,940**
(Total Includes 15,186 housed in privately operated facilities.)	
PAROLE	
Mandatory Supervision	80,619
(As of May 31, 2011)	
PROBATION	
Felony and Misdemeanor	415,321
(As of March 31, 2011)	

released on parole or mandatory supervision; conducts release and transition planning; and verifies compliance with statutory provisions of release.

Additionally, the division contracts for electronic monitoring and processing responses to violations, as well as other services. The division administers rehabilitation and reintegration programs and services through District Resource Centers and Parole Offices, and coordinates the Interstate Compact for Adult Offender Supervision.

The Community Justice Assistance Division (CJAD) administers community supervision, also known as adult probation in Texas.

CJAD is responsible for the distribution of formula and grant funds; the development of standards, including best-practice treatment standards; approval of Community Justice Plans and budgets; conducting program and fiscal audits; and providing training and certification of community supervision officers. ☆

Correctional Institutions Division

The town listed is the nearest one to the facility, although the unit may actually be in another county. For instance, the Middleton Transfer Facility is in Jones County, but the nearest city is Abilene, which is in Taylor County. Data is current as of May 31, 2011. **SAFPF** = Substance Abuse Felony Punishment Facilities; **DDP** = Developmentally Disabled Program.

COUNTY	UNIT	NEAREST TOWN	INMATES	GENDER	EMPLOYEES	TYPE
Anderson	Beto	Tennessee Colony	3,467	Male	579	Prison
Anderson	Coffield	Tennessee Colony	4,109	Male	882	Prison
Anderson	Gurney	Tennessee Colony	1,988	Male	417	Transfer Facility
Anderson	Michael	Tennessee Colony	3,185	Male	749	Prison
Anderson	Powledge	Palestine	1,116	Male	265	Prison
Angelina	Diboll	Diboll	517	Male	118	Private Prison
Angelina	Duncan	Diboll	558	Male	131	Geriatric
Bee	Garza East	Beeville	2,265	Male	480	Transfer Facility
Bee	Garza West	Beeville	2,177	Male	441	Transfer Facility
Bee	McConnell	Beeville	2,844	Male	602	Prison
Bexar	Dominguez	San Antonio	2,125	Male	336	State Jail
Bowie	Telford	New Boston	2,772	Male	698	Prison
Brazoria	C.T. Terrell	Rosharon	1,572	Male	377	Prison
Brazoria	Clemens	Brazoria	1,147	Male	302	Prison
Brazoria	Darrington	Rosharon	1,906	Male	499	Prison
Brazoria	Ramsey	Rosharon	1,772	Male	391	Prison
Brazoria	Scott	Angleton	1,116	Male	245	Prison
Brazoria	Stringfellow	Rosharon	1,165	Male	261	Prison
Brazos	Hamilton	Bryan	1,112	Male	230	Pre-Release
Brown	Havins	Brownwood	564	Male	146	Pre-Release
Burnet	Halbert	Burnet	487	Female	123	SAFPF
Caldwell	Lockhart	Lockhart	499	Female	92	Private Prison/ Work Program
Caldwell	Lockhart PPT	Lockhart	499	Male	91	Private Pre-Parole Transfer
Cherokee	Hodge	Rusk	951	Male	285	DDP
Cherokee	Skyview	Rusk	54 441	Female Male	332	Psychiatric
Childress	Roach	Childress	1,443	Male	326	Prison
Coryell	Crain	Gatesville	1,988	Female	643	Prison
Coryell	Hilltop	Gatesville	540	Female	232	Prison
Coryell	Hughes	Gatesville	2,890	Male	666	Prison
Coryell	Mountain View	Gatesville	624	Female	280	Prison
Coryell	Murray	Gatesville	1,298	Female	309	Prison
Coryell	Woodman	Gatesville	845	Female	229	State Jail
Dallas	Dawson	Dallas	1,382 823	Female Male	360	Private State Jail
Dallas	Hutchins	Dallas	2,110	Male	356	State Jail
Dawson	Smith	Lamesa	2,139	Male	473	Prison
DeWitt	Stevenson	Cuero	1,338	Male	272	Prison
Duvall	Glossbrenner	San Diego	556	Male	123	SAFPF
El Paso	Sanchez	El Paso	961	Male	257	State Jail
Falls	Hobby	Marlin	1,327	Female	276	Prison
Falls	Marlin	Marlin	582	Male	120	Transfer Facility
Fannin	C. Moore	Bonham	1,184	Male	219	Transfer Unit
Fannin	Cole	Bonham	853	Male	202	State Jail
Fort Bend	Central	Sugar Land	809	Male	258	Prison
Fort Bend	Jester I	Richmond	306	Male	109	SAFPF
Fort Bend	Jester III	Richmond	1,105	Male	264	Prison

Prison horses graze at the Huntsville Unit in Walker County. Ron Billings photo; Texas Forest Service.

COUNTY	UNIT	NEAREST TOWN	INMATES	GENDER	EMPLOYEES	TYPE
Fort Bend	Jester IV	Richmond	10 488	Female Male	344	Psychiatric
Fort Bend	Vance	Richmond	289	Male	105	Prison
Freestone	Boyd	Fairfield	1,317	Male	271	Prison
Frio	Briscoe	Dilley	1,339	Male	271	Prison
Galveston	Hospital Galveston	Galveston	6 120	Female Male	324	Medical
Galveston	Young	Galveston	297 97	Female Male	398	Medical
Gray	Jordan	Pampa	1,006	Male	215	Prison
Grimes	Luther	Navasota	1,220	Male	286	Prison
Grimes	Pack	Navasota	1,449	Male	309	Prison
Hale	Formby	Plainview	1,073	Male	251	State Jail
Hale	Wheeler	Plainview	545	Male	110	State Jail
Harris	Kegans	Houston	659	Male	157	State Jail
Harris	Lychner	Humble	2,109	Male	357	State Jail
Hartley	Dalhart	Dalhart	1,345	Male	238	Prison
Hays	Kyle	Kyle	518	Male	97	Private Prison
Henderson	East Texas Treatment	Henderson	1,808	Male	432	Multi-Use
Hidalgo	Lopez	Edinburg	1,028	Male	236	State Jail
Hidalgo	Segovia	Edinburg	1,186	Male	211	Pre-Release
Houston	Eastham	Lovelady	2,441	Male	657	Prison
Jack	Lindsey	Jacksboro	1,028	Male	187	Private State Jail
Jasper	Goodman	Jasper	582	Male	140	Transfer Facility
Jefferson	Gist	Beaumont	2,118	Male	334	State Jail
Jefferson	Leblanc	Beaumont	1,135	Male	239	Pre-Release
Jefferson	Stiles	Beaumont	2,862	Male	655	Prison
Johnson	Estes	Venus	1,040	Male	195	Private Prison
Jones	Middleton	Abilene	2,088	Male	463	Transfer Facility
Jones	Robertson	Abilene	2,870	Male	683	Prison
Karnes	Connally	Kenedy	2,818	Male	608	Prison
La Salle	Cotulla	Cotulla	583	Male	115	Transfer Facility
Liberty	Cleveland	Cleveland	519	Male	114	Private Prison
Liberty	Henley	Dayton	547	Female	116	State Jail
Liberty	Hightower	Dayton	1,329	Male	301	Prison
Liberty	Plane	Dayton	2,169	Female	383	State Jail

COUNTY	UNIT	NEAREST TOWN	INMATES	GENDER	EMPLOYEES	TYPE
Lubbock	Montford	Lubbock	947	Male	513	Psychiatric
Madison	Ferguson	Midway	2,328	Male	605	Prison
Medina	Ney	Hondo	566	Male	124	State Jail
Medina	Torres	Hondo	1,321	Male	262	Prison
Mitchell	Wallace	Colorado City	1,373	Male	284	Prison
Mitchell	Ware	Colorado City	896	Male	198	Transfer Facility
Parker	Minerals Wells PPT	Mineral Wells	2,002	Male	268	Private Pre-Parole Transfer
Pecos	Fort Stockton	Fort Stockson	593	Male	105	Transfer Facility
Pecos	Lynaugh	Fort Stockton	1,367	Male	250	Prison
Polk	Polunsky	Livingston	2,844	Male	718	Prison
Potter	Clements	Amarillo	3,643	Male	997	Prison
Potter	Neal	Amarillo	1,676	Male	342	Prison
Rusk	B. Moore	Overton	498	Male	112	Private Prison
Rusk	Bradshaw	Henderson	1,963	Male	232	Private State Jail
San Saba	San Saba	San Saba	593	Male	117	Transfer Facility
Scurry	Daniel	Snyder	1,310	Male	257	Prison
Stephens	Sayle	Breckenridge	432	Male	144	SAFPF
Swisher	Tulia	Tulia	582	Male	115	Transfer Facility
Terry	Rudd	Brownfield	572	Male	134	Transfer Facility
Travis	Travis County	Austin	1,089	Male	230	State Jail
Tyler	Lewis	Woodville	2,164	Male	532	Prison
Walker	Byrd	Huntsville	955	Male	272	Prison
Walker	Ellis	Huntsville	2,301	Male	589	Prison
Walker	Estelle	Huntsville	3,057	Male	847	Prison
Walker	Goree	Huntsville	41 974	Female Male	320	Prison
Walker	Holliday	Huntsville	2,100	Male	412	Transfer Facility
Walker	Huntsville	Huntsville	1,573	Male	407	Prison
Walker	Wynne	Huntsville	2,598	Male	617	Prison
Wichita	Allred	Iowa Park	3,634	Male	910	Prison
Willacy	Willacy County	Raymondville	1,067	Male	151	Private State Jail
Williamson	Bartlett	Bartlett	1,041	Male	182	Private State Jail
Wise	Bridgeport	Bridgeport	519	Male	94	Private Prison
Wise	Bridgeport PPT	Bridgeport	199	Female	56	Private Pre-Parole Transfer
Wood	Johnston	Winnsboro	309	Male	142	SAFPF

TEXAS' 12 OLDEST PRISONS			
UNIT	COUNTY	DATE ESTABLISHED	TYPE
Huntsville	Walker	1849	Prison
Wynne	Walker	1883	Prison
Jester I	Fort Bend	1885	SAFPF
Vance	Fort Bend	1885	Prison
Clemens	Brazoria	1893	Prison
Goree	Walker	1907	Prison
Ramsey	Brazoria	1908	Prison
Stringfellow	Brazoria	1908	Prison
Central	Fort Bend	1909	Prison
Darrington	Brazoria	1917	Prison
Eastham	Houston	1917	Prison
Scott	Brazoria	1919	Prison

Texas State Boards and Commissions

Following is a list of appointees to state boards and commissions, as well as names of other state officials, revised to **July 15, 2011**. Information includes, where available, (1) date of creation; (2) whether the position is elective or appointive; (3) length of term; (4) compensation, if any; (5) number of members; (6) names of appointees, their hometowns and expiration of terms. In some instances the date of term expiration has passed; in such cases, no new appointment had been made by press time, and the official is continuing to fill the position until a successor can be named. Most positions marked "apptv." are appointed by the Governor. Where otherwise, appointing authority is given. Most advisory boards are not listed. Salaries for commissioners and administrators are those that were authorized by the appropriations bill passed by the 81st Legislature for the 2010–2011 biennium (2012–2013 salaries were not available from the State Auditor at press time). They are "not-to-exceed" salaries: maximum authorized salaries for the positions. Actual salaries may be less than those stated here.

Accountancy, Texas State Board of Public – (1945 with 2-yr. terms; reorganized 1959 as 9-member board with 6-yr. overlapping terms; number of members increased to 12 in 1979; increased to 15 in 1989); per diem and expenses: Chair Gregory L. Bailes, Bee Cave (1/31/11); A. Carlos Barrera, Brownsville (1/31/13); John W. (Jay) Dunbar, El Paso (1/31/11); Everett R. Ferguson, Abilene (1/31/15); James C. Flagg, College Station (1/31/15); Dorothy M. Fowler, Corpus Christi (1/31/11); Jon R. Keeney, Taylor Lake Village (1/31/15); David L. King, Lago Vista (1/31/13); Evelyn M. Martinez, San Antonio (1/31/13); Maribess L. Miller, Dallas (1/31/15); Steve D. Peña, Georgetown (1/31/13); James W. Pollard, Canadian (1/31/11); Thomas G. Prothro, Tyler (1/31/13); Catherine J. Rodewald, Dallas (1/31/11); John W. Steinberg, Marion (1/31/13). Exec. Dir. William Treacy, 333 Guadalupe, Suite 3-900, Austin 78701-3900; (512) 305-7800.

Acupuncture Examiners, Texas State Board of – (1993); apptv.; 6-yr.; per diem; 9 members: Chair Allen Cline, Austin (1/31/13); Chung-Hwei Chernly, Hurst (1/31/11); Suehing (Sue) Chiang, Sugar Land (1/31/15); Linda Wynn Drain, Lucas (1/31/13); Raymond J. Graham, Dallas (1/31/11); Terry Glenn Rascoe, Temple (1/31/11); Karen Siegel, Houston (1/31/11); Rachelle Webb, Austin (1/31/13); Rey Ximenes, Austin (1/31/15). Exec. Dir. Mari Robinson, 333 Guadalupe, Tower III, #610, Austin 78768; (512) 305-7010. *Consumer Complaints:* (800) 201-9353.

Ad Valorem Tax Rate, Board to Calculate the – Est. 1907 with 3 ex-officio members: Governor, State Comptroller of Public Accounts, and State Treasurer; consolidated in 1973 with State Tax Board; abolished by 66th Legislature (SB 621, which created the Property Tax Code), effective 1/1/82, and replaced by the Texas State Property Tax Board.

Adjutant General's Dept. – (1836 by Republic of Texas; present office established 1905); apptv.; 2-yr.; 3 members: Adjutant General, Major Gen. John F. Nichols, Spring Branch (2/1/13); ($139,140); Assistant for Army, Brig. Gen. Joyce L. Stevens, Tomball; Assistant for Air, Col. Kenneth Wisian, Weatherford. Assistants each serve a term at the pleasure of the Gov.; c/o Camp Mabry, PO Box 5218, Austin 78763-5218; (512) 782-5001.

Administrative Hearings, State Office of – Created in 1991 by 72nd Leg.; apptv.; 2-yr.; 1 member: Chief Admin. Law Judge Cathleen Parsley ($122,500). William P. Clements Building, 300 W. 15th St., Ste. 502, Austin 78701; (512) 475-4993.

Administrative Judicial Districts of Texas, Presiding Judges – Apptv.; term served concurrent with term as District Judge, subject to reappointment if re-elected to bench. No additional compensation. For names of judges, *see* Administrative Judicial Districts in index.

Aging and Disability Services Council, Department of (DADS) – (2004); apptv.; 6-yr.; 9 members: Chair Sharon Swift Butterworth, El Paso (2/1/11); Glyn S. Crane, Longview (2/1/15); John A. Cuellar, Dallas (2/1/11); Jean L. Freeman, Galveston (2/1/11); Carolyn Harvey, Tyler (2/1/15); Gary D. Newsom, Austin (2/01/13); Ann Schneider, Austin (2/1/15); J. Russell Shannon, Andrews (2/1/13); 1 vacancy. Commissioner Chris Traylor ($163,200); John H. Winters Human Services Complex, 701 W. 51st St., PO Box 149030, Austin 78714-9030; (512) 438-3011.

Agricultural Finance Authority, Texas – (1987); apptv.; 2-yr.; expenses; 2 ex-officio members: Agriculture Commissioner and Director for Institute for International Agribusiness Studies at Prairie View A&M Univeristy; 7 appt'd. members: Lisa Birkman, Round Rock (1/1/10); Ted Conover, Tyler (1/1/11); Dal DeWees, San Angelo (2/1/11); Mike Golden, Lake Jackson (1/1/10); Stanley Ray, Georgetown (1/1/11); Victoria Salin, College Station (1/1/10); Larry Shafer, Granbury (1/1/10). Robert Wood, PO Box 12847, Austin 78711; (512) 936-0273.

Alcohol and Drug Abuse, Texas Commission on – (1953 as Texas Commission on Alcoholism); abolished by House Bill 2292 and functions merged into Department of State Health Services in January 2004.

Alcoholic Beverage Commission, Texas – (1935 as Liquor Control Board; name changed in 1970); apptv.; 6-yr; per diem and expenses; administrator apptd. by commission; 3 members: Chair Jose Cuevas Jr., Midland (11/15/15); Melinda S. Fredricks, Conroe (11/15/13); Steven M. Weinberg, Colleyville (11/15/11). Administrator Alan Steen ($122,500), PO Box 13127, Austin 78711-3127; (512) 206-3333.

Alzheimer's Disease & Related Disorders, Texas Council on – (1999); apptv.; 2-yr.; 19 members: Chair Debbie Hanna, Austin (8/31/15); Ronald Devere, Austin (8/31/15); Leon Douglas, Bertram; Carlos Escobar, San Angelo; Carolyn Frazier, Huffman (8/31/13); Grayson Hankins, Odessa; Clint Hackney, Austin; Rita Hortenstine, Dallas (8/31/13); Mary M. Kenan, Houston; Jack C. Kern, Austin; Margaret Krasovec, Austin; Ray Lewis, Arlington; Audrey Deckinga, Austin; Sam Shore, Austin; Jennifer Smith, Austin; Winnie Rutledge, Austin; Michael Wilson, Austin; Bobby D. Schmidt, Austin; Mary Somerville, Austin. Project Coor. Jim Hinds; (512) 263-1943.

Angelina and Neches River Authority – (1935 as Sabine-Neches Conservation Dist.; reorganized in 1950 and name changed to Neches River Conservation Dist.; changed to present name in 1977); apptv.; expenses; 6-yr.; 9 members: Chair Julie Dowell, Bullard, (9/5/11); Jody Anderson, Lufkin (9/5/13); Louis A. Bronaugh, Lufkin (9/5/11); Dominick B. (Nick) Bruno, Jacksonville (9/5/15); Al Chavira, Jacksonville (9/5/13); Patricia E. Dickey, Crockett (9/5/11); Keith Drewery, Nacogdoches (9/5/13); James Hughes Jr., Newton (9/5/15); David King, Nacogdoches (9/5/13). Gen. Mgr. Kelley Holcomb, PO Box 387, Lufkin 75902-0387; (936) 632-7795.

Animal Health Commission, Texas – (1893 as Texas Livestock Sanitary Commission; name changed in 1959; members increased to 9 in 1973; raised to 12 in 1983); apptv.; per diem and expenses; 6-yr.; 13 members: Chair Ernesto A. Morales, Devine (9/6/13); Randy C. Brown, Lubbock (9/6/13); Reta K. Dyess, Jacksonville (9/6/11); William F. Edmiston Jr., Eldorado (9/6/13); Ken Jordan, San Saba (9/6/13); Thomas George Kezar, Dripping Springs (9/6/11); Coleman Hudgins Locke, Wharton (9/6/15); Charles E. Real, Marion (9/6/13); Ralph Simmons, Center (9/6/15); Michael Louis Vickers, Falfurrias, (9/6/11); Mark A. Wheelis, Victoria (9/6/13); Beau White, Rosanky (9/6/15); R.W. (Dick) Winters Jr., Brady (9/6/13). Exec. Dir. Dee B. Ellis ($120,000), PO Box 12966, Austin 78711-2966; (512) 719-0700.

Appraiser Licensing and Certification Board, Texas – (1991); 2-yr.; apptv.; per diem on duty; 9 members; 1 ex officio: Texas General Land Office; 8 app't'd.: Chair James B. Ratliff, Garland (1/31/11); Walker Beard, El Paso (1/31/11); Malachi Boyuls, Dallas (1/31/12); Luis F. De La Garza Jr., Laredo (1/31/12); Laurie Fontana, Houston (1/31/12); Shannon McClendon, Dripping Springs (1/31/12); Sheryl R. Swift, Galveston (1/31/11); Donna L. Walz, Lubbock (1/31/11). Commissioner Douglas E. Oldmixon ($106,500) , PO Box 12188, Austin 78711-2188; (512) 459-2232.

Architectural Examiners, Texas Board of – (1937 as 3-member board; raised to 6 members in 1951 and to 9 in 1977); apptv.; 6-yr.; per diem and expenses; 9 members: Chair Alfred Vidaurri Jr., Aledo (1/31/15); Charles H. Anastos, Corpus Christi (1/31/13); Corbett (Chase) Bearden, Austin (1/31/15); Rosemary A. Gammon, Plano (1/31/11); H.L. (Bert) Mijares Jr., El Paso (1/31/15); Brandon Pinson, Midland (1/31/13); Diane Steinbrueck, Austin (1/31/13); Peggy Lewene (Lew) Vassberg, Harlingen (1/31/11); James S. Walker II, Houston (1/31/11). Exec. Dir. Cathy L. Hendricks, PO Box 12337, Austin 78711-2337; (512) 305-9000.

Arts, Texas Commission on the – (1965 as Texas Fine Arts Commission; name changed to Texas Commission on the Arts and Humanities and members increased to 18 in 1971; name changed to present form in 1979); apptv.; 6-yr.; expenses; 17 members: Chair Patty A. Bryant, Amarillo (8/31/11); Rita E. Baca, El Paso (8/31/15); Dale W. Brock, Wichita Falls (8/31/13); Alphonse A. Dotson, Voca (8/31/13); David C. Garza, Brownsville (8/31/11); Linda Lowes Hatchel, Woodway (8/31/15); Susan Howard-Chrane, Boerne (8/31/13); Molly Hipp Hubbard, Houston (8/31/13); Patty Hayes Huffines, Austin (8/31/15); Liza B. Lewis, San Antonio (8/31/15); Paul K. McCash Jr., Texarkana (8/31/13); Jeanne Parker, Austin (8/31/13); Cobie Russell, Dallas (8/31/15); Billye Proctor Shaw, Abilene (8/31/11); Polly Sowell, Austin (8/31/11); S. Shawn Stephens, Houston (8/31/15); 1 vacancy. Exec. Dir. Gary Gibbs ($85,250), 920 Colorado St., PO Box 13406, Austin 78711-3406; (512) 463-5535.

Assistive and Rehabilitative Services Council, Department of (DARS) – (2004) apptv.; 6-yr.; 9 members: Chair Timothy J. Flannery, Seabrook (2/1/11); Lee Chayes, El Paso (2/1/13); David Coco, Austin (2/1/13); Diego Demaya, Houston (2/1/15); Berkley Dyer, Austin (2/1/15); Diane Marie Novy, Bellaire (2/1/11); Donald D. Roy, Mount Pleasant (2/1/13); Judy Scott, Dallas (2/1/15); 1 vacancy. Interim Commissioner Debra Wanser ($145,860), PO Box 12866, Austin 78711-2866; (512) 377-0800.

Athletic Trainers, Advisory Board of – (1971 as Texas Board of Athletic Trainers; name changed in 1975); expenses; 6-yr.; 5 members: Chair David J. Weir, College Station (1/31/11); Marty Akins, Austin (1/31/15); David R. Schmidt, San Antonio (1/31/13); Rebecca Spurlock, Keller (1/31/15); Michael Alan Waters, Lufkin (1/31/13); c/o Texas Dept. of State Health Services, PO Box 149347, MC 1982, Austin 78714-9347; (512) 834-6615.

The Peace Officers Memorial in Austin. Photo by Ron Billings; Texas Forest Service.

Attorney, State Prosecuting – (1923) apptd. by Court of Criminal Appeals: Lisa C. McMinn (12/31/12); ($125,000); Price Daniel Sr. Building, PO Box 12405, Austin 78711-2405; (512) 463-1660.

Auditor's Office, State – (1929); 2-yr.; apptd. by Legislative Audit Committee, a joint Senate-House committee: State Auditor John Keel, PO Box 12067, Austin 78711-2067; (512) 936-9500.

Autism and Pervasive Developmental Disorders, Texas Council on – (1987); 2-yr.; expenses; 13 members: 7 ex officio; 6 apptd. by Gov.: Chair Frank Christian McCamant, Austin (2/1/11); Rick L. Campbell, Center (2/1/11); Anna Penn Hundley, Dallas (2/1/11); Pamela Rollins, Dallas (2/1/10); Stephanie Sokolosky, Lubbock (2/1/10); Glenn Roque-Jackson, Plano (2/1/10); c/o Texas Dept. of Aging and Disability Services; Texas Council on Autism and PDD; Mail Code W-578, PO Box 149030, Austin 78714-9030; (512) 438-3512.

Banking Commissioner, State – (1923); 2-yr.; apptd. by State Finance Commission: Charles G. Cooper, 2601 N. Lamar Blvd., Austin 78705-4294; (512) 475-1300. (*See* also Finance Commission of Texas.)

Bar of Texas, State – (1939 as administrative arm of Supreme Court); 30 directors elected by membership; 3-yr. terms; expenses paid from dues collected from membership. Executive director, general counsel and immediate past chair serve as ex-officio members. Exec. Dir. Michelle Hunter, PO Box 12487, Austin 78711; (512) 427-1463.

Barbering Advisory Board, State – (1929 as 3-member Texas Board of Barber Examiners; members increased in 1975; named changed to current in 2005 and functions transferred to Texas Dept. of Licensing and Regulation); 6-yr.; apptd. by department commissioners; 5 members: Chair Linda G. Connor, Austin (9-29-11); Ronald L. Brown, Dripping Springs (9-29-15); Jennifer Grisham, Alpine (9-29-15); Jimmy Johnson, Manor (9-29-13); 1 vacancy. c/o Texas Department of Licensing and Regulation, PO Box 12884, Austin 78711-1288; (512) 463-6599.

Blind and Severely Disabled Persons, Committee on Purchases of Products of – (*See* Disabilities, Texas Council on Purchasing from People with.)

Blind, Texas Commission for the – Now the Division for Blind Services within the Department of Assistive and Rehabilitative Services (DARS) of the Health and Human Services Commission as of 3/1/04.

Blind and Visually Impaired Governing Board, Texas School for the – (1979); apptv.; 6-yr.; expenses; 9 members: Mary K. Alexander, Valley View (1/31/15); Gene I. Brooks, Austin (1/31/15); Caroline K. Daley, Kingwood (1/31/11); Bobby Druesedow, Aledo (1/31/13); Cynthia Finley, Lubbock (1/31/11); Michael E. Garrett, Missouri City (1/31/13); Michelle D. Goodwin, Fort Worth (1/31/13); Deborah Louder, San Angelo (1/31/11); Joseph Muñoz, Harlingen (1/31/15). Superintendent William Daugherty ($115,000), 1100 W. 45th St., Austin 78756-3494; (512) 454-8631.

Board of (Note: In most instances, state boards are alphabetized under key word, as **Accountancy, Texas State Board of Public.**)

Bond Review Board – (1987); composed of Governor, Lieutenant Governor, House Speaker, and Comptroller of Public Accounts; oversees debt financing for Texas' infrastructure and other public purposes, debt issuance, and debt management functions of state and local entities, and the state's private activity bond allocation; Exec. Dir. Robert C. Kline ($99,000); PO Box 13292, Austin 78711-3292; (512) 463-1741.

Brazos River Authority – (1929 as Brazos River Conservation and Reclamation District; name changed to present form in 1953); apptv.; 6-yr; expenses; 21 members: Chair Christopher D. DeCluitt, Waco (2/1/11); Christopher Steve Adams Jr., Granbury (2/1/11); Richard L. Ball, Mineral Wells (2/1/13); Grady Barr, Abilene (2/1/13); F. LeRoy Bell, Tuscola (2/1/13); Kari Belt, Gatesville (2/1/15); Peter G. Bennis, Cleburne (2/1/13); Michel (Todd) Brashears, Wolfforth (2/1/15); Col. Robert M. Christian, Jewett (2/1/11); Carolyn H. Johnson, Freeport (2/1/11); Roberta Jean Killgore, Somerville (2/1/11); Sara Lowrey Mackie, Salado (2/1/15); William Masterson, Guthrie (2/1/13); Trent McKnight, Throckmorton (2/1/15); G. Dave Scott, Richmond (2/1/13); Jon Sloan, Round Rock (2/1/11); John D. Steinmetz, Lubbock (2/1/15); Jeffery S. Tallas, Sugar Land (2/1/15); Robert E. Tesch, Georgetown (2/1/15); Mary Ward, Granbury (2/1/11); Salvatore A. Zaccagnino, Caldwell (2/1/15). Gen. Mgr./CEO Phillip J. Ford, PO Box 7555, Waco 76714-7555; (254) 761-3100.

Building and Procurement Commission, Texas – (1919; renamed Texas Facilities Commission in 2007 and some procurement duties transferred to the Comptroller of Public Accounts); *see* Facilities Commission, Texas.

Canadian River Compact Commissioner – (1951); apptv.; salary and expenses; (negotiates with New Mexico and Oklahoma regarding waters of the Canadian): vacant; Interstate Compacts Coordinator Herman Settemeyer, TCEQ, PO Box 13087, Austin 78711-3087; (512) 239-4707.

Canadian River Municipal Water Authority – (1953); 2-yr; 17 members: Glenn Bickel, Plainview (7/31/10); Jerry Carlson, Pampa (7/31/11); James O. Collins, Lubbock (7/31/11); Tom Edmonds, Borger (7/31/10); Richard Ellis, Levelland (7/31/11); Larry Hagood, Tahoka (7/31/11); William Hallerberg, Amarillo (7/31/10); Shannon Himango, Levelland (7/31/10); Glendon Jett, Borger (7/31/11); Robert Keys, Amarillo (7/31/11); Rex McKay, Pampa (7/31/10); E.R. Moore, O'Donnell (7/31/11); Dale Newberry, Lamesa (7/31/11); L.J. Richardson, Brownfield (7/31/11); Robert Rodgers, Lubbock (7/31/10); Steve Tucker, Slaton (7/31/11); Norman Wright, Plainview (7/31/11); Gen. Mgr. Kent Satterwhite, PO Box 9, Sanford 79078-0009; (806) 865-3325.

Cancer Prevention & Research Institute of Texas – (1985 as Texas Cancer Council; named changed in 2007); apptv.; 4-yr.; expenses; 11 members; 2 ex officio: Attorney General and Comptroller of Public Accounts; 9 apptd.: Chair James M. Mansour, Austin (12/4/11); Joseph S. Bailes, Austin (12/4/11); Barbara Canales, Corpus Christi (12/4/11); Faith S. Johnson, DeSoto (12/4/11), Joyce King, Plano (1/31/13); Lionel Sosa, Floresville (12/4/11);

Charles Tate, Houston (12/4/11); Phil Wilson, Austin (12/4/11); Cindy Brinker Simmons, Dallas (12/4/11). Exec. Dir. William Gimson ($214,000) PO Box 12097, Austin 78711-2097; (512) 463-3190.

Cardiovascular Disease and Stroke, Texas Council on – (1999); apptv.; 2-yr.; 15 members: 4 ex officio: Department of Assistive and Rehabilitative Services, Department of Aging and Disability Services, Texas Education Agency, Texas Department of State Health Services; 11 appt'd.: Chair Thomas E. Tenner Jr., Lubbock (2/1/15); Pamela R.W. Akins, Austin (2/1/15); Michael M. Hawkins, Austin (2/1/13); Melbert (Bob) C. Hillert Jr., Dallas (2/1/15); Deanna Hoelscher, Austin (2/1/11); Sue Pope, Willis (2/1/13); J. Neal Rutledge, Austin (2/1/11); Erica W. Swegler, Keller (2/1/11); Ann Quinn Todd, Houston (2/1/15); Louis West, Taylor (2/1/13); Clyde W. Yancy, DeSoto (2/1/15); c/o Texas Dept. of State Health Services, PO Box 149347, Austin 78714-9347; (512) 458-7200.

Cemetery Committee, Texas State – (1997); apptv.; 6-yr.; 3 members: Chair Scott P. Sayers Jr., Austin (2/1/15); James Coley Cowden, Austin (2/1/11); Deborah (Borah) Van Dormolen, Salado (2/1/13); 909 Navasota, Austin 78702; (512) 463-0605.

Central Colorado River Authority (*See* **Colorado River Authority, Central.**)

Chemist, Office of State – (1911); ex officio, indefinite term: State Chemist Timothy J. Herrman, PO Box 3160, College Station 77841-3160; (979) 845-1121.

Childhood Intervention, Interagency Council on Early – Combined 3/1/04 into Department of Assistive and Rehabilitative Services (DARS) of the Health and Human Services Commission.

Chiropractic Examiners, Texas Board of – (1949); apptv.; 6-yr.; expenses; 9 members: Chair Kenneth Mack Perkins, Conroe (2/1/11); Armando Elizarde, Harlingen (2/1/13); Janette A. Kurban, Arlington (2/1/13); Larry R. Montgomery, Belton (2/1/15); Kathleen S. Summers, Andrews (2/1/11); Cynthia Tays, Austin (2/1/13); Patrick J. Thomas, Corpus Christi (2/1/15); Tom O. Turner, San Antonio (2/1/15); Kenya Scott Woodruff, Dallas (2/1/11). Exec. Dir. Glenn Parker ($70,000), 333 Guadalupe, Ste. 3-825, Austin 78701; (512) 305-6700.

Coastal Water Authority – (1967 as Coastal Industrial Water Authority; name changed in 1985); 2-yr.; per diem and expenses; 7 members; 4 apptd. by Houston mayor; 3 apptd. by Gov.: Pres. Kurt F. Metyko, Houston (3/31/11); John Odis Cobb, Houston (3/31/12); Alan D. Conner, Dayton (3/31/12); Zebulun Nash, Houston (4/1/11); F. William Othon, Houston (3/31/11); Douglas Walker, Beach City (4/1/11); Giti Zarinkelk, Houston (4/1/11). Exec. Dir. Gary N. Oradat, 500 Dallas, One Allen Center, Ste. 2800, Houston 77002; (713) 658-9020.

Colorado River Authority, Central – (1935); apptv.; 6-yr.; per diem on duty; 9 members: Mathew K. Gaines, Coleman (2/1/11); Kimberly E. Horne, Valera (2/1/11); Patrick S. Justiss, Coleman (2/1/11); David (Lance) McWhorter, Coleman (2/1/11); Roger Nelson, Santa Anna (2/1/13); Bruce N. Pittard, Novice (2/1/11); Andrew Mark Young, Coleman (2/1/11); 2 vacancies. Operations Mgr. Lynn W. Cardinas, PO Box 964, Coleman 76834-0964; (325) 625-4398.

Colorado River Authority, Lower – (1934 as 9-member board; members increased in 1951 and 1975); apptv.; 6-yr.; per diem on duty; 15 members: Chair Timothy Timmerman, Travis Co. (2/1/13); Steve K. Balas, Colorado Co. (2/1/15); Lori A. Berger, Fayette Co. (2/1/15); Ida A. Carter, Burnet Co. (2/1/11); John C. Dickerson III, Matagorda Co. (2/1/15); Jett Johnson, Mills Co. (2/1/15); Rebecca A. Klein, Elec. Service Area (2/1/13); Tom Martine, Blanco Co. (2/1/13); Woodrow (Woody) McCasland, Llano Co. (2/1/11); Michael G. McHenry, San Saba Co. (2/1/15); Linda Raun, Wharton Co. (2/1/11); Vernon E. (Buddy) Schrader, Wharton Co. (2/1/15); Franklin (Scott) Spears Jr., Travis Co. (2/1/13); B.R. (Skipper) Wallace, Lampasas Co. (2/1/11); Kathleen H. White, Bastrop Co. (2/1/13). Gen. Man. Becky Motal, PO Box 220, Austin 78767-0220; (512) 473-3200.

Colorado River Authority, Upper – (1935 as 9-member board; reorganized in 1965); apptv.; 6-yr.; per diem and expenses; 9 members: Chair Jeffie Harmon Roberts, Robert Lee (2/1/11); Ronny Alexander, Paint Rock (2/1/15); Bill Holland, San Angelo (2/1/13); William R. Hood, Robert Lee (2/1/11); Eva Horton, San Angelo (2/1/15); A.J. Jones, Miles (2/1/11); Martin Lee, Bronte (2/1/13); John Nikolauk, Eldorado (2/1/13); Hyman Sauer, Eldorado (2/1/11). Director Chuck Brown, 512 Orient, San Angelo 76903; (325) 655-0565.

Commissioner of (*See keyword,* as **Agriculture, Commissioner of.**)

Concho River Water and Soil Conservation Authority,

Lower – Established in 1939; abolished by the 81st Texas Legislature on 9/1/09.

Consumer Credit Commissioner – Leslie L. Pettijohn, 2601 N. Lamar, Austin 78705-4207; (512) 936-7600. *Consumer Help Line: (800) 538-1579.*

Cosmetology Advisory Board, Texas – (1935 as 3-member State Board of Hairdressers and Cosmetologists; name changed and members increased in 1971; named changed to current in 2005 and functions transferred to Texas Dept. of Licensing and Regulation); apptv.; per diem and expenses; 6-yr.; 8 members: Chair Daired Ogle, Arlington (9/29/13); Rojean S. Brewer, Lubbock (9/29/13); Pamela Gold, Plano (9/29/15); Glenda Jemison, Houston (9/29/15); Clive Lamb, Dallas (9/29/11); Ron Robinson, Waco (9/29/11); Allison Leigh West, Carrollton (9/29/13); ex officio, Diane Salazar, Austin; c/o Texas Dept. of Licensing and Regulation, PO Box 12157, Austin 78711; (512) 463-6599.

Counselors, Texas State Board of Examiners of Professional – (1981); apptv.; 6-yr.; expenses; 9 members: Chair Glenda Corley, Round Rock (2/1/11); Sarah Abraham, Sugar Land (2/1/13); Brenda (Brandi) Buckner, Weatherford (2/1/15); Karen R. Burke, Austin (2/1/15); Steven D. Christopherson, Pasadena (2/1/13); Brenda S. Compagnone, Carrizo Springs (2/1/15); Michelle A. Eggleston, Amarillo (2/1/11); Leslie F. Pohl, Austin (2/1/13); Jaa A. St. Julien, Houston (2/1/11). Exec. Dir. Bobbe Alexander, c/o Texas Dept. of State Health Services, 1100 W. 49th St., PO Box 149347, Austin 78714-9347; (512) 834-6658.

Texas County and District Retirement System – (*See* **Retirement System, Texas County and District**.)

Court Administration, State Office of – (1985); apptd. by chief justice of the State Supreme Court; 1 member who also serves as executive director of the Texas Judicial Council: Admin. Dir. Carl Reynolds ($121,847) Tom C. Clark State Courts Bldg., PO Box 12066, Austin 78711-2066; (512) 463-1625.

Court Reporters Certification Board – (1977 as 9-member Texas Reporters Committee; name changed to present form and members increased in 1983); 6-yr.; expenses; 13 members (6 apptd. by State Supreme Court); Chair Ben Woodward, San Angelo (12/31/12); Attorney members: Charles Noteboom, Hurst (12/31/14); Adam Poncio, San Antonio (12/31/13). Official reporters: Tammy Adams, Houston (12/31/11); LaVearn Ivey, Houston (12/31/10). Freelance reporters: John Foster, Henderson (12/31/10); Judy Hobart, Bedford (12/31/15); Firm reps.: Donna Collins, Dallas (12/31/15); Janice Eidd-Meadows, Dallas (12/31/12); Lay members: Esther Kelly, Dallas (12/31/13); Thomas Melton, Cross Plains (12/31/11); Richard Neely, University Park (12/31/15); Krista M. Saeger, Austin (12/31/14). Dir. Michele L. Henricks, PO Box 13131, Austin 78711-3131; (512) 463-1630.

Credit Union Commission – (1949 as 3-member Credit Union Advisory Commission; name changed and members increased to 6 in 1969; increased to 9 in 1981); apptv.; 6-yr.; expenses; 9 members: Chair Gary L. Janacek, Temple (2/15/15); Thomas F. Butler, Deer Park (2/15/13); Manuel Cavazos IV, Austin (2/15/11); Dale E. Kimble, Denton (2/15/13); Robert Kyker, Richardson (2/15/15); Allyson Truax Morrow, San Benito (2/15/13); Barbara K. Sheffield, Sugar Land (2/15/11); Henry E. (Pete) Snow, Texarkana (2/15/11); A. John Yoggerst, San Antonio (2/15/15). Commissioner Harold E. Feeney ($115,000), 914 E. Anderson Ln., Austin 78752-1699; (512) 837-9236.

Crime Stoppers Advisory Council – (1981); apptv.; 4-yr.; per diem and expenses; 5 members: Chair Jorge E. Gaytan, Houston (9/1/12); Nelda L. Garcia (9/1/12); Emerson F. Lane Jr., Beaumont (9/1/12); William Randy McDaniel, Montgomery (9/1/13); Katherine Cabaniss, Houston (9/1/13); Texas State University San Marcos, 601 University Dr., San Marcos 78666-4610; (866) 220-4357.

Crime Victims' Institute Advisory Council – (1995 as function of attorney general's office; transferred to Sam Houston State University in 2003); apptv.; 2-yr.; 3 ex-officio: Attorney General, 1 member of House, 1 member of Senate; 14 appt'd. members: Victoria Camp, Austin (1/31/12); Ben M. Crouch, College Station (1/31/12); Nancy Holmes Ghigna, The Woodlands (1/31/12); Terry Gilmour, Midland (1/31/09); Rodman Goode, Cedar Hill (1/31/12); Lana Myers, Coppell (1/31/09); Stephanie Pecora, Houston (1/31/09); Henry Porretto, Galveston (1/31/12); Richard L. Reynolds, Manor (1/31/12); Stephanie Anne Schulte, El Paso (1/31/11); Debbie Unruh, Amarillo (1/31/12); Michael Valdez, Conroe (1/31/09); Mary Anne Wiley, Austin (1/31/12); Anthony York, Pearland (1/31/09). Director Glen Kercher, Criminal Justice Center, Sam Houston State University, PO Box 2296, Office A-175B, Huntsville 77341; (936) 294-1642.

Criminal Justice, Texas Board of – (1989: assumed duties of former Board of Corrections, Adult Probation Commission and Board of Pardons and Paroles); apptv; 6-yr.; expenses; 9 members: Chair Oliver J. Bell, Austin (2/1/15); John (Eric) Gambrell, Dallas (2/1/13); Charles Lewis (C.L.) Jackson, Houston (2/1/11); Janice Harris Lord, Arlington (2/1/15); R. Terrell McCombs, San Antonio (2/1/13); Tom Mechler, Amarillo (2/1/11); J. David Nelson, Lubbock (2/1/13); Leopoldo R. Vasquez III, Houston (2/1/11); Carmen Villanueva-Hiles, Palmhurst (2/1/15). Exec. Dir. Dept. of Criminal Justice: Brad Livingston ($186,300), PO Box 13084, Austin 78711-3084; (512) 475-3250.

Deaf, Texas School for the, Governing Board – (1979); apptv.; 6-yr.; expenses; 9 members: Chair Walter Camenisch III, Austin (1/31/15); Jean Andrews, Beaumont (1/31/11); Beatrice M. Burke, Temple (1/31/13); Shalia Cowan, Dripping Springs (1/31/11); Eric Hogue, Wylie (1/31/15); Tyran Lee, Humble (1/31/13); Susan K. Ridley, Sugar Land (1/31/13); Connie F. Se-fcik-Kennedy, Austin (1/31/11); Angela O. Wolf, Austin (1/31/15). Superintendent Claire Bugen ($115,000), 1102 S. Congress, Austin 78704; (512) 462-5353.

Deaf and Hard of Hearing, Texas Commission for the – Combined into Department of Assistive and Rehabilitative Services (DARS) of the Health and Human Services Commission as of 3/1/04.

Dental Examiners, State Board of – (1919 as 6-member board; increased to 9 members in 1971; increased to 12 in 1981; increased to 15 in 1991; sunsetted in 1994; reconstituted with 18 members in 1995; reduced to 15 in 2005); apptv.; 6-yr.; per diem and expenses; 15 members: Chair Tamela L. Gough, Allen (2/1/11); Steven J. Austin, Amarillo (2/1/13); Mary L. Baty, Humble (2/1/15); William R. Birdwell, Bryan (2/1/13); James W. Chancellor, Garden Ridge (2/1/15); Maxwell D. Finn, Dallas (2/1/13); Alicia Grant, Richardson (2/1/13); Whitney Hyde, Midland (2/1/15); Georgiana M. Matz, Harlingen (2/1/11); Ann G. Pauli, El Paso (2/1/11); William Lindsay Purifoy, Fort Worth (2/1/11); Rodolfo G. (Rudy) Ramos Jr., Houston (2/1/13); Jerry Romero, El Paso (2/1/13); Russel H. Schlattman II, Houston (2/1/11); Arthur Troilo III, Austin (2/1/13). Exec. Dir. Sherri Sanders Meek ($82,500), 333 Guadalupe, Tower III, #800, Austin 78701-3942; (512) 463-6400.

Depository Board, State – Abolished in May 1997.

Diabetes Council, Texas – (1983; with 5 ex officio and 6 public members serving 2-yr. terms; changed in 1987 to 3 ex officio and 8 public members; changed to present in 1991; term length changed from 4 to 6 years in 1997); 6-yr.; 16 members: 11 apptv.: Chair Victor Hugo Gonzalez, McAllen (2/1/15); Gene Fulton Bell, Lubbock (2/1/15); Neil Burrell, Beaumont (2/1/13); Timothy Cavitt, Spring (2/1/13); Maria Duarte-Gardea, El Paso (2/1/11); John Griffin, Victoria (2/1/11); Arthur E. Hernandez, Corpus Christi (2/1/15); Dora Rivas, Dallas (2/1/15); Curtis Triplitt, San Antonio (2/1/13); Melissa Wilson, Corpus Christi (2/1/15); Don Yarbrough, Garland (2/1/11); 5 ex officio: reps. from DARS-Services for the Blind; DARS-Rehabilitative Services; Dept. of Aging and Disability Services; Dept. of State Health Services; Texas Education Agency. Dir. Roger Faske, c/o Texas Dept. of State Health Services, P.O. Box 149347 Austin 78714-9347; (512) 458-7490.

Dietitians, State Board of Examiners of – (1983); apptv.; 6-yr.; per diem and expenses; 9 members: Belinda Bazan-Lara, San Antonio (9/1/11); Janet S. Hall, Georgetown (9/1/13); Brian Irons, Lubbock (9/1/13); Amy N. McLeod, Houston (9/1/13); Hawley Poinsett, Austin (9/1/11); D.A. Sharpe, Aurora (9/1/11); Christina Stirling, Brownsville (9/1/13); Elizabeth J. Tindall, Odessa (9/1/15); Mary Kate (Suzy) Weems, Waco (9/1/15). Exec. Dir. Bobbe Alexander, c/o Texas Dept. of State Health Services, PO Box 149347, Austin 78714-9347; (512) 834-6601.

Disabilities, Governor's Committee on People with – (1949 as Gov.'s Committee on Employment of the Handicapped; recreated in 1983 as Gov.'s Committee for Disabled Persons; in 1991, given current name and expanded duties); apptv.; 2-yr. and at pleasure of Gov.; 12 members: Chair Joe Bontke, Houston (2/1/11); Alan Babin Jr., Round Rock (2/1/11); Aaron Bangor, Austin (2/1/12); Rodolfo (Rudy) Becerra Jr., Nacogdoches (2/1/12); Daphne Brookins, Fort Worth (2/1/11); David A. Fowler, Katy (2/1/11); Bobby Z. Holcomb Jr., Mount Pleasant (2/1/11); Margaret Larson, Austin (2/1/12); Maureen F. McClain, Pharr (2/1/12); Brian D. Shannon, Lubbock (2/1/11); Kathy S. Strong, Garrison (2/1/12); Patty Watson, Flower Mound (2/1/11). Exec. Dir. Angi English, PO Box 12428, Austin 78711-2428; (512) 463-5739; 7-1-1 TDD.

Disabilities, Texas Council for Developmental – (1971); apptv.; 6-yr.; 27 members: 19 apptv.: Chair Brenda K. Coleman-Beattie, Austin (2/1/13); Rebecca Hunter Adkins, Lakeway (2/1/15); Kristine Bissmeyer, San Antonio (2/1/11); Kimberley A. Blackmon, Fort Worth (2/1/15); Kristen L. Cox, El Paso (2/1/15); Andrew D. Crim, Fort Worth (2/1/13); Mateo Delgado, El Paso

(2/1/13); Mary M. Durheim, McAllen (2/1/11); Marcia J. Dwyer, Plano (2/1/11); Cindy Johnston, Dallas (2/1/13); Diana Kern, Cedar Creek (2/1/15); John C. Morris, Leander (2/1/13); Dana S. Perry, Brownwood (2/1/15); Deneesa A. Rasmussen, Arlington (2/1/15); Joe Rivas, Denton (2/1/11); Lora T. Taylor, Houston (2/1/13); Richard A. Tisch, Spring (2/1/15); Susan Vardell, Sherman (2/1/13); 1 vacancy; 8 ex offico members from various state agencies. Exec. Dir. Roger A. Webb, 6201 E. Oltorf, Ste. 600, Austin 78741; (512) 437-5432.

Disabilities, Texas Council on Purchasing from People with – (1979 as 10-member Committee on Purchases of Products and Services of Blind and Severely Disabled Persons; name changed and members reduced to 9 in 1995); apptv.; expenses; 5-yr.; 9 members: Chair John W. Luna, Euless (1/31/15); Chuck Brewton, San Antonio (1/31/11); Scott D. Burford, Austin (1/31/11); Les Butler, Austin (1/31/13); James Michael Daugherty, Irving (1/31/13); Kevin M. Jackson, Austin (1/31/13); Victor Kilman, Lubbock (1/31/15); Margaret (Meg) Pfluger, Lubbock (1/31/11); Wanda White Stovall, Fort Worth (1/31/15). Exec. Dir. Kelvin Moore, PO Box 13528, Austin 78711-3528; (512) 463-3244.

Disabilities, Texas Office for Prevention of Developmental – (1991) 6-yr.; apptv.; 9 members: Chair Rep. Vicki Truitt, Keller; Richard Garnett, Fort Worth; Angelo Giardino, Houston; Ashley C. Givens, Dallas (2/1/15); Rep. Jim L. Jackson, Carrollton; Valerie Kiper, Amarillo (2/1/13); Joan Roberts-Scott, Austin; Marian Sokol, San Antonio (2/1/11); Mary S. Tijerina, San Marcos. Exec. Dir. Janet Sharkis, PO Box 12668, Austin 78711-2668; (512) 206-4544.

Disaster Recovery and Renewal, Governor's Commission for – (2008); apptv.; terms at pleasure of Gov.; 23 ex-officio members: County judges from the coastal counties of Aransas, Brazoria, Calhoun, Cameron, Chambers, Galveston, Harris, Hidalgo, Jackson, Jefferson, Kenedy, Kleberg, Liberty, Matagorda, Nueces, Orange, Refugio, San Patricio, Starr, Victoria, and Willacy along with the General Land Office Commissioner and the Agriculture Commissioner; 24 appt'd. members: Chair Robert Eckels, Houston; Ronnie Acosta, Pearland; William B. Claybar, Orange; Irma Diaz-Gonzalez, Houston; George (Trey) H. Henderson III, Lufkin; Gary L. Hockstra, Lake Jackson; Jo Ann Howard, Austin; Jerry Kane, Corpus Christi; Mary E. Kelly, Austin; William E. King, Houston; H. Thomas Kornegay, Houston; David L. Lakey, Austin; David S. Lopez, Houston; Ross D. Margraves Jr., Houston; Scott McClelland, Houston; Tracye McDaniel, Houston; Allan B. Polunsky, San Antonio; Penny Redington, Austin; Regina Rogers, Beaumont; Rolando Rubiano, Harlingen; Karen A. Sexton, Galveston; Wade E. Upton, Houston; Daniel J. Wolterman, Houston; H. Edwin Young, Houston. c/o Office of the Governor, PO Box 12428, Austin, 78711; (512) 463-2000.

Education Board, Southern Regional – (1969); apptv.; 4-yr.; 5 members: Gov. ex officio, 4 apptv.: Rep. Rob Eissler, The Woodlands (6/30/12); Rep. Geanie W. Morrison, Victoria (6/30/11); Robert P. Scott, Austin (6/30/14); Sen. Florence Shapiro, Plano (6/30/13); President Daivd Spence, 592 10th St. N.W., Atlanta, GA 30318-5790; (404) 875-9211.

Education, Commissioner of – (1866 as Superintendent of Public Instruction; 1949 changed to present name by Gilmer-Aiken Act; apptd. by Gov. since 1995; 4-yr.: Robert P. Scott ($186,300); 1701 N. Congress Ave., Austin 78701-1494; (512) 463-9734. (*See also* Education, State Board of.)

Education, State Board of – (1866; re-created in 1928 and re-formed in 1949 by Gilmer-Aikin Act to consist of 21 elective members from districts co-extensive with 21 congressional districts at that time; increased to 24 with congressional redistricting in 1971; increased to 27 with congressional redistricting in 1981; reorganized by special legislative session as 15-member apptv. board in 1984; became elective board again in 1988); expenses; 4-yr.; 15 members: **Dist. 1:** Carlos (Charlie) Garza, El Paso (1/1/13); **Dist. 2:** Mary Helen Berlanga, Corpus Christi (1/1/13); **Dist. 3:** Michael Soto, San Antonio (1/1/13); **Dist. 4:** Lawrence A. Allen Jr., Houston (1/1/13); **Dist. 5:** Ken Mercer, San Antonio (1/1/13); **Dist. 6:** Terri Leo, Spring (1/1/13); **Dist. 7:** David Bradley, Beaumont (1/1/13); **Dist. 8:** Barbara Cargill, The Woodlands (1/1/13); **Dist. 9:** Thomas Ratliff, Mount Pleasant (1/1/13); **Dist. 10:** Marsha Lane Farney, Georgetown (1/1/13); **Dist. 11:** Patricia Hardy, Weatherford (1/1/13); **Dist. 12:** George M. Clayton, Richardson (1/1/13); **Dist. 13:** Mavis B. Knight, Dallas (1/1/13); **Dist. 14:** Chair Gail Lowe, Lampasas (1/1/13); **Dist. 15:** Bob Craig, Lubbock (1/1/13). c/o Texas Education Agency, 1701 N. Congress Ave., Austin 78701-1494; (512) 463-9734.

Educator Certification, State Board for – (1995); apptv.; 6-yr.; expenses; 14 members; 3 ex officio: rep. of Comm. of Education; rep. of Comm. of Higher Education; 1 dean of a college of education; 11 apptv.: Chair Bonny L. Cain, Pearland (2/1/15); Brad W. Allard, Burleson (2/1/15); Janie Baszile, Houston (2/1/11); Laurie Bricker, Houston (2/1/13); Sandra D. Bridges, Rockwall (2/1/13); Curtis Culwell, Garland (2/1/11); Jill Harrison Druesedow, Haskell (2/1/13); Ben W. Morris, Cleburne (2/1/15); Christie Pogue, Buda (2/1/11); Judy Robison, El Paso (2/1/15); Homer Dean Treviño, Waco (2/1/13). Dir. Tabita Gutierrez, 1701 N. Congress Ave., 5th floor, Austin 78701-1494; (512) 936-8400.

Edwards Aquifer Authority – (1993); 4-yr.; expenses; 17 members (2 apptv. and 15 elected from single-member districts). Elected members: **Dist. 1:** Carol Patterson, Bexar Co. (12/1/14); **Dist. 2:** Byron Miller, Bexar Co. (12/1/12); **Dist. 3:** Lauro A. Bustamante, Bexar County (12/1/14); **Dist. 4:** Benjamin F. Youngblood, Bexar Co. (12/1/12; **Dist. 5:** Ron Ellis, Bexar Co. (12/1/14); **Dist. 6:** Susan Hughes, Bexar Co. (12/1/12); **Dist. 7:** Enrique Valdivia, Bexar Co. (12/1/14); **Dist. 8:** John Lovett Jr., Comal Co. (12/1/12); **Dist. 9:** Ronald J. Walton Sr., Comal & Guadalupe Cos. (12/1/14); **Dist. 10:** Patrick Stroka, Hays Co. (12/1/12); **Dist. 11:** Peggy Jones, Hays & Caldwell Cos. (12/1/14); **Dist. 12:** Adam Yablonski, Medina Co. (12/1/12; **Dist. 13:** Chair Luana Buckner, Medina & Atascosa Cos. (12/1/14); **Dist. 14:** Mario H. Cruz, Uvalde Co. (12/1/12); **Dist. 15:** Joe Parker, Uvalde Co. (12/1/14). Apptv. members: Austin Clary, Medina & Uvalde Cos. (12/1/12); Jerry James, South Central Texas Water Advisory Committee (12/1/12). Gen. Mgr. Karl J. Dreher, 1615 N. St. Mary's St., San Antonio 78215; (210) 222-2204.

Egg Marketing Advisory Board – Abolished May 1997.

Election Commission, State – (1973); 9 members; 4 ex officio: Chmn. of Democratic State Executive Committee; Chmn. of Republican State Executive Committee; Chief Justice of Supreme Court; Court of Criminal Appeals Presiding Judge; 5 apptv.: 1 justice of the Court of Appeals apptd. by Chief Justice of Supreme Court, 1 District Judge apptd. by presiding judge of Court of Criminal Appeals; 2 county chairmen (1 Democrat, 1 Republican, named by their parties); Secretary of State.

Emergency Communications, Commission on State – (1985 as 17-member Advisory Commission on State Emergency Communications; name changed and members reduced to 12 in 2000); apptv.; 4-yr.; expenses; 12 members: 3 ex offico: reps. of Dept. of State Health Services, Public Utilities Comm., and Dept. of Information Resources; 9 apptd.: Chair William Buchholtz, San Antonio (9/1/15); Kay Alexander, Abilene (8/31/13); James Beauchamp, Midland (8/31/13); Sue Brannon, Midland (9/1/11); Mitchell Fuller, Cedar Park (9/1/15); David A. Levy, Archer City (9/1/13); Jack D. Miller, Denton (9/1/15); Steve Mitchell, Richardson (9/1/11); Gregory Parker, New Braunfels (9/1/11). Exec. Dir. Paul Mallett ($90,750), 333 Guadalupe St., Ste. 2-212, Austin 78701-3942; (512) 305-6911.

Emergency Management Council, State – 32 members from state agencies and volunteer organizations. Texas Division of Emergency Management Chief W. Kim Kidd, P.O. Box 4087, Austin 78773-0220; (512) 424-2138.

Emergency Services Retirement System, Texas – (*See* **Retirement System, Texas Emergency Services**.)

Employment Commission, Texas – (*See* **Workforce Commission, Texas**.)

Engineers, Texas Board of Professional – (1937 as 6-member State Board of Registration for Professional Engineers; members increased to 9 in 1981; name changed to present in 1997); apptv.; per diem and expenses; 6-yr.; 9 members: Chair George Kemble Bennett, College Station (9/26/11); Carry A. Baker, Amarillo (9/26/15); Lamberto (Bobby) Balli, Houston (9/26/15); James Alan Greer, Dallas (9/26/15); Govind Nadkarni, Corpus Christi (9/26/11); Gary W. Raba, San Antonio (9/26/13); Elvira Reyna, Little Elm (9/26/13); Edward L. Summers, Austin (9/26/11); Daniel O. Wong, Houston (9/26/13). Exec. Dir. Lance Kinney, 1917 IH-35 S, Austin 78741; (512) 440-7723.

Environmental Quality, Texas Commission on – (1913 as State Board of Water Engineers; name changed in 1962 to Texas Water Commission; reorganized and name changed in 1965 to Water Rights Commission; reorganized and name changed back to Texas Water Commission in 1977 to perform judicial function for the Texas Dept. of Water Resources; name changed to Texas Natural Resource Conservation Commission in 1993; changed to present form in 2002); apptv.; 6-yr.; 3 members full-time ($150,000): Chair Bryan W. Shaw, Bryan (8/31/13); Buddy Garcia, Austin (8/31/11); Carlos Rubinstein, Austin (8/31/15). Exec. Dir. Mark Vickery ($145,200), PO Box 13087, Austin 78711-3087; (512) 239-3900.

Ethics Commission, Texas – (1991); apptv.; 4-yr.; 8 members: 2 apptd. by House Speaker, 2 apptd. by Lt. Gov, 4 apptd. by

Gov.: Chair Jim Graham, Dallas (11/19/09); James Clancy, Portland (11/19/13); Wilhelmina Delco, Austin (11/19/11); Tom Harrison, Austin (11/19/11); George H. (Trey) Henderson III, Lufkin (11/19/11); Paula M. Mendoza, Houston (11/19/07); Thomas Ramsey, Mount Vernon (11/19/13); Chase Untermeyer, Houston (11/19/13). Exec. Dir. David A. Reisman ($115,000), PO Box 12070, Austin 78711-2070; (512) 463-5800.

Facilities Commission, Texas – (2007; formerly Texas Building and Procurement Commission); apptv.; 6-yr.; 7 members: Chair Betty Reinbeck, Sealy (1/31/11); Malcolm Beckendorff, Katy (1/31/13); William Derek Darby, Houston (1/31/09); Virginia I. Hermosa, Austin (1/31/09); Victor E. Leal, Amarillo (1/31/09); Barkley J. Stuart, Dallas (1/31/11); 1 vacancies. Exec. Dir. Edward Johnson ($126,500) PO Box 13047, Austin 78711-3047; (512) 463-3446.

Family and Protective Services Advisory Council, Department of – (1991 as Dept. of Protective and Regulatory Services; reorganized to present form in 2004); apptv.; 6-yr.; 9 members: Chair Ommy Strauch, San Antonio (2/1/11); Gigi Edwards Bryant, Austin (2/1/13); Debbie Epperson, Austin (1/31/13); Theodore Paul Furukawa, San Antonio (2/1/11); Christina R. Martin, Mission (2/1/15); Imogen Papadopoulos, Houston (2/1/15); Linda Bell Robinson, Houston (2/1/13); Scott Rosenbach, Amarillo (2/1/15); Mamie Salazar-Harper, El Paso (2/1/11). Commissioner Anne Heiligenstein ($160,000), PO Box 149030, Austin 78714-9030; (512) 438-4800.

Finance Commission of Texas – (1923 as Banking Commission; reorganized as Finance Commission in 1943 with 9 members; members increased to 12 in 1983; changed back to 9 members in 1989); apptv.; 6-yr.; per diem and traveling expenses; 9 members: Chair William James White, Georgetown (2/1/12); Darby Ray Byrd Sr., Orange (2/1/12); David J. Cibrian, San Antonio (2/1/12); Riley Couch III, Frisco (2/1/12); Stacy G. London, Houston (2/1/14); Cindy F. Lyons, El Paso (2/1/10); Lori B. McCool, Boerne (2/1/14); Jonathan B. Newton, Houston (2/1/10); Paul Plunket, Dallas (2/1/14). Banking Commissioner, Randall S. James ($136,191), 2601 N. Lamar Blvd., Austin 78705; (512) 936-7640; appointee of Finance Commission. (*See also* Banking Commissioner, State.)

Fire Fighters' Pension Commissioner – (1937); apptv.; 2-yr.: Sherri Barr Walker, Pflugerville (7/1/11) ($77,000), PO Box 12577, Austin 78711-2577; (512) 936-3372. (*See also* Retirement System, Texas Emergency Services.)

Fire Protection, Texas Commission on – (1991; formed by consolidation of Fire Dept. Emergency Board and Commission on Fire Protection Personnel Standards and Education); apptv.; 6-yrs.; expenses; 13 members: Chair Christopher Connealy, Cedar Park (2/1/11); Les Bunte, Bryan (2/1/15); Elroy Carson, Ransom Canyon (2/1/11); Rhea Cooper, Lubbock (2/1/13); Yusuf Elias Farran, El Paso (2/1/15); Carl (Gene) Giles, Carthage (2/1/15); John Kelly Gillette III, Frisco (2/1/11); Joseph (Jody) Gonzalez, Krugerville (2/1/13); John W. Green, San Leon (2/1/11); Michael L. Melton, Gilmer (2/1/13); Arthur Lee Pertile III, Katy (2/1/13); Kimberley Shambley, Dallas (2/1/15); Steven C. Tull, Valley Mills (2/1/15). Exec. Dir. Gary L. Warren Sr. ($90,000), PO Box 2286, Austin 78768-2286; (512) 936-3838.

Food and Fibers Commission, Texas – Abolished Jan. 1, 2006, and duties transferred to the Texas Dept. of Agriculture Food and Fibers Research Council; PO Box 12847, Austin 78711; (512) 936-2450.

Forensic Science Commission, Texas – (2005); apptv.: 2-yr.; 9 members: 4 apptd. by Gov., 3 apptd. by Lt. Gov. and 2 apptd. by Atty. Gen.: Chair Nizam Peerwani, Fort Worth (9/1/11); Garry Adams, College Station (9/1/11); Arthur Jay Eisenberg, Fort Worth (9/1/12); Lance Evans, Fort Worth (9/1/11); Norma J. Farley, Harlingen (9/1/11); Stanley R. Hamilton, Houston (9/1/11); Jean Hampton, Houston (9/1/11); Sarah Kerrigan, Huntsville (9/1/12); one vacancy. Dir. Leigh Tomlin, 816 17th St., Huntsville 77340; (936) 294-1640.

Funeral Service Commission, Texas – (1903 as State Board of Embalming; 1935 as State Board of Funeral Directors and Embalmers; name changed to present form in 1987); apptv.; per diem and expenses; 6-yr.; 7 members: Chair Sue Evenwel, Mt. Pleasant (2/1/15); Gene Allen, Kerrville (2/1/15); Carol M. Becker, Abdo (9/1/13); Doug Carmichael, Pampa (2/1/11); Jess A. Fields Sr., Kingwood (2/1/15); Joyce M. Odom, San Antonio (2/1/11); Norberto Salinas, Mission (2/1/13). Exec. Dir. O.C. (Chet) Robbins ($55,816), 333 Guadalupe St., Ste. 2-110, Austin 78701; (512) 936-2474.

General Services Commission – Abolished in February 2002, with most functions taken over by the newly created Texas Building and Procurement Commission, which was renamed Texas Facilities Commission in 2007.

Geoscientists, Texas Board of Professional – (2001); apptv.; expenses; 6-yr.; 9 members (6 professional geoscientists, 3 public members): Chair Barbara O. Roeling, Austin (2/1/13); Yale Lynn Clark, Farmers Branch (2/1/11); Kelly Krenz-Doe, Houston (2/1/09); Charles T. (Tom) Hallmark, College Station (2/1/13); Ronald L. Kitchens, Harper (2/1/13); Glenn R. Lowenstein, Houston (2/1/11); Ben Harris, Plano (2/1/15); Justin McNamee, Rowlett (2/1/15); Gregory C. Ulmer, Houston (2/1/11). Interim Exec. Dir. Charles Horton ($57,400), 333 Guadalupe St., Tower 1, Suite 530; PO Box 13225, Austin 78711-3225; (512) 936-4400.

Guadalupe-Blanco River Authority – (1935); apptv.; per diem and expenses on duty; 6-yr.; 9 members: Chair Oscar H. Fogle, Lockhart (2/1/14); Grace G. Kunde, Seguin (2/1/15); Arlene N. Marshall, Port Lavaca (2/1/11); Myrna P. McLeroy, Gonzales (2/1/13); Frank J. Pagel, Tivoli (2/1/13); Jim Powers, Dripping Springs (2/1/14); Michael D. Schultz, Fair Oaks Ranch (2/1/15); Clifton L. Thomas Jr., Victoria (2/1/15); Tilmon Lee (T.L.) Walker, New Braunfels (2/1/09). Gen. Mgr. William E. West, 933 E. Court St., Seguin 78155; (830) 379-9718.

Guadalupe River Authority Board of Directors, Upper – (1939); apptv.; 6-yr.; 9 members: Pres. Scott S. Parker, Kerrville (2/1/13); Mike L. Allen, Kerrville (2/1/13); Harold Danford, Kerrville (2/1/17); Lester C. Ferguson, Kerrville (2/1/15); Lonnie (Pat) Holloway, Kerrville (2/1/11); D. Michael (Mike) Hughes, Ingram (2/1/17); Claudell Kercheville, Kerrville (2/1/13); Stan R. Kubenka, Kerrville (2/1/15); Lucy Wilke, Kerrville (2/1/15). Gen. Mgr. Ray Buck Jr., 125 Lehman Dr., Ste. 100, Kerrville 78028-5908; (830) 896-5445.

Guaranteed Student Loan Corporation, Texas – (1979 as non-profit corp.); apptv.; 6-yr.; 1 ex-officio member (Comptroller of Public Accounts); 10 apptv.: Ivan A. Andarza, Austin (1/31/13); Yvonne Batts, Tuscola (1/31/11); F.H. (Skip) Landis, College Station (1/31/11); Richard M. Rhodes, El Paso (1/31/15); Michael J. Savoie, Justin (1/31/11); Connie S. Sitterly, Fort Worth (1/31/13); Dora Ann Verde, San Antonio (1/31/15); Welcome W. Wilson, Houston (1/31/15); Phil W. Worley, Bruni (1/31/13); student apptee.: Wroe Jackson, Austin (1/31/11). Pres. and CEO Sue McMillin, P.O. Box 83100, Round Rock 78683-3100; (800) 252-9743.

Guardianship Certification Board – (2006); apptd. by the Texas Supreme Court; 6-yr.; 15 members: Chair Judge Gladys Burwell, Galveston (2/1/11); Barry Anderson, Arlington (2/1/13); Leah Cohen, Austin (2/1/09); Jason Armstrong, Lufkin (2/1/13); Garth Corbett, Austin (2/1/11); Raymond Costello, San Antonio (2/1/11); Carol Patrice Dabner, Dallas (2/1/009); Susan Eason, Austin (2/1/11); Don D. Ford III, Houston (2/1/11); Philip A. Grant, Round Rock (2/1/09); Marlane Meyer, McAllen (2/1/13); Gina D. Patterson, Houston (2/1/13); Kathy S. Strong, Nacogdoches (2/1/13); Patti Turner, Fort Worth (2/1/09); Robert Warach, El Paso (2/1/09). Dir. Lesley Martin Ondrechen, PO Box 12066, Austin 78711-2066; (512) 463-1635.

Gulf Coast Waste Disposal Authority – (1969); apptv.; 2-yr.; per diem and expenses on duty; 9 members: 3 apptv. by Gov., 3 by County Commissioners Courts of counties in district, 3 by Municipalities Waste Disposal Councils of counties in district. Chair Mark Schultz, Anahuac (8/31/10); Zoe Milian Barinaga, Houston (8/31/11); Ron Crowder, LaMarque (8/31/07); Randy Jarrell, Crystal Beach (8/31/10); Franklin Jones Jr., Houston (8/31/09); James A. Matthews Jr., Texas City (8/31/09); Lamont Meaux, Stowell (8/31/10); Irvin Osborne-Lee, Houston (8/31/04); Rita Standridge, Beach City (8/31/10). Gen. Mgr. Charles Ganze, 910 Bay Area Blvd., Houston 77058; (281) 488-4115.

Gulf States Marine Fisheries Commission – (1949 with members from Texas, Alabama, Florida, Louisiana and Mississippi); apptv.; 3-yr.; 3 Texas members: 2 ex officio: Texas Parks and Wildlife Dept. exec. dir. and 1 member of House; 1 apptd. by Gov.: David A. McKinney, Cypress Mill (3/17/11). Exec. Dir. Larry B. Simpson, PO Box 726, Ocean Springs, MS 39566-0726; (228) 875-5912.

Health Coordinating Council, Statewide – (1977); apptv.; 6-yr.; 17 members (4 ex officio; 13 apptd. by Gov.): Chair Ben G. Raimer, Galveston (8/1/09); Richard L. Beard, Mesquite (8/1/09); Davidica Blum, Georgetown (8/1/13); Lourdes M. Cuellar, Houston (8/1/11); James A. Endicott Jr., Harker Heights (8/1/13); Karl Alonzo Floyd, Stafford (8/1/09); Eric W. Ford, Lubbock (8/1/13); Janie Martinez Gonzalez, San Antonio (8/1/11); John Q. Gowan, Dallas (8/1/11); Ayeez A. Lalji, Sugar Land (8/1/13); Elva C. LeBlanc, Galveston (8/1/13); Lorraine O'Donnell, El Paso (8/1/11); Richard Madsen Smith, Amarillo (8/1/09). Ex-officio members include 1 each from Texas Dept. of State Health Services, Texas Dept. of Aging and Disability Services, Texas Higher Education Coordinating Board and Texas Health and Human Services Com-

mission. Proj. Dir. Connie Turney, PO Box 149347, Austin, TX 78714-9347; 512-458-7261.

Health and Human Services Commission Council – (1991); apptv.; 4-yr.; 9 members: Chair Jerry Kane, Corpus Christi (2/1/15); Kathleen O. Angel, Round Rock (2/1/11); Sharon J. Barnes, Lake Jackson (2/1/13); Maryann Choi, Georgetown (2/1/11); Rev. Manson B. Johnson, Houston (2/1/15); Leon J. Leach, Houston (2/1/13); Ronald Luke, Austin (2/1/13); Robert A. Valadez, San Antonio (2/1/11); Teresa (Terry) Wilkinson, Midland (2/1/15). Commissioner Thomas Suehs ($200,000; 2/1/11), PO Box 13247, Austin 78711-3247; (512) 424-6603.

Health and Human Services, Commissioner of – (1879 as State Health Officer; 1955 changed to Commissioner of Health; 1975 changed to Director, Texas Department of Health Resources; 1977 changed to Commissioner, Texas Dept. of Health; changed to present name in 2004); apptv.; 2-yr.: Thomas Suehs ($200,000; 2/1/11), PO Box 13247, Austin 78711-3247; (512) 424-6603.

Health Professions Council – (1993); ex officio; 14 members: 1 from Gov.'s office and 1 each from the following 13 regulating agencies: Texas Board of Chiropractic Examiners, Texas State Board of Dental Examiners, Texas Medical Board, Texas Board of Nursing, Texas Optometry Board, Texas State Board of Pharmacy, Physical Therapy Examiners Board, Texas State Board of Podiatric Medical Examiners, Texas Board of Examiners of Psychologists, Occupational Therapy Examiners Board, Texas Board of Veterinary Medical Examiners, Texas Funeral Service Commission, Texas Department of State Health Services Professional Licensing and Certification Unit. Admin. Officer John Monk, 333 Guadalupe St., Ste. 2-220, Austin 78701; (512) 305-8550.

Health Services Authority, Texas – (2007); apptv.; 2-yr.; expenses; 2 ex officio plus 11 appt'd. members: Chair Manfred Sternberg, Houston (6/15/09); Alesha Adamson, San Antonio (6/15/09); Fred Buckwold, Houston (6/15/09); Raymond F. Davis, El Paso (6/15/09); David C. Fleeger, Austin (6/15/09); Matthew J. Hamlin, Argyle (6/15/09); Edward W. Marx, Euless (6/15/09); Kathleen K. Mechler, Fredericksburg (6/15/09); Donna Montemayor, San Antonio (6/15/09); J. Darren Rodgers, Dallas (6/15/09); Stephen Yurco, Austin (6/15/09); c/o Texas Health Care Policy Council, Stephen Palmer, Health Policy Advisor, PO Box 12428, Austin 78711; (512) 463-1778.

Health Services Council, Texas Department of State – (1975); apptv.; 4-yr.; 9 members: Chair Glenda R. Kane, Corpus Christi (2/1/15); Beverly Barron, Odessa (2/1/13); Kirk Aquilla Calhoun, Tyler (2/1/11); Graciela A. Cigarroa, San Antonio (2/1/11); Lewis E. Foxhall, Houston (2/1/15); Jacinto P. Juarez, Laredo (2/1/13); Jeffrey A. Ross, Bellaire, (2/1/13); Nasruddin Rupani, Sugar Land (2/1/15); David Woolweaver, Harlingen (2/1/11). Exec. Dir. David L. Lakey ($175,000), PO Box 149347, Austin 78714-9347; (512) 458-7111.

Hearing Instruments, State Committee of Examiners in the Fitting and Dispensing of – (1969); apptv.; 6-yr.; expenses; 9 members: Chair Kenneth B. Haesly, Pasadena (12/31/11); Robert J. Gebhard Jr., Pearland (12/31/11); Carla Hoffman, Corpus Christi (12/31/15); James Jay, Temple (12/31/15); James Leffingwell, Arlington (12/31/13); Benjamin Norris, Elm Mott (12/31/13); Melissa Kay Rodriguez, El Paso (12/31/11); Cindy M. Steinbart, Round Rock (12/31/15); Amy Trost, Seguin (12/31/13). Exec. Dir. Joyce N. Parsons, c/o Texas Dept. of State Health Services, PO Box 194347, MC 1982, Austin 78714-9247; (512) 834-6784.

Higher Education Coordinating Board, Texas – (1953 as temporary board; 1955 as permanent 15-member Texas Commission on Higher Education; 1965 as Texas College and University Systems Coordinating Board; name and membership changed to present form in 1987); apptv.; 6-yr.; expenses; 9 members: Chair Fred W. Heldenfels IV, San Marcos (8/31/13); Durga D. Agrawal, Houston (8/31/15); Dennis Golden, Carthage (8/31/15); Harold W. Hahn, El Paso (8/31/13); Joe Bob Hinton, Crawford (8/31/11); James H. Lee, Houston (8/31/11); Lyn Bracewell Phillips, Bastrop (8/31/11); A.W. (Whit) Riter III, Tyler (8/31/11); one vacancy. Commissioner of Higher Education, Raymund A. Paredes, ($165,000) PO Box 12788, Austin 78711-2788; (512) 427-6101.

Higher Education Tuition Board, Texas Prepaid – (1995); apptv.; expenses; term at pleasure of Gov.; 6 members, plus 1 ex officio: State Comptroller; 2 apptd. by Gov. and 4 apptd. by Lt. Gov.: Johh C. Anderson, Plainview; Richard H. Collins, Weatherford; Joe Colonnetta, Dallas (2/1/11); Jack R. Hamilton, Houston; Harrison Keller, Austin; Stephen N. Mueller, Cypress (2/1/15); c/o Texas Guaranteed Tuition Plan, Comptroller of Public Accounts, PO Box 13407, Austin 78711-3407; (800) 445-4723.

Historian, Texas State – (2005); apptv.; 2-yr.; Light Townsend Cummins, Sherman (5/29/11); c/o Department of History, Austin College, 900 N. Grand Ave., Sherman 75090-4400; (903) 813-2359.

Historical Commission, Texas – (1953); apptv.; expenses; 6-yr.; 17 members: Chair Jon T. Hansen, El Paso (1/31/13); Thomas E. Alexander, Kerrville (2/1/15); Earl P. Broussard Jr., Austin (2/1/17); Mario Castillo, San Angelo (1/31/13); Leslie (Kirk) Courson, Perryton (2/1/15); John Crain, Dallas (1/31/13); David A. Gravelle, Dallas (1/31/13); Lisa Hembry, Dallas (1/31/13); Steven L. Highlander, Austin (2/1/15); Sheri S. Krause, Austin (2/1/15); Matthew Kreisle III, Austin (2/1/17); Tom Perini, Buffalo Gap (2/1/17); Gilbert E. Peterson, Alpine (1/31/13); Judy Richardson, Caldwell (2/1/17); Nancy Steves, San Antonio (2/1/15); Daisy Sloan White, Houston (2/1/17). Commissioner Emeritus T.R. Fehrenbach, San Antonio. Exec. Dir. Mark Wolfe ($125,000), PO Box 12276, Austin 78711-2276; (512) 463-6100.

Historical Records Advisory Board, Texas – (1976); apptv.; 3-yr.; 9 members: State Archivist; 6 apptd. by Texas State Library and Archives Commission director; 2 apptd. by Gov.: Coordinator and State Archivist Jelain Chubb, Austin; Suzanne Campbell, San Angelo; Lynn Denton, San Marcos; Margaret Harris, Houston; Shelly Henley Kelly, Houston; J.P. (Pat) McDaniel, Midland; Jennifer Boswell Pickens, Dallas; John Slate, Dallas; Bratten Thomason, Austin; c/o Texas State Library and Archives Commission, PO Box 12927, Austin 78711; (512) 463-5455.

Housing and Community Affairs, Texas Dept. of – (1979 as Texas Housing Agency; merged with Department of Community Affairs and name changed in 1991); apptv.; expenses; 6-yr.; 7 members: Chair John Paul (J. Paul) Oxer, Sugar Land (1/31/17); Leslie Bingham-Escareño, Brownsville (1/31/13); C. Kent Conine, Frisco (1/31/15); Tom H. Gann, Lufkin (1/31/15); Lowell Keig, Austin (1/31/13); Juan Sanchez Muñoz, Lubbock (1/31/17); Gloria L. Ray, San Antonio (1/31/11). Exec. Dir. Michael Gerber ($129,250), PO Box 13941, Austin 78711-3941; (512) 475-3800.

Housing Corp., Texas State Affordable – (1994); 6 yrs.; 5 members: Chair Robert Jones, Corpus Christi (2/1/15); Jeran Akers, Plano (2/1/17); William H. Dietz Jr., Waco (2/1/13); Jo Van Hovel, Temple (2/1/13); Jerry Romero, El Paso (2/1/15). Pres. David Long, PO Box 12637, Austin 78711-2637; (888) 638-3555.

Human Rights Commission, Texas – (2004 as part of the Texas Workforce Commission's Civil Rights Division); apptv.; 6-yr.; 7 members: Chair Thomas M. Anderson, Richmond (2/1/13); Michelle H. Diggs, Cedar Park (2/1/15); Toni Glover, Fort Worth (2/1/17); Shara Michalka, Dallas (2/1/17); Travis A. Morris, Pearland (2/1/15); Danny L. Osterhout, Andrews (2/1/13); Veronica Vargas Stidvent, Austin (2/1/15). Interim Dir. Jonathan Babiak, 101 E. 15th St., Rm. 144T, Austin 78778-0001; (512) 463-2642.

Industrialized Building Code Council, Texas – (1973); apptv.; 2-yr.; 12 members: Chair Robert L. Bowling IV, El Paso (2/1/13); Roland L. Brown, Mansfield (2/1/13); Joe D. Campos, Dallas (2/1/12); Randy Childers, Waco (2/1/12); Amy Dempsey, Austin (2/1/12); Martin J. Garza, San Antonio (2/1/12); Scott A. McDonald, Amarillo (2/1/13); Mark Remmert, Round Rock (2/1/12); Jesse Rider, Tyler (2/01/12); Douglas O. Robinson, Fort Worth (2/1/13); Rolando R. Rubiano, Harlingen (2/1/13); Larry E. Wilkinson, League City (2/1/13); c/o Texas Dept. of Licensing and Regulation, PO Box 12157, Austin 78711; (512) 463-6599.

Information Resources, Department of – (1981 as Automated Information and Telecommunications Council; name changed to current in 1990); 6-yr.; expenses; 10 members: 3 ex officio, 7 apptv.: Chair Charles Bacarisse, Houston (2/1/13); Ramon Baez, Southlake (2/1/15); Rosemary Martinez, Brownsville (2/1/13); Richard Moore, Goliad (2/1/15); Phillip (Keith) Morrow, Southlake (2/1/17); Robert E. Pickering Jr., Houston (2/1/15); Wanda Rohm, San Antonio (2/1/17); ex-officio members are from Health and Human Services Commission, Texas Dept. of Insurance and Texas Dept. of Transportation. Chief Technology Officer Karen Robinson ($175,000), PO Box 13564, Austin 78711-3564; (512) 475-4700.

Insurance Commissioner, Texas Dept. of – (1876 as Dept. of Insurance; 1887 as Dept. of Agriculture, Insurance, Statistics and History; 1907 as Dept. of Insurance and Banking; 1923 as Dept. of Insurance); apptv.; 2-yr.; Commissioner Eleanor Kitzman, Austin (2/1/13), ($175,000), PO Box 149104, Austin 78714-9104; (512) 463-6169.

Insurance Counsel, Office of Public – (See Public Insurance Counsel, Office of.)

Interstate Commission for Adult Offender Supervision – (1937 as Interstate Compact for the Supervision of Parolees and Probationers; 2000 as present name); 50 member states; apptv.: Rissie Owens, Huntsville (2/1/17). Compact Admin. for Texas:

Stuart Jenkins, 8610 Shoal Creek Blvd., Ste. 290, Austin 78757; (512) 406-5401.

Interstate Mining Compact Commission – (1970); 19 member states, plus 5 associate member states; ex officio or apptv., according to Gov's. choice; Texas reps. are appointed from the Texas Railroad Commission: John Caudle. Exec. Dir. Gregory E. Conrad, 445-A Carlisle Dr., Herndon, VA 22170-4802; (703) 709-8654.

Interstate Oil and Gas Compact Commission, Texas Rep. – (1935); 30 member states, plus 8 associate member states; ex officio or apptv., according to Gov's. choice; per diem and expenses. Official rep. for Texas: Victor G. Carrillo, Austin (12/31/10). Exec. Dir. Mike Smith, PO Box 53127, Oklahoma City, OK 73152; (405) 525-3556.

Jail Standards, Texas Commission on – (1975); apptv.; 6-yr.; expenses; 9 members: Chair Donna S. Klaeger, Burnet (1/31/13); Irene A. Armendariz, El Paso (1/31/15); Allen Cain, Carthage (1/31/17); Stanley D. Egger, Abilene (1/31/17); Jerry W. Lowry, New Caney (1/31/13); Larry S. May, Sweetwater (1/31/13); Gary Painter, Midland (2/1/15); Michael M. Seale, Houston (1/31/17); Tam Terry, White Deer (1/31/15). Exec. Dir. Adan Munoz Jr. ($75,350), PO Box 12985, Austin 78711-2985; (512) 463-5505.

Judicial Compensation Commission – (2007); apptv.; 6-yr.; expenses; 9 members: Chair William Strawn, Austin (2/01/15); Romulo Chavez, Spring (2/01/17); Tommy Harwell, El Paso (2/01/13); Cruz G. Hernandez, Burleson (2/01/15); Harold Jenkins, Irving (2/01/17); Patrick Mizell, Houston (2/01/13); Paul Bane Phillippi, Cedar Creek (2/01/15); Linda Russell, Houston (2/01/13); Michael Slack, Austin (2/01/17); c/o Office of Court Administration, Tom C. Clark Building, 205 W. 14th St., Ste. 600, Austin 78701; (512) 463-1625.

Judicial Conduct, State Commission on – (1965 as 9-member Judicial Qualifications Commission; name changed to present in 1977); apptv.; expenses; 6-yr.; 13 members: 6 apptd. by Supreme Court; 2 apptd. by State Bar; 5 apptd. by Gov.: Chair Jorge C. Rangel, Corpus Christi, (11/19/11); Joel Baker, Tyler (11/19/11); Tom Cunningham, Houston (11/19/13); David Gaultney, Beaumont (11/19/13); Sid L. Harle, San Antonio, (11/19/15); Martha Morales Hernandez, Diboll, (11/19/15); Patti H. Johnson, Canyon Lake (11/19/11); M. Sue Kurita, El Paso (11/19/15); Karry K. Matson, Georgetown (11/19/13); Steven L. Seider, Dallas (11/19/15); Janelle Shephard, Weatherford (11/19/11); Edward J. Spillane III, College Station (11/19/15); Diane De La Torre Threadgill, Midlothian (11/19/15). Exec. Dir. Seana B. Willing ($110,000), PO Box 12265, Austin 78711-2265; (512) 463-5533.

Judicial Council, Texas – (1929 as Texas Civil Judicial Council; name changed in 1975); 6-yr.; expenses; 22 members: 16 ex officio and 6 apptd. from general public. Public members: Richard Battle, Lakeway (6/30/15); Richard S. Figueroa, Houston (6/30/13); Allyson Ho, Dallas (6/30/13); Ashley Johnson, Dallas (6/30/17); Henry Virgil Justice III, Kerrville (6/30/17); Henry (Hank) Nuss, Corpus Christi (6/30/15). Exec. Dir. Carl Reynolds ($121,847), PO Box 12066, Austin 78711; (512) 463-1625.

Judicial Districts Board – (1985); 12 ex-officio members (term in other office); 1 apptv. (4 yrs.); ex officio: Chief Justice of Texas Supreme Court; Presiding Judge, Court of Criminal Appeals; Presiding Judge of each of 9 Administrative Judicial Districts; Gov. apptee.: Craig Enoch, Austin (12/12/14).

Judicial Districts of Texas, Administrative, Presiding Judges of – (See Administrative Judicial Districts, Presiding Judges.)

Juneteenth Cultural and Historical Commission, Texas Emancipation – (1997); apptv.; 6 yr.; expenses; 11 members: 5 ex officio, 6 apptd by Gov.: Chair Rep. Al Edwards, Houston; Vicki D. Blanton, Dallas (2/1/11); Willie Belle Boone, Houston (2/1/15); Carmen Francis, Georgetown (2/1/11); Clarence E. Glover Jr., Dallas (2/1/13); Rev. William H. Watson, Lubbock (2/1/13); PO Box 2910, Austin 78768-2910; (512) 463-0518.

Juvenile Probation Commission, Texas – (1981); apptv.; 6-yr.; expenses; 9 members: 3 District Court judges and 6 private citizens: Chair E. Ray West, Brownwood (8/31/11); Jean H. Boyd, Fort Worth (8/31/13); William Conley, Wimberley (8/31/15); Migdalia Lopez, Brownsville (8/31/15); Billy Wayne McClendon, Austin (8/31/13); Scott O'Grady, Dallas (8/31/15); Rene Ordonez, El Paso (8/31/11); Robert Shults, Houston (8/31/13); Lea R. Wright, Amarillo (8/31/11). Exec. Dir. Vicki Spriggs ($120,023), PO Box 13547, Austin 78711-3547; (512) 424-6700.

Land Board, School – (1939); 2-yr.; per diem and expenses; 3 members: 1 ex officio: Comm. of General Land Office; 2 apptd.: 1 by Atty. Gen. and 1 by Gov.: Tommy Orr, Houston (8/29/11); David S. Herrmann, San Antonio (8/31/11); c/o General Land Office, SFA Office Bldg., 1700 N. Congress Ave., Austin 78701-1495; (512) 463-5001.

Land Board, Veterans' – (Est. 1949 as 3-member ex-officio board; reorganized 1956); 4-yr.; per diem and expenses; 3 members: 1 ex officio: Comm. of General Land Office; 2 apptd.: Alan L. Johnson, Harlingen (12/29/12); Alan K. Sandersen, Missouri City (12/29/14). Exec. Sec. Paul E. Moore, PO Box 12873, Austin 78711-2873; (800) 252-8387.

Land Surveying, Texas Board of Professional – (1979; formed from consolidation of Board of Examiners of Licensed Land Surveyors, est. 1977, and State Board of Registration for Public Surveyors, est. 1955); apptv.; 6-yr.; 9 members: 1 ex officio: Comm. of General Land Office; 8 apptd.: Chair David G. (Greg) Smyth, Uvalde (1/31/13); James Allen Childress, San Saba (1/31/15); Mary Chruszczak, The Woodlands (1/31/17); Nedra J. Foster, Silsbee (1/31/15); Gerardo M. (Jerry) Garcia, Corpus Christi (1/31/17); Jon Hodde, Brenham (1/31/13); Paul P. Kwan, Houston (1/31/17); Robert H. (Bob) Price, Euless (1/31/15). Exec. Dir. Frank DiTucci ($70,000), 12100 Park 35 Circle, Bldg. A, Ste. 156, MC 230, Austin 78753; (512) 239-5263.

Lands, Board for Lease of University – (1929 as 3-member board; members increased to 4 in 1985); ex officio; term in other office; 4 members: Comm. of General Land Office, 2 members of Board of Regents of The University of Texas, 1 member Board of Regents of Texas A&M University. Sec. Sharon Burks, The University of Texas System; (432) 684-4404.

Lavaca-Navidad River Authority, Board of Directors – (1954 as 7-member Jackson County Flood Control District; reorganized as 9-member board in 1959; name changed to present form in 1969); apptv.; 6-yr.; per diem and expenses; 9 members: Jerry Adelman, Palacios (5/1/17); Jon Bradford, Edna (5/1/13); John Alcus Cotten Jr., Ganado (5/1/15); Sherry Kay Frels, Edna (5/1/13); Olivia R. Jarratt, Edna (5/1/13); Ronald Edwin Kubecka, Palacios (5/1/15); Nils P. Mauritz, Ganado (5/1/15); David Martin Muegge, Edna (5/1/17); Terri Parker, Ganado (5/1/17). Gen. Mgr. Patrick Brzozowski, PO Box 429, Edna 77957; (361) 782-5229.

Law Enforcement Officer Standards & Education, Texas Commission on – (1965); expenses; 14 members; 5 ex officio: Atty. Gen., Dir. of Public Safety, Comm. of Education, Exec. Dir. of Gov.'s Office Criminal Justice Division, and Comm. of Higher Education; 9 apptv. members: Chair Charles R. Hall, Midland (8/30/11); Steven M. Griffith, Sugar Land (8/30/13); Johnny E. Lovejoy II, San Antonio (8/30/13); James Oakley, Spicewood (8/30/11); Joseph B. Pennington, Jersey Village (8/30/15); Joel W. Richardson, Canyon (8/30/13); Patt Scheckel-Hollingsworth, Arlington (8/30/11); Ruben Villescas, Pharr (8/30/15); John Randall (Randy) Watson, Burleson (8/30/15). Exec. Dir. Timothy Braaten ($88,000), 6330 U.S. Hwy. 290 E, Ste. 200, Austin 78723-1035; (512) 936-7700.

Law Examiners, Texas Board of – (1919); 9 attorneys apptd. by Supreme Court biennially for 2-year terms expiring Sept. 30 of odd-numbered years. Compensation set by Supreme Court not to exceed $20,000 per annum: Chair John Simpson, Lubbock; Jerry Grissom, Dallas; Jerry Nugent, Austin; Al Odom, Houston; Cynthia Olsen, Houston; E. Lee Parsley, Austin; Dan Pozza, San Antonio; Michael Sokolow, Houston; Sandra Zamora. Exec. Dir. Julia Vaughan, PO Box 13486, Austin 78711-3486; (512) 463-1621.

Law Library Board, Texas State – (1971); ex officio; expenses; 3 members: Atty. Gen., Chief Justice State Supreme Court, Presiding Judge Court of Criminal Appeals. Dir. Dale Propp ($70,180), PO Box 12367, Austin 78711-2367; (512) 463-1722.

Legislative Budget Board – (1949); 10 members; 5 ex-officio: Lt. Gov.; House Speaker, Chmn., Senate Finance Comm.; Chmn., House Appropriations Comm.; Chmn., House Ways and Means Comm.; plus 5 other members of Legislature. Dir. John O'Brien, PO Box 12666, Austin 78711-2666; (512) 463-1200.

Legislative Council, Texas – (1949); 14 ex-officio members: Lt. Gov.; House Speaker; 6 senators apptd. by Lt. Gov.; 5 representatives apptd. by Speaker; Chmn., House Administration Committee. Exec. Dir. Debbie Irvine, PO Box 12128, Austin 78711-2128; (512) 463-1155.

Legislative Redistricting Board – (1951); 5 ex-officio members: Lt. Gov., House Speaker, Atty. Gen., Comptroller of Public Accounts, and Comm. of General Land Office; PO Box 12128, Austin 78711-2128; (512) 463-1155.

Legislative Reference Library – See Library, Legislative Reference.

Librarian, State – (Originally est. in 1839; present office est. 1909); apptv., indefinite term: Peggy D. Rudd ($104,500), PO Box

12927, Austin 78711-2927; (512) 463-5455.

Library and Archives Commission, Texas State – (1909 as 5-member Library and State Historical Commission; name changed to present form in 1979); apptv.; per diem and expenses on duty; 6-yr.; 7 members: Chair Sandra J. Pickett, Liberty (9/28/15); Sharon T. Carr, El Paso (9/28/11); Martha Doty Freeman, Austin (9/28/15); Larry G. Holt, College Station (9/28/15); Wm. Scott McAfee, Driftwood (9/28/13); Sally Ann Reynolds, Rockport (9/28/11); Michael C. Waters, Dallas (9/28/13). Director and Librarian Peggy D. Rudd ($104,500), PO Box 12927, Austin 78711-2927; (512) 463-5455.

Library, Legislative Reference – (1909); 3 ex-officio members: Lt. Gov., House Speaker, Chrm., House Appropriations Committee; 3 Legislative members; indefinite term. Dir. Mary Camp, Box 12488, Austin 78711-2488; (512) 463-1252.

Licensing and Regulation, Texas Department on – (1989); apptv.; 6-yr.; expenses; 7 members: Chair Frank S. Denton, Conroe (2/1/13); Mike Arismendez Jr., Shallowater (2/1/15); LuAnn Roberts Morgan, Midland (2/1/15); Fred N. Moses, Plano (2/1/15); Lillian Norman-Keeney, Taylor Lake Village (2/1/17); Ravi Shah, The Colony (2/1/17); Deborah A. Yurco, Austin (2/1/13). Exec. Dir. Willliam H. Kuntz Jr. ($135,000); PO Box 12157, Austin 78711-2157; (800) 803-9202.

Licensing Standards, Committee on– (2007); apptv.; 2-yr.; expenses; 7 members: Chair Karyn Purvis, Fort Worth (2/1/11); Dan Adams, Amarillo (2/1/11); Adriene J. Driggers, San Antonio (2/1/11); Kimberly B. Kofron, Round Rock (2/1/11); Sasha Rasco, Austin (2/1/11); Ann Stanley, Austin (2/1/11); Tivy Whitlock, Mico (2/1/11). Dept. of Family and Protective Services, PO Box 149030, Austin 78714-9030; (512) 438-4800.

Lottery Commission, Texas – (1993); 6-yrs.; apptv.; expenses; 3 members: Chair Mary Ann Williamson, Weatherford (2/1/15); J. Winston Krause, Austin (2/1/11); one vacancy. Exec. Dir. Gary Grief ($140,900), PO Box 16630, Austin 78761-6630; (512) 344-5000.

Lower Colorado River Authority – (See Colorado River Authority, Lower).

Lower Concho River Water and Soil Conservation Authority – (See Concho River Water and Soil Conservation, Lower).

Lower Neches Valley Authority – (See Neches Valley Authority, Lower).

Manufactured Housing Governing Board – (1995); apptv.; 6 yrs.; 5 members: Chair Michael H. Bray, El Paso (1/31/17); Anthony Burks, Fort Worth (1/31/17); Pablo Schneider, Richardson (1/31/13); Sheila M. Vallés-Pankratz, Mission (1/31/15), Donnie W. Wisenbaker, Sulphur Springs (1/31/13). Exec. Dir. Joe Garcia, PO Box 12489, Austin 78711-2489; (512) 475-2200.

Marriage & Family Therapists, Texas State Board of Examiners of – (1991); apptv.; 6 yrs.; per diem and transportation expenses; 9 members: Chair Sandra L. DeSobe, Houston (2/1/13); Rick Bruhn, Huntsville (2/1/17); Joe Ann Clack, Missouri City (2/1/15); George Francis IV, Georgetown (2/1/17); Michael Miller, Belton (2/1/13); Michael R. Puhl, McKinney (2/1/15); Jennifer Smothermon, Abilene (2/1/13); Sean Stokes, Denton (2/1/17); Beverly Walker Womack, Jacksonville (2/1/15). Exec. Dir. Carol Miller, Texas Dept. of Health Services, PO Box 149347, MC 1982, Austin 78714-9347; (512) 834-6657.

Medical Board, Texas – (1907 as 11-member Texas State Board of Medical Examiners; members increased to 12 in 1931, 15 in 1981,18 in 1993 and 19 in 2003; changed to present name in 2005 by Senate Bill 419); apptv.; 6-yr.; per diem on duty; 19 members: Chair Irvin E. Zeitler Jr., San Angelo (4/13/17); Michael Arambula, San Antonio (4/13/13); Julie Attebury, Amarillo (4/13/17); David Baucom, Sulphur Springs (4/13/15); Patricia S. Blackwell, Midland (4/13/13); Patrick J. Crocker, Austin (4/13/15); John D. Ellis Jr., Houston (4/13/15); Manuel G. Guajardo, Brownsville (4/13/15); J. Scott Holliday, University Park (4/13/15); Melinda C. McMichael, Austin (4/13/13); Margaret C. McNeese, Houston (4/13/13); Charles E. Oswalt III, Waco (4/13/13); Allan Shulkin, Dallas (4/13/15); Wynne M. Snoots, Dallas (4/13/15); Paulette B. Southard, Alice (4/13/11); Timothy J. Turner, Houston (4/13/15); Stanley Wang, Austin (4/13/17); Timothy Webb, Houston (4/13/13); George Willeford III, Austin (4/13/17). Exec. Dir. Mari Robinson ($121,000), PO Box 2018, Austin 78768-2018; (512) 305-7010. *Consumer Complaint Hotline: (800) 201-9353.*

Medical Physicists, Texas Board of Licensure for Professional – (1991); apptv.; 6-yrs.; 9 members: Chair Richard E. Wendt III, Houston (2/1/13); Charles Beasley, Bellaire (2/1/17); Valerie Foreman, Frisco (2/1/15); Douglas A. Johnson, College Station (2/1/13); John R. Leahy, Austin (2/1/13); James Marbach,

San Antonio (2/1/17); Pamela M. Otto, San Antonio (2/1/15); Kiran Shah, Houston (2/1/17): Alvin (Lee) Schlichtemeier (2/1/15). Exec. Sec. Ann Hammer, PO Box 149347, Austin 78714-9347; (512) 834-6655.

Midwestern State University, Board of Regents – (1959); apptv.; 6-yr.; 9 members: Chair Carol Carlson Gunn, Graford (2/25/12); Michael Bernhardt, Wichita Falls (2/25/16); J. Kenneth Bryant, Wichita Falls (2/25/16); Tiffany D. Burks, Grand Prairie (2/25/16); Charles Engleman, Wichita Falls (2/25/14); Fenton Lynwood Givens, Plano (2/25/12); Shawn G. Hessing, Fort Worth (2/25/14); Samuel M. Sanchez, Fort Worth (2/25/12); Jane W. Spears, Wichita Falls (2/25/14). Pres. Dr. Jesse W. Rogers, 3410 Taft Blvd., Wichita Falls 76308; (940) 397-4010.

Midwifery Board, Texas – (1999); apptv. by Health and Human Services Comm.; 6-yr.; travel expenses; 9 members: Susan Chick (1/1/09); Connie Carlos (1/1/11); Janet Dirmeyer (1/1/11); Laurie Fremgen (1/1/13); Charleta Guillory (1/1/13); Thalia Hufton (1/1/09); Sylyna Kennedy (1/1/11); Andrew MacLaurin (1/1/13); Barry E. Schwarz (1/1/09). c/o Texas Dept. of Health Services, PO Box 149347, Austin 78714-9347; (512) 834-4523.

Military Facilities Commission, Texas – (1935 as 3-member Texas National Guard Armory Board; reorganized in 1981 as 6-member board; name changed to present in 1997; members increased to 7 in 2003; 6-yr.; 7 members: Chair Sandra Paret, Dallas (4/30/06); Regino J. Gonzales, Galena Park (4/30/09); Delores Ann Harper, San Antonio (4/30/07); Larry W. Jackson, Temple (4/30/09); Chao-Chiung Lee, Houston (4/30/09); Jorge Perez, McAllen (4/30/05); Michael G. Taylor, Lufkin (4/30/07). Exec. Dir. John A. Wells, 2200 W. 35th St., Bldg. 64, Austin 78703-1222; (512) 782-6971.

Military Preparedness Commission, Texas– (2003); apptv.; some terms at pleasure of Gov.; 2 ex-officio members (1 Senator, 1 House Representative); 13 apptv.: Chair Paul F. Paine, Fort Worth; Dora G. Alcala, Del Rio (2/1/15); William J. (Bill) Ehrie, Abilene; Arthur Emerson, San Antonio (2/1/11); Ralph C. Gauer, Harker Heights (2/1/15); Howard C. Ham Jr., Lockhart; Ronald D. Henson, Texarkana; Alvin W. Jones, College Station (2/1/15); Loyd Neal, Corpus Christi; Charles E. Powell, San Angelo; A.F. (Tom) Thomas, El Paso (2/1/11); Eugene N. Tulich, Houston; Thomas Whaylen, Wichita Falls; PO Box 12428, Austin, 78711; (512) 463-8800.

Motor Vehicles Board, Texas Dept. of – (2009); 9 members; 6-yr.; Chair Victor Vandergriff, Arlington (2/1/15); Clifford Butler, Mount Pleasant (2/1/13); James (Jim) Campbell Jr., Sachse (2/1/11); Ramsay Gillman, Houston (2/1/13); Cheryl Johnson, Friendswood (2/1/13); Janet Marzett, Keller (2/1/15); Victor Rodriguez, McAllen (2/1/15); Marvin Rush, Seguin (2/1/11); John Walker III, Houston (2/1/11).

Municipal Retirement System, Texas (See Retirement System, Texas Municipal).

National Guard Armory Board, Texas – (See Military Facilities Commission, Texas).

Natural Resource Conservation Commission, Texas (See Environmental Quality, Texas Commission on).

Neches River Municipal Water Authority, Upper – (1953 as 9-member board; members decreased to 3 in 1959); apptv.; 6-yr.; 3 members: Jesse D. Hickman, Palestine (2/1/15); William Barry James, Palestine (2/1/13); Robert E. McKelvey, Palestine (2/1/11). Gen. Mgr. Monty D. Shank, PO Box 1965, Palestine 75802; (903) 876-2237.

Neches Valley Authority, Lower – (1933); apptv.; per diem and expenses on duty; 6-yr.; 9 members: Lonnie Arrington, Beaumont (7/28/13); Brian Babin, Woodville (7/28/13); Sue Cleveland, Lumberton (7/28/15); Jimmie Ruth Cooley, Woodville (7/28/15); Kathleen Thea Jackson, Beaumont (7/28/15); Steven M. McReynolds, Groves (7/28/15); Dade Phelan, Beaumont (7/28/11); Jordan Reese IV, Beaumont (7/28/11); James Olan Webb, Silsbee (7/28/11). Gen. Mgr. Robert Stroder, PO Box 5117, Beaumont 77726-5117; (409) 892-4011.

Nueces River Authority – (1953 as Nueces River Conservation and Reclamation District; name changed to present in 1971); apptv.; 6-yr.; per diem and expenses; 22 members: President Dan S. Leyendecker, Corpus Christi (2/1/13); W. Scott Bledsoe III, Oakville (2/1/15); Karen Bonner, Corpus Christi (2/1/11); Rebecca Bradford, Corpus Christi (2/1/13); Fernando Camarillo, Boerne (2/1/15); Manuel D. Cano, Corpus Christi (2/1/13); Joe M. Cantu, Pipe Creek (2/1/13); James T. Clancy, Portland (2/1/15); William I. Dillard, Uvalde (2/1/15); Robert M. Dullnig, San Antonio (2/1/13); John Galloway, Beeville (2/1/09); Gary Jones, Beeville (2/1/11); Yale Leland Kerby, Uvalde (2/1/11); Lindsey Alfred Koenig, Orange Grove (2/1/15); James Richard Marmion III, Carrizo Springs (2/1/11); Betty Ann Peden, Hondo (2/1/09); Scott James Petty, Hondo (2/1/13); Curtis Raabe, Poth (2/1/15); Thomas M. Reding Jr., Portland (2/1/15); Fidel R. Rul Jr., Alice (2/1/11); Roxana P. Tom, Campbellton (2/1/11); 1 vacancy. Exec. Dir. Con Mims, PO Box 349, Uvalde 78802-0349; (830) 278-6810.

Nursing, Texas Board of – (1909 as 5-member Texas Board of Nurse Examiners; members increased to 6 in 1931 and to 9 in 1981; name changed to present and members increased to 13 in 2007); apptv.; per diem and expenses; 6-yr.; 13 members: President Linda Rounds, Galveston (1/31/11); Deborah Hughes Bell, Abilene (1/31/11); Kristin K. Benton, Austin (1/31/13); Patricia Clapp, Dallas (1/31/13); Tamara Cowen, Harlingen (2/1/15); Sheri Crosby, Mesquite (2/1/15); Marilyn Davis, Sugar Land (1/31/13); Blanca Rosa (Rosie) Garcia, Corpus Christi (1/31/11); Richard Gibbs, Mesquite (1/31/13); Kathy Leader-Horn, Granbury (2/1/15); Josefina Lujan, El Paso (2/1/15); Beverly Jean Nutall, Bryan (1/31/11); Mary Jane Salgado, Eagle Pass (2/1/15). Exec. Dir. Katherine A. Thomas ($89,749), 333 Guadalupe, Suite 3-460, Austin 78701; (512) 305-7400.

Nursing Facility Administrators, Texas Board of – Abolished Sept. 1997 and responsibilities transferred to Texas Dept. of Human Services, which itself was abolished in 2004 and responsibilities transferred to Texas Dept. of Aging and Disability Services.

Occupational Therapy Examiners, Texas Board of – (1983 as 6-member board; increased to 9 in 1999); apptv.; 6-yr.; per diem and expenses; 9 members: Catherine Benavidez, Carrollton (2/1/15); Judith Ann Chambers, Austin (2/1/13); Dely De Guia Cruz, Houston (2/1/09); Kathleen Hill, Hutto (2/1/13); Stephanie Johnston, Houston (2/1/11); Pamela D. Nelon, Fort Worth (2/1/11); Todd Novosad, Austin (2/1/13); Angela Sieffert, Dallas (2/1/15); Bobby James Vasquez, Frisco (2/1/11). Exec. Dir. John Maline ($62,000), 333 Guadalupe St., Ste. 2-510, Austin 78701-3942; (512) 305-6900.

Offenders with Medical or Mental Impairments, Texas Correctional Office on – Apptv.; 6-yr.; 21 members: 11 ex officio from various state agencies; 10 apptd. by Gov.: Chair John Bradley, Georgetown (2/1/13); Ellen Cokinos, Houston (7/20/08); Joseph Gutheinz, Houston (7/20/08); Kevin E. Haynes, Ennis (2/1/11); Gabriel Holguin, San Antonio (2/1/11); Christopher C. Kirk, Bryan (10/21/11); Kathryn J. Kotria, Georgetown (2/1/13); Jan Krocker, Houston (7/20/08); John L. Moore, Denison (2/1/13); Eulon Ross Taylor, Austin (2/1/13). Dir. Dee Wilson, 8610 Shoal Creek Blvd., Austin 78757; (512) 406-5406.

Office of Injured Employee Counsel – (2005; represents the interests of workers' compensation claimants); apptv.; 2-yr.; 1 member: Public Counsel Norman Darwin ($105,000), 7551 Metro Center Dr., Ste. 100, Austin 78744-1609; (866) 393-6432.

One-Call Board of Texas – (1997; created by the Underground Facility Damage Prevention and Safety Act and serves as the board for the Texas Underground Facility Notification Corp.); apptv.; 3-yr.; 12 members: Chair Joseph F. Berry, Houston (8/31/10); Christian A. Alvarado, Austin (8/31/11); Dean D. Bernal, Austin (8/31/12); Barry Calhoun, Grapevine (8/31/09); Julio Cerda, Mission (8/31/12); Bill Daugette Jr., Huntsville (8/31/09); Judith H. Devenport, Midland (8/31/07); Jason Hartgraves, Frisco (8/31/12); John Linton, Fort Worth (8/31/10); Barbara J. Mathis, Lufkin (8/31/11); John A. Menchaca II, Austin (8/31/09); Christopher J. Rourk, Dallas (8/31/09); Rodney J. Unruh, Spring Branch (8/31/11); Janie Walenta, Quitman (8/31/12); James Wynn, Midland (8/31/11). Exec. Dir. Donald M. Ward, PO Box 9764, Austin 78766-9764; (512) 467-9764.

Optometry Board, Texas – (1921 as 6-member State Board of Examiners in Optometry; name changed to present in 1981 and members increased to 9); apptv.; per diem; 6-yr.; 9 members: Chair D. Dixon Golden, Center (1/31/15); Carolyn Carmen-Merrifield, Mansfield (1/31/11); Melvin Cleveland, Arlington (1/31/13); John Coble, Rockwall (1/31/11); James Dyess, Austin (1/31/13); Larry Fields, Carthage (1/31/11); Cynthia T. Jenkins, Irving (1/31/15); Randall N. Reichle, Houston (1/31/15); Virginia Sosa, Uvalde (1/31/13). Exec. Dir. Chris Kloeris ($68,250), 333 Guadalupe St., Ste. 2-420, Austin 78701; (512) 305-8501.

Orthotics and Prosthetics, Texas Board of – (1998 with 6 members; increased to 7 in 2003); apptv.; per diem and travel expenses; 6-yr.; 7 members: Chair Richard Michael Neider, Lubbock (2/1/13); Erin Elizabeth Berling, Coppell (2/1/13); Rebecca Hill Brou, Rockport (2/1/11); Leah F. Esparza, Austin (2/1/15); Roy McCoy, Round Rock (2/1/15); Miguel Mojica, Coppell (2/1/15); James C. Wendlandt, Austin (2/1/11). Exec. Dir. David D. Olvera, Texas Dept. of Health Services, PO Box 149347, Austin 78714-9347; (512) 834-4520.

Pardons and Paroles, Texas Board of – (1893 as Board of Pardon Advisers; changed in 1936 to Board of Pardons and

Paroles with 3 members; members increased to 6 in 1983; made a division of the Texas Dept. of Criminal Justice in 1990); apptv.; 6-yr.; 7 members (chairman, $99,500; members, $93,500 each): Chair Rissie L. Owens, Huntsville (2/1/15); Conrith Davis, Sugar Land (2/1/13); Juanita M. Gonzalez, Round Rock (2/1/15); David Gutierrez, Lubbock (2/1/15); James LaFavers, Amarillo (2/1/17); Thomas A. Leeper, Huntsville (2/1/13); Michelle Skyrme, Flint (2/1/17). *Parole Commissioners:* Pamela Freeman, Angleton; Roy Garcia, Huntsville; James Hensarling, Palestine; Elvis Hightower, Gatesville; Billy Humphrey, Huntsville; Paul Kiel, Palestine; Edgar Morales, San Antonio; Lynn Ruzicka, Angleton; Charles A. Shipman, Amarillo; Charles Speier, San Antonio; Howard Thrasher, Gatesville. Gen. Counsel Bettie L. Wells, PO Box 13401, Austin 78711-3401; (512) 406-5852.

Parks and Wildlife Commission, Texas – (1963 as 3-member board; members increased to 6 in 1971 and to 9 in 1983); apptv.; expenses; 6-yr.; 9 members: Chair Peter M. Holt, San Antonio (2/1/11); Mark E. Bivins, Amarillo (2/1/11); Rick L. Campbell, Center (2/1/15); Ralph H. Duggins, Fort Worth (2/1/13); Antonio Falcon, Rio Grande City (2/1/13); T. Dan Friedkin, Houston (2/1/11); Karen J. Hixon, San Antonio (2/1/13); Margaret Martin, Boerne (2/1/15); S. Reed Morian, Houston (2/1/15). Chairman-

The Texas Pioneer Woman statue stands in front of the Texas Supreme Court Building in Austin. Photo by Ron Billings; Texas Forest Service.

Emeritus Lee Marshall Bass, Fort Worth. Exec. Dir. Carter Smith ($130,000), 4200 Smith School Rd., Austin 78744; (512) 389-4800.

Pecos River Compact Commissioner – (1942); apptv.; 6-yr.; salary and expenses; (negotiates with New Mexico regarding waters of the Pecos): Julian W. Thrasher Jr. ($32,247), Monahans (1/23/11), PO Box 340, Monahans 79756; (432) 940-1753.

Pension Boards – For old age, blind and dependent children's assistance, *see* Health and Human Services Commission Council. *Also see,* listings under Retirement for state and municipal employee and teacher retirement systems.

Pension Review Board, State – (1979); apptv.; 6-yr.; 9 members (1 senator apptd. by Lt. Gov., 1 representative apptd. by Speaker, 7 apptd. by Gov.): Chair Richard Earl McElreath, Amarillo (1/31/13); Paul A. Braden, Dallas (1/31/15); Andrew Cable, Wimberley (1/31/13); Jerry R. Massengale, Lubbock (1/31/11); Norman W. Parrish, The Woodlands (1/31/13); Wayne R. Roberts, Austin (1/31/15); Scott D. Smith, Cedar Park (1/31/15). Exec. Dir. Paul Janssen Nicholson ($60,000), PO Box 13498, Austin 78711-3498; (512) 463-1736.

Perfusionists, Texas State Board of Examiners of – Abolished September 2005; responsibilities transferred to the Texas Dept. of Human Services, now part of the Health and Human Services Commission.

Pest Control Board, Texas Structural – Abolished August 2007; responsibilities transferred to the Texas Dept. of Agriculture, Structural Pest Control Service, Pesticide Program.

Pharmacy, Texas State Board of – (1907 as 6-member board; members increased to 9 in 1981); apptv.; 6-yr.; 9 members: Chair Jeanne D. Waggener, Waco (8/31/11); Buford T. Abeldt Sr., Lufkin (8/31/13); Rosemary F. Combs, El Paso (8/31/11); Wilson Benjamin Fry, San Benito (8/31/15); Suzan Kedron, Dallas (8/31/13); Alice G. Mendoza, Kingsville (8/31/11); Joyce Tipton, Houston (8/31/15); Charles Wetherbee, Boerne (8/31/15); Dennis Wiesner, Austin (8/31/13). Exec. Dir. Gay Dodson ($105,000), 333 Guadalupe St., Ste. 3-600, Austin 78701-3903; (512) 305-8000. *Consumer complaints: (800) 821-3205.*

Physical Therapy Examiners, Texas Board of – (1971); apptv.; 6-yr.; expenses; 9 members: Chair Karen Gordon, Port O'Connor (1/31/13); Frank Bryan Jr., Austin (1/31/13); Gary Gray, Midland (1/31/11); Kevin Lindsey, Mission (1/31/15); Phillip B.

Palmer, Abilene (1/31/11); Rene Peña, El Paso (1/31/15); Daniel Reyna, Waco (1/31/11); Melinda A. Rodriguez, San Antonio (1/31/15); Shari Waldie, Fredericksburg (1/31/13). Exec. Dir. John Maline ($62,000), 333 Guadalupe St., Ste. 2-510, Austin 78701-3942; (512) 305-6900.

Physical Therapy and Occupational Therapy Examiners, Executive Council of – (1971); apptv.; 2-yr.; expenses; 5 members: Chair Arthur Roger Matson, Georgetown (2/1/11); Stephanie Johnston, Houston (2/1/11); Pamela D. Nelon, Fort Worth (2/1/11); Daniel Reyna, Waco (2/1/11); Melinda Rodriguez, San Antonio (2/1/09). Exec. Dir. John Maline ($62,000), 333 Guadalupe St., Ste. 2-510, Austin 78701-3942; (512) 305-6900.

Physician Assistant Board, Texas – (1993 as Physician Advisory Council; changed to present name in 1995); apptv.; 6-yr.; 9 members: Chair Margaret K. Bentley, DeSoto (2/1/15); Ron Bryce, Red Oak (2/1/15); Anna Arredondo Chapman, Del Rio (2/1/11); Teralea Davis Jones, Beeville (2/1/13); Felix Koo, McAllen (2/1/11); Michael Allen Mitchell, Wichita Falls (2/1/13); Richard R. Rahr, Galveston (2/1/11); Abelino (Abel) Reyna, Waco (2/1/13); Edward W. Zwanziger, Eustace (2/1/15). Exec. Dir. Mari Robinson ($110,000), 333 Guadalupe, Tower III, #610, TX 78768; (512) 305-7010.

Consumer Complaints: (800) 201-9353.

Plumbing Examiners, State Board of – (1947 as 6-member board; members increased to 9 in 1981); apptv.; expenses; 6-yr.; Chair Tammy Betancourt, Houston (9/05/09); Enrique Castro, El Paso (9/05/11); Ricardo Jose Guerra, Austin (9/05/11); Robert Franklin Jalnos, San Antonio (9/05/09); Dave Lilley, Wichita Falls (9/05/13); Richard Allen Lord, Pasadena (9/05/09); Carol Lynne McLemore, La Marque (9/05/11); Alex Meade III, Brownsville (9/05/13); Ed Thompson, Tyler (9/05/13). Exec. Dir. Robert L. Maxwell ($70,000), PO Box 4200, Austin 78765-4200; (800) 845-6584.

Podiatric Medical Examiners, Texas State Board of – (1923 as 6-member State Board of Chiropody Examiners; name changed to State Board of Podiatry Examiners in 1967; made 9-member board in 1981; name changed to present in 1996); apptv.; 6-yr.; expenses; 9 members: Pres. Doris A. Couch, Burleson (7/10/11); Charles Jason Hubbard, Austin (7/10/15); H. Ashley Ledger, Killeen (7/10/15); James Michael Lunsford, Katy (7/10/13); Joe E. Martin Jr., College Station (7/10/13); James Michael Miller, Aledo (7/10/13); Travis Motley, Colleyville (7/10/11); Morgan Talbot, McAllen (7/10/15); Ana Urukalo, Austin (7/10/11). Exec. Dir. Hemant Makan ($55,000), PO Box 12216, Austin 78711-2216; (512) 305-7000. *Consumer Complaint Hotline: (800) 821-3205.*

Polygraph Examiners Board – (1965); apptv.; 6-yr.; 7 members: Chair Andy Sheppard, Fate (6/18/09); Elizabeth P. Bellegarde, El Paso (6/18/07); Priscilla Jane Kleinpeter, Amarillo (6/18/09); Gory Dean Loveday, Tyler (6/18/11); Lawrence D. Mann, Plano (6/18/09); Horacio Ortiz, Corpus Christi (6/18/07); Donald K. Schutte, Texarkana (6/18/11). Exec. Officer Frank Di Tucci ($49,080), PO Box 4087, Austin 78765-4087; (512) 424-2058.

Port Freeport Commission – Apptv.; 6-yr.; 6 members: James F. Brown, Lake Jackson (5/31/11); John W. Damon, West Columbia (5/31/09); J.M Lowrey, Brazosport (5/31/11); Thomas S. Perryman, Angleton (5/31/09); Ravi K. Singhania, Brazoria (5/31/13); Bill Terry, Brazosport (5/31/13). Exec. Dir. A.J. Reixach Jr., PO Box 615, Freeport 77542-0615; (800) 362-5743.

Preservation Board, State – (1983); 2-yr.; 6 members (3 ex officio: Gov., Lt. Gov., House Speaker); 3 apptv.: 1 apptd. by Gov.: Charlotte C. Foster, San Antonio (2/1/11); 1 senator apptd. by Lt. Gov.; 1 representative apptd. by Speaker. Exec. Dir. John

Sneed ($115,000), PO Box 13286, Austin 78711-3286; (512) 463-5495.

Prison Board – (*See* Criminal Justice, Texas Dept. of)

Prison Industries Oversight Authority, Private Sector – (1997); 6-yr.; expenses; 6 ex officio: Senate member, House member, Dept. of Criminal Justice, Texas Youth Comm., Texas Work Force Comm., employer liaison; 8 apptd.: Chair Jeffery R. LaBroski, Richmond (2/1/13); Sarah Abraham, Sugar Land (2/1/13); Elaine (Anne) Boatright, Smithville (2/1/15); Burnis Brazil, Richmond (2/1/15); William B. Brod, Granbury (2/1/11); S. Roxanne Carter, Canyon (2/1/15); Suzanne C. Hart, San Antonio (2/1/11); Rigoberto Villarreal, Mission (2/1/13); Employer Liaison: Randall Henderson, Austin. Admin. Robert Carter, 8610 Shoal Creek, Austin 78757; (512) 406-5310.

Private Security Bureau, Texas – (1969 as Board of Private Investigators and Private Security Agencies; reorganized in 1998 as Texas Comm. on Private Security; reestablished in 2004 as a bureau of the Texas Dept. of Public Safety); apptv.; expenses; 8 members (1 ex officio: Dir., Dept. of Public Safety); 7 apptd. members: Chair John E. Chism, Irving (1/31/15); Stella Caldera, Houston (1/31/11); Charles E. Crenshaw, Austin (1/31/13); Howard H. Johnsen, Dallas (1/31/11); Patrick A. Patterson, Boerne (1/31/15); Mark L. Smith, Dallas (1/31/11); Doris F. Washington, Arlington (1/31/13). Man. Capt. Leonard Hinojosa, PO Box 4087, Austin 78773-0001; (512) 424-7710.

Process Server Review Board – Apptv. by Texas Supreme Court; staggered terms; 9 members: Chair Carl Weeks, Austin (7/1/11); Mark P. Blenden, Bedford (7/1/11); Joe F. Brown Jr., San Antonio (7/1/09); Ron Hickman, Houston (7/1/09); Tony Lindsay, Houston (7/1/11); Connie Mayfield, Corsicana (7/1/09); Justiss Rasberry, El Paso (7/1/10); Lois Rogers, Tyler (7/1/10); Lee H. Russell, Dallas (7/1/10). Clerk Meredith Musick, PO Box 12248, Austin 78711-2248; (512) 463-2713.

Produce Recovery Fund Board – (1977 as 3-member board; members increased to 5 in 1981); apptv.; expenses; 6-yr.; 5 members: Chair Doyle (Neal) Newson III, Plains (1/31/15); Ralph Diaz, Corpus Christi (1/31/05); Steven Dexter Jones, Lubbock (1/31/01); Ly H. Nguyen, Lake Jackson (1/31/15); Byron Edward White, Arlington (1/31/01). Coor. Rick Garza, c/o Texas Dept. of Agriculture, PO Box 12847, Austin 78711-2847; (512) 936-2430.

Psychologists, Texas Board of Examiners of – (1969 as 6-member board; members increased to 9 in 1981); apptv.; 6-yr.; per diem and expenses; 9 members: Chair Timothy Branaman, Dallas (10/31/13); Donna L. Black, Houston (10/31/11); Jo Ann Campbell, Abilene (10/31/11); Carlos R. Chacón, El Paso (10/31/15); Angela A. Downes, Irving (10/31/13); Gary R. Elkins, Temple (10/31/09); Lou Ann Todd Mock, Bellaire (10/31/11); Leslie Rosenstein, Austin (10/31/15); Carl E. Settles, Killeen (10/31/09). Exec. Dir. Sherry L. Lee ($68,250), 333 Guadalupe St., Ste. 2-450, Austin 78701; (512) 305-7700.

Public Finance Authority, Texas – (1984, assumed duties of Texas Building Authority); apptv.; per diem and expenses; 6-yr.; 7 members: Chair Gary E. Wood, Austin (2/1/15); Gerald Byron Alley, Arlington (2/1/13); D. Joseph Meister, Dallas (2/1/13); Rodney K. Moore, Lufkin (2/1/15); Robert Thomas Roddy, San Antonio (2/1/11); Ruth Schiermeyer, Lubbock (2/1/13); Macedonio (Massey) Villarreal, Missouri City (2/1/11). Exec. Dir. Dwight D. Burns ($120,000), PO Box 12906, Austin 78711-2906; (512) 463-5544.

Public Insurance Counsel, Office of – (1995); apptv.; 2-yr.; 1 member: Deeia Beck (2/1/11) ($99,000), 333 Guadalupe St., Ste. 3-120; Austin 78701; (512) 322-4143.

Public Safety Commission – (1935 with 3 members; members increased to 5 in 2007); apptv.; expenses; 6-yr.; 5 members: Chair Allan B. Polunsky, San Antonio (12/31/15); Carin Marcy Barth, Houston (12/31/13); Ada Brown, Dallas (12/31/11); C. Thomas Clowe Jr., Austin (1/1/10); John Thomas Steen Jr., San Antonio (1/1/12). Interim Dir. of Texas Dept. of Public Safety, Col. Lamar Beckworth ($157,500), PO Box 4087, Austin 78773-0001; (512) 424-2000.

Public Utility Commission – (1975); apptv.; 6-yr., 3 members (chairman, $111,800; members, $109,200): Chair Barry Thomas Smitherman, Austin (9/1/13); Kenneth W. Anderson, Dallas (9/1/11); Donna L. Nelson, Austin (9/1/15). Exec. Dir. W. Lane Lanford ($115,500), PO Box 13326, Austin 78711-3326; (512) 936-7120.

Public Utility Counsel, Office of – (1983); apptv.; 2-yr.; 1 member: Sheri Sanders Givens, Round Rock (2/1/11) ($99,000); PO Box 12397, Austin 78711-2397; (512) 936-7500.

Racing Commission, Texas – (1986); apptv.; 6-yr.; per diem and expenses; 9 members; 2 ex officio: Chmn., Public Safety Commission and Comptroller of Public Accounts; 7 apptv.: Chair Rolando B. Pablos, San Antonio (2/01/11); Ronald F. Ederer, Fair Oaks Ranch (2/1/13); Scott Haywood, Austin (2/1/15); Gloria Hicks, Corpus Christi (2/1/13); Thomas Latham, Sunnyvale (2/1/15); Robert Schmidt, Fort Worth (2/1/11); Vicki Smith Weinberg, Colleyville (2/1/15). Exec. Dir. Charla Ann King ($85,536), PO Box 12080, Austin 78711-2080; (512) 833-6699.

Radiation Advisory Board, Texas – (1961); apptv.; 6-yr.; 18 members: Jesse Ray Adams, Longview (4/16/13); Bradley Bunn, Andrews (4/16/13); Bill Campbell, Fort Worth (4/16/13); Amy Clark, Floresville (4/16/15); Ana Cleveland, Denton (4/16/11); John Hageman, San Antonio (4/16/11); Bobby J. Haley, Denton (4/16/11); Ian Hamilton, Cypress (4/16/15); L.R. (Rick) Jacobi Jr., Austin (4/16/15); Nora Anita Janjan, Navasota (4/16/15); Mitch Lucas, Glen Rose (4/16/13); Melanie Marshall, Mansfield (4/16/15); Darlene Metter, San Antonio (4/16/13); Rosana G. Moreira, College Station (4/16/11); Jay Murphy, Houston (4/16/13); David Nichols, Austin (4/16/15); Kevin Raabe, Austin (4/16/11); Mark Silberman, Austin (4/16/11). Program Dir. Richard A. Ratliff, Radiation Control MC 2835, Texas Dept. of State Health Services, PO Box 149347, Austin 78714-9347; (512) 834-6679.

Radioactive Waste Disposal Compact, Texas Low-Level – (1993); apptv.; 6-yr.; expenses; 6 Texas members, plus one member each from Maine and Vermont; Texas apptees.: Chair Michael Ford, Amarillo (11/25/14); Richard Dolgener, Andrews (11/25/14); Bob Gregory, Austin (11/25/14); Kenneth L. Peddicord, College Station (11/25/14); John White, Plano (11/25/14); Robert C. Wilson, Lockhart (11/25/14). Radioactive Materials Division MC-233, Texas Commission on Environmental Quality, PO Box 13087, Austin 78711-3087; (512) 239-6466.

Railroad Commission of Texas – (1891); elective; 6-yr.; 3 members, $137,500 each: Elizabeth Ames Jones (12/31/12); David Porter (12/31/16); Barry Thomas Smitherman (12/31/12). Dir. John Tintera ($106,381), PO Box 12967, Austin 78711-2967; (512) 463-7288.

Real Estate Commission, Texas – (1949 as 6-member board; members increased to 9 in 1979); apptv.; per diem and expenses; 6-yr.; 9 members: Chair John D. Eckstrum, Conroe (1/31/11); Troy C. Alley Jr., Arlington (1/31/13); Adrian A. Arriaga, McAllen (1/31/13); Robert C. (Chris) Day, Jacksonville (1/31/13); Jaime Blevins Hensley, Lufkin (1/31/15); Joanne Justice, Arlington (1/31/11); Tom C. Mesa Jr., Houston (1/31/11); Dona Scurry, El Paso (1/31/15); Avis Wukasch, Goergetown (1/31/13). Admin. Douglas E. Oldmixon ($106,500), PO Box 12188, Austin 78711-2188; (512) 459-6544.

Real Estate Research Center Advisory Committee – (1971); apptv.; 6-yr.; 10 members; 1 ex officio: rep. of Texas Real Estate Commission; 9 apptv.: Chair D. Marc McDougal, Lubbock (1/31/11); Mona R. Bailey, North Richland Hills (1/31/13); James M. Boyd, Houston (1/31/15); Louis A. (Tony) Cortes, San Antonio (1/31/15); Jacquelyn K. Hawkins, Austin (1/31/11); Joe Bob McCartt, Amarillo (1/31/13); Kathleen McKenzie Owen, Pipe Creek (1/31/13); Barbara A. Russell, Denton (1/31/11); Ronald C. Wakefield, San Antonio (1/31/15). Dir. Gary Maler, Texas A&M University Real Estate Center, 2115 TAMU, College Station 77843-2115; (979) 845-0460.

Red River Authority of Texas – (1959); apptv.; 6-yr.; per diem and expenses; 9 members: Nathan J. (Jim) Bell IV, Paris (8/11/11); Lisa Caldwell Brent, Amarillo (8/11/11); Cole Camp, Amarillo (8/11/11); Penny Cogdell Carpenter, Silverton (8/11/13); Jerry B. Daniel, Truscott (8/11/15); Mayfield McCraw Jr., Telephone (8/11/11); George (Wilson) Scaling II, Henrietta (8/11/15); Clyde Siebman, Pottsboro (8/11/13); Cliff A. Skiles Jr., Hereford (8/11/15). Gen. Mgr. Curtis W. Campbell, PO Box 240, Wichita Falls 76307-0240; (940) 723-8697.

Red River Compact Commissioner – (1949); apptv.; 4-yr.; salary and expenses; (negotiates with Oklahoma, Arkansas and Louisiana regarding waters of the Red): William A. Abney ($24,225), El Paso (2/1/11); PO Box 1386, Marshall 75671; (903) 938-4572.

Redistricting Board, Legislative – (*See* Legislative Redistricting Board.)

Rehabilitation Commission, Texas – Combined into Department of Assistive and Rehabilitative Services (DARS) of the Health and Human Services Commission as of 3/1/04.

Residential Construction Commission, Texas – apptv.; 6-yr.; expenses; 9 members: Chair J. Paulo Flores, Dallas (2/1/11); Lewis Brown, Trinity (2/1/11); Art Cuevas, Lubbock (2/1/11); Kenneth L. Davis, Weatherford (2/1/09); Gerardo M.

(Jerry) Garcia, Corpus Christi (2/1/13); John R. Krugh, Houston (2/1/09); Steven Leipsner, Lakeway (2/1/09); Glenda C. Mariott, Bryan (2/1/13); Mickey R. Redwine, Ben Wheeler (2/1/13). Exec. Dir. A. Duane Waddill ($98,000), PO Box 13509, Austin 78711-3509; (512) 463-1040.

Retirement System of Texas, Employees – (1949); apptv.; 6-yr.; 6 members: 1 apptd. by Gov., 1 by Chief Justice of State Supreme Court, 1 by House Speaker; 3 elected by ERS members: Gov.'s apptee: Chair Cydney Donnell, College Station (8/31/12); Chief Justice's apptee: I. Craig Hester, Austin (8/31/16); Speaker's apptee: Donald E. Wood, Odessa (8/31/14). Elected members: Yolanda (Yoly) Griego, El Paso (8/31/15); Cheryl MacBride, Austin (8/31/13); Owen Whitworth, Austin (8/31/11). Exec. Dir. Ann S. Fuelberg ($300,000), PO Box 13207, Austin 78711-3207; (512) 867-7711.

Retirement System of Texas, Teacher – (1937 as 6-member board; members increased to 9 in 1973); 6-yr.; expenses; 9 members; 2 apptd. by State Board of Education, 3 apptd. by Gov., 4 apptd. by Gov. after being nominated by popular ballot of retirement system members: Chair R. David Kelly, Plano (8/31/11); Todd Barth, Houston (8/31/15); Charlotte Renee Clifton, Snyder (8/31/13); Robert P. Gauntt, Houston (8/31/13); Eric C. McDonald, Lubbock (8/31/15); Christopher Moss, Lufkin (8/31/15); Phillip M. Mullins, Austin (8/31/11); Nanette Sissney, Whitesboro (8/31/15); Linus D. Wright, Dallas (8/31/11). Exec. Dir. Ronnie Jung ($225,000), 1000 Red River, Austin 78701; (512) 542-6400.

Retirement System, Texas County and District – (1967); apptv.; 6-yr.; 9 members: Chair Robert Eckels, Houston (12/31/13); Jerry Bigham, Canyon (12/31/15); H.C. (Chuck) Cazalas, Corpus Christi (12/31/11); Daniel R. Haggerty, El Paso (12/31/15); Jan Kennady, New Braunfels (12/31/15); Bridget McDowell, Baird (12/31/13); Eddie J. Miles Jr., San Antonio (12/31/11); Kristeen Roe, Bryan (12/31/11); Robert C. Willis, Livingston (12/31/13). Exec. Dir. Gene Glass, PO Box 2034, Austin 78768-2034; (512) 328-8889.

Retirement System, Texas Municipal, – (1947); apptv.; 6-yr.; expenses; 6 members: Ben Gorzell Jr., San Antonio (2/1/13); Patricia Hernandez, Plainview (2/1/11); Carolyn M. Linér, San Marcos (2/1/13); April Nixon, Arlington (2/1/09); Roel Rodriguez, McAllen (2/1/11); H. Frank Simpson, Missouri City (2/1/09). Exec. Dir. (vacant), PO Box 149153, Austin 78714-9153; (512) 476-7577.

Retirement System, Texas Emergency Services – (1977; formerly the Fire Fighters' Relief and Retirement Fund); apptv.; expenses; 6-yr.; 9 members: Chair Francisco R. Torres, Raymondville (9/1/11); Graciela G. Flores, Corpus Christi (9/1/15); Dan Key, Friendswood (9/1/13); Ronald V. Larson, Horizon City (9/1/13); Jenny Moore, Lake Jackson (9/1/15); Maxie L. Patterson, Houston (9/1/13); Dennis Rice, Canyon (9/1/15); Don R. Shipman, Colleyville (9/1/11); Stephen Williams, Carthage (9/1/11). Commissioner Sherri Barr Walker ($77,000), PO Box 12577, Austin 78711-2577; (512) 936-3372. (*See also* Fire Fighters' Pension Commissioner.)

Rio Grande Compact Commissioner of Texas – (1929); apptv.; 6-yr.; salary and expenses; (negotiates with Colorado and New Mexico regarding waters of the Rio Grande): Patrick R. Gordon ($41,195), El Paso (6/9/13); PO Box 1917, El Paso 79950-1917; (915) 834-7075.

Rio Grande Regional Water Authority – (2003); apptv.; 4-yr.; 18 members: 12 appt'd. by Gov.; 6 appt'd. by member counties. Gov.'s apptees: Joe A. Barrera III, Brownsville (2/1/13); Dario (D.V.) Guerra Jr., Edinburg (2/1/13); Wayne Halbert, Harlingen (2/1/09); Paul Glenn Heller, Mission (2/1/11); Sonny Hinojosa, Edinburg (2/1/13); Sonia Kaniger, San Benito (2/1/13); Brian Macmanus, Rio Hondo (2/1/09); Joe Pennington, Raymondville (2/1/13); Roel Rodriguez, McAllen (2/1/11); Bobby Sparks, Valley Acres (2/1/09); Jimmie Steidinger, Donna (2/1/13); Frank (JoJo) White, Progreso Lakes (2/1/13). **County apptees:** John Bruciak, Cameron Co.; Jim Darling, Hidalgo Co.; Ricardo Gutierrez, Starr Co.; Fitzgerald G. Sanchez, Webb Co.; Frank Torres, Willacy Co.; Karran Westerman, Zapata Co. Exec. Dir. Kenneth N. Jones Jr., 311 N. 15th St., McAllen 78501-4705; (956) 682-3481.

Risk Management, State Office of – apptv.; 2-yr.; 5 members: Chair Ernest C. Garcia, Austin (2/1/09); Lloyd M. Garland, Lubbock (2/1/13); Ruben W. Hope, Montgomery (2/1/13); Kenneth N. Mitchell, El Paso (2/1/09); Ronald James Walenta, Quitman (2/1/11). Exec. Dir. Jonathan D. Bow ($95,000), PO Box 13777 Austin 78711-3777; (512) 475-1440.

Rural Affairs, Texas Department of – (2001 as Office of Rural Community Affairs; named changed to present in 2009);

apptv.; 6-yr.; 11 members: 1 ex officio, Agriculture Commissioner; 10 appt'd.: Chair Wallace Klussmann, Fredericksburg (2/1/13); Dora G. Alcala, Del Rio (2/1/15); David Alders, Nacogdoches (2/1/15); Woodrow Anderson, Colorado City (2/1/15); Mackie Bobo, Bedias (2/1/13); Charles N. Butts Sr., Lampasas (2/1/13); Remelle Farrar, Crowell (2/1/11); Charles W. Graham, Elgin (2/1/15); Bryan Tucker, Childress (2/1/11); Patrick Wallace, Athens (2/1/11). Exec. Dir. Charles S. (Charlie) Stone ($99,000), 1700 N. Congress Ave., Suite 220, Austin 78711-2877; (512) 936-6701.

Sabine River Authority of Texas – (1949); apptv.; per diem and expenses; 6-yr.; 9 members: Cary (Mac) Abney, Marshall (7/06/15); Don O. Covington, Orange (7/06/11); J.D. Jacobs Jr., Rockwall (7/06/13); David W. Koonce, Center (7/06/13); Stanley N. Mathews, Orange (7/6/11); Cliff R. Todd, Carthage (7/6/11); Connie J. Wade, Longview (7/06/15); Connie Moore Ware, Marshall (7/06/15); Clarence Earl Williams, Orange (7/06/13). Gen. Mgr. Jerry L. Clark, PO Box 579, Orange 77630; (409) 746-2192.

Sabine River Compact Commission – (1953); apptv.; 6-yr.; salary ($8,487) and expenses; (negotiates with Louisiana regarding the waters of the Sabine); 5 members – the chairman, who does not vote, is appointed by the President of United States; Texas and Louisiana each have 2 members. Texas members: Gary E. Gagnon, Mauriceville (7/12/07), Jerry F. Gipson, Longview (7/12/10); c/o P.O. Box 13087, Austin 78711; (512) 239-4707.

San Antonio River Authority – (1937); apptv., 6 yr., 12 members: Terry E. Baiamonte, Goliad Co. (11/1/09); Sara (Sally) Buchanan, Bexar Co. (11/1/11); John Flieller, Wilson Co. (11/1/09); Alois (Al) Kollodziej Jr., Wilson Co. (11/1/13); Hector Morales, Bexar Co. (11/1/11); Jeffrey Neathery, Bexar Co. (11/1/09); Gaylon J. Oehlke, Karnes Co. (11/1/13); Nazirite Ruben Perez, Bexar Co. (11/1/13); Roberto G. Rodriguez, Bexar Co. (11/1/13); H.B. (Trip) Ruckman III, Karnes Co. (11/1/09); Adair Ramsey Sutherland, Goliad Co. (11/1/13); Thomas G. Weaver, Bexar Co. (11/1/09). Gen. Mgr. Suzanne B. Scott, PO Box 839980, San Antonio 78283-9980; (210) 227-1373.

San Jacinto River Authority, Board of Directors – (1937); apptv.; expenses while on duty; 6 members: Pres. R. Gary Montgomery, The Woodlands (10/16/13); David Kleimann, Willis (10/16/13); Mary L. Rummell, Spring (10/16/09); John H. Stibbs, The Woodlands (10/16/09); Lloyd B. Tisdale, Conroe (10/16/11); Joseph V. Turner, Conroe (10/16/11). Gen. Mgr. H. Reed Eichelberger, PO Box 329, Conroe 77305; (936) 588-1111.

Savings and Mortgage Lending Commissioner – (1961); apptd. by State Finance Commission: Douglas B. Foster ($100,000), 2601 N. Lamar, Ste. 201, Austin 78705; (512) 475-1350. *Consumer Complaint Hotline: 877-276-5550.*

School Land Board – (*See* Land Board, School).

School Safety Center, Texas – (2001); apptv.; 2-yr.; 6 ex-officio members from the Texas Commissioner of Higher Education, Texas Youth Commission, Texas Education Agency, Dept. of State Health Services, Attorney General's office, and the Texas Juvenile Probation Commission; 10 appt'd. members: Chair Carl A. Montoya, Brownsville (2/1/10); Eric J. Cedarstrom, Palo Pinto (2/1/10); Amy L. Clapper, Georgetown (2/1/11); Mike Cox, Driftwood (2/1/12); Garry E. Eoff, Brownwood (2/1/12); Daniel R. Griffith II, Pflugerville (2/1/12); James R. Pendell, Clint (2/1/09); Stephen Raley, Lufkin (2/1/12); Dawn DuBose-Randell, Houston (2/1/12); Ruben Reyes, Lubbock (2/1/09); Severita Sanchez, Laredo (2/1/09); Jane A. Wetzel, Dallas (2/1/10). Associate Director Billy Jacobs, 100 N. Guadalupe Suite 140, PMB 164, San Marcos 78666; (877) 304-2727.

Securities Board, State – (Est. 1957, the outgrowth of several amendments to the Texas Securities Act, originally passed in 1913); act is administered by the Securities Commissioner, who is appointed by the board members; expenses; 6-yr.; 5 members: Chair Beth Ann Blackwood, Dallas (1/20/13); Bryan K. Brown, Pearland (1/20/11); Edward Escudero, El Paso (1/20/11); E. Wally Kinney, Dripping Springs (1/20/13); Derrick M. Mitchell, Houston (1/20/15). Commissioner Denise Voigt Crawford ($130,000), PO Box 13167, Austin 78711-3167; (512) 305-8300.

Seed and Plant Board, State – (1959); apptv.; 2-yr.; 6 members: Chair A. James Allison, Buchanan Dam (10/6/09); David Baltensperger, College Station (10/6/09); Nick Bamert, Muleshoe (10/6/11); Kelly A. Book, Bastrop (10/6/10); Robert Wright, Shallowater (10/6/09); James Wahrmund, Fredericksburg (10/6/10). Regulatory Branch Chief Ed Price, Texas Dept. of Agriculture, PO Box 12847, Austin 78711; (512) 463-7607.

Sex Offender Treatment, Council on – (1983); apptv.; expenses; 6-yr.; 7 members: Chair Frederick Liles Arnold, Plano (2/1/15); Ronnie Fanning, Woodway (2/1/11); Joseph Gutheinz, Houston (2/1/15); Alida S. Hernandez, McAllen (2/1/13); Holly A. Miller, The Woodlands (2/1/15); Aaron Paul Pierce, Rockdale (2/1/11); Dan Powers, Carrollton (2/1/13). Exec. Dir. Allison Taylor, c/o Texas Dept. of State Health Services, c/o Texas Dept. of State Health Services, PO Box 149347, Austin 78714-9347; (512) 834-4530

Skill Standards Board, Texas – (1995); apptv.; terms at pleasure of Gov.; 11 members: Chair Wayne J. Oswald, Freeport; Bruce Aumack, Austin; Gary Forrest Blagg, Grapevine; Carlos Chacón, El Paso; Andy Ellard, Dallas; Edward C. Foster Jr., Mansfield; Iria Ganious, Dallas; Erma Palmer, Houston; Linda Stegall, Houston; Whitney Wolf, San Antonio; 1 vacancy; PO Box 2241, Austin 78768-2241; (512) 936-8100.

Social Worker Examiners, Texas State Board of – (1993); apptv.; 6-yr.; per diem and travel expenses; 9 members: Chair Timothy M. Brown, Bryan (2/1/13); Jody Anne Armstrong, Abilene (2/1/15); Stewart Geise, Austin (2/1/15); Candace Guillen, La Feria (2/1/13); Kimberly Hernandez, El Paso (2/1/11); Dorinda N. Noble, San Marcos (2/1/11); Denise Pratt, Baytown (2/1/11); Nary Spears, Houston (2/1/15); Mark Talbot, McAllen (2/1/13). Exec. Dir. Charles Horton, c/o Texas Dept. of State Health Services, PO Box 149347 Austin 78714-9347; (512) 719-3521.

Soil and Water Conservation Board, Texas State – (1939); 2-yr.; 7 members: 2 apptd. by Gov.; 5 elected by district directors; **Gov.'s apptees:** Larry D. Jacobs, Montgomery (2/1/12); Joe L. Ward, Telephone (2/1/11); elected members: **Dist. 1:** Aubrey Russell, Panhandle (5/1/09); **Dist. 2:** Marty H. Graham, Rocksprings (5/1/10); **Dist. 3:** José Dodier Jr., Zapata (5/1/10); **Dist. 4:** Jerry D. Nichols, Nacogdoches (5/2/10); **Dist. 5:** Barry Mahler, Iowa Park (5/1/09). Exec. Dir. Rex Isom ($90,000), 4311 S. 31st St., Suite 125, PO Box 658, Temple 76503; (254) 773-2250.

Special Education Continuing Advisory Committee, Texas – (1997); apptv.; 4 yr.; 17 members: Lené Al-Rashid, Austin (2/1/11); Ismael (Mel) Capelo, Pasadena (2/1/13); Rose Marie Cruz, Laredo (2/1/13); Debra B. Emerson, Austin (2/1/13); Julia W. Erwin, Montgomery (2/1/13); Kathy L. Grant, Houston (2/1/11); Sherri Hammack, Austin (2/1/11); Marjie Haynes, Huntsville (2/1/11); Candance L. Hawks, Belton (2/1/13); Teresa Hernandez, San Marcos (2/1/11); Drusilla Knight-Villarreal, Corpus Christi (2/1/11); Marnie L. Mast, Austin (2/1/11); Diane Taylor, Stephenville (2/1/13); Jennifer L. Taylor, Houston (2/1/13); Paul Watson, Flower Mound (2/1/13); Shewanda Williams, Houston (2/1/11); Pam Willson, Brookesmith (2/1/13); c/o Texas Education Agency, Division of IDEA Coordination, 1701 N. Congress Ave., Austin 78701-1494; (512) 463-9414; *Parent Information Line: 1-800-252-9668.*

Speech-Language Pathology and Audiology, State Board of Examiners for – (1983); apptv.; 6-yr.; per diem and expenses; 9 members: Chair Vickie B. Dionne, Nederland (8/31/11); Patricia Elaine Brannon, San Antonio (8/31/11); Tammy Camp, Lubbock (8/31/13); Kimberly M. Carlisle, Plano (8/31/15); Kerry Ormson, Amarillo (8/31/15); Christopher Rourk, Dallas (8/31/15); Sonya Salinas, Mission (8/31/11); Leila Ramirez Salmons, Houston (8/31/13); Phillip Lee Wilson, Dallas (8/31/13). Exec. Dir. Joyce Parsons, c/o Texas Dept. of State Health Services, PO Box 149347, MC 1982, Austin 78714-9347; (512) 834-6627.

Stephen F. Austin State University, Board of Regents – (1969); apptv.; expenses; 6-yr.; 9 members: Carlos Z. Amaral, Plano (1/31/13); Richard B. Boyer, The Colony (1/31/11); Scott Coleman, Houston (1/31/15); James Hinton Dickerson, New Braunfels (1/31/11); Valerie E. Ertz, Dallas (1/31/15); John R. (Bob) Garrett, Tyler (1/31/13); Steve D. McCarty, Alto (1/31/15); James A. Thompson, Sugar Land (1/31/11); Melvin R. White, Pflugerville (1/31/11). Pres. Baker Pattillo, PO Box 13026, SFA Station, Nacogdoches 75962-3026; (936) 468-4048.

Sulphur River Basin Authority – (1985); 7 members; 6-yr.; **Region I:** Borden E. Bell Jr., Texarkana (2/1/15); Richard (Doug) Smith, Clarksville (2/1/11); **Region 2:** David T. Neeley, Mount Pleasant (2/1/15); Patricia A. Wommack, Lone Star (2/1/11); **Region 3:** Mike Russell, Powderly (2/1/13); Brad Drake, Paris (2/1/13); Kirby Hollingsworth, Mount Vernon (6/15/15); 911 N. Bishop St., Ste. C 104, Wake Village 75501; (903) 223-7887.

Sunset Advisory Commission – (1977); 12 members: 5 members of House of Representatives, 5 members of Senate, 1 public member apptd. by Speaker, 1 public member apptd. by Lt. Gov.; 2-yr.; expenses. Public members: Charles McMahen, Houston (9/1/09); Ike Sugg, San Angelo (9/1/09). Dir. Joey Long-

ley, PO Box 13066, Austin 78711-3066; (512) 463-1300.

Tax Board, State – Est. 1905; 3 ex-officio members: Comptroller, Secretary of State and State Treasurer; abolished by the 66th Legislature, effective 1/1/82, and replaced by the Texas State Property Tax Board.

Tax Professional Examiners, Texas Board of – (1977 as Board of Tax Assessor Examiners; name changed to present form 1983); apptv.; expenses; 6-yr.; 5 members: Chair Dorye Kristeen Roe, Bryan (3/1/13) James E. Childers, Canyon (3/1/11); P.H. (Fourth) Coates, Medina (3/1/11); Linda Lowes Hatchel, Woodway (3/1/15); Steve Mossman, Flower Mound (3/1/11). Exec. Dir. David E. Montoya ($60,000), 333 Guadalupe, Ste. 2-520 Austin 78701-3942; (512) 305-7300.

Teacher Retirement System – See, Retirement System, Teacher.

Texas A&M University System Board of Regents – (1875); apptv.; 6-yr.; expenses; 9 members: Chair Richard A. Box, Austin (2/1/13); Phil Adams, Bryan (2/1/15); Morris E. Foster, Salado (2/1/13); Elaine Mendoza, San Antonio (2/1/17); Judy Morgan, Texarkana (2/1/17); Jim Schwertner, Austin (2/1/15); Cliff Thomas, Victoria (2/1/17); John D. White, Houston (2/1/15); James P. Wilson, Sugar Land (2/1/13). Interim Chancellor Jay Kimbrough, PO Box 15812, College Station 77841-5013; (979) 845-9600.

Texas Southern University Board of Regents – (1947); expenses; 6-yr.; 9 members: Chair Glenn O. Lewis, Fort Worth (2/1/13); Gary Bledsoe, Austin (2/1/13); Samuel Lee Bryant, Austin (2/1/11); Dionicio (Don) Flores, El Paso (2/1/15); Richard C. Holland, Plano (2/1/13); Richard Knight Jr., Dallas (2/1/11); Curtistene McCowan, DeSoto (2/1/15); Tracye McDaniel, Houston (2/1/15); Richard Salwen, Austin (2/1/13). Pres. John M. Rudley. Exec. Dir. Karen A. Griffin 3100 Cleburne St., Hannah Hall, Rm. 104, Houston 77004; (713) 313-7992.

Texas State Technical College System Board of Regents – (1960 as Board of the Texas State Technical Institute; changed to present name in 1991); apptv.; expenses; 6-yr.; 9 members: Chair James Virgil Martin, Sweetwater (8/31/15); Penny Forrest, Waco (8/31/15); Joe M. Gurecky, Rosenberg (8/31/11); Rolf R. Haberecht, Richardson (8/31/11); Joe K. Hearne, Richardson, (8/31/11); Linda McKenna, Harlingen (8/31/15); Mike Northcutt, Longview (8/31/13); Eugene Seaman, Corpus Christi (8/31/13); Ellis Matthew Skinner II, Spicewood (8/31/13). Chancellor William Segura, TSTC System, 3801 Campus Dr., Waco 76705; (254) 867-4891.

Texas State University System Board of Regents – (1911 as Board of Regents of State Teachers Colleges; name changed in 1965 to Board of Regents of State Senior Colleges; changed to present form in 1975); apptv.; per diem and expenses; 6-yr.; 9 members: Charlie Amato, San Antonio (2/1/13); Ron Blatchley, Bryan-College Station (2/1/11); Kevin J. Lilly, Houston (2/1/15); Ron Lynn Mitchell, Horseshoe Bay (2/1/15); James David Montagne, Beaumont (2/1/15); Trisha S. Pollard, Bellaire (2/1/13); Michael Truncale, Beaumont (2/1/13); Robert (Greg) Wilkinson, Dallas (2/1/11); Donna N. Williams, Arlington (2/1/11). Chancellor Charles R. Matthews, Thomas J. Rusk Bldg., 200 E. 10th Street, Ste. 600, Austin, 78701; (512) 463-1808.

Texas Tech University Board of Regents – (1923); apptv.; expenses; 6-yr.; 9 members: Larry Keith Anders, Dallas (1/31/11); L. Frederick (Rick) Francis, El Paso (1/31/13); Mark Griffin, Lubbock (1/31/11); John Huffaker, Amarillo (1/31/15); Mickey L. Long, Midland (1/31/15); Nancy Neal, Lubbock (1/31/15); John F. Scovell, Dallas (1/31/13); Daniel T. Serna, Arlington (1/31/11); Jerry Edward Turner, Blanco (1/31/13). Chancellor Kent Hance, P.O. Box 42011, Lubbock 79409-2011; (806) 742-2161.

Texas Woman's University Board of Regents – (1901); apptv.; expenses; 6-yr.; 9 members: Sue S. Bancroft, Argyle (2/1/15); Lola Chriss, Rowlett (2/1/15); Virginia Chandler Dykes, Dallas (2/1/11); P. Mike McCullough, Dallas (2/1/13); Ann S. McGinity, Pearland (2/1/15); Cecilia May Moreno, Laredo (2/1/11); Lou Halsell Rodenberger, Baird (2/1/11); George R. Schrader, Dallas (2/1/13); Mary Pincoffs Wilson, Austin (2/1/11). Chancellor Ann Stuart, PO Box 425587, TWU Sta., Denton 76204-5587; (940) 898-3250.

Transportation Commission, Texas – (1917 as State Highway Commission; merged with Mass Transportation Commission and name changed to State Board of Highways and Public Transportation in 1975; merged with Texas Dept. of Aviation and Texas Motor Vehicle Commission and name changed to present form in 1991); apptv.; 6-yr.; 5 members ($15,914 each): Chair Deirdre Delisi, Austin (2/1/13); Ned S. Holmes, Houston

(2/1/11); Ted Houghton, El Paso (2/1/15); William Meadows, Fort Worth (2/1/13); Fred Underwood, Lubbock (2/1/15). Exec. Dir. Amadeo Saenz Jr. ($192,500), 125 E. 11th St., Austin 78701-2483; (512) 305-9509.

Trinity River Authority Board of Directors – (1955); apptv.; per diem and expenses; 6-yr.; 25 members (3 from Tarrant County, 4 from Dallas County, 3 from area-at-large and 1 each from 15 other districts): Chair Michael Cronin, Terrell (3/15/11); Harold L. Barnard, Waxahachie (3/15/11); Herschel Brannen III, Trinity (3/15/11); Karl R. Butler, Dallas (3/15/11); Patricia Carlson, Fort Worth (3/15/13); William W. Collins Jr., Fort Worth (3/15/15); Steve Cronin, Shepherd (3/15/11); Amanda B. Davis, Buffalo (3/15/11); Ronald J. Goldman, Fort Worth (3/15/15); Martha Hernandez, Burleson (3/15/11); John W. Jenkins, Hankamer (3/15/15); Keith W. Kidd, Dallas (3/15/15); Jess Laird, Athens (3/15/11); Nancy E. Lavinski, Palestine (3/15/15); David Leonard, Liberty (3/15/13); Andrew Martinez, Huntsville (3/15/13); Kevin Maxwell, Crockett (3/15/15); James W. Neale, Dallas (3/15/13); Manny Rachal, Livingston (3/15/15); Amir A. Rupani, Dallas (3/15/13); AnaLaura Saucedo, Dallas (3/15/15); Shirley K. Seale, Anahuac (3/15/15); J. Carol Spillars, Madisonville (3/15/11); Linda D. Timmerman, Streetman (3/15/13); Kim C. Wyatt, Corsicana (3/15/15). Gen. Mgr. Danny F. Vance, PO Box 60, Arlington 76004-0060; (817) 467-4343.

Tuition Board, Prepaid Higher Education – (See Higher Education Tuition Board, Texas Prepaid).

Uniform State Laws, Commission on – (1941 as 5-member Commissioners to the National Conference on Uniform State Laws; name changed to present form, members increased to 6 and term of office raised to 6 years in 1977; members increased to 9 in 2001); apptv.; 6-yr.; 9 members: Rita Arneil, Austin (9/30/12); Levi J. Benton, Houston (9/30/10); Cullen M. Godfrey, Austin (9/30/10); Debra H. Lehrmann, Colleyville (9/30/10); Peter K. Munson, Pottsboro (9/30/14); Marilyn Phelan, Lubbock (9/30/12); Rodney Wayne Satterwhite, Midland (9/30/14); Karen R. Washington, Dallas (9/30/14); Earl L. Yeakel III, Austin (9/30/12). Life members, Patrick Guillot, Dallas; Stanley Plettman, Beaumont; Leonard Reece, Austin. Exec. Dir. John Sebert, 111 N. Washington Ave., Ste. 1010, Chicago, IL, 60602; (312) 450-6600.

University of Houston System Board of Regents – (1963); apptv.; expenses; 6-yr.; 9 members: Chair Carroll Robertson Ray, Houston (8/31/11); Nandita Berry, Houston (8/31/15); Nelda Luce Blair, Houston (8/31/13); Tilman Fertitta, Houston (8/31/15); Jarvis V. Hollingsworth, Sugar Land (8/31/15); Jacob M. Monty, Houston (8/31/13); Mica Mosbacher, Houston (8/31/13); Welcome Wade Wilson Sr., Houston (8/31/11); Jim P. Wise, Houston (8/31/11). Chancellor Renu Khator; Exec. Admin. Gerry Mathisen, 4800 Calhoun, 128 E. Cullen Bldg., Houston 77204-6001; (832) 842-3446.

University of North Texas System Board of Regents – (1949); apptv.; 6-yr.; expenses; 9 members: Michael R. Bradford, Midland (5/22/15); Don A. Buchholz, Dallas (5/22/13); Charles D. Mitchell, Mesquite (5/22/11); Steve Mitchell, Richardson (5/22/15); George (Brint) Ryan, Dallas (5/22/15); Gwyn Shea, Irving (5/22/13); Alfredo (Al) Silva, San Antonio (5/22/11); C. Dan Smith, Plano (5/22/11); Jack A. Wall, Dallas (5/22/13). Chancellor Lee F. Jackson; Brd. Sec. Julia A. Boyce, 1901 Main St., Dallas, 75201; (214) 752-5533.

University of Texas System Board of Regents – (1881); apptv.; expenses; 6-yr.; 9 members: Chair William (Gene) Powell, San Antonio (2/1/15); Alex Cranberg, Austin (2/1/17); James D. Dannenbaum, Houston (2/1/13); Paul Foster, El Paso (2/1/13); Printice L. Gary, Dallas (2/1/13); Wallace Hall, Dallas (2/1/17); R. Steven Hicks, Austin (2/1/15); Brenda Pejovich, Dallas (2/1/17); Robert L. Stillwell, Houston (2/1/15). Chancellor Francisco G. Cigarroa, 201 W. Seventh St., Ste. 820, Austin, 78701-4402; (512) 499-4402.

Utility Commission, Public – (See Public Utility Commission).

Veterans Commission, Texas – (1927 as Veterans State Service Office; reorganized as Veterans Affairs Commission in 1947 with 5 members; name changed to present in 1985); apptv.; 6-yr.; per diem while on duty and expenses; 5 members: Chair Karen S. Rankin, San Antonio (12/31/09); Eliseo Cantu Jr., Corpus Christi (12/31/13); John McKinney, El Paso (12/31/13); Terrence O'Mahoney, Dallas (12/31/11); Ezell Ware Jr. (12/31/11). Exec. Dir. James E. Nier ($115,000), PO Box 12277, Austin 78711-2277; (512) 463-6564.

Veterans' Land Board – (See Land Board, Veterans').

Veterinary Medical Examiners, Texas State Board of – (1911; revised 1953; made 9-member board in 1981); apptv.; expenses on duty; 6-yr.; 9 members: Chair Bud E. Alldrege Jr., Sweetwater (8/26/15); Patrick M. Allen, Lubbock (8/26/15); Janie Allen Carpenter, Garland (8/26/11); John D. Clader, Jourdanton (8/26/13); Cynthia S. Diaz, San Antonio (8/26/11); David Wayne Heflin, Mission (8/26/11); David Kercheval, Fort Worth (8/26/13); Paul Martinez, Sonora (8/26/15); David Roseberg Jr., Mason (8/26/13). Exec. Dir. Dewey E. Helmcamp III ($65,000), 333 Guadalupe St., Ste. 3-810, Austin 78701-3942; (512) 305-7555.

Wastewater Treatment Research Council, Texas On-Site – (1987); apptv.; 11 members: Chair Janet Dee Meyers, Aubrey (9/1/10); Elaine (Anne) Boatright, Rosanky (9/1/11); Janet R. Boone, North Zulch (9/1/10); Richard D. Gerard, Livingston (9/1/10); Susan R. Johnson, Austin (9/1/10); Sockalingam (Sam) Kannappan, Houston (9/1/11); Sarah E. Kirksey, Beaumont (9/1/11); Brian L. Padden, Austin (9/1/11); Carl M. Russell Jr., Lubbock (9/1/11); William F. (Dubb) Smith III, Dripping Springs (9/1/11); Ronald J. Suchecki Jr., China Spring (9/1/10). Exec. Sec. Sandra Mota, TCEQ, Field Operations Support Division MC-235, PO Box 13087, Austin 78711-3087; (512) 239-1452.

Water Development Board, Texas – (1957; legislative function for the Texas Dept. of Water Resources, 1977); apptv.; per diem and expenses; 6-yr.; 6 members: Chair Ed Vaughn, Boerne (12/31/13); Billy R. Bradford Jr., Brownsville (12/31/15); Monte Cluck, Gruver (12/31/13); Joe M. Crutcher, Palestine (12/31/13); Thomas Weir Labatt III, San Antonio (12/31/11); Lewis McMahan, Dallas (12/31/11). Interim Exec. Admin. Melanie Callahan ($135,000), PO Box 13231, Austin 78711-3231; (512) 463-7847.

Women, Governor's Commission for – (1967); apptv.; 2-yr. term or at pleasure of Gov.; 12 members: Chair Carol Foxhall Peterson, Alpine (12/31/11); Claudia Abney, Marshall (12/31/11); Gina Bridwell, Abilene (12/31/11); Stephanie Cavender, San Antonio (12/31/11); Cris Graham, Fredericksburg (12/31/11); Cynthia Tyson Jenkins, Irving (12/31/11); Elisa (Lisa) Gonzales Lucero, Austin (12/31/11); Becky McKinley, Amarillo (12/31/11); Carmen Pagan, McAllen (12/31/11); Tresa Rockwell, Austin (12/31/11); Connie Weeks, Austin (12/31/11); Daisy Sloan White, Houston (12/31/11). Dir. Lesley Guthrie, PO Box 12428, Austin 78711; (512) 475-2615.

Workers' Compensation Commissioner, Texas – (1991); functions transferred to the Texas Dept. of Insurance Division of Workers' Compensation in 2005; apptv.; 2-yr.; Commissioner Rod A. Bordelon Jr., Austin, (2/1/11), PO Box 149104, Austin 78714-9104; (512) 463-6169.

Workforce Commission, Texas – (1936 as Texas Employment Commission; name changed 1995); apptv.; chairman, $125,000; commissioners, $115,000; 6-yr.; 3 members: Chair Tom Pauken, Dallas (2/1/15); Andres Alcantar, Austin (2/1/13), representing employers; Ronald G. Congleton, Rockwall (2/1/11), representing labor. Exec. Dir. Larry Temple ($140,000), 101 E. 15th St., Austin 78778-0001; (512) 463-2222.

Workforce Investment Council, Texas – (1993); apptv.; 19 members: 5 ex officio (directors from Economic Development and Tourism, Higher Education Coordinating Board, Texas Education Agency, Texas Health and Human Services Comm., Texas Workforce Comm.); 14 apptd.: Chair Wes Jurey, Arlington (9/1/13); James Brookes, Amarillo (9/1/11); Blas Castaneda, Laredo (9/1/13); Robert Cross, Houston (9/1/15); Carmen Olivas Graham, El Paso (9/1/11); Richard Hatfield, Austin (9/1/15); Robert Hawkins, Bellmead (9/1/11); Sharla E. Hotchkiss, Midland (9/1/11); Larry Jeffus, Garland (9/1/15); Matthew Maxfield, Brownwood (9/1/15); Paul Mayer, Garland (9/1/15); Danny Prosperie, Bridge City (9/1/13); Joyce Delores Taylor, Houston (9/1/15); 1 vacancy. Dir. Cheryl Fuller, PO Box 2241, Austin 78768; (512) 936-8100.

Youth Commission, Texas – (1949 as 9-member advisory board; reorganized in 1957 and again in 1975; in March 2007, all board members resigned and the commission was placed under conservatorship; in October 2008, the Gov. removed TYC from conservatorship); terms expire at pleasure of Gov.; per diem on duty; 6 apptv. members: Chair Scott W. Fisher, Bedford (2/1/11); Joseph Brown, Sherman (2/1/11); Larry Carroll, Midland (2/1/11); Manson B. Johnson, Houston (2/1/11); Rolando Olvera, Brownsville (2/1/11); Toni Sykora, San Antonio (2/1/11); David Teuscher, Beaumont (2/1/11). Independent Ombudsman Debbie Unruh, Amarillo (2/1/13); Exec. Dir. Cheryln K. (Cherie) Townsend ($125,000); PO Box 4260, Austin 78765; (512) 424-6073. ☆

Local Government

Texas has **254 counties,** a number that has not changed since 1931 when Loving County was organized. Loving has a population of 82, according to the 2010 U.S. Census, compared with 164 in 1970 and a peak of 285 in 1940. It is the **least-populous county** in Texas. In contrast, Harris County has the **most residents** in Texas, with a 2010 population estimate of 4,092,459.

Counties range in area from Rockwall's 148.7 square miles to the 6,192.78 square miles in Brewster, which is equal to the combined area of the states of Connecticut and Rhode Island.

The Texas Constitution makes a county a legal subdivision of the state. Each county has a commissioners court. It consists of four commissioners, each elected from a commissioner's precinct, and a county judge elected from the entire county. In smaller counties, the county judge retains judicial responsibilities

in probate and insanity cases. For names of county and district officials, see tables on pages 535–546.

There are **1,215 incorporated municipalities** in Texas that range in size from 19 residents in Los Ybañez to Houston's 2,099,451, according to the 2010 U.S. Census. More than 80 percent of the state's population lives in cities and towns, meeting the U.S. Census Bureau definition of urban areas.

Texas had 335 incorporated towns with more than 5,000 population, according to the 2010 U.S. Census. Under law, these cities may adopt their own charters (called **home rule**) by a majority vote. Cities of less than 5,000 may be chartered only under the **general law.** Some home-rule cities may show fewer than 5,000 residents because population has declined since adopting home-rule charters. **Home-rule cities are marked in this list by a single-dagger symbol (†) after the name.** ☆

Mayors and City Managers of Texas Cities

This list was compiled from questionnaires sent out after the May 10, 2011, municipal elections. It includes the name of each city's mayor, as well as the name of the city manager, city administrator, city coordinator, or other managing executive for munipalities having that form of government. If a town's mail goes to a post office in a different town, the mailing address is included. If the Texas Almanac received no response to the questionnaire, the information is from other official sources..

— A —

Abbott.................................Harry G. Nors
Abernathy....................Darrell Stephens
  City Mgr., Mike Cypert
Abilene (†) ....Norm Archibald
  City Mgr., Larry D. Gilley
Ackerly............................ Mary Schuelke
Addison (†)............................ Todd Meier
  City Mgr., Ron Whitehead
Adrian .... Finis Brown
Agua Dulce...........................Carl Vajdos
Alamo (†) ....Rudy Villarreal
  City Mgr., Luciano Ozuna Jr.
Alamo Heights (†) (6116 Broadway, San
  Antonio 78209)...........Louis R. Cooper
  City Mgr., J. Mark Browne
Alba.......................................Orvin Carroll
Albany...................................Sally Maxey
  City Mgr., Dave Ramone
Aledo........................... Kit Marshall
  City Admin., Ken Pfeifer
Alice (†).................. Grace Saenz-Lopez.
  City Mgr., Pete Anaya
Allen (†) ....Stephen Terrell
  City Mgr., Peter H. Vargas
Alma.............................. Scot Shepherd
Alpine (†) ....Jerry Johnson
  City Mgr., Chuy Garcia
Alto, City of ....Monty Collins
Alton ....Salvador Vela
  City Mgr., Jorge Arcaute
Alvarado ....E. Dewayne Richters
  City Mgr., Clint Davis
Alvin (†) .... Gary Appelt
  City Mgr., Terry Lucas
Alvord .... Chris Caster
  City Admin., (vacant)
Amarillo (†)....................... Paul Harpole
  City Mgr., W. Jarrett Atkinson
Ames.......................................John White
Amherst ....Harold Heller
Anahuac .... Sue Hawthorne
  City Admin., Lance Nauman
Anderson .... Gail M. Sowell
Andrews (†)..........................Robert Zap
  City Mgr., Glen E. Hackler

Angleton (†)................J. Patrick Henry
  City Admin., Michael Stoldt
Angus .... (6008 S. I-45 W, Corsicana
  75109) ....Eben Dale Stover
Anna (†) ....Darren R. Driskell
  City Mgr., Philip Sanders
Annetta ....(PO Box 1150, Aledo 76008)
  ....Bruce M. Pinckard
Annetta North.........(PO Box 1238, Aledo
  76008) .... Robert Watson
Annetta South .... (PO Box 61, Aledo
  76008) ....Gerhard Kleinschmidt
Annona ....George H. English
  City Mgr., Garry L. Watkins
Anson (†)..............................Tom Isbell
  City Mgr., Dowell Matthews
Anthony .... Art Franco
Anton ....Blake Cate
  City Mgr., Larry Conkin
Appleby (223 CR 257, Nacogdoches
  75965) ....Gerald Herbert Sr.
Aquilla........................ James Hamner Sr.
Aransas Pass (†)............. Tommy Knight
  City Mgr., Mike Sullinger
Archer City ....David A. Levy
  City Mgr., George Huffman
Arcola .... Mary Etta Anderson
Argyle ....Greg Landrum
  City Admin., Lyle Dresher
Arlington (†)................Robert N. Cluck
  City Mgr., Jim Holgersson
Arp ....Damon Nichols
Asherton..............Gilberto Gonzalez Jr.
Aspermont............................Billie Carter
  City Admin., Roger Parker
Athens (†)........................Randy Daniel
  City Mgr., Pam J. Burton
Atlanta (†).............................Keith Crow
  City Mgr., David Cockrell
Aubrey.........................Gary W. Hammett
  City Coordinator, Nancy Downes
Aurora.............(Box 558, Rhome 76078)
  ....Barbara Brammer
  City Admin., Toni Kelly-Richardson
Austin (†)........................Lee Leffingwell
  City Mgr., Marc A. Ott
Austwell...................Mustafa W. Curtess

Avery...............................Taylor Gilreath
Avinger ....Marvin E. Parvino
Azle (†)................................Russ Braudis
  City Mgr., Craig Lemin

— B —

Bailey .... John Robert Stephens
Bailey's Prairie..... (PO Box 71, Angleton
  77516) .... Randy Taylor
Baird .... Jon E. Hardwick
  City Mgr., Nancy Turnbow
Balch Springs (†)..........Carrie F. Gordon
  City Admin., Ed Morris
Balcones Heights ....Suzanne de Leon
  City Admin., Amy Buckert
Ballinger (†)......................Sam Mallory
  City Mgr., Tommy New
Balmorhea .... Rosendo Galindo
  City Mgr., Terry Upchurch
Bandera ....Horst Pallaske
  City Admin., Gene R. Foerster
Bangs.............................Martin Molotsky
Bardwell....................................Clinton Ivy
Barry ....John Wade Braly
Barstow ....James A. Collins
Bartlett............................ Arthur T. White
Bartonville .... Ron Robertson
  Town Admin., Debbie E. Millican
Bastrop (†)................................. Terry Orr
  City Mgr., Michael H. Talbot
Bay City (†)........................Mark Bricker
Bayou Vista ....Ed Flanagan
Bayside.................................. Ken Dahl
Baytown (†) .... Stephen H. DonCarlos
  City Mgr., Robert (Bob) Leiper
Bayview ....Leon A. Deason
Beach City .... Billy Combs
Bear Creek (13012 S. Madrone Trail, Aus-
  tin 78737) ....Bruce Upham
Beasley .... Kenneth Reid
Beaumont (†) .... Becky Ames
  City Mgr., Kyle Hayes
Beckville......................Gene Mothershed
Bedford (†) .... Jim Story
  City Mgr., Beverly Queen
Bedias.....................Mackie Bobo-White

Stagecoach Days, held the second Saturday of each month in Anderson, includes rides on a stagecoach around the Grimes County Courthouse and tours of Fanthorp Inn State Historic Site. Photo by Ron Billings; Texas Forest Service.

Bee Cave ....Caroline L. Murphy
City Admin., Frank L. Salvato
Beeville (†).................Jimmy Marinez Jr.
City Mgr., Tom Ginter
Bellaire (†) ....Cynthia Siegel
City Mgr., Bernard M. Satterwhite Jr.
Bellevue............................ Marvin Bigbie
Bellmead (†) .... Carl E. Swanson III
City Mgr., S.G. (Scooter) Radcliff
Bells .... Gary Martin
Bellville .... Philip B. Harrison
City Admin., Lynn S. Roberts
Belton (†).......................... Jim Covington
City Mgr., Sam A. Listi
Benavides............ Ernestina C. Gonzalez
Benbrook (†) ....Jerry B. Dittrich
City Mgr., Andy Wayman
Benjamin ....Sylinda Meinzer
City Mgr., Ronnie White
Berryville ....(PO Box 908, Frankston
75763) ....Roy Brown
City Mgr., Sharyn Harrison
Bertram...........................JoAnn Stephens
Beverly Hills (3418 Memorial Dr., Waco
76711) ....David Gonzales
Bevil Oaks ...... Rebecca (Becky) M. Ford
Big Lake...........................Cindy O'Bryan
City Admin., Evelyn Ammons
Big Sandy .... Wayne Weese
Big Spring (†) .... Tommy Duncan
City Mgr., Gary Fuqua
Big Wells .... Randall R. Matthews
City Admin., Charlene Greenhill
Bishop ....Victor Ramos
Bishop Hills (#6 Manchester Rd., Ama-
rillo 79124)......................Betty Benham
Blackwell ....Laura Rozzlle
Blanco............................. Chuck Homan
Blanket......................................Judy Eoff
Bloomburg .... Jerrell Ritchie
Blooming Grove......... Jeanette Wisdom
Blossom ....Jeremy Wilson
Blue Mound .....(301 S. Blue Mound Rd.,
Fort Worth 76131) ....Alan Hooks
Blue Ridge......................Dan Standeford

Blum...............................Elaine Edwards
Boerne (†)................. Michael D. Szhultz
City Mgr., Ron Bowman
Bogata .... Vincent Lum
Bonham (†).........................Roy V. Floyd
City Mgr., Corby D. Alexander
Bonney .... Raymond Cantu
Booker .... Jim Riggs
City Mgr., Donald R. Kerns
Borger (†) ....Jeff Brain
City Mgr., Wanda Klause
Bovina...................................Stan Miller
City Mgr., Jana Pitcock
Bowie (†)...................................Pat Polk
City Mgr., James Cantwell
Boyd......................................Brent Wilson
City Admin., John Hamilton
Brackettville .... Eduardo Esparza
Brady (†) ....Gail Lohn
City Mgr., James Minor
Brazoria, City of ....Ken Corley
City Mgr., Teresa Borders
Brazos Bend............. Vernon E. Oechsle
Brazos Country (316 Pecan Grove Rd.,
Sealy 77474) ....Charles A. Kalkomey
Breckenridge (†) .... Jimmy McKay
City Mgr., Brad Newton
Bremond............................Ricky Swick
Brenham (†)...................... Milton Y. Tate Jr.
City Mgr., Terry K. Roberts
Briarcliff................................. Robert Pigg
City Admin., Aaron Johnson
Briaroaks .... (PO Box 816, Burleson
76097) ....James Dunn
Bridge City (†) ....Kirk Roccaforte
City Mgr., Jerry D. Jones
Bridgeport ....Keith McComis
City Admin., Brandon Emmons
Broaddus..................William W. Barth
Bronte ....Gerald Sandusky
Brookshire........................ Joey Vaughn
Brookside Village ....Denise Ford
Browndell (Box 430, Brookeland
75931) ....Sheila Smith
Brownfield ....Bob Simpson

City Mgr., Eldon Jobe
Brownsboro ....Terry Mills
Brownsville ....Tony Martinez
City Mgr., Charlie Cabler
Brownwood (†)......... Stephen E. Haynes
City Mgr., Bobby Rountree
Bruceville-Eddy ...... (143 Wilcox Dr., #A,
Eddy 76524) ....Rick Eaton
City Admin., Koni Billings
Bryan (†)...........................Jason Bienski
Interim City Mgr., Kean Register
Bryson ....Sheila Birdwell
Buckholts ....Hal Senkel
Buda..............................Sarah Mangham
City Mgr., Kenneth R. Williams
Buffalo .... Royce Dawkins
Buffalo Gap .... David L. Perry
Buffalo Springs (99-B Pony Express Trl.,
Lubbock 79404)................ Velvet Keys
Bullard ....Pam Frederick
City Mgr., Larry Morgan
Bulverde ....Sarah Stevick
City Admin., Bob Hieronymus
Bunker Hill Village (11977 Memorial Dr.,
Houston 77024)...........Derry D. Essary
City Admin., Ruthie P. Sager
Burkburnett (†).........................Carl Law
Interim City Mgr., Trish Holley
Burke ...... (RR 3, Box 315, Diboll 75941)
.........................John Thomas Jones
Burleson (†)..........................Ken Shetter
City Mgr., Curtis E. Hawk
Burnet (†)........................ Gary Wideman
City Mgr., David Vaughn
Burton............................Peggy A. Felder
Byers............................Robert Lawrence
Bynum .... Lawana Jolene Custer

— C —

Cactus....................................Luiz Aguilar
City Mgr., Jeffrey G. Jenkins
Caddo Mills .... Dwayne Pattison
City Mgr., Manuel Leal
Caldwell ....Norris L. McManus
City Admin., Johnny L. Price

Callisburg .... Frances West
Calvert .... Marcus D. Greaves
Cameron (†)................Connie Anderle
  City Mgr., Ricky Tow
Campbell .... Geri Barnes
Camp Wood........................ Emma Dean
Canadian .... John Baker
  City Mgr., Colby Waters
Caney City ....Joe Barron
Canton....................... William Wilson
  City Mgr., Andy McCuistion
Canyon (†)................Quinn Alexander
  City Mgr., Glen R. Metcalf
Carbon .... Dale Walker (pro tem)
Carl's Corner.............. Carl W. Cornelius
Carmine .... Justin Flasowski
Carrizo Springs (†) ......Ralph E. Salinas
  City Mgr., Mario Martinez
Carrollton (†)..............Matthew Marchant
  City Mgr., Leonard Martin
Carthage (†)..................Carson C. Joines
  City Mgr., Brenda Samford
Cashion Community (354 Baker Rd.,
  Wichita Falls 76305)......Robyn Murphy
Castle Hills (209 Lemonwood Dr., San
  Antonio 78213).......Bruce Smiley-Kaliff
  City Mgr., Michael T. Steele
Castroville .... Robert Lee
  City Admin., Paul Hofmann
Cedar Hill (†) .... Rob Franke
  City Mgr., Alan Sims
Cedar Park (†)..................Bob Lemon
  City Mgr., Brenda Eivens
Celeste..................................Larry Godwin
Celina (†) .... Jim Lewis
  City Mgr., Jason Gray
Center (†).................... David Chadwick
  City Mgr., Chad D. Nehring
Centerville .... Noal Ray Goolsby
Chandler................................. Joye Rains
  City Admin., Jim Moffeit
Channing ....Karen Schulz
Charlotte..................Augustine R. Munoz
Chester ............................C.E. Lawrence
Chico..................................... J.D. Clark
Childress............................Barbara Jones
  City Mgr., Bryan Tucker
Chillicothe .... Wallace A. Clay
China........... Margaret (Peggy) Harkrider
China Grove ....Dennis Dunk
  City Admin., Susan Conaway
Chireno .... Mike Metteauer
Christine ....Odel Vasquez
Cibolo ....Johny Sutton
Cisco (†) ....James Maples
  City Mgr., Jim Baker
Clarendon............................. Larry Hicks
  City Admin., Lambert Little
Clarksville..........................Ann Rushing
  City Mgr., Wayne Dial
Clarksville City.....(Box 1111, White Oak
  75693) .... Larry G. Allen
  City Mgr., Billy F. Silvertooth Jr.
Claude.................................Jim Hubbard
Clear Lake Shores .... Vern Johnson
  City Admin., Paul Shelley
Cleburne (†).....................Justin Hewlett
  City Mgr., Rick Holden
Cleveland (†) ....Jill B. Kirkonis
  City Mgr., Philip Cook
Clifton .... Fred Volcansek
  City Admin., Charles McLean
Clint......................... Dale T. Reinhardt
Clute (†) .... Calvin Shiflet
  City Mgr., Kyle McCain
Clyde.............................Steve Livingston
  City Admin., Tim Atkinson
Coahoma ....Warren Wallace
Cockrell Hill.......(4125 W. Clarendon Dr.,
  Dallas 75211) ....Luis D. Carrera
  City Admin., Hector M. Saenz
Coffee City...(Box 716, Frankston 75763)
  .... Tony M. Moore

Coldspring...........................Pat Eversole
Coleman (†)...................... Nick Poldrack
  City Mgr., Larry Weise
College Station (†)..................Ben White
  City Mgr., Glenn Brown
Colleyville (†) .... David Kelly
  City Mgr., Jennifer Fadden
Collinsville.................... Carrol McKnight
Colmesneil .... Donald Baird
Colorado City (†).........Carol Sue Dakan
  City Mgr., Pete Kempfer
Columbus ....Richard Heffley
  City Mgr., David Meisell
Comanche .... Raymond W. Stepp
  City Admin., Bill Flannery
Combes .... Silvestre (Silver) Garcia
  City Mgr., Lonnie Bearden
Combine .... Keith Taylor
Commerce (†)....................Sheryl Zelhart
  City Mgr., Bill Shipp
Como.................................Jerry Radney
Conroe (†)...................... Webb K. Melder
  City Admin., Paul Virgadamo
Converse (†)..........................Al Suarez
  City Mgr., Sam Hughes
Cool (†) .. (150 FM 113 S., Millsap 76066)
  .... Dorothy Hall
Coolidge ....David Frazier
Cooper ....Thomas Scott Stegall
  City Admin., Margaret Eudy
Coppell (†).................. Douglas N. Stover
  City Mgr., Clay Phillips
Copperas Cove (†)............John Hull
  City Mgr., Andrea M. Gardner
Copper Canyon .... Sue Tejml
  Town Admin., Quentin Hix
Corinth (†) .... Paul Ruggiere
  Interim City Mgr., James Berzina
Corpus Christi (†) .... Joe Adame
  City Mgr., Ron Olson
Corral City (14007 Corral City Dr., Argyle
  76226) ....Tim Gamblin
  Town Admin., Bob Blizzard
Corrigan...........................Grimes Fortune
  City Mgr., Mandy K. Risinger
Corsicana (†)............Chuck McClanahan
  City Mgr., Connie Standridge
Cottonwood...... (Box 293, Scurry 75158)
  .... Doug Harris
Cottonwood Shores ....Janelle Long
  City Admin., Jerrial Wafer
Cotulla ....Joe Lozano
  Interim City Admin., Larry Dovalina
Cove..............(PO Box 529, Mont Belvieu
  77580) .... Lee Wiley
Covington....................... Tommy L. Elkins
Coyote Flats ....John Barnett
Crandall ....Cody Frazier
  City Mgr., Heath Kaplan
Crane .... Kelly S. Nichols
  City Admin., Dru Gravens
Cranfills Gap, City of ....Russell Algien
Crawford........................ David C. Posten
Creedmoor .... (12108 FM 1625, Austin
  78747)....................Robert L. Wilhite
  City Admin. Richard L. Crandal Jr.
Cresson.......................W.R. (Bob) Cornett
Crockett (†)...................... Wayne Mask
  City Admin., Ronald M. Duncan
Crosbyton.....................Dusty Cornelius
  City Admin., Margot Hardin
Cross Plains ....Ray Purvis
  City Admin., Debbie Gosnell
Cross Roads .... Ross Schraeder
Cross Timber .... Wava McCullough
Crowell.............................Gayle Simpson
Crowley (†) ....Billy P. Davis
  City Mgr., Truitt Gilbreath
Crystal City (†) ....Ricardo S. Lopez
  City Mgr., Alfredo Gallegos
Cuero (†)...................... Sara Post Meyer
  City Mgr., Raymond Zella Jr.
Cumby ....Jeff Strickland
Cuney.............................. Jessie Johnson

Cushing ....Bruce Richards
  City Mgr., Brian Delafield
Cut and Shoot............... Lang Thompson

— D —

Daingerfield (†) .... Lou Irvin
  City Mgr., Marty Byers
Daisetta.....................Edward Lynn Wells
Dalhart (†)....................... Kevin Caddell
  City Mgr., Greg Duggan
Dallas (†).....................Mike Rawlings
  City Mgr., Mary K. Suhm
Dalworthington Gardens..Michel Tedder
  City Admin., Melinda Brittain
Danbury .... Fred Williamson
Darrouzett.....................Paul Laughead
Dawson............. Stephen (Red) Sanders
Dayton (†)................. Steve E. Stephens
  City Mgr., David Douglas
Dayton Lakes .... (Box 1476, Dayton
  77535) .... Jerry A. Ham
Dean (6913 State Hwy. 79 N., Wichita
  Falls 76035)............. Steve L. Sicking
Decatur (†)......................Joe A. Lambert
  City Mgr., Brett Shannon
De Cordova (PO Box 5905, Granbury
  76049) ....Dick Pruitt
Deer Park (†) ....Wayne Riddle
  City Mgr., James Stokes
De Kalb ....Paul Meadows
  City Admin., Abbi Baker
De Leon (†).................... Danny Owen
  City Admin., Karen Wilkerson
Dell City ....Maria Guillen
  City Admin., Juanita R. Collier
Del Rio (†)................ Roberto Fernandez
  City Mgr., Robert Eads
Denison (†).......................Robert Brady
  City Mgr., Robert Hanna
Denton (†)..................Mark Burroughs
  City Mgr., George Campbell
Denver City (†) .... David Bruton
  City Mgr., Stan David
Deport ....Mike Francies
DeSoto (†)..................... Carl O. Sherman
  City Mgr., Tarron Richardson
Detroit.............................Travis Bronner
Devers................................ Edna Johnson
Devine.................................. Jerry Beck
  City Admin., Dora V. Rodriguez
Diboll (†) .... Bill Brown
  City Mgr., Dennis McDuffie
Dickens .... Eddy Robertson
  City Admin., Jody Taylor
Dickinson (†).............Julie Dues Masters
  City Admin., Julie M. Johnson
Dilley, City of ....Mary Ann Obregon
  City Admin., Melissa L. Gonzalez
Dimmitt (†)........................Roger Malone
  City Mgr., David Denman
Dish .... William Sciscoe
Dodd City ....Jackie Lackey
Dodson ....Steve Kane
Domino .... Marvin Campbell
Donna (†)......................David S. Simmons
  City Mgr., Oscar E. Ramirez
Dorchester...........................David Smith
Double Oak, Town of .Thomas P. Pidcock
Douglassville .... Douglass B. Heath
Dripping Springs .... Todd Purcell
  City Admin., Michelle Fischer
Driscoll .... John A. Aguilar
Dublin ....Becky Norris
  City Mgr., Jerry Guillory
Dumas (†)......................... Mike Milligan
  City Mgr., Vince DiPiazza
Duncanville....................David L. Green
  City Mgr., Kent Cagle

— E —

Eagle Lake..........................Mike Morales
  City Mgr., Keith H. Webb

Eagle Pass (†) ....Ramsey E. Cantu
City Mgr., Daniel Valenzuela
Early........................ Robert G. Mangrum
City Admin., Ken Thomas
Earth .... Brad Freeman
East Bernard ....Buck Boettcher
Eastland (†) .... Mark Pipkin
City Mgr., Ron Holliday
East Mountain (103 Municipal Dr., Gilmer
75645) ....Ronnie Hill
City Admin., Tammy Hazel
Easton, City of .... Walter Ward
East Tawakoni............James R. Thomas
Ector ....Mary Dean Norris
Edcouch ....Robert T. Schmalzried
City Admin., Ernesto Ayala Jr.
Eden................................. Eugene Spann
City Admin., Celina Hemmeter
Edgecliff Village.............Tony Dauphinot
Edgewood ....Charles Prater
Edinburg (†) ....Richard H. Garcia
City Mgr., Ramiro Garza Jr.
Edmonson...............Wendell Edmonson
Edna (†) ....Joe D. Hermes
City Mgr., Kenneth D. Knight
Edom................................Barbara Crow
El Campo (†)...............Richard A. Young
City Mgr., Mindi Snyder
El Cenizo ....Raul L. Reyes
Eldorado ....John Nikolauk
Electra (†) ....Tom Delizio
City Admin., Stephen Giesbrecht
Elgin (†) ....Marc Holm
City Mgr., Greg Vick
Elkhart .... Raymond Dunlap
El Lago.................................. Brad Emel
Elmendorf.................. Manuel Decena Jr.
City Admin., Cody D. Dailey
El Paso (†) .... John F. Cook
City Mgr., Joyce A. Wilson
Elsa (†)..........................Senovio Castillo
City Mgr., Maria Hilda Ayala
Emhouse (3825 Joe Johnson Dr., Corsi-
cana 75110)................Johnny Pattison
Emory ....Cay Frances B. House
City Admin., Clyde Smith
Enchanted Oaks (Box 5019, Mabank

75147) ....Don Warner III
Encinal...............................Javier Mancha
City Admin., Matt Peter Olivera
Ennis (†) ....Russell R. Thomas
City Mgr., Steve Howerton
Escobares ....Noel Escobar
Estelline................................Rick Manley
Euless (†).........................Mary Lib Saleh
City Mgr., Gary McKamie
Eureka...........(1305 FM 2859, Corsicana
75109) ....Barney Thomas
Eustace.............................Elicia Sanders
Evant............................ Sterling Manning
Everman (†).........James R. Stephenson
City Mgr., Donna F. Anderson

— F —

Fairchilds (8713 Fairchilds Rd., Rich-
mond 77469) .... Bob Haenel
Fairfield..Roy Hill
City Admin., Mike Gokey
Fair Oaks Ranch ....Cheryl Landman
Fairview (†)...................... Sim Israeloff
Town Mgr., John Godwin
Falfurrias ....Joe Garcia
Falls City ....Brent Houdmann
Farmers Branch (†)............... Bill Glancy
City Mgr., Gary D. Greer
Farmersville ....Robbin H. Lamkin
City Mgr., Alan Hein
Farwell ....Jimmie Mace
Fate (†)............................. Bill Broderick
City Mgr., Vicki Mikel
Fayetteville ....Ronald Pflughaupt
City Mgr., Billy J. Wasut
Ferris.................................... Rick Barrett
City Mgr., Eric Strong
Flatonia .... Scott Mica
City Mgr., vacant
Florence...........................Mary Condon
Floresville (†) ....Daniel M. Tejada
City Mgr., Andy Joslin
Flower Mound (†)..............Jody A. Smith
Town Mgr., Harlan Jefferson
Floydada..........................Bobby Gilliland
City Mgr., Gary Brown

Follett......................................Lynn Blau
City Mgr., Robert Williamson
Forest Hill (†).....................James Gosey
City Mgr., Sheyi I. Ipaye
Forney (†) ....Darren Rozell
City Mgr., Brian Brooks
Forsan.............................Roger Hudgins
Fort Stockton ....William Bill Lannom
City Mgr., Raul Rodriguez
Fort Worth (†).......................Betsy Price
Interim City Mgr., Tom Higgins
Franklin............................Charles Ellison
Frankston ....James Gouger
Fredericksburg (†)..Thomas Musselman
City Mgr., Gary Neffendorf
Freeport (†)..........Norma Moreno Garcia
City Mgr., Jeff Pynes
Freer....................................Arnoldo Cantu
Friendswood (†)........... David J.H. Smith
City Mgr., Roger Roecker
Friona.....................................J.B. Douglas
City Mgr., Patricia Phipps
Frisco (†) ....Mike Simpson
City Mgr., George A. Purefoy
Fritch...............................Kevin R. Keener
City Mgr., Ernest Terry
Frost....................................Velma Ballew
Fruitvale..............................Carl Waddell
Fulshear.......... Thomas C. Kuykendall Jr.
City Admin., C.J. Snipes
Fulton................................Russel Cole

— G —

Gainesville (†) ....Jim Goldsworthy
City Mgr., Barry Sullivan
Galena Park (†) .... R.P. (Bobby) Barrett
Gallatin ....Juanita Cotton
Galveston (†)....................... Joe Jaworski
Interim City Mgr., Brian Maxwell
Ganado ....Clinton W. Tegeler
Garden Ridge ....Jay F. Feibelman
City Admin., Nancy Cain
Garland (†)....................Ronald E. Jones
City Mgr., William E. Dollar
Garrett.................................. Matt Newsom
Garrison..............................Patsy Nugent

The historic Gruene Hall in Comal County. Photo by Ron Billings; Texas Forest Service.

Jones Creek ....George Mitchell
Jonestown.................. Deane Armstrong
City Admin., Dan Dodson
Josephine.....................Cameron Brooks
Joshua (†)..........................Joe Hollarn
City Mgr., Paulette Hartman
Jourdanton............................ Larry Pryor
City Mgr., Daniel G. Nick
Junction...................Shannon R. Bynum
Justin.......................................Greg Scott
City Admin., Mike Evans

— K —

Karnes City..........................Don Tymrak
City Admin., Larry Pippen
Katy (†)............................... Don Elder Jr.
City Admin., Johnny Nelson
Kaufman (†).....................William Fortner
City Mgr., Curtis Snow
Keene (†) .... John Ackermann
City Admin., Ismael Lopez
Keller (†) .... Pat McGrail
City Mgr., Daniel O'Leary
Kemah................................Bob Cummins
City Admin., R.W. (Bill) Kerber
Kemp.................................Donald Kile
Kempner......................... Gene Isenhour
Kendleton.......... Darryl K. Humphrey Sr.
Kenedy ....Randy Garza
City Mgr., Alexander Ford Patton
Kenefick (3564 FM 1008, Dayton 77535)
Keegan Johnson
Kennard...........................Jesse Stephens
City Admin., Mike Deckard
Kennedale (†)...................Bryan Lankhorst
City Mgr., Bob Hart
Kerens ....Jeffrey Saunders
City Admin., Cindy Scott
Kermit (†)................... Ted Westmoreland
City Mgr., Sam Watson
Kerrville (†).....................Todd A. Bock
City Mgr., Todd Parton
Kilgore (†).....................Ronnie Spradlin
Interim City Mgr., Tony Williams
Killeen (†) .... Timothy L. Hancock
Interim City Mgr., Glenn Morrison
Kingsville (†)...................Sam R. Fugate
City Mgr., Carlos R. Yerena
Kirby (†)................................Ray Martin
City Mgr., Zina Tedford
Kirbyville ....Lanette Hall
Kirvin.................................(vacancy)
Knollwood (100 Collins Dr., Sherman
75090) ....Richard R. Roelke
Knox City...................... Jeff Stanfield
City Admin., Chad Roberts
Kosse................................Ben Daniell
Kountze .... Fred E. Williams
City Admin., Roderick Hutto
Kress...................................Esther Mount
City Admin., Kenny Hughes
Krugerville ....Robert Cleversy
Krum ....Terri Wilson
Kurten ....Ronnie Vitulli
Kyle (†)................................Lucy Johnson
City Mgr., Lanny Lambert

— L —

La Coste ....Andy Keller
City Admin., C. George Salzman
Lacy-Lakeview (†).............Calvin Hodde
City Mgr., Michael Nicoletti
Ladonia............................Janis Cooper
La Feria (†) .... Stephen Page Brewer
City Mgr., Sunny K. Philip
Lago Vista (†).....................Randy Kruger
City Mgr., Bill Angelo
La Grange (†)...................Janet Moerbe
City Mgr., Shawn Raborn
La Grulla................... Brenda A. Villarreal
Laguna Vista ....Susie Houston
City Mgr., Rolando Vela

La Joya ....William R. (Billy) Leo
City Admin., Mike Alaniz
Lake Bridgeport.............. Monty Slayton
Lake City ....Jake Hoskins
Lake Dallas (†)...................Tony Marino
City Mgr., Earl Berner
Lake Jackson (†)....................Bob Sipple
City Mgr., William P. Yenne
Lakeport (207 Milam Rd., Longview
75603) .... Johnny Sammons
Lakeside (San Patricio Co.; Box 787,
Mathis 78368)..................Damon Ellis
Lakeside (Tarrant Co.) ....Patrick Jacob
Town Admin., Dianna Buchanan
Lakeside City (Box 4287, Wichita Falls
76308) .... Steve Halloway
City Admin., Sam Bownds
Lake Tanglewood (100 N. Shore Dr.,
Amarillo 79118) .... John Langford
Lakeview...............................Kelly Clark
Lakeway (†) .... Dave P. DeOme
City Mgr., Steve Jones
Lakewood Village .... Frank Jaromin
City Mgr., Angela Rangel
Lake Worth (†)................... Walter Bowen
City Mgr., Brett McGuire
La Marque (†) .... Larry E. Crow
City Mgr., Robert Ewart
Lamesa (†)...............................Dave Nix
City Mgr., Fred Vera
Lampasas (†)..............Judith A. Hetherly
City Mgr., Michael Stoldt
Lancaster (†) ....Marcus E. Knight
City Mgr., Rickey Childers
La Porte (†).....................Louis R. Rigby
City Mgr., Ron Bottoms
Laredo (†) .... Raul G. Salinas
City Mgr., Carlos R. Villarreal
Latexo ....Robert Hernandez
La Vernia........................... Harold Schott
La Villa ....Rene Castillo
City Mgr., Jaime Gutierrez
Lavon ....Norma Cooper Martin
La Ward ....Richard Koch
Lawn ....Veronica Burleson
League City (†)..................Tim Paulissen
City Admin., Marcus Jahns
Leakey ....Jesse Pendley
Leander (†) ....John D. Cowman
City Mgr., (vacant)
Leary ...... (PO Box 1799, Hooks 75561)
....James Palma Sr.
Ledbetter ....(vacancy)
Lefors ....J. Susan Oldham
Leona ....Travis J. Oden
Leonard .... Willaim J. Yoss
City Admin., George Henderson
Leon Valley ....Chris Riley
City Mgr., Manuel Longoria Jr.
Leroy.................................David Williams
Levelland (†)..............R.L. (Bo) Bowman
City Mgr., Richard A. Osburn
Lewisville (†) .... Dean Ueckert
City Mgr., Claude King
Lexington .... Robert Willrich Sr.
Liberty (†) ....Carl Pickett
City Mgr., Gary Broz
Liberty Hill ....Michele (Mike) Murphy
City Mgr., Manuel De La Rosa
Lincoln Park (110 Parker Pkwy., Aubrey
76227) ....Loretta Ray
City Mgr., Nat Parker III
Lindale ....Jim Mallory
City Mgr., Owen Scott
Linden .... Kenny R. Hamilton
Lindsay ....Donald L. Metzler
Lipan ....Mike Stowe
Little Elm (†) ....Charles Platt
City Mgr., Ivan Langford
Littlefield (†) ....Shirley Mann
City Mgr., Danny Davis
Little River-Academy (Box 521, Little
River 76554).............. Ronnie W. White
Live Oak (†) .... Mary M. Dennis

City Mgr., H. Matthew Smith
Liverpool ....Bill Strickland
Livingston ....Clarke Evans
City Mgr., Marilyn Sutton
Llano...............................Mike Reagor
City Mgr., John T. Montgomery
Lockhart (†)...................... Ray Sanders
City Mgr., Vance Rodgers
Lockney ....Rodger Stapp
City Admin., Charlotte Hooten
Log Cabin (†) .... Billy Goodwin
Lometa ....Mike McGarry
Lone Oak ....Harold Slemmons
Lone Star .... C.E. Nick Nichols
Longview (†)..........................Jay Dean
City Mgr., David Willard
Loraine....................... Ina Vay McAdams
Lorena................................Stacy Garvin
City Mgr., John Moran
Lorenzo....................... Lester C. Bownds
City Admin., Jim Lively
Los Fresnos (†).................Polo Narvaez
City Mgr., Mark W. Milum
Los Indios...................Diamantina Bennett
Los Ybañez...................Mary A. Ybañez
City Mgr., John Henry Castillo
Lott ....Annita Tindle
Lovelady .... Michael R. Broxson
Lowry Crossing (1405 S. Bridgefarmer
Rd., McKinney 75069) Derek Stephens
Lubbock (†) .... Tom Martin
City Mgr., Lee Ann Dumbauld
Lucas (†) .... Bill Carmickle
City Mgr., Robert Patrick
Lueders............................Danny Dillard
Lufkin (†) ....Jack Gorden Jr.
City Mgr., Paul Parker
Luling (†) ....Mike Hendricks
City Mgr., Robert W. Berger
Lumberton (†) ....Don Surratt
City Mgr., Steve Clark
Lyford ....Henry de la Paz Jr.
Lytle .... Mark L. Bowen

— M —

Mabank .... Larry Teague
Madisonville.......................Don F. Dean
City Mgr., Paul Catoe
Magnolia ....Jimmy Thornton
Malakoff..............................Pat Isaacson
City Admin., Glen Herriage, Ann Baker
Malone ....Ovie Kettler
Manor (†) ....Jeff Turner
City Mgr., Phil Tate
Mansfield (†)...................David L. Cook
City Mgr., Clayton W. Chandler
Manvel (†) ....Delores M. Martin
Marble Falls (†) .... George W. Russell
City Mgr., Ralph Hendricks
Marfa................................Daniel P. Dunlap
City Admin., James R. Mustard Jr.
Marietta ....Lynda Shaddix
Marion .... Glenn A. Hild
Marlin (†)........................Norman D. Erskine
City Mgr., Randall Holly
Marquez...................................Kim Smith
Marshall (†)..........William (Buddy) Power
City Mgr., Frank Johnson
Marshall Creek (Box 1070, Roanoke
76262) ....James Stimpson
Mart...............................Norman Hopping
Martindale.................... Truman Hawkins
City Admin., Nancy G. Hempel
Mason ....Brent Hinckley
City Admin., John Palacio
Matador...................................Pat Smith
Mathis (†)........................ Mario Alonzo
City Admin., Manuel Lara
Maud .... Dwight Richard Butler
Maypearl ....John Wayne Pruitt
McAllen (†) .... Richard Cortez
City Mgr., Mike R. Perez
McCamey..........................Sherry Phillips

Visitors tour the Harrison County Courthouse, the centerpiece of Marshall's Wonderland of Lights. The annual festival, which features over one million lights and hundreds of light displays, begins the night before Thanksgiving and runs through New Years Eve. Photo by Ron Billings; Texas Forest Service.

McGregor (†) ....James S. Hering
  City Mgr., Kevin Evans
McKinney (†) ....Brian S. Loughmiller
  City Mgr., Jason Gray
McLean ....Bobby Martin
McLendon-Chisholm (1248 St Hwy 205
  S Rockwall 75032) ....Gary Moody
  City Admin., David Butler
Meadow (†) ....Eloisa Cuellar
Meadowlakes ....Don Williams
  City Mgr., Johnnie Thompson
Meadows Place ..... Charles D. Jessup IV
Megargel ....Danny Fails
Melissa .... Reed Greer
  City Admin., Jason Little
Melvin ....Woody Pennington
Memphis ....Robert C. Maddox
Menard ....Barbara Hooten
  City Admin., Sharon L. Key
Mercedes (†) ....Joel Quintanilla
  City Mgr., Ricardo Garcia
Meridian ....Johnnie Haverland
  City Mgr., Marie Garland
Merkel ....Rusty Watts
  City Mgr., Donnie Edwards
Mertens ....Barbara Crass
Mertzon ....Arthur (Art) Uber
  City Admin., Scott Edmonson
Mesquite (†) ....John Monaco
  City Mgr., Ted Barron
Mexia (†) .... Troy Miller
  City Mgr., Larry Brown
Miami ....Chad Breeding
Midland (†) .... Wes Perry
  City Mgr., Courtney B. Sharp
Midlothian (†) ....Boyce L. Whatley
  City Mgr., Don Hastings
Midway (†) ........................J.W. Williams
Milano ....Billy Barnett
Mildred ....(5417 FM 637, Corsicana
  75109) ....Robert Duane Carpenter
Miles ....Juan Ornelas
Milford ....John Knight
Miller's Cove (PO Box 300 Winfield
  75493) ....Grady Hughes
Millsap ....Jamie French
Mineola ........................E.F. (Bo) Whitus
  City Admin., David Stevenson
Mineral Wells (†) ....Mike Allen

  City Mgr., Lance Howerton
Mingus ....Milo Moffit
Mission (†) ....Norberto Salinas
  City Mgr., Julio Cerda
Missouri City (†) ....Allen Owen
  City Mgr., Frank Simpson
Mobeetie ....Gordon Estes
Mobile City ..(824 Lilac, Rockwall 75087)
  .... Wanda Cooper
Monahans (†) ....David B. Cutbirth
  City Mgr., David Mills
Mont Belvieu ....Nick Dixon
  City Admin., Bryan Easum
Montgomery .... Travis Mabry
  City Admin., Brant Gary
Moody ....Michael Alton
  City Admin., Charleen Dowell
Moore Station (4818 FM 314
  S, LaRue 75770) .... Arthur T. Earl
Moran ....Mike Whitt
Morgan ....Jonathan W. Croom II
Morgan's Point ....Patricia Grimes
  City Admin., Ken Bays
Morgan's Point Resort ... James Enyeart
  City Mgr., Stacy Wayne Hitchman
Morton ....Eric Charles Silhan
  City Mgr., Brenda Shaw
Moulton ....Ervin Patek
  City Admin., Deborah Pattison
Mountain City .... (Box 1494, Buda
  78610) .... Rick Tarr
  City Mgr., Jeff Radke
Mount Calm ....Jimmy Tucker
Mount Enterprise .... Harvey L. Graves
  City Admin., Rosena J. Becker-Ross
Mount Pleasant (†)... Paul O. Meriwether
  City Mgr., Mike Ahrens
Mount Vernon .... Margaret Sears
  City Admin., Eddie Turner
Muenster ....Johnny Pagel
  City Admin., Stan Endres
Muleshoe (†) ....Cliff Black
  City Mgr., David Brunson
Mullin ....Jean Smith
Munday ....Buddy Norville
  City Admin., Dwayne Bearden
Murchison ....Mike Hill
Murphy (†) ....Bret Baldwin
  City Mgr., James Fisher

Mustang ....(Box 325, Corsicana
  75151) ....Jackie Bounds
Mustang Ridge ....Alisandro Flores

— N —

Nacogdoches (†) ....Roger Van Horn
  City Mgr., Jim Jeffers
Naples ....John R. Anthony
Nash ....David H. Slaton
  City Mgr., Elizabeth Lea
Nassau Bay (†) (1800 NASA Rd. 1, Hous-
  ton 77058) ....Donald C. Matter
  City Mgr., John D. Kennedy
Natalia (†) ....Ruberta C. Vera
  City Mgr., Beth Leonesio
Navarro (222 S. Harvard Ave., Corsicana
  75109) .... Pam Chapman
Navasota (†) ....Bert Miller
  City Mgr., Brad Stafford
Nazareth ....Ralph Brockman
Nederland (†) ...........R.A. (Dick) Nugent
  City Mgr., Chris Duque
Needville ....Delbert Wendt
Nevada .... Joe Poovey
Newark ....Matt Newby
  City Admin., Diane Rasor
New Berlin ....(275 FM 2538 Seguin
  78155) ....Gilbert Merkle
New Boston ....Johnny L. Branson
New Braunfels (†) ....Gale Pospisil
  City Mgr., Michael Morrison
Newcastle ....Stephen J. Sosinski
New Chapel Hill (14039 Cty. Rd. 220, Ty-
  ler 75707) ....Robert Whitaker
New Deal ....Emsley Baker
New Fairview ....Joe Max Wilson
New Home ....Steve Lisemby
New Hope (Box 562, McKinney 75070)
  Johnny Hamm
New London ....Dale McNeel
New Summerfield ....Jane Barrow
Newton ....Mark Bean
  City Admin., Donald H. Meek
New Waverly ....Dan Underwood
Neylandville (2469 Cty. Rd. 4311, Green-
  ville 75401) ....Kathy Wilson
Niederwald ....Reynell Smith
  City Admin., Richard L. Crandal Jr.

Nixon..............................Bonnie Chessher
City Admin., George Blanch
Nocona.......................Robert H. Fenoglio
City Mgr., Lynn Henley
Nolanville........................James Cole Sr.
Noonday ....(Box 6425, Tyler 75711)
.... Mike Turman
Nordheim.....................Katherine Payne
Normangee...........................J.C. Traylor
North Cleveland (Box 1266, Cleveland
77327) ....Robert Bartlett
Northlake ....(Box 729, Justin 76247)
...................................Peter Dewing
Town Admin., Drew Corn
North Richland Hills (†)....Oscar Treviño
City Mgr., Mark Hindman
Novice.............................. Wanda Motley

— O —

Oak Grove ... (Box 309, Kaufman 75142)
...................................Jerry G. Holder
Oak Leaf ....Craig Wilson
Oak Point...............................Jim Wohletz
City Mgr., Douglas C. Mousel
Oak Ridge (Cooke Co.; 129 Oak Ridge
Dr., Gainesville 76240).. Chad Ramsey
Oak Ridge (Kaufman Co.; Box 458,
Kaufman 75142)..........Roy W. Perkins
Oak Ridge North ....Joe Michels
City Mgr., Vicky Rudy
Oak Valley (2211 Oak Valley, Corsicana
75110)........................Beverly Pollard
Oakwood ....Vicki Stroud
O'Brien...........................Richard Garcia
Odem.................................Billy Huerta
Odessa (†) ....Larry L. Melton
City Mgr., Richard N. Morton
O'Donnell ....Scott Martinez
Oglesby ....Kenneth Goodwin
Old River-Winfree ....Joe Landry
Olmos Park (119 W. El Prado Dr., San
Antonio 78212)...........Susan O. Gragg
City Mgr., Michael W. Simpson
Olney (†) ....Brenda Stennett
City Admin., Danny C. Parker
Olton ....Mark McFadden
City Mgr., Marvin Tillman
Omaha ....Janet Blackburn
Onalaska..................................Lew Vail
Opdyke West (Box 1179, Levelland
79336) ....Wayne Riggins
Orange (†)...........William Brown Claybar
City Mgr., Shawn Oubre
Orange Grove.....................Seale Brand
City Admin., Perry R. Young
Orchard.................................Rod Pavlock
Ore City..........................Glenn Breazeale
Overton.......................John Edd Welch
City Mgr., B.J. Potts
Ovilla......................................Bill Vansyckle
City Admin., Randy Whiteman
Oyster Creek.........................Louis Guidry

— P —

Paducah.........................Gordon Melton
Paint Rock ....Duane Schniers
Palacios (†)...................John C. Sardelich
City Mgr., Charles R. Winfield
Palestine (†) ....Bob Herrington
City Mgr., Mike Ohrt
Palisades (115 Brentwood Rd., Amarillo
79118) ....Thomas B. Medlin
Palmer.................................Don Huskins
Palmhurst...........Ramiro J. Rodriguez Jr.
City Mgr., Lori A. Lopez
Palm Valley (1313 Stuart Place Rd., Har-
lingen 78552)......................Dean Vail
Palmview ....Jorge García
City Mgr., Johnn V. Alaniz
Pampa (†)...........................Brad Pingel
City Mgr., Richard Morris
Panhandle ....Dan Looten
City Mgr., Loren Brand

Panorama Village ......Howard L. Kravetz
Pantego ....Melody L. Paradise
City Mgr., Sean P. Fox
Paradise.................................Sam Starr
Paris (†) ....Arjumand Hashmi
Interim City Mgr., Gene Anderson
Parker ....Joe Cordina
City Admin., Dina J. Daniel
Pasadena (†) ....Joe Cordina
Pattison ....Bill Matthews
Patton Village (16940 Main St., Splen-
dora 77372) .... Pamela (Vikki) Muñoz
Payne Springs ....Rodney Renberg
Pearland (†)..........................Tom Reid
City Mgr., Bill Eisen
Pearsall (†).................George Cabasos
City Mgr., José G. Treviño
Pecan Gap .... Warner Cheney
Pecan Hill ....Howard Hobbs
Pecos (†)..........................Venetta Seals
Interim City Mgr., Clay McKinney
Pelican Bay ......Thomas (Sandy) Tolbert
Penelope.............................. Inez Arriola
Peñitas ....Marcos Ochoa
City Admin., Noe H. Cavazos
Perryton..............................Charles Kelly
City Mgr., David Landis
Petersburg.........................Bob Pierson
City Mgr., Bryan Grimes
Petrolia .... Cindy Armour
Petronila (2475 Cty. Rd. 69, Robstown
78380) ....Dan Burkhardt
Pflugerville (†).....................Jeff Coleman
Interim City Mgr., Lauri Gillam
Pharr (†)........Leopoldo (Leo) Palacios Jr.
City Mgr., Fred Sandoval
Pilot Point .... Janet Groff
City Admin., J.C. Hughes
Pine Forest ....(305 Nagel St., Vidor
77662)................................Joey Peno
Pinehurst (3640 Mockingbird St., Orange
77630) ........................T.W. Permenter
City Admin., Joe Parkhurst
Pine Island (20005 Pine Island Rd.,
Hempstead 77445)...........Debra Ferris
Pineland...............................Randy Burch
City Admin., Chuck Corley
Piney Point Village (7676 Woodway Dr.,
#300, Houston 77063)
...................................Karen Bresenhan
City Admin., Terri J. Johnson
Pittsburg....................Shawn Kennington
Interim City Mgr., Margaret Jackson
Plains ....Pamela K. Redman
City Admin., Terry B. Howard
Plainview (†)...............John C. Anderson
City Mgr., Greg Ingham
Plano (†) ....Phil Dyer
City Mgr., Bruce Glasscock
Pleak, Village of (6621 FM 2218 S., Rich-
mond 77469) ....Margie Krenek
Pleasanton (†).......................Bill Carroll
City Mgr., Kathy Coronado
Pleasant Valley (4006 U.S. 287 E, Iowa
Park 76367)............Raymond Haynes
City Admin., Norm Hodges
Plum Grove (Box 1358, Splendora
77372) ...............................T.W. Garrett
Point.....................................G.P. Aucoin
Point Blank................Clyde L. Chandler
Point Comfort..................Pam Lambden
Point Venture....................Richard Shinn
Ponder ....Jeff Vardell
Port Aransas (†)................Claude Brown
City Mgr., Michael Kovacs
Port Arthur (†) ....Oscar G. Ortiz
City Mgr., Steve Fitzgibbons
Port Isabel (†) ....Joe E. Vega
City Mgr., Edward Meza
Portland (†)....................David R. Krebs
City Mgr., Michael Tanner
Port Lavaca (†)...................Jack Whitlow
City Mgr., Bob Turner
Port Neches (†) .... R. Glenn Johnson

City Mgr., André Wimer
Post...............................Theressa Harp
City Mgr., Arbie Taylor
Post Oak Bend (1175 Cty. Rd. 278,
Kaufman 75142).......Raymond Bedrick
Poteet.......................Raul (Roy) Ybarra
City Admin., LaNell M. Matthews
Poth............................... Travis Pruski
Pottsboro............................Frank Budra
City Mgr., Kevin M. Farley
Powell ....Dennis Bancroft
Poynor..............................Dannie Smith
Prairie View ....Frank D. Jackson
Premont .... Dalia Gee
Presidio ....Lorenzo P. Hernandez
City Admin., Brad Newton
Primera .... Pat Patterson
City Admin., Javier Mendez
Princeton...................Steven Deffibaugh
City Admin., Lesia Thornhill
Progreso ....Omar Vela
City Admin., Alfredo (Fred) Espinosa
Progreso Lakes (Box 760, Progreso
78579) .... O.D. Emery
Prosper (†) ....Charles E. Niswanger
Town Mgr., Mike Land
Providence Village.........Brian Roberson
Putnam ....Roy Petty
Pyote...................................Willie Bates

— Q —

Quanah (†)..................... Gary Newsom
City Admin., Danny Felty
Queen City.......................Harold Martin
Quinlan ...........................R.W. Oliver
Quintana ....Wallace Neeley
Quitaque...........................Clyde Dudley
City Mgr., Maria Cruz Merrell
Quitman ....Jerry Edwards
City Admin., Mike Hall

— R —

Ralls ....D'Ann L. Reynolds
City Admin., J. Rhett Parker
Rancho Viejo...............Roberto Medrano
Town Admin., Cheryl J. Kretz
Ranger (†).............................John Casey
Rangerville (31850 Rangerville Rd., San
Benito 78586)............... Wayne Halbert
Rankin..............................Timothy Potter
Ransom Canyon ....Robert G. Englund
City Admin., Murvat Musa
Ravenna.......................Claude L. Lewis
Raymondville (†) ....Orlando A. Correa
City Mgr., Eleazar Garcia Jr.
Red Lick ....(Box 870, Nash 75569)
...................................Sheila K. Kegley
Red Oak (†).......................Alan Hugley
City Mgr., Timothy Kelty
Redwater.........................Beverly Phares
Refugio .... Ray Jaso
Reklaw..........................Harlan Crawford
Reno (Lamar Co.) ....William Heuberger
Reno (Parker Co.; 195 W. Reno Rd., Azle
76020)..............................Roen Cox
Retreat (621 N. Spikes Rd., Corsicana
75110) ....Janice Barfknecht
Rhome ....Mark Lorance
Rice ....Larry Bailey
City Admin., Tonya Roberts
Richardson (†).................Steve Mitchell
City Mgr., Bill Keffler
Richland ....Dolores Baldwin
Richland Hills (†) ....David Ragan
City Mgr., James Quin
Richland Springs ....Jerry M. Benton
Richmond....................Hilmar G. Moore
City Mgr., R. Glen Gilmore
Richwood ....Clint Kocurek
City Admin., Glenn Patton
Riesel.................................Dave Ross
Rio Bravo (1402 Centeno Ln., Laredo
78046) ....Juan G. Gonzalez

Rio Grande City (†)...Ruben O. Villarreal
City Admin., Juan F. Zuniga
Rio Hondo ....Santiago A. Saldana Jr.
City Admin., Arturo F. Prida
Rio Vista .... William Keith Hutchison
Rising Star.......................Joe Swinney
City Admin., Ron E. Watson
River Oaks (†) ....Herman D. Earwood
City Admin., Marvin Gregory
Riverside .... G. F. Rich
Roanoke ....Carl E. Gierisch Jr.
City Mgr., Jimmy Stathatos
Roaring Springs..............Corky Marshall
City Mgr., Robert Osborn
Robert Lee...........................Joe V. White
Robinson ....Bryan Ferguson
City Mgr., R.C. Fletcher
Robstown (†).............Rodrigo Ramon Jr.
City Admin., Paula Wakefield
Roby..Eli Sepeda
City Mgr., Jack W. Brown
Rochester ....Marvin Stegemoeller
City Mgr., Gregg Hearn
Rockdale (†) ....Larry Don Jones
City Mgr., Kelvin Knauf
Rockport (†) ....Charles J. (CJ) Wax
City Mgr., Thomas J. Blazek
Rocksprings ....LaWanda Goller
Rockwall (†).........................David Sweet
City Mgr., Julie Couch
Rocky Mound............(Box 795, Pittsburg
75686) ....Noble T. Smith
Rogers ....Billy Ray Crow
Rollingwood .....William C. (Bill) Hamilton
Roma (†) ....Rogelio Ybarra
City Mgr., Crisanto Salinas
Roman Forest ....Floyd O. Jackson Jr.
Ropesville..........................Victor Marrett
Roscoe ....Frank S. (Pete) Porter
City Admin., Cody Thompson
Rosebud ....Ken Hensel
City Mgr., Eric Kuykendall
Rose City .... David E. Bush
Rose Hill Acres (100 Jordan Rd., Lum-
berton 77657) ....Rick Thomisee
Rosenberg (†).................Joe M. Gurecky
City Mgr., Jack S. Hamlett
Ross...........................James L. Jaska Sr.
Rosser .... Shannon Rex Corder
Rotan ....H. Lynn Gibson
Round Mountain ....Alvin Gutierrez
Round Rock (†)..................Alan McGraw
City Mgr., Steve Norwood
Round Top ....Barnell Albers
Rowlett (†) ....John E. Harper
City Mgr., Lynda K. Humble
Roxton ....James Cooper
City Mgr., Janet Wheeler
Royse City (†).....................Jerrell Baley
City Mgr., Bill Shipp
Rule ....W.L. Wolf
Runaway Bay, City of .... A.L. (Len) Jowitt
City Admin., Mike Jump
Runge ....Cecil Franke
Rusk (†) ....Angela Raiborn
City Mgr., Mike Murray

— S —

Sabinal...........Enrique (Henry) Alvarado
Sachse (†)............................. Mike J. Felix
City Mgr., Allen Barnes
Sadler...............................Jaime Harris
Saginaw (†)......................Gary Brinkley
City Mgr., Nan Stanford
Saint Hedwig ....Mary Jo Dylla
Saint Jo (†) ....Tom Weger
Saint Paul ....Opie Walter
Salado ....Merle Stalcup
San Angelo (†) ....Alvin New
City Mgr., Harold Dominguez
San Antonio (†) ....Julián Castro
City Mgr., Sheryl L. Sculley

San Augustine ....Leroy Hughes
City Mgr., James Duke Lyons Jr.
San Benito (†) ....Joe Hernandez
City Mgr., Victor Trevino
Sanctuary ....(Box 125, Azle 76098)
....Cliff Scallan
San Diego ....Rupert Canales III
City Mgr., Ernesto Sanchez Jr.
Sandy Point.......................Curt Mowery
San Felipe...........................Bobby Byars
Sanford ....Rodney Ormon
Sanger (†) ....Thomas Muir
City Mgr., Michael Brice
San Juan (†) ....Pedro Contreras
City Mgr., Antonio (Tony) Garza
San Leanna (Box 1107, Manchaca
78652)............................Joel Chapa
City Admin., Kathleen Lessing
San Marcos (†).................Susan Narvaiz
City Mgr., Rick Menchaca
San Patricio.. (4615 Main, Mathis 78368)
.............................Lonnie Glasscock III
San Perlita.......................Oscar de Luna
San Saba ....Kenneth Jordan
City Mgr., Stan Weik
Sansom Park (5500 Buchanan St., Fort
Worth 76114).................Jim Barnett Jr.
City Mgr., Karen Boylard
Santa Anna.................Harold Fahrlender
Santa Clara ......(Box 429, Marion 78124)
..................................David D. Mueller
Santa Fe (†) ....Ralph W. Stenzel Jr.
City Mgr., Joe Dickson
Santa Rosa ....Ruben Ochoa Jr.
City Admin., Hipolito Cabrera
Savoy ....Charles Downs
Schertz (†) ....Harold D. (Hal) Baldwin
City Mgr., Don E. Taylor
Schulenburg..........Roger Moellenberndt
City Admin., Don Doering
Scotland ....Brian Vieth
Scottsville......................Walter Johnson
Scurry ....Robert N. Stewart
Seabrook (†) ....Glenn R. Royal
City Mgr., Charles W. (Chuck) Pinto
Seadrift ....Billy F. Ezell
City Mgr., Paula Moncrief
Seagoville (†) .... Sydney Sexton Jr.
City Mgr., Denny Wheat
Seagraves.................Ovidio Martinez Jr.
Sealy (†).............................. Nick Tirey
City Mgr., Chris Coffman
Seguin (†) .... Betty Ann Matthies
City Mgr., Doug Faseler
Selma .... Tom Daly
City Admin., Ken Roberts
Seminole (†) .... Wayne Mixon
City Admin., Tommy Phillips
Seven Oaks ....(Box 540, Leggett 77350)
....Anna Wallace
Seven Points ....John J. Dobbs
Seymour ....Ronald B. Reeves
City Admin., John W. Studer
Shady Shores (Box 362, Lake Dallas
75065) ....Jerry Williams
Shallowater ....Robert Olmsted
Shamrock ....Wendell Morgan
City Mgr., Johnny W. Rhodes
Shavano Park ....A. David Marne
City Mgr., Kyle H. McCain
Shenandoah ....Garry B. Watts
City Admin., Greg Smith
Shepherd ....Glenn Dillon
Sherman (†) ....Bill Magers
City Mgr., George Olson
Shiner ....Fred Henry Hilscher
Shoreacres ....Dolly Arons
City Admin., David K. Stall
Silsbee (†)....................Herbert Muckleroy
City Mgr., Charles T. (Tommy) Bartosh
Silverton ....Lane B. Garvin
City Admin., Jerry Patton
Simonton ....Daniel McJunkin
Sinton (†) ....Jessica Thomas Bates

City Mgr., Jackie Knox Jr.
Skellytown...........................Randy Ruth
Slaton (†) .... Laura Lynn Wilson
City Admin., Roger McKinney
Smiley ....Donald Janicek
Smithville.....................Mark A. Bunte
City Mgr., Price (Tex) Middlebrook IV
Smyer..........................Mary Beth Sims
Snook........................John W. See III
Snyder (†) .... Terry Martin
City Mgr., Merle Taylor
Socorro (†) .... Trini Lopez
Interim City Mgr., Manny Soto
Somerset ....Paul G. Cuellar
City Admin., Miguel Cantu
Somerville ....Tommy Thompson
City Admin., Barbara J. Pederson
Sonora ....Lemuel D. Lopez
City Mgr. Charles Graves
Sour Lake (†)..................Bruce Robinson
City Mgr., Larry Saurage
South Houston............................Joe Soto
Southlake (†) ....John Terrell
City Mgr., Shana Yelverton
Southmayd .... Tom Byler
South Mountain (107 Barton Ln., Gates-
ville 76528) .... Billy Mayhew
South Padre Island..........Bob Pinkerton
City Mgr., Dewey P. Cashwell Jr.
Southside Place (6309 Edloe St., Hous-
ton 77005) .... Pat Patterson
City Mgr., David N. Moss
Spearman ....Brian Gillispie
City Mgr., Edward Hansen
Splendora........................Carol W. Carley
Spofford .... Alex Solis
Springlake (†)..................Gaylon Conner
Springtown ....Doug Hughes
City Admin., Mark N. Krey
Spring Valley (1025 Campbell Rd., Hous-
ton 77055)................... Michael Andrews
City Admin., Richard R. Rockenbaugh
Spur ....Deborah Harris
Stafford (†) .... Leonard Scarcella
Stagecoach ....Galen Mansee
Stamford (†) .... Johnny Anders
City Mgr., Roy Rice
Stanton ....Lester Baker
City Admin., Danny Fryar
Staples ....Eddie Daffern
Star Harbor ...(Box 949, Malakoff 75148)
....Bill Kerlee
Stephenville (†) ....Nancy A. Hunter
City Admin., Mark Kaiser
Sterling City ..... Enrique (Henry) Estrada
Stinnett ....Billy Murphy
City Mgr., Mark Anderson
Stockdale..........................Johnny Stahl
City Mgr., Banks Akin
Stratford ....David Brown
City Admin., Sean Hardman
Strawn...............................David G. Day
Streetman ....Johnny A. Robinson
Sudan........................... Robert K. Sisson
Sugar Land (†) .... James A. Thompson
City Mgr., Allen Bogard
Sullivan City (†).......Rosendo Benavides
Interim City Mgr., Nestor Mata
Sulphur Springs (†)...........Craig Johnson
City Mgr., Marc Maxwell
Sundown .... Jim Winn
City Admin., T. Flemming
Sunnyvale.............................Jim Phaup
Town Mgr., Scott Campbell
Sunray ....Casey Stone
City Mgr., Greg Smith
Sunrise Beach Village ....Patricia Frain
Sunset.............................Danny Russell
Sunset Valley ....Jeff Mills
Sun Valley (800 Shady Grove Rd., Paris
75462)......................Maria Z. Wagnon
Surfside Beach ....Larry Davison
Sweeny (†) ....Kenneth Lott
City Mgr., Cindy King

Sweetwater (†) ....Gregory L. Wortham
City Mgr., Edward P. Brown

— T —

Taft .... Robert Vega
City Mgr., vacant
Tahoka ....John B. Baker
City Admin., Jerry W. Webster
Talco ...........................K.M. (Mike) Sloan
Talty (9550 Helms Trail, Ste. 500, Forney
75126) ....Larry Farthing
Town Admin., Connie Goodwin
Tatum ....Phil Cory
Taylor (†) ....Donald R. Hill
City Mgr., Jim Dunaway
Taylor Lake Village ....Jon Powell
Taylor Landing ....John J. Durkay
Teague ....Earnest G. Pack
City Admin., vacant
Tehuacana ....Herman D. East Jr.
Temple (†) ....William A. Jones III
City Mgr., David A. Blackburn
Tenaha ....George N. Bowers
Terrell (†) ....Hal Richards
City Mgr., Torry L. Edwards
Terrell Hills ....J. Bradford Camp
City Mgr., James Mark Browne
Texarkana (†)...............Stephen A. Mayo
City Mgr., F. Larry Sullivan
Texas City (†) ....Matthew T. Doyle
Texhoma ....Mel Yates
Texline ....Brad Riley
City Mgr., G.A. (Buster) Poling Jr.
The Colony (†)...................Joe McCourry
City Mgr., Troy Powell
Thompsons ....Freddie Newsome Jr.
Thorndale ....Billy Simank
City Admin., Keith Kiesling
Thornton ....James W. Jackson Jr.
Thorntonville (Box 740, Monahans
79756) ....David Mitchell
Thrall ....Troy Marx
Three Rivers ....James Liska
City Admin., Marion R. Forehand
Throckmorton ....Will Carroll
Tiki Island ....Ted C. Kennedy
Timbercreek Canyon (101 S. Timber-
creek Dr., Amarillo 79118) .. Terri Welch
City Mgr., Jamie Allen
Timpson...............................Debra Smith
Tioga ....Stanley Kemp
Tira (801 Cty. Rd. 4612, Sulphur Springs
75482) ....Floyd Payton
Toco (2103 Chestnut Dr., Brookston
75421) ....John Jason Waller
Todd Mission (21718 FM 1774, Planters-
ville 77363) ....George Coulam
Tolar ....Terry R. Johnson
Tomball (†) ....Gretchen Fagan
City Mgr., George Shackelford
Tom Bean ....Sherry E. Howard
Tool ....Leland Pitts
Toyah ....Bart F. Sanchez
Trent ....Leanna West
Trenton ....Tyler Bowman
Trinidad...................................Larry Estes
City Admin., Terri R. Newhouse
Trinity ....Lyle Stubbs
City Mgr., Phil Patchett
Trophy Club (†) ....Connie White
Town Mgr., Michael T. Slye
Troup...................................John Whitsell
City Admin., Russ Obar
Troy ....Marcy Pitts
Tulia (†) ....Pat George
City Mgr., (vacant)
Turkey ....Pat Carson
City Mgr., Lynn Gray
Tuscola ....Dale Martin (pro tem)
Tye ....Nancy Moore
Tyler (†)...............................Barbara Bass
City Mgr., Mark McDaniel

— U —

Uhland ....Daniel Heideman
Uncertain ....Sam Canup
Union Grove (RR 2, Box 196-FF,
Gladewater 75647)........Randy Simcox
Union Valley ....Chris Elliott
Universal City (†) ....John Williams
City Mgr., Ken Taylor
University Park (†) ...... W. Richard David
City Mgr., Bob Livingston
Uvalde (†) ....Cody Smith
City Mgr., Jennifer Garver

— V —

Valentine (†) ....Jesús Calderon
Valley Mills ....Rodney Nichols
Valley View ....Carl Kemplin
Van ....Billy Wilson
City Admin., Gary McDaniel
Van Alstyne ....Ruth Ann Collins
City Mgr., Bill Harrington
Van Horn...........................Okey D. Lucas
City Admin., Fran Malafronte
Vega ....Mark J. Groneman
Venus...........................Charley Grimes
City Admin., Jerry Reed
Vernon (†)...........................Jeff Bearden
City Mgr., Mitch Grant
Victoria (†) ....Will Armstrong
City Mgr., Charles E. Windwehen
Vidor (†)...................................Ray Long
City Mgr., Ricky Jorgensen
Village of the Hills ....Doug Lindgren
City Admin., Dan Roark
Vinton ....Madeleine Praino
Volente...............Justine Blackmore-Hlista
Von Ormy...............Art Martinez de Vara

— W —

Waco (†)...................................Jim Bush
City Mgr., Larry D. Groth
Waelder...................................Roy Tovar
Wake Village (†)...................Jim Green
City Admin., Micheal Burke
Waller...........................Danny Marburger
Wallis ....Carolyn Kennedy
City Admin., Charles Hinze
Walnut Springs ....Larry Stafford
Warren City (3004 George Richey Rd.,
Gladewater 75647).....Ricky J. Wallace
Waskom...................................Jesse Moore
Watauga (†) ....Henry J. Jeffries
City Mgr., Scott Neils
Waxahachie (†) ....N.B. (Buck) Jordan Jr.
City Mgr., Paul Stevens
Weatherford (†)............Dennis E. Hooks
City Mgr., Jerry Blaisdell
Webberville ....Hector Gonzales
Webster (†)...................Donna Rogers
City Mgr., Michael W. Jez
Weimar...........................Bennie Kosler
City Mgr., Randal W. Jones
Weinert ....Julian Estrada
Weir...........................Mervin Walker
Wellington ....Gary Brewer
City Mgr., Jon Sessions
Wellman...........................Karl Spuhler
Wells ...................................C.W. Williams
Weslaco (†)...................Miguel D. Wise
City Mgr., Leonardo Olivares
West...................................Tommy Muska
Westbrook ....Ramiro Fuentes
West Columbia....Laurie Beal Kincannon
City Mgr., Debbie Sutherland
Westlake ....Laura Wheat
Town Mgr., Thomas Brymer
West Lake Hills ....Dave Claunch
City Admin., Robert Wood
Weston ....Patti Harrington
Weston Lakes ....Mary Rose Zdunkewicz
West Orange (†)...............Roy McDonald

Westover Hills (5824 Merrymount, Fort
Worth 76107)..........Earle A. Shields Jr.
City Admin., James Rutledge
West Tawakoni ....Pete Yoho
City Admin., Cloy Richards
West University Place (†)....Robert Kelly
City Mgr., Michael Ross
Westworth Village (311 Burton Hill Rd.,
Fort Worth 76114) ....Anthony Yeager
City Admin., Roger Unger
Wharton (†)...........Domingo Montalvo Jr.
City Mgr., Andres Garza Jr.
Wheeler...........................Wanda Herd
White Deer...........................Dick Pierce
Whiteface............. Vernon Shellenberger
Whitehouse (†).................B.D. Jacobson
City Mgr., Ronny Fite
White Oak ....Tim Vaughn
City Coordinator, Ralph J. Weaver
Whitesboro...............W.D. (Dee) Welch
City Admin., Michael Marter
White Settlement (†)........Jerry R. Burns
City Mgr., Linda Ryan
Whitewright ....Bill Goodson
Whitney...........................Gwen Evans
City Admin., Chuck L. Upton
Wichita Falls (†)...............Glenn Barham
City Mgr., Darron Leiker
Wickett...........................Harold Ferguson
Willis (†)...........................Leonard Reed
City Mgr., James H. McAlister
Willow Park ....Brad Johnson
City Admin., Claud Arnold
Wills Point ....Deby S. Frye
City Mgr., vacant
Wilmer...................................Don Hudson
City Admin., Bobbie Jo Martinez
Wilson...........................Victor Steinhauser
Wimberley ....Bob Flocke
City Admin., Don Ferguson
Windcrest ....Jack H. Leonhardt
City Admin., Ronnie Cain
Windom ....Don Simmons
Windthorst...................Ray Vanburger
Winfield...........................John Walton
Wink...........................Gregory J. Rogers
Winnsboro...................Carolyn S. Jones
City Admin., Nina E. Browning
Winona...................................Rusty Smith
City Admin., James Bixler
Winters ....Lewis Bergman
City Mgr., Alan Hollander
Wixon Valley (9500 E. St. Hwy. 21, Bryan
77808) ....James (Jim) Soefje
Wolfe City ....Bryan Creed
Wolfforth...........................L.C. Childers
City Mgr., Darrell Newson
Woodbranch Village (58-A Woodbranch,
New Caney 77357)......Chuch Cardoza
Woodcreek...........................Eric C. Eskelund
City Admin., Pieter Sybesma
Woodloch .....(Box 1379, Conroe 77305)
...........................Diane L. Lincoln
Woodsboro.........George Hernandez Sr.
Woodson...........................Bobby Mathiews
Woodville............. Ben R. Bythewood III
City Admin., Mandy K. Risinger
Woodway (†)...........................Donald J. Baker
City Mgr., Yousry Zakhary
Wortham ....Kelly Craig
Wylie (†)...........................Eric Hogue
City Mgr., Mindy Manson

— Y —

Yantis...........................Jerry E. Miller
Yoakum (†) ....Anita R. Rodriguez
City Mgr., Calvin Cook
Yorktown ....Renee Hernandez
Interim City Admin., Robert Mendez

— Z —

Zavalla ....Hulon Miller ☆

Regional Councils of Government

Source: Texas Association of Regional Councils; www.txregionalcouncil.org/

The concept of regional planning and cooperation, fostered by enabling legislation in 1965, has spread across Texas since organization of the North Central Texas Council of Governments in 1966.

Regional councils are voluntary associations of local governments that deal with problems and planning needs that cross the boundaries of individual local governments or that require regional attention.

These concerns include criminal justice, emergency communications, job-training programs, solid-waste management, transportation, and water-quality management. The councils make recommendations to member governments and may assist in implementing the plans. Financing is provided by local, state, and federal governments.

The Texas Association of Regional Councils is at 701 Brazos, Ste. 780, Austin 78701; (512) 478-4715. Following is a list of the 24 regional councils, member counties, executive director, and contact information:

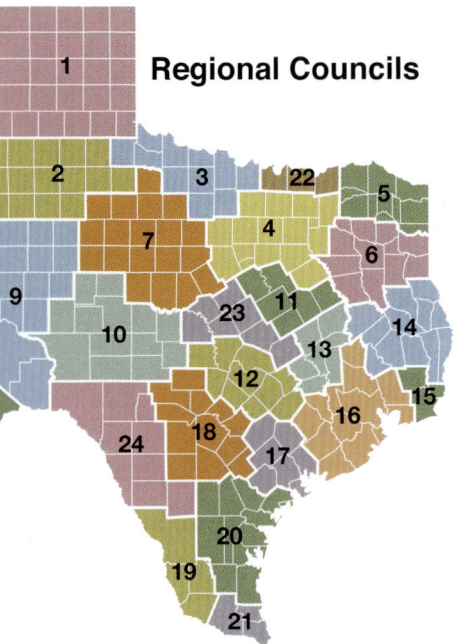

1. Panhandle Regional Planning Commission: Armstrong, Briscoe, Carson, Castro, Childress, Collingsworth, Dallam, Deaf Smith, Donley, Gray, Hall, Hansford, Hartley, Hemphill, Hutchinson, Lipscomb, Moore, Ochiltree, Oldham, Parmer, Potter, Randall, Roberts, Sherman, Swisher, and Wheeler. **Gary Pitner,** PO Box 9257, Amarillo 79105-9257; (806) 372-3381; www.prpc.cog.tx.us.

2. South Plains Association of Governments: Bailey, Cochran, Crosby, Dickens, Floyd, Garza, Hale, Hockley, King, Lamb, Lubbock, Lynn, Motley, Terry, and Yoakum. **Tim Pierce,** PO Box 3730, Lubbock 79452-3730; (806) 762-8721; www.spag.org.

3. Nortex Regional Planning Commission: Archer, Baylor, Clay, Cottle, Foard, Hardeman, Jack, Montague, Wichita, Wilbarger, and Young. **Dennis Wilde,** PO Box 5144, Wichita Falls 76307-5144; (940) 322-5281; www.nortexrpc.org.

4. North Central Texas Council of Governments: Collin, Dallas, Denton, Ellis, Erath, Hood, Hunt, Johnson, Kaufman, Navarro, Palo Pinto, Parker, Rockwall, Somervell, Tarrant, and Wise. **R. Michael Eastland,** PO Box 5888, Arlington 76005-5888; (817) 640-3300; www.nctcog.org.

5. Ark-Tex Council of Governments: Bowie, Cass, Delta, Franklin, Hopkins, Lamar, Morris, Red River, Titus, and Miller County, Ark. **L.D. Williamson,** PO Box 5307, Texarkana, Texas 75505-5307; (903) 832-8636; www.atcog.org.

6. East Texas Council of Governments: Anderson, Camp, Cherokee, Gregg, Harrison, Henderson, Marion, Panola, Rains, Rusk, Smith, Upshur, Van Zandt, and Wood. **David Cleveland,** 3800 Stone Rd., Kilgore 75662-6297; (903) 984-8641; www.etcog.org.

7. West Central Texas Council of Governments: Brown, Callahan, Coleman, Comanche, Eastland, Fisher, Haskell, Jones, Kent, Knox, Mitchell, Nolan, Runnels, Scurry, Shackelford, Stephens, Stonewall, Taylor, and Throckmorton. **Tom Smith,** 3702 Loop 322, Abilene 79602-7300; (325) 672-8544; www.wctcog.org.

8. Rio Grande Council of Governments: Brewster, Culberson, El Paso, Hudspeth, Jeff Davis, Presidio, and Doña Ana County, N.M. **Annette Gutierrez,** 1100 N. Stanton, Ste. 610, El Paso 79902; (915) 533-0998; www.riocog.org.

9. Permian Basin Regional Planning Commission: Andrews, Borden, Crane, Dawson, Ector, Gaines, Glasscock, Howard, Loving, Martin, Midland, Pecos, Reeves, Terrell, Upton, Ward, and Winkler. **Terri Moore,** PO Box 60660, Midland 79711-0660; (432) 563-1061; www.pbrpc.org.

10. Concho Valley Council of Governments: Coke, Concho, Crockett, Irion, Kimble, Mason, McCulloch, Menard, Reagan, Schleicher, Sterling, Sutton, and Tom Green. **Jeffrey Sutton,** Box 60050, San Angelo 76906-0050; (325) 944-9666; www.cvcog.org.

11. Heart of Texas Council of Governments: Bosque, Falls, Freestone, Hill, Limestone, and McLennan. **Kenneth Simons,** PO Box 20847, Waco 76712; (254) 292-1800; www.hotcog.org.

12. Capital Area Council of Governments: Bastrop, Blanco, Burnet, Caldwell, Fayette, Hays, Lee, Llano, Travis, and Williamson. **Betty Voights,** 6800 Burleson Rd., Bldg. 310, Ste. 165, Austin 78744; (512) 916-6000; www.capcog.org.

13. Brazos Valley Council of Governments: Brazos, Burleson, Grimes, Leon, Madison, Robertson, and Washington. **Tom Wilkinson Jr.,** 3991 E. 29th St., Bryan 77803; (979) 595-2800; www.bvcog.org.

14. Deep East Texas Council of Governments: Angelina, Houston, Jasper, Nacogdoches, Newton, Polk, Sabine, San Augustine, San Jacinto, Shelby, Trinity, and Tyler. **Walter G. Diggles,** 210 Premier Dr., Jasper 75951; (409) 384-5704; www.detcog.org.

15. South East Texas Regional Planning Commission: Hardin, Jefferson, and Orange. **Shaun P. Davis,** 2210 Eastex Fwy., Beaumont 77703; (409) 899-8444; www.setrpc.org.

16. Houston-Galveston Area Council: Austin, Brazoria, Chambers, Colorado, Fort Bend, Galveston, Harris, Liberty, Matagorda, Montgomery, Walker, Waller, and Wharton. **Jack Steele,** PO Box 22777, Houston 77227-2777; (713) 627-3200; www.h-gac.com.

17. Golden Crescent Regional Planning Commission: Calhoun, DeWitt, Goliad, Gonzales, Jackson, Lavaca, and Victoria. **Joe Brannan,** 120 S. Main, Ste. 210, Victoria 77901; (361) 578-1587; www.gcrpc.org.

18. Alamo Area Council of Governments: Atascosa, Bandera, Bexar, Comal, Frio, Gillespie, Guadalupe, Karnes, Kendall, Kerr, Medina, and Wilson. **Gloria C. Arriaga,** 8700 Tesoro Dr., Ste. 700, San Antonio 78217; (210) 362-5200; www.aacog.com.

19. South Texas Development Council: Jim Hogg, Starr, Webb, and Zapata. **Amando Garza Jr.,** 1002 Dicky Lane, Laredo 78044-2187; (956) 722-3995; www.stdc.cog.tx.us.

20. Coastal Bend Council of Governments: Aransas, Bee, Brooks, Duval, Jim Wells, Kenedy, Kleberg, Live Oak, McMullen, Nueces, Refugio, and San Patricio. **John P. Buckner,** PO Box 9909, Corpus Christi 78469-9909; (361) 883-5743; cbcog98.org.

21. Lower Rio Grande Valley Development Council: Cameron, Hidalgo, and Willacy. **Kenneth N. Jones Jr.,** 311 N. 15th, McAllen 78501-4705; (956) 682-3481; www.lrgvdc.org.

22. Texoma Council of Governments: Cooke, Fannin, and Grayson. **Susan B. Thomas,** 1117 Gallagher Dr., Ste. 100, Sherman 75090; (903) 813-3512; www.texoma.cog.tx.us.

23. Central Texas Council of Governments: Bell, Coryell, Hamilton, Lampasas, Milam, Mills, and San Saba. **James Reed,** PO Box 729, Belton 76513-0729; (254) 770-2200; www.ctcog.org.

24. Middle Rio Grande Development Council: Dimmit, Edwards, Kinney, La Salle, Maverick, Real, Uvalde, Val Verde, and Zavala. **Leodoro Martinez Jr.,** PO Box 1199, Carrizo Springs 78834-1199; (830) 876-3533; www.mrgdc.org. ☆

The Comanche County Courthouse was completed in 1939. Photo by Ron Billings; Texas Forest Service.

County Courts

*Each Texas county has one county court created by the Texas Constitution — a **constitutional county court** — which is presided over by the county judge (see table beginning on **page 535** for a list of county judges). In more populated counties, the Legislature has created **statutory county courts,** including courts at law, probate courts, juvenile courts, domestic relations courts, and criminal courts at law. **Following is a list of statutory county courts and judges,** as reported by county clerks as of July 2011. Other courts with jurisdiction in each county can be found on **pages 489–495**. Other county and district officials can be found on pages 535–546.*

Anderson — *Court at Law & Criminal Court at Law:* B. Jeffrey Doran. *Probate Courts No. 1:* B. Jeffrey Doran; *No. 2:* Robert D. Johnston.

Angelina — *Court at Law No. 1:* Robert Inselman; *No. 2:* Derek Flournoy.

Aransas — *Court at Law:* William Adams.

Austin — *Court at Law:* Daniel W. Leedy.

Bailey — *Probate & Juvenile courts:* Sherri Harrison. *Domestic Relations Court:* Gordon H. Green.

Bastrop — *Court at Law:* Benton Eskew.

Bee — *Probate, Domestic Relations, & Criminal Court at Law:* David Silva. *Juvenile Court:* Raul G. Casarez.

Bell — *Court at Law No. 1, Probate & Juvenile courts:* Edward S. Johnson. *Court at Law No. 2 & Criminal Court at Law:* John Mischtian.

Bexar — *Courts at Law No. 1:* John D. Fleming; *No. 2:* Jason Wolff; *No. 3:* David J. Rodriguez; *No. 4:* Sarah E. Garrahan; *No. 5:* Jason Pulliam; *No. 6:* Wayne Christian; *No. 7:* Eugenia (Genie) Wright; *No. 8:* Liza Rodriguez; *No. 9:* Walden Shelton; *No. 10:* Irene Rios; *No. 11:* Carlo Key; *No. 12:* Scott Roberts; *No. 13:* Monica Gonzalez; *No. 14:* Bill C. White; *No. 15:* Michael LaHood. *Probate Courts No. 1:* Polly Jackson Spencer; *No. 2:* Tom Rickhoff.

Bosque — *Court at Law:* David Christian.

Bowie — *Court at Law:* Jeff Addison.

Brazoria — *Courts at Law & Probate No. 1:* Jerri Lee Mills; *No. 2:* Marc W. Holder; *No. 3:* Jeremy Warren; No. 4: Lori Rickert.

Brazos — *Courts at Law No. 1:* Amanda Matzke; *No. 2:* Jim Locke.

Brooks — *Court at Law:* Joe B. Garcia.

Brown — *Court at Law, Criminal Court at Law, & Domestic Relations:* Frank Griffin. *Probate & Juvenile courts:* E. Ray West III.

The Ellis County Courthouse in Waxahachie was completed in 1896. Photo by Ron Billings; Texas Forest Service.

Burnet — *Court at Law:* W.R. Savage.

Caldwell — *Court at Law:* Edward L. Jarrett.

Calhoun — *Court at Law:* Alex R. Hernandez.

Cameron — *Court at Law No. 1:* Arturo McDonald; *No. 2:* Laura Betancourt; *No. 3:* David Gonzales III.

Cass — *Court at Law & Criminal Court at Law:* Donald Dowd; *Probabe Court:* Charles McMichael.

Cherokee — *Court at Law:* Craig A. Fletcher.

Coke — *Probate Court:* Roy Blair. *Juvenile Court:* Barbara L. Walther.

Collin — *Courts at Law No. 1:* Corinne Mason; *No. 2:* Jerry Lewis; *No. 3:* Lance S. Baxter; *No. 4:* David Rippel; *No. 5:* Dan Wilson; *No. 6:* Jay A. Bender. *Probate Court:* Weldon Copeland.

Comal — *Court at Law No. 1:* Randy C. Gray; *No. 2* Charles A. Stephens II.

Cooke — *Court at Law:* John H. Morris.

Coryell — *Court at Law:* John Lee.

Dallas — *Courts at Law No. 1:* DeMetria Benson; *No. 2:* King Fifer; *No. 3:* Sally Montgomery; *No. 4:* Ken Tapscott; *No. 5:* Mark Greenberg. *County Criminal Courts No. 1:* Dan Patterson; *No. 2:* Julia Hayes; *No. 3:* Douglas Skemp; *No. 4:* Teresa Tolle; *No. 5:* Etta J. Mullin; *No. 6:* Angela King; *No. 7:* Elizabeth Crowder; *No. 8:* Tina Yoo; *No. 9:* Peggy Hoffman; *No. 10:* Roberto Canas; *No. 11:* Elizabeth Frizell. *Probate Courts No. 1:* Brenda Thompson; *No. 2:* Chris Wilmoth; *No. 3:* Michael E. Miller. *County Criminal Courts of Appeals No. 1:* Kristin Wade; *No. 2:* Jeff Rosenfield.

Denton — *Courts at Law No. 1:* Kimberly McCary; *No. 2:* Robert Ramirez. *Probate Court:* Bonnie Robison. *Criminal Court at Law No. 1:* Jim Crouch; *No. 2:* Virgil Vahlenkamp; *No. 3:* David D. Garcia; *No. 4:* Joe Bridges; *No. 5:* Richard Podgorski.

Ector — *Courts at Law No. 1 & Juvenile Court:* J.A. (Jim) Bobo; *No. 2:* Mark D. Owens.

Ellis — *Court at Law No. 1 & Probate:* Jim Chapman; *Court at Law No. 2 & Juvenile:* A. Gene Calvert Jr.

El Paso — *Courts at Law No. 1:* Ricardo Herrera; *No. 2:* Julie Gonzalez; *No. 3:* Javier Alvarez; *No. 4:* Alejandro Gonzalez; *No. 5:* Carlos Villa; *No. 6:* M. Sue Kurita; *No. 7:* Thomas Spieczny. *Probate Court No. 1:* Patricia Chew; *No. 2:* Eduardo Gamboa. *Criminal Courts at Law No. 1:* Alma Trejo; *No. 2:* Robert An-

chondo.

Erath — *Court at Law:* Bart McDougal.

Fannin — *Court at Law, Criminal Court at Law, Probate, & Domestic Relations:* Charles Butler; *Domestic Relations & Juvenile:* Laurine J. Blake; *Probate Court No. 2:* Creta L. Carter II.

Fort Bend — *Courts at Law No. 1:* Bud Childers; *No. 2:* Jeffery McMeans; *No. 3:* Susan G. Lowery; *No. 4:* R.H. (Sandy) Bielstein.

Galveston — *Courts at Law No. 1:* John Grady; *No. 2:* Barbara Roberts; *No. 3:* Christopher Dupuya.

Grayson — *Courts at Law & Criminal Courts at Law No. 1:* James C. Henderson; *No. 2:* Carol M. Siebman.

Gregg — *Court at Law No. 1:* Rebecca Simpson. *No. 2:* Vincent Dulweber.

Guadalupe — *Court at Law No. 1:* Linda Z. Jones; *No. 2:* Frank Follis. *Juvenile Court:* Linda Z. Jones.

Harris — *Courts at Law No. 1:* R. Jack Cagle; *No. 2:* Jacqueline Lucci Smith; *No. 3:* Linda Storey; *No. 4:* Roberta Lloyd. *County Criminal Courts at Law No. 1:* Paula Goodhart; *No. 2:* Bill Harmon; *No. 3:* Natalie Fleming; *No. 4:* John Clinton; *No. 5:* Margaret Stewart Harris; *No. 6:* Larry Standley; *No. 7:* Pam Derbyshire; *No. 8:* Jay Karahan; *No. 9:* Analia Wilkerson; *No. 10:* Sherman A. Ross; *No. 11:* Diane Bull; *No. 12:* Robin Brown; *No. 13:* Don Smyth; *No. 14:* Mike Fields; *No. 15:* Jean Spradling Hughes. *Probate Courts No. 1:* Lloyd Wright; *No. 2:* Mike Wood; *No. 3:* Rory Robert Olsen; *No. 4:* Christine Riddle Butts.

Harrison — *Court at Law:* Jim Ammerman II.

Hays — *Court at Law No. 1:* Robert Updegrove; *No. 2* Linda A. Rodriguez.

Henderson — *Court at Law No 1:* D. Matt Livingston; *No 2:* Nancy Adams Perryman.

Hidalgo — *Courts at Law No. 1:* Rodolfo (Rudy) Gonzalez; *No. 2:* Jaime (Jay) Palacios; *No. 4:* Fred Garza Jr.; *No. 5:* Arnoldo Cantu; *No. 6:* Albert Garcia.

Hill — *Court at Law:* A. Lee Harris.

Hood — *Court at Law:* Vincent Messina.

Hopkins — *Court at Law:* Amy M. Smith.

Houston — *Court at Law:* Sarah Tunnell Clark.

Hunt — *Court at Law No. 1:* J. Andrew Bench; *No. 2:* R. Duncan Thomas.

Jeff Davis — *Court at Law:* George E. Grubb.

Jefferson — *Courts at Law No. 1:* Alfred S. Gerson; *No. 2:* G.R. (Lupe) Flores; *No. 3:* John Paul Davis.

Johnson — *Courts at Law No. 1:* Robert B. Mayfield III; *No. 2:* Jerry Webber.

Jones — *Criminal Court at Law:* Brooks Hagler.

Kaufman — *Court at Law No. 1 & Juvenile:* Erleigh Norville Wylie. *Court at Law No. 2:* David A. Lewis.

Kerr — *Court at Law:* Spencer W. Brown.

Kleberg — *Court at Law:* Guadalupe O. Mendoza.

Lamar — Court at Law: Bill Harris.

Liberty — *Court at Law:* Tommy Chambers.

Lubbock — *Court at Law No. 1:* Larry B. (Rusty) Ladd;

No. 2: Drue Farmer; No. 3: Judy Parker.

McLennan — Courts at Law No. 1: Mike Freeman; No. 2: Brad Cates.

Medina — Court at Law: Vivian Torres.

Midland — Courts at Law No. 1: Kyle Peeler; No. 2: Marvin Moore.

Montgomery — Courts at Law No. 1: Dennis Watson; No. 2: Claudia Laird; No. 3: Patrice McDonald; No. 4: Mary Ann Turner; No. 5: Keith Stewart.

Moore — Court at Law: Delwin McGee.

Morris — Probate Court: J.C. Jennings.

Motley — All courts: Ed D. Smith.

Nacogdoches — Court at Law: John A. (Jack) Sinz.

Nolan — Court at Law: David Hall.

Nueces — Courts at Law No. 1: Robert J. Vargas; No. 2: Lisa Gonzales; No. 3: John B. Martinez; No. 4: James E. Klager; No. 5: Brent Chesney.

Orange — Court at Law No. 1: Pat Clark; No 2: Troy Johnson.

Panola — Court at Law: Terry D. Bailey.

Parker — Court at Law No. 1: Jerry Buckner; No. 2: Ben Akers.

Polk — Court at Law: Stephen Phillips.

Potter — Court at Law No. 1: W.F. (Corky) Roberts; No. 2: Pamela Cook Sirmon.

Randall — Court at Law No. 1: James Anderson. No. 2: Ronnie Walker.

Reeves — Court at Law: Walter M. Holcombe.

Rockwall — Court at Law, Probate, & Juvenile courts: Brian Williams; Domestic Relations Court: David Rakow and Brett Hall.

Rusk — Court at Law: Chad Dean.

San Patricio — Court at Law: Richard D. Hatch III.

Smith — Courts at Law No. 1: Thomas A. Dunn; No. 2: Randall L. Rogers. No. 3: Floyd Getz. Probate Court: Joel Baker. Juvenile Court: Floyd Getz.

Starr — Court at Law: Romero Molina.

Tarrant — Courts at Law No. 1: Don Pierson; No. 2: Jennifer Rymell; No. 3: Mike Hrabal. Criminal Courts at Law No. 1: Sherry Hill; No. 2: Mike Mitchell; No. 3: Billy D. Mills; No. 4: Deborah Nekhom; No. 5: Jamie Cummings; No. 6: Molly Jones; No. 7: Cheril S. Hardy; No. 8: Daryl Coffey; No. 9: Brent A. Carr; No. 10: Phil Sorrels. Probate Courts No. 1: Steve M. King; No. 2: Pat Ferchill. Juvenile Court: Jean Boyd.

Taylor — Courts at Law No. 1: Robert Harper; No. 2: Sam Carroll.

Tom Green — Court at Law No. 1: Ben Nolan; No. 2: Penny Roberts.

Travis — Courts at Law No. 1: J. David Phillips; No. 2: Eric Shepperd; No. 3: John Lipscombe; No. 4: Mike Denton; No. 5: Nancy Hohengarten; No. 6: Brandy Mueller; No. 7: Elizabeth A. Earle; No. 8: Carlos H. Barrera. Family Relations No. 1: Susan D. Sheppard; No. 2: Leonard Saenz; No. 3: J. Andrew Hathcock.

Val Verde — Court at Law: Sergio J. Gonzalez.

Van Zandt — Court at Law & Criminal Court at Law: Randal L. McDonald; Probate & Juvenile courts: Rhita Koches.

Victoria — Courts at Law No. 1: Laura A. Weiser; No. 2: Daniel F. Gilliam.

Walker — Court at Law & Criminal Court at Law: Barbara W. Hale. Probate Court: Barbara W. Hale and Danny Pierce.

Waller — Court at Law: June Jackson.

Washington — Court at Law: Matthew Reue.

Webb — Courts at Law, Probate & Juvenile courts: Alvino (Ben) Morales and Jesús (Chuy) Garza.

Wharton — Court at Law & Probate Court: Phillip S. Spenrath. Domestic Relations Court: Randy Clapp.

Wichita — Court at Law No. 1: Gary Butler; No. 2: Greg King.

Williamson — Courts at Law No. 1: Suzanne Brooks; No. 2: Tim Wright; No. 3: Doug Arnold; No. 4: John McMaster.

Wise — Court at Law, Probate, & Criminal Court at Law: Melton D. Cude. Domestic Relations & Juvenile courts: John Fostel.

Young — Probate & Juvenile courts: Stanley H. Peavey III.

Zapata — Court at Law: Joe Rathmell. ☆

The Limestone County Courthouse in Groesbeck opened in 1924. Photo by Ron Billings; Texas Forest Service.

County Tax Appraisers

The following list of Chief Appraisers for Texas counties was furnished by the State Property Tax Division of the State Comptroller's office. It includes the mailing address for each appraiser and is current to July 2011.

Anderson—Carson Wages, PO Box 279, Palestine 75802

Andrews—Ron Huckabay, 600 N. Main St., Andrews 79714

Angelina—Tim Mayberry, PO Box 2357, Lufkin 75902

Aransas—Kevin Jamison, 601 S. Church St., Rockport 78382

Archer—Kimbra York, PO Box 1141, Archer City 76351

Armstrong—Joe Reck, PO Box 835, Claude 79019

Atascosa—Michelle Cardenas, PO Box 139, Poteet 78065

Austin—Richard Moring, 906 E. Amelia St., Bellville 77418

Bailey—Kaye Elliott, 302 Main St., Muleshoe 79347

Bandera—Wendy Graham, PO Box 1119, Bandera 78003

Bastrop—Mark Boehnke, PO Drawer 578, Bastrop 78602

Baylor—Ronnie Hargrove, 211 N. Washington, Seymour 76380

Bee—Domingo Palomo, 401 N. Washington, Beeville 78102

Bell—Marvin Hahn, PO Box 390, Belton 76513

Bexar—Michael Amezquita, PO Box 830248, San Antonio 78283

Blanco—Hollis Boatright, PO Box 338, Johnson City 78636

Borden—Kristi Harrison, PO Box 298, Gail 79738

Bosque—Rosemary Galaviz, PO Box 393, Meridian 76665

Bowie—Mike Brower, PO Box 6527, Texarkana 75505

Brazoria—Cheryl Evans, 500 N. Chenango, Angleton 77515

Brazos—Mark Price, 1673 Briarcrest Dr., #A-101, Bryan 77802

Brewster—Matt White, 107 W. Avenue E, #2, Alpine 79830

Briscoe—Pat McWaters, PO Box 728, Silverton 79257

Brooks—Mary Lou Cantu, PO Drawer A, Falfurrias 78355

Brown—Doran E. Lemke, 403 Fisk Ave., Brownwood 76801

Burleson—Carroll Brincefield, PO Box 1000, Caldwell 77836

Burnet—Stan Hemphill, PO Box 908, Burnet 78611

Caldwell—Carlton R. Pape, PO Box 900, Lockhart 78644

Calhoun—Jerry Daum, PO Box 49, Port Lavaca 77979

Callahan—Don Jones, 132 W. 4th St., Baird 79504

Cameron—Frutoso Gomez Jr., PO Box 1010, San Benito 78586

Camp—Geraldine Hull, 143 Quitman St., Pittsburg 75686

Carson—Donita Davis, PO Box 970, Panhandle 79068

Cass—Leann Lee (interim), 502 N. Main St., Linden 75563

Castro—Jerry Heller, 204 S.E. 3rd (Rear), Dimmitt 79027

Chambers—Michael Fregia, PO Box 1520, Anahuac 77514

Cherokee—Lee Flowers, PO Box 494, Rusk 75785

Childress—Terry Holley, 1710 Ave. F NW, Childress 79201

Clay—Gerald Holland, PO Box 108, Henrietta 76365

Cochran—David Greener, 109 S.E. First St., Morton 79346

Coke—Gayle Sisemore, PO Box 2, Robert Lee 76945

Coleman—Bill W. Jones, PO Box 914, Coleman 76834

Collin—Bo Daffin, 250 W. Eldorado, McKinney 75069

Collingsworth—Nancy Ellis, 800 West Ave., Rm. 104, Wellington, 79095

Colorado—Bill H. Mitchell, PO Box 10, Columbus 78934

Comal—Curtis Koehler, PO Box 311222, New Braunfels 78131

Comanche—JoAnn Hohertz, PO Box 6, Comanche 76442

Concho—Scott Sutton, PO Box 68, Paint Rock 76866

Cooke—Doug Smithson, 201 N. Dixon, Gainesville 76240

Coryell—Mitch Fast, PO Box 1058, Gatesville 76528

Cottle—Gary Zeitler (interim), PO Box 459, Paducah 79248

Crane—Janet Wilson, 511 W. 8th St., Crane 79731

Crockett—Rhonda Shaw, PO Drawer H, Ozona 76943

Crosby—Kathy Lowrie, PO Box 505, Crosbyton 79322

Culberson—Sally Carrasco, PO Box 550, Van Horn 79855

Dallam—Edward G. Carter, PO Box 579, Dalhart 79022

Dallas—Ken Nolan, 2949 N. Stemmons Fwy., Dallas 75247

Dawson—Norma J. Brock, PO Box 797, Lamesa 79331

Deaf Smith—Danny Jones, PO Box 2298, Hereford 79045

Delta—Kim Gregory, PO Box 47, Cooper 75432

Denton—Joe Rogers, PO Box 2816, Denton 76202

DeWitt—Beverly Malone, 103 E. Bailey St., Cuero 77954

Dickens—Patti Abbott, PO Box 180, Dickens 79229

Dimmit—Norma Carrillo, 404 W. Peña St., Carrizo Springs 78834

Donley—Paula Lowrie, PO Box 1220, Clarendon 79226

Duval—Rene Garza, PO Box 809, San Diego 78384

Eastland—Steve Thomas, PO Box 914, Eastland 76448

Ector—Karen McCord, 1301 E. 8th St., Odessa 79761

Edwards—Bruce Martin, PO Box 858, Rocksprings 78880

Ellis—Kathy Rodrigue, PO Box 878, Waxahachie 75165

El Paso—Dinah Kilgore, 5801 Trowbridge Dr., El Paso 79925

Erath—Jerry Lee, 1390 N. Harbin Dr., Stephenville 76401

Falls—Rosie Skiles, PO Drawer 430, Marlin 76661

Fannin—Mike Shannon, 831 W. State Hwy. 56, Bonham 75418

Fayette—Karen Schubert, PO Box 836, La Grange 78945

Fisher—Jacqueline Martin, PO Box 516, Roby 79543

Floyd—Jim Finley, PO Box 249, Floydada 79235

Foard—Jo Ann Vecera, PO Box 419, Crowell 79227

Fort Bend—Glen Whitehead, 2801 B.F. Terry Blvd., Rosenberg 77471

Franklin—Genea Burnaman, PO Box 720, Mount Vernon 75457

Freestone—Bud Black, 218 N. Mount St., Fairfield 75840

Frio—Luciano R. Gonzales, PO Box 1129, Pearsall 78061

Gaines—Gayla Harridge, PO Box 490, Seminole 79360

Galveston—Ken Wright, 600 Gulf Frwy., Ste. 113, Texas City 77591

Garza—Shirley A. Smith, PO Drawer F, Post 79356

Gillespie—David Oehler, 101 W. Main St., Unit 11, Fredericksburg 78624

Glasscock—Nancy Hillger, PO Box 89, Garden City 79739

Goliad—E.J. Bammert, PO Box 34, Goliad 77963

Gonzales—Glenda Strackbein, PO Box 867, Gonzales 78629

Gray—W. Pat Bagley, PO Box 836, Pampa 79066

Grayson—Teresa Parsons, 205 N. Travis, Sherman 75090

Gregg—Thomas Hays, 4367 W. Loop 281, Longview 75604

Grimes—Bill Sullivan, PO Box 489, Anderson 77830

Guadalupe—Jamie Osborne, 3000 N. Austin St., Seguin 78155

Hale—Nikki Branscum, PO Box 29, Plainview 79073

Hall—Marlin Felts, 512 W. Main St., Ste. 14, Memphis 79245

Hamilton—Doyle Roberts, 119 E. Henry St., Hamilton 76531

Hansford—Sonya Shieldknight, 709 W. 7th Ave., Spearman 79081

Hardeman—Jan Evans, PO Box 388, Quanah 79252

Hardin—Amador Reyna, PO Box 670, Kountze 77625

Harris—Jim Robinson, PO Box 920975, Houston 77292

Harrison—Karen Jeans, PO Box 818, Marshall 75671

Hartley—Mary M. Thompson, PO Box 405, Hartley 79044

Haskell—Wanda Hester, PO Box 467, Haskell 79521

Hays—David G. Valle, 21001 N. IH-35, Kyle 78640

Hemphill—Jason Caron, 223 Main St., Canadian 79014

Henderson—Bill Jackson, PO Box 430, Athens 75751

Hidalgo—Rolando Garza, PO Box 208, Edinburg 78540

Hill—Mike McKibben, PO Box 416, Hillsboro 76645

Hockley—Greg Kelley, PO Box 1090, Levelland 79336

Hood—Greg Stewart, PO Box 819, Granbury 76048

Hopkins—Cathy Singleton, PO Box 753, Sulphur Springs 75483

Houston—Kathryn Keith, PO Box 112, Crockett 75835

Howard—Brett McKibbin, PO Box 1151, Big Spring 79721

Hudspeth—Zedoch L. Pridgeon, PO Box 429, Sierra Blanca 79851

Hunt—Brent South, PO Box 1339, Greenville 75403

Hutchinson—Diana Hooks, PO Box 5065, Borger 79008

Irion—Byron Bitner, PO Box 980, Mertzon 76941

Jack—Kathy Conner, PO Box 958, Jacksboro 76458

Jackson—Damon D. Moore, 700 N. Wells, Ste. 101, Edna 77957

Jasper—David Luther, PO Box 1300, Jasper 75951

Jeff Davis—Zedoch L. Pridgeon, PO Box 373, Fort Davis 79734

Jefferson—Roland Bieber, PO Box 21337, Beaumont 77705

Jim Hogg—Jorge Arellano, PO Box 459, Hebbronville 78361

Jim Wells—J. Sidney Vela, PO Box 607, Alice 78333

Johnson—Jim Hudspeth, 109 N. Main, Cleburne 76033

Jones—Kim McLemore, PO Box 348, Anson 79501

Karnes—Kathey Barnhill, 915 S. Panna Maria St., Karnes City 78118

Kaufman—Chris Peace, PO Box 819, Kaufman 75142

Kendall—Gary Eldridge, PO Box 788, Boerne 78006

Kenedy—Thomas G. Denney, PO Box 39, Sarita 78385

Kent—Kay Byrd, PO Box 68, Jayton 79528

Kerr—P.H. Coates IV, PO Box 294387, Kerrville 78029

Kimble—Kandy Dick, PO Box 307, Junction 76849

King—Kala Briggs, PO Box 117, Guthrie 79236

Kinney—Gene C. Slate, PO Box 1377, Brackettville 78832

Kleberg—Ernestina Flores, PO Box 1027, Kingsville 78364

Knox—Mitzi Welch, PO Box 47, Benjamin 79505

Lamar—Phyllis Bryan, PO Box 400, Paris 75461

Lamb—Lesa Kloiber, PO Box 950, Littlefield 79339

Lampasas—Melissa Gonzales (interim), Box 175, Lampasas 76550

La Salle—Annie Garcia, PO Box 1530, Cotulla 78014

Lavaca—Pamela Lathrop, PO Box 386, Hallettsville 77964

Lee—Patricia Davis, 898 E. Richmond, Ste. 100, Giddings 78942

Leon—Jeff Beshears, PO Box 536, Centerville 75833

Liberty—Alan Conner, PO Box 10016, Liberty 77575

Limestone—Karen Wietzikoski, PO Drawer 831, Groesbeck 76642

Lipscomb—Pam Scates, PO Box 128, Darrouzett 79024

Live Oak—Willie James, PO Box 2370, George West 78022

Llano—Cindy Cowan, 103 E. Sandstone, Llano 78643

Loving—Sherlene Burrows, PO Box 352, Mentone 79754

Lubbock—Dave Kimbrough, PO Box 10542, Lubbock 79408

Lynn—Marquita Scott, PO Box 789, Tahoka 79373

Madison—Larry Krumnow, PO Box 1328, Madisonville 77864

Marion—John E. Kirkland, PO Box 690, Jefferson 75657

Martin—Marsha Graves, PO Box 1349, Stanton 79782

Mason—Ted H. Smith, PO Box 1119, Mason 76856

Matagorda—Vince Maloney, 2225 Ave. G, Bay City 77414

Maverick—Victor Perry, PO Box 2628, Eagle Pass 78852

McCulloch—Zane Brandenberger, 306 W. Lockhart, Brady 76825

McLennan—Andrew Hahn, PO Box 2297, Waco 76703

McMullen—Jesse Bryan, PO Box 38, Tilden 78072

Medina—James Garcia, 1410 Ave. K, Hondo 78861

Menard—Dianna Miller, PO Box 1008, Menard 76859

Midland—Jerry Bundick, PO Box 908002, Midland 79708

Milam—Patricia Moraw, PO Box 769, Cameron 76520

Mills—John Timmons, PO Box 565, Goldthwaite 76844

Mitchell—Linda McSpadden (interim), 2112 Hickory St., Colorado City 79512

Montague—Kim Haralson, PO Box 121, Montague 76251

Montgomery—Mark Castleschouldt, PO Box 2233, Conroe 77305

Moore—Rhonda Stafford, PO Box 717, Dumas 79029

Morris—Rhonda Hall, PO Box 563, Daingerfield 75638

Motley—Brenda Osborn, PO Box 779, Matador 79244

Nacogdoches—Gary Woods, 216 W. Hospital St., Nacogdoches 75961

Navarro—Karen Morris, PO Box 3118, Corsicana 75110

Newton—Margie L. Herrin, 109 Court St., Newton 75966

Nolan—Brenda Klepper (interim), PO Box 1256, Sweetwater 79556

Nueces—Ollie Grant, 201 N. Chaparral, Ste. 206, Corpus Christi 78401

Ochiltree—Terry Symons, 825 S. Main, Ste. 100, Perryton 79070

Oldham—Brenda Perkins, PO Box 310, Vega 79092

Orange—Michael Cedars, PO Box 457, Orange 77631

Palo Pinto—Donna Rhoades, PO Box 250, Palo Pinto 76484

Panola—Loyd Adams, 1736 Ballpark Dr., Carthage 75633

Parker—Larry Hammonds, 1108 Santa Fe Dr., Weatherford 76086

Parmer—Curby Brantley Jr., PO Box 56, Bovina 79009

Pecos—Sam Calderon, 201 S. Main St., Fort Stockton 79735

Polk—Carolyn Allen, 114 Matthews, Livingston 77351

Potter—Jim Childers, PO Box 7190, Amarillo 79114

Presidio—Irma Salgado, PO Box 879, Marfa 79843

Rains—Carrol Houllis, PO Box 70, Emory 75440

Randall—Jim Childers, PO Box 7190, Amarillo 79114

Reagan—Byron Bitner, PO Box 8, Big Lake 76932

Real—Kelley V. Shults, PO Box 158, Leakey 78873

Red River—Janet V. Tinsley, PO Box 461, Clarksville 75426

Reeves—John Huddleston, PO Box 1229, Pecos 79772

Refugio—Connie Koonce, PO Box 156, Refugio 78377

Roberts—DeAnn Williams, PO Box 458, Miami 79059

Robertson—J. Dan Brewer, PO Box 998, Franklin 77856

Rockwall—Ray Helm, 841 Justin Rd., Rockwall 75087

Runnels—Patsy Dunn, PO Box 524, Ballinger 76821

Rusk—Terry Decker, PO Box 7, Henderson 75653

Sabine—Jim Nethery, PO Box 137, Hemphill 75948

San Augustine—Jamie Doherty, 122 N. Harrison, San Augustine 75972

San Jacinto—Alan McKinley, PO Box 1170, Coldspring 77331

San Patricio—Rufino H. Lozano, PO Box 938, Sinton 78387

San Saba—Randy Henderson, 423 E. Wallace St., San Saba 76877

Schleicher—Jani Mitchell, PO Box 936, Eldorado 76936

Scurry—Larry Crooks, 2612 College Ave., Snyder 79549

Shackelford—Teresa Peacock, PO Box 2247, Albany 76430

Shelby—Robert N. Pigg, 724 Shelbyville St., Center 75935

Sherman—Teresa Edmond, PO Box 239, Stratford 79084

Smith—Michael D. Barnett, 245 South S.E. Loop 323, Tyler 75702

Somervell—Wes Rollen, 112 Allen Dr., Glen Rose 76043

Starr—Humberto Saenz Jr., 100 N. FM 3167, Ste. 300, Rio Grande City 78582

Stephens—Bun Barry (interim), PO Box 351, Breckenridge 76424

Sterling—Jeannie Gaines, PO Box 28, Sterling City 76951

Stonewall—Ozella Warner, PO Box 308, Aspermont 79502

Sutton—Mary Bustamante, 300 E. Oak St., Ste. 2, Sonora 76950

Swisher—Cindy McDowell, PO Box 8, Tulia 79088

Tarrant—Jeff Law, 2500 Handley-Ederville Rd., Fort Worth 76118

Taylor—Richard Petree, PO Box 1800, Abilene 79604

Terrell—Blain Chriesman, PO Box 747, Sanderson 79848

Terry—Ronny Burran, PO Box 426, Brownfield 79316

Throckmorton—Francis Peacock, Box 788, Throckmorton 76483

Titus—Ronny Babcock, PO Box 528, Mount Pleasant 75456

Tom Green—Bill Benson, PO Box 3307, San Angelo 76902

Travis—Patrick Brown, PO Box 149012, Austin 78714

Trinity—Susan McKinley, PO Box 950, Groveton 75845

Tyler—Eddie Chalmers, PO Drawer 9, Woodville 75979

Upshur—Sarah Pruit, 105 Diamond Loch, Gilmer 75644

Upton—Sheri Stephens, PO Box 1110, McCamey 79752

Uvalde—Alberto M. Mireles (interim), 209 N. High St., Uvalde 78801

Val Verde—Cherry Sheedy, PO Box 420487, Del Rio 78842

Van Zandt—Brenda Barnett, PO Box 926, Canton 75103

Victoria—John Haliburton, 2805 N. Navarro, Ste. 300, Victoria 77901

Walker—Raymond Kiser, PO Box 1798, Huntsville 77342

Waller—Chris Barzilla, PO Box 887, Hempstead 77445

Ward—Arlice Wittie, PO Box 905, Monahans 79756

Washington—Willy Dilworth, PO Box 681, Brenham 77834

Webb—Martin Villarreal, 3302 Clark Blvd., Laredo 78043

Wharton—Tylene Gamble, 308 E. Milam, Wharton 77488

Wheeler—Kimberly Morgan, PO Box 1200, Wheeler 79096

Wichita—Edward Trigg, PO Box 5172, Wichita Falls 76307

Wilbarger—Sandy Burkett, PO Box 1519, Vernon 76385

Willacy—Agustin Lopez, Rt. 2, Box 256, Raymondville 78580

Williamson—Alvin Lankford, 625 FM 1460, Georgetown 78726

Wilson—Edward Bridge, 1611 Railroad St., Floresville 78114

Winkler—Connie Carpenter, PO Box 1219, Kermit 79745

Wise—Michael Hand, 400 E. Business 380, Decatur 76234

Wood—Tracy Nichols, PO Box 1706, Quitman 75783

Yoakum—JoAnn Dobson, PO Box 748, Plains 79355

Young—Luke Robbins, PO Box 337, Graham 76450

Zapata—Amada Gonzalez, 2315 Stop 23A, Zapata 78076

Zavala—Yolanda Cervera, 323 W. Zavala, Crystal City 78839 ☆

Wet-Dry Counties

Source: Texas Alcoholic Beverage Commission; www.tabc.state.tx.us//

The sale of alcohol in Texas varies from one county to another. The list below shows the wet-or-dry status of counties in Texas as of July 2011.

An asterisk (*) indicates counties in which the sale of mixed beverages (liquor by the drink) is legal in all or part of the county.

In seven counties marked with a dagger (†), the sale of mixed beverages in restaurants is permitted, but the

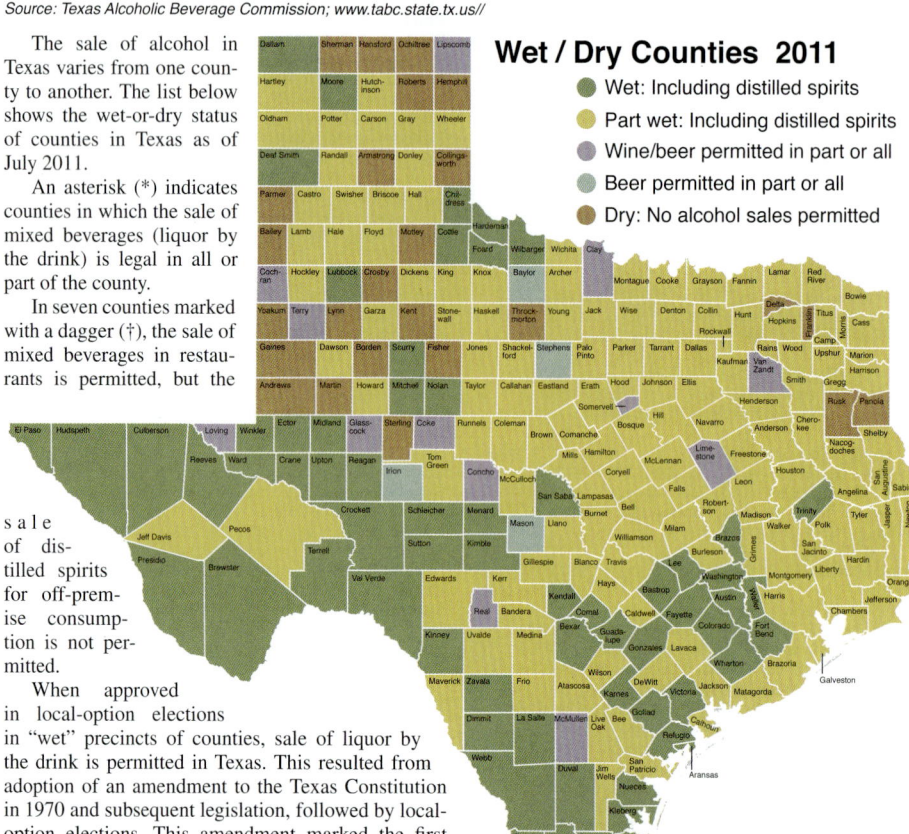

Wet / Dry Counties 2011

- 🟢 Wet: Including distilled spirits
- 🟡 Part wet: Including distilled spirits
- 🟣 Wine/beer permitted in part or all
- 🟩 Beer permitted in part or all
- 🟤 Dry: No alcohol sales permitted

© Texas Almanac 2012 – 2013

sale of distilled spirits for off-premise consumption is not permitted.

When approved in local-option elections in "wet" precincts of counties, sale of liquor by the drink is permitted in Texas. This resulted from adoption of an amendment to the Texas Constitution in 1970 and subsequent legislation, followed by local-option elections. This amendment marked the first time in 50 years that the sale of liquor by the drink was legal in Texas.

In 2011, there were 25 counties wholly dry. In 1986, there were 62 counties wholly dry.

Counties (in part or all) in Which Distilled Spirits Are Legal (212): *Anderson, *†Angelina, *Aransas, Archer, *Atascosa, *Austin, *Bandera, *Bastrop, *Bee, *Bell, *Bexar, *Blanco, *Bosque, *†Bowie, *Brazoria, *Brazos, *Brewster, Briscoe, *Brooks, *Brown, Burleson, *Burnet, *Caldwell, *Calhoun, *Callahan, *Cameron, *Camp, Carson, Cass, Castro, *Chambers, *Cherokee, *Childress, Coleman, *Collin, *Colorado, *Comal, *Comanche, *Cooke, Coryell, *Cottle, Crane, Crockett, Culberson.

Dallam, *Dallas, *Dawson, Deaf Smith, *Denton, *DeWitt, Dickens, *Dimmit, *Donley, *Duval, Eastland, *Ector, Edwards, *Ellis, *El Paso, Erath, Falls, Fannin, *Fayette, *Floyd, *Foard, *Fort Bend, Freestone, *Frio, *Galveston, *Garza, *Gillespie, *Goliad, *Gonzales, Gray, *Grayson, *Gregg, *Grimes, *Guadalupe, *Hale, Hall, Hamilton, *Hardeman, *Hardin, *Harris, Harrison, Hartley, *Haskell, *Hays, *Henderson, *Hidalgo, *Hill, *Hockley, *Hood, Hopkins, *†Houston, *Howard, *Hudspeth, *Hunt, Hutchinson, Jack, *Jackson, *Jasper, *Jeff Davis, *Jefferson, *Jim Hogg, *Jim Wells, *Johnson, *Jones.

*Karnes, *Kaufman, *Kendall, *Kenedy, *Kerr, Kimble, King, *Kinney, *Kleberg, Knox, *Lamar, Lamb, *Lampasas, *La Salle, *Lavaca, *Lee, *Leon, *Liberty, Live Oak, *Llano, *Lubbock, *†Madison, *Marion, *Matagorda, *Maverick, *McCulloch, *McLennan, *Medina, Menard, *Midland, *Milam, Mills, *Mitchell, *Montague, *Montgom-

ery, *Moore, *Morris, Nacogdoches, *Navarro, Newton, *Nolan, *Nueces.

*†Oldham, *Orange, Palo Pinto, *Parker, *Pecos, *Polk, *Potter, *Presidio, *Rains, *Randall, Reagan, Red River, *Reeves, Refugio, *Robertson, *Rockwall, Runnels, Sabine, San Augustine, San Jacinto, *San Patricio, *San Saba, Schleicher, *Scurry, Shackelford, Shelby, *Smith, *Starr, Stonewall, *Sutton, Swisher, *Tarrant, *Taylor, Terrell, Titus, *Tom Green, *Travis, Trinity, *†Tyler, Upshur, Upton, *Uvalde, *Val Verde, *Victoria, *Walker, Waller, Ward, *Washington, *Webb, *Wharton, *Wheeler, *Wichita, *Wilbarger, *Willacy, *Williamson, *Wilson, Winkler, *Wise, *†Wood, Young, *Zapata, *Zavala.

Counties in Which Only Beer Is Legal (4): Baylor, Irion, Mason, Stephens.

Counties in Which Beer and Wine Up to 14 Percent Alcohol by Volume Are Legal (13): Clay, Cochran, Coke, Concho, Glasscock, Limestone, Lipscomb, Loving, McMullen, Real, Somervell, Terry, Van Zandt.

Counties Wholly Dry (25): Andrews, Armstrong, Bailey, Borden, Collingsworth, Crosby, Delta, Fisher, Franklin, Gaines, Hansford, Hemphill, Kent, Lynn, Martin, Motley, Ochiltree, Panola, Parmer, Roberts, Rusk, Sherman, Sterling, Throckmorton, Yoakum. ☆

Texas County and District Officials — Table No. 1

County Seats, County Judges, County Clerks, County Attorneys, County Treasurers, Tax Assessors-Collectors, and Sheriffs.

See Table No. 2 on pages following this table for District Clerks, District Attorneys, and County Commissioners. Judges in county courts at law, as well as probate courts, juvenile/domestic relations courts, county criminal courts, and county criminal courts of appeal, can be found beginning on page 529. The officials listed here are elected by popular vote. An asterisk (*) before a county name marks a county whose county clerk failed to return our questionnaire; the names of officials for those counties are taken from most recent unofficial sources available to us.

County	County Seat	County Judge	County Clerk	County Attorney	County Treasurer	Assessor-Collector	Sheriff
Anderson	Palestine	Robert D. Johnston	Wanda Burke		Kim Turman	Terri Garvey	Greg Taylor
Andrews	Andrews	Richard H. Dolgener	Kenda Heckler	John L. Pool	Office abolished 11-5-1985.	Robin Harper	Sam H. Jones
Angelina	Lufkin	Wes Suiter	Jo Ann Chastain	Ed C. Jones	Deborah D. Huffman	Thelma Sherman	Kent Henson
Aransas	Rockport	C.H. (Burt) Mills Jr.	Peggy L. Friebele	Richard P. Bianchi	Dee A. Oliver	Jeri D. Cox	William (Bill) Mills
Archer	Archer City	Gary W. Beesinger	Karren Winter	R.B. (Burk) Morris	Victoria Lear	Teresa K. Martin	Staci Williams Beesinger
Armstrong	Claude	Hugh Reed	Patricia Sherrill	Randy Sherrod	Sara Messer	Joe Reck	J.R. Walker
Atascosa	Jourdanton	Diana J. Bautista	Diane Gonzales	Lucinda A. Vickers	Laura Pawelek	Barbara Schorsch	Tommy Williams
Austin	Bellville	Carolyn Cerny Bilski	Carrie Gregor	Travis Koehn	Cathleen V. Frank	Janice Kokemor	R. DeWayne Burger
Bailey	Muleshoe	Sherri Harrison	Paula Benton	Jackie Claborn	Shonda Black	Melba Clark	Richard Wills
Bandera	Bandera	Richard A. Evans	Candy Wheeler	John D. Payne	Billie J. Reeves	Mae Vion Meyer	Weldon Tucker
Bastrop	Bastrop	Ronnie McDonald	Rose Pietsch		Laurie Ingram	Linda Harmon	Terry Pickering
Baylor	Seymour	Linda Rogers	Chris Jakubicek	Trish Coleman Byars	Kevin Hostas	Jeanette Holub	Bob Elliott
Bee	Beeville	David Silva	Mirella Escamilla Davis	Michael J. Knight	Office abolished 11-2-1982.	Linda G. Bridge	Carlos Carrizales Jr.
Bell	Belton	Jon H. Burrows	Shelley Coston	Richard J. Miller	Charles Jones	Sharon Long	Dan Smith
Bexar	San Antonio	Nelson W. Wolff	Gerald C. (Gerry) Rickhoff	Office abolished.	Office abolished 11-5-1985.	Sylvia S. Romo	Amadeo Ortiz
Blanco	Johnson City	Bill Guthrie	Karen Newman	Dean C. Myane	Camille Swift	Hollis Boatright	William (Bill) R. Elsbury
Borden	Gail	Ross Sharp	Joyce Herridge		Sharlot Stone	Billy J. Gannaway	Billy J. Gannaway
Bosque	Meridian	Cole Word	Betty Spitzer Outlaw	Natalie Cobb Koehler	Diana Wellborn	Debbie Kibler	Anthony Malott
Bowie	New Boston	Sterling Lacy	Natalie Nichols		Toni Barron	Toni Barron	James Prince
Brazoria	Angleton	E.J. (Joe) King	Joyce Hudman		Brice Feasel	Ro'Vin Garrett	Charles S. Wagner
Brazos	Bryan	E. Duane Peters	Karen McQueen	Rod Anderson	Sharon L. Reynolds	Kristeen (Kristy) Roe	Christopher C. (Chris) Kirk
Brewster	Alpine	Val Clark Beard	Berta Rios-Martinez	Steve Houston	Laura Taylor Davis	Betty Jo Rooney	Ronny D. Dodson
*Briscoe	Silverton	Wayne Nance	Bena Hester	Emily Roy	Carol Ofenstein	Jon Etta Ziegler	Gene Smith
*Brooks	Falfurrias	Raul M. Ramirez	Frutoso (Pepe) Garza	Homer Mora	Mary Jo Brannon	Rey Rodriguez	Rey Rodriguez
Brown	Brownwood	E. Ray West III	Sharon Ferguson	Shane Britton	Horacio Villarreal III	Cheryl Nelson	Bobby R. Grubbs
Burleson	Caldwell	Mike Sutherland	Anna L. Schielack	Joseph J. Skrivanek III	Ann Krpoun	Curtis Doss	Alfred Dale Stroud
Burnet	Burnet	Donna Klaeger	Janet F. Parker	Eduardo (Eddie) Arredondo	Beth Andrews Bills	Sherri Frazier	W.T. Smith
Caldwell	Lockhart	Tom Bonn	Carol Holcomb		Karrie Crownover		
Calhoun	Port Lavaca	Michael J. Pfeifer	Anita Fricke		Lori D. Rangel-Pompa	Mary Vicky Gonzales	Daniel C. Law
Callahan	Baird	Roger Corn	Donna Bell	Shane Deel	Rhonda Sikes Kokena	Gloria Ann Ochoa	Burnard B. Browning
Cameron	Brownsville	Carlos H. Cascos	Joe G. Rivera		Dianne Gunter	Tammy T. Walker	John Windham
Camp	Pittsburg	Thomas Cravey	Elaine Young	Angela L. Hammonds	David A. Betancourt	Antonio Yzaguirre Jr.	Omar Lucio
Carson	Panhandle	Lewis Powers	Celeste Bichsel	Scott Sherwood	Judy Croley	Gale Burns	Alan D. McCandless
Cass	Linden	Charles L. McMichael	Jannis Mitchell		Denise Salzbrenner	Jackie Moore	Tam Terry
Castro	Dimmitt	William F. Sava	JoAnna Blanco	James R. Horton	Donna Early	Becky Watson	James D. (Troop) Estes
Chambers	Anahuac	Jimmy Sylvia	Heather H. Hawthorne	Scott Peal	Kristen M. Yorton	Pamala Rickert	Salvadore (Sal) Rivera Jr.
					Tony Sims	Margie J. Henry	Joe LaRive

County	County Seat	County Judge	County Clerk	County Attorney	County Treasurer	Assessor-Collector	Sheriff
Cherokee	Rusk	Chris Davis	Laverne Lusk	Craig D. Caldwell	Patsy J. Lassiter	Linda Little	James E. Campbell
Childress	Childress	Jay Mayden	Zona Prince	Greg Buckley	Jeanie Thomas	Kathy Dobbs	Michael Pigg
Clay	Henrietta	Kenneth Liggett	Sasha Kelton	Seth Slagle	Debra Alexander	Linda Overstreet Sellers	K.R. (Kenny) Lemons Jr.
Cochran	Morton	James St. Clair	Rita Tyson	J.C. Adams Jr.	Doris Sealy	Linda Huckabee	R. Wallace Stalcup
Coke	Robert Lee	Roy Blair	Mary Grim	Nancy Arthur	Hal Spain	Josie Dean	Wayne McCutchen
Coleman	Coleman	Joe D. Watson	Stacey Mendoza	Joe Lee Rose	Kay LeMay	Jamie Trammell	Robert Wade Turner
*Collin	McKinney	Keith Self	Stacey Kemp			Kenneth L. Maun	Terry G. Box
Collingsworth	Wellington	John A. James	Jackie Johnson	G. Keith Davis	Gina Harris	Generah Manuel	Joe Dale Stewart
Colorado	Columbus	Ty Prause	Darlene Hayek	Ken Sparks	Diane Matus	Mary Jane Poenitzsch	R.H. (Curly) Wied
*Comal	New Braunfels	Sherman Krause	Joy Streater		Renee Couch	Cathy Talcott	James R. (Bob) Holder
Comanche	Comanche	James R. (Bob) Arthur	Ruby Lesley	Craig Willingham	Sue Brown	Gay Horton Green	Jeff D. Lambert
Concho	Paint Rock	Allen Amos	Barbara K. Hoffman	Bill Campbell	Shawn L. Walston	Richard G. Doane	Richard G. Doane
Cooke	Gainesville	John O. Roane	Rebecca Lawson	Tanya S. Davis	Judy Hunter	Billie Jean Knight	Michael E. Compton
Coryell	Gatesville	John E. Firth	Barbara Simpson	Brandon Belt	Donna Medford	Justin Carothers	Johnny Burks
Cottle	Paducah	D.N. Gregory Jr.	Jan Irons	John H. Richards	Kathy Biddy	Nakia Hargrave	Kenneth A. Burns
Crane	Crane	John Farmer	Judy Crawford	Susan Loyless	Cristy Tarin	Rebecca Gonzales	Robert DeLeon
Crockett	Ozona	Fred Deaton	Debbi Puckett	Jody K. Upham	Burl J. Myers	Rhonda Shaw	Roy Glenn Sutton
Crosby	Crosbyton	David Wigley	Linda S. Jones	C. Michael Ward	Debra Riley	Anna R. Rodriguez	David E. Barker
Culberson	Van Horn	Carlos G. Urias	Linda McDonald	Stephen L. Mitchell	Susana R. Hinojos	Amalia Y. Hernandez	Oscar E. Carrillo
Dallam	Dalhart	David D. Field	Terri Banks	Jon King	Wes Ritchey	Kay Howell	Bruce Scott
Dallas	Dallas	Clay Jenkins	John F. Warren	Joe Wells	Joe Wells	John R. Ames	Lupe Valdez
Dawson	Lamesa	Allen Wells	Gloria Vera	Steven B. Payson	Julie Frizzell	Diane Hogg	Kent Parchman
Deaf Smith	Hereford	Tom Simons	David Ruland		Paula B. Price	Teresa Garth	Brent Harrison
Delta	Cooper	Herbert Brookshire	Jane Jones	Edgar J. Garrett	Bonnie Hobbs	Dawn Stewart	Gerald W. Teague
*Denton	Denton	Mary Horn	Cynthia Mitchell	Cindy Yeatts Brown	Cindy Yeatts Brown	Steve Mossman	Benny Parkey
DeWitt	Cuero	Daryl L. Fowler	Natalie Carson	Raymond H. Reese	Peggy Ledbetter	Susie Dreyer	Joe C. (Jode) Zavesky
Dickens	Dickens	Lesa Arnold	Winona Humphreys	Trey Poage	Sandy Vickrey	Sherry Hill	Jimmie Land
*Dimmit	Carrizo Springs	Francisco G. Ponce	Mario Z. Garcia	Daniel M. Gonzalez	Estanislado Z. Martinez	Melinda Vega Campos	Joel Gonzalez
Donley	Clarendon	Jack Hall	Fay Vargas		Wanda Smith	Linda Crump	Charles (Butch) Blackburn
Duval	San Diego	Abel Aragon	Elodia M. Garza	Ricardo (Rocky) O. Carrillo	Roberto Elizondo	Carlos J. Montemayor Jr.	Romeo R. Ramirez
Eastland	Eastland	Rex Fields	Cathy Jentho		Christina Dodrill	Sandra Cagle	Wayne Bradford
Ector	Odessa	Susan M. Redford	Linda Haney	Cindy Weir-Nutter	Carolyn Sue Bowen	Barbara Horn	Mark Donaldson
Edwards	Rocksprings	Souli Asa Shanklin	Sherri Gaither	Allen Ray Moody	Lupe Sifuentes-Enriquez	Lonna Trahan	Donald G. Letsinger
*Ellis	Waxahachie	Carol Bush	Cindy Polley	Patrick Wilson	Cheryl Chambers	John Bridges	Johnny Brown
El Paso	El Paso	Veronica Escobar	Delia Briones	Jo Anne Bernal	Edward A. Dion	Victor A. Flores	Richard D. Wiles
Erath	Stephenville	Tab Thompson	Gwinda Jones	Lisa Pence	Donna Kelly	Jennifer Carey	Tommy Bryant
Falls	Marlin	R. Steven Sharp	Linda Watkins	Jody Gilliam-Morris	Sandy Hodges	Bryant Hinson	Ben Kirk
Fannin	Bonham	Creta L. Carter II	Tammy Biggar	Richard Glaser	Mike Towery	Gail Young	Donnie Foster
Fayette	La Grange	Edward F. Janecka	Julie Karstedt	Peggy S. Supak	Office abolished 11-3-87.	Carol Johnson	Keith K. Korenek
Fisher	Roby	Marshal J. Bennett	Pat Thomson	Rudy V. Hamric	Kathy Davenport	Jonnye Lu Gibson	J.A. Robinson
Floyd	Floydada	Penny Golightly	Ginger Morgan	Jo Elliott		Delia G. Suarez	Paul Raissez
Foard	Crowell	Mark Christopher	Patricia (Pat) Aydelott	Daryl Halencak	Esther Kajs	Jo Ann Vecera	Mike Brown
Fort Bend	Richmond	Robert E. Hebert	Dianne Wilson	Roy L. Cordes Jr.	Jeff Council	Patsy Schultz	Milton Wright
Franklin	Mount Vernon	Paul Lovier	Betty Crane	Will Ramsay	Betty Sue Allen	Sue Ann Harper	Paul B. Fletcher Jr.

County	County Seat	County Judge	County Clerk	County Attorney	County Treasurer	Assessor-Collector	Sheriff
Freestone	Fairfield	Linda K. Grant	Linda Jarvis	Chris Martin	Debra Kay Barger	Lisa Foree	Ralph E. Billings
*Frio	Pearsall	Carlos A. Garcia	Angie Tullis	Hector M. Lozano	Anna Luna Hernández	Anna Alaniz	Lionel G. Treviño
Gaines	Seminole	Lance T. Celander	Vicki Phillips	Joe H. Nagy Jr.	Michael Lord	Susan Shaw	Jon Key
*Galveston	Galveston	Mark Henry	Dwight Sullivan	Harvey Bazaman	Kevin C. Walsh	Cheryl E. Johnson	Freddie L. Poor
Garza	Post	John Lee Norman	Jim Plummer	Mike Munk	Ruth Ann Young	Judy M. Bush	Cliff Laws
Gillespie	Fredericksburg	Mark Stroeher	Mary Lynn Rusche	Tamara Y.S. Keener	Laura Lundquist	Marissa Weinheimer	Buddy Mills
Glasscock	Garden City	Kim Halfmann	Rebecca E. Batla	Hardy L. Wilkerson	Alan J. Dierschke	Nancy Hillger	Keith Burnett
Goliad	Goliad	David Bowman	Mary Ellen Flores	Rob Baiamonte	Daphne Buelter	Anna M. Lopez	Kirby Brumby
Gonzales	Gonzales	David Bird	Eva Lee Riedel	Paul Watkins	Sheryl Barborak	Norma Jean DuBose	Glen A. Sachtleben
Gray	Pampa	Richard Peet	Susan Winborne	Joshua Seabourn	Scott Hahn	Gaye Whitehead	Don Copeland
Grayson	Sherman	Drue Bynum	Wilma Blackshear Bush		Trent Bass	John W. Ramsey	J. Keith Gary
*Gregg	Longview	Bill Stoudt	Connie J. Wade		Office abolished 1-1-88.	William Kirk Shields	Maxey Cerliano
Grimes	Anderson	Betty Shiflett	David Pasket	Jon C. Fultz	Janice Trant	Connie Perry	Donald G. Sowell
Guadalupe	Seguin	Mike Wiggins	Teresa Kiel	Elizabeth Murray-Kolb	Linda Douglass	Tavie Murphy	Arnold S. Zwicke
Hale	Plainview	Bill A. Coleman	Latrice Kemp	James (Jim) Tirey	Ida A. Tyler	Kemp Hinch	David B. Mull
*Hall	Memphis	Ray Powell	Raye Bailey	John M. Deaver II	Janet Bridges	Maribel C. Gonzales	Timothy K. Wiginton
Hamilton	Hamilton	Randy V. Mills	Debbie Rudolph	Mark C. Henkes	Debbie Eoff	Terry Payne Short	Gregg Bewley
Hansford	Spearman	Benny D. Wilson	Kim V. Vera	John L. Hutchison	Wanda Wagner	Linda Cummings	Gary Evans
Hardeman	Quanah	Ronald Ingram	Ellen London	Stanley R. Watson	Mary Ann Naylor	Darlene Gamble	Charles Mance Nelson
Hardin	Kountze	Billy Caraway	Glenda Alston	Rebecca R. Walton	Sharon Overstreet	Shirley Stephens	Ed J. Cain
Harris	Houston	Ed Emmett	Stan Stanart	Vince Ryan	Orlando Sanchez	Don Sumners	Adrian Garcia
Harrison	Marshall	Hugh Taylor	Patsy Cox		Jamie Noland	Julie R. Cox	William T. (Tom) McCool
Hartley	Channing	Ronnie Gordon	Diane Thompson	M. Shane Turner	Dinkie Parman	Franky Scott	Franky Scott
Haskell	Haskell	David C. Davis	Rhonda Moeller	Kristen L. Fouts	Janis McDaniel	Connie Benton	David Halliburton
Hays	San Marcos	Bert Cobb	Liz Q. Gonzalez		Michele Tuttle	Luanne Caraway	Gary Cutler
Hemphill	Canadian	George Briant	Lisa Johnson	Ty M. Sparks	Angie Huff	Debra L. Ford	Gary S. Henderson
*Henderson	Athens	Richard Sanders	Gwen Moffeit	Clint Davis	Michael Bynum	Milburn Chaney	Ray Nutt
Hidalgo	Edinburg	Ramon Garcia	Arturo Guajardo Jr.		Norma G. Garcia	Armando Barrera Jr.	Guadalupe (Lupe) Treviño
Hill	Hillsboro	Justin Lewis	Nicole Tanner	Mark Pratt	Becky Wilkins	Marchel Eubank	Jeffrey T. Lyon
Hockley	Levelland	Larry D. Sprowls	Irene Gonzalez Gumula	Christopher E. Dennis	Denise Bohannon	Christy Clevenger	Kevin Davis
Hood	Granbury	Darrel Cockerham	Mary Burnett	R. Kelton Conner	Kathy Davis	Teresa McCoy	Roger Deeds
Hopkins	Sulphur Springs	Chris Brown	Debbie Shirley	Dusty Hyde Rabe	Treva Watson	Debbie Pogue Jenkins	Charles (Butch) Adams
Houston	Crockett	Lonnie Hunt	Bridget Lamb	Daphne Session	Dina Herrera	Danette Millican	Darrel E. Bobbitt
Howard	Big Spring	Mark J. Barr	Donna Wright	Joshua Hamby	Teresa Thomas	Kathy A. Sayles	Stan Parker
*Hudspeth	Sierra Blanca	Becky Dean-Walker	Abigail Ortega	C.R. (Kit) Bramblett	Jennifer Canaba	Kay Scarbrough	Arvin West
Hunt	Greenville	John L. Horn	Jennifer Lindenzweig	Joel Littlefield	Delores Shelton	Barbara Wiggins	Randy Meeks
Hutchinson	Stinnett	Faye Blanks	Jan Barnes	Michael D. Milner	Kathy Sargent	Mary Lou Henderson	Guy D. Rowh
Irion	Mertzon	Tom Aiken	Cori Manning	Kenneth Greer Jr.	Carolyn Huelster	Joyce Gray	Jimmy E. Martin
Jack	Jacksboro	Mitchell G. Davenport	Shelly Clayton	Michael G. Mask	Kim Gibby	Sharon Robinson	Danny R. Nash
Jackson	Edna	Dennis Simons	Barbara Williams		Mary Horton	Donna Atzenhoffer	A.J. (Andy) Louderback
Jasper	Jasper	Mark Allen	Debbie Newman		Rene Kelley	Bobby Biscamp	Mitchell Newman
Jeff Davis	Fort Davis	George E. Grubb	Sue Blackley	Bart E. Medley	Geen Parrott	Rick McIvor	Rick McIvor
Jefferson	Beaumont	Jeff Branick	Carolyn L. Guidry		Tim Funchess	J. Shane Howard	G. Mitch Woods
Jim Hogg	Hebbronville	Guadalupe S. Canales	Zonia G. Morales	Enrique A. Garza	Gloria G. Benavides	Norma Liza S. Hinojosa	Erasmo (Kiko) Alarcon Jr.

County	County Seat	County Judge	County Clerk	County Attorney	County Treasurer	Assessor-Collector	Sheriff
Jim Wells	Alice	L. Arnoldo Saenz	J.C. Perez III	Jesusa Sánchez-Vera	Becky Dominguez	Mary Lozano	Oscar Lopez
Johnson	Cleburne	Roger Harmon	Becky Williams	Bill Moore	Debbie Rice	Scott Porter	Bob L. Alford
Jones	Anson	Dale Spurgin	LeeAnn Jennings	Chad Cowan	Amber Thompson	Mary Ann Lovelady	Larry Moore
Karnes	Karnes City	Barbara Najrar Shaw	Carol Swize	Robert L. Busselman	Vida Swierc Malone	Ann Franke	David A. Jalufka
Kaufman	Kaufman	James Bruce Wood Sr.	Laura Hughes		Johnny Countryman	Richard (Dick) Murphy	David A. Byrnes
*Kendall	Boerne	Gaylan L. Schroeder	Darlene Herrin	Don Allee	Sheryl D'Spain	James A. Hudson Jr.	Roger Duncan
Kenedy	Sarita	Louis E. Turcotte III	Veronica Vela	Jaime E. Tijerina	Cynthia M. Salinas	Eleuteria (Susie) Gonzalez	Ramon Salinas III
Kent	Jayton	Jim White	Richard Craig Harrison	Howard Freemyer	Margaret Linda McCurry	William D. (Billy) Scogin	William D. (Billy) Scogin
Kerr	Kerrville	Pat Tinley	Jannett Pieper	Rob Henneke	Mindy Williams	Diane Bolin	Wm. R. (Rusty) Hierholzer
Kimble	Junction	Andrew S. Murr	Haydee Torres	Allen J. Ahlschwede	Jolene Williams	Hilario Cantu	Hilario Cantu
King	Guthrie	Duane Daniel	Jammye D. Timmons	Marshall Capps	Traci Butler	Sadie Spitzer	Gilbert Lee (Cotton) Elliott
*Kinney	Brackettville	Tim Ward	Dora Elia Sandoval	Robert Adams	Diane Gutierrez	Martha Peña Padron	Leland K. Burgess
*Kleberg	Kingsville	Juan Escobar	Leo H. Alarcon	Delma Rios-Salazar	Priscilla Alaniz Cantu	Melissa Treviño De La Garza	Edward Mata Sr.
Knox	Benjamin	Travis Floyd	Annette Offutt	Megan Suarez	Rosie Ake	Mitzi Welch	Dean W. Homstad
Lamar	Paris	Maurice C. Superville Jr.	Kathy Marlowe	Gary Young	Shirley Fults	Haskell Maroney	Billy Joe (B.J.) McCoy
Lamb	Littlefield	James M. DeLoach	Jamee Long	Mark Yarbrough	Janice B. Wells	Brenda Goheen	Gary Maddox
Lampasas	Lampasas	Wayne L. Boultinghouse	Connie Hartmann	Larry W. Allison	Nelda DeRiso	Linda Crawford	David Whitis
La Salle	Cotulla	Joel Rodriguez Jr.	Margarita A. Esqueda	Elizabeth Martinez	Thelma R. Treviño	Elida A. Linares	Victor S. Villarreal
Lavaca	Hallettsville	Tramer J. Woytek	Elizabeth A. Kouba	John Stuart Fryer	Karen Bludau	Margaret M. Kallus	Micah C. Harmon
Lee	Giddings	Paul Fischer	Sharon Blasig	Martin Placke	Melinda (Lyndy) Krause	Suzanne Kessler	Rodney W. Meyer
Leon	Centerville	Byron Ryder	Christie Wakefield	James R. Witt Jr.	Brandi S. Hill	Louise Wilson	Jerry Wakefield
Liberty	Liberty	Craig McNair	Paulette Williams	Wesley Hinch	Kim Harris	Mark McClelland	Henry Patterson
Limestone	Groesbeck	Daniel Burkeen	Peggy Beck	William Roy DeFriend	Carol Bostain	Charlene Black	Dennis D. Wilson
Lipscomb	Lipscomb	Willis V. Smith	Kim Blau	Matthew D. Bartosiewicz	Diana Schoenhals	Kathy Fry	James Robertson
Live Oak	George West	Jim Huff	Karen Irving	Gene Chapline	Nancy Coquat	Virginia Horton	Larry R. Busby
Llano	Llano	Wayne Brascom	Bette Sue Hoy	Cheryll Mabray	Sandra Overstreet	Dexter Sagebiel	William Blackburn
Loving	Mentone	Skeet Jones	Elizabeth Jones	Roddy Harrison	Joni Lindsay	Billy Burt Hopper	Billy Burt Hopper
Lubbock	Lubbock	Thomas V. Head	Kelly J. Pinion		Sharon Gossett	Ronnie Keister	Kelly Rowe
Lynn	Tahoka	H.G. Franklin	Susan Tipton	Donnis M. Scott	Pam Miller	Sherry Pearce	Jerry Dee Franklin
Madison	Madisonville	Arthur M. Henson	Charlotte Barrett		Judy Weathers	Beverly Plumlee	Travis Neeley
Marion	Jefferson	Phil A. Parker	Vickie Smith	William K. Gleason	Terrie S. Neuville	Karen Jones	Bill McCay
Martin	Stanton	Charles T. (Corky) Blocker	Susie Graham	James L. McGilvray	Cynthia O'Donnell	Kathy Hull	John Woodward II
Mason	Mason	Jerry M. Bearden	Pam Beam	Shain V.H. Chapman	Polly McMillan	James (Buster) Nixon	James (Buster) Nixon
Matagorda	Bay City	Nate McDonald	Janet Hickl	Jill Cornelius	Amy K. Perez	Cristyn Hallmark	Gary Mathis
*Maverick	Eagle Pass	David R. Saucedo	Sara Montemayor	Ricardo Ramos	Manuel Reyes Jr.	Isamari Villarreal	Tomas S. Herrera
McCulloch	Brady	Danny Neal	Tina A. Smith	Mark Marshall	Donna Robinett	Silvia B. Campos	Earl Howell
McLennan	Waco	Jim Lewis	J.A. (Andy) Harwell		Danny Volck	A.F. (Buddy) Skeen	Larry Lynch
McMullen	Tilden	James E. Teal	Dorairene Garza	Melaine Martin	Judy Wyatt	Angel Bostwick	Bruce Thomas
Medina	Hondo	James E. Barden	Lisa J. Wernette	Kim Havel	Cynthia Alles Ivy	Loraine Neuman	Randy R. Brown
Menard	Menard	Richard Cordes	Polly Reeves	Ben Neel	Robert Bean	Tim Powell	Buck Miller
Midland	Midland	Michael R. Bradford	Cheryl Becker	Russell Malm	Mitzi Wohleking	Kathy Reeves	Gary Painter
*Milam	Cameron	Dave Barkemeyer	Barbara Vansa	Kerry Spears	Linda Acosta	Kollette Morgan	David Greene
Mills	Goldthwaite	Kirkland A. Fulk	Carolyn Foster	Keri Roberts	Terrena Busby	Douglas Storey	Douglas Storey
Mitchell	Colorado City	Ray Mayo	Debby Carlock	Ty Wood	Jennifer Rivera	Faye Lee	Patrick Toombs

County	County Seat	County Judge	County Clerk	County Attorney	County Treasurer	Assessor-Collector	Sheriff
Montague	Montague	Tommie Sappington	Glenda Henson	Ron Walker	Linda McGaughey	Sydney Nowell	Paul Cunningham
*Montgomery	Conroe	Alan B. Sadler	Mark Turnbull	David Walker	Martha Gustavsen	J.R. Moore Jr.	Tommy Gage
Moore	Dumas	J.D. (Rowdy) Rhoades	Brenda McKanna	Scott Higginbotham	Pam Cox	Nikki McDonald	J.E. (Bo) DeArmond
Morris	Daingerfield	Lynda Munkres	Vicki Camp Falls	J. Stephen Cowan	Nita Beth Traylor	Kim Thomasson	Jack. D. Martin
*Motley	Matador	James B. (Jim) Meador	Kate E. Hurt	Tom Edwards	Eva Barkley	Jo Elaine Hart	Chris O. Spence
Nacogdoches	Nacogdoches	Joe English	Carol Wilson	John Fleming	Denise Baublet	Janie Weatherly	Thomas Kerss
Navarro	Corsicana	H.M. Davenport Jr.	Sherry Dowd		Frank Hull	Russell P. Hudson	Leslie Cotten
*Newton	Newton	Truman Dougharty	Mary Cobb		Karen Fuller Pousson	Melissa J. Burks	Joe A. Walker
*Nolan	Sweetwater	Tim D. Fambrough	Patricia (Pat) McGowan	Lisa W. Peterson	Gayle Biggerstaff	Kathy Bowen	David Warren
*Nueces	Corpus Christi	Samuel L. (Loyd) Neal	Diana T. Barrera	Laura Garza Jimenez	Office abolished 11-3-87.	Ramiro (Ronnie) Canales	Jim Kaelin
Ochiltree	Perryton	Earl J. McKinley	Stacey Brown	David T. Scott	Janet Reynolds	Marsha Townsend	Terry L. Bouchard
Oldham	Vega	Don R. Allred	Becky Groneman	Kent Birdsong	Sherri Johnson	Linda Brown	David T. Medlin
*Orange	Orange	Carl K. Thibodeaux	Karen Jo Vance	John D. Kimbrough	Christy Khoury	Lynda Gunstream	Keith Merritt
Palo Pinto	Palo Pinto	David C. Nicklas	Janette K. Green	Phil Garrett	Tanya Fallin	Linda G. Tuggle	Ira Mercer
Panola	Carthage	David L. Anderson	Clara Jones		Gloria Portman	Margaret Dyer	Jack Ellett
Parker	Weatherford	Mark Riley	Jeane Brunson	John Forrest	Jim Thorp	Margorie King	Larry Fowler
Parmer	Farwell	Trey Ellis	Colleen Stover	Jeff Actkinson	Altha Herington	Bobbie Pierson	Randy Geries
Pecos	Fort Stockton	Joe Shuster	Trish King	Ori T. White	Barry McCallister	Santa Acosta	Cliff Harris
Polk	Livingston	John P. Thompson	Schelana Walker		Nola Reneau	Marion A. (Bid) Smith	Kenneth Hammack
Potter	Amarillo	Arthur Ware	Julie Smith	C. Scott Brumley	Leann Renee Jennings	Robert Miller	Brian Thomas
Presidio	Marfa	Paul Hunt	Virginia Pallarez	John Fowlkes	Mary Lane Williams	Norma Arroyo	Danny C. Dominguez
Rains	Emory	Wayne Wolfe	Linda Wallace	Robert F. Vititow	Teresa Northcutt	David Traylor	David Traylor
Randall	Canyon	Ernie Houdashell	Renee Calhoun		Glenna Canada	Dianna Sharon Hollingsworth	Joel W. Richardson
Reagan	Big Lake	Larry Isom	Terri Pullig	J. Russell Ash	Nancy Ratliff	Cynthia Aguilar	Jeff N. Garner
Real	Leakey	Garry A. Merritt	Bella A. Rubio	Bobby Jack Rushing	Vicky Cantrell	Donna Brice	James Earl Brice
Red River	Clarksville	Morris Harville	Lorie Moose Baird	Val J. Varley	Kristy Gray	Tonya R. Martin	Robert Bridges
Reeves	Pecos	Won Joo Bang	Dianne O. Florez	Alva E. Alvarez	Linda Clark	Rosemary Chabarria	Arnulfo (Andy) Gomez
Refugio	Refugio	Rene Mascorro	Ida Ramirez	Robert P. McGuill	Louise Null Aduddell	Ida M. Turner	Robert Bolcik
*Roberts	Miami	Vernon H. Cook	Toni Rankin	Leslie Standerfer	Billie J. Lunsford	DeAnn Williams	Dana Miller
*Robertson	Franklin	Jan Roe	Kathryn N. Brimhall	John C. Paschall	Mindy Turner	Carol D. Bielamowicz	Gerald Yezak
Rockwall	Rockwall	Jerry Hogan	Shelli Miller	David Peek	David Peek	Barbara Barber	Harold Eavenson
Runnels	Ballinger	Barry Hilliard	Elesa Ocker	Stuart Holden	Ann Strube	Robin M. Burgess	William A. Baird
Rusk	Henderson	Joel B. Hale	Joyce Lewis-Kugle	Micheal E. Jimerson	Karen Dobbs Vaughn	Matt B. Gabriel	Danny R. Pirtle
Sabine	Hemphill	Charles E. Watson	Janice McDaniel	Robert G. Neal Jr.	Tricia Woods Jacks	Martha Stone	Thomas N. Maddox
San Augustine	San Augustine	Samye Johnson	Diana Kovar	Wesley E. Hoyt	Pamela Smith	Regina A. Barthol	David Smith
*San Jacinto	Coldspring	Fritz Faulkner	Angelia Steele		Angie Beard	Betty Davis	James L. Walters
*San Patricio	Sinton	Terry Simpson	Gracie Alaniz-Gonzales	David Aken	Courtenay Dugat	Dalia Sanchez	Leroy Moody
*San Saba	San Saba	Byron Theodosis	Kim Wells	Tim Inman	Gayla Hawkins	Allen Brown	Allen Brown
Schleicher	Eldorado	Charlie Bradley	Peggy Williams	Clint T. Griffin	Karen Henderson	Jeanne Snelson	David R. Doran
*Scurry	Snyder	Rod Waller	Melody Appleton	Michael W. Hartman	Nelda Colvin	Jana Young	Darren Jackson
Shackelford	Albany	Ross Montgomery	Cheri Hawkins	Colton P. Johnson	Tammy Brown	Edward Miller	Edward Miller
Shelby	Center	Rick Campbell	Allison Harbison	Gary W. Rholes	Joan Rodgers	Janie Graves	Newton Johnson Jr.
*Sherman	Stratford	Terri Beth Carter	Gina Jones	Kimberly Allen	Doris Parsons	Valerie McAlister	Jack Haile
Smith	Tyler	Joel Baker	Karen Phillips	Stanley Springerley	Kelli White	Gary Barber	J.B. Smith

County	County Seat	County Judge	County Clerk	County Attorney	County Treasurer	Assessor-Collector	Sheriff
Somervell	Glen Rose	Mike Ford	Candace (Candy) Garrett	Ronald Hankins	Barbara Hudson	Darlene Chambers	Greg Doyle
Starr	Rio Grande City	Eloy Vera	Dennis D. Gonzalez	Victor Canales	Jaime U. Maldonado	Rosalinda Guerra	Rene Fuentes
*Stephens	Breckenridge	Gary L. Fuller	Jackie Ensey	Gary D. Trammel	Sharon Trigg	Terry Simmons Sullivan	Dan R. Young
Sterling	Sterling City	Ralph Sides	Susan Wyatt	William (Bill) Stroman Jr.	Wanda Foster	Joy W. Manning	Timothy A. Sanders
Stonewall	Aspermont	Ronnie Moorhead	Patricia Hoy	Trey Poage	Anya Mullen	Jim B. Ward	William M. (Bill) Mullen
Sutton	Sonora	Carla Garner	Rachel Chavez Duran	David W. Wallace	Janalyn Jones	Deedie McIntire	Joe M. Fincher
Swisher	Tulia	Harold Keeter	Brenda Hudson	J. Michael Criswell	Tricia Speed	Deborah Lemons	Emmett Benavidez
Tarrant	Fort Worth	B. Glen Whitley	Mary Louise Garcia		Office abolished 4-2-83.	Betsy Price	Dee B. Anderson
Taylor	Abilene	Downing A. Bolls Jr.	Larry G. Bevill		Lesa Hart Crosswhite	Janet Dukes	Les D. Bruce
*Terrell	Sanderson	Santiago Flores	Martha Allen	Marsha Monroe	Ana Barron	Clint McDonald	Clint McDonald
Terry	Brownfield	J.D. Wagner	Kim Carter	Ramon Gallegos	Bobbye Jo Floyd	Rexann Turrentine	Larry Gilbreath
Throckmorton	Throckmorton	Trey Carrington	Mary Susie Walraven	Jeff Mathiews	Brenda Rankin	John V. Riley	John V. Riley
Titus	Mount Pleasant	Brian Lee	Dianne Norris	John M. Cobern	Sheryl Preddy	Judy Cook	Tim Ingram
Tom Green	San Angelo	Michael D. Brown	Elizabeth McGill	Chris Taylor	Dianna Spieker	Cindy Jetton	Joe B. Hunt
*Travis	Austin	Samuel T. Biscoe	Dana DeBeauvoir	David Escamilla	Dolores Ortega-Carter	Nelda Wells Spears	Greg Hamilton
Trinity	Groveton	Doug Page	Diane McCrory	Joe Warner Bell	Jo Bitner-Bartee	Lindy Warren	Ralph Montemayor
*Tyler	Woodville	Jacques L. Blanchette	Donece Gregory		Sharon Fuller	Lynette Cruse	David Hennigan
Upshur	Gilmer	Dean Fowler	Brandy Lee		Myra Harris	Micheal L. Smith	Anthony Betterton
Upton	Rankin	Bill Eyler	LaWanda McMurray	Melanie Spratt-Anderson	Sharon Harper	Dan W. Brown	Dan W. Brown
Uvalde	Uvalde	William R. Mitchell	Ramona Esquivel Hobbs	John P. Dodson	Joni Deorsam	Margarita (Maggie) Del Toro	Charles Mendeke
Val Verde	Del Rio	Laura Allen	Generosa Gracia-Ramon	Ana Markowski-Smith	Morris L. Taylor	Beatri I. (Bea) Muñoz	Joe Frank Martinez
Van Zandt	Canton	Rhita Koches	Charlotte Bledsoe		Teri Pruitt	J.J. Minyard	R.P. (Pat) Burnett Jr.
Victoria	Victoria	Donald R. Pozzi	Robert S. Cortez		Sean K. Kennedy	Rena Scherer	T. Michael O'Connor
*Walker	Huntsville	R.D. (Danny) Pierce	Kari French		Sharon Duke	Diana McRae	Clint McRae
Waller	Hempstead	Glenn Beckendorff	Debbie Hollan	Hal Upchurch	Susan Winfree	Ellen C. Shelburne	R. Glenn Smith
Ward	Monahans	Greg M. Holly	Natrell Cain	Julie Renken	Teresa Perry-Stoner	Vicki Heflin	Mikel Strickland
Washington	Brenham	John Brieden	Beth A. Rothermel	Anna L. Cavazos Ramirez	Peggy Kramer	Dot Borchgardt	J.W. Jankowski
*Webb	Laredo	Danny Valdez	Margie Ramirez Ibarra	George A. (Trey) Maffett III	Delia Perales	Patricia Barrera	Martin Cuellar
Wharton	Wharton	Phillip S. Spenrath	Sandra K. Sanders	Misty L. Walker	Donna Thornton	Patrick L. Kubala	Jess Howell
Wheeler	Wheeler	Jerry Dan Hefley	Margaret Dorman		Nancy Emmert	Lewis Scott Porter	Joel Finsterwald
Wichita	Wichita Falls	Woodrow (Woody) Gossom Jr.	Lori Bohannon		Robert J. (Bob) Hampton	Lou H. Murdock	David Duke
Wilbarger	Vernon	Greg Tyra	Jana Kennon	Michael Baskerville	Joann Carter	Chris Quisenberry	Larry Lee
*Willacy	Raymondville	John Gonzales	Terry Flores	Bernard Ammerman	Ruben Cavazos	Elizabeth Barnhard	Larry G. Spence
Williamson	Georgetown	Dan A. Gattis	Nancy E. Rister	Jana Duty	Vivian Wood	Deborah Hunt	James R. Wilson
Wilson	Floresville	Marvin C. Quinney	Eva S. Martinez	Russell H. Wilson	Jan Hartl	Anna D. Gonzales	Joe D. Tackitt Jr.
Winkler	Kermit	Bonnie Leck	Shethelia Reed	Scott M. Tidwell	Eulonda Everest	Patti Franks	Robert L. Roberts Jr.
Wise	Decatur	Bill McElhaney	Sherry Parker-Lemon	James Stainton	Katherine Hudson	Monte Shaw	David Walker
Wood	Quitman	Bryan Jeanes	Kelley Price		Becky Burford	Carol Taylor	Bill Wansley
*Yoakum	Plains	Jim Barron	Deborah L. Rushing		Barbara Wright	Jan Parrish	Don Corzine
Young	Graham	John C. Bullock	Debra J. Taylor	Louis Dayne Miller	Ann Daily	Nancy Thomas	Bryan Walls
Zapata	Zapata	Joe Rathmell	Mary J. Villarreal-Bonoan	Said Alfonso Figueroa	Romeo Salinas	Luis Lauro Gonzalez	Sigifredo Gonzalez Jr.
Zavala	Crystal City	Joe Luna	Oralia G. Treviño		Janie Z. Rodriguez	Adriana Mata	Eusevio E. Salinas Jr.

Texas County and District Officials — Table No. 2

District Clerks, District Attorneys, and County Commissioners

See Table No. 1 on preceding pages for County Seats, County Judges, County Clerks, County Attorneys, County Treasurers, Tax Assessors-Collectors, and Sheriffs. Judges in county courts at law, as well as probate courts, juvenile/domestic relations courts, county criminal courts, and county criminal courts of appeal, can be found on page 529. An asterisk (*) before a county name marks a county whose county clerk failed to return our questionnaire; the names of officials for those counties are taken from the most recent unofficial sources available to us. If more than one district attorney is listed for a county, the district court number is listed. If no district attorney is listed, the county attorney, whose name is listed in Table No. 1, assumes the duties of that office.

County	District Clerk	District Attorney	Comm. Precinct 1	Comm. Precinct 2	Comm. Precinct 3	Comm. Precinct 4
Anderson	Janice Staples	Douglas E. Lowe	Joe W. Chaffin	Rashad Q. Mims	Kenneth Dickson	Joey Hill
Andrews	Cynthia Jones		Randy Rowe	Brad Young	Hiram Hubert	Jim Waldrop
Angelina	Reba Squyres	Clyde Herrington	Rick Harrison	Kenneth Timmons	Robert Louis Loggins	Scott Cooper
Aransas	Pam Heard	Patrick Flanigan	Jack Chaney	L.E. (Bubba) Casterline Jr.	Charles Smith	Howard Murph
Archer	Judy McLemore	Jack McGaughey	Richard Shelley	Darin Wolf	Pat Martin III	Darryl Lightfoot
Armstrong	Patricia Sherrill	Randall C. Sims	John Britten	Mike Baker	C.M. Bryant	Tom Ferris
Atascosa	Margaret Littleton	Rene M. Peña	Lon Gillespie	William (Bill) Torans	Freddie Ogden	Bill Carroll
Austin	Sue Murphy	Travis J. Koehn	David Ottmer	Robert Wayne (Bobby) Rinn	Randy Reichardt	Douglas King
Bailey	Elaine Parker	Kathryn Gurley	Floyd J. (Butch) Vandiver	C.E. Grant Jr.	Joey Kindle	Juan Chavez
Bandera	Tammy Kneuper	E. Bruce Curry	Bruce H. Eliker	Robert A. Harris	Richard Keese	Doug King
Bastrop	Sarah Loucks	Bryan Goertz	William M. Piña	Clara Beckett	John Klaus	Lee Dildy
Baylor	Chris Jakubicek	William H. Heatly	Travis Clark	John E. Nelson	Charles R. (Chuck) Morris	Jim Stout
Bee	Zenaida Silva	Martha Warner	Carlos Salazar Jr.	Dennis DeWitt	Eloy Rodriguez	Ken Haggard
Bell	Sheila Norman	Henry L. Garza	Richard Cortese	Tim Brown	Eddy Lange	John Fisher
Bexar	Donna Kay McKinney	Susan D. Reed	Sergio (Chico) Rodriguez	Paul Elizondo	Kevin A. Wolff	Tommy Adkisson
Blanco	Debby Elsbury	Sam Oatman	John F. Wood	James Sultemeier	Chris Liesmann	Paul Granberg
*Borden	Joyce Herridge	Dana W. Cooley	Monte Smith	Randy L. Adcock	Ernest Reyes	Joe T. Belew
Bosque	Juanita Miller	B.J. Shepherd	Kent Harbison	Durwood Koonsman	Gary J. Arnold	Jimmy Schmidt
Bowie	Billy Fox	Jerry Rochelle	Jack Stone	John Addington	Kelly Blackburn	Pat McCoy
Brazoria	Rhonda Cross Barchak	Jeri Yenne	Donald W. (Dude) Payne	L.M. (Matt) Sebesta	Stacy L. Adams	L.L. (Larry) Stanley
Brazos	Marc Hamlin	William R. (Bill) Turner	Lloyd Wassermann	Sammy Catalena	G. Kenny Mallard Jr.	Irma Cauley
Brewster	JoAnn Salgado	Jesse Gonzales Jr.	Asa (Cookie) Stone	Kathy Killingsworth	Ruben Ortega	Matilde Pallanez
*Briscoe	Bena Hester	Becky B. McPherson	Jimmy Burson	Dale Smith	Larry Comer	John Burson
*Brooks	Noe Guerra	Armando Berrera	Gloria Garza	Luis Arevalo	Carlos Villarreal	Jose A. (Tony) Martinez
Brown	Jan Brown	Michael Brandon Murray	Steve Adams	Joel Kelton	Richard Gist	Larry Traweek
Burleson	Joy Brymer	William E. (Bill) Parham	Frank L. Kristof	Keith Schroeder	David Hildebrand	John B. Landolt Jr.
Burnet	Casie Wills	Sam Oatman	Bill Neve	Russell Graeter	Ronny Hibler	Joe Don Dockery
Caldwell	Tina Morgan	Richard R. (Trey) Hicks III	John P. Cyrier	Fred F. Buchholtz	Ernest Madrigal	Joe Ivan Roland
Calhoun	Pamela Martin Hartgrove	Dan W. Heard	Roger C. Galvan	Vernon Lyssy	Neil E. Fritsch	Kenneth W. Finster
Callahan	Sharon Owens	Shane Deel	Harold Hicks	Bryan Farmer	Tom Windham	Cliff Kirkham
Cameron	Aurora De La Garza	Armando Villalobos	Sofia L.C. Benavides	Ernie Hernandez	David A. Garza	Dan Sanchez
Camp	Teresa Bockmon	Charles C. Bailey	Bart Townsend	Steve Hudnall	Norman Townsend	Vernon Griffin
Carson	Celeste Bichsel	Luke Inman	Mike Britten	James Martin	Paul Detten	Kevin Howell
Cass	Becky Wilbanks	Clint Allen	Brett Fitts	Danny Joe Shaddix	Paul Cothren	Darrel Godwin
Castro	JoAnna Blanco	James R. Horton	Tom McLain	Tim Elliott	W.A. (Bay) Baldridge	Dan Schmucker

County	District Clerk	District Attorney	Comm. Precinct 1	Comm. Precinct 2	Comm. Precinct 3	Comm. Precinct 4
Chambers	Patti L. Henry	Cheryl S. Lieck	Mark Huddleston	David (Bubba) Abernathy	Gary R. Nelson	Rusty Senac
Cherokee	Janet Gates	Elmer C. Beckworth Jr.	Kelly Traylor	Steven Norton	Katherine Pinotti	Byron Underwood
Childress	Zona Prince	Luke Inman	Denzil Ray	Mark Ross	Lyall Foster	Don Ray Crook
Clay	Dan Slagle	Jack McGaughey	R.L. (Lindy) Choate	Johnny Gee	John McGregor	A.J. Peek
Cochran	Rita Tyson	Gary A. Goff	Donnie B. Simpson	Margaret Allen	Stacey Dunn	Johnny Timmons
Coke	Mary Grim	Stephen Lupton	Troy Gene Montgomery	Wendell Lee	Gaylon L. Pitcock	Bobby Blaylock
Coleman	Margie Mayo	Heath Hemphill	Mark Williams	Rick Beal	Mike Stephenson	Alan Davis
*Collin	Patricia Crigger	Greg Willis	Matt Shaheen	Cheryl Williams	Joe Jaynes	Kathy Ward
Collingsworth	Jackie Johnson	Luke Inman	Dan Langford	Mike Hughs	Eddie Orr	Kirby Campbell
Colorado	Harvey Vornsand	Ken Sparks	Doug Wessels	Darrell Kubesch	Tommy Hahn	Darrell Gertson
*Comal	Katherine H. Faulkner	Jennifer Anne Tharp	Donna Eccleston	Scott Haag	Gregory Parker	Jan Kennady
Comanche	Brenda Dickey	B.J. Shepard	Gary D. (Corky) Underwood	Russell Gillette	Sherman Sides	Jimmy Dale Johnson
Concho	Barbara K. Hoffman	George E. McCrea	Trey Bradshaw	Ralph Willberg	Ernest R. Gomez	Aaron (Sonny) Browning Jr.
Cooke	Susan Hughes	Janice Warder	Gary Hollowell	B.C. Lemons	Alan Smith	Leon Klement
Coryell	Janice M. Gray	David A. Castillo	Jack Wall	Daren Moore	Don Jones	Justin Latham
Cottle	Jan Irons	David W. Hajek	Jimmy W. Sweeney	Vance Thompson	Manuel Cruz Jr.	Marvin Powe
Crane	Judy Crawford	Michael L. Fostel	Tom Brown	Dennis Young	Domingo Escobedo	Roy Hodges
Crockett	Debbi Puckett	Laurie K. English	Frank Tambunga	Pleas Childress III	Randy Branch	Eligio Martinez
Crosby	Karla Tiner	C. Michael Ward	Gary V. Jordan	Frank Mullins	Larry Wampler	Steve Henn
Culberson	Linda McDonald	Jaime Esparza	Cornelio Garibay	Rolando Gomez	Lyndon C. McDonald	Adrian Norman
Dallam	Terri Banks	David M. Green	Glenn Reagan	Corey Crabtree	Don J. Bowers	Floyd French
Dallas	Gary Fitzsimmons	Craig Watkins	Maurine Dickey	Mike Cantrell	John Wiley Price	Elba Garcia
Dawson	Pam Huse	Brian L. Kingston	Ricky Minjarez	Tony Hernandez	Nicky Goode	Foy O'Brien
Deaf Smith	Jean Schumacher Coody	Jim English	Pat Smith	Jerry O'Connor	Mike Brumley	David L. Wagner
Delta	Jane Jones	Martin Braddy	B.V. (Rip) Templeton	David Max Moody	Wayne Poole	Mark Brantley
*Denton	Sherri Adelstein	Paul Johnson	Hugh Coleman	Ron Marchant	Bobbie J. Mitchell	Andrew Eads
DeWitt	Tabeth Gardner	Michael A. Sheppard	Curtis G. Afflerbach	James B. Pilchiek Sr.	John C. Oliver	Donald R. Kuecker
Dickens	Winona Humphreys	Becky B. McPherson	Wayne Smith	Ricky West	Doc Edwards	Sheldon Parsons
*Dimmit	Maricela G. Gonzalez	Roberto Serna	Mike Uriegas	Johnny Gloria	David W. Taylor	Rodrigo (Igo) Jaime
Donley	Fay Vargas	Luke Inman	Mark White	Don Hall	Andy Wheatly	Dan Sawyer
Duval	Richard M. Barton	Heriberto Silva	Alejo C. Garcia	Rene M. Perez	Nestor Garza Jr.	Gilberto Uribe Jr.
Eastland	Carol Ann Brittain	Russell D. Thomason	Wayne Honea	John (Buzzy) Rutledge	T.J. Cummings	Robert Rains
Ector	Janis Morgan	Robert Newton Bland IV	Freddie Gardner	Greg Simmons	Dale Childers	Armando S. Rodriguez
Edwards	Sherri Gaither	Fred Hernandez	Terry Brooks	Lee Sweeten	Clifford Tuttle	Mike Grooms
*Ellis	Melanie P. Reed	Patrick Wilson	Dennis Robinson	Bill Dodson	Heath Sims	Ron Brown
El Paso	Norma Favela	Jaime E. Esparza	Anna Perez	Sergio Lewis	Willie Gandara Jr.	Daniel R. Haggerty
Erath	Wanda Pringle	Jason Cashon	Jim Pack	Herbert Brown	Joe Brown	Scot Jackson
Falls	Christi Trammel	Kathryn (Jodi) Gilliam-Morris	Milton Albright	F.A. Green	Nelson Coker	Ryan Ford
Fannin	Nancy Young	Richard Glaser	Gary Whitlock	Stanley Barker	Dewayne Strickland	Joe Strong
Fayette	Virginia Wied	Peggy S. Supak	John Saunders	Gary Weishuhn	James Kubecka	Tom Muras
Fisher	Tammy Haley	Ann Reed	Gordon Pippin	Billy Henderson	Preston Martin	Scott Feagan
Floyd	Patty Davenport	Becky B. McPherson	Mike Anderson	Lindan Morris	Nathan Johnson	Amado Morales
Foard	Patricia (Pat) Aydelott	Staley Heatly	W.N. Chatfield	Rockne Wisdom	Larry Wright	Edward Crosby
Fort Bend	Annie Rebecca Elliott	John Healey Jr.	Richard Morrison	Grady Prestage	W.A. (Andy) Meyers	James Patterson

County	District Clerk	District Attorney	Comm. Precinct 1	Comm. Precinct 2	Comm. Precinct 3	Comm. Precinct 4
Franklin	Ellen Jaggers	Martin Braddy	Danny Chitsey	Donnie Surratt	Deryl Carr	Sam Young
Freestone	Janet Chappell	Chris Martin	Luke Ward Sr.	Thomas Oakes	Stanley Gregory	Clyde E. Ridge Jr.
*Frio	Ramona B. Rodriguez	Rene M. Peña	Richard T. Hernandez	Richard Graf	Ruben Maldonado	Jose (Pepe) Flores
Gaines	Virginia Stewart	Brian L. Kingston	Danny Yocom	Donald Craig Belt	Blair Tharp	Charlie Lopez
*Galveston	Jason Murray	Jack Roady	Patrick F. Doyle	Kevin O'Brien	Stephen W. Holmes	Kenneth F. Clark
Garza	Jim Plummer	Brian L. Kingston	Gary McDaniel	Charles Morris	Ted Brannon	Jerry Benham
Gillespie	Jan Davis	E. Bruce Curry	Curtis Cameron	William A. Roeder	Calvin Ransleben	Donnie Schuch
Glasscock	Rebecca E. Batla	Hardy L. Wilkerson	Jimmy Strube	Mark L. Halfmann	Gary Jones	Michael Hoch
Goliad	Mary Ellen Flores	Michael A. Sheppard	Julian Flores	Alonza Morales	Jim Kreneck	Ted Long
Gonzales	Sandra Baker	Heather Miller	Kenneth O. (Dell) Whiddon	Donnie R. Brzozowski	Kevin T. LaFleur	Otis S. (Bud) Wuest
Gray	Sandra Burkett	Lynn Switzer	Joe Wheeley	Gary Willoughby	John Mark Baggerman	Jeff Haley
Grayson	Kelly Ashmore	Joseph D. Brown	Johnny Waldrip	David Whitlock	Jackie Crisp	Bart Lawrence
*Gregg	Barbara Duncan	Carl Dorrough	Charles W. Davis	R. Darryl Primo	Gary W. Boyd	John Mathis
Grimes	Gay Wells	Tuck Moody McLain	John Bertling	Randy Krueger	Julian Melchor Jr.	Pam Finke
Guadalupe	Debra Crow	Heather Miller	Roger Baenziger	Kyle Kutscher	Jim O. Wolverton	Judy Cope
Hale	Carla Cannon	Wally Hatch	Harold King	Mario Martinez	Kenny Kernell	Benny Cantwell
*Hall	Raye Bailey	Luke Inman	Milton Beasley	Terry Lindsey	Buddy Logsdon	James Fuston
Hamilton	Leoma Larance	B.J. Shepherd	Jim D. Boatwright	Mark Tafel	Jon Bonner	Dickie Clary
Hansford	Kim V. Vera	Mark Snider	Ira G. (Butch) Reed	David Thomas	Tim Stedje	Danny Henson
Hardeman	Ellen London	Staley Heatly	Johnny Akers	Rodger Tabor	Barry Haynes	Rodney Foster
Hardin	Pam Hartt	David Sheffield	Kenneth Riedinger	Chris Kirkendall	Ken Pelt	Bobby Franklin
Harris	Chris Daniel	Pat Lykos	El Franco Lee	Jack Morman	Steve Radack	Jerry Eversole
Harrison	Melinda Craig	Coke Solomon	Jeffrey L. Thompson	Emma Bennett	James Greer	Galen McBride
Hartley	Diane Thompson	David M. Green	David Vincent	Jim Hill	Jay Kuper	Robert (Butch) Owens
Haskell	Penny Anderson	Mike Fouts	Johnny Scoggins	Tiffen Mayfield	Kenny Thompson	Neal Kreger
Hays	Beverly Crumley	Sherri Tibbe	Debbie Gonzales Ingalsbe	Mark Jones	Will Conley	Ray Whisenant
Hemphill	Lisa Johnson	Lynn Switzer	Joe Schaef	Ed Culver	Mark Meek	Lynard G. Schafer
*Henderson	Jean Godwin	Scott McKee	Joe D. Hall	Wade McKinney	Ronny Lawrence	Ken Geeslin
Hidalgo	Laura L. Hinojosa	Rene A. Guerra	Joel Quintanilla	Hector (Tito) Palacios	Joe M. Flores	Joseph Palacios
Hill	Angelia Orr	Dan V. Dent	Danny Bodeker	Steven Sulak	Larry Wright	Harley Davis
Hockley	Dennis Price	Gary A. Goff	Curtis D. Thrash	Larry R. Carter	J.L. (Whitey) Barnett	Thomas R. Clevenger
Hood	Tonna Trumble Hitt	Robert Christian	Mike Sympson	Richard (Dick) Roan	Leonard Heathington	Steve Berry
Hopkins	Patricia Dorner	Martin Braddy	Beth B. Wisenbaker	Mike Odell	Don Patterson	Danny Evans
Houston	Carolyn Rains	Donna Gordon Kaspar	Roger Dickey	Willie E. Kitchen	Pat Perry	Kennon Kellum
Howard	Colleen Barton	Hardy L. Wilkerson	Emma (Puga) Brown	Donnie Baker	Jimmie Long	John Cline
*Hudspeth	Abigail Ortega	Jaime Esparza	Wayne West	Pati Garcia	Jim Ed Miller	Larry Breton
Hunt	Stacey Landrum	Noble Walker	Kenneth Thornton	Jay Atkins	Larry Middlebrooks	Jim Latham
Hutchinson	Robin Stroud	Mark Snider	Larry Coffman	Jerry D. Hefner	S.T. (Red) Isbell Jr.	Eddie Whittington
Irion	Cori Manning	Stephen Lupton	Wayne E. Smith	Jeff Davidson	John Nanny	Beaver McManus
Jack	Tracie Pippin	Greg Lowery	James Logan	James Brock	James L. Cozart	Terry Ward
Jackson	Sharon Mathis	Robert E. (Bobby) Bell	Wayne Hunt	Wayne Bubela	Johnny E. Belicek	Larry Deyton
Jasper	Linda Ryal	Steve Hollis	Charles Shofner Jr.	Roy Parker	Willie Stark	Vance Moss
Jeff Davis	Sue Blackley	Jesse Gonzales Jr.	Larry Francell	Kathy Bencomo	Curtis Evans	Albert Miller
Jefferson	Lolita Ramos	Tom Maness	Eddie Arnold	Brent Weaver	Michael (Shane) Sinegal	Everette (Bo) Alfred

County	District Clerk	District Attorney	Comm. Precinct 1	Comm. Precinct 2	Comm. Precinct 3	Comm. Precinct 4
Jim Hogg	Zonia G. Morales	Rudolfo Gutierrez	Antonio Flores	Abelardo Alaniz	Sandalio Ruiz	Juan Lino Ramirez
Jim Wells	R. David Guerrero	Armando G. Barrera	Zenaida Sanchez	Ventura Garcia Jr.	Oswaldo (Wally) Alanis	Javier N. Garcia
Johnson	David Lloyd	Dale Hanna	Rick Bailey	John W. Matthews	Jerry D. Stringer	Don Beeson
Jones	Lacey Hansen	Billy John Edwards	James Clawson	Mike Polk	Gaite Taylor	Steve Lollar
Karnes	Robbie Shortner	Stella Saxon	Carl Hummel	Pete Jauer	James Rosales	Tracey Schendel
Kaufman	Rhonda Hughey	Michael E. McLelland	Jerry Rowden	Ray Clark	James (J.C.) Jackson Sr.	Thomas (Tom) S. Manning
*Kendall	Kay Pugh	E. Bruce Curry	Anne Reissig	Gene Miertschin	Darrel L. Lux	Kenneth M. Rusch
Kenedy	Veronica Vela	John T. Hubert	Jose Recio	Roberto Salazar Jr.	Sarita Armstrong-Hixon	Gumecinda Gonzales
Kent	Richard Craig Harrison	Michael Fouts	Roy W. Chisum	Don Long	Tommy Stanaland	Robert Graham
Kerr	Linda Uecker	Amos Barton (198th) / E. Bruce Curry (216th)	H.A. (Buster) Baldwin	Guy R. Overby	Jonathan A. Letz	Bruce Oehler
Kimble	Haydee Torres	Amos Barton	Billy Braswell	Charles McGuire	Wylie Taff	Chad Gipson
King	Jammye D. Timmons	David W. Hajek	Reggie J. Hatfield	Larry Rush	Bobby J. Tidmore	Bob Burkett
*Kinney	Dora Elia Sandoval	Fred Hernandez	Woody Massengale	Joe Montalvo	Dennis Dodson	Pat Melancon
*Kleberg	Melissa Salinas	John T. Hubert	David Rosse	Norma Nelda Alvarez	Roy Cantu	Romeo L. Lomas
Knox	Annette Offutt	David W. Hajek	Johnny McCowan	Charles Griffith	Jimmy Urbanczyk	Johnny Birkenfeld
Lamar	Marvin Ann Patterson	Gary Young	Lawrence Malone	Lonnie Layton	Kevin Jenkins	Keith Mitchell
Lamb	Stephanie Chester	Mark Yarbrough	Rodney Smith	Kent Lewis	Danny Short	Jimmy Young
Lampasas	Terri Cox	Larry W. Allison	Robert L. Vincent Jr.	Alex Wittenburg	Lowell B. Ivey	Jack B. Cox
La Salle	Margarita A. Esqueda	René M. Peña	Chris Hinjojosa III	Ricardo Garza	Rene Benavidez	Raul Ayala
Lavaca	Sherry T. Henke	Heather Miller	Charles A. Netardus	Ronald Berckenhoff	David E. Wagner	Dennis W. Kocian
Lee	Lisa Teinert	Martin Placke	Maurice Pitts Jr.	Douglas Hartfield	Ronnie Bradshaw	Linda Kovar
Leon	Diane Oden Davis	Whitney Thompson Smith	Joey Sullivan	David Ferguson	Mark Ivey	Dean Player
Liberty	Donna Brown	Michael R. (Mike) Little	Todd Fontenot	Charlotte Warner	Melvin Hunt	Norman Brown
Limestone	Carol Sue Jenkins	William Roy DeFriend	John McCarver	William (Pete) Kirven	Morris D. Beaver	Bobby Forrest
Lipscomb	Kim Blau	Lynn Switzer	Juan Cantu	Stanley Born	Scotty Schilling	Phil Ridgway
Live Oak	Lois Shannon	Martha Warner	Richard Lee	Donna K. Mills	Jim Bassett	Emilio Garza
Llano	Joyce Gillow	Sam Oatman	Johnnie B. Heck	Linda Raschke	Thomas E. Duncan	Jerry Don Moss
Loving	Elizabeth Jones	Randall W. Reynolds	Harlan Hopper	Ysidro Renteria	Tom Jones	William (Bill) Wilkinson
Lubbock	Barbara Sucsy	Matthew D. Powell	Bill McCay	Mark E. Heinrich	Gilbert Flores	Patti Jones
Lynn	Sandra Laws	Brian L. Kingston	Keith Wied	Mike Braddock	Don Blair	Danny Martin
Madison	Joyce Batson	Brian Risinger	Ricky Driskell	Phillip Grisham	Tommy Cornelius	Sam Cole
Marion	Janie McCay	William K. Gleason	Bob Higgins	Joe McKnight	C.E. (Cecil) Bourne	Charles W. Treadwell
Martin	Susie Graham	Hardy L. Wilkerson	Jesus Garza	Valentino Sotelo	Bobby Holland	Bryan Cox
Mason	Pam Beam	Amos Barton	Wayne Hofmann	Will Frey	Stanley Toeppich	Eldon Kothmann
Matagorda	Becky Denn	Steven E. Reis	Daniel Pustka	Kent Pollard	James Gibson	David J. Woodson
*Maverick	Irene Rodriguez	Roberto Serna	Eliaz Maldonado	Rudy Heredia	Jose Luis Rosales	Cesar Flores
McCulloch	Michelle Pitcox	Amos Barton	Jim Quinn	Jerry Bratton	J.P. Murray	Brent C. Deeds
McLennan	Karen Matkin	Abel Reyna	Kelly Snell	Lester Gibson	Joe A. Mashek	Ben Perry
McMullen	Dorairene Garza	Martha Warner	Tim Teal	Murray Swaim	Paul Koonce	Maximo G. Quintanilla Jr.
Medina	Cindy Fowler	Daniel J. Kindred	Richard C. Saathoff	Larry Sittre	David Lynch	Jerry Beck
Menard	Polly Reeves	Amos Barton	Boyd Murchison	Butch Aguilar	Ed Keith	Larry Burch
Midland	Ross Bush	Teresa Clingman	Jimmy Smith	Robert R. (Robin) Donnelly	Luis D. Sanchez	Randy Prude
*Milam	Cindy Fechner	Kerry Spears	George Tomek	Kenneth Hollas	C. Dale Jaecks	Jeff Muegge
Mills	Carolyn Foster	Michael Brandon Murray	John Mann	Keith Harper	William Glen Crawford	Jason Williams

County	District Clerk	District Attorney	Comm. Precinct 1	Comm. Precinct 2	Comm. Precinct 3	Comm. Precinct 4
Mitchell	Sharon Hammond	Ann Reed	Randy Anderson	Jerry Strain	Jesse Munoz	Billy H. Preston
Montague	Lesia Darden	Jack McGaughey	Jon Kernek	James Gamblin	Steve Howard	Bob Langford
*Montgomery	Barbara Gladden Adamick	Brett W. Ligon	Mike Meador	Craig Doyal	Ed E. Chance	Ed Rinehart
Moore	Diane Hoefling	David M. Green	J. Daniel Garcia	Len Sheets	Milton Pax	Lynn Cartrite
Morris	Gwen Oney	J. Stephen Cowan	Dennis Allen	Weldon Lilley	Michael Clair	Gary Camp
*Motley	Kate E. Hurt	Becky B. McPherson	Roy G. Stephens	Donnie L. Turner	Franklin Jameson	Russell Alexander
Nacogdoches	Loretta Cammack	Nicole Lostracco	Jerry Don Williamson	Charles Thomson	Jim Elder	Elton Milstead Jr.
Navarro	Joe Hobbs	R. Lowell Thompson	Kit Herrington	Dick Martin	David (Butch) Warren	James Olsen
*Newton	Bree Neill	Robert J. Choate	William L. Fuller	Thomas Gill	Prentiss L. Hopson	Leonard Powell
*Nolan	Patti Neill	Ann Reed	Terry Willman	Terry Locklar	Tommy White	Tony Lara
*Nueces	Patsy Perez	Mark Skurka	Mike Pusley	Joe A. Gonzalez	Oscar O. Ortiz	Joe McComb
Ochiltree	Shawn Bogard	David T. Scott	Duane Pshigoda	Doug Barnes	Richard Burger	Dempsey Malaney
Oldham	Becky Groneman	Kent Birdsong	Quincy Taylor	Clay Crist	Roger Morris III	Billy Don Brown
*Orange	Vickie Edgerly	John D. Kimbrough	David Dubose	Owen Burton	John P. Dubose	Jody Crump
Palo Pinto	Janie Glover	Michael K. Burns	Beth Ray	Louis Ragle	Mike Pierce	Jeff Fryer
Panola	Debra Johnson	Danny Buck Davidson	Ronnie LaGrone	John Gradberg	Hermon E. Reed Jr.	Dale LaGrone
Parker	Sharena Gilliland	Don Schnebly	George Conley	Craig Peacock	John Roth	Dusty Renfro
Parmer	Sandra Warren	Gordon Green	Kirk Frye	James Clayton	Ronald Byrd	Lloyd Bradshaw
Pecos	Gayle Henderson	Jesse Gonzales, Jr. (83rd) Laurie English (112th)	George Riggs	Lupe Dominguez	J.H. (Jay) Kent	Santiago Cantu Jr.
Polk	Kathy E. Clifton	Lee Hon	Robert C. (Bob) Willis	Ronnie Vincent	Milton (Mitt) Purvis	C.T. (Tommy) Overstreet
Potter	Caroline Woodburn	Randall C. Sims	H.R. Kelly	Manuel Perez	Joe Kirkwood	Alphonso S. Vaughn
Presidio	Virginia Pallarez	Jesse Gonzales Jr.	Felipe A. Cordero	Eloy Aranda	Carlos Armendariz	Frank (Buddy) Knight
Rains	Deborah Traylor	Robert Vititow	Patsy Marshall	Mike Willis	Gary Mike Bishop	Sylvia Witt
Randall	Jo Carter	James A. Farren	Robert (Bob) Karrh	Mark Benton	George E. (Skip) Huskey	Buddy DeFord
Reagan	Terri Pullig	Laurie English	Jim O'Bryan	Ron Galloway	Tommy Holt	Thomas Strube
Real	Bella A. Rubio	Daniel J. Kindred	Manuel Rubio	Bryan Shackelford	Gene Buckner	Joe W. Connell Sr.
Red River	Janice Gentry	Val J. Varley	Donnie Gentry	David Barnett	Richard Harvey	John Kocurek
Reeves	Patricia Tarin	Randall W. Reynolds	Rojelio (Roy) Alvarado	Steven Kyle Taylor	Saul F. Herrera	Tony Trujillo
Refugio	Ruby Garcia	Michael A. Sheppard	Ann Lopez	Stanley D. Tuttle	Gary D. Bourland	Rodrigo Bernal
*Roberts	Toni Rankin	Lynn Switzer	Cleve Wheeler	Ken R. Gill	Kelly V. Flowers	James F. Duvall Jr.
*Robertson	Barbara Axtell	John C. Paschall	Keith Petitt	Donald Threadgill	Keith Nickelson	Robert Bielamowicz
Rockwall	Kay McDaniel	Kenda Culpepper	Jerry Wimpee	Lorie Grinnan	Dennis Bailey	David Magness
Runnels	Tammy Burleson	George McCrea	Robert H. (Bobby) Moore	Ronald Presley	James Thurman Self	Richard W. (Ricky) Strube
Rusk	Jean Hodges	Micheal E. Jimerson	W.D. (Bill) Hale	Michael Pepper	Freddy Swann	Harold Howell
Sabine	Tanya Walker	J. Kevin Dutton	Keith C. Clark	Jimmy McDaniel	Doyle Dickerson	Fayne Warner
San Augustine	Jean Steptoe	J. Kevin Dutton	Tommy Hunter	Edward Wilson	Dale Mixon	Rodney Ainsworth
*San Jacinto	Rebecca Capers	Richard Countiss	Laddie McAnally	Donnie Marrs	James (Butch) Moody	Mark Nettuno
San Patricio	Laura Miller	Patrick L. Flanigan	Nina G. Treviño	Fred P. Nardini	Alma V. Moreno	Jim Price Jr.
*San Saba	Kim Wells	Sam Oatman	Otis Judkins	Rickey Lusty	Kenley Kroll	Pat Pool
Schleicher	Peggy Williams	Stephen Lupton	Johnny F. Mayo Jr.	Lynn Meador	Kirk Griffin	Matt Brown
*Scurry	Candace Jones	Dana Cooley	Terry D. Williams	Marianne Randals	Howard Limmer	Chloanne Lindsey
Shackelford	Cheri Hawkins	Billy John Edwards	David Everett	Larry Cauble	Jimmy T. Brooks	Stan West
Shelby	Lori Oliver	Lynda Kay Russell	Roscoe McSwain	Jimmy Lout	Travis Rodgers	Bradley Allen
*Sherman	Gina Jones	David M. Green	Dana Buckles	Randy Williams	Jeff Crippen	Tommy Asher

County	District Clerk	District Attorney	Comm. Precinct 1	Comm. Precinct 2	Comm. Precinct 3	Comm. Precinct 4
Smith	Lois Rogers	D. Matt Bingham III	Jeff Warr	Cary Nix	Terry Phillips	JoAnn Hampton
Somervell	Candace (Candy) Garrett	Dale Hanna	Zach Cummings	John Curtis	Lloyd Wirt	James Barnard
Starr	Eloy R. Garcia	Heriberto Silva	Jaime M. Alvarez	Raul (Roy) Peña Jr.	Eloy Garza	Abel N. Gonzalez Jr.
*Stephens	Christie Coapland	Brenda Gray	Jerry Toland	D.C. (Button) Sikes	Joe F. High	Rickie Ray Carr
Sterling	Susan Wyatt	Stephen Lupton	Terry Wojtek	Edward J. Michulka Jr.	Deborah H. Horwood	Reed Stewart
Stonewall	Patricia Hoy	Michael Fouts	David Hoy	Jan Harris	Billy Kirk Meador	Gary Myers
Sutton	Rachel Chavez Duran	Laurie English	Miguel (Mike) Villanueva	John Wade	Milton Cavaness	Fred Perez
Swisher	Brenda Hudson	J. Michael Criswell	Lloyd Rahlfs	Joe Bob Thompson	Harvey N. Foster	Tim Reed
Tarrant	Thomas A. Wilder	Joe Shannon Jr.	Roy C. Brooks	Andy Nguyen	Gary Fickes	J.D. Johnson
Taylor	Patricia Henderson	James M. Eidson	Randall Williams	Kyle Kendrick	Stan D. Egger	Charles (Chuck) Statler
*Terrell	Martha Allen	Fred Hernandez	Yolanda G. Lopez	Michelle Marquez	Charles Stegall	Kenn Norris
Terry	Paige Lindsey	Ramon Gallegos	Mike Swain	Kirby Keesee	Narisco (Shorty) Martinez	John R. Franks
Throckmorton	Mary (Susie) Walraven	Michael Fouts	Casey Wells	John Jones	Teddy Clark	Wilton Cantrell
Titus	Debra Abston	Charles C. (Chuck) Bailey	Don Boggs	Mike Fields	Phillip Hinton	Thomas Hockaday
Tom Green	Sheri Woodfin	Stephen Lupton (51st) George McCrea (119th)	Ralph Hoelscher	Aubrey de Cordova	Steve Floyd	Yantis Green
*Travis	Amalia Rodriguez-Mendoza	Rosemary Lehmberg	Ron Davis	Sarah Eckhardt	Karen Huber	Margaret Gómez
Trinity	Cheryl Cartwright	Joe Ned Dean	Grover Worsham	Richard Chamberlin	Cecil Webb	Jimmy Brown
*Tyler	Kim Nagypal	Joe R. Smith	Martin Nash	James (Rusty) Hughes	Mike Marshall	Jack Walston
Upshur	Carolyn Bullock Parrott	William (Billy) Byrd	James Crittenden	Cole Hefner	Lloyd Crabtree	Mike Spencer
Upton	Pedro (Pete) Gomez Jr.	Laurie English	Gary N. (Pete) Jackson	Tommy Owens	W.M. (Willie) Martinez	Leon Patrick
Uvalde	Christina Ovalle	Daniel J. Kindred	Randy Scheide	Mariano Pargas Jr.	Jerry W. Bates	Raul R. Flores
Val Verde	Luz Clara Balderas	Fred Hernandez	Ramiro V. Ramon	Lewis Owens	Robert Beau Nettleton	Gustavo Flores
Van Zandt	Karen Wilson	Chris Martin	Ricky LaPrade	Virgil Melton Jr.	Duanne Harvey	Ronald G. Carroll
Victoria	Cathy Stuart	Stephen B. Tyler	Kenny Swan	Kevin M. Janak	Gary E. Burns	Clint C. Ives
*Walker	Robyn Flowers	David P. Weeks	B.J. Gaines Jr.	Ronnie White	Bobby Warren	Tim Paulsel
Waller	Patricia Spadachene	Elton Mathis	Odis Styers	Frank Pokluda	Sylvia Cedillo	Stanley Kitzman
Ward	Patricia Oyerbides	Randall W. Reynolds	Julian Florez	Larry Hanna	Dexter Nichols	Eddie Nelms
Washington	Vicki Lehmann	Bill Parham	Zeb Heckmann	Luther Hueske	Kirk Hanath	Joy Fuchs
*Webb	Esther Degollado	Isidro R. Alaniz	Frank Sciaraffa	Rosaura (Wawi) Tijerina	Gerardo (Jerry) Garza	Jaime Canales
Wharton	Nerissa House	Josh McCown	Leroy E. Dettling	D.C. (Chris) King	Philip Miller	James (Jimmy) Kainer
Wheeler	Sherri Jones	Lynn Switzer	Daryl G. Snelgrooes	Bob Hink	Hubert C. Moore	John Walker
Wichita	Patti Flores	Maureen Shelton	Ray Gonzalez	Pat Norriss	Barry Mahler	William (Bill) Presson
Wilbarger	Brenda Peterson	Staley Heatly	Richard Jacobs	Phillip Graf	Rodney Johnston	Josh Patterson
*Willacy	Gilbert Lozano	Bernard Ammerman	Eliberto Guerra	Noe Loya	Alfredo Serrato	Dora Perez
Williamson	Lisa David	John Bradley	Lisa Birkman	Cynthia Long	Valerie Covey	Ron Morrison
Wilson	Deborah Bryan	René M. Peña	Albert Gamez Jr.	Paul W. Pfeil	Ricky R. Morales	Larry A. Wiley
Winkler	Sherry Terry	Michael L. Fostel	J.R. Carpenter	James R. (Robbie) Wolf	Randy Neal	Billy Ray Thompson
Wise	Brenda Rowe	Greg Lowery	Danny White	Kevin Burns	Harry Lamance	Terry Ross
Wood	Jenica Turner	Jim Wheeler	Keith Gilbreath	Jerry Gaskill	Roger W. Pace	Jon Shirley
*Yoakum	Sandra Roblez	Bill Helwig	Woody Lindsey	Ray Marion	Chris Blundell	Tim Addison
Young	Jamye Rogers	Stephen Crawford	John L. Hawkins	Matthew Pruitt	Stacey Rogers	Jimmy R. Wiley
Zapata	Dora M. Ramos	Isidro (Chilo) Alaniz	Jose Emilio Vela	Gabriel Villarreal Jr.	Eddie Nelms	Norberto Garza
Zavala	Rachel P. Ramirez	Roberto Serna	Isidro Cantu	Raul G. Gomez	Jesse Gonzalez	Don Lindenborn

Texans in Congress

Besides the two members of the U.S. Senate allocated to each state, Texas is allocated 32 members in the U.S. House of Representatives. The term of office for members of the House is two years; the terms of all members will expire on Jan. 1, 2013. Senators serve six-year terms. Sen. Kay Bailey Hutchison's term will end in 2013. Sen. John Cornyn's term will end in 2015.

Addresses and phone numbers of the lawmakers' Washington and district offices are below, as well as the committees on which they serve. Washington **zip codes** are **20515** for members of the House and **20510** for senators. The telephone area code for Washington is **202**. On the Internet, House members can be reached through **www.house.gov/writerep**. In 2011, members of Congress received a salary of $174,000. Members in leadership positions received $193,400.

U.S. SENATE

CORNYN, John. Republican (Home: Austin); Washington Office: 517 HSOB, Washington, D.C. 20510; (202) 224-2934, Fax 228-2856. Web site, cornyn.senate.gov.

John Cornyn.

Texas Offices: 221 W. 6th Ste. 1530, **Austin** 78701, (512) 469-6034; 5001 Spring Valley Ste. 1125 E, **Dallas** 75244, (972) 239-1310; 222 E. Van Buren Ste. 404, **Harlingen** 78550, (956) 423-0162; 5300 Memorial Dr. Ste. 980, **Houston** 77007, (713) 572-3337; 1500 Broadway Ste. 1230, **Lubbock** 79401, (806) 472-7533; 600 Navarro Ste. 210, **San Antonio** 78205, (210) 224-7485; 100 E. Ferguson Ste. 1004, **Tyler** 75702, (903) 593-0905.

Committees: Armed Services, Budget, Finance, Judiciary.

Kay Bailey Hutchison.

HUTCHISON, Kay Bailey. Republican (Home: Dallas); Washington Office: 284 RSOB, Washington, D.C. 20510; (202) 224-5922, Fax 224-0776. Web site, hutchison.senate. gov.

Texas Offices: 961 Federal Bldg., 300 E. 8th St., **Austin** 78701, (512) 916-5834; 500 Chestnut Ste. 1570, **Abilene** 79602, (325) 676-2839; 10440 N. Central Expy. Ste. 1160, **Dallas** 75231, (214) 361-3500; 1906G E. Tyler St., **Harlingen** 78550, (956) 425-2253; 1919 Smith Ste. 800, **Houston** 77002, (713) 653-3456; 3133 General Hudnell Dr. Ste. 120, **San Antonio** 78226, (210) 340-2885.

Committees: Appropriations; Commerce, Science and Transportation; Rules and Administration.

U.S. HOUSE of REPRESENTATIVES

BARTON, Joe, R-Ennis, District 6; Washington Office: 2109 RHOB; (202) 225-2002; **District Offices**: 6001 West I-20 Ste. 200, Arlington 76017, (817) 543-1000; 303 N. 6th, Crockett 75835, (936) 544-8488; 2106A W. Ennis Ave. Ennis 75119, (972) 875-8488. **Committee**: Energy and Commerce.

BRADY, Kevin, R-The Woodlands, District 8; Washington Office: 301 CHOB; (202) 225-4901, Fax 225-5524. **District Offices**: 200 River Pointe Ste. 304, Conroe 77304, (936) 441-5700; 1202 Sam Houston Ave. Ste. 8, Huntsville 77340, (936) 439-9542; 420 Green Ave., Orange 77630, (409) 883-4197. **Committees**: Ways and Means, Economic.

BURGESS, Michael, R-Lewisville, District 26; Washington Office: 2241 RHOB; (202) 225-7772, Fax 225-2919. **District Offices**: 1660 S. Stemmons Fwy. Ste. 230, Lewisville 75067, (972) 434-9700; 1100 Circle Dr. Ste. 200, Fort Worth 76119, (817) 531-8454. **Committees**: Energy and Commerce, Economic.

CANSECO, Francisco, R-San Antonio, District 23; Washington Office: 1339 LHOB; (202) 225-4511; District Offices: 100 E. Ogden, Del Rio 78840; 100 S. Monroe, Eagle Pass 78852; 103 W. Callaghan, Fort Stockton 79735; 6363 DeZavala Ste. 105, San Antonio 78249 (210) 561-8855; 1313 SE Military No. 101, San Antonio 78214 (210) 922-7826. **Committee**: Financial Services.

CARTER, John, R-Round Rock, District 31; Washington Office: 409 CHOB; (202) 225-3864. District Offices: 1717 N. I-35 Ste. 303, Round Rock 78664, (512) 246-1600; 6544B S. General Bruce Dr., Temple 76502, (254) 933-1392. **Committee**: Appropriations.

CONAWAY, K. Michael, R-Midland, District 11; Washington Office: 2430 RHOB; (202) 225-3605. **District Offices**: 6 Desta Dr. Ste. 2000, Midland 79705, (432) 687-2390; 501 Center Ave. Brownwood 76801, (325) 646-1950; 104 W. Sandstone, Llano 78643, (325) 247-2826; 411 W. 8th, Odessa 79761, (866) 882-3811; 33 Twohig Ste. 307, San Angelo 76903, (325) 659-4010. **Committees**: Agriculture, Armed Services, Intelligence, Ethics.

CUELLAR, Henry, D-Laredo, District 28; Washington Office: 2463 RHOB; (202) 225-1640. **District Offices**: 602 E. Calton Rd., Laredo 78041, (956) 725-0639; 615 E. Houston Ste. 451, San Antonio 78205, (210) 271-2851; 117 E. Tom Landry, Mission 78572, (956) 424-3942; 100 S. Austin, Seguin

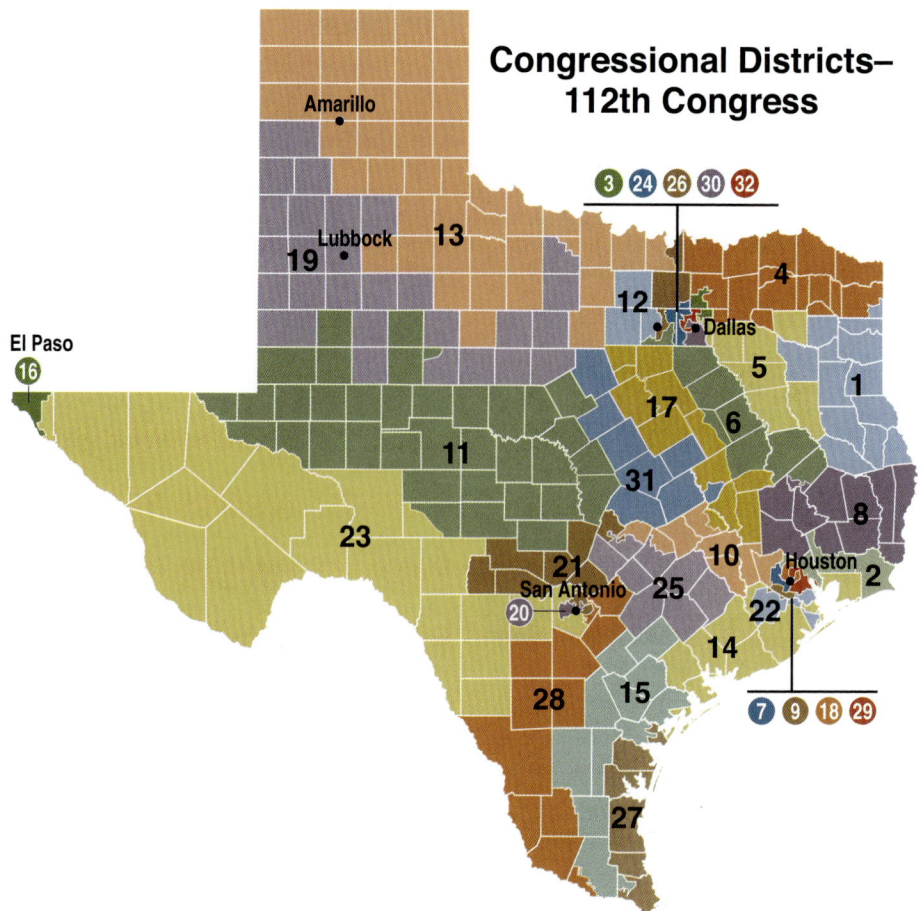

Congressional Districts– 112th Congress

Amarillo

Lubbock

El Paso ⑯

13

19

③ ㉔ ㉖ ㉚ ㉜

12

Dallas

4

5

1

17

6

11

31

10

8

23

21

San Antonio

25

Houston

2

⑳

22

14

28

15

⑦ ⑨ ⑱ ㉙

27

78155, (830) 401-0457; 100 N. FM 3167, Rio Grande City 78582, (956) 488-0952. **Committees**: Agriculture, Homeland Security.

CULBERSON, John Abney, R-Houston, District 7; Washington Office: 2352 RHOB; (202) 225-2571, Fax 225-4381; District Office: 10000 Memorial Dr. Ste. 620, Houston 77024, (713) 682-8828. **Committee**: Appropriations.

DOGGETT, Lloyd, D-Austin, District 25; Washington Office: 201 CHOB; (202) 225-4865; **District Office**: 300 E. 8th Ste. 763, Austin 78701, (512) 916-5921. **Committees**: Budget, Ways and Means.

FARENTHOLD, Blake, R-Corpus Christi, District 27; Washington Office: 2110 RHOB; (202) 225-7742; **District Offices**; 101 N. Shoreline Blvd. Ste. 300, Corpus Christi 78401, (361) 884-2222; 1805 Ruben Torres Ste. B-27, Brownsville 78521, (956) 544-8800. **Committees**: Homeland Security, Oversight and Government Reform, Transportation and Infrastructure.

FLORES, Bill, R-Waco, District 17; Washington Office: 1505 LHOB; (202) 225-6105; **District Offices**: 400 Austin Ave. Ste. 302, Waco 76701, (254)

732-0748; 1 N. Walnut Ste. 145, Cleburne 76033, (817) 774-2551; 2800 S. Texas Ave. Ste. 403, Bryan 77802, (979) 703-403. **Committees**: Natural Resources, Budget, Veterans' Affairs.

GOHMERT, Louie, R-Tyler, District 1; Washington Office: 2440 RHOB; (202) 225-3035, Fax 226-1230; **District Offices**: 1121 ESE Loop 323 Ste. 206, Tyler 75701, (903) 561-6349; 101 E. Methvin Ste. 302, Longview 75601, (903) 236-8597; 300 E. Shepherd Ste. 210, Lufkin 75901, (936) 632-3180; 102 W. Houston, Marshall 75670, (866) 535-6302; 101 W. Main Ste. 160, Nacogdoches 75961, (866) 535-6302. **Committees**: Judiciary, Natural Resources.

GONZALEZ, Charlie A., D-San Antonio, District 20; Washington Office: 1436 LHOB; (202) 225-3236, Fax 225-1915; **District Office**: 124-B Federal Building, 727 East Durango, Federal Building, San Antonio 78206, (210) 472-6195. **Committees**: Energy and Commerce, House Administration.

GRANGER, Kay, R-Fort Worth, District 12; Washington Office: 320 CHOB; (202) 225-5071, Fax 225-5683; **District Office**: 1701 River Run Rd. Ste. 407, Fort Worth 76107, (817) 338-0909. **Committee**: Appropriations.

GREEN, Al, D-Houston, District 9; Washington Office: 2201 RHOB; (202) 225-7508; **District Office:** 3003 South Loop West Ste. 460, Houston 77054, (713) 383-9234. **Committee:** Financial Services.

GREEN, Gene, D-Houston, District 29; Washington Office: 2470 RHOB; (202) 225-1688, Fax 225-9903; **District Offices:** 256 N. Sam Houston Pkwy. E. Ste. 29, Houston 77060, (281) 999-5879; 11811 I-10 East Ste. 430, Houston 77029, (713) 330-0761; 909 Decker Dr. Ste. 124, Baytown 77520, (281) 420-0502. **Committee:** Energy and Commerce.

HALL, Ralph M., R-Rockwall, District 4; Washington Office: 2405 RHOB; (202) 225-6673, Fax 225-3332; **District Offices:** 104 N. San Jacinto, Rockwall 75087, (972) 771-9118; 101 E. Pecan, Sherman 75090, (903) 892-1112; 710 James Bowie Dr., New Boston 75570, (903) 628-8309; 1800 N. Graves Ste. 101, McKinney 75069, (214) 726-9949; 320 Church Ste. 132, Sulphur Springs 75482, (903) 885-8138; 4303 Texas Blvd. Ste. 2, Texarkana 75503, (903) 794-4445. **Committee:** Science, Space and Technology (chairman).

HENSARLING, Jeb, R-Dallas, District 5; Washington Office: 129 CHOB; (202) 225-3484, Fax 226-4888. **District Offices:** 6510 Abrams Rd. Ste. 243, Dallas 75231, (214) 349-9996; 702 E. Corsicana St., Athens 77571, (903) 675-8288. **Committee:** Financial Services.

HINOJOSA, Rubén, D-Mercedes, District 15; Washington Office: 2262 RHOB; (202) 225-2531, Fax 225-5688; **District Offices:** 2864 W. Trenton Rd., Edinburg 78539, (956) 682-5545; 107 S. St. Mary's St., Beeville 78102, (361) 358-8400. **Committees:** Education and Workforce, Financial Services.

JACKSON LEE, Sheila, D-Houston, District 18; Washington Office: 2160 RHOB; (202) 225-3816, Fax 225-3317; **District Offices:** 1919 Smith Ste. 1180, Houston 77002, (713) 655-0050; 420 W. 19th St., Houston 77008, (713) 861-4070; 6719 W. Montgomery Ste. 204, Houston 77091; 3300 Lyons Ave. Ste. 301, Houston 77020, (713) 227-7740. **Committees:** Homeland Security, Judiciary.

JOHNSON, Eddie Bernice, D-Dallas, District 30; Washington Office: 2468 RHOB; (202) 225-8885, Fax 225-1477; **District Office:** 3102 Maple Ave. Ste. 600, Dallas 75201, (214) 922-8885. **Committees:** Science, Space and Technology, Transportation and Infrastructure.

JOHNSON, Sam, R-Plano, District 3; Washington Office: 1211 LHOB; (202) 225-4201, Fax 225-1485; **District Office:** 2929 N. Central Expressway, Ste. 240, Richardson 75080, (972) 470-0892. **Committee:** Ways and Means.

MARCHANT, Kenny, R-Coppell, District 24; Washington Office: 1110 LHOB; (202) 225-6605, Fax 225-0074. **District Office:** 9901 E. Valley Ranch Parkway Ste. 3035, Irving 75063, (972) 556-0162. **Committee:** Financial Services.

McCAUL, Michael, R-Austin, District 10;

Washington Office: 131 CHOB; (202) 225-2401, Fax 225-5955. **District Offices:** 5929 Balcones Dr. Ste. 305, Austin 78731, (512) 473-2357; 2000 S. Market Ste. 303, Brenham 77833, (979) 830-8497; [Katy] 1550 Foxlake Ste. 120, Houston 77084, (281) 398-1247; 990 Village Sq. Ste. B, Tomball 77375. **Committees:** Ethics, Foreign Affairs, Homeland Security, Science, Space and Technology.

NEUGEBAUER, Randy, R-Lubbock, District 19; Washington Office: 1424 LHOB; (202) 225-4005, Fax 225-9615. **District Offices:** 500 Chestnut Rm. 819, Abilene 79602, (325) 675-9779; 1510 Scurry Ste. B, Big Spring 79720, (432) 264-7592; 611 University Ave. Ste. 220, Lubbock 79401, (806) 763-1611. **Committees:** Agriculture, Financial Services, Science, Space and Technology.

OLSON, Pete, R-Sugar Land, District 22; Washington Office: 514 CHOB; (202) 225-5951, Fax 225-5241. **District Office:** 1650 Hwy 6 Ste. 150, Sugar Land 77478, (281) 494-2690; 17225 El Camino Real Ste. 447, Houston 77058, (281) 486-1095. **Committee:** Energy and Commerce.

PAUL, Ron, R-Lake Jackson, District 14; Washington Office: 203 CHOB; (202) 225-2831. **District Offices:** 122 West Way Ste. 301, Lake Jackson 77566, (979) 285-0231; 1501 Mockingbird Lane Ste. 229, Victoria 77904, (361) 576-1231. **Committees:** Financial Services, Foreign Affairs.

POE, Ted, R-Humble, District 2; Washington Office: 430 CHOB; (202) 225-6565, Fax 225-5547. **District Offices:** 505 Orleans Ste. 100, Beaumont 77701, (409) 212-1997; 1801 Kingwood Ste 340, Kingwood 77339 (281) 446-0242. **Committees:** Foreign Affairs, Judiciary.

REYES, Silvestre, D-El Paso, District 16; Washington Office: 2210 RHOB; (202) 225-4831, Fax 225-2016; **District Office:** 310 N. Mesa Ste. 400, El Paso 79901, (915) 534-4400. **Committees:** Armed Services, Veterans' Affairs.

SESSIONS, Pete, R-Dallas, District 32; Washington Office: 2233 RHOB; (202) 225-2231, Fax 225-5878; **District Office:** 12750 Merit Dr. Ste. 1434, Dallas 75251, (972) 392-0505. **Committee:** Rules.

SMITH, Lamar S., R-San Antonio, District 21; Washington Office: 2409 RHOB; (202) 225-4236, Fax 225-8628; **District Offices:** 1100 NE Loop 410 Ste. 640, San Antonio 78209, (210) 821-5024; 3536 Bee Cave Rd. Ste. 212, Austin 78746, (512) 306-0439; 301 Junction Hwy. Ste. 346C, Kerrville 78028, (830) 896-0154. **Committees:** Homeland Security, Judiciary (chairman), Science, Space and Technology.

THORNBERRY, William M. (Mac), R-Clarendon, District 13; Washington Office: 2209 RHOB; (202) 225-3706, Fax 225-3486; **District Offices:** 905 S. Fillmore Ste. 520, Amarillo 79101, (806) 371-8844; 4245 Kemp Ste. 506, Wichita Falls 76308, (940) 692-1700. **Committees:** Armed Services, Intelligence. ☆

Federal Funds to Texas by County, 2009

Texas received **$224,338,605,325** in 2009 from the federal government in direct expenditures. Below, the distribution of funds is shown by county. The first figure after the county name represents **total direct** expenditures to the county for fiscal year 2009. The second and third figures are that part of the total that went directly for **individuals**, either in **retirement** payments, such as Social Security, or **other** direct payments, principally Medicare. In the last column are direct payments other than to individuals, principally **agricultural** programs such as crop insurance. *For a more complete explanation, see end of chart. Source: Consolidated Federal Funds Report 2009, U.S. Department of Commerce.*

COUNTY	TOTAL	For INDIVIDUALS		other direct (ag., etc.)	COUNTY	TOTAL	For INDIVIDUALS		other direct (ag., etc.)
		retirement	other				retirement	other	
	(Thousands of dollars, 000)					(Thousands of dollars, 000)			
Anderson	$ 461,616	$ 174,193	$ 112,358	$ 1,542	Coryell	531,609	239,635	66,040	3,721
Andrews	83,171	31,832	25,471	4,614	Cottle	36,178	6,508	16,186	5,013
Angelina	684,004	286,125	175,221	3,797	Crane	28,687	8,598	15,774	594
Aransas	173,339	103,755	44,917	1,136	Crockett	27,663	8,807	6,688	2,691
Archer	96,115	42,909	13,062	7,018	Crosby	87,889	16,904	36,192	16,814
Armstrong	32,622	6,240	6,136	6,943	Culberson	43,820	5,997	19,950	691
Atascosa	295,030	125,143	60,798	4,740	Dallam	68,694	21,959	16,670	19,526
Austin	2,797,832	85,379	51,673	2,167	Dallas	18,142,676	4,764,939	3,067,405	75,372
Bailey	70,974	12,817	18,223	17,793	Dawson	160,226	34,453	55,609	24,342
Bandera	144,553	91,569	22,632	191	Deaf Smith	162,780	37,426	39,167	42,967
Bastrop	423,107	206,975	71,759	2,395	Delta	72,867	19,788	25,912	2,423
Baylor	65,114	16,297	16,727	11,887	Denton	2,945,454	892,795	305,406	7,668
Bee	254,567	75,331	69,501	11,379	DeWitt	204,043	57,622	60,075	3,043
Bell	8,743,237	1,075,918	299,030	19,226	Dickens	44,546	8,221	18,746	3,363
Bexar	20,050,232	5,488,274	2,524,489	100,250	Dimmit	138,136	23,103	28,506	2,798
Blanco	99,229	48,215	34,835	379	Donley	43,213	13,086	17,729	3,171
Borden	8,323	1,034	3,359	3,501	Duval	203,999	33,868	52,479	3,581
Bosque	169,893	70,870	39,247	1,631	Eastland	202,355	69,414	70,056	2,096
Bowie	1,259,168	385,172	199,571	8,300	Ector	746,309	299,681	235,014	1,912
Brazoria	1,343,571	676,791	290,405	41,441	Edwards	31,901	7,805	14,559	654
Brazos	1,254,331	320,167	156,591	9,773	Ellis	750,109	368,444	162,850	11,594
Brewster	98,601	26,842	21,874	2,946	El Paso	8,958,311	1,841,832	1,166,104	39,451
Briscoe	30,143	6,053	8,507	6,866	Erath	238,091	90,013	75,909	2,091
Brooks	205,242	22,883	26,639	1,611	Falls	224,269	54,478	53,729	10,132
Brown	343,170	142,861	102,504	2,196	Fannin	570,881	122,027	67,314	8,061
Burleson	157,804	57,449	33,473	3,473	Fayette	245,773	89,952	67,978	2,697
Burnet	323,063	181,998	71,866	1,582	Fisher	54,114	13,864	12,863	11,895
Caldwell	266,887	97,254	65,411	5,129	Floyd	91,903	17,480	21,739	22,453
Calhoun	166,666	60,779	40,228	5,681	Foard	39,337	5,539	13,067	10,232
Callahan	125,172	48,321	40,806	3,052	Fort Bend	1,660,351	717,086	39,205	196,141
Cameron	2,834,410	764,237	609,158	32,375	Franklin	72,823	30,455	22,796	412
Camp	126,808	46,703	33,128	827	Freestone	145,474	58,863	32,344	463
Carson	109,604	17,993	66,846	13,672	Frio	189,766	33,591	27,929	6,454
Cass	333,149	134,702	84,550	894	Gaines	133,792	24,762	38,549	50,944
Castro	95,395	15,249	30,470	26,111	Galveston	4,218,306	761,584	477,636	1,384,992
Chambers	238,543	49,080	50,349	51,907	Garza	46,317	12,655	15,905	6,691
Cherokee	389,018	135,398	133,245	1,463	Gillespie	190,002	112,593	48,871	2,710
Childress	79,565	20,272	27,770	9,468	Glasscock	14,093	2,296	1,161	8,228
Clay	79,717	32,466	21,097	6,487	Goliad	72,974	22,447	16,635	2,960
Cochran	53,047	8,828	17,663	17,566	Gonzales	294,065	55,873	47,761	3,531
Coke	34,260	12,752	13,904	1,995	Gray	202,763	73,425	85,587	7,001
Coleman	127,389	36,380	41,892	3,421	Grayson	881,180	409,144	227,883	10,291
Collin	3,405,268	1,249,670	266,686	22,454	Gregg	972,499	418,423	252,089	3,415
Collingsworth	59,407	10,370	14,907	9,276	Grimes	201,123	72,483	45,755	1,219
Colorado	199,304	65,919	57,279	8,279	Guadalupe	77,054	469,444	113,616	10,845
Comal	765,206	436,426	116,160	3,627	Hale	314,467	84,470	91,809	33,976
Comanche	201,931	48,626	101,214	4,054	Hall	59,131	11,403	12,678	10,773
Concho	44,781	8,504	11,883	9,563	Hamilton	77,970	29,829	26,532	1,823
Cooke	264,373	110,592	93,925	3,443	Hansford	46,650	12,676	9,364	18,756

COUNTY	TOTAL	For INDIVIDUALS		other direct (ag., etc.)
		retirement	other	
(Thousands of dollars, 000)				
Hardeman	54,823	14,531	13,692	9,124
Hardin	335,083	165,394	96,150	703
Harris	30,696,974	7,196,479	4,743,504	344,328
Harrison	525,709	171,183	109,435	3,042
Hartley	24,631	2,629	1,627	14,422
Haskell	81,991	21,786	19,090	22,088
Hays	682,360	319,633	133,121	3,737
Hemphill	27,744	7,349	6,563	1,220
Henderson	505,848	219,567	133,690	2,319
Hidalgo	4,175,094	1,126,948	999,433	58,211
Hill	363,459	128,196	75,366	22,724
Hockley	202,669	55,211	58,624	28,728
Hood	327,904	223,427	67,670	708
Hopkins	257,680	97,144	64,817	568
Houston	258,512	82,148	58,889	2,565
Howard	522,246	108,473	88,266	12,843
Hudspeth	41,053	6,382	4,788	1,334
Hunt	2,073,215	258,424	155,780	3,819
Hutchinson	154,137	68,755	47,747	6,514
Irion	14,752	5,394	2,903	1,455
Jack	50,377	23,442	15,892	833
Jackson	128,746	39,496	34,402	18,001
Jasper	335,058	118,554	90,061	767
Jeff Davis	17,758	8,371	3,215	65
Jefferson	2,363,246	742,564	678,383	86,581
Jim Hogg	85,250	11,726	16,639	1,863
Jim Wells	449,490	116,939	102,212	21,567
Johnson	781,266	433,152	178,878	3,538
Jones	171,789	55,854	40,918	22,842
Karnes	167,302	41,469	35,255	5,123
Kaufman	638,856	307,603	161,316	2,350
Kendall	261,442	166,753	34,358	998
Kenedy	4,187	805	571	1,735
Kent	10,315	2,801	2,349	2,218
Kerr	446,158	258,217	100,997	1,499
Kimble	35,363	17,271	9,570	542
King	6,897	439	343	3,203
Kinney	45,019	16,752	8,533	3,033
Kleberg	399,311	80,712	70,782	25,928
Knox	64,454	12,778	14,537	19,134
Lamar	490,447	177,062	107,372	6,967
Lamb	147,840	37,363	39,941	29,947
Lampasas	171,803	102,932	38,648	1,164
La Salle	82,382	14,564	12,861	2,847
Lavaca	222,663	79,778	64,443	2,679
Lee	101,338	44,645	21,668	348
Leon	198,836	78,803	41,006	262
Liberty	518,374	22,426	159,814	6,568
Limestone	230,646	76,025	47,663	3,906
Lipscomb	21,638	7,372	6,057	3,390
Live Oak	122,686	25,899	20,672	7,167
Llano	150,938	90,181	41,509	767
Loving	871	315	22	426
Lubbock	1,835,972	658,618	522,674	38,565
Lynn	89,685	15,703	16,697	37,771
Madison	81,884	32,368	19,510	165
Marion	118,670	37,748	21,818	280
Martin	58,401	10,265	9,581	12,679
Mason	35,962	15,427	9,751	850

COUNTY	TOTAL	For INDIVIDUALS		other direct (ag., etc.)
		retirement	other	
(Thousands of dollars, 000)				
Matagorda	833,119	103,728	64,806	14,054
Maverick	439,718	100,445	95,210	3,803
McCulloch	91,954	27,879	24,970	7,310
McLennan	1,974,130	732,456	334,948	27,084
McMullen	7,375	2,605	1,004	2,133
Medina	317,337	133,472	56,653	10,453
Menard	26,232	8,634	7,518	630
Midland	639,417	283,091	176,580	4,997
Milam	229,369	85,733	43,857	8,606
Mills	52,494	18,366	14,351	755
Mitchell	74,317	21,850	20,843	7,544
Montague	173,819	80,521	48,012	1,277
Montgomery	2,055,016	1,030,538	367,399	16,058
Moore	89,268	36,640	21,097	17,744
Morris	141,033	57,346	34,971	496
Motley	21,497	5,612	4,818	2,101
Nacgdoches	507,066	165,344	129,839	12,656
Navarro	440,535	152,709	99,713	5,995
Newton	119,685	42,807	29,871	175
Nolan	140,531	49,152	42,678	6,193
Nueces	3,433,760	976,698	611,131	90,239
Ochiltree	51,330	17,808	11,473	14,949
Oldham	20,706	5,709	3,713	5,902
Orange	992,544	283,641	199,210	344,656
Palo Pinto	203,490	89,279	59,022	992
Panola	192,559	68,930	50,954	105
Parker	534,646	306,077	101,634	1,271
Parmer	83,531	19,907	14,731	36,492
Pecos	89,671	29,304	20,986	6,304
Polk	516,916	297,499	116,908	2,270
Potter	4,084,572	518,579	257,629	6,978
Presidio	96,762	19,878	12,639	593
Rains	71,700	40,570	14,525	175
Randall	273,754	89,651	112,675	15,819
Reagan	18,881	6,433	4,554	5,386
Real	36,850	15,744	7,514	91
Red River	196,386	52,326	40,895	2,870
Reeves	108,387	27,609	25,613	1,554
Refugio	82,903	36,797	20,552	10,413
Roberts	6,433	2,153	1,659	1,498
Robertson	185,341	52,984	35,071	3,477
Rockwall	550,909	159,359	36,083	1,583
Runnels	128,482	39,344	28,239	17,414
Rusk	332,476	126,502	84,396	1,061
Sabine	147,775	67,850	38,337	223
S.Augustine	116,219	34,098	24,719	185
San Jacinto	150,783	67,626	40,401	73
San Patricio	624,478	206,439	129,708	65,181
San Saba	80,503	19,059	17,073	3,431
Schleicher	22,833	7,566	5,990	2,600
Scurry	132,716	43,577	36,979	10,029
Shackelford	27,169	10,483	7,072	3,279
Shelby	293,450	81,200	64,977	1,134
Sherman	39,201	6,856	4,899	18,250
Smith	1,696,696	653,999	342,398	11,394
Somervell	43,744	21,725	10,782	54
Starr	459,772	95,733	95,631	7,950
Stephens	75,734	28,743	24,735	1,044
Sterling	8,718	2,713	2,703	1,632

COUNTY	TOTAL	For INDIVIDUALS		other direct (ag., etc.)	COUNTY	TOTAL	For INDIVIDUALS		other direct (ag., etc.)
		retirement	other				retirement	other	
(Thousands of dollars, 000)					(Thousands of dollars, 000)				
Stonewall	21,174	5,611	4,852	5,049	Waller	228,589	72,061	64,280	3,417
Sutton	22,627	8,256	6,033	1,003	Ward	80,174	31,313	21,864	1,059
Swisher	98,324	21,926	18,811	37,240	Washington	289,143	115,671	62,483	1,399
Tarrant	8,452,393	3,760,400	1,832,290	41,361	Webb	1,707,935	374,967	299,304	10,499
Taylor	1,284,220	431,147	221,482	10,468	Wharton	382,136	111,938	91,264	27,771
Terrell	17,248	4,366	2,434	1,743	Wheeler	55,309	17,534	20,015	2,956
Terry	138,258	31,714	34,566	37,581	Wichita	1,469,414	480,336	232,672	21,903
Throckmrton	29,955	6,001	4,848	8,420	Wilbarger	143,169	41,576	42,532	20,748
Titus	214,081	76,800	59,579	406	Willacy	197,167	37,928	42,570	18,306
Tom Green	979,359	350,800	173,189	20,425	Williamson	2,099,229	828,503	158,324	16,903
Travis	17,117,618	1,846,018	848,896	114,763	Wilson	235,035	124,847	37,651	4,315
Trinity	154,864	65,655	43,384	133	Winkler	51,529	18,044	18,747	554
Tyler	177,990	77,502	51,415	275	Wise	265,246	145,955	53,320	1,057
Upshur	278,623	120,503	72,184	739	Wood	368,644	198,620	87,638	999
Upton	25,743	9,103	8,334	2,750	Yoakum	56,646	16,198	12,437	18,855
Uvalde	225,433	68,348	56,821	9,236	Young	158,224	64,725	46,070	5,771
Val Verde	576,075	125,777	59,271	3,397	Zapata	104,303	23,398	28,865	418
Van Zandt	353,873	174,469	104,867	1,609	Zavala	122,483	24,526	26,686	5,809
Victoria	596,698	258,226	150,830	9,391					
Walker	360,116	133,500	87,526	1,354					

***Total** federal government direct expenditures include: grants, salaries and wages (Postal Service, Dept. of Defense, etc.), procurement contract awards, direct payments for individuals, and other direct payments other than for individuals, such as some agriculture programs.

Retirement and disability programs include federal employee retirement and disability benefits, Social Security payments of all types, and veterans benefit payments.

Other direct payments for individuals include Medicare, excess earned income tax credits, food stamps, unemployment compensation benefit payments and lower income housing assistance, but not salaries and wages.

Other direct payments other than for individuals include crop insurance, wool and mohair loss assistance program, conservation reserve program, production flexibility payments for contract commodities and postal service funds other than salaries and procurements.

Source: Consolidated Federal Funds Report, Fiscal 2009, U.S. Department of Commerce, Bureau of the Census.

U.S. Tax Collections in Texas

*Fiscal Year	Individual Income and Employment Taxes	Corporation Income Taxes	Estate Taxes	Gift Taxes	Excise Taxes	TOTAL U.S. Taxes Collected in Texas
(1,000 of dollars) *Information for fiscal years, furnished by the Internal Revenue Service.*						
2010	$ 147,748,859	$ 24,991,374	$ 1,210,600	$ 287,181	$ 14,904,099	$ 189,142,112
2009	158,798,111	24,235,172	1,780,030	242,918	15,465,279	200,521,512
2008	178,761,539	39,971,658	1,549,767	243,043	15,150,053	235,676,058
2007	160,306,445	41,823,425	1,473,490	218,194	21,569,350	225,390,904
2006	145,758,275	37,004,514	1,135,160	136,377	20,702,545	204,736,871
2005	125,816,805	29,186,478	1,196,362	118,231	13,074,838	169,392,715
2004	118,410,514	17,127,574	1,109,558	104,214	15,939,329	152,691,189
2003	116,353,959	11,487,059	958,791	147,351	12,987,394	141,934,554
2002	117,685,965	13,702,495	1,287,937	109,064	13,654,721	146,440,182
2001	127,738,858	17,598,181	1,242,130	248,892	14,350,268	161,178,329
2000	116,094,820	20,310,672	1,176,278	269,109	14,732,513	152,583,349
1999	104,408,504	13,098,033	968,736	446,168	16,729,589	135,651,029
1998	94,404,751	14,526,238	1,300,104	247,989	11,877,230	122,356,312
1997	90,222,786	13,875,653	933,616	159,111	12,185,271	117,376,440
1996	76,863,689	12,393,992	733,282	158,237	10,418,847	101,079,028
1995	69,706,333	10,677,881	869,528	152,683	11,135,857	92,342,282
1990	52,795,489	6,983,762	521,811	196,003	5,694,006	66,191,071
1985	41,497,114	5,637,148	528,106	41,560	6,058,110	53,762,038
1980	25,707,514	7,232,486	453,830	23,722	4,122,538	37,540,089
1970	6,096,961	1,184,342	135,694	20,667	843,724	8,281,389
1960	2,059,075	622,822	70,578	10,583	209,653	2,972,712

Major Military Installations

Below are listed the major military installations in Texas in 2011. Data are taken from the U.S. Department of Defense *Base Structure Report 2010* and other sources. "Civilian" refers to Department of Defense personnel, and "other" refers to employees such as contractor personnel.

U.S. NAVY

Naval Air Station Corpus Christi
Location: Corpus Christi (est. 1941).
Address: NAS Corpus Christi, 11001 D St., Corpus Christi 78419
Main phone number: (361) 961-2384.
Personnel: 4,494 active-duty; 405 civilians.
Major units: Naval Air Training Command Headquarters; Training Air Wing 4; Marine Aviation Training Support Group; Coast Guard Air Group; Corpus Christi Army Depot (est. 1961).

Naval Air Station-Joint Reserve Base Fort Worth
Location: westside Fort Worth (est. 1994) [Carswell, est. 1942 as Fort Worth Army Air Field, closed 1993].
Address: NAS-JRB, 1215 Depot Ave., Fort Worth 76127
Main phone number: (817) 782-5000
Personnel: 4,468 active-duty; 185 civilians.
Major units: Fleet Logistics Support Squadron 59; Marine Air Group 41; 14th Marine Regiment; 36th Airlift Wing, Texas Air National Guard; 136th Airlift Wing; 301st Fighter Wing, Air Force Reserve.

Naval Air Station Kingsville
Location: Kingsville (est. 1942).
Address: NAS Kingsville, Texas 78363
Main phone number: (361) 516-6136
Personnel: 0 active-duty permanently stationed; 112 civilians.
Major units: Training Air Wing Two; Training Squadrons 21 and 22; Naval Auxiliary Landing Field Orange Grove; McMullen Target Range, Escondido Ranch.

U.S. ARMY

Fort Bliss
Location: El Paso (est. 1849).
Address: Fort Bliss, Texas 79916
Main phone number: (915) 568-2121
Personnel: 21,013 active-duty plus trainees; 2,420 civilians; 7,114 other.
Major units: 1st Armored Division; 32nd Air and Missile Defense Command; 5th Armored Brigade; Air Defense Artillery School; 11th Air Defense Artillery Brigades; 204th Military Intelligence Battalion; 76th Military Police Battalion; Biggs Army Airfield (est. 1916).

Fort Hood
Location: Killeen (est. 1942).
Address: Fort Hood, Texas 76544
Main phone number: (254) 287-2131
Personnel: 47,480 active-duty; 3,809 civilians; 13,408 other.
Major units: III Corps, Headquarters Command; First Army Division West; 1st Cavalry Division; 4th Infantry Division; 13th Sustainment Command; 89th Military Police Brigade; 3rd Armored Cavalry Regiment; 504th Military Intelligence Brigade; 21st Cavalry Brigade (Air Combat); Army Operational Test Command; Darnell Army Medical Center.

Fort Sam Houston
Location: San Antonio (est. 1878).
Address: Fort Sam Houston, Texas 78234
Main phone number: (210) 221-1211
Personnel: 15,662 active-duty; 5,024 civilians; 5,980 other.
Major units: U.S. Army North; U.S. Army South; Brooke Army Medical Center; Institute of Surgical Research; Army Medical Command; Army Medical Dept. Center and School; 5th Recruiting Brigade; 12th Brigade, Western Region (ROTC); Camp Bullis (est. 1917), training area.

Red River Army Depot
Location: 18 miles west of Texarkana (est. 1941).
Address: Red River Army Depot, Texarkana 75507
Main phone number: (903) 334-2141
Personnel: 148 active-duty; 3,991 civilians; 1,843 other.
Major unit: Defense Distribution Center; U.S. Army Tank-Automotive and Armaments Command.

U.S. AIR FORCE

Brooks City-Base
Location: San Antonio (est. 1917, in 2002 the property was conveyed to the Brooks Development Authority for commercial use, but retains military missions.).
Address: Brooks City-Base, San Antonio 78235
Main phone number: (210) 536-1110
Personnel: 723 active-duty; 1,242 civilians.
Major units: 311th Human Systems Wing; 311th Mission Support Group; School of Aerospace Medicine; Air Force Institute for Occupational Health; 59th Medical Squadron; 68th Information Operations Squadron; 710th Intelligence Flight.

Dyess Air Force Base
Location: Abilene (est. 1942 as Tye Army Airfield, closed at end of World War II, re-established in 1956).
Address: Dyess Air Force Base, Texas 79607
Main phone number: (325) 696-0212
Personnel: 5,035 active-duty; 386 civilians.
Major units: 7th Bomb Wing (Air Combat Command); 317th Airlift Group.

Goodfellow Air Force Base
Location: San Angelo (est. 1940).
Address: Goodfellow AFB, San Angelo 76908
Main phone number: (915) 654-3231
Personnel: 1,236 active-duty, approximately 1,200 trainees; 569 civilians.
Major units: 17th Training Group; 517th Training Group; 17th Medical Group. 17th Mission Support Group.

Lackland Air Force Base

Location: San Antonio (est. 1942 when separated from Kelly Field).

Address: Lackland Air Force Base, Texas 78236

Main phone number: (210) 671-1110

Personnel: 8,409 active-duty; 4,507 civilians.

Major units: 37th Training Wing; 737th Training Group; Defense Language Institute; Inter-American Air Force Academy; Kelly Field Annex (was Kelly Air Force Base, est. 1916).

Laughlin Air Force Base

Location: Del Rio (est. 1942).

Address: Laughlin Air Force Base, Texas 78843

Main phone number: (830) 298-3511

Personnel: 864 active-duty; 949 civilians.

Major unit: 47th Flying Training Wing.

Randolph Air Force Base

Location: San Antonio (est. 1930).

Address: Randolph Air Force Base, Texas 78150

Main phone number: (210) 652-1110

Personnel: 2,827 active-duty; 5,792 civilians.

Major units: 12th Flying Training Wing; 359th Medical Group; 902d Mission Support Group; Air Education and Training Command; Air Force Personnel Center; Air Force Recruiting Command; Air Force Manpower Agency.

Sheppard Air Force Base

Location: Wichita Falls (est. 1941).

Address: Sheppard Air Force Base, Texas 76311

Main phone number: (940) 676-2511

Personnel: 2,515 active-duty; 1,286 civilians.

Major units: 82nd Training Wing; 80th Flying Training Wing; NCO Academy.

TEXAS MILITARY FORCES

Camp Mabry

Location: Austin. Just west of MoPac Blvd.

Address: Box 5218, Austin, Texas 78763

Main phone number: (512) 465-5101

Web site: www.agd.state.tx.us

Personnel: 2,167 guard, 496 civilians, 257 other.

Adjutant General of Texas:

Maj. General John F. Nichols.

Major units: Joint Force Headquarters, the Standing Joint Interagency Task Force, the 36th Infantry Division, the 147th Reconnaissance Wing, 149th Fighter Wing, and the 136th Airlift Wing. Texas Air National Guard.

Texas Military Forces Museum, open Wednesday–Sunday, 10 a.m. - 4 p.m.

Tracing their history to early frontier days, the Texas Military Forces are organized into the Army and Air National Guard, the Texas State Guard.

The governor is commander-in-chief of the Texas Military Forces. This command function is exercised through the adjutant general appointed by the governor and approved by both federal and state legislative authority.

When not in active federal service, Camp Mabry, in west Austin, serves as the administative and storage headquarters. Camp Mabry was established in the early 1890s as a summer encampment of the Texas Volunteer Guard, a forerunner of the Texas National Guard. The name honors Woodford Haywood Mabry, adjutant general from 1891–1898.

The State Guard, an all-volunteer backup force, was created by the Legislature in 1941. It became an active element of the state military forces in 1965 with a mission of reinforcing the National Guard in emergencies, and replacing National Guard units called into federal service. The State Guard has a membership of approximately 2,000 personnel.

The Army National Guard is available for state and national emergencies and has been used extensively during hurricanes, tornadoes and floods. There are more than 117 Army National Guard armories throughout Texas, with many units serving in recent years in Afghanistan and Iraq.

When the military forces were reorganized following World War II, the Texas Air National Guard was added. Its units augment major Air Force commands. Approximately 3,500 men and women currently make up the Air Guard.

In 2011, Adjutant General John F. Nichols commanded a total of 23,500 soldiers, airmen and civilians.

When called into active federal service, National Guard units come within the chain of command of the Army and Air Force units. ☆

Medal of Freedom

President George H.W. Bush visits in the Oval Office with President Obama, who honored him with a Presidential Medal of Freedom in 2011 for his many years of service in public life. President Bush, who lives in Houston, was also cited for his work with President Bill Clinton to aid victims of Hurricane Katrina in 2005 and the Indian Ocean tsumani in 2004. Official White House photo.

Federal Courts in Texas

Source: The following list of U.S. appeals and district court judges and officials was compiled from court Web sites.

Texas is divided into four federal judicial districts, each of which is comprised of several divisions. Appeal from all Texas federal courts is to the **U.S. Fifth Circuit Court of Appeals** in New Orleans.

U.S. COURT OF APPEALS, FIFTH CIRCUIT

The Fifth Circuit is composed of Louisiana, Mississippi and Texas. Sessions are held in each of the states at least once a year and may be scheduled at any location having adequate facilities. U.S. circuit judges are appointed for life and received a salary of $184,500 in 2011.

Circuit Judges — Chief Judge, Edith H. Jones, Houston. **Judges:** Fortunato P. Benavides and Priscilla R. Owen, Austin; Catharina Haynes, Dallas; Carolyn Dineen King, Jerry E. Smith and Jennifer Walker Elrod, Houston; James E. Graves Jr., Leslie H. Southwick and E. Grady Jolly, Jackson, Miss.; W. Eugene Davis, Lafayette, La.; James L. Dennis and Edith Brown Clement, New Orleans; Emilio M. Garza and Edward C. Prado, San Antonio; Carl E. Stewart, Shreveport, La. **Senior Judges:** Harold R. DeMoss Jr., and Thomas M. Reavley, Houston; Will Garwood and Patrick E. Higginbotham, Austin; Rhesa H. Barksdale, Jackson, Miss.; Jacques L. Wiener Jr., New Orleans. **Clerk of Court:** Lyle W. Cayce, New Orleans.

U.S. DISTRICT COURTS

U.S. district judges are appointed for life and received a salary in 2011 of $174,000.

Northern Texas District
www.txnd.uscourts.gov

District Judges — Chief Judge, Sidney A. Fitzwater, Dallas. **Judges:** Mary Lou Robinson, Amarillo; Jorge A. Solis, Sam A. Lindsay, Barbara M.G. Lynn, David C. Godbey, Ed Kinkeade, Jane Boyle, Reed O'Connor, Dallas; John H. McBryde, Terry R. Means, Fort Worth; Sam R. Cummings, Lubbock. **Senior Judges:** A. Joe Fish, Robert B. Maloney, Royal Furgeson, Dallas. **Clerk of District Court:** Karen Mitchell, Dallas. **U.S. Attorney:** James Jacks, Dallas. **Federal Public Defender** (acting): Richard A. Anderson. **U.S. Marshal:** Randy Ely, Dallas. **Bankruptcy Judges:** Harlan D. Hale, Barbara J. Houser and Stacey G.C. Jernigan, Dallas; D. Michael Lynn and Russell F. Nelms, Fort Worth; Robert Jones, Lubbock. Court is in continuous session in each division of the Northern Texas District.

Following are the different divisions of the Northern District and the counties in each division:

Abilene Division
Callahan, Eastland, Fisher, Haskell, Howard, Jones, Mitchell, Nolan, Shackelford, Stephens, Stonewall, Taylor and Throckmorton. **Magistrate:** Phillip R. Lane, San Angelo. **Deputy-in-charge:** Marsha Elliott.

Amarillo Division
Armstrong, Briscoe, Carson, Castro, Childress, Collingsworth, Dallam, Deaf Smith, Donley, Gray, Hall, Hansford, Hartley, Hemphill, Hutchinson, Lipscomb, Moore, Ochiltree, Oldham, Parmer, Potter, Randall, Roberts, Sherman, Swisher and Wheeler. **Magistrate:** Clinton E. Averitte, Amarillo. **Deputy-in-charge:** Jeanetta Hetrick.

Dallas Division
Dallas, Ellis, Hunt, Johnson, Kaufman, Navarro and Rockwall. **Magistrates:** William F. Sanderson Jr., Jeff Kaplan, Paul Stickney, Irma C. Ramirez and Renee H. Toliver, Dallas.

Fort Worth Division
Comanche, Erath, Hood, Jack, Palo Pinto, Parker, Tarrant and Wise. **Magistrate:** Jeffrey L. Cureton, Fort Worth. **Deputy-in-charge:** Lynn Sherman.

Lubbock Division
Bailey, Borden, Cochran, Crosby, Dawson, Dickens, Floyd, Gaines, Garza, Hale, Hockley, Kent, Lamb, Lubbock, Lynn, Motley, Scurry, Terry and Yoakum. **U.S. District Judge:** Sam R. Cummings, Lubbock. **Magistrate:** Nancy M. Koenig, Lubbock. **Deputy-in-charge:** Kristy Weinheimer.

San Angelo Division
Brown, Coke, Coleman, Concho, Crockett, Glasscock, Irion, Menard, Mills, Reagan, Runnels, Schleicher, Sterling, Sutton and Tom Green. **Deputy-in-charge:** Joyce Lowe.

Wichita Falls Division
Archer, Baylor, Clay, Cottle, Foard, Hardeman, King, Knox, Montague, Wichita, Wilbarger and Young. **Magistrate:** R. Kerry Roach, Wichita Falls. **Deputy-in-Charge:** Teena McNeely.

Western Texas District
www.txwd.uscourts.gov

District Judges — Chief Judge, Fred Biery, San Antonio. **Judges:** Xavier Rodriguez, Orlando Garcia, San Antonio; Kathleen Cardone, Frank J. Montalvo, Philip R. Martinez, El Paso; Sam Sparks and Lee Yeakel, Austin; Alia Moses, Del Rio; Robert A. Junell, Midland-Odessa; Walter S. Smith Jr., Waco. **Senior Judges:** Harry Lee Hudspeth and James R. Nowlin, Austin; David Briones, El Paso. **Clerk of District Court:** William G. Putnicki, San Antonio. **U.S. Attorney:** John E. Murphy. **Federal Public Defender:** Henry J. Bemporad. **U.S. Marshal:** Robert R. Almonte, San Antonio. **Bankruptcy Judges:** Chief Judge, Ronald B. King. Judges, Craig A. Gargotta and H. Christopher Mott, Austin; Lief M. Clark, San Antonio.

Following are the different divisions of the Western District, and the counties in each division.

Austin Division
Bastrop, Blanco, Burleson, Burnet, Caldwell, Gillespie, Hays, Kimble, Lampasas, Lee, Llano, Mason, McCulloch, San Saba, Travis, Washington and Williamson. **Magistrates:** Andrew W. Austin and Robert Pitman, Austin. **Divisional Office Manager:** David O'Toole. **Bankruptcy Court Deputy-in-charge:** Maria Dozauer.

Del Rio Division

Edwards, Kinney, Maverick, Terrell, Uvalde, Val Verde and Zavala. **Magistrate:** Roberto Garcia and Victor R. Garcia, Del Rio. **Divisional Office Manager:** Rebecca Moore.

El Paso Division

El Paso County only. **Magistrates:** Robert F. Castañeda, Norbert J. Garney, David C. Guaderrama and Richard P. Mesa, El Paso. **Divisional Office Manager:** Tom Hilburger. **Bankruptcy Court Deputy-in-charge:** Julie Herrera.

Midland-Odessa Division

Andrews, Crane, Ector, Martin, Midland and Upton. Court for the Midland-Odessa Division is held at Midland, but may, at the discretion of the court, be held in Odessa. **Magistrate:** David Counts, Midland. **Divisional Office Manager:** Laura Fowler-Gonzales, Midland. **Bankruptcy Court Deputy-in-charge:** Christy L. Carouth.

Pecos Division

Brewster, Culberson, Hudspeth, Jeff Davis, Loving, Pecos, Presidio, Reeves, Ward and Winkler. **Magistrate:** B. Dwight Goains, Alpine. **Divisional Office Manager:** Karen J. White.

San Antonio Division

Atascosa, Bandera, Bexar, Comal, Dimmit, Frio, Gonzales, Guadalupe, Karnes, Kendall, Kerr, Medina, Real and Wilson. **Magistrates:** Pamela A. Mathy, John W. Primomo and Nancy Stein Nowak, San Antonio. **Divisional Office Manager:** Michael F. Oakes. **Bankruptcy Court Deputy-in-Charge:** Mary Croy, San Antonio.

Waco Division

Bell, Bosque, Coryell, Falls, Freestone, Hamilton, Hill, Leon, Limestone, McLennan, Milam, Robertson and Somervell. **Magistrate:** Jeffrey C. Manske, Waco. **Divisional Office Manager:** Mark G. Borchardt. **Bankruptcy Court Deputy-in-charge:** Bridget Hardage.

Eastern Texas District

www.txed.uscourts.gov

District Judges — Chief Judge, David J. Folsom, Texarkana. **Judges:** Ron Clark, Marcia A. Crone and Thad Heartfield, Beaumont; Michael H. Schneider and Leonard Davis, Tyler; T. John Ward, Marshall; Richard A. Schell, Sherman. **Clerk of District Court:** David J. Maland, Tyler. **U.S. Attorney:** John Malcolm Bales. **Federal Public Defender:** G. Patrick Black. **U.S. Marshal:** Gary Brown. **Bankruptcy Judges:** Chief Judge, Brenda T. Roades, Plano and William Parker, Tyler.

Following are the divisions of the Eastern District and the counties in each division:

Beaumont Division

Hardin, Jasper, Jefferson, Liberty, Newton, Orange. **Magistrates:** Earl Hines and Keith F. Giblin.

Lufkin Division

Angelina, Houston, Nacogdoches, Polk, Sabine, San Augustine, Shelby, Trinity, Tyler.

Marshall Division

Camp, Cass, Harrison, Hopkins, Marion, Morris, Upshur. **Magistrate:** Charles Everingham IV.

Sherman Division

Collin, Cooke, Delta, Denton, Fannin, Grayson, Hopkins and Lamar. **Magistrates:** Don Bush and Amos L. Mazzant.

Texarkana Division

Bowie, Franklin, Red River and Titus. **Magistrate:** Caroline M. Craven.

Tyler Division

Anderson, Cherokee, Gregg, Henderson, Panola, Rains, Rusk, Smith, Van Zandt and Wood. **Magistrates:** Judith Guthrie and John Love, Tyler.

Southern Texas District

www.txs.uscourts.gov

District Judges — Chief Judge, Ricardo H. Hinojosa, McAllen. **Judges:** Nancy F. Atlas, Keith Ellison, Vanessa Gilmore, Melinda Harmon, David Hittner, Kenneth M. Hoyt, Lynn N. Hughes, Sim Lake, Gray H. Miller, Lee H. Rosenthal, Ewing Werlein Jr., Houston; Hayden Head, Janis Jack, Corpus Christi; Hilda G. Tagle and Andrew S. Hanen, Brownsville; Randy Crane, McAllen; George P. Kazen, Micaela Alvarez and Diana Saldaña, Laredo; John D. Rainey, Victoria. **Senior Judges:** David Hittner and Ewing Werlein Jr., Houston. **Clerk of Court:** David J. Bradley, Houston. **U. S. Attorney:** José Angel Moreno, Houston. **Federal Public Defender:** Marjorie A. Meyers. **U.S. Marshal:** Elizabeth Saenz. **Bankruptcy Judges:** Chief, Marvin Isgur, Houston; Jeff Bohm, Karen K. Brown, Letitia Z. Paul, Houston; Richard S. Schmidt, Corpus Christi.

Following are the different divisions of the Southern District and the counties in each division:

Brownsville Division

Cameron and Willacy. **Magistrates:** Ronald G. Morgan, Felix Recio. **Deputy-in-charge:** Rosalina D'Venturi.

Corpus Christi Division

Aransas, Bee, Brooks, Duval, Jim Wells, Kenedy, Kleberg, Live Oak, Nueces and San Patricio. **Magistrates:** B. Janice Ellington and Brian L. Owsley. **Deputy-in-charge:** Monica Seaman.

Galveston Division

Brazoria, Chambers, Galveston and Matagorda. **Magistrate:** John R. Froeschner. **Deputy-in-charge:** Cathy Carnew.

Houston Division

Austin, Brazos, Colorado, Fayette, Fort Bend, Grimes, Harris, Madison, Montgomery, San Jacinto, Walker, Waller and Wharton. **Magistrates:** George Hanks, Frances H. Stacy, Nancy Johnson, Mary Milloy and Stephen W. Smith. **Deputy-in-charge:** Darlene Hansen.

Laredo Division

Jim Hogg, La Salle, McMullen, Webb and Zapata. **Magistrates:** J. Scott Hacker and Guillermo R. Garcia.

McAllen Division

Hidalgo and Starr. **Magistrates:** Dorina Ramos and Peter Ormsby. **Deputy-in-charge:** Sylvia S. Martinez.

Victoria Division

Calhoun, DeWitt, Goliad, Jackson, Lavaca, Refugio and Victoria. **Magistrate:** Nancy K. Johnson. **Deputy-in-charge:** Joyce Richards. ☆

The Trinity County Jail in Groveton. In 2010, both violent crime and property crime decreased in Texas compared with 2009. Photo by Ron Billings; Texas Forest Service.

Crime in Texas — 2010

Source: Texas Department of Public Safety, Austin; www.txdps.state.tx.us

Both violent crimes and property crimes decreased in 2010 compared with 2009. In addition, the **2010 overall crime rate** in Texas — the number of crimes per 100,000 population — **decreased 6 percent from 2009.** In 2010, there were 4,236.4 crimes per 100,000 people, compared with 4,507 in 2009.

The 2010 **violent crime rate** decreased 8.3 percent from 2009. The number of murders in 2010 was down 6 percent from 2009, and the number of rapes decreased 8 percent from 2009. The other two violent categories, robbery and aggravated assault, both decreased by 13.6 percent and 3.5 percent, respectively.

The 2010 **nonviolent, or property, crime rate** decreased 5.7 percent from 2009. The value of property stolen during the commission of index crimes in 2010 was more than $1.9 billion. The **value of stolen property recovered** by Texas law-enforcement agencies in 2010 was more than $492 million.

The total number of arrests in Texas decreased 5.1 percent in 2010 over 2009. The number of juvenile arrests decreased 9.3 percent, while adult arrests decreased 4.6 percent. There were 1.14 million arrests in 2010 compared with 1.2 million arrests in 2009.

The crime rate is tabulated on seven major offenses designated Index Crimes by the Federal Bureau of Investigation's **Uniform Crime Reporting program.** These seven categories include four violent offenses (murder, rape, robbery and aggravated assault) and three nonviolent crimes (burglary, larceny-theft and motor-vehicle theft). In Texas, these figures are collected by the Texas Department of Public Safety for the national UCR program. In 2010, 1,031 Texas law enforcement agencies (99.9 percent) participated in the Texas UCR program. Data are estimated for non-reporting agencies.

Arson in 2010

In 2010, reported arson offenses decreased 8.5 percent from 2009. Property damage from arson was reported at more than $167 million in 2010. There were 5,517 arsons in 2010, compared with 6,027 in 2009.

Family Violence in Texas in 2010

Family violence decreased by about 1.6 percent in 2010 over 2009. In 2010, there were 193,505 reported incidents of family violence committed against 211,769 victims by 207,474 offenders. In 2009, there were 196,713 incidents of family violence committed against 212,106 victims by 207,305 offenders. In 42.6 percent of the 2010 incidents, the relationship of victim to offender was marital. Of these victims, 16.7 percent were wives and 14.1 percent were common-law wives.

Of the remaining offenses, 15.6 percent involved parents against children or children against parents; and 41.7 involved other family or household relationships, such as grandparents, grandchildren, siblings, stepsiblings, roommates, or in-laws. The 77th Legislature amended the Texas Family Code to include violence in a "dating relationship."

There are six general categories of family violence: assault, homicide, kidnapping, robbery, forcible sex offenses, and nonforcible sex offenses. Assaults (including aggravated, simple, and intimidation) accounted for 96.8 percent of all family violence in 2010. Investigation of reports of domestic violence can be hazardous to police officers. During 2010, 358 Texas law officers were assaulted while investigating such reports.

Hate Crimes in Texas in 2010

There were 168 reported incidents of hate crime in Texas in 2010. This is an increase of 2.4 percent from the 164 incidents in 2009. These crimes involved 179 victims, 185 offenders, resulting from 171 offenses.

These crimes were motivated by race (48.5%), sexual orientation (22.5%), ethnicity or national origin (17.8%), religion (10.7%), and disability (0.5%).

Hate crimes, as defined by the Texas Hate Crimes Act, are crimes motivated by prejudice and hatred. The Texas Hate Crimes Act directs all law enforcement agencies in Texas to report bias offenses to the Texas Department of Public Safety.

Law Enforcement Deaths, Injuries

In 2010, two Texas law enforcement officers were killed in the line of duty because of criminal activity, and 13 officers were killed in duty-related accidents.

There were 4,424 officers assaulted during 2010 compared to 4,706 in 2009. This represents a decrease of 6 percent. ☆

Texas Crime History 1990–2010

Year	Murder	Rape	Robbery	Aggravated Assault	Burglary	Larceny-Theft	Motor Vehicle Theft	Rate per 100,000 Population
1990	2,388	8,746	44,316	73,860	314,346	730,926	154,387	7,823.7
1991	2,651	9,265	49,698	84,104	312,719	734,177	163,837	7,818.6
1992	2,240	9,368	44,582	86,067	268,864	689,515	145,039	7,055.1
1993	2,149	9,923	40,464	84,892	233,944	664,738	124,822	6,438.5
1994	2,023	9,101	37,639	81,079	214,698	624,048	110,772	5,873.1
1995	1,694	8,526	33,666	80,377	202,637	632,523	104,939	5,684.5
1996	1,476	8,374	32,796	80,572	204,335	659,397	104,928	5,708.3
1997	1,328	8,007	30,513	77,239	200,966	645,174	101,687	5,478.2
1998	1,343	7,914	28,672	73,648	194,872	606,805	96,614	5,110.7
1999	1,218	7,629	29,424	74,165	190,347	614,478	91,992	5,035.2
2000	1,236	7,821	30,186	73,987	188,205	634,575	92,878	4,952.4
2001	1,331	8,191	35,330	77,221	204,240	669,587	102,838	5,152.3
2002	1,305	8,541	37,599	78,713	212,702	690,028	102,943	5,196.7
2003	1,417	7,986	37,000	75,706	219,733	697,790	98,174	5,144.1
2004	1,360	8,401	35,811	75,983	220,079	696,220	93,844	5,032.0
2005	1,405	8,505	35,781	75,409	219,733	676,022	93,471	4,857.1
2006	1,385	8,407	37,221	74,624	215,754	648,083	95,750	4,599.6
2007	1,415	8,430	38,777	73,570	228,325	662,481	94,026	4,631.1
2008	1,373	8.004	37,757	76,487	230,263	654,133	85,411	4,494.7
2009	1,327	8,286	38,041	74,135	240,193	678,340	76,617	4,507.0
2010	1,247	7,626	32,865	71,561	229,269	654,484	68,220	4,236.4

Sources: Texas Department of Public Safety, Austin, and the Federal Bureau of Investigation, Washington. The crime rate is based on the 2010 Texas population of 25,145,561.

Crime Profile of Texas Counties for 2010

County	Agencies	Commissioned Personnel †	Murder	Rape	Robbery	Assault	Burglary	Larceny-Theft	Auto Theft	Total Index Crimes (see page 557 for definition)	Crime Rate per 100,000
Anderson	3	76	5	25	17	103	371	767	40	1,328	2,329.1
Andrews	2	28	0	9	0	45	111	211	10	386	2,731.0
Angelina	5	153	4	27	61	178	848	1,973	94	3,185	3,802.6
Aransas	2	72	0	8	4	23	209	450	33	727	3,040.6
Archer	3	11	0	1	0	11	33	57	2	104	1,170.6
Armstrong	1	2	0	0	0	0	11	10	1	22	1,074.2
Atascosa	5	68	0	9	7	76	268	726	51	1,137	2,496.4
Austin	5	70	5	11	4	41	178	254	27	520	1,888.3
Bailey	2	13	2	5	0	13	78	81	9	188	3,021.1
Bandera	1	28	0	0	0	13	103	105	0	221	1,063.0
Bastrop	4	118	3	22	25	336	612	1,313	91	2,402	3,123.6
Baylor	2	10	0	0	0	24	18	33	1	76	2,095.4
Bee	2	42	0	12	7	68	133	332	24	576	1,777.3
Bell ‡	14	550	13	145	359	877	3,392	6,962	386	12,134	4,170.4
Bexar	28	3,213	92	569	2,571	6,071	20,251	74,755	6,330	110,639	6,611.3
Blanco	3	7	0	1	0	20	59	67	16	163	1,762.9
Borden	1	2	0	0	0	0	2	0	0	2	343.6
Bosque ‡	5	25	0	1	0	8	60	133	8	210	1,191.6
Bowie	7	169	4	35	108	524	1,051	2,258	201	4,181	4,440.8
Brazoria	20	570	7	79	126	397	1,668	4,619	316	7,212	2,245.0
Brazos	4	392	7	73	135	467	1,512	5,510	241	7,945	4,356.5
Brewster	3	29	1	3	0	11	37	74	1	127	1,335.0
Briscoe	1	1	0	0	0	2	5	2	1	10	717.9
Brooks	2	24	1	2	3	14	77	110	3	210	2,876.7
Brown	4	74	0	12	14	146	261	742	19	1,194	3,141.8
Burleson	3	31	0	17	2	17	88	72	17	213	1,289.3
Burnet	7	113	0	12	2	61	241	643	66	1,025	2,127.2
Caldwell	4	68	0	9	12	109	207	580	37	954	2,589.6

Crime Profile of Texas Counties for 2010

County	Agencies	Commissioned Personnel †	Murder	Rape	Robbery	Assault	Burglary	Larceny-Theft	Auto Theft	Total Index Crimes (see page 557 for definition)	Crime Rate per 100,000
Calhoun	4	46	0	15	4	120	121	372	18	650	3,171.0
Callahan	3	16	0	0	0	14	60	109	18	201	1,496.1
Cameron ‡	19	654	11	101	316	916	3,572	14,254	653	19,823	4,935.5
Camp	2	17	0	8	0	15	109	175	9	316	2,453.6
Carson	2	9	0	0	1	8	9	55	5	78	1,288.6
Cass	5	46	0	19	8	63	258	424	58	830	2,862.8
Castro ‡	3	13	1	0	0	10	88	195	6	300	4,280.8
Chambers	3	49	2	7	11	44	191	428	78	761	2,656.6
Cherokee ‡	6	73	2	15	34	132	542	940	101	1,766	3,653.6
Childress	2	12	0	1	0	26	44	37	4	112	1,491.3
Clay	1	10	0	0	2	8	43	83	4	140	1,291.5
Cochran	1	8	0	0	0	0	22	46	5	73	2,561.4
Coke	1	5	0	0	0	1	15	0	1	17	522.8
Coleman	3	18	0	0	2	9	135	124	26	296	3,529.3
Collin	15	1,015	6	144	248	697	3,402	12,111	868	17,476	2,269.0
Collingsworth	1	5	0	0	0	0	0	0	0	0	0
Colorado	4	42	1	4	5	33	127	219	19	408	1,979.1
Comal	3	234	2	42	38	275	735	2,138	92	3,322	2,747.9
Comanche	3	23	0	2	3	36	105	254	6	406	3,013.2
Concho	2	9	0	2	0	2	26	13	3	46	1,302.0
Cooke	4	64	2	8	15	58	296	671	56	1,106	2,854.0
Coryell	3	94	4	6	18	152	369	1,022	42	1,613	2,207.8
Cottle	2	3	0	0	0	0	22	3	0	25	1,631.9
Crane	2	13	0	2	0	4	14	44	2	66	1,580.8
Crockett ‡	1	8	–	–	–	–	–	–	–	–	NA
Crosby	4	11	0	0	0	9	36	32	4	81	1,349.3
Culberson	1	5	0	1	0	4	0	8	2	15	670.5
Dallam	2	19	0	3	0	24	40	107	8	182	2,093.6
Dallas ‡	37	6,442	184	769	5,680	6,075	31,475	70,908	12,949	128,040	4,727.3
Dawson	2	24	1	1	2	23	73	172	13	285	2,128.3
Deaf Smith	2	33	0	3	4	62	134	319	29	551	3,014.2
Delta	1	10	0	0	3	2	39	72	5	121	2,240.3
Denton ‡	21	894	9	133	174	532	2,075	7,719	777	11,419	2,070.7
DeWitt	3	28	0	1	0	36	82	131	11	261	1,483.8
Dickens	2	4	0	0	0	2	2	1	1	6	249.6
Dimmit	1	14	0	0	5	42	55	91	11	204	2,103.3
Donley	1	6	0	0	0	9	14	25	1	49	1,347.6
Duval	3	30	2	1	3	78	105	189	22	400	3,139.2
Eastland	6	35	0	0	2	25	84	181	13	305	1,685.5
Ector	4	286	7	36	111	750	1,200	3,421	254	5,779	4,212.7
Edwards	1	4	0	0	0	3	14	17	0	34	1,855.9
Ellis	9	204	3	16	47	220	761	2,400	165	3,612	2,469.7
El Paso	10	1,511	7	222	530	2,609	2,698	16,235	1,798	24,099	3,186.4
Erath	4	80	0	17	4	56	154	582	21	834	2,291.4
Falls	4	23	0	3	4	26	126	126	16	301	1,817.3
Fannin	3	34	1	11	1	37	165	372	23	610	1,844.9
Fayette	4	40	2	4	5	17	117	263	17	425	1,853.8
Fisher	1	5	0	0	0	10	22	32	0	64	1,679.8
Floyd	3	12	1	2	2	19	58	76	7	165	2,602.5
Foard	2	3	0	0	0	1	2	4	0	7	536.4
Fort Bend ‡	11	913	20	101	317	1,034	2,576	6,783	509	11,340	2,078.6
Franklin	1	9	0	4	2	13	57	42	9	127	1,248.6
Freestone	4	38	1	3	5	37	105	172	21	344	1,765.6
Frio	3	27	1	0	2	32	126	188	12	361	2,242.2
Gaines	3	27	1	2	0	11	36	112	12	174	1,127.5
Galveston	15	811	13	144	323	542	2,383	7,257	617	11,279	3,761.8
Garza	1	9	0	0	0	2	15	18	3	38	821.4
Gillespie	2	54	1	3	0	5	63	260	7	339	1,386.2
Glasscock	1	3	0	0	0	1	3	10	0	14	1,165.7

Crime Profile of Texas Counties for 2010

County	Agencies	Commissioned Personnel †	Murder	Rape	Robbery	Assault	Burglary	Larceny-Theft	Auto Theft	Total Index Crimes (see page 557 for definition)	Crime Rate per 100,000
Goliad	1	13	0	4	0	14	21	29	2	70	997.6
Gonzales	4	37	1	9	10	88	129	278	21	536	2,728.6
Gray	2	37	0	2	11	109	194	661	50	1,027	4,677.5
Grayson	13	220	11	21	58	248	857	2,604	140	3,939	3,266.5
Gregg	5	330	13	78	149	528	1,227	4,238	536	6,769	5,322.7
Grimes	2	45	1	4	5	75	161	340	29	615	2,349.0
Guadalupe ‡	5	197	3	43	50	161	709	1,951	104	3,021	2,438.2
Hale	4	63	1	10	13	54	258	788	40	1,164	3,244.8
Hall	2	5	0	1	1	13	29	25	5	74	2,258.9
Hamilton ‡	2	13	0	1	2	21	98	79	7	208	2,600.3
Hansford	3	9	0	0	0	4	11	40	3	58	1,074.9
Hardeman	2	8	0	2	0	9	58	65	5	139	3,670.5
Hardin	5	77	1	8	11	57	232	576	73	958	1,780.3
Harris ‡	41	9,382	364	1,098	13,095	17,666	46,982	125,702	19,467	224,374	5,401.5
Harrison	5	107	3	13	32	214	556	1,089	92	1,999	3,169.3
Hartley	1	5	0	1	0	8	13	19	2	43	1,728.3
Haskell	2	7	0	1	0	5	27	27	0	60	1,236.3
Hays	4	288	5	26	42	253	730	2,747	130	3,933	2,417.9
Hemphill	1	10	0	1	1	12	7	32	3	56	1,615.7
Henderson ‡	9	139	3	45	30	203	797	1,374	184	2,636	3,327.1
Hidalgo ‡	24	1,092	35	220	546	1,633	7,699	26,119	2,548	38,800	5,118.6
Hill	5	71	1	8	8	20	246	481	26	790	2,190.4
Hockley ‡	5	44	0	14	3	82	193	383	19	694	3,131.3
Hood	3	79	1	9	5	83	260	846	70	1,274	2,430.4
Hopkins	3	54	0	7	7	43	136	261	27	481	1,384.7
Houston	3	37	1	1	3	43	152	250	33	483	2,174.3
Howard	2	60	0	17	9	174	418	1,089	61	1,768	5,392.7
Hudspeth	1	17	0	0	1	9	20	10	14	54	1,751.5
Hunt	9	151	3	27	75	260	1,169	1,858	173	3,565	4,285.9
Hutchinson ‡	3	39	1	16	7	178	153	568	47	970	4,562.6
Irion	1	4	0	0	0	1	2	15	1	19	1,096.4
Jack	2	19	0	0	2	16	56	44	8	126	1,492.0
Jackson	3	27	1	2	4	27	52	141	5	232	1,632.1
Jasper	3	47	0	10	1	99	183	464	22	779	2,281.6
Jeff Davis	1	3	0	2	0	3	5	4	0	14	621.1
Jefferson	7	568	19	114	514	849	3,140	6,931	582	12,149	5,027.6
Jim Hogg	1	20	0	0	0	10	10	15	0	35	706.4
Jim Wells	4	73	2	19	9	222	544	1,021	66	1,883	4,687.8
Johnson	7	237	5	34	33	286	844	2,671	146	4,019	2,479.4
Jones	5	25	1	4	3	51	89	176	13	337	2,602.7
Karnes	3	22	0	0	1	36	157	230	13	437	2,924.6
Kaufman ‡	7	179	2	50	47	273	1,031	1,530	218	3,151	2,969.2
Kendall	2	79	0	9	5	24	96	355	12	501	1,472.9
Kenedy	1	11	0	0	0	0	1	2	1	4	1,101.9
Kent	1	3	0	0	0	2	4	17	0	23	3,343.0
Kerr	3	103	1	8	11	68	196	830	43	1,157	2,375.5
Kimble	2	14	1	4	0	14	19	89	4	131	2,892.5
King	1	2	0	0	0	1	4	0	0	5	1,792.1
Kinney	2	6	1	0	0	6	6	6	2	21	645.4
Kleberg	3	81	1	21	15	239	477	1,053	41	1,847	6,111.8
Knox ‡	3	5	0	1	0	0	9	23	2	35	1,082.9
Lamar	4	96	2	16	28	138	568	1,441	69	2,262	4,631.1
Lamb ‡	5	34	0	3	1	52	131	244	23	454	3,497.7
Lampasas	3	37	0	10	0	11	62	221	8	312	1,545.8
La Salle	1	14	0	0	1	12	16	43	1	73	1,261.9
Lavaca	3	28	1	3	1	13	107	175	7	307	1,501.1
Lee	3	26	1	10	6	48	102	178	12	357	2,199.4
Leon	1	24	0	2	1	16	76	92	9	196	1,151.2
Liberty	4	103	4	15	38	255	693	1,765	262	3,032	3,985.3

Crime Profile of Texas Counties for 2010

County	Agencies	Commissioned Personnel †	Murder	Rape	Robbery	Assault	Burglary	Larceny-Theft	Auto Theft	Total Index Crimes (see page 557 for definition)	Crime Rate per 100,000
Limestone	4	52	2	28	7	96	284	522	25	964	4,334.3
Lipscomb	1	7	0	0	0	0	1	13	2	16	517.6
Live Oak	2	18	0	1	0	7	43	51	1	103	945.4
Llano	3	37	1	5	1	7	140	255	9	418	2,551.7
Loving	1	3	0	0	0	0	0	0	0	0	0.0
Lubbock	9	590	10	133	339	1,760	3,477	9,698	590	16,007	5,887.1
Lynn	3	12	0	2	0	3	22	39	2	68	1,196.8
Madison	2	19	2	4	7	31	88	220	24	376	2,820.3
Marion	2	20	0	8	3	43	115	164	15	348	3,407.8
Martin	2	8	0	1	1	4	32	38	8	84	2,039.8
Mason	1	4	0	1	0	1	5	30	0	37	930.8
Matagorda	4	87	2	14	13	68	405	942	22	1,466	3,987.6
Maverick	2	61	0	5	9	117	499	996	55	1,681	3,133.0
McCulloch	2	15	0	0	2	18	53	83	2	158	1,990.7
McLennan	17	540	9	119	241	905	2,532	6,710	364	10,880	4,636.9
McMullen	1	4	0	1	0	1	0	5	1	8	995.0
Medina ‡	5	60	0	9	3	73	221	494	30	830	1,855.4
Menard	1	5	1	0	0	0	2	5	1	9	428.8
Midland	3	254	3	44	69	322	1,090	2,918	180	4,626	3,487.8
Milam	4	35	0	5	2	30	130	456	19	642	2,610.9
Mills	1	6	0	0	0	2	20	31	2	55	1,107.8
Mitchell	2	12	0	4	0	10	39	149	1	203	2,185.4
Montague ‡	4	30	0	2	3	26	148	306	39	524	2,680.4
Montgomery	10	574	13	78	233	842	2,880	7,655	719	12,420	2,675.2
Moore	4	48	1	11	4	42	97	302	22	479	2,310.0
Morris	4	20	0	10	7	50	179	164	11	421	3,352.7
Motley	1	2	0	0	0	2	6	12	1	21	1,662.7
Nacogdoches	3	128	4	15	48	336	587	1,517	76	2,583	4,009.7
Navarro	3	105	0	26	30	113	583	1,268	90	2,110	4,244.2
Newton	1	12	0	0	1	9	50	80	9	149	1,104.1
Nolan	3	36	1	18	3	127	110	378	17	654	4,421.6
Nueces	8	628	18	195	413	1,668	2,993	13,120	488	18,895	5,847.5
Ochiltree	2	16	1	2	0	21	47	99	9	179	1,818.4
Oldham	1	6	0	0	0	2	3	12	2	19	903.0
Orange	7	155	1	20	70	213	986	1,867	174	3,331	4,099.4
Palo Pinto	2	51	2	24	12	86	266	629	58	1,077	3,621.4
Panola	2	37	2	7	4	51	105	263	31	463	2,006.8
Parker	5	173	3	13	23	143	611	1,301	105	2,199	1,954.2
Parmer	4	18	0	0	2	22	38	80	5	147	1,598.7
Pecos	2	35	1	14	1	54	80	257	15	422	2,612.7
Polk	4	81	3	33	16	51	356	662	52	1,173	2,500.5
Potter	4	424	13	97	241	867	2,661	7,976	657	12,512	6,092.8
Presidio ‡	3	9	0	0	1	3	18	5	2	29	388.8
Rains	1	11	0	1	2	14	47	67	5	136	1,184.5
Randall	3	109	1	6	3	36	136	336	37	555	1,619.8
Reagan	1	8	0	0	0	2	2	5	0	9	302.2
Real	1	3	0	0	0	5	8	4	0	17	585.6
Red River	3	26	0	1	1	21	99	89	10	221	1,756.5
Reeves	2	38	0	5	1	31	83	212	8	340	3,139.7
Refugio	2	21	0	2	0	11	30	37	2	82	1,147.7
Roberts	1	5	0	1	0	2	5	17	3	28	3,200.0
Robertson	4	32	1	3	4	41	125	244	21	439	2,809.8
Rockwall	4	137	1	24	6	66	253	1,046	107	1,503	1,939.4
Runnels	4	17	0	2	0	17	64	117	9	209	2,086.7
Rusk	4	82	5	8	18	134	357	688	86	1,296	2,762.1
Sabine ‡	3	11	1	3	1	25	37	63	2	132	1,300.2
San Augustine	2	12	0	1	0	22	41	78	6	148	1,739.1
San Jacinto	1	28	2	4	10	66	362	340	59	843	3,361.0
San Patricio	9	116	3	19	40	131	579	1,437	64	2,273	3,280.3

Crime Profile of Texas Counties for 2010

County	Agencies	Commissioned Personnel †	Murder	Rape	Robbery	Assault	Burglary	Larceny-Theft	Auto Theft	Total Index Crimes (see page 557 for definition)	Crime Rate per 100,000
San Saba	2	9	0	1	1	20	23	37	1	83	1,426.1
Schleicher	1	5	0	0	0	1	3	8	0	12	443.6
Scurry ‡	3	32	1	11	4	120	133	287	32	588	3,636.6
Shackelford	1	5	0	2	0	2	14	19	3	40	1,327.6
Shelby	2	34	2	4	11	60	122	407	33	639	2,376.7
Sherman	2	9	0	0	0	0	4	13	1	18	625.2
Smith ‡	11	405	13	113	129	612	1,764	5,484	401	8,516	4,110.3
Somervell	1	20	0	2	2	3	25	67	3	102	1,253.7
Starr	5	107	4	16	18	141	346	703	92	1,320	2,081.0
Stephens	2	19	1	2	1	14	49	75	6	148	1,541.5
Sterling	1	4	0	0	0	3	5	9	1	18	1,445.8
Stonewall	1	2	0	0	0	5	8	2	0	15	1,134.6
Sutton	2	9	0	2	0	5	3	30	1	41	957.0
Swisher	3	12	0	10	1	18	51	95	4	179	2,447.4
Tarrant	38	4,854	95	619	2,251	4,958	18,754	52,406	4,917	84,000	4,696.8
Taylor	6	291	4	74	113	411	1,461	3,641	206	5,910	4,436.2
Terrell	1	7	0	0	0	4	21	7	2	34	3,549.1
Terry	2	29	0	0	7	15	68	145	14	249	2,066.7
Throckmorton	1	2	0	0	0	0	5	0	0	5	319.3
Titus	2	49	2	6	12	81	323	596	36	1,056	3,481.7
Tom Green	3	244	2	58	54	188	1,123	3,235	166	4,826	4,449.0
Travis	16	2,598	48	293	1,326	2,796	10,311	40,006	2,497	57,277	5,357.0
Trinity	2	17	1	7	1	21	119	228	27	404	2,914.7
Tyler	2	25	2	13	4	76	223	175	27	520	2,541.5
Upshur ‡	5	74	2	10	5	45	219	498	50	829	2,327.5
Upton	1	11	0	1	0	1	3	17	0	22	710.4
Uvalde	3	59	1	3	9	59	299	465	6	842	3,139.9
Val Verde	2	104	1	3	19	64	212	649	37	985	2,037.8
Van Zandt	6	68	1	2	7	105	388	543	93	1,139	2,181.2
Victoria	2	107	8	44	82	363	963	2,776	134	4,370	4,971.8
Walker	2	79	2	24	56	164	474	1,089	78	1,887	2,941.2
Waller ‡	6	72	5	8	17	64	365	564	54	1,077	2,984.0
Ward	2	25	0	1	2	59	90	140	12	304	2,904.4
Washington	3	78	0	9	12	72	222	575	31	921	2,787.1
Webb	6	684	11	82	211	969	1,957	9,041	946	13,217	5,374.3
Wharton	3	99	0	4	45	122	313	705	57	1,246	3,050.5
Wheeler	2	9	1	0	3	10	20	44	7	85	1,756.6
Wichita	6	279	7	46	138	316	1,515	4,103	298	6,423	5,064.7
Wilbarger	2	29	0	6	5	51	85	281	16	444	3,315.2
Willacy ‡	5	34	0	17	11	231	317	558	16	1,150	5,646.7
Williamson	12	613	4	81	67	288	1,359	5,596	239	7,634	1,880.4
Wilson	5	50	1	5	3	30	156	394	21	610	1,469.0
Winkler	3	21	0	2	0	11	20	61	5	99	1,473.0
Wise	4	96	0	10	6	125	225	540	26	932	1,544.8
Wood	5	57	1	4	1	46	254	470	42	818	1,839.5
Yoakum	2	15	0	4	1	7	34	70	4	120	1,555.0
Young	3	39	0	11	1	21	125	312	20	490	2,764.6
Zapata	1	48	2	5	3	27	156	112	11	316	2,227.1
Zavala	2	19	0	0	1	43	44	92	7	187	1,619.5
TOTAL		54,777	1,247	7,626	32,865	71,561	229,269	654,484	68,220	1,065,272	4,236.4

* County population figures used for calculation of crime rate are the U.S. Census Bureau revised figures for 2010.

† The commissioned officers listed here are those employed by sheriffs' offices and police departments of municipalities; universities, colleges, and public-school districts; transit systems; park departments; and medical facilities. The Texas Department of Public Safety also has 3,504 commissioned personnel stationed statewide.

‡ County in which one or more law-enforcement agencies did not report data for all of 2010 to the DPS. The number of commissioned officers listed for this county does not include those employed by nonreporting agencies. The numbers of index crimes for the county includes estimates for nonreporting agencies to enable the DPS to provide comparable data for 2010.

Culture and the Arts

Sculptures in the garden of the Houston Museum of Fine Arts. Photo by Robert Plocheck.

Museums

Film and Television

Texas Medal of the Arts

Texas Institute of Letters

State Poet Laureates

State Artists, Musicians

State Historians

Texas Museums of Art, Science, History

Listed below are links to the Web pages of Texas museums. Where required some have indication of the area of emphasis of the exhibits.

Abilene
Frontier Texas! (History)
frontiertexas.com
Grace Museum (Art, History)
thegracemuseum.org
National Center for Children's Illustrated Literature
nccil.org

Addison
Cavanaugh Flight Museum
cavanaughflightmuseum.com/

Albany
Old Jail Art Center
theoldjailartcenter.org/

Alpine
Museum of the Big Bend (History)
sulross.edu/~museum/

Amarillo
Amarillo Museum of Art
amarilloart.org/
American Quarter Horse Heritage Center & Museum
aqha.com/foundation/museum/
Don Harrington Discovery Center (Science, Children's)
dhdc.org/
Texas Pharmacy Museum
ttuhsc.edu/sop/prospective/visitors/museum.aspx

Angleton
Brazoria County Historical Museum
bchm.org/

Arlington
Legends of the Game Baseball Museum
texas.rangers.mlb.com/tex/ballpark/museum.jsp

Austin
Austin Children's Museum

austinkids.org/
Austin Museum of Art
amoa.org/
Bob Bullock Texas State History Museum
thestoryoftexas.com/
Capitol Visitors Center (Historical)
tspb.state.tx.us/CVC/home/home.html
Elisabet Ney Museum (Art)
ci.austin.tx.us/elisabetney/html/main.html
French Legation Museum (History)
frenchlegationmuseum.org/
Harry Ransom Humanities Research Center (History, Literature)
hrc.utexas.edu/
Jack S. Blanton Museum of Art
blantonmuseum.org/
Jacob Fontaine Religious Museum
rootsweb.com/~txjfrm/
Jourdan-Bachman Pioneer Farms
pioneerfarms.org/
Lady Bird Johnson Wildflower Center
wildflower.org/
Lyndon B. Johnson Library
lbjlib.utexas.edu/
Mexic-Arte Museum (Art)
mexic-artemuseum.org/
O. Henry Museum (History)
ci.austin.tx.us/parks/ohenry.htm
Texas Memorial Museum (History, Natural History)
utexas.edu/tmm/
Texas Military Forces Museum
texasmilitaryforcesmuseum.org/
Texas Music Museum
texasmusicmuseum.org
Umlauf Sculpture Garden & Museum
umlaufsculpture.org
Wild Basin Wilderness Preserve
wildbasin.org/
Women and Their Work

womenandtheirwork.org/
Bay City
Matagorda County Museum
matagordacountymuseum.org/
Beaumont
Art Museum of Southeast Texas
amset.org/
Edison Museum (Science)
edisonmuseum.org/
Fire Museum of Texas
firemuseumoftexas.org/
McFaddin-Ward House (History)
mcfaddin-ward.org/
Spindletop/Gladys City Boomtown Museum (History)
spindletop.org/
Texas Energy Museum (History)
texasenergymuseum.org
Belton
Bell County Museum
bellcountytx.com/Museum/themuseum_directions.html
Big Spring
Heritage of Big Spring
bigspringmuseum.com/

Bonham
Sam Rayburn Library/Museum
cah.utexas.edu/museums/rayburn.php
Borger
Hutchinson County Historial Museum
hutchinsoncountymuseum.org/
Brownsville
Brownsville Museum of Fine Art
brownsvillemfa.org
Historic Brownsville Museum
brownsvillemuseum.org
Brownwood
Brown County Museum of History
browncountyhistory.org/
bcmoh.html
Bryan
Brazos Valley Museum of Natural

Public Libraries in Texas

The following information was furnished by the Library Development Division of the Texas State Library, Austin.

Texas public libraries continue to strive to meet the education and information needs of Texans by providing library services of high quality with oftentimes-limited resources.

Each year, services provided by public libraries increase, with more visits to public libraries and higher attendance in library programs.

The challenges facing the public libraries in Texas are many and varied. The costs for providing electronic and on-line sources, in addition to traditional library services, are growing faster than library budgets.

Urban libraries are trying to serve growing populations, while libraries in rural areas are trying to serve remote populations and provide dis-

tance learning where possible.

National rankings of public libraries are published by the National Center for Education Statistics. These rankings may be found at:
http://nces.ed.gov/globallocator.

When comparing Texas statistics to those nationally, Texas continues to rank below most of the other states in most categories, with the exception of Reference Transactions and Public Use Internet Terminals.

Complete statistical information on public libraries is available on the Texas State Library's Web page at: **www.tsl.state.tx.us**.

Many Texas public libraries have established pages on the Internet. You can find a list of Web addresses at: **www.tsl.state.tx.us/texshare/pl/texlibs.html**. ☆

History
brazosvalleymuseum.org/
Buffalo Gap
Buffalo Gap Historic Village
mcwhiney.org/buffgap/bghome.
html
Burton
Burton Cotton Gin and Museum
cottonginmuseum.org/
Canadian
River Valley Pioneer Museum
rivervalleymuseum.org/
Canyon
Panhandle-Plains Historical Museum
panhandleplains.org
Carthage
Texas Country Music Hall of Fame
& Tex Ritter Museum
carthagetexas.com/HallofFame/
index.html
Clarendon
Saints' Roost Museum (Historical)
saintsroost.org
Clifton
Bosque Museum (History)
bosquemuseum.org/
College Station
George Bush Presidential Library
bushlibrary.tamu.edu/
Stark University Center Galleries
stark.tamu.edu/
Virtual Museum of Nautical
Archaeology
ina.tamu.edu/vm.htm
Conroe
Heritage Museum of Montgomery
County
heritagemuseum.us/
Corpus Christi
Art Museum of South Texas
stia.org/
Corpus Christi Museum of Science
and History
ccmuseum.com/museum/
index.cfm
Texas State Aquarium
texasstateaquarium.org/
Texas State Museum of Asian
Cultures
asianculturesmuseum.org/
USS Lexington Museum
usslexington.com/
Corsicana
Pearce Western Art/Civil War
Museum
pearcecollections.us/
Cotulla
Brush Country Historical Museum
historicdistrict.com/museum/
Dalhart
XIT Museum (Historical)
xitmuseum.com/
Dallas
African American Museum
aamdallas.org/
Museum of the American Railroad
dallasrailwaymuseum.com
Dallas Historical Society (Fair Park)
dallashistory.org/
Dallas Museum of Art
dallasmuseumofart.org/
Dallas Museum of Natural History
natureandscience.org

The Houston Museum of Natural Sciences. Photo by Robert Plocheck.

Frontiers of Flight Museum
flightmuseum.com/
International Museum of Cultures
internationalmuseumofcultures.
org/
Meadows Museum (Art)
smu.edu/meadows/museum/
Dallas Heritage Village
dallasheritagevillage.org/
The Sixth Floor Museum (History)
jfk.org/
Denison
Red River Railroad Museum
redriverrailmuseum.org
Denton
Courthouse-on-the-Square Museum
(Historical)
dentoncounty.com/dept/main.
asp?Dept=72
UNT Art Galleries
gallery.unt.edu/
Denton County Historical Museum
dentoncountyhistoricalmuseum.
com
Dublin
Dr Pepper Bottling CompanyMuseum
dublindrpepper.com/
Edgewood
Edgewood Heritage Park and
Historical Village
vzinet.com/heritage/
Edinburg
Museum of South Texas History
mosthistory.org/
El Campo
El Campo Museum of Natural History
elcampomuseum.com/
El Paso
Centennial Museum/Chihuahuan
Desert Gardens
museum.utep.edu/
El Paso Museum of Art
elpasoartmuseum.org/
Fort Davis
Chihuahuan Desert Research
Institute and Visitor Center
cdri.org/
Fort Stockton
Annie Riggs Museum (Historical)
tourtexas.com/fortstockton/
ftstockriggs.html

Fort Worth
Amon Carter Museum (Art)
cartermuseum.org/
Cattle Raisers Museum
cattleraisersmuseum.org/
Fort Worth Museum of Science
and History
fwmuseum.org/
Kimbell Art Museum
kimbellart.org/
Log Cabin Village (Historical)
logcabinvillage.org
Modern Art Museum of Fort Worth
mamfw.org/
National Cowgirl Museum
and Hall of Fame
cowgirl.net/
Sid Richardson Collection
of Western Art
sidrmuseum.org/
Texas Civil War Museum
texascivilwarmuseum.com/
Fredericksburg
Gillespie County Historical Society
pioneermuseum.com/
National Museum of the Pacific War
nimitz-museum.org/
Galveston
Lone Star Flight Museum
lsfm.org
Offshore Energy Center/Ocean Star
(Science, Industry)
oceanstaroec.com/
Texas Seaport Museum and Tallship
"Elissa"
tsm-elissa.org/
Gilmer
Flight of Phoenix Aviation Museum
flightofthephoenix.org/
Greenville
Audie Murphy/American Cotton
Museum
cottonmuseum.com/
Henderson
The Depot Museum (Historical)
depotmuseum.com/
Houston
Blaffer Gallery, University of Houston
class.uh.edu/blaffer/
Children's Museum of Houston
cmhouston.org/

Contemporary Arts Museum
  camh.org/
Houston Center for Comtemporary
  Craft
  crafthouston.org/default.asp?ID=1
Houston Center for Photography
  hcponline.org/
Houston Fire Museum (History)
  houstonfiremuseum.org/
Houston Museum of Natural Science
  hmns.org/
Lawndale Art Center
  lawndaleartcenter.org/
The Menil Collection (Art)
  menil.org/
Museum of Fine Arts
  mfah.org/
Museum of Health and Medical
  Science
  mhms.org/
Museum of Printing History
  printingmuseum.org/

Rice University Art Gallery
  ricegallery.org/
San Jacinto Museum of History
  sanjacinto-museum.org/
Space Center Houston
  spacecenter.org/
Huntsville
Sam Houston Memorial Museum
  shsu.edu/~smm_www/
Texas Prison Museum
  txprisonmuseum.org/
Kerrville
Museum of Western Art
  museumofwesternart.org/
Kilgore
East Texas Oil Museum
  easttexasoilmuseum.com/
Lake Jackson
Lake Jackson Historical Museum
  lakejacksonmuseum.org/
Laredo
Republic of the Rio Grande Museum

webbheritage.org/riograndehistory.
  htm
Texas A&M International University
  Planetarium
  tamiu.edu/coas/planetarium/
League City
West Bay Common School
  Children's Museum (Historical)
  oneroomschoolhouse.org/
Longview
Longview Museum of Fine Arts
  lmfa.org/
Lubbock
American Museum of Agriculture
  agriculturehistory.org/
Buddy Holly Center (Historical)
  www.buddyhollycenter.org/
Museum of Texas Tech University
  (Art, Humanities, Science)
  www.depts.ttu.edu/museumttu/
National Ranching Heritage Center
  www.depts.ttu.edu/ranchhc/

State Cultural Agencies Assist the Arts

*Source: Principally, the Texas Commission on the Arts,
along with other state cultural agencies.*

Culture in Texas, as in any market, is a mixture of activity generated by both the commercial and the nonprofit sectors.

The commercial sector encompasses Texas-based profit-making businesses including commercial recording artists, nightclubs, record companies, private galleries, assorted boutiques that carry fine art collectibles and private dance and music halls. Texas also has extensive cultural resources offered by nonprofit organizations that are engaged in charitable, educational and humanitarian activities.

The Legislature has authorized five state agencies to administer cultural services and funds for the public good. The agencies are:

Texas Commission on the Arts; Texas Film Commission; Texas Historical Commission; Texas State Library and Archives Commission, and the State Preservation Board.

Although not a state agency, another organization that provides cultural services to the citizens of Texas is Humanities Texas.

The Commission on the Arts was established in 1965 to develop a receptive climate for the arts through the conservation and advancement of Texas' rich and diverse arts and cultural industries.

The Texas Commission on the Arts' primary goals are:

• provide grants for the arts and cultural industries in Texas.

• provide the financial, human, and technical resources necessary to ensure viable arts and cultural communities

• promote widespread attendance at arts and cultural performances and exhibitions in Texas.

• ensure access to arts in Texas through marketing, fund raising, and cultural tourism.

The arts commission is responsible for several initiatives including:

• Arts Education – programs that serve the curricular and training needs of the state's school districts, private schools, and home schools.

• Technology – a full service network providing a one-stop location for the arts and cultural industry of Texas.

• Marketing and Public Relations – marketing and fund-raising expertise to generate funds for agency operations and increase visibility of the arts in Texas.

• Cultural Tourism – programs that develop and promote tourism destinations featuring the arts.

Information on programs is available on the Texas Commission on the Arts at www.arts.state.tx.us or by calling (800) 252-9415 or (512) 463-5535. ☆

Performing Arts Organizations

The San Antonio Symphony. Photo by Zereshk (CC).

The Texas Commission on the Arts provides a complete listing of performing arts organizations in Texas at **www.arts.state.tx.us.** There are links arranged by category, dance, theater, music, etc.

home.htm
Science Spectrum
  sciencespectrum.com/
Lufkin
Texas Forestry Museum
  treetexas.com/
Marfa
Chinati Foundation (Art)
  chinati.org/
Marshall
Harrison County Historical Museum
  txgenes.com/TXHarrison/
  NewHome.htm
Michelson Museum of Art
  michelsonmuseum.org/
McAllen
International Museum of Art&Science
  imasonline.org/
McKinney
Heard Natural Science Museum
  heardmuseum.org/
Midland
American Airpower Heritage
  Museum/Commerative Air Force
  airpowermuseum.org/
Museum of the Southwest
  (Art, Science, Children's)
  museumsw.org/
Petroleum Museum
  petroleummuseum.org/
Mobeetie
Old Mobeetie Texas Association
  mobeetie.com/
New Braunfels
New Braunfels Sophienburg
  Museum (History)
  sophienburg.org/
Odessa
Ellen Noel Art Museum
  noelartmuseum.org/
Orange
Stark Museum of Art
  starkmuseum.org/
Panhandle
Square House Museum
  squarehousemuseum.org/
Plano
Heritage Farmstead Museum
  heritagefarmstead.org/
Port Arthur
Museum of the Gulf Coast (Historical)
  museumofthegulfcoast.org/

Port Lavaca
Calhoun County Museum (Historical)
  calhouncountymuseum.org/
Richmond
George Ranch Historical Park
  georgeranch.org/
Rockport
Texas Maritime Museum
  texasmaritimemuseum.org/
Round Top
Henkel Square (History)
  texaspioneerarts.org/
  henkel_square.html
Winedale Historical Center
  www.cah.utexas.edu/museums/
  winedale.php
San Angelo
San Angelo Museum of Fine Arts
  and Children's Art Museum
  samfa.org/

Three-dimensional art outside the Blanton Museum of Art on the campus of the University of Texas at Austin. Photo by Robert Plocheck.

San Antonio
The Alamo
  thealamo.org/
Hertzberg Circus Collection/Museum
  www.sat.lib.tx.us/Hertzberg/
  hzmain.html
Institute of Texan Cultures
  texancultures.utsa.edu/
  public/index.htm
Magic Lantern Castle Museum
  magiclanterns.org/
Museo Alameda
  thealameda.org
The McNay Art Museum
  mcnayart.org/
San Antonio Art League Museum
  saalm.org/
San Antonio Museum of Art
  samuseum.org/main/
Witte Museum (Science, Historical)
  wittemuseum.org/
San Marcos
Southwestern Writers Collection and
  Wittliff Gallery of Southwestern
  & Mexican Photography
  library.txstate.edu/swwc/
Sarita
Kenedy Ranch Museum of
  South Texas
  kenedymuseum.org/
Serbin
Texas Wendish Heritage Museum
  wendish.concordia.edu
Sherman
Red River Historical Museum
  hosting.texoma.net/rrhms/
Sulphur Springs
Southwest Dairy Center/Museum
  southwestdairyfarmers.com/
Teague
The B-RI Railroad Museum
  therailroadmuseum.com/
Temple
Railroad and Heritage Museum
  rrhm.org/

Texarkana
Museum of Regional History
  texarkanamuseums.org/
Thurber
W.K. Gordon Center for Industrial
  History of Texas
  tarleton.edu/~gordoncenter/
Tyler
Discovery Science Place
  discoveryscienceplace.com/
Smith County Historical Museum
  smithcountyhistoricalsociety.
  org/index.php
Tyler Museum of Art
  tylermuseum.org/
Victoria
Museum of the Coastal Bend
  (Historical)
  www.museumofthecoastalbend.
  org/
Waco
Dr Pepper Museum (History)
  drpeppermuseum.com/
Mayborn Museum Complex
  (History, Science)
  baylor.edu/mayborn/
Texas Ranger Hall of Fame/ Museum
  texasranger.org/
Texas Sports Hall of Fame
  tshof.org/
Washington
Star of the Republic Museum
  (Historical)
  starmuseum.org/
Weatherford
Museum of the Americas
  museumoftheamericas.com/
White Settlement
White Settlement Historical Museum
  wsmuseum.com/
Wichita Falls
Kell House Museum (History)
  wichitaheritage.org/kellhouse.html
Museum of Art
  mwsu.edu/wfma/ ☆

The old movie set of Contrabando in Big Bend Ranch State Park was used in the made-for-TV movies Streets of Laredo *and* Dead Man's Walk. *Photo by Robert Plocheck.*

Film and Television Work in Texas

Source: Texas Film Commission at governor.state.tx.us/film

For almost a century, Texas has been one of the nation's top film-making states, after California and New York.

More than 1,300 projects have been made in Texas since 1910, including **Wings**, the first film to win an Academy Award for Best Picture, which was made in San Antonio in 1927.

Texas' attractions to filmmakers are its diverse locations, abundant sunshine and moderate winter weather, and a variety of support services. The economic benefits of hosting on-location filming over the past decade are estimated at more than $2.79 billion.

Besides salaries paid to locally hired technicians and actors, as well as fees paid to location owners, the production companies do business with hotels, car rental agencies, lumberyards, restaurants, grocery stores, utilities, office furniture suppliers, gas stations, security services and florists.

All types of projects come to Texas besides feature films, including television specials, commercials, corporate films and game videos.

Many projects made in Texas originate in California studios, but Texas is also the home of many independent filmmakers who make films outside the studio system.

Some films and television shows made in Texas have become icons. **Giant**, John Wayne's **The**

Alamo, and the long-running TV series **Dallas** all made their mark on the world's perception of Texas and continue to draw tourists to their film locations.

The Texas Film Commission, a division of the Office of the Governor, markets to Hollywood Texas' locations, support services and workforce.

The commission's free services include location research, employment referrals, red-tape-cutting, and information on laws, weather, travel and other topics affecting filmmakers.

The on-line Texas Production Manual includes more than 1,200 individuals and businesses serving every facet of the film industry. ☆

Regional Commissions

Amarillo Film Office
1000 S. Polk, Amarillo 79101
(806) 374-1497
amarillofilm.org

Austin Film Office
301 Congress Ave. Ste. 200
Austin 78701, (800) 926-2282
austintexas.org

Brownsville Border Film Comm.
P.O. Box 911, City Hall
Brownsville 78520, (956) 548-6176
filmbrownsville.com

Dallas Film Commission
325 N. St. Paul Ste. 700
Dallas 75201, (214) 571-1050
filmdfw.com

El Paso Film Commission
One Civic Center Plaza
El Paso 79901, (800) 351-6024
elpasocvb.com

Houston Film Commission
901 Bagby Ste. 100
Houston 77002, (800) 365-7575
filmhouston.texaswebhost.com

Northeast Texas Film Commission
P.O. Box 247

Jefferson 75657, (903) 214-1144
netexasmovies.com

San Antonio Film Commission
203 S. St. Mary's, 2nd Floor
San Antonio 78205, (800)447-3372
filmsanantonio.com

South Padre Island Film Comm.
7355 Padre Blvd.
South Padre Island 78597
(800) 657-2373, sopadre.com

Texas Panhandle Film Commission
P.O. Box 3293, Amarillo 79116
(806) 679-1116
txpanhandlefilm.com

Recent Movies Made in Texas

Following is a partial list of recent major productions filmed in Texas, in descending order by date. The date is for the year of release of the film, while actual location shots occurred often a year or two earlier.

Location information is from the Texas Film Commission and other sources.

When only a small portion of the movie is known to have been filmed in Texas, "(part)" is listed next to the movie title.

Some of the major artists who worked on the project are listed in the column at far right.

Sources: Texas Film Commission, and online.

YEAR	MOVIE	LOCATIONS	ARTISTS
2011	The Tree of Life	Austin, Bastrop, Dallas, Houston, La Grange, Matagorda, San Marcos, Smithville, Waco	Brad Pitt, Sean Penn
2010	Predators	Bastrop, Canyon Lake, Austin	Adrien Brody, Laurence Fishburne, Topher Grace
2009	Friday the 13th	Ausitn, Bastrop, La Grange, Marshall, Wimberley	Marcus Nispel (director)
2006	No Country for Old Men (part)	Marfa	Daniel Day-Lewis
2006	There Will Be Blood (part)	Marfa, Big Bend National Park	Ethan and Joel Coen, Tommy Lee Jones
2005	The Three Burials of Melquiades Estrada	Van Horn, Monahans, Santa Elena Canyon, Lajitas, Shafter, Midland/Odessa	Tommy Lee Jones
2004	The Alamo	Dripping Springs, Wimberley, Pedernales Falls State Park, Bastrop, Austin	Dennis Quaid, Jason Patric
2004	Friday Night Lights	Odessa, Notrees, Austin, Houston	Billy Bob Thornton
2003	Texas Chainsaw Massacre	Martindale, Taylor, Austin	
2002	The Rookie	Thorndale, Taylor, Arlington, Big Lake	Dennis Quaid
2000	All the Pretty Horses	Boerne, Helotes, Pipe Creek, Big Bend	Matt Damon, Sam Shepard
2000	Miss Congeniality	Austin, San Antonio	Sandra Bullock, Michael Caine
1999	Where the Heart Is	Austin, Baylor University, Lockhart, Taylor, Kyle, Driftwood, Bastrop, Georgetown	Natalie Portman, Ashley Judd
1999	Boys Don't Cry	Greenville, Dallas area	Hilary Swank
1999	Office Space	Austin, Dallas	Jennifer Aniston, Ron Livingston
1999	Varsity Blues	Elgin, Coupland, Taylor, Georgetown	John Van Der Beek, Jon Voight
1998	Dancer, Texas Pop. 81	Fort Davis, Alpine	Breckin Meyer, Peter Facinelli
1998	Home Fries	Coupland, Taylor, Bastrop, Austin, El Paso	Drew Barrymore, Luke Wilson
1998	Hope Floats	Smithville, Austin	Sandra Bullock, Harry Connick Jr.
1998	The Newton Boys	Bertram, Martindale, Bartlett, Lockhart, Austin, San Antonio	Matthew McConaughey, Ethan Hawke
1996	Bottle Rocket	Hillsboro, Grand Prairie, Dallas	Luke and Owen Wilson, James Caan
1996	Courage Under Fire	Bertram, Bastrop, San Marcos, Austin, El Paso	Denzel Washington, Meg Ryan
1996	Lone Star	Eagle Pass, Del Rio, Laredo	Matthew McConaughey, Kris Kristofferson
1995	Apollo 13	Houston area	Tom Hanks, Kevin Bacon
1993	Dazed and Confused	Austin, Georgetown, Seguin	Richard Linklater (director), Matthew McConaughey
1993	What's Eating Gilbert Grape	Manor, Lockhart, Austin	Johnny Depp, Leonardo DiCaprio

Number of Production Projects in Texas by Year

	2001	2002	2003	2004	2005	2006	2007	2008	2009
Studio Feature Films	5	4	8	8	6	8	3	3	4
Independent Feature Films	29	25	13	22	25	37	33	24	56
TV Series	6	8	6	7	13	11	14	12	20
TV Single Episodes/Segments	7	21	12	14	1	63	38	57	53
TV Pilots	-	1	1	3	2	8	7	2	10
TV Movies	4	1	1	1	2	1	-	1	-
TV Miniseries	-	-	-	-	-	2	-	-	-
TV Specials	1	-	3	4	1	3	2	5	2
Other (documentary, music video)	2	1	2	3	1	5	7	59	99
TOTAL Film/TV projects	54	61	46	62	51	138	104	163	244

Source: Texas Film Commission (revised 2010).

Television series produced in Texas include **Friday Nights Lights** (locations include Pflugerville, Del Valle and San Marcos) and syndicated programs such as **Judge Alex**, in addition to the long-running **Austin City Limits**.

Texas Medal of the Arts Awards

Source: Texas Commission on the Arts

The Texas Medals of the Arts were presented to artists and arts patrons with Texas ties in April 2011.

The awards are administered by the Texas Cultural Trust Council. The council was established to raise money and awareness for the Texas Cultural Trust Fund, which was created by the Legislature in 1993 to support cultural arts in Texas (www.txculturaltrust. org).

The medals, awarded every two years, were first presented in 2001. A concurrent proclamation by the state Senate and House of Representatives honors the recipients, and the governor presents the awards in Austin.

2011

Lifetime Achievement Award: Barbara Smith Conrad from Center Point near Pittsburg, operatic mezzo-soprano and civil rights icon.

Music: ZZ Top of Houston, legendary band that sold over 50 million albums.

Literary: Robert M. Edsel, Dallas, author and founder/president of the Monuments Men Foundation for the Preservation of Art.

Visual arts: James Drake, Lubbock, artist.

Television: Bob Schieffer, Fort Worth, CBS news anchor.

Theater arts: Alley Theatre, Houston.

Multimedia: Ray Benson, Austin, front man for Asleep at the Wheel and co-writer of the play *A Ride with Bob* based on the life of Bob Wills.

Film: Marcia Gay Harden, UT-Austin graduate, Oscar-winning actress.

Film: Bill Paxton, Fort Worth, four-time Golden Globe nominee.

Arts education: Tom Staley, director of the Harry Ransom Center at UT-Austin.

Individual arts patron: Ernest and Sarah Butler of Austin, major donors to Austin arts groups.

Corporate arts patron: H-E-B, grocer with a long history of supporting the arts throughout Texas.

2009

A **Standing Ovation Award** was presented to former First Lady Laura Bush of Midland and Dallas.

Lifetime Achievement Award: posthumously to artist Robert Rauschenberg, born in Port Arthur.

Music: Clint Black of Katy, country music singer/songwriter.

Literary: T.R. Fehrenbach of San Antonio. Mr. Fehrenbach, born in San Benito, is the author of 18 nonfiction books, including *Lone Star: A History of Texas and Texans*.

Visual arts: Keith Carter of Beaumont, photographer.

Theater arts: Betty Buckley of Fort Worth, Tony Award winner and film actress.

Multimedia: Austin City Limits, the 30-year television series.

Film: Robert Rodriguez of Austin. Mr. Rodriguez, born in San Antonio, is a film producer and writer.

Architecture: David Lake of Austin and Ted Flato of Corpus Christi, both now working in San Antonio.

Arts education: Pianist James Dick of Round Top, founder of the International Festival-Institute there.

Individual arts patron: Edith O'Donnell of Dallas.

Corporate arts patron: Anheuser-Busch of St. Louis and Houston.

2007

Lifetime Achievement Award: Broadcast newsman Walter Cronkite of Houston.

Music: Ornette Coleman of Fort Worth, jazz saxophonist.

Dance: Alvin Ailey American Dance Theater. The late Alvin Ailey, born in Rogers, was a creator of African American dance works.

Literary: writer Sandra Brown of Waco.

Visual arts: Jesús Moroles of Corpus Christi/Rockport, sculptor.

Theater arts: actress Judith Ivey of El Paso.

Multimedia: Bill Wittliff of Taft and Austin, publisher, writer, photographer, director, producer.

Arts education: Paul Baker of Hereford/Waelder. Headed drama departments at Baylor and Trinity universities.

Individual arts patron: Diana and Bill Hobby of Houston.

Corporate arts patron: Neiman Marcus, Dallas.

Foundation arts patron: Sid W. Richardson Foundation of Fort Worth.

2005

Lifetime Achievement Award: singer Vikki Carr of El Paso.

Television/theater: actress Phylicia Rashad of Houston.

Music: singer/songwriter Lyle Lovett of Klein.

Dance: Ben Stevenson of Houston and Fort Worth.

Literary arts: Naomi Shihab Nye of San Antonio.

Visual arts: Jose Cisneros of El Paso.

Theater: Robert Wilson of Waco.

Arts education: Ginger Head-Gearheart of Fort Worth, advocate of arts education in public schools.

Individual arts patrons: Joe R. and Teresa Lozano Long of Austin, philanthropists.

Foundation arts patron: Nasher Foundation/Dallas.

2003

Lifetime Achievement: John Graves of Glen Rose, author of *Goodbye to A River*.

Media-film/television acting: Fess Parker of Fort Worth.

Music: country singer Charley Pride of Dallas.

Dance: Tommy Tune of Wichita Falls and Houston.

Theater: Enid Holm of Odessa, actress and former executive director of Texas Nonprofit Theatres.

Literary arts: Sandra Cisneros of San Antonio.

Visual arts: sculptor Glenna Goodacre of Dallas.

Folk arts: Tejano singer Lydia Mendoza of San Antonio.

Architecture: State Capitol Preservation Project of Austin, headed by Dealey Herndon.

Arts education: theater teacher Marca Lee Bircher of Dallas.

Individual arts patron: philanthropist Nancy B. Hamon of Dallas.

Corporate arts patron: Exxon/Mobil based in Irving.

Foundation arts patron: Houston Endowment Inc.

2001

Lifetime Achievement: Van Cliburn of Fort Worth.

Film: actor Tommy Lee Jones of San Saba.

Music: singer-songwriter Willie Nelson of Austin.

Dance: Debbie Allen of Houston, choreographer, director, actress and composer.

Theater: *Texas* musical-drama producer Neil Hess of Amarillo.

Literary arts: playwright Horton Foote of Wharton.

Visual arts: muralist John Biggers of Houston.

Folk arts: musician brothers Santiago Jimenez Jr. and Flaco Jimenez of San Antonio.

Architecture: restoration architect Wayne Bell of Austin.

Arts education: theater arts director Gilberto Zepeda Jr. of Pharr.

Individual arts patron: philanthropist Jack Blanton of Houston.

Corporate arts patron: SBC Communications Inc. of San Antonio.

Foundation arts patron: Meadows Foundation of Dallas. ☆

Texas Institute of Letters Awards

Each year since 1939, the **Texas Institute of Letters** (texasinstituteofletters.org/) has honored outstanding literature and journalism that is either by Texans or about Texas subjects.

Awards have been made for fiction, nonfiction, Southwest history, general information, magazine and newspaper journalism, children's books, translation, poetry and book design. The awards of recent years are listed below:

Writer/Designer: Title

2010

Jan Reid: *Comanche Sundown*

Gary Lavergne: *Before Brown: Heman Marion Sweatt, Thurgood Marshall and the Long Road to Justice*

Neil Foley: *Quest for Equality: The Failed Promise of Black-Brown Solidarity*

Bruce Machart: *The Wake of Forgiveness*

Barbara Ras: *The Last Skin*

Elyse Fenton: *Clamor*

Pamela Colloff: "Innocence Lost," *Texas Monthly*, October 2010

C.W. Smith: "Caustic," *Southwest Review*, Summer 2010

Tim Madigan: series on the surgery of a child, *Fort Worth Star-Telegram*

Julie Savasky and DJ Stout: *The Gernsheim Collection*

Diane Gonzales Bertrand: *The Party for Papa Luis/La Fiesta Para Papa Luis*

Dotti Enderle: *Crosswire*

Lon Tinkle Award (for career): C.W. Smith

2009

Scott Blackwood: *We Agreed to Meet Just Here*

Bryan Burrough: *The Big Rich: The Rise and Fall of the Greatest Texas Oil Fortunes*

John Pipkin: *Woodsburner*

Emilio Zamoro: *Claiming Rights and Righting Wrongs in Texas: Mexican Workers and Job Politics During World War II*

William Virgil Davis: *Landscape and Journey*

John Spong: "Holding Garmsir," *Texas Monthly*, January 2009.

Gwendolyn Zepeda: *Sunflowers/Girasoles*

Marjorie Kempner: "Discovered America," *Southwest Review*, Fall 2009

Lindsay Starr: *"I Do Not Apologize for the Length of This Letter": The Mari Sandoz Letters on Native American Rights, 1940–1965*

Lon Tinkle Award (for career): Larry L. King

2008

Brendan M. Greeley Jr.: *The Two Thousand Yard Stare: Tom Lea's World War II Paintings, Drawings, and Eyewitness Accounts*

Thomas Cobb: *Shavetail*

Ann Weisgarber: *The Personal History of Rachel DuPree*

Rick Bass: "Mary Katherine's First Deer" in *Gray's Sporting Journal*

Todd Benson and Guillermo Contreras: "Texas' Deadliest Export" in the *San Antonio Express-News*

Benjamin Alire Saenz: *The Perfect Season for Dreaming*

Claudia Guadalupe Martinez: *The Smell of Old Lady Perfume*

James Allen Hall: *Now You're the Enemy*

Kerry Neville Bakken: "Indignity" in *Gettysburg Review*

James M. Smallwood: *The Feud that Wasn't: The Taylor Ring, Bill Sutton, John Wesley Hardin, and Violence in Texas*

Barbara Whitehead: *Traces of Forgotten Places*

Reginald Gibbons: translator of *Sophocles, Selected Poems: Odes and Fragments*

Lon Tinkle Award (for career): Carolyn Osborn

2007

Robert Krueger and Kathleen Tobin Krueger: *From Bloodshed to Hope in Burundi: Our Embassy Years During Genocide*

John J. McLaughlin: *Run in the Fam'ly*

Todd Benson: "Breaching America" in the *San Antonio Express-News*

DJ Stout and Julie Savasky: *Reflections of a Man: The Photographs of Stanley Marcus*

Rick Bass: "The Lives of the Browns" in *Southern Review*

Rick Bass: "The Elephant"

Arturo O. Martinez: *Perdito's Way*

Naomi Shihab Nye: *I'll Ask You Three Times, Are You OK?*

Jerry Thompson: *Cortina: Defending the Mexican Name in Texas*

Cate Marvin: *Fragment of the Head of a Queen*

Lon Tinkle Award (for career): David J. Weber

2006

Lawrence Wright: *The Looming Tower: Al-Qaeda and the Road to 9/11*

Cormac McCarthy: *The Road*

Medal of Arts

Bob Schieffer, left, CBS news anchor, moderator of Face the Nation *and broadcasting hall of famer was one of the honorees who received the Texas Medal of the Arts in 2011.*

He grew up in Fort Worth and is an alumnus of Texas Christian University.

U.S. Air Force photo.

Dominic Smith: *The Mercury Visions of Louis Daguerre*
Marian Schwartz: translator of *White on Black* by Ruben Gallego
Tony Freemantle: "The Gulf Coast Revisited" in the *Houston Chronicle*
Mary Ann Jacob: *Timeless Texas*
John Sprong: "The Good Book and the Bad Book" in *Texas Monthly*
Mark Wisniewski: "Prisoners of War"
Tim Tingle: *Crossing Bok Chitto: A Choctaw Tale of Friendship and Freedom*
Heather Hepler: *Scrambled Eggs at Midnight*
Jerry Thompson: *Civil War to the Bloody End: The Life and Times of Major Samuel P. Heintzelman*
Christopher Bakken: *Goat Funeral*
Lon Tinkle Award (for career): William D. Wittliff
Special Citation: Allen Maxwell

2005

Stephen Graham Jones: *Bleed Into Me: A Bood of Stories*
Karen Olsson: *Waterloo*
Nate Blakeslee: *Tulia*
Thad Sitton and James H. Conrad: *Freedom Colonies: Independent Black Texans in the Time of Jim Crow*
John Bricuth: *As Long As It's Big*
DJ Stout and Julie Savasky: *Conjunto*
Edward Hegstrom, Tony Freemantle and Elena Vega: "One Nation: Two Worlds" in the *Houston Chronicle*
Kelly Bennett: *Not Norman: A Goldfish Story*
Pamela Porter: *The Crazy Man*
Rick Bass: "The Lives of Rocks"
Pamela Colloff: "Unholy Act" in *Texas Monthly*
Harvey Yunis: translator *Demosthenes: Speeches 18 and 19*
Lon Tinkle Award (for career): James Hoggard

2004

Steven Mintz: *Huck's Raft*
Laurie Lynn Drummond: *Anything You Say Can and Will Be Held Against You*
Bret Anthony Johnston: *Corpus Christi*
William Wenthe: *Not Till We Are Lost*
Andres Resendez: *Changing National Identities at the Frontier: Texas and New Mexico, 1800–1850*
Philip Boehm: translator of *Death in Danzig* by Stefan Chwin
Mike Nichols: *Balaam Gimble's Gumption*
Ben Fountain: "Bouki and the Cocaine"
Zanto Peabody: "The Search for Eddie Peabody" in the *Houston Chronicle*
DJ Stout and Julie Savasky: *Maps of the Imagination*
Lawrence Wright: "The Kingdom of Silence" in the *New Yorker*
Diane Stanley: *Jack and the Beanstalk*
Susan Abraham and Denise Gonzales: *Cecilia's Year*
Lon Tinkle Award (for career): T.R. Fehrenbach

2003

Betty Lou Phillips: *Emily Goes Wild*
Brian Yansky: *My Road Trip to the Pretty Girl Capital of the Word*
DJ Stout and Julie Savasky: *The Texas Cowboy Kitchen*
Steve Barthelme: "Claire"
Dick J. Reavis: articles on homelessness in the *San Antonio Express-News*
Jan Reid: "End of the River" in *Texas Monthly*
John Blair: *The Green Girls*
Jennifer Grotz: *Cusp*
Lynn Hoggard: translator of *Nelida* by Marie D'Agoult
B.H. Fairchild: *Early Occult Memory Systems of the Lower Midwest*
Jack Jackson: *Almonte's Texas*, translated by John Wheat
Don Graham: *Kings of Texas*
Robert Ford: *The Student Conductor*
Joseph Skibell: *The English Disease*
Lon Tinkle Award (for career): Bud Shrake

2002

Kathi Appelt: *Where, Where Is Swamp Bear?*
Carolee Dean: *Comfort*
Juan Rulfo: *Pedro Paramo*

Ben Fountain III: "Near-Extinct Birds of the Central Cordillera"
Mark Lisheron and Bill Bishop: "Cities of Ideas" in the *Austin American-Statesman*
Lawrence Wright: "The Man Behind Bin Laden" in the *New Yorker*
Dan Rifenburgh: *Advent*
Reginald Gibbons: *It's Time*
Kinky Friedman: *Meanwhile Back at the Ranch*
Michael Gagarin: *Antiphon the Athenian: Oratory, Law, and Justice in the Age of the Sophists*
Ray Gonzalez: *The Underground Heart: A Return to a Hidden Landscape*
Lisa Schamess: *Borrowed Light*
Rick Bass: *Hermit's Story*
Lon Tinkle Award: Shelby Hearon

2001

Carmen Bredeson: *Animals that Migrate*
Lori Aurelia Williams: *When Kambia Elaine Flew from Neptune*
Vicki Trego Hill: *Folktales of the Zapatista Revolution*
Tom McNeely: "Tickle Torture"
Mike Tolson, James Kimberly, Steve Brewer, Allan Turner: "A Deadly Distinction" in the *Houston Chronicle*
Larry L. King: "The Book on Willie Morris" in *Texas Monthly*
Ted Genoways: *Bullroarer*
Susan Wood: *Asunder*
Wendy Barker and Saranindranath Tagore: *Final Poems* by Rabindranath Tagore
Marco Perela: *Adventures of a No Name Actor*
Betje Klier: *Pavie in the Borderlands*
Larry McMurtry: *Sacagawea's Nickname: Essays on the American West*
Katherine Tannery: *Carousel of Progress*
Sarah Bird: *The Yokota Officers Club*
Lon Tinkle Award: William H. Goetzmann

2000

Rosa Shand: *The Gravity of Sunlight*
Laura Wilson: *Hutterites of Montana*
Richard V. Francaviglia: *The Cast Iron Forest*
Corey Marks: *Renunciation*
Edward Snow: *The Duino Elegies* by Rainer Maria Rilke
Glen Pourciau: "Deep Wilderness"
Pamela Colloff: "Sins of the Father"
Joe Holley: "The Hill Country: Loving It to Death"
Anne Coyle: *Crookwood*
Molly Ivins and Lou DuBose: *Shrub*
Bradley Hutchinson: *Willard Clark: Printer and Printmaker*
D.J. Stout and Julie Savasky: *John Graves and the Making of Goodbye to a River*
Lon Tinkle Award: Leon Hale

1999

Rick DeMarinis: *New and Selected Stories*
Robert Draper: *Hadrian's Walls*
Ann Rowe Seaman: *Swaggart: The Unauthorized Biography of an American Evangelist*
J.Gilberto Quezada: *Border Boss: Manuel B. Bravo and Zapata County*
Walt McDonald: "Whatever the Wind Delivers"
Jenny Lind Porter: *Verses on Death by Helinand of Froidmont*
Tracy Daugherty: *Comfort Me With Apples*
Steven and Rick Barthelme: "Good Losers"
James Hoggard: "Greetings from Cuba"
Benjamin Alire Saenz: *Grandma Fina and Her Wonderful Umbrellas/La Abuelita Fina y Sus Sombrillas Maravillosas*
Neil Barrett Jr.: *Interstate Dreams*
Margerie Adkins West: *Angels on High: Marton Varo's Limestone Angels on Bass Performance Hall*
Peter Brown: *On the Plains*
Lon Tinkle Award: Walt McDonald

(In 1983, the Texas Almanac was honored with a Special Citation.) ☆

Poets Laureate of Texas

Since 2001, a committee of seven members appointed by the governor, lieutenant governor, and speaker of the House selects the poet laureate, state artists and state musician based on recommendations from the Texas Commission on the Arts.

Earlier, the Legislature made the nominations.

The state historian is appointed by the governor and is recommended by both the Texas State Historical Association and the Texas Historical Commission.

Sources: Texas State Library and Archives; Texas Commission on the Arts; The Dallas Morning News.

1932-34	Judd Mortimer Lewis, Houston
1934-36	Aline T. Michaelis, Austin
1936-39	Grace Noll Crowell, Dallas
1939-41	Lexie Dean Robertson, Rising Star
1941-43	Nancy Richey Ranson, Dallas
1943-45	Dollilee Davis Smith, Cleburne
1945-47	DavidRiley Russell, Dallas
1947-49	Aline B. Carter, San Antonio
1949-51	Carlos Ashley, Llano
1951-53	Arthur M. Sampley, Denton
1953-55	Mildred Lindsey Raiborn, San Angelo Dee Walker, Texas City, alternate
1955-57	Pierre Bernard Hill, Hunt
1957-59	Margaret Royalty Edwards, Waco
1959-61	J.V. Chandler, Kingsville Edna Coe Majors, Colorado City, alternate
1961	Lorena Simon, Port Arthur
1962	Marvin Davis Winsett, Dallas
1963	Gwendolyn Bennett Pappas, Houston Vassar Miller, Houston, alternate
1964-65	Jenny Lind Porter, Austin Edith Rayzor Canant, Texas City, alternate
1966	Bessie Maas Rowe, Port Arthur Grace Marie Scott, Abilene, alternate
1967	William E. Bard, Dallas Bessie Maas Rowe, Port Arthur, alternate
1968	Kathryn Henry Harris, Waco Sybil Leonard Armes, El Paso, alternate
1969-70	Anne B. Marely, Austin Rose Davidson Speer, Brady, alternate
1970-71	Mrs. Robby K. Mitchell, McKinney Faye Carr Adams, Dallas, alternate
1971-72	Terry Fontenot, Port Arthur Faye Carr Adams, Dallas, alternate
1972-73	Mrs. Clark Gresham, Burkburnett Marion McDaniel, Sidney, alternate
1973-74	Violette Newton, Beaumont Stella Woodall, San Antonio, alternate
1974-75	Lila Todd O'Neil, Port Arthur C.W. Miller, San Antonio, alternate
1975-76	Ethel Osborn Hill, Port Arthur Gene Shuford, Denton, alternate
1976-77	Florice Stripling Jeffers, Burkburnett Vera L. Eckert, San Angelo, alternate
1977-78	Ruth Carruth, Vernon Joy Gresham Hagstrom, Burkburnett, alternate
1978-79	Patsy Stodghill, Dallas Dorothy B. Elfstroman, Galveston, alternate
1979-80	Dorothy B. Elfstroman, Galveston Ruth Carruth, Vernon, alternate
1980-81	Weems S. Dykes, McCamey Mildred Crabree Speer, Amarillo, alternate
1981-82	*none designated*
1982-83	William D. Barney, Fort Worth Vassar Miller, Houston, alternate
1983-87	*none designated*
1987-88	Ruth E. Reuther, Wichita Falls
1988-89	Vassar Miller, Houston
1989-93	*none designated*
1993-94	Mildred Baass, Victoria
1994-99	*none designated*
2000	James Hoggard, Wichita Falls
2001	Walter McDonald, Lubbock
2002	*none designated*
2003	Jack Myers, Mesquite
2004	Cleatus Rattan, Cisco
2005	Alan Birkelbach, Plano
2006	Red Steagall, Fort Worth
2007	Steven Fromholz, Kopperl, Sugar Land
2008	Larry Thomas, Houston
2009	Paul Ruffin, Huntsville
2010	Karla K. Morton, Denton, Fort Worth
2011	David M. Parsons, Conroe
2012	Jan Seale, McAllen

State Musicians of Texas

2003	James Dick, Round Top
2004	Ray Benson, Austin
2005	Johnny Gimble, Tyler
2006	Billy Joe Shaver, Waco
2007	Dale Watson, Pasadena, Austin
2008	Shelley King, Austin
2009	Willie Nelson, Austin, Abbott
2010	Sara Hickman, Austin
2011	Lyle Lovett, Klein
2012	Billy Gibbons (ZZ Top), Houston

State Artists of Texas

1971-72	Joe Ruiz Grandee, Arlington
1972-73	Melvin C. Warren, Clifton
1973-74	Ronald Thomason, Weatherford A.C. Gentry Jr., Tyler, alternate
1974-75	Joe Rader Roberts, Dripping Springs Bette Lou Voorhis, Austin, alternate
1975-76	Jack White, New Braunfels
July 4, 1975 –July 4, 1976	Robert Summers, Glen Rose Bicentennial Artist
1976-77	James Boren, Clifton Kenneth Wyatt, Lubbock, alternate
1977-78	Edward "Buck" Schiwetz, DeWitt County Renne Hughes, Tarrant County, alternate
1978-79	Jack Cowan, Rockport Gary Henry, Palo Pinto County, alternate Joyce Tally, Caldwell County, alternate
1979-80	Dalhart Windberg, Travis County Grant Lathe, Canyon Lake, alternate
1980-81	Harry Ahysen, Huntsville Jim Reno, Simonton, alternate
1981-82	Jerry Newman, Beaumont Raul Guiterrez, San Antonio, alternate
1982-83	Dr. James H. Johnson, Bryan Armando Hinojosa, Laredo, alternate
1983-84	Raul Gutierrez, San Antonio James Eddleman, Lubbock, alternate
1984-85	Covelle Jones, Lubbock Ragan Gennusa, Austin, alternate
1986-87	Chuck DeHaan, Graford
1987-88	Neil Caldwell, Angleton Rey Gaytan, Austin, alternate
1988-89	George Hallmark, Walnut Springs Tony Eubanks, Grapevine, alternate

	Two-dimensional	Three-dimensional
1990-91	Mondel Rogers, Sweetwater	Ron Wells, Cleveland

	Two-dimensional	Three-dimensional
1991-92	Woodrow Foster, Center	Kent Ullberg, Corpus Christi
	Harold Phenix, Houston, alternate	Mark Clapham, Conroe, alternate
1993-94	Roy Lee Ward, Hunt	James Eddleman, Lubbock
1994-95	Frederick Carter, El Paso	Garland A. Weeks, Wichita Falls
1998-99	Carl Rice Embrey, San Antonio	Edd Hayes, Humble
2000-02	none designated	
2003	Ralph White, Austin	Dixie Friend Gay, Houston
2004	Sam Caldwell, Houston	David Hickman, Dallas
2005	Kathy Vargas, San Antonio	Sharon Kopriva, Houston
2006	George Boutwell, Bosque	James Surls, Athens
2007	Lee Herring, Rockwall	David Keens, Arlington
2008	Janet Eager Krueger, Encinal	Damian Priour, Austin
2009	René Alvarado, San Angelo	Eliseo Garcia, Farmers Branch
2010	Marc Burckhardt, Austin	John Bennett, Fredericksburg
2011	Melissa Miller, Austin	Jesús Moroles, Rockport
2012	Karl Umlauf, Waco	Bill FitzGibbons, San Antonio

State Historians of Texas

2007-09	Jesús de la Teja, San Marcos
2009-11	Light Cummins, Sherman
2011-13	

National Arts Medal Honors Van Cliburn

The 2010 National Medal of Arts honored Van Cliburn, the pianist, among ten recipients.

In the award presentation, Mr. Cliburn was cited for "his contributions as one of the greatest pianists in the history of music and a persuasive ambassador for American culture."

Van Cliburn, who was raised in Kilgore, rose to world prominence at age 23 when he won the prestigious Tchaikovsky International piano competition in 1958 in Moscow.

Van Cliburn.

He is the founder of the Van Cliburn International Piano Competition which began in 1962 and is held in Fort Worth every four years.

He was honored by President George W. Bush with the Presidential Medal of Freedom in 2003.

Among the nine other artists honored at the White House ceremony in March 2011 were Quincy Jones, Harper Lee, Meryl Streep and James Taylor.

The Medal of Arts was established by Congress in 1984 to honor those who make outstanding contributions to the arts.

Each year, the National Endowment for the Arts seeks nominations from across the country. The president selects the recipients.

Previous Texas recipients include Lydia Mendoza, Tejano recording star since the 1920s; country singer George Strait, dancer Tommy Tune, as well as the *Austin City Limits* concert TV series, and dancer/actress Cyd Charisse. ☆

Holidays, Anniversaries, and Festivals, 2012 and 2013

Below are listed the principal federal and state government holidays; Christian, Jewish, and Islamic holidays and festivals; and special recognition days for 2012 and 2013. Technically, the United States does not observe national holidays. Each state has jurisdiction over its holidays, which are usually designated by its legislature. This list was compiled partially from the Texas Government Code, the U.S. Office of Personnel Management, and *Astronomical Phenomena 2012* and *Astronomical Phenomena 2013*, which are published jointly by the U.S. Naval Observatory and the United Kingdom Hydrographic Office. See the footnotes for explanations of the symbols.

2012

New Year's Day § †	Sun., Jan. 1
Epiphany	Fri., Jan. 6
Sam Rayburn Day ‡	Fri., Jan. 6
Martin Luther King Jr. Day § †	Mon., Jan. 16
Confederate Heroes Day † *	Thurs., Jan. 19
Valentine's Day	Tues., Feb. 14
Presidents' Day § † **	Mon., Feb. 20
Ash Wednesday	Wed., Feb. 22
Texas Independence Day †	Fri., March 2
Sam Houston Day ‡	Fri., March 2
Texas Flag Day ‡	Fri., March 2
Primary Election Day	Tues., March 6
César Chávez Day †	Sat., March 31
Palm Sunday	Sun., April 1
Good Friday †	Fri., April 6
Passover (Pesach), first day of ¶	Sat., April 7
Easter Day	Sun., April 8
Former Prisoners of War Recognition Day ‡	Mon., April 9
San Jacinto Day †	Sat., April 21
Mother's Day	Sun., May 13
Ascension Day	Thurs., May 17
Armed Forces Day	Sat., May 19
Shavuot (Feast of Weeks) ¶	Sun., May 27
Whit Sunday — Pentecost	Sun., May 27
Memorial Day § †	Mon., May 28
Trinity Sunday	Sun., June 3
Flag Day (U.S.)	Thurs., June 14
Father's Day	Sun., June 17
Emancipation Day in Texas (Juneteenth) †	Tues., June 19
Independence Day § †	Wed., July 4
Ramadan, first day of §§	Fri., July 20
Lyndon Baines Johnson Day †	Mon., Aug. 27
Labor Day § †	Mon., Sept. 3
Grandparents Day	Sun., Sept. 9
Rosh Hashanah (Jewish New Year) ¶	Mon., Sept. 17
Yom Kippur (Day of Atonement) ¶	Wed., Sept. 26
Sukkot (Tabernacles), first day of ¶	Mon., Oct. 1
Columbus Day § ‡	Mon., Oct. 8
Halloween	Wed., Oct. 31
Father of Texas (Stephen F. Austin) Day ‡	Sat., Nov. 3
General Election Day †	Tues., Nov. 6
Veterans Day § †	Sun., Nov. 11
Islamic New Year §§	Thurs., Nov. 15
Thanksgiving Day § † ††	Thurs., Nov. 22
First Sunday in Advent	Sun., Dec. 2
Hanukkah, first day of ¶	Sun., Dec. 9
Christmas Day § †	Tues., Dec. 25

2013

New Year's Day § †	Tues., Jan. 1
Epiphany	Sun., Jan. 6
Sam Rayburn Day ‡	Sun., Jan. 6
Confederate Heroes Day † *	Sat., Jan. 19
Inauguration Day	Sun., Jan. 20
Martin Luther King Jr. Day § †	Mon., Jan. 21
Ash Wednesday	Wed., Feb. 13
Valentine's Day	Thurs., Feb. 14
Presidents' Day § † **	Mon., Feb. 18
Texas Independence Day †	Sat., March 2
Sam Houston Day ‡	Sat., March 2
Texas Flag Day ‡	Sat., March 2
Palm Sunday	Sun., March 24
Passover (Pesach), first day of ¶	Tues., March 26
Good Friday †	Fri., March 29
Easter Day	Sun., March 31
César Chávez Day †	Sun., March 31
Former Prisoners of War Recognition Day ‡	Tues., April 9
San Jacinto Day †	Sun., April 21
Ascension Day	Thurs., May 9
Mother's Day	Sun., May 12
Shavuot (Feast of Weeks) ¶	Wed., May 15
Armed Forces Day	Sat., May 18
Whit Sunday — Pentecost	Sun., May 19
Trinity Sunday	Sun., May 26
Memorial Day § †	Mon., May 27
Flag Day (U.S.)	Fri., June 14
Father's Day	Sun., June 16
Emancipation Day in Texas (Juneteenth) †	Wed., June 19
Independence Day § †	Thurs., July 4
Ramadan, first day of §§	Tues., July 9
Lyndon Baines Johnson Day †	Tues., Aug. 27
Labor Day § †	Mon., Sept. 2
Rosh Hashanah (Jewish New Year) ¶	Thurs., Sept. 5
Grandparents Day	Sun., Sept. 8
Yom Kippur (Day of Atonement) ¶	Sat., Sept. 14
Sukkot (Tabernacles), first day of ¶	Thurs., Sept. 19
Columbus Day § ‡	Mon., Oct. 14
Halloween	Thurs., Oct. 31
Father of Texas (Stephen F. Austin) Day ‡	Sun., Nov. 3
Islamic New Year §§	Tues., Nov. 5
Veterans Day § †	Mon., Nov. 11
Thanksgiving Day § † ††	Thurs., Nov. 28
Hanukkah, first day of ¶	Thurs., Nov. 28
First Sunday in Advent	Sun., Dec. 1
Christmas Day § †	Wed., Dec. 25

§ **Federal legal public holiday.** If the holiday falls on a Sunday, the following Monday may be treated as a holiday. If the holiday falls on a Saturday, the preceding Friday may be treated as a holiday.

† **State holiday in Texas.** For state employees, the Friday after Thanksgiving Day, Dec. 24, and Dec. 26 are also holidays. *Optional holidays* are César Chávez Day, Good Friday, Rosh Hashanah, and Yom Kippur. *Partial-staffing holidays* are Confederate Heroes Day, Texas Independence Day, San Jacinto Day, Emancipation Day in Texas, and Lyndon Baines Johnson Day. State offices will be open on optional holidays and partial-staffing holidays.

‡ **State Recognition Days,** as designated by the Texas Legislature.

* **Confederate Heroes Day** combines the birthdays of Robert E. Lee (Jan. 19) and Jefferson Davis (June 3).

** **Presidents' Day** combines the birthdays of George Washington (Feb. 22) and Abraham Lincoln (Feb. 12).

¶ §§ **Jewish (¶) and Islamic (§§) holidays** are tabular, meaning they begin at sunset on the previous evening.

†† Between 1939 and 1957, Texas observed **Thanksgiving Day** on the last Thursday in November. As a result, in a November having five Thursdays, Texas celebrated national Thanksgiving on the fourth Thursday and Texas Thanksgiving on the fifth Thursday. In 1957, Texas changed the state observance to coincide with the national holiday. ☆

Health and Science

Methodist Hospital at the Texas Medical Center in Houston. Photo by Robert Plocheck.

Vital Statistics

Hospitals, Physicians

Drug Treatment

Mental Health Care

Honored Scientists

Research Funding in Texas

Computer Specialists

Death, Birth Rates Continue Trends in Texas Vital Statistics

Heart disease and cancer remained the major causes of death in 2008, the latest year for which statistical breakdowns were available from the Bureau of Vital Statistics, Department of State Health Services.

Of the 164,135 deaths, heart disease claimed 38,493 lives, and cancer claimed 35,618 lives. These two diseases have been the leading causes of death in Texas and the nation since 1950.

Cerebrovascular diseases (strokes), accidents and chronic lower respiratory diseases ranked third, fourth

and fifth, respectively. Together, these five leading causes represented 62.2 percent of all deaths.

For the first time since 1994, the number of babies born to Texas mothers declined in 2008 (405,242) from the previous year. The state's birth rate was at an all-time low of 16.7 per 1,000 population. In 1960, that figure was 25.7.

Although there was a general decrease from 1990 to 2005 in the number of abortions, there was an increasing trend since, with 78,330 abortions in 2008.

Health Care and Deaths in Texas Counties

County	2010 Physicians	2008 Hospital Beds	Total Deaths 2008	2008 Pregnancy rate*	2008 Abortions	County	2010 Physicians	2008 Hospital Beds	Total Deaths 2008	2008 Pregnancy rate*	2008 Abortions
Statewide Total	**48,897**	**61,912**	**164,135**	**91.7**	**78,330***	Collingswrth	2	15	43	93.5	0
Anderson	78	115	622	95.9	83	Colorado	27	79	254	78.2	27
Andrews	13	44	130	93.8	21	Comal	159	40	838	75.3	170
Angelina	157	345	847	86.1	139	Comanche	12	38	188	96.8	25
Aransas	15	0	345	80.2	48	Concho	2	16	39	69.0	3
Archer	1	0	79	52.5	7	Cooke	28	78	430	81.0	44
Armstrong	0	0	15	76.1	5	Coryell	23	48	372	58.5	119
Atascosa	30	67	368	81.9	83	Cottle	0	0	29	75.2	5
Austin	10	25	260	91.5	55	Crane	3	25	34	81.5	2
Bailey	5	25	50	101.7	6	Crockett	1	0	33	113.3	12
Bandera	3	0	178	65.1	27	Crosby	1	25	64	88.2	29
Bastrop	39	48	518	76.0	126	Culberson	1	14	13	85.8	0
Baylor	7	38	56	66.2	5	Dallam	6	0	55	98.8	12
Bee	24	63	223	89.5	56	Dallas	7,280	6,457	13,964	101.0	11,424
Bell	1,029	911	1,863	113.7	968	Dawson	5	29	139	113.2	23
Bexar	4,679	4,874	10,722	97.3	7,313	Deaf Smith	10	35	161	101.4	14
Blanco	5	0	111	77.3	16	Delta	1	0	74	70.6	17
Borden	0	0	2	55.6	2	Denton	691	1,020	2,548	68.4	1,653
Bosque	11	40	251	72.4	29	DeWitt	12	49	254	83.6	24
Bowie	246	621	936	71.2	39	Dickens	0	0	19	72.0	3
Brazoria	260	199	1,930	94.3	543	Dimmit	6	35	83	100.1	19
Brazos	427	410	839	68.0	618	Donley	1	0	54	70.1	7
Brewster	10	25	85	76.3	34	Duval	0	0	105	100.0	36
Briscoe	0	0	28	169.1	24	Eastland	11	36	262	73.1	16
Brooks	3	0	85	116.1	25	Ector	236	535	1,170	110.1	327
Brown	65	168	514	78.1	58	Edwards	1	0	11	84.1	5
Burleson	8	25	172	64.2	21	Ellis	106	112	941	77.1	294
Burnet	64	25	393	81.4	78	El Paso	1,119	1,846	4,524	97.2	2,253
Caldwell	19	59	257	73.4	67	Erath	40	57	281	74.1	87
Calhoun	18	25	188	90.2	32	Falls	3	32	204	57.5	36
Callahan	4	0	162	66.4	6	Fannin	22	25	422	78.5	40
Cameron	511	1,286	2,172	105.4	938	Fayette	30	50	300	78.2	24
Camp	10	24	162	83.1	15	Fisher	2	10	55	65.0	4
Carson	0	0	66	66.5	4	Floyd	8	25	72	71.3	3
Cass	13	81	405	72.1	10	Foard	0	0	19	52.0	1
Castro	6	25	64	109.5	4	Fort Bend	645	613	2,091	81.4	1,326
Chambers	10	39	224	86.9	143	Franklin	7	30	109	97.6	17
Cherokee	75	64	547	88.4	51	Freestone	12	20	199	90.8	37
Childress	10	39	71	88.6	9	Frio	9	40	94	105.2	35
Clay	4	25	104	60.3	12	Gaines	6	25	105	108.4	4
Cochran	2	12	30	98.6	2	Galveston	752	863	2,416	83.6	751
Coke	1	0	52	63.4	5	Garza	2	0	55	104.9	7
Coleman	4	25	135	82.7	5	Gillespie	69	78	322	96.2	28
Collin	1,516	1,637	2,937	76.9	1,879	Glasscock	0	0	2	82.6	2

County	Physicians 2010	Hospital Beds 2008	Total Deaths 2008	Pregnancy rate* 2008	Abortions 2008
Goliad	2	0	61	72.7	6
Gonzales	14	34	186	105.9	37
Gray	29	99	279	102.2	20
Grayson	242	436	1,267	80.5	237
Gregg	315	534	1,224	90.4	104
Grimes	14	18	248	82.8	40
Guadalupe	76	98	833	76.2	189
Hale	27	38	281	99.9	48
Hall	1	0	40	68.0	2
Hamilton	10	34	128	91.7	16
Hansford	3	20	63	109.2	2
Hardeman	5	25	23	84.2	4
Hardin	17	0	514	82.9	104
Harris	10,875	8,461	21,922	99.2	18,912
Harrison	55	132	559	71.2	14
Hartley	0	21	54	80.9	4
Haskell	2	25	95	87.9	13
Hays	182	113	739	69.0	384
Hemphill	4	19	26	118.0	4
Henderson	61	117	961	85.9	116
Hidalgo	823	2,201	3,382	114.4	1,838
Hill	18	112	416	80.4	53
Hockley	14	22	192	93.4	28
Hood	60	59	558	76.0	62
Hopkins	37	54	354	85.2	46
Houston	13	49	311	78.6	20
Howard	47	92	348	93.7	42
Hudspeth	0	0	20	69.1	3
Hunt	82	208	845	72.4	142
Hutchinson	16	25	251	80.8	21
Irion	0	0	12	37.3	0
Jack	6	17	86	82.4	9
Jackson	5	25	171	83.4	12
Jasper	32	50	422	87.8	70
Jeff Davis	1	0	13	53.5	5
Jefferson	546	1,436	2,586	89.0	736
Jim Hogg	1	0	50	111.7	14
Jim Wells	31	152	339	98.8	134
Johnson	149	48	1,163	78.1	286
Jones	9	80	210	71.1	14
Karnes	5	21	136	73.1	14
Kaufman	82	68	784	81.6	172
Kendall	50	0	283	70.7	42
Kenedy	0	0	6	96.8	1
Kent	0	0	10	50.0	0
Kerr	136	133	670	95.5	109
Kimble	3	15	57	70.5	5
King	0	0	1	–	0
Kinney	1	0	39	74.7	2
Kleberg	19	100	195	94.7	123
Knox	3	14	57	91.7	9
Lamar	104	253	612	75.9	37
Lamb	4	41	159	96.7	11
Lampasas	10	25	225	71.3	22
La Salle	3	0	44	114.9	22
Lavaca	18	50	233	80.8	18
Lee	4	0	174	73.1	22
Leon	4	0	198	86.1	16
Liberty	52	127	707	69.9	122
Limestone	21	75	298	104.3	62
Lipscomb	0	0	32	91.3	1

County	Physicians 2010	Hospital Beds 2008	Total Deaths 2008	Pregnancy rate* 2008	Abortions 2008
Live Oak	1	0	116	74.7	17
Llano	16	30	283	71.0	9
Loving	0	0	1	–	3
Lubbock	835	1,432	2,157	81.7	638
Lynn	3	19	52	90.5	7
Madison	7	25	128	92.8	2
Marion	4	0	147	79.8	4
Martin	2	20	42	101.1	8
Mason	0	0	49	66.4	3
Matagorda	34	70	334	81.7	43
Maverick	30	101	327	96.2	66
McCulloch	6	25	99	92.8	21
McLennan	477	477	2,057	80.3	637
McMullen	0	0	8	65.8	1
Medina	18	25	403	80.9	84
Menard	2	0	42	93.6	3
Midland	198	304	1,047	98.8	310
Milam	11	34	283	94.5	61
Mills	4	0	61	71.2	1
Mitchell	2	25	96	94.9	11
Montague	12	74	309	85.6	20
Montgomery	651	1,027	2,671	81.3	661
Moore	13	60	138	105.1	18
Morris	2	0	168	83.2	13
Motley	1	0	22	36.8	0
Nacgdoches	133	245	567	76.2	96
Navarro	49	148	520	85.5	95
Newton	5	0	149	59.6	9
Nolan	15	54	189	89.7	10
Nueces	809	1,444	2,581	89.3	1,212
Ochiltree	5	25	68	113.2	11
Oldham	0	0	14	56.8	0
Orange	41	113	921	80.0	130
Palo Pinto	26	42	323	87.8	37
Panola	12	37	220	76.3	3
Parker	95	74	882	73.1	173
Parmer	4	15	92	75.5	7
Pecos	11	41	125	88.3	25
Polk	42	66	597	78.2	41
Potter	493	983	1,229	91.9	175
Presidio	1	0	49	84.0	6
Rains	2	0	116	76.4	12
Randall	88	4	903	68.4	158
Reagan	1	14	30	99.0	3
Real	0	0	39	78.3	5
Red River	5	36	195	71.7	11
Reeves	10	25	118	114.3	15
Refugio	4	20	87	74.3	11
Roberts	0	0	5	67.7	1
Robertson	2	0	202	92.1	35
Rockwall	87	162	368	75.3	139
Runnels	4	37	180	70.6	8
Rusk	32	76	504	81.7	33
Sabine	3	25	166	78.7	13
S. Augustine	4	18	150	73.5	6
San Jacinto	2	0	283	73.2	27
San Patricio	22	58	526	87.7	118
San Saba	1	0	62	75.7	2
Schleicher	1	14	37	109.2	4
Scurry	11	49	170	109.8	20
Shackelford	2	0	33	69.2	4

County	Physicians 2010	Hospital Beds 2008	Total Deaths 2008	Pregnancy rate* 2008	Abortions 2008
Shelby	9	46	283	89.7	5
Sherman	0	0	21	86.4	13
Smith	757	1,140	1,860	85.4	424
Somervell	12	16	80	80.1	11
Starr	20	48	364	101.0	79
Stephens	8	33	116	98.8	16
Sterling	0	0	12	49.8	0
Stonewall	2	12	23	99.6	3
Sutton	4	12	31	108.2	12
Swisher	3	20	73	89.1	9
Tarrant	3,435	4,450	10,726	91.4	6,090
Taylor	292	594	1,205	83.8	247
Terrell	1	0	11	118.0	8
Terry	6	26	130	103.0	8
Throckmortn	2	14	17	86.6	2
Titus	51	128	269	109.1	50
Tom Green	247	395	1,072	84.6	258
Travis	2,851	2,277	4,519	86.7	3,694
Trinity	5	22	208	76.4	10
Tyler	9	25	229	77.3	48
Upshur	12	37	404	75.0	31
Upton	2	20	29	98.2	4
Uvalde	30	48	227	94.2	47
Val Verde	38	75	324	103.1	74
Van Zandt	10	24	651	75.7	66
Victoria	209	573	737	87.4	141
Walker	84	88	452	61.3	136
Waller	5	0	255	75.9	90
Ward	4	25	114	108.1	18
Washington	43	60	362	84.7	61
Webb	211	569	1,137	112.2	357
Wharton	49	126	370	84.2	52
Wheeler	7	29	47	82.3	2
Wichita	279	508	1,255	80.6	224
Wilbarger	20	47	166	88.0	18
Willacy	8	0	116	91.8	49
Williamson	481	477	1,762	84.5	805
Wilson	19	44	326	74.5	100
Winkler	3	19	66	109.3	10
Wise	67	133	474	77.6	87
Wood	33	63	583	75.7	40
Yoakum	7	22	58	108.3	10
Young	18	62	258	91.0	20
Zapata	2	0	85	120.1	32
Zavala	4	0	90	106.2	26

Sources: Texas Department of State Health Services: Vital Statistics, 2008 (by county of residence) and **Center for Health Statistics**, February 2010. **Texas Medical Board**, September 2010.
Physicians - All practicing licensed M.D.s and D.O.s.
Hospital Beds - Staffed beds not including military and veteran's hospitals. (Previous lists reported licensed beds.)
*Pregnancy Rate figured per 1,000 women age 15-44.
*Abortion total statewide includes abortions performed in Texas but county of residence unknown, plus abortions obtained outside the state by Texas residents.

Marriage and Divorce

These charts are for certain years, including 1946 when there was a significant increase in marriages after World War II as well as a significant increase in divorces. Also included are the years 1979-81 when the marriage and divorce rates reached another peak. *Source: Statistical Abstracts of the United States, National Vital Statistics System.*

Texas

Year	Total marriages	Marriage rate*	Total divorces	Divorce rate*
1940	86,500	13.5	27,500	4.3
1946	143,092	20.5	57,112	8.4
1950	89,155	11.6	37,400	4.9
1955	91,210	10.4	34,921	4.0
1960	91,700	9.6	34,732	3.6
1965	111,500	10.5	41,300	3.9
1970	139,500	12.5	51,500	4.6
1975	153,200	12.5	76,700	6.3
1979	172,800	12.9	92,400	6.9
1980	181,800	12.8	96,800	6.8
1981	194,800	13.2	101,900	6.9
1985	213,800	13.1	101,200	6.2
1990	182,800	10.5	94,000	5.5
1995	188,500	10.1	98,400	5.3
2000	196,400	9.6	85,200	4.2
2005	169,300	7.4	74,000	3.2
2006	175,000	7.5	78,100	3.3
2007	179,900	7.4	79,500	3.3
2008	177,000	7.3	79,800	3.3

*Rate per 1,000 population.

United States

Year	Total marriages	Marriage rate*	Total divorces	Divorce rate*
1940	1,595,879	12.1	264,000	2.0
1946	2,291,045	16.4	610,000	4.3
1950	1,667,231	11.1	385,144	2.6
1955	1,531,000	9.3	377,000	2.3
1960	1,523,381	8.5	393,000	2.2
1965	1,800,200	9.3	479,000	2.5
1970	2,159,000	10.6	708,000	3.5
1975	2,152,700	10.1	1,036,000	4.9
1979	2,331,300	10.6	1,181,000	5.4
1980	2,390,300	10.6	1,189,000	5.2
1981	2,422,100	10.6	1,213,000	5.3
1985	2,425,000	10.2	1,187,000	5.0
1990	2,443,000	9.8	1,182,000	4.7
1995	2,336,000	8.9	1,169,000	4.4
2000	2,329,000	8.2	**NA	4.1
2005	2,230,000	7.5	NA	3.6
2006	2,160,000	7.5	NA	3.6
2007	2,197,000	7.3	NA	3.6
2008	2,157,000	7.1	NA	3.5

**Not Available. Since 1995, the federal government no longer publishes information on the total number of divorces.

National Health Expenditures

Type of Expenditure	1990	1995	2000	2006	2007	2008
Total ($ billions)	$ 714.0	$ 1,016.5	$1,353.3	$ 2,112.5	$ 2,239.7	$ 2,338.7
Percent of gross domestic product	12.3	13.7	13.8	15.8	15.9	16.2
Private expenditures	$ 427.3	$ 551.7	$ 757.1	$ 1,136.8	$ 1,201.0	$ 1,232.0
Insurance premiums*	$ 233.7	$ 325.2	$ 455.2	$ 727.6	$ 759.7	$ 783.2
Out-of-pocket payments	$ 136.1	$ 146.3	$ 192.9	$ 254.9	$ 270.3	$ 277.8
Public expenditures	$ 286.7	$ 464.8	$ 596.1	$ 975.7	$ 1,038.7	$ 1,106.7
Percent federal of public exp.	67.6	70.4	70.0	72.7	72.7	73.8

*Covers insurance benefits and amount retained by insurance companies for expenses, additions to reserves and profits.

Source: Statistical Abstract of the United States 2011, from U.S. Centers for Medicare and Medicaid Services.

Comparison of Vital Statistics

The most current data available, with selected states; those bordering Texas and other large states. **Lowest and highest with number in bold.**

State/Country	BIRTH rate*	DEATH rate*	LIFE expectancy
Texas	16.7	6.7	77.7
Alaska	16.2	**5.1**	-
Arkansas	14.6	9.9	-
California	15.5	6.4	-
Florida	13.1	9.2	-
Georgia	15.8	7.2	-
Illinois	14.1	7.8	-
Louisiana	15.4	9.3	-
Michigan	12.4	8.6	-
New Mexico	15.5	7.9	-
New York	13.1	7.7	-
Ohio	13.2	9.3	-
Oklahoma	15.2	10.0	-
Utah	**20.8**	5.3	-
Vermont	**10.5**	8.3	-
West Virginia	13.0	**11.6**	-
United States	14.3	8.1	78.1
Afghanistan	37.8	17.4	45.0
Angola	42.9	**23.4**	**38.8**
Brazil	17.8	6.4	72.5
Canada	10.3	8.0	81.2
Germany	8.3	10.9	80.1
Italy	9.2	9.8	81.8
Japan	**7.3**	10.1	**82.3**
Mexico	19.1	4.9	76.5
Niger	**50.5**	14.1	53.4
Russia	11.1	16.1	66.3
United Arab Em.	15.9	**2.1**	76.5
United Kingdom	12.3	9.3	80.1
World	19.2	8.1	67.1

*Rates are number during 1 year per 1,000 persons. Sources: U.S. Statistical Abstract 2011; CIA World Factbook, 2011; Texas Vital Statistics Annual Report 2008. Statistics are from 2005-2009.

Life Expectancy for Texans by Group

	All	Whites	Blacks	Hispanics
Total population	77.7	77.6	73.8	79.1
Males	75.2	75.1	70.8	76.7
Females	80.2	80.1	76.5	81.4

Source: Texas Department of State Health Services, 2007.

Texas Births by Race/Ethnicity and Sex

	2007	2000	1990	1980
All Races	407,453	363,325	316,257	273,433
All Male	208,222	185,591	161,522	139,999
All Female	199,231	177,734	154,735	133,434
White Total	138,816	142,553	150,461	151,725
White Male	71,231	72,972	77,134	78,086
White Female	67,585	69,581	73,327	73,639
Black Total	46,211	41,180	43,342	38,544
Black Male	23,550	21,128	21,951	19,501
Black Female	22,661	20,052	21,391	19,043
Hispanic Total	204,419	166,440	115,576	79,324
Hispanic Male	104,215	84,750	58,846	40,475
Hispanic Female	100,204	81,690	56,730	38,849
Other* Total	18,007	13,152	6,687	3,840
Other Male	9,226	6,741	3,591	1,937
Other Female	8,781	6,411	3,287	1,903

*Other includes births of unknown race/ethnicity.
Source: Texas Department of State Health Services, 2007.

Disposition of Bodies in Texas by Percent of Deaths

Year	Burial	Cremation	Donation of body	Removal from state/other
1989	83.7	7.1	0.7	8.5
1991	83.6	8.5	1.0	7.1
1993	82.8	10.1	0.9	6.2
1995	81.7	11.6	0.8	5.8
1997	79.9	12.9	1.0	6.2
1999	78.0	14.9	0.9	6.2
2001	75.5	17.3	0.8	6.3
2003	73.1	19.7	0.9	6.2

Source: Texas Department of State Health Services.

An emergency service helicopter at the East Texas Medical Center, Tyler. Photo by Robert Plocheck.

Community Hospitals in Texas

Source: The Texas Hospital Association

– Of the 587 reporting hospitals in Texas in 2009, 428 were considered community hospitals.

(A community hospital is defined as either a non-federal, short-term general hospital or a special hospital whose facilities and services are available to the public. A hospital may include a nursing home-type unit and still be classified as short-term, provided that the majority of its patients are admitted to units where the average length-of-stay is less than 30 days.)

– These 428 hospitals employed 311,000 full-time equivalent people (FTEs) with a payroll, including benefits, of more than $21.3 billion.

– These hospitals contained some 62,000 beds.

– The average length-of-stay was 5.2 days in 2009, compared to 6.8 days in 1975. This was less than the U.S. average of 5.4 days.

– The average cost per adjusted admission in Texas was $9,580 or $1,920 per day. This was 4.6 percent less than the U.S. average of $10,045.

– There were 2,621,000 admissions in Texas, which accounted for 13,590,000 inpatient days.

– There were 36,023,000 outpatient visits in 2009, of which 9,438,000 were emergency room visits.

– Of the FTEs working in community hospitals within Texas, there were 91,000 registered nurses and 11,000 licensed vocational nurses. ☆

U.S. Medical Care: Source of Payments

Source of payment ($ in billions)	1990	1995	2000	2006	2007	2008
Hospital care, total	$ 251.6	$ 340.7	$ 417.0	$ 648.2	$ 687.6	$ 718.4
Out-of-pocket payments	$ 11.3	$ 10.4	$ 13.6	$ 21.4	$ 22.3	$ 23.2
Private health insurance	$ 97.8	$ 110.6	$ 143.6	$ 234.8	$ 246.1	$ 259.0
Federal Government	$ 101.7	$ 166.0	$ 192.9	$ 290.2	$ 307.6	$ 330.7
State/Local Government	$ 30.3	$ 39.2	$ 45.2	$ 72.4	$ 77.5	$ 78.3
Physician and clinical services, total	$ 157.5	$ 220.5	$ 288.6	$ 447.6	$ 472.6	$ 496.2
Out-of-pocket payments	$ 30.2	$ 26.0	$ 32.2	$ 46.2	$ 49.2	$ 50.1
Private health insurance	$ 67.3	$ 106.1	$ 136.8	$ 219.7	$ 232.7	$ 241.8
Federal Government	$ 38.0	$ 56.2	$ 79.0	$ 126.4	$ 132.7	$ 144.6
State/Local Government	$ 10.7	$ 14.7	$ 18.4	$ 26.6	$ 27.2	$ 27.7
Prescription drugs, total	$ 40.3	$ 60.9	$ 120.6	$ 217.0	$ 226.8	$ 234.1
Out-of-pocket payments	$ 22.4	$ 23.3	$ 33.4	$ 46.9	$ 48.9	$ 48.5
Private health insurance	$ 10.6	$ 24.4	$ 59.5	$ 96.2	$ 97.8	$ 98.5
Federal Government	$ 3.2	$ 6.6	$ 15.9	$ 58.7	$ 65.4	$ 72.5
State/Local Government	$ 4.0	$ 6.5	$ 11.8	$ 15.2	$ 14.7	$ 14.5

Source: Statistical Abstract of the United States 2011, from U.S. Centers for Medicare and Medicaid Services.

State Institutions for Mental Health Services

Source: Texas Department of State Health Services.

Mental health services are provided to some 100,000 Texans each year in various institutions. In 2010, the Texas Department of State Health Services (TDSHS) budget included $350 million for mental hospitals and $700 million for community mental health centers and substance-abuse treatment.

On Sept. 1, 2004, the TDSHS was created, bringing together:

— the Texas Department of Health,
— the Texas Department of Mental Health and Mental Retardation (MHMR),
— Commission on Alcohol and Drug Abuse,
— the Texas Health Care Information Council.

With the consolidation of the four agencies, TDSHS, with more than 11,500 employees, now includes treatment and prevention for mental illness and substance abuse in its public health framework. The Web address is: www.dshs.state.tx.us

Following is a list of state hospitals, the year each was founded and numbers of admissions of patients in fiscal year 2010.

Hospitals for Persons with Mental Illness

Austin State Hospital — Austin; 1857; 3,721 patients.

Big Spring State Hospital — Big Spring; 1937; 1,028 patients.

El Paso Psychiatric Center — El Paso; 1974; 787 patients.

Kerrville State Hospital — Kerrville; 1950; 55 patients.

North Texas State Hospital — Wichita Falls (1922) and Vernon (1969); 2,252 patients.

Rio Grande State Center — Harlingen; 1962; 1,147 patients.

Rusk State Hospital — Rusk; 1919; 972 patients.

San Antonio State Hospital — San Antonio; 1892; 1,877 patients.

Terrell State Hospital — Terrell; 1885; 2,986 patients.

Waco Center for Youth — Waco; 1979; 149 patients.

Following is a list of community mental health centers, the year each was founded, and the counties each serves.

Community Mental Health Centers

Abilene — Betty Hardwick Center; 1971; Callahan, Jones, Shackleford, Stephens and Taylor.

Amarillo — Texas Panhandle MHMR; 1968; Armstrong, Carson, Collingsworth, Dallam, Deaf Smith, Donley, Gray, Hall, Hansford, Hartley, Hemphill, Hutchinson, Lipscomb, Moore, Ochiltree, Oldham, Potter, Randall, Roberts, Sherman and Wheeler.

Austin — Austin-Travis County Center; 1967; Travis.

Beaumont — Spindletop MHMR Services; 1967; Chambers, Hardin, Jefferson and Orange.

Big Spring — West Texas Centers; 1997; Andrews, Borden, Crane, Dawson, Fisher, Gaines, Garza, Glasscock, Howard, Kent, Loving, Martin, Mitchell, Nolan, Reeves, Runnels, Scurry, Terrell, Terry, Upton, Ward, Winkler and Yoakum.

Brownwood — Center for Life Resources; 1969; Brown, Coleman, Comanche, Eastland, McCulloch, Mills and San Saba.

Bryan-College Station — MHMR Authority of Brazos Valley; 1972; Brazos, Burleson, Grimes, Leon, Madison, Robertson and Washington.

Cleburne — Johnson-Ellis-Navarro County Center; 1985; Ellis, Johnson, Navarro.

Conroe — Tri-County Services; 1983; Liberty, Montgomery and Walker.

Corpus Christi — Nueces County Community Center; 1970; Nueces.

Dallas — Dallas MetroCare; 1967; Dallas.

Denton — Denton County Center; 1987; Denton.

Edinburg — Tropical Texas Center; 1967; Cameron, Hidalgo and Willacy.

El Paso — Community Center; 1968; El Paso.

Fort Worth — MHMR of Tarrant County; 1969; Tarrant.

Galveston — Gulf Coast Center; 1969; Brazoria and Galveston.

Houston — MHMR Authority/Harris County; 1965; Harris.

Jacksonville — Anderson-Cherokee Community Enrichment Services; 1995; Anderson, Cherokee.

Kerrville — Hill Country Community Center; 1997; Bandera, Blanco, Comal, Edwards, Gillespie, Hays, Kendall, Kerr, Kimble, Kinney, Llano, Mason, Medina, Menard, Real, Schleicher, Sutton, Uvalde and Val Verde.

Laredo — Border Region Community Center; 1969; Jim Hogg, Starr, Webb and Zapata.

Longview — Sabine Valley Center; 1970; Gregg, Harrison, Marion, Panola, Rusk and Upshur.

Lubbock — Lubbock Regional Center; 1969; Cochran, Crosby, Hockley, Lubbock and Lynn.

Lufkin — Burke Center; 1975; Angelina, Houston, Jasper, Nacogdoches, Newton, Polk, Sabine, San Augustine, San Jacinto, Shelby, Trinity and Tyler.

Lytle — Camino Real Community Center; 1996; Atascosa, Dimmit, Frio, La Salle, Karnes, Maverick, McMullen, Wilson and Zavala.

McKinney — LifePath Systems; 1986; Collin.

Midland — Permian Basin Community Centers; 1969; Brewster, Culberson, Ector, Hudspeth, Jeff Davis, Midland, Pecos and Presidio.

Plainview — Central Plains Center; 1969; Bailey, Briscoe, Castro, Floyd, Hale, Lamb, Motley, Parmer and Swisher.

Portland — Coastal Plains Community; 1996; Aransas, Bee, Brooks, Duval, Jim Wells, Kenedy, Kleberg, Live Oak and San Patricio.

Rosenberg — Texana Center; 1996; Austin, Colorado, Fort Bend, Matagorda, Waller and Wharton.

Round Rock — Bluebonnet Trails Community Center; 1997; Bastroop, Burnet, Caldwell, Fayette, Gonzales, Guadalupe, Lee and Williamson.

San Angelo — MHMR Services for the Concho Valley; 1969; Coke, Concho, Crockett, Irion, Reagan, Sterling and Tom Green.

San Antonio — The Center for Health Care Services; 1966; Bexar.

Sherman — MHMR Services of Texoma; 1974; Cooke, Fannin and Grayson.

Stephenville — Pecan Valley Region; 1977; Erath, Hood, palo Pinto, Parker and Somervell.

Temple — Central Counties Center; 1967; Bell, Coryell, Hamilton, Lampasas and Milam.

Terrell — Lakes Regional Center; 1996; Camp, Delta, Franklin, Hopkins, Hunt, Kaufman, Lamar, Morris, Rockwall and Titus.

Texarkana — Northeast Texas Center; 1974; Bowie, Cass and Red River.

Tyler — Andrews Center; 1970; Henderson, Rains, Smith, Van Zandt and Wood.

Victoria — Gulf Bend Center; 1970; Calhoun, DeWitt, Jackson, Lavaca, Refugio and Victoria.

Waco — Heart of Texas Region Center; 1969; Bosque, Falls, Freestone, Hill, Limestone and McLennan.

Wichita Falls — Helen Farabee Regional Centers; 1969; Archer, Bayor, Childress, Clay, Cottle, Dickens, Foard, Hardeman, Haskell, Jack, King, Knox, Montague, Stonewall, Throckmorton, Wichita, Wilbarger and Young. ☆

Substance Abuse and Mental Health Admissions

Drug Treatment in State-Funded Programs: 2009

Primary Drug	Total Admissions	White	Black	Hispanic	Percent with no prior treatment	Average age	Percent male
			(percent)				
All Drugs	91,072	45.4	20.4	32.8	47.5	33.1	60.9
Heroin	11,368	36.5	8.0	54.4	25.3	33.6	62.4
Other opiates	5,844	77.1	7.7	14.0	38.2	33.6	42.5
Alcohol	25,288	55.3	12.6	30.4	45.9	38.5	70.1
Barbiturates	77	75.3	6.5	15.6	57.1	28.7	44.2
Other sedatives	1,348	64.5	13.6	20.8	49.0	28.9	33.9
Amphet/Methamph	7,535	84.8	2.0	11.4	46.1	33.1	44.3
Cocaine (powder)	6,611	27.0	22.5	48.9	52.6	33.0	54.0
Crack	9,623	32.2	50.6	16.2	35.4	40.3	48.5
Ecstasy	209	31.6	40.2	27.3	62.7	24.2	51.7
Marijuana	21,540	27.4	30.1	41.2	67.4	23.7	71.0

Source: Texas Department of State Health Services, 2011.

Estimated Use of Drugs in Texas and Bordering States: 2007-2008

State	Any illicit drug	Marijuana	Other than marijuana[1]	Cigarettes	Binge alcohol[2]
	Current users[3] as **percent of population**. Selected states.				
U.S. total	8.0	6.0	3.6	24.1	23.3
Texas	**6.3**	**4.4**	**3.3**	**23.4**	**23.2**
Arkansas	8.0	5.5	4.3	31.1	21.6
Louisana	7.2	5.0	3.9	26.5	23.8
Oklahoma	8.1	4.8	4.9	27.3	21.6
New Mexico	8.7	6.2	3.6	22.7	21.9

[1]Marijuana users who have also used another drug are included. [2]Binge use is defined as drinking five or more drinks on the same occasion on a least one day in the past 30 days. [3]Used drugs at least once within month.
Source: U.S. Substance Abuse and Mental Health Services Administration, National Household Survey on Drug Use and Health, 2007–2008.

Primary Diagnosis of Clients in Texas and Bordering States: 2009

State	Schizophrenia	Other Psychoses	Bipolar and Mood Disorders	No Diagnosis	All Other
	In percent of clients.				
U.S. total	14.0	3.0	44.0	8.3	30.7
Texas	**24.8**	**0.2**	**70.1**	**3.7**	**1.3**
Arkansas	13.0	3.2	51.6	3.1	29.2
Louisana	21.7	3.9	56.2	9.9	8.3
New Mexico	8.8	2.1	50.4	4.3	34.4
Oklahoma	14.4	1.6	64.2	2.2	17.6

Source: U.S. Department of Health and Human Services, Center for Mental Health Services, Uniform Reporting System, 2009.

Readmission within 180 Days of Treatment: 2007

Age	Civil* Texas	Civil U.S.	States reporting	Forensic* Texas	Forensic U.S.
	In percent of clients.				
0 to 12	16.8 %	17.9 %	19	–	–
13 to 17	13.9 %	15.6 %	27	11.1 %	8.2 %
18 to 20	18.5 %	19.7 %	47	13.2 %	11.0 %
21 to 64	20.3 %	21.8 %	51	14.0 %	11.7 %
65 to 74	14.8 %	17.1 %	36	8.0 %	14.5 %
75 and over	8.5 %	16.8 %	38	31.8 %	14.1 %
age not available	–	13.1 %	3	–	–
Total	19.4 %	20.9 %	52	14.4 %	11.6 %

Forensic services are mental health services provided to persons directed into treatment by the criminal justice system, others are listed as "Civil". Source: U.S. Department of Health and Human Services, Center for Mental Health Services, Uniform Reporting System, 2009.

Science Research Funding at Universities

The following chart shows funding for research and development by source at universities in Texas, in order of total R&D funding. The figures are from the National Science Foundation and are for fiscal year 2008.

(Thousands of dollars, $ 000)	All R&D expenditures	Federal gov.	State/local gov.	Industry	Institutional funds	All other sources
United States	$ 51,909,726	$ 31,231,220	$3,417,995	$2,870,147	$10,434,984	$ 3,954,380
Texas (statewide)	**3,744,182**	**1,950,482**	**457,214**	**234,865**	**771,485**	**390,136**
1. Texas A&M University	582,365	245,607	124,139	43,421	127,163	12,035
2. U. Texas M.D. Anderson Cancer Ctr.	558,503	194,889	149,429	40,625	100,042	73,518
3. University of Texas-Austin	493,294	324,287	20,318	42,518	80,872	25,304
4. Baylor College of Medicine	449,301	262,498	3,505	20,051	68,290	94,957
5. U. Texas Southwestern Med. Dallas	390,349	201,480	49,262	22,960	34,701	81,946
8. U. Texas Health Sci. San Antonio	201,323	121,758	4,983	5,567	50,406	18,609
6. U. Texas Health Sci. Houston	197,252	129,277	15,040	7,519	26,698	18,718
7. U. Texas Medical Branch Galveston	180,026	122,009	6,668	6,403	28,640	16,306
8. University of Houston	84,490	43,162	9,160	4,136	23,288	4,744
9. Texas A&M Health Sci. Ctr.	79,687	33,044	1,415	3,431	32,328	9,469
10. Rice University	74,254	54,959	465	2,470	9,026	7,334
11. University of Texas-Dallas	59,300	21,383	18,040	5,969	6,667	7,241
12. Texas Tech University	57,902	19,698	16,840	3,970	13,336	4,058
13. University of Texas-El Paso	48,906	26,902	1,348	3,495	17,161	0
14. University of Texas-Arlington	43,005	20,721	1,606	6,334	14,344	0
15. University of Texas-San Antonio	33,106	21,523	8,739	517	2,327	0
16. U. North Texas Health Sci. Ft.Worth	28,187	19,818	821	620	5,057	1,863
17. Texas Tech Health Science Center	24,716	8,995	1,604	1,921	9,909	2,287
18. Southern Methodist University	19,530	10,612	311	5,924	2,088	595
19. University of North Texas	15,932	8,241	232	1,059	5,278	1,122
20. Texas A&M University-Kingsville	13,519	3,364	1,426	141	7,881	707
21. Texas State University-San Marcos	11,792	2,146	1,806	884	5,397	1,559
22. Texas A&M U.-Corpus Christi	11,662	6,015	3,037	43	161	2,406
23. Prairie View A&M University	10,786	7,659	2,599	39	441	48
24. Baylor University	9,867	3,220	518	1,835	2,978	1,316
25. Tarleton State University	8,857	4,701	3,405	151	600	0
27. Stephen F. Austin State University	6,742	3,606	1,352	126	1,302	356

Colleges and universities not listed received less. Source: National Science Foundation, 2011.

Computer Specialist as Share of Workforce

The following chart shows data by selected state and by year.

STATE	Computer specialsts			As percent of workforce		
	2004	2006	2008	2004	2006	2008
United States	**2,806,910**	**2,960,460**	**3,198,050**	**2.02**	**2.05**	**2.08**
California	370,180	380,040	383,900	2.25	2.23	2.09
Colorado	74,940	76,200	79,930	3.14	3.00	2.93
Connecticut	44,120	44,160	40,900	2.57	2.50	2.18
Florida	137,740	143,450	141,320	1.71	1.i65	1.53
Georgia	94,080	89,390	86.210	2.21	1.98	1.78
Illinois	114,860	129,880	137,420	1.91	2.06	2.05
Maryland	92,40	91,040	89,900	3.34	3.15	3.00
Massachusetts	103,280	109,430	111,910	3.22	3.38	3.27
Michigan	74,600	89,280	88,980	1.59	1.89	1.80
New Jersey	114,370	116,290	121,690	2.74	2.70	2.71
New York	170,140	188,620	200,900	1.93	2.08	2.08
Pennsylvania	102,590	110,090	115,300	1.74	1.83	1.80
Texas	**209,360**	**224,330**	**245,730**	**2.00**	**2.05**	**2.10**
Virginia	151,810	169,830	171,440	4.10	4.38	4.16

Source: National Science Foundation/Division of Science Resources Statistics, 2011.

Texans in the National Academy of Sciences

Source: National Academy of Sciences

The National Academy of Sciences is a private organization of scientists and engineers dedicated to the furtherance of science and its use for the general welfare. A total of 84 scientists affiliated with Texas institutions have been named members or associates.

Established by congressional acts of incorporation, which were signed by Abraham Lincoln in 1863, the academy acts as official adviser to the federal government in matters of science or technology.

Selected to the academy in 2011 were: **Arthur L. Beaudet**, professor and chair, department of molecular and human genetics, Baylor College of Medicine, Houston; **Luis F. Parada**, professor and chair, department of developmental biology, University of Texas Southwestern Medical Center, Dallas; and **Peter J. Rossky,** professor and regents chair, department of chemistry and biochemistry, University of Texas at Austin.

Selected to the academy in 2010 was: **Allan H. MacDonald**, professor and regents chair, department of physics, University of Texas at Austin.

Election to the academy is one of the highest honors that can be accorded a scientist. As of May 2011, the number of active members was 2,113.

In addition, 418 scientists with citizenship outside the United States are nonvoting foreign associates.

In 1970, D.H.R. Barton from Texas A&M University, and, in 1997, Johann Deisenhofer of the UT Southwestern Medical Center, Dallas, were elected as foreign associates.

In 1948, Karl Folkers of UT-Austin became the first Texan elected to the science academy. ☆

Academy Member	Affiliation*	Year Elected
Perry L. Adkisson	A&M	1979
Richard W. Aldrich	UT-Austin	2008
Abram Amsel	UT-Austin	1992
Neal R. Amundson	U of H	1992
Charles J. Arntzen	A&M	1983
David H. Auston	Rice	1991
Paul F. Barbara	UT-Austin	2006
Allen J. Bard	UT-Austin	1982
Arthur L. Beaudet	Baylor Medical	2011
Brian J.L. Berry	UT-Dallas	1975
Lewis R. Binford	SMU	2001
Norman E. Borlaug	A&M	1968
Michael S. Brown	UTSWMC	1980
Karl W. Butzer	UT-Austin	1996
Luis A. Caffarelli	UT-Austin	1991
C. Thomas Caskey	Baylor Medical	1993
Joseph W. Chamberlain †	Rice	1965
C.W. Chu	U of H	1989
Melanie H. Cobb	UTSWMC	2006
F. Albert Cotton †	A&M	1967
Robert F. Curl	Rice	1997
Gerard H. de Vaucouleurs †	UT-Austin	1986
Bryce DeWitt †	UT-Austin	1990
Stephen J. Elledge	Baylor Medical	2003
Ronald W. Estabrook	UTSWMC	1979
Mary K. Estes	Baylor Medical	2007
Karl Folkers †	UT-Austin	1948
Marye Anne Fox	UT-Austin	1994
David L. Garbers	UTSWMC	1993
Wilson S. Geisler	UT-Austin	2008
Quentin H. Gibson	Rice	1982
Alfred G. Gilman	UTSWMC	1985
Joseph L. Goldstein	UTSWMC	1980
William E. Gordon	Rice	1968
Verne E. Grant †	UT-Austin	1968
Norman Hackerman †	Welch	1971
Dudley Herschbach	A&M	1967
David M. Hillis	UT-Austin	2008
Helen H. Hobbs	UTSWMC	2007
A. James Hudspeth	UTSWMC	1991
Thomas J.R. Hughes	UT-Austin	2009
James L. Kinsey	Rice	1991
Ernst Knobil †	UTHSC-Houston	1986
Jay K. Kochi †	U of H	1982
Alan M. Lambowitz	UT-Austin	2004
Alan G. MacDiarmid †	UT-Dallas	2002

Academy Member	Affiliation*	Year Elected
David J. Mangelsdorf	UT-Austin	2008
John L. Margrave †	Rice	1974
S.M. McCann	UTSWMC	1983
Allan H. MacDonald	UT-Austin	2010
Steven L. McKnight	UTSWMC	1992
David J. Meltzer	SMU	2009
Ferid Murad	UTHSC-Houston	1997
Jack Myers †	UT-Austin	1975
Eric N. Olson	UTSWMC	2000
Bert W. O'Malley	Baylor Medical	1992
Luis F. Parada	UTSWMC	2011
Kenneth L. Pike †	SIL	1985
Lester J. Reed	UT-Austin	1973
Peter J. Rossky	UT-Austin	2011
David W. Russell	UTSWMC	2006
Marlan O. Scully	A&M	2001
Richard E. Smalley †	Rice	1990
Esmond E. Snell †	UT-Austin	1955
Richard C. Starr †	UT-Austin	1976
Thomas Südhof	UTSWMC	2002
Max D. Summers	A&M	1989
Harry L. Swinney	UT-Austin	1992
John T. Tate	UT-Austin	1969
Karen K. Uhlenbeck	UT-Austin	1986
Jonathan W. Uhr	UTSWMC	1984
Roger H. Unger	UTSWMC	1986
Ellen S. Vitetta	UTSWMC	1994
Salih J. Wakil	Baylor Medical	1990
Xiaodong Wang	UTSWMC	2004
Steven Weinberg	UT-Austin	1972
D. Fred Wendorf	SMU	1987
Jean D. Wilson	UTSWMC	1983
James E. Womack	A&M	1999
Masahi Yanagisawa	UTSWMC	2003
Huda Y. Zoghbi	Baylor Medical	2004
		† Deceased

* A&M - Texas A&M University
UT-Austin - The University of Texas at Austin
U of H - University of Houston
UT-Dallas - The University of Texas at Dallas
UTSWMC - The University of Texas Southwestern
            Medical Center at Dallas
Baylor Medical - Baylor College of Medicine, Houston
Rice - Rice University
Welch - Robert A. Welch Foundation
UTHSC - Houston - The University of Texas Health
            Science Center at Houston
SIL - Summer Institute of Linguistics
SMU - Southern Methodist University

Education

Channing School in Channing, Hartley County, was built in 1931. Robert Plocheck photo.

Texas Public Schools

UIL Winning Schools for 2009–2010 & 2010–2011

Higher Education in Texas

Universities and Colleges

Texas Public Schools

Source: Texas Education Agency; www.tea.state.tx.us

Enrollment in Texas public schools reached a peak of 4,933,617 students in 2010–2011, according to the Texas Education Agency. That is an increase of almost 338,675 students over the last four years; enrollment was 4,594,942 in 2006–2007.

The seven largest districts (listed in descending order by average daily attendance) are:

School District	County	Enrollment
Houston	Harris	204,245
Dallas	Dallas	157,162
Cypress-Fairbanks	Harris	106,097
Northside	Bexar	95,581
Austin	Travis	85,697
Fort Worth	Tarrant	81,651
Fort Bend	Fort Bend	68,948

In Texas, there are 1,030 independent and common school districts and 207 charter operators. Independent school districts are administered by an elected board of trustees and deal directly with the Texas Education Agency. Common districts are supervised by elected county school superintendents and county trustees. Charter schools are discussed later in this article.

Brief History of Public Education

Public education was one of the primary goals of the early settlers of Texas, who listed in the **Texas Declaration of Independence** the failure to provide education as one of their grievances against Mexico.

As early as 1838, **President Mirabeau B. Lamar's** message to the Republic of Texas Congress advocated setting aside public domain for public schools. His interest caused him to be called the **"Father of Education in Texas."** In 1839, Congress designated three leagues of land to support public schools for each Texas county and 50 leagues for a state university. In 1840, each county was allocated one more league of land.

The Republic, however, did not establish a public school system or a university. After Texas was admitted into the Union, the 1845 Texas State Constitution advocated public education, instructing the Legislature to designate at least 10 percent of the tax revenue for schools. Further delay occurred until Gov. Elisha M. Pease, on Jan. 31, 1854, signed **the bill setting up the Texas public school system.**

The public school system was made possible by setting aside $2 million out of $10 million Texas received for relinquishing its claim to land north and west of its present boundaries **in the Compromise of 1850** (see map on page 53).

During 1854, legislation provided for state apportionment of funds based upon an annual census. Also, railroads receiving grants were required to survey alternate sections to be set aside for public-school financing. The **first school census** that year showed 65,463 students; state fund apportionment was 62 cents per student.

When adopted in 1876, the present Texas Constitution provided: "All funds, lands, and other property heretofore set apart and appropriated for the support of public schools; all the alternate sections of land reserved by the state of grants heretofore made or that may hereafter be made to railroads, or other corporations, of any nature whatsoever; one half of the pub-

Texas School Enrollment and Expenditures per Student

School Year	Enrollment	Spending per student
2009–2010	4,824,778	$11,567
2008–2009	4,728,204	11,024
2007–2008	4,651,516	10,162
2006–2007	4,576,933	9,629
2005–2006	4,505,572	9,269
2004–2005	4,383,871	8,916
2003–2004	4,311,502	7,708
2002–2003	4,239,911	7,088
2001–2002	4,146,653	6,913
2000–2001	4,059,619	6,638
1999–2000	3,991,783	6,354

Graduates and Dropouts

School Year	Graduates	*Dropouts
2008–2009	264,275	40,923
2007–2008	252,121	45,796
2006–2007	241,193	55,306
2005–2006	240,485	51,841
2004–2005	239,716	18,290
2003–2004	244,165	16,434
2002–2003	238,109	15,117
2001–2002	225,167	16,622
2000–2001	215,316	17,563
1999–2000	212,925	23,457
1998–1999	203,393	27,592

*Grades 7–12.

Personnel and Salaries

Year/ Personnel Type	Personnel (Full-Time Equivalent)*	Average Total Salaries†
2009–2010 Personnel		
Teachers	333,007	$49,544
Campus Administrators	18,543	70,723
Central Administrators	6,853	88,467
Support Staff*	58,576	57,243
Total Professionals	*416,979*	*52,207*
Educational Aides	64,701	18,596
Auxiliary Staff	178,141	22,686
Total Staff	*659,821*	*40,941*
2008–2009 Personnel		
Teachers	327,663	$48,334
Campus Administrators	18,325	69,447
Central Administrators	6,672	86,342
Support Staff*	54,476	56,563
Total Professionals	*407,135*	*51,008*
Educational Aides	62,460	18,319
Auxiliary Staff	177,220	22,238
Total Staff	*646,815*	*39,969*

*Support staff includes supervisors, counselors, educational diagnosticians, librarians, nurses/physicians, therapists, and psychologists.

†Supplements for non-teaching duties and career-ladder supplements are not included in this figure.

lic domain of the state, and all sums of money that may come to the state from the sale of any portion of the same shall constitute a **perpetual public school fund."**

More than 52 million acres of the Texas public domain were allotted for school purposes. (See table, Distribution of the Public Lands of Texas on page 498.)

The Constitution also provided for one-fourth of occupation taxes and a poll tax of one dollar for school support, and it made provisions for local taxation.

No provision was made for direct ad valorem taxation for maintenance of an available school fund, but a maximum 20-cent state ad valorem school tax was adopted in 1883 and raised to 35 cents in connection with provision of **free textbooks** in the amendment of 1918.

In 1949, the **Gilmer-Aikin Laws** reorganized the state system of public schools by making sweeping changes in administration and financing. The Texas Education Agency, headed by the governor-appointed Commissioner of Education, administers the public-school system.

The policy-making body for public education is the 15-member State Board of Education, which is elected from separate districts for overlapping four-year terms. Current membership of the board may be found in the State Government section of this Almanac.

Former First Lady Laura Bush reads to children from West Dallas Community School at Kids Vision Fest, Jan. 19, 2010, at the Dallas Public Library. The annual event is sponsored by the Essilor Vision Foundation. Photo by Elizabeth Alvarez.

Recent Changes in Public Education

Members of the 68th Legislature passed a **historic education-reform bill** in the summer of 1984. House Bill 72 came in response to growing concern over deteriorating literacy among Texas' schoolchildren over two decades, reflected in students' scores on standardized tests.

Provisions of **HB 72** raised teachers' salaries, but tied those raises to **teacher performance.** It also introduced more stringent teacher certification and initiated competency testing for teachers.

Academic achievement was set as a priority in public education with stricter attendance rules; a **no-pass, no-play rule** prohibited students who are failing courses from participating in sports and other extracurricular activities for a six-week period; and national norm-referenced testing throughout all grades was instituted to assure parents of individual schools' performance through a common frame of reference.

No-pass, no-play now requires only a three-week suspension for a failing course grade, during which time the student can continue to practice, but not participate in extracurricular activities.

The 74th Legislature passed the **Public Schools Reform Act of 1995,** which increased local control of public schools by limiting the Texas Education Agency to recommending and reporting on educational goals; overseeing charter schools; managing the permanent, foundation, and available school funds; administering an accountability system; creating and implementing the student testing program; recommending educator appraisal and counselor evaluation instruments; and developing plans for special, bilingual, compensatory, gifted and talented, vocational, and technology education.

Texas students, beginning with the Class of 1987, have been required to pass an exit-level exam, along with their courses, in order to receive a diploma from a Texas public high school. Beginning with the Class of 2005, Texas students must pass the exit-level Texas Assessment of Knowledge and Skills (TAKS) to meet this graduation requirement. TAKS, which is the most rigorous graduation test ever given to Texas students, covers English language arts, mathematics, science, and social studies.

To give Texas residents a sense of how schools are performing, the state has issued ratings for its public school districts and campuses since 1993. The system is based on state test scores and high school completion rates.

Actions of the 82nd Legislature Affecting Public Schools

The 82nd legislative session ended with no state budget and several key education-related bills still pending, bringing on the call for a special session where a handful of bills were finally passed.

HB 1, passed in the regular session, cut school funding by $4 billion and slashed another $1.3 billion in special program funding. In addition, HB 1 eliminated funding for several programs, including the Pre-Kindergarten Early Start Program, the Technology Allotment, science lab grants, new instructional facilities allotment, and middle school physical education grants.

SB 1 contains the school funding bill, including a provision that allows charter school bonds to be guaranteed by the Permanent School Fund for a AAA rating.

SB 6, the textbook bill, expands the way school districts can use funding for textbooks. It creates an Instructional Materials Allotment (IMA) which entitles a school district to an annual allotment from the state that may be used to purchase instructional materials, regardless of whether or not they are on the State Board of Education's adopted list; consumable materials; bilingual, supplemental, and state-developed open-source instructional materials; and technological equipment.

The allotment may also be used to pay for training educational personnel directly involved in student learning in the appropriate use of instructional materials, as well as salaries of employees providing technical support for technological equipment.

SB 8 is a comprehensive mandate relief bill that allows school districts to furlough teachers, reduce salaries of classroom teachers, reduce the notification time for contract termination, and allows terminations to be made based on performance evaluations rather than reverse order of seniority.

Charter Schools

Charter-school legislation in Texas provides for three types of charter schools: the home-rule school district charter, the campus or campus-program charter, and the open-enrollment charter.

As of April 2007, no district has expressed official interest in home-rule charter status, because of its complex developmental procedures. Houston, Dallas, Nacogdoches, San Antonio, Clear Creek, Colorado, Corpus Christi, and Spring Branch school districts have created campus charter schools, which are overseen by each school district's board of trustees.

Open-enrollment charter schools are public schools released from some Texas education laws and regulations. These schools are granted by the State Board of Education (SBOE). This charter contract is typically granted for five years and can be revoked if the school violates its charter.

Many charter schools have focused efforts on educating young people who are at risk of dropping out of school or who have dropped out and then returned to school. ☆

PSF Apportionment, 1854–2008

The first apportionment by Texas to public schools was for school year 1854–1855

Years	Amount of P.S.F. Distributed to Schools	Years	Amount of P.S.F. Distributed to Schools
1854–55	$ 40,587	1992–93	739,494,967
1880–81	679,317	1993–94	737,677,545
1900–01	3,002,820	1994–95	737,008,244
1910–11	5,931,287	1995–96	739,996,574
1920–21	18,431,716	1996–97	692,678,412
1930–31	27,342,473	1997–98	690,802,024
1940–41	34,580,475	1998–99	661,892,466
1950–51	93,996,600	1999–00	698,487,305
1960–61	164,188,461	2000–01	794,284,231
1970–71	287,159,758	2001–02	764,554,567
1980–81	3,042,476	2002–03	896,810,915
1985–86	807,680,617	2003–04	825,059,655
1988–89	882,999,623	2004–05	879,981,965
1989–90	917,608,395	2005–06	841,878,709
1990–91	700,276,846	2006–07	843,136,949
1991–92	739,200,044	2007–08	716,534,543

Source: Texas Education Agency.

Permanent School Fund

The Texas public school system was established and the permanent fund set up by the Fifth Legislature, Jan. 31, 1854.

Year	Total Investment Fund*	Total Income Earned by P.S.F.	Amount of P.S.F. Distributed to Schools	Year	Total Investment Fund*	Amount of P.S.F. Distributed to Schools
1854	$ 2,000,000	...	$ 40,587	1993	11,822,465,497	739,494,967
1880	3,542,126	...	679,317	1994	11,330,590,652	737,677,545
1900	9,102,873	$ 783,142	3,002,820	1995	12,273,168,900	737,008,244
1910	16,752,407	1,970,527	5,931,287	1996	12,995,820,070	762,569,466
1920	25,698,282	2,888,555	18,431,716	1997	15,496,646,498	692,678,412
1930	38,718,106	2,769,547	27,342,473	1998	16,296,199,389	690,802,024
1940	68,299,082	3,331,874	34,580,475	1999	19,615,730,341	661,892,466
1950	161,179,979	3,985,974	93,996,600	2000	22,275,586,452	698,487,305
1961	454,391,643	13,766,436	164,188,461	2001	19,021,750,040	794,284,231
1970	842,217,721	34,762,955	287,159,758	2002	17,047,245,212	764,554,567
1980	2,464,579,397	166,475,426	3,042,476	2003	18,037,320,374	896,810,915
1985	5,095,802,979	417,080,383	807,680,617	2004	19,261,799,285	825,059,655
1988	6,493,070,622	572,665,253	882,999,623	2005	21,354,333,727	879,981,967
1989	6,873,610,771	614,786,823	917,608,395	2006	22,802,708,177	841,878,709
1990	8,930,703,666	674,634,994	700,276,846	2007	25,311,835,346	843,136,949
1991	10,227,777,535	700,276,846	739,200,044	2008	23,142,393,002	716,534,543
1992	10,944,944,872	739,200,044	739,494,967	2009	20,545,271,679	716,533,764

For years before 1991, includes cash, bonds at par and stocks at book value. For years beginning with 1991, includes cash, bonds and stocks at fair value.

University Interscholastic League Winning Schools for the 2009–2010 and 2010–2011 School Years

Winners in the academic, music, and the arts categories are listed first, then winners in sports categories. A dash (—) in the box means there was no competition in that conference in that category for that year. Source: University Interscholastic League. http://www.uil.utexas.edu/

Academics

Year	Conference A	Conference AA	Conference AAA	Conference AAAA	Conference AAAAA
	Overall State Meet Academic Champions				
2009–10	Lindsay	Holliday	Argyle	Friendswood	Fort Bend Clements
2010–11	Martin's Mill	Tuscola Jim Ned	Argyle	Friendswood	Fort Bend Clements
	Accounting				
2009–10	Happy	TIE: Grandview Rosebud-Lott	Giddings	Granbury	Laredo United
2010–11	Happy	Rosebud-Lott	Longview Spring Hill	Azle	Round Rock
	Accounting Team				
2009–10	Happy	Grandview	Giddings	Granbury	Laredo United
2010–11	Happy	Rosebud-Lott	Giddings	Granbury	Fort Bend Dulles
	Calculator Applications				
2009–10	Poolville	Elkhart	Argyle	Mission Vet. Memorial	Fort Bend Clements
2010–11	Plains	New Boston	Argyle	Mission Vet. Memorial	Fort Bend Clements
	Calculator Applications Team				
2009–10	Poolville	Paris Chisum	Argyle	Mission Vet. Memorial	Galena Park N. Shore
2010–11	Lindsay	Elkhart	Argyle	Mission Vet. Memorial	Galena Park N. Shore
	Computer Applications				
2009–10	Junction	Sonora	Orangefield	Friendswood	Houston Cyprs. Woods
2010–11	Yantis	Junction	Orangefield	Friendswood	Houston Cyprs. Woods
	Computer Science				
2009–10	Houston Harmony	Irving North Hills	Somerset	Aledo	Fort Worth Paschal
2010–11	Port Aransas	Buna	Needville	Friendswood	Fort Bend Clements
	Computer Science Team				
2009–10	Houston Harmony	Wall	Wimberley	Friendswood	Fort Bend Clements
2010–11	Port Aransas	Wall	Needville	Friendswood	Fort Bend Clements
	Number Sense				
2009–10	Lindsay	Salado	Wichita Falls Hirschi	Pearland Dawson	Fort Bend Clements
2010–11	Lovelady	Daingerfield	Wichita Falls Hirschi	Pearland Dawson	Fort Bend Clements
	Number Sense Team				
2009–10	Lindsay	Salado	Wichita Falls Hirschi	Mount Pleasant	Fort Bend Clements
2010–11	Lindsay	Daingerfield	Wichita Falls Hirschi	Pearland Dawson	Fort Bend Clements
	Mathematics				
2009–10	Lindsay	Idalou	TIE: Argyle & New Boston	Port Lavaca Calhoun	Fort Bend Kempner
2010–11	Haskel	New Boston	Wichita Falls Hirschi	Pearland Dawson	Fort Bend Dulles
	Mathematics Team				
2009–10	Lindsay	Caddo Mills	New Boston	Port Lavaca Calhoun	Fort Bend Dulles
2010–11	Savoy	New Boston	Argyle	Port Lavaca Calhoun	Fort Bend Dulles
	Science				
2009–10	Canadian	White Oak	Whitney	Dallas Highland Park	Fort Bend Clements
2010–11	Canadian	Whitney	La Feria	Dallas Highland Park	Fort Worth Paschal
	Science Team				
2009–10	Canadian	Irving North Hills	TIE: La Feria & Whitney	Dallas Highland Park	Fort Bend Clements
2010–11	Avery	Whitney	La Feria	Dallas Highland Park	Fort Worth Paschal
	Social Studies				
2009–10	Lindsay	Sadler S&S Consol.	Lytle	Hereford	Katy Seven Lakes
2010–11	Lindsay	Tolar	Wimberley	Manvel	Katy Taylor
	Social Studies Team				
2009–10	San Isidro	Sadler S&S Consol.	Van	Hereford	Katy Seven Lakes
2010–11	Sabine Pass	Tolar	Wimberley	Aledo	Katy Taylor
	Current Issues & Events				
2009–10	Apple Springs	Holliday	Hidalgo Early College	SA Alamo Heights	Fort Bend Dulles
2010–11	Latexo	Vanderbilt Industrial	Wimberley	SA Alamo Heights	Katy Seven Lakes
	Current Issues & Events Team				
2009–10	Latexo	Sadler S&S Consol.	Hidalgo Early College	Aledo	Katy Seven Lakes
2010–11	Latexo	TIE: Tuscola Jim Ned Sadler S&S Consol.	Van	SA Alamo Heights	Katy Seven Lakes
	Literary Criticism				
2009–10	Martin's Mill	Eastland	Bridge City	Denton Ryan	Laredo United South
2010–11	Iraan	Eastland	Bridge City	Whitehouse	College Station A&M

Year	Conference A	Conference AA	Conference AAA	Conference AAAA	Conference AAAAA
Literary Criticism Team					
2009–10	Lockney	Eastland	Liberty	Denton Ryan	Lewisville Flower Mound
2010–11	Martin's Mill	Elkhart	Liberty	Whitehouse	Kingwood
Poetry Interpretation					
2009–10	Gail Borden Cnty.	Rogers	Seminole	Ennis	Houston Cypress Ridge
2010–11	Santa Anna	Bishop	Athens	Stephenville	San Angelo Central
Prose Interpretation					
2009–10	Tolar	Abernathy	Athens	Saginaw	Plano
2010–11	Morton	Holliday	Van	Ennis	Grand Prairie
Ready Writing					
2009–10	Tolar	Paris Chisum	Paris	Ennis	MacArthur
2010–11	Port Aransas	East Bernard	Mabank	Port Neches-Groves	Conroe The Woodlands
Speech Team					
2009–10	Tolar	Holliday	La Vernia	Hallsville	San Antonio Churchill
2010–11	Lometa	Holliday	Crandall	Austin Lake Travis	Fort Bend Dulles
Informative Speaking					
2009–10	Hull-Daisetta	Bishop	Snyder	Whitehouse	Harlingen South
2010–11	Stamford	Bishop	Crandall	Austin Lake Travis	Lewisville Flower Mound
Persuasive Speaking					
2009–10	Lometa	Holliday	Paris North Lamar	San Marcos	Carrollton Creekview
2010–11	Lometa	Holliday	Big Spring	Austin Lake Travis	Plano
Lincoln-Douglas Debate					
2009–10	Lometa	Holliday	La Vernia	Hallsville	San Antonio Churchill
2010–11	Canadian	Mount Pleasant Chapel Hill	Big Spring	Richmond Foster	Garland
Cross Examination Team Debate					
2009–10	Fort Davis	Lago Vista	Smithville	Hallsville	Fort Bend Dulles
2010–11	Rising Star	Vanderbilt Industrial	Crandall	Mercedes	Fort Bend Dulles
Spelling & Vocabulary					
2009–10	Granger	Vanderbilt Industrial	Giddings	Ennis	Katy Seven Lakes
2010–11	TIE: Granger Nicholas Salyers	Vanderbilt Industrial	Glen Rose	Friendswood	Harlingen South
Spelling & Vocabulary Team					
2009–10	Lindsay	Vanderbilt Industrial	Orangefield	Friendswood	Katy Seven Lakes
2010–11	Martin's Mill	Groveton	Giddings	Friendswood	Katy Taylor
Journalism Team					
2009–10	Nazareth	Karnes City	Carthage	Lindale	Allen
2010–11	Martin's Mill	New Boston	Lindale	Hallsville	Bryan
Editorial Writing					
2009–10	Nazareth	Karnes City	Fredericksburg	Dayton	League City Clear Creek
2010–11	Martin's Mill	Sunnyvale	Decatur	Marble Falls	Bryan
Feature Writing					
2009–10	Martin's Mill	Univ. City Randolph	La Feria	Lindale	Lewisville Marcus
2010–11	Seymour	New Boston	Carthage	Hallsville	Keller
Headline Writing					
2009–10	Nazareth	East Bernard	Hardin-Jefferson	Hallsville	Allen
2010–11	Muenster	Univ. City Randolph	Hardin-Jefferson	Bastrop	Lewisville Marcus
News Writing					
2009–10	Thrall	Salado	Carthage	Manvel	Katy Cinco Ranch
2010–11	Nazareth	Quitman	Lindale	Texarkana	Grapevine

Publications

Year	Yearbooks (Gold Awards)	Newspapers (Gold Awards)
2009–10	Burges, Duncanville, Franklin, McKinney Boyd, McKinney, McKinney North, Pleasant Grove, St. Mark's School of Texas.	Albany, Connally, Fulmore, Liberal Arts and Science Academy, Pleasant Grove, St. Mark's School of Texas, Texas, Austin Westlake.
2010–11	Connally, Duncanville, Franklin, McKinney.	Hebron, Liberal Arts and Science Academy, McCallum, St. Mark's School of Texas.

Music and Theater

Year	Conference A	Conference AA	Conference AAA	Conference AAAA	Conference AAAAA
One-Act Play					
2009–10	Medina	Salado	Paris North Lamar	Mont Belvieu Barbers Hill	Keller
2010–11	Plains	Hempstead	Van	Carrollton Creekview	Austin
State Marching Band Contest					
2009–10	Sundown	Queen City		Dripping Springs	
2010–11	—	—	Argyle	—	Lewisville Marcus

Athletics

Year	Conference A	Conference AA	Conference AAA	Conference AAAA	Conference AAAAA
Baseball					
2009–10	Windthorst	Rogers	Texarkana Pleasant Grove	Brenham	Corpus Christi Carroll
2010–11	Johnson City Johnson	Cameron Yoe	Kennedale	Wichita Falls Rider	Clute Brazoswood
Basketball, Boys					
2009–10	I: Cayuga II: Nazareth	Ponder	Lubbock Estacado	Houston Yates	Fort Bend Bush
2010–11	I: Clyde Eula II: Paducah	Idalou	Corpus Christi West Oso	Dallas Kimball	Lewisville Marcus
Basketball, Girls					
2009–10	I: Smyer II: Neches	Brock	Texarkana Liberty-Eylau	Mansfield Timberview	Houston Cypress Fairbanks
2010–11	I: Smyer II: Neches	Brock	Abilene Wylie	Canyon	Irving MacArthur
Cross Country Team, Boys					
2009–10	Plains	East Bernard	Argyle	Boerne Champion	Conroe The Woodlands
2010–11	Sundown	Luling	Lucas Lovejoy	Cedar Park	Conroe The Woodlands
Cross Country Individual, Boys					
2009–10	Sanderson	East Bernard	Lytle	Boerne Champion	Lewisville Marcus
2010–11	Water Valley	Crawford	Argyle	Brenham	Lewisville Marcus
Cross Country Team, Girls					
2009–10	Gruver	Spearman	Decatur	Humble Kingwood Park	Humble Kingwood
2010–11	Gruver	Spearman	Lucas Lovejoy	Dallas Highland Park	Humble Kingwood
Cross Country Individual, Girls					
2009–10	Round Top-Carmine	Brock	Argyle	Fort Worth Boswell	Conroe The Woodlands
2010–11	Brackettville Brackett	Luling	Lucas Lovejoy	Canyon Randall	Plano
Golf Team, Boys					
2009–10	Robert Lee	Quitman	Texarkana Pleasant Grove	Dallas Highland Park	Austin Westlake
2010–11	Robert Lee	Wall	Prosper	Austin Lake Travis	Mansfield
Golf Individual, Boys					
2009–10	Robert Lee	Millsap	Texarkana Pleasant Grove	Castroville Medina Valley	Houston Memorial
2010–11	Robert Lee	Muleshoe	Texarkana Pleasant Grove	Austin Lake Travis	Dallas Jesuit
Golf Team, Girls					
2009–10	Baird	Salado	Monahans	Montgomery	Austin Westlake
2010–11	Baird	Tuscola Jim Ned	Andrews	Montgomery	Austin Westlake
Golf Individual, Girls					
2009–10	Huckabay	Sonora	Kaufman	Frisco Wakeland	Colleyville Heritage
2010–11	Baird	Sonora	Andrews	Magnolia	Austin Westlake
Softball					
2009–10	Forsan	George West	Paris North Lamar	Waco Midway	Pearland
2010–11	Shiner	Danbury	Celina	Santa Fe	Conroe The Woodlands
Tennis, Team					
2009–10	—	—	—	Dallas Highland Park	New Braunfels
2010–11	—	—	—	Dallas Highland Park	New Braunfels
Tennis, Boys Singles					
2009–10	Mason	Kerens	Argyle	Montgomery	Austin Westlake
2010–11	Mason	Tornillo	Argyle	Texarkana Texas	Mansfield
Tennis, Boys Doubles					
2009–10	Mason	Bishop	Abilene Wylie	Boerne Champion	Tyler Lee
2010–11	Mason	Wall	Abilene Wylie	Austin Lake Travis	Conroe The Woodlands
Tennis, Girls Singles					
2009–10	Mason	Franklin	Northwest Nelson	Gregory-Portland	New Braunfels
2010–11	Mason	Sunnyvale	Wharton	Waco Midway	Northside O'Connor
Tennis, Girls Doubles					
2009–10	Mason	Florence	Abilene Wylie	Dallas Highland Park	Klein Oak
2010–11	Mason	Franklin	Abilene Wylie	Dallas Highland Park	Katy Taylor
Tennis, Mixed Doubles					
2009–10	Paint Rock	Wall	Abilene Wylie	Waco Midway	New Braunfels
2010–11	Menard	Blanco	Borger	Richardson Pearce	Houston Memorial
Track & Field, Boys Team					
2009–10	Lindsay	Daingerfield	West Orange-Stark	Lancaster	Galena Park N. Shore
2010–11	Munday	Corrigan-Camden	West Orange-Stark	Lancaster	Galena Park N. Shore

Year	Conference A	Conference AA	Conference AAA	Conference AAAA	Conference AAAAA
Track & Field, Girls Team					
2009–10	Dallas Gateway	TIE: Altair Rice Centerville	Texarkana Liberty-Eylau	Houston Westbury	Dallas Skyline
2010–11	Snook	Cameron Yoe	Texarkana Liberty-Eylau	Beaumont Ozen	DeSoto
Volleyball					
2009–10	Louise	Poth	Lucas Lovejoy	Canyon Randall	Amarillo
2010–11	Round Top-Carmine	White Oak	Lucas Lovejoy	Austin Lake Travis	Lewisville Hebron

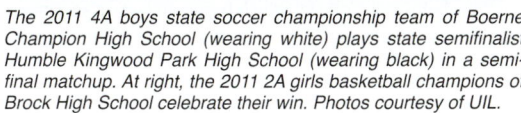

The 2011 4A boys state soccer championship team of Boerne Champion High School (wearing white) plays state semifinalist Humble Kingwood Park High School (wearing black) in a semifinal matchup. At right, the 2011 2A girls basketball champions of Brock High School celebrate their win. Photos courtesy of UIL.

	Football				
Year	6-man	A	AA	AAA	AAAA	AAAAA
2009–10	I: Garden City II: Gail Borden	I: Goldthwaite II: Cayuga	I: Pilot Point II: Daingerfield	I: Gilmer II: Carthage	I: Austin Lake Travis II: Aledo	I: Euless Trinity II: Abilene
2010–11	I: Garden City II: Richland Springs	I: Mart II: Falls City	I: Daingerfield II: Idalou	I: Henderson II: Carthage	I: Austin Lake Travis II: Aledo	I: Pearland II: Cibolo Steele

	Soccer			
	Girls		**Boys**	
Year	AAAA	AAAAA	AAAA	AAAAA
2009–10	Richardson Pearce	Conroe the Woodlands	Frisco Wakeland	Dallas Jesuit
2010–11	Frisco Wakeland	McKinney Boyd	Boerne Champion	Southlake Carroll

	Swimming & Diving, Team			
	Girls		**Boys**	
Year	AAAA	AAAAA	AAAA	AAAAA
2009–10	Dallas Highland Park	Humble Kingwood	Humble Kingwood Park	Conroe the Woodlands
2010–11	Frisco	Humble Kingwood	Humble Kingwood Park	Southlake Carroll

Wrestling, Boys	
2009–10	**Team**: Allen; **Weight Class 103**: Boyd; **112**: San Antonio Reagan; **119**: Amarillo Tascosa; **125**: Frisco Centennial; **130**: Houston Cypress Fairbanks; **135**: Houston Westside; **140**: Allen; **145**: El Paso Eastwood; **152**: Canyon Randall; **160**: Richardson Lake Highlands; **171**: Keller Central; **180**: Allen; **189**: McAllen; **215**: Conroe The Woodlands; **285**: Arlington Martin.
2010–11	**Team**: Allen; **Weight Class 103**: Lewisville Flower Mound; **112**: Canyon Randall; **119**: Amarillo Tascosa; **125**: Canyon Randall; **130**: Allen; **135**: San Antonio Reagan; **140**: Converse Judson; **145**: Arlington Martin; **152**: El Paso Eastwood; **160**: Lewisville Flower Mound; **171**: Allen; **189**: Keller Central; **215**: Henderson; **285**: Arlington Martin.
Wrestling, Girls	
2009–10	**Team**: Amarillo Caprock; **Weight Class 95**: McAllen Rowe; **102**: Amarillo Caprock; **110**: Bushland; **119**: Katy; **128**: Houston Cypress Creek; **138**: Katy Morton Ranch; **148**: Katy; **165**: Arlington Martin; **185**: Azle; **215**: Hereford.
2010–11	**Team**: Amarillo Caprock; **Weight Class 95**: Frisco Centennial; **102**: Amarillo Caprock; **110**: Clute Brazoswood; **119**: Bushland; **128**: Katy Morton Ranch; **138**: Katy Morton Ranch; **148**: El Paso Irvin; **165**: Katy Seven Lakes; **185**: Hereford; **215**: Amarillo Caprock.

Stephen F. Austin State University in Nacogdoches had a Fall 2010 enrollment of 12,954 students. Photo by Ron Billings; Texas Forest Service.

Brief History of Higher Education in Texas

The first permanent institutions of higher education established in Texas were church-supported schools, although there were some earlier efforts:

• Rutersville University was established in 1840 by Methodist minister Martin Ruter in Fayette County and was the predecessor of Southwestern University, Georgetown, established in 1843;

• Baylor University, now at Waco, was established in 1845 at Independence, Washington County, by the Texas Union Baptist Association; and

• Austin College, now at Sherman, was founded in 1849 at Huntsville by the Brazos Presbytery of the Old School Presbyterian Church.

Other historic Texas schools of collegiate rank included:

Larissa College, 1848, at Larissa, Cherokee County; McKenzie College, 1841, Clarksville; Chappell Hill Male and Female Institute, 1850, Chappell Hill; Soule University, 1855, Chappell Hill; Johnson Institute, 1852, Driftwood, Hays County; Nacogdoches University, 1845, Nacogdoches; Salado College, 1859, Salado, Bell County.

Add-Ran College, established at Thorp Spring, Hood County, in 1873, was the predecessor of present-day Texas Christian University, Fort Worth.

Texas A&M University and The University of Texas

The Agricultural and Mechanical College of Texas (now Texas A&M University), authorized by the Legislature in 1871, opened its doors in 1876 to become the first publicly supported institution of higher education.

In 1881, Texans established The University of Texas in Austin, with a medical branch in Galveston. The Austin institution opened Sept. 15, 1883, and the Galveston school opened in 1891.

First College for Women

In 1901, the 27th Legislature established the Girls Industrial College, which began classes at its campus in Denton in 1903. A campaign to establish a state industrial college for women was led by the State Grange and Patrons of Husbandry.

A bill was signed into law on April 6, 1901, creating the college. It was charged with a dual mission, which continues to guide the university today, to provide a liberal education and to prepare young women with a specialized education "for the practical industries of the age."

In 1905 the name of the college was changed to the College of Industrial Arts; in 1934, it was changed to Texas State College for Women.

Since 1957 the institution, which is now the largest university principally for women in the United States, has been the Texas Woman's University.

Historic, Primarily Black Colleges

A number of Texas schools were established primarily for blacks, although collegiate racial integration has long been the status quo.

The black-oriented institutions include state-supported Prairie View A&M University (originally established as Alta Vista Agricultural College in 1876) Prairie View; Texas Southern University, Houston; privately supported Huston-Tillotson College, Austin; Jarvis Christian College, Hawkins; Wiley College, Marshall; Paul Quinn College, originally located in Waco, now in Dallas; and Texas College, Tyler.

Predominantly black colleges that are important in the history of higher education in Texas, but which have ceased operations, include Bishop College, established in Marshall in 1881, then moved to Dallas; Mary Allen College, established in Crockett in 1886; and Butler College, originally named the Texas Baptist Academy, in 1905 in Tyler.

Recent Developments in Texas Higher Education

Source: Texas Higher Education Coordinating Board; **www.thecb.state.tx.us/**

State Appropriations

For the 2012–2013 biennium, beginning Sept. 1, 2011, and ending Aug. 31, 2013, total funding for higher education is **$21.8 billion in All Funds,** a decrease of $969.1 million, or 4.3 percent, over the 2010–2011 appropriation of $22.7 billion.

Higher education for 2012–2013 will be 12.6 percent of the total state budget, compared with 12.5 percent of the state budget for 2010–2011.

Note: The 2010-2011 base used in the calculations above includes the 5 percent budget reduction that agencies were required to take during the biennium, but not the further 2.5 percent reduction some agencies were required to make to their fiscal year 2011 budgets.

Enrollment

Enrollment in Texas public and independent, or private, colleges and universities in fall 2010 totaled 1,505,449 students, an increase of 84,456 from fall 2009.

Enrollment in the **38 public universities** increased by 25,324 students to 557,550 students. Thirty-six universities reported enrollment increases, while two reported decreases.

The state's **public community college districts and Lamar State Colleges,** which offer two-year degree programs, reported fall 2010 enrollments totaling 730,228 students, an increase of 52,839 over fall 2009.

The public **Texas State Technical College System,** which also offers two-year degree programs, reported fall 2010 enrollments totaling 13,024 students, a decrease of 2,432 students over fall 2009.

Enrollments for fall 2010 at the state's **37 independent senior colleges and universities** increased to 119,954 students, up 2,611 students from fall 2009.

The state's **two independent junior colleges** reported 1,466 students in fall 2010, an increase of 323 students from the fall 2009.

Public medical, dental, nursing, and allied **health institutions** of higher education reported enrollments totaling 20,245 students in fall 2010, up 1,599 from fall 2009.

Enrollment at **independent health-related institutions** totaled 2,690 students, down 18 students from fall 2009.

Actions of the 82nd Legislature

The 82nd Texas Legislature approved critical legislation that will change the way higher education does business. Innovative legislative strategies to improve student outcomes and increase institutional productivity were approved including:

SB 28, known as the TEXAS Grant Priority Model or the TEXAS Grant College Readiness Reform Act, will improve the state's return on investment by prioritizing awards to financially needy high school students whose academic efforts make them well-prepared to complete a college degree. (This legislation will go into effect in fall 2013.)

HB 9 moves Texas a step closer to implementing outcomes-based funding for two-year and four-year institutions of higher education by requiring the Higher Education Coordinating Board to recommend to the Legislature student success-based funding formulas that are aligned with the state's education goals and economic development needs.

HB 1000 provides a methodology for the distribution of funds from the National Research University Fund (NRUF) to emerging research universities.

HB 3025 implements cost efficiency recommendations designed to help facilitate timely degree completion by requiring students to file a degree plan not later than earning 45 semester credit hours and requiring institutions to send transcripts of eligible transfer students back to the lower division institution for the awarding of an Associate's degree, called "reverse transfer."

SB 851 will send students a clear and uniform message regarding financial aid processes and implement a statewide deadline for financial aid. The provisions of the legislation apply beginning with financial assistance awarded for the 2013–2014 academic year.

The passage of **HB 1244** will help the Coordinating Board implement changes to reform a developmental education system that is failing students. This legislation requires the Board to prescribe standards for each Texas Success Initiative assessment instrument to measure student readiness and align the delivery of developmental education. In addition, HB 1244 requires institutions to provide a range of coursework options, including online and non-course based remediation to get students on a faster track toward degree attainment.

SB 1799 and **SJR 50** help expand access during these challenging budgetary times by increasing the Coordinating Board's College Access Loans bonding capacity to meet expected loan demand. These loans are competitive and offer the lowest rates in the country, which are 5.25% for fall 2011. This legislation and constitutional amendment, upon approval of voters, will provide students additional options for paying for college.

SB 5 will eliminate unnecessary mandates on institutions of higher education and state agencies in an effort to be more efficient and remove duplicative reporting. ☆

Art students give a demonstration at the University of North Texas at Denton. Photo courtesy of UNT.

Universities and Colleges

Sources: Texas Higher Education Coordinating Board and individual institutions. Dates of establishment may differ from Brief History on page 594 because schools use the date when authorization was given rather than date of first classes. For explanation of type of institution and other symbols, see notes at end of table. www.thecb.state.tx.us

Name of Institution — Location; (*type or ownership, if private sectarian institution); date of founding; president (unless otherwise noted)	Number of Faculty †	Enrollment		
		Fall Term 2010	Summer Sessions 2010 §	Extension or Continuing Ed.
Abilene Christian University — Abilene; (3–Church of Christ); 1906 (as Childers Classical Institute; as Abilene Christian College, 1914; as university, 1976); Dr. Phil Schubert	368	4,728	1,428	NA
ALAMO COLLEGES (9) — Dr. Bruce H. Leslie, chancellor. 1978 (as San Antonio Community College District; 1982, as Alamo Community College District; current name, 2009). System consists of following colleges and presidents:	2,752	62,295	25,934	4,950
Northeast Lakeview College — San Antonio; (7); 2007; Dr. Eric Reno		1,312	NA	NA
Northwest Vista College — San Antonio; (7); 1995; Dr. Jacqueline Claunch	298	15,921	2,817	285
Palo Alto College — San Antonio; (7); 1983; Dr. Ana M. (Cha) Guzmán	337	8,965	4,307	1,516
St. Philip's College — San Antonio; (7); 1898; Dr. Adena Williams Loston	601	10,828	4,928	5,396
San Antonio College — San Antonio; (7); 1925; Dr. Robert E. Zeigler	1,051	25,269	11,461	4,337
Alvin Community College — Alvin; (7); 1949; Dr. A. Rodney Allbright	**92	5,721	2,114	491
Amarillo College — Amarillo; (7); 1929; Dr. Paul Matney, acting president	384	11,540	3,393	25,000
Amberton University — Garland; (3); 1971 (as Amber University; current name, 2001); Dr. Melinda H. Reagan	40	1,562	1,378	NA
Angelina College — Lufkin; (7); 1968; Dr. Larry Phillips	110	5,904	2,613	2,574
Angelo State University — San Angelo (*See* **Texas Tech University**)				
Arlington Baptist College — Arlington; (3–Baptist); 1939 (as Bible Baptist Seminary; name changed to current in 1965); Dr. David Bryant	20	175	80	75
Austin College — Sherman; (3–Presbyterian USA); 1849; Dr. Marjorie Hass	106	1,330	**	**
Austin Community College — Austin; (7); 1972; Dr. Stephen B. Kinslow	1,842	41,582	24,407	16,002
Austin Presbyterian Theological Seminary — Austin; (3–Presbyterian); 1902 (successor of Austin School of Theology, est. 1884); Theodore J. Wardlaw	25	255	52	388
Baptist Missionary Association Theological Seminary — Jacksonville; (3–Baptist Missionary); 1955; Dr. Charley Holmes	15	145	NA	30
Baylor College of Medicine — Houston; (5); 1903 (in Dallas; moved to Houston, 1943; Baptist until 1969); Dr. William T. Butler, interim president	3,696	1,485	NA	~17,901
Baylor University — Waco; (3–Southern Baptist); 1845 (in Independence; merged with Waco University and moved to Waco, 1887); Kenneth W. Starr	823	14,900	4,789	NA
Bee County College — Beeville (*See* **Coastal Bend College**)				
Blinn College — Brenham; (7); 1883 (as academy; jr. college, 1927); Dr. Daniel J. Holt	575	17,755	10,783	900
Brazosport College — Lake Jackson; (7); 1967; Dr. Millicent M. Valek	86	4,174	2,434	1,088
Brookhaven College — Farmers Branch (*See* **Dallas County Community College District**)				
Cedar Valley College — Lancaster (*See* **Dallas County Community College District**)				
Central Texas College — Killeen; (7); 1965; Dr. James R. Anderson, chancellor	2,316	12,737	17,477	721
Cisco College — Cisco; (7); 1909 (as Cisco Junior College, a private institution; became state school in 1939; name changed to current in 2009); Dr. Colleen Smith	195	4,745	1,435	67
Clarendon College — Clarendon; (7); 1898 (as church school; became state school in 1927); Dr. William R. Auvenshine	**69	1,583	428	376
Coastal Bend College — Beeville; (7); (1966 as Bee County College, name changed in 1999); Dr. Thomas Baynum	99	4,348	2,266	588
College of the Mainland — Texas City; (7); 1967; Dr. J. Lawrence Durrence, interim president	89	4,352	2,949	**
College of St. Thomas More, The — Fort Worth; (3–Roman Catholic); 1981 (as St. Thomas More Institute; as college, 1989); Dr. James A. Patrick, chancellor	9	45	4	NA
Collin College — McKinney; (7); 1985 (as Collin County Community College); Dr. Cary A. Israel	1,102	31,952	14,174	13,452
Concordia University Texas— Austin; (3–Lutheran Church–Missouri Synod); 1926 (as Concordia Lutheran College; current name, 1995); part of Concordia University System. Dr. Thomas Cedel	358	2,170	1,256	314
Cooke County College — Gainesville (*See* **North Central Texas College**)				
Corpus Christi State University — (*See* **Texas A&M University–Corpus Christi** under **Texas A&M University System**)				
Cy-Fair College — Houston (*See* **Lone Star College System**)				
Dallas Baptist University — Dallas; (3–Southern Baptist); 1891 (as Northwest Texas Bible College; name changed to Decatur Baptist College, 1897; moved to Dallas, name changed to Dallas Baptist College, 1965; became university, 1985); Dr. Gary R. Cook	523	5,297	2,461	NA
Dallas Christian College — Dallas; (3–Christian); 1950; Dr. Dustin D. Rubeck	60	268	116	NA
DALLAS COUNTY COMMUNITY COLLEGE DISTRICT (9) — Dr. Wright Lassiter, chancellor. System consists of following colleges and presidents:	3,163	73.183	36,448	22,186
Brookhaven College — Farmers Branch; (7); 1978; Dr. Richard D. McCrary	585	10,847	8,706	3,204
Cedar Valley College — Lancaster; (7); 1977; Dr. Jennifer B. Wimbish	†† 100	5,924	**	2,500
Eastfield College — Mesquite; (7); 1970; Dr. Jean Conway	460	10,852	8,077	2,177
El Centro College — Dallas; (7); 1966; Dr. Paul J. McCarthy	408	9,823	4,079	10,441
Mountain View College — Dallas; (7); 1970; Dr. Felix A. Zamora	382	7,975	3,786	2,631
North Lake College — Irving; (7); 1977; Dr. Herlinda M. Glassock	550	10,904	6,606	3,092

Name of Institution — Location; (*type or ownership, if private sectarian institution); date of founding; president (unless otherwise noted)	Number of Faculty †	Enrollment		
		Fall Term 2010	Summer Sessions 2010 §	Extension or Continuing Ed.
Richland College — Dallas; (7); 1972; Dr. Stephen K. Mittelstet	903	16,858	16,946	8,200
Dallas Theological Seminary — Dallas; (3–Christian); 1924 (as Evangelical Theological College; current name, 1936); Dr. Mark L. Bailey	119	2,036	1,144	493
Del Mar College — Corpus Christi; (7); 1935; Dr. Mark Escamilla	314	12,236	7,256	2,188
Eastfield College — Mesquite (*See* **Dallas County Community College District**)				
East Texas Baptist University — Marshall; (3–Baptist); 1913 (as College of Marshall; as East Texas Baptist College, 1944; as university, 1984); Dr. Samuel (Dub) Oliver	64	1,210	NA	NA
East Texas State University — Commerce (*See* **Texas A&M University–Commerce** under **Texas A&M University System**)				
East Texas State University at Texarkana — Texarkana (*See* **Texas A&M University–Texarkana** under **Texas A&M University System**)				
El Centro College — Dallas (*See* **Dallas County Community College District**)				
El Paso Community College — El Paso; (7); 1969; *five campuses:* Mission del Paso, Northwest, Rio Grande, Transmountain, and Valle Verde; Dr. Richard M. Rhodes	# 1,337	27,337	15,586	**
Episcopal Theological Seminary of the Southwest — Austin; (3–Episcopal); 1952; Dr. Doug Travis	38	109	55	NA
Frank Phillips College — Borger; (7); 1948; includes campus in Perryton; Dr. Jud Hicks	73	1,226	594	994
Galveston College — Galveston; (7); 1967; Dr. W. Myles Shelton	70	2,318	1,643	154
Grayson County College — Denison; (7); 1963; Dr. Alan Scheibmeir	¶ 104	5,034	2,128	450
Hardin-Simmons University — Abilene; (3–Southern Baptist); 1891 (as Simmons College; as Simmons University, 1925; current name, 1934); Dr. Lanny Hall	157	2,392	1,123	NA
Hill College — Hillsboro; (7); 1923 (as Hillsboro Junior College; name changed to current, 1962); Dr. Sheryl Smith Kappus	195	4,429	1,512	161
Houston Baptist University — Houston; (3–Baptist); 1960; Dr. Robert B. Sloan Jr.	139	2,564	1,052	NA
HOUSTON COMMUNITY COLLEGE (9) — Dr. Mary S. Spangler, chancellor. Houston; 1971. System consists of following colleges and presidents:	2,878	49,717	40,905	4,649
Central College — Houston; (7); Dr. William W. Harmon				
Coleman College for Health Sciences — Houston; (7); 2004; Dr. William W. Harmon, interim president	**	**	1,058	2,116
Northeast College — Houston; (7); Dr. Margaret Ford Fisher				
Northwest College — Houston; (7); Dr. Zachary R. Hodges				
Southeast College — Houston; (7); Dr. Irene M. Porcarello, interim president				
Southwest College — Houston; (7); Dr. Orfelina (Fena) Garza				
Howard College — Big Spring; (7); 1945; Dr. Cheryl T. Sparks; (*three campuses:* Big Spring, Lamesa and San Angelo, and the **Southwest Collegiate Institute for the Deaf**, Mark J. Myers, provost)	# 309	4,685	**	**
Howard Payne University — Brownwood; (3–Baptist); 1889; Dr. Lanny Hall	146	1,388	251	172
Huston-Tillotson University — Austin; (3–United Church of Christ and United Methodist); 1952 (as Huston-Tillotson College, the merger of Tillotson College, 1875, and Samuel Huston College, 1876; current name, 2005); Dr. Larry L. Earvin	71	785	146	NA
International Bible College — San Antonio; (3–Christian); 1944; Rev. David W. Cook	15	75	NA	NA
Jacksonville College — Jacksonville; (8–Missionary Baptist); 1899; Dr. Edwin Crank	27	274	171	24
Jarvis Christian College — Hawkins; (3); 1912; Dr. Cornell Thomas	**	538	**	**
Kilgore College — Kilgore; (7); 1935; Dr. William M. Holda	139	4,968		4,968
Kingwood College — Kingwood (*See* **Lone Star College System**)				
Lamar University and all branches (*See* **Texas State University System**)				
Laredo Community College — Laredo; (7); 1946; Dr. Juan L. Maldonado	337	9,994	4,480	3,545
Lee College — Baytown; (7); 1934; Dr. Dennis Topper, interim president	364	6,719	4,615	2,616
LeTourneau University — Longview; (3); 1946 (as LeTourneau Technical Institute; became 4-yr. college, 1961); Dr. Dale A. Lunsford	¶ 76	3,661	472	1,035
Lon Morris College — Jacksonville; (8–Methodist); 1854 (as Danville Academy; changed name in 1873 to Alexander Institution; name changed to present, 1923); Dr. Miles McCall	**	437	NA	NA
LONE STAR COLLEGE SYSTEM (9) — Dr. Richard Carpenter, chancellor. (Formerly North Harris Montgomery Community College District.) System consists of following colleges and presidents:	2,798	63,826	28,876	35,797
Lone Star College–Cy-Fair — Houston; (7); Dr. Audre Levy	661	16,861	9,161	683
Lone Star College–Kingwood — Humble; (7); Dr. Katherine Persson	442	9,807	4,434	5,300
Lone Star College–Montgomery — Conroe; (7); Dr. Penny Westerfeld, interim	700	11,154	**	†† 2,500
Lone Star College–North Harris — Houston; (7); Dr. Stephen C. Head	10,114	15,213		
Lone Star College–Tomball — Tomball; (7); Dr. Raymond H. Hawkins	**	10,791	4,637	**
Lubbock Christian University — Lubbock; (3–Church of Christ); 1957; Dr. L. Ken Jones	172	1,868	588	NA
McLennan Community College — Waco; (7); 1965; Dr. Johnette McKown	386	9,912	6,743	900
McMurry University — Abilene; (3–Methodist); 1923; Dr. John H. Russell	104	1,386	612	NA
Midland College — Midland; (7); 1972; Dr. Steve Thomas	290	6,344	4,513	2,404
Midwestern State University — Wichita Falls; (2); 1922; Dr. Jesse W. Rogers	¶ 224	6,093	3,997	1,422
Montgomery College — Conroe (*See* **Lone Star College System**)				
Mountain View College — Dallas (*See* **Dallas County Community College District**)				
Navarro College — Corsicana; (7); 1946; *four campuses:* Corsicana, Mexia, Midlothian and Waxahachie; Dr. Richard M. Sanchez	738	9,982	4,720	658

Name of Institution — Location; (*type or ownership, if private sectarian institution); date of founding; president (unless otherwise noted)	Number of Faculty †	Enrollment		
		Fall Term 2010	Summer Sessions 2010 §	Extension or Continuing Ed.
North Central Texas College — Gainesville; (7); 1924 (as Gainesville Jr. College; Cooke County College, 1960; present name, 1994); *four campuses:* Gainesville, Corinth, Bowie, and Flower Mound; Dr. Eddie Hadlock	372	9,402	4,343	4,434
Northeast Lakeview College — San Antonio (*See* **Alamo Colleges**)				
Northeast Texas Community College — Mount Pleasant; (7); 1984; Dr. Bradley W. Johnson	135	3,226	1,678	2,533
North Harris College — Houston (*See* **Lone Star College System**)				
North Lake College — Irving (*See* **Dallas County Community College District**)				
Northwest Vista College — San Antonio (*See* **Alamo Colleges**)				
Northwood University — Cedar Hill; (3); 1966; Dr. Kevin Fegan		57	1,135	524
Oblate School of Theology — San Antonio; (3–Roman Catholic); 1903 (formerly Scholasticate); the Rev. Ronald Rolheiser	24	166	78	**
Odessa College — Odessa; (7); 1946; Dr. Gregory Williams	191	5,211	2,858	1,934
Our Lady of the Lake University of San Antonio — San Antonio; (3–Roman Catholic); 1895 (as school for girls; as senior college, 1911; as university, 1975); *two campuses:* San Antonio and Houston; Dr. Tessa Martinez Pollock	256	2,642	**	**
Palo Alto College — San Antonio (*See* **Alamo Colleges**)				
Panola College — Carthage; (7); 1947 (as Panola Junior College; name changed, 1988); Dr. Gregory S. Powell	177	2,322	1,142	510
Paris Junior College — Paris; (7); 1924; Dr. Pamela Anglin	¶ 95	6,197	2,582	773
Parker College of Chiropractic — Dallas; (5); 1982; Dr. Dr. Fabrizio Mancini	92	913	981	424
Paul Quinn College — Dallas; (3–African Methodist Episcopal Church); 1872 (in Waco; moved to Dallas, 1990); Dr. Michael J. Sorrell	55	441	**	NA
Prairie View A&M University — Prairie View (*See* **Texas A&M University System**)				
Ranger College — Ranger; (7); 1926; Dr. James McDonald, interim president	23	1,588	398	NA
Rice University — Houston; (3); chartered, 1891; opened, 1912 (as Rice Institute; as William Marsh Rice University, 1960); Dr. David W. Leebron	741	5,456	NA	5,432
Richland College — Dallas (*See* **Dallas County Community College District**)				
St. Edward's University — Austin; (3–Catholic); 1885; Dr. George E. Martin	522	5,317	**	1,886
St. Mary's University of San Antonio — San Antonio; (3–Roman Catholic); 1852; Dr. Charles L. Cotrell	351	3,889	1,153	**
St. Philip's College — San Antonio (*See* **Alamo Colleges**)				
Sam Houston State University — Huntsville (*See* **Texas State University System**)				
San Antonio College — San Antonio (*See* **Alamo Colleges**)				
SAN JACINTO COLLEGE DISTRICT (9) — Dr. Brenda Lang Hellyer, chancellor. System consists of following colleges and presidents:	1,072	32,105	9,985	2,005
Central — Pasadena; (7); Dr. Neil Matkin		15,035		
North — Houston; (7); Dr. Allatia Harris		6,573		
South — Houston; (7); Dr. Maureen Murphy	¶ 145	10,497	**	**
Schreiner University — Kerrville; (3–Presbyterian); 1923; Dr. Charles Timothy Summerlin	94	930	125	NA
South Plains College — Levelland; (7); 1957; Dr. Kevin Sharp	289	10,153	2,500	**
South Texas College — McAllen; (7); NA; Dr. Shirley A. Reed	760	27,971	10,775	1,678
South Texas College of Law — Houston; (3); 1923; Dr. James J. Alfini	124	1,267	589	NA
Southern Methodist University — Dallas; (3–Methodist); 1911; Dr. R. Gerald Turner	¶ 656	10,965	4,458	2,186
Southwest Collegiate Institute for the Deaf — Big Spring (*See* **Howard College**)	20	120	NA	NA
Southwest Texas Junior College — Uvalde; (7); 1946; Dr. Ismael Sosa Jr.	**	6,235	**	**
Southwest Texas State University — San Marcos (*See* **Texas State University–San Marcos** under **Texas State University System**)				
Southwestern Adventist University — Keene; (3–Seventh-Day Adventist); 1893 (as Keene Industrial Academy; as Southwestern Junior College, 1916; as Southwestern Union College, 1963; as Southwestern Adventist College,1980; as university, 1996); Dr. Eric Anderson	75	894	260	289
Southwestern Assemblies of God University — Waxahachie; (3–Assemblies of God); 1927 (in Enid, Okla., as Southwestern Bible School; moved to Fort Worth and merged with South Central Bible Institute, 1941; moved to Waxahachie as Southwestern Bible Institute, 1943; as Southwestern Assemblies of God College,1963; as university, 1996); Dr. Kermit S. Bridges	96	1,702	**	NA
Southwestern Baptist Theological Seminary — Fort Worth; (3–Southern Baptist); 1908; Dr. Kenneth Hemphill	91	3,005	1,179	26
Southwestern Christian College — Terrell; (3–Church of Christ); 1948 (as Southern Bible Institute in Fort Worth; moved to Terrell and changed name, 1950); Dr. Jack Evans Sr.	20	220	NA	NA
Southwestern University — Georgetown; (3–Methodist); 1840 (merger of Rutersville College, 1840; McKenzie College, 1841; Wesleyan College, 1846; and Soule University, 1855; first named Texas University; current name, 1875); Dr. Jake B. Schrum	127	1,270	NA	NA
Stephen F. Austin State University — Nacogdoches; (2); 1921; Dr. Baker Pattillo	712	11,990	8,527	NA
Sul Ross State University — Alpine (*See* **Texas State University System**)				
Sul Ross State University–Rio Grande College — Uvalde (*See* **Texas State University System**)				
Tarleton State University — Stephenville (*See* **Texas A&M University System**)				
TARRANT COUNTY COLLEGE DISTRICT (9) — Erma Johnson Hadley, chancellor. Fort Worth; 1965 (as Tarrant County Junior College; name changed, 1999). System consists of following colleges and presidents:	1,756	58,051	7,980	21,571
Northeast Campus — Hurst; (7); Dr. Larry Darlage	412	15,899	7,130	5,553

Name of Institution — Location; (*type or ownership, if private sectarian institution); date of founding; president (unless otherwise noted)	Number of Faculty †	Enrollment		
		Fall Term 2010	Summer Sessions 2010 §	Extension or Continuing Ed.
Northwest Campus — Fort Worth; (7); Dr. Elva Concha LeBlanc	261	12,032	2,987	8,597
South Campus — Fort Worth, (7); Dr. Ernest L. Thomas		11,690		
Southeast Campus — Arlington, (7); Dr. Judith J. Carrier		13,911		
Trinity River Campus — Fort Worth, (7);		4,519		
Temple College — Temple; (7); 1926; Dr. Glenda O. Barron	261	5,966	2,065	1,163
Texarkana College — Texarkana; (7); 1927; Dr. Alan Rasco	215	4,003	1,812	4,000
Texas A&I University — Kingsville (*See* **Texas A&M University–Kingsville** under **Texas A&M University System**)				
TEXAS A&M UNIVERSITY SYSTEM (1) — Jay Kimbrough, interim chancellor. System consists of following colleges and presidents:				
Prairie View A&M University — Prairie View; (2); 1876 (as Alta Vista Agricultural College; as Prairie View State Normal Institute, 1879; as Prairie View Normal and Industrial College; as Prairie View A&M College, 1947, as branch of Texas A&M University System; current name, 1973); Dr. George C. Wright	467	8,781	3,389	NA
Tarleton State University — Stephenville; (2); 1899 (as John Tarleton College; as state-run John Tarleton Agricultural College,1917; as Tarleton State College, 1949; current name, 1973); includes campus in Killeen; Dr. F. Dominic Dottavio	535	9,340	4,489	NA
Texas A&M International University — Laredo; (2); 1970 (as Laredo State University; current name, 1993); Dr. Ray M. Keck III	284	6,853	3,398	NA
Texas A&M University — College Station; (2); 1876 (as Agricultural and Mechanical of Texas; current name,1963); includes College of Veterinary Medicine and College of Medicine at College Station; Dr. R. Bowen Loftin.	3,730	49,129	18,622	NA
Texas A&M University–Commerce — Commerce; (2); 1889 (as East Texas Normal College; as East Texas State Teachers College, 1923; as East Texas State College, 1957; university status conferred and named changed to East Texas State University, 1965; transferred to Texas A&M System, 1995); includes ETSU Metroplex Commuter Facility, Mesquite; Dr. Dan R. Jones	330	10,280	4,834	152
Texas A&M University–Corpus Christi — Corpus Christi; (2); 1973 (as upper-level Corpus Christi State University; current name, 1993; 4-year in 1994); Dr. Flavius C. Killebrew	580	10,033	4,728	NA
Texas A&M University at Galveston — Galveston; (2); 1962 (as Texas Maritime Academy; as 4-yr. Moody College of Marine Sciences and Maritime Resources, 1971); William C. Hearn, acting Vice President and CEO	170	1,867	803	NA
Texas A&M University–Kingsville — Kingsville; (2); 1925 (as South Texas Teachers College; as Texas College of Arts and Industries, 1929; as Texas A&I University, 1967; joined University of South Texas System, 1977; joined Texas A&M University System, 1993); Dr. Steven H. Tallant	471	7,134	5,443	1,312
Texas A&M University Health Science Center — (4); Includes Baylor College of Dentistry, College of Medicine, Graduate School of Biomedical Sciences, Institute of Biosciences and Technology, School of Rural Public Health, and HSC Stattelite locations; Dr. Nancy W. Dickey	1,077	1,695	NA	NA
Texas A&M University–Texarkana — Texarkana; (2); 1971 (as East Texas State University at Texarkana; transferred to Texas A&M System and name changed, 1996); Dr. Carlisle Baxter (Bix) Rathburn III	135	1,803	1,444	NA
West Texas A&M University — Canyon; (2); 1910 (as West Texas State Normal College; as West Texas State Teachers College, 1923; as West Texas State College, 1949; as West Texas State Univ., 1963; currentt name, 1993); Dr. J. Patrick O'Brien	374	7,839	4,425	191
Texas Baptist Institute-Seminary — Henderson; (3–Calvary Baptist); 1948; Dr. Ray O. Brooks	16	50	NA	20
Texas Christian University — Fort Worth; (3–Disciples of Christ); 1873 (as AddRan Male and Female College at Thorp Spring; moved to Waco, 1895; as AddRan Christian University, 1889; current name,1902; moved to Fort Worth, 1910); Dr. Victor J. Boschini Jr., chancellor	811	8,696	2,604	2,050
Texas Chiropractic College — Pasadena; (5); 1908; Dr. Richard G. Brassard	39	292	352	NA
Texas College — Tyler; (3–C.M.E.); 1894; Dr. Billy C. Hawkins	42	757	109	0
Texas College of Osteopathic Medicine — Fort Worth (*See* **University of North Texas Health Science Center at Fort Worth**)				
Texas Lutheran University — Seguin; (3–Evangelical Lutheran); 1891 (as Evangelical Lutheran College in Brenham; as Lutheran College of Seguin, 1912; as Texas Lutheran College,1932; as university, 1996); Rev. Ann M. Svennungsen	142	1,432	217	161
Texas Southern University — Houston; (2); 1926 (as Houston Colored Junior College; as 4-yr. Houston College for Negroes, mid-1930s; as Texas State University for Negroes, 1947; present name, 1951); Dr. John M. Rudley	578	9,557	2,818	50
Texas Southmost College — Brownsville (*See* **The University of Texas at Brownsville** under **University of Texas System**)				
TEXAS STATE TECHNICAL COLLEGE SYSTEM (6) — Dr. Willaim Segura, chancellor. System consists of following colleges and presidents:	534	13,024	7,551	4,089
Texas State Technical College–Harlingen — Harlingen; 1967; Dr. J. Gilbert Leal	**	5,779	**	**
Texas State Technical College–Marshall — Marshall; 1991 (as extension center; as independent college, 1999); Dr. Randall Wooten	46	949	393	246
Texas State Technical College–Waco — Waco; 1965 (as James Connally Technical Institute; current name, 1969); Dr. Elton E. Stuckly Jr.	280	4,976	2,602	88
Texas State Technical College–West Texas — Abilene, Breckenridge, Brownwood and Sweetwater; 1970; Dr. Mike Reeser	123	1,320	1,208	1,990

Name of Institution — Location; (*type or ownership, if private sectarian institution); date of founding; president (unless otherwise noted)	Number of Faculty †	Enrollment		
		Fall Term 2010	Summer Sessions 2010 §	Extension or Continuing Ed.
TEXAS STATE UNIVERSITY SYSTEM (1) — Dr. Charles R. Matthews, chancellor. System consists of following colleges and presidents:				
Lamar University — Beaumont; (2); 1923 (as South Park Junior College; as Lamar College, 1932; as Lamar State College of Technology, 1951; present name, 1971; transferred from Lamar University System, 1995); Dr. James M. Simmons	561	13,280	6,836	4,263
Lamar State College–Orange — Orange; (10); 1969 (transferred from Lamar University System, 1995; current name, 2000); Dr. J. Michael Shahan	97	2,649	694	97
Lamar State College–Port Arthur — Port Arthur; (10); 1909 (as Port Arthur College; joined Lamar University System, 1975; joined TSU System, 1995; current name, 2000); Dr. W. Sam Monroe	115	2,374	1,772	485
Lamar Institute of Technology — Beaumont; (10); (joined TSU System, 1995); Dr. Paul Szuch	162	3,243	889	650
Sam Houston State University — Huntsville; (2); 1879; Dr. James F. Gaertner	669	16,663	10,722	NA
Sul Ross State University — Alpine; (2); 1917 (as Sul Ross State Normal College; as Sul Ross State Teachers College, 1923; as Sul Ross State College, 1949; current name, 1969); Dr. R. Vic Morgan	148	2,047	1,024	NA
Sul Ross State University – Rio Grande College — Uvalde, Eagle Pass, Del Rio (2); 1973 (current name, 1995); Dr. R. Vic Morgan	30	1,092	1,020	NA
Texas State University–San Marcos — San Marcos; (2); 1903 (as Southwest Texas Normal School; as Southwest Texas State Normal College, 1918; as Southwest Texas State Teachers College, 1923; as Southwest Texas State College, 1959; as Southwest Texas State University, 1969; current name, 2003); Dr. Denise M. Trauth	1,300	32,572	17,011	1,759
TEXAS TECH UNIVERSITY SYSTEM (1) —Kent Hance, chancellor. System consists of following colleges and presidents:				
Angelo State University — San Angelo; (2); 1928 (was part of Texas State University System; joined Texas Tech system, 2007); Dr. Joseph C. Rallo	336	6,155	3,362	1,340
Texas Tech University — Lubbock; (2); 1923 (as Texas Technological College; current name, 1969); Dr. Guy Bailey	2,488	31,587	16,990	**
Texas Tech University Health Sciences Center — Lubbock; (4); 1972; Dr. John Charles Baldwin	596	2,272	**	NA
Texas Wesleyan University — Fort Worth; (3–United Methodist); 1891 (as college; current name, 1989); Dr. Harold G. Jeffcoat	266	3,202	695	NA
Texas Woman's University — Denton; (2); 1901 (as College of Industrial Arts; as Texas State College for Women, 1934; current name, 1957); Dr. Ann Stuart, chancellor	†† 700	14,008	17,000	NA
Tomball College — Tomball (*See* **Lone Star College System**)				
Trinity University — San Antonio; (3–Presbyterian); 1869 (at Tehuacana; moved to Waxahachie, 1902; to San Antonio, 1942); Dr. Dennis Ahlburg	243	2,703	356	NA
Trinity Valley Community College — Athens; (7); 1946 (as Henderson County Junior College); includes campus at Terrell; Dr. Glendon S. Forgey	124	7,594	2,500	1,400
Tyler Junior College — Tyler; (7); 1926; Dr. Mike Metke	492	11,736	3,951	1,782
University of Central Texas — Killeen (*See* **Tarleton State University** under **Texas A&M University System**)				
University of Dallas — Irving; (3–Catholic); 1956; Dr. Francis M. Lazarus	244	2,977	1,526	200
UNIVERSITY OF HOUSTON SYSTEM (1) — Dr. Renu Khator, chancellor. System consists of following colleges and presidents:				
University of Houston — Houston; (2); 1927; Dr. Renu Khator	3,036	38,752	NA	NA
University of Houston–Clear Lake — Houston; (2); 1974; Dr. William A. Staples	687	8,099	4,350	NA
University of Houston–Downtown — Houston; (2); 1948 (as South Texas College; joined University of Houston System, 1974); Dr. William V. Flores	570	12,900	7,505	2,177
University of Houston–Victoria — Victoria; (2); 1973; Dr. Tim Hudson	176	4,095	2,033	NA
University of the Incarnate Word — San Antonio; (3–Catholic); 1881 (as Incarnate Word College; current name, 1996); Dr. Louis J. Agnese Jr.	¶ 200	6,702	NA	1,012
University of Mary Hardin–Baylor — Belton; (3–Baptist); 1845; Dr. Randy O'Rear	238	2,701	742	NA
UNIVERSITY OF NORTH TEXAS SYSTEM (1) — Lee F. Jackson, chancellor. System consists of following colleges and presidents:				
University of North Texas — Denton; (2); 1890 (as North Texas Normal College; as North Texas State Teachers College, 1923; as North Texas State College, 1949; as university, 1961; current name, 1988); Dr. V. Lane Rawlins	2,098	36,067	15,823	
University of North Texas Dallas Campus — Dallas; (2); (2000); Dr. John Ellis Price, CEO		2,084		
University of North Texas Health Science Center at Fort Worth — Fort Worth; (4);1966 (as private college; part of North Texas State University, 1975; current name, 1993); Dr. Scott B. Ransom		222	1,021	777
University of St. Thomas — Houston; (3); 1947; Dr. Robert R. Ivany	273	3,246	2,106	NA
THE UNIVERSITY OF TEXAS SYSTEM (1) — Dr. Francisco G. Cigarroa, chancellor. System consists of following colleges and presidents:	18,198	201,058	**	5,951
University of Texas at Arlington, The — Arlington; (2); 1895 (as Arlington College; as state-run Grubbs Vocational College, 1917; as North Texas Agricultural and Mechanical College, 1923; as Arlington State College, 1949; current name, 1967); Dr. James D. Spaniolo	1,973	32,975	11,164	7,468
University of Texas at Austin, The — Austin; (2); 1883; Dr. William Powers Jr.	2,137	51,195	**	**

Name of Institution — Location; (*type or ownership, if private sectarian institution); date of founding; president (unless otherwise noted)	Number of Faculty †	Enrollment		
		Fall Term 2010	Summer Sessions 2010 §	Extension or Continuing Ed.
University of Texas at Brownsville, The, and Texas Southmost College — (2); 1973 (as branch of Pan American College; as University of Texas–Pan American at Brownsville, 1989; present name, 1991); Dr. Juliet V. Garcia **Texas Southmost College** — Brownsville; (7); 1926 (as Brownsville Junior College; current name, 1949); Dr. Juliet V. Garcia	¶ 216	19,923	7,653	1,651
University of Texas at Dallas, The — Richardson; (2); 1961 (as Graduate Research of the Southwest; as Southwest Center for Advanced Studies, 1967; joined UT System with current name, 1969; full undergraduate program, 1975); Dr. David Daniel	772	17,128	**	NA
University of Texas at El Paso, The — El Paso; (2); 1913 (as Texas College of Mines and Metallurgy; as Texas Western College of UT, 1949; current name, 1967); Dr. Diana S. Natalicio	1,083	22,051	8,716	2,921
University of Texas–Pan American, The — Edinburg; (2); 1927 (as Edinburg Junior College; as 4-yr. Pan American College, 1952; as Pan American University, 1971; current name, 1991); Dr. Charles Sorber, interim president	819	18,744	15,165	50
University of Texas of the Permian Basin, The — Odessa; (2); 1969 (as 2-yr., upper-level institution; expanded to 4-yr., 1991); Dr. W. David Watts	128	4,063	2,156	140
University of Texas at San Antonio, The — San Antonio; (2); 1969; Dr. Ricardo Romo	1,271	30,258	**	**
University of Texas at Tyler, The — Tyler; (2); 1971 (as Tyler State College; as Texas Eastern University, 1975; joined UT System, 1979); Dr. Rodney H. Mabry	383	6,446	2,169	NA
University of Texas Telecampus, The — 1998; Exec. Vice-Chancellor Dr. David Prior	NA	5,093	2,898	NA
University of Texas Health Science Center at Houston, The — Houston; (4); 1972; *includes* Dental Branch (1905); Graduate School of Biomedical Sciences (1963); Medical School (1970); School of Allied Health Sciences (1973); School of Nursing (1972); School of Public Health (1967); Division of Continuing Education (1958); Dr. Larry R. Kaiser	1,389	3,865	2,306	24,875
University of Texas Health Science Center at San Antonio, The — San Antonio; (4) 1968; *includes* Dental School (1970); Graduate School of Biomedical Sciences (1970); Health Science Center (1972); Medical School (1959 as South Texas Medical School of UT; present name, 1966); School of Allied Health Sciences (1976); School of Nursing (1969); Dr. William L. Henrich, interim president	1,400	2,845	NA	NA
University of Texas Health Science Center at Tyler, The — Tyler; (4); 1949 (as East Texas Tuberculosis Sanatorium; as East Texas Chest Hospital, 1971; joined UT system with current name, 1977); Dr. Kirk A. Calhoun	125	75	NA	NA
University of Texas M.D. Anderson Cancer Center, The — Houston; (4); 1941; Dr. John Mendelsohn	1,050	70	NA	2,252
University of Texas Medical Branch at Galveston, The — Galveston; (4) 1891; *includes* Graduate School of Biomedical Sciences (1952); Medical School (1891); School of Allied Health Sciences (1968); School of Nursing (1890); Dr. David L. Callender	1,885	2,338	NA	NA
University of Texas Southwestern Medical Center at Dallas, The — Dallas; (4); 1943 (as private institution; as Southwestern Medical College of UT, 1948; as UT Southwestern Medical School at Dallas, 1967; joined UT Health Science Center at Dallas, 1972); *includes* Graduate School of Biomedical Sciences (1947); School of Allied Health Sciences (1968); Southwestern Medical School (1943); Dr. Daniel Podolsky	2,223	4,327	NA	NA
Vernon College — Vernon; (7); 1970; includes Wichita Falls campus; Dr. Dusty R. Johnston	139	3,167	2,180	930
Victoria College, The — Victoria; (7); 1925; Dr. Thomas Butler	111	4,290	2,211	3,181
Wayland Baptist University — Plainview; (3–Southern Baptist); 1910; Dr. Paul Armes	329	6,039	4,516	NA
Weatherford College — Weatherford; (7); 1869 (as branch of Southwestern University; as denominational junior college, 1922; as municipal junior college, 1949); Dr. Joseph Birmingham	225	5,651	2,319	1,012
Western Texas College — Snyder; (7); 1969; Dr. Michael Dreith	72	2,307	1,099	876
Wharton County Junior College — Wharton; (7); 1946; Dr. Betty A. McCrohan	293	6,922	4,006	300
Wiley College — Marshall; (3–Methodist); 1873; Dr. Haywood L. Strickland	85	967	182	20

Key to Table Symbols

*Type: (1) Public University System   (6) Public Technical College System
       (2) Public University   (7) Public Community College
       (3) Independent Senior College or University   (8) Independent Junior College
       (4) Public Medical School or Health Science Center   (9) Public Community College System
       (5) Independent Medical, Dental or Chiropractic School   (10) Public Lower-Level Institution

NA — Not applicable

† Unless otherwise noted, faculty count includes professors, associate professors, adjunct professors, instructors and tutors, both full- and part-time, but does not include voluntary instructors.

‡ No reply received to questionnaire. Name of president and number of students enrolled in fall 2008 obtained from the institution's website or the Texas Higher Education Coordinating Board website: www.txhighereddata.org/Interactive/Institutions.cfm.

Includes faculty and enrollment at all branches or divisions.

§ Figure may combine multiple summer sessions.

¶ Full-time faculty only.

** Information not supplied by institution.

†† Approximate count.

§§ Latest figures available from institution's website were for 2008–2009 school year.

§§§ Enrollment in online courses only.

~ Number of students in extension courses or continuing education for all of fiscal year 2008.

Business

A feed store in Alice, Jim Wells County. Photo by Robert Plocheck.

Economy and Employment
Banking and Insurance
Oil and Gas
Minerals
Media
Construction
Utilities

Section Sponsored by

WORTHAM
Insurance

Texas Economy: Recovering from a Great Recession

Source: Excerpted from the State of Texas Annual Cash Report 2010, Comptroller of Public Accounts.

The Texas economy, which joined the nation in recession in fiscal 2009, began adding jobs again at the beginning of fiscal 2010. Recovery from the nation's worst recession since World War II has been lukewarm compared to other economic recoveries.

However, Texas gained 129,100 jobs during fiscal 2010. This is about 30 percent of the 431,300 jobs lost from August 2008 to September 2009. Even with slower expanison than usual, Texas accounted for more than half of the nation's 229,000 jobs added in 2010.

Not only did Texas add more jobs than any state over the year, but it also led in the rate of job growth among the 10 most populous states (five of which lost jobs over this period) as well as having faster growth than all but four of the other 40 states.

During previous bouts of economic weakness, renewed consumer spending helped bring the economy into recovery. Yet, even with job growth, the unemployment rate remains high, and wages per worker have not kept up with inflation, growing a mere 0.3 percent during the year.

As a consequence, retail sales declined markedly in the first half of the fiscal year and only eked out modest increases in the second half, yielding a second year of declining retail spending, which fell even more than in 2009.

Although the Texas economy's domestic demand for good and services remained in neutral through most of the year, Texas export markets more than recovered the severe losses in 2009.

Texas exporters faced a 16 percent sale decline in 2009, but had a 22 percent increase in 2010.

The number of oil and natural gas drilling rigs in Texas at the end of fiscal 2010 was 714. Although far from its record level, this doubling of the number from 2009 was indicative of a turnaround in the state's oil and natural gas industry. In addition to the economic impact from exploration activities with the state, Texas is the headquarters for many of the nation's oil and natural gas firms.

The broader oil and natural gas industry, which includes mining, petrochemicals, petroleum refining and oil/natural gas-related manufacturing, accounts for a 15 percent share of the total Texas economy, and this serves as a buttress for the state economy when increasing oil and natural gas prices hinder the consuming industries.

Among the Texas good-producing industries, construction was the only industry to lose jobs. A sustained weakness in the building of single-family and multi-family residences was exacerbated by tight credit and shrunken investment in business structures. Construction lost 16,600 jobs in 2010.

Texas' service-providing industries, which account for more than 84 percent of the state's total nonfarm employment, uncharacteristically under-performed the goods-producing industries in the rate of growth in 2010 but still accounted for 81 percent of the added jobs.

The education and health services industry accounted for nearly half of the employment growth in Texas during fiscal 2010. All sectors of the industry except child day-care services added jobs, with some sectors, such as home health care and ambulatory health care services (medical offices, laboratories, home health care and ambulance services) growing more than 6 percent. Overall, the industry added 57,300 jobs during fiscal 2010.

The Texas information industry lost 12,900 jobs during 2010. The industry has been losing employment since the "dot-com" bust in 2000 and has shed more than 30 percent of its workforce since then. Losses during fiscal 2010 were spread over publishers, Internet services and data services. ☆

Gross Domestic Product in Current Dollars

	Millions of $ dollars			Percent of U.S. total			GDP* 2010	
	2005	2007	2009	2005	2007	2009	European Union	14,910,000
United States	12,346,871	13,743,021	14,150,826	100.0	100.0	100.0	United States	14,720,000
1. California	1,632,822	1,883,679	1,891,363	13.2	13.5	13.4	China	9,872,000
2. Texas	979,311	1,140,030	1,144,695	7.9	8.2	8.1	Japan	4,338,000
3. New York	953,641	1,088,169	1,093,219	7.7	7.8	7.7	India	4,046,000
4. Florida	670,237	758,776	737,038	5.4	5.4	5.2	Germany	2,960,000
5. Illinois	554,099	630,277	630,398	4.5	4.5	4.5	Russia	2,229,000
6. Pennsylvania	482,413	534,620	554,744	3.9	3.8	3.9	Brazil	2,194,000
7. New Jersey	425,497	474,487	482,967	3.4	3.4	3.4	United Kingdom	2,189,000
8. Ohio	439,271	471,119	471,264	3.6	3.4	3.3	France	2,160,000
9. North Carolina	349,216	396,832	398,042	2.8	2.8	2.8	Italy	1,782,000
10. Georgia	359,694	400,967	395,194	2.9	2.9	2.8	Mexico	1,560,000

Source: Bureau of Economic Analysis, U.S. Department of Commerce.

*Estimated Gross Domestic Product in millions of U.S. dollars from the World Factbook of the CIA.

Texas Gross Domestic Product, 2001–2010, By Industry (in millions)

Industry	2001	2002	2003	2004	2005	2006	2007	2008	2009	2010
Agriculture, Forestry, Fishing/Hunting	$6,394	$7,457	$8,094	$9,878	$9,239	$7,377	$10,796	$9,780	$9,343	$9,906
% change*	(1.2)	16.6	8.5	21.0	(6.5)	(20.2)	46.3	(9.4)	(4.5)	0.7
Natural Resources and Mining	44,072	39,219	57,917	68,248	91,263	104,406	114,134	138,422	140,546	155,873
% change	(2.5)	(11.0)	47.7	19.1	33.7	14.4	9.3	21.3	1.5	10.9
Construction	40,259	41,871	43,475	45,648	51,826	56,004	55,981	58852	57,037	56,986
% change	9.2	4.0	3.8	3.7	13.5	8.1	(0.0)	5.1	(3.1)	(0.1)
Manufacturing	92,273	94,462	93,158	119,028	125,538	145,867	154,117	158,802	151,912	156,604
% change	(0.8)	2.4	(1.4)	27.6	5.5	16.2	5.7	3.0	(4.3)	3.1
Trade, Transportation, Utilities	160,789	164,723	170,757	181,596	193,039	211,185	224,491	231,317	230,987	240,644
% change	3.2	2.4	3.7	5.3	6.3	9.4	6.3	3.0	(0.1)	4.2
Information	36,992	36,531	36,040	38,545	39,599	40,638	43,536	46,333	46,669	48,627
% change	3.1	(1.2)	(1.3)	7.7	2.7	2.6	7.1	6.4	0.7	4.2
Financial Activities	125,928	128,219	133,439	137,454	145,853	154,859	165,748	171,415	171,146	177,790
% change	7.4	1.8	4.1	4.7	6.1	6.2	7.0	3.4	(0.2)	3.9
Professional and Business Services	82,195	83,937	88,719	93,307	105,004	115,343	128,501	140,779	142,571	149,610
% change	12.3	2.1	3.9	7.7	12.5	9.8	11.4	9.6	1.3	4.9
Educational and Health Services	46,797	51,380	54,761	59,440	62,343	66,232	71,121	75,924	80,666	86,609
% change	10.5	9.8	6.6	7.8	4.9	6.2	7.4	6.8	6.2	7.4
Leisure and Hospitality Services	23,993	25,492	26,479	27,877	29,755	32,485	34,557	36,773	37,322	39,105
% change	3.8	6.2	3.9	4.6	6.7	9.2	6.4	6.4	1.5	4.8
Other Private Services	18,106	18,679	19,644	19,889	21,168	22,386	23,957	25,113	25,381	26,366
% change	2.9	3.2	5.2	1.4	6.4	5.8	7.0	4.8	1.1	3.9
Government and Schools	84,448	91,512	96,326	100,759	107,439	113,518	121,650	129,973	133,859	138,523
% change	4.8	8.4	5.3	5.0	6.6	5.7	7.2	6.8	3.0	3.5
TOTAL	$762,246	$783,482	$828,809	$901,669	$982,065	$1,070,295	$1,148,590	$1,223,482	$1,227,439	$1,286,143
% change	4.8	2.8	5.8	9.1	8.9	9.0	7.3	6.5	0.3	4.8
TOTAL (in 2000 chained dollars)**	$745,325	$760,588	$770,975	$806,055	$828,417	$869,379	$907,358	$925,492	$915,305	$946,603
% change	2.5	2.0	1.4	4.8	2.8	4.9	4.4	2.0	(1.1)	3.4

*Percent change from the previous year. ** In 1996, the U.S. Department of Commerce introduced the chained-dollar measure. The new measure is based on the average weights of goods and services in successive pairs of years. It is "chained" because the second year in each pair, with its weights, becomes the first year of the next pair. *Source: 2010 Comprehensive Annual Financial Report for the State of Texas.*

Per Capita Income by County, 2009

Below are listed data for 2009 for total personal income and per capita income by county. Total income is reported in millions of dollars. The middle column indicates the percent of change in total income from 2008 to 2009.

In the far right column is the county's rank in the state for per capita income. Loving County, a unique case — with an estimated population in 2009 of only 45, leads in per capita income with $150,933. Midland County is second with $54,164.

The lowest per capita income is in Starr County, along the Rio Grande, at $16,433.

Source: Bureau of Economic Analysis, U.S. Department of Commerce.

County	Total Income ($ mil)	% change 08/09	Per capita income	Rank in State
United States	$12,168,161	−1.7	$39,635	—
Metropolitan	10,608,997	−1.9	41,223	—
Nonmetro	1,559,163	−0.6	31,402	—
Texas	$ 956,808	−1.2	$ 38,609	—
Metropolitan	863,281	−1.3	39,617	—
Nonmetro	93,527	−0.3	31,262	—
Anderson	$ 1,497	0.4	$ 26,264	229
Andrews	507	−2.1	36,062	79
Angelina	2,911	−0.5	34,787	90
Aransas	951	0.5	38,289	47
Archer	373	−1.4	41,857	24
Armstrong	78	−2.3	37,819	52
Atascosa	1,265	1.9	28,333	209
Austin	1,061	0.1	38,954	4.3
Bailey	209	−5.0	33,307	117
Bandera	735	0.8	35,729	84
Bastrop	2,028	−0.2	27,083	223
Baylor	119	−5.7	32,494	126
Bee	760	0.6	23,397	244
Bell	11,386	2.8	39,839	33
Bexar	60,220	1.0	36,465	75
Blanco	405	1.3	44,063	17
Borden	25	13.8	41,808	25
Bosque	563	0.4	31,947	139
Bowie	3,184	1.2	33,886	105
Brazoria	11,602	1.3	37,523	54
Brazos	5,247	3.1	29,151	193
Brewster	317	5.6	33,485	114
Briscoe	49	3.1	34,048	103
Brooks	192	0.9	25,985	232
Brown	1,151	2.4	30,218	175
Burleson	551	0.3	33,257	118
Burnet	1,675	−1.0	37,098	60
Caldwell	958	−0.8	25,328	235
Calhoun	648	0.3	31,479	147
Callahan	419	−0.8	31,209	154
Cameron	8,874	3.2	22,388	248
Camp	402	0.3	31,421	150
Carson	27	−1.0	37,163	57
Cass	935	2.1	32,017	137
Castro	239	−14.8	33,542	113
Chambers	1,422	5.4	45,257	13
Cherokee	1,417	0.6	29,225	192
Childress	166	7.2	21,943	249

County	Total Income ($ mil)	% change 08/09	Per capita income	Rank in State
Clay	422	1.4	38,764	44
Cochran	105	−8.0	35,980	82
Coke	96	0.2	29,006	198
Coleman	264	−0.7	31,081	155
Collin	36,323	−3.8	45,884	9
Collingsworth	93	0.3	30,402	171
Colorado	754	−0.4	36,525	72
Comal	4,241	2.0	37,028	62
Comanche	413	−2.3	30,474	169
Concho	83	1.4	23,152	246
Cooke	1,578	−5.1	40,819	27
Coryell	2,651	0.6	36,547	71
Cottle	62	7.9	39,863	32
Crane	133	−4.1	31,813	142
Crockett	119	−1.7	31,764	144
Crosby	208	0.8	34,095	101
Culberson	69	10.0	29,979	178
Dallam	221	−2.1	35,142	88
Dallas	111,323	−3.0	45,406	12
Dawson	374	2.4	27,409	219
Deaf Smith	516	−0.9	28,132	213
Delta	141	−0.4	26,126	230
Denton	25,774	0.0	39,133	42
DeWitt	599	−0.7	30,364	172
Dickens	62	7.1	25,593	234
Dimmit	252	2.9	25,836	233
Donley	118	4.1	32,200	130
Duval	342	−1.2	28,454	206
Eastland	679	−2.3	37,381	55
Ector	4,516	−4.6	33,544	112
Edwards	56	3.1	30,181	176
Ellis	4,865	0.4	32,059	135
El Paso	22,073	3.6	29,381	191
Erath	1,079	−1.7	29,830	181
Falls	436	0.5	25,998	231
Fannin	936	0.6	28,370	208
Fayette	896	−0.7	39,147	41
Fisher	116	−3.8	29,979	178
Floyd	212	−1.6	32,738	125
Foard	41	−2.9	30,956	158
Fort Bend	25,503	2.4	45,798	10
Franklin	330	−2.6	30,484	168
Freestone	575	1.1	29,669	186
Frio	393	5.1	24,333	239
Gaines	418	−6.4	27,178	222
Galveston	11,937	−1.1	41,621	26

County	Total Income ($ mil)	% change 08/09	Per capita income	Rank in State	County	Total Income ($ mil)	% change 08/09	Per capita income	Rank in State
Garza	172	−0.1	36,939	63	La Salle	138	−0.7	23,670	241
Gillespie	1,081	0.6	44,723	16	Lavaca	681	0.0	36,736	69
Glasscock	47	2.1	38,371	45	Lee	551	−1.4	33,919	104
Goliad	204	−2.4	29,071	197	Leon	547	2.3	32,325	128
Gonzales	551	−0.2	28,092	214	Liberty	2,556	0.0	33,729	109
Gray	869	−4.1	39,357	37	Limestone	668	2.6	30,868	161
Grayson	3,849	1.2	32,066	134	Lipscomb	114	−3.0	36,753	68
Gregg	5,052	−2.0	42,228	23	Live Oak	314	−3.0	28,447	207
Grimes	723	0.1	27,815	216	Llano	669	−0.3	36,634	70
Guadalupe	4,370	4.7	35,988	81	Loving	7	2.0	150,933	1
Hale	942	0.7	26,602	226	Lubbock	9,220	1.6	34,079	102
Hall	91	8.3	27,283	221	Lynn	162	5.2	28,608	201
Hamilton	276	−0.6	34,371	98	Madison	336	2.3	25,228	236
Hansford	186	−11.8	34,373	97	Marion	294	0.5	28,546	202
Hardeman	122	−5.5	31,376	152	Martin	151	3.5	32,996	123
Hardin	1,948	1.4	36,468	74	Mason	122	1.7	30,680	163
Harris	196,779	−4.0	48,337	7	Matagorda	1,124	1.5	30,409	170
Harrison	2,382	−0.8	36,763	67	Maverick	1,050	6.3	19,740	251
Hartley	201	0.0	40,469	30	McCulloch	247	−1.7	30,924	159
Haskell	173	−5.3	34,576	94	McLennan	7,530	2.2	32,265	129
Hays	4,623	0.7	29,721	185	McMullen	31	−1.7	37,723	53
Hemphill	181	−18.2	52,387	3	Medina	1,33l0	2.6	29,735	183
Henderson	2,414	−1.4	30,593	165	Menard	68	0.7	31,992	138
Hidalgo	15,200	3.6	20,509	250	Midland	7,167	−7.0	54,164	2
Hill	1,043	0.4	29,089	196	Milam	737	−2.6	29,910	180
Hockley	748	−3.4	33,567	111	Mills	153	−2.1	30,552	166
Hood	2,022	−0.6	39,293	39	Mitchell	214	1.4	22,846	247
Hopkins	1,058	1.7	30,598	164	Montague	742	−3.1	37,905	50
Houston	652	2.2	29,143	194	Montgomery	20,366	2.0	45,490	11
Howard	1,032	1.4	31,339	153	Moore	611	−2.6	29,479	188
Hudspeth	86	7.8	27,681	217	Morris	397	−1.5	31,447	148
Hunt	2,613	−1.3	31,541	146	Motley	38	−0.5	29,738	182
Hutchinson	786	1.3	36,491	73	Nacogdoches	1,804	2.3	28,141	212
Irion	83	1.7	47,608	8	Navarro	1,410	0.9	28,516	204
Jack	308	−5.7	36,300	77	Newton	360	2.9	26,377	228
Jackson	436	−3.0	30,515	167	Nolan	472	2.4	31,621	145
Jasper	1,093	0.8	31,800	143	Nueces	12,005	−1.5	37,162	58
Jeff Davis	78	1.8	34,693	92	Ochiltree	373	−9.8	38,118	49
Jefferson	9,034	0.5	37,139	59	Oldham	62	−7.4	29,139	195
Jim Hogg	173	4.5	34,642	93	Orange	2,869	0.1	35,070	89
Jim Wells	1,342	−4.0	32,740	124	Palo Pinto	930	−1.2	33,746	108
Johnson	4,850	−0.8	30,891	160	Panola	838	−2.6	35,959	83
Jones	502	−1.1	26,462	227	Parker	4,093	−2.6	35,617	86
Karnes	335	0.4	23,631	242	Parmer	281	−4.4	30,260	174
Kaufman	3,306	1.7	32,082	132	Pecos	405	−10.9	24,941	238
Kendall	1,720	1.6	50,495	4	Polk	1,726	2.0	37,098	60
Kenedy	19	−4.4	50,333	5	Potter	3,878	−1.0	31,835	141
Kent	25	7.8	35,253	87	Presidio	180	3.6	24,113	240
Kerr	2,105	−0.4	43,508	18	Rains	305	0.5	27,032	224
Kimble	142	1.7	31,384	151	Randall	4,564	1.8	39,182	40
King	12	9.4	42,483	21	Reagan	105	−11.3	34,731	91
Kinney	97	4.8	29,728	184	Real	95	3.7	32,406	127
Kleberg	982	1.9	32,036	136	Red River	366	2.0	28,679	200
Knox	107	−9.2	32,117	131	Reeves	296	3.7	26,779	225
Lamar	1,522	−0.1	31,079	156	Refugio	267	−2.5	36,937	64
Lamb	380	−2.8	28,876	199	Roberts	29	−14.3	33,218	119
Lampasas	884	4.0	42,280	22	Robertson	537	0.6	34,222	100

County	Total Income ($ mil)	% change 08/09	Per capita income	Rank in State	County	Total Income ($ mil)	% change 08/09	Per capita income	Rank in State
Rockwall	3,500	2.6	42,999	19	Trinity	393	2.9	28,271	210
Runnels	290	−1.5	28,488	205	Tyler	609	2.0	29,623	187
Rusk	1,516	−1.5	33,425	115	Upshur	1,214	−0.7	31,891	140
Sabine	341	1.9	33,425	115	Upton	123	−5.6	39,336	38
San Augustine	236	1.4	27,567	218	Uvalde	788	2.7	29,401	189
San Jacinto	783	2.1	31,443	149	Val Verde	1,358	2.6	28,202	211
San Patricio	2,256	−1.5	33,068	121	Van Zandt	1,725	−0.7	33,165	120
San Saba	160	2.1	27,331	220	Victoria	3,349	−3.1	38,151	48
Schleicher	85	−2.6	31,073	157	Walker	1,608	3.9	25,072	237
Scurry	559	−7.6	34,488	95	Waller	1,235	0.0	33,798	107
Shackelford	137	−4.5	44,846	15	Ward	354	−5.4	33,632	110
Shelby	750	1.3	27,960	215	Washington	1,322	0.9	40,185	31
Sherman	109	−13.1	37,312	56	Webb	5,624	1.0	23,294	245
Smith	7,843	−0.6	38,319	46	Wharton	1,369	−0.5	33,400	116
Somervell	290	−4.4	36,159	78	Wheeler	193	−9.7	39,532	34
Starr	1,030	6.3	16,433	254	Wichita	4,837	−2.1	37,899	51
Stephens	332	−3.0	34,442	96	Wilbarger	464	3.1	34,287	99
Sterling	42	−6.8	33,053	122	Willacy	481	0.7	23,584	243
Stonewall	55	1.9	40,777	28	Williamson	14,801	−0.2	36,040	80
Sutton	213	−5.2	49,731	6	Wilson	1,307	1.8	32,067	133
Swisher	212	−4.6	28,521	203	Winkler	247	−8.2	36,425	76
Tarrant	70,486	−1.4	39,380	36	Wise	2,008	−3.6	33,802	106
Taylor	4,712	−0.3	36,902	65	Wood	1,268	1.8	29,398	190
Terrell	38	8.6	39,461	35	Yoakum	283	−9.4	36,793	66
Terry	365	−2.9	30,072	177	Young	760	−2.4	42,742	20
Throckmorton	72	−3.8	44,949	14	Zapata	276	−0.8	19,638	252
Titus	916	2.4	30,312	173	Zavala	207	3.9	17,892	253
Tom Green	3,870	0.6	35,704	85					
Travis	41,605	−0.9	40,544	29					

Average Work Hours and Earnings

The following table compares the **average weekly earnings**, **hours worked per week** and **average hourly wage** in Texas for selected industries in January 2011 and January 2010. Figures are provided by the Texas Workforce Commission.

Industry	Avg. Weekly Earnings		Avg. Weekly Hours		Avg. Hourly Earnings	
	Jan. 11	Jan. 10	Jan. 11	Jan. 10	Jan. 11	Jan. 10
Mining and Logging	$ 719.10	$ 637.79	42.5	38.1	$ 16.92	$ 16.74
Mining (including Oil & Gas)	746.93	707.58	43.3	41.5	17.25	17.05
Manufacturing	612.98	612.99	42.1	41.7	14.56	14.70
Durable Goods	602.62	587.45	42.8	42.6	14.08	13.79
Fabricated Metal Product Mfg.	644.94	582.24	46.1	42.1	13.99	13.83
Non-Durable Goods	634.03	658.35	40.8	39.9	15.54	16.50
Trade, Transportation, Utilities						
Wholesale Trade	640.59	632.73	39.3	39.3	16.30	16.10
Machinery, Equipment, Supplies	579.96	559.87	40.5	39.4	14.32	14.21
Retail Trade						
Auto Dealers/Parts	655.59	646.38	39.0	37.8	16.81	17.10
Building Material/Garden Equip.	411.77	415.60	34.4	35.4	11.97	11.74
Food/Beverage Stores	318.55	328.49	31.2	32.3	10.21	10.17
Gasoline Stations	340.34	355.13	35.6	375	9.56	9.47
Clothing/Accessories Stores	199.40	199.50	19.1	19.0	10.44	10.50
Information						
Telecommunications	656.97	599.65	35.9	33.5	18.30	17.90

Employment in Texas by Industry

Employment in Texas reached 10,567,000 in April 2011, up from 10,313,000 in April 2010. The following table shows Texas Workforce Commission estimates of the nonagricultural labor force by industry for April 2010 and 2011. The column at the extreme right shows the percent change during the year in the number employed. *Source: Texas Workforce Commission. Additional information available at the website www.twc.state.ts.us.*

Industry	2011	2010	Chng.	Industry	2011	2010	Chng.
(in thousands, 000)				Utilities	49.5	48.3	2.5
GOODS PRODUCING	1,637.2	1,569.5	4.3	Transportation	373.2	365.2	2.2
				Air	60.2	60.4	−0.3
Mining	230.6	199.1	15.8	Trucking	110.5	104.8	5.4
Oil & Gas Extraction	84.2	80.5	4.6	Pipeline	15.7	15.2	3.3
Support Activities	132.3	109.2	21.2	Support Activities	70.4	66.7	5.5
Construction	588.7	564.2	4.3	Couriers/Messengers	34.1	33.2	2.7
Manufacturing	816.1	804.7	1.4	Warehousing/Storage	45.8	46.0	−0.4
Durable Goods	524.6	510.3	2.8	Information	184.8	196.4	−5.9
Wood Products	18.3	19.5	−6.2	Publishing	40.0	41.9	−4.5
Furniture/Fixtures	21.8	22.8	−4.4	Telecommunications	82.0	86.5	−5.2
Primary Metals	20.8	19.4	7.2	Internet/Data Search	24.3	25.7	−5.4
Fabricated Metal Industries	116.9	110.5	5.8	**Financial Activities**	622.9	620.9	0.3
Machinery	91.7	83.5	9.8	Finance/Insurance	451.5	450.9	0.1
Computers/Electronics	96.1	94.4	1.8	Credit Intermediation	237.7	237.1	0.3
Electric/Appliances	16.2	16.8	−3.6	Securities/Investments	49.1	47.7	2.9
Transportation Equipment	85.9	83.2	3.2	Insurance Carriers	153.5	156.8	−2.1
Misc. Manufacturing	25.9	27.1	−4.4	Real Estate/Rental	171.4	170.0	0.8
Non-Durable Goods	291.5	294.4	−1.0	Real Estate	116.7	116.6	0.1
Food	87.4	88.2	−0.9	Rental/Leasing	48.9	51.3	−4.7
Beverage/Tobacco	11.0	11.1	−0.9	**Professional Services**	1,318.1	1,263.9	4.3
Paper	17.3	17.6	−1.7	Scientific/Tech	576.2	568.9	1.3
Printing	27.2	28.4	−4.2	Management/Enterprises	79.0	79.0	0.0
Petroleum/Coal Products	23.8	24.5	−2.9	Administration/Support	662.9	616.0	7.6
Chemicals	69.9	70.7	−1.1	**Education/Health**	1,431.4	1,381.8	3.6
Rubber/Plastics	36.5	37.4	−2.4	Educational Services	158.5	159.0	−0.3
				Health Care	1,272.9	1,222.8	4.1
SERVICE PROVIDING	8,929.8	8,743.5	2.1	Ambulatory	607.6	574.9	5.7
				Hospitals	294.3	290.6	1.3
Trade/Transport/Utilities	2,077.6	2,027.3	2.5	Residential Care	177.6	167.4	6.1
Wholesale Trade	508.8	492.9	3.2	Social Assistance	193.4	189.9	1.8
Merchants/Durable Goods	288.4	277.4	4.0	**Leisure/Hospitality**	1,038.2	1,007.8	3.0
Merchants/Non-Durable	157.6	154.0	2.3	Accommodations	104.4	99.5	4.9
Retail Trade	1,146.1	1,120.9	2.2	Food/Drinking Places	823.9	799.6	3.0
Building/Garden Supplies	96.5	92.1	4.8	Amusements/Recreation	76.2	77.0	−1.0
General Merchandise	251.8	249.4	1.0	**Other Services**	368.8	359.7	2.5
Food/Beverage Stores	206.3	203.7	1.3	Repair/Maintenance	110.5	106.5	3.8
Motor Vehicles/Parts	148.0	140.8	5.1	Personal/Laundry	94.9	92.4	2.7
Clothing/Accessories	118.0	109.2	8.1	Religious/Civic	163.4	160.8	1.6
Furniture	35.7	37.3	−4.3	**Total Government**	1,888.0	1,885.7	0.1
Electronics/Appliances	42.1	42.0	0.2	Federal	201.2	211.0	−4.6
Gasoline Stations	67.9	68.5	−0.9	State	384.1	3827	0.4
Sporting/Books/Music	37.6	37.8	−0.5	Local	1,302.7	1,292.0	0.8
Misc. Store Retailers	58.0	55.9	3.8				
Nonstore Retailers	18.2	18.8	−3.2				
Transportation/Utilities	422.7	413.5	2.2				

Cost of Living Index for Metro Areas

The comparison standard of all values is for the **United States set at 100**. Data are an annual average for 2007. The overall composite is excluding taxes. The column at the far right refers to miscellaneous goods and services.

Metro area	Overall	Groceries	Housing	Utilities	Transport	Health	Goods/Services
Austin	94.5	89.8	80.8	94.7	99.2	98.1	105.3
Brownsville	85.9	86.4	71.4	104.7	98.4	95.9	87.2
Corpus Christi	88.2	82.0	79.9	98.2	93.3	87.4	92.8
Dallas	91.2	99.0	71.5	98.6	103.4	101.6	97.4
El Paso	93.0	112.1	78.5	95.6	99.2	100.3	94.3
Fort Worth	88.2	95.3	74.0	97.9	97.7	90.1	91.1
Houston	87.7	83.1	73.5	100.6	96.2	101.2	93.0
Lubbock	86.4	91.3	71.1	83.7	102.8	98.7	91.5
San Antonio	94.1	83.7	84.1	83.5	100.1	102.5	106.4

Source: Statistical Abstract of the United States 2009.

Largest Banks Operating in Texas by Asset Size

Source: Texas Department of Banking, Dec. 31, 2010
Abbreviations: NA, not available; N.A. National Association.

	Name	City	Class	Assets (in thousands, 000)	Loans (in thousands, 000)
1	JP Morgan Chase Bank	New York NY	National	$ 80,425,000	NA
2	Bank of America	Charlotte NC	National	71,271,000	NA
3	Comerica Bank	Dallas	State	54,933,693	$ 40,278,266
4	Wells Fargo Bank	San Francisco CA	National	47,569,000	NA
5	Wells Fargo Bank South Central N.A.	Houston	National	33,582,000	17,130,000
6	Compass Bank	Birmingham AL	State	27,263,000	8,816,927
7	Frost National Bank	San Antonio	National	17,804,466	8,063,046
8	Amergy Bank N.A.	Houston	National	10,997,445	7,639,958
9	International Bank of Commerce	Laredo	State	10,009,177	4,754,804
10	Prosperity Bank	El Campo	State	9,232,949	3,413,819
11	Capital One	New Orleans LA	National	7,491,000	NA
12	Texas Capital Bank N.A.	Dallas	National	6,330,112	4,483,203
13	Bank of Texas N.A.	Dallas	State	5,509,534	2,660,304
14	PlainsCapital Bank	Lubbock	State	5,069,412	2,993,255
15	Sterling Bank	Houston	State	5,037,149	2,862,952
16	Regions Bank	Birmingham AL	State	4,532,000	NA
17	First National Bank	Edinburg	National	3,891,104	2,658,241
18	Citibank	Las Vegas NV	National	3,627,000	NA
19	Woodforest National Bank	Houston	National	3.280.340	1.509.823
20	Southside Bank	Tyler	State	3,011,605	1,037,208
21	Amarillo National Bank	Amarillo	National	2,698,455	2,042,858
22	United Central Bank	Garland	State	2,519,058	1,649,086
23	American State Bank	Lubbock	State	2,501,627	10,094,184
24	Broadway National Bank	San Antonio	National	2,339,697	1,074,888
25	TIB Independent BankersBank	Irving	State	2,300,552	724,382
26	Inter National Bank	McAllen	National	2,113,892	997,982
27	Lone Star National Bank	Pharr	National	2,071,605	1,222,479
28	City Bank	Lubbock	State	1,959,414	1,566,338
29	American National Bank of Texas	Terrell	National	1,881,466	1,140,635
30	First Victoria National Bank	Victoria	National	1,698,653	1,264,059
31	Northern Trust	Miami FL	National	1,665,000	NA
32	Encore Bank N.A.	Houston	National	1,644,196	924,589
33	LegacyTexas Bank	Plano	State	1,563,715	1,109,501
34	Happy State Bank	Happy	State	1,385,882	937,329
35	Commun1ityBank of Texas	Beaumont	National	1,325,390	922,454
36	Inwood National Bank	Dallas	National	1,320,019	801,115
37	Patriot Bank	Houston	State	1,281,363	968,178
38	Texas Bank and Trust Co.	Longview	State	1,277,229	1,013,341
39	Extraco Banks N.A.	Temple	National	1,189,945	670,480
40	First Financial Bank N.A.	Abilene	National	1,183,576	421,286
41	MetroBank N.A.	Houston	National	1,163,323	841,703
42	American Bank of Texas	Sherman	State	1,108,348	817,799
43	North Dallas Bank & Trust Co.	Dallas	State	1,107,366	345,486
44	Austin Bank Texas N.A.	Jacksonville	National	1,099,091	815,471
45	Independent Bank	McKinney	State	1,071,483	845,660
46	Western National Bank	Odessa	National	1,036,644	576,583
47	First State Bank Central Texas	Austin	State	1,030,758	609,328
48	First National Bank Texas	Killeen	National	972,214	249,505
49	Moody National Bank	Galveston	National	958,924	450,676
50	Guaranty Bonk Bank	Mount Pleasant	State	944,842	529,883

Deposits/Assets of Commercial Banks by County

Source: Federal Reserve Bank of Dallas as of Dec. 31, 2010.
(thousands of dollars, 000)

COUNTY	Banks	Deposits	Assets	COUNTY	Banks	Deposits	Assets
Anderson	2	150,884	167,695	Donley	1	33,096	41,139
Andrews	2	471,839	518,857	Duval	2	94,544	103,245
Angelina	2	919,843	1,042,846	Eastland	1	142,064	163,934
Armstrong	1	93,708	105,653	Ector	4	1,744,910	2,016,199
Atascosa	3	195,871	232,927	Edwards	1	50,748	58,374
Austin	5	1,098,409	1,284,806	Ellis	5	742,781	869,270
Bailey	2	182,499	205,476	El Paso	3	1,158,983	1,341,212
Bandera	2	58,154	69,154	Erath	4	533,893	614,899
Bastrop	2	365,474	432,192	Fannin	2	168,526	202,388
Baylor	1	41,105	45,452	Fayette	4	718,046	790,408
Bee	1	220,989	240,762	Fisher	1	53,727	59,206
Bell	4	2,069,283	2,542,373	Floyd	1	91,321	103,170
Bexar	7	17,652,150	21,322,907	Foard	1	26,249	29,579
Blanco	3	289,455	321,718	Fort Bend	2	714,711	824,777
Bosque	2	170,060	188,763	Franklin	1	113,123	137,002
Bowie	3	520,484	600,452	Freestone	2	363,279	541,158
Brazoria	8	943,133	1,114,555	Frio	5	1,838,153	2,088,744
Brazos	2	335,334	377,397	Galveston	1	495,101	628,098
Briscoe	1	36,975	44,125	Gillespie	2	287,735	319,860
Brooks	2	107,635	122,555	Gonzales	1	17,919	20,732
Brown	2	389,228	480,377	Gray	5	1,339,644	1,562,306
Burleson	1	332,415	362,701	Grayson	6	1,695,946	1,953,648
Burnet	3	816,249	974,256	Gregg	2	244,757	271,229
Caldwell	2	184,371	207,348	Grimes	3	312,376	352,948
Calhoun	1	180,613	206,631	Guadalupe	3	253,065	295,551
Callahan	1	177,402	199,255	Hale	2	345,388	382,918
Cameron	5	906,505	1,236,321	Hall	2	92,367	102,760
Camp	1	306,744	371,695	Hamilton	1	31,739	35,759
Carson	2	38,228	42,959	Hansford	3	267,988	316,246
Cass	4	263,503	323,552	Hardeman	2	86,791	97,105
Castro	1	911,878	1,008,921	Harris	35	49,314,369	64,075,621
Chambers	2	167,469	185,379	Harrison	2	153,436	167,061
Cherokee	2	1,305,776	1,517,691	Haskell	1	56,258	64,106
Childress	1	63,535	72,456	Hemphill	2	375,514	419,512
Clay	1	84,057	94,221	Henderson	8	7,073,179	8,866,878
Coke	1	40,916	46,534	Hidalgo	2	171,243	227,652
Coleman	2	95,664	110,890	Hill	2	124,788	138,696
Collin	12	3,951,288	4,764,704	Hockley	2	364,901	406,997
Collingsworth	1	157,090	173,401	Hood	2	799,400	899,772
Colorado	4	322,977	379,864	Hopkins	3	128,824	142,286
Comal	1	243,588	280,742	Houston	2	405,467	459,655
Comanche	2	266,335	308,300	Howard	1	35,653	39,238
Concho	2	120,996	138,705	Hunt	1	175,785	192,690
Cooke	2	552,476	635,875	Hutchinson	1	36,952	41,289
Coryell	3	487,214	539,958	Irion	1	164,833	181,113
Cottle	1	55,077	60,079	Jack	2	508,216	648,769
Crockett	2	395,675	464,531	Jackson	1	54,480	59,358
Crosby	2	227,942	250,256	Jasper	1	186,759	217,714
Dallam	1	59,412	66,164	Jeff Davis	1	71,111	78,217
Dallas	36	59,750,859	79,396,344	Jefferson	1	1,255,806	1,453,183
Dawson	1	243,991	272,700	Jim Hogg	1	103,292	120,094
Deaf Smith	2	269,015	304,259	Jim Wells	1	269,288	345,505
Delta	2	57,114	65,553	Johnson	3	781,663	900,870
Denton	7	1,499,959	1,686,658	Jones	2	121,578	141,950
DeWitt	2	249,359	286,051	Karnes	2	252,395	281,203
Dickens	1	34,730	39,054	Kaufman	2	2,045,045	2,261,516
Dimmit	1	41,159	48,579	Kent	1	77,050	90,191

Total bank assets in Dallas County were $79.4 billion, down from $88.8 billion in 2008. In Harris County (Houston), assets were $64.1 billion and in Bexar County (San Antonio), assets were $21.3 billion.

Besides the major metropolitan areas, banks in three counties had assets over $10 billion, Lubbock, Wharton and Webb (Laredo).

No independent banks were reported in 46 counties: Aransas, Archer, Borden, Brewster, Cochran, Crane, Culberson, Falls, Gaines, Garza, Glasscock, Goliad, Hardin, Hartley, Hays, Hudspeth, Kendall, Kenedy, King, Kinney, Lipscomb, Loving, Madison, Marion, Maverick, McMullen, Moore, Motley, Newton, Oldham, Randall, Reagan, Real, Red River, Robertson, San Augustine, Somervell, Stephens, Terrell, Terry, Upton, Waller, Ward, Willacy, Winkler and Yoakum.

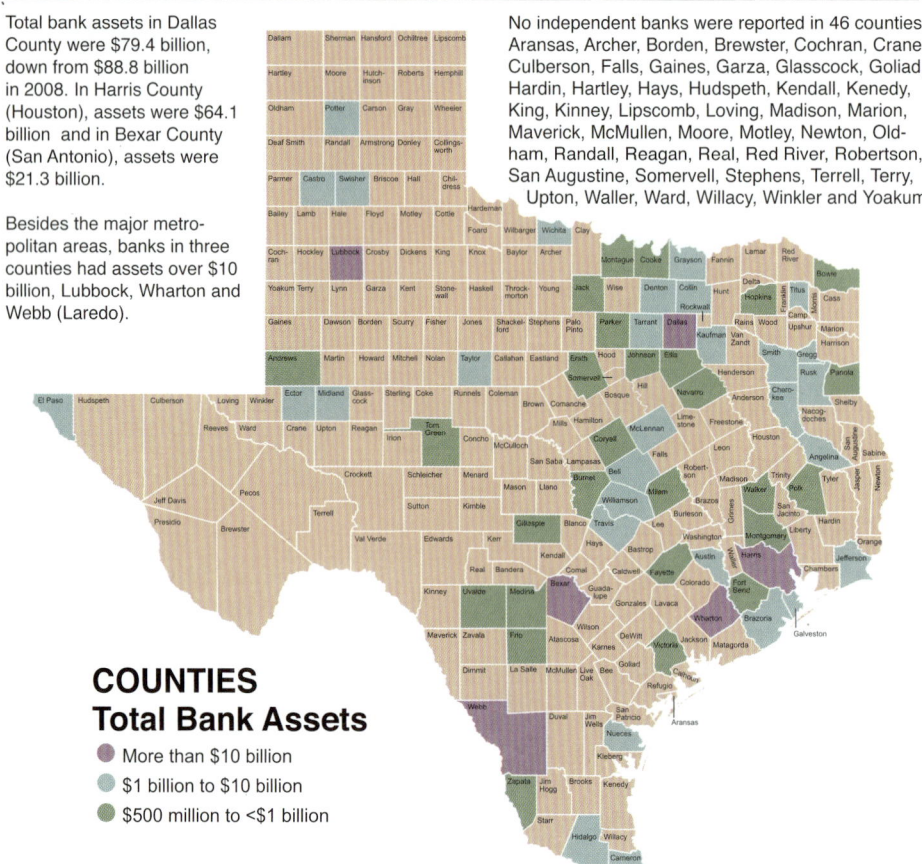

COUNTIES
Total Bank Assets

- 🔴 More than $10 billion
- 🔵 $1 billion to $10 billion
- 🟢 $500 million to <$1 billion

COUNTY	Banks	Deposits	Assets
Kerr	2	103,678	114,969
Kimble	2	67,640	79,044
Kleberg	1	304,156	368,948
Knox	1	73,921	81,870
Lamar	3	396,600	485,236
Lamb	3	318,821	354,081
Lampasas	1	91,142	106,704
La Salle	1	58,068	63,622
Lavaca	2	302,960	349,062
Lee	1	126,585	148,762
Leon	3	448,668	491,549
Liberty	2	292,921	337,480
Limestone	3	238,135	267,136
Live Oak	2	268,535	302,178
Llano	2	214,781	240,742
Lubbock	11	10,166,753	12,835,706
Lynn	1	58,161	64,588
Martin	1	74,846	85,262
Mason	2	96,260	118,508
Matagorda	1	45,466	50,815
McCulloch	2	175,477	198,025
McLennan	11	2,432,741	2,762,231
Medina	1	74,846	85,262
Menard	2	96,260	118,508
Midland	1	45,466	50,815
Milam	3	461,817	531,644

COUNTY	Banks	Deposits	Assets
Mills	1	$ 154,701	$ 179,040
Mitchell	2	93,835	106,203
Montague	1	454,490	519,561
Montgomery	3	906,600	1,027,369
Morris	3	175,438	213,626
Nacogdoches	1	355,466	408,784
Navarro	5	506,131	582,807
Nolan	3	310,466	348,057
Nueces	5	1,386,419	1,555,931
Ochiltree	1	108,001	122,404
Orange	1	105,397	119,240
Palo Pinto	3	270,405	328,061
Panola	2	495,663	565,902
Parker	3	550,013	625,385
Parmer	1	104,991	118,409
Pecos	3	235,414	263,866
Polk	3	547,143	654,064
Potter	3	3,416,021	4,066,464
Presidio	1	70,160	82,789
Rains	1	79,684	99,977
Reeves	1	141,461	157,130
Refugio	2	229,880	256,976
Roberts	1	36,792	39,990
Rockwall	2	94,927	107,827
Runnels	4	244,910	271,674
Rusk	3	1,032,211	1,167,794

COUNTY	Banks	Deposits	Assets
Sabine	1	43,068	51,248
San Jacinto	2	112,662	125,092
San Patrico	1	94,078	101,387
San Saba	1	45,692	53,792
Schleicher	1	43,730	50,449
Scurry	2	206,354	233,431
Shackelford	1	319,725	360,129
Shelby	3	424,935	474,432
Sherman	1	159,650	179,091
Smith	5	3,093,849	4,332,257
Starr	1	61,540	70,516
Sterling	1	73,662	83,323
Stonewall	1	30,710	41,786
Sutton	1	208,411	234,301
Swisher	2	1,403,627	1,616,106
Tarrant	18	3,334,066	3,917,476
Taylor	4	1,133,893	1,402,615
Throckmorton	1	26,526	29,138
Titus	2	858,780	1,070,537
Tom Green	2	497,972	578,818
Travis	6	1,124,144	1,395,300

COUNTY	Banks	Deposits	Assets
Trinity	1	44,817	48,920
Tyler	1	102,232	118,379
Upshur	18	3,334,066	3,917,476
Uvalde	4	1,133,893	1,402,615
Val Verde	1	26,526	29,138
Van Zandt	2	858,780	1,070,537
Victoria	2	497,972	578,818
Walker	2	508,174	571,054
Washington	4	341,110	393,435
Webb	4	8,285,429	12,219,107
Wharton	4	8,173,482	10,259,587
Wheeler	1	89,185	95,468
Wichita	5	1,197,431	1,391,025
Wilbarger	1	195,238	226,493
Williamson	8	1,080,067	1,216,352
Wilson	1	27,980	34,308
Wise	3	347,322	379,621
Wood	4	351,679	435,590
Young	3	327,638	379,475
Zapata	2	484,163	627,902
Zavala	1	50,282	58,274

Texas Total Bank Resources and Deposits: 1905–2010

On Dec. 31, 2010, Texas had 567 national and state banks, the lowest number since the first decade of the 20th century. In 1986, the number of independent banks in the state peaked at 1,972. In 2009, total assets were the hightest ever at nearly $317 billion. Deposits peaked in 2010 at $248.8 billion. *Source: Federal Reserve Bank of Dallas*

Date	National Banks			State Banks			Combined Total		
	No. Banks	Assets (add 000)	Deposits (add 000)	No. Banks	Assets (add 000)	Deposits (add 000)	No. Banks	Assets (add 000)	Deposits (add 000)
Sept. 30, 1905	440	$ 189,484	$ 101,285	29	$ 4,341	$ 2,213	469	$ 193,825	$ 103,498
Nov. 10, 1910	516	293,245	145,249	621	88,103	59,766	1,137	381,348	205,015
Dec. 29, 1920	556	780,246	564,135	1,031	391,127	280,429	1,587	1,171,373	844,564
Dec. 31, 1930	560	1,028,420	826,723	655	299,012	231,909	1,215	1,327,432	1,058,632
Dec. 31, 1940	446	1,695,662	1,534,702	393	227,866	179,027	839	1,923,528	1,713,729
Dec. 31, 1950	442	6,467,275	6,076,006	449	1,427,680	1,338,540	891	7,894,955	7,414,546
Dec. 31, 1960	468	10,520,690	9,560,668	532	2,997,609	2,735,726	1,000	13,518,299	12,296,394
Dec. 31, 1970	530	22,087,890	18,384,922	653	8,907,039	7,958,133	1,183	30,994,929	26,343,055
Dec. 31, 1980	641	75,540,334	58,378,669	825	35,186,113	31,055,648	1,466	110,726,447	89,434,317
Dec. 31, 1985	1,058	144,674,908	111,903,178	878	64,349,869	56,392,634	1,936	209,024,777	168,295,812
Dec. 31, 1986	1,077	141,397,037	106,973,189	895	65,989,944	57,739,091	1,972	207,386,981	164,712,280
Dec. 31, 1987	953	135,690,678	103,930,262	812	54,361,514	47,283,855	1,765	190,052,192	151,214,117
Dec. 31, 1988	802	130,310,243	106,740,461	690	40,791,310	36,655,253	1,492	171,101,553	143,395,714
Dec. 31, 1989	687	133,163,016	104,091,836	626	40,893,848	36,652,675	1,313	174,056,864	140,744,511
Dec. 31, 1990	605	125,808,263	103,573,445	578	45,021,304	40,116,662	1,183	170,829,567	143,690,107
Dec. 31, 1991	579	123,022,314	106,153,441	546	46,279,752	41,315,420	1,125	169,302,066	147,468,861
Dec. 31, 1992	562	135,507,244	112,468,203	529	40,088,963	35,767,858	1,091	175,596,207	148,236,061
Dec. 31, 1993	502	139,409,250	111,993,205	510	44,566,815	39,190,373	1,012	183,976,065	151,183,578
Dec. 31, 1994	481	140,374,540	111,881,041	502	47,769,694	41,522,943	983	188,144,234	153,403,984
Dec. 31, 1995	456	152,750,093	112,557,468	479	49,967,946	42,728,454	935	202,718,039	155,285,922
Dec. 31, 1996	432	152,299,695	122,242,990	445	52,868,263	45,970,674	877	205,167,958	168,213,664
Dec. 31, 1997	417	180,252,942	145,588,677	421	54,845,186	46,202,808	838	235,098,128	191,791,485
Dec. 31, 1998	402	128,609,813	106,704,893	395	50,966,996	42,277,367	797	179,576,809	148,982,260
Dec. 31, 1999	380	128,878,607	99,383,776	373	52,266,148	42,579,986	753	181,144,755	141,963,762
Dec. 31, 2000	358	112,793,856	88,591,657	351	53,561,550	43,835,525	709	166,355,406	132,427,182
Dec. 31, 2001	342	85,625,768	72,812,548	344	59,047,520	47,843,799	686	144,673,288	120,656,347
Dec. 31, 2002	332	95,308,420	79,183,418	337	62,093,220	49,715,186	669	157,401,640	128,898,604
Dec. 31, 2003	316	75,003,613	62,567,943	337	61,448,617	49,790,333	653	136,452,230	112,358,276
Dec. 31, 2004	311	82,333,800	67,977,669	328	69,127,411	54,950,601	639	151,461,211	122,928,270
Dec. 31, 2005	302	96,505,262	77,688,463	324	76,697,256	61,257,128	626	173,202,518	138,945,591
Dec. 31, 2006	286	97,936,270	79,389,737	322	83,910,356	66,132,394	608	181,846,626	145,522,131
Dec. 31, 2007	282	107,260,539	83,637,302	330	154,283,181	114,537,280	612	261,543,720	198,174,582
Dec. 31, 2008	267	108,816,852	84,802,191	327	164,658,101	$115,186,285	594	273,474,953	199,988,476
Dec. 31, 2009	263	153,639,579	109,552,071	318	162,958,865	120,962,911	581	316,598,444	230,514,982
Dec. 31, 2010	253	$149,498,073	$120,827,780	314	$162,772,458	$127,925,865	567	$312,270,531	$248,753,645

Texas State Banks

Consolidated Statement, Foreign and Domestic
Offices, as of Dec. 31, 2010
Source: Federal Reserve Bank of Dallas

Number of Banks	314

(thousands of dollars, 000)

Assets

Cash and balances due from banks:
Non-interest-bearing balances
and currency and coin .... $ 3,162,538
Interest-bearing balances 8,315,448
Held-to-maturity securities 8,287,451
Available-for sale securities 30,462,467
Federal funds sold in domestic offices 1,519,669
Securities purchases under agreements to resell ...127,374
Loans and lease financing receivables:
Loans and leases held for sale 894,888
Loans and leases, net of unearned income 99,001,764
Less: allowance for loan and lease losses....... 1,913,665
Loans and leases, net 97,088,099
Trading Assets 478,512
Premises and fixed assets.................................. 2,888,795
Other real estate owned 830,782
Investments in unconsolidated subsidiaries
and associated companies..................................... 30,893
Direct/indirect investments in real estate ventures........ 176
Intangible assets:
Goodwill 2,022,636
Other 153,047
Other assets 6,509,684

Total Assets .... **$ 162,772,459**

Liabilities

Deposits:
In domestic offices .... $ 127,925,868
Non-interest-bearing..................................... 34,590,547
Interest-bearing 93,335,321
In foreign offices, edge & agreement subsidiaries
and IBFs 1,470,316
Non-interest-bearing...149,203
Interest-bearing balances.............................. 3,321,113
Federal funds purchased and securities sold under
agreements to repurchase:
funds in domestic offices.......................................800,846
securities sold under agreement to repurchase .2,496,338
Trading liabilities.. 405,031
Other borrowed money (mortgages/leases).......... 8,107,599
Subordinated notes and debentures 2,021,650
Other liabilities... 1,761,080

Total Liabilities .... **$ 144,988,728**

Equity Capital

Perpetual preferred stock .... $ 7,091
Common stock... 668,718
Surplus (exclude surplus related to
preferred stock) 8,621,317
Retained earnings 8,796,443
Accumulated other comprehensive income........... –310,369
Other equity capital components................................–1,894
Total bank equity capital 17,781,306
Minority interest in cons. subsidiaries.................... 2,425

Total Equity Capital .... **$ 17,783,731**

Total liabilities, minority interest and
equity capital .... **$ 162,772,459**

Texas National Banks

Consolidated Statement, Foreign and Domestic
Offices, as of Dec. 31, 2010
Source: Federal Reserve Bank of Dallas

Number of Banks	253

(thousands of dollars, 000)

Assets

Cash and balances due from banks:
Non-interest-bearing balances
and currency and coin .... $ 3,747,544
Interest-bearing balances 9,145,903
Held-to-maturity securities................................. 2,160,723
Available-for sale securities................................ 24,088,561
Federal funds sold in domestic offices 3,420,583
Securities purchases under agreements to resell 14,052
Loans and lease financing receivables:
Loans and leases held for sale 16,427,600
Loans and leases, net of unearned income 82,035,440
Less: allowance for loan and lease losses........ 2,335,923
Loans and leases, net...................................... 79,699,517
Trading Assets 105,146
Premises and fixed assets.................................. 2,299,313
Other real estate owned 763,992
Investments in unconsolidated subsidiaries
and associated companies.......................................25,568
Direct/indirect investments in real estate ventures......... 170
Intangible assets:
Goodwill 2,078,364
Other 172,826
Other assets 5,348,211

Total Assets .... **$ 149,498,073**

Liabilities

Deposits:
In domestic offices ....$ 120,827,780
Non-interest-bearing..................................... 41,842,124
Interest-bearing 78,985,656
In foreign offices, edge & agreement subsidiaries
and IBFs 784,843
Non-interest-bearing..0
Interest-bearing balances................................. 784,843
Federal funds purchased and securities sold under
agreements to repurchase:
funds in domestic offices....................................1,169,893
securities sold under agreement to repurchase .1,781,605
Trading liabilities...96,720
Other borrowed money (mortgages/leases)..........6,964,172
Subordinated notes and debentures 160,804
Other liabilities... 778,369

Total Liabilities .... **$ 132,564,184**

Equity Capital

Perpetual preferred stock .... $ 476,760
Common stock... 515,359
Surplus (exclude surplus related to
preferred stock) 10,200,150
Retained earnings 5,484,584
Accumulated other comprehensive income............ 258,153
Other equity capital components .... –2,770
Total bank equity capital 16,932,236
Minority interest in consolidated subsidiaries 1,651

Total Equity Capital .... **$ 16,933,887**

Total liabilities, minority interest and
equity capital .... **$ 149,498,073**

Credit Unions: End of Year 2010

	#Credit Unions	State Charter	Federal Charter	Members	Percent of Pop.*	Savings (000)	Loans (000)	Assets (000)
Texas	550	206	344	7,539,545	29.9	$58,912,234	$43,230,571	$67,831,026
U.S.	7,605	3,020	4,585	92,619,205	29.6	$804,356,909	$580,035,421	$934,134,063

* Percent of population, each member counted once for every credit union they belong to. Source: Credit Union National Association.

	U.S. Credit Union History				Texas Credit Union History			
Year	# Credit Unions	Members	Savings ($ millions)	Loans ($ millions)	# Credit Unions	Members	Savings ($ millions)	Loans ($ millions)
2009	7,831	91,997,528	770,055	587,125	561	7,402,875	$ 55,070	$ 42,161
2008	8,088	90,735,249	697,972	580,101	571	7,197,177	49,335	39,092
2007	8,538	89,053,757	650,879	522,904	595	6,993,043	44,018	$ 35,984
2006	8,853	87,895,738	613,297	492,635	610	6,880,403	41,228	33,894
2005	9,198	86,987,764	591,388	449,891	625	6,832,172	40,273	32,745
2004	9,542	85,639,535	567,827	407,937	641	7,130,609	40,749	31,709
2003	9,875	84,240,057	538,033	367,065	667	7,000,010	39,148	29,199
2000	10,860	78,865,715	380,858	295,251	714	6,454,376	28,400	22,562
1995	12,230	69,305,876	278,813	198,337	819	5,360,020	20,306	14,701
1990	14,549	61,610,057	201,082	141,889	954	4,379,982	13,875	8,946
1980	21,465	43,930,569	61,724	48,703	1,379	3,202,066	4,818	3,691
1970	23,687	22,775,511	15,411	14,068	1,435	1,452,416	1,034	951
1960	20,094	12,025,393	4,976	4,376	1,159	688,517	282	265
1950	10,586	4,617,086	862	679	484	179,956	38	35

Source: Credit Union National Association.

Credit Unions in Texas

Source: Texas Credit Union Department, National Credit Union Administration and Credit Union National Association.

Credit unions are chartered at federal and state levels. The National Credit Union Administration (NCUA) is the regulatory agency for the federal-chartered credit unions in Texas.

The Texas Credit Union Department is the regulatory agency for the state-chartered credit unions. It was established in 1969 as a separate agency by the 61st Legislature. In 2010, it supervised 206 active state-chartered credit unions.

These state-chartered credit unions served 2.8 million Texans and had approximately $19.6 billion in assets in 2010.

The department is supervised by the nine-member Texas Credit Union Commission, which is appointed by the governor at staggered terms of six years, with the terms of one-third of the members expiring Feb. 15 of each odd-numbered year.

The Texas Credit Union League has been the state association for federal and state chartered credit unions since October 1934.

The league's address is 4455 LBJ Freeway Ste. 909, Farmers Branch, 75244-5998.

The address for the Texas Credit Union Department is 914 East Anderson Lane, Austin, 78752-1699. Their Web site is www.tcud.state.tx.us. ☆

Distribution of Consumer Savings
$ billions. End-of-Year 2010

	Savings	Market share
Commercial banks	$ 5,714.8	69.7%
Money Market Mutual Funds	942.0	11.5%
Credit Unions	804.4	9.8%
Savings Institutions	550.5	6.8%
US Savings Securities	188.0	2.3%
Total	$ 8,199.7	

Credit Outstanding by Lenders

	Outstanding	Market share
Commercial banks	$ 1,098.7	44.6%
Pool of Securitized Assets	130.7	5.3%
Finance Companies	518.6	21.1%
Credit Unions	255.2	10.4%
Student Loans	317.1	12.9%
Savings Institutions	86.8	3.5%
Nonfinancial business	56.2	2.3%
Total	$ 2,463.4	

Source: Credit Union National Association.

Savings and Loan Associations in Texas

This table includes all thrifts that are not also classified as banks under federal law: that is, it includes federal savings and loan associations and federal savings banks. *Source: Texas Department of Savings and Mortgage Lending.*

Year ending	Number of Institutions	Total Assets	Mortgage Loans	Cash/ Securities	Deposits	FHLB/ Borrowed Money	†Net Worth
				in thousands of dollars (000)			
Dec. 31, 2010	19	$ 53,980,441	$ 17,005,657	$ 14,230,550	$ 46,935,007	$ 987,211	$ 4,840466
Dec. 31, 2009	19	46,524,327	17,810,587	9,702,023	40,272,742	973,610	4,254,794
Dec. 31, 2008	22	87,572,855	49,816,471	31,763,898	52,606,655	27,137,730	6,582,759
Dec. 31, 2007	21	74,346,114	38,795,098	15,444,116	43,442,843	23,264,570	5,628,255
Dec. 31, 2006	20	64,692,927	22,908,898	12,709,276	39,661,286	18,817,750	4,993,335
Dec. 31, 2005	19	55,755,096	42,027,293	9,140,789	30,565,411	11,299,136	4,228,103
Dec. 31, 2004	20	51,000,806	40,740,030	6,648,858	26,526,138	12,786,086	3,647,046
Dec. 31, 2003	21	45,941,356	16,840,610	17,362,664	23,954,623	10,725,209	3,130,442
Dec. 31, 2002	24	43,940,058	31,604,285	4,900,880	23,264,510	11,662,118	3,189,629
Dec. 31, 2001	24	42,716,060	35,823,258	9,542,688	22,182,152	15,531,159	3,608,222
Dec. 31, 2000	25	55,709,391	43,515,610	1,512,444	28,914,234	17,093,369	4,449,097
Dec. 31, 1999	25	45,508,256	40,283,186	2,615,072	26,369,005	14,790,241	3,802,977
Dec. 31, 1998	30	40,021,239	35,419,110	5,236,596	21,693,469	15,224,654	3,101,795
Dec. 31, 1997	32	40,284,148	33,451,365	4,556,626	21,854,620	15,190,014	3,089,458
Dec. 31, 1996	37	54,427,896	27,514,639	5,112,995	28,053,292	20,210,616	4,345,257
Dec. 31, 1995	45	52,292,519	27,509,933	5,971,364	28,635,799	15,837,632	3,827,249
Dec. 31, 1994	50	50,014,102	24,148,760	6,790,416	29,394,433	15,973,056	3,447,110
Dec. 31, 1993	62	42,983,595	14,784,215	10,769,889	25,503,656	13,356,018	2,968,840
Dec. 31, 1992	64	47,565,516	14,137,191	14,527,573	33,299,278	10,490,144	2,917,881
Dec. 31, 1991	80	53,500,091	15,417,895	11,422,071	41,985,117	8,189,800	2,257,329
Dec. 31, 1990 §	131	72,041,456	27,475,664	20,569,770	56,994,387	17,738,041	-4,566,656
Conservatorship	51	14,952,402	6,397,466	2,188,820	16,581,525	4,304,033	-6,637,882
Privately Owned	80	57,089,054	21,078,198	18,380,950	40,412,862	13,434,008	2,071,226
Dec. 31, 1989 §	196	90,606,100	37,793,043	21,218,130	70,823,464	27,158,238	-9,356,209
Conservatorship	81	22,159,752	11,793,445	2,605,080	25,381,494	7,103,657	-10,866,213
Privately Owned	115	68,446,348	25,999,598	18,613,050	45,441,970	20,054,581	1,510,004
Dec. 31, 1988	204	110,499,276	50,920,006	26,181,917	83,950,314	28,381,573	-4,088,355
Dec. 31, 1987	279	99,613,666	56,884,564	12,559,154	85,324,796	19,235,506	-6,677,338
Dec. 31, 1986	281	96,919,775	61,489,463	9,989,918	80,429,758	14,528,311	109,807
Dec. 31, 1985	273	91,798,890	* 60,866,666	10,426,464	72,806,067	13,194,147	3,903,611
Dec. 31, 1980	318	34,954,129	$ 27,717,383	$ 3,066,791	$ 28,439,210	$ 3,187,638	$ 1,711,201

Texas Savings Banks

The savings bank charter was approved by the Legislature in 1993 and the first savings bank was chartered in 1994. Savings banks operate similarly to savings and loans associations in that they are housing-oriented lenders. Under federal law a savings bank is categorized as a commercial bank and not a thrift. Therefore savings-bank information is also reported with state and national bank information. *Source: Texas Department of Savings and Mortgage Lending.*

Year ending	Number	Total Assets	Mortgage Loans	Cash/ Securities	Deposits	FHLB/ Borrowed	Net Worth
				in thousands of dollars (000)			
Dec. 31, 2010	29	$ 8,559,443	$ 4,568,866	$ 4,164,611	$ 6,720,417	$ 332,684	$ 1,329,943
Dec. 31, 2009	29	8,372,892	4,283,372	1,237,215	6,330,896	307,494	1,201,409
Dec. 31, 2008	28	3,988,377	1,980,651	538,162	3,119,082	411,119	434,893
Dec. 31, 2007	26	9,967,678	6,471,833	1,027,709	6,162,709	2,328,467	1,372,231
Dec. 31, 2006	22	9,393,482	6,444,178	836,821	5,721,314	2,453,757	1,138,780
Dec. 31, 2005	19	8,720,497	5,605,678	985,535	5,308,639	1,967,673	1,352,882
Dec. 31, 2004	22	12,981,650	6,035,081	1,654,978	8,377,409	3,000,318	1,482,078
Dec. 31, 2003	23	17,780,413	8,396,606	3,380,565	11,901,441	3,315,544	2,422,317
Dec. 31, 2002	24	15,445,211	7,028,139	3,147,381	10,009,861	3,422,600	1,910,660
Dec. 31, 2001	25	11,956,074	5,845,605	1,305,731	8,742,372	1,850,076	1,270,273
Dec. 31, 2000	25	11,315,961	9,613,164	514,818	8,644,826	1,455,497	1,059,638
Dec. 31, 1995	13	7,348,647	5,644,591	1,106,557	4,603,026	2,225,793	519,827
Dec. 31, 1994	8	$ 6,347,505	$ 2,825,012	$ 3,139,573	$ 3,227,886	$ 2,628,847	$ 352,363

* Beginning in 1982, net of loans in process.
† Net worth includes permanent stock and paid-in-surplus general reserves, surplus and undivided profits.
§ In 1989 and 1990, the Office of Thrift Supervision, U.S. Department of the Treasury, separated data on savings and loans (thrifts) into two categories: those under the supervision of the Office of Thrift Supervision (Conservatorship Thrifts) and those still under private management (Privately Owned).

Insurance in Texas

Source: 2010 Annual Report, Texas Dept. of Insurance.

The Texas Department of Insurance reported that on Aug. 31, 2010, there were 2,721 firms licensed to handle insurance business in Texas and 327,411 insurance agents.

From 1957 to 1993, a three-member State Board of Insurance administered legislation relating to the insurance industry. This board, appointed by the governor, hired a commissioner of insurance. The establishment of the system followed discovery of irregularities in some firms. It succeeded two previous regulatory groups, established in 1913 and changed in 1927.

Under reforms in 1993-94, the board was replaced by the Texas Department of Insurance with a Com-missioner of Insurance appointed by the governor for a two-year term in each odd-numbered year and confirmed by the Texas Senate.

On Sept. 1, 2005, legislation passed by the 79th Legislature took effect, transferring functions of the Texas Workers' Compensation Commission to the Texas Department of Insurance and creating within it the Division of Worker's Compensation.

Also established was the office of Commissioner of Workers' Compensation, appointed by the governor, to enforce and implement the Texas Workers' Compensation Act. The division consists of five sections: dispute resolution, field services, legal/compliance, medical advisor, and workplace and medical services.

Companies in Texas

The following table shows the number and kinds of insurance companies licensed in Texas on Aug. 31, 2010.

Type of Insurance	Texas	Out-of-State	Total
Stock Life	105	445	550
Mutual Life	3	32	35
Stipulated Premium Life	29	0	29
Non-Profit Life	0	1	1
Stock Fire	2	3	5
Stock Fire & Casualty	108	675	783
Mutual Fire & Casualty	4	55	59
Stock Casualty	11	160	171
Mexican Casualty	0	13	13
Lloyds	54	0	54
Reciprocal Exchanges	7	16	23
Fraternal Benefit Societies	7	24	31
Title Insurance	4	23	27
Non-Profit Legal Services	2	0	2
Health Maintenance Org.	49	3	52
Risk Retention Groups	2	0	2
Multiple Employer Welfare Arrang.	4	2	6
Joint Underwriting Associations	3	3	6
Third Party Administrators	274	508	782
Workers' Comp. Self Insurance	7	0	7
Continuing Care Retirement Communities	25	4	29
Total	**700**	**1,967**	**2,667**
Local Mutual Associations	2	0	2
Local Mutual Burial Associations	2	0	2
Exempt Associations	7	0	7
Non-Profit Hospital Service	2	0	2
County Mutual Fire	24	0	24
Farm Mutual Fire	17	0	17
Total	**54**	**0**	**54**
Grand Total	**754**	**1,967**	**2,721**

Source: 2010 Annual Report, Texas Department of Insurance.

Premium Income and Losses Paid, 2008

(Texas business only)	Texas Companies	Out-of-State Companies
Legal Reserve Life Insurance Companies		
Life premiums	$727,813,578	$ 7,891,651,863
Claims & benefits paid	$2,611,836,036	$ 220,812,350,490
Accident & health premiums	$ 372,266,337	$ 11,972,736,915
Accident & health loss paid	$ 248,273,536	$ 8,569,490,297
Mutual Fire & Casualty Companies		
Premiums	$ 975,587,709	$ 3,459,691,956
Losses	$ 493,964,841	$ 2,401,464,789
Lloyds Insurance		
Premiums	$4,733,891,700	. . . .
Losses	$4,280,332,637	. . . .
Reciprocal Insurance Companies		
Premiums	$ 856,965,670	$ 594,032,588
Losses	$ 765,609,927	$ 669,811,653
Fraternal Benefit Societies		
Life Certificates Issued	8,276	19,879
Amount issued 2008	$ 208,482,510	$ 2,161,619,211
Considerations from members:		
Life	$ 88,037,034	$ 325,772,791
Accident/Health	$ 1,055,902	$ 39,869,226
Benefits paid to members:		
Life	$ 62,710,757	$ 272,791,628
Accident/Health	$ 586,639	$ 24,651,709
Insurance in force	$2,855,872,793	$20,472,514,728
Title Companies		
Premiums	$ 380,175,274	$ 869,977,183
Paid losses	$ 10,729,813	$ 43,915,176
Stock Fire, Stock Casualty, and Stock Fire & Casualty Companies		
Premiums	$2,492,240,914	$14,306,753,079
Losses	$1,953,599,039	$9,324,060993

Texas Top 5 Auto Insurers

Company	% of market
1. State Farm Mutual	18.15
2. Farmers Texas County Mutual	9.72
3. Progressive County Mutual	7.89
4. Government Employees	4.34
5. Allstate County Mutual	3.92

Texas Top 5 Homeowners Insurers

1. State Farm Lloyds	28.75
2. Allstate Texas Lloyds	9.15
3. Texas Farmers	6.34
4. United Services	4.30
5. Travelers Lloyds of Texas	3.86

Texas Top 5 Accident/Health Insurers

1. Blue Cross/Blue Shield	27.32
2. United Healthcare	14.71
3. Aetna Life	7.87
4. Humana	7.10
5. Unicare	2.28

Texas Top 5 HMOs

1. Pacificare of Texas	15.36
2. Amerigroup Texas	10.51
3. Aetna Health	6.86
4. Superior Healthplan	6.82
5. Humana	6.76

Texas Top 5 Life Insurers

1. Metropolitan Life	6.69
2. Northwestern Mutual Life	4.55
3. Lincoln National Life	4.06
4. New York Life	3.79
5. State Farm Life	3.31

Source: 2010 Annual Report, Texas Department of Insurance.

Homeowners Insurance: Average Premiums by State, 2007

The U.S. average is $822. Idaho has the least expensive at $422.

1. Florida	$ 1,534
2. Texas	**1,448**
3. Louisiana	1,400
4. District of Columbia	1,090
5. Oklahoma	1,054
6. Massachusetts	1,023
7. Mississippi	1,019
8. Rhode Island	950
9. New York	936
10. Connecticut	929

In dollars. The Texas Insurance Commissioner promulgates residential policy forms which are similar but not identical to the standard national forms. Source: U.S. Statistical Abstract 2011.

Auto Insurance: Average for Coverage by State, 2007

The U.S. average is $795. North Dakota has the least expensive at $512.

1. District of Columbia	$ 1,140
2. New Jersey	1,104
3. Louisiana	1,096
4. New York	1,047
5. Florida	1,043
6. Rhode Island	1,017
7. Delaware	1,012
8. Nevada	1,000
9. Massachusetts	981
10. Connecticut	964
18. Texas	**808**

In dollars. The figures are actually reported as 'average expenditures', which equals total premiums divided by liability car-years. A car-year is equal to 365 days of insured coverage for a single vehicle. Source: U.S. Statistical Abstract 2011.

Ten-year history, number of insurance companies operating in Texas

	2001	2002	2003	2004	2005	2006	2007	2008	2009	2010
Life/Health										
In-State	216	213	206	196	190	186	175	170	161	161
Out-of-State	625	607	580	561	552	546	529	520	514	504
subtotal	841	820	786	757	742	732	704	690	675	665
Property/Casualty										
In-State	245	243	244	245	250	248	252	250	250	243
Out-of-State	910	913	916	915	917	926	932	942	948	948
subtotal	1,155	1,156	1,160	1,160	1,167	1,174	1,184	1,192	1,198	1,191
Other*										
In-State	373	368	362	348	352	341	341	348	353	350
Out-of-State	426	436	456	462	479	485	471	486	504	515
subtotal	799	804	818	810	831	826	812	834	857	865
Grand Total	**2,795**	**2,780**	**2,764**	**2,727**	**2,740**	**2,732**	**2,700**	**2,716**	**2,730**	**2,721****

*Other includes: Non-profit legal services corporations, third party administrators, continuing care retirement communities and health maintenance organizations.

**Does not include 194 premium finance companies and their 10 branch offices.

Source: 2010 Annual Report, Texas Department of Insurance.

Construction Industry: Comparison of Awards, 1950–2009

The chart below shows the total value of construction contract awards in Texas by year: *Source Texas Contractor, 2009.*

Year	Total Awards	Year	Total Awards	Year	Total Awards
2009	$ 29,892,995,000	1997	$ 5,088,017,435	1985	$ 4,806,998,065
2008	30,790,000,000	1996	4,383,336,574	1984	3,424,721,025
2007	25,785,189,283	1995	4,771,332,413	1983	4,074,910,947
2006	20,566,889,250	1994	4,396,199,988	1982	3,453,784,388
2005	18,923,051,000	1993	5,394,342,718	1981	3,700,112,809
2004	13,014,672,068	1992	4,747,666,912	1980	3,543,117,615
2003	12,897,933,353	1991	3,926,799,801	1975	1,737,036,682
2002	7,297,909,363	1990	3,922,781,630	1970	1,458,708,492
2001	6,067,377,351	1989	4,176,355,929	1965	1,254,638,051
2000	5,232,788,835	1988	3,562,336,666	1960	1,047,943,630
1999	4,941,352,362	1987	4,607,051,270	1955	949,213,349
1998	4,951,275,224	1986	4,636,310,266	1950	1,059,457,667

Texas Non-Residential Construction

Month	Value of Contracts
April 2010	$ 1.416 billion
May 2010	1.425 billion
June 2010	1.262 billion
July 2010	0.931 billion
August 2010	1.016 billion
September 2010	2.590 billion
October 2010	0.726 billion
November 2010	0.561 billion
December 2010	2.194 billion
January 2011	0.834 billion
February 2011	0.754 billion
March 2011	1.246 billion
April 2011	1.544 billion
Change from previous year: up 20.2 percent	
Source: Texas Comptroller of Public Accounts.	

Value of Highway Awards

The chart below shows value of contracts awarded in **millions of dollars** by the Texas Department of Transportation by year.

Year	Construction awards	Maintenance awards	Total
2005	$ 4,348	$ 286	**$ 4,634**
2006	4,954	320	**5,274**
2007	3,663	298	**3,961**
2008	2,755	362	**3,116**
2009	2,664	375	**3,039**
Source: Texas Comptroller of Public Accounts.			

Texas Single-Family Building Permits

Year	No. of Dwelling Units		Avg. Value per Unit ($)	
	Units	% change	Value	% change
1981	66,161	–	$ 55,700	–
1982	78,714	19	53,800	-3
1983	103,252	31	63,400	18
1984	84,565	-18	68,000	7
1985	67,964	-20	71,000	4
1986	59,143	-13	72,200	2
1987	43,975	-26	77,700	8
1988	35,908	-18	83,900	8
1989	36,658	2	90,400	8
1990	38,233	4	95,500	6
1991	46,209	21	92,800	-3
1992	59,543	29	95,400	3
1993	69,964	18	96,400	1
1994	70,452	1	99,500	3
1995	70,421	0	100,300	1
1996	83,132	18	102,100	2
1997	82,228	-1	108,900	7
1998	99,912	22	112,800	4
1999	101,928	2	118,800	5
2000	108,782	7	127,100	7
2001	111,915	3	124,700	-2
2002	122,913	10	126,400	1
2003	137,493	12	128,800	2
2004	151,384	10	137,600	7
2005	166,203	10	144,300	5
2006	163,032	-2	155,100	7
2007	120,366	-26	169,000	9
2008	81,107	-34	174,100	3
2009	68,230	-16	167,900	-4
2010	68,170	0	$ 179,200	7
Real Estate Center at Texas A&M University, 2011.				

Federal Aid to States for Highway Trust Fund, 2008

The chart below shows dispersement of federal funds for highway construction and maintenance in **millions of dollars** in the middle column. The column at right shows dollars per capita based on estimated population. *Source: U.S. Bureau of Census.*

State	Highway Fund		State	Highway Fund		State	Highway Fund	
	Total	Per capita		Total	Per capita		Total	Per capita
U.S.	$ 34,913	$ 113	Pennsylvania	$ 1,515	$ 121	New Jersey	$ 801	$ 92
Texas	**2,578**	**106**	N. Carolina	872	94	Missouri	854	143
California	2,735	75	Ohio	1,176	102	S. Carolina	359	80
Florida	2,172	118	Michigan	988	99	Tennessee	679	109
New York	1,446	74	Georgia	1,143	118	Illinois	1,243	97

Texas Commercial Fishery Landings by Species

Species	2005 Pounds	2005 Value	2007 Pounds	2007 Value	2009 Pounds	2009 Value
Shrimp, Brown	40,441,245	$80,726,617	42,841,648	$84,258,622	65,297,755	$86,812,353
Shrimp, White	27,532,112	57,464,870	27,160,444	56,847,983	23,590,484	40,846,270
Oyster, Eastern	5,007,472	15,882,977	5,187,631	17,759,573	2,733,150	9,375,720
Snapper, Red	1,939,953	5,344,722	1,214,664	3,769,518	850,932	2,398,100
Shrimp, Dendrobranchiata	1,231,858	3,675,740	1,051,026	3,127,202	790,484	3,071,621
Crab, Blue	3,119,000	2,410,342	3,309,044	2,660,051	2,844,263	2,454,370
Drum, Black	2,077,446	1,917,329	1,684,400	1,656,699	1,610,103	1,377,472
Snapper, Vermilion	278,803	570,543	664,095	1,535,104	561,013	1,232,502
Croaker, Atlantic	58,174	415,399	54,926	417,341	63,393	484,016
Total, including others	**84,289,291**	**$172,336,642**	**84,937,097**	**$174,346,556**	**99,497,064**	**$150,231,931**

Source: National Ocean Economics Program and National Maritime Fisheries Service, 2011.

Oyster boats in Fulton Harbor in Aransas County. Photo by Robert Plocheck.

Commercial Fisheries in Texas

Total coastwide landings in 2009 were more than 99.5 million pounds, valued at more than $150 million. Shrimp accounted for most of the weight and value of all seafood landed *(see chart above)*.

The Coastal Fisheries Division of the Texas Parks and Wildlife Department manages the marine fishery resources of Texas' four million acres of saltwater, including the bays and estuaries and out to nine nautical miles in the Gulf of Mexico.

The division works toward sustaining fisheries populations at levels that are necessary to ensure replenishable stocks of commercially and recreationally important species. It also focuses on habitat conservation and restoration and leads the agency research on all water-related issues, including assuring adequate in-stream flows for rivers and sufficient freshwater inflows for bays and estuaries. ☆

Landings by State 2009

Rank	States	Pounds (000)	Dollars (000)
	Total, U.S.	7,867,333	$ 3,882,178
1	Alaska	4,064,032	1,333,536
2	Massachusetts	356,021	399,973
3	Maine	183,366	282,833
4	Louisiana	1,000,815	280,691
8	**Texas**	**99,497**	**150,232**

Source: National Maritime Fisheries Service, 2011.

U.S. Ports in 2009

Rank	Port	Fishery Landed Value Dollars (000,000)
1	New Bedford, MA	$ 249.2
2	Dutch Harbor–Unalaska, AK	159.7
3	Kodiak, AK	103.8
4	Naknekll–King Salmon AK	76.1
5	Cape May-Wildwood NJ	73.4
14	**Brownsville–Port Isabel, TX**	**41.0**

Source: NOAA Fisheries, 2011.

Top Fishing Ports for Texas in 2009

Rank	Landing Weight Port	Pounds (000)	Landed Value Port	Dollars (000)
1	Brownsville–Port Isabel	27,000	Brownsville–Port Isabel	$ 41,000
2	Galveston	22,000	Galveston	35,000
3	Palacios	20,000	Port Arthur	27,000
4	Port Arthur	16,000	Palacios	27,000

Source: NOAA Fisheries: Office of Science & Technology, 2011.

Tourism Impact Estimates by County, 2009

This analysis covers most travel in Texas including business, pleasure, shopping, to attend meetings and other destinations. Visitor **spending** is for purchases including lodging taxes and other applicable local and state taxes. **Earnings** are wages and salaries of employees and income of proprietors of businesses that receive travel expenditures. Employment associated with these businesses are listed under **jobs**. **Local tax** receipts are from hotel taxes, local sales taxes, auto rental taxes, etc, as separate from state tax receipts. *Source: Office of the Governor, Economic Development and Tourism.*

County	Spending ($000)	Earnings ($000)	Jobs	Local tax ($000)
Anderson	$ 45,050	$ 11,080	620	$ 700
Andrews	11,800	2,830	240	160
Angelina	110,380	24,600	1,400	1,520
Aransas	95,780	28,110	1,320	1,860
Archer	1,750	310	20	20
Armstrong	1,020	80	10	0
Atascosa	28,080	7,800	350	420
Austin	35,930	8,900	430	380
Bailey	3,900	1,090	70	70
Bandera	28,560	18,600	1,600	610
Bastrop	117,760	45,050	1,480	2,760
Baylor	5,570	700	30	30
Bee	26,410	6,780	370	400
Bell	365,030	93,600	4,600	6,940
Bexar	4,697,380	1,407,860	51,300	109,640
Blanco	9,950	2,550	140	1650
Borden	90	10	0	0
Bosque	12,130	5,560	180	200
Bowie	154,030	26,630	1,630	2,100
Brazoria	242,100	64,800	3,450	3,790
Brazos	325,020	78,390	4,310	5,970
Brewster	50,380	23,980	1,450	1,030
Briscoe	1,100	140	10	0
Brooks	11,840	1,790	100	150
Brown	42,220	13,200	610	840
Burleson	11,970	3,060	150	130
Burnet	60,420	21,050	940	1,360
Caldwell	24,820	5,810	190	260
Calhoun	31,100	9,740	450	620
Callahan	3,580	910	50	40
Cameron	642,260	147,960	7,410	13,790
Camp	12,580	1,110	60	40
Carson	5,500	450	30	20
Cass	19,320	5,580	390	260
Castro	2,770	540	30	30
Chambers	26,670	5,620	220	700
Cherokee	31,110	7,320	420	420
Childress	11,870	2,780	210	340
Clay	16,350	1,250	80	30
Cochran	780	170	10	10
Coke	3,120	610	70	20
Coleman	6,360	1,250	80	100
Collin	866,810	291,070	10,440	18,720
Collingswrth	2,030	380	30	20
Colorado	44,520	9,670	470	470
Comal	259,890	76,810	3,080	5,440
Comanche	11,960	2,200	130	140
Concho	1,560	1,000	40	30
Cooke	51,070	13,570	600	860
Coryell	37,930	9,890	490	580
Cottle	1,500	160	10	10

County	Spending ($000)	Earnings ($000)	Jobs	Local tax ($000)
Crane	$ 1,620	$ 300	20	$ 30
Crockett	21,250	2,000	150	100
Crosby	1,420	360	30	10
Culberson	27,620	3,780	170	280
Dallam	12,840	4,530	210	280
Dallas	6,244,900	2,223,240	61,630	164,570
Dawson	11,430	1,910	140	110
Deaf Smith	13,600	3,060	180	210
Delta	1,160	220	10	10
Denton	464,240	134,080	4,480	9,380
DeWitt	32,780	5,990	280	270
Dickens	650	190	10	10
Dimmit	13,330	1,930	110	160
Donley	5,990	1,780	120	130
Duval	9,840	1,120	70	120
Eastland	13,010	3,210	210	260
Ector	204,640	61,020	2,380	4,220
Edwards	1,040	240	10	10
Ellis	118,910	29,690	960	1,990
El Paso	1,133,200	306,360	11,570	19,500
Erath	37,980	10,010	450	580
Falls	7,250	1,550	80	100
Fannin	10,450	1,690	90	100
Fayette	32,890	6,790	420	440
Fisher	870	140	10	10
Floyd	4,650	700	40	20
Foard	320	80	10	0
Fort Bend	354,800	102,910	3,830	7,130
Franklin	7,420	1,350	100	90
Freestone	43,100	5,830	490	520
Frio	13,420	3,110	170	230
Gaines	10,950	2,100	130	120
Galveston	647,070	179,820	8,090	16,890
Garza	8,430	2,960	110	80
Gillespie	76,680	23,400	1,020	2,030
Glasscock	210	30	0	0
Goliad	7,120	1,300	60	60
Gonzales	17,160	2,510	140	150
Gray	35,940	10,290	560	610
Grayson	167,240	29,110	1,440	2,090
Gregg	194,110	50,930	2,550	3,140
Grimes	15,570	4,160	190	220
Guadalupe	101,670	37,200	1,420	1,870
Hale	49,030	11,620	840	760
Hall	2,030	280	20	20
Hamilton	5,710	1,230	60	100
Hansford	1,670	290	20	30
Hardeman	5,200	920	60	70
Hardin	34,460	7,250	450	510
Harris	7,886,610	3,898,910	92,690	201,040
Harrison	85,350	15,540	800	610

Horsemen in the Hill Country, a top destination. Photo by Ron Billings; Texas Forest Service.

Travelers' Top Destinations, 2009

Most visited sites by non-residents as percent of total. *Source: Survey for Office of Governor.*

Rank	Destination	Percent
1.	Alamo	37.65
2.	Six Flags Over Texas	14.25
3.	SeaWorld of Texas	12.69
4.	Bass Pro Shops	12.39
5.	San Antonio River Walk	12.05
6.	State Capitol	11.11
7.	Dallas Museum of Art	10.27
8.	Cabela's	9.58
9.	NASA Space Center	9.15
10.	Fort Worth Zoo	9.04
11.	Galveston Island	7.93
12.	Big Bend National Park	7.49
13.	Six Flags Fiesta Texas	7.36
14.	Hill Country	7.00
15.	Fort Worth Stockyards	6.69

Top Areas, 2009

State areas visited as a percent of total visitors, by rank. *Source: Survey for Office of Governor.*

Rank	Area	Percent
1.	Dallas-Fort Worth-Arlington	21.3
2.	Houston-Baytown-Sugar Land	17.4
3.	San Antonio	14.1
4.	Austin-Round Rock	9.9
5.	Corpus Christi	3.9
6.	Lubbock	2.7
7.	Amarillo	2.2
8.	Bryan-College Station	1.8
9.	Waco	1.7
10.	Abilene	1.7
11.	Killeen-Temple-Fort Hood	1.6
12.	Beaumont-Port Arthur	1.5
13.	Tyler	1.3
14.	El Paso	1.2
	Rural Texas	17.5

County	Spending ($000)	Earnings ($000)	Jobs	Local tax ($000)
Hartley	$ 780	$ 130	10	$ 10
Haskell	4,120	920	60	80
Hays	204,590	57,620	2,260	3,670
Hemphill	5,950	1,030	60	180
Henderson	93,680	17,270	500	810
Hidalgo	1,025,790	272,550	13,900	18,600
Hill	52,390	9,470	570	520
Hockley	20,510	5,580	360	230
Hood	55,850	14,090	520	980
Hopkins	54,070	10,340	540	510
Houston	29,440	5,970	290	230
Howard	71,590	11,720	680	910
Hudspeth	4,330	330	10	0
Hunt	89,250	21,550	720	1,100
Hutchinson	33,520	7,890	400	520
Irion	8,360	300	10	0
Jack	4,110	720	40	40

County	Spending ($000)	Earnings ($000)	Jobs	Local tax ($000)
Jackson	$ 10,100	$ 1,970	110	$ 140
Jasper	33,980	9,730	560	650
Jeff Davis	7,020	3,310	110	0
Jefferson	428,410	94,300	5,100	7,740
Jim Hogg	5,010	1,220	60	50
Jim Wells	53,340	12,480	670	470
Johnson	113,380	21,210	900	1,450
Jones	7,500	2,240	140	90
Karnes	14,490	2,460	110	100
Kaufman	105,510	17,280	620	1,070
Kendall	66,040	17,930	920	1,040
Kenedy	760	260	10	0
Kent	650	120	10	0
Kerr	84,780	34,630	1,820	1,710
Kimble	14,850	2,510	200	240
King	30	10	0	0
Kinney	5,320	1,620	90	60

County	Spending ($000)	Earnings ($000)	Jobs	Local tax ($000)
Kleberg	$ 52,440	$ 14,620	670	$ 830
Knox	3,050	530	30	40
La Salle	6,670	1,770	100	110
Lamar	57,650	16,470	720	870
Lamb	10,650	1,520	100	90
Lampasas	11,680	2,240	150	170
Lavaca	11,670	2,640	120	170
Lee	18,640	4,450	200	160
Leon	26,900	4,200	250	330
Liberty	40,960	13,710	440	560
Limestone	16,300	2,370	140	270
Lipscomb	2,130	220	10	10
Live Oak	25,170	3,160	180	270
Llano	86,650	34,330	2,120	1,880
Loving	30	0	0	0
Lubbock	552,910	179,690	7,190	8,310
Lynn	990	220	20	10
Madison	8,260	1,810	110	150
Marion	7,650	1,960	140	130
Martin	11,370	540	30	10
Mason	2,440	600	50	30
Matagorda	48,910	16,560	900	1,160
Maverick	46,010	10,600	560	860
McCulloch	13,560	1,930	160	180
McLennan	400,770	91,100	4,850	5,960
McMullen	650	130	10	0
Medina	35,350	6,800	340	320
Menard	2,420	300	20	20
Midland	271,250	65,730	3,080	3,890
Milam	25,790	6,750	340	340
Mills	2,880	550	30	40
Mitchell	7,000	1,410	60	70
Montague	16,170	4,100	310	260
Montgomery	379,560	163,490	4,670	8,760
Moore	30,700	4,980	320	520
Morris	4,670	850	50	40
Motley	600	80	10	0
Nacgdoches	73,650	20,010	1,220	1,610
Navarro	40,890	10,400	600	670
Newton	4,300	640	30	40
Nolan	18,930	5,980	360	550
Nueces	821,310	231,690	11,240	20,760
Ochiltree	16,950	3,130	200	350
Oldham	7,450	790	60	50
Orange	89,090	18,690	900	1,060
Palo Pinto	58,000	10,600	480	460
Panola	16,170	3,390	210	410
Parker	92,190	18,810	750	1,050
Parmer	4,090	580	40	30
Pecos	39,770	6,080	470	890
Polk	46,300	13,740	690	520
Potter	581,300	127,450	7,070	11,760
Presidio	8,140	1,670	60	210
Rains	5,860	1,630	60	50
Randall	92,100	17,860	1,120	1,070
Reagan	1,990	400	30	10
Real	5,300	1,700	80	50
Red River	4,180	1,150	50	40
Reeves	34,030	5,050	370	560

County	Spending ($000)	Earnings ($000)	Jobs	Local tax ($000)
Refugio	$ 17,990	$ 1,980	120	$ 140
Roberts	830	30	0	0
Robertson	20,420	3,940	250	490
Rockwall	66,460	16,380	630	1,390
Runnels	5,890	1,120	70	60
Rusk	34,430	6,730	360	480
Sabine	11,170	2,410	170	30
S.Augustne	7,760	2,080	80	100
SanJacinto	10,800	2,290	160	60
SanPatricio	92,080	20,550	1,000	1,690
San Saba	3,610	870	50	40
Schleicher	450	120	10	10
Scurry	26,320	8,830	560	420
Shackelford	1,980	1,390	80	40
Shelby	29,880	7,570	530	520
Sherman	4,600	450	40	20
Smith	282,990	68,090	3,380	4,480
Somervell	14,590	3,610	190	350
Starr	24,440	5,110	250	420
Stephens	6,330	1,560	100	100
Sterling	1,880	150	10	10
Stonewall	840	210	10	10
Sutton	7,300	1,930	160	200
Swisher	3,020	710	40	30
Tarrant	3,661,300	2,690,630	65,470	69,880
Taylor	318,380	65,470	3,280	5,740
Terrell	1,360	260	10	0
Terry	7,100	2,040	150	140
Throckmrton	2,810	160	10	0
Titus	48,020	10,100	560	740
Tom Green	166,100	51,160	3,010	2,380
Travis	3,026,910	939,330	35,990	77,740
Trinity	9,850	5,140	300	130
Tyler	9,550	2,220	140	120
Upshur	18,710	2,830	150	170
Upton	2,190	530	40	40
Uvalde	55,160	11,140	610	980
Val Verde	49,870	14,960	730	1,000
Van Zandt	41,620	8,220	450	450
Victoria	150,180	31,830	1,450	2,060
Walker	81,190	17,710	1,080	1,000
Waller	34,090	4,980	170	380
Ward	10,270	2,730	180	210
Washington	72,410	12,180	620	750
Webb	423,910	107,370	5,140	6,330
Wharton	28,600	7,750	440	480
Wheeler	17,440	3,120	210	250
Wichita	186,810	44,620	3,070	3,670
Wilbarger	18,780	4,620	290	360
Willacy	20,700	3,350	150	170
Williamson	384,090	90,240	3,740	7,400
Wilson	20,810	4,500	240	170
Winkler	3,920	690	40	50
Wise	48,020	13,550	760	820
Wood	24,120	7,960	410	250
Yoakum	4,000	870	60	50
Young	22,060	6,840	360	330
Zapata	15,830	2,790	180	170
Zavala	6,740	900	50	70

Telecommunications Trends to High-Speed, Wireless

The chart below shows the move to wireless communications, and the decline in the number of telephone land lines in Texas and nationwide. The chart also shows the growth of high-speed Internet use in the state and in the United States. *Sources: Trends in Telephone Service, Federal Communications Commission, September 2010.*

	2000	2003	2004	2005	2006	2007	2009
Mobile Wireless Telephone Subscribers (in thousands)							
Texas	6,705	10,776	12,091	14,424	16,928	18,792	21,008
U.S.	90,643	147,624	167,313	192,053	217,418	238,230	261,284
Local Telephone Lines							
Texas	13,657,444	12,717,073	11,590,497	10,945,498	10,308,842	9,692,891	8,948,577
U.S.	188,499,586	173,140,710	165,978,892	157,041,487	146,848,926	135,121,037	122,596,593
High-Speed Lines for Internet (in thousands)							
Texas	253	1,571	2,203	2,943	4,357	6,856	7,484
U.S.	4,107	22,995	31,951	42,518	65,271	100,922	102,043

Percent of U.S. Households with Internet Connections

Year	Internet			Dail-Up			High-Speed			Other		
	Rural	Urban	Total	Rural	Urban	Total	Rural	Urban	Total	Rural	Urban	Total
2003	54.1	54.8	54.6	40.4	32.3	34.3	13.2	21.8	19.9	0.4	0.5	0.4
2007	58.3	62.6	61.7	19.3	8.5	10.7	38.8	53.8	50.8	0.3	0.3	0.3
2009	63.4	70.0	68.7	8.9	3.7	4.7	54.1	65.9	63.5	0.4	0.4	0.4

Source: Trends in Telephone Service, Federal Communications Commission, September 2010.

High-Speed Lines by Technology as of January 2009 (in thousands)

	DSL	Cable Modem	Traditional Wireline	Fiber	Satellite	Fixed Wireless	Mobile Wireless	Power Line	Total
Texas	2,616	2,081	*	258	*	37	2,349	0	7,484
U.S.	30,435	41,468	711	2,881	938	488	25,117	5	102,043

* Data withheld to maintain firm confidentiality.

Summary Statistics for Natural Gas in Texas

	2002	2005	2006	2007	2008	2009
Total Supply (MMcf, million cubic feet)	7,136,599	7,058,461	6,868,572	7,485,099	7,918,414	7,770,949
Consumption (million cubic feet) delivered to consumers						
Residential	209,951	185,124	166,225	199,680	192,750	192,225
Commercial	226,273	159,972	147,366	161,199	167,129	167,357
Industrial	1,978,184	1,341,461	1,288,887	1,296,251	1,326,451	1,199,127
Vehicle Fuel	1,811	1,811	1,866	1,966	1,966	2,206
Electric Power	1,550,292	1,466,263	1,463,658	1,473,555	1,440,043	1,387,421
Number of Consumers						
Residential	3,809,370	3,984,481	4,067,508	4,155,204	4,205,412	4,245,055
Commercial	317,446	322,999	329,918	326,762	324,6i71	318,176
Industrial	9,143	9,136	8,664	11,043	5,568	8,587
Average Price for Natural Gas (dollars per Mcf, thousand cubic feet)						
Residential	$ 7.29	$ 12.48	$ 13.11	$ 12.00	$ 13.75	$ 11.19
Commercial	5.49	10.47	10.25	9.77	11.25	8.16
Industrial	3.40	7.62	6.69	6.76	8.96	4.05
Vehicle Fuel	5.67	10.52	10.07	9.76	11,53	4.88
Electric Power	3.41	8.12	6.55	6.77	8.91	3.96

Source: Federal Energy Information Administration, Natural Gas Annual 2009.

Texas Electric Grids: Demand and Capacity

- The Electric Reliability Council of Texas (**ERCOT**) operates the electric grid for 75 percent of the state.
- The Panhandle, South Plains and a small corner of Northeast Texas are under the Southwest Power Pool (**SPP**).
- El Paso and the far western corner of the Trans Pecos are under the Western Electric Coordinating Council (**WECC**).
- The southeast corner of Texas is under the **SERC** Reliability Corporation.

The councils were first formed in 1968 to ensure adequate bulk power supply.

History *(in megawatts)*						Projections			
	2002	2004	2006	2008	2009	2010	2011	2012	2013
ERCOT demand	55,833	58,531	61,214	41,063	63,518	62,412	63,532	64,947	66,514
capacity	76,849	73,850	70,664	74,274	76,280	75,181	73,075	74,733	75,435
% margin*	27.3	20.7	13.4	17.8	16.7	17.0	13.1	13.1	11.8
SPP demand	38,298	39,383	41,982	42,906	41,117	42,976	43,567	44,834	45,544
capacity	47,233	48,000	45,831	48,110	49,194	53,298	55,576	56,477	57,154
% margin	18.9	18.0	8.4	10.8	16.4	19.4	21.6	20.6	20.3
WECC demand	117,032	121,205	139,402	130,916	122,881	124,924	126,318	127,495	127,459
capacity	142,624	155,455	162,288	167,860	152,467	161,358	170,649	176,431	179,803
% margin	17.9	22.0	14.1	22.0	19.4	22.6	26.0	27.7	29.1
SERC demand	154,459	153,024	196,196	196,711	186,507	195,833	199,297	204,045	207,756
capacity	172,485	182,861	223,630	228,169	247,400	247,674	252,732	256,713	260,524
% margin	10.5	16.3	12.3	13.8	24.6	20.9	21.1	20.5	20.3
U.S. demand	696,376	692,908	776,479	744,151	713,106	739,798	751,342	764,267	775,088
capacity	833,380	875,870	891,226	909,504	916,449	934,894	958,855	980,542	992,773
% margin	16.4	20.9	12.9	18.2	22.2	20.9	21.6	22.1	21.9

Capacity Margin is the amount of unused available capability of an electric power system at summer peak load as a percentage of capacity resources. Source: Federal Energy Information Administration, 2009.

A power plant in Dallas County. Photo by Robert Plocheck.

Electric Cooperatives

Source: Texas Electric Cooperatives, 2011.

Electric cooperatives are nonprofit, consumer-owned utilities providing electric service primarily in rural areas. Rates are regulated by the Public Utility Commission of Texas.

The nation's first electric cooperative was established in 1935 at Bartlett in Central Texas. It and others were organized when investor-owned utilities neglected or refused to serve farms and rural communities. By 1940 there were 567 cooperatives in 46 states.

Today Texas is home to 65 distribution co-ops and nine generation and transmission co-ops serving nearly 3 million member-customers.

And, there are more than 286,000 miles of lines serving more than 1.6 million meters in 232 of the state's 254 counties.s. ☆

Nuclear Power Plants

	Texas	U.S.		Texas	U.S.
Units	4**	104	Units	4	104
NET GENERATION				NET SUMMER CAPACITY	
Year	Total mil. kWh	% of total	Total mil. kWh	% of total	Year	Total mil. kW	% of total	Total mil. kW	% of total

Year	Total mil. kWh	% of total	Total mil. kWh	% of total	Year	Total mil. kW	% of total	Total mil. kW	% of total
2008	40,727	10.1	806,208	19.6	2008	4.90	4.7	100.80	10.0
2006	41,264	10.3	787,219	19.4	2006	4.86	4.8	100.33	10.2
2004	40,435	10.4	788,528	19.9	2004	4.86	4.8	99.63	10.3
2002	35,618	9.2	780,064	20.2	2002	4.74	5.0	98.66	10.9

***Texas has two nuclear plants; South Texas near Bay City and Comanche Peak near Glen Rose. Each has two units.*

Wind power, old and new, near McAdoo, Dickens County. Photo by Robert Plocheck.

Wind Energy Continues Expansion in State

Source: U.S. Energy Information Administration, 2011

Texas continues to lead the nation in installed wind capacity and generation. In 2008, Texas increased its wind capacity by 65 percent, reaching 7,427 megawatts, and its wind generation by 80 percent to 16,225 thousand megawatthours. California is second in installed wind capacity.

With Texas' significant increase, wind generation was responsible for four percent of total electricity generation in the state.

By the end of 2008, U.S. installed wind capacity had grown to 24,651 MW, enough to power more than 5 million homes based on their average household consumption in 2006.

The Texas plains continues to see rapid growth in wind farms, while more recently expansion has began offshore on the Gulf Coast. ☆

Installed Wind Capacity in megawatts (MW)			
YEAR	Texas	California	U.S.
2008	7,427	2,368	24,651
2007	4,296	2,439	16,596
2006	2,739	2,376	11,575
2005	1,995	2,150	9,149
2004	1,293	2,096	6,740
2003	1,293	2,043	6,374
2002	1,096	1,822	4,685
2001	1,096	1,714	4,261
2000	181	1,646	2,566
1999	180	1,646	2,500

Source: U.S. Department of Energy and the State Energy Conservation Office, 2011.

2008 Renewable Energy Net Generation of Electricity by Source

[in millions of kilowatt-hours (381,044 represents 381,044,000,000).]

State	Total	Hydroelectric	Biomass*	Wind	Wood and derived fuels
1. Washington	82,575	77,637	168	3,657	1,113
2. California	48,912	24,128	2,362	5,385	3,484
3. Oregon	37,228	33,805	131	2,575	717
4. New York	30,042	26,723	1,513	1,251	555
5. Texas	18,679	1,039	438	16,225	976
6. Montana	10,815	10,000	NA	593	111
7. Idaho	10,111	9,363	NA	207	455
8. Alabama	9,493	6,136	34	NA	3,324
9. Maine	8,515	4,457	258	132	3,669
10. Arizona	7,400	7,266	23	NA	76
United States	381,044	254,831	17,734	55,363	37,300

*NA Not Available. *Biomass includes landfill gas and municipal solid waste biogenic. It also, includes agriculture by-products. Source: Energy Information Administration, 2010.*

Texas Oil Production History

The table shows the year of oil or gas discovery in each county, oil production in 2009 and 2010 and total oil production from date of discovery to Jan. 1, 2011. **The 16 counties omitted have not produced oil.**

The table has been compiled by the Texas Almanac from information provided in past years by the Texas Mid-Continent Oil & Gas Assoc., which used data from the U.S. Bureau of Mines and the Texas state comptroller. Since 1970, production figures have been compiled from records of the Railroad Commission of Texas. The figures in the final column are cumulative of all previously published figures. The change in sources, due to different techniques, may create some discrepancies in year-to-year comparisons among counties.

County	Year of Discovery	Production in Barrels* 2009	Production in Barrels* 2010	Total Production to Jan. 1, 2011	County	Year of Discovery	Production in Barrels* 2009	Production in Barrels* 2010	Total Production to Jan. 1, 2011
Anderson	1928	712,854	678,046	304,181,804	Crockett	1925	5,441,176	5,240,866	393,451,460
Andrews	1929	23,613,175	25,548,644	2,927,582,902	Crosby	1955	606,457	638,782	27,824,891
Angelina	1936	17,104	14,993	954,329	Culberson	1953	96,112	152,328	25,430,069
Aransas	1936	346,734	235,063	87,333,875	Dallas	1986	0	0	231
Archer	1911	1,037,496	1,039,301	500,336,552	Dawson	1934	3,923,509	3,739,466	404,654,777
Atascosa	1917	601,783	867,311	154,098,364	Delta	1984	0	0	65,089
Austin	1915	484,515	822,492	117,455,298	Denton	1937	543,017	437,925	9,160,976
Bandera	1995	1,925	1,717	31,698	DeWitt	1930	835,046	1,890,716	71,941,231
Bastrop	1913	321,136	151,952	17,880,135	Dickens	1953	1,112,685	1,009,928	24,708,321
Baylor	1924	95,859	88,872	58,597,358	Dimmit	1943	971,832	2,524,637	113,183,036
Bee	1929	521,105	522,581	111,005,339	Donley	1967	344	259	1,643
Bell	1980	0	0	446	Duval	1905	1,277,420	1,128,445	593,896,863
Bexar	1889	119,959	109,645	36,536,793	Eastland	1917	315,268	261,699	158,457,078
Borden	1949	3,526,952	3,334,943	427,696,728	Ector	1926	20,292,107	22,147,145	3,204,742,134
Bosque	2006	18	43	189	Edwards	1946	5,000	17,922	564,062
Bowie	1944	61,048	64,512	6,821,441	Ellis	1953	1,056	847	842,044
Brazoria	1902	2,382,709	2,434,511	1,285,473,786	Erath	1917	46,418	24,946	2,223,690
Brazos	1942	1,766,489	2,238,580	147,867,475	Falls	1937	2,416	4,996	864,218
Brewster	1969	0	0	56	Fannin	1980	0	0	13,281
Briscoe	1982	430	62	4,046	Fayette	1943	1,130,760	1,269,151	159,465,996
Brooks	1935	971,806	859,396	176,591,306	Fisher	1928	777,132	792,072	252,408,079
Brown	1917	106,852	132,657	53,930,994	Floyd	1952	1,885	1,558	164,904
Burleson	1938	1,903,507	1,902,981	204,111,827	Foard	1929	99,886	108,632	24,669,423
Caldwell	1922	965,910	1,070,398	287,001,370	Fort Bend	1919	1,778,770	1,842,918	702,395,846
Calhoun	1935	448,091	339,145	106,651,457	Franklin	1936	407,827	322,458	179,145,075
Callahan	1923	221,488	229,761	87,179,639	Freestone	1916	203,929	209,866	46,362,297
Cameron	1944	701	765	471,048	Frio	1934	551,332	635,054	149,203,853
Camp	1940	204,244	195,419	30,335,711	Gaines	1935	24,639,011	24,619,538	2,329,958,921
Carson	1921	268,013	251,830	181,548,740	Galveston	1922	1,234,141	1,031,542	460,923,970
Cass	1936	282,719	274,601	115,868,808	Garza	1926	3,454,802	3,183,150	356,308,305
Chambers	1916	964,660	1,178,889	914,656,626	Glasscock	1925	3,956,867	4,779,871	289,033,624
Cherokee	1926	292,500	290,866	72,413,036	Goliad	1930	541,289	435,555	86,698,903
Childress	1961	31,876	23,610	1,722,461	Gonzales	1902	204,588	693,692	45,403,900
Clay	1917	612,313	556,240	207,850,657	Gray	1925	1,065,364	1,067,851	679,173,594
Cochran	1936	3,702,283	3,625,329	525,452,437	Grayson	1930	1,049,053	1,055,105	262,613,084
Coke	1942	664,925	803,327	226,619,824	Gregg	1931	2,524,329	2,490,077	3,301,753,093
Coleman	1902	249,764	248,347	96,248,163	Grimes	1952	188,658	292,308	19,293,205
Collin	1963	0	0	53,000	Guadalupe	1922	1,055,621	998,680	210,819,037
Collingswrth	1936	1,718	1,194	1,249,266	Hale	1946	2,510,105	2,351,209	191,689,369
Colorado	1932	452,897	404,811	43,731,231	Hamilton	1938	1,613	2,167	158,397
Comanche	1918	6,993	12,210	6,013,498	Hansford	1937	335,837	301,745	40,361,639
Concho	1940	374,048	340,637	28,338,622	Hardeman	1944	1,026,104	906,164	89,624,413
Cooke	1924	2,032,033	2,830,998	400,591,996	Hardin	1893	2,287,038	1,936,305	450,682,826
Coryell	1964	0	0	1,100	Harris	1905	1,719,181	1,547,816	1,385,008,087
Cottle	1955	154,104	111,607	5,355,216	Harrison	1928	1,260,619	1,096,630	96,203,429
Crane	1926	9,425,930	8,899,979	1,798,345,864					

*Total includes condensate production.

County	Year of Discovery	Production in Barrels*		Total Production to Jan. 1, 2011	County	Year of Discovery	Production in Barrels*		Total Production to Jan. 1, 2011
		2009	2010				2009	2010	
Hartley	1937	224,788	388,920	8,751,452	Medina	1901	100,012	97,612	11,279,502
Haskell	1929	313,927	367,083	118,526,574	Menard	1946	143,708	143,092	8,080,311
Hays	1956	0	0	296	Midland	1945	13,128,775	14,731,125	688,619,405
Hemphill	1955	1,792,308	1,759,881	46,156,034	Milam	1921	362,476	400,393	23,156,259
Henderson	1934	332,501	294,343	179,787,188	Mills	1982	0	0	28,122
Hidalgo	1934	2,669,960	2,107,818	126,580,501	Mitchell	1920	3,874,784	3,984,161	245,299,426
Hill	1929	1,340	1,379	78,809	Montague	1919	3,068,549	2,873,097	302,594,802
Hockley	1937	17,500,996	16,451,786	1,741,727,344	Montgomery	1931	1,242,458	1,135,852	781,324,546
Hood	1958	495,771	320,701	1,713,359	Moore	1926	311,211	278,504	31,623,547
Hopkins	1936	265,888	281,543	91,121,539	Morris	2004	1,778	1,399	12,959
Houston	1934	779,927	739,205	60,957,737	Motley	1957	30,623	31,285	11,180,698
Howard	1925	5,483,707	6,046,866	845,451,086	Nacgdoches	1866	451,228	358,199	6,264,812
Hudspeth	2008	0	0	59	Navarro	1894	372,193	313,774	220,356,814
Hunt	1942	0	0	2,024,660	Newton	1937	695,195	585,583	67,675,558
Hutchinson	1923	823,183	780,701	535,387,207	Nolan	1939	1,146,225	1,170,952	205,071,515
Irion	1928	2,422,079	2,489,645	112,984,495	Nueces	1930	959,442	986,988	568,989,010
Jack	1923	851,646	858,132	208,403,039	Ochiltree	1951	2,045,244	2,867,472	169,554,178
Jackson	1934	1,171,976	1,071,347	687,694,865	Oldham	1957	212,783	213,481	14,679,889
Jasper	1928	899,595	799,630	38,368,140	Orange	1913	1,126,370	1,143,486	163,608,689
Jeff Davis	1980	0	0	20,866	Palo Pinto	1902	654,138	477,480	25,800,673
Jefferson	1901	4,626,552	7,789,629	560,365,859	Panola	1917	2,382,906	2,113,629	106,294,759
Jim Hogg	1921	170,869	133,990	113,635,797	Parker	1942	318,397	254,046	4,413,503
Jim Wells	1931	176,746	162,690	463,597,036	Parmer	1963	0	0	144,000
Johnson	1962	58,531	39,983	389,181	Pecos	1926	11,975,325	10,926,629	1,823,576,540
Jones	1926	760,632	708,508	225,014,492	Polk	1930	1,874,001	1,459,452	133,268,196
Karnes	1930	464,891	2,215,609	112,359,848	Potter	1925	168,733	148,640	10,833,876
Kaufman	1948	91,549	99,773	25,030,362	Presidio	1980	0	0	4,377
Kenedy	1947	292,614	340,965	40,825,442	Rains	1955	3	0	148,900
Kent	1946	3,989,935	4,282,134	595,072,471	Reagan	1923	6,359,080	7,932,531	539,208,557
Kerr	1982	0	0	78,946	Real	2003	202	466	26,740
Kimble	1939	358	371	99,845	Red River	1951	114,625	96,904	8,553,435
King	1943	1,852,204	1,551,026	187,943,458	Reeves	1939	1,143,282	1,558,777	83,990,566
Kinney	1960	0	0	402	Refugio	1920	3,734,381	3,917,807	1,343,501,377
Kleberg	1919	334,432	321,280	338,828,029	Roberts	1945	1,291,221	1,343,759	53,637,174
Knox	1946	194,471	183,020	63,395,146	Robertson	1944	1,261,314	1,168,569	32,745,049
Lamb	1945	564,609	433,822	41,302,752	Runnels	1927	571,634	519,898	150,596,882
Lampasas	1985	0	0	111	Rusk	1930	2,879,903	2,556,580	1,845,415,039
La Salle	1940	397,612	874,331	30,034,286	Sabine	1981	4,137	12,151	4,943,326
Lavaca	1941	571,679	488,929	34,437,300	S.Augustine	1947	51,850	106,459	2,695,810
Lee	1939	1,147,304	1,053,061	141,431,462	San Jacinto	1940	396,555	398,656	27,851,493
Leon	1936	698,597	609,451	67,637,671	SanPatricio	1930	1,308,375	1,081,074	492,092,275
Liberty	1904	2,503,202	2,610,649	548,649,026	San Saba	1982	0	0	32,362
Limestone	1920	164,501	161,023	120,443,534	Schleicher	1934	456,218	442,718	90,486,596
Lipscomb	1956	2,440,483	2,161,401	69,757,655	Scurry	1923	15,404,325	14,695,034	2,123,298,371
Live Oak	1930	923,162	1,445,147	89,030,257	Shackelford	1910	713,564	679,448	186,310,849
Llano	1978	0	o	647	Shelby	1917	528,713	523,742	5,137,862
Loving	1921	1,593,395	1,634,800	118,610,724	Sherman	1938	82,646	68,443	9,804,778
Lubbock	1941	1,449,478	1,505,281	77,298,360	Smith	1931	1,344,250	1,325,145	273,260,134
Lynn	1950	266,713	249,924	20,510,695	Somervell	1978	12,147	13,078	40,180
Madison	1946	626,144	1,053,961	36,710,080	Starr	1929	2,438,097	1,929,793	308,014,437
Marion	1910	171,838	168,106	56,673,334	Stephens	1916	2,262,660	2,164,952	352,822,148
Martin	1945	10,525,792	12,448,122	356,635,357	Sterling	1947	1,172,149	1,076,566	94,801,030
Matagorda	1901	1,082,923	1,005,903	286,936,023	Stonewall	1938	1,000,014	1,068,261	268,123,398
Maverick	1929	1,487,880	1,072,949	60,313,729	Sutton	1948	104,215	110,833	8,325,013
McCulloch	1938	67,259	59,891	2,227,181	Swisher	1981	0	0	6
McLennan	1902	1,161	1,008	343,967	*Total includes condensate production.				
McMullen	1922	1,592,320	1,979,197	112,727,230					

| County | Year of Discovery | Production in Barrels* | | Total Production to Jan. 1, 2011 |
		2009	2010	
Tarrant	1969	42,345	32,585	183,598
Taylor	1929	394,099	410,385	147,084,598
Terrell	1952	151,952	118,286	10,074,774
Terry	1940	4,295,573	4,470,894	463,214,475
Throckmrton	1925	588,424	553,633	224,965,557
Titus	1936	453,356	442,757	213,993,000
Tom Green	1940	688,817	542,645	95,644,307
Travis	1934	1,814	2,061	762,750
Trinity	1946	76,130	67,058	1,314,820
Tyler	1937	3,122,768	2,779,908	60,520,276
Upshur	1931	547,505	499,325	290,877,279
Upton	1925	15,833,728	16,917,140	909,411,375
Uvalde	1950	0	0	1,814
Val Verde	1935	1,537	1,200	149,828
Van Zandt	1929	646,492	569,413	555,084,585
Victoria	1931	776,240	702,304	257,564,873
Walker	1934	3,663	3,373	548,593
Waller	1934	557,036	511,091	32,629,469
Ward	1928	8,832,876	10,205,409	797,544,479

| County | Year of Discovery | Production in Barrels* | | Total Production to Jan. 1, 2011 |
		2009	2010	
Washington	1915	375,556	408,863	34,046,978
Webb	1921	1,133,026	2,424,127	168,836,693
Wharton	1925	1,903,857	1,786,479	353,626,104
Wheeler	1910	3,624,501	4,756,965	116,307,086
Wichita	1910	2,252,250	2,280,112	840,400,046
Wilbarger	1915	655,406	660,263	267,666,230
Willacy	1936	829,133	766,311	118,782,445
Williamson	1915	10,216	9,648	9,595,908
Wilson	1941	233,703	258,096	50,431,918
Winkler	1926	3,603,116	3,297,318	1,095,794,838
Wise	1942	1,336,015	1,266,182	107,606,599
Wood	1940	3,164,298	3,369,379	1,222,292,415
Yoakum	1936	22,498,025	22,277,354	2,203,920,562
Young	1917	1,299,828	1,228,211	317,044,556
Zapata	1919	447,700	305,070	49,537,567
Zavala	1937	464,454	421,390	50,545,223

Source: Railroad Commission, 2009-10 production reports.

*Total includes condensate production.

Rig Counts and Wells Drilled by Year

| Year | Rotary rigs active* | | Permits | Texas wells completed | | Wells drilled** |
	Texas	U.S.	Texas	Oil	Gas	Texas
1982	994	3,117	41,224	16,296	6,273	27,648
1983	796	2,232	45,550	15,941	5,027	26,882
1984	850	2,428	37,507	18,716	5,489	30,898
1985	680	1,980	30,878	16,543	4,605	27,124
1986	313	964	15,894	10,373	3,304	18,707
1987	293	1,090	15,297	7,327	2,542	13,121
1988	280	936	† 13,493	6,441	2,665	12,261
1989	264	871	12,756	4,914	2,760	10,054
1990	348	1,009	14,033	5,593	2,894	11,231
1991	315	860	12,494	6,025	2,755	11,295
1992	251	721	12,089	5,031	2,537	9,498
1993	264	754	11,612	4,646	3,295	9,969
1994	274	775	11,030	3,962	3,553	9,299
1995	251	723	11,244	4,334	3,778	9,785
1996	283	779	12,669	4,061	4,060	9,747
1997	358	945	13,933	4,482	4,594	10,778
1998	303	827	9,385	4,509	4,907	11,057
1999	226	622	8,430	2,049	3,566	6,658
2000	343	918	12,021	3,111	4,580	8,854
2001	462	1,156	12,227	3,082	5,787	10,005
2002	338	830	9,716	3,268	5,474	9,877
2003	449	1,032	12,664	3,111	6,336	10,420
2004	506	1,192	14,700	3,446	7,118	11,587
2005	614	1,381	16,914	3,454	7,197	11,154
2006	746	1,649	18,952	4,761	8,534	12,764
2007	834	1,769	19,994	5,084	8,643	13,778
2008	898	1,880	24,073	6,208	10,361	16,615
2009	432	1,086	12,212	5,860	8,706	14,585
2010	659	1,541	18,029	5,392	4,071	9,477

Texas Railroad Commission. *Source for rig count: Baker Hughes Inc. This is an annual average from monthly reports.
†Totals shown for 1988 and after are number of drilling permits issued; data for previous years were total drilling applications received.
Wells drilled are oil and gas well **completions and dry holes drilled/plugged.

Top Oil Producing Counties since Discovery

There are 35 counties that have produced more than 500 million barrels of oil since discovery. The counties are ranked below. The column at right lists the number of regurlar producing oil wells in the county in February 2011.

Rank	County	Barrels	Oil Wells	Rank	County	Barrels	Oil Wells
1.	Gregg	3,301,753,093	3,268	19.	Wichita	840,400,046	5,507
2.	Ector	3,204,742,134	6,096	20.	Ward	797,544,479	3,021
3.	Andrews	2,927,582,902	7,597	21.	Montgomery	781,324,546	153
4.	Gaines	2,329,958,921	3,529	22.	Fort Bend	702,395,846	313
5.	Yoakum	2,203,920,562	3,525	23.	Midland	688,619,405	5,012
6.	Scurry	2,123,298,371	2,515	24.	Jackson	687,694,865	232
7.	Rusk	1,845,415,039	1,848	25.	Gray	679,173,594	2,788
8.	Pecos	1,823,576,540	2,961	26.	Kent	595,072,471	574
9.	Crane	1,798,345,864	4,207	27.	Duval	593,896,863	669
10.	Hockley	1,741,727,344	4,275	28.	Nueces	568,989,010	194
11.	Harris	1,385,008,087	317	29.	Jefferson	560,365,859	161
12.	Refugio	1,343,501,377	638	30.	Van Zandt	555,084,585	390
13.	Brazoria	1,285,473,786	292	31.	Liberty	548,649,026	693
14.	Wood	1,222,292,415	586	32.	Reagan	539,208,557	4,268
15.	Winkler	1,095,794,838	1,709	33.	Hutchinson	535,387,207	2,979
16.	Chambers	914,656,626	181	34.	Cochran	525,452,437	1,882
17.	Upton	909,411,375	3,398	35.	Archer	500,336,552	3,016
18.	Howard	845,451,086	3,455				

Source: Texas Railroad Commission.

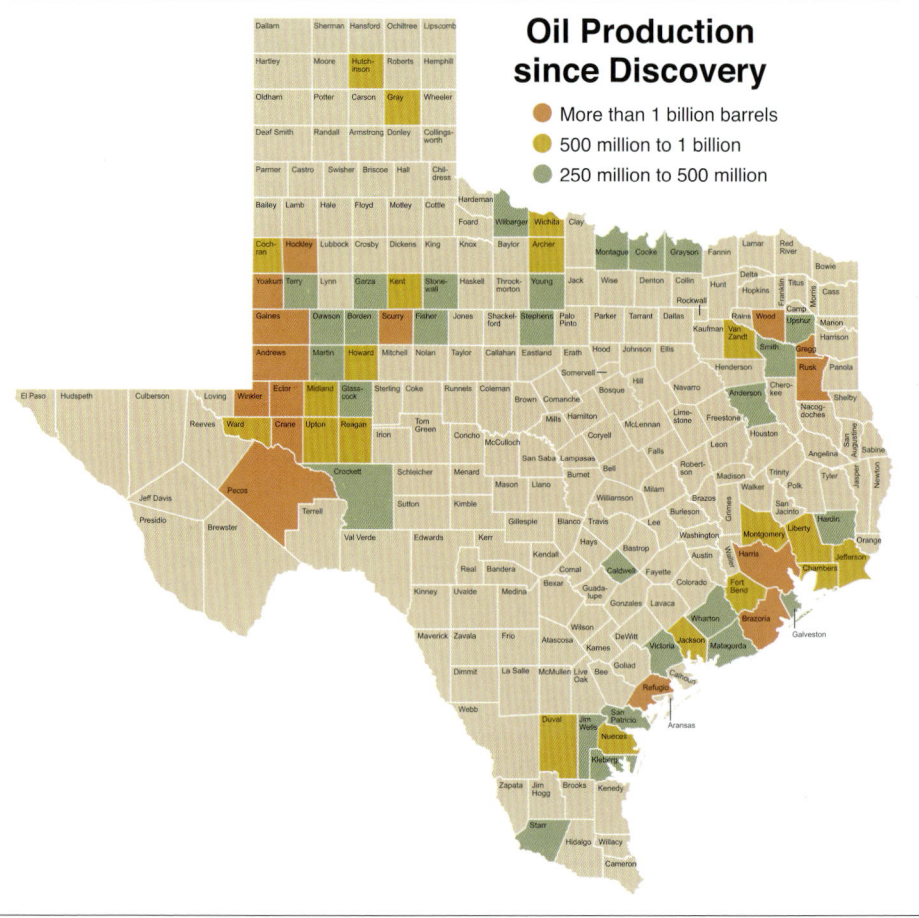

Oil Production since Discovery

- More than 1 billion barrels
- 500 million to 1 billion
- 250 million to 500 million

Oil and Gas Production by County, 2010

In 2010 in Texas, the total natural gas production from gas wells was 6,592,188,526 thousand cubic feet (MCF) and total crude oil production was 363,416,391 barrels (BBL). Total condensate was 53,389,679 barrels. Total casinghead production was 834,361,930 MCF. **Counties not listed in the chart below had no production in 2010.** *Source: Texas Railroad Commission.*

County	Oil (BBL)	Casing-head (MCF)	GW Gas (MCF)	Conden-sate (BBL)	County	Oil (BBL)	Casing-head (MCF)	GW Gas (MCF)	Conden-sate (BBL)
Anderson	623,285	3,223,202	4,994,149	54,761	Eastland	225,114	770,473	3,478,402	36,585
Andrews	25,531,505	33,225,953	1,835,207	17,139	Ector	22,139,872	41,081,909	7,164,022	7,273
Angelina	3,386	26,602	10,313,757	11,607	Edwards	17,036	0	12,647,475	886
Aransas	45,165	257,826	6,757,353	189,898	Ellis	847	0	11,103,261	0
Archer	1,039,169	415,503	17,057	132	Erath	3,376	66,011	8,004,170	21,570
Atascosa	825,537	387,479	5,072,889	41,774	Falls	4,996	0	0	0
Austin	729,486	329,067	5,907,445	93,006	Fayette	1,085,932	8,300,782	9,297,578	183,219
Bandera	1,692	0	153,675	25	Fisher	789,798	2,022,318	171,580	2,274
Bastrop	147,752	154,138	130,746	4,200	Floyd	1,558	0	0	0
Baylor	88,872	1	0	0	Foard	108,632	32,503	121,795	0
Bee	402,092	608,605	26,748,593	120,489	Fort Bend	1,637,408	2,256,650	12,202,537	205,510
Bexar	109,645	41	0	0	Franklin	299,630	166,884	1,321,795	22,828
Borden	3,334,943	3,437,707	0	0	Freestone	97,141	206,456	259,272,350	112,725
Bosque	0	0	551,261	43	Frio	632,270	561,833	1,245,627	2,784
Bowie	55,640	12,194	118,563	8,872	Gaines	24,585,692	20,205,402	12,027,585	33,846
Brazoria	1,668,920	2,256,048	26,261,745	765,591	Galveston	536,664	795,804	8,328,631	494,878
Brazos	2,172,686	7,085,506	5,164,918	65,894	Garza	3,183,150	580,774	0	0
Brooks	127,715	220,406	37,614,751	731,681	Glasscock	4,767,041	14,422043	1,002,655	12,830
Brown	130,777	387,846	986,104	1,880	Goliad	207,521	324,264	27,878,069	228,034
Burleson	1,850,062	8,189,829	2,036,903	52,919	Gonzales	686,192	586,036	739,107	7,500
Caldwell	1,070,398	368,207	11,158	0	Gray	1,056,033	2,470,402	8,103,001	11,818
Calhoun	167,763	183,539	6,543,717	171,382	Grayson	1,021,604	3,582,221	2,074,892	33,501
Callahan	225,960	286,323	845,722	3,801	Gregg	2,231,506	2,510,027	46,777,418	258,571
Cameron	610	156	133,086	155	Grimes	202,250	750,527	17,384,026	90,058
Camp	195,402	0	328,315	17	Guadalupe	998,680	71,570	84	0
Carson	245,547	1,594,207	11,518,110	6,283	Hale	2,351,209	1,294,808	0	0
Cass	258,707	405,835	742,809	15,894	Hamilton	1,383	12	135,107	784
Chambers	994,052	1,381,136	8,225,041	184,837	Hansford	281,805	1,004,344	17,991,515	19,940
Cherokee	167,736	254,187	25,378,917	123,130	Hardeman	906,164	180,778	59	0
Childress	23,610	0	0	0	Hardin	1,183,970	1,283,879	11,952,687	752,335
Clay	549,492	579,882	344,392	6,748	Harris	1,178,106	1,119,978	21,572,463	369,710
Cochran	3,624,134	2,144,916	210,141	1,195	Harrison	314,191	1,838,077	163,088,488	782,439
Coke	800,509	4,042,623	388,538	2,818	Hartley	388,920	0	1,922,687	0
Coleman	244,878	545,687	860,750	3,469	Haskell	367,038	23,857	0	0
Collingswth	1,194	17,193	1,207,894	0	Hemphill	155,762	1,919,384	135,940,270	1,604,119
Colorado	143,526	332,865	16,895,925	261,285	Henderson	262,128	6,649,433	18,229,582	32,215
Comanche	10,678	87,985	543,361	1,536	Hidalgo	52,615	162,760	152,765,493	2,055,203
Concho	388,364	295,836	567,491	2,273	Hill	1,351	0	26,541,533	28
Cooke	2,823,805	6,525,278	405,245	7,193	Hockley	16,449,829	10,503,523	79,648	1,957
Cottle	45,405	29,455	4,860,750	66,202	Hood	401	28,953	65,059,292	320,300
Crane	8,786,635	47,254,452	9,308,332	113,344	Hopkins	279,850	103,819	184,321	1,693
Crockett	4,778,089	4,567,005	89,245,259	462,777	Houston	669,735	287,403	7,110,266	69,470
Crosby	638,782	38,914	0	0	Howard	6,036,290	7,737,755	413,729	10,576
Culberson	150,368	172,290	3,959,952	1,960	Hutchinson	767,550	4,368,648	8,413,639	13,151
Dallas	0	0	6,313,239	0	Irion	2,455,028	12,193,615	2,972,643	34,617
Dawson	3,739,466	2,214,117	0	0	Jack	680,190	2,604,781	13,821,101	177,942
Denton	40,531	812,134	233,187,978	397,394	Jackson	689,399	1,014,803	13,011,050	318,948
DeWitt	159,277	71,950	44,057,619	1,731,439	Jasper	371,225	577,136	17,194,601	428,405
Dickens	1,009,928	65,388	0	0	Jefferson	892,893	1,236,338	114,074,844	6,896,736
Dimmit	1,576,445	3,015,765	9,645,275	948,192	Jim Hogg	26,966	6,144	12,586,154	107,024
Donley	0	0	14,669	259	Jim Wells	126,622	476,310	5,709,644	36,068
Duval	865,340	360,465	40,773,183	263,105	Johnson	0	0	531,780,474	39,983

County	Oil (BBL)	Casing-head (MCF)	GW Gas (MCF)	Condensate (BBL)
Jones	707,457	419,672	15,961	1,051
Karnes	1,405,468	1,649,783	15,499,768	810,141
Kaufman	99,773	27,942	0	0
Kenedy	72,654	797,429	47,370,955	268,311
Kent	4,282,134	7,116,105	0	0
Kimble	371	0	61,229	0
King	1,546,935	69,158	457,064	4,091
Kleberg	146,207	146,963	127,215,809	175,073
Knox	183,020	48	0	0
La Salle	344,077	999,868	38,419,316	530,254
Lamb	433,822	160,530	0	0
Lavaca	99,869	228,643	41,270,246	389,060
Lee	1,019,460	7,230,465	1,726,723	33,601
Leon	503,323	904,262	117,795,854	106,128
Liberty	1,369,013	1,140,780	27,953,655	1,241,636
Limestone	84,068	1,812	88,921,895	76,955
Lipscomb	1,282,877	10,040,909	52,687,443	928,524
Live Oak	378,647	350,623	32,365,727	1,066,500
Loving	1,444,353	3,403,063	77,539,600	190,447
Lubbock	1,505,281	81,692	0	0
Lynn	249,924	80,599	0	0
Madison	1,005,911	742,983	4,377,416	48,050
Marion	104,936	199,762	3,339,215	63,170
Martin	12,447,879	21,973,953	21,247	243
Matagorda	400,700	1,122,291	28,614,172	605,203
Maverick	1,061,097	303,332	2,836,845	11,852
McCulloch	59,891	473	4,139	0
McLennan	1,008	0	0	0
McMullen	1,525,272	4,183,584	24,406,666	453,925
Medina	97,612	1,467	93,114	0
Menard	143,092	9,781	10,890	0
Midland	14,436,040	37,482,000	10,222,448	295,085
Milam	400,076	315,100	79,325	317
Mills	0	0	8,211	0
Mitchell	3,984,161	483,630	0	0
Montague	2,827,307	19,730,377	404,160	45,790
Montgomery	1,069,870	1,641,785	6,392,682	65,982
Moore	275,482	2,152,092	29,793,724	3,022
Morris	1,399	0	0	0
Motley	31,285	0	0	0
Nacgdoches	6,316	134,733	113,727,303	351,883
Navarro	300,164	19,770	526,738	13,610
Newton	539,599	1,270,667	6,229,670	225,984
Nolan	1,169,100	1,724,863	391,812	1,852
Nueces	4889,974	1,281,929	27,974,339	497,014
Ochiltree	2,714,440	8,668,086	18,338,221	153,032
Oldham	213,481	0	130,127	0
Orange	425,801	1,056,878	11,314,632	717,685
Palo Pinto	379,298	6,123,645	14,413,240	98,182
Panola	276,003	2,495,414	285,808,088	1,837,626
Parker	8,174	526,064	99,659,818	245,872
Pecos	10,768,849	134,780,928	177,793,830	157,780
Polk	530,584	515,468	20,413,671	878,868
Potter	148,599	170,755	12,089,598	41
Rains	0	0	2,031,875	0
Reagan	7,904,977	36,870,926	1,438,230	27,554
Real	466	7,529	83,000	0
Red River	96,904	2,970	0	0
Reeves	1,509,286	2,775,269	27,551,559	49,491
Refugio	3,736,511	16,587,715	7,909,390	181,296
Roberts	571,347	4,827,680	53,412,034	772,412
Robertson	1,155,686	795,588	236,393,772	12,883
Runnels	518,980	2,264,804	274,547	918
Rusk	1,886,514	1,990,063	125,127,331	670,066
Sabine	12,151	31,900	344,317	0
S. Augustine	76,480	658,776	53,467,789	29,979
San Jacinto	38,354	83,449	9,827,237	360,302
San Patricio	405,310	744,333	17,355,234	675,764
Schleicher	372,612	1,445,459	11,494,634	70,106
Scurry	14,695,034	32,877,372	0	0
Shackelford	665,821	859,194	1,870,097	13,627
Shelby	408,301	4,738,958	68,070,085	115,441
Sherman	63,395	75,069	20,852,644	5,048
Smith	1,164,012	1,330,807	27,927,526	161,133
Somervell	0	0	8,288,057	13,078
Starr	332,432	763,338	96,430,714	1,597,361
Stephens	2,116,708	3,581,023	10,382,873	48,244
Sterling	1,042,277	7,530,793	4,123,062	34,289
Stonewall	1,068,261	453,545	0	0
Sutton	34,025	81,467	59,411,956	76,808
Tarrant	0	0	649,287,761	32,585
Taylor	410,040	182,608	102,124	345
Terrell	13,586	389,811	49,042,037	104,700
Terry	4,470,894	948,829	0	0
Throckmrton	552,266	1,078,591	235,501	1,367
Titus	442,757	1,619	0	0
Tom Green	526,109	1,229,290	1,574,045	16,536
Travis	2,061	0	0	0
Trinity	65,166	79,840	149,789	1,892
Tyler	305,063	455,968	27,502,687	2,474,845
Upshur	130,136	34,552	36,238,686	369,189
Upton	16,273,764	50,181,086	33,163,992	643,376
Uvalde	0	0	4,663	0
Val Verde	829	699	10,620,240	371
Van Zandt	563,062	452,913	2,959,889	6,351
Victoria	608,783	732,860	8,410,027	93,521
Walker	1,650	0	705,238	1,723
Waller	469,292	73,591	5,041,593	41,799
Ward	10,109,277	21,510,626	25,640,747	96,132
Washington	319,461	2,189,562	11,946,483	89,402
Webb	113,856	87,392	218,605,930	2,310,271
Wharton	980,581	825,419	46,359,152	805,898
Wheeler	1,345,352	5,363,425	181,526,179	3,411,613
Wichita	2,280,112	317,645	0	0
Wilbarger	660,263	49,262	6,563	0
Willacy	339,712	399,276	24,152,092	426,599
Williamson	9,648	0	0	0
Wilson	257,870	61,437	21,920	226
Winkler	3,236,747	11,828,230	20,126,667	60,571
Wise	326,011	5,264,337	230,334,313	940,171
Wood	3,340,215	2,850,463	4,956,459	29,164
Yoakum	22,274,994	23,359,907	652,199	2,360
Young	1,212,464	1,403,516	1,276,867	15,747
Zapata	22,391	25,360	226,448,812	282,679
Zavala	421,346	236,586	654,531	44

Source: Texas Railroad Commission.

Top Gas Producing Counties, 1993–2010

The top 37 natural gas-producing counties are listed in the chart below. The fourth column at the right lists the number of producing gas wells in the county in February 2011. Fifty-six counties have produced more than 500 billion cubic feet of natural gas since 1993 (see map). (**MCF** is thousand cubic feet.)

Rank	County	Gas (MCF)	Gas Wells	Rank	County	Gas (MCF)	Gas Wells
1.	Zapata	5,441,774,907	3,212	20.	Terrell	1,171,355,004	679
2.	Webb	5,003,753,701	4,934	21.	Duval	1,159,980,435	609
3.	Panola	4,681,558,491	5,236	22.	Limestone	1,114,511,278	1,157
4.	Hidalgo	4,450,434,062	1,486	23.	Brooks	1,096,032,006	430
5.	Pecos	3,410,880,542	1,398	24.	Wharton	1,021,579,514	483
6.	Freestone	3,134,085,856	2,970	25.	Gregg	1,018,429,793	1,021
7.	Starr	2,525,292,523	1,303	26.	Upshur	958,076,328	774
8.	Tarrant	2,330,645,025	2,821	27.	Nacogdoches	942,758,671	1,434
9.	Wise	2,258,604,003	4,146	28.	Moore	931,483,482	1,287
10.	Johnson	2,142,865,065	2,999	29.	Harris	864,389,692	158
11.	Crockett	2,099,171,746	5,901	30.	Nueces	829,112,652	728
12.	Hemphill	1,773,676,053	2,590	31.	Loving	814,611,852	228
13.	Denton	1,670,909,345	2,756	32.	Kenedy	801,845,120	215
14.	Rusk	1,636,237,884	2,661	33.	Ward	790,008,627	276
15.	Robertson	1,633,689,098	914	34.	Lipscomb	787,315,351	1,311
16.	Harrison	1,469,046,154	2,599	35.	Leon	761,745,670	524
17.	Lavaca	1,291,237,830	547	36.	Washington	758,242,121	174
18.	Sutton	1,276,108,385	6,000	37.	Goliad	731,519,529	510
19.	Wheeler	1,227,827,904	1,762		Source: Texas Railroad Commission.		

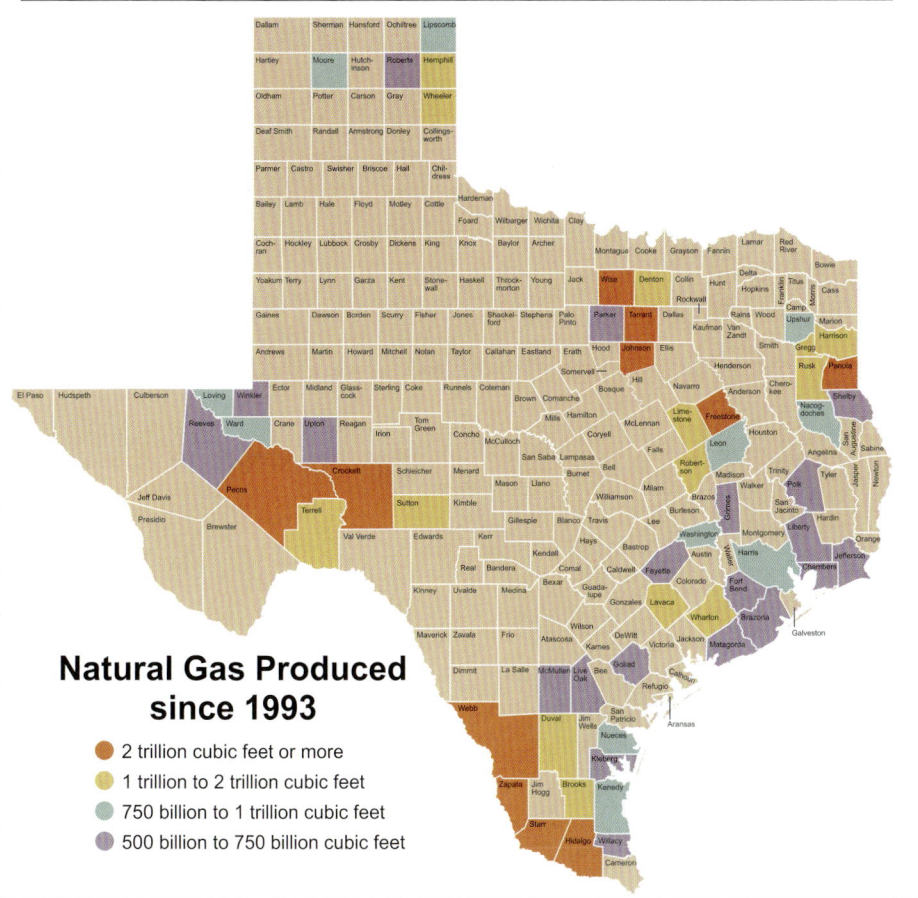

Natural Gas Produced since 1993

- 🟠 2 trillion cubic feet or more
- 🟡 1 trillion to 2 trillion cubic feet
- 🟢 750 billion to 1 trillion cubic feet
- 🟣 500 billion to 750 billion cubic feet

Offshore Production History – Oil and Gas

The cumulative offshore natural gas production as of March 1, 2011, was **4,089,103,585** thousand cubic feet (Mcf). The cumulative offshore oil production was **39,514,255** barrels.

Production in Recent Years

YEAR	Crude Oil BBL	Casing-head Mcf	Gas Well Gas Mcf	Conden-sate BBL
1996	908,743	724,651	68,159,547	212,048
1997	765,283	698,488	76,974,574	328,025
1998	586,999	611,882	60,080,329	233,044
1999	448,207	431,690	48,816,099	132,827
2000	548,046	335,415	44,086,237	220,309
2001	530,261	408,163	53,526,532	475,387
2002	1,144,389	2,404,329	54,988,278	405,577
2003	760,824	1,370,696	52,572,194	436,442
2004	442,462	325,345	46,539,253	396,096
2005	450,378	389,301	28,589,312	452,049
2006	310,625	262,049	26,870,964	295,034
2007	232,602	124,942	30,051,725	410,375
2008	210,897	120,986	42,029,079	393,594
2009	480,514	1,673,140	37,235,149	918,357

2010 Production by Area

Offshore Area	Crude Oil BBL	Casing-head Mcf	Gas Well Gas Mcf	Conden-sate BBL
Brazos-LB	0	0	2,174,490	1,719
Brazos-SB	0	0	391,626	281
Galveston-LB	0	0	2,323,557	338,658
Galveston-SB	0	0	26,007	0
High Island-LB	199,708	144,728	12,649,044	379,163
High Island-SB	25,645	0	0	0
Matagrda Is.-LB	234,183	987,331	3,795,915	7,052
Matagrda Is.-SB	0	0	502,797	6,090
Mustang Is.-LB	0	0	1,956,152	9,404
Mustang Is.-SB	17,544	27,728	3,427,971	90,504
N. Padre Is.-LB	0	0	329,678	14,759
Sabine Pass	0	0	0	0
Total	**477,080**	**1,159,787**	**27,577,237**	**843,630**

Offshore Areas

Based on a map of the Texas Railroad Commission.

Receipts by Texas from Tidelands

The Republic of Texas had proclaimed its Gulf boundaries as three marine leagues, recognized by international law as traditional national boundaries. These boundaries were never seriously questioned when Texas joined the Union in 1845. But, in 1930 a congressional resolution authorized the U.S. Attorney General to file suit to establish offshore lands as properties of the federal government. Congress returned the disputed lands to Texas in 1953, and the U.S. Supreme Court confirmed Texas' ownership in 1960. In 1978, the federal government also granted states a "fair and equitable" share of the revenues from offshore leases within three miles of the states' outermost boundary. States did not receive any such revenue until 1986.

The following table shows receipts from tidelands in the Gulf of Mexico by the Texas General Land Office to Aug. 31, 2009. It does not include revenue from bays and other submerged area owned by Texas. Source: General Land Office.

From	To	Total	Bonus	Rental	Royalty	Lease
6-09-1922	9-28-1945	$ 924,363.81	$ 814,055.70	$ 61,973.75	$ 48,334.36	...
9-29-1945	6-23-1947	296,400.30	272,700.00	7,680.00	16,020.30	...
6-24-1947	6-05-1950	7,695,552.22	7,231,755.48	377,355.00	86,441.74	...
6-06-1950	5-22-1953	55,095.04	—	9,176.00	45,919.04	...
5-23-1953	6-30-1958	54,264,553.11	49,788,639.03	3,852,726.98	623,187.10	...
7-01-1958	8-31-1959	771,064.75		143,857.00	627,207.75	...
9-01-1959	8-31-1960	983,335.32	257,900.00	98,226.00	627,209.32	...
9-01-1960	8-31-1961	3,890,800.15	3,228,639.51	68,578.00	593,582.64	...
9-01-1961	8-31-1962	1,121,925.09	297,129.88	127,105.00	697,690.21	...
9-01-1962	8-31-1963	3,575,888.64	2,617,057.14	177,174.91	781,656.59	...
9-01-1963	8-31-1964	3,656,236.75	2,435,244.36	525,315.00	695,677.39	...
9-01-1964	8-31-1965	54,654,576.96	53,114,943.63	755,050.12	784,583.21	...
9-01-1965	8-31-1966	22,148,825.44	18,223,357.84	3,163,475.00	761,992.60	...
9-01-1966	8-31-1967	8,469,680.86	3,641,414.96	3,711,092.65	1,117,173.25	...
9-01-1967	8-31-1968	6,305,851.00	1,251,852.50	2,683,732.50	2,370,266.00	...
9-01-1968	8-31-1969	6,372,268.28	1,838,118.33	1,491,592.50	3,042,557.45	...
9-01-1969	8-31-1970	10,311,030.48	5,994,666.32	618,362.50	3,698,001.66	...
9-01-1970	8-31-1971	9,969,629.17	4,326,120.11	726,294.15	4,917,214.91	...
9-01-1971	8-31-1972	7,558,327.21	1,360,212.64	963,367.60	5,234,746.97	...
9-01-1972	8-31-1973	9,267,975.68	3,701,737.30	920,121.60	4,646,116.78	...
9-01-1973	8-31-1974	41,717,670.04	32,981,619.28	1,065,516.60	7,670,534.16	...
9-01-1974	8-31-1975	27,321,536.62	5,319,762.85	2,935,295.60	19,066,478.17	...
9-01-1975	8-31-1976	38,747,074.09	6,197,853.00	3,222,535.84	29,326,685.25	...
9-01-1976	8-31-1977	84,196,228.27	41,343,114.81	2,404,988.80	40,448,124.66	...
9-01-1977	8-31-1978	118,266,812.05	49,807,750.45	4,775,509.92	63,683,551.68	...
9-01-1978	8-31-1979	100,410,268.68	34,578,340.94	7,318,748.40	58,513,179.34	...
9-01-1979	8-31-1980	200,263,803.03	34,733,270.02	10,293,153.80	155,237,379.21	...
9-01-1980	8-31-1981	219,126,876.54	37,467,196.97	13,100,484.25	168,559,195.32	...
9-01-1981	8-31-1982	250,824,581.69	27,529,516.33	14,214,478.97	209,080,586.39	...
9-01-1982	8-31-1983	165,197,734.83	10,180,696.40	12,007,476.70	143,009,561.73	...
9-01-1983	8-31-1984	152,755,934.29	32,864,122.19	8,573,996.87	111,317,815.23	...
9-01-1984	8-31-1985	140,568,090.79	32,650,127.75	6,837,603.70	101,073,959.34	...
9-01-1985	8-31-1986	516,503,771.05	6,365,426.23	4,241,892.75	78,289,592.27	$427,606,859.83
9-01-1986	8-31-1987	60,066,571.05	4,186,561.63	1,933,752.50	44,691,907.22	9,254,349.70
9-01-1987	8-31-1988	56,875,069.22	14,195,274.28	1,817,058.90	28,068,202.53	12,794,533.51
9-01-1988	8-31-1989	61,793,380.04	12,995,892.74	1,290,984.37	35,160,568.40	12,345,934.53
9-01-1989	8-31-1990	68,701,751.51	7,708,449.54	1,289,849.87	40,331,537.06	19,371,915.04
9-01-1990	8-31-1991	90,885,856.99	3,791,832.77	1,345,711.07	70,023,601.01	15,724,712.14
9-01-1991	8-31-1992	51,154,511.34	4,450,850.00	1,123,585.54	26,776,191.35	18,803,884.45
9-01-1992	8-31-1993	60,287,712.60	3,394,230.00	904,359.58	34,853,679.68	21,135,443.34
9-01-1993	8-31-1994	57,825,043.59	3,570,657.60	694,029.30	32,244,987.95	21,315,368.74
9-01-1994	8-31-1995	62,143,227.78	8,824,722.93	674,479.79	34,691,023.35	17,951,001.71
9-01-1995	8-31-1996	68,166,645.51	13,919,246.80	1,102,591.39	32,681,315.73	20,463,491.59
9-01-1996	8-31-1997	90,614,935.93	22,007,378.46	1,319,614.78	41,605,792.50	25,682,150.19
9-01-1997	8-31-1998	104,016,006.75	36,946,312.49	2,070,802.90	38,760,320.91	26,238,570.45
9-01-1998	8-31-1999	53,565,810.30	5,402,171.00	2,471,128.47	23,346,515.93	22,345,994.90
9-01-1999	8-31-2000	55,465,763.99	3,487,563.84	2,171,636.35	24,314,241.99	25,492,320.85
9-01-2000	8-31-2001	68,226,347.58	9,963,608.68	1,830,378.11	23,244,034.74	33,188,326.05
9-01-2001	8-31-2002	30,910,283.91	9,286,015.20	1,545,583.01	13,369,771.56	6,708,914.14
9-01-2002	8-31-2003	50,881,515.90	15,152,092.40	1,071,377.60	19,648,641.39	15,009,404.51
9-01-2003	8-31-2004	54,379,791.20	14,448,555.70	1,094,201.41	25,199,635.21	13,637,398.88
9-01-2004	8-31-2005	53,594,809.87	9,148,220.20	1,624,666.50	32,406,328.78	10,415,594.39
9-01-2005	8-31-2006	60,829,271.63	22,565,845.14	1,605,090.30	23,287,994.53	13,370,341.66
9-01-2006	8-31-2007	52,513,621.85	15,879,744.44	2,022,859.80	18,785,626.55	15,825,351.06
9-01-2007	8-31-2008	86,705,980.28	4,632,175.50	1,485,080.97	68,408,943.01	12,179,780.80
9-01-2008	8-31-2009	65,835,625.76	3,896,795.20	1,020,204.33	53,166,364.50	7,752,261.73
Totals		$3,773,626,896.94	$762,268,579.45	$144,984,965.30	$2,001,759,447.90	$824,613,904.19
Inside three-mile line		$ 516,162,336.77	$178,397,971.53	$38,478,525.13	$299,285,840.11	0
Between three-mile and three marine-league line		$2,390,025,290.30	$581,218,523.53	$106,333,158.98	$1,702,473,607.79	0
Outside three marine-league line		$ 827,439,269.77	$ 2,652,084.39	$ 173,281.19	0	$824,613,904.19

Petroleum Production and Income in Texas

Year	Crude Oil				Natural Gas		
	Production (thousand barrels)	Value (add 000)	Average Price per barrel (nominal)	*Average price per barrel (2005 $)	Production (million cubic feet)	Value (add 000)	Average Price (cents per **MCF)
1915	24,943	$ 13,027	$ 0 .52	NA	13,324	$ 2,594	19.5
1925	144,648	262,270	1.81	NA	134,872	7,040	5.2
1935	392,666	367,820	0.94	NA	642,366	13,233	2.1
1945	754,710	914,410	1.21	NA	1,711,401	44,839	2.6
1955	1,053,297	2,989,330	2.84	NA	4,730,798	378,464	8.0
1965	1,000,749	2,962,119	2.96	NA	6,636,555	858,396	12.9
1970	1,249,697	4,104,005	3.28	NA	8,357,716	1,203,511	14.4
1971	1,222,926	4,261,775	3.48	NA	8,550,705	1,376,664	16.1
1972	1,301,685	4,536,077	3.48	NA	8,657,840	1,419,886	16.4
1973	1,294,671	5,157,623	3.98	NA	8,513,850	1,735,221	20.4
1974	1,262,126	8,773,003	6.95	NA	8,170,798	2,541,118	31.1
1975	1,221,929	9,336,570	7.64	NA	7,485,764	3,885,112	51.9
1976	1,189,523	10,217,702	8.59	NA	7,191,859	5,163,755	71.8
1977	1,137,880	9,986,002	8.78	$ 22.73	7,051,027	6,367,077	90.3
1978	1,074,050	9,980,333	9.29	23.00	6,548,184	6,515,443	99.5
1979	1,018,094	12,715,994	12.65	28.91	7,174,623	8,509,103	118.6
1980	977,436	21,259,233	21.84	47.74	7,115,889	10,673,834	150.0
1981	945,132	32,692,116	35.06	67.14	7,050,207	12,598,712	178.7
1982	923,868	29,074,126	31.77	57.33	6,497,678	13,567,151	208.8
1983	876,205	22,947,814	29.35	50.95	5,643,183	14,672,275	260.0
1984	874,079	25,138,520	28.87	48.31	5,864,224	13,487,715	230.0
1985	860,300	23,159,286	26.80	43.52	5,805,098	12,665,114	218.0
1986	813,620	11,976,488	14.73	23.40	5,663,491	8,778,410	155.0
1987	754,213	13,221,345	17.55	27.10	5,516,224	7,612,389	138.0
1988	727,928	10,729,660	14.71	21.96	5,702,643	7,983,700	140.0
1989	679,575	12,123,624	17.81	25.62	5,595,190	8,113,026	145.0
1990	672,081	15,047,902	22.37	30.98	5,533,771	8,281,372	149.7
1991	672,810	12,836,080	19.04	25.47	5,509,990	7,713,986	140.0
1992	642,059	11,820,306	18.32	23.94	5,436,408	8,643,888	159.0
1993	572,600	9,288,800	16.19	20.70	5,606,498	7,365,800	131.4
1994	533,900	7,977,500	14.98	18.76	5,675,748	6,220,300	109.6
1995	503,200	8,177,700	16.38	20.09	5,672,105	5,305,200	093.8
1996	478,100	9,560,800	20.31	24.44	5,770,255	6,945,000	120.4
1997	464,900	8,516,800	18.66	22.07	5,814,745	8,134,200	139.9
1998	440,600	5,472,400	12.28	14.36	5,772,080	6,362,900	110.2
1999	337,100	5,855,800	17.29	19.93	5,538,929	6,789,700	122.6
2000	348,900	10,037,300	28.60	32.26	5,645,972	12,837,600	227.4
2001	325,500	7,770,500	23.41	25.82	5,668,602	13,708,700	241.8
2002	335,600	8,150,400	23.77	25.80	5,611,958	9,840,800	175.4
2003	333,300	9,708,600	29.13	30.96	5,671,689	14,797,800	260.9
2004	327,910	12,762,650	38.79	40.08	5,817,227	17,077,700	293.6
2005	327,600	12,744,600	52.61	52.61	5,700,613	16,399,400	287.7
2006	314,600	19,353,500	61.31	59.38	6,077,786	23,500,800	386.7
2007	311,830	21,341,100	68.30	64.30	6,421,375	22,968,420	357.7
2008	315,896	30,409,170	96.85	89.28	7,271,815	34,415,890	473.3
2009	349,391	18,455,530	57.40	$ 52.29	7,573,033	12,167,800	160.7
2010	363,416	$ 14,309,300	$ 76.23	NA	7,426,550	$ 7,283,300	098.1

*In chained (2005) dollars, as calculated by the federal Energy Information Administration. (NA, not available.) **MCF (thousand cubic feet).

Sources: Previously from the Texas Railroad Commission, Texas Mid-Continent Oil & Gas Association and, beginning in 1979, data are from Department of Energy. Data since 1993 are from the state comptroller. DOE figures do not include gas that is vented or flared or used for pressure maintenance and repressuring, but do include non-hydrocarbon gases.

Nonpetroleum Minerals

Source: U.S. Geological Survey and the Texas Bureau of Economic Geology.

There are many nonpetroleum, or nonfuel, minerals found in Texas. Some are currently mined, and others may have a potential for future development. Still others are minor occurrences only.

Although they are overshadowed by the petroleum, natural gas, and natural gas liquids that are produced in the state, many of the nonpetroleum minerals are, nonetheless, important to the economy. In 2007, nonfuel minerals were valued at **an estimated $3.24 billion,** representing an 7.6 percent increase from the $3.01 billion in value for 2006 and ranking Texas seventh in overall U.S. production.

The **Bureau of Economic Geology,** which functions as the state geological survey of Texas, revised the following information about nonpetroleum minerals for this edition of the Texas Almanac. Publications of the Bureau, on file in many libraries or available on the Internet, contain more detailed information. Among the items available is the Bureau map, "Mineral Resources of Texas," showing locations of resource access of many nonpetroleum minerals.

A catalog of Bureau publications is also available free on request from the Bureau Publications Sales, University Station, Box X, Austin, TX 78713-7508; (512) 471-1534. On the Web: **www.beg.utexas.edu/.**

Texas' nonpetroleum minerals are as follows:

ALUMINUM — No aluminum ores are mined in Texas, but three Texas plants process aluminum materials in one or more ways. Plants in San Patricio and Calhoun counties produce **aluminum oxide (alumina)** from imported raw ore **(bauxite),** and a plant in Milam County

reduces the oxide to aluminum.

ASBESTOS — Small occurrences of amphibole-type asbestos have been found in the state. In West Texas, **richterite,** a white, long-fibered amphibole, is associated with some of the **talc deposits** northwest of **Allamoore** in Hudspeth County. Another type, **tremo-lite,** has been found in the **Llano Uplift** of Central Texas where it is associated with **serpentinite** in eastern Gillespie and western Blanco counties. No asbestos is mined in Texas.

ASPHALT (Native) — Asphalt-bearing Cretaceous limestones crop out in Burnet, Kinney, Pecos, Reeves, Uvalde, and other counties. The most significant deposit is in southwestern Uvalde County, where asphalt occurs naturally in pore spaces of the Anacacho Limestone. The material is quarried and used extensively as **road-paving material.** Asphalt-bearing sandstones occur in Anderson, Angelina, Cooke, Jasper, Maverick, Montague, Nacogdoches, Uvalde, Zavala, and other counties.

BARITE — Deposits of a heavy, nonmetallic mineral, barite (barium sulphate), have been found in many localities, including Baylor, Brown, Brewster, Culberson, Gillespie, Howard, Hudspeth, Jeff Davis, Kinney, Llano, Live Oak, Taylor, Val Verde, and Webb counties. During the 1960s, there was small, intermittent production in the **Seven Heart Gap** area of the **Apache Mountains** in Culberson County, where barite was mined from open pits. Most of the deposits are known to be relatively small, but the Webb County deposit has not been evaluated. Grinding plants, which prepare barite mined outside of Texas for use chiefly as a **weighting agent** in well-drilling muds and as a **filler,** are located in Brownsville, Corpus Christi, El Paso, Galena Park, Galveston,

Nonfuel Mineral Production and Value

*Production as measured by mine shipments, sales, or marketable production, including consumption by producers. Production is in **thousand metric tons** and value is in **thousand dollars.***

MINERAL	2005 Production	2005 Value	2006 Production	2006 Value	2007 Production	2007 Value
Cement:						
Masonry	395	$ 48,500*	382	$ 50,700*	368	$ 52,100*
Portland	11,600	951,000*	11,300	1,070,000*	10,900	1,060,000*
Clays:						
Ball	W	7,730	W	W	W	W
Bentonite	W	W	71	4,000 r	64	3,730
Common	2,340	8,680	2,360	12,600	1,950	12,100
Gemstones, natural	NA	201	NA	202	NA	202
Gypsum, crude	824 r	9,520 r	1,010 r	10,200 r	1,180	8,200
Lime	1,610	112,000	1,650	130,000	1,620	132,000
Salt	9,600	118,000	9,570	132,000	8,950	143,000
Sand and gravel:						
Construction	80,700	472,000	99,500	603,000	95,400	651,000
Industrial	2,840	114,000	1,530	65,600	3,280	123,000
Stone:						
Crushed	137,000	820,000	139,000 r	853,000 r	145,000	972,000
Dimension	44	12,200	31	12,600	44	13,900
‡Combined values	§	41,500	§	68,200	§	72,100
**Total Texas Values	§	$2,710,000 r	§	$3,010,000 r	§	$3,240,000

* *Estimated.* r*Revised.* **NA:** *Not available.* **W:** *Withheld to avoid disclosing company proprietary data. Withheld values are included in "Combined values."* § *Not applicable.* ‡ *Combined values of brucite, clays (fuller's earth, kaolin), helium (crude, Grade–A), talc (crude), zeolites, and values indicated by symbol W.* ***Data are rounded to no more than three significant digits; may not add to totals shown.*

and Houston.

BASALT (TRAP ROCK) — Masses of basalt — a hard, dark-colored, fine-grained igneous rock — crop out in Kinney, Travis, Uvalde, and several other counties along the **Balcones Fault Zone,** and also in the Trans-Pecos area of West Texas. Basalt is quarried near Knippa in Uvalde County for use as **road-building material, railroad ballast, and other aggregate.**

BENTONITE (see **CLAYS**).

BERYLLIUM — Occurrences of beryllium minerals at several Trans-Pecos localities have been recognized for several years.

BRINE (see also **SALT, SODIUM SULPHATE**) — Many wells in Texas produce brine by solution mining of subsurface salt deposits, mostly in West Texas counties such as Andrews, Crane, Ector, Loving, Midland, Pecos, Reeves, Ward, and others. These wells in the Permian Basin dissolve salt from the Salado Formation, an enormous salt deposit that extends in the subsurface from north of the Big Bend northward to Kansas, has an east-west width of 150 to 200 miles, and may have several hundred feet of net salt thickness. The majority of the brine is used in the petroleum industry, but it also is used in water softening, the chemical industry, and other uses. Three Gulf Coast counties, Fort Bend, Duval, and Jefferson, have brine stations that produce from salt domes.

BUILDING STONE (DIMENSION STONE) — **Granite** and **limestone** currently are quarried for use as dimension stone. The granite quarries are located in Burnet, Gillespie, Llano, and Mason counties; the limestone quarries are in Shackelford and Williamson counties. Past production of limestone for use as dimension stone has been reported in Burnet, Gillespie, Jones, Tarrant, Travis, and several other counties. There also has been production of **sandstone** in various counties for use as dimension stone.

CEMENT MATERIALS — Cement is currently manufactured in Bexar, Comal, Dallas, Ector, Ellis, Hays, McLennan, Nolan, and Potter counties. Many of these plants utilize Cretaceous limestones and shales or clays as raw materials for the cement. On the Texas High Plains, a cement plant near Amarillo uses impure **caliche** as the chief raw material. Iron oxide, also a constituent of cement, is available from the iron ore deposits of East Texas and from smelter slag. **Gypsum,** added to the cement as a retarder, is found chiefly in North-Central Texas, Central Texas, and the Trans-Pecos area.

CHROMIUM — Chromite-bearing rock has been found in several small deposits around the margin of the Coal Creek **serpentinite** mass in northeastern Gillespie County and northwestern Blanco County. Exploration has not revealed significant deposits.

CLAYS — Texas has an abundance and variety of ceramic and non-ceramic clays and is one of the country's leading producers of clay products.

Almost any kind of clay, ranging from common clay used to make ordinary brick and tile to clays suitable for manufacture of specialty whitewares, can be used for ceramic purposes. **Fire clay** suitable for use as **refractories** occurs chiefly in East and North-Central Texas; **ball clay,** a high-quality plastic ceramic clay, is found locally in East Texas.

Ceramic clay suitable for quality structural clay products, such as **structural building brick, paving brick, and drain tile,** is especially abundant in East and North-Central Texas. Common clay suitable for use in the manufacture of cement and ordinary brick is found in most counties of the state. Many of the Texas clays will expand or bloat upon rapid firing and are suitable for the manufacture of lightweight aggregate, which is used mainly in concrete blocks and highway surfacing.

Nonceramic clays are utilized without firing. They are used primarily as **bleaching and absorbent clays, fillers, coaters, additives, bonding clays, drilling muds, catalysts,** and potentially as sources of alumina. Most of the nonceramic clays in Texas are **bentonites** and **fuller's earth.** These occur extensively in the Coastal Plain and locally in the High Plains and Big Bend areas. **Kaolin clays** in parts of East Texas are potential sources of such nonceramic products as **paper coaters and fillers, rubber fillers, and drilling agents.** Relatively high in alumina, these clays also are a potential source of metallic aluminum.

COAL (see also **LIGNITE**) — **Bituminous coal,** which occurs in North-Central, South, and West Texas, was a significant energy source in Texas prior to the large-scale development of oil and gas. During the period from 1895–1943, Texas mines produced more than 25 million tons of coal. The mines were inactive for many years, but the renewed interest in coal as a major energy source prompted a revaluation of Texas' coal deposits. In the late 1970s, bituminous coal production resumed in the state on a limited scale when mines were opened in Coleman, Erath, and Webb counties.

Much of the state's bituminous coal occurs in North-Central Texas. Deposits are found there in Pennsylvanian rocks within a large area that includes Coleman, Eastland, Erath, Jack, McCulloch, Montague, Palo Pinto, Parker, Throckmorton, Wise, Young, and other counties. Before the general availability of oil and gas, underground coal mines near **Thurber, Bridgeport, Newcastle, Strawn,** and other points annually produced significant coal tonnages. Preliminary evaluations indicate substantial amounts of coal may remain in the North-Central Texas area. The coal seams there are generally no more than 30 inches thick and are commonly covered by well-consolidated overburden. Ash and sulphur content are high. Beginning in 1979, two bituminous coal mine operations in North-Central Texas — one in southern Coleman County and one in northwestern Erath County — produced coal to be used as fuel by the cement industry. Neither mine is currently operating.

In South Texas, bituminous coal occurs in the Eagle Pass district of Maverick County, and bituminous **cannel coal** is present in the **Santo Tomas district** of Webb County. The Eagle Pass area was a leading coal-producing district in Texas during the late 1800s and early 1900s. The bituminous coal in that area, which occurs in the Upper Cretaceous Olmos Formation, has a high ash content and a moderate moisture and sulfur content. According to reports, Maverick County coal beds range from four to seven feet thick.

The **cannel coals** of western Webb County occur near the Rio Grande in middle Eocene strata. They were mined for more than 50 years and used primarily as a boiler fuel. Mining ceased from 1939 until 1978, when a surface mine was opened 30 miles northwest of Laredo to produce cannel coal for use as fuel in the cement industry and for export. An additional mine has since been opened in that county. Tests show that the coals of the Webb County Santo Tomas district have a high hydrogen content and yield significant amounts of gas and oil when distilled. They also have a high sulfur content. A potential use might be as a source of various petrochemical products.

Coal deposits in the Trans-Pecos country of West Texas include those in the Cretaceous rocks of the Terlingua area of Brewster County, the Eagle Spring area of Hudspeth County, and the **San Carlos** area of Presidio County. The coal deposits in these areas are believed to have relatively little potential for development as a fuel. They have been sold in the past as a soil amendment (see **LEONARDITE**).

COPPER — Copper minerals have been found in

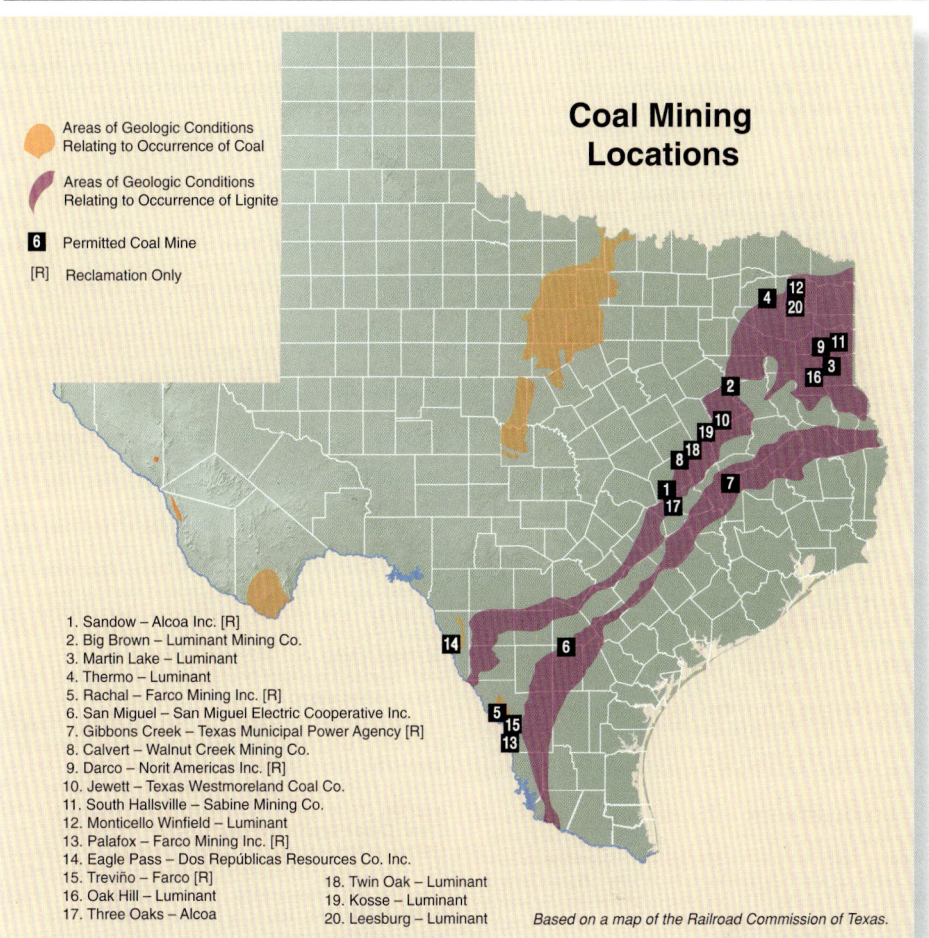

Coal Mining Locations

- Areas of Geologic Conditions Relating to Occurrence of Coal
- Areas of Geologic Conditions Relating to Occurrence of Lignite
- **6** Permitted Coal Mine
- [R] Reclamation Only

1. Sandow – Alcoa Inc. [R]
2. Big Brown – Luminant Mining Co.
3. Martin Lake – Luminant
4. Thermo – Luminant
5. Rachal – Farco Mining Inc. [R]
6. San Miguel – San Miguel Electric Cooperative Inc.
7. Gibbons Creek – Texas Municipal Power Agency [R]
8. Calvert – Walnut Creek Mining Co.
9. Darco – Norit Americas Inc. [R]
10. Jewett – Texas Westmoreland Coal Co.
11. South Hallsville – Sabine Mining Co.
12. Monticello Winfield – Luminant
13. Palafox – Farco Mining Inc. [R]
14. Eagle Pass – Dos Repúblicas Resources Co. Inc.
15. Treviño – Farco [R]
16. Oak Hill – Luminant
17. Three Oaks – Alcoa
18. Twin Oak – Luminant
19. Kosse – Luminant
20. Leesburg – Luminant

Based on a map of the Railroad Commission of Texas.

Mine Production (in short tons)

Mine	2008	Cumulative
Sandow	0	268,255,593
Big Brown	3,608,723	292,651,358
Martin Lake	7,146,063	481,792,418
Monticello-Thermo	1,764,648	53,718,837
Rachal	0	1,819,465
San Miguel	3,078,762	137,382,477
Gibbons Creek	0	85,957,570
Calvert	2,121,961	51,664,725
Darco	0	13,099,767
Jewett	6,490,558	285,295,890
South Hallsville	4,054,916	132,817,424
Monticello-Winfield	3,019,319	503,265,431
Palafox	0	10,480,075
Eagle Pass	0	0
Treviño	0	1,573,110
Oak Hill	4,311,076	164,330,644
Three Oaks	3,754,012	17,426,727
Twin Oak	0	236
Kosse	802,074	998,880
Leesburg	0	0
Little Bull Creek (Coleman Co.)	No longer permitted	857,864
Powell Bend (Bastrop Co.)	No longer permitted	3,139,750
Thurber (Erath Co.)	No longer permitted	465,984
Statewide total	40,152,112	2,507,454,209
Lignite for Electricity	40,152,112	2,479,251,903

Source: Railroad Commission of Texas, 2009.

Coal Production by State, 2009
(million short tons)

Total	United States	1,074.9
1.	Wyoming	431.1
2.	West Virginia	137.1
3.	Kentucky	107.3
4.	Pennsylvania	58.0
5.	Montana	39.5
6.	Indiana	35.7
7.	**Texas**	**35.1**

Source: U.S. Energy Information Administration.

Texas Coal Consumption
(million tons)

Year	Total	Percent from out of state
2001	96.89	52.9%
2002	99.32	55.0%
2003	104.54	53.9%
2004	105.92	56.7%
2005	105.33	56.7%
2006	103.76	56.1%
2007	104.78	60.1%

Source: U.S. Energy Information Administration.

the **Trans-Pecos** area of West Texas, in the **Llano Uplift** area of Central Texas, and in redbed deposits of North Texas. No copper has been mined in Texas during recent years, and the total copper produced in the state has been relatively small. Past attempts to mine the North Texas and Llano Uplift copper deposits resulted in small shipments.

Practically all the copper production in the state has been from the **Van Horn–Allamoore** district of Culberson and Hudspeth counties in the Trans-Pecos area. Chief output was from the **Hazel copper-silver mine** of Culberson County that yielded over 1 million pounds of copper during 1891–1947. Copper ores and concentrates from outside of Texas are processed at **smelters** in El Paso and Amarillo.

CRUSHED STONE — Texas is among the leading states in the production of crushed stone. Most production consists of **limestone;** other kinds of crushed stone produced in the state include **basalt (trap rock), dolomite, granite, marble, rhyolite, sandstone, and serpentinite.** Large tonnages of crushed stone are used as **aggregate** in concrete, as **road material,** and in the manufacture of cement and lime. Some is used as **riprap, terrazzo, roofing chips, filter material, fillers,** as well as other purposes.

DIATOMITE (DIATOMACEOUS EARTH) — Diatomite is a very lightweight siliceous material consisting of the remains of microscopic aquatic plants (diatoms). It is used chiefly as a **filter and filler;** other uses are for **thermal insulation,** as an **abrasive,** as an **insecticide carrier,** as a **lightweight aggregate,** and for other purposes. The diatomite was deposited in shallow, freshwater lakes that were present in the High Plains during portions of the Pliocene and Pleistocene epochs. Deposits have been found in Armstrong, Crosby, Dickens, Ector, Hartley, and Lamb counties. No diatomite is mined in Texas.

DOLOMITE ROCK — Dolomite rock, which consists largely of the mineral dolomite (calcium-magnesium carbonate), commonly is associated with limestone in Texas. Areas in which dolomite rock occurs include Central Texas, the Callahan Divide, and parts of the Edwards Plateau, High Plains, and West Texas. Some of the principal deposits of dolomite rock are found in Bell, Brown, Burnet, Comanche, Edwards, El Paso, Gillespie, Lampasas, Mills, Nolan, Taylor, and Williamson counties. Dolomite rock can be used as crushed stone (although much of Texas dolomite is soft and not a good aggregate material), in the manufacture of lime, and as a source of **magnesium.**

FELDSPAR — Large crystals and crystal fragments of feldspar minerals occur in the Precambrian pegmatite rocks that crop out in the **Llano Uplift** area of Central Texas — including Blanco, Burnet, Gillespie, Llano, and Mason counties — and in the **Van Horn area** of Culberson and Hudspeth counties in West Texas. Feldspar has been mined in Llano County for use as **roofing granules** and as a **ceramic material.** Feldspar is currently mined in Burnet County for use as an aggregate.

FLUORSPAR — The mineral fluorite (calcium fluoride), which is known commercially as fluorspar, occurs in both Central and West Texas. In Central Texas, the deposits that have been found in Burnet, Gillespie, and Mason counties are not considered adequate to sustain mining operations. In West Texas, deposits have been found in Brewster, El Paso, Hudspeth, Jeff Davis, and Presidio counties. Fluorspar has been mined in the **Christmas Mountains** of Brewster County and processed in Marathon. Former West Texas mining activity in the **Eagle Mountains** district of Hudspeth County resulted in the production of approximately 15,000 short tons of fluorspar during the peak years of 1942–1950. No production has been reported in Hudspeth County

since that period. Imported fluorspar is processed in Brownsville, Eagle Pass, El Paso, and Houston. Fluorspar is used in the **steel, chemical, aluminum, magnesium, ceramics, and glass industries,** and for various other purposes.

FULLER'S EARTH (see **CLAY**).

GOLD — No major deposits of gold are known in Texas. Small amounts have been found in the **Llano Uplift** region of Central Texas and in West Texas; minor occurrences have been reported on the **Edwards Plateau** and the **Gulf Coastal Plain** of Texas. Nearly all of the gold produced in the state came as a by-product of silver and lead mining at **Presidio mine,** near Shafter in Presidio County. Additional small quantities were produced as a by-product of copper mining in Culberson County and from residual soils developed from gold-bearing quartz stringers in metamorphic rocks in Llano County. No gold mining has been reported in Texas since 1952. Total **gold production** in the state from 1889–1952 amounted to more than 8,419 troy ounces, according to U.S. Bureau of Mines figures. Most of the production — at least 73 percent and probably more — came from the Presidio mine.

GRANITE — Granites in shades of red and gray and related intrusive igneous rocks occur in the **Llano Uplift** of Central Texas and in the **Trans-Pecos** country of West Texas. Deposits are found in Blanco, Brewster, Burnet, El Paso, Gillespie, Hudspeth, Llano, McCulloch, Mason, Presidio, and other counties. Quarries in Burnet, Gillespie, Llano, and Mason counties produce Precambrian granite for a variety of uses as **dimension stone** and **crushed stone.**

GRAPHITE — Graphite, a soft, dark-gray mineral, is a form of very high-grade carbon. It occurs in Precambrian schist rocks of the **Llano Uplift** of Central Texas, notably in Burnet and Llano counties. Crystalline-flake graphite ore formerly was mined from open pits in the **Clear Creek area** of western Burnet County and processed at a plant near the mine. The mill now occasionally grinds imported material. Uses of natural crystalline graphite are **refractories, steel production, pencil leads, lubricants, foundry facings, and crucibles,** as well as other purposes.

GRINDING PEBBLES (ABRASIVE STONES) — Flint pebbles, suitable for use in **tube-mill grinding,** are found in the **Gulf Coastal Plain,** where they occur in gravel deposits along rivers and in upland areas. Grinding pebbles are produced from **Frio River terrace deposits** near the McMullen–Live Oak county line, but the area is now part of the Choke Canyon Reservoir area.

GYPSUM — Gypsum is widely distributed in Texas. Chief deposits are bedded gypsum in the area east of the **High Plains,** in the **Trans-Pecos** country, and in **Central Texas.** It also occurs in **salt-dome caprocks** of the Gulf Coast. The massive, granular variety, which is known as rock gypsum, is the kind most commonly used by industry. Other varieties include **alabaster, satin spar, and selenite.**

Gypsum is one of the important industrial minerals in Texas. Bedded gypsum is produced from surface mines in Culberson, Fisher, Gillespie, Hardeman, Hudspeth, Kimble, Nolan, and Stonewall counties. Gypsum was formerly mined at **Gyp Hill salt dome** in Brooks County and at **Hockley salt dome** in Harris County. Most of the gypsum is calcined and used in the manufacture of **gypsum wallboard, plaster, joint compounds,** and other construction products. Crude gypsum is used chiefly as a **retarder in portland cement** and as a **soil conditioner.**

HELIUM — Helium is a very light, nonflammable, chemically inert gas. The **U.S. Interior Department has ended its helium operation** near Masterson in the Panhandle. The storage facility at **Cliffside gas field** near Amarillo and the 425-mile pipeline system will remain in operation until the government sells its remaining unrefined, crude helium. Helium is used in **cryogenics, welding, pressurizing and purging, leak detection, synthetic breathing mixtures,** and for other purposes.

IRON — Iron oxide (**limonite, goethite, and hematite**) and **iron carbonate (siderite)** deposits occur widely in East Texas, notably in Cass, Cherokee, Marion, and Morris counties, and also in Anderson, Camp, Harrison, Henderson, Nacogdoches, Smith, Upshur, and other counties. **Magnetite (magnetic, black iron oxide)** occurs in Central Texas, including a deposit at **Iron Mountain** in Llano County. Hematite occurs in the **Trans-Pecos** area and in the **Llano Uplift** of Central Texas. The extensive deposits of **glauconite** (a complex silicate containing iron) that occur in East Texas and the hematitic and goethitic Cambrian sandstone that crops out in the northwestern Llano Uplift region are potential sources of low-grade iron ore.

Limonite and other East Texas iron ores are mined from open pits in Cherokee and Henderson counties for use in the preparation of **portland cement,** as a **weighting agent in well-drilling fluids,** as an **animal feed supplement,** and for other purposes. East Texas iron ores also were mined in the past for use in the iron-steel industry.

KAOLIN (see **CLAY**).

LEAD AND ZINC — The lead mineral **galena (lead sulfide)** commonly is associated with zinc and silver. It formerly was produced as a by-product of West Texas silver mining, chiefly from the **Presidio mine at Shafter** in Presidio County, although lesser amounts were obtained at several other mines and prospects. Deposits of galena also are known to occur in Blanco, Brewster, Burnet, Gillespie, and Hudspeth counties.

Zinc, primarily from the mineral **sphalerite (zinc sulphide),** was produced chiefly from the **Bonanza** and **Alice Ray** mines in the **Quitman Mountains** of Hudspeth County. In addition, small production was reported from several other areas, including the **Chinati** and **Montezuma mines** of Presidio County and the **Buck Prospect** in the **Apache Mountains** of Culberson County. Zinc mineralization also occurs in association with the lead deposits in Cambrian rocks of Central Texas.

LEONARDITE — Deposits of weathered (oxidized) low-Btu value bituminous coals, generally referred to as "leonardite," occur in Brewster County. The name leonardite is used for a mixture of chemical compounds that is high in humic acids. In the past, material from these deposits was sold as **soil conditioner.** Other uses of leonardite include **modification of viscosity of drill fluids and as sorbants in water-treatment.**

LIGHTWEIGHT AGGREGATE (see **CLAY, DIATOMITE, PERLITE, VERMICULITE**).

LIGNITE — Almost all current coal production in Texas is located in the Tertiary-aged lignite belts that extend across the Texas Gulf Coastal Plain from the Rio Grande in South Texas to the Arkansas and Louisiana borders in East Texas. The Railroad Commission of Texas (RRC) reported that in 2010, **Texas produced 41.4 million short tons of lignite from 14 mines.** Cumulative production in 2010 was 1.5 billion short tons of lignite and coal. The U.S. Energy Information Administration (EIA) ranked Texas as the sixth-largest coal-producing state.

The near-surface lignite resources, occurring at depths of less than 200 feet in seams of three feet or thicker, are estimated at 23 billion short tons. **Recoverable reserves of strippable lignite** — those that can be economically mined under current conditions of price and technology — are estimated by the EIA to be 722 million short tons.

Additional lignite resources of the Texas Gulf Coastal Plain occur as deep-basin deposits. Deep-basin resources, those that occur at depths of 200 to 2,000 feet in seams of five feet or thicker, are comparable in magnitude to near-surface resources. The deep-basin lignites are a potential energy resource that conceivably could be utilized by in situ (in place) recovery methods such as underground gasification.

As with bituminous coal, lignite production was significant prior to the general availability of oil and gas. Remnants of old underground mines are common throughout the area of lignite occurrence. Large reserves of strippable lignite have again attracted the attention of energy suppliers, and Texas is now the nation's **sixth leading producer of coal,** 99 percent of it lignite. Twelve large strip mines are now producing lignite that is burned for **mine-mouth electric-power generation,** and additional mines are planned. Mines are located in Atascosa, Franklin, Freestone, Harrison, Hopkins, Leon, Limestone, McMullen, Milam, Panola, Robertson, Rusk, and Titus counties.

LIME MATERIAL — Limestones, which are abundant in some areas of Texas, are heated to produce lime (calcium oxide) at a number of plants in the state. High-magnesium limestone and dolomite are used to prepare lime at a plant in Burnet County. Other lime plants are located in Bexar, Bosque, Comal, Hill, Johnson, and Travis counties. Lime production captive to the kiln's operator occurs in several Texas counties. Lime is used in **soil stabilization, water purification, paper and pulp manufacture, metallurgy, sugar refining, agriculture, construction, removal of sulfur from stack gases,** and for many other purposes.

LIMESTONE (see also **BUILDING STONE**) — Texas is one of the nation's leading producers of limestone, which is quarried in more than 60 counties. Limestone occurs in nearly all areas of the state with the exception of most of the Gulf Coastal Plain and High Plains. Although some of the limestone is quarried for use as **dimension stone,** most of the output is crushed for uses such as **bulk building materials (crushed stone, road base, concrete aggregate), chemical raw materials, fillers or extenders, lime and portland cement raw materials, agricultural limestone, and removal of sulfur from stack gases.**

MAGNESITE — Small deposits of magnesite (natural magnesium carbonate) have been found in Precambrian rocks in Llano and Mason counties of Central Texas. At one time, there was small-scale mining of magnesite in the area; some of the material was used as **agricultural stone** and as **terrazzo chips.** Magnesite also can be calcined to form magnesia, which is used in metallurgical furnace refractories and other products.

MAGNESIUM — On the Texas Gulf Coast in Brazoria County, magnesium chloride is **extracted from sea water** at a plant in Freeport and used to produce **magnesium compounds and magnesium metal.** During World War II, high-magnesium Ellenburger dolomite rock from Burnet County was used as magnesium ore at a plant near Austin.

MANGANESE — Deposits of manganese minerals, such as **braunite, hollandite, and pyrolusite,** have been found in several areas, including Jeff Davis, Llano, Mason, Presidio, and Val Verde counties. Known deposits are not large. Small shipments have been made from Jeff Davis, Mason, and Val Verde counties, but no manganese mining has been reported in Texas since 1954.

MARBLE — Metamorphic and sedimentary marbles suitable for **monument and building stone** are found in the **Llano Uplift** and nearby areas of Central Texas and the **Trans-Pecos** area of West Texas. Gray, white, black, greenish black, light green, brown, and cream-colored marbles occur in Central Texas in Burnet, Gillespie,

Llano, and Mason counties. West Texas metamorphic marbles include the bluish-white and the black marbles found southwest of Alpine in Brewster County and the white marble from **Marble Canyon** north of Van Horn in Culberson County. Marble can be used as **dimension stone, terrazzo, and roofing aggregate,** and for other purposes.

MERCURY (QUICKSILVER) — Mercury minerals, chiefly **cinnabar,** occur in the **Terlingua district** and nearby districts of southern Brewster and southeastern Presidio counties. Mining began there about 1894, and from 1905–1935, Texas was one of the nation's leading producers of quicksilver. Following World War II, a sharp drop in demand and price, along with depletion of developed ore reserves, caused abandonment of all the Texas mercury mines.

With a rise in the price, sporadic mining took place between 1951–1960. In 1965, when the price of mercury moved to a record high, renewed interest in the Texas mercury districts resulted in the reopening of several mines and the discovery of new ore reserves. By April 1972, however, the price had declined and the mines have reported no production since 1973.

MICA — Large crystals of flexible, transparent mica minerals in igneous pegmatite rocks and mica flakes in metamorphic schist rocks are found in the **Llano Uplift area** of Central Texas and the **Van Horn area** of West Texas. Most Central Texas deposits do not meet specifications for sheet mica, and although several attempts have been made to produce West Texas sheet mica in Culberson and Hudspeth counties, sustained production has not been achieved. A mica quarry operated for a short time in the early 1980s in the Van Horn Mountains of Culberson and Hudspeth counties to mine mica schist for use as an **additive in rotary drilling fluids.**

MOLYBDENUM — Small occurrences of molybdenite have been found in Burnet and Llano counties, and **wulfenite,** another molybdenum mineral, has been noted in rocks in the **Quitman Mountains** of Hudspeth County. Molybdenum minerals also occur at **Cave Peak** north of Van Horn in Culberson County, in the **Altuda Mountain area** of northwestern Brewster County, and in association with uranium ores of the Gulf Coastal Plain.

PEAT — This spongy organic substance forms in bogs from plant remains. It has been found in the **Gulf Coastal Plain** in several localities including Gonzales, Guadalupe, Lee, Milam, Polk, and San Jacinto counties. There has been intermittent, small-scale production of some of the peat for use as a **soil conditioner.**

PERLITE — Perlite, a glassy igneous rock, expands to a lightweight, porous mass when heated. It can be used as a **lightweight aggregate, filter aid, horticultural aggregate,** and for other purposes. Perlite occurs in Presidio County, where it has been mined in the **Pinto Canyon area** north of **the Chinati Mountains.** No perlite is currently mined in Texas, but perlite mined outside of Texas is expanded at plants in Bexar, Dallas, El Paso, Guadalupe, Harris, and Nolan counties.

PHOSPHATE — Rock phosphate is present in Paleozoic rocks in several areas of Brewster and Presidio counties in West Texas and in Central Texas, but the known deposits are not large. In Northeast Texas, sedimentary rock phosphate occurs in thin conglomeratic lenses in Upper Cretaceous and Tertiary rock units; possibly some of these low-grade phosphorites could be processed on a small scale for local use as a **fertilizer.** Imported phosphate rock is processed at a plant in Brownsville.

POTASH — The potassium mineral **polyhalite** is widely distributed in the subsurface Permian Basin of West Texas and has been found in many wells in that area. During 1927–1931, the federal government drilled a series of potash-test wells in Crane, Crockett, Ector, Glasscock, Loving, Reagan, Upton, and Winkler counties. In addition to polyhalite, which was found in all of the counties, these wells revealed the presence of the potassium minerals **carnallite and sylvite** in Loving County and carnallite in Winkler County. The known Texas potash deposits are not as rich as those in the New Mexico portion of the Permian Basin and have not been developed.

PUMICITE (VOLCANIC ASH) — Deposits of volcanic ash occur in Brazos, Fayette, Gonzales, Karnes, Polk, Starr, and other counties of the Texas Coastal Plain. Deposits also have been found in the Trans-Pecos area, High Plains, and in several counties east of the High Plains. Volcanic ash is used to prepare **pozzolan cement, cleansing and scouring compounds, and soaps and sweeping compounds;** as a **carrier for insecticides,** and for other purposes. It has been mined in Dickens, Lynn, Scurry, Starr, and other counties.

QUICKSILVER (see **MERCURY**).

RARE-EARTH ELEMENTS AND METALS — The term, "rare-earth elements," is commonly applied to elements of the **lanthanide** group (atomic numbers 57 through 71) plus **yttrium.** Yttrium, atomic number 39 and not a member of the lanthanide group, is included as a rare-earth element because it has similar properties to members of that group and usually occurs in nature with them. The metals **thorium and scandium** are sometimes termed "rare metals" because their occurence is often associated with the rare-earth elements.

The majority of rare-earth elements are consumed as **catalysts** in petroleum cracking and other chemical industries. Rare earths are widely used in the **glass industry for tableware, specialty glasses, optics, and fiber optics.** Cerium oxide has growing use as a **polishing compound** for glass, gem stones, cathode-ray tube faceplates, and other polishing. Rare earths are alloyed with various metals to produce materials used in the **aeronautic, space, and electronics** industries. The addition of rare-earth elements may improve resistance to metal fatigue at high temperatures, reduce potential for corrosion, and selectively increase conductivity and magnetism of the metal.

Various members of this group, including **thorium,** have anomalous concentrations in the **rhyolitic and related igneous rocks** of the **Quitman Mountains** and the **Sierra Blanca area** of Trans-Pecos.

SALT (SODIUM CHLORIDE) (see also **BRINES**) — Salt resources of Texas are virtually inexhaustible. Enormous deposits occur in the subsurface **Permian Basin** of West Texas and in the **salt domes of the Gulf Coastal Plain.** Salt also is found in the alkali **playa lakes** of the High Plains, the **alkali flats or salt lakes in the Salt Basin** of Culberson and Hudspeth counties, and along some of the bays and lagoons of the South Texas **Gulf Coast.**

Texas is one of the leading salt-producing states. **Rock salt** is obtained from underground mines in **salt domes at Grand Saline** in Van Zandt County and **Hockley Dome** in Harris County. Salt is produced from rock salt and by solution mining as brines from wells drilled into the underground salt deposits.

SAND, INDUSTRIAL — Sands used for special purposes, due to **high silica content** or to unique physical properties, command higher prices than common sand. Industrial sands in Texas occur mainly in the **Central Gulf Coastal Plain** and in **North-Central Texas.** They include **abrasive, blast, chemical, engine, filtration, foundry, glass, hydraulic-fracturing (propant), molding, and pottery sands.** Recent production of industrial sands has been from Atascosa, Colorado, Hardin, Harris, Liberty, Limestone, McCulloch, Newton, Smith, Somervell, and Upshur counties.

SAND AND GRAVEL (CONSTRUCTION) — Sand and gravel are among the most extensively utilized resources in Texas. Principal occurrence is along the major streams and in stream terraces. Sand and gravel are important **bulk construction materials, used as railroad ballast, base materials,** and for other purposes.

SANDSTONE — Sandstones of a variety of colors and textures are widely distributed in a number of geologic formations in Texas. Some of the sandstones have been quarried for use as **dimension stone** in El Paso, Parker, Terrell, Ward, and other counties. **Crushed sandstone** is produced in Freestone, Gaines, Jasper, McMullen, Motley, and other counties for use as **road-building material, terrazzo stone, and aggregate.**

SERPENTINITE — Several masses of serpentinite, which formed from the alteration of basic igneous rocks, are associated with other Precambrian metamorphic rocks of the **Llano Uplift.** The largest deposit is the **Coal Creek serpentinite mass** in northern Blanco and Gillespie counties from which **terrazzo chips** have been produced. Other deposits are present in Gillespie and Llano counties. (The features that are associated with surface and subsurface Cretaceous rocks in several counties in or near the **Balcones Fault Zone** and that are commonly known as **"serpentine plugs"** are not serpentine at all, but are altered igneous volcanic necks and pipes, and mounds of altered volcanic ash — **palagonite** — that accumulated around the former submarine volcanic pipes.)

SHELL — Oyster shells and other shells in shallow coastal waters and in deposits along the **Texas Gulf Coast** have been produced in the past chiefly by dredging. They were used to a limited extent as raw material in the **manufacture of cement, as concrete aggregate and road base,** and for other purposes. No shell has been produced in Texas since 1981.

SILVER — During the period 1885–1952, the production of silver in Texas, as reported by the U.S. Bureau of Mines, totaled about **33 million troy ounces.** For about 70 years, silver was the most consistently produced metal in Texas, although always in moderate quantities. All of the production came from the **Trans-Pecos country** of West Texas, where the silver was mined in Brewster County (**Altuda Mountain**), Culberson and Hudspeth counties (**Van Horn Mountains and Van Horn–Allamoore district**), Hudspeth County (**Quitman Mountains and Eagle Mountains**), and Presidio County (**Chinati Mountains area, Loma Plata mine, and Shafter district**).

Chief producer was the **Presidio mine in the Shafter district,** which began operations in the late 1800s, and, through September 1942, produced more than 30 million ounces of silver — more than 92 percent of Texas' total silver production. Water in the lower mine levels, lean ores, and low price of silver resulted in the closing of the mine in 1942. Another important silver producer was the **Hazel copper-silver mine** in the **Van Horn–Allamoore district** in Culberson County, which accounted for more than 2 million ounces.

An increase in the price of silver in the late 1970s stimulated prospecting for new reserves, and exploration began near the old **Presidio mine,** near the old **Plata Verde mine** in the Van Horn Mountains district, at the Bonanza mine in the **Quitman Mountains** district, and at the old **Hazel mine.** A decline in the price of silver in the early 1980s, however, resulted in reduction of exploration and mine development in the region. The recent rise in value of silver has sparked new interest in the Shafter mining district of West Texas.

SOAPSTONE (see **TALC AND SOAPSTONE**).

SODIUM SULFATE (SALT CAKE) — Sodium sulfate minerals occur in salt beds and brines of the alkali **playa lakes** of the High Plains in West Texas. In some lakes, the sodium sulfate minerals are present in deposits a few feet beneath the lakebeds. Sodium sulfate also is found in underground brines in the Permian Basin. Current production is from brines and dry salt beds at alkali lakes in Gaines and Terry counties. Past production was reported in Lynn and Ward counties. Sodium sulfate is used chiefly by the **detergent and paper and pulp industries.** Other uses are in the **preparation of glass and other products.**

STONE (see **BUILDING STONE** and **CRUSHED STONE**).

STRONTIUM — Deposits of the mineral **celestite (strontium sulfate)** have been found in a number of places, including localities in Brown, Coke, Comanche, Fisher, Lampasas, Mills, Nolan, Real, Taylor, Travis, and Williamson counties. Most of the occurrences are very minor, and no strontium is currently produced in the state.

SULFUR — Texas is **one of the world's principal sulfur-producing areas.** The sulfur is mined from deposits of native sulfur, and it is extracted from sour (sulfur-bearing) natural gas and petroleum. **Recovered sulfur** is a growing industry and accounted for approximately 60 percent of all 1987 sulfur production in the United States, but only approximately 40 percent of Texas production. Native sulfur is found in large deposits in the caprock of some of the **salt domes** along the Texas Gulf Coast and in some of the surface and subsurface Permian strata of West Texas, notably in Culberson and Pecos counties.

Native sulfur obtained from the underground deposits is known as **Frasch sulfur,** so-called because of Herman Frasch, the chemist who devised the method of drilling wells into the deposits, melting the sulfur with superheated water, and forcing the molten sulfur to the surface. Most of the production now goes to the users in molten form.

Frasch sulfur is produced from only one Gulf Coast salt dome in Wharton County and from West Texas underground Permian strata in Culberson County. Operations at several Gulf Coast domes have been closed in recent years. During the 1940s, acidic sulfur earth was produced in the **Rustler Springs district** in Culberson County for use as a **fertilizer and soil conditioner.** Sulfur is recovered from sour natural gas and petroleum at plants in numerous Texas counties.

Sulfur is used in the preparation of **fertilizers and organic and inorganic chemicals, in petroleum refining,** and for many other purposes.

TALC AND SOAPSTONE — Deposits of talc are found in the Precambrian metamorphic rocks of the **Allamoore area** of eastern Hudspeth and western Culberson counties. Soapstone, containing talc, occurs in the Precambrian metamorphic rocks of the **Llano Uplift** area, notably in Blanco, Gillespie, and Llano counties. Current production is from surface mines in the **Allamoore area.** Talc is used in **ceramic, roofing, paint, paper, plastic, synthetic rubber,** and other products.

TIN — Tin minerals have been found in El Paso and Mason counties. Small quantities were produced during the early 1900s in the Franklin Mountains north of El Paso. **Cassiterite (tin dioxide)** occurrences in Mason County are believed to be very minor. The **only tin smelter in the United States,** built at **Texas City** by the federal government during World War II and later sold to a private company, processes tin concentrates from ores mined outside of Texas, tin residues, and secondary tin-bearing materials.

TITANIUM — The titanium mineral **rutile** has been found in small amounts at the **Mueller prospect** in Jeff Davis County. Another titanium mineral, **ilmenite,** occurs in sandstones in Burleson, Fayette, Lee, Starr, and several other counties. Deposits that would be consid-

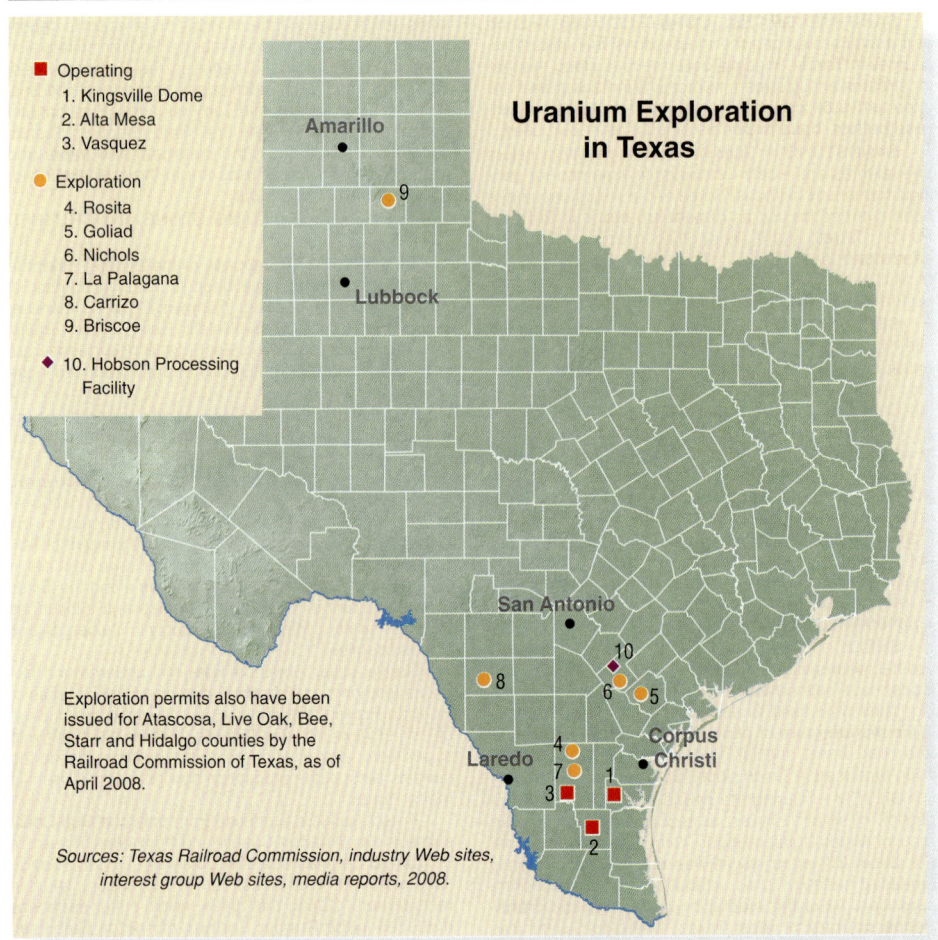

Uranium Exploration in Texas

- ■ Operating
  1. Kingsville Dome
  2. Alta Mesa
  3. Vasquez

- ● Exploration
  4. Rosita
  5. Goliad
  6. Nichols
  7. La Palagana
  8. Carrizo
  9. Briscoe

- ◆ 10. Hobson Processing Facility

Exploration permits also have been issued for Atascosa, Live Oak, Bee, Starr and Hidalgo counties by the Railroad Commission of Texas, as of April 2008.

Sources: Texas Railroad Commission, industry Web sites, interest group Web sites, media reports, 2008.

ered commercial under present conditions have not been found.

TRAP ROCK (see **BASALT**).

TUNGSTEN — The tungsten mineral **scheelite** has been found in small deposits in Gillespie and Llano counties and in the **Quitman Mountains** in Hudspeth County. Small deposits of other tungsten minerals have been prospected in the **Cave Peak area** north of Van Horn in Culberson County.

URANIUM — Uranium deposits were discovered in the **Texas Coastal Plain** in 1954 when abnormal radioactivity was detected in the Karnes County area. A number of uranium deposits have since been discovered within a belt of strata extending more than 250 miles from the middle Coastal Plain southwestward to the Rio Grande.

Various uranium minerals also have been found in other areas of Texas, including the **Trans-Pecos**, the **Llano Uplift**, and the **High Plains**. With the exception of small shipments from the High Plains during the 1950s, all the uranium production in Texas has been from the Coastal Plain. Uranium has been obtained from surface mines extending from northern Live Oak County, southeastern Atascosa County, across northern Karnes County, and into southern Gonzales County. Uranium is produced by in-situ leaching, brought to the surface through wells, and stripped from the solution at recovery operations.

In 1999, uranium mining shut down because of

decreased value and demand. Production resumed in Texas in late 2004, when inventories were depleted and market prices rose to economic levels that allowed resumption of production. A total of 1.38 million pounds (606.5 tons) of eU_3O_8 was produced in South Texas in 2007.

VERMICULITE — Vermiculite, a mica-like mineral that expands when heated, occurs in Burnet, Gillespie, Llano, Mason, and other counties in the **Llano Uplift** region. It has been produced at a surface mine in Llano County. Vermiculite, mined outside of Texas, is exfoliated (expanded) at plants in Dallas, Houston, and San Antonio. Exfoliated vermiculite is used for **lightweight concrete aggregate, horticulture, insulation,** and other purposes.

VOLCANIC ASH (see **PUMICITE**).

ZEOLITES — The zeolite minerals **clinoptilolite** and **analcime** occur in Tertiary lavas and tuffs in Brewster, Jeff Davis, and Presidio counties in West Texas. Clinoptilolite also is found associated with Tertiary tuffs in the southern Texas Coastal Plain, including deposits in Karnes, McMullen, and Webb counties, and currently is produced in McMullen County. Zeolites, sometimes called "**molecular sieves,**" can be used in **ion-exchange processes to reduce pollution,** as a catalyst in **oil cracking,** in obtaining **high-purity oxygen and nitrogen** from air, in **water purification,** and for many other purposes.

ZINC (see **LEAD AND ZINC**). ☆

Texas Newspapers, Radio & Television Stations

In the list of print and broadcast media, below, frequency of publication of subscription newspapers is indicated after the names by the following codes: (D) daily, (S) semiweekly, (TW) triweekly, (BW) biweekly, (SM) semimonthly, (M) monthly; all others are weeklies. The radio and TV stations are those with valid operating licenses as of July 2011. Not included are those with only construction permits or with applications pending. Newspaper Source: 2011 Texas Newspaper Directory, Texas Press Association, Austin; Broadcast Media Source: Federal Communications Commission website: http://transition.fcc.gov/mb/audio/index.html.

Abilene — Newspaper: Abilene Reporter-News (D). **Radio-AM:** KSLI, 1280 kHz; KWKC, 1340; KYYW, 1470; KZQQ, 1560. **Radio-FM:** KGNZ, 88.1 MHz; KACU, 89.7; KAGT, 90.5; KAQD, 91.3; KULL, 92.5; KFGL, 100.7; KEAN, 105.1; KKHR, 106.3; KEYJ, 107.9. **TV:** KXVA-Ch. 15; KTAB-Ch. 24; KRBC-Ch. 29.

Alamo — Radio-FM: KJAV, 104.9 MHz.

Alamo Heights — Radio-AM: KDRY, 1100 kHz.

Albany — Newspaper: Albany News.

Aledo — Newspaper: The Community News.

Alice — Newspaper: Alice Echo-News Journal (TW). **Radio-AM:** KOPY, 1070 kHz. **Radio-FM:** KIFR, 88.3 MHz; KOPY, 92.1; KNDA, 102.9.

Allen — Newspaper: The Allen American. **Radio-FM:** KESN, 103.3 MHz.

Alpine — Newspaper: Alpine Avalanche. **Radio-AM:** KVLF, 1240 kHz. **Radio-FM:** KALP, 92.7 MHz.

Alvarado — Newspapers: Alvarado Post; Alvarado Star.

Alvin — Newspaper: Alvin Sun. **Radio-AM:** KTEK, 1110 kHz. **Radio-FM:** KACC, 89.7 MHz. **TV:** KFTH-Ch. 36.

Amarillo — Newspaper: Amarillo Globe-News (D). **Radio-AM:** KGNC, 710 kHz; KIXZ, 940; KTNZ, 1010; KZIP, 1310; KDJW, 1360; KPUR, 1440. **Radio-FM:** KJRT, 88.3 MHz; KXLV, 89.1; KACV, 89.9; KAVW, 90.7; KXRI, 91.9; KQIZ, 93.1; KMXJ, 94.1; KXSS, 96.9; KGNC, 97.9; KPRF, 98.7; KBZD, 99.7; KXGL, 100.9; KATP, 101.9; KRGN, 102.9; KJJP, 105.7. **TV:** KVII-Ch. 7; KACV-Ch. 8; KFDA-Ch. 10; KCIT-Ch. 15; KAMR-Ch. 19.

Anahuac — Newspaper: The Progress.

Andrews — Newspaper: Andrews County News (S). **Radio-AM:** KACT, 1360 kHz. **Radio-FM:** KACT, 105.5 MHz.

Anna — Newspaper: The Anna-Melissa Tribune.

Anson — Newspaper: Western Observer. **Radio-FM:** KTLT, 98.1 MHz.

Aransas Pass — Newspapers: Aransas Pass Progress; The Coastal Bend Herald. **Radio-FM:** KKWV, 88.1 MHz.

Archer City — Newspaper: Archer County News. **Radio-FM:** KPMA, 91.9 MHz.

Arlington — Radio-FM: KLTY, 94.9 MHz. **TV:** KPXD-Ch. 42.

Aspermont — Newspaper: Stonewall County Courier.

Athens — Newspaper: Athens Daily Review (D). **Radio-AM:** KLVQ, 1410 kHz. **Radio-FM:** KATG, 88.1 MHz.

Atlanta — Newspaper: Atlanta Citizens Journal (S). **Radio-AM:** KPYN, 900 kHz. **Radio-FM:** KNRB, 100.1 MHz.

Austin — Newspapers: Austin American-Statesman (D); Austin Business Journal; Daily Texan (D); Texas Observer (M); West Austin News; Westlake Picayune. **Radio-AM:** KLBJ, 590 kHz; KVET, 1300; KFON, 1490. **Radio-FM:** KAZI, 88.7 MHz; KMFA, 89.5; KUT, 90.5; KVRX, 91.7; KLBJ, 93.7; KKMJ, 95.5; KVET, 98.1; KASE, 100.7; KPEZ, 102.3. **TV:** KTBC-Ch. 7; KXAN-CH. 21; KLRU-Ch. 22; KVUE-CH. 33; KEYE-Ch. 43; KNVA-Ch. 49.

Azle — Newspaper: Azle News. **Radio-FM:** KTCY,101.7 MHz.

Baird — Newspapers: Baird Banner; Callahan County Star. **Radio-FM:** KORQ, 95.1 MHz.

Balch Springs — Radio-AM: KSKY, 660 kHz.

Ballinger — Newspaper: Ballinger Ledger. **Radio-AM:**

KRUN, 1400 kHz. **Radio-FM:** KKCN, 103.1 MHz.

Bandera — Newspapers: The Bandera Bulletin; Bandera County Courier. **Radio-FM:** KEEP, 103.1 MHz.

Bartlett — Newspaper: Tribune-Progress.

Bastrop — Newspaper: Bastrop Advertiser (S). **Radio-FM:** KHIB, 88.5 MHz; KLZT, 107.1.

Bay City — Newspaper: The Bay City Tribune (S). **Radio-FM:** KEDR, 88.1 MHz; KZBJ, 89.5; KXGJ, 101.7; KMKS, 102.5.

Baytown — Newspaper: Baytown Sun (D). **Radio-AM:** KWWJ, 1360 kHz. **TV:** KUBE-Ch. 41.

Beaumont — Newspaper: The Beaumont Enterprise (D). **Radio-AM:** KLVI, 560 kHz; KZZB, 990; KIKR, 1450. **Radio-FM:** KLBT, 88.1 MHz; KGHY, 88.5; KTXB, 89.7; KVLU, 91.3; KQXY, 94.1; KYKR, 95.1; KFNC, 97.5; KTCX, 102.5; KQQK, 107.9. **TV:** KBMT-Ch. 12; KFDM-Ch. 21; KITU-Ch. 33.

Bee Cave — Radio-FM: KTXX, 104.9 MHz.

Beeville — Newspaper: Beeville Bee-Picayune (S). **Radio-AM:** KIBL, 1490 kHz. **Radio-FM:** KVFM, 91.3 MHz; KTKO, 105.7; KRXB, 107.1.

Bellaire — Radio-AM: KGOW, 1560 kHz.

Bells — Radio-FM: KMKT, 93.1 MHz.

Bellville — Newspaper: Bellville Times. **Radio-AM:** KULF, 1090 kHz.

Belton — Newspaper: The Belton Journal. **Radio-AM:** KTON, 940 kHz. **Radio-FM:** KOOC, 106.3 MHz. **TV:** KNCT-Ch. 46.

Benavides — Radio-FM: KXTM, 107.7 MHz.

Benbrook — Radio-FM: KDXX, 107.1 MHz.

Big Lake — Newspaper: Big Lake Wildcat. **Radio-FM:** KPDB, 98.3 MHz; KWTR, 104.1.

Big Sandy — Newspaper: Big Sandy–Hawkins Journal. **Radio-FM:** KTAA, 90.7 MHz.

Big Spring — Newspaper: Big Spring Herald (D). **Radio-AM:** KBYG, 1400 kHz; KBST, 1490. **Radio-FM:** KPBD, 89.3 MHz; KBCX, 91.5; KBTS, 94.3; KBST, 95.7. **TV:** KWAB-Ch. 33.

Bishop — Newspaper: Kingsville Record and Bishop News. **Radio-FM:** KMZZ, 106.9 MHz.

Blanco — Newspaper: Blanco County News. **TV:** KNIC-Ch. 18.

Bloomington — Radio-FM: KHVT, 91.5 MHz; KLUB, 106.9.

Boerne — Newspapers: Boerne Star (S). **Radio-AM:** KBRN, 1500 kHz.

Bogata — Newspaper: Bogata News–Talco Times.

Bonham — Radio-AM: KFYN, 1420 kHz.

Booker — Newspaper: Booker News.

Borger — Newspaper: Borger News-Herald (D). **Radio-AM:** KQTY, 1490 kHz. **Radio-FM:** KASV, 88.7 MHz; KQFX, 104.3; KQTY, 106.7. **TV:** KEYU-Ch. 31.

Bovina — Radio-FM: KKNM, 96.5 MHz.

Bowie — Newspaper: Bowie News (S). **Radio-AM:** KNTX, 1410 kHz.

Brackettville — Newspaper: The Brackett News.

Brady — Newspaper: Brady Standard-Herald. **Radio-AM:** KNEL, 1490 kHz. **Radio-FM:** KNEL, 95.3 MHz.

Breckenridge — Newspaper: Breckenridge American (S). **Radio-AM:** KROO, 1430 kHz. **Radio-FM:** KQXB, 89.9 MHz; KLXK, 93.5.

Bremond — Newspaper: The Bremond Press.

Brenham — Newspaper: Brenham Banner-Press (D). **Radio-AM:** KWHI, 1280 kHz. **Radio-FM:** KUBJ, 89.7 MHz; KLTR, 94.1; KTTX, 106.1.

Bridgeport — **Newspaper:** Bridgeport Index. **Radio-FM:** KBOC, 98.3 MHz.

Brookshire — **Newspaper:** The Times Tribune. **Radio-AM:** KCHN, 1050 kHz.

Brownfield — **Newspaper:** Brownfield News (S). **Radio-AM:** KKUB, 1300 kHz. **Radio-FM:** KPBB, 88.5 MHz; KMLU, 90.7; KTTU, 104.3.

Brownsboro — **Newspaper:** Chandler & Brownsboro Statesman.

Brownsville — **Newspaper:** The Brownsville Herald (D). **Radio-AM:** KVNS, 1700 kHz. **Radio-FM:** KBNR, 88.3 MHz; KKPS, 99.5. **TV:** KVEO-Ch. 24.

Brownwood — **Newspaper:** Brownwood Bulletin (D). **Radio-AM:** KXYL, 1240 kHz; KBWD, 1380. **Radio-FM:** KPBE, 89.3 MHz; KBUB, 90.3; KHBW, 91.7; KQBZ, 96.9; KPSM, 99.3; KOXE, 101.3.

Bruni — **Radio-FM:** KMAE, 106.5 MHz.

Bryan — **Newspaper:** The Eagle (D). **Radio-AM:** KTAM, 1240 kHz; KAGC, 1510. **Radio-FM:** KORA, 98.3 MHz; KNFX, 99.5; KKYS, 104.7. **TV:** KAMU-Ch.12; KYLE-Ch. 28; KBTX-Ch. 50.

Buda — **Newspaper:** Hays Free Press. **Radio-FM:** KROX, 101.5 MHz.

Buffalo — **Newspapers:** Buffalo Express; The Buffalo Press.

Bullard — **Newspaper:** Bullard Banner News.

Buna — **Newspaper:** The Buna Beacon.

Burkburnett — **Newspaper:** Burkburnett Informer Star. **Radio-FM:** KYYI, 104.7 MHz.

Burleson — **Newspaper:** Burleson Star (S). **Radio-AM:** KCLE, 1460 kHz.

Burnet — **Newspapers:** Burnet Bulletin; Citizens Gazette. **Radio-AM:** KRHC, 1340 kHz. **Radio-FM:** KBEY, 92.5 MHz.

Bushland — **Radio-FM:** KTXP, 91.5 MHz.

Byrne — **Radio-FM:** KLRW, 88.5 MHz.

Caldwell — **Newspaper:** Burleson County Tribune. **Radio-FM:** KALD, 91.9 MHz; KAPN, 107.3.

Callisburg — **Radio-FM:** KPFC, 91.9 MHz.

Cameron — **Newspaper:** The Cameron Herald. **Radio-AM:** KTAE, 1330 kHz. **Radio-FM:** KMIL, 105.1 MHz.

Campbell — **Radio-FM:** KRVA, 107.1 MHz.

Camp Wood — **Radio-FM:** KAYG, 99.1 MHz.

Canadian — **Newspaper:** Canadian Record.

Canton — **Newspapers:** Canton Herald; Van Zandt News. **Radio-AM:** KRDH, 1510 kHz.

Canyon — **Newspaper:** The Canyon News (S). **Radio-AM:** KZRK, 1550 kHz. **Radio-FM:** KWTS, 91.1 MHz; KPUR, 107.1; KZRK, 107.9.

Carrizo Springs — **Newspaper:** Carrizo Springs Javelin. **Radio-AM:** KBEN, 1450 kHz. **Radio-FM:** KCZO, 92.1 MHz; KAJP, 93.5.

Carrollton — **Radio-FM:** KJON, 850 kHz.

Carthage — **Newspaper:** The Panola Watchman (S). **Radio-AM:** KGAS, 1590 kHz. **Radio-FM:** KTUX, 98.9 MHz; KGAS, 104.3.

Castroville — **Newspaper:** Castroville News Bulletin.

Cedar Lake — **Radio-FM:** KQVI, 89.9 MHz.

Cedar Park — **Newspaper:** Hill Country News Weekender. **Radio-FM:** KGSR, 93.3 MHz.

Celina — **Newspaper:** The Celina Record.

Center — **Newspaper:** The Light & Champion (TW). **Radio-AM:** KDET, 930 kHz. **Radio-FM:** KQBB, 100.5 MHz.

Centerville — **Newspaper:** Centerville News. **Radio-FM:** KUZN, 105.9 MHz.

Charlotte — **Radio-FM:** KSAQ, 102.3 MHz.

Chico — **Newspaper:** Chico Texan.

Childress — **Newspaper:** The Childress Index (S). **Radio-AM:** KCTX, 1510 kHz. **Radio-FM:** KFCH, 89.5 MHz; KCTX, 96.1.

Cisco — **Newspaper:** Cisco Press (S).

Clarendon — **Newspaper:** Clarendon Enterprise. **Radio-FM:** KEFH, 99.3 MHz.

Clarksville — **Newspaper:** Clarksville Times. **Radio-AM:** KCAR, 1350 kHz. **Radio-FM:** KGAP, 98.5 MHz.

Claude — **Newspaper:** The Claude News. **Radio-FM:** KARX, 95.7 MHz.

Clear Lake — **Newspaper:** The Bay Area Citizen.

Cleburne — **Newspaper:** Cleburne Times-Review (D). **Radio-AM:** KHFX, 1140 kHz.

Cleveland — **Newspaper:** Cleveland Advocate. **Radio-FM:** KTHT, 97.1 MHz.

Clifton — **Newspaper:** Clifton Record. **Radio-FM:** KWOW, 104.1 MHz.

Clute — **Newspaper:** The Facts (D).

Clyde — **Newspaper:** Clyde Journal.

Coahoma — **Radio-FM:** KXCS, 105.5 MHz.

Cockrell Hill — **Radio-AM:** KRVA, 1600 kHz.

Coleman — **Newspaper:** Chronicle & Democrat-Voice. **Radio-AM:** KSTA, 1000 kHz. **Radio-FM:** KXYL, 102.3 MHz.

College Station — **Newspaper:** The Battalion (D). **Radio-AM:** KZNE, 1150 kHz; WTAW, 1620. **Radio-FM:** KEOS, 89.1 MHz; KLGS, 89.9; KAMU, 90.9; KNDE, 95.1. **TV:** KAMU-Ch. 12.

Colorado City — **Newspaper:** Colorado City Record. **Radio-AM:** KVMC, 1320 kHz. **Radio-FM:** KAUM, 107.1 MHz.

Columbus — **Newspapers:** The Banner Press Newspaper; Colorado County Citizen. **Radio-FM:** KULM, 98.3 MHz.

Comanche — **Newspaper:** Comanche Chief. **Radio-AM:** KCOM, 1550 kHz. **Radio-FM:** KYOX, 94.3 MHz.

Comfort — **Newspaper:** The Comfort News. **Radio-FM:** KGSX, 95.1 MHz.

Commerce — **Newspaper:** Commerce Journal. **Radio-FM:** KETR, 88.9 MHz; KYJC, 91.3.

Conroe — **Newspaper:** The Courier (D). **Radio-AM:** KJOJ, 880 kHz; KYOK, 1140. **Radio-FM:** KAFR, 88.3 MHz; KHPT, 106.9. **TV:** KPXB-Ch. 32; KTBU-Ch. 42.

Converse — **Radio-AM:** KTMR, 1130 kHz.

Cooper — **Newspaper:** Cooper Review. **Radio-FM:** KPCO, 89.9 MHz.

Coppell — **Newspaper:** Citizens' Advocate.

Copperas Cove — **Newspaper:** Copperas Cove Leader-Press (S). **Radio-FM:** KSSM, 103.1 MHz.

Corpus Christi — **Newspapers:** Corpus Christi Caller-Times (D); Coastal Bend Legal & Business News (D). **Radio-AM:** KCTA, 1030 kHz; KCCT, 1150; KSIX, 1230; KKTX, 1360; KUNO, 1400; KEYS, 1440. **Radio-FM:** KKLM, 88.7 MHz; KEDT, 90.3; KBNJ, 91.7; KMXR, 93.9; KBSO, 94.7; KZFM, 95.5; KLTG, 96.5; KRYS, 99.1.**TV:** KIII-Ch. 8; KZTV-Ch. 10; KRIS-Ch. 13; KEDT-Ch. 23; KORO-Ch. 27; KUQI-Ch. 38.

Corrigan — **Newspaper:** Corrigan Times.

Corsicana — **Newspapers:** Corsicana Daily Sun (D); Navarro County Times. **Radio-AM:** KAND, 1340 kHz.

Crane — **Newspaper:** Crane News. **Radio-AM:** KXOI, 810 kHz. **Radio-FM:** KMMZ, 101.3 MHz.

Creedmoor — **Radio-AM:** KZNX, 1530 kHz.

Crockett — **Newspaper:** Houston County Courier (S). **Radio-AM:** KIVY, 1290 kHz. **Radio-FM:** KCKT, 88.5 MHz; KIVY, 92.7; KBHT, 93.5.

Cross Plains — **Newspaper:** Cross Plains Review.

Crowell — **Newspaper:** Foard County News.

Crowley — **Newspaper:** Crowley Star.

Crystal Beach — **Radio-FM:** KSTB, 101.5 MHz; KPTY, 105.3.

Crystal City — **Newspaper:** Zavala County Sentinel. **Radio-FM:** KHER, 94.3 MHz.

Cuero — **Newspaper:** Cuero Record. **Radio-FM:** KTLZ, 89.9 MHz.

Cypress — **Radio-AM:** KYND, 1520 kHz.

Daingerfield — **Newspaper:** The Bee. **Radio-AM:** KNGR, 1560 kHz.

Dalhart — **Newspaper:** Dalhart Texan (TW). **Radio-AM:** KXIT, 1240 kHz. **Radio-FM:** KTDA, 91.7 MHz; KPPC, 96.3.

Dallas — Newspapers: The Dallas Morning News (D); Dallas Business Journal; Daily Commercial Record (D); Park Cities News; Park Cities People; Texas Jewish Post; Texas Lawyer. **Radio-AM:** KLIF, 570 kHz; KGGR, 1040; KRLD, 1080; KFXR, 1190; KTCK, 1310; KNIT, 1480. **Radio-FM:** KNON, 89.3 MHz; KERA, 90.1; KCBI, 90.9; KKXT, 91.7; KZPS, 92.5; KBFB, 97.9; KLUV, 98.7; KJKK, 100.3; WRR, 101.1; KDMX, 102.9; KKDA, 104.5; KRLD, 105.3. **TV:** WFAA-Ch. 9; KERA-Ch. 14; KDAF-Ch. 32; KDFW-Ch. 35; KDFI-Ch. 36; KXTX-Ch. 40; KDTX-Ch. 45.

Decatur — Newspaper: Wise County Messenger (S). **Radio-FM:** KDKR, 91.3 MHz; KRNB, 105.7. **TV:** KMPX-Ch. 30.

Deer Park — Radio-FM: KAMA, 104.9 MHz.

De Kalb — Newspaper: De Kalb News (S).

De Leon — Newspapers: De Leon Free Press.

Dell City — Newspaper: Hudspeth County Herald.

Del Mar Hills — Radio-AM: KVOZ, 890 kHz.

Del Rio — Newspaper: Del Rio News-Herald (D). **Radio-AM:** KTJK, 1230 kHz; KWMC, 1490. **Radio-FM:** KDLI, 89.9 MHz; KDLK, 94.1; KTDR, 96.3.

Del Valle — Radio-AM: KIXL, 970 kHz.

Denison — Radio-FM: KYFB, 91.5 MHz.

Denton — Newspaper: Denton Record-Chronicle (D). **Radio-FM:** KFZO, 99.1 MHz; KHKS, 106.1. **TV:** KDTN-Ch. 43.

Denver City — Newspaper: Denver City Press.

Deport — Newspaper: Deport Times-Blossom Times.

DeSoto — Newspapers: Focus Daily News (D).

Detroit — Newspaper: Detroit Weekly.

Devine — Newspaper: Devine News. **Radio-FM:** KRPT, 92.5 MHz.

Diboll — Newspaper: Diboll Free Press. **Radio-AM:** KSML, 1260 kHz. **Radio-FM:** KAFX, 95.5 MHz.

Dilley — Radio-FM: KVWG, 95.3 MHz; KLMO, 98.9.

Dimmitt — Newspaper: Castro County News. **Radio-AM:** KDHN, 1470 kHz. **Radio-FM:** KNNK, 100.5 MHz.

Doss — Radio-FM: KGLF, 88.1 MHz.

Dripping Springs — Newspapers: Dripping Springs Century News; The News-Dispatch. **Radio-FM:** KLLR, 91.9 MHz.

Dublin — Newspaper: Dublin Citizen. **Radio-FM:** KSTV, 93.1 MHz.

Dumas — Newspaper: Moore County News-Press (S). **Radio-AM:** KDDD, 800 kHz. **Radio-FM:** KDDD, 95.3 MHz.

Eagle Lake — Newspaper: Eagle Lake Headlight.

Eagle Pass — Radio-AM: KEPS, 1270 kHz. **Radio-FM:** KEPI, 88.7 MHz; KEPX, 89.5; KINL, 92.7. **TV:** KVAW-Ch. 18.

East Bernard — Newspaper: East Bernard Express.

Eastland — Newspaper: Eastland Telegram (S). **Radio-FM:** KQXE, 91.1 MHz; KATX, 97.7.

Eden — Newspaper: The Eden Echo.

Edgewood — Newspaper: Edgewood Enterprise.

Edinburg — Radio-AM: KURV, 710 kHz. **Radio-FM:** KOIR, 88.5 MHz; KBFM, 104.1; KVLY, 107.9.

Edna — Newspaper: Jackson County Herald-Tribune. **Radio-FM:** KIOX, 96.1 MHz.

El Campo — Newspaper: El Campo Leader-News (S). **Radio-AM:** KULP, 1390 kHz. **Radio-FM:** KNTE, 96.9 MHz.

Eldorado — Newspaper: Eldorado Success. **Radio-FM:** KOPE, 88.9 MHz; KLDE, 104.9.

Electra — Newspaper: Electra Star-News. **Radio-FM:** KOLI, 94.9 MHz.

Elgin — Newspaper: Elgin Courier. **Radio-FM:** KXXS, 92.5 MHz.

El Paso — Newspaper: El Paso Times (D). **Radio-AM:** KROD, 600 kHz; KTSM, 690; KAMA, 750; KQBU, 920; KXPL, 1060; KHRO, 1150; KVIV, 1340; KHEY, 1380; KELP, 1590; KSVE, 1650. **Radio-FM:** KTEP, 88.5 MHz; KKLY, 89.5; KVER, 91.1; KOFX, 92.3; KSII,

93.1; KINT, 93.9; KYSE, 94.7; KLAQ, 95.5; KHEY, 96.3; KBNA, 97.5; KTSM, 99.9; KPRR, 102.1. **TV:** KVIA-Ch. 7; KTSM-Ch. 9; KCOS-Ch. 13; KFOX-CH. 15; KDBC-Ch. 18; KSCE-Ch. 39; KTFN-Ch. 51.

Emory — Newspaper: Rains County Leader.

Encinal — Radio-FM: KELT, 102.5 MHz.

Ennis — Newspaper: Ennis Daily News (D).

Escobares — Radio-FM: KERG, 104.7 MHz.

Fabens — Radio-FM: KPAS, 103.1 MHz.

Fairfield — Newspapers: Freestone County Times; The Fairfield Recorder. **Radio-FM:** KNES, 99.1 MHz.

Falfurrias — Newspaper: Falfurrias Facts. **Radio-AM:** KLDS, 1260 kHz. **Radio-FM:** KDFM, 103.3 MHz; KPSO, 106.3.

Fannett — Radio-FM: KZFT, 90.5 MHz.

Farmersville — Newspaper: Farmersville Times. **Radio-AM:** KFCD, 990 kHz. **Radio-FM:** KXEZ, 92.1 MHz.

Farwell — Newspaper: State Line Tribune. **Radio-AM:** KMUL, 830 kHz; KIJN, 1060. **Radio-FM:** KIJN, 92.3 MHz; KICA, 98.3. **TV:** KPTF-Ch. 18.

Ferris — Newspaper: The Ellis County Press. **Radio-AM:** KDFT, 540 kHz.

Flatonia — Newspaper: The Flatonia Argus.

Floresville — Newspaper: Wilson County News. **Radio-FM:** KJMA, 89.7 MHz; KTFM, 94.1.

Flower Mound — Radio-FM: WBAP, 96.7 MHz.

Floydada — Newspaper: Floyd County Hesperian-Beacon. **Radio-AM:** KFLP, 900 kHz. **Radio-FM:** KFLP, 106.1 MHz.

Forney — Newspaper: Forney Messenger.

Fort Davis — Newspaper: Jeff Davis County Mt. Dispatch.

Fort Stockton — Newspaper: Fort Stockton Pioneer. **Radio-AM:** KFST, 860 kHz. **Radio-FM:** KRAF, 88.3 MHz; KFST, 94.3.

Fort Worth — Newspapers: Fort Worth Business Press; Commercial Recorder (D); Fort Worth Star-Telegram (D); Texas Jewish Post. **Radio-AM:** WBAP, 820 kHz; KFJZ, 870; KHVN, 970; KFLC, 1270; KKGM, 1630. **Radio-FM:** KTCU, 88.7 MHz; KLNO, 94.1; KSCS, 96.3; KEGL, 97.1; KPLX, 99.5; KDGE, 102.1; KMVK, 107.5. **TV:** KFWD-Ch. 9; KTVT-Ch. 11; KTXA-Ch. 29; KXAS-Ch. 41.

Franklin — Newspaper: Franklin News Weekly. **Radio-FM:** KJXJ, 103.9 MHz.

Frankston — Newspaper: The Frankston Citizen. **Radio-FM:** KOYE, 96.7 MHz.

Fredericksburg — Newspaper: Standard-Radio Post. **Radio-AM:** KNAF, 910 kHz. **Radio-FM:** KBLC, 91.5 MHz; KNAF, 105.7. **TV:** KCWX-Ch. 5.

Freeport — Radio-FM: KJOJ, 103.3 MHz.

Freer — Newspaper: Freer Press. **Radio-FM:** KPBN, 90.7 MHz; KBRA, 95.9.

Friendswood — Newspapers: Friendswood Journal; Friendswood Reporter News.

Friona — Newspaper: Friona Star. **Radio-FM:** KGRW, 94.7 MHz.

Frisco — Newspaper: The Frisco Enterprise. **Radio-AM:** KATH, 910 kHz.

Fritch — Newspaper: The Eagle Press.

Fulshear — Newspaper: Fulshear Times.

Gail — Newspaper: Borden Star.

Gainesville — Newspaper: Gainesville Daily Register (D). **Radio-AM:** KGAF, 1580 kHz. **Radio-FM:** KSOC, 94.5 MHz.

Galveston — Newspaper: Galveston County Daily News (D). **Radio-AM:** KGBC, 1540 kHz. **Radio-FM:** KOVE, 106.5 MHz. **TV:** KLTJ-Ch. 23; KTMD-Ch. 48.

Ganado — Radio-FM: KHTZ, 104.7 MHz.

Gardendale — Radio-FM: KFZX, 102.1 MHz.

Garland — Radio-AM: KAAM, 770 kHz. **TV:** KUVN-Ch. 23.

Garrison — Newspaper: Garrison In The News.

Gatesville — Newspaper: Gatesville Messenger and Star Forum (S). **Radio-FM:** KVLW, 88.1 MHz.

Georgetown — Newspapers: Sunday Sun; Williamson County Sun. **Radio-FM:** KHFI, 96.7 MHz; KLJA, 107.7.

George West — Radio-FM: KGWT, 93.5 MHz.

Giddings — Newspaper: Giddings Times & News. **Radio-FM:** KANJ, 91.1 MHz.

Gilmer — Newspaper: Gilmer Mirror (S). **Radio-AM:** KOFY, 1060 kHz. **Radio-FM:** KFRO, 95.3 MHz.

Ginger — Radio-FM: KYFA, 91.5 MHz.

Gladewater — Newspaper: Gladewater Mirror. **Radio-AM:** KEES, 1430 kHz.

Glen Rose — Newspapers: Glen Rose Newspaper; Glen Rose Reporter. **Radio-FM:** KTFW, 92.1 MHz.

Goldsmith — Radio-FM: KTXO, 94.7 MHz.

Goldthwaite — Newspaper: Goldthwaite Eagle.

Goliad — Newspaper: The Texan Express. **Radio-FM:** KHMC, 95.9 MHz.

Gonzales — Newspaper: Gonzales Inquirer (S). **Radio-AM:** KCTI, 1450 kHz. **Radio-FM:** KZAR, 88.1 MHz; KMLR, 106.3.

Gorman — Newspaper: Gorman Progress.

Graford — Newspaper: Lake Country Sun.

Graham — Newspaper: The Graham Leader (S). **Radio-AM:** KSWA, 1330 kHz. **Radio-FM:** KWKQ, 94.7 MHz.

Granbury — Newspaper: Hood County News (S). **Radio-AM:** KPIR, 1420 kHz.

Grand Prairie — Radio-AM: KKDA, 730 kHz.

Grand Saline — Newspaper: Grand Saline Sun.

Grandview — Newspaper: Grandview Tribune.

Grapeland — Newspaper: The Messenger (S).

Greenville — Newspaper: Herald-Banner (D). **Radio-AM:** KGVL, 1400 kHz. **Radio-FM:** KTXG, 90.5 MHz; KIKT, 93.5. **TV:** KTAQ-Ch. 46.

Gregory — Radio-FM: KPUS, 104.5 MHz.

Groesbeck — Newspaper: Groesbeck Journal.

Groom — Newspaper: Groom News.

Groves — Radio-FM: KCOL, 92.5 MHz.

Groveton — Newspaper: Groveton News.

Gun Barrel City — Newspaper: Cedar Creek Pilot.

Hale Center — Newspaper: Hale Center American.

Hallettsville — Newspaper: Hallettsville Tribune-Herald. **Radio-AM:** KHLT, 1520 kHz. **Radio-FM:** KTXM, 99.9 MHz.

Haltom City — Radio-FM: KLIF, 93.3 MHz.

Hamilton — Newspaper: Hamilton Herald-News. **Radio-AM:** KCLW, 900 kHz. **Radio-FM:** KHHG, 107.7 MHz.

Hamlin — Newspaper: Hamlin Herald. **Radio-FM:** KCDD, 103.7 MHz.

Hardin — Radio-FM: KGBV, 90.7 MHz.

Harker Heights — Radio-FM: KUSJ, 105.5 MHz.

Harlingen — Newspaper: Valley Morning Star (D). **Radio-AM:** KGBT, 1530 kHz. **Radio-FM:** KMBH, 88.9 MHz; KFRQ, 94.5; KBTQ, 96.1. **TV:** KGBT-Ch. 31; KLUJ-Ch. 34; KMBH-Ch. 38.

Hart — Newspaper: Hart Beat. **Radio-FM:** KKFC, 89.3 MHz.

Haskell — Newspaper: Haskell Free Press. **Radio-FM:** KVRP, 97.1 MHz.

Hearne — Newspaper: Hearne–Robertson County News. **Radio-FM:** KEDC, 88.5 MHz; KVJM, 103.1.

Hebbronville — Newspapers: Hebbronville View; Jim Hogg County Enterprise. **Radio-FM:** KAZF, 91.9 MHz; KEKO, 101.7.

Helotes — Radio-FM: KONO, 101.1 MHz.

Hemphill — Newspaper: The Sabine County Reporter. **Radio-AM:** KPBL, 1240 kHz. **Radio-FM:** KTHP, 103.9 MHz.

Hempstead — Newspaper: Waller County News-Citizen. **Radio-FM:** KTWL, 105.3 MHz.

Henderson — Newspaper: Henderson Daily News (D). **Radio-AM:** KWRD, 1470 kHz.

Henrietta — Newspaper: Clay County Leader.

Hereford — Newspaper: Hereford Brand (D). **Radio-AM:** KPAN, 860 kHz. **Radio-FM:** KRLH, 90.9 MHz; KJNZ, 103.5; KPAN, 106.3.

Hewitt — Newspaper: Hometown News. **Radio-FM:** KDRW, 106.7 MHz.

Hico — Newspaper: Hico News Review.

Highland Park — Radio-AM: KVCE, 1160 kHz. **Radio-FM:** KVIL, 103.7 MHz.

Highlands — Newspaper: Highlands Star/Crosby Courier.

Highland Village — Radio-FM: KWRD, 100.7 MHz.

Hillsboro — Newspaper: Hillsboro Reporter (S). **Radio-AM:** KHBR, 1560 kHz. **Radio-FM:** KBRQ, 102.5 MHz.

Holliday — Radio-FM: KGVB, 90.9 MHz; KWFB, 100.9.

Hondo — Newspaper: Hondo Anvil Herald. **Radio-AM:** KCWM, 1460 kHz. **Radio-FM:** KZIC, 89.9 MHz; KMFR, 105.9.

Honey Grove — Newspaper: The Weekly Gazette.

Hooks — Radio-FM: KPWW, 95.9 MHz.

Hornsby — Radio-FM: KOOP, 91.7 MHz.

Houston — Newspapers: Houston Business Journal; Houston Chronicle (D); Daily Court Review (D); Houston Forward Times; Jewish Herald-Voice. **Radio-AM:** KILT, 610 kHz; KTRH, 740; KBME, 790; KEYH, 850; KPRC, 950; KLAT, 1010; KNTH, 1070; KQUE, 1230; KXYZ, 1320; KCOH, 1430; KMIC, 1590. **Radio-FM:** KUHF, 88.7 MHz; KPFT, 90.1; KTSU, 90.9; KUHA, 91.7; KKRW, 93.7; KTBZ, 94.5; KKHH, 95.7; KHMX, 96.5; KBXX, 97.9; KODA, 99.1; KILT, 100.3; KLOL, 101.1; KMJQ, 102.1; KLTN, 102.9; KRBE, 104.1; KHCB, 105.7. **TV:** KUHT-Ch. 8; KHOU-Ch. 11; KTRK-Ch. 13; KTXH-Ch. 19; KETH-Ch. 24; KRIV-Ch. 26; KPRC-Ch. 35; KIAH-Ch. 38; KZJL-Ch. 44.

Howe — Newspaper: Texoma Enterprise. **Radio-FM:** KHYI, 95.3 MHz.

Hubbard — Newspaper: Hubbard City News.

Hudson — Radio-FM: KZXL, 96.3 MHz.

Humble — Radio-AM: KGOL, 1180 kHz. **Radio-FM:** KSBJ, 89.3 MHz.

Huntington — Radio-FM: KSML, 101.9 MHz.

Hunt — Radio-FM: KRZS, 99.9 MHz.

Huntsville — Newspaper: Huntsville Item (D). **Radio-AM:** KM2XVL, 1220 kHz; KHCH, 1410; KHVL, 1490. **Radio-FM:** KSHU, 90.5 MHz; KSAM, 101.7.

Hurst — Radio-AM: KMNY, 1360 kHz.

Hutto — Radio-FM: KYLR, 92.1 MHz.

Idalou — Newspaper: Idalou Beacon. **Radio-FM:** KRBL, 105.7 MHz.

Ingleside — Newspaper: Ingleside Index. **Radio-FM:** KAJE, 107.3 MHz.

Ingram — Newspaper: West Kerr Current. **Radio-FM:** KTXI, 90.1 MHz; KSYY, 96.5.

Iowa Park — Newspaper: Iowa Park Leader. **Radio-FM:** KXXN, 96.3 MHz.

Irving — Newspaper: The Irving Rambler. **TV:** KSTR-Ch. 48.

Jacksboro — Newspapers: Jacksboro Gazette-News; The Jack County Herald. **Radio-FM:** KJKB, 95.5 MHz.

Jacksonville — Newspaper: Jacksonville Daily Progress (D). **Radio-AM:** KEBE, 1400 kHz. **Radio-FM:** KBJS, 90.3 MHz; KLJT, 102.3; KOOI, 106.5. **TV:** KETK-Ch. 22.

Jasper — Newspaper: The Jasper Newsboy. **Radio-AM:** KCOX, 1350 kHz. **Radio-FM:** KTXJ, 102.7 MHz; KJAS, 107.3.

Jefferson — Newspaper: Jefferson Jimplecute. **Radio-FM:** KHCJ, 91.9 MHz; KJTX, 104.5.

Jewett — Newspaper: Jewett Messenger.

Johnson City — Newspaper: Johnson City Record-Courier. **Radio-FM:** KFAN, 107.9 MHz.

Joshua — Newspaper: Joshua Star.

Jourdanton — Radio-FM: KLEY, 95.7 MHz.

Junction — Newspaper: Junction Eagle. **Radio-AM:**

KMBL, 1450 kHz. **Radio-FM:** KOOK, 93.5 MHz.

Karnes City — **Newspaper:** The Karnes Countywide. **Radio-AM:** KAML, 990 kHz. **Radio-FM:** KHHL, 103.1 MHz.
Katy — **Newspaper:** Katy Times. **TV:** KYAZ-Ch. 47.
Kaufman — **Newspaper:** The Kaufman Herald.
Keene — **Newspaper:** Keene Star. **Radio-FM:** KJRN; 88.3 MHz.
Kempner — **Radio-FM:** KHLE, 106.9 MHz.
Kenedy — **Radio-AM:** KAML, 990 kHz. **Radio-FM:** KTNR, 92.1 MHz.
Kerens — **Newspaper:** Kerens Tribune. **Radio-FM:** KRVF, 106.9 MHz.
Kermit — **Newspaper:** The Winkler County News. **Radio-AM:** KERB, 600 kHz. **Radio-FM:** KERB, 106.3 MHz.
Kerrville — **Newspapers:** Kerrville Daily Times (D); Hill Country Community Journal. **Radio-AM:** KERV, 1230 kHz. **Radio-FM:** KKER, 88.7 MHz; KHKV, 91.1; KRNH, 92.3; KRVL, 94.3; KKVR, 106.1. **TV:** KMYS-Ch. 32.
Kilgore — **Newspaper:** Kilgore News Herald (S). **Radio-AM:** KDOK, 1240 kHz. **Radio-FM:** KZLO, 88.7 MHz; KKTX, 96.1.
Killeen — **Newspaper:** Killeen Daily Herald (D). **Radio-AM:** KRMY, 1050 kHz. **Radio-FM:** KNCT, 91.3 MHz; KIIZ, 92.3. **TV:** KAKW-Ch. 13.
Kingsville — **Newspaper:** Kingsville Record & Bishop News (S). **Radio-AM:** KINE, 1330 kHz. **Radio-FM:** KTAI, 91.1 MHz; KKBA, 92.7; KFTX, 97.5.
Kirbyville — **Newspaper:** Kirbyville Banner.
Knox City — **Newspaper:** Knox County News.
Kress — **Newspaper:** Kress Chronicle.
Krum — **Radio-FM:** KNOR, 93.7 MHz.
Kyle — **Newspaper:** Hays Free Press.

La Feria — **Newspaper:** La Feria News.
La Grange — **Newspaper:** The Fayette County Record (S). **Radio-AM:** KVLG, 1570 kHz. **Radio-FM:** KBUK, 104.9 MHz.
Lake Dallas — **Newspaper:** The Lake Cities Sun. **TV:** KAZD-Ch. 39.
Lake Jackson — **Radio-FM:** KYBJ, 91.1 MHz; KGLK, 107.5.
Lakeway — **Newspaper:** Lake Travis View.
Lamesa — **Newspaper:** Lamesa Press Reporter (S). **Radio-AM:** KPET, 690 kHz. **Radio-FM:** KBKN, 91.3 MHz; KTXC, 104.7.
Lampasas — **Newspaper:** Lampasas Dispatch Record (S). **Radio-AM:** KCYL, 1450 kHz.
La Porte — **Radio-FM:** KHJK, 103.7 MHz.
Laredo — **Newspaper:** Laredo Morning Times (D). **Radio-AM:** KLAR, 1300 kHz; KLNT, 1490. **Radio-FM:** KHOY, 88.1 MHz; KBNL, 89.9; KJBZ, 92.7; KQUR, 94.9; KRRG, 98.1; KNEX, 106.1. **TV:** KVTV-Ch. 13; KLDO-Ch. 19.
Laughlin AFB — **Radio-FM:** KDRX, 106.9 MHz.
La Vernia — **Newspaper:** La Vernia News.
League City — **Radio-AM:** KHCB, 1400 kHz.
Leakey — **Radio-FM:** KBLT, 104.3 MHz.
Leander — **Radio-FM:** KXBT, 98.9 MHz.
Leonard — **Newspaper:** Leonard Graphic.
Levelland — **Newspaper:** Levelland & Hockley County News-Press (S). **Radio-AM:** KLVT, 1230 kHz. **Radio-FM:** KJDL, 105.3 MHz.
Lewisville — **Radio-FM:** KESS, 107.9 MHz.
Lexington — **Newspaper:** Lexington Leader.
Liberty — **Newspaper:** The Vindicator. **Radio-FM:** KSHN, 99.9 MHz.
Liberty Hill — **Newspaper:** The Liberty Hill Independent.
Lindale — **Newspapers:** Lindale News & Times.
Linden — **Newspaper:** Cass County Sun.
Lindsay — **Newspaper:** Lindsay Letter.
Little Elm — **Newspaper:** The Little Elm Journal.
Littlefield — **Newspaper:** Lamb County Leader-News

(S). **Radio-AM:** KZZN, 1490 kHz.
Livingston — **Newspaper:** Polk County Enterprise (S). **Radio-AM:** KETX, 1440 kHz. **Radio-FM:** KETX, 92.3 MHz.
Llano — **Newspapers:** Llano County Journal; The Llano News. **Radio-FM:** KAJZ, 96.3 MHz; KITY, 102.9. **TV:** KBVO-Ch. 27.
Lockhart — **Newspaper:** Lockhart Post-Register. **Radio-AM:** KFIT, 1060 kHz.
Lometa — **Radio-FM:** KACQ, 101.9 MHz.
Longview — **Newspaper:** Longview News-Journal (D). **Radio-AM:** KFRO, 1370 kHz. **Radio-FM:** KYKX, 105.7 MHz. **TV:** KFXK-Ch. 31; KCEB-Ch. 51.
Lorena — **Radio-FM:** KYAR, 98.3 MHz.
Lorenzo — **Radio-FM:** KKCL, 98.1 MHz.
Los Ybañez — **Radio-FM:** KBXJ, 98.5 MHz.
Lovelady — **Radio-FM:** KHMR, 104.3 MHz.
Lubbock — **Newspaper:** Lubbock Avalanche-Journal (D). **Radio-AM:** KRFE, 580 kHz; KFYO, 790; KJTV, 950; KKAM, 1340; KJDL, 1420; KBZO, 1460; KDAV, 1590. **Radio-FM:** KTXT, 88.1 MHz; KOHM, 89.1; KAMY, 90.1; KKLU, 90.9; KXTQ, 93.7; KFMX, 94.5; KLLL, 96.3; KQBR, 99.5; KONE, 101.1; KZII, 102.5; KEJS, 106.5. **TV:** KCBD-Ch. 11; KPTB-Ch. 16; KTXT-Ch. 39; KLBK-Ch. 40.
Lufkin — **Newspaper:** Lufkin Daily News (D). **Radio-AM:** KRBA, 1340 kHz. **Radio-FM:** KLDN, 88.9 MHz; KSWP, 90.9; KAVX, 91.9; KAGZ, 93.9; KYBI, 100.1; KYKS, 105.1. **TV:** KTRE-Ch. 9.
Luling — **Newspaper:** Luling Newsboy and Signal. **Radio-FM:** KAMX, 94.7 MHz.
Lumberton — **Radio-AM:** KSET, 1300 kHz.
Lytle — **Newspapers:** Leader News; Medina Valley Times. **Radio-FM:** KZLV, 91.3 MHz.

Mabank — **Newspaper:** The Monitor (S). **Radio-AM:** KTXV, 890 kHz.
Madisonville — **Newspaper:** Madisonville Meteor. **Radio-AM:** KMVL, 1220 kHz. **Radio-FM:** KHML, 91.5 MHz; KAGG, 96.1; KMVL, 100.5; KKLB, 107.7.
Malakoff — **Newspaper:** Malakoff News. **Radio-FM:** KCKL, 95.9 MHz.
Manor — **Radio-AM:** KELG, 1440 kHz.
Marble Falls — **Newspapers:** The Highlander (S); The River Cities Sunday Tribune. **Radio-FM:** KBMD, 88.5 MHz.
Marfa — **Newspaper:** The Big Bend Sentinel. **Radio-FM:** KRTS, 93.5 MHz.
Marion — **Radio-AM:** KBIB, 1000 kHz.
Markham — **Radio-FM:** KKHA, 92.5 MHz.
Marlin — **Newspaper:** The Marlin Democrat. **Radio-FM:** KRMX, 92.9 MHz.
Marshall — **Newspaper:** Marshall News Messenger (D). **Radio-AM:** KCUL, 1410 kHz; KMHT, 1450. **Radio-FM:** KBWC, 91.1 MHz; KCUL, 92.3; KMHT, 103.9.
Mart — **Newspaper:** Mart Messenger. **Radio-FM:** KSUR, 88.9 MHz.
Mason — **Newspaper:** Mason County News. **Radio-FM:** KOTY, 95.7 MHz; KYRT, 97.7; KZZM, 101.7; KHLB, 102.5.
Matador — **Newspaper:** Motley County Tribune.
Mathis — **Newspaper:** Mathis News.
McAllen — **Newspaper:** The Monitor (D). **Radio-AM:** KRIO, 910 kHz. **Radio-FM:** KHID, 88.1 MHz; KVMV, 96.9; KGBT, 98.5. **TV:** KNVO-Ch. 49.
McCamey — **Radio-FM:** KPBM, 95.3 MHz.
McCook — **Radio-FM:** KCAS, 91.5 MHz.
McGregor — **Newspaper:** McGregor Mirror & Crawford Sun.
McKinney — **Newspapers:** McKinney Courier-Gazette (D); Collin County Commercial Record. **Radio-FM:** KNTU, 88.1 MHz.
McQueeney — **Radio-FM:** KLTO, 97.7 MHz.
Melissa — **Newspaper:** The Anna-Melissa Tribune.
Memphis — **Newspaper:** Hall County Herald. **Radio-FM:**

KLSR, 105.3 MHz.
Menard — Newspaper: Menard News and Messenger.
Mercedes — Newspaper: Mercedes Enterprise. **Radio-FM:** KTEX, 100.3 MHz.
Meridian — Newspaper: Meridian Tribune. **Radio-FM:** KOME, 95.3 MHz.
Merkel — Newspaper: Merkel Mail. **Radio-AM:** KMXO, 1500 kHz. **Radio-FM:** KHXS, 102.7 MHz.
Mertzon — Radio-FM: KMEO, 91.9 MHz.
Mesquite — Radio-FM: KEOM, 88.5 MHz.
Mexia — Newspaper: The Mexia News (TW). **Radio-AM:** KLRK, 1590 kHz. **Radio-FM:** KWBT, 104.9 MHz.
Miami — Newspaper: Miami Chief.
Midland — Newspaper: Midland Reporter-Telegram (D). **Radio-AM:** KCRS, 550 kHz; KWEL, 1070; KLPF, 1150; KMND, 1510. **Radio-FM:** KPBJ, 90.1 MHz; KVDG, 90.9; KNFM, 92.3; KZBT, 93.3; KQRX, 95.1; KCRS, 103.3; KCHX, 106.7. **TV:** KUPB-Ch. 18.
Midlothian — Newspaper: Midlothian Mirror.
Miles — Newspaper: Miles Messenger.
Mineola — Newspaper: Mineola Monitor. **Radio-FM:** KMOO, 99.9 MHz.
Mineral Wells — Newspaper: Mineral Wells Index (D). **Radio-AM:** KVTT, 1110 kHz. **Radio-FM:** KFWR, 95.9 MHz.
Mirando City — Radio-FM: KBDR, 100.5 MHz.
Mission — Newspaper: Progress-Times. **Radio-AM:** KIRT, 1580 kHz. **Radio-FM:** KQXX, 105.5 MHz.
Missouri City — Radio-AM: KBRZ, 1460 kHz.
Monahans — Newspaper: The Monahans News (S). **Radio-AM:** KCKM, 1330 kHz. **Radio-FM:** KBAT, 99.9 MHz.
Morton — Newspaper: Morton Tribune. **Radio-FM:** KQOA, 91.1 MHz; KPGA, 91.9.
Moulton — Newspaper: Moulton Eagle.
Mount Pleasant — Newspaper: Daily Tribune (D). **Radio-AM:** KIMP, 960 kHz. **Radio-FM:** KYZQ, 88.3 MHz.
Mount Vernon — Newspaper: Mount Vernon Optic-Herald.
Muenster — Newspaper: Muenster Enterprise. **Radio-FM:** KZZA, 106.7 MHz.
Muleshoe — Newspaper: Muleshoe Journal. **Radio-FM:** KMUL, 103.1 MHz.
Munday — Newspaper: The Munday Courier.
Murphy — Newspaper: Murphy Monitor.

Nacogdoches — Newspaper: Nacogdoches Daily Sentinel (D). **Radio-AM:** KSFA, 860 kHz. **Radio-FM:** KSAU, 90.1 MHz; KJCS, 103.3; KTBQ, 107.7. **TV:** KYTX-Ch. 18.
Naples — Newspaper: The Monitor.
Natalia — Radio-FM: KYRQ, 90.3 MHz.
Navasota — Newspaper: The Navasota Examiner. **Radio-AM:** KWBC, 1550 kHz. **Radio-FM:** KWUP, 92.5 MHz.
Nederland — Radio-AM: KBED, 1510 kHz.
Needville — Newspaper: The Gulf Coast Tribune.
New Boston — Newspaper: Bowie County Citizen Tribune (S). **Radio-AM:** KLBW, 1530 kHz. **Radio-FM:** KEWL, 95.1 MHz; KZRB, 103.5; KTTY, 105.1.
New Braunfels — Newspaper: Herald-Zeitung (D). **Radio-AM:** KGNB, 1420 kHz. **Radio-FM:** KNBT, 92.1 MHz.
New Deal — Radio-FM: KLZK, 97.3 MHz.
Newton — Newspaper: Newton County News.
New Ulm — Newspaper: New Ulm Enterprise. **Radio-FM:** KNRG, 92.3 MHz.
Nixon — Newspaper: Cow Country Courier.
Nocona — Newspaper: Nocona News.
Nolanville — Radio-FM: KLFX, 107.3 MHz.
Normangee — Newspaper: Normangee Star.

Odem — Newspaper: Odem-Edroy Times. **Radio-FM:** KMJR, 98.3 MHz.

Odessa — Newspaper: Odessa American (D). **Radio-AM:** KFLB, 920 kHz; KOZA, 1230; KRIL, 1410. **Radio-FM:** KBMM, 89.5 MHz; KLVW, 90.5; KOCV, 91.3; KMRK, 96.1; KMCM, 96.9; KODM, 97.9; KHKX, 99.1; KQLM, 107.9. **TV:** KOSA-Ch. 7; KPEJ-Ch. 23; KWWT-Ch. 30; KPBT-Ch. 38; KMLM-Ch. 42.
O'Donnell — Newspaper: O'Donnell Index-Press.
Olney — Newspaper: The Olney Enterprise.
Olton — Newspaper: Olton Enterprise.
Orange — Newspaper: The Orange Leader (D). **Radio-AM:** KOGT, 1600 kHz. **Radio-FM:** KKMY, 104.5 MHz; KIOC, 106.1.
Ore City — Radio-FM: KAZE, 106.9 MHz.
Overland — Radio-FM: KKVI, 89.9 MHz.
Overton — Newspaper: Overton Press. **Radio-FM:** KPXI, 100.7 MHz.
Ozona — Newspaper: Ozona Stockman. **Radio-FM:** KYXX, 94.3 MHz.

Paducah — Newspaper: Paducah Post.
Paint Rock — Newspaper: Concho Herald.
Palacios — Newspaper: Palacios Beacon. **Radio-FM:** KROY, 99.7 MHz.
Palestine — Newspaper: Palestine Herald Press (D). **Radio-AM:** KNET, 1450 kHz. **Radio-FM:** KYFP, 89.1 MHz; KYYK, 98.3.
Pampa — Newspaper: The Pampa News (D). **Radio-AM:** KGRO, 1230 kHz. **Radio-FM:** KAVO, 90.9 MHz; KOMX, 100.3; KDRL, 103.3.
Panhandle — Newspaper: Panhandle Herald White Deer News.
Paris — Newspaper: Paris News (D). **Radio-AM:** KZHN, 1250 kHz; KPLT, 1490. **Radio-FM:** KHCP, 89.3 MHz; KOYN, 93.9; KBUS, 101.9; KPLT, 107.7.
Pasadena — Newspaper: The Pasadena Citizen (S). **Radio-AM:** KIKK, 650 kHz; KLVL, 1480. **Radio-FM:** KFTG, 88.1 MHz; KKBQ, 92.9.
Pearland — Newspapers: Pearland Journal; Pearland Reporter News.
Pearsall — Newspaper: Frio-Nueces Current. **Radio-AM:** KVWG, 1280 kHz. **Radio-FM:** KSAG, 103.3 MHz; KSAH, 104.1.
Pecan Grove — Radio-AM: KREH, 900 kHz.
Pecos — Newspaper: Pecos Enterprise (S). **Radio-AM:** KIUN, 1400 kHz. **Radio-FM:** KPKO, 91.3 MHz; KGEE, 97.3; KPTX, 98.3.
Perryton — Newspaper: Perryton Herald (S). **Radio-AM:** KEYE, 1400 kHz. **Radio-FM:** KEYE, 96.1 MHz.
Pflugerville — Newspaper: Pflugerville Pflag. **Radio-AM:** KOKE, 1600 kHz.
Pharr — Newspaper: Advance News Journal. **Radio-AM:** KVJY, 840 kHz.
Pilot Point — Newspaper: Pilot Point Post-Signal. **Radio-FM:** KZMP, 104.9 MHz.
Pittsburg — Newspaper: Pittsburg Gazette. **Radio-FM:** KGWP, 91.1 MHz; KPIT, 91.7; KSCN, 96.9; KMPA, 103.1.
Plains — Radio-FM: KPHS, 90.3 MHz.
Plainview — Newspaper: Plainview Daily Herald (D). **Radio-AM:** KVOP, 1090 kHz; KREW, 1400. **Radio-FM:** KPMB, 88.5 MHz; KBAH, 90.5; KWLD, 91.5; KRIA, 103.9; KKYN, 106.9.
Plano — Newspaper: Plano Star Courier (S). **Radio-AM:** KMKI, 620 kHz.
Pleasanton — Newspaper: Pleasanton Express. **Radio-AM:** KWMF, 1380 kHz.
Pleasant Valley — Radio-FM: KZAM, 98.7 MHz.
Point Comfort — Radio-FM: KJAZ, 94.1 MHz.
Port Aransas — Newspaper: Port Aransas South Jetty.
Port Arthur — Newspaper: The Port Arthur News (D). **Radio-AM:** KDEI, 1250 kHz; KOLE, 1340. **Radio-FM:** KQBU, 93.3 MHz; KTJM, 98.5.
Port Isabel — Newspaper: Port Isabel/South Padre Press (S). **Radio-FM:** KNVO, 101.1 MHz.
Portland — Newspaper: Portland News; The Coastal

Bend Herald. **Radio-FM:** KSGR, 91.1 MHz; KLHB, 105.5.

Port Lavaca — Newspaper: Port Lavaca Wave (S). **Radio-FM:** KITE, 93.3 MHz.

Port Neches — Radio-AM: KBPO, 1150 kHz.

Port O'Connor — Radio-FM: KHPO, 91.9 MHz.

Post — Newspaper: Post Dispatch. **Radio-FM:** KSSL, 107.3 MHz.

Prairie View — Radio-FM: KPVU, 91.3 MHz.

Premont — Radio-FM: KLBD, 88.1 MHz; KMFM, 100.7.

Presidio — Newspaper: The International Presidio Paper.

Princeton — Newspaper: Princeton Herald.

Quanah — Newspaper: Quanah Tribune-Chief. **Radio-AM:** KOLJ, 1150 kHz.

Quinlan — Newspaper: The Quinlan-Tawakoni News.

Quitaque — Newspaper: Valley Tribune.

Quitman — Newspaper: Wood County Democrat.

Ralls — Newspaper: Crosby County News. **Radio-AM:** KCLR, 1530 kHz.

Ranger — Newspaper: Ranger Times (S). **Radio-FM:** KWBY, 98.5 MHz.

Rankin — Newspaper: Pecos River Dispatch.

Raymondville — Newspaper: Chronicle/Willacy County News. **Radio-AM:** KSOX, 1240 kHz. **Radio-FM:** KBUC, 102.1 MHz; KBIC, 105.7.

Red Oak — Newspapers: Ellis County Chronicle; Red Oak Record.

Refugio — Newspaper: Refugio County Press. **Radio-FM:** KRIK, 100.5 MHz; KOUL, 103.7; KYRK, 106.1.

Reno — Radio-FM: KLOW, 98.9 MHz.

Richardson — Radio-AM: KKLF, 1700 kHz.

Richmond — Radio-AM: KRTX, 980 kHz.

Riesel — Newspaper: Riesel Rustler.

Rio Grande City — Radio-FM: KRGX, 95.1 MHz; KQBO, 107.5. **TV:** KTLM-Ch. 40.

Rising Star — Newspaper: Rising Star.

Robert Lee — Newspaper: Observer/Enterprise.

Robinson — Radio-FM: KWPW, 107.9 MHz.

Robstown — Newspaper: Nueces County Record-Star. **Radio-AM:** KROB, 1510 kHz. **Radio-FM:** KLUX, 89.5 MHz; KSAB, 99.9; KMIQ, 104.9.

Rockdale — Newspaper: Rockdale Reporter. **Radio-FM:** KRXT, 98.5 MHz.

Rockport — Newspapers: Rockport Pilot (S); The Coastal Bend Herald. **Radio-FM:** KKPN, 102.3 MHz.

Rocksprings — Newspaper: Texas Mohair Weekly.

Rockwall — Newspaper: Rockwall County News.

Rollingwood — Radio-AM: KJCE, 1370 kHz.

Roma — Newspaper: South Texas Reporter. **Radio-FM:** KRIO, 97.7 MHz.

Rosebud — Newspaper: Rosebud News.

Rosenberg — Newspaper: Rosenberg Herald & Texas Coaster (D). **Radio-AM:** KRTX, 980 kHz. **TV:** KXLN-Ch. 45.

Rotan — Newspaper: Rotan Advance-Star-Record.

Round Rock — Newspaper: Round Rock Leader (TW). **Radio-FM:** KNLE, 88.1 MHz; KFMK, 105.9.

Rowena — Newspaper: Rowena Press.

Rowlett — Newspaper: The Rowlett Lakeshore Times.

Rudolph — Radio-FM: KTER, 90.7 MHz.

Rusk — Newspaper: Cherokeean Herald. **Radio-AM:** KTLU, 1580 kHz. **Radio-FM:** KWRW, 97.7 MHz.

Sachse — Newspaper: Sachse News.

Saint Jo — Newspaper: Saint Jo Tribune.

Salado — Newspaper: Salado Village Voice.

San Angelo — Newspaper: San Angelo Standard-Times (D). **Radio-AM:** KGKL, 960 kHz; KKSA, 1260; KCRN, 1340. **Radio-FM:** KNAR, 89.3 MHz; KNCH, 90.1; KLTP, 90.9; KDCD, 92.9; KCRN, 93.9; KIXY, 94.7; KGKL, 97.5; KELI, 98.7; KCLL, 100.1; KWFR, 101.9; KMDX, 106.1; KSJT, 107.5. **TV:** KLST-Ch. 11; KSAN-

Ch. 16; KIDY-Ch. 19.

San Antonio — Newspapers: San Antonio Business Journal; Commercial Recorder (D); Express-News (D); Hart Beat (TW); Today's Catholic (BW). **Radio-AM:** KTSA, 550 kHz; KSLR, 630; KKYX, 680; KTKR, 760; KONO, 860; KRDY, 1160; WOAI, 1200; KZDC, 1250; KAHL, 1310; KCOR, 1350; KCHL, 1480; KEDA, 1540. **Radio-FM:** KPAC, 88.3 MHz; KSTX, 89.1; KSYM, 90.1; KYFS, 90.9; KRTU, 91.7; KROM, 92.9; KXXM, 96.1; KAJA, 97.3; KISS, 99.5; KCYY, 100.3; KQXT, 101.9; KJXK, 102.7; KZEP, 104.5; KXTN, 107.5. **TV:** KLRN-Ch. 9; KSAT-Ch. 12; KHCE-Ch. 16; KABB-Ch. 30; KVDA-Ch. 38; KENS-Ch. 39; KWEX-Ch. 41; WOAI-Ch. 48.

San Augustine — Newspaper: San Augustine Tribune. **Radio-FM:** KDET, 92.5 MHz.

San Benito — Newspaper: San Benito News (S). **Radio-FM:** KHKZ, 106.3 MHz.

San Diego — Radio-FM: KUKA, 105.9 MHz.

Sanger — Newspaper: Sanger Courier. **Radio-FM:** KVRK, 89.7 MHz; KTDK, 104.1.

San Juan — Radio-AM: KUBR, 1210 kHz.

San Marcos — Newspaper: San Marcos Daily Record (D). **Radio-AM:** KUOL, 1470 kHz. **Radio-FM:** KTSW, 89.9 MHz; KBPA, 103.5.

San Saba — Newspaper: San Saba News & Star. **Radio-AM:** KNVR, 1410 kHz. **Radio-FM:** KNUZ, 106.1 MHz.

Santa Fe — Radio-FM: KJIC, 90.5 MHz.

Savoy — Radio-FM: KQDR, 107.3 MHz.

Schertz — Radio-FM: KBBT, 98.5 MHz.

Schulenburg — Newspaper: Schulenburg Sticker.

Seabrook — Radio-FM: KROI, 92.1 MHz.

Seadrift — Radio-FM: KMAT, 105.1 MHz.

Seagoville — Newspaper: Suburbia News.

Seagraves — Newspaper: Tri County Tribune.

Sealy — Newspaper: The Sealy News. **Radio-FM:** KQLC, 90.7 MHz.

Seguin — Newspaper: Seguin Gazette-Enterprise (D). **Radio-AM:** KWED, 1580 kHz. **Radio-FM:** KSMG, 105.3 MHz.

Seminole — Newspaper: Seminole Sentinel (S). **Radio-AM:** KIKZ, 1250 kHz. **Radio-FM:** KSEM, 106.3 MHz.

Seymour — Newspaper: Baylor County Banner. **Radio-AM:** KSEY, 1230 kHz. **Radio-FM:** KSEY, 94.3 MHz.

Shamrock — Newspaper: County Star-News.

Shepherd — Newspaper: San Jacinto News-Times.

Shenandoah — Radio-AM: KRCM, 1380 kHz.

Sherman — Newspaper: Herald Democrat (D). **Radio-AM:** KJIM, 1500 kHz. **TV:** KXII-Ch. 20.

Shiner — Newspaper: The Shiner Gazette.

Silsbee — Newspaper: Silsbee Bee. **Radio-FM:** KAYD, 101.7 MHz.

Silverton — Newspaper: Briscoe County News.

Sinton — Newspaper: San Patricio County News. **Radio-AM:** KDAE, 1590 kHz. **Radio-FM:** KNCN, 101.3 MHz.

Slaton — Newspaper: Slaton Slatonite. **Radio-FM:** KJAK, 92.7 MHz.

Smithville — Newspaper: Smithville Times.

Snyder — Newspaper: Snyder Daily News (D). **Radio-AM:** KSNY, 1450 kHz. **Radio-FM:** KGWB, 91.1 MHz; KLYD, 98.9; KSNY, 101.5. **TV:** KPCB-Ch. 17.

Somerset — Radio-AM: KYTY, 810 kHz.

Somerville — Radio-FM: KUTX, 88.1 MHz.

Sonora — Newspaper: Devil's River News. **Radio-FM:** KHOS, 92.1 MHz.

South Padre Island — Radio-FM: KESO, 92.7 MHz; KZSP, 95.3.

Spearman — Newspaper: Hansford County Reporter-Statesman. **Radio-FM:** KTOT, 89.5 MHz; KXDJ, 98.3.

Springtown — Newspaper: Springtown Epigraph. **Radio-FM:** KSQX, 89.1 MHz.

Spur — Newspaper: Texas Spur.

Stamford — Newspapers: The New Stamford American; The Stamford Star. **Radio-AM:** KVRP, 1400 kHz. **Radio-FM:** KLGD, 106.9 MHz.

Stanton — Newspaper: Martin County Messenger. **Radio-FM:** KFLB, 88.1 MHz; KKJW, 105.9.
Stephenville — Newspaper: Stephenville Empire Tribune (D). **Radio-AM:** KSTV, 1510 kHz. **Radio-FM:** KQXS, 89.1 MHz; KEQX, 89.7; KTRL, 90.5.
Sterling City — Radio-FM: KNRX, 96.5 MHz.
Stratford — Newspaper: Stratford Star.
Sulphur Bluff — Radio-FM: KETE, 99.7 MHz.
Sulphur Springs — Newspaper: News-Telegram (D). **Radio-AM:** KSST, 1230 kHz. **Radio-FM:** KGPF, 91.1 MHz; KZRF, 91.9; KSCH, 95.9.
Sweetwater — Newspaper: Sweetwater Reporter (D). **Radio-AM:** KXOX, 1240 kHz. **Radio-FM:** KXOX, 96.7. **TV:** KTXS-Ch. 20.

Taft — Newspaper: Taft Tribune.
Tahoka — Newspaper: Lynn County News. **Radio-FM:** KMMX, 100.3 MHz; KAMZ, 103.5.
Tatum — Newspaper: Trammel Trace Tribune. **Radio-FM:** KZQX, 100.3 MHz.
Taylor — Newspaper: Taylor Daily Press (D). **Radio-AM:** KWNX, 1260 kHz. **Radio-FM:** KLQB, 104.3 MHz.
Teague — Newspaper: Teague Chronicle.
Temple — Newspaper: Temple Daily Telegram (D). **Radio-AM:** KTEM, 1400 kHz. **Radio-FM:** KVLT, 88.5 MHz; KBDE, 89.9; KLTD, 101.7. **TV:** KCEN-Ch. 9.
Terrell — Newspaper: Terrell Tribune (S). **Radio-AM:** KPYK, 1570 kHz.
Terrell Hills — Radio-AM: KLUP, 930 kHz. **Radio-FM:** KTKX, 106.7 MHz.
Texarkana — Newspaper: Texarkana Gazette (D). **Radio-AM:** KCMC, 740 kHz; KTFS, 940; KKTK, 1400. **Radio-FM:** KTXK, 91.5 MHz; KTAL, 98.1; KKYR, 102.5. **TV:** KTAL-Ch. 15.
Texas City — Radio-AM: KYST, 920 kHz.
Thorndale — Newspaper: Thorndale Champion. **Radio-FM:** KLGO, 99.3 MHz.
Three Rivers — Newspaper: The Progress. **Radio-FM:** KEMA, 94.5 MHz.
Throckmorton — Newspaper: Throckmorton Tribune.
Timpson — Newspaper: Timpson & Tenaha News.
Tomball — Radio-AM: KSEV, 700 kHz.
Tom Bean — Radio-FM: KLAK, 97.5 MHz.
Trenton — Newspaper: Trenton Tribune.
Trinity — Newspaper: Trinity Standard.
Tulia — Newspapers: Swisher County News; Tulia Herald. **Radio-AM:** KTUE, 1260 kHz. **Radio-FM:** KBTE, 104.9 MHz.
Tuscola — Newspaper: Jim Ned Journal (BW).
Tye — Radio-FM: KBCY, 99.7 MHz.
Tyler — Newspapers: Tyler Morning Telegraph (D). **Radio-AM:** KTBB, 600 kHz; KGLD, 1330; KYZS, 1490. **Radio-FM:** KVNE, 89.5 MHz; KGLY, 91.3; KTBB, 92.1; KTYL, 93.1; KNUE, 101.5; KKUS, 104.1. **TV:** KLTV-Ch. 7.

Umbarger — Radio-FM: KRBG, 88.7 MHz.
Universal City — Radio-AM: KSAH, 720 kHz.
University Park — Radio-AM: KTNO, 1440 kHz; KZMP, 1540.
Uvalde — Newspaper: Uvalde Leader-News (S). **Radio-AM:** KVOU, 1400 kHz. **Radio-FM:** KBNU, 93.9 MHz; KUVA, 102.3; KVOU, 104.9. **TV:** KPXL-Ch. 26.

Valley Mills — Newspaper: Valley Mills Progress.
Valley View — Radio-FM: KQFZ, 89.1 MHz.
Van — Newspaper: Van Banner.
Van Alstyne — Newspaper: Van Alstyne Leader.
Van Horn — Newspaper: Van Horn Advocate. **Radio-FM:** KVHR, 91.5 MHz.
Vega — Newspaper: Vega Enterprise.
Vernon — Newspaper: Vernon Daily Record (D). **Radio-AM:** KVWC, 1490 kHz. **Radio-FM:** KVED, 88.5 MHz; KVWC, 103.1.
Victoria — Newspaper: Victoria Advocate (D). **Radio-**

AM: KVNN, 1340 kHz; KNAL, 1410. **Radio-FM:** KAYK, 88.5 MHz; KXBJ, 89.3; KVRT, 90.7; KQVT, 92.3; KVIC, 95.1; KTXN, 98.7; KBAR, 100.9; KIXS, 107.9. **TV:** KAVU-Ch. 15.
Vidor — Newspaper: Vidor Vidorian.

Waco — Newspapers: The Suburban Courier. The Waco Citizen; Waco Tribune-Herald (D); **Radio-AM:** KBBW, 1010 kHz; KWTX, 1230; KRZI, 1660. **Radio-FM:** KBCT, 94.5; KBGO, 95.7; KWTX, 97.5; WACO, 99.9; KWBU, 103.3. **TV:** KDYW-Ch 20; KXXV-Ch. 26; KWKT-Ch. 44; KWTX-Ch. 53.
Wake Village — Radio-FM: KHTA, 92.5 MHz.
Wallis — Newspaper: Wallis News-Review.
Waskom — Radio-FM: KQHN, 97.3 MHz.
Waxahachie — Newspaper: Waxahachie Daily Light (D). **Radio-AM:** KBEC, 1390 kHz.
Weatherford — Newspaper: Weatherford Democrat (D). **Radio-AM:** KZEE, 1220 kHz. **Radio-FM:** KMQX, 88.5 MHz; KYQX, 89.5.
Weimar — Newspaper: Weimar Mercury.
Wells — Radio-FM: KVLL, 94.7 MHz.
Wellington — Newspaper: Wellington Leader.
Weslaco — Radio-AM: KRGE, 1290 kHz. **TV:** KRGV-Ch. 13.
West — Newspaper: The West News.
West Lake Hills — Radio-AM: KTXZ, 1560 kHz.
West Odessa — Radio-FM: KFRI, 88.7 MHz.
Wharton — Newspaper: Wharton Journal-Spectator (S). **Radio-AM:** KANI, 1500 kHz.
Wheeler — Newspaper: The Wheeler Times. **Radio-FM:** KLXL, 88.3 MHz; KPDR, 90.3.
Whitehouse — Newspaper: Tri County Leader. **Radio-FM:** KISX, 107.3 MHz.
White Oak — Newspaper: White Oak Independent. **Radio-FM:** KZTK, 99.3 MHz.
Whitesboro — Newspaper: Whitesboro News-Record. **Radio-FM:** KMAD, 102.5 MHz.
Whitewright — Newspaper: Whitewright Sun.
Whitney — Newspaper: Lake Whitney Views (M).
Wichita Falls — Newspaper: Times-Record-News (D). **Radio-AM:** KWFS, 1290. **Radio-FM:** KMCU, 88.7 MHz; KMOC, 89.5; KZKL, 90.5; KNIN, 92.9; KLUR, 99.9; KWFS, 102.3; KQXC, 103.9; KBZS, 106.3. **TV:** KJTL-Ch. 15; KAUZ-Ch. 22; KFDX-Ch. 28.
Willis — Radio-FM: KVST, 99.7 MHz.
Wills Point — Newspaper: Wills Point Chronicle.
Wimberley — Newspaper: Wimberley View (S).
Winfield — Radio-FM: KALK, 97.7 MHz.
Winnie — Newspaper: The Hometown Press. **Radio-FM:** KKHT, 100.7 MHz.
Winnsboro — Newspaper: Winnsboro News. **Radio-FM:** KWNS, 104.7 MHz.
Winona — Radio-FM: KBLZ, 102.7 MHz.
Winters — Newspaper: Winters Enterprise. **Radio-FM:** KFNA, 96.1 MHz.
Wixon Valley — Radio-FM: KBXT, 101.9 MHz.
Wolfe City — Newspaper: Wolfe City Mirror.
Wolfforth — Radio-FM: KAIQ, 95.5 MHz. **TV:** KLCW-Ch. 43.
Woodville — Newspaper: Tyler County Booster. **Radio-AM:** KWUD, 1490 kHz.
Wylie — Newspaper: The Wylie News. **Radio-AM:** KHSE, 700 kHz.

Yoakum — Newspaper: Yoakum Herald-Times. **Radio-FM:** KYKM, 92.5 MHz.
Yorktown — Newspaper: Yorktown News-View. **Radio-FM:** KGGB, 96.3 MHz.

Zapata — Newspaper: Zapata County News. **Radio-FM:** KBAW, 93.5 MHz; KJJS, 103.9. ☆

Transportation

Interstate 10 near Van Horn, Culberson County. Photo by Robert Plocheck.

Highways
Railroads
Aviation
Ports
Freight Gateways
Foreign Trade Zones
Consulates

Freight Railroads in Texas

In Texas in 2008 there were 44 railroad companies operating, carrying 384 million tons of freight. A complete list of railroads is in the Counties section on page 233. *Source: Association of American Railroads.*

Railroads in State	Miles Operated
Class I *(3 – see chart at right)*	12,130
Regional (2)	1,058
Local (19)	741
Switching & Terminal (20)	1,003
Total	**14,982**
Total excluding trackage rights*	**10,743**

Railroads in State	Miles Operated
Class I	
Union Pacific Railroad Co.	6,331
BNSF Railway Co.	4,941
Kansas City Southern Railway Co.	908

*Trackage rights — track provided by another railroad. Numbers in parentheses represent the number of railroad companies in each category.

Freight Traffic in Texas by Kind – 2008							
Carloads originated		Tons		**Carloads terminated**		Tons	
Chemicals	393,847	34.1 million		Coal	565,975	67.2 million	
Gravel, crushed stone	174,506	17.9 million		Gravel, crushed stone	312,934	32.6 million	
Petroleum products	99,152	8.8 million		Farm products	246,710	25.6 million	
Intermodal	504,560	8.5 million		Chemicals	273,608	23.4 million	
Farm products	64,641	5.0 million		Food products	157,318	12.0 million	
All Other	708,283	22.3 million		All Other	1,540,003	49.5 million	
Total	**1,944,989**	**96.6 million**		**Total**	**3,096,548**	**210.3 million**	

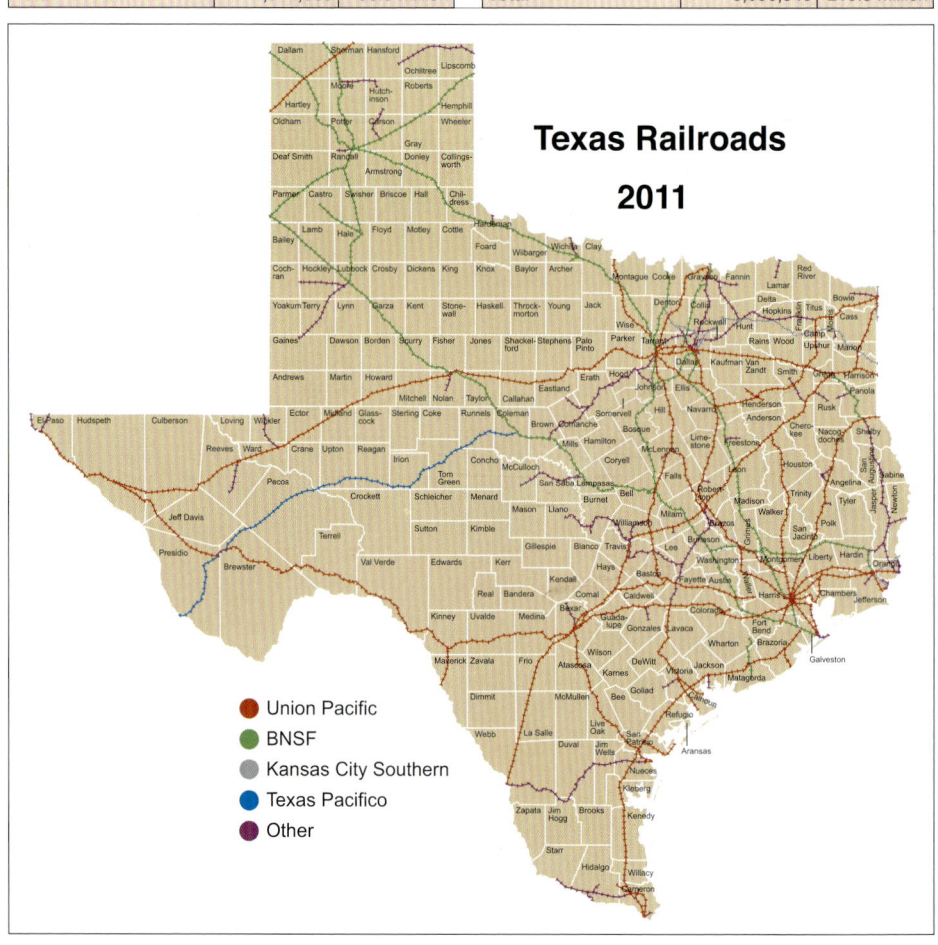

Texas Railroads 2011

- Union Pacific
- BNSF
- Kansas City Southern
- Texas Pacifico
- Other

Artwork on an underpass in Bryan. Photo by Ron Billings; Texas Forest Service.

Highway Miles, Construction, Maintenance, Vehicles: 2010

Texans drove more than 21.5 million motor vehicles in 2010 over 300,000 miles of roadways, including city- and county-maintained roads. That driving is calculated to have included more than 464 million miles driven daily on the 192,000 miles of state-maintained highways alone.

The Texas Department of Transportation (TxDOT) is responsible for state highway construction and maintenance, motor vehicles titles and registration, commercial trucking, automobile dealer licensing and the state's 12 official Texas Travel Information Centers and 100 safety rest areas.

The following mileage, maintenance and construction figures (listed by county) refer only to roads that are maintained by the state: Interstates, U.S. highways, state highways, farm-to-market roads and some loops around urban areas. Not included are city- or county-maintained streets and roads. A lane mile is one lane for one mile; i.e., one mile of four-lane highway equals four lane miles. Source: Texas Department of Transportation, 2011.

County	Vehicles Registered	Lane Miles of Highway	Vehicle Miles Driven Daily	State Construction Expenditures	Combined Construction Maintenance Expenditures	State Net Receipts	County Net Receipts	Total Vehicle Registration Fees
Anderson	49,740	971	1,124,234	$ 11,728,269	$20,985,881	$ 2,072,942	$ 985,533	$ 3,058,474
Andrews	17,040	545	510,957	2,228,417	7,460,686	822,032	429,376	1,251,407
Angelina	83,478	929	2,042,803	12,351,224	24,899,997	3,914,183	1,507,639	5,421,822
Aransas	24,948	203	419,307	604,932	1,969,544	915,800	545,779	1,461,579
Archer	11,653	547	323,090	3,955,009	7,004,376	243,978	457,326	701,304
Armstrong	2,800	378	349,643	824,220	6,870,396	3,941	161,733	165,673
Atascosa	39,511	1,010	1,331,317	6,265,086	14,805,284	1,456,034	843,337	2,299,372
Austin	37,851	613	1,248,861	5,022,617	13,565,655	1,559,163	809,537	2,368,700
Bailey	6,689	490	198,285	288,516	1,744,441	77,460	386,452	463,912
Bandera	25,677	417	397,609	1,173,202	3,792,304	764,765	626,100	1,390,864
Bastrop	72,852	809	1,901,906	2,840,260	14,955,520	3,049,897	1,329,811	4,379,709
Baylor	4,606	499	160,432	1,771,429	3,699,189	10,755	249,791	260,546
Bee	21,659	655	531,164	7,897,496	16,274,842	694,403	620,379	1,314,782
Bell	267,380	1,506	5,746,501	91,448,811	121,383,020	12,197,410	4,790,944	16,988,354
Bexar	1,362,454	3,341	26,877,750	82,664,927	189,136,062	70,833,858	23,204,609	94,038,467
Blanco	14,634	462	515,296	860,146	3,495,773	479,875	431,935	911,810
Borden	1,120	344	52,309	58,044	1,060,638	1,458	46,080	47,539
Bosque	22,045	696	437,825	1,426,582	5,558,400	589,567	606,432	1,195,998

County	Vehicles Registered	Lane Miles of Highway	Vehicle Miles Driven Daily	State Construction Expenditures	Combined Construction Maintenance Expenditures	State Net Receipts	County Net Receipts	Total Vehicle Registration Fees
Bowie	89,932	1,203	2,680,895	32,146,059	57,515,399	3,884,245	1,620,755	5,505,000
Brazoria	286,072	1,317	4,377,928	72,477,957	100,527,278	13,879,641	4,333,877	18,213,518
Brazos	131,112	944	3,009,831	31,326,456	58,593,622	6,449,996	2,472,625	8,922,621
Brewster	10,688	608	236,540	2,114,856	5,861,622	266,926	364,593	631,518
Briscoe	2,351	326	50,964	250,957	1,201,147	4,939	143,301	148,241
Brooks	7,110	317	563,039	23,383,852	29,444,721	106,793	265,475	372,268
Brown	41,826	768	737,910	1,939,331	8,060,567	1,691,380	899,086	2,590,466
Burleson	22,239	522	642,408	4,286,744	9,614,473	729,226	625,412	1,354,638
Burnet	50,681	804	1,253,489	6,227,440	11,713,290	2,088,676	1,040,613	3,129,289
Caldwell	34,054	602	878,881	7,761,730	14,216,276	1,293,428	754,059	2,047,487
Calhoun	21,504	405	409,730	1,061,350	6,255,332	867,307	604,013	1,471,320
Callahan	16,911	746	804,155	1,561,583	11,328,025	471,821	600,083	1,071,904
Cameron	267,139	1,748	6,002,954	35,895,595	57,867,340	12,753,113	6,730,590	19,483,703
Camp	16,447	264	273,830	1,651,069	5,713,760	832,771	574,556	1,407,327
Carson	7,847	775	748,567	2,035,860	5,899,862	86,794	396,011	482,805
Cass	35,383	986	882,482	12,336,357	23,149,107	1,170,930	758,789	1,929,719
Castro	8,500	534	247,131	1,277,385	7,262,328	163,954	470,318	634,272
Chambers	40,551	815	2,511,788	5,152,902	25,195,408	1,678,064	825,444	2,503,508
Cherokee	45,982	1,149	1,118,695	3,066,619	11,135,328	1,764,754	926,128	2,690,882
Childress	6,671	479	330,046	2,817,114	5,183,326	41,752	326,968	368,720
Clay	13,675	784	720,068	1,414,164	7,659,520	242,301	549,402	791,703
Cochran	3,467	468	90,643	312,224	1,345,484	7,551	210,046	217,597
Coke	4,520	368	165,225	165,032	1,685,953	16,366	221,215	237,581
Coleman	11,584	754	329,129	4,165,341	8,973,587	137,714	475,512	613,226
Collin	635,865	1502	7,405,968	115,220,381	142,720,480	31,222,973	11,520,962	42,743,935
Collingsworth	3,416	445	89,379	1,287,283	3,995,920	5,761	190,037	195,797
Colorado	27,952	755	1,458,966	4,503,629	9,360,179	1,103,678	687,976	1,791,653
Comal	122,620	681	3,281,774	24,658,176	43,128,509	6,395,060	2,335,620	8,730,681
Comanche	16,903	740	438,072	3,303,336	8,053,815	458,729	568,441	1,027,169
Concho	3,545	481	212,841	1,943,572	3,542,238	6,468	182,786	189,255
Cooke	48,804	847	1,536,349	4,254,592	19,443,625	2,568,790	994,762	3,563,552
Coryell	55,654	683	926,431	8,164,162	18,681,829	2,034,706	999,307	3,034,013
Cottle	1,844	390	69,519	393,552	1,881,448	3,753	99,422	103,175
Crane	4,765	318	196,852	22,783	936,430	127,115	232,460	359,575
Crockett	5,357	783	487,561	2,516,419	4,240,207	56,898	278,112	335,010
Crosby	6,386	568	168,865	504,929	2,667,832	29,382	333,117	362,499
Culberson	2,226	751	715,896	1,953,272	10,329,503	3,461	129,097	132,558
Dallam	7,336	644	360,382	9,114,872	10,544,715	137,678	453,633	591,310
Dallas	1,903,004	3326	38,317,279	443,542,056	535,345,206	104,274,812	30,954,265	135,229,077
Dawson	12,000	712	384,470	578,497	2,462,546	268,612	582,985	851,596
Deaf Smith	19,971	603	389,031	1,277,627	6,975,037	968,620	641,292	1,609,912
Delta	6,750	343	160,666	1,070,237	5,222,246	79,043	278,792	357,836
Denton	524,981	1526	9,250,240	237,225,649	253,554,529	26,185,271	8,600,968	34,786,239
Dewitt	22,925	669	467,403	1,471,044	5,800,153	713,266	618,116	1,331,382
Dickens	3,209	469	95,126	164,637	2,306,584	4,638	157,613	162,252
Dimmit	8,728	507	292,762	1,029,662	3,594,581	216,551	357,378	573,929
Donley	3,698	454	503,314	2,018,721	4,959,724	8,793	206,067	214,860
Duval	12,342	629	395,320	2,285,141	9,926,566	327,259	460,499	787,758
Eastland	24,437	1022	1,031,027	1,706,716	11,852,641	1,244,874	651,176	1,896,051
Ector	135,853	961	1,821,018	3,187,582	6,666,515	8,012,942	2,709,311	10,722,252
Edwards	3,095	499	84,138	193,877	2,093,688	4,865	157,690	162,555
Ellis	157,851	1513	4,596,773	17,513,169	52,268,235	7,846,948	2,421,713	10,268,661
El Paso	585,616	1634	10,306,475	42,905,822	74,008,312	29,463,989	8,854,573	38,318,562
Erath	38,002	821	1,035,855	1,700,141	6,564,178	1,487,681	833,156	2,320,838
Falls	16,628	736	692,786	12,250,228	18,705,409	385,440	550,943	936,383
Fannin	36,416	970	696,984	924,124	6,504,883	1,321,006	854,139	2,175,146
Fayette	32,539	1032	1,406,720	2,060,330	12,163,264	1,094,109	742,337	1,836,447
Fisher	4,918	555	139,685	264,034	1,897,503	7,643	249,297	256,939
Floyd	7,513	703	173,967	425,438	3,411,774	80,621	390,031	470,652

County	Vehicles Registered	Lane Miles of Highway	Vehicle Miles Driven Daily	State Construction Expenditures	Combined Construction Maintenance Expenditures	State Net Receipts	County Net Receipts	Total Vehicle Registration Fees
Foard	1,646	298	50,188	25,847	995,937	2,564	81,222	83,786
Fort Bend	452,884	1189	6,381,175	24,979,073	42,897,032	23,133,700	7,598,995	30,732,696
Franklin	12,120	338	435,588	152,042	3,013,250	237,290	414,353	651,642
Freestone	24,771	826	1,495,558	1,869,737	11,198,549	902,938	647,883	1,550,821
Frio	12,651	759	845,595	1,572,821	8,300,111	293,052	485,978	779,030
Gaines	17,812	667	469,521	645,118	2,250,352	704,179	424,351	1,128,530
Galveston	258,471	1,067	4,809,948	26,179,583	48,541,624	12,091,576	3,919,579	16,011,155
Garza	5,265	460	357,903	328,758	1,370,588	65,089	256,042	321,131
Gillespie	31,747	690	701,435	792,669	6,981,340	1,048,223	757,247	1,805,470
Glasscock	2,347	294	190,123	224,286	828,657	3,117	105,531	108,648
Goliad	8,691	531	293,522	924,620	3,246,742	90,011	334,983	424,994
Gonzales	21,830	886	1,103,238	1,593,281	5,982,784	708,762	608,886	1,317,648
Gray	25,023	759	634,475	490,819	3,638,566	937,705	694,383	1,632,087
Grayson	125,003	1,205	2,818,855	5,406,873	29,454,395	5,817,652	2,074,201	7,891,853
Gregg	127,751	798	2,574,624	14,015,834	28,886,154	7,248,512	2,291,163	9,539,676
Grimes	30,545	615	881,886	3,499,332	8,822,615	1,059,442	704,491	1,763,932
Guadalupe	120,925	924	2,690,502	12,958,350	25,318,939	5,531,233	1,936,633	7,467,867
Hale	30,837	1,054	740,472	2,145,508	9,486,278	1,250,765	751,577	2,002,342
Hall	3,505	457	213,580	1,049,094	5,570,290	6,319	196,643	202,961
Hamilton	11,321	582	288,545	867,692	4,059,395	171,315	480,199	651,514
Hansford	7,065	525	123,346	370,182	2,336,925	96,925	395,080	492,005
Hardeman	4,549	465	348,054	708,023	3,816,489	7,744	266,009	273,753
Hardin	58,501	575	1,315,761	1,544,635	6,182,755	2,525,423	1,228,854	3,754,277
Harris	3,115,974	4,776	54,923,250	204,627,667	369,701,506	171,409,759	55,543,414	226,953,173
Harrison	69,883	1,185	2,529,476	7,923,069	24,573,615	3,140,299	1,276,265	4,416,565
Hartley	6,043	540	310,504	1,884,003	6,817,636	140,491	356,055	496,546
Haskell	6,875	673	203,524	112,973	2,928,932	51,689	367,984	419,673
Hays	138,054	695	3,624,670	18,359,586	33,724,688	6,651,395	2,364,566	9,015,961
Hemphill	5,820	386	206,102	843,999	4,338,724	78,773	297,847	376,620
Henderson	85,599	1,015	1,634,872	9,685,920	28,922,608	3,625,900	1,373,106	4,999,006
Hidalgo	484,192	2,309	10,060,738	46,386,484	85,571,826	25,542,318	12,228,500	37,770,818
Hill	41,132	1,076	2,189,335	27,973,782	42,845,615	1,616,757	847,564	2,464,321
Hockley	25,614	752	584,581	867,102	3,858,533	1,136,624	677,124	1,813,749
Hood	60,703	396	1,050,076	3,789,379	7,328,215	2,727,910	1,218,436	3,946,346
Hopkins	39,222	964	1,422,783	7,397,643	16,489,213	1,579,124	853,977	2,433,101
Houston	23,944	863	591,093	2,246,023	14,905,097	709,871	626,780	1,336,651
Howard	29,155	859	880,055	5,360,803	15,429,031	1,046,728	735,871	1,782,599
Hudspeth	3,597	827	1,095,883	1,086,542	3,520,046	5,829	182,147	187,976
Hunt	88,371	1,320	2,405,925	21,520,481	37,729,606	3,788,963	1,567,488	5,356,451
Hutchinson	26,917	474	357,842	1,767,915	3,545,923	1,096,927	645,504	1,742,431
Irion	3,255	246	120,324	423,489	3,332,874	53,497	187,826	241,323
Jack	11,723	576	336,143	1,322,963	3,840,825	427,524	451,141	878,664
Jackson	16,538	636	844,591	1,102,473	8,105,762	422,775	540,644	963,419
Jasper	40,700	775	1,122,269	6,822,008	21,104,606	1,543,267	844,441	2,387,708
Jeff Davis	3,179	468	207,969	381,010	3,151,462	57,921	167,002	224,923
Jefferson	213,831	1,126	5,297,274	16,927,127	45,469,575	10,801,097	3,581,497	14,382,593
Jim Hogg	5,113	289	204,371	186,247	743,664	105,375	266,000	371,375
Jim Wells	40,889	708	1,098,733	8,379,230	16,678,737	2,127,056	915,804	3,042,860
Johnson	158,676	953	3,258,698	12,430,043	34,439,670	7,915,778	2,460,204	10,375,982
Jones	17,888	1,011	466,226	1,425,611	5,913,437	596,219	619,441	1,215,660
Karnes	13,159	696	345,792	2,247,996	8,899,853	207,111	514,645	721,756
Kaufman	100,082	1,197	3,480,679	5,072,733	23,002,230	4,351,438	1,799,692	6,151,130
Kendall	48,331	453	1,001,464	1,125,675	5,784,396	2,110,708	1,288,680	3,399,388
Kenedy	868	188	487,140	1,795,550	2,788,868	1,105	36,856	37,961
Kent	1,192	325	50,508	58,870	1,385,000	3,701	58,016	61,717
Kerr	54,924	707	1,097,234	4,458,120	14,544,433	2,310,845	1,083,307	3,394,151
Kimble	6,568	684	478,902	724,301	7,307,199	65,572	295,613	361,185
King	647	205	70,826	259,220	1,065,702	622	36,693	37,316
Kinney	3,525	407	172,403	552,775	1,961,917	44,843	158,900	203,743

Texas Toll Roads

Facilities	Authority	2006	2007	2008	2009
Roads		(**Tolls collected** in thousands of dollars, 000)			
Camino Colombia Toll Road	TxDOT	$ 566	$ 574	$ 668	$ 668*
Central Texas Toll Facilities[1]	Central Texas Turnpike System and Regional Mobility Authority	–	25,413	99,837	98,745
Fort Bend Toll Road	Fort Bend County Toll Road Authority	11,643	15,622	15,155	15,000*
Harris County Toll Facilities[2]	Harris County Toll Road Authority	354,460	391,569	428,022	455,548
North Texas Toll Facilities	North Texas Tollway Authority	200,865	212,805	241,609	290,800
Total roadway tolls collected in Texas		**$ 567,534**	**$ 645,983**	**$ 785,291**	**$ 860,761**

[1]Including U.S. 183A. [2]Including Jesse Jones Memorial Toll Bridge. *Estimate.
Sources: Highway Statistics annual, Federal Highway Administration, and regional toll authories.

County	Vehicles Registered	Lane Miles of Highway	Vehicle Miles Driven Daily	State Construction Expenditures	Combined Construction Maintenance Expenditures	State Net Receipts	County Net Receipts	Total Vehicle Registration Fees
Kleberg	26,109	373	750,109	1,658,725	6,248,305	1,054,273	665,062	1,719,335
Knox	4,709	467	119,286	59,310	1,537,490	40,337	284,854	325,191
Lamar	52,440	990	1,073,332	2,989,746	12,751,377	2,326,734	1,066,618	3,393,352
Lamb	14,208	805	402,388	1,152,754	4,331,645	380,458	550,070	930,528
Lampasas	23,912	502	499,410	2,051,572	3,629,326	758,385	722,661	1,481,047
La Salle	5,681	648	606,458	2,544,529	6,564,686	142,266	243,550	385,816
Lavaca	26,177	658	494,646	1,561,491	5,807,632	847,590	639,914	1,487,504
Lee	21,982	531	622,379	1,695,195	5,741,012	768,460	584,857	1,353,317
Leon	23,229	839	1,287,096	1,893,209	14,152,123	784,749	593,860	1,378,608
Liberty	75,730	823	1,909,795	9,864,510	25,297,904	3,631,351	1,312,198	4,943,549
Limestone	24,796	771	673,444	7,623,642	19,964,326	782,938	651,397	1,434,336
Lipscomb	4,037	412	94,392	241,644	1,547,809	7,747	252,047	259,794
Live Oak	13,031	1,000	1,149,185	8,323,788	14,532,760	282,605	520,372	802,976
Llano	25,079	499	433,499	422,444	4,095,238	735,745	658,524	1,394,269
Loving	256	67	17,424	-	179,546	263	16,882	17,145
Lubbock	223,416	1,724	3,505,429	54,661,407	71,250,783	11,950,101	3,989,321	15,939,422
Lynn	6,487	715	324,783	576,395	3,049,689	33,630	324,532	358,163
Madison	13,236	575	876,408	760,801	4,290,071	401,919	508,421	910,340
Marion	11,444	323	307,960	10,430,573	14,832,156	206,456	464,007	670,463
Martin	6,297	574	426,204	2,721,515	6,175,082	54,850	393,269	448,119
Mason	5,971	423	165,697	217,933	2,101,956	51,918	260,133	312,051
Matagorda	37,712	689	716,178	3,087,143	9,099,890	1,443,826	825,523	2,269,349
Maverick	37,315	477	699,763	30,835,206	45,298,098	1,686,678	784,301	2,470,979
McCulloch	9,956	608	269,600	1,531,632	3,190,216	136,921	458,904	595,825
McLennan	206,545	1,690	5,617,602	56,607,832	93,066,091	10,167,090	3,313,521	13,480,611
McMullen	2,270	317	110,270	415,184	2,110,950	21,499	112,357	133,855
Medina	46,774	766	1,139,997	2,338,637	14,677,718	1,836,185	987,807	2,823,992
Menard	3,084	348	123,881	327,922	1,416,950	14,799	137,791	152,591
Midland	150,367	1,034	2,229,557	10,121,198	33,482,106	9,511,750	2,501,199	12,012,949
Milam	29,327	691	864,292	2,731,876	8,852,059	922,406	689,810	1,612,216
Mills	7,083	451	235,066	840,966	4,070,757	43,715	334,434	378,149
Mitchell	8,038	662	507,801	1,049,778	5,509,472	85,858	378,424	464,282
Montague	25,798	849	723,666	856,841	8,818,476	932,349	675,975	1,608,325
Montgomery	408,296	1,199	7,867,244	97,702,053	109,548,204	20,575,443	5,993,089	26,568,531
Moore	21,890	467	462,398	1,351,765	8,180,019	998,044	586,181	1,584,225
Morris	14,998	357	436,323	1,013,067	4,971,828	384,863	442,266	827,128
Motley	1,721	331	56,329	411,241	3,863,345	2,513	82,673	85,187
Nacogdoches	56,627	975	1,753,770	3,903,007	21,317,965	2,335,126	1,141,961	3,477,087
Navarro	48,819	1,191	2,011,287	9,571,539	26,357,008	2,035,251	999,187	3,034,438
Newton	15,334	551	399,495	1,356,275	11,120,276	274,598	535,302	809,899

County	Vehicles Registered	Lane Miles of Highway	Vehicle Miles Driven Daily	State Construction Expenditures	Combined Construction Maintenance Expenditures	State Net Receipts	County Net Receipts	Total Vehicle Registration Fees
Nolan	15,703	694	829,703	427,005	3,798,988	437,430	557,348	994,778
Nueces	269,639	1,504	5,339,125	27,685,542	71,884,433	13,966,773	4,390,695	18,357,468
Ochiltree	13,223	430	233,548	1,086,656	5,665,713	491,778	537,574	1,029,352
Oldham	2,926	468	563,410	220,805	2,285,167	24,313	177,709	202,022
Orange	83,600	620	2,486,957	22,851,614	38,706,974	3,597,542	1,382,549	4,980,091
Palo Pinto	34,414	829	888,177	1,277,348	7,715,597	1,423,623	728,557	2,152,180
Panola	31,404	769	1,129,548	3,925,965	13,968,743	1,394,998	490,549	1,885,547
Parker	127,767	878	3,072,472	5,748,324	16,391,363	6,200,920	2,273,268	8,474,188
Parmer	10,953	612	358,850	996,053	2,969,958	242,025	513,376	755,401
Pecos	17,356	1,679	958,241	1,595,946	9,289,670	745,146	571,456	1,316,602
Polk	58,055	861	1,688,058	3,462,003	16,794,328	2,954,784	1,188,262	4,143,046
Potter	100,093	896	2,595,103	4,339,243	14,804,735	5,241,612	1,778,968	7,020,580
Presidio	7,993	545	193,142	354,000	3,329,046	135,200	335,954	471,153
Rains	13,773	268	269,248	252,901	3,273,148	322,380	449,805	772,185
Randall	122,308	898	1,248,545	2,150,708	9,225,533	5,960,346	2,332,344	8,292,689
Reagan	4,121	320	122,588	490,273	1,106,538	77,437	255,239	332,675
Real	4,285	296	105,511	789,934	3,910,797	45,141	201,841	246,983
Red River	15,489	750	381,162	773,543	6,327,361	273,452	514,196	787,648
Reeves	9,986	1,178	663,558	2,137,463	7,008,227	152,573	466,903	619,476
Refugio	8,252	465	667,785	1,094,625	6,668,470	147,261	348,255	495,516
Roberts	1,448	257	91,357	306,973	881,512	2,572	73,771	76,343
Robertson	18,756	651	918,194	6,576,713	14,933,435	486,759	599,822	1,086,581
Rockwall	75,685	347	1,715,662	12,304,010	16,222,153	3,678,419	1,303,162	4,981,581
Runnels	13,193	731	341,640	5,831,255	7,641,658	355,299	512,715	868,014
Rusk	52,830	1,182	1,362,728	2,076,968	10,139,952	2,222,006	995,205	3,217,211
Sabine	13,404	484	292,085	765,036	6,618,111	265,275	460,731	726,006
SanAugustine	9,862	545	284,960	1,296,810	12,666,628	147,152	430,080	577,233
San Jacinto	26,931	519	736,465	3,992,910	16,353,721	919,420	683,868	1,603,288
San Patricio	62,878	974	1,850,576	5,281,253	16,060,225	2,761,168	1,267,484	4,028,652
San Saba	7,718	436	144,741	628,386	2,302,856	70,277	372,962	443,239
Schleicher	4,249	361	142,494	61,175	901,136	34,589	206,539	241,129
Scurry	20,871	682	562,356	1,176,575	9,594,310	980,977	629,823	1,610,800
Shackelford	4,746	353	152,543	152,752	3,148,183	65,138	253,257	318,395
Shelby	28,287	876	860,498	2,655,319	13,589,665	1,058,421	714,291	1,772,712
Sherman	3,163	429	231,716	3,214,828	5,581,502	6,327	202,509	208,836
Smith	205,297	1,609	4,782,946	43,962,860	68,667,614	9,809,932	3,739,876	13,549,809
Somervell	10,252	198	275,246	20,181	1,148,430	269,000	311,559	580,559
Starr	46,299	524	1,099,739	5,420,428	12,783,333	1,883,406	924,854	2,808,260
Stephens	11,741	561	217,730	769,512	4,630,195	345,114	443,539	788,653
Sterling	2,103	283	179,334	20,400	944,150	7,861	89,682	97,543
Stonewall	2,314	329	83,740	277,019	2,731,806	2,623	132,951	135,574
Sutton	6,787	591	457,375	231,908	1,916,360	170,733	305,443	476,175
Swisher	7,413	806	347,784	370,119	3,977,286	71,559	380,284	451,843
Tarrant	1,479,482	3,197	29,868,670	301,538,428	388,566,755	80,306,372	23,635,218	103,941,590
Taylor	123,529	1,207	2,208,628	12,585,203	26,150,946	5,991,107	2,196,071	8,187,178
Terrell	1,507	374	86,469	719,490	1,398,636	2,221	65,581	67,803
Terry	12,210	630	405,814	471,765	2,078,807	269,059	534,872	803,931
Throckmorton	2,300	341	55,329	822,479	5,507,220	3,067	116,775	119,842
Titus	30,357	539	985,625	1,568,467	11,299,425	1,233,989	784,485	2,018,473
Tom Green	107,199	1,024	1,557,512	15,731,732	25,630,060	5,046,225	2,045,704	7,091,928
Travis	949,068	2,055	17,090,788	62,777,935	130,869,922	41,158,776	14,165,899	55,324,675
Trinity	15,988	443	334,863	1,593,113	6,603,431	386,846	507,074	893,921
Tyler	22,299	521	557,757	839,743	6,237,393	572,867	608,426	1,181,294
Upshur	42,995	787	935,191	1,754,916	11,341,326	1,503,700	859,974	2,363,673
Upton	4,250	391	165,650	262,828	1,408,605	61,139	191,581	252,720
Uvalde	25,132	748	660,268	1,550,670	9,265,519	1,091,090	619,896	1,710,986
Val Verde	42,657	713	492,720	9,027,251	14,616,892	1,786,018	892,897	2,678,915
Van Zandt	61,933	1,162	1,962,022	3,638,756	12,016,889	2,372,822	1,072,965	3,445,787
Victoria	86,189	905	1,923,910	3,181,044	13,012,997	4,352,295	1,605,635	5,957,930

County	Vehicles Registered	Lane Miles of Highway	Vehicle Miles Driven Daily	State Construction Expenditures	Combined Construction Maintenance Expenditures	State Net Receipts	County Net Receipts	Total Vehicle Registration Fees
Walker	49,510	797	2,243,194	2,552,205	14,584,083	1,904,424	1,011,428	2,915,853
Waller	43,484	584	1,709,980	12,432,757	21,140,716	1,765,250	897,491	2,662,740
Ward	13,132	664	448,084	823,465	3,148,949	513,795	312,015	825,810
Washington	40,958	658	1,110,624	2,428,842	10,180,028	1,822,835	904,705	2,727,540
Webb	162,394	1,131	2,622,009	44,737,776	58,923,149	9,361,973	2,876,627	12,238,599
Wharton	46,308	883	1,529,177	6,021,963	15,905,854	2,230,296	949,584	3,179,879
Wheeler	7,731	672	633,833	258,747	2,839,913	104,199	392,761	496,960
Wichita	115,536	1,123	1,827,537	9,458,005	22,274,586	5,398,623	1,991,642	7,390,265
Wilbarger	13,882	727	560,715	2,790,835	8,316,311	275,813	556,681	832,494
Willacy	14,546	510	463,895	761,297	3,638,027	348,343	537,082	885,425
Williamson	342,959	1,639	6,994,320	18,433,779	38,706,922	17,120,990	6,329,804	23,450,794
Wilson	45,956	749	819,985	1,986,957	5,133,450	1,701,645	893,775	2,595,420
Winkler	7,909	294	157,016	317,955	2,957,952	224,780	316,197	540,977
Wise	78,934	871	2,312,061	10,323,651	26,209,530	4,278,923	1,410,333	5,689,257
Wood	50,543	900	838,817	6,131,679	12,945,232	1,892,063	976,613	2,868,676
Yoakum	9,988	431	219,554	797,260	2,014,799	247,743	491,131	738,874
Young	23,981	706	312,902	918,856	6,680,560	872,309	648,686	1,520,995
Zapata	12,334	255	412,414	4,627,758	10,747,646	413,217	346,056	759,274
Zavala	8,330	542	285,313	578,597	2,861,838	169,612	354,291	523,902
Total	21,556,233	193,334	464,484,787	3,030,749,729	5,471,611,579	1,044,783,623	409,935,518	1,454,719,141

Bob's Oil Well is a roadside attraction in Matador at the intersection of U.S. 62/70 and Texas 70. The old gas station opened in the 1930s and closed in the 1950s. Photo by Robert Plocheck.

Driver Licenses

The following list shows the number of licensed drivers by year for Texas and for all the states. Sources are the Texas Department of Public Safety and the Federal Highway Administration.

Year	Texas licensed drivers	Total U.S. licensed drivers
2010	16,808,359	NA
2009	16,602,416	210,000,000
2008	16,511,156	208,320,681
2007	16,330,825	205,741,845
2006	16,096,985	202,810,438
2005	15,831,852	200,548,972
2004	15,562,484	198,888,912
2003	15,091,776	196,165,666
2002	14,639,132	194,295,633
2001	14,303,799	191,275,719
2000	14,024,305	190,625,023
1999	13,718,319	187,170,420
1998	13,419,288	184,980,177
1997	12,833,603	182,709,204
1996	12,568,265	179,539,340
1995	12,369,243	176,628,482
1990	11,136,694	167,015,250
1985	10,809,078	156,868,277
1980	9,287,286	145,295,036
1975	7,509,497	129,790,666
1970	6,380,057	111,542,787
1965	5,413,887	98,502,152
1960	4,352,168	87,252,563
1955	3,874,834	74,685,949
1950	2,687,349	59,322,278

Motor Vehicles Crashes, Losses in Texas

| Year | Number killed | Number injured | Crashes by Kind | | | | Vehicle Miles Traveled | | Economic loss (000,000) |
			Fatal	Injury	Non-injury	Total	Number (000,000)	Deaths per 100 mill miles	
1960	2,254	127,980	1,842	71,100	239,300	312,242	46,353	4.9	$ 350
1965	3,028	186,062	2,460	103,368	365,160	470,988	* 52,163	5.8	498
1966	3,406	208,310	2,784	115,728	406,460	524,972	55,261	**6.2**	557
1970	3,560	223,000	2,965	124,000	886,000	1,012,965	* 68,031	5.2	1,042
1971	3,594	224,000	2,993	124,000	890,000	1,016,993	70,709	5.1	1,045
1972	· 3,688	† 128,158	3,099	83,607	346,292	432,998	76,690	4.8	1,035
1973	3,692	132,635	3,074	87,631	373,521	464,226	80,615	4.6	1,035
1974	3,046	123,611	2,626	83,341	348,227	434,194	78,290	3.9	1,095
1975	3,429	138,962	2,945	92,510	373,141	468,596	84,575	4.1	1,440
1976	3,230	145,282	2,780	96,348	380,075	479,203	91,279	3.5	1,485
1977	3,698	161,635	3,230	106,923	393,848	504,001	96,998	3.8	1,960
1978	‡ 3,980	178,228	‡ 3,468	117,998	§ 304,830	426,296	102,624	3.9	2,430
1979	4,229	184,550	3,685	122,793	322,336	448,814	101,909	4.1	2,580
1980	4,424	185,964	3,863	123,577	305,500	432,940	103,255	4.3	3,010
1981	4,701	206,196	4,137	136,396	317,484	458,017	111,036	4.2	3,430
1982	4,271	204,666	3,752	135,859	312,159	451,770	* 124,910	3.4	3,375
1983	‡3,823	208,157	‡3,328	137,695	302,876	443,899	129,309	3.0	3,440
1984	3,913	220,720	3,466	145,543	293,285	442,294	137,280	2.9	¶ 3,795
1985	3,682	231,009	3,270	151,657	300,531	452,188	143,500	2.6	3,755
1986	3,568	234,120	3,121	154,514	298,079	452,593	150,474	2.4	3,782
1987	3,261	226,895	2,881	146,913	246,175	395,969	151,221	2.2	3,913
1988	3,395	238,845	3,004	152,004	237,703	392,711	152,819	2.2	4,515
1989	3,361	243,030	2,926	153,356	233,967	390,249	159,679	2.1	4,873
1990	3,243	262,576	2,882	162,424	216,140	381,446	163,103	2.0	4,994
1991	3,079	263,430	2,690	161,470	207,288	371,448	162,780	1.9	5,604
1992	3,057	282,025	2,690	170,513	209,152	382,355	162,769	1.9	6,725
1993	3,037	298,891	2,690	178,194	209,533	390,417	167,988	1.8	¶ 11,784
1994	3,142	326,837	2,710	192,014	219,890	414,614	172,976	1.8	12,505
1995	3,172	334,259	2,790	196,093	152,190	351,073	183,103	1.7	13,005
1996	3,738	350,397	3,247	204,635	§ 90,261	298,143	187,064	2.0	¶ 7,766
1997	3,508	347,881	3,079	205,595	97,315	305,989	194,665	1.8	7,662
1998	3,576	338,661	3,160	202,223	102,732	308,115	201,989	1.8	8,780
1999	3,519	339,448	3,106	203,220	105,375	311,701	213,847	1.6	8,729
2000	3,775	341,097	3,247	205,569	110,174	318,990	210,340	1.8	9,163
2001	3,739	340,554	3,319	207,043	113,596	323,958	216,276	1.73	9,348
2002	3,826	315,061	3,544	196,211	113,089	** 324,651	215,873	1.77	¶ 21,100
2003	3,823	308,543	3,372	190,926	§ 245,607	†† 460,025	218,209	1.75	20,700
2004	3,725	288,715	3,286	180,556	245,000	447,691	229,345	1.62	19,400
2005	3,559	293,583	3,157	184,093	257,532	464,541	234,232	1.52	19,200
2006	3,523	272,779	3,120	173,861	243,970	439,027	236,852	1.49	20,400
2007	3,463	267,305	3,098	173,052	264,098	459,689	241,746	1.43	20,600
2008	3,477	243,547	3,116	159,760	257,154	438,996	234,593	1.48	22,900
2009	3,108	234,704	2,807	154,685	251,850	428,273	232,055	1.34	$ 20,300

(Note: The highest death rate was in 1966 at 6.2.)

*Method of calculating vehicle miles traveled revised. Last changed in 1982 by TxDOT.

†In August 1967, amended estimating formula received from National Safety Council (NCS). Starting 1972, actual reported injuries are listed rather than estimates.

‡Change in counting fatalities. In 1978, counted when injury results in death within 90 days of accident. In 1983, counted when injury results in death within 30 days.

§Change in counting Non-injury accidents. For 1996–2002, only crashes having at least **one vehicle towed** were tabulated.

¶Economic loss formula changed. Last changed in 2002, when figures are calculated using NCS Average Calculable Cost on a per death basis figure for the year identified. Figures are rounded to the nearest hundred million. For 1996–2001, only property damage in crashes having at least one vehicle towed was tabulated.

**Beginning with 2002 data, the "Total" crash figure includes "Unknown Severity Crashes" which are not included on this chart. Prior to 2002 these crashes were counted in the Non-injury or Injury category.

††Beginning with 2003 crashes, only those resulting in injury or death or damage to property to the apparent extent of $1,000 are tabulated.

Source: Texas Department of Transportation (TxDOT) since 2001. Earlier statistics are from the Texas Department of Public Safety (DPS).

U.S. Freight Gateways, 2008

[**In millions of dollars** (243,910 represents $243,910,000,000)]. Top gateways ranked by value of shipments, with Texas gateways highlighted. *Source: U.S. Bureau of Transportation Statistics, National Transportation Statistics, annual.*

Rank	Port	Mode	Total trade	Exports	Imports	Exports as a percent of total
1	Los Angeles, CA	Water	243,910	34,823	209,086	14.3%
2	Port of New York/New Jersey, NY/NJ	Water	185,385	50,568	134,817	27.3%
3	John F. Kennedy, NY	Air	167,966	85,516	82,450	50.9%
4	Houston, TX	Water	147,695	68,821	78,873	46.6%
5	Detroit, MI	Land	120,168	66,454	53,714	55.3%
6	Laredo, TX	Land	115,759	53,929	61,830	46.6%
7	Chicago, IL	Air	97,180	35,822	61,358	36.9%
8	Long Beach, CA	Water	91,537	31,599	59,938	34.5%
9	Port Huron, MI	Land	81,223	35,215	46,008	43.4%
10	Buffalo-Niagara Falls, NY	Land	80,838	40,330	40,508	49.9%
11	Los Angeles, CA	Air	78,292	41,323	36,970	52.8%
12	Charleston, SC	Water	62,332	22,281	40,051	35.7%
13	Savannah, GA	Water	58,987	22,838	36,150	38.7%
14	Norfolk, VA	Water	53,950	23,927	30,023	44.4%
15	San Francisco, CA	Air	52,758	26,598	26,161	50.4%
16	New Orleans, LA	Water	49,765	25,348	24,417	50.9%
17	New Orleans Customs District, LA	Air	49,585	22,252	27,333	44.9%
18	El Paso, TX	Land	48,174	20,156	28,018	41.8%
19	Baltimore, MD	Water	45,312	16,126	29,187	35.6%
20	Philadelphia, PA	Water	43,176	5,039	38,137	11.7%
21	Anchorage, AK	Air	41,443	10,194	31,249	24.6%
22	Miami, FL	Air	40,036	29,208	10,828	73.0%
23	Seattle, WA	Water	39,989	9,940	30,049	24.9%
24	Dallas-Fort Worth, TX	Air	39,488	16,403	23,085	41.5%
25	Oakland, CA	Water	38,698	12,400	26,299	32.0%
31	Corpus Christi, TX	Water	29,685	4,965	24,721	16.7%
35	Texas City, TX	Water	22,726	3,264	19,462	14.4%
38	Hidalgo, TX	Land	22,149	9,853	12,296	44.5%
39	Beaumont, TX	Water	21,338	2,847	18,490	13.3%

Border Crossings at U.S. Ports of Entry, 2009-2010

Below are statistics for selected states as to incoming border traffic at ports of entry into the United States. *Data are from the U.S. Bureau of Transportation Statistics.* (**Total in thousands**. Percent of U.S. total listed with states.)

Entering at border (thousands 000)	U.S. total	Texas	%	California	%	New York	%	Arizona	%	Michigan	%
2009											
Vehicle passengers	194,526	72,273	37.2	48,911	25.1	18,031	9.3	17,579	9.0	12,013	6.2
Personal vehicles	97,003	35,585	36.7	26,536	27.4	8,245	8.5	7,388	7.6	6,440	6.6
Pedestrians	41,695	18,847	45.2	14,124	33.9	247	0.6	8,067	19.3	17	0.0
Trucks	9,312	2,856	30.7	1,027	11.0	1,398	15.0	344	3.7	1,868	20.1
Containers (truck)	6,626	1,797	27.1	621	9.4	1,542	23.7	265	4.0	1,542	23.3
2010											
Vehicle passengers	152,519	53,356	35.0	45,611	29.9	18,189	11.9	14,726	9.7	12,251	8.0
Personal vehicles	92,920	31,349	33.7	25,260	27.2	8,573	9.2	6,651	7.2	6,566	7.1
Pedestrians	40,310	17,156	42.6	14,740	36.6	262	0.6	7,648	19.0	17	0.0
Trucks	10,187	3,194	31.4	1,089	10.7	1,452	14.3	373	3.7	2,165	21.3
Containers (truck)	7,346	2,149	29.3	678	9.2	1,145	15.6	291	4.0	1,805	24.6

Foreign Consulates in Texas

In the list below, these abbreviations appear after the name of the city: (CG) Consulate General; (C) Consulate; (VC) Vice Consulate. The letter "H" before the designation indicates honorary status. Compiled from "Foreign Consular Offices in the United States," U.S. Dept. of State, Summer 2007, and recent Internet sources.

Albania: Houston (HC); 10 Waterway Ct., Ste. 401, The Woodlands, 77380. (281) 548-4740.

Angola: Houston (CG); 3040 Post Oak Blvd., Ste. 780, 77056. (713) 212-3840.

Argentina: Houston (CG); 3050 Post Oak Blvd., Ste. 1625, 77056. (713) 871-8935.

Australia: Houston (HC); 4623 Feagan St., 77007. (713) 782-6009.

Austria: Houston (HCG); 1717 Bissonet St., Ste 306, 77005. (713) 526-0127.

Bangladesh: Houston (HCG); 35 N. Wynden Dr., 77056. (713) 621-8462.

Barbados: Houston (HC); 3027 Sleepy Hollow Dr., Sugar Land 77479. (832) 725-5566.

Belgium: Houston (HC); 2009 Lubbock St., 77007. (713) 426-3933.
Fort Worth (HC); 6201 South Fwy., 76134. (817) 551-8389.
San Antonio (HC); 106 S. St. Mary's, Ste. 200, 78205. (210) 271-8820.

Belize: Houston (HCG); 7101 Breen, 77086. (713) 999-4484.
Dallas (HC); 1315 19th St., Ste. 2A, Plano, 75074. (972) 579-0070.

Bolivia: Houston (HCG); 800 Wilcrest, Ste. 100, 77042 (713) 977-2344.
Dallas (HC); 1881 Sylvan Ave., Ste. 110, 75208. (214) 571-6131.

Botswana: Houston (HC); 10000 Memorial Dr., Ste. 400, 77024. (713) 680-1155.

Brazil: Houston (CG); 1233 West Loop South, Ste. 1150, 77027. (713) 961-3063.

Cameroon: Houston (HC); 1319 Gamma, Crosby 77532. (713) 499-3502.

Canada: Dallas (CG); 750 N. Saint Paul, Ste. 1700, 75201. (214) 922-9806.
Houston (C); 5847 San Felipe St., Ste. 1700, 77057. (713) 821-1442.
San Antonio (HCG); 106 S. St. Mary's, Ste. 800, 78205. (210) 299-3525.

Chile: Houston (CG);1360 Post Oak Blvd., Ste. 1130, 77056; (713) 963-9066.
Dallas (HC); 3500 Oak Lawn, Apt. 200, 75219. (214) 528-2731.

China: Houston (CG); 3417 Montrose, Ste. 700, 77006. (713) 524-0780.

Colombia: Houston (CG); 5851 San Felipe, Ste. 300, 77057; (713) 527-8919.

Costa Rica: Houston (CG); 3000 Wilcrest, Ste. 112, 77042. (713) 266-0484.
Austin (C); 1730 E. Oltorf, 78741. (512) 445-0023.
Dallas (HC); 7777 Forest Lane, Ste. B-445, 75230. (972) 566-7020.

Cyprus: Houston (HCG); 320 S. 66th St., 77011. (713) 928-2264.

Czech Republic: Houston (HC); 11748 Heritage Pkwy., West, 76691. (713) 629-6963.

Denmark: Dallas (HC); 2100 McKinney Ave., Ste. 700, 75201. (214) 661-8399.
Houston (HC); 4545 Post Oak Place, Ste. 347, 77027. (713) 622-9018.

Ecuador: Houston (CG); 4200 Westheimer, Ste. 218, 77027. (713) 622-1787.
Dallas (HCG); 7510 Acorn Lane, Frisco, 75034. (972) 712-9107.

Egypt: Houston (CG); 1990 Post Oak Blvd., Ste. 2180, 77056. (713) 961-4915.

El Salvador: Dallas (CG); 1555 W. Mockingbird Lane, Ste. 216, 75235.
Houston (CG); 1702 Hillendahl Blvd. 77055. (713) 270-6239.

Ethiopia: Houston (HC); 9301 Southwest Freeway, Ste. 250, 77074. (713) 271-7567.

Fiji: Dallas (HC); 3400 Carlisle, Ste. 310, 75204. (214) 954-9993.

Finland: Dallas (HC); 1601 Elm, Ste. 3000, 75201. (214) 999-4472.
Houston (HC); 14 Greenway Plaza, Ste. 22R, 77046. (713) 552-1722.

France: Houston (CG); 777 Post Oak Blvd. Ste. 600, 77056. (713) 572-2799.
Austin (HC); 515 Congress Ave, 78701. (512) 480-5605.
Dallas (HC); 12720 Hillcrest, Ste. 730, 75230. (972) 789-9305.
San Antonio (HC); X Route 1, 78209. 78209. (210) 659-3101.

Georgia: Houston (HC); 3040 Post Oak Blvd., Ste. 700, 77056. (281) 633-3500.

Germany: Houston (CG); 1330 Post Oak Blvd., Ste. 1850, 77056. (713) 627-7770.
Corpus Christi (HC); 615 N. Upper Broadway, Ste. 630,78477. (361) 884-7766.
Dallas (HC); 325 N. St. Paul, Ste. 2300, 75201. (214) 748-8500.
San Antonio (HC); 310 S. St. Mary's, 78205. (210) 226-1788.

Ghana: Houston (HC); 3434 Locke Lane, 77027. (713) 960-8806.

Greece: Houston (CG); 520 Post Oak Blvd., Ste. 450, 77027. (713) 840-7522.

Guatemala: Houston (CG); 3013 Fountain View, Ste 210, 77057. (713) 953-9531.
San Antonio (HC); 4840 Whirlwind, 78217.

Guyana: Houston (HC); 1810 Woodland Park Dr., 77077. (713) 497-4466.

Haiti: Houston (HC); 3535 Sage Rd., 77027.

Honduras: Houston (CG); 5433 Westheimer Rd., Ste. 325, 77056. (713) 667-4693.

Hungary: Houston (HCG); 2221 Potomac B, 77057. (713) 977-8604.

Iceland: Dallas (HC); 17910 Windflower, Apt. 2201, 75252. (214) 540-9135.
Houston (HC); 2348 W. Settler's Way, The Woodlands, 77380. (713) 367-2777.

India: Houston (CG); 1990 Post Oak Blvd., Ste 600, 77056. (713) 626-2148.

Indonesia: Houston (CG); 10900 Richmond Ave., 77042.

Ireland: Houston (HC); 2630 Sutton Ct., 77027. (713) 961-5363.

Israel: Houston (CG); 24 Greenway Plz., Ste. 1500, 77046. (713) 627-3780.

Italy: Houston (CG); 1300 Post Oak Blvd., Ste. 660, 77056. (713) 850-7520.
Dallas (HVC); 6255 W. Northwest Hwy., Apt. 304, 75225. (214) 368-4113.

Ivory Coast: Houston (HCG); 412 Hawthorne, 77006. (713) 529-4928.

Jamaica: Houston (HC); 7737 Southwest Fwy., Suite 580, 77074. (713) 541-3333.
Dallas (HC); 3068 Forest Lane, 75234. (972) 396-7969.

Japan: Houston (CG); 909 Fannin, Ste. 3000,

77010. (713) 652-2977.

Dallas (HCG); 5819 Edinburgh St., 75252.
(972) 713-8683.

Korea: Houston (CG); 1990 Post Oak Blvd., Ste. 1250,
77056. (713) 961-0186.

Dallas (HC); 13111 N. Central Expy., 75243. (214)
454-1112.

Kyrgyzstan: Houston (HCG); 15600 Barkers Landing Rd.,
Apt. 1, 77079. (281) 920-1841.

Latvia: Houston (HC); 5847 San Felipe, Ste. 3400,
77057. (713) 785-0807.

Lebanon: Houston (HC); 2400 Augusta Dr., Ste. 308,
77057. (713) 526-1141.

Lesotho: Austin (HC); 7400 Valburn Dr., 78731.

Lithuania: Houston (HC); 4030 Case, 77005
(713) 665-4218.

Luxembourg: Fort Worth (HC); 48 Valley Ridge Rd.,
76107. (817) 738-8600.

Malaysia: Houston (HC); 700 Louisiana, Floor 46,
77002. (713) 222-1470.

Malta: Houston (HCG); 2602 Commonwealth, 77006.
(713) 654-7900.

Dallas (HC); PO Box 830688, SM-24, Richardson,
75083. (972) 883-4785.

Austin (HC); 3925 W. Braker Lane, Ste. 300, 78759.
(512) 305-0612.

Mexico: Austin (CG); 800 Brazos, Ste. 330, 78701.
(512) 478,2803.

Brownsville (C); 301 Mexico Blvd., Ste. F3, 78520.
(956) 542-4431.

Corpus Christi (C); 800 N. Shoreline, Ste. 410,
78401.

Dallas (CG); 8855 N. Stemmons Fwy, 75247.
(214) 522-9740.

Del Rio (C); 2398 Spur 239, 78840.
(830) 774-5031.

Eagle Pass (C); 2252 E. Garrison, 78852.
(830) 773-9255.

El Paso (CG); 910 E. San Antonio Ave., 79901.
(915) 533-3644.

Houston (HC); 4507 San Jacinto St., 77004.
(713) 271-6800.

Laredo (CG); 1612 Farragut St., 78040.
(956) 723-6369.

McAllen (C); 600 S. Broadway, 78501.
(956) 686-0243.

Midland (C); 511 W. Ohio St., Ste. 121, 79701.

Presidio (C); 6717 Kelley Addition 1 Hwy, 79845.
(915) 229-2788.

San Antonio (CG); 127 Navarro St., 78205. (210)
227-9145.

San Antonio (Office of Mexican Attorney General);
613 NW Loop 410 Ste. 610, 78216.
(210) 344-1131.

Monaco: Dallas (HC); 8350 N. Central Expressway,
Ste. 1900, 75206. (214) 234-4124.

Mongolia: Houston (HCAgent); 1221 Lamar, Ste. 1201,
77010. (713) 759-1922.

Nambia: Houston (HC); 1330 Post Oak Blvd., Ste. 2200,
77056. (713) 965-5119.

Netherlands: Houston (CG); 2200 Post Oak Blvd.,
Ste. 610, 77056. (713) 622-8000.

New Zealand: Houston (HC); 246 Warrenton Dr.,
77024. (713) 973-8680.

Nicaragua: Houston (CG); 8989 Westheimer, Ste. 103,
77063. (713) 789-2762.

Norway: Houston (CG); 2777 Allen Parkway, Ste. 1185,
77019. (713) 521-2900.

Dallas (HC); 5500 Caruth Haven Lane, 75225.
(214) 750-4222.

Pakistan: Houston (C); 11850 Jones Rd. 77070.
(2810 890-8525.

Panama: Houston (CG); 24 Greenway Plaza, Ste. 1307,

77046. (713) 622-4451.

Papua New Guinea: Houston (HCG); 4900 Woodway Dr.
Ste. 1200, 77056. (713) 966-2500.

Peru: Houston (CG); 5177 Richmond Ave., Ste.
695, 77056. (713) 355-9571.

Dallas (CG); 1500 Marilla, Rm D, 75201.

Poland: Houston (HC); 35 Harbor View, Sugar Land,
77479. (281) 565-1507.

Portugal: Houston (HC); 4544 Post Oak Place, Ste. 350,
77027. (713) 759-1188.

Qatar: Houston (CG); 1990 Post Oak Blvd, Ste. 810,
77056. (713) 355-8221.

Romania: Dallas (HC); 220 Ross Ave., Ste. 2200,
75201. (214) 740-8608.

Houston (HC); 4265 San Felipe, Ste. 220, 77027.
(713) 629-1551.

Russia: Houston (CG); 1333 West Loop South, Ste. 1300,
77027. (713) 337-3300.

Saint Kitts/Nevis: Dallas (HC); 6336 Greenville Ave.,
75206.

Saudi Arabia: Houston (CG); 5718 Westheimer, Ste.
1500, 77057. (713) 785-5577.

Senegal: Houston (CG); 9701 Richmond, Ste. 212, 77042.

Singapore: Houston (HCG); 600 Travis, Ste. 370, 77002.
(713) 512-4488.

Slovenia: Houston (HC); 2925 Briar Park, Floor 7,
77042. (713) 430-7350.

South Africa: Dallas (HC); 400 S. Zang, Ste. 806, 75208.

Spain: Houston (CG); 1800 Bering Dr., Ste. 660,
77057. (713) 783-6200.

Corpus Christi (HC); 7517 Yorkshire Blvd., 78413
(361) 994-7517.

Dallas (HC); 5499 Glen Lakes Dr., Ste. 209, 75231.
(214) 373-1200.

El Paso (HC); 420 Golden Springs Dr., 79912.
(915) 534-0677.

San Antonio (HC); 8350 Delphian, 78148.

Sweden: Houston (HC); 2909 Hillcroft, Ste. 515, 77057.
(713) 953-1417.

Dallas: (HC); 6600 LBJ Fwy, Ste. 183, 75240.
(972) 991-8013.

Switzerland: Houston (CG); 11922 Taylorcrest, 77024.
(713) 467-9889.

Dallas (HC); 2651 N. Harwood, Ste. 455, 75201.
(214) 965-1025.

Syria: Houston (HCG); 5433 Westheimer Rd., Ste. 1020,
77056. (713) 622-8860.

Thailand: Houston (HCG); 600 Travis St., Ste. 2800,
77002. (713) 229-8733.

Dallas (HCG); 1717 Main St., Ste. 4100,
75201.

El Paso (HCG); 4401 N. Mesa, Ste. 204, 79902.
(915) 533-5757.

Trinidad/Tobago: Houston (HC); 2400 Augusta, Ste. 250,
77057. (713) 840-1100.

Tunisia: Dallas (HC); 4227 N. Capistrano Dr., 75287.
(972) 267-4191.

Houston (HC); 12527 Mossycup, 77024.
(713) 935-9427.

Turkey: Houston (CG); 1990 Post Oak Blvd., Ste.1300,
77056. (713) 622-5849.

Ukraine: Houston (HC); 2934 Fairway Dr., Sugar Land,
77478. (281) 242-2842.

United Kingdom: Houston (CG); 1000 Louisiana St.,
Ste. 1900, 77002. (713) 659-6270.

Dallas (C); 2911 Turtle Creek, Ste. 940, 75219.
(214) 637-3600.

San Antonio (HC); 254 Spencer Lane, 78201.
(210) 735-9393.

Uruguay: Houston (HCG); 1220 S. Ripple Creek Dr.,
77057. (713) 974-7855.

Venezuela : Houston (CG); 2925 Briar Park Dr., Ste. 900,
77027. (713) 961-5141. ☆

Foreign Trade Zones in Texas

Source: U.S. Department of Commerce.

Foreign-trade-zone status endows a domestic site with certain customs privileges, causing it to be considered outside customs territory and therefore available for activities that might otherwise be carried on overseas.

Operated as public utilities for qualified corporations, the zones are established under grants of authority from the Foreign-Trade Zones board, which is chaired by the U.S. Secretary of Commerce. Zone facilities are available for operations involving storage, repacking, inspection, exhibition, assembly, manufacturing and other processing.

A foreign-trade zone is especially suitable for export processing or manufacturing operations when foreign components or materials with a high U.S. duty are needed to make the end product competitive in markets abroad.

Source: U.S. Department of Commerce

There were 33 Foreign-Trade Zones in Texas as of June 2011.

Amarillo, FTZ 252
City of Amarillo
801 S. Fillmore, Ste. 2205, Amarillo 79101

Athens, FTZ 269
Athens Economic Development Corp.
100 W. Tyler St., Athens 75751

Austin, FTZ 183
FTZ of Central Texas Inc.
210 Barton Springs, Ste. 400, Austin 78041

Beaumont, FTZ 115
Port Arthur, FTZ 116
Orange, FTZ 117
FTZ of Southeast Texas Inc.
P.O. Drawer 2297, Beaumont 77704

Bowie County, FTZ 258
Red River Redevelopment Authority
107 Chapel Lane, New Boston 75570

Brownsville, FTZ 62
Brownsville Navigation District
1000 Foust Road, Brownsville 78521

Calhoun/Victoria Counties FTZ 155
Calhoun-Victoria FTZ Inc.
P.O. Drawer 397, Point Comfort 77978

Conroe, FTZ 265
City of Conroe
PO Box 3066, Conroe 77305

Corpus Christi, FTZ 122
Port of Corpus Christi Authority
1305 N. Shoreline Blvd.
Corpus Christi 78403

Dallas/Ft.Worth, FTZ 39
D/FW International Airport Board
Drawer 619428, D/FW Airport 75261

Dallas/Fort Worth, FTZ 168
FTZ Operating Company of Texas
P.O. Box 742916, Dallas 75374

Eagle Pass, FTZ 96
Maverick County Development Corp.
P.O. Box 3693, Eagle Pass 78853

Edinburg, FTZ 251
City of Edinburg
602 W. University Dr., Ste. B
Edinburg 78539

Ellis County, FTZ 113
Ellis County Trade Zone Corp.
P.O. Box 788
Midlothian 76065

El Paso, FTZ 68
City of El Paso
501 George Perry, Ste. I,
El Paso 79906

El Paso, FTZ 150
Westport Economic Dev. Corp.
1865 Northwestern Dr.. El Paso 79912

Fort Worth, FTZ 196
Alliance Corridor Inc.
13600 Heritage Pkwy., Ste. 200
Fort Worth 76177

Freeport, FTZ 149
Port Freeport
200 W. 2nd, Ste. 301, Freeport 77541

Galveston, FTZ 36
Port of Galveston
P.O. Box 328, Galveston 77553

Gregg County, FTZ 234
Gregg County
269 Terminal Circle, Longview 75603

Harris County, FTZ 84
Port of Houston Authority
111 East Loop North, Houston 77029

Laredo, FTZ 94
Laredo International Airport
5210 Bob Bullock Loop, Laredo 78041

Liberty County, FTZ 171
Liberty Co. Economic Dev. Corp.
P.O. Box 857, Liberty 77575

Lubbock, FTZ 260
City of Lubbock
1500 Broadway, 6th Floor,
Lubbock 79401

McAllen, FTZ 12
McAllen Economic Dev. Corp.
6401 South 33rd St., McAllen 78501

Midland, FTZ 165
City of Midland
P.O. Box 60305, Midland 79711

San Antonio, FTZ 80
City of San Antonio
P.O. Box 839966, San Antonio 78283

Starr County, FTZ 95
Starr County Industrial Foundation
P.O. Box 502, Rio Grande City 78582

Texas City, FTZ 199
Texas City Harbor FTZ Corp.
P.O. Box 2608, Texas City 77592

Waco, FTZ 246
City of Waco
P.O. Box 1220, Waco 76703

Weslaco, FTZ 156
City of Weslaco
255 S. Kansas Ave., Weslaco 78596

A barge carrying loaded containers in the Houston Ship Channel. Photo by Robert Plocheck.

Annual Tonnage Handled by Major/Minor Texas Ports

Table below gives consolidated tonnage (x1,000) handled by Texas ports. All figures are in short tons (2,000 lbs.). Note that " - " indicates no commerce was reported, "0" means tonnage reported was less than 500 tons. *Source: U.S. Corps of Engineers.*

Port	2009	2008	2005	2000	1995	1990	1985
Beaumont	67,716	69,484	78,887	76,894	20,937	26,729	26,842
Brownsville	4,693	5,669	5,105	3,268	2,656	1,372	1,443
Corpus Christi	68,240	76,775	77,637	81,164	70,218	60,165	41,057
Freeport	27,363	29,842	33,602	28,966	19,662	14,526	12,918
Galveston	9,792	9,781	8,008	10,402	10,465	9,620	7,792
Houston	211,341	212,208	211,666	186,567	135,231	126,178	90,669
Matagorda Channel (Port Lavaca)	6,951	10,318	11,607	10,552	9,237	6,097	4,366
Port Arthur	33,804	31,753	26,385	20,524	49,800	30,681	15,755
Sabine Pass	753	1,214	641	910	231	631	547
Texas City	52,633	52,606	57,839	58,109	50,403	48,052	33,441
Victoria Channel	1,952	2,862	3,224	5,104	4,624	3,740	3,414
Anahuac	-	-	-	-	-	0	53
Aransas Pass	241	-	128	6	181	169	10
Arroyo Colorado	287	704	791	837	994	765	692
Port Isabel	19	0	-	5	130	269	280
Cedar Bayou	945	1,455	1,172	1,002	473	219	219
Chocolate Bayou	1,022	3,085	3,537	3,488	3,480	3,463	4,077
Clear Creek	-	-	-	-	-	0	0
Colorado River	506	464	501	445	576	476	480
Dickinson	385	591	688	904	657	556	195
Double Bayou	3	-	257	0	-	0	21
Greens Bayou	5,251	6,628	3,768	0	0	0	0
Harbor Island (Port Aransas)	1	12	10	151	209	na	na
Liberty Channel	-	-	-	-	-	0	0
Orange	623	677	627	681	693	710	648
Palacios	7	16	-	-	-	0	10
Port Mansfield	-	-	-	-	20	102	204
Rockport	-	-	-	-	-	644	0
San Bernard River	438	589	773	633	653	534	519
Other Ports	0	0	0	0	0	0	307
TOTAL*	451,843	473,342	487,100	452,991	371,021	335,312	245,959

Excludes duplication.

Foreign/Domestic Commerce: Breakdown for 2009

Data below represent inbound and outbound tonnage for major ports. Note that "-" means no tonnage was reported. *Does not include Canadian. Source: U.S. Corps of Engineers*
(All figures in short tons x1000)

Port	Foreign*		Domestic				
			Coastwise		Internal		Local
	Imports	Exports	Receipts	Shipments	Receipts	Shipments	
Beaumont	35,937	6,407	310	1,637	8,117	12,427	1,938
Brownsville	2,916	216	407	-	487	632	4
Corpus Christi	39,507	10,875	544	3,825	3,937	7,065	2,064
Freeport	21,040	2,143	121	215	2,260	1,428	2
Galveston	1,106	3,437	76	1,456	2,253	1,325	139
Houston	84,013	63,297	1,717	3,384	26,743	17,013	14,515
Matagorda Chl. (Port Lavaca)	3,718	1,485	-	261	146	984	-
Port Arthur	14,249	9,864	167	1,399	3,271	3,274	56
Sabine Pass	0	0	37	197	89	430	-
Texas City	31,579	4,775	351	1,972	5,584	7,800	449
Victoria	-	-	-	-	314	1,638	-

Gulf Intracoastal Waterway by Commodity (Texas portion)

(All figures in short tons x1000) *Source: U.S. Army Corps of Engineers*

Commodity	2009	2008	2005	2000	1995
Coal	88	172	335	121	162
Petroleum products	46,757	42,946	39,538	34,816	40,496
Chemicals	15,461	17,271	20,668	21,382	26,818
Raw materials	2,496	4,725	4,898	5,822	6,544
Manufactured goods	1,118	2,717	2,449	2,301	2,056
Food, farm products	518	378	473	960	1,216
Total	67,010	69,145	69,549	66,440	78,386

U.S. ports ranked by tonnage, 2009
(x1,000)

1. S. Louisiana......... 212,581
2. **Houston 211,341**
3. New York 144,690
4. Long Beach 72,500
5. **Corpus Christi...... 68,240**
6. New Orleans.......... 68,126
7. **Beaumont............. 67,715**
8. Huntington, WV 59,172
9. Los Angeles........... 58,406
10. **Texas City........... 52,632**

States ranked by tonnage, 2009
(x1,000)

1. **Texas.................. 451,843**
2. Louisiana 449,274
3. California 201,814
4. New Jersey.......... 155,569
5. Illinois...................119,078
6. Washington.......... 107,009
7. Florida................. 98,091
8. Pennsylvania 90,846
9. Ohio...................... 90,628
10. Kentucky............. 86,042

Aviation: Enplanements, Service Decline

Air transportation is a vital and vigorous part of the Texas economy, and Texans are major users of air transportation. The state's airport system ranks as one of the busiest and largest in the nation.

The state's 47,949 active pilots represent 8.07 percent of the nation's pilots. The number of active general aviation aircraft in the state total 19,416, 8.67 percent of the nation's total. Collectively they flew nearly 2.04 million hours.

In 2009, Texas' commercial service airports with scheduled passenger service enplaned 66,106,914 passengers, a decrease of 6.5 percent over the last two years. Scheduled carriers served 27 Texas airports in 25 Texas cities, and more than 90 percent of the state's population lived within 50 miles of an airport with scheduled air passenger service.

Dallas/Fort Worth International, Dallas Love Field, Houston George Bush Intercontinental, and Houston's William P. Hobby together accounted for 81 percent of the passengers, or 53,453,994 enplanements.

Twenty-seven airports continue to provide commercial service to Texas communities including the Texarkana Regional Airport which is physically located in Arkansas. Scheduled passenger traffic (air carrier and commuters) decreased from 2007 to 2009 breaking a trend that began in 2002.

Twenty-six airports saw their enplanements decrease with only one airport, Killeen-Fort Hood/Gray, experiencing an increase. Of these 26 airports, 15 of them experienced double-digit losses ranging from 10 percent to 37 percent. Four airports saw decreases of 20 percent or more including Southeast Regional in Beaumont (-36.89%), Del Rio (-20.33%), Texarkana Regional (-21.97%), and Victoria Regional (-30.76%).

Air service continues to be an area of concern for some communities as the airlines have worked to remove excess capacity from the system in an effort to return to profitability. This has been exacerbated by the global economic recession that officially began in late 2007. None of the 25 cities served by the airlines have seen their air service completely eliminated but some have experienced a decrease in the level of service.

Airlines, to generate additional revenue, have instituted fees for services typically included in ticket prices. These have included baggage fees, meals, and priority boarding, among others. While fuel prices are below their 2008 levels, they have increased somewhat since their 2009 drop.

General aviation had enjoyed strong growth in recent years but it now faces serious challenges precipitated by the sharp economic decline. Total aircraft shipments peaked in 2007 and billings peaked in 2008.

Public Administration

Source: Texas Transportation Institute

In 1945, the Texas Aeronautics Commission (TAC) was created and directed by the legislature to foster and assist in the development of aeronautics within the state, and to encourage the establishment of airports and air navigational facilities.

The commission's first annual report of Dec. 31, 1946, stated that Texas had 592 designated airports and 7,756 civilian aircraft.

In 1989, the TAC became the Texas Department of Aviation (TDA). And on Sept. 1, 1991, when the Texas Department of Transportation (TxDOT) was created and the TDA became the Aviation Division within the department.

The primary responsibilities of the Aviation Division include providing engineering and technical services for constructing and maintaining aeronautical facilities in the state. It is also responsible for long-range planning on the statewide system of airports and applying for and disbursing federal funds.

One of TxDOT's goals is to develop a statewide system of airports that will provide adequate air access to the population and economic centers of the state.

In the Texas Airport System Plan, TxDOT has identified 292 airports and two heliports that are needed to meet the forecast aviation demand and to maximize access by aircraft to the state's population, business, and agricultural and mineral resource centers.

Of these 292 airports, 27 are commercial service airports, 24 are reliever airports, and 241 are general aviation airports.

Commercial service airports provide scheduled passenger service. Reliever airports are a special class of general aviation airports designated by the Federal Aviation Administration (FAA).

They provide alternative landing facilities in the metropolitan areas separate from the commercial service airports, and, together with the business service, provide access for business and executive turbine-powered aircraft.

The community service and basic service airports provide access for single- and multi-engine, piston-powered aircraft to smaller communities throughout the state. Some community service airports are also capable of accommodating light jets.

TxDOT is charged by the legislature with planning and implementing improvement projects at the general aviation airports. In carrying out these responsibilities, TxDOT channels the Airport Improvement Program (AIP) funds provided by the FAA.

Since 1993, TxDOT has participated in the FAA's state block grant demonstration program. Under this program, TxDOT assumes most of the FAA's responsibility for the administration of the AIP funds.

The Aviation Facilities Development Program (AFDP) oversees planning and research, assists with engineering and technical services, and provides financial assistance through state grants to public bodies operating airports.

The 81st Legislature appropriated funds to TxDOT who subsequently allocated a portion of those funds to the Aviation Division. TxDOT allocated approximately $16 million annually for the 2010-2011 biennium to the Aviation Division to help implement and administer the AFDP.

A terminal at Austin-Bergstrom International Airport. Photo by LoneStarMike (CC)

Worldwide aircraft shipments shipments were down to 2,015 from 2,274 in 2009, 3,967 in 2008 and 4,270 in 2007. This is down significantly from the all-time high set in 2007.

Billings for general aviation aircraft worldwide were a slightly different story in 2010. Total billings increased from $19.465 billion in 2009 to $19.705 billion in 2010 after dropping from an all-time high of $24.766 billion in 2008.

This slight year-over-year increase is due to an increase in turbine aircraft billings, which make up the vast majority of total billings.

Airplane shipments for those manufactured in the U.S. showed a decline in 2010 dropping to 1,334 from 1,585 in 2009 and 3,079 in 2008. Billings also decreased to $7.875 billion from $9.082 in 2009 and $13.348 billion in 2008.

In both worldwide and U.S. manufacturing, turbine aircraft continued to show a decline in shipments in 2010 with double-digit decreases from 2009, while piston shipments experienced more modest decreases over the same period.

Overall, shipments decreased 11.39 percent and 15.84 percent for aircraft manufactured worldwide and in the U.S., respectively. Billings, however, increased 1.23 percent for aircraft manufactured worldwide but decreased 13.29 percent for U.S. manufactured aircraft.

Billings of U.S manufactured aircraft exported out of the country increased 5.53 percent from 2009 to 2010 while shipments decreased 5.87 percent. U.S. exports accounted for 51.6 percent of the total U.S. manufactured shipments and 61.8 percent of the billings, both all-time highs.

It is clear the global marketplace is significant to U.S. aircraft manufacturers and will also add to its challenges as the global economy works to recover.

Business aviation has long been a leader in the industry and that is not expected to change. While very light jets and air taxi companies once dominated the talk of the industry, this is no longer the case.

Several small jet manufacturers as well as companies that planned on utilizing these aircraft have gone bankrupt, suspended operations, or both.

The earlier focus on very light jets and the potential of air taxi services has given way to improving the operating efficiencies of a range of business jets to better meet the needs of their customers no matter their utilization.

New technology and innovation continue to drive general aviation both in terms of aircraft and how they operate in the airspace as well as on and around the airport environment.

This includes new flight information and navigations systems in the cockpit to new satellite and ground based augmentation systems that enhance the current global positioning system allowing for improved approaches to airports. These enhancements have provided for a safer and more efficient air transportation system.

Additionally, the most recent study of general aviation in Texas showed that it plays a large role in the state's economy.

The economic impact of general aviation in Texas includes total employment of 61,943 jobs, a total payroll of $2,514,708,000, and total economic output of $8,738,586,000.

Sources: Federal Aviation Administration, General Aviation and Part 135 Activity Survey - CY2009; General Aviation Manufacturer's Association 2010 General Aviation Statistical Databook and Industry Outlook; FAA Terminal Area Forecasts 2010; Texas Department of Transportation, Aviation Division; FAA Aerospace Forecasts 2011-2031; Wilbur Smith Associates, 2007.

Passenger Enplanement by Airport

Airport	1999	2001	2003	2005	2007	Percent change*	2009
Abilene	48,624	57,645	46,166	75,414	90,507	-10.01	81,451
Amarillo	435,758	440,018	384,829	442,327	455,539	-11.12	404,903
Austin	3,235,560	3,595,173	3,157,961	3,600,331	4,112,023	-2.26	4,019,088
Beaumont	100,684	78,215	43,931	55,484	35,352	-36.89	22,310
Brownsville	71,530	74,411	60,087	73,361	91,262	-15.15	77,438
Brownwood**	1,475	2,232	2,008	603	-	-	-
College Station	92,691	85,875	67,459	84,039	89,830	-18.22	73,462
Corpus Christi	451,999	425,847	358,843	413,363	418,674	-15.48	353,868
D/FW	28,077,898	26,929,286	24,601,481	27,960,344	28,395,711	-6.51	26,548,401
Dallas/Love	3,415,785	3,552,419	2,783,787	2,977,048	3,912,856	-5.32	3,704,594
Del Rio	889	0	0	7,638	17,386	-20.33	13,851
El Paso	1,664,123	1,618,128	1,418,974	1,614,404	1,676,738	-11.16	1,489,619
Harlingen	465,516	461,067	392,733	429,541	442,117	-15.35	374,232
Houston/Bush	15,026,663	16,693,056	15,934,088	18,638,471	20,717,170	-7.47	19,168,962
Houston/Hobby	4,222,144	4,265,890	3,691,967	3,947,543	4,219,867	-4.45	4,032,037
Houston/Ellington	46,520	31,775	45,748	3,021	-	-	-
Killeen†	86,649	98,574	92,106	-	-	-	-
Fort Hood/Gray†	-	15,176	3,159	153,930	193,722	4.39	202,226
Laredo	88,969	82,215	73,210	93,541	110,971	-9.61	100,308
Longview	28,888	31,436	29,022	23,250	26,076	-7.19	24,201
Lubbock	565,173	552,726	504,916	545,377	575,774	-7.32	533,635
McAllen	307,325	306,259	263,431	341,910	411,431	-12.35	360,608
Midland	486,709	452,889	399,334	439,507	489,845	-11.00	435,979
San Angelo	40,400	49,140	42,688	63,785	69,738	-13.51	60,315
San Antonio	3,384,107	3,434,894	3,121,545	3,521,538	3,907,118	-2.51	3,809,114
Texarkana	40,506	34,799	25,634	33,573	35,280	-21.97	27,530
Tyler	73,845	65,336	53,854	81,723	77,117	-5.11	73,177
Victoria	20,585	16,835	10,775	11,115	8,829	-30.76	6,113
Waco	61,668	62,228	49,915	70,942	75,496	-12.42	66,116
Wichita Falls	54,453	51,286	39,608	47,126	46,297	-6.31	43,376
Total	**62,597,136**	**63,564,830**	**57,699,259**	**65,750,249**	**70,702,726**	**-6.50**	**66,106,914**

*Percent change 2007 to 2009. **Not a commercial airport. †Killeen-Fort Hood Regional/Robert Gray AAF replaced Killeen Municipal as the commercial service airport in the area. Calendar year data. Source: FAA Terminal Area Forecast 2010.

Texas Air History

Passengers enplaned in Texas by scheduled carriers. (Texarkana not included.) Fiscal year data. *Source: Federal Aviation Administration.*

1950	1,169,051
1955	2,434,814
1960	3,113,582
1965	5,757,689
1970	10,256,691
1975	13,182,957
1980	26,282,723
1985	40,719,223
1990	49,317,619
1995	57,166,515
1999	62,558,165
2000	65,109,179
2001	63,531,077
2002	57,638,423
2003	57,675,118
2004	62,835,571
2005	65,718,669
2006	69,254,682
2007	70,682,651
2008	69,906,579
2009	66,088,575

Leading U.S. Routes, 2009

Rank	Route	Daily Passengers*
1.	New York to-from Los Angeles	4,106
2.	New York to-from Fort Lauderdale	4,093
3.	New York to-from Chicago	3,914
4.	New York to-from Orlando	3,675
5.	New York to-from San Francisco	3,140
17.	**Dallas/Fort Worth** to-from **Houston**	1,694
18.	**Dallas/Fort Worth** to-from New York	1,684

*Average/Each Way. Includes all commercial airports in a metro area.
Source: Air Transport Association.

Leading U.S. Airlines, 2009

Rank	Airline	Passengers	Planes
1.	Delta	108,600,000	740
2.	**Southwest**	101,300,000	537
3.	**American**	85,700,000	608
4.	United	56,000,000	360
5.	US Airways	51,000,000	349
6	**Continental**	43,900,000	337
7.	AirTran	24,000,000	138
8.	JetBlue	22,400,000	151
9.	SkyWest	21,200,000	294
10.	**American Eagle**	16,000,000	223

*Source: Air Transport Association. Note: Texas-based airlines in bold type.
SkyWest data is from July 2010. Scheduled service only.*

Agriculture

Hay bales dot a field in Angelina County. Photo by Ron Billings; Texas Forest Service.

Principal Crops

Vegetable Crops

Fruits and Nuts

Livestock and Their Products

Longhorns in Burleson County. Livestock and livestock products accounted for 64.2 percent of the $16.573 billion in cash receipts from farm marketings in 2009. Photo by Ron Billings; Texas Forest Service.

Agriculture in Texas

Information was provided by Texas AgriLife Extension specialists, Texas Agricultural Statistics Service, U.S. Department of Agriculture, and U.S. Department of Commerce. John Robinson, Professor and Extension Specialist–Cotton Marketing, Texas AgriLife Extension Service, and Caroline Gleaton, Office Associate, coordinated the information. All references are to Texas unless otherwise specified.

The Importance of Agriculture to the Texas Economy

Agribusiness is the combined phases of food and fiber production, processing, transporting, and marketing. Most of this article is devoted to the phase of production on farms and ranches.

Agriculture is one of the most important industries in Texas. Many businesses, financial institutions, and individuals are involved in providing supplies, credit, and services to farmers and ranchers, and in processing and marketing agricultural commodities.

Texas agriculture is a strong industry. **Receipts from farm and ranch marketings in 2010 were estimated at $20 billion, compared with $16.6 billion in 2009.**

With the increasing demand for food and fiber throughout the world, the potential for further growth is favorable. Agricultural exports are also important to the U.S. trade balance, which means that agriculture in Texas will play an even greater role in the future.

Major efforts of research and educational programs by the Texas A&M University System are directed toward developing the state's agricultural industry to its fullest potential. The goal is to capitalize on natural advantages that agriculture has in Texas because of the relatively warm climate, productive soils, and availability of excellent export and transportation facilities.

Texas Farms

The number and nature of farms have changed over time. The number of farms in Texas has decreased from 420,000 in 1940 to 247,500 in 2010, with an average size of 527 acres. Average value per farm of all farm assets, including land and buildings, has increased from $20,100 in 1950 to $816,646 in 2009. The number of small farms is increasing, but part-time farmers operate them.

Mechanization of farming continues as new and larger machines replace manpower. Although machinery price tags are high relative to times past, machines are technologically advanced and efficient. Tractors, mechanical harvesters, and numerous cropping machines have virtually eliminated menial tasks that for many years were traditional to farming.

Revolutionary agricultural chemicals have appeared along with improved plants and animals. Many of the natural hazards of farming and ranching have been reduced by better use of weather information, machinery, and other improvements; but rising costs, labor availability, and high-energy costs have added to concerns of farmers and ranchers. Changes in Texas agriculture in the last 50 years include:

1. More detailed record keeping that assists in management and marketing decisions;

2. More restrictions on choice or inputs/practices;

3. Precision agriculture will takes on new dimensions through the use of satellites, computers, Global Positioning Systems (GPS), and other high-tech tools to help producers manage inputs, such as seed, fertilizers, pesticides, and water.

Farms have become fewer, larger, specialized, and much more expensive to own and operate, but far more productive. The number of small farms operated by part-time farmers is increasing. Land ownership is becoming more of a lifestyle used mostly for recreational purposes. The number of non-farm landowners is increasing.

Irrigation has become an important factor in crop production. Crops and livestock have made major changes in production areas, as in the concentration of cotton on the High Plains and increased livestock production in Central and East Texas.

Pest and disease control methods have improved, and herbicides are relied upon for weed control.

Feedlot finishing, commercial broiler production, artificial insemination, improved pastures and brush control, and reduced feed requirements have greatly increased livestock and poultry efficiency. Biotechnology and genetic engineering promise new breakthroughs in reaching even higher levels of productivity. Horticultural plant and nursery businesses have expanded. Improved wildlife management has increased deer, turkey, and other wildlife populations. The use of land for recreation and ecotourism is growing.

Ranchers and farmers are better educated and informed, and more science- and business-oriented. Today, agriculture operates in a global, high-tech, consumer-driven environment.

Cooperation among farmers in marketing, promotion, and other fields has increased.

Agricultural producers also have become increasingly dependent on off-the-farm services to supply production inputs, such as feeds, chemicals, and credit.

Agribusiness

Texas farmers and ranchers have developed considerable dependence on agribusiness. With many producers specializing in the production of certain crops and livestock, they look beyond the farm and ranch for supplies and services. On the input side, they rely on suppliers of production needs and services and, on the output side, they need assemblers, processors, and distributors. The impact of production agri-

culture and related businesses on the Texas economy is about $44.6 billion annually.

Since 1940, the proportion of Texans whose livelihood is linked to agriculture has changed greatly. In 1940, about 23 percent were producers on farms and ranches, and about 17 percent were suppliers or were engaged in assembly, processing, and distribution of agricultural products. The agribusiness alignment in 2008 was less than 2 percent on farms and ranches, with

Cash Receipts for Commodities, 2005–2009

Commodity *	2005	2006	2007	2008	2009	Percent of 2009
(All values in thousands of dollars)						
All Commodities:	16,619,150	16,142,518	18,900,695	19,501,878	16,573,054	100.00%
Livestock & products	10,547,325	10,229,947	11,386,144	11,403,421	10,640,865	64.21%
Crops, fruits & others	6,071,825	5,912,571	7,514,551	8,098,457	5,932,189	35.79%
Livestock & Products	10,547,325	10,229,947	11,386,144	11,403,421	10,640,865	64.21%
Cattle & calves	7,342,832	7,326,211	7,630,837	7,230,267	6,938,721	41.87%
Broilers	1,436,644	1,198,800	1,404,552	1,592,246	1,650,227	9.96%
Milk, wholesale	982,107	948,556	1,449,723	1,568,743	1,172,129	7.07%
Eggs, chicken	238,798	254,055	373,500	462,283	347,480	2.10%
Hogs	104,010	107,060	93,888	131,744	129,461	0.78%
Sheep and lambs	53,350	35,927	38,646	28,711	37,964	0.23%
Wool	5,328	4,459	5,445	4,872	3,640	0.02%
Mohair	3,750	4,400	3,840	3,116	2,077	0.01%
Other livestock †	380,506	350,479	385,713	381,439	359,166	2.17%
Crops:	6,071,825	5,912,571	7,514,551	8,098,457	5,932,189	35.79%
Corn	364,344	534,638	736,200	1,252,502	1,002,127	6.05%
Cotton lint	1,708,033	1,719,255	1,581,745	1,762,729	963,537	5.81%
Sorghum grain	203,464	189,563	488,119	572,788	376,553	2.27%
Wheat	277,257	189,016	690,418	850,777	324,534	1.96%
Hay	254,627	326,220	688,115	393,347	262,925	1.59%
Cottonseed	256,411	216,326	343,341	315,407	225,092	1.36%
Rice	97,200	103,738	108,611	175,738	163,798	0.99%
Peanuts	175,500	96,258	162,597	200,376	129,658	0.78%
Potatoes	72,104	91,334	67,026	82,361	96,529	0.58%
Onions	149,327	89,424	186,520	82,163	86,155	0.52%
Watermelons	74,214	62,195	35,834	52,592	47,986	0.29%
Soybeans	45,973	34,145	28,189	44,515	43,095	0.26%
Sugarcane for sugar	54,241	48,130	34,164	35,497	36,363	0.22%
Cabbage	41,499	42,454	41,472	46,122	32,400	0.20%
Cucumbers	11,068	15,866	15,290	21,484	22,833	0.14%
Sunflower	17,522	17,205	6,449	12,801	21,123	0.13%
Peppers, chili	10,199	5,250	12,192	13,883	18,701	0.11%
Dry beans	4,042	5,146	6,933	9,242	12,768	0.08%
Carrots, fresh	20,010	12,338	8,400	7,800	8,294	0.05%
Cantaloupes	34,206	20,236	14,040	6,732	6,960	0.04%
Tomatoes, fresh	8,625	5,709	6,020	8,008	6,451	0.04%
Squash	5,320	12,269	14,700	12,690	6,412	0.04%
Honeydew melons	2,187	5,642	7,462	5,538	4,410	0.03%
Corn, sweet	2,642	2,367	3,848	3,542	3,432	0.02%
Oats	3,839	2,564	8,182	7,015	3,083	0.02%
Sweet potatoes	4,546	3,233	3,174	3,088	2,492	0.02%
Spinach, fresh	3,234	4,682	2,400	3,432	1,936	0.01%
Other crop ‡	360,753	401,942	523,870	569,973	575,459	3.47%
Fruits & Nuts:						
Pecans	95,850	75,310	77,600	32,650	89,250	0.54%
Grapefruit	83,596	56,367	54,460	31,460	40,577	0.24%
Peaches	14,047	1,230	11,115	13,230	7,220	0.04%
Oranges	11,431	15,632	11,017	1,673	5,170	0.03%
Grapes	10,625	3,855	4,751	4,804	3,554	0.02%
Other fruits and nuts	8,670	8,185	19,255	14,956	17,043	0.10%
Other Farm Income:						
Greenhouse/nursery	1,585,219	1,494,847	1,511,042	1,447,542	1,284,269	7.75%

*Commodities are listed in order of importance for 2009 by crop items and by livestock items.
† For 2005–2009, includes milkfat, turkey eggs, equine, goats, goat milk, catfish, honey, farm chickens and other poultry, and livestock.
‡ For 2005–2009, includes miscellaneous vegetables and other field crops.
Source: 2009 Texas Agricultural Statistics, USDA/Texas Agricultural Statistics Service, October 2010; various issues of Texas Agriculture Statistics, Texas Agricultural Cash Receipts, and Price Statistics, USDA/TASS.

about 15 percent of the labor force providing production or marketing supplies and services, and retailing food and fiber products.

Cash Receipts

Farm and ranch **cash receipts in 2009 totaled $16.573 billion.** With estimates of $1.407 billion for government payments, $1.977 billion of non-cash income, and $1.806 billion of other farm-related income included, realized gross farm income totaled $21.763 billion. With farm production expenses of $19.639 billion, net farm income totaled $2.124 billion. The value of inventory adjustment was –$261.3 million.

Percent of Income from Products

Livestock and livestock products accounted for 64.2 percent of the $16.573 billion cash receipts from farm marketings in 2009, with the remaining 35.8 percent from crops. Receipts from livestock have trended up largely because of increased feeding operations and reduced crop acreage associated with farm programs and low prices. However, these relationships change because of variations in commodity prices and volume of marketings.

Meat animals (cattle, hogs, and sheep) accounted for 42.9 percent of total cash receipts received by Texas farmers and ranchers in 2009. Most of these receipts were from cattle and calf sales. Dairy products made up 7.1 percent of receipts; poultry and eggs, 12.5 percent; and miscellaneous livestock, 1.7 percent.

Cotton and cottonseed accounted for 7.2 percent of total receipts; feed crops, 9.9 percent; food grains, 3.0 percent; vegetables, 3.1 percent; greenhouse/nursery products, 7.6 percent; oil crops, 1.2 percent; fruits and nuts, 0.98 percent; and other crops, 2.8 percent.

Texas' Rank Among the States

Measured by cash receipts for farm and ranch marketings, **Texas ranked third in 2009,** behind California and Iowa, first and second, respectively.

Texas normally leads all other states in numbers of farms and ranches, farm and ranch land, cattle slaughtered, cattle on feed, calf births, sheep and lambs, goats, cash receipts from livestock marketings, cattle and calves, beef cows, wool production, mohair production, and exports of fats, oils, and greases. The state also usually leads in production of cotton.

Texas' Agricultural Exports

The value of Texas' share of **agricultural exports in fiscal year 2009 was $4.8 billion:**

Cotton accounted for $1.39 billion of the exports; feed grains and products, $378.8 million; wheat and products, $284.6 million; fats, oil, and greases, $114.0 million; rice, $144.7 million; cottonseed and products, $52.8 million;

Hides and skins, $248.0 million; live animals and meat, excluding poultry, $709.5 million; fruits, $59.3 million; peanuts and products, $48.3 million; soybeans and products, $25.0 million;

Realized Gross Income* and Net Income from Farming, 1980–2009

Year	**Realized Gross Farm Income	Farm Production Expenses	Net Change In Farm Inventories	***Total Net Farm Income	***Total Net Income Per Farm
	— Millions of Dollars —				Dollars
1980	9,611.4	9,081.1	–542.5	456.9	2,331.0
1981	11,545.7	9,643.1	699.9	1,902.6	9,756.8
1982	11,404.5	10,008.2	–127.8	1,396.3	7,197.6
1983	11,318.1	9,778.9	–590.7	1,539.2	7,933.8
1984	11,692.6	10,257.3	186.1	1,435.3	7,398.3
1985	11,375.3	9,842.8	–9.0	1,532.5	7,981.9
1986	10,450.1	9,272.8	–349.0	1,177.3	6,196.6
1987	12,296.6	10,038.7	563.2	2,257.9	12,010.1
1988	12,842.3	10,331.7	–128.4	2,510.6	13,076.2
1989	12,843.1	10,328.4	–798.6	2,514.7	12,962.1
1990	14,421.5	11,012.9	343.9	3,408.6	17,391.0
1991	14,376.4	11,270.3	150.0	3,106.1	15,767.0
1992	14,482.5	10,617.6	464.1	3,864.9	19,519.8
1993	15,817.0	11,294.6	197.0	4,522.5	20,745.4
1994	15,394.5	11,134.7	107.7	4,259.9	19,363.0
1995	15,678.9	12,537.3	243.7	3,141.6	14,151.3
1996	15,025.0	12,006.6	–290.1	3,018.4	13,475.1
1997	16,430.7	12,718.5	709.2	3,712.3	16,498.9
1998	15,506.0	12,047.4	–817.1	3,458.6	15,269.7
1999	17,469.5	12,441.9	196.0	5,027.6	22,099.3
2000	16,810.1	12,707.8	–50.2	4,102.3	17,968.9
2001	18,089.1	13,106.6	113.4	4,982.5	21,795.7
2002	16,567.7	11,372.8	436.8	5,195.1	22,686.0
2003	20,105.7	13,687.6	–137.7	6,418.1	28,026.6
2004	21,826.4	14,343.8	539.0	7,482.5	32,674.7
2005	21,928.5	15,371.6	306.7	6,556.8	28,507.8
2006	20,329.6	16,010.9	–753.8	4,318.7	18,777.0
2007	24,734.4	19,801.2	948.6	4,933.2	19,932.1
2008	23,876.0	20,311.5	–868.3	3,564.5	14,402.0
2009	21,763.2	19,639.2	–330.0	2,124.0	8,581.8

*Details for items may not add to totals because of rounding.
**Cash receipts from farm marketings, government payments, value of home consumption, and gross rental value of farm dwellings.
***Farm income of farm operators.
Note: A positive value of inventory change represents current-year production not sold by Dec. 31. A negative value is an offset to production from prior years included in current-year sales. Starting in 1977, farms with production of $1,000 or more used to figure income.
Source: "Economic Indicators of the Farm Sector, State Financial Summary, 1985, 1987, 1989, 1993," USDA/ERS; "Farm Business Economics Report," August 1996; "Texas Agricultural Statistics Service, October 2010"; ERS Briefing Room.

Export Shares of Commodities

Commodity*	2006	2007	2008	2009	2009 % of U.S. Total
	Millions of Dollars				
Rice	78.6	67.2	126.7	144.7	6.00
Cotton & Linters	1,247.0	1,823.6	1,631.7	1,389.8	38.31
Fats, Oils & Greases	80.0	111.3	178.7	114.0	16.69
Hides & Skins	314.9	321.7	341.1	248.0	16.43
Live Animals & Meat (other than poultry)	419.4	510.9	740.0	709.5	7.97
Feed Grains	259.6	482.5	834.1	378.8	3.16
Poultry & Products	154.3	193.7	266.6	289.4	5.97
Fruits & Preps	63.4	71.7	61.7	59.3	1.04
Vegetables	56.3	48.6	55.3	57.9	1.10
Wheat & Flour	153.8	538.2	603.1	284.6	3.31
Soybeans	9.6	14.2	32.6	25.0	0.14
Cottonseed	34.8	71.9	76.8	52.8	39.38
Peanuts	33.4	47.0	54.6	48.3	14.71
Tree Nuts	35.3	33.3	40.4	36.4	1.04
Dairy Products	5.7	12.3	21.8	13.4	0.57
† All Other	697.3	861.8	976.6	895.2	4.69
Total	**3,643.3**	**5,210.0**	**6,041.7**	**4,747.0**	**4.91**

Totals may not add due to rounding.
*Commodity and related preparations.
† Sunflower-seed oil, feeds and fodders, seeds, sugar, and tropical products, minor oilseeds, essential oils, beverages other than juice, nursery and greenhouse, wine, and vegetable products.
Source: FATUS, Foreign Agricultural Trade of the United States, various issues, website: www.ers.usda.gov for 2009 data. USDA/ERS.

A farm worker floods dry rows of dirt before cotton is planted on Deputy Farms in El Paso County. Although sprinkler irrigation is used on about 65 percent of the total irrigated acreage in Texas, furrow methods continue to be used on much of the remaining irrigated land. Photo by Richard Michael Pruitt.

Vegetables and products, $57.9 million; poultry and products, $289.4 million; dairy products, $13.4 million; and miscellaneous and other products, $895.2 million.

In 2008, Texas' exports of $6.042 billion of farm and ranch products was an increase over $5.210 billion in 2007 and $3.643 billion in 2006.

Hunting

The management of wildlife as an economic enterprise through leasing for hunting makes a significant contribution to the economy of many counties. Leasing the right of ingress on a farm or ranch for the purpose of hunting is the service marketed. After the leasing, the consumer — the hunter — goes onto the land to seek the harvest of the wildlife commodity. **Hunting lease income to farmers and ranchers in 2010 was estimated at $558 million,** an increase over $504 million in 2008.

The demand for hunting opportunities is growing, while the land capable of producing huntable wildlife is decreasing. As a result, farmers and ranchers are placing more emphasis on wildlife management practices to help meet requests for hunting leases.

Irrigation

Agricultural irrigation in Texas peaked in 1974 at 8.6 million acres. Over the next 20 years, irrigation declined due to many factors including poor farm economics, falling water tables, and conversion to more efficient technologies. Total irrigated area fluctuates from year to year with current estimates at about **6 million acres.** This puts Texas third in the nation, behind California and Nebraska, in agricultural irrigation.

Although some irrigation is practiced in nearly every county of the state, about 50 percent of the total irrigated acreage is on the High Plains. Other concentrated areas of irrigation are the Gulf Coast rice-producing area, the Lower Rio Grande Valley, the Winter Garden area of South Texas, the Trans-Pecos area of West Texas, and the peanut-producing area in North-Central Texas that is centered around Erath, Eastland, and Comanche counties.

Sprinkler irrigation is used on about 65 percent of the total irrigated acreage, with surface irrigation methods, primarily **furrow and surge methods,** being used on the remaining irrigated area. Texas farmers lead the nation in the adoption of efficient irrigation technologies, particularly **LEPA** (low energy precision application) and **LESA** (low elevation spray application) **center pivot systems,** both of which were developed by Texas AgriLife Research and the Texas AgriLife Extension Service.

The use of **drip irrigation** continues to increase but still accounts for less than 10 percent of the total irrigated acreage. Drip irrigation is routinely used on vegetables and tree crops, such as citrus, pecans, and peaches. Some drip irrigation of cotton, forages, and turfgrass is being practiced in West Texas. Farmers continue to experiment with drip irrigation, but the relatively high costs and management requirements are limiting more widespread use.

Agricultural irrigation uses about 60 percent of all fresh water in the state, and landscape irrigation accounts for about 40 percent of total municipal water use. Texas is one of only a handful of states that require a state irrigator's license for the design and installation of landscape and residential irrigation systems. **New regulations went into effect January 2009** that require all cities of 20,000 persons or larger to have irrigation inspectors, and for irrigation dealers to meet new design and installation requirements. However, no license or certification is required for the design or installation of agricultural irrigation systems.

To meet future water demand for our rapidly growing cities and industries, several regions of the state are looking at water transfers from agriculture. In recent years, major water transfer projects have been proposed; however, significant environmental and legal obstacles exist, and the viability of such projects is not known.

Water utilities in San Antonio also have water

transfer programs with irrigators in the Edwards Aquifer region. The effects of such transfers on farm and rural economies are uncertain.

In about 20 percent of the irrigated area, water is delivered to farms by irrigation and other types of water districts, and by river authorities through canals and pipelines. Many of these delivery networks are aging, in poor condition, and have high seepage losses.

Approximately 80 percent of the state's irrigated acreage is supplied with water pumped from wells. Surface water sources supply the remaining area. Declining groundwater levels in several of the major aquifers is a serious problem, particularly in the Ogallala Aquifer in the Texas High Plains, and the southern portion of the Carizo-Wilcox formation. As the water level declines, well yields decrease and pumping costs increase. *See Major Aquifers of Texas, page 84.*

Texas common law grants the landowner with broad rights to exploit the underlying groundwater. Laws and regulations governing groundwater use enacted in Texas over the last 50 years attempt to recognize the landowner's right to beneficially use the water, while giving water districts certain powers to manage and restrict water use. Legal battles are ongoing between these two interests.

Irrigation is an important factor in the productivity of Texas agriculture. The value of crop production from irrigated acreage is 50–60 percent of the total value of all crop production, although only about 30 percent of the state's total harvested cropland acreage is irrigated.

Principal Crops

The value of crop production in Texas is less than 40 percent of the total value of the state's agricultural output. Cash receipts from farm sales of crops are reduced somewhat because some grain and roughage is fed to livestock on farms where produced. Drought and low prices also have reduced receipts in recent years.

Receipts from all Texas crops totaled $5.932 billion in 2009; $8.098 billion in 2008; and $7.515 billion in 2007.

Cotton, corn, grain sorghum, and wheat account for a large part of the total crop receipts. In 2009, cotton contributed about 16.2 percent of the crop total; corn, 16.9 percent; grain sorghum, 6.3 percent; and wheat, 5.5 percent. Hay, cottonseed, vegetables, peanuts, rice, and soybeans are other important cash crops.

Value of Cotton and Cottonseed 1900–2010

Crop Year	Upland Cotton Production (Bales)	Upland Cotton Value	Cottonseed Production (Tons)	Cottonseed Value
	(All Figures in Thousands)			
1900	3,438	$157,306	1,531	$20,898
1910	3,047	210,260	1,356	31,050
1920	4,345	376,080	1,934	41,350
1930	4,037	194,080	1,798	40,820
1940	3,234	162,140	1,318	31,852
1950	2,946	574,689	1,232	111,989
1960	4,346	612,224	1,821	75,207
1970	3,191	314,913	1,242	68,310
1980*	3,320	1,091,616	1,361	161,959
1981	5,645	1,259,964	2,438	207,230
1982	2,700	664,848	1,122	90,882
1983	2,380	677,443	1,002	162,324
1984	3,680	927,360	1,563	157,863
1985	3,910	968,429	1,635	102,156
1986	2,535	560,945	1,053	82,118
1987	4,635	1,325,981	1,915	157,971
1988	5,215	1,291,651	2,131	238,672
1989	2,870	812,784	1,189	141,491
1990	4,965	1,506,182	1,943	225,388
1991	4,710	1,211,789	1,903	134,162
1992	3,265	769,495	1,346	145,368
1993	5,095	1,308,396	2,147	255,493
1994	4,915	1,642,003	2,111	215,322
1995	4,460	1,597,037	1,828	201,080
1996	4,345	1,368,154	1,784	230,136
1997	5,140	1,482,787	1,983	226,062
1998	3,600	969,408	1,558	204,098
1999	5,050	993,840	1,987	160,947
2000	3,940	868,061	1,589	162,078
2001	4,260	580,723	1,724	159,470
2002	5,040	967,680	1,855	191,065
2003	4,330	1,199,237	1,616	202,000
2004	7,740	1,493,510	2,895	301,080
2005	8,440	1,879,757	2,869	289,739
2006	5,800	1,288,992	2,066	243,776
2007	8,250	2,391,840	2,861	443,409
2008	4,450	935,568	1,547	351,192
2009	4,620	1,328,342	1,634	254,904
2010	8,050	3,083,472	2,791	429,814

* Beginning in 1971, the basis for cotton prices was changed from 500 pound gross weight to 480 pound net weight bale; to compute comparable prices for previous years multiply price times 1.04167.
Sources: "Texas Agricultural Facts," Crop Value Annual Summary, February 2011 and "Texas Ag Statistics," Texas Agricultural Statistics Service, Austin, Texas, annual summary, March 2011. Also, Texas Cottonseed Crushers historical records; U.S. Commerce Dept.; and USDA.

The leading counties in production for 2009 were Hartley, Dallam, Castro, Sherman, and Parmer.

Corn

Interest in corn production throughout the state has increased since the 1970s as yields improved with new varieties. Once the principal grain crop, corn acreage declined as plantings of grain sorghum increased. Only 500,000 acres were harvested annually until the mid-1970s, when development of new hybrids occurred.

Harvested acreage was 2.08 million in 2010; 1.96 million in 2009; and 2.03 million in 2008. Yields for the corresponding years (2010–2008) were 145, 130, and 125 bushels per acre, respectively.

Most of the acreage and yield increase has occurred in Central and South Texas. **In 2010, corn ranked second in value among the state's crops.** It was valued at $1.5 billion in 2010; $1.0 billion in 2009; and $1.2 billion in 2008. The grain is largely used for livestock feed, but other important uses are in food products.

Cotton

Cotton has been a major crop in Texas for more than a century. Since 1880, Texas has led all states in cotton production in most years, and today the annual Texas cotton harvest amounts to approximately a fourth of total production in the United States. The annual Texas cotton crop has averaged 5.54 million bales since 1996.

Value of upland cotton produced in Texas in 2010 was $3.083 billion. Cottonseed value in 2010 was $429.8 million, making the **value of the Texas crop around $3.513 billion.**

Upland cotton was harvested from 5.35 million acres in 2010, and **American-Pima** from 16,500 acres, for a total of 5.367 million acres. Yield for upland cotton in 2010 was 722 pounds per harvested acre, with American-Pima yielding 931 pounds per acre. Cotton acreage harvested in 2009 totaled 3.5 million, with a yield of 634 pounds per acre for upland cotton and 836 pounds per acre for American-Pima.

Total cotton production amounted to 8.082 million bales in 2010 and 4.651 million in 2009. Counties leading in production of upland cotton in 2009 included Hale, Lubbock, Gaines, Dawson, Hockley, Crosby, and Floyd.

Cotton is the raw material for processing operations at gins, oil mills, compresses, and a small number of textile mills in Texas. Cotton in Texas is machine harvested. Field storage of harvested seed cotton has become common practice as gins decline in number. **Most of the Texas cotton crop is exported.** China, Turkey, Mexico, and various Pacific Rim countries are major buyers. With the continuing development of fiber-spinning technology and the improved quality of Texas cotton, the export demand for Texas cotton has grown. Spinning techniques can efficiently produce high-quality yarn from relatively strong short or longer staple upland cotton with fine mature fiber.

Forest Products

For information on Texas forest products, **see Texas Forest Resources, page 107.**

Grain Sorghum

Grain sorghum in 2010 **ranked sixth in dollar value.** Much of the grain is exported, as well as being used in livestock and poultry feed throughout Texas. Ethanol production is a more recent demand source for Texas sorghum.

Total production of grain sorghum in 2010 was 119 million hundredweight (cwt.), with a 3,920 pound per acre yield. With an average price of $7.75 per cwt., the total value reached $516.5 million.

Texas Crop Production 2010

Crop	Harvested Acres (000)	Yield Per Acre	Unit	Total Production (000)	Value (000)
Beans, dry edible	19	1,210	lb.,cwt.	229	6,962
Corn, grain	2,080	145	bu.	301,600	1,477,840
Corn, silage	140	18	ton	2,520	—
Cotton, American-Pima	16.5	931	lb./bale	32	—
Cotton, Upland	5,350	722	lb., bale	8,050	3,083,472
Cottonseed	—	—	ton	2,791	429,814
Grapefruit *	—	—	box	5,600	—
Hay, Alfalfa	120	5	ton	600	109,200
Hay, Other	5,100	2	ton	10,200	1,132,200
Hay, all	5,220	2	ton	10,800	1,241,400
Oats	80	52	bu.	4,160	17,472
Oranges †	—	—	box	1,635	—
Peaches (utilized)	—	—	ton	13	27,300
Peanuts	163	3,600	lb.	586,800	159,610
Pecans	—	—	lb.	70,000	134,200
Potatoes (all)	12.9	289	cwt.	3,729	12,090
Rice	188	7,160	lb., cwt.	13,468	157,576
Sorghum, grain	1,700	70	lb., cwt.	119,000	516,460
Sorghum, silage	80	14	ton	1,120	—
Soybeans	185	30	bu.	5,550	55,500
Sugar cane	52	33	ton	1,716	††
Sunflowers	71	1,351	lb.	95,950	21,468
Sweet potatoes	1	120	cwt.	120	—
Vegetables (commercial):					
Fresh market ‡	59.1	—	cwt.	13,450	337,249
Processing §	14.6	—	cwt.	18,968	23,863
Wheat, winter	3,750	34	bu.	127,500	643,875
Total of Listed Crops	**24,402.1**	**—**	**—**	**—**	**9,587,551**

Grapefruit, Texas 80-lb./box, reflects 09/10 crop year. †Oranges, Texas 85-lb./box, reflects 09/10 crop year. ††Sugarcane value will be published February 2012. ‡Total Texas fresh market vegetables include: Bell peppers, cabbage, cantaloupes, carrots, chile peppers, cucumbers, honeydew melons, onions, spinach, squash, sweet corn, tomatoes and watermelons. §Total Texas processing vegetables include carrots, cucumbers, snap beans, and spinach. Source: ATexas Ag Facts Annual Summary@, TASS/USDA, 3/4/2011.

Research associate Mark Arnold, with the Cotton Entomology Research Program, Texas Agricultural Experiment Station in Lubbock, releases marked boll weevils on freshly harvested cotton. Recapture of weevils a day later enables researchers to determine survival rate. Photo by Tom Sappington; USDA.

In a greenhouse at the Cropping Systems Research Laboratory in Lubbock, soil scientist Veronica Acosta-Martinez (left) and plant physiologist Gloria Burow compare the response of sorghum varieties undergoing water stress. Photo by Stephen Ausmus; USDA.

In 2009, 2.05 million acres of grain sorghum were harvested, yielding an average of 2,688 pounds per acre for a total production of 98.4 million cwt. It was valued at $6 per cwt., for a total value of $330.6 million. In 2008, 3.05 million acres were harvested with an average of 2,912 pounds per acre, or 158.6 million cwt. The season's average price was $6.91 per cwt. for a total value of $613.72 million.

Although grown to some extent in all counties where crops are important, the largest concentrations are in the High Plains, Coastal Bend, and the Lower Rio Grande Valley areas. Counties leading in production in 2009 were Willacy, Hidalgo, Cameron, Matagorda, Ochiltree, and Lamb.

Research continues to develop high-yielding hybrids resistant to diseases and insect damage. *A history of grain sorghum appeared in the 1972–1973 edition of the Texas Almanac and can be found at www. TexasAlmanac.com/archive.*

Hay, Silage, and Other Forage Crops

A large proportion of Texas' agricultural land is devoted to forage crop production. This acreage produces forage needs and provides essentially the total feed requirements for most of the state's large domestic livestock population as well as game animals.

Approximately 87.2 million acres of pasture and rangeland, which are primarily in the western half of Texas, provide **grazing for beef cattle, sheep, goats, horses, and game animals.** An additional 7.8 million acres are devoted to cropland used only for pasture or grazing. The average annual acreage of forage land used for hay, silage, and other forms of machine-harvested forage is around 5 million acres.

Hay accounts for a large amount of this production with some corn and sorghum silage being produced. The most important hay crops are **annual and perennial grasses and alfalfa.** Production in 2010 totaled 10.8 million tons of hay from 5.22 million harvested acres at a yield of 2.0 tons per acre. **Value of hay was $1.241 billion,** or $126 per ton. In 2009, 8.25 million tons of hay was produced from 4.62 million harvested acres at a yield of 1.8 tons per acre. The value in 2009 was $937.2 million or $124 per ton. In 2008, the production of hay was 9.211 million tons from 4.430 million harvested acres with a value of $1.01 billion, or $119 per ton, at a yield of 2.08 tons per acre.

Alfalfa hay production in 2010 totaled 600,000 tons with 120,000 acres harvested with a yield of 5.0 tons per acre. At a value of $182 per ton, total value was $109.2 million. In 2009, 600,000 tons of alfalfa hay was harvested from 120,000 acres at a yield of 5 tons per acre. Value was $111 million, or $185 per ton. Alfalfa hay was harvested from 130,000 acres in 2008, producing an average of 4.70 tons per acre for total production of 611,000 tons valued at $112.42 million.

An additional sizable acreage of annual forage crops is grazed, as well as much of the small grain acreage. Alfalfa, sweet corn, vetch, arrowleaf clover, grasses, and other forage plants also provide income as seed crops.

Nursery Crops

The trend to increase production of nursery crops continues to rise as transportation costs on long-distance hauling increases. This has resulted in a marked increase in the production of container-grown plants within the state. This increase is noted especially in the production of **bedding plants, foliage plants, sod, and the woody landscape plants.**

Plant rental services have become a multi-million dollar business. This relatively new service provides the plants and maintains them in office buildings, shopping malls, public buildings, and even in some homes for a fee. The response has been good as evidenced by the growth of companies providing these services.

The interest in plants for interior landscapes is popular among all age groups, as both retail nurseries and florist shops report that people of all ages are buying their plants—from the elderly in retirement homes to high school and college students in dormitory rooms and apartments.

Texas AgriLife Extension specialists estimated cash receipts from nursery crops in Texas to be around $1.6 billion in 2010. Texans are creating colorful and green surroundings by improving their landscape plantings.

Oats

Oats are grown extensively in Texas for winter pasture, hay, silage, and greenchop feeding, and some acreage is harvested for grain.

Of the 550,000 acres planted to oats in 2010, 80,000 acres were harvested. The average yield was 52 bushels per acre. Production totaled 4.16 million bushels with a value of $17.5 million. In 2009, 600,000 acres were planted. From the plantings, 60,000 acres were harvested, with an average yield of 47 bushels per acre for a total production of 2.82 million bushels. Average price per bushel was $4.51, and total production value was $12.72 million.

Texas farmers planted 600,000 acres of oats in

Lemont rice, the first high-yielding semidwarf rice variety, was released in 1983 by the USDA's Agricultural Research Service and the Texas Experiment Station at Texas A&M University. Photo by David Nance; USDA.

2008. They harvested 100,000 acres that averaged 50 bushels per acre for a total production of 5 million bushels at an average price of $4 per bushel. The estimated value was $20 million. Most of the acreage was used for grazing.

Almost all oat grain produced in Texas is utilized as feed for livestock within the state. A small acreage is grown exclusively for planting seed.

Leading oat grain-producing counties in 2009 were Hamilton, McLennan, Cooke, Uvalde, Coryell, and Hill.

Peanuts

Peanuts are grown on more than 250,000 acres in Texas. Well over three-fourths of the annual production is from irrigated acreage. **Texas ranked second nationally in production of peanuts in 2010.** Among Texas crops, peanuts rank ninth in value.

Until 1973, essentially all of the Texas acreage was planted to the **Spanish type,** which was favored because of earlier maturity and better drought tolerance than other types. The Spanish variety is also preferred for some uses due to its distinctive flavor. The **Florunner variety,** a runner market type, is now planted on a sizable proportion of the acreage where soil moisture is favorable. The variety is later maturing but better yielding than Spanish varieties under good-growing conditions. Florunner peanuts have acceptable quality to compete with the Spanish variety in most products.

In 2010, peanut production totaled 586.8 million pounds from 163,000 harvested acres, yielding 3,600 pounds per acre. At 27.2 cent per pound, value of the crop was estimated at $159.61 million. In 2009, peanut production amounted to 506.85 million pounds from 165,000 acres planted and 155,000 harvested. Average yield of 3,270 pounds per acre and average price of 23.1 cents per pound combined for a 2009 value of $117.1 million.Production in 2008 amounted to 834.9 million pounds of peanuts from 257,000 acres planted and 253,000 acres harvested, or an average of 3,300 pounds per harvested acre. At 24 cents per pound, the crop was valued at $200.4 million.

Leading counties in peanut production in 2009 included Gaines, Yoakum, Terry, Frio, Collingsworth, Andrews, and Donley.

Rice

Rice, which is grown in about 20 counties on the Coastal Prairie of Texas, ranked third in value among Texas crops for a number of years. However, in 2010, cotton, corn, hay, wheat, and grain sorghum outranked rice.

Rice farms are highly mechanized, producing rice through irrigation and using airplanes for much of the planting, fertilizing, and application of insecticides and herbicides.

Texas farmers grow **long- and medium-grain rice** only. The Texas rice industry, which has grown from 110 acres in 1850 to a high of 642,000 acres in 1954, has been marked by significant yield increases and improved varieties. Record production was in 1981, with 27.24 million cwt. harvested. Highest yield was 7,770 pounds per acre in 2009.

Several different types of rice milling procedures are in use today. The simplest and oldest method produces a product known as regular milled white rice, the most prevalent on the market today.

During this process, rice grains are subjected to additional cleaning to remove chaff, dust, and foreign seed, and then husks are removed from the grains. This results in a product that is the whole unpolished grain of rice with only the outer hull and a small amount of bran removed. This product is called **brown rice** and is sometimes sold without further treatment other than grading. It has a delightful nutlike flavor and a slightly chewy texture.

When additional layers of the bran are removed, the rice becomes white in color and begins to appear as it is normally recognized at retail level. The removal of the bran layer from the grain is performed in a number of steps using two or three types of machines. After the bran is removed, the product is ready for classification as to size. Rice is more valuable if the grains are not broken. In many cases, additional vitamins are added to the grains to produce what is called **"enriched rice."**

Another process may be used in rice milling to produce a product called **parboiled rice.** In this process, the rice is subjected to a combination of steam and pressure prior to the time it is milled. This process gelatinizes the starch in the grain, which aids in the retention of much of the natural vitamin and mineral content. After cooking, parboiled rice tends to be fluffy, more separate, and plump.

Still another type of rice is **precooked rice,** which is actually milled rice that, after milling, has been cooked. Then the moisture is removed through a dehydration process. Precooked rice requires a minimum of preparation time since it needs merely to have the moisture restored.

The United States produces only a small part of the world's total rice, but it is **one of the leading exporters.** American rice is popular abroad and is exported to more than 100 foreign countries.

Texas rice production in 2010 totaled 13.47 million cwt. from 188,000 harvested acres, with a yield of 7,160 pounds per acre. The crop value totaled $157.6 million. Rice production was 13.2 million cwt. in 2009 on 170,000 harvested acres, yielding 7,770 pounds per acre. Total value in 2009 was $170.3 million. Rice production was 11.9 million cwt. in 2008 on 172,000 harvested acres. Production in 2008 was valued at $186.3 million, with a yield of 6,900 pounds per acre. Counties leading in production in 2009 included Wharton, Colorado, Matagorda, Brazoria, Jackson, and Jefferson.

Soybeans

Production is largely in the areas of the Upper Coast, irrigated High Plains, and Red River Valley of Northeast Texas. Soybeans are adapted to the same general soil climate conditions as corn, cotton, or grain sorghum, provided moisture, disease, and insects are not limiting factors. The major counties in soybean production in 2009 were Fannin, Lamar, Wharton, Delta, Ochiltree, and Matagorda.

In low-rainfall areas, yields have been too low or inconsistent for profitable production under dryland conditions. **Soybeans' need for moisture in late summer** minimizes economic crop possibilities in the Blacklands and Rolling Plains. In the Blacklands, cotton root rot seriously hinders soybean production. Limited moisture at critical growth stages may occasionally prevent economical yields, even in high-rainfall areas of Northeast Texas and the Coastal Prairie.

Because of day length sensitivity, soybeans should be planted in Texas during the long days of May and June to obtain sufficient vegetative growth for optimum yields. Varieties planted during this period usually cease vegetative development and initiate reproductive processes during the hot, usually dry months of July and August. When moisture is insufficient during the blooming and fruiting period, yields are drastically reduced. In most areas of the state, July and August rainfall is insufficient to permit economical dryland production. The risk of dryland soybean production in the Coastal Prairie and Northeast Texas is considerably less when compared to other dryland areas because moisture is available more often during the critical fruiting period.

The 2010 soybean crop totaled 5.55 million bushels and was **valued at $55.5 million,** or $10 per bushel. Of the 205,000 acres planted, 185,000 were harvested with an average yield of 30 bushels per acre. In 2009, the Texas soybean crop averaged 25 bushels per acre from 190,000 acres harvested.

Total production of 4.75 million bushels was valued at $44 million, or $9.25 per bushel. In 2008, the Texas soybean crop averaged 24.5 bushels per acre from 205,000 acres harvested. Total production of 5.02 million bushels was valued at $46.5 million, or $9.25 per bushel.

Sugarcane

Sugarcane is grown from seed cane planted in late summer or fall. It is harvested 12 months later and milled to produce **raw sugar and molasses.** Raw sugar requires additional refining before it is in final form and can be offered to consumers.

The **sugarcane grinding mill operated at Santa Rosa, Cameron County,** is considered one of the most modern mills in the United States. Texas sugarcane-producing counties are Cameron, Hidalgo, and Willacy.

At a yield of 33 tons per acre, sugarcane production in 2010 totaled 1.72 million tons from 52,000 harvested acres. In 2009, 39,700 acres were harvested for total production of 1.43 million tons valued at $31.8 million. The yield was 35.9 tons per acre. In 2008, 39,200 acres were harvested, from which 1.4 million tons of sugarcane were milled. The yield averaged 35.5 tons per acre for a total value of $35.5 million.

Sunflowers

Sunflowers constitute **one of the most important annual oilseed crops** in the world. The cultivated types, which are thought to be descendants of the common wild sunflower native to Texas, have been successfully grown in several countries including Russia, Argentina, Romania, Bulgaria, Uruguay, Western Canada, and portions of the northern United States. Extensive trial plantings conducted in the Cotton Belt states since 1968 showed sunflowers have considerable potential as an oilseed crop in much of this area, including Texas.

This crop exhibits good cold and drought tolerance, is adapted to a wide range of soil and climate conditions, and tolerates higher levels of hail, wind, and sand abrasion than other crops normally grown in the state.

In 2010, sunflower production totaled 96 million pounds and was harvested from 71,000 acres at a yield of 1,351 pounds per acre. With an average price

A field of sunflowers bloom in early April in Cameron County. In 2010, sunflower production totaled 96 million pounds and was harvested from 71,000 acres The crop was valued at $21.5 million. Photo by Christy de la Garza.

of $22.40 per cwt., **the crop was valued at $21.5 million.** In 2009, 118,000 of the 135,000 acres planted to sunflowers were harvested with an average yield of 1,100 pounds per acre. Total production of 130 million pounds was valued at $25.3 million, or $19.50 per cwt.

In 2008, of 101,000 acres planted to sunflowers, 87,000 acres were harvested, yielding 1,062 pounds per acre for a total yield of 92.4 million pounds valued at $18.3 million, or $19.80 per cwt. The leading counties in production in 2009 were Lamb, Lynn, Hale, Bailey, Yoakum, and Dallam.

Reasons for growing sunflowers include the need for an additional cash crop with low water and plant nutrient requirements, the development of sunflower hybrids, and interest by food processors in **Texas sunflower oil,** which has high oleic acid content. Commercial users have found many advantages in this high oleic oil, including excellent cooking stability, particularly for use as a deep-frying medium for potato chips, corn chips, and similar products.

Sunflower meal is a high-quality protein source free of nutritional toxins that can be included in rations for swine, poultry, and ruminants (cud-chewing animals). The hulls constitute a source of roughage, which can also be included in livestock rations.

Wheat

Wheat for grain is **one of the state's most valuable cash crops.** In 2010, wheat was exceeded in value by cotton, corn, and hay. Wheat pastures also provide considerable winter forage for cattle that is reflected in the value of livestock produced.

Texas wheat production totaled 127.5 million bushels in 2010, and yield averaged 34 bushels per acre. Planted acreage totaled 5.7 million acres and 3.75 million acres were harvested. With an average price of

$5.05 per bushel, **the 2010 wheat value totaled $644 million.** In 2009, Texas wheat growers planted 6.4 million acres and harvested 2.45 million acres. The yield was 25 bushels per acre, with total production of 61.3 million bushels. At $5.27 per bushel, the crop's value was $323 million.

Texas wheat growers planted 5.8 million acres in 2008 and harvested grain from 3.3 million acres. The yield was 30 bushels per acre for a total production of 99 million bushels, valued at $750.4 million.

Leading wheat-producing counties, based on 2009 production, were Hansford, Ochiltree, Sherman, Dallam, Castro, Hartley, and Moore. The leading counties, based on acreage planted in 2009 were Deaf Smith, Hansford, Parmer, Ochiltree, Castro, Wilbarger, and Swisher.

Wheat was **first grown commercially in Texas near Sherman about 1833.** The acreage expanded greatly in North-Central Texas after 1850 because of rapid settlement of the state and introduction of the well-adapted Mediterranean strain of wheat. A major family flour industry was developed in the Fort Worth-Dallas-Sherman area between 1875 and 1900.

Now, around half of the state acreage is planted on the High Plains and about a third of this is irrigated. Most of the Texas wheat acreage is of the hard red winter class. Because of the development of varieties with improved disease resistance and the use of wheat for winter pasture, there has been a sizable expansion of acreage in Central and South Texas.

Most all wheat harvested for grain is used in some phase of the milling industry. The better-quality hard red winter wheat is used in the production of **commercial bakery flour.** Lower grades and varieties of soft red winter wheat are used in family flours. By-products of milled wheat are used for feed.

Vegetable Crops

Some market vegetables are produced in almost all Texas counties, but most of the commercial crop comes from about 200 counties. Hidalgo County is the leading Texas county in vegetable acres harvested, followed by Parmer and Uvalde counties. Other leading producing counties are: Hale, Frio, Yoakum, Zavala, Hudspeth, and Gaines.

Texas is one of the eight leading states in the production of fresh market vegetables. Nationally in 2010, Texas ranked eighth in production, exceeded by California, Florida, Arizona, Georgia, Washington, Oregon, and New York, and seventh in value of fresh-market vegetables. Texas had 3.1 percent of the

production, and 3 percent of the value of fresh-market vegetables produced. Onions were the number one cash crop, with watermelons second. Other vegetables leading in value of production for 2010 were cabbage, chile peppers, squash, cantaloupes, and carrots.

In 2010, **total vegetable production of 32.4 million cwt. was valued at $361.1 million** from 59,100 acres harvested. In 2009, Texas growers harvested total commercial vegetable crops valued at $221.6 million from 75,500 acres with a production of 15.7 million cwt. Texas growers harvested 15.6 million cwt. of commercial vegetable crops from 74,400 acres in 2008, valued at $276.6 million.

Onions

Onion production in 2010 totaled 2.8 million cwt. from 9,100 harvested acres and was valued at $161.3 million, at a yield of 330 cwt. per acre. In 2009, 32 million cwt. of onions were harvested from 9,700 acres and valued at $48 million, at a yield of 315 cwt. per acre. In 2008, total of 2.7 million cwt. of onions were produced from 9,600 harvested acres and valued at $44.4 million, yielding 335 cwt. per acre.

Carrots

Carrot production in 2010 totaled 338,000 cwt. from 1,300 harvested acres at a yield of 260 cwt. per acre.

Production was valued at $8.62 million. In 2009, carrots were harvested from 1,200 acres with a value of $8.3 million. At a yield of 270 cwt. per acre, 2009 production was 324,000 cwt. Carrot production was valued at $7.8 million in 2008 from 1,300 acres harvested. Production was 312,000 cwt. at a yield of 240 cwt. per acre.

The winter carrot production from South Texas accounts for about three-fourths of total production during the winter season.

All Potatoes

In 2010, all potatoes were harvested from 12,900 acres with production of 3.72 million cwt. valued at $12.1 million at a yield of 289 cwt. per acre. All potatoes were

Children find ripe strawberries at Gnismer Farms in Arlington on an April morning, the month when that fruit typically peaks in Texas. Many farms and orchards around the state invite the public to pick their own produce. For locations by region and best times to pick, see www.PickYourOwn.org. Photo by Evans Caglage.

harvested from 13,700 acres with production of 4.44 million cwt. valued at $22.7 million in 2009, yielding 324 cwt. per acre. This compares with 15,400 acres harvested and valued at $84.9 million in 2008, with production of 4.6 million cwt. and a yield of 299 cwt. per acre.

Cantaloupes & Honeydews

Cantaloupe production in 2010 totaled 297,000 cwt. from 2,700 harvested acres. It was valued at $9.3 million at a yield of 110 cwt. per acre. In 2009, cantaloupes were harvested from 2,400 acres for total production of 240,000 cwt. valued at $7 million, yielding 100 cwt. per acre. Of the 1,800 harvested acres in 2008, 198,000 cwt. cantaloupes were produced at a yield of 110 cwt. per acre and were valued at $6.7 million.

Honeydew production in 2010 totaled 219,000 cwt. and was valued at $5.8 million at a yield of 365 cwt. per acre. In 2009, 210,000 cwt. of honeydew melons were harvested from 600 acres for total value of $4.4 million, yielding 350 cwt. per acre. Honeydew melons valued at $5.54 million were harvested on 700 acres in 2008, producing a yield of 270 cwt. per acre for a total production of 189,000 cwt.

Cabbage

In 2010, 7,800 acres of cabbage were harvested and yielded total production of 2.5 million cwt. that was valued at $50.42 million. Yield was 320 cwt. per acre.

In 2009, 7,500 acres of cabbage were harvested yielding total production of 2.4 million cwt., or 320 cwt. per acre, valued at $32.4 million. The 7,100 acres of cabbage harvested in Texas in 2008 brought a value of $46.1 million. At a yield of 320 cwt. per acre, total production was 2.27 million cwt.

Watermelons

Watermelon production in 2010 was 6.23 million cwt. from 24,900 acres with a value of $52.3 million, yielding 250 cwt. per acre.

In 2009, at a yield of 280 cwt. per acre, 5.9 million cwt. watermelons were harvested from 20,900 acres and valued at $48 million. Watermelon production was 6.05 million cwt. from 19,500 acres in 2008, with a value of $52.6 million at a yield of 310 cwt. per acre.

Tomatoes

Commercial tomatoes are marketed throughout the year from Texas partly as a result of recent increases in **greenhouse production during the winter.** Numbers were not reported for 2010.

In 2009, 800 harvested acres of tomatoes at a yield of 140 cwt. per acre produced 112,000 cwt. of tomatoes with a value of $6.5 million. In 2008, 1,000 acres of tomatoes were harvested, producing 130,000 cwt. at a yield of 130 cwt. per acre for a value of $8 million.

Sweet Potatoes

In 2010, 120,000 cwt. sweet potatoes were harvested from 1,000 acres at a yield of 120 cwt. per acre. Sweet potatoes in 2009 produced 130,000 cwt. from 1,300 harvested acres with a value of $2.2 million. Yield was 100 cwt. per acre. This compared with 210,000 cwt. produced at a yield of 140 cwt. from 1,500 harvested acres valued at $3 million in 2008.

Spinach

Spinach production is primarily concentrated in the **Winter Garden** area of South Texas.

The 2010 production value of spinach was estimated at $4.4 million. Production of 190,000 cwt. was harvested from 1,000 acres with a yield of 190 cwt. per acre. In 2009, 600 acres were harvested with a value of $1.94 million. At a yield of 146 cwt. per acre, production was 88,000 cwt. The 1,100 acres, harvested in 2008, produced 132,000 cwt. at a yield of 120 cwt. per acre and valued at $3.4 million.

Cucumbers

In 2010, 1,100 acres of cucumbers were harvested. Production totaled 156,000 cwt. and was valued at $4.1

million. The 2010 yield was 142 cwt. per acre. In 2009, 1,100 acres of cucumbers were harvested with a value of $3.16 million. Production was 117,000 cwt. with a yield of 106 cwt. per acre. At a yield of 104 cwt. per acre, the 104,000 cwt. cucumber crop in Texas during 2008 was harvested from 1,000 acres and valued at $2.4 million.

Sweet Corn

In 2010, 162,000 cwt. of sweet corn was harvested from 2,700 acres. Value of production was estimated at $3.6 million, with a yield of 60 cwt. per acre.

In 2009, 156,000 cwt. of sweet corn was produced from 2,400 harvested acres at a yield of 65 cwt. per acre and valued at $3.4 million. Sweet corn was harvested in Texas in 2008 from 2,400 acres and valued at $3.5 million. Production was 161,000 cwt. at a yield of 67 cwt. per acre.

Vegetables for Processing

In 2010, 1.9 million cwt. of cucumbers, carrots, snap beans, and spinach for processing were harvested from 14,600 acres and valued at $24 million. In 2009, 19,600 acres were harvested and valued at $33.5 million ,with a production of 2.65 million cwt. In 2008, 22,100 acres were harvested and valued at $31.7 million, producing 2.9 million cwt.

Vegetable Production 2010

Crop	Harvested Acres (000)	Yield Per Acre, Cwt.	Production (000) Cwt.	Value (000)
Cabbage	7,800	320	2,496	50,419
Cantaloupes	2,700	110	297	9,266
Carrots	1,300	260	338	8,619
Chile Peppers ‡	5,400	51	276	20,460
Cucumbers	1,100	142	156	4,056
Honeydew Melons	600	365	219	5,804
Onions, Spring	8,600	310	2,666	154,628
Onions, Summer	500	350	175	6,685
Spinach	1,000	190	190	4,370
Squash	1,700	100	170	13,056
Sweet Corn	2,700	60	162	3,564
Watermelons	24,900	250	6,225	52,290
Total Fresh Market*	*59,100*	*—*	*13,450*	*337,249*
Processed †	14,600	—	18,968	23,863
Total Vegetables	**73,700**	**—**	**32,418**	**361,112**

* Includes some quantities processed.
† Carrots, cucumbers, snap beans, and spinach.
‡ Chile peppers are defined as all peppers, excluding bell peppers. Estimates include both fresh and dry product combined.
Source: "Texas Ag Facts," Texas Agricultural Statistics Service/USDA. February 2011.

Fruits and Nuts

Texas is noted for producing a wide variety of fruits. The pecan is the only commercial nut crop in the state. The pecan is native to most of the state's river valleys and is the Texas state tree. Citrus is produced commercially in the three southernmost counties in the Lower Rio Grande Valley. Peaches represent the next most important Texas fruit crop. There is also an increasing interest in growing apples.

Citrus

Texas ranks with Florida, California, and Arizona as leading states in the production of citrus. Most of the Texas production is in Cameron, Hidalgo, and Willacy counties of the Lower Rio Grande Valley. In the 2009–2010 growing season, **grapefruit** production was estimated at 5.6 million boxes. Grapefruit production in 2008–2009 was 5.5 million boxes at $6.64 per box for a total value of $36.5 million. Production in 2007–2008 was 6 million boxes at $6.83 per box with a value of $41 million.

Production of **oranges** in 2009–2010 was 1.64 million boxes. In 2008–2009, production was 1.5 million boxes at $6.82 per box for a total value of $10 million. Production was 1.8 million boxes in 2007–2008 at $5.35 per box for a value of $9.6 million.

Peaches

Primary production areas are East Texas, the Hill Country, and the West Cross Timbers. Production varies substantially due to adverse weather conditions. Low-

The 2010 Texas peach crop was valued at $27.3 million. Photo by Kye R. Lee.

chilling varieties for early marketings are being grown in Atascosa, Frio, Webb, Karnes, and Duval counties.

The Texas peach crop's utilized production totaled 13,000 tons in 2010 for a value of $27.3 million, or $2,100 per ton. In 2009, utilized production was 3,800 tons. Value of production was $7.2 million, or $1,900 per ton. In 2008, utilized production was 6,300 tons that was valued at $13.2 million, or $2,100 per ton.

The demand for high-quality Texas peaches greatly exceeds the supply. Texas ranked ninth nationally in utilized peach production in 2010. Leading Texas counties in production are Gillespie, Parker, Montague, Comanche, Limestone, and Eastland.

Pecans

The pecan, **the state tree,** is one of the most widely distributed trees in Texas. It is native to over 150 counties and is grown commercially in some 30 other counties.

The pecan is also widely used as a dual-purpose yard tree. The commercial plantings of pecans have accelerated in Central and West Texas, with many of the new orchards being irrigated. Many new pecan plantings are being established under trickle-irrigation systems.

In 2010, utilized pecan production totaled 70 million pounds and was valued at $134.2 million or $1.92 per pound. In 2009, 60 million pounds were produced. Total value was estimated at $89.3 million, as price averaged at $1.49 per pound. The 2008 crop totaled 30 million pounds valued at $32.7 million or $1.09 per pound.

Nationally, Texas ranked first in utilized pecan production in 2010, followed by Georgia and New Mexico. Leading Texas counties in pecan production are Hood, El Paso, Pecos, San Saba, Mills, Comanche, Wharton, and Gonzales.

Dairy cows and beef cattle graze at the Truth Farm in Hunt County. Cattle and calves dominate livestock production in Texas, contributing around 41.9 percent of cash receipts each year. Photo by Natalie Caudill.

Livestock and Their Products

Livestock and their products accounted for about 64.2 percent of the agricultural cash receipts in Texas in 2009. The state **ranks first nationally** in all cattle, beef cattle, cattle on feed, sheep and lambs, wool, goats, and mohair.

Meat animals account for around 42.9 percent of cash receipts from marketings of livestock and their products. Sales of livestock and products in 2009 totaled $10.64 billion, down from $11.40 billion in 2008.

Cattle and calves dominate livestock production in Texas, contributing around 41.9 percent of cash receipts from livestock and products each year. The Jan. 1, 2011, inventory of all cattle and calves in Texas totaled 13.3 million head, valued at $11.44 billion, compared to 13.3 million as of Jan. 1, 2010, valued at $10.11 billion.

On Jan. 1, 2011, the **sheep and lamb** inventory stood at 880,000 head, valued at $113.5 million, compared with 830,000 head as of Jan. 1, 2010, valued at $83 million. Sheep and lambs numbered 3.21 million on Jan. 1, 1973, down from a high of 10.83 million in 1943. Sheep and lamb production fell from 148.3 million pounds in 1973 to 32.4 million pounds on Jan. 1, 2011. Wool production decreased from 26.4 million pounds valued at $23.2 million in 1973 to 3.6 million pounds valued at $5.74 million in 2010. Production was 3.5 million pounds in 2009 valued at $3.64 million. The price of wool per pound was 88 cents in 1973, $1.04 in 2009, and $1.58 in 2010.

Lamb prices averaged $134 per cwt. as of Jan. 1, 2011, $109 per cwt. in 2010, and $98.20 per cwt. in 2009. The average price of sheep was $52 per cwt. as of Jan. 1, 2011, $34.70 in 2010, and $30.20 in 2009.

Mohair production in Texas has dropped from a 1965 high of 31.6 million pounds to 730,000 pounds in 2010. Production was valued at $3.1 million or $4.20 per pound. In 2009, production was 700,000 pounds valued at $2.2 million or $3.10 per pound. Mohair production in 2008 was 820,000 pounds valued at $3.12 million or $3.80 per pound.

Beef Cattle

Raising beef cattle is the most extensive agricultural operation in Texas. In 2009, 41.9 percent of total cash receipts from farm and ranch marketings — $6,938,721 of $16,573,054 — came from cattle and calves, compared with $7,230,267 of $19,501,880 in 2008 (37.1 percent) and $7,630,837 of $18,900,694 in 2007 (40.4 percent). The next leading commodity is broilers.

Nearly all of the 254 counties in Texas derive more revenue from cattle than from any other agricultural commodity, and those that don't usually rank cattle second in importance.

Within the boundaries of Texas are **14.4 percent of all the cattle in the United States,** as are 16.3 percent of the beef breeding cows, and 13.5 percent of the calf crop as of the Jan. 1, 2011, inventory.

The number of all cattle in Texas on Jan. 1, 2011, and Jan. 1, 2010 totaled 13.3 million, compared with 13.6 million in 2009.

Calves born on Texas farms and ranches as of Jan. 1, 2011, totaled 4.8 million compared with 4.75 million as of Jan. 1, 2010; and 4.8 million as of Jan. 1, 2009.

Sale of cattle and calves at approximately 145 livestock auctions inspected by the Texas Animal Health Commission totaled 4.4 million head in 2010; 4.53 million head in 2009; and 4.16 million in 2008. The number of cattle and calves shipped into Texas totaled 1.37 million head in 2010; 1.85 million head in 2009, and 2 million head in 2008.

Livestock Industries

A large portion of Texas livestock is sold through local **auction markets.** In 2009, the Texas Animal Health Commission reported 145 livestock auctions. Auctions sold 4.4 million head of cattle and calves; 27,000 hogs; and 869,000 sheep and goats in 2010. This compared with 4.53 million cattle and calves; 28,000 hogs; and 928,000 sheep and goats in 2009. Figures for 2008 were 4.2 million cattle and calves; 32,000 hogs; 1.03 million sheep and goats.

During 2010, the commission reported 871503 cattle and calves shipped from Texas to other states and 1.37 million shipped in; compared with 813,145 shipped out and 1.85 million shipped in during 2009; and 720,000 shipped out and 2 million shipped in during 2008. (Figures exclude cattle shipped directly to slaughter, where no health certificates are required.)

Texas shipped out 72,756 sheep and lambs and shipped in 11,425 during 2010; compared with 62,132 shipped out and 21,779 shipped in during 2009; and 26,000 shipped out and 12,000 shipped in during 2008.

Feedlot Production

Feedlot production of livestock, mainly cattle, is a major industry in Texas. Annual fed cattle marketings totaled 5.73 million for 1,000 and over feedlot capacity (head) in 2008. Texas lots marketed a total of 5.7 million head of grain-fed cattle in 2007, compared with 5.78 million in 2006; and 5.76 million in 2005. **In recent years, more cattle have been fed in Texas than any other state in the United States.** Future state-level numbers will only be published in conjunction with the Census of Agriculture every five years.

During 2008, there were 128 feedlots in Texas with capacity of 1,000 animals or more. This compared with 128 in 2007, 130 in 2006, and 130 in 2005.

Slaughter plants in Texas numbered 103 in 2010. This compared with 111 in 2009 and 121 in 2008. In 2009, the number of federally inspected cattle slaughtered in Texas totaled 6.6 million cattle, 352,000 hogs, 21,000 sheep and lambs, and 43,000 calves. Those 2009 figures compared with 6.72 million cattle, 369,000 hogs, 5,000 sheep and lambs, and 19,000 calves in 2008; and 6.1 million cattle, 357,000 hogs, 3,000 sheep and lambs, and 11,000 calves in 2007.

Feeding of cattle in commercial feedlots is a major economic development that has stimulated the establishment and expansion of beef slaughtering plants. Most of this development is in the Northern High Plains area of Northwest Texas. This area alone accounts for around 91 percent of the cattle fed in the state as of Jan. 1, 2009.

Total feedlot marketings represented about 26 percent of total U.S. fed cattle marketings in Jan. 1, 2009. Large amounts of capital are required for feedlot operations, which has forced many lots to become custom feeding facilities.

Feedlots are concentrated on the High Plains largely because of extensive supplies of corn, sorghum, and other feed. Beef breeding herds have increased the most in East Texas, where acreage for grazing is abundant.

Texas Cattle Marketed by Size of Feedlots, 1965–2007

| Year | Feedlot Capacity (head) | | | | | | Total |
	Under 1,000	1,000– 1,999	2,000– 3,999	4,000– 7,999	8,000– 15,999	16,000 & Over	
	Cattle Marketed — 1,000 head —						
1965	104	108	205	324	107	246	1,094
1970	98	53	112	281	727	1,867	3,138
1975	50	22	51	134	485	2,325	3,067
1976	60	33	62	170	583	3,039	3,947
1977	146	22	38	206	604	3,211	4,277
1978	80	20	50	242	697	3,826	4,915
1979	54	19	46	227	556	3,543	4,445
1980	51	18	47	226	533	3,285	4,160
1981	50	20	50	220	510	3,110	3,960
1982	55	20	60	210	540	3,190	4,075
1983	100	20	80	130	490	3,580	4,400
1984	60	20	180	150	540	4,140	5,090
1985	70	10	20	170	620	4,140	5,030
1986	90	10	40	180	550	4,390	5,260
1987	90	20	35	170	625	4,375	5,255
1988	30	15	35	185	650	4,120	5,035
1989	40	15	40	165	675	3,810	4,745
1990	35	24	56	180	605	3,940	4,840
1991	35	25	45	225	500	4,250	5,080
1992	50	10	25	140	505	4,065	4,795
1993	30	20	70	160	640	4,370	5,290
1994	14	13	55	173	725	4,680	5,660
1995	12	24	43	166	630	4,665	5,540
1996	NA	17	43	180	460	4,800	5,500
1997	NA	17	48	250	485	5,000	5,800
1998	NA	10	20	140	420	5,470	6,060
1999	NA	10	20	140	385	5,510	6,065
2000	NA	8	17	125	470	5,570	6,190
2001	NA	8	22	90	450	5,460	6,030
2002	NA	10	15	85	390	5,480	5,980
2003	NA	10	15	75	420	5,450	5,970
2004*	NA	20		485		5,180	5,685
2005	NA	20		475		5,260	5,755
2006	NA	25		470		5,280	5,755
2007	NA	20		400		5,265	5,685

Number of feedlots with 1,000 head or more capacity is number of lots operating any time during the year. Number under 1,000 head capacity and total number of all feedlots is number at end of year.
* Beginning in 2004 report, cattle marketed as 1,000–3,999 and 4,000–15,999 in feedlot capacity.
Source: "Texas Agricultural Facts, 1997," Texas Agricultural Statistics Service, September 1998. Numbers for 1986, 1987, 1988, 1989, 1990, 1991, 1992.: 1993 Texas Livestock Statistics, Bulletin 252, August 1994; Cattle on Feed annual summary, USDA/NASS, February 2009.

Dairying

The state's dairy industry is spread out across the with the trend toward larger operations. As of Jan. 1, 2010, inventory, leading counties in milk production are Erath, Parmer, Deaf Smith, Castro, Hopkins, Hartley, and Lamb, which combined, produce 58 percent of the milk in the state, with Erath producing 14 percent of the total.

All the milk sold by Texas dairy farmers is marketed under the terms of **Federal Marketing Orders.** Most Texas dairymen are members of one of four marketing cooperatives. Associate Milk Producers, Inc., is the largest, representing the majority of the state's producers.

Texas dairy farmers received an average price for milk of $17.10 per hundred pounds in 2010, $13.30 in 2009, and $18.70 in 2008. A total of 8.803 billion pounds of milk was sold to plants and dealers in 2010, bringing in cash receipts from milk to dairy farmers of $1.505 billion. This compared with 8.814 billion pounds sold in 2009 that brought in $1.172 billion in cash receipts. In 2008, Texas dairymen sold 8.389 billion pounds of milk, which brought in cash receipts of $1.569 billion.

The annual average number of milk cows in Texas

Sheep and lambs in Texas numbered 880,000 head on Jan. 1, 2011, and were valued at $113.5 million. This flock is in Coryell County. Photo by Ron Billings; Texas Forest Service.

was 425,000 head as of the Jan. 1, 2011, inventory. This compared with 410,000 head as of Jan. 1, 2010, and 430,000 as of Jan. 1, 2009.

Average milk production per cow in the state has increased steadily over the past several decades. The average milk production per cow was 21,375 pounds in 2010; 20,898 pounds in 2009; and 20,134 pounds in 2008. Total milk production in Texas was 8.828 billion pounds in 2010; 8.840 billion pounds in 2009; and 8.416 billion pounds in 2008.

There were 1,200 operations reporting milk cows in Texas in 2007. In 2006, 1,300 operations reported milk cows, and in 2005, 1,500 operations reported milk cows in Texas.

Dairy Manufacturing

The **major dairy products** manufactured in Texas include condensed, evaporated and dry milk, creamer, butter, and cheese. However, this data are not available because of the small number of manufacturing plants producing these products.

Frozen Desserts

Production of frozen desserts in Texas totaled 82.2 million gallons in 2009. The 2008 production amounted to 89.5 million gallons, and 90.1 million in 2007. Production for regular ice cream in Texas in 2009 amounted to 48.2 million gallons, compared to 59.13 million in 2008, and 61.5 million gallons in 2007.

Regular ice cream mix produced in Texas in 2009 amounted to 27 million gallons; 31.9 million in 2008; and 33.1 million in 2007.

Sherbet mix in Texas totaled 634,000 gallons in 2009; 616,000 gallons in 2008; and 916,000 gallons in 2007. Sherbet production in 2009 totaled 987,000 gallons. This compared with 2008 sherbet production of 946,000 gallons, and 1,299,000 gallons in 2007.

Goats and Mohair

Goats in Texas numbered 1.08 million on Jan. 1, 2011. This compares with 1.11 million on Jan. 1, 2010, and 1.12 million on Jan. 1, 2009. They had a value of $108.3 million or $98 per head in 2010; and $130 million or $116 per head in 2009.

The goat herd consists of **Angora goats for mohair production.** Angora goats totaled 110,000 as of Jan. 1, 2011; 100,000 as of Jan. 1, 2010; and 120,000 as of Jan. 1, 2009. **Spanish goats** and others numbered 970,000 as of Jan. 1, 2011; 1.01 million as of Jan. 1, 2010; and 1 million as of Jan. 1, 2009.

Mohair production during 2010 totaled 730,000 pounds. This compares with 700,000 in 2009, and 820,000 pounds in 2008. Average price per pound in 2010 was $4.20 from 120,000 goats clipped for a total value of $3.07 million. In 2009, producers received $3.10 per pound from 110,000 goats clipped for a total value of $2.8 million. In 2008, producers received $3.80 per pound from 130,000 goats clipped for a total value of $3.12 million.

Over half of the world's mohair and over 66 percent of the U.S. clip are produced in Texas. The leading Texas counties in Angora goats as of Jan. 1, 2010, are Edwards, Val Verde, Crockett, Gillespie, Kendall, and Schleicher.

Horses

Nationally, Texas ranks as **one of the leading states in horse numbers** and is the headquarters for many national horse organizations. The largest single breed registry in America, the American Quarter Horse Association, has its headquarters in Amarillo. The National Cutting Horse Association and the American Paint Horse Association are both located in Fort Worth. In addition to these national associations, Texas also has active state associations that include Palominos,

Arabians, Thoroughbreds, Appaloosa, and Ponies.

Horses are still used to support the state's giant beef cattle and sheep industries. However, the largest horse numbers within the state are **near urban and suburban areas where they are mostly used for recreation activities,** such as horse shows, trail rides, play days, rodeos, polo, and horse racing.

In some areas, residential subdivisions have been developed within the state to provide facilities for urban and suburban horse owners.

Poultry and Eggs

Poultry and eggs annually contributed about 11.6 percent to the average yearly cash receipts (including government payments) of Texas farmers in 2009. On Jan. 1, 2010, **Texas ranked sixth among the states in broilers produced, fifth in eggs produced, and seventh in hens.**

In 2009, cash receipts to Texas producers from the production of poultry and eggs totaled $2.078 billion. This compares with $2.142 billion in 2008, and $1.856 in 2007.

Value of production from eggs was $395.1 million in 2010. This compares with $347.5 million in 2009, and $462.3 million in 2008. Eggs produced in 2010 totaled 4.81 billion, compared with 4.99 bil-

Texas ranks fifth among the states in eggs produced, with a value of $395 million. Photo by Johnny Hanson.

lion in 2009, and 4.95 billion in 2008. The average price received per dozen in 2010 was 98.5 cents, compared with 83.6 cents in 2009, and $1.12 in 2008.

Broiler production in 2010 totaled 653.5 million birds, compared with 668.7 million in 2009, and 641 million in 2008. Value of production from broilers totaled $622 million in 2010; $1.65 billion in 2009; and $1.592 billion in 2008. Price per pound averaged 48.2 cents in 2010, 45.7 cents in 2009, and 46.0 cents in 2008.

Sheep and Wool

Sheep and lambs in Texas numbered 880,000 head on Jan. 1, 2011, compared to 830,000 as of Jan. 1, 2010, and 870,000 as of Jan. 1, 2009. All sheep were valued at $113.5 million or $129 per head on Jan. 1, 2011, compared with $83 million or $100 per head as of Jan. 1, 2010, and $87.9 million or $101 per head as of Jan. 1, 2009.

Breeding ewes one year old and over numbered 525,000 as of Jan. 1, 2011; 510,000 as of Jan. 1, 2010; and 520,000 as of Jan. 1, 2009. Replacement lambs less than one year old totaled 125,000 head as of Jan. 1, 2011; 105,000 as of Jan. 1, 2010; and 100,000 as of Jan. 1, 2009. Sheep and lamb operations in Texas were estimated to be 8,700 as of Jan. 1, 2007;

Sheep and Wool Production
1850–2011

Year	Sheep *Number	Sheep Value	Wool Production (lbs)	Wool Value	Year	Sheep *Number	Sheep Value	Wool Production (lbs)	Wool Value
1850	100,530	N A	131,917	N A	1986	1,850,000	107,300,000	16,400,000	13,284,000
1860	753,363	N A	1,493,363	N A	1987	2,050,000	133,250,000	16,400,000	19,844,000
1870	1,223,000	$2,079,000	N A	N A	1988	2,040,000	155,040,000	18,200,000	35,854,000
1880	6,024,000	12,048,000	N A	N A	1989	1,870,000	133,445,000	18,000,000	27,180,000
1890	4,752,000	7,128,000	N A	N A	1990	2,090,000	133,760,000	17,400,000	19,662,000
1900	2,416,000	4,590,000	9,630,000	N A	1991	2,000,000	108,000,000	16,700,000	13,861,000
1910	1,909,000	5,536,000	8,943,000	$1,699,170	1992	2,140,000	111,280,000	17,600,000	16,896,000
1920	3,360,000	33,600,000	22,813,000	5,019,000	1993	2,040,000	118,320,000	17,000,000	11,050,000
1930	6,304,000	44,758,000	48,262,000	10,135,000	1994	1,895,000	106,120,000	14,840,000	15,582,000
1940	10,069,000	49,413,000	79,900,000	23,171,000	1995	1,700,000	100,300,000	13,468,000	15,488,000
1950	6,756,000	103,877,000	51,480,000	32,947,000	1996	1,650,000	108,900,000	9,900,000	8,316,000
1960	5,938,000	85,801,000	51,980,000	21,832,000	1997	1,400,000	100,800,000	10,950,000	11,607,000
1970	3,708,000	73,602,000	30,784,000	11,082,000	1998	1,530,000	122,400,000	9,230,000	5,815,000
1973	3,214,000	64,280,000	26,352,000	23,190,000	1999	1,350,000	95,850,000	7,956,000	3,898,000
1974	3,090,000	80,340,000	23,900,000	15,535,000	2000	1,200,000	94,800,000	7,506,000	3,678,000
1975	2,715,000	63,803,000	23,600,000	14,868,000	2001	1,150,000	92,000,000	6,003,000	3,122,000
1976	2,600,000	81,900,000	22,000,000	17,380,000	2002	1,130,000	88,140,000	5,950,000	4,046,000
1977	2,520,000	93,240,000	21,000,000	17,220,000	2003	1,040,000	82,160,000	5,600,000	5,040,000
1978	2,460,000	111,930,000	18,500,000	15,355,000	2004	1,100,000	105,600,000	5,600,000	5,712,000
1979	2,415,000	152,145,000	19,075,000	18,503,000	2005	1,070,000	112,350,000	5,550,000	5,328,000
1980	2,400,000	138,000,000	18,300,000	17,751,000	2006	1,090,000	124,260,000	4,900,000	4,459,000
1981	2,360,000	116,820,000	20,500,000	24,600,000	2007	1,050,000	111,300,000	4,500,000	5,445,000
1982	2,400,000	100,800,000	19,300,000	16,212,000	2008	960,000	97,920,000	4,200,000	4,872,000
1983	2,225,000	86,775,000	18,600,000	15,438,000	2009	870,000	87,870,000	3,500,000	3,640,000
1984	1,970,000	76,830,000	17,500,000	16,100,000	2010	830,000	83,000,000	3,630,000	5,735,000
1985	1,930,000	110,975,000	16,200,000	13,284,000	2011	880,000	113,520,000	NA	NA

NA = not available
Source: "1985 Texas Livestock, Dairy and Poultry Statistics," USDA Bulletin 235, June 1986.; "Texas Agricultural Facts" Annual Summary, Crop and Livestock Reporting Service, various years; "1993 Texas Livestock Statistics," Texas Agricultural Statistics Service, Bulletin 252, August 1994; "Texas Agricultural Statistics, 2009," October 2010; "Texas Ag Fact," February and March 2011.

7,300 as of Jan. 1, 2006; and 7,200 as of Jan. 1, 2005.

Texas wool production in 2010 was 3.63 million pounds from 505,000 sheep. Value totaled $5.74 million or $1.58 per pound. This compared with 3.5 million pounds of wool from 495,000 sheep valued at $3.64 million or $1.04 per pound in 2009; and 4.2 million pounds from 600,000 sheep valued at $4.87 million or $1.16 per pound in 2008.

Most sheep and lambs in Texas are concentrated in the **Edwards Plateau** area of West Central Texas and nearby counties. As of Jan. 1, 2010, the 10 leading counties are Crockett, Val Verde, Tom Green, Schleicher, Gillespie, Pecos, Concho, Edwards, Mills, and Sutton. Sheep production is largely dual purpose, for both wool and lamb production.

San Angelo long has been the largest sheep and

wool market in the nation, and the center for wool and mohair warehouses, scouring plants, and slaughterhouses.

Swine

Texas had 660,000 head of swine on hand, Dec. 1, 2010 — only 1 percent of the U.S. swine herd. Swine producers in the state produce about 600,000 head marketed annually.

Although the number of farms producing hogs has steadily decreased, **the size of production units has increased substantially.** There is favorable potential for increased production.

In 2010, 1 million head of hogs were marketed in Texas, producing 154.4 million pounds of pork valued at $50.20 per 100 pounds, or $78.3 million. In 2009, 1.76 million head of hogs were marketed, producing 302.6 million pounds of pork valued at $114,.7 million, or $37.60 per 100 pounds. Comparable figures for 2008 were 1.7 million head marketed, and 323.6 million pounds of pork produced with a value of $128.7 million, or $40.50 per 100 pounds. ✩

Goats and Mohair
1900–2011

Year	Goats		Mohair	
	Number	Farm Value	Production (lbs)	Value
1900	627,000	$924,000	961,000	$268,000
1910	1,135,000	2,514,000	1,998,000	468,000
1920	1,753,000	9,967,000	6,786,000	1,816,000
1930	2,965,000	14,528,000	14,800,000	4,995,000
1940	3,300,000	10,560,000	18,250,000	9,308,000
1950	2,295,000	13,082,000	12,643,000	9,735,000
1960	3,339,000	29,383,000	23,750,000	21,375,000
1970	2,572,000	19,033,000	17,985,000	7,032,000
1980	1,400,000	64,400,000	8,800,000	30,800,000
1981	1,380,000	53,130,000	10,100,000	35,350,000
1982	1,410,000	57,810,000	10,000,000	25,500,000
1983	1,420,000	53,250,000	10,600,000	42,930,000
1984	1,450,000	82,215,000	10,600,000	48,160,000
1985	1,590,000	76,797,000	13,300,000	45,885,000
1986	1,770,000	70,977,000	16,000,000	40,160,000
1987	1,780,000	82,592,000	16,200,000	42,606,000
1988	1,800,000	108,180,000	15,400,000	29,876,000
1989	1,850,000	100,270,000	15,400,000	24,794,000
1990	1,900,000	93,100,000	14,500,000	13,775,000
1991	1,830,000	73,200,000	14,800,000	19,388,000
1992	2,000,000	84,000,000	14,200,000	12,354,000
1993	1,960,000	84,280,000	13,490,000	11,197,000
1994	1,960,000	74,480,000	11,680,000	30,602,000
1995	1,850,000	81,400,000	11,319,000	20,940,000
1996	1,900,000	89,300,000	7,490,000	14,606,000
1997	1,650,000	70,950,000	6,384,000	14,556,000
1998	1,400,000	71,400,000	4,650,000	12,044,000
1999	1,350,000	71,550,000	2,550,000	9,384,000
2000	1,300,000	74,100,000	2,346,000	10,088,000
2001	1,400,000	105,000,000	1,716,000	3,775,000
2002	1,250,000	106,250,000	1,944,000	3,110,400
2003	1,200,000	110,400,000	1,680,000	2,856,000
2004	1,200,000	115,200,000	1,620,000	3,402,000
2005	1,270,000	138,430,000	1,250,000	3,750,000
2006	1,310,000	140,170,000	1,100,000	4,400,000
2007	1,300,000	150,800,000	960,000	3,840,000
2008	1,185,000	120,870,000	820,000	3,116,000
2009	1,120,000	129,920,000	700,000	2,170,000
2010	1,110,000	108,290,000	730,000	3,066,000
2011	1,080,000	NA	NA	NA

NA = not available.
Source:"1985 Texas Livestock, Dairy and Poultry Statistics," USDA, Bulletin 235, June 1986; "Texas Agricultural Facts," Crop and Livestock Reporting Service, various years; "1993 Texas Livestock Statistics," Texas Agricultural Statistics Service, Bulletin 252, August 1994; "Texas Agricultural Statistics, 2009," October 2010; "Texas Ag Facts," February and March 2011.

Hog Production
1960–2009

Year	Production (1,000 Pounds)	Avg. Market Wt. (Pounds)	Avg. Price Per Cwt. (Dollars)	Gross Income (1,000 Dollars)
1960	288,844	228	$14.70	$44,634
1970	385,502	241	22.50	75,288
1980	315,827	259	35.90	111,700
1981	264,693	256	41.70	121,054
1982	205,656	256	49.60	112,726
1983	209,621	256	45.20	95,343
1984	189,620	262	45.50	95,657
1985	168,950	266	43.40	72,512
1986	176,660	269	47.30	82,885
1987	216,834	NA	50.60	103,983
1988	236,658	NA	41.30	100,029
1989	224,229	NA	39.90	93,178
1990	196,225	NA	48.20	92,222
1991	207,023	NA	45.10	97,398
1992	217,554	NA	36.40	79,436
1993	221,130	NA	39.90	90,561
1994	224,397	NA	35.10	78,394
1995	221,323	NA	35.50	81,509
1996	203,761	NA	45.90	93,526
1997	224,131	NA	47.40	106,238
1998	270,977	NA	30.70	83,190
1999	274,572	NA	27.50	71,604
2000	328,732	NA	36.60	115,105
2001	260,825	NA	39.10	105,217
2002	223,441	NA	28.70	67,255
2003	197,876	NA	33.60	67,998
2004	202,199	NA	44.90	90,349
2005	223,375	NA	45.40	105,989
2006	259,989	NA	40.80	109,318
2007	273,213	NA	39.70	95,581
2008	317,446	NA	40.50	133,488
2009	303,688	NA	37.60	131,049

NA = not available.
Source: "1985 Texas Livestock, Dairy and Poultry Statistics," USDA, Bulletin 235, June 1986, pp. 32, 46; 1991 "Texas Livestock Statistics"; USDA, "Meat Animals – Prod., Dips., & Income," April 2010 and April 2011; "1993 Texas Livestock Statistics," Bulletin 252, Texas Agricultural Statistics Service, August 1994; "Texas Agricultural Facts, 2009," October, 2010; "Texas Ag Facts," various years.

Appendix

Morning in Roberts County in the Panhandle. Photo by Robert Plocheck.

Pronunciation Guide
Texas Obituaries
Index of Entries

Texas Pronunciation Guide

Texas' rich cultural diversity is reflected nowhere better than in the names of places. Standard pronunciation is used in many cases, but purely colloquial pronunciation often is used, too.

In the late 1940s, George Mitchel Stokes, a graduate student at Baylor University, developed a list of pronunciations of 2,300 place names across the state. Stokes earned his doctorate and served as director of the speech division in the communications studies department at Baylor University. He retired in 1983.

In the following list based on Stokes longer list, pronunciation is by respelling and diacritical marking. Respelling is employed as follows: "ah" as in the exclamation, ah, or the "o" in tot; "ee" as in meet; "oo" as in moot; "yoo" as in use; "ow" as in cow; "oi" as in oil; "uh" as in mud.

Note that ah, uh and the apostrophe(') are used for varying degrees of neutral vowel sounds, the apostrophe being used where the vowel is barely sounded. Diacritical markings are used as follows: bāle, băd, lĕt, rīse, rĭll, ōak, brōōd, fŏŏt.

The stressed syllable is capitalized. Secondary stress is indicated by an underline as in Atascosa — ăt uhs KŌ suh.

A

Abbott — Ă buht
Abernathy — Ă ber nă thĭ
Abilene — ĂB uh leen
Acala — uh KĀ luh
Ackerly — ĂK er lĭ
Acme — ĂK mĭ
Acton — ĂK t'n
Acuff — Ā kuhf
Adamsville — Ă d'mz vĭl
Addicks — Ă dĭks
Addielou — ă dĭ LŌŌ
Addison — A di s'n
Adkins — ĂT kĭnz
Adrian — Ā drĭ uhn
Afton — ĂF t'n
Agua Dulce — ah wuh DŌŌL sĭ
Agua Nueva — ah wuh nyōō Ā vuh
Aiken — Ā kĭn
Alamo — ĂL uh mō
Alamo Heights — ăl uh mō HĪTS
Alanreed — ĂL uhn reed
Alba — ĂL buh
Albany — AWL buh nĭ
Albert — ĂL bert
Aledo — uh LEE dō
Alexander — ĕl ĭg ZĂN der
Alfred — ĂL frĕd
Algoa — ăl GŌ uh
Alice — Ă lĭs
Alief — Ā leef
Allen — Ă lĭn
Allenfarm — ălĭn FAHRM
Alleyton — Ă lĭ t'n
Allison — ĂL uh s'n
Alma — AHL muh
Alpine — ĂL pīn
Altair — awl TĂR
Alta Loma — ăl tuh LŌ muh
Alto — ĂL tō
Altoga — ăl TŌ guh
Alvarado — ăl vuh RĀ dō
Alvin — ĂL vĭn
Alvord — ĂL vord
Amarillo — ăm uh RĬL ō
Amherst — AM herst
Ammannsville — ĂM 'nz vĭl
Anahuac — ĂN uh wăk
Anderson — ĂN der s'n
Andice — ĂN dīs
Andrews — ĂN drōōz
Angelina — ăn juh LEE nuh
Angleton — ĂNG g'l t'n
Anna — ĂN uh
Annona — ă NŌ nuh
Anson — ĂN s'n
Antelope — ĂNT uh lōp
Anton — ĂNT n
Appleby — Ă p'l bĭ
Apple Springs — ă p'l SPRĬNGZ
Aquilla — uh KWĬL uh
Aransas — uh RĂN zuhs
Aransas Pass — uh răn zuhs PĂS
Arbala — ahr BĀ luh
Arcadia — ahr KĀ dĭ uh
Archer — AHR cher
Archer City — ahr cher SĬT ĭ
Arcola — ahr KŌ luh
Argo — AHR gō
Argyle — ahr GĪL
Arlington — AHR lĭng t'n
Arneckeville — AHR nĭ kĭ vĭl
Arnett — AHR nĭt
Arp — ahrp
Artesia Wells — ahr tee zh' WĔLZ
Arthur City — ahr ther SĬT ĭ
Asherton — ĂSH er t'n
Aspermont — ĂS per mahnt
Atascosa — ăt uhs KŌ suh
Athens — Ă thĕnz
Atlanta — ăt LĂN tuh
Atlas — ĂT l's
Attoyac — AT uh yăk
Aubrey — AW brĭ
Augusta — aw GUHS tuh
Austin — AWS t'n
Austonio — aws TŌ nĭ ō
Austwell — AWS wĕl
Avalon — ĂV uhl n
Avery — Ā vuh rĭ
Avinger — Ă vĭn jer
Avoca — uh VŌ kuh
Axtell — ĂKS t'l
Azle — Ā z'l

B

Bagwell — BĂG w'l
Bailey — BĀ lĭ
Baileyboro — BĀ lĭ ber ruh
Baileyville — BĀ lĭ vĭl
Baird — bărd
Bakersfield — BĀ kers feeld
Balch Springs — bawlch or bawlk SPRĬNGZ
Ballinger — BĂL ĭn jer
Balmorhea — băl muh RĀ
Bandera — băn DĔR uh
Bangs — băngz
Banquete — băn KĔ tĭ
Barclay — BAHRK lĭ
Bardwell — BAHRD w'l
Barker — BAHR ker
Barksdale — BAHRKS dāl
Barnhart — BAHRN hahrt
Barnum — BAHR n'm
Barry — BĂ rĭ
Barstow — BAHRS tō
Bartlett — BAHRT lĭt
Bassett — BĂ sĭt
Bastrop — BĂS trahp
Batesville — BĀTS v'l
Batson — BĂT s'n
Baxter — BĂKS ter
Bay City — ba SĬT ĭ
Baylor — BĀ ler
Bayside — BĀ sīd
Baytown — BĀ town
Beasley — BEEZ lĭ
Beaukiss — bō KĬS
Beaumont — BŌ mahnt
Bebe — bee bee
Beckville — BĔK v'l
Becton — BĔK t'n
Bedias — BEE dīs
Bee — bee
Beehouse — BEE hows
Beeville — BEE vĭl
Belcherville — BĔL cher vĭl
Bell — bĕl
Bellaire — bĕl ĂR
Bellevue — BĔL vyōō
Bellmead — bĕl MEED
Bells — bĕlz
Bellville — BĔL vĭl
Belmont — BĔL mahnt
Belton — BĔL t'n

Diacritical markings are used as follows: bāle, băd, lĕt, rīse, rĭll, ōak, brōōd, fŏŏt. The stressed syllable is capitalized. Secondary stress is indicated by an underline as in Atascosa — ăt uhs KŌ suh.

Ben Arnold — běn AHR n'ld
Benavides — <u>běn</u> uh VEE d's
Ben Bolt — běn BŌLT
Benbrook — BĬN brook
Benchley — BĚNCH lĭ
Bend — běnd
Ben Franklin — běn FRĂNGk lĭn
Ben Hur — běn HER
Benjamin — BĚN juh m'n
Bennett — BĚN ĭt
Bentonville — BĚNT n vĭl
Ben Wheeler — bĭn HWEE ler
Berclair — ber KLĂR
Bertram — BERT r'm
Bessmay — běs MĀ
Best — běst
Bettie — BĚT ĭ
Bexar — BA är or băr
Beyersville — BĪRZ vĭl
Biardstown — BĂRDZ t'n
Bigfoot — BĬG foot
Big Lake — bĭg LĀK
Big Sandy — bĭg SĂN dĭ
Big Spring — bĭg SPRĬNG
Big Wells — bĭg WĚLZ
Birdville — BERD vĭl
Birome — bī RŌM
Birthright — BERTH rīt
Bishop — BĬ sh'p
Bivins — BĬ vĭnz
Black — blăk
Blackfoot — BLĂK foot
Blackwell — BLĂK w'l
Blair — blăr
Blanchard — BLĂN cherd
Blanco — BLĂNG kō
Blanket — BLĂNG kĭt
Bleakwood — BLEEK wood
Bledsoe — BLĚD sō
Blessing — BLĚ sĭng
Blewett — BLOO ĭt
Blooming Grove — <u>bloo</u> mĭng GRŌV
Bloomington — BLOOM ĭng t'n
Blossom — BLAH s'm
Blue Grove — bloo GRŌV
Blue Ridge — bloo RĬJ
Bluff Dale — BLUHF dāl
Bluffton — BLUHF t'n
Blum — bluhm
Boerne — BER nĭ
Bogata — buh GŌ duh
Boling — BŌL ĭng
Bolivar — BAH lĭ ver
Bomarton — BŌ mer t'n
Bonham — BAH n'm
Bonita — bō NEE tuh
Bonney — BAH nĭ
Bonus — BŌ n's
Bon Wier — bahn WEER
Booker — BOO ker
Boonsville — BOONZ vĭl
Booth — booth
Borden — BAWRD n
Borger — BŌR ger
Bosque — BAHS kĭ

Sculpture along U.S. 90 outside Marfa. Photo by Robert Plocheck.

Boston — BAWS t'n
Bovina — bō VEE nuh
Bowie — BOO Ĭ
Boxelder — bahks ĚL der
Boyce — bawĭs
Boyd — boĭd
Brachfield — BRĂCH feeld
Bracken — BRĂ kĭn
Brackettville — BRĂ kĭt vĭl
Bradford — BRĂD ferd
Bradshaw — BRĂD shaw
Brady — BRĂ dĭ
Brandon — BRĂN d'n
Brashear — bruh SHĬR
Brazoria — bruh ZŌ rĭ uh
Brazos — BRĂZ uhs
Breckenridge — BRĚK uhn rĭj
Bremond — <u>bree</u> MAHND
Brenham — BRĚ n'm
Brewster — BROO ster
Brice — brīs
Bridgeport — BRĬJ pōrt
Briggs — brĭgz
Briscoe — BRĬS kō
Britton — BRĬT n
Broaddus — BRAW d's
Brock — brahk
Bronson — BRAHN s'n
Bronte — brahnt
Brookeland — BROOK l'nd
Brookesmith — BROOK smith
Brooks — brooks
Brookshire — BROOK sher
Brookston — BROOKS t'n
Brown — brown
Browndel — brown DĚL
Brownfield — BROWN feeld
Brownsboro — BROWNZ <u>buh</u> ruh
Brownsville — BROWNZ vĭl
Brownwood — BROWN wood
Bruceville — BROOS v'l
Brundage — BRUHN dĭj
Bruni — BROO nĭ
Brushy Creek — bruh shĭ KREEK
Bryan — BRĪ uhn
Bryans Mill — brī 'nz MĬL
Bryarly — BRĪ er lĭ
Bryson — BRĪ s'n

Buchanan Dam — buhk hăn uhn DĂM
Buckholts — BUHK hōlts
Buckhorn — BUHK hawrn
Buda — BYOO duh
Buena Vista — <u>bwā</u> nuh VEES tuh
Buffalo — BUHF uh lō
Buffalo Gap — <u>buhf</u> uh lō GĂP
Buffalo Springs — <u>buhf</u> uh lō SPRĬNGZ
Bula — BYOO luh
Bullard — BOOL erd
Bulverde — bool VER dĭ
Buna — BYOO nuh
Burkburnett — <u>berk</u> ber NET
Burkett — BER kĭt
Burkeville — BERK vĭl
Burleson — BER luh s'n
Burlington — BER lĭng t'n
Burnet — BER nět
Burton — BERT n
Bushland — BOOSH l'nd
Bustamante — <u>buhs</u> tuh MAHN tĭ
Butler — BUHT ler
Byers — BĬ erz
Bynum — BĬ n'm
Byrd — berd

C

Cactus — KĂK t's
Caddo Mills — <u>kă</u> dō MĬLZ
Calallen — kăl ĂL ĭn
Calaveras — kăl uh VĚR's
Caldwell — KAHL wěl
Calhoun — kăl HOON
Call — kawl
Calliham — KĂL uh hăm
Callisburg — KĂ lĭs berg
Call Junction — kawl JUHNGK sh'n
Calvert — KĂL vert
Camden — KĂM dǐn
Cameron — KĂM uh r'n
Camilla — kuh MEEL yuh
Camp — kămp
Campbell — KĂM uhl
Campbellton — KĂM uhl t'n
Camp Wood — kămp WOOD

Diacritical markings are used as follows: bāle, băd, lět, rīse, rĭll, ōak, brood, foot. The stressed syllable is capitalized. Secondary stress is indicated by an underline as in Atascosa — <u>ăt</u> uhs KŌ suh. TEXAS ALMANAC ©.

Canadian — <u>kuh</u> NĂ dĭ uhn
Candelaria — kăn duh LĔ rĭ uh
Canton — KĂNT n
Canyon — KĂN y'n
Caplen — KĂP lĭn
Caps — kăps
Caradan — KĂR uh dăn
Carbon — KAHR b'n
Carey — KĂ rĭ
Carlisle — KAHR lĭl
Carlsbad — KAHR uhlz băd
Carlton — KAHR uhl t'n
Carmine — kahr MEEN
Carmona — <u>kahr</u> MŌ nuh
Caro — KAH rō
Carrizo Springs — kuh <u>ree</u> zuh
SPRĬNGZ
Carrollton — KĂR 'l t'n
Carson — KAHR s'n
Carthage — KAHR thĭj
Cash — kăsh
Cason — KĂ s'n
Cass — kăs
Castell — kăs TĔL
Castro — KĂS trō
Castroville — KĂS tro vĭl
Catarina — kăt uh REE nuh
Cat Spring — kăt SPRĬNG
Caviness — KĂ vĭ nĕs
Cayuga — kă YŌŌ guh
Cedar Bayou — <u>see</u> der BĪ ō
Cedar Creek — <u>see</u> der KREEK
Cedar Hill — <u>see</u> der HĬL
Cedar Lake — <u>see</u> der LĂK
Cedar Lane — <u>see</u> der LĂN
Cedar Park — <u>see</u> der PAHRK
Cedar Valley — <u>see</u> der VA lĭ
Cee Vee — <u>see</u> VEE
Celeste — suh LĔST
Celina — suh LĪ nuh
Center — SENT er
Center City — sĕn ter SĬT ĭ
Center Point — sĕn ter POINT
Centerville — sĕn ter vĭl
Centralia — sĕn TRĂL yuh
Chalk — chawlk
Chalk Mountain — chawlk
MOWNT n
Chambers — CHĂM berz
Chandler — CHĂND ler
Channelview — <u>chăn</u> uhl VYŌŌ
Channing — CHĂN ĭng
Chapman Ranch — chăp m'n
RĂNCH
Chappell Hill — chă p'l HĬL
Charco — CHAHR kō
Charleston — CHAHR uhls t'n
Charlie — CHAHR lĭ
Charlotte — SHAHR l't
Chatfield — CHĂT feeld
Cheapside — CHEEP sīd
Cheek — cheek
Cherokee — CHĔR uh <u>kee</u>
Chester — CHĔS ter
Chico — CHEE kō
Chicota — chĭ KŌ tuh
Childress — CHĬL drĕs

Chillicothe — <u>chĭl</u> ĭ KAH thĭ
Chilton — CHĬL t'n
China — CHĪ nuh
China Spring — chī nuh SPRĬNG
Chireno — sh' REE nō
Chisholm — CHĬZ uhm
Chita — CHEE tuh
Chocolate Bayou — <u>chah</u> kuh līt
BĪ ō
Choice — chois
Chriesman — KRĬS m'n
Christine — krĭs TEEN
Christoval — krĭs TŌ v'l
Cibolo — SEE bō lō
Circle Back — SER k'l băk
Circleville — SER k'l vĭl
Cisco — SĬS kō
Cistern — SĬS tern
Clairemont — KLĂR mahnt
Clairette — klăr ĭ ĔT
Clarendon — KLĂR ĭn d'n
Clareville — KLĂR vĭl
Clarksville — KLAHRKS vĭl
Clarkwood — KLAHRK wōōd
Claude — klawd
Clawson — KLAW s'n
Clay — klā
Clayton — KLĂT n
Clear Lake — KLĬR lăk
Clear Spring — klĭr SPRĬNG
Cleburne — KLEE bern
Clemville — KLĔM vĭl
Cleveland — KLEEV l'nd
Clifton — KLĬF t'n
Cline — klīn
Clint — klĭnt
Clodine — klaw DEEN
Clute — klōōt
Clyde — klīd
Coahoma — kuh HŌ muh
Cockrell Hill — kahk ruhl HĬL
Coke — kōk
Coldspring — KŌLD sprĭng
Coleman — KŌL m'n
Colfax — KAHL făks
Collegeport — kah lĭj PŌRT
College Station — <u>kah</u> lĭj STĂ sh'n
Collin — KAH lĭn
Collingsworth — KAH lĭnz werth
Collinsville — KAH lĭnz vĭl
Colmesneil — KŌL m's neel
Colorado — <u>kahl</u> uh RAH dō
Colorado City — kah luh <u>rā</u> duh
SĬT ĭ or kah luh <u>rah</u> duh SĬT ĭ
Columbus — kuh LUHM b's
Comal — KŌ măl
Comanche — kuh MĂN chĭ
Combes — kōmz
Comfort — KUHM fert
Commerce — KAH mers
Como — KŌ mō
Comstock — KAHM stahk
Concan — KAHN kăn
Concepcion — kuhn sep sĭ ŌN
Concho — KAHN chō
Concord — KAHN kawrd
Concrete — kahn KREET

Cone — kōn
Conlen — KAHN lĭn
Conroe — KAHN rō
Converse — KAHN vers
Conway — KAHN wā
Cooke — kōōk
Cookville — KŌŌK vĭl
Coolidge — KŌŌ lĭj
Cooper — KŌŌ per
Copeville — KŌP v'l
Coppell — kahp pĕl or kuhp PĔL
Copperas Cove — kahp ruhs KŌV
Corbett — KAWR bĭt
Cordele — kawr DĔL
Corinth — KAH rĭnth
Corley — KAWR lĭ
Corpus Christi — <u>kawr</u> p's KRĬS tĭ
Corrigan — KAWR uh g'n
Corsicana — <u>kawr</u> sĭ KĂN uh
Coryell — kō rĭ ĔL
Cost — kawst
Cottle — KAH t'l
Cotton Center — <u>kaht</u> n SĔNT er
Cotton Gin — KAHT n jĭn
Cottonwood — KAHT n wōōd
Cotulla — kuh TŌŌ luh
Coupland — KŌP l'n
Courtney — KŌRT nĭ
Covington — KUHV ĭng t'n
Coy City — koi SĬT ĭ
Craft — kräft
Crafton — KRĂF t'n
Crandall — KRĂN d'l
Crane — krān
Cranfills Gap — krăn f'lz GĂP
Crawford — KRAW ferd
Creedmore — KREED mōr
Cresson — KRĔ s'n
Crisp — krĭsp
Crockett — KRAH kĭt
Crosby — KRAWZ bĭ
Crosbyton — KRAWZ bĭ t'n
Cross — kraws
Cross Cut — KRAWS kuht
Cross Plains — kraws PLĂNZ
Cross Roads — KRAWS rōdz
Crow — krō
Crowell — KRŌ uhl
Crowley — KROW li
Crystal City — krĭs t'l SĬT ĭ
Crystal Falls — krĭs t'l FAWLZ
Cuero — KWĔR o
Culberson — KUHL ber s'n
Cumby — KUHM bĭ
Cuney — KYŌŌ nĭ
Cunningham — KUHN ĭng hăm
Currie — KER rĭ
Cushing — KŌŌ shĭng
Cuthand — KUHT hănd
Cyclone — SĪ klōn
Cypress — SĪ prĕs

D

Dabney — DĂB nĭ
Dacosta — duh KAHS tuh
Dacus — DĂ k's

Diacritical markings are used as follows: bāle, băd, lĕt, rīse, rĭll, ōak, brōōd, fōōt. The stressed syllable is capitalized. Secondary stress is indicated by an underline as in Atascosa — <u>ăt</u> uhs KŌ suh. TEXAS ALMANAC ©.

Daingerfield — DĂN jer feeld
Daisetta — dā ZĚT uh
Dalby Springs — dĂl bĭ SPRĬNGZ
Dale — dāl
Dalhart — DĂL hahrt
Dallam — DĂL uhm
Dallas — DĂ luhs
Damon — DĂ m'n
Danbury — DĂN bĕrĭ
Danciger — DĂN sĭ ger
Danevang — DĂN uh văng
Darrouzett — dăr uh ZĚT
Davilla — duh VĬL uh
Dawn — dawn
Dawson — DAW s'n
Dayton — DĀT n
Deadwood — DĚD wŏŏd
Deaf Smith — dĕf SMĬTH
Deanville — DEEN vĭl
DeBerry — duh BĚ rĭ
Decatur — dee KĀT er
Deer Park — dĭr PAHRK
De Kalb — dĭ KĂB
De Leon — da lee AHN
Del Rio — dĕl REE ō
Delta — DĚL tuh
Del Valle — dĕl VĂ lĭ
Delwin — DĚl wĭn
Denhawken — DĬN haw kĭn
Denison — DĚN uh s'n
Denning — DĚN ĭng
Dennis — DĚ nĭs
Denton — DĚNT n
Denver City — dĕn ver SĬT ĭ
Deport — dĭ PŌRT
Derby — DER bĭ
Desdemona — dĕz dĭ MŌ nuh
DeSoto — dĭ SŌ tuh
Detroit — dee TROIT
Devers — DĚ vers
Devine — duh VĬN
Dew — dyŏŏ
Deweyville — DYŎŎ ĭ vĭl
DeWitt — dĭ WĬT
Dewville — DYŎŎ vĭl
Dexter — DĚKS ter
D'Hanis — duh HĂ nĭs
Dialville — DĬ uhl vil
Diboll — DĬ bawl
Dickens — DĬK Ĭnz
Dickinson — DĬK ĭn s'n
Dike — dĭk
Dilley — DĬL i
Dilworth — DĬL werth
Dimebox — dīm BAHKS
Dimmit — DĬM ĭt
Dinero — dĭ NĚ rō
Direct — duh RĚKT
Dixon — DĬK s'n
Dobbin — DAH bĭn
Dobrowolski — dah bruh WAHL skĭ
Dodd City — dahd SĬT ĭ
Dodge — DAH j
Dodson — DAHD s'n
Donie — DŌ nĭ
Donley — DAHN lĭ

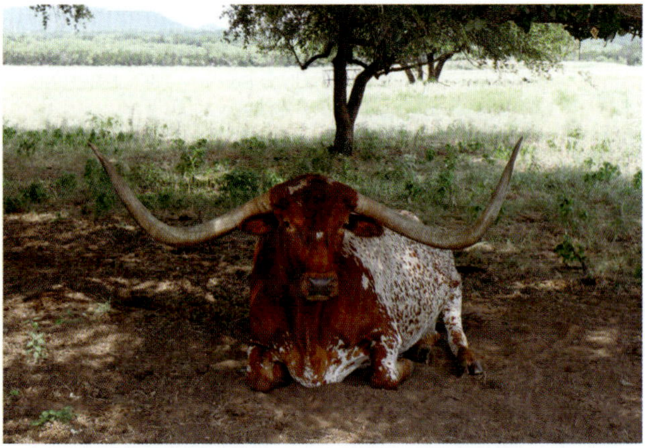

A longhorn, near Possum Kingdom Lake. Photo by Robert Plocheck.

Donna — dah nuh
Doole — DOO lĭ
Dorchester — dawr CHĚS ter
Doss — daws
Doucette — DŌŌ sĕt
Dougherty — DAHR tĭ
Douglass — DUHG l's
Douglassville — DUHG lĭs vĭl
Downing — DOWN ĭng
Downsville — DOWNZ vĭl
Dozier — DŌ zher
Draw — draw
Driftwood — DRĬFT wŏŏd
Dripping Springs — drĭp ĭng SPRĬNGZ
Driscoll — DRĬS k'l
Dryden — DRĬD n
Dublin — DUHB lĭn
Duffau — DUHF ō
Dumas — DŌŌ m's
Dumont — DYŎŎ mahnt
Dundee — DUHN dĭ
Dunlap — DUHN lăp
Dunlay — DUHN lĭ
Dunn — duhn
Durango — duh RĂNG gō
Duval — DŌŌ vawl

E

Eagle — EE g'l
Eagle Lake — ee g'l LĀK
Eagle Pass — ee g'l PĂS
Earth — erth
East Bernard — eest ber NAHRD
Easterly — EES ter lĭ
Eastland — EEST l'nd
Easton — EES t'n
Ector — ĔK ter
Edcouch — ĕd KOWCH
Eddy — E di
Eden — EED n
Edge — ĕj
Edgewood — ĔJ wŏŏd
Edinburg — ĔD n berg
Edmonson — ĔD m'n s'n

Edna — ED nuh
Edom — EE d'm
Edroy — ĔD roi
Edwards — ĔD werdz
Egan — EE g'n
Egypt — EE juhpt
Elbert — ĔL bert
El Campo — ĕl KĂM pō
Eldorado — ĕl duh RĂ duh
Electra — ĭ LĔK truh
Elgin — ĔL gĭn
Eliasville — ee LĬ uhs vĭl
El Indio — ĕl ĬN dĭ ō
Elkhart — ĔLK hahrt
Ellinger — ĔL ĭn jer
Elliott — ĔL ĭ 't
Ellis — ĔL uhs
Elmendorf — ĔLM 'n dawrf
Elm Mott — ĕl MAHT
Elmo — ĔL mō
Eloise — ĔL o eez
El Paso — ĕl PĂS ō
Elsa — ĔL suh
Elysian Fields — uh lee zh'n FEELDZ
Emhouse — ĔM hows
Emory — ĔM uh rĭ
Encinal — ĕn suh NAHL
Encino — ĕn SEE nō
Energy — ĔN er jĭ
Engle — ĔN g'l
English — ĬNG glĭsh
Enloe — ĔN lō
Ennis — ĔN ĭs
Enochs — EE nuhks
Eola — ee Ō luh
Era — EE ruh
Erath — EE răth
Esperanza — ĕs per RĂN zuh
Estelline — ĔS tuh leen
Etoile — ĭ TOIL
Etter — ĔT er
Eula — YŎŎ luh
Euless — YŎŎ lĭs
Eureka — yŏŏ REE kuh

Merchandising, in Menard. Photo by Robert Plocheck.

Eustace — YŌŌS t's
Evadale — EE vuh däl
Evant — EE vänt
Evergreen — Ĕ ver green
Everman — Ĕ ver m'n

F

Fabens — FĀ b'nz
Fairbanks — FĂR bangks
Fairfield — FĂR feeld
Fairlie — FĂR lee
Fair Play — fär PLĀ
Fairview — FĂR vyōō
Fairy — FĀ rĭ
Falfurrias — fäl FYŌŌ rĭ uhs
Falls — fawlz
Falls City — fawlz SĬT ĭ
Fannett — fä NĔT
Fannin — FĂN ĭn
Fargo — FAHR gō
Farmers Branch — fahr merz BRĂNCH
Farmersville — FAHRM erz vĭl
Farnsworth — FAHRNZ werth
Farrar — FĂR uh
Farrsville — FAHRZ vĭl
Farwell — FAHR w'l
Fashing — FĂ shĭng
Fate — fāt
Fayette — fä ĔT
Fayetteville — FĀ uht vĭl
Fentress — FĔN trĭs
Ferris — FĔR ĭs
Field Creek — feeld KREEK
Fieldton — FEEL t'n
Fife — fif
Fischer — FĬ sher
Fisher — FĬSH er
Fisk — fĭsk
Flagg — flăg
Flat — flăt
Flatonia — flä TŌN yuh

Flint — flĭnt
Flomot — FLŌ maht
Florence — FLAH ruhns
Floresville — FLŌRZ vil
Florey — FLŌ ri
Floyd — floid
Floydada — floi DĀ duh
Fluvanna — flōō VĂN uh
Flynn — flĭn
Foard — förd
Foard City — förd SĬT ĭ
Fodice — FŌ dĭs
Follett — fah LĔT
Fordtran — förd TRĂN
Forest — FAW rĕst
Forestburg — FAW rĕst berg
Forney — FAWR nĭ
Forreston — FAW rĕs t'n
Forsan — FŌR sän
Fort Bend — fört BĔND
Fort Chadbourne — fört CHĂD bern
Fort Davis — fört DĀ vĭs
Fort Griffin — fört GRĬF ĭn
Fort Hancock — fört HĂN kahk
Fort McKavett — fört muh KĂ vĕt
Fort Stockton — fört STAHK t'n
Fort Worth — fört WERTH
Fowlerton — FOW ler t'n
Francitas — frän SEE t's
Franklin — FRĂNGK lĭn
Frankston — FRĂNGS t'n
Fred — frĕd
Fredericksburg — FRĔD er rĭks berg
Fredonia — free DŌN yuh
Freeport — FREE pört
Freer — FREE er
Freestone — FREE stŏn
Frelsburg — FRĔLZ berg
Fresno — FRĔZ nō
Friday — FRĪ dĭ
Friendswood — FRĔNZ wŏŏd

Frio — FREE ō
Friona — free Ō nuh
Frisco — FRĬS kō
Fritch — frĭch
Frost — frawst
Fruitland — FRŌŌT länd
Fruitvale — FRŌŌT väl
Frydek — FRĪ dĕk
Fulbright — FŌŌL brĭt
Fulshear — FUHL sher
Fulton — FŌŌL t'n

G

Gail — gāl
Gaines — gānz
Gainesville — GĂNZ vuhl
Galena Park — guh lee nuh PAHRK
Gallatin — GĂL uh t'n
Galveston — GĂL vĕs t'n
Ganado — guh NĀ dō
Garceno — gahr SĀ nō
Garciasville — gahr SEE uhs vĭl
Garden City — GAHRD n sĭt ĭ
Gardendale — GAHRD n däl
Garden Valley — gahrd n VĀ lĭ
Garland — GAHR l'nd
Garner — GAHR ner
Garrett — GĂR ĭt
Garrison — GĂ rĭ s'n
Garwood — GAHR wŏŏd
Gary — GĒ rĭ
Garza — GAHR zuh
Gatesville — GĂTS vil
Gause — gawz
Gay Hill — gä HĬL
Geneva — juh NEE vuh
Georgetown — JAWRJ town
George West — jawrj WĔST
Geronimo — juh RAH nĭ mō
Giddings — GĬD ĭngz
Gillespie — guh LĔS pĭ
Gillett — juh LĔT
Gilliland — GĬL ĭ l'nd
Gilmer — GĬL mer
Ginger — JĬN jer
Girard — juh RAHRD
Girvin — GER vĭn
Gladewater — GLĀD wah ter
Glasscock — GLĂS kahk
Glazier — GLĀ zher
Glen Cove — glĕn KŌV
Glendale — GLĔN däl
Glenfawn — glĕn FAWN
Glen Flora — glĕn FLŌ ruh
Glenn — glĕn
Glen Rose — GLĔN rōz
Glidden — GLĬD n
Gober — GŌ ber
Godley — GAHD lĭ
Golden — GŌL d'n
Goldfinch — GŌLD fĭnch
Goldsboro — GŌLZ buh ruh
Goldsmith — GŌL smith
Goldthwaite — GŌLTH wät
Goliad — GŌ lĭ ăd
Golinda — gō LĬN duh

Gonzales — guhn ZAH l's
Goodland — GO͝OD l'n
Goodlett — GO͝OD lĕt
Goodnight — GO͝OD nīt
Goodrich — GO͝OD rĭch
Gordon — GAWRD n
Gordonville — GAWRD n vĭl
Goree — GŌ ree
Gorman — GAWR m'n
Gouldbusk — GO͝OLD buhsk
Graford — GRĀ ferd
Graham — GRĀ 'm
Granbury — GRĂN bĕ rĭ
Grandfalls — grănd FAWLZ
Grand Saline — grăn suh LEEN
Grandview — GRĂN vyo͞o
Granger — GRĀN jer
Grapeland — GRĀP l'nd
Grapevine — GRĀP vīn
Grassland — GRĂS l'nd
Grassyville — GRĂ sĭ vĭl
Gray — grā
Grayburg — GRĀ berg
Grayson — GRA s'n
Green — green
Greenville — GREEN v'l
Greenwood — GREEN wo͝od
Gregg — grĕg
Gregory — GRĔG uh rĭ
Grimes — grīmz
Groesbeck — GRŌZ bĕk
Groom — gro͞om
Groveton — GRŌV t'n
Grow — grō
Gruene — green
Gruver — GRO͝O ver
Guadalupe — gwah duh LO͝O pĭ or gwah duh LO͝O pā
Guerra — GWĔ ruh
Gunter — GUHN ter
Gustine — GUHS teen
Guthrie — GUHTH rĭ
Guy — gī

H

Hackberry — HĂK bĕ rĭ
Hagansport — HĀ gĭnz pōrt
Hainesville — HĀNZ v'l
Hale — hāl
Hale Center — hāl SĔNT er
Hall — hawl
Hallettsville — HĂL ĕts vĭl
Hallsville — HAWLZ vĭl
Hamilton — HĂM uhl t'n
Hamlin — HĂM lĭn
Hammond — HĂM 'nd
Hamon — HĂ m'n
Hamshire — HĂM sher
Handley — HĂND lĭ
Hankamer — HĂN kăm er
Hansford — HĂNZ ferd
Happy — HĂ pĭ
Hardeman — HAHR duh m'n
Hardin — HAHRD n
Hare — hăr
Hargill — HAHR gĭl
Harleton — HAHR uhl t'n
Harlingen — HAHR lĭn juhn
Harper — HAHR per
Harris — HĂ rĭs
Harrison — HĂ rĭ s'n
Harrold — HĂR 'ld
Hart — hahrt
Hartburg — HAHRT berg
Hartley — HAHRT lĭ
Harwood — HAHR wo͝od
Haskell — HĂS k'l
Haslam — HĂZ l'm
Haslet — HĂS lĕt
Hasse — HĂ sĭ
Hatchell — HĂ ch'l
Hawkins — HAW kĭnz
Hawley — HAW lĭ
Hays — hāz
Hearne — hern
Heath — heeth
Hebbronville — HĔB r'n vĭl
Hebron — HEE br'n
Hedley — HĔD lĭ
Heidenheimer — HĪD n hīmer
Helena — HĔL uh nuh
Helotes — hĕl Ō tĭs
Hemphill — HĔMP hĭl
Hempstead — HĔM stĕd
Henderson — HĔN der s'n
Henly — HĔN lĭ
Henrietta — hĕn rĭ Ĕ tuh
Hereford — HER ferd
Hermleigh — HER muh lee
Hewitt — HYO͝O ĭt
Hicks — hĭks
Hico — HĪ kō
Hidalgo — hĭ DĂL gō
Higgins — HĬ gĭnz
High — hī
Highbank — HĪ băngk
High Island — hī Ī l'nd
Highlands — HĪ l'ndz
Hightower — HĪ tow er
Hill — hĭl
Hillister — HĬL ĭs ter
Hillsboro — HĬLZ buh ruh
Hindes — hīndz
Hiram — HĪ r'm
Hitchcock — HĬCH kahk
Hitchland — HĬCH l'nd
Hobson — HAHB s'n
Hochheim — HŌ hīm
Hockley — HAHK lĭ
Holland — HAHL 'nd
Holliday — HAH luh dā
Hondo — HAHN dō
Honey Grove — HUHN ĭ grōv
Honey Island — huhn ĭ Ī l'nd
Honey Springs — huhn ĭ SPRĬNGZ
Hood — ho͝od
Hooks — ho͝oks
Hopkins — HAHP kĭnz
Houston — HYO͝OS t'n or YO͝OS t'n
Howard — HOW erd
Howe — how
Howland — HOW l'nd
Hubbard — HUH berd
Huckabay — HUHK uh bĭ
Hudspeth — HUHD sp'th
Huffman — HUHF m'n
Hufsmith — HUHF smĭth
Hughes Springs — hyo͞oz SPRĬNGZ
Hull — huhl
Humble — UHM b'l
Hungerford — HUHNG ger ferd
Hunt — huhnt
Hunter — HUHNT er
Huntington — HUHNT ĭng t'n
Huntsville — HUHNTS v'l
Hurlwood — HERL wo͝od
Hutchins — HUH chĭnz
Hutchinson — HUH chĭn s'n
Hutto — HUH tō
Hye — hī
Hylton — HĬL t'n

I

Iago — ī Ā gō
Idalou — Ī duh lo͞o
Imperial — ĭm PĬR ĭ uhl
Inadale — Ī nuh dāl
Independence — ĭn duh PĔN d'ns
Indian Creek — ĭn dĭ uhn KREEK
Indian Gap — ĭn dĭ uhn GĂP
Industry — ĬN duhs trĭ
Inez — ī NĔZ
Ingleside — ĬNG g'l sīd
Ingram — ĬNG gr'm
Iola — ī Ō luh
Iowa Park — ī uh wuh PAHRK
Ira — Ī ruh
Iraan — ī ruh ĂN
Iredell — Ī ruh dĕl
Ireland — Ī rĭ l'nd
Irene — ī REEN
Irion — ĬR i uhn
Ironton — ĪRN t'n
Irving — ER vĭng
Italy — ĬT uh lĭ
Itasca — ī TĂS kuh
Ivan — Ī v'n
Ivanhoe — Ī v'n hō

J

Jack — jăk
Jacksboro — JĂKS buh ruh
Jackson — JĂK s'n
Jacksonville — JĂK s'n vĭl
Jamestown — JĀMZ town
Jardin — JAHRD n
Jarrell — JĂR uhl
Jasper — JĂS per
Jayton — JĀT n
Jean — jeen
Jeddo — JĔ dō
Jeff Davis — jĕf DĀ vĭs
Jefferson — JĔF er s'n
Jericho — JĔ rĭ kō
Jermyn — JER m'n
Jewett — JO͝O ĭt
Jiba — HEE buh
Jim Hogg — jĭm HAWG

Diacritical markings are used as follows: bāle, băd, lĕt, rīse, rĭll, ōak, bro͞od, fo͝ot. The stressed syllable is capitalized. Secondary stress is indicated by an underline as in Atascosa — ăt uhs KŌ suh.

Jim Wells — jǐm WĔLZ
Joaquin — waw KEEN
Johnson — JAHN s'n
Johnson City — jahn s'n SĬT ǐ
Johntown — JAHN town
Johnsville — JAHNZ vǐl
Joinerville — JOI ner vǐl
Jolly — JAH lǐ
Jollyville — JAH lǐ vǐl
Jonah — JŌ nuh
Jones — jōnz
Jonesboro — JŌNZ buh ruh
Jonesville — JŌNZ vǐl
Josephine — JŌ suh feen
Joshua — JAH sh' wa
Jourdanton — JERD n t'n
Joy — joi
Joyce — jawǐs
Juliff — JŌO lǐf
Junction — JUHNGK sh'n
Juno — JŌO nō
Justiceburg — JUHS tǐs berg
Justin — JUHS tǐn

K

Kalgary — KĂL gĕ rǐ
Kamay — KĀ ǐm ā
Kanawha — KAHN uh wah
Karnack — KAHR näk
Karnes — kahrnz
Karnes City — kahrnz SĬT ǐ
Katemcy — kuh TĔM sǐ
Katy — KĀ tǐ
Kaufman — KAWF m'n
Keechi — KEE chǐ
Keene — keen
Kellerville — KĔL er vǐl
Kemah — KEE muh
Kemp — kĕmp or kǐmp
Kemp City — kĕmp SĬT ǐ
Kempner — KĔMP ner
Kendalia — kĔn DĀL yuh
Kenedy — KĔN uh dǐ
Kennard — kuh NAHRD
Kennedale — KĔN uh däl
Kent — kĕnt
Kerens — KER 'nz
Kermit — KER mǐt
Kerr — ker
Kerrville — KER vǐl
Kildare — KǏL där
Kilgore — KǏL gōr
Killeen — kuh LEEN
Kimble — KǏM b'l
King — kǐng
Kingsbury — KǏNGZ bĕ rǐ
Kingsland — KǏNGZ l'nd
Kingsmill — kǐngz MǏL
Kingston — KǏNGZ t'n
Kingsville — KǏNGZ vǐl
Kinney — KǏN ǐ
Kirby — KER bǐ
Kirbyville — KER bǐ vǐl
Kirkland — KERK l'nd
Kirvin — KER vǐn
Kleberg — KLĀ berg
Klondike — KLAHN dǐk

Knickerbocker — NǏK uh bah ker
Knippa — kuh NǏP uh
Knott — naht
Knox — nahks
Knox City — nahks SĬT ǐ
Kosciusko — kuh SHŌOS kō
Kosse — KAH sǐ
Kountze — kōōntz
Kress — kres
Krum — kruhm
Kurten — KER t'n
Kyle — kǐl

L

La Blanca — lah BLAHN kuh
La Coste — luh KAWST
Ladonia — luh DŌN yuh
LaFayette — lah fǐ ĔT
La Feria — luh FĔ rǐ uh
Lagarto — luh GAHR tō
La Gloria — lah GLŌ rǐ uh
La Grange — luh GRĀNJ
La Grulla — lah GRŌŌL yuh
Laguna — luh GŌŌ nuh
Laird Hill — lärd HǏL
La Joya — luh HŌ yuh
Lake Creek — läk KREEK
Lake Dallas — läk DĂL uhs
Lake Jackson — läk JĂK s'n
Laketon — LĂK t'n
Lake Victor — läk VǏK ter
Lakeview — LĂK vyōō
Lamar — luh MAHR
La Marque — luh MAHRK
Lamasco — luh MĂS kō
Lamb — läm
Lamesa — luh MEE suh
Lamkin — LĂM kǐn
Lampasas — läm PĂ s's
Lancaster — LĂNG k's ter
Land City — län SĬT ǐ
Laneville — LĂN vǐl
Langtry — LĂNG trǐ
Lanier — luh NǏR
La Paloma — lah puh LŌ muh
La Porte — luh PŌRT
La Pryor — luh PRǏ er
Laredo — luh RĀ dō
Lariat — LĂ rǐ uht
Larue — luh RŌŌ
LaSalle — luh SĂL
Lasara — luh SĔ ruh
Lassater — LĂ sǐ ter
Latch — lĂch
Latexo — luh TĔKS ō
Lavaca — luh VĂ kuh
La Vernia — luh VER nǐ uh
La Villa — lah VǏL uh
Lavon — luh VAHN
La Ward — luh WAWRD
Lawn — lawn
Lawrence — LAH r'ns
Lazbuddie — LĂZ buh dǐ
League City — leeg SĬT ǐ
Leakey — LĀ kǐ
Leander — lee ĂN der

Leary — LǏ er ǐ
Ledbetter — LĔD bĕt er
Lee — lee
Leesburg — LEEZ berg
Leesville — LEEZ vǐl
Lefors — lǐ FŌRZ
Leggett — LĔ gǐt
Leigh — lee
Lela — LEE luh
Lelia Lake — leel yuh LĀK
Leming — LĔ mǐng
Lenorah — lĕ NŌ ruh
Leo — LEE ō
Leon — lee AHN
Leona — lee Ō nuh
Leonard — LĔN erd
Leon Springs — lee ahn SPRǏNGZ
Leroy — LEE roi
Levelland — LĔ v'l länd
Levita — luh VǏ tuh
Lewisville — LŌO ǐs vǐl
Lexington — LĔKS ǐng t'n
Liberty — LǏB er tǐ
Liberty Hill — lǐ ber tǐ HǏL
Lillian — LǏL yuhn
Limestone — LǏM stōn
Lincoln — LǏNG k'n
Lindale — LǏN däl
Linden — LǏN d'n
Lindenau — lǐn duh NOW
Lindsay — LǏN zǐ
Lingleville — LǏNG g'l vǐl
Linn — lǐn
Lipan — lǐ PĂN
Lipscomb — LǏPS k'm
Lissie — LǏ sǐ
Little Elm — lǐt l ĔLM
Littlefield — LǏT uhl feeld
Little River — lǐt uhl RǏV er
Live Oak — LǏV ōk
Liverpool — LǏ ver pōōl
Livingston — LǏV ǐngz t'n
Llano — LĂ nō
Locker — LAH ker
Lockett — LAH kǐt
Lockhart — LAHK hahrt
Lockney — LAHK nǐ
Lodi — LŌ dǐ
Lohn — lahn
Lolita — lō LEE tuh
Loma Alto — lō muh ĂL tō
Lometa — lō MEE tuh
London — LUHN d'n
Lone Grove — lōn GRŌV
Lone Oak — LŌN ōk
Long Branch — lawng BRĂNCH
Long Mott — lawng MAHT
Longview — LAWNG vyōō
Longworth — LAWNG werth
Loop — lōōp
Lopeno — lō PEE nō
Loraine — lō RĀN
Lorena — lō REE nuh
Los Angeles — laws AN juh l's
Los Ebanos — lōs ĔB uh nōs
Los Fresnos — lōs FRĔZ nōs
Los Indios — lōs ǏN dǐ ōs

Mural at Baird, Callahan County. Photo by Robert Plocheck.

Losoya — luh SAW yuh
Lott — laht
Louise — LŌŌ eez
Lovelady — LUHV lā dĭ
Loving — LUH vĭng
Lubbock — LUH buhk   or   LUH b'k
Lueders — LŌŌ derz
Luella — lōō ĔL uh
Lufkin — LUHF kĭn
Luling — LŌŌ lĭng
Lund — luhnd
Lutie — LŌŌ tĭ
Lyford — LĪ ferd
Lynn — lĭn
Lyons — LĪ 'nz
Lytton Springs — lĭt n SPRĬNGZ

M

Mabank — MĀ băngk
Macune — muh KŌŌN
Madison — MĂ dĭ s'n
Madisonville — MĂ duh s'n vĭl
Magnolia — măg NŌL yuh
Magnolia Springs — măg nol yuh
  SPRĬNGZ
Malakoff — MĂL uh kawf
Malone — muh LŌN
Malta — MAWL tuh
Manchaca — MĂN shăk
Manchester — MĂN chĕs ter
Manheim — MĂN hĭm
Mankins — MĂN kĭnz
Manor — MĂ ner
Mansfield — MĂNZ feeld
Manvel — MĂN v'l
Maple — MĂ puhl
Marathon — MĂR uh th'n
Marble Falls — mahr b'l FAWLZ
Marfa — MAHR fuh
Margaret — MAHR guh rĭt
Marietta — mĕ rĭ Ĕ tuh
Marion — MĔ rĭ uhn

Markham — MAHR k'm
Marlin — MAHR lĭn
Marquez — mahr KĀ
Marshall — MAHR sh'l
Mart — mahrt
Martin — MAHRT n
Martindale — MAHRT n dāl
Martinsville — MAHRT nz vĭl
Maryneal — mā rĭ NEEL
Marysville — MĂ rĭz vĭl
Mason — MĀ s'n
Matador — MĂT uh dōr
Matagorda — măt uh GAWR duh
Mathis — MĂ thĭs
Maud — mawd
Mauriceville — maw REES vĭl
Maverick — MĂV rĭk
Maxey — MĂKS ĭ
Maxwell — MĂKS w'l
May — mā
Maydell — MĂ dĕl
Maypearl — mā PERL
Maysfield — MĀZ feeld
McAdoo — MĂK uh dōō
McAllen — măk ĂL ĭn
McCamey — muh KĂ mĭ
McCaulley — muh KAW lĭ
McCoy — muh KOI
McCulloch — muh KUH luhk
McFaddin — măk FĂD n
McGregor — muh GRĔ ger
McKinney — muh KĬN ĭ
McLean — muh KLĀN
McLennan — muhk LĔN uhn
McLeod — măk LOWD
McMahan — măk MĂN
McMullen — măk MUHL ĭn
McNary — măk NĂ rĭ
McNeil — măk NEEL
McQueeney — muh KWEE nĭ
Meadow — MĔ dō
Medicine Mound — mĕd uhs n

MOWND
Medill — mĕ DĬL
Medina — muh DEE nuh
Megargel — muh GAHR g'l
Melissa — muh LĬS uh
Melrose — MĔL rōz
Melvin — MĔL vĭn
Memphis — MĔM fĭs
Menard — muh NAHRD
Mendoza — mĕn DŌ zuh
Mentone — mĕn TŌN
Mercedes — mer SĀ deez
Mercury — MER kyuh ri
Mereta — muh RĔT uh
Meridian — muh RĬ dĭ uhn
Merit — MĔR ĭt
Merkel — MER k'l
Mertens — mer TĔNZ
Mertzon — MERTS n
Mesquite — muhs KEET
Mexia — muh HĂ uh
Meyersville — MĪRZ vĭl
Miami — mĭ ĂM uh or mĭ ĂM ĭ
Mico — MEE kō
Middleton — MĬD uhl t'n
Midfields — MĬD feeldz
Midland — MĬD l'nd
Midlothian — mĭd LŌ thĭ n
Midway — MĬD wā
Milam — MĪ l'm
Milano — mĭ LĂ nō
Mildred — MĬL drĕd
Miles — mīlz
Milford — MĬL ferd
Miller Grove — mĭl er GRŌV
Millersview — MĬL erz vyōō
Millett — MĬL ĭt
Millheim — MĬL hĭm
Millican — MĬL uh kuhn
Mills — mĭlz
Millsap — MĬL săp
Minden — MĬN d'n

Mineola — mĭn ĭ Ō luh
Mineral — MĬN er uhl
Mineral Wells — mĭn er uhl WĔLZ
Minerva — mĭ NER vuh
Mingus — MĬNG guhs
Minter — MĬNT er
Mirando City — mĭ răn duh SĬT ĭ
Mission — MĬSH uhn
Mission Valley — mĭsh uhn VĂ lĭ
Missouri City — muh zōŏr uh SĬT ĭ
Mitchell — MĬ ch'l
Mobeetie — mō BEE tĭ
Moline — mō LEEN
Monahans — MAH nuh hănz
Monaville — MŌ nuh vĭl
Monkstown — MUHNGKS town
Monroe — MAHN rō
Monroe City — mahn rō SĬT ĭ
Montague — mahn TĀG
Montalba — mahnt ĂL buh
Mont Belvieu — mahnt BĔL vyōō
Montell — mahn TĔL
Montgomery — mahnt GUHM er ĭ
Monthalia — mahn THĂL yuh
Moody — MŌŌ dĭ
Moore — mōr
Morales — muh RAH lĕs
Moran — mō RĂN
Morgan — MAWR g'n
Morgan Mill — mawr g'n MĬL
Morse — mawrs
Morton — MAWRT n
Moscow — MAHS kow
Mosheim — MŌ shīm
Moss Bluff — maws BLUHF
Motley — MAHT lĭ
Moulton — MŌL t'n
Mound — mownd
Mountain Home — mownt n HŌM
Mount Calm — mownt KAHM
Mount Enterprise — mownt
  ĔN ter prīz
Mount Pleasant — mownt PLĔ z'nt
Mount Selman — mownt SĔL m'n
Mount Sylvan — mownt SĬL v'n
Mount Vernon — mownt VER n'n
Muenster — MYŌŌNS ter
Muldoon — muhl DŌŌN
Muleshoe — MYŌŌL shōō
Mullin — MUHL ĭn
Mumford — MUHM ferd
Munday — MUHN dĭ
Murchison — MER kuh s'n
Murphy — MER fĭ
Mykawa—mĭ KAH wuh
Myrtle Springs — mert I SPRĬNGZ

N

Nacogdoches — năk uh DŌ chĭs
Nada — NĀ duh
Naples — NĀ p'lz
Nash — năsh
Natalia — nuh TĂL yuh
Navarro — nuh VĂ rō
Navasota — năv uh SŌ tuh

Nazareth — NĂZ uh r'th
Neches — NĀ chĭs
Nederland — NEE der l'nd
Needville — NEED vĭl
Nelsonville — NĔL s'n vĭl
Neuville — NYŌŌ v'l
Nevada — nuh VĀ duh
Newark — NŌŌ erk
New Baden — nyōō BĀD n
New Berlin — nyōō BER lin
New Boston — nyōō BAWS t'n
New Braunfels — nyōō BRAHN f'ls
  or BROWN fĕlz
Newby — NYŌŌ bĭ
New Caney — nyōō KĀ nĭ
Newcastle — NYŌŌ kăs uhl
New Gulf — nyōō GUHLF
New Home — NYŌŌ hōm
New Hope — nyōō HŌP
Newlin — NYŌŌ lĭn
New London — nyōō LUHN d'n
Newman — NYŌŌ m'n
Newport — NYŌŌ pōrt
New Salem — nyōō SĀ I'm
Newsome — NYŌŌ s'm
New Summerfield — nyōō
  SUHM er feeld
Newton — NYŌŌT n
New Ulm — nyōō UHLM
New Waverly — nyōō WĀ ver lĭ
New Willard — nyōō WĬL erd
Nimrod — NĬM rahd
Nineveh — NĬN uh vuh
Nixon — NĬKS uhn
Nocona — nō KŌ nuh
Nolan — NŌ l'n
Nolanville — NŌ l'n vĭl
Nome — nōm
Noonday — NŌŌN dā
Nopal — NŌ păl
Nordheim — NAWRD hīm
Normandy — NAWR m'n dĭ
Normangee — NAWR m'n jee
Normanna — nawr MĂN uh
Northrup — NAWR thr'p
North Zulch — nawrth ZŌŌLCH
Norton — NAWRT n
Novice — NAH vĭs
Nueces — nyōō Ā sĭs
Nugent — NYŌŌ j'nt
Nursery — NER suh rĭ

O

Oakalla — ō KĂL uh
Oak Grove — ōk GRŌV
Oak Hill — ōk HĬL
Oakhurst — ŌK herst
Oakland — ŌK I'nd
Oakville — ŌK vĭl
Oakwood — ŌK wŏŏd
O'Brien — ō BRĪ uhn
Ochiltree — AH k'l tree
Odell — Ō dĕl or ō DĔL
Odem — Ō d'm
Odessa — ō DĔS uh
O'Donnell — ō DAH n'l

Oenaville — ō EEN uh v'l
Oglesby — Ō g'lz bĭ
Oilton — OIL t'n
Oklaunion — ōk luh YŌŌN y'n
Olden — ŌL d'n
Oldenburg — ŌL dĭn berg
Oldham — ŌL d'm
Old Glory — ōld GLŌ rĭ
Olivia — ō LĬV ĭ uh
Olmito — awl MEE tuh
Olmos Park — ahl m's PAHRK
Olney — AHL nĭ
Olton — ŌL t'n
Omaha — Ō muh haw
Omen — Ō mĭn
Onalaska — uhn uh LĂS kuh
Oplin — AHP lĭn
Orange — AHR ĭnj
Orangefield — AHR ĭnj feeld
Orange Grove — AHR ĭnj GRŌV
Orchard — AWR cherd
Ore City — ōr SĬT ĭ
Osceola — ō sĭ Ō luh
Otey — Ō tĭ
Otis Chalk — ō tĭs CHAWLK
Ottine — ah TEEN
Otto — AH tō
Ovalo — ō VĂL uh
Overton — Ō ver t'n
Owens — Ō ĭnz
Ozona — ō ZŌ nuh

P

Paducah — puh DYŌŌ kuh
Paige — pāj
Paint Rock — pānt RAHK
Palacios — puh LĂ sh's
Palestine — PAL uhs teen
Palito Blanco — p' lee to
  BLAHNG kō
Palmer — PAH mer
Palo Pinto — pă lō PĬN tō
Paluxy — puh LUHK sĭ
Pampa — PĂM puh
Pandora — păn DŌR uh
Panhandle — PĂN hăn d'l
Panna Maria — păn uh
  muh REE uh
Papalote — pah puh LŌ tĭ
Paradise — PĂR uh dīs
Paris — PĂ rĭs
Parker — PAHR ker
Parmer — PAH mer
Parnell — pahr NĔL
Parsley Hill — pahrs lĭ HĬL
Pasadena — păs uh DEE nuh
Patricia — puh TRĬ shuh
Patroon — puh TRŌŌN
Pattison — PĂT uh s'n
Pattonville — PĂT n vĭl
Pawnee — paw NEE
Paxton — PĂKS t'n
Peacock — PEE kahk
Pearl — perl
Pearland — PĂR lănd
Pearsall — PEER sawl

Peaster — PEES ter
Pecan Gap — pǐ kahn GĂP
Pecos — PĀ k's
Penelope — puh NĚL uh pǐ
Penitas — puh NEE t's
Pennington — PĚN ǐng t'n
Penwell — PĬN wĕl
Peoria — <u>pee</u> Ō rǐ uh
Percilla — per SĬL uh
Perrin — PĚR ǐn
Perry — PĚ rǐ
Perryton — PĚ rǐ t'n
Peters — PEET erz
Petersburg — PEET erz <u>berg</u>
Petrolia — puh TRŌL yuh
Petteway — PĚT uh wā
Pettit — PĚT ĭt
Pettus — PĚT uhs
Petty — PĚT ǐ
Pflugerville — FLŌŌ ger vǐl
Pharr — fahr
Phelps — fĕlps
Phillips — FĬL uhps
Pickton — PĬK t'n
Pidcoke — PĬD kŏk
Piedmont — PEED mahnt
Pierce — PĬ ers
Pilot Point — pǐ l't POINT
Pine Forest — <u>pīn</u> FAW rĕst
Pine Hill — pīn HĬL
Pinehurst — PĬN herst
Pineland — PĬN land
Pine Mills — pīn MĬLZ
Pine Springs — pīn SPRĬNGZ
Pioneer — pǐ uh NĬR
Pipecreek — pǐp KREEK
Pittsburg — PĬTS berg
Placedo — PLĂS ǐ dō
Placid — PLĂ sǐd
Plains — plānz
Plainview — PLĀN vyōō
Plano — PLĀ nō
Plantersville — PLĂN terz vǐl
Plaska — PLĂS kuh
Plateau — plă TŌ
Pleasant Grove—<u>plĕ</u> z'nt GRŌV
Pleasanton — PLĔZ uhn t'n
Pledger — PLĔ jer
Plum — pluhm
Point — point
Pointblank — pint BLĂNGK
Polk — pōlk
Pollock — PAHL uhk
Ponder — PAHN der
Ponta — pahn TĀ
Pontotoc — PAHNT uh tahk
Poolville — PŌŌL vǐl
Port Aransas — pōrt uh RĂN zuhs
Port Arthur — pōrt AHR ther
Port Bolivar — <u>pōrt</u> BAH lǐ ver
Porter Springs — <u>pōr</u> ter SPRĬNGZ
Port Isabel — pōrt ĬZ uh bĕl
Portland — PŌRT l'nd
Port Lavaca — <u>pōrt</u> luh VĂ kuh
Port Neches — pōrt NĂ chǐs
Port O'Connor — pōrt ō KAH ner

The house/sculpture of the late Robert Bruno in Ransom Canyon outside Lubbock. Photo by Robert Plocheck.

Posey — PŌ zǐ
Post — pōst
Postoak — PŌST ōk
Poteet — pō TEET
Poth — pōth
Potosi — puh TŌ sǐ
Potter — PAHT er
Pottsboro — PAHTS buh ruh
Pottsville — PAHTS vǐl
Powderly — POW der lǐ
Powell — POW w'l
Poynor — POI ner
Prairie Dell — prĕr ǐ DĔL
Prairie Hill — prĕr ǐ HĬL
Prairie Lea — prĕr ǐ LEE
Prairie View — prĕr ǐ VYŌŌ
Prairieville — PRĔR ǐ vǐl
Premont — PREE mahnt
Presidio — pruh SĬ dǐ ō
Priddy — PRĬ dǐ
Primera — <u>pree</u> MĚ ruh
Princeton — PRĬNS t'n
Pritchett — PRĬ chǐt
Proctor — PRAHK ter
Progreso — prō GRĚ sō
Prosper — PRAHS per
Purdon — PERD n
Purley — PER lǐ
Purmela — per MEE luh
Putnam — PUHT n'm
Pyote — PĬ ōt

Q

Quail — kwāl
Quanah — KWAH nuh
Queen City — kween SĬT ǐ
Quemado — kuh MAH dō
Quihi — KWEE <u>hee</u>
Quinlan — KWĬN l'n
Quintana — kwǐn TAH nuh
Quitaque — KĬT uh kwa
Quitman — KWĬT m'n

R

Rainbow — RĂN bō
Rains — rānz

Ralls — rahlz
Randall — RĂN d'l
Randolph — RĂN dahlf
Ranger — RĂN jer
Rangerville — RĂN jer vǐl
Rankin — RĂNG kǐn
Ratcliff — RĂT klǐf
Ravenna — rǐ VĚN uh
Rayburn — RĀ bern
Raymondville — RĀ m'nd vǐl
Raywood — RĀ wōōd
Reagan — RĀ g'n
Real — REE awl
Realitos — <u>ree</u> uh LEE t's
Redford — RĔD ferd
Red Oak — RĔD ōk
Red River — rĕd RĬ ver
Red Rock — rĕd RAHK
Red Springs — rĕd SPRĬNGZ
Red Water — RĔD wah ter
Reeves — reevz
Refugio — rĕ FYŌŌ rǐ ō
Reilly Springs — <u>rǐ</u> lǐ SPRĬNGZ
Reklaw — RĔK law
Reno — REE nō
Rhineland — RĬN l'nd
Rhome — rōm
Rhonesboro — RŌNZ buh ruh
Ricardo — rǐ KAHR dō
Rice — rīs
Richards — RĬCH erdz
Richardson — RĬCH erd s'n
Richland — RĬCH l'nd
Richland Springs — <u>rǐch</u> l'nd SPRĬNGZ
Richmond — RĬCH m'nd
Ridge — rǐj
Ridgeway — RĬJ wā
Riesel — REE s'l
Ringgold — RĬNG gōld
Rio Frio — <u>ree</u> ō FREE ō
Rio Grande City — ree ō grahn dǐ or ree ō grän SĬT ǐ
Rio Hondo — <u>ree</u> ō HAHN dō
Riomedina — <u>ree</u> ō muh DEE nuh

Rios — REE ōs
Rio Vista — <u>ree</u> ō VĬS tuh
Rising Star — rī zǐng STAHR
River Oaks — rī ver ŌKS
Riverside — RĬ ver sǐd
Riviera — ruh VĬR uh
Roane — rōn
Roanoke — RŌN ōk or
  RŌ uh <u>nōk</u>
Roans Prairie — rōnz PRĔR Ĭ
Roaring Springs — rōr ǐng
  SPRĬNGZ
Robert Lee — rah bert LEE
Roberts — RAH berts
Robertson — RAH bert s'n
Robinson — RAH bǐn s'n
Robstown — RAHBZ town
Roby — RŌ bǐ
Rochelle — rō SHĔL
Rochester — RAH chĕs ter
Rockdale — RAHK dāl
Rock Island — rahk Ĭ l'nd
Rockland — RAHK l'nd
Rockport — rahk PŌRT
Rocksprings — rahk SPRĬNGZ
Rockwall — rahk WAWL
Rockwood — RAHK wōōd
Roganville — RŌ g'n vǐl
Rogers — RAH jerz
Roma — RŌ muh
Romayor — rō MĀ er
Roosevelt — RŌŌ suh v'lt
Ropesville — RŌPS vǐl
Rosanky — rō ZĂNG kǐ
Roscoe — RAHS kō
Rosebud — RŌZ b'd
Rose Hill — rōz HĬL
Rosenberg — RŌZ n berg
Rosenthal — RŌZ uhn thawl
Rosewood — RŌZ wōōd
Rosharon — rō SHĔ r'n
Rosita — rō SEE tuh
Ross — raws
Rosser — RAW ser
Rosston — RAWS t'n
Rossville — RAWS vǐl
Roswell — RAHZ w'l
Rotan — rō TĂN
Round Rock — ROWND rahk
Round Top — ROWN tahp
Rowena — rō EE nuh
Rowlett — ROW lǐt
Roxton — RAHKS t'n
Royalty — ROI uhl tǐ
Royse City — roi SĪT ǐ
Royston — ROIS t'n
Rugby — RUHG bǐ
Ruidosa — <u>ree</u> uh DŌ suh
Rule — rōōl
Runge — RUHNG ǐ
Runnels — RUHN 'lz
Rural Shade — rōōr uhl SHĀD
Rusk — ruhsk
Rutersville — RŌŌ ter vǐl
Rye — rī

S

Sabinal — SĂB uh năl
Sabine — suh BEEN
Sabine Pass — suh <u>been</u> PĂS
Sabinetown — suh <u>been</u> TOWN
Sachse — SĂK sǐ
Sacul — SĂ k'l
Sadler — SĂD ler
Sagerton — SĀ ger t'n
Saginaw — SĂ guh naw
Saint Jo — sănt JŌ
Saint Paul — sănt PAWL
Salado — suh LĀ dō
Salesville — SĀLZ vǐl
Salineno — suh LEEN yō
Salmon — SĂL m'n
Salt Gap — sawlt GĂP
Saltillo — săl TĬL ō
Samfordyce — săm FOR dis
Sample — SĂM p'l
Samnorwood — săm NAWR wōōd
San Angelo — <u>săn</u> ĂN juh lō
San Antonio — <u>săn</u> ăn TŌ nǐ ō
San Augustine — <u>săn</u> AW g's teen
San Benito — săn buh NEE tuh
Sanderson — SĂN der s'n
Sandia — săn DEE uh
San Diego — <u>săn</u> dǐ Ā gō
Sandy Point — săn dǐ POINT
San Elizario — săn ĕl ǐ ZAH rǐ ō
San Felipe — <u>săn</u> fuh LEEP
Sanford — SĂN ferd
San Gabriel — săn GĀ brǐ uhl
Sanger — SĂNG er
San Jacinto — <u>săn</u> juh SĬN tuh
  or juh SĬN tō
San Juan — săn WAHN
San Marcos — <u>săn</u> MAHR k's
San Patricio — <u>săn</u> puh TRĬSH ǐ ō
San Perlita — <u>săn</u> per LEE tuh
San Saba — <u>săn</u> SĂ buh
Santa Anna — <u>săn</u> tuh ĂN uh
Santa Elena — săn tuh LEE nuh
Santa Maria — <u>săn</u> tuh
  muh REE uh
Santa Rosa — <u>săn</u> tuh RŌ suh
Santo — SĂN tō
San Ygnacio — <u>săn</u> ǐg NAH sǐ ō
Saragosa — <u>sĕ</u> ruh GŌ suh
Saratoga — <u>sĕ</u> ruh TŌ guh
Sargent — SAHR juhnt
Sarita — suh REE tuh
Saspamco — suh SPĂM kō
Satin — SĂT n
Savoy — suh VOI
Schattel — SHĂT uhl
Schertz — sherts
Schleicher — SHLĪ ker
Schroeder — SHRĀ der
Schulenburg — SHŌŌ lǐn berg
Schwertner — SWERT ner
Scotland — SKAHT l'nd
Scottsville — SKAHTS vǐl
Scranton — SKRĂNT n
Scurry — SKUH rǐ
Scyene — sǐ EEN

Seabrook — SEE brōōk
Seadrift — SEE drǐft
Seagoville — SEE gō vǐl
Seagraves — SEE grāvz
Seale — seel
Sealy — SEE lǐ
Sebastopol — suh BĂS tuh pōōl
Sebastian — suh BĂS tǐ 'n
Security — sǐ KYŌŌR ǐ tǐ
Segno — SĔG nō
Segovia — sǐ GŌ vǐ uh
Seguin — sǐ GEEN
Selfs — sĕlfs
Selma — SĔL muh
Seminole — SĔM uh nōl
Seymour — SEE mōr
Shackelford — SHĂK uhl ferd
Shady Grove — shā dǐ GRŌV
Shafter — SHĂF ter
Shallowater — SHĂL uh wah ter
Shamrock — SHĂM rahk
Shannon — SHĂN uhn
Sharp — shahrp
Sheffield — SHĒ feeld
Shelby — SHĔL bǐ
Shelbyville — SHĔL bǐ vǐl
Sheldon — SHĔL d'n
Shepherd — SHĒ perd
Sheridan — SHĒ rǐ dn
Sherman — SHER m'n
Sherwood — SHER wood
Shiner — SHĪ ner
Shiro — SHĪ rō
Shive — shīv
Sidney — SĬD nǐ
Sierra Blanca — sǐer ruh
  BLĂNG kuh
Siloam — suh LŌM
Silsbee — SĬLZ bǐ
Silver Lake — sǐl ver LĀK
Silverton — SĬL ver t'n
Silver Valley — sǐl ver VĂ lǐ
Simms — sǐmz
Simonton — SĪ m'n t'n
Singleton — SĬNG g'l t'n
Sinton — SĬNT n
Sipe Springs — SEEP sprǐngz
Sisterdale — SĬS ter dāl
Sivells Bend — sǐ v'lz BĔND
Skellytown — SKĔ lǐ town
Skidmore — SKĬD mōr
Slaton — SLĀT n
Slayden — SLĀD n
Slidell — slī DĔL
Slocum — SLŌ k'm
Smiley — SMĪ lǐ
Smith — smǐth
Smithfield — SMĬTH feeld
Smithland — SMĬTH l'nd
Smithson Valley — smǐth s'n VĂ lǐ
Smithville — SMĬTH vǐl
Smyer — SMĪ er
Snook — snōōk
Snyder — SNĪ der
Somerset — SUH mer sĕt
Somervell — SUH mer vĕl
Somerville — SUH mer vǐl

Diacritical markings are used as follows: bāle, băd, lĕt, rīse, rĭll, ōak, brōōd, fōōt. The stressed syllable is capitalized. Secondary stress is indicated by an underline as in Atascosa — <u>ăt</u> uhs KŌ suh. TEXAS ALMANAC ©.

Sonora — suh NŌ ruh
Sour Lake — sowr LĀK
South Bend — sowth BĔND
South Bosque — sowth BAHS kĭ
South Houston — sowth HYŌŌS t'n
Southland — SOWTH l'nd
Southmayd — sowth MĀD
South Plains — sowth PLĀNZ
Spade — spād
Spanish Fort — spă nĭsh FŌRT
Sparenberg — SPĂR ĭn berg
Speaks — speeks
Spearman — SPĬR m'n
Spicewood — SPĬS wŏŏd
Splendora — splĕn DŌ ruh
Spofford — SPAH ferd
Spring — sprĭng
Springdale — SPRĬNG dāl
Springlake — sprĭng LĀK
Springtown — SPRĬNG town
Spur — sper
Spurger — SPER ger
Stacy — STĀ sĭ
Stafford — STĀ ferd
Stamford — STĂM ferd
Stanton — STĂNT n
Staples — STĀ p'lz
Starr — stahr
Stephens — STEE vĕnz
Stephenville — STEEV n vĭl
Sterley — STER lĭ
Sterling — STER lĭng
Sterling City — <u>ster</u> lĭng SĬT ĭ
Stiles — stĭlz
Stinnett — stĭ NĔT
Stockdale — STAHK dāl
Stoneburg — STŌN berg
Stoneham — STŌN uhm
Stone Point — stōn POINT
Stonewall — STŌN wawl
Stout — stowt
Stowell — STO w'l
Stranger — STRĀN jer
Stratford — STRĂT ferd
Strawn — strawn
Streeter — STREET er
Streetman — STREET m'n
Study Butte — styŏŏ dĭ BYŌŌT
Sublime — s'b LĬM
Sudan — SŌŌ dăn
Sugar Land — SHŎŎ ger länd
Sullivan City — <u>suh</u> luh v'n
   SĬT ĭ
Sulphur Bluff — suhl fer BLUHF
Sulphur Springs — suhl fer
   SPRĬNGZ
Summerfield — SUHM er <u>feeld</u>
Sumner — SUHM ner
Sundown — SUHN down
Suniland — SUH nĭ länd
Sunny Side — SUH nĭ sĭd
Sunray — SUHN rā
Sunset — SUHN sĕt
Sutherland Springs — <u>suh</u> ther l'nd
   SPRĬNGZ
Sutton — SUHT n
Swan — swahn

Sweeny — SWEE nĭ
Sweet Home — sweet HŌM
Sweetwater — SWEET wah ter
Swenson — SWĔN s'n
Swift — swĭft
Swisher — SWĬ sher
Sylvester — <u>sil</u> VES ter

T

Taft — täft
Tahoka — tuh HŌ kuh
Talco — TĂL kō
Talpa — TĂL puh
Tanglewood — TĂNG g`l wŏŏd
Tankersley — TĂNG kers lĭ
Tarrant — TAR uhnt
Tarzan — TAHR z'n
Tascosa — täs KŌ suh
Tatum — TĀ t'm
Tavener — TĂV uh ner
Taylor — TĀ ler
Teague — teeg
Tehuacana — <u>tuh</u> WAW kuh nuh
Telephone — TĔL uh fōn
Telferner — TĔLF ner
Tell — tĕl
Temple — TĔM p'l
Tenaha — TĔN uh haw
Tennyson — TĔN uh s'n
Terlingua — TER lĭng guh
Terrell — TĔR uhl
Terrell Hills — <u>ter</u> uhl HILZ
Terry — TĔR ĭ
Texarkana — tĕks ahr KĂN uh
Texas City — <u>tĕks</u> ĕz SĬT ĭ
Texhoma — tĕks Ō muh
Texline — TĔKS lĭn
Texon — tĕks AHN
Thalia — THĀL yuh
The Grove — th' GRŌV
Thicket — THĬ kĭt
Thomaston — TAHM uhs t'n
Thompsons — TAHMP s'nz
Thorndale — THAWRN dāl
Thornton — THAWRN t'n
Thorp Spring — thawrp SPRING
Thrall — thrawl
Three Rivers — <u>three</u> RĬ verz
Throckmorton — THRAHK mawrt n
Thurber — THER ber
Tilden — TĬL d'n
Timpson — TĬM s'n
Tioga — tĭ Ō guh
Titus — TĬT uhs
Tivoli — tĭ VŌ luh or tĭ VŌ lĭ
Tokio — TŌ kĭ ō
Tolar — TŌ ler
Tolbert — TAHL bert
Tolosa — tuh LŌ suh
Tomball — TAHM bawl
Tom Bean — <u>tahm</u> BEEN
Tom Green — <u>tahm</u> GREEN
Tool — tŏŏl
Topsey — TAHP sĭ
Tornillo — tawr NEE yō
Tow — tow
Toyah — TOI yuh

Toyahvale — TOI yuh vāl
Trawick — TRĀ wĭk
Travis — TRĂ vĭs
Trent — trĕnt
Trenton — TRĔNT n
Trickham — TRĬK uhm
Trinidad — TRĬN uh dăd
Trinity — TRĬN ĭ tĭ
Troup — trŏŏp
Troy — TRAW ĭ
Truby — TRŌŌ bĭ
Trumbull — TRUHM b'l
Truscott — TRUHS k't
Tucker — TUHK er
Tuleta — tŏŏ LEE tuh
Tulia — TŌŌL yuh
Tulsita — tuhl SEE tuh
Tundra — TUHN druh
Tunis — TŌŌ nĭs
Turkey — TER kĭ
Turlington — TER lĭng t'n
Turnersville — TER nerz vĭl
Turnertown — TER ner town
Turney — TER nĭ
Tuscola — tuhs KŌ luh
Tuxedo — TUHKS ĭ dō
Twin Sisters — <u>twĭn</u> SĬS terz
Twitty — TWĬ tĭ
Tye — tī
Tyler — TĬ ler
Tynan — TĬ nuhn

U

Uhland — YŌŌ l'nd
Umbarger — UHM bahr ger
Union — YŌŌN y'n
Upshur — UHP sher
Upton — UHP t'n
Urbana — <u>er</u> BĂ nuh
Utley — YŌŌT lĭ
Utopia — yŏŏ TŌ pĭ uh
Uvalde — yŏŏ VĂL dĭ

V

Valdasta — văl DĂS tuh
Valentine — VĂL uhn tīn
Valera — vuh LĬ ruh
Valley Mills — vă lĭ MĬLZ
Valley Spring — vă lĭ SPRĬNG
Valley View — vă lĭ VYŌŌ
Van — văn
Van Alstyne — văn AWLZ <u>teen</u>
Vancourt — VĂN kōrt
Vanderbilt — VĂN der bĭlt
Vanderpool — VĂN der pŏŏl
Van Horn — văn hawrn
Van Vleck — văn VLĔK
Van Zandt — văn ZĂNT
Vashti — VĂSH tĭ
Vaughan — vawn
Vega — VĀ guh
Velasco — vuh LĂS kō
Venus — VEE n's
Vera — VĬ ruh
Verhalen — ver HĂ lĭn
Veribest — VĔR ĭ bĕst

Vernon — VER n'n
Vickery — VĬK er ĭ
Victoria — vĭk TŌ rĭ uh
Vidor — VĪ der
Vienna — vee ĔN uh
View — vyōō
Village Mills — vĭl ĭj MĬLZ
Vincent — VĬN s'nt
Vinegarone — vĭn er guh RŌN
Vineyard — VĬN yerd
Violet — VĪ ō lĕt
Voca — VŌ kuh
Von Ormy — vahn AHR mĭ
Voss — vaws
Votaw — VŌ taw

W

Waco — WĀ kō
Wadsworth — WAHDZ werth
Waelder — WĔL der
Waka — WAH kuh
Walberg — WAWL berg
Waldeck — WAWL dĕk
Walker — WAWL ker
Wall — wawl
Waller — WAW ler
Wallis — WAH lĭs
Wallisville — WAH lĭs vĭl
Walnut Springs — wawl n't
    SPRĬNGZ
Walton — WAWL t'n
Warda — WAWR duh
Ward — wawrd
Waring — WĂR ĭng
Warren — WAW rĭn
Warrenton — WAW rĭn t'n
Washburn — WAHSH bern
Washington — WAHSH ĭng t'n
Waskom — WAHS k'm
Wastella — wahs TĔL uh
Watauga — wuh TAW guh
Water Valley — wah ter
    VĂ lĭ
Waxahachie — wawks uh HĂ chĭ
Wayland — WĀ l'nd
Weatherford — WĔ ther ferd
Weaver — WEE ver
Webb — wĕb
Webberville — WĔ ber vĭl
Webster — WĔBS ter
Weches — WEE chĭz
Weesatche — WEE săch
Weimar — WĪ mer
Weinert — WĪ nert
Weir — weer
Welch — wĕlch
Welcome — WĔL k'm
Weldon — WĔL d'n
Wellborn — WĔL bern
Wellington — WĔL ĭng t'n
Wellman — WĔL m'n
Wells — wĕlz
Weser — WEE zer
Weslaco — WĔS luh kō
West — wĕst
Westbrook — WĔST brŏŏk

Family on the Canadian River hiking trail. Photo by Robert Plocheck.

Westfield — WĔST feeld
Westhoff — WĔS tawf
Westminster — wĕst MĬN ster
Weston — WĔS t'n
Westover — WĔS tō ver
Westphalia — wĕst FĀL yuh
West Point — wĕst POINT
Wetmore — WĔT mōr
Wharton — HWAWRT n
Wheeler — HWEE ler
Wheelock — HWEE lahk
White Deer — HWĪT Deer
Whiteface — HWĪT fās
Whiteflat — hwīt FLĂT
Whitehouse — HWĪT hows
Whitesboro — HWĪTS buh ruh
Whitewright — HWĪT rīt
Whitharral — HWĪT här uhl
Whitney — HWĪT nĭ
Whitsett — HWĪT sĭt
Whitson — HWĪT s'n
Whitt — hwĭt
Whon — hwahn
Wichita — WĬCH ĭ taw
Wichita Falls — wĭch ĭ taw
    FAWLZ
Wickett — WĬ kĭt
Wiergate — WEER găt
Wilbarger — WĬL bahr ger
Wildorado — wĭl duh RĂ dō
Willacy — WĬL uh sĭ
Williamson — WĬL yuhm s'n
Willis — WĬ lĭs
Wills Point — wĭlz POINT
Wilmer — WĬL mer
Wilson — WĬL s'n
Wimberley — WĬM ber lĭ
Winchester — WĬN ches ter
Windom — WĬN d'm
Windthorst — WĬN thr'st
Winfield — WĬN feeld
Wingate — WĬN găt
Wink — wĭngk
Winkler — WĬNGK ler

Winnie — WĬ nĭ
Winnsboro — WĬNZ buh ruh
Winona — wĭ NŌ nuh
Winterhaven — WĬN ter hā v'n
Winters — WĬN terz
Wise — wīz
Wizard Wells — wĭ zerd WĔLZ
Woden — WŌD n
Wolfe City — wŏŏlf SĬT ĭ
Wolfforth — WŎŎL forth
Wood — wŏŏd
Woodbine — WŎŎD bīn
Woodlake — wŏŏd LĀK
Woodland — WŎŎD l'nd
Woodlawn — wŏŏd LAWN
Woodrow — WŎŎD rō
Woodsboro — WŎŎDZ buh ruh
Woodson — WŎŎD s'n
Woodville — WŎŎD v'l
Wortham — WERTH uhm
Wright City — rĭt SĬT ĭ
Wrightsboro — RĬTS buh ruh
Wylie — WĪ lĭ

Y

Yancey — YĂN sĭ
Yantis — YĂN tĭs
Yoakum — YŌ k'm
Yorktown — YAWRK town
Young — yuhng
Youngsport — YUHNGZ pōrt
Ysleta — īs LĔT uh

Z

Zapata — zuh PAH tuh
Zavalla — zuh VĂL uh
Zephyr — ZĔF er
Zuehl — ZEE uhl

Obituaries: July 2009–June 2011

Adams, Randall Dale, 61; former death row inmate, one of the first from Dallas to be exonerated, released from prison in 1989 following an outcry brought on by the documentary *The Thin Blue Line*; in Ohio, Oct. 30,2010.

Baker, Paul, 98; legendary theatre figure in Texas, headed drama departments at Baylor and Trinity, founding artistic director of Dallas Theater Center; in Waelder, Oct, 25, 2009.

Ballas, George C. Sr., 85; Houston entrepreneur and dance studio owner who invented the Weed Eater in 1971 after watching the whirling soap brushes at a car wash; in Houston, June 25, 2011.

Banner, Bob, 89; Ennis native who after SMU went on to produce TV shows beginning with *Kukla, Fran & Ollie* and going on to *The Carol Burnett Show, Gary Moore Show, Candid Camera* and many others; in Woodland Hills, Calif., June 15, 2011.

Bellard, Emory, 83; creator of the wishbone offense in college football, head coach at Texas A&M in the 1970s and at Mississippi State; in Georgetown, Feb. 10, 2011.

Bivins, Teel, 61; served in state Senate for 15 years, was U.S. ambassador to Sweden 2004–06; in Amarillo, Oct. 26, 2009.

Bock, Harry, 80; Lithuania native survived a Nazi concentration camp, became known for his Dallas jewelry business, Bachendorf's, and for his radio commercials; in Dallas, July 12, 2010.

Borlaug, Norman, 95; Nobel Prize-winning plant scientist and father of the "green revolution" that

increased crop yields worldwide, distinguished professor at Texas A&M; in Dallas, Sept. 12, 2009.

Box, Harold, 81; Commerce native was dean of the UT architecture school 1976–92 where he raised a $6 million endowment; in Austin, May 8, 2011.

Bragan, Bobby, 92; manager of three major league teams, nicknamed "Mr. Baseball," associated with the Fort Worth Cats beginning in the 1940s; in Fort Worth, Jan. 21, 2010.

Breazeale, George, 80; sports writer for the *Austin American-Statesman* for 45 years, he was considered the authority on high school sports in Central Texas; in Austin, Sept 25, 2010.

Breeden, Leon, 88; longtime director of jazz studies at the University of North Texas in Denton beginning in 1959, making it an international mecca for jazz training, raised in Wichita Falls; in Dallas, Aug. 11, 2010.

Briscoe, Dolph; 87; scion of Southwest Texas ranch family who served as governor during the oil boom years of 1972–78, restored credibility of state government following the Sharpstown scandal; in Uvalde, June 27, 2010.

Briscoe, Frank, 84; a power in Houston politics for three decades, Harris County district attorney 1961-66, ran for mayor twice; in Richmond, Jan. 4, 2011.

Brockett, Oscar, 87; UT professor whose 1968 book, "History of the Theatre," became a standard text for students over the last four decades; in Austin, Nov. 6, 2010.

Buckley, James H. "Jim" Jr., 83; co-founded the Texas Famous

Chili Co. in the 1950s, selling refrigerated bricks at supermarkets throughout the region; in Fort Worth, June 12, 2010.

Buckmeyer, Jerry, 76; Overton native, federal judge beginning in 1979, ruled for open housing and single-member council districts in Dallas; in San Marcos, Sept. 21, 2009.

Burns, Stoney, 68; a leading voice for 1960s Dallas counterculture when he was editor of the alternative newspaper *Dallas Notes*; in Dallas, April 28, 2011.

Buss, Frances, 92; rose from receptionist at CBS in 1941 to be a director in early television, helped establish the talk show, game show and cooking show as TV staples, raised in Dallas; in Hendersonville, N.C. Jan. 19, 2010.

Butler, Roy, 83; businessman who headed the Austin school board for many years and was mayor of Austin 1971–75; in Austin, Nov. 13, 2009.

Byers, W.B. "Bo," 90; longtime political reporter and bureau chief in Austin for the *Houston Chronicle*; in Austin, May 23, 2010.

Caldeiro, Fernando "Frank," 51; astronaut since 1996, Argentina native; in League City after battling a brain tumor for two years, Oct. 3, 2009.

Carpenter, Liz, 89; author, women's rights activist and humorist was aide to Lyndon Johnson and press secretary to Lady Bird during the White House years; in Austin, March 20, 2010.

Catto, Jessica Hobby, 72; patron of charities, noted conservationist, daughter of Oveta Culp Hobby and former Gov. William P. Hobby;

Gov. Dolph Briscoe, left, Texas State Library photo. Liz Carpenter, above, LBJ Library photo.

in Aspen, Colo., Oct, 1, 2009.

Chapman, Gary, 58; UT-Austin professor who was a visionary thinker on the influence of technology and computers on society and public policy; from a heart attack Dec. 14, 2010, while kayaking in Guatemala.

Cisneros, Jose, 99; known for pen-and-ink illustrations depicting the people and culture of the Southwest, awarded the National Humanities Medal in 2001; in El Paso, Nov. 14, 2009.

Clements, Bill, 94; Dallas oilman who in 1978 became the first Republican elected governor since Reconstruction, elected to another four-year term in 1986; in Dallas, May 29, 2011.

Cryer, Sherwood, 81; started in 1971 the honky-tonk Gilley's in Pasadena made famous by the movie *Urban Cowboy*, his partnership with Mickey Gilley broke up later; in Pasadena, Aug. 13, 2009.

Dean, Jimmy, 81; country singer raised in Plainview, smash hit "Big Bad John," hosted variety TV show, entrepreneur known for sausage brand; in Virginia, June 13, 2010.

De La Vina, Gustavo, 70; Edinburg native joined the Border Patrol in 1970 in Eagle Pass, served as chief of the Border Patrol 1997–2004; in the Balkans where he was serving as a private adviser, Oct. 26, 2009.

DeYoung, Helen, 81; founder of *The Greensheet* in Houston in 1970, the tabloid advertiser reached 650,000 circulation and expanded to three other Texas cities; in Houston, March 31, 2010.

Dillon, David, 68; for 25 years the architecture critic at *The Dallas Morning News*, considered on of the country's foremost writers on

the subject; in Amherst, Mass., June 3, 2010.

Duncan, Dan, 77; founded one of the largest energy services companies in the U.S., raised in Center, became Houston's richest man worth an estimated $9 billion; in Houston, March 29, 2010.

Dupey, Michael J., 64; considered the founder of arts and crafts superstore concept, started Michaels in Dallas in 1976; in Dallas, May 1, 2010.

Dupree, Cornell Jr., 68; R&B guitarist discovered by King Curtis in 1962, backed Sam Cooke, Roberta Flack, Fats Domino and others; in Fort Worth, May, 8, 2011.

Ellis, Herb, 88; Farmersville native was jazz guitar vitruoso who played with Ella Fitzgerald, was a member of the Oscar Peterson Trio in the 1950s, attended UNT-Denton; in Los Angeles, March 28, 2010.

Fearing, Kelly, 92; modernist painter taught art at UT-Austin 1947–87, one of the last of the Fort Worth Circle of artists; in Austin, March 13, 2011.

Franks, Zarko, 89; reporter for the *Houston Chronicle* beginning in 1945, covered crime and sports, was city editor, family emigrated from Yugoslavia when he was 6; in Houston, Dec. 2, 2010.

Gardner, Carl, 83; Tyler native was original lead singer of the R&B group the Coasters who had No. 1 hit "Yakety Yak" in 1958, also "Charlie Brown"; in Florida, June 12, 2011.

Garrett, Jenkins, 95; Fort Worth lawyer and philanthropist, accumulated one of the most comprehensive collections of Texas historical artifacts, president of the Texas State Historical Assn. 1988–89; in Fort Worth, Jan. 27, 2010.

Garrison, Sam, 88; one of the Tuskegee airmen, the first all black fighter squadron in the segregated U.S. Armed Forces in World War II; in Tyler, May, 26, 2011.

Gentling, Scott, 68; Fort Worth artist best known for the 1986 book *Of Birds and Texas*, which he did with his twin Stuart who died in 2006; in Fort Worth, Feb. 8, 2011.

Gilmore, Kathleen Kirk, 95; authority on Spanish colonial archaeology, spent decades in finding the location of the French explorer La Salle's fort on Garcitas Creek; in Dallas, March 18, 2010.

Glaze, Bob, 82; legislator from East Texas for 12 years as a conservative Democrat beginning in 1990, worked for child health care; in Gilmer, June 25, 2010.

Gochman, Arthur, 79; Houston lawyer-businessman who built the Academy chain of sports stores, champion of school funding equity; in Oct. 25, 2010.

Goetzmann, William H., 80; Pulitzer Prize-winning historian for *Exploration and Empire*, chair of the UT department of American Studies for 16 years; in Austin, Sept. 7, 2010.

Gordon, William E., 92; electrical engineer who designed the world's largest radio telescope, provost and vice president of Rice University 1980–86; in Ithaca, N.Y., Feb. 16, 2009.

Greenhill, Joe, 96; longest-serving member of the Texas Supreme Court 1957–82, chief justice from 1972; in Austin, Feb. 11, 2011.

Harte, Edward H., 88; son of co-founder of Harte-Hanks Newspapers, publisher of *Corpus Christi Caller-Times*, philanthopist and ardent conservationist; in Maine, May, 18, 2011.

Hollingsworth, James F., 91; in the

Gov. Bill Clements, above, with wife Rita, at his inauguration in 1979, Texas State Library photo. Norman Borlaug, right.

Army for 36 years through World War II, Korea and Vietnam, called the most decorated military officer to come out of Texas A&M; in San Antonio, March 9, 2010.

Hosty, James P., 86; was FBI agent in Dallas when told in October 1963 to investigate Lee Harvey Oswald as a potential spy, one of 12 agents reprimanded for investigative improprieties after the Warren Commission's report; in Kansas City, June 10, 2011.

Howell, Deborah, 68; San Antonio native was one of the first women to lead a big U.S. newspaper at the *St. Paul Pioneer Press*; Jan. 1, 2010, while vacationing in New Zealand.

Jefferson, Mildred, 84; Pittsburg (Tx.) native, physician who was a national figure in the anti-abortion movement, the first African-American woman to graduate from Harvard Medical School; in Cambridge, Mass., Oct. 15, 2010.

Jordan, Esteban "Steve," 71; conjunto accordionist credited with introducing elments of jazz, pop, rock and blues into the traditional polka genre; in San Antonio, Aug. 13, 2010.

Justice, William Wayne, 89; East Texas federal judge who wrote the decisions integrating Texas schools, reforming state prisons and opening classrooms to children of illegal immigrants; in Austin, Oct. 13, 2009.

Kennard, Don, 81; champion of state parks and education, represented Fort Worth in Texas House 1953–62, state Senate 1962–73; in Austin, March 17, 2011.

Kelsey, John R. Jr., 88; Deport native, physician who was co-founder of the Kelsey-Sebold Clinics in Houston in the late 1950s; in

Houston, July 21, 2010.

Kelton, Elmer, 83; famed Western novelist wrote more than 60 books mostly set in West Texas, spent most of his life as a journalist writing about livestock and ranches, first for the *San Angelo Standard-Times*; in San Angelo, Aug. 22, 2009.

Kinch, Sam Jr., 70; covered state and national politics for 40 years in Austin and Washington, many for *The Dallas Morning News*; in Austin, Feb. 1, 2011.

Kuempel, Edmund, 67; esteemed veteran Republican legislator since 1983 from Seguin, oversaw Capitol restoration in the 1990s; in Austin, Nov. 4, 2010.

Lipscomb, Al, 86; Dallas political and civil rights leader, city council member for 15 years; in Dallas, June 18, 2011.

Long, Emma, 98; Austin's first female city council member in 1948, liberal firebrand served until 1969 when she was defeated after proposing a fair housing ordinance; in Austin, Jan. 16, 2011.

Lounge, John M., 64; astronaut who flew on three shuttle missions, including the first after the 1986 Challenger disaster; in Houston, March 1, 2011.

Manges, Clinton, 87; South Texas rancher and oil tycoon, confidant and friend to state officials including Jim Mattox and Bob Bullock; in San Antonio, Sept. 23, 2010.

Marzio, Peter C., 67; elevated to national esteem the Houston Museum of Fine Arts where he was director for nearly 30 years; in Houston, Dec. 9, 2010.

Mashek, John W., 77; reporter from 1955 at *The Dallas Morning News* who sent him to Washington in 1960 to cover the Texas

congressional delegation, headed Southwest bureau for *U.S. News & World Report;* in Rockville, Md., Nov. 3, 2009.

Matson, Ollie, 80; NFL star for 14 years was born and raised to age 14 in Trinity, Olympic medalist in track in 1952; in Los Angeles, Feb. 19, 2011.

Matthews, E.O. "Coots," 86; part of the Boots and Coots oil well firefighting business, helped put out Kuwaiti oil fires following the first Gulf war; in Humble, March 31, 2010.

Matthiesen, Leroy T., 88; Catholic bishop in the Panhandle for 17 years, in 1981 counseled Catholics to leave their jobs at the local Pantex plant that assembled nuclear weapons; in Amarillo, March 22, 2010.

McKenzie, W.A. "Billy Mac," 87; Houston Reagan grad, lawyer who served as Texas A&M regent 1981–93, Republican stalwart was chairman when George H.W. Bush chose College Station for his presidential library; April 18, 2010.

Meaux, Huey P., 82; the "Crazy Cajun" created his own music industry in Houston where he was producer for the Sir Douglas Quintet, Freddy Fender and others; in Winnie, April 23, 2011.

Meredith, Don, 72; Dallas Cowboys quarterback whose charm and wit brought fame as commentator for Monday Night Football where he always acknowledged his parents, Jeff and Hazel, back in Mount Vernon; in Santa Fe, N.M., Dec. 5, 2010.

Mooney, Ralph, 82; played pedal steel guitar for Merle Haggard, Buck Owens and Waylon Jennings and wrote "Crazy Arms"; in Kennedale, March 20, 2011.

Mosbacher, Robert A., 82; Houston oilman prominent in Republican politics, U.S. secretary of commerce for longtime friend President George H.W. Bush; in Houston, Jan. 24, 2010.

Newcomb, William W. Jr., 88; UT professor of anthropology who focused on the rock art of Texas, led the Texas Memorial Museum for 21 years; in Austin, Feb. 8, 2010.

Obledo, Mario, 78; Hispanic rights leader born in San Antonio, earned law degree at St. Mary's University, co-founded the Mexican Amercian Legal Defense Fund, awarded Presidential Medal of Freedom in 1998; in Sacremento, Calif., Aug. 18, 2010.

O'Quinn, John, 68; flamboyant Houston lawyer who won billions in cases involving breast implants,

Pinetop Perkins at the Fort Lauderdale blues festival, 2006. Carl Lender (CC).

tobacco and pharmaceuticals; in Houston, Oct. 29, 2009.

Parker, Fess, 85; TV's Davy Crockett and Daniel Boone, actor was born in Fort Worth and grew up in San Angelo; in California, March 18, 2010.

Parker, Walt, 92; was a five-term legislator who helped development of the University of North Texas, worked decades as NFL referee; in Denton, Jan. 22, 2010.

Perkins, Pinetop, 97; boogie-woogie piano player, one of the last surviving members of the first Delta bluesmen; in Austin, where he spent his last years, on March 21, 2011.

Perry, Malcolm O., 80; surgeon who attended President Kennedy and Lee Harvey Oswald at Parkland Hospital in 1963; in Tyler, Dec. 5, 2009.

Pillsbury, Edmund P., 66; director of the Kimbell Art Museum in Fort Worth 1980-98, a specialist in Italian Renaissance art; in rural Kaufman County, March 25, 2010.

Powers, Melvin Lane, 68; acquitted in the 1964 stabbing and clubbing death of the husband of Candace Mossler, his aunt who he allegedly was having an affair with; in Houston, Oct. 8, 2010.

Prather, Hugh, 72; Dallas native was author of self-help books including *Notes to Myself,* which has sold over 5 million copies; in Tuscon, Nov. 15, 2010.

Purcell, Graham, 92; Archer City native was congressman from Northwest Texas 1961–73; in Wichita Falls, June 11, 2011.

Reid, Frances, 95; Wichita Falls native who played family matriarch Alice Horton on the soap opera *Days of Our Lives* for more than 40 years; in Beverly Hills, Calif., Feb 3, 2010.

Roach, Joe, 49; Houston Republican was prosecutor, three-term city council member and advocate for people with disabilities; a dwarf, he died of an undisclosed illness in Houston, April 18, 2011.

Rubottom, R. Richard, 98; diplomant who helped shape U.S. policy to Cuba and Latin America in the late 1950s, SMU professor; in Austin, Dec. 6, 2010.

Sakowitz, Ann, 96; matriarch of the Houston retail family, San Antonio native attended Rice University, patron of the arts; in Houston, Jan. 18, 2010.

Samuels, Joseph, 95; a leader in the Jewish community in Houston where he was from 1973 publisher of the *Jewish Herald-Voice;* in Houston, Jan. 19, 2011.

Sanborn, Eunice G., 114; according to Gerontology Research Group, the world's oldest person when she died; in Jacksonville, Jan. 31, 2011.

Sherman, Cecil, 82; Fort Worth native, Baylor graduate became national leader of the theological moderates in the losing battle with conservatives of the Southern Baptist Convention; in Richmond, Va., April 17, 2010.

Shivers, Robin, 53; launched a charity to provide health insurance for Austin musicians, daughter-in-law of former Gov. Allan Shivers; in Austin, unexpectedly of unknown causes, Oct. 26, 2009.

Simpson, James P., 87; former FBI agent and lawyer who helped close down illegal gambling in Galveston in the late 1950s; in Austin, Nov. 27, 2010.

Stumberg, Louis, 87; San Antonio businessman who in 1946 launched with this father and brother Patio brand frozen Mexican dinners; in San Antonio, May 3, 2011.

Swayze, Patrick, 57; movie star and dancer was native of Houston, his mother started the city's Jazz Ballet Company, track and field star at Waltrip High School; from pancreatic cancer, in Los Angeles, Sept. 14, 2009.

Vandergriff, Tom, 84; longtime Arlington mayor first elected in 1951 who transformed the city by luring General Motors, the Texas Rangers and the tourist industry, Tarrant County judge until 2006; in Fort Worth, Dec. 30, 2010. His wife, Anna Waynette, 82, preceded him in death, July 3, 2009.

Vela, Ruben, 72; famed conjunto accordionist called "King of the Dance Hall Sound," known for pioneering a choppy, staccato style;

in Harlingen, March 9, 2010.

Wagner, Helen, 91; Lubbock native played mild-mannered Nancy Hughes on the soap opera *As the World Turns* for more than 50 years; in Mount Kisco, N.Y., May 1, 2010.

Weber, David J., 69; historian of the Southwest who focused on the relationship between Mexico and the United States, professor at SMU in Dallas; in Gallup, N.M., Aug. 20, 2010.

Widman, Ralph Jr. "Buddy," 90; voice of sports play-by-play at Dallas' WFAA in 1940s–1960s; in Arlington, Nov. 17, 2009.

Wier, Rusty, 65; singer-songwriter was a Texas music legend, part of the Austin scene of the 1970s, wrote "Don't It Make You Want to Dance"; in Driftwood, Oct. 9, 2009.

Wilkerson, David, 79; Lindale resident was evangelical minister and author of *The Cross and the Switchblade,* founder of Teen Challenge International and the Times Square Church in New York; in Cuney, April 7, 2011.

Wilson, Charlie, 76; congressman from East Texas for twelve terms, his advocacy for the Afghan struggle against the Soviet Army was the subject of *Charlie Wilson's War;* in Lufkin, Feb. 10, 2010.

Yarborough, Don, 83; liberal Democrat was three-time candidate for governor in the 1960s, his challenge to incumbent John Connally was one of the reasons President John F. Kennedy came to Texas in November 1963; in Houston, Sept. 23, 2009.

Zapalac, Willie, 89; 1946 Aggie football captain, assistant to Bear Bryant with the Junction Boys in the mid-1950s, also coached with Darrell Royal and Bum Phillips; in Austin, May 18, 2010. ☆

Charlie Wilson, above. Patrick Swayze, right, Alan Light photo (CC).

ADVERTISER INDEX

GENERAL INDEX

For cities and towns not listed in the index, see lists on pages 421–447 and pages 518–527. For full information about cities, see "Cities and towns" entry in this index. For full information about counties, also look under the cities and towns in the county, as well as the "Counties" index entry. Page numbers in *italics* refer to photographs and captions of photographs.

For CITIES and TOWNS not listed in the Index, see complete list on pages 421–447.

Big Boggy National Wildlife Refuge, 114
Big Creek Reservoir, 98
Biggers, John, 570
Biggs Field, 284
Big Lake, 97
Big Lake (town), 371, 423, 519
Big Lake Bottom Wildlife Management Area, 116, 117
Big Sandy, 399, 423, 519
Big Spring, 318, 423, 519
Big Spring State Park, 167, 170
Big Thicket National Preserve, *105*, 180-181
Big Wells, 278, 423, 519
Biomass, 626
Bipolar disorder, 583
Bircher, Marca Lee, 570
Birds and birding
  bird sighting centers, 188-189
  Coastal Birding Trail, 185, 189
  endangered species of, 118
  hunting license for game birds, 187
  map of bird sighting regions, 188
  state bird, 15, 21
  in state parks, 166-179, 188-189
  in wildlife refuges, 114-115, *188*
  World Birding Center, 188
Births
  comparative rankings with other states, 17, 580
  by county, 232-415
  international statistics on, 580
  by race/ethnicity, 580
  by sex, 580
  state statistics, 15, 577, 580
Bishop, 362, 423, 519
Bishop Hills, 368, 423, 519
Bison, *119*, 120
Bivins, Teel, 702
Bivins Lake, 98
Black, Clint, 570
Black bean lottery, 50, 177
Black-capped vireos, 169, 174, 176
Black colleges, 31, 594
Black Creek Lake, 183
Black Gap Wildlife Management Area, 116, 117
Black Kettle National Grassland, 112, 183
Blackland Belt, 69, 70, 71, 82, 104
Blackland Prairie soils, 82
Blacks
  births, 580
  as Buffalo Soldiers, 172, 181
  as Civil War soldiers, 31
  discrimination against and segregation of, 56, 58, 60-61, 64
  drug treatment by types of drugs, 583
  education of, 31, 55, 56, 64, 594
  life expectancy, 580
  monument to, 473
  as musicians, 36
  organizations for, 61
  as politicians, 58, 65
  population statistics, 15, 418

as prisoners, 500
during Reconstruction, 55-56, 473
in Texas Legislature, 31, 65, 473
Texas Revolution and, 48
violence against, 53, 56, 60-61
voting rights for, 55, 56, 58, 61, 64
in World War I, 60
Blackwell, 262, 361, 423, 519
Blanco (town), 244, 423, 519
Blanco Canyon, 72, *290*
Blanco County, map, profile, 244
Blanco State Park, 167, 170
Blanket (town), 251, 423, 519
Blanton, Jack, 570
Blind, Commission for, 505
Blind and Visually Impaired, School for, 505
Blinn College, 596
Blizzards, 137-139. *See also* Snowfall and snowstorms
Bloomburg, 257, 423, 519
Blooming Grove, 360, 423, 519
Blossom, 336, 423, 519
Blowout Cave, 119
Bluebonnets, 15, 21, *103*, 175, *347*
"Bluebonnets" (song), 22
Blue Elbow Swamp-Tony Houseman Wildlife Management Area, 116, 117
Blue Lacy dog, 21-22
Blue Mound, 390, 391, 423, 519
Blue Ridge, 263, 423, 519
Blue topaz (state gem), 22
Blum, 315, 423, 519
Board of Education. *See* Education, State Board of
Board of Insurance. *See* Insurance, State Board of
Boards and commissions, 504-517
Bobcats, 120
Bob Sandlin, Lake, 98, 171, 174
Boca Chica State Park, 170
Bock, Harry, 702
Boerne, 330, 423, 519
Bogata, 372, 423, 519
Bolivar Peninsula, 295
Bolivia, consular office, 663
Bolo tie, 23
Bond Review Board, 505
Bonham, 287, 423, 519
Bonham, Lake, 98
Bonham State Park, 167, 170
Bonney, 247, 423, 519
Booker, 341, 363, 423, 519
Boquillas Canyon, 74, 88
Borden County, map, profile, 244
Borger, 321, 423, 519
Borlaug, Norman, 702
Bosner, Paul, 39
Bosque County, map, profile, 245
Botswana, consular office, 663
Boundary lines of Texas, 68, 87-89, 91, 92
Bouton Lake, 182
Bovina, 366, 423, 519
Bowie, James, 46-47
Bowie (town), 355, 423, 519
Bowie County, map, profile, 246
Bowles, Philip, 49

Bowser, Erbie, 36
Box, Harold, 702
Boyd, 412, 424, 519
Bracken Cave, 119
Brackettville, 334, 424, 519
Brady, Kevin, 455, 458, 547
Brady, 349, 424, 519
Brady Creek Reservoir, 98
Bragan, Bobby, 702
Brandy Branch Reservoir, 98
Branson, David, 30
Braunig (Victor), Lake, 98
Brazil, consular office, 663
Brazoria (town), 247, 424, 519
Brazoria County, 419
  map, profile, 247
Brazoria National Wildlife Refuge, 114
Brazoria Reservoir, 98
Brazos Bend, 316, 424, 519
Brazos Bend State Park, 167, *168*, 170
Brazos Country (town), 238, 424, 519
Brazos County, 419
  map, profile, 248
Brazosport, 247, 424
Brazosport College, 596
Brazos River, 82, 87, 89, 90, 93
Brazos River Authority, 90, 505
Brazos Santiago, 54
Brazos Valley Council of Governments, 528
Bread (state), 21
Breadth and length of Texas, 68
Breazeale, George, 702
Breckenridge, 387, 424, 519
Breeden, Leon, 702
Bremond, 375, 424, 519
Brenham, 405, 424, 519
Breweries, 177
Brewster County, map, profile, 249
Briarcliff, 397, 424, 519
Briaroaks, 327, 424, 519
Bridge City, 364, 424, 519
Bridgeport, 412, 424, 519
Bridgeport, Lake, 91, 98
Brine, 638
Briscoe, Dolph, 65, 702
Briscoe, Frank, 702
Briscoe County, map, profile, 250
Broaddus, 378, 424, 519
Brockett, Oscar, 702
Bronte, 262, 424, 519
Brooks City-Air Force Base, 243, 553
Brooks County, map, profile, 250
Brookshire, 404, 424, 519
Brookside Village, 247, 424, 519
Brown, Sandra, 570
Brown County, map, profile, 251
Browndell, 323, 424, 519
Brownfield, 394, 424, 519
Brownsboro, 313, 424, 519
Brownsville, 255, 424, 519
  Brownsville-Harlingen MSA (metro area), 420
  during Civil War, 30-31, *32*, 54
Brownwood, 251, 424, 519
Brownwood, Lake, 98, 171, 174
Bruceville-Eddy, 286, 350, 424, 519
Bruno, Robert, house/sculpture,

For CITIES and TOWNS not listed in the Index, see complete list on pages 421–447.

For CITIES and TOWNS not listed in the Index, see complete list on pages 421–447.

For CITIES and TOWNS not listed in the Index, see complete list on pages 421–447.

For CITIES and TOWNS not listed in the Index, see complete list on pages 421–447.

For CITIES and TOWNS not listed in the Index, see complete list on pages 421–447.

For CITIES and TOWNS not listed in the Index, see complete list on pages 421–447.

For CITIES and TOWNS not listed in the Index, see complete list on pages 421–447.

For CITIES and TOWNS not listed in the Index, see complete list on pages 421–447.

For CITIES and TOWNS not listed in the Index, see complete list on pages 421–447.

For CITIES and TOWNS not listed in the Index, see complete list on pages 421–447.

For CITIES and TOWNS not listed in the Index, see complete list on pages 421–447.

For CITIES and TOWNS not listed in the Index, see complete list on pages 421–447.

For CITIES and TOWNS not listed in the Index, see complete list on pages 421–447.

For CITIES and TOWNS not listed in the Index, see complete list on pages 421–447.

For CITIES and TOWNS not listed in the Index, see complete list on pages 421–447.

For CITIES and TOWNS not listed in the Index, see complete list on pages 421–447.

For CITIES and TOWNS not listed in the Index, see complete list on pages 421–447.

For CITIES and TOWNS not listed in the Index, see complete list on pages 421–447.

For CITIES and TOWNS not listed in the Index, see complete list on pages 421–447.

Texas Lakes

Bodies of water with a normal capacity of 5,000 acre-feet or larger. Italicized reservoirs usually dry.

● PANHANDLE PLAINS
1. Palo Duro Reservoir
2. Lake Rita Blanca
3. Lake Meredith
4. Bivins Lake
5. Buffalo Lake
6. Mackenzie Reservoir
7. Greenbelt Lake
8. Baylor Creek Lake
9. White River Lake
10. Lake Alan Henry
11. Lake J.B. Thomas
12. Sulphur Springs Draw Reservoir
13. Natural Dam Lake
14. Red Draw Reservoir
15. Lake Colorado City
16. Champion Creek Reservoir
17. Mitchell County Reservoir
18. Lake Sweetwater
19. E.V. Spence Reservoir
20. Oak Creek Reservoir
21. O.C. Fisher Lake
22. Twin Buttes Reservoir
23. Lake Nasworthy
24. Lake Ballinger/ Moonen
25. O.H. Ivie Reservoir
26. Hords Creek Lake
27. Lake Winters
28. Lake Abilene
29. Lake Coleman
30. Lake Brownwood
31. Lake Clyde
32. Lake Kirby
33. Lake Fort Phantom Hill
34. Lake Stamford
35. Lake Davis
36. Truscott Brine Lake
37. Santa Rosa Lake
38. Lake Electra
39. Lake Kemp
40. Lake Diversion
41. Lake Kickapoo
42. North Fork Buffalo Creek Reservoir
43. Lake Wichita
44. Lake Arrowhead
45. Millers Creek Reservoir
46. Lake Cooper/Olney
47. Lake Graham
48. Lost Creek Reservoir
49. Possum Kingdom Lake
50. Hubbard Creek Reservoir
51. Lake Daniel
52. Lake Cisco
53. Lake Palo Pinto
54. Lake Leon
55. Proctor Lake

● BIG BEND
56. Red Bluff Reservoir
57. Balmorhea Lake
58. Imperial Reservoir
59. Amistad International Reservoir

● HILL COUNTRY
60. Brady Creek Reservoir
61. Lake Buchanan
62. Inks Lake
63. Lake Lyndon B. Johnson
64. Lake Marble Falls
65. Lake Travis
66. Lake Austin
67. Town Lake
68. Lake Walter E. Long
69. Lake Georgetown
70. Granger Lake
71. Canyon Lake
72. Medina Lake

● PRAIRIES AND LAKES
73. Lake Nocona
74. Hubert H. Moss Lake
75. Lake Texoma
76. Randell Lake
77. Valley Lake
78. Lake Bonham
79. Coffee Mill Lake
80. Pat Mayse Lake
81. Lake Crook
82. River Crest Lake
83. Big Creek Reservoir
84. Cooper Lake
85. Lake Sulphur Springs
86. Lake Cypress Springs
87. Greenville City Lakes
88. Lake Tawakoni
89. Terrell City Lake
90. Lake Lavon
91. Lake Ray Hubbard
92. Lake Kiowa
93. Lake Ray Roberts
94. Lewisville Lake
95. Grapevine Lake
96. North Lake
97. White Rock Lake
98. Mountain Creek Lake
99. Joe Pool Reservoir
100. Lake Arlington
101. Lake Worth
102. Eagle Mountain Lake
103. Lake Weatherford
104. Lake Amon G. Carter
105. Lake Bridgeport
106. Lake Mineral Wells
107. Benbrook Lake
108. Lake Granbury
109. Squaw Creek Reservoir
110. Lake Pat Cleburne
111. Lake Waxahachie
112. Bardwell Lake
113. Cedar Creek Reservoir
114. Forest Grove Reservoir
115. Lake Athens
116. Trinidad Lake
117. Lake Halbert
118. Richland-Chambers Reservoir
119. Fairfield Lake
120. Navarro Mills Lake
121. Aquilla Lake
122. Lake Whitney
123. Lake Waco
124. Tradinghouse Creek Reservoir
125. Lake Creek Lake
126. Belton Lake
127. Stillhouse Hollow Lake
128. Alcoa Lake
129. Lake Limestone
130. Twin Oaks Reservoir
131. Camp Creek Lake
132. Bryan Lake
133. Gibbons Creek Reservoir
134. Somerville Lake
135. Lake Bastrop
136. Fayette County Reservoir
137. Lake Dunlap
138. Lake Gonzales
139. Eagle Lake

● PINEYWOODS
140. Wright Patman Lake
141. Monticello Reservoir
142. Lake Winnsboro
143. Lake Bob Sandlin
144. Welsh Reservoir
145. Ellison Creek Reservoir
146. Lake O' the Pines
147. Johnson Creek Reservoir
148. Caddo Lake
149. Lake Fork Reservoir
150. Lake Quitman
151. Lake Holbrook
152. Lake Hawkins
153. Gilmer Reservoir
154. Lake Gladewater
155. Eastman Lakes
156. Brandy Branch Reservoir
157. Lake Cherokee
158. Martin Creek Lake

Dallam
Hartley 2
Oldham
Deaf Smith
Parmer   Castro
Bailey   Lamb
Coch-ran   Hockley
Yoakum   Terry
Gaines
Andrews
Ector   Mi
El Paso   Hudspeth   Culberson   56 Loving   Winkler
Reeves   Ward   Crane   Up
58
57
Jeff Davis   Pecos
Presidio   Brewster   Terr